COPYRIGHT
CASES AND COMMENTARY
ON THE CANADIAN AND
INTERNATIONAL LAW

Second Edition

Barry Sookman

Steven Mason

Carys Craig

CARSWELL®

ISBN 978-0-7798-5535-3

A cataloguing record for this publication is available from Library and Archives Canada.

Composition: Computer Composition of Canada LP

Printed in Canada by Thomson Reuters.

TELL US HOW WE'RE DOING

Scan the QR code to the right with your smartphone to send your comments regarding our products and services.
Free QR Code Readers are available from your mobile device app store.
You can also email us at carswell.feedback@thomsonreuters.com

 **THOMSON REUTERS**

CARSWELL, A DIVISION OF THOMSON REUTERS CANADA LIMITED

One Corporate Plaza
2075 Kennedy Road
Toronto, Ontario
M1T 3V4

Customer Relations
Toronto 1-416-609-3800
Elsewhere in Canada/U.S. 1-800-387-5164
Fax 1-416-298-5082
www.carswell.com
E-mail www.carswell.com/email

ACKNOWLEDGEMENTS

We would like to thank the great number of individuals who have helped to make this book a reality. We wish to convey our gratitude to our partners at McCarthy Tétrault who have provided us with the support for the creation of this book. We would also like to express our thanks to a number of people who have helped us research and compile this book, including Kate Findlay and Ryan Prescott. Finally, we appreciate the efforts made by our legal assistants, Marija Blazanin and Nicolina Accardo and by Carswell's Lisa Gordon and Erica Malone.

TABLE OF CONTENTS

Chapter 1

INTRODUCTION

Most individuals encounter copyrighted works on a daily basis by reading a book, using computer software, listening to music on an Ipod, or watching a movie. Copyright is ever present in our daily lives. Its legal protection is also an important — and increasingly contentious — social, cultural and economic concern.

Copyright law creates incentives to produce and disseminate works. It does so by giving authors a series of exclusive rights such as the right to reproduce works and to communicate them to the public. Copyright law also has limitations and exceptions to promote a balance between what can be controlled by exclusive rights and what can be freely used without restrictions imposed by copyright holders.

Copyright law was first established by the *Statute of Anne*, a British statute enacted in 1710. This statute bestowed upon authors for the first time the right to benefit from the reproduction of their works. The Canadian *Copyright Act* first came into force in 1924.[1] Since then it has been amended many times to deal with developing technologies. Copyright law is now a complex, challenging and important area of the law.

This casebook provides extracts from the leading cases on copyright. Copyright laws operate territorially. However, increasingly, countries around the world are faced with common challenges and seek to solve them in a harmonious and consistent manner. Accordingly, this casebook refers to leading Canadian and international jurisprudence to help illustrate the challenges, concepts and divergent approaches to copyright issues that shape this area of law.

1. Basic Concepts and Rationale for Protecting Copyright

Why protect copyright? This section explores this important question. There are economic, social and philosophical reasons for doing so. The rationales for providing authors with legal protection have important consequences for fundamental concepts relating to copyright.

---

[1]   Online: <http://www.canadianheritage.gc.ca/progs/ac-ca/progs/pda-cpb/faq-info/index_e.cfm>.

**International Bureau of WIPO, "Basic Notions
of Copyright and Related Rights".[2]**

BASIC NOTIONS OF COPYRIGHT

A. Introduction

1. Copyright legislation is part of the body of law known as "intellectual property," which protects the interests of creators by giving them property rights over their creations. These rights of property are recognized under the laws of most countries in order to stimulate human intellectual creativity, to make the fruits of such creativity available to the public, and to ensure that international trade in goods and services protected by intellectual property rights is allowed to flourish on the basis of a smoothly functioning system of harmonized national laws.

2. In countries with Latin-based languages, the expression "intellectual property" referred only to copyright. In the international sphere, however, the expression referred to both industrial property and copyright, reflecting the evolution of the two international unions created at the end of 19th century to protect both types of intellectual property: the Paris Union created by the Paris Convention for the Protection of Industrial Property of 1883 and the Berne Union, established under the Berne Convention for the Protection of Literary and Artistic Works of 1886. Under each Convention, a secretariat called the "International Bureau" was created for purposes of administration, and the two secretariats were combined in 1893. The resulting combined secretariat was known under various names, the last of which was "United International Bureaux for the Protection of Intellectual Property," known under its French acronym BIRPI, which became what is now WIPO.

3. Today, the expression "intellectual property" is used even more broadly, to refer to all creations of the human mind. Article 2 (viii) of the Convention Establishing the World Intellectual Property Organization does not define intellectual property as such, but gives the following list of the subject matter protected by intellectual property rights: literary, artistic and scientific works; performances of performing artists, phonograms, and broadcasts; inventions in all fields of human endeavor; scientific discoveries; industrial designs; trademarks, service marks, and commercial names and designations; protection against unfair competition; and "all other rights resulting from intellectual activity in the industrial, scientific, literary or artistic fields."

4. The most direct source of protection for intellectual property is national laws. Other sources include legal instruments of regional bodies composed of groups of countries (such as the directives of the European Union), bilateral and plurilateral agreements among countries which contain provisions on intellectual property (such as the North American Free Trade Agreement), and multilateral agreements, such as the Berne Convention and the recent Agreement on the

---

2   Online: <http://www.wipo.int/export/sites/www/copyright/en/activities/pdf/international_
protection.pdf>.

Trade Related Aspects of Intellectual Property Rights (the TRIPS Agreement), concluded under the Uruguay Round of negotiations under the former GATT (now the World Trade Organization).

1. "Property"

5. In order to gain a fuller understanding of the term "intellectual property," it may be useful to approach it in terms of the notion of "property" in general. The most important feature of property is that the owner of the property may use it as he wishes; nobody else can lawfully use his property without his authorization. The property owner may be a human being or a legal entity, such as a corporation.

6. Roughly speaking, there are three types of property. One is property consisting of movable things, such as a wristwatch, a car, or furniture in a home. In some legal systems, this is known as "movable property." No one except the owner of the wristwatch, the car or the furniture can use these items of property. This legal right is referred to as "exclusive," because the owner has the "exclusive" right to use his property. Naturally, the proprietor may authorize others to use the property, but without such authorization, use by others is illegal.

7. The second type of property is immovable property, or as it is sometimes known, real property. Land and things permanently fixed on it, such as houses, are immovable property, because they cannot be lifted or moved.

8. The third type of property is intellectual property, which protects the creations of the human mind, the human intellect. This is why this kind of property is called "intellectual" property.

2. "Intellectual" Property

9. As noted above, intellectual property has been divided into two branches, namely "industrial" property, which includes inventions (patents), trademarks, industrial designs, and geographic indications of source, and "copyright," which protects literary and artistic works as well as creations in the field of so-called "related rights." While other types of intellectual property also exist, for present purposes it is helpful to explore the distinction between industrial property and copyright, in particular, the basic difference between inventions and literary and artistic works.

10. A patent is an exclusive right granted for an invention, which is a product or a process that provides a new way of doing something, or offers a new technical solution to a problem. Protection of inventions under patent law does not require that the invention be represented in a physical embodiment. Protection accorded to inventors is, therefore, protection against any use of the invention without the authorization of the owner. Even a person who later makes the same invention independently, without copying or even being aware of the first inventor's work, must obtain authorization before he can exploit it.

11. Literary and artistic works include books, music, works of fine arts such as paintings and sculptures, and technology-based works such as computer programs and electronic databases. Copyright law protects only the form of expression of ideas, not the ideas themselves. The creativity protected by copyright law is creativity in the choice and arrangement of words, musical notes, colors and shapes. Copyright law protects the owner of property rights in literary and artistic works against those who "copy" or otherwise take and use the form in which the original work was expressed by the author.

12. From this basic difference between inventions and literary and artistic works, it follows that the legal protection provided to each also differs. Since protection under patent law gives a monopoly right in the exploitation of an invention, such protection is short in duration-usually about 20 years. The fact that the invention is protected must also be made known to the public — there must be an official notification that a specific, fully described invention is the property, for a fixed number of years, of a specific owner; in other words, the protected invention must be disclosed in an official register, open to the public, and the owner must ensure that his invention appears in the register.

13. Legal protection of literary and artistic works under copyright prevents only unauthorized use of the expressions of ideas. Without protection under a patent, a person who has disclosed to the public an invention cannot prevent third parties from using that invention. Therefore, the duration of protection can be much longer than in the case of the protection of inventions, without damage to the public interest. Also, the law can be (and, in most countries, is) simply declaratory, i.e., the law may state that the author of an original work has the right to prevent other persons from copying or otherwise using his work. Under copyright, in general, registration of works is not a condition for protection.

B. Copyright

14. What has been said so far has been an introduction. The next part of this paper will explain the general structure of copyright law, and will be divided into the following sections: (1) the works protected by copyright; (2) the rights granted to the owner of copyright; (3) limitations on such rights; (4) duration of copyright (5) ownership and transfer of copyright; and (6) enforcement of rights.

1.   Protected Works

15. Article 2 of the Berne Convention reads in part as follows:

> "The expression 'literary and artistic works' shall include every production in the literary, scientific and artistic domain, whatever may be the mode or form of its expression, such as books, pamphlets and other writings; lectures, addresses, sermons and other works of the same nature; dramatic or dramatico-musical works; choreographic works and entertainments in dumb show; musical compositions with or without words; cinematographic works to which are assimilated works expressed by a process analogous to cinematography; works of drawing, painting, architecture, sculpture, engraving and lithography; photographic works, to which are assimilated works expressed by a process analogous to photography; works of

applied art; illustrations, maps, plans, sketches and three-dimensional works relative to geography, topography, architecture or science. Translations, adaptations, arrangements of music and other alterations of a literary or artistic work shall be protected as original works without prejudice to the copyright in the original work. Collections of literary or artistic works such as encyclopaedias and anthologies which, by reason of the selection and arrangement of their contents, constitute intellectual creations shall be protected as such, without prejudice to the copyright in each of the works forming part of such collections."

16. From this provision, it may be seen that copyright applies to "every production in the literary, scientific and artistic domain, whatever may be the mode or form of its expression." The expression "literary and artistic works" is a general concept to be understood, for the purposes of copyright protection, as including every original work of authorship, irrespective of its literary or artistic merit.

17. All countries which are members of the Berne Convention, and many other countries, provide protection under their copyright laws to the categories of works contained in the preceding list, which illustrates and gives examples of what is meant by the expression "every production in the literary, scientific and artistic domain." The list is not intended to limit the modes or forms of expression which are protected by copyright law. It is not an exhaustive list. Other modes or forms of expression of works in the literary, scientific and artistic domain, not included in the list, are protected also by many copyright laws.

18. Computer programs are a good example of a type of work which is not included in the list contained in the Berne Convention, but which is undoubtedly included in the notion of a "production in the literary, scientific and artistic domain" within the meaning of Article 2 of the Convention; indeed, computer programs are protected under the copyright laws of a number of countries, and under the TRIPS Agreement. A computer program is a set of instructions which controls the operations of a computer in order to enable it to perform a specific task, such as the storage and retrieval of information. A computer program is produced by one or more human authors but, in its final "mode or form of expression," it can be understood directly only by a machine (the computer), not by humans. Another, recent example of a type of work not listed in Article 2 of the Berne Convention, but which is clearly included in the notion of a creation "in the literary, scientific and artistic domain," is multimedia productions. While no acceptable legal definition has been developed, there is a consensus that the combination of sound, text and images in a digital format which is made accessible by a computer program, embodies an original expression of authorship sufficient to justify the protection of multimedia productions under the umbrella of copyright.

2.   Rights Protected

19. Earlier in this lecture, it was noted that there are three kinds of property — movable property, immovable property and intellectual property — and that the most important feature of property is that the owner may use it exclusively, i.e., as he wishes, and that nobody else can lawfully use it without his authorization.

When we say that the owner of property can use it "as he wishes" we do not, of course, mean that he can use it regardless of the legally recognized rights and interests of other members of society. For example, the owner of a car may use it "as he wishes," but this does not mean that he may drive his car recklessly and create danger to others, nor that he may disregard traffic regulations.

20. Copyright is a branch of intellectual property. The owner of copyright in a protected work may use the work as he wishes, and may prevent others from using it without his authorization. Thus, the rights granted under national laws to the owner of copyright in a protected work are normally "exclusive rights" to authorize others to use the work, subject to the legally recognized rights and interests of others.

21. There are two types of rights under copyright, economic rights, which allow the owner of rights to derive financial reward from the use of his works by others, and "moral rights," which allow the author to take certain actions to preserve the personal link between himself and the work. Moral rights will be discussed later in this paper.

22. The next question, which we must examine, is what is meant by "using" a work protected by copyright. Most copyright laws state that the author or owner of rights has the right to "authorize or prevent" certain acts in relation to a work. Such acts include the following: reproduction of the work (making copies); public performance of the work; broadcasting or other communication to the public of the work; translation of the work; and adaptation of the work.

a.   Right of reproduction and related rights

23. The right of the owner of copyright to prevent others from making copies of his works is the most basic right under copyright. For example, the making of copies of a protected work is the act performed by a publisher who wishes to distribute copies of a text -based work to the public, whether in the form of printed copies or digital media such as CD-Roms. Likewise, the right of a phonogram producer to manufacture and distribute compact discs (CDs) containing recorded performances of musical works is based, in part, on the authorization given by the composers of such works to reproduce their compositions in the recording. Therefore, the right to control the act of reproduction is the legal basis for many forms of exploitation of protected works.

24. Other rights are recognized in national laws in order to ensure that the basic right of reproduction is respected. For example, some laws include a right to authorize distribution of copies of works; obviously, the right of reproduction would be of little economic value if the owner of copyright could not authorize the distribution of the copies made with his consent. The right of distribution is usually subject to exhaustion upon first sale or other transfer of ownership of a particular copy, which means that, after the copyright owner has sold or otherwise transferred ownership of a particular copy of a work, the owner of that copy may dispose of it without the copyright owner's further permission, for example, by giving it away or even by reselling it. Another right which is

achieving wider and wider recognition, including in the TRIPS Agreement, is the right to authorize rental of copies of certain categories of works, such as musical works included in phonograms, audiovisual works, and computer programs. The right of rental is justified because technological advances have made it very easy to copy these types of works; experience in some countries has shown that copies were made by customers of rental shops, and therefore, that the right to control rental practices was necessary in order to prevent abuse of the copyright owner's right of reproduction. Finally, some copyright laws include a right to control importation of copies as a means of preventing erosion of the principle of territoriality of copyright; that is, the legitimate economic interests of the copyright owner would be endangered if he could not exercise the rights of reproduction and distribution on a territorial basis.

25. There are some acts of reproducing a work which are exceptions to the general rule, because they do not require the authorization of the author or other owner of rights; these are known as "limitations" on rights. The subject of limitations on rights will be discussed later in this presentation, but it bears mention here that an area of major concern at present relates to the scope of a limitation, traditionally present in copyright laws, which allows individuals to make single copies of works for private, personal and non-commercial purposes. The emergence of digital technology, which creates the possibility of making high-quality, unauthorized copies of works which are virtually indistinguishable from the source (and thus a perfect substitute for the purchase of, or other legitimate access to, authorized copies), has called into question the continued justification for such a limitation on the right of reproduction.

b. Rights of public performance, broadcasting and communication to the public

26. Under numerous national laws, a "public performance" is considered any performance of a work at a place where the public is or can be present, or at a place not open to the public, but where a substantial number of persons outside the normal circle of a family and its closest social acquaintances is present. On the basis of the right of public performance, the author or other owner of copyright may authorize live performances of a work, such as the presentation of a play in a theater or an orchestra performance of a symphony in a concert hall. Public performance also includes performance by means of recordings; thus, musical works embodied in phonograms are considered "publicly performed" when the phonograms are played over amplification equipment in such places as discotheques, airplanes, and shopping malls.

27. The right of "broadcasting" covers the transmission by wireless means for public reception of sounds or of images and sounds, whether by radio, television, or satellite. When a work is "communicated to the public," a signal is distributed, by wire or wireless means, which can be received only by persons who possess the equipment necessary to decode the signal. An example of "communication to the public" is cable transmission.

28. Under the Berne Convention, authors have the exclusive right of authorizing public performance, broadcasting and communication to the public of their

works. Under some national laws, the exclusive right of the author or other owner of rights to authorize broadcasting is replaced, in certain circumstances, by a right to equitable remuneration, although such a limitation on the broadcasting right is less and less common.

29. In recent years, the rights of broadcasting, communication to the public and public performance have been the subject of much discussion. New questions have arisen as a result of technological developments, in particular digital technology, which has produced what is referred to as the "convergence" of telecommunications and computer technology. These developments have blurred the legal distinctions between the traditional forms of making works available to the public by incorporeal means, such as broadcasting, communication to the public and public performance. Discussions will continue in an effort to adapt the legal definitions of such uses to new technological and commercial realities.

c.   Translation and adaptation rights

30. The acts of translating or adapting a work protected by copyright also require the authorization of the owner of rights. "Translation" means the expression of a work in a language other than that of the original version. "Adaptation" is generally understood as the modification of a work to create another work, for example adapting a novel to make a motion picture, or the modification of a work to make it suitable for different conditions of exploitation, e.g., by adapting an instructional textbook originally prepared for higher education into an instructional textbook intended for students at a lower level.

31. Translations and adaptations are works protected by copyright. Therefore, in order to reproduce and publish a translation or adaptation, authorization must be obtained from both the owner of the copyright in the original work and of the owner of copyright in the translation or adaptation.

32. In recent years, the scope of the right of adaptation has been the subject of discussion, because of the increased possibilities for adapting and transforming works which are embodied in digital format. With digital technology, manipulation of text, sound and images by the user is quick and easy; discussions have focused on the appropriate balance between the rights of the author to control the integrity of the work by authorizing modifications, on the one hand, and the rights of users to make changes which seem to be part of a normal use of works in digital format, on the other hand.

d.   Moral rights

33. The Berne Convention requires Member countries to grant to authors: (i) the right to claim authorship of the work (sometimes called the right of "paternity"); and (ii) the right to object to any distortion, mutilation or other modification of, or other derogatory action in relation to, the work which would be prejudicial to the author's honor or reputation (sometimes called the right of "integrity"). These rights, which are generally known as the moral rights of authors, are required to be independent of the economic rights and to remain with the author

even after he has transferred his economic rights. It is worth noting that moral rights are only accorded to human authors; even if someone else is the owner of economic rights in a work (for example, a film producer or a publisher), only the individual creator has moral interests at stake.

3. Limitations on Rights

34. The first limitation is the exclusion from copyright protection of certain categories of works. In some countries, works are excluded from protection if they are not fixed in tangible form; for example, a work of choreography would only be protected once the movements were written down in dance notation or recorded on videotape. In some (but not all) countries, moreover, the texts of laws, court and administrative decisions are excluded from copyright protection.

35. The second category of limitations on the rights of authors and other owners of copyright concerns particular acts of exploitation, normally requiring the authorization of the owner of rights, which may, under circumstances specified in the law, be done without authorization. There are two basic types of limitations in this category: (1) "free uses," which are acts of exploitation of works which may be carried out without authorization and without an obligation to compensate the owner of rights for the use, and (2) "non-voluntary licenses", under which the acts of exploitation may be carried out without authorization, but with the obligation to compensate the owner of rights.

36. Examples of free uses include the making of quotations from a protected work, provided that the source of the quotation, including the name of the author, is mentioned and that the extent of the quotation is compatible with fair practice; use of works by way of illustration for teaching purposes; and use of works for the purpose of news reporting. In respect of a free use for reproduction, the Berne Convention contains a general rule, rather than an explicit limitation: Article 9(2) provides that member States may provide for free reproduction in "special cases" where the acts do not conflict with normal exploitation of the work and do not unreasonably prejudice the legitimate interests of the author. As noted above, numerous laws contain provisions allowing reproduction of a work exclusively for the personal, private and non-commercial use of human individuals; the ease and quality of individual copying made possible by recent technology has led some countries to narrow the scope of such provisions, including through systems which allow certain copying but incorporate a mechanism for payment to owners of rights for the prejudice to their economic interests resulting from the copying.

37. In addition to specific free uses enumerated in national laws, the laws of some countries recognize the concept known as "fair use" or "fair dealing", which allows use of works without the authorization of the owner of rights, taking into account factors such as the following: the nature and purpose of the use, including whether it is for commercial purposes; the nature of the work used; the amount of the work used in relation to the work as a whole; and the likely effect of the use on the potential commercial value of the work.

38. As noted above, "non-voluntary licenses" allow use of works in certain circumstances without the authorization of the owner of rights, but require that compensation be paid in respect of the use. Such licenses are called "non-voluntary" because they are allowed in the law, and do not result from the exercise of the exclusive right of the copyright owner to authorize particular acts. Nonvoluntary licenses were usually created in circumstances where a new technology for the dissemination of works to the public had emerged, and where the national legislator feared that owners of rights would prevent the development of the new technology by refusing to authorize use of works. This was true of two non-voluntary licenses recognized in the Berne Convention, which allow the mechanical reproduction of musical works and broadcasting. It should be noted, however, that the justification for nonvoluntary licenses is called increasingly into question, since effective alternatives now exist for making works available to the public based on authorizations given by the owners of rights, including in the form of collective management of rights.

4.   Duration of Copyright

39. Copyright does not continue indefinitely. The law provides for a period of time, a duration, during which the rights of the copyright owner exist. The period or duration of copyright begins from the moment when the work has been created, or, under some national laws, when it has been expressed in a tangible form. The period of duration continues, in general, until some time after the death of the author. The purpose of this provision in the law is to enable the author's successors to benefit economically from exploitation of the work after the author's death.

40. In countries which are party to the Berne Convention, and in many other countries, the duration of copyright provided for by national law is, as a general rule, the life of the author and not less than 50 years after his death. The Berne Convention also establishes periods of protection for works in respect of which the duration cannot be based on the life of a single human author, for example, anonymous, posthumous and cinematographic works. It should be noted that a trend exists in certain national laws toward lengthening of the duration of copyright. For example, a recent directive of the European Union requires that, as from July 1, 1995, the duration of copyright under the national laws of the member States be fixed at 70 years following the death of the author.

Andrew Gowers, *Review of Intellectual Property*[3] (Norwich, UK: HM Treasury, 2006)

(See page 16 for Endnotes.)

DEFINITION

WHAT IS INTELLECTUAL PROPERTY?

1.1 Property is simply a bundle of rights to own, use and prevent others from using something, for example a plot of land, a car or a house. Intellectual Property (IP) is a bundle of rights that protects applications of ideas and information that have commercial value.[1] IP rights give creators certain exclusive rights over the knowledge and information they create (e.g. the text of a book) to prevent others using it without permission.

Knowledge is non-rivalrous

1.2 Unlike physical property, knowledge, ideas and creations are partial 'public goods'. Knowledge is inherently non-rivalrous. That means one person's possession, use and enjoyment of the good is not diminished by another's possession, use and enjoyment of the good. As Thomas Jefferson said: "he who receives an idea from me, receives instruction himself without lessening mine ... as he who lights his taper at mine, receives light without darkening me".[2] By contrast, physical property is typically rivalrous, with one person's consumption preventing simultaneous consumption by another. Privatising property gives rights over it to a legal individual, creating a legal barrier which prevents others from accessing it. IP confers a set of time-limited legal rights over the expression and use of certain ideas. Although the knowledge protected by the IP remains non-rivalrous, the legal force of IP rights prevents others from using it.

1.3 IP serves three principal functions: to incentivise knowledge (and hence wealth) creation; to accumulate knowledge in a culture; and to protect a distinctive identity. But those rights must be balanced in order to achieve these three aims. Listening to the radio, buying a branded product, taking a medicine and storing food in a fridge are all possible because inventions and creations have been incentivised through the IP system.

IP rights provide incentives to create knowledge

1.4 Ideas are expensive to produce but cheap to copy. The fixed costs of producing knowledge are high. Hollywood blockbusters can costs hundreds of millions of dollars to make and R&D for drugs can cost billions of pounds. At the same time, the marginal costs of production, both for drugs and for digital files, are very low. Without protection, others will free ride on the creator's initial investment and sell the invention or creation at a much lower cost. If the innovator

---

3   (London, Nov. 2006), online: <http://www.hm-treasury.gov.uk/media/53F/C8/pbr06_gowers_report_755.pdf>.

knows that someone else can do this easily, there will be no financial incentive to innovate in the first instance. Clearly, wealth generation is only one motivation for creativity. For example, Wilfred Owen's poetry written during the First World War was motivated by a desire to communicate his experience of war. But without protection there would be no economic incentive to fund innovation or creativity.

1.5   IP rights create legal barriers to accessing or using knowledge or information by granting exclusive rights to inventors and creators. These exclusive rights prevent others from free riding on investment and enable the rights owner to exploit their knowledge or creativity on the market — thus creating incentives to innovate.

IP rights help to develop public knowledge

1.6   As every creator 'stands on the shoulders of giants', it follows that the more knowledge that is available, the more others can develop and progress. Much of the value from the inventions and creativity protected by IP can only be realised if that knowledge is widely accessible to others. To secure an IP right, the idea must be made public, thereby adding to the common stock of knowledge available for progress.

1.7   Largely for this reason, IP rights are more limited than physical property rights. Patent applications are required to 'lay open' the details of an invention as a condition of grant and the requirement of disclosure enables others to improve upon existing inventions. After the patent protection ends, the invention becomes public. For example, Aspirin was patented in 1899 by the pharmaceutical company Bayer and became a proprietary drug for treating headaches. The structure of the molecule was published along with the patent, but only the company owning the patent had the right to manufacture the drug. The patent expired in 1917 and its formula is now publicly and freely available, allowing research, manufacture or sale of Aspirin by anyone. If IP rights do not sufficiently secure the ownership of the invention, either the investment will not be made or alternative tools, such as trade secrets, will be used. In either case, the public stock of knowledge available for future inventors and creators is diminished.

The costs of IP and the need for balance

IP rights entail a trade-off

1.8   The very essence of IP rights entails a trade-off. On the one hand, IP rights provide economic incentives to innovate, but on the other, the exclusive rights that they confer to achieve this allow monopoly prices and associated welfare losses and prevent access by other innovators. In the short run, this information is largely privatised. In the long run, information protected by IP rights falls into the public domain and enables follow-on innovation. So there is a trade-off between incentives on one side and costs to consumers and limited access for follow-on innovators on the other. It is therefore crucial to have the right balance in the system.

1.9 Achieving this balance is made more difficult by the vocabulary used to discuss IP policy and practice. Copyright infringement through unauthorised copying and distribution of music and video across the Internet is likened to stealing by some, and to sharing by others. Those who seek to prevent others from using a patented invention without permission are branded 'trolls'. Those who copy and distribute material illegally are called 'pirates'. And the problem of 'orphan' works, which arises where copyright owners are untraceable, perhaps provokes an easy sympathy.

WHAT ARE THE FORMS OF INTELLECTUAL PROPERTY?

1.10 Several different forms of IP rights have evolved to protect different applications of knowledge. The four most common are patents, copyright, designs and trade marks; Chart 1.1 summarises the applications to which different rights apply. In practice the situation is more complex, encompassing different forms of a right (e.g. unregistered and registered designs), and some other rights that are of their own kind (e.g. semi-conductor rights). These rights are described in more detail below.

Patents protect useful ideas

1.11 A patent is a set of exclusive rights granted by the state to a person for a fixed period of time (twenty years in the UK) in exchange for the regulated, public disclosure of certain details of an invention. The exclusive right granted to a patentee is a negative right that prevents others from making, using, selling, offering to sell or importing the claimed invention. However, the right itself does not give the patentee the right to make, use or sell the invention, and the patentee must still comply with other laws and regulations. Products eligible for patent protection must:

- be novel; the invention must never have been made public in any way, anywhere in the world, before the priority date (normally the date on which an application for a patent is filed);

- involve an inventive step; an invention involves an inventive step if, when compared with what is already known, it would not be obvious to someone skilled in the relevant art;

- be capable of industrial application; an invention must be capable of being made or used in some kind of industry; and

- not be 'excluded'; an invention is not patentable if it is: a discovery; a scientific theory or mathematical method; an aesthetic creation such as a literary, dramatic or artistic work; a scheme or method for performing a mental act, games or business methods; the presentation of information; or a computer program; but these things are only excluded when the claim relates to them 'as such'.

1.12 The requirements that an invention must meet in order to be patentable aim to achieve the balance between access and incentive described above. For example, a mathematical theory might be useful and capable of industrial application, as in recent advances in number theory for cryptography, but it would be unpatentable because of the potential benefits that might accrue from the basic 'building blocks' of research being publicly available.

. . .

Copyright protects original expression

1.14 Where a work is protected by copyright it cannot legally be reproduced, distributed, communicated to the public, lent, rented out or publicly performed without the consent of the owner. Copyright subsists in a wide range of creative or artistic forms or 'works', including poems, plays and other literary works, movies, choreographic works, musical compositions, audio recordings, paintings, drawings, sculptures, software, radio and television broadcasts.

1.15 There is no official register for copyright in the UK. Copyright comes into effect automatically and without any necessary process as soon as something that can be protected is created and 'fixed' in some way, e.g. on paper, on film, as a sound recording, or as an electronic record on the Internet. Copyright law covers the way in which the work is expressed, rather than the idea behind the work. So Dan Brown's *The Da Vinci Code* was recently found not to have infringed the copyright of an earlier book which contained many of the theories found in *The Da Vinci Code*. Drawing on ideas of other copyrighted works does not infringe those copyrights.

1.16 Exceptions to copyright exist to rectify two problems. The first is transaction costs. There are uses of copyright protected material for which it would be too costly and too time consuming to clear the rights, for example in a book review. Second, there are issues of equity. Copyright prevents the copying and communication of literary works. In the absence of exceptions, copying a text into Braille would be infringing copyright. To deal with such cases 'fair dealing' legislation exists, which creates a space in which it is not illegal to infringe copyright. Exemptions include: news reporting and criticism; copying for blind users; copying for non-commercial private research under library privilege; copying for preservation; and copying and communication for education.

History of copyright

1.17 Copyright was first established in the Statute of Anne in 1710, which declared that copyright comes into existence with the act of composition by an author[3] and is accorded to the author. The author could then transfer their right to a publisher for fourteen years, which could be extended for another fourteen years should the author still be alive. In 1774, the House of Lords ruled in *Donaldson v. Beckett* that perpetual copyright was illegal: they concluded that no natural law of copyright existed and that copyright was a purely statutory right created for the utilitarian purpose of encouraging literary efforts.[4] However, throughout the nineteenth and twentieth centuries, copyright was extended and the scope of protection was broadened under pressure from publishers and as a result of international harmonisation. The principal piece of domestic legislation currently governing copyright is the Copyright, Designs and Patents Act 1988.

Trade marks protect distinctive identity

1.18 A trade mark is a badge of origin for goods or services; it can be a word, name, logo, colour, sound or shape. Once registered it gives the right to prevent others from using the same or similar marks on the same or similar products. By providing a distinctive identity for a product or service, trade marks lower the search costs for consumers by providing them with information about the nature and quality of the product; this also gives brands an incentive to build up good reputations and to develop brand loyalty.

1.19 Trade marks lose protection when they cease being used or become generic, i.e. when a brand name comes to stand for a general class of items. For example 'escalator' and 'gramophone' were both marks that were afforded protection. In Austria, Sony no longer has exclusive rights to the term 'Walkman', and in Australia 'Linux' is no longer eligible for protection. Firms are keen for their trade marks not to become generic: Google recently wrote to media outlets warning against inappropriate use of its trade mark for fear of losing protection for its brand.

1.20 Marking of goods for various purposes, including distinguishing them from those of other traders, dates back to ancient times. In the nineteenth century people began to think of marks, which had become distinctive to a trader's goods and so attracted valuable goodwill, as a type of property. The Trade Marks Act 1905 gave the first statutory definition of a 'trade mark'. The principal legislation governing UK trade marks is the Trade Marks Act 1994.[5]

. . .

OTHER METHODS OF INCENTIVISE INNOVATION

1.40 While this report principally deals with IP rights, they are only one method of spurring innovation. As Table 1.1 below indicates, other commercial strategies like confidentiality agreements and being first to market are often perceived to be more important. The examples given below are important not only in their own right, but also because they illustrate the balance that IP strikes (as described earlier in the chapter) between private incentives and public accessibility.

Secrecy

1.41 The main mechanism used as an alternative to formal IP is the trade secret. Examples of knowledge protected by trade secrets include: a formula; practice; process; pattern; or compilation of information which is protected so that the holder can gain economic benefits derived from the secrecy of the information. Unlike patents, designs or copyright, trade secrets are protected without any disclosure. In addition, reasonable efforts must be taken to keep the information a secret, such as Non-Disclosure Agreements for new employees. The most famous example of a trade secret is Coca-Cola, which has not patented its recipe. While there are provisions to protect the owner if the secret is uncovered by improper or unlawful means, the state provides little protection if the trade secret is exposed through reverse engineering or independent duplication.

. . .

Endnotes to Gowers Review of Intellectual Property

1   Intellectual Property: Patents, Copyright, Trade Marks and Allied Rights, Cornish W. and Llewelyn D., 2003.
2   Letter to Isaac McPherson, Jefferson T., 13 August 1813.
3   The Reading Nation in the Romantic Period, St Clair W., 2004.
4   (1774) 4 EURR 2407 Law Professors' Amici Brief in "MPAA v. 2600" CaseBrief Amicus Curiae in Support of Defendants-Appellants, Supporting Reversal; Universal v. Reimerdes (Jan. 26, 2001) see Understanding the Copyright Clause, Patterson L.R., *Journal of the Copyright Society*, 2000.
5   In 1995 the European Community introduced Community Trade Marks with (EC) Regulation No. 40/94 on the Community Trade Mark.

Economic Council of Canada, *Report on Intellectual and Industrial Property*, (Ottawa: Industry Canada, 1971)

(See page 21 for Endnotes.)

. . .

CHAPTER 2

INNOVATION, INFORMATION AND KNOWLEDGE

In order for its economy to grow and develop satisfactorily, a society must be innovative; to be innovative, it must be well-informed; and to be well-informed, it must be good at the production, distribution and use of knowledge. This statement can be amplified and qualified in a number of ways: knowledge is desirable for other ends besides economic growth and development, and knowledge alone does not guarantee innovation and, economic advancement. The statement nevertheless expresses a set of relationships that is of great significance for economic policy and that constitutes both a starting point and a necessary background and context for the present Report.

CHAPTER 3

ECONOMIC SIGNIFICANCE OF INTELLECTUAL AND INDUSTRIAL PROPERTY

Patents, copyrights, trademarks and registered industrial designs are part of a class of policy tools used to improve society's "total information system" in sectors in which the production and distribution of knowledge might otherwise be inadequate. They are, in short, incentive devices, designed to elicit more of certain kinds of "learning" or knowledge creation and certain kinds of knowledge processing. In the case of patents and registered industrial designs, the knowledge to be produced is not in itself the ultimate objective, but is rather an "intermediate input". It must be incorporated into a "total innovative process" and utilized as technical information in order that out of the succession of research, development, invention, pilot plant, etc., there eventually comes a new or improved product or process capable of benefiting society.

In the case of copyright it is the conveyance of information to a broader public that is aimed at — the presentation of knowledge in such highly processed and accessible forms as books, plays, films and musical compositions. Another innovative process, running from author to publisher to printer to bookseller, is required. Trademarks also aim at the presentation of information — in this case, flows of product information to final consumers and other buyers. These flows are chiefly valuable in helping buyers to achieve greater confidence and a saving of time in their purchases of goods and services.

All four of these devices work in essentially the same way. The state creates an incentive for individuals and firms to do more of certain things by granting them limited rights in intangibles — in ideas, expressions of ideas and the goodwill of enterprises.

It is sometimes argued that in doing this, the state is not merely granting rights for incentive purposes, but is instead defining, validating and protecting fundamental rights that were in some sense already there. The character of the rights involved in intellectual and industrial property is not an easy question, and countries have differed in the legal approaches that they have taken to it. The economic nature of these rights is discussed somewhat further in Appendix A. Suffice it to say here that the "fundamental-rights" view of intellectual and industrial property is difficult to square with the history of these laws in Britain and Canada (see notably the discussion of the origins of British and Canadian copyright law at the beginning of Chapter 7), or with the scope of their application in almost any country where they exist. For example, patent, copyright and design protection has always been specifically limited in time, as would presumably not be the case if the fundamental-rights view was carried as far as its own logic and internal consistency would allow it to be taken. Again, many highly important areas of knowledge production and processing have always been excluded from the grant of rights. No patent was ever issued, for instance, on Einstein's theory of relativity or on the General Motors divisional system of large-scale business organization, although each in its sphere was an epoch-making discovery.

From a fundamental-rights viewpoint and possibly other viewpoints, this may all look exceedingly messy and inconsistent; but when the incentive viewpoint is adopted, much of the seeming inconsistency drops away. What society appears to do is to use the policy instrument of intellectual and industrial property rights in certain parts only of the total information system — in parts where there is widely agreed to be a serious problem of underproduction and underprocessing of knowledge, and where this particular kind of incentive, by itself or in association with others, seems likely to be an appropriate means of improving the situation.

. . .

The copyright system is a way of dealing with the same problem in another area. The author and publisher of a book or other work commit resources to the processing of knowledge into widely accessible form; but if neither copyright nor a substitute for it exists, and if copying technology permits other persons profitably to copy the book and make no contribution to the original costs of the author and first publisher, the latter may not consider the game worth the candle. Similar logic supports the laws protecting industrial designs and trademarks.

The amount of incentive provided to knowledge production and information processing by the laws of intellectual and industrial property, as compared with the situation in their absence, is not a measurable quantity. Clearly, however, it varies a great deal from case to case, depending on many factors. If an invention can easily be kept secret, patent protection will not have much effect on the incentive to produce it and may not indeed be sought. Much also hangs on the likely strength of demand for the projected product or process. If a process is peculiar to the needs of one firm, or if a new product is likely to enjoy only a modest market, patent protection may provide little extra incentive to go ahead. The case is obviously quite different, however, if at the end of the line are foreseen a booming demand and a cluster of envious competitors.

Society, through government, normally provides incentives to private parties in the hope of receiving benefits, and this is true in the present instance. A better dynamic allocation of resources is the goal, with a larger proportion of productive factors flowing into certain kinds of knowledge production and processing and into associated innovative investments. But most incentive policies have significant social costs as well as benefits, and this too is clearly true here. All of the principal forms of intellectual and industrial property have long been recognized to have such costs, and good policy-making requires that these be taken into account along with the benefits. They should be borne in mind when deciding, firstly, whether a sector of the total information system stands in need of state-provided incentives, and secondly, if it does, what particular kinds of incentive would be most suitable.

The laws of intellectual and industrial property are really a kind of compromise in the face of a dilemma. Ideally, a total information system should work rapidly and efficaciously both on the learning and knowledge-producing side and on the side of distribution and use. Ideally, the moment a valuable invention is placed in a store of knowledge anywhere in Canada, it should be made fully available — at least, to the extent justified when the cost of moving and relearning the knowledge by the most efficient available means is taken into account — to every Canadian enterprise whose economic performance might be improved by it. A quick and wide spreading of benefits among manufacturers, consumers and others would then be assured. The problem is how to do this while preserving an acceptable rate of knowledge production. Intellectual and industrial property laws come down on the side of promoting knowledge production, while deliberately imposing some check on knowledge use (compared with what would happen in a wide-open, non-proprietary free-for-all) in order to provide more incentive at the production stage.

In a description of the benefits and costs to society of the patent system and other types of intellectual and industrial property, the benefits may be more easily summarized because they are more obvious. It is widely accepted that parts of the total information system do suffer from an underlying tendency towards under-production. The provision of incentives can rectify this and the gains of more production can be readily perceived. That is, more of certain kinds of knowledge will be produced; more of certain kinds of information-processing will take place; more of certain kinds of innovation will occur. Greater numbers of new and better-designed products and processes and more book titles and films, etc., will appear. All this will tend to promote the achievement of a number of social goals.

But there is, inevitably, another side to the story, unfavourable to the attainment of social goals. The granting of limited monopoly rights has more than one kind of consequence. As already indicated, the incentive to knowledge production and information processing is achieved by means of a sacrifice on the distributional side. The higher returns provided to knowledge producers and processors and their innovative associates arise from higher prices to the users of the products involved (and therefore in smaller sales and output of them) than would prevail under other circumstances. Individually, each of the new books, films and other products will be scarcer and more expensive than it would be if some more efficient and less socially costly form of incentive could be brought into play.

There is a sense in which one can say that an optimally "efficient" law of intellectual and industrial property would be highly flexible, tailoring the term and other characteristics of each patent or other grant of right to the incentive needs of each recipient. More powerful incentives (and therefore more extensive rights) might be deemed necessary in some fields than in others. However, this would involve formidable administrative difficulties and costs,[1] and it is probably no coincidence that while most countries' systems contain provisions for the modification of rights under certain circumstances (e.g. via compulsory licensing), they are not to any important extent "tailored" in the fashion described above. Where countries wish to favour particular areas of knowledge production and innovation, they normally use other methods.[2]

As things stand, the costs and uncertainties of incentives under intellectual and industrial property laws, including the difficulty of working out on average an appropriate set of limitations on the grant of exclusive rights, have led some informed observers to consider such drastic steps as the total abandonment of the patent system in favour of other incentive devices. We do not in this Report advocate the abandonment by Canada of patents or any of the other three classes of intellectual and industrial property. It seems to us that they have a useful role to play in the future, particularly if they can be more accurately aimed at the chief social and economic goals towards which they are in principle directed. We do, however, take into account, at appropriate points, their costs and their benefits, and the various available alternatives to them. Neither patents nor any other single incentive device should be regarded as sacred, for this will surely impede the achievement of a good mixture of policies.

. . .

Before proceeding to recommendations regarding copyright, a word is in order about what may be termed the "noneconomic" aspects and implications of the subject. We are fully conscious that copyright relates more to the cultural and artistic side of life than does any other form of intellectual and industrial property. We gave some attention to this side of life in our broad survey of innovation and information in Chapter 2, and it has not been forgotten in the formulation of recommendations for the present chapter.

The problem is essentially one of bringing into the analysis, in some workable way, a number of the more important noneconomic goals and aspirations that appear to be widely held by Canadians, even though these goals have not yet been subjected to nearly as much thoughtful specification and systematic study as they deserve to be. What we have done on the basis of considerable, though necessarily largely impressionistic, evidence is to wrap these various goals and aspirations into one and assume that most Canadians desire for their country (full account being taken of its fundamentally bilingual and bicultural character) a strong and distinctive cultural identity. We have further assumed that, for this, most Canadians would be willing to pay some as yet undetermined economic price.

We would immediately add to this assumption an important qualification to the effect that the cultural identity sought should as quickly as possible become a sturdy and viable entity, capable of holding its own in the world without shame or inordinate special protection. A member of his creative staff once said of a certain television producer, "He doesn't want it good, he wants it Thursday." We assume that most Canadian information-users want the domestic portion of their requirements to be both Canadian and good. To reduce the matter to a concrete example, any decision-maker responsible for foisting upon Canadian students a third-rate textbook simply because it is written and produced in Canada should consider himself overdue for an interview with his conscience and a careful contemplation of the long forward shadow cast by the quality of education. More generally, he might think too of the points made earlier about the feedback characteristics of information flows and knowledge production. Low-grade cultural parochialism does no service to the cause of a durable and creative Canadian nationalism — quite the contrary.

It is sometimes implied that where cultural goals are important, economic analysis, with its base associations of the market place, should take a back seat. But this involves a serious misconception of the proper and useful role of economic analysis. It may well be true that in the final analysis, economics is much more concerned with means than with ends, and that the really fundamental "achievement goals" of a society are largely, if not wholly, noneconomic in nature. It is also true, however, that, in practice, means can have an enormous influence on ends, whether for good or ill, and that as a result the systematic analysis of economic means is indispensable both in the specification of social goals and the planning of how to achieve them. In the case of cultural goals, among others, economic analysis can be of great help in bringing about a clearer identification of the goals in the first place, and then in planning for their attainment by the shortest, least costly and most perseverance-inducing route.

It is particularly important that the relevance of cultural goals in a policy-planning situation should not be used as a smoke screen behind which material interests and conflicts between private and social interests are allowed to shelter unexamined. In an increasingly service-oriented and knowledge-based society, cultural matters in the broadest sense are to a growing extent what economic life is all about. They must not fail to be studied in their economic as well as their other aspects.

Endnotes to Economic Council of Canada, *Report on Intellectual and Industrial Property*, 1971

1   If one had all the information necessary to make such a system work, one would probably, in the process, have invented a new incentive system better than the patent system or any of the alternatives to it that have been suggested up to now. But the cost of obtaining that much information might well be prohibitive.

2   For example, if a country wished to encourage innovations such as pollution-control devices, with strongly positive "external" effects on the quality of life, ...

Industry Canada & Canadian Heritage, *Framework for Copyright Reform*[4] (Ottawa: Industry Canada, 2001)

Economic Policy Objective

The *Copyright Act* is an important framework law that affects many sectors of the Canadian economy. It represents a powerful lever to promote innovation, entrepreneurship and success in the new economy. Copyright protection rewards the creation and dissemination of knowledge and cultural content, and facilitates access to this knowledge and content.

The importance of copyright is highlighted in the January 2001 Speech from the Throne, where the Government indicated that it:

> *"will provide better copyright protection for new ideas and knowledge [...] It will ensure that Canadian laws and regulations remain among the most modern and progressive in the world, including those for intellectual property and competitiveness. [...] The focus of our cultural policies for the future must be on excellence in the creative process, diverse Canadian content, and access to the arts and heritage for all Canadians."*

The *Copyright Act* impacts on the development of Internet content, the use of electronic commerce by business and consumers, and on the growth of a wide range of cultural and information-based industries. In 2000, the gross domestic product (GDP) of the copyright-related sectors (publishing, film, sound recording, broadcasting, visual arts, software, etc) was estimated at \$65.9B,

---

4   (Ottawa: Industry Canada, 2001), online: Industry Canada <http://strategis.ic.gc.ca/epic/internet/incrp-prda.nsf/en/rp01101e.html>.

accounting for 7.4% of Canadian GDP. Between 1992 and 2000, these sectors grew at an average annual rate of 6.6%, compared to 3.3% for the rest of the Canadian economy. Together, they represent the third most important contributor to Canada's economic growth.

Cultural Policy Objective

The *Copyright Act* provides protection to creators and other rights holders in the form of exclusive rights over the communication, reproduction and other uses of their works. It is therefore seen as the foundation for creative endeavour. The creation of Canadian cultural content and the availability of diverse choices for Canadians depend on adequate copyright protection and effective enforcement and administration of copyright.

The Government is committed to ensuring that copyright law promotes both the creation and the dissemination of works. The objective of the *Copyright Act* is also to ensure appropriate access for all Canadians to works that enhance the cultural experience and enrich the Canadian social fabric. Access is assured through various means: by establishing simple rights clearance mechanisms; by devising alternate schemes that recognize copyright, e.g. the private copying regime; by allowing specific exemptions to aid users such as libraries, schools and archives to fulfill their vital institutional roles in Canadian society; and by other means that favour the circulation of information and cultural content for and by Canadians. Access is therefore an important public policy objective to consider when reviewing the copyright framework.

Another important public policy consideration for the Government is Canada's international commitments in relation to copyright. In an increasingly interconnected world where the borders between markets are rapidly diminishing, Canada must ensure that its copyright law promotes appropriate availability of copyright works by taking into account the level of protection as defined by international agreements.

Canadian Heritage, *The Economic Contribution of Copyright Industries to the Canadian Economy by Wall Communications Inc.*[5] (Ottawa: Industry Canada, 2004)

The Value Added (GDP) of Canadian Copyright Based Industries

Much like the findings in studies from other countries, Canada's copyright-based industries have seen a significant growth in the last decade. Core CB industries have grown from a value-added of $19,598 million dollars in 1991 to $39,561 million in 2002. When non-core industries are added, the totals become $26,987 million in 1991 and $53,408 million in 2002.

---

5   (Ottawa: Canadian Heritage, 2004), online: Canadian Heritage <http://www.pch.gc.ca/progs/ac-ca/progs/pda-cpb/pubs/index>.

Calculated as a percentage of economy-wide GDP, CB industries have steadily increased their contribution to the economy. The 1991 contribution of 3.87% grew to 5.38% by 2002.

. . .

Two conclusions can be drawn when comparing growth in the CB industries with growth in the overall economy. First, the variability in growth from year to year is more extreme in the CB industries. Second, average annual rate of growth for the CB industries was approximately twice the rate of the general economy. Overall, the CB industries grew at an average annual rate of 6.46% between 1991 and 2002. This compares with an economy-wide average annual growth over the period of 3.27%.

Comparing the contribution of CB industries to other industries, CB industries now provide a significant contribution to overall GDP, contributing more than accommodation and food, agriculture, or mining.

Contribution of Copyright Based Industries
Compared to Selected Other Industries, 2002

Industry	2002 Annual Growth Rate	GDP 1997 Chained $
Copyright Based	6.5 %	53.4 billion
Agriculture, Forestry, Fishing and Hunting	-3.4 %	20.5 billion
Mining and Oil and Gas Extraction	1.9 %	37.4 billion
Utilities	4.2 %	28.3 billion
Accommodation and Food Services	4.7 %	23.5 billion
Retail Trade	1.9 %	53.9 billion

Source: The Daily, January 31, 2003 Statistics Canada, and Wall Communications Inc.

Employment in Copyright Based Industries

Much like the GDP data, the employment numbers reflect the increasing importance of CB industries to the overall economy. From roughly 500,000 employees in 1991, the CB industries reached almost 900,000 employees by 2002.

. . .

Compared to the Canadian economy, the CB industries outperformed the economy in general growing at more than three times the overall rate. Between 1991 and 2002, employment in the CB industries grew at about 5.3% while the national economy only grew at 1.4%. As should be expected, the growth rate of the economy displays less volatility than the CB industries.

2. Judicial Perspectives on Protecting Copyright

(a) Historical Perspective

Canadian copyright law has traditionally been built on the historical foundations and theoretical framework of UK copyright legislation, and in particular the UK 1911 *Copyright Act*. That legislation consistently protected the labours of authors either as an end in itself, or at the very least, as the primary goal of copyright.[6] Canadian copyright legislation historically was interpreted by the Supreme Court of Canada and other appellate courts as having the same purpose.[7] In this regard, the Act and its English counterpart have often been construed so as to protect the value of authors' copyrights in their works and to prevent persons from unfairly availing themselves of their labours without their consent. Under this perspective, authors' rights were interpreted broadly so that rights granted were not lightly defeated or affected by the rights or interests of others. The extracts that follow give some indication of the prevalence and significance, in common law copyright, of this philosophical (Lockean) commitment to protecting the fruits of the authors' labour against defendants who sought to reap what they did not sow. Divergent strands of reasoning can be discerned, however, in the judgments of the Lords in the next case, where concerns about the nature of authorship and the public interest also arise.

Walter v. Lane, [1900] A.C. 539 (U.K. H.L.)

Earl of Halsbury L.C., Lord Davey, Lord James of Hereford, Lord Brampton and Lord Robertson.

1900 Aug. 6.

The action was brought by the appellants, who were the proprietors of *The Times* newspaper, to restrain the respondent from publishing in book form speeches of Lord Rosebery delivered upon various occasions, which speeches, it was admitted, were taken without alteration from verbatim reports taken down in shorthand by reporters employed by the appellants for that purpose, and afterwards published by them in their newspaper.

It was admitted that the respondent had taken the speeches, without the knowledge or consent of the appellants, from the reports which appeared in *The Times*:

---

6   See, for example, *Ladbroke (Football) Ltd. v. William Hill (Football) Ltd.*, [1964] 1 All E.R. 465 (H.L.); *L.B. (Plastics) Ltd. v. Swish Products Ltd.*, [1979] R.P.C. 551 (U.K. H.L.); *Walter v. Lane*, [1900] A.C. 539 (U.K. H.L.); *MacMillan & Co. Ltd. v. Cooper* (1923), 40 T.L.R. 186 (India P.C.).

7   See, *Bishop v. Stevens*, [1990] 2 S.C.R. 467; *Théberge v. Galerie d'Art du Petit Champlain inc.*, [2002] S.C.R. 336, (at para.141); *Vigneux v. Canadian Performing Rights Society*, [1943] S.C.R. 348, reversed [1945] A.C. 108 (Canada P.C.); *Canadian Assn. of Broadcasters v. SOCAN* (1994), 58 C.P.R. (3d) 190 (Fed. C.A.).

That Lord Rosebery had taken no steps to retain his own copyright in the speeches:

That if the reporters were the "authors" within the meaning of the Copyright Act 1842, they had validly assigned their copyright in the reports to the appellants.

North, J, granted the injunction as prayed, but this judgment was reversed, as above mentioned, on the ground that a reporter who merely reproduced a verbatim report of the speech of another person was not the "author" of it, within the meaning of the Copyright Act 1842. The plaintiffs appealed.

EARL OF HALSBURY L.C.

My Lords, I should very much regret it if I were compelled to come to the conclusion that the state of the law permitted one man to make profit and to appropriate to himself the labour, skill, and capital of another. And it is not denied that in this case the defendant seeks to appropriate to himself what has been produced by the skill, labour, and capital of others. In the view I take of this case I think the law is strong enough to restrain what to my mind would be a grievous injustice. The law which I think restrains it is to be found in the Copyright Act, and that Act confers what it calls copyright — which means the right to multiply copies — which it confers on the author of books first published in this country.

That the publications in question, namely, reports of Lord Rosebery's speeches, are simply copies of what was first printed in *The Times* newspaper is not denied. And further, it has not been and cannot be denied that they were originally, as in The Times, a sheet or sheets of letterpress, and came within the definition of the Act as a book. The speeches, therefore, and the sheets of letterpress in which they were contained, were books first published in this country; and I confess upon looking at the definition and the right conferred I am wholly unable to discover why they are not protected by the statute from being pirated by unauthorized persons.

. . .

The question here is solely whether this book (to use the language of the statute), printed and published and existing as a book for the first time, can be copied by some one else than the producers of it (I avoid the use of the word "author"), by those who have not produced it themselves but have simply copied that which others have laboured to create by their own skill and expenditure.

My Lords, I cannot help thinking that underlying the argument which has been addressed to us there is something of the contention which was boldly made nearly half a century ago in the case of Maclean v. Moody in the Court of Session, where, relying on the preamble, the advocate argued that the object of the statute of Victoria was to encourage literary merit, that the intellectual labour constituting authorship was alone thereby protected, and that there could be no authorship without an author. Lord Deas refused to accept such an argument, and expressed the opinion that the Act did not confine the privilege to cases in which there was a known author. But it appears to me that, although it may be true that a preamble may be a guide to the general objects of the statute, it undoubtedly is unquestioned law that it can neither restrict nor limit express enactment. And though I think in these compositions there is literary merit and intellectual labour, yet the statute seems to me to require neither, nor originality either in thought or in language.

. . .

My Lords, if I have not insisted upon the skill and accuracy of those who produce in writing or print spoken words, it is not because I think the less of those qualities, but because, as I have endeavoured to point out, neither the one nor the other are conditions precedent to the right created by the statute. That right, in my view, is given by the statute to the first producer of a book, whether that book be wise or foolish, accurate or inaccurate, of literary merit or of no merit whatever.

I must notice one supposed difficulty in this view very persistently urged at the bar. It is said that in the view I have suggested there would be as many copyrights as reporters. I do not see the difficulty. Each reporter is entitled to report, and each undoubtedly would have a copyright in his own published report; but where is the difficulty? Suppose a favourite view — a dozen artists take, each independently, his own representation of it. Is there any reason why each should not have his own copyright? Or even a photograph, where each photograph, if taken from the same point and in the same state of the light, would be identical in all respects. There is of course no copyright in the view itself, but in the supposed picture or photograph there is. And in truth there is a confusion of thought between the difficulty of proof of the piracy and the existence of piracy. Here, as I have said before, no such difficulty arises, since it is admitted that the report of these speeches is not the result of independent labour, but is simply taken from *The Times*.

My Lords, I think the judgment of North J. was right, and that the only answer sought to be given to it by the Court of Appeal was the restricted use of the word "author" with which I have endeavoured to deal. I therefore move your Lordships that the judgment of the Court of Appeal be reversed with costs, and the judgment of North J. restored.

. . .

LORD DAVEY.

[The appellants] seek only to prevent the respondent from multiplying copies of their own report of the speech and availing himself for his own profit of the skill, labour, and expense by means of which that report was produced and published. ... In my opinion the reporter is the author of his own report. He it was who brought into existence in the form of a writing the piece of letterpress which the respondent has copied. I think also that he, and he alone, composed his report. The materials for his composition were his notes which were his own property aided to some extent by his memory and trained judgment. Owing to the perfection which the art of shorthand writing has attained in recent years, memory and judgment bear a less important part in the composition of a report of a speech than was formerly the case. But the question whether the composer has copyright in his report does not seem to me to depend on, or to vary inversely as, his skill in stenography. Nor, as it appears to me, does the fact that the subject matter of the report had been made public property, or that no originality or literary skill was demanded for the composition of the report, have anything to do with the matter.

. . . Copyright has nothing to do with the originality or literary merits of the author or composer. It may exist in the information given by a street directory: Kelly v. Morris or by a list of deeds of arrangement: Cate v. Devon and Exeter Constitutional Newspaper Co. or in a list of advertisements: Lamb v. Evans. I think those cases right, and the principle on which they proceed directly applicable to the present case. It was of course open to any other reporter to compose his own report of Lord Rosebery's speech, and to any other newspaper or book to publish that report; but it is a sound principle that a man shall not avail himself of another's skill, labour, and expense by copying the written product thereof. To quote the language of North J. in another case:

> "For the purposes of their own profit they desire to reap where they have not sown, and to take advantage of the labour and expenditure of the plaintiffs in procuring news for the purpose of saving labour and expense to themselves."

… For these reasons I agree with my noble and learned friend in thinking that the judgment of the Court of Appeal should be reversed, and that of North, J, restored.

LORD JAMES OF HEREFORD:

… Now what is it that a reporter does? Is he a mere scribe, does he produce original matter, or does he produce the something which I have mentioned which entitles him to be regarded as an author within the Act? I think that from a general point of view a reporter's art represents more than mere transcribing or writing from dictation. To follow so as to take down the words of an ordinary, and certainly of a rapid speaker, is an art requiring considerable training, and does not come within the knowledge of ordinary persons. Even amongst professional reporters many different degrees of skill exist. Some reporters can take down the words of a speaker however rapidly he speaks, others less practised or proficient cannot, as the term is, "keep up with" the rapid speaker. Apart from the dealing with the rapidity of speech, there are some reporters whose ears and thoughts and hands never fail them, and they therefore produce reports of complete accuracy. On the other hand, reporters less skilled may be so deficient in this quality of accuracy as to produce reports which certainly tend to perturb the speakers whom they have endeavoured to report. Thus there seems to be a degree of skill in one class of reporters over the other. Again, one reporter may possess knowledge apart from stenography which may confer upon him the power of producing a report not within the capability of another of the same calling. Supposing a speech were delivered in a language little used, such as Persian or Turkish, only a reporter acquainted with such a language would be able to report it. Does the work resulting from such special knowledge mean nothing? The proprietor of a journal may have paid highly for obtaining a special report of this almost unreportable speech. May he not make a claim for protection against a rival journalist who seeks to make equal use of the report thus obtained? It may also be that the report has been obtained under circumstances of peculiar difficulty on the one hand, or of advantageous conditions on the other. Thus, if a reporter attended a meeting of Anarchists intended to be secret and made public their speeches, or if in former times a man had secreted himself in one of the Houses of Parliament and taken down the words of different speakers, may it not be contended that the reporters were doing something more than merely transcribing? After taking such matters as those into consideration, I have after some doubt come to the conclusion that a reporter of a speech under the conditions existing in this case is the meritorious producer of the something necessary to constitute him an author within the meaning of the Copyright Act of 1842, and that, therefore, the judgment of the Court of Appeal should be reversed.

LORD BRAMPTON:

... The reporters who represented *The Times,* with whom alone I have now to deal, were undoubtedly gentlemen of education, great ability, and long and varied experience in the duties of their vocation. They wrote the descriptive parts of their reports from personal observation. The speeches they took down in shorthand, word for word, transcribed them verbatim in longhand, carefully corrected and revised and punctuated them, so that when they appeared in the columns of *The Times* they might, as perfectly as printed words could do, convey to the readers all that was to be seen or heard upon those occasions. From these reports all that appeared in *The Times* was first published to the world. It is obvious that the preparation of them involved considerable intellectual skill and brain labour, beyond the mere mechanical operation of writing. That the reports so published were "books" within the meaning of the Copyright Act is undisputed; the great contention throughout the case has been whether the reporters were the "authors" of them....

... I do not agree that the question of the authorship of a book depends upon the literary quality of it. If a person chooses (and many do) to compose and write a volume devoid of the faintest spark of literary or other merit, I see no legal reason why he should not, if he desires, become the first publisher of it, and register his copyright, worthless and insignificant as it would be. The statute has prescribed no standard of merit in a book as a condition to entitle its author to become the proprietor of copyright in it, and, even if such standard were prescribed, I should think that the merits of the book ought to be determined having regard to the contents of the book itself, without inquiring as to whether any of the component parts of it emanated from the brain of some person other than the author of the book. ...True it is that the reporter was not the author of the speech, but he was the composer and author of the book. Without his brain and handiwork the book would never have had existence, and the words of Lord Rosebery would have remained unrecorded save in the memories of the comparatively few who were present on those occasions. In the descriptive passages of his report the language is his own; and although, as regards the speeches, he has given great value to his work by introducing verbatim the language of Lord Rosebery, he was strictly within his rights in so doing, and was clearly acting with the full sanction of his lordship, in order that, by its publication in the *Times,* the thousands of readers of that journal might be truthfully and accurately informed of those intellectual and interesting utterances of Lord Rosebery which they had not been privileged to hear. I think, for the reasons which I have given, that the proprietors of the *Times* have copyright in the articles and reports in question. I am therefore of opinion that the judgment of the Court of Appeal should be reversed, and the decision of North, J, restored, with costs.

LORD ROBERTSON:

...The case before your Lordships is a case of shorthand reporting, pure and simple. It so happens that Lord Rosebery's speeches are so conceived and expressed as to require on the part of the reporter nothing but literal accuracy in order to their presentation to the public as literary compositions. In so saying I am in no way disparaging the gifts of the shorthand writer, and, as the nature of his work is really of the essence of the present controversy, I dwell on it for a moment. The reporters of the *Times* are educated gentlemen, as are many other practitioners of the art of stenography, while there are reporters less highly equipped in knowledge of literature and history. What is the difference between the educated and the less educated in reporting, let us say, Lord Rosebery? ... [T]he contribution which education enables the good reporter to make to the speech is of a purely negative kind—he does not interfere, but faithfully acts as conduit. In fact, the merit of the reports now before your Lordships is that they present the speaker's thoughts untinctured by the slightest trace or colour of the reporter's mind. These observations apply to the stage of taking down in shorthand what the speaker says. The next stage—copying out the notes—is purely clerical work. Now, I recognize the skill of the stenographer; I find that, for the reasons which I have mentioned, an educated man is the better qualified to be a faithful reporter. But I fail entirely to see how, in the widest sense of the term "author", we are in the region of authorship. A very striking illustration of the subject is obtained by remembering who, or rather what, is the rival of a good stenographer—it is the phonograph. In reporting the kind of speech of which I am speaking—the speech of allusion and of phrase—the phonograph, which has no literary taste, good or bad, and no intellect, great or small, will record Lord Rosebery's speeches better than the best of reporters. The appellants think that if the owner of a phonograph publishes the speech as taken down by the phonograph he is the author of the report and entitled to copyright. I should have thought (and think) this a *reductio ad absurdum* of the whole argument of the appellants. When it is remembered that there is no manner of composition, as the term is generally used, even in the sense of arrangement, by a shorthand reporter, I find it difficult to understand what attribute of an author belongs to him. Some of the judicial decisions have indeed applied the words of the Act to very pedestrian efforts of the mind. But, although time-tables and furniture catalogues are not great things, there has been structure and arrangement on the part of the maker. I think that the recording by stenography the words of another is in a different region from the making up a time-table. I do not say that it is lower or higher, but in a different plane, because there is no construction. …The word "author", occurring as it does, not in the preamble, but in the enacting section, seems to me to present a criterion consistent with the widest application of the Act to all who can claim, as embodying their own thought, whether humble or lofty, the letterpress of which they assert the authorship. The fact that the man who speaks in public is not a competitor with the reporter for copyright has not the slightest effect in altering the intellectual relation of the reporter to the words of the speech, nor does it render less inappropriate the result of holding the statute to confer on the stenographer a reward which has no relation whatever to his art. For these reasons I am unable to concur in the judgment proposed.

MacMillan & Co. Ltd. v. Cooper (1923), 40 T.L.R. 186 (India P.C.)

JUDICIAL COMMITTEE OF THE PRIVY COUNCIL

Lord Atkinson, Lord Shaw, Lord Wrenbury, Lord Carson and Sir Robert Younger

25, 26, 29, 30 October, 14 December 1923

LORD ATKINSON

Copyright is therefore a statutory right. Section 1(1) of the Act enacts in respect of what it may be acquired. Subsection (2) of the same section defines its meaning. Section 2 deals with the methods by which it may be protected, and the moral basis on which the principal of those protective provisions rests is the Eighth Commandment, "Thou shalt not steal". It is for this reason that Lord Halsbury begins his judgment in *Walter v Lane* [1900] AC 539; (1900) 83 LT Rep 289 with the following words:

> I should very much regret if I were compelled to come to the conclusion that the state of the law permitted one man to make a profit and to appropriate to himself the labour, skill, and capital of another. And it is not denied that in this case the defendant seeks to appropriate to himself what has been produced by the skill, labour and capital of others. In the view I take of this case I think the law is strong enough to restrain what to my mind would be a grievous injustice.

It will be observed that it is the product of the labour, skill, and capital of one man which must not be appropriated by another, not the elements, the raw material, if one may use the expression, upon which the labour and skill and capital of the first have been expended. To secure copyright for this product it is necessary that the labour, skill, and capital expended should be sufficient to impart to the product some quality or character which the raw material did not possess, and which differentiates the product from the raw material. This distinction is well brought out in the judgment of that profound and accomplished lawyer and great and distinguished judge, Story J, in the case of *Emerson v*

Davies decided in the United States. Some of the points decided are stated in the headnote to be first, that:

> Any new and original plan, arrangement or combination of materials, will entitle the author to a copyright therein, whether the materials themselves be new or old. Second, that whosoever by his own skill, labour and judgment writes a new work may have a copyright therein, unless it be directly copied or evasively imitated from another's work. Third, that to constitute piracy of a copyright it must be shown that the original has been either substantially copied or to be so imitated as to be a mere evasion of the copyright.

Ladbroke (Football) Ltd. v. William Hill (Football) Ltd., [1964] 1 All E.R. 465 (H.L.)

Lord Reid and Lord Evershed Lord Hodson, Lord Devlin and Lord Pearce

1963 Nov. 18, 20, 21, 25, 26, 27, 28 1964 Jan. 21

LORD DEVLIN

My lords, I think that this appeal can be determined on quite a short point. It is an important point and one that has led to a difference of judicial opinion. The respondents are bookmakers who devoted a great deal of time, skill and experience to the preparation of a fixed odds betting coupon for football matches. There is an infinity of ways of betting on the results of the 54 League matches that are played every Saturday during the season. . . .

. . .

It was argued on behalf of the appellants, still on the analogy of the sale of goods, that a decision against them would amount to grave interference with freedom of trade. There is no copyright in business methods. If a wine merchant, it was argued, selected a dozen different wines as having in combination a special appeal, and arranged the bottles together in a shop window, there was nothing to prevent a rival trader copying the arrangement. Ought it to make any difference if, instead of a shop window arrangement, the merchant makes a list?

My Lords, I think, with respect, that this argument is based upon a fundamental misapprehension of the law of copyright. The law does not impinge upon freedom of trade; it protects property. It is no more an interference with trade than is the law against larceny. Free trade does not require that one man should be allowed to appropriate without payment the fruits of another's labour, whether they are tangible or intangible. The law has not found it possible to give full protection to the intangible. But it can protect the intangible in certain states, and one of them is when it is expressed in words and print. The fact that that protection is of necessity limited is no argument for diminishing it further; and it is nothing to the point to say that either side of the protective limits a man can obtain gratis whatever his ideas of honesty permit him to pick up.

I would therefore dismiss the appeal.

. . .

In such cases the courts have looked to see whether the compilation of the unoriginal material called for work or skill or expense. If it did, it is entitled to be considered original and to be protected against those who wish to steal the fruits of the work or skill or expense by copying it without taking the trouble to compile it themselves. So the protection given by such copyright is in no sense a monopoly, for it is open to a rival to produce the same result if he chooses to evolve it by his own labours.

Vigneux v. Canadian Performing Rights Society, [1943] S.C.R. 348, reversed [1945] A.C. 108 (Canada P.C.)

Duff C.J.C., Rinfret, Davis, Kerwin and Taschereau JJ.

Judgment: May 4, 1943

Duff C.J.C. — (concurred in by Davis J.):

1 The Copyright Act was enacted in the year 1921 and it may almost be described as having given legal effect to a code of copyright law. The Act provides that rights existing on the 1st of July, 1924, of the kinds specified in the first column of the first Schedule of the Act, shall be converted into the rights defined oppositely in the second column of the Schedule. The Schedule is in these words: —

. . .

3 I have reproduced the Schedule because I think it is important to realize that the rights included in copyright are rights dependent upon statutory enactments which in effect came into force in the year 1924. The right with which we are more particularly concerned is that which is given by sec. 3, "the sole right ... to perform ... the work or any substantial part thereof in public." At common law the author of a musical or dramatic work had the right to prevent its performance in public so long as it remained unpublished, but the right disappeared upon publication. This, of course, was unfair, but the Statute of Anne did not help the author and it was not until about one hundred years ago that the authors of musical works obtained some statutory relief. By the English Copyright Act of 1911 the law was put upon its present footing and the sole right of public performance was vested in copyright owners generally. The right is not limited to the cases of musical and dramatic works; in this respect the Canadian Act of 1921 follows the English Act. The right is a statutory right resting upon the enactments of the statute of 1921, which in effect came into force in 1924 and, as we shall see, the statutory provisions, which it is our duty now to consider, are provisions which must be read and construed as part of the enactments of the Copyright Act of 1921.

. . .

7 Under this plan the dealer in performing rights has his sole right to perform any particular musical composition in public qualified by a statutory license vested in everybody who pays or tenders to the dealer a fee, charge or royalty which has been fixed by the Copyright Appeal Board and notified in the Canada Gazette. That seems like a revolutionary change, but it is evident that the legislature realized in 1931 that this business in which the dealers were engaged is a business affected with a public interest; and it was felt to be unfair and unjust that these dealers should possess the power so to control such performing rights as to enable them to exact from people purchasing gramophone records and sheets of music and radio receiving sets such tolls as it might please them to exact. It is of the first importance, in my opinion, to take notice of this recognition by the legislature of the fact that these dealers in performing rights, which rights are the creature of statute, are engaged in a trade which is affected with a public interest and may, therefore, conformably to a universally accepted canon, be properly subjected to public regulation. It is not out of place here to call attention to an observation of Lord Justice Lindley in *Hanfstaengl v. Empire Palace*, [1894] 3 Chancery, p. 128: —

> Copyright, like patent right, is a monopoly restraining the public from doing that which, apart from the monopoly, it would be perfectly lawful for them to do. The monopoly is itself right and just, and is granted for the purpose of preventing persons from unfairly availing themselves of the work of others, whether that work be scientific, literary, or artistic. The protection of authors, whether of inventions, works of art, or of literary compositions, is the object to be attained by all patent and copyright laws. The Acts are to be construed with reference to this purpose. On the other hand, care must always be taken not to allow them to be made instruments of oppression and extortion.

8 This passage expresses the raison d'etre of the enactments under consideration.

Bishop v. Stevens, [1990] 2 S.C.R. 467

Lamer C.J. and La Forest, L'Heureux-Dubé, Gonthier and McLachlin JJ.

Judgment: March 30, 1990
Judgment: August 16, 1990

. . .

McLachlin J.:

. . .

21 This distinction between the right to perform and the right to record a work is unsurprising in light of the object and purpose of the Act. As noted by Maugham J., in *Performing Right Society, Ltd. v. Hammond's Bradford Brewery Co.*, [1934] 1 Ch. 121, at p. 127, "the Copyright Act, 1911, was passed with a single object, namely, the benefit of authors of all kinds, whether the works were

literary, dramatic or musical". See also Article 1 of the Revised Berne Convention, cited above. A performance is by its very nature fleeting, transient, impermanent. When it is over, only the memory remains. A composer who authorizes performance of his work for a period of time has not irrevocably given up control over how the work is presented to the public. He may choose at a future time to withdraw his authorization, and be the sole interpreter of his own work, or he may place conditions on his authorization. He may control the frequency of performance, and choose the audiences which are to hear his work. Other performers might copy his performances without authorization, but the public nature of performance is such that this will likely come to his attention. Furthermore, no imitation of a performance can be a precise copy. A recording, on the other hand, is permanent. It may be copied easily, privately, and precisely. Once a work has been recorded, the recording takes on a life of its own. This is why, from a composer's point of view, the right to control the circumstances under which the first recording is made is crucial. Once the composer has made or authorized a recording of his work, he has irrevocably given up much of his control over its presentation to the public. These are the reasons why the rights to perform and to record are recognized as distinct in the Act, and why in practice a composer may wish to authorize performances but not recordings of his work.

BMG Canada Inc. v. John Doe, 2005 FCA 193

Noël J.A., Richard C.J., Sexton J.A.

Heard: April 20-21, 2005
Judgment: May 19, 2005
Docket: A-203-04

. . .

Sexton J.A.:

• • •

40 The reasoning in *Glaxo* and *Norwich* is compelling. Intellectual property laws originated in order to protect the promulgation of ideas. Copyright law provides incentives for innovators–artists, musicians, inventors, writers, performers and marketers–to create. It is designed to ensure that ideas are expressed and developed instead of remaining dormant. Individuals need to be encouraged to develop their own talents and personal expression of artistic ideas, including music. If they are robbed of the fruits of their efforts, their incentive to express their ideas in tangible form is diminished.

41 Modern technology such as the Internet has provided extraordinary benefits for society, which include faster and more efficient means of communication to wider audiences. This technology must not be allowed to obliterate those personal property rights which society has deemed important. Although privacy

concerns must also be considered, it seems to me that they must yield to public concerns for the protection of intellectual property rights in situations where infringement threatens to erode those rights.

42 Thus, in my view, in cases where plaintiffs show that they have a *bona fide* claim that unknown persons are infringing their copyright, they have a right to have the identity revealed for the purpose of bringing action. However, caution must be exercised by the courts in ordering such disclosure, to make sure that privacy rights are invaded in the most minimal way.

(b) Modern Perspective

Canadian courts have now departed from emphasizing the primary importance of authors' rights to a vision of copyright law as concerned with balancing the public interest in economic and cultural development against the interests of individuals in securing a fair and equitable return for their intellectual efforts. The current interpretative analysis seeks to find an appropriate balance between promoting the public interest in the encouragement and dissemination of works and obtaining a "just reward" for the creator. In contrast to the US approach, the balance is not presented as entirely instrumental in nature; it is not aimed, solely, at furthering the public interest such that authors' rights become merely the means to social ends. Rather, the public interest must be weighed against the author's right to reward, to "prevent someone other than the creator from appropriating whatever benefits may be generated."[8] While a commitment to protect the authorial right persists, it is not regarded as akin to an absolute ownership right. The Supreme Court of Canada has stated that the public policy behind copyright lies not only in recognizing the authors' rights, but also in recognizing their "limited nature."[9] The utilitarian approach typically associated with US copyright policy is indeed evident in this balancing exercise, and is captured in the Court's observation that "in crassly economic terms, it would be as inefficient to overcompensate artists and authors for the right of reproduction, as it would be self-defeating to under compensate them." Further, the Court admonished that "excess control by holders of copyrights and other forms of intellectual property may unduly limit the ability of the public domain to incorporate and embellish creative innovation in the long-term interests of

---

8   *Galerie d'Art du Petit Champlain inc. c. Théberge* (2002), (sub nom. *Théberge v. Galerie d'Art du Petit Champlain inc.*) 17 C.P.R. (4th) 161 (S.C.C.); *Society of Composers, Authors & Music Publishers of Canada v. Canadian Assn. of Internet Providers*, 2004 SCC 45 (S.C.C.).

9   *Galerie d'Art du Petit Champlain inc. c. Théberge* (2002), (sub nom. *Théberge v. Galerie d'Art du Petit Champlain inc.*) 17 C.P.R. (4th) 161 (S.C.C.), *CCH Canadian Ltd. v. Law Society of Upper Canada*, 2004 SCC 13 (S.C.C.).

society as a whole or create practical obstacles to proper utilization."[10] Thus, the Supreme Court of Canada has articulated an understanding of copyright policy that endorses the idea of creators' rights, economic utilitarianism, public interest theory and a positive role for the public domain. Some may view this as a happy compromise; others may regard it as an uneasy truce. No one doubts that the balance is a fragile one.

United Artists Pictures Inc. v. Pink Panther Beauty Corp. (1998), 80 C.P.R. (3d) 247 (Fed. C.A.), leave to appeal allowed (1998), 235 N.R. 399 (note) (S.C.C.)

Isaac C.J., Linden, McDonald JJ.A.

Heard: January 22, 1998
Judgment: March 30, 1998
Docket: A-365-96

. . .

Linden J.A.:

. . .

16 The question posed by the existence of intellectual property regimes has been defined as one of where to draw the line between the right to copy and the right to compete. This is a question about what is truly worthy of the status of property and what is in reality an element of the marketplace which should be open to all competitors to use in their efforts to succeed. I find this question a profitable one to keep in mind. For example, Henderson discusses the rationale behind protection for certain things and not others. He wrote:

> The main reason that we do not protect ideas *per se* is because they are commonplace. To protect an idea at its preliminary or "bare idea" stage could stultify economic progress. And, most importantly, ideas, *per se*, are relatively useless.

17 When deciding property issues it is always a matter of balancing the public right to competition with the private right to ownership. I do not find that this is limited to questions of intellectual property; an owner does not have unlimited rights with respect to personality or realty. Consideration of the public interest is advanced through statute and through the common law (e.g. the tort of nuisance). When considering these types of questions the Court must be cognizant of the fact that the market relies on individuals who, through their labour and ingenuity, bolster the strength of our economy. That strength benefits us all. We must be careful when we determine property rights so that the line is drawn fairly between the right to the exclusive use of an idea and the right of individuals to

---

10   *Galerie d'Art du Petit Champlain inc. c. Théberge* (2002), (sub nom. *Théberge v. Galerie d'Art du Petit Champlain inc.)* 17 C.P.R. (4th) 161 (S.C.C.), *CCH Canadian Ltd. v. Law Society of Upper Canada*, 2004 SCC 13 (S.C.C.).

compete and earn a livelihood. This dilemma is neatly summarized by Madame Justice McLachlin when she says:

> We must stop thinking of intellectual property as an absolute and start thinking of it as a function–as a process, which, if it is to be successful, must meet diverse aims: the assurance of a fair reward to creators and inventors and the encouragement of research and creativity, on the one hand; and on the other hand, the widest possible dissemination of the ideas and products of which the world, and all the individuals in it, have such great need.

Théberge v. Galerie d'Art du Petit Champlain inc., [2002] S.C.R. 336

McLachlin C.J.C., L'Heureux-Dubé, Gonthier, Iacobucci, Major, Binnie, LeBel JJ.

Heard: October 11, 2001
Judgment: March 28, 2002
Docket: 27872

. . .

Binnie J.:

. . .

III. The Content of the Respondent's Rights Under the Copyright Act

11 The Act provides the respondent with both economic and "moral" rights to his work. The distinction between the two types of rights and their respective statutory remedies is crucial.

12 Generally speaking, Canadian copyright law has traditionally been more concerned with economic than moral rights. Our original Act, which came into force in 1924, substantially tracked the English *Copyright Act, 1911* (U.K.), 1 & 2 Geo. 5, c. 46. The principal economic benefit to the artist or author was (and is) the "sole right to produce or reproduce the work or any substantial part thereof in any material form whatever" (s. 3(1)) for his or her life plus fifty years (s. 6). The economic rights are based on a conception of artistic and literary works essentially as articles of commerce. (Indeed, the initial *Copyright Act, 1709* (U.K.), 8 Anne, c. 19, was passed to assuage the concerns of printers, not authors.) Consistently with this view, such rights can be bought and sold either wholly or partially, and either generally or subject to territorial limitations, and either for the whole term of the copyright or for any part thereof (s. 13(4)). The owner of the copyright, thus, can be, but need not be, the author of the work. It was the respondent's economic rights in enumerated works that were the subject matter of an assignment to two poster manufacturers, Éditions Galerie L'Imagerie É.G.I. Ltée (herein "É.G.I.") by contract dated October 29, 1996, and New York Graphic Society, Ltd. by contract dated February 3, 1997.

. . .

27 On this view, it does not matter that the appellants were multiple offenders at "ink transfers" or that they were commercial entities participating in the resale market. The copyright infringement occurred at the moment of "reproduction" in each instance, and would have been similarly objectionable, according to my colleague's approach, if done to a single copy by the individual appellant to hang in his own living-room.

28 In my view, with respect, this expansive reading of the s. 3(1) economic rights tilts the balance too far in favour of the copyright holder and insufficiently recognizes the proprietary rights of the appellants in the physical posters which they purchased. Adoption of this expanded interpretation would introduce the *civiliste* conception of "*droit de destination*" into our law without any basis in the *Copyright Act* itself, and blur the distinction between economic and moral rights imposed by Parliament.

. . .

A.   The Present Balance Between the Economic Interest of the Copyright Holder and the Proprietary Interest of the Purchasing Public Would be Significantly Altered to the Public's Detriment

30 The *Copyright Act* is usually presented as a balance between promoting the public interest in the encouragement and dissemination of works of the arts and intellect and obtaining a just reward for the creator (or, more accurately, to prevent someone other than the creator from appropriating whatever benefits may be generated). The elements of this balance are discussed in more detail by J. S. McKeown, *Fox Canadian Law of Copyright and Industrial Designs* (3rd ed. 2000), at p. 3. See also D. Vaver, *Intellectual Property Law*: Copyright, Patents, Trade-marks (1997), at p. 22. This is not new. As early as 1769 it was said by an English judge:

> It is wise in any state, to encourage letters, and the painful researches of learned men. The easiest and most equal way of doing it, is, by securing to them the property of their own works....

> He who engages in a laborious work, (such, for instance, as Johnson's Dictionary,) which may employ his whole life, will do it with more spirit, if, besides his own glory, he thinks it may be a provision for his family.

> (*Millar v. Taylor* (1769), 4 Burr. 2303, 98 E.R. 201 (Eng. K.B.), *per* Willes J., at p. 218.)

31 The proper balance among these and other public policy objectives lies not only in recognizing the creator's rights but in giving due weight to their limited nature. In crassly economic terms it would be as inefficient to overcompensate artists and authors for the right of reproduction as it would be self-defeating to undercompensate them. Once an authorized copy of a work is sold to a member of the public, it is generally for the purchaser, not the author, to determine what happens to it.

32 Excessive control by holders of copyrights and other forms of intellectual property may unduly limit the ability of the public domain to incorporate and embellish creative innovation in the long-term interests of society as a whole, or create practical obstacles to proper utilization. This is reflected in the exceptions to copyright infringement enumerated in ss. 29 to 32.2, which seek to protect the public domain in traditional ways such as fair dealing for the purpose of criticism or review and to add new protections to reflect new technology, such as limited computer program reproduction and "ephemeral recordings" in connection with live performances.

33 This case demonstrates the basic economic conflict between the holder of the intellectual property in a work and the owner of the tangible property that embodies the copyrighted expressions.

. . .

E.   The Proposed Test Would Undermine the Distinction Between Moral Rights and Economic Rights Contrary to Legislative Intent

57 As previously noted, s. 28.2(1) of the Act provides that even a purchaser of the tangible object may not "distor[t], mutilat[e] *or otherwise modif[y]*" (emphasis added) the work "to the prejudice of the honour or reputation of the author". It seems clear, at least by negative implication, that a modification of a work by the purchaser which does *not* "prejudice ... the honour or reputation of the author" was intended by Parliament to be within the purchaser's rights.

58 In addition, as a secondary point, s. 28.2(3) of the Act provides that a change in "the physical ... structure containing a work ... shall not, by that act alone, constitute a distortion, mutilation or other modification of the work". To the extent a change in substrate can be said to change the "physical structure" containing the respondent's work, it does not "by that act alone" amount to a violation of a moral right either.

59 The separate structures in the Act to cover economic rights on the one hand and moral rights on the other show that a clear distinction and separation was intended. Professor Ysolde Gendreau is one of those who have drawn attention to this rather rigid compartmentalisation:

> Unfortunately, the present text of the *Copyright Act* does little to help the promotion of the fusion of moral rights with the economic prerogatives of the law, since there is no comprehensive definition of copyright that embodies both. Section 3 of the Act, which is drafted as a definition of copyright, only refers to the economic dimension of copyright. Moral rights are defined and circumscribed in entirely distinct sections. This absence of cohesion leads to the separate mention of "copyright" and "moral rights" whenever Parliament wants to refer to both aspects of copyright law and to the near duplication of the provision on remedies for moral rights infringements.
>
> (Y. Gendreau, "Moral Rights" in G. F. Henderson, ed., *Copyright and Confidential Information Law of Canada* (1994), 161, at p. 171)

(See also R. G. Howell, L. Vincent, and M. D. Manson, *Intellectual Property Law: Cases and Materials* (1999), at p. 383.) This is not to say that moral rights do not have an economic dimension (e.g., there may be an economic aspect to being able to control the personality-invested "moral" rights of integrity and attribution) or to deny that there is a moral rights aspect to copyright (e.g., a critic may reproduce parts of the text of a book when reviewing it, but it will be considered a breach of the author's economic rights unless his or her authorship is attributed). However, in terms of remedies, the distinction in the Act between the two sets of rights is clear.

60 My view is that Parliament intended modification without reproduction to be dealt with under the provisions dealing with moral rights rather than economic rights. To adopt a contrary view, i.e., to treat the modification of the substrate here as the violation of an economic right, would allow copyright holders other than the artist to complain about modification (despite the non-assignability of moral rights). It would allow an artist who objected to a "modification" of an authorized reproduction both to sidestep the independent evaluation of a judge in unleashing a pre-judgment seizure in Quebec, and to sidestep at a trial anywhere in Canada the important requirement of showing prejudice to honour or reputation in order to establish an infringement of moral rights.

61 Could the *economic* rights of the sculptor of the descending geese at the Eaton Centre be said to be infringed (quite apart from his *moral* rights) because the seasonal "combination" of geese plus Christmas ribbons could be considered a "reproduction"? The be-ribboned flock incorporated the original artistic work in more than "substantial part", no doubt, but there was no "reproduction" in any legal sense, any more than there was "reproduction" when the appellants in this case contributed blank canvas to the "combination" of ink layer and canvas. The sculptor rightly invoked his moral rights against the Eaton Centre, not economic rights.

. . .

Gonthier J.:

I.   Introduction

81 The issue in this case involves the validity of a seizure before judgment under s. 38(1) of the Copyright Act, R.S.C. 1985, c. C-42 (C.A.), and art. 734(1) of the Quebec Code of Civil Procedure, R.S.Q., c. C-25 (C.C.P.). The only matter before this Court is the seizure of the canvas-backed reproductions of the paper posters that embody the respondent artist's works. In order to dispose of that question, however, we must first determine whether the process of transferring a poster onto canvas can give rise to an infringement of the exclusive rights conferred by the C.A. and thereby constitute a form of copyright infringement.

. . .

B. Copyright

(1) Introduction

112 Even though our legislation derives from the common law, it is important to recall the origin and significance of copyright. In 1777, P.-A. Caron de Beaumarchais, who founded the Société des Auteurs, stated:

> [TRANSLATION] It is said in the theatre lobby that it is not noble for authors to write for the worthless pursuit of money, they who pride themselves on their claim to fame. Indeed, they are right, fame is appealing. But they forget that nature condemns us to dine 365 times in order to bask in glory merely for a year. For the authors, they are not defending a privilege, but the sacred right of all rights to retain ownership of their works... .

> (M. Pagnol, Preface, in J. Boncompain, *Le droit d'auteur au Canada* (1971), at p. 9.)

113 In Canada, it is settled law that the sole source of copyright is the *C.A.*, which "simply creates rights and obligations upon the terms and in the circumstances set out in the statute": *Compo Co. v. Blue Crest Music Inc.* (1979), [1980] 1 S.C.R. 357 (S.C.C.), at p. 373, cited in *Bishop v. Stevens*, [1990] 2 S.C.R. 467 (S.C.C.), at p. 477. Nonetheless, the Act is framed in somewhat general terms and must be applied in diverse and even unprecedented situations. As Normand Tamaro pointed out (*Le droit d'auteur: Fondements et principes* (1994), at p. 5):

> [TRANSLATION] In fact, although Canada's *Copyright Act* was enacted in 1921, the manner in which it is interpreted is modern, and allows the development of new techniques and modern theories surrounding the creative act to be taken into consideration.

In the event of disagreement regarding the meaning of specific provisions, it will be up to the courts to interpret them, referring to the ordinary meaning of the words and the purpose and spirit of the Act (*Rizzo & Rizzo Shoes Ltd. (Re)*, [1998] 1 S.C.R. 27 (S.C.C.), at para. 21).

114 In Canada, the first real *Copyright Act* was enacted in 1921 and came into force in 1924, although canvases were already protected by *The Copyright Act of 1875*, S.C. 1875, c. 88, an Act validated by the British Parliament by *The Canada Copyright Act*, 1875 (U.K.), 38 & 39 Vict., c. 53. (For an analysis of the sources of copyright in Canada, see P.-E. Moyse, "La nature du droit d'auteur: droit de propriété ou monopole?" (1998), 43 *McGill L.J.* 507.) The Act of 1921 was designed to enable Canadian authors to benefit from the protection provided by the provisions of the Berne Convention, which was adopted in 1886 and ratified by Great Britain on behalf of Canada. The purpose of the Convention was to establish an international code and to create a Union of States "for the protection of the rights of authors in their literary and artistic works" (*Revised Berne Convention*, art. 1). Generally, copyright enables the owner to prevent the unauthorized plagiarism and distribution of an original work. It is therefore these acts themselves that are prohibited, without regard to their purpose, be it mercenary or otherwise. In some respects, copyright is also similar to a real

right; *inter alia*, it is an exclusive right that can be set up against anyone. The intangible subject-matter that it protects distinguishes it, however, from a right in a material thing. In short, given the *sui generis* nature of copyright, we must be circumspect in proposing any analogy to other rights.

115 Moreover, the purpose of copyright is not to protect the ideas or opinions expressed by the creator, but rather the various means and forms by which those ideas are communicated (J.S. McKeown, *Fox, Canadian Law of Copyright and Industrial Designs* (3rd ed. 2000), at p. 60; *Cartwright v. Wharton* (1912), 25 O.L.R. 357 (Ont. H.C.); *Stevenson v. Crook*, [1938] Ex. C.R. 299 (Can. Ex. Ct.), at p. 307; *L.B. (Plastics) Ltd. v. Swish Products Ltd.*, [1979] R.P.C. 551 (U.K. H.L.)). In other words, it is the formal expression of those ideas or opinions that is protected by copyright.

116 Moreover, it is important to recall that Canadian copyright law derives from multiple sources and draws on both common law tradition and continental civil law concepts. As Moyse observes, *supra*, at p. 562:

> [TRANSLATION] What the term "copy-right" very certainly reveals is the actual function of copyright. It is an exclusive right and, as it applies to the part that relates to the commercial exploitation of the work, a true monopoly on reproduction. ...Canadian law inherited that aspect while remaining receptive to the French doctrines, particularly because of Quebec's influence. This does great credit to our law since the Canadian Parliament is more inclined than any other legislature to stay attuned to external developments in order to mould its own rules. ...
>
> ... Thus, in Canadian statutes, the intention is to establish both a right that is centered on the person of the author, this being derived from the civil structures of the right of ownership, and a definitely dynamic right centered on its economic function, which reflects the theories underlying the concept of monopoly [.]

Canadian statutes must therefore be interpreted in light of their historical context, domestic case law and legislative developments, and international conventions.

(2) Infringement: The Rights At Issue

(a) Copyright and Moral Rights

117 The *C.A.* provides protection for both copyright, defined by s. 3(1), and the author's moral rights, in particular in ss. 14.1 and 14.2. While the intended purposes of those rights overlap in some respects, they are nonetheless completely different legal instruments in terms of both their definition and their scope.

118 Copyright protects against the unlawful appropriation and distribution of creative expression. With respect to a work, that right includes (s. 3(1) *C.A.*) the right: (i) "to produce or reproduce the work or any substantial part thereof in any material form whatever", (ii) "to perform the work or any substantial part thereof in public", and (iii) "to publish the work or any substantial part thereof", as well as a series of other rights derived from those fundamental rights (s. 3(1) *C.A.*). Copyright is a patrimonial right that may be assigned, as provided in s. 13(4) *C.A.*

119 J. Herman, in "Moral Rights and Canadian Copyright Reform: The Impact on Motion Picture Creators" (1989-1990), 20 *R.D.U.S.* 407, at p. 411, analyses and defines the purpose of the concept of copyright and its relationship with society as follows:

> The relationship between the artist and society may be characterized in straight-forward economic terms: society places demands on its members to share with it the fruits of their intellectual labour. Artists supply those demands; however, if society recognizes an artist's right of ownership of his intellectual work, he may set conditions and exact a price for the society's consumption of it. Copyright confers in the creator a monopoly to exploit his work in public for his own economic self-interest.

120 Moral rights, inspired by the continental civil law concept of *droit d'auteur*, are concerned primarily with protecting the integrity and paternity of the work (s. 14.1(1) *C.A.*), which is then regarded as an extension of the author's personality. These are extra-patrimonial rights, which, by definition, are not assignable (s. 14.1(2) *C.A.*). (For an analysis on the scope and application of moral rights in Canada, see: E. Colas, "Le droit moral de l'artiste sur son oeuvre" (1981), 59 *Can. Bar Rev.* 521; M. Goudreau, "Le droit moral de l'auteur au Canada" (1994), *R.G.D.* 403.)

121 Furthermore, my colleague, Binnie J., suggests that this case arises out of the conceptual differences between "the *droit d'auteur* of the continental *civiliste* tradition and the English copyright tradition" (para. 6). I cannot subscribe to that view. The disposition of this case is determined solely by the aspects that derive from the English concept of copyright. The concepts of moral rights, as I will explain later, are inapplicable to the facts of this case.

122 In other words, the subject-matter of copyright, unlike moral rights, is a right in the work and not a personal right. As Stephen Stewart accurately observed in his text entitled *International Copyright and Neighbouring Rights* (2nd ed. 1989), the key factor is the work, including its material support, and not the idea expressed by the work (at pp. 7-8):

> It is simply the right to prevent the copying of physical material and its object is to protect the owner of the copyright against <u>any reproduction or use of that material which he has not authorised</u>. Copyright, in its essence is a negative concept. It is the right to prevent people from dealing with something that is yours and has been improperly taken by someone else. <u>It focuses on the material support rather than on the creation</u>. Copyright, as the word suggests, was in its origin <u>a right to prevent copying</u>, that is reproduction. [Emphasis added.]

123 Furthermore, in *Apple Computer Inc. v. Mackintosh Computers Ltd.* (1986), [1987] 1 F.C. 173 (Fed. T.D.), at p. 200, Reed J. accurately stated the purpose of the *C.A.*:

> [T]he purpose of the Copyright Act is and always has been to grant a monopoly. No distinction is made therein as to the purpose of the work created — for entertainment, instruction or other purposes. The legislation historically, in my view had two purposes: to encourage disclosure of works for the "advancement

of learning", and to protect and reward the intellectual effort of the author (for a limited period of time) in the work.

In light of those observations, if we are to determine whether infringement has occurred, we must examine the concept of reproduction.

. . .

141   The primary purpose of s. 3(1) C.A. is to enable the author to profit from his or her work. Despite the fact that the legislation was written early in the last century, Parliament's use of general terms allows the C.A. to evolve and adapt to new social and technological circumstances.

Euro Excellence Inc. v. Kraft Canada Inc., [2007] 3 S.C.R. 20

Abella J., Bastarache J., Binnie J., Charron J., Deschamps J., Fish J., LeBel J., McLachlin C.J.C., Rothstein J.

Heard: January 16, 2007
Judgment: July 26, 2007
Docket: 31327

Rothstein J.:

1   I have read the reasons of Bastarache J. While I agree with his conclusion, I am respectfully unable to agree with his analysis. I have three main concerns with his reasons.

(1) The Concerns

2   This Court has repeatedly adopted Driedger's approach to statutory interpretation:

> Today there is only one principle or approach, namely, the words of an Act are to be read in their entire context and in their grammatical and ordinary sense harmoniously with the scheme of the Act, the object of the Act, and the intention of Parliament. (E. A. Driedger, *Construction of Statutes* (2nd ed. 1983), at p. 87; see also *Bell ExpressVu Ltd. Partnership v. Rex*, [2002] 2 S.C.R. 559, 2002 SCC 42 (S.C.C.), at para. 26; *CCH Canadian Ltd. v. Law Society of Upper Canada*, [2004] 1 S.C.R. 339, 2004 SCC 13 (S.C.C.), at para. 9.)

3   I am concerned that Bastarache J.'s approach in this case is inconsistent with this Court's approach to statutory interpretation. The "modern" or "purposive" approach requires that the words of the statute "in their grammatical and ordinary sense" be read harmoniously with the objects of the Act. It does not, however, give judges licence to substitute their policy preferences for those of Parliament. This Court has consistently held that "copyright is a creature of statute and the rights and remedies provided by the *Copyright Act* are exhaustive": see *CCH*, at para. 9; *Galerie d'art du Petit Champlain inc. c. Théberge*, [2002] 2 S.C.R. 336, 2002 SCC 34 (S.C.C.), at para. 5; *Bishop v. Stevens*, [1990] 2 S.C.R. 467 (S.C.C.), at p. 477; *Compo Co. v. Blue Crest Music Inc.* (1979),

[1980] 1 S.C.R. 357 (S.C.C.), at pp. 372-73. In my respectful view, Bastarache J.'s reasons depart from this doctrine.

. . .

7 To support his argument for the "incidental" approach to copyright law, Bastarache J. introduces a concept of "legitimate economic interests" to read down rights expressly granted by the Copyright Act. The term "legitimate economic interest" was used by this Court in Théberge, but in a different context. The legitimate economic interest described in Théberge was the right of the creator of an artistic work to receive a reward for that work. The issue in Théberge was whether the transferring of an artistic work from a paper backing to a canvas backing constituted reproduction contrary to the "legitimate economic interests" of the artist. Binnie J., for the majority, found that reproduction did not occur on the facts of that case. Binnie J.'s holding relied on the concepts of originality and reproduction, which are firmly rooted in the words of the Copyright Act.

8 In this case, Bastarache J. expands the concept of "legitimate economic interest" to exclude logos on wrappers from the domain of copyright. I find no authority in the Act or in our jurisprudence for Bastarache J.'s theory of "legitimate economic interests". As this Court has often stated, "the rights and remedies provided by the Copyright Act are exhaustive": CCH, at para. 9. I would not depart from this approach by introducing a new equitable doctrine of "legitimate economic interest" to read down the legislation.

9 I accept, of course, that the Copyright Act is to be given a purposive interpretation. However, I distinguish between an approach that is rooted in the words of the Act and the approach taken by my colleague Bastarache J. that involves reading words into the legislation that are at odds with Parliament's intent. Section 64 of the Copyright Act, which can be found, along with the other relevant provisions of the Copyright Act, in the Appendix, addresses the very issue that is fundamental to my colleague's approach: can a work of art appearing on a label and receiving trade-mark protection also be the subject of copyright protection? Parliament concluded that works can receive concurrent copyright and trade-mark protection.

. . .

Bastarache J.:

1. Introduction

57 Can a chocolate bar be copyrighted because of protected works appearing on its wrapper? In particular, can s. 27(2) of the Copyright Act, R.S.C. 1985, c. C-42, which prohibits parallel importation into Canada of copyrighted works, be used by the respondent Kraft Canada Inc. to prevent the appellant, Euro-Excellence Inc., from, in the words of s. 27(2), importing, for the purpose of selling, renting, distributing or trading, genuine Toblerone and Côte d'Or chocolate bars into Canada, without obscuring the logos of those chocolate bars, on the basis that the logos are copyrighted? I conclude that it cannot. Both s. 27(2) and the

Copyright Act as a whole are about the protection of copyrighted works, not about the importation and sale of consumer goods in general. The merely incidental presence of the copyrighted works on the wrappers of the chocolate bars does not bring the chocolate bars within the protections offered by the Copyright Act. This appeal is allowed for the reasons set out below.

. . .

2.   The Purpose of the Copyright Act

76 In Galerie d'art du Petit Champlain inc. c. Théberge, [2002] 2 S.C.R. 336, 2002 SCC 34 (S.C.C.), Binnie J. set out the dual objectives of the Copyright Act, at paras. 30-31:

> The Copyright Act is usually presented as a balance between promoting the public interest in the encouragement and dissemination of works of the arts and intellect and obtaining a just reward for the creator...
>
> The proper balance among these and other public policy objectives lies not only in recognizing the creator's rights but in giving due weight to their limited nature.
>
> As the Chief Justice noted in CCH, at para. 10, applications of the Copyright Act should attempt "to maintain an appropriate balance between these two goals". It is also important to keep in mind Justice Binnie's holding in Théberge which limits copyright protection to the "legitimate economic interests" of the copyright holder (para. 38 (emphasis added)).

77 The CCH decision recognized the "limited nature" of the rights of a copyright holder in two important ways: in its definition of originality and in its treatment of fair dealing.

78 The Copyright Act protects original works only. In CCH, the Chief Justice held that, to be considered original in the sense required by the Act, a work must be the result of "an exercise of skill and judgment" (para. 16). This standard is consistent with the purpose of the Act, in that it provides a just reward for the labour of the creator; a "creativity" standard of originality was rejected insofar as it required novelty or uniqueness for copyright protection and failed to take account of the division between copyright and patent: CCH, at para. 24. However the skill and judgment standard does not provide a reward for all types of labour: the "sweat of the brow" standard of originality was rejected in CCH because it fails to take account of the "knowledge, developed aptitude or practised ability" and "capacity for discernment or ability to form an opinion or evaluation" which are the special hallmarks of the types of labour which produce the type of works protected by the Copyright Act (CCH, at paras. 16 and 24).

79 The CCH decision recognized the limited nature of the rights of a copyright holder in its treatment of fair dealing, which recognized that, unlike other exceptions, fair dealing is an essential part of copyright protection, and therefore that fair dealing is constitutive of the idea of the wrong in copyright law. Not every substantial reproduction of a copyrighted work counts as an infringement of copyright. This logic is clarified by Professor Abraham Drassinower in his article "Taking User Rights Seriously", in M. Geist, ed., In the Public Interest:

The Future of Canadian Copyright Law (2005), 462. As Drassinower writes, at p. 470, "Fair dealing stands for the proposition that responding to another's work in one's own does not mean that one's work is any less one's own. Thus the defendant who makes out the fair dealing defence is an author in her own right." This is consistent with the understanding of copyright discussed above: sometimes a substantial reproduction of a copyrighted work will not be an infringement, because copyright protection is limited to protection of legitimate economic interests which are the result of an exercise of skill and judgment, and that protection must not be extended beyond its proper limits.

80 The CCH decision thus confirms that in order to protect the essential balance which lies at the heart of copyright law, care must be taken to ensure that copyright protection is not allowed to extend beyond the legitimate interests of a copyright holder. Copyright will not be granted to works which are not the result of an exercise of skill and judgment, which is the special kind of labour for which copyright is the appropriate protection. Similarly, once copyright is granted in a given work, the protection that it provides must not be extended beyond its natural limits, and must take proper account of user rights such as the right to deal fairly with a copyrighted work. It is useful to note here that, while copyright protection results from an action of an individual — that is, the exercise of skill and judgment in creating an original work — that protection inheres in the work created, rather than its creator. In this manner, a copyrighted work is a form of property which may be transferred or licensed to others. But the rights transferred to a licensee must be limited in the same way as those of the original creator of the work to the legitimate economic interests resulting from the exercise of skill and judgment.

81 This Court's recent decision in Society of Composers, Authors & Music Publishers of Canada v. Canadian Assn. of Internet Providers, [2004] 2 S.C.R. 427, 2004 SCC 45 (S.C.C.), confirms this purposive interpretation of the Act. In that case, Binnie J. wrote, at para. 116: "'Caching'is dictated by the need to deliver faster and more economic service, and should not, when undertaken only for such technical reasons, attract copyright liability" (emphasis added). While "caching" is certainly an instance of substantial reproduction, it is a technical process only; as such it does not consist in an attempt to appropriate the legitimate economic interests of the copyright holder, and therefore does not constitute infringement.

82 The logic of this view of copyright has also been held to extend to other forms of intellectual property. In Kirkbi AG v. Ritvik Holdings Inc. / Gestions Ritvik Inc., [2005] 3 S.C.R. 302, 2005 SCC 65 (S.C.C.), LeBel J., for the Court, noted, at para. 37, the importance of "basic and necessary distinctions between different forms of intellectual property and their legal and economic functions". He then went on to review the purposes of trade-marks and patents, noting that "[p]atent rights focus on the patented product or process", but that "[i]n the case of trade-marks, the focus shifts from the product itself to the distinctiveness of its marketing": see paras. 38 and 39. This focus on the fundamental natures and purposes of different sorts of intellectual property protections and the necessary

divisions between them suggests that each form of protection relies on some core normative notion which must ground the economic interests claimed. Thus, a trade-mark, which protects distinctiveness of marketing and goodwill, cannot be leveraged to extend protection to products themselves, which is usually granted by patent.

83 The approach in Kirkbi is consistent with the principle of statutory interpretation which requires coherent interpretation of statutes in pari materia: see P.-A. Côté, The Interpretation of Legislation In Canada (3rd ed. 2000), at pp. 342 ff. According to this principle, the Copyright Act ought not only to be interpreted with an eye to the internal coherence of its own scheme; it must also not be interpreted in a fashion which is inconsistent with the Trade-marks Act, R.S.C. 1985, c. T-13. Trade-mark law protects market share in commercial goods; copyright protects the economic gains resulting from an exercise of skill and judgment. If trade-mark law does not protect market share in a particular situation, the law of copyright should not be used to provide that protection, if that requires contorting copyright outside its normal sphere of operation. The protection offered by copyright cannot be leveraged to include protection of economic interests that are only tangentially related to the copyrighted work. This Court's decision in Astrazeneca Canada Inc. v. Canada (Minister of Health), [2006] 2 S.C.R. 560, 2006 SCC 49 (S.C.C.), which was based on a simultaneous interpretation of "two regulatory systems with sometimes conflicting objectives" (para. 12), is also consistent with the principle.

84 With this view of the purpose of the Act, which provides us with a principled fulcrum on which we may undertake copyright's balance, we may turn now to an examination of the purpose of s. 27(2) of the Act.

The Purpose of Section 27(2)(e) of the Copyright Act

85 The Act protects only the legitimate economic interests of copyright holders. It protects the economic benefits of skill and judgment; it does not protect all economic benefits of all types of labour. Section 27(2) of the Act is meant to prohibit secondary infringement resulting from the wrongful appropriation of the gains of another's skill and judgment by way of the acts enumerated in paras. (a) to (c). Conversely, other economic interests — although they may seem to be closely associated with the interests legitimately protected as emanating from that skill and judgment — are not protected. In particular, if a work of skill and judgment (such as a logo) is attached to some other consumer good (such as a chocolate bar), the economic gains associated with the sale of the consumer good must not be mistakenly viewed as the legitimate economic interests of the copyright holder of the logo that are protected by the law of copyright.

86 Thus s. 27(2)(e) is meant to protect copyright holders from the unauthorized importation of works which are the result of their skill and judgment. It is not meant to protect manufacturers from the unauthorized importation of consumer goods on the basis of their having a copyrighted work affixed to their wrapper, this work being merely incidental to their value as consumer goods.

87 I should note here that, contrary to what was argued before this Court at the hearing, s. 27(2) is not meant to protect manufacturers from the importation of counterfeit versions of their consumer goods. The laws of trade-mark and passing off provide protection to manufacturers who fear the importation of cheap imitations of their products with a copy of the logo of the real product affixed to them. Indeed, this protection is central to the purpose of trade-mark law, as identified by LeBel J. in Kirkbi, at para. 39: "Trade-marks seek to indicate the source of a particular product, process or service in a distinctive manner, so that, ideally, consumers know what they are buying and from whom." While it is certainly true that one work can be the subject of both copyright and trade-mark protection (see s. 64(3)(b) of the Act), it is equally certain that different forms of intellectual property protect different types of economic interests. To ignore this fact would be to ignore the "basic and necessary distinctions between different forms of intellectual property and their legal and economic functions", as noted by LeBel J. at para. 37 of Kirkbi.

88 This interpretation of s. 27(2) respects copyright's insistence that only legitimate economic interests receive copyright protection. To allow s. 27(2) to protect all interests of manufacturers and distributors of consumer goods would upset the copyright balance. Far from ensuring a "just reward" for creators of copyrighted works, it would allow a copyright to be leveraged far beyond the use intended by Parliament, allowing rights to be artificially enlarged into protection over consumer goods. This undue expansion of copyright would certainly be a failure to give heed to Binnie J.'s insistence, at para. 31 of Théberge, that the law give due weight to the limited nature of the rights of a copyright holder.

. . .

Abella J.:

110 On the first issue, I agree with the conclusion reached by Rothstein J. There is nothing in the Act to endorse a restrictive definition of "sell". Section 64(3) (b) of the Act extends copyright protection to trademarks and labels. When a product is sold, title to its wrapper is also transferred to the purchaser. The Act is indifferent as to whether the sale of the wrapper is important to the consumer.

111 Like Bastarache J., I agree with the trial judge that the logos are copyrighted works. I respectfully disagree with his view, however, that no infringement is made out because the elephant and bear logos are incidental to the chocolate bars and are therefore not protected by s. 27(2). To inject an exception for logos on the basis that they are "incidental" would be to introduce unnecessary uncertainty, inviting case-by-case judicial explorations into the uncharted area of what is "merely" incidental, "somewhat" incidental, or not incidental at all. Such an approach also takes insufficient account of the reality that many products are, to a significant extent, sold on the basis of their logo or packaging.

112 Nor do I share the view that s. 27(2)(e), which on its face appears to me to be applicable, "protects only the legitimate economic interests of copyright holders", that is, "the unauthorized importation of works which are the result of their skill and judgment" (paras. 85-86). It seems to me, with respect, that

once a work falls within s. 27(2)(a) to (c) and otherwise meets the requirements established by the Act as prerequisites to copyright protection, there is no scope for a judicially created limit to that protection based on what might — or might not — be a "legitimate economic interest". I do not believe that Galerie d'art du Petit Champlain inc. c. Théberge, [2002] 2 S.C.R. 336, 2002 SCC 34 (S.C.C.), stands for such a proposition.

SOCAN v. Bell Canada, 2012 SCC 36, (sub nom. Society of Composers, Authors and Music Publishers of Canada v. Bell Canada) [2012] 2 S.C.R. 326 (S.C.C.)

Coram: McLachlin C.J. and LeBel, Deschamps, Fish, Abella, Rothstein, Cromwell, Moldaver and Karakatsanis JJ.

Reasons for Judgment: (paras. 1 to 50) Abella J. (McLachlin C.J. and LeBel, Deschamps, Fish, Rothstein, Cromwell, Moldaver and Karakatsanis JJ. concurring)

[8] In *Théberge v. Galerie d'Art du Petit Champlain inc.*, [2002] 2 S.C.R. 336, this Court noted that copyright requires "a balance between promoting the public interest in the encouragement and dissemination of works of the arts and intellect and obtaining a just reward for the creator" (para. 30).

[9] *Théberge* reflected a move away from an earlier, author-centric view which focused on the exclusive right of authors and copyright owners to control how their works were used in the marketplace: see, e.g. *Bishop v. Stevens*, [1990] 2 S.C.R. 467, at pp. 478-79. Under this former framework, any benefit the public might derive from the copyright system was only "a fortunate by-product of private entitlement": Carys J. Craig, "Locke, Labour and Limiting the Author's Right: A Warning against a Lockean Approach to Copyright Law" (2002), *28 Queen's L.J.* 1, at pp. 14-15.

[10] *Théberge* focused attention instead on the importance copyright plays in promoting the public interest, and emphasized that the dissemination of artistic works is central to developing a robustly cultured and intellectual public domain. As noted by Professor David Vaver, both protection and access must be sensitively balanced in order to achieve this goal: *Intellectual Property Law: Copyright, Patents, Trade-marks* (2nd ed. 2011), at p. 60.

[11] *CCH* confirmed that users' rights are an essential part of furthering the public interest objectives of the *Copyright Act*. One of the tools employed to achieve the proper balance between protection and access in the Act is the concept of fair dealing, which allows users to engage in some activities that might otherwise amount to copyright infringement. In order to maintain the proper

balance between these interests, the fair dealing provision "must not be interpreted restrictively": *CCH*, at para. 48.

Reference re Broadcasting Act, S.C. 1991 (Canada), 2012 SCC 68 (S.C.C.)

Coram: McLachlin C.J. and LeBel, Deschamps, Fish, Abella, Rothstein, Cromwell, Moldaver and Karakatsanis JJ.

Reasons for Judgment: (paras. 1 to 83) Rothstein J. (McLachlin C.J. and LeBel, Fish and Moldaver JJ. concurring)

Joint Dissenting Reasons: (paras. 84 to 126) Abella and Cromwell JJ. (Deschamps and Karakatsanis JJ. concurring)

. . .

[36] The *Copyright Act* is concerned both with encouraging creativity and providing reasonable access to the fruits of creative endeavour. These objectives are furthered by a carefully balanced scheme that creates exclusive economic rights for different categories of copyright owners in works or other protected subject matter, typically in the nature of a statutory monopoly to prevent anyone from exploiting the work in specified ways without the copyright owner's consent. It also provides user rights such as fair dealing and specific exemptions that enable the general public or specific classes of users to access protected material under certain conditions. (See, e.g., *Théberge v. Galerie d'Art du Petit Champlain inc.*, 2002 SCC 34, [2002] 2 S.C.R. 336, at paras. 11-12 and 30; *Mattel, Inc. v. 3894207 Canada Inc.*, 2006 SCC 22, [2006] 1 S.C.R. 772, at para. 21; D. Vaver, *Intellectual Property Law: Copyright, Patents, Trade-marks* (2nd ed. 2011), at pp. 34 and 56.) Among the categories of subject matter protected by copyright are the rights of broadcasters in communication signals (see ss. 2 "copyright" and 21 of the *Copyright Act*). In addition, "program[s]" within the meaning of the *Broadcasting Act*, are often pre-recorded original content which may constitute protected works, namely "dramatic work[s]" or "compilation[s]" thereof, under the *Copyright Act*: see, e.g., discussion in J. S. McKeown, *Fox on Canadian Law of Copyright and Industrial Designs* (4th ed. loose-leaf), at para. 15:3(a).

. . .

Phonographic Performance Company of Australia Limited v. Commonwealth of Australia, [2012] HCA 8 (H.C.A.)

French CJ, Gummow, Hayne, Heydon, Crennan, Kiefel and Bell JJ

. . .

[94] The copyright given to authors and makers of records was, as Augustine Birrell said of the copyright granted by the Statute of Anne of 1709[46],

"qualified and time-limited property"[47]. Although the categories of protected works were much enlarged by the time of the 1911 Act, speaking generally the 1911 Act, like the Statute of Anne, took into account and balanced the interests of authors[48], entrepreneurs[49] and the public. The public's interest lay in the dissemination of copyright works, including dissemination on reasonable terms. Any detailed consideration of the historical context of the Statute of Anne supports this construction of its intent and its provisions[50]. Further, presaging compulsory licence schemes, the prices of books under the Statute of Anne were regulated to ensure that they were "just and reasonable"[51] and the uses by, and rights of, nominated libraries and universities in respect of copyright works were preserved[52].

[97] Exceptions to infringement, which include fair dealings or fair uses and compulsory licence provisions, constitute qualifications of or limitations upon a copyright owner's exclusive rights to do acts within the copyright, during the term of a copyright. In each case, such provisions reflect a specific public interest in obtaining access to the subject matter of copyright on some reasonable basis, a topic about which more will be said later.

. . .

Eldred v. Ashcroft, 123 S.Ct. 1505 (U.S. Sup. Ct. 2003)

Argued Oct. 9, 2002.

Decided Jan. 15, 2003. Rehearing Denied March 10, 2003. See 538 U.S. 916, 123 S.Ct. 1505

Ginsbury J:

. . .

[4] Petitioners dominantly advance a series of arguments all premised on the proposition that Congress may not extend an existing copyright absent new consideration from the author. They pursue this main theme under three headings. Petitioners contend that the CTEA's extension of existing copyrights (1) overlooks the requirement of "originality," (2) fails to "promote the Progress of Science," and (3) ignores copyright's *quid pro quo.*

Petitioners' "originality" argument draws on *Feist Publications, Inc. v. Rural Telephone Service Co.,* 499 U.S. 340, 111 S.Ct. 1282, 113 L.Ed.2d 358 (1991). In *Feist,* we observed that "[t]he *sine qua non* of copyright is originality,"*id.,* at 345, 111 S.Ct. 1282, and held that copyright protection is unavailable to "a narrow category of works in which the creative spark is utterly lacking or so trivial as to be virtually nonexistent,"*id.,* at 359, 111 S.Ct. 1282. Relying on *Feist,* petitioners urge that even if a work is sufficiently "original" to qualify for copyright protection in the first instance, any extension of the copyright's duration is impermissible because, once published, a work is no longer original.

Feist, however, did not touch on the duration of copyright protection. Rather, the decision addressed the core question of copyrightability, *i.e.,* the "creative spark" a work must have to be eligible for copyright protection at all. Explaining the originality requirement, *Feist* trained on the Copyright Clause words "Authors" and "Writings." *Id.,* at 346-347, 111 S.Ct. 1282. The decision did not construe the "limited Times" for which a work may be protected, and the originality requirement has no bearing on that prescription.

More forcibly, petitioners contend that the CTEA's extension of existing copyrights does not "promote the Progress of Science" as contemplated by the preambular language of the Copyright Clause. Art. I, § 8, cl. 8. To sustain this objection, petitioners do not argue that the Clause's preamble is an independently enforceable limit on Congress' power. See 239 F.3d, at 378 (Petitioners acknowledge that "the preamble of the Copyright Clause is not a substantive limit on Congress' legislative power."(internal quotation marks omitted)). Rather, they maintain that the preambular language identifies the sole end to which Congress may legislate; accordingly, they conclude, the meaning of "limited Times" must be "determined in light of that specified end." Brief for Petitioners 19. The CTEA's extension of existing copyrights categorically fails to "promote the Progress of Science," petitioners argue, because it does not stimulate the creation of new works but merely adds value to works already created.

As petitioners point out, we have described the Copyright Clause as "both a grant of power and a limitation,"*Graham v. John Deere Co. of Kansas City,* 383 U.S. 1, 5, 86 S.Ct. 684, 15 L.Ed.2d 545 (1966), and have said that "[t]he primary objective of copyright" is "[t]o promote the Progress of Science,"*Feist,* 499 U.S., at 349, 111 S.Ct. 1282. The "constitutional command," we have recognized, is that Congress, to the extent it enacts copyright laws at all, create a "system" that "promote[s] the Progress of Science." *Graham,* 383 U.S., at 6, 86 S.Ct. 684.[FN18]

> FN18. Justice STEVENS' characterization of reward to the author as "a secondary consideration" of copyright law, *post,* at 793, n. 4 (internal quotation marks omitted), understates the relationship between such rewards and the "Progress of Science." As we have explained, "[t]he economic philosophy behind the [Copyright] [C]lause ... is the conviction that encouragement of individual effort by personal gain is the best way to advance public welfare through the talents of authors and inventors." *Mazer v. Stein,* 347 U.S. 201, 219, 74 S.Ct. 460, 98 L.Ed. 630 (1954). Accordingly, "copyright law *celebrates* the profit motive, recognizing that the incentive to profit from the exploitation of copyrights will redound to the public benefit by resulting in the proliferation of knowledge.... The profit motive is the engine that ensures the progress of science." *American Geophysical Union v. Texaco Inc.,* 802 F.Supp. 1, 27 (S.D.N.Y.1992), aff'd, 60 F.3d 913 (C.A.2 1994). Rewarding authors for their creative labor and "promot[ing] ... Progress" are thus complementary; as James Madison observed, in copyright "[t]he public good fully coincides ... with the claims of individuals." The Federalist No. 43, p. 272 (C. Rossiter ed.1961). Justice BREYER's assertion that "copyright statutes must serve public, not private, ends,"*post,* at 803, similarly misses the mark. The two ends are

not mutually exclusive; copyright law serves public ends by providing individuals with an incentive to pursue private ones.

. . .

Closely related to petitioners' preambular argument, or a variant of it, is their assertion that the Copyright Clause "imbeds a quid pro quo." Brief for Petitioners 23. They contend, in this regard, that Congress may grant to an "Autho[r]" an "exclusive Right" for a "limited Tim[e]," but only in exchange for a "Writin[g]."

Congress' power to confer copyright protection, petitioners argue, is thus contingent upon an exchange: The author of an original work receives an "exclusive Right" for a "limited Tim[e]" in exchange for a dedication to the public thereafter. Extending an existing copyright without demanding additional consideration, petitioners maintain, bestows an unpaid-for benefit on copyright holders and their heirs, in violation of the *quid pro quo* requirement.

We can demur to petitioners' description of the Copyright Clause as a grant of legislative authority empowering Congress "to secure a bargain-this for that." *Id.,* at 16; see *Mazer v. Stein,* 347 U.S. 201, 219, 74 S.Ct. 460, 98 L.Ed. 630 (1954) ("The economic philosophy behind the clause empowering Congress to grant patents and copyrights is the conviction that encouragement of individual effort by personal gain is the best way to advance public welfare through the talents of authors and inventors in 'Science and useful Arts.' "). But the legislative evolution earlier recalled demonstrates what the bargain entails. Given the consistent placement of existing copyright holders in parity with future holders, the author of a work created in the last 170 years would reasonably comprehend, as the "this" offered her, a copyright not only for the time in place when protection is gained, but also for any renewal or extension legislated during that time.[FN21] Congress could rationally seek to "promote ... Progress" by including in every copyright statute an express guarantee that authors would receive the benefit of any later legislative extension of the copyright term. Nothing in the Copyright Clause bars Congress from creating the same incentive by adopting the same position as a matter of unbroken practice. See Brief for Respondent 31-32.

> FN21. Standard copyright assignment agreements reflect this expectation. See, *e.g.,* A. Kohn & B. Kohn, Music Licensing 471 (3d ed.1992-2002) (short form copyright assignment for musical composition, under which assignor conveys all rights to the work, "including the copyrights and proprietary rights therein and in any and all versions of said musical composition(s), and any renewals and extensions thereof (whether presently available *or subsequently available as a result of intervening legislation)*" (emphasis added)); 5 M. Nimmer & D. Nimmer, Copyright § 21.11[B], p. 21-305 (2002) (short form copyright assignment under which assignor conveys all assets relating to the work, "including without limitation, copyrights and renewals and/or extensions thereof"); 6 *id.,* § 30.04[B][1], p. 30-325 (form composer-producer agreement under which composer "assigns to Producer all rights (copyrights, rights under copyright and otherwise, whether now or hereafter known) and all renewals and extensions (as may now or hereafter exist)").

Neither *Sears, Roebuck & Co. v. Stiffel Co.,* 376 U.S. 225, 84 S.Ct. 784, 11 L.Ed.2d 661 (1964), nor *Bonito Boats, Inc. v. Thunder Craft Boats, Inc.,* 489

U.S. 141, 109 S.Ct. 971, 103 L.Ed.2d 118 (1989), is to the contrary. In both cases, we invalidated the application of certain state laws as inconsistent with the federal patent regime. *Sears,* 376 U.S., at 231-233, 84 S.Ct. 784; *Bonito,* 489 U.S., at 152, 109 S.Ct. 971. Describing Congress' constitutional authority to confer patents, *Bonito Boats* noted: "The Patent Clause itself reflects a balance between the need to encourage innovation and the avoidance of monopolies which stifle competition without any concomitant advance in the 'Progress of Science and useful Arts.' "*Id.,* at 146, 109 S.Ct. 971. *Sears* similarly stated that "[p]atents are not given as favors ... but are meant to encourage invention by rewarding the inventor with the right, limited to a term of years fixed by the patent, to exclude others from the use of his invention." 376 U.S., at 229, 84 S.Ct. 784. Neither case concerned the extension of a patent's duration. Nor did either suggest that such an extension might be constitutionally infirm. Rather, *Bonito Boats* reiterated the Court's unclouded understanding: "It is for Congress to determine if the present system" effectuates the goals of the Copyright and Patent Clause. 489 U.S., at 168, 109 S.Ct. 971. And as we have documented, see *supra,* at 779-781, Congress has many times sought to effectuate those goals by extending existing patents.

We note, furthermore, that patents and copyrights do not entail the same exchange, and that our references to a *quid pro quo* typically appear in the patent context. See, *e.g., J.E.M. Ag Supply, Inc. v. Pioneer Hi-Bred International, Inc.,* 534 U.S. 124, 142, 122 S.Ct. 593, 151 L.Ed.2d 508 (2001) ("The disclosure required by the Patent Act is 'the *quid pro quo* of the right to exclude.' " (quoting *Kewanee Oil Co. v. Bicron Corp.,* 416 U.S. 470, 484, 94 S.Ct. 1879, 40 L.Ed.2d 315 (1974))); *Bonito Boats,* 489 U.S., at 161, 109 S.Ct. 971 ("the *quid pro quo* of substantial creative effort required by the federal [patent] statute"); *Brenner v. Manson,* 383 U.S. 519, 534, 86 S.Ct. 1033, 16 L.Ed.2d 69 (1966) ("The basic *quid pro quo*... for granting a patent monopoly is the benefit derived by the public from an invention with substantial utility."); *Pennock v. Dialogue,* 2 Pet. 1, 23, 7 L.Ed. 327 (1829) (If an invention is already commonly known and used when the patent is sought, "there might be sound reason for presuming, that the legislature did not intend to grant an exclusive right," given the absence of a "*quid pro quo*."). This is understandable, given that immediate disclosure is not the objective of, but is *exacted from,* the patentee. It is the price paid for the exclusivity secured. See *J.E.M. Ag Supply,* 534 U.S., at 142, 122 S.Ct. 593. For the author seeking copyright protection, in contrast, disclosure is the desired objective, not something exacted from the author in exchange for the copyright. Indeed, since the 1976 Act, copyright has run from creation, not publication. See 1976 Act § 302(a); 17 U.S.C. § 302(a).

Further distinguishing the two kinds of intellectual property, copyright gives the holder no monopoly on any knowledge. A reader of an author's writing may make full use of any fact or idea she acquires from her reading. See § 102(b). The grant of a patent, on the other hand, does prevent full use by others of the inventor's knowledge. See Brief for Respondent 22; *Alfred Bell & Co. v. Catalda Fine Arts,* 191 F.2d 99, 103, n. 16 (C.A.2 1951) (The monopoly granted by a copyright "is not a monopoly of knowledge. The grant of a patent does prevent full use being made of knowledge, but the reader of a book is not by the copyright laws prevented from making full use of any information he may acquire from his reading."(quoting W. Copinger, Law of Copyright 2 (7th ed.1936))). In light of these distinctions, one cannot extract from language in our patent decisions-language not trained on a grant's duration-genuine support for petitioners' bold view. Accordingly, we reject the proposition that a *quid pro quo* requirement stops Congress from expanding copyright's term in a manner that puts existing and future copyrights in parity.[FN22]

> FN22. The fact that patent and copyright involve different exchanges does not, of course, mean that we may not be guided in our "limited Times" analysis by Congress' repeated extensions of existing patents. See *supra,* at 779-781. If patent's *quid pro quo* is more exacting than copyright's, then Congress' repeated extension of existing patents without constitutional objection suggests even more strongly that similar legislation with respect to copyrights is constitutionally permissible.

---

3. Technological Neutrality

As evolving technologies challenge traditional applications of long-standing legal doctrine, a commitment to "technological neutrality" has emerged as an important, if ambiguous, guiding principle in recent copyright jurisprudence.

Entertainment Software Assn. v. SOCAN, 2012 SCC 34 (S.C.C.)

Coram: McLachlin C.J. and LeBel, Deschamps, Fish, Abella, Rothstein, Cromwell, Moldaver and Karakatsanis JJ.

Joint Reasons for Judgment: (paras. 1 to 44) Abella and Moldaver JJ. (McLachlin C.J. and Deschamps and Karakatsanis JJ. concurring)

Dissenting Reasons: (paras. 45 to 128) Rothstein J. (LeBel, Fish and Cromwell JJ. concurring)

. . .

[4] The focus of this appeal is on the meaning of the word "communicate" in s. 3(1)(f), a term which is not defined in the Act. The Society of Composers, Authors and Music Publishers of Canada (SOCAN), which administers the right to "communicate" musical works on behalf of copyright owners, applied to the Board for a tariff under this provision to cover downloads of musical works over the Internet. The Entertainment Software Association and the Entertainment Software Association of Canada (collectively, ESA), which represent a broad coalition of video game publishers and distributors, objected to the tariff, arguing that "downloading" a video game containing musical works did not amount

to "communicating" that game to the public by telecommunication under s. 3(1) (f). Instead, a "download" is merely an additional, more efficient way to deliver copies of the games to customers. The downloaded copy is identical to copies purchased in stores or shipped to customers by mail, and the game publishers already pay copyright owners reproduction royalties for all of these copying activities.

[5] We agree with ESA. In our view, the Board's conclusion that a separate, "communication" tariff applied to downloads of musical works violates the principle of technological neutrality, which requires that the *Copyright Act* apply equally between traditional and more technologically advanced forms of the same media: Robertson v. Thomson Corp., [2006] 2 S.C.R. 363, at para. 49. The principle of technological neutrality is reflected in s. 3(1) of the Act, which describes a right to produce or reproduce a work "in any material form whatever". In our view, there is no practical difference between buying a durable copy of the work in a store, receiving a copy in the mail, or downloading an identical copy using the Internet. The Internet is simply a technological taxi that delivers a durable copy of the same work to the end user.

[6] This argument is echoed by David Vaver in his book, Intellectual Property Law: Copyright, Patents, Trade-marks (2nd ed. 2011), where he appears to criticize the Board's decision in this particular case:

> In principle, *substitute delivery systems* should compete on their merits: either both or neither should pay. Copyright law should strive for technological neutrality.
>
> . . .
>
> In the past, whether a customer bought a sound recording or video game physically at a store or ordered it by mail made no difference to the copyright holder: it got nothing extra for the clerk's or courier's handover of the record to the customer. Now, because of the telecommunication right, *copyright holders can and do charge extra for electronic delivery of identical content acquired off websites.* [Emphasis added; pp. 172-73.]

[7] ESA's argument is also consistent with this Court's caution in *Théberge v. Galerie d'Art du Petit Champlain inc.*, [2002] 2 S.C.R. 336, that the balance in copyright between promoting the public interest in the encouragement and dissemination of works and obtaining a just reward for the creator requires recognizing the "limited nature" of creators' rights:

> The proper balance among these and other public policy objectives lies not only in recognizing the creator's rights but in giving due weight to their limited nature. In crassly economic terms *it would be as inefficient to overcompensate artists and authors for the right of reproduction as it would be self-defeating to undercompensate them.* Once an authorized copy of a work is sold to a member of the public, it is generally for the purchaser, not the author, to determine what happens to it. [Emphasis added; para. 31.]

[8] The traditional balance between authors and users should be preserved in the digital environment: Carys Craig, "Locking Out Lawful Users: Fair Dealing and Anti-Circumvention in Bill C-32", in Michael Geist, ed., *From "Radical*

Extremism" to "Balanced Copyright": Canadian Copyright and the Digital Agenda (2010), 177, at p. 192.

[9] SOCAN has never been able to charge royalties for copies of video games stored on cartridges or discs, and bought in a store or shipped by mail. Yet it argues that identical copies of the games sold and delivered over the Internet are subject to both a fee for reproducing the work and a fee for communicating the work. The principle of technological neutrality requires that, absent evidence of Parliamentary intent to the contrary, we interpret the *Copyright Act* in a way that avoids imposing an additional layer of protections and fees based solely on the *method of delivery* of the work to the end user. To do otherwise would effectively impose a gratuitous cost for the use of more efficient, Internet-based technologies.

[10] The Board's misstep is clear from its definition of "download" as "a file containing data… the user is meant to keep as his own" (para. 13). The Board recognized that downloading is a copying exercise that creates an exact, durable copy of the digital file on the user's computer, identical to copies purchased in stores or through the mail. Nevertheless, it concluded that delivering a copy through the Internet was subject to two fees — one for reproduction and one for communication — while delivering a copy through stores or mail was subject only to reproduction fees. In coming to this conclusion, the Board ignored the principle of technological neutrality.

. . .

Rogers Communications Inc. v. SOCAN, 2012 SCC 35 (S.C.C.)

Coram: McLachlin C.J. and LeBel, Deschamps, Fish, Abella, Rothstein, Cromwell, Moldaver and Karakatsanis JJ.

Reasons for Judgment: (paras. 1 to 57) Rothstein J. (McLachlin C.J. and LeBel, Deschamps, Fish, Cromwell, Moldaver and Karakatsanis JJ. concurring)

Concurring reasons: (paras. 58 to 88) Abella J.

. . .

[36] The right to communicate to the public is historically linked to traditional media that operated on a broadcasting, or "push", model. As pointed out by the appellants, the predecessor to s. 3(1)(f) guaranteed copyright holders an exclusive right to communicate literary, dramatic, musical or artistic works by *radio-communication*. The predecessor section was introduced in 1931, implementing Article 11bis of the *Berne Convention for the Protection of Literary and Artistic Works*, 828 U.N.T.S. 221 (Rome Revision of 1928): J. S. McKeown, *Fox on Canadian Law of Copyright and Industrial Designs*, (4th ed. (loose-leaf), at p. 21-86); *Composers, Authors and Publishers Assoc. of Canada Ltd. v. CTV Television Network Ltd.*, [1968] S.C.R. 676, at p. 681. Radio-communications were

understood to include transmissions by microwave over the airwaves: *Canadian Admiral Corp. v. Rediffusion, Inc.*, [1954] Ex. C.R. 382. As such, the radio-communication right extended to radio and traditional over-the-air television broadcasting, notably leaving transmissions by cable outside of copyright protection.

[37] This technology-specific communication right was amended to the technologically neutral right to "communicate . . . to the public by telecommunication" to reflect the obligations entered into by Canada under NAFTA (*Canada-United States Free Trade Agreement Implementation Act*, S.C. 1988, c. 65, ss. 61 and 62). The change from radio-communication to telecommunication meant that Canadian cable companies which previously escaped any payment of royalties under the "radio-communication" right, were now caught by the Act: S. Handa, *Copyright Law in Canada* (2002), at p. 320.

[38] The historic relationship between the right to communicate to the public and broadcasting-type, "push" technologies, and the 1988 amendment in particular, is evidence that the Act has evolved to ensure its continued relevance in an evolving technological environment. The historic relationship does not support reading into the Act restrictions which are not apparent from and are even inconsistent with the neutral language of the Act itself.

[39] In addition, this Court has long recognized in the context of the reproduction right that, where possible, the Act should be interpreted to extend to technologies that were not or could not have been contemplated at the time of its drafting: *Apple Computer Inc. v. Mackintosh Computers Ltd.*, [1987] 1 F.C. 173 (T.D.), aff'd [1988] 1 F.C. 673 (C.A.), aff'd [1990] 2 S.C.R. 209. That the Act was to apply to new technologies was recently reaffirmed in *Robertson v. Thomson Corp.*, 2006 SCC 43, [2006] 2 S.C.R. 363, at para. 49, per LeBel and Fish JJ.:

> Media neutrality is reflected in s. 3(1) of the *Copyright Act* which describes a right to produce or reproduce a work "in any material form whatever". Media neutrality means that the *Copyright Act* should continue to apply in different media, including more technologically advanced ones. . . . [I]t exists to protect the rights of authors and others as technology evolves.

Although the words "in any material form whatever" qualify the right to "produce or reproduce the work" in s. 3(1), the same principle should guide the application of the neutral wording of the right to "communicate . . . to the public by telecommunication". The broad definition of "telecommunication" was adopted precisely to provide for a communication right "not dependent on the form of technology" (*SOCAN v. CAIP*, at para. 90).

[40] Ultimately, in determining the extent of copyright, regard must be had for the fact that "[t]he *Copyright Act* is usually presented as a balance between promoting the public interest in the encouragement and dissemination of works of the arts and intellect and obtaining a just reward for the creator" (*Théberge v. Galerie d'Art du Petit Champlain inc.*, 2002 SCC 34, [2002] 2 S.C.R. 336, at para. 30). This balance is not appropriately struck where the existence of copyright protection depends merely on the business model that the alleged infringer

chooses to adopt rather than the underlying communication activity. Whether a business chooses to convey copyright protected content in a traditional, "broadcasting" type fashion, or opts for newer approaches based on consumer choice and convenience, the end result is the same. The copyrighted work has been made available to an aggregation of individuals of the general public.

. . .

4. International Treaties Related to Copyright/Copyright Territoriality

Canada is a party to many international conventions and international trade agreements pertaining to copyright. These include the *Berne Convention for the Protection of Literary and Artistic* Works[11] the *Universal Copyright Convention*,[12] the *International Convention for the Protection of Performers, Producers of Phonograms and Broadcasting Organizations* (the *Rome Convention*),[13] the *WIPO Copyright Treaty* and the *WIPO Performances and Phonograms Treaties* (the Internet Treaties),[14] the *Canada-United States Free Trade Agreement* (FTA)[15] the *North American Free Trade Agreement* (*NAFTA*)[16] and the *World Trade Organization Agreement on Trade-Related Aspects of Intellectual Property Rights* (*TRIPs*).[17] These instruments are often used as an aid in construing the Act.[18] In cases of ambiguity, courts will favour a construction of the Act which accords with a treaty Canada has ratified, over an interpretation which is inconsistent with obligations undertaken in such documents.[19]

---

[11]   Canada first joined the *Berne Convention* in 1923 and ratified the 1971 version of the *Berne Convention* on September 28, 1998.

[12]   This convention was adopted in 1952. Canada adhered to the convention on August 10, 1962.

[13]   This convention was adopted in 1961 and was ratified by Canada on June 4, 1998.

[14]   These were signed by Canada in 1997 and came into force in 2002. Canada has not yet ratified these treaties.

[15]   This came into force 1988 and resulted in amendments to the Copyright Act.

[16]   This came into force, for the most part, on January 1, 1994.

[17]   This came into force in Canada on January 1, 1996.

[18]   *Tele-Direct (Publications) Inc. v. American Business Information Inc.* (1997), 76 C.P.R. (3d) 296 (Fed. C.A.); *C.A.P.A.C. v. CTV Television Network* (1968), 68 D.L.R. (2d) 98 (S.C.C.); *Bishop v. Steven's*, [1990] 2 S.C.R. 467. Copies of these treaties are contained in the Appendix.

[19]   *SOCAN v. Canadian Association of Internet Providers*, 2004 SCC 45.

Harvard College v. Canada, [2002] 4 S.C.R. 45

Arbour J., Bastarache J., Binnie J., Gonthier J., Iacobucci J., L'Heureux-Dubé

J., LeBel J., Major J., McLachlin C.J.C

Judgment: December 5, 2002
Heard: May 21, 2002
Docket: 28155

. . .

Binnie J.:

. . .

B. International Scope of Intellectual Property Law

12 Intellectual property has global mobility, and states have worked diligently to harmonize their patent, copyright and trademark regimes. In this context, the Commissioner's approach to this case sounds a highly discordant note. Intellectual property was the subject matter of such influential agreements as the *International Convention for the Protection of Industrial Property* (*Paris Convention*) as early as 1883. International rules governing patents were strengthened by the *European Patent Convention* in 1973, and, more recently, the World Trade Organization *Agreement on Trade-Related Aspects of Intellectual Property Rights* (TRIPS) in 1994. Copyright was the subject of the *Berne Convention for the Protection of Literary and Artistic Works* in 1886, revised by the *Berlin Convention of 1908* and the *Rome Convention* of 1928. The *Universal Copyright Convention* was concluded in 1952. Legislation varies of course, from state to state, but broadly speaking Canada has sought to harmonize its concepts of intellectual property with other like-minded jurisdictions.

13 The mobility of capital and technology makes it desirable that comparable jurisdictions with comparable intellectual property legislation arrive (to the extent permitted by the specifics of their own laws) at similar legal results: *Galerie d'art du Petit Champlain inc. c. Théberge*, 2002 SCC 34 (S.C.C.), at para. 6.

14 The appellant Commissioner's definition of *un*patentable "higher life forms" includes not only animals but also plants and seeds. Genetically modified foods are controversial, but these are not controversies that should be dealt with by judicial exclusion of "higher life forms" from the definition of "an invention". Parliament itself has clearly signalled its limited view of the role and function of the *Patent Act*. In 1993, it repealed the prohibition in the former s. 27(3) of the *Patent Act* against patenting "an invention that has an illicit object in view". It thereby made it clear that granting a patent is not an expression of approval or disapproval. At that time, Parliament did *not* add a provision, present in the *European Patent Convention* and in many civil law systems and international agreements, that patents will not be granted for inventions whose use or exploitation would be inconsistent with *ordre public*, public morality, or environmental or health protection. That type of provision would open the door to value judgments in assessing

patentability. Parliament did not endorse such an approach, even though the 1993 amendments were introduced to bring Canadian patent law into compliance with various international agreements. Parliament thereby signalled, however passively, that these important aspects of public policy would continue to be dealt with by regulatory regimes outside the *Patent Act*.

The internationalization of copyright is exemplified by the analysis of the territorial scope of the *Copyright Act* in the Tariff 22 case by the Supreme Court of Canada.

SOCAN v. Canadian Association of Internet Providers, 2004 SCC 45

Arbour J., Bastarache J., Binnie J., Deschamps J., Fish J., Iacobucci J., LeBel J., Major J., McLachlin C.J.C.

Heard: December 3, 2003
Judgment: June 30, 2004
Docket: 29286

Binnie J.:

1 This appeal raises the difficult issue of who should compensate musical composers and artists for their Canadian copyright in music downloaded in Canada from a foreign country via the Internet. In an era when it is as easy to access a website hosted by a server in Bangalore as it is to access a website with a server in Mississauga, where is the protection for the financial rights of the people who created the music in the first place? Who, if anyone, is to pay the piper?

2 The Internet "exists", notionally, in cyberspace. It has been described as a "fascinating exercise in symbiotic anarchy"; see G. S. Takach, *Computer Law* (2nd ed. 2003), at p. 30. It is not contained by national boundaries. The Internet thus presents a particular challenge to national copyright laws, which are typically territorial in nature.

3 The answer to this challenge proposed by the respondent, the Society of Composers, Authors and Music Publishers of Canada ("SOCAN"), is to seek to impose liability for royalties on the various Internet Service Providers located in Canada irrespective of where the transmission originates. There is no doubt that such an imposition, from SOCAN's perspective, would provide an efficient engine of collection.

4 The appellants, on the other hand, representing a broad coalition of Canadian Internet Service Providers, resist. Their basic argument is that none of them, as found by the Copyright Board, regulate or are even in the usual case *aware* of the content of the Internet communications which they transmit. Like a telephone company, they provide the medium, but they do not control the message.

5 Parliament has spoken on this issue. In a 1988 amendment to the *Copyright Act*, R.S.C. 1985, c. C-42, it made it clear that Internet intermediaries, as such, are not to be considered parties to the infringing communication. They are service providers, not participants in the *content* of the communication. In light of Parliament's legislative policy, when applied to the findings of fact by the Copyright Board, I agree with the Board's conclusion that as a matter of law the appellants did not, in general, "communicate" or "authorize" the communication of musical works in Canada in violation of the respondent's copyright within the meaning of the *Copyright Act*.

6 SOCAN sought a judicial review of the Board's decision by the Federal Court of Appeal, which essentially upheld the Board's exclusion of the appellants from copyright liability where they perform a pure intermediary function. However, the court, in a 2-1 majority decision, also held that where an Internet Service Provider in Canada creates a "cache" of Internet material, even for purely technical reasons, they are no longer a mere intermediary but a communicator and thus become a participant in the copyright infringement. A contrary conclusion was reached by Sharlow J.A., dissenting in part, who agreed with the Copyright Board that to cache for the purpose of enhancing Internet economy and efficiency does not constitute infringement. I agree with the dissent on this point. To that extent, the appeal should be allowed.

7 The respondent's cross-appeal seeking to hold Internet intermediaries liable for copyright royalties even where serving only as a conduit should be dismissed.

. . .

IV. Analysis

40 This Court has recently described the *Copyright Act* as providing "a balance between promoting the public interest in the encouragement and dissemination of works of the arts and intellect and obtaining a just reward for the creator (or, more accurately, to prevent someone other than the creator from appropriating whatever benefits may be generated)" (*Galerie d'art du Petit Champlain inc. c. Théberge*, [2002] 2 S.C.R. 336, 2002 SCC 34 (S.C.C.), at para. 30, *CCH Canadian Ltd. v. Law Society of Upper Canada*, [2004] 1 S.C.R. 339, 2004 SCC 13 (S.C.C.), at para. 10). The capacity of the Internet to disseminate "works of the arts and intellect" is one of the great innovations of the information age. Its use should be facilitated rather than discouraged, but this should not be done unfairly at the expense of those who created the works of arts and intellect in the first place.

41 The issue of the proper balance in matters of copyright plays out against the much larger conundrum of trying to apply national laws to a fast-evolving technology that in essence respects no national boundaries. Thus in *Citron v. Zündel* (2002), 41 C.H.R.R. D/274 (Can. Human Rights Trib.), the Canadian Human Rights Tribunal wrestled with jurisdiction over an alleged hate Web site supplied with content from Toronto but posted from a host server in California. In *Earth Future Lottery, Re*, [2003] 1 S.C.R. 123, 2003 SCC 10 (S.C.C.), the issue was whether sales of tickets from an Internet lottery in Prince Edward Island

constituted gambling "in the province" when almost all of the targeted on-line purchasers resided elsewhere. The "cyber libel" cases multiply. In *Braintech Inc. v. Kostiuk* (1999), 171 D.L.R. (4th) 46 (B.C. C.A.), the British Columbia Court of Appeal refused to enforce a Texas judgment for Internet defamation against a B.C. resident where the B.C. resident's only connection with Texas was "passive posting on an electronic bulletin board" (para. 66). There was no proof that anyone in Texas had actually looked at it. On the other hand, in *Dow Jones & Co. v. Gutnick* (2002), 194 A.L.R. 433, [2002] H.C.A. 56 (Australia H.C.), the High Court of Australia accepted jurisdiction over a defamation action in respect of material uploaded onto the defendant's server in New Jersey and downloaded by end users in the State of Victoria. The issue of global forum shopping for actions for Internet torts has scarcely been addressed. The availability of child pornography on the Internet is a matter of serious concern. E-Commerce is growing. Internet liability is thus a vast field where the legal harvest is only beginning to ripen. It is with an eye to this broader context that the relatively precise questions raised by the Copyright Board must be considered.

. . .

1 Canada's Legislative Reach

54 While the Parliament of Canada, unlike the legislatures of the Provinces, has the legislative competence to enact laws having extraterritorial effect, it is presumed not to intend to do so, in the absence of clear words or necessary implication to the contrary. This is because "[i]n our modern world of easy travel and with the emergence of a global economic order, chaotic situations would often result if the principle of territorial jurisdiction were not, at least generally, respected"; see *Tolofson v. Jensen*, [1994] 3 S.C.R. 1022 (S.C.C.), at p. 1051, *per* La Forest J.

55 While the notion of comity among independent nation States lacks the constitutional status it enjoys among the provinces of the Canadian federation (*Morguard Investments Ltd. v. De Savoye*, [1990] 3 S.C.R. 1077 (S.C.C.), at p. 1098), and does not operate as a limitation on Parliament's legislative competence, the courts nevertheless presume, in the absence of clear words to the contrary, that Parliament did not intend its legislation to receive extraterritorial application.

56 Copyright law respects the territorial principle, reflecting the implementation of a "web of interlinking international treaties" based on the principle of national treatment (see D. Vaver, *Copyright Law* (2000), at p. 14).

57 The applicability of our *Copyright Act* to communications that have international participants will depend on whether there is a sufficient connection between this country and the communication in question for Canada to apply its law consistent with the "principles of order and fairness ... that ensure security of [cross-border] transactions with justice"; see *Morguard Investments Ltd.*, *supra*, at p. 1097; see also *Unifund Assurance Co. of Canada v. Insurance Corp. of British Columbia*, [2003] 2 S.C.R. 63, 2003 SCC 40 (S.C.C.), at para. 56; R. Sullivan, *Sullivan and Driedger on the Construction of Statutes* (4th ed. 2002), at pp. 601-602.

58 Helpful guidance on the jurisdictional point is offered by La Forest J. in *R. v. Libman*, [1985] 2 S.C.R. 178 (S.C.C.). That case involved a fraudulent stock scheme. U.S. purchasers were solicited by telephone from Toronto, and their investment monies (which the Toronto accused caused to be routed through Central America) wound up in Canada. The accused contended that the crime, if any, had occurred in the United States, but La Forest J. took the view that "[t] his kind of thinking has, perhaps not altogether fairly, given rise to the reproach that a lawyer is a person who can look at a thing connected with another as not being so connected. For *everyone knows that the transaction in the present case is both here and there*" (at p. 208 (emphasis added)). Speaking for the Court, he stated the relevant territorial principle as follows (at pp. 212-13):

> I might summarize my approach to the limits of territoriality in this way. As I see it, all that is necessary to make an offence subject to the jurisdiction of our courts is that a significant portion of the activities constituting that offence took place in Canada. As it is put by modern academics, it is sufficient that there be a "real and substantial link" between an offence and this country... [Emphasis added.]

59 So also, in my view, a telecommunication from a foreign state to Canada, or a telecommunication from Canada to a foreign state, "is both here and there". Receipt may be no less "significant" a connecting factor than the point of origin (not to mention the physical location of the host server, which may be in a third country). To the same effect, see *Canada (Human Rights Commission) v. Canadian Liberty Net*, [1998] 1 S.C.R. 626 (S.C.C.), at para. 52; *Kitakufe v. Oloya*, [1998] O.J. No. 2537 (Ont. Gen. Div.). In the factual situation at issue in *Citron v. Zündel Earth Future Lottery*, *supra*, for example, the fact that the host server was located in California was scarcely conclusive in a situation where both the content provider (Zundel) and a major part of his target audience were located in Canada. The *Zündel* case was decided on grounds related to the provisions of the *Canadian Human Rights Act*, but for present purposes the object lesson of those facts is nevertheless instructive.

60 The "real and substantial connection" test was adopted and developed by this Court in *Morguard Investments Ltd.*, *supra*, at pp. 1108-1109, *Hunt v. T & N plc*, [1993] 4 S.C.R. 289 (S.C.C.), at pp. 325-6 and 328, and *Tolofson*, *supra*, at p. 1049. The test has been reaffirmed and applied more recently in cases such as *Holt Cargo Systems Inc. v. ABC Containerline N.V. (Trustees of)*, [2001] 3 S.C.R. 907, 2001 SCC 90 (S.C.C.), at para. 71, *Spar Aerospace Ltd. v. American Mobile Satellite Corp.*, [2002] 4 S.C.R. 205, 2002 SCC 78 (S.C.C.), *Unifund*, *supra*, at para. 54, and *Beals v. Saldanha*, [2003] 3 S.C.R. 416, 2003 SCC 72 (S.C.C.). From the outset, the real and substantial connection test has been viewed as an appropriate way to "prevent overreaching ... and [to restrict] the exercise of jurisdiction over extraterritorial and transnational transactions" (La Forest J. in *Tolofson*, *supra*, at p. 1049). The test reflects the underlying reality of "the territorial limits of law under the international legal order" and respect for the legitimate actions of other states inherent in the principle of international comity (*Tolofson*, at p. 1047). A real and substantial connection to Canada is sufficient to support the application of our *Copyright Act* to international Internet

transmissions in a way that will accord with international comity and be consistent with the objectives of order and fairness.

61 In terms of the Internet, relevant connecting factors would include the *situs* of the content provider, the host server, the intermediaries and the end user. The weight to be given to any particular factor will vary with the circumstances and the nature of the dispute.

62 Canada clearly has a significant interest in the flow of information in and out of the country. Canada regulates the reception of broadcasting signals in Canada wherever originated; see *Bell ExpressVu Ltd. Partnership v. Rex*, [2002] 2 S.C.R. 559, 2002 SCC 42 (S.C.C.). Our courts and tribunals regularly take jurisdiction in matters of civil liability arising out of foreign transmissions which are received and have their impact here; see *WIC Premium Television Ltd. v. General Instrument Corp.* (2000), 8 C.P.R. (4th) 1 (Alta. C.A.); *World Stock Exchange, Re* (2000), 9 A.S.C.S. 658 (Alta. Securities Comm.).

63 Generally speaking, this Court has recognized as a sufficient "connection" for taking jurisdiction, situations where Canada is the country of transmission (*Libman, supra*) *or* the country of reception (*Canada v. Liberty Net, supra*). This jurisdictional posture is consistent with international copyright practice.

64 In a recent decision of the European Commission involving "simulcasting", a model reciprocal agreement approved by the Commission was based on the country-of-destination principle. The decision commented that according to the principle "*which appears to reflect the current legal situation in copyright law*, the act of communication to the public of a copyright protected work takes place *not only* in the country of origin (emission-State) but also in all the States where the signals can be *received* (reception-States)" (at para. 21 (emphasis added)), EC, *Commission Decision of 8 October 2002 relating to a proceeding under Article 81 of the EC Treaty and Article 53 of the EEA Agreement*, Case No. COMP/C2/38.014 IFPI ("the Simulcasting decision")

65 Canada is a signatory but not yet a party to the WIPO Copyright Treaty. This treaty responded to the development of the Internet and other on-demand telecommunications technology. Article 8 provides that:

> ...authors of literary and artistic works shall enjoy the exclusive right of authorizing any communication to the public of their works, by wire or wireless means, including the making available to the public of their works in such a way that members of the public may access these works from a place and at a time individually chosen by them.

The "making available" right is generally exercised at the point of transmission. This does not deny the interest of the country of reception but avoids, as a matter of policy, a "layering" of royalty obligations in different countries that are parties to the *WCT*.

66 In 2000, the European Commission issued what is known as its *E-Commerce Directive*; see *Directive 2000/31 EC of the European Parliament and of the Council of June 8, 2000 on certain legal aspects of information society services,*

in particular electronic commerce, in the Internal Market ("Directive on electronic commerce"), [2000] O.J. L.178/1. Its purpose was to ensure the free movement among Member States of "information society services", defined as "any service normally provided for remuneration, at a distance, by means of electronic equipment ... and at the individual request of a recipient of a service" (Preamble, clause 17). The *E-Commerce Directive* preferred as a matter of policy the law of the Member State on whose territory the service provider is established (art. 3(1)). It was thought that *"[i]nformation society services should be supervised at the source of the activity* ... to that end, it is necessary to ensure that the competent authority provides such protection not only for the citizens of its own country but for all Community citizens" (Preamble, clause (22) (emphasis added)). The Directive notes that the place where a service provider is established should be determined by the case law of the European Court of Justice, which holds that the proper *situs* is not the place where the technology is, or the place where the person accessing the service is, but rather where the service provider's centre of activities is (Preamble, clause (19)); see G. J. H. Smith, *Internet Law and Regulation* (3rd ed. 2002), at p. 269.

67 Supranational organizations such as the European Commission may thus allocate responsibility among their member States whether the state of transmission or the state of reception as a matter of policy. In the absence of such regional or international arrangements, the territorial nature of copyright law must be respected.

68 National practice confirms that *either* the country of transmission *or* the country of reception may take jurisdiction over a "communication" linked to its territory, although whether it chooses to do so is a matter of legislative or judicial policy; see generally M. V. Pietsch, "International Copyright Infringement and the Internet: An Analysis of the Existing Means of Enforcement" (2001-2002), 24 *Hastings Comm. & Ent. L.J.* 273.

a.   The United States

69 At present there is authority in the United States for taking copyright jurisdiction over both the sender of the transmission out of the United States and the receiver in the United States of material from outside that country.

70 In *N.F.L. v. PrimeTime 24 Joint Venture*, 211 F.3d 10 (U.S. 2nd Cir., 2000), the U.S. defendant caused satellite transmission of NFL football games from the U.S. to Canada. The court found this to violate the NFL's U.S. copyright even though the broadcasts were being sent to the satellite and thence to Canada for Canadian viewers. The United States was the *country of transmission*. It was held sufficient to constitute U.S. copyright infringement that a significant step in the telecommunication had taken place in the United States (at p. 13):

> ...it is clear that PrimeTime's uplink transmission of signals captured in the United Sates is a step in the process by which NFL's protected work wends its way to a public audience. In short, PrimeTime publicly displayed or performed material in which the NFL owns the copyright. Because PrimeTime did not have authorization to make such a public performance, PrimeTime infringed the NFL's copyright.

71 At the same time, some U.S. courts take the view that U.S. copyright is also breached when the U.S. is the *country of reception*. Thus in *Los Angeles News Service v. Conus Communications Co.*, 969 F. Supp. 579 (U.S. C.D. Cal., 1997), the plaintiff had videotaped riots that occurred in Los Angeles in connection with the Rodney King assault case. The CBC broadcast some of the footage in Canada. Inevitably, some homes in border States saw the CBC broadcast. The plaintiff alleged breach of U.S. copyright. The CBC moved to dismiss the U.S. proceeding for lack of jurisdiction, but was unsuccessful. The court held, at pp. 583-84:

> Under the plain language of the Act, the subject footage was "displayed" on televi-sion sets within the United States within the meaning of the Copyright Act. To find otherwise would leave a substantial loophole in the copyright laws. Broadcasters could deliberately transmit potentially infringing material from locations across the U.S. borders for display in the United States without regard to the rights of copyright owners set forth in the U.S. Copyright Act.

72 Equally, in *N.F.L. v. TVRadioNow Corp.*, 53 U.S.P.Q.2d 1831 (U.S. W.D. Pa., 2000), the court found that a Web site in Canada that "streamed" U.S. cable television through the Internet with worldwide availability infringed the U.S. transmission rights of the copyright owners despite the fact that the defendant was located in Canada and arguably was not in violation of Canadian copyright laws.

b.   Australia

73 Australia has recently adopted the *Copyright Amendment (Digital Agenda) Act 2000* to implement its obligations under the WIPO treaties. The definition of "communication to the public" appears to apply Australian copyright law to communications entirely within Australia, those originating within Australia and received by an end user outside Australia, and those originating outside Austra-lia but received by an end user in Australia:

> **10. Interpretation**
>
> (1) In this Act, unless the contrary intention appears
>
> > **communicate** means make available online or electronically transmit (whether over a path, or a combination of paths, provided by a material substance or otherwise) a work or other subject-matter.
> >
> > **to the public** means to the public within or outside Australia. [Emphasis added.]

74 The definition of "to the public" seems to permit Australian copyright hold-ers to exact royalties on both communication from Australia of material directed to overseas audiences as well as overseas communications received in Australia.

c.   France

75 An analysis of liability in France suggests that "[c]ourts will likely assert jurisdiction not only over transmissions *from France*, but also transmissions *into*

France that are alleged to cause damage" (emphasis added); see D. J. Gervais, "Transmissions of Music on the Internet: An analysis of the Copyright Laws of Canada, France, Germany, Japan, the United Kingdom, and the United States" (2001), 34 *Vand. J. Transnat'l L.* 1363, at p. 1376. In *UEJF v. Yahoo! Inc.*, Trib. gr. inst. Paris, May 22, 2000, the court ordered Yahoo! Inc., a U.S. based Internet company, to block access by French users to an Internet auction offering Nazi paraphernalia because [translation] "the harm is suffered in France". (The U.S. courts refused to give effect in the United States to the French court order, not on jurisdictional grounds as such, but based on First Amendment rights; see *Yahoo!, Inc. v. La Ligue Contre Le Racisme et L'Antisemitisme*, 145 F.Supp.2d 1168 (U.S. N.D. Cal., 2001)).

76 Accordingly, the conclusion that Canada *could* exercise copyright jurisdiction in respect both of transmissions originating here and transmissions originating abroad but received here is not only consistent with our general law (*Libman, supra*, and *Canada v. Liberty Net, supra*) but with both national and international copyright practice.

77 This conclusion does not, of course, imply imposition of automatic copyright liability on foreign content providers whose music is telecommunicated to a Canadian end user. Whether or not a real and substantial connection exists will turn on the facts of a particular transmission (*Braintech, supra*). It is unnecessary to say more on this point because the Canadian copyright liability of foreign content providers is not an issue that arises for determination in this appeal, although, as stated, the Board itself intimated that where a foreign transmission is aimed at Canada, copyright liability might attach.

78 This conclusion also raises the spectre of imposition of copyright duties on a single telecommunication in both the State of transmission and the State of reception, but as with other fields of overlapping liability (taxation for example), the answer lies in the making of international or bilateral agreements, not in national courts straining to find some jurisdictional infirmity in either State.

. . .

LeBel J.:

I. Introduction

134 Among the difficult issues raised by this appeal is how to determine, under the Copyright Act, R.S.C. 1985, c. C-42, whether an Internet communication occurs in Canada. I have read my colleague Binnie J.'s reasons and, although I agree with his judgment in all other respects and with his disposition of the appeal, I respectfully disagree with his analysis of the localization issue. My disagreement is confined to the appropriate test for determining the location of an internet communication under the Copyright Act and does not touch on determining liability. For the reasons that follow, I would affirm the Board's determination that an Internet communication occurs within Canada when it originates from a server located in Canada.

. . .

B. Communication Within Canada

145 Given that Parliament did not intend the Act to have effect outside Canada, when does a communication occur *within* Canada for the purpose of s. 3(1)(*f*)? Any choice between the location of the end user, host server or content provider, or all three, will be somewhat arbitrary and will import its own set of problems. Each choice has its own supporters and critics; for an overview of positions, see A. P. Reindl, "Choosing Law in Cyberspace: Copyright Conflicts on Global Networks" (1997-1998), 19 *Mich. J. Int'l L.* 799.

146 I share the Board's view that a communication occurs within Canada where it originates from a host server located in Canada. In this way, the copyrighted works physically exist within Canadian territory and thus attract the protection of s. 3(1)(*f*). This does not mean that the host server provider is liable; it is the content provider who is liable for an infringing communication. The Board's approach, as I have observed, provides a straightforward and logical rule for locating communications occurring within Canada that will be readily applicable by the Board in setting tariffs, by the courts in infringement proceedings, and by solicitors in providing advice to their clients.

147 With respect, I disagree with the approach taken by Binnie J. Turning first to the real and substantial connection test, it is my view that a test that was developed by this Court to deal with the exigencies of the Canadian federation should not be lightly transposed as a rule of statutory construction. The real and substantial connection test grew out of the recognition and enforcement of judgments between sister provinces as well as the appropriate assumption of jurisdiction by a court in one province over matters affecting another province, and was more recently applied to the recognition and enforcement of foreign judgments from outside Canada: see *Morguard, supra*; *Beals v. Saldanha*, [2003] 3 S.C.R. 416, 2003 SCC 72 (S.C.C.). There is no constitutional imperative raised in this appeal, unlike interprovincial cases (*Hunt v. T & N plc*, [1993] 4 S.C.R. 289 (S.C.C.)), though international comity is implicated. The real and substantial connection test is not a principle of legislative jurisdiction; it applies only to courts.

148 The only question is whether Parliament intended the Act to have effect beyond Canada. The principle of territoriality operates at the level of a rebuttable presumption that Parliament does not intend the Act to operate beyond Canada's borders. Moreover, copyright law is territorial in nature and thus limited to its enacting State. The territoriality principle has been incorporated into a number of international treaties, to which Canada is a signatory: see e.g. *Berne Convention for the Protection of Literary and Artistic Works*, 1886 ("*Berne Convention*"); *Agreement on Trade-Related Aspects of Intellectual Property Rights*, 1994 ("TRIPS") (1869 U.N.T.S. 299); World Intellectual Property Organization *Copyright Treaty*, 1996 ("*WCT*"); and World Intellectual Property Organization *Performances and Phonograms Treaty*, 1996 ("*PPT*").

149 Article 5 of the *Berne Convention* calls for the territorial treatment of copyright; however, the *Berne Convention* does not specifically address the

communication of works over the Internet. Canada is a signatory to the *WCT*, but it is not yet party to the treaty; it has yet to ratify it. The Board refused to interpret the Act in light of the *WCT* because the *WCT* is "not binding in Canada since it has been signed but not ratified by the Canadian Government" (at p. 448). I disagree. Although Canada has not ratified the treaty, this does not mean that it should not be considered as an aid in interpreting the Act. Article 8 of the *WCT* provides:

> **[Right of Communication to the Public]**
>
> Without prejudice to the provisions of Articles 11(1)(ii), 11bis(1)(i) and (ii), 11ter(1)(ii), 14(1)(ii) and 14bis(1) of the Berne Convention, authors of literary and artistic works shall enjoy the exclusive right of authorizing any communication to the public of their works, by wire or wireless means, including the making available to the public of their works in such a way that members of the public may access these works from a place and at a time individually chosen by them. [Emphasis added.]

The purpose of art. 8 of the *WCT* is to harmonize domestic copyright laws in the party States with respect to the right of communication of copyrighted works. We should not ignore that fact.

150 As McLachlin C.J. recently held, even though international norms are generally not binding without domestic implementation, they are relevant in interpreting domestic legislation: see *R. v. Sharpe*, [2001] 1 S.C.R. 45, 2001 SCC 2 (S.C.C.), at para. 175. Parliament is presumed not to legislate in breach of a treaty, the comity of nations and the principles of international law. This rule of construction is well established: see *Daniels v. White*, [1968] S.C.R. 517 (S.C.C.), at p. 541. Although the *Copyright Act* has not yet been amended to reflect the signing of the *WCT*, I believe this cannon of interpretation is equally applicable to the case at bar.

151 How to interpret the meaning of "communicate" in s. 3(1)(*f*) in the context of the Internet so as to best respect the principle of territoriality in the *Berne Convention*? In my opinion, the host server test adopted by the Board has the benefit of clearly complying with the territoriality requirement of international copyright law. It also accords with the *WCT* communication right (art. 8), which includes "the making available to the public of their works in such a way that members of the public may access these works from a place and at a time individually chosen by them"; copyrighted works are made available on the Internet when they are posted on a host server. Before they are posted on a host server, they are not available to the public.

152 The real and substantial connection test proposed by Binnie J. is inconsistent with the territoriality principle in that it may reach out and grasp content providers located in Bangalore who post content on a server in Hong Kong based only on the fact that the copyrighted work is retrieved by end users in Canada. Unlike a broadcaster, a content provider does not know in advance which territories will receive its transmissions. Placing an emphasis on the end user is also inconsistent with the "making available" right in the *WCT*. A danger with

Binnie J.'s approach is that it could result in a layering of royalty obligations between States. This danger is particularly acute with the Internet: content posted on a server is usually accessible from anywhere on the globe. With respect, to say that asserting jurisdiction over communications originating elsewhere but received in Canada accords with national and international copyright practice overstates the case. A review of various national laws demonstrates precious little harmonization in law or practice.

Chapter 2

WHAT COPYRIGHT PROTECTS AND PRE-REQUISITES TO PROTECTION

1. The Intangible Work

The subject matter of copyright is the intangible work of original expression. Inherent in the concept of *"intellectual* property" is the notion that the intellectual subject to which rights attach exists separately from the physical manifestation or embodiment of that subject. While copyright's intangible work must find expression in a tangible medium in order for rights to vest (see Section 4 below), it is with the intangible thing that the law of copyright is truly concerned. The following case illustrates this important distinction.

Dickens v. Hawksley, [1935] Ch. 267 (Eng. Ch. Div.)

COURT OF APPEAL

1934 June 6, 7; July 23.

LORD HANWORTH M.R., ROMER and MAUGHAM L.JJ.

LORD HANWORTH M.R. A number of interesting points are involved in this appeal, but before discussing them it is important to state the facts with some care. Charles Dickens, the well known novelist and writer, wrote for his children the story of the life of Jesus Christ, which was known in his family as "The Life of Our Lord" or "The New Testament" or "The Life of Christ." He died on June 9, 1870, and at that time this story was in manuscript in his own hand and had never been published. By the terms of his will, which was dated May 12, 1869, he made (inter alia) the following bequest to his sister-in-law, Georgina Hogarth: "I also give to the said Georgina Hogarth all my private papers whatsoever and wheresoever." The will was duly proved, and under the terms of the above bequest Miss Hogarth took possession of the manuscript. By his said will Charles Dickens gave "to my dear and trusty friend John Forster .... such manuscripts of my published works as may be in my possession at the time of my decease." Thereafter he devised all his real and personal estate to Georgina Hogarth and John Forster, upon trust at their, his or her uncontrolled and irresponsible direction to "proceed to an immediate sale or conversion into money of the said real and personal estate (including my copyrights) or defer and postpone any sale or conversion into money till such time or times as they, he or she shall think fit, and in the meantime may manage and let the said real and personal estate (including my copyrights) in such manner in all respects as I myself could do if I were living and acting therein; it being my intention that the trustees or trustee for the time being of this my will shall have the fullest power over the said real and personal estate which I can give them, him or her." He directed that the residue of his estate and the annual income of it should be held in trust for all his children, and that his daughter Mary, to whom he had previously left an annuity, "as regards my copyrights and the produce and profits thereof," should, notwithstanding the previous provision made for her, share with his other children therein.

Georgina Hogarth died on April 19, 1917, and by her will which was dated July 25, 1908, and a codicil dated October 20, 1915, she bequeathed her manuscript of "The Life of Christ" to Sir Henry Fielding Dickens and his wife for their lives, and upon the death of the survivor of them to Sir Henry Fielding Dickens absolutely. The manuscript thus came into the possession of Sir Henry Fielding Dickens, who was the last surviving son of Charles Dickens and died on December 21, 1933. By his will he explained why the manuscript had never been published while in his possession and left the question of its publication after his death to be decided by a majority of his surviving children.

By a deed of assignment dated February 6, 1934, the widow of Sir Henry Fielding Dickens, with the assent of his surviving children who were parties to the deed, in her capacity as executrix of Sir Henry Fielding Dickens and also as executrix and trustee of the estate of Charles Dickens, sold and assigned the copyright, but not the manuscript, of "The Life of Christ" to the Associated Newspapers, Limited, for a large sum of money. The latter company afterwards published the work in a daily newspaper and have now published it as a book under the title "The Life of Christ" by Charles Dickens.

ROMER L.J. The first question to be determined upon this appeal is whether upon the true construction of the will of Charles Dickens the manuscript of "The Life of Christ" passed to Georgina Hogarth by virtue of the bequest to her of all the testator's private papers whatsoever and wheresoever. Bennett J. answered this question in the affirmative, and in my opinion he was plainly right in so doing. The manuscript was written by Charles Dickens for the benefit of his children and with no thought of its ever being published to the world. It had not even a title, "The Life of Christ" being merely one of several names by which it was known in the family. The manuscript remained in his possession until his death, though he caused a few copies of it to be made by Miss Georgina Hogarth. But these copies, except for one that was given to a friend of the family, were given exclusively to his sons or some of them. In these circumstances it seems clear that the manuscript was one of Charles Dickens' private papers. The cross-appeal on this point must, therefore, be dismissed.

The next question is whether there passed to Georgina Hogarth, together with the manuscript, what has been called the common law "copyright" in the work, that is to say, the sole right of first printing and publishing the same for sale. That such a right was vested in Dickens at the date of his death is clearly established by numerous authorities of which it is sufficient to mention *Millar v. Taylor*. It was indeed said by Wightman J. in *Jefferys v. Boosey* that so far as he was aware there had never been any decision to the contrary. Whether at common law the sole right of making copies ever survived publication, and whether, even if it did, the common law right did not become extinguished by statutory copyright where that existed, were questions that gave rise to much conflict of judicial opinion. But there is no doubt that in the case of an unpublished literary work the author and those claiming through him had the sole right of publication. In cases where the author himself retains possession of the manuscript, it matters not whether this right flows from such possession or from a right in the literary composition apart from and independent of such possession. But the question is one of vital importance where the manuscript is in the possession of some person other than the author. This, of course, usually happens in the case of letters. The manuscript is in the physical possession of the recipient of the letter. It has nevertheless been established by numerous authorities that the writer of the letters may restrain publication. This right exists quite independently of there being any such breach of trust or confidence in making the publication as would induce a Court of equity to interfere. The publication is a breach of a common law right. In *Millar v. Taylor* Willes J. said this in speaking of the manuscript of a literary work: "Suppose the original, or a transcript, was given or lent to a man to read, for his own use; and he publishes it; it would be a violation of the author's *common law right to the copy*. This never was doubted; and has often been determined." He then referred to four cases in Chancery that had been cited in argument which included that of *Pope v. Curl*. (3) Speaking of this case Willes J. said (2): "Lord Hardwicke thought, 'sending a letter transferred the *paper* upon which it was wrote, and *every use* of the contents, *except* the *liberty* and *profit of publishing*.' When *express consent* is not proved, the *negative is implied* as a tacit condition." The observations made by Lord Mansfield in delivering judgment in the same case are of the greatest importance as they are of the highest authority: "From premises either expressly admitted, or which cannot and therefore never have been denied, conclusions follow, in my apprehension, decisive upon all the objections raised to the property of an author, in the copy of his own work, by the common law. I use the word 'copy,' in the technical sense in which that name or term has been used for ages, to signify an incorporeal right to the sole printing and publishing of somewhat intellectual, communicated by letters. It has all along been expressly admitted 'that by the common law an author is entitled to the copy of his own work until it has been once printed and published by his authority,' and 'that the four cases in Chancery, cited for that purpose, are agreeable to the common law; and the relief was properly given, in consequence of the legal right.' The property in the copy, thus abridged, is equally an incorporeal right to print a set of intellectual ideas or modes of thinking, communicated in a set of words and sentences and modes of expression. It is equally detached from the manuscript, or any other physical existence whatsoever," and he added a little later: "No disposition, no transfer of paper upon which the composition is written, marked, or impressed, (though it gives the power to print and publish) can be construed a conveyance of the copy without the author's express consent 'to print and publish'; much less against his will. The property of the copy, thus narrowed, may equally go down from generation to generation, and possibly continue for ever: though neither the author nor his representatives should have any manuscript whatsoever of the work, original duplicate, or transcript." It is plain that the words "though it gives the power to print and publish" in this passage means "though it gives the opportunity to print and publish."

These observations of Willes J. and Lord Mansfield have not, so far as I am aware, ever been questioned in any later case. There is no doubt a passage in the speech of Lord Brougham in *Jefferys v. Boosey* (1) which seems at first sight to indicate his opinion that, if an author desires to prevent a person to whom he has given or lent his manuscript, from publishing the contents to the world, he must impose an express condition to that effect, differing in this respect from the opinions of both Lord Mansfield and Willes J. But Lord Brougham was merely concerned with showing that the author's common law right did not survive publication and he ought not, I think, to be regarded as having laid it down that, where an author gives or lends his manuscript to a person, there is not in general implied a condition that the manuscript shall not be used to defeat that common law right of the author to what Lord Mansfield called his "copy." It was held in *Millar v. Taylor* that copy exists as an incorporeal right independently of the manuscript and I can find nothing in Lord Brougham's speech that indicates his disagreement with this view. But, if this be so, it is difficult to see why the copy should pass with a gift of the manuscript unless it is in terms expressly made to do so. Confirmation of this view seems to me to be afforded by *Caird v. Sime*, in which the right of a professor to restrain the publication of lectures delivered by him in his class room was upheld by the House of Lords. In that case Lord Watson said: "The author of a lecture on moral philosophy, or of any other original composition, retains a right of property in his work which entitles him to prevent its publication by others until it has, with his consent, been communicated to the public." If such consent is not to be implied by the delivery of a lecture in a class room I cannot see why it should be implied by the delivery of the manuscript of a literary composition to some friend or acquaintance of the author. As Lord Halsbury L.C. said in the same case: "It is not denied, and it cannot in the present state of the law be denied, that an author has a proprietary right in his unpublished literary productions. It is further incapable of denial that that proprietary right may still continue notwithstanding some kind of communication to others." In *Mansell v. Valley Printing Co.* Cozens-Hardy M.R., after quoting these two passages from the speeches of Lord Halsbury and Lord Watson, said: "The law thus laid down is based upon property, irrespective of implied contract or breach of duty. It does not depend upon property in the paper or MS. It is an incorporeal property." In the same case Farwell L.J. said: "The only question is what is the extent and nature of an author's right at common law in his own work before publication, apart from any title to the corporeal paper or canvas on which it is written or delineated. I am of opinion that it is an incorporeal right of property giving to the author the fullest rights not only of exclusion, but also of actual enjoyment so far as they are compatible with non-publication." Fletcher Moulton L.J. said much to the same effect in *Macmillan & Co. v. Dent*: "Now it is beyond question that the common law recognized in an author a property in his composition so long as he kept it to himself. But that property was lost by publication. It was not necessarily lost by communication. He might hand the manuscript of his composition to a friend confidentially, or he might even give the manuscript to a friend without the transaction having any confidential character, and the law did not hold that by doing so he must necessarily have denuded himself of his property in the literary composition itself. It thus contemplated a property in a composition independently of the property in the manuscript in which that composition was to be found."

In view of these authorities I am of opinion that the bequest to Miss Georgina Hogarth of the manuscript of "The Life of Christ" did not pass to her the incorporeal right of Charles Dickens in the composition. That right would, therefore, have passed under the gift in his will of his residuary estate even though such estate had been referred to merely in general terms. ...

---

2. Copyright is a Creature of Statute

The history of copyright law and the prevalence of rights-based justifications for the copyright interest could appear to imply that authors' exclusive rights exist independently of statute. However, the Supreme Court has stated that copyright law is purely statutory; it is neither tort law nor property law in classification. It simply creates rights and obligations upon the terms and in the circumstances set out in the statute and the rights and remedies it provides are exhaustive.[1]

While this may be so, the *Copyright Act* cannot be said to offer answers to every question it provokes; the task of interpreting the *Act* often demands principled or analogical reasoning, which necessarily looks beyond the confines of the legal text.

---

[1]   *Compo Co. v. Blue Crest Music Inc.* (1997), [1980] 1 S.C.R. 357 at 372-3; *Bishop v. Stevens*, [1990] 2 S.C.R. 467.

Compo Co. Ltd. v. Blue Crest Music Inc., [1980] 1 S.C.R. 357

Supreme Court of Canada

Laskin C.J. and Martland, Ritchie, Pigeon, Dickson, Beetz, Estey, Pratte and McIntyre JJ.

Judgment: January 29, 1979
Judgment: January 30, 1979
Judgment: October 2, 1979

The judgment of the Court was delivered by Estey J.:

1 Arising out of a rather complex set of facts is the simple issue as to whether a person who presses phonograph records thereby infringes the exclusive rights granted by s. 3 of the Copyright Act, R.S.C. 1970, c. C-30, to the holder of the copyright in the musical work in question when such pressing is done without the consent of the copyright owner or without a statutory licence under s. 19 of the Copyright Act.

2 The essential facts are these. The appellant Compo Company Limited (the defendant in these proceedings), hereinafter referred to as Compo, entered into a contract with Canusa Records Inc., hereinafter referred to as Canusa, whereby Compo would press records for Canusa. In the sequence of production of these records, Canusa first caused to be produced by other contractors a master tape on which was recorded a French version of a copyrighted musical work, namely the song "There Goes My Everything". From this tape other contractors produced a master acetate which is an aluminum disc coated with a cellulose acetate on which is cut in fine grooves a tract which when placed in audio reproduction equipment would produce an audio representation of the aforementioned musical work. Compo, utilizing the master acetate, produced a series of moulds and stampers or dies which they ultimately used in stamping equipment to produce the records in quantities as ordered by Canusa.

3 We are not here concerned with the detailed participation in the production of this master acetate by various other persons starting with the musicians and culminating in the engineers and technicians who actually produced the master acetate. It should be noted, however, that in this transitional stage, there is produced a tape recording of the musical work from which the stamping device is ultimately produced. By playing this tape recording, the musical work could be acoustically performed but the purpose of the tape is entirely technical and transitional in the sequence of events from the performance of the musical works in the recording studio by musicians to the delivery of the record for retail sale.

4 Canusa obtained no licence from the holders of the mechanical rights in the copyrighted work; nor did it obtain a statutory licence under s. 19 of the Copyright Act. Similarly, Compo, as the presser of these records held no licence or grant of right either contractual or statutory for the production of these records. It was found at trial that Canusa had committed a breach of the right of the

respondent under the Copyright Act and the question now raised in these proceedings is whether Compo has done so as well.

5 Courts in this technical field of copyright have found it prudent to make their judicial answers congruent with the legal issues raised in the proceeding at hand leaving, so far as possible, analogies, examples and hypothetical questions to another day. I propose to follow this principle and therefore expressly refrain from deciding such questions as whether or not there may be in law two "makers" of a single record for the purpose of these sections of the Copyright Act. Mr. Hughes for the respondent in answer to a question from the Bench put it very well when he said that copyright law is neither tort law nor property law in classification, but is statutory law. It neither cuts across existing rights in property or conduct nor falls between rights and obligations heretofore existing in the common law. Copyright legislation simply creates rights and obligations upon the terms and in the circumstances set out in the statute. This creature of statute has been known to the law of England at least since the days of Queen Anne when the first copyright statute was passed. It does not assist the interpretive analysis to import tort concepts. The legislation speaks for itself and the actions of the appellant must be measured according to the terms of the statute.

33 In the context of s. 3 of the *Copyright Act* the verb "to make" includes the direct sense of physically causing the record to come into being. It may also include the general activity of bringing about the production of the record and the indirect actions associated therewith, but that phase of the meaning of the word is not, in these proceedings, directly applicable. In my view, the person who by means of stampers, dies or other devices and procedures, forms plastics and other materials into discs, and imprints thereon grooves and tracks "by means of which the work may be mechanically performed", has thereby within the meaning of s. 3(1)(*d*) made a record.

34 There may be persons involved in one or more stages in the production chain leading to the creation of the record as the end product who have, in the sense of s. 3, thereby 'made a record'. Conversely, there may be persons who, through a coordinating role analogous to that of a general contractor, will be deemed in some circumstances to have made the record even though they may not have physically themselves brought into being either the record or any material, intermediate tool, or piece of equipment in the production of the record. None of these questions need on this appeal be determined. Sufficient it be to determine, as I have done, that Compo did indeed make the record in breach of the respondents' sole right as the owners of the copyright, so to do. I therefore would dismiss the appeal with costs.

Bishop v. Stevens, [1990] 2 S.C.R. 467

Supreme Court of Canada

Lamer C.J. and La Forest, L'Heureux-Dubé, Gonthier and McLachlin JJ.

Judgment: March 30, 1990
Judgment: August 16, 1990
Docket: 20695

The judgment of the Court was delivered by *McLachlin J.*:

1 The principal issue in this case is whether the right to broadcast a musical work in accordance with the *Copyright Act*, R.S.C. 1970, c. C-30 (now R.S.C., 1985, c. C-42), includes the incidental right to make an "ephemeral" recording beforehand for the sole purpose of facilitating the broadcast.

2 The appellant Télé-Métropole Inc. operates a television broadcasting business. The respondent Bishop is a musician, who composed the music and lyrics to a song entitled "Stay". He sent a copy, with the appropriate forms, to the Performing Rights Society (PRS) of Great Britain, which is an association for the protection and enforcement of music copyrights held by its members. That association is affiliated with a similar association in Canada, the Composers, Authors and Publishers Association of Canada (CAPAC), which administers rights held by PRS and its members within Canada. CAPAC is a "performing rights society" as contemplated by s. 48 (now s. 66) of the *Copyright Act*, and is entitled to collect fees for performing rights of its members and affiliates according to a scale published in the Canada Gazette. These fees are then passed on to the copyright holder.

3 Stevens, a singer, subsequently heard a performance of the song, and had inconclusive discussions with the respondent about the possibility of recording it. Without entering into any agreement with the respondent, Stevens recorded the song, in both English and French (under the title "Ne t'en vas pas" (*sic*)). To publicize the recording, Stevens arranged with the appellant to appear on television shows that feature popular music. Performances of the song were broadcast by the appellant on two occasions, in each case using a prerecorded tape. The appellant, though unaware that the song was written by the respondent and not by Stevens, gave due notification and paid the appropriate fees to CAPAC, and the payments for the broadcast performances were eventually forwarded through PRS to the respondent. No specific arrangements, however, were made regarding the prerecordings used in the broadcast.

4 Subsequent to the broadcasts, the respondent entered into an agreement with the Canadian Musical Reproduction Rights Agency Ltd. (CMRRA), an organization for the protection of reproduction rights in music held by its members. By the terms of the agreement, CMRRA had the non-exclusive right to administer the reproduction rights in the respondent's work, including the right to take legal action (with the respondent's consent) to collect monies due or to enforce his rights.

5 The respondent and CMRRA brought an action against several defendants including Stevens and the appellant. By the time of the trial, only the appellant remained as defendant. The complaint against the appellant was that it had infringed the respondent's copyright by recording the song without first obtaining his permission, though the recording was intended to be used only to effect the later broadcasts (which the parties agreed involved only performing rights that the appellant had properly paid for). The appellant claimed that the right to broadcast the performances included the incidental right to make an "ephemeral" recording for the sole purpose of facilitating the broadcasts.

Issue I: Does the Right to Broadcast a Performance Include the Right to Make Ephemeral Recordings?

18 Analysis of these arguments must begin by emphasizing that copyright law is purely statutory law, which "simply creates rights and obligations upon the terms and in the circumstances set out in the statute": *Compo Co. v. Blue Crest Music Inc.*, [1980] 1 S.C.R. 357, at p. 373, *per* Estey J. First and foremost, then, this case is a matter of statutory interpretation. It is clear from an examination of s. 3(1) that it lists a number of distinct rights belonging to the copyright holder. As stated in *Ash v. Hutchinson & Co. (Publishers), Ltd.*, [1936] 2 All E.R. 1496 (C.A.), at p. 1507, *per* Greene L.J.:

> Under the Copyright Act, 1911 [on which the Canadian Act was based], s. 1(2), the rights of the owner of copyright are set out. A number of acts are specified, the sole right to do which is conferred on the owner of the copyright. The right to do each of these acts is, in my judgment, a separate statutory right, and anyone who without the consent of the owner of the copyright does any of these acts commits a tort; if he does two of them, he commits two torts, and so on.

See also *Compo Co. v. Blue Crest Music Inc.*, *supra*, at p. 373.

19 The right to perform (including radio broadcast), and the right to make a recording, are separately enumerated in s. 3(1). They are distinct rights in theory and in practice, as is evident from a description of the licensing system by which musicians obtain payment for use of their works:

> Two main assignments occur. Both are a significant step towards earning income from transferring copyright. One is the assignment of the performing right to a performing rights society. The terms of the assignment are technically negotiable. However, both PROCAN and CAPAC, which are discussed below, have standard forms for assigning performing rights which are seldom amended. The second assignment is of the remainder of the copyright, that is, all copyright except the performing right, which was previously assigned to the performing rights society, to a music publisher. Upon assignment, the publisher becomes the owner of the copyright, and usually through its agent reproduction rights agency, licenses specific copyright uses thereby generating income. This is a skeletal outline of the voluntary aspect of the transfer system in relation to the music business.

. . .

> Reproduction rights agencies are generally agents for music publishers as owners of musical copyrights. They license reproduction rights, which are essentially all of the musical copyrights other than the performing right.

(P. Sanderson, *Musicians and the Law in Canada* (1985), at pp. 22 and 24.) Thus the rights to perform and to record a work are considered sufficiently distinct that they are generally assigned separately, and administered by different entities.

Reference re Broadcasting Act, S.C. 1991 (Canada), 2012 SCC 68 (S.C.C.)

Coram: McLachlin C.J. and LeBel, Deschamps, Fish, Abella, Rothstein, Cromwell, Moldaver and Karakatsanis JJ.

Reasons for Judgment: (paras. 1 to 83) Rothstein J. (McLachlin C.J. and LeBel, Fish and Moldaver JJ. concurring)

Joint Dissenting Reasons: (paras. 84 to 126) Abella and Cromwell JJ. (Deschamps and Karakatsanis JJ. concurring)

. . .

[4] Broadcasters acquire, create and produce television programming, and are licensed by the CRTC to serve a certain geographic area within the reach of their respective signal transmitters. BDUs, such as cable or satellite television service providers, pick up the over-the-air signals of broadcasters and distribute them to the BDUs' subscribers for a fee. Even though broadcasters' signals are free to anyone equipped with a television and an antenna, more than 90 percent of Canadians receive these signals as part of their cable service (transcript, at p. 2).

[5] BDUs must be licensed by the CRTC pursuant to s. 9 of the *Broadcasting Act*. Under the current regulatory model, the CRTC requires BDUs to provide certain benefits to broadcasters, in the nature of mandatory carriage and contributions to a local programming improvement fund accessible by certain local television stations. However, the broadcasters do not receive fees directly from the BDUs for the carriage of their signals.

[6] As noted by the Federal Court of Appeal ("FCA"), 2011 FCA 64, 413 N.R. 312, at para. 6, the CRTC has concluded that the existing model does not adequately deal with recent changes to the broadcasting business environment, which have caused advertising revenues for broadcasters to fall, while the revenues of BDUs have increased. As the FCA observed, the CRTC has concluded that this has resulted in a significant shift in their relative market positions and a financial crisis for broadcasters.

[7] As a solution, the CRTC seeks to implement what it terms a "value for signal regime". This regime would permit broadcasters to negotiate with BDUs the terms upon which the BDUs may redistribute their signals. These are its main features:

- Broadcasters would have the right, every three years, to choose either to negotiate with BDUs for compensation for the right to retransmit the broadcaster's programming services, or to continue to operate under the existing regulatory regime;

- A broadcaster who participates in the value for signal regime would forego all existing regulatory protections, including, for example, mandatory distribution of its signals as part of the basic package of BDU television services, and the right to require a BDU to delete a non-Canadian program and substitute it with the comparable program of the broadcaster, where the two programs are simultaneously broadcast and retransmitted by the BDU;

- The CRTC would only involve itself in the negotiations for the value for signal regime if the parties do not negotiate in good faith or if they request the CRTC to arbitrate;

- If no agreement is reached between the broadcaster and the BDU on the value of the distribution of the local television's programming services, the broadcaster could require the BDU to delete any program owned by the broadcaster or for which it has acquired exclusive contractual exhibition rights from all signals distributed by the BDU in the broadcaster's market.

The proposed regime is fully described in *Broadcasting Regulatory Policy CRTC 2010-167* (2010) ("2010 Policy") (A.R., vol. II, at p. 1).

[8] The BDUs disputed the jurisdiction of the CRTC to implement such a regime on the basis that it conflicts with specific provisions in the *Copyright Act*. As a result, the CRTC referred the following question to the FCA:

> Is the Commission empowered, pursuant to its mandate under the *Broadcasting Act*, to establish a regime to enable private local television stations to choose to negotiate with broadcasting distribution undertakings a fair value in exchange for the distribution of the programming services broadcast by those local television stations? ...

(1) Connection Between the *Broadcasting Act* and the *Copyright Act*

[34] Even if jurisdiction for the proposed value for signal regime could be found within the text of the *Broadcasting Act*, that would not resolve the question in this reference as the *Broadcasting Act* is part of a larger statutory scheme that includes the *Copyright Act* and the *Telecommunications Act*. As Sunny Handa et al. explain, the *Telecommunications Act* and the *Radiocommunication Act*, R.S.C. 1985, c. R-2, are the main statutes governing carriage, and the *Broadcasting Act* deals with content, which is "the object of 'carriage'" (S. Handa et al., Communications Law in Canada (loose-leaf), at §3.21). In Bell ExpressVu, at para. 52, Justice Iacobucci also considered the *Copyright Act* when interpreting a provision of the *Radiocommunication Act*, saying that "there is a connection between these two statutes". Considering that the *Broadcasting Act* and the

Radiocommunication Act are clearly part of the same interconnected statutory scheme, it follows, in my view, that there is a connection between the *Broadcasting Act* and the *Copyright Act* as well. The three Acts (plus the Telecommunications Act) are part of an interrelated scheme.

[35] Indeed, the *Broadcasting Act* regulates "program[s]" that are "broadcast" for reception by the Canadian public (see s. 2(1), definitions of "broadcasting" and of "program"), with a view to implementing the Canadian broadcasting policy described in s. 3(1) of the Act. Generally speaking, "[t]he *Broadcasting Act* is primarily concerned with the programmed content delivered by means of radio waves or other means of telecommunication to the public" (Handa at al., at §5.5).

[36] The *Copyright Act* is concerned both with encouraging creativity and providing reasonable access to the fruits of creative endeavour. These objectives are furthered by a carefully balanced scheme that creates exclusive economic rights for different categories of copyright owners in works or other protected subject matter, typically in the nature of a statutory monopoly to prevent anyone from exploiting the work in specified ways without the copyright owner's consent. It also provides user rights such as fair dealing and specific exemptions that enable the general public or specific classes of users to access protected material under certain conditions. (See, e.g., *Théberge v. Galerie d'Art du Petit Champlain inc.*, 2002 SCC 34, [2002] 2 S.C.R. 336, at paras. 11-12 and 30; *Mattel, Inc. v. 3894207 Canada Inc.*, 2006 SCC 22, [2006] 1 S.C.R. 772, at para. 21; *D. Vaver, Intellectual Property Law: Copyright, Patents, Trade-marks* (2nd ed. 2011), at pp. 34 and 56.) Among the categories of subject matter protected by copyright are the rights of broadcasters in communication signals (see ss. 2 "copyright" and 21 of the *Copyright Act*). In addition, "program[s]" within the meaning of the *Broadcasting Act*, are often pre-recorded original content which may constitute protected works, namely "dramatic work[s]" or "compilation[s]" thereof, under the *Copyright Act*: see, e.g., discussion in J. S. McKeown, *Fox on Canadian Law of Copyright and Industrial Designs* (4th ed. loose-leaf), at para. 15:3(a).

[37] Although the Acts have different aims, their subject matters will clearly overlap in places. As Parliament is presumed to intend "harmony, coherence, and consistency between statutes dealing with the same subject matter" (*R. v. Ulybel Enterprises Ltd.*, 2001 SCC 56, [2001] 2 S.C.R. 867, at para. 52; Sullivan, at pp. 325-26), two provisions applying to the same facts will be given effect in accordance with their terms so long as they do not conflict.

[38] Accordingly, where multiple interpretations of a provision are possible, the presumption of coherence requires that the two statutes be read together so as to avoid conflict. Lamer C.J. wrote in *Pointe-Claire (City) v. Quebec (Labour Court)*, [1997] 1 S.C.R. 1015, at para. 61:

> There is no doubt that the principle that statutes dealing with similar subjects must be presumed to be coherent means that interpretations favouring harmony among those statutes should prevail over discordant ones.

[39] In addition, "[o]rdinarily, . . . an Act of Parliament must prevail over inconsistent or conflicting subordinate legislation" (*Friends of the Oldman*

River Society v. Canada (Minister of Transport), [1992] 1 S.C.R. 3, at p. 38). Consequently, as it would be impermissible for the CRTC, a subordinate legislative body, to implement subordinate legislation in conflict with another Act of Parliament, the open-ended jurisdiction-conferring provisions of the *Broadcasting Act* cannot be interpreted as allowing the CRTC to create conflicts with the *Copyright Act*.

[40] It is therefore necessary to first determine if a conflict arises.

(2) Types of Conflict

[41] For the purposes of statutory interpretation, conflict is defined narrowly. It has been said that overlapping provisions will be given effect according to their terms, unless they "cannot stand together" (*Toronto Railway Co. v. Paget* (1909), 42 S.C.R. 488, at p. 499 per Anglin J.).

[42] In *Lévis (City) v. Fraternité des policiers de Lévis Inc.*, 2007 SCC 14, [2007] 1 S.C.R. 591, the Court was concerned with incoherence between provisions of two statutes emanating from the same legislature. Bastarache J., writing for the majority, defined conflict, at para. 47:

> The test for determining whether an unavoidable conflict exists is well stated by Professor Côté in his treatise on statutory interpretation:
>
>> According to case law, two statutes are not repugnant simply because they deal with the same subject: application of one must implicitly or explicitly preclude application of the other.
>
> (P.-A. Côté, *The Interpretation of Legislation in Canada* (3rd ed. 2000), at p. 350)
>
> Thus, a law which provides for the expulsion of a train passenger who fails to pay the fare is not in conflict with another law that only provides for a fine because the application of one law did not exclude the application of the other (*Toronto Railway Co. v. Paget* (1909), 42 S.C.R. 488). Unavoidable conflicts, on the other hand, occur when two pieces of legislation are directly contradictory or where their concurrent application would lead to unreasonable or absurd results. A law, for example, which allows for the extension of a time limit for filing an appeal only before it expires is in direct conflict with another law which allows for an extension to be granted after the time limit has expired (*Massicotte v. Boutin*, [1969] S.C.R. 818). [Emphasis added.]

[43] Absurdity also refers to situations where the practical effect of one piece of legislation would be to frustrate the *purpose* of the other (*Lévis*, at para. 54; Sullivan, at p. 330).

[44] This view is not inconsistent with the approach to conflict adopted in federalism jurisprudence. For the purposes of the doctrine of paramountcy, this Court has recognized two types of conflict. Operational conflict arises when there is an *impossibility of compliance* with both provisions. The other type of conflict is incompatibility of purpose. In the latter type, there is no impossibility of dual compliance with the letter of both laws; rather, the conflict arises because applying one provision would frustrate the purpose intended by Parliament in another.

See, e.g., *British Columbia (Attorney General) v. Lafarge Canada Inc.*, 2007 SCC 23, [2007] 2 S.C.R. 86, at paras. 77 and 84.

[45] Cases applying the doctrine of federal paramountcy present some similarities in defining conflict as either operational conflict or conflict of purpose (*Friends of the Oldman River Society*, at p. 38). These definitions of legislative conflict are therefore helpful in interpreting two statutes emanating from the same legislature. The CRTC's powers to impose licensing conditions and make regulations should be understood as constrained by each type of conflict. Namely, in seeking to achieve its objects, the CRTC may not choose means that either operationally conflict with specific provisions of the *Broadcasting Act*, the *Radiocommunication Act, the Telecommunications Act*, or the *Copyright Act*; or which would be incompatible with the purposes of those Acts.

(3) The Allocation of Rights Under the Copyright Act

(a) *Section 21*

[46] The BDUs contend that the CRTC's proposed value for signal regime conflicts with the retransmission regimes specifically established in ss. 21(1)(c) and 31(2) of the *Copyright Act*.

[47] It is necessary to describe the *Copyright Act*'s regimes at some length. It will become apparent from this description that, in my respectful view, the analysis of the *Copyright Act* conducted by the majority of the FCA is problematic.

[48] The BDUs first submit that s. 21(1) of the *Copyright Act* conflicts with the value for signal regime. Section 21(1) grants broadcasters a limited copyright in the over-the-air signals they broadcast. This copyright gives the broadcaster the sole right to authorize or to do four acts in relation to a communication signal or any substantial part of it:

> (a) to fix it;
>
> (b) to reproduce any fixation of it that was made without the broadcaster's consent;
>
> (c) to authorize another broadcaster to retransmit it to the public simultaneously with its broadcast; and
>
> (d) in the case of a television communication signal, to perform it in a place open to the public on payment of an entrance fee, and to authorize any act described in paragraph (a), (b) or (d).

[49] The aspect relevant for this appeal is in para. (c). Under this paragraph, a broadcaster has the sole right to authorize another *broadcaster* to retransmit simultaneously a communication signal. Section 2 of the *Copyright Act* defines "broadcaster" as

> a body that, in the course of operating a broadcasting undertaking, broadcasts a communication signal in accordance with the law of the country in which the broadcasting undertaking is carried on, but excludes a body whose primary activity in relation to communication signals is their retransmission.

[50] The underlined portion of the definition refers to BDUs. BDUs are not a "broadcaster" within the meaning of the *Copyright Act* because their primary activity in relation communication signals is their retransmission. Thus, the broadcaster's s. 21(1)(c) right to authorize, or not authorize, another broadcaster to simultaneously retransmit its signals does not apply against BDUs. In other words, under s. 21 of the *Copyright Act*, a broadcaster's exclusive right does not include a right to authorize or prohibit a BDU from retransmitting its communication signals.

(b) *Section 31*

[51] In addition to their s. 21 rights in communication signals, broadcasters may hold other retransmission rights under the *Copyright Act*. As mentioned, a pre-recorded television program is often copyright subject matter that can be protected as an original "dramatic work" or a "compilation" thereof (s. 2 of the *Copyright Act*). The broadcaster, as a corporation, may hold copyright in the pre-recorded program or compilation of programs carried in its signals, either as the employer of the author of such a work or as an assignee of copyright from the original author.

[52] The *Copyright Act* seeks to regulate the economic rights in communication signals, as well as the retransmission of works by BDUs. The BDUs contend that the value for signal regime would conflict with the retransmission regime for works set out in s. 31 of the *Copyright Act*. The proposed regime would enable broadcasters to control the simultaneous retransmission of programs, by granting them the right to require deletion of any program in which they own or control the copyright from all signals distributed by the BDU, if no agreement is reached on compensation for the simultaneous retransmission of the broadcaster's programming services.

[53] The *Copyright Act* in s. 3(1)(f) confers on the owner of copyright in a work the exclusive right to communicate it to the public by telecommunication. Section 3(1)(f) provides:

> 3. (1) For the purposes of this Act, "copyright", in relation to a work, means the sole right . . .
>
> (f) in the case of any literary, dramatic, musical or artistic work, to communicate the work to the public by telecommunication,
>
> . . .

"Telecommunication", in s. 2 of the Act, is broadly defined to include

> any transmission of . . . intelligence of any nature by wire, radio, visual, optical or other electromagnetic system.

[54] These general words would at first blush confer on the copyright owner, including a broadcaster in that capacity, the right to control the retransmission of the works in which it holds copyright. However, s. 31(2) of the *Copyright Act* proceeds in detailed fashion to circumscribe the right of copyright owners to control the retransmission of literary, dramatic, musical or artistic works carried

in signals. "Signal" is defined for the purposes of s. 31(2) to mean "a signal that carries a literary, dramatic, musical or artistic work and is transmitted for free reception by the public by a terrestrial radio or terrestrial television station" (see s. 31(1)). Section 31(1) defines "retransmitter" as "a person who performs a function comparable to that of a cable retransmission system . . .".

[55] Section 31(2) provides:

> It is not an infringement of copyright for a retransmitter to communicate to the public by telecommunication any literary, dramatic, musical or artistic work if
>
> (a) the communication is a retransmission of a local or distant signal;
>
> (b) the retransmission is lawful under the *Broadcasting Act*;
>
> (c) the signal is retransmitted simultaneously and without alteration, except as otherwise required or permitted by or under the laws of Canada;
>
> (d) in the case of the retransmission of a distant signal, the retransmitter has paid any royalties, and complied with any terms and conditions, fixed under this Act; and
>
> (e) the retransmitter complies with the applicable conditions, if any, referred to in paragraph (3)(b).

[56] Read together, ss. 31(1) and 31(2) create an exception to the exclusive right of the copyright owners of literary, dramatic, musical or artistic works to control the communication of their works to the public by telecommunication. The exception, or user's right, in effect, entitles BDUs to retransmit those works without the copyright owners' consent, where the conditions set out in paras. (a) through (e) are met. Paragraph (b) provides that the retransmission must be lawful under the *Broadcasting Act*. I will come back to the meaning of this particular condition.

[57] In the case of works carried in distant signals only, the section provides copyright owners with a right to receive royalties as payment for the simultaneous retransmission of those works by a BDU. The royalties are determined by the Copyright Board, on the basis of tariffs filed by collective societies, pursuant to the regime detailed in ss. 71 to 74 of the *Copyright Act*. Under s. 31(2), works carried in local signals attract no royalty when retransmitted in accordance with all conditions of that section. The Governor in Council has defined "local signal" as the signal of a terrestrial station reaching all or a portion of the service area of a retransmitter. A "distant signal" is a signal that is not a local signal. See ss. 1 and 2 of Local Signal and Distant Signal Regulations, SOR/89-254.

[58] It bears underlining that, in the case of works carried in both local and distant signals, the copyright owner has *no right to prohibit* the simultaneous retransmission of the work; recourse is limited to receiving through a collective society the prescribed royalty, but only for the simultaneous retransmission of works carried in distant signals (ss. 76(1) and 76(3) of the *Copyright Act*). On the one hand, the copyright owner is granted a general right to retransmit the work. This retransmission right is part of the right, under s. (3)(1)(f), to

communicate the work by telecommunication to the public. On the other hand, the owner's general right to retransmit is restricted by a carve-out in s. 31(2) of the *Copyright Act*, which effectively grants to a specific class of retransmitters two retransmission rights. The first right lets these users simultaneously retransmit without a royalty payment, works carried in a local signal. The second right lets them simultaneously retransmit works carried in distant signals, but only subject to the payment of royalties under a form of compulsory licence regime (*Copyright Act*, s. 31(2)(a) and (d)). Both user rights are, subject to s. 31(2), beyond the owner's control.

[59] In sum, under the *Copyright Act*'s retransmission regimes for communication signals and for works:

- Broadcasters have a limited exclusive right in their signals (s. 21);

- Broadcasters do not have an exclusive right in signals against BDUs;

- BDUs have the right to simultaneously retransmit works carried in local signals without authorization and without payment to the copyright owner;

- Owners of copyright in those works, including broadcasters in that capacity, do not have the right to block retransmission of local or distant signals carrying their works;

- The Copyright Board has jurisdiction to value the compulsory licence royalty for the simultaneous retransmission of works carried in distant signals;

(4) Finding Conflict

[60] The CRTC's proposed value for signal regime would enable broadcasters to negotiate compensation for the retransmission by BDUs of their signals or programming services, regardless of whether or not they carry copyright protected "work[s]", and regardless of the fact that any such works are carried in local signals for which the *Copyright Act* provides no compensation. Importantly, contrary to the retransmission regimes of the *Copyright Act*, the value for signal regime proposed by the CRTC would grant individual broadcasters, should they elect to be governed by this regime, the *right to prohibit* the simultaneous retransmission of their programs.

[61] As mentioned, the presumption of coherence between related Acts of Parliament requires avoiding an interpretation of a provision that would introduce conflict into the statutory scheme. In this case, the presumption of coherence requires that if the CRTC's proposed regulatory regime would create such conflict with the specific expressions of Parliament's intent under the *Copyright Act*, it must be ultra vires. Sections 21 and 31(2) of the *Copyright Act* are relevant.

[62] First, the value for signal regime conflicts with s. 21(1) of the *Copyright Act* because it would grant broadcasters a retransmission authorization right against BDUs that was withheld by the scheme of the *Copyright Act*.

[63] Looking only at the letter of the provision, s. 21 expressly speaks only to the relationship between a broadcaster and another broadcaster and not the relationship between a broadcaster and a retransmitter. As such, it is arguable that nothing in s. 21 purports to prevent another regulator from regulating the terms for carriage of a broadcaster's television signal by the BDUs, leaving it open to the CRTC, provided it is authorized to do so under the *Broadcasting Act*, to establish a value for signal regime without conflicting with s. 21.

[64] However, s. 21 cannot be considered devoid of its purpose. This Court has characterized the purpose of the *Copyright Act* as a balance between authors' and users' rights. The same balance applies to broadcasters and users. In Théberge, Binnie J. recognized that the *Copyright Act*

> . . . is usually presented as a balance between promoting the public interest in the encouragement and dissemination of works of the arts and intellect and obtaining a just reward for the creator (or, more accurately, to prevent someone other than the creator from appropriating whatever benefits may be generated). [para. 30]

(See also *CCH Canadian Ltd. v. Law Society of Upper Canada*, 2004 SCC 13, [2004] 1 S.C.R. 339, at paras. 10 and 23.)

[65] This point was reiterated in *Society of Composers, Authors and Music Publishers of Canada v. Canadian Assn. of Internet Providers*, 2004 SCC 45, [2004] 2 S.C.R. 427. In that case, the Court considered whether, for the purposes of the *Copyright Act*, Internet Service Providers "communicate [works] to the public" when such works are requested by their subscribers — thereby infringing copyright in such works. The Court was required to interpret s. 2.4(1)(b) of the *Copyright Act*, which provides that

> a person whose only act in respect of the communication of a work or other sub-ject-matter to the public consists of providing the means of telecommunication necessary for another person to so communicate the work or other subject-matter does not communicate that work or other subject-matter to the public.

[66] In rejecting the argument that s. 2.4(1)(b), as an exemption, should be read narrowly, the majority, *per* Binnie J., held that

> . . . under the *Copyright Act*, the rights of the copyright owner and the limitations on those rights should be read together to give "the fair and balanced reading that befits remedial legislation". [para. 88]

The Court recognized that "[s]ection 2.4(1)(b) is not a loophole but an important element of the balance struck by the statutory copyright scheme" (para. 89). The Court therefore confirmed its earlier teaching in *Théberge* that the policy balance established by the *Copyright Act* is maintained also by "giving due weight to [the] limited nature" of the rights of creators (*Théberge*, at para. 31).

[67] In my view, s. 21(1) represents the expression by Parliament of the appropriate balance to be struck between broadcasters' rights in their communication signals and the rights of the users, including BDUs, to those signals. It would be incoherent for Parliament to set up a carefully tailored signals retransmission right in the *Copyright Act*, specifically excluding BDUs from the scope of

the broadcasters' exclusive rights over the simultaneous retransmission of their signals, only to enable a subordinate legislative body to enact a functionally equivalent right through a related regime. The value for signal regime would upset the aim of the *Copyright Act* to effect an appropriate "balance between promoting the public interest in the encouragement and dissemination of works of the arts and intellect and obtaining a just reward for the creator" (*Théberge*, at para. 30).

[68] Second, while the conflict of the proposed regime with s. 21 is sufficient to render the regime *ultra vires*, further conflict arises in my opinion between the value for signal regime and the retransmission rights in works set out in s. 31 of the *Copyright Act*.

[69] As discussed above, s. 31 creates an exception to copyright infringement for the simultaneous retransmission by a BDU of a work carried in local signals. However, the value for signal regime envisions giving broadcasters deletion rights, whereby the broadcaster unable to agree with a BDU about the compensation for the distribution of its programming services would be entitled to require any program to which it has exclusive exhibition rights to be deleted from the signals of any broadcaster distributed by the BDU. As noted above, "program[s]" are often "work[s]" within the meaning of the *Copyright Act*. The value for signal regime would entitle broadcasters to control the simultaneous retransmission of works, while the *Copyright Act* specifically excludes it from the control of copyright owners, including broadcasters.

[70] Again, although the exception to copyright infringement established in s. 31 on its face does not purport to prohibit another regulator from imposing conditions, directly or indirectly, on the retransmission of works, it is necessary to look behind the letter of the provision to its purpose, which is to balance the entitlements of copyright holders and the public interest in the dissemination of works. The value for signal regime would effectively overturn the s. 31 exception to the copyright owners' s. 3(1)(f) communication right. It would disrupt the balance established by Parliament.

[71] The recent legislative history of the *Copyright Act* supports the view that Parliament made deliberate choices in respect of copyright and broadcasting policy. The history evidences Parliament's intent to facilitate simultaneous retransmission of television programs by cable and limit the obstacles faced by the retransmitters.

[72] Leading up to the 1997 amendment to the *Copyright Act* (Bill C-32), under which s. 21 was introduced, broadcasters made submissions to the Standing Committee on Canadian Heritage seeking signal rights. They contended that they should be granted the right to authorize, or refuse to authorize, the retransmission of their signals by others, including BDUs. The broadcasters, in fact, argued expressly against the narrow right that Parliament eventually adopted as s. 21(1)(c). See, for example, submissions of CTV to Standing Committee on Canadian Heritage, "Re: Bill C-32" (August 30,1996) (A.R., vol. VII, at p. 68); submissions of WIC Western International Communications Ltd. (1996)

(A.R., vol. VII, at p. 15); submissions of the British Columbia Association of Broadcasters, "Bill C-32, the Copyright Reform Legislation" (August 28, 1996) (A.R., vol. VII, at p. 20); submissions of the Canadian Association of Broadcasters, "Clause by Clause Recommendations for Amendments to Bill C-32" (November 27, 1996) (A.R., vol. VII, at p. 77). In addition, although this section has not been amended since 1997, ongoing consultations between Parliament and the broadcasters show continued requests from the latter to include the right to authorize BDU retransmissions. See, for example, submissions of CTV-globemedia, "Re: Government's 2009 Copyright Consultations" (September 11, 2009) (A.R., vol. IX, at pp. 35-37); Canadian Association of Broadcasters, "A Submission to the House of Commons Standing Committee on Canadian Heritage With Respect to A Statutory Review of the *Copyright Act*" (September 15, 2003) (A.R., vol. IX, at p. 28).

[73] Notwithstanding successive amendments to the *Copyright Act*, Parliament has not amended s. 21 in the fashion requested by the broadcasters. Parliament's silence is not necessarily determinative of legislative intention. However, in the context of repeated urging from the broadcasters, Parliament's silence strongly suggests that it is Parliament's intention to maintain the balance struck by s. 21 (see Tele-Mobile Co. v. Ontario, 2008 SCC 12, [2008] 1 S.C.R. 305, at para. 42, per Abella J.).

[74] The same purposeful balancing is evidenced in the legislative history of the s. 31 regime for the retransmission of *works*. The predecessor to the current s. 3(1)(f) guaranteed copyright holders an exclusive right to communicate works by radio *communication*. Jurisprudence interpreted the radio communication right as excluding transmissions by cable: *Canadian Admiral Corp. v. Rediffusion, Inc.*, [1954] Ex. C.R. 382. Section 3(1)(f) was amended in 1988 to confer the exclusive right to "communicate the work to the public by telecommunication" to reflect the obligations entered into by Canada under the *Free Trade Agreement between the Government of Canada and the Government of the United States of America*, Can. T.S. 1989 No. 3 (see *Canada-United States Free Trade Agreement Implementation Act*, S.C. 1988, c. 65, ss. 61 and 62; see also *Rogers Communications Inc. v. Society of Composers, Authors and Music Publishers of Canada*, 2012 SCC 35, at paras. 36-37 and McKeown, at para. 3:2(b)). The change from radio communication to telecommunication meant that cable companies were now liable for copyright infringement when they communicate copyright-protected works to the public.

[75] However, at the same time, Parliament specifically addressed the question of whether the simultaneous retransmission of works carried in local and distant television signals should require the consent of the copyright owner: it adopted the compulsory licence and exception regime by way of ss. 31 and 71 to 76 of the *Copyright Act* (*Canada-United States Free Trade Agreement Implementation Act*, s. 62). Studies on the same question had preceded this enactment; there, too, a major concern was that copyright owners "should not be permitted to stop retransmission because this activity is too important to Canada's communications system" (Standing Committee on Communications and Culture. *A*

Charter of Rights for Creators: Report of the Sub-Committee on the Revision of Copyright (1985), at p. 80 (A.R., vol. III, at p. 118); Government Response to A Charter of Rights for Creators (February 1986) (A.R., vol. III, at p. 127)).

[76] The value for signal regime would rewrite the balance between the owners' and users' interests as set out by Parliament in the *Copyright Act*. Because the CRTC's value for signal regime is inconsistent with the purpose of the *Copyright Act*, it falls outside of the scope of the CRTC's licensing and regulatory jurisdiction under the *Broadcasting Act*.

[77] I said earlier that I would come back to s. 31(2)(b) of the *Copyright Act*. The majority of the FCA concluded that there is no incoherence between the value for signal regime and the *Copyright Act* because of s. 31(2)(b) of the *Copyright Act*. This section provides that in order for the exception to copyright to apply, the retransmission must be "lawful under the *Broadcasting Act*". The majority appears to have thought this was sufficient to ground the CRTC's jurisdiction to implement the value for signal regulatory regime.

[78] In my respectful opinion, this provision cannot serve to authorize the CRTC acting under the *Broadcasting Act* to effectively amend the very heart of the balance of the retransmission regime set out in s. 31(2). Section 31(2)(b) is not a so-called Henry VIII clause that confers jurisdiction on the CRTC to promulgate, through regulation or licensing conditions, subordinate legislative provisions that are to prevail over primary legislation (see Sullivan, at pp. 342-43). Absent specific indication, Parliament cannot have intended by s. 31(2)(b) to empower a subordinate regulatory body to disturb the balance struck following years of studies. The legislative history does not lend support to this argument; indeed, the history confirms Parliament's deliberate policy choice in enacting the compulsory licence and exception, or user's rights, regime under s. 31(2). A general reference to "lawful under the *Broadcasting Act*" cannot authorize the CRTC, acting under open-ended jurisdiction-conferring provisions, to displace the specific direction of Parliament in the *Copyright Act*.

[79] In any case, the conflict found between the value for signal regime and s. 21 is sufficient. It could not be overcome even on a different reading of s. 31(2)(b) of the *Copyright Act*.

[80] There is one final point to be made. Section 89 of the *Copyright Act* provides:

> 89. No person is entitled to copyright otherwise than under and in accordance with this Act or any other Act of Parliament, but nothing in this section shall be construed as abrogating any right or jurisdiction in respect of a breach of trust or confidence.

[81] The deliberate use of the words "this Act or any other Act of Parliament" rather than "this Act or any other enactment" means that the right to copyright must be found in an Act of Parliament and not in subordinate legislation promulgated by a regulatory body. "Act" and "enactment" are defined in s. 2 of the *Interpretation Act*, R.S.C. 1985, c. I-21, where

> "Act" means an Act of Parliament;

and

> "enactment" means an Act or regulation or any portion of an Act or regulation.

The definitions confirm that Parliament did not intend that a subordinate regulatory body could create copyright by means of regulation or licensing conditions.

[81] Contrary to s. 89, the value for signal regime would create a new type of copyright by regulation or licensing condition. Sections 2 and 21 of the *Copyright Act* define copyright in a communication signal to include the sole right to authorize another broadcaster to retransmit it to the public simultaneously with its broadcast. Authorizing simultaneous retransmission is then an aspect of copyright, although the right under the *Copyright Act* is limited to authorizing only specific defined entities, other broadcasters. In light of the legislative history discussed above, this limitation on copyright appears to be the result of a specific Parliamentary choice not to change the balance struck in the *Copyright Act* between broadcasters and BDUs. The value for signal regime would create a new right to authorize retransmission (and correspondingly prevent retransmission if agreement as to compensation is not achieved), in effect, amending the copyright conferred by s. 21. Thus the value for signal regime would create a new type of copyright and would do so without the required Act of Parliament, contrary to s. 89.

[82] My colleagues assert that there are functional differences between copyright and the proposed regulatory scheme. With respect, the differences that they point to do not alter the fundamental functional equivalence between the proposed regime and a copyright. Section 21 of the *Copyright Act* empowers broadcasters to prohibit the retransmission of their signals if certain conditions are met; the value for signal regime does exactly the same thing. My colleagues are correct that the CRTC cannot, through the value for signal regime, amend s. 21 of the *Copyright Act*. However that is precisely what the proposed regime does. Parliament could have imposed conditions that are the same, or similar to the value for signal regime in s. 21 in the same way it imposed limits in s. 31 on the copyright it granted in respect of retransmission of works, had it intended broadcasters to have such a right. Describing this new right granted to broadcasters under the value for signal regime as a series of regulatory changes does not alter the true character of the right being created. Not calling it copyright does not remove it from the scope of s. 89. If that type of repacking was all that was required, s. 89 would not serve its intended purpose of restricting the entitlement to copyright to grants under and in accordance with Acts of Parliament.

David Vaver,[1] "Chocolate, Copyright and Confusion: Intellectual Property and the Supreme Court of Canada" (2008)

(See page 97 for Endnotes.)

OSGOODE HALL REVIEW OF LAW AND POLICY

VOLUME 1 APRIL 2008 ISSUE 1 NO. 5

. . .

The second broader point Estey J. made causes even more difficulty. It involves how intellectual property law relates to the general law. Accepting an argument put by counsel, Estey J. said that:

> ...[C]opyright law is neither tort law nor property law in classification, but is statutory law. It neither cuts across existing rights in property or conduct nor falls between rights and obligations heretofore existing in the common law. Copyright legislation simply creates rights and obligations upon the terms and in the circumstances set out in the statute. ... The legislation speaks for itself and the actions of the appellant must be measured according to the terms of the statute.[2]

That statement is fine as far as it goes: owners and users should not have powers beyond what Parliament has conferred. But what if the legislation does not "speak for itself", as it often does not? Intellectual property laws are not passed in a vacuum. They are only partial codes set against the backdrop of the general law. To suggest the solution to every intellectual property problem can be found within the four corners of the statute, without recourse to the baggage of general law the drafters expected readers would bring with them when looking at the statutes, is disingenuous.

Take, for example, the proposition that copyright law is not "property law in classification". This may be a useful reminder not to apply the rules dealing with tangible property such as cars or chocolate bars mechanically to copyright or other intellectual property. But suppose the question is whether a contract, will, or statute that refers to "property" includes a copyright. Can one just say "No, it does not, because copyright is not 'property law in classification, but is statutory law'"? I think not. The way the Copyright Act contours the right gives it many of the characteristics of what we think of as property: rights to exclude third parties, the power to transfer and license, property-like remedies for infringement.[3] So copyright or other intellectual property rights are capable of being characterized as property under a contract, will or statute.[4]

The second question is more crucial: is this form of property meant to be caught by the language of this particular contract, will, or statute? The first question — is it capable of being so caught? — involves construing the intellectual property statute. The second — is it in fact so caught? — involves construing the particular contract, will, or statute that refers to property. It is perfectly possible to conclude that intellectual property is property within the meaning of one document, but not property within the meaning of another. It might not be property that is capable of being stolen under the Criminal Code, as the Court convincingly demonstrated in 1988.[5] It might very well be property under a will, where the testator disposes of his land to one set of beneficiaries and his personal property to another.[6] It may or may not be property under a provincial statute that lets sheriffs seize personal property for non-payment of a judgment debt; provincial courts have reached different results in interpreting their execution statutes, depending on a close reading of the history and purpose of those Acts.[7]

So perhaps before the 1990s the judges were wise to stick closely to what they had to decide and not venture into larger questions. For when they did, they created problems for both themselves and lower courts. The Estey dictum keeps cropping up in various guises in later Court decisions: for example, in such statements as that "the rights and remedies provided by the Copyright Act are exhaustive".[8] Such statements are potentially mischievous.

For example, some intellectual property statutes — e.g., the Copyright Act — require assignments of the right to be in writing; otherwise they say the transaction is of no effect. Some lower courts, relying on the Estey dictum, take those provisions quite literally. No effect means no effect; an oral assignee or exclusive licensee is a legal non-entity: he gets no right at all.[9] But suppose I pay $1m on a handshake for a copyright and spend another $1m developing and marketing it. Is it really possible that the seller can pocket the $1m and say I have nothing at all — except a right to a refund, and maybe not even that — simply because we only shook hands and didn't think to have the seller scribble down and sign the magic words: "I hereby assign you all my copyright in X"? Have we not progressed beyond the "primitive stage of formalism when the precise word was the sovereign, and every slip was fatal"?[10] Commonwealth courts, including civilian jurisdictions such as Scotland, have long said that the intellectual property statutes deal only with legal rights and remedies; equity steps in where legal rules fail to go.[11] An oral assignment for value does create rights: the assignee can go to court to get his title formalized by asking for an order compelling the seller to sign a transfer; in default, a court official can sign in the seller's place.[12] Even before then, oral assignees have got interlocutory injunctions against infringers, but no final injunction without first getting a signed assignment or joining the assignor. Despite some favourable dicta in the Supreme Court,[13] I do not know that any lower federal court has clearly recognized such equitable rights in an intellectual property case, and a number of decisions oppose the idea.[14] I do not know if the argument for such rights was plainly put to the court. What is clear is that Supreme Court statements to the effect that the language of the intellectual property statute is the beginning and end of rights and obligations under it wrongly dissuade counsel from making such arguments, and lower courts from accepting them.

Endnotes to David Vaver, "Chocolate, Copyright and Confusion: Intellectual Property and the Supreme Court of Canada"

1 Professor Emeritus of Intellectual Property and Information Technology Law, University of Oxford. This paper is a revised version of the James L. Lewtas Lecture delivered at Osgoode Hall Law School on October 24, 2007. A webcast is archived at mms://media.osgoode.yorku.ca/events/LewtasLecture-Oct242007.wmv. A version in French is in progress for publication.

2 Compo, supra note 16, 372-73

3 Other states make the point explicitly: e.g., in the U.K., subs. 1(1) of the Copyright, Designs and Patents Act 1988 provides: "Copyright is a property right...". So do other UK intellectual property statutes: e.g., s. 30(1) of the Patents Act 1977: "Any patent or application for patent is personal property (without being a thing in action)..."The phrase in parentheses – "without being a thing in action" – is somewhat mystical: is there a tertium quid between a chose in possession and a chose in action? The idea is presumably to oust the operation of the usual provisions on assigning things in action in s. 136 of the Law of Property Act 1925 (U.K.) – mirroring provincial provisions such as s. 36 of the Law and Equity Act, R.S.B.C. 1996, c. 253– in favour of the special assignment provisions of the Patents Act R.S.C. 1985, c. P-4.

4 See e.g., Planet Earth Productions Inc. v. Rowlands (1990), 69 D.L.R. (4th) 715, 73 O.R. (2d) 505 (H.C.J.) [Planet Earth].

5 Stewart, supra note 12.

6 Re Dickens, [1935] Ch. 267 (C.A.).

7 Planet Earth, supra note 25, holding copyright to be personal property under Ontario's Execution Act; criticized in Vaver, "Can Intellectual Property be Taken to Satisfy a Judgment Debt?" (1991), 6 Banking & Finance L.Rev. 255.

8 See e.g., Canadian Assn of Internet Providers v. SOCAN, 2004 SCC 45, [2004] 2 S.C.R. 427 at para. 85, 240 D.L.R. (4th) 193 [Internet Providers].

9 Jeffrey Rogers Knitwear Productions Ltd v. R.D. International Style Collections Ltd (1986), 19 C.P.R. (3d) 217 (Fed. T.D.) [Jeffrey Rogers]; Masterfile Corp. v. World Internett Corp. (2001), 16 C.P.R. (4th) 139 (Fed. T.D.) [Masterfile].

10 Wood v. Duff-Gordon, 222 N.Y. 88 at 91 (C.A. 1917), Cardozo C.J., (on implying terms in contracts).

11 Performing Right Society Ltd v. London Theatre of Varieties Ltd, [1924] A.C. 1 (H.L.), the principle of which has been often applied in the Commonwealth outside Canada: see, e.g., Lakeview Computers plc v. Steadman, 1999 WL 1048310 (C.A.); Griggs Group Ltd v. Evans, [2004] F.S.R. 673 (Ch.), aff'd [2005] EWCA 11 [Griggs]; Comprop Ltd v. Moran, [2002] Jersey L.R. 222 at paras. 31-33 & 38 (Royal Ct.); Sheldon v. Metrokane, [2004] FCA 19 at paras. 47 & 55 (Aust. Fed. Ct.); Tayplan Ltd v. D & A Contracts, [2005] ScotCS CSOH 17, para. 7 ("If I assign a thing which is not mine, I assign all the rights I have to make it mine. ... The law implies that a cedent confers on his

assignee everything which is necessary to make the assignation effectual");
cf. the inconclusive discussion in Downing v. General Synod of the Church of
England in Canada, (1943) 553, O.R. 652 (C.A.).

12 Seanix Technology Inc. v. Ircha (1998), 78 C.P.R. (3d) 443 (B.C. S.C.);
Csak v. Aumon (1990), 69 D.L.R. (4th) 567 at 570 (Ont. H.C.J.); Peck v.
Powell, (1885) 11 S.C.R. 494.

13 In Webb & Knapp, supra note 5, Abbott J. in his dissent (Ritchie J. concurring) recognized that an unwritten intention to transfer copyright constituted an equitable assignment; the majority (by Hall J.) did not disapprove,
holding only that the parties lacked this intention. The Supreme Court has
elsewhere accepted that the beneficial owner of a right is its owner "in
reality" even though, until a writing is signed, the right is formally held in
the assignor's name: Pecore v. Pecore, 2007 SCC 17, [2007] 1 S.C.R. 795
at para. 4. See also Bau- und Forschungsgesellschaft Thermoform AG v.
Chang (1991), 60 B.C.L.R. (2d) 90, 37 C.P.R. (3d) 349 (C.A.), enforcing
equitable interest in patent; Teledyne Industries Inc. v. Lido Industrial Products Ltd (1982), 68 C.P.R. (2d) 204, 227 (Fed. T.D.), holding that the federal
court may exercise all the powers of a court of equity.

14 Jeffrey Rogers, supra note 30; Masterfile, supra note 30.

---

3. Originality

(a) The Evolution of Originality

Pursuant to Section 5(1) of the *Copyright Act*, copyright shall subsist in
"every original literary, dramatic, musical and artistic work." In order to be the
subject-matter of copyright, a work must therefore be "original." The question of whether a work is worthy of protection is one of fact and degree, to be
judged by considering the work as a whole.[2] The originality requirement does
not mean that a work must be the expression of original or inventive thought.
The measure of originality is not one requiring comparison to pre-existing
works; rather it is an inquiry into the process by which the author brought the
work into being. It is thus possible for two identical works to be "original" for
the purposes of copyright law, provided that each was independently produced. Nor does copyright require any particular quality or merit as such;
historically, it was sufficient to obtain protection that there had been labour,
skill, time, ingenuity, selection, *or* mental effort expended in the production
of the work.[3] The originality required could have been of the lowest order,[4]
demanding nothing beyond the mere "sweat of the brow." By contrast, the
Continental *droit d'auteur* system has traditionally required something in the

---

[2]   *Ladbroke (Football) Ltd. v. William Hill (Football) Ltd.*, [1964] 1 All E.R. 465 (U.K. H.L.).
[3]   *Underwriters' Survey Bureau Ltd. v. American Home Fire Assurance Co.*, [1939] 4
D.L.R. 89 (Can. Ex. Ct.).
[4]   *Commercial Signs v. General Motors Products of Canada Ltd.*, [1937] O.W.N. 58 (Ont.
H.C.), affirmed 1937 CarswellOnt 309 (Ont. C.A.).

way of creativity, demonstrating the personality of the author, for rights to be acquired. In 1991, the US Supreme Court adopted a similar standard, although rationalized on more instrumental grounds.[5] Of course, disagreement over the threshold requirement for protection reflects a deeper tension between competing theories of copyright and its purpose.

As the following excerpts reveal, competing conceptions of originality have long been the source of confusion and inconsistency in the Anglo-Canadian jurisprudence, particularly with respect to compilation works. Indeed, in Canada, the United Kingdom and elsewhere in the Commonwealth, the case law regarding compilations has failed on any consistent basis to distinguish between skill and judgment, on the one hand, and the labour and capital necessary to bring a work into existence on the other. The weight of judicial authority has been to confer protection on compilations based upon the labour, time and expense expended in assembling facts; or in the skill, judgment and knowledge involved in selecting or arranging them; or both.[6]

Ladbroke (Football) Ltd. v. William Hill (Football) Ltd., [1964] 1 All E.R. 465 (H.L.)

Lord Reid and Lord Evershed Lord Hodson, Lord Devlin and Lord Pearce

1963 NOV. 18, 20, 21, 25, 26, 27, 28 1964 JAN. 21

. . .

LORD REID

Their Lordships took time for consideration.

January 21, 1964. My Lords, the respondents are well known bookmakers. Each week during the football season they have for many years sent out to their clients — referred to as punters — a fixed odds football betting coupon. The appellants are also old-established bookmakers. They decided to enter this field of betting in 1959 and began to send out coupons which closely resembled the

---

5   *Feist Publications Inc. v. Rural Telephone Service Co.*, 499 U.S. 340 (Kan., 1991)

6   *British Columbia Jockey Club v. Standen (Winbar Publications)* (1985), 22 D.L.R. (4th) 467 (B.C. C.A.); *Underwriters' Survey Bureau Ltd. v. American Home Fire Assurance Co.*, [1939] 4 D.L.R. 89 (Can. Ex. Ct.); *Cuisenaire v. South West Imports Ltd.* (1967), 54 C.P.R. 1 (Can. Ex. Ct.), affirmed (1968), 57 C.P.R. 76 (S.C.C.); *Fourgons Transit Inc. c. Fourgons Ramco Inc.* (1989), 22 C.I.P.R. 165 (Fed. T.D.); *G.A. Cramp & Sons Ltd. v. Frank Smythson Ltd.*, [1944] A.C. 329 (U.K. H.L.). *Ladbroke (Football) Ltd. v. William Hill (Football) Ltd.*, [1964] 1 W.L.R. 273 (U.K. H.L.); *Weetman v. Baldwin*, 2001 CarswellBC 2499 (B.C. Prov. Ct.); *Football League Ltd. v. Littlewoods Pools Ltd.*, [1959] 2 All E.R. 546 (Eng. Ch. Div.); *Hogg v. Scott* (1874), L.R. 18 Eq. 444 (Eng. Ch.); *Kelly v. Morris* (1866), L.R. 1 Eq. 697 (Eng. Ch.); *Morris v. Ashbee* (1868), L.R. 7 Eq. 34 (Eng. Ch. Div.); *Bookmakers' Afternoon Greyhound Services Ltd. v. Gilbert (Staffordshire) Ltd.*, [1994] F.S.R. 723 (Eng. Ch. Div.); *R. v. Laurier Office Mart Inc.* (1994), 58 C.P.R. (3d) 403 (Ont. Prov. Div.), affirmed (1995), 63 C.P.R. (3d) 229 (Ont. Gen. Div.); *Desktop Marketing Systems Pty Ltd. v. Telstra Corporation Limited*, [2002] F.C.A.F.C. 112 (Aust. C.A.).

respondents' coupons. The respondents claim copyright in their coupons and allege infringement by the appellants. The appellants maintain that only certain parts of the respondents' coupons are copyright and they deny infringement. The decision of Lloyd-Jacob J. in favour of the appellants was reversed by the Court of Appeal (Lord Denning M.R. and Donovan L.J., Diplock L.J. dissenting) and an injunction was granted. The appellants now seek to have the order of Lloyd-Jacob J. restored.

A coupon is a sheet of paper on which are printed various lists of forthcoming matches between well-known teams. One called "Nothing Barred" is a full list of some 50 matches. The others are shorter lists of matches selected by the bookmaker from the full list. The bets offered in respect of these lists vary in character. From some the punter must pick a certain number of winners. From others he must pick so many home or away wins or draws or a combination of these. And there are other kinds of bets offered. The variety of bets offered is very great. The respondents' coupon contained 16 lists, each with an appropriate name and we were told that no less than 148 different varieties of bet were offered if one adds up all those offered under each list. Naturally the odds offered differ widely — from as low as 5-2 to as high as 20,000-1. And the respondents have one list of peculiar difficulty where they offer £ 100,000 for twopence.

It is not disputed that a vast amount of skill, judgment, experience and work has gone into building up the respondents' coupon. There is keen competition in this field. If the bookmaker selects matches too easy to forecast, or offers too favourable odds, he may lose very large sums. If his selections of types of bet, matches and odds do not appeal to punters they will go to rival firms. It appears that the respondents have not altered the general form of their coupon since 1951. They only occasionally alter the odds offered for each type of bet. What is new each week is the selection of the matches which are to go into the lists.

When the appellants decided to enter this field they had to devise a suitable form of coupon. Their manager who was given this task was formerly employed by the respondents, but it appears that he tried to devise a form of coupon substantially different from the respondents' coupon. The coupons of some 20 other firms in the business were produced at the trial, and, while they have a general similarity, they vary very much in the nature of their lists and the variety of bets offered in respect of many of the lists. Most of them were studied by the appellants' manager, but his proposals were rejected by the appellants' managing director, who adopted a form closely similar to the respondents' coupon. The respondents had 16 lists: the appellants' coupon contains 15 of these lists, all of which appear in the same order as in the respondents' coupon. Moreover, the varieties of bets offered by the appellants in each of these 15 lists are almost identical with the offers by the respondents in their corresponding list. It is true that, with, I think, one exception, each of these lists is to be found in one or more of the other bookmakers' coupons and some are to be found in almost all of them. But the appellants do not suggest that the close resemblance between their coupon and the respondents' coupon is fortuitous. They admit that a good deal was simply copied from the respondents, and they say that they were entitled to do that. By no means everything was copied. For some of the lists they devised new names or headings, and the learned trial judge has found that they worked out for themselves the hundred or more different odds offered in respect of the various kinds of bet. And it was impossible to copy the selections of matches: the selections must be from the matches to take place in the following week, so there would not be time for one bookmaker to copy from the coupon of another matter which alters every week.

The first question to be determined is whether or to what extent copyright attaches to these coupons. The respondents say that a coupon must be regarded as a single work and that as such it is protected by copyright. The appellants seek to dissect the coupon. They would not only dissect it into the 16 lists, but they would further dissect each list into heading, selection of matches, and statement of odds offered for the various kinds of bets. They admit that there is copyright in the selection and in the statements of odds offered: they can safely do that because there they did not copy. But they deny any copyright as regards the rest of the coupon.

The Copyright Act, 1956, provides, by section 2, that copyright shall subsist in every original literary work and, by section 48, that literary work includes any written table or compilation. I have no doubt that the coupon must be treated as a single compilation. The appellants' dissection theory is derived from some statements in infringement cases and I must, therefore, examine at this point the law regarding infringement. Copyright gives the exclusive right to do certain things including "reproducing the work in any material form" (section 2 (5)), and reproduction includes reproduction of a substantial part of the work (section 49 (1)). Broadly, reproduction means copying, and does not include cases where an author or compiler produces a substantially similar result by independent work without copying. And, if he does copy, the question whether he has copied a substantial part depends much more on the quality than on the quantity of what he has taken. One test may be whether the part which he has taken is novel or striking, or is merely a commonplace arrangement of ordinary words or well-known data. So it may sometimes be a convenient short cut to ask whether the part taken could by itself be the subject of copyright. But, in my view, that is only a short cut, and the more correct approach is first to determine whether the plaintiffs' work as a whole is "original" and protected by copyright, and then to inquire whether the part taken by the defendant is substantial.

A wrong result can easily be reached if one begins by dissecting the plaintiffs' work and asking, could section A be the subject of copyright if it stood by itself, could section B be protected if it stood by itself, and so on. To my mind, it does not follow that, because the fragments taken separately would not be copyright, therefore the whole cannot be. Indeed, it has often been recognised that if sufficient skill and judgment have been exercised in devising the arrangements of the whole work, that can be an important or even decisive element in deciding whether the work as a whole is protected by copyright.

The appellants relied on cases where it has been held that in general the title of a work is not copyright. Those cases are dealt with by Lord Wright in the judgment of the Privy Council in Francis Day & Hunter Ltd. v. Twentieth Century Fox Corporation Ltd., and I think that he rightly expressed the principle when he said:

> "The copying which is complained of is the use of the title, and that is too unsubstantial on the facts of this case to constitute an infringement."

None of the decisions cited in argument appears to me to conflict with the view that you must first decide whether the plaintiffs' work as a whole is entitled to copyright and then see whether the part taken is a substantial part. The only apparent exception would seem to be a case such as Leslie v. J. Young & Sons, where a compilation was treated as consisting of severable parts, one of which was held to be original work and copyright while the rest was not.

The appellants' main argument was based on quite a different ground. They deny that the respondents' coupon is an original compilation. There is no dispute about the meaning of the term "original."

> "The word 'original' does not in this connection mean that the work must be the expression of original or inventive thought. Copyright Acts are not concerned with the originality of ideas, but with the expression of thought, and, in the case of 'literary work,' with the expression of thought in print or writing. The originality which is required relates to the expression of the thought. But the Act does not require that the expression must be in an original or novel form, but that the work must not be copied from another work — that it should originate from the author."

Per Peterson J. in University of London Press Ltd. v. University Tutorial Press Ltd. And it is not disputed that, as regards compilation, originality is a matter of degree depending on the amount of skill, judgment or labour that has been involved in making the compilation.

. . .

LORD HODSON

My lords, the first question is whether copyright subsists in the plaintiffs' fixed odds football coupons. The second is whether the defendants have, if the answer to the first question is in the affirmative, infringed the plaintiffs' copyright by appropriating a substantial part of their labours by the publication of similar coupons.

. . .

If the plaintiffs have employed more than negligible skill and labour in their selection of 16 lists containing varieties of bets which they offer to their customers they are entitled to be protected in respect of their coupons as being original compilations.

The evidence shows that this section was a highly skilled matter involving, as the learned Master of the Rolls said, selections from an infinity of choice and much expenditure of time, money and effort. I agree, therefore, with the majority of the Court of Appeal that the plaintiffs' coupons are entitled to protection as compilations, for the amount of skill and labour employed is not to be regarded as negligible.

. . .

LORD PEARCE

My Lords, the question whether the plaintiffs are entitled to copyright in their coupon depends on whether it is an original literary work. The words "literary work" include a compilation. They are used to describe work which is expressed in print or writing irrespective of whether it has any excellence of quality or style of writing (*per* Peterson J. in University of London Press Ltd. v. University Tutorial Press Ltd. The word "original" does not demand original or inventive thought, but only that the work should not be copied but should originate from the author.

B.C. Jockey Club v. Standen Winbar Publications (1985), 66 B.C.L.R. 245

British Columbia Court of Appeal

Nemetz C.J.B.C., Macdonald and Hutcheon JJ.A.

Judgment: September 25, 1985
Docket: Vancouver No. CA000589

Macdonald J.A. (Nemetz C.J.B.C. concurring):

1 This is an appeal from a judgment [reported at [1983] 4 W.W.R. 537, 73 C.P.R. (2d) 164, 146 D.L.R. (3d) 693] declaring that the appellant, through publishing the "Vancouver Sporting Special News", infringed the copyright of the respondents in their publication "Overnight Entries, Exhibition Park".

2 "Overnight" is published by British Columbia Jockey Club for each day of racing. It contains the following:

3 (a) the date of the race, and the race day number;

4 (b) order of races;

5 (c) length of each race;

6 (d) purses;

7 (e) class of horse eligible for each race;

8 (f) entries by post position;

9 (g) last date upon which each horse ran;

10 (h) assigned weight for each entry or "handicap";

11 (i) originally assigned jockeys;

12 (j) weather and track condition at the time Overnight Entries, Exhibition Park is prepared;

13 (k) time of first race of the day;

14 (l) combination of races for the "Daily Double", the "Quinella", the "Exactor", the "Triactor", and the "Sweep Six" races.

15 A good deal of work has to be performed before publication of the "Overnight". With respect to that work, the judge took the following from the statement of agreed facts:

> In performing these tasks a substantial amount of skill, knowledge and experience is employed and paid for by the Club to produce races which are of a high quality and are likely to be entertaining to the public. Overnight embodies in written form all the pre-set factors of each race for each racing day. It is prepared for the purposes of providing information in written form in respect of each race for use by licensed horse owners and their employees, trainers and jockeys. It informs such persons if, when and where they have been accepted to participate in a race. It provides information to the media and to Colwood in respect of the races to be run the next racing day. The Club has been and continues to be put to considerable time and expense in accumulating information and in creating a unique set of races. It publishes the information in its condition book, in Overnight, and in its Official Programme. Each edition of Overnight is an entirely novel list of horses and other information in respect of each race.

16 In publishing the "Special News", the appellant reproduced from "Overnight", with respect to each race, the following information: the order of races, the distance of races, the list of horses in each race, the jockeys for each horse, and the assigned weights. With respect to some races, he also took from "Overnight" certain conditions of the races: the purses, the claiming prices, and the post positions of some of the horses. The form of the "Special News" is not at all similar to that of the "Overnight". And the "Special News" contains a good deal of additional information contributed by the skill and experience of the appellant as a handicapper. He lists the horses in the order of his preference and gives his comments with respect to each. Then he makes a general comment with respect to each race.

. . .

18 The basis for the judge's finding of infringement appears in these passages from his reasons [p. 545]:

> But in my opinion the defendant in the case at bar has done more than copy information from Overnight. He has appropriated the results of the labour and skills of the Club which has gone into the compilation of the information which the Club has developed and published.

. . .

The judge expressed his conclusion in these passages [p. 548]:

> In my opinion the facts here show that the defendant has made a substantial use of all the essential facts compiled by the Club.

Although he adopted that information to his own style and added information of his own, the defendant nevertheless appropriated a substantial amount of the work, skill, judgment and knowledge of the Club. The copyright of the Club does not reside solely in the order of the information which it has compiled. Although the defendant has rearranged and republished that information in a different style, he nevertheless continued to appropriate a substantial part of the Club's original work.

19 Now if the governing principle is as I stated it earlier, and inviolable, then the judge did indeed err. This is para. 2.65 of the Laddie, Prescott and Vitoria text, upon which he relied:

2.65 A compilation is a work consisting of a collection of materials, and its merit normally resides in the painstaking labour which has been expended in assembling the facts (as in the case of a directory); or in the skill, judgment and knowledge involved in selecting those things which are to be included (as in the case of an anthology); or both. Consequently the copyright in such a work may be infringed by appropriating an undue amount of the material, although the language employed be different or the order of the material be altered. Were the law otherwise copyrights in compilations would be of little or no value. The point is succinctly stated in two dicta which have frequently been approved: "No man is entitled to avail himself of the previous labours of another for the purpose of conveying to the public the same information"; and "The true principle in all these cases is that the defendant is not at liberty to use or avail himself of the labour which the plaintiff has been at for the purpose of producing his work; that is, in fact, merely to take away the result of another man's labour or, in other words, his property".

. . .

22 The judge quoted from the speeches of Lord Reid and Lord Evershed in the *Ladbroke (Football) Ltd.* case, supra, italicizing certain passages for emphasis. There the defendants copied from the plaintiff's coupon 15 out of the 16 lists arranging them in the same order as they appeared in the plaintiff's coupon, in many cases with the same headings and almost identical varieties of wager, and with similar explanatory notes. So I am unable to see how that decision supports the respondents' case. But it is not authority against it.

. . .

24 As, in my view, the judge was not wrong in relying upon the paragraph in the Laddie, Prescott and Vitoria text, I would dismiss the appeal.

Under United States law, "industrious collection" or "sweat of the brow" alone are insufficient to render a work original for copyright purposes. In the following case, the United States Supreme Court held that to qualify as a copyrightable compilation three elements are required: (1) the collection and assembly of pre-existing material, facts, or data; (2) the selection, coordination, or arrangement of those materials; and (3) the creation of an "original" work of authorship that is not so mechanical or routine, entirely typical, or obvious as to require no creativity whatsoever. It is now settled that "originality" in the United States is a "constitutional requirement," according to which a work must possess "at least some minimal degree of creativity" in order to attract copyright.

Feist Publications Inc. v. Rural Telephone Services Co., 499 U.S. 340 (U.S. Sup. Ct. 1991)

Supreme Court of the United States

. . .

Justice O'CONNOR delivered the opinion of the Court.

This case requires us to clarify the extent of copyright protection available to telephone directory white pages.

I

Rural Telephone Service Company, Inc., is a certified public utility that provides telephone service to several communities in northwest Kansas. It is subject to a state regulation that requires all telephone companies operating in Kansas to issue annually an updated telephone directory. Accordingly, as a condition of its monopoly franchise, Rural publishes a typical telephone directory, consisting of white pages and yellow pages. The white pages list in alphabetical order the names of Rural's subscribers, together with their towns and telephone numbers. The yellow pages list Rural's business subscribers alphabetically by category and feature classified advertisements of various sizes. Rural distributes its directory free of charge to its subscribers, but earns revenue by selling yellow pages advertisements.

Feist Publications, Inc., is a publishing company that specializes in area-wide telephone directories. Unlike a typical directory, which covers only a particular calling area, Feist's area-wide directories cover a much larger geographical range, reducing the need to call directory assistance or consult multiple directories. The Feist directory that is the subject of this litigation covers 11 different telephone service areas in 15 counties and contains 46,878 white pages listings-compared to Rural's approximately 7,700 listings. Like Rural's directory, Feist's is distributed free of charge and includes both white pages and yellow pages. Feist and Rural compete vigorously for yellow pages advertising.

As the sole provider of telephone service in its service area, Rural obtains subscriber information quite easily. Persons desiring telephone service must apply to Rural and provide their names and addresses; Rural then assigns them a telephone number. Feist is not a telephone company, let alone one with monopoly status, and therefore lacks independent access to any subscriber information. To obtain white pages listings for its area-wide directory, Feist approached each of the 11 telephone companies operating in northwest Kansas and offered to pay for the right to use its white pages listings.

Of the 11 telephone companies, only Rural refused to license its listings to Feist. Rural's refusal created a problem for Feist, as omitting these listings would have left a gaping hole in its area-wide directory, rendering it less attractive to potential yellow pages advertisers. In a decision subsequent to that which we review here, the District Court determined that this was precisely the reason Rural refused to license its listings. The refusal was motivated by an unlawful purpose "to extend its monopoly in telephone service to a monopoly in yellow pages advertising." *Rural Telephone Service Co. v. Feist Publications, Inc.,* 737 F.Supp. 610, 622 (Kan.1990).

Unable to license Rural's white pages listings, Feist used them without Rural's consent. Feist began by removing several thousand listings that fell outside the geographic range of its area-wide directory, then hired personnel to investigate the 4,935 that remained. These employees verified the data reported by Rural and sought to obtain additional information. As a result, a typical Feist listing includes the individual's street address; most of Rural's listings do not. Notwithstanding these additions, however, 1,309 of the 46,878 listings in Feist's 1983 directory were identical to listings in Rural's 1982-1983 white pages. App. 54 (¶ 15-16), 57. Four of these were fictitious listings that Rural had inserted into its directory to detect copying.

Rural sued for copyright infringement in the District Court for the District of Kansas taking the position that Feist, in compiling its own directory, could not use the information contained in Rural's white pages. Rural asserted that Feist's employees were obliged to travel door-to-door or conduct a telephone survey to discover the same information for themselves. Feist responded that such efforts were economically impractical and, in any event, unnecessary because the information copied was beyond the scope of copyright protection. The District Court granted summary judgment to Rural, explaining that "[c]ourts have consistently held that telephone directories are copyrightable" and citing a string of lower court decisions. 663 F.Supp. 214, 218 (1987). In an unpublished opinion, the Court of Appeals for the Tenth Circuit affirmed "for substantially the reasons given by the district court." App. to Pet. for Cert. 4a, judgt. order reported at 916 F.2d 718 (1990). We granted certiorari, 498 U.S. 808, 111 S.Ct. 40, 112 L.Ed.2d 17 (1990), to determine whether the copyright in Rural's directory protects the names, towns, and telephone numbers copied by Feist.

II

A

[1] This case concerns the interaction of two well-established propositions. The first is that facts are not copyrightable; the other, that compilations of facts generally are. Each of these propositions possesses an impeccable pedigree. That there can be no valid copyright in facts is universally understood. The most fundamental axiom of copyright law is that "[n]o author may copyright his ideas or the facts he narrates." *Harper & Row, Publishers, Inc. v. Nation Enterprises,* 471 U.S. 539, 556, 105 S.Ct. 2218, 2228, 85 L.Ed.2d 588 (1985). Rural wisely

concedes this point, noting in its brief that "[f]acts and discoveries, of course, are not themselves subject to copyright protection." Brief for Respondent 24. At the same time, however, it is beyond dispute that compilations of facts are within the subject matter of copyright. Compilations were expressly mentioned in the Copyright Act of 1909, and again in the Copyright Act of 1976.

There is an undeniable tension between these two propositions. Many compilations consist of nothing but raw data-*i.e.,* wholly factual information not accompanied by any original written expression. On what basis may one claim a copyright in such a work? Common sense tells us that 100 uncopyrightable facts do not magically change their status when gathered together in one place. Yet copyright law seems to contemplate that compilations that consist exclusively of facts are potentially within its scope.

[2][3] The key to resolving the tension lies in understanding why facts are not copyrightable. The *sine qua non* of copyright is originality. To qualify for copyright protection, a work must be original to the author. See *Harper & Row, supra,* at 547-549, 105 S.Ct., at 2223-2224. Original, as the term is used in copyright, means only that the work was independently created by the author (as opposed to copied from other works), and that it possesses at least some minimal degree of creativity. 1 M. Nimmer & D. Nimmer, Copyright §§ 2.01 (1990) (hereinafter Nimmer). To be sure, the requisite level of creativity is extremely low; even a slight amount will suffice. The vast majority of works make the grade quite easily, as they possess some creative spark, "no matter how crude, humble or obvious" it might be. *Id.,* § 1.08. Originality does not signify novelty; a work may be original even though it closely resembles other works so long as the similarity is fortuitous, not the result of copying. To illustrate, assume that two poets, each ignorant of the other, compose identical poems. Neither work is novel, yet both are original and, hence, copyrightable. See *Sheldon v. Metro-Goldwyn Pictures Corp.,* 81 F.2d 49, 54 (CA2 1936).

Originality is a constitutional requirement. The source of Congress' power to enact copyright laws is Article I, § 8, cl. 8, of the Constitution, which authorizes Congress to "secur[e] for limited Times to Authors ... the exclusive Right to their respective Writings." In two decisions from the late 19th century-*The Trade-Mark Cases,* 100 U.S. 82, 25 L.Ed. 550 (1879); and *Burrow-Giles Lithographic Co. v. Sarony,* 111 U.S. 53, 4 S.Ct. 279, 28 L.Ed. 349 (1884)-this Court defined the crucial terms "authors" and "writings." In so doing, the Court made it unmistakably clear that these terms presuppose a degree of originality.

In *The Trade-Mark Cases,* the Court addressed the constitutional scope of "writings." For a particular work to be classified "under the head of writings of authors," the Court determined, "originality is required." 100 U.S., at 94. The Court explained that originality requires independent creation plus a modicum of creativity: "[W]hile the word *writings* may be liberally construed, as it has been, to include original designs for engraving, prints, &c., it is only such as are *original,* and are founded in the creative powers of the mind. The writings which are to be protected are *the fruits of intellectual labor,* embodied in the form of books, prints, engravings, and the like." *Ibid.* (emphasis in original).

In *Burrow-Giles,* the Court distilled the same requirement from the Constitution's use of the word "authors." The Court defined "author," in a constitutional sense, to mean "he to whom anything owes its origin; originator; maker." 111 U.S., at 58, 4 S.Ct., at 281 (internal quotation marks omitted). As in *The Trade-Mark Cases,* the Court emphasized the creative component of originality. It described copyright as being limited to "original intellectual conceptions of the author,"111 U.S., at 58, 4 S.Ct., at 281, and stressed the importance of requiring an author who accuses another of infringement to prove "the existence of those facts of originality, of intellectual production, of thought, and conception." *Id.,* at 59-60, 4 S.Ct., at 281-282.

[4] The originality requirement articulated in *The Trade-Mark Cases* and *Burrow-Giles* remains the touchstone of copyright protection today. See *Goldstein v. California,* 412 U.S. 546, 561-562, 93 S.Ct. 2303, 2312, 37 L.Ed.2d 163 (1973). It is the very "premise of copyright law." *Miller v. Universal City Studios, Inc.,* 650 F.2d 1365, 1368 (CA5 1981). Leading scholars agree on this point. As one pair of commentators succinctly puts it: "The originality requirement is *constitutionally mandated* for all works." Patterson & Joyce, Monopolizing the Law: The Scope of Copyright Protection for Law Reports and Statutory Compilations, 36 UCLA L.Rev. 719, 763, n. 155 (1989) (emphasis in original) (hereinafter Patterson & Joyce). Accord, *id.,* at 759-760, and n. 140; Nimmer § 1.06 ("[O]riginality is a statutory as well as a constitutional requirement"); *id.,* § 1.08 ("[A] modicum of intellectual labor ... clearly constitutes an essential constitutional element").

It is this bedrock principle of copyright that mandates the law's seemingly disparate treatment of facts and factual compilations. "No one may claim originality as to facts." *Id.,* § 2.11, p. 2-157. This is because facts do not owe their origin to an act of authorship. The distinction is one between creation and discovery: The first person to find and report a particular fact has not created the fact; he or she has merely discovered its existence. To borrow from *Burrow-Giles,* one who discovers a fact is not its "maker" or "originator." 111 U.S., at 58, 4 S.Ct., at 281. "The discoverer merely finds and records." Nimmer § 2.03[E]. Census takers, for example, do not "create" the population figures that emerge from their efforts; in a sense, they copy these figures from the world around them. Denicola, Copyright in Collections of Facts: A Theory for the Protection of Nonfiction Literary Works, 81 Colum.L.Rev. 516, 525 (1981) (hereinafter Denicola). Census data therefore do not trigger copyright because these data are not "original" in the constitutional sense. Nimmer § 2.03. The same is true of all facts-scientific, historical, biographical, and news of the day. "[T]hey may not be copyrighted and are part of the public domain available to every person." *Miller, supra,* at 1369.

[5][6] Factual compilations, on the other hand, may possess the requisite originality. The compilation author typically chooses which facts to include, in what order to place them, and how to arrange the collected data so that they may be used effectively by readers. These choices as to selection and arrangement, so long as they are made independently by the compiler and entail a minimal

degree of creativity, are sufficiently original that Congress may protect such compilations through the copyright laws. Nimmer §§ 2.11, 3.03; Denicola 523, n. 38. Thus, even a directory that contains absolutely no protectible written expression, only facts, meets the constitutional minimum for copyright protection if it features an original selection or arrangement. See *Harper & Row,* 471 U.S., at 547, 105 S.Ct., at 2223. Accord, Nimmer § 3.03.

[7][8] This protection is subject to an important limitation. The mere fact that a work is copyrighted does not mean that every element of the work may be protected. Originality remains the *sine qua non* of copyright; accordingly, copyright protection may extend only to those components of a work that are original to the author. Patterson & Joyce 800-802; Ginsburg, Creation and Commercial Value: Copyright Protection of Works of Information, 90 Colum.L.Rev. 1865, 1868, and n. 12 (1990) (hereinafter Ginsburg). Thus, if the compilation author clothes facts with an original collocation of words, he or she may be able to claim a copyright in this written expression. Others may copy the underlying facts from the publication, but not the precise words used to present them. In *Harper & Row,* for example, we explained that President Ford could not prevent others from copying bare historical facts from his autobiography, see 471 U.S., at 556-557, 105 S.Ct., at 2228-2229, but that he could prevent others from copying his "subjective descriptions and portraits of public figures." *Id.,* at 563, 105 S.Ct., at 2232. Where the compilation author adds no written expression but rather lets the facts speak for themselves, the expressive element is more elusive. The only conceivable expression is the manner in which the compiler has selected and arranged the facts. Thus, if the selection and arrangement are original, these elements of the work are eligible for copyright protection. See Patry, Copyright in Compilations of Facts (or Why the "White Pages" Are Not Copyrightable), 12 Com. & Law 37, 64 (Dec. 1990) (hereinafter Patry). No matter how original the format, however, the facts themselves do not become original through association. See Patterson & Joyce 776.

[9] This inevitably means that the copyright in a factual compilation is thin. Notwithstanding a valid copyright, a subsequent compiler remains free to use the facts contained in another's publication to aid in preparing a competing work, so long as the competing work does not feature the same selection and arrangement. As one commentator explains it: "[N]o matter how much original authorship the work displays, the facts and ideas it exposes are free for the taking.... [T]he very same facts and ideas may be divorced from the context imposed by the author, and restated or reshuffled by second comers, even if the author was the first to discover the facts or to propose the ideas." Ginsburg 1868.

It may seem unfair that much of the fruit of the compiler's labor may be used by others without compensation. As Justice Brennan has correctly observed, however, this is not "some unforeseen byproduct of a statutory scheme." *Harper & Row,* 471 U.S., at 589, 105 S.Ct., at 2245 (dissenting opinion). It is, rather, "the essence of copyright," *ibid.,* and a constitutional requirement. The primary objective of copyright is not to reward the labor of authors, but "[t]o promote the Progress of Science and useful Arts." Art. I, § 8, cl. 8. Accord,

Twentieth Century Music Corp. v. Aiken, 422 U.S. 151, 156, 95 S.Ct. 2040, 2044, 45 L.Ed.2d 84 (1975). To this end, copyright assures authors the right to their originalexpression, but encourages others to build freely upon the ideas and information conveyed by a work. *Harper & Row, supra,* 471 U.S., at 556-557, 105 S.Ct., at 2228-2229. This principle, known as the idea/expression or fact/expression dichotomy, applies to all works of authorship. As applied to a factual compilation, assuming the absence of original written expression, only the compiler's selection and arrangement may be protected; the raw facts may be copied at will. This result is neither unfair nor unfortunate. It is the means by which copyright advances the progress of science and art.

This Court has long recognized that the fact/expression dichotomy limits severely the scope of protection in fact-based works. More than a century ago, the Court observed: "The very object of publishing a book on science or the useful arts is to communicate to the world the useful knowledge which it contains. But this object would be frustrated if the knowledge could not be used without incurring the guilt of piracy of the book." *Baker v. Selden,* 101 U.S. 99, 103, 25 L.Ed. 841 (1880). We reiterated this point in *Harper & Row:*

> "[N]o author may copyright facts or ideas. The copyright is limited to those aspects of the work-termed 'expression'-that display the stamp of the author's originality.

> "[C]opyright does not prevent subsequent users from copying from a prior author's work those constituent elements that are not original-for example ... facts, or materials in the public domain-as long as such use does not unfairly appropriate the author's original contributions." 471 U.S., at 547-548, 105 S.Ct., at 2223-2224 (citation omitted).

[10] This, then, resolves the doctrinal tension: Copyright treats facts and factual compilations in a wholly consistent manner. Facts, whether alone or as part of a compilation, are not original and therefore may not be copyrighted. A factual compilation is eligible for copyright if it features an original selection or arrangement of facts, but the copyright is limited to the particular selection or arrangement. In no event may copyright extend to the facts themselves.

. . .

III

[14] There is no doubt that Feist took from the white pages of Rural's directory a substantial amount of factual information. At a minimum, Feist copied the names, towns, and telephone numbers of 1,309 of Rural's subscribers. Not all copying, however, is copyright infringement. To establish infringement, two elements must be proven: (1) ownership of a valid copyright, and (2) copying of constituent elements of the work that are original. See *Harper & Row,* 471 U.S., at 548, 105 S.Ct., at 2224. The first element is not at issue here; Feist appears to concede that Rural's directory, considered as a whole, is subject to a valid copyright because it contains some foreword text, as well as original material in its yellow pages advertisements. See Brief for Petitioner 18; Pet. for Cert. 9.

[15] The question is whether Rural has proved the second element. In other words, did Feist, by taking 1,309 names, towns, and telephone numbers from Rural's white pages, copy anything that was "original" to Rural? Certainly, the raw data does not satisfy the originality requirement. Rural may have been the first to discover and report the names, towns, and telephone numbers of its subscribers, but this data does not "'ow[e] its origin' " to Rural. *Burrow-Giles,* 111 U.S., at 58, 4 S.Ct., at 281. Rather, these bits of information are uncopyrightable facts; they existed before Rural reported them and would have continued to exist if Rural had never published a telephone directory. The originality requirement "rule[s] out protecting ... names, addresses, and telephone numbers of which the plaintiff by no stretch of the imagination could be called the author." Patterson & Joyce 776.

Rural essentially concedes the point by referring to the names, towns, and telephone numbers as "preexisting material." Brief for Respondent 17. Section 103(b) states explicitly that the copyright in a compilation does not extend to "the preexisting material employed in the work."

[16][17] The question that remains is whether Rural selected, coordinated, or arranged these uncopyrightable facts in an original way. As mentioned, originality is not a stringent standard; it does not require that facts be presented in an innovative or surprising way. It is equally true, however, that the selection and arrangement of facts cannot be so mechanical or routine as to require no creativity whatsoever. The standard of originality is low, but it does exist. See Patterson & Joyce 760, n. 144 ("While this requirement is sometimes characterized as modest, or a low threshold, it is not without effect") (internal quotation marks omitted; citations omitted). As this Court has explained, the Constitution mandates some minimal degree of creativity, see *The Trade-Mark Cases,* 100 U.S., at 94; and an author who claims infringement must prove "the existence of ... intellectual production, of thought, and conception." *Burrow-Giles, supra,* 111 U.S., at 59-60, 4 S.Ct., at 281-282.

The selection, coordination, and arrangement of Rural's white pages do not satisfy the minimum constitutional standards for copyright protection. As mentioned at the outset, Rural's white pages are entirely typical. Persons desiring telephone service in Rural's service area fill out an application and Rural issues them a telephone number. In preparing its white pages, Rural simply takes the data provided by its subscribers and lists it alphabetically by surname. The end product is a garden-variety white pages directory, devoid of even the slightest trace of creativity.

Rural's selection of listings could not be more obvious: It publishes the most basic information-name, town, and telephone number-about each person who applies to it for telephone service. This is "selection" of a sort, but it lacks the modicum of creativity necessary to transform mere selection into copyrightable expression. Rural expended sufficient effort to make the white pages directory useful, but insufficient creativity to make it original.

We note in passing that the selection featured in Rural's white pages may also fail the originality requirement for another reason. Feist points out that Rural did not truly "select" to publish the names and telephone numbers of its subscribers; rather, it was required to do so by the Kansas Corporation Commission as part of its monopoly franchise. See 737 F.Supp., at 612. Accordingly, one could plausibly conclude that this selection was dictated by state law, not by Rural.

[18] Nor can Rural claim originality in its coordination and arrangement of facts. The white pages do nothing more than list Rural's subscribers in alphabetical order. This arrangement may, technically speaking, owe its origin to Rural; no one disputes that Rural undertook the task of alphabetizing the names itself. But there is nothing remotely creative about arranging names alphabetically in a white pages directory. It is an age-old practice, firmly rooted in tradition and so commonplace that it has come to be expected as a matter of course. See Brief for Information Industry Association et al. as *Amici Curiae* 10 (alphabetical arrangement "is universally observed in directories published by local exchange telephone companies"). It is not only unoriginal, it is practically inevitable. This time-honored tradition does not possess the minimal creative spark required by the Copyright Act and the Constitution.

We conclude that the names, towns, and telephone numbers copied by Feist were not original to Rural and therefore were not protected by the copyright in Rural's combined white and yellow pages directory. As a constitutional matter, copyright protects only those constituent elements of a work that possess more than a *de minimis* quantum of creativity. Rural's white pages, limited to basic subscriber information and arranged alphabetically, fall short of the mark. As a statutory matter, 17 U.S.C. § 101 does not afford protection from copying to a collection of facts that are selected, coordinated, and arranged in a way that utterly lacks originality. Given that some works must fail, we cannot imagine a more likely candidate. Indeed, were we to hold that Rural's white pages pass muster, it is hard to believe that any collection of facts could fail.

Because Rural's white pages lack the requisite originality, Feist's use of the listings cannot constitute infringement. This decision should not be construed as demeaning Rural's efforts in compiling its directory, but rather as making clear that copyright rewards originality, not effort. As this Court noted more than a century ago, "'great praise may be due to the plaintiffs for their industry and enterprise in publishing this paper, yet the law does not contemplate their being rewarded in this way.'" Baker *v. Selden,* 101 U.S., at 105.

The judgment of the Court of Appeals is

Reversed.

In the next case, Canada's Federal Court of Appeal appeared to follow the US lead in *Feist* by endorsing a creativity threshold for originality. For a time, it looked likely that this case would settle the debate between competing conceptions of originality in Canada, and would have the added advantage of harmonizing

Canadian law with that of the United States and much of Europe. It is interesting that the Court points to international law in support of its ruling, particularly as the NAFTA language of "intellectual creations" was omitted from the implementing Canadian legislation. It should also be noted that NAFTA established a minimal baseline for protection; there is nothing in the agreement that would prevent Canada from protecting more than it is obligated to protect (i.e., industrious collections as well as intellectual creations).[7]

Teledirect (Publications) Inc. v. American Business Information Inc.
(1997), 221 N.R. 113

Federal Court of Appeal

Denault, Décary JJ.A. and Chevalier D.J.

Heard: October 6 and 7, 1997
Judgment: October 27, 1997
Docket: A-553-96

The judgment of the court was delivered by *Décary J.A.*:

1 The main issue in this appeal is whether copyright subsists in the compilation of information contained in Yellow Pages directories ("the Yellow Pages") published by Tele-Direct (Publications) Inc. ("the appellant"), an affiliate of Bell Canada. The American Business Information, Inc. ("the respondent") has conceded that the Yellow Pages, when taken as a whole and given the visual aspects of the pages and their arrangement, enjoy the protection of copyright.

2 In essence, the appellant, who itself is conceding that it does not claim copyright in the subscriber information given to it by Bell Canada (the subscriber information consists of the heading description of the business and the name, address and telephone number of the business), claims copyright in respect of the organization of the subscriber information received in a disorganized state from Bell Canada and in respect of the collection of additional data such as facsimile numbers, trade-marks and number of years in operation which the appellant itself obtains from Bell Canada's customers.

. . .

9 Compilations have been known to the Canadian law of copyright for ages, but it is only recently that they have been formally defined in the Act.

10 Prior to the 1993 *North American Free Trade Agreement Implementation Act* (NAFTA Implementation Act), compilations were only protected in so far as they could be characterized as "literary works".

---

[7]   See Myra Tawfik, "Decompiling the Federal Court of Appeal's NAFTA Argument in *Teledirect (Publications) Inc. v. American Business Information Inc.* — From Facts to Fiction", 33 Ottawa L. Rev. 147 (2001–2002).

11 In order to implement the North American Free Trade Agreement [*North American Free Trade Agreement Between the Government of Canada, the Government of the United Mexican States and the Government of the United States of America*, [1994] Can. T.S. No. 2] (NAFTA), the *Copyright Act* was substantially amended. "Artistic work", "dramatic work", "literary work" and "musical work" were from now on to include, respectively, "compilations of artistic works", "any compilation of dramatic works", "compilations of literary works" and "any compilation [of any work of music or musical composition]" (subsection 53(2) of the NAFTA Implementation Act). . . .

Furthermore, a definition of "compilation" was added to section 2 of the *Copyright Act* by subsection 53(3) of the NAFTA Implementation Act. It reads as follows:

2. "compilation" means

> (*a*) a work resulting from the selection or arrangement of literary, dramatic, musical or artistic works or of parts thereof, or
>
> (*b*) a work resulting from the selection or arrangement of data;

. . .

13 ...[T]he addition of the definition of "compilation" in so far as it relates to "a work resulting from the selection or arrangement of data" appears to me to have decided the battle which was shaping up in Canada between partisans of the "creativity" doctrine" according to which compilations must possess at least some minimal degree of creativity" and the partisans of the "industrious collection" or "sweat of the brow" doctrine" wherein copyright is a reward for the hard work that goes into compiling facts.

14 The definition of "compilation" must be interpreted in relation to the context in which it was introduced. Simply put, it was introduced as a result of the signature of the North American Free Trade Agreement and with the specific purpose of implementing it. It is therefore but natural when attempting to interpret the new definition to seek guidance in the very words of the relevant provision of NAFTA which the amendment intends to implement. The applicable provision is Article 1705 which reads as follows:

Article 1705: Copyright

> 1.   Each Party shall protect the works covered by Article 2 of the Berne Convention, including any other works that embody original expression within the meaning of that Convention. In particular:
>
> (a)   all types of computer programs are literary works within the meaning of the Berne Convention and each Party shall protect them as such; and
>
> (b)   compilations of data or other material, whether in machine readable or other form, which by reason of the selection or arrangement of their contents constitute intellectual creations, shall be protected as such.

The protection a Party provides under subparagraph (b) shall not extend to the data or material itself, or prejudice any copyright subsisting in that data or material.

. . .

15 Clearly, what the parties to the Agreement wanted to protect were compilations of data that "embody original expression within the meaning of [the Berne] Convention" and that constitute "intellectual creations". The use of these last two words is most revealing: compilations of data are to be measured by standards of intellect and creativity. As these standards were already present in Anglo-Canadian jurisprudence — as we shall see later — I can only assume that the Canadian government in signing the Agreement and the Canadian Parliament in adopting the 1993 amendments to the *Copyright Act* expected the Court to follow the "creativity" school of cases rather than the "industrious collection" school.

. . .

17 All in all, apart from the possible qualifications one might wish to make with respect to some earlier decisions, I have come to the conclusion that the 1993 amendments did not alter the state of the law of copyright with respect to compilations of data. The amendments simply reinforce in clear terms what the state of the law was, or ought to have been: the selection or arrangement of data only results in a protected compilation if the end result qualifies as an original intellectual creation. I shall therefore, as have counsel and the Trial Judge, use the post-1993 amendments terminology as if it had applied throughout the years at issue in these proceedings.

18 Another impact of the 1993 amendments may well be that more assistance can henceforth be sought from authoritative decisions of the United States courts when interpreting these very provisions that were amended or added in the *Copyright Act* in order to implement NAFTA. I do not wish to be interpreted as saying that Canadian courts, when interpreting these provisions, should move away from following the Anglo-Canadian trend. I am only suggesting that where feasible without departing from fundamental principles, Canadian courts should not hesitate to adopt an interpretation that satisfies both the Anglo-Canadian standards and the American standards where, as here, it appears that the wording of Article 1705 of NAFTA and, by extension, of the added definition of "compilation" in the Canadian *Copyright Act* , tracks to a certain extent the wording of the definition of "compilation" found in the United States *Copyrights Act*. I note that contrary to what happened in Canada, the United States did not find it necessary in order to implement NAFTA to amend the definition of "compilation" which they already had in their legislation.

. . .

b)   the test of originality

28 Essentially, for a compilation of data to be original, it must be a work that was independently created by the author and which displays at least a minimal degree of skill, judgment and labour in its overall selection or arrangement. The threshold is low, but it does exist. If it were otherwise, all types of selections or arrangements would automatically qualify, for they all imply some degree of intellectual effort, and yet the Act is clear: only those works which are original are protected. There can therefore be compilations that do not meet the test. Counsel for the appellant has put a great, if not disproportionate emphasis on the amount of labour that went into the main compilation it has made, and has said little of the required labour, let alone the skill and judgment expanded in the development of the sub-compilation. His position is best described in paragraph 129 of his Memorandum of fact and law:

> 129. [...] What the trial judge appears inadequately to assess is whether there was sufficient originality in the cumulative work of TELE-DIRECT in:
>
> > i) organizing the subscribers information received in a disorganized state from BELL CANADA;
> >
> > ii) verifying BELL CANADA's determination of headings and, where necessary, making appropriate corrections;
> >
> > iii) arranging for businesses to appear under more than one heading;
> >
> > iv) collecting and adding to data supplied by BELL CANADA such information as facsimile numbers, trade-marks, years of establishing and any other information that ABI copies from the **YELLOW PAGES** directories of TELE-DIRECT whenever the information is available in these directories.

29 It is true that in many of the cases we have been referred to, the expression "skill, judgment *or* labour" has been used to describe the test to be met by a compilation in order to qualify as original and, therefore, to be worthy of copyright protection. It seems to me, however, that whenever "or" was used instead of" and", it was in a conjunctive rather than in a disjunctive way. It is doubtful that considerable labour combined with a negligible degree of skill and judgment will be sufficient in most situations to make a compilation of data original. One should always keep in mind that one of the purposes of the copyright legislation, historically, has been "to protect and reward the *intellectual* effort of the *author* (for a limited period of time) in the work" (my emphasis). The use of the word "copyright" in the English version of the Act has obscured the fact that what the Act fundamentally seeks to protect is "le droit d'auteur". While not defined in the Act, the word "author" conveys a sense of creativity and ingenuity. I do not read these cases which have adopted the "sweat of the brow" approach in matters of compilations of data as having asserted that the amount of labour would in itself be a determinative source of originality. If they did, I suggest that their approach was wrong and is irreconcilable with the standards of intellect and creativity that were expressly set out in NAFTA and endorsed in the 1993 amendments to the *Copyright Act* and that were already recognized in Anglo-Canadian law.

30 *Cramp & Sons* is a good illustration in the House of Lords of the indifferent use of the words "or" and "and" in the application of the" skill, judgment and/or labour test"; yet no one will argue that the proper test was that defined by Lord Porter:

> [...] It is conceded that, if the work, labour and skill required to make the selection and to compile the tables which form its items are negligible, then no copyright can subsist in it. Whether enough work, labour and skill is involved, and what its value is, must always be a question of degree [...]

31 As noted by Lord MacMillan in *Cramp & Sons*, "on questions of degree different minds may naturally reach different conclusions". McGillis J. found on the facts that there was not a sufficient degree of originality in the sub-compilation. I have reached the same conclusion.

32 Commenting on Lord Mansfield's statement in *Sayre v. Moore* (1785), 1 East 361n, 102 E.R. 139 (Eng. K.B.) to the effect that

> We must take care to guard against two extremes equally prejudicial: the one, that men of ability, who have employed their time for the service of the community, may not be deprived of their just merits, and the reward of their ingenuity and labour; the other, that the world may not be deprived of improvements, nor the progress of the arts be retarded,

Professor Siebrasse observed that "intellectual property law must strike a balance between protecting the new products of inventive labour and allowing these to be freely available so as to form the basis for future progress". In the case at bar, it can hardly be said that the sub-compilation was a "new product of inventive labour" to use the learned professor's words or that it amounted to an "intellectual creation" within the meaning of Article 1705 of NAFTA. The compilation of the in-column listings is of such an obvious and commonplace character as to be unworthy of copyright protection. Certain compilations of routine data are so mechanical as to be devoid of a creative element.

. . .

39 In view of my finding that no copyright can be claimed by the appellant, I do not find it necessary to examine the issue of infringement. I do not therefore endorse nor disapprove the observations and findings made in that regard by the Trial Judge.

40 I would therefore dismiss the appeal with costs.

(b) The Current Test for Originality

As the following case of *CCH Canadian v. Law Society of Upper Canada* progressed through Canada's courts, it seemed to encapsulate the debate around originality in Canada. Excerpts from each level of court are included below to highlight the significant swing between extreme positions on the meaning of originality and its application to the facts. While the Trial Division limited copyright to works that demonstrated "imagination" or a "creative spark," the Court of Appeal required nothing more than that the work be "not copied." The case thus provided the opportunity for Canada's highest court to settle the longstanding debate between sweat-of-the-brow and creativity. It did so by arriving at what appears to be a compromise position: drawing on the idea of copyright's "balance," the Court concluded that an original work involves the exercise of skill and judgment that is not so trivial as to be purely mechanical. By "skill," the Court referred to, "the use of one's knowledge, developed or practiced ability in producing the work." By "judgment," the court meant, "the use of one's capacity for discernments or ability to form an opinion or evaluation by comparing different possible options in producing the work." Questions remain as to how this standard will be applied by the Canadian courts. How does it differ from the US creativity standard in purpose or effect? Does it establish a standard that is truly in between labour and creativity? Does it invite subjective inquiry into the quality of a work or the attributes of the author? How will it avoid the problems of a sweat-of-the-brow approach when it comes to ensuring that facts (even those discovered or generated through skill and judgment) remain in the public domain?

CCH Canadian Ltd. v. Law Society of Upper Canada

**1999 CarswellNat 2123, [1999] F.C.J. No. 1647 (Fed. T.D.),
additional reasons 2000 CarswellNat 168 (Fed. T.D.),
reversed 2002 CarswellNat 1000 (Fed. C.A.)
Federal Court of Canada–Trial Division
Toronto, Ontario
November 9, 1999**

GIBSON J. (Reasons for Order): —

INTRODUCTION

1 These actions were commenced by Statements of Claim each filed the 2nd of July, 1993. The actions involve allegations of infringements of copyrights owned by the plaintiffs. The alleged infringements result from the photocopying policies and activities of the defendant in supplying for the legal profession and the judiciary, limited copies of legal materials published by the plaintiffs and held in the defendant's "Great Library" at Osgoode Hall in Toronto.

. . .

THE ISSUES

11 In keeping with the revised reliefs claimed by the plaintiffs, counsel for the plaintiffs defined the issues in these actions in the following terms:

  – PLAINTIFFS' OWNERSHIP OF COPYRIGHT

1. Is copyright, other than any copyright owned by the Crown or a judge, capable of subsisting in whole or in part in any of the following publications which involve additions to statutory instruments and judicial decisions:

   (a) a reported judicial decision (with headnote, running heads and other matter added by a publisher) published in a volume containing other reported judicial decisions,…

   (b) a headnote (with catchwords, statement of the case and conclusion) in a reported judicial decision,…

   (c) an annotated statutory instrument (containing commentary, citations and summaries of relevant case law),…

   (d) a case summary (comprised of a citation together with a brief synopsis of a judicial decision),…

   (e) a topical case index,

   (f) a textbook or monograph on legal issues,

   . . .

ANALYSIS AND CONCLUSIONS

1) Subsistence of Copyright

   . . .

116 The object and purpose of the Copyright Act is to benefit authors, albeit that in benefiting authors, it is capable of having a substantially broader-based public benefit through the encouragement of disclosure of works for the advancement of learning or, as in this case, the wider dissemination of law. In Bishop v. Stevens[53], Madame Justice McLachlin, for the Supreme Court, wrote:

> – As noted by Maugham J., in Performing Right Society, Ltd. v. Hammond's Bradford Brewery Co., [1934] 1 Ch. 121 (C.A.) at p. 127, "the Copyright Act, 1911, was passed with a single object, namely, the benefit of authors of all kinds, whether the works were literary, dramatic or musical ...": see also art. 1 of the Revised Berne Convention, ...

117 Madame Justice Reed of this Court wrote in Apple Computer Inc. v. Mackintosh Computers Ltd.[54]:

> – ...the purpose of the Copyright Act is and always has been to grant a monopoly. No distinction is made therein as to the purpose of the work created — for entertainment, instruction or other purposes. The legislation historically, in my view had two purposes: to encourage disclosure of works for the "advancement of learning", and to protect and reward the intellectual effort of the author (for a limited period of time) in the work.

118 The Federal Court of Appeal has recently held that the Copyright Act should be interpreted in light of its object and purpose.

119 Copyright is said to comprise a "bundle" of incorporeal or intangible economic rights of authors of works and certain "neighbouring" rights of performers, makers of sound recordings and broadcasters.[56]

120 ...[C]opyright law, a "creature of statute", has been known to the law of England at least since the days of Queen Anne and many of the principles underlying even the current United Kingdom statute remain applicable in Canada. Thus, United Kingdom case law and that of other nations whose copyright laws are derived from the United Kingdom tradition can generally be relied on with impunity. By contrast, copyright legislation of the United States has developed through a different tradition and therefore American case law must be carefully scrutinized. Once again, in Compo v. Blue Crest, Mr. Justice Estey wrote at page 8:

> – The United States Copyright Act, both in its present and earlier forms, has, of course, many similarities to the Canadian Act, as well as to the preexisting Imperial Copyright Act. However, United States Court decisions, even where the factual situations are similar, must be scrutinized very carefully because of some fundamental differences in copyright concepts which have been adopted in the legislation of that country.

That this caveat may recently have been diluted by legislative change, as commented on by the Federal Court of Appeal in Tele-Direct, will be discussed later in these reasons.

121 Copyright subsists in every original literary work, subject to the terms of the Copyright Act. For the purposes of this action, I place particular emphasis on the word "original" in the foregoing statement of general principle, a word that is an integral element of the definition "every original literary, dramatic, musical and artistic work" in section 2 of the Copyright Act....

124 I turn to the issue of "originality" which is at the heart of copyright. As Madame Justice McLachlin wrote in Slumber-Magic in the quotation that appears in footnote 71:

> – The basis of copyright is the originality of the work in question. So long as work, taste and discretion have entered into the composition, that originality is established.

Thus, at least at the time Madame Justice McLachlin, then of the British Columbia Supreme Court, was writing originality did not require that the work be an expression of original or inventive thought. However, at least in respect of compilations, Madame Justice McLachlin went on to note, "...the originality requisite to copyright is a matter of degree depending on the amount of skill, judgment or [and] labour that has been involved..." . In University of London Press, Limited v. University Tutorial Press, Limited, Mr. Justice Peterson wrote at pages 608-609:

> – The word "original" does not in this connection mean that the work must be the expression of original or inventive thought. Copyright Acts are not concerned with the originality of ideas, but with the expression of thought, and, in the case of "literary work", with the expression of thought in print or writing. The originality which is required relates to the expression of

the thought. But the Act does not require that the expression must be in an original or novel form, but that the work must not be copied from another work–that it should originate from the author.

125 Professor David Vaver wrote in Copyright in Legal Documents:

–   Quantitative and qualitative tests for originality are notoriously unpredictable and to avoid them wherever possible is a good idea. As a legal technique, it might be better instead to accept all legal documents a person produces, without slavishly copying a prior form, as original to that person. Judges could then concentrate more on the real questions at stake: not how high the copyright threshold should be, but rather when, by whom, and how far copyright should be asserted.

126 In Interlego A.G. v. Tyco Industries Inc.[74], Lord Oliver of Aylmerton wrote:

–   Originality in the context of literary copyright has been said in several well known cases to depend upon the degree of skill, labour and judgment involved in preparing a compilation. ... Similarly in the speeches of Lord Reid and Lord Hodson ... it is stressed that the amount of skill, judgment or labour is likely to be decisive in the case of compilations. To apply that, however, as a universal test of originality in all copyright cases is not only unwarranted by the context in which the observations were made but palpably erroneous. Take the simplest case of artistic copyright, a painting or a photograph. It takes great skill, judgment and labour to produce a good copy by painting or to produce an enlarged photograph from a positive print, but no one would reasonably contend that the copy painting or enlargement was an "original" artistic work in which the copier is entitled to claim copyright. Skill, labour or judgment merely in the process of copying cannot confer originality. [citations omitted]

127 I detect a difference of view between the words of Lord Oliver of Aylmerton just quoted and the advice of Professor Vaver to accept all legal documents a person produces, without slavishly copying a prior form, as original and to then concentrate, not on how high the copyright threshold should be, but rather when, by whom, and how far copyright should be asserted. That being said, I recognize that Lord Oliver uses an example of what Professor Vaver would most likely describe as "slavish copying", while Professor Vaver's advice is related to circumstances where there has not been a "slavish copying". Neither Lord Oliver nor Professor Vaver provide much guidance as to how far one should go in following their reasoning where the copying is somewhat less than "slavish".

128 Not surprisingly, counsel for the defendant urged that the proximity to "slavish copying" exhibited in the evidence before the Court, at least in respect of reasons for judgment, is very close. Furthermore, in the face of the alleged existence of Crown copyright, counsel for the defendant urged that the plaintiffs own no copyright in individual case reports, including enhancements that they publish, and notwithstanding the Reproduction of Federal Law Order that is reproduced in paragraph 35 of the Agreed Statement of Facts that appears earlier in these reasons. Counsel for the defendant urged that the individual case reports published by the plaintiffs are "derivative works", that is to say, they are works substantially derived from pre-existing works that are protected by copyright such that no copyright exists in the "derivative works" themselves. It seems to me that this is simply a different way of urging that the plaintiffs' published reasons for judgment simply lack originality.

. . .

131 In Tele-Direct (Publications) Inc. v. American Business Information Inc.[75], Mr. Justice Décary, by reference to the 1993 amendments to the Copyright Act and to Article 1705 of the NAFTA Agreement to which the 1993 amendments were related, wrote at pages 31 and 32:

> – Clearly, what the parties to the Agreement wanted to protect were compilations of data that "embody original expression within the meaning of [the Berne] Convention" and that constitute "intellectual creations". The use of these last two words is most revealing: compilations of data are to be measured by standards of intellect and creativity. As these standards were already present in Anglo-Canadian jurisprudence–... I can only assume that the Canadian Government in signing the Agreement and the Canadian Parliament in adopting the 1993 amendments to the Copyright Act expected the Court to follow the "creativity" school of cases rather than the "industrious collection" school. [citations omitted]

Mr. Justice Décary continued at pages 37 and 38:

> – It is doubtful that considerable labour combined with a negligible degree of skill and judgment will be sufficient in most situations to make a compilation of data original. One should always keep in mind that one of the purposes of the copyright legislation, historically, has been "to protect and reward the intellectual effort of the author (for a limited period of time) in the work" (my emphasis). The use of the word "copyright" in the English version of the Act has obscured the fact that what the Act fundamentally seeks to protect is "le droit d'auteur". While not defined in the Act, the word "author" conveys a sense of creativity and ingenuity. [citations omitted]

While Justice Décary was dealing with the issue of copyright in a compilation in the Tele-Direct case, I am satisfied that much the same could be said with equal force in respect of a claim of copyright in edited reasons for judgment, both alone and in conjunction with "enhancements" such as a unique style of cause, catchlines, running heads, headnotes, lists of cases and other authorities cited and parallel citations.

132 In Édutile Inc. v. Automobile Protection Assn.[76], Mr. Justice Dubé, on the question of originality and again in the context of a compilation, cited Édition Hurtubise HMH Ltée v. Cégep André Laurendeau[77] where Mr. Justice Tessier, in translation, wrote:

> – What are the tests for determining whether a work is original? Quite obviously, it must above all else be the result of a creative effort and must not be a copy. The creative aspect requires a certain personal effort on the author's part together with knowledge, skill, time, reflection, judgment

and imagination. The author must expend his or her intellectual energy to
the extent required by the nature and anticipated content of the work.

This expansion of the traditional criteria of judgment, skill and labour, is, in my
view, an admirable expression of the creativity aspect inherent in the concept of
originality.

133 Finally, and with some trepidation given the concerns earlier acknowledged
in these reasons regarding reliance on American jurisprudence in the field of
copyright law, I wish to turn to Matthew Bender & Company v. West Publishing
Co. where the subject matter was similar to that now before this Court. West,
like the plaintiffs, is a law publisher. Circuit Judge Jacobs wrote:

> According to West, the required originality and creativity inhere in four elements
> of the case reports that HyperLaw intends to copy:
>
> i)   the arrangement of information specifying the parties, court, and date of
>   decision;
>
> ii) the selection and arrangement of the attorney information;
>
> iii) the arrangement of information related to subsequent procedural develop-
>   ments such as amendments and denials of rehearing; and
>
> iv) the selection of parallel and alternative citations.

Each element either adds or rearranges pre-existing facts, in themselves unprotectable, and so West is not entitled to protection for these elements of its case reports
unless it demonstrates creativity in the selection or arrangement of those facts. ...

. . .

The creative spark is missing where:

> industry conventions or other external factors so dictate selection that any person
> composing a compilation of the type at issue would necessarily select the same
> categories of information,... or (ii) the author made obvious, garden-variety, or
> routine selections,...

. . .

Thus, when it comes to the selection or arrangement of information, creativity
inheres in making non-obvious choices from among more than a few options.
... However, selection from among two or three options, or of options that have
been selected countless times before and have become typical, is insufficient.
Protection of such choices would enable a copyright holder to monopolize widely-used expression and upset the balance of copyright law.

In sum, creativity in selection and arrangement therefore is a function of (i) the
total number of options available, (ii) external factors that limit the viability of
certain options and render others non-creative, and (iii) prior uses that render
certain selections "garden variety."......

West's editorial work entails considerable scholarly labor and care, and is of
distinct usefulness to legal practitioners. Unfortunately for West, however,

creativity in the task of creating a useful case report can only proceed in a narrow groove. Doubtless, that is because for West or any other editor of judicial opinions for legal research, faithfulness to the public-domain original is the dominant editorial value, so that the creative is the enemy of the true.

134 I am satisfied that the last quoted paragraph is particularly apt on much of the evidence before me.

135 A further cautionary note: in at least three places in the Bender v. West decision from which the foregoing quotation is taken, reliance is placed on Feist Publications, Inc. v. Rural Telephone Service Co., Inc. In Hager v. E.C.W. Press Ltd., Madame Justice Reed notes:

> Interestingly, there is now a Bill before the United States Congress ... to overrule the decision of the United States Supreme Court in Feist..., a decision in that country that had a result similar to Tele-Direct in this. There is debate among both United States and Canadian authors as to whether the Feist decision is limited to database type cases or will have wider ramifications....

136 Madame Justice Reed in Hager also casts doubt on the impact of the Tele-Direct decision on the elements of creativity and originality. Madame Justice Reed writes at pages 310 and 311:

> Counsel argues that even if the words of an interviewee were previously copyrightable by the interviewer, as set out in the Express Newspapers and Gould Estate cases, the recent decision of the Federal Court of Appeal in Tele-Direct has overruled that jurisprudence. As noted above, it is argued that the elements of creativity and originality that are now required for copyright protection cannot exist in the quoted words of another. In addition, as I understand the argument, it is that the Tele-Direct decision has turned Canadian copyright law, at least insofar as it is relevant for present purposes, from its previous alignment with the law of the United Kingdom towards an alignment with that of the United States.
>
> I do not interpret the Tele-Direct decision as having such a broad effect. In both the United States and Canada, jurisprudence has defined the requirement that copyright be granted in an "original" work, as meaning that the work originate from the author and that it not be copied from another. In the United States this was initially the result of case law; the statutory requirement of "originality" was only added in 1976. The requirement that a work be "original" has been a statutory requirement in Canada since 1924 when the Copyright Act... enacted in 1921 ... came into force. That Act was largely copied from the United Kingdom Copyright Act, 1911. I am not persuaded that the Federal Court of Appeal intended a significant departure from the pre-existing law. In the absence of an express decision from the Court of Appeal to the contrary, I think the law as set out in Express Newspapers and Gould Estate is still the law.
>
> One reason for being cautious about not over-extending the Tele-Direct decision is that it deals with an entirely different type of work from those in issue in this case. It deals with a compilation of data ... . The appropriate test to be applied when copyright is claimed for works that consists of compilations of data has been a difficult area. This is because such works are not likely to exhibit, on their face, indicia of the author's personal style or manner of expression. [citations omitted]

137 I am satisfied that the types of works here at issue, particularly edited and enhanced versions of reasons for judgment, are more akin to the works at issue in Tele-Direct than they are to those at issue before Madame Justice Reed in Hager. That being said, they are not as akin to the works at issue in Tele-Direct as were the works that were before me in Ital-Press Ltd. v. Giuseppina Sicoli et al where I adopted an interpretation of "originality" closer to that preferred by Madame Justice Reed in Hager. I rely entirely upon the evidence before me and on the extensive and sophisticated nature of the argument before me, both in writing and orally, in this matter, in adopting for the purpose of this matter a broader interpretation of "originality" than I did in Ital-Press .

138 Against the foregoing, and taking into account all of the evidence before the Court in this matter, I reach the following conclusions regarding the subsistence of copyright based on the statement of issues that appears earlier in these reasons. I will repeat the relevant elements of the issue statement here for ease of reference:

> Is copyright, other than any copyright owned by the Crown or a judge, capable of subsisting in whole or in part in any of the following publications which involve additions to statutory instruments and judicial decisions:
>
> (a) a reported judicial decision (with headnote, running heads and other matter added by a publisher) published in a volume containing other reported judicial decisions,
>
> . . .

139 To the extent that the question relates to the three decisions cited, not merely as examples but as the subject matter of the question, my answer is "no". While the evidence before the Court demonstrates, beyond a doubt, that the preparation of the reported judicial decisions, including the headnote, catch-lines, parallel citations, running heads and other matter added by the publisher, in respect of the three decisions in question, involved extensive labour, skill and judgment, I am satisfied that the whole process, particularly those elements involving skill and judgment, lacked the "imagination" or "creative spark" that I determine to now be essential to a finding of originality. I am satisfied that editorially enhanced judicial decisions should be measured by a standard of intellect and creativity in determining whether they give rise to copyright, in the same way as compilations of data might be said to be measured following the decision of the Federal Court of Appeal in Tele-Direct. Article 2 of The Berne Convention, 1971, I am satisfied, clearly reaches to the form of alterations of literary works represented by the case reports here at issue, but those case reports simply lack the "original expression" and fail to constitute the "intellectual creations" contemplated by that Article and, more particularly, Article 1705 of NAFTA as reproduced in the Tele-Direct decision. To revert, once again with some trepidation, to the words of Bender v. West which I am satisfied are equally apt under Canadian law to the facts of this matter:

West's editorial work entails considerable scholarly labor and care, and is of distinct usefulness to legal practitioners. Unfortunately for West, however, creativity in the task of creating a useful case report can only proceed in a narrow groove. Doubtless, that is because for West or any other editor of judicial opinions for legal research, faithfulness to the public-domain original is the dominant editorial value, so that creativity is the enemy of the true.

140 Here, whether or not the reasons for judgment in issue can be descried as opinions for legal research, faithfulness to the original, whether or not in the public domain, is the dominant editorial value and thus, the creative "is the enemy of the true".

> Is copyright, other than any copyright owned by the Crown or a judge, capable of subsisting in whole or in part in any of the following publications which involve additions to statutory instruments and judicial decisions:
>
> > (b) a headnote (with catchwords, statement of the case and conclusion) in a reported judicial decision,...

141 Once again, subject to the limitations expressed in my answer to the first issue question, my conclusion is "no" and I reach that conclusion for the same reasons I reached a negative answer in respect of the reported judicial decisions of the same three cases.

> Is copyright, other than any copyright owned by the Crown or a judge, capable of subsisting in whole or in part in any of the following publications which involve additions to statutory instruments and judicial decisions:...
>
> > (d) a case summary (comprised of a citation together with a brief synopsis of a judicial decision),
> >
> > (e) a topical case index,...

142 Once again, subject to the limitations expressed in my answer to the first issue question, my conclusion is "no" and I reach that conclusion for the same reasons I reached a negative answer in respect of the reported judicial decisions referred to in the first issue question.

> Is copyright, other than any copyright owned by the Crown or a judge, capable of subsisting in whole or in part in any of the following publications which involve additions to statutory instruments and judicial decisions:
>
> > (f) a textbook or monograph on legal issues,...

143 I reach an opposite conclusion with respect to the annotated statutory instrument containing commentary, citations and summaries of relevant case law, that is Martin's Ontario Criminal Practice 1999, and with respect to the textbooks or monographs of legal issues, that are Economic Negligence and Forensic Evidence in Canada. I am satisfied on the evidence before me that these publications reflect the degree of originality, creativity and ingenuity appropriate to the existence of copyright.

144 I decline any invitation to generalize on the basis of the foregoing answers and conclusions.

CCH Canadian Ltd. v. Law Society of Upper Canada

(2002), 212 D.L.R. (4th) 385 (Fed. C.A.), reversed 2004 CarswellNat 446 (S.C.C.)
Federal Court of Appeal

Linden, Rothstein and Sharlow JJ.A.
Heard: October 23-25, 2001.
Judgment: May 14, 2002.

Linden J.A.:

I.   Introduction

… In essence, the Publishers assert that copyright subsists in their material, and that the Law Society infringes those copyrights through its custom photocopying service and by making free-standing copiers available in the Great Library. Notably however, the Publishers allow reproductions by certain persons for limited purposes. For example, they expressly grant a license to lawyers to make copies to submit in judicial proceedings, to judges to use in judicial proceedings and to anyone to use in parliamentary proceedings. The Law Society denies all liability.

. . .

II.   The Issues

A.   Subsistence of Copyright

. . .

15 … [T]his Court must decide whether the Trial Judge erred in concluding that copyright does not subsist in the reported judicial decisions, the headnotes, the case summary and the topical index. If copyright does subsist in these works, there is no dispute with the Trial Judge's finding that such copyright would be owned by the Publisher of each respective work.

. . .

III.   Analysis

22 Copyright law is statutory law, based upon the *Copyright Act*, R.S.C., 1985, c. C-42, and its relevant amendments (the "*Act*") (see *Compo Co. v. Blue Crest Music Inc.* (1979), [1980] 1 S.C.R. 357 (S.C.C.), at 372-3 ("*Compo*")). However, case law, both domestic and foreign, guides this Court's interpretation of the *Act*. This Court might be guided by British jurisprudence, since Canadian copyright law was historically based upon, and still closely resembles British law (see J.S. McKeown, *Fox, Canadian Law of Copyright and Industrial Designs*, 3rd ed. (Scarborough: Carswell, 2000) at 38-39 ("*Fox*"). On the other hand, the Supreme Court of Canada has indicated that American jurisprudence must be carefully scrutinized, because there are important differences between Canadian and American copyright policy and legislation (*Compo, supra* at 367). Canadian courts must always be careful not to upset the balance of rights as it exists under the Canadian *Act*.

23 Broadly speaking, the purposes of Canadian copyright law are to benefit authors by granting them a monopoly for a limited time, and to simultaneously encourage the disclosure of works for the benefit of society at large (see *Apple Computer Inc. v. Mackintosh Computers Ltd.* (1986), [1987] 1 F.C. 173 (Fed. T.D.), at 200 (abridged version), var'd (1987), [1988] 1 F.C. 673 (Fed. C.A.), aff'd [1990] 2 S.C.R. 209 (S.C.C.) ("*Apple Computer*"); see also *Galerie d'art du Petit Champlain inc. c. Théberge*, 2002 SCC 34 (S.C.C.), at para. 30). Copyright law should recognize the value of disseminating works, in terms of advancing science and learning, enhancing commercial utility, stimulating entertainment and the arts and promoting other socially desirable ends. In order to realize these benefits, however, creators must be protected from the unauthorized exploitation of their works to guarantee sufficient incentives to produce new and original works. The person who sows must be allowed to reap what is sown, but the harvest must ensure that society is not denied some benefit from the crops. Perhaps Lord Mansfield best characterized the tension over two centuries ago when, in the case of *Sayre v. Moore* (1785), 102 E.R. 139 (Eng. K.B.), he stated:

> ... we must take care to guard against two extremes equally prejudicial; the one, that men of ability, who have employed their time for the service of our community, may not be deprived of their just merits, and the reward of their ingenuity and labour; the other, that the world may not be deprived of improvements, nor the progress of the arts be retarded.

The challenge facing this Court, and copyright law generally, is to find a fair and appropriate equilibrium that achieves both goals.

A.   Does Copyright Subsist in the Publishers' Works?

1.   The Standard of Originality

. . .

26 The first issue now before this Court is whether "imagination or creative spark" is indeed "essential to a finding of originality", and whether the Publishers' materials should indeed be "measured by a standard of intellect and creativity in determining whether they give rise to copyright".

27 In my view, the Trial Judge misinterpreted this Court's decision in *Tele-Direct (Publications) Inc. v. American Business Information Inc.* (1997), [1998] 2 F.C. 22 (Fed. C.A.) ("*Tele-Direct*"), and other jurisprudence as shifting the standard of originality away from the traditional Anglo-Canadian approach. Neither Article 2 of the *Berne Convention for the Protection of Literary and Artistic Works*, Paris Revision, 24 July 1971, 161 U.N.T.S. 18338 (the "*Berne Convention*"), nor Article 1705 of the *North American Free Trade Agreement*, 17 December 1992, Can T.S. 1994 No. 2 ("NAFTA"), require a more onerous standard for copyright protection than already contained in the *Act*. In addition, there are significant differences between Anglo-Canadian copyright law and the American standard of originality that was applied in *Matthew Bender & Co. v.*

West Publishing Co., 158 F.3d 674 (U.S. 2nd Cir. N.Y., 1998). Whether or not the Publishers' works are "original" depends upon the meaning of that term in its statutory context, as explained by existing Anglo-Canadian jurisprudential principles.

28 As Chief Justice McLachlin (as she now is) stated in *Bishop v. Stevens* , [1990] 2 S.C.R. 467 (S.C.C.), at 477, the task is "first and foremost ... a matter of statutory interpretation". The *Act* contains no express requirement of creative spark or imagination; the only prerequisite to protection (relevant to this discussion) is that a work be original. In fact, the *Act*, which has been the sole source of copyright protection in Canada since its inception in 1921 (see *Fox, supra* at 34-56), contains no mention whatsoever of any requirement other than, or in addition to originality. The Supreme Court of Canada has refused to imply exemptions in addition to those Parliament expressly chose to include in the *Act* (see *Bishop v. Stevens, supra* at 480-1). Similarly, this Court should not erect barriers to copyright protection that Parliament itself has declined to construct. Therefore, this Court will not insert an additional requirement of creative spark or imagination into the *Act*, and instead will focus on the *Act*'s only relevant prerequisite in this case, which is that the work be "original".

29 Admittedly, it is difficult if not impossible to assess originality without some interpretative framework. Consequently, the proper interpretation of the word "original" has been the subject of much discussion within the case law.

30 The British case of *University of London Press v. University Tutorial Press Ltd.*, [1916] 2 Ch. 601 (Eng. Ch. Div.) (*"University of London Press "*), is perhaps one of the oldest and most frequently cited cases regarding originality in Anglo-Canadian copyright law. With respect to copyright in a professor's examination papers, that case established (at 608-9) that "the Act does not require that the expression must be in an original or novel form, but that the work must not be copied from another work — that it should originate from the author." Here, the word "original" was interpreted to mean independently created and not copied.

31 British courts built on this foundation and embraced assorted incarnations of the phrases "skill, judgment or labour", "knowledge, labour, judgment or skill" and "skill, labour and capital" to aid in the application of the concept of originality. These phrases guided the determination of the fundamental question, which is whether the work is something new or simply a copy of another work. As Lord Oliver of Aylmerton explained in *Interlego (Attorney General) v. Tyco Industries Inc.* (1988), [1989] 1 A.C. 217 (England P.C.) (*"Interlego"*), great skill, judgment and labour is required to produce a good copy of a painting, but nobody could reasonably say that the second painting is original. He said (at 262-3, emphasis added): "[s]kill, judgment or labour *merely in the process of copying* cannot confer originality".

32 The phrases mentioned above are often invoked in the context of compilations, which are a distinct type of work. No doubt this is because a compilation by definition might include some material that has been created by someone else. The underlying question in such a case is whether the compilation is

original or merely a rearranged copy of existing works (see for example *Ladbroke (Football) Ltd. v. William Hill (Football) Ltd.*, [1964] 1 All E.R. 465 (U.K. H.L.) ("*Ladbroke*"); *G.A. Cramp & Sons Ltd. v. Frank Smythson Ltd.* , [1944] 2 All E.R. 92 (U.K. H.L.); and *MacMillan & Co. v. Cooper* (1923), 51 Ind. App. 109 (India P.C.)).

33 Canadian courts have generally parallelled the British approach. The traditional Canadian standard has been summarized as follows:

> The requirement of originality means that the <u>product must originate from the author</u> in the sense that it is the result of a substantial degree of skill, industry or experience employed by the author. ... The effective meaning of the requirement of originality is that <u>the work must not be copied from another</u> ....

(see *Fox*, *supra* at 118, emphasis added, citing *Langlois v. Vincent* (1874), 2 Can. Com. R. 164 (Que. S.C.); *Canadian Admiral Corp. v. Rediffusion Inc.* (1954), 20 C.P.R. 75 (Can. Ex. Ct.) ("*Canadian Admiral*"); *Kilvington Brothers Ltd. v. Goldberg* (1957), 16 Fox Pat. C. 164 (Ont. H.C.); *Horn Abbot Ltd. v. W.B. Coulter Sales Ltd.* (1984), 1 C.I.P.R. 97 (Fed. T.D.); *Lifestyle Homes Ltd. v. Randall Homes Ltd.* (1991), 34 C.P.R. (3d) 505 (Man. C.A.)).

34 Chief Justice McLachlin considered the originality requirement when she was a Trial Judge in British Columbia, and decided that copyright subsisted in the arrangement of an advertising brochure for adjustable beds. In *Slumber-Magic Adjustable Bed Co. v. Sleep-King Adjustable Bed Co.* (1984), 3 C.P.R. (3d) 81 (B.C. S.C.), at 84 ("*Slumber-Magic*"), she adopted the British jurisprudence regarding originality in compilations, commenting:

> So long as work, taste and discretion have entered into the composition, that originality is established. In the case of a compilation, the originality requisite to copyright is a matter of degree depending on the amount of skill, judgment or labour that has been involved in making the compilation. ... [T]he court should canvas the degree of industry, skill or judgment which has gone into the over-all arrangement.

Notably, the now Chief Justice of Canada realized that the concept of originality was inherently broad and used a variety of terms to describe it, including work, taste, discretion, skill, judgment, industry and labour. She found these ideas helpful to assess originality, but did not suggest that one phrase or another was the exclusive test.

35 The now Chief Justice of this Court, Richard J. (as he then was), stated in *U & R Tax Services Ltd. v. H & R Block Canada Inc.* (1995), 62 C.P.R. (3d) 257 (Fed. T.D.), at 264 (footnote omitted):

> Industriousness ('sweat of the brow') as opposed to creativity is enough to give a work sufficient originality to make it copyrightable. The meaning of the word 'original' was succinctly stated by Cameron J. in *Canadian Admiral Corp. v. Rediffussion Inc.*: 'For a work to be 'original' it must originate from the author; it must be the product of his labour and skill and must be the expression of his thought.'

Importantly, the sweat of the brow exerted by U&R Tax Services to create its tax form was directed at selecting the content from among earlier government forms, draft releases and other information and arranging the layout of the form, not at merely copying existing materials. As Lord Oliver noted, one who sweats to produce what is, in essence, a copy cannot be rewarded with copyright protection. Richard J. also did not suggest that "sweat of the brow" would make a work original if poured into merely copying another work. Rather, the phrase "sweat of the brow" referred to the effort required to distinguish an original work from a mere copy. Richard J. differentiated between "sweat of the brow" and "creativity" since, as will be discussed below, the latter term might connote novelty, a quality with which copyright law is not concerned.

36 Thus, the classic Anglo-Canadian precondition to copyright is that a work must be independently produced and not copied from another person. Where a work, such as a compilation, is produced by selecting and arranging existing material originality can be established if the new work is more than simply a rearranged copy of existing materials. Producing a work that is not, in essence, a copy of existing material will require effort that is most often referred to as skill, judgment or labour. The Trial Judge in this case interpreted *Tele-Direct* as altering the classic Anglo-Canadian standard of originality and adding new requirements of "imagination" and "creative spark". In this, he was mistaken.

37 The first point to note about *Tele-Direct* is that involved sub-compilations of routine data, whereas this case concerns materials that are considerably more complex. ...

38 In *Tele-Direct* this Court considered whether NAFTA, *supra*, required some change in our understanding of copyright protection for compilations of data. To deal with that possibility, this Court set forth an extensive discussion of that agreement and its impact on compilations (at paras 14-15, footnotes omitted).

. . .

39 A close reading of this passage indicates that the Court's focus was on the addition of the definition of "compilation" to section 2 of the *Act*, particularly regarding compilations of data. This portion of the Court's reasons makes no mention whatsoever of the proper meaning of the word "original", which is contained in section 5 of the *Act*, and which this Court must now interpret.

40 As the commentary surrounding the implementation of the NAFTA amendments demonstrates, the mandate was to ensure among signatories protection for *forms* of expression, such as compilations of literary works and of data, not to alter the *standard* upon which those forms are protected (see Canada, *House of Commons Debates* (31 March 1993); Canada, *House of Commons Debates* (27 May 1993); Canada, Legislative Committee on Bill C-115, An Act to Implement NAFTA, *Minutes, Proceedings and Evidence of the Legislative Committee on Bill C-115, An Act to Implement NAFTA*, (5 November 1993) and accompanying submissions; and *Fox, supra* at 44-46). Therefore, the copyright provisions in NAFTA were not intended to alter the standard of originality in Canadian

copyright law. Neither NAFTA nor the *Berne Convention, supra* impose a higher standard of originality than was already present under Canadian law.

41 As the *Fox* textbook, *supra*, points out, the World Intellectual Property Organization's *Guide to the Berne Convention for the Protection of Literary and Artistic Works*, 1971 (Geneva, W.I.P.O., 1978), states:

> ... the very concept of copyright from a philosophical, theoretical and pragmatic point of view differs [sic] from country to country, since each has its own legal framework influenced by social and economic factors. To define it in a manner binding on all member countries would be difficult, if not impossible.

This recognizes expressly that signatories to the *Berne Convention* may award copyright based upon standards unique to each country.

42 Even if NAFTA and the *Berne Convention* were somehow intended to alter the prerequisites for copyright protection in member countries, those instruments would set minimum standards (see *Fox, supra* at 138). A more onerous standard of originality deprives owners of the copyright protection that the signatories to these agreements intended to guarantee. Their purpose is frustrated, rather than promoted by implying additional requirements of creativity, imagination or creative spark into the *Act*, as the Trial Judge did.

43 Furthermore, neither Article 2 of the *Berne Convention* nor Article 1705 say anything about "creative spark" or "imagination". They merely require that member states recognize and protect compilations as "intellectual creations". To me, the use of the phrase "intellectual creation" does not necessarily mandate a test of originality involving "creative spark" or "imagination". Article 2 of the *Berne Convention*, and the definition of "every literary ... work" in section 2 of the *Act*, both use the word "production", spurning the notion that any creative spark is required. In fact, even if "intellectual creation" did imply a requirement of "creative spark", Parliament chose not to include those words in the definition of a "compilation" set out in section 2, or in any other section of the *Act*. Had Parliament intended to affect any change to the standard for copyright protection, it could have done so.

44 Importantly, in *Tele-Direct* the classic Anglo-Canadian test of originality was described (at para. 28, emphasis added) as follows:

> [F]or a compilation of data to be original, it must be a work that was <u>independently created</u> by the author and which displays at least a <u>minimal degree of skill, judgment and labour in its overall selection or arrangement</u>.

In my view, this is an admirable summary and an accurate representation of the Canadian standard, which did, in fact, resolve the matter. The Court merely affirmed (at para. 7) the factual finding of McGillis J. (the trial judge in that case) that Tele-Direct "exercised only a minimal degree of skill, judgement or labour in its overall arrangement which is insufficient to support a claim of originality in the compilation so as to warrant copyright protection."

45 This Court in *Tele-Direct* also suggested that the phrase "skill, judgment or labour" was intended to be used in the conjunctive, rather than disjunctive sense. The Court observed (at para. 29) that "[i]t is doubtful that considerable labour combined with a negligible degree of skill and judgment will be sufficient in most situations to make a compilation of data original." Notably, this observation resembles Lord Oliver's sentiments in *Interlego, supra*, where he concluded that labour merely in the process of copying is insufficient to establish originality. I also do not think that labour alone will usually suffice to demonstrate originality, since an investment of labour alone is often indicative of slavish copying. If one employs labour alone without any degree of skill or judgment the result will typically be, in essence, a mere copy and will be unoriginal for that reason.

. . .

47 After *Tele-Direct*, this Court also decided the case of *Édutile Inc. v. Automobile Protection Assn. (APA)* (2000), 6 C.P.R. (4th) 211 (Fed. C.A.), rev'g (1997), 81 C.P.R. (3d) 338 (Fed. T.D.), leave to appeal to S.C.C. refused [2000] C.S.C.R. No. 302 (S.C.C.) (*"Édutile"*). The reasons quoted the passages from *Tele-Direct* regarding the impact of NAFTA on compilations of data. However, the issue was resolved (at para. 14) using the traditional test of originality, as articulated and relied on in *Tele-Direct* to the effect that "[s]uch a work was independently created by the author and displayed at least a minimal degree of skill, judgment and labour in its overall selection or arrangement." The fact that *Édutile* was ultimately decided on the basis of the classic Anglo-Canadian interpretation of originality further demonstrates that *Tele-Direct* did not introduce an additional precondition to copyright protection under Canadian law.

48 On the other hand, the American threshold for copyright protection, which the Trial Judge mistakenly adopted, does contain requirements of both originality and creativity. According to the United States Supreme Court in *Harper & Row Publishers Inc. v. Nation Enterprises*, 471 U.S. 539 (U.S. N.Y., 1985), at 547-9, a work "must be original to the author". The United States Supreme Court has also interpreted Article I, § 8, cl. 8 of the U.S. Constitution as requiring "independent creation plus a modicum of creativity" (see *Feist Publications Inc. v. Rural Telephone Service Co.*, 499 U.S. 340 (U.S. Kan., 1991) (*"Feist"*), citing *Trade-Mark Cases, Re*, 100 U.S. 82 (U.S. S.C., 1879); *Burrow-Giles Lithographic Co. v. Sarony*, 111 U.S. 53 (U.S. Sup. Ct., 1884)). In *Feist* the U.S. Supreme Court stated (at 345) that "original, as the term is used in copyright means only that the work was independently created by the author (as opposed to copied from other works), and that it possesses at least some minimal degree of creativity."

49 *Matthew Bender v. West Publishing Co., supra*, expanded on the American standard in the context of legal publications. The following passages were among those cited by the Trial Judge:

> The creative spark is missing where:
>
> > (i) industry conventions or other external factors so dictate selection that any person composing a compilation of the type at issue would necessarily select the same categories of information, ... or

> (ii) the author made obvious, garden-variety, or routine selections, ...
>
> ...West's editorial work entails considerable scholarly labor and care, and is of distinct usefulness to legal practitioners. Unfortunately for West, however, creativity in the task of creating a useful case report can only proceed in a narrow groove. Doubtless, that is because for West or any other editor of judicial opinions for legal research, faithfulness to the public-domain original is the dominant editorial value, so that the creative is the enemy of the true.

50 The dramatic statement that concludes this passage is somewhat facile. It ignores the possibility that truth can always be expressed in a creative, and certainly in an original way. Often, creativity and truth are allies in the task of expressing facts, history, news and the even the law. The creative may illuminate the true, it may explain the true and it may certainly adorn the true, all of which situations may give rise to copyright in original expression.

51 Interestingly, there is substantial controversy over whether or not the U.S. Supreme Court in *Feist* correctly affirmed the American requirement of creativity, as it merely accepted the American common-law standard without exploring the consequences of the codification of the originality requirement (see R. VerSteeg, "Sparks in the Tinderbox: *Fiest*, "Creativity," and the Legislative History of the 1976 Copyright Act" (1995) 56 U. Pitt. L.R. 549). Commentators have alerted us to the potential implications of the U.S. Supreme Court's decision in *Feist* (see for example J.R. Boyarski, "The Heist of Feist: Protections for Collections of Information and the Possible Federalization of 'Hot News'" (1999), 21 Cardozo Law Review 871; J.C. Ginsburg, "No 'Sweat'? Copyright and Other Protection of Works of Information After *Feist v. Rural Telephone*" (1992), 92 Colum. L. Rev. 338; R.A. Gorman, "the *Feist* case: Reflections on a Pathbreaking Copyright Decision" (1992), 18 Rutgers Computer & Tech. L.J. 731; J. Litman, "After *Feist*" (1992) 17 U. Dayton L. Rev. 607; J.P. McDonald, "The Search for Certainty" (1992) 17 U. Dayton L. Rev. 331; N. Siebrasse, "Copyright in Facts and Information: Feist Publications is Not, and Should Not Be, the Law in Canada", (1994) 11 C.I.P.R. 191; and A.C. Yen, "The Legacy of *Feist*: Consequences of the Weak Connection Between Copyright and the Economics of Public Goods" (1991), 52 Ohio St. L.J. 1343). In addition, I note that there have been efforts in the United States to repeal the effect of the U.S. Supreme Court's decision (see the *Collections of Information Antipiracy Act*, 106 H.R. 354).

52 As noted above, the Supreme Court of Canada has warned that "United States Court decisions ... must be scrutinized very carefully because of some fundamental differences in copyright concepts ..." (*Compo, supra* at 367). The wisdom in that advice is well demonstrated in this case, where the American principle sought to be imported is based upon an unstable foundation that has not yet been tested thoroughly. Although the Trial Judge prefaced his remarks with a disclaimer that he proceeded with some trepidation, he failed to conduct any substantive analysis of the American standard of originality. Therefore, he inadvertently entangled the standard set out in *Feist* and applied in *Bender v. West* with the Canadian touchstone of originality. As discussed above, there is

no universal requirement of "creative spark" or "imagination" in Anglo-Canadian copyright law.

Summary of the Meaning of "Original"

53 It is widely accepted that an "original" work must be independently produced and not copied. In attempts to further explain this cornerstone of copyright law, different judges and commentators have described the word "original" with a host of words and phrases mentioned above, including various combinations of the terms "labour", "judgment", "skill", "work", "industry", "effort", "taste" or "discretion" (see for example *Ladbroke Football, supra* and *Slumber-Magic, supra*). To me, these are all possible ingredients in the recipe for originality, which may be altered to suit the flavour of the work at issue. Each term may help to determine whether a work is, in fact, original, but it is mistake to treat any of these words as if they were statutory requirements. These are not, in themselves, prerequisites to copyright protection, but rather evidence of the sole prerequisite, originality. To determine whether or not the materials in issue are "original" works, a principled and reasoned approach based upon evidence is required, not reliance on a particular word or phrase that merely seeks to explain the concept of originality.

54 Moreover, I am not convinced that a substantial difference exists between an interpretation of originality that requires intellectual effort, whether described as skill, judgment and/or labour or creativity, and an interpretation that merely requires independent production. As discussed above, any skill, judgment and/or labour must be directed at an exercise other than mere copying for the result to be an original work (see *Interlego, supra* at 262-3; *Tele-Direct, supra* at para. 29). Clearly, therefore, the crucial requirement for a finding of originality is that the work be more than a mere copy. The vast majority of works that are not mere copies will normally require the investment of some intellectual effort, whatever that may be labelled. Works that are entirely devoid of such effort are, almost inevitably, simply copies of existing material.

. . .

56 Even where "creativity" has been employed as a label for the intangible effort required to distinguish an original work from a mere copy, courts have emphasized that the standard is extremely low. British, Canadian and American jurisprudence has firmly established that copyright law is unlike patent law in that novelty or non-obviousness are not required, and that courts must not subjectively judge the quality or merit of an author's work (see *Fox, supra* at 112-14). In *Apple Computer, supra* (F.C.A.), Hugessen J.A. stated that the sole distinguishing characteristic of literary work is that it be print or writing. In *Ladbroke, supra*, the court noted that aesthetic quality or virtue is not required for copyright protection. In *University of London Press , supra*, it was said that copyright could subsist "... irrespective of the question whether the quality or style is high"(*supra*, at 608). The House of Lords held in *Walter v. Lane*, [1900] A.C. 539 (U.K. H.L.), at 549 that copyright could subsist in a book whether it was "wise or foolish, accurate or inaccurate, of literary merit or of no merit

whatever", and (at 558) that a work "devoid of the faintest spark of literary or other merit" may have a copyright, "worthless and insignificant as it would be". American law also warns against judges constituting themselves judges of worth (see U.S. House Report No. 1476 (1976), 94th Cong., 2d Sess. 51; and *Bleistein v. Donaldson Lithographing Co.*, 188 U.S. 239 (U.S. S.C., 1903) (per Justice Holmes at 251)).

57 To ignore this basic axiom is to intrude on the domain of critics and become appraisers of merit instead of arbiters of originality. It is not necessary for a copyright work to evince qualities of novelty, ingenuity, innovation, genius, merit, virtue, beauty, brilliance, imagination, creative spark and other such attributes, for copyright law is not necessarily concerned with them. Of course, most, if not all "creative" and "imaginative" works would be original, but not all original works must be "creative" or "imaginative"; those attributes, though praiseworthy, are not mandatory characteristics of every original work.

58 Moreover, the lack of objectivity implicit in a requirement of "creativity" makes a coherent application of such a standard impossible (see D. Vaver, *Copyright Law*, (Toronto: Irwin Law, 2000) at 61-3, VerSteeg, *supra* at 562-565; Yen, *supra* at 1345-1346; and E.R. York, *"Warren Publishing Inc. v. Microdos Data Corp: Continuing the Stable Uncertainty in Factual Compilations"* (1999) 74 *Notre Dame Law Review* 565). Inevitably, judges will be forced to create their own definitions of creativity, resulting in substantial uncertainty and further jeopardizing the public benefit that accrues from the production of new and original works. The fact that an objective and coherent definition of "creative" is elusive at best and that "creativity" can sometimes connote qualities that are not required of an "original" work makes it preferable to avoid such unpredictable labels when assessing originality.

59 Admittedly, the public interest in the dissemination of works may be a policy reason to impose a high standard of "creativity" as a prerequisite to copyright protection. There is also the concern that overprotection of certain works will thwart social and scientific progress by precluding persons from building upon earlier works. However, I would suggest that copyright monopolies are better controlled through the avenues that Parliament has established than through the imposition of an arbitrary and subjective standard of "creative spark" or "imagination". As will be discussed below, a fair interpretation of user rights can counteract the apparent imbalance potentially generated by a low threshold (see Vaver, *Copyright Law*, *supra* at 169-70). For example, the fair dealing provisions of the *Act* provide a mechanisms whereby user rights are better considered.

2. The Publisher's Works

60 Having dismissed the notion that imagination or creative spark is essential to a finding of originality, I must now determine whether the Publishers' materials are, in fact, original works.

. . .

a.   The Reported Judicial Decisions

. . .

70 The Trial Judge found (at para. 139) "beyond a doubt, that the preparation of these reported judicial decisions ... involved extensive labour, skill and judgment". In my opinion, the skill, judgment and labour invested in these reported judicial decisions demonstrates that they are far more than mere copies and they are, therefore, original works in which copyright subsists.

71 Originality stems, in part, from the Publishers' selection of the elements of each reported judicial decision. The Publishers might have chosen to include any of a variety of different categories of data regarding a particular set of reasons. Although some of the Publishers' selections may also be made by other publishers, the selections are not all dictated by necessity, and there is no evidence to indicate that these particular selections have merely been copied from other sources. Furthermore, each Publisher might arrange the elements in any number of ways, depending upon their unique goals, style or preference. These reported judicial decisions are original notwithstanding that the respective Publishers may have selected the same types of elements for other reported judicial decisions and each Publisher arranges the elements of their compilations consistently. The *Act* does not require that a work be in a novel form.

72 Most importantly each Publisher has incorporated independently composed features, such as the summary of the facts, reasons and conclusions and the catchlines. To me, these elements put the matter beyond doubt, and by adding independently composed features to the compilation, each Publisher has significantly strengthened its claim of originality in the overall work. Although copyright may subsist in an original compilation of unoriginal material, it is generally far easier to demonstrate originality in a compilation that includes substantial independently composed features. That is, unlike routine compilations of data, these reported judicial decisions do display some indicia of their authors' style or manner of expression.

73 In particular, the summaries of the facts, reasons and conclusions could have been long or short, technical or simple, dull or dramatic, well-written or confusing; the organization and presentation might have varied greatly. I take judicial notice of the fact that in the past Canadian headnotes have been authored by some of the greatest legal minds in our country such as the late Chief Justice Bora Laskin, Dean Cecil A. Wright and other well-respected academics and practitioners including the witnesses professors Dunlop and Feldthusen. It is doubtful that such distinguished scholars would have devoted their time and effort to mundane copying. The independently composed features are obviously more than simply abridged copies of the reasons for judgment.

74 The Trial Judge correctly noted that the value of these features resides in their faithfulness to the reasons for judgment. However, it is not relevant that the ideas expressed in these elements of the reported judicial decisions may not be original, as copyright law is only concerned only with the originality of an expression, not ideas. In *University of London Press*, Mr. Justice Peterson wrote:

The word "original" does not in this connection mean that work must be the expression of original or inventive thought. Copyright Acts are not concerned with the originality of ideas, but with the expression of thought in print or writing. The originality which is required relates to the expression of the thought.

75 Naturally, if a Publisher has chosen to include, for example, a list of cases cited in the reasons, then all cases cited will inevitably be listed. Therefore, two independently produced compilations that may appear similar in some ways are both entitled to copyright protection. In this respect, the U.S. 2nd Circuit Court of Appeals' apprehension that to grant copyright protection to common selections would enable a copyright holder to monopolize widely-used expression was misguided (see *Bender v. West, supra*). The Publishers do not monopolize information in the sense that they can preclude others from independently producing similar materials; they merely acquire the right to preclude others from copying their works.

76 In sum, I am satisfied that copyright subsists in each of these reported judicial decisions.

b.   The Headnotes

. . .

78 For the reasons discussed above, I have no doubt that these headnotes are original and qualify for independent copyright protection under the *Act*. Indeed, I would repeat that, in my mind, the headnotes are essential to establishing originality in the reported judicial decision as a whole. Although the question does not arise in this particular case, there is some doubt whether, without the headnote, a Publisher could support a claim for copyright protection in judicial reasons alone, which seem to be merely copied and edited.

c.   The Case Summary

. . .

80 Although the information contained within this summary is necessarily derived from the case that it summarizes, that information could have been expressed in any number of ways, much like the independently composed features of the reported judicial decisions. This condensation of judicial reasons required significant skill and judgment in its composition and discretion in its presentation. Its concise style does not affect its originality. This is clearly more than simply an abridged copy of the reasons for judgment upon which it is based. In my view, this particular work is, therefore, sufficiently original to be protected under section 5 of the *Act*.

d.   The Topical Index

. . .

82 I have also concluded that the topical index is original. Its authors exhibited skill and judgment in selecting and arranging its elements. They selected cases that they judged to be binding or persuasive authority concerning the GST. Although the topical index is arranged alphabetically, there are significant cross-references to other headings within the index, and important decisions were required as to where certain information ought to appear. Moreover, the authors have added considerable independently composed material to this compilation by incorporating their own summaries relevant cases. That these summaries are extremely brief, usually only a few words, does not diminish the claim of originality, but rather enhances it. It is no easy task to summarize an entire decision into a single phrase, which might have be done in an infinite number of ways. By selecting which cases to include, independently composing extremely brief summaries of the decisions, and arranging and cross-referencing the topics, the Publishers have demonstrated that the topical index is an original work.

K. Sharlow J.A.: I agree.

Rothstein J.A. (Concurring):

Introduction

180 I have had the opportunity of reading the reasons of my colleague Linden J.A. I am in agreement with his conclusions. However, my analytical approach to the issues of originality and infringement differ from my colleague's. Consequently, I have prepared these concurring reasons.

. . .

209 I am of the opinion that Gibson J. was correct in holding that the Annotated Statute, the Textbook and Monograph were original. The Law Society does not dispute these findings and I need not dwell on them further. However, in my respectful view, Gibson J. erred in finding that the Headnotes, the Case Summary and the Reported Judicial Decisions were not original.

210 I commence my analysis of originality by reference to the fundamental principles of originality.

211 First, copyright law protects expressions of ideas, but not ideas themselves. In *University of London Press v. University Tutorial Press Ltd.* , [1916] 2 Ch. 601 (Eng. Ch. Div.), at 608, Mr. Justice Peterson wrote:

> The word "original" does not in this connection mean that work must be the expression of original or inventive thought. Copyright Acts are not concerned with the originality of ideas, but with the expression of thought in print or writing. The originality which is required relates to the expression of the thought.

(See also *Canadian Admiral Corp. v. Rediffusion Inc.* (1954), 20 C.P.R. 75 (Ex. Ct.); and *Prism Hospital Software Inc. v. Hospital Medical Records Institute* (1994), 57 C.P.R. (3d) 129 (B.C. S.C.)). When considering whether the legal materials in question are original, therefore, the focus is on originality of the expression of thought and not on originality of the thought itself.

212 Second, there can be no copyright in facts. This point is well-settled and was set out by Lord Erskine in *Matthewson v. Stockdale* (1806), 12 Ves. Jun. 270 (Eng. Ch.), at 273:

> All human events are equally open to all, who wish to add or improve the materials, already collected by others; making an original work. No man can monopolize such a subject [...].

See also *Deeks v. Wells* (1930), [1931] O.R. 818 (Ont. H.C.), affirmed at 831 (Ont. C.A.) and [1931] 4 D.L.R. 533 (Ont C.A.), affirmed (1932), [1933] 1 D.L.R. 353 (Ontario P.C.); and *Zamacoïs v. Douville* (1943), 3 Fox Pat. C. 44 (Exch. Ct.) at 66.

213 Third, the work in question must originate from its author and not be copied. *University of London Press, supra,* established (at 608-9) that:

> [T]he Act does not require that the expression must be in an original or novel form, but that the work must not be copied from another work — that it should originate from the author.

214 Fourth, something in addition to not being copied is required. What this additional requirement is has been the subject of some disagreement in the jurisprudence. One school of thought is that the monopoly which flows from a finding of copyright will only be justified if some intellectual effort is expended by the author. This line of authority uses terminology such as skill, judgment and/or labour. See for example *Ladbroke (Football) Ltd. v. William Hill (Football) Ltd.,* [1964] 1 All E.R. 465 (U.K. H.L.); *G.A. Cramp & Sons Ltd. v. Frank Smythson Ltd.,* [1944] 2 All E.R. 92 (U.K. H.L.) and *Slumber-Magic Adjustable Bed Co. v. Sleep-King Adjustable Bed Co.* (1984), 3 C.P.R. (3d) 81 (B.C. S.C.).

215 The other school of thought is that, at least in respect of compilations, only time and/or expense is necessary. See for example the early white pages business directory cases of *Kelly v. Morris* (1866), L.R. 1 Eq. 697; *Morris v. Ashbee* (1868), L.R. 7 Eq. 34 (Eng. Ch. Div.); and *Morris v. Wright* (1870), 5 Ch. App. 279 (Eng. C.A.). This jurisprudence is the basis of the "sweat of the brow" or "industrious collection" approach as discussed by Finkelstein J. at paragraph 50 *et seq.* of his detailed analysis of the two approaches in *Telstra Corporation Ltd. v. Desktop Marketing Systems Pty Ltd.* (2001), 51 I.P.R. 257 (Australia Fed. Ct.). Industrious collection has also found favour in Canada, see for example *U & R Tax Services Ltd. v. H & R Block Canada Inc.* (1995), 97 F.T.R. 259 (Fed. T.D.).

216 From my review of the jurisprudence, it appears that the intellectual effort standard has been applied to all types of literary works, while the industrious collection standard has generally been applied only to compilations of facts, such as white page directories, or other public domain material.

217 In the 1997 decision of this Court in *Tele-Direct (Publications) Inc. v. American Business Information Inc.* (1997), [1998] 2 F.C. 22 (Fed. C.A.), Décary J.A. rejected the industrious collection school of thought for compilations of data. He reached this conclusion based on Article 1705 of the NAFTA and consequential changes to the Canadian *Copyright Act,* including the introduction of

the current "compilation" definition (pursuant to an *Act to Implement the North American Free Trade Agreement*, S.C. 1993, c. 44). As a result of these changes, and having regard to United States jurisprudence (see *Feist Publications Inc. v. Rural Telephone Service Co.*, 111 S. Ct. 1282 (U.S. Kan., 1991)), Décary J.A. concluded that compilations of data required at least a minimal level of creativity to be original.

218   Gibson J. appears to have read *Tele-Direct*, *supra*, as creating some new and higher standard of originality than the intellectual effort represented by terminology such as skill judgment and labour. This higher standard appears to be represented in Gibson J.'s reasons by such terminology as "imagination", "creative spark" and "intellect and creativity". However, I read *Tele-Direct*, *supra*, as merely re-iterating the requirement that some intellectual effort will be necessary in order for a work to qualify as original. Indeed, a key passage of Décary J.A.'s reasons, at paragraph 28, confirms that skill, judgment and labour are the proper factors to consider:

> For a compilation of data to be original, it must be a work that was independently created by the author and which displays at least a minimal degree of skill, judgment and labour in its overall selection and arrangement. The threshold is low, but it does exist. [Emphasis added]

Therefore, I do not think that *Tele-Direct*, *supra*, created a new or different standard of originality. The analysis still involves whether sufficient intellectual effort has been expended by the author.

219   I recognize that *Tele-Direct*, *supra*, may be read to eliminate the industrious collection approach to originality that has sometimes been used for compilations. I also recognize that debate continues over whether industrious collection or creativity is the better approach for determining the originality of compilations (see the discussion of the competing views in *Telstra*, *supra*, at paragraph 43 *et seq.*). However, I am mindful of the words of Estey J. in *Compo Co. Ltd.*, *supra*, at page 372, not to decide copyright cases on broader grounds than necessary:

> Courts in this technical field of copyright have found it prudent to make their judicial answers congruent with the legal issues raised in the proceeding at hand leaving, so far as possible, analogies, examples and hypothetical questions to another day.

Therefore, given that I am not here concerned with compilations, it is not necessary to enter the debate involving compilations. I am satisfied that originality outside of compilations has always required evidence of some level of intellectual effort and that, in that context, *Tele-Direct*, *supra*, is consistent with this position.

220   How much intellectual effort is required will vary upon the circumstances of each case. In *Telstra*, *supra*, Finkelstein J. noted at paragraph 64:

> The cases have not defined with any precision what amount of intellectual effort, labour etcetera is required to justify copyright. "In every case it must depend largely on the special facts of that case, and must in each case be very much a question of degree"; *Macmillan and Co. Ltd. v. Cooper* (1923), 40 T.L.R. 186, at

190. What is not clear is whether the intellectual effort, labour, etc., must be more than negligible or whether it must be substantial; see *Kalamazoo (Aust) Pty. Ltd. v. Compact Business Systems Pty. Ltd.* (1985), 84 F.L.R. 101, at 120-1; 5 R.P.R 213, at 233-4 where the cases expressing the competing views are collected.

221 In sum, for purposes of this case, in the context of the legal material at issue here, I think that whether a work is original will be guided by the following principles:

1. The focus is on expression and not ideas or facts.
2. The work must originate from the author and not be copied.
3. Some intellectual effort is required. The necessary degree of intellectual effort will vary with the circumstances.

. . .

Conclusion

298

1. The Reported Judicial Decisions, the Headnotes, the Case Summary, the Annotated Statute, the Textbook and the Monograph constitute works for the purposes of copyright.
2. These legal materials are original within the meaning of the *Copyright Act* and copyright subsists in them.
3. The 1997 G.S.T.C. topical index is a substantial part of the 1997 G.S.T.C. Book. The Book is original and copyright subsists in it.

CCH Canadian Ltd. v. Law Society of Upper Canada

[2004] 1 S.C.R. 339 (S.C.C.)
Supreme Court of Canada

Arbour J., Bastarache J., Binnie J., Deschamps J., Iacobucci J., LeBel J., Major J., McLachlin C.J.C.

Heard: November 10, 2003

Judgment: March 4, 2004

The Chief Justice:

I.   Introduction — The Issues To Be Determined

. . .

4 The key question that must be answered in this appeal is whether the Law Society has breached copyright by either (1) providing the custom photocopy service in which single copies of the publishers' works are reproduced and sent to patrons upon their request or by (2) maintaining self-service photocopiers and

copies of the publishers' works in the Great Library for use by its patrons. To answer this question, the Court must address the following sub- issues:

> (1) Are the publishers' materials "original works" protected by copyright?

. . .

II.   Analysis on Appeal

. . .

9 In Canada, copyright is a creature of statute and the rights and remedies provided by the *Copyright Act* are exhaustive: see *Galerie d'art du Petit Champlain inc. c. Théberge*, [2002] 2 S.C.R. 336, 2002 SCC 34 (S.C.C.), at para. 5; *Bishop v. Stevens*, [1990] 2 S.C.R. 467 (S.C.C.), at p. 477; *Compo Co. v. Blue Crest Music Inc.* (1979), [1980] 1 S.C.R. 357 (S.C.C.), at p. 373. In interpreting the scope of the *Copyright Act*'s rights and remedies, courts should apply the modern approach to statutory interpretation whereby "the words of an Act are to be read in their entire context and in their grammatical and ordinary sense harmoniously with the scheme of the Act, the object of the Act, and the intention of Parliament": *Bell ExpressVu Ltd. Partnership v. Rex*, [2002] 2 S.C.R. 559, 2002 SCC 42 (S.C.C.), at para. 26, citing E.A. Driedger, *Construction of Statutes* (2nd ed. 1983), at p. 87.

10 Binnie J. recently explained in *Théberge , supra*, at paras. 30-31, that the *Copyright Act* has dual objectives:

> The *Copyright Act* is usually presented as a balance between promoting the public interest in the encouragement and dissemination of works of the arts and intellect and obtaining a just reward for the creator... The proper balance among these and other public policy objectives lies not only in recognizing the creator's rights but in giving due weight to their limited nature. In interpreting the *Copyright Act*, courts should strive to maintain an appropriate balance between these two goals. ... ...

(1)   Are the Publishers' Materials "Original Works" Covered by Copyright?

(a)   The Law

14 Section 5 of the *Copyright Act* states that, in Canada, copyright shall subsist "in every *original* literary, dramatic, musical and artistic work" (emphasis added). Although originality sets the boundaries of copyright law, it is not defined in the *Copyright Act*. Section 2 of the *Copyright Act* defines "every original literary ... work" as including "every original production in the literary ... domain, whatever may be the mode or form of its expression". Since copyright protects only the expression or form of ideas, "the originality requirement must apply to the expressive element of the work and not the idea": S. Handa, *Copyright Law in Canada* (2002), at p. 209.

15 There are competing views on the meaning of "original" in copyright law. Some courts have found that a work that originates from an author and is more

than a mere copy of a work is sufficient to ground copyright. See, for example, *University of London Press v. University Tutorial Press Ltd.*, [1916] 2 Ch. 601 (Eng. Ch. Div.); *U & R Tax Services Ltd. v. H & R Block Canada Inc.* (1995), 62 C.P.R. (3d) 257 (Fed. T.D.). This approach is consistent with the "sweat of the brow" or "industriousness" standard of originality, which is premised on a natural rights or Lockean theory of "just desserts", namely that an author deserves to have his or her efforts in producing a work rewarded. Other courts have required that a work must be creative to be "original" and thus protected by copyright. See, for example, *Feist Publications Inc. v. Rural Telephone Service Co.* (1991), 499 U.S. 340 (U.S. Kan.) ; *Tele-Direct (Publications) Inc. v. American Business Information Inc.* (1997), [1998] 2 F.C. 22 (Fed. C.A.). This approach is also consistent with a natural rights theory of property law; however it is less absolute in that only those works that are the product of creativity will be rewarded with copyright protection. It has been suggested that the "creativity" approach to originality helps ensure that copyright protection only extends to the expression of ideas as opposed to the underlying ideas or facts. See *Feist Publications Inc., supra*, at p. 353.

16 I conclude that the correct position falls between these extremes. For a work to be "original" within the meaning of the *Copyright Act*, it must be more than a mere copy of another work. At the same time, it need not be creative, in the sense of being novel or unique. What is required to attract copyright protection in the expression of an idea is an exercise of skill and judgment. By skill, I mean the use of one's knowledge, developed aptitude or practised ability in producing the work. By judgment, I mean the use of one's capacity for discernment or ability to form an opinion or evaluation by comparing different possible options in producing the work. This exercise of skill and judgment will necessarily involve intellectual effort. The exercise of skill and judgment required to produce the work must not be so trivial that it could be characterized as a purely mechanical exercise. For example, any skill and judgment that might be involved in simply changing the font of a work to produce "another" work would be too trivial to merit copyright protection as an "original" work.

17 In reaching this conclusion, I have had regard to: (1) the plain meaning of "original"; (2) the history of copyright law; (3) recent jurisprudence; (4) the purpose of the *Copyright Act*; and (5) that this constitutes a workable yet fair standard.

(i)   The Plain Meaning of "Original"

18 The plain meaning of the word "original" suggests at least some intellectual effort, as is necessarily involved in the exercise of skill and judgment. The *Concise Oxford Dictionary* (7th ed. 1982), at p. 720, defines "original" as follows:

> 1. *a* .... existing from the first, primitive, innate, initial, earliest; ... **2.** that has served as pattern, of which copy or translation has been made, not derivative or dependant, first-hand, not imitative, novel in character or style, inventive, creative, thinking or acting for oneself.

"Original's" plain meaning implies not just that something is not a copy. It includes, if not creativity *per se*, at least some sort of intellectual effort. As Professor Gervais has noted, "[w]hen used to mean simply that the work must originate from the author, originality is eviscerated of its core meaning. It becomes a synonym of 'originated,' and fails to reflect the ordinary sense of the word": D.J. Gervais, "*Feist* Goes Global: A Comparative Analysis of the Notion of Originality in Copyright Law" (2002), *49 J. Copyright Soc'y U.S.A.* 949, at p. 961.

(ii) History of Copyright

19 The idea of "intellectual creation" was implicit in the notion of literary or artistic work under the *Berne Convention for the Protection of Literary and Artistic Works* (1886), to which Canada adhered in 1923, and which served as the precursor to Canada's first *Copyright Act*, adopted in 1924. See S. Ricketson, *The Berne Convention for the Protection of Literary and Artistic Works: 1886-1986* (1987), at p. 900. Professor Ricketson has indicated that in adopting a sweat of the brow or industriousness approach to deciding what is original, common law countries such as England have "depart[ed] from the spirit, if not the letter, of the [Berne] Convention" since works that have taken time, labour or money to produce but are not truly artistic or literary intellectual creations are accorded copyright protection: Ricketson, *supra*, at p. 901.

20 In the international context, France and other continental civilian jurisdictions require more than mere industriousness to find that a work is original. "Under the French law, originality means both the intellectual contribution of the author and the novel nature of the work as compared with existing works": Handa, *supra*, at p. 211. This understanding of originality is reinforced by the expression "*le droit d'auteur*"–literally the "*author's* right" — the term used in the French title of the *Copyright Act*. The author must contribute something intellectual to the work, namely skill and judgment, if it is to be considered original.

(iii) Recent Jurisprudence

21 Although many Canadian courts have adopted a rather low standard of originality, i.e., that of industriousness, more recently, some courts have begun to question whether this standard is appropriate. For example, the Federal Court of Appeal in *Tele-Direct (Publications) Inc. , supra*, held, at para. 29, that those cases which had adopted the sweat of the brow approach to originality should not be interpreted as concluding that labour, in and of itself, could ground a finding of originality. As Décary J.A. explained: "If they did, I suggest that their approach was wrong and is irreconcilable with the standards of intellect and creativity that were expressly set out in NAFTA and endorsed in the 1993 amendments to the *Copyright Act* and that were already recognized in Anglo-Canadian law." See also *Édutile Inc. v. Automobile Protection Assn. (APA)*, [2000] 4 F.C. 195 (Fed. C.A.), at para. 8, adopting this passage.

22 The United States Supreme Court explicitly rejected the "sweat of the brow" approach to originality in *Feist Publications Inc. , supra*. In so doing, O'Connor

J. explained at p. 353 that, in her view, the "sweat of the brow" approach was not consistent with the underlying tenets of copyright law:

> The "sweat of the brow" doctrine had numerous flaws, the most glaring being that it extended copyright protection in a compilation beyond selection and arrangement — the compiler's original contributions — to the facts themselves. Under the doctrine, the only defense to infringement was independent creation. A subsequent compiler was "not entitled to take one word of information previously published," but rather had to "independently wor[k] out the matter for himself, so as to arrive at the same result from the same common sources of information."... "Sweat of the brow" courts thereby eschewed the most fundamental axiom of copyright law–that no one may copyright facts or ideas.

As this Court recognized in *Compo Co., supra*, at p. 367, U.S. copyright cases may not be easily transferable to Canada given the key differences in the copyright concepts in Canadian and American copyright legislation. This said, in Canada, as in the United States, copyright protection does not extend to facts or ideas but is limited to the expression of ideas. As such, O'Connor's J. concerns about the "sweat of the brow" doctrine's improper extension of copyright over facts also resonate in Canada. I would not, however, go as far as O'Connor J. in requiring that a work possess a minimal degree of creativity to be considered original. See *Feist, supra*, at pp. 345 and 358.

(iv) Purpose of the Copyright Act

23 As mentioned, in *Galerie d'art du Petit Champlain inc. c. Théberge, supra*, this Court stated that the purpose of copyright law was to balance the public interest in promoting the encouragement and dissemination of works of the arts and intellect and obtaining a just reward for the creator. When courts adopt a standard of originality requiring only that something be more than a mere copy or that someone simply show industriousness to ground copyright in a work, they tip the scale in favour of the author's or creator's rights, at the loss of society's interest in maintaining a robust public domain that could help foster future creative innovation. See J. Litman, "The Public Domain" (1990), 39 *Emory L.J.* 965, at p. 969, and C.J. Craig, "Locke, Labour and Limiting the Author's Right: A Warning against a Lockean Approach to Copyright Law" (2002), 28 *Queen's L.J.* 1. By way of contrast, when an author must exercise skill and judgment to ground originality in a work, there is a safeguard against the author being overcompensated for his or her work. This helps ensure that there is room for the public domain to flourish as others are able to produce new works by building on the ideas and information contained in the works of others.

(v) Workable, Yet Fair Standard

24 Requiring that an original work be the product of an exercise of skill and judgment is a workable yet fair standard. The "sweat of the brow" approach to originality is too low a standard. It shifts the balance of copyright protection too far in favour of the owner's rights, and fails to allow copyright to protect the public's interest in maximizing the production and dissemination of intellectual

works. On the other hand, the creativity standard of originality is too high. A creativity standard implies that something must be novel or non-obvious–concepts more properly associated with patent law than copyright law. By way of contrast, a standard requiring the exercise of skill and judgment in the production of a work avoids these difficulties and provides a workable and appropriate standard for copyright protection that is consistent with the policy objectives of the *Copyright Act*.

(vi) Conclusion

25 For these reasons, I conclude that an "original" work under the *Copyright Act* is one that originates from an author and is not copied from another work. That alone, however, is not sufficient to find that something is original. In addition, an original work must be the product of an author's exercise of skill and judgment. The exercise of skill and judgment required to produce the work must not be so trivial that it could be characterized as a purely mechanical exercise. While creative works will by definition be "original" and covered by copyright, creativity is not required to make a work "original".

(b) Application of the Law to these Facts

26 At trial, the respondent publishers claimed copyright in eleven works: three reported judicial decisions; the three headnotes preceding these decisions; the Annotated *Martin's Ontario Criminal Practice 1999*; a case summary; a topical index; the textbook *Economic Negligence* (1989); and the monograph "Dental Evidence", being chapter 13 in *Forensic Evidence in Canada* (1991). Gibson J. held that the publishers' works should be judged against a standard of intellect and creativity in order to determine if they were original. Based on this standard of originality, the trial judge found that the publishers only had copyright in the Annotated *Criminal Practice*, the textbook and the monograph. He concluded that the remaining eight works were not original and, therefore, were not covered by copyright ((1999), [2000] 2 F.C. 451 (Fed. T.D.)).

27 On appeal, the Law Society did not challenge the trial judge's findings with respect to the three works in which he found copyright did exist, with the exception of questioning whether the monograph constituted a "work" within the meaning of the *Copyright Act*. The Federal Court of Appeal adopted the "sweat of the brow" approach to originality and found that if a work was more than a mere copy, it would be original. On this basis, Linden J.A., writing for the majority, held that all of the remaining works were original and therefore covered by copyright ([2002] 4 F.C. 213 (Fed. C.A.)). The Law Society appeals, contending that the headnotes, case summary, topical index and reported judicial decisions are not "original" within the meaning of the *Copyright Act* and, therefore, are not covered by copyright.

28 As stated, in order to be original, a work must have originated from the author, not be copied, and must be the product of the exercise of skill and

judgment that is more than trivial. Applying this test, all of the works in question are original and therefore covered by copyright.

(i)   Headnotes

29 The Federal Court of Appeal held that "headnotes", defined as including the summary of the case, catchlines, statement of the case, case title and case information, are more than mere copies and hence "original" works in which copyright subsists. It found that the headnotes are more than simply an abridged version of the reasons; they consist of independently composed features. As Linden J.A. explained, at para. 73, the authors of the headnotes could have chosen to make the summaries "long or short, technical or simple, dull or dramatic, well written or confusing; the organization and presentation might have varied greatly".

30 Although headnotes are inspired in large part by the judgment which they summarize and refer to, they are clearly not an identical copy of the reasons. The authors must select specific elements of the decision and can arrange them in numerous different ways. Making these decisions requires the exercise of skill and judgment. The authors must use their knowledge about the law and developed ability to determine legal *ratios* to produce the headnotes. They must also use their capacity for discernment to decide which parts of the judgment warrant inclusion in the headnotes. This process is more than just a mechanical exercise. Thus the headnotes constitute "original" works in which copyright subsists.

(ii)   Case Summary

31 For substantially the same reasons as given for headnotes, the case summary is also covered by copyright. A summary of judicial reasons is not simply a copy of the original reasons. Even if the summary often contains the same language as the judicial reasons, the act of choosing which portions to extract and how to arrange them in the summary requires an exercise of skill and judgment.

(iii) Topical Index

32 The topical index is part of the book *Canada GST Cases*, (1997). It provides a listing of cases with short headings to indicate the main topics covered by the decision and very brief summaries of the decisions. The Federal Court of Appeal held that the index was original in that it required skill and effort to compile. I agree. The author of the index had to make an initial decision as to which cases were authorities on GST. This alone is a decision that would require the exercise of skill and judgment. The author also had to decide which headings to include and which cases should fall under which headings. He or she had to distill the essence of the decisions down to a succinct one-phrase summary. All of these tasks require skill and judgment that are sufficient to conclude that the topical index is an "original" work in which copyright subsists.

(iv) Reported Judicial Decisions

33 The reported judicial decisions, when properly understood as a *compilation* of the headnote and the accompanying edited judicial reasons, are "original" works covered by copyright. Copyright protects originality of *form* or expression. A compilation takes existing material and casts it in a different form. The arranger does not have copyright in the individual components. However, the arranger may have copyright in the form represented by the compilation. "It is not the several components that are the subject of copyright, but the over-all arrangement of them which the plaintiff through his industry has produced": *Slumber-Magic Adjustable Bed Co. v. Sleep-King Adjustable Bed Co.* (1984), 3 C.P.R. (3d) 81 (B.C. S.C.), at p. 84; see also *Ladbroke (Football) Ltd. v. William Hill (Football) Ltd.*, [1964] 1 All E.R. 465 (U.K. H.L.), at p. 469.

34 The reported judicial decisions here at issue meet the test for originality. The authors have arranged the case summary, catchlines, case title, case information (the headnotes) and the judicial reasons in a specific manner. The arrangement of these different components requires the exercise of skill and judgment. The compilation, viewed globally, attracts copyright protection.

35 This said, the judicial reasons in and of themselves, without the headnotes, are not original works in which the publishers could claim copyright. The changes made to judicial reasons are relatively trivial; the publishers add only basic factual information about the date of the judgment, the court and the panel hearing the case, counsel for each party, lists of cases, statutes and parallel citations. The publishers also correct minor grammatical errors and spelling mistakes. Any skill and judgment that might be involved in making these minor changes and additions to the judicial reasons are too trivial to warrant copyright protection. The changes and additions are more properly characterized as a mere mechanical exercise. As such, the reported reasons, when disentangled from the rest of the compilation–namely the headnote–are *not* covered by copyright. It would not be copyright infringement for someone to reproduce only the judicial reasons.

36 In summary, the headnotes, case summary, topical index and compilation of reported judicial decisions are all works that have originated from their authors and are not mere copies. They are the product of the exercise of skill and judgment that is not trivial. As such, they are all "original" works in which copyright subsists. The appeal of these findings should be dismissed....

IceTV Pty Limited v. Nine Network Australia Pty Limited, [2009] HCA 14 (H.C.A.)

French CJ, Crennan and Kiefel JJ.

per Gummow, Hayne and Heydon JJ.

...

45. Not every piece of printing or writing which conveys information will be subject to copyright. For a long time, and precisely because compilations often contain facts, it has been commonplace to enquire what skill and labour was required in the preparation of a compilation[60]. That question has arisen in the context of considering whether copyright subsists at all in a compilation as well as being relevant to a later inquiry as to the "quality" of any material taken from a copyrighted work.

46. In *Feist Publications Inc v Rural Telephone Service Co Inc* [61] the Supreme Court of the United States considered the compatibility of two propositions: first, that compilations of facts are generally copyrightable, and secondly, that facts were not copyrightable. This case involves the same tension between those two propositions. "Originality" was a constitutional requirement that was the source of Congress's power to "secur[e] for limited Times to Authors ... the exclusive Right to their respective Writings"[62]. It was recognised, however, that copyright in a factual compilation is necessarily "thin"[63] because the standard for originality should not be such that copyright owners have a monopoly on facts or information. Ultimately the decision turned in a significant degree on the view that "[t]he primary objective of copyright is not to reward the labor of authors, but '[t]o promote the Progress of Science and useful Arts.'"[64] The exclusion of ideas and information from copyright protection has been codified in the United States[65].

47. Much has been written about differing standards of originality in the context of the degree or kind of "skill and labour" said to be required before a work can be considered an "original" work in which copyright will subsist[66]. "Industrious collection" or "sweat of the brow", on the one hand, and "creativity", on the other, have been treated as antinomies in some sort of mutually exclusive relationship in the mental processes of an author or joint authors. They are, however, kindred aspects of a mental process which produces an object, a literary work, a particular form of expression which copyright protects. A complex compilation or a narrative history will almost certainly require considerable skill and labour, which involve both "industrious collection" and "creativity", in the sense of requiring original productive thought to produce the expression, including selection and arrangement, of the material[67].

48. It may be that too much has been made, in the context of subsistence, of the kind of skill and labour which must be expended by an author for a work to be an "original" work. The requirement of the Act is only that the work originates with an author or joint authors from some independent intellectual effort. Be that as it may, as noted previously, since the subsistence of copyright need not

be considered in this appeal, the relevance of skill and labour to that inquiry need not be considered further.

...

187. One final point should be made. This concerns the submission by the Digital Alliance that this Court consider the Full Court's decision in Desktop Marketing[196] and, to the contrary of Desktop Marketing, affirm that there must be some "creative spark"[197] or exercise of "skill and judgment"[198] before a work is sufficiently "original" for the subsistence of copyright.

188. It is by no means apparent that the law even before the 1911 Act was to any different effect to that for which the Digital Alliance contends. It may be that the reasoning in Desktop Marketing with respect to compilations is out of line with the understanding of copyright law over many years. These reasons explain the need to treat with some caution the emphasis in Desktop Marketing upon "labour and expense" per se and upon misappropriation. However, in the light of the admission of Ice that the Weekly Schedule was an original literary work, this is not an appropriate occasion to take any further the subject of originality in copyright works.

---

4. Fixation

A work, in order to be protected, must exist, at least for some period of time, in some concrete or non-evanescent form.[8] While the fixation doctrine does perform an evidentiary burden insofar as it enables the identification of the protected work, it is thus a substantive requirement that must be met in order for copyright to vest. The particular material form that a fixation takes is not significant, and in light of the desirability of media neutrality, it should include anything from print forms to audio-visual recordings and digital storage.

The Act does not contain an express requirement that works be fixed; it is a judge-made rule. The Act does, however, contain a few express acknowledgements of the concept in the definitions of "computer program," "dramatic work" (s. 2) and performers' performance (s. 15). The latter example constitutes the only exception to the rule; performers have a neighbouring "copyright" in an unfixed performance allowing them to control its public performance and fixation.

The fixation requirement was codified in the US Copyright Act, 17 U.S.C. §102(a), in the following, technology-neutral terms: "Copyright protection subsists... in original works of authorship fixed in any tangible medium of expression, now known or later developed, from which they can be perceived, reproduced, or otherwise communicated, either directly or with the aid of a machine or device." §101 explains that "a work is fixed in a tangible

---

8   *Canadian Admiral Corp. Ltd. v. Rediffusion Inc.*, [1954] Ex. C.R. 382 (Ex. Ct.); *Théberge v. Galerie d'Art du Petit Champlain inc.* (2002), 17 C.P.R. (4th) 161 (S.C.C.).

medium of expression when its embodiment in a copy or phonorecord, by or under the authority of the author, is sufficiently permanent or stable to permit it to be perceived, reproduced, or otherwise communicated for a period of more than transitory duration."

There remain some uncertainties around the application of the fixation doctrine. First, it is unclear, in Canada, who must fix the work and under what conditions in order to perfect the copyright. The US definition requires the fixer to be the author or someone acting on her authority, such that an unauthorized third party fixation will not suffice. It is also uncertain whether simultaneous fixation (e.g. fixing a work only as it is performed) is always sufficient protection against simultaneous unauthorized copying (see s. 3(1.1)). Finally, we might ask precisely what amounts to a sufficient permanence or materiality in the context of digital technologies and digital memory. Indeed, one would be forgiven for wondering whether this requirement is merely a remnant of a pre-digital era.

Canadian Admiral Corp. Ltd. v. Rediffusion Inc., [1954] Ex. C.R. 382 (Ex. Ct.)

Cameron J.

Judgment: May 21, 1954

. . .

3 The plaintiff is a company incorporated under the Dominion Companies Act, having its principal place of business at the Township of Toronto, in Ontario. It is engaged in the manufacture of television receiving sets, some of which are sold by dealers throughout the Province of Quebec. For the purpose of advertising its wares, the plaintiff decided to sponsor the telecast of the football games to be played in the Autumn of 1952 by the Montreal Football Club Inc., which operates a rugby football team called "The Alouettes" in the Inter-Provincial Football Union.

4 Accordingly, the plaintiff entered into an agreement with that football club (which I shall hereafter refer to as 'The Alouettes') on August 19, 1952, (ex. 1) and thereby, for the consideration mentioned, it was agreed that the plaintiff should have (a) the exclusive right to *live* telecasts of the six football games to be played by the Alouettes in Montreal; and (b) an option to purchase the exclusive right to televise films in Montreal of the six games to be played by the Alouettes away from Montreal.

5 By an agreement dated August 27, 1952, between the Canadian Broadcasting Corporation and the plaintiff, the former for the consideration specified (a), agreed to furnish the personnel and all the facilities and equipment necessary to produce and telecast from Delorimier Stadium, Montreal over its television station CBFT Montreal the football games to be played by the Alouettes in Montreal during the 1952 season; (b) assigned and transferred to the plaintiff

exclusively all of its right, title and interest in the copyright and any other property rights in the live telecast productions of the said games; and (c), agreed to supply the necessary facilities and the station time to telecast films provided by the plaintiff of the six games to be played by the Alouettes away from Montreal, such facilities to be available on the dates specified, namely, six days after the games were actually played. It was also agreed that the Broadcasting Corporation would not make available such telecast productions and film telecasts by direct wire to any other person, firm or corporation.

6 Dow Brewery Ltd. had acquired certain rights entitling it to make movie films of the league games to be played by the Alouettes away from Montreal in 1952. By an agreement dated September 11, 1952, (ex. 3) Dow transferred and assigned to the plaintiff exclusively, all its rights to televise over station CBFT or to distribute by wire service within the Province of Quebec, films or any part thereof of such games, such films, however, not to be televised by the plaintiff until the Friday following the dates when the games were played. The plaintiff was authorized to obtain from Dow's supplier one black-and-white copy of the film of each such game. By a supplementary agreement between the said parties dated October 17, 1952, (ex. 3) it was agreed that the rights granted to the plaintiff by the agreement of September 12 should include "the exclusive right to distribute and perform the television broadcasts of such films after receiving the same through the ether, by wire service or rediffusion."

7 The agreement between the plaintiff and the Broadcasting Corporation was duly carried out. The plaintiff sponsored the live telecast over station CBFT of the first four games played at Montreal. The plaintiff also obtained from Dow a cinematographic film of each of the first four games played by the Alouettes away from Montreal, furnished them to the Broadcasting Corporation, and telecasts thereof, without the assistance of a commentator, took place over station CBFT on the agreed dates. It is established that prior to the first of the four live telecasts and again prior to the first of the four film telecasts, the plaintiff, in writing, notified the defendant or its solicitors, of the rights which the plaintiff had acquired and forbade the defendant to rediffuse any of such telecasts. The defendant's solicitors, in each case, replied that their client could not agree that the relaying of the telecast programmes over their rediffusion circuits, in any way infringed the legal rights of the plaintiff.

8 By the agreement filed at the trial (ex. 5) it is admitted that the effect of the two agreements between the plaintiff and Dow Breweries was to vest in the plaintiff whatever copyright the latter had in the films of the games played by the Alouettes away from Montreal; that such cinematographic films were produced for valuable consideration by Briston Films Ltd. for Dow and were taken by employees of Briston Films Ltd.; and that the plaintiff by virtue of its agreement with Dow was entitled to and did obtain a black-and-white film of each of such games from Briston Films Ltd. to be used for telecast over station CBFT.

9 It is alleged that the defendant took each of the said telecasts off the ether and rediffused the same to its various subscribers and to its showroom and

sales office at 1650 Berri Street, Montreal, and that thereby the defendant has infringed the copyright of the plaintiff in both the live and film telecasts. ...

. . .

26 S. 2(g), *supra*, defines "dramatic work" and one of the requirements is that "the scenic arrangements or acting form of the work is fixed in writing or otherwise". In Copinger and James' work on *Law of Copyright*, 8th Ed., it is said at p. 24:

> The 'making' of a work is *prima facie* the production of a material thing — a manuscript, a picture or negative, and, in the case of a lecture or speech, of the literary work which is the subject-matter of copyright from which the lecture or speech was delivered.

27 In the same work the author, in discussing the "nature of copyright states at p. 2:

> When, however, any material has embodied those ideas, then the ideas, through that corporeity, can be recognized as a species of property by the common law. The claim is not to ideas, but to the order of words, and this order has a marked identity and a permanent endurance.

28 I have given careful consideration to the terms of The Copyright Act and more particularly to the provisions of s. 2 and 3, and the conclusion seems inescapable — at least to me — that for copyright to subsist in a "work" it must be expressed to some extent at least in some material form, capable of identification and having a more or less permanent endurance. All the works included in the definitions of "artistic work" and literary work" (s. 2(b) and (n)) have a material existence; "musical works" by s. 2(p) must be printed, reduced to writing or otherwise graphically produced or reproduced. Likewise, in regard to "dramatic works" there is the requirement which I have noted, namely, that the scenic arrangements or acting form must be fixed in writing or otherwise. "Cinematographic productions" which are also dramatic works are obviously "fixed otherwise", since as will be noted later, they involve the making of films.

29 Now on this point it is not necessary to consider to what extent the scenic arrangement or acting form must be *fixed* in writing or otherwise. It is sufficient to say that in the present case nether Renaud nor any of his associates had fixed anything in writing or otherwise, or had anything whatever to do with the scenic arrangements of the acting form of the players participating in the football match. By the very nature of the spectacle, nothing of that sort could have been planned in advance or fixed in writing or in any other manner whatsoever. Renaud stated that very clearly at the conclusion of his cross-examination when in referring to the live telecasts of the football matches, he said: "It is an 'ad lib' production, because you can't prepare it, you can't control your subject at all; you have no authority over a football player".

30 In commenting on s. 35 of the English Copyright Act, 1911, Russell-Clarke in his work on *Copyright and Industrial Designs* (1951), said in reference to these words, at p. 39:

Writing is the method mentioned in the definition, and is the most obvious method, as by this means the nature of the work can be readily ascertained by a series of directions to be followed by those taking part. Another possible method of fixing would be by photographic means, or by a series of verbal directions embodied in some form of record. Mere spoken words, however, such as oral directions by a stage manager or producer, not reduced to a definite ascertainable form, which can be referred to at any time, cannot be sufficient to create a copyright. Quite apart from the above statutory requirements as to fixing created by the words of the definition, from a practical point of view, the law will not intervene to protect something which is not definite and ascertainable.

31 As authority for that proposition, the author relies on the case of *Tate v. Thomas*, [1921] 1 Ch. 503.

32 For these reasons, I think that the plaintiff must fail on this point.

Gould Estate v. Stoddart Publishing Co. (1998), 39 O.R. (3d) 545 (Ont. C.A.) Ontario Court of Appeal

Finlayson, Krever and Weiler JJ.A.

Heard: April 16-17, 1998
Judgment: May 6, 1998
Docket: CA C25822, C25823

. . .

The judgment of the court was delivered by *Finlayson J.A.*:

1 This is an appeal from two summary judgments of the Honourable Mr. Justice Lederman dismissing Action No. 95-CQ-62384 (the "Photograph Action") and the other dismissing Action No. 95-CU-92931 (the "Words Action"). The motions judge held that there was no basis in law for either action.

2 The two actions concern a book entitled "Glenn Gould: Some Portraits of the Artist as a Young Man" that was published by the respondent Stoddart Publishing Co. Limited ("Stoddart") in 1995 without the consent of or compensation to the appellants, the Estate of Glenn Gould and Glenn Gould Limited. The book contains photographs of the late Glenn Gould taken by the late Jock Carroll with captions and an accompanying narrative written by Carroll. The narrative is based on notes and audio tape recordings of interviews of Gould by Carroll in the spring of 1956 during an extended photo-opportunity agreed to by Gould. The photographs were taken and the interviews conducted for the purposes of an article that Carroll was to write and submit to Weekend Magazine for publication. The article headed "I Don't Think I'm At All Eccentric" was in fact published. It contains nine photographs of Gould and a narrative that contains many quotations attributed to Gould.

3 At issue in this appeal is whether the respondent Carroll was entitled, for his own exclusive benefit, to later exploit commercially the photographs he took

of Gould in 1956 and to use his notes and tapes of his interviews at that time to write other articles on Gould notwithstanding that such later use of the photographs and interviews had never been discussed with or agreed to by Gould or his successors or assigns.

. . .

The facts

6 The late Glenn Gould was a world-famous concert and recording pianist who died in 1982. Stephen Posen is the executor of Gould's estate. Glenn Gould Limited is the owner of the rights to the use of the name Glenn Gould pursuant to an assignment of those rights from Gould in 1961. In 1956, the late Jock Carroll was a freelance writer associated with Weekend Magazine as a writer and photographer. Carroll died on August 4, 1995.

7 In the early spring of 1956, Gould's agent, Walter Homburger, approached Carroll to enquire whether Carroll would be interested in interviewing Gould and taking photographs of him for a story in Weekend Magazine. Carroll, after consultation with his editor at Weekend Magazine, agreed.

8 Gould and Carroll met on several occasions for interviews and picture taking. Initial meetings took place at Massey Hall, Homburger's office, Gould's home and along the boardwalk in Toronto's Beaches. Gould had already planned a private trip to Nassau and invited Carroll to travel with him in order to continue with the interviews and photo-taking opportunities. Carroll accepted the invitation and paid his own expenses for which he was reimbursed by Weekend Magazine. During these occasions, Carroll took approximately 400 photographs of Gould and made notes and audio tape recordings of numerous interviews. Carroll retained all the photographs, notes and tape recordings.

. . .

22 The motions judge did address the issue of copyright with respect to the oral conversations that occurred between Gould and Carroll. The appellants submitted that what they described as "transcriptions" of these conversations in the text of the book in question was the subject of copyright and that copyright had been retained by Gould. The motions judge did not agree. In rejecting this submission, he referred to a number of authorities and set out an extended quotation from *Falwell v. Penthouse International Ltd.*, 215 U.S.P.Q. 975 (U.S. W.D. Va. 1981) at p. 977. The court in *Falwell* held that the Reverend Jerry Falwell had no copyright in unstructured remarks that he made in an interview with members of the media. Such a claim presupposed that every utterance he made was a valuable property right. Relying upon this authority, the motions judge concluded:

> Here too, the nature of the interview, conducted in informal settings–at an empty Massey Hall, at the home of Gould's mother and on vacation in the Bahamas–was such that it was intended to be casual, to catch the spontaneity of Gould when he was relaxing. The conversation between the two men was the kind that Gould would have with a friend. Indeed Gould and Carroll remained friends for a short while afterwards. Gould was not delivering a structured lecture or dictating to

Carroll. Rather, Carroll engaged Gould in easy going conversation out of which emerged comments which provided insights into Gould's character and personal life. Gould was making offhand comments that he knew could find their way into the public domain. This is not the kind of disclosure which the *Copyright Act* intended to protect.

23 I agree with this conclusion, but I question its limits. It is evident from this record that Gould did not have a copyright with respect to his oral utterances or in the "transcriptions" of them, to use the appellants' phrase. To the contrary, Carroll as the author of the text and captions in the book was the owner of the copyright in the very written material the appellants are attempting to suppress.

---

5. Publication

The term "publication" in relation to any work is defined as "making copies of the work available to the public" but does not include the performance in public of a literary, dramatic or musical work, the delivery in public of a lecture, or the communication of a work to the public by telecommunication, or the exhibition in public of an artistic work. The concept of publication is used as one of the eligibility conditions for copyright to subsist in a work. It is different from the exclusive right in s. 3(1) to publish a work.

Infabrics Ltd. v. Jaytex Ltd., [1982] A.C. 1 (H.L.)

House of Lords

Before: Lord Wilberforce, Lord Edmund-Davies, Lord Fraser of Tullybelton, Lord Scarman, Lord Roskill

17th — 19th February and 26 March 1981

. . .

Lord Wilberforce:

This appeal is concerned with an artistic work designed by the third respondent, the copyright in which belongs to the first respondent, and which is claimed to have been infringed by the appellants.

The work consists of an attractive drawing in colours of three racehorses with jockeys engaged in a close finish at a winning post, this drawing being repeated at spaced intervals. It has become known as "Past the Post" though that point had in fact not been reached.

Put very shortly the essential facts are that a representative of the appellants saw the design in Hong Kong at the premises of a company called TAL and selected it from a number of others. The appellants then ordered a quantity of cloth to be printed with the design and arranged with a shirt maker, also in Hong Kong, to make it up into shirts and export them to the United Kingdom. The appellants then arranged for the shirts to be put on the market and sold by retailers. They sold well in the King's Road, Chelsea.

The claim as framed and as presented at the trial was based on infringement of copyright by importation from Hong Kong and sale in this country of shirts made from cloth bearing the Past the Post design which would have infringed the copyright if the cloth had been made in the United Kingdom. It was based upon section 5 of the Copyright Act 1956 which requires, as a condition of liability for infringement, knowledge that the making of the cloth constituted an infringement of the copyright or would have done so if the cloth had been made in the United Kingdom.

The appellants denied any such knowledge and the trial took place upon that issue. It was held by Whitford J. that until 5 March 1975, a fortnight after a warning letter had been sent, the appellants had no such knowledge, but that after that date they had. The appellants accepted the latter finding, and an inquiry as to damages was ordered.

In their speech in reply, after the appellants' (defendants') case had been closed, counsel for the respondents contended for the first time that the appellants were liable for infringement on the basis of "publishing" the work, under section 1 and section 3 (5) (b) of the Act. They obtained leave to amend their statement of claim by inserting the following paragraph:

> "5. Further or alternatively the defendants have infringed the said copyright work (*sic*) by publishing the same by their aforesaid acts of sale and distribution of shirts bearing the said design."

> The reference to "aforesaid acts" is to those acts of sale and distribution in the United Kingdom as to which Whitford J. had held the appellants not liable for infringement on the ground of lack of knowledge. In view of the late stage at which this claim was introduced, no additional evidence was called to support it. In particular, and this may well have been fatal, no evidence was called, or was available, that the artistic work was unpublished at the date of the alleged publication by the appellants.

. . .

The section dealing with artistic works is section 3 (literary, dramatic and musical works are dealt with in section 2). By section 3 (5) the acts restricted by the copyright in an artistic work are:

> "(*a*) reproducing the work in any material form;" (not relied on)

> (*b*) publishing the work;

> (*c*) . . .

> (*d*) . . ."

There is no definition of "publishing" in this section, and there are great difficulties in extracting the meaning of the word from the rest of the Act.

There are three suggested meanings:

The first (accepted by the Court of Appeal) is that publishing consists of the issue of reproductions of the work to the public.

The second (contended for by the respondents) is that publishing is what is done by a publisher.

The third (contended for by the appellants) is that publishing means making public, in the Territory, a work which had not previously been made public in the Territory. I shall examine these in order.

1. The interpretation of the Court of Appeal is based upon section 49 (2) (c) of the Act which reads, together with the introductory and closing words of section 49 (2):

> "With regard to publication, the provisions of this subsection shall have effect for the purposes of this Act, that is to say, —
>
> . . .
>
> (c) subject to the preceding paragraphs, a literary, dramatic or musical work, or an edition of such a work, or an artistic work, shall be taken to have been published if, but only if, reproductions of the work or edition have been issued to the public;
>
> . . .
>
> and in determining for the purposes of paragraph (c) of this subsection, whether reproductions of a work or edition have been issued to the public, the preceding subsection shall not apply."

Reference back to subsection (1) of the section unfortunately leads to an intricate piece of drafting which can only be approximately summarised by saying that reproduction includes reproduction of a substantial part of a work, but even this is qualified by a proviso referring to several other sections. It is this labyrinthine quality, which pervades the whole Act, that makes it so extraordinarily difficult to interpret. However, I think that we can take it that paragraph (c) applies only to the issue of reproductions of the whole work.

The question then is, whether the Court of Appeal was right in treating this sub-section 2 (c) as a definition of "publishing" in section 3 (5) (b). The respondents did not support this approach, and I think that this was inevitable. In the first place, if the interpretation were right, it would follow that a retail seller of a copyright work would be regarded as publishing it — a novel consequence and one contrary to the well-accepted distinction between primary and secondary infringement. Moreover, it would be difficult to reconcile with the requirement of knowledge which section 5 imposes with regard to selling. Would a selling publisher be entitled to the defence of ignorance or not? More importantly, per-haps, if section 49 (2) (c), together with the closing words, were to apply to "publishing" in section 3 (5) (b), it would not be an infringement under section 1 (2) to publish a substantial part of the work. This would be paradoxical, and also contrary to section 49 (1) as above summarised. In my opinion, the correct view of section 49 (2) (c), on which I think both sides agree, is that it is not a defini-tion of "publishing" for the purposes of the Act — it is indeed not cast in the form of a definition — but is a provision relating to the words in section 3 (3) (and similarly in s. 2 (2)) "Where an original artistic work has been published, then . . . copyright shall subsist in the work . . ." In other words, it is dealing with subsistence of copyright, and stating a rule as to the time of publication, a matter of importance in relation to the subsistence of copyright. The conclusion, through this regrettably opaque reasoning, is that the Court of Appeal's approach cannot be supported.

2. The respondents' contention is that publishing means what a publisher does. I should say of this, first, that even if this were correct there would still be difficulties in the respondents' way. As I have explained, evidence which might have been borne directly on the question whether what the appellants did amounts to publishing in this sense was not called and I think it far from clear, on the existing material, that the appellants did anything amounting to publishing, sc. acting as publishers of the design.

But in any event I cannot accept the meaning offered. In relation to copyright, whether under common law or statute, "publishing" and "publication" are fundamental expressions meaning making available to the public, and it would take a great deal of contextual restraint to force them into a narrower and special meaning. Mr. Blanco White ingeniously tried to overcome this initial difficulty by deriving the word "published" in the Act of 1911 (the predecessor of the Act of 1956) from the Berne Copyright Convention of 1886 with reference to which the Act of 1911 was no doubt drafted. The word there used in the French authentic text and translated by "published" is *edite* — a word which seems to suggest what is done by an *editeur* — *i.e.* a publisher. But even in the Convention the word is used in various contexts with various meanings, and so is "published" in the Act of 1911. Indeed, section 1 (3) provides that for purposes of the Act publication means the issue of copies to the public. So I do not think that the Convention indication is a strong one.

In the Act of 1956 itself, Mr. Blanco White was able to point to some contexts in which "publishing" or "publisher" may refer to what is done by a "publisher." The clearest of these is section 7 (7). But that section does not apply to artistic works, and has to be regarded as a special compartment on its own — it relates to libraries and archives. Section 15, again, is of a specialised character — it relates to published editions of literary, dramatic or musical works. It may be true that in relation to such productions — *i.e.* to editions of literary, dramatic or musical works — the person who gives the work to the public would normally be a "publisher," but I find that insufficient reason for imposing that meaning on "publishing, etc." throughout the Act. In my opinion this suggested meaning cannot stand before the strong *prima facie* leaning which must exist, in the context of copyright, to interpret publication as making available to the public something unpublished.

3. The appellants' submission is, for these reasons, *prima facie* convincing. All through the history of copyright, under the Common Law, and through the legislation over 280 years, there has been the well-known contrast between unpublished works and published works. The distinction lies at the roots of the

law. The Act of 1911 was drafted wholly in line with these traditional concepts. Section 1 (1) paragraphs (a) and (b) deal respectively with a published work, and an unpublished work. Under section 1 (2) the position is clear. Copyright is the sole right to produce or reproduce the work in any material form, etc.: and "if the work is unpublished, to publish the work or any substantial part thereof," and by section 1 (3) publication "means the issue of copies of the work to the public." By section 2 infringement is linked to the rights defined in section 1, so publication of *an unpublished work* is infringement. The position is then perfectly plain: if that Act applied to the present case, the appellants could not be guilty of infringement by publishing. The question is whether the Act of 1956 has changed this. As with all other questions, the complexity and obscurity of the Act makes any answer difficult and a certain answer impossible. It is at least permissible to start from the point that (*a*) it is unlikely that the law as to and the distinction between published and unpublished works would have been changed without some clear indication; (*b*) it is implausible that a person who escapes secondary infringement liability through lack of knowledge should be condemned for primary infringement irrespective of knowledge. The result of the respondents' contention indeed would be to take away almost entirely the protection, in respect of lack of knowledge, given by section 5 (3) and (4) notwithstanding that these provisions substantially reproduce the terms of section 2 (2) of the 1911 Act conferring similar protection. As against this — and the main difficulty for the appellants — there is the unqualified reference in section 3 (5) (b) to "publishing" contrasted with the reference in the Act of 1911 section 1 (2) to publishing the work if unpublished.

The explanation of this change suggested by the appellants, and which I accept, is this. There has been a significant change in the 1956 Act, as compared with the Act of 1911, regarding the scope of copyright. Under the Act of 1911, section 1 (1), copyright subsisted in a published work only if the work was published within the countries to which the Act extended (the Territory). So "publishing" in that context clearly meant making public in the territory a work not previously made public in the territory.

The 1956 Act, section 3 (3) (*b*), enabled copyright of, *inter alia*, an artistic work to subsist even though the work was not published in the Territory, if the author was a qualified person. This made it inappropriate to preserve in section 3 (5) (b) an express condition that the work must have been unpublished, since if such words had been inserted, the qualified person above referred to could not have prevented publication in the Territory or sued for infringement in the event of such publication. When, however, it is a matter of dealing with infringement, the relevant provisions (in 1 (1) and (2)) are concerned only with publication in the Territory. In such a context, in accordance with the accepted meaning of the words, publishing can only mean making public what had not previously been made public in the Territory. Since it is not shown that the design in this case had not previously been so made public, the case based on publishing must fail. In my opinion, therefore, the respondents fail to establish any infringement as regards acts done before 5 March 1975.

It is now becoming increasingly common for works to be accessed and distributed through electronic networks such as the Internet. In fact, the electronic purchasing and distribution of copyrighted materials may someday supplement or ultimately replace traditional sales channels such as record or video stores. Is a work distributed electronically published under the Act?

---

6. Scope of Protection

(a) Idea/Expression Dichotomy

It is a basic principle of copyright law that copyright protection extends to expression in a work and not to ideas, procedures, methods of operation or mathematical concepts as such.[9] An author has no copyright in basic ideas or information, but only in his form of expression of them. The idea/expression dichotomy is a feature of copyright law not only in Canada and other Commonwealth countries, but also in the United States where, it has been observed, it is applied with greater rigor than in English/Canadian law.[10]

A difficulty frequently arising in an infringement action is to ascertain the degree of detail, or conversely, the level of abstraction, to apply in defining what the idea is and what the expression is. The difficulty is to determine just where the basic concept ends and the exercise of expressing the concept begins. The "idea" of any work can always be defined in such detail that the description of the expression adds nothing to the "idea" thus allowing a defendant to engage in all but verbatim copying. Conversely, if the idea is so abstractly stated, the creation of many original works in which there is treatment of the same topic could be rendered infringing.

There is no litmus-paper test by which to apply the idea/expression distinction, and it is often a vexing question to distinguish what is the idea and what is its expression. It is an ill-defined boundary and there is no general formula by which to establish the line between the general idea and the author's expression of the idea. The basic idea (or concept) is not necessarily simple — it may be complex. It may be something innovative; or it may be commonplace, utilitarian or banal. The way the author treats the subject, the forms he uses to express the basic concept, may range from the crude and simplistic to the ornate, complicated — and involving the collation and application of a great number of constructive ideas.[11] Ultimately, in difficult cases, the line to be drawn will be informed by the policy objectives underlying the

9   *Delrina Corp. v. Triolet Systems Inc.* (2002), 17 C.P.R. (4th) 289 (Ont. C.A.).
10 *Delrina Corp. v. Tiolet Systems Inc.* (2002), 17 C.P.R. (4th) 289 (Ont. C.A.); *IBCOS Computers Ltd. v. Barclay's Mercantile Highland Finance Ltd.*, [1994] F.S.R. 275 (Ch.D.).
11 L.B. (Plastics) Ltd. v. Swish Products Ltd., [1979] R.P.C. 551 (H.L.).
12 *Baigent v. The Random House Group Ltd. (The Da Vinci Code)*, [2006] E.W.H.C. 719 (Ch) (7 April 2006).

Act. "The line to be drawn is to enable a fair balance to be struck between protecting the rights of the author and allowing development of works."[12]

Article 9, TRIPS Agreement

Relation to the Berne Convention

1. Members shall comply with Articles 1 through 21 of the Berne Convention (1971) and the Appendix thereto. However, Members shall not have rights or obligations under this Agreement in respect of the rights conferred under Article 6*bis* of that Convention or of the rights derived therefrom.

2. Copyright protection shall extend to expressions and not to ideas, procedures, methods of operation or mathematical concepts as such.

US Copyright Act 1976, 17 U.S.C.

Sect. 102. Subject matter of copyright: In general

(b) In no case does copyright protection for an original work of authorship extend to any idea, procedure, process, system, method of operation, concept, principle, or discovery, regardless of the form in which it is described, explained, illustrated, or embodied in such work.

---

i. Distinguishing Idea from Expression

Nichols v. Universal Pictures Corporation

45 F.2d 119 (2d Cir., 1930)

Circuit Court of Appeals, Second Circuit

L. Hand:

The plaintiff is the author of a play, "Abie's Irish Rose," which it may be assumed was properly copyrighted under section five, subdivision (d), of the Copyright Act, *17 USCA § 5*(d). The defendant produced publicly a motion picture play, "The Cohens and The Kellys," which the plaintiff alleges was taken from it. As we think the defendant's play too unlike the plaintiff's to be an infringement, we may assume, arguendo, that in some details the defendant used the plaintiff's play, as will subsequently appear, though we do not so decide. It therefore becomes necessary to give an outline of the two plays.

"Abie's Irish Rose" presents a Jewish family living in prosperous circumstances in New York. The father, a widower, is in business as a merchant, in which his son and only child helps him. The boy has philandered with young women, who to his father's great disgust have always been Gentiles, for he is obsessed with a passion that his daughter-in-law shall be an orthodox Jewess. When the play opens the son, who has been courting a young Irish Catholic girl, has already married her secretly before a Protestant minister, and is concerned to soften the blow for his father, by securing a favorable impression of his bride, while concealing her faith and race. To accomplish this he introduces her to his father at his home as a Jewess, and lets it appear that he is interested in her, though he conceals the marriage. The girl somewhat reluctantly falls in with the plan; the father takes the bait, becomes infatuated with the girl, concludes that they must marry, and assumes that of course they will, if he so decides. He calls in a rabbi, and prepares for the wedding according to the Jewish rite.

Meanwhile the girl's father, also a widower, who lives in California, and is as intense in his own religious antagonism as the Jew, has been called to New York, supposing that his daughter is to marry an Irishman and a Catholic. Accompanied by a priest, he arrives at the house at the moment when the marriage is being celebrated, but too late to prevent it, and the two fathers, each infuriated by the proposed union of his child to a heretic, fall into unseemly and grotesque antics. The priest and the rabbi become friendly, exchange trite sentiments about religion, and agree that the match is good. Apparently out of abundant caution, the priest celebrates the marriage for a third time, while the girl's father is inveigled away. The second act closes with each father, still outraged, seeking to find some way by which the union, thus trebly insured, may be dissolved.

The last act takes place about a year later, the young couple having meanwhile been abjured by each father, and left to their own resources. They have had twins, a boy and a girl, but their fathers know no more than that a child has been born. At Christmas each, led by his craving to see his grandchild, goes separately to the young folks' home, where they encounter each other, each laden with gifts, one for a boy, the other for a girl. After some slapstick comedy, depending upon the insistence of each that he is right about the sex of the grandchild, they become reconciled when they learn the truth, and that each child is to bear the given name of a grandparent. The curtain falls as the fathers are exchanging amenities, and the Jew giving evidence of an abatement in the strictness of his orthodoxy.

"The Cohens and The Kellys" presents two families, Jewish and Irish, living side by side in the poorer quarters of New York in a state of perpetual enmity. The wives in both cases are still living, and share in the mutual animosity, as do two small sons, and even the respective dogs. The Jews have a daughter, the Irish a son; the Jewish father is in the clothing business; the Irishman is a policeman. The children are in love with each other, and secretly marry, apparently after the play opens. The Jew, being in great financial straits, learns from a lawyer that he has fallen heir to a large fortune from a great-aunt, and moves into a great house, fitted luxuriously. Here he and his family live in vulgar ostentation, and here the Irish boy seeks out his Jewish bride, and is chased away by the angry father. The Jew then abuses the Irishman over the telephone, and both become hysterically excited. The extremity of his feelings makes the Jew sick, so that he must go to Florida for a rest, just before which the daughter discloses her marriage to her mother.

On his return the Jew finds that his daughter has borne a child; at first he suspects the lawyer, but eventually learns the truth and is overcome with anger at such a low alliance. Meanwhile, the Irish family who have been forbidden to see the grandchild, go to the Jew's house, and after a violent scene between the two fathers in which the Jew disowns his daughter, who decides to go back with her husband, the Irishman takes her back with her baby to his own poor lodgings. The lawyer, who had hoped to marry the Jew's daughter, seeing his plan foiled, tells the Jew that his fortune really belongs to the Irishman, who was also related to the dead woman, but offers to conceal his knowledge, if the Jew will share the loot. This the Jew repudiates, and, leaving the astonished lawyer, walks through the rain to his enemy's house to surrender the property. He arrives in great dejection, tells the truth, and abjectly turns to leave. A reconciliation ensues, the Irishman agreeing to share with him equally. The Jew shows some interest in his grandchild, though this is at most a minor motive in the reconciliation, and the curtain falls while the two are in their cups, the Jew insisting that in the firm name for the business, which they are to carry on jointly, his name shall stand first.

It is of course essential to any protection of literary property, whether at common-law or under the statute, that the right cannot be limited literally to the text, else a plagiarist would escape by immaterial variations. That has never been the law, but, as soon as literal appropriation ceases to be the test, the whole matter is necessarily at large, so that, as was recently well said by a distinguished judge, the decisions cannot help much in a new case. *Fendler v. Morosco, 253 N.Y. 281, 292, 171 N.E. 56.* When plays are concerned, the plagiarist may excise a separate scene [*Daly v. Webster, 56 F. 483* (C.C.A. 2); *Chappell v. Fields, 210 F. 864* (C.C.A. 2); *Chatterton v. Cave, L.R. 3 App. Cas. 483];* or he may appropriate part of the dialogue (*Warne v. Seebohm, L.R. 39 Ch. D. 73).* Then the question is whether the part so taken is "substantial," and therefore not a "fair use" of the copyrighted work; it is the same question as arises in the case of any other copyrighted work. *Marks v. Feist, 290 F. 959* (C.C.A. 2); *Emerson v. Davies, Fed. Cas. No. 4436, 3 Story, 768, 795-797.* But when the plagiarist does not take out a block in situ, but an abstract of the whole, decision is more troublesome. Upon any work, and especially upon a play, a great number of patterns of increasing generality will fit equally well, as more and more of the incident is left out. The last may perhaps be no more than the most general statement of what the play is about, and at times might consist only of its title; but there is a point in this series of abstractions where they are no longer protected, since otherwise the playwright could prevent the use of his "ideas," to which, apart from their expression, his property is never extended. *Holmes v. Hurst, 174 U.S. 82, 86, 19 S. Ct. 606, 43 L. Ed. 904; Guthrie v. Curlett, 36 F.(2d) 694* (C.C.A. 2). Nobody has ever been able to fix that boundary, and nobody ever can. In some cases the question has been treated as though it were analogous to lifting a portion out of the copyrighted work (Rees v. Melville, MacGillivray's Copyright Cases [1911-1916], 168); but the analogy is not a good one, because, though the skeleton is a part of the body, it pervades and supports the whole. In such cases we are rather concerned with the line between expression and what is expressed. As respects plays, the controversy chiefly centers upon the characters and sequence of incident, these being the substance.

We did not in *Dymow v. Bolton, 11 F.(2d) 690*, hold that a plagiarist was never liable for stealing a plot; that would have been flatly against our rulings in *Dam v. Kirk La Shelle Co., 175 F. 902, 41 L.R.A. (N.S.) 1002, 20 Ann. Cas. 1173*, and *Stodart v. Mutual Film Co., 249 F. 513*, affirming my decision in (D.C.) *249 F. 507*; neither of which we meant to overrule. We found the plot of the second play was too different to infringe, because the most detailed pattern, common to both, eliminated so much from each that its content went into the public domain; and for this reason we said, "this mere subsection of a plot was not susceptible of copyright." But we do not doubt that two plays may correspond in plot closely enough for infringement. How far that correspondence must go is another matter. Nor need we hold that the same may not be true as to the characters, quite independently of the "plot" proper, though, as far as we know, such a case has never arisen. If Twelfth Night were copyrighted, it is quite possible that a second comer might so closely imitate Sir Toby Belch or Malvolio as to infringe, but it would not be enough that for one of his characters he cast a riotous knight who kept wassail to the discomfort of the household, or a vain and foppish steward who became amorous of his mistress. These would be no more than Shakespeare's "ideas" in the play, as little capable of monopoly as Einstein's Doctrine of Relativity, or Darwin's theory of the Origin of Species. It follows that the less developed the characters, the less they can be copyrighted; that is the penalty an author must bear for marking them too indistinctly.

In the two plays at bar we think both as to incident and character, the defendant took no more — assuming that it took anything at all — than the law allowed. The stories are quite different. One is of a religious zealot who insists upon his child's marrying no one outside his faith; opposed by another who is in this respect just like him, and is his foil. Their difference in race is merely an obbligato to the main theme, religion. They sink their differences through grandparental pride and affection. In the other, zealotry is wholly absent; religion does not even appear. It is true that the parents are hostile to each other in part because they differ in race; but the marriage of their son to a Jew does not apparently offend the Irish family at all, and it exacerbates the existing animosity of the Jew, principally because he has become rich, when he learns it. They are reconciled through the honesty of the Jew and the generosity of the Irishman; the grandchild has nothing whatever to do with it. The only matter common to the two is a quarrel between a Jewish and an Irish father, the marriage of their children, the birth of grandchildren and a reconciliation.

If the defendant took so much from the plaintiff, it may well have been because her amazing success seemed to prove that this was a subject of enduring popularity. Even so, granting that the plaintiff's play was wholly original, and assuming that novelty is not essential to a copyright, there is no monopoly in such a background. Though the plaintiff discovered the vein, she could not keep it to herself; so defined, the theme was too generalized an abstraction from what she wrote. It was only a part of her "ideas."

Nor does she fare better as to her characters. It is indeed scarcely credible that she should not have been aware of those stock figures, the low comedy Jew and Irishman. The defendant has not taken from her more than their prototypes have contained for many decades. If so, obviously so to generalize her copyright, would allow her to cover what was not original with her. But we need not hold this as matter of fact, much as we might be justified. Even though we take it that she devised her figures out of her brain de novo, still the defendant was within its rights.

There are but four characters common to both plays, the lovers and the fathers. The lovers are so faintly indicated as to be no more than stage properties. They are loving and fertile; that is really all that can be said of them, and anyone else is quite within his rights if he puts loving and fertile lovers in a play of his own, wherever he gets the cue. The plaintiff's Jew is quite unlike the defendant's. His obsession is his religion, on which depends such racial animosity as he has. He is affectionate, warm and patriarchal. None of these fit the defendant's Jew, who shows affection for his daughter only once, and who has none but the most superficial interest in his grandchild. He is tricky, ostentatious and vulgar, only by misfortune redeemed into honesty. Both are grotesque, extravagant and quarrelsome; both are fond of display; but these common qualities make up only a small part of their simple pictures, no more than any one might lift if he chose. The Irish fathers are even more unlike; the plaintiff's a mere symbol for religious fanaticism and patriarchal pride, scarcely a character at all. Neither quality appears in the defendant's, for while he goes to get his grandchild, it is rather out of a truculent determination not to be forbidden, than from pride in his progeny. For the rest he is only a grotesque hobbledehoy, used for low comedy of the most conventional sort, which any one might borrow, if he chanced not to know the exemplar.

The defendant argues that the case is controlled by my decision in *Fisher v. Dillingham (D.C.) 298 F. 145.* Neither my brothers nor I wish to throw doubt upon the doctrine of that case, but it is not applicable here. We assume that the plaintiff's play is altogether original, even to an extent that in fact it is hard to believe. We assume further that, so far as it has been anticipated by earlier plays of which she knew nothing, that fact is immaterial. Still, as we have already said, her copyright did not cover everything that might be drawn from her play; its content went to some extent into the public domain. We have to decide how much, and while we are as aware as any one that the line, whereever it is drawn, will seem arbitrary, that is no excuse for not drawing it; it is a question such as courts must answer in nearly all cases. Whatever may be the difficulties a priori, we have no question on which side of the line this case falls. A comedy based upon conflicts between Irish and Jews, into which the marriage of their children enters, is no more susceptible of copyright than the outline of Romeo and Juliet.

The plaintiff has prepared an elaborate analysis of the two plays, showing a "quadrangle" of the common characters, in which each is represented by the emotions which he discovers. She presents the resulting parallelism as proof of infringement, but the adjectives employed are so general as to be quite useless. Take for example the attribute of "love" ascribed to both Jews. The plaintiff has depicted her father as deeply attached to his son, who is his hope and joy; not so, the defendant, whose father's conduct is throughout not actuated by any affection for his daughter, and who is merely once overcome for the moment by her distress when he has violently dismissed her lover. "Anger" covers emotions aroused by quite different occasions in each case; so do "anxiety," "despondency" and "disgust." It is unnecessary to go through the catalogue for emotions are too much colored by their causes to be a test when used so broadly. This is not the proper approach to a solution; it must be more ingenuous, more like that of a spectator, who would rely upon the complex of his impressions of each character.

We cannot approve the length of the record, which was due chiefly to the use of expert witnesses. Argument is argument whether in the box or at the bar, and its proper place is the last. The testimony of an expert upon such issues, especially his cross-examination, greatly extends the trial and contributes nothing which cannot be better heard after the evidence is all submitted. It ought not to be allowed at all; and while its admission is not a ground for reversal, it cumbers the case and tends to confusion, for the more the court is led into the intricacies of dramatic craftsmanship, the less likely it is to stand upon the firmer, if more naive, ground of its considered impressions upon its own perusal. We hope that in this class of cases such evidence may in the future be entirely excluded, and the case confined to the actual issues; that is, whether the copyrighted work was original, and whether the defendant copied it, so far as the supposed infringement is identical.

Decree affirmed.

Designers Guild Ltd. v. Russell Williams (Textiles) Ltd., [2000] 1 W.L.R. 2416 (U.K. H.L.)

Lord Bingham of Cornhill Lord Hoffmann Lord Hope of Craighead Lord Millett Lord Scott of Foscote

Lord Hoffmann

6.   Ideas and expression

It is often said, as Morritt L.J. said in this case, that copyright subsists not in ideas but in the form in which the ideas are expressed. The distinction between expression and ideas finds a place in the Agreement on Trade-Related Aspects of Intellectual Property Rights (TRIPS) (O.J. 1994 L. 336 p. 213), to which the United Kingdom is a party (see article 9.2: "Copyright protection shall extend to expressions and not to ideas…"). Nevertheless, it needs to be handled with care. What does it mean? As Lord Hailsham of St. Marylebone said in *L.B. (Plastics) Ltd v. Swish Products Ltd* [1979] R.P.C. 551, 629, "it all depends on what you mean by 'ideas'."

Plainly there can be no copyright in an idea which is merely in the head, which has not been expressed in copyrightable form, as a literary, dramatic, musical or artistic work. But the distinction between ideas and expression cannot mean anything so trivial as that. On the other hand, every element in the expression of an artistic work (unless it got there by accident or compulsion) is the expression of an idea on the part of the author. It represents her choice to paint stripes rather than polka dots, flowers rather than tadpoles, use one colour and brush technique rather than another, and so on. The expression of these ideas is protected, both as a cumulative whole and also to the extent to which they form a "substantial part" of the work. Although the term "substantial part" might suggest a quantitative test, or at least the ability to identify some discrete part which, on quantitative or qualitative grounds, can be regarded as substantial, it is clear upon the authorities that neither is the correct test. *Ladbroke (Football) Ltd. v. William Hill (Football) Ltd.* [1964] 1 W.L.R. 273 establishes that substantiality depends upon quality rather than quantity (Lord Reid at p. 276, Lord Evershed at p. 283, Lord Hodson at p. 288, Lord Pearce at p. 293). And there are numerous authorities which show that the "part" which is regarded as substantial can be a feature or combination of features of the work, abstracted from it rather than forming a discrete part. That is what the judge found to have been copied in this case. Or to take another example, the original elements in the plot of a play or novel may be a substantial part, so that copyright may be infringed by a work which does not reproduce a single sentence of the original. If one asks what is being protected in such a case, it is difficult to give any answer except that it is an idea expressed in the copyright work.

My Lords, if one examines the cases in which the distinction between ideas and the expression of ideas has been given effect, I think it will be found that they support two quite distinct propositions. The first is that a copyright work may express certain ideas which are not protected because they have no connection with the literary, dramatic, musical or artistic nature of the work. It is on this ground that, for example, a literary work which describes a system or invention does not entitle the author to claim protection for his system or invention as such. The same is true of an inventive concept expressed in an artistic work. However striking or original it may be, others are (in the absence of patent protection) free to express it in works of their own: see *Kleeneze Ltd. v. D.R.G. (U.K.) Ltd.* [1984] F.S.R. 399. The other proposition is that certain ideas expressed by a copyright work may not be protected because, although they are ideas of a literary, dramatic or artistic nature, they are not original, or so commonplace as not to form a substantial part of the work. *Kenrick & Co. v. Lawrence & Co.* (1890) 25 Q.B.D. 99 is a well-known example. It is on this ground that the mere notion of combining stripes and flowers would not have amounted to a substantial part of the plaintiff's work. At that level of abstraction, the idea, though expressed in the design, would not have represented sufficient of the author's skill and labour as to attract copyright protection.

Generally speaking, in cases of artistic copyright, the more abstract and simple the copied idea, the less likely it is to constitute a substantial part. Originality, in the sense of the contribution of the author's skill and labour, tends to lie in the detail with which the basic idea is presented. Copyright law protects foxes better than hedgehogs. In this case, however, the elements which the judge found to have been copied went well beyond the banal and I think that the judge was amply justified in deciding that they formed a substantial part of the originality of the work.

---

ii. Procedures, Processes, Systems and Methods of Operation

Baker v. Selden (1879), 101 U.S. 99 (U.S.Ohio)

Supreme Court of the United States
October Term, 1879

. . .

2. The difference between a copyright and letters-patent stated and illustrated.

MR. JUSTICE BRADLEY delivered the opinion of the court.

Charles Selden, the testator of the complainant in this case, in the year 1859 took the requisite steps for obtaining the copyright of a book, entitled 'Selden's Condensed Ledger, or Book-keeping Simplified,' the object of which was to exhibit and explain a peculiar system of book-keeping. In 1860 and 1861, he took the copyright of several other books, containing additions to and improvements upon the said system. The bill of complaint was filed against the defendant, Baker, for an alleged infringement of these copyrights.

. . .

The book or series of books of which the complainant claims the copyright consists of an introductory essay explaining the system of book-keeping referred to, to which are annexed certain forms or banks, consisting of ruled lines, and headings, illustrating the system and showing how it is to be used and carried out in practice. This system effects the same results as book-keeping by double entry; but, by a peculiar arrangement of columns and headings, presents the entire operation, of a day, a week, or a month, on a single page, or on two pages facing each other, in an account-book. The defendant uses a similar plan so far as results are concerned; but makes a different arrangement of the columns, and uses different headings. If the complainant's testator had the exclusive right to the use of the system explained in his book, it would be difficult to contend that the defendant does not infringe it, notwithstanding the difference in his form of arrangement; but if it be assumed that the system is open to public use, it seems to be equally difficult to contend that the books made and sold by the defendant are a violation of the copyright of the complainant's book considered merely as a book explanatory of the system. Where the truths of a science or the methods of an art are the common property of the whole world, any author has the right to express the one, or explain and use the other, in his own way. As an author, Selden explained the system in a particular way. It may be conceded that Baker makes and uses account-books arranged on substantially the same system; but the proof fails to show that he has violated the copyright of Selden's book, regarding the latter merely as an explanatory work; or that he has infringed Selden's right in any way, unless the latter became entitled to an exclusive right in the system.

The evidence of the complainant is principally directed to the object of showing that Baker uses the same system as that which is explained and illustrated in Selden's books. It becomes important, therefore, to determine whether, in obtaining the copyright of his books, he secured the exclusive right to the use of the system or method of book-keeping which the said books are intended to illustrate and explain. It is contended that he has secured such exclusive right, because no one can use the system without using substantially the same ruled lines and headings which he was appended to his books in illustration of it. In other words, it is contended that the ruled lines and headings, given to illustrate the system, are a part of the book, and, as such, are secured by the copyright; and that no one can make or use similar ruled lines and headings, or ruled lines and headings made and arranged on substantially the same system, without violating the copyright. And this is really the question to be decided in this case. Stated in another form, the question is, whether the exclusive property in a system of book-keeping can be claimed, under the law or copyright, by means of a book in which that system is explained? The complainant's bill, and the case made under it, are based on the hypothesis that it can be.

. . .

There is no doubt that a work on the subject of book-keeping, though only explanatory of well-known systems, may be the subject of a copyright; but, then, it is claimed only as a book. Such a book may be explanatory either of old systems, or of an entirely new system; and, considered as a book, as the work of an author, conveying information on the subject of book-keeping, and containing detailed explanations of the art, it may be a very valuable acquisition to the practical knowledge of the community. But there is a clear distinction between the book, as such, and the art which it is intended to illustrate. The mere statement of the proposition is so evident, that it requires hardly any argument to support it. The same distinction may be predicated of every other art as well as that of book-keeping. A treatise on the composition and use of medicines, be they old or new; on the construction and use of ploughs, or watches, or churns; or on the mixture and application of colors for painting or dyeing; or on the mode of drawing lines to produce the effect of perspective,-would be the subject of copyright; but no one would contend that the copyright of the treatise would give the exclusive right to the art or manufacture described therein. The copyright of the book, if not pirated from other works, would be valid without regard to the novelty, or want of novelty, of its subject-matter. The novelty of the art or thing described or explained has nothing to do with the validity of the copyright. To give to the author of the book an exclusive property in the art described therein, when no examination of its novelty has ever been officially made, would be a surprise and a fraud upon the public. That is the province of letters-patent, not of copyright. The claim to an invention or discovery of an art or manufacture must be subjected to the examination of the Patent Office before an exclusive right therein can be obtained; and it can only be secured by a patent from the government.

The difference between the two things, letters-patent and copyright, may be illustrated by reference to the subjects just enumerated. Take the case of medicines. Certain mixtures are found to be of great value in the healing art. If the discoverer writes and publishes a book on the subject (as regular physicians generally do), he gains no exclusive right to the manufacture and sale of the medicine; he gives that to the public. If he desires to acquire such exclusive right, he must obtain a patent for the mixture as a new art, manufacture, or composition of matter. He may copyright his book, if he pleases; but that only secures to him the exclusive right of printing and publishing his book. So of all other inventions or discoveries.

The copyright of a book on perspective, no matter how many drawings and illustrations it may contain, gives no exclusive right to the modes of drawing described, though they may never have been known or used before. By publishing the book, without getting a patent for the art, the latter is given to the public. The fact that the art described in the book by illustrations of lines and figures which are reproduced in practice in the application of the art, makes no difference. Those illustrations are the mere language employed by the author to convey his ideas more clearly. Had he used words of description instead of diagrams (which merely stand in the place of words), there could not be the slightest doubt that others, applying the art to practical use, might lawfully draw the lines and diagrams which were in the author's mind, and which he thus described by words in his book.

The copyright of a work on mathematical science cannot give to the author an exclusive right to the methods of operation which he propounds, or to the diagrams which he employs to explain them, so as to prevent an engineer from using them whenever occasion requires. The very object of publishing a book on science or the useful arts is to communicate to the world the useful knowledge which it contains. But this object would be frustrated if the knowledge could not be used without incurring the guilt of piracy of the book. And where the art it teaches cannot be used without employing the methods and diagrams used to illustrate the book, or such as are similar to them, such methods and diagrams are to be considered as necessary incidents to the art, and given therewith to the public; not given for the purpose of publication in other works explanatory of the art, but for the purpose of practical application.

Of course, these observations are not intended to apply to ornamental designs, or pictorial illustrations addressed to the taste. Of these it may be said, that their form is their essence, and their object, the production of pleasure in their contemplation. This is their final end. They are as much the product of genius and the result of composition, as are the lines of the poet or the historian's period. On the other hand, the teachings of science and the rules and methods of useful art have their final end in application and use; and this application and use are what the public derive from the publication of a book which teaches them. But as embodied and taught in a literary composition or book, their essence consists only in their statement. This alone is what is secured by the copyright. The use by another of the same methods of statement, whether in words or illustrations, in a book published for teaching the art, would undoubtedly be an infringement of the copyright.

Recurring to the case before us, we observe that Charles Selden, by his books, explained and described a peculiar system of book-keeping, and illustrated his method by means of ruled lines and blank columns, with proper headings on a page, or on successive pages. Now, whilst no one has a right to print or publish his book, or any material part thereof, as a book intended to convey instruction in the art, any person may practise and use the art itself which he has described and illustrated therein. The use of the art is a totally different thing from a publication of the book explaining it. The copyright of a book on book-keeping cannot secure the exclusive right to make, sell, and use account-books prepared upon the plan set forth in such book. Whether the art might or might not have been patented, is a question which is not before us. It was not patented, and is open and free to the use of the public. And, of course, in using the art, the ruled lines and headings of accounts must necessarily be used as incident to it.

The plausibility of the claim put forward by the complainant in this case arises from a confusion of ideas produced by the peculiar nature of the art described in the books which have been made the subject of copyright. In describing the art, the illustrations and diagrams employed happen to correspond more closely than usual with the actual work performed by the operator who uses the art. Those illustrations and diagrams consist of ruled lines and headings of accounts; and it is similar ruled lines and headings of accounts which, in the application of the art, the book-keeper makes with his pen, or the stationer with his press; whilst in most other cases the diagrams and illustrations can only be represented in concrete forms of wood, metal, stone, or some other physical embodiment. But the principle is the same in all. The description of the art in a book, though entitled to the benefit of copyright, lays no foundation for an exclusive claim to the art itself. The object of the one is explanation; the object of the other is use. The former may be secured by copyright. The latter can only be secured, if it can be secured at all, by letters-patent.

The remarks of Mr. Justice Thompson in the Circuit Court in *Clayton* v. *Stone & Hall* (2 Paine, 392), in which copyright was claimed in a daily price-current, are apposite and instructive. He says: 'In determining the true construction to be given to the act of Congress, it is proper to look at the Constitution of the United

States, to aid us in ascertaining the nature of the property intended to be protected. 'Congress shall have power to promote the progress of science and useful arts, by securing for limited times to authors and inventors the exclusive right to their writings and discoveries.'The act in question was passed in execution of the power here given, and the object, therefore, was the promotion of science; and it would certainly be a pretty extraordinary view of the sciences to consider a daily or weekly publication of the state of the market as falling within any class of them. They are of a more fixed, permanent, and durable character. The term 'science' cannot, with any propriety, by applied to a work of so fluctuating and fugitive a form as that of a newspaper or price-current, the subject-matter of which is daily changing, and is of mere temporary use. Although great praise may be due to the plaintiffs for their industry and enterprise in publishing this paper, yet the law does not contemplate their being rewarded in this way: it must seek patronage and protection from its utility to the public, and not a work of science. The title of the act of Congress is, 'for the encouragement of learning,' and was not intended for the encouragement of mere industry, unconnected with learning and the sciences. . . . We are, accordingly, of opinion that the paper in question is not a book the copyright to which can be secured under the act of Congress.'

The case of *Cobbett* v. *Woodward* (Law Rep. 14 Eq. 407) was a claim to copyright in a catalogue of furniture which the publisher had on sale in his establishment, illustrated with many drawings of furniture and decorations. The defendants, being dealers in the same business, published a similar book, and copied many of the plaintiff's drawings, though it was shown that they had for sale the articles represented thereby.

The court held that these drawings were not subjects of copyright. Lord Romilly, M. R., said: 'This is a mere advertisement for the sale of particular articles which any one might imitate, and any one might advertise for sale. If a man not being a vendor of any of the articles in question were to publish a work for the purpose of informing the public of what was the most convenient species of articles for household furniture, or the most graceful species of decorations for articles of home furniture, what they ought to cost, and where they might be bought, and were to illustrate his work with designs of each article he described,-such a work as this could not be pirated with impunity, and the attempt to do so would be stopped by the injunction of the Court of Chancery; yet if it were done with no such object, but solely for the purpose of advertising particular articles for sale, and promoting the private trade of the publisher by the sale of articles which any other person might sell as well as the first advertiser, and if in fact it contained little more than an illustrated inventory of the contents of a warehouse, I know of no law which, while it would not prevent the second advertiser from selling the same articles, would prevent him from using the same advertisement; provided he did not in such advertisement by any device suggest that he was selling the works and designs of the first advertiser.'

Another case, that of *Page* v. *Wisden* (20 L. T. N. S. 435), which came before Vice-Chancellor Malins in 1869, has some resemblance to the present. There a copyright was claimed in a cricket scoring-shett, and the Vice-Chancellor held that it was not a fit subject for copyright, partly because it was not new, but also because 'to say that a particular mode of ruling a book constituted an object for a copyright is absurd.'

These cases, if not precisely in point, come near to the matter in hand, and, in our view, corroborate the general proposition which we have laid down.

In *Drury* v. *Ewing* (1 Bond, 540), which is much relied on by the complainant, a copyright was claimed in a chart of patterns for cutting dresses and basques for ladies, and coats, jackets, &c., for boys. It is obvious that such designs could only be printed and published for information, and not for use in themselves. Their practical use could only be exemplified in cloth on the tailor's board and under his shears; in other words, by the application of a mechanical operation to the cutting of cloth in certain patterns and forms. Surely the exclusive right to this practical use was not reserved to the publisher by his copyright of the chart. Without undertaking to say whether we should or should not concur in the decision in that case, we think it cannot control the present.

The conclusion to which we have come is, that blank account-books are not the subject of copyright; and that the mere copyright of Selden's book did not confer upon him the exclusive right to make and use account-books, ruled and arranged as designated by him and described and illustrated in said book.

The decree of the Circuit Court must be reversed, and the cause remanded with instructions to dismiss the complainant's bill; and it is

So ordered.

Moreau v. St. Vincent, [1950] Ex. C.R. 198 (Ex. Ct.)

Exchequer Court of Canada

Thorson P.

Judgment: February 15, 1950

Thorson P.:

1 This is an action for infringement of copyright. The facts are not in dispute. The plaintiff is a partner and manager of a firm carrying on business in Montreal under the firm name of L'Information Sportive, its business being the publication and sale of a weekly sports paper called "L'Information Sportive". On October 2, 1947, the plaintiff and his associates, who were then Louis Daniel, J.L. Letourneux and Ch.-Roger Poitras, applied to the Commissioner of Patents for the registration of a copyright under the Copyright Act, R.S.C. 1927, chapter 32, in what they called "Concours: Recrutement d'Abonnés", declaring that for the purpose of promoting subscriptions to the paper "L'Information Sportive" they had devised a system of distribution of prizes to subscribers for which

they requested the grant of copyright, and on October 6, 1947, the Commissioner issued a certificate that copyright in a literary unpublished work called "L'Information Sportive" by the plaintiff and his associates had been registered in their names ...

2 ... After the registration of the copyright the firm commenced to publish its paper "L'Information Sportive" and to conduct a weekly competition for prizes to its subscribers which it called "Concours: Recrutement d'Abonnés" the details of which were published in each issue. The paper was sold for 25 cents per copy and a numbered receipt was issued to the purchaser of each copy.

3 The plaintiff stated that he had devised the competition in order to promote the sale of the paper, and had used three elements in an original arrangement of them. The elements said to have been thus brought together were described in the letters from L'Information Sportive to the Commissioner of Patents, dated October 2, 1947, to which I have referred, and also in the paper. The elements forming the system on which the competitions were based were three, namely, a numbered subscription receipt, a copy of the paper with two lists of sports clubs, one giving the results of contests already had and compilations of numbers from such results and another giving the scheduled contests for the following week the results of which were to serve as the basis of the compilation of numbers for the competition of that week, and a questionnaire or quiz relating to sports topics to be answered by the holders of subscription receipts carrying numbers corresponding to those compiled from the results of the sports contests given in the first list in the paper. The details and conditions for each competition appeared in substantially the same form on page 9 of each issue of "L'Information Sportive", except, of course, for necessary differences, such as the names of the sports clubs selected, the results of the contests and the questions in the quiz. Likewise, the receipts continued to be issued in the same form, the only difference being in their numbers.

4 The defendant was in the employ of L'Information Sportive as a distributor of its paper under a contract with it for one year, dated December 30, 1947, subject to cancellation on thirty days' notice. On May 12, 1948, he sent a telegram of resignation effective on June 27, 1948. On the same day he filed a declaration of carrying on business under the firm name of "Loisir Favori." And on the same day his solicitors forwarded his request for the registration of a copyright in an original literary unpublished work called "Loisir Favori", and copyright in the said work was registered on May 13, 1948, and a certificate to that effect sent to him. On July 3, 1948, the defendant commenced the publication of a weekly leaflet called "Mots Croisés", which he sold at 25 cents a copy, the purchaser receiving a numbered receipt. The leaflet contained a number of cross-word puzzles. With each issue the defendant conducted a competition called "Quizz général de la publication Loisir Favori Enrg.", the details of which were published in the leaflet. The defendant did not hesitate to solicit distributors and vendors of the paper "L'Information Sportive" to handle his leaflet and several of them did so. Some of them said that their customers preferred it. Moreover, the defendant sold his leaflet in the same area as "L'Information Sportive" had

previously found its market. The result was that the sales of "L'Information Sportive", which had been approximately 50,000 copies per week, had by September 12, 1948, been reduced by over 14,000 copies per week.

. . .

6 The plaintiff alleges, inter alia, that the defendant's "Quizz général de la publication Loisir Favori Enrg." is a plagiarism of his "Concours: Recrutement d'Abonnés" and an infringement of his copyright ...

. . .

10 It is plain from the statement of claim and the evidence that the plaintiff has misconceived the nature of his copyright and the extent of the protection that it affords. While it was stated that the object of the competitions, both that of the defendant as well as that of the plaintiff, was to promote the sale of their respective publications, I could not help feeling that the parties were primarily concerned with the success of their competitions rather than the sale of their publications. I find it difficult, to say the least, to believe that any one would pay 25 cents for a copy of either "L'Information Sportive" or "Mots Croisés" if that was all he was getting. What the so-called purchaser of the paper or leaflet was really doing was buying a chance to win a prize in the so-called competition. It seems clear to me that what the plaintiff was really seeking was protection of his competition against the encroaching competition run by the defendant. Undoubtedly, it was this competition that ate into the profits he had made from his own competition when he was exclusively in the field. Thus, what the plaintiff was attempting to protect was the arrangement or system for conducting a competition that he said be had devised. Unfortunately for him, the law of copyright does not give him any such protection. Just as an author has no copyright in the ideas he has expressed even although they are original, but only in his expression of them, so also no person has any copyright in an arrangement or system or scheme or method for doing a particular thing even if he devised it himself. It is only in his description or expression of it that his copyright subsists. This principle was tersely put by Lindley L.J. in the leading case of Hollinrake v. Truswell, [1894] 3 Ch. D. 420 at 427 as follows:

> Copyright, however, does not extend to ideas, or schemes, or systems, or methods; it is confined to their expression; and if their expression is not copied the copyright is not infringed.

and there has never been any departure from this principle. I am, therefore, of the view that in seeking to protect his system for conducting a competition from encroachment by the defendant the plaintiff was attempting to use the law of copyright for a purpose to which it is not applicable. He claimed more than the law permits.

11 If the plaintiff has any copyright it must be in some original literary work. He was hard pressed on his cross-examination to identify the literary work to the protection of which his copyright is restricted and appeared to be torn between the description of his arrangement given in the letter of October 2,

1947, to the Commissioner of Patents in which the request for registration of a copyright was first made and the text giving the details and conditions of his "Concours: Recrutement d'Abonnés" that appeared on page 9 of each issue of "L'Information Sportive", but counsel for the plaintiff in an able argument contended that the literary work in which the plaintiff had his copyright consisted of the article or writing on page 9 of each issue of "L'Information Sportive" together with the subscription receipt that went with it. It was in these two documents that the plaintiff expressed and described his arrangement and system for conducting his competition. I see no reason why this identification of the literary work in which the plaintiff has his copyright should not be accepted. It is only for this work, and not for any ideas or any arrangement or system for conducting a competition expressed or described in it, that the plaintiff has any protection. If he is to succeed in an action for infringement of copyright he must show that his literary work has been copied. It will not be enough to prove that his ideas have been adopted or that his arrangement or system has been used.

. . .

13 There is, in my judgment, no doubt that the defendant's competition was similar in its essential principles to that conducted by the plaintiff. He made use of similar elements, namely, a numbered receipt, lists of clubs and the results of sports contests and a questionnaire and his arrangement of the elements and his system of conducting his competition were likewise similar. And it may well be that he acquired his knowledge of the arrangement and system he used for his competition from the expression and description contained in the plaintiff's literary work. If he did, there is nothing in the law of copyright that prevents him from so doing.

14 To succeed in his claim the plaintiff must show that the defendant copied, not his ideas or his arrangement or system, but his literary work. This, in my opinion, he cannot do. Counsel made much of certain facts and actions of the defendant prior to embarking on his own publication as indicative of his intentions. Undoubtedly, he was thoroughly familiar with the details of the plaintiff's competition and very deliberate in his preparations to leave the employ of "L'Information Sportive" and start a competition of his own. It is clear that he was concerned with the extent of the plaintiff's rights under his copyright for he made a special trip to the Copyright Office at Ottawa to enquire about the matter. Then he began to solicit distributors and vendors to see whether they would handle his publication if he brought one out. Then on the same day as he sent his telegram of resignation he registered his declaration of firm name and applied for registration of his own copyright. Then he had a discussion with Mr. Robert in which he questioned the value of the plaintiff's copyright and asked him to go in with him. Then they consulted two lawyers whose views as to the protection given by the plaintiff's copyright differed. Far from indicating an intention to infringe the plaintiff's copyright these actions of the defendant suggest carefulness on his part not to do so. Obviously, there must be similarities between the defendant's "Quizz général de la publication Loisir Favori Enrg." and the plaintiff's "Concours: Recrutement d'Abonnés" to the extent that both are based

on an arrangement of elements and a system for conducting a competition that are essentially the same but a comparison of the two literary works show that the former is not a copy of the latter. The lists of the clubs are different and the results of the sports contests are set out differently; the texts of the conditions and rules for the two competitions are not the same; the questions in the plaintiff's questionnaire relate to sports, whereas those in the defendant's quizz are of a general nature. The receipts likewise, although necessarily similar in that both are receipts, are different in text, type and appearance. Nor can the fact that in one issue of the plaintiff's paper the word "engagement" was used erroneously for "agencement" and a similar error appears on the back of the defendant's leaflet in the form of "engensement" outweigh the other evidence of difference. And while I have not overlooked the fact that copying need not be word for word if there is colourable imitation, I am also of the view that there should be no anxiety to find copying in a case such as this and thereby indirectly give protection to a system of competition such as that conducted by the plaintiff when the law does not give it directly.

15   Under the circumstances, I have no hesitation in finding that the defendant has not copied the plaintiff's literary work or otherwise infringed his copyright and that the plaintiff's action must be dismissed with costs.

Judgment accordingly.

Cuisenaire v. South West Imports Ltd., [1969] S.C.R. 208

Supreme Court of Canada

Cartwright C.J.C. and Fauteux, Martland, Ritchie and Hall JJ.

Judgment: December 20, 1968

. . .

Ritchie J.:

2   The actions were for the infringement of the plaintiff's alleged copyright in two sets of "coloured rods of uniform square at centre cross section and of ten different lengths and colours for the teaching of the science of arithmetic in primary school grades". The issues raised by the "special case" were:

. . .

3   The rods in question were made in conformity with a system or method of teaching arithmetic which is fully described in a book written by the appellant and entitled *Les Nombres en Couleurs*, and, as has been indicated, they were referred to in the plaintiff's pleadings as "works". Paragraph 8 of the Statement of Claim reads as follows:

Each of the said works is an original production in the scientific domain and is one of the works referred to by the expression 'every literary, dramatic, musical and artistic work' in section 4(1) of the *Copyright Act*.

The relevant provisions of the *Copyright Act*, R.S.C. 1952 Ch. 55 read as follows:

> 4. (1) Subject to the provisions of this Act, copyright shall subsist in Canada for the term hereinafter mentioned, *in every original literary, dramatic, musical and artistic work,*
>
> . . .

The italics are my own.

4 Section 2.(v) provides that:

> 'every original literary, dramatic, musical and artistic work' includes every original production in the literary, *scientific* or artistic *domain*, whatever may be the mode or form of its expression, such as books, pamphlets, and other writings, lectures, dramatic or dramatico-musical works, musical works or compositions with or without words, illustrations, sketches, and *plastic works* relative to geography, topography, architecture, or *science*.

The italics are my own.

5 In aid of the construction which appellant's counsel seeks to place upon these sections of the statute, he relies upon the presumption which he contends is created by s. 20(3) of the Act which reads:

> 20.(3) In any action for infringement of copyright in any work, in which the defendant puts in issue either the existence of the copyright, or the title of the plaintiff thereto, then, in any such case,
>
> (a) the work shall, unless the contrary is proved, be presumed to be a work in which copyright subsists; and
>
> (b) the author of the work shall, unless the contrary is proved, be presumed to be the owner of the copyright;
>
> . . .

6 The question which lies at the threshold of this appeal is whether the rods in question are things in which copyright can be had, and if that question is answered in the negative, it does not appear to me to be necessary to comment on the close analysis to which the learned trial judge has subjected the various statutory provisions.

. . .

8 Even if Mr. Cuisenaire's method of teaching could be considered as an "original production ... in the ... scientific domain" within the meaning of s.2(v) of the Act, the originality consisted in the ideas as they were expressed in his book and in my opinion the rods are merely devices which afford a practical means of employing the method and presenting it in graphic form to young children. The "original" work or production, whether it be characterized as literary, artistic or

scientific, was the book. In seeking to assert a copyright in the "rods" which are described in his book as opposed to the book itself, the appellant is faced with the principle stated by Davey L.J. in the case of *Hollinrake v. Truswell*, [1894] 3 Chancery 420 at 428, where he says:

> No doubt one may have copyright in the description of an art; but, having described it, you give it to the public for their use; and there is a clear distinction between the book which describes it, and the art or mechanical device which is described.

This principle was discussed and adopted by President Thorson in the Exchequer Court of Canada in *Moreau v. St. Vincent*, [1950] Ex. C.R. 198 at page 203, 10 Fox Pat. C. 194 at 198, where he said:

> It is, I think, an elementary principle of copyright law that an author has no copyright in ideas but only in his expression of them. The law of copyright does not give him any monopoly in the use of the ideas with which he deals or any property in them, even if they are original. His copyright is confined to the literary work in which he has expressed them. The ideas are public property, the literary work is his own. Every one may freely adopt and use the ideas but no one may copy his literary work without his consent.

This principle is recognized by Dr. Fox in the 2nd Edition (1967) of his work *The Canadian Law of Copyright and Industrial Designs* where he says, at page 45:

> Not only is it not required that there should be any originality in the idea of the work, but a novel idea as distinct from the form in which the idea is expressed is not capable of being the subject of copyright protection.

I have considered the many Canadian cases cited by Dr. Fox, all of which appear to illustrate this principle.

9 What is alleged in the present case is that the respondent has distributed to school trustees and others sets of rods which are substantially the same as those which the appellant claims to have made and that the respondent has thereby "without consent of the plaintiff reproduced and authorized the reproduction of the said works or a substantial part thereof ..." What has in fact happened is that the respondent has adopted and used the idea contained in the appellant's literary work and I find that its actions come directly within the language employed by President Thorson in the above quoted excerpt from his reasons for judgment. The matter is graphically illustrated by the brief quotation from the reasons for judgment of Page J. in *Cuisenaire v. Reed*, [1963] V.R. 719, cited by the learned trial judge, where the question at issue was whether the use and distribution of "rods" made in conformity with the directions contained in the present appellant's book, constituted a breach of copyright under the *Copyright Act* then in force in Australia. Page J. said, at page 735:

> Were the law otherwise, every person who carried out the instructions in the handbook in which copyright was held to subsist in *Meccano Ltd. v. Anthony Hordern and Sons Ltd.* (1918), 18 S. R. (N.S.W.) 606, and constructed a model in accordance with those instuctions, would infringe the plaintiff's literary copyright. Further, as Mr. Fullager put it, everybody who made a rabbit pie in accordance with

the recipe of *Mrs. Beeton's Cookery Book* would infringe the literary copyright in that book.

10 For these reasons I do not think that the "rods" in question are things in which copyright can be had and I would accordingly dismiss this appeal with costs.

Appeal dismissed with costs.

The Bulman Group Ltd. v. Alpha One-Write Systems Ltd. B.C. Ltd.
(1982), 16 B.L.R. 16 (F.C.)

Federal Court of Canada — Trial Division

Collier J.

Heard: January 19-22, 1982
Judgment: January 22, 1982
Docket: T-4572-78

. . .

Collier J.:

1 The plaintiff sues for copyright infringement in respect of nine business forms. The forms have identifying numbers. They are set out in Sched. A to the statement of claim. The forms are for use in the keeping of books of account in businesses, particularly in what was called "One Write" systems. The forms are designed in such a way that when combined with related forms and carbons, records are created in one writing, rather than in two or three separate, basically repetitive writings, in various books.

2 Addy J., in *Bulman Group Ltd. v. Alpha One-Write Systems, B.C. Ltd.* (1980), 54 C.P.R. (2d) 171 described generally the forms, and their use, as follows, at pp. 174-75:

> The accounting forms in issue, to which the copyright refers, are basically part of what is termed a 'one-write' system, the purpose being to avoid the necessity of repeating entries for bookkeeping and accounting purposes in various books of account and other financial documents required by a business. Several forms of different colours to facilitate recognition, with coinciding vertical and horizontal lines forming rectangular spaces for entries of figures, are fixed together temporarily on a board with small pegs which protrude through holes in the forms to keep the columns and lines perfectly aligned. When an entry is made on the top form, the same entry is automatically transferred by carbon imprint on the other forms underneath, thus, obviating the repetition of entries by other manual or mechanical means. Each form can then be removed and placed in its proper binder or sent out to third parties as the case may be. For instance, the first series of four forms in issue are part of a pay-roll system. The first form is an 'earnings record card' for each employee, the second is a 'payroll journal sheet,' the third is a 'pay-advice sheet' and the fourth is a 'salary cheque form' attached to a stub containing

the breakdown of earnings, various deductions, benefits, non-taxable allowances, etc. All of these four forms contain in a vertical column the same headings or sub-headings such as 'earnings', 'regular and overtime', 'gross earnings', 'paid benefits', 'deduction': 'U.I.C.', 'income tax', 'Canada pension' etc. In other words, all the required headings to break down and show in detail all of the particulars of an employee's earnings and benefits, the disposition which has been made of same and also whether they are taxable or non-taxable are shown and transferred by the one entry on the top one of the four forms. The other three forms in issue are part of two different systems, one being a 'cheque-writing system' which includes blank cheque forms and the other an 'accounts-payable system'. Basically, the idea is the same, although there is much less writing on the forms of these two last-mentioned categories. For instance, the 'accounts-payable form' pertaining to the 'accounts-payable system' merely has seven columns with the words 'date', 'detail', 'reference', 'discount', 'debit', 'credit' and 'balance' along an horizontal line with vertical columns under each of the headings. At the top of the page are the words 'name and address', 'account number' and 'sheet number'.

. . .

18   The South African case, *Kalamazoo Div. (Pty.) Ltd. v. Gay*, [1978] S.A.L.R. 184, was cited to me. The business forms there seem quite similar to some of those in issue here. The only question was whether copyright subsisted in the forms. If it did, infringement was conceded.

19   Mr. Buchanan frankly stated that, to give effect to his contention, I would likely have to distinguish the *Kalamazoo* case, disregard it, or consider it wrongly decided.

20   The *Kalamazoo* case, in my view, is correct in law. I follow it in finding for the plaintiff in this case. I refer to the following passages:

21   At pp. 188-89:

> The question for decision in this case is whether copyright subsists in the applicant's forms. Mr. Ipp, on behalf of the respondent, conceded that, if such copyright subsists, then it has been infringed. He advanced two main grounds, however, in support of the argument that the documents in question were not susceptible of copyright. In the first place he submitted that where documents form an integral part of a system they are not capable of copyright. Reliance for this proposition was placed on *Hollinrake v. Truswell*, [1894] 3 Ch. 420. In that case the plaintiff claimed copyright in a cardboard pattern sleeve containing upon it scales, figures and descriptive words for adapting it to sleeves of any dimensions. It was held that it was not capable of copyright as a 'map, chart, or plan' within the meaning of the Copyright Act then in force in England. I do not consider that *Hollinrake's* case is of assistance in the present matter. The facts there were entirely different. The so-called sleeve chart in respect of which copyright protection was sought was held to be in truth a measuring instrument, like a scaled ruler. It consisted of a piece of cardboard, so curved as to represent the parts of the arm above and below the elbow, with the following words printed on it: 'Top curve line; under curve line; under arm curves; measure round the thick part of the arm; measure round the thick part of the elbow; measure round the knuckles of the hand.' Lord Herschell LC pointed out that the words and figures on the chart do not in combination

convey any intelligible idea, nor could they be of the slightest use to anyone, apart from the cardboard upon which they were printed.

> They are not merely directions for the use of the cardboard, which is in truth a measuring apparatus, but they are a part of that very apparatus itself, without which it cannot be used, and except in connection with which they are absolutely useless.

LINDLEY LJ said [at p. 426]:

> The character of what is published is the test of copyright. If what is published is not separately published, is not a publication complete in itself, but is only a direction on a tool or machine, to be understood and used with it, such direction cannot, in my opinion, be severed from the tool or machine of which it is really part, and cannot be monopolized by its inventor under the *Copyright Act*.

The following description of the object which the Court had before it in *Hollinrake's* case was given by DAVEY LJ [at p. 428]:

> The sleeve chart before us gives no information or instruction ... It is a representation of the shape of a lady's arm, or more probably of a sleeve designed for a lady's arm, with certain scales for measurement upon it. It is intended, not for the purpose of giving information or pleasure, but for practical use in the art of dressmaking. It is, in fact, a mechanical contrivance, appliance or tool, for the better enabling a dressmaker to make her measurements for the purpose of cutting out the sleeve of a lady's dress, and is intended to be used for that purpose.

It will be seen that in the *Hollinrake* case the Court had to deal with a situation entirely different from the one presently before me. Here the applicant's forms are not printed on any instrument, apparatus, mechanical contrivance or tool, of which they are part and parcel or of which they form an integral, indivisible part. Nor can it be said that the forms do not convey any intelligible idea or that they cannot be of the slightest use to anyone, apart from an instrument to which they belong. They are publications complete in themselves and not only directions on a tool or machine from which they cannot be severed. In the circumstances and on the facts of this case I do not think that the *Hollinrake* case can be used as authority for the proposition that no copyright can subsist in respect of the applicant's forms. I also do not agree with the suggestion by counsel for the respondents that what applicant is in effect claiming in this case is copyright in a system.

And at p. 191:

> Mr. Ipp argued that whatever labour or judgment was involved in connection with the production of the applicant's forms was expended not on the compilation of the forms as such but rather on the development and proper functioning of an office system in connection with which the forms are used. I do not agree. It seems to me that the amount of labour, skill and judgment bestowed by Mr. Barr on the compilation of the forms themselves is sufficiently substantial to attract copyright. In any event I do not consider that the fact that the forms were designed and intended for use in an office system such as that described by Mr. Barr means that they can no longer be regarded as proper subject-matter for copyright. In developing his argument Mr. Ipp contended, if I understood him correctly, that the

skill, labour and ingenuity expended by Mr. Barr was directed to the production of information or the creation of a system and not to the preparation or production of the forms. He referred to the principle that there can be no copyright in information or ideas and argued, in effect, that Mr. Barr was not basically concerned with the production of documents but with information leading to a system which he wanted to put into operation. I do not think there is any substance in this argument. Mr. Barr's activities were not directed to the production of noncopyright information to be made available to the public but to the production of compilations of a particular kind, designed and arranged in a particular way and containing and expressing information in a particular manner. A somewhat similar argument to the one addressed to me in this case was advanced by counsel and rejected by the Court in *Football League Ltd. v. Littlewoods Pools Ltd.*, [[1959] Ch. 637, [1959] 2 All E.R. 546], a case to which Mr. Ipp referred. See further [*Ladbroke (Football) Ltd. v. William Hill Ltd.*, [1964] 1 W.L.R. 273, [1964] 1 All E.R. 465 (H.L.)] where many of the aspects that arise in this case were considered and where Lord Reid made the interesting observation [at pp. 470 ff.] that the cases where copyright has been denied to a compilation are comparatively few.

22 The plaintiff is entitled to succeed in this action.

(b) Merger

i. U.S. Merger Doctrine

In some circumstances it is so difficult to distinguish between an idea and its expression that the two are said to merge. In such instances, rigorously protecting the expression will confer a monopoly over the idea itself. To prevent this consequence, courts in the United States have developed the merger doctrine. Under the concept of merger, if the idea and the author's particular way of expressing that idea cannot be separated, or the idea can be expressed in only a very limited number of ways, then others should not be barred from copying the expression. This result ensures that the author's zone of exclusivity does not encompass ideas or information that belong in the public domain. In this sense, the doctrine can be said to prioritize the public domain over the author's right to control what may be minimally original expression.

Morrissey v. Procter & Gamble Company

379 F.2d 675 (1st Cir., 1967)

United States Court of Appeals for the First Circuit

Aldrich, Chief Judge.

This is an appeal from a summary judgment for the defendant. The plaintiff, Morrissey, is the copyright owner of a set of rules for a sales promotional contest of the 'sweepstakes' type involving the social security numbers of the participants. Plaintiff alleges that the defendant, Procter & Gamble Company, infringed, by copying, almost precisely, Rule 1. In its motion for summary judgment, based upon affidavits and depositions, defendant denies that plaintiff's Rule 1 is copyrightable material, and denies access. The district court held for the defendant.

. . .

The second aspect of the case raises a more difficult question. Before discussing it we recite plaintiff's Rule 1, and defendant's Rule 1, the italicizing in the latter being ours to note the defendant's variations or changes.

'1. Entrants should print name, address and social security number on a boxtop, or a plain paper. Entries must be accompanied by * * * boxtop or by plain paper on which the name * * * is copied from any source. Official rules are explained on * * * packages or leaflets obtained from dealer. If you do not have a social security number you may use the name and number of any member of your immediate family living with you. Only the person named on the entry will be deemed an entrant and may qualify for prize. 'Use the correct social security number belonging to the person named on entry * * * wrong number will be disqualified.' (Plaintiff's Rule)

'1. Entrants should print name, address and Social Security number on a Tide boxtop, or on (a) plain paper. Entries must be accompanied by Tide boxtop (any size) or by plain paper on which the name 'Tide' is copied from any source. Official rules are available on Tide Sweepstakes packages, or on leaflets at Tide dealers, or you can send a stamped, self-addressed envelope to: Tide 'Shopping Fling' Sweepstakes, P.O. Box 4459, Chicago 77, Illinois. 'If you do not have a Social Security number, you may use the name and number of any member of your immediate family living with you. Only the person named on the entry will be deemed an entrant and may qualify for a prize. 'Use the correct Social Security number, belonging to the person named on the entry — wrong numbers will be disqualified.' (Defendant's Rule)

The district court, following an earlier decision, Gaye v. Gillis, D.Mass., 1958, 167 F.Supp. 416, took the position that since the substance of the contest was not copyrightable, which is unquestionably correct, Baker v. Selden, 1879, 101 U.S. 99, 25 L.Ed. 841; Affiliated Enterprises v. Gruber, 1 Cir., 1936, 86 F.2d 958; Chamberlin v. Uris Sales Corp., 2 Cir., 1945, 150 F.2d 512, and the substance was relatively simple, it must follow that plaintiff's rule sprung directly from the substance and 'contains no original creative authorship.' 262 F.Supp. at 738. This does not follow. Copyright attaches to form of expression, and defendant's own proof, introduced to deluge the court on the issue of access, itself established that there was more than one way of expressing even this simple substance. Nor, in view of the almost precise similarity of the two rules, could defendant successfully invoke the principle of a stringent standard for showing infringement which some courts apply when the subject matter involved admits of little variation in form of expression. E.g., Dorsey v. Old Surety Life Ins. Co.,

10 Cir., 1938, 98 F.2d 872, 874, 119 A.L.R. 1250 ('a showing of appropriation in the exact form or substantially so.'); Continental Casualty Co. v. Beardsley, 2 Cir., 1958, 253 F.2d 702, 705, cert. denied, 358 U.S. 816, 79 S.Ct. 25, 3 L.Ed.2d 58 ('a stiff standard for proof of infringement.').

Nonetheless, we must hold for the defendant. When the uncopyrightable subject matter is very narrow, so that 'the topic necessarily requires,' Sampson & Murdock Co. v. Seaver-Radford Co., 1 Cir., 1905, 140 F. 539, 541; cf. Kaplan, An Unhurried View of Copyright, 64-65 (1967), if not only one form of expression, at best only a limited number, to permit copyrighting would mean that a party or parties, by copyrighting a mere handful of forms, could exhaust all possibilities of future use of the substance. In such circumstances it *679 does not seem accurate to say that any particular form of expression comes from the subject matter. However, it is necessary to say that the subject matter would be appropriated by permitting the copyrighting of its expression. We cannot recognize copyright as a game of chess in which the public can be checkmated. Cf. Baker v. Selden, supra.

Upon examination the matters embraced in Rule 1 are so straightforward and simple that we find this limiting principle to be applicable. Furthermore, its operation need not await an attempt to copyright all possible forms. It cannot be only the last form of expression which is to be condemned, as completing defendant's exclusion from the substance. Rather, in these circumstances, we hold that copyright does not extend to the subject matter at all, and plaintiff cannot complain even if his particular expression was deliberately adopted.

Affirmed.

Herbert Rosenthal Jewelry Corp. v. Kalpakian, 446 F.2d 738 (9th Cir., 1971)

United States Court of Appeals, Ninth Circuit

Browning, Circuit Judge:

Plaintiff and defendants are engaged in the design, manufacture, and sale of fine jewelry.

Plaintiff charged defendants with infringing plaintiff's copyright registration of a pin in the shape of a bee formed of gold encrusted with jewels. A consent decree was entered, reciting that the parties had agreed to a settlement of the action and entry of the decree. It provided that plaintiff's copyright of the jeweled bee was "good and valid in law," that defendants had manufactured a jeweled bee "alleged to be similar," and that defendants were enjoined from infringing plaintiff's copyright and from manufacturing or selling copies of plaintiff's jeweled bee pin.

Later plaintiff filed a motion for an order holding defendants in contempt of the consent decree. The district court, after an evidentiary hearing, found that while defendants had manufactured and sold a line of jeweled bee pins, they designed their pins themselves after a study of bees in nature and in published works and did not copy plaintiff's copyrighted bee. The court further found that defendants' jeweled bees were "not substantially similar" to plaintiff's bees, except that both "do look like bees." The court concluded that defendants had neither infringed plaintiff's copyright nor violated the consent decree, and entered a judgment order denying plaintiff's motion. We affirm.

I

Both in this court and below, the parties have assumed that defendants are bound by their concession of the validity of plaintiff's copyright in the consent decree. Although we accept that assumption for purposes of this litigation, we expressly save the question whether the line of cases upon which the assumption is based, *see* Siebring v. Hansen, 346 F.2d 474, 477 (8th Cir. 1965), and cases cited, survived Lear, Inc. v. Adkins, 395 U.S. 653, 89 S.Ct. 1902, 23 L.Ed.2d 610 (1969), and in this circuit, Massillon-Cleveland-Akron Sign Co. v. Golden State Advertising Co., 444 F.2d 425 (9th Cir. 1971). See also, Blonder-Tongue Laboratories, Inc. v. University of Illinois Foundation, 402 U.S. 313, 91 S.Ct. 1434, 28 L.Ed.2d 788 (1971).

II

Plaintiff contends that its copyright registration of a jeweled bee entitles it to protection from the manufacture and sale by others of any object that to the ordinary observer is substantially similar in appearance. The breadth of this claim is evident. For example, while a photograph of the copyrighted bee pin attached to the complaint depicts a bee with nineteen small white jewels on its back, plaintiff argues that its copyright is infringed by defendants' entire line of a score or more jeweled bees in three sizes decorated with from nine to thirty jewels of various sizes, kinds, and colors.

Although plaintiff's counsel asserted that the originality of plaintiff's bee pin lay in a particular arrangement of jewels on the top of the pin, the elements of this arrangement were never identified. Defendants' witnesses testified that the "arrangement" was simply a function of the size and form of the bee pin and the size of the jewels used. Plaintiff's counsel, repeatedly pressed by the district judge, was unable to suggest how jewels might be placed on the back of a pin in the shape of a bee without infringing plaintiff's copyright. He eventually conceded, 'not being a jeweler, I can't conceive of how he might rearrange the design so it is dissimilar.'

If plaintiff's understanding of its rights were correct, its copyright would effectively prevent others from engaging in the business of manufacturing and selling jeweled bees. We think plaintiff confuses the balance Congress struck between protection and competition under the Patent Act and the Copyright Act.

The owner of a patent is granted the exclusive right to exploit for a period of seventeen years (a maximum of fourteen years for design patents) the conception that is the subject matter of the patent. 35 U.S.C. §§ 154, 173. The grant of this monopoly, however, is carefully circumscribed by substantive and procedural protections. To be patentable the subject matter must be new and useful, and represent a nonobvious advance — one requiring "more ingenuity and skill than that possessed by an ordinary mechanic acquainted with the business"; an advance that would not be obvious to a hypothetical person skilled in the art and charged with knowledge of all relevant developments publicly known to that point in time. Graham v. John Deere Co., 383 U.S. 1, 86 S.Ct. 684, 15 L.Ed.2d 545 (1966). A patent is granted only after an independent administrative inquiry and determination that these substantive standards have been met. 35 U.S.C. § 131. This determination is subject to both administrative and court review. 35 U.S.C. §§ 134, 141, 145, 146.

Copyright registration, on the other hand, confers no right at all to the conception reflected in the registered subject matter. "Unlike a patent, a copyright gives no exclusive right to the art disclosed; protection is given only to the expression of the idea — not the idea itself." Mazer v. Stein, 347 U.S. 201, 217, 74 S.Ct. 460, 470, 98 L.Ed. 630 (1954). Accordingly, the prerequisites for copyright registration are minimal. The work offered for registration need only be the product of the registrant. So long as it is not a plagiarized copy of another's effort, there is no requirement that the work differ substantially from prior works or that it contribute anything of value. "The copyright protects originality rather than novelty or invention." *Id.* at 218, 74 S.Ct. at 471. A copyright is secured simply by publishing the work with the required notice, 17 U.S.C. § 10, and registration is accomplished simply by filing a claim and depositing copies of the work with the Register of Copyrights, 17 U.S.C. §§ 11, 13. There is no administrative investigation or determination of the validity of the claim. A certificate is refused only if the object falls outside the broad category of matter subject to copyright registration. 17 U.S.C. §§ 4-5. A copyright affords little protection. It confers "only 'the sole right of multiplying copies.' Absent copying there can be no infringement of copyright." Mazer v. Stein, *supra*, 347 U.S. at 218, 74 S.Ct. at 471. Because the registrant's protection is limited and the social cost therefore small, the life of the copyright is long and, under current proposals, potentially even longer — now twenty-eight years plus a renewal period of twenty-eight more, 17 U.S.C. § 24, and, under Copyright Revision Bill § 543, 91st Congress, 1st Session, the life of the author plus fifty years.

Obviously a copyright must not be treated as equivalent to a patent lest long continuing private monopolies be conferred over areas of gainful activity without first satisfying the substantive and procedural prerequisites to the grant of such privileges.

Because copyright bars only copying, perhaps this case could be disposed of on the district court's finding that defendants did not copy plaintiff's bee pin. It is true that defendants had access to plaintiff's pin and that there is an obvious similarity between plaintiff's pin and those of defendants. These two facts constitute strong circumstantial evidence of copying. But they are not conclusive, Overman v. Loesser, 205 F.2d 521, 523 (9th Cir. 1953); Nimmer on Copyright §§ 139.4, 141.2, and there was substantial evidence to support the trial court's finding that defendant's pin was in fact an independent creation. Defendants testified to independent creation from identified sources other than plaintiff's pin. The evidence established defendants' standing as designers of fine jewelry and reflected that on earlier occasions they had designed jeweled pins in the form of living creatures other than bees, including spiders, dragonflies, and other insects, birds, turtles, and frogs. Any inference of copying based upon similar appearance lost much of its strength because both pins were lifelike representations of a natural creature. Moreover, there were differences between defendants' and plaintiff's bees — notably in the veining of the wings.

Although this evidence would support a finding that defendants' bees were their own work rather than copied from plaintiff's, this resolution of the problem is not entirely satisfactory, particularly in view of the principle that copying need not be conscious, but "may be the result of subconscious memory derived from hearing, seeing or reading the copyrighted work at some time in the past." Howell's Copyright Law 129 (4th ed. 1962). See Sheldon v. MetroGoldwyn Pictures Corp., 81 F.2d 49, 54 (2d Cir. 1936); Harold Lloyd Corp. v. Witwer, 65 F.2d 1, 16 (9th Cir. 1933). It seems unrealistic to suppose that defendants could have closed their minds to plaintiff's highly successful jeweled bee pin as they designed their own.

A finding that defendants "copied" plaintiff's pin in this sense, however, would not necessarily justify judgment against them. A copyright, we have seen, bars use of the particular "expression" of an idea in a copyrighted work but does not bar use of the "idea" itself. Others are free to utilize the "idea" so long as they do not plagiarize its "expression." As the court said in Trifari, Krussman & Fishel, Inc. v. B. Steinberg-Kaslo Co., 144 F.Supp. 577, 580 (S.D.N.Y.1956), where the copyrighted work was a jeweled pin representing a hansom cab, "though an alleged infringer gets the idea of a hansom cab pin from a copyrighted article there can be no infringement unless the article itself has been copied. The idea of a hansom cab cannot be copyrighted. Nevertheless plaintiff's expression of that idea, as embodied in its pin, can be copyrighted." Or as Judge Hand put it in Sheldon v. Metro-Goldwyn Pictures Corp., supra, 81 F.2d at 54, "defendants were entitled to use, not only all that had gone before, but even the plaintiffs' contribution itself, if they drew from it only the more general patterns; that is, if they kept clear of its 'expression." See also Millworth Converting Corp. v. Slifka, 276 F.2d 443, 445 (2d Cir. 1960).

The critical distinction between "idea" and "expression" is difficult to draw. As Judge Hand candidly wrote, 'Obviously, no principle can be stated as to when an imitator has gone beyond copying the 'idea,' and has borrowed its "expression." Peter Pan Fabrics, Inc. v. Martin Weiner Corp., 274 F.2d 487, 489 (2d Cir. 1960). At least in close cases, one may suspect, the classification the court selects may simply state the result reached rather than the reason for it. In our view, the difference is really one of degree as Judge Hand suggested in his striking "abstraction" formulation in Nichols v. Universal Pictures Corp., 45 F.2d 119, 121 (2d Cir. 1930). The guiding consideration in drawing the line is the preservation of the balance between competition and protection reflected in the patent and copyright laws.

What is basically at stake is the extent of the copyright owner's monopoly — from how large an area of activity did Congress intend to allow the copyright owner to exclude others? We think the production of jeweled bee pins is a larger private preserve than Congress intended to be set aside in the public market without a patent. A jeweled bee pin is therefore an 'idea' that defendants were free to copy. Plaintiff seems to agree, for it disavows any claim that defendants cannot manufacture and sell jeweled bee pins and concedes that only plaintiff's particular design or "expression" of the jeweled bee pin 'idea' is protected under its copyright. The difficulty, as we have noted, is that on this record the 'idea' and its 'expression' appear to be indistinguishable. There is no greater similarity between the pins of plaintiff and defendants than is inevitable from the use of jewel-encrusted bee forms in both.

When the "idea" and its "expression" are thus inseparable, copying the "expression" will not be barred, since protecting the "expression" in such circumstances would confer a monopoly of the "idea" upon the copyright owner free of the conditions and limitations imposed by the patent law. Baker v. Selden, 101 U.S. 99, 103, 25 L.Ed. 841 (1879); Morrissey v. Procter & Gamble Co., 379 F.2d 675, 678-679 (1st Cir. 1967); Crume v. Pacific Mut. Life Ins. Co., 140 F.2d 182, 184 (7th Cir. 1944). See also Continental Cas. Co. v. Beardsley, 253 F.2d 702, 705-706 (2d Cir. 1958).

Affirmed.

---

ii. Merger in Canada

At one time there was doubt as to whether the merger doctrine applied in Canada or the extent of its application. While Canadian courts do not ordinarily expressly state they apply the "merger" doctrine in separating the protectable from the non-protectable parts of a work, it is clear that those aspects of a work which are commonplace and must necessarily be used as incident to an idea, system or process have never been protectable under Anglo-Canadian copyright law.[13]

Kilvington Bros. Ltd. v. Goldberg (1957), 16 Fox Pat. C. 164 (Sup. Ct.)

Judson J.

Judgment: 1957

. . .

Judson J.:

1 The plaintiff is a limited company which manufactures and sells tombstones. The defendant partnership is in the same business. The defendant Sniderman purchased a tombstone from the Goldbergs. It is alleged that this tombstone is a reproduction of a design in which the plaintiff claims copyright.

2 In 1950 or 1951 one C.E. Ridsdale, a designer employed by the plaintiff, drew the design (Ex. 1) upon which the claim is based. If copyright exists in the design, it belongs to the plaintiff as a work made in the course of Ridsdale's employment. Ex. 1 is a drawing to scale. It shows an oblong tombstone of greater length than height. The face has three panels, the centre panel being a sunken one. In this centre panel there is a lamp and a flame. Above the flame there is a symbol of the star of David. The top is known in the trade as a peaked top. Such a tombstone as this is intended for a double grave. This is the reason for the double raised panels with the centre sunken panel. One side is meant to have the inscription for the male members of the family, the other for the female members.

3 The tombstone made by the Goldberg firm for Mr. Sniderman has the characteristics that I have just described, with this difference: The star of David is at the top of the right hand panel, instead of being over the flame in the centre sunken panel. The left hand panel at the top has a carving of a seven-branched candelabra called the Menorah. Twenty or twenty-five photographs of tombstones from cemeteries in Toronto were filed as exhibits. These show that tombstones having these characteristics are commonly known in the business and have been so known for a long time. Nevertheless, the plaintiff claims copyright in its design as an original artistic work.

. . .

7 There are many similarities between Goldberg's work and the plaintiff's design, but once the customer decides on a certain type of tombstone these are inevitable. The top, the two raised panels, the sunken panel with the lamp and flame and the symbolism are conventional. The height of the stone is governed by the regulations of the cemetery. This, to a certain extent, determines the proportions of the work. There are also differences, and in my opinion significant differences — particularly in the flame and the lamp. Goldberg says that he drew these freehand and did not copy them from the plaintiff's work. His evidence is supported by the physical result, and I accept it as I do the rest of his evidence in denial of copying. The similarities are plain to be seen but they do not enable me to draw an inference of copying. Tombstone workers working on a task of this kind are working with common ideas and with only a limited field for the expression of these ideas. It is not surprising that the results are similar. The plaintiff cannot, by making a design embodying conventional ideas, obtain a monopoly of the use of these ideas. Others are entitled to use these ideas provided they do so by going to the common source and do not copy the plaintiff's

---

13   *Designers Guild Ltd. v. Russell Williams (Textiles) Ltd.*, [2000] 1 W.L.R. 2416 (H.L.) at pp. 2422-2423;

expression. There is, therefore, no infringement of copyright and the action fails at this point.

. . .

Action dismissed with costs.

Les Promotions Antiques v. Hardcraft Industries (1987), 13 C.I.P.R. 194
(F.C.)

Federal Court of Canada — Trial Division

Strayer J.

Heard: May 21, June 29 and 30, 1987
Judgment: August 10, 1987
Docket: No. T-1013-87

. . .

***Strayer J.*:**

1 This was an application for an interlocutory injunction to prevent the defendants and their retailer customers from marketing the ROTAWASH and AUTO PAL brushes by use of packaging like that of the plaintiff's or in such way as to cause confusion between those brushes and the plaintiff's brush or to pass off the defendants' brushes as the plaintiff's.

. . .

5 ... As for the instructions it is of course apparent that the defendants have copied the instructions which appear on the back of plaintiff's package. There now appears to be some doubt as to the authorship of those instructions. Further there could be a serious legal dispute as to whether such instructions, simple and brief as they are, can be the subject of copyright. I am somewhat persuaded by the reasoning in an American decision, *Morrissey v. Procter & Gamble Co.*, 379 F. 2d 675 (U.S. C.A., 1st Circ., 1967) in which it was said that there could not be copyright in a set of instructions for a mail-in contest. As the subject itself is not the subject of copyright and is very narrow in its nature so that only one or a very limited number of ways exist to describe it, such description or instructions cannot be the subject of copyright or this would preclude others from using or engaging in the subject itself. I would distinguish cases such as that relied on by the plaintiff, *B.C. Jockey Club v. Standen (Winbar Publications)*, 66 B.C.L.R. 245, [1985] 6 W.W.R. 683, 8 C.P.R. (3d) 283, *(sub nom. B.C. Jockey Club v. Standen)* 22 D.L.R. (4th) 467 (B.C. C.A.), as in that case the original material produced by the plaintiff involved a large measure of labour, skill, and judgment. Such is not the case here. While of course I need not, and do not, decide the validity of the copyright claim, it is relevant to observe that the legal position is far from clear which militates against the plaintiff obtaining an interlocutory injunction.

· · ·

8 Having regard to all these factors, I have concluded that I should exercise my discretion at this time against granting an interlocutory injunction.

Application refused.

Apple Computer Inc. v. Mackintosh Computers Ltd. (1986), 28 D.L.R. (4th) 178 (F.C.T.D.), affirmed 18 C.P.R. (3d) 129 (Fed. C.A.), affirmed 30 C.P.R. (3d) 257 (S.C.C.)

Federal Court of Canada — Trial Division

Reed J.

**Heard: January 21-24, 28-31, February 3-7 and 10, 1986
Judgment: April 29, 1986
Docket: Nos. T-1232-84 and T-1235-84**

· · ·

Reed J.:

1 The issue for decision in this case is a narrow but important one: is a computer program when embodied in a silicon chip in the computer a subject matter in which copyright exists?

· · ·

Expression — Idea — Merger

53 It is argued that copyright does not extend to computer programs because (1) copyright protects the expression of the idea not the idea expressed and (2) a computer program as embodied in a ROM chip exhibits a merger of the idea and the expression of that idea.

54 Counsel for the defendants relies heavily on the decision in: Cuisenaire v. South West Imports Ltd., [1968] 1 Ex. C.R. 493, 37 Fox Pat. C. 93, 54 C.P.R. 1 (Ex. Ct.) as affirmed [1969] S.C.R. 208, 40 Fox Pat. C. 81, 57 C.P.R. 76 (S.C.C.), and in Cuisenaire v. Reed, [1963] V.R. 719 (S.C. of Victoria). Those cases involved a publication by the plaintiff (a book) in which a new method of teaching arithmetic was described. The method used a number of wooden rods of varying lengths and colours, all having a uniform thickness (one centimetre square). The book set out a table describing the number of rods required, their respective lengths and colours. There was no indication that the book contained any diagrams or illustrations of the rods. I reproduce part of the editor's note at 37 Fox Pat. C. 93 at 95:

> It will be noted that, ... the plaintiff did not allege that his copyright in his book was being infringed but only his copyright in his rods. ... If the rods in issue had been copied from illustrations in the plaintiff's book, the result might well have

been different, for it is trite law that infringement exists where a copyright work is reproduced 'in any material form whatsoever'.

55 The claim before the Canadian Courts focused on subs. 2(v) of the Canadian Copyright Act, R.S.C. 1952, c. 55:

> 'every original literary, dramatic, musical and artistic work' includes every original production in the literary, scientific or artistic domain *whatever may be the mode or form of its expression, such as* books, pamphlets, and other writings, lectures, dramatic or dramatico-musical works, musical works or compositions with or without words, illustrations, sketches, and plastic works relative to geography, topography, architecture or science;

(underlining added) The plaintiff argued that it was not necessary to demonstrate that his rods were artistic, literary, musical or dramatic because as long as they were "original productions in the scientific domain" they were to be considered as falling within the scope of works protected by copyright. Both the Exchequer Court and the Supreme Court rejected that argument.

56 The plaintiff claimed that even if the rods could not be said to fall within the Act pursuant to s. 2, they were nevertheless literary or artistic works or works of artistic craftsmanship. That argument was rejected by both Canadian Courts on the same ground as it had been by the Australian Court in Cuisenaire v. Reed. Mr. Justice Noel, at trial [p. 117 Fox Pat. C.], quoted from the judgment of Mr. Justice Pape, in Cuisenaire v. Reed at pp. 735- 36:

> ... Where, as here, you have a literary copyright in certain tables or compilations, there is in my view no infringement of the copyright in those tables or compilations unless that which is produced is itself something in the nature of a table or compilation which, whether it be in two dimensions or three dimensions, and whatever its material form, reproduces those tables. Were the law otherwise, every person who carried out the instructions in the handbook in which copyright was held to subsist in Meccano Ltd. v. Anthony Hordern and Sons Ltd. (1918), 18 S.R. (N.S.W.) 606, and constructed a model in accordance with those instructions, would infringe the plaintiff's literary copyright. Further, as Mr. Fullagar put it, everybody who made a rabbit pie in accordance with the recipe in *Mrs. Beeton's Cookery Book* would infringe the literary copyright in that book. ...

(underlining added)

57 The Supreme Court upheld the judgment of Mr. Justice Noel on essentially the same ground. The Court noted at p. 84, that the original work was the plaintiff's book and that in seeking to assert a copyright in the rods which were described in the book, as opposed to the book itself, the appellant was faced with the principle that an author has no copyright in ideas but only in his expression of them. Reference was made to the application of this principle in Hollinrake v. Truswell, [1894] 3 Ch. 420 at 428 (C.A.) and Moreau v. St. Vincent, 10 Fox Pat. C. 194, [1950] Ex. C.R. 198 at 203, 12 C.P.R. 32, [1950] 3 D.L.R. 713.

58 In Hollinrake v. Truswell, it was sought to assert copyright in a "sleeve chart" designed to operate as a pattern for cutting out sleeves. The Court held

that "The thing is in truth a measuring instrument: it is no more a chart or plan within the Copyright Act than is a scaled ruler..." (Lindley L.J. at p. 425).

59 In Moreau v. St. Vincent, the plaintiff alleged the defendant had breached his copyright in "Concours: Recrutement d'Abonnés". This title referred to a weekly competition which was designed to increase the circulation of the plaintiff's paper "L'Information Sportive". The competition involved a subscription receipt held by the purchaser of the paper; a questionnaire relating to sports topics to be answered by holders of subscription receipts carrying certain numbers and conditions; and, terms of the contest set out in the paper. The defendant commenced publication of a weekly leaflet called "Mots croisés" which contained a competition called "Quizz Général de la Publication Loisir Favori Enrg." The Court rejected the plaintiff's claim that this activity infringed his copyright. The Court stated that the plaintiff had misconceived the nature of copyright and was really seeking protection of his contest against an encroaching competitor who was running a contest of a similar nature. But, there was no copying of the relevant written texts — it was the idea of running a contest along generally similar lines which was copied.

60 It appears from these cases that the principle that copyright covers the expression of ideas but not the ideas themselves is used in the jurisprudence to cover at least two different situations. It is used in cases such as Hollinrake and Cuisenaire to indicate that the "work" for which copyright is sought is not of a type (eg: literary, artistic) that falls within the Act. In Cuisenaire v. Reed, it was held that the rods themselves as physical objects were not a type of work covered by the Act. It is used in cases such as Moreau to indicate that the two works in issue are not, in fact, similar — there has been no substantial copying. Thus in making Mrs. Beeton's rabbit pie, there is no substantial copying of the recipe book — the instructions found therein have been followed but the book has not been copied.

61 Neither of these applications of the idea-expression principle apply in the present case. The program as originally written is copyrightable subject-matter. There has in fact been copying — the code read from the defendants' chips is the same as that which can be read from the plaintiffs' chips. I do not see that the decision in the Cuisenaire case in any way assists the defendants in this case. The computer program when written is clearly a literary work. What is more, its embodiment in a silicon chip retains the form of expression of the original work. The program in its source code version can be retrieved (read) by a process of translation or translations from the ROM chip. There was no such relationship between the words in the book "Nombres en Couleurs" and the rods which were in issue in the Cuisenaire case. No part of the text of the book could be retrieved or "read" from the rods.

62 Counsel argues that in copying the ROM the defendants are doing no more than following the recipe prescribed by the program, ie: making Mrs. Beeton's apple pie. I think a closer analogy is that what they are doing is copying the recipe book.

63   What then of counsel's argument that a computer program exhibits a merger of the idea and the expression of the idea and therefore it is not copyrightable. I have considerable difficulty with this argument from a number of points of view. In the first place, if this argument is valid then it is difficult to understand why the concession was made that the assembly code version of the program is copyrightable. Surely if there is a merger of idea and expression, it exists not only in the machine code version of the program but also in the written assembly code version as well. Secondly, the exact scope of the legal rule (if one exists) that when there is a merger of the idea with its expression, copyright protection does not operate, is not at all clear. And, thirdly, the evidence that there is a multitude of forms of expression in which any given program can be written seems to me to demonstrate that there is no merger of the idea and the expression of the idea with respect to the programs in issue.

64   The Cuisenaire, Hollinrake and Moreau decisions do not stand for the proposition, urged by counsel, that when there exists a merger of the idea and the expression thereof this renders the work uncopyrightable. I have not been referred to any United Kingdom, Australian or Canadian case where that rule has been applied as the ratio of the case. Counsel's argument in the present case seems to be that there is a merger of idea and expression because there can be only one pattern in the ROM chip: i.e. one way of structuring that chip to enable it to replicate the plaintiffs' program. But this clearly cannot be a case of merger rendering the device uncopyrightable because the same can equally be said of every record or cassette tape.

65   I cannot disguise the fact that in seeking to apply the alleged merger rule I have considerable difficulty; it seems to me that many works which are clearly copyrightable exhibit a merger of the idea they convey and the expression thereof: a poem, a play, a painting, a map, a chart. It is only if the idea communicated by such works is described in highly abstract, remote and general terms that one could say there is no merger of the idea they convey and the expression in which that idea is conveyed. In addition, the word "idea" itself is of varying definition.

66   Examples given in argument of the application of the merger principle are formulations such as $E = mc^2$, the phythogorean theorem, or various algebraic proofs. It may be that these examples demonstrate nothing more than that the particular idea being expressed is really information about the external world (recognizing that $E = mc^2$ is in fact a hypothesis) and that factual information is something which copyright does not protect. I see an analogy, for example, between a statement such as "the Prime Minister of Canada met with the President of the United States on March 17" and "the square on the hypotenuse of a right-angled triangle is equal to the sum of the squares on the other two sides". Neither of these phrases as such, apart from a larger text in which they might appear, would be subject of copyright. The example of algebraic proofs leads, it seems to me, to an almost philosophical discussion of the nature of intellectual thought. It is a discussion which a higher Court than this may find it necessary to consider but which I consider it sufficient to deal with by noting that a computer program is not similar to any of the examples cited. It is not a statement

reporting a fact. It is not comparable to an algebraic proof. It is a creation in the same way that an instruction book is a creation. While copyright would not prevent someone making Mrs. Beeton's rabbit pie (indeed it was to encourage people to do so that Mrs. Beeton's Book of Household Management was first published), it does prevent someone copying the book itself. The order in which the recipes are listed, the form and expression in which they are couched are properly the subject of copyright. This order, form, pattern of expression of the plaintiffs' program is retained in the ROM and is copied when the defendants copy the ROM.

67 There is another branch of the merger doctrine which has prevailed in the United States and which it is necessary to consider. It would appear to have originated with the decision in Baker v. Selden, 101 U.S. 99 (1879), a case referred to in several "commonwealth" decisions, but without reliance on the full scope of the decision given therein. Baker v. Selden dealt with copyright claimed in a book which described a new system of accounting and particularly accounting forms (consisting of certain ruled lines and headings) contained in the book. The Court found that the defendant's use of the book and development of his own forms did not breach the plaintiff's copyright: i.e. there was no substantial copying. But the Court went further and drew a distinction between works of science or instruction and other types of works. It held that where a useful art could only be employed by using the forms or diagrams by which it was explained there would be no copyright in such forms and diagrams.

68 The Court thus proceeded to lay down a much broader rule than was necessary for the purpose of the case: it held that the forms in the books were not protected by copyright. There is no doubt that this conclusion was in part at least shaped by the wording of congressional legislative authority under the United States Constitution. This has given the United States copyright law a form and development particular to that country.

69 The Baker v. Selden decision, even in the United States, however, has been criticized as wrongly decided: Nimmer on Copyright (1985), vol. 1, para. 2.18. This criticism proceeds in part on the basis that it is simply inaccurate to think that expositions on science or the useful arts require that any particular form provided in the original exposition must be followed in order to avail oneself of the "idea" of the work. All such works it is noted can be expressed in a variety of forms.

70 This development of copyright law is not one that has been adopted in this country, as far as I know. Indeed rejection thereof would seem to be implicit in the Court of Appeal's decision in Bulman Group Ltd. v. Alpha One-Write Systems B.C. Ltd., supra, and in the subsequent decision of the Trial Division Bulman Group Ltd. v. "One Write" Accounting Systems Ltd., supra. At issue in those cases was the copyrightability of accounting forms. Initially the claim for copyright in such forms was rejected by the Trial Division on an application for an interlocutory injunction. The Court of Appeal overturned that decision indicating that there was a seriously arguable case. Following full trial of the

issue, copyright was held to exist (this decision was not appealed to the Court of Appeal).

71 In any event, I have not been persuaded that there is a merger of the idea and the expression thereof in a computer program. The fact that a program can be written in a variety of different forms, that the same programmer would not write a program the same way if he or she were to start anew a second time, that the programmer is indifferent to the medium in which the program is embodied, all indicate that computer programs do not fall within the *merger* exception to copyrightable subject matter (if such exception exists).

Apple Computer Inc. v. Mackintosh Computers Ltd. (1990), 71 D.L.R. (4th) 95 (S.C.C.)

Supreme Court of Canada

Cory J.:

1 The issue raised in this appeal is whether a computer program, originating in copyrightable written form, continues to be protected by copyright when it is replicated in the circuitry of a silicon chip.

. . .

14 I agree with the conclusion reached by the trial judge and the Court of Appeal that the programs embodied in the silicon chip are protected under the *Copyright Act*. Indeed, there is little I can or would wish to add to Reed J.'s excellent reasons.

15 Like Reed J. and for the same reasons that were expressed by her, I am of the opinion that the programs embedded in the silicon chip are a reproduction of the programs in assembly language and as such are protected by copyright under s. 3(1) of the *Copyright Act*. In addition, I agree with her that these programs constitute a form of expression that is conceptually and functionally unique and cannot be regarded as a merger of idea and expression. Since the programs contained in the silicon chip are therefore protected under the Act, it is unnecessary for me to determine whether the silicon chips can be regarded as a translation under s. 3(1)(*a*) or a contrivance under s. 3(1)(*d*).

… Appeal dismissed.

Delrina Corp. v. Triolet Systems Inc. (2002), 17 C.P.R. (4th) 289 (Ont. C.A.)

Ontario Court of Appeal

Morden, Carthy, MacPherson JJ.A.

Heard: September 19-21, 2001
Judgment: March 1, 2002
Docket: CA C03375

. . .

Morden J.A.:

. . .

48 With respect to merger, the trial judge made the following statement at page 41 in his enumeration of "some general principles applicable to the law of copyright":

> If an idea can be expressed in only one or in a very limited number of ways, then copyright of that expression will be refused for it would give the originator of the idea a virtual monopoly on the idea. In such a case, it is said that the expression merges with the idea and thus is not copyrightable.

49 The merger doctrine developed in U.S. case law has been subjected to criticism in England (*IBCOS Computers Ltd. v. Barclays Mercantile Highland Finance Ltd.*, [1994] F.S.R. 275 (Eng. Ch. Div.) at 290-92 and Canada *Apple Computer Inc. v. Mackintosh Computers Ltd.* (1986), 10 C.P.R. (3d) 1 (Fed. T.D.) at 21-27, aff'd (1987), 18 C.P.R. (3d) 129 (Fed. C.A.); aff'd [1990] 2 S.C.R. 209 (S.C.C.).) In *IBCOS Computers Ltd.*, Jacob J. said at p. 291:

> The true position is that where an 'idea' is sufficiently general, then even if the original work embodies it, the mere taking of that idea will not infringe. But if the 'idea' is detailed, then there may be infringement. It is a question of degree.

50 The merger question was raised in rather stark form in *Apple Computer Inc.* This was not a case of infringement based on an alleged substantial reproduction of the plaintiff's work but one of an outright copying of the whole work. One of the defendant's defences was the general submission that "a computer program exhibits a merger of the idea and the expression of the idea and therefore is not copyrightable" (p. 24).

51 Reed J. was of the view that there were several difficulties with this argument. One of them was that the assembly code version of the program in question had been conceded to be copyrightable. I do not think that the court's rejection of the merger argument that computer programs, generally, are not entitled to copyright necessarily forecloses its application to a particular element in a program in the course of a substantial reproduction analysis. As *IBCOS Computers Ltd.* said "[i]t is a question of degree."

52 The merger notion is a natural corollary of the idea/expression distinction which, as I have said, is fundamental in copyright law in Canada, England and

the United States. Clearly, if there is only one or a very limited number of ways to achieve a particular result in a computer program, to hold that that way or ways are protectable by copyright could give the copyright holder a monopoly on the idea or function itself.

(c) Stock Devices

i. U.S. Scenes a faire Doctrine

There is authority in the United States that the "scenes a faire" doctrine excludes from protection those elements of a work that are stock, standard or commonplace devices employed in the relevant genre or in relation to a particular topic. Like the merger doctrine, the purpose of the scenes a faire doctrine is to ensure that copyright does not create an effective monopoly that unduly limits the creative expressions of others.

Cain v. Universal Pictures Co., 47 F. Supp. 1013 (S.D. Cal., 1942)

District Court, S.D. California Central Division

December 14, 1942

YANKWICH, District Judge.

The plaintiff, James M. Cain, is a wellknown writer who has written several novels, among which, perhaps, the best known is "The Postman Always Rings Twice", and a large number of short stories and stories for film production. In 1937, he wrote a novel called "Serenade".... Universal Pictures Corporation, Inc., is a corporation engaged in the production of motion pictures. On Novembers 22, 1938, the plaintiff sold to the film corporation, for the sum of $17,500, a story entitled "Modern Cinderella". ...The motion picture was completed on July 15, 1939, and released on August 11, 1939, under the title "When Tomorrow Comes".

...The plaintiff, in his complaint, charges that the motion picture infringes "Serenade". More particularly, he claims that the church sequence in the motion picture is copied from the church sequence in the book. He seeks damages, accounting of profits and injunctive relief against further exhibition of the motion picture.

. . .

One need not deny originality to "Serenade". There can be no claim of similarity of subject or of characterization between the book as a whole and the motion picture. ...Plaintiff, himself, concedes as much when he limits the alleged infringement to the church sequence. But, here again, there is no similarity....

It is not claimed that the choice of the church as a refuge in storm lends itself to the assertion of copyrightable originality. Houses of worship have been asylums since their very beginning. At one time, the legal privilege of sanctuary attached to churches. And he who entered one of them acquired immunity against the law.

The other small details, on which stress is laid, such as the playing of the piano, the prayer, the hunger motive, as it called, are inherent in the situation itself. They are what the French call "scenes a faire". Once having placed two persons in a church during a big storm, it was inevitable that incidents like these and others which are, necessarily, associated with such a situation should force themselves upon the writer in developing the theme. Courts have held repeatedly that similarities and incidental details necessary to the environment or setting of an action are not the material of which copyrightable originality consists. See Bachman v. Belasco, D.C.N.Y.1913, 224 F. 815; Underhill v. Belasco, D.C.N.Y.1918, 254 F. 838; Bein v. Warner Bros. Pictures, Inc., 2 Cir., 1939, 105 F.2d 969, 971; London v. Biograph Co., 2 Cir., 1916, 231 F. 696; Seltzer v. Sunbrock, D.C.Cal.1938, 22 F.Supp. 621, 628; De Montijo v. 20th Century Fox Film Corp., D.C.Cal.1941, 40 F.Supp. 133.

So I need not draw any parallelisms between the scene in the plaintiff's book and similar scenes in similar locale, which may occur to me as a student of literature....

. . .

Judgment will, therefore, be for the defendants that plaintiff take nothing by his Complaint against the defendants or any of them.

---

ii. Stock Devices in Anglo-Canadian Law

Commonwealth case law, while eschewing the United States term "scenes a faire" applies similar principles to avoid protecting commonplace standard, stock devices, common tools of the trade, standard, and commonly used techniques that are indispensable, or at least standard, in the treatment of a given topic.[14]

Collins v. Rosenthal (1974), 14 C.P.R. (2d) 143 (Fed. T.D.)

Federal Court of Canada – Trial Division
Toronto, Ontario

Collier J.

Heard: February 26-28, 1974
Judgment: May 24, 1974

. . .

1 COLLIER J.: — The plaintiffs are the joint authors of a publication entitled 1971 Individual Income Tax Tables Ontario, British Columbia and Nova Scotia. It was first sold to the public in early February, 1972. The defendants produced a publication entitled Individual Graduated Tax Tables for 1971 British Columbia, Nova Scotia, Ontario. It was first sold to the public in early March, 1972. For convenience, I shall refer to the plaintiffs' publication as the "plaintiffs' tax tables", and to the defendants' publication as the "defendants' tax tables". It was conceded at the outset of the trial that the plaintiffs had copyright in their tax tables. Their work was registered in the Copyright Office on February 17, 1972. The plaintiffs allege their tax tables have been copied by the defendants and claim the usual remedies in respect of infringement.

2 The defence is simply that there has been no infringement of the plaintiffs' work; the ideas in the two publications may be substantially the same or almost identical, but there can be no copyright in ideas; the defendants did not in fact copy from the plaintiffs; their publication was the result of their own labours.

. . .

12 In this case, I think the great similarity in the two tables is easily explicable. The common source material of the plaintiffs and Rosenthal was the limited government tax tables, and more important, the T-1 tax return. When one examines the return, particularly the portion headed "Detailed Tax Calculation", the similar order and headings of the columns chosen by these competing parties, becomes immediately apparent. To assist quickly the preparer of the return, there is no other logical arrangement. The order in the tables follows the order of calculations required in the form. The condensed wording of the headings in the tables obviously comes from the wording in the return.

13 I do not find anything piratical in the use of $5.00 increments. More accuracy in the tax calculation is achieved by that use. The separation into groupings of five is a very common technique. The selection of Ontario, British Columbia, and Nova Scotia seems to me to be a logical choice to anyone preparing a table. The largest sales market was in Ontario. Next came British Columbia. Nova Scotia happened to have the same 1971 rate of provincial tax. The size of

---

14 *Hutton v. Canadian Broadcasting Corp.* (1989), 29 C.P.R. (3d) 398 at 435-436 (Alta. Q.B.), affirmed (1992), 41 C.P.R. (3d) 45 (Alta. C.A.); Overseas *Enterprises Ltd. v. Feathers Publishing & Marketing* (1990), 34 C.P.R. (3d) 78 (Fed. T.D.); *Nova Productions Limited v. Mazooma Games Ltd.*, [2006] E.W.H.C. 24 (Ch) (20 January 2006).

the printing paper, and the somewhat different method of opening the book and reading from it, were, according to the evidence, dictated by the size of paper used by the computers in the print-outs, and the number of columns required. Apart from cost, the inclusion of additional provinces and setting out other provincial tax rates is dictated by the number of printing dimensions or positions available on the particular computer.

Hutton v. Canadian Broadcasting Corp. (1989), 41 C.P.R. (3d) 45 (Alta. C.A.)

Alberta Court of Queen's Bench

MacCallum J.

Judgment: December 20, 1989

The plaintiffs and the defendant co-produced a television series entitled "Star Chart", in which the plaintiff, H, registered copyright. The defendant cancelled the series after nineteen programs, pursuant to the provisions of the contract between the parties. One year later, the defendant produced and aired a series entitled "Good Rockin' Tonite". The plaintiffs brought a copyright infringement action in which they alleged that the defendant's series copied the plaintiff H's concept and creative elements. There was evidence that the production of a pilot program in preparation for the launching of a complete series was standard in the industry and that no such pilot was produced for Good Rockin' Tonite. Star Chart focussed on the "Music Central" theme, creating the illusion that the host and his assistants were gathering information for the countdown by means of a computer. In Good Rockin' Tonite, the host was the same, but he was no longer acting as a character. As opposed to Star Chart, Good Rockin' Tonite contained interviews and did not create the illusion of live performances.

. . .

11 The background to the Hutton claim should be briefly explained. Douglas Hutton conceived and produced a program called "Star Tracks". He persuaded the C.B.C. to co-produce with him the series S.C. based upon Star Tracks. He retained the copyright in S.C. which he registered as a dramatic work. The C.B.C. cancelled the series, as it was contractually entitled to, after nineteen programs.

12 About 3 years after cancellation of S.C. the C.B.C. produced and aired G.R.T. a program which, at the time of trial, was still being shown. Hutton alleges that the first 298 episodes of G.R.T. copied his concept and creative elements, and that the C.B.C. thereby breached his copyright.

. . .

15 *Summary* — I have found that S.C. grew out of a discussion between an American distributor and Douglas Hutton and it traces its origins back to the Canadian show Hot Pops and the British show Top of the Pops. Hutton produced

a pilot called Star Tracks. He showed it to the C.B.C. and together they reworked the pilot to co-produce S.C. in which Hutton owned the copyright.

I have found that G.R.T. was created by personnel of the C.B.C. in response to a perceived need for a program which resembled an earlier C.B.C. program called Rockin Doc.

16 Bearing in mind Hutton's contention that G.R.T. is nothing more than a cheap 1983 version of S.C., it is of interest to inquire into the genesis of these programs.

. . .

54 *Summary* — Although there are some similarities in structure between the two programs, I find the similarity to be, in the main, typical to the genre and that the programs are essentially dissimilar.

55 Many examples of S.C. and G.R.T. programs were shown at the trial as a means of comparing and contrasting the two. Hutton also put forward what it says is a more objective and scientific means of comparison, in the form of an analysis of the two programs based upon a detailed viewing of them and upon examination of the scripts and formats for each show.

56 The weight of such evidence depends first of all upon the confidence I have in the accuracy of the work done by the analysts, and, secondly, the appropriateness of the criteria used by them. The analysts were clerical personnel from the offices of counsel for Hutton, acting on the instructions of an expert, whose evidence I will review later. One of the clerical persons was Mrs. Diane Mah, who spent 230 hours reviewing tapes of the two programs. I am satisfied that she saw a representative sampling, by viewing eight shows of the U.S. version of S.C., 15 shows of the Canadian version and 77 shows of G.R.T.

57 Mah made a very large number of observations (Exhibits 166-168) and, for the most part, I am satisfied as to their accuracy. She viewed programs of S.C. which were aired between May and September 1980, and of G.R.T. which were aired between October 1983 and January 1988. In her analysis she was told what to look for, one example being the role the host played in each show. She invariably said: "Video Disc Jockey". She did not invent this term. She had the definition before her (Exhibit 164) of Mr. Jack McGaw, an expert called by the plaintiff. The C.B.C. objected to her use of this term on the ground that she was not qualified to say what a video disc jockey was. I do not think that her use of the term is objectionable because she used it as a shorthand way of describing what she observed the host to be doing. What matters is that she saw him, in each show, doing six things which comprise McGaw's definition.

58 The analysis was of course centered on the manner of presenting the performers rather than upon their performances, the quality of which has nothing to do with this lawsuit. From her work (Exhibits 166-168), I am able to draw certain conclusions as to points of similarity and distinction between the two shows.

59 What we are looking for when addressing the issue of copyright infringement is "substantial similarity". I will go farther and say that what we are looking for

is substantial similarity as a whole. One cannot evaluate the mode of expression simply by dissecting the program and numerically reciting the similarities and dissimilarities. That process is helpful, of course, but in itself it does not answer the question of whether one program is substantially similar to the other, viewed in its entirety.

60 I will refer first of all to those characteristics which I find, on the basis of the Mah observations, to be similar. Then I will move to those in which I find dissimilarity:

61 (i) The host was not only similar, but in fact was the same man throughout S.C. and 125 episodes of G.R.T.

62 Had he been hired as host of G.R.T. to do the same things that he did in S.C. because the producers wanted to do basically the same show, this fact would be very significant. The evidence is, however, to the contrary, indicating that he was hired because he was the best qualified person available, that he was the natural choice for the job, and that there was nobody else in the Vancouver area at the time as well qualified as he. I do not think that there was any obligation upon the producers of G.R.T. to hire a different host than the one they had for S.C. simply because they wanted to ensure that there was no similarity between the shows. What, therefore, is obviously similar in terms of host is only coincidentally and not deliberately so, and the similarity is relatively unimportant.

63 (ii) The number of commercial breaks was roughly proportional to the lenght of each program and therefore similar. The Evidence Is That this simply a standard of the industry and I find the similarity therefore to be unimportant.

64 (iii) Both shows featured countdowns. These were more varied in G.R.T. than in S.C. (example: top ten, top 20, album, singles) but their use was similar. Countdowns are standard fare in pop music shows, so the similarity is not important.

65 A comparison was made between the use of video clips as opposed to the showing of full videos in each show. The observations demonstrate a similar proportion, but I see nothing very significant about this.

66 (iv) The number of videos shown in each show is also compared and the results demonstrate similarity, but again I do not consider this to be important.

67 (v) The comparisons show that in both G.R.T. and S.C. the host acted as a video disc jockey within McGaw's definition, meaning that: the V.J. was very knowledgeable about the music business; he introduced videos of pre-recorded musical performances; he spoke directly to the camera/television viewer and did not appear with the studio audience; he did not perform musical material himself; he did not appear on stage with any artist in performance; and his delivery was largely scripted in both shows, although some ad-libbing was done in G.R.T.

68 The role of the host was therefore similar, but one must remember the additional tasks which were assigned to the host in G.R.T. in connection with interviews and trivia contests and the like, none of which he was expected to do in S.C.

69 (vi) The tone of both programs was lively, enthusiastic and "hip", and to this extent the programs were similar, but I have viewed a great number of pop music shows in the course of the evidence and I can think of only one, featuring a female host operating in a livingroom setting, where the tone was any different.

70 Both programs were similar in the use of natural hairstyling for the host, a characteristic upon which I place no importance.

71 (vii) In respect to the delivery of information at the introduction to videos which was done by the host in both shows, I calculate that the introductions were long versus short on a ratio of 5 to 1. Chart-related information in the introductions was common to both shows but more extensively used in G.R.T., and only occasionally on ei ther show did the host make editorial comment on music or about any personal experiences with the performers. In these respects, therefore, the shows were similar, but the similarity, as I find from the evidence, is a function of the type of material available (mainly through record company biographies) to the host to use as information. The observations demonstrated similarity with respect to the introduction of the videos in both programs where the host was usually seen to speak directly to the camera/viewer. Sometimes in G.R.T. instead of doing this, his voice would be heard over the introduction to the musical number. Although there is basic similarity here, it is not a matter of great significance.

72 (viii) Both programs utilized a screen upon which performances would appear and several television monitors upon which images, often of the same person or scene, would be shown. In both shows the host, when first seen by the viewer, would deliver a monologue in front of or beside the screen and monitors. In G.R.T. he sometimes did so from the library part of the set in which there was no screen or monitors. The shows were similar in this respect, but it must be remembered that the screen and monitors formed a very prominent part of both sets.

73 (ix) Observations demonstrated that the programs were similar in the use of casual wardrobe for the host. It must be said, however, that the host wardrobe in S.C. was more costume-like or "flashier" than the sort of street or casual wear we saw used in G.R.T. In a general sense, however, the wardrobe was similar in both shows.

74 The shows were similar in their use of straight cuts, rear screen transitions, T.V. monitor transitions, dissolves, and the playing of more than one video back to back. These things, however, are simply standard devices used in television to transfer from the continuity part of the program to the performance part and vice versa.

. . .

84 *Summary* — I find that the sets of S.C. and G.R.T. were similar only in their use of front projection screens, monitors and a desk, table, or console at

which the host sat from time to time. Apart from these items there were major differences.

85 The S.C. set was brightly lit and brightly coloured. It had "a high tech" look. There were rows of coloured lights which blinked and "chased". There were flashing numbers. The console at which the host and the two young women were seated from time to time was in two different sections and had rows of switches. All three persons could be seated at the console at the same time. The screen, which appeared on the center wall of this computer-like room, had the appearance of a window through which one viewed the videotaped performances. When the videotapes were not being played, one usually saw a star or outer space motif with twinkling or swirling stars. The lines of the set were clearly defined and there was a notable absence of incidental items to be seen.

86 The G.R.T. set consisted of two rooms connected by a door through which the host was seen to move occasionally. One room contained a desk, screen and monitors, and from this location the host generally showed the video performances on the screen. The second room was a den or library which contained comfortable furniture, many items of personal memorabilia, a coffee maker, books and records. Here the host conducted interviews with his guests. The wall and floor decoration in both rooms was consistent, and the lighting was low. Subdued colours were used on the walls and on the furniture. In the control room where the screen and monitors were found, the host's desk was apparently a working item, covered with papers and pencils. There was a typewriter. I make these findings from observing many programs shown in evidence. They are obvious to anybody who sees the tapes. The many experts in the trial also testified as to what they saw in the sets and some of them attached great symbolic importance to items such as the colour of a telephone, the authoritarian stature of a desk, or the presence of a coffee maker. I must say that they were more alive to subliminal stimuli than I was.

87 Not surprisingly, the designer of the G.R.T. set, Richard Cook, was in the best position to know what motivated its design. While noting his past association both as an employee and a contractor for the C.B.C., I detected no hint of bias in his testimony and he gave the following evidence, which I accept.

88 Cook was approached by Ken Gibson, the producer of G.R.T., to design the first set for G.R.T. He and Gibson viewed some tapes of S.C. because Gibson told him that he wanted Cook to have a clear idea of what was not wanted on the G.R.T. set. Gibson and Cook thought that the S.C. set was vulgar and a little ridiculous. They wanted to avoid this at all cost, wishing instead to create a comfortable low key environment for Mulligan, the host of G.R.T. This was corroborated by Gibson, as we shall see in discussing his evidence below.

89 They came up with a two area concept — a host area or den for interviews and a connecting control room. They decided on the use of the front projection screen because it was an available technology. They decided to use earth tones and to create a homey atmosphere. They wanted the control room to relate to the coziness of the host area. They decided to use static lighting of low intensity.

The G.R.T. set was intended to reflect the casual, informal and relaxed personality of Mulligan and to this end the latter "dressed" the library or den with many of his personal items to lend a homey look. These features were to be in contrast to the cold clinical impression conveyed by the S.C. set and to its bright chasing and flashing lights.

90   It was said that the G.R.T. graphics were an imitation of the star fields which were frequently seen on S.C. But from the evidence of Gordon Gill, who was the first director of G.R.T., I accept that the design which appeared on the G.R.T. screen from time to time was created by a graphic artist in response to Gill's instruction to create a late night feel. The artist created a moonscape and Gill accepted it.

91 Mulligan was the host on all S.C. shows and his impressions of that set are valuable. In evaluating his evidence one cannot, of course, lose sight of the fact that he was at one time a party defendant in the action but, in general, I found his evidence to be trustworthy.

92 He said that a lot of work went into the S.C. set and that it had the look of a starship — the "Star Trek" sort of thing — bright and visually active. He said that it had the feel of a command centre on a starship complete with electronic gear which, except for the monitors, was not functional. The phones were dead and so was the 2 inch reel-to-reel tape seen on the desk. The "command centre" concept gave the illusion that the music chart information was being collected there and then by the two female assistants. They purported to switch to live "stages" for performances, except that the women were never seen with the performers. I have one reservation about this evidence and that is that I believe he carries the illusion of a starship a little too far. His own comportment as host and his manner of dress were too casual to impart any real sense of command and apart from the physical appearance of the set, no effort was made in S.C. to tell the audience that the host and the women were in a starship.

93 With reference to the G.R.T. set, I accept that the working typewriter and coffee maker were there at his insistence. I accept that Mulligan wanted, and got, a "junkier" set for G.R.T. than he had in S.C. and that he wanted a lived-in feel with as little "glitz" as possible. He wanted it to be down-lit and to give the impression of a late night experience. He wanted and got a library where a guest could be interviewed in comfort. He wanted a working typewriter where he could do revisions as they went along and a working phone to the director. He said that the set measured up to his expectations. Mulligan had a good deal of input into this set which I find represented a significant change from S.C.

94 The evidence of Gill and Gibson regarding the dissimilarities in the sets was corroborated by that of Professor Robert Gardner, an expert called by the C.B.C.

95 G.R.T. producer Gibson spoke of the decision to use the screen, monitors and desk. He said that he was told to come up with something like the program Rockin Doc which had a large screen. He liked this idea. The device was very popular in 1983 and people were used to seeing screens in bars for the showing

of rock videos. As for the monitors, Gibson had used them in the past. He really wanted a large bank of them, but budgetary considerations prevented this. Mulligan wanted, and received, a desk as a work area. I accept this.

96 Hutton's experts Jack McGaw and Paul Taylor (for Taylor's substance of opinion see Exhibit 197) both said that the S.C. and G.R.T. sets were similar. Their opinions focussed on the use of screens, monitors and a desk. For the reasons I have expressed above, I find that despite the common use of these devices, the sets as a whole were quite different.

97 I conclude that while there was similarity in function between the two sets, there was no striking similarity in appearance.

· · ·

12) Stock Devices

176 *Summary* — I have concluded that the use of stock devices in both S.C. and G.R.T. lends an air of similarity to the programs but does not support the allegation of copying.

177 Some of the similarities demonstrated between S.C. and G.R.T. are common constituent elements of any television program of the genre. Consequently, the fact that they appear in G.R.T. does not prove copying from S.C.

178 I find from the evidence of the witnesses that the following devices, which were common to both S.C. and G.R.T. are also commonly used as stock devices in television:

> 1. *Hitting the post* — this describes a method of introducing a musical performance in which the anouncer's voice is heard over an instrumental introduction and the announcer stops speaking just as the vocal performance commences;
>
> 2. *Infinity shots* — a repetition of the same image on multiple screens or monitors;
>
> 3. *Bumper to commercial* — a common form of transition from continuity to commercial;
>
> 4. *Tease to commercial* — a promise of things to come, it is commonly used to persuade the audience to stay with the program through the commercial;
>
> 5. *Opening montage* — a glimpse of performances to come;
>
> 6. *Countdowns* — the process of counting down the top ten, twenty, etc. songs by means of visual or musical clips, or both, culminating in the no. 1 song;
>
> 7. *Screen* — a common transition device between the host and the video;
>
> 8. *Desk* — a common prop used by a host.

179 The use of these devices no doubt lends an air of similarity to S.C. and G.R.T. The fact is, however, that such devices were in common use long before either of these two shows were aired and remain in common use in the industry. Their appearance in S.C. and G.R.T. therefore lends little assistance in deciding the issue of substantial similarity between the two programs.

13) Conclusion of Experts

180 *Summary* — The evidence of many experts called by both the plaintiff and the defendant contained useful observations and helpful opinions. It has not, however, changed my preliminary assessment that G.R.T. and S.C. are not substantially similar.

181 I have reviewed the evidence of the participants in the events in light of the issue of similarity. Their evidence, together with my own viewing of the video tapes during the course of their testimony, leads me to the conclusion that while much similarity exists between the two programs in terms of technique and subject matter, there are important differences in the mode of expression. A major difference lies in the distinction between G.R.T. as a rock magazine video show and S.C. as a high tech, dramatically con trived rock (or pop) video show.

182 I must say that the contribution of the experts to this trial was welcome insofar as their evidence concerned matters which truly required expertise to interpret. A great deal of what they had to say, however, might be termed over-kill. A rock video show is neither the most sublime nor the most complicated of artistic creations and one would have thought that the C.B.C. would have been hard pressed to find expert opinion which differed very much from that expressed by the expert witnesses for Hutton. Not so. The C.B.C. produced three experts whose opinions on the issue of substantial similarity are altogether different. If this proves anything, it is that the issue of substantial similarity is a highly subjective one which, in large measure, the trier of fact must decide for himself.

. . .

4) *Substantiality*

225 In *Bagge v. Miller*, [1920] MacG. Cop. C. 179, a decision of Russell J. of the English Chancery Division, it is stated at p. 188:

> To adopt the language of the present Master of the Rolls in the case of *Rees v. Melville*, 'In a dramatic work both the plot (including in that word the idea and the arrangement of the incidents) and the dialogue and working out of the play must be regarded in order to see whether one play is a reproduction of the other or of a substantial part of it, and regard must also be had to the extent to which both plays include stock incidents ...'

Counsel for the defendant urges that in this case the requirement of substantiality has not been met.

226 It must be acknowledged that there is appreciable similarity between the words of the two productions, at least between the words of S.C. and the first 125 programs of G.R.T., which were all written by the same person. It cannot be said that these words were unimportant and trifling in relation to their effect upon the whole composition. However, the similarity did not extend to all the words, only to those which had to do with the background material to the videos. These cannot be properly said, in my opinion, to be part of any dramatic incident, but rather are merely factual and informative. It is only the words relating to the

bogus gathering of chart information which are part of any dramatic conceit, and these are not repeated in G.R.T.

227 Another element of similarity between S.C. and G.R.T. is the presence of the same host who uses his knowledge, looks and voice on both shows to similar effect. In fact I find that he was chosen for both shows because of these qualities.

228 Copyright legislation, however, should not be taken to impose unreasonable restrictions on the right to work. As stated in *Hepworth Manufacturing Co. Ltd. v. Ryott*, [1918-19] All E.R. Rep. 1019, [1920] 1 Ch. 1 at 12 (C.A.):

> [A] man's aptitudes, his skill, his dexterity and his manual or mental ability may not nor ought to be relinquished by an employee. They are not his master's property, they are his own, they are himself.

Hutton did not own the skills which Mulligan brought to the task and the producer Gibson had put these skills to work long before Hutton came on the scene.

229 Mulligan wrote the introductions to videos for both shows using the same source, i.e., material-trade magazines and record company biographies. Thus the similarity in the scripts between the two programs is practically inevitable given the author's personal writing style and the clichés of the business.

230 Common stock elements to both programs such as teasers, bumpers, montages, countdowns, screens and monitors are nothing more than the tools of the trade in the pop music business and are not indicators of substantial or striking similarity. All of these items were in common use by 1983 when G.R.T. came on the air.

(d) News and History

As we have seen, copyright does not protect facts or ideas but is limited to the expression of ideas. From this basic axiom it follows that copyright protects neither the news of the day nor the facts of history as such. A news article can enjoy protection as an original literary work, for example, but the information it conveys will remain beyond the scope of the copyright owner's control. In this context, again, the difficulty lies with distinguishing between the non-protectable information, facts or theories and the protectable expression thereof. Where is the line between the facts reported and the manner of the reporting? Should it matter if the facts are "true" or merely the result of speculation or historical theorizing? When does the choice of which facts to report in a news story, or which events to include in an historical account, amount to an original selection requiring skill and judgment that copyright will protect? Are there circumstances in which the law should prevent the use of laboriously researched facts by a competitor or "free-rider" in spite of this general rule?

International News Service v. Associated Press, 248 U.S. 215, 39 S. Ct. 68 (1918)

Supreme Court of the United States

Mr. Justice PITNEY delivered the opinion of the Court:

The parties are competitors in the gathering and distribution of news and its publication for profit in newspapers throughout the United States. The Associated Press, which was complainant in the District Court, is a co-operative organization, incorporated under the Membership Corporations Law of the state of New York, its members being individuals who are either proprietors or representatives of about 950 daily newspapers published in all parts of the United States. That a corporation may be organized under that act for the purpose of gathering news for the use and benefit of its members and for publication in newspapers owned or represented by them, is recognized by an amendment enacted in 1901 (Laws N. Y. 1901, c. 436). Complainant gathers in all parts of the world, by means of various instrumentalities of its own, by exchange with its members, and by other appropriate means, news and intelligence of current and recent events of interest to newspaper readers and distributes it daily to its members for publication in their newspapers. The cost of the service, amounting approximately to $3,500,000 per annum, is assessed upon the members and becomes a part of their costs of operation, to be recouped, presumably with profit, through the publication of their several newspapers. Under complainant's by-laws each member agrees upon assuming membership that news received through complainant's service is received exclusively for publication in a particular newspaper, language, and place specified in the certificate of membership, that no other use of it shall be permitted, and that no member shall furnish or permit any one in his employ or connected with his newspaper to furnish any of complainant's news in advance of publication to any person not a member. And each member is required to gather the local news of his district and supply it to the Associated Press and to no one else.

Defendant is a corporation organized under the laws of the state of New Jersey, whose business is the gathering and selling of news to its customers and clients, consisting of newspapers published throughout the United States, under contracts by which they pay certain amounts at stated times for defendant's service. It has widespread news-gathering agencies; the cost of its operations amounts, it is said, to more than $2,000,000 per annum; and it serves about 400 newspapers located in the various cities of the United States and abroad, a few of which are represented, also, in the membership of the Associated Press.

The parties are in the keenest competition between themselves in the distribution of news throughout the United States; and so, as a rule, are the newspapers that they serve, in their several districts.

. . .

The bill was filed to restrain the pirating of complainant's news by defendant in three ways: First, by bribing employees of newspapers published by complainant's members to furnish Associated Press news to defendant before publication, for transmission by telegraph and telephone to defendant's clients for publication by them; second, by inducing Associated Press members to violate its by-laws and permit defendant to obtain news before publication; and, third, by copying news from bulletin boards and from early editions of complainant's newspapers and selling this, either bodily or after rewriting it, to defendant's customers.

. . .

In considering the general question of property in news matter, it is necessary to recognize its dual character, distinguishing between the substance of the information and the particular form or collocation of words in which the writer has communicated it.

No doubt news articles often possess a literary quality, and are the subject of literary property at the common law; nor do we question that such an article, as a literary production, is the subject of copyright by the terms of the act as it now stands. In an early case at the circuit Mr. Justice Thompson held in effect that a newspaper was not within the protection of the copyright acts of 1790 (1 Stat. 124) and 1802 (2 Stat. 171). Clayton v. Stone, 2 Paine, 382, Fed. Cas. No. 2,872. But the present act is broader; it provides that the works for which copyright may be secured shall include 'all the writings of an author,' and specifically mentions 'periodicals, including newspapers.' Act of March 4, 1909, c. 320, §§ 4 and 5, 35 Stat. 1075, 1076 (Comp. St. 1916, §§ 9520, 9521). Evidently this admits to copyright a contribution to a newspaper, notwithstanding it also may convey news; and such is the practice of the copyright office, as the newspapers of the day bear witness. See Copyright Office Bulletin No. 15 (1917) pp. 7, 14, 16, 17.

But the news element — the information respecting current events contained in the literary production — is not the creation of the writer, but is a report of matters that ordinarily are publici juris; it is the history of the day. It is not to be supposed that the framers of the Constitution, when they empowered Congress 'to promote the progress of science and useful arts, by securing for limited times to authors and inventors the exclusive right to their respective writings and discoveries' (Const. art. 1, § 8, par. 8), intended to confer upon one who might happen to be the first to report a historic event the exclusive right for any period to spread the knowledge of it.

We need spend no time, however, upon the general question of property in news matter at common law, or the application of the copyright act, since it seems to us the case must turn upon the question of unfair competition in business. And, in our opinion, this does not depend upon any general right of property analogous to the common-law right of the proprietor of an unpublished work to prevent its publication without his consent; nor is it foreclosed by showing that the benefits of the copyright act have been waived. We are dealing here not with restrictions upon publication but with the very facilities and processes of publication. The peculiar value of news is in the spreading of it while it is fresh; and it is evident that a valuable property interest in the news, as news, cannot be maintained by keeping it secret. Besides, except for matters improperly disclosed, or published in breach of trust or confidence, or in violation of law, none of which is involved in this brance [sic] of the case, the news of current events may be regarded as common property. What we are concerned with is the business of making it known to the world, in which both parties to the present suit are engaged. That business consists in maintaining a prompt, sure, steady, and reliable service designed to place the daily events of the world at the breakfast table of the millions at a price that, while of trifling moment to each reader, is sufficient in the aggregate to afford compensation for the cost of gathering and distributing it, with the added profit so necessary as an incentive to effective action in the commercial world. The service thus performed for newspaper readers is not only innocent but extremely useful in itself, and indubitably constitutes a legitimate business. The parties are competitors in this field; and, on fundamental principles, applicable here as elsewhere, when the rights or privileges of the one are liable to conflict with those of the other, each party is under a duty so to conduct its own business as not unnecessarily or unfairly to injure *236 that of the other. Hitchman Coal & Coke Co. v. Mitchell, 245 U. S. 229, 254, 38 Sup. Ct. 65, 62 L. Ed. 260, L. R. A. 1918C, 497, Ann. Cas. 1918B, 461.

Obviously, the question of what is unfair competition in business must be determined with particular reference to the character and circumstances of the business. The question here is not so much the rights of either party as against the public but their rights as between themselves. See Morison v. Moat, 9 Hare, 241, 258. And, although we may and do assume that neither party has any remaining property interest as against the public in uncopyrighted news matter after the moment of its first publication, it by no means follows that there is no remaining property interest in it as between themselves. For, to both of them alike, news matter, however little susceptible of ownership or dominion in the absolute sense, is stock in trade, to be gathered at the cost of enterprise, organization, skill, labor, and money, and to be distributed and sold to those who will pay money for it, as for any other merchandise. Regarding the news, therefore, as but the material out of which both parties are seeking to make profits at the same time and in the same field, we hardly can fail to recognize that for this purpose, and as between them, it must be regarded as quasi property, irrespective of the rights of either as against the public.

In order to sustain the jurisdiction of equity over the controversy, we need not affirm any general and absolute property in the news as such. The rule that a court of equity concerns itself only in the protection of property rights treats any civil right of a pecuniary nature as a property right (In re Sawyer, 124 U. S. 200, 210, 8 Sup. Ct. 482, 31 L. Ed. 402; In re Debs, 158 U. S. 564, 593, 15 Sup. Ct. 900, 39 L. Ed. 1092); and the right to acquire property by honest labor or the conduct of a lawful business is as much entitled to protection as the right to guard property already acquired (Truax v. Raich, 239 U. S. 33, 37-38, 36 Sup. Ct. 7, 60 L. Ed. 131, L. R. A. 1916D, 545, Ann. Cas. 1917B, 283; Brennan v. United Hatters, 73 N. J. Law, 729, 742, 65 Atl. 165, 9 L. R. A. [N. S.] 254, 118 Am. St. Rep. 727, 9 Ann. Cas. 698; *237 Barr v. Essex Trades Council, 53 N. J.

Eq. 101, 30 Atl. 881). It is this right that furnishes the basis of the jurisdiction in the ordinary case of unfair competition.

The question, whether one who has gathered general information or news at pains and expense for the purpose of subsequent publication through the press has such an interest in its publication as may be protected from interference, has been raised many times, although never, perhaps, in the precise form in which it is now presented.

. . .

Not only do the acquisition and transmission of news require elaborate organization and a large expenditure of money, skill, and effort; not only has it an exchange value to the gatherer, dependent chiefly upon its novelty and freshness, the regularity of the service, its reputed reliability and thoroughness, and its adaptability to the public needs; but also, as is evident, the news has an exchange value to one who can misappropriate it.

The peculiar features of the case arise from the fact that, while novelty and freshness form so important an element in the success of the business, the very processes of distribution and publication necessarily occupy a good deal of time. Complainant's service, as well as defendant's, is a daily service to daily newspapers; most of the foreign news reaches this country at the Atlantic seaboard, principally at the city of New York, and because of this, and of time differentials due to the earth's rotation, the distribution of news matter throughout the country is principally from east to west; and, since in speed the telegraph and telephone easily outstrip the rotation of the earth, it is a simple matter for defendant to take complainant's news from bulletins or early editions of complainant's members in the eastern cities and at the mere cost of telegraphic transmission cause it to be published in western papers issued at least as warly as those served by complainant. Besides this, and irrespective of time differentials, irregularities in telegraphic transmission on different lines, and the normal consumption of time in printing and distributing the newspaper, result in permitting pirated news to be placed in the hands of defendant's readers sometimes simultaneously with the service of competing Associated Press papers, occasionally even earlier.

Defendant insists that when, with the sanction and approval of complainant, and as the result of the use of its news for the very purpose for which it is distributed, a portion of complainant's members communicate it to the general public by posting it upon bulletin boards so that all may read, or by issuing it to newspapers and distributing it indiscriminately, complainant no longer has the right to control the use to be made of it; that when it thus reaches the light of day it becomes the common possession of all to whom it is accessible; and that any purchaser of a newspaper has the right to communicate the intelligence which it contains to anybody and for any purpose, even for the purpose of selling it for profit to newspapers published for profit in competition with complainant's members.

The fault in the reasoning lies in applying as a test the right of the complainant as against the public, instead of considering the rights of complainant and defendant, competitors in business, as between themselves. The right of the purchaser of a single newspaper to spread knowledge of its contents gratuitously, for any legitimate purpose not unreasonably interfering with complainant's right to make merchandise of it, may be admitted; but to transmit that news for commercial use, in competition with complainant — which is what defendant has done and seeks to justify — is a very different matter. In doing this defendant, by its very act, admits that it is taking material that has been acquired by complainant as the result of organization and the expenditure of labor, skill, and money, and which is salable by complainant for money, and that defendant in appropriating it and selling it as its own is endeavoring to reap where it has not sown, and by disposing of it to newspapers that are competitors of complainant's members is appropriating to itself the harvest of those who have sown. Stripped of all disguises, the process amounts to an unauthorized interference with the normal operation of complainant's legitimate business precisely at the point where the profit is to be reaped, in order to divert a material portion of the profit from those who have earned it to those who have not; with special advantage to defendant in the competition because of the fact that it is not burdened with any part of the expense of gathering the news. The transaction speaks for itself and a court of equity ought not to hesitate long in characterizing it as unfair competition in business.

The underlying principle is much the same as that which lies at the base of the equitable theory of consideration in the law of trusts — that he who has fairly paid the price should have the beneficial use of the property. Pom. Eq. Jur. § 981. It is no answer to say that complainant spends its money for that which is too fugitive or evanescent to be the subject of property. That might, and for the purposes of the discussion we are assuming that it would furnish an answer in a common-law controversy. But in a court of equity, where the question is one of unfair competition, if that which complainant has acquired fairly at substantial cost may be sold fairly at substantial profit, a competitor who is misappropriating it for the purpose of disposing of it to his own profit and to the disadvantage of complainant cannot be heard to say that it is too fugitive or evanescent to be regarded as property. It has all the attributes of property necessary for determining that a misappropriation of it by a competitor is unfair competition because contrary to good conscience.

The contention that the news is abandoned to the public for all purposes when published in the first newspaper is untenable. Abandonment is a question of intent, and the entire organization of the Associated Press negatives such a purpose. The cost of the service would be prohibited if the reward were to be so limited. No single newspaper, no small group of newspapers, could sustain the expenditure. Indeed, it is one of the most obvious results of defendant's theory that, by permitting indiscriminate publication by anybody and everybody for purposes of profit in competition with the news-gatherer, it would render publication profitless, or so little profitable as in effect to cut off the service by rendering the cost prohibitive in comparison with the return. The practical needs and requirements of the business are reflected in complainant's by-laws which have been referred to. Their effect is that publication by each member must be deemed not by any means an abandonment of the news to the world for any and all purposes, but a publication for limited purposes; for the benefit of the readers of the bulletin or the newspaper as such; not for the purpose of making merchandise of it as news, with the result of depriving complainant's other members of their reasonable opportunity to obtain just returns for their expenditures.

It is to be observed that the view we adopt does not result in giving to complainant the right to monopolize either the gathering or the distribution of the news, or, without complying with the copyright act, to prevent the reproduction of its news articles, but only postpones participation by complainant's competitor in the processes of distribution and reproduction of news that it has not gathered, and only to the extent necessary to prevent that competitor from reaping the fruits of complainant's efforts and expenditure, to the partial exclusion of complainant and in violation of the principle that underlies the maxim 'sic utere tuo,' etc.

. . .

The decree of the Circuit court of Appeals will be *affirmed.*

In the next case, the assertion that "there can be no copyright in the facts of history or in their chronological sequence" seems sound. The plaintiff's selection of historical facts, however, spanning from the creation of the sun to the World War, was largely replicated in Wells' book. Given the possibility of copying by Wells, together with close parallels in the language and structure of the books, one can understand why Florence Deeks was motivated to spend her life pursuing this case — seeking justice for what she regarded as a great travesty. (For a fascinating historical account of this case, see Brian Mckillop, *The Spinster and the Prophet: Florence Deeks, H.G. Wells, and the Mystery of the Purloined Past* (Macfarlane Walter & Ross, 2001).

Deeks v. Wells, [1931] O.R. 818 (Ont. H.C.)

Ontario Appellate Division – Latchford, C.J., Riddell, Masten, and Orde, Jj.A.

Raney, J.: The plaintiff is the author of the manuscript of an unpublished book, "The Web," the theme of which is feminism in history. The scope of her work is worldwide, and ante-dates the advent of man upon the earth; the manuscript is necessarily voluminous. The defendant Wells is the author of many well known books, including a work having the title, "The Outline of History". This is also a history of the world and is more voluminous than the plaintiff's manuscript.

After about four year's work, the plaintiff completed her manuscript in 1918, and early in August of that year she submitted it, looking to its publication, to the defendant the MacMillan Company of Toronto, in whose custody it remained for several months. Miss Deeks says it was returned to her in April, 1919; the company's records indicate that it was returned in February, 1919. It is not important for the purposes of this action to determine which is the correct date. At all events the manuscript was with the MacMillan Company of Toronto, or under its control, for six months beginning with August, 1918.

Mr. Wells began the writing of his book in the late autumn of 1918, some two or three months after Miss Deeks' manuscript was left with the MacMillan Company in Toronto. Before beginning to write, Mr. Wells had offered the publication rights of his book for Great Britain to the MacMillan Company of England and that company had declined the offer. Then he arranged for publication in England by the Newnes Company, and for publication on this side of the Atlantic by the MacMillan Company of New York. Incidentally, the MacMillan Company of England controls both the MacMillan Company of New York and the MacMillan Company of Canada.

Between August, 1918, and February, 1919, there was time enough for the forwarding of Miss Deeks' manuscript to England, its use by Mr. Wells and its return to Toronto. That is the plaintiff's theory of what actually happened; but there is no evidence that the manuscript was sent to England, or that Mr. Wells or any one else in England knew of its existence, or that the MacMillan Company of Toronto, or any one else in Toronto, knew that Mr. Wells was writing, or had it in mind to write, a history of the world. In the absence of such evidence, the plaintiff seeks to make her case by pointing to similarities in the two works which, she says, are so significant as to leave no manner of doubt that Mr. Wells had access to her manuscript.

The plaintiff is not able to point to any paragraph in "The Outline of History" that corresponds verbally with any paragraph in her manuscript, or even to any sentence; but she alleges that the general plan of Mr. Wells' book establishes the use of her manuscript, and she points to the use of many ideas and words used by her that were afterwards used by him. The absence of identical paragraphs or sentences, or even of phrases, only goes to establish, she says, the care that was taken by the pirate to conceal the source of his ideas and language.

. . .

Orde, J.A.: I agree that this appeal must be dismissed. The plaintiff sets up two distinct causes of action, one an infringement of her copyright, the other, breach of trust.

As to the first, the simplest test to apply is that suggested by myself during the argument. If the plaintiff's work "The Web" had already been published and distributed throughout the world as widely, say, as "The Encyclopaedia Britannica," could an action for an infringement of the plaintiff's copyright by reason of anything appearing in "The Outline of History" have possibly succeeded, even if it were proved that the defendant Wells had made use of a published copy of "The Web" in writing his book? There can be no copyright in the facts of history or in their chronological sequence. Had " The Web" been published, the defendant Wells was as free to consult and use it in the preparation of his work as the plaintiff was to consult and use " The Encyclopaedia Britannica" or any other publication as a source of information. Infringement of copyright in such cases must, as a general rule, consist of the copying of the words of another in the order in which he has used them. The use of the same historical facts or of the same ideas is not enough. Appeal dismissed with costs.

The following cases explore the limits of copyright in fact-based works (or those that purport to be such). Having presented a work as historical fact or theory, the plaintiffs in the following cases were unable to control creative re-uses of the theory by downstream authors.

Nash v. CBS, INC., et al.

United States Court of Appeals, Seventh Circuit

Decided April 23, 1990

John Dillinger, Public Enemy No. 1, died on July 22, 1934, at the Biograph Theater in Chicago. He emerged from the air conditioned movie palace into a sweltering evening accompanied by two women, one wearing a bright red dress. The "lady in red", Anna Sage, had agreed to betray his presence for $10,000. Agents of the FBI were waiting. Alerted by Polly Hamilton, the other woman, Dillinger wheeled to fire, but it was too late. A hail of bullets cut him down, his .45 automatic unused. William C. Sullivan, *The Bureau* 30-33 (1979). Now a national historic site, the Biograph bears a plaque commemorating the event. It still shows movies, and the air conditioning is no better now than in 1934.

Jay Robert Nash believes that Dillinger did not die at the Biograph. In *Dillinger: Dead or Alive?* (1970), and *The Dillinger Dossier* (1983), Nash maintains that Dillinger learned about the trap and dispatched Jimmy Lawrence, a small-time hoodlum who looked like him, in his stead. The FBI, mortified that its set-up had no sting, kept the switch quiet. Nash points to discrepancies between Dillinger's physical characteristics and those of the corpse: Dillinger had a scar on his upper lip and the corpse did not; Dillinger lacked a tooth that the corpse possessed; Dillinger had blue eyes, the corpse brown eyes; Dillinger's eyebrows were thicker than those of the corpse. Although Dillinger's sister identified the dead man, Nash finds the circumstances suspicious, and he is struck by the decision of Dillinger's father to encase the corpse in concrete before burial. As part of the cover- up, according to Nash, the FBI planted Dillinger's fingerprints in the morgue. After interviewing many persons connected with Dillinger's gang and the FBI's pursuit of it, Nash tracked Dillinger to the west coast, where Dillinger married and lay low. Nash believes that he survived at least until 1979. *The Dillinger Dossier* contains pictures of a middle-aged couple and then an elderly man who, Nash believes, is Dillinger in dotage. Nash provides capsule versions of his conclusions in his *Bloodletters and Badmen: A Narrative Encyclopedia of American Criminals from the Pilgrims to the Present* (1973), and his expose *Citizen Hoover* (1972).

Nash's reconstruction of the Dillinger story has not won adherents among historians — or the FBI. Someone in Hollywood must have read *The Dillinger Dossier*, however, because in 1984 CBS broadcast an episode of its *Simon and Simon* series entitled *The Dillinger Print*. *Simon and Simon* featured brothers Rick and A.J. Simon, private detectives in San Diego. The district court summarized the episode:

> The opening scene of The [Dillinger] Print shows Ty Becker, a retired FBI agent, telling his grandchildren about Dillinger's life and the shooting outside the Biograph Theater on July 22, 1934. Ty also mentions that he doubts Dillinger was the man who was shot that night and vows to track him down some day. After the grandchildren leave with his daughter Addie, an intruder breaks into Ty's home, steals an old gun which once belonged to Dillinger, and kills Ty with the gun.
>
> Concerned that the police would regard Ty's death as a typical murder incident to burglary rather than related to moonlighting she suspected he was performing for the FBI, Addie hires the Simons. Next, Addie goes to the bank to remove her father's safety deposit box. While she is in the vault, a masked man, wearing 1930s-style spectator shoes, shoots tear gas into the bank and steals Ty's safety deposit box. The Simons arrive at the bank soon thereafter and pick up the thief's gun, which turns out to be the Dillinger gun stolen from Ty's house. Police investigation later reveals that the gun bears the fresh fingerprint of John Dillinger.
>
> The Simons are next seen purchasing newspapers which are carrying the story that Dillinger may be alive. As the Simons discuss the case, A.J. reads from a book entitled "Twentieth Century Desperadoes." He implies that some evidence supports the idea Dillinger is alive and relates to Rick several physical discrepancies between Dillinger and the corpse described in the 1934 autopsy. Nash cites the same discrepancies in his books.
>
> Numerous Dillinger impostors soon come forward, and the FBI enters the case. However, FBI Agent Kinneman, who is a friend of A.J.'s, informs the Simons that Ty Becker was not working for the FBI at the time of his death.
>
> The scene then switches to a health club. As A.J. and Kinneman are playing racquetball, a man wearing a trench coat and spectator shoes enters the club and, from the viewing area, sprays a salvo of bullets over A.J. and Kinneman. Afterwards, A.J. solemnly swears revenge against Dillinger or whoever tried to shoot him.
>
> The next day, the Simons visit the police station and discover that " leads" regarding Dillinger's whereabouts have poured in from all over the world. They agree to check out a few leads, including one that takes them to a dentist in San Diego. The dentist rejects the Simons' suggestion that Dillinger lives in his house and attributes the police tip to a crazy woman who lives across the street.
>
> The Simons and Addie then pay a visit to Ty Becker's old secretary, who informs them that Ty was working on an internal FBI investigation at the time he was killed. Immediately thereafter, the Simons and Addie receive a call from Kinneman, who tells them that " there is more truth to this" Dillinger affair than anyone had imagined and that the Simons should meet him at a closed-down theater.
>
> When the Simons and Addie enter the theater, a gangster documentary is playing. Kinneman and a man wearing spectator shoes shoot at the trio. The Simons eventually kill the man in spectator shoes. They then subdue Kinneman, who admits to

killing Ty Becker in order to stop the internal investigation which, it turns out, was directed at Kinneman, and to leaving the fake Dillinger fingerprint on the gun at the bank.

In the penultimate scene, the FBI thanks the Simons for their help in arresting Kinneman and solving the Dillinger mystery. Rick nevertheless insists Dillinger may be alive and perhaps living in Oregon.... The episode closes with a teaser: the dentist, one of the leads whom the Simons had interviewed earlier in the program, is seen pushing his elderly father in a wheelchair and admonishing him to refrain from discussing the "old days in Chicago" anymore.

Nash filed this suit seeking damages on the theory that *The Dillinger Print* violates his copyrights in the four books setting out his version of Dillinger's escape from death and new life on the west coast. The district court determined that the books' copyrighted material consists in Nash's presentation and exposition, not in any of the historical events. CBS then moved for summary judgment, conceding for this purpose both access to Nash's books and copying of the books' factual material. The court granted this motion, holding that *The Dillinger Print* did not appropriate any of the material protected by Nash's copyrights.

CBS's concession removes . . . the questions whether the copier used matter that the copyright law protects and, if so, whether it took "too much" .... These latter questions have proven especially difficult when, as in this case, the copier works in a medium different from the original.

Learned Hand, whose opinions still dominate this corner of the law, observed in *Nichols v. Universal Pictures Corp.*, that all depends on the level of abstraction at which the court conceives the interest protected by the copyright. If the court chooses a low level (say, only the words the first author employed), then a copier may take the plot, exposition, and all other original material, even though these may be the most important ingredients of the first author's contribution. As a practical matter this would mean that anyone could produce the work in a new medium without compensating the original author, despite the statute's grant to the author of the privilege to make "derivative works" . If on the other hand the court should select a high level of abstraction, the first author may claim protection for whole genres of work ("the romantic novel" or, more modestly, any story involving doomed young lovers from warring clans, so that a copyright on *Romeo and Juliet* would cover *West Side Story* too). Even a less sweeping degree of abstraction creates a risk of giving copyright protection to "the idea" although the statute protects only "expression".

Sometimes called the "abstractions test", Hand's insight is not a "test" at all. It is a clever way to pose the difficulties that require courts to avoid either extreme of the continuum of generality. It does little to help resolve a given case, even when melded with Hand's further observation, in cases such as *Peter Pan Fabrics Inc. v. Martin Weiner Corp.*, that one may ask what the "ordinary observer" would think are the essential parts of the two works' "aesthetic appeal". ...Who is the "ordinary" observer, and how does this person choose the level of generality? Ordinary observers, like reasonable men in torts, are fictitious characters of the law, reminders that judges must apply objective tests rather than examine their own perceptions. They do not answer the essential question: at what level of generality? After 200 years of wrestling with copyright questions, it is unlikely that courts will come up with the answer any time soon, if indeed there is "an" answer, which we doubt.

Hand returned again and again to the opposing forces that make the formulation of a single approach so difficult. Intellectual (and artistic) progress is possible only if each author builds on the work of others. No one invents even a tiny fraction of the ideas that make up our cultural heritage. Once a work has been written and published, any rule requiring people to compensate the author slows progress in literature and art, making useful expressions "too expensive", forcing authors to re-invent the wheel, and so on. Every work uses scraps of thought from thousands of predecessors, far too many to compensate even if the legal system were frictionless, which it isn't. Because any new work depends on others even if unconsciously, broad protection of intellectual property also creates a distinct possibility that the cost of litigation — old authors trying to get a "piece of the action" from current successes — will prevent or penalize the production of new works, even though the claims be rebuffed. Authors as a group therefore might prefer limited protection for their writings — they gain in the ability to use others' works more than they lose in potential royalties. See William M. Landes & Richard A. Posner, *An Economic Analysis of Copyright Law,* 18 J. Legal Studies 325, 332-33, 349-59 (1989).

Yet to deny authors all reward for the value their labors contribute to the works of others *also* will lead to inefficiently little writing, just as surely as excessively broad rights will do. The prospect of reward is an important stimulus for thinking and writing, especially for persons such as Nash who are full-time authors. Before the first work is published, broad protection of intellectual property seems best; after it is published, narrow protection seems best. At each instant some new works are in progress, and every author is simultaneously a creator in part and a borrower in part. In these roles, the same person has different objectives. Yet only one rule can be in force. This single rule must achieve as much as possible of these inconsistent demands. Neither Congress nor the courts has the information that would allow it to determine which is best. Both institutions must muddle through, using not a fixed rule but a sense of the consequences of moving dramatically in either direction.

If Nash had written a novel that another had translated into a screenplay, this would be a difficult case. Although *The Dillinger Print* is substantially original, it does not matter that almost all of the second author's expression is new. "[N] o plagiarist can excuse the wrong by showing how much of his work he did not pirate." *Sheldon v. Metro-Goldwyn Pictures Corp.* (L. Hand, J.). The TV drama took from Nash's works the idea that Dillinger survived and retired to the west coast, and employed many of the ingredients that Nash used to demonstrate that the man in the Cook County morgue was not Dillinger. CBS even used one of Nash's books as a prop: "Twentieth Century Desperadoes" in *The Dillinger Print* is a ringer for Nash's *Bloodletters and Badmen.* To see that *The Dillinger Print* is in a sense a "derivative work" , we need only imagine how we would react if Nash had written a short story based on the premise that Dillinger was really a woman masquerading as a man, and CBS had used a switch in sex roles as the centerpiece of a drama. In such an event we would need to decide, as Hand did in *Sheldon* whether the portions CBS took over were qualitatively so important that the original author's market would be diminished excessively by a rule allowing similar appropriations in the regular course.

Nash does not portray *The Dillinger Dossier* and its companion works as fiction, however, which makes all the difference. The inventor of Sherlock Holmes controls that character's fate while the copyright lasts; the first person to conclude that Dillinger survived does not get dibs on history. If Dillinger survived, that fact is available to all. Nash's rights lie in his expression: in his words, in his arrangement of facts (his deployment of narration interspersed with interviews, for example), but not in the naked "truth". *The Dillinger Print* does not use any words from *The Dillinger Dossier* or Nash's other books; it does not take over any of Nash's presentation but instead employs a setting of its own invention with new exposition and development. Physical differences between Dillinger and the corpse, planted fingerprints, photographs of Dillinger and other gangsters in the 1930s, these and all the rest are facts as Nash depicts them. (Nash did not take the photographs and has no rights in them; *The Dillinger Print* used the photos but not Nash's arrangement of them.)

The cases closest to ours are not plays translated to the movie screen (as in *Sheldon*) but movies made from speculative works representing themselves as fact. For example, Universal made a motion picture based on the premise that an idealistic crewman planted a bomb that destroyed the dirigible *Hindenburg* on May 6, 1937. The theory came straight from A.A. Hoehling's *Who Destroyed the Hindenburg?* (1962), a monograph based on exhaustive research. The motion picture added sub-plots and development, but the thesis and the evidence adduced in support of it could be traced to Hoehling. Nonetheless, the Second Circuit concluded that this did not infringe Hoehling's rights, because the book placed the facts (as opposed to Hoehling's exposition) in the public domain. *Hoehling v. Universal City Studios, Inc.* See also *Miller v Universal City Studios* (facts about a notorious kidnapping are not protected by copyright). Cf. *Musto v. Meyer* (idea for *The Seven Per Cent Solution* derived from article in medical journal).

Hoehling suggested that "[t]o avoid a chilling effect on authors who contemplate tackling an historical issue or event, broad latitude must be granted to subsequent authors who make use of historical subject matter, including theories or plots". As our opinion in *Toksvig* shows, we are not willing to say that "anything goes" as long as the first work is about history. *Toksvig* held that the author of a biography of Hans Christian Andersen infringed the copyright of the author of an earlier biography by using portions of Andersen's letters as well as some of the themes and structure. *Hoehling* rejected *Toksvig*, concluding that "[k]nowledge is expanded ... by granting new authors of historical works a relatively free hand to build upon the work of their predecessors." With respect for our colleagues of the east, we think this goes to the extreme of looking at incentives only *ex post*. The authors in *Hoehling* and *Toksvig* spent years tracking down leads. If all of their work, right down to their words, may be used without compensation, there will be too few original investigations, and facts will not be available on which to build.

In *Toksvig* the first author, who knew Danish, spent three years learning about Andersen's life; the second author, who knew no Danish, wrote her biography in less than a year by copying out of the first book scenes and letters that the original author discovered or translated. Reducing the return on such effort, by allowing unhindered use, would make the initial leg-work less attractive and so less frequent. Copyright law does not protect hard work (divorced from expression), and hard work is not an essential ingredient of copyrightable expression; to the extent *Toksvig* confuses work or ideas with expression, it has been justly criticized.... See also *Eisenschiml v. Fawcett Publications, Inc.* (recognizing both that any two treatments of the same historical subject will be similar because the facts limit the author's freedom, and that a scholar is entitled to use a predecessor's work). We need not revisit *Toksvig* on its own facts to know that it is a mistake to hitch up at *either* pole of the continuum between granting the first author a right to forbid all similar treatments of history and granting the second author a right to use anything he pleases of the first's work....

Authors of fiction do not (necessarily) need greater incentives than authors of non-fiction. Users of and elaborators on works of non-fiction are not (necessarily) more easily dissuaded than are those who use or elaborate on works of fiction. Decisions such as *Hoehling* do not come straight from first principles. They depend, rather, on the language of what is now 17 U.S.C. s. 102(b): "In no case does copyright protection for an original work ... extend to any idea, ... or discovery, regardless of the form in which it is described, explained, illustrated, or embodied in such work." Long before the 1976 revision of the statute, courts had decided that historical facts are among the "ideas" and "discoveries" that the statute does not cover. *International News Service v. Associated Press.* This is not a natural law; Congress could have made copyright broader (as patent law is). But it is *law,* which will come as no surprise to Nash. His own books are largely fresh expositions of facts looked up in other people's books. Consider the introduction to the bibliography in *Murder, America: Homicide in the United States from the Revolution to the Present* 447 (1980):

The research for this book was done in libraries and archives throughout the United States, in addition to interviews and lengthy correspondence. The author's own files, exceeding more than a quarter of a million separate entries and a personal crime library of more than 25,000 volumes, were heavily employed.

The producers of *Simon and Simon* used Nash's work as Nash has used others': as a source of facts and ideas, to which they added their distinctive overlay. As the district court found, CBS did no more than s. 102(b) permits. Because *The Dillinger Print* uses Nash's analysis of history but none of his expression, the judgment is

AFFIRMED.

Baigent v. Random House Group Ltd., [2007] EWCA Civ 247 (Eng. C.A.)

Court of Appeal, Civil Division

Mummery, Rix and Lloyd LJJ

28 March 2007

LORD JUSTICE LLOYD:

Introduction

1. The Claimants are two of the three authors of a book published in 1982, The Holy Blood and the Holy Grail (HBHG). The Defendant is the publisher in the UK of a book written by Dan Brown, the Da Vinci Code (DVC), first published in 2003. The Claimants' contention is that, in writing DVC, Mr Brown infringed their copyright by copying a substantial part of HBHG in the course of writing six chapters of DVC. The case came to trial over 11 days in February and March 2006 before Mr Justice Peter Smith. In his judgment, delivered on 7 April 2006, he dismissed the claim: [2006] EWHC (Ch) 719. He also refused permission to appeal, but on the Claimants' application to the Court of Appeal, I granted permission to appeal on 13 June 2006.

2. It is not in dispute that HBHG is an original literary work in which copyright subsists, nor that the Claimants are two of the joint holders of the copyright. No point arises from the failure of the third, Mr Lincoln, to join them in bringing the proceedings. By virtue of section 16 of the Copyright, Designs and Patents Act 1988, it is an infringement of the Claimants' copyright for another person, without their licence, to copy HBHG or any substantial part of it, directly or indirectly. The Claimants' case is that Mr Brown derived the majority of six chapters of DVC from HBHG, that in so doing he copied part of HBHG, and that what he copied was a substantial part of HBHG.

3. The judge appears to have held that the six chapters were largely derived from HBHG, but he rejected the claim of copying....

4. The claim for breach of copyright is in some respects unusual, but it has to be tested by reference to the same principles as would be relevant in a more conventional case. If material is found in a later work which is also in an earlier copyright work, and it is shown that the author of the later work had access to the earlier work, an inference of copying is raised. Then it has to be considered whether there was in fact any copying, in relation to which the later author may say that he obtained the material from his own unaided efforts or from a different source. If it is found that any of the material common to both works was copied from the earlier work, then the question arises whether what was copied was a substantial part of the earlier work.

5. If the copyright work in question is a literary work, the allegation will normally be that part of the text of the earlier work was copied, exactly or with some modification, in the creation of the later work. In the present case that is not what is alleged as the basis for the claim in copyright infringement. What is said to have been copied is a theme of the copyright work. Copyright does not subsist in ideas; it protects the expression of ideas, not the ideas themselves. No clear principle is or could be laid down in the cases in order to tell whether what is sought to be protected is on the ideas side of the dividing line, or on the expression side.

. . .

9. Each of the two books in question contains a great deal of material which is not in the other. It was necessary for the Claimants to identify what they said had been copied, and to identify the material which they relied on as supporting their allegation of copying. It was all the more necessary for this to be done, and done clearly, given the non-textual nature of the infringement which they alleged. The judge referred to the history of the Claimants' attempts to formulate their case in this respect. I do not need to go further back than the Claimants' Voluntary Supplemental Schedule (VSS) and an order made by Lewison J on 27 October 2005. In paragraph 3 of the Amended Particulars of Claim the Claimants allege that HBHG "expresses a central theme", set out in an Annex to the statement of case. (It is also set out as an Appendix to this judgment.) The VSS sets out the Central Theme in 15 elements, and identifies in separate columns in relation to each element the passages relied on in each work for showing that the particular element is in it....

[Appendix–The Central Theme]

Points 10, 11 and 13 are in italics to show that they were held not to be in DVC. Point 14 is underlined to show that it was held not to be in HBHG.

1.	Jesus was of royal blood, with a legitimate claim to the throne of Palestine
2.	Like any devout Jew of the time, and especially like a Rabbi and any royal or aristocratic claimant, he would have been married.
3.	As expected of any Jew at the time, he would have children.
4.	At some time after the crucifixion, Jesus' wife, the figure known as Mary Magdalene, fled the Holy Land and found refuge in one of many Judaic communities then scattered around the south of France. When she fled the Holy Land, the Magdalene might have been pregnant with Jesus' offspring, or such offspring might already have been born and brought with her. We concluded from studying the Grail Romances and early manuscripts that Mary Magdalene fled the Holy Land with the Sangraal and that by turning Sangraal into 'Sang Raal' or 'Sang Réal' we suggested that Mary Magdalene fled with the royal blood.

5. We considered what the Holy Grail was, whether the Holy Grail was a cup or whether the Grail was in some way related to Mary Magdalene and the Sang Real. We concluded that the Grail would have been at least two things simultaneously. On the one hand it would have been Jesus's bloodline and descendants and it would have been quite literally the vessel that contained Jesus's blood. In other words it would have been the womb of the Magdalene and by extension the Magdalene herself.

6. In a Judaic community in the South of France, the bloodline of Jesus and the Magdalene would have been perpetuated for some five centuries–not a particularly long time, so far as royal and aristocratic blood lines are concerned.

7. Towards the end of the 5th century, Jesus' bloodline intermarried with that of the royal line of the Franks. From this union, there issued the Merovingian dynasty.

8. In the meantime, the Roman Empire in the fourth century AD, under the auspices of Constantine, had adopted "Pauline" Christianity as its officially sanctioned and tolerated form of Christianity. This was done as a matter of convenience to foster unity; and once "Pauline" Christianity became the official orthodoxy, all other forms of Christianity became, by definition, heresies. By the end of the century Christianity had become the official religion of the Roman Empire. The Church's dogmatic religious stance thus benefited from the support of secular authority.

9. When the Merovingian dynasty grew weaker under Clovis' successors, the Church reneged on its pact and colluded in the assassination of Dagobert II, last of the Merovingian rulers. Although Dagobert died and the Merovingians were deposed, Dagobert's son, Sigisbert, survived and perpetuated the Merovingian bloodline through a number of noble houses. Towards the end of the 11th century, the Merovingian blood line emerged on the central stage of history in the person of Godfroi de Bouillon, Duke of Lorraine.

10. *When Godfroi embarked on the first crusade in 1099, he was, in effect seeking to reclaim his birthright and heritage, the throne of Palestine to which his ancestors had possessed a claim a thousand years before.*

11. *Godfroi surrounded himself with a circle of counsellors, who were endowed with the Abbey situated on Mount Sion in Jerusalem and became known as the Ordre de Sion, or, subsequently, the Prieuré de Sion (Priory of Sion).*

12. The Ordre or Prieuré de Sion created the Knights Templar as their administrative and executive arm.

13. *In the mid-12th century, members of the Ordre de Sion established themselves in France, from where they subsequently spread out to own properties across the whole of Europe. When the Holy Land was lost, France became the Prieuré's primary base and headquarters.*

14. The Prieuré continued to act as protectors and custodians of the Merovingian bloodline, the "blood royal" or "sang réal", the so-called "Holy Grail" .

15. During its early history — until the 14th century — the Grand Masters of the Prieuré were drawn from a network of interlinked families, all of whom could claim Merovingian descent. From the 14th century on, the Prieuré (according to its purported statutes, which Brown would appear not to have seen) would, for complicated reasons, move outside the family. Grand Masters would then be, on occasion, illustrious names — Leonardo, for example, Botticelli, Sir Isaac Newton, Victor Hugo, Debussy, Cocteau. Sometimes, however, the names would be rather more obscure, like Charles Nodier. In any case, all "outsiders" listed as Grand Masters still have close connections with the network of families claiming Merovingian descent.

10. In the course of the trial the formulation of the Claimants' case underwent further scrutiny and clarification. They confirmed that they did not rely on any special feature by way of the architecture of the Central Theme, or the collocation of the several elements in it, other than the natural chronological sequence of the elements.

11. In section K of his judgment, paragraphs 272 to 292, the judge compared the two books by reference to the fifteen Central Theme elements. He came to the conclusion that elements 10, 11 and 13 were not to be found in DVC, and that element 14 was not to be found in HBHG. On that basis, those four elements were to be disregarded as regards any question of copying. In effect, the judge was there going through the task of establishing whether the material said to have been copied was (a) in the copyright work itself and, if so, (b) also in the work alleged to infringe that copyright.

12. As regards the other eleven elements, since they were to be found in both works, and since it was not denied that Mr Brown had access to HBHG when he was writing DVC, an inference of copying arose, so that the evidence had to be examined as to how the common material got into DVC.

. . .

14. The Claimants' case for showing that Mr Brown infringed their copyright relied on four different factors. The first was the presence in DVC of the Central Theme elements which they said were in HBHG as a central theme. The second was nine examples of language similarity, too minor to constitute a substantial part in themselves, but relied on to show that Mr Brown had HBHG at hand when writing DVC and did copy something from it. The third was a number of references to HBHG in material used by Mr Brown and his wife: there is a prominent reference to HBHG in the text of DVC itself. Fourthly, they relied on two supporting arguments, of minor significance in themselves.

15. The Defendant did not suggest that Mr Brown had not used HBHG. It did deny that he had derived any of the Central Theme elements from it rather than

from other books. Part of its case was that all the relevant Central Theme elements were already present in a Synopsis which Mr Brown wrote at an early stage, the case being that he did not have access to HBHG at all at that stage. The judge did not accept the proposition that Mr Brown did not have at least indirect access to HBHG at that stage, but he appears to have held that the Synopsis was written without any use of HBHG. On the other hand he also appears to have held that HBHG was used as a, or the, principal source at the later stage of writing the text of the relevant part of DVC itself.

16. The Defendant also contended that, if anything was taken from HBHG in the course of writing DVC, it was at too high a level of abstraction and generality; in other words, it was on the wrong side of the line between ideas and the expression of ideas. It was also said to be not a substantial part of the copyright work, principally for the same reason.

. . .

The two books

19. With that by way of introduction, I must now say something about the two books, and about the way in which DVC was written....

20. The books are very different one from the other. HBHG is described by the Claimants as a work of historical conjecture. It draws on a good deal of pre-existing material, for example about the Cathars and the Albigensian Crusade, about the Knights Templar and, farther back in time, about the Merovingian kings. It draws on writings about the Holy Grail, and on material concerned with the early history of the Christian Church. The material is presented as the story of a quest on the part of the authors, describing how their investigation of one mystery led them to explore other aspects of history, and to form conjectures and hypotheses of which, by the end of their work, they had become convinced. The judge at paragraph 46 describes the authors' thesis as being at the far end of conjecture, but nothing turns on how realistic or plausible their conclusions may be. By contrast DVC is a thriller, but one which draws on some themes similar to and overlapping with the content of HBHG to add interest, colour and tension.

. . .

The use made of HBHG in writing DVC: the judge's findings

. . .

99. Although the judge did not express his reasoning in these terms, it seems to me that his judgment can be analysed as proceeding as follows.

    i) There is relevant material in HBHG which is also to be found in DVC, namely eleven of the Central Theme elements.

    ii) Mr Brown had access to HBHG at the time when he wrote the parts of DVC which include this common material. It is not in dispute that Mr Brown used HBHG at this stage.

iii) Mr Brown based relevant parts of DVC (the Langdon/Teabing lectures) on material in HBHG.

iv) Nevertheless, what he took from HBHG amounted to generalised propositions, at too high a level of abstraction to qualify for copyright protection, because it was not the product of the application of skill and labour by the authors of HBHG in the creation of their literary work. It lay on the wrong side of the line between ideas and their expression.

v) In any event (this being the judge's principal ground for decision) although the relevant eleven Central Theme elements were to be found in both books, the claim depended on showing that the Central Theme propounded was a central theme of HBHG, sufficient to qualify as a substantial part of the work, albeit as a combination of features obtained by abstraction, as described by Lord Hoffmann in paragraph 24 of *Designers' Guild*, and this assertion by the Claimants was not justified, because the Central Theme was not a theme of HBHG at all, but rather was no more than a selection of features of HBHG collated for forensic purposes rather than emerging from a fair reading of the book as a whole....

100. In my judgment it has not been shown that the judge was wrong in the conclusions to which he came. On the contrary, it seems to me that he was entitled to come to those conclusions. I would therefore dismiss this appeal.

LORD JUSTICE RIX

101. I agree with the judgments of Lord Justice Lloyd and Lord Justice Mummery and with their reasons....

103. It remains true that a copyright work can be copied and substantially so in other than discretely linguistic ways, as Lord Hoffmann observed at para 24 of *Designers' Guild*. That is what, in one sense, occurred in *Ravenscroft v. Herbert and New English Library Limited* [1980] RPC 193, but in that case there was wholesale pillaging of not only theme (and "a single theme" at that, see page 198, line 25) but also incident and language (see at 200/203), which on any view has not occurred here.

104. ... Lord Justice Lloyd's review of the contents of HBHG itself demonstrates some of the difficulties in the way of the claimants' case.

105. Those difficulties can also be identified by both macro and micro illustrations. On the macro level, I would underline the failure of the claimants themselves in their evidence at trial to support their forensic case about the Central Theme. On the micro level, I would point, merely as examples, to element 1 ("Jesus was of royal blood, with a legitimate claim to the throne of Palestine" (sic)), which might be described as an idea fully in the world, with a pedigree back to Matthew; and to element 8 ("the Roman Empire in the fourth century AD, under the auspices of Constantine, had adopted 'Pauline' Christianity ... By the end of the century Christianity had become the official religion of the Roman Empire..."), which is concerned with a view of history which, whether accurately elaborated or not, is hardly original; and whose place in any theme is not obviously explicable. If the individual elements are concerned with ideas rather than their expression, and the structure which binds them together is

merely chronological, the judge's view of the Central Theme as falling on the wrong side of the line (for the purposes of establishing copyright infringement) between ideas and their expression is well understandable.

106. The test of copyright infringement is an objective one. As Lord Justice Lloyd has pointed out, it is not necessary to prove a guilty mind to establish liability, and it is no defence to prove an innocent mind if in fact a substantial part of a copyright work has been copied. Nevertheless, it may be observed that in writing the Langdon/Teabing lectures Mr Brown has acknowledged the use of HBHG as a source for the lectures' ideas in HBHG both cryptically, since Leigh Teabing is an anagram of Messrs Baigent and Leigh, and straightforwardly, when he has Teabing show HBHG to Sophie, describing it as "perhaps the best-known tome" on the subject and recording its claim to be "The Acclaimed International Bestseller" . That is not the mark of an author who thought that he was making illegitimate use of the fruits of someone else's literary labours, but of one who intended to acknowledge a debt of ideas, which he has gone on to express in his own way and for his own purposes.

LORD JUSTICE MUMMERY

107. I agree with the judgment of Lloyd LJ. The Claimants have not satisfied me that the decision of Peter Smith J was wrong. I would also dismiss the appeal.

. . .

136. On the issue of "a substantial part" it is nothing to the point that copyright does not subsist in the Central Theme or its 15 points or elements as an original literary work. It was not in dispute that copyright subsists in HBHG. It was not claimed that the Central Theme or its elements were a copyright work. The issue was whether the copyright in the work HBHG was infringed by copying the Central Theme. The statutory requirement of substantial copying necessitated an evaluation by the court of the part copied in DVC in relation to HBHG as a whole.

137. However, for the reasons given by Lloyd LJ I am satisfied that in this case the judge reached the right conclusion on substantiality.... Reading the judgment as a whole and in the context of the way in which the case was pleaded, the judge proceeded on the basis that the copying was not substantial, because it was of ideas expressed in HBHG rather than of the form or manner in which ideas were expressed.

138. Incidentally, I question the accuracy of the description of the matters in the VSS as "the Central Theme" or as "Central Theme Points". In ordinary usage a "theme" of a literary work simply describes what it is about in general terms. I would not normally regard a list of individual assertions of actual or virtual history contained in HBHG (such as that the Roman Empire under Constantine adopted Pauline Christianity as officially sanctioned religion or as to the creation of the Knights Templar as an arm of the Priory of Sion) as themes or as theme points.

139. In the VSS "Theme Points" is not the same use as, for example, "theme" in the expression "theme tune" , which may consist of an entire musical work or a substantial part of it. In his choice of words the pleader in this case may well have had in mind understandable copyright law reasons for describing his points as themes or theme points rather than as ideas, facts or items of information.

E. Infringement and substantial part

145. ...[I] t is not necessary for the actual language of the copyright work to be copied or even for similar words to be used tracking, like a translation, the language of the copyright work. It is sufficient to establish that there has been substantial copying of the original collection, selection, arrangement, and structure of literary material, even of material that is not in itself the subject of copyright.

146. It is not, however, sufficient for the alleged infringing work simply to replicate or use items of information, facts, ideas, theories, arguments, themes and so on derived from the original copyright work.

147. I agree with Lloyd LJ that no clear principle can be laid down on how or where to draw the line between the legitimate use of the ideas expressed and the unlawful copying of their expression.

148. A judgment has to be reached by careful attention to the facts of each particular case....

153. I appreciate that the Central Theme and its elements particularised in the VSS are important to the Claimants. They are by-products of their years of research, discussion and speculation. Viewed objectively, however, in the context of the necessary and sufficient conditions for infringement, they are not "a substantial part" of HBHG. They are not substantial in the copyright sense, any more than a fact or theory that took a lifetime to establish, or a discovery that cost a fortune to make.

154. The position is that the individual elements of the Central Theme Points distilled from HBHG in the VSS are not of a sufficiently developed character to constitute a substantial part of HBHG. In the words of the judge they are "too generalised" to be a substantial part of HBHG. They are an assortment of items of historical fact and information, virtual history, events, incidents, theories, arguments and propositions. They do not contain detailed similarities of language or "architectural" similarities in the detailed treatment or development of the collection or arrangement of incidents, situations, characters and narrative, such as is normally found in cases of infringement of literary or dramatic copyright. The 11 aspects of the Central Theme in DVC are differently expressed, collected, selected, arranged and narrated.

155. Of course, it takes time, effort and skill to conduct historical research, to collect materials for a book, to decide what facts are established by the evidence and to formulate arguments, theories, hypotheses, propositions and conclusions. It does not, however, follow, as suggested in the Claimants' submissions, that the use of items of information, fact and so on derived from the assembled material

is, in itself, "a substantial part" of HBHG simply because it has taken time skill and effort to carry out the necessary research.

156. The literary copyright exists in HBHG by reason of the skill and labour expended by the Claimants in the original composition and production of it and the original manner or form of expression of the results of their research. Original expression includes not only the language in which the work is composed but also the original selection, arrangement and compilation of the raw research material. It does not, however, extend to clothing information, facts, ideas, theories and themes with exclusive property rights, so as to enable the Claimants to monopolise historical research or knowledge and prevent the legitimate use of historical and biographical material, theories propounded, general arguments deployed, or general hypotheses suggested (whether they are sound or not) or general themes written about.

157. The reported cases in which infringement claims have succeeded in relation to historical works or semi-historical works do not assist the Claimants' case. They are decisions by experienced Chancery judges at first instance correctly applying well established general principles to the particular facts of the case. For example in *Ravenscroft v. Herbert* [1980] RPC 193 Brightman J found that there was copying of a substantial part of a work of non-fiction (The Spear of Destiny) in the form of a novel. To an appreciable extent they were competing works. The defendant's novel was alleged to contain as many as 50 instances of deliberate language copying, as well as copying of the same historical characters, historical incidents and interpretation of the significance of historical events.

158. *Harman Pictures NV v. Osborne* [1967] 1 WLR 723 is another well known example of a case in which the author of a historical work (The Reason Why) obtained an interlocutory injunction in a copyright claim against the writer of a film script, which had much in common with the original copyright work in its selection of incidents and quotations supplemented by some alterations and additions attributed to other sources. Goff J found "many similarities of detail" in John Osborne's film script (page 735) and he was impressed by "the marked similarity of the choice of incidents ... and by the juxtaposition of ideas" for which there was a lack of explanation on the defendant's side.

159. In my judgment, the judge rightly held that the Claimants have not established that a substantial part of HBHG has been copied, either as to the original composition and expression of the work or as to the particular collection, selection and arrangement of material and its treatment in HBHG.

Chapter 3

SUBJECT MATTER

1. Works and Related Subject Matter

For copyright to subsist in a work, the work must fall into one of the enumerated categories of works protected under the *Copyright Act*.[1] Section 2 of the Act states that "every original literary, dramatic, musical, and artistic work includes every original production in the literary, scientific or artistic domain, whatever may be the mode or form of its expression, such as compilations, books, pamphlets, and other writings, lectures, dramatic, or dramatico-musical works, musical works, translations, illustrations, sketches, and plastic works relative to geography, topography, architecture or science." This list of works is taken, with minor changes, from Article II of *The Berne Convention*, which was signed at Rome on June 2, 1928, to which Canada has adhered.

It is clear that copyright protects an enormous range of intellectual expression, from poetry to software, from paintings to buildings and beyond. Remarkably — and some would say problematically — the protection it offers to these widely disparate expressive forms is determined by consistent application of the same fundamental principles and legal doctrine. There is no doubt, however, that from both a principled and practical perspective, each one of copyright's various subject matters presents a unique set of challenges when it comes to the application of the "one-size-fits-all" legal rules. In this chapter, we will canvass copyright's subject-matter categories, examining their definitions, limits, and the particular problems that they present.

One question that arises repeatedly in the jurisprudence is whether, and to what extent, the subject-matter category itself imposes a qualitative threshold or substantive standard that works must meet in order to be regarded as such. What does it mean for something to be "literary" in nature? What is "art or "artistic-ness" and should it matter for the purposes of the law? What is music, and by whose ears should it be judged? What is the difference between the Swan Lake ballet and a perfectly planned football play?

As we will see, courts have been reluctant to craft definitions of copyright's subject-matter; but if one of the goals of copyright law is to encourage a particular kind of expressive creativity, why should it be inappropriate to

---

[1] Section 89, *Cuisenaire v. South West Imports Ltd.* (1967), 54 C.P.R. 1 (Ex. Ct.), affirmed (1968), 57 C.P.R. 76 (S.C.C.).

define the kind of expression it is meant to encourage? Does it not seem strange that copyright law protects art, for example, but refuses to define it?

Cuisenaire v. South West Imports Ltd. (1967), [1968] 1 Ex. C.R. 493, affirmed (1968), 57 C.P.R. 76 (S.C.C.)

Exchequer Court of Canada

Noel J.

Judgment: December 7, 1967

In an action for infringement of copyright, the plaintiff claimed to be the author of two works, namely, (1) a set of ten coloured rods and (2) a set of 241 coloured rods of different lengths, for the teaching of the science of arithmetic in primary school grades. The rods were cut from lengths of wood one square centimeter in cross-section and in lengths ranging from one to ten centimeters. Each of the ten rods had a characteristic colour according to its length. The plaintiff also published an explanatory book but did not claim that any part of his copyright in the book was being infringed by the defendant but that his book was being used to demonstrate the defendant's rods. The plaintiff claimed that the rods, considered by themselves, were a work in which copyright subsisted as an artistic work or a work of artistic craftsmanship.

. . .

30   Section 2(v) of the Canadian *Copyright Act* reads as follows:

2. In this Act,

. . .

> (v) *"every original literary, dramatic, musical and artistic work"* includes every *original production in the* literary, *scientific* or artistic *domain, whatever may be the mode or form of its expression,* such as books, pamphlets, and other writings, lectures, dramatic or dramatico-musical works, musical works or compositions with or without words, illustrations, sketches, and plastic works relative to geography, topography, architecture or science. (The emphasis is mine).

. . .

36   The position of counsel for the plaintiff is that it is not even necessary to say whether the works are artistic, literary, musical or dramatic because as long as such works are *original productions in the scientific domain,* they are within the expression "every original literary, dramatic, musical and artistic work". He, in other words, takes the position that he does not have to say any more than that these works are an original production in the scientific domain and need not say whether they are artistic, literary, dramatic or musical.

37   The defendant, on the other hand, submits that section 2(v) should be interpreted as if the words "in one or other of these categories" were inserted therein

to read as follows: "every original literary, dramatic, musical and artistic work includes every original production" *in one or other of these categories* "in the literary, scientific or artistic domain" even if in order to do so one must make a repetition and read into the text of the section additional words.

38 There was apparently nothing novel in saying that copyright could subsist in scientific works as there were areas under the law prior to 1931 in which scientific works were protected. As a matter of fact, a literary work in the scientific domain was always protected as a literary work as well as certain artistic works in the scientific domain such as charts and the question here is whether the inclusion of section 2(v) into our Act in 1931 with the words "*includes every original production in the literary, scientific or artistic domain whatever may be the mode or form of its expression ...*" (which are of a descriptively wide scope) has extended the classes of matters that can be the subject of copyright under the Act to a point where it could comprise any original production in the scientific field.

. . .

53 I will first deal with plaintiff's submission that any production in the scientific domain under section 2(v) can be a proper subject matter of copyright and that this is what his rods are as they are at least a partial expression of his scientific work which is his book *Les nombres en couleur*.

54 I believe that in order to deal properly with section 2(v) of our Act, some consideration should be given to the manner in which it came into the Act as well as to its wording and the inclusion therein of the word scientific which I must say is somewhat confusing. I should mention that the word scientific was in the Canadian Act as far back as the year 1875 and remained therein until the year 1924 when that statute was repealed (*cf. Revised Statutes*, 1875-1886 and 1906 chapter 70). The expression used in those statutes was "literary, scientific and artistic works". The statute from 1924 to 1931 did not have the word "scientific" in it and this word returned in 1931 when, as already mentioned, section 2(v) was taken from the Rome Convention of 1928, the words "musical and dramatic" were added to the term "artistic and literary works" and the whole was inserted in the interpretation section of the Act probably, as I have already indicated, in an attempt to comply with the obligations undertaken by Canada as a member of the Convention.

55 The manner in which the addition of section 2(v) came about and the somewhat confusing language used therein (by which I refer to the word "scientific" between the words literary and artistic) indicate, I believe, that not too much thought could have been given at the time to its possible effect on the subject matter of copyright in this country.

56 It therefore is at least an ambiguous section and considerable caution should, I believe, be exercised as a matter of construction in interpreting the language used so as to avoid absurd results and so as to avoid concluding that it involves a substantial change in the law that could not have been intended by Parliament.

57 Before an interpretation is given to this section which would lead to an absurdity or to a construction which would produce impractical or incongruous results (such as that products such as penicillin or tetracyclin, or IBM computers or telephone switchboard with complicated wirings with a colour code in the wiring that are ordinarily proper subject matters of inventions could, in addition to being patented be also copyrighted, and thereby given a longer life) a very close look should, I believe, be taken at this section with a view to restricting it to reasonable proportions and to giving it a meaning in conformity with the object of the *Copyright Act* and in accordance with the generally accepted scheme of the protection that is to be given to industrial rights in this country. Indeed, when words used are ambiguous and uncertain, one must resist an interpretation which would lead to a very substantial change in the character of the subject matter involved.

58 Should I give this section the wide interpretation claimed by the plaintiff so that it covers everything that can be described, as an original production in the scientific field or as purely utilitarian which would indeed involve giving protection under our Copyright Act to objects which have been held in the past not to be the proper subject of a copyright (such as in *Hollinrake v. Truswell*, [1894] 3 Ch.D. 420) where a cardboard pattern sleeve containing upon it scales, figures and descriptive words for adapting it to sleeves for any dimensions were held to be not "copyrightable" although it might be the subject of a patent as an instrument or tool) and would considerably expand the law in this regard. I must, I am afraid, hold after a careful consideration of this matter, that the law cannot be extended in this manner by such an ambiguous provision.

59 I am also of the view that the subject matter of copyright must remain in line with the general nature of the works defined in sections 2(b) and 2(n) and with the examples given therein as well as in section 2(v) which all put a limitation on the meaning that would otherwise be given to them and I should add that plaintiff's rods do not fall into any class illustrated by these examples.

60 I must, therefore, conclude that section 2(v) of the Act has not altered the law in any substantial way, if at all, and that it is still necessary to find that the work in which copyright is claimed is an "original literary, dramatic, musical or artistic work" in the normal meaning of those words and in the light of the definitions in section 2 of the Act.

61 Indeed the only reasonable solution I can arrive at is that the Act only protects those original literary, dramatic, musical and artistic works referred to in section 4(1) of the Act and it therefore follows that it is still necessary before section 2(v) comes into operation to find that the work falls in one or the other of these four categories.

62 If such is the case, the question may well be asked what section 2(v) can mean as it should not be presumed that Parliament has spoken uselessly. I should think that the most that it can mean is that it may, within any one of those four categories, give a more extended meaning to the works included therein because of the words "whatever may be the mode or form of its expression" or because

of the examples given in the subsection, than was considered right under the statute as it stood immediately before section 2(v) was put in.

63 Whatever such an extended meaning may be, it cannot, in any event, assist the plaintiff here as his rods clearly do not fall in the category of a dramatic or musical work nor of a literary work nor even in the category of an artistic work with which I will deal later.

. . .

70 I now turn to plaintiff's contention that if his rods are not original productions in the scientific domain, as contemplated by section 2(v) of the Act, they are either artistic works or works of artistic craftsmanship under section 2(b) of the Act. This section reads as follows:

> 2. In this Act,
>
> . . .
>
> (b) "artistic work" includes works of painting, drawing, sculpture and artistic craftsmanship, and architectural works of art and engravings and photographs;

71 Here again I must disagree with this submission. In my view, plaintiff's rods are physically little more than tools or counters to be used for a particular purpose. Although they are coloured in a manner such as to interest or please children, the same as blocks for instance, they were never intended primarily as an article regarded as artistic or beautiful in itself even if the artistic requirements required here are not too great. Indeed, even if artistic merit is not a matter of importance in copyright law, the word artistic must still be given its ordinary meaning although, may I add, there could be considerable debate as to the merit of a particular work.

72 It is true, as pointed out by counsel for the plaintiff, that there is originality in the colouring and size, selection and arrangement within the sets and the choice of the colours may well have been arrived at with a view to applying the method he conceived to teach children arithmetic. It is, however, the artistic work itself which is entitled to protection and not the idea behind it. These rods indeed are tools and nothing more, the same as colours, for instance, are tools in teaching children how to paint. They can take on meaning only when considered and integrated with a concept itself which in itself is not entitled to protection. The only relationship between the rods which exists here is by reference to Cuisenaire's theory where it can be seen that there is a connection between the colours denoting certain families of significantly related mathematical values which, however, cannot really be considered as an artistic arrangement. Furthermore, although these coloured rods set out orderly in a box could be considered as an artistic arrangement, there is no claim to such arrangement here and it is difficult to see how colour through these rods could confer copyright on the works even if all these things are claimed in combination.

73 An artistic work, in my view, must to some degree at least, be a work that is intended to have an appeal to the aesthetic senses not just an incidental appeal,

such as here, but as an important or one of the important objects for which the work is brought into being. The plaintiff's rods may have a certain attraction to children, but this, in my view, is a very secondary purpose which, I am afraid, is not a sufficient basis for a finding that the rods are artistic.

74 I must, therefore, conclude that plaintiff's rods are not and cannot be held to be artistic works under the Act.

2. Literary Works

The term "literary work" is defined in the Act to include "tables, computer programs, and compilations of literary works."[2] Literary merit is not required for a work to be a literary work and many works in print or in writing are capable of being literary works.

Some judicial attempts have been made to craft a more substantive standard for "literary works" in order to exclude subject matter that belongs more appropriately in the realm of trade-mark or patent law. However, the inclusion of machine-readable computer software in the "literary" category has tested the boundaries of "literariness"; it seems clear that the "literary works" category can act as a virtual catch-all for anything that could be regarded as original expression for which the benefits of copyright protection might be sought. In *North West Marine Technology, Inc. v. Crosby*, [1996] B.C.J. No. 2203, it was accepted by the B.C. court that even a binary coding system for tagging and tracking fish might qualify as copyrightable subject matter: "As technology changes and advances, there will undoubtably be many new forms of expression, and many of them will be of a form that warrants protection by copyright." (At para. 60). The *US Copyright Act 1976* defines "literary works" in the following, expansive terms: "'Literary works are works, other than audiovisual works, *expressed in words, numbers, or other verbal or numerical symbols or indicia*, regardless of the nature of the material objects, such as books, periodicals, manuscripts, phonorecords, film, tapes, disks, or cards, in which they are embodied."

Hollinrake v. Truswell, [1894] 3 Ch. 420 (C.A.)

Court of Appeal

Lord Herschell, L.C., Lindleyand Davey, L.JJ.

1894 July 9; Aug. 8.

1894.   Aug. 8. LORD HERSCHELL, L.C.: —

This action was brought by the Plaintiff as assignee under an assignment in writing of the 1st of February, 1891, from one *Edmund George Kendall*, "of the copyright in a book, to wit, a map, chart, or plan entitled the 'Cosmopolitan

---

2   S.C. 1993, c. 44, s. 53(2).

Sleeve Chart, 1886."' The copyright and assignment were both duly registered at *Stationers' Hall*. The Plaintiff alleged that the Defendant had infringed his copyright in the "Cosmopolitan Sleeve Chart" by the printing, publishing, and sale of a large number of sleeve charts called the "*Ideal*," such sleeve charts being copies of the Plaintiffs "*Cosmopolitan Sleeve Chart*." ...

The words and figures for which the Plaintiff is alleged to have obtained such protection consist of the words "top curve line; under curve line; under arm curves; measure round the thick part of the arm; measure round the thick part of the elbow; measure round the knuckles of the hand;" together with certain curved lines in connection with the words "under arm curves" and certain scales of inches and half-inches in connection with the words "measure round the thick part of the arm," and "measure round the thick part of the elbow." All these are printed on a piece of cardboard, so curved as to represent the parts of the arm above and below the elbow, which is called the "*Cosmopolitan Sleeve Chart*."

. . .

Now, I have to observe, in the first place, that no one could claim a monopoly of the use of such a sentence as "measure round the thick part of the arm," or of a half-inch scale. And the words and figures found on the "chart" do not in combination convey any intelligible idea, nor could they be of the slightest use to any one, apart from the cardboard upon which they are printed. The object of the Copyright Act was to prevent any one publishing a copy of the particular form of expression in which an author conveyed ideas or information to the world. These may be retained by any one, though the book, map, or chart which embodied them has passed out of his possession. If he were to commit to memory the contents of the book, or the information disclosed by the map or chart, he would be as much in possession of the author's ideas or information as if the book, map, or chart were physically in his hands. But this is not the case with the words or figures upon the sleeve chart. They are intended to be used, and can only be of use, in connection with that upon which they are inscribed. They are not merely directions for the use of the cardboard, which is in truth a measuring apparatus, but they are a part of that very apparatus itself, without which it cannot be used, and except in connection with which they are absolutely useless.

I think it is clear, therefore, that what the Plaintiff has sought to protect under the Act for the protection of literary productions is not a literary production, but an apparatus for the use of which certain words and figures must necessarily be inscribed upon it. It is quite true that, notwithstanding the words of the preamble, the protection of copyright may be obtained for works which cannot be said, in the ordinary sense of the term, to have literary merit. Compilations, such as the Post Office Directory, have, no doubt, properly been held to be the subject of copyright; but there is, as I have pointed out, a marked distinction between these and the claim of protection under the Copyright Actfor words and figures inscribed on and necessarily forming part of an apparatus or tool. ...

. . .

LINDLEY, L.J.: —

The evidence shews that what is on the cardboard is not intended simply to be understood by persons who wish to learn how to cut out sleeves, but that the cardboard itself is intended for use in cutting them out. This at once distinguishes this particular thing from every publication which is generally understood to come under the definition of the word "book" in the Act 5 & 6 Vict. c. 45, s. 2- viz., "volume, part or division of a volume, pamphlet, sheet of letterpress, sheet of music, map, chart, or plan separately published." The learned Judge considered that this thing was a map, chart, or plan; but, if so, it is a very peculiar one, for the use of it lies, not in the information conveyed by it, but in such information combined with the material on which the information is printed. The thing is in truth a measuring instrument: it is no more a chart or plan within the Copyright Act than is a scaled ruler such as is found in any mathematical instrument case. Such a thing may possibly, if novel and useful, be a good subject-matter for a patent. But I cannot bring myself to hold that it is a map, chart, or plan within the meaning of the Copyright Act.

. . .

DAVEY, L.J.: —

... I agree with the learned Judge below that a "map" is not confined to what is popularly known as a map — viz., a geographical map — and that a "chart" is not confined to what is popularly called a chart — viz., a map of a portion of the seas shewing the rocks, soundings, and suchlike information for the use of navigators. But I cannot agree with him that the cardboard before us is either a map, plan, or chart within the Act. There may, no doubt, be an anatomical or physiological plan, shewing the structure and distribution of the muscles and bones of the human arm, or any other part of the human frame, which would be protected by the Copyright Act. But this so-called chart does not seem to me to be of that character, or to be the proper subject of copyright. The preamble of the Act recites that it is expedient "to afford greater encouragement to the production of literary works of lasting benefit to the world": and although I agree that the clear enactment of a statute cannot be controlled by the preamble, yet I think that the preamble may be usefully referred to for the purpose of ascertaining the class of works it was intended to protect.

Now, a literary work is intended to afford either information and instruction, or pleasure, in the form of literary enjoyment. The sleeve chart before us gives no information or instruction. It does not add to the stock of human knowledge or give, and is not designed to give, any instruction by way of description or otherwise; and it certainly is not calculated to afford literary enjoyment or pleasure. It is a representation of the shape of a lady's arm, or more probably of a sleeve designed for a lady's arm, with certain scales for measurement upon it. It is intended, not for the purpose of giving information or pleasure, but for practical use in the art of dressmaking. It is, in fact, a mechanical contrivance, appliance or tool, for the better enabling a dressmaker to make her measurements for the purpose of cutting out the sleeve of a lady's dress, and is intended to be used for that purpose. In my opinion it is no more entitled to copyright as a literary work than the scale attached to the barometer in Davis v. Comitti [FN23]. The Plaintiff is really seeking a monopoly of her mode of measuring for sleeves of dresses under the guise of a claim to literary copyright.

Exxon Corp. v. Exxon Insurance Consultants International Ltd., [1981] 3 All E.R. 241

Court of Appeal

Stephenson and Oliver L.JJ. and Sir David Cairns

1981 June 11, 12

Graham J.

1981 Jan. 13, 14, 16, 22

STEPHENSON L.J.

The claim relevant to this appeal is made first of all under paragraph 19 of the statement of claim, which reads as follows:

> "The word 'Exxon' is an original literary work falling within the provisions of section 2 (1) of the Copyright Act 1956 and the first plaintiff is the owner of the copyright therein and the second, third and fourth plaintiffs licensees thereof."

The defendant company was formed in 1977 and it is alleged in para graph 21 of the statement of claim that it "has, without the licence or consent of the plaintiffs, adopted the name 'Exxon' as part of its corporate name." Then, in paragraph 22, the statement of claim alleges:

> "Further the defendant has, without the licence or consent of the plaintiffs, repro-duced and/or authorised the reproduction of the plaintiffs' copyright work 'Exxon' in the defendant's corporate name"

and then, in paragraph 23:

> "By reason of the matters referred to ... the defendant has infringed the plaintiffs' copyright in the word 'Exxon' and threatens to continue to do so."

. . .

In his judgment Graham J. p. 129A-B posed the basic question, and in my judg-ment posed it rightly, as being the question

> "whether it is proper to construe 'original literary work' in the Copyright Act 1956, section 2, as covering a single invented word even if considerable time and work were expended on it and, if so, whether the word 'Exxon' here is such a work. There are, I think, no decided cases which deal specifically with the precise point that I have to decide. The answer, therefore, must in the end depend upon the proper construction of the words in the Act according to general principles and on the facts of the case."

He answered the question in this way, at pp. 130G-D–131D:

> "As I have already stated, the question that I have to decide is, shortly stated, whether 'Exxon' is an 'original literary work' within section 2? I do not think it is. What is it then?, one may ask. It is a word which, though invented and therefore original, has no meaning and suggests nothing in itself. To give it substance and meaning, it must be accompanied by other words or used in a particular context or juxtaposition. When used as part of any of the plaintiffs' corporate names, it clearly has a denominative characteristic as denoting the company in question. When used, as I assume it is, with the plaintiffs' goods, it would clearly have the effect of denoting origin or quality. It is in fact an invented word with no meaning, which is a typical subject for trade mark registration, and which no doubt, with adequate user, is capable also of becoming, if it has not already become, distinctive of the plaintiffs and their goods at common law. It is not in itself a title or distinguishing name and, as I have said, only takes on meaning or significance when actually used with other words, for example indicating that it is the name of a company, or in a particular juxtaposition as, for example, upon goods.

> "Nothing I have said above is intended to suggest that I consider that a word which is used as a title can, as a matter of law, never in any circumstances be the subject of copyright, and I would disagree with dicta in previous cases to the contrary effect. Such a word would, however, I think, have to have qualities or characteristics in itself, if such a thing is possible, which would justify its recognition as an original literary work rather than merely as an invented word. It may well turn out not to be possible in practice, but, as at present advised, I consider that the mere fact that a single word is invented and that research or labour was involved in its invention does not in itself, in my judgment, necessarily enable it to qualify as an original literary work within section 2 of the Act."

Graham J. then went on to consider an analogy with Lewis Carroll's nonsense poem, "Jabberwocky" and came to the conclusion, at pp. 131H–132D, that the words "Jabberwock" or "Jabberwocky," if used alone without any poem, could not form the subject of copyright, the legal reason being, said Graham J.:

> "that the word alone and by itself cannot properly be considered as a ' literary *work* ,' the subject of copyright under the Act. It becomes part of a 'literary work' within the Act when it is embodied in the poem, but it is the poem as a composition which is a work within the Act and not the word itself."

I have quoted extensively from Graham J.'s judgment in order to adopt it gratefully. It seems to me that he asked the right question and gave it the right answer; but I would be doing less than justice to Mr. Price's vigorous argument on behalf of the plaintiffs if I left the matter there.

. . .

The question, therefore, is whether this word "Exxon" is an "original literary work." It was invented, as the statement of claim alleges, after research and testing to find a suitable word, apparently over a period of more than a year. It is therefore difficult, if not impossible, to say that it is not original. It was invented and devised by and originated with the first plaintiff. Is it an "original literary work"? Mr. Price submitted that it is. He said that the Act of 1842, by its preamble, was concerned to protect literary works of lasting benefit to the world, but such literary works were confined by the Act, as is clear from all its sections, to printed books; there is no such limitation in copyright in literary works since 1911 in this country. What is now protected as an original literary work is anything which can be, and has been, written down for the first time; any combination of letters thought out and written down; any tangible product of intellectual endeavour. Mr. Price referred us to Webster's Dictionary, in which "work" is defined in one place as

> "... something produced or accomplished by effort, exertion, or exercise of skill ... something produced by the exercise of creative talent or expenditure of creative effort..."

> He said that this word satisfies those conditions. It does not matter how much work went into it, subject, perhaps, to the principle de minimis lex non curat; it does not matter how poor the quality of the work is; if it was the result, or the product, of creative effort, the exercise of some skill and effort, it is a work, and if it is a work which is written down and consists of letters, it is a literary work. If you take the phrase "original literary work" to pieces, this word "Exxon" is original for the reason that I have given, it is literary and it is a work. Why, then, is it not an "original literary work"? But he conceded, although he submitted that it is helpful to split the phrase up into its three component words, that it is the expression as a whole in the context of the Act which has to be construed. "Literary" is given a broader meaning in the Act of 1956 than it was given in the Act of 1842, and that broader meaning must colour and extend the meaning of "work. " Some skill and care having been exerted in inventing this word by selecting these four letters out of the alphabet of 26, the word qualifies as an "original literary work." Admittedly there is no authority for treating such a word as the subject of copyright, but Mr. Price submitted that in its plain and natural meaning this one word, meaningless though it is unless applied to a company or to goods, is an "original literary work."

The only help which I have found in the authorities cited by Mr. Price is the judgment of Peterson J. in University of London Press Ltd. v University Tutorial Press Ltd. [1916] 2 Ch. 601 which Graham J. cited. In that case, Peterson J. had to consider whether examination papers were the subject of copyright under section 1 (1) of the Copyright Act 1911, which provided, exactly in the way provided by section 2 of the Act of 1956, for copyright in "every original literary, dramatic, musical and artistic work." Peterson J. pointed out, at p. 608, that under the Act of 1842 which protected books:

> "many things which had no pretensions to literary style acquired copyright; for example, a list of registered bills of sale, a list of foxhounds and hunting days, and trade catalogues; and I see no ground for coming to the conclusion that the present Act was intended to curtail the rights of authors. In my view the words 'literary work' cover work which is expressed in print or writing, irrespective of the question whether the quality or style is high. The word 'literary' seems to be used in a sense somewhat similar to the use of the word ' literature' in political or electioneering literature and refers to written or printed matter. Papers set by examiners are, in my opinion, 'literary work' within the meaning of the present Act."

Peterson J. said, at pp. 609-610:

> "The objections with which I have dealt do not appear to me to have any substance, and, after all, there remains the rough practical test that what is worth copying is prima facie worth protecting."

Those observations of Peterson J. were approved by Lord Reid, Lord Hodson and Lord Pearce in Ladbroke (Football) Ltd. v. William Hill (Football) Ltd. [1964] 1 W.L.R. 273, where their Lordships were concerned with the originality of certain football coupons and with the question whether a substantial part of them had been copied. So there is nothing in the decision in that case which assists either Mr. Price's argument, or this court in considering what the right answer to the question is; but the majority of their Lordships indicated their approval of what Peterson J. had said in the London University Press case.

I think Mr. Price was also entitled to rely on the "code" case of D. P. Anderson & Co. Ltd. v. Lieber Code Co. [1917] 2 K.B. 469. In that case Mr. Worrall had selected from an enormous number of words 100,000 five-letter words to form a suitable code for cabling purposes and Bailhache J. was pressed with the argument that, these words being meaningless, except so far as they were fixed with the arbitrary meaning which the deviser of the code gave them in the so-called "Empire cipher code," they could not be literary, or a literary work. Bailhache J. rejected that argument and said, at p. 471:

> "The words — I call them so for want of a better name — are for use for telegraphic purposes, and to each of them a meaning can be attached by the person sending the message and also by the addressee, provided, of course, he is informed of the meaning attached to it by the sender."

and he came to the conclusion that copyright did exist and that the defendants had infringed it, although it was a copyright in those very numerous and meaningless code words — meaningless only in the sense which I have described.

Mr. Price also referred us to observations made by Megarry J. in British Northrop Ltd. v. Texteam Blackburn Ltd. [1974] R.P.C. 57 in which he said, at p. 68:

> "I do not think that the mere fact that a drawing is of an elementary and commonplace article makes it too simple to be the subject of copyright."

He also referred us to an observation of Whitford J. in Karo Step Trade Mark [1977] R.P.C. 255, 273:

> "No doubt a drawing may be so simple that it cannot be said to be 'a work' — for example, a straight line or a circle — for the word 'work' itself carries with it the idea of the exercise of some degree of skill and labour; but I am unable to accept the submission of counsel for Mrs. Bishop that the artistic part of this device is of so simple a nature that no copyright can reside in it."

With those observations I do not, of course, quarrel, but I do not find them of much assistance in deciding whether this word "Exxon" qualifies as an original literary work, when I give those words in their context as ordinary a meaning as I can.

I find rather more assistance in the last case to which Mr. Mummery referred us; in particular, the observations of Davey L.J. in the case of Hollinrake v. Truswell

[1894] 3 Ch. 420. That case was concerned with copyright in a cardboard pattern sleeve with scales and figures and descriptive words on it. In his judgment Davey L.J. said, at pp. 427-428:

> "The preamble of the Act" that was referring to the Act of 1842 "recites that it is expedient 'to afford greater encouragement to the production of literary works of lasting benefit to the world:' and although I agree that the clear enactment of a statute cannot be controlled by the preamble, yet I think that the preamble may be usefully referred to for the purpose of ascertaining the class of works it was intended to protect. Now, a literary work is intended to afford either information and instruction, or pleasure, in the form of literary enjoyment. The sleeve chart before us gives no information or instruction. It does not add to the stock of human knowledge or give, and is not designed to give, any instruction by way of description or otherwise; and it certainly is not calculated to afford literary enjoyment or pleasure. It is a representation of the shape of a lady's arm, or more probably of a sleeve designed for a lady's arm, with certain scales for measurement upon it. It is intended, not for the purpose of giving information or pleasure, but for practical use in the art of dressmaking. It is, in fact, a mechanical contrivance, appliance or tool, for the better enabling a dressmaker to make her measurements for the purpose of cutting out the sleeve of a lady's dress, and is intended to be used for that purpose. In my opinion it is no more entitled to copyright as a literary work than the scale attached to the barometer in the case of Davis v. Comitti (1885) 52 L.T.(N.S.) 539."

He agreed with Lindley L.J., I think, that the plaintiffs in that case were attempting to use the Copyright Act 1842 for a purpose to which it was not properly applicable. Mr. Price said that those observations as to what is a literary work must be considered in the light of the preamble to the Act of 1842, to which Davey L.J. expressly referred. The words do, however, appeal to me as stating the ordinary meaning of the words "literary work." I would have thought, unaided or unhampered by authority, that unless there is something in the context of the Act which forbids it, a literary work would be something which was intended to afford either information and instruction, or pleasure in the form of literary enjoyment, whatever those last six words may add to the word "pleasure." Mr. Price has not convinced me that this word "Exxon" was intended to do, or does do, either of those things; nor has he convinced me that it is not of the essence of a literary work that it should do one of those things. Nor has he convinced me that there is anything in the Act, or in what Peterson J. said about the words in the earlier Act, or in any authority, or in principle, which compels me to give a different construction from Davey L.J.'s to the words "literary work." As I have already said, I agree with the way in which Graham J. put the matter; I am not sure whether this can be said to be a "work" at all, I am clearly of the opinion that it cannot be said to be a "literary work." I therefore agree with Graham J. and I would dismiss this appeal.

OLIVER L.J.

I entirely agree. Section 2 of the Act of 1956 provides that copyright should subsist in every "original literary work," and in essence Mr. Price's submissions were very simple. First, he said that the name "Exxon" is undoubtedly original;

it had not been thought of before or, so far as is known, used before; it is an artificial word, which does not appear in any known language. It is, he said, literary; it is composed of letters and it is written, typed or printed. It is a "work" because work or effort went into its invention, and its selection as a suitable name for the plaintiff group which had no meaning, offensive or otherwise, in any other language. But "original literary work" as used in the statute is a composite expression, and for my part I do not think that the right way to apply a composite expression is, or at any rate is necessarily, to ascertain whether a particular subject matter falls within the meaning of each of the constituent parts, and then to say that the whole expression is merely the sum total of the constituent parts. In my judgment it is not necessary, in construing a statutory expression, to take leave of one's common sense, and the result to which Mr. Price sought to drive us is one which, to my mind, involves doing just that.

Stephenson L.J. has already referred to the judgment of Davey L.J. in Hollinrake v. Truswell [1894] 3 Ch. 420, 428, where he said: "Now, a literary work is intended to afford either information and instruction, or pleasure, in the form of literary enjoyment." Admittedly, that was said in relation to the preamble of the Act of 1842, which referred to affording "encouragement to the production of literary works of lasting benefit to the world." But it does seem to me, as it seems to Stephenson L.J., that what Davey L.J. said was a fair summary of what the expression means in ordinary language. We have been referred to a number of cases in which copyright has been successfully claimed in, for instance, examination papers, football coupons and tables of ciphers; but all these — and I do not exclude the case of the telegraphic code in D. P. Anderson & Co. Ltd. v. Lieber Code Co. [1917] 2 K.B. 469 - seem to me to fall fairly within Davey L.J.'s commonsense formulation. But that for which protection is sought in the instant case does not appear to me to have any of the qualities which commonsense would demand. It conveys no information; it provides no instruction; it gives no pleasure that I can conceive; it is simply an artificial combination of four letters of the alphabet which serves a purpose only when it is used in juxtaposition with other English words, to identify one or other of the companies in the plaintiffs' group. Whether, as might perhaps be the case if one followed up the suggestion made in the judgment of Graham J., the insertion of the extra "x" was to avoid the risk of involving the Bishop of Exeter in proceedings for infringement every time he wrote to "The Times" newspaper, I do not pause to inquire. I am clearly of the opinion that Graham J. arrived at the correct conclusion when he held that this was not an "original literary work " in which copyright subsists, and I agree that the appeal should be dismissed.

The Bulman Group Ltd. v. Alpha One — Write Systems B.C. Ltd. (1980), 54 C.P.R. (2d) 171, reversed (1981), 54 C.P.R. (2d) 179 (Fed. C.A.)

Federal Court of Appeal

Pratte, LeDain, JJ., and Verchere, D.J.

Heard: March 30, 1981
Judgment: April 2, 1981
Docket: A-883-80

LeDain, J.:

1 This is an appeal from an order of the Trial Division dismissing an application for an interlocutory injunction in an action for alleged infringement of copyright in certain accounting forms on the ground that the forms are not proper subject matter for copyright.

5 ... the trial judge held that the accounting forms were not literary works within the meaning of the *Copyright Act*, R.S.C. 1970, c. C-30. Section 4(1) of the Act provides that "Subject to this Act, copyright shall subsist in Canada for the term hereinafter mentioned, in every original literary, dramatic, musical and artistic work", and section 2 defines literary work as follows:

> 2. In this Act
>
> "literary work" includes maps, charts, plans, tables and compilations;

6 The learned trial judge based this conclusion on the view that as a matter of law a literary work must be informative, and that the accounting forms did not meet this requirement. That this was clearly and emphatically the single ground of his decision is indicated by the following passages from his reasons:

> It is of some importance to note that not only in section 4 but throughout the Act, "literary works" are linked with dramatic musical and artistic works. It is settled law that the literary merit of a work need not be high and indeed might be minimal or, to all intents and purposes, non-existent, especially in the case of a compilation. There still remains, however, the essential element of conveying special information of some kind. The work must of itself possess either aesthetic or informative value. In other words, to be the subject of copyright it is not always necessary that the work have literary quality or merit in the sense of aesthetic quality or virtue. It might be a trade directory (*Lamb v. Evans*) or a compilation of some sort as long as some original skill and judgment is required in its preparation. But it is essential, however, that of itself, it be informative and not merely part of a system which permits someone else to gather, insert and convey information more efficiently.
>
> However, they are not only part of the system but, with the peg board, constitute the system itself. They do not convey nor are they intended to convey information by themselves for they constitute essentially and exclusively a tool or method by which information can be speedily and efficiently recorded. They do not constitute a literary work even under the extended meaning given those words by section 2 of the Act for there remains in that definition the concept of "literary" in the sense that it must at least be informative as a work in itself and not designed merely as a repository of information to be supplied.

I therefore conclude that, because they are not informative and are merely part of a system, the object of which is use rather than information, the forms are not proper material for copyright.

. . .

10 The appellant contends that the individual accounting forms are protected by copyright as compilations within the definition of literary work. In my opinion, that contention, on the basis of what has been recognized by the courts as compilations in decisions that were cited by the trial judge, is at the very least a seriously arguable one. I am further of the respectful opinion that it is at the very least doubtful that the trial judge was correct in holding that a work must be informative in order to be a literary work within the meaning to the Act, and that the contrary is seriously arguable. We were not referred to any authority to support this conclusion of the trial judge. As counsel for the appellant submitted, the requirement that a work be informative, at least in the sense used by the trial judge, might prevent a compilation of questions, such as found in a survey, from being a literary work that could be protected by copyright. I am further of the view that even if the trial judge were correct in law in applying this criterion, there is a serious question, for the reason indicated by the appellant, whether the accounting forms are in fact informative. This question could only be properly determined upon the basis of the evidence adduced at trial.

11 For these reasons I am of the opinion that an interlocutory injunction should not have been refused on the ground that the accounting forms were not proper subject matter for copyright. I would allow the appeal, set aside the order of the Trial Division and grant an interlocutory injunction in the terms sought by the appellant's application.

---

3. Artistic Works

(a) What are Artistic Works?

An "artistic work" is defined in the Act to include "paintings, drawings, maps, charts, plans, photographs, engravings, sculptures, works of artistic craftsmanship, architectural works, and compilations of artistic works." The term "artistic work" is used as a general description of works which find expression in a visual medium as opposed to works of literary, musical or dramatic expression.

Kenrick & Company v. Lawrence & Company (1890), L.R. 25 Q.B.D. 99

Queen's Bench Division

Wills, J.

1890 April 21, 24

. . .

1890. April 24. WILLS, J.

The plaintiffs in this case are A. J. Kenrick and F. T. Jefferson, trading in partnership at West Bromwich as the Free Press Company. They are printers and publishers. During the pendency of the partnership it occurred to Mr. Jefferson that it was very difficult without a picture to convey to a voter who cannot read, in respect to parliamentary and other elections at which voting is effected by means of a cross put in a certain place on a piece of paper, how he is to vote; and it occurred to him that a card or paper on which there should be a picture of a hand holding a pencil and in the act of completing a cross within the proper square upon the paper would be likely to sell. He is unable to draw himself, but he drew upon a piece of paper the proper lines dividing a representation of the ballot paper into the proper spaces, and told a Mr. Bott, an artist in the employment of himself and his partner, to draw a hand carrying a pencil and in the act of finishing a cross enclosed in a square. The artist made him a sketch, which he directed the artist to alter as to the position of the hand, and this drawing so arrived at Mr. Jefferson registered under 25 & 26 Vict. c. 68, as a drawing of which he, Mr. Jefferson, was the author, and of which his firm were the proprietors.

The defendant has published a similar card, with a hand in a slightly different position, also holding a pencil in the act of finishing a cross upon the proper spot in a voting paper, and I have no doubt that he took the suggestion from the plaintiffs' card. The plaintiffs complain of this as an infringement of their copyright under the Act. It was in evidence that more than a million copies of the card of the plaintiffs have been sold since the year 1885, and that they have been used at nearly every election in the kingdom. It was urged, probably with truth, that such a card was practically the only mode of instructing the illiterate voter how to record his vote, and it is obvious that if the privilege of instructing the illiterate voter how to vote, by the only vehicle by which the act of voting can be represented to the eye, and the instructions how to vote and whom to vote for can be brought home to him, be vested in the plaintiffs for seven years beyond the termination of a life which may very well subsist for half a century longer — for Mr. Jefferson is now only thirty-six years of age — and be their monopoly, it is difficult to put an adequate value upon their property in such a right. If that period should shortly arrive, which to many politicians appears to be a kind of constitutional millennium, when all the remaining ignorance, male and female, of the three kingdoms shall be swept into the electoral fold, the amount of political power which may become vested in the plaintiffs or their assignees will be greater than it is possible to estimate, and the destinies of the country may be placed in the hands of the fortunate owner of the talisman. A prospect is open which may be described in well-known language as a "potentiality of wealth beyond the dreams of avarice," and legislation might even be necessary to prevent so potent an engine of political power from becoming vested in an infant or a madman, an official receiver, or a trustee in bankruptcy, or from being bought or sold at auction, or remaining permanently the heritage of any one political party. The importance of the question raised in this particular instance cannot, therefore, be put too high, and justifies the elaborateness and seriousness with which the case was opened by Mr. Aston, and which, until I came to reflect upon the constitutional aspect of the case, I confess I thought a little exaggerated.

The first question which arises is, what is and what is not the nature of the right conferred under the Act upon the author by the registration of the drawing of which he is the author. It is perhaps easier to say what it is not than to give a satisfactory definition of what it is, and I think that I am upon very safe ground in saying that the mere choice of subject can rarely, if ever, confer upon the author of the drawing an exclusive right to represent the subject, and certainly where the subject chosen is merely the representation to the eye of a simple operation which must be performed by every person who records a vote there cannot possibly be an exclusive right to represent in a picture that operation. It may well be that something special in the way of artistic treatment even of this simple operation, if it existed, might be the subject of copyright; but nothing of the kind has been suggested or exists in the present case, and if it does exist without being discovered it has not been imitated, for there is nothing which by any flight of imagination can be called artistic about either the plaintiffs' or the defendants' representation of a hand making the mark of a cross. It may be also that even the coarsest, or the most commonplace, or the most mechanical representation of the commonest object is so far protected on registration that an exact reproduction of it, such as photography for instance would produce, would be an infringement of copyright. But in such a case it must surely be nothing short of an exact literal reproduction of the drawing registered that can constitute the infringement, for there seems to me to be in such a case nothing else that is not the common property of all the world. It is possible that in this case the proprietors of the drawing registered may have a right to be protected from a reproduction of their picture of a hand drawing a cross in which every line, dot, measurement, and blank space shall be rendered exactly as in the original, or in which the variations from such minute agreement shall be microscopic. But I cannot see how they can possibly make a higher claim, or say that because they have registered a drawing of a hand pencilling a cross within a square that no other person in the United Kingdom is at liberty to draw a hand pencilling a cross within a square for perhaps the next half century. The plaintiff, Mr. Jefferson, put his case as high as that proposition, for he said he might wish to claim applications of the picture to subjects other than the voting cards. It is obvious that unless there be a copyright in the *subject*, any other person who wishes to draw a hand pencilling a cross within a square cannot help producing something so like the plaintiffs' design as to look very like a colour-able imitation of it. Now, it may or may not be very shabby conduct on the part of the defendant to wish to represent a hand pencilling a cross within a square, notwithstanding that the plaintiffs were first in the field, and notwithstanding that but for the picture used by the plaintiffs they might never have thought of making theirs; but I cannot see why they should be precluded, for the next fifty years perhaps, from representing in a picture the act which every voter performs when he records his vote simply because one of the plaintiffs first thought of doing so — any more than if a new article of commerce were introduced of extensive distribution and very simple and definite shape and proportions, and a drawing of it were made for one firm, all other persons should be precluded from making a drawing which, if it truthfully represented the same thing, must be exceedingly like the first drawing, nor, even though the draftsman of the second drawing might never have seen the original article, or might have derived his knowledge of its existence and aspect solely from the first drawing. If a new and very simple tea-caddy were represented first by A. in a drawing which he registered, I cannot conceive that he could during his whole life prevent B. from drawing the same tea-caddy, and even from drawing it from his recollection of A.'s picture, nor that A. could claim copyright, except in the extremely limited and useless sense in which I have suggested that possibly a copyright might exist for a registered drawing of even such a subject. In the present instance, what the plaintiffs claim is really a right to prevent any one else from drawing the same subject as that of his drawing. If he has a copyright in the subject there is a colour-able imitation, because the subject is not altered by changing the position of the hand and adding the indications of a shirt sleeve. But it is clear that there is no copyright in the subject. As for the manner of treating the *subject*, there can be no copyright in that, for if the thing to be represented be represented at all, it is impossible to treat it in any other way. It seems to me, therefore, that although every drawing of whatever kind may be entitled to registration, the degree and kind of protection given must vary greatly with the character of the drawing, and that with such a drawing as we are dealing with the copyright must be confined to that which is special to the individual drawing over and above the idea — in other words, the copyright is of the extremely limited character which I have endeavoured to describe. A square can only be drawn as a square, a cross can only be drawn as a cross, and for such purposes as the plaintiffs' drawing was intended to fulfil there are scarcely more ways than one of drawing a pencil or the hand that holds it. If the particular arrangement of square, cross, hand, or pencil be relied upon it is nothing more than a claim of copyright for the *subject*, which in my opinion cannot possibly be supported.

I have endeavoured to discuss this part of the subject without putting any limitation upon the kind or nature of the drawing for which copyright may be claimed. But it is clear that in the opinion of Bowen, L.J., in Nottage v. Jackson, the statute relates only to works of art of some sort or other. He says: "Parliament treats photography as a fine art. It puts it on a level for the purposes of registration with paintings and drawings" (at page 636). It would be absurd to speak of such drawings as those in the present case as works of art. Possibly it would be a more correct view of his Lordship's judgment to say that he considered that it was the product of the artistic faculty that was intended to be primarily, at all events, the subject of copyright — the thing to be protected by the Act. The difference, after all, is one rather of words than of practical effect. The title of the statute is, "An Act for amending the law relating to copyright in works of fine arts and for repressing the commission of fraud in the production and sale of such works." The title of a statute does not go for much in construing it; but I do not know that it is to be absolutely disregarded. The cases on the subject are collected and their effect stated in Master Wilberforce's very careful and able treatise on Statute Law, at pages 272-276. The title of Lord Campbell's Act was certainly referred to as not without significance in a considered judgment of the Court of Queen's Bench in Blake v. Midland Ry. Co. As far as it goes, the title would certainly seem to point to the notion that it is the product of the artistic faculty, which is the primary thing to be protected. And although it might not be right on that account to cut down the generality of the expression "every drawing," yet it may serve to point to the character of the protection intended. The phrase "artistic faculty" which I have used is vague enough; but here, again, it is easier to say what is not the product of any artistic faculty than to define what is so; and here it is easy to pronounce that no such faculty has been exercised. No kind of value is given to the article produced by reason of its being a pleasing, a particularly accurate, or a tasteful representation upon paper of the object represented, or by reason of that object itself or the method of treating it appealing in any way to imagination, affection, memory, or association. It has less even of such properties than the geometrical figures which illustrate a proposition of Euclid, and the kind of moral claim, if I may so speak, which such a drawing has to protection is far more of the nature which attaches to a trade design than to that which belongs to a work of art — a production which has merit or value as and in its character of a drawing, a painting, or a photograph, and not simply because it conveys by way of a picture a description or direction which could be just as well put into words, if words were not to many people a sealed book.

Without going further, therefore, my judgment would be for the defendant.

DRG Inc. v. Datafile Ltd., [1988] 2 F.C. 243

Federal Court of Canada — Trial Division

Reed J.

Heard: October 21, 1987
Judgment: November 20, 1987
Docket: Application No. T-1334-86

Reed J.:

1 The issue in this case is whether certain labels which the respondent has registered under the *Copyright Act*, R.S.C. 1970, c. C-30, are properly the subject of copyright. The applicant seeks to expunge those registrations.

. . .

6 The labels are designed to be stuck on a file folder and folded over its edge. Thus, in an open filing system the colours on the edge of the file give an easy indication as to the letters or numbers of the file and any misfiling which might occur. The letters and numbers on the label are of a size and shape which make them easily visible to persons seeking a specific file. Mr. Barber chose a standard type face for the letters and numbers and chose to have them reverse printed (ie: the letters and numbers left white). The digit or letter, as the case may be, was then outlined in black. This design created a label having a greater degree of clarity and ease of recognition than had been the case with his earlier labels. His expert witness, Karen Okada, rather pithily described the visual impact of the labels:

> A Datafile label ... impacts *its numeric message via modes* (i.e. the colour and the digit itself), *merged into one presentation*. The arrangement is such that the eye focuses immediately on the digit. The colour does not interfere with the digit, and at the same time the digit does not detract from the colour.

· · ·

8 I will deal first with the argument that the work is not a proper subject matter for copyright because it lacks the characteristics of an "artistic work". The following passage is cited from *Burke v. Spicers Dress Designs*, [1936] Ch. D. 400, [1936] 1 All E.R. 99 (Ch.) at 408 [Ch. D.] to support this contention:

> [T]he meaning of the term 'artistic' as indicated in the Oxford English Dictionary, is that which pertains to an artist. An artist is defined in the same dictionary as: 'One who cultivates one of the fine arts in which the object is mainly to gratify the aesthetic emotions by perfection of execution whether in creation or representation.'

It is suggested that criteria such as the following must be applied: (1) is the work in question a work of art? (2) did the artist have a conscious intention to create a work of art? (3) would a substantial section of the public genuinely admire and value the thing for its appearance and get intellectual or emotional pleasure from it? In support of these propositions are cited: *Merlet v. Mothercare, P.L.C.*, [1986] R.P.C. 115, (1984) *Times* April 18 (C.A.) and *George Hensher Ltd. v. Restawhile Upholstery (Lancs.) Ltd.*, [1976] A.C. 64, [1974] 2 All E.R. 420, [1975] R.P.C. 31 (H.L.). Counsel's position is that the application of criteria such as those above does not involve a determination of whether or not a work has artistic merit or not. He argues that the question of merit is irrelevant, but that the predominant criterion to be applied is the intention of the artist. Thus, in this case, he argues: the author of the work intended to create a utilitarian object, not a work of art, and therefore, the work produced is not an artistic work and should not be protected by copyright.

9 I have considerable difficulty with this argument. In the first place the cases cited, *Burke*, supra, *Merlet*, supra, and *Hensher*, supra, all deal with works of "artistic craftsmanship" and all deal with the United Kingdom copyright legislation. Two of the cases, *Merlet* and *Hensher*, relate to section 3(1) of the *Copyright Act, 1956* (U.K. 4 & 5 Eliz. 2), c. 74. That section specifically indicates

that a different test is applicable to works of artistic craftsmanship from that applicable to other types of artistic works covered by the legislation:

> In this Act 'artistic work' means a work of any of the following descriptions, that is to say, —
>
> (a) the following, *irrespective of artistic* quality, namely paintings, sculptures, drawings, engravings and photographs;
>
> (b) works of architecture, being either buildings or models for buildings;
>
> (c) works of artistic craftsmanship, not falling within either of the preceding paragraphs.

[underlining added]

The applicable Canadian legislative provision is of course drafted differently (it follows the pre-1957 United Kingdom text):

> 'artistic work' includes works of painting, drawing, sculpture and artistic craftsmanship, and architectural works of art and engravings and photographs;

The *Burke* case, *by way of dicta*, indicates that the Courts may be required to determine whether a work is "artistic" in relation to works of artistic craftsmanship, but the ratio of that case relates to authorship. Copyright was refused to the first maker of the dress in question on the ground that the maker had not in fact been the author of the design but had copied a design originally set out in a sketch drawn by someone else.

10 As I understand counsel's argument it is that the category "artistic works", in the Canadian *Copyright Act*, requires determination of "artistic"- ness (i.e. some assessment of the intention of the author and whether he or she intended to create a work of art). If this is not so, as a general rule, then, he would argue that non-enumerated artistic works, i.e., those which cannot be classified as paintings, drawings, sculptures, engravings, or photographs, at least, must meet such a test. (Works of artistic craftsmanship and architectural works of art would also be included in the category of works which must meet such a test by virtue of the wording of the statute.)

11 Thus counsel argues either the whole category of artistic works must meet an "artistic" test and the respondent's labels do not qualify, or, non-enumerated types of artistic works (as well as the enumerated categories of architecture and craftsmanship) must meet such a test and the respondent's works fall within the non-enumerated category. In either event, it is argued the works do not meet the test of "artistic"-ness. It will be noted that this argument is based on a view of the statutory definition of "artistic works" as one which deems paintings, drawings, sculptures, engravings and photographs to be artistic, but which requires that proof be given as to the "artistic"-ness of other types of works. It is immediately obvious that these arguments are based on the assumption that the adjective "artistic", as it applies to the whole category of "artistic works", is being used in the same sense as it is used in the phrase "artistic craftsmanship".

12 Requiring Courts to determine what is "artistic", be it with respect only to works of craftsmanship, architecture and unenumerated works, or with respect to the broader category of all "artistic works", is not a happy situation. For example, I note that the attempt of the House of Lords to do so in the *Hensher* case, with respect to a work of craftsmanship, led to findings which can be summarized as follows. Lord Reid expressed the view that a thing is artistic if any substantial section of the public genuinely admires and values it for its appearance and gets pleasure or satisfaction, whether emotional or intellectual, from looking at it (p. 78 [A.C.]). Lord Morris of Borth-Y-Gest expressed the view that: distinctive features of design and skill in workmanship or distinctive characteristics of shape, form and finish would not make a work artistic without "something additional and different"; the object must be judged as a thing in itself, regardless of the opinions of the creator or prospective owner; the question must be asked, "Does it have the character or virtue of being artistic?" and the Court should rely on the testimony of expert witnesses (pp. 81-82 [A.C.]). Viscount Dilhorne expressed the view that the words "works of artistic craftsmanship" should be given their ordinary and natural meaning and that a Judge should rely on expert witnesses but that it was not enough that one segment of the public might find the work artistic (pp. 86-87 [A.C.]). Lord Simon [of Glaisdale] held that artistic merit was irrelevant to a determination of whether a work of artistic craftsmanship existed; rather, one should ask whether the work was one produced by an individual who was an artist-craftsman, and to determine this the views of experts (i.e., other artist-craftsmen) should be called (p. 94 [A.C.]). Lord Kilbrandon expressed the view that the intention of the creator to create a work of art, not the reaction of others, was the primary test (p. 96 [A.C.]). He also noted that between the two lower Court judgments, the lawyers for the parties and the five decisions in the House of Lords, nine different tests, as to what is meant by "artistic" and how it should be determined, had been rejected.

13 Another attempt to define "artistic", or rather "work of art" as it relates to the architectural field is found in the decision *Hay & Hay Construction Co. v. Sloan*, [1957] O.W.N. 445, 16 Fox Pat. C. 185, 27 C.P.R. 132, 12 D.L.R. (2d) 397 (Ont. H.C.). In that case it was held that the Court was not required to decide whether a building was good or bad in an aesthetic sense, but rather it should consider the intention of the creator. It was held that if there had been an intention to create a thing of beauty or delight and there existed originality in the sense described in *Chabot v. Davies*, [1936] 3 All E.R. 221 (Ch.), then the building was a proper subject for copyright.

14 To turn then to the definition of "artistic works" as set out in s. 2 of the *Copyright Act*, I forebear from stating whether "artistic"-ness must be determined by the Courts for works of craftsmanship and architecture. It is not necessary to discuss this issue, although it must be noted that the text of Canadian statutes mirrors that of the 1911 Act of the United Kingdom [*Copyright Act*, 1911 (U.K., 1 & 2 Geo. 5), c. 46], where jurisprudence has seemed to indicate that such is required. Also the *Hay* case, noted above, has accepted this view and struggled to find an appropriate test.

15 Even if works of craftsmanship and architecture must be measured against some test of "artistic"-ness (as set out in the *Hensher, Merlet* or *Hay* cases) I do not accept that the category of artistic works in general must meet such a test. I do not accept that the word "artistic" in reference to "artistic works" is being used in the same sense as the word "artistic" in reference to "works of artistic craftsmanship", that is, if in the latter case "artistic"-ness requires a determination along the lines of that attempted in *Hensher, Merlet* or *Hay*. In my view the phrase "artistic work" is used merely as a generic description of the type of works which follow. It is used as a general description of works which find expression in a visual medium as opposed to works of literary, musical or dramatic expression.

16 Specifically, then, with respect to the respondent's label designs, first of all, it is my view that they fall within the enumerated classes of works set out in the definition of artistic works. They come within the category of "engravings"; that concept is expanded by s. 2, to include:

> ... etchings, lithographs, woodcuts, prints and other *similar works* not being photographs;

[underlining added] Mr. Barber, in para. 22 of his affidavit, states "each of the labels ... is a coloured print, printed on white paper in a printing press by printing plates or engravings." That evidence has not been challenged.

17 If I am wrong in this and the respondent's work, which I would characterize as a graphic design, does not fall within the specifically enumerated category "engravings", then I would hold that it falls within the general category of artistic works as being analogous to an engraving. For the reasons given above it is my view that in either case, it is not necessary to ascertain "artistic"-ness along the lines of the investigation undertaken by the House of Lords in the *Hensher* case, or even to ascertain such by reference to a more restrained basis, as counsel would suggest, by determining whether the intention of the author at the time of creation was to create a work of art. In this regard I note that not only is this intention test a difficult one to apply, it is certainly not required with respect to works such as drawings or photographs (where the only intention may be to record a specific event). The respondent's work is a graphic design reproduced by a printing process. As such it is an artistic work for purposes of copyright and no higher standard of originality is required than the case of literary copyright: *University of London Press, Ltd. v. University Tutorial Press, Ltd.*, [1916] 2 Ch. D. 601 (Ch.) at p. 610.

18 What then of the argument that the work is not protected by copyright because it is primarily designed to serve a functional purpose. The decision in *Hollinrake v. Truswell*, [1894] 3 Ch. D. 420, 7 R. 568 (C.A.) and *Cuisenaire v. South West Imports Ltd.*, [1969] S.C.R. 208, 40 Fox Pat. C. 81, 57 C.P.R. 76 (S.C.C.), affirming [1968] 1 Ex. C.R. 493, 37 Fox Pat. C. 93, 54 C.P.R. 1 (Ex. Ct.) are cited. In *Hollinrake v. Truswell*, supra, a sleeve pattern was held not to be a proper subject for copyright because the letters or characters thereon were not separately publishable:

[I]t is not a publication complete in itself, but is only a direction on a tool or machine, to be understood and used with it, such direction cannot, in my opinion, be severed from the tool or machine of which it is really part. [Ch. D. 426]

. . .

When the real character of the thing is ascertained, it proves to be a measuring tool or instrument. [Ch. D. 426]

. . .

The plaintiff is really seeking a monopoly of her mode of measuring for sleeves of dresses under the guise of a claim to literary copyright.

[Ch. D. 428] And in *Cuisenaire v. South West Imports Ltd.*, supra:

[T]he rods are merely devices which afford a practical means of employing the method and presenting it in graphic form to young children. The 'original' work or production, whether it be characterized as literary, artistic or scientific, was the book. In seeking to assert a copyright in the 'rods' which are described in his book as opposed to the book itself, the appellant is faced with the principle stated by Davey L.J. in the case of *Hollinrake v. Truswell*. ...

[S.C.R., 211]

19 Counsel argues that the labels identified in the respondent's copyright registration are nothing more than devices or tools for the implementation of a colour coded filing system and, as such, are not properly the subject matter of copyright.

20 Both the *Hollinrake* and *Cuisenaire* cases are easily distinguishable from the case at Bar. *Hollinrake* dealt with something called a "sleeve chart" which the Court characterized as a measuring instrument (similar to a ruler). It was held that the letters and figures in the instrument were part of the measuring instrument and did not constitute a literary production. Similarly, in the *Cuisenaire* case the coloured rods were held to be tools for the implementation of the appellant's teaching technique but which could not be related to either an artistic or literary work. I note that in the decision by Mr. Justice Noël at pp. 23-24 [C.P.R.] he draws a distinction between the rods and flash cards used as educational aids in teaching arithmetic. The flash cards bore words, numbers and pictures:

The cards in the above case were, however, a literary or graphic work and, of course, there is that difference with the instant case where plaintiff's rods could not be related to either an artistic or literary work unless they could be said to be reproductions of the written instructions contained in plaintiff's book *Les nombres en couleur* which contains a table, and in another case, a series of plain and coloured circles which are numbered and set out in the form of a chart. This, however, they cannot be as these rods are not in the nature of a table or compilation and, therefore, do not reproduce the written instructions in his book.

With respect to the claim for artistic copyright, Mr. Justice Noël said, at pp. 21-22 [C.P.R.]:

These rods indeed are tools and nothing more, the same as colours, for instance, are tools in teaching children how to paint. They can take on meaning only when considered and integrated with a concept itself which in itself is not entitled to protection. [C.P.R. 21]

. . .

An artistic work, in my view, must to some degree at least, be a work that is intended to have an appeal to the aesthetic senses not just an incidental appeal, such as here, but as an important or one of the important objects for which the work is brought into being.

[C.P.R. 22]

21 In the present case it is not the labels themselves which are claimed to be the subject of copyright (it is the design thereon). It is not the file folder, not the label, for which copyright is claimed. It is the graphic design. In my view, this is similar to the flash cards mentioned by Mr. Justice Noël. Despite counsel's argument to the contrary, it is not the colour coded filing system which is being protected by copyright. It is the design of the label. Indeed, there is nothing to prevent the applicant from designing labels compatible with the respondent's filing system, providing it does not copy the respondent's labels. I note in this regard that the simpler a copyrighted work is, the more exact must be the copying in order to constitute infringement.

22 It is true that, in designing the labels, functionality was a very important consideration. Their effectiveness (and the desire of the applicant to copy them) no doubt arises from the fact that their design features (balance, shape, colour, letter and number size, etc.) combine to make a particularly effective visual presentation. But I cannot hold that because function and design, in this case, coalesce (necessarily coalesce) the design, thereby becomes unprotectable by copyright. I note that many items specifically listed in the *Copyright Act* may be designed primarily to serve functional purposes: maps, charts, photographs, architectural buildings, works of artistic craftsmanship. I quote from Lord Simon in the *Hensher* case, at p. 93:

> And in one purchaser alone the motives may be so mixed that it is impossible to say what is the primary inducement to acquisition or retention.

[A.C.] The label design was created to serve a functional purpose. That does not deprive it of the character of an "artistic work" nor of copyright protection.

Lucasfilm Ltd v. Ainsworth, [2011] UKSC 39 (U.K. S.C.)

Lord Phillips, President, Lord Walker, Lady Hale, Lord Mance, Lord Collins

1. The first Star Wars film (later renamed "Star Wars Episode IV — A New Hope" in order to provide for "prequels" as well as sequels) was released in the United States in 1977. It was an enormous commercial success. It won an Oscar for best costume design. This appeal is concerned with intellectual property rights in various artefacts made for use in the film. The most important of

these was the Imperial Stormtrooper helmet to which the trial judge (Mann J) referred in his judgment ([2008] EWHC 1878 (Ch), [2009] FSR 103, paras [2] and [121]):

> "One of the most abiding images in the film was that of the Imperial Stormtroopers. These were soldiers clad in white armour, including a white helmet which left no part of the face uncovered... The purpose of the helmet was that it was to be worn as an item of costume in a film, to identify a character, but in addition to portray something about that character — its allegiance, force, menace, purpose and, to some extent, probably its anonymity. It was a mixture of costume and prop."

The parties are agreed that for the purposes of this final appeal the helmet can be taken as the paradigm case that will be decisive of the outcome.

2. The facts are set out in the judge's clear and thorough judgment. For present purposes a brief summary will suffice. The film's story-line and characters were conceived by Mr George Lucas. Between 1974 and 1976 Mr Lucas's concept of the Imperial Stormtroopers as threatening characters in "fascist white-armoured suits" was given visual expression in drawings and paintings by an artist, Mr Ralph McQuarrie, and three-dimensional form by Mr Nick Pemberton (a free-lance scenic artist and prop-maker) and Mr Andrew Ainsworth (who is skilled in vacuum-moulding in plastic). Mr Pemberton made a clay model of the helmet, which was adapted several times until Mr Lucas was happy with it. Mr Ainsworth produced several prototype vacuum-moulded helmets. Once Mr Lucas had approved the final version Mr Ainsworth made 50 helmets for use in the film. These events all took place in England. Although Mr Lucas and his companies are based in California he had come to live in England while the film was made at Elstree (there was also filming on location in Tunisia).

3. The first appellant is a Californian corporation owned by Mr Lucas. The second appellant is an English company owned by Mr Lucas. The third appellant is a Californian corporation responsible for the group's licensing activities; it is wholly owned by the first appellant. Between them these three companies own copyrights in the artistic works created for the Star Wars films, and they can be referred to generally as "Lucasfilm". Apart from the huge commercial success of the Star Wars films, Lucasfilm has built up a successful licensing business which includes licensing models of Imperial Stormtroopers and their equipment. This litigation has come about because in 2004 Mr Ainsworth, the principal respondent in this appeal, used his original tools to make versions of the Imperial Stormtrooper helmet and armour, and other artefacts that it is not necessary to detail, for sale to the public. The second respondent is a private company owned by Mr Ainsworth but for practical purposes Mr Ainsworth can be treated as the only respondent.

4. Mr Ainsworth sold some of the goods that he produced (to the value of at least $8,000 but not more than $30,000) in the United States. In 2005 Lucasfilm sued Mr Ainsworth in the United States District Court, Central District of California, and in 2006 it obtained a default judgment for $20m, $10m of which represented triple damages under the Lanham Act. The whole judgment remains

unsatisfied. Lucasfilm also commenced proceedings in the Chancery Division of the English High Court. The re-amended particulars of claim put forward a variety of claims under English law, including infringement of copyright (paras (1) to (10) of the prayer for relief); a claim for enforcement of the United States judgment to the extent of $10m (para (11)); and claims under United States copyright law (paras (12) to (17)).

5. The trial occupied 17 days during April and May 2008. In his judgment delivered on 31 July 2008 Mann J dismissed all Lucasfilm's claims based on English copyright law (together with some other claims that are no longer pursued). He held that the helmet made by Mr Ainsworth was a substantial reproduction of original work carried out by Mr McQuarrie and other persons working for Lucasfilm. But the English copyright claims failed because the helmet was not a work of sculpture and Mr Ainsworth had defences (to a claim that he was reproducing Mr McQuarrie's work) under sections 51 and 52 of the Copyright Designs and Patents Act 1988 ("the 1988 Act"). The judge also dismissed Mr Ainsworth's counterclaim based on his own claim to copyright in the helmet.

6. The judge held that the United States judgment was unenforceable for want of personal jurisdiction over Mr Ainsworth and his company. But he held that Lucasfilm's United States copyright claims were justiciable in England and that Mr Ainsworth and his company had infringed those rights.

7. The Court of Appeal ([2009] EWCA Civ 1328, [2010] Ch 503) agreed with the judge that the United States judgment is unenforceable, and there is no further appeal on that point. The Court of Appeal also agreed with the judge that any intellectual property rights in the helmet belong to Lucasfilm, and this Court has refused Mr Ainsworth permission to cross-appeal on that point. The issues that are open in this Court are whether the helmet was a sculpture and the defences under sections 51 and 52 of the 1988 Act (on all of which the Court of Appeal agreed with the judge) and justiciability in England of the United States copyright claims (on which the Court of Appeal disagreed with the judge). The issues on sections 51 and 52 arise only if the helmet was a sculpture (and so an artistic work) within the meaning of the 1988 Act. In the Court of Appeal Lucasfilm abandoned its alternative contention that the helmet qualified as an artistic work because it was a work of artistic craftsmanship.

Part I: English copyright law issues

Current statutory provisions

8. The Court has been taken to the full legislative history but it is better to start with the current legislation, that is the 1988 Act. Under section 1(1)(a) copyright is a property right which subsists in original literary, dramatic, musical or artistic works. Other works, including films, come in under section 1(1)(b) and (c). By section 4(1) "artistic work" means, for copyright purposes,

> "(a) a graphic work, photograph, sculpture or collage, irrespective of artistic quality,

(b) a work of architecture being a building or a model for a building, or

(c) a work of artistic craftsmanship."

By section 4(2) "sculpture" includes a cast or model made for purposes of sculpture.

9. Sections 51 and 52 are in Part I, Chapter III of the 1988 Act (acts permitted in relation to copyright works). Chapter III contains a variety of exemptions from liability on general grounds, including fair dealing (sections 29-31) and educational, archival and other public purposes (sections 32-50). Section 62 contains a general exemption for buildings, sculpture and works of artistic craftsmanship on permanent public display.

10. Section 51 (design documents and models) as amended provides as follows:

"(1) It is not an infringement of any copyright in a design document or model recording or embodying a design for anything other than an artistic work or a typeface to make an article to the design or to copy an article made to the design.

(2) Nor is it an infringement of the copyright to issue to the public, or include in a film or communicate to the public, anything the making of which was, by virtue of subsection (1), not an infringement of that copyright.

(3) In this section —

'design' means the design of any aspect of the shape or configuration (whether internal or external) of the whole or part of an article, other than surface decoration; and

'design document' means any record of a design, whether in the form of a drawing, a written description, a photograph, data stored in a computer or otherwise."

11. Section 52 (effect of exploitation of design derived from artistic work) provides as follows:

(1) This section applies where an artistic work has been exploited, by or with the licence of the copyright owner, by -

(a) making by an industrial process articles falling to be treated for the purposes of this Part as copies of the work, and

(b) marketing such articles, in the United Kingdom or elsewhere.

(2) After the end of the period of 25 years from the end of the calendar year in which such articles are first marketed, the work may be copied by making articles of any description, or doing anything for the purpose of making articles of any description, and anything may be done in relation to articles so made, without infringing copyright in the work.

(3) Where only part of an artistic work is exploited as mentioned in subsection (1), subsection (2) applies only in relation to that part.

(4) The Secretary of State may by order make provision —

(a) as to the circumstances in which an article, or any description of article, is to be regarded for the purposes of this section as made by an industrial process;

(b) excluding from the operation of this section such articles of a primarily literary or artistic character as he thinks fit.

(5) An order shall be made by statutory instrument which shall be subject to annulment in pursuance of a resolution of either House of Parliament.

(6) In this section —

(a) references to articles do not include films; and

(b) references to the marketing of an article are to its being sold or let for hire or offered or exposed for sale or hire."

12. These two sections operate so as to limit (in different ways) the influence of literary or artistic copyright on other persons' freedom to make and market three-dimensional objects. Section 51 applies where the end-product of a design document or model is not an artistic work. It provides a more principled answer to the problem to which the House of Lords gave a radical and controversial solution in *British Leyland Motor Corporation Ltd v Armstrong Patents Co Ltd* [1986] AC 577 while the Bill which became the 1988 Act was before Parliament. Section 52 applies (subject to exceptions specified by the Secretary of State) where there is an artistic work, but that work has been exploited (with the consent of the copyright owner) by industrial production of copies to be marketed.

13. The Copyright (Industrial Process and Excluded Articles) (No 2) Order 1989 (SI 1989/1070) ("the 1989 Order"), made under section 52(4) of the 1988 Act, provides (para 2) for an article to be regarded as made by an industrial process if it is one of more than 50 articles which are to be treated as copies of a particular artistic work (and are not together a set). The Order also provides (para 3(1)(a)) for the exclusion from section 52 of "works of sculpture, other than casts or models used or intended to be used as models or patterns to be multiplied by any industrial process."

Legislative history: before the 1911 Act

14. These provisions (and especially sections 51 and 52) are difficult to understand without reference to their legislative history. Unfortunately the history is itself quite complicated. The *Copyright Act* 1911 ("the 1911 Act") was (as Lord Bridge observed in *British Leyland* [1986] AC 577, 619) "the first attempt to provide a comprehensive code of copyright protection". Section 1(1) of the 1911 Act was in terms similar to those of section 1(1)(a) of the 1988 Act, (except that the words "irrespective of artistic quality" did not appear in the 1911 Act), and it may give the impression of embodying a well-proportioned symmetrical principle providing equal protection to every form of human creativity. Any such impression would be misleading. When the 1911 Act was passed there had already been two centuries of legislative history, starting with the *Copyright Act*

1709 ("the 1709 Act"), and for most of that time it was the protection of printed words — published literary works — that was the law's principal concern. Moreover the original legislative purpose of laws on literary copyright was the protection of the commercial interests of stationers (the early publishers) and booksellers, and the control of unlicensed (and possibly subversive) publications, rather than the vindication of the legal and moral rights of authors. There are useful summaries of the history of English copyright law in *Copinger and Skone James on Copyright*, 16th ed (2010), paras 2-08 to 2-42, and *Cornish, Llewelyn and Aplin, Intellectual Property: Patents, Copyright, Trade Marks and Allied Rights*, 7th ed (2010), paras 10-01 to 10-41.

15. The 1709 Act protected literary works, books and other writings. During the 18th century protection was extended (by statute) to engravings and (by a liberal interpretation of the 1709 Act) to musical and dramatic compositions. Three-dimensional works of art were brought within the scope of copyright by a statute enacted in 1798, 38 Geo III c 71, but it was very badly drafted and offered little practical protection (Lord Ellenborough said in *Gahagan v Cooper* (1811) 3 Camp 111, 113 that "The statute seems to have been framed with a view to defeat its own object"). This Act was replaced by the Sculpture *Copyright Act* 1814 ("the 1814 Act"). The class of protected works was described in discursive terms, starting with

> "any new and original sculpture, or model, or copy, or cast of the human figure or human figures, or of any bust or busts, or of any part or parts of the human figure, clothed in drapery or otherwise,"

> and continuing in broader terms, referring to "any matter being subject of invention in sculpture." The sculpture was required to bear the maker's name and the date when it was made. Paintings, drawings and photographs were not protected until the Fine Arts *Copyright Act* 1862 ("the 1862 Act"). The 1862 Act required registration as a condition of protection. Architectural works were not protected until the 1911 Act (which also introduced works of "artistic craftsmanship" into the definition of "artistic work" in section 35 of that Act).

16. The 1814 Act remained in force until the coming into force of the 1911 Act, and was until then the only statute that gave long-term copyright protection to any three-dimensional works. During the 19th century the rapid expansion of mechanical mass-production produced an obvious need for industrial designers and manufacturers to be protected against unfair competition by copying of their designs. Parliament decided that protection should be provided by a new right which was (rather confusingly, as the Court of Appeal said in para [24] of its judgment) called copyright, but which differed in two respects from literary and artistic copyright. First, the proprietor was required to register his design. Second, the period of protection was much shorter. Those were the essential features of the scheme introduced by the Copyright of Designs Act 1839, repealed and replaced by the Designs Act 1842. Earlier legislation granting copyright to the design of a range of printed textiles was repealed and replaced by the new system of registration, but copyright in sculpture under the 1814 Act was preserved.

17. The law as to registered designs was amended by the Copyright of Designs Act 1850, was further amended and consolidated by Part III of the Patents, Designs and Trade Marks Act 1883 ("the 1883 Act") and finally (as regards legislation before the 1911 Act) was further amended by the Patents and Designs Act 1907 ("the 1907 Act"). Most of the detail of this history is irrelevant for present purposes. But it is to be noted that although the periods of protection for registered designs were progressively extended, they were always much shorter than the period for literary or artistic copyright. It is also to be noted that after an uncertain start in the early statutes, a design for a work of sculpture was excluded from the statutory definition of "design" (section 60 of the 1883 Act and section 93 of the 1907 Act).

18. Only one judicial decision on the 1814 Act calls for mention, that is *Britain v Hanks Bros & Co* (1902) 86 LT 765. Wright J held that copyright protection as sculpture was available to what the report refers to as "toy metal models of soldiers on horseback, or mounted yeomen." The models were designed and made by William Britain, a partner in the plaintiff firm. The report does not say how large the models were, but they were evidently large enough for each to have stamped on it the maker's name and the date of its manufacture. There was expert evidence, which the judge accepted, that the models were "artistic productions, in that the anatomy is good, and that the modelling shows both technical knowledge and skill." The judge seems to have regarded the case as near the borderline, but was prepared to hold that the models were entitled to protection.

19. The Court of Appeal observed (para [59]) that it is "difficult . . . to take too much from this case." A minor point in the appellants' case is that that is just what the Court did (para [82]) in describing the *Britain* models as "highly crafted models designed to appeal to the collector but which might be played with by his children."

Legislative history: the 1911 Act and afterwards

20. The introduction by the 1911 Act of full copyright protection for "a work of artistic craftsmanship" was ascribed by Lord Simon, in *George Hensher Ltd v Restawile Upholstery (Lancs) Ltd* [1976] AC 64, 89-91, to the influence of the Arts and Crafts movement inspired by William Morris and John Ruskin. Lord Simon's view (at p 91) was that the expression is a composite phrase which must be construed as a whole, and that view has had recent support from the High Court of Australia (*Swarbrick v Burge* (2007) 232 CLR 336).

21. Section 22 of the 1911 Act provided as follows:

"(1) This Act shall not apply to designs capable of being registered under the Patents and Designs Act 1907, except designs which, though capable of being so registered, are not used or intended to be used as models or patterns to be multiplied by any industrial process.

(2) General rules under section 86 of the Patents and Designs Act 1907 may be made for determining the conditions under which a design shall be deemed to be used for such purposes as aforesaid."

The test for production by an industrial process was (by rule 89 of the Designs Rules 1920, and so far as now material) the same as that in the 1989 Order (mentioned in para [13] above).

22. The effect of the double negative in section 22(1) can be more easily understood, as Viscount Maugham observed in *King Features Syndicate Inc v O & M Kleeman Ltd.* [1941] AC 417, 427, if it is rewritten:

> "This Act shall apply to designs capable of being registered under [the 1907 Act], which are not used or intended to be used as models or patterns to be multiplied by any industrial process. With that exception this Act shall not apply to designs capable of being registered under [the 1907 Act]."

The main issue in that case (which was concerned with "Popeye" dolls derived from published comic strips enjoying artistic copyright) was the time at which the intention of use for industrial production had to be formed. The Lords decided that the intention must have been there from the start.

23. The Patents and Designs Act 1919 amended the 1907 Act by substituting for the definition in section 93 of the 1907 Act a new definition of "design" which referred to features applied "by any industrial process" and did not make an express exception for a design for a sculpture. Because of the way that section 22 of the 1911 Act was framed, this had the effect of withdrawing from works of sculpture their specially privileged position in relation to mass-production of copies. Its effect was illustrated by *Pytram Ltd v Models (Leicester) Ltd* [1930] 1 Ch 639. The Boy Scouts Association commissioned a model of a wolf-cub's head which was to be used to produce a permanent mould for the production of large numbers of papier-maché models to be attached to the top of wooden poles. Clauson J dismissed the plaintiff's claim to copyright in the original model. He accepted that the model was a work of sculpture, but it was not automatically exempt from registration under the 1907 Act as amended, and it did not come within the exception in section 22(1) because (p 647) "The whole point in the preparation of this model was to enable the plaintiffs to supply totem poles in large quantities."

24. After the second world war there was a legislative shift back again. In 1947 the Swan Committee recommended that works of sculpture should again be excluded from registrable designs. The Registered Designs Act 1949 provided (section 1(3) and (4)) for exclusions from registration of articles which were primarily literary or artistic in character. Rule 26(1) of the Designs Rules 1949 (SI 1949/2368) excluded "works of sculpture other than casts or models used or intended to be used as models or patterns to be multiplied by any industrial process." This wording (now reproduced in the 1989 Order) followed section 22(1) of the 1911 Act and must be construed in line with the House of Lords' decision on that section in *King Features*.

25. The 1911 Act was repealed by the *Copyright Act* 1956 ("the 1956 Act"). Section 10 of the 1956 Act (special exception in respect of industrial designs) restated the boundaries between copyright and design right. As amended by the Design *Copyright Act* 1968, section 10(3) set a 15-year limit on copyright

protection for any work in respect of which a corresponding design could have been registered under the 1949 Act. But section 10(4) made an exception for designs excluded from registration by rules made under the 1949 Act; and rule 26 of the Designs Rules 1949 has now been replicated by rule 26 of the Registered Designs Rules 1989.

26. The 1956 Act introduced the words "irrespective of artistic quality" into para (a) of its definition of "artistic work" in section 3(1). This was, it seems, as a result of maps, charts and plans being reclassified by the 1956 Act as artistic rather than literary works. The new wording sits rather uneasily with "works of artistic craftsmanship" in para (c) of the same definition. In *Hensher* [1976] AC 64, 94, Lord Simon suggested an explanation which some may not find wholly convincing. But it is common ground that in copyright cases the court is not concerned with passing judgment on the merits of either literary or artistic works.

27. The Court of Appeal drew two general conclusions from its own survey of the legislative history (which occupies paras [21] to [39] of the judgment). The first ([40] and [41]) was that there is little or no assistance as to the meaning of "sculpture" in the 1988 Act to be derived from the relationship between copyright and registered design rights. The second ([42] and [43]) is that "design" and "artistic work" are different concepts. Apart from unregistered design right (introduced by Part III of the 1988 Act), design right statutes are concerned with features that have visual appeal. Copyright protection depends on a work falling within a particular category specified in the 1988 Act: "It does not depend upon a further analysis or identification of its design features."

The meaning of "sculpture"

28. Both the judge and the Court of Appeal undertook a full review of English and Commonwealth authority as to the meaning of "sculpture". They rightly concluded that some first-instance decisions gave them no real assistance, and it is unnecessary to go into them again. The judgments that call for discussion are (in chronological order) those of the Court of Appeal of New Zealand in *Wham-O Manufacturing Co v Lincoln Industries Ltd* [1985] RPC 127, [1984] 1 NZLR 641; of Falconer J in *Breville Europe Plc v Thorn EMI Domestic Appliances Ltd* [1995] FSR 77; of Laddie J in *Metix (UK) Ltd v G H Maughan (Plastics) Ltd* [1997] FSR 718; and of Angel J (sitting in the Supreme Court of the Northern Territory) in *Wildash v Klein* (2004) 61 IPR 324.

29. Before discussing these four cases it is appropriate to make a further brief reference to the decision of the House of Lords in *Hensher* [1976] AC 64. Since Lucasfilm is no longer contending that the helmet is a work of artistic craftsmanship it is unnecessary to make much further reference to *Hensher,* which Mann J discussed at some length, drawing attention to the difficulty of identifying the true principle of the decision. The reason why that contention has been abandoned is stated (para 22(2) of the appellants' printed case) to be that section 4(1)(c) of the 1988 Act is intended to comprise articles whose purpose is primarily functional, and which cannot therefore qualify as sculpture. The

relative significance of the functional and the artistic is central to this appeal. The speeches in *Hensher*, difficult though they are, show a general inclination to start with the ordinary meaning of the words of the statute (see Lord Reid at p 78, Lord Morris at p 81, Viscount Dilhorne at pp 86-87, Lord Simon at p 91 and Lord Kilbrandon at p 97), however much they differed as to the application of that principle. The same approach is called for in relation to the meaning of "sculpture".

30. In *Wham-O* the Court of Appeal of New Zealand was concerned with frisbees (light plastic discs used in outdoor games because of their aerodynamic qualities). Lincoln made and marketed in New Zealand frisbees which were alleged to infringe Wham-O's copyright in design drawings, wooden models, moulds and the final plastic moulded products. The relevant parts of the *Copyright Act* 1962 of New Zealand were similar but not identical to those of the 1988 Act. At first instance Moller J held that the wooden models were copyright as sculptures and that the moulds and final products were engravings. The Court of Appeal upheld this result, while holding that the final products were not sculptures (a point left open by the judge). Much of the judgment is taken up with reasoning leading to the rather surprising conclusion that the moulds and final products were engravings. The finding that the wooden model of a frisbee — and that alone — was a sculpture seems to have been based mainly on the fact that only the model had been made by hand, and the moulds and final products had been made industrially. Davison CJ stated ([1985] RPC 127, 157):

> "It seems to us inappropriate to regard utilitarian objects such as plastic flying discs, manufactured as toys, by an injection moulding process, as items of sculpture for the purposes of the *Copyright Act*."

31. The *Breville* case was concerned with sandwich toasters. Copyright was claimed for plaster shapes made for the production of die-cast moulds of the heating plates (which were required to have the same scalloped shape as was to be impressed on the toasted sandwiches). Falconer J held that there had been no infringement, but went on to express the view that the plaster shapes were protected by copyright. He stated (at p 94):

> "I do not see why the word 'sculpture' in section 3 of the *Copyright Act* 1956 should not receive its ordinary dictionary meaning except in so far as the scope of the word is extended by section 48(1) which provides that 'sculpture' includes any cast or model made for purposes of sculpture."

In reaching this conclusion he relied on the part of the *Wham-O* decision which recognised copyright in the wooden model of a frisbee. He also relied on the Concise Oxford Dictionary's definition of "sculpture":

> "Art of forming representations of objects etc or abstract designs in the round or in relief by chiselling stone, carving wood, modelling clay, casting metal, or similar processes; a work of sculpture."

32. Falconer J was a very experienced intellectual property judge but in *Breville* he seems to have overlooked the significance of the words "for purposes of

sculpture" in the statute and the significance of the first word, "Art", in the dictionary definition. That was the view of the Court of Appeal (para [66]):

> "The same ['far removed from the creation of expressive form'] goes for the plastic shapes considered by Falconer J in the *Breville* case [1995] FSR 77. No ordinary citizen — indeed no ordinary lawyer — would regard a sandwich toaster or any part of it as a work of sculpture — even if it did produce 'scalloped' sandwiches. So why should a copyright lawyer take a different view? A total or almost total emphasis on the manner of creation, as in the *Breville* case and *Wham-O* case [1985] RPC 127 produces a result which offends common sense and in our view is wrong. There must, as Mann J said, be some element of artistic expression however unsuccessful."

33. The point about "for purposes of sculpture" is underlined by some observations earlier in the judgment of the Court of Appeal (paras [49] and [50], and again at para [70]) as to the word "sculpture" being applicable both to a process and to a product (terms familiar to intellectual property lawyers). Over the centuries statues and other works of art cast in metal have been produced by what is basically a three-stage process: first by making a model in clay or some other malleable material; then by taking a mould from the model; and then by casting, that is, pouring molten metal into the mould to produce the work of art (followed no doubt by appropriate finishing). Copyright protection is therefore extended (currently by section 4(2) of the 1988 Act) to a cast or model made for purposes of sculpture. But not every product of industrial casting or moulding is sculpture. As the Court of Appeal observed (para [50]):

> "Casting or moulding is an industrial process commonly used where the end product is made of plastic or metal of some kind. It is used in the production of millions of ordinary household objects, none of which would usually be described as sculptures. A motor car is but one obvious example. Some would have qualified for protection as registered designs so as to be excluded under section 22(1) of the 1911 Act. But would they have qualified as 'sculpture'?".

34. *Metix* can be taken more shortly. It was a case in which Laddie J rightly rejected a claim to artistic copyright in moulds used for making cartridges used in conjunction with flow mixers (the judge described them as looking like double-barrelled hyperdermic syringes). Laddie J, another very experienced intellectual property judge made some general observations (at pp 721-722):

> "The law has been bedevilled by attempts to widen out the field covered by the *Copyright Act*s. It is not possible to say with precision what is and what is not sculpture, but I think Mr Meade was close to the heart of the issue. He suggested that a sculpture is a three-dimensional work made by an artist's hand. It appears to me that there is no reason why the word 'sculpture' in the 1988 Act, should be extended far beyond the meaning which that word has to ordinary members of the public."

Mr Meade's formulation as recorded by Laddie J seems to be the only suggested definition or near-definition that has not attracted adverse comment from any quarter.

35. *Wildash v Klein* (2004) 61 IPR 324, like *Metix*, is of interest not so much for what it decides as for its discussion of general issues (including the notion of copying of part, which is not an issue here). The case was an unfortunate dispute between two women, each of whom made craftwork depicting local wildlife for sale at markets. Initially they cooperated but later each accused the other of copyright infringement. The craftworks were made of wire but also (and here the summaries in the judgments below are rather sparse) glass rods, glass nuggets, copper foil and other materials. The judge held that they were sculptures or, alternatively, works of artistic craftsmanship. The judge cited the Court of Appeal of New Zealand in *Wham-O* ("sculpture should in some way express in three-dimensional form an idea of the sculptor") and also Laddie J in *Metix*. In connection with copying the judge also cited Lord Hoffmann's cryptic observation about foxes and hedgehogs in *Designers Guild Ltd v Russell Williams (Textiles) Ltd* [2000] 1 WLR 2416, 2423, describing it as an allusion to an essay written in 1953 by Sir Isaiah Berlin; in fact Sir Isaiah was alluding, as has Professor Ronald Dworkin in his latest book, *Justice for Hedgehogs* (2011), to a saying attributed to Archilochus in the 7th century BC.

"πολλ' οιδ'αλωπηξ, αλλ'εχινος έν μεγα

(the fox knows many things, but the hedgehog one big thing.)"

The judgments of Mann J and the Court of Appeal

. . .

42. In this Court the appellants have challenged the reasoning of the judge and the Court of Appeal. Mr Sumption QC said that it was eccentric of the judge to describe the helmet's purpose as utilitarian, and that the Court of Appeal could find it to have a functional purpose only by treating it as having the same functional purpose as a real helmet "within the confines of a film".

43. This is quite a puzzling point. The Star Wars films are set in an imaginary, science-fiction world of the future. War films set in the past (Paths of Glory, for instance, depicting the French army in the first world war, or Atonement depicting the British Expeditionary Force at Dunkirk) are at least based on historical realities. The actors and extras in the trenches or on the beaches may be wearing real steel helmets, or (because real steel helmets of the correct style are unobtainable in sufficient numbers) they may be wearing plastic helmets painted khaki. In either case the helmets are there as (in the judge's words) "a mixture of costume and prop" in order to contribute to the artistic effect of the film as a film. They are part of a production process, as Laddie J said in *Metix* at p 721, citing Whitford J in *Davis (J & S)(Holdings) Ltd v Wright Health Group Ltd* [1988] RPC 403, 410-412. In this case the production process was the making of a full-length feature film.

44. It would not accord with the normal use of language to apply the term "sculpture" to a 20th century military helmet used in the making of a film, whether it was the real thing or a replica made in different material, however great its

contribution to the artistic effect of the finished film. The argument for applying the term to an Imperial Stormtrooper helmet is stronger, because of the imagination that went into the concept of the sinister cloned soldiers dressed in uniform white armour. But it was the Star Wars film that was the work of art that Mr Lucas and his companies created. The helmet was utilitarian in the sense that it was an element in the process of production of the film.

45. Those were the concurrent findings of both the judge and the Court of Appeal, in paras [121] and [80] of their respective judgments. The type of judgmental conclusion that often has to be reached in intellectual property cases — on issues such as obviousness, inventiveness, and copying — are matters on which appellate courts should be slow to interfere with the judgment of the trial judge. In *Designers Guild* [2000] 1 WLR 2416, 2423-2424, Lord Hoffmann observed that there were two reasons for this. The first is that the judge has, and the appellate court has not, seen and heard the witnesses. Lord Hoffmann continued,

> "Secondly, because the decision involves the application of a not altogether precise legal standard to a combination of features of varying importance, I think that this falls within the class of case in which an appellate court should not reverse a judge's decision unless he has erred in principle: see *Pro Sieben Media AG v Carlton UK Television Ltd* [1991] 1 WLR 605, 612-613. I agree with Buxton LJ in *Norowzian v Arks Ltd (No 2)* [2000] FSR 363, 370 when he said: 'where it is not suggested that the judge has made any error of principle a party should not come to the Court of Appeal simply in the hope that the impression formed by the judges in this court, or at least two of them, will be different from that of the trial judge.'"

That applies with extra force in the case of a second appeal. To the same effect are Lord Hoffmann's observations in *Biogen Inc v Medeva plc* [1997] RPC 1, 45, which are too well known to need repetition.

46. The Court of Appeal (para [78]) relied on Lord Hoffmann's observations in *Designers Guild*, and in our view it was right to do so. During the 17 days of the trial Mann J heard evidence about the helmet and the other artefacts from numerous different witnesses. Long and thorough as his judgment is, he may not have recorded every nuance that contributed to his conclusion. He did not err in law or reach an obviously untenable conclusion, and the Court of Appeal was right to uphold his decision on this point.

47. We would uphold the judgments below very largely for the reasons that they give. But (at the risk of appearing humourless) we are not enthusiastic about the "elephant test" in para [77] of the Court of Appeal's judgment ("knowing one when you see it"). Any zoologist has no difficulty in recognising an elephant on sight, and most could no doubt also give a clear and accurate description of its essential identifying features. By contrast a judge, even one very experienced in intellectual property matters, does not have some special power of divination which leads instantly to an infallible conclusion, and no judge would claim to have such a power. The judge reads and hears the evidence (often including expert evidence), reads and listens to the advocates' submissions, and takes

what the Court of Appeal rightly called a multi-factorial approach. Moreover the judge has to give reasons to explain his or her conclusions.

48. There is one other matter to which the Court of Appeal attached no weight, but which seems to us to support the judge's conclusion. It is a general point as to the policy considerations underlying Parliament's development of the law in order to protect the designers and makers of three-dimensional artefacts from unfair competition. After reviewing the legislative history the Court of Appeal took the view (para [40]) that there was no assistance to be obtained from the relationship between copyright and registered design right. We respectfully disagree, especially if the relatively new unregistered design right is also taken into account. It is possible to recognise an emerging legislative purpose (though the process has been slow and laborious) of protecting three-dimensional objects in a graduated way, quite unlike the protection afforded by the indiscriminate protection of literary copyright. Different periods of protection are accorded to different classes of work. Artistic works of art (sculpture and works of artistic craftsmanship) have the fullest protection; then come works with "eye appeal" (*AMP Inc v Utilux Pty Ltd* [1971] FSR 572); and under Part III of the 1988 Act a modest level of protection has been extended to purely functional objects (the exhaust system of a motor car being the familiar example). Although the periods of protection accorded to the less privileged types have been progressively extended, copyright protection has always been much more generous. There are good policy reasons for the differences in the periods of protection, and the Court should not, in our view, encourage the boundaries of full copyright protection to creep outwards.

Sections 51 and 52

49. The appellants accept that if the helmet did not qualify as a sculpture within the meaning of the 1988 Act, then Mr Ainsworth had a defence under section 51 to any infringement claim based on Mr McQuarrie's graphics, and section 52 does not arise. The Court of Appeal dealt with these sections, for completeness, in paras 83 to 98 of its judgment. It is unnecessary to cover the same ground again. We would dismiss the appeal so far as it is based on the English law of copyright.

(b) Works of Artistic Craftsmanship

In the *DRG* case above, Justice Reed accepted that it may be appropriate to measure "works of artistic craftsmanship" in particular against some test of "artistic-ness." Even if the word "artistic" in reference to "artistic works" is understood to be a generic description of works that find expression in a visual medium, the word "artistic" in reference to "works of artistic craftsmanship" could be regarded as an explicit qualification, limiting the kinds of works of craftsmanship that copyright will protect. In the next cases, we see attempts to formulate tests for "artistic-ness" in this context. The *Cuisenaire* case was ultimately decided by the Supreme Court on the grounds that the rods, as teaching devices, were not "things in which copyright can be had." (See Chapter 2). At the Exchequer Court, Justice Noel questioned whether the rods could be considered "artistic" in light of their intended purpose. The *George Henscher* case underscores the difficulties inherent in making this determination — each Lord has a somewhat different understanding of what "artistic-ness" requires.

Cuisenaire v. South West Imports Ltd., [1968] 1 Ex. C.R. 493, 54 C.P.R. 1 (Can. Ex. Ct.)

Exchequer Court of Canada

Noel J.:

. . .

24 The plaintiff herein had a rather difficult task in that he was faced by a decision in Australia in *Cuisenaire v. Reed*, [1963] V.R. 719, where Pape J. held that his rods could not be the subject of copyright because the Australian *Copyright Act* (based on the *Imperial Copyright Act* of 1911) did not protect works of craftsmanship *per se*, but only of artistic craftsmanship and that his rods were not artistic. Pape J. also held that as no special skill or training was required to cut the strips of wood in predetermined lengths, and to colour them, no craftsmanship was involved in their production and they were not works of "artistic craftsmanship" within the definition of the Act.

25 The allegation in the Australian case was that the defendant, by making the rods, had infringed the plaintiff's book or books by constructing in three dimensions articles in accordance with the directions in the tables in the book and that, therefore, these rods were part of the work.

26 The plaintiff, in the present instance, has taken a different position and claims that these rods, considered by themselves, are a work in which copyright subsists as an artistic work or as a work of artistic craftsmanship, although they must be considered against the background of their development and are part of a larger overall work, his book.

27 As a matter of fact, the plaintiff, by the amended statement of facts, deliberately excluded, in describing the works on which he relies, his literary work *Les nombres en couleurs* as well as any reference to the system, relying only on two single works, the two set of rods, one of 10 and the other of 241 pieces, and merely mentioning that the rods are "for the teaching of the science of arithmetic in primary school grades". Pape J. in the Australian case held that the rods were not artistic on two main grounds which were (1) that the definition of "artistic" in section 2(b) is an exhaustive definition and although it uses only the word "includes" it means "means and includes" and, therefore, the artistic works

contemplated are restricted to "painting, drawing, sculpture" even if "artistic" here is a generic label which was intended to include subject-matters possessing no elements of artistic quality at all and (2) that "artistic" with the word craftsmanship had a narrower meaning, does not fall within the wider scope of artistic as defined above and must have an artistic element. He also held that the plaintiff's works were not works of craftsmanship.

28 I should point out here that the definitions of "artistic work" and "literary work" as set out hereunder are exactly the same in the Canadian statute as they were in the Australian statute that Pape J. had under consideration. They are:

2. In this Act, ...

(b) "artistic work" includes works of painting, drawing, sculpture and artistic craftsmanship, and architectural work of art and engravings and photographs;

. . .

(n) "literary works" includes maps, charts, plans, tables and compilations;

. . .

70 I now turn to plaintiff's contention that if his rods are not original productions in the scientific domain, as contemplated by section 2(v) of the Act, they are either artistic works or works of artistic craftsmanship under section 2(b) of the Act. This section reads as follows:

2. In this Act, ...

(b) "artistic work" includes works of painting, drawing, sculpture and artistic craftsmanship, and architectural works of art and engravings and photographs;

71 Here again I must disagree with this submission. In my view, plaintiff's rods are physically little more than tools or counters to be used for a particular purpose. Although they are coloured in a manner such as to interest or please children, the same as blocks for instance, they were never intended primarily as an article regarded as artistic or beautiful in itself even if the artistic requirements required here are not too great. Indeed, even if artistic merit is not a matter of importance in copyright law, the word artistic must still be given its ordinary meaning although, may I add, there could be considerable debate as to the merit of a particular work.

72 It is true, as pointed out by counsel for the plaintiff, that there is originality in the colouring and size, selection and arrangement within the sets and the choice of the colours may well have been arrived at with a view to applying the method he conceived to teach children arithmetic. It is, however, the artistic work itself which is entitled to protection and not the idea behind it. These rods indeed are tools and nothing more, the same as colours, for instance, are tools in teaching children how to paint. They can take on meaning only when considered and integrated with a concept itself which in itself is not entitled to protection. The only relationship between the rods which exists here is by reference to Cuisenaire's theory where it can be seen that there is a connection between the colours denoting certain families of significantly related mathematical values which,

however, cannot really be considered as an artistic arrangement. Furthermore, although these coloured rods set out orderly in a box could be considered as an artistic arrangement, there is no claim to such arrangement here and it is difficult to see how colour through these rods could confer copyright on the works even if all these things are claimed in combination.

73 An artistic work, in my view, must to some degree at least, be a work that is intended to have an appeal to the aesthetic senses not just an incidental appeal, such as here, but as an important or one of the important objects for which the work is brought into being. The plaintiff's rods may have a certain attraction to children, but this, in my view, is a very secondary purpose which, I am afraid, is not a sufficient basis for a finding that the rods are artistic.

74 I must, therefore, conclude that plaintiff's rods are not and cannot be held to be artistic works under the Act.

75 Neither can they be held to be works of artistic craftsmanship because they are not artistic and for the additional reason given by Pape J. in *Cuisenaire v. Reed* (*supra*) in that no craftsmanship was involved in their production.

76 Neither are these rods plastic works relative to science under section 2(v) as although plastic here is not used in the scientific or polyethylene sense all the definitions of plastic suggest that it must be something that is or has been mouldable or pliable material and, of course, wood is not of that nature. Nor can these rods be assimilated in any way with the artistic meaning of plastic, which involves the art of shaping or modeling such as in the art of sculpture or ceramics.

77 It follows that plaintiff's rods are not a proper subject matter of copyright under the Act and his action must, therefore, fail....

George Hensher Ltd v Restawile Upholstery (Lancs) Ltd., [1976] AC 64

House of Lords

LORD REID: The appellants manufacture upholstered chairs and settees. Sales of their old types were falling off and they proposed to design a completely new type. After much consideration they evolved a prototype or "mock-up". This consisted of a light frame with upholstery nailed on so as to look like a chair. It was too flimsy to be used as a chair but served as a model for chairs which were copied from it and sold. Once the new type was in production the prototype was destroyed.

This new type proved to be popular and sold well. Several other manufacturers copied the appellants' products. The appellants thought that this was an infringement of their rights and they took action. Only the respondents maintained that they were not infringing the appellants' rights.

The appellants did not register any design under the Registered Designs Act 1949. They maintain that the respondents have infringed their copyright. Section (3) (2) of the Copyright Act, 1956, provides that copyright shall subsist in every original artistic work, and section 3(1) provides;

> "3-(1) In this Act "artistic work" means a work of any of the following descriptions, that is to say;
>
> "(a) the following, irrespective of artistic quality, namely paintings, sculptures, drawings, engravings and photographs;
>
> "(b) works of architecture, being either buildings or models for buildings;
>
> "(c) works of artistic craftsmanship, not falling within either of the preceding paragraphs."

The appellants maintain that the prototype of their furniture was a "work of artistic craftsmanship" within the meaning of section 3(1)(c). The respondents admit that the prototype was a work of craftsmanship but deny that it was of "artistic craftsmanship".

It is common ground that we must consider the prototype and not the furniture put on the market by the appellants. Apparently this is because the articles put on the market were not works of craftsmanship. But if there was copyright in the prototype then the furniture put on the market by the appellants was copied from it, and the respondents" products were copied from the furniture which the appellants put on the market. The respondents do not deny that this would be infringement of that copyright.

The respondents have not taken the point that such a prototype however artistic could not be a "work of artistic craftsmanship", and the point was not argued. But I feel bound to say that I have great doubt about this matter. A work of craftsmanship suggests to me a durable useful handmade object and a work of artistic craftsmanship suggests something, whether of practical utility or not, which its owner values because of its artistic character. It appears to me to be difficult to bring within the terms or the intention of the statute an object which, however artistic it might appear to be, is only intended to be used as a step in a commercial operation and has no value in itself. I express no concluded opinion on this matter, on which the decision of this case can be of no authority. This case must I think be decided on the assumption that a real chair similar to those put on the market had been made by craftsmanship.

Section 3(1) is difficult to understand unless one takes account of its origin. The Copyright Act, 1911, covered artistic works. Section 35 contains a definition. "Artistic work" includes works of painting, drawing, sculpture" and artistic craftsmanship, and architectural works of art and engravings "and photographs". "Architectural work of art" is defined as meaning any building or structure having an artistic character or design. This brought in artistic craftsmanship and buildings for the first time. It would seem that paintings, drawings, sculpture, engravings and photographs were protected whether they had any artistic character or not, but works of craftsmanship had to be of "artistic" craftsmanship and buildings must have an "artistic" character or design. There is no further explanation of what is meant by "artistic".

The 1956 Act in section 3(1)(a) makes explicit that the works to which it refers need have no artistic quality. Section 3(1)(b) removes the need for any artistic character or design in buildings. But section 3(1)(c) preserves the limitation that there must be "artistic" craftsmanship.

The word "artistic" is not an easy word to construe or apply not only because it may have different shades of meaning but also because different people have different views about what is artistic. One may have a word which substantially everyone understands in much the same way. Recently we had to consider such a word — "insulting" (Brutus v. Cozens [1973] A.C. 854). Then the matter can and, indeed, must be left to the judge or jury for further explanation will confuse rather than clarify.

But here two questions must be determined. What precisely is the meaning of "artistic" in this context and who is to judge of its application to the article in question? There is a trend of authority with which I agree that a court ought not to be called on to make an aesthetic judgement. Judges have to be experts in the use of the English language but they are not experts in art or aesthetics. In such a matter my opinion is of no more value than that of anyone else. But I can and must say what in my view is the meaning of the word "artistic".

I think we must avoid philosophic or metaphysical argument about the nature of beauty, not only because there does not seem to be any consensus about this but also because those who are ignorant of philosophy are entitled to have opinions about what is artistic. I think that by common usage it is proper for a person to say that in his opinion a thing has an artistic character if he gets pleasure or satisfaction or it may be uplift from contemplating it. No doubt it is necessary to beware of those who get pleasure from looking at something which has cost them a great deal of money. But if unsophisticated people get pleasure from seeing something which they admire I do not see why we must say that it is not artistic because those who profess to be art experts think differently. After all there are great differences of opinion among those who can properly be called experts.

It is I think of importance that the maker or designer of a thing should have intended that it should have an artistic appeal but I would not regard that as either necessary or conclusive. If any substantial section of the public genuinely admires and values a thing for its appearance and gets pleasure or satisfaction, whether emotional or intellectual, from looking at it, I would accept that it is artistic although many others may think it meaningless or common or vulgar.

I think that it may be misleading to equate artistic craftsmanship with a work of art. "Work of art" is generally associated more with the fine arts than with craftsmanship and may be setting too high a standard. During last century there was a movement to bring art to the people. I doubt whether the craftsman who set out with that intention would have regarded all their products as works of art, but they were certainly works or artistic craftsmanship whether or not they were useful as well as having an artistic appeal.

I am quite unable to agree with the view of the Court of Appeal that "there must at least be expected in an object or work that its utilitarian or functional appeal should not be the primary inducement to its acquisition or retention". The whole conception of artistic craftsmanship appears to me to produce things which are both useful and artistic in the belief that being artistic does not make them any less useful. A person who only wants, or has only room for, one of a particular kind of household object may be willing to pay more to get one which he regards as artistic; if a work of craftsmanship it is none the less of artistic craftsmanship because his primary purpose is to get something useful.

But on the other hand, I cannot accept the Appellants" submission or the view of Graham, J. Many people — probably too many — buy things on eye appeal or because they are of a new or original design. But they would not claim that therefore they thought that their purchase had artistic merit. They might say that they were not interested in art or that they would have liked to have bought an artistic object but that there was none to be had, at least at a price they could pay. It is notorious that manufacturers go to great expense in providing packaging which will catch the eye of customers. But the customer does not regard the packaging as artistic — he throws it away.

In the present case I find no evidence at all that anyone regarded the Appellants" furniture as artistic. The Appellants" object was to produce something which would sell. It was, as one witness said, "a winner" and they succeeded in their object. No doubt many customers bought the furniture because they thought it looked nice as well as being comfortable. But looking nice appears to me to fall considerably short of having artistic appeal. I can find no evidence that anyone felt or thought that the furniture was artistic in the sense which I have tried to explain. I am therefore of opinion that this appeal should be dismissed.

LORD MORRIS OF BORTH-Y-GEST: ...I consider that in its place in the phrase "work of artistic craftsmanship" the word "artistic" will be well understood. As a word it can only stand on and by its own strength. It needs no interpretation. That is not to say that there will not be differences of opinion as to whether some particular work of craftsmanship does or does not measure up to the standard which must be reached before the use of the word "artistic" is warranted. But that is only because in this field personal judgment has to be formed: there are no absolute standards: there can be no scientific precision in measurement. Nor can there be unanimity in conclusion through a general consensus of opinion among those whose views command respect will surely be firm ground on which judgment in a court of law can be based.

If by reference to a dictionary it is thought that one sense in which the word "artists" is understood is that of denoting "one who cultivates one of the fine arts which please by perfection of execution" then there are conveyed some of the conceptions which the word "artistic" suggests. But I would not seek to formulate any kind of judicial*181 definition of a word which needs no such aid. If it is asked whether works which possess distinctive features of design and skill in workmanship or works which possess distinctive characteristics of shape, form and finish all qualify to be called artistic I would say that the word artistic calls for something additional and different. If it is asked whether there is artistry if there is an appeal to the eye I would say that something more is needed. In any event, and apart from this, such questions would tend to suggest or to impose a clamp of rigidity and restriction in definition where none is needed....

VISCOUNT DILHORNE: ...How, then, is the phrase to be interpreted? An "artistic work" is no more and no less that a work of art. Every work of art is an artistic work and vice versa. How does one distinguish between what is a work of art and what is not? Various tests have been suggested. In the Court of Appeal, Russell, L.J. said:

> "In our judgment if it can be said of a work of craftsmanship that it is an object which would be expected to be acquired or retained rather for its functional utility than for any appeal to aesthetic taste, it is not within the scope of the phrase "other works of artistic craftsmanship". Mere originality in points of design aimed at appealing to the eye as commercial selling points will not, in our judgment, suffice,"

and

> "in order to qualify as a work of artistic craftsmanship, there must at least be expected in an object or work that its utilitarian or functional appeal should not be the primary inducement to its acquisition or retention".

The Court of Appeal agreed with Noel, J.'"s rejection in Cuisenaire v. South West Imports Ltd. [1968] 1 Ex. C.R. 493 (Can:) of the idea that because a work or object was partly functional or utilitarian, it could not be an artistic work.

While I agree with the rejection of that idea and I agree that mere originality in design does not make a thing an artistic work of art, I do not think that whether or not a work is to be regarded as artistic depends on whether or not the primary inducement for its acquisition or retention is its functional character. To determine the primary possession of an article seems to me a very difficult and uncertain test for any court to apply: and I do not think that the words "works of artistic craftsmanship" are to be interpreted as involving the application of any such test. A Work which is one of artistic craftsmanship does not, I think, lose that character on account of its functional qualities....

So in my view it is simply a question of fact whether a work is one of artistic craftsmanship. Questions of fact are often difficult to decide but juries have to decide them....

. . .

LORD SIMON OF GLAISDALE: ... The significant feature of this part of the law before 1911 was that the artistic works given copyright protection were works of fine art. This accorded with the almost universal concept current in 1862: a work of art was a product of the fine arts and primarily an easel painting. But almost from the moment of the Fine Arts Copyright Act 1862, there was a reaction, which came to be known as the Arts and Crafts movement. ... These are no more than a handful of key events; but they put beyond doubt what it was that prompted Parliament in 1911 to give copyright protection to 'works of artistic craftsmanship' — namely, the Arts and Crafts movement with its emphasis on the applied or decorative arts.

For the essence of the Arts and Crafts ideology was that 'art' did not mean merely, or even primarily, the fine arts. Art was a way of life, standing in contrast to the prevailing life of industrialism and commercialism, which was seen as a threat to mankind's spiritual and physical well-being. 'On every hand', Carlyle had written, 'the living artisan is driven from his workshop, to make room for a speedier inanimate one'. So the handicraftsman must be restored to his creative role in society. Moreover, his creation, wherever appropriate, should be a work of art — creation par excellence; and the artist must in turn be a craftsman....

...'[W]orks of artistic craftsmanship' is a composite phrase which must be construed as a whole. There is nothing to suggest that any of the words is used in other than one of its ordinary senses. A work of craftsmanship, even though it cannot be confined to handicraft, at least presupposes special training, skill and knowledge for its production: see *Cuisenaire v Reed* and *Cuisenaire v South West Imports Ltd* ([1968] 1 Ex CR 493 at 514). 'Craftsmanship', particularly when considered in its historical context, implies a manifestation of pride in sound workmanship — a rejection of the shoddy, the meretricious, the facile. But the craftsmanship — not the work itself — must, in addition, be artistic.

. . .

It is, my Lords, I confess, easier to question the criteria put forward by others than to propound one's own. The attempt must nevertheless be made. I start by re-emphasising that the statutory phrase is not 'artistic work of craftsmanship', but 'work of artistic craftsmanship'; and that this distinction accords with the social situation in which Parliament was providing a remedy. It is therefore misleading to ask, first, is this a work produced by a craftsman, and secondly, is it a work of art? It is more pertinent to ask, is this the work of one who was in this respect an artist-craftsman? It follows that the artistic merit of the work is irrelevant. ...Not only is artistic merit irrelevant as a matter of statutory construction, evaluation of artistic merit is not a task for which judges have any training or general aptitude. Words are the tools and subject-matter of lawyers; but even in matters of literary copyright the court will not concern itself with literary merit: *Walter v Lane*. Since the tribunal will not attempt a personal aesthetic judgment (Stewart J in *Hay v Sloan* ((1957) 16 Fox Pat C 185 at 190)) it follows again, that whether the subject-matter is or is not a work of artistic-craftsmanship is a matter of evidence; and the most cogent evidence is likely to be either from those who are themselves acknowledged artist-craftsmen or from those who are concerned with the training of artist-craftsmen — in other words, expert evidence. In evaluating the evidence, the court will endeavour not to be tied to a particular metaphysics of art, partly because courts are not naturally fitted to weigh such matters, partly because Parliament can hardly have intended that the construction of its statutory phrase should turn on some recondite theory of aesthetics — though the court must, of course, in its task of statutory interpretation, take cognisance of the social-aesthetic situation which lies behind the enactment, nor can counsel be prevented from probing the reasons why a witness considers the subject-matter to be or not to be a work of artistic craftsmanship. It is probably enough that common experience tells us that artists have vocationally an aim and impact which differ from those of the ordinary run of humankind. Given the craftsmanship, it is the presence of such aim and impact — what Stewart J ((1957) 16 Fox Pat C 185 at 190) called 'the intent of the creator and its result' — which will determine that the work is one of artistic craftsmanship.

Against this construction of the statutory phrase, the result of the instant appeal cannot be in doubt: there was no, or certainly no adequate, evidence that the prototype of the Bronx chair was a work of artistic craftsmanship. ... If it were permissible to express a personal view, I would agree with the Court of Appeal that Henshers' suites are perfectly ordinary pieces of furniture. It would be an entire misuse of language to describe them or their prototypes as works of artistic craftsmanship.

LORD KILBRANDON: ...Whether a given object is a work of artistic craftsmanship can be posed as a question of fact, but only after the meaning of the work 'artistic' has been determined; what that meaning is, is a question of law, since it involves a decision of what Parliament meant by the word Parliament used. I do not believe that it is possible, as matter of law or of exegesis, to arrive at a comprehensive definitive interpretation of such a familiar English word, so as to be armed with a test which will enable one, by the application of it, at a glance, to exclude all that does not properly fall within the scope of the simple word itself. It is, indeed, seldom that a simple word can, by translation into some easier or more difficult phrase, be rendered the more capable of furnishing such a test. But it is quite plain, in my opinion, that you cannot get on without exercising, in any case in which this kind of dispute arises, the judicial function of holding whether the facts bring the object within the meaning of the statutory definition. You will get no assistance, until you have exercised that judicial function, by asking the opinion of an expert; if he says, 'I regard that object as artistic', the next question which must be asked in order to make his last answer intelligible is, 'What do you mean by artistic?' That question is incompetent, because the answer would be irrelevant. Since the word is a word of common speech, it requires, and permits of, no interpretation by experts. It is for the judge to determine whether the object falls within the scope of the common meaning of the word.

. . .

...In the result I have failed, perhaps inevitably, to find a substitute formula which will replace the word 'artistic', and be one which will serve to qualify as artistic or non-artistic any given piece of craftsmanship. I do not think it is necessary to do so. I would put it in this way, that in my opinion the common meaning of the word 'artistic' does not permit that word to be used as a description of the craftsmanship involved in the production of the prototype 'Bronx' chair, having regard to all the evidence of the circumstances surrounding its manufacture....Your Lordships' House has been offered 'definitions' of the word 'artistic' framed by each of Graham J, counsel for the appellants together with two by counsel for the respondents, and has rejected them all. In addition, I rather gather that there is no definition framed by a member of the appellate committee which is altogether acceptable to any other member; this means that each of their Lordships has rejected, or at least refrained from adopting, nine solutions of the problem. It may be that Copinger is right when he says:

> 'Copyright law is, in essence, concerned with the negative right of preventing the copying of physical material existing in the field of literature and the arts. Its object is to protect the writer and the artist from the unlawful reproduction of his material.'

Since ample protection is provided aliunde for those preparing designs for commercial reproduction, it would not be doing any injustice were it made clear that the Copyright Act is not concerned to protect, eg, the Bronx prototype.

I would dismiss the appeal.

(c) Architectural Works

Hay & Hay v. Sloan (1957), 27 C.P.R. 132

Supreme Court of Ontario

Stewart J.

Judgment: July 16, 1957

Stewart J.:

1 The plaintiff Hay is a builder and sole proprietor of the plaintiff corporation. In 1954 he designed a house to sell at the now modest price of $12,500.00, including the lot. The ground plan was a rather conventional disposition of the available space but such space was used to the best advantage by making an otherwise undistinguished ground plan into a split level house. The exterior was pleasing, using a cottage — instead of a gable — roof and a very attractive disposition of windows, doors and treatment of exterior building materials.

2 After the prototype had been built it was seen by the defendant Shanks, who wished to acquire one like it. He was dealing with the defendant Sloan, a real estate agent, and it was first thought that he might buy a lot from the plaintiff and erect one of the latter's house upon it. Shanks, however, preferred a lot on a different locality and, through Sloan, attempted to obtain permission to copy the original house known as Belaire. Permission was refused by Hays but, notwithstanding this, the lot was purchased by Shanks, through Sloan, from the defendant Kukura, who built upon it a residence which was an almost exact copy of the Belaire. In spite of the use of somewhat different materials and some very minor variations the facade of the house built for Shanks was a deliberate copy of the plaintiff's plan. I also find that the plaintiff warned Sloan that, in the event

of his persisting in copying his house, he would institute action against him and was told that there was nothing he, Hay, could do about it. This is confirmed by the evidence of Shanks who states that he was assured by Sloan that Shanks would not be adversely affected by Hay's proposed action. It is significant to note that various minor changes were made in the Belaire during the course of construction and that even these changes have been incorporated in the building erected for Shanks.

3 The plaintiff now sues for damages and for an injunction restraining all the defendants from copying his plan. The defences may be summarized as follows: —

(1) That no copy was in fact made, and with this I have already dealt.

(2) That such a house is not the proper subject matter of copyright.

(3) That the ground plan (which it is admitted is not capable of being copyrighted) imposes upon the builder the facade.

(4) That the plaintiff's plan had no artistic quality or design within the meaning of The Copyright Act.

4 Counsel submits as to the second argument that, in a fairly small house, the costs of which is kept to a minimum, the greatest possible use of standard and prefabricated material is made and that therefore a standard result is achieved. He submits that it therefore follows that any real expression of originality or artistic quality or design is impossible and hence that there can be no copy rights. It must be obvious that size is not only no criterion of artistic value but that it cannot even be considered. The jewellery of Faberge and Cellini are as artistically valid as Cheop's Pyramid or the Temple at Karnak and, artistically speaking, there may be "infinite riches in a little room". Nor can the cost of construction be a consideration. I see no reason to suppose a Cape Cod Cottage or a small but beautifully designed Country Georgian House to be of less architectural merit than the costly cube which today expresses the success of a large corporation. That neither size nor value affects the right to copyright in the artistic quality of architectural designs was held in the case of *Blake v. Warren*, MacGilivrary copyright cases, 1928- 1935, at p. 268 where subsidy houses were held to be the proper subject matter of copyright provided that they had in fact some artistic quality.

5 Thirdly, counsel for the defendants submitted that the ground plan of the house imposed a necessary arrangement of voids and solids and that therefore if two houses were built with the same ground plan the facade would of necessity be almost identical. It is clear that copyright of floor plans under the architectural sections of The Copyright Act is not possible although subsection (n) of Section 2 defines "literary work" as including maps, charts and plans. I do not agree that the exterior of a building is automatically dependent upon its ground plan, and one of the architects said, and I agree, that if six architects were to enter a competition for the design of a house upon a given ground plan, it being split level and with a cottage roof, the facade of each house would be quite different

in effect. The final argument of counsel for the defence, that the Belaire has no artistic character or design, stems from the definition under Section 2(a) of The Copyright Act of Architectural Works of Art, which is defined as being "any building or structure having an artistic quality or design in respect of such character or design ... but the protection afforded by this act is confined to the artistic character and design and does not extend to processes or methods of construction". It was said that it was for the trial Judge to decide whether the building was artistic or inartistic and that the wording of the Act requires such a decision. It is gratifying to think that those who drafted this act were content to leave such aesthetic responsibility to the judiciary, but it is, I think, dangerous to assume such intention. While juries are occasionally faced with such problems as in the case of *Whistler v. Ruskin* and Lord Chancellors or Boards of Censors may be saddled with the duty of protecting an innocent and pure-minded public from impropriety in the arts, yet legislators in the past have, probably not unwisely, refrained from appointing judges to act as *arbitriarium* perhaps due to the fact that they, like Gilberts' learned statesmen, "do not itch to interfere in matters which they do not understand", and, for other reasons, I do not believe that this was the intention of the legislators. The good art of today is almost invariably the bad Art of tomorrow, for aesthetic standards and values change from generation to generation. The admirer of Fragonard would scarcely concede merit to Mondrian's rectangles. He who rejoices in the stately periods of Sir Thomas Brown would probably find the prosody of Gertrude Stein intolerable. Orff and Offenbach, save in the unusually electric, do not attract the same disciples nor for that matter would Martha Graham and Gypsy Rose Lee. In this last antithesis I may be wrong. The legal approach is, as a rule, to elevate precedent and to view innovations somewhat askance. The function of the Judge has always been to weigh evidence and propound existing law. In the arts evidence of aesthetic values is, as a rule, merely the heated opinion of prejudiced adherents. *Whistler's* case is an interesting and entertaining example of the futility of attempting to make aesthetic judgments on opinion evidence, a fact which the plaintiff vitriolically demonstrates in his "the Gentle Act of Making Enemies". Artistic values cannot be weighed, for no universally acceptable unit or artistic laws retained their sanctity for a protracted period of time. I think it unlikely that any legislature would be so addle-pated as to appoint the judiciary to decide whether Frank Lloyd Wright, Palladio, Pheidias, Corbusier or the plaintiff had produced buildings of artistic character or design in the sense that they are artistically good or artistically bad. The art of architecture has never been more happily described than by Vetruvius' phrase — *firmitas, utilitas, venusta*. Assuming an equal capacity to produce *firmitas* and *utilitas* the distinction between the good and the mediocre architect is the degree in which he produces the quality of *venusta*. This is frequently translated "beauty" but is, I think, more happily, and equally properly, translated as "delight", and the experience of it will depend, as I have indicated, upon the person, the age, and the place. Therefore, to interpret the Act properly, the tribunal should not attempt to exercise a personal aesthetic judgment but to consider the intent of the creator and its result. Suppose a man were to build himself a pig-pen garnished with fretted ginger-bread and with four lovely turrets, yet firm and commodious. Let it stand in its multicoloured horror a mid-Victorian blot upon the landscape. Let us assume that no contemporary could accept this edifice as anything but an architectural excrescence of the most loathsome kind, yet to its creator it would well be a thing of beauty and to its inhabitants a porcine paradise. An attempt has been made to produce *venustua* and some originality displayed. This, in my view, is sufficient to render such building the subject matter of copyright. The work must, of course, be original as this is required by Section 4, sub-section (1) which refers to every "original ... artistic work", and artistic work by section 2(b) includes architectural works of art. The question of what is original was dealt with in the case of *Chabot v. Davies* , [1936] 3 All E.R. 221 where at page 225 Crossman, J., says, quoting from the judgment of Peterson, J., in the case of *University of London Press Limited v. University Tutorial Press Limited*, [1916] 2 Ch. 601 —

> the word 'original' does not in this connection mean that the work must be the expression of original or inventive thought. Copyright Acts are not concerned with the originality of ideas, but with the expression of thought, and, in the case of 'literary work,' with the expression of thought in print or writing. The Originality which is required relates to the expression of the thought. But the Act does not require that the expression must be in an original or novel form, but that the work must not be copied from another work — that it should originate from the author.

6   That the Belaire was of an original design is stated by one Hunter MacKenzie, an Ontario land surveyor, who stated that the outward appearance of the house is quite different to anything that he had seen before. Frederick W.J. Davies, an architect and an excellent witness, said that there were many distinctive features in the Belaire such as the fact that it was of split level, the position and relationship of the brick to the clapboard the positioning of windows in good proportion and that in general the balance of the voids and solids was harmonious and well done. He found the entire facade pleasing and that it had "something that others don't have". In cross-examination he said that the designer had attempted to produce good design, good proportion and good use of material and that this is the true artistry of architecture. His evidence was corroborated by another architect one Kelvin R. Sills. I therefore find that the Belaire has artistic character and design within the meaning of The Copyright Act, and that it is an original artistic work.

Chancellor Management Inc. v. Oasis Homes Ltd. (2002), 19 C.P.R. (4th) 480

Alberta Court of Queen's Bench

Fraser J.

Fraser J.:

INTRODUCTION

1 This Judgment follows the trial of an action arising from an alleged breach of copyright or of contract or both. In this action the Plaintiff, Chancellor Management Inc., operating as Chancellor Homes ("Chancellor"), seeks a declaration that it is the owner of the architectural work represented by the plans for a show home titled "the Cartier" ("the Plans"). Chancellor also seeks: an injunction to enjoin the Defendants Oasis Homes Ltd. ("Oasis") a housebuilder, and John Haddon Design Ltd. ("Haddon Design"), a design firm, from using or reproducing the Plans; damages; and other related remedies.

2 The action arises as a result of Chancellor hiring Haddon Design to design the Plans. Chancellor alleges that it instructed Haddon Design, through its principal, John Haddon ("Haddon"), to incorporate certain unique features into the Plans. Chancellor claims authorship to those features and submits that they are not common to other homes. It claims a copyright to the Plans on that basis.

3 Haddon Design, also claims authorship of the majority of the unique features over which Chancellor claims authorship. Additionally, Haddon Design claims authorship of other aspects of the Plans, such as dimensions, placement of windows and a multitude of other details which were necessary components of the Plans. Haddon Design also relies on presumptions within the *Copyright Act*, R.S.C. 1985, c. C-42 ("the *Act*") and an alleged contract between it and Chancellor to support its claim to ownership of copyright in the Plans.

4 Oasis is also a home builder. It bought a copy of the Plans from Haddon Design and built a show home based on them which opened in mid-April 1999. Oasis argues that the Plans do not attract the protection of the *Act*. In the alternative, it states that Haddon Design is the owner of the copyright. In the further alternative, it submits that if copyright exists in the Plans and Chancellor owns that copyright, it was not infringed by Oasis.

. . .

ANALYSIS

1. Does copyright exist in the Plans?

20 Chancellor submits that a copyright can exist in house plans. It relies on section 5(1) of the Act; *Hay v. Sloan* (1957), 12 D.L.R. (2d) 397 (Ont. H.C.); and *Randall Homes Ltd. v. Harwood Homes Ltd.*, [1987] 4 W.W.R. 705 (Man. Q.B.), as support for that proposition. For house plans to become subject to copyright protection, Chancellor argues, that the design elements in the plans, either alone or in combination with other elements, must be "original". Originality in this

context, it submits, is established by proving that a party's expressions contributed to a work and that those expressions originated from him or her and were not copied.

21 Chancellor concedes that some of these design elements it claims authorship over are not new. However, it maintains that these elements in the combination in which they exist in the Plans have an original character.

22 Oasis acknowledges that copyright may exist in house plans, however, it takes the position that a house plan must be unique before it will be protected by copyright. In that regard Oasis relies on *Randall Homes, supra; Hay, supra; Viceroy Homes Ltd. v. Ventury Homes Inc.* (1991), 34 C.P.R. (3d) 385 (Ont. Gen. Div.), aff'd (1996), 69 C.P.R. (3d) 459 (Ont. C.A.); and *Lifestyle Homes Ltd. v. Randall Homes Ltd.* (1991), 34 C.P.R. (3d) 505 (Man. C.A.), aff'g (1990), 30 C.P.R. (3d) 76 (Man. Q.B.). In that regard it states that it is the court that must decide whether the house design is sufficiently distinctive, so as to obtain protection under the *Act*. The Cartier, it submits, is not unique in that sense.

. . .

24 Haddon Design submits that it is not necessary for a court to find a work unique in order for copyright to attach. It argues that the only requirement is that the work, as a whole, be original. Originality, it submits, exists where a court finds that the requisite labour, skill and imagination went into a work. It states that there was a sufficient degree of all of those qualities employed in the creation of the Plans so as to make them original. On that basis, Haddon Designs argues that the Plans are subject to copyright protection.

25 Section 2 of the *Act* defines "artistic work" to include "plans" and "architectural works". "Architectural works" is defined in that section as "any building or structure or any model of a building or structure". Section 5(1) states:

> 5.(1) Subject to this Act, copyright shall subsist in Canada, for the term hereinafter mentioned, in every *original* literary, dramatic, musical and artistic work . . . [Emphasis added.]

26 Subsection 34(3) of the *Act* sets out the following presumption:

> 34(3) In any action for infringement of copyright in any work in which the defendant puts in issue either the existence of the copyright or the title of the plaintiff thereto,
>
> (a) the work shall, unless the contrary is proved, be presumed to be a work in which copyright subsists . . .

27 Thus, the *Act* makes clear that house plans may be subject to copyright protection, so long as they are original. What constitutes "original" in this context and whether an element of uniqueness is also required before copyright protection will obtain, as Oasis suggests, remains in issue.

28 The requirements of originality and uniqueness have been considered in a number of cases. In *Hay, supra*, the Ontario High Court found that "originality" was required in order for a work to be protected by copyright. It held that the

requirement of originality relates to the expression of thought, in that it must not be copied, but must originate from the author. The Court also found that one should consider the intent of the creator rather than exercise a personal aesthetic judgement, in determining whether an architectural work of art possesses sufficient artistic character and design so as to attract the protection of the *Act*. In determining whether the subject house satisfied those requirements, the Court reviewed evidence to the effect that: the outward appearance of the house was "quite different"; that "there were many distinctive features and that it had "something that others don't have".

29 Scott C.J.M, in the dissent in *Lifestyle Homes, supra*, held that originality did not require a brand new idea. Rather, he found that the relevant question was whether the plans were sufficiently distinctive and were an original product. The majority, in *Lifestyle Homes*, per Hubband J.A., quoted with approval from *Blake v. Warren* (1931), Mac G.C.C. 268 (Eng. K.B.) in considering what constituted an "original architectural work of art":

> There must be something apart from the common stock of ideas. There must be something that strikes the eye as uncommon.

30 The Court in *Randall Homes, supra*, in considering whether a home could possess originality or uniqueness, stated:

> I cannot agree that there can be no artistic work in a home, for once in a while a designer can come up with a quite creative, original design which creates a home with flair, artistic panache, an appeal with unique qualities in form, appearance and function, not simply a copy from the neighbour's home, but a fundamental creation of his own talents.

31 In *Viceroy Homes, supra*, Potts J., of the Ontario General Division, held that both originality and uniqueness were required in order to attract the protection of the *Act*. The Court noted that the definition of "architectural work of art" required that a structure possess "artistic character or design". The Court then determined that the cases had consistently found that artistry includes an element of uniqueness. The Court defined the term "unique" as meaning distinctive. As to "originality", the Court found that a number of cases including *Hay, supra*; and *Randall Homes, supra*, found that that term referred to:

> the overall concern of the Copyright Act with the idea that work must not be copied and 'that it should originate from the author'.

32 Potts J. in *Viceroy Homes, supra*, also cited H.G. Fox, *The Canadian Law of Copyright and Industrial Designs*, 2nd ed. (Toronto: Carswell, 1967) at 41, wherein the author states:

> The effective meaning of the requirement of originality is that the work must not be copied from another, or must not have been in the public domain.

33 "Original" was similarly defined in *Canadian Admiral Corp. v. Rediffusion Inc.*, [1954] Ex. C.R. 382 (Can. Ex. Ct.) at p. 398:

> For a work to be "original" it must originate from the author; it must be the product of his labour and skill and it must be the expression of his thoughts.

34 I accept the definition of originality set out in *The Canadian Law of Copyright and Industrial Design*; *Canadian Admiral Corp.*, *supra*; and *Viceroy Homes, supra* — that the work must be the work of the author and not simply a copy of someone else's production. In my view the Plans satisfy the criteria of originality in that sense.

35 I find further that house plans are not required to be unique, in the sense that the elements contained therein have never been seen before, in order to engage copyright protection. Whether a work is required to be unique in the sense that it is distinctive, however, is not as clear. In that regard, I would note that the definition of "architectural work of art" was amended in 1993. Before that time, section 2 defined "architectural work of art" as:

> any building or structure *having an artistic character or design*, in respect of that character or design, or any model for the building or structure, but the protection afforded by this Act is confined to the artistic character and design, and does not extend to processes or methods of construction. [Emphasis added.]

36 In the 1995 version of the *Act*, which is under consideration here, "architectural work" was defined as meaning any building or structure or any model of a building or structure. Without determining whether the scope of that definition would include plans, I note that the 1995 definition no longer required an element of "artistic character or design". This materially distinguishes the cases cited by Oasis in support of its position that distinctiveness is required before copyright can exist in house plans. In other words, distinctiveness may no longer be required in order for house plans to be subject to copyright under the definition of "architectural work".

37 In the circumstances of the present case, however, I need not finally determine this issue as I find that the Plans are sufficiently distinctive to satisfy any requirement in that regard. Specifically, I find that the various design elements used in the combination set out in the Plans are unique in the sense that they are distinctive.

38 Given my finding in this regard, I need not comment on whether an artistic element is required in an architectural work or plans in order for those works to become subject to copyright under the general definition of "artistic work". I would, however, note the judgement of Reed J. in *DRG Inc. v. Datafile Ltd.* (1987), 18 C.P.R. (3d) 538 (Fed. T.D.); affd(1991), 35 C.P.R. (3d) 243 (Fed. C.A.), wherein she expressly declined to state whether "artistic"-ness must be found in architecture in order to satisfy the definition of "artistic work". As to other works enumerated under "artistic works", however, she concluded that "artistic" was merely a general description used for works which find expression in a visual medium.

39 I wish to emphasize that, although I have found the Plans to be distinctive as a result of the combination of the various design elements over which both

Haddon Design and Chancellor claim ownership, it is the Plans as a whole, not their constituent parts, which attract copyright protection in this case. In this regard I note the judgement of McLaughlin J., as she then was, in *Slumber-Magic Adjustable Bed Co. v. Sleep-King Adjustable Bed Co.* (1984), 3 C.P.R. (3d) 81 (B.C. S.C.), at 84:

> It is well established that compilations of material produced by others may be protected by copyright, provided that the arrangement of the elements taken from other sources is the product of the plaintiff's thought, selection and work. It is not the several components that are the subject of the copyright, but the over-all arrangement of them which the plaintiff through his industry has produced. . . In the case of a compilation, the originality requisite to copyright is a matter of degree depending on the amount of skill, judgement, or labour that has been involved in making the compilation: *Ladbroke (Football), Ltd. v. William Hill (Football), Ltd.*, [1964] 1 All E.R. 465 (H.L.). Where copyright is claimed in a compilation it is not the correct approach to dissect the work in fragments and, if the fragments are not entitled to copyright, then deduce that the whole compilation is not so entitled; rather, the court should canvas the degree of industry, skill or judgement which has gone into the over-all arrangement [cites omitted.]

40 Although *Slumber-Magic* is not directly on point, I find it instructive. I acknowledge that partial copyright may exist in some cases: J.S. McKeown, *Fox Canadian Law of Copyright and Industrial Designs*, 3rd ed. (Scarborough: Carswell, 2000) at 63. However, in the case at bar, the pleadings and the entire case were argued on the basis that it was the Plans as a whole which were the subject of copyright, not simply those design elements which the parties both claim to have authored. Further, it is the combination of these design elements which is subject to copyright and that combination exists in the Plans as a whole.

41 Accordingly, I find that the presumption at subsection 34(3)(a) applies to the Plans. I find further that Oasis has failed to rebut that presumption and, as a result, the Plans are subject to copyright protection.

(d) Industrial Design

Given the broad definition of "origin artistic expression" for copyright purposes, there is an overlap between copyright and industrial design protection. An industrial design is essentially an artistic work — visual features of shape, configuration, pattern or ornament — applied to a "useful article" (any article with a utilitarian function ranging from, e.g. a lamp or teapot to an item of clothing or a car) (see section 64(1)). Copyright does not give full protection to such "applied artwork." Pursuant to section 64(2) of the *Act*, when the useful article is mass-produced (which is determined, rather arbitrarily, by whether it is reproduced in a quantity of more than fifty) then the copyright owner can no longer bring an infringement claim in respect of the artistic work — protection must be sought under the *Industrial Design Act* (R.S.C., 1985, c. I-9). This is subject to the exceptions found in section

64(3), which include graphic representations applied to the face of an article (i.e. two-dimensional design features), trade-marks, and architectural works. What qualifies as "functional" is not always clear, as the following case demonstrates.

Pyrrha Design Inc. v. 623735 Saskatchewan Ltd., 2004 CarswellNat 5920, [2004] F.C.J. No. 2084 (F.C.A.)

Federal Court of Appeal

Vancouver, British Columbia

Linden, Létourneau and Sharlow JJ.A.

December 13, 2004

1 **LINDEN J.A.**: — The main issue on this appeal is whether the Motions Judge was correct in granting summary judgment dismissing the claim of the appellants for copyright infringement in relation to certain jewellery designs.

2 On March 26, 2002 the appellants issued a Statement of Claim alleging that the respondents had infringed copyright in certain of their jewellery designs. The appellants claimed liability and damages with respect to the infringement. The respondents filed a Statement of Defence dated May 2, 2002 denying liability. On September 25, 2003, the respondents filed a Notice of Motion seeking summary judgment dismissing the claim on the basis of section 64 of the Copyright Act, R.S.C. 1985 c. C-42.

3 The Motions Judge found that the jewellery in issue "clearly" was a "useful article", pursuant to section 64(2) of the Copyright Act, and held that the action should be dismissed since no relevant issues remained to be decided.

4 In my view, this decision was not correct in law and must be set aside, allowing the matter to proceed to trial on the merits.

Facts

5 The appellant, Pyrrha Design Inc., is a jewellery design company, based in Vancouver, B.C. and owned by the appellants Danielle Wilmore and Wade Papin, who are designers for Pyrrha. The respondent, 623735 Saskatchewan Ltd., carrying on business as SpareParts, is based in Saskatchewan with stores in various parts of Canada, including one in metropolitan Vancouver, British Columbia. Daniel Mysak is the President of SpareParts.

6 Pyrrha makes rings, earrings and pendants featuring vibrantly coloured fibre-optic glass stones, some resembling a cat's eye, set in chunky cast sterling silver mountings of modern character. The appellants believe that the respondents are infringing their copyright in their original jewellery items by copying them and offering them for sale.

Analysis

7 The relevant section of the *Copyright Act* is as follows:

64(1) In this section and section 64.1,

"article" means any thing that is made by hand, tool or machine;

"design" means features of shape, configuration, pattern or ornament and any combination of those features that, in a finished article, appeal to and are judged solely by the eye;

"useful article" means an article that has a utilitarian function and includes a model of any such article;

"utilitarian function", in respect of an article, means a function other than merely serving as a substrate or carrier for artistic or literary matter.

(2) Where copyright subsists in a design applied to a useful article or in an artistic work from which the design is derived and, by or under the authority of any person who owns the copyright in Canada or who owns the copyright elsewhere,

(a) the article is reproduced in a quantity of more than fifty, or

(b) where the article is a plate, engraving or cast, the article is used for producing more than fifty useful articles,

it shall not thereafter be an infringement of the copyright or the moral rights for anyone

(c) to reproduce the design of the article or a design not differing substantially from the design of the article by

(i) making the article, or

(ii) making a drawing or other reproduction in any material form of the article, or

(d) to do with an article, drawing or reproduction that is made as described in paragraph (c) anything that the owner of the copyright has the sole right to do with the design or artistic work in which the copyright subsists.

8 This legislation provides, therefore, that copyright may exist in a design of a useful article, but if that useful article is produced in a quantity of more than 50, it is not an infringement of the copyright for others to reproduce similar articles. In other words, where copyright exists in such articles produced in what might be considered commercial quantities, an action for copyright infringement may not lie, but the remedy, if any, must depend upon the registration system under the *Industrial Design Act*, R.S.C. I-9.

9 In this case, it was admitted, for purposes of the summary judgment motion, that there was copyright in the design of the jewellery and that more than 50 copies were produced by the appellant. The sole disputed matter is whether these items are denied the protection of the *Copyright Act* because the jewellery was a "useful article", which is defined as "an article that has a utilitarian function", which in turn is defined as a "function other than merely serving as a

substrate or carrier for artistic or literary matter". (See section 64(1), *Copyright Act, supra.*)

10 The Motions Judge was persuaded that the jewellery in issue was a "useful article". The primary argument advanced by the respondent to support the Judge's conclusion is that, as jewellery is "to be worn", it is "functional". Rings are worn on fingers, earrings are worn on ears and necklaces are worn around the neck "to give a visual effect". Hence, it is argued, they have a function "other than merely acting as a substrate or carrier for a design". All jewellery that is capable of being worn, it is urged, is functional, and, hence, denied the protection of the *Copyright Act*, if produced in a quantity of more than fifty.

11 The appellants, on the other hand, contend that the wearing of jewellery does not by itself make it useful, any more than the hanging of a painting on a wall makes it useful. Jewellery is unlike clothing in that it does not provide warmth or protection. It is worn mainly because of the way it looks, its attractive appearance. If the respondent is right, suggests the appellants, any sculpture adorning a lobby or a painting decorating a wall would also be considered useful and would lose their copyright protection if more than 50 copies were made.

12 In this case, it was agreed that the test to decide whether summary judgment should be issued is that there must be a "lack of genuine issue" to be tried. (See Tremblay-Lamer J in *Granville Shipping Co. v. Pegasus Lines Ltd.* [1996] 2 F.C. 853 (F.C.T.D.).)

13 In my view, it is not clear that there was no genuine issue to be tried in this case. The issue of whether articles of the kind involved here are useful in copyright law has not been litigated before in Canada. Significant consequences flow from such a decision. It is necessary, in deciding such a question, to have more evidence about the jewellery's usefulness or lack thereof, including evidence from the artistic and cultural milieu. This difficult issue should not have been decided in a summary way. The appellants deserve a day in Court to fully defend their rights to copyright in their jewellery.

14 There is something amounting to a genuine issue raised by the appellants' analysis, for otherwise every work of art could be considered useful merely because it can be enjoyed as an adornment. It is not enough to hold without evidence that because jewellery is worn it is ipso facto useful. It is doubtful whether the usefulness of a work of art can be determined solely by its existence; there must be a practical use in addition to is esthetic value. Some items of jewellery that are worn may be useful whereas others may not be. For example, a tie pin or cuff links may be useful types of jewellery holding clothing together, while other objects such as a brooch or an earring may be purely ornamental and not useful at all, valuable only for their own intrinsic merit as works of art. Further, a sculpture may be created merely to be observed and admired or it may be made to be used as a paper weight. This issue is a genuine one deserving of a full trial on viva voce evidence.

15 There was much discussion about the case of *Datafile Ltd. v. DRG Inc.* [1991] F.C.J. No. 144 (F.C.A.) but it is clear that the reasons in that case were based on earlier legislation that has since been altered. In the earlier legislation, section 46 of the Copyright Act had stated that "This act does not apply to designs capable of being registered under the Industrial Design Act". This restriction no longer appears in the current legislation (see section 64). It is obvious, therefore, that it is now possible for the Copyright Act to apply to the designs capable of being registered under the Industrial Design Act, that is, dual protection may now be possible in some situations.

16 The appeal should be allowed and the Motions Judge's decision should be set aside so that the case may proceed to a full and fair trial on all the evidence. Costs in the cause.

---

4. Dramatic Works

Dramatic Works are defined in the Act as including (a) any piece for recitation, choreographic work or mime, the scenic arrangement or acting form of which is fixed in writing or otherwise (b) any cinematographic work, and (c) any compilation of dramatic works. "Choreographic work" includes "any work of choreography, whether or not is has a story line." The term "cinematographic work" includes any work expressed by a process analogous to cinematography, whether or not accompanied by a sound track.

While *any* original cinematographic work, with or without dramatic character, will be protected as such, the usual copyright duration of fifty years following the death of the author applies only to cinematographic works in which "the arrangement or acting form or the combination of incidents represented give the work a dramatic character." In all other cases, the duration of copyright will be limited to fifty years from the end of the calendar year in which it is first published (or, if unpublished, from the year of its making) in accordance with section 11.1 of the *Act*. As with copyright's other subject-matter categories, courts have struggled to articulate what it is that gives a work "dramatic" character.

Kantel v. Grant, [1933] Ex. C.R. 84

Exchequer Court of Canada

The President

The President, now delivered the following judgment:

1 This is an action for infringement, by the defendants, of a copyright alleged to subsist in a dramatic sketch, a work of which the plaintiff claims to be the author. Throughout the trial the work in question was referred to as a "sketch,"

and it will be convenient to continue the use of that term in designating the subject matter in which copyright is said to subsist. It would appear desirable first to state the facts as appearing from the evidence.

. . .

3 The plaintiff's statement of claim purports to set forth an outline of the sketch prepared by Kantel, and perhaps reference should be made to this. The title of the sketch is Uncle Bob's Sunshine Club. First, there is reproduced a phonograph record suggesting a train in motion, and there is announced the arrival of what is described as the Sunshine Special, from the Land of Happiness, having as passengers Uncle Bob and Happy Harry who will entertain the members of Uncle Bob's Sunshine Club. Happy Harry, a dummy, is described as a child who lives in the Land of Happiness and is brought thence by Uncle Bob in a little black bag. Uncle Bob, who says Hello to the children tuned in, sings a greeting song set to the tune of "Heigho Everybody Heigho," the words of which song Kantel claims to have composed. A conversation then follows between Uncle Bob — who is the person broadcasting — and Happy Harry, the former speaking in his ordinary voice, and the latter supposedly in a thin falsetto; the subject of the conversation relates to personal events in the lives of individual children, either fictitious, or derived from letters received by Uncle Bob from children who have already actually listened to the presentation of the sketch. Then a simple nursery song is sung by Uncle Bob or Happy Harry, followed by further conversation between Uncle Bob and Happy Harry and somewhat similar to that just mentioned, and then follows another nursery song. Conversation then ensues between Uncle Bob and Happy Harry in reference to individual children whose birthday falls, or is supposed to fall on that day, and a birthday song prepared by Kantel is sung by Uncle Bob to the tune of "Good Morning Merry Sunshine," followed by another selected nursery song which is sung by either Uncle Bob or Happy Harry. There then follows a conversation between Uncle Bob and Happy Harry, on the subject of the conduct of children, Happy Harry being presented as a model of what a good child should be, and this is followed by another nursery song. Then follows a conversation relating to named children who are ill, and a special song, prepared by Kantel, is sung for sick children to the tune of "The Old Oaken Bucket," or "Yankee Doodle," and another nursery song follows. An appeal is then made by Uncle Bob and Happy Harry to the children listening to the broadcast to become members of the Sunshine Club. Uncle Bob then sings a parting song, prepared by Kantel, and set to the same tune as the opening song. Uncle Bob and Happy Harry then say good-bye and indicate they are about to entrain on the Sunshine Special to travel back to the Land of Happiness; the announcer calls "All Aboard for the Sunshine Special," and the same train phonograph record as in the opening is reproduced. It is then announced that Uncle Bob and Happy Harry will return to-morrow at the same hour.

. . .

11 Copyright subsists "in every original literary, dramatic, musical and artistic work," and, I think, the sketch in question must be held to constitute a dramatic work within the meaning of copyright law, and was, I think, fixed in writing

sufficiently to say it was a dramatic composition capable of being published or performed and in which the dramatic element was present. The original manuscript, and even Exhibit A, grouped a series of predetermined incidents, songs, dialogues, and for want of a better name what I would call talks, in a fixed sequence, which gave to the sketch in its entirety the elements and characteristics of a dramatic composition. Had the performance of the sketch, as in the case of Uncle Don's performance in a shop in Philadelphia, been on the stage, the dramatic element would be more clearly realized than when communicated by radio. "The word 'original' does not in this connection mean that the work must be the expression of original or inventive thought. Copyright Acts are not concerned with ideas or the originality of ideas — in which there is no copyright; it is the language in which the idea is expressed which is the only thing protected, and it is that to which 'original' in the Act relates; the Act does not require that the expression must be in an original or novel form, but that the work must not be copied from another work — that it should originate from the author." See *University of London v. University Tutorial Press*, in which case, I might observe, it was held that copyright subsisted even in examination papers. In *British Broad-Casting Co. v. Wireless League Gazette Publishing Co.*, it was held that there was copyright in the compilation of advance daily radio programs published for the ensuing week, on the ground that the compilation required very considerable work and was not a mere collection of what had already been prepared. Literary skill or originality is not necessary for a copyright, and does not depend on whether the material collected consists of matters which are *publici juris*, or whether such materials show literary skill or originality, either in thought or in language, or anything more than industrious collection. *Jewellers Circular Pub. Co. v. Keystone Pub. Co.* The Courts appear to be extremely liberal in their construction of what constitutes copyright, and also as to what constitutes a dramatic work. The sketch may have contained some ideas that were not quite original with Kantel, it may have embodied some ideas of Auld and Pogue, but the complete sketch is, I think, original in the sense that it gave expression to ideas in language and form which no one else, so far as I know, had done before. The fact that the original manuscript was departed from daily is not, I think, fatal to the plaintiff. In the presentation of a dramatic work, in whatever form, it is open to the performer to depart from the literal text of the work. Whatever the merits of the sketch, and it is not claimed to be of a high dramatic or literary order, it interested a section of the juvenile public for some months, and the work involved some labour, talent and judgment. From a perusal of decided cases wherein copyright in works has been upheld, I am led to the conclusion that there is enough of original literary and dramatic work in the sketch to support the plaintiff's claim to copyright, though, I must confess, I was inclined in the other direction during the progress of the trial.

Hutton v. Canadian Broadcasting Corp. (1989), 27 C.I.P.R. 12 (Alta. Q.B.), affirmed (1992), 41 C.P.R. (3d) 45 (Alta. C.A.)

Alberta Court of Queen's Bench

MacCallum J.

The plaintiffs and the defendant co-produced a television series entitled "Star Chart", in which the plaintiff, H, registered copyright. The defendant cancelled the series after nineteen programs, pursuant to the provisions of the contract between the parties. One year later, the defendant produced and aired a series entitled "Good Rockin' Tonite". The plaintiffs brought a copyright infringement action in which they alleged that the defendant's series copied the plaintiff H's concept and creative elements. There was evidence that the production of a pilot program in preparation for the launching of a complete series was standard in the industry and that no such pilot was produced for Good Rockin' Tonite. Star Chart focussed on the "Music Central" theme, creating the illusion that the host and his assistants were gathering information for the countdown by means of a computer. In Good Rockin' Tonite, the host was the same, but he was no longer acting as a character. As opposed to Star Chart, Good Rockin' Tonite contained interviews and did not create the illusion of live performances.

. . .

MacCallum J.:

2)   Dramatic Work

214 Copyright law in Canada is codified and there being no copyright apart from the Act, it is argued that the fact that the plaintiff chose to register S.C. as a "dramatic work" has some important implications. First, if the program is not truly a "dramatic work" it is not entitled to copyright protection and second, even if it is a dramatic work, G.R.T. most certainly is not and therefore does not meet the test of substantial similarity and is not an infringement.

215 Was S.C. truly a "dramatic work" and entitled as such to protection under the Act? By reference to s. 2:

> 'dramatic work' includes ... any cinematograph production where the arrangement or acting form or the combination of incidents represented give the work an original character

216 Apart from the fiction of Music Central, I should think that neither the arrangement, nor the acting form, nor the combination of incidents involved in the presentation of rock videos by a host was original in character.

217 I am referred to *Seltzer v. Sunbrock*, 22 F. Supp. 621 at 628 (S.D. Cal., 1938):

> The courts, in determining what constitutes a dramatic composition have emphatically stated that there must be a story, a thread of consecutively related events — either narrated or presented by dialogue or action or both...

Attempts have been made to extend the protection afforded dramas under the Act to other forms of compositions spectacular in nature and theatrical in presentation, but lacking the story element...

The courts likewise have clung to first principles and have refused to extend the definition of a 'drama' to include other forms of composition having no bona fide plot or story ...

It is essential to such a composition that it should tell some story. The plot may be simple. It may be but the narrative or representation of a single transaction; but it must repeat or mimic some action, speech, emotion, passion or character, real or imaginary. And when it does, it is the ideas thus expressed which become subject of copyright...

218 Professor Peacock described Music Central as the place where the viewer was told that information was gathered and charted. This was the dramatic conceit of the program. According to the defendant's expert Dr. Gardner, whose evidence I accept on this point, S.C. might be considered as a primitive form of dramatic work in which the S.C. team gathers the latest chart information from coast to coast using high tech equipment and at the end of the program tells the audience which numbers are the top ten by presenting the countdown. There is a high tech environment, Music Central, inhabited by three characters who play parts in the drama. Donna Marie and Louise gather information for Mulligan, giving it to him at the end of the program and he, in turn, gives it to the audience. There is an effort to build suspense by announcing at the start that the chart information will be gathered and then counted down at the end of the program. The Music Central concept permits the host to introduce, and the television viewers to see, performances of S.C. guests who are performing pop music. Viewers are taken by the screen or monitor to the "star stages" where the performance is ongoing, complete with applause.

219 On the basis of the Peacock, Gardner and Jacobson evidence, I find the concept of Music Central, with the female assistants busily gathering information for host Mulligan by means of computer, and the introduction of performances on three different star stages, lent enough dramatic incident and seminal story-line to qualify it as a "dramatic work".

220 I adopt the opinions of Gardner and Jacobson to the effect that there is no equivalent in G.R.T. to the S.C. story line. The character setting and implementation of G.R.T. are quite different.

221 I find that it would be stretching any definition of "dramatic work" to say that G.R.T. was such because there we find no attempt at pretence or story-line or dramatic incident. We simply have a presentation of rock videos by a host trying to be himself, and featuring various other elements such as interviews and trivia contests. Whatever else is common to both S.C. and G.R.T, it is not those elements which made S.C. a "dramatic work".

222 We read the following at p. 631 of *Seltzer v. Sunbrock*, supra, on the subject of what constitutes infringement:

> In order to infringe, under the *Copyright Act*, the production on the stage must obviously tell the same story as the copyrighted drama. If it tells another story or acts another sequence of events, it is outside the protection afforded the registered work...

223 S.C. tells the story of Mulligan and his two assistants gathering chart information for the countdown. It is a story which is perhaps incidental to the playing of rock videos, but it is the only thing in my view which lends dramatic incident to the programs. By contrast, G.R.T. tells no story at all.

Green v. Broadcasting Corp. of New Zealand, [1989] R.P.C. 469

Court of Appeal Wellington

15, 16 March; 22 September 1988

Somers, Casey and Gallen JJ

SOMERS J.

The appellant, Mr Hugh H Green, was the author, producer and compere of a television talent quest produced and transmitted in the United Kingdom under the name "Opportunity Knocks" from the early 1960s until 1978. In 1979 he brought an action against the respondent, the Broadcasting Corporation of New Zealand, claiming that by its production and transmission in New Zealand of a similar television talent quest under the same name in 1978 it passed off its programme as his, or as an adaptation authorised and approved by him. Mr Green also claimed that the Corporation by its transmission had infringed his copyright in the title "Opportunity Knocks" and to scripts and the dramatic format of his programme.

. . .

The Judge also rejected the claim to copyright in the dramatic format of Mr Green's English programme. He considered this too vague a concept for protection under the Act and if capable of exact formulation could only subsist if reduced to writing.

But these conclusions, that there was no sufficient script to found copyright and no relevant copyright in format, were said to be erroneous. It is necessary therefore to consider the evidence and then the conclusions which ought to be drawn.

I am afraid I must disagree with the Judge's finding, set out above, that the catchphrases and references to the sponsors were excluded from such script as existed and that the clapometer does not lend itself to such incorporation. The passage in the evidence of Mr Green cited by the Judge seems to me with respect to indicate the contrary. Mr Green said that he wrote the scripts "because we would have what we would call the introductions, our stock phrases . . . The other part of the writing dealt with interviews . . .". The reference to "other" part of the writing indicates that which had been first mentioned was itself in writing and not, as the Judge held, excluded. In another part of his evidence Mr Green said "So far as there were scripts I wrote them. . . . So far as there were introductions in shows over that period, I wrote them and conceived them". In cross-examination the following passage appears:

> "Do you say that that introduction is a formula which cannot be used by anybody anywhere else in the world without your consent? — I have been so advised legally.

> "Is there any written record of what you claim to own in the sense that a script which has become available in New Zealand before 1975? — May I understand you completely is that a script before 1975.

> "Which you claim you own and which has been used as a script in New Zealand. — The script of 'Opportunity Knocks' has continuously been the same for the catchphrases, the interviews each week with the artists has differed, the script for the past 17 years and long before 1975 contained particularly the end of the show beginning with the words 'Make your mind up time' using the clapometer and bringing back the five people. I would also if I might be permitted to turn to front page of the script (p 280) which is the way the show has always run for us . . ."

Script p 280 is the front page of the running order of TV2's programme "Opportunity Knocks" for 10 June 1978.

The evidence in my view justifies the conclusion that Mr Green's scripts included the title, the various catchphrases (which as time went by became a standard and expected part of the entertainment), recorded the names of the competitors or entrants together with the nature of their act, the names of the sponsors and the general order of appearances and happenings, and specifically referred to the "clapometer". They must, as did the Corporation's scripts, have indicated the sequence of events, musical interludes and the like. They did not include the details of interviews for they were ad lib, nor, obviously, details of the particular performance of each competitor.

The various catchphrases referred to included the words "For X Opportunity Knocks", this being the introduction of each competitor, and the words "Make your mind up time" used after all competitors had performed their act and the sponsor for each interviewed as a call to the studio audience and television viewers to prepare to select the best act. A short part of each act was shown in response to which the studio audience would applaud, the decibel rating being recorded on the clapometer which was visible to all.

I think it may be said therefore that each written script contained the skeleton outline or framework of the manner in which a type of talent quest would be conducted. The competitors, the sponsors and their interviews, would change from programme to programme but the general form or structure was, on the evidence set out, in the script for the first and second programmes. The latter and subsequent programmes differed from the first for in these there was at the beginning a brief review of the immediately preceding programme, the announcement of its winner and a repetition of that winner's act as part of the current programme. Upon the evidence the format was adhered to thereafter in all future scripts. I think, however, that it would be necessary to see a show before its whole could be appreciated; in particular the essence of the sponsorship could not, as I understand the evidence, have been fully apprehended from the script.

As no written script was produced reliance was placed by the appellant on s 3(8) of the Copyright Act 1962 which provides:

> "References in this Act to the time at which, or the period during which, a literary, dramatic, or musical work was made are references to the time or period at or during which it was first reduced to writing or some other material form."

It was submitted that the filming of "Opportunity Knocks" in the United Kingdom was the reduction of the work to a material form with the consequence that copyright ran from the end of the year in which it was first broadcast under s 8(1)(a).

There is much force in the submission that writing is but one method of giving a work the degree of certainty necessary to justify the monopoly conferred by the Act and that the same security can be obtained by fixing in other tangible forms. The point has not, so far as I am aware, been the subject of any considered decision but has the support of writers of textbooks — see Copinger and Skone James on Copyright (12th ed, 1980) para 164; Laddie, Prescott and Vitoria, The Modern Law of Copyright (1980) paras 2.12 and 2.14-2.17; Ricketson, The Law of Intellectual Property (1984) paras 3.13 and 5.36. Assuming it to be correct, however, I do not think it advances the appellant's case.

The scripts, as I understand them, could not constitute a dramatic work. They could not themselves be acted or performed which I take to be the essence of such a work for they were no more than a general scheme for a proposed entertainment. The actual telecast programme to which each script was the guide may have been a dramatic work. But copyright in the performance (assuming it to have been reduced to material form) is not claimed by Mr Green nor was it suggested that any one of his many telecast productions was actually copied.

Nor can situations or scenic effects by themselves apart from the words and incidents of a dramatic work be the subject of dramatic copyright. That topic is discussed in Tate v Fullbrook [1908] 1 KB 821 at pp 829, 832 and 834. They may be protected as part of a whole dramatic work and similarity may evidence an intention to steal a work.

I am of opinion that Mr Green's script or scripts cannot support a claim of copyright in a dramatic work. Nor do I think there can be a claim for "format" which is not either a dramatic or literary work itself or perhaps a combination of both. The monopoly conferred by the Copyright Act can only be maintained where the conditions of its grant are complied with.

The question remains whether the script or scripts is, or are, literary works.

FWS Joint Sports Claimants v. Canada Copyright Board,

36 C.P.R. (3d) 483 (Fed. C.A.), leave to appeal to S.C.C. refused (1992), 88 D.L.R. (4th) vi (note) (S.C.C.)

Federal Court of Canada — Court of Appeal

Mahoney, MacGuigan and Linden, JJ.A.

Linden J.A.:

9 The third issue argued by FWS was whether there is a copyright in the playing of a sports game. The Board decided there was no such copyright, although there was in the television production of a game. It also held that there was copyright in the coaches' written play books and game plans, as well as in the team crests and uniform designs, but that these were not used by the cable operators. As for the playing of the game itself, even though it is played as much as possible in accordance with those plans, the Board found that this was not copyrightable, since it was not a "choreographic work, because, unlike dance, a sporting event is for the most part a random series of events. The unpredictability of the action is inconsistent with the concept of choreography."

10 I agree with the Board. Even though sports teams may seek to follow the plays as planned by their coaches, as actors follow a script, the other teams are dedicated to preventing that from occurring and often succeed. As well, the opposing team tries to follow its own game plan, which, in turn, the other team tries to thwart. In the end, what transpires on the field is usually not what is planned, but something that is totally unpredictable. That is one of the reasons why sports games are so appealing to their spectators. No one can forecast what will happen. This is not the same as a ballet, where, barring an unforeseen accident, what is performed is exactly what is planned. No one bets on the outcome of a performance of *Swan Lake*. Ballet is, therefore, copyrightable, but team sports events, despite the high degree of planning now involved in them, are not. (See Fox, *The Canadian Law of Copyright and Industrial Designs* (2nd ed., 1967), page 139; *Nimmer on Copyright* (1990), at page 2-138; *Canadian Admiral Corpn. Ltd. v. Rediffusion Inc.*, [1954] Ex.C.R. 382, at page 400.) A "mere spectacle standing alone" cannot be copyrighted. (See *Tate v. Fulbrook*, [1908] 1 K.B. 821 (C.A.), at page 832.) It is necessary for copyright not to have "changing materials" that are "lacking in certainty" or "unity". (See *Green v Broadcasting Corp of New Zealand*, [1989] 2 All ER 1056 (P.C.), at page 1058 *per* Lord Bridge), even though some variations could be permitted (see *Kantel, Frederick W. v. Frank E. Grant et al.*, [1933] Ex.C.R. 84, at page 95; see also *Wilson v. Broadcasting Corporation of New Zealand*, [1990] 2 N.Z.L.R. 565 (H.C.)). The unpredictability in the playing of a football or hockey game is so pervasive, despite the high degree of planning, that it cannot be said to be copyrightable. The American cases are not helpful here, given the different

statutory provisions and jurisprudence. (See, for example, *Baltimore Orioles, Inc. v. Major League Baseball*, 805 F. 2d 663 (7th Circ. 1986).)

---

5. Musical Works

"Musical work" is defined in section 2 of the *Act* as meaning "any work of music or musical compilation, with or without words, and includes any compilation thereof." Prior to amendments in 1993, the definition of "musical work" referred to "any combination of melody and harmony, or either of them, printed, reduced to writing or otherwise graphically produced or reproduced." The requirement of reduction to print or writing stemmed originally from the time when copyright protected only "books," such that music could qualify only in the form of printed notation. Also, until the invention of sound recording, written notation was, of course, the only way that music could be fixed in physical form. Prompting the elimination of the reference to print or writing was the case of *CTV Television Network Ltd. v. Canada (Copyright Board)*, (*sub nom.* Reseau de Television CTV Ltee v. Canada) [1993] 2 F.C. 115 (Fed. C.A.), leave to appeal refused 1993 CarswellNat 2473 (S.C.C.). It was held in that case that CTV was not communicating "musical works" to the public within the meaning of section 3(1)(f) because what was communicated was not the graphic notation as such but rather a performance or "acoustic representation" thereof. It is now understood that the "musical work" is the original musical composition itself, as fixed in any manner whatsoever. The amended definition also settled a debate by clarifying that the lyrics of a song are part of the musical work and not a separate literary work. Finally, the definition no longer requires anything in the way of melody or harmony. While avoiding the need for unduly subjective or qualitative assessments of the musical work, the resultant definition is tautological and leaves us wondering what a "work of music" is — or is not.

Need Intellectual Property be Everywhere?
Against Ubiquity and Uniformity

David Vaver
(Spring, 2002) 25 Dalhousie L.J. 1

Some have called intellectual property law the most boring subject known to man but, boring or not, intellectual property (IP) is omnipresent and certainly much more talked about than once was the case. Twenty years ago, the press ran few IP-related stories. Today, no week or sometimes even day goes by without a paper or news magazine coming out with one.

. . .

Consider the following example. A few months ago, a musical group called The Planets issued a record album which included a track titled "One Minute Silence," attributed on the cover to John Cage and one of the group's members, Mike Batt. The title was quite accurate: the track comprised a minute's silence. When the record was released, the publishers of John Cage's "work" entitled 4'33" complained that Batt had infringed the copyright owned by Cage's estate. Cage's score reads thus on an otherwise blank page: "4'33" FOR ANY INSTRUMENT OR COMBINATION OF INSTRUMENTS."[33] The publisher, the alleged "right" holder, argued not only that Cage's work had copyright but also that Batt had infringed that copyright by his inclusion of a performance of a substantial part of the piece on the record.

This all sounds quite amusing, except that the publisher seemed to be in earnest and the case in fact settled "without prejudice" on Batt's paying Cage's estate an undisclosed sum, widely reported as [pounds] 100,000, although Batt says it was less. Unfortunately, U.K. and other Western laws, as currently structured, allow such jokes to be plausibly and seriously played. Modern copyright legislation deliberately leaves the definition of a musical work vague. Standards of infringement are similarly vague: a "substantial part" of the work cannot be reproduced, but "substantiality" is treated as a question of "fact and degree," which gives lawyers and courts plenty of scope for fuzzy argument and reasoning.

A newspaper columnist, dealing with the Cage/Batt imbroglio, had this comment on the infringement issue:

> My totally uninformed opinion is that one minute of silence is as different from 4 minutes and 33 seconds of silence as Florida is from Alaska. If a pianist sits at the keyboard for a minute and doesn't play a note, you might not be sure if he is doing so intentionally or if he is simply daydreaming about Reese Witherspoon. When the pianist sits motionless for 4 minutes and 33 seconds, however, you can be pretty sure that he is making some sort of artistic statement. Either that or he's dead.[34]

That's not bad for a "totally uninformed opinion." An argument along these lines is certainly on track on the issue of substantiality.

To cap matters, Batt now says he has registered copyrights "on all "silent musical seconds" from one second up to 10 minutes" — except for 4'33". "I've got him [Cage] hemmed in," Batt is reported as saying, "he can't move an inch, and he will be breaching my copyright if his piece is performed and overruns by a second or two."[35] Silence can indeed be golden.

Cage died in 1992. His estate can therefore continue to claim copyright in 4'33" throughout the world until the end of 2042 and in some countries even until the end of 2062. Perhaps the claim will be exploded before then as a mere bubble. Music presupposes sound, and Cage's work is the antithesis of that. It may be merely an unprotected "idea" rather than the protected "expression" of an idea. So it may have no U.K. copyright.

Even if Cage's work is copyright, consider the question of infringement. Cage's claim would have been difficult had Batt not attributed the track on his album to Cage. Having "produced" "his" 4'33", Cage has no monopoly over silences of this or any length, at best, only over those silences that reproduce his. Veterans observing a minute's silence on Remembrance Day can do so regardless of Cage. They "create" their own silences; they do not re-create Cage's. Silence pre-dates Cage.

Even were a particular period of silence attributed to Cage, one returns to the point that Cage's work is, if the expression of an idea, a simple expression. Judges say that the simpler an expression, the more exact must the copy be before it can be labelled as "substantial." Mike Batt's instincts in claiming copyrights in longer and shorter silences may have a legal basis: 4'30" silence might infringe Cage's copyright; 1 minute or 10 minutes probably would not.

One could argue that a law that pressures musicians to buy off claims such as Cage's is absurd and cannot morally be imposed on other states. A more modest argument against ubiquity and uniformity is also available. Just because one country is willing, for its own reasons, to protect a particular activity does not mean that another country need accept that decision. Even if Cage's work were protected by copyright in the U.K., Canada need not extend it a Canadian copyright, nor need any another country do so under its law. That is indeed the current position under international law for copyright.

. . .

Copyright in musical works presents many challenging questions of law and policy. How do we determine when similarities between two musical works are the result of copying and when they are simply the result of features common to a particular genre or indicative of a shared compositional technique, for example? What kinds of similarities might constitute unlawful copying? A similarity of musical ideas, non-original melodies, commonplace rhythms, generic chord progressions — all of these may be recognizable to the average listener comparing two works, but none should produce a finding of infringement. Should musicians be able to reference other works of cultural significance without infringing the copyright in those works? How should copyright law treat the digital sampling that is such a vital component of modern music-making? The picture becomes increasingly complex as we add into the mix the rights not only of composers, but also of performers and sound recording makers. The following cases tackle some of these important questions.

Gondos v. Hardy (1982), 64 C.P.R. (2d) 145 (Ont. H.C.)

Ontario High Court of Justice

Carruthers J.

May 7, 1982

CARRUTHERS J.: — The above styled actions have been tried as one. They both involve claims based upon an alleged infringement of copyright of a musical work.

. . .

Generally speaking, the plaintiff alleges that portions of his original musical composition, which he titled, Variations on a Theme in A Minor ("Variations"), and sometimes referred to as "Variations on a Theme" and "Theme and Variations", were copied or performed by the defendants in contravention of the provisions of the Copyright Act, R.S.C. 1970, c. C-30, s. 1 ("the Act").

In action No. 60735/80 ("first action"), the plaintiff claims that a musical composition, ultimately entitled "The Homecoming", written and performed by Hagood Hardy ("Hardy") and published by Hagood Hardy Productions ("Productions") in 1972, contains 16 bars or measures of Variations. In action No. 60736/ 80 ("second action"), the plaintiff claims that a musical composition known as "Moment of Love", written and published by the defendants Rudy and Jerry Toth sometime after May of 1975, contains eight bars or measures of Variations. In his testimony at trial, the plaintiff described The Homecoming and Moment of Love as being identical to Variations. I think it is clear from all of the evidence and the position taken by counsel that, in fact, the position of the plaintiff is that those bars or measures in question do not constitute the whole of the works of the defendants, but only the melodies or themes thereof. It is not maintained on behalf of the plaintiff that The Homecoming contains the bars or measures claimed to be found in Moment of Love, or that those alleged to be in Moment of Love are found in The Homecoming.

In each of the actions, the defendants can be said to generally deny the position taken by the plaintiff against them. Specifically, while admitting that The Homecoming was written in Toronto, Ontario, in or about the month of July, 1972, Hardy and Productions deny that any part of any work of the plaintiff was copied in so doing. They also specifically deny that prior to his writing the music for The Homecoming, Hardy had previously seen or heard Variations or met the plaintiff as alleged, or at all. They deny that Variations was written prior to 1972. …The defendants Toth…specifically deny that they had ever met, spoken to, or heard of the plaintiff or Variations prior to the music for Moment of Love being written or first recorded in 1970. In the counterclaim brought on behalf of the defendants Jerry and Rudy Toth, it is alleged that the plaintiff, in composing his work, copied from Moment of Love, and that this constitutes an infringement of the copyright which they maintain subsists in that work. None of the parties suggest that any of the musical works under consideration in this action are not or cannot be that in which copyright may subsist in accordance with the provisions of the Act.

. . .

I think it is only fair to look upon the plaintiff's case as being a complaint that the melody of The Homecoming and that of Moment of Love were copied from his work Variations, whether it be as stated in ex. 1 or otherwise. Furthermore, and as the case unfolded at trial, the position of the plaintiff is not that the copying occurred as a result of that which is written in ex. 1 being seen by either Hardy or Rudy Toth. As I have noted above, there is no suggestion that at any time, apart from those copies about which specific evidence was led, there was any publication of the plaintiff's written work in any form that could be or, in fact, did come into the possession of any of the defendants. The allegation of copying then, as I understand it from what was said on behalf of the plaintiff and, in particular, in argument by his counsel, is that the work of the plaintiff was heard on occasion or occasions by the defendants and, thereafter, copied. To my mind, it is for this reason that much time was spent at trial considering a comparison between the principal melody of Variations with that of The Homecoming and the melody contained in variation one with that of Moment of Love.

. . .

I have also considered a number of the reported authorities British, American and Canadian, including opinions of text writers to which I was referred by counsel. From these, I have drawn a number of legal principles which I adopt and apply in reaching my decision in this case. One, of great persuasive authority, is a decision of the English Court of Appeal, Francis, Day & Hunter Ltd. et al. v. Bron (trading as Delmar Publishing Co.) et al., [1963] 2 All E.R. 16. At p. 27, Diplock L.J. states:

> First, as to the law; ... it is well established that to constitute infringement of copyright in any literary, dramatic or musical work there must be present two elements: First, there must be sufficient objective similarity between the infringing work and the copyright work, or a substantial part thereof, for the former to be properly described, not necessarily as identical with, but as a reproduction or adaptation of the latter; secondly, the copyright work must be the source from which the infringing work is derived ... But, while the copyright work must be the source from which the infringing work is derived, it need not be the direct source; ... there must be a causal connexion between the copyright work and the infringing work. To borrow an expression once fashionable in the law of negligence, the copyright work must be shown to be a causa sine qua non of the infringing work.

Some of the authorities, and particularly the American, in discussing copying, refer to it as being either conscious or unconscious. Whether it be found to be one or the other, none of the authorities suggest that there can be an infringement without a causal connection between the work in which copyright is claimed to subsist and the alleged infringing work or works. At p. 28 of the Francis, Day case, Diplock L.J. says:

> If the existence of the copyright work has no causal connexion with the production
> of the alleged infringing work, even though the latter be identical with the former,
> there is no infringement of copyright.

If there is found to be no causal connection and, therefore, no copying, either
conscious or unconscious, then, any similarities, however strong, which are
found to exist between the works must be deemed a coincidence. The word
"copying", in its ordinary usage, connotes a conscious, intended, or deliberate
act. Unconscious copying occurs, then, in the absence of any of these elements,
but, of necessity, with the required evidence of de facto familiarity with the
work alleged to be copied. As is stated by Diplock L.J. on p. 27, after referring
to subconscious copying:

> We know not whether it is rare or common, general or idiosyncratic, nor indeed
> whether it is possible to remember, not a mere isolated phrase, but a "substantial
> part of" the remembered work without remembering that one is remembering.

The most recent case in which a finding of infringement of copyright was made
on the basis of "unconscious copying" is an American one, Bright Tunes Music
Corp. v. Harrisongs Music, Ltd. et al. (1976), 420 F. Supp. 177. In that case, it
was claimed that the song "My Sweet Lord" was plagiarized from an earlier one
"He's So Fine". District Judge Owen, of the United States District Court, S. D.
New York, found both works [p. 180] "virtually identical except for one phrase".
The use of an identical grace note in the same place was considered significant.
George Harrison, the composer of My Sweet Lord, denied consciously copying
He's So Fine, and his position was accepted by Judge Owen. However, he found
that Harrison was aware of He's So Fine because of the extent of its popularity
in both the United States and England at a time when other songs, either written
by Harrison or played by the group of which he was a member, the Beatles, were
also popular in both those countries. Owen J. says at pp. 180-1:

> What happened? I conclude that the composer, in seeking musical materials to
> clothe his thoughts, was working with various possibilities. As he tried tried this
> possibility and that, there came to the surface of his mind a particular combination
> that pleased him as being one he felt would be appealing to a prospective listener;
> in other words, that this combination of sounds would work. Why? Because his
> subconscious knew it already had worked in a song his conscious mind did not
> remember. Having arrived at this pleasing combination of sounds, the recording
> was made, the lead sheet prepared for copyright and the song became an enormous
> success. Did Harrison deliberately use the music of He's So Fine? I do not believe
> he did so deliberately. Nevertheless, it is clear that My Sweet Lord is the very
> same song as He's So Fine with different words; and Harrison had access to He's
> So Fine. This is, under the law, infringement of copyright, and is no less so even
> though subconsciously accomplished.

Judge Owen, in concluding as he did, was following earlier American decisions
which had been outstanding for many years. One was particularly applicable,
namely: Fred Fisher, Inc. v. Dillingham et al. (1924), 298 F. 145, a decision of District Judge Learned Hand of the same court, made in 1924. Judge Hand accepted
the position of the famous composer Jerome Kern that he was quite unconscious

of any plagiarism in composing the accompaniment to the refrain of "Kalua". It was claimed, and found, by Judge Hand that his work contained a musical figure identical to that of the other work "Dardanella" which could not be the result of coincidence. The work in which copyright was claimed there had attained popularity prior to Kern's composition being written. Judge Hand said at p. 147:

> Whether he unconsciously copied the figure, he cannot say, and does not try to. Everything registers somewhere in our memories, and no one can tell what may evoke it. On the whole, my belief is that, in composing the accompaniment to the refrain of "Kalua," Mr. Kern must have followed, probably unconsciously, what he had certainly often heard only a short time before.

In the present case, several witnesses, with varying degrees of interest, knowledge, or training in music, were called on behalf of the plaintiff to express their opinions as to the composer or author of certain work or works and the similarities existing between them.

. . .

The position taken on behalf of the plaintiff is that the similarity between the works is so striking that the only conclusion to be reached is that the works of the defendants were copied from that of the plaintiff. I am prepared to accept that all of these witnesses, and as I have said, with one going back as far as 1962, heard the plaintiff play, on a variety of occasions and times thereafter, a melody similar to that heard on the playing of ex. 7. I am also prepared to find, and I do not think there is any disagreement between the parties on this fact, that the melodies which the plaintiff purports to be his are similar to those claimed by the defendants to be theirs. This is particularly so with the comparison between the principal melody of Variations and that of The Homecoming. For the purpose of this judgment, I am even prepared to say that they are strikingly similar, to my ear, whereas, the similarity between variation one and Moment of Love, again, to my ear, and I think, to those of others testifying at trial, is less. I arrive at this conclusion mindful of statements which have been made on several prior occasions that the question of infringement involves a determination of whether the substance of the original work is taken or not by the ear as well as by the eye.

. . .

As I have noted above, it is the plaintiff's position that the melody of Moment of Love was copied from variation one of ex. 1. It was also the position of the plaintiff, at least at the commencement of trial, that the defendants Toth were all involved in the scheme by which this copying was made, and that, central to it, was the recording ex. 7. The plaintiff alleged that Chris Toth, son of Rudy Toth, and a fellow employee of the plaintiff at Deerhurst Inn in the summer of 1975, obtained a copy of ex. 7 for his father. In addition, the plaintiff maintained that Chris Toth had heard him play Variations on a number of occasions at Deerhurst Inn and that, through his hearing of Variations being performed and the playing of the record, was able to assist the defendant Rudy Toth, who also heard the record, compose Moment of Love. Chris Toth denies ever purchasing or obtaining or having in his possession a copy of ex. 7, or to seeing it at any time in his home or cottage, which is close to Deerhurst Inn. Chris Toth also denies ever recalling hearing the plaintiff play Variations at any time or anywhere, and maintains he is not possessed of the ability to translate into musical notes that which he hears or has heard. In any event, the specific theory of the plaintiff in so far as all the Toths are concerned was significantly weakened, if not destroyed when the plaintiff adopted as part of his own case the evidence of Rudy Toth that he wrote Moment of Love some four years or more prior to the plaintiff making the record from which he claims it was copied. In any event, I accept all of the evidence of the defendants Toth, and in particular, wherever it conflicts with any of that given by or on behalf of the plaintiff.

During the course of the trial, it became apparent to all that the action as against Chris Toth could not succeed.

. . .

In so far as the defendants Hardy and Productions are concerned, the plaintiff does not make any allegation of conscious copying on their part. At this point, I raise the question of why Productions is a defendant in this action. There appears to be no evidence to involve it in any infringement of any copyright which the plaintiff has in Variations. In so far as Hardy is concerned, the plaintiff's cause of action against him rests upon an allegation of unconscious copying. The plaintiff's position in this respect is that Hardy heard the plaintiff perform Variations on one occasion, as a result of which the alleged plagiarism occurred. The plaintiff testified that on Friday evening, September 25, 1970, while performing as a pianist at Sutton Place Hotel, he played Variations as his "second last piece" of the evening. When he finished his performance, and in the process of leaving the room where he was playing, he stopped at a table where two men and a girl were seated. One of the men asked him: "What was the second last piece played?" The plaintiff testified that his response was: "It's one of my own. It's a classic." The conversation ended with the other man saying: "It's very nice." About a year later, while the plaintiff and his wife were attending another cocktail bar in the City of Toronto to hear a long time acquaintance play piano, the plaintiff testified he recognized the man he spoke to on that occasion in September, 1970, as the defendant Hagood Hardy, who was playing at the cocktail bar with his musical group then known as The Montage. Hardy, apart from denying in evidence generally that he had ever seen or met the plaintiff or heard or seen any of the plaintiff's music, specifically denied that he met the plaintiff or heard him play at the Sutton Place Hotel, either as the plaintiff claims or otherwise. Hardy called evidence as to his activities on that date in September. He was involved in a recording session that would have kept him in a studio until close to 9:00 p.m. Without the evidence of the defendant Hardy in this respect, I would not be prepared to accept that of the plaintiff. The plaintiff's evidence on this point, like the rest, is highly improbable, not credible and I specifically reject it. I accept the evidence of the defendant Hardy, in any event, wherever it conflicts with that of the plaintiff.

Counsel for the plaintiff urges me to conclude that the similarity between the work of the plaintiff and Hardy and the plaintiff and Toth is so similar that I should conclude copying from that fact, even in the absence of evidence from which I can find or infer copying, whether conscious or unconscious. Having disposed of the allegation of conscious copying against Toth, and in light of the fact that no such allegation was made against Hardy, I am, therefore, left, as I have said before, to deal with unconscious copying in respect of both Hardy and Toth.

The law is clear that in order to substantiate a finding of infringement on the basis of unconscious copying, there must be evidence of access or a causal connection between the works. Counsel for the plaintiff asked me to consider that this is not the law, and maintained that it is that a strong or striking similarity, as in the present case, alone, is sufficient to support a conclusion of infringement. In this respect, he is able to refer me to one authority only, and that is a 1972 paper prepared by Jeffrey G. Sherman entitled: "Musical Copyright Infringement: The Requirement of Substantial Similarity". From my reading of that paper, I must conclude that the learned author, although making this suggestion, does not refer to any authority in support. Counsel for the plaintiff referred me to one case; but a reading of it discloses it to be a judgment reached on default of a defence and, consequently, not of much persuasive authority, in any event, to offset what otherwise appears to be a well-entrenched principle of law. To support unconscious copying on the part of the defendants Hardy and Toth, plaintiff's counsel referred me to the fact that they, like the plaintiff, worked extensively in and about Toronto and that, accordingly, I should infer that at some time, at some place, they heard the plaintiff's work. This I will not do in this case.

I accept the evidence of Rudy Toth that he had never heard of the plaintiff's work prior to his writing Moment of Love in 1970. I have already said I accept Hardy's evidence that he had no opportunity to be influenced by the plaintiff's work in composing The Homecoming. Having rejected, then, that the defendant Hardy and the defendant Rudy Toth copied any part of the work of the plaintiff, the similarity which I have found to exist between them must, of necessity, be the result of coincidence. As I have noted above, Dr. McIntyre had expressed the opinion that the similarities which existed between the works of the defendants and that of the plaintiff were such that the one had to have influenced the writing of the others. In saying this, he made no mention that the similarities could be due to coincidence. To my mind, the effective result of Dr. McIntyre's testimony is that a striking similarity exists between the works, and that, his exercise shows this to exist in the passages which he has isolated for consideration. As I have said before, I accept that similarity does exist, but I do not agree that this means that the one has to have influenced the other. I accept the evidence of Dr. Ciamaga that the similarities in the melodies of the works under consideration do not, without something more, permit a conclusion that one influenced the others. I was impressed by Dr. Ciamaga's testimony concerning musical cliches or common place, and the support of his position in this respect given by two, obviously, talented and knowledgeable musicians, Dale and Riley. They had put together the cassette upon which the 11 pieces, which Dr. McIntyre was asked to comment upon, are contained. Dr. McIntyre's reaction to the playing of those pieces I have noted above. The first, which he described as "strikingly similar" to the melodies of the plaintiff and Hardy, was a piece "Je ne Songeais pas a Rose", composed in 1969 by a Belgian. The second, which Dr. McIntyre described as being "strikingly similar", was a passage from the song "What Was Good Enough for Me", composed in 1967. The third I have already noted he recognized as being the theme from "The Fox". The fourth, which Dr. McIntyre did not recognize or find similar in any way, was a passage from Vivaldi, who lived between 1675 and 1741. To my ear, the passage from Vivaldi alone would be sufficient to support the opinions of the witnesses Ciamaga, Dale and Riley. I found it to be very similar to the melodies of the works of the plaintiff and Hardy. I do not need to comment on the balance of the passages found on that cassette except to say that those which are intended to relate to the melody of Moment of Love are not very similar, to my ear. The playing of those passages that are similar is relevant, not to support any defence of public domain, which was not raised in this action, but rather, the issue of coincidence. In this respect, for the purposes of this judgment, I am prepared to find that all of the works have the required degree of originality necessary to give rise to a claim for copyright. That the defendant Rudy Toth wrote Moment of Love in 1970 as he did, in the complete absence of the work of the plaintiff, in itself, provides an example of coincidence for he was not in any way involved with or connected to Hardy. I think that a general statement, well applied to the circumstances of these actions, is that which was made by Circuit Judge Learned Hand in Darrell v. Joe Morris Music Co., Inc., et al. (1940), 113 F. 2d 80:

> "It must be remembered that, while there are an enormous number of possible permutations of the musical notes of the scale, only a few are pleasing; and much fewer still suit the infantile demands of the popular ear. Recurrence is not therefore an inevitable badge of plagiarism."

… Actions dismissed.

EMI Songs Australia Pty Ltd v. Larrikin Music Publishing Pty Ltd., [2011] FCAFC 47

INTRODUCTION

[1] The principal question in these two appeals is whether recordings of performances of an iconic Australian musical work known as "Down Under", performed by a group known as "Men At Work", involved the reproduction in a material form of a substantial part of another iconic Australian musical work, "Kookaburra Sits in the Old Gum Tree" (Kookaburra), so as to constitute infringement of the copyright subsisting in Kookaburra under the Copyright Act 1968 (Cth) (the Copyright Act). Larrikin Music Publishing Pty Ltd (Larrikin), a respondent in both appeals, is the owner of the copyright in Kookaburra. Larrikin contends that the copyright has been infringed by EMI Songs Australia Pty Ltd and EMI Music Publishing Australia Pty Ltd (together the EMI Companies), the first and second appellants in both appeals, and by Mr Colin Hay and Mr Ronald Strykert, respectively an appellant and a respondent in one of the appeals.

. . .

THE WORKS IN QUESTION

[9] In considering whether an alleged infringing work constitutes an infringement of a musical work, it is necessary to regard music as a language, with its own vocabulary and structure. Music must be understood, by analogy, in the way in which traditional language is understood.

[10] It is important to identify precisely the relevant work in which copyright subsists. The Copyright Act offers no definition of musical work. The musical work in which copyright subsists is an abstract concept. That concept may be indicated or evidenced by a notated musical score or a sound recording. However, the musical score or sound recording is not the musical work.

[11] It is necessary, when identifying the precise work in which copyright subsists, to identify also that part of the musical work that manifests its originality. A melody, excerpt or phrase in a completed work is capable of manifesting originality. However, the copying of musical ideas and commonplace building blocks and motifs from a musical work, which are not themselves original, will not normally constitute infringement of that musical work (see, for example, Ronald S Rosen, *Music and Copyright* (Oxford University Press, 2008) at 2-3).

[12] It is convenient to describe separately each of the musical works in issue in the appeals.

Kookaburra

[13] Kookaburra was written and composed by Ms Marion Sinclair. It was published in 1934 in the Girl Guides publication, "Three Rounds by Marion Sinclair", in the form set out in Sch 1 to these reasons. As notated in Sch 1, the music of Kookaburra is in the key of F major. Dr Andrew Ford, a composer, writer and broadcaster, who gave evidence before the primary judge, transposed Kookaburra into the key of D major. Dr Ford's transposition, which was referred to as Example A, is set out in Sch 2 to these reasons. Aside from the transposition, the versions of Kookaburra in Schs 1 and 2 exhibit several small differences. However, the differences are irrelevant for present purposes.

[14] Kookaburra, clearly enough, is a short musical work. When notated as shown in Sch 1, it consists of eight bars. In Sch 2, it consists of only four bars. The parties consistently described Kookaburra as a four-bar work.

[15] Kookaburra was published with lyrics, which provide the title of the work and indicate that it was intended to be sung to those lyrics. There is no separate musical accompaniment shown in Sch 1. Kookaburra was published as a "Round in 4 Parts". That indicates that it was to be sung by four voices or four groups of voices, such that each of the parts is continuously repeated. When sung as a round, the four phrases shown in Sch 1 would be progressively heard over the top of each other. Thus, even if Kookaburra were sung through as a round only once, it would consist of seven bars rather than four. The notation of

Kookaburra set out in Sch 3 to these reasons illustrates how Kookaburra might be sung through as a round three times.

[16] It was not disputed that Kookaburra was an original composition, although there was no evidence as to the degree of skill involved in its composition, other than that skill was involved in writing the work as a round. Dr Ford described writing a round as "a tricky and rather amusing business", because all the phrases have to fit on top of each other. By that he should probably be understood as saying that, as well as each phrase making independent sense as a melody, the phrases must be capable of harmonising against each other.

Down Under

[17] Down Under was composed in 1978 by Messrs Hay and Strykert and was originally arranged to be performed as a duet. Mr Hay initially composed the lyrics, verses, choruses and chord structure of the work on his acoustic guitar. The bass line was composed by Mr Strykert, who added some guitar embellishments. Mr Hay jotted down the original version of Down Under in his notebook in about May 1978. As originally written, Down Under's musical elements did not include the flute phrase described below, which is critical for the present appeals. Messrs Hay and Strykert began to perform Down Under live in clubs and other venues around Melbourne in 1978.

[18] The performance group Men at Work was formed in 1979. Men at Work started as a trio, consisting of Messrs Hay and Strykert and a third person playing drums. Mr Greg Ham joined Men at Work in the middle of 1979. Mr Ham is classically trained and can play and read music. He plays a number of instruments, including the flute.

[19] The lyrics, vocal melody, chords and bass line were already established when Mr Ham first heard Down Under. Mr Ham sought to complement those elements with another instrumental part, especially one that would consolidate the tongue-in-cheek nature of Down Under. Mr Ham added flute phrases, which incorporated a part of Kookaburra. Mr Ham was aware of Kookaburra, having apparently heard it when at primary school in Australia in the late 1950s. His aim in adding the flute phrase to Down Under was to inject the song with Australian flavour. He said that the flute phrase fitted rhythmically into Down Under, and to the percussion section at the start of the song, which, in the 1981 Recording, is played on beer bottles with different amounts of water in them. Mr Ham described the flute phrase as an "Aussie cliché melody", and said that he thought of it as an "Irish/Australian style melody".

[20] The 1979 Recording is of an arrangement of Down Under, in the key of B minor, performed by Men at Work. It was published on the B side of a seven inch single recording titled Key Punch Operator. The version of Down Under in the 1979 Recording included the relevant flute phrases.

[21] By 1980, Men at Work had grown to five musicians and were performing regularly at venues around Melbourne. The songs that they performed included

Down Under. The version of Down Under that they performed live was close to, though not identical to, the version in the 1979 Recording. No two live performances, of course, were identical to each other.

[22] The 1981 Recording is of a further performance of Down Under by Men at Work, recorded as part of an album entitled Business as Usual. The version of Down Under in the 1981 Recording also includes the relevant flute phrases, though it differs from the version in the 1979 Recording in some respects. The version of Down Under in the 1981 Recording is also in the key of B minor. It is described as having a strong "ska/reggae feel" and a recurring rhythmic motif in the guitar. It is arranged for vocals, guitar, bass, percussion and flute. The version of Down Under in the 1981 Recording is ninety-three bars long. It, too, is different from the versions that were performed live.

[23] Dr Ford identified what he called the basic hook of Down Under, which he referred to as Example C when notated. The basic hook is as follows:

Example C: 'Down Under' basic hook

Dr Ford identified the basic hook as an element of a longer, four-bar hook in Down Under, which is first heard in an incomplete form, and which, when notated in this form, he referred to as Example D. The longer hook is as follows:

Example D: 'Down Under' extended hook (first appearance)

Dr Ford said that, in bar 1 of Example D, the flute plays a version of the basic hook, but with two extra notes. The flute is silent in bar 2. Bar 3 contains the basic hook, and bar 4 presents the first quotation from Kookaburra, namely, the second phrase of Kookaburra.

[24] The full version of the longer hook was referred to by Dr Ford as Example E when notated, and is as follows:

Example E: 'Down Under' extended hook (subsequent appearances)

Dr Ford said that bars 1 and 3 of Example E present the basic hook, while bars 2 and 4 present direct quotes from the first and second phrases respectively of Kookaburra.

[25] Examples C, D and E are played on the flute in the respective versions of Down Under in which they appear. Example E appears once in the 1979 Recording. In the 1981 Recording, Example D appears once and Example E twice. Thus the pattern of notes from Kookaburra appears in five out of the ninety-three bars of the version of Down Under in the 1981 Recording. Each bar is separated from the others by material that is not derived from Kookaburra.

[26] The EMI Companies attach some significance to the fact that any resemblance between any part of Kookaburra and the versions of Down Under in the Impugned Recordings went unnoticed by the general public, as well as by Larrikin, for more than 20 years, notwithstanding that both were well known iconic Australian compositions. Larrikin has owned the copyright in Kookaburra since 1990, but did not perceive the resemblance until it was pointed out in the course of a popular television panel programme in 2007, in which participants were invited to listen to one of the Impugned Recordings, and to identify the iconic piece of music, a passage from which was said to be reproduced in the Impugned Recording.

. . .

DEVELOPMENT OF COPYRIGHT

[28] The word *substantial* is susceptible of some degree of ambiguity, and its meaning for the purposes of s 14 of the Copyright Act will be influenced by its context. The relevant context includes the development of copyright protection for specific kinds of works (see *IceTV Pty Ltd v Nine Network Australia Pty Ltd* (2009) 239 CLR 458 (*IceTV*) at [154]). Accordingly, I shall first say something about the history of copyright in musical works.

[29] Just as nature abhors a vacuum, so the law abhors a monopoly. Copyright is an exception to the law's abhorrence of monopolies (see *IceTV* at [28]). Copyright legislation strikes a balance of competing interests and competing policy considerations. Relevantly, it is concerned with rewarding authors of original literary, artistic and musical works with commercial benefits, having regard to the fact that such works in turn benefit the public (see *IceTV* at [24]).

[30] The Romans disliked monopolies just as much as common lawyers. The Emperor Zeno, at the end of the fifth century, provided that no-one was to be permitted to monopolise the sale of certain commodities. Zeno's measure stipulated that, should anyone practice monopoly, he would be deprived of all his property and sentenced to perpetual exile, and that those venturing to fix the prices of their merchandise or bind themselves by any illegal contracts of that kind would be punished by a fine. Further, any tribunal that did not enforce the laws as to monopolies was also to be punished by a fine (see Justinian's Code, Book 4 Title 59).

[31] However, the Romans recognised no exception for copyright. They recognised no monopoly in the result of literary, artistic or musical effort. Rather, the Romans were concerned only with ownership of the physical embodiment of a

literary, artistic or musical work. That is to say, they analysed the question in terms of accessio and specificatio. Thus, writing on paper or parchment, even in letters of gold, accedes to or becomes part of the paper or parchment by the doctrine of accessio. For example, if an author writes a poem, history or speech on another's paper or parchment, that other person remains the owner of the paper or parchment. However, if the paper or parchment is in the possession of the author and the owner seeks to recover it, that owner will be required to compensate the author for the loss of the writing, assuming that the author acquired possession of the paper or parchment in good faith (see *Justinian's Institutes* Book 2.1.33). On the other hand, if the owner is in possession of the paper or parchment, the author has no claim against the owner. The requirement to give compensation as a condition of obtaining possession of the paper or parchment indicates that Roman jurists recognised some proprietary interest in the work that was done. There was nothing to stop the author from writing the poem, history or speech down on another paper or parchment. Nor, of course, was there anything to stop the owner of the paper or parchment from copying the work and distributing the copies by sale or otherwise.

[32] The position under Roman law was different if someone paints a picture on another's board or canvas. A picture or painting by a famous artist was regarded as being of far greater value than the canvas or board on which it was painted. The Roman jurists regarded it as ridiculous to say that the paint acceded to the board or canvas, irrespective of the quality of the painting or picture. However, where the original owner of the canvas or board has possession of the painting or picture, and the painter claims return of the painting, the painter will be required to compensate the owner of the board for the value of the board or canvas. Even if the painter is in possession, the owner of the board or canvas is given an action to recover its value (*Institutes* 2.1.34).

[33] The question of a sculptor who uses somebody else's bronze, silver or gold to make an artistic work is dealt with by Roman law under the rubric of specificatio, making a new thing or species out of different materials. If the maker owns the materials, no difficulty arises. However, when somebody else's materials are used, the position varies. If the new thing can be turned back into its materials, its owner is the one who owned the materials. If not, its maker is its owner. The completed artistic work, made from bronze, silver or gold, can be turned back into raw bronze, silver or gold. Hence the owner of the materials is the owner of the work. However, things such as wine, oil or grain cannot be made back into grapes, olives or corn. Hence, the wine, oil or grain belongs to the maker, subject to rights of compensation for the loss of materials. On the other hand, when the maker uses materials belonging both to the maker and to someone else, the maker is regarded as the owner of the product, having contributed not only the work but also part of the materials (*Institutes* 2.1.25). Thus, the Romans did recognise that the author of or maker of a thing had an interest in the product by reason of the effort in producing the product. Nevertheless, that was not a proprietary right that could be alienated by the author or maker, separately from the alienation of the object.

[34] Of course, the problems of multiple copying and reproduction that began with the invention of printing, and were exacerbated by the development of digitalisation and dissemination by means of the internet, were not problems known to the Romans. Printing technology provided the first realistic opportunity for authors to realise the potential economic benefits of their work. That led to intervention by the state.

[35] For example, in 1469, the Governors of Venice granted to John of Spira, a printer, the exclusive rights to publish both Cicero's and Pliny's letters for five years. Others in Venice and elsewhere quickly began seeking and securing the exclusive privilege to publish particular works in specific localities. The mid-to-late fifteenth century witnessed a rise in the creation of copyright, taking the guise of an exclusive right granted by the state to a publisher.

[36] By the early sixteenth century, the English Crown had begun granting to individual printers exclusive rights to publish specific books. A Royal Charter of 1556 gave the Stationers' Company, a printers' guild that dominated all publishing in London at the time, exclusive and perpetual rights in books that were duly registered with it. However, the rights granted by the Royal Charter had nothing to do with rewarding authors. Rather, the grant was much more concerned with the control of the press by the Crown. The Charter made it clear that church and state were never to be subjected to heresy, scandal or descent. Nevertheless, the result was that publishers enjoyed a state-sanctioned monopoly over what appeared in print.

[37] In that context, the Westminster Parliament enacted the Statute of Anne (8 Anne c. 19), which came into force in 1710, giving the authors or proprietors of books the sole liberty of printing and reprinting for the term of 14 years, renewable once if the author was still living. The privilege was not automatic. Authors and publishers had to apply for it, pay a fee and register the relevant work. The Statute of Anne is the significant forebear of English, and, therefore, Australian copyright legislation.

[38] The Statute of Anne did not deal with musical works as such. However, the monopoly extended to a book that recorded a musical work as sheet music. By s 20 of the Copyright Act 1842 (5 & 6 Vict. c. 45) (the 1842 Act), the sole liberty of representing a musical composition, performing a musical composition, or causing or permitting a musical composition to be represented or performed, was to endure and be the property of the author for the term provided for the duration of copyright in books. In the 1842 Act, *book* was defined as including a sheet of music.

[39] By s 1(1) of the Copyright Act 1911 (UK) (the 1911 Act), copyright was to subsist in, relevantly, every original musical work. Under s 1(2) of the 1911 Act, copyright was defined as the sole right to produce or reproduce the work, or *any substantial part thereof*, in any material form whatsoever and to perform the work, or any substantial part thereof, in public. That was the first statutory recognition of copyright in a substantial part of a work. Copyright was also to include the sole right, in the case of a musical work, to make any contrivance by

means of which the work might be mechanically performed or delivered. There was no definition of musical work in the 1911 Act. However, s 19(2) provided that it would not be an infringement of copyright in any musical work to make contrivances by means of which the work might be mechanically performed, if the contrivances had previously been made with the consent or acquiescence of the owner of the copyright, notice had been given of intention to make the contrivances and the applicable royalty had been paid. Section 19(2)(ii) further provided that, for the purposes of that provision, a musical work was to be deemed to include any words so closely associated therewith as to form part of the same work. Section 8 of the Copyright Act 1912 (Cth) (the 1912 Act) provided that the 1911 Act was to be in force in Australia from 1 July 1912.

THE RELEVANT STATUTORY PROVISIONS

[40] The Copyright Act replaced the 1912 Act. Under s 13(1) of the Copyright Act, an act comprised in the copyright in a work, including a musical work, is any act that, under the Copyright Act, the owner of the copyright has the exclusive right to do. …Under s 14, a reference to the doing of an act in relation to a work includes a reference to the doing of that act in relation to a substantial part of the work and a reference to a reproduction of a work includes a reference to a reproduction of a substantial part of the work.

SOME LEGAL PRINCIPLES

[45] Certain musical works, such as operas, may be regarded as containing or consisting of several smaller, discrete works. Copyright may subsist in an air or melody and may be infringed by copying part of that air or melody, as well as by copying the whole of the air or melody. There will be an infringement if that in which the whole meritorious part of the original work consists is incorporated in a new work (see *D'Almaine v Boosey* (1835) 1 Y & C Ex 288 at 301-2).

[46] The copyright in an original work will also be infringed by the taking from that work, without any material alteration, of all of the bars that consecutively form an entire air or melody. On the other hand, to take the bars in a different order, or broken by the intersection of other bars, will not necessarily be an infringement. Infringement depends upon whether the air or melody taken is substantially the same as the original. The mere adaptation of an air or melody, by transferring it from one instrument to another, does not alter the original subject, if the ear tells one it is the same. The adaptation or accompaniment does not change it. There will be infringement where the original work, though adapted to a different purpose from that of the original, can still be recognised by the ear (see *D'Almaine v Boosey* at 302).

[47] Infringement does not depend upon whether the actual notes are taken (*Austin v Columbia Graphophone Company Ltd* [1917-1923] MacG Cop Cas 398 at 408). Determining infringement is not a question of note for note comparison, but of whether the substance of the original copyright work is taken

(see *Austin v Columbia* at 415). There will be infringement where a new work is arrived at by way of imitation and appropriation (see *Austin v Columbia* at 421).

[48] In order to establish infringement of copyright in a musical work, it must be shown that the work said to have been infringed has been copied or that a substantial part of it has been copied (see *G Ricordi & Co (London) Ltd v Clayton & Waller Ltd* [1928-1935] MacG Cop Cas 154 at 162). The originality of a particular musical work may be due, not to the sequence of the notes, but to the treatment, accentuation and orchestration by the composer. It is the musical work as a whole that is entitled to the protection of copyright. It may be that the part that is taken is so small a part of the original music work as not to constitute an infringement, because it is not a substantial part of the musical work in which copyright subsists. While eight bars of a particular air, constituting about a quarter of the work, may form a substantial part of that work, there may be no infringement if the eight bars in question are not the most distinctive or important part of the original air (see *G Ricordi & Co* at 162).

[49] When dealing with the word *substantial* in the context of infringement of copyright in a musical work, it is appropriate to consider whether or not the amount of the copyright musical work that is taken is so slender that it would be impossible to recognise it (see *Hawkes & Son (London) Ltd v Paramount Film Service Ltd* [1934] 1 Ch 593 at 604). However, even though the alleged infringement is not very prolonged in its reproduction, there will nevertheless be infringement if what is reproduced is a substantial, vital and essential part of the original (*Hawkes v Paramount* at 606). Further, there will be infringement if the bars of a musical work that are taken contain what constitutes the principal air or melody of the copyright work, which anyone who heard the alleged infringing work would recognise as being the essential air or melody of the copyright work (see *Hawkes v Paramount* at 609).

[50] It may be appropriate, in determining whether one musical work infringes the copyright in another, to analyse the musical features and structure of each, stating points of similarity or difference (see *Francis Day & Hunter Ltd v Bron* [1963] 1 Ch 587 at 609-10). For example, the following may be compared:

(ii) the structure of two works;

(ii) whether particular bars of the copyright work are an essential part of that work, and whether the theme of those bars has been borrowed in the alleged infringing work;

(ii) whether the theme of the copyright work, despite being built up of musical commonplaces or clichés, combines those devices originally;

(ii) whether there is a noticeable correspondence, on a note for note comparison, between the two works;

(ii) whether the harmonic structure of parts of the two works is the same;

(ii) the importance of time and/or rhythm in each work.

In such a comparison, the question is whether the degree of similarity can be said to be definite or considerable (see *Francis Day* at 610).

. . .

THE ISSUES IN THE APPEALS AND THE CROSS-APPEAL

[62] The principal question in the appeals is whether the Impugned Recordings involved a reproduction of a substantial part of Kookaburra. If they did, both appeals should be dismissed. If they did not, both appeals should be allowed and orders should be made accordingly.

. . .

INFRINGEMENT BY THE IMPUGNED RECORDINGS

[66] In the light of the principles summarised above, the correct approach in an action for an infringement of copyright in a musical work may be summarised as follows:

> (ii) Identification of the work in which copyright subsists. That arises from s 32, which directs attention to the copyright work. There must be a work that, relevantly, is an original musical work. There must also be the requisite connection with Australia.
>
> (ii) Identification, in the alleged infringing work, of the part taken, derived or copied from the copyright work. That directs attention to the alleged infringing work and requires an inquiry as to what it reproduces from the copyright work. Reproduction requires there to be both sufficient objective similarity between the two works and a causal link between the two works.
>
> (ii) Determination of whether the part taken constitutes a substantial part of the copyright work. That is a primarily qualitative matter. The question is whether the alleged infringement reproduces that which made the copyright work an original musical work. However, the Copyright Act recognises that there may be some measure of appropriation that does not constitute infringement.

(See *Elwood Clothing Pty Ltd v Cotton On Clothing Pty Ltd* (2008) 172 FCR 580 at [41] and [42]).

. . .

Comparison between Kookaburra and Relevant Versions of Down Under

[82] In the light of the legal principles summarised above, the question is whether the evidence established that, having regard to Kookaburra as a whole, there was a reproduction of a substantial part of it in the particular use made in the Impugned Recordings of two of its phrases, without either lyrics or any relationship in the nature of a round. It is important to have regard to the part said to have been taken from Kookaburra, not only as it appears in Kookaburra as originally published, but also in the context in which it appears in the

Impugned Recordings. Regard must be had to the whole of each work in making that assessment, and attention must be given to what it was that constituted Kookaburra as an original work. On the other hand, in order for there to be infringement, it is not necessary that the part of Kookaburra taken constitute a substantial part of the Impugned Recordings.

[83] There was evidence before the primary judge that the composition of Kookaburra as a round involved some skill and originality. The EMI Companies and Mr Hay contend that the evidence established no skill or originality other than that required to compose Kookaburra as a round. There was no express evidence to the effect that the four phrases shown in Sch 1, by themselves, constituted original works or, taken in isolation, constituted original parts of works. However, I consider that each of Kookaburra's phrases, having been brought to fruition through the application of skill and originality in writing Kookaburra as a round, consequently manifests the application of skill and originality.

[84] Even accepting the limited evidence of originality before the primary judge, I do not consider that reproduction of a substantial part of Kookaburra requires reproduction of Kookaburra as a round. The limitation of originality to a work's composition as a round does not mean that performance of that work as a round is necessary in order to reproduce that which gives the work its originality. I consider that the Impugned Recordings, in reproducing the first two phrases of Kookaburra, thereby reproduced that which constitutes Kookaburra as an original work.

[85] There was no suggestion that the effort involved in the composition of Kookaburra's four phrases was so slight that no copyright would subsist in them, standing alone. It is clear enough that there was skill and originality involved in the composition of those bars as a stand-alone piece of music. Dr Ford said that Kookaburra's first two bars (or phrases), being the parts reproduced in the Impugned Recordings, are its "signature". That proposition, if accepted, is independent of any performance of Kookaburra as a round. Certainly, the complete work evidenced by the notation in Sch 1 may, on a fair analysis, for the reasons indicated above, involve more than four discrete phrases. Nevertheless, reproducing two of the four phrases shown in Sch 1 involves reproduction of at least a part of the musical work first published in 1934, being, though brief, an important and significant part whose composition may be said to have involved skill and originality. I consider that those phrases constituted an essential air or melody of the copyright work. To the extent that the contentions of the EMI Companies and Mr Hay conflate Kookaburra's brevity and relative simplicity with a lack of originality, they ought not to be accepted.

[86] A consideration of the similarities and differences between Kookaburra and the versions of Down Under in the Impugned Recordings gives the impression that there is, within the versions of Down Under in each of the Impugned Recordings, with respect to the critical features of a musical work, an adoption of the individual effort that Ms Sinclair bestowed upon Kookaburra, which gave to it its distinct characteristics and individuality. There is a reasonably ready aural

perception that the versions of Down Under in the Impugned Recordings contain a recognisable part of Kookaburra. A similarity between part of Kookaburra and the flute phrase is clearly perceptible. True it is that that similarity went largely unnoticed for in excess of 20 years, notwithstanding that each work is said to be an iconic Australian work. Nevertheless, the question is one of objective similarity. The aural resemblance need not be resounding or obvious. The relevant test is not the effect upon a casual listener of the whole of the versions of Down Under in the Impugned Recordings. Sensitised though the primary judge may have been to the similarity, it is not erroneous to direct oneself to the relevant parts of the works, to listen to the works a number of times, and to accept the assistance of the views of experts, in determining the question of objective similarity. In those respects, I do not consider that the primary judge erred.

[87] Further, the issue of who first noticed the infringement, and when, is not of itself relevant to the question of objective similarity. That question is to be determined by reference to aural perception and, though its resolution may depend somewhat on expert evidence, evidence of the lack of subjective perceptions of persons connected with the owner of the copyright is not of assistance in resolving it.

[88] Certainly, Kookaburra was published as a four-part round to be performed with lyrics, and is not reproduced in that manner in the Impugned Recordings. Further, it is integral to Kookaburra, as published, that the phrases will be progressively sung over the top of each other, building up to a four-voice texture. In that form, Kookaburra can be said to have seven aurally unique bars, only one of which, the first, is reproduced in the Impugned Recordings. In the versions of Down Under in the Impugned Recordings, on the other hand, the notes from Kookaburra appear only as part of the phrases that make up an ornamental flute line.

[89] However, those dissimilarities in the structures of the respective works are not determinative. As I have said, the reproduction of the melody of Kookaburra in the form in which it was published, as shown in Sch 1, is a reproduction of that which constitutes Kookaburra as an original work, or gives it its creativity. Kookaburra would make perfect sense as a work if sung as one linear melody. That is one possible realisation of the musical work that was first published by Ms Sinclair and that is evidenced in Sch 1. As Down Under itself shows, a musical work may exist in multiple versions, and musical scores are not necessarily coterminous with the works they represent.

[90] There are limited features of similarity between Kookaburra and Down Under in terms of key, harmony, tempo and rhythm. Kookaburra was written in a major key. The relevant bars in the Impugned Recordings appear as part of an overall work in a minor key. The harmony in Kookaburra arises both from its character as a round, and the implied harmonies suggested by casting its melody in a specific key. The versions of Down Under in the Impugned Recordings have a highly distinctive harmony, arising from the voice of Mr Hay, singing very different lyrics, and the mix of instruments. While, as a result, the bars in question in the Impugned Recordings may, in some sense, sound different from Kookaburra, the melody is nevertheless clearly recognisable. Dr Ford described

the change in underlying harmony as "a bit like shining a different light" on the relevant melodic phrase. Although, as the primary judge observed, that might differentiate the listener's impressions of the same notes in the two works, I do not consider that it meaningfully detracts from the objective similarity between the works.

[91] Kookaburra, as published, has no indications of tempo or rhythm, and the relevant versions of Down Under have their own highly distinctive tempo and rhythm. However, it is implicit in what appears in Sch 1 that the work must be sung at a tempo suited to the capabilities of the human voice, especially as regards enunciation and breathing. The versions of Down Under plausibly reproduce the melody at such a tempo. Further, the phrases of Kookaburra, as reproduced in the Impugned Recordings, do not alter Kookaburra's underlying rhythmic pulse or tactus.

[92] It is true that the works do not represent similar musical genres or styles. Kookaburra is a folk melody, children's song or nursery rhyme, while Down Under was characterised as a rock anthem, and is influenced by ska and/or reggae. There is no similarity between the respective natures and objects of the works. Nevertheless, such quotation of Kookaburra as appears in the versions of Down Under in the Impugned Recordings was intended to be perceived by listeners as just that, namely, a quotation, or a reproduction, of part of Kookaburra, and the musical genres or styles associated with Kookaburra. Neither the existence of the quotation or reproduction, nor its capacity to be discerned, is affected by casting it as a tribute or reference to an Australian cliché or iconic melody. The flute phrases in the Impugned Recordings are a clear departure from the genre of a rock anthem, and therefore distinguish the part taken from Kookaburra from the other parts and musical elements of Down Under. The listener will hear a reproduction of part of Kookaburra.

[93] It is also true that there is only a limited similarity of notes. Only five of the ninety-three bars in the 1981 Recording contain notes in the flute phrases that are similar to any part of Kookaburra. The first phrase in Sch 1 mirrors the flute phrase in bars 23 and 51, and the second phrase in Sch 1 mirrors the flute phrase in bars 5, 25 and 53 of that version of Down Under. However, in assessing objective similarity, quantity is secondary to quality. When one compares the relevant bars of Sch 1 with the relevant bars of the versions of Down Under in the Impugned Recordings, there is a very close similarity, if not a complete identity. While the appearances of phrases from Sch 1 may be sparse in the overall context of the Impugned Recordings, the flute is the dominant musical element when the phrases do appear.

[94] It is true that the relevant phrases from Kookaburra, when reproduced in the Impugned Recordings, appear separately and interspersed with other musical material. In the 1981 Recording, on the first occasion when the flute phrase appears, the fourth bar is similar to the first phrase of Sch 1, but no other bars of Kookaburra appear. On the second and third occasions, the second and fourth bars of the flute phrase are similar to the first and third phrases of Sch 1, but are

not consecutive. The basic hook of Down Under is interpolated. Similar observations are applicable to the version of Down Under in the 1979 Recording. However, the consistent reproduction of the melodic excerpt from Kookaburra as a discrete whole is a much more significant consideration, which, together with the other matters outlined above, suggests that the air or melody taken is substantially the same as in Kookaburra.

[95] There was no evidence before the primary judge that the EMI Companies, Mr Hay, Mr Strykert or Mr Ham took any part of Kookaburra with the intention of taking advantage of the skill and labour of Ms Sinclair in composing Kookaburra, in order to save effort on their part. Certainly, no advantage was taken of Kookaburra as a round. Mr Hay was open regarding the tribute made to Kookaburra. Mr Ham said in an affidavit, which was not read, but relevant parts of which were tendered by Larrikin, that he recognised the melody that he referenced as "an Australian cliché". He did not identify it as Kookaburra as such. No inference was available from the failure to call Mr Ham beyond what was apparent on the face of the affidavit. Consequently, neither the evidence of Mr Hay nor that of Mr Ham supported a finding that there was any animus furandi.

[96] In any event, I do not consider that there is any requirement that there be a finding of animus furandi before there will be infringement.

[97] A four-part round is a musical idea, explicable in the abstract. That idea is not capable of copyright protection, just as other musical ideas and commonplace building blocks and motifs, such as bare musical genres, harmonic clichés and the like, are not capable of copyright protection. However, the specific melodies or phrases that constitute the expression of the idea of a four-part round will, in total, constitute an original musical work. Further, each melody or phrase may, by virtue of its importance in the overall schema of such an original musical work, constitute a substantial part of that work. I consider that the first two phrases of Kookaburra's melody, as published by Ms Sinclair in the form shown in Sch 1, constitute a substantial part of Kookaburra.

Conclusion as to Infringement

[98] In all of the circumstances, and taking all of the matters set out above into account, I consider that both Impugned Recordings reproduce a substantial part of Kookaburra. Accordingly, there has been an infringement of copyright. However, I have some disquiet about that conclusion in the circumstances of this case.

[99] The better view of the taking of the melody from Kookaburra is not that the melody was taken, animus furandi, in order to save effort on the part of the composer of Down Under, by appropriating the results of Ms Sinclair's efforts. Rather, the quotation or reproduction of the melody of Kookaburra appears by way of tribute to the iconicity of Kookaburra, and as one of a number of references made in Down Under to Australian icons.

[100] If, as I have concluded, the relevant versions of Down Under involve an infringement of copyright, many years after the death of Ms Sinclair, and

enforceable at the behest of an assignee, then some of the underlying concepts of modern copyright may require rethinking. While there are good policy reasons for encouraging the intellectual and artistic effort that produces literary, artistic and musical works, by rewarding the author or composer with some form of monopoly in relation to his or her work (see *Ice TV* at [24]), it may be that the extent of that monopoly, both in terms of time and extent of restriction, ought not necessarily be the same for every work. For example, it is arguably anomalous that the extent of the monopoly granted in respect of inventions under the Patents Act 1990 (Cth), being a limited period following disclosure, is significantly less than the monopoly granted in respect of artistic, literary or musical works, being a fixed period following the death of the author or composer, irrespective of the age of the author or composer at the time of publication.

[101] Of course, the significance of the anomalous operation of the Copyright Act can be addressed in terms of the remedies and relief granted in respect of infringement. Nevertheless, one may wonder whether the framers of the Statute of Anne and its descendants would have regarded the taking of the melody of Kookaburra in the Impugned Recordings as infringement, rather than as a fair use that did not in any way detract from the benefit given to Ms Sinclair for her intellectual effort in producing Kookaburra.

CONCLUSION

[104] I consider that both appeals should be dismissed.

Newton v. Diamond, 388 F.3d 1189
United States Court of Appeals for the Ninth Circuit
November 4, 2003

SCHROEDER, Chief Judge:

This appeal raises the difficult and important issue of whether the incorporation of a short segment of a musical recording into a new musical recording, i.e., the practice of "sampling," requires a license to use both the performance and the composition of the original recording.

...

Background and Procedural History

The plaintiff and appellant in this case, James W. Newton, is an accomplished avant-garde jazz flutist and composer. In 1978, he composed the song "Choir," a piece for flute and voice intended to incorporate elements of African-American gospel music, Japanese ceremonial court music, traditional African music, and classical music, among others. According to Newton, the song was inspired by his earliest memory of music, watching four women singing in a church in rural Arkansas. In 1981, Newton performed and recorded "Choir" and licensed all rights in the sound recording to ECM Records for $ 5000. The license covered only the sound recording, and it is undisputed that Newton retained all rights to the composition of "Choir." Sound recordings and their underlying compositions are separate works with their own distinct copyrights. 17 U.S.C. § 102(a) (2), (7).

The defendants and appellees include the members of the rap and hip-hop group Beastie Boys, and their business associates. In 1992, Beastie Boys obtained a license from ECM Records to use portions of the sound recording of "Choir" in various renditions of their song "Pass the Mic" in exchange for a one-time fee of $ 1000. Beastie Boys did not obtain a license from Newton to use the underlying composition.

The portion of the composition at issue consists of three notes, C — D flat — C, sung over a background C note played on the flute. The score to "Choir" also indicates that the entire song should be played in a "largo/senza-misura" tempo, meaning "slowly/without-measure." The parties disagree about whether two additional elements appear in the score. First, Newton argues that the score contains an instruction that requires overblowing the background C note that is played on the flute. Second, Newton argues that multiphonics are part of the composition because they are necessarily created when a performer follows the instructions on the score to simultaneously play the flute note and sing the vocal notes. Because we review the district court's grant of summary judgment to the Beastie Boys, we must construe the evidence in Newton's favor. We therefore assume that these two elements are part of the "Choir" composition. As we will discuss more fully below, there are other elements that are part of Newton's performance that was captured in the sound recording, but that do not appear in the score.

The dispute between Newton and Beastie Boys centers around the copyright implications of the practice of sampling, a practice now common to many types of popular music. Sampling entails the incorporation of short segments of prior sound recordings into new recordings. The practice originated in Jamaica in the 1960s, when disc jockeys (DJs) used portable sound systems to mix segments of prior recordings into new mixes, which they would overlay with chanted or 'scatted' vocals. *See* Robert M. Szymanski, *Audio Pasitiche: Digital Sampling, Intermediate Copying, Fair Use*, 3 U.C.L.A. Ent. L. Rev. 271, 277 (Spring 1996). Sampling migrated to the United States and developed throughout the 1970s, using the analog technologies of the time. *Id.* The digital sampling involved here developed in the early 1980s with the advent of digital synthesizers having MIDI (Musical Instrument Digital Interface) keyboard controls. These digital instruments allowed artists digitally to manipulate and combine sampled sounds, expanding the range of possibilities for the use of prerecorded music. Whereas analog devices limited artists to "scratching" vinyl records and "cutting" back and forth between different sound recordings, digital technology allowed artists to slow down, speed up, combine, and otherwise alter the samples. *See id.*

Pursuant to their license from ECM Records, Beastie Boys digitally sampled the opening six seconds of Newton's sound recording of "Choir." Beastie Boys repeated or "looped" this six-second sample as a background element throughout "Pass the Mic," so that it appears over forty times in various renditions of the song. In addition to the version of "Pass the Mic" released on their 1992 album, "Check Your Head," Beastie Boys included the "Choir" sample in two remixes, "Dub the Mic" and "Pass the Mic (Pt. 2, Skills to Pay the Bills)." It is unclear whether the sample was altered or manipulated, though Beastie Boys' sound engineer stated that alterations of tone, pitch, and rhythm are commonplace, and Newton maintains that the pitch was lowered slightly.

. . .

Whether Defendants' Use was De Minimis

We may affirm the grant of summary judgment on any basis supported by the record and need not reach each ground relied upon by the district court. ... Assuming that the sampled segment of the composition was sufficiently original to merit copyright protection, we nevertheless affirm on the ground that Beastie Boys' use was de minimis and therefore not actionable.

For an unauthorized use of a copyrighted work to be actionable, the use must be significant enough to constitute infringement. *See Ringgold v. Black Entertainment TV*, 126 F.3d 70, 74–75 (2d Cir. 1997). This means that even where the fact of copying is conceded, no legal consequences will follow from that fact unless the copying is substantial. *See Laureyssens v. Idea Group, Inc.*, 964 F.2d 131, 140 (2d Cir. 1992); 4 Melville B. Nimmer & David Nimmer, Nimmer on Copyright § 13.03[A], at 13-30.2. The principle that trivial copying does not constitute actionable infringement has long been a part of copyright law. Indeed, as Judge Learned Hand observed over 80 years ago: "Even where there is some copying, that fact is not conclusive of infringement. Some copying is permitted. In addition to copying, it must be shown that this has been done to an unfair extent." *West Publ'g Co. v. Edward Thompson Co.*, 169 F. 833, 861 (E.D.N.Y. 1909). This principle reflects the legal maxim, *de minimis non curat lex* (often rendered as, "the law does not concern itself with trifles"). *See Ringgold*, 126 F.3d at 74–75.

A leading case on de minimis infringement in our circuit is *Fisher v. Dees*, 794 F.2d 432 (9th Cir. 1986), where we observed that a use is de minimis only if the average audience would not recognize the appropriation. *See id.* at 434 n.2 ("[A] taking is considered de minimis only if it is so meager and fragmentary that the average audience would not recognize the appropriation."). This observation reflects the relationship between the de minimis maxim and the general test for substantial similarity, which also looks to the response of the average audience, or ordinary observer, to determine whether a use is infringing. *See, e.g., Cavalier v. Random House, Inc.*, 297 F.3d 815, 822 (9th Cir. 2002); *Castle Rock Entm't, Inc. v. Carol Publ'g Group, Inc.*, 150 F.3d 132 (2d Cir. 1998) ("Two works are substantially similar where 'the ordinary observer, unless he set out to detect the disparities, would be disposed to overlook them, and regard

[the] aesthetic appeal [of the two works] as the same.'" (quoting *Arica Inst., Inc. v. Palmer*, 970 F.2d 1067, 1072 (2d Cir. 1992) (quoting *Peter Pan Fabrics, Inc. v. Martin Weiner Corp.*, 274 F.2d 487, 489 (2d Cir. 1960) (L. Hand, J.)))). To say that a use is de minimis because no audience would recognize the appropriation is thus to say that the use is not sufficiently significant.

...

This case involves not only use of a composition, as was the case in *Fisher*, but also use of a sound recording of a particular performance of that composition. Because the defendants were authorized to use the sound recording, our inquiry is confined to whether the unauthorized use of the composition itself was substantial enough to sustain an infringement claim. Therefore, we may consider only Beastie Boys' appropriation of the song's compositional elements and must remove from consideration all the elements unique to Newton's performance. Stated another way, we must "filter out" the licensed elements of the sound recording to get down to the unlicensed elements of the composition, as the composition is the sole basis for Newton's infringement claim....

In filtering out the unique performance elements from consideration, and separating them from those found in the composition, we find substantial assistance in the testimony of Newton's own experts. ... Newton's experts, however, reveal the extent to which the sound recording of "Choir" is the product of Newton's highly developed performance techniques, rather than the result of a generic rendition of the composition. As a general matter, according to Newton's expert Dr. Christopher Dobrian, "the contribution of the performer is often so great that s/he in fact provides as much musical content as the composer." This is particularly true with works like "Choir," given the improvisational nature of jazz performance and the minimal scoring of the composition. Indeed, as Newton's expert Dr. Oliver Wilson explained:

> The copyrighted score of "Choir", as is the custom in scores written in the jazz tradition, does not contain indications for all of the musical subtleties that it is assumed the performer-composer of the work will make in the work's performance. The function of the score is more mnemonic in intention than prescriptive.

And it is clear that Newton goes beyond the score in his performance. For example, Dr. Dobrian declared that "Mr. Newton blows and sings in such a way as to emphasize the upper partials of the flute's complex harmonic tone, [although] such a modification of tone color is not explicitly requested in the score." Dr. Dobrian also concludes that Newton "uses breath control to modify the timbre of the sustained flute note rather extremely" and "uses portamento to glide expressively from one pitch to another in the vocal part." Dr. Dobrian concedes that these elements do not appear in the score, and that they are part of Newton's performance of the piece.

A crucial problem with the testimony of Newton's experts is that they continually refer to the "sound" produced by the "Newton technique." A sound is protected by copyright law only when it is "fixed in a tangible medium." 17 U.S.C. § 102(a). Here, the only time any sound was fixed in a tangible medium was when a particular performance was recorded. Newton licensed the recording at issue to ECM Records over twenty years ago, and ECM Records in turn licensed the interest in the recording to the Beastie Boys. Newton's copyright extends only to the elements that he fixed in a tangible medium — those that he wrote on the score. Thus, regardless of whether the average audience might recognize the "Newton technique" at work in the sampled sound recording, those performance elements are beyond consideration in Newton's claim for infringement of his copyright in the underlying composition.

Once we have isolated the basis of Newton's infringement action — the "Choir" composition, devoid of the unique performance elements found only in the sound recording — we turn to the nub of our inquiry: whether Beastie Boys' unauthorized use of the composition, as opposed to their authorized use of the sound recording, was substantial enough to sustain an infringement action. In answering that question, we must distinguish between whether there is a high enough degree of similarity between the works to establish copying, and whether that copying is substantial enough to constitute infringement. ... The practice of music sampling will often present cases where the degree of similarity is high. Indeed, unless the sample has been altered or digitally manipulated, it will be identical to the sampled portion of the original recording. Yet as Nimmer explains, "[if] the similarity is only as to nonessential matters, then a finding of no substantial similarity should result." 4 Nimmer § 13.03[A][2], at 13–48.... This reflects the principle that the substantiality requirement applies throughout the law of copyright, including cases of music sampling, even where there is a high degree of similarity.

The high degree of similarity between the works here (i.e., "Pass the Mic" and "Choir"), but the limited scope of the copying, place Newton's claim for infringement into the class of cases that allege what Nimmer refers to as "fragmented literal similarity." 4 Nimmer § 13.03[A][2], at 13–45. Fragmented literal similarity exists where the defendant copies a portion of the plaintiff's work exactly or nearly exactly, without appropriating the work's overall essence or structure. *Id.* Because the degree of similarity is high in such cases, the dispositive question is whether the copying goes to trivial or substantial elements. Substantiality is measured by considering the qualitative and quantitative significance of the copied portion in relation to the plaintiff's work as a whole. *See, e.g., Worth v. Selchow & Righter Co.*, 827 F.2d 569, 570 n. 1 (9th Cir. 1987) ("The relevant inquiry is whether a substantial portion of the protectible material in the *plaintiff's* work was appropriated — not whether a substantial portion of *defendant's* work was derived from plaintiff's work."); *Jarvis v. A&M Records*, 827 F. Supp. 282, 289-90 (D.N.J. 1993); 4 Nimmer § 13.03[A][2], at 13–47 to 48 & n.97. This focus on the sample's relation to the plaintiff's work as a whole embodies the fundamental question in any infringement action, as expressed more than 150 years ago by Justice Story: whether "so much is taken[] that the value of the original is sensibly diminished, or the labors of the original author are substantially to an injurious extent appropriated by another." *Folsom v. Marsh*, 9 F. Cas. 342, 348, F. Cas. No. 4901 (C.C. Mass. 1841). Courts also focus on the relationship to the plaintiff's work because a contrary rule that measured the significance of the copied segment in the defendant's work would allow an unscrupulous defendant to copy large or qualitatively significant portions of another's work and escape liability by burying them beneath non-infringing material in the defendant's own work, even where the average audience might recognize the appropriation. *Cf. Sheldon v. Metro-Goldwyn Pictures Corp.*, 81 F.2d 49, 56 (2d Cir. 1936) ("It is enough that substantial parts were lifted; no plagiarist can excuse the wrong by showing how much of his work he did not pirate."). Thus, as the district court properly concluded, the fact that Beastie Boys "looped" the sample throughout "Pass the Mic" is irrelevant in weighing the sample's qualitative and quantitative significance. *See Newton*, 204 F. Supp. 2d at 1257.

On the undisputed facts of this record, no reasonable juror could find the sampled portion of the composition to be a quantitatively or qualitatively significant portion of the composition as a whole. Quantitatively, the three-note sequence appears only once in Newton's composition. It is difficult to measure the precise relationship between this segment and the composition as a whole, because the score calls for between 180 and 270 seconds of improvisation. When played, however, the segment lasts six seconds and is roughly two percent of the four-and-a-half-minute "Choir" sound recording licensed by Beastie Boys. Qualitatively, this section of the composition is no more significant than any other section. Indeed, with the exception of two notes, the entirety of the scored portions of "Choir" consist of notes separated by whole- and half-steps from their neighbors and is played with the same technique of singing and playing the flute simultaneously; the remainder of the composition calls for sections of improvisation that range between 90 and 180 seconds in length.

The Beastie Boys' expert, Dr. Lawrence Ferrara, concludes that the compositional elements of the sampled section do not represent the heart or the hook of the "Choir" composition, but rather are "simple, minimal and insignificant." The sampled section may be representative of the scored portions of the composition as Newton's expert's contend. Newton has failed to offer any evidence, however, to rebut Dr. Ferrara's testimony and to create a triable issue of fact on the key question, which is whether the sampled section is a qualitatively significant portion of the "Choir" composition as a whole. Instead, Newton's experts emphasize the uniqueness of the "Newton technique," which is found throughout the "Choir" composition and in Newton's other work.

Newton nevertheless maintains that the testimony of his experts creates a genuine issue of material fact on the substantiality of the copying. To the extent the expert testimony is relevant, it is not helpful to Newton. On the key question of whether the sample is quantitatively or qualitatively significant in relation to the composition as a whole, his experts are either silent or fail to distinguish between the sound recording, which was licensed, and the composition, which was not. Moreover, their testimony on the composition does not contain anything from which a reasonable jury could infer the segment's significance in relation to the composition as a whole. In contrast, Dr. Ferrara stated that the sampled excerpt from the "Choir" composition "is merely a common, trite, and generic three-note sequence, which lacks any distinct melodic, harmonic, rhythmic or structural elements." He described the sequence as "a common building block tool" that "has been used over and over again by major composers in the 20th century, particularly in the '60s and '70s, just prior to James Newton's usage."

Because Newton conceded that "Choir" and "Pass the Mic" "are substantially dissimilar in concept and feel, that is, in [their] overall thrust and meaning" and failed to offer any evidence to rebut Dr. Ferrara's testimony that the sampled section is not a quantitatively or qualitatively significant portion of the "Choir" composition, the Beastie Boys are entitled to prevail on summary judgment. On the undisputed facts of this case, we conclude that an average audience would not discern Newton's hand as a composer, apart from his talent as a performer, from Beastie Boys' use of the sample. The copying was not significant enough to constitute infringement. Beastie Boys' use of the "Choir" composition was de minimis. There is no genuine issue of material fact, and the grant of summary judgment was appropriate.

Conclusion

Because Beastie Boys' use of the sound recording was authorized, the sole basis of Newton's infringement action is his remaining copyright interest in the "Choir" composition. We hold that Beastie Boys' use of a brief segment of that composition, consisting of three notes separated by a half-step over a background C note, is not sufficient to sustain a claim for infringement of Newton's copyright in the composition "Choir". We affirm the district court's grant of summary judgment on the ground that Beastie Boys' use of the composition was de minimis and therefore not actionable.

DISSENT

GRABER, Circuit Judge, dissenting:

I respectfully dissent. The majority has laid out correctly the legal principles that apply in this case, and I agree with the majority's assumption that the sampled portion of "Choir" qualifies as "original" and therefore is copyrightable. Maj. op. at 15783. However, on the record before us, a finder of fact reasonably could find that Beastie Boys' use of the sampled material was not de minimis. Therefore, summary judgment is inappropriate.

As the majority observes, a use is de minimis only if an average audience would not recognize the appropriation. *Fisher v. Dees*, 794 F.2d 432, 434 n.2 (9th Cir. 1986). The majority is correct that James Newton's considerable skill adds many recognizable features to the performance sampled by Beastie Boys. Even after those features are "filtered out," however, the composition, standing alone, is distinctive enough for a fact-finder reasonably to conclude that an average audience would recognize the appropriation of the sampled segment and that Beastie Boys' use was therefore not de minimis.

Newton has presented evidence that the compositional elements of "Choir" are so compositionally distinct that a reasonable listener would recognize the sampled segment even if it were performed by the featured flautist of a middle school orchestra. It is useful to begin by observing that the majority's references to the sampled segment of "Choir" as a "3 note sequence" are overly simplified. The sampled segment is actually a three-note sequence sung above a fingered held C note, for a total of four separate tones. Even passages with relatively few notes may be qualitatively significant. The opening melody of Beethoven's Fifth Symphony is relatively simple and features only four notes, but it certainly is compositionally distinctive and recognizable.

. . .

Newton presented a letter from Professor Christopher Dobrian of the University of California, Irvine, which concludes:

> Applying traditional analysis to this brief excerpt from Newton's "Choir"—i.e., focusing solely on the notated pitches—a theorist could conclude (erroneously, in my opinion) that the excerpt contains an insignificant amount of information because it contains a simple "neighboring-tone" figure: C to D-flat and back to C. . . . If, on the other hand, one considers the special playing technique *described in the score* (holding one fingered note constant while singing the other pitches) and the resultant complex, expressive effect that results, it is clear that the "'unique expression" of this excerpt is not solely in the pitch choices, but is actually in those particular pitches performed in that particular way on that instrument. These components in this particular combination are not found anywhere else in the notated music literature, and they are *unique and distinctive* in their sonic/musical result.

Professor Dobrian is not talking about Newton's performance of the sampled portion. Rather, he is speaking of the distinctiveness of the underlying composition. The "playing technique" is not a matter of personal performance, but is a built-in feature of the score itself. In essence, Dobrian is stating that *any* flautist's performance of the sampled segment would be distinctive and recognizable, because the score itself is distinctive and recognizable.

... A fact-finder would be entitled to find either that the sampled passage is trivial and trite (Beastie Boys' expert) or, instead, that it is "unique and distinctive" in the musical literature (Newton's expert).

Because Newton has presented evidence establishing that reasonable ears differ over the qualitative significance of the composition of the sampled material, summary judgment is inappropriate in this case. Newton should be allowed to present his claims of infringement to a fact-finder. I therefore dissent from the majority's conclusion to the contrary.

––––––––––––––––––––––––––––

6. Sound Recordings, Broadcast Signals and Other Neighbouring Rights

International Bureau of WIPO, "Basic Notions of Copyright and Related Rights"

. . .

II. BASIC NOTIONS OF RELATED RIGHTS

52. This part of the lecture is dedicated to the subject of what are called "related rights," or more correctly, "rights related to copyright." The purpose of related rights is to protect the legal interests of certain persons and legal entities who either contribute to making works available to the public or produce subject matter which, will not qualify as "works" under the copyright systems of all countries, but express creativity or technical and organizational skill sufficient to justify recognition of a copyright-like property right. The law of related rights deems that the productions which result from the activities of such persons and entities are deserving of legal protection in themselves, as they are "related" to the protection of works of authorship under copyright. Some laws make clear, however, that the exercise of related rights should leave intact and in no way affect the protection of copyright.

53. Traditionally, related rights have been granted to three categories of beneficiaries: performers, producers of phonograms and broadcasting organizations. The expression "neighboring rights" is also used to refer to such rights. The rights of performers are recognized because their creative intervention is necessary to give life, for example, to musical works, dramatic and choreographic works, and motion pictures, and because they have a justifiable interest in legal protection of their individual interpretations. The rights of producers of phonograms are recognized because their creative, financial and organizational resources are necessary to make recorded sound available to the public in the form of commercial phonograms, and because of their legitimate interest in having the legal resources necessary to take action against unauthorized uses, whether it be through the making and distribution of unauthorized copies (piracy) or in the form of unauthorized broadcasting or communication to the public of their phonograms. Likewise, the rights of broadcasting organizations are recognized because of their role in making works available to the public, and in light of their justified interest in controlling the transmission and retransmission of their broadcasts.

54. The first organized international response to the need for legal protection of the three categories of related rights beneficiaries was the conclusion, in 1961, of the Rome Convention, or more specifically, the "International Convention for the Protection of Performers, Producers of Phonograms and Broadcasting Organizations." Unlike most international conventions, which follow in the wake of national legislation and are intended to synthesize existing laws, the Rome Convention was an attempt to establish international regulations in a new field where few national laws existed at the time. This meant that most States would have to draft and enact laws before adhering to the Convention. Since the

adoption of the Convention in 1961, a large number of States have legislated in matters related to the Convention, and a number of others are considering such legislation; indeed, the laws of many such States exceed the minimum levels of protection established by the Convention. While there is a widespread view that it is out-of-date and in need of revision or replacement by a new set of international norms in the field of related rights, the Rome Convention remains the international benchmark for protection in this field: for example, the European Union has required that all its Member States adhere to the Convention, and it was the basis for inclusion of provisions on the rights of performers, producers of phonograms and broadcasting organizations in the TRIPS Agreement (even though the levels of protection are not the same).

55. The rights granted to the three beneficiaries of related rights in national laws are as follows, although not all rights may be granted in the same law. *Performers* are provided the rights to prevent fixation (recording), broadcasting and communication to the public of their live performances without their consent, and the right to prevent reproduction of fixations of their performances under certain circumstances; the rights in respect of broadcasting and communication to the public may be in the form of equitable remuneration rather than a right to prevent. Due to the personal nature of their creations, some national laws also grant performers moral rights, which may be exercised to prevent unauthorized uses of their name and image, or modifications to their performances which present them in an unfavorable light. *Producers of phonograms* are granted the rights to authorize or prohibit reproduction, importation and distribution of their phonograms and copies thereof, and the right to equitable remuneration for broadcasting and communication to the public of phonograms. *Broadcasting organizations* are provided the rights to authorize or prohibit rebroadcasting, fixation and reproduction of their broadcasts. Under some laws, additional rights are granted: for example, in the countries of the European Union, producers of phonograms and performers are granted a right of rental in respect of phonograms (and, in respect of performers, audiovisual works), and some countries grant specific rights over cable transmissions. Under the TRIPS Agreement, likewise, producers of phonograms (as well as any other right holders in phonograms under national law) are granted a right of rental.

56. As in the case of copyright, the Rome Convention and national laws contain limitations on rights allowing, for example, private use, use of short excerpts in connection with the reporting of current events, and use for teaching or scientific research, of protected performances, phonograms, and broadcasts. Some countries allow the same kinds of limitations on related rights as their laws provide in connection with protection of copyright, including the possibility of non-voluntary licenses.

57. The duration of protection of related rights under the Rome Convention is 20 years from the end of the year (1) the fixation (recording) is made, in the case of phonograms and performances included in phonograms; (2) the performance took place, as regards performances not incorporated in phonograms; or (3) the broadcast took place, for broadcasts. In the TRIPS Agreement, the rights of

performers and producers of phonograms are to be protected for 50 years from the date of the fixation or the performance, and the rights of broadcasting organizations for 20 years from the date of the broadcast. It is to be noted that many national laws which protect related rights grant a longer term than the minima contained in the Rome Convention.

58.   In terms of enforcement of rights, remedies for infringement or violation of related rights are, in general, similar to those available to owners of copyright described above, namely, conservatory or provisional measures; civil remedies; criminal sanctions; measures to be taken at the border; and measures, remedies and sanctions against abuses in respect of technical devices.

See also sections 15 to 26 of the *Copyright Act.*

Sound v. Motion Picture Theatre Associations of Canada, Re, 2012 SCC 38 (S.C.C.)

Coram: McLachlin C.J. and LeBel, Deschamps, Fish, Abella, Rothstein, Cromwell, Moldaver and Karakatsanis JJ.

Reasons for Judgment: (paras. 1 to 53) LeBel J. (McLachlin C.J. and Deschamps, Fish, Abella, Rothstein, Cromwell, Moldaver and Karakatsanis JJ. concurring)

[1]   This appeal concerns the interpretation of the definition of "sound recording" in s. 2 of the Copyright Act, R.S.C. 1985, c. C-42 ("Act"), and specifically, the interpretation of the undefined term "soundtrack" used in that definition. The Act provides that performers and makers of sound recordings are entitled to remuneration for the performance in public or the communication to the public by telecommunication of their published sound recordings, except for retransmissions. Ultimately, the question this Court must answer is whether the broadcasting of sound recordings incorporated into the soundtrack of a cinematographic work can be subject to a tariff under the Act or whether such broadcasts are excluded by virtue of the definition of "sound recording" in s. 2.

[2]   The appellant, Re:Sound, argues that the word "soundtrack" as used in s. 2 refers only to the aggregate of sounds accompanying a cinematographic work and not to the soundtrack's constituent parts. In its view, since pre-existing sound recordings incorporated into a soundtrack are constituent parts of the soundtrack and not the aggregate of sounds accompanying the work, they do not fall within the scope of the word "soundtrack" as used in s. 2.

[3]   For the reasons that follow, the appeal must be dismissed. A proper application of the principles of statutory interpretation leads to the conclusion that the appellant's argument is untenable.

II.   Facts and Judicial History

A. *Background*

[4] Re: Sound is a collective society authorized by the Copyright Board of Canada ("Board") to collect equitable remuneration pursuant to s. 19(1) of the Act for the performance in public or communication to the public by telecommunication of published sound recordings of musical works.

[5] On March 28, 2008, Re:Sound — formerly the Neighbouring Rights Collective of Canada — filed two tariff proposals (Tariffs 7 and 9), under s. 67.1(1) of the Act, for the performance in public or the communication to the public by telecommunication, in Canada, of published sound recordings embodying musical works and performers' performances of such works. In Tariff 7, it claimed royalties for the use of sound recordings embodied in a movie by motion picture theatres and other establishments exhibiting movies. Tariff 9 targeted the use of sound recordings in programs broadcast by commercial over-the-air, pay, specialty and other television services.

[6] The respondents objected to the proposed tariffs on the ground that the Act's definition of "sound recording" excludes soundtracks of cinematographic works. The definition of "sound recording" in s. 2 reads as follows:

> "sound recording" means a recording, fixed in any material form, consisting of sounds, whether or not of a performance of a work, but excludes any soundtrack of a cinematographic work where it accompanies the cinematographic work;

[7] Re: Sound submitted that a proper interpretation of the definition of "sound recording" does not exclude a pre-existing sound recording that is incorporated into a soundtrack. Rather, it argued, the purpose of the exclusion was to combine rights in the visual features of a cinematographic production with rights in the audio features of the same cinematographic production, and to protect those rights in a new work defined as a "cinematographic work".

[8] According to the respondents, Re:Sound had no legal claim to equitable remuneration under the Act by virtue of the plain meaning of the word "soundtrack" used in the definition of "sound recording". The respondents sought a determination of the following preliminary issue:

> Is anyone entitled to equitable remuneration pursuant to section 19 of the Copyright Act when a published sound recording is part of the soundtrack that accompanies (a) a motion picture that is performed in public [or] (b) a television program that is communicated to the public by telecommunication?

The Board answered "no", refused to certify the tariffs and ordered them struck from the proposed statement of royalties as published in the Canada Gazette, Part I, on May 31, 2008. On judicial review, the Federal Court of Appeal upheld that decision. Re:Sound now appeals to this Court.

. . .

[25] The main issue in this appeal involves the application of well-known principles of statutory interpretation. The question this Court must resolve is the

following: Do pre-existing sound recordings incorporated into a soundtrack fall within the meaning of the undefined term "soundtrack" used in the definition of "sound recording" in s. 2 of the Act? In other words, in view of the fact that only a "sound recording" can be the subject of a tariff under s. 19, can the reproduction of a pre-existing sound recording that is part of a soundtrack of a cinematographic work be the subject of a tariff when the soundtrack accompanies the cinematographic work?

[26] For the reasons that follow, I conclude that, irrespective of the standard of review, the Board was correct in its interpretation of the word "soundtrack". Consequently, a pre-existing sound recording that is part of a soundtrack cannot be the subject of a tariff when the soundtrack accompanies the cinematographic work.

. . .

[28] Under s. 19 of the Act, the appellant is entitled to collect equitable remuneration on behalf of performers and makers of sound recordings when their recordings are performed in public or communicated to the public by telecommunication. The right to collect these royalties was added to the Act in 1997 as part of a package of "neighbouring rights" in sound recordings which can be distinguished from traditional copyrights held by creators of musical works such as composers and lyricists (S.C. 1997, c. 24). These new neighbouring rights were introduced by Parliament to comply with Canada's obligations under the Rome Convention. In addition to Article 12 of the Rome Convention, which establishes the right to equitable remuneration where a published phonogram "is used directly for broadcasting or for any communication to the public", Article 10 provides that "[p]roducers of phonograms shall enjoy the right to authorise or prohibit the direct or indirect reproduction of their phonograms."

[29] As I mentioned above, the right to collect royalties on behalf of performers and makers of sound recordings, although provided for in s. 19, is dependent on the definition of "sound recording" in s. 2 of the Act. This definition has a bearing on the limits of the right. Unless what is being performed or communicated to the public by telecommunication is a "sound recording", the right to collect royalties on that performance or communication will not be triggered.

[30] The relevant sections of the Act read:

2. In this Act, . . .

"sound recording" means a recording, fixed in any material form, consisting of sounds, whether or not of a performance of a work, but excludes any soundtrack of a cinematographic work where it accompanies the cinematographic work;

. . .

19. (1) Where a sound recording has been published, the performer and maker are entitled, subject to section 20, to be paid equitable remuneration for its performance in public or its communication to the public by telecommunication, except for any retransmission.

(2) For the purpose of providing the remuneration mentioned in subsection (1), a person who performs a published sound recording in public or communicates it to the public by telecommunication is liable to pay royalties

(a) in the case of a sound recording of a musical work, to the collective society authorized under Part VII to collect them; . . .

[31] As I noted above, the word "soundtrack" used in the definition of "sound recording" is not defined.

D. *Statutory Interpretation*

[32] This Court has reiterated on many occasions that the object of statutory interpretation is to establish Parliament's intent by reading the words of the provisions in question in their entire context and in their grammatical and ordinary sense, harmoniously with the scheme of the Act, the object of the Act and the intention of Parliament (Rizzo & Rizzo Shoes Ltd. (Re), [1998] 1 S.C.R. 27, citing E. A. Driedger, Construction of Statutes (2nd ed. 1983), at p. 87).

[33] Although statutes may be interpreted purposively, the interpretation must nevertheless be consistent with the words chosen by Parliament. Moreover, the legislative history can be of great assistance in discerning Parliament's intent with respect to a particular wording in a statute.

[34] In the instant case, the statutory interpretation process must begin with the words of s. 2.

[35] According to s. 2, a "sound recording" is a recording consisting of sounds, "but excludes any soundtrack of a cinematographic work where it accompanies the cinematographic work". Therefore, a "soundtrack" is a "sound recording" except where it accompanies the motion picture. Otherwise, the exclusion would be superfluous.

[36] When it accompanies the motion picture, therefore, the recording of sounds that constitutes a soundtrack does not fall within the definition of "sound recording" and does not trigger the application of s. 19. A pre-existing sound recording is made up of recorded sounds. The Act does not specify that a pre-existing recording of "sounds" that accompanies a motion picture cannot be a "soundtrack" within the meaning of s. 2. In my view, a pre-existing sound recording cannot be excluded from the meaning of "soundtrack" unless Parliament expressed an intention to do so in the Act. It could have done this by, for example, excluding only "the aggregate of sounds in a soundtrack".

[37] The legislative history confirms this interpretation.

[38] In its decision in the case at bar, the Board referred to some instructive comments made at the Standing Committee on Canadian Heritage hearing with respect to the provisions at issue. It quoted these comments and summarized their importance as follows (at para. 36):

. . . the definition of "sound recording" was amended at the Committee stage so as to ensure that while a soundtrack would not be a sound recording and therefore would not attract equitable remuneration when accompanying a movie or television program, the soundtrack would be a sound recording and would attract equitable remuneration when it was played separate from the movie or program. The following comments made at the Standing Committee on Canadian Heritage hearing are instructive:

> Mr. Abbott [M.P.]: [. . .] As [the bill] stands at present, a soundtrack that is now available on a CD would not qualify for rights. Is that right?
>
> Mr. Bouchard [Heritage]: As it is now.
>
> Mr. Abbott: However, the addition of the words "where it accompanies" would then qualify it for neighbouring rights. Is that correct?
>
> Ms. Katz: Yes, that's correct.
>
> [. . .]
>
> Mr. Richstone [Justice]:

I'd just like to point out that, as you see in the bill, you have the words "integral part". That raises a lot of concern on a technical level with a lot of people. What is the integral part? Is that integral part. . .? Are you going to apply a conceptual test, or are you going to apply a physical test?

Often the soundtrack of a film is not physically an integral part of the film if it's played at the same time. So the word that is chosen is "accompanies". You find that word in U.S. legislation and in other Commonwealth legislation.

When the soundtrack accompanies a cinematographic work, it is a part of the cinematographic work. When it doesn't accompany a cinematographic work — i.e., it is separately marketed, sold, exploited, performed, whatever, as a sound recording — then it's protected as a sound recording. [Emphasis deleted; text in brackets in original.]

[39] These comments confirm that the word "accompanies" qualifies a soundtrack on a CD for remuneration under s. 19, whereas such a soundtrack would not otherwise attract remuneration under that section. It is difficult to imagine that the comment regarding "a soundtrack that is now available on a CD" might concern a CD containing "the entire collection of sounds accompanying the movie as a whole", which is the interpretation of "soundtrack" the appellant urges this Court to adopt. If the appellant's interpretation is correct, the CD in question would have to include not only the pre-existing recordings, but also all the dialogue, sound effects, ambient music and noises in the motion picture. It could not contain only the pre-existing sound recordings used in the movie.

[40] The appellant's interpretation must be rejected.

E.   *Comparative Law and International Rules*

[41] The appellant argues that support for its position can be found in foreign jurisprudence. In actual fact, the foreign jurisprudence makes it clear that significant differences exist between Canadian copyright legislation and the foreign legislation on which those decisions are based.

[42] The U.K. Copyright Act, 1956, c. 74, contains a definition for "sound recording" that is fundamentally different from the definition in the Canadian Act. The relevant portion of s. 12(9) reads,

> In this Act "sound recording" means the aggregate of the sounds embodied in, and capable of being reproduced by means of, a record of any description, other than a sound-track associated with a cinematograph film;

[43] The Australian Copyright Act 1968, No. 63, defines "sound recording" as "the aggregate of the sounds embodied in a record" (s. 10). "Cinematograph film" is defined as

> the aggregate of the visual images embodied in an article or thing so as to be capable by the use of that article or thing . . . and includes the aggregate of the sounds embodied in a sound-track associated with such visual images; [s. 10]

[44] These definitions — unlike the one in the Canadian Act — include the concept of an "aggregate" of sounds. The distinction between the Canadian and foreign legislation is clear enough to discount any persuasive value that the cases in which this concept was applied might otherwise have had.

[45] The decision the appellant relies on most heavily is that of the High Court of Australia in *Phonographic Performance Co. of Australia Ltd. v. Federation of Australian Commercial Television Stations*, [1998] HCA 39, 195 C.L.R. 158. In that case, the court was faced with a similar issue. The court held, on the basis of the definitions in the Australian Act, that "[w]hat the Act deems not to be a sound recording is the aggregate of sounds that is recorded in a particular form: a sound-track" (para. 22 (emphasis added)). However, the legislation in question in that case was different and, what is more, the court was deeply divided on the issue, with two judges dissenting.

[46] In the case at bar, the appellant's arguments are substantially the same as the ones advanced in the Australian case, and it asks this Court to reach the same conclusion as the majority of the High Court of Australia. However, that case is not a precedent that this Court is required to follow, nor is it compelling here. As the Court of Appeal noted in the instant case, the foreign cases the appellant relies on are of no assistance and serve only to highlight the differences in the legislation.

[47] The appellant also argues that the Act is incompatible with the Rome Convention.

[48] As I mentioned above, the Rome Convention provides that "[p]roducers of phonograms shall enjoy the right to authorise or prohibit the direct or indirect reproduction of their phonograms" (Article 10). The appellant submits that producers of soundtracks would be denied this right if a pre-existing sound recording is deemed to be a soundtrack and that the effect of the Court of Appeal's interpretation is therefore that the Act is in breach of the Rome Convention.

[49] The appellant is overlooking Article 3 of the Rome Convention, which defines a "phonogram" as "any exclusively aural fixation of sounds of a

performance or of other sounds". Thus, excluding a soundtrack from the definition of "sound recording" where the soundtrack accompanies the cinematographic work is consistent with the Rome Convention, since this exclusion is not for "exclusively aural fixation[s]".

[50] Contrary to the appellant's assertion, a "ripped" (reproduced) recording of a pre-existing sound recording that accompanies a motion picture would be subject to copyright. As the Court of Appeal pointed out, once a pre-existing sound recording is extracted from a soundtrack accompanying a cinematographic work, it once again attracts the protection offered for sound recordings. There is therefore no violation of the Rome Convention.

[51] As this Court noted in *National Corn Growers Assn. v. Canada (Import Tribunal)*, [1990] 2 S.C.R. 1324: ". . . where the text of the domestic law lends itself to it, one should also strive to expound an interpretation which is consonant with the relevant international obligations" (p. 1371). In the case at bar, the Board's interpretation is consonant with Canada's obligations under the Rome Convention.

IV. Conclusion

[52] The Board made no error in finding that the word "soundtrack" includes pre-existing sound recordings and that such recordings are accordingly excluded from the definition of "sound recording" when they accompany a cinematographic work. This interpretation of the word "soundtrack" is consistent with the scheme of the Act, the intention of Parliament and Canada's international obligations. Contrary to the appellant's suggestion, it does not lead to absurd results.

[53] For these reasons, the appeal is dismissed with costs.

Appeal dismissed with costs.

Reference re Broadcasting Act, S.C. 1991 (Canada), 2012 SCC 68 (S.C.C.)
(pre-emption)

Coram: McLachlin C.J. and LeBel, Deschamps, Fish, Abella, Rothstein, Cromwell, Moldaver and Karakatsanis JJ.

Reasons for Judgment: (paras. 1 to 83) Rothstein J. (McLachlin C.J. and LeBel, Fish and Moldaver JJ. concurring)

Joint Dissenting Reasons: (paras. 84 to 126) Abella and Cromwell JJ. (Deschamps and Karakatsanis JJ. concurring)

[1] The Canadian Radio-television and Telecommunications Commission ("CRTC") has authority under the *Broadcasting Act*, S.C. 1991, c. 11, to regulate and supervise the Canadian broadcasting system. In 2010, the CRTC sought to introduce a market-based value for signal regulatory regime, whereby private local television stations (referred to as such or as "broadcasters") could

choose to negotiate direct compensation for the retransmission of their signals by broadcasting distribution undertakings ("BDUs"), such as cable and satellite companies. The new regime would empower broadcasters to authorize or prohibit BDUs from retransmitting their programming services. The reference question in this appeal is whether the CRTC has jurisdiction to implement the proposed regime.

[2] The *Broadcasting Act* grants the CRTC wide discretion to implement regulations and issue licences with a view to furthering Canadian broadcasting policy as set out in the *Broadcasting Act*. However, these powers must be exercised within the statutory framework of the *Broadcasting Act*, and also the larger framework including interrelated statutes. This scheme includes the *Copyright Act*, R.S.C. 1985, c. C-42: Bell ExpressVu Limited Partnership v. Rex, 2002 SCC 42, [2002] 2 S.C.R. 559, at paras. 44-52. As such, the CRTC, as a subordinate legislative body, cannot enact a regulation or attach conditions to licences under the *Broadcasting Act* that conflict with provisions of another related statute.

[3] In my opinion, the value for signal regime does just that and is therefore ultra vires.

II. Facts and Procedural History

[4] Broadcasters acquire, create and produce television programming, and are licensed by the CRTC to serve a certain geographic area within the reach of their respective signal transmitters. BDUs, such as cable or satellite television service providers, pick up the over-the-air signals of broadcasters and distribute them to the BDUs' subscribers for a fee. Even though broadcasters' signals are free to anyone equipped with a television and an antenna, more than 90 percent of Canadians receive these signals as part of their cable service (transcript, at p. 2).

[5] BDUs must be licensed by the CRTC pursuant to s. 9 of the *Broadcasting Act*. Under the current regulatory model, the CRTC requires BDUs to provide certain benefits to broadcasters, in the nature of mandatory carriage and contributions to a local programming improvement fund accessible by certain local television stations. However, the broadcasters do not receive fees directly from the BDUs for the carriage of their signals.

[6] As noted by the Federal Court of Appeal ("FCA"), 2011 FCA 64, 413 N.R. 312, at para. 6, the CRTC has concluded that the existing model does not adequately deal with recent changes to the broadcasting business environment, which have caused advertising revenues for broadcasters to fall, while the revenues of BDUs have increased. As the FCA observed, the CRTC has concluded that this has resulted in a significant shift in their relative market positions and a financial crisis for broadcasters.

[7] As a solution, the CRTC seeks to implement what it terms a "value for signal regime". This regime would permit broadcasters to negotiate with BDUs the

terms upon which the BDUs may redistribute their signals. These are its main features:

- Broadcasters would have the right, every three years, to choose either to negotiate with BDUs for compensation for the right to retransmit the broadcaster's programming services, or to continue to operate under the existing regulatory regime;

- A broadcaster who participates in the value for signal regime would forego all existing regulatory protections, including, for example, mandatory distribution of its signals as part of the basic package of BDU television services, and the right to require a BDU to delete a non-Canadian program and substitute it with the comparable program of the broadcaster, where the two programs are simultaneously broadcast and retransmitted by the BDU;

- The CRTC would only involve itself in the negotiations for the value for signal regime if the parties do not negotiate in good faith or if they request the CRTC to arbitrate;

- If no agreement is reached between the broadcaster and the BDU on the value of the distribution of the local television's programming services, the broadcaster could require the BDU to delete any program owned by the broadcaster or for which it has acquired exclusive contractual exhibition rights from all signals distributed by the BDU in the broadcaster's market.

The proposed regime is fully described in Broadcasting Regulatory Policy CRTC 2010-167 (2010) ("2010 Policy") (A.R., vol. II, at p. 1).

[8] The BDUs disputed the jurisdiction of the CRTC to implement such a regime on the basis that it conflicts with specific provisions in the *Copyright Act*. As a result, the CRTC referred the following question to the FCA:

> Is the Commission empowered, pursuant to its mandate under the *Broadcasting Act*, to establish a regime to enable private local television stations to choose to negotiate with broadcasting distribution undertakings a fair value in exchange for the distribution of the programming services broadcast by those local television stations?

. . .

B.   *The Larger Statutory Scheme — Conflict with the Copyright Act*

(1)   Connection Between the Broadcasting Act and the Copyright Act

[34]   Even if jurisdiction for the proposed value for signal regime could be found within the text of the *Broadcasting Act*, that would not resolve the question in this reference as the *Broadcasting Act* is part of a larger statutory scheme that includes the *Copyright Act* and the Telecommunications Act. As Sunny Handa et al. explain, the Telecommunications Act and the Radiocommunication Act,

R.S.C. 1985, c. R-2, are the main statutes governing carriage, and the *Broadcasting Act* deals with content, which is "the object of 'carriage'" (S. Handa et al., Communications Law in Canada (loose-leaf), at §3.21). In Bell ExpressVu, at para. 52, Justice Iacobucci also considered the *Copyright Act* when interpreting a provision of the Radiocommunication Act, saying that "there is a connection between these two statutes". Considering that the *Broadcasting Act* and the Radiocommunication Act are clearly part of the same interconnected statutory scheme, it follows, in my view, that there is a connection between the *Broadcasting Act* and the *Copyright Act* as well. The three Acts (plus the Telecommunications Act) are part of an interrelated scheme.

[35] Indeed, the *Broadcasting Act* regulates "program[s]" that are "broadcast" for reception by the Canadian public (see s. 2(1), definitions of "broadcasting" and of "program"), with a view to implementing the Canadian broadcasting policy described in s. 3(1) of the Act. Generally speaking, "[t]he *Broadcasting Act* is primarily concerned with the programmed content delivered by means of radio waves or other means of telecommunication to the public" (Handa at al., at §5.5).

[36] The *Copyright Act* is concerned both with encouraging creativity and providing reasonable access to the fruits of creative endeavour. These objectives are furthered by a carefully balanced scheme that creates exclusive economic rights for different categories of copyright owners in works or other protected subject matter, typically in the nature of a statutory monopoly to prevent anyone from exploiting the work in specified ways without the copyright owner's consent. It also provides user rights such as fair dealing and specific exemptions that enable the general public or specific classes of users to access protected material under certain conditions. (See, e.g., *Théberge v. Galerie d'Art du Petit Champlain inc.*, 2002 SCC 34, [2002] 2 S.C.R. 336, at paras. 11-12 and 30; *Mattel, Inc. v. 3894207 Canada Inc.*, 2006 SCC 22, [2006] 1 S.C.R. 772, at para. 21; D. Vaver, *Intellectual Property Law: Copyright, Patents, Trade-marks* (2nd ed. 2011), at pp. 34 and 56.) Among the categories of subject matter protected by copyright are the rights of broadcasters in communication signals (see ss. 2 "copyright" and 21 of the *Copyright Act*). In addition, "program[s]" within the meaning of the *Broadcasting Act*, are often pre-recorded original content which may constitute protected works, namely "dramatic work[s]" or "compilation[s]" thereof, under the *Copyright Act*: see, e.g., discussion in J. S. McKeown, Fox on Canadian Law of Copyright and Industrial Designs (4th ed. loose-leaf), at para. 15:3(a).

[37] Although the Acts have different aims, their subject matters will clearly overlap in places. As Parliament is presumed to intend "harmony, coherence, and consistency between statutes dealing with the same subject matter" (*R. v. Ulybel Enterprises Ltd.*, 2001 SCC 56, [2001] 2 S.C.R. 867, at para. 52; Sullivan, at pp. 325-26), two provisions applying to the same facts will be given effect in accordance with their terms so long as they do not conflict.

[38] Accordingly, where multiple interpretations of a provision are possible, the presumption of coherence requires that the two statutes be read together so as

to avoid conflict. Lamer C.J. wrote in *Pointe-Claire (City) v. Quebec (Labour Court)*, [1997] 1 S.C.R. 1015, at para. 61:

There is no doubt that the principle that statutes dealing with similar subjects must be presumed to be coherent means that interpretations favouring harmony among those statutes should prevail over discordant ones.

[39] In addition, "[o]rdinarily, . . . an Act of Parliament must prevail over inconsistent or conflicting subordinate legislation" (Friends of the Oldman River Society v. Canada (Minister of Transport), [1992] 1 S.C.R. 3, at p. 38). Consequently, as it would be impermissible for the CRTC, a subordinate legislative body, to implement subordinate legislation in conflict with another Act of Parliament, the open-ended jurisdiction-conferring provisions of the Broadcasting Act cannot be interpreted as allowing the CRTC to create conflicts with the Copyright Act.

[40] It is therefore necessary to first determine if a conflict arises.

(2) Types of Conflict

[41] For the purposes of statutory interpretation, conflict is defined narrowly. It has been said that overlapping provisions will be given effect according to their terms, unless they "cannot stand together" (*Toronto Railway Co. v. Paget* (1909), 42 S.C.R. 488, at p. 499 per Anglin J.).

[42] In *Lévis (City) v. Fraternité des policiers de Lévis Inc.*, 2007 SCC 14, [2007] 1 S.C.R. 591, the Court was concerned with incoherence between provisions of two statutes emanating from the same legislature. Bastarache J., writing for the majority, defined conflict, at para. 47:

> The test for determining whether an unavoidable conflict exists is well stated by Professor Côté in his treatise on statutory interpretation:
>
>> According to case law, <u>two statutes are not repugnant simply because they deal with the same subject: application of one must implicitly or explicitly preclude application of the other</u>.
>
> (P.-A. Côté, *The Interpretation of Legislation in Canada* (3rd ed. 2000), at p. 350)
>
> Thus, a law which provides for the expulsion of a train passenger who fails to pay the fare is not in conflict with another law that only provides for a fine because the application of one law did not exclude the application of the other (*Toronto Railway Co. v. Paget* (1909), 42 S.C.R. 488). <u>Unavoidable conflicts, on the other hand, occur when two pieces of legislation are directly contradictory or where their concurrent application would lead to unreasonable or absurd results</u>. A law, for example, which allows for the extension of a time limit for filing an appeal only before it expires is in direct conflict with another law which allows for an extension to be granted after the time limit has expired (*Massicotte v. Boutin,* [1969] S.C.R. 818). [Emphasis added.]

[43] Absurdity also refers to situations where the practical effect of one piece of legislation would be to frustrate the *purpose* of the other (*Lévis*, at para. 54; Sullivan, at p. 330).

[44] This view is not inconsistent with the approach to conflict adopted in federalism jurisprudence. For the purposes of the doctrine of paramountcy, this Court has recognized two types of conflict. Operational conflict arises when there is an *impossibility of compliance* with both provisions. The other type of conflict is incompatibility of purpose. In the latter type, there is no impossibility of dual compliance with the letter of both laws; rather, the conflict arises because applying one provision would frustrate the purpose intended by Parliament in another. See, e.g., *British Columbia (Attorney General) v. Lafarge Canada Inc.*, 2007 SCC 23, [2007] 2 S.C.R. 86, at paras. 77 and 84.

[45] Cases applying the doctrine of federal paramountcy present some similarities in defining conflict as either operational conflict or conflict of purpose (*Friends of the Oldman River Society*, at p. 38). These definitions of legislative conflict are therefore helpful in interpreting two statutes emanating from the same legislature. The CRTC's powers to impose licensing conditions and make regulations should be understood as constrained by each type of conflict. Namely, in seeking to achieve its objects, the CRTC may not choose means that either operationally conflict with specific provisions of the *Broadcasting Act*, the *Radiocommunication Act*, the *Telecommunications Act*, or the *Copyright Act*; or which would be incompatible with the purposes of those Acts.

(3) The Allocation of Rights Under the Copyright Act

(a) *Section 21*

[46] The BDUs contend that the CRTC's proposed value for signal regime conflicts with the retransmission regimes specifically established in ss. 21(1)(c) and 31(2) of the *Copyright Act*.

[47] It is necessary to describe the *Copyright Act*'s regimes at some length. It will become apparent from this description that, in my respectful view, the analysis of the *Copyright Act* conducted by the majority of the FCA is problematic.

[48] The BDUs first submit that s. 21(1) of the *Copyright Act* conflicts with the value for signal regime. Section 21(1) grants broadcasters a limited copyright in the over-the-air signals they broadcast. This copyright gives the broadcaster the sole right to authorize or to do four acts in relation to a communication signal or any substantial part of it:

> (a) to fix it;
>
> (b) to reproduce any fixation of it that was made without the broadcaster's consent;
>
> (c) to authorize another broadcaster to retransmit it to the public simultaneously with its broadcast; and
>
> (d) in the case of a television communication signal, to perform it in a place open to the public on payment of an entrance fee, and to authorize any act described in paragraph (a), (b) or (d).

[49] The aspect relevant for this appeal is in para. (c). Under this paragraph, a broadcaster has the sole right to authorize another broadcaster to retransmit

simultaneously a communication signal. Section 2 of the *Copyright Act* defines "broadcaster" as

> a body that, in the course of operating a broadcasting undertaking, broadcasts a communication signal in accordance with the law of the country in which the broadcasting undertaking is carried on, but excludes a body whose primary activity in relation to communication signals is their retransmission.

[50] The underlined portion of the definition refers to BDUs. BDUs are not a "broadcaster" within the meaning of the *Copyright Act* because their primary activity in relation communication signals is their retransmission. Thus, the broadcaster's s. 21(1)(c) right to authorize, or not authorize, another broadcaster to simultaneously retransmit its signals does not apply against BDUs. In other words, under s. 21 of the *Copyright Act*, a broadcaster's exclusive right does not include a right to authorize or prohibit a BDU from retransmitting its communication signals.

(b) *Section 31*

[51] In addition to their s. 21 rights in communication signals, broadcasters may hold other retransmission rights under the *Copyright Act*. As mentioned, a pre-recorded television program is often copyright subject matter that can be protected as an original "dramatic work" or a "compilation" thereof (s. 2 of the *Copyright Act*). The broadcaster, as a corporation, may hold copyright in the pre-recorded program or compilation of programs carried in its signals, either as the employer of the author of such a work or as an assignee of copyright from the original author.

[52] The *Copyright Act* seeks to regulate the economic rights in communication signals, as well as the retransmission of works by BDUs. The BDUs contend that the value for signal regime would conflict with the retransmission regime for works set out in s. 31 of the *Copyright Act*. The proposed regime would enable broadcasters to control the simultaneous retransmission of programs, by granting them the right to require deletion of any program in which they own or control the copyright from all signals distributed by the BDU, if no agreement is reached on compensation for the simultaneous retransmission of the broadcaster's programming services.

[53] The *Copyright Act* in s. 3(1)(f) confers on the owner of copyright in a work the exclusive right to communicate it to the public by telecommunication. Section 3(1)(f) provides:

> 3. (1) For the purposes of this Act, "copyright", in relation to a work, means the sole right . . .
>
> (f) in the case of any literary, dramatic, musical or artistic work, to communicate the work to the public by telecommunication,
>
> . . .

"Telecommunication", in s. 2 of the *Act*, is broadly defined to include any transmission of . . . intelligence of any nature by wire, radio, visual, optical or other electromagnetic system.

[54] These general words would at first blush confer on the copyright owner, including a broadcaster in that capacity, the right to control the retransmission of the works in which it holds copyright. However, s. 31(2) of the *Copyright Act* proceeds in detailed fashion to circumscribe the right of copyright owners to control the retransmission of literary, dramatic, musical or artistic works carried in signals. "Signal" is defined for the purposes of s. 31(2) to mean "a signal that carries a literary, dramatic, musical or artistic work and is transmitted for free reception by the public by a terrestrial radio or terrestrial television station" (see s. 31(1)). Section 31(1) defines "retransmitter" as "a person who performs a function comparable to that of a cable retransmission system . . .".

[55] Section 31(2) provides:

> It is not an infringement of copyright for a retransmitter to communicate to the public by telecommunication any literary, dramatic, musical or artistic work if
>
> > (a) the communication is a retransmission of a local or distant signal;
> >
> > (b) the retransmission is lawful under the *Broadcasting Act*;
> >
> > (c) the signal is retransmitted simultaneously and without alteration, except as otherwise required or permitted by or under the laws of Canada;
> >
> > (d) in the case of the retransmission of a distant signal, the retransmitter has paid any royalties, and complied with any terms and conditions, fixed under this Act; and
> >
> > (e) the retransmitter complies with the applicable conditions, if any, referred to in paragraph (3)(b).

[56] Read together, ss. 31(1) and 31(2) create an exception to the exclusive right of the copyright owners of literary, dramatic, musical or artistic works to control the communication of their works to the public by telecommunication. The exception, or user's right, in effect, entitles BDUs to retransmit those works without the copyright owners' consent, where the conditions set out in paras. (a) through (e) are met. Paragraph (b) provides that the retransmission must be lawful under the *Broadcasting Act*. I will come back to the meaning of this particular condition.

[57] In the case of works carried in distant signals only, the section provides copyright owners with a right to receive royalties as payment for the simultaneous retransmission of those works by a BDU. The royalties are determined by the Copyright Board, on the basis of tariffs filed by collective societies, pursuant to the regime detailed in ss. 71 to 74 of the *Copyright Act*. Under s. 31(2), works carried in local signals attract no royalty when retransmitted in accordance with all conditions of that section. The Governor in Council has defined "local signal" as the signal of a terrestrial station reaching all or a portion of the service area of a retransmitter. A "distant signal" is a signal that is not a local signal. See ss. 1 and 2 of Local Signal and Distant Signal Regulations, SOR/89-254.

[58] It bears underlining that, in the case of works carried in both local and distant signals, the copyright owner has no right to prohibit the simultaneous retransmission of the work; recourse is limited to receiving through a collective society the prescribed royalty, but only for the simultaneous retransmission of works carried in distant signals (ss. 76(1) and 76(3) of the *Copyright Act*). On the one hand, the copyright owner is granted a general right to retransmit the work. This retransmission right is part of the right, under s. (3)(1)(f), to communicate the work by telecommunication to the public. On the other hand, the owner's general right to retransmit is restricted by a carve-out in s. 31(2) of the *Copyright Act*, which effectively grants to a specific class of retransmitters two retransmission rights. The first right lets these users simultaneously retransmit without a royalty payment, works carried in a local signal. The second right lets them simultaneously retransmit works carried in distant signals, but only subject to the payment of royalties under a form of compulsory licence regime (*Copyright Act*, s. 31(2)(a) and (d)). Both user rights are, subject to s. 31(2), beyond the owner's control.

[59] In sum, under the *Copyright Act*'s retransmission regimes for communication signals and for works:

- Broadcasters have a limited exclusive right in their *signals* (s. 21);

- Broadcasters do not have an exclusive right in *signals* against BDUs;

- BDUs have the right to simultaneously retransmit works carried in local signals without authorization and without payment to the copyright owner;

- Owners of copyright in those works, including broadcasters in that capacity, do not have the right to block retransmission of local or distant signals carrying their works;

- The Copyright Board has jurisdiction to value the compulsory licence royalty for the simultaneous retransmission of works carried in distant signals;

(4) Finding Conflict

[60] The CRTC's proposed value for signal regime would enable broadcasters to negotiate compensation for the retransmission by BDUs of their signals or programming services, regardless of whether or not they carry copyright protected "work[s]", and regardless of the fact that any such works are carried in local signals for which the *Copyright Act* provides no compensation. Importantly, contrary to the retransmission regimes of the *Copyright Act*, the value for signal regime proposed by the CRTC would grant individual broadcasters, should they elect to be governed by this regime, the *right to prohibit* the simultaneous retransmission of their programs.

[61] As mentioned, the presumption of coherence between related Acts of Parliament requires avoiding an interpretation of a provision that would introduce conflict into the statutory scheme. In this case, the presumption of coherence

requires that if the CRTC's proposed regulatory regime would create such conflict with the specific expressions of Parliament's intent under the *Copyright Act*, it must be ultra vires. Sections 21 and 31(2) of the *Copyright Act* are relevant.

[62] First, the value for signal regime conflicts with s. 21(1) of the *Copyright Act* because it would grant broadcasters a retransmission authorization right against BDUs that was withheld by the scheme of the *Copyright Act*.

[63] Looking only at the letter of the provision, s. 21 expressly speaks only to the relationship between a broadcaster and another broadcaster and not the relationship between a broadcaster and a retransmitter. As such, it is arguable that nothing in s. 21 purports to prevent another regulator from regulating the terms for carriage of a broadcaster's television signal by the BDUs, leaving it open to the CRTC, provided it is authorized to do so under the *Broadcasting Act*, to establish a value for signal regime without conflicting with s. 21.

[64] However, s. 21 cannot be considered devoid of its purpose. This Court has characterized the purpose of the *Copyright Act* as a balance between authors' and users' rights. The same balance applies to broadcasters and users. In *Théberge*, Binnie J. recognized that the *Copyright Act*

> . . . is usually presented as a balance between promoting the public interest in the encouragement and dissemination of works of the arts and intellect and obtaining a just reward for the creator (or, more accurately, to prevent someone other than the creator from appropriating whatever benefits may be generated). [para. 30]

(See also *CCH Canadian Ltd. v. Law Society of Upper Canada*, 2004 SCC 13, [2004] 1 S.C.R. 339, at paras. 10 and 23.)

[65] This point was reiterated in *Society of Composers, Authors and Music Publishers of Canada v. Canadian Assn. of Internet Providers*, 2004 SCC 45, [2004] 2 S.C.R. 427. In that case, the Court considered whether, for the purposes of the *Copyright Act*, Internet Service Providers "communicate [works] to the public" when such works are requested by their subscribers — thereby infringing copyright in such works. The Court was required to interpret s. 2.4(1)(b) of the *Copyright Act*, which provides that

> a person whose only act in respect of the communication of a work or other subject-matter to the public consists of providing the means of telecommunication necessary for another person to so communicate the work or other subject-matter does not communicate that work or other subject-matter to the public.

[66] In rejecting the argument that s. 2.4(1)(b), as an exemption, should be read narrowly, the majority, *per* Binnie J., held that

> . . . under the *Copyright Act*, the rights of the copyright owner and the limitations on those rights should be read together to give "the fair and balanced reading that befits remedial legislation". [para. 88]

The Court recognized that "[s]ection 2.4(1)(b) is not a loophole but an important element of the balance struck by the statutory copyright scheme" (para. 89). The Court therefore confirmed its earlier teaching in *Théberge* that the policy balance established by the *Copyright Act* is maintained also by "giving due weight to [the] limited nature" of the rights of creators (Théberge, at para. 31).

[67] In my view, s. 21(1) represents the expression by Parliament of the appropriate balance to be struck between broadcasters' rights in their communication signals and the rights of the users, including BDUs, to those signals. It would be incoherent for Parliament to set up a carefully tailored signals retransmission right in the *Copyright Act*, specifically excluding BDUs from the scope of the broadcasters' exclusive rights over the simultaneous retransmission of their signals, only to enable a subordinate legislative body to enact a functionally equivalent right through a related regime. The value for signal regime would upset the aim of the *Copyright Act* to effect an appropriate "balance between promoting the public interest in the encouragement and dissemination of works of the arts and intellect and obtaining a just reward for the creator" (*Théberge*, at para. 30).

[68] Second, while the conflict of the proposed regime with s. 21 is sufficient to render the regime ultra vires, further conflict arises in my opinion between the value for signal regime and the retransmission rights in works set out in s. 31 of the *Copyright Act*.

[69] As discussed above, s. 31 creates an exception to copyright infringement for the simultaneous retransmission by a BDU of a *work* carried in local signals. However, the value for signal regime envisions giving broadcasters deletion rights, whereby the broadcaster unable to agree with a BDU about the compensation for the distribution of its programming services would be entitled to require any program to which it has exclusive exhibition rights to be deleted from the signals of any broadcaster distributed by the BDU. As noted above, "program[s]" are often "work[s]" within the meaning of the *Copyright Act*. The value for signal regime would entitle broadcasters to control the simultaneous retransmission of works, while the *Copyright Act* specifically excludes it from the control of copyright owners, including broadcasters.

[70] Again, although the exception to copyright infringement established in s. 31 on its face does not purport to prohibit another regulator from imposing conditions, directly or indirectly, on the retransmission of works, it is necessary to look behind the letter of the provision to its purpose, which is to balance the entitlements of copyright holders and the public interest in the dissemination of works. The value for signal regime would effectively overturn the s. 31 exception to the copyright owners' s. 3(1)(f) communication right. It would disrupt the balance established by Parliament.

[71] The recent legislative history of the *Copyright Act* supports the view that Parliament made deliberate choices in respect of copyright and broadcasting policy. The history evidences Parliament's intent to facilitate simultaneous retransmission of television programs by cable and limit the obstacles faced by the retransmitters.

[72] Leading up to the 1997 amendment to the *Copyright Act* (Bill C-32), under which s. 21 was introduced, broadcasters made submissions to the Standing Committee on Canadian Heritage seeking signal rights. They contended that they should be granted the right to authorize, or refuse to authorize, the retransmission of their signals by others, including BDUs. The broadcasters, in fact, argued expressly against the narrow right that Parliament eventually adopted as s. 21(1)(c). See, for example, submissions of CTV to Standing Committee on Canadian Heritage, "Re: Bill C-32" (August 30,1996) (A.R., vol. VII, at p. 68); submissions of WIC Western International Communications Ltd. (1996) (A.R., vol. VII, at p. 15); submissions of the British Columbia Association of Broadcasters, "Bill C-32, the Copyright Reform Legislation" (August 28, 1996) (A.R., vol. VII, at p. 20); submissions of the Canadian Association of Broadcasters, "Clause by Clause Recommendations for Amendments to Bill C-32" (November 27, 1996) (A.R., vol. VII, at p. 77). In addition, although this section has not been amended since 1997, ongoing consultations between Parliament and the broadcasters show continued requests from the latter to include the right to authorize BDU retransmissions. See, for example, submissions of CTV-globemedia, "Re: Government's 2009 Copyright Consultations" (September 11, 2009) (A.R., vol. IX, at pp. 35-37); Canadian Association of Broadcasters, "A Submission to the House of Commons Standing Committee on Canadian Heritage With Respect to A Statutory Review of the *Copyright Act*" (September 15, 2003) (A.R., vol. IX, at p. 28).

[73] Notwithstanding successive amendments to the *Copyright Act*, Parliament has not amended s. 21 in the fashion requested by the broadcasters. Parliament's silence is not necessarily determinative of legislative intention. However, in the context of repeated urging from the broadcasters, Parliament's silence strongly suggests that it is Parliament's intention to maintain the balance struck by s. 21 (see *Tele-Mobile Co. v. Ontario*, 2008 SCC 12, [2008] 1 S.C.R. 305, at para. 42, per Abella J.).

[74] The same purposeful balancing is evidenced in the legislative history of the s. 31 regime for the retransmission of works. The predecessor to the current s. 3(1)(f) guaranteed copyright holders an exclusive right to communicate works by radio communication. Jurisprudence interpreted the radio communication right as excluding transmissions by cable: *Canadian Admiral Corp. v. Rediffusion, Inc.*, [1954] Ex. C.R. 382. Section 3(1)(f) was amended in 1988 to confer the exclusive right to "communicate the work to the public by telecommunication" to reflect the obligations entered into by Canada under the Free Trade Agreement between the Government of Canada and the Government of the United States of America, Can. T.S. 1989 No. 3 (see *Canada-United States Free Trade Agreement Implementation Act*, S.C. 1988, c. 65, ss. 61 and 62; see also *Rogers Communications Inc. v. Society of Composers, Authors and Music Publishers of Canada*, 2012 SCC 35, at paras. 36-37 and McKeown, at para. 3:2(b)). The change from radio communication to telecommunication meant that cable companies were now liable for copyright infringement when they communicate copyright-protected works to the public.

[75] However, at the same time, Parliament specifically addressed the question of whether the simultaneous retransmission of works carried in local and distant television signals should require the consent of the copyright owner: it adopted the compulsory licence and exception regime by way of ss. 31 and 71 to 76 of the *Copyright Act* (*Canada-United States Free Trade Agreement Implementation Act*, s. 62). Studies on the same question had preceded this enactment; there, too, a major concern was that copyright owners "should not be permitted to stop retransmission because this activity is too important to Canada's communications system" (Standing Committee on Communications and Culture. *A Charter of Rights for Creators: Report of the Sub-Committee on the Revision of Copyright* (1985), at p. 80 (A.R., vol. III, at p. 118); Government Response to A Charter of Rights for Creators (February 1986) (A.R., vol. III, at p. 127)).

[76] The value for signal regime would rewrite the balance between the owners' and users' interests as set out by Parliament in the *Copyright Act*. Because the CRTC's value for signal regime is inconsistent with the purpose of the *Copyright Act*, it falls outside of the scope of the CRTC's licensing and regulatory jurisdiction under the *Broadcasting Act*.

[77] I said earlier that I would come back to s. 31(2)(b) of the *Copyright Act*. The majority of the FCA concluded that there is no incoherence between the value for signal regime and the *Copyright Act* because of s. 31(2)(b) of the *Copyright Act*. This section provides that in order for the exception to copyright to apply, the retransmission must be "lawful under the *Broadcasting Act*". The majority appears to have thought this was sufficient to ground the CRTC's jurisdiction to implement the value for signal regulatory regime.

[78] In my respectful opinion, this provision cannot serve to authorize the CRTC acting under the *Broadcasting Act* to effectively amend the very heart of the balance of the retransmission regime set out in s. 31(2). Section 31(2)(b) is not a so-called Henry VIII clause that confers jurisdiction on the CRTC to promulgate, through regulation or licensing conditions, subordinate legislative provisions that are to prevail over primary legislation (see Sullivan, at pp. 342-43). Absent specific indication, Parliament cannot have intended by s. 31(2)(b) to empower a subordinate regulatory body to disturb the balance struck following years of studies. The legislative history does not lend support to this argument; indeed, the history confirms Parliament's deliberate policy choice in enacting the compulsory licence and exception, or user's rights, regime under s. 31(2). A general reference to "lawful under the *Broadcasting Act*" cannot authorize the CRTC, acting under open-ended jurisdiction-conferring provisions, to displace the specific direction of Parliament in the *Copyright Act*.

[79] In any case, the conflict found between the value for signal regime and s. 21 is sufficient. It could not be overcome even on a different reading of s. 31(2)(b) of the *Copyright Act*.

[80] There is one final point to be made. Section 89 of the *Copyright Act* provides:

> 89. No person is entitled to copyright otherwise than under and in accordance with this Act or any other Act of Parliament, but nothing in this section shall be construed as abrogating any right or jurisdiction in respect of a breach of trust or confidence.

The deliberate use of the words "this Act or any other Act of Parliament" rather than "this Act or any other enactment" means that the right to copyright must be found in an Act of Parliament and not in subordinate legislation promulgated by a regulatory body. "Act" and "enactment" are defined in s. 2 of the Interpretation Act, R.S.C. 1985, c. I-21, where

> "Act" means an Act of Parliament;

> and

> "enactment" means an Act or regulation or any portion of an Act or regulation.

The definitions confirm that Parliament did not intend that a subordinate regulatory body could create copyright by means of regulation or licensing conditions.

[81] Contrary to s. 89, the value for signal regime would create a new type of copyright by regulation or licensing condition. Sections 2 and 21 of the *Copyright Act* define copyright in a communication signal to include the sole right to authorize another broadcaster to retransmit it to the public simultaneously with its broadcast. Authorizing simultaneous retransmission is then an aspect of copyright, although the right under the *Copyright Act* is limited to authorizing only specific defined entities, other broadcasters. In light of the legislative history discussed above, this limitation on copyright appears to be the result of a specific Parliamentary choice not to change the balance struck in the *Copyright Act* between broadcasters and BDUs. The value for signal regime would create a new right to authorize retransmission (and correspondingly prevent retransmission if agreement as to compensation is not achieved), in effect, amending the copyright conferred by s. 21. Thus the value for signal regime would create a new type of copyright and would do so without the required Act of Parliament, contrary to s. 89.

[82] My colleagues assert that there are functional differences between copyright and the proposed regulatory scheme. With respect, the differences that they point to do not alter the fundamental functional equivalence between the proposed regime and a copyright. Section 21 of the *Copyright Act* empowers broadcasters to prohibit the retransmission of their signals if certain conditions are met; the value for signal regime does exactly the same thing. My colleagues are correct that the CRTC cannot, through the value for signal regime, amend s. 21 of the *Copyright Act*. However that is precisely what the proposed regime does. Parliament could have imposed conditions that are the same, or similar to the value for signal regime in s. 21 in the same way it imposed limits in s. 31 on the copyright it granted in respect of retransmission of works, had it intended broadcasters to have such a right. Describing this new right granted to broadcasters under the value for signal regime as a series of regulatory changes does not alter the true character of the right being created. Not calling it copyright does

not remove it from the scope of s. 89. If that type of repacking was all that was required, s. 89 would not serve its intended purpose of restricting the entitlement to copyright to grants under and in accordance with Acts of Parliament.

---

7. Computer Programs and Video Games

(a) Computer Programs

The term "computer program" is defined in the Act as "a set of instructions or statements, expressed, fixed, embodied or stored in any manner, that is to be used directly or indirectly in a computer in order to bring about a specific result."[3] Computer programs in source and object codes are now protected as literary works under the Act.

**Apple Computer Inc. v. Mackintosh Computers Ltd., [1987] 1 F.C. 173
(Fed. T.D.), varied (1987), 44 D.L.R. (4th) 74 (Fed. C.A.) per MacGuigan J.
(C.A.), affirmed [1990] 2 S.C.R.**

Federal Court of Canada — Trial Division

Reed J.

**Heard: January 21-24, 28-31, February 3-7 and 10, 1986
Judgment: April 29, 1986**

Reed J.:

1 The issue for decision in this case is a narrow but important one: is a computer program when embodied in a silicon chip in the computer a subject matter in which copyright exists?

. . .

40 The defendants do not dispute the fact that the written assembly language code versions of the programs fall within s. 4(1) and s. 2 of the Copyright Act, R.S.C. 1970, c. C-30:

> ... copyright shall subsist ... in every original literary, dramatic, musical and artistic work...

> 'literary work' includes maps, charts, plans, tables and compilations;

Writings in the form of alphanumeric code have obviously been included within the definition of compilation.

. . .

---

3   S.C. 1993, c. 44, s. 1(3).

42 The computer programs, however, were not copied by the defendants in their written form. The copying which occurred was from the chips directly. Chips identical (with the exceptions already noted) to those in the Apple II & computer containing Autostart ROM and Applesoft were made using an EPROM "burner". It is not necessary to explain the process involved suffice it to say that the programs in the defendants' chips were identical to the plaintiffs' programs except for the minor difference noted on pp. 168-69, supra.

. . .

46 The issue is whether a computer program, which originates as a written test (in the normal and usual sense of those terms) but which has a dimension (as appears from the facts set out above) which is not traditional to associate with such texts, continues to be covered by copyright when it is converted into its electrical code version or, more precisely in this case, when it is embodied in a device designed to replicate that code.

. . .

Copyright Act — Statutory Interpretation

72 Section 3 of the Copyright Act provides:

> ... 'copyright' means the sole right *to produce or reproduce the work or any substantial part thereof in any material form whatever* ...

(underlining added) These opening words are followed by a list of specific examples, infra, pp. 187-88. The question, then, is whether these opening words of s. 3 encompass the embodiment of the plaintiffs' program in the ROM chip.

73 No one disputes, of course, that when the present Copyright Act was originally enacted by Parliament in 1921, S.C. 1921, c. 24, no thought could have been given to computer programs and whether they would be covered by the provisions of the Act. This is not a relevant consideration, since the only question is whether the terms of the Act as drafted can fairly be said to cover such programs as encoded in the ROM chip.

74 The legislative history of the present s. 3 of the Copyright Act is of some assistance in this regard. The 1842 United Kingdom Copyright Act, 1842 (U.K., 5 & 6 Vict.), c. 45, which applied initially to Canada as well, provided:

> 'Copyright' shall be construed to mean the sole and exclusive liberty of printing or otherwise multiplying copies of any ... 'book'.

"Book" was defined as including "every Volume, Part or Division of a Volume, pamphlet, sheet of letter press, sheet of music, map, chart, or plan. ..."

75 In Boosey v. Whight, [1899] 1 Ch. 836, affirmed [1900] 1 Ch. 122 (C.A.), the question arose as to whether perforated sheets created for use in player pianos were copies of the relevant sheet music for the purposes of the Act. It was argued, by the plaintiff, that one could take the perforated sheets and write out the notes of music therefrom in ordinary musical notation providing one

understood the method or pattern of making the perforations. The defendant argued, on the other hand, that: the piano rolls were not covered by the terms of the 1842 Act; music boxes and barrel-organs which operated on the same principle had long been known; the Legislature had not intended "sheet of music" to cover this type of apparatus for the mechanical reproduction of music. The Courts agreed with the defendants' representations. Mr. Justice Stirling, at trial stated [pp. 841-42 [1899] 1 Ch.]:

> ... I think it is possible that, with considerable trouble, a person might so far master the scheme according to which the perforations are made as to be able to read the notes thereby denoted, but this is not shown in any case to have been done. ... It also appears to me that for this purpose the rolls constitute an extremely cumbrous system of writing music, hardly available without the use of some mechanism which at present does not exist. Upon the whole, I think it is highly improbable that any one would ever go to the trouble of acquiring the art of reading these rolls.

> ... The copyright conferred by that Act [of 1842] appears to me to be the exclusive liberty of multiplying copies of something in the nature of a book. The rolls, so far as they contain perforations, are, in fact, used simply as parts of a machine for the production of musical sounds, not for the purpose of a book. ...

The Court of Appeal in upholding this decision agreed: that the then Copyright Act treated a sheet of music as if it were a book; that a perforated sheet which became part of a musical instrument to play the music is different from a sheet of music which "appeals to the eye", that the defendants' perforated sheets were part of a "mechanical contrivance" for producing musical notes.

76 This decision was followed in several subsequent decisions, on both sides of the Atlantic ocean: Newmark v. National Phonograph Co. (1907), 23 T.L.R. 439 (K.B.); Monckton v. Gramophone Co. (1912), 106 L.T. 84 (C.A.); White-Smith Music Publishing Co. v. Apollo Co., 209 U.S. 1, 14 Ann. Cas. 628, 28 S. Ct. 319, 52 L. Ed. 655 (U.S. N.Y., 1908).

77 The United Kingdom copyright legislation (which still applied at that time to Canada) was amended in 1911 (Copyright Act, 1911 (U.K., 1 & 2 Geo. 5), c. 46). The new provisions in the legislation of 1911 read:

> 1(2) ... 'copyright' means the right to produce or reproduce the work or any substantial part thereof *in any material form whatsoever*, to a perform or in the case of a lecture to deliver the work ... and shall include the right, —

> a) to produce, reproduce, perform, or publish any translation of the work; ...

> d) in the case of a literary, dramatic, or musical work, to make any record, perforated roll, cinematograph film, or other contrivance by means of which the work may be mechanically performed or delivered.

(underlining added) And subs. 19(1) was added:

> Copyright shall subsist in records, perforated rolls, and other contrivances by means of which sounds may be mechanically reproduced ...

These subsections were eventually carried forward into the Canadian legislation and appear in almost identical form as s. 3 and subs. 4(3) of the present Act.

78 Counsel for the plaintiffs argues that the opening words of s. 1(2), now s. 3 of the Act, "were purposely drafted broadly enough to encompass new technologies which had not been thought of when the Act was drafted. I agree.

79 It seems clear that the 1911 amendments did away with any requirement that in order to be covered by copyright the copy or reproduction of the work had to a be in a human readable form. Equally, I think the 1911 amendments did away with any rule which would deny copyright protection to a work merely because the copy or reproduction could be characterized as being part of a machine.

80 The piano rolls in Boosey v. Whight were removable parts comparable to the modern day record, cassette or video tape. The ROM chips are removable with relative ease but they are not intended to be removed. They are not removable in the same manner as a floppy disc or a cassette is removable. The ROM chip is meant to be left in the machine on a permanent basis. However, the legislation draws no distinction on this basis. Accordingly, I think it is irrelevant, in the present case, whether the program is encoded in a floppy disc, on a punch card or in a ROM chip. The copyrightability issue does not differ merely on the basis of the medium in which the program is found.

81 I can see no difference at a physical level between a device such as a record which "contains" a musical work by virtue of the grooves impressed therein, and a ROM chip which "contains" a program by virtue of the pattern of conductive and non-conductive areas created therein. In my view the opening words of s. 3 clearly cover the plaintiffs' program as embodied in a ROM chip. Such embodiment is surely the production or reproduction of the work in a material form, just as a record or a cassette tape is a production or reproduction of a work in a material form. (I have not overlooked the fact that there is a separate section in the Act which covers copyright in records.)

82 In my view the requirement of "readability" or "appearance to the eye" found in the jurisprudence requires no more than that there be a method by which the work in which copyright is claimed and the work which is alleged to infringe can be visually compared for the purpose of determining whether copying has occurred. Since in this case the programs can be "read" out of ROM and so compared, this requirement is met. I adopt in this regard the reasoning of Mr. Justice Megarry in Thrustcode Ltd. v. W.W. Computing Ltd., [1983] F.S.R. 502 at 505 (Ch. Div.):

> ... For computers, as for other things, what must be compared are the thing said to have been copied and the thing said to be an infringing copy. If these two things are invisible, then normally they must be reproduced in visible form, or in a form that in some way is perceptible, before it can be determined whether one infringes the other.

> ... Normally, ... what will be needed is a print-out or other documentary evidence of the program alleged to have been copied, and of the alleged infringing program, or sufficient parts of each.

And those of Mr. Justice Fox in the Computer Edge case, supra, at p. 237:

> ... In my view it does not matter, if it be the fact, that the code cannot be seen, ... The adaptation of the work is rendered perceptible with a machine. It is sufficient that the code has its existence in, and is ascertainable from, the chips.

83 For cases which have dealt with the creation of a work in a material form different from that in which it originated see: Chabot v. Davies, [1936] 3 All E.R. 221 (Ch.D.) (a store front built from plans thereof); King Features Syndicate Inc. v. O. & M. Kleeman Ltd., [1941] A.C. 417, [1941] 2 All E.R. 403 (H.L.) (brooches and dolls from a Popeye cartoon); Dorling v. Honnor Marine, [1965] Ch. 1, [1964] 1 All E.R. 241, [1963] 2 Lloyd's Rep. 455, [1964] R.P.C. 160 (C.A.) (boats from plans); and Bayliner Marine Corp. v. Doral Boats Ltd. (1985), 5 C.I.P.R. 268, 5 C.P.R. (3d) 289 (Fed. T.D.) [reversed (1986), 67 N.R. 139 (Fed. C.A.)]. These cases also demonstrate that a copy of a reproduction which reproduction exists in a different material form from the original is still an infringement of copyright in the original. The reasoning found in these cases is applicable to the present situation although I note that the plaintiff does not claim copyright in the ROM chip itself as a device but only in the program encoded therein. In this respect it differs from the three-dimensional cases cited above. In my view, this strengthens rather than weakens the plaintiff's claim to copyright.

84 As I understand counsel's argument it is that even if the reproduction itself does not have to be in human readable form there is a requirement that the *purpose* for which that reproduction is made must ultimately be to communicate the work to human beings. A record or cassette when used with a machine produces sounds for human listening while the ROM chip does not so communicate to humans as its *primary* function. As noted above, it *can* be used to so communicate and for certain limited purposes is so used, but that is not its *primary* purpose.

85 It is argued that the requirement that the primary purpose of the work be to communicate to human beings in order for copyright to exist is found in both the context of the Act and in the wording of specific sections thereof. The context argument is one that has found favour with some Courts. I note particularly the dissenting decision of Mr. Justice Sheppard in the Computer Edge case, supra, at p. 277. His remarks were addressed to the meaning of the words translation and adaptation in the Australian Copyright Act but it is the approach which counsel urges on this Court:

> ... There seems to be running through these various provisions [of the Act] the idea or notion that what is the subject of copyright (whether a work or an adaptation thereof) will, although not immediately published and perhaps never published, be capable of being published and thus being seen or heard. The very idea of publishing is that something should be seen or heard. ...

86 It is argued that even if the context of the Act does not make it clear that computer programs in their machine code version fall outside the Act, the textual

wording of pertinent sections does so indicate. Section 2 and s. 3 are referred to. Section 2 states:

> 'every original literary, dramatic, musical and artistic work' includes every original production in the literary, scientific or artistic domain *whatever may be the mode or form of its expression, such as* books, pamphlets, and other writings, lectures, dramatic or dramatico-musical works, musical works or compositions with or without words, illustrations, sketches, and plastic works relative to geography, topography, architecture or science;

(underlining added) And s. 3:

> 3. (1) For the purposes of this Act, 'copyright' means the sole right to produce or reproduce the work or any substantial part thereof *in any material form whatever*, to perform, or in the case of a lecture to deliver the work or any substantial part thereof in public; if the work is unpublished to publish the work or any substantial part thereof; *and includes* the sole right
>
> > (a) to produce, reproduce, perform or publish any translation of the work;
> >
> > (b) in the case of a dramatic work, to convert it into a novel or other non-dramatic work;
> >
> > (c) in the case of a novel or other non-dramatic work, or of an artistic work, to convert it into a dramatic work, by way of performance in public or otherwise;
> >
> > (d) in the case of a literary, dramatic, or musical work, to make any record, perforated roll, cinematograph film, or other contrivance by means of which the work may be mechanically performed or delivered;
> >
> > (e) in the case of any literary, dramatic, musical or artistic work, to reproduce, adapt and publicly present such work by cinematograph, if the author has given such work an original character; but if such original character is absent the cinematographic production shall be protected as a photograph;
> >
> > (f) in case of any literary, dramatic, musical or artistic work, to communicate such work by radio communication;
>
> and to authorize any such acts as aforesaid.

(underlining added)

87 The general words, both "whatever may be the mode or form of its expression" in s. 2 and "in any material form whatever" in s. 3, it is said, must be interpreted by reference to the particular examples which follow in each case. That is, in the case of s. 2 "books, pamphlets ..." and in the case of s. 3 the particular forms of production or reproduction itemized by each of subss. (a) to (f). It is argued that the principle of statutory interpretation noscitur a sociis is applicable.

88 In my view counsel's arguments based on the context of the Act and on the specific wording of the sections thereof are conclusively answered by s. 3 itself. Section 3 provides that "copyright means the sole right to produce or reproduce the work ... *in any material form whatever*". In my view that clearly covers

the program as embodied in the ROM chip. To find otherwise, it seems to me, would require reading words into s. 3 of the Copyright Act which are not there.

89 With respect to the argument based on the principle noscitur a sociis, that principle is only applicable to cut down the general words of a statutory provision when it is clear that Parliament did not intend a broad one. Parliament's intention in the case of s. 3, and perhaps also s. 2, is very clear. The enumerations are used as examples. The general wording is said to "include" the specifics. In that context, the principle noscitur a sociis can have no role to play.

90 It is also argued that it is clear that the opening words of s. 3 were not intended to cover works in "*any*" material form because if this were so there would have been no need to include in the Act subs. 3(1)(d). The text of subs. 3(1)(d) itself indicates, it is said, that only contrivances which communicate to human beings were meant to be covered by the Act. This last is based in part on the fact that "delivery" in s. 2 of the Act only refers to delivery in relation to a lecture and that "performance" is defined as meaning any acoustic or visual representation. In this regard, counsel for the defendants argues that application programs which cause a text or graphics to be displayed on the screen, or which result in sounds being emitted or music being played are covered by copyright. In his view they are contrivances (in the chip version) by means of which the work may be mechanically delivered.

91 The argument based on subs. 3(1)(d) I find unconvincing. It has a two-edged quality. It can equally be asked why, if Parliament only intended to cover records or contrivances which utter sounds or communicate to humans, the opening words of s. 3 were drafted so broadly. The references to the definition sections are not persuasive. They only purport to define one particular aspect of delivery as it relates to lectures; no all-inclusive definition is given of that word. The definition of performance is irrelevant since no one has suggested that it applies in the present case. Also, I have difficulty with the distinction counsel makes between programs which result in something being displayed on the screen and those (such as ROM) which do not. When "something" is displayed on the screen it is not the program (ie: it is not the original or a hexadecimal version thereof which is displayed). The program remains invisible unless disassembled by the translation processes similar to that used to "read" the ROM.

92 In addition, I think there is merit in the argument that the ROM chip, whatever the interpretation of the opening words of s. 3, can be said to fall within para. 3(1)(d) as a contrivance by means of which the work may be delivered. The program (as noted above) can be delivered to the screen of the monitor, or as a print-out to be read by human beings. I do not find it necessary to decide whether "delivery" to the CPU satisfies para. 3(1)(d).

Apple Computer Inc. v. Mackintosh Computers Ltd., [1988] 1 F.C. 673
(Fed. C.A.)

Federal Court of Canada, Appeal Division

Mahoney, Hugessen and MacGuigan JJ.

Heard: September 28-30, October 1, 1987
Judgment: October 13, 1987
Docket: Nos. A-275-86; A-276-86

Hugessen J.:

26 The appellants have, in popular parlance, pirated two computer programs used by the respondents in their Apple II+ computer. It is common ground that the programs in question, when written, as they originally were, in letters, symbols and figures known as 6502 assembly code, were original literary works subject to copyright and that the copyright therein vests in respondent Apple Computer Inc. But the appellants have not copied the programs written in assembly code. They have not copied any writing at all. What they have done is reproduce, apparently by mechanical means, the electrical circuitry of a silicon chip in which, by the magic of computer science, the programs are embodied. The question at issue is to know whether the appellants have infringed the respondents' copyright in the original assembly code programs.

. . .

41 At first blush, it would seem obvious that when one produces or reproduces a work the result of that operation must necessarily also be a work. The only kinds of works in which copyright can subsist in accordance with s. 4 of the Act are literary, dramatic, musical and artistic works. The only category into which the respondents' programs in assembly code could possibly fit is that of literary works and it is indeed common ground that they are such works.

42 The sole distinguishing characteristic of a literary work is not its quality as literature or art but simply that it be in print or writing. As early as 1916, within 5 years of the passage of the U.K. *Copyright Act*, 1911 (U.K., 1 & 2 Geo. 5), c. 46, upon which our act is modeled, it was said in *University of London Press Ltd. v. University Tutorial Press Ltd.*, [1916] 2 Ch. 601:

> Although a literary work is not defined in the Act, s. 35 [in Canada, s. 2] states what the phrase includes; the definition is not a completely comprehensive one, but the section is intended to show what, amongst other things, is included in the description 'literary work,' and the words are ' "Literary work" includes maps, charts, plans, tables, and compilations.' It may be difficult to define 'literary work' as used in this Act, but it seems to be plain that it is not confined to 'literary work' in the sense in which that phrase is applied, for instance, to Meredith's novels and the writings of Robert Louis Stevenson. In speaking of such writings as literary works, one thinks of the quality, the style, and the literary finish which they exhibit. Under the Act of 1842, which protected 'books,' many things which had no pretensions to literary style acquired copyright: for example, a list of registered bills of sale, a list of foxhounds and hunting days, and trade catalogues; and I see

no ground for coming to the conclusion that the present Act was intended to curtail the rights of authors. In my view the words 'literary work' cover work which is expressed in print or writing, irrespective of the question whether the quality or style is high. The word 'literary' seems to be used in a sense somewhat similar to the use of the word 'literature' in political or electioneering literature and refers to written or printed matter. Papers set by examiners are, in my opinion, 'literary work' within the meaning of the present Act.

(per Peterson J., at p. 608). That statement found approval in the House of Lords in *Ladbroke (Football) Ltd. v. William Hill (Football) Ltd.*, [1964] 1 All E.R. 465, [1964] 1 W.L.R. 273.

43 It seems to me to follow from the foregoing that when a literary work is produced or reproduced the result must necessarily be a literary work, i.e., expressed in print or writing.

44 The difficulty which this raises in the present case is obvious. The respondents' copyright is in the assembly code version of the programs. Clearly that version is expressed in print or writing. When the program is reproduced in either binary or hexadecimal notation, the result being in figures and letters is also in print or writing and hence a literary work. When, however, the binary code version is transposed into open-and-closed electrical circuits embodied in a silicon chip, the latter contains no print or writing and hence cannot be said to be a literary work.

45 Does this mean that the production of the chip embodying programs does not constitute an infringement of the copyright? I think not. We have already seen that the statute defines copyright as being, amongst other things, the sole right to produce or reproduce in any material form. It is, in my opinion, possible to read those words as including by necessary implication the sole right to produce the means of reproduction of the work or, to put the matter another way, the sole right to produce anything used or intended to be used to reproduce the work. When the opening words of subs. 3(1) are read in the context of the remainder of that subsection and of other sections of the *Copyright Act*, it is my view that such interpretation is not only possible but is required.

. . .

MacGuigan J.:

56 These cases, which were argued together, are concerned with copyright in computer programs as embodied in silicon chips.

. . .

68 On the statutory argument she held, at pp. 194-8 F.C., pp. 30-4 C.P.R. [pp. 185-89 C.I.P.R.]:

In my view the opening words of section 3 clearly cover the plaintiffs' program as embodied in a ROM chip. Such embodiment is surely the production or reproduction of the work in a material form, just as a record or a cassette tape is a production or reproduction of a work in a material form. (I have not overlooked the fact that there is a separate section in the Act which covers copyright in records.)

In my view the requirement of 'readability' or 'appearance to the eye' found in the jurisprudence requires no more than that there be a method by which the work in which copyright is claimed and the work which is alleged to infringe can be visually compared for the purpose of determining whether copying has occurred. Since in this case the programs can be 'read' out of ROM and so compared, this requirement is met. I adopt in this regard the reasoning of Mr. Justice Megarry in *Thrustcode Ltd. v. W.W. Computing Ltd.*, [1983] F.S.R. 502 (Ch.D.) at page 505:

> ... for computers, as for other things, what must be compared are the thing said to have been copied and the thing said to be an infringing copy. If these two things are invisible, then normally they must be reproduced in visible form, or in a form that in some way is perceptible, before it can be determined whether one infringes the other.

> Normally ... what will be needed is a print-out or other documentary evidence of the program alleged to have been copied, and of the alleged infringing program, or sufficient parts of each.

. . .

As I understand counsel's argument it is that even if the reproduction itself does not have to be in human readable form there is a requirement that the *purpose* for which that reproduction is made must ultimately be to communicate the work to human beings. A record or cassette when used with a machine produces sounds for human listening while the ROM chip does not so communicate to humans as its *primary* function. As noted above, it *can* be used to so communicate and for certain limited purposes is so used, but that is not its *primary* purpose....

In my view counsel's arguments based on the context of the Act and on the specific wording of the sections thereof are conclusively answered by section 3 itself. Section 3 provides that ' "copyright" means the sole right to produce or reproduce the work.... *in any material form whatever*'. In my view that clearly covers the program as embodied in the ROM chip. To find otherwise, it seems to me, would require reading words into section 3 of the *Copyright Act* which are not there....

The argument based on paragraph 3(1)(*d*) I find unconvincing. It has a two-edged quality. It can equally be asked why, if Parliament only intended to cover records or contrivances which utter sounds or communicate to humans, the opening words of section 3 were drafted so broadly. The references to the definition sections are not persuasive. They only purport to define one particular aspect of delivery as it relates to lectures; no all inclusive definition is given of that word. The definition of performance is irrelevant since no one has suggested that it applies in the present case. Also, I have difficulty with the distinction counsel makes between programs which result in something being displayed on the screen and those (such as ROM) which do not. When 'something' is displayed on the screen it is not the program (i.e.: it is not the original or hexadecimal version thereof which is displayed). The program remains invisible unless disassembled by the translation processes similar to that used to 'read' the ROM.

69 On the fourth argument, she found no compelling policy reasons for refusing the extend copyright protection in this case, at pp. 200-01 F.C., pp. 35-6 C.P.R. [p. 191 C.I.P.R.]:

With respect to the first argument, the purpose of the *Copyright Act* is and always has been to grant a monopoly. No distinction is made therein as to the purpose of the work created — for entertainment, instruction or other purposes. The legislation historically, in my view had two purposes: to encourage disclosure of works for the 'advancement of learning', and to protect and reward the intellectual effort of the author (for a limited period of time) in the work. A book is an article of commerce, as is a map or a chart. The interpretation of the legislation which the defendants urge, based on a view that the Act was not intended to interfere with commerce, is both not accurate and would add a gloss to the statute which its wording does not bear.

With respect to the second argument, as I read the authorities and references to which I have been referred by counsel they indicate that computer programs are not *per se* patentable but that an apparatus or process that meets the standards of novelty and unobviousness required by the *Patent Act*, R.S.C. 1970, c. P-4, will not be disqualified from patent protection merely because a computer is used to operate the apparatus or implement the process. In addition, I do not see that over-lapping areas of the law are particularly unusual (reference need only be made to the fields of tort and contract). Nor do I see it as the role of the courts to frame decisions to avoid such results. In addition, I would note that the present case does not deal with a special purpose program. It concerns the operation of a general purpose computer, although I must admit that I do not, at the moment, see any rationale for distinguishing between the two. I note that Mr. Justice Megarry in the *Thrustcode* case did not think it necessary to draw such a distinction.

70 Finally, adverted to the trend both abroad and in Canada to extend copyright protection in such cases, at p. 203 F.C., p. 38 C.P.R. [p. 193 C.I.P.R.]:

There are a growing number of cases in jurisdictions where the copyright law is not too dissimilar from our own which have held that computer programs in their machine code version are protected by the copyright law applicable existing in that jurisdiction. [*Sega Enterprises Limited v. Richards*, [1983] F.S.R. 73 (Ch. D.); *Thrustcode Limited v. W.W. Computing Ltd.*, supra, p. 194; *Northern Office Microcomputers (Pty) Ltd. v. Rosenstein*, [1982] F.S.R. 124 (S.C. South Africa); *Apple Computer Inc. v. Computer Edge Pty Ltd.*, [(1984), 53 A.L.R. 225].] Not only is there such a trend abroad, but a similar phenomenon can also be discerned in this country. [*Apple Computer Inc. v. Computermat Inc.* (1983), 1 C.I.P.R. 1 (Ont. H.C.); *Apple Computer Inc. v. Minitronics of Canada Ltd. et al.* (1985), 7 C.P.R. (3d) 104 (F.C.T.D.) affirmed (1985), 8 C.P.R. (3d) 431 (F.C.A.); *Société (La) d'Informatique R.D.G. Inc. v. Dynabec Ltée et al.* (1984) 6 C.P.R. (3d) 299 (Que. S.C.); *F & I Retail Systems Ltd. v. Thermo Guard Automotive Products Canada Ltd. et al.* (unreported decision of the Supreme Court of Ontario of June 26, 1984); *Logo Computer Systems Inc. c. 115778 Canada Inc. et al.* (unreported decision of the Quebec Superior Court of October 25, 1983); *Nintendo of America Inc. v. Coinex Video Games Inc.*, [1983] 2 F.C. 189 (C.A.), which deals with the issue in a peripheral way; *Spacefile Ltd. v. Smart Computing Systems Ltd. et al.* (1983), 75 C.P.R. (2d) 281 (Ont. H.C.).] ...

71 The learned trial Judge was quite right in her analysis of the trend in the case law up to that time, and had it not been for the decision of the High Court of Australia in *Computer Edge Pty Ltd. v. Apple Computer Inc.* (1986), 65 A.L.R. 33, released the week after her decision, it might not have been necessary for

this Court to add to her reasons for judgment at all. However, in the *Computer Edge* case, the Australian Court held by a 3-2 margin that there was no infringement of copyright in an identical case. The appellants in argument before this Court relied heavily on the three majority judgments in that case, particularly that of Deane J.

72 All four of the Australian High Court Judges who decided the question held that the source or assembly programs were copyrightable. In the cases at Bar that point is admitted by the appellants.

73 Both Gibbs C.J. and Brennan J. in the majority held that under the Australian *Copyright Act*, 1968, the object programs embodied in the ROMs as well as the source programs were required to be literary works, and that they were not because they were not "written". Deane J. agreed with respect to the object programs. Mason and Wilson JJ. in dissent agreed that the object programs had to be themselves literary works but disagreed that they had to be in writing.

74 This Court must certainly accept the interpretation of the 1968 Australian legislation, which follows the English Act of 1956 [Copyright Act, 1956 (U.K., 4 & 5 Eliz. 2), c. 74], by the highest Court in that country as final, but that is not to say that the Canadian Act, which follows rather the English legislation of 1911, should be interpreted in the same way. The Australian Act differs from ours in establishing a fragmented series of copyright rights rather than a simple comprehensive statement.

75 However, to my mind the principal distinguishing feature of the cases at Bar from the *Computer Edge* decision is expressed in the following comment by Mason and Wilson JJ. at p. 45:

> Whether it is the series of electrical impulses stored in the ROMs or the written description in binary or hexadecimal notation that is truly the object program, is not entirely clear. *However, the case has been conducted on the footing that it is the former rather than the latter....* We propose to deal with the case on this footing as no issue is raised with respect to it in this court.

(emphasis added) It is true that Gibbs C.J. applies his conclusion that the object programs were not literary works both to the dynamic sequence of electrical impulses and to the static pattern of circuits. But Brennan J. seems to approach the matter only in terms of a computer in operation. He says, for example, at pp. 54-5:

> The electrical charges which constitute the object programs cannot be seen or touched or heard or, if they can, they do not communicate the letters of the original literary work, the source programs. Nor, for that manner, do the electrical charges communicate the letters or figures by which an object program may be represented.... 6502 Assembly Language is not a language; it is a code. Even if the code were thought to be susceptible of 'translation' into another language, it was not so translated; the electrical charges which constitute the object programs are clearly not a language. To describe such electrical charges — no doubt helpfully enough for the purposes of computer science — as 'machine readable language' is to make metaphor serve as reality. The machine has no comprehension of thought which it is the essential purpose of language to convey, and the fact that a microprocessor

is activated by a sequence of electrical charges in a predictable way does not mean that it has understood and executed some command.

76 Deane J. was even more radical. He said, at p. 60:

> The programming of a ROM is done electrically. Its effect is essentially functional rather than visual and the program state of a ROM is ascertained not by visual observation but by actual electrical operation.

77 And again, at p. 63:

> The re-arrangement of electrons in a programmed ROM is not visible to the human eye. The programmed ROM may be used as a switching device in a functioning computer to produce a print out or visual display of something which could, for relevant purposes, preferably be called a 'literary work.' Of itself however, and regardless of how widely one construes the phrase, the arrangement (or series) of electrons or electrical charges in the silicon chip does not constitute a 'literary work.' It is not written. It is not in a comprehensible language. It cannot be read. It cannot even be seen. Nor is it designed or produced to be read or seen.

> It is, and was designed and produced to be, an attribute of a functioning part of an operating machine.

The closest that Brennan and Deane JJ. came to considering the static pattern of circuits in the chips as a language was in relation to the visual display or printout which they are capable of producing. Deane J. described as "an inversion of logic" (at p. 63) the contention that such a product could be a translation or reproduction protected by copyright.

78 Deane J.'s approach appears to me to be the more radical because he refuses to view programmed chips as anything more than "an attribute of a functioning part of an operating machine". For him "the program state of a ROM is ascertained ... by actual electrical operation". There is therefore no static point of view possible, only the dynamic viewpoint of an operating machine.

79 The appellants accepted this approach and added to it a further refinement. It is common ground that computer programs can be categorized by function as either application programs or operating system programs. Application programs perform a specific task for the user, such as word processing, checkbook balancing, or playing a game, whereas operating system programs manage the internal functions of the computer or facilitate use of application programs. It is also common ground that the two computer programs in question in the cases at Bar are operating system programs.

80 The appellants' ultimate contention was that, regardless of the law with respect to application programs, operating systems programs are not a proper subject of copyright since they are entirely a process or method of operation.

81 In my view it is not necessary for this Court to decide whether, seen in a dynamic or process approach, the ROM chips are the subject of copyright. All that is necessary in the cases at Bar is to note that such an approach is inconsistent with the findings of the trial Judge, which are not successfully challenged.

82 The evidence of the respondents' witnesses, which was accepted by the trial Judge, was that the programs in question are permanently encoded on chips that are permanent storage devices within the Apple II+.

. . .

84 The appellants did not succeed before us in casting doubt on the software perspective adopted by the trial Judge. Indeed, the point of view that the programmed chips are only attributes of a functioning part of an operating machine seems to fly in the face of common sense. The original programs registered were works at rest, as it were, not in operation. When a comparison is to be made for purposes of establishing whether the memory chips are either reproductions or translations of the original works, it is only reasonable that they, also, should be taken in their static state. Moreover, the activity which occurs in an operating computer originates from the CPU, not from the memory chips, and by looking into the latter one cannot see the operation of the CPU. One can, however, under examination by an elecron microscope, discover the pattern of the electric circuits, and so read the code, which turns out to be an exact replica of the assembly code, though in a different material form.

85 I am strengthened in my approach by the fact that the programs of the appellants which give rise to the allegations of infringement of copyright are themselves produced and sold in a static state and should therefore be compared on the same basis.

Apple Computer, Inc. v. Mackintosh Computers Ltd., [1990] 2 S.C.R. 209

Supreme Court of Canada

Dickson C.J. and Lamer, Wilson, La Forest, L'Heureux-Dubé, Sopinka, Gonthier, Cory and McLachlin JJ.

Judgment: February 26, 1990
Judgment: June 21, 1990

Cory J.:

. . .

14 I agree with the conclusion reached by the trial judge and the Court of Appeal that the programs embodied in the silicon chip are protected under the *Copyright Act*. Indeed, there is little I can or would wish to add to Reed J.'s excellent reasons.

15 Like Reed J. and for the same reasons that were expressed by her, I am of the opinion that the programs embedded in the silicon chip are a reproduction of the programs in assembly language and as such are protected by copyright under s. 3(1) of the *Copyright Act*. In addition, I agree with her that these programs constitute a form of expression that is conceptually and functionally unique and cannot be regarded as a merger of idea and expression. Since the programs

contained in the silicon chip are therefore protected under the Act, it is unnecessary for me to determine whether the silicon chips can be regarded as a translation under s. 3(1)(*a*) or a contrivance under s. 3(1)(*d*).

16 Finally, like MacGuigan J., I do not believe that the Australian *Computer Edge* decision should be applied in Canada. That decision characterizes the program embedded in the silicon chip in a manner which accords with the electrical processes that underlie its operation. Rather, the appropriate approach is to view the silicon chip program as embodying a set of instructions in machine code which are designed to move information and perform other specified tasks. I agree with MacGuigan J. that the silicon chip should be viewed as a static object encoded with written instructions rather than as constituting a dynamic interchange of electrical impulses. It follows that the program embodied in the silicon chip is properly subject to protection by copyright and the unauthorized copying of that program constitutes a violation of copyright.

Computer Associates Intern., Inc. v. Altai, Inc., 982 F.2d 693 (2d Cir., 1992)

Before Altimari, Mahoney and WALKER, Circuit Judges

In recent years, the growth of computer science has spawned a number of challenging legal questions, particularly in the field of copyright law. As scientific knowledge advances, courts endeavor to keep pace, and sometimes — as in the area of computer technology — they are required to venture into less than familiar waters. This is not a new development, though. "From its beginning, the law of copyright has developed in response to significant changes in technology." Sony Corp. v. Universal City Studios, Inc., 464 U.S. 417, 430, 104 S.Ct. 774, 782, 78 L.Ed.2d 574 (1984).

Article I, section 8 of the Constitution authorizes Congress "[t]o promote the Progress of Science and useful Arts, by securing for limited Times to Authors and Inventors the exclusive Right to their respective Writings and Discoveries." The Supreme Court has stated that "[t]he economic philosophy behind the clause ... is the conviction that encouragement of individual effort by personal gain is the best way to advance public welfare...." Mazer v. Stein, 347 U.S. 201, 219, 74 S.Ct. 460, 471, 98 L.Ed. 630 (1954). The author's benefit, however, is clearly a "secondary" consideration. See United States v. Paramount Pictures, Inc., 334 U.S. 131, 158, 68 S.Ct. 915, 929, 92 L.Ed. 1260 (1948). "[T]he ultimate aim is, by this incentive, to stimulate artistic creativity for the general public good." Twentieth Century Music Corp. v. Aiken, 422 U.S. 151, 156, 95 S.Ct. 2040, 2044, 45 L.Ed.2d 84 (1975).

Thus, the copyright law seeks to establish a delicate equilibrium. On the one hand, it affords protection to authors as an incentive to create, and, on the other, it must appropriately limit the extent of that protection so as to avoid the effects of monopolistic stagnation. In applying the federal act to new types of cases, courts must always keep this symmetry in mind. Id.

Among other things, this case deals with the challenging question of whether and to what extent the "non-literal" aspects of a computer program, that is, those aspects that are not reduced to written code, are protected by copyright. While a few other courts have already grappled with this issue, this case is one of first impression in this circuit. As we shall discuss, we find the results reached by other courts to be less than satisfactory. Drawing upon long-standing doctrines of copyright law, we take an approach that we think better addresses the practical difficulties embedded in these types of cases. In so doing, we have kept in mind the necessary balance between creative incentive and industrial competition.

This appeal comes to us from the United States District Court for the Eastern District of New York, the Honorable George C. Pratt, Circuit Judge, sitting by designation. By Memorandum and Order entered August 12, 1991, Judge Pratt found that defendant Altai, Inc.'s ("Altai"), OSCAR 3.4 computer program had infringed plaintiff Computer Associates' ("CA"), copyrighted computer program entitled CA-SCHEDULER. Accordingly, the district court awarded CA $364,444 in actual damages and apportioned profits. Altai has 697*697 abandoned its appeal from this award. With respect to CA's second claim for copyright infringement, Judge Pratt found that Altai's OSCAR 3.5 program was not substantially similar to a portion of CA-SCHEDULER called ADAPTER, and thus denied relief. Finally, the district court concluded that CA's state law trade secret misappropriation claim against Altai had been preempted by the federal Copyright Act. CA appealed from these findings.

Because we are in full agreement with Judge Pratt's decision and in substantial agreement with his careful reasoning regarding CA's copyright infringement claim, we affirm the district court's judgment on that issue. However, we vacate the district court's preemption ruling with respect to CA's trade secret claim, and remand the case to the district court for further proceedings.

BACKGROUND

We assume familiarity with the facts set forth in the district court's comprehensive and scholarly opinion. See Computer Assocs. Int'l., Inc. v. Altai, Inc., 775 F.Supp. 544, 549-55 (E.D.N.Y.1991). Thus, we summarize only those facts necessary to resolve this appeal.

I.   COMPUTER PROGRAM DESIGN

Certain elementary facts concerning the nature of computer programs are vital to the following discussion. The Copyright Act defines a computer program as "a set of statements or instructions to be used directly or indirectly in a computer in order to bring about a certain result." 17 U.S.C. § 101. In writing these directions, the programmer works "from the general to the specific." Whelan Assocs., Inc. v. Jaslow Dental Lab., Inc., 797 F.2d 1222, 1229 (3d Cir.1986), cert. denied, 479 U.S. 1031, 107 S.Ct. 877, 93 L.Ed.2d 831 (1987). See generally Steven R. Englund, Note, Idea, Process, or Protected Expression?: Determining the Scope of Copyright Protection of the Structure of Computer

Programs, 88 MICH.L.REV. 866, 867-73 (1990) (hereinafter "Englund"); Peter S. Menell, An Analysis of the Scope of Copyright Protection for Application Programs, 41 STAN. L.REV. 1045, 1051-57 (1989) (hereinafter "Menell"); Mark T. Kretschmer, Note, Copyright Protection For Software Architecture: Just Say No!, 1988 COLUM.BUS.L.REV. 823, 824-27 (1988) (hereinafter "Kretschmer"); Peter G. Spivack, Comment, Does Form Follow Function? The Idea/Expression Dichotomy In Copyright Protection of Computer Software, 35 U.C.L.A.L.REV. 723, 729-31 (1988) (hereinafter "Spivack").

The first step in this procedure is to identify a program's ultimate function or purpose. An example of such an ultimate purpose might be the creation and maintenance of a business ledger. Once this goal has been achieved, a programmer breaks down or "decomposes" the program's ultimate function into "simpler constituent problems or 'subtasks,'" Englund, at 870, which are also known as subroutines or modules. See Spivack, at 729. In the context of a business ledger program, a module or subroutine might be responsible for the task of updating a list of outstanding accounts receivable. Sometimes, depending upon the complexity of its task, a subroutine may be broken down further into sub-subroutines.

Having sufficiently decomposed the program's ultimate function into its component elements, a programmer will then arrange the subroutines or modules into what are known as organizational or flow charts. Flow charts map the interactions between modules that achieve the program's end goal. See Kretschmer, at 826.

In order to accomplish these intra-program interactions, a programmer must carefully design each module's parameter list. A parameter list, according to the expert appointed and fully credited by the district court, Dr. Randall Davis, is "the information sent to and received from a subroutine." See Report of Dr. Randall Davis, at 12. The term "parameter list" refers to the form in which information is passed between modules (e.g. for accounts receivable, the designated time frame and particular customer identifying number) and the information's actual content (e.g. 698*698 8/91-7/92; customer No. 3). Id. With respect to form, interacting modules must share similar parameter lists so that they are capable of exchanging information.

"The functions of the modules in a program together with each module's relationships to other modules constitute the 'structure' of the program." Englund, at 871. Additionally, the term structure may include the category of modules referred to as "macros." A macro is a single instruction that initiates a sequence of operations or module interactions within the program. Very often the user will accompany a macro with an instruction from the parameter list to refine the instruction (e.g. current total of accounts receivable (macro), but limited to those for 8/91 to 7/92 from customer No. 3 (parameters)).

In fashioning the structure, a programmer will normally attempt to maximize the program's speed, efficiency, as well as simplicity for user operation, while taking into consideration certain externalities such as the memory constraints of the computer upon which the program will be run. See id.; Kretschmer, at 826;

Menell, at 1052. "This stage of program design often requires the most time and investment." Kretschmer, at 826.

Once each necessary module has been identified, designed, and its relationship to the other modules has been laid out conceptually, the resulting program structure must be embodied in a written language that the computer can read. This process is called "coding," and requires two steps. Whelan, 797 F.2d at 1230. First, the programmer must transpose the program's structural blue-print into a source code. This step has been described as "comparable to the novelist fleshing out the broad outline of his plot by crafting from words and sentences the paragraphs that convey the ideas." Kretschmer, at 826. The source code may be written in any one of several computer languages, such as COBAL, FORTRAN, BASIC, EDL, etc., depending upon the type of computer for which the program is intended. Whelan, 797 F.2d at 1230. Once the source code has been completed, the second step is to translate or "compile" it into object code. Object code is the binary language comprised of zeros and ones through which the computer directly receives its instructions. Id. at 1230-31; Englund, at 868 & n. 13.

After the coding is finished, the programmer will run the program on the computer in order to find and correct any logical and syntactical errors. This is known as "debugging" and, once done, the program is complete. See Kretschmer, at 826-27.

II. FACTS

CA is a Delaware corporation, with its principal place of business in Garden City, New York. Altai is a Texas corporation, doing business primarily in Arlington, Texas. Both companies are in the computer software industry — designing, developing and marketing various types of computer programs.

The subject of this litigation originates with one of CA's marketed programs entitled CA-SCHEDULER. CA-SCHEDULER is a job scheduling program designed for IBM mainframe computers. Its primary functions are straightforward: to create a schedule specifying when the computer should run various tasks, and then to control the computer as it executes the schedule. CA-SCHEDULER contains a sub-program entitled ADAPTER, also developed by CA. ADAPTER is not an independently marketed product of CA; it is a wholly integrated component of CA-SCHEDULER and has no capacity for independent use.

Nevertheless, ADAPTER plays an extremely important role. It is an "operating system compatibility component," which means, roughly speaking, it serves as a translator. An "operating system" is itself a program that manages the resources of the computer, allocating those resources to other programs as needed. The IBM System 370 family of computers, for which CA-SCHEDULER was created, is, depending upon the computer's size, designed to contain one of three operating systems: DOS/VSE, MVS, or CMS. As the district court noted, the general rule is that "a 699*699 program written for one operating system, e.g., DOS/VSE, will not, without modification, run under another operating system such as MVS." Computer Assocs., 775 F.Supp. at 550. ADAPTER's function is to translate the language of a given program into the particular language that the computer's own operating system can understand.

The district court succinctly outlined the manner in which ADAPTER works within the context of the larger program. In order to enable CA-SCHEDULER to function on different operating systems, CA divided the CA-SCHEDULER into two components:

- a first component that contains only the task-specific portions of the program, independent of all operating system issues, and

- a second component that contains all the interconnections between the first component and the operating system.

In a program constructed in this way, whenever the first, task-specific, component needs to ask the operating system for some resource through a "system call", it calls the second component instead of calling the operating system directly.

The second component serves as an "interface" or "compatibility component" between the task-specific portion of the program and the operating system. It receives the request from the first component and translates it into the appropriate system call that will be recognized by whatever operating system is installed on the computer, e.g., DOS/VSE, MVS, or CMS. Since the first, task-specific component calls the adapter component rather than the operating system, the first component need not be customized to use any specific operating system. The second, interface, component insures that all the system calls are performed properly for the particular operating system in use.

Id. at 551. ADAPTER serves as the second, "common system interface" component referred to above.

A program like ADAPTER, which allows a computer user to change or use multiple operating systems while maintaining the same software, is highly desirable. It saves the user the costs, both in time and money, that otherwise would be expended in purchasing new programs, modifying existing systems to run them, and gaining familiarity with their operation. The benefits run both ways. The increased compatibility afforded by an ADAPTER-like component, and its resulting popularity among consumers, makes whatever software in which it is incorporated significantly more marketable.

Starting in 1982, Altai began marketing its own job scheduling program entitled ZEKE. The original version of ZEKE was designed for use in conjunction with a VSE operating system. By late 1983, in response to customer demand, Altai decided to rewrite ZEKE so that it could be run in conjunction with an MVS operating system.

At that time, James P. Williams ("Williams"), then an employee of Altai and now its President, approached Claude F. Arney, III ("Arney"), a computer programmer who worked for CA. Williams and Arney were longstanding friends, and had in fact been co-workers at CA for some time before Williams left CA to work for Altai's predecessor. Williams wanted to recruit Arney to assist Altai in designing an MVS version of ZEKE.

At the time he first spoke with Arney, Williams was aware of both the CA-SCHEDULER and ADAPTER programs. However, Williams was not involved in their development and had never seen the codes of either program. When he asked Arney to come work for Altai, Williams did not know that ADAPTER was a component of CA-SCHEDULER.

Arney, on the other hand, was intimately familiar with various aspects of ADAPTER. While working for CA, he helped improve the VSE version of ADAPTER, and was permitted to take home a copy of ADAPTER'S source code. This apparently developed into an irresistible habit, for when Arney left CA to work for Altai in January, 1984, he took with him copies of 700*700 the source code for both the VSE and MVS versions of ADAPTER. He did this in knowing violation of the CA employee agreements that he had signed.

Once at Altai, Arney and Williams discussed design possibilities for adapting ZEKE to run on MVS operating systems. Williams, who had created the VSE version of ZEKE, thought that approximately 30% of his original program would have to be modified in order to accommodate MVS. Arney persuaded Williams that the best way to make the needed modifications was to introduce a "common system interface" component into ZEKE. He did not tell Williams that his idea stemmed from his familiarity with ADAPTER. They decided to name this new component-program OSCAR.

Arney went to work creating OSCAR at Altai's offices using the ADAPTER source code. The district court accepted Williams' testimony that no one at Altai, with the exception of Arney, affirmatively knew that Arney had the ADAPTER code, or that he was using it to create OSCAR/VSE. However, during this time period, Williams' office was adjacent to Arney's. Williams testified that he and Arney "conversed quite frequently" while Arney was "investigating the source code of ZEKE" and that Arney was in his office "a number of times daily, asking questions." In three months, Arney successfully completed the OSCAR/VSE project. In an additional month he developed an OSCAR/MVS version. When the dust finally settled, Arney had copied approximately 30% of OSCAR's code from CA's ADAPTER program.

The first generation of OSCAR programs was known as OSCAR 3.4. From 1985 to August 1988, Altai used OSCAR 3.4 in its ZEKE product, as well as in programs entitled ZACK and ZEBB. In late July 1988, CA first learned that Altai may have appropriated parts of ADAPTER. After confirming its suspicions, CA secured copyrights on its 2.1 and 7.0 versions of CA-SCHEDULER. CA then brought this copyright and trade secret misappropriation action against Altai.

Apparently, it was upon receipt of the summons and complaint that Altai first learned that Arney had copied much of the OSCAR code from ADAPTER. After Arney confirmed to Williams that CA's accusations of copying were true, Williams immediately set out to survey the damage. Without ever looking at the

ADAPTER code himself, Williams learned from Arney exactly which sections of code Arney had taken from ADAPTER.

Upon advice of counsel, Williams initiated OSCAR's rewrite. The project's goal was to save as much of OSCAR 3.4 as legitimately could be used, and to excise those portions which had been copied from ADAPTER. Arney was entirely excluded from the process, and his copy of the ADAPTER code was locked away. Williams put eight other programmers on the project, none of whom had been involved in any way in the development of OSCAR 3.4. Williams provided the programmers with a description of the ZEKE operating system services so that they could rewrite the appropriate code. The rewrite project took about six months to complete and was finished in mid-November 1989. The resulting program was entitled OSCAR 3.5.

From that point on, Altai shipped only OSCAR 3.5 to its new customers. Altai also shipped OSCAR 3.5 as a "free upgrade" to all customers that had previously purchased OSCAR 3.4. While Altai and Williams acted responsibly to correct Arney's literal copying of the ADAPTER program, copyright infringement had occurred.

After CA originally instituted this action in the United States District Court for the District of New Jersey, the parties stipulated its transfer in March, 1989, to the Eastern District of New York where it was assigned to Judge Jacob Mishler. On October 26, 1989, Judge Mishler transferred the case to Judge Pratt who was sitting in the district court by designation. Judge Pratt conducted a six day trial from March 28 through April 6, 1990. He entered judgment on August 12, 1991, and this appeal followed.

DISCUSSION

While both parties originally appealed from different aspects of the district court's judgment, Altai has now abandoned its appellate claims. In particular, Altai has conceded liability for the copying of ADAPTER into OSCAR 3.4 and raises no challenge to the award of $364,444 in damages on that score. Thus, we address only CA's appeal from the district court's rulings that: (1) Altai was not liable for copyright infringement in developing OSCAR 3.5; and (2) in developing both OSCAR 3.4 and 3.5, Altai was not liable for misappropriating CA's trade secrets.

CA makes two arguments. First, CA contends that the district court applied an erroneous method for determining whether there exists substantial similarity between computer programs, and thus, erred in determining that OSCAR 3.5 did not infringe the copyrights held on the different versions of its CA-SCHEDULER program. CA asserts that the test applied by the district court failed to account sufficiently for a computer program's non-literal elements. Second, CA maintains that the district court erroneously concluded that its state law trade secret claims had been preempted by the federal Copyright Act. See 17 U.S.C. § 301(a). We shall address each argument in turn.

I.   COPYRIGHT INFRINGEMENT

In any suit for copyright infringement, the plaintiff must establish its owner-ship of a valid copyright, and that the defendant copied the copyrighted work. See Novelty Textile Mills, Inc. v. Joan Fabrics Corp., 558 F.2d 1090, 1092 (2d Cir.1977); see also 3 Melville B. Nimmer & David Nimmer, Nimmer on Copy-right § 13.01, at 13-4 (1991) (hereinafter "Nimmer"). The plaintiff may prove defendant's copying either by direct evidence or, as is most often the case, by showing that (1) the defendant had access to the plaintiff's copyrighted work and (2) that defendant's work is substantially similar to the plaintiff's copyright-able material. See Walker v. Time Life Films, Inc., 784 F.2d 44, 48 (2d Cir.), cert. denied, 476 U.S. 1159, 106 S.Ct. 2278, 90 L.Ed.2d 721 (1986).

For the purpose of analysis, the district court assumed that Altai had access to the ADAPTER code when creating OSCAR 3.5. See Computer Assocs., 775 F.Supp. at 558. Thus, in determining whether Altai had unlawfully copied protected aspects of CA's ADAPTER, the district court narrowed its focus of inquiry to ascertaining whether Altai's OSCAR 3.5 was substantially similar to ADAPTER. Because we approve Judge Pratt's conclusions regarding substan-tial similarity, our analysis will proceed along the same assumption.

As a general matter, and to varying degrees, copyright protection extends beyond a literary work's strictly textual form to its non-literal components. As we have said, "[i]t is of course essential to any protection of literary property ... that the right cannot be limited literally to the text, else a plagiarist would escape by immaterial variations." Nichols v. Universal Pictures Co., 45 F.2d 119, 121 (2d Cir.1930) (L. Hand, J.), cert. denied, 282 U.S. 902, 51 S.Ct. 216, 75 L.Ed. 795 (1931). Thus, where "the fundamental essence or structure of one work is duplicated in another," 3 Nimmer, § 13.03[A][1], at 13-24, courts have found copyright infringement. See, e.g., Horgan v. Macmillan, 789 F.2d 157, 162 (2d Cir.1986) (recognizing that a book of photographs might infringe ballet cho-reography); Twentieth Century-Fox Film Corp. v. MCA, Inc., 715 F.2d 1327, 1329 (9th Cir.1983) (motion picture and television series); Sid & Marty Krofft Television Prods., Inc. v. McDonald's Corp., 562 F.2d 1157, 1167 (9th Cir.1977) (television commercial and television series); Sheldon v. Metro-Goldwyn Pic-tures Corp., 81 F.2d 49, 55 (2d Cir.), cert. denied, 298 U.S. 669, 56 S.Ct. 835, 80 L.Ed. 1392 (1936) (play and motion picture); accord Stewart v. Abend, 495 U.S. 207, 238, 110 S.Ct. 1750, 1769, 109 L.Ed.2d 184 (1990) (recognizing that motion picture may infringe copyright in book by using its "unique setting, characters, plot, and sequence of events"). T his black letter proposition is the springboard for our discussion.

A.   Copyright Protection for the Non-literal Elements of Computer Programs

It is now well settled that the literal elements of computer programs, i.e., their source and object codes, are the subject of copyright protection. See Whelan, 797 F.2d at 1233 (source and object code); CMS Software Design Sys., Inc. v. Info Designs, Inc., 785 F.2d 1246, 1247 (5th Cir.1986) (source code); Apple

Computer, Inc. v. Franklin Computer Corp., 714 F.2d 1240, 1249 (3d Cir.1983), cert. dismissed, 464 U.S. 1033, 104 S.Ct. 690, 79 L.Ed.2d 158 (1984) (source and object code); Williams Elecs., Inc. v. Artic Int'l, Inc., 685 F.2d 870, 876-77 (3d Cir.1982) (object code). Here, as noted earlier, Altai admits having copied approximately 30% of the OSCAR 3.4 program from CA's ADAPTER source code, and does not challenge the district court's related finding of infringement.

In this case, the hotly contested issues surround OSCAR 3.5. As recounted above, OSCAR 3.5 is the product of Altai's carefully orchestrated rewrite of OSCAR 3.4. After the purge, none of the ADAPTER source code remained in the 3.5 version; thus, Altai made sure that the literal elements of its revamped OSCAR program were no longer substantially similar to the literal elements of CA's ADAPTER.

According to CA, the district court erroneously concluded that Altai's OSCAR 3.5 was not substantially similar to its own ADAPTER program. CA argues that this occurred because the district court "committed legal error in analyzing [its] claims of copyright infringement by failing to find that copyright protects expression contained in the non-literal elements of computer software." We disagree.

CA argues that, despite Altai's rewrite of the OSCAR code, the resulting program remained substantially similar to the structure of its ADAPTER program. As discussed above, a program's structure includes its non-literal components such as general flow charts as well as the more specific organization of inter-modular relationships, parameter lists, and macros. In addition to these aspects, CA contends that OSCAR 3.5 is also substantially similar to ADAPTER with respect to the list of services that both ADAPTER and OSCAR obtain from their respective operating systems. We must decide whether and to what extent these elements of computer programs are protected by copyright law.

The statutory terrain in this area has been well explored. See Lotus Dev. Corp. v. Paperback Software Int'l, 740 F.Supp. 37, 47-51 (D.Mass.1990); see also Whelan, 797 F.2d at 1240-42; Englund, at 885-90; Spivack, at 731-37. The Copyright Act affords protection to "original works of authorship fixed in any tangible medium of expression...." 17 U.S.C. § 102(a). This broad category of protected "works" includes "literary works," id. at § 102(a)(1), which are defined by the Act as

> works, other than audiovisual works, expressed in words, numbers, or other verbal or numerical symbols or indicia, regardless of the nature of the material objects, such as books, periodicals, manuscripts, phonorecords, film tapes, disks, or cards, in which they are embodied.

17 U.S.C. § 101. While computer programs are not specifically listed as part of the above statutory definition, the legislative history leaves no doubt that Congress intended them to be considered literary works. See H.R.Rep. No. 1476, 94th Cong., 2d Sess. 54, reprinted in 1976 U.S.C.C.A.N. 5659, 5667 (hereinafter "House Report"); Whelan, 797 F.2d at 1234; Apple Computer, 714 F.2d at 1247.

The syllogism that follows from the foregoing premises is a powerful one: if the non-literal structures of literary works are protected by copyright; and if computer programs are literary works, as we are told by the legislature; then the non-literal structures of computer programs are protected by copyright. See Whelan, 797 F.2d at 1234 ("By analogy to other literary works, it would thus appear that the copyrights of computer programs can be infringed even absent copying of the literal elements of the program."). We have no reservation in joining the company of those courts that have already ascribed to this logic. See, e.g., Johnson Controls, Inc. v. Phoenix Control Sys., Inc., 886 F.2d 1173, 1175 (9th Cir.1989); Lotus Dev. Corp., 740 F.Supp. at 54; Digital Communications Assocs., Inc. v. Softklone Distrib. Corp., 659 F.Supp. 449, 455-56 (N.D.Ga.1987); Q-Co Industries, Inc. v. Hoffman, 625 F.Supp. 608, 615 (S.D.N.Y.1985); SAS Inst., Inc. v. S & H Computer Sys., Inc., 605 F.Supp. 816, 829-30 (M.D.Tenn.1985). However, that conclusion does not end our analysis. We must determine the scope of copyright protection that extends to a computer program's non-literal structure.

As a caveat, we note that our decision here does not control infringement actions regarding categorically distinct works, such as certain types of screen displays. These items represent products of computer programs, rather than the programs themselves, and fall under the copyright rubric of audiovisual works. If a computer audiovisual display is copyrighted separately as an audiovisual work, apart from the literary work that generates it (i.e., the program), the display may be protectable regardless of the underlying program's copyright status. See Stern Elecs., Inc. v. Kaufman, 669 F.2d 852, 855 (2d Cir.1982) (explaining that an audiovisual works copyright, rather than a copyright on the underlying program, extended greater protection to the sights and sounds generated by a computer video game because the same audiovisual display could be generated by different programs). Of course, the copyright protection that these displays enjoy extends only so far as their expression is protectable. See Data East USA, Inc. v. Epyx, Inc., 862 F.2d 204, 209 (9th Cir.1988). In this case, however, we are concerned not with a program's display, but the program itself, and then with only its non-literal components. In considering the copyrightability of these components, we must refer to venerable doctrines of copyright law.

1) Idea vs. Expression Dichotomy

It is a fundamental principle of copyright law that a copyright does not protect an idea, but only the expression of the idea. See Baker v. Selden, 101 U.S. 99, 25 L.Ed. 841 (1879); Mazer v. Stein, 347 U.S. 201, 217, 74 S.Ct. 460, 470, 98 L.Ed. 630 (1954). This axiom of common law has been incorporated into the governing statute. Section 102(b) of the Act provides:

In no case does copyright protection for an original work of authorship extend to any idea, procedure, process, system, method of operation, concept, principle, or discovery, regardless of the form in which it is described, explained, illustrated, or embodied in such work.

17 U.S.C. § 102(b). See also House Report, at 5670 ("Copyright does not preclude others from using ideas or information revealed by the author's work.").

Congress made no special exception for computer programs. To the contrary, the legislative history explicitly states that copyright protects computer programs only "to the extent that they incorporate authorship in programmer's expression of original ideas, as distinguished from the ideas themselves." Id. at 5667; see also id. at 5670 ("Section 102(b) is intended ... to make clear that the expression adopted by the programmer is the copyrightable element in a computer program, and that the actual processes or methods embodied in the program are not within the scope of copyright law.").

Similarly, the National Commission on New Technological Uses of Copyrighted Works ("CONTU") established by Congress to survey the issues generated by the interrelationship of advancing technology and copyright law, see Pub.L. No. 93-573, § 201, 88 Stat. 1873 (1974), recommended, inter alia, that the 1976 Copyright Act "be amended ... to make it explicit that computer programs, to the extent that they embody the author's original creation, are proper subject matter for copyright." See National Commission on New Technological Uses of Copyrighted Works, Final Report 1 (1979) (hereinafter "CONTU Report"). To that end, Congress adopted CONTU's suggestions and amended the Copyright Act by adding, among other things, a provision to 17 U.S.C. § 101 which defined the term "computer program." See Pub.L. No. 96-517, § 10(a), 94 Stat. 704*704 3028 (1980). CONTU also "concluded that the idea-expression distinction should be used to determine which aspects of computer programs are copyrightable." Lotus Dev. Corp., 740 F.Supp. at 54 (citing CONTU Report, at 44).

Drawing the line between idea and expression is a tricky business. Judge Learned Hand noted that "[n]obody has ever been able to fix that boundary, and nobody ever can." Nichols, 45 F.2d at 121. Thirty years later his convictions remained firm. "Obviously, no principle can be stated as to when an imitator has gone beyond copying the 'idea,' and has borrowed its 'expression,'" Judge Hand concluded. "Decisions must therefore inevitably be ad hoc." Peter Pan Fabrics, Inc. v. Martin Weiner Corp., 274 F.2d 487, 489 (2d Cir. 1960).

The essentially utilitarian nature of a computer program further complicates the task of distilling its idea from its expression. See SAS Inst., 605 F.Supp. at 829; cf. Englund, at 893. In order to describe both computational processes and abstract ideas, its content "combines creative and technical expression." See Spivack, at 755. The variations of expression found in purely creative compositions, as opposed to those contained in utilitarian works, are not directed towards practical application. For example, a narration of Humpty Dumpty's demise, which would clearly be a creative composition, does not serve the same ends as, say, a recipe for scrambled eggs — which is a more process oriented text. Thus, compared to aesthetic works, computer programs hover even more closely to the elusive boundary line described in § 102(b).

The doctrinal starting point in analyses of utilitarian works, is the seminal case of Baker v. Selden, 101 U.S. 99, 25 L.Ed. 841 (1879). In Baker, the Supreme

Court faced the question of "whether the exclusive property in a system of bookkeeping can be claimed, under the law of copyright, by means of a book in which that system is explained?" Id. at 101. Selden had copyrighted a book that expounded a particular method of bookkeeping. The book contained lined pages with headings intended to illustrate the manner in which the system operated. Baker's accounting publication included ledger sheets that employed "substantially the same ruled lines and headings...." Id. Selden's testator sued Baker for copyright infringement on the theory that the ledger sheets were protected by Selden's copyright.

The Supreme Court found nothing copyrightable in Selden's bookkeeping system, and rejected his infringement claim regarding the ledger sheets. The Court held that:

The fact that the art described in the book by illustrations of lines and figures which are reproduced in practice in the application of the art, makes no difference. Those illustrations are the mere language employed by the author to convey his ideas more clearly. Had he used words of description instead of diagrams (which merely stand in the place of words), there could not be the slightest doubt that others, applying the art to practical use, might lawfully draw the lines and diagrams which were in the author's mind, and which he thus described by words in his book.

The copyright of a work on mathematical science cannot give to the author an exclusive right to the methods of operation which he propounds, or to the diagrams which he employs to explain them, so as to prevent an engineer from using them whenever occasion requires.

Id. at 103.

To the extent that an accounting text and a computer program are both "a set of statements or instructions ... to bring about a certain result," 17 U.S.C. § 101, they are roughly analogous. In the former case, the processes are ultimately conducted by human agency; in the latter, by electronic means. In either case, as already stated, the processes themselves are not protectable. But the holding in Baker goes farther. The Court concluded that those aspects of a work, which "must necessarily be used as incident to" the idea, system or process that the work describes, are also not copyrightable. 101 U.S. at 104. Selden's ledger sheets, therefore, enjoyed no copyright protection because they were "necessary incidents to" the system of accounting that he described. Id. at 103. From this reasoning, we conclude that those elements of a computer program that are necessarily incidental to its function are similarly unprotectable.

While Baker v. Selden provides a sound analytical foundation, it offers scant guidance on how to separate idea or process from expression, and moreover, on how to further distinguish protectable expression from that expression which "must necessarily be used as incident to" the work's underlying concept. In the context of computer programs, the Third Circuit's noted decision in Whelan has, thus far, been the most thoughtful attempt to accomplish these ends.

The court in Whelan faced substantially the same problem as is presented by this case. There, the defendant was accused of making off with the non-literal structure of the plaintiff's copyrighted dental lab management program, and employing it to create its own competitive version. In assessing whether there had been an infringement, the court had to determine which aspects of the programs involved were ideas, and which were expression. In separating the two, the court settled upon the following conceptual approach:

> [T]he line between idea and expression may be drawn with reference to the end sought to be achieved by the work in question. In other words, the purpose or function of a utilitarian work would be the work's idea, and everything that is not necessary to that purpose or function would be part of the expression of the idea.... Where there are various means of achieving the desired purpose, then the particular means chosen is not necessary to the purpose; hence, there is expression, not idea.

797 F.2d at 1236 (citations omitted). The "idea" of the program at issue in Whelan was identified by the court as simply "the efficient management of a dental laboratory." Id. at n. 28.

So far, in the courts, the Whelan rule has received a mixed reception. While some decisions have adopted its reasoning, see, e.g., Bull HN Info. Sys., Inc. v. American Express Bank, Ltd., 1990 Copyright Law Dec. (CCH) ¶ 26,555 at 23,278, 1990 WL 48098 (S.D.N.Y.1990); Dynamic Solutions, Inc. v. Planning & Control, Inc., 1987 Copyright Law Dec. (CCH) ¶ 26,062 at 20,912, 1987 WL 6419 (S.D.N.Y.1987); Broderbund Software Inc. v. Unison World, Inc., 648 F.Supp. 1127, 1133 (N.D.Cal.1986), others have rejected it, see Plains Cotton Co-op v. Goodpasture Computer Serv., Inc., 807 F.2d 1256, 1262 (5th Cir.), cert. denied, 484 U.S. 821, 108 S.Ct. 80, 98 L.Ed.2d 42 (1987); cf. Synercom Technology, Inc. v. University Computing Co., 462 F.Supp. 1003, 1014 (N.D.Tex.1978) (concluding that order and sequence of data on computer input formats was idea not expression).

Whelan has fared even more poorly in the academic community, where its standard for distinguishing idea from expression has been widely criticized for being conceptually overbroad. See, e.g., Englund, at 881; Menell, at 1074, 1082; Kretschmer, at 837-39; Spivack, at 747-55; Thomas M. Gage, Note, Whelan Associates v. Jaslow Dental Laboratories: Copyright Protection for Computer Software Structure — What's the Purpose?, 1987 WIS. L.REV. 859, 860-61 (1987). The leading commentator in the field has stated that "[t]he crucial flaw in [Whelan's] reasoning is that it assumes that only one 'idea,' in copyright law terms, underlies any computer program, and that once a separable idea can be identified, everything else must be expression." 3 Nimmer § 13.03(F), at 13-62.34. This criticism focuses not upon the program's ultimate purpose but upon the reality of its structural design. As we have already noted, a computer program's ultimate function or purpose is the composite result of interacting subroutines. Since each subroutine is itself a program, and thus, may be said to have its own "idea," Whelan's general formulation that a program's overall purpose equates with the program's idea is descriptively inadequate.

Accordingly, we think that Judge Pratt wisely declined to follow Whelan. See Computer Assocs., 775 F.Supp. at 558-60. In addition to noting the weakness in the Whelan definition of "program-idea," mentioned above, Judge Pratt found that Whelan's synonymous use of the terms "structure, sequence, and organization," see Whelan, 797 F.2d at 1224 n. 1, demonstrated a flawed understanding of a computer program's method of operation. See Computer Assocs., 775 F.Supp. at 559-60 (discussing the distinction between a program's "static structure" and "dynamic structure"). Rightly, the district court found Whelan's rationale suspect because it is so closely tied to what can now be seen — with the passage of time — as the opinion's somewhat outdated appreciation of computer science.

2) Substantial Similarity Test for Computer Program Structure: Abstraction-Filtration-Comparison

We think that Whelan's approach to separating idea from expression in computer programs relies too heavily on metaphysical distinctions and does not place enough emphasis on practical considerations. Cf. Apple Computer, 714 F.2d at 1253 (rejecting certain commercial constraints on programming as a helpful means of distinguishing idea from expression because they did "not enter into the somewhat metaphysical issue of whether particular ideas and expressions have merged"). As the cases that we shall discuss demonstrate, a satisfactory answer to this problem cannot be reached by resorting, a priori, to philosophical first principals.

As discussed herein, we think that district courts would be well-advised to undertake a three-step procedure, based on the abstractions test utilized by the district court, in order to determine whether the non-literal elements of two or more computer programs are substantially similar. This approach breaks no new ground; rather, it draws on such familiar copyright doctrines as merger, scenes a faire, and public domain. In taking this approach, however, we are cognizant that computer technology is a dynamic field which can quickly outpace judicial decisionmaking. Thus, in cases where the technology in question does not allow for a literal application of the procedure we outline below, our opinion should not be read to foreclose the district courts of our circuit from utilizing a modified version.

In ascertaining substantial similarity under this approach, a court would first break down the allegedly infringed program into its constituent structural parts. Then, by examining each of these parts for such things as incorporated ideas, expression that is necessarily incidental to those ideas, and elements that are taken from the public domain, a court would then be able to sift out all non-protectable material. Left with a kernel, or possible kernels, of creative expression after following this process of elimination, the court's last step would be to compare this material with the structure of an allegedly infringing program. The result of this comparison will determine whether the protectable elements of the programs at issue are substantially similar so as to warrant a finding of infringement. It will be helpful to elaborate a bit further.

Step One: Abstraction

As the district court appreciated, see Computer Assocs., 775 F.Supp. at 560, the theoretic framework for analyzing substantial similarity expounded by Learned Hand in the Nichols case is helpful in the present context. In Nichols, we enunciated what has now become known as the "abstractions" test for separating idea from expression:

> Upon any work ... a great number of patterns of increasing generality will fit equally well, as more and more of the incident is left out. The last may perhaps be no more than the most general statement of what the [work] is about, and at times might consist only of its title; but there is a point in this series of abstractions where they are no longer protected, since otherwise the [author] could prevent the use of his "ideas," to which, apart from their expression, his property is never extended.

Nichols, 45 F.2d at 121.

While the abstractions test was originally applied in relation to literary works such as novels and plays, it is adaptable to computer programs. In contrast to the Whelan approach, the abstractions test "implicitly recognizes that any given work may consist of a mixture of numerous ideas and expressions." 3 Nimmer § 13.03[F], at 13-62.34-63.

As applied to computer programs, the abstractions test will comprise the first step in the examination for substantial similarity. Initially, in a manner that resembles reverse engineering on a theoretical plane, a court should dissect the allegedly copied program's structure and isolate each level of abstraction contained within it. This process begins with the code and ends with an articulation of the program's ultimate function. Along the way, it is necessary essentially to retrace and map each of the designer's steps — in the opposite order in which they were taken during the program's creation. See Background: Computer Program Design, supra.

As an anatomical guide to this procedure, the following description is helpful:

At the lowest level of abstraction, a computer program may be thought of in its entirety as a set of individual instructions organized into a hierarchy of modules. At a higher level of abstraction, the instructions in the lowest-level modules may be replaced conceptually by the functions of those modules. At progressively higher levels of abstraction, the functions of higher-level modules conceptually replace the implementations of those modules in terms of lower-level modules and instructions, until finally, one is left with nothing but the ultimate function of the program.... A program has structure at every level of abstraction at which it is viewed. At low levels of abstraction, a program's structure may be quite complex; at the highest level it is trivial.

Englund, at 897-98; cf. Spivack, at 774.

Step Two: Filtration

Once the program's abstraction levels have been discovered, the substantial similarity inquiry moves from the conceptual to the concrete. Professor Nimmer suggests, and we endorse, a "successive filtering method" for separating protectable expression from non-protectable material. See generally 3 Nimmer § 13.03[F]. This process entails examining the structural components at each level of abstraction to determine whether their particular inclusion at that level was "idea" or was dictated by considerations of efficiency, so as to be necessarily incidental to that idea; required by factors external to the program itself; or taken from the public domain and hence is nonprotectable expression. See also Kretschmer, at 844-45 (arguing that program features dictated by market externalities or efficiency concerns are unprotectable). The structure of any given program may reflect some, all, or none of these considerations. Each case requires its own fact specific investigation.

Strictly speaking, this filtration serves "the purpose of defining the scope of plaintiff's copyright." Brown Bag Software v. Symantec Corp., 960 F.2d 1465, 1475 (9th Cir.) (endorsing "analytic dissection" of computer programs in order to isolate protectable expression), cert. denied, ___ U.S. ___, 113 S.Ct. 198, 121 L.Ed.2d 141 (1992). By applying well developed doctrines of copyright law, it may ultimately leave behind a "core of protectable material." 3 Nimmer § 13.03[F][5], at 13-72. Further explication of this second step may be helpful.

(a) Elements Dictated by Efficiency

The portion of Baker v. Selden, discussed earlier, which denies copyright protection to expression necessarily incidental to the idea being expressed, appears to be the cornerstone for what has developed into the doctrine of merger. See Morrissey v. Proctor & Gamble Co., 379 F.2d 675, 678-79 (1st Cir.1967) (relying on Baker for the proposition that expression embodying the rules of a sweepstakes contest was inseparable from the idea of the contest itself, and therefore were not protectable by copyright); see also Digital Communications, 659 F.Supp. at 457. The doctrine's underlying principle is that "[w]hen there is essentially only one way to express an idea, the idea and its expression are inseparable and copyright is no bar to copying that expression." Concrete Machinery Co. v. Classic Lawn Ornaments, Inc., 843 F.2d 600, 606 (1st Cir.1988). Under these circumstances, the expression is said to have "merged" with the idea itself. In order not to confer a monopoly of the idea upon the copyright owner, such expression should not be protected. See Herbert Rosenthal Jewelry Corp. v. Kalpakian, 446 F.2d 738, 742 (9th Cir.1971).

CONTU recognized the applicability of the merger doctrine to computer programs. In its report to Congress it stated that:

> [C]opyrighted language may be copied without infringing when there is but a limited number of ways to express a given idea.... In the computer context, this means that when specific instructions, even though previously copyrighted, are the only and essential means of accomplishing a given task, their later use by another will not amount to infringement.

CONTU Report, at 20. While this statement directly concerns only the application of merger to program code, that is, the textual aspect of the program, it reasonably suggests that the doctrine fits comfortably within the general context of computer programs.

Furthermore, when one considers the fact that programmers generally strive to create programs "that meet the user's needs in the most efficient manner," Menell, at 1052, the applicability of the merger doctrine to computer programs becomes compelling. In the context of computer program design, the concept of efficiency is akin to deriving the most concise logical proof or formulating the most succinct mathematical computation. Thus, the more efficient a set of modules are, the more closely they approximate the idea or process embodied in that particular aspect of the program's structure.

While, hypothetically, there might be a myriad of ways in which a programmer may effectuate certain functions within a program, — i.e., express the idea embodied in a given subroutine — efficiency concerns may so narrow the practical range of choice as to make only one or two forms of expression workable options. See 3 Nimmer § 13.03[F][2], at 13-63; see also Whelan, 797 F.2d at 1243 n. 43 ("It is true that for certain tasks there are only a very limited number of file structures available, and in such cases the structures might not be copyrightable...."). Of course, not all program structure is informed by efficiency concerns. See Menell, at 1052 (besides efficiency, simplicity related to user accommodation has become a programming priority). It follows that in order to determine whether the merger doctrine precludes copyright protection to an aspect of a program's structure that is so oriented, a court must inquire "whether the use of this particular set of modules is necessary efficiently to implement that part of the program's process" being implemented. Englund, at 902. If the answer is yes, then the expression represented by the programmer's choice of a specific module or group of modules has merged with their underlying idea and is unprotected. Id. at 902-03.

Another justification for linking structural economy with the application of the merger doctrine stems from a program's essentially utilitarian nature and the competitive forces that exist in the software marketplace. See Kretschmer, at 842. Working in tandem, these factors give rise to a problem of proof which merger helps to eliminate.

Efficiency is an industry-wide goal. Since, as we have already noted, there may be only a limited number of efficient implementations for any given program task, it is quite possible that multiple programmers, working independently, will design the identical method employed in the allegedly infringed work. Of course, if this is the case, there is no copyright infringement. See Roth Greeting Cards v. United Card Co., 429 F.2d 1106, 1110 (9th Cir. 1970); Sheldon, 81 F.2d at 54.

Under these circumstances, the fact that two programs contain the same efficient structure may as likely lead to an inference of independent creation as it does to one of copying. See 3 Nimmer § 13.03[F][2], at 13-65; cf. Herbert Rosenthal 709*709 Jewelry Corp., 446 F.2d at 741 (evidence of independent creation may stem from defendant's standing as a designer of previous similar works). Thus, since evidence of similarly efficient structure is not particularly probative of copying, it should be disregarded in the overall substantial similarity analysis. See 3 Nimmer § 13.03[F][2], at 13-65.

We find support for applying the merger doctrine in cases that have already addressed the question of substantial similarity in the context of computer program structure. Most recently, in Lotus Dev. Corp., 740 F.Supp. at 66, the district court had before it a claim of copyright infringement relating to the structure of a computer spreadsheet program. The court observed that "the basic spreadsheet screen display that resembles a rotated `L' ..., if not present in every expression of such a program, is present in most expressions." Id. Similarly, the court found that "an essential detail present in most if not all expressions of an electronic spreadsheet — is the designation of a particular key that, when pressed, will invoke the menu command system." Id. Applying the merger doctrine, the court denied copyright protection to both program elements.

In Manufacturers Technologies, Inc. v. Cams, Inc., 706 F.Supp. 984, 995-99 (D.Conn.1989), the infringement claims stemmed from various alleged program similarities "as indicated in their screen displays." Id. at 990. Stressing efficiency concerns in the context of a merger analysis, the court determined that the program's method of allowing the user to navigate within the screen displays was not protectable because, in part, "the process or manner of navigating internally on any specific screen displays ... is limited in the number of ways it may be simply achieved to facilitate user comfort." Id. at 995.

The court also found that expression contained in various screen displays (in the form of alphabetical and numerical columns) was not the proper subject of copyright protection because it was "necessarily incident to the idea[s]" embodied in the displays. Id. at 996-97. Cf. Digital Communications, 659 F.Supp. at 460 (finding no merger and affording copyright protection to program's status screen display because "modes of expression chosen ... are clearly not necessary to the idea of the status screen").

We agree with the approach taken in these decisions, and conclude that application of the merger doctrine in this setting is an effective way to eliminate non-protectable expression contained in computer programs.

(b) Elements Dictated By External Factors

We have stated that where "it is virtually impossible to write about a particular historical era or fictional theme without employing certain `stock' or standard literary devices," such expression is not copyrightable. Hoehling v. Universal City Studios, Inc., 618 F.2d 972, 979 (2d Cir.), cert. denied, 449 U.S. 841, 101 S.Ct. 121, 66 L.Ed.2d 49 (1980). For example, the Hoehling case was an infringement suit stemming from several works on the Hindenberg disaster. There we concluded that similarities in representations of German beer halls, scenes depicting German greetings such as "Heil Hitler," or the singing of certain German songs would not lead to a finding of infringement because they were "`indispensable, or at least standard, in the treatment of'" life in Nazi Germany. Id. (quoting Alexander v. Haley, 460 F.Supp. 40, 45 (S.D.N.Y.1978)). This is known as the scenes a faire doctrine, and like "merger," it has its analogous application to computer programs. Cf. Data East USA, 862 F.2d at 208 (applying scenes a faire to a home computer video game).

Professor Nimmer points out that "in many instances it is virtually impossible to write a program to perform particular functions in a specific computing environment without employing standard techniques." 3 Nimmer § 13.03[F][3], at 13-65. This is a result of the fact that a programmer's freedom of design choice is often circumscribed by extrinsic considerations such as (1) the mechanical specifications of the computer on which a particular program is intended to run; (2) compatibility requirements of other programs with which a program is designed to operate in conjunction; (3) computer manufacturers' design standards; (4) demands of the industry being serviced; and (5) widely accepted programming practices within the computer industry. Id. at 13-66-71.

Courts have already considered some of these factors in denying copyright protection to various elements of computer programs. In the Plains Cotton case, the Fifth Circuit refused to reverse the district court's denial of a preliminary injunction against an alleged program infringer because, in part, "many of the similarities between the ... programs [were] dictated by the externalities of the cotton market." 807 F.2d at 1262.

In Manufacturers Technologies, the district court noted that the program's method of screen navigation "is influenced by the type of hardware that the software is designed to be used on." 706 F.Supp. at 995. Because, in part, "the functioning of the hardware package impact[ed] and constrain[ed] the type of navigational tools used in plaintiff's screen displays," the court denied copyright protection to that aspect of the program. Id.; cf. Data East USA, 862 F.2d at 209 (reversing a district court's finding of audiovisual work infringement because, inter alia, "the use of the Commodore computer for a karate game intended for home consumption is subject to various constraints inherent in the use of that computer").

Finally, the district court in Q-Co Industries rested its holding on what, perhaps, most closely approximates a traditional scenes a faire rationale. There, the court denied copyright protection to four program modules employed in a teleprompter program. This decision was ultimately based upon the court's finding that "the same modules would be an inherent part of any prompting program." 625 F.Supp. at 616.

Building upon this existing case law, we conclude that a court must also examine the structural content of an allegedly infringed program for elements that might have been dictated by external factors.

(c) Elements taken From the Public Domain

Closely related to the non-protectability of scenes a faire, is material found in the public domain. Such material is free for the taking and cannot be appropriated by a single author even though it is included in a copyrighted work. See E.F. Johnson Co. v. Uniden Corp. of America, 623 F.Supp. 1485, 1499 (D.Minn.1985); see also Sheldon, 81 F.2d at 54. We see no reason to make an exception to this rule for elements of a computer program that have entered the public domain by virtue of freely accessible program exchanges and the like. See 3 Nimmer § 13.03[F][4]; see also Brown Bag Software, 960 F.2d at 1473 (affirming the district court's finding that "'[p]laintiffs may not claim copyright protection of an ... expression that is, if not standard, then commonplace in the computer software industry.'"). Thus, a court must also filter out this material from the allegedly infringed program before it makes the final inquiry in its substantial similarity analysis.

Step Three: Comparison

The third and final step of the test for substantial similarity that we believe appropriate for non-literal program components entails a comparison. Once a court has sifted out all elements of the allegedly infringed program which are "ideas" or are dictated by efficiency or external factors, or taken from the public domain, there may remain a core of protectable expression. In terms of a work's copyright value, this is the golden nugget. See Brown Bag Software, 960 F.2d at 1475. At this point, the court's substantial similarity inquiry focuses on whether the defendant copied any aspect of this protected expression, as well as an assessment of the copied portion's relative importance with respect to the plaintiff's overall program. See 3 Nimmer § 13.03[F][5]; Data East USA, 862 F.2d at 208 ("To determine whether similarities result from unprotectable expression, analytic dissection of similarities may be performed. If ... all similarities in expression arise from use of common ideas, then no substantial similarity can be found.").

3) Policy Considerations

We are satisfied that the three step approach we have just outlined not only comports with, but advances the constitutional policies underlying the Copyright Act. Since any method that tries to distinguish idea from expression ultimately impacts on the scope of copyright protection afforded to a particular type of work, "the line [it draws] must be a pragmatic one, which also keeps in consideration 'the preservation of the balance between competition and protection....'" Apple Computer, 714 F.2d at 1253 (citation omitted).

CA and some amici argue against the type of approach that we have set forth on the grounds that it will be a disincentive for future computer program research and development. At bottom, they claim that if programmers are not guaranteed broad copyright protection for their work, they will not invest the extensive time, energy and funds required to design and improve program structures. While they have a point, their argument cannot carry the day. The interest of the copyright law is not in simply conferring a monopoly on industrious persons, but in advancing the public welfare through rewarding artistic creativity, in a manner that permits the free use and development of non-protectable ideas and processes.

In this respect, our conclusion is informed by Justice Stewart's concise discussion of the principles that correctly govern the adaptation of the copyright law to new circumstances. In Twentieth Century Music Corp. v. Aiken, he wrote:

The limited scope of the copyright holder's statutory monopoly, like the limited copyright duration required by the Constitution, reflects a balance of competing claims upon the public interest: Creative work is to be encouraged and rewarded, but private motivation must ultimately serve the cause of promoting broad public availability of literature, music, and the other arts.

The immediate effect of our copyright law is to secure a fair return for an "author's" creative labor. But the ultimate aim is, by this incentive, to stimulate artistic creativity for the general public good.... When technological change has rendered its literal terms ambiguous, the Copyright Act must be construed in light of this basic purpose.

422 U.S. 151, 156, 95 S.Ct. 2040, 2043-44, 45 L.Ed.2d 84 (1975) (citations and footnotes omitted).

Recently, the Supreme Court has emphatically reiterated that "[t]he primary objective of copyright is not to reward the labor of authors...." Feist Publications, Inc. v. Rural Tel. Serv. Co., ___ U.S. ___, ___, 111 S.Ct. 1282, 1290, 113 L.Ed.2d 358 (1991) (emphasis added). While the Feist decision deals primarily with the copyrightability of purely factual compilations, its underlying tenets apply to much of the work involved in computer programming. Feist put to rest the "sweat of the brow" doctrine in copyright law. Id. at ___, 111 S.Ct. at 1295. The rationale of that doctrine "was that copyright was a reward for the hard work that went into compiling facts." Id. at ___, 111 S.Ct. at 1291. The Court flatly rejected this justification for extending copyright protection, noting that it "eschewed the most fundamental axiom of copyright law — that no one may copyright facts or ideas." Id.

Feist teaches that substantial effort alone cannot confer copyright status on an otherwise uncopyrightable work. As we have discussed, despite the fact that significant labor and expense often goes into computer program flow-charting and debugging, that process does not always result in inherently protectable expression. Thus, Feist implicitly undercuts the Whelan rationale, "which allow[ed] copyright protection beyond the literal computer code ... [in order to] provide the proper incentive for programmers by protecting their most valuable efforts...." Whelan, 797 F.2d at 1237 (footnote omitted). We note that Whelan was decided prior to Feist when the "sweat of the brow" doctrine still had vitality. In view of the Supreme 712*712 Court's recent holding, however, we must reject the legal basis of CA's disincentive argument.

Furthermore, we are unpersuaded that the test we approve today will lead to the dire consequences for the computer program industry that plaintiff and some amici predict. To the contrary, serious students of the industry have been highly critical of the sweeping scope of copyright protection engendered by the Whelan rule, in that it "enables first comers to `lock up' basic programming techniques as implemented in programs to perform particular tasks." Menell, at 1087; see also Spivack, at 765 (Whelan "results in an inhibition of creation by virtue of the copyright owner's quasi-monopoly power").

To be frank, the exact contours of copyright protection for non-literal program structure are not completely clear. We trust that as future cases are decided, those limits will become better defined. Indeed, it may well be that the Copyright Act serves as a relatively weak barrier against public access to the theoretical interstices behind a program's source and object codes. This results from the hybrid nature of a computer program, which, while it is literary expression, is also a highly functional, utilitarian component in the larger process of computing.

Generally, we think that copyright registration — with its indiscriminating availability — is not ideally suited to deal with the highly dynamic technology of computer science. Thus far, many of the decisions in this area reflect the courts' attempt to fit the proverbial square peg in a round hole. The district court, see Computer Assocs., 775 F.Supp. at 560, and at least one commentator have suggested that patent registration, with its exacting up-front novelty and non-obviousness requirements, might be the more appropriate rubric of protection for intellectual property of this kind. See Randell M. Whitmeyer, Comment, A Plea for Due Processes: Defining the Proper Scope of Patent Protection for Computer Software, 85 Nw.U.L.REV. 1103, 1123-25 (1991); see also Lotus Dev. Corp. v. Borland Int'l, Inc., 788 F.Supp. 78, 91 (D.Mass.1992) (discussing the potentially supplemental relationship between patent and copyright protection in the context of computer programs). In any event, now that more than 12 years have passed since CONTU issued its final report, the resolution of this specific issue could benefit from further legislative investigation — perhaps a CONTU II.

In the meantime, Congress has made clear that computer programs are literary works entitled to copyright protection. Of course, we shall abide by these instructions, but in so doing we must not impair the overall integrity of copyright law. While incentive based arguments in favor of broad copyright protection are perhaps attractive from a pure policy perspective, see Lotus Dev. Corp., 740 F.Supp. at 58, ultimately, they have a corrosive effect on certain fundamental tenets of copyright doctrine. If the test we have outlined results in narrowing the scope of protection, as we expect it will, that result flows from applying, in accordance with Congressional intent, long-standing principles of copyright law to computer programs. Of course, our decision is also informed by our concern that these fundamental principles remain undistorted.

(b) Computer Screen Displays and Video Games

The user interface of a computer program, also sometimes called the "look and feel" of the program, is generally the design of the video screen and the manner in which information is presented to the user. User interfaces employed in computer programs include all the devices by which the human user can interact with the computer in order to accomplish the task the computer is programmed to perform.

A significant amount of the creative work in designing a computer program is in the conceptualization of the program and its user interface, rather than in its encoding. In fact, creating a suitable user interface is often a more difficult intellectual task, requiring greater creativity, originality, and insight, than converting the user interface design into instructions to the machine. Software publishers, particularly in the United States, have litigated to protect the "look and feel" of their programs, on the basis that their creation is dictated primarily by artistic and aesthetic considerations. Are computer screen displays protected in Canada?

Harmony Consulting Ltd. v. G.A. Foss Transport Ltd., 2012 FCA 226 (F.C.A.)

REASONS FOR JUDGMENT

GAUTHIER J.A.

. . .

Screen Display and the Number of Users

[75] The trial Judge says in her Reasons that she does not need to decide if Foss exceeded the number of users allowed in the license agreements because such breach would not, in her view, constitute an infringement of a right protected pursuant to subsection 3(1) of the Act.

[76] I agree with the trial judge that the *Act* does not give the owner of the copyrights an exclusive right to use the copyrighted work. In that respect, the rights of a copyright owner differ from those granted to the owner of a patent or a trademark.

[77] The trial judge does not discuss the two cases relied upon by Harmony when it says that she erred in dismissing its argument that screen displays on more than five users' monitors is an unauthorized reproduction of its copyrighted works: *Delrina Corp v Triolet Systems Inc.* (1993), 9 B.L.R. (2d) 140, 47 C.P.R. (3d) 1 (Ont. Gen. Div.), (*Delrina* Ont. Gen. Div.), aff'd 2002 CanLII 11389 (ON CA), (2002), 58 O.R. (3d) 339, 156 O.A.C. 166 (O.C.A.) , (*Delrina* O.C.A.), and the Federal Court decision of *Équipe de recherche opérationnelle en santé Inc. v. Conseillers en gestion & informatique C.G.I. Inc.*, 2004 FC 178 (CanLII), 2004 FC 178, 258 F.T.R. 172 , (Eros).

[78] Obviously, I am dealing here with the arguments regarding Harmony's copyrighted programs that were actually used by Foss (the Dip Forecasting and the Railmaster).

[79] Though the arguments were not put very clearly either orally or in writing (see paragraphs 59-62 of Appellant's Memorandum of Fact and Law), I understand Harmony to be saying that, based on *Delrina* O.C.A., the screen display is a reproduction of the copyrighted object code of the licensed programs in a different material form (visual display) (Eros).

[80] Harmony's counsel also referred to the screen displays as works of art (presumably artistic works) at the hearing. Thus, I understand Harmony to also argue on appeal that the reproduction on the user's monitor at Foss is a reproduction of the copyrighted forms (distinct artistic works) included in its computer programs.

[81] Having reviewed the transcripts of the arguments before the trial judge, I could find only two relevant passages, albeit exceedingly brief, dealing with these issues:

> In chief
>
> On the issue of display screens, I've included two cases in our Book of Authorities, tabs 13 and 14, where Justices of the Ontario High Court of Justice held that copyright subsists in display screens and software (page 03278 of Appeal Book vol. 10 at tab10).
>
> In reply
>
> My lady, any change in the display screen is a reproduction. There is copyright in display screens. Gemologists, the Del Rena (sic) cases, make that clear. Every time you make a change to a computer program you are replacing the former program with the new one. That's a reproduction (page 03641 of Appeal Book vol. 11 at tab 11).

[82] I mention this because the issue of copyrights in screen displays has never been addressed by this Court. It is a subject of importance that may have far reaching implications. A single example will suffice to illustrate the point. It is now common for individual users to have multiple screens connected to their computer open at the same time. Should these consumers buy more than one license for the programs that they use?

[83] In my view, this Court should be careful not to address anything more than is absolutely necessary where such matter was not fully argued before either court and there is clearly a lack of evidence and findings supporting the argument, as in this case.

[84] Certainly, the argument based on Eros that forms included in these programs qualify as distinct artistic works was not made before the judge, and she made no findings in that respect. Harmony did not refer to any particular

evidence on this point in its Memorandum of Fact and Law. In my view, this argument should not be entertained by this Court.

[85] I shall now address briefly Harmony's argument based on Delrina Ont. Gen. Div., particularly paragraph 28 therein.

[86] It is worth noting that the Ontario Court of Appeal overtly declined to express any opinion with respect to the statements that Harmony now relies upon. The Court of Appeal did not opine on these statements essentially because they were obiter, considering the judge's findings of fact (Delrina O.C.A. at paragraph 6).

[87] The passage highlighted by Harmony in the Delrina Ont. Gen. Div. decision reads as follows:

> By using the instructions in the manual, and touching the required keys on the terminal keyboard, the user of the program causes the computer to create a screen display in form and content dictated by the way it was programmed by the object code. The screen display so produced is the reproduction of the object code in a different "material form". I am here talking about the style and format of the screen display, not the individual numbers the computer may fill in on the screen when asked to do so by the operator of the program.

[88] With respect, I cannot agree that a screen display is simply a reproduction of the object code. A computer program is defined in section 2 of the *Act* as:

> "computer program" means a set of instructions or statements, expressed, fixed, embodied or stored in any manner, that is to be used directly or indirectly in a computer in order to bring about a specific result;

[89] In my view, the screen display on a user monitor is the result of such a set of instructions rather than a reproduction of the set of instruction in another form. To use the analogy of the Supreme Court of *Canada in Cuisenaire v. South West Imports Ltd.*, 1968 CanLII 122 (SCC), [1969] S.C.R. 208, 2 D.L.R. (3d) 430, the screen display is the rabbit pie rather than the recipe (the recipe being the set of instructions).

[90] This distinction between the two is especially clear when one considers that Mr. Chari explained, in the course of his cross examination (see pages 01887-01889 of Appeal Book vol. 7 at tab 2), that what goes on behind the screen display is quite different, even though particular screen displays for each product are very similar in that essentially the same form is used.

Lotus Development Corp. v. Borland International Inc., 49 F.3d 807
(1st Cir. 1995)

U.S. Court of Appeals First Circuit
No. 93-2214

Decided March 9, 1995

Stahl, J.

This appeal requires us to decide whether a computer menu command hierarchy is copyrightable subject matter. In particular, we must decide whether, as the district court held, plaintiff-appellee Lotus Development Corporation's copyright in Lotus 1-2-3, a computer spreadsheet program, was infringed by defendant-appellant Borland International, Inc., when Borland copied the Lotus 1-2- 3 menu command hierarchy into its Quattro and Quattro Pro computer spreadsheet programs.

I. Background

Lotus 1-2-3 is a spreadsheet program that enables users to perform accounting functions electronically on a computer. Users manipulate and control the program via a series of menu commands, such as "Copy," "Print," and "Quit." Users choose commands either by highlighting them on the screen or by typing their first letter. In all, Lotus 1-2-3 has 469 commands arranged into more than 50 menus and submenus.

Lotus 1-2-3, like many computer programs, allows users to write what are called "macros." By writing a macro, a user can designate a series of command choices with a single macro keystroke. Then, to execute that series of commands in multiple parts of the spreadsheet, rather than typing the whole series each time, the user only needs to type the single pre- programmed macro keystroke, causing the program to recall and perform the designated series of commands automatically. Thus, Lotus 1-2-3 macros shorten the time needed to set up and operate the program.

Borland released its first Quattro program to the public in 1987, after Borland's engineers had labored over its development for nearly three years. Borland's objective was to develop a spreadsheet program far superior to existing programs, including Lotus 1-2-3. In Borland's words, " [f]rom the time of its initial release . . . Quattro included enormous innovations over competing spreadsheet products."

. . .

D.   The Lotus Menu Command Hierarchy: A "Method of Operation"

Borland argues that the Lotus menu command hierarchy is uncopyrightable because it is a system, method of operation, process, or procedure foreclosed from copyright protection by 17 U.S.C. Section 102(b). Section 102(b) states: "In no case does copyright protection for an original work of authorship extend to any idea, procedure, process, system, method of operation, concept, principle, or discovery, regardless of the form in which it is described, explained, illustrated, or embodied in such work." Because we conclude that the Lotus menu command hierarchy is a method of operation, we do not consider whether it could also be a system, process, or procedure.

We think that "method of operation," as that term is used in Section 102(b), refers to the means by which a person operates something, whether it be a car, a food processor, or a computer. Thus a text describing how to operate something would not extend copyright protection to the method of operation itself; other people would be free to employ that method and to describe it in their own words. Similarly, if a new method of operation is used rather than described, other people would still be free to employ or describe that method.

[2] We hold that the Lotus menu command hierarchy is an uncopyrightable "method of operation." The Lotus menu command hierarchy provides the means by which users control and operate Lotus 1-2-3. If users wish to copy material, for example, they use the "Copy" command. If users wish to print material, they use the "Print" command. Users must use the command terms to tell the computer what to do. Without the menu command hierarchy, users would not be able to access and control, or indeed make use of, Lotus 1-2-3's functional capabilities.

The Lotus menu command hierarchy does not merely explain and present Lotus 1-2-3's functional capabilities to the user; it also serves as the method by which the program is operated and controlled. The Lotus menu command hierarchy is different from the Lotus long prompts, for the long prompts are not necessary to the operation of the program; users could operate Lotus 1-2-3 even if there were no long prompts. The Lotus menu command hierarchy is also different from the Lotus screen displays, for users need not "use" any expressive aspects of the screen displays in order to operate Lotus 1-2-3; because the way the screens look has little bearing on how users control the program, the screen displays are not part of Lotus 1-2-3's "method of operation." The Lotus menu command hierarchy is also different from the underlying computer code, because while code is necessary for the program to work, its precise formulation is not. In other words, to offer the same capabilities as Lotus 1-2-3, Borland did not have to copy Lotus's underlying code (and indeed it did not); to allow users to operate its programs in substantially the same way, however, Borland had to copy the Lotus menu command hierarchy. Thus the Lotus 1-2-3 code is not a uncopyrightable "method of operation."

The district court held that the Lotus menu command hierarchy, with its specific choice and arrangement of command terms, constituted an "expression" of the "idea" of operating a computer program with commands arranged hierarchically into menus and submenus. *Borland II*, 799 F. Supp. at 216. Under the district court's reasoning, Lotus's decision to employ hierarchically arranged command terms to operate its program could not foreclose its competitors from also employing hierarchically arranged command terms to operate their programs, but it did foreclose them from employing the specific command terms and arrangement that Lotus had used. In effect, the district court limited Lotus 1-2-3's "method of operation" to an abstraction.

Accepting the district court's finding that the Lotus developers made some expressive choices in choosing and arranging the Lotus command terms, we nonetheless hold that that expression is not copyrightable because it is part of Lotus 1-2-3's "method of operation." We do not think that "methods of operation" are limited to abstractions; rather, they are the means by which a user operates something. If specific words are essential to operating something, then they are part of a "method of operation" and, as such, are unprotectable. This is so whether they must be highlighted, typed in, or even spoken, as computer programs no doubt will soon be controlled by spoken words.

The fact that Lotus developers could have designed the Lotus menu command hierarchy differently is immaterial to the question of whether it is a "method of operation." In other words, our initial inquiry is not whether the Lotus menu command hierarchy incorporates any expression. Rather, our initial inquiry is whether the Lotus menu command hierarchy is a "method of operation." Concluding, as we do, that users operate Lotus 1-2-3 by using the Lotus menu command hierarchy, and that the entire Lotus menu command hierarchy is essential to operating Lotus 1-2-3, we do not inquire further whether that method of operation could have been designed differently. The "expressive" choices of what to name the command terms and how to arrange them do not magically change the uncopyrightable menu command hierarchy into copyrightable subject matter.

Our holding that "methods of operation" are not limited to mere abstractions is bolstered by *Baker v. Selden*. In *Baker*, the Supreme Court explained that the teachings of science and the rules and methods of useful art have their final end in application and use; and this application and use are what the public derive from the publication of a book which teaches them. . . . The description of the art in a book, though entitled to the benefit of copyright, lays no foundation for an exclusive claim to the art itself. The object of the one is explanation; the object of the other is use. The former may be secured by copyright. The latter can only be secured, if it can be secured at all, by letters-patent.

Baker v. Selden, 101 U.S. at 104-05. Lotus wrote its menu command hierarchy so that people could learn it and use it. Accordingly, it falls squarely within the prohibition on copyright protection established in *Baker v. Selden* and codified by Congress in Section 102(b).

In many ways, the Lotus menu command hierarchy is like the buttons used to control, say, a video cassette recorder ("VCR"). A VCR is a machine that enables one to watch and record video tapes. Users operate VCRs by pressing a series of buttons that are typically labelled "Record, Play, Reverse, Fast Forward, Pause, Stop/Eject." That the buttons are arranged and labeled does not make them a "literary work," nor does it make them an "expression" of the abstract "method of operating" a VCR via a set of labeled buttons. Instead, the buttons are themselves the "method of operating" the VCR.

When a Lotus 1-2-3 user chooses a command, either by highlighting it on the screen or by typing its first letter, he or she effectively pushes a button. Highlighting the "Print" command on the screen, or typing the letter "P," is analogous to pressing a VCR button labeled "Play."

Just as one could not operate a buttonless VCR, it would be impossible to operate Lotus 1-2-3 without employing its menu command hierarchy. Thus the Lotus command terms are not equivalent to the labels on the VCR's buttons, but are instead equivalent to the buttons themselves. Unlike the labels on a VCR's buttons, which merely make operating a VCR easier by indicating the buttons' functions, the Lotus menu commands are essential to operating Lotus 1-2-3. Without the menu commands, there would be no way to "push" the Lotus buttons, as one could push unlabeled VCR buttons. While Lotus could probably have designed a user interface for which the command terms were mere labels, it did not do so here. Lotus 1-2-3 depends for its operation on use of the precise command terms that make up the Lotus menu command hierarchy.

One might argue that the buttons for operating a VCR are not analogous to the commands for operating a computer program because VCRs are not copyrightable, whereas computer programs are. VCRs may not be copyrighted because they do not fit within any of the Section 102(a) categories of copyrightable works; the closest they come is "sculptural work." Sculptural works, however, are subject to a "useful-article" exception whereby "the design of a useful article . . . shall be considered a pictorial, graphic, or sculptural work only if, and only to the extent that, such design incorporates pictorial, graphic, or sculptural features that can be identified separately from, and are capable of existing independently of, the utilitarian aspects of the article." 17 U.S.C. Section 101. A "useful article" is "an article having an intrinsic utilitarian function that is not merely to portray the appearance of the article or to convey information."*Id.* Whatever expression there may be in the arrangement of the parts of a VCR is not capable of existing separately from the VCR itself, so an ordinary VCR would not be copyrightable.

Computer programs, unlike VCRs, are copyrightable as "literary works." 17 U.S.C. Section 102(a). Accordingly, one might argue, the "buttons" used to operate a computer program are not like the buttons used to operate a VCR, for they are not subject to a useful-article exception. The response, of course, is that the arrangement of buttons on a VCR would not be copyrightable even without a useful-article exception, because the buttons are an uncopyrightable "method of operation." Similarly, the "buttons" of a computer program are also an uncopyrightable "method of operation."

That the Lotus menu command hierarchy is a "method of operation" becomes clearer when one considers program compatibility. Under Lotus's theory, if a user uses several different programs, he or she must learn how to perform the same operation in a different way for each program used. For example, if the user wanted the computer to print material, then the user would have to learn not just one method of operating the computer such that it prints, but many different methods. We find this absurd. The fact that there may be many different ways to operate a computer program, or even many different ways to operate a computer program using a set of hierarchically arranged command terms, does not make the actual method of operation chosen copyrightable; it still functions as a method for operating the computer and as such is uncopyrightable.

Consider also that users employ the Lotus menu command hierarchy in writing macros. Under the district court's holding, if the user wrote a macro to shorten the time needed to perform a certain operation in Lotus 1-2-3, the user would be unable to use that macro to shorten the time needed to perform that same operation in another program. Rather, the user would have to rewrite his or her macro using that other program's menu command hierarchy. This is despite the fact that the macro is clearly the user's own work product. We think that forcing the user to cause the computer to perform the same operation in a different way ignores Congress's direction in Section 102(b) that "methods of operation" are not copyrightable. That programs can offer users the ability to write macros in many different ways does not change the fact that, once written, the macro allows the user to perform an operation automatically. As the Lotus menu command hierarchy serves as the basis for Lotus 1-2-3 macros, the Lotus menu command hierarchy is a "method of operation."

In holding that expression that is part of a "method of operation" cannot be copyrighted, we do not understand ourselves to go against the Supreme Court's holding in *Feist*. In *Feist*, the Court explained:

The primary objective of copyright is not to reward the labor of authors, but to promote the Progress of Science and useful Arts. To this end, copyright assures authors the right to their original expression, but encourages others to build freely upon the ideas and information conveyed by a work.

Feist, 499 U.S. at 349-50 (quotations and citations omitted). We do not think that the Court's statement that "copyright assures authors the right to their original expression" indicates that all expression is necessarily copyrightable; while original expression is necessary for copyright protection, we do not think that it is alone sufficient. Courts must still inquire whether original expression falls within one of the categories foreclosed from copyright protection by Section 102(b), such as being a "method of operation."

We also note that in most contexts, there is no need to "build" upon other people's expression, for the ideas conveyed by that expression can be conveyed by someone else without copying the first author's expression. In the context of methods of operation, however, "building" requires the use of the precise method of operation already employed; otherwise, "building" would require dismantling, too. Original developers are not the only people entitled to build on the methods of operation they create; anyone can. Thus, Borland may build on the method of operation that Lotus designed and may use the Lotus menu command hierarchy in doing so.

Our holding that methods of operation are not limited to abstractions goes against *Autoskill*, 994 F.2d at 1495 n.23, in which the Tenth Circuit rejected the defendant's argument that the keying procedure used in a computer program was an uncopyrightable "procedure" or "method of operation" under Section 102(b). The program at issue, which was designed to test and train students with reading deficiencies, *id.* at 1481, required students to select responses to the program's queries "by pressing the 1, 2, or 3 keys."*id.* at 1495 n.23. The Tenth Circuit held that, "for purposes of the preliminary injunction, . . . the record showed that [this] keying procedure reflected at least a minimal degree of creativity," as required by *Feist* for copyright protection. *Id.* As an initial matter, we question whether a programmer's decision to have users select a response by pressing the 1, 2, or 3 keys is original. More importantly, however, we fail to see how "a student select [ing] a response by pressing the 1, 2, or 3 keys,"*id.*, can be anything but an unprotectable method of operation.

. . .

Most of the law of copyright and the "tools" of analysis have developed in the context of literary works such as novels, plays, and films. In this milieu, the principal problem — simply stated, if difficult to resolve — is to stimulate creative expression without unduly limiting access by others to the broader themes and concepts deployed by the author. The middle of the spectrum presents close cases; but a "mistake" in providing too much protection involves a small cost: subsequent authors treating the same themes must take a few more steps away from the original expression.

The problem presented by computer programs is fundamentally different in one respect. The computer program is a *means* for causing something to happen; it has a mechanical utility, an instrumental role, in accomplishing the world's work. Granting protection, in other words, can have some of the consequences of *patent* protection in limiting other people's ability to perform a task in the most efficient manner. Utility does not bar copyright (dictionaries may be copyrighted), but it alters the calculus.

Of course, the argument *for* protection is undiminished, perhaps even enhanced, by utility: if we want more of an intellectual product, a temporary monopoly for the creator provides incentives for others to create other, different items in this class. But the "cost" side of the equation may be different where one places a very high value on public access to a useful innovation that may be the most efficient means of performing a given task. Thus, the argument for extending protection may be the same; but the stakes on the other side are much higher.

It is no accident that patent protection has preconditions that copyright protection does not — notably, the requirements of novelty and non-obviousness — and that patents are granted for a shorter period than copyrights. This problem of utility has sometimes manifested itself in copyright cases, such as *Baker v. Selden*, 101 U.S. 99 (1879), and been dealt with through various formulations that limit copyright or create limited rights to copy. But the case law and doctrine addressed to utility in copyright have been brief detours in the general march of copyright law.

Requests for the protection of computer menus present the concern with fencing off access to the commons in an acute form. A new menu may be a creative work, but over time its importance may come to reside more in the investment that has been made by *users* in learning the menu and in building their own mini-programs — macros — in reliance upon the menu. Better typewriter keyboard layouts may exist, but the familiar QWERTY keyboard dominates the market because that is what everyone has learned to use. *See* P. David, *CLIO and the Economics of QWERTY*, 75 Am. Econ. Rev. 332 (1985). The QWERTY keyboard is nothing other than a menu of letters.

Thus, to assume that computer programs are just one more new means of expression, like a filmed play, may be quite wrong. The "form" — the written source code or the menu structure depicted on the screen — look hauntingly like the familiar stuff of copyright; but the "substance" probably has more to do with problems presented in patent law or, as already noted, in those rare cases where copyright law has confronted industrially useful expressions. Applying copyright law to computer programs is like assembling a jigsaw puzzle whose pieces do not quite fit.

Navitaire Inc. v. Easy Jet Airline Co. Ltd., [2004] EWHC 1725

High Court (Chancery Division)

(Pumfrey J.):

This was an action for infringement of copyright in computer software which implemented a "ticketless" airline booking system. The claimant owned the copyright in the various works that went to make up the source code of a system called "OpenRes". The first defendant ("easyJet") was a well known low-cost airline, and the second defendant ("BulletProof") was a software developer located in California.

In November 1996 easyJet had taken a licence of the OpenRes system. Under the licence agreement the claimant supplied an interface to the world-wide web in the form of a program called "TakeFlight" which was then integrated into easyJet's website. By 1999 the website had become of primary importance, and easyJet wanted to modify TakeFlight to add new routes and destinations and special offers and promotions, and to add foreign-language versions which were not available. The claimant was reluctant or unable to provide the means for easyJet to write its own internet booking screen for its website.

As a consequence of its deteriorating relationship with the claimant, and perhaps because the internet system used would have incurred a charge for each transaction handled, easyJet decided to develop its own booking system (called "eRes") in place of OpenRes and engaged BulletProof to write the code in consultation with its own information technology department. easyJet wanted a system that was substantially indistinguishable from OpenRes in the appearance that the running software presented to the user, whether an agent in a call centre or a private individual seeking to make a booking by use of the world-wide web. By February 2000, BulletProof had successfully demonstrated that its proposed approach was capable of giving what easyJet required to achieve this far-from-simple goal. The eRes system eventually went live in December 2001 and was the subject of the present action for copyright infringement.

The case advanced by the claimant had its origin in the suggestion that the "business logic" of OpenRes had been appropriated, and was based on the fact that the functions of OpenRes and eRes were identical to the user so far as the aspects of the system of interest to easyJet were concerned. The claimant did not suggest that easyJet or BulletProof had ever had access to the source code of the OpenRes system, although there were minor allegations of infringement by copying of certain code and an allegation in respect of databases. None of the underlying software of eRes resembled that of OpenRes in any way, save that it acted on identical or very similar inputs and produced very similar results. The claimant nevertheless alleged that the copyright in OpenRes had been infringed by so-called non-textual copying. There were three aspects of this alleged infringement. The first was the adoption of the look and feel of the running OpenRes software. The second was a detailed copying of many of the individual commands entered by the user to achieve particular results. The third was the copying of certain of the results in the form of screen displays and of reports displayed on the screen in response to prescribed instructions.

. . .

The user interface screen was a standard green screen (VT100) providing 80 single-character columns and 24 rows for display. (It displayed only printable characters and was not capable of displaying complex graphics.) The claimant contended that because the OpenRes code displayed the data in a particular layout with particular fixed data (such as column titles) the screen layout was a separate artistic or literary copyright work for each display, and because the fixed data and the layout appeared in the same place on the eRes screen that artistic or literary work had necessarily been copied. It did not matter that the work could not be discerned from the code. The work was a design for an essentially transient object, a computer display. It was recorded in the software which, when executed, displayed it. It was therefore a copyright work, and any other similar screen copied from the first transient display infringed the copyright.

The claimant also alleged infringement of the copyright in the displays on Microsoft Windows GUI screens of a module enabling the database administrator to make long-term alterations to the database by providing a new fare structure or a new flight schedule, and on the copyright in the original designs of the icons on certain buttons on the screens. The claimant contended that the GUI screens were copyright works as they stood and that certain of them had been copied.

. . .

The screens

95 The screens are obviously part of the user interface. The degree of similarity varies, and in my view the GUI screens raise different issues from those raised by the VT100 screens. There are 26 screens in all, and my analysis is set out in **Annexe 5** ([304-317]).

96 The VT100 is a character-based terminal, that is, it displays only printable characters. It provides 80 single-character columns and 24 rows for the display. As I endeavour to show in **Annexe 5**, one can see some of the layouts, at least, in the code because they are character-based, a good example being the baggage count display (item 11). The inference I draw from this is that the character-based displays are properly to be viewed as tables and so literary in character for the purposes of copyright (s.3(1)(a) of the 1988 Act above). They are, in my view, "ideas which underlie its interfaces" in the sense used in Art.1(2) of the Directive: they provide the static framework for the display of the dynamic data which it is the task of the software to produce.

97 The GUI screens stand in a different position. The Directive is concerned only with the protection of computer programs as literary works, and I do not read it as having any impact on relevant artistic copyrights. It is certainly possible to view the GUI screens as tables, because they are "drawn" by selecting from a palette of available objects things such as command buttons, toggle buttons, checkboxes, scrolling lists and so forth and moving them around on a form until a satisfactory layout is concerned. The "interface builder" program provides "stubs" for the routines that will be executed when the user selects or clicks on one of these objects, and it is the task of the programmer to provide the necessary code to ensure that the right thing happens when the user presses (for example) the OK button. Although composed of elements made available by the manufacturer of the interface builder program, I can see that the screen resulting from such an operation might properly be considered to be an artistic work. What the programmer ultimately produces is code that depends upon a large number of complex graphic routines that draw the background, the boxes and the shading in the places selected, and act appropriately when the mouse moves over them or they are selected. The programmer does not write this code: it is the scaffolding for his or her own window design.

98 In my judgment, the better view is that the GUI screens are artistic works. They are recorded as such only in the complex code that displays them, but I think that this is strictly analogous to more simple digital representations of graphic works. The code constructs the screen from basic elements, and is so arranged to give a consistent appearance to the individual elements. I think, nonetheless, that to arrange a screen certainly affords the opportunity for the exercise of sufficient skill and labour for the result to amount to an artistic work. I consider that the GUI screens satisfy this requirement. There is force in the suggestion that they present a uniform appearance in layout of the elements, and

so contribute to a uniformity of interface. On the whole this is sufficient skill and labour to entitle the screens sued on to artistic copyright.

99 In the result, therefore, the action fails so far as the VT100 screens are concerned, but succeeds so far as the GUI screens are concerned. The icons are plainly copyright works, albeit minor, and the action succeeds in respect of them as well.

No authoritative decision has yet explored in any detail the basis for protection of the audio-visual aspects of video games in Canada. Some works expressed in a visual medium are clearly protected in Canada. For example, copyright subsists in Canada in "cinematographic works." These are defined to include "any work expressed by any process analogous to cinematography".[4] The term "cinematography" generally has three characteristics: it has a sequence of images, it is recorded on material, and it is capable of being shown as a moving picture.[5] Do video games fit into this definition?

Would video games be protected as artistic works? The visual effects of many games have artistic merit. To the extent that a video game incorporates pre-existing literary, artistic, musical or dramatic works would it be protected as a compilation?

Nintendo Co. Ltd. v. Golden China TV-Game Centre (1993), 28 I.P.R. 313 (Sup. Ct. S. Africa)

Hartzenberg J

28 October 1993

Hartzenberg J.

The applicant, one of the largest manufacturers and distributors of video games in the world, if not the largest, seeks to interdict the respondents from dealing in some forty video games which it contends are copies of games created, developed and manufactured by itself under the name "Nintendo". The word "dealing" is used to encompass all of the following conduct by the respondents: importing, selling, letting, hiring, offering or exposing for sale or hire or distributing the aforesaid video games. The first three and the fifth respondents are importers and distributors of video games and the fourth and sixth to the sixteenth respondents are in the retail market where the selling and/or hiring out of video games constitute one line of their respective businesses.

. . .

------

4   S.C. 1993, c. 44, s. 53(2).
5   *Spelling Goldberg Productions Inc. v. B P C Publishing Ltd.*, [1981] R.P.C. 283.

The first basis for the application is a claim of copyright infringement either of the games as "cinematograph films" or alternatively of the artistic, literary and musical work which allegedly form some of the component works of the video games in question. In the alternative the applicant maintains that the respondents' conduct constitutes unfair competition. There is a third basis which is somewhat narrower based on the registered trade marks of the applicant in the names "Donkey Kong" and "Mario Bros Device" both in classes 9 and 28. There is also a prayer for delivery-up of the so-called infringing games in terms of s 24(1) of Act 98 of 1978, the Copyright Act.

. . .

To understand what the issues are it is necessary to explain the way in which a video game is played, how such a game is created and how copies thereof are made.

It is played by means of a machine, or console known as a games machine which, in turn, is connected to a domestic television set. The games are stored in silicon micro-chips known as read only memory chips ("ROMs"). The ROMs are capable of causing images to appear on a television screen and sounds to emanate from a speaker when an electric current is passed through them, which give the appearance of a moving picture. The video game cartridges containing ROM chips can be interchangeably inserted into the games machine so that different games can be played on the equipment. The console is also electronically connected to hand-operated controls which are used to control, to an extent, the playing of the game which is displayed on the television screen. The standard controls have a four-directional cross-shaped switch with which the player regulates the direction of characters or objects such as balls or cars, etc. The standard controls may be substituted by alternate controls such as joy sticks or joy pads which serve the same function as the standard controls. The standard control also has two round buttons marked A and B that are also used to control some of the game play. For instance in action games these buttons can be operated to cause a game character to make a specific type of movement like jumping, ducking or flying or other movements. In sports games the buttons can be used to cause the swinging of a bat or the throwing of a punch or ball or to increase or decrease the speed of for instance a racing car. The standard control also contains "select" and "start" buttons that are used to select certain options in the game like teams and team members in sports games and options available in adventure games. They are used to initiate the game play. During the play there is interaction between the player(s), the equipment and the game displayed on the screen.

The applicant maintains that there are three basic phases in the creation, design and development of its video games. The first phase is the creation phase which includes an initial determination of the basic concept of the game, the primary game characters and their interactions, the theme, overall "story" and sequence of the game, the basic lay-out of the background and the primary items. After this phase, an analysis is conducted to evaluate whether the game will be fun and interesting and sufficiently challenging. Also, a determination is made by the applicant as to whether the game is technically feasible, ie can be success-fully programmed. Thereafter the development of the game begins.

The design and development phase is conducted under the direction and super-vision of the team leader. It involves various different stages including the cre-ation and designing of the numerous component works that make up and are ultimately integrated into the composite game. The composite works are alleged to include game characters, items, backgrounds or environments, screen texts and/or wording, sounds (music and sound effects) and the game play sequence. The game characters are drawn on paper or fixed on magnetic disc including the characters shown in all their different positions, poses, configurations and forms. It is the applicant's case that these works are in the nature of artistic works in terms of the Copyright Act and constitute part of the visual compo-nents of the games.

The "items" are things such as weapons, tools, sporting equipment and the like which are drawn on paper or fixed on magnetic disc (including their different positions, poses, configurations and forms). It is also alleged that these works are in the nature of artistic works and are part of the visual components of the game.

The backgrounds or environments of the games are things such as scenery, "worlds" and playing fields. They are also drawn on paper or fixed on magnetic disc. That includes all the different configurations, forms and positions of the background. It is also maintained that they are in the nature of artistic works and are part of the visual components of the game.

In the case of some of the games screen texts and/or wording appear on the screen when the game is played. They are also written or fixed on paper or on magnetic disc and it is also alleged that they are in the nature of literary or artistic works. The allegation is likewise that they comprise part of the visual components of the game.

The sounds comprising of the music and the sound effects are written or fixed on paper or on magnetic tapes or disc. It is alleged that they are in the nature of musical works or sound recordings and that they constitute the audio compo-nents of the games.

The game-play sequences are made up of specifications, notes, "maps", "story boards" and the like. They, in unencoded form, define the contents and story of each game and the game-play sequences by indicating how the various compo-nent works are to be integrated together in a sequential progression to constitute each game. It is alleged that these game-play sequences are in fact the video games in unencoded form.

During the design and development phase new items and characters may be developed. The story is evolved and expanded. Detailed game-play sequences are designed using specifications, notes and story boards. The manner in which the characters and items move and interact with each other and their background is choreographed. As part of this process the music and sound effects are also designed and integrated into the game.

The programming phase involves the writing of a computer program for the video game. The purpose of the computer program is to enable a video game which incorporates the component works to be played and operated. The computer program controls the visual display of the component works and allows the player to manipulate the character and items. During the development of the game the degree of difficulty of the game is continuously balanced with the level of fun achieved in playing it. A successful video game has to be not only entertaining but also of the requisite difficulty in challenge so that the game cannot be instantly mastered by the player and become boring.

The component works, as has been said, are drawn on paper or fixed on magnetic disc. The fixing thereof on magnetic disc occurs after the drawing thereof when they are converted into computer data so that each character, item or background can be electronically displayed on a television screen. Sometimes sophisticated computer programs known as "paint programs" are utilised by the designers so that drawings of whatever nature can take place directly on a computer screen. The applicant alleges that the paint programs have been developed by itself and that the data generated during the drawing of a paint program can be retained on disc, revised, copied and otherwise used directly.

When a video game character is shown on screen to be running, the character's legs, feet and arms appear to move. To create this effect, many individual drawings of the character must be made in a manner similar to drawing the many individual frames required for the making of an animated cartoon. Many drawings of game characters are therefore produced in the design and development of a game.

In an adventure or action game the characters commonly travel through a number of different background "worlds" each with many different sections. All games have backgrounds of one form or another, while each section may have a unique setting such as mountains, desert, outer space, underground or inside a castle. Creating the background of a game usually involves a number of designers who work under the direction and supervision of the game director. The background is initially and usually drawn on paper. Different forms, configurations or positions of the background may exist and each must be separately drawn and recorded.

Adventure and action video games include numerous items such as weapons, sprites, aids, physical enhancement devices and the like that are used, collected or encountered by the game characters. Video games also include traps and obstacles that must be overcome or avoided by the main character during movement, using the articles that I have referred to as "items". The game designers determine the nature, location, manner, using and other aspects of the items. They are also drawn on paper or may be created by the use of computer programs. They are also drawn and recorded in different configurations, poses, forms, etc.

In the video game cartridge the visual components of the game including the characters, items, background and text are stored in a CH-ROM chip. It is an integrated circuit. It is one of two ROMs contained in the game cartridge. The music and other sound effects are also important aspects of a successful video game. It is therefore necessary that the music or sound effects composer has to liaise with the game designer to create appropriate music and sound effects and to incorporate those effects into the game. The second ROM chip (the P-ROM) contains those elements. It also contains the program which operates the functioning and display of the game. Also stored in the CH-ROM chips are the so-called character charts. It is necessary to plan and indicate where and at what "addresses" all the different component, artistic and literary works (including the works in their various configurations, poses and the like) are to be stored in the CH-ROMs. That is done on the character charts.

Just before the final completion of the video game the efforts of the designer, artists and sound effects composer will be on magnetic discs. They are then debugged and transposed to the two ROM chips. The game is then ready to be reproduced.

Scott on behalf of the third respondent describes the manufacture of a ROM roughly as follows. It involves the production of what is known as custom masks. The masks can be designed by mask designers either manually, like engineering drawings, on paper or by an automatic process involving the use of a computer aided design program. The result is a drawing of a mask on a sheet of paper or some other material. It illustrates the mask on what is a very large scale relative to the actual mask which is needed for the factory process. The drawing is then photographically reduced by several orders of magnitude and the mask is made from the final photographic negative. A set of such masks is used, one at a time, to lay out on several successive layers of silicon the pattern of electronically activated zones or areas which the ROM designer wants to demarcate and use for the various types of components which are to be incorporated in the ROM, such as resisters, capacitators, transistors, etc. The masks also determine the area in which material is to be altered or removed when the layer to which the mask is applied is later exposed to a processing material such as etching fluid. Every layer takes the form of a wafer or strip of silicon semi-conductor material. The superimposed layers constitute the body of the chip. The final layering step is not one of electronic activation but involves the deposit of a thin body or layer of metal on top of the electronic activated silicon layers. Where the underlying layer has been provided with an etched aperture corresponding to an aperture in the mask applied to that layer the metal deposited in the apertures forms an electrical connection between layers. In this way the numerous diodes, transistors, resisters, capacitators and other components which the chip incorporates are interconnected or "wired up" into a complex circuit through which electrical impulses can flow when the circuit is used.

He describes the copying of a ROM more or less as follows: by making certain electrical measurements of a ROM and applying certain computer engineering and programming skills it is possible to construct a computer program stored magnetically on a computer disc or equivalent storage medium which corresponds either exactly or approximately to a computer program according to which the ROM was in the first place designed. The process of taking the electrical measurements is sometimes called, in the anthropomorphic language of electronics, reading the ROM. With that as basis the copier can set up a manufacturing operation to produce copies of the original ROM. It can also be done by "peeling" the ROM. The ROM is stripped into its component layers. Each layer is then observed and measured and identical or similar layers to those used for the manufacture of the original ROM are then made. They are again superimposed. The result will also be a copy of the original ROM.

Before the advent of video games there were games known as "arcade" games. These games were played in public places like arcades and cafes. They were played on large games machines or "consoles". To play a game a coin had to be inserted into a slot in the machine. The applicant developed some arcade games and some of the games in issue in this case are based on the earlier arcade versions of the applicant's games.

Some of the component works which form part of the applicant's video games were based on earlier works not of the applicant's origination. Examples are the characters in the "Popeye" video game (Popeye, Olive Oyl, Wimpy and Brutus), the general concept of the game "Tetris" and the soccer field background in the game "Soccer". The applicant alleges and it is not contradicted that the other works have been used by the applicant with the authority of the owners of the copyright therein. The applicant maintains that the specific forms or versions of the component works as authorised and created by the applicant are original.

The applicant's main contention is that a video game, thus created, is a cinematograph film within the definition thereof in terms of the Act. The definition reads;

> "Cinematograph film" means the first fixation by any means whatsoever on film or any other material of a sequence of images capable, when used in conjunction with any mechanical, electronic or other device, of being seen as a moving picture and of reproduction, and includes the sounds embodied in a sound track associated with the film.

The "author" of a cinematograph film is defined in the Act as follows:

> "Author", in relation to — a cinematograph film, means the person by whom the arrangements for the making of the film were made;

The only copyright protection which an author enjoys in this country is that afforded to him by the Act. Section 2(1) of the Act is emphatic that in order to be eligible for copyright cinematograph films are to be original.

In order to prove that each one of the games is "original", as the word is interpreted in the Act, affidavits by the team leaders of every game have been filed. The team leader of each game states that he supervised over the creation of that particular game. He states who the designer or designers were, who the programmer or programmers were and who the composer or composers of the music or sound effects were. He states the time which it took to create that game. He states that all the people involved were Japanese citizens and most of them employed by the applicant. There were Japanese citizens employed by other Japanese companies which companies did specific things in respect of some games on commission. The team leaders state that each one of the games was created in Japan. They state that there are literally thousands of original drawings in respect of each game. Examples were annexed to the papers but because they are being stored on magnetic disc which can be reproduced only on equipment common in Japan, but which are not compatible with the equipment used in this country and because of the great volume thereof it is stated that it will be impracticable to annex each drawing to the papers. In each case it is stated that a considerable amount of original work was done by the team. The team leader personally observed that being done. That allegation is also made in respect of the games "Popeye", "Tetris" and "Soccer". There is in any event not the slightest suggestion that any one of the games is a copy of a similar game except in the cases where the applicant's video games are based on its earlier arcade games.

It is the applicant's contention that in order to enjoy the protection of the Act it is necessary for the applicant to establish that each one of the games which it seeks to protect constitutes:

    (a) the first fixation by any means whatsoever on film or any other material;

    (b) of a sequence of images;

    (c) capable, when used in conjunction with any mechanical, electronic or other device of being seen as a moving picture and of reproduction.

The applicant summarises its submission in respect of a cinematograph film as follows: it has a sequence of images, it is fixed on material and it is capable of being shown as a moving picture. It is the applicant's contention that each one of the video games in question has those characteristics. I have been referred to many reported cases in a number of different countries inter alia to the judgment in *Spelling Goldberg Productions Inc v B P C Publishing Ltd* [1981] RPC 283. At 287 the learned judge said:

> Thus a cinematograph film has three characteristics. It has a sequence of images, it is recorded on material, and it is capable of being shown as a moving picture.

(The definition of "cinematograph film" under discussion in that case reads as follows:

> Any sequence of visual images recorded on material of any description (whether translucent or not) so as to be capable, by the use of that material, (a) of being shown as a moving picture, or (b) of being recorded on other material (whether translucent or not), by the use of which it can be so shown.)

Although the two definitions are not identical those three characteristics are also the three characteristics of a cinematograph film in terms of the South African definition.

There is such a fundamental difference in approach between the parties that in effect two different cases were argued. The respondents deny that a video game is or can be a cinematograph film. They went into the minutest detail to explain how integrated circuits are created, what a computer is, and what in their view in a video game is eligible for copyright protection. They criticised the applicant for submitting evidence of team leaders and designers explaining what artistic work is contained in each one of the video games accusing it of clouding the issue with irrelevant material. They contended that the only component of the video game which is eligible for copyright protection is the program contained in the P-ROM which enables the player to manipulate the game. They accused the applicant of deliberately failing to place any evidence before the court as to how such a program is created and in particular by whom and where each one of the programs was created. It is their contention that as it is clear from the applicant's affidavits, that in the case of thirty-three of the forty games, the programmers were not employed by the applicant but employed by other Japanese companies, commissioned by the applicant to manufacture the programs, the applicant cannot have any copyright in the programs. It is their contention further that as the only aspect of the video game eligible for copyright protection is the program, the true investigation is if the computer programs really fall within the definition of a "literary work" in terms of the Act or not. They maintain that a video game is a sui generis form of intellectual property which, unfortunately for the applicant, the legislature has thus far failed to protect.

To develop this argument Mr Bowman dissected everything said on behalf of the applicant since October 1991. He says that there was a complete change in the applicant's approach as to what exactly qualifies for protection in terms of the Act and what not. One thing is clear. In the very first letters written on behalf of the applicant to the various respondents it was stated emphatically that the applicant claims copyright in the games because they are cinematograph films. In the alternative it was the applicant's contention that the component works are also protected in terms of the Act. It is so that the applicant claimed protection of the computer programs as such. At present the applicant does not claim any protection in respect of these programs. To that extent its approach changed. Apart from that its case is still as it was in the very first instance, ie that it is entitled to protection because the video games are cinematograph films. It is also still the applicant's case that the component works are also infringed.

The respondents argue that in the first place the video games are contained in the ROM chips. It is alleged that those chips are three-dimensional and a form of computer hardware, or at least what is known as "firmware", ie some program which is first written as software but has to be repeated so often that it is encoded into a ROM chip and really forms part of the hardware. It is alleged that there is nothing in such a chip which makes it eligible to protection in terms of the Act. A second leg of the respondents' defence is that the program in the P-ROM chip is actually the only thing which could possibly claim protection in terms of the Act. The respondents contend, however, that it is not eligible for protection as it is the basis of a video game and the legislature has so far not extended the provisions of the Act to video games. My attention was drawn to the Draft Designs Bill which was published in *Government Gazette* 13328 of 28 June 1991 as Notice 588 of 1991 — wherein "functional design" is defined to include "an integrated circuit topography, as mask work and a series of mask works". It is argued that only if that draft bill is enacted will the owner of a video game be entitled to protection. In my view the investigation at this stage is if a video game is a cinematograph film in terms of the Act and not if the proposed Designs Act may afford protection to the owner of a video game if and when enacted.

The respondents further say that even if it is eligible for protection in terms of the Act the applicant is not entitled to such protection as the programmers were not directly employed by the applicant (in the case of thirty-three of the forty games in question). The respondents' case further is that if those defences are without substance then on a common sense analysis of what a conventional cinematograph film is a video game cannot possibly be a cinematograph film. It is argued that the length of a cinematograph film is constantly the same. As was graphically illustrated during the hearing of the matter by the son of Mr Bowman for the respondents the length of a video game is absolutely variable. If the player possesses no skills and fails to take any positive or avoiding action the game lasts an extremely short time and ends abruptly whereas when the game player is experienced he can manipulate the game to last for hours. On the other hand in the "tract" mode and even if it lasts only a short time (at a guess between half a minute and a minute) the same sequence is always repeated.

Another argument is that in the case of a conventional cinematograph film there is not the slightest suggestion of manipulation of the game by a player. It is further argued that the definition of cinematograph film requires a "first fixation" of images and that in this case the fixation in the ROM chip cannot possibly be a "first" fixation. It is also said that the sequence of images cannot be reproduced. There is merely a transient sequence of images which will vary on each occasion. Furthermore attention is drawn to the deliberate change by the legislature of the words "any sequence of images" in the 1965 Act to "a sequence of images" in the 1978 Act. The argument is therefore that a cinematograph film is one only sequence of images and not one of a myriad of possible sequences of images.

The logical way to approach the matter in my view is to look at the definition of cinematograph film and to see if a video game falls within the definition or not. It is wrong to look for similarities and differences between video games and conventional cinematograph films. It is then to be ascertained if in the case of a video game there is a first fixation of a sequence of images. In my view there can be little doubt that that is so. The applicant was at pains to explain that literally thousands of images are stored in the CH-ROM. By causing them to appear in quick succession they give the impression of movement as in the case of an animated cartoon. The word "fixation" according to the *Oxford Dictionary* is the "process of being fixated". There is no dispute that a video game can be played over and over again and that some of the images are caused to be seen every time when the game is played as a moving picture. It is of course so that the picture is not every time the same. I fail to see how those images can be reproduced unless they have first been fixated in the CH-ROM.

The Act is not very particular whereon the images are to be fixated. It can be a film or "any other material". The concept is extremely wide and in my view wide enough to include a CH-ROM chip. In my view it is also clear that what has been fixated in each case is "a sequence of images". In the case of each one of these games there are many possibilities. If the game player chooses to do so he or she enters one plane or another plane in some cases or he or she rides on one motorbike or another motorbike and so on. Once the player has made an election of that kind there are various things which will happen to the character depending upon what the player does. Every one of those things which happen is shown on the screen for one reason only and that is that there is a large sequence of images stored from which smaller sequences are selected which are then shown on the screen. For example when in the game "Excitebike" the speed is too high the motorcycle will every time overheat and exactly the same sequence of the stored images is shown on the screen. That indicates to me that there is a sequence of images and that a particular portion thereof is selected when that scene is depicted on the screen. I do not read the definition to be as narrow as to require that the whole stored sequence is to be capable of being seen every time. In *Stern Electronics Inc v Harold Kaufman and Omni Video Games Inc* 669 Federal Reporter 2nd series 852 the second circuit of the United States Court of Appeals held that the repetitive sequence of substantial portions of sights and sounds of video games qualifies for copyright protection. (In that case it was necessary for the court to interpret the definition of "audio visual works" which reads as follows:

> Works that consist of a series of related images which are extrinsically intended to be shown by the use of machines or devices such as projectors, viewers or electronic equipment, together with accompanying sounds, if any, regardless of the nature of the material objects, such as films, or tapes, in which the works are embodied.)

That definition refers to "a series of... images" and not to "any series". Although it is of course not binding on me I agree with the reasoning of the court on this aspect.

The next question to be asked is if the sequence of images is capable of being seen as a moving picture and of reproduction when used in conjunction with any mechanical, electronic or other device. Here again the phrase "when used in conjunction with any mechanical, electronic or other device" is extremely wide. Mr Wilkins, the engineer who made an affidavit on behalf of the respondents, describes what happens as follows:

> It is not accurate to say, as Mr Taho (one of the deponents for the applicant) does, that the sequence of images seen on the screen and the sound effects that accompany them are determined by the equipment. They are determined by the player's interaction with the equipment. The equipment (of which the games cartridge is a part) determines what components of the images will be seen. The player, by his

actions in manipulating the controls of the machine, enters data into the machine and so determines the way in which play will proceed. This intervention of the player correspondingly determines the way in which the components of the images are combined and the sequence taken by the images. Some very brief sequences are fixed, in the sense that if, for instance, a bullet hits a duck in the game "Duck Hunt", the duck always falls to the ground, but the frequency and position of such events in the sequence is determined by the actions of the player. The position of the falling duck on the screen is also determined by this interaction of the player with the equipment.

The more experienced the player is the more of the images will be caused to be seen on the screen. During the playing of one game an experienced player can conceivably cause all the stored images to be shown as moving pictures on the screen. In most instances that will not happen. The definition does not require the images to be seen as a whole. It requires it to be seen as a moving picture. When a video game is played that happens every time. The images are capable of reproduction. After all, the games can be played over and over again. The applicant made equipment and game's cartridges available to me. I know that the games "Donkey Kong", "Tetris" and "Golf" can be played over and over and that the images remain the same. I must confess that the skill of the player does not necessarily improve dramatically when a game is played for a second or subsequent time. Thereto must be added that the picture shown in the "tract" mode is always the same.

But was the fixation of images, the sound and the computer program the "first" fixation for the purposes of the definition of cinematograph film? In many instances the images were first drawn by hand and thereafter transposed to a computer and stored on magnetic tape before they were fixated in the ROM chips. By the same token many images were created by means of a paint program and stored on magnetic tape. It is understandable that the respondents argue that in the case of handdrawn images on paper the first fixation was on paper and in the case of the drawing thereof on a computer screen the first fixation was on that screen. When exactly a work is created is not always easy to ascertain. In the work *Handbook of South African Copyright Law* the author O H Dean has this to say on 1-15 to 16:

The moment of birth of a work can depending on the circumstances be a difficult moment to pinpoint. Many types of works go through several stages of development before being cast in their final form, whereafter they are exploited or reproduced in derivative forms: For instance an artistic work used as the design printed on a textile may be conceived ahd embodied by the artist in a rough drawing; thereafter he may develop it into a fully fledged painting, which painting is transformed into a textile design. Which version is the work? At what stage is the work born? Each case will be determined by its own facts but generally, we submit that "the work" is the final complete version which is ready for utilisation or commercial exploitation. It is this version which forms the basis of any copyright infringement proceedings when the author's finished product or derivative articles are copied or are otherwise misappropriated. In the example we have quoted "the work" would be the fully fledged painting; the rough drawing is simply a stage in the development of the work and is not a complete work in the sense that it is ready for utilisation or commercial exploitation while the textile design represents the manner of exploitation of the painting and is a derivative work of the painting. It may be that the textile design could constitute a separate and independent work the originality of which lies not in the conception of the design applied to the textile but rather in the transformation of the painting into a textile design.

In this particular case the whole object of the applicant's exercise was to create video games which can be commercially exploited. If it was not for that aim the applicant would certainly not have paid designers to create thousands of cartoon-like images nor would it have paid composers to compose music. It would also not have paid programmers to write programs which will cause the images and sound to be visible and audible. Until such time as the whole video game with all its component works have been fixated in the CH-ROM and the P-ROM it is not commercially exploitable. In my view this is a case where the birth of the game is easily ascertainable as when the game was fixated in the ROMs. I am therefore satisfied that the fixation was a "first" fixation for the purposes of the definition of cinematograph film.

Nova Productions Ltd v. Mazooma Games Ltd, [2007] EWCA Civ 219 (CA (Civ Div), 2007)

THE CHANCELLOR OF THE HIGH COURT LORD JUSTICE JACOB

and LORD JUSTICE LLOYD

Lord Justice Jacob:

1. Nova appeals from the dismissal by Kitchin J of its actions for infringement of copyright against Mazooma (and others) and against Bell-Fruit, [2006] EWHC 24 (Ch); [2006] RPC 379. The copyright works relied on are Nova's computer game based on pool and called "Pocket Money". The defendants' games are respectively called "Jackpot Pool" and "Trick Shot." Nova's case was argued by Mr Martin Howe QC, that of the defendants by Mr Henry Carr QC.

2. The kinds of copyright work originally relied upon were:

    i)   Artistic works being the bitmap graphics and the frames generated and displayed to the user;

    ii) Literary works, being Mr Jones' [Nova's designer] design notes and the program which he wrote to implement the game;

    iii) A dramatic work embodied in the game itself;

    iv) Film copyright.

3. Below, Nova relied upon the first three types. Having regard to the decision in *Norowzian v Arks* [1998] FSR 394 it merely reserved its position in relation

to film copyright for possible argument on appeal. In the event it chose not to do so. It has also abandoned its dramatic work case. So we only have to consider the cases advanced based on artistic and literary works.

4. The relevant legislation is rather lengthy. I set it out in an Appendix so as to get to the issues sooner. So far as the facts are concerned Kitchin J had to deal with more than we do. None of his factual findings is challenged. A fuller account of them than is necessary here can be found in his judgment and the Annex to it showing relevant screens of the various games. We had the advantage of actually seeing the games and the moving images involved and also a DVD of them. These helped, but actually, having read in advance the Judge's extremely clear description with the Annex, I at least, saw just what I expected to see.

Key Findings of fact

Generally

5. First some general findings applicable to both actions. I set them out in the words of the Judge:

> (1) ... the visual appearance and the rules of Pocket Money, Trick Shot and Jackpot Pool are all very different. There are certainly similarities between them which I address below. Nevertheless, each of the games looks and, to my mind, plays in a very different way, [136].

6. I pause to interpolate that it is a remarkable feature of this case that it is unnecessary actually to know how any of the games concerned are played or even what they are other than computer games based on pool. Moreover although the two defendants' games are very different from each other as well as from the claimants', both are said to infringe the same copyrights. This is because the allegation is at such a general level.

7. Moving back to the findings:

> (2) It is not contended that the defendants ever had access to or copied the code itself, [129].

> (3) the use of a power meter was extremely common practice in games design and to have the power level pulsing was an obvious way to implement the feature and so permit the player to select what level of force he wishes to use. .... having a pulsing bar going from left to right was a common choice by numerous games designers and ... the colour scheme involving the use of yellow changing to red was also a common choice as it conveyed to the player the strength of the shot, [151].

> (4) the idea of having a visual indication of the direction of the shot was commonplace. .... nearly all two dimensional and three dimensional pool games produced over the last 20 years have had some form of dashed or dotted or solid view line projecting from the cue ball for aiming purposes. .... having an aiming or view line was a simple or common idea, [149].

> (5) .... it was desirable to have dots or crosses as opposed to a solid view line to avoid the problem of aliasing, [136].

(6) Further, it was common ground ... that having the cue rotate around the cue ball was an obvious, common and functional way of showing the player how to direct the shot [144]. ... the majority of computer pool games in the last 20 years show a cue pointing at the cue ball and rotating around it under player control. It is fundamental to a pool game to show the direction of a shot, and generally speaking it is usual to show the cue rotating around the cue ball to indicate this. .... this feature was commonplace, [145].

(7) Showing the table in plan view is commonplace, [140] and [141].

(8) Showing the pulsing power level by an animation cycle in which (i) the cue moves away from and towards the cue ball, and (ii) a bar graphic varies with the power level [is not commonplace but] was one of the obvious ways to implement the commonplace idea of having a pulsing power meter in a pool game, [155].

(9) Having values associated with pockets was very common in video pool games, [162].

Extent of "copying" generally

8. The Judge of course had to consider in detail the features of Pocket Money said to have been copied into Trick Shot and Jackpot Pool respectively. This he did at [138–197] for Trick Shot and at [172-197] for Jackpot Pool. In each case the claimants had listed a number of features which they alleged had been copied. The Judge found that none of these features had been copied actually as implemented in Pocket Money. However a few had been "inspired" or "affected" by Pocket Money. I turn to consider these in the case of each game complained of.

"Copying" by Trick shot

9. 12 features were alleged to be similar and to have been copied. In the result the Judge found that most of the features of similarity relied upon owed nothing to Pocket Money at all. They were the result of the designers' of Trick Shot own work based on their general experience and what was commonplace. His findings in relation to the surviving features were summarised conveniently by Mr Howe as follows, using the Judge's numbering:

(1) Theme of pool: general idea in part inspired by PM.

(4) Cue moves round ball under rotary controller: idea of rotary controller inspired by PM but movement of cue round ball not derived from PM.

(7) Animation cycle: idea of synchronising cue with power meter probably derived from PM.

(8) Values near/in pockets: general idea inspired by PM, implemented very differently.

"Copying" by Jackpot Pool

10. Mr Howe's summary of the features found by the Judge was:

(1) Theme of pool: inspired by PM.

(4) Row of sighting dots: affected by PM in that it led to shortening of line of dots.

(6) Animation of cycle: synchronise pulsing cue with pulsing power meter.

(9) Graphic of money travelling across screen: not as pleaded derived but idea of coin graphic moving across screen probably inspired by PM.

The case on artistic works

Identify the copyright work — a series?

11. First one must identify the artistic work relied upon and then decide whether it has been reproduced by copying of the work as a whole or of any substantial part of it. That is the effect of s.3(1) and s.16(1) of the Act. It is an aspect of UK copyright law untouched by any EU harmonisation.

12. First then, what is the artistic work? It was common ground that the individual frames stored in the memory of a computer were "graphic works" with the meaning of the Act (Judgment [100-104]). But the actual appearance of individual frames between Pocket Money and the alleged infringements are very different (see Judgment Annex). Regarded just as pictures — as "graphic works" in the words of the Act — they are obviously very different. Save for the fact that they are of a pool table with pocket, balls and a cue, nothing of the defendants' screens as single frames can be said to be a substantial reproduction of a corresponding screen in Pocket Money. Both before the Judge and us Mr Howe accepted that "each of the defendants had done their own drawings of cues and billiard balls" and did not contend for infringement at the level of individual screen graphics.

13. Mr Howe invited us to find that there was in effect a further kind of artistic work, something beyond individual freeze-frame graphics. This was said to be because there is a series of graphics which show the "in-time" movement of cue and meter. So, it was said, that what the defendants had done was to:

> create "a dynamic 're- posing' of the Claimant's version — one in which the detail of the subjects had changed, but an essential artistic element of the original was carried through to the Defendants.

This was said to involve extra skill and labour beyond just that involved in creating the individual frames.

14. The Judge was prepared to accept:

> that "in time" movement of the cue and meter must be considered as being reflected in a series of still shots and like must be compared with like,

but nonetheless held there was no infringement.

15. Mr Carr, by a respondents' notice, challenged that assumption. He submitted that a series of still images, whether created by drawing for a cartoon film or by a computer, was not in itself anything more than a series of frames, each of which would have its own copyright and no more. No "extra" copyright work or

protection is created by having a series. Putting it another way, a series of stills is just that.

16. I think that must be right. "Graphic work" is defined as including all the types of thing specified in s.4(2) which all have this in common, namely that they are static, non-moving. A series of drawings is a series of graphic works, not a single graphic work in itself. No-one would say that the copyright in a single drawing of Felix the Cat is infringed by a drawing of Donald Duck. A series of cartoon frames showing Felix running over a cliff edge into space, looking down and only then falling would not be infringed by a similar set of frames depicting Donald doing the same thing. That is in effect what is alleged here.

17. This reasoning is supported by the fact that Parliament has specifically created copyright in moving images by way of copyright in films. If Mr Howe were right, the series of still images which provides the illusion of movement would itself create a further kind of copyright work protecting moving images. It is unlikely that Parliament intended this.

18. So I think the case on artistic works falls at the first hurdle, given the concession that there is no frame-for-frame reproduction.

Reproduction of a substantial part

19. If it got as far as the second hurdle, the case would fall there too — no reproduction of a substantial part. The Judge so held at [245] for Trick Shot and [252] for Jackpot Pool. Mr Howe first has to overcome the difficulty that he is asking us on appeal to take a different view from that of the trial judge as to what amounts to a "substantial part". That brings him right up against the clear direction from the House of Lords in *Designer Guild v Russell Williams* [2001] FSR 113 that the Court of Appeal should be very chary of doing so.

20. Thus Lord Bingham (with whom the rest of the House agreed) said:

> It was not for the Court of Appeal to embark on the issue of substantiality afresh, unless the judge had misdirected himself, which in my opinion he had not, [6]

See also Lord Hoffmann at [29].

21. Mr Howe contended that the Judge had indeed misdirected himself — in two ways, on the facts and as a matter of law. As to the facts, he relied upon a passage in the evidence of Mr Starling, the designer of Jackpot Pool. It was about the "animation" cycle". The judge records this:

> [231] In early December Mr Wilson and Mr Burns arranged for Pocket Money to be brought into the office where it stayed for five or six days. Mr Starling played the game solidly for one day and reached the conclusion that it was not sufficiently skill based. He wanted to produce a game which was more realistic. He recalled finding the level of control obtained by the rotary controller impressive.

> [232] Under cross examination he accepted that he definitely noticed other aspects of the game. In particular, he limited the length of the line of dots of the sight line having seen Pocket Money and he also noticed the combination of cue,

line of dots and cue pulsing in and out in time with the power meter. He accepted that having seen the game he "tied the features that I already had in my mind into the game" and that this "solved all the problems".

22. The submission was that that which "solved all the problems" must be a substantial part of Pocket Money. Mr Howe developed the argument:

> When you talk about an idea that consists in essence of using a number of features in combination, it is possible to look at that from two points of view. One is to say it is just the idea of combining things. The other way to look at it is to say what you have created by way of expression in the program is a combination of features, and that combination is what you should look at. Ask whether that is a substantial part of the copyright work if that combination is reproduced in the defendant's work.

Thus, it was argued, the combination represented a significant part of Mr Jones' skill and labour and must be a substantial part of the work created by him.

23. The submission applied also to the case on literary works. I reject it for reasons given in more detail in relation to them (in short, idea not expression) but even as a matter of alleged misdirection by the judge it must fail — for the Judge clearly took the answer into consideration. So where is the misdirection?

24. Moreover the answer must be seen in context. The "combination" is actually just a construct of Mr Howe's argument. After all the idea of a cue moving round a ball, of a pulsing power meter, of a sight line indicated by dots or crosses were all commonplace. And the Judge held that Mr Starling knew about all of them before he saw Pocket Money and they had already been developed by him for his game (Judgment [231]). All that was "taken" by Mr Starling was a shortened row of dots (he already had one) and synchronisation of the pulsing cue with the power meter.

25. As to the law, Mr Howe relied upon what was said by Lord Scott in *Designers Guild*:

> There had been no direct evidence of copying and the judge's finding had been based on the extensive similarities between *Ixia* and *Marguerite*. These similarities, coupled with the opportunity to copy and in the absence of any acceptable evidence from RWT as to an independent provenance for *Marguerite*, had led the judge to conclude, on a balance of probabilities, that *Marguerite* had been copied from *Ixia*. If the similarities between the two works were sufficient to justify the inference that one had been copied from the other, there was, in my judgment, no further part for the concept of substantiality to play

26. Mr Howe tried to elevate this into a general principle — that whenever copying has been found it must follow that a substantial part has been taken. I cannot agree. In many cases a coincidence in the copyright work and the alleged infringement of small, unimportant, details is an indication of copying. Thus the "reverse countersink" in *LB Plastics v Swish* [1979] RPC 551 and the misspellings in *Ibcos v Barclays* proved the copying. But no-one would say that those details alone meant that a substantial part of the copyright work had been taken — they are the starting point for a finding of infringement, not the end

point. Lord Scott's observations must be taken as concerned with the facts of *Designers Guild* itself, not as laying down any general principle. Actually that is clear from what he said, referring as he did to "<u>the</u> [my emphasis] two works." After all in that case it was the overall appearance of the two works which led to the inference of overall copying — an inference which the defendants failed to rebut. And the two designs were not just similar overall, one would serve as a substitute for the other. Here the judge has expressly rejected nearly all of the allegations of copying, leaving just a rump of a few ideas which were "derived from or inspired by the copyright work", albeit implemented in very different ways. And the games, being different from one another, are not competitive in the sense that one would do as a substitute for the other.

The case on a literary work

27. Accordingly I think the appeal in relation to artistic works fails. I turn to that in relation to the literary work. This involves EU law since it is based on the Software Directive of 1991. Pursuant to that Directive as implemented in the UK, copyright can subsist in a computer program and its preparatory design material. It was common ground that the UK legislation must be interpreted in accordance with the Directive, see *Marleasing* [1990] I ECR 4135.

28. The UK Act, drafted with the traditional, but wholly unhelpful way of re-wording a Directive, sets out "a computer program" and "preparatory design work for a computer program" as though they are entirely different types of work in which literary copyright can subsist. What the Directive actually says is: "the term 'computer programs' shall include their preparatory design material." That may not be quite the same thing — the EU legislation appears to contemplate just one copyright in a computer program, not two, one in the preparatory work and the other in the program itself. I do not think anything turns on the difference here. But one can think of cases where it might. Suppose for example different authors for the program and its preparatory material. When does the copyright expire — on different dates depending on the death of the respective author? Or suppose different dealings in the "two" copyrights — is that possible given that the Directive supposes only one copyright? The re-wording, as it nearly always does, throws up room for wholly unnecessary uncertainty and argument.

29. Fortunately nothing turns on the difference of language here. I should, in passing, mention one other difference of language pointed out by Mr Howe. The Directive defines "restricted acts" as reproduction "in any form, in part or in whole" (Art 4(a)). The UK Act does not say "in part or in whole". It uses the well-established language "in relation to the work as a whole or any <u>substantial</u> part", s.16(3)(a). Mr Howe wisely decided that he could not make any point based on this difference of language. He accepted that although the Directive did not say "substantial part" its meaning must be so limited. Otherwise it would require the copying of insubstantial parts to be an infringement — which is so absurd as to be assuredly wrong.

30. With those preliminary observations I can turn to the main arguments. The Judge found against the claimants on two distinct, although related, bases, applicable to both alleged infringements:

> [247] [The similarities found to have been derived] are cast at such a level of abstraction and are so general that I am quite unable to conclude that they amount to a substantial part of the computer program. They are ideas which have little to do with the skill and effort expended by the programmer and do not constitute the form of expression of the literary works relied upon.

> [248] Further, application of the principles explained by Pumfrey J in *Navitaire* leads to the same conclusion. Nothing has been taken in terms of program code or program architecture. Such similarities that exist in the outputs do not mean that there are any similarities in the software. Further, what has been taken is a combination of a limited number of generalised ideas which are reflected in the output of the program. They do not form a substantial part of the computer program itself. Consideration of Article 1(2) of the Software Directive confirms this position. Ideas and principles which underlie any element of a computer program are not protected by copyright under the Directive.

Mere idea, not expression

31. Mr Howe had to face the formidable objection created by Art. 1.2 of the Directive and recitals 13 and 15. To my mind these provisions are abundantly clear. The well-known dichotomy between an idea and its individual expression is intended to apply and does to copyright in computer software. When I say "well-known" I mean not just known to copyright lawyers of one country but well-known all over the world. Recital 15 refers to the protection of the expression of ideas as being "in accordance with the legislation and jurisprudence of the Member States and the international copyright conventions" and is clearly a reference to this dichotomy. The TRIPS agreement of 1994 likewise recognises this dichotomy, see particularly Art, 9.2.

32. Mr Howe suggested that the dichotomy was intended to apply only to ideas which underlie an element of a program — what he called a "building block". He cited (as did the Judge) what Lord Hoffmann said about the dichotomy outside the context of computer programs in *Designers Guild*:

> [25] My Lords, if one examines the cases in which the distinction between ideas and the expression of ideas has been given effect, I think it will be found that they support two quite distinct propositions. The first is that a copyright work may express certain ideas which are not protected because they have no connection with the literary, dramatic, musical or artistic nature of the work. It is on this ground that, for example, a literary work which describes a system or invention does not entitle the author to claim protection for his system or invention as such. The same is true of an inventive concept expressed in an artistic work. However striking or original it may be, others are (in the absence of patent protection) free to express it in works of their own: see *Kleeneze Ltd. v. D.R.G. (U.K.) Ltd.* [1984] F.S.R. 399 . The other proposition is that certain ideas expressed by a copyright work may not be protected because, although they are ideas of a literary, dramatic or artistic nature, they are not original, or so commonplace as not to form a

substantial part of the work. *Kenrick & Co. v. Lawrence & Co.* (1890) 25 Q.B.D. 99 is a well-known example. It is on this ground that the mere notion of combining stripes and flowers would not have amounted to a substantial part of the plaintiff's work. At that level of abstraction, the idea, though expressed in the design, would not have represented sufficient of the author's skill and labour as to attract copyright protection.

33. As regards the first proposition I said much the same thing in *Ibcos Computers v. Barclays Mercantile* [1994] FSR 275 at p.291:

> The true position is that where an "idea" is sufficiently general, then even if an original work embodies it, the mere taking of that idea will not infringe. But if the "idea" is detailed, then there may be infringement. It is a question of degree. The same applies whether the work is functional or not, and whether visual or literary. In the latter field the taking of a plot (i.e. the "idea") of a novel or play can certainly infringe if that plot is a substantial part of the copyright work. As Judge Learned Hand said (speaking of the distinction between "idea" and "expression"): "Nobody has ever been able to fix that boundary and nobody ever can, *Nichols v Universal Pictures* (1930) 45 F. (2d) 119"

34. Mr Howe then submitted that the "idea" of the cue pulsing with the power-meter could not be discounted within Lord Hoffmann's first category because here we are concerned with copyright in a computer program. You cannot say the "idea" has no connection with the nature of the work. Nor did it fall within the second category because it was not held "commonplace," merely "obvious." He sought to bolster the argument by reference to the *travaux préparatoires* to the Directive. At the very least, he submitted, the position was unclear and that we should refer some questions to the European Court of Justice pursuant to Art. 234 of the Treaty.

35. I reject all of that. First I think the fact that we are considering a computer program copyright does not in any way preclude a mere "idea" as to what the program should do from being excluded as having nothing to do with the nature of the work. The nature of the work is a computer program having all the necessary coding to function. The general idea is only faintly related to that — no different from the relationship of the general idea of a plastic letter-box draught excluder to the artistic works consisting of the drawings for a particular excluder in the *Kleeneze* case. Indeed I have to say that, as Mr Howe waxed lyrical about the combination of features in the animation, he sounded more like counsel in a patent case than one in a copyright case. Not all of the skill which goes into a copyright work is protected — the obvious example being the skill involved in creating an invention which is then described in a literary work. An idea consisting of a combination of ideas is still just an idea. That is as true for ideas in a computer program as for any other copyright work.

36. Nor am I impressed by Mr Howe's attempt to limit the dichotomy to "building blocks". He sought to do this by reference to recital 14 which refers to "logic, algorithms and programming languages" as comprising "ideas and principles." I see no reason to suppose that Art. 13 is thereby limited. Art 14 is clearly drawn

on the basis that the basic position of Art.13 — no protection for ideas and principles — applies also to those specified matters.

37. The same conclusion is reached if one considers TRIPS. Although normally a UK Act is not to be construed by reference to a later international Treaty, I note that Lord Hoffmann considered TRIPS to be of relevance to our domestic copyright law in *Designers Guild* (see [23]). Here the position is much clearer because we are dealing with EU law. The ECJ has held that TRIPS (to which the EU as well as its Member States is a party) is relevant to the construction of earlier EU legislation concerned with intellectual property. In *Schieving-Nijstad v Groeneveld* Case C-89/99 (13th September 2001) the court said:

> [30] In the field of trade marks, to which TRIPs is applicable and in respect of which the Community has already legislated, the Court has jurisdiction to interpret Article 50 of TRIPs — as, indeed, it has previously had occasion to do (see *Hermés* [[1998] ECR I-3603], and Joined Cases C-300/98 and C-392-98 *Dior and Others* [2000] ECR I-11307). It is therefore appropriate to recapitulate the principles laid down in that case-law."

> [35] Nevertheless, it is apparent from the Court's case-law, in a field which TRIPs applies and in respect of which the Community has already legislated, the judicial authorities of the Member States are required by virtue of Community law, when called upon to apply national rules with a view to ordering provisional measures for the protection of rights falling within such a field, to do so as far as possible in the light of the wording and purpose of Article 50 of TRIPs (see *Hermés*, paragraph 28, and *Dior and Others*, paragraph 47).

38. Mr Howe sought to escape from the fact that we should construe the UK Act in accordance with the Directive which should be construed so far as possible as to conform to TRIPS by a further submission: that TRIPS was only concerned with minimum standards for intellectual property rights and that its signatories were free to provide for greater rights. So, he said, the EU could provide that copyright protection extended to ideas if it so wanted. Now it is in general true that a party to TRIPS can provide more extensive protection than called for TRIPS, see Art.1. But the concluding words of the first sentence of Art.1 add "provided that such protection does not contravene the provisions of this Agreement". Art. 9.2 positively provides that "copyright protection shall extend to expressions and <u>not to</u> ideas etc. as such". So in this instance TRIPS lays down a positive rule as to the point beyond which copyright protection may not go. To protect by copyright mere ideas as such would contravene TRIPS. The Software Directive must be construed so as to conform to TRIPS and so must be construed as not to protect ideas as such.

39. As to the *travaux* Mr Howe took us through the following:

> i) the original Commission "Proposal for a Council Directive on the legal protection of computer programs" COM(88) 816 final —SYN 183, submitted on 5th January 1989 (89/C91/05);

> ii) the amended proposal COM (90) 509 final — SYN 183 (1990/C 320/11), submitted on 18th October 1990; and

iii) the Opinion of the Economic and Social Committee.

40. Mr Howe was unable to point to any clear unequivocal statement anywhere suggesting that copyright in computer programs should extend to ideas. Given that state of affairs it would be a waste of time to set out all the material in detail. It is sufficient to record that the submission is based on an argument by implication from unexplained alterations from the original proposal. In particular the original proposal did not use the expression "element of a computer program" in proposed Art.1.2 but merely to "the ideas, principles, logic, algorithms or programming languages." I cannot extract from this any intention to extend protection to ideas provided they are not "elements."

41. I am reinforced in my view by the fact that the Economic and Social Committee (whose report is specifically recited in the Directive as being a document to which the Council had regard in making the Directive) clearly did not think the proposal was limited as suggested by Mr Howe. It said tersely:

> "There is no dispute that 'ideas and principles' are outside the protection of the law of copyright."

42. So there is no help for Mr Howe in the *travaux*. I would add generally that *travaux preparatoires*, if not bang on the point, seldom help. If the meaning of the ultimate document is ambiguous, or obscure, then, even if the *travaux* are admissible, there is no point in trawling through them unless they are clear as to what was intended and meant. Constructing arguments around unexplained changes, passages in themselves ambiguous, or mere possible hints as to what would have been intended if the actual point in issue had actually been addressed, is just a waste of time. I said in *Dyson v Qualtex* [2006] EWCA Civ 166, [2006] RPC 769:

> [11] …. In the context of construing an international treaty by reference to the travaux préparatoires to find a definite legal intention Lord Steyn said: "Only a bull's-eye counts" (*Effort Shipping v Linden Management* [1988] AC 605 at 625). Much the same goes for trying to ascertain such an intention from a White Paper which precedes legislation.

That is equally applicable to all documents which fall to be construed in the light of admissible *travaux*. There is no point in relying upon *travaux* which are not directly in point — you just substitute the puzzle posed by the actual language to be construed by another puzzle about other language at first or even second remove.

43. So I reject Mr Howe's "only ideas which are elements are excluded" argument. Actually I do not see, even if it had been right, why the animation cycle should not be regarded as "an element". After all it is not the game itself. It is an element of the game and so of its computer program. That it is only an element is shown by the fact that it could be transposed to any other snooker/pool computer game as an element of that game.

44. Accordingly I think the appeal on literary copyright fails on the simple ground that what was found to have inspired some aspects of the defendants' game is just

too general to amount to a substantial part of the claimants' game. The Judge's evaluation, far from being wrong in principle, was right when he said:

> They are ideas which have little to do with the skill and effort expended by the programmer and do not constitute the form of expression of the literary works relied upon.

45. I also think the appeal fails on the more specific basis (also accepted by the Judge) of the principles applied by Pumfrey J in *Navitaire v easyJet* [2004] EWHC 1725 (Ch), [2006] RPC 111.

46. The facts there were stronger than in the present cases, yet the claimants lost. easyJet wanted to substitute its existing airline booking program with another because it had fallen out with Navitaire, the owner of the copyright in the existing program. It commissioned the second defendant to produce a substitute which would look and feel like its predecessor. So far as possible users were not to notice any difference when they used the new program. Without in any way using or even having access to the source code of Navitaire, this was achieved.

47. Pumfrey J held that there was infringement of the artistic copyright in some of the "buttons" of the claimants' program (see p.131 of the RPC report). But he rejected the main claim. He said:

> "125. This does not answer the question with which I am confronted, which is peculiar, I believe, to computer programs. The reason it is a new problem is that two completely different computer programs can produce an identical result: not a result identical at some level of abstraction but identical at any level of abstraction. This is so even if the author of one has no access at all to the other but only to its results. The analogy with a plot is for this reason a poor one. It is a poor one for other reasons as well. To say these programs possess a plot is precisely like saying that the book of instructions for a booking clerk acting manually has a plot: but a book of instructions has no theme, no events, and does not have a narrative flow. Nor does a computer program, particularly one whose behaviour depends upon the history of its inputs in any given transaction. It does not have a plot, merely a series of pre-defined operations intended to achieve the desired result in response to the requests of the customer.
>
> 126. The view in favour of Navitaire's case is expressed concisely by the authors of *The Modern Law* in paragraph 34.64 (I have assumed that when they speak of 'obtains…from the original program' they do not mean obtain directly, but indirectly from watching the program work):
>
> > For instance, the writing of a financing program may require as part of the task a careful elucidation of the relevant tax regulations — so that they may be reduced to a series of unambiguous statements — and it will be evident to any lawyer that this alone will probably involve a very large amount of work. A competitor might write a program of his own in a different computer language and arranged in a different way and with many improvements of his own but if he obtains the rules for calculating the tax from the original program instead of working these out for himself it is hard to see why he should not be considered a plagiarist.

127. There is a counter-example that throws some light on the nature of the problem. Take the example of a chef who invents a new pudding. After a lot of work he gets a satisfactory result, and thereafter his puddings are always made using his written recipe, undoubtedly a literary work. Along comes a competitor who likes the pudding and resolves to make it himself. Ultimately, after much culinary labour, he succeeds in emulating the earlier result, and he records his recipe. Is the later recipe an infringement of the earlier, as the end result, the plot and purpose of both (the pudding) is the same? I believe the answer is no.

129. The questions in the present case are both a lack of substantiality and the nature of the skill and labour to be protected. Navitaire's computer program invites input in a manner excluded from copyright protection, outputs its results in a form excluded from copyright protection and creates a record of a reservation in the name of a particular passenger on a particular flight. What is left when the interface aspects of the case are disregarded is the business function of carrying out the transaction and creating the record, because none of the code was read or copied by the defendants. It is right that those responsible for devising OpenRes envisaged this as the end result for their program: but that is not relevant skill and labour. In my judgment, this claim for non-textual copying should fail.

130. I do not come to this conclusion with any regret. If it is the policy of the Software Directive to exclude both computer languages and the underlying ideas of the interfaces from protection, then it should not be possible to circumvent these exclusions by seeking to identify some overall function or functions that it is the sole purpose of the interface to invoke and relying on those instead. As a matter of policy also, it seems to me that to permit the 'business logic' of a program to attract protection through the literary copyright afforded to the program itself is an unjustifiable extension of copyright protection into a field where I am far from satisfied that it is appropriate."

48. Mr Howe attacked that. I quote his skeleton argument:

"this analogy is a poor one. The reason is that the first chef has deployed two quite distinct types of skill and labour. The first is the skill of devising a recipe, a skill which on no view forms part of the skill and labour protected by copyright in literary works. The second is skill and labour in reducing the recipe he has devised to written form. A copyist who copies from his pudding rather than from his recipe book may appropriate the former skill and labour but none of the latter.

By contrast, a copyist who copies the function of a computer program to write his own program to achieve the same results is clearly appropriating part of the skill and labour expended in designing the program.

49. He further developed the argument basing himself on recital 7 of the Directive. This says "'computer program' … also includes preparatory design work leading to the development of a computer program provided that the nature of the preparatory work is such that a computer program can result from it at a later stage". He asked us to suppose a case where there are two clear stages in the making of a program — a first stage where the designer sets out all the things he wants the program to be able do and a second stage (which may be by a different person) where the actual program code is written. Mr Howe contended that the first stage was intended to be protected as such, even if it consisted only of ideas

as to what the program should do. Going back to the analogy, the "preparatory work" for the program is like the skill of devising the recipe and the actual program writing like the reduction of the recipe to written form. The difference, he submitted, is that for computer programs, unlike the recipe, the preparatory work is to be protected.

50. I reject the argument. The reason is simple. The Directive does not say that mere ideas by way of preparatory design work are to be protected. As I have said it makes it clear that for computer programs as a whole (which includes their preparatory design work) ideas are not to be protected. What is protected by way of preparatory design work is that work as a literary work — the expression of the design which are to go into the ultimate program, not the ideas themselves.

51. So for example, if Mr Jones had actually written a description of the pulsing, rotating cue, and synchronised power meter his description would (if not too trivial at least) be protected as a literary work. People could not copy that. But they could use the same idea. Similarly and more generally, a written work consisting of a specification of the functions of an intended computer program will attract protection as a literary work. But the functions themselves do not. Of course to someone familiar with the prior English law it is self-evident that copyright could subsist in such a description. The fact that a work can get copyright even if mundane, is old and familiar to an English lawyer. But the Directive needed to say that protection as a literary work should be provided for preparatory design work because not all Member States under their existing laws necessarily provided that. That is the whole point of the Directive — and the clear reason for it is recited in Art. 1.

52. So I think Mr Howe's attack on *Navitaire* fails. The reasoning in *Navitaire* provides a second reason for dismissing this appeal. Pumfrey J was quite right to say that merely making a program which will emulate another but which in no way involves copying the program code or any of the program's graphics is legitimate.

53. Finally Mr Howe suggested the law was sufficiently uncertain as to warrant a reference being made to the European Court of Justice. No less than 6 elaborate draft questions were supplied. I do not think it is necessary to make any reference to resolve this case. It is wholly unrealistic to suppose that the European Court of Justice would hold that copyright protection was to be given to ideas at such a high level of abstraction as those in this case.

54. I would only add this. Both sides submitted that this case had significance for the computer games (and computer program writing) industry. Mr Howe submitted that if the decision below is upheld there is no effective protection for games against copying of the game where a party copies the rules of a game but not its graphics. Mr Carr submitted that that not all things are covered by copyright, that most if not every work is, to some extent, influenced or derived from other works. So it is very important that copyright is not allowed to intervene to stifle the creation of works that are actually very different, as the individual games are here.

55. I agree with Mr Carr. If protection for such general ideas as are relied on here were conferred by the law, copyright would become an instrument of oppression rather than the incentive for creation which it is intended to be. Protection would have moved to cover works merely inspired by others, to ideas themselves.

Lord Justice Lloyd:

56. I agree.

Chancellor of the High Court:

57. I also agree.

APPENDIX — THE LEGISLATION

For "artistic works"

58. So far as is relevant here, s.4(1) of the Copyright, Designs and Patents Act defines artistic works and graphic work as follows:

> **4.** — (1) In this Part "artistic work" means —
>
> (a) a graphic work, …., irrespective of artistic quality,
>
> (2) In this Part —
>
> . . .
>
> "graphic work" includes —
>
> (a) any painting, drawing, diagram, map, chart or plan, and
>
> (b) any engraving, etching, lithograph, woodcut or similar work;

59. Additionally s. 9(3) provides:

> 3 — In the case of a literary, dramatic, musical or artistic work which is computer-generated, the author shall be taken to be the person by whom the arrangements necessary for the creation of the work are undertaken.

And s.178 reads:

> "Computer-generated", in relation to a work, means that the work is generated by computer in circumstances such that there is no human author of the work.

For "Literary Works"

60. Section 3(1) of the Act (as amended by the Copyright (Computer Programs) Regulations (1992)) provides so far as is relevant:

> **3(1)** In this Part:
>
> "literary work" means any work, other than a dramatic or musical work, which is written, spoken or sung, and accordingly includes:
>
> . . .

(b) a computer program,

(c) preparatory design material for a computer program

. . .

For Infringement

61. Section 16 of the Act provides:

16 The acts restricted by copyright in a work

(1) The owner of the copyright in a work has, in accordance with the following provisions of this Chapter, the exclusive right to do the following acts in the United Kingdom —

(a) to copy the work (see section 17);

(3) References in this Part to the doing of an act restricted by the copyright in a work are to the doing of it —

(a) in relation to the work as a whole or any substantial part of it

62. Section 17 expands on the meaning of "to copy"

17 Infringement of copyright by copying

(1) The copying of the work is an act restricted by the copyright in every description of copyright work; and references in this Part to copying and copies shall be construed as follows.

(2) Copying in relation to a literary, dramatic, musical or artistic work means reproducing the work in any material form. This includes storing the work in any medium by electronic means.

The Software Directive 91/250/EEC

63. The 1992 Regulations implement Council Directive 91/250/EEC of 14 May 1991 on the Legal Protection of Computer Programs ("the Directive"). It follows (and was not disputed) that these provisions of the Act must be interepreted in accordance with the Directive. I therefore set out its relevant recitals (adding numbers) and provisions:

1. Whereas computer programs are at present not clearly protected in all Member States by existing legislation and such protection, where it exists, has different attributes;

4. Whereas certain differences in the legal protection of computer programs offered by the laws of the Member States have direct and negative effects on the functioning of the common market as regards computer programs and such differences could well become greater as Member States introduce new legislation on this subject;

5. Whereas existing differences having such effects need to be removed and new ones prevented from arising, while differences not adversely affecting the functioning of the common market to a substantial degree need not be removed or prevented from arising;

6. Whereas the Community's legal framework on the protection of computer programs can accordingly in the first instance be limited to establishing that Member States should accord protection to computer programs under copyright law as literary works and, further, to establishing who and what should be protected, the exclusive rights on which protected persons should be able to rely in order to authorize or prohibit certain acts and for how long the protection should apply;

7. Whereas, for the purpose of this Directive, the term 'computer program' shall include programs in any form, including those which are incorporated into hardware; whereas this term also includes preparatory design work leading to the development of a computer program provided that the nature of the preparatory work is such that a computer program can result from it at a later stage;

13. Whereas, for the avoidance of doubt, it has to be made clear that only the expression of a computer program is protected and that ideas and principles which underlie any element of a program, including those which underlie its interfaces, are not protected by copyright under this Directive;

14. Whereas, in accordance with this principle of copyright, to the extent that logic, algorithms and programming languages comprise ideas and principles, those ideas and principles are not protected under this Directive;

15. Whereas, in accordance with the legislation and jurisprudence of the Member States and the international copyright conventions, the expression of those ideas and principles is to be protected by copyright;

20. Whereas the unauthorized reproduction, translation, adaptation or transformation of the form of the code in which a copy of a computer program has been made available constitutes an infringement of the exclusive rights of the author;

Article 1

Object of protection

1. In accordance with the provisions of this Directive, Member States shall protect computer programs, by copyright, as literary works within the meaning of the Berne Convention for the Protection of Literary and Artistic Works. For the purposes of this Directive, the term 'computer programs' shall include their preparatory design material.

2. Protection in accordance with this Directive shall apply to the expression in any form of a computer program. Ideas and principles which underlie any element of a computer program, including those which underlie its interfaces, are not protected by copyright under this Directive.

3. A computer program shall be protected if it is original in the sense that it is the author's own intellectual creation. No other criteria shall be applied to determine its eligibility for protection.

Article 4

Restricted Acts

Subject to the provisions of Articles 5 and 6, the exclusive rights of the rightholder within the meaning of Article 2, shall include the right to do or to authorize:

(a) the permanent or temporary reproduction of a computer program by any means and in any form, in part or in whole. Insofar as loading, displaying, running, transmission or storage of the computer program necessitate such reproduction, such acts shall be subject to authorization by the rightholder;

. . .

TRIPS

64. Also of importance in the debate are Arts. 1 and 9 of TRIPS (The Agreement on Trade-related Aspects of Intellectual Property Rights which forms Annex 1C to the Agreement establishing the World Trade Organisation signed in Morocco on 15th April 1994 by representatives of the Community and its Member States).

Art. 1. Members shall give effect to the provisions of this Agreement. Members may, but shall not be obliged to, implement in their law more extensive protection that is required by this Agreement, provided that such protection does not contravene the provisions of this Agreement. Members shall be free to determine the appropriate method of implementing the provisions of this Agreement within their own legal system and practice.

Art. 9.1 Members shall comply with Articles 1 through 21 of the Berne Convention (1971) and the Appendix thereto. However, Members shall not have rights or obligations under this Agreement in respect of the rights conferred under Article 6*bis* of that Convention or of the rights derived therefrom.

Art. 9.2 Copyright protection shall extend to expressions and not to ideas, procedures, methods of operation or mathematical concepts as such.

Chapter 4

AUTHORSHIP

1. Authorship

The term "author" is not defined in the Act, but generally it is the person who writes, draws or composes the work, or is otherwise responsible for putting it into a concrete form.[1] The concept of authorship reflects the essential nature of copyright in works under the Act. Copyright protects original forms of expression, and the author is the person who originates the particular form of the expression. The concepts of "author" and "original work" are therefore correlative; each one connotes the other. A person who merely suggests certain ideas without contributing anything to the expressive form of the work will not be the author of the work. Rather, the author is the person who expresses the ideas in a work in an original form.

Ateliers Tango Argentin Inc. v. Festival d'Espagne d'Amerique Latine Inc.
(1997), 84 C.P.R. (3d) 56

Crête J.

Judgment rendered: October 31, 1997

. . .

CRETE J. (translation):-Does the plagiarizing of a photograph used to advertise a dance troupe and tango school constitute copyright infringement and if so, what damages can be claimed by the author and user of the photograph at issue?

These are the issues before the court in the present suit.

The facts of the case are as follows.

Juan Felipe Argaez is a professional photographer employed by a Montreal hospital. He makes ends meet as a freelance photographer.

Mr. Argaez also has a passion for dance. He takes tango lessons at a specialized school, the Ateliers Tango Argentin. This school is affiliated with a professional dance troupe which presents tango shows in Montreal and elsewhere in Canada under the name of Grafiti Tango. The two organizations are directed by Joseph Bain, who is a dancer, choreographer, artistic director and dance instructor.

---

[1] *Dubois v. System de Gestion ed d'Analyse de Données Média/Média-Source Canada Inc.* (1991), 41 C.P.R. (3d) 92 (Que. S.C.).

During June 1992, Mr. Bain asked Mr. Argaez to take photos that were to be used for the purposes of introducing and promoting his dance troupe and tango school. He was seeking a distinctive image, designed to express visually the features that are particular to tango culture, a form of dance which developed in the streets and on the sidewalks of certain "barrios" of Buenos Aires towards the end of the last century.

Ateliers Tango Argentin and Mr. Argaez entered into an agreement pursuant to which Mr. Argaez was to provide his services as a photo-grapher in order to produce a certain number of photographs. Ateliers Tango Argentin obtained the right, for a period of five years, to use the photos which Mr. Argaez had taken for them. In exchange for his services, Mr. Argaez would receive $2000 for pro-ducing the photos and $2000 for allowing the tango school and dance troupe, over a period of five years, to use the photos that he had taken. It was agreed that the school would provide Mr. Argaez the equivalent of $4000 in tango lessons in exchange for his services and the use of his photos.

After several days of research in order to find the ideal location for producing the requested photos, Mr. Argaez settled on a section of Prince Arthur Street near St. Louis Square in Montreal.

Early in the morning of the photo session, he painted the word TANGO in graf-fiti on the walls which were to be used as background for the photos.

Mr. Argaez brought a male and female dancer from the GrafJiti Tango dance troupe as well as Mr. Bain and Danielle Sturk, the cofounder of the school and dance troupe.

The photo session lasted between three and four hours. Mr. Argaez took approx-imately fifteen snapshots, each of which represented one worhan and three men in a form of fixed choreography.

Using the photos taken by Mr. Argaez, Ateliers Tango Argentin selected one in particular which was to become the image of the tango school and dance troupe, their business card, their "brand name" in the large sense of the expression.

This black and white photo showed the back of a woman in the foreground, slightly swaying, wearing a dark-coloured, very short dress. Her right arm is behind her back, extended towards the ground, the hand open, a bracelet on her wrist. The left arm is perpendicular to the right arm, the left hand gripping onto the right forearm. The posture is one of both challenge and provocation.

The woman faces three men with their backs to the wall under the word TANGO drawn by Mr. Argaez. They are all wearing white shirts and dark-coloured pants. The man in the centre is squatting between the two others who remain upright.

For his photo, Mr. Argaez used the posts and chains typical of this particular location on Prince Arthur Street. They serve as background suggesting a barrier which is both physical and psychological between the woman and the three men.

The photo selected by Ateliers Tango Argentin was used shortly thereafter as an image representing the troupe and school in various newspapers including

Le Devoir, The Mirror and L'Express d'outremont. It was primarily used to announce events and shows. Also, 5000 copies were printed out in the form of postcards and used for various promotional purposes. An enlargement of the photo decorated the walls of the dance studio of the school and the troupe on St. Lawrence Boulevard. In sum, the photo became the visual representation par excellence that Ateliers Tango Argentin had wished to acquire for its school and dance troupe. See Mr. Argaez's photo attached as Schedule I to this judgment.

During the summer of 1993, a certain Antonio Grediaga Bueno approached Mr. Bain with a view to inviting the GrafJiti Tango troupe to participate in a Festival, which he was organizing and which was to present various shows the following autumn under the name of Festival d 'Espagne et d'Amérique Latine.

During the course of negotiations between Mr. Bueno and Mr. Bain, the latter delivered to the organizer of the Festival a sample of the photo taken the previous year by Mr. Argaez for Ateliers Tango Argentin in a postcard format.

However, negotiations between the two men did not prove fruitful, and Mr. Bueno was obliged to find other participants to ensure a "tango" presence at his Festival.

At the time of preparation of the promotional material for his Festival, Mr. Bueno first wished to use the photo delivered to him by Mr. Bain, but Madame Françoise Chartrand, his production director, immediately advised him that this was prohibited as the photo did not belong to him. Another colleague, Chantal Chevrier, then suggested that he retain the services of a certain Bruce McNeil, a professional photographer she knew.

Mr. Bueno and Mr. McNeil met during August. Mr. Bueno asked Mr. McNeil to produce a photo similar to the one which Mr. Bain had recently given to him. Mr. Bueno gave Mr. McNeil a photocopy of the Ateliers Tango Argentin postcard, stating that he did not have the negative but that the photo belonged to him.

Mr. McNeil proposed taking other photos at different locations, but Mr. Bueno insisted: he wanted to recreate the same image, the same atmosphere, the same concept as in the photo taken by Mr. Argaez. He was careful, however, not to inform Mr. McNeil that the photo was taken by Mr. Argaez and that it had been given to him by Mr. Bain.

The day of the photo session, Mr. McNeil brought with him one woman and three men who were to pose for the shoot. They went to the exact location on Prince Arthur where Mr. Argaez had written TANGO in graffiti the preceding year. They had to wait for Mr. Bueno who insisted on being present. Upon his arrival, Mr. Bueno did not like the dress worn by the woman hired by Mr. McNeil, They therefore had to purchase another one. Finally, Mr. Bueno insisted that the four models assume exactly the same posture as in the Ateliers Tango Argentin photo. The camera angle was also identical. Mr. McNeil proceeded with the shoot.

The photos which were the result of that shoot were used shortly thereafter by the Festival d'Espagne et d'Amérique Latine in all its advertising for tango activities: posters put up throughout the city of Montreal and other locations where the Festival was scheduled to appear (Quebec City and Sherbrooke); programs given to spectators; promotional brochures; advertisements in various newspapers. See the photo which appeared on posters and in Festival programs attached as Schedule II to this judgment.

Alerted by what they considered to be piracy of their image and their photo, Ateliers Tango Argentin and Juan Felipe Argaez served formal notice on the Festival and its promoter Mr. Bueno to cease any distribution of the photos taken by Mr. McNeil. These formal notices were ignored: the advertising and photos continued to circulate up until the end of the Festival in October 1993.

. . .

The defendants Grediaga and Gingras deny Mr. Argaez's claim to copyright ownership on the ground that the physical person who pressed the button on the camera when the photos were taken was not Mr. Argaez himself, but Danielle Sturk, the spouse of Mr. Bain and co-director of Ateliers Tango Argentin. It is true that the evidence discloses that Mr. Argaez was not the person who actually took the photo, as he was one of the three males who appeared in the photo. Ms. Sturk took the picture, acting on Mr. Argaez's instructions.

The claim of the defendants is ill-founded. In fact, Ms. Sturk only participated in the photo session as a simple assistant, acting under the artistic direction of Mr. Argaez. The author is the person who conceives, who expresses ideas, who composes, who creates the work as a result of his labour, his qualities and his personal efforts.' There is no doubt therefore that the true creator and inventor of the work is Mr. Argaez and not Ms. Sturk, who was only working as an assistant under the direction of Mr. Argaez. Furthermore, he is the professional photographer whose name appears on the reverse of the photo (Exhibit P-1).

John Maryon International Ltd. v. New Brunswick Telephone Co. Ltd.
(1982), 24 C.C.L.T. 146 (N.B. C.A.)

New Brunswick Court of Appeal

Hughes C.J.N.B., Richard C.J.Q.B. and La Forest J.A.

Heard: December 1-4, 1981
Judgment: September 10, 1982
Addendum: October 20, 1982
Docket: 41/81/CA

. . .

The judgment of the Court was delivered by _La Forest J.A._:

Background

1 In early 1970 the New Brunswick Telephone Company, Limited (N.B. Tel) learned that plans had been approved by the City of Moncton for the construction

of the Place L'Assomption development, a new high-rise business complex in the heart of the city. This development would block the transmission of micro-wave messages to and from N.B. Tel's 135-foot steel tower located in down-town Moncton. As a result, N.B. Tel decided to build a new and higher tower, and in June 1970 it invited several consulting engineers to submit proposals for the construction of the new tower. Ultimately, John Maryon International Ltd. (which I shall call Maryon International) was selected as consultant to design and arrange for its construction. On August 25, 1970 it was authorized to pre-pare final design plans for the structure, the actual engineering design work to be done by an associated company, John Maryon and Partners Limited (which I shall call Maryon Partners). A written contract dated November 24, 1970 was signed under which Maryon International agreed to manage the project, its ser-vices to include:

> the organization and coordination of all aspects of the project, the establishment of design criteria in consultation with the client, preparation of final working drawings and project specifications, and control and supervision of construc-tion, all as described in more detail [in the contract], so that the desired program would be completed to the satisfaction of the client.

2 Construction work had in fact already started on September 21, 1970, when excavation for the foundation was begun. The slip form method of construc-tion, whereby concrete is poured into forms continuously moving upwards, was recommended and used in constructing the tower shaft. The slip form began on November 4, 1970 and was finished on November 20, 1970. Other aspects of the work proceeded with similar celerity, and the tower was completed and fully operational by the following summer. It was officially opened at the beginning of June 1971.

3 The tower was thus described by the trial Judge [33 N.B.R. (2d) 543 at 551-52, 80 A.P.R. 543]:

> The tower as built has an octagonally shaped concrete foundation which is 56 feet wide and 5 feet thick. The tower itself consists of a reinforced concrete shaft which rises to a height of 350 feet above ground elevation. It is circular in cross section and has a diameter of 20 feet. The wall of the tower shaft is 12 inches thick. Forming part of the shaft wall are 4 equally spaced semi-circular nibs each having a radius of 2 feet, which extend to a height of 246 feet. There are 5 cantile-vered antennae platforms located in the top 94 feet of the tower having a diameter of 32 feet which project 6 feet from the outside face of the tower shaft. There is a pierced wall or turret, 8 feet 9 inches high, at the top of the tower to which it was planned to attach a 51 foot broadcast antenna.

4 The first intimation of trouble came in June 1971 when the tower crew, which was charged with continuous routine work on the tower, reported cracks, espe-cially in the interior of the tower shaft. Mr. John Maryon (the president of Maryon International and Maryon Partners) visited the tower later that month but in his report of June 25 he expressed no concern. In particular, the cracks in the shaft had, in his view, "virtually no effect on the strength or stiffness of the tower".

5 However, subsequent events were to increase N.B. Tel's concerns about the stability of the tower. Two members of the tower crew testified that the hairline cracks running up and down a portion of the interior of the east and west faces of the shaft appeared to lengthen and widen between 1971 to 1974. During heavy rain storms there was dampness and water within the tower, as well as dampness and discolouration of the concrete adjacent to the cracks. Small pieces of concrete broke off, or spalled, inside the tower adjacent to the larger cracks. There were as well three large spalls, one in the interior at the 235 foot level, one on the underside of the third platform, two of them apparently resulting from frozen conduits and one from the freezing of water which had entered the tower along an uncapped hollow jack rod. Radial cracks were also found in the platforms, some of which penetrated right through the platforms. However, the tower crew found no cracks on the outside of the tower shaft when they inspected it using bosun's chairs.

6 So. N.B. Tel again asked Mr. Maryon to examine the tower. He did so in April or May of 1974 and reported his findings on May 30, 1974. Again he reassured N.B. Tel that the vertical cracking on the inside face of the tower had no significant structural implications. Such cracks, he stated, were not unusual for this type of tower because it moves under changing atmospheric conditions; the major significance of the cracks, he asserted, was cosmetic although there was some potential danger to workers from falling concrete. He therefore recommended removing loose materials and filling the larger voids with epoxy. He further advised N.B. Tel about the large spalls, the spalling at the top of the platforms, the problems related to the electrical outlet boxes and conduits, and concluded:

> We trust that these recommendations cover the essential problems being experienced. We recognize that the cracking referred to appears unsightly and is potentially dangerous to workers in the tower but would reiterate that it has no real adverse structural significance. Further as all indications suggest that there is no cracking at the outside of the tower, no deterioration of the reinforcing steel can result. Should staining at the inside of the tower ever occur however, please notify us immediately as it might be necessary to provide the outside of the tower with a watertight film. At present, we do not feel such a coating is necessary or warranted.

> When we have made analysis of the material which broke loose at the 230 foot level in the tower, we will send you a further subsidiary report to this one. The repair at this level can however proceed without this report if you wish to carry it out in the immediate future.

7 Mr. Maryon may well have been confident about the structure of the tower. He knew, as all the experts at the trial confirmed, that all concrete cracks. This is principally owing to shrinkage and atmospheric conditions. In this case, the outside of the tower is affected by the heat of the sun while the inside is sheltered, and different portions outside are subjected to varying degrees of heat at different times of the day and season. So different parts of the tower move in reaction to these forces and the tower cracks. Indeed, Mr. Maryon testified that he intended the tower to crack internally much in the manner it did. Such cracks, he stated, permit the structure "to breathe", i.e., the cracks afford the

tower necessary flexibility as the cracks open and close in reaction to changing atmospheric conditions.

8 But Mr. Maryon at no time informed N.B. Tel that the structure was designed to crack in this way, and it remained concerned about the structural adequacy of the tower. On May 31, 1974 its solicitor and one of its engineers inspected the tower with the tower crew, and following the report of this inspection N.B. Tel retained Mr. John Bickley, a civil engineer with expertise in concrete technology, to make an independent investigation of the tower. After a preliminary inspection on June 5, 1974, Mr. Bickley verbally reported his opinion that the tower showed significant signs of distress and should be investigated. He recommended that an independent structural engineering firm be employed to conduct the investigation, and from three such firms proposed N.B. Tel selected Nicolet, Carrier and Dressel of Montreal. The member of that firm principally involved with the matter was Dr. Franz Knoll, an expert in structural engineering who numbered among his accomplishments the design of the C.N. Tower in Toronto, the highest manmade structure in the world.

9 Following his investigation, Dr. Knoll reported that there were serious problems respecting the shaft, the platforms and the foundation. As a result of this investigation and the recommendations flowing from it, N.B. Tel undertook extensive repairs to remedy these alleged problems at a cost of $997,874.44 (compared to the estimated $500,000 cost of the tower and the actual $291,000 paid to Maryon International and Maryon Partners). N.B. Tel then began an action against Maryon International and Maryon Partners for this expenditure claiming that they were in breach of their contracts in failing to ensure the adequacy of the design of the tower for its intended purpose. It further claimed that Maryon Partners was negligent in the preparation of the design and plans and specifications of the tower, and that Maryon Partners failed to ensure that all the materials were installed in conformity with the plans and specifications and in a good and workmanlike manner. N.B. Tel also brought action against Dineen Construction (Atlantic) Ltd., which actually carried out the construction, for breach of contract and negligence in carrying out this task, but this action was dismissed and no appeal was taken from it, so it need not be referred to further.

10 Maryon International and Maryon Partners (to which I shall collectively refer as the Maryon companies) defended the action on the grounds that there were no inadequacies or defects of design, and that if N.B. Tel suffered any damage, it failed to mitigate it. The Maryon companies also counterclaimed and Mr. Maryon brought action against N.B. Tel on a variety of grounds but the only ones seriously pursued were for infringement of copyright in the tower design and for loss of business.

11 The trial Judge held that the Maryon companies were in breach of their contractual duty to use the reasonable care and skill that would ordinarily be expected of professional engineers in the circumstances, and awarded damages against them in the amount of $786,084.12, with costs. The action had been framed both in tort and in contract, but the trial Judge rejected the claim in tort

and based his judgment wholly on the contract claim. This determination was not directly questioned on appeal, but as will be seen it is latent in one of the grounds of cross-appeal.

. . .

Copyright

140 In addition to entering a defence, the Maryon companies also counterclaimed against N.B. Tel for substantial damages for breach of contract, infringement of copyright, loss of business and slander of title. Only the counterclaims for infringement of copyright and loss of business were addressed at trial, and in its post-trial brief counsel for the Maryon companies asserted that Mr. Maryon was the author and owner of the copyright. In a second action, Mr. Maryon claimed substantial damages for breach of copyright in the design of the tower of which he claims to be either the sole author and owner, or in the alternative to be a tenant in common with Mr. Fred Chatwin, N.B. Tel's consulting architect. The infringement of copyright, it is alleged, arose from the fact that N.B. Tel unilaterally and materially altered the design of the tower as a result of which he suffered serious harm. The trial Judge dismissed the counterclaim and the second action on the basis that Mr. Maryon was not the author of the design of the tower, but that Mr. Chatwin was. Mr. Maryon now appeals on the following grounds:

1. The learned trial Judge erred in finding, at law, that Mr. Chatwin was the sole author of the design of the Moncton Tower.

2. The learned trial Judge erred in omitting to find that the copyright was owned by either John Maryon or International.

141 Copyright is governed by the Copyright Act, R.S.C. 1970, c. C-30. By virtue of s. 4 of the Act copyright subsists in every original, literary, dramatic or artistic work, including by virtue of s. 2 architectural works of art. The author of a work is the original owner of the copyright (s. 12(1)), and he may deal with this right in much the same way as any other chose in action. Section 3(1) defines the rights comprised in a copyright in a non-exhaustive way. Generally it is the sole right to produce or reproduce the work or a substantial part of it in any form, but as will be seen later the law also affords protection to the author against certain interferences with the right.

142 To succeed, therefore, Mr. Maryon had to establish that the tower is an artistic work, or more specifically an architectural work of art; that it was original; that he was the author; and that the action of N.B. Tel in placing a girdle around the tower for the purpose of repairing it constituted an interference with his copyright. Maryon International, which it was asserted is the owner of the copyright, must additionally establish that fact.

143 In view of the opinion I have reached respecting the authorship of any copyright in the tower, it is unnecessary for me to determine whether the tower as first constructed was an artistic or original work within the meaning of the Copyright Act.

144 The term author is not defined in the Act, but reference was made to the statement in Fox, The Canadian Law of Copyright and Industrial Designs (2nd ed., 1967), p. 239 that it is the person who actually writes, draws or composes a work. However, this idea must not be carried too far. The cases reveal that the person who "actually writes" must not be equated to a mere scribe or amanuensis: see Univeristy of London Press Ltd. v. Univeristy Tutorial Press Ltd., [1916] 2 Ch. 601. On the other hand, a person who merely gives ideas to a person is not the author: see Commercial Signs v. Gen. Motors Products (Can.) Ltd., [1937] O.W.N. 58, [1937] 2 D.L.R. 310 at 800 [affirmed without written reasons [1937] 2 D.L.R. 800 (C.A.)]. Rather, the author would seem to be the person who expresses the ideas in an original or novel form: see University of London Press Ltd. v. University Tutorial Press Ltd., supra, at p. 608. Transferred to the architectural field, the stonemason was not the author of the gothic cathederal; nor was the cleric who dreamed of an edifice reaching toward heaven. A more homely example is the relationship of the architect to the builder. The present situation resembles this but is more involved. In the case of a physical structure, I would have thought the author of the copyright was the person who had devised the characteristics that made the structure artistically distinctive.

145 The problem is made more difficult by the fact that in addition to the copyright in the structure itself (see Meikle v. Maufe, [1941] 3 All E.R. 144), copyright in a literary work may exist in the plans for the tower. And here there are two sets of plans — the final design of the structure prepared by Mr. Chatwin (of which he is the author) and the detailed structure plans (of which Mr. Maryon or at least someone in the employ of Maryon International is the author).

146 We may now look at the manner in which the trial Judge arrived at his conclusion that Mr. Chatwin was the author of the design of the tower. He notes [at pp. 625-26]:

> The evidence established that Mr. Chatwin was first contacted by N.B. Tel in the late spring or early summer of 1970 and at that time prepared a sketch of a steel tower, 350 feet high. In the latter part of July, at the request of Mr. Smith of N.B. Tel, Mr. Chatwin attended a meeting with Mr. Maryon and Mr. Smith. Mr. Smith described the nature of Mr. Chatwin's engagement to be to help him 'in setting out and selecting a design that would be architecturally pleasing and attractive'. At that meeting, Mr. Maryon produced the sketch of a triangular tower which he had designed to go in at the Bell Canada Pharmacy Avenue location in Toronto. Also at that meeting, Mr. Chatwin was asked to prepare designs for a triangular and a circular tower, which he did in August, 1970.
>
> At a meeting held around the end of August, 1970, attended by Messrs. Smith, Maryon and Chatwin, the circular tower design was agreed upon due to reasons of economy during slip forming. Additionally, the lower platform shown on Mr. Chatwin's plan was raised at the request of N.B. Tel. It is clear Mr. Chatwin was responsible for the appearance of the Tower, including the four nibs and the scalloped platforms, and that it was his firm that prepared a model of the Tower for presentation to the City of Moncton for the necessary regulatory approvals. It is equally clear that Mr. Maryon had considerable involvment with respect to the diameter and shape of the Tower and the wind resistance.

It was Mr. Chatwin's evidence that the concept of a concrete Tower was Mr. Maryon's although he refused to agree that the concept of a cylindrical Tower was Mr. Maryon's. It was also Mr. Chatwin's evidence that his firm was the author of the final design which came into existence some time shortly after the meeting held in late August. It was Mr. Chatwin's position that his firm had designed the structure architecturally and that Mr. Maryon was the author of the structural design. Mr. Chatwin had never seen the drawing of a cylindrical tower with fins and hexagonal platforms which was prepared by Mr. Maryon and is dated July, 1970.

Upon consideration, if the design of the Moncton Tower does have the requisite artistic character or design so as to come within the definition of an 'architectural work of art', I am not persuaded by the evidence that Mr. Maryon was the author of it as he asserts that he is. Rather, on a balance of the probabilities of the case, I conclude and find that Mr. Chatwin was the author of the design of the Moncton Tower.

147 It will be evident from this that the trial Judge was clearly of the view that it was Mr. Chatwin who was responsible for devising any characteristics that made the tower artistically distinctive, and that may have been interfered with by the remedial work. Of course, Mr. Maryon made suggestions, sometimes for aesthetic but more often for structural reasons, but as noted above, the author is the person who finds expression for these suggestions in the product. Mr. Chatwin clearly stated that Mr. Maryon's contribution in this regard was no more than is usual for a structural engineer. One need only look at Mr. Chatwin's final design to see that the structure as built was obviously that designed by Mr. Chatwin. It is true that Mr. Chatwin's original design was for a steel tower and that the suggestion that it be a concrete tower was made by Mr. Maryon, but the trial Judge held that Mr. Chatwin, not Mr. Maryon, was responsible for the final design of the structure.

148 It is also true, of course, that Mr. Maryon or at least Maryon International had to devise a detailed structural design to construct the tower (and to that design, of course, he or it has the copyright), but it is the tower as conceived by Mr. Chatwin that was built. In fact the structural design appears to have been based on processes devised by others. The major defence of the Maryon companies to the action for negligence, in fact, was that he relied on Dr. Leonhardt's structural concepts.

149 I, therefore, conclude that the trial Judge was right in finding that Mr. Chatwin, and not Mr. Maryon, was the author of the design of the tower. I am fortified in this conclusion by the final words of the definition of an "architectural work of art" as it appears in the Copyright Act. It reads as follows:

2. In this Act

'architectural work of art' means any building or structure having an artistic character or design, in respect of such character or design, or any model for such building or structure, *but the protection afforded by this Act is confined to the artistic character and design, and does not extend to processes or methods of construction.*

[The underlining is mine.]

150 This is sufficient to dispose of the appeal. It also disposes of the counter-claim, for Maryon International's claim of ownership is dependant on the question of authorship. But even if Mr. Maryon was the author of the design, I do not think he could recover. It is true, as his counsel argued, that the extent to which copyright material may be altered is not unfettered; the Court may imply terms in a contract limiting such alteration. This is pointed out by Judson J., giving the judgment of the Supreme Court of Canada, in Netupsky v. Dom. Bridge Co., [1972] S.C.R. 368 at 378, [1972] 1 W.W.R. 420, 3 C.P.R. (2d) 1, 24 D.L.R. (3d) 484. But that case is really authority for the proposition that Courts will imply terms limiting the right under a copyright in order to permit repair of a structure.

While not framed explicitly in terms of an authorship issue, the following case addresses the troublesome question of authorship of interviews. Can it be said that interviewer is the author of the interview as a whole, including the words of the interviewee? Does the interviewee have no claim to have authored the words that she spoke? Under what conditions might the interviewer resemble the mere scribe who fixes the original expression of the interviewee with her authority or on her behalf such that the copyright should reside with interviewee alone? In what context might an interview more appropriately be regarded as a work of joint authorship? It bears emphasis that determining authorship for the purposes of copyright cannot simply be a matter of who pushes the pen. The late Justice Laddie explained this best in *Fylde Microsystems Ltd v. Key Radio Systems Ltd*, [1998] F.S.R. 449:

> In my view, to have regard merely to who pushed the pen is too narrow a view of authorship. What is protected by copyright in a drawing or a literary work is more than just the skill of making marks on paper or some other medium. It is both the words or lines and the skill and effort involved in creating, selecting or gathering together the detailed concepts, data or emotions which those words or lines have fixed in some tangible form which is protected. It is wrong to think that only the person who carries out the mechanical act of fixation is an author.

Hager v. ECW Press Ltd., [1999] 2 F.C. 287, 85 C.P.R. (3d) 289 (Fed. T.D.)

Federal Court of Canada – Trial Division

Reed, J.:

1 This claim is brought by the plaintiff Barbara Hager against the defendants ECW Press Ltd., Dallas Williams (a pseudonym used by Michael Holmes) and General Distribution Services Limited. They are respectively the publisher, author, and distributor of a book entitled *Shania Twain: On My Way*. The plaintiff alleges that sixteen major passages from a chapter of her book *Honour Song: a Tribute* were incorporated into the defendants' book, thereby infringing her copyright.

Background Facts

2 In April 1996, Barbara Hager was in the process of writing a book about individuals of Canadian aboriginal heritage who have become well known. She sought and was given time to interview the popular country singer and song writer Shania Twain. The book she was writing was eventually published in September 1996. It contained a nine page chapter on Shania Twain, called "*Shania Twain: Buckskin and Cowboy Boots*".

3 While the chapter on Shania Twain included information from a number of sources, it was based primarily on Barbara Hager's interviews with Shania Twain. These were private interviews in which no one else participated. The first was by telephone from Vancouver. The second was an in person interview for which Ms. Hager flew to Los Angeles paying the necessary expenses. On this occasion she not only interviewed Shania Twain but also was allowed "to shadow" her for half a day, and then interview her for approximately two hours.

4 Prior to both interviews Barbara Hager prepared questions that she wanted to ask in keeping with the theme of the chapter she planned to write. She took notes of the telephone conversation including the responses to the prepared questions. She taped the in-person interview, with Ms. Twain's permission. In Barbara Hager's view the interview was a personal and unique interchange between her and Ms. Twain because they were of a similar age, came from similar backgrounds, and in their childhood and teen years had had similar experiences.

5 At about the same time, April 1996, Mr. Lecker of ECW Press Ltd. approached Michael Holmes (Dallas Williams) and suggested that he write a book about Shania Twain. Mr. Holmes was a part-time employee of ECW Press Ltd.; he was the poetry editor. While ECW Press Ltd. was originally a publisher of primarily scholarly works, it had changed direction in recent years so that it was now also producing books for the popular commercial market. The book on Shania Twain was to be one such. It was described by Mr. Holmes, in June 1996, in some promotional material he wrote before he wrote the book, as "a detailed and revealing account of the life, passion, and determination behind Twain's Cinderella story."

6 Mr. Holmes collected as much published material as he could concerning Shania Twain and from it began putting together his book. He did few original interviews because he found people would charge. For example, David Hartt, a member of one of Twain's first teenage bands, wanted $7,000 to be interviewed. Mr. Holmes states that he did not obtain a copy of Ms. Hager's book until May 5, 1997, at which time he incorporated parts of it into his book. Mr. Holmes kept no drafts of his text so exactly how and when it was prepared cannot be verified by references to drafts. He did not seek, nor did his publisher seek, permission from Ms. Hager or from her publisher Raincoast Books Distribution Inc. to use any part of *Honour Song*.

. . .

8 Barbara Hager purchased a copy of the Holmes (Williams) book on December 1, 1997. On noting the similarities between parts of its text and her own, she

contacted her publisher to see if permission had been given for such use. When she was told that it had not she contacted her literary agent, Carolyn Swayze, who in turn contacted Mr. Lecker.

9 Ms. Hager subsequently wrote to Mr. Lecker setting out her complaints. These are essentially the ones that constitute the basis of the present action:

> I'm sending you the 19 pages in Williams' book that contain excerpts from my chapter on Shania Twain in *Honour Song*. I'm also sending you a copy of my chapter which cross-references the sections that were reprinted in the Williams book. Almost every single direct quote from my interview with Twain that was in *Honour Song*, appears in the ECW book. In addition, a significant amount of the narrative portions in my book appear in the Williams book, however, they have undergone varying degrees or rewriting from the original manuscript. In some cases, the "paraphrased sections" (as in the section on Shania's relationship to Canadian singer Lawrence Martin on page 127) have only a few words changed from my version, and even have the same sentence structure. I consider this reuse of my writing to constitute plagiarism.

> . . .

20 It is now necessary to assess the defendants' claim that no breach of copyright occurred because the direct quotations from Shania Twain are not the proper subject of copyright ...

Defendants' Position

21 The defendants argue that, while Mr. Holmes took parts of Barbara Hager's book, this does not constitute copyright infringement because he took mainly quotations of Shania Twain's words, words used by her in the interviews given to Ms. Hager. It is argued that such quotations are not subject to copyright. Furthermore, the defendants argue that Mr. Holmes only took facts, not the mode of expression in which those facts were recounted by Ms. Hager...

22 The defendants rely heavily on the recent Federal Court of Appeal decision in *Tele-Direct (Publications) Inc. v. American Business Information Inc.* (1997), [1998] 2 F.C. 22 (Fed. C.A.), leave to appeal denied (1998), 228 N.R. 200 (note) (S.C.C.). They argue that there was neither creativity nor originality on the part of Barbara Hager in recounting the words used by Shania Twain during the interview and therefore Ms. Hager cannot assert copyright therein. It is argued that the *Tele-Direct (Publications) Inc.* decision has altered the pre-existing jurisprudence, if it ascribed copyright to the interviewer, and that it is now appropriate to consider the United States jurisprudence relating to originality for the purposes of the present fact situation.

23 I will refer briefly (1) to some of the Anglo-Canadian jurisprudence upon which counsel for the plaintiff relied, (2) to some of the mainly American jurisprudence to which counsel for the defendants has referred, (3) to the *Tele-Direct* decision, (4) to the arguments relating to lack of copyright in facts, ...

Quotations from Interviews–Anglo-Canadian Jurisprudence

24 The Anglo-Canadian jurisprudence upon which counsel for the plaintiff relies is: *Walter v. Lane*, [1900] A.C. 539 (U.K. H.L.); *Express Newspapers plc v. News (U.K.) Ltd.*, [1990] 3 All E.R. 376 (Eng. Ch. Div.); *Gould Estate v. Stoddart Publishing Co.* (1996), 30 O.R. (3d) 520 (Ont. Gen. Div.), affirmed (1998), 80 C.P.R. (3d) 161 (Ont. C.A.). These cases demonstrate that under Anglo-Canadian law, insofar as private interviews are concerned, it is the person who reduces the oral statements to a fixed form that acquires copyright therein. That individual is considered to be the originator of the work.

25 In *Walter v. Lane*, it was held that copyright *in the verbatim reports of public speeches* given by the Earl of Roseberry, that were taken down by reporters for *The Times*, belonged to the proprietors of *The Times*, the reporters having assigned their copyright to the proprietors. While counsel for the defendants argues that this is no longer good law for a number of reasons, one being that it pre-dates the 1911 amendment to the *U.K. Copyright Act*, at which time the word "original" was added to the *Act*, the jurisprudence does not support that contention. For example, in *Sands & McDougall Pty Ltd. v. Robinson* (1917), 23 C.L.R. 49 (Australia H.C.) there is a discussion of the validity of *Walter v. Lane* in light of the 1911 amendments to the U.K. Copyright Act which were appended to the Australian Act.

26 It was argued in *Sands & McDougall Pty Ltd.* that the law now required inventive ingenuity as well as authorship in the sense used in *Walter v. Lane*. The Australian High Court rejected the argument at page 55, quoting from *Walter v. Lane*: "[t]rue it is that the reporter was not the author of the speech; but he was the composer and author of the book ... Without his brain and handiwork the book would never have had existence." The Court noted that the two expressions "author" and "original work" had always been correlative and that the dictionary definition of author was "the person who originates or gives existence to anything." The Court held that the *Copyright Act 1911*, which was enacted in part to implement the Berlin Convention of 1908, did not intend to alter the pre-existing law as set out in *Walter v. Lane*. In that context the reporter of the speech had been found to be the author of the report, and because it had not existed before, the reporter had "originated" the report.

27 More recent jurisprudence has dealt with private interviews, a situation closer to that in issue in this case. In the *Express Newspapers plc* case, although the decision was based on another aspect of the dispute between the parties, the Court made it clear at pages 379 and 381 that it was the reporters who held the copyrights in the quotations taken down by them in the course of exclusive interviews they conducted with the respective celebrities they were writing about, not the interviewees:

> Each of the original stories is made up of two elements. First, there is the news story as such; second, there are the quotations of the words used by the person interviewed.

...the recorder of spoken words [has] a copyright in the record of those words as distinct from the words recorded.

28 In the *Gould Estate* case, the Estate of the late Glenn Gould sought to prevent the publication, by the defendant Carroll, of a book on Glenn Gould when he was a young man. It contained photographs and a narrative. Carroll had taken the photographs and conducted an interview with Glenn Gould in 1956, in order to produce an article for a weekend magazine. Carroll kept the photographs and his notes and tapes of the interview. In 1995 he decided to use these to produce the book that the Estate sought to enjoin. The narrative portion of the book was comprised of extracts from the defendant's conversations with Glenn Gould, which the defendant had recorded in 1956. The Estate argued that copyright in the oral conversations recorded by Carroll rested with the Estate, not with him. This argument was rejected by Mr. Justice Lederman of the General Division, at page 216, on the ground that oral statements are not expressed in material form and, except in the case of an amanuensis, the speaker has no copyright therein. The greater part of this decision focussed on the tort of appropriation of personality.

. . .

30 The Ontario Court of Appeal held that it was Carroll, not Gould's Estate, that held the copyright in the interviews with Gould. In agreeing with the trial judge that Gould did not hold a copyright in his oral statements because such statements were not the kind of disclosure the *Copyright Act* intended to protect—they were not in material form—the Court of Appeal stated at 169-170 that it was the defendant who owned the copyright therein:

> [para23] ...It is evident from this record that <u>Gould did not have a copyright with respect to his oral utterances</u> or in the "transcriptions" of them, to use the appellants' phrase. <u>To the contrary, Carroll</u> as the author of the text and captions in the book <u>was the owner of the copyright in the very written material the appellants are attempting to suppress.</u>

> [para24] Once it is established that Carroll owned the unrestricted copyright in the photographs and the written material in the book, there is nothing else to decide....
> [Underlining added.]

Quotations from Interviews — American Jurisprudence

31 I turn then to the jurisprudence on which the defendants' counsel relies. Most of the U.S. jurisprudence respecting quotations from interviews relates to the fair use provisions of that country's copyright law (17 U.S.C. § 107). Counsel for the defendants relies particularly on the following cases for the proposition that an interviewer does not have copyright in the statements of an interviewee: *Rokeach v. Avco Embassy Pictures Corp.*, 197 U.S.P.Q. 155 (U.S. D. N.Y. 1978), *Suid v. Newsweek Magazine*, 503 F. Supp. 146 (U.S. D.D.C. 1980). ...

32 The *Rokeach* decision dealt with a play that had been written by the defendant about an insane English earl who during part of the play believes himself to be Christ. The plaintiff had written a scientific research study, in the field of abnormal psychology, that dealt with three patients each of whom believed he

was Christ. For the purposes of this study, Rokeach, and more commonly his research assistants, recorded and subsequently transcribed sessions in which the three patients were present. The defendant borrowed some ideas from the report of this study, one being the confrontation between two delusional Christs. He also used several phrases and words that were reported as having been said by the patients, in order to give his play authenticity. The Court held that copyright does not protect ideas, concepts, and themes; that the two works bore virtually no resemblance to each other, and that the copying was in any event de minimus; and if subject to copyright, which the Court did not believe to be the case, the copying would fall under the fair use exception. In discussing the use that had been made of the actual words spoken by the patients to each other, to Rokeach, or to his research assistants, the Court stated at page 161 that Rokeach could not claim copyright in these words because he did not create them.

33 In the *Suid* case, the plaintiff alleged copyright infringement by News-week Magazine in a book he had written about John Wayne. Infringement was claimed in quotations from two interviews the author had conducted, one with Michael Wayne, the other with William Wellman. The Court held at 148, citing the *Rokeach* decision, that the plaintiff would not have copyright in the inter-view quotations unless he had obtained copyright assignments from the two interviewees. In the case of the Wayne quotations, the Court refused to consider a consent granted by Wayne to use the quotations as sufficient for the purpose of assigning copyright. An assignment of copyright had been obtained for the Wellman quotations, however, it had not been registered and thus copyright could not be claimed. The Court was of the opinion that with respect to the Wellman quotations fair use would apply because it had never been intended that the interview would have commercial value, and in any case, the amount taken was insubstantial.

. . .

36 Reference can be made as well to the descriptions of this area of United States law that are found in several journals and texts. In K. Dunlap, *Copyright Protection for Oral Works: Expansion of the Copyright Law into the Area of Conversations*, (1973) 20 Bulletin of the Copyright Society of the U.S.A. 285, the pre-1976 situation is described. It discusses the protection of oral statements under state "common law" of copyright. In V. L. Ruhga, *Ownership of Inter-views: A Theory for Protection of Quotations*, (1988) 67 Nebr. L. Rev. 675 at 684, the author describes the jurisprudence respecting the post-1976 statutory copyright in quotations as being split:

> When dealing with statutory copyright, courts have split on the issue of interview ownership. Some courts advocate interviewer ownership of the copyright. Others maintain that the interviewer and the interviewee separately own their respective contributions, unless otherwise agreed. Generally, the court's view of ownership determines the degree of copyright protection available. [Footnotes omitted.]

The article is concerned with the interviewee being able to control the use that is made of an interview, beyond use by the first interviewer. Such use can, of course, be controlled by contract.

37 In A.S. Hirsch, *Copyrighting Conversations: Applying the 1976 Copyright Act to Interviews*, (1982) 31 Am. Univ. L. Rev. 1071 at 1082-1083, it is suggested that interviews constitute works of joint authorship:

Under the contemporaneous intent standard, an interview qualifies as a joint work because the interviewer and interviewee meet with each other for the express purpose of conducting an interview. This goal is a manifestation of their intent to merge their respective contributions into one work, thereby establishing a work of joint authorship. Furthermore, because interviews necessitate interaction between two people, individual efforts on the part of either the interviewer or the interviewee cannot produce the same result. A participant in a conversation, therefore, should be considered a joint author of comments made by coparticipants. This proposition has been recognized by some courts. Therefore, although there is precedent supporting a finding that either the interviewer or interviewee individually owns the copyright in an interview, the better view is that the combined effort creates a work of joint authorship. [Footnotes omitted.]

38 And in *Latman's The Copyright Law*, 6th ed. (Washington: BNA Books, 1986) at 115, n. 3 the position of the United States Copyright Office is described as being that copyright in an interview can be held in part by the interviewee or interviewer or entirely by one or the other depending upon the agreement between them:

...with respect to interviews, the Copyright Office has stated:

A work consisting of an interview often contains copyrightable authorship by the person interviewed and the interviewer. Each has the right to claim copyright in his or her own expression in the absence of an agreement to the contrary. Where an application for such a work names only the interviewee or the interviewer as the author and claimant, and where the nature of authorship is described as "entire text," it is unclear whether the claim actually extends to the entire work, or only to the text by the interviewee or interviewer. In any case where the extent of the claim is not clear, the Copyright Office must communicate with the applicant for clarification.

Compendium II of Copyright Office Practices §317.

An application naming only the interviewer or interviewee as the author but listing "text" instead of "entire text" as the nature of authorship will be interpreted as asserting a claim only for the interviewer or interviewee's portion of the interview.

Effect of Tele-Direct Decision

39 Counsel for the defendants argues that the jurisprudence in *Walter v. Lane*, *Express Newspapers plc* and *Gould Estate* cases, as well as being distinguishable because none of it deals directly with a second person taking the quoted words of an interviewee, is no longer good law in Canada because it is all based on the premise that copyright law protects an author's labour....

40 Counsel argues that even if the words of an interviewee were previously copyrightable by the interviewer, as set out in the *Express Newspapers plc* and

Gould Estate cases, the recent decision of the Federal Court of Appeal in *Tele-Direct (Publications) Inc.* has overruled that jurisprudence....

41 .... I am not persuaded that the Federal Court of Appeal intended a significant departure from the pre-existing law. In the absence of an express decision from the Court of Appeal to the contrary, I think the law as set out in *Express Newspapers* and *Gould Estate* is still the law.

. . .

Summary of Conclusions re: Copyright Infringement

. . .

68 While the decisions in *Express Newspapers plc* and *Gould Estate* do not deal directly with a dispute between an interviewer and a third party who has copied the words of an interviewee, the statements in those cases that the interviewer holds the copyright are unequivocal. I consider them to state the law applicable to the circumstances of this case. The quoted words of Ms. Twain cannot be divorced from the context in which they were spoken. They were elicited by Ms. Hager in response to questions she had framed. They were not made to the public at large. She chose the parts of her interview with Shania Twain that would be incorporated into the monograph she wrote. If she had not created the work *Shania Twain: Buckskin and Cowboy Boots*, the quoted words would not have been available for copying.

69 It was made very clear in the *Slumber-Magic Adjustable Bed Co.* decision, referred to above, and in other cases, that when assessing copyright protection one must not dissect the work into fragments. It is not appropriate then to fragment Barbara Hager's work and treat the quotes as independent parts. Barbara Hager's work required each of (1) skill, (2) judgment and (3) labour for its creation. ...

71 I conclude that Michael Holmes breached Barbara Hager's copyright in her chapter "*Shania Twain: Buckskin and Cowboy Boots*," when he copied parts of it into his book *Shania Twain: On My Way*. ...

Action allowed.

---

2. Joint Authorship

Under the *Copyright Act*, copyright can subsist in a "work of joint authorship". A "work of joint authorship" is defined to mean "a work produced by the collaboration of two or more authors in which the contribution of one author is not distinct from the contribution of the other author or authors."[2] For a work to be a "work of joint authorship" there must be some working together in furtherance of a common or pre-concerted joint design to produce the work; each joint author must contribute significant original expression so as

---

2   Section 2.

to be considered an "author" of the resultant work; the contributions of each author must not be distinct from the contributions of the other authors; each of the joint authors must intend that their contributions be merged into a unitary whole; and finally, if the *Neudorf* case is followed, each joint author must intend the other to be the joint author of the work.[3]

The Act does not specifically address the scope of the required contribution that must be made by a person in order to qualify as an author of the work. Since the Act requires that the work be created by the collaboration of more than one "author", a person whose contribution in making the work falls short of what is required to constitute such a person an author for copyright purposes cannot be a joint author of the work.[4] A person who merely suggests certain ideas for a work without contributing anything to the form of the work cannot, therefore, be a joint author of the work.[5] For co-authorship to exist, it is not necessary that each author should contribute equally, provided that the contribution is not negligible.[6]

Notably, in the United States, joint owners of copyright in a work can deal freely and independently with that work subject only to an obligation to account for profits; in the United Kingdom and, it seems, in Canada, joint owners of copyright must act in concert or obtain permission from all owners before exercising an exclusive right. A defendant's claim of joint authorship in the United States can therefore function as a complete answer to a copyright infringement claim in a way that it cannot in the United Kingdom or Canada (although it could form the basis of a counter-claim alleging infringement by the plaintiff). This important difference might suggest that Canadian courts should follow the lead of the UK courts when making joint authorship determinations.

Neudorf v. Nettwerk Productions Ltd. (1999), 3 C.P.R. (4th) 129 (B.C. S.C.)

Cohen J.

. . .

I. THE PLAINTIFF'S CLAIMS

[1] A phonograph record containing performances by the defendant Sarah McLachlan ("McLachlan") was commercially released in Canada by the defendant record company Nettwerk Productions Ltd. ("Nettwerk") in September 1988 under the title "Touch." Touch was later commercially re-released on compact disc in Canada in January 1989 by Nettwerk, and in the United States in April 1989 by Arista Records Inc., an American corporation. The compact disc liner notes ("liner notes") list the following songwriting credits:

---

3   *Neudorf v. Nettwerk Productions Ltd.* (1999), 8 C.P.R. (4th) 154 (B.C. S.C.).
4   *Kantel v. Frank E. Grant, Nisbet & Auld Ltd.*, [1933] Ex. C.R. 84 (Ex. Ct.).
5   *Thrustcode Ltd. v. W.W. Computing Ltd.*, [1983] F.S.R. 502 (Ch.D.).
6   *Levy v. Rutley* (1871), 24 L.T. 621 (C.P.).

All songs by Sarah McLachlan except "Steaming," music by Sarah McLachlan &
Darren Phillips, lyrics, by Sarah McLachlan; and "Uphill Battle," music by Darren
Phillips & Sarah McLachlan.

[2] This is an action for a declaration of co-ownership of copyright in four of
the musical works which appear on Touch, namely "Strange World," "Steaming," "Vox," and "Sad Clown" ("the songs"). The plaintiff, Darryl Neudorf,
claims that he co-authored the songs and seeks remedies for breach of copyright
arising out of the defendants' use of the songs. He also seeks remedies for unjust
enrichment in relation to the defendants' use of the songs and in relation to the
services he provided to the defendants in the nature of pre-production and production. Finally, the plaintiff claims damages for breach of contract in relation to
the services he provided on McLachlan's second record, "Solace."

II. BACKGROUND

[3] In the mid-1980s, the defendants Mark Jowett ("Jowett"), Terry McBride
("McBride") and Rick Arboit, three friends then in their twenties, formed Nettwerk and the defendant Nettoverboard Publishing ("Nettoverboard"), the publishing arm of Nettwerk. They were, and remain, the shareholders, officers and
directors of Nettwerk, and partners in Nettoverboard.

[4] In 1985 Jowett, while on a national tour with his then band MOEV, met
McLachlan in Halifax. At the time, she was a teenager in a Halifax band that
opened for MOEV. Jowett was so impressed with her ability to sing and play
guitar that he invited her to join MOEV. She declined the invitation and decided
instead to finish high school. Upon graduation she enrolled at an art college in
Halifax.

[5] In 1987, during McLachlan's second semester, McBride, while in Halifax
touring with the band Skinny Puppy, met with McLachlan and on the spot offered
her a five-album recording contract with Nettwerk, which she accepted. She also
entered into a five-year music publishing contract wherein she agreed to assign
ownership of copyright in compositions authored by her to Nettoverboard.

[6] In September 1987, at the age of 19, McLachlan moved to Vancouver to
begin work on the Touch project. Throughout the fall of 1987 she lived in an
apartment in the west end of Vancouver, writing songs on her own, as well as
with a musician by the name of Darren Phillips ("Phillips").

[7] The plaintiff is a musician who, in the summer of 1982, was the drummer
for a Vancouver band called 54-40. He initially came to know Jowett when
Jowett was working at a Vancouver record store that the plaintiff frequented.
The plaintiff was a fan of MOEV and over time he and Jowett became very
close friends. In the fall of 1985, shortly after the plaintiff left 54-40, Jowett
asked him to join MOEV on a national tour. In 1986, the plaintiff moved to
Toronto and commenced work at a computer music based studio.

[8] Some time in the summer or fall of 1987, there were several long-distance
telephone conversations between the plaintiff and Jowett which led to Jowett

inviting the plaintiff to come to Vancouver to work on the Touch project. The plaintiff accepted the offer in return for his airfare, accommodation and a weekly per diem.

[9] The plaintiff arrived in Vancouver around the middle of January 1988 and set up a small pre-production recording set in the space at the back of Nettwerk's office. The plaintiff's first meeting with McLachlan took place in this space, while he was setting up the equipment. Shortly thereafter, the plaintiff and McLachlan began working together on the Touch project. On March 4, 1988 the Touch project moved to the Limited Vision recording studio. The parties' working relationship continued until the end of March 1988, when the plaintiff left the Touch project. He returned to Toronto in early April. It was during this period of time that the plaintiff claims to have co-written the songs.

. . .

IV. THE TEST FOR JOINT AUTHORSHIP

[14] Section 2 of the *Copyright Act*, R.S.C. 1985, c. C-42 (the "*Act*") defines a "work of joint authorship," as follows:

> ... a work produced by the collaboration of two or more authors in which the contribution of one author is not distinct from the contribution of the other author or authors[.]

[15] Section 13(1) of the *Act* provides that the author of a work shall be the first owner of the copyright therein.

(i) THE ELEMENT OF CONTRIBUTION

[16] The *Act* provides that a claimant of joint authorship must have contributed to the work as an "author." This term is not defined in the *Act*. However, in *John Maryon International Ltd. v. New Brunswick Telephone Co. Ltd.* reflex, (1982), 141 D.L.R. (3d) 193 (N.B. C.A.), a case dealing with, *inter alia*, the authorship of the design of a tower, La Forest J.A. (as he then was), at p. 244, wrote, as follows:

> The term "author" is not defined in the Act, but reference was made to the statement in Fox, *The Canadian Law of Copyright*, 2nd ed., p. 239, that it is the person who actually writes, draws or composes a work. However, this idea must not be carried too far. The cases reveal that the person who "actually writes" must not be equated to a mere scribe or amanuensis: see *University of London Press Ltd. v. University Tutorial Press Ltd.*, [1916] 2 Ch. 601. On the other hand, a person who merely gives ideas to a person is not the author: see *Commercial Signs v. General Motors Products of Canada Ltd. et al.*, [1937] 2 D.L.R. 310, [1937] O.W.N. 58; affirmed [1937] 2 D.L.R. 800 (Ont. C.A.). Rather, the author would seem to be the person who expresses the ideas in an original or novel form: see *University of London Press Ltd. v. University Tutorial Press Ltd.*, *supra*, at p. 608.

[17] And in *Grignon v. Roussel* reflex, (1991), 38 C.P.R. (3d) 4 (F.C.T.D.), a case dealing with the alleged infringement of the copyright in a musical work, the court, at p. 7, said, as follows:

[F]irst, no one may claim copyright to an idea: it must have taken material form of some kind if it is to be protected by copyright. Secondly, the work created must be original or at least be of an innovative nature: no one may copy an existing work... [T]he registration of a work is not necessary to provide copyright protection for its author.

[18] Therefore, authorship has two basic requirements: originality, and expression.

[19] Originality is not defined in the *Act*. However, with the possible exception of a work that deals with a compilation of data (see *Tele-Direct (Publications) Inc. v. American Business Information Inc.* 1997 CanLII 6378 (F.C.A.), (1997), 76 C.P.R. (3d) 296 (F.C.A.); *Hager v. ECW Press Ltd.* 1998 CanLII 9115 (F.C.), (1998), 85 C.P.R. (3d) 289 (F.C.T.D.)), the meaning of the word "original" appears now to be well-settled by the oft-cited statement of law set out in *University of London Press Ltd. v. University Tutorial Press Ltd.*, [1916] 2 Ch. 601. That case dealt with the issue of whether copyright subsisted in certain examination papers as "original literary work." At pp. 608-9, the court said, as follows:

The word 'original' does not in this connection mean that the work must be the expression of original or inventive thought. Copyright Acts are not concerned with the originality of ideas, but with the expression of thought... The originality which is required relates to the expression of the thought. But the Act does not require that the expression must be in an original or novel form, but that the work must not be copied from another work — that it should originate from the author.

[20] In my opinion, I can rely upon the *University of London Press* definition of originality to find that all the plaintiff in the instant case must prove on this point is that whatever expressions he claims to have contributed to the songs originated from him and were not copied.

[21] Several Canadian authorities have dealt with the element of contribution in the context of a claim to joint authorship. In *Kantel v. Grant*, [1933] Ex. C.R. 84, the plaintiff prepared a radio sketch for the defendant's advertising campaign. The defendant suggested the general outline of the work. The court held that the plaintiff was the sole author of the sketch, he having given it form and expression, although certain ideas had been suggested by the defendant.

. . .

[25] In his written submission, plaintiff's counsel in the instant case stated that *Maryon*, and other cases dealing with authorship, made a distinction between a situation where someone merely suggested an idea, and where someone was involved in the actual expression of an idea. He gave the example: if person A wrote an original song and person B heard it and said to person A, "I think that this song needs a bridge," the mere suggestion of the idea of a bridge would not make person B an author. He claimed that if, on the other hand, person B not only suggested the idea but was involved in the actual writing of the bridge, then person B would be an author of the bridge. He argued that while the plaintiff at times suggested an idea, it was clear from the evidence that he was involved in the actual expression or writing of ideas as well. I think this position is flawed.

[26] The issue before me is not whether the plaintiff was "involved in the actual expression or writing of ideas." Rather, the issue is whether the plaintiff himself contributed original expressions to the songs. Only then would he be able to meet the test for joint authorship under s. 2 of the *Act*. Mr. Maryon was "involved" in the expression of an idea, but did not himself express the idea, and so did not acquire a copyright interest in Mr. Chatwin's expression of it. Indeed, in the instant case, if it turns out that all the plaintiff contributed to the songs were suggestions and ideas, then the facts and the result in *Maryon* weigh strongly against a finding in favour of the plaintiff.

[27] Another point raised in *Maryon* is that the person who expresses ideas in a tangible form must be distinguished from a mere scribe. At p. 244, the court stated, "The cases reveal that the person who 'actually writes' must not be equated to a mere scribe or amanuensis." Plaintiff's counsel submitted that *Maryon* supported the view that the songwriting process between the plaintiff and McLachlan was one where McLachlan was, at times, acting as a mere scribe. As examples, he pointed to McLachlan's evidence at trial, and at examination for discovery, when she described situations where she would be playing or singing and the plaintiff would tell her to "go there" or "try this." He said that while the evidence showed that McLachlan certainly did the actual writing in relation to the songs, in those situations where the plaintiff suggested notes or chords to McLachlan as she was singing or playing, she must be viewed more as a scribe. I disagree with this submission.

[28] In my view, McLachlan could not be considered a mere scribe if what the plaintiff was communicating to her were ideas, or suggestions. A reason that an amanuensis or scribe is not the author of expression is that he exercises no authority or control over the recording, but is instead a verbatim recorder. To the extent that the plaintiff's contributions were ideas or suggestions, this means that McLachlan was free to accept or reject them. This is antithetical to claiming that in those situations her status was that of a mere scribe or amanuensis.

[29] In *Royal Doulton Tableware Ltd. v. Cassidy's Ltd.* reflex, (1984), 1 C.P.R. (3d) 214 (F.C.T.D.), the plaintiff asserted ownership of copyright in a floral pattern as applied to china tableware. The defendant suggested to the plaintiff that a rose floral design might have a market in Canada. The plaintiff did some paintings for such a design. These paintings were shown to the defendant who suggested that the "sprays" of roses should be "spread out somewhat so as to occupy more of the top surface of the tableware." The plaintiff modified the design accordingly. The defendant was satisfied and placed an order for tableware bearing the design. The court concluded that the plaintiff was the author of the pattern. At p. 230, the court said, as follows:

> I conclude that Mr. Johnson was the author of the pattern and that copyright subsists therein in Canada by virtue of s-s. 4(1) of the *Copyright Act*, R.S.C. 1970, c. C-30. At the time of the making of the work Mr. Johnson was a British subject, resident within Her Majesty's realms and territories in 1967, and the work was first published within such realms and territories, namely, in England or Canada. Further, by virtue of s-s. 12(3), because Mr. Johnson was in the employment of

Paragon and the work was made in the course of that employment, Paragon was the first owner of the copyright and remains so. I do not accept that Mr. Robertson's suggestions and advice, helpful as they may have been, rendered him the author of the pattern. It was the skill and experience of Mr. Johnson, who testified that during his career he had made perhaps 2,000 such sketches of possible patterns, which created an aesthetically pleasing design, albeit that it was in reaction to Mr. Robertson's marketing idea.

[30] In *Boudreau v. Lin* 1997 CanLII 12369 (ON S.C.), (1997), 75 C.P.R. (3d) 1 (Ont. Gen. Div.), the plaintiff, a university student, submitted a term paper to the defendant, his professor. The professor made corrections and suggested revisions to the paper, some of which were incorporated into the paper by the plaintiff. The defendant made several further minor revisions, replaced the student's name with his own name and the name of another professor, and published and presented the paper, all without the plaintiff's knowledge. The plaintiff brought an action for copyright infringement. The defendant claimed to be a co-author of the paper. The court found that the plaintiff was the sole author of the work. At p. 8, Métivier J., dealing with the defendant's contribution, said, as follows:

> I find as a fact that the professor offered editorial suggestions, and, on a conceptual level, that he attempted to direct the student in his paper to a less technical and more management-oriented view, as befitted a course of study in the Masters of Business Administration program. But, it was clear from the evidence, the professor was neither the originator nor the developer of any substantive ideas or concepts. His contributions consisted of general comments that were directed to polishing the paper and were those which one expects from a professor who is editing and discussing a paper written by a student. None of the changes he proposed affected the substance of the paper.

[31] At p. 9, the court said, as follows:

> I now consider whether Professor Lin's changes, improvements and editing added enough to the paper to make him a co-author. I am guided by the decision in the case of *Dion v. Trottier* (1986), 9 C.I.P.R. 258 (Que. S.C.), where the plaintiff sued for recognition of his input into a published work, authored by his former wife. The court held that one must look at the nature of the contribution as well as its importance. In the cited case, involving a story written by Trottier, the author's ex-husband had corrected her grammar, added certain words, summarized, altered the structure of the text, improved the literary style and rewritten much of what his former wife had written. The published version incorporated parts of both the original and the rewritten version.

> The court found that while the plaintiff's version had "some utility and a certain value", the basis of the story, the vocabulary, the rhythm, the magnitude, the sensibility and truthfulness, were all the result of the defendant's labours and so the plaintiff's case was dismissed. One can see from this brief outline of the analysis that Professor Lin's contribution to the authorship of the paper in the case at bar came nowhere close to duplicating such efforts–efforts which were rejected as constituting joint authorship.

[32] Turning to the English authorities, section 10(1) of the *Copyright, Designs and Patents Act 1988* (U.K.), 1988, c. 48, defines "a work of joint authorship" in virtually identical words to s. 2 of the *Act*. It provides, as follows:

> ... a work produced by the collaboration of two or more authors in which the contribution of each author is not distinct from that of the other author or authors.

[33] The English and Canadian cases are consistent in requiring that a putative joint author contribute expression and not merely ideas to the work. For example, in *Stuart v. Barrett*, [1994] E.M.L.R. 448 (Ch.D.), the plaintiff was a drummer who had been invited to join a popular music group of which the defendants were already members. The plaintiff alleged that he co-authored various songs. The headnote reports that the court held, *inter alia*, that "a person with an original idea was not the author of any work composed by another who made use of that idea unless the person with the idea contributed to the form of the work."

[34] Section 101 of the U.S. *Copyright Act of 1976*, 17 U.S.C. §§ 101 *et seq.*, defines joint authorship, as follows:

> A 'joint work' is a work prepared by two or more authors with the intention that their contributions be merged into inseparable or interdependent parts of a unitary whole.

[35] In the United States, there has been a debate over whether it is sufficient for a joint author to merely contribute ideas as opposed to expressions. Competing approaches have been posited by two American scholars on the law of copyright: the "*de minimis*" approach advocated by Professor Nimmer and the "copyrightable" approach advocated by Professor Goldstein. The *de minimis* approach requires only that the resulting work be copyrightable. The copyrightable approach requires that each author's contribution be copyrightable.

[36] Various circuits of the federal courts in the United States have come to differing conclusions as to the standard required in order to meet the contribution element. The more recent trend in the cases is towards the acceptance of the copyrightable approach. In *Childress v. Taylor*, 945 F.2d 500 (2d Cir. 1991), where the defendant actress claimed to be a joint author with the plaintiff playwright, the court struggled with the issue of why the contributions of all joint authors needed to be copyrightable. The court, at p. 506, stated, "An individual creates a copyrightable work by combining a non-copyrightable idea with a copyrightable form of expression; the resulting work is no less a valuable result of the creative process simply because the idea and the expression came from two different individuals." Notwithstanding this view, the court endorsed the copyrightable approach, stating at p. 507:

> The insistence on copyrightable contributions by all putative joint authors might serve to prevent some spurious claims by those who might otherwise try to share the fruits of the efforts of a sole author of a copyrightable work, even though a claim of having contributed copyrightable material could be asserted by those so inclined.

The court summarized at p. 507:

> It seems more consistent with the spirit of copyright law to oblige all joint authors to make copyrightable contributions, leaving those with non-copyrightable contributions to protect their rights through contract.

[37] Hence, I think it is now well-established by the body of law in Canada and England, and for that matter in the United States, that to satisfy the test for joint authorship a putative joint author must contribute original expression, not merely ideas, to the creation of the work. Even involvement in the expression of ideas is not enough to satisfy the element of contribution.

[38] It is not necessary for a putative joint author to prove that any of the ideas embodied in the work originated from him. In the English case of *Godfrey v. Lees*, [1995] E.M.L.R. 307 (Ch.D.), the plaintiff worked with a band in composing several musical works and claimed to be a joint author of the works. The court, in considering an issue of estoppel, commented that the following view held by the defendants was wrong:

> [T]he band believed that it was the person who had the idea for the song who was regarded in law as the composer. Since the plaintiff had not had the idea for any of the songs, the defendants clearly assumed that he, the plaintiff, could not claim to be the composer or author of any of them whereas they, or whoever among them had had the idea, could.

[39] Indeed, the notion that a joint author need not have been the originator of the ideas embodied in the work is completely consistent with the rule that copyright does not exist in ideas. As long as the claimant contributes original expression to the work, he may be a joint author, regardless of the source of the ideas being expressed. Applying this principle to the instant case, even if McLachlan was the one who came up with all of the ideas for the songs, this in itself would not be fatal to the plaintiff's claim of joint authorship. The test, as discussed above, is not whether the plaintiff came up with the ideas for the songs, but whether he gave the ideas original expression.

[40] The case law also provides that the contribution of joint authors to the work need not be equal. In *Levy v. Rutley*, [1871] W.L.R. 976 (C.A.), the seminal English case on joint authorship, which I discuss in greater detail later in these reasons, Byles J. at p. 977 stated that two or more persons could be joint authors "although one person had contributed a very small amount of work to the execution[.]" And at the same page, Keating J. agreed with Byles J., adding that to be joint authors, "it is not necessary that each should contribute the same amount of labour."

[41] H.G. Fox, *The Canadian Law of Copyright and Industrial Design*, 2d ed. (Toronto: Carswell, 1967) ("Fox"), relying on *Levy v. Rutley*, at p. 244, states that in a work of joint authorship, the contribution of each joint author need not be equal and different portions of the work may be the sole production of either one.

[42] The rule of not requiring equal contribution is still followed in England. For example, in *Godfrey v. Lees, supra*, the court said, as follows:

> It is not necessary that [a joint author's] contribution to the work is equal in terms of either quantity, quality or originality to that of his collaborators.

[43] However, even though the contribution of one joint author need not be equal to that of the other joint authors, it appears that the contribution of each joint author must nevertheless be significant or substantial. For example, in *Godfrey v. Lees, supra*, the court said, as follows:

> What the claimant to joint authorship of a work must establish is that he has made a significant and original contribution to the creation of the work...

[44] In that case, the plaintiff claimed that he was a joint author of six songs that appeared on the defendants' record albums. One of the songs was a 48-bar work, and the plaintiff's contribution to this song consisted of composing six bars out of the 48 bars. The court held that this was sufficient for the claimant to be considered a joint author of the work. The court wrote, as follows:

> Nor is it in dispute that the plaintiff wrote the orchestral arrangement which accompanies the version that links the two half of the work in its recorded form as heard on track 11 of the 1992 compact disc... The main orchestral contribution to the work is in bars 24 to 29 of this 48 bar work. Those bars form a linking sequence and constitute an integral part of the work. In my view the plaintiff's contribution is sufficient in importance and originality to qualify him as a joint author of the work. The fact that when composing the six bar orchestral link the plaintiff took the basic melodic and harmonic lines from the song does not deprive the plaintiff of a share in the authorship of the work in the form in which I heard it. The link passage is, to my ear, an original and cleverly worked adaptation of the song's melodic line.

[45] And, in *Cala Homes (South) Ltd. v. Alfred McAlpine Homes East Ltd.*, [1995] E.W.J. No. 66 (Ch.D.), a case which dealt with the issue of joint authorship of architectural plans, the court, at paragraph 45, held, as follows:

> [W]here two or more people collaborate in the creation of a work and each contributes a significant part of the skill and labour protected by the copyright, then they are joint authors.

[46] There is no bright line test for what constitutes a significant or substantial contribution. I think that the test must include both quantitative and qualitative considerations of the contribution of the joint authors. For example, one must look at the amount and importance of the expressions to the work as a whole. And, while a claimant need not contribute a major part of the work to be considered a joint author, "someone who tinkered with and improved the work of another might not have done enough to show joint authorship." (See *Stuart v. Barrett, supra*.)

[47] Accordingly, while the plaintiff in the instant case need not show that his contributions to the songs were equal to McLachlan's contributions, he must show that his contributions to the songs were significant or substantial in order for him to qualify as a joint author.

. . .

(ii) THE ELEMENT OF COLLABORATION

. . .

[64] Joint authorship was introduced to the English jurisprudence by *Levy v. Rutley, supra*. At the time of its introduction, neither the U.K. nor the Canadian copyright legislation included a definition of a "work of joint authorship." The current definition in the *Act* dates from the 1921 Act, and essentially copied the terms of the U.K. Act of 1911.

[65] In *Levy v. Rutley*, the plaintiff employed a third party, Wilkes, to write a play. The third party prepared a manuscript. The plaintiff made some alterations and additions but the plot remained the same. The third party then agreed to assign his copyright in the work to the plaintiff. A receipt for part payment on the assignment stated that it was for the third party's share as "co-author" with the plaintiff. The assignment was never executed, nor the balance paid. The third party died. Subsequently, the defendants staged the play, as altered by the plaintiff. The plaintiff brought an action "to recover penalties," but the court dismissed his claim on the basis that he was not a joint author of the play. At p. 977, Byles J. said, as follows:

> It is admitted that Wilkes wrote most of the play, and that the plaintiff made only some small alterations; he cannot therefore be said to have been the sole author. If there were an execution by two or more persons of one common design for a dramatic piece, it might constitute joint authorship, although one person had contributed a very small amount of work to the execution–but here there is nothing to show any common design between Wilkes and the plaintiff, and on those grounds I am of opinion that the verdict should be entered for the defendant.

> (my emphasis)

[66] At the same page, Keating J. agreed, and added, as follows:

> I entirely agree with my brother Byles that to be joint authors, although it is not necessary that each should contribute the same amount of labour, yet there must be joint labour in carrying out a common design. Here Wilkes wrote a complete play, and without his cooperation the plaintiff added some scenes and incidents. Can this make him joint author of the whole piece? Even if an author should complete a play, upon a design of his own, there might possibly be joint authorship, if another suggested alterations which he agreed to adopt. If they agreed to rearrange the play together there might be joint authorship, although the common design was not commenced till after the completion of an original design by one of them. But here there was no common design whatever. Under these circumstances, I think there was no evidence of the plaintiff being joint author, and therefore the rule must be made absolute.

> (my emphasis)

[67] And finally, at the same page, Montague Smith J. agreed, and added, as follows:

> There may be some difficulty in deciding what constitutes joint authorship. Although one of the persons should actually write a much greater part of the work than the other, still they might, if there was co-operation in carrying out the

same design, possibly be considered joint authors. Here, Wilkes wrote a complete play; and Levy, considering it might be improved, added a scene and made various alterations. The main plot remained the same. There seems to have been no agreement originally that they should be joint authors. If there had been a joint re-modelling of the piece, they might have been joint authors, but here there is no evidence of such a proceeding. Reliance is placed upon the words of the receipt. It might be evidence that they considered themselves to be co-authors at that time; but the statement did not make them so – it was not an admission binding on third persons, and was not, as I think, warranted by the facts.

(my emphasis)

[68] There is a dearth of Canadian law on the meaning of the word "collaboration" in s. 2 of the *Act*. However, the Canadian and English authorities have interpreted the statutory definitions of joint authorship to require a common design. At p. 244, after referring to the definition of joint authorship in the *Act*, Fox states, "Joint authors are those who engage in the production of a work by joint labour in prosecution of a preconcerted joint design ...", citing Keating J. in *Levy v. Rutley*.

[69] In *Godfrey v. Lees, supra*, the plaintiff brought a claim for co-authorship of certain musical works. In 1969, the plaintiff had joined or been associated with the four defendants, in the band in which the four defendants had been members since 1966. The court noted that the plaintiff's claim was "confined to the six works in the versions in which they were performed on these two albums." The court also found that the plaintiff worked with the band upon their invitation to him to join them "for the purpose of working with the band as an orchestral arranger of a number of its songs" and that he carried out this role. The court stated the applicable test, as follows:

> What the claimant to joint authorship of a work must establish is that he has made a significant and original contribution to the creation of the work and that he has done so pursuant to a common design. See, for example, Stuart v. Barrett & ors [1994] EMLR 448.

[70] In *Stuart v. Barrett, supra*, the plaintiff was a drummer who had been invited to join a group of which the defendants were already members. The plaintiff alleged that he was a joint author of a number of songs composed while he was a member of the group. According to the headnote, the court concluded, as follows:

> By common design the members of the group had composed songs with each of them making contributions which could not be separated one from another. Composing was a joint enterprise for the mutual benefit of the members of the group. The plaintiff was therefore a joint author and was entitled to 25 per cent of the copyright in the music of the songs composed while he was a member of the group.

[71] Neither Fox, *Stuart v. Barrett* nor **Godfrey v. Lees** expanded upon the test for joint authorship beyond the scope of its introduction into the common law by *Levy v. Rutley*. However, in my opinion, the authorities, at the very least, have settled that to satisfy the test for joint authorship a putative joint author must

establish that he has made a contribution of significant original expression to the work at the time of its creation, and that he has done so pursuant to a common design (or, in other words, some form of shared intent).

[72] I turn next to review the development of the law of joint authorship in the United States. Originally, the U.S. copyright legislation did not refer to, nor define joint authorship. The definition of joint authorship was imported into the American common law by Learned Hand J. directly from *Levy v. Rutley*, in the case of *Maurel v. Smith*, 220 F. 195 (S.D.N.Y. 1915), aff'd 271 F. 211 (2d Cir. 1921).

. . .

[75] When the definition of joint authorship was introduced into the United States copyright legislation it included an express requirement of "intention" thereby restoring the focus on the joint authors' intention at the time of creation of the work. Courts in the United States have equated the requirement of intention in s. 101 with collaboration. Since collaboration is an element in s. 2 of the *Act*, I am therefore of the view that the American cases interpreting s. 101 are germane to my determination of the appropriate test for joint authorship in this jurisdiction.

[76] In holding that I view the American cases as a source of guidance to me, I am not unmindful of the caution expressed in *Compo Co. Ltd. v. Blue Crest Music Inc.* (1979), 45 C.P.R. (2d) 1 (S.C.C.), a case dealing with the infringement of copyright in a musical work, where, at p. 8, the court said, as follows:

> The United States *Copyright Act*, both in its present and earlier forms, has, of course, many similarities to the Canadian Act, as well as to the pre-existing Imperial *Copyright Act*. However, United States Court decisions, even where the factual situations are similar, must be scrutinized very carefully because of some fundamental differences in copyright concepts which have been adopted in the legislation of that country.

[77] However, despite these cautionary words from the Supreme Court of Canada, in *Tele-Direct (Publications) Inc.*, *supra* at p. 311 (footnote 8), the Federal Court of Appeal noted, as follows:

> In [*Compo Co. Ltd. v. Blue Crest Music Inc.*], Estey J. has observed that United States decisions "must be scrutinized very carefully because of some fundamental differences in copyright concepts which have been adopted in the legislation of that country" but he did not discourage Canadian courts to "find some assistance in examining the experience in the United States" [citation omitted]. I take these observations as referring only to authoritative decisions of the United States courts.

[78] The leading American authority interpreting "joint work" is *Childress v. Taylor*, *supra*. In that case, the plaintiff playwright alleged infringement of copyright in a play she wrote. The defendant actress claimed to be a joint author of the play by, *inter alia*, providing research material to the plaintiff, discussing with the plaintiff the inclusion of certain general scenes and characters in the play, and speaking with the plaintiff on a regular basis about the progress of the play. The court affirmed the trial judge's decision that the plaintiff was the sole author of the play.

[79] The court squarely addressed the nature of the intent requirement that must be met by each putative author at the time the contribution was created. At pp. 505-506, the court discussed joint authorship in the following terms:

> The Copyright Act defines a "joint work" as
>
> > a work prepared by two or more authors with the intention that their contributions be merged into inseparable or interdependent parts of a unitary whole.
>
> 17 U.S.C. § 101. As Professor Nimmer has pointed out, this definition is really the definition of a work of joint authorship. See 1 *Nimmer on Copyright* § 6.01 (1991). The definition concerns the *creation* of the work by the joint authors, not the circumstances, in addition to joint authorship, under which a work may be *jointly owned*, for example, by assignment of an undivided interest. The distinction affects the rights that are acquired. Joint authors hold undivided interests in a work, like all joint owners of a work, but joint authors, unlike other joint owners, also enjoy all the rights of authorship, including the renewal rights applicable to works in which a statutory copyright subsisted prior to January 1, 1978. *See* 17 U.S.C. § 304.
>
> Some aspects of the statutory definition of joint authorship are fairly straightforward. Parts of a unitary whole are "inseparable" when they have little or no independent meaning standing alone. That would often be true of a work of written text, such as the play that is the subject of the pending litigation. By contrast, parts of a unitary whole are "interdependent" when they have some meaning standing alone but achieve their primary significance because of their combined effect, as in the case of the words and music of a song. Indeed, a novel and a song are among the examples offered by the legislative committee reports on the 1976 Copyright Act to illustrate the difference between "inseparable" and "interdependent" parts. *See* H.R.Rep. No. 1476, 94th Cong., 2d Sess. 120 (1976) ("*House Report*"), *reprinted in* 1976 U.S.C.C.A.N. 5659, 5736; S.Rep. No. 473, 94th Cong., 2d Sess. 103-04 (1975) ("Senate Report").
>
> The legislative history also clarifies other aspects of the statutory definition, but leaves some matters in doubt. Endeavoring to flesh out the definition, the committee reports state:
>
> > [A] work is "joint" if the authors collaborated with each other, or if *each* of the authors prepared his or her contribution with the knowledge and *intention* that it would be merged with the contributions of other authors as "inseparable or interdependent parts of a unitary whole." The touchstone here is the *intention, at the time the writing is done*, that the parts be absorbed or combined into an integrated unit....
>
> *House Report* at 120; *Senate Report* at 103 (emphasis added). This passage appears to state two alternative criteria–one focusing on the act of collaboration and the other on the parties' intent. However, it is hard to imagine activity that would constitute meaningful "collaboration" unaccompanied by the requisite intent on the part of both participants that their contributions be merged into a unitary whole, and the case law has read the statutory language literally so that the intent requirement applies to all works of joint authorship. *See, e.g., Weissmann v. Freeman*, 868 F.2d 1313, 1317-19 (2d Cir.1989); *Eckert v. Hurley Chicago Co., Inc.*, 638 F.Supp. 699, 702-03 (N.D.Ill.1986).

[80] This last passage dealing with the committee reports held that the mere act of collaboration in the sense of "fusion of effort" (the *12th Street Rag* doctrine) was not enough, and that the intent to merge one's contributions into a unitary whole was required. But the intent to merge requirement was not all. At. p. 507 the court continued, as follows:

> There remains for consideration the crucial aspect of joint authorship–<u>the nature of the intent that must be entertained by each putative joint author at the time the contribution of each was created</u>. The wording of the statutory definition appears to make relevant only the state of mind regarding the unitary nature of the finished work–an intention "that their contributions be merged into inseparable or interdependent parts of a unitary whole." However, an inquiry so limited would extend joint author status to many persons who are not likely to have been within the contemplation of Congress. For example, a writer frequently works with an editor who makes numerous useful revisions to the first draft, some of which will consist of additions of copyrightable expression. Both intend their contributions to be merged into inseparable parts of a unitary whole, yet very few editors and even fewer writers would expect the editor to be accorded the status of joint author, enjoying an undivided half interest in the copyright in the published work. Similarly, research assistants may on occasion contribute to an author some protectable expression or merely a sufficiently original selection of factual material as would be entitled to a copyright, yet not be entitled to be regarded as a joint author of the work in which the contributed material appears. <u>What distinguishes the writer-editor relationship and the writer-researcher relationship from the true joint author relationship is the lack of intent of both participants in the venture to regard themselves as joint authors</u>.

(my emphasis)

[81] In footnote 6 on p. 507, the court acknowledged that in some situations the editor or researcher will be the employee of the "primary" author, in which case the "work made for hire" doctrine would ensure that copyright in the contributions would inure with the writer in any event. The court then said, "But in many situations the editor or researcher will be an independent contractor or an employee of some person or entity other than the primary author, in which event a claim of joint authorship would not be defeated by the 'work made for hire' doctrine."

. . .

[93] In my opinion, the common law definition of joint authorship, the statutory definitions of joint authorship in Canada, England and the United States, and the judicial interpretation of the statutory definitions all confirm that mutual intent is a prerequisite for a finding of collaboration. As to the importation of the requirement of an intent to co-author into Canadian copyright law, plaintiff's counsel's position on the court's findings in *Childress v. Taylor* was that given the legislative history behind the definition of "joint work," and the unique jurisprudence which flowed from the definition, that case should not be relied upon to determine the test for joint authorship in Canada. I disagree with this position. I have concluded that the intent to co-author requirement mandated by the *Childress v. Taylor* line of cases should be part of the test for joint authorship under s. 2 of the *Act* for the reasons that follow.

[94] First, the creation of the intent to co-author requirement in *Childress v. Taylor* happened despite the statutory definition of joint authorship in s. 101, not because of it. The court looked beyond the language of the section and moved on to review policy considerations in the application of the section. In particular, the court could not accept that Congress intended to extend joint authorship to, for example, editors and researchers. It was for this reason that the court created the intent to co-author requirement. In light of this background, I think that the difference in wording between the American and Canadian statutory definitions of joint authorship becomes irrelevant to my consideration of whether intent to co-author should also be a requirement under s. 2 of the *Act*.

[95] Secondly, I agree with the rationale for the policy expressed by the court in *Childress v. Taylor* to the effect that a person should not be elevated to the status of joint author unless each of the collaborators intended the other to be a joint author of the work. In my opinion, this standard accommodates the competing demands advanced by persons claiming ownership in a creative work and pays heed to the important warning stated in *Childress v. Taylor* at p. 504: "Care must be taken to ensure that true collaborators in the creative process are accorded the perquisites of co-authorship and to guard against the risk that a sole author is denied exclusive authorship status simply because another person rendered some form of assistance. Copyright law best serves the interests of creativity when it carefully draws the bounds of 'joint authorship' so as to protect the legitimate claims of both sole authors and co-authors."

[96] In the result, I find that the test for joint authorship that should be applied to the facts in the instant case is, as follows:

> (i) Did the plaintiff contribute significant original expression to the songs? If yes,

> (ii) Did each of the plaintiff and McLachlan intend that their contributions be merged into a unitary whole? If yes,

> (iii) Did each of the plaintiff and McLachlan intend the other to be a joint author of the songs?

. . .

VI. Application of the Test for Joint Authorship to the Songs

1. "Steaming"

(i) Did the Plaintiff Contribute Significant Original Expression?

. . .

[117] As for the verse vocal melody, McLachlan in her answers to interrogatories said that she "collaborated on verse melody with Darryl Neudorf in the early spring of 1988." In chief, she said that she remembered the plaintiff suggesting a melody line for this song and that she took what he gave her and developed it. When asked what the plaintiff's contribution was to this song, she replied, "Well, I would say that he helped to collaborate on verse, melody." In cross-examination, she said that she felt that the contribution was rather minor in the

sense that a melody was already in place, but when asked by plaintiff's counsel if she was suggesting that the change was insignificant, she said, "I don't think it was completely insignificant."

[118] Based upon the plaintiff's evidence, and McLachlan's concession about the plaintiff's contribution, I am satisfied that the plaintiff contributed original expression to the verse vocal melody of this song. And, quite apart from McLachlan's concession, I think the plaintiff's contribution to the verse vocal melody was a contribution of significant original expression to the song. The verse vocal melody is the first part that one hears after the instrumental intro, and it is repeated twice more in the song ("you never wanted time to end ..." and "Lying awake in these restless dreams..."). Although the verse vocal melody is not heard in the second half of the song, it is nonetheless, I think, an important component of the whole song.

. . .

(ii) Did Each of the Plaintiff and McLachlan Intend that their Contributions be Merged Into a Unitary Whole?

[121] This was not a case where McLachlan unilaterally took the plaintiff's contribution to the verse vocal melody and merged it into "Steaming" without the plaintiff's co-operation or consent. Neither was this a case where the plaintiff unilaterally made his contribution to "Steaming" without McLachlan's co-operation or consent. Here, the plaintiff made a contribution of significant original expression to the verse vocal melody, which McLachlan accepted and merged into the song. Both the plaintiff and McLachlan clearly intended that the plaintiff's contribution to the verse vocal melody would be merged into the song.

[122] And, while the evidence is that McLachlan embellished the plaintiff's contribution to the verse vocal melody, in my opinion, the embellishment does not detract from the shared intent between the parties to merge the plaintiff's contribution into this song. Therefore, I find that the plaintiff has satisfied the second prong of the test for joint authorship.

(iii) Did Each of the Plaintiff and McLachlan Intend the Other to be a Joint Author?

[123] While I am satisfied that the plaintiff and McLachlan shared an intent to merge the plaintiff's contribution to the verse vocal melody into the song, I am not so satisfied that they shared an intent to co-author the song. In my opinion, there is no subjective or objective evidence to support a conclusion by me that the plaintiff and Mclachlan formed the intent to regard each other as joint authors of "Steaming."

. . .

[129] From Jowett's and McLachlan's evidence, it is plain that the plaintiff was not introduced into the Touch project with any intention by them that the plaintiff would co-author the songs with McLachlan, nor did McLachlan consider

herself to be co-writing the songs with the plaintiff. However, even if I give greater weight to the testimony of the plaintiff on this issue, in my view his testimony cannot support a conclusion that the plaintiff and McLachlan regarded each other as co-authors.

. . .

[136] In my opinion, the plaintiff's evidence establishes that he did not regard his role in the project as that of co-author of the songs. Rather, he described his role as nurturing and teaching McLachlan, being a guiding and disciplinary force, helping manifest the songs, collaborating with the musicians, recording the demos, and getting the songs ready for the recording studio.

. . .

[151] Accordingly, given the evidence of McLachlan and Jowett regarding the plaintiff's role on the Touch project; the plaintiff's own description of his role on the Touch project; the fact that when Touch was released the plaintiff was not listed in the liner notes as a joint author of the songs; and the fact that it was not until many years after the release of Touch that for the first time the plaintiff claimed to the defendants that he was a co-author of the songs, I find that the plaintiff has not proven, on a balance of probabilities, that he and McLachlan shared an intent to co-author the song "Steaming." Therefore, his claim for a declaration of co-ownership of copyright in this song is dismissed.

. . .

XI. Summary

[231] The plaintiff has proven that he made a contribution of original expression to the verse vocal melody in the song "Steaming." However, he has failed to satisfy the test for joint authorship because he did not prove a mutual intent to co-author this song with McLachlan. The plaintiff has failed to prove that he contributed original expression to "Vox," "Sad Clown" or "Strange World." Accordingly, his claim to co-ownership of copyright in the songs must be dismissed. As well, his unjust enrichment claim must be dismissed.

Neugebauer v. Labieniec, 2009 FC 666 (F.C.), reversed 2010 CarswellNat 3299 (F.C.A.)

The Honourable Madam Justice Simpson

[1] This case involves an application to expunge a Certificate of Registration of Copyright (Registration No. 1,039,825) registered at the Canadian Intellectual Property Office on July 12, 2006, in connection with a literary work in the Polish language entitled *Gesi puch* (the Book). The Registration at issue identifies both the Applicant and the Respondent as the owners and authors of the Book.

The application is brought pursuant to subsection 57(4) of the Copyright Act, R.S.C. 1985, c. C-42 (the Act).

THE PARTIES

[2] The Applicant, Henry Neugebauer, was born in Poland in 1926 and has lived in Canada since the 1950s. He is a Holocaust survivor and was 13 years old when the Germans occupied Poland in 1939. The Book is based on his life story, particularly his experiences during the Holocaust. The Applicant has no writing experience and is not familiar with matters such as computer layouts, cover design and the process of printing and publishing a book. The Applicant says that he is fluent in English and Polish.

[3] The Respondent, Anna M. Labieniec, is a writer and journalist who has lived and worked in Canada for twelve years. She speaks and works in Polish and is fluent only in that language. Accordingly, the Respondent was assisted by a translator at the hearing of this application. In addition to her claim to have jointly authored the Book, the Respondent has written and published six books, four as general editor, one as a joint author, and one as an author. She also claims to have authored several hundred interviews as well as reports in print and for radio and television.

[4] The Respondent was briefly represented during a motion to adjourn these proceedings, but was self-represented during the hearing on the merits. Unfortunately, as a result of her decision to represent herself, her record was not complete. For example, although in her affidavit of December 23, 2008 she described thirty pages of transcription which she alleged she prepared, she was not permitted to introduce them during the hearing because they had not been exhibited to her affidavit. As well, I have disregarded evidence she provided during her submissions which was not included in her affidavits.

THE FACTS

[5] The Applicant says that a document entitled "Confirmation of Oral Agreement" dated September 1, 2005 (the First Agreement) reflected the intention of the parties to create a book with the Applicant as the author and the Respondent as the editor. The Applicant further submits that the parties are bound by the terms respecting "authorship" in the First Agreement because the Respondent failed to demonstrate a modification of that agreement or a material change in the parties' intentions.

[6] The Respondent denies that the First Agreement related to a Book. She says that it provided that she would prepare an edited transcription of the Applicant's tape-recorded recollections of his Holocaust experiences. The recordings were in Polish and the transcription was also to be in that language.

[7] The Respondent says that a separate oral contract was made dealing with the writing of the Book as joint authors (the Second Agreement) and that the Applicant's conduct supports their joint authorship of the Book.

[8] For the reasons below, I have concluded that the Respondent is credible and that there was a Second Agreement under which she and the Applicant agreed to jointly author the Book.

The First Agreement

[9] The parties did not know one another prior to their discussions about the First Agreement. Based on a favourable recommendation, the Applicant contacted the Respondent in August 2005.

[10] On September 1, 2005, the parties signed the First Agreement. It was a one page personal service contract which had been drafted in English by the Respondent's husband, J. Bogdan Pasziewicz. Mr. Pasziewicz explained the terms of the First Agreement to the parties in Polish before they signed it. It identifies the Applicant as author and the Respondent as editor. Her duties were to "[t]ransfer from tape recording to written media (Polish)"and "[e]dit and shape the materials to literary form".

[11] The First Agreement makes no mention of a book, but rather refers to the work as an"edition" or "memoires". The word "Memoires" appears over the Applicant's name on the top left corner of the page and again under the heading "miscellaneous"as follows: "Author gives the rigts [sic] to the editor to use parts of memoires in her future works". The word "edition" appears twice under the heading "miscellaneous" as follows: "Edition shall remain the property of the Author" and "Author shall have final approval over edition".

[12] Mr. Pasziewicz's affidavit said that he explained to the parties that "[t]he material is called Memoirs" and that:

> The result of transferring the recordings onto paper, the printed version of it (edition) belongs to the author of the tapes. Such author has the right to ask for a correction of the printed version in cases when he would not like to reveal some secrets from his life in print. He gives Anna Labieniec the right to use parts of his history in her journalistic work, without separate permission. The last clause was the main concern for Mr. Neugebauer.

[13] The Respondent asserts that the content of the tape recordings was "a chaotic accumulation of non-sequitur information about the Applicant's life" with no chronology. She also said that the language was difficult to understand. Given her difficulty with the materials provided, the Respondent requested interviews with the Applicant in order to complete her transcription of the Applicant's tapes. She also undertook some independent research to fill in gaps in the material. In the end, she provided the Applicant with thirty pages of material.

[14] I have concluded that the First Agreement was a limited contract for the transcription and editing and shaping of the material on the Applicant's tapes into an organized written form in Polish. Because the First Agreement provides for a fee of only $2,000.00, two months for the completion of the work, and makes no provision regarding copyright or royalties, I have accepted the Respondent's evidence that it did not deal with a book.

The Second Agreement

[15] The Respondent asserts that the Applicant was satisfied with the thirty page transcription under the First Agreement but stated that he also dreamt of writing a book. The Respondent says that the Applicant wanted her to write a book of approximately 240 pages based on his life. He was to be the main character. At this point, the parties orally made the Second Agreement providing that they would be joint authors of the Book. The Second Agreement also provided that the Applicant would pay for the first printed edition and thus receive the whole income from that edition, but that profits from future editions and any translations would be divided between the parties.

The Book

[16] The Book was first published in Toronto on May 5, 2006. It is 224 pages in length and has a paper jacket. The front of the jacket prominently displays the names of both parties, with the Applicant's name above and in slightly larger type than the Respondent's. The publishing information on the second page of the Book shows copyrights for both individuals. The inside front flap of the jacket includes the Applicant's photo and provides information about his background. It also notes that "[h]e told his story to [the Respondent], Polish author and journalist who live in Canada". The Respondent translated the first sentence on the back of the jacket as follows:

> "Gesi puch" ("Goos Down") [*sic*] of Henry Neugebauer and Anna Labieniec is a story based on true events, seen through the eyes of teenager, history of the Holocaust in Sosnowiec.

[17] The Applicant acknowledges that the Respondent wrote every word in the Book. I have accepted the Respondent's submission that she took the Applicant's disjointed information and created a narrative. I have rejected the Applicant's submission that the Respondent merely edited and organized his narrative. I have also concluded that the Respondent included original material in the Book about events which were not actually based on the Applicant's recollections. She created this material to expand his story to make the Book.

[18] The Applicant says that, at the time the Book was printed by a printer arranged by the Respondent, he was unaware that any reference was being made to the Respondent as either an author or copyright owner. The Applicant states that before the printing he was shown some items on Mr. Paszkiewicz's computer, but that he could not see anything as he was not wearing his glasses. He also states that he was not given paper material to review, despite having asked for it. He asserts: that everything was rushed and unorganized at the printing house; that he was only given a few pages to look at; that he was not given sufficient time to review the cover of the book; and that no one pointed out to him "the small passages about copyright, rights being attributed to the Sooni Project and other such details that are in the printed version of *Gesi Puch*".

[19] The Applicant also says that when he saw the layout of the Book, he thought he was sufficiently represented as the author by such things as his name

being larger on the cover, his forward introducing the Book, his picture and biography on the front flap of the jacket cover, and "the fact that *Gesi Puch* is the autobiography of [his] life".

[20] On the other hand, the Respondent says that the Applicant liked the design of the Book and approved of her name on the cover as joint author. Further, although she didn't agree, he wanted her to have her photograph on the back flap of the cover. The Respondent and Marek Kornas, the owner and operator of Nova Printing, both deposed that the Applicant participated in all decisions and approved all consecutive stages of the work throughout the printing process which took three weeks. They say that, during that period, the Applicant took the jacket and the text of the work home and never objected to any aspect of the material. They also say in late April 2006, the Applicant attended at the printing shop and carefully examined the Book and the cover and approved the content of both.

[21] Based on the above submissions, I have rejected the Applicant's claims that he was unaware of the copyright and authorship information in the Book before it was printed.

Publication of the Book

[22] The Applicant submits that the conduct of the parties after a work is published should not be treated as evidence of their intentions. However, in *Drapeau c. Girard*, 2003 CanLII 5575 (QC CA), [2003] R.J.Q. 2539 at para. 9, the Quebec Court of Appeal held that parties post-publication behaviour was relevant to issues of authorship and joint authorship. Accordingly, I will examine that behaviour.

[23] The first promotional event for the Book took place in Toronto on May 5, 2006 at the Artus bookstore. According to Teresa Budzillo, the owner and manager of Artus, the event was planned in a meeting involving herself, the Applicant and the Respondent, wherein the Applicant "introduced himself as a co-author of the book *Gesi puch* written by Anna Labieniec". Ms. Budzillo and the Respondent said that the public reading on May 5, 2006 was attended by writers and journalists as well as readers and the Applicant's close family members.

[24] Ms. Budzillo described the event, in part, as follows:

> Anna Labieniec talked about the process of writing the book, and about the difficulties which she had to overcome in order to convey in words the way of thinking of the man raised in different from Christian culture, and express the character's traumatic experience in the face of extermination. [...]During the reading, Mr. Neugebauer repeatedly thanked Anna Labieniec for writing a beautiful book about him and his lot. He presented her with a bouquet of roses. Ms. Labieniec and Mr. Neugebauer jointly signed the books for the readers.

[25] Marek Kusiba, a writer and journalist who attended the event, said that the parties were both asked for autographs by several purchasers. However, the

Applicant asserts that the parties signed the Book not as joint authors, but as author and editor and says that they co-signed at the Toronto book launch only because the Respondent had many friends in attendance. However, because they also signed the Book together in Poland, I have not accepted this explanation.

[26] The Applicant gave the Respondent an autographed copy of the Book. The Respondent translated the autograph from Polish into English as follows: "For Ms. Ania for writing beautiful book with thanks. Henry Neugebauer." The Applicant does not contest the translation, rather he asserts that he meant to express his gratitude for her editorial assistance. The Applicant's counsel said that the Applicant meant to thank the Respondent for editing the Book, and that the Court should not put too much weight on his choice of words. However, I have taken his words at face value and am comfortable that, if she had been an editor, his note of thanks would have reflected that fact. In reaching this conclusion, I am mindful that the Applicant was aware of the distinction between an author and an editor when he signed the First Agreement.

[27] I have found the evidence about the promotional reading at Studio 102 in Lodz, Poland on May 26, 2006 to be particularly useful. The Respondent provides a translation of the portion of the reading that was videotaped and the Applicant does not contest the Respondent's translation. The Respondent clearly described herself as an author of the Book without objection from the Applicant.

[28] Based on all the evidence, including photographs of the Respondent autographing the Book with the Applicant in Toronto and Poland, I have determined that the parties signed together on at least two occasions. In light of this conduct at the promotional events and particularly Ms. Budzillo's evidence that he identified himself as "co-author" with the Respondent, I also reject the Applicant's submission that these signings were not as co-authors. Accordingly, I find that the parties held themselves out as joint authors during the promotion of the Book.

Events Leading up to This Proceeding

[29] The Applicant testified that on his return from Europe, his daughter (now deceased) alerted him to her belief that the Respondent was claiming joint authorship in the Book. He was apparently surprised and enraged and took corrective action, including publishing a newspaper advertisement identifying himself as the Book's sole author.

[30] Ms. Budzillo says that in late June 2006, she discovered that the Applicant had replaced the promotional posters in her store which bore the names of both parties with ones that bore only his name. She took them down and requested a meeting with the Applicant. She also says that the Respondent informed her that the Applicant's lawyer had written to her accusing her of unlawfully presenting herself as co-author of the Book and threatening litigation. Ms. Budzillo says that, in their meeting, the Applicant gave her no reason for his conduct. She informed him that she considered his behaviour scandalous and ungrateful and she refused to sell the Book. She returned the unsold copies to the Applicant.

[31] The Respondent says that the Applicant's story about discovering her claim to joint authorship from his daughter is untrue. She says that his conduct is explained by the fact that she had the contacts needed to arrange the promotional tour inPoland and, once it was over, the Applicant had no further need of her. She also says he was motivated to deny her joint authorship by the prospect that he would have to pay her if the Book was republished or translated.

[32] The Respondent registered the Book with the Canadian Intellectual Property Office on July 12, 2006. The registration identified the Respondent and the Applicant as owners and authors of the Book.

[33] In October 2007, the Applicant submitted an independent Application for Registration of Copyright in the Book to the Canadian Intellectual Property Office, which was registered on November 2, 2007. This registration identifies the Applicant as the sole owner and author of the Book.

ISSUES

[34] Against this background, the following questions require consideration:

1. Did the Respondent's contribution to the Book constitute "authorship" under the Act?

2. Did the parties'respective contributions to the Book constitute "joint authorship"?

Issue 1–Authorship

[35] The parties disagree about the Respondent's creative contribution to the Book. While the Applicant asserts that the Respondent did not contribute to the creative or intellectual process of writing the Book, characterizing her contribution as merely editorial, the Respondent asserts that the intellectual and creative process of writing the Book was all her own.

[36] The Applicant correctly notes that although the word "author" is not defined in the Act, cases have indicated that it conveys a sense of creativity and ingenuity. The Applicant further cites the New Brunswick Court of Appeal's decision in *New Brunswick Telephone Company* in this regard. It states:

> The word author must "not be equated to a mere scribe or amanuensis." Nor can a person who shared or gives to another person be considered an author. Rather, it is the individual who "expressed the ideas in an original or novel form" that is considered the author.

> *New Brunswick Telephone Company, Limited v. John Maryon International Limited* reflex, [1982] N.B.J. No. 387, [1982] 141 D.L.R. (3d) 193 at 244 (N.B.C.A.).

[37] I have concluded that, in this case, the Respondent contributed sufficient originality and expression to claim authorship of the Book and have rejected the Applicant's submission that the Book is simply the Respondent's transcription of the Applicant's narrative with minor improvements to flow, editing of vocabulary and crafting. In my view, the Applicant did not provide the Respondent with

sufficient personal recollections to allow her to write a book. This is why her affidavit describes over a dozen scenes based on her imagination and research in order to fill out the Book. The Respondent takes issue with only one of her claims and says he told her about drinking whale oil.

[38] Canadian cases have consistently maintained that copyright law does not protect ideas, concepts and facts, but rather the expression of these ideas, concepts and facts in an original form. The Applicant maintains that all the Respondent's created events are "loosely base on my life and or [*sic*] the lives of those like me who endured the Holocaust". I find this to be an admission that these events were not simply the Respondent's edited transcription of a narrative authored by the Applicant.

[39] In *Gould Estate v. Stoddart Publishing Co.* 1996 CanLII 8209 (ON SC), (1996), 30 O.R. (3d) 520 (Gen. Div.), aff'd 1998 CanLII 5513 (ON CA), (1998), 80 C.P.R. (3d) 161 (Ont. C.A.). Glenn Gould, who was the subject of the literary work, contributed substantially to the content of the work in the form of statements given in interviews. However, the author was held to be the person who conducted interviews and performed the creative task of assembling his statements into a literary work. Accordingly, *Gould* states that people do not have copyright in a work simply because they are its subjects or respond to questions in interviews. Following *Gould, Hager v. ECW Press Ltd.,* 1998 CanLII 9115 (FC), [1999] 2 F.C. 287, 85 C.P.R. (3d) 289, at para. 24, noted that:

> Under Anglo-Canadian law, insofar as private interviews are concerned, it is the person who reduces the oral statements to a fixed form that acquires copyright therein. That individual is considered to be the originator of the work.

Issue 2: Joint Authorship

[40] The Applicant also contests the Respondent's factual and legal entitlement to joint authorship.

[41] Section 2 of the Act defines "work of joint authorship" as follows:

"work of joint authorship" *«oeuvre créée en collaboration »*	*«oeuvre créée en collaboration »* "*work of joint authorship*"
"work of joint authorship" means a work produced by the collaboration of two or more authors in which the contribution of one author is not distinct from the contribution of the other author or authors;	*«oeuvre créée en collaboration »* Oeuvre exécutée par la collaboration de deux ou plusieurs auteurs, et dans laquelle la part créée par l'un n'est pas distincte de celle créée par l'autre ou les autres.

[42] Thus, the statutory definition involves two precise requirements: there must be collaboration and the contributions must not be distinct.

[43] I have concluded that, under the Second Agreement, there was collaboration which contributed towards a unitary whole and that the parties intended that their contributions be joined in furtherance of a common design. I have accepted

the Respondent's evidence that the Applicant agreed that they would be joint authors of the Book. I am persuaded that the Respondent is a joint author by the evidence of the bookstore owner who asserted that the Applicant introduced himself to her as the "co-author" of the Book written by the Respondent and by the Applicant's post-publication conduct.

[44] I have reached this conclusion under both the conventional test for joint authorship as well as the expanded test introduced by the British Columbia Supreme Court its decision *Neudorf v. Nettwerk Productions Ltd.* 1999 CanLII 5293 (BC SC), (1999), 3 C.P.R. (4th) 129 (B.C.S.C.) at para. 24 (*Neudorf*). *Neudorf* followed American law, which imposes a requirement that collaborators intend to regard each other as joint authors, instead of the Canadian and British precedents, which impose no such requirement.

[45] *Levy v. Rutley* (1871) 6 L.R. 976 (CP) 1870-71 523 [*Levy v. Rutley*] continues to be cited as the leading authority on the constituent elements of joint authorship under English and Canadian law. For example, Normand Tamaro, *The 2009 Annotated Copyright Act* (Toronto: Carswell, 2008), at pp. 189-191, cites this judgment as establishing the following three important elements concerning work of joint authorship:

> First, the existence of a work of joint authorship is established by the facts and by the law, and is not based on the parties' intentions.
>
> [...]
>
> Second, the contributions of each of the parties need not be equal, though each must be substantial.
>
> [...]
>
> Third, even if one contribution may be qualitatively and quantitatively inferior to the other, there must be a joint labour in carrying out a common design.
>
> [my emphasis]

[46] In contrast to the joint authorship element of "contribution", which has been considered in numerous Canadian cases, Mr. Justice Cohen said in *Neudorf* at para. 68 that"[t]here is a dearth of Canadian law on the meaning of the word "collaboration"in the definition of joint authorship in s. 2 of the Act."

[47] After describing some of the Canadian and English authorities, Mr. Justice Cohen concluded at para. 71 that:

> Neither Fox, Stuart v. Barrett nor Godfrey v. Lees expanded upon the test for joint authorship beyond the scope of its introduction into the common law by Levy v. Rutley. However, in my opinion, the authorities, at the very least, have settled that to satisfy the test for joint authorship a putative joint author must establish that he has made a contribution of significant original expression to the work at the time of its creation, and that he has done so pursuant to a common design (or, in other words, some form of shared intent).
>
> [my emphasis]

[48] In introducing the requirement for shared intention, Justice Cohen drew on American legislation and precedents.

[49] Section 101 of the U.S. *Copyrights Act* of 1976, 17 U.S.C., the legislative definition of a "joint work" in force in the U.S. at the time *Neudorf* was decided, provided as follows:

> A "joint work" is a work prepared by two or more authors with the intention that their contributions be merged into inseparable or interdependent parts of a unitary whole.

[50] Justice Cohen also relied on *Childress v. Taylor*, 945 F.2d 500 (2d Cir. 1991) (*Childress*), which he treated as the leading American authority interpreting the American statutory definition of "joint work". It established the following three-prong test:

1) each of the collaborators intended the other to be a joint author of the work;
2) each author's work was independently copyrightable; and
3) each author intended that his work be merged into inseparable or interdependent parts of the whole.

[51] Although the *Neudorf* test has been used at the trial level in Quebec, Ontario and Nova Scotia (see *Drapeau c. Carbone 14*, [2000] J.Q. no 1171 (QCCS) (Locus Para. 55); *Saxon c. Communications Mont-Royal inc.*, [2000] J.Q. no 5634 (QCCS) (Locus Para. 75); *Dolmage v. Erskine* 2003 CanLII 8350 (ON SC), (2003), 23 C.P.R. (4th) 495 (ONSupCtJus) (Locus Para. 45); and *Wall v. Horn Abbot Ltd.*, 2007 NSSC 197 (CanLII), 2007 NSSC 197 (Locus Paras. 498-506), it has not, in my view, been applied at the appellate level. In particular, I have not accepted the Applicant's submission that it was relied on by the Quebec Court of Appeal in *Drapeau c. Girard*, [2003] J.Q. no 13044, 127 A.C.W.S. (3d) 533. As I read that decision, the Court relied on the conventional test for joint authorship found in *Levy v. Rutley*.

[52] Given this background, I have decided not to follow *Neudorf*'s articulation of the appropriate test for joint authorship under s. 2 of the Act. However, as previously mentioned, even if I had followed *Neudorf*, my conclusion on the issue of joint authorship would have been the same.

Aalmuhammed v. Lee, 202 F. 3d 1227 (9th Cir. 2000)

United States Court of Appeals, Ninth Circuit.

No. 99-55224.

Submitted April 19, 1999.

. . .

KLEINFELD, Circuit Judge:

This is a copyright case involving a claim of coauthorship of the movie *Malcolm X.* We reject the "joint work" claim but remand for further proceedings on a quantum meruit claim.

I. FACTS

In 1991, Warner Brothers contracted with Spike Lee and his production companies to make the movie *Malcolm X,* to be based on the book, *The Autobiography of Malcolm X.* Lee co-wrote the screenplay, directed, and co-produced the movie, which starred Denzel Washington as Malcolm X. Washington asked Jefri Aalmuhammed to assist him in his preparation for the starring role because Aalmuhammed knew a great deal about Malcolm X and Islam. Aalmuhammed, a devout Muslim, was particularly knowledgeable about the life of Malcolm X, having previously written, directed, and produced a documentary film about Malcolm X.

Aalmuhammed joined Washington on the movie set. The movie was filmed in the New York metropolitan area and Egypt. Aalmuhammed presented evidence that his involvement in making the movie was very extensive. He reviewed the shooting script for Spike Lee and Denzel Washington and suggested extensive script revisions. Some of his script revisions were included in the released version of the film; others were filmed but not included in the released version. Most of the revisions Aalmuhammed made were to ensure the religious and historical accuracy and authenticity of scenes depicting Malcolm X's religious conversion and pilgrimage to Mecca.

Aalmuhammed submitted evidence that he directed Denzel Washington and other actors while on the set, created at least two entire scenes with new characters, translated Arabic into English for subtitles, supplied his own voice for voice-overs, selected the proper prayers and religious practices for the characters, and edited parts of the movie during post production. Washington testified in his deposition that Aalmuhammed's contribution to the movie was "great" because he "helped to rewrite, to make more authentic." Once production ended, Aalmuhammed met with numerous Islamic organizations to persuade them that the movie was an accurate depiction of Malcolm X's life.

Aalmuhammed never had a written contract with Warner Brothers, Lee, or Lee's production companies, but he expected Lee to compensate him for his work. He did not intend to work and bear his expenses in New York and Egypt gratuitously. Aalmuhammed ultimately received a check for $25,000 from Lee, which he cashed, and a check for $100,000 from Washington, which he did not cash.

During the summer before *Malcolm X* 's November 1992 release, Aalmuhammed asked for a writing credit as a co-writer of the film, but was turned
down. When the film was released, it credited Aalmuhammed only as an "Islamic Technical Consultant," far down the list. In November 1995, Aalmuhammed
applied for a copyright with the U.S. Copyright Office, claiming he was a co-
creator, co-writer, and co-director of the movie. The Copyright Office issued
him a "Certificate of Registration," but advised him in a letter that his "claims
conflict with previous registrations" of the film.

On November 17, 1995, Aalmuhammed filed a complaint against Spike Lee,
his production companies, and Warner Brothers, (collectively "Lee"), as well as
Largo International, N.V., and Largo Entertainment, Inc. (collectively "Largo"),
and Victor Company of Japan and JVC Entertainment, Inc. (collectively "Victor"). The suit sought declaratory relief and an accounting under the Copyright
Act. In addition, the complaint alleged breach of implied contract, quantum
meruit, and unjust enrichment, and federal (Lanham Act) and state unfair competition claims. The district court dismissed some of the claims under Rule 12(b)
(6) and the rest on summary judgment.

II. ANALYSIS

A. Copyright claim

Aalmuhammed claimed that the movie *Malcolm X* was a "joint work" of which
he was an author, thus making him a co-owner of the copyright.[FN2] He sought
a declaratory judgment to that effect, and an accounting for profits. He is not
claiming copyright merely in what he wrote or contributed, but rather in the
whole work, as a co-author of a "joint work."[FN3] The district court granted
defendants summary judgment against Mr. Aalmuhammed's copyright claims.
We review de novo.[FN4]

> FN2. 17 U.S.C. §§ 101, 201(a).

> FN3. Cf. *Thomson v. Larson,* 147 F.3d 195, 206 (2nd Cir.1998).

> FN4. *See Covey v. Hollydale Mobilehome Estates,* 116 F.3d 830, 834 (9th
> Cir.1997), *amended by,* 125 F.3d 1281 (1997).

[1] Defendants argue that Aalmuhammed's claim that he is one of the authors of
a joint work is barred by the applicable statute of limitations. A claim of authorship of a joint work must be brought within three years of when it accrues.[FN5]
Because creation rather than infringement is the gravamen of an authorship
claim, the claim accrues on account of creation, not subsequent infringement,
and is barred three years from "plain and express repudiation" of authorship.[FN6]

> FN5. *See* 17 U.S.C. § 507(b); *Zuill v. Shanahan,* 80 F.3d 1366, 1371 (9th
> Cir.1996), *cert. denied,* 519 U.S. 1090, 117 S.Ct. 763, 136 L.Ed.2d 710 (1997).

> FN6. *Zuill,* 80 F.3d at 1371.

[2] The movie credits plainly and expressly repudiated authorship, by listing
Aalmuhammed far below the more prominent names, as an "Islamic technical

consultant." That repudiation, though, was less than three years before the lawsuit was filed. The record leaves open a genuine issue of fact as to whether authorship was repudiated before that. Aalmuhammed testified in his deposition that he discussed with an executive producer at Warner Brothers his claim to credit as one of the screenwriters more than three years before he filed suit. Defendants argue that this discussion was an express repudiation that bars the claim. It was not. Aalmuhammed testified that the producer told him "there is nothing I can do for you," but "[h]e said we would discuss it further at some point." A trier of fact could construe that communication as leaving the question of authorship open for further discussion. That leaves a genuine issue of fact as to whether the claim is barred by limitations, so we must determine whether there is a genuine issue of fact as to whether Aalmuhammed was an author of a "joint work."

[3][4] Aalmuhammed argues that he established a genuine issue of fact as to whether he was an author of a "joint work," *Malcolm X*. The Copyright Act does not define "author," but it does define "joint work":

A "joint work" is a work prepared by two or more authors with the intention that their contributions be merged into inseparable or interdependent parts of a unitary whole.[FN7]

> FN7. 17 U.S.C. § 101.

"When interpreting a statute, we look first to the language."[FN8] The statutory language establishes that for a work to be a "joint work" there must be (1) a copyrightable work, (2) two or more "authors," and (3) the authors must intend their contributions be merged into inseparable or interdependent parts of a unitary whole. A "joint work" in this circuit "requires each author to make an independently copyrightable contribution" to the disputed work.[FN9] *Malcolm X* is a copyrightable work, and it is undisputed that the movie was intended by everyone involved with it to be a unitary whole. It is also undisputed that Aalmuhammed made substantial and valuable contributions to the movie, including technical help, such as speaking Arabic to the persons in charge of the mosque in Egypt, scholarly and creative help, such as teaching the actors how to pray properly as Muslims, and script changes to add verisimilitude to the religious aspects of the movie. Speaking Arabic to persons in charge of the mosque, however, does not result in a copyrightable contribution to the motion picture. Coaching of actors, to be copyrightable, must be turned into an expression in a form subject to copyright.[FN10] The same may be said for many of Aalmuhammed's other activities. Aalmuhammed has, however, submitted evidence that he rewrote several specific passages of dialogue that appeared in *Malcolm X,* and that he wrote scenes relating to Malcolm X's Hajj pilgrimage that were enacted in the movie. If Aalmuhammed's evidence is accepted, as it must be on summary judgment, these items would have been independently copyrightable. Aalmuhammed, therefore, has presented a genuine issue of fact as to whether he made a copyrightable contribution. All persons involved intended that Aalmuhammed's contributions would be merged into interdependent parts of the movie as a unitary whole.

Aalmuhammed maintains that he has shown a genuine issue of fact for each element of a "joint work."

> FN8. *Richardson v. United States,* 526 U.S. 813, 119 S.Ct. 1707, 1710, 143 L.Ed.2d 985 (1999).
>
> FN9. *Ashton-Tate Corp. v. Ross,* 916 F.2d 516, 521 (9th Cir.1990).
>
> FN10. *See Ashton-Tate Corp. v. Ross,* 916 F.2d 516, 521 (9th Cir.1990).

[5] But there is another element to a "joint work." A "joint work" includes "two or more authors."[FN11] Aalmuhammed established that he contributed substantially to the film, but not that he was one of its "authors." We hold that authorship is required under the statutory definition of a joint work, and that authorship is not the same thing as making a valuable and copyrightable contribution. We recognize that a contributor of an expression may be deemed to be the "author" of that expression for purposes of determining whether it is independently copyrightable. The issue we deal with is a different and larger one: is the contributor an author of the joint work within the meaning of 17 U.S.C. § 101.

> FN11. 17 U.S.C. § 101.

By statutory definition, a "joint work" requires "two or more authors."[FN12] The word "author" is taken from the traditional activity of one person sitting at a desk with a pen and writing something for publication. It is relatively easy to apply the word "author" to a novel. It is also easy to apply the word to two people who work together in a fairly traditional pen-and-ink way, like, perhaps, Gilbert and Sullivan. In the song, "I Am the Very Model of a Modern Major General," Gilbert's words and Sullivan's tune are inseparable, and anyone who has heard the song knows that it owes its existence to both men, Sir William Gilbert and Sir Arthur Sullivan, as its creative originator. But as the number of contributors grows and the work itself becomes less the product of one or two individuals who create it without much help, the word is harder to apply.

> FN12. 17 U.S.C. § 101.

Who, in the absence of contract, can be considered an author of a movie? The word is traditionally used to mean the originator or the person who causes something to come into being, or even the first cause, as when Chaucer refers to the "Author of Nature." For a movie, that might be the producer who raises the money. Eisenstein thought the author of a movie was the editor. The "auteur" theory suggests that it might be the director, at least if the director is able to impose his artistic judgments on the film. Traditionally, by analogy to books, the author was regarded as the person who writes the screenplay, but often a movie reflects the work of many screenwriters. Grenier suggests that the person with creative control tends to be the person in whose name the money is raised, perhaps a star, perhaps the director, perhaps the producer, with control gravitating to the star as the financial investment in scenes already shot grows.[FN13] Where the visual aspect of the movie is especially important, the chief cinematographer might be regarded as the author. And for, say, a Disney animated movie like "The Jungle Book," it might perhaps be the animators and the composers of the music.

FN13. *See* Richard Grenier, *Capturing the Culture,* 206-07 (1991).

The Supreme Court dealt with the problem of defining "author" in new media in *Burrow-Giles Lithographic Co. v. Sarony.*[FN14] The question there was, who is the author of a photograph: the person who sets it up and snaps the shutter, or the person who makes the lithograph from it. Oscar Wilde, the person whose picture was at issue, doubtless offered some creative advice as well. The Court decided that the photographer was the author, quoting various English authorities: "the person who has superintended the arrangement, who has actually formed the picture by putting the persons in position, and arranging the place where the people are to be-the man who is the effective cause of that"; " 'author' involves originating, making, producing, as the inventive or master mind, the thing which is to be protected"; "the man who really represents, creates, or gives effect to the idea, fancy, or imagination."[FN15] The Court said that an "author," in the sense that the Founding Fathers used the term in the Constitution,[FN16] was "'he to whom anything owes its origin; originator; maker; one who completes a work of science or literature.'"[FN17]

FN14. *Burrow-Giles Lithographic Co. v. Sarony,* 111 U.S. 53, 61, 4 S.Ct. 279, 28 L.Ed. 349 (1884).

FN15. *Id.* at 61, 4 S.Ct. 279 (quoting *Nottage v. Jackson,* 11 Q.B.D. 627 (1883)).

FN16. U.S. Const. Art. 1, § 8, cl. 8.

FN17. *Burrow-Giles,* 111 U.S. at 58, 4 S.Ct. 279 (quoting Worcester).

Answering a different question, what is a copyrightable "work," as opposed to who is the "author," the Supreme Court held in *Feist Publications* that "some minimal level of creativity" or "originality" suffices.[FN18] But that measure of a "work" would be too broad and indeterminate to be useful if applied to determine who are "authors" of a movie. So many people might qualify as an "author" if the question were limited to whether they made a substantial creative contribution that that test would not distinguish one from another. Everyone from the producer and director to casting director, costumer, hairstylist, and "best boy" gets listed in the movie credits because all of their creative contributions really do matter. It is striking in *Malcolm X* how much the person who controlled the hue of the lighting contributed, yet no one would use the word "author" to denote that individual's relationship to the movie. A creative contribution does not suffice to establish authorship of the movie.

FN18. *Feist Publications, Inc. v. Rural Telephone Service Co., Inc.,* 499 U.S. 340, 345, 111 S.Ct. 1282, 113 L.Ed.2d 358 (1991).

Burrow-Giles, in defining "author," requires more than a minimal creative or original contribution to the work.[FN19] *Burrow-Giles* is still good law, and was recently reaffirmed in *Feist Publications.*[FN20] *Burrow-Giles* and *Feist Publications* answer two distinct questions; who is an author, and what is a copyrightable work.[FN21] *Burrow-Giles* defines author as the person to whom the work owes its origin and who superintended the whole work, the "master mind."[FN22] In a movie this definition, in the absence of a contract to the contrary, would generally limit authorship to someone at the top of the screen credits, sometimes the producer, sometimes the director, possibly the star, or the screenwriter-someone who has artistic control. After all, in *Burrow-Giles* the lithographer made a substantial copyrightable creative contribution, and so did the person who posed, Oscar Wilde, but the Court held that the photographer was the author.[FN23]

FN19. *Burrow-Giles Lithographic Co. v. Sarony,* 111 U.S. 53, 58, 4 S.Ct. 279, 28 L.Ed. 349 (1883).

FN20. *Feist Publications, Inc. v. Rural Telephone Service Co., Inc.,* 499 U.S. 340, 346, 111 S.Ct. 1282, 113 L.Ed.2d 358 (1991).

FN21. *See Burrow-Giles Lithographic Co. v. Sarony,* 111 U.S. 53, 4 S.Ct. 279, 28 L.Ed. 349 (1884); *Feist Publications, Inc. v. Rural Telephone Service Co., Inc.,* 499 U.S. 340, 111 S.Ct. 1282, 113 L.Ed.2d 358 (1991).

FN22. *Burrow-Giles,* 111 U.S. at 61, 4 S.Ct. 279 (quoting *Nottage v. Jackson,* 11 Q.B.D. 627 (1883)).

FN23. *Id.* at 61, 4 S.Ct. 279.

The Second and Seventh Circuits have likewise concluded that contribution of independently copyrightable material to a work intended to be an inseparable whole will not suffice to establish authorship of a joint work.[FN24] Although the Second and Seventh Circuits do not base their decisions on the word "authors" in the statute, the practical results they reach are consistent with ours. These circuits have held that a person claiming to be an author of a joint work must prove that both parties intended each other to be joint authors.[FN25] In determining whether the parties have the intent to be joint authors, the Second Circuit looks at who has decision making authority, how the parties bill themselves, and other evidence.[FN26]

FN24. *Thomson v. Larson,* 147 F.3d 195, (2nd Cir.1998); *Erickson v. Trinity Theatre, Inc.,* 13 F.3d 1061 (7th Cir.1994); *Childress v. Taylor,* 945 F.2d 500 (2d Cir.1991).

FN25. *Thomson,* 147 F.3d at 202-05.

FN26. *Id.*

In *Thomson v. Larson,* an off-Broadway playwright had created a modern version of *La Boheme,* and had been adamant throughout its creation on being the sole author.[FN27] He hired a drama professor for "dramaturgical assistance and research," agreeing to credit her as "dramaturg" but not author, but saying nothing about "joint work" or copyright.[FN28] The playwright tragically died immediately after the final dress rehearsal, just before his play became the tremendous Broadway hit, *Rent.*[FN29] The dramaturg then sued his estate for a declaratory judgment that she was an author of *Rent* as a "joint work," and for an accounting.[FN30] The Second Circuit noted that the dramaturg had no decision making authority, had neither sought nor was billed as a co-author, and that the defendant entered into contracts as the sole author.[FN31] On this reasoning, the Second Circuit held that there was no intent to be joint authors by the putative parties and therefore it was not a joint work.[FN32]

FN27. *Id.* at 197.

FN28. *Id.*

FN29. *Id.* at 198.

FN30. *Id.*

FN31. *Id.* at 202-04.

FN32. *Id.* at 202-24.

[6] Considering *Burrow-Giles,* the recent cases on joint works[FN33] (especially the thoughtful opinion in *Thomson v. Larson*[FN34]), and the Gilbert and Sullivan example, several factors suggest themselves as among the criteria for joint authorship, in the absence of contract. First, an author "superintend[s]"[FN35] the work by exercising control.[FN36] This will likely be a person "who has actually formed the picture by putting the persons in position, and arranging the place where the people are to be-the man who is the effective cause of that,"[FN37] or "the inventive or master mind" who "creates, or gives effect to the idea."[FN38] Second, putative coauthors make objective manifestations of a shared intent to be coauthors, as by denoting the authorship of *The Pirates of Penzance* as "Gilbert and Sullivan."[FN39] We say objective manifestations because, were the mutual intent to be determined by subjective intent, it could become an instrument of fraud, were one coauthor to hide from the other an intention to take sole credit for the work. Third, the audience appeal of the work turns on both contributions and "the share of each in its success cannot be appraised."[FN40] Control in many cases will be the most important factor.

FN33. *See Thomson v. Larson,* 147 F.3d 195, (2nd Cir.1998); *Erickson v. Trinity Theatre, Inc.,* 13 F.3d 1061 (7th Cir.1994); *Childress v. Taylor,* 945 F.2d 500 (2nd Cir.1991).

FN34. *Thomson v. Larson,* 147 F.3d 195 (2nd Cir.1998).

FN35. *Burrow-Giles v. Sarony,* 111 U.S. at 61, 4 S.Ct. 279 (quoting *Nottage v. Jackson,* 11 Q.B. div. 627 (1883)).

FN36. *Thomson,* 147 F.3d at 202.

FN37. *Burrow-Giles v. Sarony,* 111 U.S. at 61, 4 S.Ct. 279 (quoting *Nottage v. Jackson,* 11 Q.B. Div. 627 (1883)).

FN38. *Id.*

FN39. *Cf. Thomson v. Larson,* 147 F.3d 195, 202 (2nd Cir.1998).

FN40. *Edward B. Marks Music Corp. v. Jerry Vogel Music Co., Inc.,* 140 F.2d 266, 267 (2nd Cir.1944) (Hand, J.) *modified by,* 140 F.2d 268 (1944).

The best objective manifestation of a shared intent, of course, is a contract saying that the parties intend to be or not to be co-authors. In the absence of a contract, the inquiry must of necessity focus on the facts. The factors articulated in this decision and the Second and Seventh Circuit decisions cannot be reduced to a rigid formula, because the creative relationships to which they apply vary too much. Different people do creative work together in different ways, and even among the same people working together the relationship may change over time as the work proceeds.

Aalmuhammed did not at any time have superintendence of the work.[FN41] Warner Brothers and Spike Lee controlled it. Aalmuhammed was not the person "who has actually formed the picture by putting the persons in position, and arranging the place...."[FN42] Spike Lee was, so far as we can tell from the record. Aalmuhammed, like Larson's dramaturg, could make extremely helpful recommendations, but Spike Lee was not bound to accept any of them, and the work would not benefit in the slightest unless Spike Lee chose to accept them. Aalmuhammed lacked control over the work, and absence of control is strong evidence of the absence of co-authorship.

> FN41. *See Burrow-Giles v. Sarony,* 111 U.S. 53, 61, 4 S.Ct. 279, 28 L.Ed. 349 (1883).

> FN42. *Id.*

Also, neither Aalmuhammed, nor Spike Lee, nor Warner Brothers, made any objective manifestations of an intent to be coauthors. Warner Brothers required Spike Lee to sign a "work for hire" agreement, so that even Lee would not be a co-author and co-owner with Warner Brothers. It would be illogical to conclude that Warner Brothers, while not wanting to permit Lee to own the copyright, intended to share ownership with individuals like Aalmuhammed who worked under Lee's control, especially ones who at the time had made known no claim to the role of co-author. No one, including Aalmuhammed, made any indication to anyone prior to litigation that Aalmuhammed was intended to be a co-author and co-owner.

Aalmuhammed offered no evidence that he was the "inventive or master mind" of the movie. He was the author of another less widely known documentary about Malcolm X, but was not the master of this one. What Aalmuhammed's evidence showed, and all it showed, was that, subject to Spike Lee's authority to accept them, he made very valuable contributions to the movie. That is not enough for co-authorship of a joint work.

The Constitution establishes the social policy that our construction of the statutory term "authors" carries out. The Founding Fathers gave Congress the power to give authors copyrights in order "[t]o promote the progress of Science and useful arts."[FN43] Progress would be retarded rather than promoted, if an author could not consult with others and adopt their useful suggestions without sacrificing sole ownership of the work. Too open a definition of author would compel authors to insulate themselves and maintain ignorance of the contributions others might make. Spike Lee could not consult a scholarly Muslim to make a movie about a religious conversion to Islam, and the arts would be the poorer for that.

> FN43. U.S. Const. Art. 1, § 8, cl. 8.

The broader construction that Aalmuhammed proposes would extend joint authorship to many "overreaching contributors,"[FN44] like the dramaturg in *Thomson,* and deny sole authors "exclusive authorship status simply because another person render[ed] some form of assistance."[FN45] Claimjumping by research assistants, editors, and former spouses, lovers and friends would endanger authors who talked with people about what they were doing, if creative copyrightable contribution were all that authorship required.

> FN44. *Thomson,* 147 F.3d at 200 (internal quotations omitted).

> FN45. *Id.* at 202 (citing *Childress v. Taylor,* 945 F.2d 500, 504 (1991)).

[7] Aalmuhammed also argues that issuance of a copyright registration certificate to him establishes a prima facie case for ownership. A prima facie case could not in any event prevent summary judgment in the presence of all the evidence rebutting his claim of ownership. "The presumptive validity of the certificate may be rebutted and defeated on summary judgment."[FN46] The Copyright Office stated in its response to Aalmuhammed's application for copyright (during the pendency of this litigation) that his claims "conflict with previous registration claims," and therefore the Copyright Office had "several questions" for him. One of the questions dealt with the "intent" of "other authors," i.e., Warner Brothers. The evidence discussed above establishes without genuine issue that the answers to these questions were that Warner Brothers did not intend to share ownership with Aalmuhammed.

> FN46. *S.O.S., Inc. v. Payday, Inc.,* 886 F.2d 1081, 1086 (9th Cir.1989).

Because the record before the district court established no genuine issue of fact as to Aalmuhammed's co-authorship of *Malcolm X* as a joint work, the district court correctly granted summary judgment dismissing his claims for declaratory judgment and an accounting resting on co-authorship.

. . .

---

3. Authorship in Computer Aided/Computer Generated Works

Substantial questions involving copyright are raised by works created, in whole or in part, by the use of programmed computers. Increasingly, works are created using interactive computing technologies. In many cases the processing done by the programmed machines would constitute an original literary, musical, or artistic work if it were done by a human being. The *Copyright Act* requires that the author of a work be a human being.[7] The interactive nature of computing technologies, however, can make it difficult to separate the user's contribution to the final product from the contribution of the technology to the work's originality.

---

[7] S. 5(1).

To date there has been no consensus on the question of who is the author of a work created using an interactive computing device. A person who creates a work using a computer as tool (a computer-aided work) can be an author as such person is responsible for giving form or expression to it.[8] However, a person who uses a computer to create a work where the creative contribution of the person is negligible or completely lacking (a computer-generated work) probably cannot be an author for copyright purposes.[9]

As a computer cannot be an author under the *Copyright Act* because it is not a human being, the dispute over authorship is between four parties: (i) the programmer, (ii) the provider of the data, (iii) the user, and (iv) the investor or owner, or some combination thereof.[10]

Express Newspapers Plc v. Liverpool Daily Post & Echo Plc, [1985] 3 All E.R. 680 (Ch. D.)

Before: Mr. Justice Whitford

19 February 1985

. . .

Whitford J.:

The plaintiffs, Express Newspapers Plc, seek interlocutory relief against four defendants, who are all concerned in the publication of newspapers, the particular newspapers which the defendants publish being newspapers circulating in the provinces, as I understand it. The plaintiffs' action arises out of a competition which they have been running since September of last year, which is called "Millionaire of the Month." It was in fact a successor to a previous competition which was running from September 1983 for a year, also arranged by the plaintiffs, known as "Millionaires' Club."

The nature of this competition is very fully explained in the affidavit of Mr. Shott, sworn for the plaintiffs on 14 December 1984. The Millionaires' Club having been successful, the plaintiffs decided in February of last year that they would like to run some fresh competition, and they engaged the services of a company, Simco Limited, who are in the field of devising promotional schemes of one kind and another. What they wanted was some kind of novel idea, which would be simple, would guarantee that somebody could win £1 million, and would involve this: that a person taking part in the competition would examine one of the plaintiffs' papers — the Sunday Express, the Daily Express or the Star — to check whether or not they had been lucky enough to win. A scheme was thought up. Without

---

8   *Express Newspapers Plc v. Liverpool Daily Post & Echo Plc*, [1985] F.S.R. 306 (Ch.D.).

9   *Payen Components South Africa Ltd. v. Bovic Gaskets Co.* (1995), 33 I.P.R. 406 (S.Africa C.A.).

10 Stephen Hewitt, "Copyright Claims to Computer Output in the UK," [1983] 11 E.I.P.R. 308.

going into too much detail, what it involved was this. Cards were prepared in very large numbers. They were distributed at random; a specimen is exhibit NRS. 3 to Mr. Shott's affidavit. These cards each carried a five-letter code, which could be revealed by scraping away some covering of paper.

At the start of the operation during the first two weeks in September over 20 million cards were distributed; and as many again have apparently been distributed since; in fact some distribution of these cards is still going on.

If you have got a card and you have scraped off the covering of paper, you can find out whether you have won a prize or not by looking in one of the three newspapers that I have named. With each issue of the papers in question there are published combinations of letters which will inform you whether you have won a prize or not. You can of course buy a paper, but you can look at somebody else's copy if you have the opportunity, or you can go to the reading room of a public library or some other place where any one of these papers is available. In the result of course, as Mr. Shott makes plain in his affidavit, to take part in this competition you do not have to buy a newspaper. Entry to the scheme is free; if you get a card, then you can take part.

There is no need to go into great detail about it, but the way in which you ascertain whether you have a prize or not can be readily understood by looking at another of the exhibits to Mr. Shott's first affidavit, exhibit NRS.4, which shows a typical entry — in this case it is in the Daily Express for Friday 28 September — where at the top right of the page you see the legend "Match your Card Here," with underneath a square containing twenty-five letters set out in rows of five. There are also two separate rows of five letters, one of which is seen above the Large Crossword and the other of which is seen under the words "Here's How to Win the Prize of a Lifetime"; and your chances depend on your finding upon the card that you have been sent, in the case of the letters above the Large Crossword, the corresponding letters — TMGFB — which may win you a Citroen Visa or, in the case of "Here's How to Win the Prize of a Lifetime," the letters O W M Q U, the chance to enter a draw, or, in the case of a match against the five-by-five squares, the twenty-five letters, either the letters running from top to bottom in the vertical line, when five sequences will win you £100, or from left to right — that is on the horizontal line — when five sequences will bring you £1,000, or, from the bottom left to top right along the diagonal, which could bring you £50,000, or from top left to bottom right, which will bring you £50,000. You may then reach a position where you can go on at some later stage to win £1 million.

What the defendants have done that is the subject of complaint is this. They are copying day by day into their various publications the grid and the two sequences of five letters, which in themselves provide additional prizes apart from what you can make out of reading some appropriate line of the grid.

If these grids and these sequences of five letters can be said to be copyright works, I do not understand it to be argued on the defendants' side that what they have done would not be an infringement. The defendants, however, say that there is here disclosed no copyright work. The Copyright Act 1956 provides for the giving of protection under the Act in respect of a variety of works. The only relevant heading so far as the present proceedings are concerned is "literary works." By the definition section, "literary work" includes tables; and it was not suggested by Mr. Jeffs, on the defendants' side, that a table could not be the subject of protection. It is of course accepted, because it is easily established by reference to one of a number of well-known authorities, that mathematical tables can acquire copyright protection as "literary work." They do so because their compilation — and compilations in themselves are by definition "literary work" — involves the exercise of skill and labour, or possibly maybe only labour.

That a great deal of skill and, indeed, a good deal of labour went into the production of the grid and the two separate sequences of five letters is, to my mind, quite plainly established from the evidence of Mr. Ertel, who is with an American corporation, Amphora Enterprises Inc., who were saddled with the task of preparing these grid patterns and sequences to be used in the plaintiffs' competition. Mr. Ertel's affidavit sets out in detail what he has had to do and the steps that had to be taken. He describes how participants in the competition look at the grid and see if they can match certain patterns of letters and in the same way see if they can match the sequence of five letters. He describes the difficulties that are involved in preparing these grids and five-letter sequences if you are going to arrive at a situation in which you do not get so many winning lines that the whole thing is going to become hopelessly uneconomic from the point of view of the person running the competition. He describes the constraints with which he was necessarily faced in ensuring that a sufficient number of possible winning combinations emerged to make the game attractive, without producing such a number of combinations to make the whole thing hopelessly uneconomic. He goes to some length to point out the difficulties of achieving these results. He describes also how the effort had to be made to introduce a system of some sort of check codes to avoid frauds.

What Mr. Ertel says is that he started off by seeing whether he could work out these grids by just writing down appropriate sequences of letters. It soon became apparent to him that, although this could be done, and done without too much difficulty when just producing a small number of grids, if you are going to produce sufficient for a year's supply or something of that order, it becomes a very different matter indeed. It was immediately apparent to him that the labour involved in doing this could be immensely reduced by writing out an appropriate computer program and getting the computer to run up an appropriate number of varying grids and letter sequences.

Mr. Ertel did all this. He programmed his computer; he ran out the results; he checked the results; and the steps which he had to take in this regard, which are set out in paragraphs 10 to 16 in particular of his affidavit, show that indeed the preparation of these grids and sequences of five letters involved a great deal of skill and labour.

A point was taken by Mr. Jeffs on the question of the employment of a computer, the suggestion of Mr. Jeffs being that, whatever might be the position of anything that was done before the computer was employed, although he was prepared to accept that computer programs might well be copyright works, the result produced as a consequence of running those programs was not a work of which it could truly be said that Mr. Ertel was the author.

I reject this submission. The computer was no more than the tool by which the varying grids of five-letter sequences were produced to the instructions, via the computer programs, of Mr. Ertel. It is as unrealistic as it would be to suggest that, if you write your work with a pen, it is the pen which is the author of the work rather than the person who drives the pen.

Payen Components South Africa Ltd. v. Bovic Gaskets Co. (1995), 33 I.P.R. 406 (S.Africa C.A.)

Supreme Court of South Africa — Appellate Division

Corbett CJ, Hefer, Steyn, F H Grosskopf and Schutz JJA

9, 25 May 1995

. . .

Schutz JA.

The appellant (Payen, applicant below) and the first respondent (Bovic, first respondent below) are competitors in the market for gaskets used in assembling and repairing motor vehicles. The customary aspersions are cast. Payen complains that Bovic's products are of inferior quality and that it does not keep a full range of gaskets, which allows it to concentrate on the more lucrative part of the market. The result is that it undercuts Payen. Bovic counters by ascribing Payen's higher prices to inefficiency, and charges that Payen is trying to establish a monopoly. However all that may be, the legal grounds on which Payen relies to curb Bovic's activities are copyright, unlawful competition, and, lastly and faintly, contract. There is no reliance on trade mark or passing off, although many expressions associated with these disciplines are used. Resort to the Merchandise Marks Act and the Trade Practices Act was abandoned in this court.

The second respondent (Bodell, second respondent below) is a 50% member and the controlling force in Bovic. Three further persons were cited as respondents below but the claims against them were abandoned in this court, so that their participation in these proceedings is now confined to their claim for costs.

The activity of which Payen complains is the use by Bovic in its price lists and catalogues and on the wrappers containing its gaskets of the Payen code for identifying the huge range of gaskets in use in South Africa. Each code consists of five digits, the first two being letters and the other three numbers. The first letter indicates the type of gasket, so that, for instance, all cylinder head gaskets commence with an A or a B. To give examples of complete codes, AF 240 denotes a cylinder head gasket for an Alfa Romeo 1300, and CJ 494, a head set for a Nissan L 185. There is nothing novel about such a system, but its utility is such that Bovic contends that it has become the language of the trade when identifying gaskets, so much so that it is necessary for any trader to use it (so it is contended).

Copyright work?

First, the facts. Payen's essentially uncontested case is based on the evidence of five witnesses, Ellis, Thomas and Butler who depose to the code's English origins, and Parker-Nance and Galloway who describe its South African adaptations and accretions.

Companies not only enjoy perpetual succession but some also undergo changes of name and parentage. The "Payen Group" in the United Kingdom is a good example, which tends to render the exposition following rather tortuous.

Coopers Mechanical Joints Ltd (CMJ) was a subsidiary of another Payen Group company, namely Engineering Components Ltd (EC). The coding system for gaskets in use in 1970, although partly computer based, was unsatisfactory in several respects. One Machin, the management services manager of EC, tackled the problem first. What he did was to work out the mathematical basis for what was to become the new Payen coding system. He prepared a table of significance (the table) which contains an outline of the later system, although there were some departures from the outline. The table is skeletonic in form and is in no sense the final embodiment of the work. No copyright was claimed in it. It is neither a catalogue nor a price list.

The next step was taken by one Butler, the chief systems analyst working at EC under Machin. Using the table he "devised a computer program for allocating new reference numbers in place of the old" (the program). That is all that we are told about this important step.

Thomas took over the coordination of the project in October 1971. The old numbers were grouped in accordance with the classes of gasket, which were described. This data which was to be fed into the computer was then meticulously checked and re-arranged. Then, to quote the words of Thomas, also echoed by Butler, "the data was entered into the computer to generate new numbers in accordance with (the) program devised by Mr Butler". That is all we are told about this other important step. Although the bulk of the new numbers was generated in this way, a significant part was formulated manually. This was done "by the staff of the Payen technical department" where the old number was not in the standard format. This technical department appears to have been that of EC.

The next important step is not expressly stated at all, namely the printing out by the computer of the list of new numbers. However, I suppose that it is implicit in the narration. What followed next, after many months, was two lists giving cross-references from the old numbers to the new, and the new to the old (the lists). They were first used internally and were then published in February and

April 1972. Although there is confusion and contradiction in the affidavits it seems that it is the originals that no longer survive, not the printed ones. Five named persons prepared these lists. They were all British subjects employed by EC and CMJ. The lists were necessary for the transitional period.

They were used for the preparation of the first master catalogue, which was published in October 1972. The format was that of the old catalogue but the numbers were new. Four other named persons prepared it. They too were British subjects and employees of EC or CMJ. All the later catalogues were based on the 1972 master.

After a master list had been entered into the computer it was thereafter kept up to date. This work was done by Butler and employees of EC, CMJ and Coopers Payen Ltd (CP — the new name for CMJ after 1980, and thus still a subsidiary of EC).

As both South Africa and the United Kingdom give effect to the Berne Convention the various Payen companies and their employees are to be treated as if they were here.

Although there is a challenge on the point by Bovic, I think that it is obvious from the recitation of the facts so far that the preparation of the new English catalogue involved much labour and at least some skill.

On 11 March 1988 EC and CP (formerly CMJ) assigned copyright and rights of a like nature in the numbering system to Payen International Ltd (PI). EC is the wholly owned subsidiary of PI. What was not ceded was Butler's program. What was ceded was the "original works" consisting of the table, the 1972 and later catalogues, the computer printout of the summer of 1971 (here mentioned with Butler as the author), and the "New Reference/Old Reference". This last pair and the printout are shown as having been authored by Butler and being no longer in existence. Their best available reference is given as the "Interchange Lists February and April 1972". This last no doubt refers to the published cross-reference lists, whereas the "New Reference/Old Reference" presumably refers to the original manuscript or part manuscript form.

Although Payen (the applicant — Payen Components South Africa Ltd, a subsidiary of PI's holding company Turner and Newall Ltd) has been the exclusive licensee of the numbering system for a long time, a written licensing agreement was concluded with PI (by now the copyright holder) only in 1989. Nemo dat quod non habet. Payen's rights can be no better than PI's rights.

Parker-Nance has been involved in the production of the South African version of the catalogues and price lists using the new system since the first local edition in 1973. It had to be adapted to the South African market and has had to be kept up to date. Doing this has entailed "a vast amount of work". Among other things he has to keep abreast of new models as also modifications. New gaskets are referred either to CP in the United Kingdom or Components Eastern Ltd ("our Far East associate") depending on the country of origin of the new engine. Numbers are allocated by the one or other of those companies. The new numbers are then included in the catalogue. Nothing more is said about the nature of the association with the Far East associate. One additional task has had to be undertaken in South Africa, namely the translation of the material into Afrikaans.

The catalogue cum price list is a kind as may qualify as a "literary work" in the generous sense that that phrase is used in copyright law. Moreover it has been "written down" in a material form. Further, there has been enough labour and skill expended both in England and South Africa for the same to be "original", in the sense of copyright law.

Mr Ginsburg, for Bovic, raises two contentions, both related to authorship. The first goes along these lines. Except in those cases where the law provides otherwise, for copyright to subsist it must be possible to identify a human author. Here there was no human author, as the author was a computer. Even though a computer program may qualify as a literary work, Butler's program cannot be relied upon because it has not been infringed. It is a completely different work from the printout or its successors. That, no doubt, is why it has not been relied upon by Payen. Nor has it even been assigned to PI. The program, so the argument proceeds, was the thing that mattered. It was what made or allowed the computer to do what it did. It was the "author" of the printout. Butler was merely the author of the program not the printout. This argument is not dependent upon its being only in 1992 that separate provision was made in our statutes for copyright protection for computer programs, which before qualified, if they qualified at all, as "literary works" in the ordinary way: *Northern Office Micro Computers Pty Ltd v Rosenstein* 1981 (4) SA 123(C).

Mr Ginsburg relies on one English case, *Express Newspapers Plc v Liverpool Daily Post & Echo Plc* [1985] 1 WLR 1089 (Ch); FSR 306 and two foreign textbooks, Laddie, Prescott and Vitoria, *The Modern Law of Copyright*, p 94 and Dworkin, *Blackstone's Guide to the Copyright Designs and Patents Act 1988* p 47. A distinction is drawn between "computer aided" and "computer generated" works. In the former case the computer is a mere tool like a pen or word processor. In the latter the work of creation is performed by the computer itself with relatively little human input. Perhaps it should be noted that the computer which Butler used was used in 1971 when computers had not yet been taught to do all the remarkable things they now do.

Dworkin describes a computer generated work in these terms (op cit p 47):

> The computer-generated category is really aimed at more sophisticated devices such as those now beginning to be marketed whereby a computer can produce to order an original piece of music in the style of a known composer.

And again at pp 185-6:

> There is now a crucial distinction between a computer-aided work, as in the above case (the *Express Newspapers* case), and a computer-generated work. The latter work is one which is created without expenditure of significant human skill and effort in the completed work. For example, the compilation of new crossword puzzles, moves generated by computer chess programs or computer-generated original pieces of music in the style of a known composer. The steps to be taken by the

operator of the machine may be so trivial that it is difficult on normal principles to say that he or she is the author. The real creative work is done by the person who devises the original computer program, but it would be inconvenient and misleading to treat that programmer in all cases as the owner of the copyright in the new works which his program produces, eg in all the new music produced by the various programs which are sold to the public.

Laddie, op cit, says at p 94:

> There may be cases where the real work has been done by the computer, the human contribution being too trivial or not sufficiently related to the work that has emerged. Suppose a computer linked directly to a large number of meteorological instruments and programmed automatically to print out a weather chart on demand. It seems factually wrong to contend that the deviser of the program is the "author" of the chart. He may have died many years ago, the program may have been bought in from an independent software house, yet every day quite different charts are printed out. (It is true that the programmer's labour and ingenuity are in a sense responsible for the chart; but in that sense so are the efforts of the designers of the computer itself; for that matter, so are those of the inventor of the barometer.) It is perhaps even more artificial to argue that the operator is the author: the only skill and labour he had employed is ensuring that the flow or programs and data to the machine is maintained. It might be said that the real author is the owner or hirer of the computer who has expended the capital in setting up and operating the system; but such a person is probably a body corporate, and if considered to be the "author", would enjoy a potentially perpetual copyright.

The *Express* case was concerned with a competition entitled "Millionaire of the Month" published in three newspapers with a view to increasing circulation. Numerous cards, each carrying a five-letter code, were distributed free and at random to members of the public. In order to see whether or not they had won a prize those taking part in the competition could check the cards against grids containing 25 letters and two separate rows of five letters which were published daily. Various prizes were offered to lucky winners. Another newspaper copied the scheme as it was, and an infringement action was brought. The manner in which the scheme had been prepared for the plaintiff was fully explained in the affidavits. What had to be done was to produce a large number of combinations which would suffice for a year or so, while at the same time ensuring that there would not be too many winners. The description proceeds (at 1093C):

> What Mr Ertel says is that he started off by seeing whether he could work out these grids by just writing down appropriate sequences of letters. It soon became apparent to him that, although this could be done, and done without too much difficulty when just producing a small number of grids, if you are going to produce sufficient for a year's supply or something of that order, it becomes a very different matter indeed. It was immediately apparent to him that the labour involved in doing this could be immensely reduced by writing out an appropriate computer program and getting the computer to run up an appropriate number of varying grids and letter sequences.
>
> Mr Ertel did all this. He programmed his computer; he ran out the results; he checked the results; and the steps which he had to take in this regard show that

indeed the preparation of these grids and sequences of five letters involved a great deal of skill and labour.

The point taken before Whitford J and the manner in which he disposed of it are contained in these words (at 1093):

> A point was taken by Mr Jeffs on the question of the employment of a computer, the suggestion of Mr Jeffs being that, whatever might be the position of anything that was done before the computer was employed, although he was prepared to accept that computer programs might well be copyright works, the result produced as a consequence a running those programs, was not a work of which it could truly be said that Mr Ertel was the author.

> I reject this submission. The computer was no more than the tool by which the varying grids of five-letter sequences were produced to the instructions, via the computer programs, of Mr Ertel. It is unrealistic as it would be to suggest that, if you write your work with a pen, it is the pen which is the author of the work rather than the person who drives the pen.

The distinction between computer generated and computer aided works drawn in these writings seems to me to be valid and such as should be recognised here. It may be of importance in cases where ownership and duration of copyright are in issue, and bears upon this case because the question whether copyright did nor did not vest in 1971 or 1972 must be decided with reference to the Copyright Act 63 of 1964: see s 43 of the Copyright Act 98 of 1978 as interpreted in *Appleton v Harnischfeger Corp* 1995 (2) SA 247(A) at 260E and 261G-H.

This brings me back to the facts. Has Payen proved that there was a human author, in other words that the printout was not computer generated? In answering this question it is necessary first to observe that the facts set out by Payen are extremely sparse at some critical points. Also that computer literacy is not to be assumed in persons over 50, as most judges are. Copyright is a technical subject and it is essential that a party trying to prove it establishes the technical points necessary for his claim: *Vagar (t/a Rajshree Release) v Transavalon Pty Ltd (t/a Avalon Cinema)* 1977 (3) SA 766(W) at 775C.

However, I consider that enough evidence has been produced. After the computer had received the data what remained was essentially an arithmetic function including the requirement that there should be no duplication.

Mr Ginsburg's second point was that Payen has not proved what the original "work" was, a matter sometimes interwoven with the paramount question of identifying the author, as is pointed out in Dean, *Handbook of South African Copyright Law*, 1-15. It is true that Mr Puckrin, for the applicant, had difficulty in pinpointing at what point the original work came into existence, and there were even contradictions in his argument. This is not surprising given the sketchiness of the affidavits at some places. But there is, I think enough, just enough, to get him home. The first printout was the basis of all that followed. What was added or changed thereafter was done by employees of the assignors or of Payen. Problems that might have arisen if this had not been so do not arise. Nor do I think that the fact that later numbers are supplied by CP or Components

Eastern Ltd affects the result. There is clearly a need for international uniformity in numbers. The process seems to be no more or no less than adding or removing items in a railway timetable on the basis of information supplied. What Payen is doing is maintaining an up-to-date compilation.

For these reasons I consider that Payen has proved copyright in its catalogue cum price list.

. . .

Telstra Corporation Limited v Phone Directories Company Pty Ltd, [2010] FCAFC 149

Judges: KEANE CJ, PERRAM AND YATES JJ

Date of judgment: 15 December 2010

KEANE CJ:

1 In Australia copyright is a creature of the *Copyright Act 1968* (Cth) (the Act). The monopoly in copyright subsists only insofar as the Act provides. Because the terms of the Act reflect the intention of the *Berne Convention for the Protection of Literary and Artistic Works* to protect the rights of authors, copyright subsists in a literary work only by virtue of the authorship of that work by an individual or individuals. It may be that if the author of a work is the employee of another person, ownership of the copyright may vest in the employer; but copyright in a literary work can subsist only if it originates from an individual. This case highlights the difficulty confronting a claim to copyright in a literary work which is compiled by an automated process.

2 In these proceedings, the learned trial judge determined, as an issue separate from the other issues in the case, the question whether copyright subsists under the Act in the White Pages Directory (WPD) and the Yellow Pages Directory (YPD) published by Telstra Corporation Limited and Sensis Pty Ltd (the appellants). The question concerned regional WPDs and YPDs dating back to the year 2000 for 11 different regional areas of Australia. Her Honour determined the question in the negative.

3 The appellants' case is that each WPD and YPD is an original literary work. In particular, each directory is said to be a compilation consisting of the expression of the information in individual listings in their particular form and arrangement and in the overall arrangement of the individual listings, and, additionally in the case of the YPD, in the cross-referencing of the information under subject matter headings.

4 Numerous individuals, some identified and some not, contributed to the work preparatory to the compilation of each of the WPDs and YPDs, but the

compilations were brought into the form in which they were published primarily by an automated computerised process. No claim was made by the appellants to copyright in the computer database or software.

5 The trial judge approached the determination of the question by reference to the decision of the High Court of Australia in *IceTV Pty Limited v Nine Network Australia Pty Limited* (2009) 239 CLR 458. Her Honour held at [2010] FCA 44 at [5]:

> For the reasons that follow, copyright does not subsist in any Work. None is an original literary work. By way of summary:
>
> 1. among the many contributors to each Work, the Applicants have not and cannot identify who provided the necessary authorial contribution to each Work. The Applicants concede there are numerous non-identified persons who "contributed" to each Work (including third party sources);
>
> 2. even if the human or humans who "contributed" to each Work were capable of being identified (and they are not), much of the contribution to each Work:
>
>   2.1 was not "independent intellectual effort" (*IceTV* 254 ALR 386 at [33]) and further or alternatively, "sufficient effort of a literary nature" (*IceTV* 254 ALR 386 at [99]) for those who made a contribution to be considered an author of the Work within the meaning of the Copyright Act;
>
>   2.2 further or alternatively, was anterior to the Work first taking its "material form" (*IceTV* 254 ALR 386 at [102]);
>
>   2.3 was not the result of human authorship but was computer generated;
>
> 3. the Works cannot be considered as "original works" because the creation of each Work did not involve "independent intellectual effort" (*IceTV* 254 ALR 386 at [33]) and / or the exercise of "sufficient effort of a literary nature": *IceTV* 254 ALR 386 at [99]; see also *IceTV* 254 ALR 386 at [187]-[188].

6 In this Court, the principal argument of the appellants is that, because each directory is a literary work published in Australia, the only question to be answered is whether it is an original literary work; this question can be answered, they say, without identifying any particular author much less all the authors. That is said to be because copyright in a work first published in Australia can subsist by virtue of s 32(2)(c) of the Act if the work is original in the sense of not being a copy. The appellants contend that it can be inferred that intellectual effort of some kind was applied by some individual or individuals in the production of each directory so that it can be said to be an original literary work. They argue that, neither the decision in *IceTV*, nor the reasons given by the High Court in that case, compels, or points to, a different conclusion in this case.

7 The principal contention of the respondents is that the directories were compiled, not by the individuals engaged to facilitate the process, but by a computerised process of storing, selecting, ordering and arranging the data to produce the directories in the form in which they were published.

8 In my respectful opinion, the principal contention of the respondents should be accepted, and the decision of the trial judge should be upheld for that reason.

...

31 The trial judge concluded that the compilation of the directories was essentially an automated process. Her Honour said at [334]-[335]:

> [A]lthough the Applicants tendered 91 affidavits from individuals who were said to be "authors" of one or more of the Works, the affidavits did not cover the range of people who would have made a contribution to the Works or cover the entire period the subject of the claim. Moreover, some of the 91 individuals had a limited (or non-existent) role in contributing to the Sample Directories and of those who did contribute, the nature of the contribution was certainly not of a nature to be described as "independent intellectual effort" or "sufficient effort of a literary nature".
>
> Moreover, these affidavits made clear that there are substantial parts of the directories that do not have human authors...are automated to the extent that human involvement is minor...or have authors who cannot be ascertained (for example, much of the rollover component of the directories...).

32 In relation to whether the directories were original works, the automated nature of the process again loomed large. The trial judge said at [340]-[344]:

...

> Authorship and originality are correlatives. The question of whether copyright subsists is concerned with the particular form of expression of the work. You must identify authors, and those authors must direct their contribution (assessed as either an "independent intellectual effort" of a "sufficient effort of a literary nature") to the particular form of expression of the work. Start with the work. Find its authors. They must have done something, howsoever defined, that can be considered original. The Applicants have failed to satisfy these conditions. Whether originality be the product of some "independent intellectual effort" and / or the exercise of "sufficient effort of a literary nature", or involve a "creative spark" or the exercise of "skill and judgment", it is not evident in the claim made by the Applicants.

33 The trial judge rejected an alternative claim by the appellants that the directories were the product of joint authorship on the part of all the individuals whose efforts contributed to the production process. Her Honour said, at [337]-[338]:

> ...Even if the authors of the Works could be identified with sufficient clarity and certainty (and they cannot), the people suggested to be the authors of the Works did not exercise "independent intellectual effort" and / or "sufficient effort of a literary nature". A majority of the creation process of the WPD and the YPD was heavily automated. Human intervention was regulated and controlled according to either the various computer systems in place including the Rules...Further, the contribution of the people suggested to be authors of the Works was anterior to the work taking its material form. Very few people had any part to play in the final presentation of the Works or the *particular form of expression of the information*. Those people, again, could not have been said to have exercised "independent intellectual effort" and / or "sufficient effort of a literary nature"... (Original emphasis.)

...

89 The compilation of the directories was overwhelmingly the work of the Genesis Computer System or its predecessors. The selection of data and its arrangement in the form presented in each directory occurred only at "the book extract" or "book production" process. The compilations which emerged from the operation of the computer system do not originate from an individual or group of individuals. Indeed, none of the individuals who contributed to the production of the directories had any conception of the actual form in which they were finally expressed.

90 In my respectful opinion, the decision of the trial judge must be upheld on the basis that the findings of primary fact made by her Honour establish that the WPDs and YPDs are not compiled by individuals but by the automated processes of the Genesis Computer System or its predecessors. That being so, it is neither necessary nor relevant to seek to come to a conclusion as to the sufficiency of the intellectual effort deployed by those individuals who provide data input to the computerised database. Their activities are not part of the activity of compilation: they do not select, arrange and present that data in the form in which it is published.

JOINT AUTHORSHIP

91 I respectfully agree with the trial judge that the directories cannot be regarded as a work of joint authorship.

92 The contributions of individuals discussed in her Honour's findings may have been precursors to the compilation of the directories but they were not part of the actual compilation. Moreover, the work of these individuals was not collaborative. It was, no doubt, organised to facilitate the production of the directories but this organisation was not collaboration of the kind contemplated by the definition of joint authorship, and the contribution of each of the groups of individuals referred to earlier was made quite separately.

CONCLUSION AND ORDERS

95 In my respectful opinion, the decision of the trial judge was correct.

96 The reasons of the High Court in *IceTV* authoritatively establish that the focus of attention in relation to the subsistence of copyright is not upon a general concern to prevent misappropriation of skill and labour but upon the protection of copyright in literary works which originate from individuals. In this case copyright was said to subsist in the directories as compilations, but the directories were not compiled by individuals.

97 In *IceTV* the High Court recognised, at [52] and [135]-[139], that this focus may give rise to a perception of injustice on the part of those whose skill and labour has been appropriated. Whether or not that means that legislative reform of the kind adopted in the European Union by the Directive of the European Parliament and of the Council on the Legal Protection of Databases is warranted is a matter for the legislature. This Court can give effect to the statutory monopoly conferred by the Act only in conformity with the terms of the Act.

The appeal must be dismissed with costs.

YATES J:

129 I agree that the appeal should be dismissed.

130 In my view the primary judge was correct in concluding that the relevant compilations in the White Pages Directories (WPDs) and the Yellow Pages Directories (YPDs) for particular regions, as published by the appellants, were not original literary works for copyright purposes. The primary judge advanced a number of reasons for coming to that conclusion, including that much of the contribution to each work was not the result of human authorship but was computer-generated: at [5(2.3)]. In my view that finding alone justified the conclusion to which her Honour came on the question of copyright subsistence and is determinative of this appeal.

...

134 In relation to works, an author is, under Australian law, a human author. So much is made clear (if it be doubted) by s 33 of the Act which conditions the duration of copyright on the year of the author's death....

135 Significantly authorship (as it is understood in the context of works) plays no role in relation to the subsistence of copyright in subject-matter other than works. In that milieu the *making* of the subject-matter can play a central role: see ss 89(2), 90(2) and 91 of the Act in relation to sound recordings, cinematograph films, television broadcasts and sound broadcasts, which fix on the *making* of the relevant subject-matter by a qualified person who may be, in this context, a body corporate incorporated under a law of the Commonwealth or of a State. First publication in Australia can also play a role in relation to the subsistence of copyright in that subject-matter: see ss 89(3) and 90(3). In the case of published editions of works, copyright will subsist if the first publication of the edition took place in Australia or if the publisher was a qualified person (including a qualified person that is a body corporate) at the date of the first publication of the edition: see s 92(1).

136 Under United Kingdom copyright legislation, specific recognition is given to works that are computer-generated. In the case of literary, dramatic, musical or artistic works that are computer-generated, the author is taken to be the person by whom the arrangements necessary for the creation of the work were undertaken: see s 9(3) of the *Copyright, Designs and Patents Act 1988* (UK). This conceptual framework is akin to that adopted in Australian copyright law with respect to subject-matter other than works. However, it has no corresponding recognition in Australian copyright law as it pertains to works.

...

164 The starting point must be the identification of the alleged copyright work. That starting point is critical because it is only at that point that one can ask and then consider the question: is this an *original* work? It is only by looking back from that vantage point that one can identify and assess the nature and quality

of the acts that can be said to contribute to the material form of the work for which copyright is claimed. In the case of a compilation the relevant acts are of those who gather or organise the collection of material and who select, order or arrange its fixation in material form: *Ice TV* at [99]; see also *Waterlow Publishers Ltd v Rose* (1989) 17 IPR 493 at 500. Of necessity, those acts must be the acts of an author or authors.

...

166 In my view the work of the second appellant's employees is relevant to the consideration of whether each work, as a compilation, was an original literary work for copyright purposes. However, as I have noted, this work was more in the nature of collecting, entering and manipulating data to provide the fabric (the Genesis Computer System database) out of which each identified compilation in the WPDs and YPDs was to be fashioned. In this sense it can be seen that those activities contributed to the making of each claimed copyright work. However, significantly, the selection, ordering and arrangement of information to fix the compilation in its material form was computer-generated by the Genesis Computer System.

167 Contrary to the appellants' submission, the Genesis Computer System was not a mere tool utilised by the second appellant's employees for this purpose. To describe the functioning of the system in this way obscures the fact that the activities carried out by the Genesis Computer System in the "Book Extract" process were transformative steps that were obviously fundamental to the making of the compilation in each case. It was those activities that resulted in each compilation taking the form that it did. Those activities replaced what would otherwise have been, no doubt, the extensive work of individuals deploying their respective intellectual resources and capacities to select, order and arrange the listings as they appeared in each WPD or YPD, albeit in accordance with specifically mandated rules and procedures. When carried out by individuals, activities of this kind undoubtedly would have been of an authorial nature and would have been counted as an essential contribution to the making of the compilation in each case. However, in the present case, these activities, essentially, were not those of an author for copyright purposes. The appellants, no doubt for good commercial reasons, effectively supplanted the involvement of authors in carrying out those transformative steps.

168 In this connection it is not to the point that the second appellant's employees were also involved (as the appellants submitted) in selecting, customising, maintaining and operating the computer systems that were deployed in the production of the directories, including particularly in relation to the "Book Extract" process. Those activities are akin to educating, training or instructing individuals, and maintaining a sufficient number of them, to carry out the discrete activities of selecting, ordering and arranging material to create the individual compilations. However, the two bodies of activity should not be confused for one another. It may well be, of course, that the activities of the second appellant's employees, in this regard, have resulted in the creation of other works (for example, a computer

program or a compilation of computer programs) that are protected by copyright. However, no such claims have been made in this proceeding.

169 No doubt questions of fact and degree are involved in forming a judgment about whether a work is an original work for copyright purposes: see, for example, the effect of the authorities summarised in *Desktop Marketing* by Lindgren J at [160] (proposition 7). Similar questions arise in forming a judgment about authorship: *IceTV* at [99]. Leaving aside the possibility of non-authorial contributions that are, overall, and in context, insignificant or inconsequential, it is essential to a finding of originality for copyright purposes that the work be one that is properly characterised as originating from an author or authors. In my view, the compilations claimed in this case cannot bear that characterisation. The contribution of the essentially computer-generated "Book Extract" process was of such overwhelming significance to the expression in material form of each compilation that none of the compilations can be properly characterised, overall, as a work that originates from an author or authors, even though elements of authorial contribution are present. It follows, in my view, that none of the works can be an original work for copyright purposes. Thus copyright cannot subsist in those works.

...

Chapter 5

MORAL RIGHTS

Authorship gives rise to copyright, as we have seen, but it is also the basis of a separate species of "moral right" that vests in the author. The economic rights that copyright protects treat the work as an object to be owned, exploited or alienated as the owner so chooses. Moral rights, in contrast, recognize the author's work as an extension of the author, as an embodiment of her will or personality, that deserves protection and remains inherently tied to the author notwithstanding the ownership or transfer of economic rights. The concept of the author's moral right eschews pure utilitarianism in favour of a more romantic notion of authorial dignity as the source of entitlement. Consequently, moral rights occupy an interesting position in copyright law and policy, exemplifying the tension between competing visions of copyright's purpose. Whereas moral rights, which descend from the civil tradition, fit harmoniously with the notion of the "droit d'auteur", they bear an uneasy relationship to the more instrumental common law copyright system. As such, moral rights have not flourished to the same extent in common law jurisdictions, where protection has been more limited and more controversial. Because Canada's original copyright legislation substantially tracked the *British Copyright Act 1911*, it has traditionally been more concerned with economic than moral rights.[1] However, Canada's mixed common-civil law tradition has ensured the continued relevance of the latter as an important component of the copyright "balance".

It is generally considered that moral rights comprise four characteristics: (1) the right to disclosure, (2) the right to the respective name which is also referred to as paternity rights, (3) the right to respect of the work or the right to the integrity thereof, and finally, (4) the right to retract or withdraw subject to compensating the assignee for any losses incurred. The Canadian Act however, only recognizes the right to integrity and paternity rights.[2] The Act expressly confers upon authors of works the right to "the integrity of the work" and the right, where reasonable in the circumstances, "to be associated with the work as its author by name or under a pseudonym and the right to remain anonymous".[3]

An author's right to the integrity of a work is infringed only if the work, to the prejudice of the honour or reputation of the author, (a) is distorted, mutilated, or otherwise modified; or (b) is used in association with a product, service, cause or institution. The section does not require the plaintiff to

---

1   *Théberge v. Galerie d'Art du Petit Champlain inc.* (2002), 17 C.P.R. (4th) 161 (S.C.C.).
2   *Desputeaux v. éditions Shouette* (1987) Inc., (2001), 16 C.P.R. (4th) 77, [2001] J.Q. No. 1510, [2001] R.J.Q. 945, (C.A.), leave to appeal allowed (2001), 2001 CarswellQue 2452, (note) (S.C.C.).
3   *Copyright Act*, s. 14.1(1). (3).

prove prejudice to his honour or reputation; rather, it must be proved that the work was distorted, mutilated or otherwise modified "to the prejudice of the honour or reputation of the author". This provision has been interpreted as being a subjective criterion — the author's opinion — in assessing whether an infringement is prejudicial. However, whether a distortion, mutilation or other modification is prejudicial to an author's honour or reputation also requires an objective evaluation of the prejudice based on public or expert opinion. It seems clear, at least by negative implication, that a modification of a work which does not in fact prejudice the honour or reputation of the author was intended by Parliament not to infringe the author's moral rights.

Moral rights in a work may not be assigned by an author but may be waived in whole or in part.[4] Under the Act, an assignment of copyright in a work does not by that act alone constitute a waiver of any moral rights.[5]

Theberge v. Galerie d'art due Petit Champlain, 2002 SCC 34

Supreme Court of Canada

McLachlin C.J.C., L'Heureux-Dubé, Gonthier, Iacobucci, Major, Binnie, LeBel JJ.

Heard: October 11, 2001
Judgment: March 28, 2002

. . .

Binnie J.:

. . .

2   Claude Théberge, a well-established Canadian painter with an international reputation, seeks to stop the appellants, who amongst other things produce poster art, from transferring authorized reproductions of his artistic works from a paper substrate (or support) to a canvas substrate for purposes of resale. In my opinion, for the reasons which follow, the appellants did not thereby "copy" the respondent's artistic works. They purchased lawfully reproduced posters of his paintings and used a chemical process that allowed them to lift the ink layer from the paper (leaving it blank) and to display it on canvas. They were within their rights to do so as owners of the physical posters (which lawfully incorporated the copyrighted expression). At the end of the day, no new reproductions of the respondent's works were brought into existence. Nor, in my view, was there production (or reproduction) of a new artistic work "in any material form" within the meaning of s. 3(1) of the *Copyright Act*. What began as a poster, authorized by the respondent, remained a poster.

---

4   Section 14.1(2).
5   Section 14.1(3).

3 Nevertheless, on August 19, 1999, the respondent arranged to have the bailiff seize canvas-backed reproductions from the appellants without ever satisfying a judge that the appellants had violated the *Copyright Act*. Although seizure before judgment is designed purely as a conservation measure divorced from the merits of the case, the appellants claim that the seizure of their inventory caused them a significant loss, both in sales and reputation. The respondent has not proceeded with his action on the merits since the date of the seizure two and a half years ago.

4 I find myself in respectful disagreement with the conclusion of my colleague Gonthier J. In my view, the seizure was not authorized by the *Copyright Act*. The pre-judgment seizure provisions of Article 734 of the Quebec *Code of Civil Procedure*, R.S.Q., c. C-25 were thus not an available remedy. The seizure was therefore wrongful. I would allow the appeal.

I. The Nature of Copyright

5 Copyright in this country is a creature of statute and the rights and remedies it provides are exhaustive: *Compo Co. v. Blue Crest Music Inc.* (1979), [1980] 1 S.C.R. 357 (S.C.C.), at p. 373; *R. v. Stewart*, [1988] 1 S.C.R. 963 (S.C.C.); *Bishop v. Stevens*, [1990] 2 S.C.R. 467 (S.C.C.), at p. 477.

6 This is not to say that Canadian copyright law lives in splendid isolation from the rest of the world. Canada has adhered to the *Berne Convention for the Protection of Literary and Artistic Works* (1886) and subsequent revisions and additions, and other international treaties on the subject including the *Universal Copyright Convention* (1952). In light of the globalization of the so-called "cultural industries", it is desirable, within the limits permitted by our own legislation, to harmonize our interpretation of copyright protection with other like-minded jurisdictions. That being said, there are some continuing conceptual differences between the *droit d'auteur* of the continental *civiliste* tradition and the English copyright tradition, and these differences seem to lie at the root of the misunderstanding which gave rise to the present appeal.

7 I acknowledge, at the outset, that there is a significant difference in appearance between a paper-backed poster and a canvas-backed poster. The question is whether for present purposes creating this difference by mechanical transfer from one substrate or backing to another violates the Act. The respondent must find authority for the seizure in the *Code of Civil Procedure* read in light of the *Copyright Act*. If he cannot find authority in the legislation, then it does not exist and the seizure was wrongful.

II. The Respondent's Copyright

8 The respondent easily meets the first hurdle, which is to satisfy the statutory requirements for a copyright. There is no doubt that his talent is embodied in artistic works of great originality. These works were protected by copyright from the moment of their expression, without any requirement of registration or other formality on his part. The protection extends not only to the original

painting ("artistic work") but also to subsequent copies which embody the work. The respondent is thus entitled to the full measure of protection the Act allows. The question, however, is whether he went too far in obtaining a seizure before judgment of works which he, necessarily viewing the matter in his own interest, found to be infringing.

9 In my view, with respect, my colleague Gonthier J. gives too little scope to the property rights of the purchaser who owns the poster, i.e., the physical object incorporating the copyrighted expression, and excessive rights to the artist who authorized the printing and sale of the poster purchased.

10 More specifically, I think that if modification of these posters were to give rise to any legitimate objection on the part of the artist, it must be as a result of violation of his "moral" right to the integrity of his work. In that regard, however, my colleague Gonthier J. and I are in agreement that seizure before trial is not a remedy available in an action based on the alleged breach of the artist's "moral" right in a work.

III. The Content of the Respondent's Rights Under the Copyright Act

11 The Act provides the respondent with both economic and "moral" rights to his work. The distinction between the two types of rights and their respective statutory remedies is crucial.

12 Generally speaking, Canadian copyright law has traditionally been more concerned with economic than moral rights. Our original Act, which came into force in 1924, substantially tracked the English *Copyright Act, 1911* (U.K.), 1 & 2 Geo. 5, c. 46. The principal economic benefit to the artist or author was (and is) the "sole right to produce or reproduce the work or any substantial part thereof in any material form whatever" (s. 3(1)) for his or her life plus fifty years (s. 6). The economic rights are based on a conception of artistic and literary works essentially as articles of commerce. (Indeed, the initial *Copyright Act, 1709* (U.K.), 8 Anne, c. 19, was passed to assuage the concerns of printers, not authors.) Consistently with this view, such rights can be bought and sold either wholly or partially, and either generally or subject to territorial limitations, and either for the whole term of the copyright or for any part thereof (s. 13(4)). The owner of the copyright, thus, can be, but need not be, the author of the work. It was the respondent's economic rights in enumerated works that were the subject matter of an assignment to two poster manufacturers, Éditions Galerie L'Imagerie É.G.I. Ltée (herein "É.G.I.") by contract dated October 29, 1996, and New York Graphic Society, Ltd. by contract dated February 3, 1997.

13 We are told that all of the reproductions at issue here were printed by É.G.I., art. 19 of whose contract with the respondent provided that:

> [TRANSLATION] 19- Free use of the product
>
> The product is offered for sale without restriction as to use, i.e. it may be framed, laminated or combined with other products and such uses shall not be considered

to have generated products or sub-products other than those provided for in this contract.

14 The appellants were not party to this contract, but I agree with my colleague Gonthier J. that its terms may nevertheless be relevant in determining to what extent the respondent assigned away his economic rights under the *Copyright Act*, and to what extent he still holds them. É.G.I., it is noted, is not a party to this proceeding. The only *economic* rights the respondent can assert under the Act are those rights that he has retained. Accepting, as I do, my colleague's interpretation of the É.G.I. contract to the effect that the respondent (rather than É.G.I.) retained the right to bring this action, the respondent must still establish a breach by the appellants of s. 3(1) of the Act.

15 Moral rights, by contrast, descend from the civil law tradition. They adopt a more elevated and less dollars and cents view of the relationship between an artist and his or her work. They treat the artist's *oeuvre* as an extension of his or her personality, possessing a dignity which is deserving of protection. They focus on the artist's right (which by s. 14.1(2) is not assignable, though it may be waived) to protect throughout the duration of the economic rights (even where these have been assigned elsewhere) both the integrity of the work and his or her authorship of it (or anonymity, as the author wishes).

16 The *civiliste* tradition surfaced at an early date in this Court in *Le Sueur v. Morang & Co.* (1911), 45 S.C.R. 95 (S.C.C.), where Fitzpatrick C.J. approached the interpretation of a contract between a publisher and the author of an unpublished work on William Lyon Mackenzie with the civil law notions of "*droit moral*" in mind, at pp. 97-98:

> I cannot agree that the sale of the manuscript of a book is subject to the same rules as the sale of any other article of commerce, *e.g.*, paper, grain or lumber. The vendor of such things loses all dominion over them when once the contract is executed and the purchaser may deal with the thing which he has purchased as he chooses. It is his to keep, to alienate or to destroy. But ... [a]fter the author has parted with his pecuniary interest in the manuscript, he retains a species of personal or moral right in the product of his brain.

17 The important feature of moral rights in the present statute is that the integrity of the work is infringed only if the work is modified *to the prejudice of the honour or reputation of the author* (s. 28.2(1)). Given the importance of this condition in construing the scheme of the Act as a whole, I set out the relevant provisions:

> 28.2 (1) The author's right to the integrity of a work is infringed only if the work is, <u>to the prejudice of the honour or reputation of the author,</u>
>
> · (a) distorted, mutilated <u>or otherwise modified</u>; or
>
> (b) used in association with a product, service, cause or institution.
>
> (2) In the case of a painting, sculpture or engraving, the prejudice referred to in subsection (1) shall be deemed to have occurred as a result of any distortion, mutilation or other modification of the work.
>
> (3) For the purposes of this section,

(a) a change in the location of a work, the physical means by which a work is exposed or the physical structure containing a work, or

(b) steps taken in good faith to restore or preserve the work

shall not, by that act alone, constitute a distortion, mutilation or other modification of the work. [Emphasis added.]

28.2 (1) Il n'y a violation du droit à l'intégrité que si l'oeuvre est, d'une manière préjudiciable à l'honneur ou à la réputation de l'auteur, déformée, mutilée ou autrement modifiée, ou utilisée en liaison avec un produit, une cause, un service ou une institution.

(2) Toute déformation, mutilation ou autre modification d'une peinture, d'une sculpture ou d'une gravure est réputée préjudiciable au sens du paragraphe (1).

(3) Pour l'application du présent article, ne constitue pas nécessairement une déformation, mutilation ou autre modification de l'oeuvre un changement de lieu, du cadre de son exposition ou de la structure qui la contient ou toute mesure de restauration ou de conservation prise de bonne foi. [Emphasis added.]

Thus, in *Snow v. Eaton Centre Ltd.* (1982), 70 C.P.R. (2d) 105 (Ont. H.C.), a sculptor successfully objected to the Eaton Centre festooning with Christmas ribbons his creation of a flight of 60 Canada geese that are forever poised to land inside the south entrance of a downtown shopping mall in Toronto. The artist's counsel said, at p. 106, that his client:

> ... [was] adamant in his belief that his naturalistic composition has been made to look ridiculous by the addition of ribbons and suggests [that] it is not unlike dangling earrings from the Venus de Milo.

18 Thus, even though the flying geese had been sold and paid for, the artist was able to reach across the ownership divide to take action against a successor owner not for infringing his *economic* rights but for violating his *moral* rights, i.e., for perpetrating what both he and the judge regarded as an attack on the artistic integrity of the descending flock.

19 The evidence here suggests that, at least in some instances, the respondent's name was deleted and was no longer on the posters when they were offered for resale. The respondent could have asserted a moral right to be publicly identified with his artistic work in this respect.

IV. The Respondent's Complaint

20 The respondent made it clear in his evidence that his real complaint is more properly characterized as the alleged infringement of his "moral" rights and its potential impact on the market for his works.

> [TRANSLATION] **Q.** Is it not true, Mr. Théberge, that your position is that the canvas-backed reproductions that are now being made of your works are unlawful because you do not authorize them and especially because you are not paid a royalty for each reproduction that is made?

A. I would never want a penny for those works. Do you know why? Shall I tell you why?

Q. Tell me why.

A. Because, first and foremost, it is once again a dilution of my work; it is an abusive commercialization of my work, without authorization; it is a manipulation of the work because, in many cases, my signature does not appear on the reproduction; it is an anonymization, if I can use that word without being scholarly. There is no Théberge on my work, it is not signed. Turn it around and there is nothing on the back. Where does it come from, who sells it? Not a word. These things are all over the place. And, furthermore, the final argument, Mr. Charia, is that clients and friends of mine call me, they won't accept it anymore and they are asking me whether I am a party to the distribution of these things.

Q. So, is it ...

A. Being a party to the distribution of these things means that they assume that I hatched a plot in which I am a participant. I'm getting money, royalties or ... that I make money off of it — "otherwise, it's just not possible. How can you allow such a thing, Mr. Théberge?" So there are clients who have originals, who have paid eight thousand dollars ($8,000), nine thousand dollars ($9,000) that they find reproduced on canvas all over, in slightly smaller or medium sizes, or depending on the size, and for forty dollars ($40), sixty dollars ($60), eighty dollars ($80) or one hundred and twenty dollars ($120).... Me, Claude Théberge, the artist, I have nothing whatsoever to do with it, and want to put a stop to it. It's just unreal. And especially, if I accepted money for that manoeuvre, I wouldn't dare look myself in the mirror, Sir.

Q. So, this morning, it is your testimony, Mr. Théberge, that it is not a question of money ...

A. Absolutely not.

21 Apart from the complaint of non-attribution (which is a moral rights issue), it seems the respondent as an artist simply wishes to stop the appellants from catering to the market for canvas-backed reproductions that apparently exists. To do so, however, he must as a litigant demonstrate a statutory right that overrides what the owners of the authorized poster could otherwise do with their tangible property.

22 Moral rights act as a continuing restraint on what purchasers such as the appellants can do with a work once it passes from the author, but respect must be given to the limitations that are an essential part of the moral rights created by Parliament. Economic rights should not be read so broadly that they cover the same ground as the moral rights, making inoperative the limits Parliament has imposed on moral rights.

23 To the extent the respondent is suggesting that observers cannot tell the difference between the original painting and a poster reproduction on a canvas substrate, I think he perhaps does them all a disservice. In any event, he has enabled the appellants to do what they are doing by authorizing the creation of

up to 10,000 paper-backed posters, some of which they have duly purchased on the open market.

. . .

E. The Proposed Test Would Undermine the Distinction Between Moral Rights and Economic Rights Contrary to Legislative Intent

57 As previously noted, s. 28.2(1) of the Act provides that even a purchaser of the tangible object may not "distor[t], mutilat[e] *or otherwise modif[y]*" (emphasis added) the work "to the prejudice of the honour or reputation of the author". It seems clear, at least by negative implication, that a modification of a work by the purchaser which does *not* "prejudice ... the honour or reputation of the author" was intended by Parliament to be within the purchaser's rights.

58 In addition, as a secondary point, s. 28.2(3) of the Act provides that a change in "the physical ... structure containing a work ... shall not, by that act alone, constitute a distortion, mutilation or other modification of the work". To the extent a change in substrate can be said to change the "physical structure" containing the respondent's work, it does not "by that act alone" amount to a violation of a moral right either.

59 The separate structures in the Act to cover economic rights on the one hand and moral rights on the other show that a clear distinction and separation was intended. Professor Ysolde Gendreau is one of those who have drawn attention to this rather rigid compartmentalisation:

> Unfortunately, the present text of the *Copyright Act* does little to help the promotion of the fusion of moral rights with the economic prerogatives of the law, since there is no comprehensive definition of copyright that embodies both. Section 3 of the Act, which is drafted as a definition of copyright, only refers to the economic dimension of copyright. Moral rights are defined and circumscribed in entirely distinct sections. This absence of cohesion leads to the separate mention of "copyright" and "moral rights" whenever Parliament wants to refer to both aspects of copyright law and to the near duplication of the provision on remedies for moral rights infringements.
>
> (Y. Gendreau, "Moral Rights" in G. F. Henderson, ed., *Copyright and Confidential Information Law of Canada* (1994), 161, at p. 171)

(See also R. G. Howell, L. Vincent, and M. D. Manson, *Intellectual Property Law: Cases and Materials* (1999), at p. 383.) This is not to say that moral rights do not have an economic dimension (e.g., there may be an economic aspect to being able to control the personality-invested "moral" rights of integrity and attribution) or to deny that there is a moral rights aspect to copyright (e.g., a critic may reproduce parts of the text of a book when reviewing it, but it will be considered a breach of the author's economic rights unless his or her authorship is attributed). However, in terms of remedies, the distinction in the Act between the two sets of rights is clear.

60 My view is that Parliament intended modification without reproduction to be dealt with under the provisions dealing with moral rights rather than economic rights. To adopt a contrary view, i.e., to treat the modification of the substrate here as the violation of an economic right, would allow copyright holders other than the artist to complain about modification (despite the non-assignability of moral rights). It would allow an artist who objected to a "modification" of an authorized reproduction both to sidestep the independent evaluation of a judge in unleashing a pre-judgment seizure in Quebec, and to sidestep at a trial anywhere in Canada the important requirement of showing prejudice to honour or reputation in order to establish an infringement of moral rights.

61 Could the *economic* rights of the sculptor of the descending geese at the Eaton Centre be said to be infringed (quite apart from his *moral* rights) because the seasonal "combination" of geese plus Christmas ribbons could be considered a "reproduction"? The be-ribboned flock incorporated the original artistic work in more than "substantial part", no doubt, but there was no "reproduction" in any legal sense, any more than there was "reproduction" when the appellants in this case contributed blank canvas to the "combination" of ink layer and canvas. The sculptor rightly invoked his moral rights against the Eaton Centre, not economic rights.

F. A "Droit de Destination" Would Be Introduced into our Law Without any Basis in the Copyright Act

62 It is not altogether helpful that in the French and English versions of the Act the terms "copyright" and "droit d'auteur" are treated as equivalent. While the notion of "copyright" has historically been associated with economic rights in common law jurisdictions, the term "droit d'auteur" is the venerable French term that embraces a bundle of rights which include elements of both economic rights and moral rights. As Professor Strowel observes:

> [TRANSLATION] The expressions "droit d'auteur" and "copyright" speak volumes in themselves. It has been pointed out that the distinction between the copyright tradition and the "droit d'auteur" tradition is based on a question of terminology: where the followers of the first tradition, the British and their spiritual heirs, talk about "copyright" to refer to a right that derives from the existence of a "copy," an object in itself, the followers of the second tradition talk about "author's right" (droit d'auteur) to refer to a right that stems from intellectual effort or activity brought to bear by an author, a creator. This is the fundamental difference: on the one hand, a right that is conceived of by reference to the author, the creative person, and, on the other, by reference to the copy of the work, the product of the creative activity that is protected against copying.

> (A. Strowel, *Droit d'auteur et copyright — Divergences et convergences: étude de droit comparé*, Paris, L.G.D.J., 1993, at pp. 19-20.)

63 Under the *civiliste* tradition, and particularly in France, the right of reproduction was interpreted to include not only the right to make new copies of the work (reproduction *stricto sensu*) but also what is called by French jurists the

"right of destination" (*droit de destination*). The right of destination gives the author or artist the right to control to a considerable extent the use that is made of authorized copies of his or her work: see generally A. Lucas and H.-J. Lucas, *Traité de la propriété littéraire & artistique* (1994), at p. 235; F. Pollaud-Dulian, *Le droit de destination : Le sort des exemplaires en droit d'auteur* (1989). See also Crim., January 28, 1888, *Bull. crim.*, No. 46, p. 68; Crim., December 2, 1964, *Bull. crim.*, No. 320, p. 672; Crim., October 7, 1977, *bull. crim.*, No. 315, p. 801; Civ. 1er, May 5, 1976, *Bull. civ.*, No. 161, p. 128; Paris, March 18, 1987, D. 1988. Somm. 209, note Colombet; Civ. 1er, April 19, 1988, *Bull. civ.*, No. 112, p. 76; Paris, April 27, 1945, *Gaz. Pal.*, 1945, p. 192.

64 The "*droit de destination*" applies in other *civiliste* jurisdictions. Thus in *Hovener/Poortvliet*, HR January 19, 1979, NJ 412, brought to our attention by counsel for the respondent, the Netherlands Supreme Court found a violation of the *droit d'auteur* where a purchaser of an authorized art calendar cut out the pictures, stuck them to coasters, and resold them. This was regarded by the court as an altogether new and different "publication". In *Frost v. Olive Series Publishing Co.* (1908), 24 T.L.R. 649 (Eng. Ch. Div.), by contrast, the English court did not regard as an infringement the cutting out of pictures from books, pasting them on cards, and reselling. "[The recirculation of] objects already in existence is not reproduction in a material form": Laddie, et al., *supra*, at p. 614.

65 It seems to me that the respondent is pursuing a form of "*droit de destination*" in this case. But, under our *Copyright Act*, the "right of destination" as such does not exist. Generally, the copyright holder does not by virtue of his or her *economic* rights retain any control over the subsequent uses made of authorized copies of his work by third party purchasers. Where in specified situations the Act gives the copyright holder some power to control or benefit from subsequent uses of authorized copies of his work, the relevant provisions are narrowly framed to apply only to very specific forms of reproduction, as in the case of sound recordings (s. 15(1)) or computer programs (s. 3(1)(*h*)). If a general right to control subsequent usage existed, it would not have been necessary to make specific provision in these cases.

. . .

VI. Conclusion with Respect to the Substantive Issue

74 My conclusion is that in this case the respondent is asserting a moral right in the guise of an economic right, and the attempt should be rejected.

75 If the respondent's argument were correct in principle, of course, the absence of authority would not prevent his success. It is in the nature of the subject that intellectual property concepts have to evolve to deal with new and unexpected developments in human creativity. The problem here is that the respondent's submission ignores the balance of rights and interests that lie at the basis of copyright law.

Morans and Co. v. LeSueur (1911), 45 S.C.R. 95

Supreme Court of Canada

Sir Charles Fitzpatrick C.J. and Davies, Idington, Duff and Anglin JJ.

Judgment: March 20, 1911
Judgment: October 3, 1911

The Chief Justice:

1 Once it is admitted, as it is by both parties here, that the manuscript Life of Mackenzie which the respondent was commissioned to write was originally intended for publication in book form in the series then being published by the appellant and known as "Makers of Canada," such an intention based on the facts revealed by the evidence implies a tacit agreement to publish the manuscript, if accepted; and, the manuscript having been rejected as unsuitable for the purpose for which it was intended, no property in it passed and the respondent was entitled to ask that the contract be rescinded and the manuscript returned upon the repayment of the money consideration which he had received.

2 I cannot agree that the sale of the manuscript of a book is subject to the same rules as the sale of any other article of commerce, *e.g.*, paper, grain or lumber. The vendor of such things loses all dominion over them when once the contract is executed and the purchaser may deal with the thing which he has purchased as he chooses. It is his to keep, to alienate or to destroy. But it will not be contended that the publisher who bought the manuscript of "The Life of Gladstone," by Morley, or of Cromwell by the same author, might publish the manuscript, having paid the author his price, with such emendations or additions as might perchance suit his political or religious views and give them to the world as those of one of the foremost publicists of our day. Nor could the author be denied by the publisher the right to make corrections, in dates or otherwise, if such corrections were found to be necessary for historical accuracy; nor could the manuscript be published in the name of another. After the author has parted with his pecuni ary interest in the manuscript, he retains a species of personal or moral right in the product of his brain. Lyon Caen, note to Sirey, 1881.1.25.

3 What I have said is sufficient to show that what is called literary property has a character and attributes of its own and that such a contract as we are now called upon to consider must be interpreted and the rights of the parties determined with regard to the special nature of the thing which is the subject of the contract. *Cox v. Cox.* An ancient manuscript or a papyrus might have by reason of its antiquity or the circumstances surrounding its discovery some intrinsic monetary value. But what may be the value to the writer or to the publisher of the manuscript in question here, so long as it is allowed to remain in the pigeonhole of the latter? What was the consideration for the payment of $500? Not the paper on which the manuscript is written; its value is destroyed for all commercial purposes. Not the paper with the writing on it; that can have no value without publication, except for the purposes suggested by Mr. Justice Meredith. The only way in which the appellant can legitimately recoup himself for his expenditure must be by the publication of

the manuscript, and in this I find an additional reason for holding that publication was an implied term of the contract.

4 In the absence of English authorities on the subject, I referred to the French books which treat at great length of such contracts as we are now considering. The majority of French writers, and among them some of the most eminent, such as Pardessus, held that the obligation to publish is always to be considered as an implied term in every contract for the purchase of the manuscript of a book; but admitting with the minority that a contract might be drawn which would transfer the whole property in the manuscript to the purchaser so that it would be in his power to retain it in his possession for his own personal use, all the French authorities admit that where, as in the present case, the parties have chosen to leave so much to intendment and implication, the court should give to the contract a construction wide enough to include the obligation to publish, that being, generally speaking, the more probable intention of the parties, as it was in this case their admitted intention at the inception of their negotiations.

5 See Pandectes Francaises, vbo. Propriété littéraire, Nos. 1912 and 1913. Pouillet, Propriété littéraire, 2nd ed., No. 308.

6 In conclusion, therefore, I hold that, as argued on behalf of the respondents and as found in both courts below, the conditions which together made up the consideration moving to the respondent were the payment of the stipulated price, $500, in instalments of $250 each, and the publication of the work in and as part of the series, "Makers of Canada." The respondent fully performed his contract when he wrote and delivered the manuscript and if, in the exercise of his undoubted right, the appellant properly rejected it as unsuitable for the purpose for which it was intended, viz., publication in the "Makers of Canada" series, then both parties were free to rescind the contract altogether and the respondent upon the return of so much of the consideration as he had received was entitled to have the manuscript returned to him. It cannot be denied that by the appellant's refusal the respondent was deprived of the chief consideration which moved him to write the manuscript, that is the benefit to his literary reputation resulting from publication. Tindal C.J. in *Planché v. Colburn.*

7 It is unnecessary for me to go over in detail the evidence of the contract and the correspondence, all of which must be taken into consideration, as well as the standard form of contract used by the publisher with all his contributors. In the judgment of the Court of Appeal and in the notes of my brother judges all that is useful is discussed with much ability.

8 For the short reasons which I have just given and for those more fully set out by Mr. Justice Meredith in the Court of Appeal, I would confirm the judgments below and dismiss this appeal with costs.

Snow v. The Eaton Centre (1982), 70 C.P.R. (2d) 105 (Ont. H.C.)

Ontario High Court of Justice

O'Brien J.

Judgment: December 8, 1982

O'Brien J.:

1 The application in this motion relies solely on s. 12(7) of the *Copyright Act*, R.S.C. 1970, c. C-30, and in particular that part which gives the author the right to restrain any distortion, mutilation or other modification of his work that would be prejudicial to his honour or reputation.

2 The distortion or modification complained of is that of attaching ribbons to the necks of the 60 geese forming a sculpture known as "flight stop", a work of the plaintiff sold to the defendants and paid for by them and a Wintario grant.

3 The geese were be-ribboned by the defendants without the knowledge or consent of the plaintiff. The plaintiff, an artist of international reputation takes the position that the work as presently displayed is prejudicial to his honour and reputation. Counsel advise there are no cases which interpret s. 12(7) of the *Copyright Act.*

4 The defendants argue that the plaintiff's complaint is not one which comes within s. 12(7) but if it does, that section is unconstitutional. The Attorneys-General of Canada and Ontario have been notified of this application and hearing but are not intervening at this stage of the proceedings. The defendants further submit s. 12(7) should be looked at in a manner similar to a libel or slander action. I am not persuaded the section of the Act is unconstitutional. In my view the use of the word "independently" in s. 12(7) merely indicates the rights conferred by that section are in addition to the author's right of copyright. I reject the argument that I interpret s. 12(7) as suggested, in my view, the section gives rights greater than those based on libel or slander.

5 It is conceded that the sculpture is a "work" within the meaning of the *Copyright Act*. I believe the words "prejudicial to his honour or reputation" in s. 12(7) involve a certain subjective element or judgment on the part of the author so long as it is reasonably arrived at.

6 The plaintiff is adamant in his belief that his naturalistic composition has been made to look ridiculous by the addition of ribbons and suggests it is not unlike dangling earrings from the Venus de Milo. While the matter is not undisputed, the plaintiff's opinion is shared by a number of other well respected artists and people knowledgeable in his field.

7 The plaintiff does not seek to interfere with the Christmas advertising campaign of the defendants other than to have the ribbons removed from the necks of the geese.

8 I am satisfied the ribbons do distort or modify the plaintiff's work and the plaintiff's concern this will be prejudicial to his honour or reputation is reasonable under the circumstances.

9 Application granted. Ribbons to be removed by Monday, December 6, 1982 at 9 a.m. If the matter goes no further costs to the plaintiff in any event. If the matter proceeds, costs at discretion of trial judge.

Prise de Parole Inc. v. Gvérin, éditeur Ltée (1995), 66 C.P.R. (3d) 257 (F.C.T.D.)

Federal Court of Canada — Trial Division

Denault, J.

Judgment: November 27, 1995

Denault J.:

1 In 1992 the defendant Guérin, éditeur Ltée ("Guérin") published a collection for schools entitled *Libre expression* containing a number of stories, including a substantial extract from the work *La vengeance de l'orignal*, a protected and duly registered original work within the meaning of the *Copyright Act*, R.S.C. 1985, c. C-42 ("the Act"). The author of this work, Doric Germain, had assigned the exclusive right to print and publish it and to negotiate his copyright to Prise de parole Inc. ("Prise de parole").

2 It is clear that in the case at bar the defendant has infringed the plaintiffs' rights by publishing an extract from *La vengeance de l'orignal* without their authorization and that it must compensate them. The instant dispute relates essentially to the remedies and damages to which the plaintiffs are entitled.

3 A brief summary of the facts will be helpful. Doric Germain, a professor at Hearst University, is the author of a number of novels, including *La vengeance de l'orignal*, the work that is the subject of the instant case. This novel, which is for a teenage audience, was written in 1979 and published in 1980 by Prise de parole pursuant to an agreement (May 9, 1980) between the author and his publisher. At that time, Prise de parole obtained the exclusive right to print and publish this work. In this contract, Doric Germain also assigned his publisher the exclusive right to negotiate his copyright.

4 In 1981 Prise de parole began marketing the work in Grade 9 and 10 classes in Franco-Ontarian schools. This launch was very successful considering the limited market it reached. Between 1981 and 1991, an average of 1,000 copies of *La vengeance de l'orignal* were sold every year. However, sales of this novel slowed when, in May 1992, the defendant published its *Libre expression* school collection containing substantial extracts from Doric Germain's original work. As the textbook states, this collection was intended for Grade 8 students. About a third of Doric Germain's novel was reproduced word for word in the

defendant's collection. These extracts were also reproduced in the teaching guide published by the defendant for teachers. After the defendant's textbook came out, sales of *La vengeance de l'orignal* dropped off drastically as a result of the fact that the *Libre expression* collection was for Grade 8 students and Doric Germain's work was for Grade 9 students.

5   In 1993 Doric Germain and Prise de parole instituted this action alleging that the defendant had infringed their rights under sections 14.1, 28.1 and 27(1) and (4) of the Act. In the *Libre expression* collection, the author of *La vengeance de l'orignal* is identified — his photograph is even reproduced — and it is stated that this story is published by Prise de parole. However, in the author's submission the defendant greatly impaired his work by cutting several descriptions of northern Ontario, the habits of people from that region and their hunting and fishing methods — all elements for which his work is known — and by eliminating the novel's subplot relating to the activities and schemes of a game warden. He argued that the defendant published such a clumsy adaptation of his novel that he would have preferred his name not to be associated with the *Libre expression* collection. For its part, Prise de parole's primary allegation is that the defendant published this extract without its authorization, thereby infringing its rights.

. . .

Whether Doric Germain's moral rights were infringed

24   Under section 14.1(1) of the Act the author of a work has, subject to section 28.2, the right to the integrity of his or her work: these are moral rights. The Act also provides in section 14.1(2) that an author's moral rights may not be assigned but may be waived in whole or in part. The evidence does not show that in the case at bar Doric Germain waived his moral rights. To be able to make a claim based on the right to the integrity of his or her work, the author must show, as stated in section 28.2(1) of the Act, that the work was distorted, mutilated or otherwise modified to the prejudice of the author's honour or reputation. I note that section 28.2(1) does not require the plaintiff to prove prejudice to his honour or reputation; rather, it must be proved that the work was distorted, mutilated or otherwise modified "to the prejudice of the honour or reputation of the author" ("d'une manière préjudiciable à l'honneur ou à la réputation de l'auteur"). In my view, this nuance justifies the use of a subjective criterion — the author's opinion — in assessing whether an infringement is prejudicial.

25   It has, moreover, been recognized by the courts that this concept has a highly subjective aspect that in practice only the author can prove. In *Snow*, the court ruled as follows:

> I believe the words "prejudicial to his honour or reputation" in s. 12(7) [of the *Copyright Act*, R.S.C. 1970, c. C-30] involve a certain subjective element or judgment on the part of the author so long as it is reasonably arrived at.

26   However, in my view the assessment of whether a distortion, mutilation or other modification is prejudicial to an author's honour or reputation also requires an objective evaluation of the prejudice based on public or expert opinion. In

Snow the applicant proved this. In the case at bar, the evidence certainly shows that Doric Germain felt frustrated by the publication of a shortened version of his work. During his testimony, he talked at length about the changes the defendant had made to his work: a substantial amount of his novel was reproduced but with essential omissions such as the subplot and a number of details about northern Ontario that were an important part of his original work; in addition, the order in which the plot was presented was altered and the novel's divisions and subdivisions were left out or changed. In short, the author clearly demonstrated that his work was distorted, mutilated or otherwise modified.

27 It must still be determined whether the work was distorted to the prejudice of the author's honour and reputation. Doric Germain expressed his great disappointment at seeing his work so distorted that he would have preferred his name not to be associated with the defendant's collection. He also stated that he is well known in his circle, has a good reputation as an author and has already written four novels. He received a grant from the Ontario Arts Council, was invited by the province of Ontario to the Salon international du livre in Le Mans, France in 1989 and had his photograph published on the cover of *Liaison*, the main arts journal in Ontario. He was invited to tour Manitoba schools and at that time gave radio and television interviews. He is often asked to give lectures in schools, although when asked by counsel for the defendant whether the number of lectures he was asked to give fell after the publication of the *Libre expression* collection, he acknowledged that [TRANSLATION] "I don't think it did any harm." Doric Germain also acknowledged that he had not been ridiculed or mocked by his colleagues or the newspapers and that he had not personally heard any complaints after the *Libre expression* collection was published.

28 In short, although the author has shown that his novel was substantially modified without his knowledge and that he was shocked and distressed by this, the evidence has not shown that, objectively, as required by section 28.2(1) of the Act, his work was modified to the prejudice of his honour or reputation. Since this has not been proven, the plaintiff is not entitled to moral damages.

Nintendo of America Inc. v. Camerica Corp. (1991), 34 C.P.R. (3d) 193, (Fed. T.D.), affirmed (1991), 36 C.P.R. (3d) 352 (Fed. C.A.)

Federal Court Trial Division

Rouleau J.

Judgment: January 28, 1991

Rouleau, J:

1 This is an application for an interlocutory injunction restraining the defendants from infringing the plaintiffs' copyright in Nintendo Games and from infringing Nintendo's trade-marks. It also seeks to restrain the defendants from selling, importing, advertising, manufacturing, etc., their product known

as "Game Genie", a hardware tool designed for use with home video games. The remedies are sought pending final judgment in this action for copyright and trademark infringement.

2 The plaintiff, Nintendo of America Inc. ("Nintendo") is a company existing under the laws of the State of Washington and is the largest subsidiary of Nintendo Co. Ltd ("Nintendo Japan"), a one hundred year old company incorporated pursuant to the laws of Japan. Nintendo is engaged in the business of distributing video game products, including home video games and coin-operated video games. From 1981 through 1985, the principal business of Nintendo was the distribution of coin-operated video games. Beginning in late 1985, Nintendo introduced the Nintendo Entertainment System ("NES"), a revolutionary video game system designed for use in the home. Since 1986, Nintendo's principal business has been the marketing and distribution of NES hardware and software cartridges for home use. In Canada, Mattel Canada Inc. ("Mattel") is Nintendo's exclusive distributor of the NES and video game cartridges for the NES which are developed by Nintendo Japan.

3 The co-plaintiff in this proceeding, Shigeru Miyamoto, is a leading designer of video games for Nintendo Japan. Mr Miyamoto first started designing video games in 1980 with the creation of a game entitled Donkey Kong. He was responsible for the game design and artwork, including creating the game story, the game characters and scenery. Donkey Kong was a very popular video game for Nintendo both as an arcade game and subsequently as a home video game. Its popularity led to a number of game sequels including Donkey Kong Jr. and Donkey Kong 3. Over two million copies of the Donkey Kong series of games have been sold worldwide. For the Donkey Kong game, Mr. Miyamoto created the game character called Mario, who is also the central game character in the very popular and highly successful Nintendo game series Super Mario Bros.

4 In Super Mario Bros., Mr. Miaymoto worked as both the game designer and producer to create the general concept and theme of the game. He made sketches of the characters, concept drawings of the scenery, decided on the attributes and movements of the characters and then worked in conjunction with other employees of Nintendo in relation to computer programming, composing the game music and various other items. For the sequel games, Super Mario Bros. 2, Super Mario Bros. 3, and the upcoming Super Mario Bros. 4 game, Mr. Miyamoto acted as the game producer responsible for the complete production of the game. His task was to work with a team of several game directors to create the game story, theme, sketches and characters for the game.

5 The defendant Camerica Corporation ("Camerica"), a Canadian corporation with its head offices located in Unionville, Ontario, has three main divisions: a gift division, a furniture division and an electronics division. The fastest growing division of the company is the electronics division which accounts for approximately sixty percent of Camerica's annual sales, which in 1989 exceeded $11.5 million. Roughly thirty percent of that figure was derived from the sale of Game Genie, the product in dispute in these proceedings. In addition, Camerica is a distributor of

video game cartridges for the NES for between fifteen and twenty percent of all Nintendo licensees in Canada. Approximately, forty percent of the revenues of the electronics division are derived from the sale of these video games.

6 The leadership role of Nintendo in the home video game industry is not disputed. In the early 1980's the market was flooded with low quality, non-challenging video game cartridges which led to massive consumer dissatisfaction. The resulting consumer malaise was evidenced by the public's refusal to purchase additional games. As a result, the industry suffered a major decline in 1982 and 1983. It was Nintendo's opinion, when it entered the home video game industry in 1985, that the market collapse had resulted from the failure of video game manufacturers to ensure the games being offered were of high quality. In the past, consumers had often paid for software only to discover the games to be poorly conceived and of poor quality resulting in mastery of the games with minimal effort.

7 In late 1985, Nintendo introduced the Nintendo Entertainment System ("NES"), a video game system designed for use in the home, which has become a major commercial success in both Canada and the United States. Since 1985, the plaintiff has sold over twenty million NES Control Decks and tens of millions of game cartridges. Most of the games require a player to master a number of levels or "worlds" of increasingly difficult and creative game play.

8 In many of these games, the game player guides an action character through levels of increasing difficulty where various obstacles must be overcome. The character's ability to overcome these obstacles depends upon the attributes (such as jumping, running, etc.) with which he is endowed. The action figure is controlled by the game player, but only in certain repetitive moves on the screen. The player guides the figure through the various worlds or levels by helping him pick up useful objects and weapons along the way. If the character's enemies defeat him, the game play ends. The game player can then start a new game to try to progress to the finish or complete the highest level of the game. A player's skill is heightened by practising various techniques and uncovering secrets which enable him or her to continue playing further and further into the game. The Super Mario Bros. series and The Legend of Zelda series are designed to be played for one hundred hours or more depending on a players's level of skill: NES video games are devised so that only a very skilled player, over a considerable period of time, can reach the end of the game.

9 In December 1989, the defendant Camerica began marketing and advertising a product called Game Genie. This device is a hardware tool which allows a video game player to choose certain game play characteristics such as the number of lives an action figure may lose before a game ends; how much time, energy or ammunition an action figure has to overcome; the number of obstacles or enemies an action figure will face; and on what world or level the action will start. The device was demonstrated at the Consumer Electronics Show in Las Vegas in January of 1990 and since then has been advertised in trade magazines. Camerica commenced selling Game Genie to retailers and large distributors in

January of 1990, manufacturing began that March and the first shipment to customers occurred in early June, 1990.

10 The Game Genie is a cartridge-like pack that connects between the video game cartridge and the game deck. It introduces its own startup screen, called the "Code Screen" when the game deck is powered up. On this screen the video game player may enter special codes from examples listed in the Codebook, the manual sold with Game Genie, and thereby modify game-play features. The player can also program his own codes. A maximum of three codes may be entered each time a game is played to control up to three of the games' operating parameters. For every code entered by the player, the Game Genie blocks the value for a single data byte sent by the game cartridge to the central processing unit in the Nintendo controller and replaces it with a new value. For example, if the cartridge sends a data byte setting the number of lives for the action character at 3, the Game Genie might, depending on the code chosen by the player, substitute the value 6, thereby giving the character 6 lives rather than 3 in which to complete the game. The player is also able to modify the color of certain features in the audio-visual display, change the speed at which the action character moves, allow the character to float above obstacles and alter myriad other attributes of the Nintendo game.

11 Although the Game Genie permits the player to alter certain game play characteristics, it does not enable changes to be made to the fundamental game action content. It does not, for instance, change the object of the game: if the object is to defeat an evil villain and rescue a princess, that remains the object of the game. Neither does it; change the appearance of game action figures, enemies, obstacles and situations that are encountered during game play or settings of the game; allow for the creation of a new game action figure or visual object; permit a player to create a "power" for an action figure that the action figure does not have or cannot create during game play. Therefore, it does not create the "power" to become "big" or to "shoot" if the power is not part of the game. Likewise, if an action figure can only walk, run and jump, Game Genie does not enable a player to create displays showing the action figure kicking, crawling or swimming.

12 The Game Genie does not make any change in the data which is stored in the game cartridge. Its interception and substitution of data occurs only as long as it is attached to the game cartridge and the controller's power is on. The individual changes that a player makes through entering codes alter the audio-visual display temporarily but do not change it or the Nintendo game permanently.

13 The Game Genie comes packaged in a box within which is the cartridge and the Codebook. The front, back, top and both sides of the package display the Camerica trademark and also state that the Game Genie works on many game titles for the Nintendo Entertainment System. The NES trademark appears on the packaging in this context. The front and back of the box state, in both French and English, that Game Genie is a product of Camerica and is "not manufactured, distributed or endorsed by Nintendo of America Inc." The Nintendo trademark appears within this disclaimer.

14 The Codebook, which is contained within the package and is not accessible to consumers unless they purchase the product, bears the Camerica trademark on the front cover, back cover and the spine. The back cover and the first page of the Codebook state that the Game Genie "works on many game titles for the Nintendo Entertainment System" and displays the NES trademark. The following statements also appears on the back cover and first page: "Game Genie is a product of Camerica Corp. and is not manufactured, distributed or endorsed by Nintendo of America Inc. Nintendo, Nintendo Entertainment System and Control Deck are trademarks of Nintendo of America Inc. Game Genie and Camerica are trademarks of Camerica Corp.". Listed within the Code Book are numerous video games which are compatible with Game Genie, many of which are not Nintendo game titles.

15 The plaintiffs bring this application on three grounds. First, they submit the defendants are infringing Nintendo's copyright in the Nintendo Games by the marketing and distribution of the product Game Genie contrary to the provisions of the *Copyright Act*, R.S.C. 1985, c. C-42, in particular section 3.1. Second, it is asserted the defendants have infringed the moral rights of the co-plaintiff, Mr. Miyamoto, as the author of a work protected by copyright, contrary to sections 14.1, 28.1 and 28.2 of the Act. Third, the plaintiffs argue that the defendants have used Nintendo's registered trademarks in a manner likely to depreciate the value of the goodwill associated with those trademarks contrary to Section 22 of the *Trade Marks Act*, R.S.C. 1985, c. T-13.

. . .

21 The second argument advanced by the plaintiffs relates to sections 14.1(1) and 28.2 of the *Copyright Act* which pertain to the moral rights of a creator or author of a work. The Act now specifically grants to the author of a work a statutory right to "the integrity of the work". Pursuant to section 28.2, that right is infringed if, to the prejudice of the author's honour or reputation, his work is distorted, mutilated or otherwise modified or if his work is used in association with a product, service, cause or institution.

22 It is submitted that the co-plaintiff Shigeru Miyamoto is an author of video games, with an international reputation for producing excellent and challenging games. Mr. Miyamoto's affidavit evidence states his opinion that Game Genie destroys his work by changing and mutilating the movements of the game characters, the scenery, the colours, and other features of his video games and has a detrimental effect on game play. He also states that his honour and reputation as a game creator are prejudiced by the use of Game Genie and that by offering it for sale to retailers, with the intention that it be sold to the general public, the defendant Camerica has authorized and induced infringements of Mr. Miyamoto's moral rights by others.

. . .

25 In spite of the exhaustive evidence submitted by both sides during the course of the hearing before me and the myriad of authorities relied upon by counsel, it must be emphasized that my role, in disposing of an interlocutory motion of

this nature, is not to make any precise determinations on either the facts or the law. Indeed, in cases embracing intricate and complex questions of law which exact detailed argument, it is not only exceedingly difficult, but also imprudent to attempt to decide the merits of the claim.

Chapter 6

OWNERSHIP, ASSIGNMENTS AND LICENSES

Ownership of intellectual property carries with it important rights. Yet it is surprising how many agreements related to the development of intellectual property fail to adequately address issues related to ownership. Consequently numerous disputes related to ownership have arisen in Canada and around the world. The cases highlight why it is desirable that parties involved in the development of works provide clearly in their contracts who is to own the copyright and exploitation rights of the developed work at each stage. In the absence of agreements which expressly address the ownership of copyright in works, the principles discussed below will apply.

1. Works Made in the Course of Employment and by Contractors

The author of a work is generally the first owner of the copyright therein. However, where the author of a work is in the employment of some other person under a contract of service or apprenticeship and the work is made in the course of his employment, in the absence of any agreement to the contrary, the first owner of the copyright is the employer and not the employee.[1] It is not necessary for there to be any transfer agreement or licence, either written or oral. In such circumstances, copyright vests in the employer by operation of law. The agreement to the contrary may be express or implied and also need not be in writing.[2]

Difficult questions frequently emerge as to whether a person is under a contract of service or a contract for services. The issue can be particularly challenging when the employee is very skilled such as where that person exercises a high degree of professional skill and expertise in the performance of his or her duties.

---

[1] Section 13(3).
[2] *Dolmage v. Erskine* (2003), 23 C.P.R. (4th) 495 (Ont. S.C.J.).

University of London Press Ltd. v. University Tutorial Press Ltd., [1916] 2 Ch. 601 (Ch. D.)

Peterson J.

1916 July 13, 14, 18, 19, 26.

. . .

...On February 24, 1915, the Senate of the University of London passed a resolution that "it be made a condition of the appointment of every examiner that any copyright possessed by him in examination papers prepared by him for the University shall be vested in the University, provided that the foregoing shall not apply to copyright in drawings; and that it be a further condition of such appointment that the University will raise no objection to the use by any such examiner, without payment, of the material of any paper set by him for any purpose except the republication of such paper as a whole, and that the University shall, without payment, have the right of reproduction of any drawing included in such paper." Examiners were subsequently appointed for the matriculation examinations to be held in September, 1915, and January and June, 1916. Among the examiners so appointed were Professor Lodge and Mr. Jackson, who were the examiners for the purpose of setting the examination papers in mathematics. The appointment was communicated to the examiners by letter of May 19 informing them that they "were this day elected to the office of examiner in mathematics" — or as the case might be — "in this University for the matriculation examinations in September, 1915, and January and June, 1916." Enclosed was a copy of the resolution as to copyright. The duties and salaries of the examiners were fixed. The examiners were not on the staff of the University. They were employed, for the particular examinations for which they were appointed, to prepare the examination papers on the subjects in respect of which they were respectively appointed. The papers were prepared in the examiners' own time. They were free, subject to a syllabus and having regard to the knowledge required from students, to choose their own questions. They perused the answers of students and awarded marks. They were paid a lump sum as salary. They were not bound to give their services exclusively to the London University. The examiners thus appointed prepared examination papers for September, 1915, and January, 1916. On July 26, 1915, the University entered into an agreement with the University of London Press, Limited, the plaintiff company, by which it was agreed that as and when after August 31, 1915, the University should from time to time prepare and issue or cause to be prepared and issued any examination papers (other than papers not material to this report) the University agreed (subject to the provisions and conditions thereinafter contained) from time to time to assign and make over to the Press Company all such copyright and rights of publication (if any) as the University might have in such respective papers (other than those as aforesaid) for the period of six years from the date of publication thereof respectively, with a proviso for a further period in absence of notice. By an indenture of January 13, 1916, made between the University and the University of London Press, Limited, in pursuance of the agreement of July 26, 1915, and for the consideration mentioned, the University purported to assign to the

Press Company all the copyright and rights of publication of the University in the papers of which particulars were contained in a schedule for the period and subject to the terms and conditions contained in the agreement. The schedule included the matriculation examination for January, 1916. The University of London Press, Limited, proceeded in January to publish the examination papers for the examination of January, 1916. In the same month the defendant company, the University Tutorial Press, Limited, issued a publication in which were included sixteen out of forty-two matriculation papers of January, 1916. The papers were not copied from the publication of the University of London Press, Limited, but were taken from copies of the examination papers supplied by students. Amongst the sixteen papers taken were three which were set by Professor Lodge and Mr. Jackson, one in arithmetic and algebra, another in geometry, and a third in more advanced mathematics. In addition to the papers so published the University Tutorial Press, Limited, published in the same book the answers to the questions in some of the papers, including the arithmetic and algebra paper and the geometry paper, but did not publish any answers to the questions in more advanced mathematics; and, further, made some criticisms on the way in which the papers had been set. On February 24, 1916, the University of London Press, Limited, commenced this action against the Tutorial Press, Limited, for infringement of copyright, and, objection being taken that the plaintiff company was not entitled to sue, Professor Lodge and Mr. Jackson were, in the course of the proceedings, joined as co-plaintiffs.

. . .

July 26. PETERSON J.

. . .

The next question is, In whom did the copyright in the examination papers vest when they had been prepared? This problem must be solved by the determination of the effect of s. 5 of the Act of 1911. The author, by that section, is the first owner of the copyright, subject only to the exceptions contained in the Act. The only relevant exception is to be found in s. 5, sub-s. 1 (b). [His Lordship read the section so far as relevant, and continued:] The examiners were no doubt employed by the University of London, and the papers were prepared by them in the course of their employment. But, in order that s. 5, sub-s. 1 (b), should be applicable, the examiners must have been "under a contract of service or apprenticeship"; and accordingly the plaintiffs contend that the papers were prepared by the examiners in the course of their employment under a contract of service, and that, therefore, the copyright in the papers belonged to the University of London. The meaning of the words "contract of service" has been considered on several occasions, and it has been found difficult, if not impossible, to frame a satisfactory definition for them. In Simmons v. Heath Laundry Co., in which the meaning of these words in the Workmen's Compensation Act, 1906, was discussed, Fletcher Moulton L.J. pointed out that a contract of service was not the same thing as a contract for service, and that the existence of direct control by the employer, the degree of independence on the part of the person who renders services, the place where the service is rendered, are all matters to be considered in determining whether there is a contract of service. As Buckley L.J. indicated in the same case, a contract of service involves the existence of a servant, and imports that there exists in the person serving an obligation to obey the orders of the person served. A servant is a person who is subject to the commands of his master as to the manner in which he shall do his work. A person who is employed by a company at a fixed annual salary to supply weekly articles for a periodical is not a servant within s. 209 of the Companies Consolidation Act, 1908: In re Beeton & Co.; nor can a visiting physician of a hospital who, for an annual salary, undertakes to exercise his judgment, skill, and knowledge in determining whether a patient can safely be discharged be properly described as a servant: Evans v. Liverpool Corporation. In Byrne v. Statist Co. the meaning of the words in s. 5 of the Copyright Act, 1911, was considered in the case of a person, permanently employed on the editorial staff of a newspaper, who was specially employed by the proprietors to translate and summarize a speech. He did the work in his own time and independently of his ordinary duties, and it was held that in doing so he did not act under a contract of service. In the present case the examiner was employed to prepare the papers on the subject in respect of which he was elected or appointed examiner. He had to set papers for September, 1915, and January and June, 1916, and his duty also comprised the perusal of the students' answers, and the consideration of the marks to be awarded to the answers. For this he was to be paid a lump sum. He was free to prepare his questions at his convenience so long as they were ready by the time appointed for the examination, and it was left to his skill and judgment to decide what questions should be asked, having regard to the syllabus, the book work, and the standard of knowledge to be expected at the matriculation examination. It is true that the University issued instructions to examiners for the conduct of the examination, but these instructions are only regulations framed with a view to securing accuracy in the system of marking. Professor Lodge and Mr. Jackson were regularly employed in other educational establishments and were not part of the staff of the London University, and it was not suggested that the other examiners were on the staff of the University. In my judgment it is impossible to say that the examiner in such circumstances can be appropriately described as the servant of the University, or that he prepared these papers under a contract of service.

. . .

The plaintiffs' next contention was that the copyright in the papers vested at once in the University by virtue of the fact that the examiners were employed on the terms that the copyright should belong to the University, who thereby became equitable assignees of the copyright; and Grace v. Newman was cited in support of this argument. Grace v. Newman seems to be one of those cases which under the present Act would come within s. 5, sub-s. 1 (b), but, however that may be, the present question must be determined by the provisions of the Act of 1911. Sect. 5 declares that, subject to the provisions of the Act, the author shall be the first owner of the copyright, and that every assignment of a copyright must be in writing, signed by the owner or his agent. The only exceptions from the rule that the author is the first owner are the cases mentioned in s. 5, sub-s. 1 (a) and (b), which do not cover the present case. The examiner was the first owner, and he has not assigned the copyright in writing signed by him or his agent. The copyright therefore remains in the examiners, subject to the obligation under the contract of employment to assign it to the University or as it may direct. The copyright was vested in the examiners, but the University was equitably entitled to it subject to the restrictions contained in the proviso to s. 5, sub-s. 2. The University assigned its rights to the plaintiff company, which is now equitably entitled to the copyright. In order to sue for infringement of the copyright, the plaintiff company must either obtain a proper assignment of the copyright or join the examiners, who are the legal owners of the copyright, as parties. It has not obtained an assignment, but it has in the course of the action joined Professor Lodge and Mr. Jackson as co-plaintiffs. The plaintiffs can therefore sue for infringement of the copyright in the papers prepared by Professor Lodge and Mr. Jackson, but, in the absence of the other examiners, the action fails in respect of the copyright in the papers which were composed by them.

. . .

Beloff v. Pressdram Ltd. [1973] 1 All E.R. 241 (Ch. D.)

In the High Court of Justice — Chancery Division

Before: Mr. Justice Ungoed-Thomas

. . .

UNGOED — THOMAS, J.

— This is an action for infringement of copyright. The plaintiff is Political and Lobby Correspondent of the Observer newspaper, which is owned by Observer Ltd. The first defendant, Pressdram Ltd., is the publisher and the second defendant, Leo Thorpe Ltd., is the printer of Private Eye magazine. The infringement alleged is by the reproduction in an article in Private Eye of an internal Observer office memorandum written by the Plaintiff. The alleged infringement is in the case of Pressdram by publishing and in the case of Leo Thorpe by printing. There is also a subsidiary claim against Pressdram for conversion in respect of copies of the article infringing the plaintiff's alleged copyright. The relief as claimed before me is, as against both defendants, for an injunction against future infringement and damages for breach of copyright, together with, in the case of Pressdram only, statutory and aggravated and exemplary damages, damages for conversion and delivery up of infringing material.

It is common ground that (1) copyright subsists in the memorandum, and if the plaintiff is entitled to sue for the alleged infringement of such copyright; (2) damages for such infringement are nominal (apart from statutory, aggravated or exemplary damages), (3) there is by Pressdram such conversion as is alleged for which damages would (as I agree) be most conveniently assessed by enquiry, and (4) there should be the usual order for delivery up by Pressdram of infringing material.

The main issues as they emerged before me are: (1) Whether the plaintiff is the owner of the copyright in the memorandum and, if so, whether she is entitled to sue in respect of the alleged infringement. (2) Whether the defendants establish their statutory defence under section 6 of the Copyright Act. 1956) which I shall refer to as the defence of fair dealing) or their defence of publication in the public interest, which in the argument in this case has been interwoven with the defence of fair dealing. (3) If the answer to (1) is Yes and (2) is No, whether the plaintiff is entitled to statutory, aggravated or exemplary damages in respect of the infringement.

Is the plaintiff the owner of the copyright in the memorandum and is she entitled to sue for the alleged infringement?

This question raises five subsidiary issues. (1) Was the copyright originally vested in the Observer Ltd. or the plaintiff? If it was so vested in the Observer Ltd., (2) was a duly proved purported assignment by the editor of the Observer on behalf of Observer Ltd. of the copyright, together with any accrued rights of action therein, to the plaintiff before the commencement of these proceedings made with the authority of Observer Ltd.? Or, if not, (3) would such assignment nevertheless be valid on the ground that the editor of the Observer represented to the plaintiff that he was authorised to make the assignment on behalf of Observer Ltd. and that the plaintiff relied upon such representation? (4) Was the assignment ineffective on the ground that it was not a bona fide assignment of copyright? (5) Is the plaintiff incapable for lack of notice to the defendants in accordance with section 136 of the Law of Property Act, 1925 of suing, in this action as constituted, in respect of the alleged infringement?

These five issues turn partly on law and partly on fact, but insofar as any of them turns on fact, the issue of fact falls within a small and separate ambit. It will therefore be convenient to deal with this main question separately from the other two main questions which have substantial issues of fact in common.

(1) Was the copyright originally vested in Observer Ltd. or the plaintiff? I will deal first with the law.

The copyright subsisted in the memorandum as an unpublished literary work and both the plaintiff and Observer Ltd. were qualified to own the copyright in it. (See Copyright Act, 1956, sections 1(1)(5)(a), 2(1)(5), 49(2)(3)(a)).

The original ownership of the copyright in this case is governed by section 4, subsections (1) and (4). These subsections read:

"(1) Subject to the provisions of this section, the author of a work shall be entitled to any copyright subsisting in the work by virtue of this Part of this Act.

(4) Where . . . a work is made in the course of the author's employment by another person under a contract of service or apprenticeship, that other person shall be entitled to any copyright subsisting in the work by virtue of this Part of this Act".

So if this case falls within subsection (4) the original copyright was in Observer Ltd. Otherwise it was in the plaintiff.

The memorandum was clearly made in the course of the plaintiff's employ-ment by Observer Ltd.: nor was this disputed. The only question is whether the plaintiff's employment was under a contract of service. If yes, the copyright originally vested in Observer Ltd.; if no, it vested in the plaintiff.

The distinction, familiar to lawyers, is between contract of service and contract for services. In applying this distinction there appears to have been a tendency in the past towards considering, and therefore describing, contracts of service in terms of occupations of a lowly character — not surprisingly, because it was in such occupations that contracts of service were most apt to occur. This tendency may well have been accentuated by the concern with such occupations, of stat-utes in whose setting contracts of service were from time to time considered. Thus Simmons v. Heath Laundry Company [1910] 1 K.B. 543 provides judicial quotations familiar in text books and in the courts on judicia of contracts of service. But that was a case under the Workmen's Compensation Act which was providing compensation for workmen. The material words were:

"Workman . . . means any person who has entered into or works under a contract of service or apprenticeship with an employer whether by way of manual labour, clerical work or otherwise".

And the distinguished members of the Court of Appeal who decided that case made it clear that the contract of service with which they were dealing was a contract of service "under the Act". In re Ashley & Smith Ltd. Mac. C.C. (1917-23) 54 a contract of service was considered in the context of provision of pref-erential payments for "clerks, servants, workmen and labourers" on the winding up of a company under the Companies' Act. In Simmons v. Heath Laundry Co. (supra) Fletcher Moulton, L.J. said at page 549:

"These facts, although very simple, raise a question of law of considerable importance and difficulty. It turns substantially on the scope which is to be given to the phrase 'contract of service' in the Act. It is true that as a matter of law it is not every contract of service that constitutes a person a workmen under the Act, since under the definition clause it must be 'a contract of service or appren-ticeship with an employer whether by way of manual labour, clerical work, or otherwise.' But I do not feel called upon to limit the generality of the word 'oth-erwise' in such a way as to exclude all contracts in respect of teaching".

At page 549-50:

"The greater the amount of direct control exercised over the person ren-dering the services by the person contracting for them the stronger the grounds for holding it to be a contract of service, and similarly the greater the degree of independence of such control the greater the probability that the services ren-dered are of the nature of professional services and that the contract is not one of service. The place where the services are rendered, i.e. whether at the residence of the person rendering the services or not, will also be an element in deciding the case, but is not in my opinion decisive".

And Buckley, L.J. said at page 552:

"A person employed to exercise his skill may or may not be a servant. The football player in Walker v. Crystal Palace Football Club [1910] 1 K.B. 87 was held to be a workman, that is, to be employed under a contract of service, notwithstanding that in certain respects it was his duty to exercise his own judgment uncontrolled by anybody. On the other hand in Bagnall v. Levinstein Ltd. [1907] 1 K.B. 531 a skilled chemist was held not to be a workman notwithstanding that his employment involved manual labour".

And at page 553:

"The question to be answered is, Was he employed as a workman or was he employed as a skilled adviser? I do not know whether it is possible to approach more closely to an answer to the question as to what is a contract of service under this Act than to say that in each case the question to be asked is what was the man employed to do; was he employed upon the terms that he should within the scope of his employment obey his master's orders, or was he employed to exercise his skill and achieve an indicated result in such manner as in his judgment was most likely to ensure success? Was his contract a contract of service within the meaning which an ordinary person would give to the words? Was it a contract under which he would be appropriately described as the servant of the employer?

Parts of these passages are quoted in In re Ashley & Smith referred to in Copinger, 11th Edition, paragraph 326, under the heading "What is a contract of service?" These passages bring out the way in which the test of control and contracts of service of a lowly nature have been associated with each other, as contrasted with contracts for professional or similarly skilled services. So counsel's original submission for the plaintiff was that "a contract of service means a contract for domestic, manual or clerical service whose execution is superintended by some higher official or employee".

But nowadays professional and similarly skilled persons are widely engaged under what are recognised as contracts of service. So I come to recent authorities which are rich in statements of principle and of relevant factors and in references to employment which, in the circumstances of particular cases, have been held to be, or not to be, under contracts of service.

In Stevenson Jordan and Harrison Ltd. v. MacDonald and Evans (1952) T.L.R. 101, it was held that some work done by an accountant was within a contract of service and some work done by him was outside it. Lord Denning said at pages 110 and 111:

"The test usually applied is whether the employer has the right to control the manner of doing the work. Thus in Collins v. Herts County Council [1947] K.B. 598 Hilbery, J. said:

'The distinction between a contract for services and a contract of service can be summarised in this way: In the one case the master can order or require what is to be done, while in the other case he can not only order or require what is to be done but how it shall be done'.

But in Cassidy v. Ministry of Health [1951] 2 K.B. 543 Somervell, L.J. pointed out that that test is not universally correct. There are many contracts of service where the master cannot control the manner in which the work is to be done, as in the case of a captain of a ship. Somervell, L.J. went on to say:

"One perhaps cannot get much beyond this 'Was the contract a contract of service within the meaning which an ordinary person would give under the words?'"

I respectfully agree. As my Lord has said, it is almost impossible to give a precise definition of the distinction. It is often easy to recognize a contract of service when you see it, but difficult to say wherein the difference lies. A ship's master, a chauffeur, and a reporter on the staff of a newspaper are all employed under a contract of service; but a ship's pilot, a taximan, and a newspaper contributor are employed under a contract for services".

Then Lord Denning goes on to the test which he indicates:

"One feature which seems to run through the instances is that, under a contract of service, a man is employed as part of the business, and his work is done as an integral part of the business; whereas, under a contract for services, his work, although done for the business, is not integrated into it but is only accessory to it".

In Morren v. Swinton and Pendlebury Borough Council, [1965] 1 W.L.R. 576 Lord Parker, L.C.J. held that an engineer was employed under a contract of service. Lord Parker observed at pages 581 to 582:

"The cases have over and over again stressed the importance of the factor of superintendence and control, but that it is not the determining test is quite clear. In Cassidy v. Ministry of Health [1951] 2 K.B. 543 Somervell, L.J. referred to this matter, and instanced as did Lord Denning in the later case of Stevenson, Jordan & Harrison v. McDonald & Evans (1952) T.L.R. 101 that clearly superintendence and control cannot be the decisive test when one is dealing with a professional man, or a man of some particular skill and experience. Instances of that have been given in the form of the master of a ship, an engine driver, or a professional architect, or as in this case, a consulting engineer. In such cases there can be no question of the employer telling him how to do work, therefore the absence of control and direction in that sense can be of little, if any, use as a test".

Then he goes on:

"In my judgment here all the other considerations point to a contract of service".

Then I omit some lines, and he continues with reference to the engineer in that case:

"... he was appointed by the respondents, they had the right to dismiss him, he was paid such matters of subsistence allowance, National Insurance contributions and holidays, and in addition there was provision for one month's notice. Pausing there, it seems to me that looked at on those facts, the only possible inference is that he was engaged under a contract of service. How different is the contract with Kaufman, who is not paid a subsistence allowance, or National Insurance contributions and is not entitled to holidays. Further there is no provision for termination of his services or service by notice".

In Whittaker v. Minister of Pensions and National Insurance [1967] 1 Q.B. 156, it was held that a trapeze artiste, who also undertook to help in moving the circus from place to place and to act as usherette, was employed under the one contract of service. Mocatta, J. at page 167 said:

"It seems clear, therefore, from the more recent cases that persons possessed of a high degree of professional skill and expertise, such as surgeons and civil engineers, may nevertheless be employed as servants under contracts of service, notwithstanding that their employers can, in the nature of things, exercise extremely little, if any, control over the way in which such skill is used. The test of control is, therefore, not as determinative as used to be thought to be the case, though no doubt it is still of value in that the greater the degree of control exercisable by the employer, the more likely it is that the contract is one of service".

In Market Investigations Ltd. v. Minister of Social Security [1969] 2 Q.B. 173 it was held that a part — time interviewer engaged by a market research company was under a contract of service. Cooke, J. observed at page 184:

"The observations of Lord Wright, of Denning, L.J. and of the judges of the Supreme Court suggest that the fundamental test to be applied is this: 'Is the person who has engaged himself to perform these services performing them as a person in business on his own account?' If the answer to that question is 'yes' then the contract is a contract for services. If the answer is 'no', then the contract is a contract of service. No exhaustive list has been compiled and perhaps no exhaustive list can be compiled of the considerations which are relevant in determining that question, nor can strict rules be laid down as to the relative weight which the various considerations should carry in particular cases. The most that can be said is that control will no doubt always have to be considered, although it can no longer be regarded as the sole determining factor: and that factors which may be of importance are such matters as whether the man performing the services provides his own equipment, whether he hires his own helpers, what degree of financial risk he takes, what degree of responsibility for investment and management he has, and whether and how far he has an opportunity of profiting from sound management in the performance of his task".

And at page 188:

"The opportunity to deploy individual skill and personality is frequently present in what is undoubtedly a contract of service. I have already said that the right to work for others is not inconsistent with the existence of a contract of service. Mrs. Irving did not provide her own tools or risk her own capital, nor did her opportunity of profit depend in any significant degree on the way she managed her work".

It thus appears, and rightly in my respectful view, that, the greater the skill required for an employee's work, the less significant is control in determining whether the employee is under a contract of service. Control is just one of many factors whose influence varies according to circumstances. In such highly skilled work as that of the plaintiff it seems of no substantial significance.

The test which emerges from the authorities seems to me, as Lord Denning said, whether on the one hand the employee is employed as part of the business and his work is an integral part of the business, or whether his work is not integrated into the business but is only accessory to it, or, as Cooke, J. expressed it, the work is done by him in business on his own account.

The only documents produced relating to the nature of the plaintiff's employment were two letters of 1947 and 1948 and two statements by the Observer Ltd. directed to the plaintiff under the Contracts of Employment Act, 1963 and the Industrial Relations Act, 1971.

The first letter, dated 19th September, 1947 was from the Observer editor to the plaintiff confirming her appointment as Paris correspondent with a yearly salary and expenses. It reads:

"We are very pleased to hear that you are willing to become Paris correspondent for the Observer and the Observer Foreign News Service.

You have done excellent work for us on the Paris Conference, and I am happy to confirm your appointment, as from November 2nd, 1947, and for an initial period of six months, at the rate of £750 a year, plus expenses incurred on our behalf. We hope it will be possible, as you indicate, to keep the expenses within reasonable limits.

In addition to full week-end coverage for the Observer, and the occasional provision of Profile, obituary and Notebook material as the needs arise, we shall require a minimum of one article a week, by mail or telephone, for Servob. (Hitherto we have stipulated two Servob articles weekly from our correspondents, but in practice one is usually sufficient. We should, however, like to be able to call on you for additional Servob articles in special circumstances, which would include occasions like the Paris Conference). Your name will be used on all Servob contributions; for the Observer our customary rule is that correspondents' names are used on major pieces (leader-page articles, Notebooks, important and exclusive news stories), but not necessarily on all items of straightforward reporting: and we shall prefer to apply this rather flexible rule to you, too.

I understand you will be in London next month: we shall be happy to see you then to discuss any further aspects of your appointment".

The second letter is dated the 15th October 1948 and made a different appointment upon different terms. It appointed the plaintiff to the staff of the Observer,
first in London and then in Washington for some years, on a full-time basis at a
yearly salary of £1,200 in London and a salary with living allowance elsewhere.
As far as it is material it reads:

"This is to inform you officially that we would like you to come back to
London at the end of November and to join our staff on a whole-time basis. We
would want you to leave for Washington at the end of December and to remain
there for at least one year and more probably for several years.

I suggested to you that we should ensure your future by giving you a contract for five years. I am quite confident that you can be an asset to this paper
for much longer than that, but would like to ask you if a three year promise of
employment would satisfy you. The reason for asking this is simply that five
years is much longer than we promise any of the other members of the staff and
might therefore cause some indignation amongst them. The promise of employment would be subject to your being willing to write whenever the paper might
need you most and not necessarily in Washington all the time.

The financial terms of our offer are a combined salary-cum-living allowance while in Washington of £2,000 per annum; when elsewhere your salary
would be at £1,200 with an additional living allowance if outside Britain.

We will, of course, have to talk over details of office accommodation,
travel expenses, etcetera with you before you go to Washington".

The two statutory statements came after the plaintiff's appointment as Political
and Lobby Correspondent of the Observer. The first is addressed to the plaintiff under the Contracts of Employment Act, and states that the Act requires
the Observer Ltd. to state certain of the main terms and conditions on which it
employs "you Nora Leah Beloff as at August 1, 1964". It states the commencement of employment as 1947, the rate of remuneration as £3,000 per year, the
normal hours of work, "subject to day to day circumstances," as 10.00 a.m. to
6.00 p.m. Tuesday to Friday, "and as required by the Head of your Department
on Saturday". "Your employment is subject to six months' notice on either side"
and "Your paid holiday entitlement is four weeks per calendar year" with Bank
holiday, with the provision that, "All holiday dates are to be settled by agreement with the Head of your Department/ the Manager": and that sickness payments are considered individually.

The second statement is described as a supplementary statement and is headed
by reference to the 1963 Act as amended by the Industrial Relations Act, 1971.
It is addressed to the plaintiff and includes a statement that she is entitled to
receive, and required to give notice of termination of employment under her
contract, or national agreements entered into by her Trade Union or in accordance with the above Acts.

The plaintiff said she assumed that she was in the Observer as a result of the
1947 letter, but that she did not remember signing it. She was in Washington

for the Observer from 1949 to 1950 as contemplated by the 1948 letter, and I have no doubt that those letters stated the terms under which she immediately thereafter entered upon her work for the Observer.

She said, however, that she must have received the statutory statements but that she did not think that she read them. It is of course clear that her work was not regulated by any specified hours; that she worked late hours, and had more than four weeks' holiday. It was submitted for the plaintiff that the statements were documents issued by the Observer Ltd. and that she was not bound by them. But she recognised that she must have received them, although she might not have read them; and it does at any rate seem that even after the coming into force of the Industrial Relations Act, 1971 her employers did not contemplate her as being outside the Act. But I do not rely on these statements in deciding whether or not the plaintiff was under a contract of service.

The Editor of the Observer said in evidence in answer to a question whether he could direct the plaintiff to New York or elsewhere, that it was for him to allocate jobs: and since 1948, before her appointment as Political and Lobby Correspondent, she was directed not only to Washington and to Moscow, but to cover Common Market negotiations, and since that appointment she has also done some foreign assignments for the Observer.

Like many journalists, such as Mr. Howard, Editor of the New Statesman, who gave evidence, she has broadcast and appeared on television. And she has written on occasions for certain other papers such as the Atlantic Monthly and Punch, and she has had leaves from the Observer to write books. But these incidents do not appear to have affected the permanent basis of her salaried employment with the Observer, and appear to have been, in the case of leaves for writing books at any rate, with the consent of the Observer. Indeed, leave itself tends to indicate a permanent full-time job on the staff.

In 1964 the plaintiff was appointed Political and Lobby Correspondent of the Observer, and she has since done that job interspersed with the foreign assignments for the Observer as I have mentioned. As the accredited Lobby Correspondent for the Observer she holds a very important and regular position in the Observer organisation, and, so far as I know, she is the only person in the Observer organisation who holds such a position. It means that she has on behalf of the Observer the advantages essential to a great national newspaper, of special access to the House of Commons, of arrangements available to the group of Lobby Correspondents, including various forms of help and briefings which are important, not only for writing informed articles but also for obtaining news items earlier than would otherwise be available for the Observer. This means, of course, that it is essential for the Observer that she keeps in constant touch with Parliament at all hours when any such advantages are likely to be gained by doing so. Her work as Lobby Correspondent, as she explained, is not just the production of an article but also the reporting of political news. This work includes news and other coverage of Parliamentary occurrences for the Observer, including in particular briefings, news and other advantages which, as

I have indicated, the Lobby Correspondent is appointed by his paper to obtain and supply. The job of Political and Lobby Correspondent for the Observer is essential for and woven into its political coverage. Such a paper as the Observer without its accredited Lobby Correspondent is hardly conceivable.

The plaintiff writes for the Observer a weekly article headed "Politics-Nora Beloff": it is usually on one theme. She also writes profiles, and on the major speeches of politicians, and she even writes leaders. The Editor described her as "a very active member of the general editorial staff" and said that she shared in the editorial responsibility of the newspaper. She is a regular attendant at weekly and ad hoc editorial meetings presided over by the Editor and whose wide scope is indicated by the functions of those who attend — deputy and assistant editors, chief reporters, the Business Editor, the Leader Writer, the News Editor, and others as advisable from time to time. The plaintiff said its purpose was to plan the paper for the next issue, to look ahead and to have a general discussion and exchange ideas. She said that her article for the following issue was very often discussed. The Editor said that she tells him what she is going to write and that discussion only arises if it overlaps with something else. The Editor has certainly some strong-minded persons attending these meetings and, as might be expected from his experience and wisdom, he said that "my government is as a rule consensual". The plaintiff said that she was free to decline to write on a suggested topic. Of course, she could not be forced to do so, nor can I imagine Mr. Astor attempting to force her. The editorial meetings are for discussion, without power of decision; that rests solely with the Editor, and not the less so, although as a rule consensually exercised by him.

I come to other recognised indications of contract of service, in addition to her substantial regular salary for her full-time job and her holidays. Apart from an electric typewriter, which the plaintiff has at home, the plaintiff does not provide any equipment of her own which she uses for her work. All the Observer's resources are available to her to carry out her job. She has an office in the Observer building, and a secretary who is provided by the Observer. She does not use her own capital for the job, nor is her remuneration affected by the financial success of otherwise of the Observer. In addition to P.A.Y.E. deductions, deduction for the pension scheme to which she belongs is also made by the Observer from her salary. All these indications are in favour of her contract being a contract of service.

The submission relied on for a contrary conclusion was, as I have indicated, that such contracts were limited to contracts to do lowly tasks under supervision. But this became clearly unsustainable, and at a later stage it was submitted that the overriding consideration was whether the plaintiff produced an article every week or worked full-time for the Observer or, as it was put, whether she was a contributor and not a reporter. But this submission clearly fails on the facts which I have stated — her job was full-time and was far from being limited to a weekly article and in fact included reporting Parliamentary events. Nor (in accordance with, e.g. Market Investigations Ltd. v. Minister of Social Security [1969] 2 Q.B. 173 at 176C) does a full-time contract of service exclude some television and broadcasting appearances and the writing of such articles as she wrote for Punch and Atlantic Monthly.

I have increasingly in the course of this case, as the relevant facts came to be deployed, inclined to the conclusion which I now firmly hold that the plaintiff's job is "an integral part of the business" of the Observer and its organisation and that the plaintiff's contract with the Observer Ltd. is a contract of service. My conclusion, therefore, is that the copyright in the memorandum originally vested in the Observer Ltd. and not in the plaintiff.

The Supreme Court of Canada has since set out the appropriate test for determining the existence of an employment relationship in the context of assessing vicarious liability for a tortious act. It could be argued that the interests of justice and fairness as between the parties are likely to be some-what different in this context than in the context of a copyright dispute (where finding employment may deprive the weaker party of rights that he or she would otherwise enjoy). Nevertheless, it seems likely that the test articulated in the next case will be followed for the purposes of determining whether section 13(3) of the Copyright Act applies.

671122 Ontario Ltd. v. Sagaz Industries Canada Inc., [2001] 2 S.C.R. 983 (S.C.C.)

Supreme Court of Canada

2001: June 19 / 2001: September 28

Present: McLachlin C.J. and Iacobucci, Major,

Bastarache, Binnie, Arbour and LeBel JJ.

MAJOR J.: —

. . .

36 Various tests have emerged in the case law to help determine if a worker is an employee or an independent contractor. The distinction between an employee and an independent contractor applies not only in vicarious liability, but also to the application of various forms of employment legislation, the availability of an action for wrongful dismissal, the assessment of business and income taxes, the priority taken upon an employer's insolvency and the application of contractual rights (Flannigan, supra, at p. 25). Accordingly, much of the case law on point while not written in the context of vicarious liability is still helpful.

37 The Federal Court of Appeal thoroughly reviewed the relevant case law in Wiebe Door Services Ltd. v. M.N.R., [1986] 3 F.C. 553. As MacGuigan J.A. noted, the original criterion of the employment relationship was the control test

set out by Baron Bramwell in Regina v. Walker (1858), 27 L.J.M.C. 207, and adopted by this Court in Hôpital Notre-Dame de l'Espérance v. Laurent, [1978] 1 S.C.R. 605. It is expressed as follows: "the essential criterion of employer-employee relations is the right to give orders and instructions to the employee regarding the manner in which to carry out his work" (Hôpital Notre-Dame de l'Espérance, supra, at p. 613).

38   This criterion has been criticized as wearing "an air of deceptive simplicity" (Atiyah, supra, at p. 41). The main problems are set out by MacGuigan J.A. in Wiebe Door, supra, at pp. 558-59:

A principal inadequacy [with the control test] is its apparent dependence on the exact terms in which the task in question is contracted for: where the contract contains detailed specifications and conditions, which would be the normal expectation in a contract with an independent contractor, the control may even be greater than where it is to be exercised by direction on the job, as would be the normal expectation in a contract with a servant, but a literal application of the test might find the actual control to be less. In addition, the test has broken down completely in relation to highly skilled and professional workers, who possess skills far beyond the ability of their employers to direct.

39   An early attempt to deal with the problems of the control test was the development of a fourfold test known as the "entrepreneur test". It was set out by W. O. Douglas (later Justice) in "Vicarious Liability and Administration of Risk I" (1928-1929), 38 Yale L.J. 584, and applied by Lord Wright in Montreal v. Montreal Locomotive Works Ltd., [1947] 1 D.L.R. 161 (P.C.), at p. 169:

In earlier cases a single test, such as the presence or absence of control, was often relied on to determine whether the case was one of master and servant, mostly in order to decide issues of tortious liability on the part of the master or superior. In the more complex conditions of modern industry, more complicated tests have often to be applied. It has been suggested that a fourfold test would in some cases be more appropriate, a complex involving (1) control; (2) ownership of the tools; (3) chance of profit; (4) risk of loss. Control in itself is not always conclusive.

40   As MacGuigan J.A. notes, a similar general test, known as the "organization test" or "integration test" was used by Denning L.J. (as he then was) in Stevenson Jordan and Harrison, Ltd. v. Macdonald, [1952] 1 The Times L.R. 101 (C.A.), at p. 111:

One feature which seems to run through the instances is that, under a contract of service, a man is employed as part of the business, and his work is done as an integral part of the business; whereas, under a contract for services, his work, although done for the business, is not integrated into it but is only accessory to it.

41   This decision imported the language "contract of service" (employee) and "contract for services" (independent contractor) into the analysis. The organization test was approved by this Court in Co-operators Insurance, supra (followed in Mayer, supra), where Spence J. observed that courts had moved away from the control test under the pressure of novel situations, replacing it instead with a

type of organization test in which the important question was whether the alleged servant was part of his employer's organization (from Fleming, supra, at p. 416).

42 However, as MacGuigan J.A. noted in Wiebe Door, the organization test has had "less vogue in other common-law jurisdictions" (p. 561), including England and Australia. For one, it can be a difficult test to apply. If the question is whether the activity or worker is integral to the employer's business, this question can usually be answered affirmatively. For example, the person responsible for cleaning the premises is technically integral to sustaining the business, but such services may be properly contracted out to people in business on their own account (see R. Kidner, "Vicarious liability: for whom should the 'employer' be liable?" (1995), 15 Legal Stud. 47, at p. 60). As MacGuigan J.A. further noted in Wiebe Door, if the main test is to demonstrate that, without the work of the alleged employees the employer would be out of business, a factual relationship of mutual dependency would always meet the organization test of [page1003] an employee even though this criterion may not accurately reflect the parties' intrinsic relationship (pp. 562-63).

43 Despite these criticisms, MacGuigan J.A. acknowledges, at p. 563, that the organization test can be of assistance:

> Of course, the organization test of Lord Denning and others produces entirely acceptable results when properly applied, that is, when the question of organization or integration is approached from the persona of the "employee" and not from that of the "employer," because it is always too easy from the superior perspective of the larger enterprise to assume that every contributing cause is so arranged purely for the convenience of the larger entity. We must keep in mind that it was with respect to the business of the employee that Lord Wright [in Montreal] addressed the question "Whose business is it?"

44 According to MacGuigan J.A., the best synthesis found in the authorities is that of Cooke J. in Market Investigations, Ltd. v. Minister of Social Security, [1968] 3 All E.R. 732 (Q.B.D.), at pp. 737-38 (followed by the Privy Council in Lee Ting Sang v. Chung Chi-Keung, [1990] 2 A.C. 374, per Lord Griffiths, at p. 382):

> The observations of LORD WRIGHT, of DENNING, L.J., and of the judges of the Supreme Court in the U.S.A. suggest that the fundamental test to be applied is this: "Is the person who has engaged himself to perform these services performing them as a person in business on his own account?". If the answer to that question is "yes", then the contract is a contract for services. If the answer is "no" then the contract is a contract of service. No exhaustive list has been compiled and perhaps no exhaustive list can be compiled of considerations which are relevant in determining that question, nor can strict rules be laid down as to the relative weight which the various considerations should carry in particular cases. The most that can be said is that control will no doubt always have to be considered, although it can no longer be regarded as the sole determining factor; and that factors, which may be of importance, are such matters as whether the man performing the services provides his [page1004] own equipment, whether he hires his own helpers, what degree of financial risk he takes, what degree of responsibility for investment and management he has, and whether and how far he has an opportunity of profiting from sound management in the performance of his task.

. . .

46 In my opinion, there is no one conclusive test which can be universally applied to determine whether a person is an employee or an independent contractor. Lord Denning stated in Stevenson Jordan, supra, that it may be impossible to give a precise definition of the distinction (p. 111) and, similarly, Fleming observed that "no single test seems to yield an invariably clear and acceptable answer to the many variables of ever changing employment relations ..." (p. 416). Further, I agree with MacGuigan J.A. in Wiebe Door, at p. 563, citing Atiyah, supra, at p. 38, that what must always occur is a search for the total relationship of the parties:

> [I]t is exceedingly doubtful whether the search for a formula in the nature of a single test for identifying a contract of service any longer serves a useful purpose.... The most that can profitably be done is to examine all the possible factors which have been referred to in these cases as bearing on the nature of the relationship between the parties concerned. Clearly not all of these factors will be relevant in all cases, or have the same weight in all cases. Equally clearly no magic formula can be propounded for determining which factors should, in any given case, be treated as the determining ones.

47 Although there is no universal test to determine whether a person is an employee or an independent contractor, I agree with MacGuigan J.A. that a persuasive approach to the issue is that taken by Cooke J. in Market Investigations, supra. The central question is whether the person who has been engaged to perform the services is performing them as a person in business on his own account. In making this determination, the level of control the employer has over the worker's activities will always be a factor. However, other factors to consider include whether the worker provides his or her own equipment, whether the worker hires his or her own helpers, the degree of financial risk taken by the worker, the degree of responsibility for investment and management held by the worker, and the worker's opportunity for profit in the performance of his or her tasks.

48 It bears repeating that the above factors constitute a non-exhaustive list, and there is no set formula as to their application. The relative weight of each will depend on the particular facts and circumstances of the case.

In addition to establishing whether a person is an employee for the purposes of section 13(3), it is necessary to establish whether the work at issue was produced in the course of his or her employment. Works produced in the employee's personal time for purposes other than the performance of obligations under the employment contract typically fall outside of the operation of s. 13(3).

Hannis v. Teevan, (1998), 81 C.P.R. (3d) 496 (Ont. C.A.), additional reasons at (1998), 81 C.P.R. (3d) 496 at 514 (Ont. C.A.)

Ontario Court of Appeal

McKinlay, Goudge and Southey (ad hoc) JJ.A.

Heard: April 7-8, 1998
Judgment: June 18, 1998[FN*]
Docket: CA C21503

. . .

The judgment of the court was delivered by *Southey J.* (ad hoc):

1 This is an appeal by the plaintiff from the decision of Mr. Justice McDermid, dated March 17, 1995, dismissing the claims of the plaintiff arising out of the termination of his employment by The University of Western Ontario (the "University") for cause and without notice on October 16, 1986. The plaintiff had been employed since 1972 as the Director of the Social Science Computing Laboratory (the "SSCL") at the University and as an Adjunct Professor without tenure.

2 The claims against the University were for wrongful dismissal, infringement and other remedies arising out of copyrights in computer software claimed by the plaintiff, damages for inducing breach of contract and a declaration that the University held certain property in trust for him. The claims against the defendants Teevan and Bjerring were abandoned at the opening of trial. The plaintiff did not appeal the dismissal by the learned trial judge of his claims against the other individual defendants. The claim for inducing breach of contract was not pressed in this court, with the result that the appeal related only to the claims for wrongful dismissal and the claims arising out of copyright.

3 The plaintiff was dismissed because of his continued use for his own purposes of the University's computer, allegedly without the consent or knowledge of the University. ...:

. . .

Copyright in Tycho/Hasp

44 The only issue respecting copyright raised on appeal related to the appellant's claim of copyright in TYCHO/HASP. TYCHO/HASP was a computer software system which enabled multiple users of a mini-computer to obtain computing services from, and exchange information with a remote main frame computer.

45 Mr. Roland made 3 submissions without elaboration in oral argument. Those submissions were:

    1.   The TYCHO/HASP system was the personal research project of the appellant, notwithstanding the contrary finding of the learned trial judge, because the appellant said it was his personal research project, and it had been accepted as such.

2. The University is estopped from denying the copyright of the appellant in the software, because he had relied on his belief in the existence of copyright while marketing the software over a 10-year period.

3. The appellant had paid approximately $190,000 to his consultants to write the software, and had taken assignments of copyright from them.

46 None of these three points is telling, in my opinion. As to the first, determination of the issue of copyright does not depend on whether or not the system is labelled as the personal research project of the appellant. As to the second, the elements necessary in law for an estoppel were not present. There was no representation by the University and no detrimental reliance by the appellant. As to the third, the appellant received substantial net pecuniary benefit from marketing and servicing the software, despite payments to those whom he described as consultants. The assignments of copyright from them were ineffective, because they themselves had no copyright in the software for reasons to be explained below.

47 I turn then to the points raised in the appellant's factum. The first is that the learned trial judge failed to consider that the University had infringed the appellant's copyright in certain design notes, drawings and diagrams. The documents in question were handwritten design notes, drawings and diagrams prepared by the appellant in 1968 before he commenced employment at the University. We were not referred to evidence sufficient to prove that TYCHO/HASP constituted an infringement of the appellant's copyright, if any, in the contents of those documents. It is significant that the documents, which were the basis of the appellant's claim respecting TYCHO/HASP, were not proferred in his evidence in chief, but were put to him in cross-examination by counsel for the University. They were marked as Exhibits 13A and 13B. The appellant admitted in cross-examination that he never showed these documents to anyone at the University. The TYCHO/HASP software reflected the idea in the 1968 notes, but did not copy any form of expression in them, as would be necessary for infringement of copyright.

48 The learned trial judge relied on the evidence of an independent expert in computer technology, Mr. W.G. Hutchinson, in finding that it was a "long way" from exhibits 13A and B to the source code for TYCHO/HASP. In my judgment, the evidence amply supports the following finding by the learned trial judge:

> The "idea" is at one extreme of the process, and the source code is at the other end. In between, there are many steps or phases, including the preparation of functional and technical design specifications, the use of computer programming languages to write the code, assembling it in machine language, execution and testing. The skills required to accomplish all these tasks are usually not resident in one person. To go from what is incorporated in Exhibits 13A and B to the finished programme known as TYCHO/HASP would require a significant amount of analysis, planning, and programming by experienced communications programmers. Such programming ability is highly skilled in nature and would likely require someone with a degree in computer science. Dr. Hanis did not possess this ability.

Therefore, I reject any suggestion by Dr. Hanis that he had "created" TYCHO/HASP before coming to UWO and that he merely "implemented" his "original work" after his arrival. I find that Dr. Hanis had an idea, which Mr. Kushnir took and used to write most of the source code for TYCHO/HASP under Dr. Hanis' direction.

49 The second point raised in the appellant's factum is that the learned trial judge failed to consider that the appellant was an employer of the consultants who developed the source code for TYCHO/HASP and had obtained from them assignments of the copyright to which they were entitled under s. 13(3) of the *Copyright Act*, R.S.C. 1985, c. C-42. The relevant portions of s. 13 read as follows:

> 13(1) Subject to this Act, the author of a work shall be the first owner of the copyright therein.
>
> . . .
>
> (3) Where the author of a work was in the employment of some other person under a contract of service or apprenticeship and the work was made in the course of his employment by that person, the person by whom the author was employed shall, in the absence of any agreement to the contrary, be the first owner of the copyright....
>
> (4) The owner of the copyright in any work may assign the right, either wholly or partially, and either generally or subject to territorial limitations, and either for the whole term of the copyright or for any other part thereof, and may grant any interest in the right by licence, but no assignment or grant is valid unless it is in writing signed by the owner of the right in respect of which the assignment or grant is made, or by his duly authorized agent.

50 Although the appellant had obtained assignments of copyright from his consultants, who were the authors of the TYCHO/HASP software, those assignments, in my judgment, conveyed no ownership to the appellant for two reasons:

1. The consultants were all employees of the University, so that the University was the owner of the copyright in their work under s. 13(3). No records were kept to establish that these authors produced the software outside of the course of their employment by the University.

2. The appellant emphasized that the authors were independent contractors, or independent consultants, as opposed to persons under a contract of service with him, so that he did not become the owner of copyright in their work because of the operation of s. 13.

51 The third point raised in the appellant's factum is that the learned trial judge failed to consider that the University assigned copyright to the appellant. The assignment was said to be contained in correspondence between the appellant and the University in 1976. The correspondence consisted of a letter, dated March 29, 1976, from the appellant to Dean Kymlicka and a letter dated June 28, 1976, from A.K. Adlington, Vice-President, Administration and Finance, to

Dean Kymlicka, with copy to the appellant, approving the proposal contained in the appellant's letter.

52 The appellant stated in his letter that in the course of developing the Computing Laboratory from "ground zero" he had developed certain software which he had decided to supply in modified and extended versions with the requisite consulting services "to very limited numbers of sites on the following basis". The provisions relevant to copyright are the first two, which read as follows:

1. As the author, I intend to exercise copyright ownership over the software and modification and extensions thereto under section E-X-1 of the Faculty Handbook.

2. In order to proceed in a clearcut fashion, I have invested in the establishment of a firm, Tycho Research Associates, (P.O. Box #415, Station 'B', London, Ontario). Tycho is presently an individual proprietorship, but will be incorporated if and when activity should warrant the expense. Ownership of the software copyrights is held by Tycho and Tycho will contract with interested clients for the supply of modified versions of RSTS/UT200 or RSTS/HASP and the prerequisite consulting services.

53 The short answer to the third point in the appellant's factum is that the letter of March 29, 1976, did not contain any words of conveyance or transfer of any copyright interest from the University to the appellant. The appellant in his letter did not recognize that the University owned the copyright of which he was seeking an assignment. Instead, he asserted in the letter that he owned the copyright in the software and would licence it to the University.

54 For the foregoing reasons, I see no error in the decision of the learned trial judge denying the copyright interest in TYCHO/HASP claimed by the appellant.

---

2. Crown Copyright

Section 12 of the *Act* states that, "Without prejudice to any rights of privileges of the Crown, where any work is, or has been, prepared or published by or under the direction or control of Her Majesty or any government department, the copyright in the work shall, subject to any agreement with the author, belong to Her Majesty and in that case shall continue for the remainder of the calendar year of the first publication of the work and for a period of fifty years following the end of that calendar year." This stands in stark contrast to the US law, which denies copyright protection to any work "prepared by an officer or employee of the United States Government as part of that person's official duties." (17 U.S.C. § § 101, 105.) Because Crown copyright subsists for fifty years following the year of publication, it would seem that there is no temporal limit to copyright in unpublished works belonging to the Crown. In the next case, the Federal Court of Appeal insists that the position of the Crown as plaintiff in a copyright action "even if it be 'unusual', is no more relevant than the colour of a litigant's hair." This worked in the Crown's favour in Lorimer (while arguably running counter to the public interest in open and accessible democratic governance). The refusal to accord special status to the Crown worked to its disadvantage, however, in the recent case of *Manitoba v. CCLA*, below, where the Court of Appeal ruled that the Act also *binds* the Crown.

R. v. James Lorimer & Co. (1983), 77 C.P.R. (2d) 262 (Fed. C.A.)

Federal Court of Appeal.

Heald, Ryan and Mahoney JJ.

MAHONEY J.: — This is an appeal and cross-appeal from a judgment of the trial division which found the respondent had infringed the appellant's copyright in a certain work but denied the appellant costs as well as the injunctive relief and exemplary damages sought and dismissed the respondent's counterclaim without costs. The learned trial judge found that the Crown owned the copyright in its work. He rejected the defenses of fair dealing, violation of Charter freedoms and public interest. He characterized the infringing work as an abridgement and the respondent's conduct as deliberate and a "blatant disregard" of the appellant's rights . The infringement was done for a "primarily commercial" purpose. It is agreed the appellant suffered no economic loss. The findings of fact by the learned trial judge are amply supported by the evidence and are not to be disturbed.

The Copyright Act, R.S.C. 1970, c. C-30, provides:

> 11. Without prejudice to any rights or privileges of the Crown, where any work is, or has been, prepared or published by or under the direction of control of Her Majesty or any governmental department, the copyright in the work shall, subject to any agreement with the author, belong to Her Majesty and in such case shall continue for a period of fifty years from the date of the first publication of the work.

The work subject of the Crown copyright here is a report entitled "The State of Competition in the Canadian Petroleum Industry". The content of the work is the statement of evidence prepared by the Director of Investigation and Research under the Combines Investigation Act, R.S.C. 1970, c. C-23, submitted to the Restrictive Trade Practices Commission pursuant to s. 18(1) of that Act ensuing upon an inquiry instituted on application under s. 7(1). The appellant caused the 1,748 page work to be published in seven volumes and offered for public sale at $70 a set, $10 a volume (ex. A-1). The respondent's infringing work is an abridgement of the Crown's work consisting, in the words of its publisher's introduction, of:

> ... the full text of Volume I — the findings and recommendations of the Director regarding the oil industry, together with much of the supporting discussion

and information from Volumes II-VI. In the interests of keeping this volume to a reasonable length, some of the more technical sections have been omitted. But conclusions and summaries from all sections of the report have been reprinted ...

In this volume, the original volume, chapter and section heads from the full report have been retained, as have their letter and numerical designations.

Footnote numbers from the original report have been retained. Readers wishing to obtain footnote references can find them in Volume VII of the full report.

The infringing work, a single, 626 page volume, was retailed at $14.95 (exs. A-2 and A-3).

Dealing first with the appeal, the first point in issue is the refusal to grant the relief sought, which was:

(a) a permanent injunction enjoining and restraining the Defendant company, its officers, servants, agents and employees from producing or reproducing substantial portions of the Report of Robert J. Bertrand, Q.C., Director of Investigation and Research, Combines Investigation Act, entitled "The State of Competition in the Canadian Petroleum Industry" in a book entitled "Canada's Oil Monopoly" or in any other form whatsoever;

(b) a mandatory injunction requiring the Defendant company, its officers, servants, agents and employees to immediately deliver up to the Plaintiff all plates used or itended to be used for the production of the book entitled "Canada's Oil Monopoly";

(c) a mandatory injunction requiring the Defendant company, its officers, servants, agents and employees to immediately deliver up to the Plaintiff all copies of the book entitled "Canada's Oil Monopoly" which are presently in its possession or control;...

(e) an accounting of all monies received by the Defendant company from the publication and sale of the book entitled "Canada's Oil Monopoly" and payment over to the Plaintiff of the resulting profits from such publication and sale;

(f) exemplary damages;

The learned trial judge, after reviewing the evidence found

All of that seems to confirm that Mr. Lorimer knew and acted at all times in a manner consistent with a person who knew that what he was doing was on the face of it an infringement of the plaintiff 's copyright, and that he should either secure the consent or permission of someone to go ahead with it or expect to negotiate some kind of licence or royalty, and I therefore conclude that, if the copyright laws are to mean anything, then this defendant ought not to have done what it did in publishing this report in the form it did without the consent of the plaintiff.

In denying exemplary damages and substituting what is, in effect, a compulsory licence for the injunctive relief, the learned trial judge said:

...In terms of remedy, the plaintiff does not seek any accounting profits. I am relieved, therefore, of the burden of examining into the profit and loss information of the defendant company. I do not think that justice is served by having this court attempt or either of the parties attempt at this time to withdraw from circulation or from publication a further distribution of copies of this work. It is not a situation, in other words, of the plaintiff 's original work in its distribution or sale that the fact the plaintiff 's economic position is adversely effected. Obviously, we have circumstances which mitigate the infringement of copyright to some extent. In the first place, the Crown is an unusual plaintiff and really is not greatly interested in income or revenue from this work. It could never approach the cost of the inquiry which ran for several years and undoubtedly cost many millions of dollars. The printing cost associated with the work was set upon the evidence by a very rough gauge to somehow cover printing costs which, I am sure, did not take place. So, the importance of the revenue or the significance of the revenue to this plaintiff is very minimal. Furthermore, I repeat that the defendant's publication did not then and certainly now is not having any adverse effect on further distribution or sales of the plaintiff 's original work and, therefore, I see no purpose in ordering a recall or injunction by enjoining the defendant from further sales of this work at this time.

It not being, therefore, a situation in which the Plaintiff should be compensated or even seeks compensation in the sense of loss of revenues from the sale of its own work, and not being one where I feel at this time the distribution of the plaintiff 's work is adversely affected by the presence of the defendant's work in the market-place, that injunction is not a proper remedy.

Again turning to the essential element of the defendant's transgression of the civil law, it is that it went ahead and did it without seeking permission what it, in my opinion, either knew or should have known could not be done properly without permission or could not be done without some consequences without permission. It is, in my opinion, therefore, an appropriate case for compensation not by way of injunction or damages either exemplary or punitive, but rather by way of royalty.

...In exercising his discretion to refuse the injunctive relief, the learned trial judge found persuasive the facts that the infringement had not adversely affected distribution and sales of the appellant's infringed work nor adversely affected the revenue deriving from its sales as well as the unusual character of the appellant as a plaintiff. The characterization of the Crown as an "unusual plaintiff " lies, I take it, in his finding of fact that it was not much interested in income or revenue from its work and not, I trust, in a generalization that the Crown is to be treated differently than other litigants.

The Act is clear. Infringement does not require that the infringing work compete in the market-place with that infringed; it requires only that the infringer do something that the copyright owner alone has the right to do. It follows that, where infringement of copyright has been established, the owner of the copyright is prima facie entitled to an injunction restraining further infringement. It likewise follows that, where the infringing work is found to include any substantial part of a work in which copyright subsists, the copyright owner is to be deemed owner of all copies of the infringing work and all production plates and is prima facie entitled to the assistance of the court in gaining possession of them. The onus is on the infringer to establish grounds upon which the court may properly exercise its discretion against granting such relief: Massie & Renwick, Ltd. v. Underwriters' Survey Bureau et al., [1937] 2 D.L.R. 213, [1937] S.C.R. 265. Those grounds must lie in the conduct of the copyright owner, not in the conduct or motives of the infringer. The fact that the copyright owner has suffered no damages as a result of the infringement is not a basis for refusing an injunction: Bouchet v. Kyriacopoulos (1964), 45 C.P.R. 265, 27 Fox Pat. C. 91.

A computation of damages based on an appropriate royalty is acceptable where the copyright owner does not prove he would have made the sales the infringer did: Dominion Manufacturers Ltd. v. Electrolier Mfg. Co. Ltd., [1939] 2 D.L.R. 482, [1939] Ex. C.R. 204. However, I find no authority for requiring a copyright owner to acquiesce in a continuing infringement against payment of a royalty. That is tantamount to the imposition of a compulsory licence. In the absence of legislative authority, the court has no power to do that.

I am of the opinion that the learned trial judge applied wrong principles and erred in law in denying the relief sought in paras. (a), (b) and (c) of the prayer for relief and substituting for that relief a royalty on the future sale of infringing copies.

The question of exemplary damages is more difficult. In addition to what has already been quoted, the learned trial judge characterized the respondent's conduct as a "blatant disregard of what was obviously the right of the Plaintiff under our copyright laws ...". He also found that "the Defendant's purpose was primarily commercial". Taken as a whole, the findings of fact are expressed in terminology that would lead one to think that an award of exemplary damages was in the offing.

. . .

The grounds for refusing exemplary damages, unlike the grounds for refusing injunctive relief, are to be found in the conduct and motives of the infringer. The absence of economic injury and the "unusual" nature of the Crown as a plaintiff are not good reasons to deny the Crown exemplary damages. The language of the reasons for judgment is difficult to reconcile with the conclusion that this is not an appropriate case for exemplary damages. It is manifest that the learned trial judge, notwithstanding his characterization of the unquestionably deliberate infringement, motivated by the respondent's marketing considerations, as "blatant", did not find it warranted punishment, nor did he see deterrence as a desirable object. It cannot be said that he clearly erred in so exercising his discretion and I do not feel it open to substitute my view of such an infringement for his.

In denying the appellant costs, the learned trial judge had the following to say:

> Turning to the question of costs, I am not going to award costs, which would normally follow the event, and I have given that very extensive thought. The Crown has been justified in its pursuit of the interpretation of the copyright law as it applies to his position and has been successful. The defendant in infringing the copyright law here, as I have said repeatedly, did without permission what it should have known required permission. However, it did not unfairly deal with the work, put together a fair abridgement of it, and that is upon all of the evidence, and now having been put in a position of paying the royalties that it would have on its own evidence expected to pay if it had got the permission, I don't feel it is a case where the defendant needs to be punished beyond that point by the assumption of the costs that would normally follow such a judgment.

Here again I allude to the unusual position of the plaintiff in this matter, being the Crown. Of course, there are a number of elements that are singular to this case. In the ownership of this work, in the protection of it, it is, after all, somewhat extraordinary that we are dealing here with the protection of copyright in a work which is the obligation of the owner, and the owner does so, but it is its obligation to see that it receives the widest possible dissemination and, in concluding that the defendant in this matter went about without permission to publish a version that would be more accessible to the public, he was vindicated in that judgment by the number of purchases that would indeed have been higher had the legal difficulties not intervened, and also that the defendant did a fair abridgement of the work and, finally, that perhaps the treatment that I have given to the costs in the matter can be taken as a reflection that the defendant can at least partially be forgiven for assuming, because of the public nature of the document involved, that the stance in respect to copyright would be somewhat less stringent than would be expected in a private work.

I have said again and again that does not excuse the defendant for its blatant disregard of what was obviously the right of the plaintiff under our copyright laws, but I think it is a situation in which the Crown is able, without adversity, to bear its own costs and that I think it is a proper circum- stance to allow a proper case to not further burden the Defendant in this matter by bearing the costs of both parties.

The Copyright Act provides:

> 20(2) The costs of all parties in any proceedings in respect of the infringement of copyright shall be in the absolute discretion of the court.

That absolute discretion is, nevertheless, to be exercised judicially....

It is trite law that costs are not awarded to punish an unsuccessful party. There was a time when the "rule of dignity" dictated that the Crown neither asked nor paid costs in the ordinary course of events. That time is long past and the position of the Crown, even if it be "unusual", is no more relevant than the colour of a litigant's hair. With respect, none of the reasons given for denying the appellant costs have anything to do with the case nor any facts connected with it or leading up to it. I say that specifically of any assumption the respondent may have felt entitled to make as to the appellant's reaction to the infringement. An innocent invasion of another's rights may be a different matter but I fail to see that a deliberate invasion in the expectation that the aggrieved party will acquiesce is a fact justifying an exercise of discretion to the detriment of the aggrieved party. The appellant had a clear right of action; neither it nor its subject-matter were trivial. The Attorney-General proceeded in this court immediately, expeditiously and economically. The appellant was entirely successful at trial in all respects but obtaining a remedy the law provided. There was no proper basis for a judicial exercise of discretion denying the appellant costs.

The cross-appeal is concerned with defences raised by the respondent and rejected at trial and with the dismissal of the counterclaim. The first defence was that of fair dealing. ...The respondent says its abridgment was a fair dealing for the purposes of review. After considering the authorities, the learned trial judge concluded that such fair dealing "... requires as a minimum some dealing with the work other than simply condensing it into an abridged version and reproducing it under the author's name." The trial judge was right.

The second defence was that of public interest which is posed in the respondent's memorandum of fact and law in the following terms: Did the respondent's publication further the disclosure to the public of facts and material relating to alleged misdeeds or other matters of a serious nature that are of importance to the country and to the public's welfare, such that the defence of public interest applies on the facts of this particular case?

Three copyright decisions were cited in support of the defence. In Hubbard et al. v. Vosper et al., [1972] 2 Q.B. 84 (C.A.), the alleged copyright infringement involved confidential documents of the Church of Scientology and, in Beloff v. Pressdram Ltd. et al., [1973] R.P.C. 765 (Ch. Div.), the work subject of copyright was an unpublished document. Both deal with public interest in the context of information that ought to be public and is not, which is certainly not the situation here. The learned trial judge found:

> The extent of the disclosure in the report was very great. There was no suggestion that the public was suffering under any deprivation on the part of the authors of this report or those responsible for its distribution. Free copies were given out in very large numbers, put in libraries across the country and, therefore, there is not in the circumstances of this case any justification that relates to some concern that the public might not be fully informed of the subject matter of this industry. Furthermore, it seems to me that Mr. Lorimer knew that.

I have no doubt that a defence of public interest as enunciated in the English cases is available in proper circumstances against an assertion of Crown copyright. However, the facts here do not support its application and the learned trial judge was right to reject it....

The third defence was based on the Canadian Charter of Rights and Freedoms, which provides:

> 1. The Canadian Charter of Rights and Freedoms guarantees the rights and freedoms set out in it subject only to such reasonable limits prescribed by law as can be demonstrably justified in a free and democratic society.
>
> 2. Everyone has the following fundamental freedoms:
>
>> (b) freedom of thought, belief, opinion and expression, including freedom of the press and other media of communication;

Again, I agree with the learned trial judge that there is no merit in this defence. If, indeed, the constraints on infringement of copyright could be construed as an unjustified limitation on an infringer's freedom of expression in some circumstances, this is not among them. So little of its own thought, belief, opinion and expression is contained in the respondent's infringing work that it is properly to be regarded as entirely an appropriation of the thought, belief, opinion and expression of the author of the infringed work. ...

I would allow the appeal and dismiss the cross-appeal with costs here and in the Trial Division.... .

David Vaver, "Copyright & The State in Canada and the U.S."

10 I.P.J. 187 (1996)

In Canada, the government has copyright in the works it produces; in the US, the government does not. ... Reading the Canadian provision, one is immediately struck by the obscurity of the opening words: "without prejudice to any rights or privileges of the Crown". What rights or privileges are these? On investigation, we find this refers to the ancient royal prerogative: the crown's "sole right of printing a somewhat miscellaneous collection of works, no catalogue of which appears to be exhaustive." This non-exhaustive catalogue — which in the 17th century was said to encompass *everything written* — is said today to include statutes, orders-in-council, proclamations, admiralty charts, and (some even say) judicial decisions. The right is conveniently said to be perpetual (so it would cover statutes long ago repealed) and not to lapse through non-use or non-assertion.

The next striking thing is the breadth of the following phrase in section 12. On top of the prerogative power, this allocates copyright to the crown in "any work [that] is, or has been, prepared or published by or under the direction or control of Her Majesty or a government department." If those "or"s are truly conjunctive, that phrase of 24 words potentially includes 24 classes of material. Unsurprisingly, it appears wide enough for the government to publish a work prepared by a freelancer, divesting her copyright and revesting a new 50-year copyright in the government!

To cap matters, we find that, if section 12 fails it, the government can rely on the parts of the *Copyright Act* applying to private sector employers. It is on this theory that it has claimed the copyright in all creative work produced by prisoners serving their sentence. Recently, an inmate served his time, opened an art business and wanted to reclaim a painting he had done in jail as part of his rehabilitation. A federal judge decided the government owned both the painting and its copyright. Not only had the inmate been an involuntary tenant of Her Majesty, but also (unbeknownst to him) an employee of Her Majesty paid at the rate of $6 per day. His employer therefore owned copyright in his job output. The artist could not even photograph his painting without the leave of the government.

Small wonder that section 12 has attracted abuse such as "legislative monstrosity" and "atrocious drafting", nor that as recently as 1981 a study by Barry Torno bore the title *Crown Copyright in Canada: a Legacy of Confusion*. For to understand what copyrights the federal and provincial governments could claim at the end of the 20th century, Torno had to retreat into mid 17th century Britain to the time of the restoration of Charles II, well before the passage of England's first copyright law in 1710. Not surprisingly, he found confusion then, let alone now, about exactly what the ancient law was or meant at a time when the role of the monarchy was changing and, with it, the extent of its despotic power. An exercise like this is only for the dedicated antiquarian, masochist or crown lawyer — of which I am none. Sadly, nothing has changed in the 14 years since Torno wrote. The "legislative monstrosity" with its "atrocious drafting" sits there in its pristine glory and, in the waning years of Elizabeth II, decisions made by Charles II's judges are still relied on by the governments of Canada and the provinces to support their claims of copyright. The smell of the crumbling pages of 17th century law reports hangs over the dancing pixels on the electronic highway.

. . .

WHY COPYRIGHT FOR CANADIAN GOVERNMENT WORKS?

Why then does the Canadian government exercise copyright over its works? Looking at section 12 of the *Copyright Act* and the treasury board rules implementing it, we may posit the following:

(a) If Ordinary Citizens Can Have Copyright in Their Works, So Should Governments

Arguments for equality and equal protection are often attractive, but they founder here because:

- the Crown is already treated *better* than everyone else: e.g., it retains its perpetual prerogative power, and it automatically allocates to itself copyrights that freelancers would hold had they been hired in the private sector;
- the ascription of formal equality to the Crown overlooks the *substantive* inequality between the government and the people: ask any defendant on criminal legal aid;
- as noted earlier, the government would still produce virtually
- everything it produces now without the spur of copyright;
- the government can make or break this equality at a stroke: after all, government copyright is created and maintained by the government; no private person has this power.

A variant of this argument is that no creative work — including government works — should be excepted from copyright protection, for to do so would open the door to arguments that *some other* creative work should also be excepted and so would put the whole copyright edifice in danger of collapse. Slippery slope "reasoning" of this sort substitutes slogans for careful policy analysis. It sidesteps basic questions such as whether all creative work deserves protection and, if so, what levels of protection might be desirable. It assumes full protection for everything is copyright's perfect and natural state. It has been responsible for the present situation, under which material as diverse as routine letters, business forms and computer programs attracts identical types and lengths of copyright protection. Only lunatics, legislators, lawyers or lobbyists could reach conclusions like this with equanimity.

(b) The Government Has Copyright to Ensure Accuracy

This was a major reason given for the royal prerogative over printing legislation or the authorized religious writings. People had to know how to behave legally and morally: where would society be if someone printed the Ten Commandments or the Criminal Code without all those "nots"?

These fears may have been realistic at a time when the state tried to enforce morality through blasphemy and sedition laws, but they are not so now. Government control or licensing does not guarantee accuracy, any more than unlicensed private sector publishing guarantees inaccuracy.

On government accuracy: we all no doubt have our favourite example of mistakes by official printers. My favourite in this context is a passage in the official report of Canada's Supreme Court in the leading copyright case of *Underwriters' Survey Bureau Ltd. v. Massie & Renwick Ltd.*, issued under the aegis of the King's Printer of Canada. Because of a series of editing errors, the report makes the Chief Justice of Canada, Sir Lyman Duff, look as if he has plagiarized a former Lord Chancellor of England! Is it not piquant that a decision on copyright, over which the Crown itself claims copyright ostensibly to ensure accuracy, is reported in a way that is not only misleading but also defamatory of the chief judicial officer of the land? It took the private sector publishers of the Court's decision, who transcribed it accurately, to resurrect the Chief Justice's honour.

As to private sector inaccuracy: the market should take care of that. A publisher with a record of inaccuracy will be shunned by those for whom accuracy is critical. Informal sanctions also encourage accuracy. For example, courts may accept only the government printer's version of legislation as authentic evidence, and in the past have refused to accept citations to law reporters with a reputation for imprecision.

(c) Government Copyright Helps Prevent Material from Being Used Inappropriately

This appears a major worry according to the Treasury Board Manual, which states that permission to copy government material can be refused if the copy would

- be in an undignified context;
- be considered as an unfair or misleading selection;
- be used for advertising purposes in an undesirable manner;
- be used in a context that may prejudice or harm a third party;
- be considered inappropriate by the institution in question for legal or other specifiable reasons!"

It is hard to imagine conditions like these surviving parliamentary scrutiny. What counts as an "undignified" context, or "undesirable" advertising? What business is it of the government that a third party may be "prejudiced or harmed" (can't she look after her own interests)? What is "inappropriate for legal or other specifiable reasons"? If a publication is illegal, it may be dealt with on that ground. Is the vagueness of "inappropriate for ... specifiable reasons" tolerable in a democracy?

Assume an artist takes the *Copyright Act* and, after copying it, proceeds to do unspeakable things to it in the name of art. If this activity is not proscribed by the ordinary criminal or civil law, why should copyright–designed to protect the economic interests of authors and distributors–be the government's weapon of choice? If the artist is foolish enough to seek the government's permission to do her art, how could a prior restraint on free speech be justified morally, let alone under the *Canadian Charter of Rights and Freedoms*?

(d) The Government Should Be Able to Make Money Off Its Works

This at least is plausible, and probably has history on its side. Note. that, of all the departments of government with a possible interest in Crown copyright, it is the Treasury Board that has produced the rules for its administration.

Now governments are free to decide that some of their services should break even or make a profit. Even in the U.S., postage stamp designs and compilations of "standardized scientific and technical reference data" can be copyrighted. So a business wanting to make a textile design from a postage stamp or to use StatsCan data can hardly complain if it has to ask for a licence or pay for these private for-profit uses. But isolated examples like these hardly justify across-the-board control of all government material.

(e) Government Copyright Can Be Used to Advance General Economic Welfare

The government, could advance economic or social welfare by encouraging or discouraging particular activities through giving or withholding copyright permission, and charging or not charging royalties. So the Treasury Board rules offer preferential treatment to

- uses that "assist in the achievement of program objectives" of a department;
- non-profit organizations;
- Canadian publishers reproducing statutes, statutory orders and regulations and judicial decisions.

Except for the boost to Canadian law publishing, no coherent policy emerges from this. The general rule–permission must be sought, it can be denied, and royalties are anyway payable–does nothing to maximize the use of government material to help the economy or society.

Whether the government can be trusted even to recognize when an activity may "assist in the achievement of program objectives" is doubtful. Take the case of the report on competition in the petroleum industry issued by the Competition Director in 1981. This seven-volume report was tabled in Parliament and then published for $70. Many free copies were nonetheless distributed, including to public libraries. Along came a small publisher called Lorimer who thought a one-volume condensed version of the report would sell well. But speed was essential lest his project turn into Canadian history. Lorimer spoke with department officials but was met with foot-dragging. So he decided to go ahead anyway. He spent 2 weeks cutting and pasting, and issued the condensed version at $14.95 another 2 weeks later. Meanwhile Lorimer wrote to the Minister of Supply and Services offering 8 per cent royalty on retail sales of his book. The Ministry's lawyer wrote back refusing permission and complaining that the use of the Competition Director's name on the cover of Lorimer's book suggested the director had also authored the abridgment. Lorimer corrected that by covering the director's name with stickers carrying his publishing company's name. This was still not good enough. Instead of giving him a medal for making the report available cheaply to a wider audience cheaply, the government took Lorimer to court for copyright infringement and got an injunction, damages at 8 per cent on past sales, delivery up of all existing stocks, and the costs of the action."

The government admitted it had not lost anything by Lorimer's publication and that widest possible dissemination of the report was an important goal. But all this was set aside to establish the principle of full control over government publications. Whether publications like Lorimer's are any more possible today because of speedier clearance is uncertain. What is certain is that such versions would more likely occur if pre-clearance was unnecessary. The greater distribution of information that would result would surely "assist in the achievement of program objectives" more than any fallout from the occasional unworthy republication.

(f)   The Government Has "the Right or Privilege" to Control Disclosure or Publication of Its Works

This may historically be the real reason for Crown copyright. Crown copyright comes from and is justified by a particular non-democratic conception of government. Look at how section 12 opens: by telling us the "rights or privileges of the Crown" are retained. Note, *first*, the absence of any reference to preserving the rights or privileges of the people. Why? Because they had none to retain. It is the government, not the public, that has rights and privileges over disclosure and publication of government works. Note, *second*, the absence of any reference to *duties*: the crown has *rights* and *privileges*, but no *duties*. It takes no Hohfeld to recognize that the government owes no-one a duty to disclose or publish anything it does not want to.

Taken together, these two silences reveal much about how the legislative and the executive arms of government view their relationship with the people. While the US *Copyright act* talks of extending copyright to "nationals and domiciliaries" of the US and other nations, the Canadian *Copyright act* extends copyright to "citizens, residents and *subjects*". This is the relationship section 12 reflects: that of CROWN and subject, of monarchical government, under which the crown through its delegates does what it thinks best for its people, and the people as the crown's subjects accept this as the best because the crown can do no (or perhaps today, not much) wrong. Under this theory, a government that decides not to publish does so because it has decided the public interest favours secrecy.

The judges are supposedly there to mediate the public interest — but in practice this means backing the government unless it has gone egregiously wrong in its calculation of that interest. In the rare case where a British court overrode copyright and allowed a publication to occur in the public interest — significantly not a case involving a government document — one of the judges cautioned that the decision should not be treated as a "mole's charter": "there is a world of difference," he intoned, "between what is in the public interest and what is of interest to the public."

If one were designing new coats of arms for judges, this would be as good a motto as any; for few Canadian courts take the public interest defence seriously. Consider *Lorimer*: while Jerome ACJ there said "the copyright laws ought not be used to assist the suppression of information when it is in the public interest that that information be made known", he did not recognize any public interest in making published information more widely available. Still he was willing to let the abridgment continue, so long as the publisher paid an 8% royalty; this view did not hold on appeal, where an injunction issued.

1)

. . .

Canada's law should be clarified to reflect the imperatives of a modern democracy, not the ancient hierarchy of Crown and subject. In particular:

- The federal government should consider freeing some, if not all, classes of work from copyright. Federal, provincial and municipal laws, the proceedings of legislative bodies, and decisions of judges and administrative tribunals are obvious candidates. In the US this legal material, because it is in the public domain, has been made more accessible at cheaper cost than would otherwise have been the case.
- If copyright must be retained for some material for specifiable strategic reasons, those works should be identified and a clear rationale for protection given. One should start from the presumption that government works should be in the public domain, unless there is very good reason to the contrary.
- Copyright law should not be used to prevent disclosure of unpublished material.
- The long duration of protection for private sector works need not apply to government works.
- The government should no longer assert, through the royal prerogative, perpetual copyright over an unascertained, not easily ascertainable, and unclosed category of works. This uncertainty is in nobody's interest. The federal and provincial prerogative power in respect of copyright should be repealed.

Reprographic Reproduction 2005-2014, Re, 2013 FCA 91 (F.C.A.)

GAUTHIER J.A.

[1] The governments of the Provinces of Manitoba, New Brunswick, Nova Scotia, Prince Edward Island and Saskatchewan (the Applicants) seek judicial review of the decision of Copyright Board of Canada (the Board) dismissing their objection that the Board has no jurisdiction to establish a tariff that would apply to them in respect of the reprographic reproduction of copyrighted works in the repertoire of the Canadian Copyright Licensing Agency, operating as "Access Copyright" (Access).

[2] Before the Board, the Applicants and a number of other provinces and territories who are not parties to this application argued that by virtue of section 17 of *the Interpretation Act, R.S.C. 1985, c. I-21*, they are entirely immune from the Copyright Act, R.S.C. 1985, c. C-42 (the *Act*) and therefore would not be subject to the proposed tariffs for the years 2005-2009 and 2010-2014 filed by Access for certification by the Board pursuant to section 70.15(1) of the *Act*. Section 17 of the *Interpretation Act* reads as follows:

17. No enactment is binding on Her Majesty or affects Her Majesty or Her Majesty's rights or prerogatives in any manner, except as mentioned or referred to in the enactment.	**17.** Sauf indication contraire y figurant, nul texte ne lie Sa Majesté ni n'a d'effet sur ses droits et prérogatives.

[3] The Board concluded that the *Act*, construed contextually, is intended to bind the Crown, and on that basis rejected the Applicants' claim of Crown immunity.

[4] The Applicants challenge this finding. For the reasons that follow, I have concluded that their application should be dismissed.

BACKGROUND

[5] On March 31, 2004 and March 31, 2009 Access filed with the Board proposed tariffs relating to the reproduction of published works in its repertoire by employees of all provincial and territorial governments (with the exception of Quebec). All these provinces and territories filed timely written objections with the Board.

[6] Further to a joint request by all those concerned, the Board agreed to hear a preliminary challenge to its statutory power under the *Act* to consider the proposed tariffs. In the course of this challenge, the Applicants argued that the presumption of Crown immunity applies and the *Act* does not bind them.

[7] The Board released its decision dismissing this challenge on January 5, 2012, with accompanying reasons on March 15, 2012 (Reasons). Since then, the Board has proceeded to hear the parties' representations on the merits, and the Applicants have participated in the said hearing on a without prejudice basis.

[8] As mentioned, some of the original objectors before the Board have decided not to challenge the decision under review. Also, Access did not seek the Board's approval for a tariff in respect of the federal government or the provinces of Ontario, British Columbia, and Quebec. Ontario, British Columbia and the federal government have each made an agreement with Access. The province of Quebec has done the same with the parallel collective societies in Quebec.

[9] The factual underpinning of the Applicants' claim for Crown immunity is set out in a jointly filed Statement of Agreed Facts.

[10] At this stage, it is worth noting that the Applicants have long standing policies and practices whereby they abide by the provisions of the *Act* by seeking authorization and paying royalties to copyright holders. They emphasize that they intend to continue these practices, which they consider to be voluntary.

The Board's decision

[11] First, the Board rejected the argument of Access that the Applicants' claim for Crown immunity conflicts with the common law principle that there can be no expropriation without just compensation. It held that the common law cannot overcome the clear statutory language of section 17 of the *Interpretation Act*. In its view, the fact that the Applicants would be prejudiced if the proposed tariffs were approved and imposed on them is sufficient to entitle them to assert their claim to Crown immunity.

[12] Relying in part on *R. v. Eldorado Nuclear Ltd.*, 1983 CanLII 34 (SCC), [1983] 2 S.C.R. 551 (*Eldorado*), the Board noted at paragraph 23 of the Reasons that section 17 of the *Interpretation Act* creates a presumption that the Crown is not bound by any statute, but that presumption is rebutted where it can be demonstrated that there exists a contrary intention to bind the Crown.

[13] After agreeing with the parties that "there are no expressly binding words which establish that the Crown is bound by the *Act*" (paragraph 28 of the Reasons), the Board proceeded with a contextual analysis of the *Act*, as required by the modern rule of statutory interpretation, to determine whether there are other provisions from which it might be inferred that the Crown is intended to be bound by the *Act*.

[14] The Applicants relied on section 12 of the *Act*, which reads as follows:

12. Without prejudice to any rights or privileges of the Crown, where any work is, or has been, prepared or published by or under the direction or control of Her Majesty or any government department, the copyright in the work shall, subject to any agreement with the author, belong to Her Majesty and in that case shall continue for the remainder of the calendar year of the first publication of the work and for a period of fifty years following the end of that calendar year.

12. Sous réserve de tous les droits ou privilèges de la Couronne, le droit d'auteur sur les œuvres préparées ou publiées par l'entremise, sous la direction ou la surveillance de Sa Majesté ou d'un ministère du gouvernement, appartient, sauf stipulation conclue avec l'auteur, à Sa Majesté et, dans ce cas, il subsiste jusqu'à la fin de la cinquantième année suivant celle de la première publication de l'œuvre.

[15] Section 12 appears in Part I of the *Act*, which defines the rights of copyright holders. After carefully and thoroughly considering the legislative history and evolution of section 12, the Board rejected the Applicants' argument that section 12 should be read as expressly providing for Crown immunity from the *Act*. The Board's analysis began with a recognition of the history of Crown copyright under the Crown prerogative particularly its right to print and publish. This right goes back hundreds of years, and includes the right to print and publish statutes, court decisions, and authorized versions of the Bible, among other things. The Board expressed the view that, "Crown copyright under the Crown prerogative is wider in scope and duration than what section 12 provides" (see paragraph 50 of the Reasons). It then reasoned that section 12 must be read in context with section 89, which provides in part that "[n]o person is entitled to copyrights otherwise than under and in accordance with this *Act*". In the absence of the opening phrase of section 12, section 89 would operate to eliminate all remaining common law copyright held by the Crown. The Board concluded that the words "without prejudice to any right or privilege of the Crown" in section 12 of the *Act* are necessary to maintain that common law Crown prerogative, and the scope of section 12 should be limited accordingly.

[16] The Board noted that Parliament introduced an exception targeting an emanation of the federal Crown in 1987, and added a large number of very specific exceptions for both the federal and provincial Crowns in 1997 (see paragraph 66 of the Reasons). Thus, apart from section 12, the *Act* contains a score or more of exceptions that expressly benefit the Crown such as those that benefit the Crown at large (for example, paragraph 45.1(b) and subsection 32.1(1); see paragraph 60 of the Reasons), those that benefit educational institutions (for example, subsection 29.4(2) and section 30.3; see paragraphs 61-63 of the Reasons) and those that concern Library and Archives Canada (for example, section 30.3; see paragraphs 64-65 of the Reasons).

[17] The Board then held at paragraph 66 of its Reasons:

> The number and the detailed nature of these exceptions seem to indicate a purposeful, explicit intention on the part of Parliament to identify and circumscribe activities that do not infringe copyright. If the Crown benefited from an overall

immunity from the *Act*, why would Parliament spend so much time and effort in crafting these exceptions?

[18] The Board rejected the Applicants' argument that these exceptions were adopted out of an abundance of caution or as historical incidents, as in *Alberta Government Telephones v. Canadian Radio-Television & Telecommunications Commission*, 1989 CanLII 78 (SCC), [1989] 2 S.C.R. 225 (*AGT*). The Board distinguished *AGT*, where a single, somewhat unclear reference to "government railways" could be explained away in this manner.

[19] The Board then drew upon *R. v. Ouellette*, 1980 CanLII 9 (SCC), [1980] 1 S.C.R. 568 (*Ouellette*), and concluded at paragraph 68 of the Reasons:

> [...] when analysing the whole of the *Act* contextually, we are irresistibly drawn to a logical conclusion that the Act generally binds the Crown.

[20] The Board went on to consider the implications of a finding that the Crown is immune from the *Act*. In its view, this would mean that the Board would have to reject on its own motion any tariff filed in respect of any emanation of the Crown, unless immunity had been waived. This would also mean that Crown corporations such as Telefilm, the National Film Board, and the CBC could use copyrighted works without regard to the rights of their authors or copyright holders. This would leave a significant gap in the enforcement of copyright by rights holders which, in the Board's view, supports the logical implication that the Crown must be bound (paragraph 73 of the Reasons).

[21] The Board added at paragraph 75 of the Reasons that the *Act* would make no sense unless it bound the Crown, given the reach of government action in the copyright market and the extent to which governments must rely on the *Act* to enforce their own copyrights. That said, the Board noted that excluding the Crown and its agents from the reach of the *Act* would not totally frustrate the *Act* (See *Friends of the Oldman River Society v. Canada (Minister of Transport)*, 1992 CanLII 110 (SCC), [1992] 1 S.C.R. 3 (*Oldman River*)). This finding should, however, be considered together with the Board's statement at paragraph 28 of the Reasons that "it will not be necessary to decide whether there would be a resulting absurdity were the Crown not so bound", given that Parliament's intention is revealed when the provisions are read in the context of other provisions.

[22] Having so concluded, the Board stated that no further analysis would be required to dismiss the preliminary objection. Nevertheless, given the importance of the legal issues involved, the Board explained that it would be useful to comment on whether in any event the Applicants had waived their immunity either in relation to the totality of the provisions contained in the *Act*, or alternatively, in relation to certain of its provisions.

[23] The Board considered the applicable legal principles set out in *Sparling v. Québec (Caisse de dépôt & placement)*, 1988 CanLII 26 (SCC), [1988] 2 S.C.R. 1015 (*Sparling*), and then noted that the conduct of the Applicants since the first adoption of the *Act* spoke volumes. The Applicants' behaviour, coupled with the

fact that they have enjoyed benefits under sections 3, 15, 18 and 21 of the *Act* and exercised their rights in relation to a number of related provisions, showed that they had waived Crown immunity (see paragraph 82 of the Reasons). This did not mean that, in the future, the Applicants could not reclaim their immunity if any, but that simply, at this stage, they could not do so.

THE ISSUES

[24] The Applicants submit that the Board erred in law when it concluded that the *Act* binds them by necessary implication. In that respect, they advance four main points:

> a. the Board misapplied *AGT* by failing to abide by the Supreme Court of Canada's direction that the necessary implication exception should be narrowly confined (*AGT* at page 277);
>
> b. the Board erred by finding that the presence of exceptions that benefit the Crown necessarily imply that the Crown is bound by the *Act*;
>
> c. the Board erred by reading words into section 12 of the *Act* in order to restrict the introductory words of that section to a Crown prerogative relating to the printing and publishing of works; and

d. the Board erred by considering the possible consequences of a finding that the Crown is immune to the *Act*.

[25] With respect to the Board's *obiter* that the Applicants had waived their immunity, if indeed they were immune from the *Act*, the Applicants claim that the Board misunderstood the test to be applied. They argue that the Board failed to appreciate that there must be a sufficient nexus between the benefits and the burdens involved to apply this doctrine. They advance that the Board misapplied the said test to the facts of this matter, failing to appreciate that the Applicants' practice of voluntarily respecting the rights of copyright holders was simply the result of the Crown trying to act as a good citizen, as was found by the Ontario Court of Appeal in *Collège d'arts appliqués & de technologie La Cité collégiale v. Ottawa (City)* 1998 CanLII 1632 (ON CA), (1998), 37 O.R. (3d) 737 (OCA) at paragraph 19. Given the conclusion I have reached on the other grounds of appeal, I do not consider it necessary to consider this issue, and I have not done so.

ANALYSIS

[26] As this application for judicial review concerns a question of law of general application in respect of the *Act*, the standard of review is correctness (*Rogers v. Society of Composers, Authors and Music Publishers of Canada*, 2012 SCC 35 (CanLII), 2012 SCC 35 at paragraphs 10 and 20).

[27] Before considering the issues, it is worth noting that, at the hearing, the Applicants confirmed that they are not relying on any constitutional argument in this case. They also confirmed that despite what appears in paragraph 69 of the Board's Reasons, they were and still are seeking a declaration that they are

immune from the *Act* as a whole, not only in respect of the proposed tariffs in the current proceeding before the Board.

[28] The principles to be applied in determining whether the Crown is immune from a particular statute on the basis of section 17 of the *Interpretation Act* are now well established. In *Oldman River*, the most recent pronouncement of the Supreme Court on this issue, Laforest J. summarized the situation as follows, at pages 52-53:

> However, any uncertainty in the law on these points was put to rest by this Court's recent decision in *Alberta Government Telephones, supra*. After reviewing the authorities, Dickson C.J. concluded, at p. 281:
>
>> In my view, in light of *PWA [Her Majesty in right of the Province of Alberta v. Canadian Transportation Commission*, 1977 CanLII 150 (SCC), [1978] 1 S.C.R. 61] and *Eldorado [supra]*, the scope of the words "mentioned or referred to" must be given an interpretation independent of the supplanted common law. However, the qualifications in *Bombay [Province of Bombay v. Municipal Corporation of Bombay*, [1947] A.C. 58] are based on sound principles of interpretation which have not entirely disappeared over time. It seems to me that the words "mentioned or referred to" in s. 16 [now s. 17 of the *Interpretation Act*] are capable of encompassing: (1) expressly binding words ("Her Majesty is bound"); (2) a clear intention to bind which, in *Bombay* terminology, "is manifest from the very terms of the statute", in other words, an intention revealed when provisions are read in the context of other textual provisions, as in *Ouellette, supra*; and, (3) an intention to bind where the purpose of the statute would be "wholly frustrated" if the government were not bound, or, in other words, if an absurdity (as opposed to simply an undesirable result) were produced. These three points should provide a guideline for when a statute has clearly conveyed an intention to bind the Crown.
>
> In my view, this passage makes it abundantly clear that a contextual analysis of a statute may reveal an intention to bind the Crown if one is irresistibly drawn to that conclusion through logical inference.

[29] Thus, once the Board acknowledged in its analysis that there is no section stating clearly that "this *Act* shall bind her Majesty" (first prong of the exception), it had to consider, through a purposive and contextual statutory analysis, whether it could discern a clear parliamentary intention to bind the Crown (second prong of the exception). Only if it were unable to find such a clear intention would it have to proceed to the next step of determining whether the third prong of the exception provided for in relation to section 17 applies (frustration or absurdity).

[30] To rebut the presumption in section 17 of the *Interpretation Act*, there must be a clear parliamentary intention to bind the Crown, or, to use the words of La Forest J. in *Oldman River*, one must be irresistibly drawn, through logical inference, to the conclusion that there is an intention to bind the Crown. The search for parliamentary intention must be undertaken though a contextual interpretation of the statute. In my view, the Board understood this and applied the proper approach when it undertook its task.

[31] As always, context matters. *AGT* did not change the law in *Ouellette*. On the contrary, it confirmed it (see *AGT* at pages 279-280). Different results occur when the courts interpret different statutes within their different contexts. I do not agree with the applicants that the Board gave too much weight to the exceptions targeting the Crown or its agents in this case.

[32] I turn now to a detailed consideration of the provisions of the *Act* which are relevant to the issues in this case. I begin with the objectives of the *Act* which were described in *Reference re Broadcasting Act, S.C. 1991 (Canada)*, 2012 SCC 68 (CanLII), 2012 SCC 68 at paragraph 36 as follows:

> **36** The *Copyright Act* is concerned both with encouraging creativity and providing reasonable access to the fruits of creative endeavour. These objectives are furthered by a carefully balanced scheme that creates exclusive economic rights for different categories of copyright owners in works or other protected subject matter, typically in the nature of a statutory monopoly to prevent anyone from exploiting the work in specified ways without the copyright owner's consent. It also provides user rights such as fair dealing and specific exemptions that enable the general public or specific classes of users to access protected material under certain conditions. (See, e.g., *Théberge v. Galerie d'Art du Petit Champlain inc.*,2002 SCC 34 (CanLII), 2002 SCC 34, [2002] 2 S.C.R. 336, at paras. 11-12 and 30; *Mattel,Inc. v. 3894207 Canada Inc.*, 2006 SCC 22 (CanLII), 2006 SCC 22, [2006] 1 S.C.R. 772, at para. 21; D. Vaver, *Intellectual Property Law: Copyright, Patents, Trade-marks* (2nd ed. 2011), at pp. 34 and 56). ...

[33] Section 12 of the *Act* is an important part of the contextual analysis. As mentioned above, it is found in Part I of the *Act*. Part I is entitled"Copyright and Moral Rights in Works". It deals with the rights attached to copyrighted works, the owners, and the duration of said copyright. Part III of the *Act* is entitled "Infringement of Copyright and Moral Rights and Exceptions to Infringement", and it is where one finds a score or more of exceptions that quite explicitly relate or apply to the Crown (federal and provincial).

[34] Having carefully examined the wording of section 12 in its overall context, including the structure of the *Act*, its legislative history and evolution, and other provisions, such as section 89, I agree with the Board that the words "[w]ithout prejudice to any right or privilege of the Crown" set out in section 12 are intended to refer to and preserve the Crown's rights and privileges of the same general nature as copyright that may not fall within the meaning of the rest of this provision. These rights and privileges could otherwise be excluded by the general principle set out in section 89 which provides that no person is entitled to copyright otherwise than under and in accordance with the *Act* or any other Act of Parliament.

[35] I turn now to the various exceptions or user rights set out in Part III in favour of the Crown and its agents. However, a few preliminary comments are appropriate.

[36] First, the Applicants appear to say that these exceptions should all be disregarded as the Court should deduce the legislator's intention from the first version of the *Act*, adopted in 1921.

[37] Like the Board, I believe that section 17 must be applied to construe the *Act* as it now stands. In fact, the Applicants included in Volume IV of their record the most recent amendments to the *Act*, which came into force in June of 2012. These include a number of additional exceptions dealing with new technologies, among other things, as well as detailed provisions in respect of available remedies that, in my view, confirm Parliament's intention as expressed by the Board when construing the *Act* before them.

[38] Second, the Board noted that the parties felt that the parliamentary debates shed little light on the meaning of section 12 or on the immunity issue *per se*. However, I observe that the debates indicate that there was a strong opposition to the large number of exceptions targeting the Crown or its agents included in Bill C-32 which was adopted in 1997. These exceptions were seen to be an unwarranted limitation of rights of copyright holders under the *Act* in favour of governmental organizations (*House of Commons Debates*, (4 June 1997) at 3442-3443 (Mr. Louis Plamondon (Richelieu, BQ)), at 3460 (Mrs. Suzanne Tremblay (Rimouski-Témiscouata, BQ), and at 3461-3462 (Mrs. Christiane Gagnon (Québec, BQ)). There is no reference anywhere to the fact that these exceptions did not really constitute a restriction on the rights of copyright holders given that, in any event, the federal and provincial Crowns and their agents were immune, and these provisions were included out of an abundance of caution. This would certainly have quelled all protest. Instead, the Parliamentary Secretary to the Deputy Prime Minister and the Minister of Canadian Heritage responsible for the Bill stated early on that the exceptions were proposed for reasons of public interest and that they responded to real concerns (*House of Commons Debates*, (13 March 1997) at 9031 (Mr. Guy H. Arseneault (Parliamentary Secretary to Deputy Prime Minister and Minister of Canadian Heritage, Lib.)).

[39] That said, aside from the high number of exceptions noted by the Board, many are very detailed. They are also subject to conditions which would be illogical in the absence of a clear intent to otherwise bind the Crown. A few illustrations will suffice to clarify what I mean here.

[40] For my first illustration I will use one of the exceptions dealing with educational institutions. The definition of "educational institution" (at section 2 of the *Act*)is particularly clear. It includes:

"educational institution" means	« établissement d'enseignement » :
. . .	[...]
(c) a department or agency of any order of government, or any non-profit body, that controls or supervises education or training referred to in paragraph (a) or (b), or	c) ministère ou organisme, quel que soit l'ordre de gouvernement, ou entité sans but lucratif qui exerce une autorité sur l'enseignement et la formation visés aux alinéas a) et b);

[41] The exception set out in subsection 29.7 provides:

29.7 (1) Subject to subsection (2) and section 29.9, it is not an infringement of copyright for an educational institution or a person acting under its authority to

(*a*) make a single copy of a work or other subject-matter at the time that it is communicated to the public by telecommunication; and

(*b*) keep the copy for up to <u>thirty days</u> to decide whether to perform the copy for educational or training purposes.

(2) An educational institution that has not destroyed the copy by the expiration of the thirty days <u>infringes copyright in the work or other subject-matter unless it pays any royalties, and complies with any terms and conditions, fixed under this</u> Act <u>for the making of the copy.</u>

(3) It is not an infringement of copyright for the educational institution or a person acting under its authority to perform the copy in public for educational or training purposes on the premises of the educational institution before an audience consisting primarily of students of the educational institution <u>if the educational institution pays the royalties and complies with any terms and conditions fixed under this</u> Act <u>for the performance in public.</u>

[Emphasis added]

29.7 (1) Sous réserve du paragraphe (2) et de l'article 29.9, les actes ci-après ne constituent pas des violations du droit d'auteur s'ils sont accomplis par un établissement d'enseignement ou une personne agissant sous l'autorité de celui-ci :

a) la reproduction à des fins pédagogiques, en un seul exemplaire, d'une œuvre ou de tout autre objet du droit d'auteur lors de leur communication au public par télécommunication;

b) la conservation de l'exemplaire <u>pour une période maximale de trente jours afin d'en déterminer la valeur du point de vue pédagogique.</u>

(2) L'établissement d'enseignement <u>qui n'a pas détruit l'exemplaire à l'expiration des trente jours viole le droit d'auteur s'il n'acquitte pas les redevances ni ne respecte les modalités fixées sous le régime de la présente loi pour la reproduction.</u>

(3) L'exécution en public, devant un auditoire formé principalement d'élèves de l'établissement, de l'exemplaire dans les locaux de l'établissement et à des fins pédagogiques, par l'établissement ou une personne agissant sous l'autorité de celui-ci, ne constitue pas une violation du droit d'auteur <u>si l'établissement acquitte les redevances et respecte les modalités fixées sous le régime de la présente loi pour l'exécution en public.</u>

[mon souligné]

[42] Further on, the legislator provides that the institution will not have the right to the exception set out in subsection 29.7(1) where the communication to the public by telecommunication was obtained by illegal means (section 29.8 of the *Act*).

[43] This is only one of many similar exceptions targeting emanations of the Crown, but it is sufficient to show how far we are from the scenario described by Dickson C.J.C. in *AGT* at pages 281-282. In our case, the exceptions cannot be explained away.

[44] A further illustration is found in the additional provisions added to the *Act* in 2012. The legislator provides at subsection 41.1(1) that no person shall attempt to circumvent technological protection measures relating to copyrighted works. Further, subsection 41.2 provides that:

41.2 If a court finds that <u>a defendant that is a library, archive or museum or an educational institution</u> has contravened subsection 41.1(1) and the defendant satisfies the court that it was not aware, and had no reasonable grounds to believe, that its actions constituted a contravention of that subsection, the plaintiff is not entitled to any remedy other than an injunction.	**41.2** Dans le cas où <u>le défendeur est une bibliothèque, un musée, un service d'archives ou un établissement d'enseignement</u> et où le tribunal est d'avis qu'il a contrevenu au paragraphe 41.1(1), le demandeur ne peut obtenir qu'une injonction à l'égard du défendeur si celui-ci convainc le tribunal qu'il ne savait pas et n'avait aucun motif raisonnable de croire qu'il avait contrevenu à ce paragraphe.
[Emphasis added]	[Mon souligné]

[45] Then, in a totally different context, paragraph 45(1)(b) of the *Act* provides that it is lawful for a person to do the following:

45. (1) Notwithstanding anything in this Act, it is lawful for a person . . . (*b*) to import for use by a department of the Government of Canada or a province copies of a work or other subject-matter made <u>with the consent of the owner of</u> <u>the copyright in the country where it was made;</u> . . .	**45.** (1) Malgré les autres dispositions de la présente loi, il est loisible à toute personne : [...] b) d'importer, pour l'usage d'un ministère du gouvernement du Canada ou de l'une des provinces, des exemplaires — produits <u>avec le consentement du titulaire du droit d'auteur dans le pays de production</u> — d'une œuvre ou d'un autre objet du droit d'auteur; [...]
[Emphasis added]	[Mon souligné]

[46] Turning back to the 1997 additions to the *Act*, subsection 30.3(1) sets out another scenario where an educational institution, library, archive or museum's

actions will not constitute infringement. However, this scenario is subject to strict conditions set out in subsection 30.3(2):

30.3 (1) An educational institution or a library, archive or museum does not infringe copyright where

. . .

(2) Subsection (1) only applies if, in respect of a reprographic reproduction,

(*a*) the educational institution, library, archive or museum <u>has entered into an agreement with a collective society that is authorized by copyright owners to grant licences on their behalf;</u>

(*b*) <u>the Board</u> has, in accordance with section 70.2, <u>fixed the royalties and related terms and conditions in respect of a licence;</u>

(*c*) <u>a tariff has been approved in accordance with section 70.15;</u> or

(*d*) a collective society has filed a proposed tariff in accordance with section 70.13.

[Emphasis added]

30.3 (1) Un établissement d'enseignement, une bibliothèque, un musée ou un service d'archives ne viole pas le droit d'auteur dans le cas où :

[…]

(2) Le paragraphe (1) ne s'applique que si, selon le cas, en ce qui touche la reprographie :

a) ils ont conclu une <u>entente avec une société de gestion</u> habilitée par le titulaire du droit d'auteur à octroyer des licences;

b) <u>la Commission a fixé</u>, conformément à l'article 70.2, <u>les redevances et les modalités afférentes à une licence;</u>

c) <u>il existe déjà un tarif pertinent homologué en vertu de l'article 70.15;</u>

d) une société de gestion a déposé, conformément à l'article 70.13, un projet de tarif.

[Mon souligné]

[47] In my view, the references in the *Act* to very strict conditions, to tariffs fixed by the Board, to the consent of the copyright owners, and to the power of the court when the defendant is an "educational institution", including a federal or provincial government department, all point to only one logical and plausible conclusion as to the intent of Parliament: the Crown is bound.

[48] I have considered that the *Act*, unlike other statutes such as the Patent Act, R.S.C., 1985, c. P-4, s.2.1, does not contain an "expressly binding" clause at the beginning, as was recommended in the 1985 report entitled *A Charter of Rights for Creators*. I am still irresistibly drawn to the conclusion that Parliament clearly intended to bind the federal and provincial Crowns by the express language of the *Act* and through logical inference.

[49] It is not necessary in my view to consider the argument advanced by Access regarding whether any other interpretation of the *Act* would result in a breach of Canada's international obligations under NAFTA, TRIPS or any other international convention ratified and implemented in Canada. This is especially so when one considers that this argument was not fully developed before us.

[50] In the circumstances, there is also no need to consider whether granting immunity would result in a frustration of the *Act* as a whole or in an absurdity.

[51] Access had argued that Crown immunity should not even be in play, as immunity from the *Act* and the tariffs would constitute expropriation without compensation. As noted earlier, the Board rejected this argument. Given that I have found that the Crown is bound by the *Act*, I express no opinion on this point.

[52] In light of the foregoing, I propose that this application be dismissed with costs.

---

3. Copyright Assignments

Copyright is in the nature of a chose in action; it is an incorporeal right. The owner of the copyright in a work may assign the right and any interest in the right by licence, but no assignment or grant is valid unless it is in writing signed by the owner of the right or by his duly authorized agent.[3] The various rights of the copyright owner can be divided up and transferred as the owner so chooses. An assignment is absolute; the assignor has no remaining claim to the particular right assigned, although he or she may continue to hold other rights in relation to the same work. The Canadian Act does not contemplate an assignment of copyright that may take effect at a future date.[4]

Although not completely settled, it is arguable that the writing requirement does not apply to an agreement to assign a copyright, which may be an express oral agreement or an agreement implied from conduct.[5] A binding and enforceable agreement to assign a copyright is effective as an equitable assignment which may be carried into execution by an order for specific performance or by a vesting order transferring the legal title to the equitable owner.[6] In this regard there is a difference between an equitable assignment of a legal interest in a copyright which need not be in writing and a legal assignment of an interest in a copyright which must be.[7]

---

[3]   *Copyright Act*, s. 13(4).
[4]   *Master File Corp. v. Internett Corp.* (2001), 16 C.P.R. (4th) 139 (Fed. T.D.).
[5]   *Delta Hotels v. Backus-Naur et al.*, 2013 ONSC 582.
[6]   *Lakeview Computers plc v. Steadman* [1999] E.W.J. No. 6192 (Eng. C.A.); *Cyprotex Discovery Limited v. The University of Sheffield*, [2003] E.W.H.C. 760 (T.C.C.), affirmed [2004] EWCA Civ 380 (Eng. C.A.).
[7]   *Lakeview Computers plc v. Steadman* [1999] E.W.J. No. 6192 (Eng.C.A.); *Robam Jig Tool Co Ltd & Elkadort Lt v Taylor & Ors*, [1979] FSR 130; *Telephonic Communicators Ingemational Pty. Ltd v. Motor Solutions Australia Pty. Ltd.*, [2004] F.C.A. 942 (21 July 2004).

Downing v. General Synod Church of England in Canada, [1943] 3 D.L.R. 553 (C.A.)

ONTARIO
[COURT OF APPEAL]

Robertson C.J.O., Gillanders, and Laidlaw JJ.A.

19th July 1943.

. . .

ROBERTSON C.J.O.: —

1. An appeal from the judgment of Roach J., dated 7th January 1943, after the trial of the action without a jury, at Toronto. The action is in respect of a copyright.

2. John Merbecke, who lived in Tudor times, and was organist of St. George's, Windsor, set to music the office of Holy Communion, in the reign of Edward VI. The music written by Merbecke was to be sung in unison, and he wrote no accompaniment for it. There have been frequent publications of Merbecke's music, with organ accompaniment, in recent times, by musicians of high standing. Dr. Healey Willan, resident in Toronto, and eminent throughout Canada as an organist and a composer, was engaged, in 1933, in preparing an edition of this music of Merbecke's that would represent what he believed to be the proper way in which it should be sung, and in providing an organ accompaniment for it. A friend of Dr. Willan's, Canon Pilcher, now Coadjutor Bishop of Sydney, Australia, but then Canon Precentor of St. Alban's Cathedral, in Toronto, urged him to publish the edition of Merbecke's music on which he was engaged, with his organ accompaniment. This led to a discussion of the matter of a publisher. Dr. Pilcher was acquainted with the plaintiff and knew that the latter had some connection with Oxford University Press. This circumstance was attractive to Dr. Willan and a meeting was arranged at the plaintiff's shop to discuss the matter of publication. There was one meeting, and perhaps more, at plaintiff's shop, Dr. Pilcher being present with Dr. Willan. In the result the plaintiff was to have Dr. Willan's setting of Merbecke's Holy Communion music published. Some little confusion or misunderstanding existed after Dr. Willan had left his manuscript with the plaintiff, as to the relation of Oxford University Press to the publication. The plaintiff was only a sales agent for Oxford University press, and had no authority to make a contract for publication by them, and it was Oxford University Press that Dr. Willan desired as his publisher. He had had them in that relation before. Dr. Willan recalls very little of his interviews with the plaintiff, and Dr. Pilcher remembers even less, but there are letters written by the plaintiff to Oxford University Press forwarding the manuscript, and, making some allowance for the fact that the plaintiff was rather keen on having this work, particularly as he suspected a competitor of trying to get it away from him, his letters written at the time indicate, at least, what he desired to have, and thought he would get. Oxford University Press were requested to have the music engraved and printed for him, and at his cost. In a second latter it is apparent

that there were misunderstandings, particularly as to whether Oxford University Press or the plaintiff was to be the publisher. Dr. Willan wanted the former, but the letter says, "I am going to stand to my guns and possession is a factor that Willan cannot get around." In the third of three letters written by the plaintiff within a week, he informed Oxford University Press that after another interview with Dr. Willan and Canon Pilcher everything had been arranged to the satisfaction of all. He proceeded to say in the letter that the work, of course, would be copyrighted by him, and his own edition published in the ordinary way, the English edition to be arranged entirely by Oxford University Press. He suggested that he transfer to Oxford University Press all rights of sale in Great Britain and her colonies and all other countries excepting Canada, Newfoundland and the United States, they being the only markets he had access to. No payment was to be required for these rights, but Oxford University Press was to be responsible directly to Dr. Willan for royalties on all copies sold of the British edition.

3. Whether all of the foregoing was intended to be a statement of what had been agreed upon with Dr. Willan, or whether it was the plaintiff's own idea of desirable working arrangements, based upon a somewhat less definite understanding with Dr. Willan, the letter itself does not make clear. The plaintiff says, in his evidence, that "the agreement was finally agreed to that he was to assign to me all copyright and other rights for all countries which he agreed to do." Dr. Willan, in his evidence, admits that he did not greatly care about the matter, as he could not see anything in the way of financial return of any value because of other editions of Merbecke's Holy Communion on the market. However, he prepared his manuscript and, with Dr. Pilcher, took it to the plaintiff. Dr. Willan says that he understood it was to be issued by Oxford University Press, but he says that he cannot remember definitely the terms at all.

4. It was in July 1933 that the plaintiff wrote the letters to Oxford University Press that I have referred to. There was more correspondence with them later in the year. Proofs were sent out for revision, and Dr. Willan revised them and made suggestions. The invoice of Oxford University Press to the plaintiff covering 1998 copies of the completed work as engraved and printed, is dated 18th January 1934, and the plaintiff made his first sales on 1st February. The cost to him was (STERLING)17-1-6.

5. Up to this time there was nothing in writing between Dr. Willan and the plaintiff. Oxford University Press had very briefly responded to the plaintiff's first letter of July 1933, by saying, "Of course we will put Mr. Healey Willan's MS in hand, many thanks for sending it." There were also other letters later, making their arrangements with the plaintiff a little more definite. Dr. Willan, however, had not even been asked to put his arrangement in writing, or to sign anything.

6. The plaintiff says, in evidence, that the verbal agreement he made with Dr. Willan was not put in writing. He further says that he had an assignment in writing from Dr. Willan of all rights for all countries, but that this document is lost. The date of that assignment he says was 6th April 1934. That alleged assignment in writing is the basis of the plaintiff's title, and it is specifically pleaded in the

statement of claim, and no other assignment or agreement with Dr. Willan is alleged.

7. There is a good deal of evidence that bears in one way or another upon the fact of this assignment in writing, and it will be necessary to consider it in some detail, and the finding of the learned trial judge as well. I defer all of that until I have stated what conduct of the defendants the plaintiff complains of in this action.

8. In February 1936 a committee of the General Synod of the Church of England in Canada entered into a contract with Oxford University Press for the publication by the latter of a revised Book of Common Praise. The publisher undertook, as a term of the contract, to acquire and arrange, for the use and purpose of such revised hymn book, and any and every edition thereof, the copyright of in and to such hymns and tunes as might be required for the purpose thereof. The publisher further undertook to take all necessary steps to see that the copyright of the said revised hymn book should be vested in the Synod. It was agreed that the publisher should have the sole, exclusive right to print and publish, and should print and publish and bind the revised hymn book in certain styles, sizes and bindings, and the publisher agreed to pay to the treasurer of the Synod annually the royalties by a schedule attached.

9. It was desired that certain tunes of which Dr. Willan was the composer, and certain parts of his setting of Merbecke's Holy Communion, should be included in the revised hymn book, and after some negotiation between a representative of the Synod's committee, and Mr. Clarke, the manager at Toronto of Oxford University Press, and Dr. Willan, the latter gave a letter, dated 15th February 1938 to Mr. Clarke giving his permission to use the desired tunes and arrangements in the revised hymn book, and stating that, so far as the writer knew, no one else had any rights in these tunes. Under some general verbal arrangement between Dr. Willan and Mr. Clarke that Dr. Willan would be fairly compensated for anything of his that was used, Oxford University Press later paid Dr. Willan 3 guineas in respect of those parts of his setting of Merbecke's Holy Communion that were used in the hymn book.

10. The revised hymn book was published under the agreement already mentioned, in September 1938, and it contained the parts of Dr. Willan's setting of Merbecke's Holy Communion for which Dr. Willan had given permission. There have been sales of the hymn book throughout Canada, and it can be purchased on the market, and continues to be sold. This, the plaintiff claims, is an infringement of the copyright of which he alleges that he is the owner by assignment from Dr. Willan.

11. The plaintiff alleges that both Oxford University Press and the General Synod had notice of his ownership of the copyright, the former by reason of the plaintiff's correspondence with it in 1933 and 1934, in regard to the separate publication of Dr. Willan's Merbecke, and the Synod by reason of the member of its committee who negotiated with Dr. Willan having had, in the negotiations, a copy of the plaintiff's publication of 1934, on which appeared the words "Copyright, 1934, by The Anglo-Canadian Music Co., Toronto, Canada."

12. The plaintiff brought his action in December 1940, against the Church of England in Canada, the General Synod, and Oxford University Press, claiming an injunction, damages and other relief. The Church of England in Canada was eliminated as a party to the action by a consent order. The General Synod gave a third party notice to Oxford University Press, claiming indemnity against liability to the plaintiff. Oxford University Press gave a third party notice to Dr. Willan, claiming, in turn, to be indemnified by him against any liability in respect of the plaintiff's claim. By the judgment of the learned trial judge, the defendants are restrained from printing, publishing or causing to be printed or published, or selling or causing to be offered for sale or distribution in Canada, those parts of Dr. Willan's setting of Merbecke's Holy Communion that are included in the revised hymn book. The defendants are ordered to pay the plaintiff damages, to be fixed by reference to the Master. Oxford University Press is ordered to deliver to the plaintiff all plates used by it in printing those parts of the said musical composition already enumerated. The defendants were further ordered to pay the plaintiff's costs of the action and of the reference. The General Synod was granted indemnity from Oxford University Press for such sum as it should be required to pay the plaintiff for damages and costs, and Oxford University Press was ordered to pay the General Synod costs of the third party proceedings between them. Dr. Willan, as a third party, was ordered to pay Oxford University Press such sum as it might be required to pay to the plaintiff or to the General Synod by way of damages and costs, and also the costs of Oxford University Press of the third party proceedings taken against Dr. Willan. Appeals are taken against this judgment by the General Synod, by Oxford University Press, and by Dr. Willan.

13. I shall now return to consider the question whether Dr. Willan did in fact make the assignment in writing of the copyright that the plaintiff relies upon. It is the basis of the action.

14. The Copyright Act, R.S.C. 1927, c. 32, as amended, provides in s. 12, subs. 1, that, subject to the provisions of this Act, the author of a work shall be the first owner of the copyright therein. Then subs. 2 is as follows: —

> "The owner of the copyright in any work may assign the right, either wholly or partially, and either generally or subject to territorial limitations, and either for the whole term of the copyright or for any other part thereof, and may grant any interest in the right by license, but no such assignment or grant shall be valid unless it is in writing signed by the owner of the right in respect of which the assignment or grant is made, or by his duly authorized agent."

15. The plaintiff is specific in, and as a consequence, is restricted by, his evidence as to the occasion and manner of obtaining an assignment in writing. He says he prepared the document, personally, on a typewriter, and, having prepared it, he gave it to Canon Pilcher, no one else being present, and that Canon Pilcher took it away, and a short time later he brought it back signed; that is, there was a signature on it. He was asked, "Do you know whether or not it was Dr. Willan's signature?" To this he answered, "No, I couldn't have sworn it was Dr. Willan's signature, but there was no occasion for anybody else to sign it." The signature

was written in ink, but he could not swear whether there was a witness's name on the document. It was brought back to him by Canon Pilcher a few days later. The date in the document, he says, was 6th April 1934.

16. This document is lost, the plaintiff says. He says that he kept his "documents, assignments and so forth, in a vault in the Bank of Commerce on Yonge Street." He discontinued the box some time late in 1937 or early in 1938, and the contents were all carried over from the vault to his office, and he did not check them then, and he thinks it may have been lost in transit or after it got to the office. When he went to find it, he could not find it.

17. Dr. Willan flatly denies that such an incident occurred as the plaintiff describes. He admits that his recollection of his interview with the plaintiff, in regard to the publication of his work, is vague, and while he admits that he probably would have executed an assignment of copyright to the plaintiff had he been asked to do so, he not only does not recall having done so at any time, and, to the best of his knowledge and belief, never did sign such a document, but on the question of the specific incident of signing such a document brought to him by Dr. Pilcher for signature, he definitely and emphatically denies it. The evidence of Dr. Pilcher was taken on commission at Sydney, Australia. He recalls the matter of an edition of Merbecke, and of visiting the plaintiff with Dr. Willan at the plaintiff's shop, but he has no recollection whatever of taking any document from the plaintiff to Dr. Willan. He does not remember any occasion of being present when Dr. Willan signed a document in connection with Merbecke, nor has he any recollection whatever of taking any document from Dr. Willan to the plaintiff.

. . .

31. Neither the plaintiff nor any one else gave evidence that Dr. Willan had in fact signed the assignment of copyright of 6th April 1934, upon which the action is founded, and Dr. Willan denied it. I can find nothing in the subsequent events to support a presumption that Dr. Willan did in fact sign such a document, in the absence of direct evidence of any witness to the fact, that the conclusion could be reached that Dr. Willan signed the document as alleged. If the learned trial judge had had the sworn testimony of a witness to support his finding, and had accepted the evidence of that witness, that finding would have been hard to overcome. There being no such evidence, however, and the learned trial judge having, in his reasons for judgment, overlooked both its absence and Dr. Willan's positive denial, any opinion based upon subsequent events, and the part played in them by Dr. Willan, is open to review. With respect, I am of opinion that his finding that Dr. Willan executed an assignment of his copyright, as the plaintiff alleges, should be reversed. Having regard to the conduct of both the plaintiff and Dr. Willan, it affords, in my opinion, no support for the plaintiff's contention. In this connection I should mention the submission made by counsel for the General Synod that the issue to be tried being between the plaintiff and the defendant, the conduct and the letters of Dr. Willan, subsequent to his grant of the licence or permit to use his compositions in the hymn book, were not admissible in evidence against the defendants in weighing the validity of his grant — that there was not then an

identity of interest. I have not found it necessary to consider the point in view of the conclusion I have reached upon all the evidence.

32. This conclusion is fatal to the action as brought, and it becomes unnecessary to go into the question of notice that would otherwise arise under s. 40(3) of The Copyright Act.

33. A good deal was said on the argument of the appeal, and appears in memoranda submitted by counsel since, in regard to the question whether or not there was an equitable assignment under which the plaintiff can claim. The question, I think, was raised first by the Court in the course of argument for the appellants. No case of that kind is raised on the pleadings, and no such case was tried. There may be also a good deal of doubt whether, under our present Copyright Act, an action for the relief granted here can be maintained on a mere equitable assignment. I have already quoted subs. 2 of s. 12 as to the statutory requirements for a valid assignment. S. 40 no longer contains, in subs. 3, the words "no grantee shall maintain any action under this Act, unless his and each such prior grant has been registered", which were held fatal to the claim of an assignee with an unregistered assignment, in Canadian Performing Right Society, Limited v. Famous Players Canadian Corporation, Limited, [1929] A.C. 456, [1929] 1 D.L.R. 1. This was amended by c. 8, s. 9 of the statutes of 1931. S. 45, however, provides as follows: —

> "No person shall be entitled to copyright or any similar right in any literary, dramatic, musical or artistic work otherwise than under and in accordance with the provisions of this Act, or of any other statutory enactment for teh time being in force, but nothing in this section shall be construed as abrogating any right or jurisdiction to restrain a breach of trust or confidence."

This would seem to leave but little remedy to one with only an equitable assignment, for which the Act makes no provision. No doubt an equitable assignment of a chose in action results in the creation of a sort of trust on the part of the assignor for the benefit of his assignee, and a writing is not necessary to its creation. The assignor would, however, be a necessary party to such an action, and Dr. Willan is only a third party. The relief available, moreover, if s. 45 fixes its limits, would only be the restraint of a breach of trust.

34. In the circumstances, I have not thought it was open to the Court on this appeal to enter upon the consideration of any question resting upon, or relating to, an equitable assignment, and no opinion is, therefore, expressed upon it.

35. An important, and possibly difficult, question necessary to be determined would be whether the parties ever agreed upon the definite terms of any assignment of the copyright, or whether they existed in the mind of the plaintiff alone.

36. The appeal should be allowed and the action dismissed. The defendants are entitled to their costs of action and appeal against the plaintiff. The third parties

are entitled to their costs, as third parties, of the action and appeal, against the party who brought them in, respectively.

Lakeview Computers plc v. Steadman, [1999] E.W.J. No. 6192 (Eng. C.A.)

(Transcript: Smith Bernal)

26 November 1999

. . .

MUMMERY LJ:

. . .

Background

Between 1986 and 1988 Mr Charles Steadman devised the LM computer software package as it later came to be known. He is experienced in computer technology and with both hardware and software application. In that period he was a sole trader (using the name 'Lakeview Computer Services') and was the author and, as such, the first owner of any copyright material written or created by him at that time.

In 1988 he and his brother, Mr Matthew Steadman, formed Lakeview in which they held equal shareholdings. It was incorporated under the name Lakeview Computer Services Limited on 1 November 1988 'on carry on the business' (in Mr Charles Steadman's own words). It has since then carried on the business of producing and distributing computer systems and software, including the LM software and a compiler called LIL. The LM software was exploited and marketed as a comprehensive integrated accounting and business management package. Licences to use the LM software were granted in a standard non-exclusive form to customers of Lakeview. The LM software package was dealt with by Lakeview as if it were its principal asset and expressly on terms that the intellectual propery rights remained with Lakeview. Mr Charles Steadman assserts that this was done with his permission. But there was never any written copyright assignment or licence made by Mr Charles Steadman in respect of the LM software in favour of the company.

In 1994 it became a public company and its name was changed to its present name. Mr Charles Steadman continued to own 50% of the shares and his brother and sister-in-law the other 50%. Both brothers remained directors. It has 35 employees and a turnover of £4.2m. Mr Charles Steadman supplied to the company his technical computer expertise by continuing to develop the LM software for the company based on the programs written while he was a sole trader and in which he now claims to have retained the copyright. Mr Matthew Steadman supplied the business acumen and commercial expertise.

Unfortunately they fell out in 1998. Mr Charles Steadman agreed to leave Lakeview. He received £850,000. He signed the following documents:

(a) On 14 July 1998 he and his brother signed an agreement following a meeting. Their signatures were witnessed by a Mr Morris and a Mr Brown who had attended the meeting. In addition to the cancellation of his employment contract and the sale of his shares in Lakeview, Mr Charles Steadman agreed to:

Rescind intellectual property rights to Lakeview software in all versions and platforms."

(b) A share acquisition Agreement dated 30 July 1998 contained an undertaking by him in clause 2.3 in which he acknowledged that:

. . . he has no proprietary interest in any intellectual property rights ('IPR') now or at any time vested in the Company and that all IPR developed or acquired by him during his employment by the Company belongs to the Company."

(c) A Consultancy Agreement also dated 30 July 1998 under which his company, Studiodrive, agreed to provide Lakeview with services, including the development of 'appropriate software' to meet the requirements of clients of Lakeview advised on Year 2000 tasks and issues. That agreement expired on 31 July 1999.

On 23 April 1999 Lakeview's solicitors wrote to Mr Charles Steadman referring to the agreements and alleging that he and his company Studiodrive had departed from the terms of the Consultancy Agreement and had misused Lakeview's IPR other than for the purpose of that agreement. A series of undertakings were requested, including an undertaking not to service, maintain, adapt, modify or upgrade any Lakeview software currently used by or in the possession of Roberto Neckware or Spheric Engineering (both customers of Lakeview) or with any other Lakeview customer, past or present.

In his reply of 29 April 1999 Mr Charles Steadman wrote:

You allege that I have used Lakeview's . . . IPR, specifically the source code of the software LM (and other related software packages), and the compiler known as LIL, both of which belong to Lakeview. I have not done so. I have also made it very clear to both Spheric and Roberto that I no longer represent Lakeview, and that I cannot modify their software in any way or use the LIL compiler to modify their existing software or create new software. I have been in the computer software industry for many years and I am extremely aware of the rights of the owners of any software package, and the resultant limitations of what I can and cannot do without those rights."

He added that he understood that he could not make modifications to the LM software which would require either or both the source code and the compiler and that, although he was authorised to modify data belonging to customers of Lakeview, he was not authorised to modify the programs that belong to Lakeview and that Lakeview was the 'software author' of the programs licensed to its customers. He denied that he had misused Lakeview's IPR in any way, that he had any copies in any form of Lakeview's source code, compiler or any other related items that make up Lakeview's IPR or that he had made or retained any copies of that material.

In a later witness statement he denied copying or reproducing any part of the software supplied to customers of Lakeview or interfering with the source code of the Lakeview computer program. But he disputed the claim that intellectual property rights in respect of the original Lakeview LM programs written by him prior to the incorporation of the company were or had ever been vested in Lakeview.

The Proceedings

In the Claim Form, as amended on 9 August 1999, Lakeview seeks a declaration that it is the owner of the copyright in the Lakeview software as defined in Sch 1 to the Particulars of Claim. ...

In his Defence Mr Steadman denied that Lakeview is the owner of the copyright in the computer programme known as LM and denied the existence of a program known as LIL. Although this application is solely concerned with the copyright title issue it should be noted that other claims are made by Lakeview for breach of contract, breach of fiduciary duty and misuse of confidential information all of which are advanced, in the view of Mr Charles Steadman, to prevent him from competing with Lakeview.

. . .

I would grant permission to appeal, allow the appeal, make the declaration that Lakeview is the beneficial owner of the copyright in the LM computer software and grant a final injunction restraining Mr Steadman and Studiodrive from copying the LM computer software or any substantial part thereof, save that this shall not prevent him from acting as an adviser for customers of Lakeview who are licensed users of the LM software and that he acts at all times within the terms of any such licence.

My reasons for this conclusion can be briefly stated as follows:

(1) On his undisputed evidence Mr Charles Steadman developed the LM software package between 1986 and 1988 while the sole proprietor of the business 'Lakeview Computer Services'. He was the sole author and therefore the first owner of the copyright in the programs.

(2) Lakeview was formed to carry on the business under the name Lakeview Computer Services Limited. His brother joined him in the business when the company was incorporated and they held the shares in equal proportions. There is no evidence that Mr Charles Steadman dealt with the LM software copyrights separately from the affairs of the company after 1988. Further development on the LM programs by Mr Charles Steadman took place and their use was licensed by the company and not by him personally.

(3) Although no 'formal agreement' was concluded in writing for the transfer to Lakeview of the legal title to the copyright in the programs developed by Mr Charles Steadman pre-1988 while a sole trader, it does not follow, as

asserted by Mr Steadman, that he still held the beneficial interest in the copyright in that material. Mr Wright correctly submits on his behalf that under s.90 of the Copyright, Designs and Patents Act 1988 an assignment of copyright has to be in writing. Subsection (3) provides that:

An assignment of copyright is not effective unless it is in writing signed by or on behalf of the assignor."

That provision does not, however, apply to an agreement to assign copyright, which may be an express oral agreement or an agreement implied from conduct. A binding and enforceable agreement to assign is effective as an equitable assignment which may be carried into execution by an order for specific performance or by a vesting order transferring the legal title to the equitable owner.

Mr Wright's further contention that an equitable assignment of copyright must be in writing is also misconceived. It arises out of a confusion between (a) an equitable assignment of a legal interest in copyright and (b) a legal assignment of an equitable interest in copyright. In this case Lakeview relies on the former, which need not be in writing, not on the latter.

(4) The evidence of Mr Charles Steadman points to conduct from which the implication of an agreement to assign the pre-1988 copyright to Lakeview is irresistible. Lakeview was formed after Mr Steadman had established a business in the course of which Mr Steadman had created the LM software. The company was formed to carry on that business which Mr Charles Steadman then ceased to carry on as a sole trader.

After its incorporation the company employed Mr Steadman to carry out further development on the software and marketed it. As he recognised in the agreements of July 1998, the company was certainly entitled to the IPR in the software produced while he was employed by the company. It is unconvincing to suggest, as his counsel, Mr Wright, did, that the beneficial interest in the underlying copyright in the LM software was retained by Mr Steadman after the company was formed and began to employ Mr Steadman to develop and to produce computer software based on the LM programs. Lakeview would be left in the vulnerable position of a non-exclusive oral licensee of the underlying pre-incorporation material. It is even less convincing to argue that Mr Steadman still retained copyright in the LM software after he had received £850,000 on leaving Lakeview and signing the agreements dealing with IPR rights. The contention that the agreements were not final, binding and enforceable against him has no real prospect of success at trial.

Fisher v. Brooker, [2009] UKHL 41 (H.L.)

Appellate Committee Lord Hope of Craighead, Lord Walker of Gestingthorpe, Baroness Hale of Richmond, Lord Mance, Lord Neuberger of Abbotsbury

Per LORD NEUBERGER OF ABBOTSBURY

. . .

My Lords,

29. This appeal concerns the ownership of the musical copyright in the song "A Whiter Shade of Pale", which was recorded by the band Procol Harum during April 1967 and first released as a single by Decca records under licence from Essex Music Ltd ("Essex") on 12 May 1967. As Blackburne J said in his judgment at first instance, it was "one of the most successful popular songs of the late 1960s", and it is "no exaggeration to say that with the passage of time the song has achieved something approaching cult status" – [2006] EWHC 3239 Ch, paras 1 and 3.

The factual background

30. The relevant facts, as found by the judge or were common ground, are as follows. The music in its original form was composed in early 1967 by the band's lead singer and pianist, Gary Brooker, around lyrics written by the band's manager, Keith Reid. Mr Brooker then recorded a demonstration tape of himself singing the song as he had composed it, accompanying himself on the piano. He played this tape to Mr Platz, the managing director of Essex, who told him that he considered it to be "a certain hit".

31. On the following day, 7 March 1967, Mr Brooker and Mr Reid entered into a written agreement with Essex ("the assignment"), whereby they assigned to Essex "all the Copyright as defined by the Copyright Act 1956... in the words and music of the composition 'A Whiter Shade of Pale' [and another song] ... absolutely". In the assignment, Essex agreed to pay Mr Brooker and Mr Reid specified percentages (normally 50% between them) of the sheet music and mechanical royalties, and of the synchronisation, performing, broadcasting and rediffusion fees, receivable in connection with the song. Mr Brooker and Mr Reid also recorded in the assignment that they would share the payments due to them thereunder equally. Around 17 March 1967, the song was registered with the Performing Rights Society ("the PRS") and with the Mechanical Copyright Protection Society ("the MCPS"). These two societies collect, and distribute, to the persons entered in their records as the copyright owners, any royalties due in respect of works registered with them.

32. Shortly thereafter, Matthew Fisher joined the band as organist, and, together with Mr Brooker and the other members of the band (Bobby Harrison, Ray Royer, and Dave Knight), he rehearsed and added to the music of the song, so that it evolved into its final form ("the 12 work") which the band recorded in

April 1967 ("the first recording"). Crucially for present purposes, Mr Fisher composed the familiar organ solo at the beginning of the work, and the organ melody which is a counterpoint throughout most of the four minutes during which the work lasts. The recording of the work was released on 12 May 1967 as a "single" record on the Decca label, under Essex's licence, and it became an instant "hit".

33. On 16 May 1967, the five members of the band, effectively acting through Mr Reid (therein "the manager") entered into a further contract ("the recording contract") with Essex. The effect of this contract was to enable Essex to exploit any recording made by the band over the period of a year (subject to renewal by Essex a maximum of four times). In return, Essex was to pay the members of the band a specified royalty in respect of every record of any such recording which was manufactured. The main purpose of the recording contract from the point of view of Essex was that it operated as "the consent required by section 1 of the Dramatic and Musical Performers Protection Act 1958" – clause 3(a). Unfortunately, there are two clauses with that assignation, so I shall refer to it as clause 3(ii)(a). By the first clause 3(a) – "clause 3(i)(a)" – the band members granted to Essex "the right to manufacture... sell, lease, license or otherwise use or dispose of .... records embodying the performances to be recorded hereunder ....". Further by what I shall for consistency's sake refer to as clause 3(i)(e), the members of the band also granted to Essex "the right to incorporate in records to be made hereunder instrumentations, orchestrations and arrangements owned by the manager at the time of recording them". It has been common ground that the recording contract applies to the first recording.

34. Thereafter, over the next two years or so, apart from enjoying great acclaim in connection with the work, the band recorded other songs (with words written by Mr Reid and music composed by Mr Brooker, sometimes together with Mr Fisher), whose musical and lyrical copyrights were assigned to Essex in the same form, and on the same terms, as the assignment.

35. In his evidence, Mr Fisher said that, during 1967, he had raised the question of his having a share in the rights in respect of the music with Mr Brooker and Mr Reid, but had been rebuffed or ignored by them. He explained that he had not wanted to push his claim as he feared that, if he did so, he would be asked to "say goodbye to a career in ... a number one pop group". In 1969, however, Mr Fisher did indeed leave the band, which by then had accrued certain debts. A relatively 13 informal agreement was reached whereby the remaining members agreed to release (or, more accurately, I think, to indemnify) Mr Fisher from any liability in respect of such debts in return for his waiving any right to certain specified royalties (not including any copyright royalties in respect of the work).

36. Despite leaving the band, Mr Fisher was invited to play with them at various functions from time to time between 1969 and 2003. On a couple of occasions during that period, once in 1971 and once in 1991, Mr Fisher contended that he was entitled to certain royalties which he was not receiving, but he never suggested that he was entitled to any money in respect of the exploitation of the work.

37. In or about 1993, Essex's rights under the assignment and the recording contract were purportedly assigned to Onward Music Ltd ("Onward"), and Onward was registered with the PRS and MCPS as the owner of the copyright in the work. Meanwhile, the first recording was proving very successful, resulting in substantial royalties, which were collected by the PRS and MCPS and distributed to Essex (or their successors), as they were registered with the societies as owners of the copyright, and Mr Brooker and Mr Reid were then paid their shares under the terms of the assignment.

38. Quite apart from the first recording, the work has been extraordinarily successful over the 38 years since it was first released. It has been the subject of many articles and interviews, and has a dedicated following, as can be seen from the number of websites devoted to the work and the band. There are over 770 versions of the work performed by other groups, and themes of the work (especially the introductory bars) are available, and popular, as mobile telephone ring tones.

39. During April and May 2005, Mr Fisher, through his solicitors wrote to Essex and Mr Brooker (together "the respondents") notifying them of his claim to a share of the musical copyright in the work, explaining the grounds for his claim, threatening proceedings if his claim was not acknowledged, and putting forward terms of settlement. Those terms were rejected; accordingly, Mr Fisher began proceedings on 31 May 2005, and they came before Blackburne J, who gave a judgment which was largely favourable to Mr Fisher – [2005] EWHC 3239 Ch. However, on appeal, the respondents substantially succeeded: Mummery LJ and Sir Paul Kennedy set aside two of the three 14 declarations made at first instance, although David Richards J dissented – [2008] Bus LR 1123.

The issues before the judge and the Court of Appeal

40. The judge had to decide a number of issues, only some of which are now raised in your Lordships' House. First, there was the question whether a fair trial was possible, bearing in mind the passage of time between the composition of the work and the issue of Mr Fisher's claim. Although the judge rightly described Mr Fisher's silence about his claim between 1967 and 2004 as "remarkable" and "quite extraordinary", he concluded that a fair trial was possible — [2006] EWHC 3239 Ch, paras 16 and 17, and 24. This conclusion was strongly challenged by the respondents on appeal, but the Court of Appeal rightly upheld the judge on this point — [2008] Bus LR 1123, para 43. There is no appeal on this point by the respondents.

41. Secondly, the judge had to determine whether, and if so to what extent, Mr Fisher could, in principle, claim any share of the musical copyright in the work. He decided that "Mr Fisher's instrumental introduction (i.e the organ solo ... as repeated) is sufficiently different from what Mr Brooker had composed on the piano to qualify in law, and by quite a wide margin, as an original contribution to the work"–[2006] EWHC 3239 Ch, para 42. Consequently, he held that "Mr Fisher qualifies to be regarded as a joint author of the work"–ibid. After considering various arguments raised by the respondents, the judge concluded that "Mr

Fisher's interest in the work should be reflected by according to him a 40% share in the musical copyright" — ibid, para 98. Rightly, the Court of Appeal had little difficulty in dismissing the respondents' appeal on this issue — [2008] Bus LR 1123, para 44. The respondents do not seek to appeal further on this issue.

42. The third issue was whether, nonetheless, Mr Fisher had no right to claim a share of the musical copyright owing to the circumstances in which he made his contribution to the work. In effect, the respondents argued that, given that the song in its original form had been recorded, and the musical copyright in it had been assigned to Essex, in March 1967, Mr Fisher impliedly assigned to Essex any interest he acquired in the musical copyright in the work. The judge rejected that argument — [2006] EWHC 3239 Ch, para 63. However, the Court of Appeal, or at least the majority, left the point open — [2008] Bus LR 1123, para 100. This "implied assignment" argument is raised by the respondents by way of cross-appeal.

43. The fourth issue was whether Mr Fisher had lost his right to maintain his claim to an interest in the musical copyright by virtue of the recording contract. The judge held that the agreement "did not purport to take from Mr Fisher any copyright interest he had in the musical composition", and therefore rejected the argument — [2006] EWHC 3239 Ch, para 66. The Court of Appeal, or at least the majority, left the point open — [2008] Bus LR 1123, para 111. The respondents maintain their case in this House on this issue by way of cross-appeal.

44. The fifth issue was whether Mr Fisher had lost his interest in the copyright as a result of estoppel, laches or acquiescence. The respondents failed on this issue before the judge — [2006] EWCA Civ 3239, para 82. The Court of Appeal accepted that the judge was entitled to come to this conclusion, and that they could not interfere — [2008] Bus LR 1123, paras 67 (Mummery LJ, with whom Sir Paul Kennedy agreed) and 117 (David Richards J). On this "laches, estoppel or acquiescence" issue, the respondents maintain their case by crossappealing.

45. The sixth issue at first instance was whether Mr Fisher could claim his share of the monies paid out by the PRS and the MCPS in respect of the work during the six years before the issue of proceedings (it being rightly accepted by Mr Fisher that any claim going further back would be time-barred). The monies collected by the societies had been paid to Essex, or, since 1993, Onward, as the copyright owner registered with the societies, and the appropriate share in accordance with the assignment had then been paid to Mr Reid and Mr Brooker. The judge rejected this claim, on the basis that "for so long as Mr Fisher chose not to make ... his claim [and] allowed the societies to account to the [respondents], ... he must be taken to have gratuitously licensed the exploitation of his copyright" — [2006] EWHC 3239 Ch, para 94. The judge went on to find that this implied licence was revoked when the letter before action was sent to the respondents in May 2005 — ibid. There was no appeal to the Court of Appeal by Mr Fisher on this finding.

46. The final matter to be considered by Blackburne J was the nature of the relief to be accorded to Mr Fisher. The judge refused an injunction restraining

Essex from exploiting the musical copyright in the work, as there was no evidence of the respondents seeking to do so "in defiance of any interest in it which Mr Fisher is able to establish" — [2006] EWHC 3239 Ch, para 88. There was no appeal by Mr Fisher on this issue.

47. However, the judge granted declarations in these terms:

> "1. [Mr Fisher] is a co-author of ... 'A Whiter Shade of Pale' as recorded by ... Procol Harum ('the work') and released as a single on 12 May 1967.
>
> 2. [Mr] Fisher is a joint owner in the musical copyright in the work, with a share of 40%.
>
> 3. The [respondents'] licence to exploit the work was revoked on 31 May 2005".

Allowing the respondents' appeal, the majority of the Court of Appeal held that it was unconscionable, in all the circumstances, for Mr Fisher to have revoked the implied licence, and that "the defences of acquiescence and laches operated to disentitle [Mr] Fisher from the exercise of the court's discretion to grant the second and third declarations" — [2008] Bus LR 1123, para 85. Accordingly, they held that the licence continued and the second and third declarations should be set aside — ibid, para 89. David Richards J dissented — ibid, para 140. Mr Fisher's appeal against the setting aside of the second and third declarations raises a point which I regard as an aspect of the laches, estoppel, and acquiescence issue.

48. Accordingly, there are three matters to be considered, namely the implied assignment issue, the recording contract issue, and the laches, estoppel and acquiescence issue. In relation to the first two of these matters, it is right to mention that there was some discussion whether the rights granted to Essex under the assignment or the recording contract were assignable, at least without the consent of the other parties to the agreement. This point, which is of particular apparent force in the case of the recording contract (given that, as pointed out by my noble and learned friend, Baroness Hale of Richmond, it describes itself as concerned with "personal services"), was not decided by Blackburne J or by the Court of Appeal and was only lightly touched on in argument in this House. Although it would be desirable to resolve all issues between the two parties, I do not consider that this is one which we can properly determine at this stage. For present purposes I am prepared to proceed on the assumption that Onward effectively stands in the shoes of Essex. Was there an implied assignment?

49. The respondents contend that the circumstances in which the work came into existence are consistent only with the copyright in the work becoming vested solely in Essex, and, in particular, with Mr Fisher having impliedly assigned his interest in the musical copyright to Essex. The essence of this argument is that Essex had taken an absolute assignment of the musical (and lyrical) copyright in the song in its original form, and was intending, and was intended by the members of the band, to exploit the song as developed for the first recording and released in May 1967, i.e. as the work. Accordingly, runs the argument, it must

have been intended by Essex and by all members of the band, including Mr Fisher, that Essex would be the sole owner of the copyright in the work.

50. This argument is based on implication, which is normally invoked in order to give rise to an unexpressed term into an existing contract. However, it is clear, as a matter of principle, commercial reality, and indeed authority, that an unexpressed contract can arise by way of implication. In order to succeed in such an argument, it is, of course, necessary for the well established requirements for implication to be satisfied. Thus, in this case, the respondents have to show that, at the time of the alleged assignment, (a) it would have been obvious to Mr Fisher (as well as Essex) that his interest in the musical copyright was being, or had to be, assigned to Essex, or, which may amount to the same thing, (b) the commercial relationship between the parties could not sensibly have functioned without such an assignment.

51. In my judgment, this argument faces a number of insurmountable problems. First, it assumes that Mr Fisher knew that the song in its original form had been recorded and that the copyright had been assigned to Essex. He may have known these facts as at the time the work was recorded in April 1967 or when it was released in May 1967, but he did not say that he did and it was not put to him that he did. In this connection, it is relevant to mention that he had not, by that time, effected any assignment to Essex of copyright in relation to other musical works, so it could not be said that he must have been aware of Essex's usual practice. Where a party contends for an implied term or an implied contract, it is up to that person to establish the relevant factual foundation for his case. Indeed, the fact that these points were not put to Mr Fisher is scarcely surprising, as the contention was not pleaded, although it was advanced before the judge in argument, albeit in somewhat different terms from the way it is now put.

52. Secondly, the fact that the recording contract was only entered into on 16 May 1967, about a month after the work was first recorded, and four days after the release of the recording, undermines the notion that, before that date, Mr Fisher had impliedly assigned his interest in the musical copyright to Essex. The date of the recording contract shows that, as one would have expected, the members of the band were content to leave it to Essex, an experienced record and publishing company, to produce the relevant documentation for them to execute as and when appropriate. That is scarcely consistent with the alleged implied assignment having taken place before 16 May 1967. The unattractiveness of the respondents' argument is reinforced by the fact, identified by Baroness Hale, that one is here concerned with five musicians, all of whom were in their early twenties, and a highly experienced music recording and publishing company, on whom they were no doubt relying.

53. Thirdly, having heard the evidence, the judge found that the question of what was to be done in relation to any interest in the musical copyright in the work as a result of additions to the original song "was left at large" — [2006] EWHC 3239 Ch, para 63. The question whether there was an implied contract is one of inference rather than primary fact, but it is a question which, at least in this case,

turned to a significant extent on the precise factual circumstances, which were very much for the trial judge to evaluate. It is also true that those circumstances had arisen nearly 40 years earlier, and some of the important witnesses (in particular the relevant employees of Essex, including Mr Platz) were dead, but there was a significant amount of relevant oral evidence. In my judgment, there would have been no warrant for an appellate tribunal interfering with the clear and carefully considered conclusion reached by the judge on this issue.

54. Finally, there is the point that, even if there was some sort of implied contract, it is very unlikely to have been an outright free assignment of Mr Fisher's interest in the musical copyright. First, such an arrangement would have been more than was necessary to give business efficacy: all that would have been needed was a licence by Mr Fisher, as someone with a share of the copyright in the work, permitting Essex to exploit the first recording. Secondly, particularly in the light of the terms of the assignment, it would very probably have been appropriate to include provision for a reasonable payment, or quantum meruit, in respect of any implied assignment or licence. In the light of the other problems this argument faces, it is unnecessary and inappropriate to expand on this aspect.

---

4. Licenses and Implied Licenses

Unlike assignments, which transfer ownership of a right in a work, licenses are generally merely permissive in nature; a license grants to the licensee permission to exercise the right that is licensed. A general license represents the consent of the copyright owner — whether express or implied — to perform an act in relation to the work that would otherwise be infringing. A sole license permits only one party (in addition to the owner-licensor) to exercise the relevant right. In either case, the license need not be in writing. In contrast, an exclusive license, like an assignment, must be in writing and signed (see section 13(4)). This is because an exclusive license is not only permissive, but actually constitutes a grant of an interest in the copyright (see section 13(7)). As defined in section 2.7, an exclusive license "is an authorization to do any act that is subject to copyright to the exclusive of all others *including the copyright owner*...." As such, an exclusive license resembles an assignment, although it may be limited in duration or subject to certain ongoing obligations in a way that assignments, as absolute transfers of the right, typically are not.

Licenses to a work can be express or implied, and except in the case of exclusive licenses, need not be in writing. The circumstances in which licenses can arise and their scope has been the subject of considerable litigation.

Ray v. Classic FM Plc [1998] EWHC Patents 333

Hearing: 23rd February – 2nd March 1998
Judgment: 18th March 1998

. . .

1. I have before me an action by the writer and broadcaster on classical music Mr Robin Ray ("the Plaintiff") against the commercial radio station broadcasting popular classical music Classic FM Plc ("the Defendant"). At issue is the entitlement of the parties to the intellectual property rights in five documents containing proposals how the tracks on the Defendant's music recordings should be categorised ("the Five Documents"); in a catalogue of over 50,000 items of classical music (using the above categories) compiled by the Plaintiff over a five year period ("the Catalogue"); and in a database ("the Database") in which the contents of the Five Documents and of the Catalogue are substantially reproduced.

2. Whilst the Plaintiff was engaged to provide services to the Defendant under what was termed a Consultancy Agreement ("the Consultancy Agreement"), he prepared the Five Documents and the Catalogue as a preliminary step to the incorporation by the Defendant of the material contained in the Database. The Defendant compiled the Database using the proprietary software known as Selector for the purpose of providing an automated and programmed system for the selection of the music to be played on its radio station. Differences arose between the Plaintiff and the Defendant during the currency of the Consultancy Agreement as to the entitlement of the Defendant to exploit the Database by making copies and granting licences to foreign radio stations to use those copies, and these differences resulted in the commencement of these proceedings. It is common ground that the Defendant is entitled to use, and make copies of, the Database for the purpose of broadcasting from its radio station in the United Kingdom. The dispute is as to whether the Defendant has further and, if so, what rights. The Defendant claims that it is entitled to exploit the Database by making copies for use by foreign licencees and the Defendant has done so. The Plaintiff contends that he is sole owner of the copyright in the Five Documents and the Catalogue and that, as the Five Documents and the Catalogue are reproduced in the Database, as such owner he is entitled to prevent the Defendant doing so.

3. This litigation springs from the failure of the parties (and more particularly the advisers who were then acting for them) at the time that the parties entered into the Consultancy Agreement to consider, or provide for, the intellectual property rights that would arise in the course of the engagement of the Plaintiff. The expensive lesson of this litigation is the vital necessity for provision for these rights in such agreements.

FACTS

4. From October/November 1988 to early 1991 the Plaintiff was closely involved with a group of investors in bids for a franchise to provide classical music broadcasts and for this purpose provided assistance in preparing and providing programme material. His great asset was that he was nationally famous for his

encyclopaedic knowledge of classical music. If the bids had been successful, he would have been appointed and employed by the successful bidder as Artistic Director. These bids however failed, and when another group of investors (through the Defendant) mounted a bid for a licence which on the 30th September 1991 proved successful, the Plaintiff sought from them the same post. Their management structure, however, had no place for the post of Artistic Director and they were unwilling to afford this role to the Plaintiff. The Plaintiff and his agent, Mr Wilkinson, pressed for the Plaintiff's employment as Artistic Director with a job description which included the assumption of "overall responsibility for the station's music policy, programming and schedules". But Mr Bernard, the chairman of the Defendant's interim management committee, made clear that no such responsibility and no such executive role could be considered before the appointment of the Defendant's Chief Executive (which took place in 1992) and that the only position that could then be offered was a short term position as freelance music adviser under a consultancy agreement, that this would only be a temporary measure for a few months, and that meanwhile his position and future could be reviewed. Under the Consultancy Agreement he would make his distinct contribution to the musical content of the Defendant's broadcasts.

. . .

6. It is to be noted that the Consultancy Agreement made no express provision in respect of the intellectual property rights in the work created by the Plaintiff as such consultant for the Defendant. It is common ground that neither party addressed their mind to this question, and neither did their advisers. That is the genesis of this dispute and litigation.

. . .

11. During the period after the 31st January 1992 the Plaintiff applied himself in preparing and supplying to the Defendant the succeeding instalments of the Catalogue. The Consultancy Agreement contemplated him doing this work on his own. He selected the works to be included in the library, he assessed their popularity and included in the instalments at least the bulk of the information required under each of the categories. After the second of the instalments of the Catalogue (and accordingly from about March 1992 to June 1997), in order to have more time for the critical task of selecting the tracks for the library and assessing their popularity, the Plaintiff was enabled to omit from the instalments he prepared and supplied details in respect of a number of categories which could safely be delegated to others: the task of providing this information was assumed by staff employed by the Defendant for this purpose and most particularly Miss Anna Gregory. The importance of the contribution by the Defendant's staff is not to be compared with that of the Plaintiff. It is common ground that the research and labour of the staff was sufficient to entitle the Defendant to copyright in the documents or the Database where that contribution is to be found. The fact that the Defendant's representatives made this separate contribution to the project cannot however be relevant to the question whether the Plaintiff is sole author of the Five Documents and the Catalogue, the contents of which it supplemented.

12. The Defendant collaborated with RCS in adapting the Selector software for use for a classical music radio station and were responsible for entering the Plaintiff's selections and data and the data collected by the Defendant's representatives onto the Selector software. It is common ground that the Defendant is entitled (jointly with RCS) to copyright in the Database.

. . .

THE ISSUES

14. There can be no doubt that copyright subsists in the Five Documents, the Catalogue and the Database. It is likewise clear that the Plaintiff was either author or joint author of the Five Documents and the Catalogue and that the Defendant and RCS are joint authors of the Database. The Defendant conceded in the course of the trial that the Five Documents and the Catalogue are reproduced in the Database. (There are a number of versions of the Database, but the Defendant had earlier agreed that, if any version of the Database substantially reproduced the Five Documents or the Catalogue, no point is to be taken that there is only insubstantial reproduction in any other version of the Database in existence now or at any earlier stage). Since the Database reproduces the Five Documents and Catalogue, if the copyright in those documents is vested in the Plaintiff and if the Defendant made the copies of the Database for purposes of exploitation abroad without the consent of the Plaintiff, this conduct constituted an infringement of that copyright.

15. The Plaintiff contends that the copyright in the Five Documents and the Catalogue is vested in him alone as sole author, and that the consent that he implicitly gave under the Consultancy Agreement was limited to use of the Database for the purposes of the Defendant's radio station in the United Kingdom and therefore did not extend to this use. The Plaintiff further contends that, even if the Defendant was a joint author of the Five Documents and the Catalogue, the making of copies of the Database for the purpose of exploitation abroad required his consent as joint author.

16. The Defendant by way of answer contends that: (1) on any basis the Defendant was joint author of the Five Documents and the Catalogue, and that as joint owner of the copyright therein the Defendant was entitled to do what it did without the consent of the Plaintiff; (2) in any event the Plaintiff and the Defendant were joint authors of the Database, and any copyright in the Five Documents and the Catalogue vested in the Plaintiff was subsumed or merged in their joint copyright in the Database, and the Defendant as joint owner of the copyright in the Database was entitled to make copies for purposes of exploitation abroad as it did; (3) under the provisions of the Consultancy Agreement any copyright vested in the Plaintiff as author passed to the Defendant at law or in equity or alternatively the Defendant was granted a licence which was extensive enough to permit the user complained of; and (4) that the Plaintiff is estopped from maintaining the claim made in this action.

17. The issues accordingly are: (1) whether the Defendant was a joint author with the Plaintiff of the Five Documents and Catalogue and whether the Plaintiff

was a joint author of the Database. This involves the determination of what is required as a matter of law to constitute a person a joint author and whether these conditions are satisfied; (2) (if the answer to (1) in respect of the Five Documents and the Catalogue is in the affirmative) whether the Defendant as joint owner of the copyright was entitled to make the copies for the purpose for which it did without the consent of the Plaintiff; (3) (if the answer to (1) in respect of the Database is in the affirmative), whether any copyright of the Plaintiff in the Five Documents and Catalogue was subsumed or merged in the copyright in the Database; (4) whether the Consultancy Agreement constituted a contract of employment which vested legal ownership of the copyright in the Five Documents and Catalogue in the Defendant as documents created by the Plaintiff in the course of his employment by the Defendant; (5) (if the Consultancy Agreement did not constitute a contract of employment), whether the Defendant is nonetheless the owner in equity as a result of an implied term of the Consultancy Agreement; and (6) whether the Plaintiff is estopped from maintaining its claim in this action. For the purposes of (4) and (5) above, it is common ground that the First Document, though it ante-dated the Consultancy Agreement, should be treated in the same way as the rest of the Five Documents, i.e. as though it came into existence after the Consultancy Agreement had been executed.

. . .

JOINT AUTHORSHIP

(a) Law

26. Sections 9(1) and 10(1) of the Copyrights Designs and Patents Act 1988 ("theAct") provides as follows:

9(1) "In this Part, 'author' in relation to a work, means the person who creates it"

10(1) "In this Part a work of joint authorship means a work produced by the collaboration of two or more authors in which the contribution of each author is not distinct from that of the other author or authors."

27. A joint author is accordingly a person (1) who collaborates with another author in the production of a work; (2) who (as an author) provides a significant creative input; and (3) whose contribution is not distinct from that of the other author. He must contribute to the "production" of the work and create something protected by copyright which finds its way into the finished work: see Cala Homes (South) Limited v. Alfred McAlpine [1995] FSR 818 ("Cala"). Copyright exists, not in ideas, but the written expression of ideas. A joint author must participate in the writing and share responsibility for the form of expression in the literary work. He must accordingly do more than contribute ideas to an author: he must be an author (or creator) of the work in question. It is not enough that he thought up the plot of a play or made suggestions for a comic routine to be included (see Tate v. Thomas [1921] 1 Ch 503); or indeed that he passed on his reminiscences to a ghost writer (see Evans v. E Hulton & Co Ltd [1923-8] MCC 51). It is not sufficient that there is established to have been a division of labour between two parties in the project of writing a book if one

alone is entirely responsible for the skill and labour of authorship of the book: see Fylde Microsystems Ltd v. Key Radio Systems Ltd unreported, Laddie J. 11th February 1998.

28. In Cala Laddie J. held that there is no restriction on the way in which a joint author's contribution may be funnelled into the finished work, and in particular that there is no requirement that each of the authors must have exercised penmanship. There is no reason why penmanship should be insisted on any more in case of joint authors than in the case of a sole author, who may dictate his work to a scribe. But in my judgment what is required is something which approximates to penmanship. What is essential is a direct responsibility for what actually appears on the paper. Accordingly in Cala, where a director of Cala provided a very detailed input (including much of the design features) in plans which architects were instructed to prepare and through regular briefing and vetting sessions with the architects ensured that the plans accorded with Cala's "image", he was held to be a joint author with the architects of the plans they prepared. As it appears to me, the architects in that case were in large part acting as "scribes" for the director. In practice such a situation is likely to be exceptional.

(b) Fact

29. The evidence in this case establishes to my full satisfaction that the Defendant was not (as claimed by the Defendant) a joint author of the Five Documents and the Catalogue and that the Plaintiff was not (again as claimed by the Defendant) a joint author of the Database.

30. As regards the Five Documents and the Catalogue, there is no doubt that on the 6th December 1991 and on later occasions there were meetings between the Plaintiff and representatives of the Defendant when discussions took place as to the categories to be adopted and as to the contents of the Catalogue, and that the Defendant's representatives initiated and developed a number of ideas which the Plaintiff incorporated in the Five Documents and the Catalogue. But the Plaintiff was solely responsible as author for the writing of the Five Documents and the Catalogue and the way the ideas were expressed in them. He was not, as submitted by the Defendant, "the team scribe". The fact that the documents in part (and in fact only in a relatively small, though significant, part) reflect the Defendant's representatives' input is totally insufficient to make the Defendant joint author.

31. By parity of reason, the Plaintiff, who had no part on the preparation of the Database beyond the contribution of material which was included, was in no wise a collaborator in its production. He was right in disclaiming any joint authorship.

CONSEQUENCES OF JOINT AUTHORSHIP

32. Since I have held that there was no joint authorship either of the Five Documents and the Catalogue or the Database, the questions raised as to the consequences of joint authorship can be answered quite briefly.

(a) Joint Authorship of Copyright in the Five Documents and the Catalogue

33. It is common ground that joint authors hold copyright in the subject of the joint authorship as tenants in common entitled in equal shares. The Defendant contends that, if it was a joint author of the copyright in the above Five Documents and the Catalogue, as tenant in common it was entitled to exploit the copyright in the way it has because: (i) such exploitation did no damage to the copyright; and, (ii) the only right of the Plaintiff as co-owner is to an account of the profits earned.

34. It is unnecessary to consider whether the use made of the copyright material did any damage, for it is quite clear that, even if the Defendant was joint author of the Five Documents and Catalogue, joint ownership could not without the consent of the Plaintiff justify the making of copies for the purpose of exploitation of the copyright abroad. The 1988 Act itself provides in Section 16(2) that it is an infringement of copyright to do any of the restricted acts (which include making copies) without the consent of the "copyright owner", and Section 173(2) expressly provides that in case of joint owners this means the consent of all the owners. This result is in accord with the decision in Cescinsky v. George Routledge [1916] 2 KB 325 and the view expressed by Laddie J. in Cala (at p.836). I reject the Defendant's submission that the Defendant as a joint owner is free to do a restricted act so long as he accounts to the Plaintiff as its joint owner for a share of the profits, or that the right of the Plaintiff is limited to claiming an account: the Plaintiff is entitled to sue for infringement, claiming damages and an injunction.

(b) Joint Authorship of the Database

35. Mr Watson proffered the novel suggestion that, because the Five Documents and the Catalogue were prepared as preliminary stages to the creation of the Database, the copyright of the Plaintiff in the Five Documents and Catalogue was subsumed in and merged in the copyright jointly owned by the Plaintiff with the Defendant in the Database. This suggestion finds no support in any authority or textbook; this is perhaps not surprising since it is wholly repugnant to the basic principles of the law of copyright. Where a work goes through successive stages in writing in the course of its creation or development, the copyright in the earlier of the writing subsists whatever the use later made of the material contained in it (see e.g. Cala at p.827). It is, I think, a kindness to Mr Watson to say no more on this (no doubt his solitary) lapse into heresy.

CONTRACT OF EMPLOYMENT OR FOR SERVICES

36. It is of importance in this case whether the Consultancy Agreement constitutes a contract of employment or for services because, if the contract was of employment, under Section 11(2) of the 1988 Act copyright in works created in the course of employment (subject to any agreement to the contrary) vest in the employer. There are accordingly raised in this case two questions. The first is whether the Consultancy Agreement was a contract of employment. The second is whether, if the Consultancy Agreement was a contract of employment, there was an agreement excluding the operation of Section 11(2).

(a) Nature of Contract

37. It is explicitly stated in the Consultancy Agreement (as in the correspondence between the parties immediately preceding it) that the parties intended the relationship between the parties to be that of the Plaintiff as an independent contractor providing services to the Defendant and not that of employee and employer. That is a relevant, but not decisive, consideration. It is necessary to look at the terms of the contract as a whole concentrating on the substantive rights and obligations of the parties and decide whether they are more or less strongly indicative of one form of relationship than the other: see Barnett v. Brabyn [1996] STC 716.

38. Far from the terms being incompatible with a contract for services rather than service or indeed indicative of a contract for service, they are, as it seems to me both compatible with and indicative of a contract for services. A positive indication that this is a contract for services is to be found in Clauses 3.1.2, 3.1.3 and 6.2 which expressly contemplate and make provision for the Plaintiff to have other business commitments imposing on him obligations of confidentiality and indeed commitments which may reasonably be expected to have precedence over the affairs of the Defendant. It is perhaps significant that the contract, when made, was intended to be short term, providing a temporary role to be reviewed on appointment of the chief executive. I find no contra-indication in the obligations assumed to furnish services. The Plaintiff has agreed to make his expert services and advice in the field of classical music available to the Defendant at the fee of £200 plus VAT per day. There is no contra-indication in the substantial commitment as to the hours to be worked. Save when he is required to attend meetings, he is free to provide them where (e.g. at home) and at times of his own choosing. (It may be noted that Clause 8 requires him to work from home during the first 5 months). He is subject to no supervision or control by the Defendant. The Defendant has placed reliance on Clause 2.6 which requires him to provide such other services "as could reasonably be expected to be performed by the head of music of a radio station as may from time to time be required of him." This clause confers on the Defendant an option to require extensive services, but they are to be provided as a freelance consultant and not as employee.

39. The obligation to provide the specified advice and services is in my view entirely apposite to a contract for services and there is no reason why effect should not be given to the parties expressed intention that their relationship should not be that of employer and employee.

(b) Agreement to the Contrary

40. The Plaintiff has submitted that, even if the Consultancy Agreement constitutes a contract of employment, copyright does not vest in the Defendant as employer because there is an agreement to the contrary. The agreement is said to be constituted by the express provision of the Consultancy Agreement that the contract shall be a contract for services, and not of employment, i.e. a contract to which Section 11(2) has no application.

41. This is a subtle and beguilingly attractive argument, but I cannot accept it. The agreement contemplated by Section 11(2), if it is to obviate the application of the section, must satisfy two requirements: (I) it must be an agreement that, notwithstanding the existence of a contract of employment, the title to copyright in works created during the course of the contract shall not vest in the employer; and (2) the agreement must be a legally effective one. Neither of those conditions are satisfied in this case. First the express term of the Consultancy Agreement purports to provide, not that the title to the copyrights shall vest in the Plaintiff notwithstanding the fact that a contract of employment is thereby created between the Plaintiff and the Defendant, but that a contract of employment shall not be created. Secondly the express term that a contract of employment shall not be created is legally ineffective if the substantive provisions of the Consultancy Agreement in law do give rise to the existence of a contract of employment: the reason is that the parties, by agreeing such substantive provisions, have in law impliedly agreed that there shall be a contract of employment, and the implied agreement to this effect is inconsistent with and overrides the express agreement to the contrary. In short there is a conflict between the expressions of what the parties have agreed, and the expression of agreement that there be a contract of employment constituted by the choice of the substantive provisions of the agreement prevails over the express of agreement as to the legal effect of those substantive provisions: the latter agreement is legally without effect and for all practical purposes is to be treated as deleted.

IMPLIED GRANT BY COMMISSION

(a) <u>Law</u>

42. As an alternative to the claim based on Section 11(2) of the 1988 Act, the Defendant claims that by commissioning the Plaintiff to provide the Five Documents and the Catalogue under the terms of the Consultancy Agreement the Defendant has become in equity entitled to require the Plaintiff to assign to the Defendant the copyright in the works created in the course of the consultancy.

43. There has been cited to me a considerable number of authorities where a copyright, brought into existence by a person ("the Contractor") pursuant to a contract for services with another ("the Client"), has been held to belong in equity to the Client. One example is Massine v de Basil [1936-45] MCC 233. What was at issue in that case was the copyright in the plaintiff's choreography for a ballet intended to form part of the repertoire of the defendant's ballet company. The Court of Appeal held that the contract between the defendant and the plaintiff was that of employer and employee, and accordingly the copyright vested in the defendant as employer. But the Court also held that, even if the contract was not one of employment but for services, it was an implied term of the contract that the plaintiff as Contractor would assign the copyright to the defendant as Client. The Court emphasised that the ballet was a composite work of which the elements were the music, the story, the choreography or notation of the dancing, the scenery and the costumes, and held that it must necessarily have

been intended that the copyright in the whole ballet and each of its component elements should be in the Client.

44. The issue in every such case is what the Client under the contract has agreed to pay for and whether he has "bought" the copyright. The alternatives in each case are that the Client has bought the copyright, some form of copyright licence or nothing at all. It is common ground in this case that by implication the Consultancy Agreement at the least confers on the Defendant a licence to use the copyright material for the purposes of its radio station. The issue is whether the Defendant impliedly bought the copyright or a more extensive licence than the limited licence conceded.

45. The general principles governing the respective rights of the Contractor and Client in the copyright in a work commissioned by the Client appear to me to be as follows:

(1) the Contractor is entitled to retain the copyright in default of some express or implied term to the contrary effect;

(2) the contract itself may expressly provide as to who shall be entitled to the copyright in work produced pursuant to the contract. Thus under a standard form Royal Institute of British Architects ("RIBA") contract between an architect and his client, there is an express provision that the copyright shall remain vested in the architect;

(3) the mere fact that the Contractor has been commissioned is insufficient to entitle the Client to the copyright. Where Parliament intended the act of commissioning alone to vest copyright in the Client e.g. in case of unregistered design rights and registered designs, the legislation expressly so provides (see Section 215 of the 1988 Act and Section 1(a) of the Registered Designs Act 1949 as amended by the 1988 Act). In all other cases the Client has to establish the entitlement under some express or implied term of the contract;

(4) the law governing the implication of terms in a contract has been firmly established (if not earlier) by the decision of the House of Lords in Liverpool City Council v. Irwin [1977] AC 239 ("Liverpool"). In the words of Lord Bingham MR in Philips Electronique v. BSB [1995] EMLR 472 ("Philips") at 481, the essence of much learning on implied terms is distilled in the speech of Lord Simon of Glaisdale on behalf of the majority of the Judicial Committee of the Privy Council in BP Refinery (Westernport) Pty Ltd v. The President, Councillors and Ratepayers of the Shire of Hastings (1978) 52 ALJR 20 at 26:

"Their Lordships do not think it necessary to review exhaustively the authorities on the implication of a term in a contract which the parties have not thought fit to express. In their view, for a term to be implied, the following conditions (which may overlap) must be satisfied: (1) it must be reasonable and equitable; (2) it must be necessary to give business efficacy to the contract, so that no term will be implied if the contract is effective without it; (3) it must be so obvious that 'it goes without saying'; (4) it must be capable of clear expression; (5) it must not contradict any express term of the contract."

2. Lord Bingham added an explanation and warning:

"The courts' usual role in contractual interpretation is, by resolving ambiguities or reconciling apparent inconsistencies, to attribute the true meaning to the language in which the parties themselves have expressed their contract. The implication of contract terms involves a different and altogether more ambitious undertaking: the interpolation of terms to deal with matters for which, ex hypothesi, the parties themselves have made no provision. It is because the implication of terms is so potentially intrusive that the law imposes strict constrains on the exercise of this extraordinary power.

. . .

The question of whether a term should be implied, and if so what, almost inevitably arises after a crisis has been reached in the performance of the contract. So the court comes to the task of implication with the benefit of hindsight, and it is tempting for the court then to fashion a term which will reflect the merits of the situation as they then appear. Tempting, but wrong."

> (5) where (as in the present case) it is necessary to imply the grant of some right to fill a lacuna in the contract and the question arises how this lacuna is to be filled, guidance is again to be found in Liverpool. The principle is clearly stated that in deciding which of various alternatives should constitute the contents of the term to be implied, the choice must be that which does not exceed what is necessary in the circumstances (see Lord Wilberforce at p.245 F-G). In short a minimalist approach is called for. An implication may only be made if this is necessary, and then only of what is necessary and no more;
>
> (6) accordingly if it is necessary to imply some grant of rights in respect of a copyright work, and the need could be satisfied by the grant of a licence or an assignment of the copyright, the implication will be of the grant of a licence only;
>
> (7) circumstances may exist when the necessity for an assignment of copyright may be established. As Mr Howe has submitted, these circumstances are, however, only likely to arise if the Client needs in addition to the right to use the copyright works the right to exclude the Contractor from using the work and the ability to enforce the copyright against third parties. Examples of when this situation may arise include: (a) where the purpose in commissioning the work is for the Client to multiply and sell copies on the market for which the work was created free from the sale of copies in competition with the Client by the Contractor or third parties; (b) where the Contractor creates a work which is derivative from a pre-existing work of the Client, e.g. when a draughtsman is engaged to turn designs of an article in sketch form by the Client into formal manufacturing drawings, and

the draughtsman could not use the drawings himself without infringing the underlying rights of the Client; (c) where the Contractor is engaged as part of a team with employees of the Client to produce a composite or joint work and he is unable, or cannot have been intended to be able, to exploit for his own benefit the joint work or indeed any distinct contribution of his own created in the course of his engagement: see Nichols Advanced Vehicle Systems Inc v. Rees [1979] RPC 127 at 139 and consider Sofia Bogrich v. Shape Machines unreported, 4th November 1994 and in particular page 15 of the transcript of the judgment of Aldous J. In each case it is necessary to consider the price paid, the impact on the Contractor of assignment of copyright and whether it can sensibly have been intended that the Contractor should retain any copyright as a separate item of property;

(8) if necessity requires only the grant of a licence, the ambit of the licence must be the minimum which is required to secure to the Client the entitlement which the parties to contract must have intended to confer upon him. The amount of the purchase price which the Client under the contract has obliged himself to pay may be relevant to the ambit of the licence. Thus in Stovin-Bradford v. Volpoint Properties Ltd [1971] 1 Ch 1007, where the Client agreed to pay only a nominal fee to his architect for the preparation of plans, he was held to have a licence to use the plans for no purpose beyond the anticipated application for planning permission. By contrast in Blair v. Osborne & Tompkins [1971] 21 QB 78, where the client was charged the full RIBA scale fee, his licence was held to extend to using the plans for the building itself. Guidance as to the approach to be adopted is provided in a passage in the judgment of Jacobs J. in Beck v. Montana Construction Pty [1964-5] NSWR 229 at 235 cited with approval by Widgery LJ in Blair v. Osborne & Tompkins supra at p.87:

"it seems to me that the principle involved is this; that the engagement for reward of a person to produce material of a nature which is capable of being the subject of copyright implies a permission, or consent, or licence in the person giving the engagement to use the material in the manner and for the purpose in which and for which it was contemplated between the parties that it would be used at the time of the engagement."

(9) the licence accordingly is to be limited to what is in the joint contemplation of the parties at the date of the contract, and does not extend to enable the Client to take advantage of a new unexpected profitable opportunity (consider Meikle v. Maufe [1941] 3 All ER 144).

46. These statements of principle accord with a number of cases where the Client has been refused an assignment of copyright and granted only a licence (see e.g. Cooper v. Stephens [1895] 1 Ch 567); and a number of other cases where the licence granted to the Client has been limited to use the copyright work for the purposes for which it was commissioned (see e.g. Stovin-Bradford

v. Volpoint Properties Ltd [1971] 1 Ch 1007). These statements may appear difficult to reconcile with the actual decisions in a number of the cases where a term has been implied into a contract for services for the assignment of copyright by the Contractor to the client. Some of the cases cited as instances where an obligation to assign has been implied may in fact have only decided that a licence should be implied: see e.g. Harold Drabble v. Hycolite Mfg. Co [1923-8] MCC 322; and in others the exact relationship of the Contractor and Client is not clear: see Merchant Adventurers Ltd v. Grew [1973] RPC 1, (a case where the Contractor supported the Client's claim against the infringer). It is however to be noted that: (1) in most, if not all, of those where a term has been implied for assignment, assumed that, if a term was to be implied conferring rights on the Client, that term should be that there should be an assignment. The alternative implication of a licence was not considered (see e.g. Ironside v. AG [1988] RPC 197); and (2) it was not until the Copyright Act 1956 that an exclusive licence could be granted conferring rights of action against third party infringers: before that date in order to confer a right of action against infringers it was necessary to assign the copyright. These authorities accordingly afford limited guidance today where the issue raised is whether the necessary implication is of an assignment or some form of licence. Indeed today it may be rare that necessity requires an assignment and the grant of an exclusive licence will not suffice.

(b) Facts

47. It is common ground that upon the true construction of the Consultancy Agreement some form of right in respect of the intellectual property rights in the Five Documents and the Catalogues must have been intended in favour of the Defendant, for without it the contract for the provision of his services by the Plaintiff would be without purpose or value: the Defendant could make no use and obtain no benefit from their product. The question raised is the content of the implication. The Plaintiff says that the implication should be of a licence limited to use of the Database and the making of copies for the purpose of the Defendant's existing business. The Defendant says that the implication should be of a grant of the copyright in the Five Documents and the Catalogue or at the least of a licence broad enough to permit the making of copies for the purposes of exploitation of the copyright abroad.

48. It seems quite clear to me upon the true construction of the Consultancy Agreement in its matrix of facts that the limits of what was contemplated at the date of the Consultancy Agreement were that the Plaintiff's work would be used for the purpose of enabling the Defendant to carry on its business as set out in Recital A, namely to broadcast in the United Kingdom. The only necessary implication to give purpose and effect to the Consultancy Agreement is accordingly the grant of a licence to the Defendant to use the copyright material for the indefinite future for this purpose and for this purpose only. No limitation should be implied, as none can reasonably have been contemplated, as to the countries in which the broadcast could be received or as to the manner of transmission (i.e. terrestrial or satellite). As Mr Howe put it, what the Defendant was "buying" under the Consultancy Agreement was the Plaintiff's distinctive help and

expertise in getting the Defendant's United Kingdom national station's play-list "up and running". The "purchase price" for this purpose was the daily rate of "200 agreed to be paid for each day that he provided his services, and not the sum of "250,000 in fact later earned and paid reflecting the days that he worked. Such a figure and such a lengthy and extensive use of his services were not in the contemplation of the parties when the Consultancy Agreement was signed. It is necessarily to be implied from the intended distinctiveness of the Plaintiff's contribution that the Plaintiff is to grant no licence to any competitor of the Defendant intending to be broadcast in the United Kingdom. This implication is perhaps reinforced by the confidentiality obligation assumed by the Plaintiff under Clause 9.1 of the Consultancy Agreement, which affords protection to the Defendant against public disclosure of the contents of the Five Documents and the Catalogue, save and insofar as they may have fallen into the public domain.

49. The Defendant can accordingly make copies of the Database if this was reasonably required for carrying on the business of a broadcaster in the United Kingdom, but cannot do so for the purpose of exploiting the Database abroad. The making of the copies in question in this case accordingly constituted an infringement of the Plaintiff's copyright.

50. Mr Watson has invited my sympathy for the Defendant saying that the parties cannot have intended so limited a licence as the return for some "250,000 in fees paid to the Plaintiff for his services and tempted me (with the benefit of hindsight) to fashion an implied term which might reflect the merits of this dispute as they may now appear to the Court. I cannot deny the existence of a temptation to do so, but (as Lord Bingham has pointed out in Philips) I must not accede.

Robertson v. Thomson Corp., [2006] 2 S.C.R. 363

Supreme Court of Canada

Heard: December 6, 2005

**Present: McLachlin C.J. and Major, Bastarache, Binnie,
LeBel, Deschamps, Fish, Abella and Charron JJ.
Rehearing: April 18, 2006
Present: McLachlin C.J. and Bastarache, Binnie, LeBel,
Deschamps, Fish, Abella, Charron and Rothstein JJ.**

Judgment: October 12, 2006.

. . .

LeBEL AND FISH JJ.: —

. . .

II. Background

6 At its core, this case concerns the competing rights of freelance authors and newspaper publishers. The Copyright Act establishes a regime of layered rights. Freelance authors who write newspaper articles retain the copyright in their work while the publisher of the newspaper acquires a copyright in the newspaper.

7 It is undisputed that freelance authors have the right to reproduce their individual works. The extent and scope of a publisher's right to reproduce those same articles as part of its right to reproduce its newspaper is less clear.

8 Advancements in computer technology have drastically altered the newspaper reality. Newspapers, once synonymous with the printed word, can now be stored and displayed electronically. The electronic databases in question archive thousands upon thousands of newspaper articles. Like a stream in constant flux, these databases are continuously growing and therefore changing. Search engines enable users to sift through these articles at lightning speed with the click of a mouse. These advancements, however, like most others, carry with them new challenges. One of these challenges is to evaluate the rights of newspaper publishers in this evolving technological landscape.

9 For well over a century, newspapers have archived back issues. Initially, as the motions judge observed, this was achieved by keeping them in a library — sometimes referred to in newspaper parlance as a "morgue". With the advent of microfilm and microfiche, past editions were archived using photographic imaging technology. Currently, newspapers are archived in electronic form. The subject electronic databases, however, do more than simply archive back issues.

10 The transfer of articles from their newspaper format and environment to Info Globe Online [page371] and CPI.Q, unlike the conversion to microfilm or microfiche, is no mere conversion of the newspaper from the print realm to the electronic world. As we will explain, the result is a different product that infringes the copyrights of freelance authors whose works appear in those databases. We begin with a review of the factual and judicial history.

III. Factual History

11 Heather Robertson is a freelance author. In 1995, she wrote two articles that were published in the Globe. One, a book excerpt, was the subject of a written agreement between the Globe and the publisher of Robertson's book; the other, a book review, was written under oral agreement with Robertson. Copyright was not addressed in either case. Subsequently, in 1996, it became the practice of the Globe to enter into written agreements with freelance authors expressly granting it certain electronic rights in freelance work. The agreement was later modified to expand the electronic rights clause. These agreements are not at issue in this case.

12 The Globe is one of Canada's leading national newspapers and has been produced in both print and electronic editions since the late 1970s. The named respondents on the appeal are: The Thomson Corporation, Thomson Canada Limited, Thomson Affiliates, Information Access Company and Bell Globemedia Publishing Inc., the current publisher of the Globe (collectively, the "Publishers").

13 Ms. Robertson objects to the presence of her articles in three databases: Info Globe Online, CPI.Q and the CD-ROMs (collectively, the "electronic databases"). The use of freelance articles in the daily internet edition of the Globe is not in issue before us.

14 Info Globe Online is a commercial database that has existed since April 1979, with stories going back to November 1977. It provides subscribers [page372] with access to stories from the Globe for a fee. It also allows subscribers to find articles in many other newspapers, news wire services, magazines and reference databases. Subscribers can search by key word and retrieve articles electronically. The subscriber may display, read, download, store, or print the articles.

15 CPI.Q is the electronic version of the Canadian Periodical Index. The Canadian Periodical Index indexes selected newspaper articles from various newspapers. It is available at libraries and is routinely used in research. In 1987, it became available electronically. CPI.Q is an enhanced form of the original index. It allows subscribers to search the electronic archives of indexed periodicals by key word and to retrieve articles electronically. Once an article is displayed, it is possible to print it as well.

16 The CD-ROMs, each containing the Globe and several other Canadian newspapers from a calendar year, have been available since 1991. Users can navigate using search engines and retrieve and print articles. Notably, the content of the CD-ROM is fixed and finite and users are able to view a paper as a single day's edition.

17 The electronic databases all omit the advertisements, some tables, photographs, artwork, photo captions, birth and death notices, financial tables, weather forecasts and some design elements from the original print edition.

18 Robertson's action against the Publishers for copyright infringement was certified as a class action, with the class consisting of all contributors to the Globe other than those who died on or before December 31, 1943: Robertson v. Thomson Corp. (1999), 43 O.R. (3d) 161 (Gen. Div.), at p. 168. Robertson brought a motion for partial summary [page373] judgment and an injunction restraining the use of her works in the databases. She sought judgment for two individual class members: herself and Cameron Smith, a former employee of the Globe.

. . .

B. The Remaining Issues

[para 54] provides: Section 13(4) of the Copyright Act

13....

(4) The owner of the copyright in any work may assign the right, either wholly or partially, and either generally or subject to limitations relating to territory, medium or sector of the market or other limitations relating to the scope of the assignment, and either for the whole term of the copyright or for any other part thereof, and may grant any interest in the right by licence, <u>but no assignment or grant is valid unless it is in writing signed by the owner of the right in respect of which the assignment or grant is made, or by the owner's duly authorized agent.</u>

[para 55]   Section 13(7) of the Copyright Act states:

13. ...

(7) For greater certainty, it is deemed always to have been the law that <u>a grant of an exclusive licence in a copyright constitutes the grant of an interest in the copyright by licence.</u>

56 We are satisfied that Weiler J.A. was correct in concluding that only an exclusive licence must be in writing. If Parliament intended for any type of non-exclusive licence to be deemed a "grant of an interest" requiring a written contract, it could have explicitly provided so just as it did for exclusive licences in s. 13(7). In our view, the following passage from the Ontario Superior Court of Justice decision in Ritchie v. Sawmill Creek Golf & Country Club Ltd. (2004), 35 C.P.R. (4th) 163, correctly states the matter:

> The "grant of an interest" referred to in s. 13(4) is the transfer of a property right as opposed to a permission to do a certain thing. The former gives the licensee the capacity to sue in his own name for infringement, the latter provides only a defence to claims of infringement. To the extent there was any uncertainty as to the meaning of "grant of an interest" and whether this section applied to non-exclusive licences, the issue was resolved in 1997 when the Copyright Act was amended to include s. 13(7) ... . [para. 20]

57 There was conflicting evidence before the motions judge regarding the scope of such an alleged implied licence. The content of these licences is a live issue that should go to trial, as ordered by the motions judge.

58 If it is determined that freelance authors have in fact impliedly licensed the Globe the right to republish their articles in the electronic databases, this decision will, of course, be of less practical significance. Parties are, have been, and will continue to be, free to alter by contract the rights established by the Copyright Act.

59 With respect to the second issue on the appeal, we find that employees of the Globe, including Cameron Smith, should not have been certified as members of the class because they have no cause of action.

. . .

62 When a staff member writes an article for a newspaper, magazine or similar periodical during the course of his or her employment, s. 13(3) of the Copyright Act provides that copyright vests with the employer while the employee is given a right to restrain publication of the work (other than in a newspaper, magazine or similar periodical). Thus, even when freelance authors have a cause of action for copyright infringement, staff writers have no cause of action unless they previously exercised their right to restrain publication. In this case, Cameron Smith never attempted to restrain publication of his articles. And, no evidence was introduced indicating that other staff members exercised such a right.

63 It is therefore unnecessary for the purposes of this case to determine whether the electronic databases constitute "newspapers, magazines or similar periodicals" within the meaning of s. 13(3) of the Copyright Act. We have already found that Info Globe Online and CPI.Q do not constitute reproductions of a substantial part of the underlying print newspapers because they are works of a different nature. Without so deciding, it follows, we believe, for essentially the same reasons, that these same databases cannot be characterized as newspapers, magazines or similar periodicals for purposes of s. 13(3).

. . .

Acohs Pty Ltd. v. Ucorp Pty Ltd.

[2012] FCAFC 16 (F.C.A.)

JACOBSON, NICHOLAS AND YATES JJ

IMPLIED LICENCE

Introduction

88. After having found that copyright subsisted in the Acohs-authored MSDSs, and after having dealt with a separate issue about whether the appellant had assigned the relevant copyright, in certain cases, to particular MISs (an issue to which we will also return), the primary judge turned to the question of whether the identified Acohs-authored MSDSs had been reproduced by the respondents without the licence of the appellant: see s 36 of the Copyright Act. As we have noted, the appellant's case, in that regard, was that the first respondent had reproduced the MSDSs and that the second respondent had authorised those reproductions.

89. Although formally denying the allegation that they had "copied ... the copyright works", the respondents do not appear to have strenuously contested the fact that the first respondent had reproduced, in the copyright sense, the MSDSs relevant to this appeal. Indeed, the primary judge recorded (at [87]) that "the respondents did not dispute the proposition that, if the HTML source code was,

and if the MSDSs themselves were, original literary works, they had reproduced them in material form". The primary judge made no separate, express finding about authorisation.

90. The main area of contest was whether the first respondent's acts in reproducing the MSDSs were done without the appellant's licence. As finally argued, this defence had two components.

91. First, the onus of proving that the first respondent's impugned acts were done without the appellant's licence, rested on the appellant. The respondents contended that the appellant had not discharged that onus. The primary judge (at [131]) accepted that contention. We shall return to consider whether his Honour erred in that regard.

92. Secondly, the respondents contended that the impugned acts were done pursuant to an implied licence granted to the appellant's customers, that is to say, the MISs who issued the MSDSs created by the appellant. It is necessary to say something more about this component of the respondents' defence.

93. In their last filed defence, which was before the amendment to paragraph 8(b) introduced by the seventh further amended statement of claim (see above at [60]-[61]), the respondents, in response to the allegation that they had infringed the alleged copyright in the layout, presentation and appearance of each Infosafe MSDS, pleaded that:

> (a) the appellant "has impliedly granted to [the appellant's MISs] an unconditional, irrevocable licence to use any copyright of [the appellant] in the templates that is [sic] reproduced in the MSDS created by or at the direction of the [the appellant's MISs]"; and

> (b) "the alleged copyright works were reproduced pursuant to a licence given by [the appellant] to [the appellant's MISs] to reproduce and licence [sic] the further reproduction of the alleged copyright works for the purpose of ensuring the ready availability and accessibility of the MSDS[s], which licence is to be implied by law and/or so as to give business efficacy to the agreements between [the appellant] and [the appellant's MISs] with respect to the creation and transcription of MSDS[s] ...".

94. As to the allegation in (b) above, the respondents specifically relied on the following facts, matters and circumstances arising under the State and Territory legislative regimes:

> (a) The MIS of each identified Infosafe MSDS is responsible for ensuring that each MSDS contains accurate and current information and that the MSDS is provided or made available to any person to whom the substance the subject of the MSDS is supplied (other than for retail sale) and to any employer on request for the provision by the employer to its employees.

> (b) Each such MIS who is also an employer to which a hazardous substance (the subject of each identified Infosafe MSDS) has been supplied is responsible for ensuring that it has obtained a current MSDS and made it readily accessible to any employee who has the potential to be exposed to the substance.

(c) The layout, presentation and appearance of the MSDS is substantially pre-scribed by the requirements of the 1994 code and the 2003 code.

(d) The layout, presentation and appearance of each MSDS is also substantially determined by the MIS depending upon the substance that is the subject of the MSDS.

(e) Each relevant MIS pays the appellant a fee for the appellant to perform the services and/or provide the software applications in relation to the creation of the MSDS in accordance with the MIS's directions, so as to enable the MIS to meet its obligations referred to above.

95. The point of present relevance is that the implied licence relied upon by the respondents was said to be one granted by the appellant to the particular MIS at whose direction an MSDS was created by the appellant.

96. In its reply, the appellant:

(a) admitted that "an implied licence exists from [the appellant] to its customers for such customers to use MSDSs for the purpose of compliance with the vari-ous regulations but such implied licence goes no further and in particular does not extend to permission for customers to provide such MSDSs to a commercial competitor of [the appellant] at no cost and for such competitor's own commercial benefit"; and

(b) admitted that "there is an implied licence to [the appellant's] customers to view and store such MSDS[s] and make them available to their own customers in order to comply with their obligations under the regulatory regime but nothing more".

97. In context, the reference in the reply to the appellant's "customers" must be taken to be a reference to the MIS at whose direction a particular MSDS was created by the appellant.

98. The primary judge treated these parts of the pleadings as extending to the amendment to paragraph 8(b) of the seventh further amended statement of claim. This appears to reflect the manner in which the parties conducted this part of the case. No issue arises on this appeal about his Honour adopting that course. The only question that arises is the scope of the implied licence on which the respondents relied and, in particular, whether the respondents' impugned acts fell within that scope.

99. As to those acts, the respondents pleaded that, so as to enable its customers to comply with their obligations under the various legislative regimes, the first respondent obtained MSDSs (created by persons other than itself) from employ-ers (who obtained MSDSs from MISs and provided them to the first respon-dent), from MISs (upon the request of an employer), and from the websites of MISs in both hard copy and a variety of electronic formats, and compiled and made available to its own customers, in a conveniently searchable form, such MSDSs in the format in which they had originally been provided. Their defence makes clear (subject to certain qualifications that are not relevant for present purposes) that such MSDSs included those that had been created using the Info-safe system.

100. The respondents' defence does not make clear who their "customers" are and, in particular, whether they are MISs, employers or occupiers and the like who are required, under the legislative regimes, to obtain MSDSs and make them readily accessible to employees who could be exposed to the products in question.

101. The primary judge found (at [128]) that the first respondent continuously searched the Internet for MSDSs generally, and that its activities in that regard were not confined to the satisfaction of requests by, or to the needs of, its existing customers.

102. In that connection the primary judge (at [20]) made the following finding:

> ... When [the first respondent] is required to give access to an MSDS of which it has not been the author for the relevant MIS, it will locate the MSDS on the Internet (and/or by direct communication with the MIS), download the MSDS as an entity and then store it as part of the Collection, from where any of its non-MIS customers who might require access to the MSDS could, under appropriate commercial relationships with [the first respondent], achieve that access. Necessarily, such an MSDS will be identical in content and appearance to the "original" MSDS from which it was derived.

103. The primary judge also appears to have accepted (at [93]) that most of the MSDSs in the Collection had been added without any particular request from a customer and that the first respondent obtained such MSDSs by "trawling" the Internet to find them. This evidence was in fact given by the second respondent in the course of cross-examination.

104. It is clear from these findings that the first respondent's "customers" include non-MIS customers with whom the first respondent enters into arrangements to provide MSDSs from the Collection.

105. It is also important to note that, in support of their case that there was an implied licence, the respondents relied upon the judgment of Merkel J in *Acohs Pty Ltd v R A Bashford Consulting Pty Ltd* (1997) 37 IPR 542. As it happens, the second respondent was a respondent in that proceeding who had cross-claimed against the present appellant alleging copyright infringement of 43 MSDSs that had been transcribed by the appellant and added to the CDB as Infosafe MSDSs. In that case Merkel J upheld the present appellant's defence to that cross-claim. His Honour found that, by transcribing the MSDSs and storing the relevant data in the CDB and by thereafter making them available for a fee, the present appellant was acting pursuant to an implied licence.

106. In the present case, the primary judge recorded (at [128]) that the appellant did not ask him to depart from *Bashford*, either in point of principle or at the level where Merkel J held that the "industrial use" and the "library use" of MSDSs were implicitly licensed by the copyright owner. We describe these particular uses later in these reasons.

107. Be that as it may, it is nevertheless important for us to discuss the reasoning and ultimate finding on the question of implied licence in *Bashford* for

two reasons. The first reason is that the appellant argued that the respondents' impugned acts fell outside the scope of the implied licence found in that case. The second matter, which we will discuss further below, is that the primary judge (at [141]) accepted that the content of the implied licence which he found in the present case was broader than that recognised by Merkel J in *Bashford.*

108. The apparent acceptance by the parties of the correctness of *Bashford* has important ramifications for this appeal. As the parties conducted both the trial before the primary judge and the present appeal on that basis, the occasion does not arise for us to proceed otherwise than in accordance with, and to the extent of, that acceptance. In so proceeding, we do not wish to be taken as endorsing the correctness of all aspects of that decision.

The reasoning and ultimate finding in Bashford

109. In *Bashford* Merkel J took as his starting point the statement of principles discussed by Jacobs J in *Beck v Montana Constructions Pty Ltd* (1963) WN (NSW) 1578 with respect to implied licences.

110. Beck was a case involving the copyright in architects' plans. In that case architects were engaged to prepare sketch plans for a building to be erected on certain land. The clients who had commissioned the architects later sold the land, with the plans. The purchaser of the land then engaged another architect to prepare further plans. Those plans were found to be a substantial reproduction of the sketch plans. The original architects sued the purchaser and its architect for infringement of the copyright in the sketch plans.

111. In dealing with the question of whether there was an implied licence, Jacobs J identified two steps. The first step was to determine whether the original client obtained the right to use the copyright work in the manner in which it was ultimately used. The second step was to determine whether the purchaser of the land (in circumstances where it had been held out to the purchaser that plans were available and approved) had obtained that same right.

112. As to the first step, Jacobs J (at 1581) said:

> The question raised is quite a broad one because it applies not only to architects but would apply for instance to artists who are engaged to prepare a particular work which would of its nature be reproduced, for instance a cartoon for a tapestry or a mosaic, or which would apply to persons who prepared written material with the intention that it should be used in a particular manner. It seems to me that the principle involved is — that the engagement for reward of a person to produce material of a nature which is capable of being the subject of copyright implies a permission or consent or licence in the person making the engagement to use the material in the manner and for the purpose in which and for which it was contemplated between the parties that it would be used at the time of the engagement. It seems to me that this must be regarded as a principle of general application.

113. Later (at 1582) his Honour said:

> I think it is a principle which can be found to be applied in a number of cases. It relates to permission or consent to what must have been taken to have been within

the contemplation of the parties at the time of the engagement. After all, it must be borne in mind that it is the engagement which brings the copyright material into existence.

When that principle is applied in the present case it seems to me to be inevitable that one should conclude that the payment for sketch plans includes a permission or consent to use those sketch plans for the purpose for which they were brought into existence, namely, for the purpose of building a building in substantial accordance with them and for the purpose of preparing any necessary drawings as part of the task of building the building.

114. As to the second step, his Honour (at 1581) said:

Assuming the right of the owner of land to make use of sketch plans for the purpose of erecting a building substantially in accordance with that sketch I think that when he sells the land and holds out to the purchaser that plans are available and approved from all authorities and shows those plans to the purchaser then on the sale of the land there should be implied an agreement collateral to the sale of the land whereby the vendor grants to the purchaser such right as he has to the use of the plans. This assumes that the right, that is to say, the licence, permission or consent, however it is described, is assignable and that depends on the implied terms of grant of the original licence, permission or consent. It therefore seems to me that subject to the first matter then the second question may be answered in the affirmative.

115. In *Bashford*, Merkel J (at 559) took *Beck* as establishing a principle that, if copyright material is produced for a particular purpose, there is an implied permission, consent or licence to use that material to carry out that purpose. This general statement of the principle had been articulated earlier by Young J in *R & A Bailey & Co Ltd v Boccaccio Pty Ltd* (1986) 4 NSWLR 701 at 711 and adopted by Beaumont J in *De Garis v Neville Jeffress Pidler Pty Limited* (1992) 37 FCR 99 at 110. However, his Honour recognised (at 559-560) the importance of identifying, with precision, the particular purpose for which the copyright work was brought into existence and whether use for that purpose was restricted to the person to whom the licence was granted. In that connection his Honour also identified the importance of an associated question, namely whether the licence could be "transferred". It is clear that his Honour (at 562) saw the answer to that associated question as being closely related to the scope of the purpose for which the copyright work was created.

116. His Honour (at 560-561) reasoned that the licence considered in *Beck* was implied by law to a particular class of contract as opposed to one implied to give business efficacy to a particular contract: see, in that regard, *Castlemaine Tooheys Ltd v Carlton & United Breweries Ltd* (1987) 10 NSWLR 468 at 486-487; cf *Devefi Pty Ltd v Mateffy Pearl Nagy Pty Ltd* (1993) 113 ALR 225 at 239-241. His Honour nevertheless concluded (at 565) that, if he was in error in that regard, such a licence would be implied, in any event, in each particular contract for the commissioning of each MSDS, as a term necessary to give business efficacy to the contract.

117. His Honour (at 562) saw the contract of engagement before him as an "open contract" (that is, one not dealing with the ambit of the licence or with the terms on which an assignment of that licence might be effected). His Honour saw the contract of engagement as being one "to prepare written material, being MSDSs, with the intention that they be used for a particular purpose, being the provision of ready access to the information contained in the MSDSs for safety related purposes". His Honour concluded that the licence was one that permitted or consented to the use of the MSDSs to carry out those purposes. This purpose was determined objectively by reference to the contract entered into by the parties and the regulatory and factual matrix in which the transaction took place. His Honour said (at 562):

> There is little difficulty in ascertaining the relevant matrix in the present case. The MSDSs were commissioned by manufacturers and importers to be in the Worksafe Australia standards format for use, inter alia, as set out in the standards. Bialkower accepted that he was commissioned to prepare MSDSs which would be distributed by manufacturers and importers on the sale of their products in accordance with the standards. They were commissioned in relation to substances, including hazardous substances, for the purpose of ensuring the ready availability and accessibility of the MSDSs for safety related purposes for or at any workplace in Australia at which the substances are or will be stored, used or transported.

118. His Honour also said (at 564):

> In the regulatory and factual matrix to which I have referred, there is little difficulty in identifying the manner in which the parties contemplated that the Chemwatch MSDSs commissioned by manufacturers and importers were to be provided. The availability and accessibility of the MSDSs for or at workplaces was to be in a photocopy or microfiche format or from a computer database. The reproduction or copying of the MSDSs in any of these formats may be commissioned by a manufacturer, importer, supplier, retailer, a public emergency service or by or for any employer from contractors engaged for the purpose if for any reason that is not achieved "in house".

119. His Honour (at 564) concluded:

> I am satisfied that, in accordance with *Beck*, an accurate copying, reproduction or adaptation of any of the 43 Chemwatch MSDSs in the manner and for the safety related purposes to which I have referred falls within the implied licence of Bialkower.

120. The implied licence thus found by Merkel J was one that extended, in the first instance, to manufacturers, importers, suppliers, retailers, employers and to any other person requiring an MSDS for the safety related purposes for which it was prepared. However, his Honour said (at 564-565) that, if he was in error in that regard, he would reach the same conclusion as that reached in *Beck* in respect of the right to "transfer" the licence, namely that it must inevitably be implied in the contract of engagement that the MIS who commissioned the MSDSs had the right to "transfer" that right to retailers, employers and other persons requiring MSDSs for the same safety related purposes.

121. It is clear that the implied licence pleaded by the respondents in the present case was one in favour of the appellant's customers (namely, each MIS who commissioned the creation or transcription of its relevant MSDSs), and not other persons. However, in accordance with Merkel J's alternative formulation, the respondents also pleaded that each such MIS had the right, in turn, "to reproduce and licence [sic] the further reproduction of the alleged copyright works for the purpose of ensuring the ready availability and accessibility of the MSDS".

122. The implied licence admitted on the pleadings by the appellant did not go that far. However, on appeal the appellant accepted that an MIS's contractual rights would be "sufficiently protected" by the implication of a licence that permitted the MIS and any employer or occupier who used the relevant product to reproduce and to authorise others to reproduce the necessary MSDS on their behalf. Nevertheless, in expressing that acceptance, the appellant submitted that any implied licence in the contract for the creation of the copyright works should not be wider than necessary to avoid undermining the rights conferred under the contract: *Byrne v Australian Airlines Limited* [1995] HCA 24; (1995) 185 CLR 410 at 450; *Concrete Pty Limited v Parramatta Design & Developments Pty Ltd* [2006] HCA 55; (2006) 229 CLR 577 at [59].

123. When Merkel J came to examine the impugned use of the MSDSs in the case before him against the background of his findings about the nature and scope of the implied licence, he identified two uses which he referred to as the "industrial use" and the "library use".

124. The "industrial use" referred to the acts of transcribing MSDSs to form part of the Infosafe system. These acts were described as having been specifically commissioned by an MIS or employer using the hazardous or other products the subject of the MSDSs and having access to the system. This use was found by Merkel J (at 565) to fall within the implied licence he had found.

125. The "library use" referred to the acts of maintaining MSDSs (including the transcribed MSDSs) on the CDB and making them available as a "library", for a fee, to public emergency or safety organisations, as well as to the Commonwealth Surgeon-General for use by sections of the Defence Forces using chemicals.

126. His Honour considered it to be "less clear" that the "library use" was within the implied licence he had found. Nevertheless his Honour (at 565) concluded that this use fell within the safety related purposes for which the relevant MSDSs were brought into existence, saying:

> The sole function of the library use is to ensure that public emergency services or organisations can provide instant access to MSDSs for safety related purposes to those in need of that information. The only reason for any of these entities to obtain or provide access to an MSDS is that such access is necessary for that entity to provide safety information to those in need of it, as a result of using the chemical the subject of the MSDS.

127. His Honour therefore found the "library use" to fall within the implied licence.

128. It should be noted at this juncture that the appellant distinguished the "industrial use" and the "library use" found by Merkel J from the impugned use in the present case. In the present case the primary judge recorded the appellant's contention (at [128]) as follows:

> [The appellant] says that the evidence discloses, at least for the main part, that [the first respondent] reproduces MSDSs, and places them into the Collection, not on the specific request of users of the substances involved (employers, occupiers etc), but at its own initiative and as part of its own commercial operation, entirely with a view to stocking the Collection with every MSDS available in the electronic universe, so as to be in a position to market its services by reference to the claim that the Collection has no equal in the range of MSDSs which it contains.

129. It is now convenient to turn to the primary judge's reasons and conclusions on the question of implied licence in the present case.

The primary judge's findings

130. The primary judge (at [136]) reasoned that, in considering the scope of the implied licence, the focus must be upon the use to which the MSDSs copied into the Collection might ultimately be put.

131. The primary judge found that the storage of the MSDSs in the Collection by the first respondent was in contemplation that access to them would, later if not sooner, be required by its customers, present or future. The primary judge reasoned that, seen in this way, the first respondent's purpose in reproducing and storing Infosafe MSDSs was to facilitate the "industrial use" of those MSDSs. Implicitly the primary judge treated these facilitative steps as tantamount to the "industrial use" found in *Bashford*.

132. The primary judge (at [137]) also considered that the first respondent's copying and storing of MSDSs fell within the "library use" found in *Bashford*. In so reasoning, the primary judge recognised that, in *Bashford*, the MSDSs were only placed in the CDB after they had been altered or transcribed for a particular customer. However, the primary judge considered this to be a distinction without a difference. The primary judge observed that if the relevant purpose relates to a later use of a particular MSDS, it was beside the point that the initial creation of the document had a different purpose. His Honour (at [137]) said:

> The question was (and still is): what was the purpose for which the "library" was stocked with MSDSs? If it was to make them available to those who would or might require access to them in connection with their responsibilities under the regulations, that purpose should, in my view, give rise to a *Bashford*-type implied licence.

133. In short, the primary judge reasoned that the steps taken by the first respondent to reproduce and store in the CDB an MSDS created by a third party in contemplation that one of the first respondent's existing or potential customers might later require such a copy of that MSDS from the first respondent, were

covered by an implied licence granted by the copyright owner, of which the first respondent had the present benefit.

134. In support of this approach, the primary judge (at [139]) referred to the fact that, in some Australian jurisdictions, an MIS is required to provide an MSDS to any person who "reasonably requires a copy"; or to "any member of the public who requests a copy"; or "on request". The primary judge reasoned that provisions of this kind made it more difficult to confine the implied licence in the way the appellant had contended: if any person could obtain a copy of an MSDS, there was no reason why that person could not be the first respondent.

135. The primary judge (at [141]) concluded:

> Either because the ultimate purpose of such copying would inevitably be the "industrial use", or because [the first respondent's] activities fell squarely within the "library use", I consider that the implied licence extends to it.

The parties' submissions

136. On appeal the appellant accepted that an implied licence existed. In that connection it submitted that there was nothing to stop the first respondent "from making or obtaining a copy of an Infosafe MSDS on behalf of an employer or occupier customer who actually requires a copy" and who "does enjoy the benefit of an implied licence from [the appellant]".

137. However, although accepting that an implied licence existed, the appellant submitted that the primary judge erred in three respects concerning the scope of that licence.

138. First, it submitted that the primary judge failed to have proper regard to the requirement of "necessity".

139. Secondly, it submitted that the primary judge erred in considering that the "purpose" in respect of the use of the MSDSs was one imposed by law rather than seen as a question of fact.

140. Thirdly, it submitted that the primary judge erred in extending the benefit of the implied licence to the first respondent when it was not a party to or otherwise privy to rights under the contracts of engagement between the appellant and its customers who were MISs.

141. The respondents answered these submissions in the following way.

142. First, they submitted that the primary judge followed and applied the principles in *Beck* and that, to the extent that "necessity" is the foundation for the implication, that requirement is involved in the test in *Beck*. In any event, they submitted that "necessity" is not the sole basis upon which terms will be implied by law in a class of contracts.

143. Secondly, they disputed that the primary judge considered the question of "purpose" without regard to questions of fact. In that connection they pointed to the primary judge's acceptance (at [135]) of Merkel J's observation in *Bashford*

that the content of the licence was informed by "the regulatory and factual matrix in which the transaction took place": *Bashford* at 562.

144. Thirdly, as to the question of whether the primary judge erred in extending the licence to the first respondent, the respondents submitted that the implied licence must extend to service providers "given their legitimate role in assisting MIS[s], employers and occupiers to meet their obligations under the regulations". In this connection the respondents pointed to the concerns of large organisations dealing with large numbers of substances, large numbers of employees or large numbers of work sites.

Consideration

145. In our view there can be no doubt that, in the context of Australian copyright law, a licence will only be implied when there is a necessity to do so. This principle was made clear in the unanimous judgment in *Copyright Agency Limited v State of New South Wales* [2008] HCA 35; (2008) 233 CLR 279 at [92] (*CAL*), which also cited in that regard *Concrete* at [13]-[14] (per Gummow A-CJ) and [96] (per Kirby and Crennan JJ); *Byrne* at 450 (per McHugh and Gummow JJ); and *Breen v Williams* (1996) 186 CLR 71 at 91 (per Dawson and Toohey JJ), at 102-103 (per Gaudron and McHugh JJ) and at 124 (per Gummow J).

146. In the present case the parties treated the licence as arising as a matter of law in a particular class of contract between an MIS and a service provider, such as the appellant or the first respondent: cf *Concrete* at [18]. "Necessity", in that context, means necessary for the reasonable or effective operation of all contracts of that particular class lest the enjoyment of rights be "rendered nugatory, worthless, or, perhaps, be seriously undermined": *Byrne* at 450; see also *Concrete* at [59].

147. The implication of such terms is to be distinguished from terms implied in the circumstances of the particular case to give business efficacy to the contract. In that latter category of case the terms implied are unique to the particular contract in question, depending upon the form of the contract, the express terms and the surrounding circumstances: *Byrne* at 448. In those cases, the implication is taken to reflect the actual intention of the parties. In cases of contracts of a particular class, wider considerations are at play and the term is implied as a legal incident of such contracts: *Byrne* at 448; *Esso Australia Resources Limited v Plowman* (1995) 183 CLR 10 at 30; *Castlemaine Tooheys* at 487-489.

148. The decision in *Beck* must be read subject to the requirement that a licence will only be implied when there is a necessity to do so, although, having made that observation, we would add that Jacobs J's treatment in *Beck* of the implication of licences is consistent with that approach.

149. The respondents' submissions tended to treat the requirement of necessity in a somewhat attenuated way, especially in submitting that "necessity" is not the sole basis upon which a licence would or could be implied in the present case. In our view that submission cannot be accepted in light of the unequivocal statement of the High Court in *CAL*.

150. We should add that, although the respondents' defence pleaded, as an alternative, the existence of an implied licence to give business efficacy to the agreements between the appellant and its MIS customers, the parties did not contend on appeal that, under that theory, a different result would ensue in the present case. Indeed, the parties' submissions did not seek to differentiate between the two possible bases for implying a licence raised in this case.

151. It is in this context that the appellant's second submission concerning "purpose" falls to be determined. The primary judge plainly proceeded on the basis that the case before him was one concerning a licence implied as a legal incident of a particular class of contract, not to give business efficacy to a particular contract or to particular contracts. It is not suggested that his Honour was in error in so approaching the matter. However, the appellant's submission on "purpose", focusing as it does on particular facts, appears to be directed to a licence implied to give business efficacy. If so, that submission is misdirected insofar as it was also sought to be related to the question of whether a licence should be implied to contracts of a class. In any event, the "facts" to which the appellant points in that regard are really no more than the facts of "contemplated use" common to all contracts of engagement between an MIS and a service provider for the creation of MSDSs. It is plain that the primary judge took into account the relevant factual matrix concerning the creation of MSDSs and their use in the relevant circumstances. In the end, we do not see the appellant's second submission as establishing any error in the approach taken by the primary judge in this regard. It seems to us that the real focus of attention for the purposes of this aspect of the appeal lies in the first and third submissions made by the appellant.

152. As the primary judge acknowledged (at [141]), the content or scope of the implied licence he found was broader than that recognised by Merkel J in *Bashford*. Both the "industrial use" and the "library use" described by Merkel J were, in the case of transcribed MSDSs, limited to where a person having the benefit of an implied licence to reproduce, or to authorise others to reproduce, an MSDS, requested a service provider, such as the first respondent, to carry out that work on its behalf. The appellant makes no complaint about such conduct. But here the primary judge found that the first respondent also copies (reproduces) MSDSs in anticipation that users will at some point engage it to provide access to a suite of MSDSs in the Collection. The primary judge justified these antecedent acts by looking to the ultimate purpose for which such reproduced MSDSs would be put. In so doing his Honour erred by attributing to the first respondent, in reproducing these MSDSs, consents or permissions it did not then have and might never have. In these cases, therefore, the first respondent, without the licence of the copyright owner (relevantly, the appellant), did an act comprised in the copyright, and thereby infringed that copyright.

153. We can see no reason of necessity why a licence in favour of a service provider to engage in these antecedent or anticipatory acts should be implied in contracts of engagement to create an MSDS, to which the service provider is not a party. While arguments of convenience or expediency might be advanced for the availability of such a facility, these alone would not justify the implication,

by law, of a licence to that effect. No different answer is required in the present case if the matter is approached by considering whether such a licence should be implied in each contract of engagement to give business efficacy to that contract.

154. In our view, therefore, the implied licence did not extend to the first respondent's reproduction of the Acohs-authored Infosafe MSDSs or its communication or supply of those works in the absence of a request for those works for safety related purposes.

ABSENCE OF LICENCE

The primary judge's findings

155. It is necessary for us to return to the first component of the respondents' defence, which was that the appellant had not discharged the onus of showing that the impugned acts were done without its licence. This issue arose in the context where, at least at the time of final submissions, the parties agreed that an implied licence existed, but the scope of that licence was disputed. The primary judge dealt with the issue on the basis that the availability to the first respondent of an implied licence to reproduce the Infosafe MSDSs turned upon whether a request to copy (reproduce) a particular MSDS had been received by the first respondent from a customer who had present regulatory obligations to provide or to have access to the MSDS in question (that is, in circumstances which all parties accepted were covered by an implied licence).

156. In this connection the primary judge found (at [128]) that there was a question as to the identification of the appellant's MSDSs that had been reproduced by the first respondent "without the present needs of any customer in mind". That is to say, there was a question as to the identification of those Infosafe MSDSs that had been reproduced by the first respondent pursuant to a request (and hence covered by the agreed implied licence) and those MSDSs that had been reproduced by the first respondent in anticipation of receiving such a request.

157. The primary judge appears to have accepted the general tenor of the evidence given by the second respondent that the first respondent receives "four or five thousand" requests each week to add MSDSs to the Collection. The second respondent also gave evidence that the first respondent was "routinely provided with copies of Infosafe MSDS[s] by [the first respondent's] customers so that those customers can access the MSDS[s] using the Chemwatch [that is, the first respondent's] system". A limited number of examples of correspondence containing such requests were in evidence.

158. The primary judge found (at [131]) that many of the Infosafe MSDSs copied by the first respondent were copied upon the requests of customers. His Honour also found that many were copied in the absence of such requests. His Honour found that the evidence was not such as to fairly raise an inference that "any particular MSDS was copied in the latter, rather than the former, situation".

159. In this connection the primary judge stressed that, although it lay principally within the first respondent's power to deal with the matter by evidence,

it was not its burden to establish the existence of an implied licence in any instance, but for the appellant to prove the contrary.

160. It followed from the primary judge's findings as to what his Honour saw as shortcomings in the appellant's evidentiary case, that it had not discharged its onus of establishing that the Infosafe MSDSs in suit (of which there were approximately 72,000) had been reproduced by the first respondent without its licence.

The parties' submissions

161. The appellant contended that the primary judge's conclusion that it had failed to discharge its onus of proof was attended by two errors: first, that the primary judge failed to have any or any sufficient regard to the principle that evidence is to be weighed according to the proof which is in the power of one party to produce and in the power of the other to contradict; secondly, the primary judge's finding that many of the Infosafe MSDSs had been copied at the request of customers was not supported by the evidence.

162. Neither of these matters was identified as a ground of appeal in the amended notice of appeal on which the appellant ultimately proceeded. The respondents raised no objection to this omission and we heard argument on both matters. In the circumstances we propose to deal with both contentions as if they had been formally raised as grounds of appeal.

163. Reduced to its essence, the appellant's submission was that, having established a case that many MSDSs had been reproduced by the first respondent without a customer request, an evidentiary burden was cast upon the first respondent to show which of the MSDSs it had reproduced pursuant to such a request. It submitted that this information was peculiarly within the knowledge or means of the respondents, rather than the appellant. It submitted that the generalised evidence given by the second respondent on this question was not sufficient to discharge that burden.

164. The respondents, on the other hand, submitted that the primary judge expressly took into account the fact that it lay principally within their power to deal with the question of the extent of customer requests by evidence. They submitted, however, that the primary judge can be taken to have held that any evidentiary burden borne by them had been discharged. They submitted that, in any event, this was not a case in which the respondents could or ought reasonably to have called evidence to establish the existence of a request in respect of each MSDS the subject of the appellant's claim, given the number of such MSDSs in issue.

165. With respect to the second alleged error, they submitted that it was open to the primary judge to find that "many" of the MSDSs reproduced by the first respondent were copied at the request of customers. In that connection they pointed to the fact that this finding was based on the primary judge's favourable credit findings in respect of the second respondent.

Consideration

166. In our view the appellant has not established error on the part of the primary judge in concluding that many of the Infosafe MSDSs copied by the first respondent were copied upon the requests of customers. In arriving at that conclusion, the primary judge gave particular emphasis to the second respondent's evidence. Although acknowledging that the second respondent was "only generally familiar with the detailed process by which MSDSs were copied", the primary judge accepted the second respondent as a witness of truth. Importantly, the primary judge considered the second respondent's evidence, in light of the size of the first respondent's operations, to be inherently probable. These subsidiary findings were matters of judgment based upon the primary judge's overall evaluation and appreciation of the evidence before him. The appellant has not established any sound basis to interfere with those findings. Those findings entitled the primary judge to come to the broadly-stated conclusion which the appellant now challenges. However, it is important to note the limitations of that conclusion: except by reference to a very small number of examples, the respondents did not identify which Infosafe MSDSs had been reproduced by the first respondent acting pursuant to a customer's request.

167. It is also important to note that the primary judge's broadly-stated conclusion does not in any way gainsay his Honour's acceptance (at [93]) of the following evidence that was given by the second respondent under cross-examination:

> And is it the case that most of the MSDSs in the Collection have been added without any particular request from a customer? — I think that's probably a fair estimate.

> And the way you get them is simply to trawl the Internet to find MSDSs? — That's right.

> Yes. And any MSDSs you find then get put into the Collection? — I think that's probably true, yes.

> Yes, and they are put in the Collection in the form in which you find them? — That's right.

> Which could be HTML or PDF or Word or other forms? — True.

168. The real issue on this part of the appeal is whether the primary judge was in error in concluding, in effect, that the appellant could not succeed, in any event, because its evidentiary case did not rise to the level of establishing which of the Infosafe MSDSs had been reproduced by the first respondent in circumstances where no present request to reproduce the MSDS had been made by a person impliedly authorised by the appellant to make that request.

169. It is without question that the appellant had the onus of proving infringement. However, that onus was one to be discharged upon the whole of the evidence: *Purkess v Crittenden* [1965] HCA 34; (1965) 114 CLR 164 at 168. It was the respondents who raised, by their pleaded defence, the existence of an implied licence, in answer to the appellant's allegations of infringement. The defence pleaded was, in terms, somewhat more limited than that found by the primary judge. As we have noted, it was pleaded as a licence to the appellant's

customers (not to either of the respondents) to reproduce and license the further reproduction of the alleged copyright works. In those circumstances, any lawful consent or permission for the first respondent to reproduce an Infosafe MSDS or for the second respondent to authorise the first respondent to do so, could only derive from a customer having the benefit of such a licence, hence the importance of identifying whether a particular MSDS was reproduced by the first respondent acting pursuant to such a request.

170. It is in these particular circumstances that the appellant sought to invoke the common law principle stated by Lord Mansfield in *Blatch v Archer* [1774] EngR 2; (1774) 1 Cowp 63 at 65; [1774] EngR 2; 98 ER 969 at 970 that all evidence is to be weighed according to the proof which is in the power of one side to have produced, and in the power of the other side to have contradicted. In *Medtel Pty Ltd v Courtney* [2003] FCAFC 151; (2003) 130 FCR 182 Branson J at [76] (with whom Jacobson J at [81] agreed) observed that s 140 of the *Evidence Act 1995* (Cth), which is concerned with the standard of proof in civil proceedings, is to be understood as incorporating that common law rule.

171. Here, in response to the respondents' pleaded defence that they could avail themselves of a licence implied by law in favour of the appellant's customers, the appellant had established that most of the MSDSs in the Collection had been added without any particular request from a customer. It was within the power of the respondents, who, in furtherance of their defence, either knew or must be taken as having the means of identifying which of the Infosafe MSDSs had been added to the Collection upon the requests of customers, to place that evidence before the Court. They did not do so. Rather, they sought to rely merely upon the fact that requests had been made, without going further, except in the limited cases that were exemplified. The evidentiary landscape, in that regard, was somewhat similar to the "ominous rumbling references" described by Windeyer J in *The Commissioner of Taxation of the Commonwealth of Australia v Casuarina Pty Ltd* [1970] HCA 30; (1970) 127 CLR 62 at 72 when dealing, in an appeal against the Commissioner of Taxation's assessment of taxation (in which the taxpayer bears the onus of proof), with a particular instance of the evidentiary burden placed upon the Commissioner to raise a particular matter in evidence so as to enable the taxpayer to deal with that issue in discharge of the taxpayer's overall burden of proof.

172. It was for the respondents to make good the evidentiary foundation for their defences in relation to the copyright works on which they had been sued for infringement. This included not only the factual matrix necessary to establish the existence and scope of the licence on which they relied, but also the identification of the specific reproductions that fell within that licence.

173. By adducing evidence merely sufficient to enable the conclusion to be drawn that many of the Infosafe MSDSs in the Collection had been reproduced upon the requests of customers, without identifying (except in a very limited number of cases) which MSDSs had been so reproduced, the respondents did not thereby effectively throw upon the appellant the evidentiary burden of

establishing the identity of those MSDSs. The identity of those MSDSs could only have been known to the respondents. In effect the respondents sought to place upon the appellant the burden of making good or filling gaps in the respondents' evidentiary case in ways that were essential to completing the respondents' defence to copyright infringement.

174. For these reasons, the primary judge erred in finding, effectively, that the appellant had failed to discharge its onus of proof to negative the existence of a licence in favour of the respondents in respect of the Infosafe MSDSs reproduced by the first respondent.

175. It follows from this conclusion that the primary judge ought to have held that, except in the very limited number of cases shown by the respondents, the evidence fell short of establishing that any particular MSDS in the Collection had been reproduced with the permission or consent of the appellant (that is, within the limits of the implied licence defence). In those circumstances, the primary judge should have further held that, on the whole of the evidence, the appellant's case on infringement of the Acohs-authored MSDSs (except in the very limited number of cases shown by the respondents) had been established to the required standard.

The right of an exclusive licensee to sue for copyright infringement was considered by the Supreme Court in the *Euro-Excellence* case.

Kraft Canada Inc. v. Euro Excellence Inc., 2007 SCC 37 (S.C.C.)

Abella J., Bastarache J., Binnie J., Charron J., Deschamps J., Fish J., LeBel J., McLachlin C.J.C., Rothstein J.

Heard: January 16, 2007
Judgment: July 26, 2007

KCI is the exclusive Canadian distributor of Côte d'Or and Toblerone chocolate bars in Canada for its parent companies KFB and KFS. Notwithstanding the exclusivity agreements, Euro continued to import and distribute Côte d'Or and Toblerone bars which it had acquired in Europe. In 2002, in order to allow KCI to mount the present case, KFB registered three Côte d'Or logos in Canada as copyrighted artistic works and granted KCI an exclusive licence in the works as used in association with confectionary products. KFS did the same with two Toblerone logos. KCI then called upon Euro to cease and desist distribution of any product to which the copyrighted works were affixed. When Euro refused, KCI brought an action against Euro alleging that it had engaged in secondary infringement under s. 27(2) of the *Copyright Act* by importing copies of KFS and KFB's copyrighted works into Canada for sale or distribution. KCI does not rely on its rights as a trade-mark holder. At trial, KCI was awarded $300,000 in damages and Euro was restrained from selling, distributing, exposing or offering for sale any copies of the copyrighted logos. It was also ordered to render the product non-infringing. KCI's motion for reconsideration was refused. The Federal Court of Appeal refused an appeal on the merits, but referred the matter of damages back to the trial judge. On hearing further submissions, the trial judge confirmed his original award.

The reasons of Binnie, Deschamps and Rothstein JJ. were delivered by

1 ROTHSTEIN J.

Licensing Under the Copyright Act

26 This case turns on the nature and scope of an exclusive licensee's rights under the *Copyright Act.* An exclusive licence under copyright law exists when the following conditions are met: (a) the copyright owner (the licensor) permits another person (the licensee) to do something within the copyright; (b) the licensor promises not to give anyone else the same permission for the duration of the licence; and (c) the licensor itself promises not to do those acts that have been licensed to the licensee for the duration of the licence: *Copyright Act*, s. 2.7; see also D. Vaver, "The Exclusive Licence in Copyright" (1995), 9 *I.P.J.* 163, at pp. 164-65. The parties agree that the agreements between Kraft Canada and the Kraft parent companies are exclusive licence agreements.

27 Under the common law, a licensee does not enjoy property rights: "A licence is merely a permission to do that which would otherwise amount to trespass" (B. H. Ziff, *Principles of Property Law* (4th ed. 2006), at p. 270). In contrast, an assignee receives a property interest from the original owner and steps into the shoes of the owner with respect to those rights assigned. As the recipient of a property interest, the assignee enjoys a right against the world, including the right to sue others (including the assignor) in trespass. The licensee's rights, on the other hand, are contractual, and the licensee is empowered only to sue the owner for breach of contract; it cannot sue in trespass: Ziff, at p. 270; R. E. Megarry, *A Manual of the Law of Real Property* (8th ed. 2002), at p. 475; see also *Thomas v. Sorrell* (1673), Vaughan 330, 124 E.R. 1098, at p. 1109.

28 A contextual reading of the *Copyright Act* reveals that Parliament has preserved the traditional distinction between assignees and licensees with some modification. Under the present Act, there is a distinction between "assignee", "licensee" and "exclusive licensee". An assignee possesses full ownership rights in the copyright with respect to the rights assigned. A non-exclusive licensee has no property rights in the copyright, and enjoys only contractual rights *vis-à-vis* the owner-licensor. As a result, it cannot sue for infringement. An exclusive licensee, on the other hand, has a limited property interest in the copyright. For reasons explained below, this limited property interest enables the exclusive licensee to sue third parties for infringement but precludes the exclusive licensee from suing the owner-licensor for infringement.

29 Under the Act, the nature of the assignee's interest in the copyright is clear. Section 13(5) states expressly that assignees of copyright are, with the exception of moral rights, on equal footing with the original copyright owner:

> Where, under any partial assignment of copyright, the assignee becomes entitled to any right comprised in copyright, the assignee, with respect to the rights so assigned, and the assignor, with respect to the rights not assigned, shall be treated for the purposes of this Act as the owner of the copyright, and this Act has effect accordingly.

The assignee of an interest in copyright is a copyright owner, and thus enjoys rights against the world, including the right to sue the assignor for infringement. This is because the assignor is no longer the owner of the copyright with respect to the right assigned. This is further reflected by the fact that, under s. 36(2), the assignee is not required to join the assignor as co-plaintiff in an action for copyright infringement. In light of these provisions, I have no difficulty in concluding that an assignee, as a holder of a full property interest in copyright, can sue the assignor for copyright infringement.

30 The status of copyright licensees is different. Parliament has manifested its intent to preserve a distinction between assignees and licensees. There is no provision analogous to s. 13(5) that purports to put licensees or exclusive licensees on equal footing with copyright owners.

31 The Act does however elevate "exclusive licensees" above mere licensees. Exclusive licensees are not licensees in the common law sense because exclusive licensees under the Act do have a limited proprietary interest in the copyright that has been licensed to them. The rights of exclusive licensees are set out in ss. 2.7, 13(4), 13(6) and 13(7) of the Act. These provisions do not state expressly whether or not an exclusive licensee can sue the licensor for infringement. However, by necessary implication, they enable exclusive licensees to sue third parties but not the owner-licensor for copyright infringement.

32 Section 2.7 defines "exclusive licence" as "an <u>authorization</u> to do any act that is subject to copyright to the exclusion of all others including the copyright owner". The deliberate choice of the term *authorization* is inconsistent with the granting of property or ownership rights. In *CCH*, at para. 38, this Court agreed that "authorize" meant "sanction, approve and countenance". This is consistent with the common law definition of licence (i.e., permission to do something that would otherwise amount to an infringement).

33 Section 36(2) further suggests that an exclusive licensee does not possess a full property interest in the copyright. Section 36(1) enables exclusive licensees to sue for infringement, but s. 36(2) states that where "a person other than the copyright owner", namely the exclusive licensee, sues for infringement, "the copyright owner must be made a party to those proceedings ...". In the present case, KFB and KFS were joined as co-plaintiffs throughout the proceedings. The requirement of joining the licensor to an infringement action suggests that the exclusive licensee does not have a full property interest in the copyright. If the exclusive licensee held a full property interest, it should not need to join the owner in an

action for infringement because a property interest — which is a right against the world — implies the right to sue for infringement in one's own name.

34 I recognize that other provisions of the Act suggest that exclusive licensees can acquire a property interest in the copyright. However, I am of the opinion that the property interest so acquired is limited and does not include an interest that defeats the ownership interest of the licensor or that could constitute the licensor an infringer of its own copyright.

35 Section 13(4) states:

> The owner of the copyright in any work may assign the right, either wholly or partially, and either generally or subject to limitations relating to territory, medium or sector of the market or other limitations relating to the scope of the assignment, and either for the whole term of the copyright or for any other part thereof, and may grant any interest in the right by licence, but no assignment or grant is valid unless it is in writing signed by the owner of the right in respect of which the assignment or grant is made, or by the owner's duly authorized agent.

Section 13(7) was enacted in 1997 to clarify the meaning of s. 13(4) with respect to exclusive licensees. It states that

> For greater certainty, it is deemed always to have been the law that a grant of an exclusive licence in a copyright constitutes the grant of an interest in the copyright by licence.

The use of the term "grant of an interest" in ss. 13(4) and 13(7) would seem to refer to the granting of a property right. This language stands out in comparison to s. 2.7, which suggests that an exclusive licence is not a "grant of an interest" but rather a non-proprietary "authorization" to do something that would otherwise amount to infringement.

36 The "grant of an interest" referred to in ss. 13(4) and 13(7) meant "grant of a property interest": *Robertson v. Thomson Corp.*, [2006] 2 S.C.R. 363, 2006 SCC 43. At para. 56 of that case, the majority of this Court adopted the following passage from *Ritchie v. Sawmill Creek Golf & Country Club Ltd.* (2004), 35 C.P.R. (4th) 163 (Ont. S.C.J.), at para. 20:

> The "grant of an interest" referred to in s. 13(4) is the transfer of a property right as opposed to a permission to do a certain thing. The former gives the licensee the capacity to sue in his own name for infringement, the latter provides only a defence to claims of infringement. To the extent there was any uncertainty as to the meaning of "grant of an interest" and whether this section applied to non-exclusive licences, the issue was resolved in 1997 when the *Copyright Act* was amended to include s. 13(7). ... [Emphasis added.]

According to this Court's decision in *Robertson*, the Act permits licensors to convey a *property interest* in the copyright to the exclusive licensee. However, neither *Robertson* nor the words of the Act delineate the precise scope of the exclusive licensee's property interest.

37 In my view, the exclusive licensee's property interest in the copyright is limited. An exclusive licence is not a complete assignment of copyright. The

owner-licensor retains a residual ownership interest in the copyright. The owner-licensor's residual ownership interest precludes it from being liable for copyright infringement. An owner-licensor is liable to its exclusive licensee for breach of the licensing agreement but not for copyright infringement.

38 In para. 75, Bastarache J. suggests that I have read down the words of s. 2.7 in order to reach this conclusion. And the Kraft companies argued that the words "to the exclusion of all others including the copyright owner" means that the exclusive licensee has standing to sue the owner-licensor for infringement. I would respectfully disagree with both. Section 2.7 must be interpreted with an eye to the other provisions of the Act. Section 2.7 states:

> For the purposes of this Act, an exclusive licence is an authorization to do any act that is subject to copyright to the exclusion of all others including the copyright owner, whether the authorization is granted by the owner or an exclusive licensee claiming under the owner.

39 An exclusive licence is an "authorization to do any act that is subject to copyright". Under s. 2 of the Act,

> "copyright" means the rights described in
>
> (a) section 3, in the case of a work,
>
>   . . .
>
> Section 3 includes, *inter alia*, the right to produce and reproduce a work.

40 Section 2.7 is a definitional section, which enshrines the common law definition of exclusive licence in the *Copyright Act.* Section 2.7 defines an exclusive licence as an authorization to do any act that is a right described in s. 3 to the exclusion of all others including the copyright owner (i.e., the right to produce and reproduce a work to the exclusion of all others including the copyright owner). But it says nothing about the consequences of violating that exclusive right. Those consequences and remedies for a violation of an exclusive licence are dealt with in other provisions of the Act, e.g. ss. 27(1) and 36(1). As discussed above, when the definitional and liability provisions are read in context, the necessary conclusion is that an exclusive licensee may sue third parties for infringement, but not the owner of the copyright who is liable only for breach of contract.

41 Comparing the treatment of exclusive licensees and assignees under the Act supports this conclusion. If the exclusive licensee could sue the owner-licensor for infringement, then the rights of exclusive licensees would be identical to those of assignees. However, Parliament has clearly manifested its intent to treat exclusive licensees differently from copyright owners and assignees. First, Parliament used express language in putting assignees on equal footing with copyright owners, but refrained from doing the same with exclusive licensees (s. 13(5)). Second, unlike assignees, the exclusive licensee lacks the capacity to sue for infringement alone; it must join the owner-licensor as a party (s. 36(2)). Third, the language of s. 2.7 defining "exclusive licence" as an "authorization" suggests an interest short of ownership. These are all reasons why the Canadian *Copyright Act* should be interpreted so that an exclusive licensee's property interest in a copyright is limited,

such that the exclusive licensee does not have a right against the licensor-owner for infringement of the copyright owned by the licensor-owner.

42 The U.S. and the U.K. copyright regimes are helpful in elucidating the Canadian approach. Under U.S. copyright law, exclusive licensees have the right to sue the owner-licensor for infringement. U.K. copyright law, by contrast, does not permit exclusive licensees to sue the owner-licensor for infringement.

U.S. Copyright Law

43 Under U.S. copyright law, "the licensor may be liable to the exclusive licensee for copyright infringement, if the licensor exercises rights that have theretofore been exclusively licensed": M. B. Nimmer and D. Nimmer, *Nimmer on Copyright* (loose-leaf ed.), vol. 3, at pp. 12–58 and 12–59; *United States Naval Institute v. Charter Communications, Inc.*, 936 F.2d 692 (2d Cir. 1991), at p. 695; *Architectronics, Inc. v. Control Systems, Inc.*, 935 F.Supp. 425 (S.D.N.Y. 1996), at p. 434.

44 However, there are some notable differences between the American and the Canadian statutes. Under the U.S. Act (17 U.S.C. § 101), a "transfer of copyright ownership" is defined as

> an assignment, mortgage, exclusive license, or any other conveyance, alienation or hypothecation of a copyright or of any of the exclusive rights comprised in a copyright, whether or not it is limited in time or place of effect, but not including a nonexclusive license.

Unlike the Canadian Act, the U.S. statute appears to put exclusive licensees on equal footing with assignees. Under U.S. copyright law, there would be no functional difference between an "exclusive license" and an "assignment". The two terms had emerged from the 1909 Act, which had put assignees but not exclusive licensees on equal footing with copyright owners. That distinction has since been eliminated under the current Act: Nimmer, at pp. 10–1 to 10–22. Because exclusive licensees are equated with copyright owners, the exclusive licensee can sue for infringement as an owner, which means that it can sue even the owner-licensor for copyright infringement.

U.K. Copyright Law

45 Under the *Copyright, Designs and Patents Act 1988* (U.K.), 1988, c. 48, the exclusive licensee lacks the capacity to sue the copyright owner-licensor. Under s. 101(1) of the U.K. Act,

> [a]n exclusive licensee has, except against the copyright owner, the same rights and remedies in respect of matters occurring after the grant of the licence as if the licence had been an assignment.

U.K. commentators have taken this provision to mean that "[t]he exclusive licensee may sue in his own name to restrain infringements occurring after the grant of the licence as if the licence had been an assignment", and that "[e]xcept as against the owner of the right he has the same rights and remedies for infringement of the right as if the licence had been an assignment": H. Laddie et al., *The Modern Law of Copyright and Designs* (3rd ed. 2000), vol. 1, at p. 905; see also L. Bently and B. Sherman, *Intellectual Property Law* (2nd ed. 2004), at pp. 254-55. Consequently, the exclusive licensee is able to sue third parties but not the owner-licensor for infringement: *Griggs Group Ltd v. Evans*, [2004] F.S.R. 31, [2003] EWHC 2914 (Ch), at para. 58.

46 Although our Act is not explicit as is the U.K. Act in this regard, a contextual reading of the Canadian Act reveals that exclusive licensees lack the capacity to sue the owner-licensor for infringement. Our Act shares a number of similarities with the U.K. Act, including common origins. In Canada, *The Copyright Act, 1921*, S.C. 1921, c. 24, the precursor to the current Act, was based largely on the British *Copyright Act, 1911*, 1 & 2 Geo. 5, c. 46. Since the 1921 Act was enacted, there have been successive rounds of amendments, but our provisions on licensing and assignments are more similar to that of the U.K. than to the U.S.

47 Unlike the U.S. statute, which puts exclusive licensees on equal footing with assignees, the Canadian and U.K. Acts preserve the distinction between exclusive licensees and assignees. Whereas the U.S. statute permits transfers of copyright ownership by way of exclusive licence, the U.K. Act states that a transfer of ownership in copyright can occur only "by assignment, by testamentary disposition or by operation of law, as personal or moveable property" (s. 90(1)). Similarly, s. 13(5) of the *Canadian Act* states that only the assignee "shall be treated for the purposes of this Act as the owner of the copyright". On their face, the Canadian and U.K. statutes do not permit transfer of copyright ownership by exclusive licence.

48 Moreover, the Canadian and U.K. Acts define exclusive licence in similar terms. Section 92(1) of the U.K. Act states:

> In this Part an "exclusive licence" means a licence in writing signed by or on behalf of the copyright owner authorising the licensee to the exclusion of all other persons, including the person granting the licence, to exercise a right which would otherwise be exercisable exclusively by the copyright owner.

This definition is almost identical to s. 2.7 of the Canadian Act. These similarities between the the Canadian and U.K. Acts suggest that our Parliament has created a copyright licensing regime similar to that of the U.K. If our Parliament had wanted exclusive licensees to be able to sue the owner-licensor for infringement, it would have put exclusive licensees on equal footing with assignees (as the U.S. Congress has done under its Act) or given exclusive licensees this right in the words of the legislation. The fact that our Parliament has retained a distinction between exclusive licensees and assignees suggests that exclusive licensees under our Act have a limited property interest in the copyright that falls short of ownership. The procedural machinery of the Act enables the exclusive licensee to sue third parties for infringement. However, the owner-licensor is liable to the exclusive licensee only in contract.

. . .

16 Bastarache J., at para. 75, suggests that on my reading of the Act, the Kraft companies could have circumvented the purposes of the Act by calling their agreements "assignments" rather than "exclusive licences". However, the distinction between assignments and exclusive licences is important and meaningful. By granting an assignment, the copyright owner intends to bestow upon the assignee the full panoply of rights and interests reserved for copyright owners. An exclusive licence, by contrast, permits owners to convey to licensees a more limited interest in the copyright. In my respectful view, an approach that conflates exclusive licences and assignments must be rejected. By enabling copyright owners to grant an interest in copyright either by assignment or exclusive licence, Parliament intended to provide copyright owners with two qualitatively different mechanisms by which to transfer their interests in whole or in part. Disregarding the distinctions between the two would lead to an unjustifiable narrowing of the owner's options in dealing with its interest.

. . .

Fish J.:

52 I agree with the reasons of Justice Rothstein and would dispose of the appeal as he suggests.

. . .

The reasons of Bastarache, LeBel and Charron JJ. were delivered by

BASTARACHE J. –

. . .

75 Thus, to properly interpret s. 27(2), we need to turn to an examination of the scheme and object of the Copyright Act. My colleague Rothstein J., at para. 4 of his reasons, would require a precise statutory provision to determine the scope of the protection afforded under s. 27(2). He believes that I am introducing a concept of legitimate interests to read down rights afforded by the Copyright Act (para. 7), that I am even introducing a new equitable doctrine (para. 8) or trying to substitute my policy preferences to those of Parliament (para. 3). I am simply applying our rules of statutory interpretation consistently to determine legislative intent and must, in doing so, give proper attention to the legislative context by looking at the provisions under scrutiny, the Act in general and the other legislative provisions that apply to related concepts. Rothstein J. does recognize in his own reasons that this legislation has to be interpreted in its proper legislative context and that it is not true that this Act is worded in such a way that no inferences have to be made. At paras. 34, 35, and 37 for instance, he finds that an exclusive licensee's property interest is limited, and restricts the application of ss. 13(6) and 36(1), ascribing a particular meaning and scope to the word "authorization" in s. 2.7, where the legislator clearly said that an exclusive licensee could do any act that is subject to copyright to the exclusion of all others "including the copyright owner". At para. 31, he speaks of limitations on the rights of exclusive licensees that are found by "necessary implication". I think the purpose of s. 27(2) is determinative and that I need not deal with the

licensing issue. I would however agree with Abella J. that the language of s. 2.7 is perfectly clear (para. 114), that a grant is a grant (para. 115), and that the grant in the present case is for an exclusive licence giving the "sole and exclusive right" to the copyright (para. 123). That right can be enforced under s. 36(1). It is obvious to me that Rothstein J. must therefore be wrong when he states at para. 22 that hypothetical infringement has not been made out. The Kraft parent companies in Europe could not have made a copy of the work in Canada without infringing the copyright. Furthermore, I see no legal justification for limiting the right of the licensee to a claim in contract (para. 27); this would be a clear contradiction of the terms of s. 36(1). Still I see no point in pursuing this course when the reasons of Rothstein J. clearly imply that the purpose of the Act could be circumvented by an assignment of the copyright rather than by the granting of a licence.

The reasons of McLachlin C.J. and Abella J. were delivered by

107 Abella J. – The central issue in this appeal is whether an exclusive licensee of a copyright can claim remedies under the *Copyright Act*, R.S.C. 1985, c. C-42, when the copyrighted work is displayed on the label of a product imported in circumstances envisioned by s. 27(2) of the Act.

108 Like the trial judge and the Federal Court of Appeal, it is my view that Kraft Canada Inc. has the right to seek remedies under the Act to prevent Euro-Excellence from selling or distributing the copyrighted works....

109 Resolving this appeal depends on the ans wers to two questions. First, is the copyrighted work being "sold" or "distributed" when it is printed on the wrapper of a consumer product? Second, can an exclusive licensee in Canada claim protection against secondary infringement when the copyrighted work was produced by the owner-licensor?

110 On the first issue, I agree with the conclusion reached by Rothstein J. There is nothing in the Act to endorse a restrictive definition of "sell". ...

. . .

113 The answer to the second question depends on how one defines the rights of exclusive licensees. Copyright law in Canada, as Estey J. stated in *Compo Co. v. Blue Crest Music Inc.*, [1980] 1 S.C.R. 357, at pp. 372-73, is:

> [N]either tort law nor property law in classification, but is statutory law. It neither cuts across existing rights in property or conduct, nor falls between rights and obligations heretofore existing in the common law. Copyright legislation simply creates rights and obligations upon the terms and in the circumstances set out in the statute.

Copyright today remains an exclusively statutory creation: *Théberge*; *Bishop v. Stevens*, [1990] 2 S.C.R. 467; *CCH Canadian Ltd. v. Law Society of Upper Canada*, [2004] 1 S.C.R. 339, 2004 SCC 13.

114 In my view, the clear language of the Act is determinative. "Exclusive licence" is defined in s. 2.7:

... an authorization to do any act that is subject to copyright <u>to the exclusion of all others including the copyright owner</u>, whether the authorization is granted by the owner or an exclusive licensee claiming under the owner.

115 Clarification of the nature and quality of the rights enjoyed by an exclusive licensee is found in a combination of ss. 13(4), 13(6), 13(7) and 36(1) of the Act, which state:

13. . . .

(4) The owner of the copyright in any work <u>may assign the right</u>, either wholly or partially, and either generally or subject to limitations relating to territory, medium or sector of the market or other limitations relating to the scope of the assignment, and either for the whole term of the copyright or for any other part thereof, <u>and may grant any interest in the right by licence</u>, but no assignment or grant is valid unless it is in writing signed by the owner of the right in respect of which the assignment or grant is made, or by the owner's duly authorized agent.

. . .

(6) For greater certainty, it is deemed always to have been the law that a right of action for infringement of copyright may be assigned in association with the assignment of the copyright <u>or the grant of an interest in the copyright by licence</u>.

(7) For greater certainty, it is deemed always to have been the law that a <u>grant of an exclusive licence in a copyright constitutes the grant of an interest in the copyright by licence</u>.

. . .

36. (1) Subject to this section, the owner of any copyright, or <u>any person</u> or persons <u>deriving any right</u>, title or interest by assignment or grant in <u>writing from the owner</u>, <u>may</u> individually for himself or herself, as a party to the proceedings in his or her own name, <u>protect and enforce any right that he or she holds</u>, and, to the extent of that right, title and interest, is <u>entitled to the remedies provided by this Act</u>.

116 Under s.13(4) and s.13(6), the owner of a copyright is free to divest itself of *any* interest in the copyright, in whole or in part, either by assignment *or* by licence: J.S. McKeown, *Fox on Canadian Law of Copyright and Industrial Designs* (4th ed. (loose- leaf)), at p. 19-24.

117 A copyright holder's ability to alienate its interest either through licensing or assignment is perfectly consistent with the statutory scheme. Vertical and horizontal divisibility is, arguably, a hallmark of copyright: see *Bouchet v. Kyriacopoulos* (1964), 45 C.P.R. 265 (Ex. Ct.). And, as Binnie J. noted in *Théberge*, at para. 12, the economic objectives of copyright law are furthered through the transferability of either full or partial copyright interests.

118 Section 13(7) clarifies that an exclusive licence is the grant of a proprietary interest in the copyright itself: see *Robertson v. Thomson Corp.*, [2006] 2 S.C.R. 363, 2006 SCC 43, at para. 56. And s. 36(1) stipulates that any such grant of an interest in the copyright can be protected through the remedies provided in the Act.

119 The effect of s. 13(7) is to limit the distinction between the rights of assignees and exclusive licensees: McKeown, at p. 19-25 ; T. Scassa, "Using Copyright Law to Prevent Parallel Importation: A Comment on *Kraft Canada, Inc. v. Euro Excellence, Inc.*" (2006), 85 *Can. Bar. Rev.* 409, at p. 416; N. Tamaro, *The 2006 Annotated Copyright Act* (2006). The interest granted under s. 13(7) therefore includes a right, under s. 36(1), to protect that interest as against all others, including the owner-licensor, by availing itself of the remedies in the Act.

120 In other words, when the owner-licensor transfers an interest to the exclusive licensee, that licensee becomes, under the Act, the owner of a defined interest in the copyright: see *Éditions de la Table ronde s.a. v. Cousture*, [1995] Q.J. No. 1519 (QL) (S.C.), and *Dynabec Ltée v. Société d'Informatique R.D.G. Inc.* (1985), 6 C.P.R. (3d) 322 (Que. C.A.).

121 Where the owner of a copyright has granted an exclusive licence, therefore, it has, to the extent of the duration, territorial scope, and terms of that licence, temporarily granted that interest in the copyright to the exclusive licensee.

122 The scope of the precise interest granted is shaped by the terms of the licensing agreement: see *Fonds Gabrielle Roy v. Éditions internationales Alain Stanké Ltée*, [1993] Q.J. No. 2525 (QL) (S.C.); and *British Actors Film Co. v. Glover*, [1918] 1 K.B. 299, at p. 307. In this case, the agreement stated:

2.01 The Licensor grants to the Licensee the sole and exclusive right and licence in the Territory to produce, reproduce and adapt the Works or any substantial part thereof, in any material form whatever, and to use and publicly present the Works in association with the manufacture, distribution or sale in Canada of confectionery products, including, but not limited to, chocolate.

123 This is the grant of the "sole and exclusive right", in Canada, to "produce", "reproduce", "adapt", "use", "distribute" and "sell" the products. These terms, read together with the rights granted to an exclusive licensee in ss. 2.7 and 13(7), as well as the rights in s. 36(1) to protect and enforce its rights and interests through remedies provided by the Act, give the exclusive licensee the right to invoke the Act for copyright infringement not only against third parties, but, as s. 2.7 confirms, against the owner-licensor as well.

124 The trial judge, not unreasonably, treated this exclusive licence as an assignment: *Kraft Canada Inc. v. Euro Excellence Inc.*, [2004] 4 F.C.R. 410, 2004 FC 652, at para. 39. However, even as an exclusive licence, the proprietary interest clearly extends to the production and distribution of copyrighted works in Canada.

125 I accept that exclusive licences are distinct from assignments under the Act. This difference is recognized in s. 13(5) of the Act, dealing with partial assignments of copyright:

(5) Where, under any partial assignment of copyright, the assignee becomes entitled to any right comprised in copyright, the assignee, with respect to the rights so assigned, and the assignor, with respect to the rights not assigned, shall be treated for the purposes of this Act as the owner of the copyright, and this Act has effect accordingly.

This provision is interpretive in nature, clarifying that a partial assignee enjoys complete control over what was assigned to it, while the assignor retains ownership rights in what was not assigned.

126 As Rothstein J. notes, there is no analogous provision with respect to licensees. But, in my view, the absence of such a provision does not derogate from the rights the Act *does* unambiguously assign to exclusive licensees.

127 An exclusive licence which did not prevent others, including the owner-licensor, from performing the acts addressed in the licensing agreement, would no longer be exclusive. It would also render meaningless the statutory definition found in s. 2.7 of an exclusive licensee as the holder of rights "to the exclusion of all others including the copyright owner".

128 While an owner-licensor is, technically, still the owner of the copyright, it is nonetheless liable to an exclusive licensee if it breaches the copyright interest it has granted. Otherwise, the owner-licensor could continue to assert that despite having granted an exclusive interest in its copyright, it was free to compete with the exclusive licensee without fear of attack from the Act's remedial tentacles. The legislation, in my view, contradicts such immunity from the statute and, on the contrary, clearly entitles an exclusive licensee to sue for secondary infringement, even where the work was reproduced by the owner-licensor.

129 Copyright confers a limited monopoly to "produce or reproduce" the work in any material form whatever. In this case, KCI purchased the exclusive licence to the copyrighted work precisely because it wanted copyright on chocolate bar wrappers. Euro-Excellence purchased chocolate bars with labels displaying the copyrighted works; it imported those works into Canada after being notified of KCI's Canadian copyright interest; its purpose in importing the chocolate bars and the wrappers was to sell them or distribute them by way of trade. A s. 27(2) (*e*) infringement is therefore made out. KCI is entitled to the remedies provided by the Act.

130 I would dismiss the appeal and, as requested by KCI, return the matter to Harrington J. for a reassessment of damages.

---

5. Registration

Under the *Copyright Act*, copyright in a work does not depend on registration, but arises automatically from original authorship. An action for infringement may be brought even where the plaintiff has not registered the work under the Act. Registration nevertheless provides certain important rights to copyright owners. A certificate of registration of copyright in a work is evidence that copyright subsists in the work and that the person registered is the owner of the copyright in it.[8] Registration also prevents a defendant from pleading and proving at trial "innocent infringement", which is a defence to the plaintiff's claim for damages in an infringement action.[9]

The registration of copyright often takes on greater importance when rights are obtained through assignment or grant, particularly in cases where there are multiple parties claiming rights in relation to a single work. While registration is not *per se* constitutive of the right, a race to the register can effectively determine ownership of a right that has been the subject of a "double grant." The Act states that, "Any assignment of copyright, or any licence granting an interest in a copyright, shall be adjudged void against any subsequent assignee or licensee for valuable consideration without actual notice, unless the prior assignment or licence is registered in the manner prescribed by the act before the registering of the instrument under which the subsequent assignee or licensee claims." The Act prescribes that any assignment of copyright or licence granting an interest shall be adjudged void against any subsequent assignee or licensee for valuable consideration without actual notice, unless the prior assignment or licence is registered in the manner prescribed by the Act before the registering of the instrument under which the subsequent assignee or licensee claims.[10]

Circle Film Enterprises v. Canadian Broadcasting Corp., [1959] S.C.R. 602

Supreme Court of Canada

1959: January 30 / 1959: May 27.

Present: Taschereau, Cartwright, Fauteux, Abbott and Judson JJ.

. . .

The judgment of the Court was delivered by

JUDSON J.: — The appellant, who claims to be the owner of the copyright in a religious film named "Golgotha", sued the respondent for infringement. The film was based upon a scenario written in 1934 by Canon Joseph Raymond, a citizen of France. All rights of film adaptation of the scenario and all television rights are claimed by the appellant, whose title depends upon a long series of assignments, most of which were executed in France. In the first place, the appellant asserts that its title is proved under s. 36(2) of the Copyright Act by virtue of the production of a certificate of registration of copyright under that Act. The respondent in its statement of defence put the ownership of the copyright in issue and asserts that s. 20, subs. (3), operates in its favour and that under this subsection the author is presumed to be the owner of the copyright. The first question, therefore, is one of the interaction of these two sections of the Copyright Act. There can, of course, be no possible conflict when the plaintiff is

---

8   Section 53(2).
9   Section 39.
10   Section 57(3).

the author of the work in which copyright is claimed, but in this case the plaintiff is admittedly not the author and the plaintiff's title is put in issue.

The judgment under appeal [[1957] 28 C.P.R. 5, 17 Fox Pat. C. 15.] holds that if s. 20(3) applies and the plaintiff is not the author but an assignee, he must prove his chain of title from the author down, and that he cannot discharge the onus of proof by the mere production of a certificate of registration under s. 36(2) of the Act, such registration being insufficient to constitute the contrary proof required by s. 20, subs. (3), of the Act. The attack on this proposition is the central point of the appeal. Section 20, subs. (3) reads:

> 20. (3) In any action for infringement of copyright in any work, in which the defendant puts in issue either the existence of the copyright, or the title of the plaintiff thereto, then, in any such case,
>
>> II. the work shall, unless the contrary is proved, be presumed to be a work in which copyright subsists; and
>>
>> III. the author of the work shall, unless the contrary is proved, be presumed to be the owner of the copyright;...

Section 36(2) reads:

> 36. (2) A certificate of registration of copyright in a work shall be prima facie evidence that copyright subsists in the work and that the person registered is the owner of such copyright.

The difficulty results from the amendment to the Copyright Act enacted by 1931 c. 8, s. 7, which repealed the old section having to do with presumptions in favour of the plaintiff in a copyright action. The old section of the Act had been in force since 1921 and was in terms identical with the English legislation. From 1921 to 1931 the Canadian Copyright Act provided:

> In any action for infringement of copyright in any work, the work shall be presumed to be a work in which copyright subsists and the plaintiff shall be presumed to be the owner of the copyright, unless the defendant puts in issue the existence of the copyright, or, as the case may be, the title of the plaintiff,...

In this form, if the presumption stands, not being put in issue by the defence, there is no conflict between ss. 20(3) and 36(2). If the presumption disappears, by being put in issue, then certain other presumptions, not relevant here but having a plain and recognizable function, appear. Why the legislation was changed to make the author the presumed owner when the title of the plaintiff is put in issue, I do not know. It seems to add nothing to the rights of an author and it may be a serious handicap to any other plaintiff. A plaintiff, if it is an assignee, may meet the presumption by proving its chain of title but where, as in this case, the plaintiff claims through a number of mesne assignments, most of which were executed in a foreign country, the burden of proof may become intolerably heavy. The important question is whether it can meet that presumption by the production of a certificate of registration under s. 36(2), which certifies that copyright in the work in question, the author of which is Canon Joseph

Raymond of Paris, France, was registered on the 5th day of February, 1952, in the name of the Circle Film Enterprises Incorporated, the plaintiff in this action.

Registration first came into Canadian copyright legislation in the Act of 1921. It disappeared from the English legislation in 1911. It is permissive in character and the subsistence of copyright in no way depends upon registration, but its proof and proof of ownership are plainly intended to be facilitated by the enactment of s. 36(2). That this was the object of s. 36(2) is indicated in the judgment of this Court in Massie & Renwick Ltd. v. Underwriters' Survey Bureau Ltd. [[1940] S.C.R. 218 at 238, 3 C.P.R. 184, 1 D.L.R. 625.], per Duff C.J., when he said:

> Certificates of registration have been produced for these plans which, under sections 36(2) and 37(6), constitute prima facie evidence that copyright subsists in the work and that the persons registered were the owners of such copyright. This prima facie case has not been met.

Is it met in the present case by the appeal to the presumption mentioned in s. 20(3)(b) that the author is presumed to be the owner of the copyright? I take the operation of a presumption of this kind to be as stated by Wigmore on Evidence, 3rd ed., s. 2491(2):

> It must be kept in mind that the peculiar effect of a presumption "of law" (that is, the real presumption) is merely to invoke a rule of law compelling the jury to reach the conclusion in the absence of evidence to the contrary from the opponent. If the opponent does offer evidence to the contrary (sufficient to satisfy the judge's requirement of some evidence), the presumption disappears as a rule of law, and the case is in the jury's hands free from any rule.

In spite of the difficulty created in 1931 when the presumption in favour of the plaintiff was changed to a presumption in favour of the author, my opinion is that a certificate of registration under s. 36(2) is evidence to show that the author in this case is not the owner. There is no evidence apart from the statutory presumption in s. 20(3)(b) that he is the owner. The case therefore, on the interrelation of these two sections, comes to the tribunal of fact merely with this evidence, that the plaintiff is, prima facie, and the author is not, the owner of the copyright in question. This is evidence to the contrary within s. 20(3)(b) and with its production, the presumption has disappeared as a rule of law. There is only one piece of evidence and that is the certificate of registration. There are no evidentiary facts behind s. 20(3)(b) which, of their own weight, can lead to an inference of ownership of the copyright remaining with the author. In a case where there is evidence to contradict the certificate, then its weight may be affected, but in the absence of any such evidence, its weight is not to be minimized because no proof of title is required in the application for registration and because the Copyright Office assumes no responsibility for the truth of the facts asserted in the application and conducts no independent examination. A plaintiff who produces this certificate has adduced some evidence in support of his case, sufficient to compel the tribunal of fact to act in his favour in the absence of any evidence to contradict it.

In my opinion, therefore, by the production of this certificate and in the absence of any evidence to the contrary, the plaintiff in this case has satisfied the burden of proof, both the primary burden — that which rests upon a plaintiff as a matter of substantive law and is sometimes referred to as the risk of non-persuasion — and also the secondary burden, that of adducing evidence; Smith v. Nevins [[1925] S.C.R. 619 at 638, [1924] 2 D.L.R. 865.] and Ontario Equitable v. Baker [[1926] S.C.R. 297 at 308, 2 D.L.R. 289.]. On this ground the dismissal of the action should be set aside and judgment entered for the plaintiff.

Drolet c. Stiftung Gralsbotchaft, 2009 FC 17 (F.C.)

. . .

[217] Because Canada is a signatory of the Berne Convention [*Berne Convention for the Protection of Literary and Artistic Works* (Paris Act of July 24, 1971 as amended on September 28,1979), [1988] Can. T.S. No. 18], the legal protection afforded by copyright takes effect as soon as the work is created. Registering the copyright with the Copyright Office is therefore not mandatory although it creates a certain number of presumptions. More specifically, subsection 53(2) provides that "[a] certificate of registration of copyright is evidence that the copyright subsists and that the person registered is the owner of the copyright." This means that the person challenging the existence of a copyright bears the burden of proof and must provide credible evidence to rebut this presumption: see *Grignon v. Roussel* (1991), 38 C.P.R. (3d) 4 (F.C.T.D.), at page 7; *Wall v. Horn Abbot Ltd.*, 2007 NSSC 197 (CanLII), 2007 NSSC 197, 256 N.S.R. (2d) 34, at paragraph 481.

. . .

[243] Having found that the Stiftung validly granted a sublicence to Mr. Kaufmann to translate the work of Oskar Ernst Bernhardt, I must now determine whether the Stiftung is indeed the owner of the rights in the translations done by Mr. Kaufmann at its request. In support of its position, the Stiftung first cited subsection 53(2) of the *Copyright Act*. This provision states that the copyright registration certificate "is evidence that the copyright subsists and that the person registered is the owner of the copyright." This presumption appears to me to be quite weak in the circumstances, however, as the defendants registered their copyright certificate very late. In fact, as I have already pointed out, the defendants registered this certificate only after being granted leave by Justice Pinard to amend their defence and to file a counterclaim in copyright infringement. In such a context, the presumption loses much of its weight. As the Court of Appeal held in *CCH Canadian Ltd. v. Law Society of Upper Canada*, 2002 FCA 187 (CanLII), 2002 FCA 187, [2002] 4 F.C. 213, at paragraph 63:

> Generally, the weight to be afforded to these certificates should not be minimized by the fact that the Copyright Office assumes no responsibility for the truth of the facts contained in the application and conducts no examination (see *Circle Film*

Enterprises Inc. v. Canadian Broadcasting Corporation, 1959 CanLII 74 (SCC), [1959] S.C.R. 602, at pages 606–607). However, the Trial Judge pointed out that nearly all of the registrations were obtained within the few months preceding the trial of this matter. To me, the fact that these certificates were obtained seemingly only in contemplation of litigation diminishes their persuasiveness. Therefore, although these certificates may support a finding that copyright subsists in the Publishers' works as described on the certificates, I do not find them particularly compelling.

[244] The books published by the Stiftung in 1990 under the titles *In the Light of Truth*, volumes II and III, contain the usual copyright notice and logo (©) indicating that the Stiftung is the owner of the copyright:

. . .

In the following case, the court considers the limits of the "double grant" rule in subsection 57(3) when rights are bequeathed by will. The case also raises the interesting issue of "reversion." This significant (and widely under-appreciated) limitation on the assignment or grant of copyright is found in section 14(1) of the Act, which applies to restrict the effective duration of assignments or grants of an interest in copyright in cases where the author was first owner of copyright. In such cases, the rights assigned or granted by the author revert to the author's estate after a period of twenty-five years following the death of the author, notwithstanding any agreement to the contrary. Originally considered the "Dickens" provision in the United Kingdom, the reversionary interest was intended to ensure that an author's beneficiaries could reap some benefit from the success of a work the rights to which were transferred during the author's lifetime. Owners of copyright may, however, be surprised to discover that the rights they acquired lawfully and for value have suddenly transferred by operation of law back to the author's estate.

Kelley Estate v. Roy, 2002 CarswellNat 2421, [2002] F.C.J. No. 1258 (Fed. T.D.)

Federal Court of Canada–Trial Division

Toronto, Ontario

September 12, 2002

GIBSON J.: —

INTRODUCTION

1 These reasons arise out of an application pursuant to various provisions of the Copyright Act, and Part V of the Federal Court Rules, 1998 whereby, in an Amended Notice Of Application, the applicant seeks the following reliefs:

1. A declaration that Theresia Winkler is the owner of the copyright in the books authored by the late Thomas P. Kelley entitled "The Black Donnellys", first published in Canada in April 1954 and "Vengeance of the Black Donnellys" first published in Canada in November 1962 (collectively, the "Books") and that Theresia Winkler is entitled to the income generated by the sale of the Books;

2. A declaration that the copyright registration, serial number 254758 dated October 15, 1974 as registered to Pagurian Press Limited is invalid and that said registration be expunged;...

6. Alternatively to the damages and profits sought, statutory damages as may be elected by the Applicant before final judgment;

5 In an amended Memorandum of Fact and Law only filed on behalf of the applicant on the 15th of July, 2002, the ...claim for a declaration of ownership of copyright is extended, or at least clarified, to include the "reversionary interest" and a claim is added for an Order that Firefly "...remit the royalties held by it to [the applicant]", a relief that would appear to flow logically from a declaration that the applicant is the owner of copyright, if such a declaration were granted....

THE PARTIES

6 The applicant is the executor or "estate administrator" designated in the will of the late Thomas P. Kelley who died on the 14th of February, 1982. Mr. Kelley's wife predeceased him on the 1st of February, 1982. By reason of the death of Mrs. Kelley before the death of her husband, the applicant who, as landlady to the Kelleys, had taken a benevolent interest in their welfare, was the only named beneficiary in the will of Mr. Kelley. Mr. Kelley's will was duly probated.

7 Mr. Kelley was the author of a number of books, among them The Black Donnellys and Vengeance of the Black Donnellys (collectively, the "Donnelly Books"), both earlier referred in the first quoted relief as originally claimed by the applicant. It is the identity of the owner of copyright in the Donnelly Books and the right to royalties flowing from that ownership that is the central issue in this matter.

8 It was not in dispute before me that, at all relevant times, Samuel Roy was a businessman residing in Toronto, Ontario. He was the principal shareholder and director of Saroy Film Productions of Canada Limited, a company incorporated pursuant to the laws of Ontario with a principal place of business or head office in Toronto. Samuel Roy Enterprises was at all relevant times the business style of three (3) corporations incorporated pursuant to the laws of Ontario and also having their principal places of business in Toronto. As earlier noted, the corporations comprising Samuel Roy Enterprises were Falwyn Developments Limited, Elane Holdings Limited and Aztec Investments Limited. Mr. Roy was at all relevant times a director and officer of each of those three (3) corporations.

9 Firefly Books Ltd. was at all relevant times a company incorporated pursuant to the laws of Ontario with a principal place of business in Willowdale, Ontario.

It carried on, and apparently continues to carry on, the business of publishing and distributing books.

10 Edperbrascan Corporation ("Edperbrascan") is apparently a successor corporation to a number of corporations including Pagurian Press Limited which, on the 15th of October, 1974, registered copyright in the published literary work, The Black Donnellys[3]. Evidence before me indicates that Pagurian Press first printed The Black Donnellys in July of 1978 and reprinted it in May 1980 and again in August 1982[4]. Pagurian Press first printed Vengeance of The Black Donnellys in January, 1975, twice reprinted it and printed a revised edition in September, 1988.[5] The same evidence indicates that the Pagurian Corporation Limited, as of 1986 in respect of The Black Donnellys and as of 1988 in respect of Vengeance of the Black Donnellys, claimed its copyright "...under agreement with Saroy Film Productions of Canada" and that "over 1 million copies" of The Black Donnellys had been sold when Pagurian Press Limited was engaged in publishing it. The relationship among Pagurian Press Limited, Pagurian Press and Pagurian Corporation Limited went unexplained. I have assumed for purposes of my decision that nothing turns on it.

PUBLICATION HISTORY OF THE DONNELLY BOOKS

11 Prior to its publication by Pagurian Press Limited, evidence before the Court indicates that The Black Donnellys was first printed by Harlequin Books Limited in April 1954, and was reprinted by Harlequin some fourteen (14) times. It was later printed by Greywood Publishing Limited in July 1969 and reprinted by Greywood some six (6) times. Finally preceding the involvement of Pagurian Press Limited, The Black Donnellys was printed by Modern Canadian Library Limited, first in June 1974 and later on four (4) subsequent dates. It was apparently also published in the United States and England.

12 Vengeance of the Black Donnellys was first printed by Harlequin Books Limited in November, 1962. It was reprinted by Harlequin some six (6) times. It was later printed by Greywood Publishing Limited in July, 1969. Greywood reprinted it six (6) times. I was referred to no evidence before the Court indicating the extent of its distribution or indicating that it was published outside Canada.

13 Evidence in the public domain, but not before the Court, indicates that the saga of The Black Donnellys whether based on Mr. Kelley's book or otherwise, continues to receive popular exposure. The following brief reference is drawn from page 40 of the issue of Maclean's magazine for the 22nd of April, 2002:

In Blyth [Ontario], at the renowned summer theatre festival, the bloody saga of the Black Donnellys plays out under the stars in June.

THE BACKGROUND

14 The late Thomas P. Kelley was apparently a quite prolific but, at least in the later years of his life, a somewhat impecunious author. By letter agreement dated the 13th of August, 1968, Mr. Kelley granted to Saroy Film Productions

of Canada Limited an option "...to acquire from [him] the sole and exclusive publishing, motion picture and allied rights throughout the world in and to those certain full length books written by [him] entitled "THE BLACK DONNEL- LYS" and "VENGEANCE OF THE BLACK DONNELLYS..."[7]. By letter dated the 15th of October, 1968,[8] Saroy Film Productions of Canada Limited exer- cised its option. In the result, a formal agreement of assignment[9] took effect in consideration of a one-time payment to Mr. Kelley by Saroy Film Productions of Canada Limited.

15 Two provisions of the agreement of assignment are central for the purposes of these reasons. The first reads as follows:

> FIRST: The Owner [Mr. Kelley] now sells and grants to the Purchaser [Saroy Film Productions of Canada Limited] exclusively all motion picture rights (including all sound, musical, and talking motion picture rights) now or hereafter known throughout the world in the Property [the Donnelly Books] (and all component parts thereof as above defined), forever. Included among the rights so conveyed are the following rights (but their enumeration shall not be deemed to limit the grant first above made):

16 The second relevant provision reads as follows:

> EIGHTH: No rights granted herein shall remain in or revert back to Owner regard- less of the time when any picture or pictures are made from the Property, and regardless whether or not any picture at all is made from the Property. Purchaser intends to produce a motion picture or pictures from the Property, but does not obligate itself to do so or to make any other use of the Property.

17 While both of the above quoted provisions speak generally to motion picture rights, it was not in dispute before me that Mr. Kelley's assignment of copyright in the Donnelly Books to Saroy Film Productions of Canada Limited purported to extend to publication rights as well as to motion picture rights.

18 Many years after the death of Mr. Kelley, the applicant, as executor and ben- eficiary of Mr. Kelley's estate, began to pursue an interest in the arrangement, whatever it might have been, between Mr. Kelley and the Roy respondents. Her enquiries of the Roy respondents, both directly and through her granddaughter, were effectively stonewalled. It was only after this proceeding was commenced that Samuel Roy produced a brief affidavit to which he annexed the documents constituting the agreement of assignment with Mr. Kelley.

19 In 1992, apparently after Pagurian Press Limited had ceased printing and publication of the Donnelly Books, Samuel Roy approached the president of Firefly with a view to having Firefly publish new editions of the Donnelly Books. Firefly agreed to publish new editions of the Books under license from Saroy Film Productions of Canada Limited, subject to receiving confirmation from Samuel Roy that Pagurian Press Limited was releasing any publication rights it had to the Donnelly Books. Firefly's concern in this regard was appar- ently satisfied by vague assurances from Samuel Roy. Firefly commenced printing and publication and from time to time remitted royalties to Saroy Film Productions of Canada Limited.

20 When the applicant brought to the attention of Firefly her interest in the Donnelly Books, Firefly immediately ceased distribution of the Donnelly Books and withheld distribution of accumulated royalties then held by it, pending settlement of any dispute. Firefly cooperated with the applicant by supplying to her information and documentation available to it relating to its publication and distribution of the Donnelly Books, ostensibly under licence from Saroy Film Productions of Canada Limited.

21 On the 14th of March, 2000, the applicant registered her interest, as "owner", of the copyright in the Donnelly Books.

22 This proceeding followed.

RELEVANT PROVISIONS OF THE COPYRIGHT ACT

23 The relevant provisions of the Copyright Act, which are extensive, are reproduced in a schedule to these reasons.

THE ISSUES

24 The issues identified in the Amended Memorandum of Fact and Law filed on behalf of the applicant are the following:

a)   whether the applicant is the owner of the copyright, including the reversionary interest, in the Donnelly Books;

b)   whether the Pagurian Registration of copyright should be expunged; and

c)   whether the applicant is entitled to statutory damages and/or an Order for payment to her of unpaid royalties....

25 The issues identified in the Amended Memorandum of Fact and Law filed on behalf of Firefly, to some extent overlapping with those identified on behalf of the applicant, are the following:

a)   is the applicant the owner of the copyright in the Donnelly Books?

b)   does Firefly's publication of the Donnelly Books under licence from Saroy Film Productions of Canada Limited infringe the applicant's copyright in the Donnelly Books;

c)   does the applicant have any entitlement to the royalties being withheld by Firefly which are payable by Firefly under its licence Agreement with Saroy Film Productions of Canada Limited in respect of the period from May 1, 1999?...

26 The only issue identified in the Memorandum of Fact and Law filed on behalf of the Roy respondents is whether copyright interest in the Donnellys Books passed by the agreement between Saroy Film Productions of Canada Limited and Mr. Kelley or was such agreement ineffectual, leaving the copyright interest in the Donnelly Books to pass by will to the applicant.

ANALYSIS

. . .

b)   The Pagurian Copyright Registration

39   Subsection 55(1) of the Act, also set out in the Schedule, provides that application for registration of copyright in a work may be made by or on behalf the author of the work, the owner of the copyright in the work, an assignee of the copyright, or a person to whom an interest in the copyright has been granted by licence.

40   Subsection 57(4) of the Act provides that this Court may, on application of the Registrar of Copyrights or of any interested persons, order rectification of the Register of Copyrights by, among other things, expunging any entry wrongly made in or remaining on the Register.

41   Edperbrascan, as successor to Pagurian Press Limited, filed no materials on this application and failed to appear at hearing to support Pagurian's copyright registration of the published literary work, The Black Donnellys, which registration is dated the 15th of October, 1974.

42   Subsection 53(2) of the Act provides that a certificate of registration of copyright is evidence that the copyright subsists and that the person registered in the owner of the copyright. In Circle Films Enterprises Inc. v. Canadian Broadcasting Corp.[10], Mr. Justice Judson, for the Court, wrote at page 215:

> In a case where there is evidence to contradict the certificate, then its weight may be affected, but in the absence of any such evidence, its weight is not to be minimized because no proof of title is required in the application for registration and because the Copyright Office assumes no responsibility for the truth of the facts asserted in the application and conducts no independent examination. A plaintiff who produces this certificate has adduced some evidence in support of his case, sufficient to compel the tribunal of fact to act in his favour in the absence of any evidence to contradict it.

43   Here, I am satisfied that there is evidence to contradict Pagurian's certificate of registration. It was not in dispute before me that Mr. Kelley was the author of The Black Donnellys. The evidence before the Court demonstrates that there may be some doubt whether the late Mr. Kelley, and through him, the applicant, or the Roy respondents, is or are the owners of copyright in The Black Donnellys. But there is no evidence other than the registration in favour of Pagurian Press Limited, and the bald assertion on the introductory pages of the Pagurian edition of The Black Donnellys that is an exhibit to the affidavit of Juliet Fernandes sworn the 26th of October, 2000[11] to support the certificate.

44   I am satisfied on the totality of the evidence before the Court that the presumption in favour of Pagurian created by subsection 53(2) of the Act is overcome by the evidence contradicting that presumption. In the result, an Order will go expunging the certificate of registration of copyright in The Black Donnellys, dated the 15th of October, 1974 in favour of Pagurian Press Limited.

c)   As between Saroy Film Productions of Canada Limited and the Applicant, who is the owner of copyright in the Donnelly Books?

45 Section 6 of the Act provides that, except as otherwise expressly provided in the Act, the term for which copyright subsists is the life of the author, the remainder of the calendar year in which the author dies, and a period of fifty (50) years following the end of that calendar year. No other term is expressly provided by the Act in respect of works such as the Donnelly Books.

46 Counsel for the applicant urged that the assignment of copyright in the Donnelly Books from Mr. Kelley to Saroy Film Productions of Canada Limited was void as against the applicant by virtue of subsection 57(3) of the Act and/or subsection 14(1) of the Act or, in the alternative, was void as against the applicant with respect to the "reversionary term" of copyright. On the facts of this matter, the reversionary term would be the balance of the calendar year that is twenty-five (25) years from the year of death of the author, 1982, and the remaining twenty-five (25) years of the term of copyright following that year. Each of these submissions will be examined in turn.

i)   Subsection 57(3) of the Act–when an assignment or licence is void

47 Subsection 57(3) of the Act provides that an assignment, among other things, of copyright shall be adjudged void against any subsequent assignee or licensee for valuable consideration without actual notice, unless the prior assignment is registered as provided in the Act before registration of the subsequent assignment or licence for valuable consideration without actual notice. This provision raises directly the question of whether the applicant can be said to be an assignee or licensee for valuable consideration without actual notice, from Mr. Kelley as the first holder of copyright in the Donnelly Books.

48 I take it as uncontested that, at the time of Mr. Kelley's death, the applicant had no notice, actual or otherwise, of the assignment of copyright in the Donnelly Books from Mr. Kelley to Saroy Film Productions of Canada Limited. But there remains the question of whether the applicant, as executor and sole surviving named beneficiary of the will of Mr. Kelley, can be said to be an assignee or licensee for valuable consideration of copyright in the Donnelly Books. I am satisfied that the short answer to that question is "she cannot".

49 Mr. Kelley's will consisted of a stationer's form with certain of the blanks filled in. It directed that all of his "...just debts and funeral and Testamentary expenses be paid and satisfied by my Executor...", the applicant. It is noteworthy that it did not transfer or assign, let alone licence, to the applicant, as executor, all of his "...Real and Personal Estate..." to be dealt with as directed. Rather, after directing the applicant to pay and satisfy his just debts and funeral and testamentary expenses, the applicant "...Devise[d] and Bequeath[ed] the Real and Personal Estate of which I may die possessed in the manner following, that is to say:" -

    To my wife Ethel Grace Kelley

All income from my Books and any money received from any other source, such as Movies, etc.

To be paid to my wife.

In the event of her death all moneyies [sic] shall be paid to [the applicant] from the sales to my Books or from any other source.

Once again, I am satisfied that the bequest to the applicant could in no sense be interpreted as an assignment, let alone a licence to the applicant since Mr. Kelley's wife had predeceased him, of any copyright in the Donnelly Books that remained in Mr. Kelley. I further note that the blank space following the introduction of the residual clause in Mr. Kelley's will form remained just that, a blank space.

50 Further, even if the applicant were found to be an assignee or a licensee, either as Executor or as beneficiary under Mr. Kelley's will, I am satisfied that it could not be said to be an assignment or licence "for valuable consideration". In support of an argument that it was such an assignment or licence "for valuable consideration", counsel referred me to Deglman v. Guaranty Trust, et al[13]. I am satisfied that that case is entirely distinguishable. At page 729, Mr. Justice Cartwright, for the majority, noted:

> The appeal was argued on the assumption, that there was an oral contract made between the respondent and the late Laura Constantineau Brunet under the terms of which the former was to perform certain services in consideration whereof the latter was to devise No. 548 Besserer Street to him... .

While, as I have earlier noted in these reasons, the applicant, as landlady to the Kelleys, took a benevolent interest in their welfare in their declining years, there is no evidence whatsoever before me that a contract, express or implied, oral or otherwise, existed between the applicant and Mr. Kelley that led to him identifying the applicant as his executor and sole surviving named beneficiary.

51 The applicant cannot succeed on the basis of subsection 57(3).

ii) Subsection 14(1) of the Act–whether a grant of an interest is wholly inoperative

52 Subsection 13(4) of the Act provides that the owner of copyright in any work may assign that right, "...either for the whole term of the copyright or for any other part thereof," and may grant any interest in the right by licence. The same subsection provides that any such assignment or grant is valid only if it is in writing and duly executed.

53 Subsection 14(1) of the Act, on its face, acts as a limitation on subsection 13(4). For ease of reference, subsection 14(1) is repeated here in full:

> 14. (1) Where the author of a work is the first owner of the copyright therein, no assignment of the copyright and no grant of any interest therein, made by him, otherwise than by will, after June 4, 1921, is operative to vest in the assignee or grantee any rights with respect to the copyright in the work beyond the expiration

of twenty-five years from the death of the author, and the reversionary interest in the copyright expectant on the termination of that period shall, on the death of the author, notwithstanding any agreement to the contrary, devolve on his legal representatives as part of the estate of the author, and any agreement entered into by the author as to the disposition of such reversionary interest is void.

54 Counsel for the applicant urged that the underlined words in the closing three (3) lines of subsection 14(1) of the Act must be read as rendering any agreement, otherwise valid under subsection 13(4) of the Act, entirely void where it purports to assign the reversionary interest as described in subsection 14(1). Counsel urged this interpretation on two (2) grounds: first, because if the closing words are not so read, they would be purely duplicative of the earlier words in the subsection that I have emphasized; and secondly, because only such an interpretation accords with the grammatical structure of the closing words.

55 By contrast, counsel for Firefly urged that subsections 13(4) and 14(1) of the Act must be read together and that the interpretation urged on behalf of the applicant would be entirely inconsistent with the objective of subsection 13(4) and the objectives of the Act, read as a whole. Counsel for Firefly referred me to two (2) passages from Chappell & Co. Ltd. v. Redwood Music Ltd.,[14] commenting on a provision equivalent to subsection 14(1) of the Act in the United Kingdom legislation. At page 823, Lord Salmon wrote:

> I agree with the Court of Appeal that the object of the proviso was to safeguard authors and their heirs from the consequences of any imprudent disposition which authors might make of the fruits of their talent and originality.

> To this end, the proviso enacts that an assignment of a copyright by its first owner shall not be operative beyond 25 years after his death; and the copyright shall then devolve for its remaining 25 years on his legal personal representatives as part of his estate.

At pages 825 and 826, Lord Russell of Killowen wrote:

> The proviso (a) enacts that no such assignment or grant by licence can operate to vest in the assignee or grantee any right or interest in the copyright extending in time beyond the expiration of 25 years from the death of the author of the work, (b) enacts that the reversionary interest for the remaining 25 years of the copyright term shall on the author's death devolve on his legal representative as part of his estate and (c) enacts that any agreement by the author as to the disposition of such reversionary interest shall be null and void. Thus it is made impossible for the author either to assign or license, or to contract to assign or license, in manner extending into the reversionary 25 year period, though his legal personal representatives (or a beneficiary after assent) can do so at any time after the author's death.

56 Counsel for the applicant urged that the foregoing passages should not be relied on because the facts underlying the Chappell decision are substantially different from the facts of this matter. I am satisfied that the factual differences are irrelevant and that the two (2) quoted passages are highly relevant to the interpretation of subsection 14(1) of the Act. I will interpret subsection 14(1) in a manner consistent with the interpretation provided by the quoted passages. I am satisfied that the interpretation urged on behalf of the applicant would simply

not be consistent with the scheme of the Act as a whole and, more particularly, with the scheme of subsections 13(4) and 14(1) of the Act, read together.

iii) Subsection 14(1) of the Act, the reversionary interest

57 I am satisfied that provisions from the assignment from Mr. Kelley to Saroy Film Productions of Canada Limited that are quoted earlier in these reasons do purport to assign copyright, at least in respect of motion pictures, and I am satisfied more broadly, in relation to the reversionary period. To the extent that they purport to do so, they are void with respect to the reversionary interest. With respect to the term of copyright from the date of assignment to the commencement of the reversionary period as defined in subsection 14(1), I find the assignment from Mr. Kelley to Saroy Film Productions of Canada Limited to be valid under subsection 13(4) of the Act.

58 Pursuant to subsection 14(1) of the Act, the reversionary interest devolves upon the applicant as Mr. Kelley's legal representative, as part of the estate of Mr. Kelley. I was not called upon in the terms of the issues identified before me, or indeed in explicit terms in the argument before me, under the terms of Mr. Kelley's will, to determine the impact of the devolution of the reversionary interest on the applicant, as the sole named beneficiary. I decline to undertake any such analysis and, indeed, I entertained very serious doubts whether I have the jurisdiction to do so.

59 In the result, I determine that as between Saroy Film Productions of Canada Limited and the applicant, Saroy Film Productions of Canada Limited is the owner of copyright in the Donnellys Books to the date that is 25 years from the death of Mr. Kelley, that is to say February 14th, 2007. Thereafter, by virtue of subsection 14(1) of the Act, the reversionary interest in the copyright in the Donnelly Books devolves upon the applicant as his executor.

d)   The Applicant's Entitlement to Statutory Damages and to Withheld Royalties

60 In light of my conclusions to this point, it follows that the applicant has no entitlement to statutory damages, as provided for in subsection 38.1(1) of the Act. Equally, it follows that the applicant has no entitlement to royalties withheld by Firefly after it received notice of the applicant's claimed interest in copyright in the Donnelly Books.

e)   Infringement by Firefly

61 Once again given my findings to this point, I conclude that Firefly, through its publication and distribution of the Donnelly Books, has infringed no copyright interest of the applicant.

f)   Reliefs other than Costs

62 A declaration will go that copyright registration Serial No. 254758 dated October 15, 1974, as registered to Pagurian Press Limited, is invalid. Such registration will be expunged under paragraph 57(4)(b) of the Act as an entry wrongly made in or remaining on the Register of Copyrights.

63 A further declaration will go that, as between the applicant and the respondents, Saroy Film Productions of Canada Limited is the owner by assignment of copyright in the Donnelly books for a term commencing with the date of the assignment of copyright in those books from Mr. Kelley to Saroy Film Productions of Canada Limited, and continuing to the 14th of February, 2007. Thereafter, for the balance of the term of copyright in the Donnelly Books as provided by section 6 of the Act, copyright devolves on the applicant, as Mr. Kelley's legal representative, as part of Mr. Kelley's estate.

Chapter 7

EXCLUSIVE RIGHTS AND INFRINGEMENT OF COPYRIGHT

The *Copyright Act* confers exclusive rights on copyright holders that enable them to control what is done with their works. Any unlicensed use of protected works which violates an exclusive right is *prima facie* infringement. The scope of the exclusive rights conferred by the Act is often tested in difficult circumstances, revealing the uncertain boundaries of copyright and its subject matter. As the cases in this section demonstrate, how we understand the nature and scope of the copyright interest is key to identifying whether a particular act infringes a particular right of the copyright owner.

1. Introducing Infringement

(a) Structure of Rights in Section 3(1)

Entertainment Software Assn. v. SOCAN, 2012 SCC 34 (S.C.C.)

. . .

[41] In our view, the Court in Bishop merely used this quote to emphasize that the rights enumerated in s. 3(1) are distinct. Bishop does not stand for the proposition that a single activity (i.e., a download) can violate two separate rights at the same time. This is clear from the quote in Ash v. Hutchinson, which refers to "two acts". In Bishop, for example, there were two activities: 1) the making of an ephemeral copy of the musical work in order to effect a broadcast, and 2) the actual broadcast of the work itself. In this case, however, there is only one activity at issue: downloading a copy of a video game containing musical works.

[42] Nor is the communication right in s. 3(1)(f) a sui generis right in addition to the general rights described in s. 3(1). The introductory paragraph defines what constitutes "copyright". It states that copyright "means" the sole right to produce or reproduce a work in any material form, to perform a work in public, or to publish an unpublished work. This definition of "copyright" is exhaustive, as the term "means" confines its scope. The paragraph concludes by stating that copyright "includes" several other rights, set out in subsections (a) through (i). As a result, the rights in the introductory paragraph provide the basic structure of copyright. The enumerated rights listed in the subsequent subparagraphs are simply illustrative: Sunny Handa, Copyright Law in Canada (2002), at p. 195;

see also *Apple Computer Inc. v. Mackintosh Computers Ltd.*, [1987] 1 F.C. 173 (T.D.), at p. 197. The rental rights in s. 3(1)(i) referred to by Justice Rothstein, for example, can fit comfortably into the general category of reproduction rights.

. . .

(b) Copyright is a Negative Right

JT International SA v. Commonwealth, [2012] HCA 43 (H.C.A.)

36. It is a common feature of the statutory rights asserted in these proceedings that they are negative in character. As Laddie, Prescott and Vitoria observed[68]:

> "Intellectual property is ... a purely negative right, and this concept is very important. Thus, if someone owns the copyright in a film he can stop others from showing it in public but it does not in the least follow that he has the positive right to show it himself."

In *Pacific Film Laboratories Pty Ltd v Federal Commissioner of Taxation*[69], Windeyer J spoke of the essential nature of a copyright:

> "It is not a right in an existing physical thing. It is a negative right, as it has been called, a power to prevent the making of a physical thing by copying."

To similar effect, in relation to patents, was the observation of Lord Herschell LC in *Steers v Rogers*[70], quoted with approval by the plurality in *The Grain Pool of Western Australia v The Commonwealth*[71]:

> "The truth is that letters patent do not give the patentee any right to use the invention — they do not confer upon him a right to manufacture according to his invention. That is a right which he would have equally effectually if there were no letters patent at all; only in that case all the world would equally have the right. What the letters patent confer is the right to exclude others from manufacturing in a particular way, and using a particular invention."

37. The Commonwealth submitted that the property rights associated with the registered trade marks, design, patents and copyright asserted by JTI and BAT involve "a statutory assurance of exclusive use, not a positive right or authority to use." On that basis the imposition of restrictions on their use would take nothing away from the rights granted. Therefore, it was submitted, no property had been taken by the TPP Act. BAT stigmatised that argument as formalistic, observing that rights of exclusion are of the essence of all proprietary rights[72]. Plainly, not all property rights are defined only by rights of exclusion. In law the term "property" generally refers to "a legal relationship with a thing"[73] and in many cases is helpfully described as "a bundle of rights"[74]. However, BAT correctly submitted that rights to exclude others from using property have no substance if all use of the property is prohibited.

38. The Commonwealth's submission points to a characteristic of the plaintiffs' asserted rights which may be relevant in determining, inter alia, whether or not they can be said to have been the subject of acquisition in terms of any benefit that could be said to have accrued to the Commonwealth. That consideration does not involve an acceptance of the proposition that rights were not taken in the sense that JTI and BAT were deprived of their ability to enjoy the fruits of their statutory monopolies.

39. BAT complained of acquisition of its goodwill. The concept of goodwill as property, and its characterisation as property or a proprietary right, arise in different contexts, discussed at length in the joint judgment in *Federal Commissioner of Taxation v Murry*[75]. As their Honours pointed out[76]:

> "Goodwill is correctly identified as property, therefore, because it is the legal right or privilege to conduct a business in substantially the same manner and by substantially the same means that have attracted custom to it." (footnote omitted)

Goodwill is derived from the use of the assets and other elements or attributes of a business. It may have different aspects or components corresponding to its sources. Goodwill derived from the use of a trade mark, registered or unregistered, or from a particular get-up, may be protected by an action for passing off. Lockhart J observed in *Conagra Inc v McCain Foods (Aust) Pty Ltd*[77]:

> "It is now beyond argument that the plaintiff's right which the law of passing off protects is a proprietary right in the goodwill or reputation of his business likely to be injured by the defendant's conduct."

That cause of action serves the purpose, which is its "underlying rationale", of preventing commercial dishonesty[78].

40. It has rightly been said that "[t]here is no 'property' in the accepted sense of the word in a get-up"[79]. The rights associated with a particular get-up, which may also be viewed as a species of common law trade mark, are the rights to protect goodwill by passing off actions or the statutory cause of action for misleading or deceptive conduct where another has made unauthorised use of the get-up in a way which satisfies the relevant criteria for liability. The get-up rights asserted by JTI and BAT and the other non-statutory rights are, like their statutory equivalents, exclusive rights which are negative in character and support protective actions against the invasion of goodwill.

. . .

(c) Territoriality And Copyright

SOCAN v. Canadian Assn. of Internet Providers, 2004 SCC 45 (S.C.C.) at p. 628

1 BINNIE J. — This appeal raises the difficult issue of who should compensate musical composers and artists for their Canadian copyright in music downloaded

in Canada from a foreign country via the Internet. In an era when it is as easy to access a website hosted by a server in Bangalore as it is to access a website with a server in Mississauga, where is the protection for the financial rights of the people who created the music in the first place? Who, if anyone, is to pay the piper?

2 The Internet "exists", notionally, in cyberspace. It has been described as a "fascinating exercise in symbiotic anarchy"; see G. S. Takach, *Computer Law* (2nd ed. 2003), at p. 30. It is not contained by national boundaries. The Internet thus presents a particular challenge to national copyright laws, which are typically territorial in nature.

3 The answer to this challenge proposed by the respondent, the Society of Composers, Authors and Music Publishers of Canada ("SOCAN"), is to seek to impose liability for royalties on the various Internet Service Providers located in Canada irrespective of where the transmission originates. There is no doubt that such an imposition, from SOCAN's perspective, would provide an efficient engine of collection.

4 The appellants, on the other hand, representing a broad coalition of Canadian Internet Service Providers, resist. Their basic argument is that none of them, as found by the Copyright Board, regulate or are even in the usual case *aware* of the content of the Internet communications which they transmit. Like a telephone company, they provide the medium, but they do not control the message.

5 Parliament has spoken on this issue. In a 1988 amendment to the *Copyright Act*, R.S.C. 1985, c. C-42, it made it clear that Internet intermediaries, as such, are not to be considered parties to the infringing communication. They are service providers, not participants in the *content* of the communication. In light of Parliament's legislative policy, when applied to the findings of fact by the Copyright Board, I agree with the Board's conclusion that as a matter of law the appellants did not, in general, "communicate"or "authorize" the communication of musical works in Canada in violation of the respondent's copyright within the meaning of the *Copyright Act*.

6 SOCAN sought a judicial review of the Board's decision by the Federal Court of Appeal, which essentially upheld the Board's exclusion of the appellants from copyright liability where they perform a pure intermediary function: [2002] 4 F.C. 3. However, the court, in a 2-1 majority decision, also held that where an Internet Service Provider in Canada creates a "cache"of Internet material, even for purely technical reasons, they are no longer a mere intermediary but a communicator and thus become a participant in the copyright infringement. A contrary conclusion was reached by Sharlow J.A., dissenting in part, who agreed with the Copyright Board that to cache for the purpose of enhancing Internet economy and efficiency does not constitute infringement. I agree with the dissent on this point. To that extent, the appeal should be allowed.

7 The respondent's cross-appeal seeking to hold Internet intermediaries liable for copyright royalties even where serving only as a conduit should be dismissed.

I.   Facts

8 The Internet is a huge communications facility which consists of a world-wide network of computer networks deployed to communicate information. A"content provider" uploads his or her data, usually in the form of a website, to a host server. The content is then forwarded to a destination computer (the end user). End users and content providers can connect to the Internet with a modem under contract with an Internet Service Provider.

9 An Internet transmission is generally made in response to a request sent over the Internet from the end user (referred to as a "pull"). The host server provider transmits content (usually in accordance with its contractual obligation to the content provider). The content at issue here is the copyrighted musical works in SOCAN's repertoire.

10 In its decision dated October 27, 1999 ((1999), 1 C.P.R. (4th) 417, at p. 441), the Copyright Board provided a succinct description of an Internet transmission:

> First, the file is incorporated to an Internet-accessible server. Second, upon request and at a time chosen by the recipient, the file is broken down into packets and transmitted from the host server to the recipient's server, via one or more routers. Third, the recipient, usually using a computer, can reconstitute and open the file upon reception or save it to open it later; either action involves a reproduction of the file, again as that term is commonly understood.

11 The respondent, SOCAN, is a collective society recognized under s. 2 of the Copyright Act, to administer "performing rights" in Canada including those of (1) its Canadian member composers, authors and music publishers, and (2) foreign composers, authors and music publishers whose interest is protected by a system of reciprocal agreements with counterpart societies here and in other countries. Essentially, SOCAN administers in Canada "the world repertoire of copyright protected music".

12 In 1995, SOCAN applied to the Copyright Board for approval of Tariff 22 applicable to Internet telecommunications of copyrighted music. Tariff 22 would require a licence and a royalty fee

> to communicate to the public by telecommunication, in Canada, musical works forming part of SOCAN's repertoire, by a telecommunications service to sub-scribers by means of one or more computer(s) or other device that is connected to a telecommunications network where the transmission of those works can be accessed by each subscriber independently of any other person having access to the service . . . .

13 Recognizing that there might be many participants in any Internet commu-nication, the Board convened a Phase I hearing to "determine which activities on the Internet, if any, constitute a protected use targeted in the tariff" (p. 424).

14 SOCAN initially argued that "virtually everyone involved in the Internet transmission chain is liable [to pay royalties] for the communication, including those who provide transmission services, operate equipment or software used

for transmissions, provide connectivity, provide hosting services or post content" (p. 426).

15 SOCAN now disclaims any intent to target the Backbone Service Providers, which are the entities that do not retail Internet services to individual subscribers but provide the facilities and long distance connections including fibre optics and telephone lines that support the Internet.

16 The appellants, on the other hand, stand at the portals of the Internet. They operate the infrastructure provided by the Backbone Service Providers. They retail access to the Internet both to content providers and to end user subscribers. Familiar examples include Bell Globemedia's"Sympatico" service and the Rogers "Hi-Speed Internet" service. As such, according to SOCAN, they are not passive conduits like the Backbone Service Providers but active participants in the alleged acts of copyright infringement.

17 The Internet operates by means of a series of protocols that enable higher level applications such as the World Wide Web to operate. Transmission control protocol ("TCP") is the most common protocol and it controls most of the applications used on the Internet. The TCP resides in both host server and end user computers and it controls the sending and receipt of packets transmitted over the Internet. However, routers and other intermediate points on the Internet have no involvement in TCP operation.

18 A content provider may store files on its own computer, but it may also purchase space on a "host server" operated by an Internet Service Provider under commercial arrangements that include storing, making available and transmitting Web site content to end users. Once a musical work or other content has been posted on a host server, it is possible for any person with a computer and an arrangement with an Internet Service Provider to access the work on demand from anywhere in the world via the Internet.

19 The Copyright Board found that Internet Service Providers who "host" Web sites for others are generally neither aware of nor control the content of the files stored in memory; however, in some cases they do warn content providers not to post illegal content (e.g., criminal pornography, defamatory material, copyright infringing materials, viruses, etc.), and will usually retain a master "root" password that allows them to access all the files on the server. The contract generally reserves to the host server provider the authority to periodically review for content posted in breach of their agreement and to remove such files. The existence of such means of control, and the host server provider's discretion in whether or not to exercise them, justifies the imposition of liability for a copyright licence on host servers, according to SOCAN.

20 The host server breaks the content down into units of data called"packets" consisting of a series of bytes (typically no more than 1500). Each packet has a destination address attached to it in the form of a "header". The host server transmits the packets to a router which reads the address in the packet's header and performs computations to determine the most appropriate transmission

route over which to send the packet to its destination. The router does not access the data portion of the packet. The various packets are forwarded from router to router and may follow different transmission routes along the way until they reach the Internet Service Provider at the receiving end which, under contract to the end user, transmits the packets to a computer operated by the end user. The result is the reconstitution on the end user's computer of all that is required to view or, in the case of music, "to play"the work, either at that time or later if the work is saved on the end user's computer.

21 It is evident that a single corporate entity like Rogers, Bell or AT&T Canada can play a variety of roles in Internet transmission. The Board's analysis therefore focussed on what functions attract copyright liability. To the extent a particular entity performs a specified function, it may be liable for copyright infringement in respect of the functionunless licensed.

22 The appellants initially argued against copyright liability on the theory that intermediaries only handle "packets" of incomplete music in computer coded compressed form, which may be sent or received out of order. In their view they were not communicating the musical works as such, and thus could not be guilty of copyright infringement. This was rejected by the Copyright Board on the basis that the fragmentation into packets was dictated by "the technical exigencies of the Internet" (at p. 447):

> While some intermediaries may not be transmitting the entire work or a substantial part of a work, all of the packets required to communicate the work are transmitted from the server on which the work is located to the end user. Consequently, the work is communicated.

The correctness of this finding is no longer contested.

23 A particular issue arose in respect of the appellants' use of"caching". When an end user visits a Web site, the packets of data needed to transmit the requested information will come initially from the host server where the files for this site are stored. As they pass through the hands of an Internet Service Provider, a temporary copy may be made and stored on its server. This is a cache copy. If another user wants to visit this page shortly thereafter, using the same Internet Service Provider, the information may be transmitted to the subsequent user either directly from the Web site or from what is kept in the cache copy. The practice of creating "caches" of data speeds up the transmission and lowers the cost. The subsequent end user may have no idea that it is not getting the information directly from the original Web site. Cache copies are not retained for long periods of time since, if the original files change, users will get out-of-date information. The Internet Service Provider controls the existence and duration of caches on its own facility, although in some circumstances it is open to a content provider to specify no caching, or an end user to program its browser to insist on content from the original Web site.

24 SOCAN argued that where a cache copy is made on a computer located in Canada and then retransmitted, there is a distinct violation in Canada of

copyright protection. This, as stated, is the issue that divided the Federal Court of Appeal.

25 The Board was also required to consider the potential copyright infringement of "hyperlinks", particularly when the link is automatic. Automatic links employ an embedded code in the Web page that automatically instructs the browser, upon obtaining access to the first site, to download a file from a second site. The user does not need to do anything but visit the initial site before information from the second site is "pulled". A different legal issue may arise where the user must take action, such as to click the mouse button over the hyperlink, in order to obtain access to the information from the second site.

26 While much of the Internet discussion focussed on music available on the World Wide Web, Tariff 22 may also apply to copyrighted music sent by e-mail or displayed on business bulletin boards or other Internet applications.

50 None of the parties is challenging the Board's view of the facts themselves. It is the legal significance of the facts that is in issue. In my view, accordingly, the decision of the Board on the legal questions at issue in this appeal should be reviewed on a correctness standard.

C. Application and Scope of the Copyright Act

51 The Federal Court of Appeal was unanimous in its conclusion that copyright infringement occurs in Canada where there is a real and substantial connection between this country and the communication at issue. Evans J.A. stated, at para. 191:

> In my opinion, therefore, the Copyright Board erred in law when it ignored all connecting factors other than the location of the host server for the purpose of identifying communications that occur in Canada and can therefore attract liability to pay a royalty to SOCAN.

52 I agree with the general proposition that the Board erred in holding that the only relevant connection between Canada and the communication is the location of the host server. As a matter of international law and practice, as well as the legislative reach of our Parliament, Canada's jurisdiction is not so limited.

53 It is a different issue, however, whether Canada intended to exerciseits copyright jurisdiction to impose copyright liability on every participant in an Internet communication with "a real and substantial connection" to Canada. This second issue raises questions of statutory interpretation of the Copyright Act.

1.   Canada's Legislative Reach

54 While the Parliament of Canada, unlike the legislatures of the Provinces, has the legislative competence to enact laws having extraterritorial effect, it is presumed not to intend to do so, in the absence of clear words or necessary implication to the contrary. This is because "[i]n our modern world of easy travel and with the emergence of a global economic order, chaotic situations would often result if the principle of territorial jurisdiction were not, at least

generally, respected"; see Tolofson v. Jensen, [1994] 3 S.C.R. 1022, at p. 1051, per La Forest J.

55 While the notion of comity among independent nation States lacks the constitutional status it enjoys among the provinces of the Canadian federation (Morguard Investments Ltd. v. De Savoye, [1990] 3 S.C.R. 1077, at p. 1098), and does not operate as a limitation on Parliament's legislative competence, the courts nevertheless presume, in the absence of clear words to the contrary, that Parliament did not intend its legislation to receive extraterritorial application.

56 Copyright law respects the territorial principle, reflecting the implementation of a "web of interlinking international treaties" based on the principle of national treatment (see D. Vaver, Copyright Law (2000), at p. 14).

57 The applicability of our Copyright Act to communications that have international participants will depend on whether there is a sufficient connection between this country and the communication in question for Canada to apply its law consistent with the "principles of order and fairness . . . that ensure security of [cross-border] transactions with justice"; see Morguard Investments, supra, at p. 1097; see also Unifund Assurance Co. v. Insurance Corp. of British Columbia, [2003] 2 S.C.R. 63, 2003 SCC 40, at para. 56; Sullivan and Driedger on the Construction of Statutes (4th ed. 2002), at pp. 601-2.

58 Helpful guidance on the jurisdictional point is offered by La Forest J. in Libman v. The Queen, [1985] 2 S.C.R. 178. That case involved a fraudulent stock scheme. U.S. purchasers were solicited by telephone from Toronto, and their investment monies (which the Toronto accused caused to be routed through Central America) wound up in Canada. The accused contended that the crime, if any, had occurred in the United States, but La Forest J. took the view that "[t]his kind of thinking has, perhaps not altogether fairly, given rise to the reproach that a lawyer is a person who can look at a thing connected with another as not being so connected. For everyone knows that the transaction in the present case is both here and there" (p. 208 (emphasis added)). Speaking for the Court, he stated the relevant territorial principle as follows (at pp. 212-13):

> I might summarize my approach to the limits of territoriality in this way. As I see it, all that is necessary to make an offence subject to the jurisdiction of our courts is that a <u>significant portion of the activities constituting that offence</u> took place in Canada. As it is put by modern academics, it is sufficient that there be a "real and substantial link" between an offence and this country . . . . [Emphasis added.]

59 So also, in my view, a telecommunication from a foreign state to Canada, or a telecommunication from Canada to a foreign state, "is both here and there". Receipt may be no less "significant" a connecting factor than the point of origin (not to mention the physical location of the host server, which may be in a third country). To the same effect, see Canada (Human Rights Commission) v. Canadian Liberty Net, [1998] 1 S.C.R. 626, at para. 52; Kitakufe v. Oloya, [1998] O.J. No. 2537 (QL) (Gen. Div.). In the factual situation at issue in Citron v. Zundel, supra, for example, the fact that the host server was located in California was scarcely conclusive in a situation where both the content provider

(Zundel) and a major part of his target audience were located in Canada. The Zundel case was decided on grounds related to the provisions of the Canadian Human Rights Act, but for present purposes the object lesson of those facts is nevertheless instructive.

60 The "real and substantial connection" test was adopted and developed by this Court in Morguard Investments, supra, at pp. 1108-9; Hunt v. T&N plc, [1993] 4 S.C.R. 289, at pp. 325-26 and 328; and Tolofson, supra, at p. 1049. The test has been reaffirmed and applied more recently in cases such as Holt Cargo Systems Inc. v. ABC Containerline N.V. (Trustees of), [2001] 3 S.C.R. 907, 2001 SCC 90, at para. 71; Spar Aerospace Ltd. v. American Mobile Satellite Corp., [2002] 4 S.C.R. 205, 2002 SCC 78; Unifund, supra, at para. 54; and Beals v. Saldanha, [2003] 3 S.C.R. 416, 2003 SCC 72. From the outset, the real and substantial connection test has been viewed as an appropriate way to "prevent overreaching . . . and [to restrict] the exercise of jurisdiction over extraterritorial and transnational transactions" (La Forest J. in Tolofson, supra, at p. 1049). The test reflects the underlying reality of "the territorial limits of law under the international legal order" and respect for the legitimate actions of other states inherent in the principle of international comity (Tolofson, at p. 1047). A real and substantial connection to Canada is sufficient to support the application of our Copyright Act to international Internet transmissions in a way that will accord with international comity and be consistent with the objectives of order and fairness.

61 In terms of the Internet, relevant connecting factors would include the situs of the content provider, the host server, the intermediaries and the end user. The weight to be given to any particular factor will vary with the circumstances and the nature of the dispute.

62 Canada clearly has a significant interest in the flow of information in and out of the country. Canada regulates the reception of broadcasting signals in Canada wherever originated; see Bell ExpressVu Limited Partnership v. Rex, [2002] 2 S.C.R. 559, 2002 SCC 42. Our courts and tribunals regularly take jurisdiction in matters of civil liability arising out of foreign transmissions which are received and have their impact here; see WIC Premium Television Ltd. v. General Instrument Corp. (2000), 8 C.P.R. (4th) 1 (Alta. C.A.); Re World Stock Exchange (2000), 9 A.S.C.S. 658.

63 Generally speaking, this Court has recognized, as a sufficient"connection" for taking jurisdiction, situations where Canada is the country of transmission (Libman, supra) or the country of reception (Liberty Net, supra). This jurisdictional posture is consistent with international copyright practice.

64 In a recent decision of the European Commission involving"simulcasting", a model reciprocal agreement approved by the Commission was based on the country-of-destination principle. The decision commented that according to the principle "which appears to reflect the current legal situation in copyright law, the act of communication to the public of a copyright protected work takes place not only in the country of origin (emission-State) but also in all the States where

the signals can be received(reception-States)": Commission Decision of 8 October 2002 relating to a proceeding under Article 81 of the EC Treaty and Article 53 of the EEA Agreement (Case No. COMP/C2/38.014 _IFPI "Simulcasting"), para. 21 (emphasis added).

65 Canada is a signatory but not yet a party to the WIPO Copyright Treaty. This treaty responded to the development of the Internet and other on-demand telecommunications technology. Article 8 provides that:

> . . . authors of literary and artistic works shall enjoy the exclusive right of authorizing any communication to the public of their works, by wire or wireless means, including the making available to the public of their works in such a way that members of the public may access these works from a place and at a time individually chosen by them.

The "making available" right is generally exercised at the point of transmission. This does not deny the interest of the country of reception but avoids, as a matter of policy, a "layering" of royalty obligations in different countries that are parties to the WIPO Copyright Treaty.

66 In 2000, the European Commission issued what is known as its E-Commerce Directive; see Directive 2000/31/EC of the European Parliament and of the Council of 8 June 2000 on certain legal aspects of information society services, in particular electronic commerce, in the Internal Market ("Directive on electronic commerce"), [2000] O.J. L. 178/1. Its purpose was to ensure the free movement among Member States of "information society services",defined as "any service normally provided for remuneration, at a distance, by means of electronic equipment . . . and at the individual request of a recipient of a service" (Preamble, clause 17). The E-Commerce Directive preferred as a matter of policy the law of the Member State on whose territory the service provider is established (art. 3(1)). It was thought that "[i]nformation society services should be supervised at the source of the activity . . . to that end, it is necessary to ensure that the competent authority provides such protection not only for the citizens of its own country but for all Community citizens" (Preamble, clause 22 (emphasis added)). The Directive notes that the place where a service provider is established should be determined by the case law of the European Court of Justice, which holds that the proper situs is not the place where the technology is, or the place where the person accessing the service is, but rather where the service provider's centre of activities is (Preamble, clause 19); see G. J. H. Smith, Internet Law and Regulation (3rd ed. 2002), at p. 269.

67 Supranational organizations such as the European Commission may thus allocate responsibility among their member States _ whether the state of transmission or the state of reception _ as a matter of policy. In the absence of such regional or international arrangements, the territorial nature of copyright law must be respected.

68 National practice confirms that either the country of transmission or the country of reception may take jurisdiction over a"communication" linked to its territory, although whether it chooses to do so is a matter of legislative or judicial

policy; see generally M. V. Pietsch, "International Copyright Infringement and the Internet: An Analysis of the Existing Means of Enforcement" (2001-2002), 24 Hastings Comm. & Ent. L.J. 273.

(a) The United States

69 At present there is authority in the United States for taking copyright jurisdiction over both the sender of the transmission out of the United States and the receiver in the United States of material from outside that country.

70 In National Football League v. PrimeTime 24 Joint Venture, 211 F.3d 10 (2d Cir. 2000), the U.S. defendant caused satellite transmission of NFL football games from the U.S. to Canada. The court found this to violate the NFL's U.S. copyright even though the broadcasts were being sent to the satellite and thence to Canada for Canadian viewers. The United States was thecountry of transmission. It was held sufficient to constitute U.S. copyright infringement that a significant step in the telecommunication had taken place in the United States (at p. 13):

> . . . it is clear that PrimeTime's uplink transmission of signals captured in the United Sates is a step in the process by which NFL's protected work wends its way to a public audience. In short, PrimeTime publicly displayed or performed material in which the NFL owns the copyright. Because PrimeTime did not have authorization to make such a public performance, PrimeTime infringed the NFL's copyright.

71 At the same time, some U.S. courts take the view that U.S. copyright is also breached when the U.S. is the country of reception. Thus in Los Angeles News Service v. Conus Communications Co., 969 F.Supp. 579 (C.D. Cal. 1997), the plaintiff had videotaped riots that occurred in Los Angeles in connection with the Rodney King assault case. The CBC broadcast some of the footage in Canada. Inevitably, some homes in border States saw the CBC broadcast. The plaintiff alleged breach of U.S. copyright. The CBC moved to dismiss the U.S. proceeding for lack of jurisdiction, but was unsuccessful. The court held, at pp. 583-84:

> Under the plain language of the Act, the subject footage was"displayed" on television sets within the United States within the meaning of the Copyright Act. To find otherwise would leave a substantial loophole in the copyright laws. Broadcasters could deliberately transmit potentially infringing material from locations across the U.S. borders for display in the United States without regard to the rights of copyright owners set forth in the U.S. Copyright Act.

72 Equally, in National Football League v. TVRadioNow Corp., 53 USPQ2d 1831 (W.D. Pa. 2000), the court found that a Web site in Canada that"streamed" U.S. cable television through the Internet with worldwide availability infringed the U.S. transmission rights of the copyright owners despite the fact that the defendant was located in Canada and arguably was not in violation of Canadian copyright laws.

(b) Australia

73 Australia has recently adopted the Copyright Amendment (Digital Agenda) Act 2000 to implement its obligations under the WIPO treaties. The definition of "communication to the public" appears to apply Australian copyright law to communications entirely within Australia, those originating within Australia and received by an end user outside Australia, and those originating outside Australia but received by an end user in Australia:

> 10. Interpretation
>
> (1) In this Act, unless the contrary intention appears:
>
> . . .
>
> *communicate* means make available online or electronically transmit (whether over a path, or a combination of paths, provided by a material substance or otherwise) a work or other subject-matter.
>
> . . .
>
> *to the public* means to the public <u>within or outside</u> Australia. [Emphasis added.]
>
> (*Copyright Act 1968* (Australia), No. 63 of 1968, s. 10(1), as amended by the *Copyright Amendment (Digital Agenda) Act 2000*, Sch.1, ss. 6 and 16)

74 The definition of "to the public" seems to permit Australian copyright holders to exact royalties on both communication from Australia of material directed to overseas audiences as well as overseas communications received in Australia.

(c) France

75 An analysis of liability in France suggests that "[c]ourts will likely assert jurisdiction not only over transmissions from France, but also transmissions into France that are alleged to cause damage" (emphasis added); see D. J. Gervais, "Transmissions of Music on the Internet: An Analysis of the Copyright Laws of Canada, France, Germany, Japan, the United Kingdom, and the United States" (2001), 34 Vand. J. Transnatl. L. 1363, at p. 1376. In UEJF v. Yahoo! Inc., Trib. gr. inst. Paris, May 22, 2000, the court ordered Yahoo! Inc., a U.S. based Internet company, to block access by French users to an Internet auction offering Nazi paraphernalia because [translation] "the harm is suffered in France". (The U.S. courts refused to give effect in the United States to the French court order, not on jurisdictional grounds as such, but based on First Amendment rights; see Yahoo! Inc. v. Ligue contre le racisme et l'antisémitisme, 145 F.Supp.2d 1168 (N.D. Cal. 2001).)

76 Accordingly, the conclusion that Canada could exercise copyright jurisdiction in respect both of transmissions originating here and transmissions originating abroad but received here is not only consistent with our general law (Libman, supra, and Liberty Net, supra), but with both national and international copyright practice.

77 This conclusion does not, of course, imply imposition of automatic copyright liability on foreign content providers whose music is telecommunicated to a Canadian end user. Whether or not a real and substantial connection exists will turn on the facts of a particular transmission (Braintech,supra). It is unnecessary to say more on this point because the Canadian copyright liability of foreign content providers is not an issue that arises for determination in this appeal, although, as stated, the Board itself intimated that where a foreign transmission is aimed at Canada, copyright liability might attach.

78 This conclusion also raises the spectre of imposition of copyright duties on a single telecommunication in both the State of transmission and the State of reception, but as with other fields of overlapping liability (taxation for example), the answer lies in the making of international or bilateral agreements, not in national courts straining to find some jurisdictional infirmity in either State.

Public Performance of Musical Works, Re, 2010 FCA 348 (F.C.A.), leave to appeal refused 2011 CarswellNat 4155 (S.C.C.)

[1] Sharlow J.A.: These are two applications for judicial review of a decision of the Copyright Board of Canada [Board] dated April 8, 2009 (corrected May 6, 2009). The decision, reported as Satellite Radio Services — SOCAN (2005-2009); NRCC (2007-2010); CMRRA/SODRAC Inc. (2006-2009), certified certain royalty tariffs pursuant to section 70.15 [as enacted by S.C. 1997, c. 24, s. 46] of the Copyright Act, R.S.C., 1985, c. C-42, payable by Sirius Canada Inc. (Sirius) and Canadian Satellite Radio Inc. (XM Canada) in relation to their satellite radio services.

[2] The tariffs as certified are payable for the use of the repertoires of three collective societies: Society of Composers, Authors and Music Publishers of Canada (SOCAN) for the communication of musical or dramatico-musical works (2005 — 2009); Neighbouring Rights Collective of Canada (NRCC) for the communication of published sound recordings embodying musical works and performers' performances of such works (2007 — 2010); and CMRRA/SODRAC Inc. (CSI) for the reproduction of musical works (2006 — 2009).

[3] It was undisputed before the Board that SOCAN and NRCC were entitled to communication royalties from Sirius and XM Canada, the only dispute being the amount. It was also undisputed that CSI was entitled to certain reproduction royalties, but the extent of its entitlement was in dispute. The present applications, one by Sirius (A-209-09) and the other by CSI (A-210-09), challenge the Board's determination of a number of legal issues relating to the royalty entitlement of CSI. The applications were heard together. These reasons address both applications.

Facts

[4] The specific facts relating to each of the issues raised in these applications are set out with the analysis of each issue. The general background relating to

the satellite radio services offered by Sirius and XM Canada during the years relevant to these applications is described by the Board in paragraphs 8 to 26 of its decision. The accuracy of that description is undisputed and it is reproduced here (footnotes omitted):

> The satellite radio services industry originated in the United States. XM Satellite Radio (XM) launched its operation on September 25, 2001 and Sirius Satellite Radio (Sirius U.S.) launched its operation on July 1, 2002. They were the first and remain the largest operators in the world.

XM uses two high-powered geostationary satellites that rotate in synchronization with the earth and provide blanket coverage of the entire U.S. mainland and southern Canada. Sirius uses three satellites that move around the earth in an elliptical orbit. These satellites are called geosynchronous and orbit above the equator for 16 hours a day and below the equator for 8 hours permitting the satellite to sleep and conserve energy.

The multiplex signal sent by satellite to the mobile receivers is encrypted so that only those receivers equipped with a decryption key which permits the unscrambling of the signal can receive and play the signal.

The American services were able to expand into Canada by forming exclusive partnerships with Canadian corporations. On June 16, 2005, the Canadian Radio-television and Telecommunications Commission (CRTC) issued broadcasting licences to [XM Canada] and Sirius to offer satellite radio services across Canada. [XM Canada] launched its operation on November 22, 2005 and Sirius on December 1, 2005.

At the end of 2004, XM reported over 3.2 million subscribers, and Sirius U.S. had reached the one million subscriber level. At the time of the hearing, Sirius and [XM Canada] had 200,000 and 120,000 subscribers respectively. By the summer of 2008, those numbers had increased to 750,000 and 440,000. Satellite radio services quickly penetrated the market. It took Sirius U.S. 3.6 years to have 5,000,000 units in the hands of American customers, while DVDs took 2.5 years to reach the same amount, MP3 players 4.8 years, cellular phones 10 years and satellite television 10.6 years.

For our purposes, the infrastructure and operations of the two American services, on which the Canadian services rely, are fairly similar. In order to provide an uninterrupted radio broadcast service, the U.S. satellite services augment their satellite signal through the use of a network of ground transmitters. This technique, which is said to create "space diversity", prevents signal dropouts. With this combined infrastructure, the satellite services are able to deliver all of their programming to all subscribers, regardless of their location in North America at the time of reception.

In terms of programming content, although each satellite service has developed its own micro-niche programming, both offer a large selection of commercial-free music channels covering a wide range of genres as well as channels of news, children's programs, sports, comedy, talk and traffic. Additionally, a subscription to the satellite services offers the following innovative features: text display providing artists' name, songs' title, scores, stock quotations, a tagging mechanism alerting listeners when a song or an artist is playing on another channel, temporary and permanent recording options, pause and replay of live radio content, Internet service delivery of some audio channels over the Web as a streaming service as well as allowing the receiver to be used as a MP3 player.

Programming of the U.S. services is created and delivered using a content management system (CMS) located at their main broadcast studio. The objective of this system is to store once and deliver many times.

[XM Canada] uses a CMS provided by Delat Digital Media System. [XM Canada] produces and delivers 12 channels originating in Canada at studios located in Toronto and Montreal. Music directors at these two sites select the music to be used which is then injected in the system using functions of the Delat workstations located in these two cities. These workstations are directly connected to the main Delat CMS located in Washington, D.C. by a fibre optic line (OC3 line).

Sirius uses a CMS called Nex Gen but does not produce any programming in Canada. All Sirius' content in Canada is produced by Canadian third-party content providers. These providers generate and deliver the content to the Sirius master control centre located in New York City.

XM has a complex of 82 studios in Washington as well as studios in New York, Nashville and Chicago. Sirius U.S. is based out of New York and has other studios in Los Angeles and Memphis. Programming is not typically delivered live, with the obvious exception of live sporting events. Essentially, before programming can be uplinked to the satellites for delivery, programming directors must store a copy of all music and audio files required onto the main server. These files are compressed, encoded and combined to complete the process commonly referred to as "multiplexing". Selection and scheduling of programming content are done using specialized software that instructs the main server when and in what order it must play the various music or audio files. The server also serves the alternative delivery channels, including Internet and cellular phone streaming services.

Although the Canadian satellite services rely heavily on their U.S. partner's programming, the terms of their CRTC licence require them to include in their subscription package a minimum of content produced in Canada. Accordingly, out of the 130 channels [XM Canada] offers, 13 are produced in Canada while out of the 110 channels Sirius offers, 11 are produced in Canada. The Satellite Radio Services differ slightly in the way they create and deliver their Canadian content. It is useful, in light of the legal issues raised, to highlight the distinctive features of each Service.

[XM Canada] creates its own programming. A digital communication link from the Canadian offices to the U.S. infrastructure allows the work stations in Canada to send instructions directly to the servers and the scheduling software sitting in U.S. headquarters in Washington. Thus, [XM Canada] programming is conceived and controlled in Canada but produced from Washington.

[XM Canada] receives audio content in the form of CDs or through DMDS-Musicrypt service provided by the sound recording industry. When dealing with a new CD, the production team makes a copy directly on the server in the U.S. using the digital connection, without making any back up or archival copies. New music obtained through DMDS-Musicrypt is received as digital audio files from a server that sits in Canada. In this case, an intermediary copy of the file is stored on a work station located in Canada. If the Canadian production team selects the song, then that file is "transferred" onto the main server in Washington via the digital communication link.

When it comes time to scheduling program content, the programming director instructs the U.S. scheduling software to play specific songs and recorded voice elements in a certain order and at the appropriate time; the Washington server plays them off its local hard drives, combining the Canadian channels with the American ones into the common multiplex signal that is sent up to the satellite.

Unlike [XM Canada], Sirius does not produce any programming itself; it acquires all of its Canadian content from Canadian third-party content providers. Standard Radio Inc. provides Sirius with a Canadian rock music channel called Iceberg 95 created in studios located in Toronto. The content is available in CD and DMDS-Musicrypt. The music is scheduled from Toronto, loaded onto the Sirius master server where it is encoded and digitized for delivery to the server's master control centre in New York City. Astral Media provides Sirius with two Canadian rock music channels, Rock Velours and Énergie, pursuant to a subcontract with Standard Radio. The programming is created in Montreal using the same technology used by Standard Radio. The music is scheduled from Montreal on a six-hour loop for broadcast each day by a program called Music Master. Content providers store the music files and create the programming on a server located in their respective broadcast studio. Again, if musical works are provided on a CD, a digital copy is made on the content provider's server. If musical works are provided through DMDS-Musicrypt, a digital link to that service is used to copy that file onto the Canadian server. Sirius' Canadian content providers do not make archival copies of musical works.

Sirius' content providers use a specialized scheduling software that is part of their server complex to determine which songs and other recorded voice elements will be played and when. When it is time for a show to air, the scheduling system automatically plays it off the copies on the Canadian servers. That output is linked by communication lines to the U.S. facility, combined with the other American channels and uplinked to the satellites. The content used on the Canadian originated signals is never actually stored on the Sirius U.S. server.

In both cases, once the programming has been multiplexed and uplinked to the satellites, programming is delivered to the subscribers' respective receivers in Canada and the U.S. The Satellite Services' management system tells the Canadian receivers which channels a subscriber is entitled to receive and the U.S. satellite services' management system does the same for its American subscribers. Although the signal that Canadian subscribers receive holds all the channels offered by both the U.S. and Canadian Satellite Services, because the signal is encrypted, they will only have access to a subset of channels.

[35] CSI asserts a number of challenges to the Board's decision. Its challenges fall into two general categories. The first category relates to the determination of the location of the copying of a work and whether an infringing authorization can occur in relation to a copy made outside Canada. The second category relates to the copies of broadcast content made in the four-, six- or ten-second buffer memory found in all satellite radio receivers.

(1) The location of the copying of a work, and the authorization of copying outside Canada

[36] A copy of each work available for broadcast by Sirius and XM Canada resides in a main server located in the United States. When Sirius and XM Canada instruct their scheduling software to play a specific work, the instruction is sent to the United States main server, and the track for that work is uplinked from the United States main server to the satellite for transmission to Canada in the course of their Canadian broadcast activities.

[37] Some of the electronic copies of works residing in the United States main server are created by transmission from a party located in the United States based on instructions from Sirius and XM Canada. Others are transmitted from the Canadian studios of XM Canada as a step in the programming of its Canadian channels.

[38] Programming entails the selection of works, some obtained in the form of CDs and some by direct electronic transfer from DMDS-Musicrypt to XM Canada's computer in Canada. Once the XM Canada music director in Canada selects a work to be added to the XM Canada playlist, he or she engages a technological device that causes the electronic music file to be transferred from Canada to a main server located in the United States, where it remains permanently available for uplink to the satellite and transmission to Canada.

[39] The issues raised by CSI in relation to the copies of works residing in the United States main server are whether the Board erred in law when it concluded that: (a) the Board has no jurisdiction to impose a royalty tariff in respect of a copy of a work made in the United States as a direct result of an act taken by XM Canada in Canada; (b) the Board has no jurisdiction to impose a royalty tariff in respect of XM Canada's authorization in Canada of the making in the United States of a copy of a work; (c) Sirius and XM Canada did not authorize the copying in the United States of any works.

[40] The Board concluded that, when an electronic copy of a work is transmitted to and stored on the United States main server solely as a result of the act of a person in Canada, the copying occurs in the United States and therefore the Board has no jurisdiction to impose a royalty tariff in respect of that copying. In reaching that conclusion, the Board reasoned that the act of reproduction occurs in the place where the creation of the copy is completed, so that an electronic

copy of a work comes into existence in the United States when it is received by the server located in the United States. Therefore, that copy is made in the United States even if the mechanism by which the copy was created was activated in Canada.

[41] CSI argues that where the copying is initiated in Canada, the act of copying occurs in Canada because there is no person outside Canada who can be held responsible for it. This argument assumes that the making of the copy in these circumstances cannot be subject to the copyright laws of the United States, and that the owner of the United States server who permits it to be used as the repository for copies of musical works cannot be held liable under the copyright laws of the United States. This Court was referred to nothing in the record and no jurisprudence that could support this assumption, and I see no basis for accepting it.

[42] CSI also relies on the decision of eBay Canada Ltd. v. M.N.R., 2008 FCA 348, [2010] 1 F.C.R. 145, at paragraph 52, for the proposition that information stored on a computer in the United States is in law capable of being located in Canada for the purpose of section 231.6 [as am. by S.C. 2000, c. 30, s. 177] of the Income Tax Act, R.S.C., 1985 (5th Supp.), c. 1. CSI argues that, based on the reasoning in that case, the electronic copy of a musical work stored on the United States server may be treated as being located in Canada for the purposes of the Copyright Act.

[43] Nothing in eBay compels the conclusion that, for the purposes of the Copyright Act, an electronic copy of a musical work stored in a server in a particular country is also located in another country merely because there is a person in that other country who can access the copy. I would reject any such interpretation because it would necessarily mean that a specific copy of a work may, at the same moment, be within the territorial scope of the Copyright Act and the territorial scope of any number of the copyright laws of any number of other countries. That would not be consistent with the well established and well understood territorial limitation of the Copyright Act (see the Tariff 22 case, at paragraph 56).

[44] Nor can I accept the argument of CSI that the copying occurred in both Canada and the United States, so that the location of the copying for purposes of the Copyright Act should be determined on the basis of the "real and substantial connection" test as applied in the Tariff 22 case. The Tariff 22 case required a determination, for the purposes of the Copyright Act, of the location of a communication initiated in one country and received in another. Given that a communication cannot be complete without both a sender and receiver, it was necessary to adopt a principled basis for choosing whether the communication would be situated at the location of the sender or the location of the receiver. The principle applied in that case — the real and substantial connection test — is not required to determine the location of the act of copying where, as in this case, the completed copy exists only in one location.

[45] I agree with the Board that the making of a copy is not complete until it exists in some material form (see subsection 3(1) of the Copyright Act). I also agree that the electronic copies of works stored in the United States main server are outside the Board's jurisdiction, even if the copying was initiated in Canada. I am compelled to conclude that CSI's challenge to that aspect of the Board's decision cannot succeed.

[46] CSI argues in the alternative that a person who initiates, in Canada, the making of an electronic copy of a work in the United States has authorized the copying, and has thereby infringed in Canada the copyright attached to the work by virtue of the closing words of subsection 3(1) of the Copyright Act. The Board, based on its interpretation of subsection 3(1), concluded that the act of authorizing in Canada is not actionable under the Copyright Act where the primary infringement occurs outside Canada. I agree.

[47] As I interpret the closing words of subsection 3(1), the authorization of a particular act infringes copyright only if the authorized act is itself an act of infringement. Therefore, when the Board concluded correctly that it has no jurisdiction to impose a royalty tariff in relation to the copying of a work located in the United States, it was compelled to conclude that it has no jurisdiction to impose a royalty tariff in relation to the authorization of that copying, even if the authorization took place in Canada.

[48] CSI also argues that the Board should have concluded that Sirius and XM Canada authorize the copying of all musical works on the United States servers, including copies created by the act of a person in the United States. That argument too must fail, based on the interpretation of subsection 3(1) of the Copyright Act set out in the previous paragraph.

Lucasfilm Ltd v. Ainsworth, [2011] UKSC 39 (U.K. SC 2011)

Lord Phillips, President
Lord Walker
Lady Hale
Lord Mance
Lord Collins

1. The first Star Wars film (later renamed "Star Wars Episode IV — A New Hope" in order to provide for "prequels" as well as sequels) was released in the United States in 1977. It was an enormous commercial success. It won an Oscar for best costume design. This appeal is concerned with intellectual property rights in various artefacts made for use in the film. The most important of these was the Imperial Stormtrooper helmet to which the trial judge (Mann J) referred in his judgment ([2008] EWHC 1878 (Ch), [2009] FSR 103, paras [2] and [121]):

"One of the most abiding images in the film was that of the Imperial Stormtroopers. These were soldiers clad in white armour, including a white helmet which left no part of the face uncovered... The purpose of the helmet was that it was to be worn as an item of costume in a film, to identify a character, but in addition to portray something about that character — its allegiance, force, menace, purpose and, to some extent, probably its anonymity. It was a mixture of costume and prop."

The parties are agreed that for the purposes of this final appeal the helmet can be taken as the paradigm case that will be decisive of the outcome.

2. The facts are set out in the judge's clear and thorough judgment. For present purposes a brief summary will suffice. The film's story-line and characters were conceived by Mr George Lucas. Between 1974 and 1976 Mr Lucas's concept of the Imperial Stormtroopers as threatening characters in "fascist white-armoured suits" was given visual expression in drawings and paintings by an artist, Mr Ralph McQuarrie, and three-dimensional form by Mr Nick Pemberton (a freelance scenic artist and prop-maker) and Mr Andrew Ainsworth (who is skilled in vacuum-moulding in plastic). Mr Pemberton made a clay model of the helmet, which was adapted several times until Mr Lucas was happy with it. Mr Ainsworth produced several prototype vacuum-moulded helmets. Once Mr Lucas had approved the final version Mr Ainsworth made 50 helmets for use in the film. These events all took place in England. Although Mr Lucas and his companies are based in California he had come to live in England while the film was made at Elstree (there was also filming on location in Tunisia).

3. The first appellant is a Californian corporation owned by Mr Lucas. The second appellant is an English company owned by Mr Lucas. The third appellant is a Californian corporation responsible for the group's licensing activities; it is wholly owned by the first appellant. Between them these three companies own copyrights in the artistic works created for the Star Wars films, and they can be.

4. referred to generally as "Lucasfilm". Apart from the huge commercial success of the Star Wars films, Lucasfilm has built up a successful licensing business which includes licensing models of Imperial Stormtroopers and their equipment. This litigation has come about because in 2004 Mr Ainsworth, the principal respondent in this appeal, used his original tools to make versions of the Imperial Stormtrooper helmet and armour, and other artefacts that it is not necessary to detail, for sale to the public. The second respondent is a private company owned by Mr Ainsworth but for practical purposes Mr Ainsworth can be treated as the only respondent.

5. Mr Ainsworth sold some of the goods that he produced (to the value of at least $8,000 but not more than $30,000) in the United States. In 2005 Lucasfilm sued Mr Ainsworth in the United States District Court, Central District of California, and in 2006 it obtained a default judgment for $20m, $10m of which represented triple damages under the Lanham Act. The whole judgment remains unsatisfied. Lucasfilm also commenced proceedings in the Chancery Division of the English High Court. The re-amended particulars of claim put forward a variety of claims under English law, including infringement of copyright (paras

(1) to (10) of the prayer for relief); a claim for enforcement of the United States judgment to the extent of $10m (para (11)); and claims under United States copyright law (paras (12) to (17)).

6. The trial occupied 17 days during April and May 2008. In his judgment delivered on 31 July 2008 Mann J dismissed all Lucasfilm's claims based on English copyright law (together with some other claims that are no longer pursued). He held that the helmet made by Mr Ainsworth was a substantial reproduction of original work carried out by Mr McQuarrie and other persons working for Lucasfilm. But the English copyright claims failed because the helmet was not a work of sculpture and Mr Ainsworth had defences (to a claim that he was reproducing Mr McQuarrie's work) under sections 51 and 52 of the Copyright Designs and Patents Act 1988 ("the 1988 Act"). The judge also dismissed Mr Ainsworth's counterclaim based on his own claim to copyright in the helmet.

7. The judge held that the United States judgment was unenforceable for want of personal jurisdiction over Mr Ainsworth and his company. But he held that Lucasfilm's United States copyright claims were justiciable in England and that Mr Ainsworth and his company had infringed those rights.

8. The Court of Appeal ([2009] EWCA Civ 1328, [2010] Ch 503) agreed with the judge that the United States judgment is unenforceable, and there is no further appeal on that point. The Court of Appeal also agreed with the judge that any intellectual property rights in the helmet belong to Lucasfilm, and this Court has refused Mr Ainsworth permission to cross-appeal on that point. The issues that are open in this Court are whether the helmet was a sculpture and the defences under sections 51 and 52 of the 1988 Act (on all of which the Court of Appeal agreed with the judge) and justiciability in England of the United States copyright claims (on which the Court of Appeal disagreed with the judge). The issues on sections 51 and 52 arise only if the helmet was a sculpture (and so an artistic work) within the meaning of the 1988 Act. In the Court of Appeal Lucasfilm abandoned its alternative contention that the helmet qualified as an artistic work because it was a work of artistic craftsmanship.

50. The appellants accept that if the helmet did not qualify as a sculpture within the meaning of the 1988 Act, then Mr Ainsworth had a defence under section 51 to any infringement claim based on Mr McQuarrie's graphics, and section 52 does not arise. The Court of Appeal dealt with these sections, for completeness, in paras 83 to 98 of its judgment. It is unnecessary to cover the same ground again. We would dismiss the appeal so far as it is based on the English law of copyright.

Part II: Whether a claim against a defendant domiciled in England for infringement of a foreign copyright is justiciable

The decision of the Court of Appeal and the issue on the appeal

51. The issue on this aspect of the appeal is a narrow one, whether the English court may exercise jurisdiction in a claim against persons domiciled in England

for infringement of copyright committed outside the European Union in breach of the copyright law of that country. That issue has raised two questions. The first question is whether a claim for infringement of a foreign copyright is non-justiciable. The second question only arises if the answer to the first question is in the affirmative: the question would then arise whether the English court is in any event required to accept jurisdiction by virtue of Council Regulation (EC) No 44/2001 on jurisdiction and the enforcement of judgments in civil and commercial matters (the Brussels I Regulation), article 2, which provides that, subject to the terms of the Regulation, persons domiciled in a Member State shall be sued in the courts of that Member State.

52. The Court of Appeal decided that the claim for breach of the United States copyright was non-justiciable. It held that the rule in *British South Africa Co v Companhia de Moçambique* [1893] AC 602 that the English court has no jurisdiction to entertain an action for the determination of the title to, or the right to possession of, foreign land, or the recovery of damages for trespass to such land, was an example of a general principle which applied not only to foreign land, but also to claims for infringement of foreign intellectual property rights, including copyright, irrespective of whether issues of title or validity were involved; and irrespective of whether the rights required registration (such as trade marks or registered designs) or not. It also held that article 2 of the Brussels I Regulation did not require the English court to exercise jurisdiction.

53. The substantial question on this aspect of the appeal is whether, as Lucasfilm contends, the Court of Appeal was wrong, as a matter of law and policy, to extend to foreign copyrights the common law rule in the *Moçambique* case that actions for damages for infringement or invasion of property rights in foreign land are not justiciable.

The foreign land rule and its application to intellectual property: British South Africa Co v Companhia de Moçambique and Potter v Broken Hill Pty Co Ltd

54. Some legal archaeology is necessary for an understanding of how the law developed to the point where the English courts, at first instance and in the Court of Appeal, decided that claims for infringement of foreign copyright were not justiciable in England.

British South Africa Co v Companhia de Moçambique

55. The decision in the *Moçambique* case is the authoritative foundation for the rule that the English court "has no jurisdiction to entertain an action for (1) the determination of the title to, or the right to the possession of, any immovable situate out of England ... or (2) the recovery of damages for trespass to such immovable" (*Dicey, Conflict of Laws*, 1st ed (1896), pp 214-215, Rule 39). The rule has for long been subject to an exception where there is a contract, or an equity, between the parties, which the courts of equity will enforce: ibid, p 216; *Penn v Lord Baltimore* (1750) 1 Ves Sen 444.

56. As the House of Lords noted, in the United States there is a similar local action rule (based on *Livingston v Jefferson*, 15 Fed Cas 660 (CCD Va, 1811), Marshall CJ on circuit) for actions to determine title: see *Hay, Borchers & Symeonides, Conflict of Laws*, 5th ed (2010), para 7.7. But the current prevailing view in the United States is that the local action rule does not apply to actions for trespass to foreign land: Restatement Second, *Conflict of Laws*, section 87 (1971). It seems also that that part of the rule which denies jurisdiction for trespass to foreign land had no counterpart outside common law countries (*Rabel, Conflict of Laws: A Comparative Study*, 2nd ed, (1960) vol 2, p 47; *Wolff, Private International Law*, 2nd ed (1950), p 92; and for the position in France see Audit, *Droit International Privé*, 6th ed (2010), para 346), and, as will be seen, although the House of Lords refused to reconsider the trespass rule, it no longer applies at least as regards land in other Member States of the European Union.

57. The speeches of Lord Herschell LC and Lord Halsbury (and, in the Court of Appeal, of Lord Esher MR, whose dissenting judgment was upheld in the House of Lords) are substantially based on *Story's Conflict of Laws*. The essence of the decision is that jurisdiction in relation to land is local (that is, the claim has a necessary connection with a particular locality) as opposed to transitory (where such a connection is not necessary) and that it is contrary to international law, or comity, for one state to exercise jurisdiction in relation to land in another state. Lord Esher MR said ([1892] 2 QB 358, 398):

> "...an action quare clausum fregit cannot be entertained by an English Court in respect of an alleged wrongful entry on land situated abroad; and ... the ground of the inability is ... no consent of other nations by way of comity to the exercise of such jurisdiction can be inferred."

58. Lord Herschell LC and Lord Halsbury relied in particular on Story's quotation (*Story, Conflict of Laws*, section 553, from the 1st edition in 1834 to the 8th edition in 1883) of a translation of a passage in Vattel's *Droit des Gens*, which concluded that, in the case of an action relating to an estate in land, or to a right annexed to such an estate: [1893] AC at 622, 631:

> "in such a case, inasmuch as property of the kind is to be held according to the laws of the country where it is situated, and as the right of granting it is vested in the ruler of the country, controversies relating to such property can only be decided in the state in which it depends."

59. In *Hesperides Hotels Ltd v Aegean Turkish Holidays Ltd* [1979] AC 508 Lord Wilberforce said (at p 537) that the foreign land rule involved "possible conflict with foreign jurisdictions, and the possible entry into and involvement with political questions of some delicacy;" and Viscount Dilhorne said (at p 541) that: "Questions of comity of nations may well be involved".

60. The leading cases all involved unusual factual situations in which the claim had major political ramifications, and in which, therefore, issues of international law and comity were engaged. The Moçambique company was a Portuguese company (with substantial British ownership) effectively in control of Mozambique and Cecil Rhodes' British South Africa Co was effectively in control of

Southern Rhodesia. The *Moçambique* case was a battle between them over mines in territories which were claimed by Portugal. In *Hesperides Hotels* the plaintiffs were Greek Cypriot hotel owners who were seeking to establish that their hotels in Northern Cyprus had been illegally requisitioned by the authorities of the unrecognised Turkish Federated State of North Cyprus. Similarly, in the leading case on the related, and more general, principle that the courts will not adjudicate upon the transactions of foreign sovereign states, *Buttes Gas and Oil Co v Hammer (No 3)* [1982] AC 888, Occidental Petroleum was endeavouring to establish that Buttes and the Ruler of Sharjah had fraudulently deprived Occidental of the benefit of its oil concession in the neighbouring emirate of Umm al Qaywayn.

Potter v Broken Hill Pty Co Ltd

61. It is inevitable that any discussion of the justiciability of claims for infringement of foreign intellectual property rights must begin with the influential decision in *Potter v Broken Hill Pty Co Ltd* [1905] VLR 612, affd (1906) 3 CLR 479, which is generally (but not entirely accurately) regarded as based on an extension of the *Moçambique* rule to actions for infringement of patents. At a time when patents were granted by the several States in Australia, Potter obtained a patent in Victoria for the separation of metals from sulphide ores and a patent for the same process in New South Wales. Potter claimed that (as well as a threatened infringement of the Victorian patent in Victoria) the defendant company (now BHP Billiton) had infringed the New South Wales patent at its mine in New South Wales. Broken Hill denied novelty and utility, but also said that an action for the infringement in New South Wales of a New South Wales patent was not justiciable in the Victorian courts. The question of justiciability was argued as a preliminary matter before the Full Court of the Supreme Court of Victoria, which decided by a majority that the claim was not justiciable, and an appeal to the High Court of Australia was dismissed.

62. As already mentioned, the decision is generally regarded as based on the *Moçambique* rule. Although the *Moçambique* rule is one of the elements in the conclusion of the High Court, an examination of the way in which the case was argued, and of the reasoning of the High Court, shows that it is a decision extending the act of state doctrine to foreign patents. There are four strands to the conclusions reached by the Full Court and the High Court of Australia. The first strand is in the judgment of Hodges J (with whom Hood J concurred) in the Full Court. That strand is based on that aspect of the *Moçambique* rule which turns on the distinction between local and transitory actions. He considered that the patent had a definite locality: Potter claimed in effect that in no building and on no land in New South Wales could the company use his invention. It was a claim made in respect of a defined area, the whole of which was outside the jurisdiction of the court in Victoria.

63. The second strand is found only in the judgment of Hood J in the Full Court, but it finds an echo in later English decisions, and that is that the action was precluded by what became known as the first branch of the rule in *Phillips v Eyre*

(1870) LR 6 QB 1, namely that an act done abroad was only actionable in England if it was actionable as a tort according to English law, that is, was an act, which if done in England, would be a tort. The rule as then understood showed what became the first limb of the rule as the second limb in these terms: "An act done in a foreign country is a tort if it is *both* (1) wrongful according to the law of the country where it was done, *and*, (2) wrongful according to English law, ie, is an act which, if done in England, would be a tort" (*Dicey, Conflict of Laws*, 1st ed (1896), Rule 175, p 659). Hood J considered that the rule was not satisfied because Potter could not show that, if the act had been committed in Victoria, it would have been actionable there, because infringement of a New South Wales patent in Victoria was not actionable in Victoria: the act of Broken Hill, " 'using and working' certain alleged inventions in New South Wales — even though it be wrong by the law of that State, would not be actionable if committed here" (at p 631).

64. The third strand is found in the reliance on the *Moçambique* case by the High Court of Australia. Both Griffiths CJ and Barton J said that the question did not depend on the distinction between local and transitory actions. They (and the third member of the court, O'Connor J) took their inspiration from those parts of the speeches in the House of Lords, and of the dissenting judgment of Lord Esher MR in the Court of Appeal, which emphasised that rights in immovables were created by the exercise of the sovereign power of the State, and that controversies relating to such property could only be decided in that State. So also, they reasoned, the comity of nations required a similar rule for patents: especially (1906) 3 CLR 479, 495, 502.

65. The appeal was first argued in November 1905, but the report shows (at p 486) that on 27 February 1906:

> "The matter was, at the desire of the Court, further argued on the point whether the Courts of one State can enquire into the propriety or validity of an attempted exercise of the sovereign power of another State."

66. As a result there is a fourth, and decisive, strand in the decision, namely the act of state doctrine. The classic statement of the act of state doctrine was enunciated by Fuller CJ in the United States Supreme Court in *Underhill v Hernandez*, 168 US 250, 252 (1897):

> "Every sovereign State is bound to respect the independence of every other sovereign State, and the Courts of one country will not sit in judgment on the acts of the government of another done within its own territory. Redress of grievances by reason of such acts must be obtained through the means open to be availed of by sovereign powers as between themselves."

67. This principle had its origin, as appears clearly from the decision of the lower court in that case, in the decision of the House of Lords in *Duke of Brunswick v Duke of Hanover* (1848) 2 HLC 1, 17, in which it was said: "the courts of this country cannot sit in judgment upon an act of a sovereign, effected by virtue of his sovereign authority abroad ...": see *Underhill v Hernandez*, 65 F 577 (2d Cir 1895). As re-stated by the United States Supreme Court, the act of

state doctrine was re-imported into English law in *Luther v Sagor* [1921] 3 KB 532 (CA).

68. All three members of the High Court of Australia quoted and applied *Underhill v Hernandez* and it is the act of state doctrine, rather than the *Moçambique* rule, which is the essential foundation of the judgments in the High Court. Thus Griffith CJ said that if a government had granted a monopoly in respect of an alleged invention which was not new, the government must have been misled: at pp 498-499. Barton J thought that the whole subject matter of the action was excluded from the cognizance or competence of Victoria, and its courts could not sit in judgment to determine whether such rights were validly granted: at p 503. O'Connor J said that a court could not enquire into the validity of a patent, any more than it could enquire into the validity of a concession granted by the Czar: at p 513.

69. Consequently the effect of the decision in *Potter v Broken Hill Pty Co Ltd* was to apply the *Moçambique* rule and, especially, the act of state doctrine to actions for patent infringement. It received no attention in the English case-law until it was mentioned by Lord Wilberforce in *Hesperides Hotels Ltd v Aegean Turkish Holidays Ltd* [1979] AC 508, 536 as authority for the proposition that the *Moçambique* rule applied in Australia. It was only from the 1980s that it came to be regarded as a significant authority in the field of transnational intellectual property litigation: *Def Lepp Music v Stuart-Brown* [1986] RPC 273; *Tyburn Productions Ltd v Conan Doyle* [1991] Ch 75 (both copyright cases).

Subsequent developments

70. There have been major developments since the decisions in the *Moçambique* case and *Potter v Broken Hill Pty Co Ltd*, which have to a significant extent undermined them, and to which it is now necessary to turn.

71. The questions to which these developments are relevant are these: (1) whether there is a distinction between actions to determine title and/or validity and actions for infringement of rights; (2) whether there is a distinction between actions for infringement which raise issues of title and/or validity and actions for infringement which do not; (3) whether there is a distinction between intellectual property rights which require registration or prior examination and those which do not, and in particular whether there is a relevant distinction between copyright and other intellectual property rights, especially patents; (4) whether the conflict of laws rules relating to tortious conduct abroad have undermined the older decisions; and (5) whether the act of state doctrine has any relevance to actions for infringement of intellectual property rights.

The Moçambique rule

72. To the extent that the principles in *Potter v Broken Hill Pty Co Ltd* were based on that part of the rule in the *Moçambique* case which precluded actions for damages for infringement of property rights (in that case damages for trespass), they have been fatally undermined so far as English law is concerned.

That part of the rule was confirmed by the House of Lords in *Hesperides Hotels Ltd v Aegean Turkish Holidays Ltd* [1979] AC 508. The House of Lords not only refused an invitation to depart from that part of the rule, but also extended it by holding that it applied when no question of title was involved. Lord Wilberforce said (at p 541) that questions of comity might well be involved, and it had to be for Parliament to change the law.

73. That invitation was taken up, and that part of the *Moçambique* rule was abolished by section 30(1) of the Civil Jurisdiction and Judgments Act 1982, which came into force in 1982, and provides:

> "The jurisdiction of any court in England . . . to entertain proceedings for trespass to, or any other tort affecting, immovable property shall extend to cases in which the property in question is situated outside that part of the United Kingdom unless the proceedings are principally concerned with a question of the title to, or the right to possession of, that property."

74. There was a parallel development in European law which also confirms, broadly, that the foreign land principle in the European Union is concerned only with actions to establish title. That development began with the Brussels Convention on jurisdiction and the enforcement of judgments in civil and commercial matters, which was signed in 1968 and came into force for the six original EEC Member States in 1973. The Brussels Convention was enacted into United Kingdom law by the 1982 Act and the relevant provisions came into force in 1987, and are now contained in the Brussels I Regulation (Council Regulation (EC) No 44/2001). The effect is that the *Moçambique* rule has been superseded, as regards land in other Member States, by what is now Article 22(1) of the Brussels I Regulation.

75. Article 22(1) (formerly article 16(1)(a) of the Brussels Convention) provides that the courts of the Member State in which the property is situated have exclusive jurisdiction, regardless of domicile,

"in proceedings which have as their object rights in rem in immovable property or tenancies of immovable property."

76. The European Court has confirmed that what is now article 22(1) must not be given an interpretation broader than is required by its objective: and that actions for damages based on infringement of rights in rem or on damage to property in which rights in rem exist do not fall within its scope: Case C-343/04 *Land Oberösterreich v CEZ as* [2006] ECR I-4557, para [26] et seq.

77. The consequence is that in the United Kingdom the trespass aspect of the *Moçambique* rule has no application as regards land in other Member States, and (subject to the controversial question of the applicability of article 2) can only apply to land outside the Member States where a question of title is involved: see *Dicey, Morris & Collins, Conflict of Laws*, 14th ed (2006), vol 2 paras 23-025-23-027.

The rule in Phillips v Eyre

78. As has been seen, in *Potter v Broken Hill Pty Co Ltd*, in the Full Court of the Supreme Court of Victoria, Hood J considered that the action was precluded by the first branch of the rule in *Phillips v Eyre*, ie that Potter could not show that, if the act had been committed in Victoria, it would have been actionable there, because infringement of a New South Wales patent in Victoria was not actionable in Victoria. The effect of the first limb of the rule in intellectual property cases was expressed in *Dicey & Morris, Conflict of Laws*, 12th ed (1993) (the last edition before the law was changed), vol 2, at p 1516:

> "Nor can the holder of a French patent, trade mark or copyright sue in England for its infringement in France. Since the French patent, trade mark or copyright is territorial in its operation and the act complained of would not be a tort if committed in England, it cannot be brought within [the first limb of the rule in *Phillips v Eyre*]."

79. In consequence it was held in *Tyburn Productions Ltd v Conan Doyle* [1991] Ch 75 that it was not possible to bring an action in England for infringement (or, as in that case, an action for a declaration of non-infringement) of United States copyright. The first limb of the rule in *Phillips v Eyre* was also employed by Sir Nicolas Browne-Wilkinson V-C in *Def Lepp Music v Stuart-Brown* [1986] RPC 273 to deny a claim in England for breach of a United Kingdom copyright in the Netherlands, but a shorter answer to the claim would have been that United Kingdom copyrights are purely territorial and do not, by United Kingdom law, confer any rights abroad: see, eg *Norbert Steinhardt & Son Ltd v Meth* (1960) 105 CLR 440.

80. But the rule in *Phillips v Eyre* was first eroded by case-law and then abolished by statute. Following the lead of Lord Wilberforce and Lord Hodson in *Boys v Chaplin* [1971] AC 356, in *Red Sea Insurance Co Ltd v Bouygues SA* [1995] 1 AC 190 the Privy Council decided that the first limb of the rule in *Phillips v Eyre* could be displaced so that an issue might be governed by the law of the country which with respect to that issue had the most significant relationship with the occurrence and with the parties. That exception was applied in *Pearce v Ove Arup Partnership Ltd* [2000] Ch 403, in which the Court of Appeal held that a claim in England for infringement of a Dutch copyright was not defeated by the first limb of the rule in *Phillips v Eyre*, because the issues had the most significant relationship with the Netherlands. Accordingly, the court held that Dutch law was the applicable law and not the combination of English law and Dutch law required by *Phillips v Eyre*. In *KK Sony Computer Entertainment v Van Veen* (2006) 71 IPR 179 (High Court of New Zealand), MacKenzie J held (in reasoning which is not entirely clear) that, in a claim for infringement of United Kingdom and Hong Kong copyrights, the first limb of the rule in *Phillips v Eyre* was satisfied.

81. The rule in *Phillips v Eyre* was abolished by the Private International Law (Miscellaneous Provisions) Act 1995. In principle the law of the place of infringement applies: 1995 Act, section 11(1). Consequently, so far as English proceedings are concerned, that basis for the decisions in *Potter v Broken Hill*

Pty Co Ltd and *Tyburn Productions Ltd v Conan Doyle* has disappeared, and the rule in *Phillips v Eyre* is no impediment to actions in England for infringement of foreign intellectual property rights.

The act of state doctrine

82. In the United States the act of state doctrine has been used as a basis for non-justiciability of foreign trade mark and patent rights. The Court of Appeals for the Second Circuit held in *Vanity Fair Mills Inc v T Eaton Co Ltd*, 234 F 2d 633, 646 (2d Cir 1956), cert den, 352 US 871 (1956) that a United States federal court should not rule on the validity of a Canadian trade mark because (among other reasons) the act of state doctrine precluded determination of the acts of a foreign sovereign done within its own territory, and to rule on validity would create conflicts with Canadian administrative and judicial officers.

83. The act of state doctrine was also invoked more recently in the United States as a ground for refusing to allow the addition of claims for infringement of parallel foreign patents to claims for infringement of United States patents, in litigation in which validity was in issue: *Voda v Cordis Corp*, 476 F 3d 887 (Fed Cir 2007). The majority of the court (Gajarsa CJ, Prost CJ concurring) said (at p 904):

> "the act of state doctrine may make the exercise of supplemental jurisdiction over foreign patent infringement claims fundamentally unfair. As "a *'principle of decision* binding on federal and state courts alike,'" the act of state doctrine "requires that, in the process of deciding, the acts of foreign sovereigns taken within their own jurisdictions shall be deemed valid." *W S Kirkpatrick & Co, Inc v Envtl Tectonics Corp, Int'l*, 493 U.S. 400, 406, 409 ... (1990) ... In this case, none of the parties or amicus curiae have persuaded us that the grant of a patent by a sovereign is not an act of state. ... Therefore, assuming arguendo that the act of state doctrine applies, the doctrine would prevent our courts from inquiring into the validity of a foreign patent grant and require our courts to adjudicate patent claims regardless of validity or enforceability."

84. The act of state doctrine was held not to apply where, in a dispute arising out of a patent licence, the issue was one of interpretation of the patent, and not of validity: *Fairchild Semiconductor Corpn v Third Dimension (3D) Semiconductor Inc*, 589 F Supp 2d 84, 98 (D Me 2008).

85. So also, in the case of copyright infringement, it has been held that the act of state doctrine has no application because there is no need to pass on the validity of acts of foreign government officials. In *London Film Productions, Ltd v Intercontinental Communications, Inc*, 580 F Supp 47, 49 (SDNY 1984) the District Court held that the plaintiff could sue for infringement of its foreign copyright in films. The court accepted Professor Nimmer's view that the act of state doctrine was not engaged: in adjudicating an infringement action under a foreign copyright law there was no need to pass upon the validity of acts of foreign governmental officials, since foreign copyright laws did not generally incorporate administrative formalities which had to be satisfied to create or perfect a copyright. In *Frink America, Inc v Champion Road Machinery Ltd*, 961 F Supp 398 (NDNY 1997) it was held that dismissal of a claim for infringement of

Canadian copyright was not warranted because US and Canada were signatories to the Berne Convention, which bars administrative formalities, and therefore there was no question of passing on acts of foreign government. Contrast *ITSI TV Productions, Inc v California Authority of Racing Fairs, Inc*, 785 F Supp 854, 866 (ED Cal 1992).

86. But in the Commonwealth *Potter v Broken Hill Pty Co Ltd* appears to stand alone in using the act of state doctrine as an impediment to actions for infringement of foreign intellectual property rights. In *Voda v Cordis Corpn*, above, Circuit Judge Newman, dissenting, rightly pointed out (at p 914) that not every governmental action and not every ministerial activity is an act of state. In *Mannington Mills, Inc v Congoleum Corpn*, 595 F 2d 1287, 1293 — 94 (3d Cir 1979) the Court of Appeals for the Third Circuit was "unable to accept the proposition that the mere issuance of patents by a foreign power constitutes … an act of state."

87. It has been said that the grant of a national patent is "an exercise of national sovereignty" (Jenard Report on the Brussels Convention (OJ 1979 C59 pp 1, 36), and the European Court has emphasised that the issue of patents necessitates the involvement of the national administrative authorities (Case C-4/03 *Gesellschaft für Antriebstechnik mbH & Co KG (GAT) v Lamellen und Kupplungsbau Beteiligungs KG (LuK)* [2006] ECR I-6509, para [23]). But in England the foreign act of state doctrine has not been applied to any acts other than foreign legislation or governmental acts of officials such as requisition, and it should not today be regarded as an impediment to an action for infringement of foreign intellectual property rights, even if validity of a grant is in issue, simply because the action calls into question the decision of a foreign official.

European law and intellectual property rights

88. Two important developments in European law have undermined any argument that there is a substantial policy reason for the view that actions for infringement of intellectual property rights cannot be brought outside the State in which they are granted or subsist.

89. First, article 22(4) of the Brussels I Regulation (formerly article 16(4) of the Brussels Convention) provides that, in proceedings concerned with the registration or validity of patents, trade marks, designs, or other similar rights required to be deposited or registered, the courts of the Member State in which the deposit or registration has been applied for, has taken place or is deemed to have taken place, have exclusive jurisdiction irrespective of the domicile of the defendant. This is an exception to the general domicile rule of jurisdiction, and has to be construed strictly. It applies only to intellectual property rights which are required to be deposited or registered, and does not apply to infringement actions in which there is no issue as to validity.

90. The European Court has emphasised that article 22(4) is only concerned with cases in which a question of validity arises. It has made the following points: the basis for article 22(4) is that the courts of the Contracting State in

which the deposit or registration has been applied for or made are best placed to adjudicate upon cases in which the dispute itself concerns the validity of the patent or the existence of the deposit or registration; but it does not apply in proceedings which do not concern the validity of the intellectual property right or the existence of the deposit or registration and these matters are not disputed by the parties, for example, a patent infringement action, in which the question of the validity of the patent allegedly infringed is not called into question; it would apply if the question of validity were raised by way of defence in infringement proceedings; the concern for the sound administration of justice is all the more important in the field of patents since, given the specialised nature of this area, a number of Contracting States have set up a system of specific judicial protection, to ensure that these types of cases are dealt with by specialised courts; the exclusive jurisdiction is also justified by the fact that the issue of patents necessitates the involvement of the national administrative authorities: Case C-4/03 *Gesellschaft für Antriebstechnik mbH & Co KG (GAT) v Lamellen und Kupplungsbau Beteiligungs KG (LuK)* **[2006] ECR I-6509**, para [16] et seq.

91. Article 22(4) does not in terms apply to intellectual property rights outside the Member States. It is not necessary for present purposes to delve into the question whether it may be applied by analogy (or "reflexively") to non-Member States. What it shows is that there is a fundamental distinction between intellectual property claims which involve the registration or validity of intellectual property rights which are required to be deposited or registered, and those which are not.

92. The second relevant piece of European legislation does not apply to the present proceedings because it came into force only on 11 January 2009, but it also shows clearly that there is no European public policy against the litigation of foreign intellectual property rights. Regulation (EC) No 864/2007 of the European Parliament and of the Council on the law applicable to non-contractual obligations (Rome II) applies wherever in the world a tort was committed. It plainly envisages that actions may be brought in Member States for infringement of foreign intellectual property rights, including copyright. Recital (26) states:

> "Regarding infringements of intellectual property rights, the universally acknowledged principle of the lex loci protectionis should be preserved. For the purposes of this Regulation, the term 'intellectual property rights' should be interpreted as meaning, for instance, copyright, related rights, the sui generis right for the protection of databases and industrial property rights."

93. As regards choice of law, article 8 provides:

"Infringement of intellectual property rights

> 1. The law applicable to a non-contractual obligation arising from an infringement of an intellectual property right shall be the law of the country for which protection is claimed.

> 2. In the case of a non-contractual obligation arising from an infringement of a unitary Community intellectual property right, the law applicable shall, for any

question that is not governed by the relevant Community instrument, be the law of the country in which the act of infringement was committed.

. . ."

Other proposals

94. These developments in European law are mirrored in proposals within the American Law Institute, which favour adjudication of foreign intellectual property rights, at least where issues of validity are not in issue. The American Law Institute's *Intellectual Property: Principles Governing Jurisdiction, Choice of Law, and Judgments in Transnational Disputes* (2008) apply to transnational civil disputes which involve (inter alia) copyrights, patents, trademarks, and other intellectual property rights (section 102) and note the controversy over the question of the justiciability of intellectual property rights (Reporters' Notes 4 and 5). Section 211 provides that the court must have subject-matter and personal jurisdiction. Comment *b* states:

> "There is substantial sentiment that issues regarding the validity of a registered right, particularly a patent right, should be adjudicated in the courts of the State in which the right is registered. Only this State is competent to cancel the registration. ... Nonetheless, the Principles do not include a blanket prohibition on the adjudication of matters involving a foreign State's registered rights, because separating adjudication of validity from infringement can have substantive ramifications. Separate resolutions can prevent a court from hearing all of the evidence relevant to the action and from using its understanding of how a technology is utilized to inform its decision on the scope of the right. Bifurcating validity and infringement can also increase the parties' costs."

95. The draft Principles for Conflict of Laws in Intellectual Property, 2011, prepared by the European Union Max Planck Group on Conflict of Laws in Intellectual Property contain no specific provision for actions for infringement of foreign rights abroad, but it is implicit in the Principles that they envisage such actions: (a) the primary rule of jurisdiction in the Principles is habitual residence (Part 2, section 1), and (b) the primary law applicable to infringement is the law of the State for which protection is sought (Part 3, section 6).

The English and foreign authorities on justiciability of intellectual property claims

96. A number of distinguished judges have expressed the view that the English court cannot, or should not, exercise jurisdiction in claims for infringement of foreign intellectual property rights, such as patents (*Mölnlycke AB v Procter & Gamble Ltd* [1992] 1 WLR 1112, 1118, per Dillon LJ; *Plastus Kreativ AB v Minnesota Mining and Manufacturing Co* [1995] RPC 438, 447, per Aldous J) or trade marks (*LA Gear Inc Ltd v Gerald Whelan & Sons Ltd* [1991] FSR 670, 674, per Mummery J). But prior to the decision of the Court of Appeal in the present proceedings the only directly relevant decisions were the decisions of Vinelott J in *Tyburn Productions Ltd v Conan Doyle* [1991] Ch 75, of Laddie J in *Coin Controls Ltd v Suzo International (UK) Ltd* [1999] Ch 33, and of the Court of Appeal in *Pearce v Ove Arup Partnership Ltd* [2000] Ch 403.

97. In *Tyburn Productions Ltd v Conan Doyle* [1991] Ch 75 Vinelott J applied the *Moçambique* rule in the light of *Potter v Broken Hill Pty Co Ltd* to what was in effect a prospective negative declaration relating to potential copyright infringement in the United States. The action was by a television company for a declaration that the daughter of Sir Arthur Conan Doyle had no rights under the copyright, unfair competition, or trademark laws of the United States to prevent the company from distributing a Sherlock Holmes television film. It was conceded on behalf of the television company that no distinction could be drawn for the purpose of the case law between patents and other intellectual property rights including copyright. Vinelott J also supported his conclusion by reliance on the first limb of the rule in *Philips v Eyre*: infringement of an American copyright was not a tort in English law and the first limb could not be satisfied. In *R Griggs Group Ltd v Evans* [2004] EWHC 1088 (Ch), [2005] Ch 153, Vinelott J's decision was criticised by Mr Peter Prescott QC, sitting as a Deputy High Court judge, who distinguished it by applying the exception to the *Moçambique* rule whereby jurisdiction could be exercised if there were a contract or an equity between the parties: the judge allowed an amendment to a pleading on the basis that the court in the exercise of its equitable in personam jurisdiction could order a person who had acquired property situate abroad with sufficient notice of an earlier obligation to transfer the property to another to assign that property to its equitable owner, and that it would not be a breach of comity to adjudicate in personam on rights to foreign intellectual property (copyright) arising out of a contract.

98. Patents were the subject of the decision of Laddie J in *Coin Controls Ltd v Suzo International (UK) Ltd* [1999] Ch 33, in which he held that the court had no jurisdiction to try claims for infringement of German and Spanish patents for two reasons: the first was that the claims were not justiciable under the *Moçambique/Potter v Broken Hill Pty Co Ltd* principles. The second was that the claims were concerned with validity and within what is now article 22(4) of the Brussels I Regulation.

99. In *Pearce v Ove Arup Partnership Ltd* [2000] Ch 403 Mr Pearce claimed that the defendants had infringed his English and Dutch copyrights in his drawings and plans for a town hall by copying them in designing the Kunsthal in Rotterdam. There was no issue about existence or validity of the copyrights. The sole factual question was whether his drawings and plans had been copied. On the question of the justiciability of the claim for infringement of the Dutch copyright, the court had personal jurisdiction over the defendants by virtue of their domicile in England (because they were additional parties for the purposes of what is now article 6(1) of the Brussels I Regulation). It was not suggested that what is now article 22(4) applied, since the proceedings were for infringement of copyright and no question of deposit or registration arose. The effect of what is now article 22(1)) was that the *Moçambique* rule no longer applied within the Member States, and that where proceedings in relation to intellectual property fell outside what is now article 22(1), the general rules of jurisdiction applied, and there was no room for an objection of non-justiciability. The common law rule of choice of law applied because the relevant events occurred before section

11 of the Private International law (Miscellaneous Provisions) Act 1995 came into force in 1996, but (as mentioned above) the court disapplied the first limb of the rule in *Phillips v Eyre* in favour of the law of the country which with respect to that issue had the most significant relationship with the occurrence and with the parties, which was Dutch law.

Foreign authorities

100. In the United States the local action rule has been used as a ground for refusal to add claims for infringement of foreign patents to a United States patent infringement action: *Voda v Cordis Corp*, 476 F 3d 887 (Fed Cir 2007), discussed above in connection with the act of state doctrine. The majority said (at pp 901-902):

> "the local action doctrine informs us that exercising supplemental jurisdiction in this case appears to violate our own norms of what sovereigns ordinarily expect. Courts derived the local action doctrine from the distinction between local and transitory actions beginning with *Livingston v Jefferson,* written by Justice John Marshall riding Circuit. 15 F. Cas. 660 (C.C.D.Va. 1811). … [T]he local action doctrine served to prevent courts from adjudicating claims for trespass or title to real property.

> The territorial limits of the rights granted by patents are similar to those conferred by land grants. A patent right is limited by the metes and bounds of the jurisdictional territory that granted the right to exclude. …

> Therefore, a patent right to exclude only arises from the legal right granted and recognized by the sovereign within whose territory the right is located. It would be incongruent to allow the sovereign power of one to be infringed or limited by another sovereign's extension of its jurisdiction. …"

101. Claims for infringement of foreign copyright have been held in New Zealand and South Africa to be non-justiciable. In *Atkinson Footwear Ltd v Hodgskin International Services Ltd,* (1994) 31 IPR 186 (High Court of New Zealand) Tipping J followed the *Tyburn Productions Ltd* decision and in *Gallo Africa Ltd v Sting Music (Pty) Ltd* [2010] ZASCA 96, 2010 (6) SA 329 the Supreme Court of Appeal of South Africa applied the decision of the Court of Appeal in the present case. But in *KK Sony Computer Entertainment v Van Veen* (2006) 71 IPR 179 MacKenzie J in the High Court of New Zealand declined to follow *Atkinson Footwear* and held that a claim for infringement of foreign intellectual property rights (in that case breach of United Kingdom and Hong Kong copyright in PlayStation 2) was justiciable if no question of the existence or validity of those rights was in issue.

Conclusions on the justiciability question

102. The issue on this appeal is a very narrow one because the appellants do not take issue with the application of the *Moçambique* rule to intellectual property so far as it is limited to patents and other intellectual property rights dependent on the grant or authority of a foreign State, and to cases where what is in issue is the validity of the patent, as opposed to its infringement.

103. As recorded by Mann J, the trial judge ([2008] EWHC 1878 (Ch), [2009] FSR 103, at [272]), the dispute relating to the United States copyright was as follows. The subsistence of copyright and ownership of all drawings was accepted by Mr Ainsworth, although the existence of some drawings was disputed. Infringement was denied so far as some drawings are concerned, on the footing that they were not copied, or not copied closely enough. Because three dimensional items were produced, it was argued that under United States law there was no infringement because copyright in the drawings would not be infringed by the production of a utilitarian or functional device. Lucasfilm claimed copyright in physical helmets and armour, which was disputed by Mr Ainsworth because they were said to be functional or utilitarian. According to the judge, at one stage it had also been suggested that if there was copyright it was vested in Mr Ainsworth and not in Lucasfilm, but this point was not ultimately persisted in.

104. Although at trial the infringement arguments sometimes merged into a subsistence argument, the substantial dispute has always been about the ownership of the relevant copyrights and their infringement rather than about their subsistence.

105. Were these claims justiciable? Mr Ainsworth argued that the principle behind the *Moçambique* rule (as extended in *Hesperides* to include actions in which no issue of title arises) still subsists and applies to claims for infringement of all foreign intellectual property rights, including copyright, because such claims are essentially "local" and must be brought in the place where the rights have been created, irrespective as to whether there is any claim to title. But to describe the claims as "local" is simply to beg the question whether as a matter of law they must be brought in the place where the rights originate and are effective.

106. We have come to the firm conclusion that, in the case of a claim for infringement of copyright of the present kind, the claim is one over which the English court has jurisdiction, provided that there is a basis for in personam jurisdiction over the defendant, or, to put it differently, the claim is justiciable. It is clear that much of the underpinning of the *Moçambique* rule and the decision in *Potter v Broken Hill Pty Co Ltd* has been eroded. All that is left of the *Moçambique* rule (except to the extent that it is modified by the Brussels I Regulation) is that there is no jurisdiction in proceedings for infringement of rights in foreign land where the proceedings are "principally concerned with a question of the title, or the right to possession, of that property." So also article 22(1) of the Brussels I Regulation does not apply to actions for damages for infringement of rights in land.

107. The basis for what remains of the rule was said by the House of Lords in the *Moçambique* case to be that controversies should be decided in the country of the situs of the property because the right of granting it was vested in "the ruler of the country" and in the *Hesperides* case to be the maintenance of comity and the avoidance of conflict with foreign jurisdictions. It is possible to see

how the rationale of the *Moçambique* rule can be applied to patents, at any rate where questions of validity are involved. For example the claims might touch on the validity of patents in sensitive areas, such as armaments, and that no doubt is part of the rationale for article 22(4) of the Brussels I Regulation. But it is very difficult to see how it could apply to copyright. It is true that copyright can involve delicate political issues. Thus in a very different context Brightman J had to deal with the international consequences for copyright protection of the *samizdat* circulation in the Soviet Union of Solzhenitsyn's *August 1914* without having been passed by the Soviet censor: *Bodley Head Ltd v Flegon* [1972] 1 WLR 680. But such cases can be dealt with by an application of the principles of public policy in appropriate cases.

108. Nor do the additional matters relied on in *Potter v Broken Hill Pty Co Ltd* lead to any different conclusion. The rule in *Phillips v Eyre* has gone. There is no room for the application of the act of state doctrine in relation to copyright in this case, even if (contrary to the view expressed above) actions of officials involved with registration and grant of intellectual property rights were acts of state. The requirement to apply for copyright registration in the United States is limited to the "copyright in any United States work" which in practice means that published works first published outside the United States are exempted from compliance with US registration provisions. In the present case the copyrights were treated as United States works and were registered. Registration is a pre-requisite to proceedings in the United States: United States Copyright Act, section 411. But the unchallenged evidence before the judge in this case was that registration was not a prerequisite to subsistence but only to suit, and it was possible to register at the time of suit. Consequently the provision is purely procedural. That has been confirmed recently by the United States Supreme Court, which has held that federal courts have subject matter jurisdiction to approve a class action settlement where some of the authors are not registered, because section 411 is not a jurisdictional rule: *Reed Elsevier Inc v Muchnick*, 130 S Ct 1237 (2010).

109. There is no doubt that the modern trend is in favour of the enforcement of foreign intellectual property rights. First, article 22(4) of the Brussels I Regulation only assigns exclusive jurisdiction to the country where the right originates in cases which are concerned with registration or validity of rights which are "required to be deposited or registered" and does not apply to infringement actions in which there is no issue as to validity. This can rarely, if ever, apply to copyright. Second, the Rome II Regulation also plainly envisages the litigation of foreign intellectual property rights and, third, the professional and academic bodies which have considered the issue, the American Law Institute and the Max Planck Institute, clearly favour them, at any rate where issues of validity are not engaged.

110. There are no issues of policy which militate against the enforcement of foreign copyright. States have an interest in the international recognition and enforcement of their copyrights, as the Berne Convention on the International Union for the Protection of Literary and Artistic Works shows. Many of the

points relied on by the Court of Appeal to justify the application of the *Moçambique* rule in this case as a matter of policy would apply to many international cases over which the English court would have jurisdiction and would in principle exercise it, especially the suggestion that questions of foreign law would have to be decided. It was also said by the Court of Appeal that enforcement of foreign intellectual property law might involve a clash of policies such that a defendant may be restrained by injunction from doing acts in this country which are lawful in this country. But such an injunction will be granted only if the acts are anticipated to achieve fruition in another country, and there is no objection in principle to such an injunction. Nor is there any objection in principle, as the Court of Appeal thought, to a restraint on acts in another country. Extra-territorial injunctions are commonly granted here against defendants subject to the in personam jurisdiction. The Court of Appeal also thought that it was relevant that there was no international regime for the mutual recognition of copyright jurisdiction and of copyright judgments, but this is no reason for the English court refusing to take jurisdiction over an English defendant in a claim for breach of foreign copyright.

111. It follows that *Tyburn Productions Ltd v Conan Doyle* was wrongly decided and that on this aspect the decision of the Court of Appeal in these proceedings cannot stand.

The Owusu v Jackson point

112. If the Court of Appeal was right to hold that the claim was in principle non-justiciable, a further question would arise whether nevertheless, in the light of the decision of the European Court in Case C-281/02 *Owusu v Jackson* [2005] ECR I-1383, the English court must grant a remedy against Mr Ainsworth, who is domiciled in England for the purposes of what is now Article 2 of the Brussels I Regulation. In *Owusu v Jackson* the European Court decided that an action in England arising out of events in Jamaica could not be stayed as against an English defendant in favour the Jamaican courts on the ground of forum non conveniens. That was because the English defendant was domiciled in a Member State for the purposes of article 2, and the assignment of jurisdiction to that State applied also as between Contracting and non-Contracting States (now Member and non-Member States). In this case the Court of Appeal distinguished *Owusu v Jackson* on the basis that it did not apply to cases where the English court held that it had no subject-matter jurisdiction.

113. Lucasfilm argues that it would be inconsistent with the *Owusu* principle for the English court to decline to decide a particular issue on the ground that it is not justiciable under English law, because (in particular) the Brussels I Regulation is concerned with subject-matter jurisdiction as well as personal jurisdiction; it is concerned with achieving the uniform application of common principles regarding jurisdiction across the European Community, and it would not be consistent with that object if national courts were able to decline jurisdiction on principles of non-justiciability. Although in argument it was stressed that the argument was one of lack of jurisdiction rather than non-justiciability, in substance the real

point of the argument is that if Lucasfilm were right, then the Brussels I Regulation would require the English court to adjudicate on other matters which have hitherto been regarded as non-justiciable, such as "the transactions of foreign sovereign states" which were held to be non-justiciable in *Buttes Gas and Oil Co v Hammer (No 3)* [1982] AC 888, 931; and that to require the English court to so adjudicate would be contrary to international law (or, perhaps more accurately, put the United Kingdom in breach of international law).

114. In view of the conclusion on the main point, this issue (on which a reference to the European Court might be required) does not arise and there is no need to express a view on it.

115. We would therefore allow the appeal on the justiciability issue.

(d) Onus of Proof

Harmony Consulting Ltd. v. G.A. Foss Transport Ltd., 2012 FCA 226 (F.C.A.)

. . .

[28] The trial judge found that, in order to succeed in its action, Harmony had to establish all of the elements set out in subsection 27(1) of the Act (all the relevant provisions of the Act are set out in Appendix "A" to my reasons). Thus, she said that Harmony had to persuade her, on a balance of probabilities, that:

- It owned the copyrights in the computer programs at issue;
- Foss'actions constituted an infringement of its exclusive rights (subsection 3 (1)); and
- Such actions were done without its consent.

[29] Harmony argues that the trial judge misplaced the burden of proof with respect to the element of consent. Relying on the decision of the Federal Court in *Aga Khanv. Tajdin*, 2011 FC 14 (CanLII), 2011 FC 14, 329 D.L.R. (4th) 521, *(Aga Khan)*, aff'd 2012 FCA 12 (CanLII), 2012 FCA 12, 426 N.R. 190 *(Aga Khan F.C.A.)*, Harmony says that consent is a defence and, as such, the burden of establishing it rests on Foss. It submits that the trial judge misconstrued an earlier decision of this Court: *Positive Attitude Safety System Inc. v. Albian Sands Energy Inc.*, 2005 FCA 332 (CanLII), 2005 FCA 332, [2006] 2 F.C.R. 50 *(Positive)*. In its view, this Court never intended to shift the burden of proof to the plaintiff in that case. I cannot agree.

[30] In *Aga Khan F.C.A.*, this Court confirmed the Federal Court decision in *Aga Khan*, noting expressly that the Federal Court's statements with respect to the burden of proof would not constitute an overriding error in the particular circumstances of that case. It is now important, in my view, to reaffirm an earlier statement of this Court on this question.

[31] Writing for the Court in *Positive*, Justice Pelletier held that infringement is defined in the Act in terms of the absence of consent and, consequently, proof of infringement requires proof of lack of consent (see paragraph 39). In my view, this statement can only mean that the plaintiff bears the burden of persuasion with respect to the lack of consent. This is in line with the general principle that a plaintiff must establish on a balance of probabilities all the necessary elements of its claim.

[32] The following extract from a brief article published by David Vaver in reaction to the Federal Court decision in *Aga Khan* summarizes perfectly my thoughts on the matter:

> Burden of proof rules allocate the costs and risks of gathering and presenting evidence, and help filter good cases from the bad. They should not be "impractical and unduly burdensome" on plaintiffs and should advance the purposes of the law involved. The *Copyright Act* has special burden of proof rules that give a plaintiff the benefit of presumptions on authorship, copyright and title if the defendant contests them, and presumptions of copyright subsistence and ownership where the right is registered. The latter presumptions satisfy the plaintiff's initial burden to produce some evidence on the issue; they do not shift his legal burden of proof. There is no presumption about consent and no reason to imply one, let alone a more draconian reversal of the legal onus of proof. It is rarely a chore for a plaintiff to prove he gave no express consent: he knows best whether he did or not. And even if it is a chore, that is a small price to pay for a right that stops people for sometimes over a century from doing what they would otherwise be free to do.

A defendant who says he has the plaintiff's *implied* consent equally puts this point in issue, but then it seems reasonable for the defendant to plead and prove the facts on which he relies, and the inferences to be drawn from them. The plaintiff can then produce whatever tends to rebut this case. That does not change the ultimate legal burden of proof, which remains on the plaintiff throughout. Only the evidentiary burden shifts to the defendant: he needs to produce some evidence of consent or the plaintiff's *prima facie* case succeeds. If, on weighing the evidence, the court is satisfied the plaintiff gave no implied consent, he wins. If the defendant does show implied consent, the plaintiff fails to discharge his onus and loses. In theory, if the evidence is left in a state where the court is unsatisfied that the plaintiff did *not* grant implied consent, the plaintiff also loses. Few cases ever stand on that knife-edge but some can, as this Note later shows.

David Vaver, "Consent or No Consent: The Burden of Proof in Intellectual Property Infringement Suits", (2001) 23 I.P.J. 147 at 148-149.

. . .

2. Reproductions

(a) What is a Reproduction?

The owner of a copyright has the sole right to produce or reproduce the work or any substantial part thereof in any material form whatsoever.[1] The right to reproduce the work is one of the most important rights conferred by the Act. The primary purpose of this right is to enable the author to profit from his or her work by exploiting it for his or her own economic self-interest.[2] The reproduction right is especially important given the ease with which works of all forms can be scanned or otherwise converted into digital form, manipulated in a computer, and transmitted instantly over networks including the Internet to unlimited numbers of users.

A variety of unauthorized acts can constitute infringement of copyright by reproduction, unless otherwise excused as coming within one or more statutory exemptions from infringement such as "fair dealing" for one of the prescribed statutory purposes. Copying of protected subject matter from one material form into another will obviously implicate the reproduction right, but so can a variety of other activities. In the absence of permission or an available defence, for example, a person may not make alterations or modifications to the work, if such activity involves substantial reproduction of the work, without being liable for infringement of copyright.[3] Some modern examples of reproduction may include loading a computer program into a computer memory without a licence, scanning a printed work into a digital file, digitizing works, including photographs, motion pictures, or sound recordings, digital sampling of musical works, and the uploading and downloading of computer files.

The historical scope of the notion of "reproduction" is usually defined as the act of producing additional or new copies of the work in a material form. In *Théberge*, the Supreme Court clarified that multiplication of copies is a necessary consequence of this physical conception of reproduction.[4]

The Act does not, however, recognize only literal, physical, mechanical reproduction. The legal concept has broadened over time to recognize metaphorical copying (transformation to another medium) as well as methods of reproduction undreamt of in earlier periods, such as evanescent and virtual copies in electronic formats. Transformation of a work from two dimensions to three dimensions or vice versa may also infringe copyright even though the physical reproduction of the original expression of that work has not been mechanically copied. Equally, translations or transformations into another medium may be infringement. The Act does not expressly protect derivative works, as does the U.S. legislation. The reproduction right is, however, broad enough to cover many derivative works. Examples of what might

---

[1] Section 3(1).
[2] *Théberge v. Galerie d'Art du Petit Champlain inc.* (2002), 17 C.P.R. (4th) 161 (S.C.C.) at para. 141, 119 per Gonthier in dissent.
[3] See section 3.7(e).
[4] *Théberge v. Galerie d'Art du Petit Champlain inc.*, 2002 SCC 34.

be called derivative works listed in sections 3.3(1)(a) to (1)(e) of the Act are consistent with the notion of reproduction because they all imply the creation of new copies or manifestations of the work or a substantial part thereof.

The concept of reproduction involves two elements: resemblance to, and actual use of, the copyright work. Two elements are required to make out a cause of action for infringement by reproduction: first, the reproduction must be either of the entire work or of a substantial part (or, as it is sometimes said, there must be sufficient objective similarity between the infringing work and the copyrighted work, or a substantial part thereof), and second, there must be some causal connection between the copyrighted work and the infringing work. In other words, the copyrighted work must be the source from which the copy is derived.[5]

Théberge v. Galerie d'Art du Petit Champlain inc., 2002 SCC 34

McLachlin C.J.C., L'Heureux-Dubé, Gonthier, Iacobucci, Major, Binnie, LeBel JJ.

Heard: October 11, 2001
Judgment: March 28, 2002
Docket: 27872

Binnie J.:

1 We are required in this appeal to determine the extent to which an artist, utilizing the statutory rights and remedies provided by the Copyright Act, R.S.C. 1985, c. C-42, can control the eventual use or display of an authorized reproduction of his or her work in the hands of a third party purchaser.

2 Claude Théberge, a well-established Canadian painter with an international reputation, seeks to stop the appellants, who amongst other things produce poster art, from transferring authorized reproductions of his artistic works from a paper substrate (or support) to a canvas substrate for purposes of resale. In my opinion, for the reasons which follow, the appellants did not thereby "copy" the respondent's artistic works. They purchased lawfully reproduced posters of his paintings and used a chemical process that allowed them to lift the ink layer from the paper (leaving it blank) and to display it on canvas. They were within their rights to do so as owners of the physical posters (which lawfully incorporated the copyrighted expression). At the end of the day, no new reproductions of the respondent's works were brought into existence. Nor, in my view, was there production (or reproduction) of a new artistic work "in any material form" within the meaning of s. 3(1) of the Copyright Act. What began as a poster, authorized by the respondent, remained a poster.

---

5 *Prism Hospital Software Inc. v. Hospital Medical Records Institute* (1994), 57 C.P.R. (3d) 129 (B.C. S.C.).

3 Nevertheless, on August 19, 1999, the respondent arranged to have the bailiff seize canvas-backed reproductions from the appellants without ever satisfying a judge that the appellants had violated the Copyright Act. Although seizure before judgment is designed purely as a conservation measure divorced from the merits of the case, the appellants claim that the seizure of their inventory caused them a significant loss, both in sales and reputation. The respondent has not proceeded with his action on the merits since the date of the seizure two and a half years ago.

4 I find myself in respectful disagreement with the conclusion of my colleague Gonthier J. In my view, the seizure was not authorized by the Copyright Act. The pre-judgment seizure provisions of Article 734 of the Quebec Code of Civil Procedure, R.S.Q., c. C-25 were thus not an available remedy. The seizure was therefore wrongful. I would allow the appeal.

. . .

B. The Proposed Test Would Depart from the General Principle that Breach of Copyright Requires Copying

42 The historical scope of the notion of "reproduction" under the Copyright Act should be kept in mind. As one would expect from the very word "copy right", "reproduction" is usually defined as the act of producing additional or new copies of the work in any material form. Multiplication of the copies would be a necessary consequence of this physical concept of "reproduction". In Underwriters' Survey Bureau Ltd. v. Massie & Renwick Ltd., [1940] S.C.R. 218 (S.C.C.), at p. 227, Duff C.J. viewed copyright law as essentially about protecting the right to multiply copies of a work:

> I think there can be no doubt that material of that character was subject matter for copyright and, not being published, the exclusive right of multiplying copies of it, or of publishing it, was a right which the common law, prior to the statute of 1921, gave primarily to the authors of it. [Emphasis added.]

See also Tom Hopkins International Inc. (Tom Hopkins Champions Unlimited) v. Wall & Redekop Realty Ltd. (1984), 1 C.P.R. (3d) 348 (B.C. S.C.). In Underwriters' Survey Bureau Ltd. v. Massie & Renwick Ltd. (1936), [1937] Ex. C.R. 15 (Can. Ex. Ct.), Maclean J., for the Exchequer Court, defined copyright as (at p. 20):

> ... the right to multiply copies of a published work, or the right to make the work public and still retain the beneficial interest therein. [Emphasis added.]

43 More pertinent still is the Ontario case of Fetherling v. Boughner (1978), 40 C.P.R. (2d) 253 (Ont. H.C.), relied on by the motions judge in this case, which dealt with a similar fact situation. Southey J. concluded in his oral judgment, at p. 256:

> The second question is whether the transfer process constitutes copying. My conclusion, after listening to the argument of counsel, but without hearing any evidence, is that such process does not constitute copying, because it involves the transfer physically of the picture on the copy of The Canadian from which the

> defendant's product is made. After such transfer there was no picture on the page of The Canadian. I am satisfied that the defendant would have been entitled to purchase a copy of The Canadian; cut out one of the strip photographs; paste it on a piece of paper; put a border around it; frame it; and sell it, without infringing copyright, just as she would have been entitled to sell the issue of The Canadian itself and just as any person, who purchases the work of an artist, is entitled to resell that work, or a piece of it. In my view that is essentially what was done by the defendant in this case.

See also to the same effect: No Fear Inc. v. Almo-Dante Mfg. (Canada) Ltd. (1997), 76 C.P.R. (3d) 414 (Fed. T.D.).

44 A similar understanding of "reproduction" is reflected in decisions under the English Act on which s. 3(1) of our Act is based, i.e., the physical making of something which did not exist before (Laddie et al., supra, at p. 614). As stated by the Earl of Halsbury in Walter v. Lane, [1900] A.C. 539 (U.K. H.L.), at p. 545:

> The law which I think restrains it is to be found in the Copyright Act, and that Act confers what it calls copyright — which means the right to multiply copies — which it confers on the author of books first published in this country. [Emphasis added.]

45 My colleague takes the view (at para. 139) that reproduction does not necessarily imply multiplication of the thing reproduced. In this connection, he refers to Apple Computer Inc. v. Mackintosh Computers Ltd. (1986), [1987] 1 F.C. 173 (Fed. T.D.), affirmed (1987), [1988] 1 F.C. 673 (Fed. C.A.), affirmed [1990] 2 S.C.R. 209 (S.C.C.). In that case, however, multiplication was admitted ((1987), [1988] 1 F.C. 673 (Fed. C.A.), at p. 697). The issue was not the meaning of reproduction but whether a computer silicon chip could be the subject matter of copyright protection. The computer program at issue was multiplied when reproduced in the form of a ROM chip. When the process was complete, the original written text of the program still existed, as did the subsequent renditions of it in code within the plaintiff's systems as well as the new reproduction etched in the memory cells of the defendant's chip (p. 12 of the trial judgment as reported in (1986), 10 C.P.R. (3d) 1). In Apple Computer Inc. the copyright issue was whether literal multiplication might nevertheless not constitute a "reproduction" for purposes of the Copyright Act. The facts here pose the opposite question, namely whether there is "reproduction" without multiplication.

46 My colleague also cites Cie générale des établissements Michelin — Michelin & Cie v. CAW — Canada (1996), [1997] 2 F.C. 306 (Fed. T.D.). In that case, the defendant union, in an organized campaign against Michelin, reproduced in its leaflets Michelin's "fanciful happy marshmallow-like" man shown stomping on the head of a worker. The union denied substantial reproduction of Michelin's copyrighted figure because of minor differences in the rendition ("qualitative" differences). The defence was rejected. There was, accordingly, reproduction, but there was also multiplication of the copyrighted image in each of the union's leaflets.

47 This is not to say that the Act recognizes only literal physical, mechanical reproduction. The legal concept has broadened over time to recognize what might be called metaphorical copying (transformation to another medium, e.g. books to films). It is recognized that technologies have evolved by which expression could be reproduced in ways undreamt of in earlier periods, such as evanescent and "virtual" copies in electronic formats. Transformation of an artistic work from two dimensions to three dimensions, or vice versa, will infringe copyright even though the physical reproduction of the original expression of that work has not been mechanically copied. Equally, translations or transformations into another medium may be infringements of economic rights. Nevertheless, the important evolution of legal concepts in the field of copyright is not engaged by the facts here. This is a case of literal physical, mechanical transfer in which no multiplication (metaphorical or otherwise) takes place.

48 It is of interest that our courts have not given an independent meaning to "produce" as distinguished from "reproduce" in s. 3(1) of the Act. Nor have the courts done so under the English Act. In fact, in that country, the word "produce" was thought to be of such little consequence that it was eliminated from the Act by amendment in 1956 (H. G. Richard et al., ed., Canadian Copyright Act Annotated (loose-leaf ed.), vol. 3, at p. 3-7). See also C. Brunet, "Copyright: The Economic Rights", in Copyright and Confidential Information Law of Canada, (G. F. Henderson, ed.), (1994), 129, at pp. 136- 37, and McKeown, supra, at p. 421.

49 The U.S. legislation expressly incorporates a definition of "derivative work", as happens for example when a cartoon character is turned into a puppet, or a tragic novel is turned into a musical comedy. In such circumstances there is, in a sense, "Aproduction" rather than a reproduction. However, the examples of what might be called derivative works listed in ss. 3(1)(a) to (e) of our Act are consistent with the notion of reproduction because they all imply the creation of new copies or manifestations of the work. In the application of the ink transfer method, however, there is no derivation, reproduction or production of a new and original work which incorporates the respondent's artistic work.

50 Even if one were to consider substitution of a new substrate to be a "fixation", the fact remains that the original poster lives on in the "re-fixated" poster. There is no multiplication and fixation alone is not an infringement of the original work.

C. There Was No Reproduction "in Substantial Part"

51 My colleague relies on the respondent's exclusive right under s. 3(1) to produce or reproduce his work "or any substantial part thereof in any material form whatever" (para. 142). Under this provision, an infringer does not escape liability by reproducing a substantial part of the artistic work as opposed to the whole of it. An individual who copies a novel does not avoid the penalties set out for infringement simply by changing a few words and, likewise, an individual cannot copy with impunity simply by changing the medium. A playwright would be liable if he or she put on the stage a substantial part (but not the whole) of a

copyrighted novel. There would clearly be reproduction of that part, i.e., the part of the novel in which intellectual property subsists. After the production, the novel would still exist intact, as would the new play. Here the layer of inks, in which resides the artistic content, rests intact and there is no such multiplication of a "substantial part" of the poster.

52 If the respondent's attempt to extend the concept of reproduction "in substantial part" to situations where there is no multiplication were correct, one would expect to find decided cases in support of his thesis but none have been brought to our attention.

G. The Proposed Test Would Conflict with Precedent from other Comparable Jurisdictions

66 Reference has already been made to the English "note card" case, Frost, supra. Comparable issues relating to the production or reproduction for the purposes of copyright law have also arisen in the United States, including cases of techniques similar to the ink transfer process used by the appellants in the present appeal. For example, in C.M. Paula Co. v. Logan, 355 F. Supp. 189 (U.S. N.D. Tex., 1973), the allegations of copyright infringement were directed at the defendant's transferral of various copyrighted designs from Paula Company greeting cards and note pads to ceramic plaques produced and sold by the defendant. The Paula Company described as follows the process employed by the defendant (at p. 190):

> [T]he process... involves the use of acrylic resin, emulsions, or similar compounds which act as a transfer medium to strip the printed indicia from the original surface on which it is printed, whereupon the image carrying film is applied to another article, such as the plaster base of a wall plaque. In effect, a decal picture is created.

67 The United States District Court concluded that there was no violation of the plaintiff's copyright (at p. 191):

> The process utilized by defendant that is now in question results in the use of the original image on a ceramic plaque; such process is not "Areproduction or duplication".

> The Court believes that plaintiff's characterization of the print thus used as a decal is appropriate. Each ceramic plaque sold by defendant with a Paula print affixed thereto requires the purchase and use of an individual piece of artwork marketed by the plaintiff. For example, should defendant desire to make one hundred ceramic plaques using the identical Paula print, defendant would be required to purchase one hundred separate Paula prints. The Court finds that the process here in question does not constitute copying.

68 Reference should also be made in this connection to Peker v. Masters Collection, 96 F. Supp.2d 216 (U.S. Dist. Ct. S.D. N.Y., 2000) where the New York District Court ruled that the mere transfer of the ink from one support to another represents only a re-displaying of the poster image — similar to framing or lamination — that does not amount to "reproduction" of the work. However, in that case, once mounted, the defendant employed specially trained "artists" to apply

oil paint in brushstrokes to the image, attempting to match the color and style of the original painting. The court held that this additional copying amounted to an unauthorized reproduction of the original work. (There was no attempt in our case to replicate brushstrokes.)

69   The "ink transfer" method appears not to have stirred much comment in other common law jurisdictions, including Australia and New Zealand.

H.   The U.S. Concept of a ARecast, Transformed or "dapted" Derivative Work Would Be Introduced into our Law without any Legislative Basis

70   Of relevance to the present discussion is the fact that the United States legislation, apart from entitling the copyright holder to control the "reproduction" of his work, allows the copyright holder the right to authorize (or prohibit) the creation of "derivative works". The concept is formally defined in s. 101 of the United States Code, Title 17, as follows:

> A "derivative work" is a work based upon one or more preexisting works, such as a translation, musical arrangement, dramatization, fictionalization, motion picture version, sound recording, art reproduction, abridgment, condensation, <u>or any other form in which a work may be recast, transformed, or adapted</u>. A work consisting of editorial revisions, annotations, elaborations, or other modifications which, as a whole, represent an original work of authorship, is a "derivative work". [Emphasis added.]

71   The concept of a derivative work is found in the Berne Convention, and in the copyright legislation of the United States, England, Australia, New Zealand and Canada. All these provisions reflect a common progression in copyright legislation from a narrow protection against mere literal physical copying to a broader view which allows the copyright owner control over some changes of medium and adaptations of the original work. While the idea of "derivative works" therefore has parallels in other jurisdictions, including Canada, the American statutory language is particularly expansive, including in particular the words "any other form in which a work may be recast, transformed, or adapted", that have no precise counterpart in Canadian legislation.

72   The poster art industry in the United States has been actively litigating the broad statutory "derivative works" provision against owners of the material objects that embody the copyrighted work. In Mirage Editions, Inc., supra, for example, the copyrighted image was applied to a ceramic tile. The 9th Circuit Court of "ppeals ruled that the ceramic was an infringing Anew" derivative work, a conclusion expressly rejected by the 7th Circuit Court of Appeals in Lee v. A.R.T. Co., 125 F.3d 580 (U.S. 7th Cir., 1997), which concluded that the fixation did not infringe the copyright. Easterbrook J., for the Seventh Circuit, reasoned that "an alteration that includes (or consumes) the original lacks economic significance" (125F. 3d, at p. 581). He further found that there was no distinction between framing works of art, an acceptable practice under copyright law, and more permanent methods of display, such as re-fixing the art work on tile. The 9th Circuit has taken a different view: see Mirage Editions Inc., supra. These cases and their progeny typically turn on conflicting interpretations of the words "recast, transformed or adapted" in the U.S. statutory definition, but

even under that more expansive U.S. definition of "derivative works" the Seventh Circuit concluded that permanently mounting the artwork on tile did not "recast, transform, or adapt" the work. If these words appeared in our Act, there would presumably be a similar battle of statutory construction here, with the respondent saying the work was "recast, transformed or adapted", and the appellants denying that characterization, but the conflict between the scope of the copyright holders' economic rights to control the end uses of his work and the purchasers' rights as owners of the material object is the same. In the absence of the "recast, transformed or adapted" language (or equivalent) in our Act, however, the respondent is unable to rely on it as an additional basis of copyright liability. As Estey J. noted in Compo Co., supra, at p. 367:

> ... United States court decisions, even where the factual situations are similar, must be scrutinized very carefully because of some fundamental differences in copyright concepts which have been adopted in the legislation of that country.

73 I should note that while there is no explicit and independent concept of "derivative work" in our Act, the words "produce or reproduce the work... in any material form whatever" in s. 3(1) confers on artists and authors the exclusive right to control the preparation of derivative works such as the union leaflet incorporating and multiplying the Michelin man in the Michelin case, supra. See generally, McKeown, supra, at p. 64. In King Features Syndicate Inc. v. O. & M. Kleemann Ltd., [1941] A.C. 417 (U.K. H.L.), under a provision in the English Act similar to s. 3(1) of our Act, the plaintiff's copyright in the cartoon character "Popeye the Sailor" was held to be infringed by an unauthorized doll, i.e., the two dimensional character was reproduced without authorization in a new three-dimensional form. See also W. J. Braithwaite, "Derivative Works in Canadian Copyright Law" (1982), 20 Osgoode Hall L.J. 191, at p. 203. To the extent, however, that the respondent seeks to enlarge the protection of s. 3(1) by reading in the general words "recast, transformed or adapted" as a free-standing source of entitlement, his remedy lies in Parliament, not the courts.

VI. Conclusion with Respect to the Substantive Issue

74 My conclusion is that in this case the respondent is asserting a moral right in the guise of an economic right, and the attempt should be rejected.

75 If the respondent's argument were correct in principle, of course, the absence of authority would not prevent his success. It is in the nature of the subject that intellectual property concepts have to evolve to deal with new and unexpected developments in human creativity. The problem here is that the respondent's submission ignores the balance of rights and interests that lie at the basis of copyright law.

· · ·

Gonthier J. [in dissent]:

100 In my opinion, there is only one real issue in this case: whether the canvas-backed reproductions of the artist's paintings constitute infringement within the

meaning of the C.A. As I will explain in greater detail in the analysis, the validity of the seizure before judgment of the canvas-backed reproductions depends entirely on the answer to that question. If we conclude that the canvas-backed reproductions are infringing copies, the respondent is deemed to be the owner of the items under s. 38 C.A. The seizure would then be valid. If, however, we reach the contrary conclusion, the seizure must be set aside.

VI. Analysis

A. Seizure Before Judgment

(1) Interaction between art. 734(1) C.C.P. and s. 38(1) C.A.

101 Article 734(1) C.C.P. allows a plaintiff to seize before judgment the movable property which he has a right to revendicate. Section 38(1) C.A. provides that "the owner of the copyright in a work... may recover possession of all infringing copies of that work... and take proceedings for seizure of those copies... before judgment if, under the law of Canada or of the province in which those proceedings are taken, a person is entitled to take such proceedings, as if those copies... were the property of the copyright owner".

102 The fate of the revendication and seizure is therefore inextricably tied to the determination of the issue of infringement. If the canvas-backed reproductions constitute infringing copies of the respondent's works, the respondent is entitled to revendicate them under s. 38(1) C.A. That right of revendication will then serve as the basis for the right of seizure before judgment under art. 734(1) C.C.P. (see, for example, Tri-Tex Co. c. Gideon, [1999] R.J.Q. 2324 (Que. C.A.); 2946-1993 Québec inc. c. Sysbyte Telecom Inc., 2001 CarswellQue 1411 (Que. S.C.)).

103 The determination of the infringement issue in this case is relevant in determining whether the affidavit in support of the application for a writ of seizure (art. 738 C.C.P.) was sufficient. This is a moot point having regard to the veracity of the relevant facts alleged in the affidavit. The appellants' admissions relating to the transfer onto canvas of some paper-backed reproductions of the respondent's works have alone eliminated any uncertainty on that point.

104 A decision with respect to the sufficiency of the affidavit in support of a seizure before judgment is not, strictly speaking, a decision on the merits of the case. The judge who analyses the issue of sufficiency must nonetheless examine the logical connection between the facts alleged and the right to seize before judgment (Stopponi c. Bélanger, [1988] R.D.J. 33 (Que. C.A.), at p. 37).

105 In this case, however, the question of the connection between the facts and the right to seize is completely indistinguishable from the question of the infringement of the respondent's copyright. This is so by reason of s. 38(1) C.A., which states that "the owner of the copyright in a work... may recover possession of all infringing copies of that work... and take proceedings for seizure of those copies... before judgment if, under the law of Canada or of the province in which those proceedings are taken, a person is entitled to take such proceedings, as if those copies... were the property of the copyright owner" (emphasis added).

"Infringing", as defined by s. 2 C.A., requires an infringement of the copyright. In other words, in order to conclude that the process of transferring onto canvas gives rise to an act of infringement, it must first be established that it constitutes a copyright infringement.

106 In short, in order for the facts in the affidavit to meet the sufficiency requirement in the C.C.P., they must establish that an infringement has occurred. The issues of sufficiency and copyright infringement therefore involve the same elements of fact and law. Since the relevant facts were admitted, the legal issue is all that remains to be decided. That issue is a narrow one, and calls for a determination of whether the process of transferring onto canvas amounts to infringement.

. . .

(b) Copy made in contravention of this Act

124 Section 38(1) C.A. provides:

> 38. (1) Subject to subsection (2), the <u>owner of the copyright</u> in a work or other subject-matter may
>
> > (a) recover possession of all <u>infringing copies</u> of that work or other subject-matter, and of all plates used or intended to be used for the production of infringing copies, and
> >
> > (b) take proceedings for seizure of those copies or plates before judgment if, under the law of Canada or of the province in which those proceedings are taken, a person is entitled to take such proceedings, as if those copies or plates were the property of the copyright owner. [Emphasis added.]

125 A seizure under s. 38(1) C.A. therefore requires that there be infringing copies of works or of any other subject-matter of copyright. As I explained earlier, the outcome of this case depends entirely on the determination of the question of infringement.

126 Section 2 C.A. defines infringing as:

> (a) <u>in relation to a work in which copyright subsists, any copy, including any colourable imitation, made or dealt with in contravention of this Act,</u>
>
> (b) in relation to a performer's performance in respect of which copyright subsists any fixation or copy of a fixation of it made or dealt with in contravention of this Act,
>
> (c) in relation to a sound recording in respect of which copyright subsists, any copy of it made or dealt with in contravention of this Act, or
>
> (d) in relation to a communication signal in respect of which copyright subsists, any fixation or copy of a fixation of it made or dealt with in contravention of this Act. [Emphasis added.]

127 The expression "or other subject-matter" in s. 38(1) C.A. refers to the concepts of performance, sound recording and communication signal referred to in paras. (b), (c) and (d) of the definition of "infringing" (McKeown, supra, at p. 667). It also appears from the wording of the various paragraphs that make up

that definition that in order for a copy to be infringing, it must have an unlawful aspect.

128 "Infringing", in relation to a work in which copyright subsists, is defined in s. 2 C.A. as "any copy, including any colourable copy, made or dealt with in contravention of this Act". Infringement can therefore arise from two distinct sources: (i) a copy made in contravention of the C.A. or (ii) a copy dealt with in contravention of that Act.

129 In the case of a copy made in contravention of the Act, it is the act of copying itself that is unlawful. What that element of the definition is referring to is copies of works made in contravention of s. 3(1) C.A., which prohibits the production or reproduction of a work in any material form whatever.

130 In the case of a copy dealt with in contravention of the Act, the copy itself was not necessarily an infringement of the C.A. Rather, it was dealt with in contravention of that Act. We might then ask whether the expression "copy dealt with in contravention of this Act" requires the commission of acts that are contrary to s. 3(1) C.A. (s. 27 C.A.), or whether it can refer to a copy that resulted solely in an infringement of the author's moral rights (s. 28.1 C.A.).

131 The respondent maintains that a copy that infringes moral rights results in infringement, while the appellants maintain that only an infringement of the copyright under s. 3 C.A. (the right to produce, reproduce, perform or publish) can do that. With all due respect, I am of the view that an appropriate interpretation of the Act leads to the conclusion that a mere infringement of moral rights cannot constitute infringement. An infringement of the copyright defined in s. 3 C.A. is required.

132 First, infringement of a work, in its most common sense, is synonymous with plagiarism or unlawful appropriation. Generally speaking, we consider that infringing therefore requires copying or unlawful appropriation regardless of any other concurrent wrongful act (for example, an infringement of moral rights). In my view, it is that definition that has been adopted in the Act.

133 Section 38(1) C.A. provides that the owner of the copyright may recover possession of all infringing copies of that work or other subject-matter. This means that the right to recover possession of infringing copies is given to the owner of the copyright and not to the author himself or herself. The owner of the copyright and the author may be one and the same person or two different persons. In the latter case, it would be illogical for a copyright owner other than the author himself or herself to be entitled to recover possession of copies of a work the reproduction of which was an infringement only of the author's moral rights. Although, as I observed earlier, those rights attach solely to the person of the author and may not be assigned, the expanded interpretation of the expression "copy dealt with in contravention of [the] Act" proposed by the respondent would lead to just that outcome.

134 Furthermore, the definition of infringement cited refers to "a work in which copyright subsists". It also seems that only where there is an infringement of

copyright will the measures described in s. 38(1) C.A. be justified. Therefore, in the case of a work, a "copy dealt with in contravention of [the] Act" refers only to a copy dealt with in contravention of s. 3(1) C.A. The statutory history of the provisions in question confirms that conclusion: the provisions relating to moral rights were added in 1985 (R.S.C. 1985, c. 10 (4th Supp.)), while the meaning of s. 38(1) C.A. and of the definition of "infringing" have always been the same, for all practical purposes, since the Act was enacted in 1921.

135 Nevertheless, as I will explain later in the analysis, I am of the view that in this case the appellants unlawfully reproduced the respondent's works in a material form in breach of s. 3(1) C.A. A more in-depth analysis is therefore required in order to determine the scope of s. 3(1) C.A.

(c) Application of s. 3(1) C.A.

136 Section 3(1) C.A. provides:

> 3. (1) For the purposes of this Act, "copyright", in relation to a work, means the sole right to produce or reproduce the work or any substantial part thereof in any material form whatever, to perform the work or any substantial part thereof in public or, if the work is unpublished, to publish the work or any substantial part thereof... [Emphasis added.]

137 I find that there are three distinct concepts in this subsection, which are crucial in resolving this case. First, s. 3(1) confers the "sole right to produce or reproduce"; second, it protects the work in its entirety or "any substantial part thereof"; third, it specifies that the protection applies to the work "in any material form whatever." Let us examine what these concepts mean.

(i) The sole right to produce or reproduce: definition

138 My colleague, Binnie J., accepts the appellants' arguments and adopts a narrow interpretation of the concept of reproduction. Reproduction can only occur if there is multiplication. With respect, I do not agree with that interpretation. It is suggested that the verb "reproduce" implies an increase in the total number of copies. At first glance, that is not an interpretation that is readily supported by the ordinary meaning of that verb. I note that the Canadian Oxford (1998) defines it as follows:

> ... 1. produce a copy or representation of 2.... cause to be seen or heard etc. again...
> 5.... give a specified quality or result when copied.... [Emphasis added.]

139 It appears that the primary and essential meaning of the word "reproduce" as it appears in s. 3(1) C.A. is "produce a copy of" or "cause to be seen again" or "give a specified quality or result when copied". Accordingly, in order for a work to be reproduced, there is no requirement whatsoever to establish that there has been an increase in the total number of copies of the work. The nature of the protection that copyright confers confirms that interpretation.

140 As Reed J. stated in Apple Computer Inc., supra, at p. 193, affirmed (1987), [1988] 1 F.C. 673 (Fed. C.A.), and by this Court, [1990] 2 S.C.R. 209 (S.C.C.), which we would recall adopted the reasons of Reed J. in their entirety, the

concept of reproduction must be interpreted broadly. The legislation is written in general terms so as to include new reproduction technologies:

> [T]he opening words of subsection 1(2), now section 3 of the Act, were purposely drafted broadly enough to encompass new technologies which had not been thought of when the Act was drafted.

141 The primary purpose of s. 3(1) C.A. is to enable the author to profit from his or her work. Despite the fact that the legislation was written early in the last century, Parliament's use of general terms allows the C.A. to evolve and adapt to new social and technological circumstances.

(ii) Reproduction of a substantial part of the work

142 To grasp the essence of the concept of reproduction, the Act must be read bearing in mind that Parliament did not protect the right only to reproduce the work as a whole but also to reproduce a substantial part of the work. Parliament does not speak in vain, and if it specified in s. 3(1) that it is prohibited to reproduce not only a work in its entirety but also "a substantial part thereof", we must therefore consider not only the quantitative aspect, but also the qualitative aspect. As Teitelbaum J. pointed out in Cie générale des établissements Michelin — Michelin & Cie v. CAW — Canada (1996), [1997] 2 F.C. 306 (Fed. T.D.), at para. 50:

> The term "substantial part" is not defined in the Copyright Act. <u>Case law has held that the quality more than the simple quantity of the reproduction is key</u>: Justice Richard in U & R Tax Services Ltd. v. H & R Block Canada Inc. (1995), 62 C.P.R. (3d) 257 (F.C.T.D.), at pages 268-269, stated that the reproduction of a substantial part is a question of fact in which the Court will consider whether the alleged infringer has taken the distinctive traits of the original work. [Emphasis added.]

143 An analysis of the qualitative aspect is therefore an essential element of the analysis under s. 3(1) C.A. If we consider only the quantitative aspect, any individual could in fact appropriate a substantial part of a work and reproduce it on a large scale, and claim that the work had not been multiplied and therefore the C.A. had been complied with. Such a restrictive interpretation would be contrary to the aim and purpose of the C.A. As Tamaro, supra, at p. 93, pointed out in his text on copyright:

> [TRANSLATION] The right to reproduce the work or a substantial part thereof means to recreate the work in a modified form. <u>This brings us back to the concept of "substantial part of a work", which implies that the right to reproduce a work includes the right to reproduce it in all its essential parts.</u> [Emphasis added.]

144 The narrow analysis, limited as it is to the quantitative aspect, is therefore not consistent with a teleological interpretation of the protection given to a substantial part of the work. The qualitative aspect of a work is protected by s. 3(1) C.A., and a restrictive analysis based solely on multiplication of the work could not provide the work with the necessary protection and would ignore the concept of "substantial part thereof", which is protected by s. 3(1) C.A.

(iii) Reproduce in any material form whatever

145 In the view of Binnie J. "[t]he process began with a single poster and ended with a single poster" (para. 38). I do not agree with that view. The concept of "work" refers to any materialized and original form of expression (Tamaro, supra, at p. 84). The work is, so to speak, the physical outcome of the creative process. Fixation of the work in a medium is a condition sine qua non of the production of a work. Therefore, "producing" a work refers to the initial materialization and "reproducing" it refers to any subsequent material fixation that is modelled (in the causal sense) on its first fixation.

146 "Reproduc[ing] [a] work... in any material form whatever" therefore simply means "rematerializing" what already existed in a first, original material form. A person who models a subsequent materialization on the original materialization therefore reproduces the work in a material form and has therefore produced the work a second time.

147 Since material fixation is essential for the production of a work, it is also essential for reproduction of the work. Fixation of the work in a new medium is therefore the fundamental element of the act of "reproduc[ing]... in any material form whatever". However, while the work is an original creation, the reproduction of the work is necessarily not. Reproducing a work therefore consists mainly of the subsequent non-original material fixation of a first original material fixation. That type of conduct amounts to plagiarism and constitutes an infringement of the rights of the copyright owner under s. 3(1) C.A.

148 It may be pointed out that the expressions "reproduce a work" and "reproduce a work in any material form" are pleonastic since in all cases, reproducing a work involves a new materialization derived from the original one. However, s. 3(1) does not say only "reproduce... in a material form"; rather, it says "reproduce [a] work... in any material form whatever" (emphasis added). That is an appropriate and carefully worded recognition that a work may be reproduced even if the new medium is different.

149 Having regard to the foregoing, it is clear that multiplication of the number of copies of a work is not an essential element of the act of "reproduc [ing]... in any material form whatever". It does not matter that the process which produces a new materialization eliminates another; all that matters is that a new act of fixation occurs. Therefore, what we must count in order to determine whether a work has been reproduced is not the total number of copies of the work in existence after the rematerialization, but the number of materializations that occurred over time.

150 On that point, the analysis by Hugessen J.A. made in Apple Computer Inc. v. Mackintosh Computers Ltd. (1987), [1988] 1 F.C. 673 (Fed. C.A.), at p. 693, of the concept of "in any material form whatever" is directly relevant to the disposition of this case:

> We have already seen that the statute defines copyright as being, amongst other things, the sole right to produce or reproduce in any material form. It is, in my opinion, possible to read those words as including by necessary implication the sole right to produce the means of reproduction of the work or, to put the matter

another way, the sole right to produce anything used or intended to be used to reproduce the work. When the opening words of subsection 3(1) are read in the context of the remainder of that subsection and of other sections of the Copyright Act, it is my view that such interpretation is not only possible but is required. [Emphasis added.]

151 That is the only interpretation that is compatible with the three elements that we analysed in relation to s. 3(1) C.A. As Tamaro, supra, at p. 93, said:

> [TRANSLATION] If it were otherwise, anyone would be entitled to make a new material fixation of a work, in a modified form, or a fixation of the work on a different medium. That is no longer the case and the owner of the right to reproduce a work has the sole right to authorize an adaptation of the work; in that case, we refer, for example, to a derivative work, an adaptation or a reproduction that has been transformed.

152 Furthermore, whether we are dealing with an unlawful reproduction is a question of fact that must be determined based on the facts in each case. In Ladbroke (Football) Ltd. v. William Hill (Football) Ltd., [1964] 1 W.L.R. 273 (U.K. H.L.), at p. 283, Lord Evershed pointed out:

> [W]hat amounts in any case to substantial reproduction... cannot be defined in precise terms but must be a matter of fact and degree. It will, therefore, depend, not merely on the physical amount of the reproduction, but on the substantial significance of that which is taken. [Emphasis added.]

153 It is useful to recall that a reproduction of an article derived from the work is also an unlawful reproduction. In King Features Syndicate Inc. v. O. & M. Kleeman Ltd., [1940] 2 All E.R. 355 (Eng. Ch. Div.), at p. 359, Simonds J. said:

> It must be immaterial whether the infringing article is derived directly or indirectly from the original work. The standard is objective. The question is whether or not the original work, or a substantial part thereof, has been reproduced. If it has been, then it is no answer to say that it has been copied from a work which was itself, whether licensed or unlicensed, a copy of the original. For this proposition there is ample authority... in Ex p. Beal:
>
> > When the subject of a picture is copied, it is of no consequence whether that is done directly from the picture or through intervening copies.
>
> This view of copyright law has never, I think been doubted, and is plain common sense. [Citations omitted.]

154 Therefore, contrary to what my colleague, Binnie, J., says, at para. 65, I am of the view that based on s. 3(1) C.A., the analysis is the same whether the reproduction was made from an original work or a copy. In both cases, we must determine whether there has been a reproduction of the work or a substantial part of the work.

155 It is also important to distinguish between the medium, which is protected by s. 3(1) C.A. and is inextricably connected to the work, and the concept of "structure" in s. 28.2(3) C.A. My colleague interprets the English version of s. 28.2(3)(a), which provides: "a change in... the physical structure containing a

work... shall not, by that act alone, constitute... modification of the work", and holds that a modification of the work is an infringement of an author's moral rights rather than his or her economic rights (paras. 17 and 60). I cannot agree with that view. Such an interpretation would be contrary to the intent of Parliament. First, we need to compare the two versions of s. 28.2(3):

> 28.2 ...
>
> (3) For the purposes of this section,
>
>> (a) a change in the location of a work, the physical means by which a work is exposed <u>or the physical structure containing a work</u>, or
>>
>> (b) steps taken in good faith to restore or preserve the work
>
> <u>shall not, by that act alone,</u> constitute a distortion, mutilation or other modification of the work. [Emphasis added.]
>
> 28.2 ...
>
> (3) Pour l'application du présent article, <u>ne constitue pas nécessairement</u> une déformation, mutilation ou autre modification de l'oeuvre un changement de lieu, du cadre de son exposition <u>ou de la structure qui la contient</u> ou toute mesure de restauration ou de conservation prise de bonne foi. [Je souligne.]

156 Two comments must be made. First, my colleague places the emphasis on the expression "shall not". A comparative analysis shows that Parliament emphasizes, rather, "shall not by that act alone", which corresponds to "ne constitue pas nécesssairement" in the French version. By using the negative, it allows authors to show that a change in structure can amount to a modification of the work and cause prejudice to the author's honour or reputation, therefore infringing his or her moral rights.

157 Second, my colleague seems to want to give the concept of "physical structure containing a work", which Parliament rendered as "la structure qui contient [l'oeuvre]", a meaning that cannot stand up to an analysis of the concept of "work" ("oeuvre" in French). In my opinion, by referring to the concept of physical structure rather than medium (s. 3(1) C.A.), Parliament is making a vital distinction and is instead referring, in s. 28.2(3) C.A., to a physical structure that is superimposed onto the work. As Binnie J. pointed out in his analysis of copyright, copyright protects only works, not ideas. As I explained earlier, a work necessarily includes the medium. A change to the medium is prohibited by s. 3(1) C.A., while a change to a physical structure containing the work will be prohibited by s. 28.2(3) if the author establishes that the new physical structure causes prejudice to the integrity of his or her work.

158 In determining the meaning of "reproducing in any material form whatever", it is completely irrelevant that the consequence of one materialization destroys another. Obviously, when a person reproduces a work and at the same time destroys a copy of it, we assume that the person derives some benefit from doing so. In this case, for example, the appellants sold the canvas-backed reproductions of the respondent's works at a much higher price than the paper-backed

reproductions. However, there would be unlawful reproduction even if the re-materialization process resulted in an economic loss as a result of the destruction of another copy.

(3) Transfer to canvas and infringement

159 We must now address the issue on which the entire case is predicated: whether transferring a poster representing a work onto canvas constitutes infringement. In order for infringement to have occurred, there must have been an infringement of the copyright conferred under s. 3(1) C.A. Section 27 C.A. defines such an infringement as "[doing], without the consent of the owner of the copyright, anything that by this Act only the owner of the copyright has the right to do". In short, in order for infringement to have occurred, a work must have been plagiarized or unlawfully appropriated. In the case of a painting, infringement will occur, inter alia, when the painting as a whole or any substantial part thereof is reproduced in any material form whatever, in the words of s. 3(1) C.A.

160 The respondent had given his publishers, in particular É.G.I., very detailed authorization for the reproduction of his works. The evidence established that the posters that were transferred onto canvas by the appellants were all purchased from É.G.I.

161 The appellants argued that transferring the paper-backed reproductions of the respondent's works onto canvas was not an infringement of the respondent's copyright. They submitted, first, that the contract between the respondent and É.G.I. allowed the works to be reproduced in any material form whatsoever. Second, they argued that transferring posters onto canvas did not ultimately result in an increase in the total number of copies of the work, and accordingly, they had not reproduced the works, in any material form whatever, in breach of s. 3(1) C.A.: they had merely transferred the image represented from one medium to another, and this was not contrary to the Act.

162 We must therefore first determine the scope of the reproduction rights that were granted, which will at the same time establish the scope of the rights that the respondent retained. That determination calls for a simultaneous examination of certain provisions of the Act and the terms of the contract between the respondent and ÉGI. We will then need to determine whether transferring an image from one medium to another amounts to "produc [ing] or reproduc[ing] the work or any substantial part thereof in any material form whatever" within the meaning of s. 3(1) C.A.

Francis Day & Hunter Ltd. v. Bron (Trading as Delmar Publishing Co.), [1963] 2 W.L.R. 868 (C.A.)

Willmer L.J., Upjohn L.J. and Diplock L.J.

1963 Feb. 20, 21, 22, 25.

WILLMER L.J.

This is an appeal from a judgment of Wilberforce J., given on July 27, 1962, whereby he dismissed an action brought by the plaintiffs for infringement of their copyright in a song called "In a Little Spanish Town" (to which I will refer hereafter as "Spanish Town"). This was composed in 1926, and (as has been admitted by the defendants) was extensively exploited in the United States of America and elsewhere by the publication of sheet music, by the distribution of gramophone records and by broadcasting. Unlike many popular songs, "Spanish Town" appears to have retained its popularity over the years. Records published in this country (some of them quite recently) were played to us during the course of the hearing; and, speaking for myself, I was readily able to recognise the tune as a familiar one which I had heard on frequent previous occasions.

The defendants are the publishers of another song called "Why," which was composed in 1959 by Peter de Angelis. "Spanish Town" is written in 3/4 time, and "Why" in 4/4 time. There are a number of other differences between the two works which were the subject of a good deal of evidence by musical experts on both sides. But when the two songs were played to us, it was immediately apparent, to me at any rate, that the effect on the ear was one of noticeable similarity. This is a matter which is not without importance, for, as was pointed out by Astbury J. in Austin v. Columbia Gramophone Co. Ltd., "Infringement of copyright in music is not a question of note for note comparison," but falls to be determined "by the ear as well as by the eye."

. . .

Mr. Arnold conceded that reproduction could possibly be the result of a subconscious process. But he went on to submit that reproduction within the section could mean nothing short of identity. Reproduction, under section 49, may be of a substantial part; but there is no suggestion in the Act of any such thing as a "substantial reproduction." In the present case it cannot be said that there is anything approaching identity between the plaintiffs' work and that of de. Angelis. Consequently, Mr. Arnold submitted, there could be no infringement of the plaintiffs' copyright, whether conscious or unconscious, by way of reproduction.

I find myself quite unable to accept this submission, for I can find no warrant for the suggestion that reproduction, within the meaning of the section, occurs only when identity is achieved. This not only offends against common sense, but is, I think, contrary to authority. In Austin v. Columbia Gramophone Company Ltd. the headnote reads: "Infringement of copyright in music is not a question of note for note comparison, but of whether the substance of the original copyright work is taken or not." In the course of his judgment in that case Astbury J. quoted from the earlier case of D'Almaine v. Boosey, where it was laid down that "it must depend on whether the air taken is substantially the same with the original." I accept that as a correct statement of the principle.

UPJOHN L.J.

I agree with the judgment which has just been delivered.

When Mr. Foster opened this appeal, he invited us in the name of international comity to say that a right of property (that is, copyright) which is the subject of international convention must be protected in a most special and unique way. We were invited to say that if similarity of the alleged infringing work to the original work was established as a fact, and if it was further established that the alleged infringer had had some access to the original work, then although a denial of conscious plagiarism was accepted, we were bound, as an irrebuttable presumption of law, to say that the alleged infringer must have unconsciously copied the original work. The doctrine was said to be necessary to protect the author of the original work, for otherwise (so it was argued) any infringer could escape the consequences of plagiarism by denying that he had done so. Alternatively, it was said that if some undefined higher degree of similarity between the two works could be proved — something higher than is necessary to prove similarity in fact — then that would be sufficient to establish a similarity from which we were bound to infer unconscious copying.

Apart from the appeal to international comity, no authority and no textbook has been cited in support of this remarkable doctrine. Copyright is statutory, and depends upon section 2 of the Copyright Act, 1956. No hint of this doctrine appears there.

As to international comity, while it is true that in the United States of America a number of authorities (to some of which I shall have occasion to refer later) accept the doctrine that subconscious or unconscious copying may be inferred in a proper case and operate as a breach of copyright, not one of those authorities gives any support to this alleged and startling doctrine. The authorities in question in each case treated the question of unconscious copying as purely a question or inference of fact which might be drawn in the circumstances of a particular case, and not as a presumption of law. We were not referred to the laws of any other convention country, and the relevant paragraph (No. 4) of the Brussels Convention itself lends no support to the doctrine. I therefore reject this submission.

The truth is that the plaintiff in a copyright action must show that a substantial part of the original work has been reproduced; see section 2 (5) and section 49 of the Copyright Act, 1956; and, although not expressed in the Act, it is common ground that such a reproduction, in the words of Mr. Skone James, must be causally connected with the work of the original author. If it is an independent work, then, though identical in every way, there is no infringement. If a true infringer wrongly persuades the court that it is his own unaided work, the plaintiff fails, as do other plaintiffs when fraudulent defendants unhappily succeed (as, no doubt, they sometimes do) in persuading the court that they have not been fraudulent. The question, therefore, in this case is whether there has been a breach of section 2 (5); that subsection has been read by my Lord, and I will not read it again.

This is really a question of fact and nothing else, which depends on the circumstances of each case; but it is a question of fact which must be taken in two stages. The first stage is objective, and the second stage subjective. The first question is whether in fact the alleged infringing work — which for the sake of brevity I will inaccurately call the defendant's work, for though the composer was a witness, he was not a defendant — is similar to the work of the original author — which again for the sake of brevity I will, with equal inaccuracy, call the plaintiff's work. Is it then proper to draw the inference that the defendant's work may have been copied from the plaintiffs' work? This is purely an objective question of fact, and depends in large degree upon the aural perception of the judge, but also upon the expert evidence tendered to him; but it is essentially a jury question. A defendant might in theory go into the witness-box and say that he had deliberately made use of the plaintiff's work, but that it is not an infringement, either because he did not make use of a substantial part of the plaintiff's work, or that, though the plaintiff's work has been utilised, he has been able so to alter it that it cannot properly be described as a reproduction. The onus is on the plaintiff to prove the contrary as a matter of purely objective fact, and if he cannot do so then the morally dishonest defendant will escape the consequence of the allegation of infringement. No such question arises in this case. At this stage similarity has been found by Wilberforce J., and that is not challenged before us. For myself, I think that perhaps I would have used rather stronger adjectives than "definite" or "considerable" similarity, which were the words used by the judge; the adjective "close" would be more appropriate, but nothing, I think, turns upon that matter.

The next stage is the subjective stage and is equally a question of fact, though, of course, the degree of similarity is most important in reaching this subjective conclusion. The question at this stage, put bluntly, is: has the defendant copied the plaintiff's work, or is it an independent work of his own? Mr. Skone James, in an attractive argument, agrees that the plaintiff, in order to succeed, must prove a causal connection between his work and the defendant's work; but he submits that, providing that upon a proper inference from the known facts, it is right to assume that the alleged infringing work was derived from the plaintiff's work, it matters not whether it was done consciously or unconsciously. There is, he submits, no difference in principle between a conscious act of piracy and an unconscious act of piracy; all that must be established is a causal connection.

While conscious acts of piracy may be established in the witness-box, unconscious acts of piracy must clearly be a matter of inference from surrounding circumstances. The alleged infringing work may be an identical reproduction of the original work with all its idiosyncrasies, and all the same mistakes. Theoretically and mathematically, that may be a complete coincidence, and both works may be the product of entirely independent brains; but the judge has to judge of these matters on the balance of probabilities; and such an identical reproduction may lead him to reject the evidence of the defendant, who otherwise appears to be an honest witness. Much less than complete identity may properly lead the judge, on the balance of probabilities, to reject the evidence of an apparently honest witness on this question. This is a question of pure fact in every case. It does not arise in this case for Wilberforce J. accepted the author's evidence that he did not consciously derive the composition of "Why" from "In a Little Spanish Town," and that has not been challenged before us.

At this stage, therefore, the question is whether, on the facts of the case, it is proper to infer that de Angelis has derived "Why" unconsciously from the plaintiff's work, which he had heard at some earlier time. This again is purely a question of the proper inference of fact to be drawn from all the relevant and admissible known facts. There may be cases which, if the circumstances do not justify the conclusion that the defendant, in denying conscious plagiarism, is not telling the truth, yet justify the conclusion that he must have heard the plaintiff's tune, and subconsciously reproduced it.

I do not pause to recapitulate the facts of this case in any detail for they have been set out in much meticulous detail in Wilberforce J.'s judgment, and also by Willmer L.J., that I do not repeat them. I draw the conclusion that although, as I have already stated, the resemblance is a close one, that resemblance, in the circumstances of this case, is little evidence of conscious or unconscious copying.

Wilberforce J. said: "Thirdly, the theme of 'Spanish Town' is made up of common-place elements, or, as some witnesses have called them, cliches. The first six notes are a commonplace enough series; they are found in an Austrian country dance and in a song, 'Let Us Sing Merrily.' The device of repetition, of resting for two bars on a long note and of repetition in sequence, are the commonest tricks of composition. But many writers of great music have used clichès to produce masterpieces; indeed, some of them have found in the commonplace character of their basic phrase their stimulus. Professor Nieman gave some interesting examples from the music of Mozart, and most writers of popular songs use, and can use, nothing else. No example was given of precisely this combination having been used in other compositions, though it was apparent that the musical dictionaries and the experience of the witnesses had been thoroughly combed."

Having heard the arguments of counsel, accompanied by very helpful demonstrations on the piano, I reach the conclusion of fact that, apart altogether from de Angelis's denial of conscious plagiarism, which was accepted, it is not a mere legal or mathematical possibility, but a real live practical possibility that the defendant's composition of "Why" is an independent composition. This practical possibility again does not conclude the matter, for the defendant's composition may nevertheless be the result of unconscious memory. But first it is necessary to establish the probability that the defendant has heard the plaintiff's composition.

Wilberforce J. had to deal with a difficult situation as to whether de Angelis had heard, or even played, as a youth in a dance band, the plaintiff's composition. I think it is possible that, although in perfect good faith he stated the contrary, de Angelis did hear the music, and possibly played it in his early youth. Each case must depend upon its own facts, and it is not possible to lay down any criteria. But it does seem to me that where, for the reasons I have given, there is evidence from the music itself that there is a real practical possibility of independent composition by the defendant, it requires quite strong evidence to support the view that there may have been unconscious copying. To my mind, the possibility that the defendant had heard it, or even played it in his early youth, is a quite insufficient ground upon which it would be proper to draw the inference of unconscious copying. It may be that in the future medical evidence will be available to guide us upon this point, but in the absence of acceptable and probative medical evidence I think it requires quite strong evidence, in a case such as this — where, as I have already pointed out, independent composition is a real practical possibility — to establish, as a matter of probability, that de Angelis's subconscious ego guided his hand.

The cases in the United States to which we have been referred offer some instructive comparison on their facts, although I do not lose sight of the fact, of course, that cases are only authorities for legal propositions; but, nevertheless, I think the cases cited are helpful. In the first case, that of Fred Fisher Inc. v. Dillingham,[FN31] that great judge, Judge Learned Hand, in giving the famous composer, Jerome Kern, the benefit of the doubt, said[FN32]: "On the whole, my belief is that, in composing the accompaniment to the refrain of 'Kalua,' Mr. Kern must have followed, probably unconsciously, what he had certainly often heard only a short time before." That is in marked contrast to the facts of this case.

FN31   298 Fed. 145.

FN32   Ibid. 147.

Then, in a rather different case, Edwards and Deutsch Lithographing Co. v. Boorman,[FN33] the plaintiffs prepared, printed, published and distributed certain discount tables, the copyright work. The defendants published very similar tables. But there it was established that the defendants had sold and handled the plaintiffs' publications for years, and on that the inference was drawn of unconscious copying. Again the facts of that case are very different from the one before us.

FN33   15 Fed. (2nd Series) 35.

Wilberforce J. put the relevant points to himself quite accurately, and my Lord has read that part of his judgment; and his summary, which I will venture to repeat, was this: "In this case, after taking account of the respective character and similarities of the two works as previously discussed, and relating this to the fact that there is no direct evidence that Mr. Peter de Angelis even knew the work 'Spanish Town' before he composed 'Why,' I have come to the conclusion that I have not sufficient factual material from which to draw an inference that he had sufficient knowledge or memory of 'Spanish Town' at the date of composition, to justify me in finding, against his express denial, that in composing 'Why' he copied, without knowing that he did so, ' Spanish Town,' or a part of 'Spanish Town.'" I entirely agree with that conclusion of fact reached by Wilberforce J.

That makes it unnecessary to decide the really interesting question in this case whether Mr. Skone James is right when he says there is no difference in law between conscious and unconscious copying. It seems to me that that is an interesting question upon which I express no opinion, for, as I have said, it does not arise. Mr. Skone James, in support of his argument, has pointed out that an infringer may be entirely ignorant of knowledge of plagiarism; normally the printer and publisher will also be guilty of infringement though they have no reason even to suspect that any plagiarism can be suggested.

This, however, does not meet my difficulty. You do not necessarily have to show knowledge or suspicion of plagiarism against every defendant, but the plaintiff always has to prove that the alleged infringement is not the independent work of the alleged infringing author or composer, but is causally connected with the plaintiff's work.

The real question is this: can it be said to be an "act" of reproduction, for the purposes of section 2 (5) of the Copyright Act, 1956, if the alleged infringing work is not the conscious act of the infringer? It has been argued that Luxmoore J. in Ricordi's case[FN34] expressed the view that subconscious copying could be an infringement of copyright; but I do not think that he intended to express any view on the law at all. For my part, I think that this question, therefore, remains entirely open.

FN34 (1930) Macg.C.C. (1928-1935) 154.

I agree that this appeal must be dismissed.

DIPLOCK L.J.

This appeal seems to me to turn entirely upon a question of fact: was the judge entitled, notwithstanding the similarities between the melodies of the plaintiffs' song "In a Little Spanish Town" and the defendants' song "Why," to refuse to infer that the composer of the latter work copied it from the former work?

It is conceded on the one hand (as is obvious to the ear) that the two works show considerable similarities, and on the other hand that the composer of "Why " did not intentionally copy it from "In a Little Spanish Town'"; but it was found by Wilberforce J. that the composer of "Why" must at some time and in some circumstances have heard "In a Little Spanish Town"; and it is contended by the plaintiffs that the only proper inference of fact is that he must have stored it in his memory and reproduced it without being aware that he was performing an exercise of recollection and not an act of independent creation.

To this assumed mental feat there has been applied the conveniently ambiguous term "subconscious copying"; and we have heard much argument as to whether, if it is established, it constitutes an infringement of the copyright in the work which has been unconsciously copied. For my part, I think that the law is perfectly clear, and that such difficulties as there are in this appeal are solely due to the absence of any factual information about the mental process involved in "subconscious copying." We know not whether it is rare or common, general or idiosyncratic, nor indeed whether it is possible to remember, not a mere isolated phrase, but a "substantial" part of the remembered work without remembering that one is remembering.

First, as to the law; and for this purpose I will assume that it is established that the composer of "Why" did in fact use his recollection of "a substantial part of" the melody of "In a Little Spanish Town " as the model for his own composition, although he was unaware that he was doing so, and genuinely thought that "Why" was his own independent creation. The word "to copy" is not used at all in the Copyright Act, 1956, nor was it in the Copyright Act, 1911. Nevertheless, it is well established that to constitute infringement of copyright in any literary, dramatic or musical work, there must be present two elements: first, there must be sufficient objective similarity between the infringing work and the copyright work, or a substantial part thereof, for the former to be properly described, not necessarily as identical with, but as a reproduction or adaptation of the latter; secondly, the copyright work must be the source from which the infringing work is derived. The necessity for the second element was expressly laid down by the Court of Appeal in Purefoy Engineering Co, Ltd. v. Sykes Boxall & Co. Ltd.,[FN35] and is, indeed, implicit in all thee compilation cases, including the recent case in this court of William Hill (Football) Ltd. v. Ladbrokes (Football) Ltd.,[FN36] where tables of betting odds were unanimously held not to infringe the copyright in substantially identical tables because the authors of the later tables, although very familiar with the earlier tables, had, in fact, worked out the odds for themselves. But while the copyright work must be the source from which the infringing work is derived, it need not be the direct source: see Hanfstaengl v. Empire Palace Ltd.[FN37] Mr. Skone James, I think put it with his usual accuracy when he said there must be a causal connection between the copyright work and the infringing work. To borrow an expression once fashionable in the law of negligence, the copyright work must be shown to be a causa sine qua non of the infringing work.

FN35 (1955) 72 R.P.C. 89, C.A.

FN36 The Times, Dec. 20, 1962.

FN37 [1894] 2 ch. 1; 63 L.J.Ch. 417; 10 T.L.R. 229, C.A.

The necessity for a causal connection between the copyright work and the infringing work, although well established under the Copyright Act, 1911, either as being implicit in the legal concept of "copyright," or in the word "reproduce," is, I think, more easily deduced from the wording of the current Copyright Act of 1956. Section 1 (1) defines "copyright" in relation to a work as the exclusive right to do and to authorise other persons to do certain acts "in relation to that work"; and subsection (2) defines "infringement " as the doing of any of those acts by a person who is not the owner of the copyright or his licensee. The acts, which are defined in section 2, and include "reproducing the work in any material form," if they are to constitute infringement must thus be done "in relation to the work," an expression which connotes a causal connection between the copyright work and the act relied upon as an infringement. If the existence of the copyright work has no causal connection with the production of the alleged infringing work, even though the latter be identical with the former, there is no infringement of copyright.

It is, however, in my view, equally clear law that neither intention to infringe, nor knowledge that he is infringing on the part of the defendant, is a necessary ingredient in the cause of action for infringement of copyright. Once the two elements of sufficient objective similarity and causal connection are established, it is no defence that the defendant was unaware (and could not have been aware) that what he was doing infringed the copyright in the plaintiff's work. This is expressly recognised by sections 17 and 18 of the Copyright Act, 1956, which restrict the remedies available against an innocent infringer, but recognises his liability. Thus under section 18, which gives to the copyright owner remedies in conversion and detinue in respect of infringing copies of his work, a defendant who "believed and had reasonable grounds for believing that they were not infringing copies "is relieved of any liability in damages, but not of his liability to deliver up any infringing copies in his possession.

"Unconscious copying" in the sense in which it has been used in the argument postulates, first, such objective similarity between the copyright work and the alleged infringing work that the latter may properly be said to reproduce the former; secondly, that there is a causal connection between the copyright work and the alleged infringing work; thirdly, that the composer of the alleged infringing work believed (and may indeed have had reasonable grounds for believing) that there was no such causal connection. The first two, if established, in my view constitute breach of copyright; the third is irrelevant on liability although it may be relevant on remedy.

The real difficulty in this case is not one of law, but of fact. It involves an inquiry into the working of the human mind. It may well be that this is a matter upon which expert evidence is admissible; but cases in English courts are normally conducted upon the tacit assumption that where no question of disease of the mind is involved, the ordinary man, whether sitting in the jury-box or on the bench: is capable of determining (where it is relevant) what went on in the defendant's mind.

The present case was so conducted before Wilberforce J. No expert evidence was called as to how the human memory or musical creative faculties work; no investigation was made into the mental idiosyncrasies of the composer of "Why" or his methods of composition. Wilberforce J. was left to draw the inference of "subconscious copying" from the evidence (1) of the similarities between the melodies of "In a Little Spanish Town" and "Why" as explained by the conflicting evidence of expert musicians; (2) of the likelihood of the composer of "Why" having at some time heard "In a Little Spanish Town"; and (3) of his denial that he had consciously copied "In a Little Spanish Town."

On this state of the evidence, there were three possible explanations of the similarities: conscious copying, unconscious copying, coincidence. The first Wilberforce J. rejected. He accepted the denial of the composer of "Why." This is a finding of primary fact, and it depends ultimately on credibility. The appellants do not seek to disturb it. This reduces the possible explanations to two: unconscious copying, or coincidence. Wilberforce J. did not reject the possibility that "unconscious copying" of musical works can occur. He proceeded to consider, in the light of the conflicting expert evidence, which was the more probable explanation of the similarities, unconscious copying, or coincidence. The relevant similarities were to be found in the first eight bars of the melody of "In a Little Spanish Town" which, it is common ground, do constitute a substantial part of that musical work. They are described clearly (and it is conceded accurately) in Wilberforce J.'s judgment.

The rival contentions, supported by expert evidence, may be summarised thus: The plaintiffs, conceding that the first bar by itself was a musical cliche in which there was no copyright, contended that the similarities in the use made of the cliche in eight successive bars in each of the two works were too great to be explained by coincidence. The defendants contended that, once a composer of popular songs had decided to use, as a basis of the theme of a popular song, the musical cliche contained in the first bar, the use which was in fact made of it in both "Why" and "In a Little Spanish Town" in the succeeding bars was a device by no means uncommon in musical composition, and the similarities were readily explicable by coincidence. Wilberforce J. was not satisfied that the similarities were due to unconscious copying. This, no doubt, was an inference of fact, but one which depends, in part at least, upon the degree of conviction which the evidence of the respective experts carried, and thus one with which an appellate court should be slow to interfere. No attempt has been made to demonstrate that he has overlooked or misunderstood any of the evidence.

How, then, is the case for the appellants put? The procedure of the English courts, says Mr. Foster, is ill-adapted to deal with such esoteric problems as "subconscious copying." It places too heavy a burden upon those who seek to establish that it has occurred. Copyright is an international proprietary right, and English law should keep in step with foreign law. They order these things better in more sophisticated (though unspecified) jurisdictions. But the only foreign law to which we have actually been referred is to be found in the United States cases which my brethren have discussed; and there, it seems, the matter is dealt with in the same unsophisticated way as that in which Wilberforce J. dealt with this case, without making it impossible for the courts to find (where the evidence, so warrants) that unconscious copying has taken place.

Faced with the difficulty that "unconscious copying" is by definition not susceptible of direct proof in the present state of psychological techniques, it must always be a matter of inference from other facts, Mr. Foster's first bold submission was, that if the plaintiff proves (1) the presence of the necessary element of objective similarity between the copyright work and the alleged infringing work; and (2) the mere possibility of access to the copyright work by the author of the alleged infringing work, there is an irrebuttable presumption (that is, a presumption of law) that the author of the alleged infringing work unconsciously copied the copyright work; or, put more briefly, what cannot be proved must be presumed. With all respect, this is bad logic as well as bad law. For, unless "the law is an ass" — which I must ex officio irrebuttably presume it is not — the essential, though unexpressed, premise of this proposition is that the similarities cannot be due to coincidence; proof of possibility of access is thus unnecessary; access as well as unconscious copying can be irrebuttably presumed. But this is merely a roundabout way of saying that proof of a causal connection between the copyright work and the alleged infringing work is not a necessary element in infringement of copyright; and that is not the law.

Mr. Foster's alternative submission (although I understood it to be presented as one of law) was, I think, upon analysis merely one as to the proper inferences of fact to be drawn from varying degrees of similarity between the copyright work and the alleged infringing work. The degree of objective similarity is, of course, not merely important, indeed essential, in proving the first element in infringement, namely, that the defendant's work can properly be described as a reproduction or adaptation of the copyright work; it is also very cogent material from which to draw the inference that the defendant has in fact copied, whether consciously or unconsciously, the copyright work. But it is not the only material. Even complete identity of the two works may not be conclusive evidence of copying, for it may be proved that it was impossible for the author of the alleged infringing work to have had access to the copyright work. And, once you have eliminated the impossible (namely, copying), that which remains (namely, coincidence) however improbable, is the truth; I quote inaccurately, but not unconsciously, from Sherlock Holmes.

No useful purpose can thus be served by seeking to classify degrees of similarity into categories which must be taken to be sufficient to prove unconscious copying where access to the copyright work by the author of the alleged infringing work is proved (1) as a certainty; (2) as a probability; (3) as a possibility, and (4) as an impossibility. That is not how questions of fact are decided in courts of law, or anywhere else.

The answer, as Wilberforce J. said at the conclusion of an impeccable summary of the evidence, "can only be reached by a judgment of fact upon a number of composite elements." Those elements on which the judge directed himself have already been read by my Lord, and I need not repeat them.

I agree that it is impossible for this court, which has not heard the evidence or seen the witnesses, to say that Wilberforce J. came to a wrong conclusion of fact.

The Cartoon Network LP v. CSC Holdings, Inc., 536 F.3d. 121 (2nd Cir. August 4, 2008)

United States Court of Appeals

JOHN M. WALKER, JR., *Circuit Judge:*

Defendant-Appellant Cablevision Systems Corporation ("Cablevision") wants to market a new "Remote Storage" Digital Video Recorder system ("RS-DVR"), using a technology akin to both traditional, set-top digital video recorders, like TiVo ("DVRs"), and the video-on-demand ("VOD") services provided by many cable companies. Plaintiffs-Appellees produce copyrighted movies and television programs that they provide to Cablevision pursuant to numerous licensing agreements. They contend that Cablevision, through the operation of its RS-DVR system as proposed, would directly infringe their copyrights both by making unauthorized reproductions, and by engaging in public performances, of their copyrighted works. The material facts are not in dispute. Because we conclude that Cablevision would not directly infringe plaintiffs' rights under the Copyright Act by offering its RS-DVR system to consumers, we reverse the district court's award of summary judgment to plaintiffs, and we vacate its injunction against Cablevision.

BACKGROUND

Today's television viewers increasingly use digital video recorders ("DVRs") instead of video cassette recorders ("VCRs")to record television programs and play them back later at their convenience. DVRs generally store recorded programming on an internal hard drive rather than a cassette. But, as this case demonstrates, the generic term "DVR" actually refers to a growing number of different devices and systems. Companies like TiVo sell a stand-alone DVR device that is typically connected to a user's cable box and television much like a VCR. Many cable companies also lease to their subscribers "set-top storage DVRs," which combine many of the functions of a standard cable box and a stand-alone DVR in a single device.

In March 2006, Cablevision, an operator of cable television systems, announced the advent of its new "Remote Storage DVR System." As designed, the RS-DVR allows Cablevision customers who do not have a stand-alone DVR to record cable programming on central hard drives housed and maintained by Cablevision at a" remote" location. RS-DVR customers may then receive playback of those programs through their home television sets, using only a remote control and a standard cable box equipped with the RS-DVR software. Cablevision notified its content providers, including plaintiffs, of its plans to offer RS-DVR, but it did not seek any license from them to operate or sell the RS-DVR.

Plaintiffs, which hold the copyrights to numerous movies and television programs, sued Cablevision for declaratory and injunctive relief. They alleged that Cablevision's proposed operation of the RS-DVR would directly infringe their exclusive rights to both reproduce and publicly perform their copyrighted works.

I. Operation of the RS-DVR System

Cable companies like Cablevision aggregate television programming from a wide variety of "content providers" — the various broadcast and cable channels that produce or provide individual programs — and transmit those programs into the homes of their subscribers via coaxial cable. At the outset of the transmission process, Cablevision gathers the content of the various television channels into a single stream of data. Generally, this stream is processed and transmitted to Cablevision's customers in real time. Thus, if a Cartoon Network program is scheduled to air Monday night at 8 pm, Cartoon Network transmits that program's data to Cablevision and other cable companies nationwide at that time, and the cable companies immediately re-transmit the data to customers who subscribe to that channel.

Under the new RS-DVR, this single stream of data is split into two streams. The first is routed immediately to customers as before. The second stream flows into a device called the Broadband Media Router ("BMR"), id. at 613, which buffers the data stream, reformats it, and sends it to the "Arroyo Server," which consists, in relevant part, of two data buffers and a number of high-capacity hard disks. The entire stream of data moves to the first buffer (the "primary ingest buffer"), at which point the server automatically inquires as to whether any customers want to record any of that programming. If a customer has requested a particular program, the data for that program move from the primary buffer into a secondary buffer, and then onto a portion of one of the hard disks allocated to that customer. As new data flow into the primary buffer, they overwrite a corresponding quantity of data already on the buffer. The primary ingest buffer holds no more than 0.1 seconds of each channel's programming at any moment. Thus, every tenth of a second, the data residing on this buffer are automatically erased and replaced. The data buffer in the BMR holds no more than 1.2 seconds of programming at any time. While buffering occurs at other points in the operation of the RS-DVR, only the BMR buffer and the primary ingest buffer are utilized absent any request from an individual subscriber.

I. The Buffer Data

It is undisputed that Cablevision, not any customer or other entity, takes the content from one stream of programming, after the split, and stores it, one small piece at a time, in the BMR buffer and the primary ingest buffer. As a result, the information is buffered before any customer requests a recording, and would be buffered even if no such request were made. The question is whether, by buffering the data that make up a given work, Cablevision "reproduce[s]" that work "in copies," 17 U.S.C. § 106(1), and thereby infringes the copyright holder's reproduction right.

"Copies," as defined in the Copyright Act, "are material objects... in which a work is fixed by any method... and from which the work can be... reproduced." Id. § 101. The Act also provides that a work is "'fixed' in a tangible medium of expression when its embodiment... is sufficiently permanent or stable to permit it to be... reproduced... for a period of more than transitory duration." Id. (emphasis added).

We believe that this language plainly imposes two distinct but related requirements: the work must be embodied in a medium, i.e., placed in a medium such that it can be perceived, reproduced, etc., from that medium (the "embodiment requirement"), and it must remain thus embodied "for a period of more than transitory duration" (the "duration requirement"). See 2 Melville B. Nimmer & David Nimmer, Nimmer on Copyright § 8.02[B][3], at 8-32 (2007). Unless both requirements are met, the work is not "fixed" in the buffer, and, as a result, the buffer data is not a "copy" of the original work whose data is buffered.

The district court mistakenly limited its analysis primarily to the embodiment requirement. As a result of this error, once it determined that the buffer data was "[c]learly... capable of being reproduced," i.e., that the work was embodied in the buffer, the district court concluded that the work was therefore "fixed" in the buffer, and that a copy had thus been made. Cablevision I, 478 F. Supp. 2d at 621-22. In doing so, it relied on a line of cases beginning with MAI Systems Corp. v. Peak Computer Inc., 991 F.2d 511 (9th Cir. 1993). It also relied on the United States Copyright Office's 2001 report on the Digital Millennium Copyright Act, which states, in essence, that an embodiment is fixed "[u]nless a reproduction manifests itself so fleetingly that it cannot be copied." U.S. Copyright Office, DMCA Section 104 Report 111 (Aug. 2001) ("DMCA Report") (emphasis added), available at http://www.copyright.gov/reports/studies/dmca/sec-104-report-vol-1.pdf.

The district court's reliance on cases like MAI Systems is misplaced. In general, those cases conclude that an alleged copy is fixed without addressing the duration requirement; it does not follow, however, that those cases assume, much less establish, that such a requirement does not exist. Indeed, the duration requirement, by itself, was not at issue in MAI Systems and its progeny. As a result, they do not speak to the issues squarely before us here: If a work is only "embodied" in a medium for a period of transitory duration, can it be "fixed" in that medium, and thus a copy? And what constitutes a period "of more than transitory duration"?

In MAI Systems, defendant Peak Computer, Inc., performed maintenance and repairs on computers made and sold by MAI Systems. In order to service a customer's computer, a Peak employee had to operate the computer and run the computer's copyrighted operating system software. See MAI Sys., 991 F.2d at 513. The issue in MAI Systems was whether, by loading the software into the computer's RAM[FN6], the repairman created a "copy" as defined in § 101. See id. at 517. The resolution of this issue turned on whether the software's embodiment in the computer's RAM was "fixed," within the meaning of the same section. The Ninth Circuit concluded that

> FN6. To run a computer program, the data representing that program must be transferred from a data storage medium (such as a floppy disk or a hard drive) to a form of Random Access Memory ("RAM") where the data can be processed. The data buffers at issue here are also a form of RAM.

> By showing that Peak loads the software into the RAM and is then able to view the system error log and diagnose the problem with the computer, MAI has adequately shown that the representation created in the RAM is "sufficiently permanent or stable to permit it to be perceived, reproduced, or otherwise communicated for a period of more than transitory duration."

Id. at 518 (quoting 17 U.S.C. § 101).

The MAI Systems court referenced the "transitory duration" language but did not discuss or analyze it. The opinion notes that the defendants "vigorously" argued that the program's embodiment in the RAM was not a copy, but it does not specify the arguments defendants made. Id. at 517. This omission suggests that the parties did not litigate the significance of the "transitory duration" language, and the court therefore had no occasion to address it. This is unsurprising, because it seems fair to assume that in these cases the program was embodied in the RAM for at least several minutes.

Accordingly, we construe MAI Systems and its progeny as holding that loading a program into a computer's RAM can result in copying that program. We do not read MAI Systems as holding that, as a matter of law, loading a program into a form of RAM always results in copying. Such a holding would read the "transitory duration" language out of the definition, and we do not believe our sister circuit would dismiss this statutory language without even discussing it. It appears the parties in MAI Systems simply did not dispute that the duration requirement was satisfied; this line of cases simply concludes that when a program is loaded into RAM, the embodiment requirement is satisfied — an important holding in itself, and one we see no reason to quibble with here[FN6].

> FN6. The same reasoning also distinguishes this court's opinion in Matthew Bender & Co. v. West Publishing Co., 158 F.3d 693 (2d Cir. 1998). Language in that opinion, taken out of context, suggests that the definition of "fixed" imposes only an embodiment requirement: "Under § 101's definition of 'copies,' a work satisfies the fixation requirement when it is fixed in a material object from which it can be perceived or communicated directly or with the aid of a machine." Id. at 702. Like the MAI Systems cases, Matthew Bender only addresses the embodiment requirement: specifically, whether West's copyrighted arrangement of judicial opinions was "embedded" in a CD-ROM compilation of opinions when the cases were normally arranged differently but could be manipulated by the user to replicate West's copyrighted arrangement. Id. at 703. The opinion merely quotes the duration language without discussing it, see id. at 702; that case therefore does not compel us to conclude that the definition of "fixed" does not impose a duration requirement.

At least one court, relying on MAI Systems in a highly similar factual setting, has made this point explicitly. In Advanced Computer Services of Michigan, Inc. v. MAI Systems Corp., the district court expressly noted that the unlicensed user in that case ran copyrighted diagnostic software "for minutes or longer," but that the program's embodiment in the computer's RAM might be too ephemeral to be fixed if the computer had been shut down "within seconds or fractions of a second" after loading the copyrighted program. 845 F. Supp. 356, 363 (E.D. Va. 1994). We have no quarrel with this reasoning; it merely makes explicit the reasoning that is implicit in the other <u>MAI Systems</u> cases. Accordingly, those cases provide no support for the conclusion that the definition of "fixed" does not include a duration requirement. <u>See Webster v. Fall</u>, 266 U.S. 507, 511 (1924) ("Questions which merely lurk in the record, neither brought to the attention of the court nor ruled upon, are not to be considered as having been so decided as to constitute precedents.").

Nor does the Copyright Office's 2001 DMCA Report, also relied on by the district court in this case, explicitly suggest that the definition of "fixed" does not contain a duration requirement. However, as noted above, it does suggest that an embodiment is fixed "[u]nless a reproduction manifests itself so fleetingly that it cannot be copied, perceived or communicated." <u>DMCA Report, supra</u>, at 111. As we have stated, to determine whether a work is "fixed" in a given medium, the statutory language directs us to ask not only 1) whether a work is "embodied" in that medium, but also 2) whether it is embodied in the medium "for a period of more than transitory duration." According to the Copyright Office, if the work is capable of being copied from that medium <u>for any amount of time</u>, the answer to both questions is "yes." The problem with this interpretation is that it reads the "transitory duration" language out of the statute.

We assume, as the parties do, that the Copyright Office's pronouncement deserves only <u>Skidmore</u> deference, deference based on its "power to persuade." <u>Skidmore v. Swift & Co.</u>, 323 U.S. 134, 140 (1944). And because the Office's interpretation does not explain why Congress would include language in a definition if it intended courts to ignore that language, we are not persuaded.

In sum, no case law or other authority dissuades us from concluding that the definition of "fixed" imposes both an embodiment requirement and a duration requirement. <u>Accord CoStar Group Inc. v. LoopNet, Inc.</u>, 373 F.3d 544, 551 (4th Cir. 2004) (while temporary reproductions "may be made in this transmission process, they would appear not to be 'fixed' in the sense that they are 'of more than transitory duration'"). We now turn to whether, in this case, those requirements are met by the buffer data.

Cablevision does not seriously dispute that copyrighted works are "embodied" in the buffer. Data in the BMR buffer can be reformatted and transmitted to the other components of the RS-DVR system. Data in the primary ingest buffer can be copied onto the Arroyo hard disks if a user has requested a recording of that data. Thus, a work's "embodiment" in either buffer "is sufficiently permanent or stable to permit it to be perceived, reproduced," (as in the case of the ingest buffer) "or otherwise communicated" (as in the BMR buffer). 17 U.S.C. § 101. The result might be different if only a single second of a much longer work was placed in the buffer in isolation. In such a situation, it might be reasonable to conclude that only a minuscule portion of a work, rather than "a work" was embodied in the buffer. Here, however, where every second of an entire work is placed, one second at a time, in the buffer, we conclude that the work is embodied in the buffer.

Does any such embodiment last "for a period of more than transitory duration"? Id. No bit of data remains in any buffer for more than a fleeting 1.2 seconds. And unlike the data in cases like MAI Systems, which remained embodied in the computer's RAM memory until the user turned the computer off, each bit of data here is rapidly and automatically overwritten as soon as it is processed. While our inquiry is necessarily fact-specific, and other factors not present here may alter the duration analysis significantly, these facts strongly suggest that the works in this case are embodied in the buffer for only a "transitory" period, thus failing the duration requirement.

Against this evidence, plaintiffs argue only that the duration is not transitory because the data persist "long enough for Cablevision to make reproductions from them." Br. of Pls.-Appellees the Cartoon Network et al. at 51. As we have explained above, however, this reasoning impermissibly reads the duration language out of the statute, and we reject it. Given that the data reside in no buffer for more than 1.2 seconds before being automatically overwritten, and in the absence of compelling arguments to the contrary, we believe that the copyrighted works here are not "embodied" in the buffers for a period of more than transitory duration, and are therefore not "fixed" in the buffers. Accordingly, the acts of buffering in the operation of the RS-DVR do not create copies, as the Copyright Act defines that term. Our resolution of this issue renders it unnecessary for us to determine whether any copies produced by buffering data would be de minimis, and we express no opinion on that question.

(b) Reproduction of Collective Works and Compilations

One area that has generated some apparent confusion is the reproduction of compilations and collective works. According to subsection 2.1(2) of the Act, "the mere fact that a work is included in a compilation does not increase, decrease or otherwise affect the protection conferred by this Act in respect of the copyright in the work or the moral rights in respect of the work." In a collective work that includes the work of several authors (see s. 2), there may be a separate copyright interest in each individual component of the collective work, as well as the copyright interest that exists in the collective work itself. Each copyright interest exists independently of the others, and the compiler does not, by virtue of his or her compilation, acquire any rights to the underlying works. Similarly, the copyright owner of a work included in a compilation does not, by virtue of that inclusion, have any right over the compilation per se. This should mean that neither the owner of the compilation nor the owner of the contribution can reproduce the other's work without permission (or beyond the scope of the permission originally obtained).

Due to the effective "layering" of rights, however, questions may arise as to whose work is being reproduced and whose rights are implicated by activities in relation to the compilation and/or parts thereof. Endorsing the controversial *Allen v. Toronto Star* decision (below), and perhaps informed by the US approach to collective works (see 17.U.S.C. §201(c)), Canadian copyright law on this issue recently took a surprising turn with the Supreme Court's ruling in *Robertson v. Thomson Corp.* The ruling, which the UK courts have declined to follow, seems to imply that, having obtained the original consent of an author to include his or her work in a compilation, the owner of copyright in the compilation has a positive right to reproduce the compilation or a substantial part thereof in any manner or medium.

Allen v. Toronto Star Newspapers Ltd., (1997), 78 C.P.R. (3d) 115 (Ont. Div. Ct.)

Ontario Court (General Division), Divisional Court

Court File No. 740/95

O'Driscoll, Flinn and Sedgwick JJ.

SEDGWICK J.: — This is an appeal by the defendant (Toronto Star) from a judgment of the Ontario Court of Justice (General Division) released on October 13, 1995 ((1995), 26 O.R. (3d) 308, 129 D.L.R. (4th) 171, 63 C.P.R. (3d) 517), in favour of the plaintiff (Allen) for $900 general damages for infringement of copyright in a photograph. This appeal comes to the Divisional Court under ss. 19(1)(a) of the Courts of Justice Act, R.S.O. 1990, c. C.43.

Allen is a freelance photographer. His services were engaged by Saturday Night, a magazine with nation-wide circulation, to shoot a cover photo of a national political figure, Sheila Copps, M.P., then a member of an active group of opposition Members of Parliament known as the "Rat Pack".

The cover of the November 1985 issue of Saturday Night bore a photograph of Ms. Copps dressed in leathers astride a motorcycle, identified by counsel as a Harley-Davidson. The photo used on the cover was taken by Allen in the course of his engagement by Saturday Night. On March 11, 1990, the Toronto Star, a daily newspaper, published a feature article about Ms. Copps, then a candidate for the national leadership of her party. The article was illustrated by two photographs. Oneof them was a photo of the cover of the November 1985 issue of Saturday Night. The other was a photo of Ms. Copps in 1990 in more conventional clothing speaking in Toronto to a group identified in the newspaper as Chinese Canadians.

The publication by the Toronto Star of that photograph resulted in this action being brought by Allen on October 16, 1991, for infringement of his copyright in the 1985 photo of Ms. Copps. Allen was successful at trial. The learned trial judge concluded (supra, p. 316):

> . . . by reproducing the Saturday Night magazine cover of November 1985 the defendant infringed the copyright in the photograph owned by Allen and accordingly I will be awarding damages for such infringement.

Allen was awarded general damages in the amount of $900, calculated to be the amount of the fee to which he would have been entitled for the use of the photograph, according to the learned trial judge's view of the evidence as to the custom of the industry. Allen was awarded pre-judgment interest on that amount in accordance with section 128 of the Courts of Justice Act, from October 16, 1991 to October 26, 1995, together with his party/party costs fixed at $10,400 (plus G.S.T.). Allen's claim for aggravated or exemplary damages in the amount of $10,000 was dismissed.

Saturday Night has not objected to the reproduction of its November 1985 cover.

The Toronto Star appeals this judgment on three grounds:

> (1) its reproduction of the 1985 magazine cover did not infringe the admitted copyright interest of Allen in the 1985 Copps photo itself, or any copyright interest in the magazine cover;

> (2) its reproduction of the 1985 magazine cover does not infringe any copyright interest in the photo or the cover because the "fair dealing" defence set out in s. 27(2)(a) of the Copyright Act, R.S.C. 1985, c. C-42 (then in force), applies;

> (3) if the "fair dealing" defence does not apply, then s. 27(2) (a) of the Copyright Act infringes s. 2(b) of the Canadian Charter of Rights and Freedoms and should be interpreted and applied in a manner consistent with s. 2(b) of the Charter.

There is no cross-appeal by Allen against the dismissal of his claim for aggravated or exemplary damages.

(1) Copyright Ownership

The Toronto Star acknowledges that Allen owns the copyright in the 1985 photograph of Ms. Copps. However, it asserts that Allen is not the owner of the separate and distinct copyright which exists in the entire cover of the November 1985 issue of Saturday Night. Any copyright in the entire cover would belong to the magazine Saturday Night, which has not objected to the reproduction of the cover by the Toronto Star.

The learned trial judge rejected this submission. He stated that if he accepted it (supra, p. 316):

> . . . I would be indulging in hair splitting of a somewhat advanced nature which I am not prepared to do as clearly the photograph dominates the Saturday Night cover.

Copyright may subsist in original literary, dramatic, musical or artistic works and may subsist in collective works, in which works or parts of works of different authors or contributors are incorporated.

Copyright may subsist separately in a compilation of elements which may themselves individually be the subject of copyright. The issue of ownership of copyright in the compilation itself was considered by McLachlin J. (as she then was) in Slumber-Magic Adjustable Bed Co. v. Sleep-King Adjustable Bed Co. (1984), 3 C.P.R. (3d) 81 (B.C.S.C.).

In that case, the issue was whether copyright subsisted in the plaintiff's advertising brochure even though a number of the elements of the brochure (including photographs) were similar to those found in the brochures of competitors (the defendants). The court held that it did. McLachlin J. concluded (p. 85):

> ... the fact that elements of the [the plaintiff's] brochure were similar to elements of other brochures, does not negate the fact that it has copyright in the arrangement of ideas, original or otherwise, which was solely the product of its own work, skill and judgment.

She explained (pp. 84-5):

> The question is whether the plaintiff had copyright in the brochure? In my opinion, it did. The defendants suggest that there is no copyright in the brochure because it used ideas and elements which are also found in the brochures of other competitors. That, however, does not defeat a claim for copyright. It is well established that compilations of material produced by others may be protected by copyright, provided that the arrangement of the elements taken from other sources is the product of the plaintiff's thought, selection and work. It is not the several components that are the subject of the copyright, but the over-all arrangement of them which the plaintiff through his industry has produced. The basis of copyright is the originality of the work in question. So long as work, taste and discretion have entered into the composition, that originality is established. In the case of a compilation, the originality requisite to copyright is a matter of degree depending on the amount of skill, judgment or labour that has been involved in making the compilation: Ladbroke (Football), Ltd. v. William Hill (Football), Ltd., [1964] 1 All E.R. 465 (H.L.). Where copyright is claimed in a compilation it is not the correct approach to dissect the work in fragments and, if the fragments are not entitled to copyright, then deduce that the whole compilation is not so entitled; rather, the court should canvas the degree of industry, skill or judgment which has gone into the over-all arrangement: Ladbroke, supra. See also T.J. Moore Co. Ltd. v. Accessoires de Bureau de Quebec Inc. (1973), 14 C.P.C. (2d) 113 (Fed. Ct. T.D.); Jarrold v. Houlston (1857), 3 K & J. 708, 69 E.R. 1294 (Ch. Div.); MacMillan & Co., Ltd. v. Cooper (1923), 40 T.L.R. 186 (P.C.).

The proposition that arrangements of common ideas may be copyright is subject to certain limitations. First, it appears that the compiler can claim no copyright unless he or she had a right to use materials constituting his compilation: T.J. Moore Co. Ltd. v. Accessoires de Bureau de Quebec Inc., supra, at p. 116. Secondly, in so far as component ideas may be in the public domain, they themselves may be copied with impunity, without breaching the compiler's copyright, which rests not in the components, but in the over-all arrangement: Fox, The Canadian Law of Copyright and Industrial Designs, 2nd ed. (1967), p. 118.

In our view, the issue whether copyright may subsist in a magazine cover as distinct from its constituent elements is governed by the same considerations. Indeed, in the courts of the United States, magazine covers have been expressly held to be the proper subject of copyright: Conde Nast Publications, Inc. v. Vogue School of Fashion Modelling Inc., 94 U.S.P.Q. 101 (U.S. Fed. Dist. Ct., So. Dist. N.Y., 1952) at 106-7; Reader's Digest Association, Inc. v. Conservative Digest Inc., 3 U.S.P.Q. 1276 (U.S. Ct. App., D.C. Circuit, 1987) at 1280.

In the law of copyright, the statutory requirement of originality does not imply inventive originality. It is enough that the work is the production of something in a new form as a result of the skill, labour and judgment of the author: Express Newspapers plc v. News (UK) Ltd., [1990] 3 All E.R. 376 (Ch. Div.) at 381; Sands and Macdougall Pty Ltd. v. Robinson (1917), 23 C.L.R. 49 (H.C. Aust.); Walter v. Lane, [1900] A.C. 539 (H.L.).

In the case before us, the terms were oral of Allen's engagement by Saturday Night to shoot the cover photo of Ms. Copps. Both parties presented evidence at trial as to the custom of the industry as to the usual terms of such engagements as well as to the way in which a magazine cover is created and produced, and as to ownership of copyright in the cover.

Allen was engaged by Saturday Night to shoot the cover photo of Ms. Copps for its November 1985 issue. The idea for the photograph of Ms. Copps in leathers astride a motorcycle originated with Saturday Night. The photo was to highlight the point of a feature article about her in that issue. Allen was given detailed instructions as to Saturday Night's requirements for the cover photo. Ms. Copps cooperated with Allen during the photo shoot.

The photo used on the magazine cover (one of many taken by Allen during two film shoots) was selected by the art director of Saturday Night. The photo chosen was integrated into the cover by the art director in consultation with the editor of Saturday Night. The cover, including its layout and type sizes, styles and positioning, as well as the cover text, was the work of the art director in consultation with the editor.

Allen was not involved in, and had no control over, this process by which the magazine cover was created. His photo of Ms. Copps became a part of the cover, which was the very purpose for which it was taken under the terms of his engagement by Saturday Night. He was acknowledged in the November 1985 issue as the cover photographer.

In his view, Allen had granted Saturday Night the "first rights" to the photograph:

He [the art director] has the right to use my transparency in any way, shape or form he feels fit to put onto that cover for his first time usage. [Trial Proceedings, Vol. I, p. 145, 1. 22-4.]

After the photos were taken and the cover photo chosen by the art director, Allen received $1,800 from Saturday Night in payment. He also received back the original photographs and transparencies. He did not request or receive the printing plates used by Saturday Night to reproduce the cover.

As to the owner of copyright in the photograph, Allen retained the right to use or permit others to use the photo after its first use by Saturday Night. His consent would be required to any subsequent use of the photo. In fact, he received payments from several newspapers and periodicals for subsequent uses of the photo. We agree that the terms of Allen's engagement by Saturday Night constitute an "agreement to the contrary" within the meaning of s. 13(2) of the Copyright Act and that Allen is the owner of copyright in the photograph.

That Allen owns copyright in the photograph is not contested by the Toronto Star. That Allen owns or has a copyright interest in the cover of Saturday Night is strenuously contested. Witnesses who testified at trial were divided in their views as to the custom of the industry in matters of copyright in magazine covers.

Some stated that the cover belongs to the publisher and that the consent of the cover photographer is not sought or required to reproduce the cover for promotional, news or other purposes. Once a magazine cover is published, some witnesses considered it to be in the public domain as part of an historical record, so that no one's consent is sought or required to reproduce the cover for any purpose. This was the view of witnesses now or formerly employed by Saturday Night, Toronto Star, Globe & Mail, Toronto Life — all newspapers or periodicals.

In evidence, Allen stated his "position" that the consent of the cover photographer is required to reproduce the magazine cover, although he acknowledged that he was not given the printing plates for the magazine cover after publication. Another photographer (Patrick Lacroix) agreed, a third (Steve Pigeon) said no one owned the cover, although another (Nigel Dickson) acknowledged that the magazine owns the cover, and George Haroutian, a publisher and art director, agreed that if he wanted to use a magazine cover, he would contact only the magazine, letting them get necessary clearances for the cover (Trial Proceedings, Vol. II, p. 141, 1. 17-23; p. 143, 1. 27-32).

On March 11, 1990, the Toronto Star chose to illustrate its feature article on Ms. Copps with a reproduction of the November 1985 Saturday Night cover reduced in size. The article appeared on an inside page of an inside section of the newspaper. The Toronto Star did not reproduce the photo alone, but as a part of the magazine cover which is, in our view, entitled to be recognized as an original artistic work created and produced by the work, skill and judgment of Saturday Night.

The magazine cover is a separate and distinct artistic work from the photograph in this case. The photo is one component of the cover, and an important one in creating the overall effect of the cover which Saturday Night intended to create. The photo tells part of the story, but by itself is not meaningful without the linkage of words and imagery associating Ms. Copps with her role in Parliament at that time as a member of the "Rat Pack". It is the overall effect of the cover which fulfils the statutory requirement of originality for purposes of copyright in this case. Saturday Night bargained with Allen for the taking of the photo it ultimately chose for the cover of its November 1985 issue and used the photo in the way it was authorized to do by Allen, according to his own evidence.

Allen's copyright in the photograph is not infringed by the reproduction of the entire magazine cover in the March 11, 1990 edition of the Toronto Star and, in our view, Allen does not own or have a legal interest in the copyright in the magazine cover.

Robertson v. Thomson Corp., [2006] 2 S.C.R. 363

Supreme Court of Canada

Abella J., Bastarache J., Binnie J., Charron J., Deschamps J., Fish J., LeBel J., Major J., McLachlin C.J.C., Rothstein J.

Heard: December 6, 2005 — April 18, 2006
Judgment: October 12, 2006
Docket: 30644

LeBel, Fish JJ.:

I. Introduction

1 The central issue on this appeal is whether newspaper publishers are entitled as a matter of law to republish in electronic databases freelance articles they have acquired for publication in their newspapers — without compensation to the authors and without their consent. In our view, they are not. Their copyright over the newspapers they publish gives them no right to reproduce, otherwise than as part of *those* collective works — their newspapers — the freelance articles that appeared in them.

2 Pursuant to the *Copyright Act*, R.S.C. 1985, c. C-42, newspaper publishers own the copyright in their newspapers and have a right to reproduce a newspaper or a substantial part of that newspaper but do not have the right, without the consent of the author, to reproduce individual freelance articles. Info Globe Online and CPI. Q are vast electronic databases. They are compilations of individual articles presented outside the context of the collective work of which they were a part. The resulting collective work presented to the public is not simply the collective works joined together — it is a collective work of a different kind.

3 In our view, therefore, *The Globe and Mail* ("*Globe*") cannot republish freelance articles in the Info Globe Online or CPI. Q electronic databases. The right to reproduce a collective work under the *Copyright Act* does not carry with it the right to republish freelance articles as part of an entirely different collective work.

4 On the other hand, we believe the CD-ROMs are a valid exercise of the *Globe*'s right to reproduce its collective work. The CD-ROMs can be viewed as collections of daily newspapers in a way that Info Globe Online and CPI. Q cannot.

5 For these reasons and the reasons set forth below, we would dismiss the appeal and dismiss the cross-appeal except with respect to the CD-ROMs.

II. Background

6 At its core, this case concerns the competing rights of freelance authors and newspaper publishers. The *Copyright Act* establishes a regime of layered rights. Freelance authors who write newspaper articles retain the copyright in their work while the publisher of the newspaper acquires a copyright in the newspaper.

7 It is undisputed that freelance authors have the right to reproduce their individual works. The extent and scope of a publisher's right to reproduce those same articles as part of its right to reproduce its newspaper is less clear.

8 Advancements in computer technology have drastically altered the newspaper reality. Newspapers, once synonymous with the printed word, can now be stored and displayed electronically. The electronic databases in question archive thousands upon thousands of newspaper articles. Like a stream in constant flux, these databases are continuously growing and therefore changing. Search engines enable users to sift through these articles at lightning speed with the click of a mouse. These advancements, however, like most others, carry with them new challenges. One of these challenges is to evaluate the rights of newspaper publishers in this evolving technological landscape.

9 For well over a century, newspapers have archived back issues. Initially, as the motions judge observed, this was achieved by keeping them in a library — sometimes referred to in newspaper parlance as a "morgue". With the advent of microfilm and microfiche, past editions were archived using photographic imaging technology. Currently, newspapers are archived in electronic form. The subject electronic databases, however, do more than simply archive back issues.

10 The transfer of articles from their newspaper format and environment to Info Globe Online and CPI. Q, unlike the conversion to microfilm or microfiche, is no mere conversion of the newspaper from the print realm to the electronic world. As we will explain, the result is a different product that infringes the copyrights of freelance authors whose works appear in those databases. We begin with a review of the factual and judicial history.

III. Factual History

11 Heather Robertson is a freelance author. In 1995, she wrote two articles that were published in the *Globe*. One, a book excerpt, was the subject of a written agreement between the *Globe* and the publisher of Robertson's book; the other, a book review, was written under oral agreement with Robertson. Copyright was not addressed in either case. Subsequently, in 1996, it became the practice of the *Globe* to enter into written agreements with freelance authors expressly granting it certain electronic rights in freelance work. The agreement was later modified to expand the electronic rights clause. These agreements are not at issue in this case.

12 The *Globe* is one of Canada's leading national newspapers and has been produced in both print and electronic editions since the late 1970s. The named respondents on the appeal are: The Thomson Corporation, Thomson Canada

Limited, Thomson Affiliates, Information Access Company and Bell GlobeMedia Publishing Inc., the current publisher of the *Globe* (collectively, the "Publishers").

13 Ms. Robertson objects to the presence of her articles in three databases: Info Globe Online, CPI.Q and the CD-ROMs (collectively, the "electronic databases"). The use of freelance articles in the daily internet edition of the *Globe* is not in issue before us.

14 Info Globe Online is a commercial database that has existed since April 1979, with stories going back to November 1977. It provides subscribers with access to stories from the *Globe* for a fee. It also allows subscribers to find articles in many other newspapers, news wire services, magazines and reference databases. Subscribers can search by key word and retrieve articles electronically. The subscriber may display, read, download, store, or print the articles.

15 CPI. Q is the electronic version of the Canadian Periodical Index. The Canadian Periodical Index indexes selected newspaper articles from various newspapers. It is available at libraries and is routinely used in research. In 1987, it became available electronically. CPI.Q is an enhanced form of the original index. It allows subscribers to search the electronic archives of indexed periodicals by key word and to retrieve articles electronically. Once an article is displayed it is possible to print it as well.

16 The CD-ROMs, each containing the *Globe* and several other Canadian newspapers from a calendar year, have been available since 1991. Users can navigate using search engines and retrieve and print articles. Notably, the content of the CD-ROM is fixed and finite and users are able to view a paper as a single day's edition.

17 The electronic databases all omit the advertisements, some tables, photographs, artwork, photo captions, birth and death notices, financial tables, weather forecasts and some design elements from the original print edition.

18 Robertson's action against the Publishers for copyright infringement was certified as a class action, with the class consisting of all contributors to the *Globe* other than those who died on or before December 31, 1943: *Robertson v. Thomson Corp.* (1999), 43 O.R. (3d) 161 (Ont. Gen. Div.), at p. 168. Robertson brought a motion for partial summary judgment and an injunction restraining the use of her works in the databases. She sought judgment for two individual class members: herself and Cameron Smith, a former employee of the *Globe*.

. . .

A. Cross-Appeal: the Main Issue

30 Section 13(1) of the *Copyright Act* states: "Subject to this Act, the author of a work shall be the first owner of the copyright therein." And, s. 2.1(2) of the *Copyright Act* confirms that "[t]he mere fact that a work is included in a compilation does not increase, decrease or otherwise affect the protection conferred by this Act in respect of the copyright in the work". Accordingly, Robertson, as

the author of her freelance works, is the owner of the copyright in those articles. The same is true for other freelance authors.

31 A publisher does not have any rights in freelance articles themselves but has another, distinct, copyright in the daily newspapers in which the freelance articles appear. Newspapers are included in the definition of "collective work" in accordance with s. 2 of the *Copyright Act*. A newspaper can also be characterized as a "compilation" pursuant to s. 2 of the *Copyright Act*, which defines "compilation" as a work resulting from "selection or arrangement". We are thus confronted with two different but overlapping copyrights.

. . .

33 Plainly, freelance authors have the right to reproduce, and authorize the reproduction of, their articles. Similarly, as the holders of the copyright in their newspapers, the Publishers are entitled to "produce or reproduce the work or any substantial part thereof in any material form whatever".

34 The real question then is whether the electronic databases that contain articles from the *Globe* reproduce the newspapers or merely reproduce the original articles. It is open to the Publishers to reproduce a substantial part of the collective work in which they have a copyright; it is a violation of the *Copyright Act* for the Publishers to reproduce, without consent, the individual works with respect to which an author owns the copyright. The answer to this question lies in the determination of whose "originality" is being reproduced: the freelance author's alone or the Publishers'as a collective work?: see *Allen v. Toronto Star Newspapers Ltd.* (1997), 36 O.R. (3d) 201 (Ont. Div. Ct.).

35 "Originality" is the foundation stone of copyright. Section 5 of the *Copyright Act* states that copyright shall subsist "in every original literary, dramatic, musical and artistic work". This was explained by McLachlin C.J., for the Court, in *CCH Canadian Ltd. v. Law Society of Upper Canada*, [2004] 1 S.C.R. 339, 2004 SCC 13 (S.C.C.):

> For a work to be "original" within the meaning of the *Copyright Act*, it must be more than a mere copy of another work. At the same time, it need not be creative, in the sense of being novel and unique. What is required to attract copyright protection in the expression of an idea is an exercise of skill and judgment. [para. 16]

36 More specifically, McLachlin C.J. addressed originality as it relates to compilations — in that case, judicial decisions:

> The reported judicial decisions, when properly understood as a *compilation* of the headnote and the accompanying edited judicial reasons, are "original" works covered by copyright. Copyright protects originality of *form* or expression. A compilation takes existing material and casts it in different form. The arranger does not have copyright in the individual components. However, the arranger may have copyright in the form represented by the compilation. "It is not the several components that are the subject of the copyright, but the over-all arrangement of them which the plaintiff through his industry has produced": *Slumber-Magic Adjustable Bed Co. v. Sleep-King Adjustable Bed Co.* (1984), 3 C.P.R. (3d) 81 (B.C.S.C.), at

p. 84; see also *Ladbroke (Football) Ltd. v. William Hill (Football) Ltd.*, [1964] 1 All E.R. 465 (H.L.), at p. 469.

> The reported judicial decisions here at issue meet the test for originality. The authors have arranged the case summary, catchlines, case title, case information (the headnotes) and the judicial reasons in a specific manner. The arrangement of these different components requires the exercise of skill and judgment. The compilation, viewed globally, attracts copyright protection. [Emphasis in original; paras. 33-34.]

37 Similarly, the Publishers have a copyright in their newspapers, each an original collection of different components reflecting the exercise of skill and judgment. Section 2 of the *Copyright Act*, as noted above, defines a compilation as an original work that is created as a result of selection or arrangement. This same conception of originality underlies the inclusion of the newspapers in the definition of collective work. We note that the use of the disjunctive "or" in s. 2 is significant. The *Copyright Act* does not require originality in both the selection and arrangement. Similarly, and with all due respect to Weiler J.A.'s contrary finding, we agree with the Publishers that a reproduction of a compilation or a collective work need not preserve *both* the selection and arrangement of the original work to be consistent with the Publisher's reproduction rights.

38 Section 3 of the *Copyright Act* provides the copyright owner with the right to reproduce a work *or* a substantial part thereof. It follows that a substantial part of a newspaper may consist only of the original selection so long as the essence of the newspaper is preserved, i.e., that which embodies the originality of the collective work that is capable of attracting copyright. In *Édutile Inc. v. Automobile Protection Assn. (APA)*, [2000] 4 F.C. 195 (Fed. C.A.), the Federal Court of Appeal stated:

> To determine whether a "substantial part" of a protected work has been reproduced, it is not the quantity which was reproduced that matters as much as the quality and nature of what was reproduced....
>
> It seems clear that APA appropriated a "substantial part", indeed the very essence, of Édutile's work ... [Emphasis added; paras. 22-23.]

39 There is much originality in a newspaper: the editorial content, the selection of articles, the arrangement of articles, the arrangement of advertisements and pictures, and the fonts and styles used. But the true essence of the originality in a newspaper is its editorial content. It is the selection of stories, and the stories themselves, that resonate in the hearts and minds of readers.

40 The task of determining whether this essence has been reproduced may be difficult. Indeed, it is largely a question of degree. At a minimum, however, the editorial content of the newspaper must be preserved and presented *in the context* of that newspaper.

41 We again agree with the Publishers that their right to reproduce a substantial part of the newspaper includes the right to reproduce the newspaper without advertisements, graphs and charts, or in a different layout and using different

fonts. But it does not follow that the articles of the newspaper can be decontex-tualized to the point that they are no longer presented in a manner that maintains their intimate connection with the rest of that newspaper. In Info Globe Online and CPI. Q, articles from a given daily edition of the *Globe* are stored and pre-sented in a database together with thousands of other articles from different periodicals and different dates. And, these databases are expanding and chang-ing daily as more and more articles are added. These products are more akin to databases of individual articles rather than reproductions of the *Globe*. Thus, in our view, the originality of the freelance articles is reproduced; the originality of the newspapers is not.

42 The Publishers argue that the connection with the original newspaper is not lost in the databases because the articles in Info Globe Online and CPI. Q contain references to the newspaper they were published in, the date they were published and the page number where the article appeared. We do not share this view. Rather, we agree with the United States Supreme Court's finding in *Tasini* where the same argument was canvassed and rejected. Ginsburg J., for the majority, stated:

> One might view the articles as parts of a new compendium — namely, the entirety of works in the Database. In that compendium, each edition of each periodical rep-resents only a minuscule fraction of the ever-expanding Database. The Database no more constitutes a "revision" of each constituent edition than a 400-page novel quot-ing a sonnet in passing would represent a "revision" of that poem.... The massive whole of the Database is not recognizable as a new version of its every small part.

> Alternatively, one could view the Articles in the Databases "as part of" no larger work at all, but simply as individual articles presented individually. That each arti-cle bears marks of its origin in a particular periodical (less vivid marks in NEXIS and NYTO, more vivid marks in GPO) suggests the article was previously part of that periodical. But the markings do not mean the article is currently reproduced or distributed as part of the periodical. The Databases'reproduction and distribution of individual Articles — simply as individual Articles — would invade the core of the Authors'exclusive rights under §106. [Footnote omitted, underlining added, italics in original; p. 500- 501.]

43 Weiler J.A. correctly pointed out that caution must be adhered to when referencing *Tasini* in the Canadian context due to differences in the applicable governing legislation. Pursuant to the U.S. *Copyrights Act*, 17 U.S.C. §201(c) (2000), the publisher does not have a separate copyright in the collective work but has only the "privilege of reproducing and distributing the contribution as part of that particular collective work, any revision of that collective work, and any later collective work in the same series". Nonetheless, we find the reasoning in the foregoing passage, which simply describes the nature of the decontextual-ization that occurs in similar databases, compelling and applicable.

44 This decontextualization is critical to the disposition of this case. As Weiler J.A. observed, "In this vast storehouse of information, the collective work that is the Globe is fragmented, submerged, overwhelmed and lost" (para. 82). In

our view, date and page references do not change this — they merely provide historical information, as the U.S. Supreme Court observed.

45 The Publishers also argue that the Court should focus on *input* rather than *output*. This was also the view of Blair J.A. in his dissenting opinion. According to this reasoning, a substantial part of the print edition of each day's *Globe* (excluding pictures, advertisements, tables and charts) is stored in an electronic file. Blair J.A. found that this electronic data, *input* into the databases, which represents the electronic reproduction of the print daily. He therefore concluded that the electronic file contains the editorial content of the newspaper and is therefore a "reproduction" within the meaning of s. 3(1) of the *Copyright Act*, regardless of what use it is put to afterwards.

46 With respect, we believe this approach prematurely terminates the analysis. And the manner in which Blair J.A. framed the question — by asking whether the *electronic version* of the *Globe* in the electronic databases is a reproduction of the *Globe* — presupposes an answer in favour of the Publishers. It is not the electronic data that is presented to the public but the finished product, i.e., the databases. We cannot avoid comparing the original collective work with the finished collective work when determining whether there has been a reproduction. As Megarry V.C., put it in *Thrusteode Ltd. v. W.W. Computing Ltd.*, [1983] F.S.R. 502, cited with approval by Mahoney J.A. in *Apple Computer Inc. v. Mackintosh Computers Ltd.* (1987), [1988] 1 F.C. 673 (Fed. C.A.), aff'd [1990] 2 S.C.R. 209 (S.C.C.): "For computers, as for other things, what must be compared are the thing said to have been copied and the thing said to be an infringing copy" (p. 505).

47 Viewed "globally", to use the language of this Court in *CCH*, Info Globe Online and CPI. Q are different selections than the selections that they incorporate. They are compilations of individual articles presented outside of the context of the original collective work from where they originated. The resulting collective work presented to the public is not simply each of the collective works joined together — it has become a collective work of a different nature.

48 To be clear, this analysis is not predicated on the ability of a user to search by key word. We agree with both Weiler J.A. and Blair J.A. that the search mechanism which enables a user to isolate individual articles is not determinative. The focus of our analysis firmly remains on what the *Globe* presents to the user; not on how the user makes use of it. In this sense, the input/output dichotomy is misleading. Moreover, we are mindful of the principle of media neutrality under the *Copyright Act* and agree that the principle precludes a finding of copyright infringement merely because it is possible to search with more efficient tools than in the past. That being said, focussing exclusively on input in the name of media neutrality takes the principle too far and ultimately, turns it on its head.

49 Media neutrality is reflected in s. 3(1) of the *Copyright Act* which describes a right to produce or reproduce a work "in any material form whatever". Media neutrality means that the *Copyright Act* should continue to apply in different media, including more technologically advanced ones. But it does not mean that

once a work is converted into electronic data anything can then be done with it. The resulting work must still conform to the exigencies of the *Copyright Act*. Media neutrality is not a license to override the rights of authors — it exists to protect the rights of authors and others as technology evolves.

50 Recent developments in international agreements on copyright have not changed these principles. On the contrary, they recognize and apply them.

51 Notwithstanding the foregoing, we part ways with Weiler J.A. regarding the CD-ROMs. In our view, the CD-ROMs are a valid exercise of the *Globe*'sright to reproduce its collective works (or a substantial part thereof) pursuant to s. 3(1) of the *Copyright Act*. The CD-ROMs, like Info Globe Online and CPI.Q, do not contain advertisements, pictures or colour and are presented in a different medium and format than the print edition. The critical distinction, however, is that the CD-ROMs preserve the linkage to the original daily newspaper.

52 The user of the CD-ROM is presented with a collection of daily newspapers which can be viewed separately. When viewing an article on CD-ROM after searching for a particular edition, the other articles from that day's edition appear in the frame on the right hand side of the screen. To pass muster, a reproduction does not need to be a replica or a photographic copy. But it does need to remain faithful to the essence of the original work. And, in our view, the CD-ROM does so by offering users, essentially, a compendium of daily newspaper editions.

53 In our view, the fact that the CD-ROM includes other newspapers is not fatal. The essential characteristic of the newspaper is not lost when it is present-ed together on a CD with a discrete number of other newspapers, each of which is viewable as a separate and distinct paper. Moreover, as we indicated above, the ability to search by key word does not make the CD-ROM reproduction any less of a reproduction.

. . .

Abella J.:

65 The basic right of every copyright holder, according to s. 3(1) of the *Copyright Act*, R.S.C. 1985, c. C-42, is to "produce or reproduce the work or any substantial part thereof in any material form whatever".

66 At issue in this appeal are online databases into which the publishers place all articles selected by them for inclusion in each day's edition of their newspapers. An article's date, page and headline in the printed version of those newspapers appear on every article.

67 I agree with LeBel and Fish JJ. that the appeal should be dismissed and that the cross-appeal should be allowed in connection with the CD-ROM issue. I have a different view, with respect, of the application of the *Copyright Act* to Info Globe Online and CPI. Q and would allow the cross-appeal in connection with them as well. In my view, these databases reproduce a "substantial part" of the publishers' "work", and are, as a result, within the right of reproduction conferred by s. 3(1) of the Act. It follows that the employees cannot

restrain publication of their individual works in those databases under s. 13(3) since that publication continues to be "part of a newspaper, magazine or similar periodical".

Analysis

. . .

70 The public interest is particularly significant in the context of archived newspapers. These materials are a primary resource for teachers, students, writers, reporters, and researchers. It is this interest that hangs in the balance between the competing rights of the two groups of creators in this case, the authors and the publishers.

71 The aftermath of the litigation in *New York Times Co. v. Tasini*, 533 U.S. 483 (U.S.S.C. 2001), is instructive. Freelance authors had sued the New York Times for copyright infringement arising out of the inclusion of articles written by them in online databases. They were successful. The New York Times Co.'s response was to remove all of the affected articles from its online databases: D. P. Bickham, "Extra! Can't Read All About It: Articles Disappear After High Court Rules Freelance Writers Taken Out of Context In *New York Times Co. v. Tasini* " (2001), 29 *W. St. U. L. Rev.* 85, at p. 102. Its response is not surprising, since "[t]he economic calculus runs sharply in favor of deletion", with publishers having "virtually no economic upside to retaining freelance articles in the electronically available archived editions, and substantial economic downside": C. S. Sims and M. J. Morris, "*Tasini* and Archival Electronic Publication Rights of Newspapers and Magazines" (2001), 18:4 *Comm. Law.* 9, at p. 15.

72 The detrimental impact of such a ruling may be even more profound in Canada since, under s. 13(3) of the *Copyright Act*, the publisher's employees have the right to prevent republication of their articles in online databases if those databases are found not to be a "newspaper". In my view, such a ruling is not mandated by the Act. The publishers own the copyright in their newspaper which, for purposes of the *Copyright Act*, is a "collective work". A newspaper is also a "compilation", which is defined by the Act to include "a work resulting from the selection or arrangement of data". The key is in the disjunctive. Either the selection *or* the arrangement of data is sufficient to constitute a copyrighted "work".

73 The most fundamental right conferred by the publisher's copyright is the right to produce *and reproduce* the copyrighted work. Copyright in relation to a work, as described in s. 3, means "the sole right to produce or reproduce the work or any substantial part thereof in any material form whatever". The right contains two key features. The first is that in Canada, unlike the narrower privilege conferred under the American *Copyrights Act*, 17 U.S.C. § 201(c) (2000), the holder of the copyright may reproduce not only the work, but also a "substantial part thereof".

74 The second is that, like its American counterpart, Canada's *Copyright Act* is media neutral: the right is to reproduce the work in "any material form whatever". Those are the words that inform the concept of "media neutrality". The

publisher's right to contribute to the online databases at issue here stands or falls on the meaning of those words.

75 The concept of media neutrality is how Parliament chose to come to grips with potential technological developments. On its face, the media neutrality protection found in s. 3(1) is a simple concept. As Gonthier J. pointed out in *Galerie d'art du Petit Champlain inc.* , s. 3(1) offers "an appropriate and carefully worded recognition that a work may be reproduced *even if* the new medium is different" (para. 148 (emphasis in original)).

76 The words "any material form whatever" in s. 3(1) should be taken to mean what they say: the author's exclusive right to reproduce a "substantial part" of a copyrighted work is not limited by changes in form or output made possible by a new medium. A media neutral *Copyright Act* ensures that such transformations in form do not erode the content of the copyright protection: see *Apple Computer Inc. v. Mackintosh Computers Ltd.* (1986), [1987] 1 F.C. 173 (Fed. T.D.), at p. 33, judgment subsequently aff'd [1990] 2 S.C.R. 209 (S.C.C.).

77 Under a media neutral *Copyright Act*, mere visual comparison of the work and the item said to be a reproduction of that work may be deceptive. The conversion of a work from one medium to another will necessarily involve changes in the work's visual appearance, but these visual manifestations do not change the content of the right.

78 As Binnie J. discussed in *Galerie d'art du Petit Champlain inc.* , at para. 47, the *Copyright Act*'s understanding of the right to reproduce is not limited to "only literal physical, mechanical reproduction", and the concept of reproduction has broadened to recognize that "technologies have evolved by which expression could be reproduced in ways undreamt of in earlier periods, such as evanescent and 'virtual' copies in electronic formats".

79 The *Copyright Act* was designed to keep pace with technological developments to foster intellectual, artistic and cultural creativity. In applying the *Copyright Act* to a realm that includes the Internet and the databases at issue in this case, courts face unique challenges, but in confronting them, the public benefits of this digital universe should be kept prominently in view. As Professor Michael Geist observes:

> The Internet and new technologies have unleashed a remarkable array of new creativity, empowering millions of individuals to do more than just consume our culture, instead enabling them to actively and meaningfully participate in it.
>
> (M. Geist, *Our Own Creative Land: Cultural Monopoly & The Trouble With Copyright* (2006), at p. 9)

80 The source of every copyright, as this Court discussed in CCH, subsists in a work as long as it is "original". Regardless of whether the work in question is individual or collective, the inquiry into whether a work has been reproduced for purposes of s. 3 must focus on whether the "originality" that conferred copyright in relation to that work has been preserved in what is said to be a reproduction.

81 In *CCH*, originality was held to encompass the exercise of "skill and judgment" by an author: see para. 16. Every copyrighted work — individual or collective — is the product of the exercise of skill and judgment. In determining, therefore, whether a work like a newspaper, or "any substantial part thereof", has been reproduced, what will be determinative is the extent to which the item said to be a reproduction contains within it, in qualitative rather than quantitative terms, a substantial part of the skill and judgment exercised by the creator of the work: see *Édutile Inc. v. Automobile Protection Assn. (APA)*, [2000] 4 F.C. 195 (Fed. C.A.), at para. 22.

82 The right of reproduction adheres equally to the benefit of authors of individual works and to those of collective works or compilations. In considering the publisher's right of reproduction, the majority says that the line between the rights of individual authors and the rights of authors of collective works should be drawn on the basis of whose originality is being reproduced. This suggests that the databases in question reproduce only one group's originality. This, with respect, seems to me to contradict the essence of collective works and compilations, which inherently contain the "originality" of both the authors of individual works as well as of the creator of the collective work or compilation. Any reproduction of a collective work will necessarily involve the reproduction of *both* sets of originality.

83 Yet this does not bar the creator of a collective work, such as a newspaper, from reprinting the newspaper. On the contrary, creators of collective works, like authors of individual works, have the "sole right" under s. 3 to produce and reproduce their works, which in the case of the former will necessarily include the originality of contributing authors: see, for example, *Allen v. Toronto Star Newspapers Ltd.* (1997), 36 O.R. (3d) 201 (Ont. Div. Ct.). This continuing right of use of the individual authors' originality creates no unfairness to those authors since, as McLachlin J. observed in *Slumber-Magic Adjustable Bed Co. v. Sleep-King Adjustable Bed Co.* (1984), 3 C.P.R. (3d) 81 (B.C. S.C.), at pp. 84-85, the ability to produce a collective work in the first place depends on the individual authors' authorization to use the materials that form the compilation.

84 In the context of a collective work, the question is whether the author of a collective work or compilation has reproduced the work, or a "substantial part" of the work, accepting that doing so will necessarily involve substantial reproduction of the "originality" of individual authors. Framing the issue, as the majority does, as "whether newspaper publishers are entitled ... to republish in electronic databases freelance articles they have acquired for publication in their newspapers" (para. 1), presupposes the conclusion that the publishers have "republis[hed] ... freelance articles", rather than the collective work — the newspaper — over which they unquestionably have a right of reproduction.

85 If the publishers were to convert every article from a given day's edition into electronic form by placing each article in its own electronic file, marking each electronic article with its page and date of appearance, and transferring all of those files onto a disk or attaching them all to an e-mail, the resulting bundle

of electronic articles would clearly constitute an electronic reproduction of "any substantial part [of that day's newspaper] in any material form whatever".

86 If media neutrality is to have any meaning, it must permit the publishers to convert their daily print edition into electronic form. The means by which the publishers do so is to remove advertisements, photographs, and other aspects of the arrangement of the articles from the newspaper, then place each article in its own electronic file. Each story is dated and includes a section, page number, headline and by-line, and is identified as appearing in *The Globe and Mail*.

87 Ms. Robertson concedes that the electronic daily edition in existence in 1995 does not infringe the copyright held by individual freelance authors. In substance, there is no difference between the actual electronic daily edition and a bundle of electronic articles from a given day's paper (each in their own file). Because both contain every article selected by the editors for inclusion in the newspaper, and because the text of every article in the electronic edition is as it appears in the newspaper, the skill and judgment of the newspaper's editors exercised in selecting and editing the articles are fully contained in either form of electronic reproduction.

88 Whether it is presented in an e-mail as an "electronic daily edition", or consists of a bundle of files on a disk, this electronic edition contains a substantial part of the skill and judgment exercised by the publishers in creating that day's newspaper. It is a reproduction of the print edition in electronic form. That is precisely what media neutrality protects. As discussed by Stevens J. in his compelling dissent in *Tasini* :

> No one doubts that the New York Times has the right to reprint its issues in Braille, in a foreign language, or in microform, even though such revisions might look and feel quite different from the original. Such differences, however, would largely result from the different medium being employed. Similarly, the decision to convert the single collective work newspaper into a collection of individual ASCII files can be explained as little more than a decision that reflects the different nature of the electronic medium. Just as the paper version of the New York Times is divided into "sections" and "pages" in order to facilitate the reader's navigation and manipulation of large batches of newsprint, so too the decision to subdivide the electronic version of that collective work into individual article files facilitates the reader's use of the electronic information. The barebones nature of ASCII text would make trying to wade through a single ASCII file containing the entire content of a single edition of the New York Times an exercise in frustration. [Footnote omitted; pp. 512-13.]

89 Given how unwieldy it would be to view an entire newspaper as a single stream of electronic text, the individual article provides the "logical unit" by which to divide the newspaper into manageable pieces: *Tasini, per* Stevens J., at p. 513, fn. 9. There is, consequently, nothing colourable about the publishers' decision to use individual articles as the more practical and more easily accessible unit of organization for an electronic version.

90 The analysis is unchanged if a number of these hypothetical electronic editions are collected together. This is simply the electronic analogy to stacking print editions of a newspaper on a shelf.

91 Having concluded that a collection of electronic articles from one day's edition of the newspaper constitutes a reproduction of that day's newspaper, I have difficulty seeing how the integration of the electronic reproduction into a database containing similarly organized versions of other periodicals causes the electronic version to lose its character as a reproduction of a newspaper and, correspondingly, to lose its protection under s. 3.

92 The ultimate question to be asked is whether the database contains a reproduction of a substantial part of the skill and judgment exercised by the publishers in creating the newspaper. If an "electronic edition" reproduces the publishers' skill and judgment and is, on that basis, a reproduction of the publishers' newspaper, there is no reason why the nature of the database in which the electronic editions are housed should change the designation and character of those editions. This too was addressed by Stevens J. in *Tasini*:

> A microfilm of the New York Times for October 31, 2000, does not cease to be a revision of that individual collective work simply because it is stored on the same roll of film as other editions of the Times or on a library shelf containing hundreds of other microfilm periodicals. Nor does § 201(c) compel the counterintuitive conclusion that the microfilm version of the Times would cease to be a revision simply because its publishers might choose to sell it on rolls of film that contained a year's editions of both the New York Times *and* the Herald-Tribune. Similarly, the placement of our hypothetical electronic revision of the October 31, 2000, New York Times within a larger electronic database does nothing to alter either the nature of our original electronic revision or the relationship between that revision and the individual articles that exist as "part of" it. [Emphasis in original; pp. 517-18.]

93 The database is, as Blair J.A. described it, better seen as an electronic archive, "just as a traditional library consists of a collection of books, newspapers, journals, periodicals and a plethora of printed materials" (para. 149). As he rightly observed, "[n]o one suggests ... that a library must be a newspaper before the copyright of a newspaper publisher in the newspapers found in the library is protected" (para. 149). The loss of "context" emphasized by the majority underlines the form, not the substance, of the databases, and, in my respectful view, is, as a result, inconsistent with the media neutral approach mandated by s. 3 of the *Copyright Act*.

94 This conclusion is reinforced by international copyright treaties to which Canada is a party, and which elaborate on the principle of media neutrality. In interpreting the *Copyright Act*'s application to new technologies, it is instructive to examine these treaties, including the *Berne Convention for the Protection of Literary and Artistic Works* (1886) and the *WIPO Copyright Treaty* (1996), CRNR/DC/94: see *Galerie d'art du Petit Champlain inc.* , at para. 71, and *SOCAN*, at para. 97.

95 Article 9 of the *Berne Convention* guarantees authors a right of reproduction of works "in any manner or form", which the WIPO *Guide to the Copyright and Related Rights Treaties Administered by WIPO and Glossary of Copyright and Related Rights Terms* (2003), at p. 55, develops as follows:

> BC9.6. The text of the Berne Convention does not contain any complete and explicit definition of "reproduction". Certain elements of the concept of reproduction may, however, be identified in it. A good example is the clarification offered in Article 9(3) [sound or visual recordings deemed to be reproductions] ... which makes it obvious that it is not a condition that, on the basis of the reproduction, the copy of the work be directly perceivable; it is sufficient if the reproduced work may be made perceivable through appropriate equipment. (See also *Apple Computer*, F.C.T.D., at para. 81.)

96 Applying the WIPO Guide language to the newspaper context, "the work" is the publisher's exercise of skill and judgment in selecting and editing the articles included in the newspaper. The entirety of the publishers' newspapers, minus certain arrangement features, remains "perceivable", as opposed to visually replicated, in the database because every article selected and edited by the publishers is contained in the database and marked as such.

97 That there is no loss of copyright by virtue of reproduction in digital storage form, such as databases, is further confirmed by an Agreed Statement concerning Art. 1(4) of the WIPO Treaty which is set out in a footnote to that article:

> The reproduction right, as set out in Article 9 of the Berne Convention, and the exceptions permitted thereunder, fully apply in the digital environment, in particular to the use of works in digital form. It is understood that the storage of a protected work in digital form in an electronic medium constitutes a reproduction within the meaning of Article 9 of the Berne Convention.

Just as individual authors do not lose copyright in their articles by virtue of their inclusion in an electronic database, newspaper publishers do not lose their right to reproduce their newspaper, including the articles that comprise it, by doing the same.

98 The fact that the actual newspaper page is not fully or identically reproduced in the database, and the articles are therefore presented in a different form from a *paper* newspaper, is irrelevant. It is not the physical manifestation of the work that governs, it is whether the product perceivably reproduces the exercise of skill and judgment by the publishers that went into the creation of the work.

99 The argument that, in order to remain within their right of reproduction, the publishers must enter the entirety of each newspaper into the database as an unwieldy stream of continuous text, rather than permitting each article to be viewed separately, finds no conceptual home in the *Copyright Act*. So long as a "substantial part" of the work is ultimately reproduced, the publisher's entitlement under our media neutral *Copyright Act* is to be able to adjust the form of its work to suit the exigencies of new media technologies.

100 The exercise of skill and judgment producing the work — the newspaper — namely, the selection, editing and arrangement of articles, is what gives rise to the publishers' copyright in the work. The databases reproduce fully both the publishers' selection and editing of the articles appearing in the newspaper, as well as some of the arrangement. This being the case, the databases reproduce the newspaper. In my view, any difference between the print and database versions of the newspaper is attributable to the digital "form" alone, and thus does not detract from the publisher's right to reproduce its newspaper in the online databases.

101 I would therefore dismiss the appeal, allow the cross-appeal, and dismiss the class action.

Appeal dismissed, cross-appeal allowed in part, MCLACHLIN C.J., BINNIE, ABELLA *and* CHARRON JJ., *dissenting in part on the cross-appeal.*

Grisbrook v. MGN Ltd., [2010] EWCA Civ 1399 (CA (Civ Div), 2010)

9 December 2010

The Chancellor:

Introduction

The appellant, MGN Ltd ("MGN"), is and at all material times has been the publisher of, amongst other well known newspapers, the Daily Mirror. The respondent, Mr Alan Grisbrook ("Mr Grisbrook"), is and has since 1974 been a well known freelance photographer. Between 1981 and 1997 Mr Grisbrook, like many other freelance photographers, supplied MGN with a large number of photographs for publication in the Daily Mirror and the other daily newspapers published by them. The basis on which he and the others did so was well established and included the following features:

(1) the decision whether or not to use the photograph then or thereafter was for MGN alone;

(2) it was for the photographer to ascertain whether his photograph had been used and, if it had, to claim payment;

(3) the amount to be paid was agreed between the photographer and MGN in accordance with the then going rate known to both of them;

(4) such payment covered use in the edition in which it was published, however many copies were printed, but subsequent use in a paper produced for a different day generated a further, albeit lower, fee;

(5) photographs used or retained for possible future use were retained in the MGN Picture Library.

There was no written agreement between MGN and Mr Grisbrook recording these features or any of them but it is common ground that copyright in each photograph was retained by Mr Grisbrook, MGN was entitled to publish it in one or more of its daily publications and Mr Grisbrook was entitled to be paid for each such publication. By a letter dated 13th October 1997 Mr Grisbrook terminated any licence to MGN to use his photographs.

In or about 1993 MGN's hard copy picture library was moved to Watford. At the same time MGN established a digital picture library called FastFoto so that its editorial staff in Canary Wharf might have electronic access to its picture library. In 1998 MGN established the website <mirrorpix.com> as a means of marketing its picture library online. In addition to its picture library that website also held digital copies of various front pages of MGN newspapers.

In 1998 Mr Grisbrook commenced proceedings against MGN claiming £161,238 as licence fees in respect of the use of his photographs between 1982 and October 1997. In 1999 he commenced a second action against MGN in respect of alleged infringement of copyright by offering for sale on <mirrorpix.com> some of Mr Grisbrook's photographs. The actions were subsequently consolidated and compromised by means of a Tomlin Order made on 9th December 2002. That order contained an undertaking by MGN that:

> "...they will not infringe the Claimant's copyright in photographs taken by the Claimant (whether by their servants or agents or any of them or otherwise howsoever)..."....

By an application notice issued in the consolidated action in April 2008 Mr Grisbrook sought the sequestration of the assets of MGN for its contempt constituted by the breach of its undertaking to the court contained in the Tomlin Order. The breach originally relied on was the infringement of Mr Grisbrook's copyright by the sale or offering for sale of his photographs via its websites <architext.com>, <mydailymirror.com> and <mirrorarchive.co.uk>. This was amended on 17th July 2008 so as to aver that MGN had:

> "(a) reproduced the Claimant's photographs in a database known as "MirrorPix" and further communicated them to the public contrary to section 20 of the Copyright Designs and Patents Act 1988 by making the said database available to the public by electronic transmission in such a way that members of the public may access it from a place and a time individually chosen by them, by means of the Defendant's website mirrorpix.com.

> (b) reproduced the Claimant's photographs without the Claimant's consent in the form of a database or databases comprising reproductions of back numbers of the Defendants' newspapers.

> (c) communicated the Claimant's photographs to the public contrary to section 20 of the Copyright Designs and Patents Act 1988 by making the said database available to the public by electronic transmission in such a way that members of the public may access it from a place and at a time individually chosen by them, by means of the Defendant's websites mydailymirror.com, mirrorarchive.co.uk and arcitext.com.

(d) sold and/or offered for sale from the said database photographs taken by the Claimant, the subject of his copyright, via its said websites mydailymirror.com, mirrorarchive.co.uk, and arcitext.com."

The application was heard by Patten LJ over two days in November 2008 and three in July 2009. ...Patten LJ made no order on the application for the committal of MGN, its directors or officers. Instead his order contained a recital of concessions made by Mr Grisbrook and made two declarations. The concessions were:

"that MGN is entitled (1) for archival purposes to copy, retain, and store copies of the photographs in which he owns the copyright as incorporated in previously published editions of the Defendants' publications ("the photographs as published by MGN") in electronic form or in any other form used from time to time in the publishing industry and (2) to use the same for its internal purposes and (3) to make the same available to third parties as part of the MGN archive but only non-commercially, and as permitted by law."

The declarations are

"1. That the making available to the public through the websites "mydailymirror.com" "arcitext.com" and "mirrorarchive.com" of photographs the copyright in which was vested in the Claimant constituted an infringement of the copyright in such photographs.

2. That such copyright was infringed by the acts referred to in declaration 1 irrespective of whether the photographs were incorporated alone or when forming part of a reproduction of a printed page of a published newspaper."

MGN now appeals with the permission of Etherton LJ. Before Patten LJ there were four principal issues. They were (1) whether on the construction of the Tomlin Order the undertaking extended to the acts complained of, (2) whether the licence to MGN from Mr Grisbrook authorised those acts so as to preclude any infringement of Mr Grisbrook's copyright and, consequently, of MGN's undertaking, (3) whether the copyright of Mr Grisbrook in his own photographs was subsumed into the copyright of MGN in the newspaper in which Mr Grisbrook had consented to their publication and (4) whether MGN was entitled to defend the allegation of contempt by relying on the public interest defence preserved by s.173(3) Copyright, Designs and Patents Act 1988. Patten LJ answered the first in the affirmative and the other three in the negative. Before this court the argument was effectively limited to the second issue, namely whether the licence Mr Grisbrook granted to MGN when he handed over the original photograph extended to making them available to the public through <mydailymirror.com> <arcitext.com> and <mirrorarchive.com> either individually or as part of the newspaper as a whole....

The relevant statutory provisions

. . .

It is also necessary to consider the position of MGN in relation to each edition of the Daily Mirror as published. It is not disputed that it constituted a compilation the copyright in which, as a literary work, vested in MGN pursuant to ss.2 and

48(1) of the 1956 Act and s.3(1)(a) of the 1988 Act. It follows that in relation to its newspaper MGN was entitled to prevent the protected acts relating to a literary work for which the 1956 Act and the 1988 Act provided.

Before Patten LJ it had been submitted for MGN that the inclusion of Mr Grisbrook's photographs, with his consent, in the published edition of the Daily Mirror precluded him from asserting his own copyright in any way which was inconsistent with the exploitation by MGN of its separate copyright in its literary work. Counsel for MGN had relied on the decision of the Supreme Court of Canada in **Robertson v The Thomson Corporation** [2006] SCC 43. This submission was rejected by Patten LJ. In paragraph 67 of his judgment he concluded:

> "The concept of a "collective work" (as opposed to a compilation) is not a feature of the 1988 Act and there may be provisions in the Canadian Act which give such works a measure of special protection. But the decision is, I think, inconsistent with English law which, so far as I am aware, has never treated copyright in a compilation as providing a defence to a claim for infringement brought by someone whose own copyright material has been included without his consent. The rights of copyright owners are governed by the 1988 Act and there is nothing in the Act which limits the rights under s.16 of someone in the position of Mr Grisbrook in the event that his work is included in a newspaper or other compilation. He retains the exclusive right to copy the work save to the extent that he licenses the publishers to do so. MGN are not therefore assisted by the Canadian decision."

MGN does not appeal from that conclusion. It follows that Mr Grisbrook is entitled to assert his copyright in the photograph so as to inhibit the exploitation of its copyright in the newspaper by MGN unless he is to be treated as having consented to it.

The contents of the websites

. . .

<mirrorarchive.co.uk>

This website was established in April 2007. It was described by Patten LJ in paragraph 38 of his judgment in these terms:

> "mirrorarchive.co.uk is owned by MGN and was set up as a beta test site in April 2007....Subscribers will be able to access and download the whole or selected pages of all Daily Mirror newspapers published since 1903. The database therefore stores electronically in pdf format complete copies of all such papers. It is not limited to front pages. ...It is intended to be a commercial operation."

It follows that such website will include, as part of the published newspaper, such photographs of Mr Grisbrook as were originally reproduced in it.

This website was part of the original and amended complaint contained in the Application Notice. It is also comprised in the first declaration made by Patten LJ. Of all the websites this one raises most clearly the issue which concerns MGN. If each contributor, like Mr Grisbrook, is entitled to complain of the inclusion on the website of his copyright work as part of the published newspaper, then, in the absence of more formal and clearer licences, MGN will be practically unable to exploit its copyright in the newspapers as a whole online by means of their inclusion in a website.

Judgment of Patten LJ

Patten LJ then referred at some length to the judgment of Lightman J in **Robin Ray v Classic FM plc** [1998] FSR 622. He concluded in paragraph 65:

> "It seems to me that the approach of Lightman J is consistent with the fact that any licence represents a derogation from or relaxation of the copyright owner's statutory rights. It must therefore be for the defendant to justify (absent express agreement) the basis for extending the licence to cover what would otherwise be separate acts of infringement. Although that test is, in my judgment, satisfied in respect of the compilation of the database and its use for archive purposes, its exploitation through the back numbers websites seems to me to be a different kind of operation which was not contemplated at the time when the licence was granted and cannot be said to have been necessary to regulate the rights of the parties at that time. For these reasons, I take the view that Mr Grisbrook's copyright in his photographs has been or would be infringed by the operation of the back number websites."

It is clear from this passage that the principle applied by Patten LJ is that the extent of the licence granted by Mr Grisbrook to MGN for each photograph is to be that contemplated at the time the licence was granted and what is necessary to regulate the rights of the parties at that time. The issues on this appeal are (1) whether Patten LJ deduced the correct principle by which to ascertain the ambit of the licence granted by Mr Grisbrook to MGN and, if so, (2) whether he applied it correctly to the facts as found by him.

The submissions for the parties and my conclusion

. . .

...A website operates over a global area, its coverage is greatly in excess of anything MGN could have reached with hard copy newspapers. It enables a member of the public to read it before deciding whether he wants a hard copy and the production of hard copies by the public far in excess of anything MGN could have produced. The extent of the market and the costs incurred in reaching it are quite different to those of the hard copy newspapers of the past. There is no need to emphasise the differences further. The suggestion that an intention may be imputed to Mr Grisbrook and MGN from their conduct in relation to Mr Grisbrook's photographs in the period 1981 to 1997 that MGN should be entitled without further charge to exploit the copyright of Mr Grisbrook in his photographs by inclusion on their websites is, to my mind, unacceptable. Newspapers are essentially ephemeral and, save for the enthusiastic collector, retain no long lasting status: the parties will have intended that they would be treated as daily papers are generally treated, that is to say, read and replaced with the following day's edition. To incorporate the pictures into the website is to provide a permanent and marketable record easily available world-wide which could well reduce the value of the further use by Mr Grisbrook of the photographs over which it is common ground he possesses the copyright. That is why, to my mind, this is not just a question of degree but of kind.

Counsel for MGN contend that the judge failed to take account of the fact that MGN owned the copyright in the newspaper as a whole. It cannot be suggested that he was unaware of the existence and ownership of MGN of copyright in its newspaper for that was the subject matter of paragraphs 66 and 67. In the passage from paragraph 67 I have quoted in paragraph 11 above Patten LJ made it clear that copyright in the compilation does not affect the rights of the owner of copyright in its parts unless he licenses its further publication. The existence of such overlapping copyrights demonstrates the need for the compiler to obtain sufficient licences from his contributors.

. . .

For all these reasons I would dismiss this appeal....

(c) Translations

Keatley Surveying Ltd. v. Teranet Inc., 2012 ONSC 7120 (Ont. S.C.J.), additional reasons 2013 CarswellOnt 2587 (Ont. S.C.J.)

. . .

2.   The Alleged Use — Translations

[116] The statement of claim alleges that Teranet infringed the surveyors copyright in the plans of survey through various uses. It is Teranet's position that one of the uses as pleaded (translation) is not an infringement in law and must be struck (Teranet narrowed its position to this one use during oral argument).

[117] The relevant parts of the statement of claim are as follows:

> 23. In clear breach of the Class' copyrights, the Defendant or its agents made unauthorized copies of the Surveyors' Works deposited in the registry offices, without notifying the Class. The unauthorized copies were *translated into a digital format*, transmitted to the Defendant's data-receiving centre by telecommunication and stored in the Defendant's electronic database ....

> 25. Copies *of the Surveyors' Works were translated into various digital formats, including Portable Document Folder (PDF) and Tagged Image File Format (TIFF), as well as being reformatted for printing in hard copy. Each format is an unauthorized translation of the original Surveyors' Works filed in the relevant registry office.*

> . . .

> 27. The Defendant infringed the Class' copyright in the Surveyors' Works by doing things, without the consent of the Class, that the Class has the exclusive right to do, including:

> . . .

(c) producing or reproducing or publishing *translations* of the Surveyors' Works

[Emphasis added.]

[118] The right of a copyright holder to create a translation of a work is established by section 3(1)(a) of the *Copyright Act* as follows:

> 3. (1) For the purposes of this Act, "copyright", in relation to a work, means the sole right to produce or reproduce the work or any substantial part thereof in any material form whatever, to perform the work or any substantial part thereof in public or, if the work is unpublished, to publish the work or any substantial part thereof, and includes the sole right
>
> (a) to produce, reproduce, perform or publish any *translation* of the work,

[Emphasis added.]

[119] What is a translation? The word "translation" is not defined in the *Copyright Act*. However, there is case law and authoritative texts that discuss the meaning of this word as used in the Act. In essence these sources confirm that the word "translation" is used in the Act in its "primary sense of the turning of something from one human language into another." (John S. McKeown, *Fox on Canadian Law of Copyright and Industrial Designs*, 4th ed., looseleaf (Toronto: Carswell, 2003) at 21:9; David Vaver, *Copyright Law* (Toronto: Irwin Law, 2000) at 130). In order to constitute a "translation", the resulting work must also be original.

[120] This interpretation of "translation" was applied in *Apple Computer, Inc. v. Mackintosh Computers Ltd.*, reflex, [1988] 1 F.C. 673 at para. 3 (C.A.), aff'd 1990 CanLII 119 (SCC), [1990] 2 S.C.R. 209. In *Apple* the issue was "whether a person who duplicates a computer chip thereby infringes the exclusive rights granted by section 3 of the *Copyright Act*". The facts were as follows, at para. 26:

> The appellants ... pirated two computer programs used by the respondents in their Apple II+ computer. It is common ground that the programs in question, when written, as they originally were, in letters, symbols and figures known as 6502 assembly code, were original literary works subject to copyright and that the copyright therein vests in respondent Apple Computer, Inc. But the appellants have not copied the programs written in assembly code. They have not copied any writing at all. What they have done is reproduce, apparently by mechanical means, the electrical circuitry of a silicon chip in which, by the magic of computer science, the programs are embodied. The question at issue is to know whether the appellants have infringed the respondents' copyright in the original assembly code programs.

[121] Two of the Federal Court of Appeal judges discussed the meaning of "translation", at paras. 17 and 38:

> I agree with the learned Trial Judge that the conversion of a text into Morse Code or shorthand does not result in a different literary work and that the text, so converted, does retain the character of the original. That, however, does not lead to the conclusion that such conversion is translation for purposes of the Act. A person knowledgeable of Morse Code or the particular shorthand system could read the

converted version and what would be heard would be the original text verbatim. Such a conversion is not, in my opinion a translation within the contemplation of the *Copyright Act*. It is rather a reproduction of the original, the making of which was equally the exclusive right of the owner of the copyright in that original.

. . .

In the first place, I cannot accept, as the Trial Judge seems to have done, that the appellants' chips were a "translation" of the respondents' programs, contrary to paragraph 3(1)(a). In my view, "translation" is used here in its primary sense of the turning of something from one human language into another. To give it its extended meaning of an expression in another medium or form of representation seems to me to be at variance with the fundamental principle that copyright subsists not in the idea expressed but in the form of its expression. That principle in turn finds application in the well-known rule that a translation is itself an original literary work and the subject of copyright, and this regardless of whether the work translated is itself subject to copyright. The rendering of a literary work in code, for example, Morse or Braille, is, I think, properly characterized as a reproduction of the work, not as a translation. Indeed, since the respondents' programs originated in code, I do not see how one can properly speak of their translation at all. The fact that both machine and assembly codes are called "languages" is simply an example of the anthropomorphic phenomenon to which I referred at the outset.

[122] The statement of claim alleges that copies of the plans of survey "were translated into various digital formats, including Portable Document Folder (PDF) and Tagged Image File Format (TIFF)". Following *Apple*, I conclude that scanning the plans of survey to create a digital format is not a translation within the meaning of s. 3(1)(a) of the *Copyright Act*. The resulting digital plan of survey is not an original work, as there is no "skill and judgment" involved in simply scanning the plans of survey. It is therefore plain and obvious that there is no infringement of copyright for "translating copies" of the plans of survey by converting the plans into digital formats. As a result, those parts of the statement of claim dealing with translation to advance an infringement cause of action will fail and must be struck.

[123] Subject to the parts of the claim dealing with translation that are struck, Keatley has satisfied the s. 5(1)(a) criterion.

(d) Establishing Infringement

In order to succeed in an action for infringement of copyright by reproduction the following inquiries must be made: (1) what are the work or works in which the plaintiff claims copyright?; (2) is each such work "original"?; (3) was there copying from that work?; and (4) if there was copying, has a substantial part of that work been reproduced? The plaintiff must prove the reproduction of either the entire work or of a substantial part. The plaintiff must also prove some causal connection between the copyrighted work and the infringing work. In other words, the copyrighted work must be the source from which the copy is derived.

The question of whether copying (that is, a causal nexus between the copyright owner's work and that of the alleged infringer) is established, is not the same as the question of whether, once copying has been established, the whole or substantial part of the copyright owner's work has been appropriated. The two issues will often overlap. Nevertheless, they are discrete issues and the answer to one does not necessarily produce an answer to the other.

To determine whether the work is an independent work or has been produced by copying, the plaintiff must prove that the defendant has directly or indirectly made an unlawful use of the plaintiff's copyright work. It is not necessary to show that the defendant has copied directly from the plaintiff's work. It is sufficient for the plaintiff to establish some chain of causation linking the plaintiff's copyright work and the allegedly infringing copy. What must be shown is that either directly or indirectly copyright work is the causa sine qua non of the infringing work. This is because copyright law protects only against copying and not against similarity per se.

In determining whether the part of a work copied is a substantial part of the copyright work, the plaintiff first has to establish that its work as a whole is "original" and protected by copyright. The plaintiff will then have to prove that the part of its work copied by the defendant is substantial, having regard to the protectable and not the unprotectable parts of it. In determining whether the part taken by the defendant is substantial, the Court must first identify the part of the copyright work which is alleged to have been reproduced and decide whether it constitutes a substantial part of the original expression in the work.

The copyright concept of "substantial similarity", a term often used in the U.S., is not consistently used with a single, settled meaning in the law of copyright. This phrase is used in at least two distinct but related senses. Substantial similarity can refer to the likeness between two works sufficient to give rise to an inference, when supported by evidence of access, that the defendant as a factual matter used the plaintiff's work as a starting point for his own. This likeness has been referred to a "probative similarity". A plaintiff must also show that the copying amounts to an improper appropriation by demonstrating that substantial similarity to protected material exists between the two works. "Substantial similarity" in this prong of the analysis is used as a term of art to describe the unlawful nature of the similarities between two works.

The presence of a "substantial similarity" requirement in both prongs of the analysis — actual copying and whether the copying constitutes an improper appropriation — creates the potential for unnecessary confusion, especially because a plaintiff need not prove substantial similarity in every case in order to prove actual copying. Copying may be established either by direct evidence of copying or by indirect evidence, including access to the copyrighted work, similarities that are probative of copying between the works, and expert testimony. In this context, "substantial similarity" simply means sufficient similarity of a given element of a work to an element in the allegedly infringing work to support a reasoned inference that more probably than not the element was copied from the copyrighted work. Copying in this context as a prong of substantial similarity is limited to the purely factual issue of whether the defendant used the plaintiff's work as a starting point for his own.

A plaintiff must also show that the copying amounts to an improper appropriation by demonstrating that substantial similarity to protected material exists between the two works. To show unlawful appropriation, the plaintiff must prove substantial similarity between copied copyrightable elements of the allegedly infringed work in the allegedly infringing work. "Substantial similarity," as used here indicates a degree of objective similarity between the allegedly infringing material and what is copyrightable (that is, the copyrightable part or parts). Thus, the copying must be extensive enough to be "substantial." Establishment of similarity, therefore, has a double significance. It can help to prove copying as a matter of fact, but it is also necessary in order to show that which is alleged to infringe is sufficiently similar as a matter of law to the original to justify a finding of infringement.

The dual usage of the term "substantial similarity" must be born in mind in considering the significance of resemblances between a plaintiff's and a defendant's work. A defendant who has copied from a plaintiff's work as a factual matter such as by employing the plaintiff's ideas, procedures or techniques may not have copied as a legal matter. For, if the defendant has not copied something protected by the copyright laws — specifically, the plaintiff's expression of his ideas — then his copying will not subject him to liability. The copying/unlawful appropriation dichotomy reflects the fact that the copyright laws do not protect basic ideas, procedures, and concepts, but only the expressions of them. Copying can occur when a defendant uses the former; unlawful appropriation, however, requires the reproduction of expression as well. However, the copying of even unprotected elements can have a probative value in determining whether the defendant copied the plaintiff's work as a matter of fact. Therefore, the presence in the allegedly infringing work of parts of the plaintiff's work that are not protected by copyright can nevertheless be evidence of copying as a matter of fact.

Francis Day & Hunter Ltd. and Another v. Bron and Another, [1963] 2 W.L.R. 868 (C.A.)

Willmer L.J., Upjohn L.J. and Diplock L.J.

1963 Feb. 20, 21, 22, 25.

WILLMER L.J.

This is an appeal from a judgment of Wilberforce J., given on July 27, 1962, whereby he dismissed an action brought by the plaintiffs for infringement of their copyright in a song called "In a Little Spanish Town" (to which I will refer hereafter as "Spanish Town"). This was composed in 1926, and (as has been admitted by the defendants) was extensively exploited in the United States of

America and elsewhere by the publication of sheet music, by the distribution of gramophone records and by broadcasting. Unlike many popular songs, "Spanish Town" appears to have retained its popularity over the years. Records published in this country (some of them quite recently) were played to us during the course of the hearing; and, speaking for myself, I was readily able to recognise the tune as a familiar one which I had heard on frequent previous occasions.

The defendants are the publishers of another song called "Why," which was composed in 1959 by Peter de Angelis. "Spanish Town" is written in 3/4 time, and "Why" in 4/4 time. There are a number of other differences between the two works which were the subject of a good deal of evidence by musical experts on both sides. But when the two songs were played to us, it was immediately apparent, to me at any rate, that the effect on the ear was one of noticeable similarity. This is a matter which is not without importance, for, as was pointed out by Astbury J. in Austin v. Columbia Gramophone Co. Ltd., "Infringement of copyright in music is not a question of note for note comparison," but falls to be determined "by the ear as well as by the eye."

. . .

Mr. Arnold conceded that reproduction could possibly be the result of a subconscious process. But he went on to submit that reproduction within the section could mean nothing short of identity. Reproduction, under section 49, may be of a substantial part; but there is no suggestion in the Act of any such thing as a "substantial reproduction." In the present case it cannot be said that there is anything approaching identity between the plaintiffs' work and that of de. Angelis. Consequently, Mr. Arnold submitted, there could be no infringement of the plaintiffs' copyright, whether conscious or unconscious, by way of reproduction.

I find myself quite unable to accept this submission, for I can find no warrant for the suggestion that reproduction, within the meaning of the section, occurs only when identity is achieved. This not only offends against common sense, but is, I think, contrary to authority. In Austin v. Columbia Gramophone Company Ltd. the headnote reads: "Infringement of copyright in music is not a question of note for note comparison, but of whether the substance of the original copyright work is taken or not." In the course of his judgment in that case Astbury J. quoted from the earlier case of D'Almaine v. Boosey, where it was laid down that "it must depend on whether the air taken is substantially the same with the original." I accept that as a correct statement of the principle.

UPJOHN L.J.

I agree with the judgment which has just been delivered.

When Mr. Foster opened this appeal, he invited us in the name of international comity to say that a right of property (that is, copyright) which is the subject of international convention must be protected in a most special and unique way. We were invited to say that if similarity of the alleged infringing work to the original work was established as a fact, and if it was further established that the alleged infringer had had some access to the original work, then although a denial of conscious plagiarism was accepted, we were bound, as an irrebuttable presumption of law, to say that the alleged infringer must have unconsciously copied the original work. The doctrine was said to be necessary to protect the author of the original work, for otherwise (so it was argued) any infringer could escape the consequences of plagiarism by denying that he had done so. Alternatively, it was said that if some undefined higher degree of similarity between the two works could be proved — something higher than is necessary to prove similarity in fact — then that would be sufficient to establish a similarity from which we were bound to infer unconscious copying.

Apart from the appeal to international comity, no authority and no textbook has been cited in support of this remarkable doctrine. Copyright is statutory, and depends upon section 2 of the Copyright Act, 1956. No hint of this doctrine appears there.

As to international comity, while it is true that in the United States of America a number of authorities (to some of which I shall have occasion to refer later) accept the doctrine that subconscious or unconscious copying may be inferred in a proper case and operate as a breach of copyright, not one of those authorities gives any support to this alleged and startling doctrine. The authorities in question in each case treated the question of unconscious copying as purely a question or inference of fact which might be drawn in the circumstances of a particular case, and not as a presumption of law. We were not referred to the laws of any other convention country, and the relevant paragraph (No. 4) of the Brussels Convention itself lends no support to the doctrine. I therefore reject this submission.

The truth is that the plaintiff in a copyright action must show that a substantial part of the original work has been reproduced; see section 2 (5) and section 49 of the Copyright Act, 1956; and, although not expressed in the Act, it is common ground that such a reproduction, in the words of Mr. Skone James, must be causally connected with the work of the original author. If it is an independent work, then, though identical in every way, there is no infringement. If a true infringer wrongly persuades the court that it is his own unaided work, the plaintiff fails, as do other plaintiffs when fraudulent defendants unhappily succeed (as, no doubt, they sometimes do) in persuading the court that they have not been fraudulent. The question, therefore, in this case is whether there has been a breach of section 2 (5); that subsection has been read by my Lord, and I will not read it again.

This is really a question of fact and nothing else, which depends on the circumstances of each case; but it is a question of fact which must be taken in two stages. The first stage is objective, and the second stage subjective. The first question is whether in fact the alleged infringing work — which for the sake of brevity I will inaccurately call the defendant's work, for though the composer was a witness, he was not a defendant — is similar to the work of the original author — which again for the sake of brevity I will, with equal inaccuracy, call the plaintiff's work. Is it then proper to draw the inference that the defendant's work may have been copied from the plaintiffs' work? This is purely an objective question of fact, and depends in large degree upon the aural perception of the judge, but also upon the expert evidence tendered to him; but it is essentially a jury question. A defendant might in theory go into the witness-box and say that he had deliberately made use of the plaintiff's work, but that it is not an infringement, either because he did not make use of a substantial part of the plaintiff's work, or that, though the plaintiff's work has been utilised, he has been able so to alter it that it cannot properly be described as a reproduction. The onus is on the plaintiff to prove the contrary as a matter of purely objective fact, and if he cannot do so then the morally dishonest defendant will escape the consequence of the allegation of infringement. No such question arises in this case. At this stage similarity has been found by Wilberforce J., and that is not challenged before us. For myself, I think that perhaps I would have used rather stronger adjectives than "definite" or "considerable" similarity, which were the words used by the judge; the adjective "close" would be more appropriate, but nothing, I think, turns upon that matter.

The next stage is the subjective stage and is equally a question of fact, though, of course, the degree of similarity is most important in reaching this subjective conclusion. The question at this stage, put bluntly, is: has the defendant copied the plaintiff's work, or is it an independent work of his own? Mr. Skone James, in an attractive argument, agrees that the plaintiff, in order to succeed, must prove a causal connection between his work and the defendant's work; but he submits that, providing that upon a proper inference from the known facts, it is right to assume that the alleged infringing work was derived from the plaintiff's work, it matters not whether it was done consciously or unconsciously. There is, he submits, no difference in principle between a conscious act of piracy and an unconscious act of piracy; all that must be established is a causal connection.

While conscious acts of piracy may be established in the witness-box, unconscious acts of piracy must clearly be a matter of inference from surrounding circumstances. The alleged infringing work may be an identical reproduction of the original work with all its idiosyncrasies, and all the same mistakes. Theoretically and mathematically, that may be a complete coincidence, and both works may be the product of entirely independent brains; but the judge has to judge of these matters on the balance of probabilities; and such an identical reproduction may lead him to reject the evidence of the defendant, who otherwise appears to be an honest witness. Much less than complete identity may properly lead the judge, on the balance of probabilities, to reject the evidence of an apparently honest witness on this question. This is a question of pure fact in every case. It does not arise in this case for Wilberforce J. accepted the author's evidence that he did not consciously derive the composition of "Why" from "In a Little Spanish Town," and that has not been challenged before us.

At this stage, therefore, the question is whether, on the facts of the case, it is proper to infer that de Angelis has derived "Why" unconsciously from the plaintiff's work, which he had heard at some earlier time. This again is purely a question of the proper inference of fact to be drawn from all the relevant and admissible known facts. There may be cases which, if the circumstances do not justify the conclusion that the defendant, in denying conscious plagiarism, is not telling the truth, yet justify the conclusion that he must have heard the plaintiff's tune, and subconsciously reproduced it.

I do not pause to recapitulate the facts of this case in any detail for they have been set out in much meticulous detail in Wilberforce J.'s judgment, and also by Willmer L.J., that I do not repeat them. I draw the conclusion that although, as I have already stated, the resemblance is a close one, that resemblance, in the circumstances of this case, is little evidence of conscious or unconscious copying.

Wilberforce J. said: "Thirdly, the theme of 'Spanish Town' is made up of common-place elements, or, as some witnesses have called them, cliches. The first six notes are a commonplace enough series; they are found in an Austrian country dance and in a song, 'Let Us Sing Merrily.' The device of repetition, of resting for two bars on a long note and of repetition in sequence, are the commonest tricks of composition. But many writers of great music have used clichès to produce masterpieces; indeed, some of them have found in the commonplace character of their basic phrase their stimulus. Professor Nieman gave some interesting examples from the music of Mozart, and most writers of popular songs use, and can use, nothing else. No example was given of precisely this combination having been used in other compositions, though it was apparent that the musical dictionaries and the experience of the witnesses had been thoroughly combed."

Having heard the arguments of counsel, accompanied by very helpful demonstrations on the piano, I reach the conclusion of fact that, apart altogether from de Angelis's denial of conscious plagiarism, which was accepted, it is not a mere legal or mathematical possibility, but a real live practical possibility that the defendant's composition of "Why" is an independent composition. This practical possibility again does not conclude the matter, for the defendant's composition may nevertheless be the result of unconscious memory. But first it is necessary to establish the probability that the defendant has heard the plaintiff's composition.

Wilberforce J. had to deal with a difficult situation as to whether de Angelis had heard, or even played, as a youth in a dance band, the plaintiff's composition. I think it is possible that, although in perfect good faith he stated the contrary, de Angelis did hear the music, and possibly played it in his early youth. Each case must depend upon its own facts, and it is not possible to lay down any criteria. But it does seem to me that where, for the reasons I have given, there is evidence from the music itself that there is a real practical possibility of independent composition by the defendant, it requires quite strong evidence to support the view that there may have been unconscious copying. To my mind, the possibility that the defendant had heard it, or even played it in his early youth, is a quite insufficient ground upon which it would be proper to draw the inference of unconscious copying. It may be that in the future medical evidence will be available to guide us upon this point, but in the absence of acceptable and probative medical evidence I think it requires quite strong evidence, in a case such as this — where, as I have already pointed out, independent composition is a real practical possibility — to establish, as a matter of probability, that de Angelis's subconscious ego guided his hand.

The cases in the United States to which we have been referred offer some instructive comparison on their facts, although I do not lose sight of the fact, of course, that cases are only authorities for legal propositions; but, nevertheless, I think the cases cited are helpful. In the first case, that of Fred Fisher Inc. v. Dillingham, that great judge, Judge Learned Hand, in giving the famous composer, Jerome Kern, the benefit of the doubt, said: "On the whole, my belief is that, in composing the accompaniment to the refrain of 'Kalua,' Mr. Kern must have followed, probably unconsciously, what he had certainly often heard only a short time before." That is in marked contrast to the facts of this case.

Then, in a rather different case, Edwards and Deutsch Lithographing Co. v. Boorman, the plaintiffs prepared, printed, published and distributed certain discount tables, the copyright work. The defendants published very similar tables. But there it was established that the defendants had sold and handled the plaintiffs' publications for years, and on that the inference was drawn of unconscious copying. Again the facts of that case are very different from the one before us.

Wilberforce J. put the relevant points to himself quite accurately, and my Lord has read that part of his judgment; and his summary, which I will venture to repeat, was this: "In this case, after taking account of the respective character and similarities of the two works as previously discussed, and relating this to the fact that there is no direct evidence that Mr. Peter de Angelis even knew the work 'Spanish Town' before he composed 'Why,' I have come to the conclusion that I have not sufficient factual material from which to draw an inference that he had sufficient knowledge or memory of 'Spanish Town' at the date of composition, to justify me in finding, against his express denial, that in composing 'Why' he copied, without knowing that he did so, ' Spanish Town,' or a part of 'Spanish Town.'" I entirely agree with that conclusion of fact reached by Wilberforce J.

That makes it unnecessary to decide the really interesting question in this case whether Mr. Skone James is right when he says there is no difference in law between conscious and unconscious copying. It seems to me that that is an interesting question upon which I express no opinion, for, as I have said, it does not arise. Mr. Skone James, in support of his argument, has pointed out that an infringer may be entirely ignorant of knowledge of plagiarism; normally the printer and publisher will also be guilty of infringement though they have no reason even to suspect that any plagiarism can be suggested.

This, however, does not meet my difficulty. You do not necessarily have to show knowledge or suspicion of plagiarism against every defendant, but the plaintiff always has to prove that the alleged infringement is not the independent work of the alleged infringing author or composer, but is causally connected with the plaintiff's work.

The real question is this: can it be said to be an "act" of reproduction, for the purposes of section 2 (5) of the Copyright Act, 1956, if the alleged infringing work is not the conscious act of the infringer? It has been argued that Luxmoore J. in Ricordi's case expressed the view that subconscious copying could be an infringement of copyright; but I do not think that he intended to express any view on the law at all. For my part, I think that this question, therefore, remains entirely open.

I agree that this appeal must be dismissed.

DIPLOCK L.J.

This appeal seems to me to turn entirely upon a question of fact: was the judge entitled, notwithstanding the similarities between the melodies of the plaintiffs' song "In a Little Spanish Town" and the defendants' song "Why," to refuse to infer that the composer of the latter work copied it from the former work?

It is conceded on the one hand (as is obvious to the ear) that the two works show considerable similarities, and on the other hand that the composer of "Why " did not intentionally copy it from "In a Little Spanish Town'"; but it was found by Wilberforce J. that the composer of "Why" must at some time and in some circumstances have heard "In a Little Spanish Town"; and it is contended by the plaintiffs that the only proper inference of fact is that he must have stored it in his memory and reproduced it without being aware that he was performing an exercise of recollection and not an act of independent creation.

To this assumed mental feat there has been applied the conveniently ambiguous term "subconscious copying"; and we have heard much argument as to whether, if it is established, it constitutes an infringement of the copyright in the work which has been unconsciously copied. For my part, I think that the law is perfectly clear, and that such difficulties as there are in this appeal are solely due to the absence of any factual information about the mental process involved in "subconscious copying." We know not whether it is rare or common, general or idiosyncratic, nor indeed whether it is possible to remember, not a mere isolated phrase, but a "substantial" part of the remembered work without remembering that one is remembering.

First, as to the law; and for this purpose I will assume that it is established that the composer of "Why" did in fact use his recollection of "a substantial part of" the melody of "In a Little Spanish Town " as the model for his own composition, although he was unaware that he was doing so, and genuinely thought that "Why" was his own independent creation. The word "to copy" is not used at all in the Copyright Act, 1956, nor was it in the Copyright Act, 1911. Nevertheless, it is well established that to constitute infringement of copyright in any literary, dramatic or musical work, there must be present two elements: first, there must be sufficient objective similarity between the infringing work and the copyright work, or a substantial part thereof, for the former to be properly described, not necessarily as identical with, but as a reproduction or adaptation of the latter; secondly, the copyright work must be the source from which the infringing work is derived. The necessity for the second element was expressly laid down by the Court of Appeal in Purefoy Engineering Co, Ltd. v. Sykes Boxall & Co. Ltd., and is, indeed, implicit in all thee compilation cases, including the recent case in this court of William Hill (Football) Ltd. v. Ladbrokes (Football) Ltd., where tables of betting odds were unanimously held not to infringe the copyright in substantially identical tables because the authors of the later tables, although very familiar with the earlier tables, had, in fact, worked out the odds for themselves. But while the copyright work must be the source from which the infringing work is derived, it need not be the direct source: see Hanfstaengl v. Empire Palace Ltd. Mr. Skone James, I think put it with his usual accuracy when he said there must be a causal connection between the copyright work and the infringing work. To borrow an expression once fashionable in the law of negligence, the copyright work must be shown to be a causa sine qua non of the infringing work.

The necessity for a causal connection between the copyright work and the infringing work, although well established under the Copyright Act, 1911, either as being implicit in the legal concept of "copyright," or in the word "reproduce," is, I think, more easily deduced from the wording of the current Copyright Act of 1956. Section 1 (1) defines "copyright" in relation to a work as the exclusive right to do and to authorise other persons to do certain acts "in relation to that work"; and subsection (2) defines "infringement " as the doing of any of those acts by a person who is not the owner of the copyright or his licensee. The acts, which are defined in section 2, and include "reproducing the work in any material form," if they are to constitute infringement must thus be done "in relation to the work," an expression which connotes a causal connection between the copyright work and the act relied upon as an infringement. If the existence of the copyright work has no causal connection with the production of the alleged infringing work, even though the latter be identical with the former, there is no infringement of copyright.

It is, however, in my view, equally clear law that neither intention to infringe, nor knowledge that he is infringing on the part of the defendant, is a necessary ingredient in the cause of action for infringement of copyright. Once the two elements of sufficient objective similarity and causal connection are established, it is no defence that the defendant was unaware (and could not have been aware) that what he was doing infringed the copyright in the plaintiff's work. This is expressly recognised by sections 17 and 18 of the Copyright Act, 1956, which restrict the remedies available against an innocent infringer, but recognises his liability. Thus under section 18, which gives to the copyright owner remedies in conversion and detinue in respect of infringing copies of his work, a defendant who "believed and had reasonable grounds for believing that they were not infringing copies "is relieved of any liability in damages, but not of his liability to deliver up any infringing copies in his possession.

"Unconscious copying" in the sense in which it has been used in the argument postulates, first, such objective similarity between the copyright work and the alleged infringing work that the latter may properly be said to reproduce the former; secondly, that there is a causal connection between the copyright work and the alleged infringing work; thirdly, that the composer of the alleged infringing work believed (and may indeed have had reasonable grounds for believing) that there was no such causal connection. The first two, if established, in my view constitute breach of copyright; the third is irrelevant on liability although it may be relevant on remedy.

The real difficulty in this case is not one of law, but of fact. It involves an inquiry into the working of the human mind. It may well be that this is a matter upon which expert evidence is admissible; but cases in English courts are normally conducted upon the tacit assumption that where no question of disease of the mind is involved, the ordinary man, whether sitting in the jury-box or on the bench: is capable of determining (where it is relevant) what went on in the defendant's mind.

The present case was so conducted before Wilberforce J. No expert evidence was called as to how the human memory or musical creative faculties work; no investigation was made into the mental idiosyncrasies of the composer of "Why" or his methods of composition. Wilberforce J. was left to draw the inference of "subconscious copying" from the evidence (1) of the similarities between the melodies of "In a Little Spanish Town" and "Why" as explained by the conflicting evidence of expert musicians; (2) of the likelihood of the composer of "Why" having at some time heard "In a Little Spanish Town"; and (3) of his denial that he had consciously copied "In a Little Spanish Town."

On this state of the evidence, there were three possible explanations of the similarities: conscious copying, unconscious copying, coincidence. The first Wilberforce J. rejected. He accepted the denial of the composer of "Why." This is a finding of primary fact, and it depends ultimately on credibility. The appellants do not seek to disturb it. This reduces the possible explanations to two: unconscious copying, or coincidence. Wilberforce J. did not reject the possibility that "unconscious copying" of musical works can occur. He proceeded to consider, in the light of the conflicting expert evidence, which was the more probable explanation of the similarities, unconscious copying, or coincidence. The relevant similarities were to be found in the first eight bars of the melody of "In a Little Spanish Town" which, it is common ground, do constitute a substantial part of that musical work. They are described clearly (and it is conceded accurately) in Wilberforce J.'s judgment.

The rival contentions, supported by expert evidence, may be summarised thus: The plaintiffs, conceding that the first bar by itself was a musical cliche in which there was no copyright, contended that the similarities in the use made of the cliche in eight successive bars in each of the two works were too great to be explained by coincidence. The defendants contended that, once a composer of popular songs had decided to use, as a basis of the theme of a popular song, the musical cliche contained in the first bar, the use which was in fact made of it in both "Why" and "In a Little Spanish Town" in the succeeding bars was a device by no means uncommon in musical composition, and the similarities were readily explicable by coincidence. Wilberforce J. was not satisfied that the similarities were due to unconscious copying. This, no doubt, was an inference of fact, but one which depends, in part at least, upon the degree of conviction which the evidence of the respective experts carried, and thus one with which an appellate court should be slow to interfere. No attempt has been made to demonstrate that he has overlooked or misunderstood any of the evidence.

How, then, is the case for the appellants put? The procedure of the English courts, says Mr. Foster, is ill-adapted to deal with such esoteric problems as "subconscious copying." It places too heavy a burden upon those who seek to establish that it has occurred. Copyright is an international proprietary right, and English law should keep in step with foreign law. They order these things better in more sophisticated (though unspecified) jurisdictions. But the only foreign law to which we have actually been referred is to be found in the United States cases which my brethren have discussed; and there, it seems, the matter is dealt with in the same unsophisticated way as that in which Wilberforce J. dealt with this case, without making it impossible for the courts to find (where the evidence, so warrants) that unconscious copying has taken place.

Faced with the difficulty that "unconscious copying" is by definition not susceptible of direct proof in the present state of psychological techniques, it must always be a matter of inference from other facts, Mr. Foster's first bold submission was, that if the plaintiff proves (1) the presence of the necessary element of objective similarity between the copyright work and the alleged infringing work; and (2) the mere possibility of access to the copyright work by the author of the alleged infringing work, there is an irrebuttable presumption (that is, a presumption of law) that the author of the alleged infringing work unconsciously copied the copyright work; or, put more briefly, what cannot be proved must be presumed. With all respect, this is bad logic as well as bad law. For, unless "the law is an ass" — which I must ex officio irrebuttably presume it is not — the essential, though unexpressed, premise of this proposition is that the similarities cannot be due to coincidence; proof of possibility of access is thus unnecessary; access as well as unconscious copying can be irrebuttably presumed. But this is merely a roundabout way of saying that proof of a causal connection between the copyright work and the alleged infringing work is not a necessary element in infringement of copyright; and that is not the law.

Mr. Foster's alternative submission (although I understood it to be presented as one of law) was, I think, upon analysis merely one as to the proper inferences of fact to be drawn from varying degrees of similarity between the copyright work and the alleged infringing work. The degree of objective similarity is, of course, not merely important, indeed essential, in proving the first element in infringement, namely, that the defendant's work can properly be described as a reproduction or adaptation of the copyright work; it is also very cogent material from which to draw the inference that the defendant has in fact copied, whether consciously or unconsciously, the copyright work. But it is not the only material. Even complete identity of the two works may not be conclusive evidence of copying, for it may be proved that it was impossible for the author of the alleged infringing work to have had access to the copyright work. And, once you have eliminated the impossible (namely, copying), that which remains (namely, coincidence) however improbable, is the truth; I quote inaccurately, but not unconsciously, from Sherlock Holmes.

No useful purpose can thus be served by seeking to classify degrees of similarity into categories which must be taken to be sufficient to prove unconscious copying where access to the copyright work by the author of the alleged infringing work is proved (1) as a certainty; (2) as a probability; (3) as a possibility, and (4) as an impossibility. That is not how questions of fact are decided in courts of law, or anywhere else.

The answer, as Wilberforce J. said at the conclusion of an impeccable summary of the evidence, "can only be reached by a judgment of fact upon a number of composite elements." Those elements on which the judge directed himself have already been read by my Lord, and I need not repeat them.

I agree that it is impossible for this court, which has not heard the evidence or seen the witnesses, to say that Wilberforce J. came to a wrong conclusion of fact.

IBCOS Computers Ltd. v. Barclay's Mercantile Highland Finance Ltd., [1994] F.S.R. 275 (Ch. D.)

Before: Mr. Justice Jacob

17-21, 24-28, 31 January to 3 February 1994, 24 February 1994

JACOB J.:

These are three actions. The plaintiffs say the defendants have infringed their copyright in respect of computer programs and have acted in breach of confidence by using the "source code" of their programs. The plaintiffs' program is called ADS ("Agricultural Dealer System"); that of the defendants, Unicorn and, in the second action, a 1993 version of Unicorn which I shall call Unicorn 2. The third action is in respect of Unicorn. It was started shortly before the trial out of an abundance of caution — the plaintiffs were concerned about a possibility that the first and third defendants might have a defence of lack of relevant state of mind as of the date of the writ in the first action. In the end, because of a concession by Mr. Kelman, counsel for those defendants, the third action became otiose save on one point. The concession was that those defendants, by selling Unicorn to customers were authorising those customers to run the program, and so would be liable if Unicorn infringed. Since that was obviously so from the outset I cannot understand why there was no admission in the defence.

. . .

Logically therefore the claim in copyright calls to be tested in the following order:

(1) What are the work or works in which the plaintiff claims copyright?

(2) Is each such work "original"?

(3) Was there copying from that work?

(4) If there was copying, has a substantial part of that work been reproduced?

I have set forth the tests which are taken directly from the statute because not only is this what the law requires but because by doing this one can avoid aphorisms such as "there is no copyright in an idea" or "prima facie what is worth copying is worth protecting." The courts have used these in the past but they can only serve as a guide. There are dangers in departing from the Act too far. For instance the latter aphorism, taken literally, would mean that all a plaintiff ever had to do was to prove copying. Originality, appropriate subject matter for copyright and a taking of a substantial part would all be proved in one go. One would not need the Act if the aphorism represented the law. It proves too much.

I therefore propose to follow that order, so far as I can, on what are clearly very messy and partly inchoate facts.

Was there copying?

For infringement there must be copying. Whether there was or not is a question of fact. To prove copying the plaintiff can normally do no more than point to bits of his work and the defendant's work which are the same and prove an opportunity of access to his work. If the resemblance is sufficiently great then the court will draw an inference of copying. It may then be possible for the defendant to rebut the inference — to explain the similarities in some other way. For instance he may be able to show both parties derived the similar bits from some third party or material in the public domain. Or he may be able to show that the similarity arises out of a functional necessity — that anyone doing this particular job would be likely to come up with similar bits. So much is common ground between the parties. The concept of sufficient similarities shifting the onus onto the defendant to prove non-copying is well recognised in copyright law. Thus Lord Wilberforce in L.B. Plastics v. Swish[FN14] asked whether the inference of copying:

FN14 Supra. At 621.

could be displaced by evidence from the respondents showing how in fact they had arrived at their design and that they had not done so by copying?

Actually I think the proposition is not so much one of law as of plain rational thought.

It should be noted that at this stage (namely "Was there copying?") both the important and the unimportant bits of the works being compared count. Indeed it is often identity of trivial matter which traps a copyist. As Hoffman J. observed in Billhofer Maschinenfabrik Gmb H v. Dixon & Co. Ltd.[FN15]:

FN15 [1990] F.S.R. 105 at 123.

It is the resemblances in inessentials, the small, redundant, even mistaken elements of the copyright work which carry the greatest weight. This is because they are least likely to have been the result of independent design.

What then is the position here? Is there an inference of copying? I have no doubt that there is. It is overwhelming. There are bits of ADS in Unicorn which cannot really be explained in any other way. It would be burdensome in this judgment to set out all the similarities which raise the inference. They were all well identified in Mr. Turner's report for the plaintiffs before the trial began. I find it surprising that the defendant's experts did not seem to have addressed or faced up to these resemblances. Only at moments in the witness box did Mr. Kenny (the better of the defendant's experts) seem to recognise that there were real difficulties in the way of a case of independent design.

. . .

"Substantial part": general considerations

There is a danger in jumping from a conclusion that there was copying to a conclusion that a substantial part of a work has been taken. It is all too easy to say that a defendant who has lied about copying must have taken a lot. Of course it is likely in most cases that this is so. But the court must always go on to look at the further question of whether a substantial part was copied. In relation to conventional kinds of work this it can do reasonably readily. Even in the case of technical drawings it is possible to examine the parties' drawings to see whether a substantial part of the plaintiff's work is to be found in the defendant's. A good example of the right way to go about the problem is the Billhofer case. Even though there was copying (betrayed by the inessential details) there was no taking of sufficient visual features of the copyright drawing. In a computer program case, however, the court cannot so readily assess the question of substantial part unaided by expert evidence. I believe I should therefore be largely guided by such evidence. Before turning to this I should mention some other considerations.

Designers Guild Ltd. v. Russell Williams (Textiles) Ltd., [2000] 1 W.L.R. 2416 (U.K. H.L.)

Lord Millett

My Lords,

The first step in an action for infringement of artistic copyright is to identify those features of the defendant's design which the plaintiff alleges have been copied from the copyright work. The court undertakes a visual comparison of the two designs, noting the similarities and the differences. The purpose of the examination is not to see whether the overall appearance of the two designs is similar, but to judge whether the particular similarities relied on are sufficiently close, numerous or extensive to be more likely to be the result of copying than of coincidence. It is at this stage that similarities may be disregarded because they are commonplace, unoriginal, or consist of general ideas. If the plaintiff demonstrates sufficient similarity, not in the works as a whole but in the features which he alleges have been copied, and establishes that the defendant had prior access to the copyright work, the burden passes to the defendant to satisfy the judge that, despite the similarities, they did not result from copying.

Even at this stage, therefore, the inquiry is directed to the similarities rather than the differences. This is not to say that the differences are unimportant. They may indicate an independent source and so rebut any inference of copying. But differences in the overall appearance of the two works due to the presence of features of the defendant's work about which no complaint is made are not material. In the present case the disposition of the flowers and (except in one instance) the colourways of the defendants' design are very different from those of the plaintiffs' design. They were not taken from the copyright work, and the plaintiffs make no complaint in respect of them. They make a significant difference to the overall appearance of the design. But this is not material where the complaint is of infringement of copyright and not passing off.

Once the judge has found that the defendants' design incorporates features taken from the copyright work, the question is whether what has been taken constitutes all or a substantial part of the copyright work. This is a matter of impression, for whether the part taken is substantial must be determined by its quality rather than its quantity. It depends upon its importance to the copyright work. It does not depend upon its importance to the defendants' work, as I have already pointed out. The pirated part is considered on its own (see Ladbroke (Football) Ltd. v William Hill (Football) Ltd. [1964] 1 W.L.R. 273, 293 per Lord Pearce) and its importance to the copyright work assessed. There is no need to look at the infringing work for this purpose.

JHP Ltd. v. BBC Worldwide Ltd., [2008] F.S.R. 29 at 726 (Ch.)

Hearing Dates: 16 APRIL 2008

Norris J.:

. . .

28. The principles which have directed my consideration of the evidence on this issue are these:-

(a) the legal burden lies upon JHP to establish copying;

(b) given that the BBCW writing team had undoubted access to each of the Books, if there is a sufficient degree of similarity between the text of any of those Books and the text of the Guide then an inference of copying may be drawn;

(c) an evidential burden is then thrust upon the BBC to demonstrate independent creation (or derivation from a common source);

(d) a sufficient degree of similarity may be established not simply by direct copying but also by "altered copying" (and in the instant case Ms Mulcahy submitted that significant parts of the Guide constituted "camouflage and gloss" and asked me to look behind that and see the text of the original Books);

(e) if copying is established that copying will only amount to an infringement of copyright in the relevant Book if what has been taken comprises a substantial part of that Book (when assessed in relation to that Book as a whole) for the purposes of section 16(3) of CDPA 1988 (see Designers Guild v Russell Williams Textiles Ltd [2001] FSR 113 at 125 per Lord Millett at paras 41-43);

(f) that is always a question of fact and degree and involves an assessment of the importance (in terms of quantity and/or quality) of the copied part to the recognition and appreciation of the copyright work because "what is protected is the skill and labour devoted to making the "artistic work" itself, not the skill and labour devoted to developing some idea or invention communicated or depicted by the "artistic work"...." (per Buckley LJ in Catnic Components (1982) RPC 183 at 222 cited in Johnstone Safety v Cook [1990] FSR 161 at 176-178);

(g) although Ms Mulcahy referred me to the practical test that "what was worth copying was prima facie worth protecting", so that I should start with a bias towards anything that was "copied" being "substantial", I have not found that test useful. I think it tends to confuse questions of "copying" with questions of "substantiality", and to proceed upon the premise that if the text was "worth" copying for the Guide it was prima facie a substantial part of the relevant Book (which seems to me to focus on the importance of the text to the Guide rather than on the importance of the text to the whole of the relevant Book);

(h) a part of the relevant Book which by itself has no originality will not normally be a substantial part of the copyright, and copying it into the Guide will not make it so (see Warwick Films v Eisinger [1969] 1 Ch 508 at 533g-534b).

. . .

(e) What is a Substantial Part?

The question of whether the defendant has, to use the words of the statute, reproduced "the work or any substantial part thereof," involves a question of fact and degree that must depend on the circumstances of each particular case. Some small amount of copying of a copyright work is permissible because simply to copy is not a legal wrong. Whether there has been *prima facie* unlawful copying depends upon whether a substantial part of the copyright work has been copied. What amounts in any case to a substantial reproduction cannot be defined in precise terms. It will depend not merely on the amount reproduced, but on the substantial significance of that which is taken.[6] If there has been copying, the question of whether the copying is substantial or not depends more on the quality than on the quantity of what has been taken, and on the prejudice to the interests of the copyright owner arising therefrom.[7] It is a question which will not be determined solely by any process of arithmetic, because it is not only the quantity copied that is important, but the value of what has been reproduced as well.

It is often said that the test of whether there has been a reproduction of a substantial part is whether the essential features and substance of the copyright work have been taken. Whether the part taken is essential or vital to the plaintiff's work is sometimes assessed by whether it would be recognizable to the average lay observer familiar with the work. Some Commonwealth courts attempt to ascertain whether a substantial part of the copyright work has been taken by asking whether there has been "unfair copying" of one work in the creation of another. This method of assessing whether a substantial part of the plaintiff's work has been taken is premised on a common view held by courts in the Commonwealth that the basis of the protection conferred by copyright "is that one man must not be permitted to appropriate the result of another's labour".[8] Under this approach, copyright can be infringed by an overborrowing of the skill, labour, expense, and judgment which went into the copyright work. Since copyright protects only the skill and judgment of the author that is expended in devising the form in which the work is expressed, this analysis directs attention to how much of the skill and judgment of the author in producing the original expressive form of the work has been taken in the making of what appears, on an objective assessment, to be a substantial reproduction — or as some courts have put it, whether there has been an unlawful appropriation of expression.[9] The analysis, therefore, focuses on the originality of the part taken and its importance in relation to the protected work as a whole.[10]

---

6   *Ladbroke (Football) Ltd. v. William Hill (Football) Ltd.*, [1964] 1 All E.R. 465 (H.L.).
7   *Ibid.*
8   *L. B. (Plastics) Ltd. v. Swish Products Ltd.*, [1979] R.P.C. 551 (H.L.) per Lord Wilberforce.
9   *Théberge v. Galerie d'Art du Petit Champlain inc.*, 2002 SCC 34.
10 *CCH Canadian Ltd. v. Law Society of Upper Canada* (2002), 18 C.P.R. (4th) 161 (Fed.C.A.).

**Hawkes & Son (London) Ltd. v. Paramount Film Service Ltd.,
[1934] Ch. 593 (C.A.)**

Lord Hanworth M.R., Slesser and Romer L.JJ.

1934 April 26, 30.

Eve J.

1934 March 6, 20.

LORD HANWORTH M.R.

This action is brought by the plaintiffs, who confessedly are the owners of the copyright in a musical work entitled "Colonel Bogey." It is a musical march. The action is brought against two defendants —

. . .

These defendants... went down on a very interesting occasion to Holbrook in Suffolk, the place to which the Naval School has been removed from Greenwich, when the opening of the school was honoured by the presence of His Royal Highness the Prince of Wales, and on that occasion took a film showing the arrival of His Royal Highness, his proceeding to the grounds of the school, and then a march past which took place before him, when the boys marched past to the tune of "Colonel Bogey." Other things are shown, such as, for instance, the school itself and the buildings, and there are other incidents of the arrival of His Royal Highness when cheering takes place, and finally at his departure, when the boys of the school rest their arms on the rigging and give him a rousing cheer from the main arm.

The plaintiffs say, and it is not disputed, that they are the owners of the copyright in this musical march "Colonel Bogey," and that in the course of this film this march has been played and reproduced; it is reproduced to the extent, I think, of some 28 or more bars, and it takes something like 50 seconds to one minute to reproduce. On the other hand, the defendants say that it is quite true that this march has been reproduced in the film, but it was reproduced only as incidental to the other features of the day which were portrayed in this film; that it was entirely subordinate to the general purpose of the film; and that in any case the march, and this part of the march, played a subsidiary part, and only a subsidiary part, in this picture film; and they suggest that it would be a hampering of trade, if they were restrained from this kind of reproduction, more especially because the film itself is what is called a news film, that is to say, a film which is taken of some incidents of a day's proceedings, and afterwards shown at a picture theatre for a short time, and that the value of the film depends upon its rapid production in the course of the next few days.

We have to look at the Copyright Act, 1911, to see whether the plaintiffs are entitled to the injunction which they seek against the Olympic Kinematograph Laboratories, Ld. With regard to their claim against the distributing company, that company is, as I understand, in close association with the second defendants, and Mr. Archer says that it matters very little what is the precise position of the Paramount Film Service, Ld., in the matter, because there could be no separation of costs, and any order against the Olympic Kinematograph Laboratories, Ld., would practically carry with it the subsidiary service rendered in distribution by the first-named defendants. Now first of all let me point out that there is no question here, on the evidence before us, of the attitude of the plaintiffs being one under which they wish to place a serious or real impediment on the work that is being done, and legitimately done, by the defendants. They do not at all intend or desire to hamper trade. All that they say is this: that if this reproduction of a copyright musical march is allowed or is sought by the defendants, then, on a payment, that licence can be granted. I do not think there is much in the plea of the defendants that the rapidity with which they have to reproduce these new films makes it difficult, or indeed impossible, for them to obtain a licence from the owners of the musical copyright. Some system could no doubt be arranged whereby, if there is a possibility of some infringement of copyright, there could be a licence applicable to the occasion, so as to avoid any damage to the plaintiffs or other owners of copyright.

I turn therefore simply to look at the statute, and I bear in mind two or three points which have been rightly called to our attention. It is quite plain from what Lindley L.J. said in Hanfstaengl v. Empire Palace[FN11] that we have to consider the statute upon broad lines; to bear in mind the necessity for the protection of authors whether of musical or of literary compositions. The Acts have to be construed with reference to that purpose, and they are not to be made the instruments of oppression and extortion. On the other hand, as the learned Lord Justice says, "the intention of an infringer is immaterial, " and as Slesser L.J. has pointed out, Parker J. said in Weatherby & Sons v. International Horse Agency and Exchange, Ld.[FN12], that the right of the owner of a copyright is not determined or measured by the amount of actual damage to him by reason of the infringement; copyright is a right of property, and he is entitled to come to the Court for the protection of that property, even though he does not show or prove actual damage. Lindley L.J. says this[FN13]: "Guided by the foregoing considerations.... I ask myself whether these sketches are such copies of the plaintiff's pictures, or such reproductions of the designs thereof, as are struck at by the statute which confers copyright in such pictures." That was his test.

FN11 [1894] 3 ch. 109, 128.

FN12 [1910] 2 Ch.. 297, 305.

FN13 [1894] 3 Ch. 109, 129.

Now applying all that has been culled from the various authorities to which our attention has been drawn, I refer to the Act to see what are the rights of the plaintiffs and the corresponding rights by way of defence of the defendants. There is no doubt that, the plaintiffs are the owners of the copyright in this march, and that means under sub-s. 2 of s. 1 of the Copyright Act, 1911, that they have the sole right to produce or reproduce the work or any substantial part thereof, and to perform it; and that includes also the sole right to make any record by means of which the work may be mechanically performed or delivered, and to authorize any such acts as aforesaid. It is plain that the second defendants have made a record, by the contrivance of which the "Colonel Bogey" march may be mechanically performed, and they have in so doing infringed the right of the owner of the copyright. But it is said, first, that there is no substantial part of this musical work taken, and that the cases show that we must look into the question of the degree and what was the nature of the reproduction. In one case to which Lindley L.J. refers, he points out that in that case a worsted work copy of an engraving was held not to be an infringement of the copyright therein. On the other hand, photographs of pictures have been held to infringe the copyright, although there is a vast difference between a photographic reproduction and the picture itself. Therefore, when one deals with the word "substantial," it is quite right to consider whether or not the amount of the musical march that is taken is so slender that it would be impossible to recognize it.

In order that we might give the defendants every chance, we decided to go and see this film reproduced, and we have done so this morning, and it appeared plain to us that there is an amount taken which would be recognized by any person. We have evidence before us which must not he overlooked — evidence "that certain small exhibitors do, if they can get hold of news films, use the sound track for the purpose of what we call a non-synchronous interlude, and that sort of thing," and "in the case of some of the smaller theatres, it was probably just a means of getting over the coming in and going out of the people; and they do not worry very much about the value of that sound."

Having considered and heard this film, I am quite satisfied that the quantum that is taken is substantial, and although it might be difficult, and although it may be uncertain whether it will be ever used again, we must not neglect the evidence that a substantial part of the musical copyright could be reproduced apart from the actual picture film.

. . .

SLESSER L.J.

I am of the same opinion. The learned judge has come to the conclusion that no substantial part of the work has been reproduced. He continues: "It appears that the whole work would take a band about four minutes to play, and that the part recorded on the news reel takes 20 seconds." The learned judge, no doubt, in coming to the conclusion that no substantial part of the film has been reproduced, was not unmindful of the history of the words "substantial part "which appear in the Copyright Act, 1911, and which are an essential ingredient if the plaintiffs are to succeed or have judgment found in their favour. Those words, as Mr. Macgillivray has pointed out, had not appeared before that time in any statute, but they are words which are derived from several of the cases in which learned judges have used either those particular words or language similar. It is to be observed that in the old Copyright Act (5 & 6 Vict. c. 45), under which Bradbury v. Hotten[FN14] and Chatterton v. Cave[FN15] and other cases fell to be decided, there is no such distinction. It is there provided by s. 15 "That if any person shall in any part of the British dominions.... print or cause to be printed either for sale or exportation any book in which there shall be subsisting copyright": no distinction is there made between the whole of the book and a substantial part of it, and, of course, the literal reading of those words would of necessity have produced absurdities, and the learned judges in several cases were at pains to point out that where the statute says "any book," it means any essential, vital or substantial part of the book as words, all of which appear in different judgments. The matter is put perhaps most clearly, or as clearly as anywhere else, by Lord Hatherley in Chatterton v. Cave[FN16], where he says: "if the quantity taken be neither substantial nor material, if, as it has been expressed by some judges, 'a fair use' only be made of the publication, no wrong is done and no action can be brought." The learned Lord in his speech there uses the words "neither substantial nor material," and the words "a fair use only be made," in apposition, and it is in that sense, I think, that before the Act of 1911 the matter has to be considered.

FN14 R. 8 Ex. 1.

FN15 3 App. Cas. 483.

FN16 3 App. Cas. 483, 492.

Mr. Archer is perfectly right when he points out that the authorities indicate that other matters beyond mere quantity may and have to be looked at; indeed it is a criticism, I think, if I may respectfully make it, of the judgment in this case, that the only ground on which the learned judge held that no substantial part had been reproduced was that the whole work would take not more than four minutes to play, and the part recorded on the news reel took 20 seconds. I agree with my Lord that this reproduction is clearly a substantial part of "Colonel Bogey," looked at from any point of view, whether it be quantity, quality, or occasion. Any one hearing it would know that it was the march called "Colonel Bogey," and though it may be that it was not very prolonged in its reproduction, it is clearly, in my view, a substantial, a vital, and an essential part which is there reproduced. That being so, it is clear to my mind that a fair use has not been made of it; that is to say, there has been appropriated and published in a form which will or may materially injure the copyright, that in which the plaintiffs have a proprietary right. As is pointed out by Sir W. Page Wood V.-C. in Scott v. Stanford: "If, in effect, the great bulk of the plaintiff's publication — a large and vital portion of his work and labour — has been appropriated and published in a form which will materially injure his copyright, mere honest intention on the part of the appropriator will not suffice, as the Court can only look at the result, and not at the intention in the man's mind at the time of doing the act complained of, and he must be presumed to intend all that the publication of his work effects." So far, therefore, it is clear that a substantial part has been appropriated; or to use the language before the Act of 1911 I should have held in accordance with the authorities that there had not been a fair use made of the matter.

Ladbroke (Football) Ltd. v. William Hill (Football) Ltd. [1964] 1 W.L.R. 273 (H.L.)

Lord Reid and Lord Evershed Lord Hodson, Lord Devlin and Lord Pearce

1963 Nov. 18, 20, 21, 25, 26, 27, 28 1964 Jan. 21

LORD PEARCE

My Lords, the question whether the plaintiffs are entitled to copyright in their coupon depends on whether it is an original literary work. The words "literary work" include a compilation. They are used to describe work which is expressed in print or writing irrespective of whether it has any excellence of quality or style of writing (Perrson J. in University of London Press Ltd. v. University Tutorial Press Ltd.[FN44]. The word "original" does not demand original or inventive thought, but only that the work should not be copied but should originate from the author.[FN45]

> FN44 [1916] 2 Ch. 601, 608.

> FN45 [1916] 2 Ch. 601, 608.

In deciding therefore whether a work in the nature of a compilation is original, it is wrong to start by considering individual parts of it apart from the whole, as the appellants in their argument sought to do. For many compilations have nothing original in their parts, yet the sum total of the compilation may be original. (See, for instance, the case of Palgrave's Golden Treasury referred to by the Privy Council in Macmillan & Co. Ltd. v. K. & J. Cooper[FN46].

> FN46 36 L.R. 51 Ind.App. 109; 93 L.J. P.C. 113.

In such cases the courts have looked to see whether the compilation of the unoriginal material called for work or skill or expense. If it did, it is entitled to be considered original and to be protected against those who wish to steal the fruits of the work or skill or expense by copying it without taking the trouble to compile it themselves. So the protection given by such copyright is in no sense a monopoly, for it is open to a rival to produce the same result if he chooses to evolve it by his own labours. (See Kelly v. Morris.)

. . .

In my opinion, the majority of the Court of Appeal rightly held that the plaintiffs had established copyright in the coupon.

Did the defendants reproduce a substantial part of it? Whether a part is substantial must be decided by its quality rather than its quantity. The reproduction of a part which by itself has no originality will not normally be a substantial part of the copyright and therefore will not be protected. For that which would not attract copyright except by reason of its collocation will, when robbed of that collocation, not be a substantial part of the copyright and therefore the courts will not hold its reproduction to be an infringement. It is this, I think, which is meant by one or two judicial observations that "there is no copyright" in some unoriginal part of a whole that is copyright. They afford no justification, in my view, for holding that one starts the inquiry as to whether copyright exists by dissecting the compilation into component parts instead of starting it by regarding the compilation as a whole and seeing whether the whole has copyright. It is when one is debating whether the part reproduced is substantial that one considers the pirated portion on its own.

In the present case the learned judge found that there was deliberate copying, but he did not decide whether the part copied was substantial. The majority of the Court of Appeal thought that it was. I agree with them. There are many things which are common to many coupons. But the plaintiffs' coupon had an individuality. The defendants clearly modelled their coupon on the plaintiffs' coupon and copied many of the things that give it this individuality. I cannot regard these thinks taken together as other than substantial. There is force in the words of Peterson J. in the case of University of London Press Ltd. v. University Tutorial Press Ltd.[FN55] that "what is worth copying is prima facie worth protecting."

FN55 [1916] 2 Ch. 601, 610.

U & R Tax Services Ltd. v. H. & R. Block Canada Inc. (1995), 62 C.P.R. (3d) 257 (Fed. T.D.)

Richard J.

Judgment: June 20, 1995
Docket: Doc. T-891-89

Richard J.:

Background

3 U&R is a Canadian company involved in the business of income tax education and preparation. H&R is a multinational company and industry leader in the same field. Both businesses consist of providing income tax education, preparation and discounting services. U&R was the largest competitor of the defendant, but a distant second, having approximately 100 offices to H&R's 878 offices, and only 35% of the defendant's market share in 1988.

4 In 1988, H&R's corporate structure was headed by a Vice-President, Canada. Below him were three regional directors. The Western Regional Director was Gary Douglas. Twenty-one district managers reported to Mr. Douglas, including the two Winnipeg district managers, David Grant (Winnipeg District 1) and Jill Parker (Winnipeg District 2).

5 The literary work in which copyright is claimed by U&R is described as the "U&R 1988 T1 General Draft Form" and was used as a teaching tool for the plaintiff's tax education courses. One of the two authors of this form, Evelyn Jacks, gave evidence at the trial. During her testimony, she stated that she had been employed by U&R as Director of Education and, together with Shirley Smith, another employee, co-authored the U&R 1988 T1 General Draft Form.

Ms. Jacks testified that she was the author of more than twelve books on Canadian income tax and over fifty professional development courses, that she was a syndicated columnist for the Winnipeg Free Press for several years, and that she also contributed to other publications on income tax matters.

Nature of the business

6 Both parties provide tax education courses. Materials for these courses are prepared in the Spring and Summer, the instructors are training in late August, and the courses for the public and for alumni (former students) are held during the months of September to January. Prior to that, the U&R and H&R would have advertised their services and placed their supply orders based on the anticipated number of students. Some of the successful graduates from the tax courses are hired as employees to carry on the provision of tax preparation and discounting services. The educational courses constitute the primary source of recruitment of employees for both parties. Both the plaintiff and the defendant also sell franchises to carry on the business of tax preparation and discounting. Potential franchisees are also recruited from the tax education student body. The most important tool in both the tax education and the preparation/discounting aspects of the business is the T1 General form.

. . .

Infringement of the Work

25 As part of its strategy for 1988 and upon completion of its draft form, U&R commenced its advertising and marketing efforts. These efforts included a cross-Canada media tour by Ms. Jacks, promoting U&R as the only company to possess such a draft 1988 T1 General return and newspaper advertisements indicating that U&R had "Reformed Tax Reform", that it was the only company that has a 1988 T1 General return, and that it would be teaching the changes to the income tax law on the new form.

26 Four witnesses addressed the issue of access by H&R to U&R's form: Richard and Joan McConachy, David Grant, and Jill Parker. Richard McConachy had access to U&R's 1988 educational materials by virtue of being an instructor for the plaintiff's courses. Richard McConachy testified that he had U&R's materials at home, that he never gave this material to his wife, that he doubted whether she accessed his materials, and that the whole issue of H&R copying U&R's form was a "joke". Near the end of the 1988 tax year, Mr. McConachy left U&R to join H&R as a tax preparer.

27 Joan McConachy, the wife of Richard McConachy, was an instructor of H&R's educational course. Mrs. McConachy testified that she only had access to U&R's T1 General draft because her husband's materials were at home. Mrs. McConachy testified that she took only the T1 General draft form to an instructor's meeting and that she had never given this or any other material to David Grant, H&R's district manager for Winnipeg District 1.

28 David Grant also testified and indicated that Joan McConachy had provided him with not only a copy of the T1 General draft form, but U&R's teaching

manual as well. He indicated that he received this material from Mrs. McConachy, not at the instructors' course, but while alone in his office. Mr. Grant further testified that Mrs. McConachy indicated to him that she had been given this material by her husband, Richard McConachy.

29 Both of H&R's district managers for Winnipeg, David Grant and Jill Parker, said that they believed that U&R's T1 General draft form was in fact a government form. David Grant indicated that he had received from H&R's training department a Revenue Canada draft of the 1988 T1 General return at a time prior to receiving U&R's form. Mr. Grant alleges that he was under the impression that both forms were government forms. When it was pointed out that Revenue Canada's draft looked more official than U&R's draft, in that the former had a Canadian flag appearing at the top of the first page, Mr. Grant explained that he did not closely review any T1's because he had seen many of them. Following that answer, however, Mr. Grant could not explain how he could have scrutinized U&R's form closely enough to notice a small reference to "U&R worksheet" appearing three quarters of the way down the page on Schedule 1 and take steps to delete that reference before photocopying the form. Mr. Grant never checked with the plaintiff as to whether it was U&R's form. Further, although he testified that he did ask his regional director why this "government form" was only available from an outside source and not made available to him from within H&R's organization, who presumably would have received it legitimately from the government, Mr. Grant testified that he could not recall how Mr. Douglas responded to this question.

30 Jill Parker also testified that although she thought the form emanated from U&R, it was a government form. This testimony was inconsistent with her answers on examination-for-discovery held in 1992. At that time, Mrs. Parker indicated that she knew that the form was U&R's form, that David Grant had told her as much, and that she knew clearly that the form was not a government form. When confronted with this evidence from the examination-for-discovery, Mrs. Parker indicated that that evidence was true then and now.

31 Both David Grant and Jill Parker were aware that copyright was being claimed in all of U&R's course materials and understood that this meant that third parties could not copy any of those materials without the permission of the plaintiff. David Grant further testified that he was aware that copyright could subsist in a form such as U&R's form and that if the form in issue was U&R's form, then the plaintiff could claim copyright in such a form.

32 In or about mid-September, 1988, upon receiving U&R's form from Mrs. McConachy, David Grant cut out the reference to U&R in Schedule 1 and made photocopies of the tax jacket. David Grant distributed and used copies of U&R's modified form at the instructors' meeting held on or about September 16, 1988. Jill Parker, as district manager for Winnipeg 2, received from David Grant a copy of U&R's form, as modified by David Grant. Mrs. Parker authorized the photocopying of the U&R's modified form for distribution and use at the instructors' meeting for Winnipeg District 2 held on or about October 14, 1988.

33 U&R's form was used to perform exercises and prepare H&R's instructors to teach the 1988 tax changes to the students in Winnipeg District 1 and District 2. Sometime in the fall of 1988, and at least as early as the end of October and beginning of November, 1988, David Grant altered U&R's form by adding the "H&R BLOCK" logo to the top of the form, as already modified by himself earlier. The instructors then distributed both versions of U&R's form, as modified by David Grant with and without the H&R Block logo superimposed on the form, to all the students in both the basic and intermediate tax courses. The students used these forms to perform exercises and learn the income tax law changes for 1988. Overall, 831 students and instructors of H&R used 1,930 copies of U&R's form. The defendant continued to use the form in Winnipeg District 1 and District 2 after November 1988, when the official Revenue Canada form became available. This use continued until January 1989.

34 Section 2 of the Copyright Act defines "infringing" as: "when applied to a copy of a work in which copyright subsist, means a copy, including any colourable imitation, made, or imported in contravention of this Act." Subsection 3(1) of the Copyright Act defines the rights of the owner of copyright:

> 3(1) For purposes of this Act, "copyright" means the sole right to produce or reproduce the work or any substantial part thereof in any material form whatever, to perform, or in the case of a lecture to deliver, the work or any substantial part thereof in public or, if the work is unpublished, to publish the work or any substantial part thereof...

Under section 27 of the Copyright Act, copyright is deemed to be infringed by any person who, without the copyright owner's consent, inter alia, does anything that the Act gives the owner the sole right to do:

> 27(1) Copyright in a work shall be deemed to be infringed by any person who, without the consent of the owner of the copyright, does anything that, by this Act, only the owner of the copyright has the right to do.

35 In order to find copyright infringement, a plaintiff must prove copying of the work or a substantial part thereof and access to the copyright protected work. In this instance, the defendant has admitted to copying a portion of U&R's form and the enquiry is therefore directed to whether the copying was "substantial" within the meaning given to that the term by the courts: "[w]hat constitutes a "substantial part" is a question of fact and, in this respect, the courts have given more emphasis on the quality of what was taken from the original work rather than the quantity." Some of the matters that have been considered by Courts in the past include:

> (a) the quality and quantity of the material taken;
>
> (b) the extent to which the defendant's use adversely affects the plaintiff's activities and diminishes the value of the plaintiff's copyright;
>
> (c) whether the material taken is the proper subject-matter of a copyright;
>
> (d) whether the defendant intentionally appropriated the plaintiff's work to save time and effort; and

(e) whether the material taken is used in the same or a similar fashion as the plaintiff's.

36 In my view, H&R copied a substantial portion of U&R's form. The form they used for at least four months was U&R's form with only a very minor deletion and the addition of the H&R Block Logo. Also, the material taken was used for the same purpose that U&R created it for, to teach the new tax changes.

Prism Hospital Software Inc. v. Hospital Medical Records Institute (1994), 97 B.C.L.R. (2d) 201 (B.C. S.C.)

Parrett J.

Heard: November 4-8, 14-15, 18-22, 25-27, December 2-4, 6, 9-13, 1991, January 6-7, 9-10, 13-17, February 3-7, 10-14, 17-18 and July 9, 1992 Judgment: August 23, 1994 Docket: Doc. Vancouver C872267

Parrett J.:

. . .

614 In his text Computer Law: Acquiring and Protecting Information Technology, vol. 1 (Toronto: Carswell, 1989), Barry Sookman writes at p. 3-186:

> The right to reproduce the work encompasses a wide variety of acts of reproduction by any process for the indefinite multiplication of copies, whether mechanically or otherwise. The concept of reproduction involves two elements: resemblance to, and actual use of, the copyright work. Two elements are required to make out a cause of action for infringement by reproduction: first, the reproduction must be either of the entire work or of a substantial part (or, as it is sometimes said, there must be sufficient objective similarity between the infringing work and the copyrighted work, or a substantial part thereof), and second, there must be some causal connection between the copyrighted work and the infringing work. In other words, the copyrighted work must be the source from which the copy is derived. In Apple Computer Inc. v. Mackintosh Computers Ltd. Hugessen J. stated that the sole right of reproduction includes, by necessary implication, the sole right to produce the means of reproduction of the work, and the sole right to produce anything used or intended to be used to reproduce the work. [footnotes omitted]

615 The use of the phrase "substantial part" is derived in part from the language of s. 3(1) which refers to the "... sole right to produce or reproduce the work or any substantial part thereof in any material form whatever..." but there is a second aspect to the phrase as well. It is a rare case in which proof of actual copying is available; in those cases where it is not, an evidentiary test can be applied through the comparison of the original and the impugned work. Where this comparison demonstrates the existence of a substantial part of the original work or "sufficient objective similarity" between the two the evidentiary burden has been met and the inference of copying may be drawn.

616 To be actionable the copying must be of the expression, in effect, the author's original or literary work not the ideas, concepts or underlying facts.

. . .

624 In order to succeed in a copyright infringement action the plaintiff must demonstrate that the defendant has made an unlawful use of the plaintiff's copyright work. It is not necessary to demonstrate actual copying direct from the plaintiff's work if the surrounding circumstances are such as to meet the evidentiary test and permit the inference previously discussed to be drawn. In the end what must be demonstrated is that either directly or indirectly through his actions the defendant has taken the fruits of the plaintiff's labour.

. . .

639 The next question is whether or not the allegedly infringing work is substantially similar to the Prism software. In the determination of what constitutes "substantial" it is not necessary to prove a particular percentage or quantity of code, indeed, in terms of numbers the amount copied may be small, that affords no defence. In Breen v. Hancock House Publishers Ltd. (1985), 6 C.I.P.R. 129, Mr. Justice Joyal of our Federal Court found that [p. 133]:

> Although the proportion of cribbing from the plaintiff's work to the total of the author's work was quantitatively small, the qualitative aspect indicated to me that it was more than "fair dealing" and that it constituted an appropriation by the author of the skill and time and talent of the plaintiff. As a result, the plaintiff was entitled to an injunction.

640 In the United States a similar approach emerged in SAS Institute Inc. v. S. & H. Computer Systems, 605 F. Supp. 816 (1985), where a District Court found that forty-four examples of copying in 186,000 lines of source code was not trivial.

641 The approach to this issue is to assess the evidence on a qualitative rather than a quantitative interpretation of the word substantial. The area of judgment involves an assessment of the work as a whole and a determination of the importance of the portions of the work found to be similar.

CCH Canadian Ltd. v. Law Society of Upper Canada, 212 D.L.R. (4th) 385 (Fed. C.A.)

Linden J.A., Rothstein J.A., Sharlow J.A.

Heard: October 23-25, 2001
Judgment: May 14, 2002

Linden J.A.:

I. Introduction

1 CCH Canadian Ltd., Thomson Canada Ltd. (which carries on business as Carswell Thomson Professional Publishing) and Canada Law Book Inc. (hereinafter

"the Publishers") produce legal materials. The Law Society of Upper Canada (hereinafter "the Law Society") is a statutory, non-profit corporation that governs the legal profession in the province of Ontario. As part of its mandate to serve and assist its members and other researchers, the Law Society operates the Great Library at Osgoode Hall in Toronto. The Great Library has one of the largest collections of legal materials in Canada.

2 Upon request from lawyers, articling students, the judiciary or other authorized researchers the Law Society will photocopy legal materials from the Great Library's collection. Library users can pick up photocopies or have them forwarded by mail or facsimile. The photocopying service is intended to be carried out in accordance with the Law Society's "Access to the Law Policy", which states:

. . .

II. The Issues

A. Subsistence of Copyright

7 At trial, the Publishers submitted eleven specific items in which they assert copyright subsists. This case deals with copyright subsistence in only those specific materials. However, I recognize that this case will guide the results in similar cases, and I have approached the issues with that in mind.

8 First, the Publishers assert copyright in following three reported judicial decisions:

> a. Meyer v. Bright (1992), as published in 94 D.L.R. (4th) 648 (Ont. Gen. Div.) by Canada Law Book,
>
> b. R. v. C.I.P. Inc. (1992), as published in 71 C.C.C. (3d) 129 (S.C.C.) by Canada Law Book and
>
> c. Hewes v. Etobicoke (City) (1993), as published in 93 C.L.L.C. 14,042 (Ont. C.A.) by CCH Canadian Ltd..

9 Each reported judicial decision contains reasons for judgment, which are written by a judge or judges but edited by the Publishers to conform with their preferred style. Each of these reported judicial decisions also includes material composed by the Publishers, including a summary of the facts, reasons and conclusions contained in the judicial reasons, point-form "catchlines" that highlight topics and issues considered in the case, a "statement of case" that very briefly states the issue or issues addressed by the Court and an indexing case title that succinctly states the parties involved. In addition, the reported judicial decisions contain information about the judicial reasons, such as the date of the judgment, the Court and panel that decided the case; counsel for each party; lists of cases, statutes and rules and regulations referred to; parallel citations; and other notes regarding the decision or the status of any appeals. Several reported judicial decisions are typically compiled into published volumes, which themselves are usually parts of a series of reported judicial decisions. However, neither volumes nor series of reported judicial decisions are at issue in this case. The Trial Judge

found that copyright does not subsist in any of these reported judicial decisions, and the Publishers appeal from that finding.

10 Second, the Publishers assert copyright in three headnotes, which accompany but are submitted as independent of the reported judicial decisions of:

a. Meyer v. Bright (1992), as published in 94 D.L.R. (4th) 648 (Ont. Gen. Div.) by Canada Law Book,

b. R. v. C.I.P. Inc. (1992), as published in 71 C.C.C. (3d) 129 (S.C.C.) by Canada Law Book and

c. Hewes v. Etobicoke (City) (1993), as published in 93 C.L.L.C. 14,042 (Ont. C.A.) by CCH Canadian Ltd..

11 It is difficult for me to ascertain precisely what the Publishers mean when they use the term "headnote". At times, they use the term to connote only a summary of the facts, reasons and conclusions from a case. Generally, however, the Publishers indicate that a headnote also includes "catchlines" and a "statement of case". The latter use suggests that a headnote is everything in a reported judicial decision other than the edited judicial reasons, such as the summary, catchlines, statement of case, indexing title and other information about the reasons for judgment. That is how I have considered these headnotes. According to the Trial Judge, copyright does not subsist in any of the headnotes. The Publishers appeal from that conclusion. The Law Society does not submit that copyright can never subsist in any headnote, but asserts that copyright does not subsist in these particular headnotes.

12 Third, the Publishers assert copyright in the case summary of Confederation Life Insurance Co. v. Shepherd, McKenzie, Plaxton, Little & Jenkins (1992), as published in (1992), 37 A.C.W.S. (3d) 141 (Ont. Gen. Div. [Commercial List]) by Canada Law Book. The case summary is a concise, point-form summary of the facts, reasons and conclusions of the case upon which it is based. The Trial Judge found that no copyright subsists in the case summary, and the Publishers take issue with that finding.

13 Fourth, the Publishers assert copyright in the consolidated topical index that appears in Canada GST Cases, [1997] G.S.T.C., as published by Carswell Thomson Professional Publishing. The topical index lists and cross-references topics with extremely brief summaries of the issues or conclusions in cases relevant to the goods and services tax (GST). The Trial Judge denied copyright protection for the topical index to [1997] G.S.T.C., and the Publishers appeal from that conclusion.

14 The Publishers also assert copyright in the annotated statute, E.L. Greenspan & M. Rosenberg, Martin's Ontario Criminal Practice 1999 (Aurora: Canada Law Book, 1998), the textbook, B. Feldthusen, Economic Negligence: The Recovery of Pure Economic Loss, 2nd ed. (Toronto: Carswell, 1989), and the monograph by S.L. Kogon, "Dental Evidence", as it appears as chapter 13 in G.M. Chayko, E.D. Gulliver & D.V. Macdougall, Forensic Evidence in Canada (Aurora: Canada Law Book, 1991). The Trial Judge found that copyright does subsist in the annotated

statute, textbook and monograph. These conclusions have not been appealed, however, the Law Society objects to the characterization of the monograph as a "work" in itself, separate from the book in which it appears.

15 Thus, this Court must decide whether the Trial Judge erred in concluding that copyright does not subsist in the reported judicial decisions, the headnotes, the case summary and the topical index. If copyright does subsist in these works, there is no dispute with the Trial Judge's finding that such copyright would be owned by the Publisher of each respective work.

B. Infringement of Copyright

16 The Publishers allege that, through its custom photocopying service, the Law Society infringes their exclusive right to reproduce and communicate their works to the public by telecommunication. The Publishers also allege that by providing free-standing photocopiers the Law Society infringes their exclusive right to authorize others to reproduce their works. Finally, the Publishers allege that the Law Society is liable for selling, distributing and possessing infringing copies of their works.

· · ·

a. Reproduction of a Work or a Substantial Part Thereof

92 Subsection 3(1) grants the copyright holder the exclusive right to "reproduce the work or any substantial part thereof". There is no dispute that a photocopy constitutes a reproduction. To photocopy an entire work is to "reproduce the work", as described in subsection 3(1). One who reproduces an entire work will, therefore, be prima facie liable for copyright infringement. The phrase, "any substantial part thereof" is only relevant if less than an entire work has been produced or reproduced.

93 Given my earlier conclusions regarding the subsistence of copyright in the reported judicial decisions, the headnotes, the case summary, the topical index, the monograph, there are no specific examples before this Court of reproductions of less than entire works. The fact that, for example, the monograph amounts only to 4.5% of the pages in the book in which it appears is not relevant, nor is the fact that the reported judicial decision of Meyer v. Bright is one of 62 decisions reported in 94 D.L.R. (4th).

94 Notably, the Law Society publishes the following notice in its own publication, the Ontario Reports:

> Copies of individual decisions appearing in this report may be made for the purposes of research, private study, review, criticism, or use in court, tribunal and government proceedings.

The fact that the Law Society feels the need to grant permission to copy individual decisions implies that it believes such activity might otherwise constitute infringement. If a copy of an individual decision was a reproduction of anything less than an entire work or a substantial part of a work, anyone could make copies of them for any purpose at all, and no permission would be needed.

Therefore, the Law Society's argument that a copy of a single Reported Judicial Decision is not of a substantial part of a work contradicts its own notice in the Ontario Reports.

95 Although the specific reproductions at issue before this Court were of entire works, I suspect that if the Law Society reproduced only a headnote rather than an entire reported judicial decision, such reproduction would be of a substantial part of a work. An investigation into substantiality is not a purely quantitative exercise (see Édutile, supra at para. 22; Ladbroke, supra at 469, 473; and Vaver, Copyright Law, supra at 145). Clearly, an overwhelming proportion of the skill, judgment and labour invested in compiling reported judicial decisions is directed at creating the headnotes. For that reason, I also suspect that if the Law Society reproduced only the edited reasons for judgment from a reported judicial decision, such reproduction may not be of a substantial part of a work. Although the reasons for judgment are certainly significant and indeed form the basis of the reported judicial decision, the Publishers have invested relatively little effort in distinguishing that portion of their work from a mere copy of the underlying judicial reasons. Qualitatively, the Publishers invest an insubstantial amount of effort into edited reasons for judgment, as compared to headnotes. Thus, a headnote, which may be relatively brief compared to an entire reported judicial decision, may constitute a substantial part, whereas edited judicial reasons, which may be considerably longer than a headnote, may be an insubstantial part.

96 Similarly, if I am mistaken that the topical index to [1997] G.S.T.C., for example, is an independent work, then I would suggest it is nevertheless a substantial part of the reporter in which it appears. Whether the index is protected as a work itself, or as a substantial part of a larger work, the result is the same. Its author has invested substantial skill, judgment and labour in its composition, and that effort ought to be protected by copyright law.

97 In general, however, I decline to specify and particular percentage of a work that delineates the substantial from the insubstantial, as the Law Society has attempted to do in its Access to the Law Policy. In some circumstances, a small number of very important pages may be substantial, whereas other times, a larger number of unimportant pages may be insubstantial. Such a determination can only be made in the context of a particular reproduction.

France Animation, s.a. c. Robinson, 2011 QCCA 1361

COURT OF APPEAL

THE HONOURABLE FRANCE THIBAULT, J.A.

BENOÎT MORIN, J.A.

FRANÇOIS DOYON, J.A.

1. Background

...

[3] The respondent Claude Robinson is an artist. In the summer of 1982, he drew the first sketches of the characters in a projected children's television series that would be called *Robinson Curiosité*. He defined the characters and their personalities in written form. Between 1982 and 1985, he refined his project.

[4] On October 16, 1985, the Copyright Office issued a registration certificate for *Robinson Curiosité* indicating Mr. Robinson as the author of the work and the respondent Les productions Nilem inc. (hereinafter Nilem), a business corporation of which Mr. Robinson is the sole shareholder, as the owner.

[5] As of 1985, the respondents took additional steps to promote and start production on their work, *Robinson Curiosité*: a partnership with Pathonic, a television production company, a contract with Cinar to mandate it to solicit the U.S. market, meetings with representatives from Columbia Pictures and the Disney Channel, participating in the MIP-TV international trade show in 1986 and 1987 in Cannes, a new partnership with a Quebec film production company, Les Productions SDA ltée (hereinafter SDA), SDA's incorporation of two business corporations, and so on.

[6] Unfortunately, the respondents' considerable efforts did not bear fruit. The two business corporations incorporated by SDA were dissolved on December 12, 1990, and the *Robinson Curiosité* project was put on the back-burner.

[7] In December of 1994, Mr. Robinson gave a presentation on his project to his spouse and to some friends and associates. They persuaded him to reactivate the project. In this context, he gave a few presentations, including one that led to interest from a company named Philips. That company wrote to him on April 24, 1995: "As you are aware, Philips ... has recently created a catalog of software titles entitled... Following our investigation, we believe that your project for a collection of CD-i/CD-ROM titles based on "Robinson Curiosity" possesses all the necessary criteria to participate in this market program." In addition, Mr. Robinson prepared a project which he presented to a representative from Toys "R" Us.

[8] Nothing came of these new possibilities because in early September of 1995, the first episode was broadcast in Quebec of *Robinson Sucroë*, a work produced by Cinar, France Animation, and Ravensburger. The respondents and their new partners felt that there was too much resemblance between *Sucroë* and *Curiosité*. As a result, plans to develop *Robinson Curiosité* were suspended.

[9] For the purpose of the appeal, it is unnecessary to relate in detail the steps taken by the respondents to develop the *Robinson Curiosité* project or to describe the stages involved in creating *Robinson Sucroë*, which debuted in 1992. In this regard, the timeline drawn up by the trial judge may be consulted (paragraphs 22 to 205 of the judgment).

[10] A formal demand was served on Cinar, Mr. Weinberg, Micheline Charest, and all the partners in the coproduction and distribution of *Robinson Sucroë*. A complaint was filed with the Royal Canadian Mounted Police.

[11] On July 16, 1996, the respondents brought a suit against the appellants. The suit was divided into two parts. The first dealt with the infringement of their copyright and moral rights in the work *Robinson Curiosité*, in violation of the *Copyright Act*.[1] The second part of the suit had to do with the extracontractual liability of certain persons whom the respondents accused of disloyal conduct toward them, in violation of the obligations of the *Civil Code of Québec*. In addition to injunctive-type conclusions, the respondents claimed damages from the appellants for psychological harm, infringement of their moral rights, infringement of their copyright, and loss of profits. Finally, they sought punitive damages and reimbursement for solicitor-client fees.

...

2. Trial judgment

[13] At the end of an 83-day trial, the trial judge granted the respondents' lawsuit in part.

[14] In a detailed judgment, the judge found that the appellants had had access to *Robinson Curiosité* (paragraphs 250 to 404).

[15] His assessment of the evidence also led him to state that *Robinson Curiosité* is an original work (paragraphs 405 to 436) and that *Robinson Sucroë* presents substantial similarities with this work (paragraphs 502 to 685).

[16] Finally, the judge considered that the appellants had not established that *Robinson Sucroë* was an independent work in such a way as to refute the evidence of infringement. He therefore found that the respondents' work had been infringed (paragraphs 686 to 827).

...

[19] In terms of damages, the judge awarded the respondents $5,224,293: $607,489 to compensate them for copyright infringement (paragraphs 994 to 1005), $1,716,804 for reimbursement of the profits earned by the appellants (paragraphs 1006 to 1030), $400,000 for psychological harm (paragraphs 959 to 993), $1,000,000 for punitive damages (paragraphs 1036 to 1073) and $1,500,000 for extrajudicial fees (paragraphs 1074 to 1103).

3. Grounds for appeal

[20] In their factums, the appellants outline various grounds that can be grouped under the following headings: ...

3. Definition of the respondents' work and its original nature.

4. Substantial reproduction in *Robinson Sucroë* of the respondents' work.

5. Evidence of independent creation.

...

4. Analysis

...

3. <u>Definition of the respondents' work and its original nature</u>.

[41] The trial judge found that the work is original and that it is protected by the *Copyright Act*. The appellants write that he omitted a preliminary stage, that of defining the work [TRANSLATION]:

Defining the work that is allegedly plagiarized is a preliminary stage that is essential for determining copyright infringement. It requires identifying its substance because only reproducing the substance can lead to a finding of infringement...

[42] The Court does not share this point of view.

[43] There is no indication that the court, in a preliminary stage, must identify the substance of the work in order to determine whether there has been infringement by copying a significant, a substantial part of the original work. Doing so would reduce the content of the work, unduly restrict the scope of the protection granted by the *Copyright Act* and could, for no reason, limit the exercise aimed at identifying the number of similarities likely to be accepted. Therefore, it is not the substance of the work that must be compared to the copy, but the overall work to determine if there has been substantial reproduction of it in the copy.

[44] In *Avanti*,[11] Paul-Arthur Gendreau J.A. wrote [TRANSLATION]:

> Two particular elements of the quote from the judgment of McLachlin J. are interesting for resolving the case at bar. First, when characterizing the work, an essential and demanding task, the court must use a comprehensive approach to determine whether the work produced is novel and original and not just a mere compilation of various fragments. This facilitates the definition of what constitutes an essential and substantial part of the work. Second, this classification must be done by studying the work from the perspective of the amount of labour and creativity involved on the author's part. Thus, a substantial part of a work will be one which has an important place in the work as a whole and which results from the work of the artist, writer, filmmaker, playwright, etc.

[45] The court must therefore consider the originality of the work, without which, of course, there can be no infringement of the *Copyright Act*. It then carries out a comparative analysis to determine whether there are similarities between the original work and the copy, similarities that must involve aspects that have a significant place in the original work as a whole. This is emphasized by the Federal Court of Appeal in *Tele-Direct (Publications) Inc. v. American Business Information, Inc.*:[12]

21 The principles in that regard have been set out by Lord Reid in *Ladbroke (Football) Ltd. v. William Hill (Football) Ltd.*:

The appellants' dissection theory is derived from some statements in infringement cases and I must, therefore, examine at this point the law regarding infringement. Copyright gives the exclusive right to do certain things including "reproducing the work in any material form" (section 2(5)), and reproduction includes reproduction of a substantial part of the work (section 49(1)). Broadly, reproduction means copying, and does not include cases where an author or compiler produces a substantially similar result by independent work without copying. And, if he does copy, the question whether he has copied a substantial part depends much more on the quality than on the quantity of what he has taken. One test may be whether the part which he has taken is novel or striking, or is merely a commonplace arrangement of ordinary words or well-known data. <u>So it may sometimes be a convenient short cut to ask whether the part taken could by itself be the subject of copyright. But, in my view, that is only a short cut, and the more correct approach is first to determine whether the plaintiffs' work as a whole is "original" and protected by copyright, and then to inquire whether the part taken by the defendant is substantial.</u>

<u>A wrong result can easily be reached if one begins by dissecting the plaintiffs' work and asking, could section A be the subject of copyright if it stood by itself, could section B be protected if it stood by itself,</u> and so on. To my mind, it does not follow that, because the fragments taken separately would not be copyright, therefore the whole cannot be. Indeed, it has often been recognised that if sufficient skill and judgment have been exercised in devising the arrangements of the whole work, that can be an important or even decisive element in deciding whether the work as a whole is protected by copyright. [Emphasis added.]

[46] In the present case, the *Copyright Act* protects the expression of ideas that emerge from the skill and judgment of Mr. Robinson and which can be found in Exhibits P-18, P-27, P-30 and P-210. We must therefore examine the substantiality of the similarities with regard to the work as a whole and not with regard to the parts classified as substantial beforehand, to find out whether there has been substantial borrowing from the work.

[47] The trial judge supports his finding that this is overall an original work, including P-18, by referring to several aspects of the evidence.

[48] He refers to the testimony of Seth Willenson, from Cinar U.S., who, 15 years after being interested in the project, still recognized Mr. Robinson's work in looking at Exhibit P-18. In the judge's eyes, the work had [TRANSLATION] "so much style and character" that the witness still remembered it despite the passage of time.

...

[50] In paragraph 429 of his judgment, the judge repeats the description of the work as given in the formal notice sent to the defendants [TRANSLATION]:

1. Children's television program format, each show lasting thirty minutes (30 min), using live and animated formats;
2. One main character, ROBINSON CURIOSITÉ:

The character is bearded, near-sighted, and curious; he is a journalist, explorer, and communicator. He is keenly interested in all kinds of discoveries and experiments; his relationships with others are like those of a child; he can be generous, sulky, impatient, cheeky, likeable, curious, clumsy, hot-headed, starry-eyed, carefree, thoughtless, a cook, sometimes sweet, exuberant, and absent-minded;

3. Supporting characters, including the following:

    3.1 VENDREDI FÉRIÉ (HOLIDAY):
    Scientific mind, teacher, inventor, he is calm and kindly disposed toward Robinson;

    3.2 BOUM BOUM (TIPTOES):
    Typical overweight guy in appearance, both insecure and very helpful to the point of being annoying; generous, exuberant but also sulky; finds it hard to make himself understood;

    3.3 CHARLIE
    Gruff, spineless bachelor, an adventurer; he is narrow-minded and determined; awkward with women; the worst smells don't bother him at all; he sets great store by what his parents might think of him; has a means of transportation.

    3.4 LÉON:
    Small, loves playing tricks and is easy to spot in spite of all his disguises;

    3.5 PARESSEUX (LAZYBONES):
    He is slow; speaks slowly; he is glassy-eyed, slack-jawed; lazy, a scapegoat; likes music and vegetarian cooking;

    3.6 GERTRUDE:
    She is from a large family and is determined, independent, and dainty in her gestures; although she has a stable temperament, she sometimes has mood swings; she has an innate sense of organization, discipline at work is essential to her; she has an enviable femininity and a booming voice; defender of the oppressed; she doesn't suffer fools gladly; she has also travelled extensively.

4. Main theme: the adventures of Robinson Curiosité on a south-sea island, with abundant vegetation, a volcano and, to the north-east, a semi-circular beach; this island where the action takes place is inhabited and located near another, smaller island; it stays in contact with the continent;

5. Concerning the artistic and visual expression of the WORK:
Photographic and artistic documentation of Robinson Curiosité's expressions and movements; drawings of the other characters; an artistic and visual description of the island and its inhabitants, its vegetation and its other components; hundreds of comic strips with different incidents; drawings in the form of boards and posters;

6. Positioning studies in terms of teaching, business, and art;

7. ...

8. Concerning the dramatic and literary expression of the WORK:

fifty-two (52) synopses and eighty-two (82) themes for shows, including the following:

- Robinson opens an advertising agency;
- The time-travelling machine;
- Robinson makes a movie;
- Tourism;
- The Olympic Games;
- Elections on the island;
- The symphony orchestra;
- Eruption of the volcano;
- BOUM BOUM's birthday;
- Finding it hard to get up.

[51] He found that the work *Robinson Curiosité*, including P-18, is an original work within the meaning of the *Copyright Act*.

[52] The appellants did not demonstrate a palpable and overriding error in the judge's analysis and his conclusion. Among the original aspects of the work *Robinson Curiosité*, Robinson, unlike the hero of the work *Robinson Crusoe* by Daniel Defoe, is not alone on his island.[13] He lives with several people, including Vendredi Férié, who is the polar opposite of the classic Friday. There is also a very detailed and specific description of the personalities of the dozen or so characters who live on the island, and especially their relations with each other in the framework of scripts that illustrate all these dynamics, which are an essential part of the work. Finally, all the drawings in the work must also be retained as the original expression of an idea.

[53] As the author Tamaro[14] wrote, citing the aforementioned judgment in *Avanti* [TRANSLATION]:

> All in all, case law concerning fictitious characters can be summed up in an idea expressed by an American judge: the less developed a character is, the less chance its author can claim copyright. An author is thus penalized for not sufficiently developing a character.

[54] In the present case, the author Claude Robinson has sufficiently drawn his characters, their personalities, their relations, and their environment for him to be entitled to the protection of the *Copyright Act*.

4. Substantial reproduction in Robinson Sucroë of the respondents' work

[55] Section 2 of the *Copyright Act*[15] defines infringing in relation to a work in the following manner:

> "*infringing*" means
>
> (a) when applied to a copy of a work in which copyright subsists, any copy, <u>including any colourable imitation</u>, made or imported in contravention of this Act [Emphasis added.]

[56] The *Copyright Act* then describes actions that may be carried out only by the owner of the copyright:

> 3. (1) For the purposes of this Act, "copyright" means the sole right <u>to produce or reproduce the work or any substantial part thereof</u> in any material form whatever, to perform, or in the case of a lecture to deliver, the work or any substantial part thereof in public or, if the work is unpublished, to publish the work or any substantial part thereof... [Emphasis added.]

[57] Infringing is not limited to an exact or slavish copy of the work, since it can be a colourable imitation inasmuch as it reproduces, if not all, at least a substantial part of the work.

[58] What is substantial or significant in a work?

[59] First, it is not really a matter of quantity. Rather, it is a matter of quality, although both aspects remain important:

> 21 There was no reproduction here of the protected work. However, was there reproduction of a "substantial part" of the work?

> 22 To determine whether a "substantial part" of a protected work has been reproduced, it is not the quantity which was reproduced that matters as much as the quality and nature of what was reproduced. In *Beauchemin v. Cadieux*, Blanchet J. cited with approval at page 281 this passage from Pouillet, *Propriété littéraire*, No. 507 [TRANSLATION]:

>> It would be risky to confine oneself to determining the number or extent of the borrowings: it is their quality and nature that should be looked at.

> To enter upon a simple calculation of percentages or proportions in order to determine whether there was an infringement would be to unduly minimize the protection given to copyright. In a copyright matter a part may be as important as the whole, and this seems especially relevant when we are considering arrangements of data which are in the public domain.[16]

[60] The author Tamaro points out the trend in case law in this regard [TRANSLATION]:

> Noting, in the development of case law, that great importance had to be attributed to the result of the author's labour, the courts are now turning toward the criterion of the qualitative importance of the borrowings instead of contenting themselves with tallying the number of borrowings.[17]

[61] It goes without saying, moreover, that an infringing copy is assessed first by its similarities, since, for instance, the use of a known important character from a comic strip may be enough, even if there are numerous differences in the rest of the copy. Overall, the similarities make it possible to determine whether a substantial part of a work has been borrowed, while the differences could, for example, support a claim of independent creation.

[62] The trial judge was therefore justified in examining the existence of similarities and basing himself on the expert testimony of Charles Perraton,[18] whose mandate was in fact to identify, as the case might be, resemblances and similarities between *Robinson Curiosité* and *Robinson Sucroë*.

[63] The appellants, who would like the court to examine and weigh the similarities and differences concurrently, refer to certain judgments that do not, however, support their claim. Thus, whether it is in *Cummings v. Global Television Network*,[19] *Hutton v. Canadian Broadcasting Corp. (CBC)*,[20] *Shaker v. MGM Distribution*,[21] or *Preston v. 20th Century Fox Canada Ltd.*[22] neither the originality of the work nor the presence of substantial similarities was demonstrated.

[64] As already mentioned, the *Copyright Act* states that colourable imitation is still infringement. In other words, differences may sometimes be used to camouflage an infringing copy, but does not eliminate it.

[65] However, we must not go to extremes and conclude that the purpose of every difference is to camouflage infringement. As Buffoni J. wrote [TRANSLATION]:

> 36 Certainly, the Act proscribes what it calls "colourable imitation". And case law provides many examples of defendants who tried in vain to disguise their plagiarism by putting, as the classic aphorism goes, enough similarities to confuse the buyers, and enough differences to confound the court.

> 37 But we cannot infer from this that an accumulation of differences automatically amounts to as many acts of concealment. Otherwise, the argument becomes circular: carried through to its end, it would mean that the more a competitor tries to stand out by expressing a common idea in a different way, the more he is trying to [TRANSLATION] "disguise" his misdemeanour.[23]

[66] In sum, the differences may have no impact if the borrowing remains substantial. Conversely, the result may also be a novel and original work simply inspired by the first. Everything is therefore a matter of nuance, degree, and context, such that, on this subject as on many others, it is a question of fact that is first and foremost a matter for the trial judge.[24]

[67] It must also be said that, if there is substantial reproduction, the infringement remains despite a significant intellectual effort on the part of the infringer:

> 57 Thus, the true test for infringement is whether the act complained of is only an act that the copyright owner could do under subsection 27(1), including reproduction of the original or a substantial part of the work. The expenditure of some mental labour is not enough to trump the fact that there has been reproduction of a substantial part of a work. Persons who adapt novels into musicals or films also expend mental effort but if there is reproduction of a substantial part of the original, there is still infringement if the consent of the copyright owner has not been obtained.[25]

[68] Thus, even if the infringer, thanks to his skill, has produced an [TRANSLATION] "improved" version of the original work, which some could claim in this case, it does not change the reality: the infringement remains and the author is entitled to the protection of the *Copyright Act*.

[69] The appellants also submit that the trial judge erred in refusing to take into account the fact that many similarities can be explained by the common source of inspiration for the two works – *Robinson Crusoe*. This argument must be dismissed.

[70] The trial judge, on the contrary, acknowledged that certain similarities could be explained by the common source of inspiration. However, he characterized them as minor and rightly did not give them much importance. In reality, the similarities accepted by the judge to find that there was substantial reproduction of Mr. Robinson's work are in no way similarities that may be explained by the common source material: Daniel Defoe's work, *Robinson Crusoe*. For instance, it goes without saying that the existence of other residents on the island, or the reassuring presence of a companion so entirely different from the classic Friday could not be similarities resulting from the same source material.

[71] As for the admissibility of the report and testimony of the expert Perraton, the appellants are once again going down the wrong path.

[72] It is true that expert testimony is generally not necessary to allow a court to determine whether there has been substantial reproduction of a work. Having an ordinary, reasonable person compare two works should normally enable a court to reach a conclusion without the help of an expert, as it did in *Avanti*, quoted above.

[73] On this matter, expert testimony does not answer different rules of eligibility, which Rothstein J. points out, in the context of a trade-mark lawsuit:

[75] Tendering expert evidence in trade-mark cases is no different than tendering expert evidence in other contexts. This Court in *R. v. Mohan*, 1994 CanLII 80 (SCC), [1994] 2 S.C.R. 9, set out four requirements to be met before expert evidence is accepted in a trial: (a) relevance; (b) necessity in assisting the trier of fact; (c) the absence of any exclusionary rule; and (d) a properly qualified expert...[26]

[74] This testimony must therefore be necessary, which is not always the case in matters of infringement since, very often, the judge is just as well placed to determine whether there has been substantial reproduction of the work. In sum, the criterion of necessity must be examined with regard to the circumstances of the case at bar while ensuring that this testimony does not distract the court from the analysis it must undertake. That is what Rothstein J. points out in *Masterpiece*, particularly in paragraphs 77, 79, and 93. How does this apply to the present case?

[75] The very particular situation that was before the trial judge must be taken into consideration.

[76] On the one hand, there was a work that was still only a project, in development, and on the other, a completed television series that had been produced and broadcast. Two works at very different stages of development had to be compared. It made comparing them all the more difficult, notably because *Robinson*

Curiosité was made up of a set of many documents, texts, and drawings that then had to be examined and compared to *Robinson Sucroë*, a completed work. Incidentally, the respondents' claims deal not only with certain graphic aspects of the work, but also with its literary aspects, particularly in relation to the characters. The judge could have taken on the exercise and examined each aspect of the two works without the aid of an expert. That would have meant devoting an excessive number of hours to it, however, while an expert could also sort and analyze the various elements of the works for the purpose of comparison. This was a much more efficient way to proceed, as long, of course, as the judge remained the only decision-maker.

[77] In sum, part of the expert Perraton's report consisted in support work for the court, which could have done the work itself. This is nothing new. In many cases, for instance, the parties have recourse to an accountant to sort information and carry out mathematical operations that the judge could do as well, but proceeding this way saves precious time.

[78] However, there is another reason that justifies the testimony of the expert Perraton here.

[79] Indeed, his report involves two separate methods of comparison. First, there is the [TRANSLATION] "visible" form of a work. This is the part of the work that can be seen directly, either in the choice of shapes, colours, layout, and such, or in the choice of words and how they are expressed. In sum, it is the concrete and common way to examine a work, by considering what the senses permit us to discover directly. It can be said that this is in all likelihood the aspect of a work to which case law refers when it prescribes that ordinary persons should be able to see the similarities for themselves between two works.

[80] The report however deals with another method of comparison which, unlike the first, may require explanations likely to help the court to make a comparison. This is the [TRANSLATION] "intelligible" form of a work. The expert Perraton explains that this involves [TRANSLATION] "its structure and composition and the way its elements are arranged: characters, interactions between them, time period, actions, and so on. These are things that are not perceived directly, but can be drawn from the perceptible form. It is the understanding of the dynamics, the atmosphere and the motivations that make up the work."

[81] In short, the ordinary observer is aware of what he perceives and can therefore easily compare the two works in this regard. This is much less the case when it comes to what he does not perceive directly, which justifies having an expert to make a comparison of the "intelligible" form of the work. The expert Perraton, for example, made a connection and established a resemblance between two characters by examining and comparing their physical appearance, their personality traits, and their relations with the other characters, to suggest that even if one is an animal and the other a human being,[27] the second is a reproduction of the first. Whether or not this proposal is accepted, it may be concluded that a court would find it more difficult, without the help of an expert,

to make such a connection between an animal and a person. This is another reason justifying the admissibility of the expert Perraton's testimony.

[82] The appellants also argue that the trial judge unreservedly espoused the expert's theory and, to all intents and purposes, abdicated his role. This is not at all the case.

[83] The trial judge amply explains why he accepted the expert Perraton's testimony, his methodology, and most of his findings. The appellants do not point out any palpable and overriding error in this respect. Furthermore, the judge set aside certain aspects of the report and the testimony, which once again shows that he examined everything properly, accepting part of the testimony and rejecting part of it. He therefore made an independent analysis of the similarities identified by the expert Perraton. He concluded that some were significant and others were not. He therefore disagreed with some of the findings in the report. As a result, if the judge accepted a large part of the report, it was only after analyzing it and making the findings of fact that he considered necessary. That was his role and there is nothing to justify the Court's intervention in this regard.

[84] The judge therefore noted a number of similarities between the two works and expressed himself at length on this aspect in his judgment.

[85] He accepted those which he classified as substantial. However, it must be noted that the criterion applicable is not the number of substantial similarities, but rather the substantial reproduction of the work, or substantial borrowing from it. In spite of this formulation used by the judge, the appellants have not convinced the Court that there was an error of law. Indeed, the judge's result is in accordance with the rule. It is necessary to proceed in stages and question whether there are similarities before finding that there has been substantial reproduction or borrowing.

[86] And now, let us consider these similarities.

[87] As the judge wrote, the framework and the story are not at issue:

[TRANSLATION]

From the outset, the plaintiff has admitted that it was not the story that was reproduced; rather, it was the main characters and their personalities as well as certain drawings that were reproduced.

[88] In his opinion, the evidence established a number of substantial similarities with respect to both the graphic aspect of the work and the personality traits of a number of the characters and their interactions. He found that there was substantial reproduction from *Robinson Curiosité*.

...

[100] Without citing the judgment word for word, the main similarities accepted were as follows:

- The main character, **Robinson**: graphic resemblance and similar personalities: both are sulky, childish, moody, in the process of developing, clumsy, naive, versatile, messy, curious, kind, and generous, but sometimes hot-tempered and impatient;

- **Vendredi Férié** and **Mercredi**: graphic resemblance, resemblance of names[28] and similar personalities: father figures and therefore paternalistic in their interactions with Robinson, scientific, intelligent, erudite, knowledgeable, ingenious, good at explaining, kindly;

- **Boum Boum** and **Duresoirée** (her real name being Hildegarde Van Boum Boum): two characters that are physically large[29] with similar personalities: sulky, irritable, emotional. It should also be noted that, in the first synopsis of *Robinson Sucroë* ([TRANSLATION] The treasure hunt)*, the name Duresoirée was given to a pachyderm;

- **Gertrude** and **Gladys**: graphic resemblance (young, pretty, tall, thin, and elegant; both have freckles) and similar personalities: strong-willed women with very definite ideas, independent, self-sufficient;

- **Charlie le pilote** and **Courtecuisse**: graphic resemblance and similar personalities: sloppy, strange and repulsive tastes in food, gruff, but lose their heads when in the presence of either Gertrude (for the one) or Duresoirée (for the other);

- **Paresseux** and **Dimanchemidi**: graphic resemblance and similar personalities: eyes half-open, very lazy, always sleeping or struggling to stay awake, very slow movements, talk slowly, slack-jawed;

- **Général Schloup** and **Capitaine Brisk**: graphic resemblance (tall, thin, elegant, slender faces and hollow cheeks) and similar personalities: dishonest, bossy;

- **Léon le Caméléon** and **Petitevacances**: no graphic resemblance, but similar personalities: mischievous, like to play tricks and disguise themselves, they can change their appearance in spite of certain traits by which they can be recognized; they often help Robinson;

- The **main house**: an L-shaped bungalow, topped by a slender tube that serves as a chimney and an observatory, or a cone-shaped observation tower with a telescope, a retractable dome, lit by a skylight, along with a porch covered by an awning supported by bamboo trunks, as can be seen in another drawing from *Robinson Curiosité*;

- Numerous **duplications**; i.e., the infringer uses the same borrowing on more than one occasion for different characters.

- **Vehicles used for transportation**;

- The **logo** used in both works.

[101] One might disagree with some of the similarities accepted by the judge (for instance, the graphic resemblance between Boum Boum and Duresoirée). It remains that the evidence allowed him to find that there was substantial reproduction of Mr. Robinson's work, even if the plot was not in question and even if *Robinson Sucroë* as a finished product contains a great many new elements that

are distinct from *Robinson Curiosité*. It is the accumulation of perceptible and intelligible elements that is determinative here.

[102] Finally, the appellant's other criticisms cannot be accepted either. It is therefore inaccurate to say that the judge erred by not setting aside similarities that were from the public domain. He did this in paragraphs 620 and 621 of the judgment, amongst others. He also set aside the similarities particular to children's programs, which the appellants had brought to his attention.[30] As for the time period in which the adventure of *Robinson Sucroë* takes place, it is not relevant since the respondents do not claim any reproduction of the storyline.

[103] In conclusion, even if the Court does not share all the reasons for the trial judgment, it is not convinced by the appellants that the judge committed a reviewable error by finding that there was substantial reproduction of the work *Robinson Curiosité*, except as regards music rights, which we will later see.

5. Evidence of independent creation

[104] It must be noted that the purpose of proving independent creation is to refute evidence of infringement:[TRANSLATION]

> [40] With respect for the contrary opinion, I think that the appellant could be partly right concerning this aspect: in truth, case law recognizes that in the absence of direct or contrary evidence, circumstantial evidence resulting from a substantial number of similarities, if not of identical expressions, formulas, and terms or errors common to both texts, may indeed create a presumption of infringement (*Cadieux v. Beauchemin*). The presumption then reverses the burden on the defendant to establish that he has not infringed the work of the plaintiff and that his work constitutes an independent creation.[31]

[105] The burden of proof was incumbent on the appellants....

> We must therefore go beyond the step of mere pernickety harping over everything seen and heard by the judge at trial, to identify in the judgment an obvious weakness with respect to the evidence (hence its palpable nature), a weakness likely to falsify all or part of the formal judgment (hence its overriding nature).[32]

[106] This is all the more true when, as in the present case, the judge's findings are based on his assessment of the credibility of the appellants' witnesses. The judge devoted some 136 paragraphs to analyzing this issue and raised a number of troubling elements in the version given by these witnesses.

It is not necessary to list all of his conclusions....

[110] The appellants maintain that the judge seemed to suggest that the evidence of access to Claude Robinson's work prohibits proof of independent creation [TRANSLATION]:

> [802] One thing is certain: Izard had access to the plaintiff's work and the representatives from CINAR also required changes. Izard orchestrated all literary production and was in charge of Caillon. Considering his contamination as a result of his certain access to the plaintiff's work, he cannot claim to be independent and to direct an independent production.

[111] If the judge had refused to consider evidence of independent production based solely on the fact that Mr. Izard had access to the work, this would have been an error of law. But this excerpt does not have the meaning given it by the appellants. In fact, the judge's entire analysis of the claim of independent creation, which is quite long (paragraphs 680 to 822), shows that he certainly did not want to reject it on this ground. In reality, in this excerpt, which comes from the last part of his analysis, the judge is instead trying to show the complete absence of evidence of independent creation. The choice of words is perhaps not the best, but here again one fact is undeniable: the judge does not believe the witnesses, to a point where there cannot be a preponderance of proof of independent creation.

[112] Following this exercise, the judge concluded, in paragraphs 823 to 826:[TRANSLATION]

> [823] In *Problèmes de droit d'auteur en éducation,* the authors write:
>
>> [TRANSLATION] What is well established, however, is the fact that the literal reproduction of a work in its entirety always constitutes infringement. However, when the reproduction covers only part of a protected work, the judge will refuse to consider the quantitative criterion and will retain the qualitative criterion instead. The qualitative criterion expresses the idea that when the very essence, substance, or vital part of a protected work is reproduced, there is infringement. This situation may occur even if what is reproduced is only a few lines of a text that is otherwise important or a single character from a comic strip, or a few bars from a piece of music. Each time, judges will strive to situate the reproduction vis-à-vis the original work as a whole. If they find that the reproduction repeats the very essence of the original work, they will conclude that there is infringement.[33]
>
> [824] Considering the existence of substantial similarities, including:
>
> • Drawings for the main character Curiosité;
>
> • The L-shaped house and its observation tower;
>
> • The personalities of the main characters disguised as humans, such as Boum Boum as Duresoirée; Paresseux as Dimanchemidi, Léon the chameleon as Petitevacances;
>
> • The disguising of Vendredi Férié as Mercredi, of Charlie as Courtecuisse, and of Schloup as Brisk;
>
> [825] Considering Dr. Perraton's conclusion, which the Court adopts and which reads as follows [TRANSLATION]:
>
>> By systematically identifying similarities and the observed and inferred connections between characters and their relationships, or the spacial-temporal context and elements of the storyline that organize the action, the comparative analysis is in fact sufficiently exhaustive to answer the initial question in the affirmative: yes, there are similarities and connections between Robinson Curiosité and Robinson Sucroë that can be seen not only in quantity, through the reproduction of visible forms, but also and above all in quality through the reproduction of the intelligible form.

[826] The Court finds that the defendants have reproduced the essence, substance, and vital part of the work Curiosité.

[113] The appellants have not shown that this finding is unreasonable. It is based on the evidence and does not proceed from a palpable and overriding error of law or fact....

(f) Non-literal Copying

A reproduction need not copy the exact "literal" expression in a work. Non-literal copying and "colourable imitation" can also be infringing. The challenge is to distinguish between the unlawful copying of protected, non-literal expression and the lawful copying of unprotected ideas. Establishing whether non-literal copying is *prima facie* infringing therefore requires careful attention to the idea-expression dichotomy examined in Chapter 2.

King Features Syndicate (Inc.) v. Kleemann (O. & M.) Ltd., [1941] 2 A.C. 417 (H.L.)

VISCOUNT MAUGHAM.

My Lords, this is an appeal from the Court of Appeal (England) who on July 8, 1940 (Scott and Clauson L.JJ., Luxmoore L.J. dissenting), reversed a judgment of Simonds J., delivered on March 25, 1940, and dismissed the action. The action was brought for alleged infringement of the appellants' copyright in certain artistic works, namely, sketches portraying a fictitious character known as "Popeye, the Sailor," by the importation and sale of certain dolls and brooches. It was admitted that copyright had at one time subsisted in sketches relied on by the appellants, and that the appellants, or one of them, was the owner of them, and it was also admitted that the respondents had imported and sold the dolls and brooches in question. It was originally contended by the respondents that neither the dolls nor the brooches constituted a reproduction in a material form of any of the sketches relied on and that consequently there was no infringement. Relief was granted to the appellants by Simonds J., both in respect of the dolls and the brooches. The Court of Appeal differed as to the brooches, holding that these were not a reproduction of any of the sketches. As to the dolls, the Court of Appeal held that they did constitute a reproduction of one particular sketch, but they held (by a majority) that the copyright, or at least the right to restrain infringement of it in this case, was taken away as the result of the operation of s. 22 of the Copyright Act, 1911.

The respondents were content before your Lordships to accept the view of the Court of Appeal, and they no longer contend that the dolls are not a reproduction in a material form of that sketch. They supported the view of the Court of Appeal as to the brooches, and as to the effect of the section to which I have referred.

. . .

Before considering the effect of this section, I will deal with the other two questions raised by the respondents. The first is whether, assuming that the appellants are entitled to copyright in the drawings, the brooches are colourable reproductions in three dimensions of any substantial part of the original drawings. It is not now contended that a figure in three dimensions which reproduces an original artistic work (within the meaning of the Copyright Act, 1911) may not be an infringement of a drawing. On this point I have nothing to add to that which Simonds J. and Clauson L.J. have said. There remains the question whether the figure of "Popeye" on the brooches does or does not reproduce any substantial part of the drawings. The question is one of fact. When, as in this case, the copy or the reproduction is not exact the court must examine the degree of resemblance. It is impossible to lay down any useful test of what constitutes a copy or a colourable imitation of such a work. I think, as Lord Watson seems to have thought in the not very different case of Hanfstaengl v. Baines & Co., that the language of Bayley J. in West v. Francis, though not always applicable, gives some assistance in determining what resemblance constitutes copying. Bayley J. said: "A copy is that which comes so near to the original as to give to every person seeing it the idea created by the original." Lord Shand, in Hanfstaengl v. Baines & Co., remarked that, in comparing the works and keeping in view the idea and general effect created by the original, there was "such a degree of similarity as would lead one to say that the alleged infringement is a copy or reproduction of the original or the design — having adopted its essential features and substance." Those were remarks made in reference to the Fine Arts Copyright Act, 1862, and there is in the Act of 1911 no reference to the design of the work as there was in the earlier Act. I think that makes no difference, and it seems to me that the remarks of Lord Watson and Lord Shand are applicable to the present case. Accepting those views, and not without some hesitation, I have arrived at the conclusion, agreeing with Simonds J. and differing with respect from the Court of Appeal, that the brooches, like the dolls, on the hypothesis that copyright is established, are infringements of drawing No. 3 in the set of drawings published in the New York Evening Journal on June 17, 1929.

. . .

LORD WRIGHT.

My Lords, of the various general questions which were agitated and decided in the courts below one alone has been raised before your Lordships. It is a question of some importance because it involves determining what is the construction of s. 22 of the Copyright Act, 1911, so far as it is relevant to the facts of the case.

I must, however, before discussing that question of principle, state my conclusion on a limited issue of fact on which the respondents succeeded in the Court of Appeal but failed before Simonds J. Three classes of the respondents' productions were said to infringe the appellants' copyright in the sketches of "Popeye, the Sailor." These were the brooches, the dolls, the mechanical toys. The two latter classes were held by the unanimous decision of the Court of Appeal to be actionable infringements apart from the defence based on s. 22. The first class, the brooches, were held by the Court of Appeal not to be copied from the appellants' sketches, directly or indirectly. It was rightly not questioned in this House that under s. 1 of the Copyright Act, 1911, the sole right to produce or reproduce the sketches or any substantial part thereof in any material form whatsoever would cover a reproduction of a substantial part of the sketches or any of them in three-dimensional form, as by the dolls or the mechanical toys. In the case of these it was not contested before this House that the dolls or the toys were reproductions of a substantial part of the sample sketch selected, though in a different medium, namely plaster, and in coloured threedimensional figures as contrasted with the flat published sketch in plain black and white. But the respondents supported the view of the Court of Appeal that with regard to the brooches no copying, whether direct or indirect, was made out. This is a question of fact. No evidence of the actual operation of copying or of its absence has been given. The respondents called no evidence. The issue must thus be determined simply on the basis of a comparison between the brooches (which may be treated as all of the same design notwithstanding some minor variations in the actual examples) and the selected sketch, which was No. 3 of the sketches published by the New York Evening Journal on January 17, 1929. The test to be applied is purely visual, the sketch and the brooch being compared oculis subjecta fidelibus. It is not material that the respondents were stealing the idea of "Popeye, the Sailor," or availing themselves for commercial profit of the popularity acquired by that figure. The appellants' copyright is in the actual sketch, not in the idea. There would be no infringement if the respondents had independently produced a similar figure without copying the sketch directly or indirectly. The question is whether there was copying of the actual sketch. Here the only evidence of actual copying, direct or indirect, is similarity with regard to the figure, which is a substantial part of the sketch, between the copyright work and the alleged infringement. I think, however, that, where there is substantial similarity, that similarity is prima facie evidence of copying which the party charged may refute by evidence that, notwithstanding the similarity, there was no copying but independent creation. In the present case, on a careful comparison of the brooches and the sketch, I find substantial similarity between the different editions of the brooch and sketch No. 3, sufficient to raise a prima facie case of actual copying. The respondents have called no evidence to rebut that prima facie case. I agree, accordingly, with Simonds J. in finding that copying is proved in respect of the brooches, equally with the dolls and toys.

. . .

LORD PORTER.

Your Lordships have, therefore, to determine whether the brooch sufficiently resembles any of the fifty-five sketches so as to afford prima facie evidence that it is a reproduction in a material form of one of them. Counsel for the appellants stated that he was content to rely on the resemblance to figure 3 in strip 1 of those put in. For myself, I think the resemblance is sufficient. It repeats the salient features. The cap, face, nose, chin, mouth and pipe, swollen forearms, baggy trousers and feet are all there. This is the subsidiary point on which all the members of the Court of Appeal differed from the learned judge and held that the brooches were not a reproduction of sketch 3, or, indeed, of the figure in any of the fifty-five strips. I prefer the view of Simonds J., and, in coming to that conclusion, I have not forgotten two arguments of the respondents' counsel.

In the present case he contended that the brooch had not been proved to have been copied from any one of the fifty-five strips, and that there were a very large number of other strips not proved to be the subject of copyright from which it might have been copied. Obviously if the brooch were a reproduction of something not in itself the subject of copyright it could not be an infringement. But if the respondents desire to rely on this argument they must prove it. None of the other strips was produced and there was no evidence that the brooch resembled any one of them whereas there is a marked resemblance to those produced. Secondly, it is argued that Simonds J. applied the wrong test. He asks, it is said: Could this be recognized as a new material form of the essential "Popeye"? instead of asking: Is this a copy of a material sketch? Bayley J. in West v. Francis [FN19] defined a copy as "that which comes so near to the original as to give to every person seeing it the idea created by the original." This definition was criticized by Lord Watson in Hanfstaengl v. Baines [FN20], where he pointed out that the idea created by a picture or drawing does not necessarily form an element in the original work or its design which is protected by copyright. The same idea which is suggested by the copyright work may be expressed by another painting or drawing which is in no sense a copy and does not borrow its design. No doubt, if the learned judge had asked himself whether the essential idea of "Popeye" had been utilized in the dolls and brooches, instead of asking whether one or more of the material sketches had been copied, he would have applied the wrong test. But I do not understand him to have come to his conclusion because he thought that the idea of "Popeye" had been copied. He meant, I think, only that the brooch sufficiently resembled the figure as drawn in any one of the strips relied on, the salient features being practically identical in each.

Preston v. 20th Century Fox Canada Ltd. (1990), 38 F.T.R. 183 (Fed. T.D.), affirmed (1994), 53 C.P.R. (3d) 407 (Fed. C.A.)

MacKay J.

Judgment: November 9, 1990
Docket: Doc. T-142-85

MacKay, J. reasons for judgment:

1 In this action, the plaintiff, who describes himself as a writer, producer and entrepreneur in the entertainment industry, residing in Calgary, Alberta, seeks

a variety of remedies against the defendants based on alleged infringement of copyright claimed by the plaintiff in a literary work entitled Space Pets.

2 The basis of the claim of the plaintiff is that the defendants used the work said to have been created by the plaintiff without the latter's knowledge, consent or authority in a motion picture entitled Return of the Jedi and in a television series Ewok Adventure and in various other forms and mediums.

3 The defendant, George Lucas, is a well-known motion picture producer, writer and director of films, a major shareholder and Chairman of the Board of the corporate defendant Lucasfilm Ltd., who resides in California. The correct legal names of the defendant corporations are Twentieth Century-Fox Canada Limited and Lucasfilm Ltd. The former carries on business in Alberta and elsewhere in Canada as a distributor of motion pictures and the latter has its head office in California in the United States of America.

4 The defendants together are the producers and distributors, among other films, of a series of films known as the Star Wars trilogy, the third film in this series being Return of the Jedi. That film, and others in the Star Wars series, were very successful at the box office and together with the marketing of related wares and merchandise, they led to very significant financial success in the late 1970's and early 1980's.

. . .

6 It may be helpful before setting out issues, reviewing the evidence, and settling essential facts to describe in summary outline the case that the testimony of the parties portrays.

7 The plaintiff Preston claims that he wrote an unspecified number of pages, some fifteen to twenty-five pages, of notes, in his handwriting, which were designed as a story line for the script of a television or movie film. These he gave to his friend Mr. David Hurry, for whose abilities as a script writer he had a high regard. He asked Hurry to produce a script from his, Preston's, notes and to send that to the defendant George Lucas in care of 20th Century Fox Film Corp. in Los Angeles, California, a well-known American firm in the business of producing and distributing films, and apparently the parent of the Canadian corporate defendant in this action. Hurry claims to have been uninterested in working on anyone's writing but his own but after some badgering by Preston, he did as he had been asked. Hurry's evidence is that Preston gave him about 25 pages of handwritten notes that were hard to decipher in places and that from the notes he produced the script entitled Space Pets the copy of which, entered in evidence, is headed by that title followed by the words "by Dean Preston Scripted by D. Hurry". Using his employer's mail room facilities he put the envelope containing the letter and the script through the stamp machine and left the envelope with outgoing mail to be sent by regular mail to the address provided by Preston. A copy of a covering letter, attached to the copy of the script, is dated October 20, 1978 and Hurry testifies that it, with the script, was sent then or shortly thereafter. The script included among its characters two small furry animal species with primitive human characteristics named Olaks and Ewoks who

live on a previously unexplored planet in space. No reply or acknowledgement was received from the addressee and the script was not returned.

8 Lucasfilm Ltd. and George Lucas were at that time involved in production of the Star Wars trilogy, specifically in planning the second film in that series, The Empire Strikes Back, and George Lucas was also at that time working on the screenplay for another film, Raiders of the Lost Ark, and was the executive producer of yet another film, More American Graffiti. For some years Lucasfilm had a policy and practice to return all unsolicited scripts or materials, other than mail that was deemed to be fan mail, and to isolate George Lucas from reception of all incoming mail. There is no record of the script Space Pets having been received from David Hurry in 1978, or at any other time.

9 For the third film of the trilogy, Return of the Jedi, active planning began about June or July 1980, production was under way from January 1982 to April or May 1983, and release for distribution to theatres was made May 25, 1983. Small furry animal creatures with certain human characteristics, living on the planet Endor, were featured in the final third of the film. The name for these creatures is not heard in the film but it does appear in the credits at its end which lists among other players some under the heading of Ewoks, the same name as appeared in the Preston-Hurry script Space Pets. These creatures became widely known as Ewoks as a result of the film, at least one television production, and marketing of a variety of merchandise, books and pamphlets, all under the authorization of the defendants.

Issues

10 These circumstances raise a number of issues if the plaintiff is to succeed in his claim based on infringement of copyright. These are:

1) Did George Lucas copy the character of the Ewok or, as was argued at trial, significant other features from the script Space Pets? To conclude that there was copying it is essential to compare the similarities in the script and the film Return of the Jedi, which was the focus of discussion relating to the alleged copying. Of course, to conclude that the script Space Pets was copied it is also necessary to conclude by implication that the script was received by Twentieth Century-Fox at its Los Angeles address and that it found its way to George Lucas or one of his staff and was used without authorization in the film, that is, that the defendant Lucas had access to the script.

2) Can copyright exist in the name Ewok and the description of the Ewok character as depicted in the script? As a general rule, courts have not recognized copyright in a name itself, while recognizing that it may be possible to claim copyright in a name which has sufficient character delineation and is widely known.

3) Was Preston the author of the script Space Pets so that he could claim copyright in it as an artistic work? It is trite law that there can be no copyright in an idea but only in the form given to ideas in artistic works. Thus, determination of this issue depends upon the evidence of the relationship of Preston and Hurry respectively in the production of the script Space Pets.

11 I propose to return to these issues, the evidence and the law relating to them, after setting out more fully the background of this action.

. . .

58 I turn now to my assessment of the specific detailed similarities that were the focus of attention at trial. After carefully considering the evidence adduced, including the testimony at trial, the following summarizes my conclusions about detailed similarities.

59 First, I dismiss some similarities because they could not be evidence of copying from the script by Lucas, since these appear in Return of the Jedi as a continuing saga in the trilogy after first appearing in Star Wars, released in 1977 before the script Space Pets was written, or in The Empire Strikes Back, planning for which was well under way and for which filming began within a few months of the date of Hurry's letter accompanying the script. Thus, even though there are differences in their respective roles in the script and the film, it is of no consequence that the script included four human principal characters, one woman and three men, and so did the film (though there were also many other human characters including principals in the film and not in the script). For the same reason the alleged similarity between one human principal in the script (Chi Chi Gomez) and one in the film (Lando Calrissian), is of no consequence, for the latter was first featured in The Empire Strikes Back. Moreover, the role of Lando in relation to the Ewoks is very different in the film, for he is not involved with them in any way until the final scenes, whereas Gomez in the script is involved with them throughout their part in the story.

60 Some other similarities I tend to discount also, for their presence in the film is traceable to the 1974 original script by Lucas, "The Star Wars". Thus, the general concept of a primitive species, furry creatures with some human character-istics, living in a forest and with primitive weapons including spears and bows and arrows is traceable to the original script. So is the concept of small one or two rider vehicles, "speeder bikes" in the film, "landspeeders" in the script of 1974, and "God cycles" in the Preston-Hurry script of 1978.

61 Other similarities prove to be general without allowing for differences in detail provided by the script Space Pets and the film. Thus, the primitive Ewoks are biped, small furry creatures. Yet in the script they are less than three feet tall, long haired, dark, with faces like a panda with large white patches beneath the eyes, and in the film they are three and a half to four or a little more feet tall, short haired and of many hues, some striped, with a face unlike a bear's, with no white patches beneath their eyes but with large yellow eyes. Their garments in the script include heavy body armour of tree bark with skirt-styled lower halves in pieces linked by tough vines and they wear helmets of wood or hollowed skulls of larger animals. In the film they wear no such armour or skirts, and only three Ewoks are seen with bird or animal head dresses on their heads but all wear leather helmets exposing the ears, designed to hide the velcro fastening of costume and head piece. Their weapons are said to be similar and in the sense of being primitive weapons that is so. In the script the Ewoks use "a spinner type weapon thrown by hand and made from round pieces of wood with spikes

sticking out at the edge, a large crossbow affair that takes several Ewoks to load and fire, and slings with which they are very accurate". They are also depicted in one scene with spears. Only the spears and slings of this group of weapons are used in the film, though a catapult, a weapon used by the Olaks in the script, is used by Ewoks in the film with some other weapons, including a hang-glider, not mentioned in the script. Not among their weapons, but generally similar features which on closer examination are different are the Little God Riders of the script ("small battery powered kiddie cycles" which in testimony Preston described as having wheels) and the "speeder bikes" of the film (two seater, airborne, apparently jet propelled vehicles without wheels).

62 A sedan chair is used in both the script (for a throne and to transport the Ewok chieftain) and the film (to transport and honour the droid/automaton character C-3PO, deemed by the Ewoks as a special being, and to permit Luke Skywalker to demonstrate his powers of levitation). In the script a vine net trap falls in a forest clearing but does not trap the human explorers who neverthe-less are soon surrounded by Ewoks. In the film a vine net trap does fall and traps the exploring party of humans and droids who break free but are soon surrounded by Ewoks. The voices of the Ewoks are said to be similar in script and film. In the script the voice is "high, squeaky...when passed through the language interpretor, (Langread) comes out sounding similar to the voices used by David Seville of Chipmonk fame" which enables the heroes and the audience to understand them. In the film they also have high voices, but only C-3PO can understand them and he translates for others what they have said. Their voices range in pitch and are not otherwise intelligible even as voices akin to those "of Chipmonk fame". Finally, there is similarity in their forest dwellings, in tree huts joined by platforms or walkways but as earlier noted this scene in the film was from a setting used in 1978, before the date of Hurry's letter, for filming of a television special program.

63 Many of the detailed similarities, in my view, can be traced to the common store of folklore about primitive species with human characteristics upon which Lucas was as free to draw as were Preston and Hurry. Yet drawing upon a com-mon store of information does not in itself answer to the claim of infringement. It is the expression of ideas, not the ideas themselves, that is the subject of copy-right. It is entirely possible that two or more authors, composers, dramatists or other artists may draw upon a common store of information for ideas and each may have copyright in his or her expression of those ideas. But if while drawing upon the common information base, one should copy the expression in literary or dramatic form of another author copyright may be infringed.

Conclusion concerning similarities alleged

64 Under the Copyright Act, copyright is the sole right to produce or repro-duce a literary, dramatic, musical or artistic work or any substantial part of it in any form whatever, copyright is vested first in the author of the work, and infringement is deemed when any person without the consent of the owner of

the copyright does anything that only the owner has the right to do. (The Act, sections 3(1) and (2), 13(1) and 27(a)).

65 Here there is no suggestion that the defendants simply reproduced by film the script Space Pets; rather the claim is that without consent of the plaintiff they incorporated a substantial part of the script in Return of the Jedi. Thus the consideration of similarities claimed between the script and the film.

66 There appears a dearth of Canadian jurisprudence on the test for assessing substantial similarity. Authorities from England and from the United States are helpful for, though the legislation differs in some respects from the Act in Canada, it appears in both cases to be based on similar concepts and principles. Substantial similarity is not to be measured only by the quantity of matter reproduced from a copyrighted work, though that may be a significant factor. Of more import may be the quality of matter reproduced. At least in the case of literary or dramatic works assessing similarities may depend upon a number of factors. In the recent Canadian decision, Hutton et al. v. Canadian Broadcasting Corp., MacCallum J. refers to the test for substantial similarity developed by the Ninth Circuit, in California, of the United States Court of Appeals and by the District Court for the Southern District of New York (within the Second Circuit of the U.S. Court of Appeals). Two more recent decisions of each Court provide a current overview of the tests as evolved within these two circuits of the U.S. Court of Appeals. From the two step test developed in the Ninth Circuit and from the single step test of the Second Circuit certain factors for assessing substantial similarity are suggested. These factors include plot, themes, dialogue, mood, setting or scenes, pace, sequence and characters, so far as these are within the recognized limits of copyright in the protected work. In assessing these factors, a decision ultimately for the trier of fact, the test is ultimately whether the average lay observer, at least one for whom the work is intended, would recognize the alleged copy as having been appropriated from the copyrighted work.

67 In my view it is helpful to consider these factors in assessing substantial similarity alleged here in the script and the film. I have already noted that there is no claim to similarity in plot or dialogue, and the previous outlines of the two productions, I believe, clearly indicate no similarity in themes, in mood, pace or sequence. Similarity is claimed in relation to setting or scenes, those involving a net trap of vines, the forest habitat and houses of the Ewoks in both, but it is my view that those scenes in themselves are not subject to copyright or protected by it for they are standard aspects of productions concerning primitive species or primitive humans, drawn from a common pool of folklore.

68 It is my view, after careful consideration of the similarities alleged, that the average lay observer, the average person in the respective intended audiences would find no substantial similarity in the script and the film. I conclude that, while there are some general similarities in details depicting the Ewoks, there is not substantial similarity between the script Space Pets and the film Return of the Jedi.

69 This would be sufficient to dispose of any claim that the defendants infringed any right of the plaintiff under subsection 3(1)(d) of the Act but further consideration must be given to the question of whether the Ewok character, as developed in the script Space Pets, is subject to copyright and the author's right to produce or reproduce that character is protected under subsection 3(1)(d) or (e) of the Act, and if so whether that character was substantially reproduced in the film.

Baigent v. The Random House Group Ltd., [2006] EWHC 719 (Ch.)

Peter Smith J.

7 April 2006

. . .

Judgment

Peter Smith J:

A Setting The Scene

1 *Introduction*

1. The two Claimants Michael Baigent and Richard Leigh claim that the novel The Da Vinci Code ("DVC") is an infringement of their copyright in their book The Holy Blood and The Holy Grail ("HBHG").

2. The Claimants are two of the three authors of HBHG. The third author, Henry Lincoln is not a claimant and does not participate in the claim. No point is taken about his non participation. Nor is there any claim that the Claimants' title to sue in respect of their interests in that copyright by reason that they had been two of the three joint holders copyright.

3. DVC was written by Dan Brown who lives and works in America. The Claimants' case is that in writing DVC he produced a book which is an infringing copy of HBHG. The Defendant to the proceedings is The Random House Group Ltd ("Random") which is responsible for the publication of DVC in the United Kingdom. Dan Brown is not a Defendant, but Random relied upon his witness statements and his evidence in this action. In reality Mr Brown is on trial over the authorship of DVC.

. . .

149. By section 16 (3) CDPA88 copying a copyright work is an infringement if the work or "a substantial part of it" has been copied. The Claimants' case is not that a substantial part of the text of HBHG has been copied but there has nevertheless been copying of a substantial part of the work to produce an altered copy or a colourable imitation.

150. There have been a number of important decisions concerning copying of the nature alleged in this case (i.e. non-textual). Before I analyse those however

I should make some preliminary observations. First it is necessary to identify features that have been allegedly copied. In this case it is said that the Central Themes are the features allegedly copied.

151. The differences between the two copyright works are not relevant and while the copied features must be a substantial part of the copyright work relied upon there is no need for them to be a substantial part of the Defendant's work (see Lord Millet Designers Guild v Russell Williams (textiles) Ltd [2001] FSR 11 citing Warwick Film Productions Ltd v Eisinger [1969] 1 Ch 508.

152. There is much in DVC that is the original (in the non copyright sense) effort of Mr Brown with the assistance of his wife Blythe. There is much in the text and plot of DVC which is not in HBHG. The part that is copied from HBHG must be a substantial part of it but it does not have to be a substantial part in DVC.

153. ...Copyright protection is not confined to the literal text in literary work and changing a few immaterial words in a work that is otherwise the same will not escape liability as they rightly observe. At the other end of the spectrum however they acknowledge copyright should not protect against the borrowing of an idea contained in a work. The courts will not protect "works" through this extreme level of abstraction. An extreme level of abstraction was shown in paragraph 111 of the Defendant's opening skeleton argument. There they say that if there was any scheme of the 15 central points it is that Jesus was father of a bloodline which married into the Merovingians in France and his descendants who have been protected since the Middle Ages by a secret society have a claim to the throne of Palestine. As the Claimants set out in their closing submissions, the extreme points are easy to identify but there is a point on the spectrum which the complexity of the expression warrants protection. The line to be drawn is to enable a fair balance to be struck between protecting the rights of the author and allowing literary development. That seems to me to be a fair stance to take.

. . .

24 *Green v Broadcasting Corporation*

155. However as part of the assessment of the level of abstraction it seems to me clear that there must be certainty in the subject matter of such monopoly given by copyright in order to avoid justice to the rest of the world see IPC Media paragraph 7 referring to Green v Broadcasting Corporation New Zealand [1989] RPC 700.

156. The Claimants criticised that submission (see paragraph 57 of their closing submissions). I do not accept the criticism is valid. What the Defendants are saying is that if what is asserted to be infringed is so general that it cannot be certain that would lead to a conclusion that it is such a level of abstraction that no protection should be afforded to it. It is important to appreciate the context in which the Defendant raised this issue, namely the uncertainty created by the Claimants' own inability clearly to state what the Central Theme is by reason of their changes of the Central Theme. The point is that if the Claimants do not know with certainty what their Central Theme is how can anybody else possibly

know? The fact that the Defendants have conceded (with the reservation) copyright in HBHG as a whole is nothing to the point. It is for the Claimants to establish that what has been copied is a substantial part of HBHG and in this context that means a substantial part of the Central Theme in a way which seeks to exploit for the Defendant's own benefit the Claimants' work in producing it.

25 *Authorities In Non-Textual Infringement Cases*

157. It is particularly important when a literary work is dealing with actual events to see what it is alleged is protectable and what is infringed.

158. In Harman Pictures NV v Osborne [1967] 1 WLR 723 the Plaintiffs owned the copyright in a reproduction in cinemagraphic form of a book "The Reason Why" dealing with the Charge of the Light Brigade and the events connected with it. Discussions ensued between them and the Defendants about the possibility of purchase of the Plaintiffs rights or a joint production based on the reason why but they came to nothing. Later the Plaintiff discovered the Defendants intended to produce on their own account a film called "The Charge of the Light Brigade" based on a screenplay written by John Osborne the first Defendant (a well known author). The Plaintiffs issued a writ claiming that there was a marked similarity in the choice of incidents in the book and the screenplay although besides any similarities there were many dissimilarities. They applied for an interlocutory injunction. In the course of giving judgment Goff J dealt with the situation where ideas or schemes or systems or methods are sought to be protected see:-

> "It is common ground that there can be an original work entitled to protection although the subject matter is not original, but is for example, as in the present case, some well-known event in history. The precise amount of knowledge, labour, judgment or literary skill or taste which the author of any book or other compilation must bestow upon its composition in order to acquire copyright in it within the meaning of the Copyright Act, 1911, cannot be defined in precise terms: per Lord Atkinson in Macmillan & Co. Ltd. v. Cooper. There is, however, no dispute that Mrs. Woodham-Smith displayed all these qualities in amply sufficient measure and acquired copyright in her book, whilst the plaintiffs' title to the film rights by assignment is also not disputed. What is much more difficult is whether the plaintiffs have made out a sufficient prima facie case of infringement, or rather intended infringement, and before considering the facts, I must refer at some length to the relevant law.
>
> There is no copyright in ideas or schemes or systems or methods: it is confined to their expression...
>
> One must, however, be careful not to jump to the conclusion that there has been copying merely because of similarity of stock incidents, or of incidents which are to be found in historical, semi-historical and fictional literature about characters in history, see Poznanski v. London Film Production Ltd. In such cases the plaintiffs, and that includes the plaintiffs in the present case, are in an obvious difficulty because of the existence of common sources, as was emphasised in the case of Pike v. Nicholas..."

159. On the facts Goff J granted the interlocutory injunction.

26 *Ravenscroft*

160. The next case is probably the most important in the area of the present litigation Ravenscroft v Herbert [1980] RPC 193. This was a claim by the author of a non-fiction book called The Spear of Destiny. He alleged that the First Defendant James Herbert a well known author in writing a novel entitled The Spear had infringed his copyright. The central feature of both books was a spearhead which forms part of the Hapsburg Treasure exhibited in Vienna. It is described in the museum guide as The Holy Lance. After the 13th century it was venerated as the lance with which the side of Jesus was pierced at the crucifixion. It is said that the spear had been carried in important battles as an emblem and the victories were attributed to its power. The Plaintiff's book combined historical facts and a great deal of mysticism and purports to tell the story of the spear from the earliest times down to the end of the Second World War.

161. Mr Herbert's book is a thriller which weaves an improbable story it is alleged of neo Hitler terrorism in England around the supposed post war exploits of the spear. The Judge (Brightman J as he then was) was plainly unimpressed with the book. For example the fact that the spear is apparently in Vienna is dealt with by Mr Herbert simply describing that as a useless replica.

162. The Plaintiff's allegation was that Mr Herbert was alleged to have made extensive use of the Plaintiff's non fiction work in order to paint in a backcloth of apparent truth against which his own fiction story can be narrated. The question for decision in the case was whether he made a legitimate or illegitimate use of the Plaintiffs work.

163. The Plaintiff's book is summarised in the judgment. The judgment then went on to consider how Mr Herbert came to write The Spear. He discovered the Plaintiff's book, bought it, read it and thought it would make a splendid theme for a novel. He duly produced a novel which is summarised in the judgment and plainly did not as I say impress Brightman J "One must not underestimate the commercial attraction of the rubbish which I have attempted to describe. The book is written with much inventiveness and a racy flow of language and incident and the numerous scenes of violence exercise a strong appeal to certain readers. The Defendants novels have enjoyed great financial success. Mr Herbert does not think of himself as a serious novelist".

164. I make no such comments about either book in the present case as this is not as I have said a quest for truth of the speculative conjectures or an exercise in literary criticism of either book.

165. Mr Herbert conceded that he used the Plaintiff's book for the source of much of the material.

166. There were numerous examples of significant textual copying (up to 50). The Judge concluded that Mr Herbert had the Plaintiff's book in front of him when writing his own book (a point which Mr Rayner James QC attempted to put repeatedly to Mr Brown in cross examination). He also acknowledged he had no independent knowledge of medieval history and did no research of his

own and as the Judge observed there was much language copying from one book to the other in the Defendants writing of (for example) the prologue. The prologue contains a long list of Emperors of the Roman Empire and the Holy Roman Empire and others (vis Alaric the Visigoth and Theodoric the Visigoth) who held the spear and were successful. These were identical reproductions of the Plaintiffs record save the Roman General Aetius and apparently St Francis of Assisi. I suppose the naming of Aetius is superfluous if the spear is held by Theodoric the Visigoth bearing in mind the result of the Battle of Chalons (as I prefer to call it). Perhaps the dying Theodoric passed it on to Aetius.

167. General Patton emerges in the story but that is not surprising given his apparent interest in mystical things and the surprising manner of his death. As the Judge pointed out the question to decide is the question of fact whether there has been substantial copying of The Spear of Destiny amounting to an infringement of the Plaintiff's rights. The first question is whether there has been copying and secondly whether the copying is substantial. That factual decision on the facts of that case has no significance in the present dispute. Thus merely because an author of a work of non fiction successfully sued an author of fiction based on his non fictional book provides me with no assistance whatsoever.

168. The judgment is important however in the analysis as between facts and ideas and copyright claims which involve facts or ideas. Thus at page 203 he said this:-

> "Mr. Laddie, for the defendants, rightly says that an author has no copyright in his facts, nor in his ideas, but only in his original expression of such facts or ideas. He submitted that in deciding whether copying is substantial there are four principal matters to be taken into account. First, the volume of the material taken, bearing in mind that quality is more important than quantity; secondly, how much of such material is the subject-matter of copyright and how much is not; thirdly, whether there has been an animus furandi on the part of the defendant; this was treated by Page-Wood V.C. in Jarrold v. Houlston (1857) 3 K & J. 708 as equivalent to an intention on the part of the defendant to take for the purpose of saving himself labour; fourthly, the extent to which the plaintiff's and the defendant's books are competing works.

> Copyright protects the skill and labour employed by the plaintiff in production of his work. That skill and labour embraces not only language originated and used by the plaintiff, but also such skill and labour as he has employed in selection and compilation. The principles are clear from the cases. There is a helpful summary of the authorities in Harman Pictures N.V. v. Osborne ([1967] 1 W.L.R. 723). For my purposes it is sufficient to cite two passages from that case which are taken from earlier authority:

> ... another person may originate another work in the same general form, provided he does so from his own resources and makes the work he so originates a work of his own by his own labour and industry bestowed upon it. In determining whether an injunction should be ordered, the question, where the matter of the plaintiff's work is not original, is how far an unfair or undue use has been made of the work? If, instead of searching into the common sources and obtaining your subject-matter from thence, you avail yourself of the labour of your predecessor, adopt his

arrangements and questions, or adopt them with a colourable variation, it is an illegitimate use".

This appears at page 730 of the report.

There is also this passage:

In the case of works not original in the proper sense of the term, but composed of, or compiled or prepared from materials which are open to all, the fact that one man has produced such a work does not take away from anyone else the right to produce another work of the same kind, and in doing so to use all the materials open to him. But as the law has been precisely stated by Hall V.C. in Hogg v. Scott, the true principle in all these cases is that the defendant is not at liberty to use or avail himself of the labour which the plaintiff has been at for the purpose of producing his work, that is, in fact, merely to take away the result of another man's labour or, in other words, his property"': see page 732.

In this case the judge was confronted with the well-known book by Mrs. Cecil Woodham Smith entitled The Reason Why and also the script for a motion picture written by John Osborne. The question which the judge posed was this (at page 736):

> ... did John Osborne work independently and produce a script which, from the nature of things, has much in common with the book, or did he proceed the other way round and use the book as a basis, taking his selection of incidents and quotations therefrom, al-beit omitting a number and making some alternations and additions, by reference to the common sources and by some reference to other sources?

That is the same test as was stated by Buckley L.J. in Elanco Products Ltd. v. Mandops (Agrochemical Specialists) Ltd. [1979] F.S.R. 46 which was heard on motion for interim relief. The facts, briefly, were that the plaintiffs had invented a herbicide and had carried out trials in order to discover how the product could best be used. Various research establishments had also conducted their own field trials. The results of both the plaintiffs' trials and of the independent trials had been published in certain scientific journals. The plaintiffs marketed the herbicide in tins with which they included a leaflet compiled by the plaintiffs which set out detailed instructions on how the herbicide should be used, upon what crops and when, and what weeds it would best control. The plaintiffs claimed copyright in the leaflet and asserted that it was a compilation of what they regarded as relevant information extracted from all the available literature and especially from their own. After the patent had expired the defendants began to sell the same herbicide with a leaflet which was alleged to be similar to the plaintiffs'. The substantial defence raised by the defendants was that they were entitled to take any information available to the public including that contained in the plaintiffs' literature provided that they did not adopt the same form or the same language, that is to say provided that they did not just copy the plaintiffs' literature. Buckley L.J. said this at page 57:

> "As I understand the law in this case, the defendants were fully entitled to make use of any information of a technical or any other kind, which was available to them in the public domain, for the purpose of compiling their label and their trade literature, and they were not entitled to copy the plaintiffs' label or trade literature thereby making use of the plaintiffs' skill and judgment and saving themselves the trouble, and very possibly the cost, of

assembling their own information, either from their own researches or from
sources available in documents in the public domain and thereby making
their own selection of material to put into that literature and producing their
own label and trade literature".

The main thrust of Mr. Laddie's argument was that the plaintiff intended his book
to be read as a factual account of historical events, that the defendant accepted it as
fact and did no more than repeat certain of those facts. The plaintiff cannot claim
a monopoly in historical facts. The law of copyright does not preclude another
author from writing upon the same theme. It is perfectly legitimate for another
person to contrive a novel about the Hofburg spear, even about its supposed ancestry and supernatural powers. Otherwise one would be driven to the conclusion that
the plaintiff has a monopoly of the facts. Members of the public are entitled to use
The Spear of Destiny as a historical work of reference. Mr. Laddie conceded that
if the plaintiff had research and selected which facts to use, and had expended substantial labour in making that selection, and a substantial amount of his labour had
been taken by the defendant, then there might be infringement. In the present case,
he submitted, the plaintiff's facts were selected by history or by Dr. Stein and not
by the plaintiff. In the result, there had been no reproduction of the plaintiff's book
in relation to a substantial part thereof. In the course of his copying the defendant
confined himself to those matters which are represented in the plaintiff's book as
historical facts, whether their origin is to be found in documented history or in the
meditations of Dr. Stein.

In developing his argument Mr. Laddie drew a distinction between historical
works and works of fiction. He said that if any author writes a history book he
obtains copyright, but what amounts to an infringement of that copyright, i.e. substantial reproduction, depends to a great extent upon whether all the defendant has
taken is historical facts or amounts to more than that. The degree of user which
would amount to an infringement is different in the case of a historical work than
in the case of a work of fiction. There is more freedom to copy in the case of the
historical work.

I am inclined to accept that a historical work is not to be judged by precisely the
same standards as a work of fiction. The purpose of a novel is usually to interest
the reader and to contribute to his enjoyment of his leisure. A historical work may
well have that purpose, but the author of a serious and original historical work may
properly be assumed by his readers to have another purpose as well, namely to add
to the knowledge possessed by the reader and perhaps in the process to increase
the sum total of human experience and understanding. The author of a historical
work must, I think, have attributed to him an intention that the information thereby
imparted may be used by the reader, because knowledge would become sterile if it
could not be applied. Therefore, it seems to me reasonable to suppose that the law
of copyright will allow a wider use to be made of a historical work than of a novel
so that knowledge can be built upon knowledge."

169. There is a further observation on Mr Laddie's submissions at page 206:-

"In my judgment, Mr. Laddie's proposition must not be pressed too far. It is, I
think, clear from the authorities that an author is not entitled, under the guise of
producing an original work, to reproduce the arguments and illustrations of another
author so as to appropriate to himself the literary labours of that author: see Pike
v. Nicholas (1870) L.R. 5 Ch. App. 251, Ladbroke (Football) Ltd. v. William Hill

[1964] 1 W.L.R. 273 and the passages, which I have already read, from the Harman Pictures N.V. case.

Mr. Sheridan, for the plaintiff, invites me to view the matter in a different light. He submits that the plaintiff's work is not a historical work of the conventional type, because it is not a chronology. It is not a continuous methodical record of public events (which is the primary dictionary definition of "history"). The plaintiff's book is poles away from history. It is disjointed and unmethodical (no offensive criticism is intended of the literary technique that he employs) being composed of a variety of different events, recollections, quotations, philosophy, meditations and so on, designed to support the theory in which the plaintiff had come to believe. Vast areas of history are left out by the plaintiff in his attempt to persuade the reader that the Hofburg Spear has the ancestry and attributes which the plaintiff believes are to be ascribed to it. The book is a very personal insight into history. What the plaintiff has done is to select events from history and from his recollection of the meditations of Dr. Stein in order to present to the reader the credentials of the Hofburg Spear.

I accept Mr. Sheridan's analysis of the nature of the plaintiff's work.

There was a suggestion by Mr. Laddie that some distinction should be drawn in the present case because much of what the defendant copied from The Spear of Destiny was merely information derived by the plaintiff from Dr. Stein. I do not think it matters whether the source of the plaintiff's book was painstaking research into documented history or painstaking recording and recollection of what Dr. Stein had told him. It was also suggested that a distinction should be drawn on the ground that The Spear of Destiny was, since the death of Dr. Stein, the only possible source of certain of the facts brought to light by the meditation of Dr. Stein. It does not, however, seem to me that the paucity of sources of information excuses the defendant from taking the trouble of assembling his own information and making his own selection of material. If that is not practicable, he can always apply to the plaintiff for a licence".

170. Not surprisingly the Claimants rely upon this case as being a strong pointer in their favour. Less surprisingly and equally understandable in its context is Mr Baldwin QC's reliance upon parts of the judgment for the defence (he was second junior Counsel on behalf of the Defendants).

171. First it seems to me that it is accepted that an author has no copyright in his facts nor in his ideas but only in his original expression of such facts or ideas. Original in that context does not mean novel of course.

172. Second the purpose of copyright is to protect the skill and labour employed by the Plaintiff in the production of his work.

173. Third in the case of works not original in the proper sense of the term but composed or compiled from materials which are open to all the fact that one man has produced such a work does not take away from anyone else the right to produce another work of the same kind "and in doing so to use all the materials open to him". What he cannot do however is avail himself of the labour of the Plaintiff.

174. Subject to what I say in the next paragraph where a book is intended to be read as a factual historical event and that the Defendant accepts it as fact and did

no more than repeat certain of those facts the Plaintiff cannot claim a monopoly in those historical facts. It is accordingly perfectly legitimate for another person to contrive a novel based on those facts as otherwise a Claimant would have a monopoly of the facts. This was an argument put forward by Mr Laddie (page 205 above line 18). It seems to me that the Judge accepted that argument as far as it went (see the bottom of that page and on to page 206). This seems to me to mirror what the Claimants actually expected to occur when they published their book. I do not see Brightman J as such rejecting Mr Laddie's submis-sions.

175. It is true (page 206 above) that he accepted that Mr Laddie's proposition must not be pressed too far as he rightly set out in that part of his judgment although the historical contents and the ar-guments can be used they cannot be used through the medium of appropriating the literary labours of the original author.

176. In other words the facts and the themes and the ideas cannot be protected but how those facts, themes and ideas are put together (this is the Claimants' "architecture" argument) can be. It follows from this that the Claimants must show that there is a putting together of facts, themes and ideas by them as a result of their efforts and it is that which Mr Brown has copied. I should say on passing that there is no claim based on collocation.

Designers Guild

177. The next important decision is The Designers Guild case.

178. This was a claim by the Plaintiff to enforce its copyright in the artwork for the fabric design Ixia. The infringement complained of was the creation of the Defendants own design Marguerite. There were two issues namely what had the designers of Marguerite copied from Ixia and second did what had been copied amount to the whole or substantial part of Ixia. At first instance the trial judge (Mr Lawrence Collins Q.C as he then was) examined all the circumstances and the witnesses and disbelieved essentially the Defendants and concluded that they had used Ixia (despite their pro-tests to the contrary). On the second issue he rejected the Defendants submissions based on a dissec-tion of the Ixia design and suggestions that they lacked originality and concluded that what hap-pened amounted to a copying of a substantial part of Ixia.

179. On appeal the Judge's findings as to copying were not challenged; the only issue was substantiality. The Court of Appeal overturned the Judge's view as to substantiality on the basis of three rea-sons namely visual comparison, dissec-tion and ideas rather than expression.

180. Visual comparison has nothing to do with the present case.

181. Second dissection is relevant in the sense that the copied features must not be dealt with piecemeal but the copying as a whole and the cumulative effect (as the Judge had done at first instance) must be considered. However, as Lord Hoffman pointed out (paragraph 22) "if there had been no findings anything that had been copied except the notion of flowers and stripe, the conclusion in the

Court of Appeal would have been unexceptionable, with this involved ignoring the findings of fact, both in their detail and their cumulative effect".

182. The key part of the judgment as regards to the present case concerns and observations on "ideas and expressions". Lord Hoffman said this (paragraph 23):

"Ideas and expression

23 It is often said, as Morritt L.J. said in this case, that copyright subsists not in ideas but in the form in which the ideas are expressed. The distinction between expression and ideas finds a place in the Agreement on Trade-Related Aspects of Intellectual Property Rights (TRIPS) ([1994] O.J. L336/213), to which the United Kingdom is a party (see Article 9.2: "Copyright protection shall extend to expressions and not to ideas..."). Nevertheless, it needs to be handled with care. What does it mean? As Lord Hailsham of St Marylebone said in L.B. (Plastics) Ltd v. Swish Products Ltd [1979] R.P.C. 551 at 629, "it all depends on what you mean by 'ideas'".

24 Plainly there can be no copyright in an idea which is merely in the head, which has not been expressed in copyrightable form, as a literary, dramatic, musical or artistic work, but the distinction between ideas and expression cannot mean anything so trivial as that. On the other hand, every element in the expression of an artistic work (unless it got there by accident or compulsion) is the expression of an idea on the part of the author. It represents her choice to paint stripes rather than polka dots, flowers rather than tadpoles, use one colour and brush technique rather than another, and so on. The expression of these ideas is protected, both as a cumulative whole and also to the extent to which they form a "substantial part" of the work. Although the term "substantial part" might suggest a quantitative test, or at least the ability to identify some discrete part which, on quantitative or qualitative grounds, can be regarded as substantial, it is clear upon the authorities that neither is the correct test. Ladbroke (Football) Ltd v. William Hill (Football) Ltd [1964] 1 W.L.R. 273 establishes that substantiality depends upon quality rather than quantity (Lord Reid at 276, Lord Evershed at 283, Lord Hodson at 288, Lord Pearce at 293), and there are numerous authorities which show that the "part" which is regarded as substantial can be a feature or combination of features of the work, abstracted from it rather than forming a discrete part. That is what the judge found to have been copied in this case. Or to take another example, the original elements in the plot of a play or novel may be a substantial part, so that copyright may be infringed by a work which does not reproduce a single sentence of the original. If one asks what is being protected in such a case, it is difficult to give any answer except that it is an idea expressed in the copyright work.

25 My Lords, if one examines the cases in which the distinction between ideas and the expression of ideas has been given effect, I think it will be found that they support two quite distinct propositions. The first is that a copyright work may express certain ideas which are not protected because they have no connection with the literary, dramatic, musical or artistic nature of the work. It is on this ground that, for example, a literary work which describes a system or invention does not entitle the author to claim protection for his system or invention as such. The same is true of an inventive concept expressed in an artistic work. However striking or original it may be, others are (in the absence of patent protection) free to express it in works of their own: see Kleeneze Ltd v. D.R.G. (U.K.) Ltd [1984] F.S.R. 399. The other proposition is that certain ideas expressed by a copyright

work may not be protected because, although they are ideas of a literary, dramatic or artistic nature, they are not original, or so commonplace as not to form a substantial part of the work. Kenrick & Co. v. Lawrence & Co. (1890) 25 Q.B.D. 99, is a well-known example. It is on this ground that the mere notion of combining stripes and flowers would not have amounted to a substantial part of the plaintiff's work. At that level of abstraction, the idea, though expressed in the design, would not have represented sufficient of the author's skill and labour as to attract copyright protection.

26 Generally speaking, in cases of artistic copyright, the more abstract and simple the copied idea, the less likely it is to constitute a substantial part. Originality, in the sense of the contribution of the author's skill and labour, tends to lie in the detail with which the basic idea is presented. Copyright law protects foxes better than hedgehogs. In this case, however, the elements which the judge found to have been copied went well beyond the banal and I think that the judge was amply justified in deciding that they formed a substantial part of the originality of the work."

183. Lord Millet criticised the Court of Appeal in effect for attempting by considering that whilst copying had occurred a substantial part of the expression of the idea had not (paragraphs 34-35):

"34 The Court of Appeal began by making a visual comparison of the two designs. Their initial reaction was that it did not look as if the defendants' design involved the copying of a substantial part of the copyright work. As Morritt L.J. put it at para. 30:

On the broadest level they just do not look sufficiently similar.

Recognising that it would not be right to reach a concluded view "on so subjective and unanalytical approach alone", they proceeded to conduct a detailed analysis of the judge's findings of fact and recorded the many differences of detail in those features of the defendants' design which the judge had found to have been copied from the copyright work. This only served to confirm their initial impression. They concluded that, while the defendants had copied the idea of the copyright work and adopted the same techniques, they had not copied a substantial part of the expression of the idea. They accordingly allowed the defendants' appeal.

35 It is difficult to avoid the impression that the Court of Appeal were not persuaded that the defendants had copied the copyright work at all. Unable to reverse the judge's unchallenged findings that they had, they thought that if the defendants had copied any features of the copyright work they could not have copied very much. By adopting this approach they not only went behind the judge's unchallenged findings of fact, which they were not entitled to do, but rejected his finding of substantiality which, being essentially a matter of impression, an appellate court should always be very slow to do".

184. He also gave guidance as to how a claim of the present type should be approached (paragraphs 38-41):

"38 An action for infringement of artistic copyright, however, is very different. It is not concerned with the appearance of the defendant's work but with its derivation. The copyright owner does not complain that the defendant's work resembles his, his complaint is that the defendant has copied all or a substantial part of the copyright work. The reproduction may be exact or it may introduce deliberate variations — involving altered copying or colourable imitation as it is sometimes called. Even where the copying is exact, the defendant may incorporate the copied features into a larger work much and perhaps most of which is original or derived from other sources. But while the copied features must be a substantial part of the copyright work, they need not form a substantial part of the defendant's work: see Warwick Film Productions Ltd v. Eisinger [1969] Ch. 508. Thus the overall appearance of the defendant's work may be very different from the copyright work, but it does not follow that the defendant's work does not infringe the plaintiff's copyright.

39 The first step in an action for infringement of artistic copyright is to identify those features of the defendant's design which the plaintiff alleges have been copied from the copyright work. The court undertakes a visual comparison of the two designs, noting the similarities and the differences. The purpose of the examination is not to see whether the overall appearance of the two designs is similar, but to judge whether the particular similarities relied on are sufficiently close, numerous or extensive to be more likely to be the result of copying than of coincidence. It is at this stage that similarities may be disregarded because they are commonplace, unoriginal, or consist of general ideas. If the plaintiff demonstrates sufficient similarity, not in the works as a whole but in the features which he alleges have been copied, and establishes that the defendant had prior access to the copyright work, the burden passes to the defendant to satisfy the judge that, despite the similarities, they did not result from copying.

40 Even at this stage, therefore, the inquiry is directed to the similarities rather than the differences. This is not to say that the differences are unimportant. They may indicate an independent source and so rebut any inference of copying, but differences in the overall appearance of the two works due to the presence of features of the defendant's work about which no complaint is made are not material. In the present case the disposition of the flowers and (except in one instance) the colourways of the defendants' design are very different from those of the plaintiffs' design. They were not taken from the copyright work, and the plaintiffs make no complaint in respect of them. They make a significant difference to the overall appearance of the design, but this is not material where the complaint is of infringement of copyright and not passing off.

41 Once the judge has found that the defendants' design incorporates features taken from the copyright work, the question is whether what has been taken constitutes all or a substantial part of the copyright work. This is a matter of impression, for whether the part taken is substantial must be determined by its quality rather than its quantity. It depends upon its importance to the copyright work. It does not depend upon its importance to the defendants' work, as I have already pointed out. The pirated part is considered on its own (see Ladbroke (Football) Ltd v. William Hill (Football) Ltd [1964] 1 W.L.R. 273 at 293, per Lord Pearce) and its importance to the copyright work assessed. There is no need to look at the infringing work for this purpose".

185. Finally Lord Scott stated that the court should consider whether the Defendant "has incorporated substantial part of the independent skill, labour etc contributed by the original author in creating the copyright work and that that test is based on the principle" a copier is not at liberty to appropriate the benefit of anothers skill and labour" (paragraph 64).

...

41 The Task of Analysis

255. ...Copyright should not protect against the borrowing of an idea contained in a work. It is necessary to strike a fair balance between protecting the rights of the author and allowing literary development. It is that fair balance which is in question in my view in this case. Of course it is dependant on the facts of any particular case.

256. Having read the Central Theme as I have said I am unable to find the Central Theme expressed as such in HBHG.

257. The reason is obvious from a reading of the Central Themes individually and as a whole. They consist of a series of generalised ideas, assertions or facts. Some are incredibly general....

258. As I have said as a Central Theme they cannot as a whole or individually be found in HBHG. It has many other facts, ideas or assertions which are not in the Central Theme. It is quite wrong to assert that HBHG has very little apart from the Central Theme.

42 Central Themes, What Are They?

259. Even if there is a Central Theme as alleged by the Claimants in HBHG its expression in the Central Theme it is merely an expression of a number of facts and ideas at a very general level. There is nothing in them in my view that goes beyond that proposition. It follows therefore that the Central Theme as expressed is not such as to justify being protected against copying.

260. In this context I follow the accepted submissions of Mr Laddie in *Ravenscroft* and the expansion in Lord Hoffman's speech in *Designer Guild.* When a book is put forward as being a non fictional book and contains a large number of facts and ideas it is always going to be a difficult exercise in trying to protect against copying of those facts and ideas because as such they cannot be protected. It is the effort and time that has gone into the way in which those ideas and facts are presented that is capable of protection.

...

Delrina Corp. v. Triolet Systems Inc. (2002), 17 C.P.R. (4th) 289
(Ont. C.A.)

Morden, Carthy, MacPherson JJ.A.

Heard: September 19-21, 2001

Judgment: March 1, 2002

Docket: CA C03375

Morden J.A.:

1 There are two appeals before this court, both commenced by the plaintiff, Delrina Corporation, which carries on business as Carolian Systems (Carolian). In the first appeal, Carolian appeals from the dismissal of its action by O'Leary J. against the defendants Triolet Systems Inc. and Brian Duncombe. In this action Carolian alleged that the defendants' computer software program, known as Assess, infringed its copyright in its program known as Sysview. In the second appeal, Carolian appeals from a judgment of O'Leary J. assessing the defendants' damages under Carolian's undertaking to pay damages given to obtain an interlocutory injunction restraining the defendants from selling, giving away, or marketing Assess. I shall deal first with the appeal concerned with the dismissal of Carolian's action.

2 Carolian raises four grounds of appeal, all of which allege errors of law on the part of the trial judge. In the circumstances, I do not think it is necessary to set out the facts in detail. They are comprehensively stated in the trial judge's reasons for judgment, which are reported at (1993), 47 C.P.R. (3d) 1 (Ont. Gen. Div.). My references to pages in the trial judge's reasons are to the pages in this report.

3 The respondent Duncombe was employed by Carolian for the period from January 1984 to December 1985 to improve Carolian's performance monitoring program called Sysview. The purpose of this program was to allow a skilled operator of a Hewlett-Packard HP 3000 computer to assess the efficiency of the operation of this computer. Duncombe completely rewrote Sysview for Carolian.

4 After leaving Carolian in 1985, Duncombe began to design Assess in January 1986. Assess was designed to be functionally similar to Sysview in order to compete directly with Sysview for the same customers. I shall refer to further facts where they are relevant to a particular ground of appeal.

The Grounds of Appeal

> 1. The learned trial judge erred in defining "copying" as only including copying which Duncombe committed while having Sysview before him, including its source code, when he created Assess.

> 2. The learned trial judge erred in excusing the many similarities between Sysview and Assess as being attributable to a collection of factors which are irrelevant in copyright law. These factors included: (a) Duncombe deliberately designing Assess to be similar to Sysview; and (b) Duncombe being the author of both programs.

3. The learned trial judge erred in denying copyrightability to much of Sysview. The learned trial judge made this error, in large part, by applying United States authorities on the copyrightability of computer programs without regard to the significant differences between the copyright statutes and the development of copyright law in the two countries [the United States and Canada]. Based on these authorities, the learned trial judge ignored the fact that Sysview met the standard set under the Copyright Act of being "original".

4. The learned trial judge erred in: (a) drawing an adverse inference that Carolian did not produce a privileged expert's report because it would not have been helpful to Carolian; and (b) finding that Fitzpatrick J. might have declined to award an interlocutory injunction had he been made aware of the Aronoff report.

. . .

1. The trial judge's use of 'copying'

8 Carolian submits that the trial judge erred in defining "copying" as only including copying which Duncombe committed while having Sysview before him, including its source code, when he created Assess.

9 The key passage in the trial judge's reasons relating to this ground is as follows:

> In using the word "copying", Campbell [a principal of Carolian] uses it in the literal sense. He means that Duncombe had a copy of Sysview before him, including its source code, when he created Assess and that he copied from it when it benefitted his work to do so — which was most of the time. Campbell is not talking about copying from memory that Duncombe might have had for some portions of the source code, the display screens, and other portions of Sysview from having created it from scratch while at Carolian. I also in these reasons use "copying" in the literal sense I have just described (p. 9).

10 It is not in issue that "copying" in the law of copyright clearly goes beyond copying from something which is physically before the person who copies. It includes copying from memory, even subconscious memory: Gondos v. Hardy (1982), 64 C.P.R. (2d) 145 (Ont. H.C.) at 159-61, 167; Boudreau v. Lin (1997), 75 C.P.R. (3d) 1 (Ont. Gen. Div.) at 10; Shewan v. Canada (Attorney General) (1999), 87 C.P.R. (3d) 475 (Ont. S.C.J.) at 496-97; and Bright Tunes Music Corp. v. Harrisongs Music Ltd., 420 F. Supp. 177 (U.S. Dist. Ct. 1976) at 181.

11 The issue with respect to this error relates to the extent to which it affects the trial judge's ultimate conclusions on copyright infringement. It is a troublesome point but I am satisfied that, when the reasons are read as a whole, it can be seen that the trial judge's essential findings were not based on the view that copying from memory could not be a basis of copyright infringement. As my reasons will indicate, the main basis for explaining similarities between Assess and Sysview is that features common to both programs are not capable of copyright protection.

12 Further, if the trial judge was of the view that copying protectable expression from memory was excusable, he would not have felt obliged to canvass in the detail that he did what Carolian submitted to be intrinsic evidence of copying. He rejected Carolian's submission.

13 Further still, near the end of this canvass, the trial judge said:

> Finally, I accept Duncombe's evidence that he created Assess without copying Sysview in any way (p. 18). (Emphasis added.)

14 For these reasons, I would not give effect to this ground of appeal.

. . .

19 I would not give effect to this ground of appeal.

3. Error in denying copryrightability to much of Sysview

20 Carolian submits that the trial judge erred in denying copyrightability to much of Sysview. According to this submission, the learned trial judge made this error, in large part, by applying United States authorities on the copyrightability of computer programs without regard to the significant differences between the copyright statutes and the development of copyright law in Canada and the United States. Following U.S. authorities, the learned trial judge ignored the fact that Sysview met the standard set under the Copyright Act of being "original".

21 I should mention, at the outset of this part of my reasons, that the evidence the trial judge relied upon showed, in his view, both that the portions of Sysview which Carolian submitted proved copyright infringement by the defendants were not entitled to copyright protection and, in fact, had not been copied by Duncombe from Sysview. On this the trial judge said:

> We have then Burkowski [an expert witness called on behalf the plaintiff] and other witnesses for the plaintiff saying that certain parts of Assess were copied from Sysview but making no attempt at establishing that Carolian had copyright in the parts of Sysview that were copied. We have Sieler [the defendants' expert] saying that the portions of Sysview, that Burkowski and others referred to, were not copied by Duncombe in creating Assess, and in many cases that the similarities are accounted for by being the logical or only way of accomplishing the particular task at hand, or that the routine came from the public domain or was dictated by the make-up of the HP3000 or other like reasons — all of which in addition to explaining away copying, also deny copyrightability (p. 38).

. . .

> Sieler lists many reasons for similarities between Sysview and Assess without the suggestion of copying arising, but reasons which likewise establish that those parts of Sysview under [re]view are not copyrightable (p. 41).

22 Carolian advanced several specific arguments under this ground of appeal. One fundamental argument was that the trial judge erred in dissecting Sysview into parts and then determining that each of these parts was not entitled to copyright protection. The proper approach, Carolian submits, is, first, to determine whether Sysview as a whole is entitled to copyright and then to determine whether the part reproduced by the defendants is a substantial part of the whole. This latter step involves looking at the quality and quantity of what has been taken. Carolian submitted that the law is "neatly encapsulated" in Ladbroke (Football) Ltd. v. William Hill (Football) Ltd., [1964] 1 All E.R. 465 (U.K. H.L.).

23 I shall deal with this basic submission now. The House of Lords' decision in Ladbroke (Football) Ltd. clearly supports the propositions advanced by Carolian, but I think that the major answer to the appeal on this point is that the trial judge, in his decision of the case, did not run afoul of these propositions. In fairness to Carolian, I acknowledge that there are several general statements in the trial judge's reasons at pp. 27-46 which would tend to support its position. However, in his actual decision on the issue of infringement, the trial judge engaged in what I consider to be a proper analysis relating to whether the defendants reproduced a substantial part of Sysview. I shall elaborate.

24 The reasons of Lord Pearce in Ladbroke (Football) Ltd. at p. 481 are in point:

> Did the appellants reproduce a substantial part of it? Whether a part is substantial must be decided by its quality rather than its quantity. The reproduction of a part which by itself has no originality will not normally be a substantial part of the copyright and therefore will not be protected. For that which would not attract copyright except by reason of its collocation will, when robbed of that collocation, not be a substantial part of the copyright and therefore the courts will not hold its reproduction to be an infringement. It is this, I think, which is meant by one or two judicial observations that "there is no copyright" in some unoriginal part of a whole that is copyright. They afford no justification, in my view, for holding that one starts the inquiry as to whether copyright exists by dissecting the compilation into component parts instead of starting it by regarding the compilation as a whole and seeing whether the whole has copyright. It is when one is debating whether the part reproduced is substantial that one considers the pirated portion on its own. [Emphasis added]

25 This approach has been followed in John Richardson Computers Ltd. v. Flanders, [1993] F.S.R. 497 (Eng. Ch. Div.) at 548 and in Prism Hospital Software Inc. v. Hospital Medical Records Institute (1994), 57 C.P.R. (3d) 129 (B.C. S.C.) at 272-73.

26 The trial judge in his reasons at pp. 71-82 carefully examined similarities between Sysview and Assess upon which Carolian relied and concluded that none of them involved parts of Sysview that were entitled to copyright protection or that, in fact, were copied by Duncombe from Sysview. This analytical approach is fully supportable under the emphasized passages in Ladbroke (Football) Ltd. set forth above. While it would have been preferable if the trial judge had avoided using "copyrightable" in considering the elements of Assess alleged to be similar to Sysview (the word applies more accurately to a work as a whole), I think that he properly considered whether those elements were entitled to copyright protection.

27 In Ladbroke (Football) Ltd., the plaintiff alleged that the defendant had infringed its copyright in a football betting coupon which was a "compilation" form of "literary work" under the applicable legislation. The first line of defence was that the plaintiff did not have copyright in the coupon as a whole. In pursuing this position the defendants argued that "the coupons could be dissected and that on analysis no copyright attached to any of their component parts and

accordingly no protection is available" (p. 475). This approach was rejected by the House of Lords.

28 In the present case, the trial judge at no place in his reasons expressed the view that there was no copyright in Sysview as a whole and, for the purpose of these reasons, I am prepared to assume that Carolian had copyright in the work as a whole. It was sufficient for the trial judge to examine those elements of Assess which Carolian alleged were similar to elements of Sysview, with a view to determining whether Assess was a substantial reproduction of Sysview. If the elements of Assess Carolian alleged were similar to Sysview were not capable of copyright protection, Carolian cannot rely on those similarities to establish copyright infringement.

29 I accept that the reproduction of a particular arrangement of elements that are not themselves protectable can constitute copyright infringement if that arrangement is original. However, in this case the trial judge found that all of the alleged similarities between Sysview and Assess, including similarities in the arrangement of elements, were dictated by functional considerations or otherwise not protectable by copyright. Given this finding, it could hardly be concluded that Assess was a substantial reproduction of Sysview, even if the Sysview elements, by reasons of their collocation with other parts of Sysview, were part of a work which was entitled to copyright as a whole.

30 The foregoing relates to the particular similarities upon which Carolian relied. The trial judge also looked at the aggregate of what was alleged to be copied. First, with respect to the user interface (which includes the display screens and keyboard commands) he held, contrary to the submission of the defendants, that it was legally capable of being protected by copyright (pp. 27-31) but found that, on the evidence, no substantial part was "copyrightable" (pp. 44 and 46). Second, with respect to the source code part of the program, he was satisfied that portions of it were not copyrightable but, more importantly, that none of it (apart, unwittingly, from a de minimus 40 lines out of a total of 14,000 lines — pp. 29 and 31) was copied by Duncombe (pp. 39 and 46). On this point he made the following significant finding:

> After examining the source code for both Sysview and Assess, Sieler stated:
>
> > In the clearest possible terms, I want to state: I do not believe that the source for Sysview was altered into the source code for Assess.... Both Sysview and Assess show rigid, but different, coding disciplines.
>
> No independent expert has come forward to say that the Assess source code was copied from Sysview. Accordingly, the evidence of Sieler goes a long way in convincing me that Duncombe, in creating Assess did not copy from the Sysview source code (p. 39).

31 The foregoing, in my view, addresses one important aspect of Carolian's submission on this part of the appeal. I turn now to other aspects of the submission.

32 These aspects all relate, in various ways, to what Carolian submits is the trial judge's incorrect application of the term "original" in copyright law, specifically,

that the trial judge ignored the fact that Sysview met the standard under the Copyright Act of being original. This error, according to the submission, stems from the trial judge's reliance on U.S. authorities as opposed to Canadian and English authorities.

33 It is a fundamental feature of the copyright law in all three countries that it protects only original expression. It does not protect the idea underlying the expression. Frequent reference has been made to the following statement of Thorson P. in Moreau v. St. Vincent, [1950] Ex. C.R. 198 (Can. Ex. Ct.) at 203.

> It is... an elementary principle of copyright law that an author has no copyright in ideas but only in his expression of them. The law of copyright does not give him any monopoly in the use of the ideas with which he deals or any property in them, even if they are original. His copyright is confined to the literary work in which he expressed them. The ideas are public property, the literary work is his own. Everyone may freely adopt and use the ideas but no one may copy his literary work without his consent.

34 Although the idea/expression dichotomy is a common feature of copyright law in the three countries, it has been observed that it is applied with greater rigour in the United States, with the effect of enlarging the idea aspect of a work and, correspondingly, reducing the expression aspect. The result is a narrowing of the scope of copyright protection. The submitted wider protection afforded under the English/Canadian approach is based on some recognition of the skill and labour in the creation of the work:

> While Anglo-Canadian copyright law also places significant emphasis on the idea/ expression distinction, this principle has not been applied with the same rigour. Canadian and British courts have been willing to depart from this principle and grant copyright protection based on the skill and labour used in the creation of a work. This departure has created some doctrinal tension. In choosing to protect skill and labour, British and Canadian courts have accorded a certain degree of protection to ideas.

Michael F. Morgan, "Canadian Copyright and Computer Software: Back to the Future?" (1995), 12 C.I.P.R. 162 at 173-4.

35 Accepting that there may be this difference in the law, it has been recognized in Anglo-Canadian law that the non-protection of ideas embraces the view that there is no copyright in any arrangement, system, scheme or method for doing a particular thing or process. Several English and Canadian decisions in support of this statement are set forth in Sookman, Computer, Internet, and Electronic Commerce Law (1991-) p. 3-151 at footnote 644.117.

36 I refer also to the World Trade Organization ("WTO") Agreement on Trade Related Aspects of Intellectual Property Rights ("TRIPS") which was incorporated into Canadian law by S.C. 1994, c. 47, s. 8. It provides in Art. 9.2 that "[c]opyright protection shall extend to expressions and not to ideas, procedures, methods of operation or mathematical concepts as such." (Emphasis added.) I refer to the emphasized words as showing what, authoritatively, falls outside the

scope of protectable expression. Cf. Apotex Inc. v. Wellcome Foundation Ltd. (2000), 10 C.P.R. (4th) 65 (Fed. C.A.) at 84.

37 The foregoing discussion on the scope of protectable expression in "original" works relates to Carolian's objection to what it submits was the trial judge's application of the U.S. doctrine of "merger" and the "abstraction — filtration — comparison" method of determining the protectable expression in the course of determining whether there has been a substantial reproduction. I shall return to these matters. I turn now to another objection, of a different order, which Carolian has raised with respect to the meaning the trial judge gave to "original" in copyright law.

38 Carolian objected to the following statement in the trial judge's reasons:

> In my view, Sysview, as rewritten and improved by Duncombe, is not the inspired, elusive solution to some unrelenting, intractable problem relating to the performance monitoring of a HP3000 computer (p. 26).

39 The trial judge made this statement during his consideration of Carolian's claim based on breach of a fiduciary obligation by Duncombe, which is no longer in issue in this proceeding, and not in a copyright law part of the case. With respect to the latter, he stated the law correctly:

> Perhaps the next most fundamental principle is that to give rise to copyright, the work must be original, that is to say, it must not have been copied by the author from another work, whether that other work was protected by copyright or was in the public domain and free for the taking (p. 32).

> . . .

> Copyright exists in original literary works. There is no copyright in what the author has copied from something already in the public domain or from the work in which another holds the copyright (p. 41).

These statements are in accord with the leading authority, University of London Press v. University Tutorial Press Ltd., [1916] 2 Ch. 601 (Eng. Ch. Div.) at 608.

40 Carolian also raised a procedural issue relating to the originality of Sysview. Carolian submitted that the trial judge misplaced the legal burden of proof relating to the existence of copyright. The Copyright Act, s. 34.1(1)(a) provides that "Copyright shall be presumed, unless the contrary is proved." There are passages of some generality in the trial judge's reasons which misstate the law on this issue. For example: "For Carolian to succeed on its copyright infringement claim, it must, of course, first establish it has copyright which subsists in Sysview or some material portion of it" (p. 27).

41 It is clear, however, that when the trial judge dealt with the issues on which the case turned, relating to copyright protectability in the parts of Sysview which Carolian alleged were copied, he came to a determinate conclusion that Sysview had no protection:

> In my view, Sieler's evidence in regard to each of the examples of alleged copying I have just reviewed, while relevant to the issue of copying, establishes if accepted (and I accept it) that those portions of Sysview's interface referred to in those examples were not copyrightable ... At the same time, Sieler has convinced me that for many of the reasons that parts of the user interface are not copyrightable, for those same reasons portions of the source code are not copyrightable. Little will be accomplished by identifying those portions of the Sysview source code that are not copyrightable since I have concluded that in any event none of it was copied by Duncombe (p. 46).

This shows that the trial judge's findings did not flow from any error in the application of the proper burden of proof.

42 I return to the substantive application of the requirement of originality. As I have indicated, the appellant submitted that the trial judge, in applying U.S. authorities, erred in applying the doctrine of merger and the "abstraction — filtration — comparison" method of determining whether certain portions of a work are entitled to copyright protection. Both these issues relate to the idea/expression dichotomy which I have earlier discussed.

43 The trial judge in his reasons (at pp. 57-65) referred extensively to Computer Associates International Inc. v. Altai Inc., 23 U.S.P.Q.2d 1241 (U.S. 2nd Cir. N.Y. 1992) which discussed and applied the "abstraction — filtration — comparison" method. However, following this, he said at (p. 37) "[w]hether a Canadian court should adopt the abstraction — filtration — comparison method in deciding an action for copyright infringement or some other similar method" it was clear that "some method must be found to weed out or remove from copyright protection those portions which, for the various reasons already mentioned, cannot be protected by copyright". This indicates that the trial judge did not necessarily apply the abstraction — filtration — comparison method, assuming it, for the moment, to be "wrong." Further, I see nothing wrong with his general "weeding-out" observation.

44 Before referring to the trial judge's analysis of the evidence relating to the parts of Assess which Carolian alleged were similar to parts of Sysview, I will say something more on " the law" relating to the abstraction — filtration — comparison method, which is described in some detail in the trial judge's reasons at pages 33-37. As I have said, it is a method of determining whether a part of a work is entitled to copyright protection in the process of determining whether a defendant has substantially reproduced a plaintiff's work.

45 In John Richardson Computers Ltd. v. Flanders, [1993] F.S.R. 497 (Eng. Ch. Div.) Ferris J. generally approved the "abstraction — filtration — comparison method." He said at p. 392:

> But at the stage at which the substantiality of any copying falls to be assessed in an English case the question which has to be answered, in relation to the originality of the plaintiff's program and the separation of an idea from its expression, is essentially the same question as the United States court was addressing in Computer Associates. In my judgment it would be right to adopt a similar approach in England.

46 The method did not find quite the same favour in the subsequent English decision of IBCOS Computers Ltd. v. Barclays Mercantile Highland Finance Ltd., [1994] F.S.R. 275 (Eng. Ch. Div.) when Jacob J. said, after referring to John Richardson Computers Ltd., at p. 302:

> For myself I do not find the route of going via United States case law particularly helpful. As I have said, United Kingdom copyright cannot prevent the copying of a mere general idea but can protect the copying of a detailed "idea." It is a question of degree where a good guide is the notion of overborrowing of the skill, labour and judgment which went into the copyright work.

47 It can be seen from the foregoing that there are differences of view on the method or process to be followed in performing a substantial reproduction analysis. I do not think that a hard-edged question of law is necessarily involved. I shall return to this after I have addressed the question of "merger".

. . .

53 I have set forth and, to some extent, dealt with Carolian's submissions relating to the trial judge's application of U.S. law. I deal now with the trial judge's specific reasons for concluding that Assess was not a substantial reproduction of Sysview.

54 The trial judge addressed, at pp. 41-46, the parts of Sysview which Carolian alleged were copied in Assess. As part of this analysis he was obliged to consider the defendants' evidence that these parts were not entitled to copyright protection and, in fact, had not been copied. I say at the outset that his rather detailed canvass of the points of alleged similarities between Sysview and Assess shows that the source of similarities was not Sysview but, rather, other sources. Many were dictated by Hewlett Packard's operating system or reflected common programming practices. They were not the original expression of Sysview.

55 The following is an outline of the trial judge's canvass:

> (a) The fact that some of the "names" of items on which the measurement interface will report were the same in Sysview and Assess was not significant because they were "the obvious or logical or customary words to use" (pp. 41- 42).

> (b) A number of programming problems may only be solved in one or two ways, accounting for similarities between Sysview and Assess. For example, the data respecting how to determine the processor time (CPU) used by a process is kept in only one location and there is only one basic approach to retrieving it (p. 42).

> (c) Similar lines of source code in Sysview and Assess are common throughout the HP3000 community (p. 42).

> (d) With respect to the method of terminal input/output (use of centralized routines), because all well-written programs have centralized terminal input/output, Assess would be expected to have this (p. 42).

> (e) Respecting the technique used to log program information and determine file names, the predominant means of obtaining process information in both Sysview and Assess is similar to that found in SOO, an early contributed library program (pp. 42-43).

(f) With respect to similarities in the technique to gather information about the system, the predominant means of logging information system information in both Sysview and Assess is the Measurement Interface, documented by Hewlett Packard. It is not proprietary to Sysview (p. 43).

(g) Respecting similarities in screen layouts and similar information, many of the displays are similar to SOO and the similarity of the information is accounted for because it comes from the same source, the Measurement Interface. Further, other performance monitors, OPT and Probe, would produce similar information (p. 43).

(h) Small chunks of code in Sysview and Assess are very similar but are also similar to publicly available code (p. 43).

(i) Much of the similar design structures come from the design of the Measurement Interface and some of the design of both programs is similar to the functions of the OPT programs (p. 43).

(j) The common screen handling approach is the same as that used by OPT (pp. 43-44).

(k) Respecting the similarities in the screen displays, much of this is accounted for by the Hewlett Packard manual and the order provided for by the HP Measurement Interface — and the content is similar to that in SOO, OPT or other previously existing monitor tools (p. 44).

(l) Similarities in keyboard commands are accounted for by being generic to users of HP 3000 computers, by sharing an approach used by OPT and many spreadsheets which existed before either Sysview or Assess, by being the logical command to accomplish a particular purpose, and by being the simplest for the user (p. 44).

(m) Other similarities in parts of the user interface are accounted for by both being similar to OPT and SOO or one or the other (pp. 44-46).

56 The foregoing is based on the evidence before the trial judge, particularly the expert evidence of Mr. Sieler, whose evidence the trial judge preferred to that of Carolian's expert witness. I do not think that the analysis shows any denial of copyright protection to ideas reflecting skill and labour on the part of Carolian which would attract protection under what is said to be the less rigorous English application of the idea/expression dichotomy.

57 I would not give effect to this ground of appeal.

---

3.   Perform in Public

(a)   What is a Performance?

In Canada, the owner of a copyright has the exclusive right to perform the work or any substantial part thereof in public. The term "performance" is defined as "any acoustic or visual representation of a work, performer's performance, sound recording or communication signal, including a representation made by means of any mechanical receiving instrument, radio set or television receiving set."[11] The right is based on, and designed to implement, Article 11 of the Berne Convention of 1886 as revised in Berlin in 1908. That Article stated that the Convention "shall apply to the public representation of dramatic or dramatico musical works, and to the public performance of musical works, whether such works be published or not."

Although the Act does not mention digital or other computer technology by name in the definition of the term "performance", the definition and the case law which have interpreted the term show an intent that this portion of the Act be interpreted broadly to cover new technologies and clearly support the conclusion that a digital transmission of a musical work or a digital representation of dramatic action in a dramatic work, whether through computers or otherwise, is capable of invoking the right of performance in public.

The definition of "performance" in the Act is a very broad one, particularly as it relates to acoustic representations of works.[12] It has been held that the word "any" applies to acoustic representations produced by any technical means.[13]

Canadian Cable Television Association v. Canada (Copyright Board)
(1993), 46 C.P.R. 3(d) 359 (Fed. C.A.)

Heald, Desjardins and Létourneau JJ.

Heard: December 7 — 10, 1992
Judgment: January 5, 1993

. . .

The judgment of the Court was delivered by **LETOURNEAU J.:** —

This is an appeal by the Canadian Cable TV Association (CCTA) from a decision of a judge of the Trial Division dismissing an application to prohibit the Copyright Board from taking further proceedings with respect to Tariff No. 17 proposed by the respondent societies PROCAN and CAPAC under s. 67 of the Copyright Act (R.S.C., c. C-30).

The Facts

The appellant is a corporation composed of some 619 cable television licensees and system operators in Canada. Its self-described role is to promote its members' interests and to reconcile those interests with the interests of cable

---

11 See section 2.
12 *Canadian Cable Television Assn. v. Canada (Copyright Board)* (1993), 46 C.P.R. (3d) 359 (Fed. C.A.).
13 *Canadian Cable Television Assn. v. Canada (Copyright Board)* (1993), 46 C.P.R. (3d) 359 (Fed. C.A.); *Chappell & Co. Ltd. v. Associated Radio Co. of Australia Ltd.*, [1925] V.L.R. 350 (Sup. Ct. Vict.).

television subscribers and the general public. It holds a distribution undertaking license.

The respondent Societies, the Performing Rights Organization of Canada Limited (PROCAN) and Composers, Authors and Publishers Association of Canada Limited (CAPAC), are performing rights societies currently in the process of merging. They own and administer the performance rights to a variety of musical works in Canada. The Societies grant licences for the performance of those works in Canada and collect and distribute royalties pursuant to statements of royalties certified by the Copyright Board.

Pursuant to statements of proposed tariffs filed by the respondent societies, the Copyright Board published proposed Tariff No. 17 in the Canada Gazette on September 30, 1989. Tariff No. 17 required a "transmitter" of "non-broadcast services to its subscribers" to pay a fee for "a licence to perform or to communicate by telecommunication" a work over which the Societies have the "power to grant a performing licence".

"Non-broadcast services" are those that do not originate from a regular television broadcasting station and include such speciality services as "Much Music" and "Arts and Entertainment". CCTA transmit these services to their subscribers via electrical signals over a closed circuit network. There are apparently 7 million subscribers to cable television in Canada; 97% of which are residential customers and 6.3 million of whom subscribe from CCTA members. The remainder are commercial subscribers such as rental and hotel units, hospitals, schools, restaurants and bars.

After the CCTA filed objections to the proposed tariff, the Copyright Board convened a pre-hearing conference on May 23, 1990. At the outset, the CCTA stated its belief that Tariff No. 17 was unenforceable against cable television systems because their transmissions do not involve any of the acts involved in s. 3 of the Copyright Act as the transmissions are not public performances of musical works nor a communication of same to the public. On this basis, CCTA indicated that it was preparing an application for a prohibition order. The Board responded that, in the absence of court decisions to the contrary, it intended to proceed. On June 14, 1990, the CCTA obtained an order of the Federal Court staying the Board from any consideration of Tariff No. 17 until final disposition of the matter. On January 16, 1991, the learned Trial Division judge finally dismissed the application for prohibition.

The Substantive Issues

This appeal raises three issues under s. 3 of the Copyright Act with respect to the appellant's transmission of musical works to its subscribers. This Court is called upon to determine whether the appellant CCTA communicates musical works to the public, whether it performs musical works in public and whether it authorizes the performance of such works. These are the alleged foundation for Tariff No. 17 which is the subject of this attack by way of prohibition.

. . .

Whether appellant CCTA performs musical works in public within the meaning of s. 3(1) of the Copyright Act

The appellant first submits that it does not perform musical works because it does not, as required by the definition of "performance" in s. 2 of the Act, broadcast an acoustic representation of a melody or harmony. Under the Act, performance means "any acoustic representation of a work or any visual representation of any dramatic action in a work, including a representation made by means of any mechanical instrument or by radio communication". What it transmits, appellant says, are electrical signals to individual subscribers' premises. Such signals are electro-magnetic waves which are completely distinct from acoustic or sound waves and cannot be heard at any time during their distribution to subscribers' premises. While the acoustic or sound waves are generated by compression of air or some other medium, electro-magnetic waves are generated by a change in an electric or magnetic field. In the words of the appellant, a cable system is simply a medium for the transmission of electrical signals to the subscribers' premises and their transmission of non-broadcast services by cable television systems to individual subscribers' premises is through a closed circuit network as opposed to being propagated through space by radio waves.

I do not think this whole case ought to depend on whether it is this kind or that kind of waves which are transmitted to the subscribers. The definition of "performance" in s. 2 speaks of any acoustic representation. It does not speak of acoustic waves as opposed to electro-magnetic waves or vice-versa. When a subscriber turns on the television set and listens to the music broadcasted or transmitted by the appellant, it is an acoustic representation of a melody that he or she gets: it is the very performance of a musical work as contemplated by the Act.

Furthermore, the definition of "performance" covers "any" acoustic representation. The fact that it goes on to add that it includes a representation made by means of any mechanical instrument or radio communication does not limit the generality of the word "any" and surely does not limit it to the type of radio communication defined by s. 35(1) of the Interpretation Act. The word "includes" is generally not limitative and is certainly not apt in this context to limit Parliament's intention to cover all kinds of acoustic representations. It is merely illustrative of the fact that it applies as well to acoustic representations by technological means. The words "by means of any mechanical instrument or radio communication" in the definition of performance are nothing more than mere surplusage for greater certainty. As is often the case, however, in legislative drafting, it creates more ambiguity than certainty, especially when the reasons for introducing such precision have long been forgotten. The words "radio communication" appear to have been introduced in 1931 to avoid endless litigation and to ensure that performance would extend to new technological means.

The appellant also contends that, should this Court find that its transmission amounts to a performance, such performance is not a public performance as 97% of all cable television subscribers in Canada are residential subscribers and the transmission is to the private homes of the various subscribers.

I would have thought on a mere common sense basis that when the Prime Minister of Canada addresses the nation, either from his home or his private office, and reaches the citizens in their homes by means of radio and television, he appears in public and performs in public. I would have been content to leave it at that had it not been for early conflicting decisions on this issue.

In the case of Canadian Admiral Corporation Ltd. v. Rediffusion, Inc., the Court held that radio or television broadcasts do not amount to performances in public when received in private homes. Cameron J. wrote:

> Counsel for the plaintiff, however, submits that even if one such "view" in the privacy of the owner's home does not constitute a performance in public, that in cases where a large number of people, each having a terminal unit in his home, performs the work by operating the terminal units, that such would constitute a performance in public. He says that from the point of view of the owner, a large number of such performances would constitute an interference with the owner's right of making copies of his work and might cause him to lose part of his potential market. I am unable to agree with that submission. I cannot see that even a large number of private performances, solely because of their numbers, can become public performances. The character of the individual audiences remains exactly the same; each is private and domestic, and therefore not "in public". Moreover, in telecasting the films, I think the plaintiff desired to have the telecasts seen by as many people as were within range and possessed the necessary receiving equipment in order that they might be informed of its product; so that I do not think that what was done by the defendant in so far as the private homes and apartments are concerned, interfered with his potential market in any way. It was stated and not denied that the films, including the commercial announcements of the plaintiff, were rediffused as a whole.

> I find, therefore, that the performances in the homes and apartments of the subscribers of the defendant company were not performances "in public".

With respect, I prefer and adopt the contrary views expressed by English, Indian and Australian authorities. They are consistent with our Act. They take a realistic view of the impact and effect of technological developments and they are consistent with the plain and usual meaning of the words "in public", that is to say openly, without concealment and to the knowledge of all. In Messager v. British Broadcasting Company Limited, an opera was played for a few friends in a private studio but was transmitted by wireless telephony to the general public. Called upon to decide whether this amounted to a public performance for the purpose of the English Copyright Act whose definition was analogous to ours, McCardie J. wrote:

> In my view, however, the defendants, in doing what they did, clearly gave a public performance. Instead of gathering the public into a vast assembly room, they set in motion certain ether waves knowing that millions of receiving instruments in houses and flats were tuned to the waves sent forth, and knowing and intending also that acoustic representation of the opera would thereby be given to an enormous number of listeners. If I did not hold this to be a public performance by the defendants I should fail to recognize the substance and reality of the matter and also the object and intent of the Copyright Act.

In Chappell Co. Ltd v. Associated Radio Co. of Australia Ltd, Cussen J. wrote for the Court:

> A performance, in our judgment, is no less public because the listeners are unable to communicate with one another or are not assembled within an enclosure or gathered together in some open stadium or park or other public place. Nor can a performance, in our judgment, be deemed private because each listener may be alone in the privacy of his home. Radio-broadcasting is intended and in fact does reach a very much larger number of the public at the moment of the rendition than any other medium of performance.

This is certainly even truer of a transmission by means of television. I am satisfied that the transmission of non-broadcast services by the appellant to its numerous subscribers, when it relates to musical works, is a performance in public within the meaning of s. 3(1) of the Copyright Act.

. . .

(b) What is a "Public"?

The Act does not confer any right upon copyright owners to perform a work in private. For a performance to be infringing, it must be "in public". There is no precise definition of the term "in public" in the Act. However, a substantial body of case law exists on the interpretation of the term. The word "public" is used in the Act in contradiction to the word "private". If the act is purely domestic or quasi domestic or private, or a matter of family and household concern only, it is not an act in public. The word "public" has been defined to mean "openly, without concealment and the knowledge of all".[14] It has also been interpreted to mean "in a place, situation, location, or state open to public view or access; openly, publicly; opposed to in private".[15]

Certain tests have been established by the courts to determine when a performance is "in public". A leading test in determining who is the public is to examine the character of the audience.[16] This inquiry asks whether or not the act complained of as an infringement would, if done by the copyright owner himself, have been an exercise by him of the statutory right conferred by the Act. The key question under this test is whether the audience in relation to the owner of the copyright may properly be described as the owner's public or part of his public. Another test is to determine whether the performance occurred as an adjunct to some commercial activity.[17]

---

[14] *Canadian Cable Television Assn. v. Canada (Copyright Board)* (1993), 46 C.P.R. (3d) 359 (Fed. C.A.).

[15] *Australasian Performing Right Assn. Ltd. v. Commonwealth Bank of Australia* (1992), 25 I.P.R. 157 (Aust. Fed. Ct.).

[16] *Jennings v. Stephens*, [1934] 1 Ch. 469 (C.A.).

[17] *Australasian Performing Right Assn. Ltd. v. Commonwealth Bank of Australia* (1992), 25 I.P.R. 157 (Aust. Fed. Ct.).

A performance takes place in public wherever the acoustic or visual rendering of the work takes place. The performance may be rendered perceptible in a private place and extend far beyond that area into areas that are public. For example, the original performance may be in a studio, which is generally private, and be transmitted in one or more ways to be received and acoustically or visually represented in a place which is in public. Examples of what have been held to be performances "in public" include: performances in social clubs frequented by members and guests, restaurants, hotel lobbies, dining rooms and lounges, places of employment such as factories or offices and public shops, as well as showing movies to guests of a hotel in the privacy of their rooms, broadcasting of musical works over radio, transmission of non-broadcast services over cable systems to private subscribers, and television broadcasts of a performance of music.

In assessing the applicability of the right to perform a work in public in these contexts, it should be noted that the Act contains a specifically enumerated right of communicating a work to the public by telecommunication.[18] Pursuant to section 2.3, the act of communicating a work to the public by telecommunication does not constitute the act of performing or delivering the work in public, nor does it constitute an authorization to do the act of performing or delivering the work in public. The Supreme Court of Canada recently ruled, in the *Entertainment Software Association* case below, that the communication right should be understood as a category of performance right.

Canadian Admiral Corp. Ltd. v. Rediffusion Inc., [1954] 14 Fox Pat. C. 114 (Can. Ex. Ct.)

Cameron J.

Judgment: May 21, 1954

Cameron J.:

1 This is an action for infringement of copyright, taken under the provisions of The Copyright Act, R.S.C. 1927, c. 32, as amended. In its Statement of Claim, the plaintiff also claimed an injunction and damages under the Unfair Competition Act, but at the opening of the trial these claims were dropped. By its Statement of Defence, the defendant in para. 22 alleged that for the reasons therein stated, the plaintiff had deprived itself of any right to relief in the action, but, at the trial, that paragraph, by consent, was struck out.

2 At the trial there was filed an agreement (ex. 5) in which, for the purposes of this action, the parties agreed on a substantial number of matters; there is little dispute as to the remaining facts.

---

18   Section 3(1)(f).

3 The plaintiff is a company incorporated under the Dominion Companies Act, having its principal place of business at the Township of Toronto, in Ontario. It is engaged in the manufacture of television receiving sets, some of which are sold by dealers throughout the Province of Quebec. For the purpose of advertising its wares, the plaintiff decided to sponsor the telecast of the football games to be played in the Autumn of 1952 by the Montreal Football Club Inc., which operates a rugby football team called "The Alouettes" in the Inter-Provincial Football Union.

4 Accordingly, the plaintiff entered into an agreement with that football club (which I shall hereafter refer to as 'The Alouettes') on August 19, 1952, (ex. 1) and thereby, for the consideration mentioned, it was agreed that the plaintiff should have (a) the exclusive right to live telecasts of the six football games to be played by the Alouettes in Montreal; and (b) an option to purchase the exclusive right to televise films in Montreal of the six games to be played by the Alouettes away from Montreal. The parties hereto have agreed that that agreement was duly executed and delivered by the parties thereto, that it was carried out according to its tenor, and that the option was taken up.

5 By an agreement dated August 27, 1952, between the Canadian Broadcasting Corporation and the plaintiff, the former for the consideration specified (a), agreed to furnish the personnel and all the facilities and equipment necessary to produce and telecast from Delorimier Stadium, Montreal over its television station CBFT Montreal the football games to be played by the Alouettes in Montreal during the 1952 season; (b) assigned and transferred to the plaintiff exclusively all of its right, title and interest in the copyright and any other property rights in the live telecast productions of the said games; and (c), agreed to supply the necessary facilities and the station time to telecast films provided by the plaintiff of the six games to be played by the Alouettes away from Montreal, such facilities to be available on the dates specified, namely, six days after the games were actually played. It was also agreed that the Broadcasting Corporation would not make available such telecast productions and film telecasts by direct wire to any other person, firm or corporation.

6 Dow Brewery Ltd. had acquired certain rights entitling it to make movie films of the league games to be played by the Alouettes away from Montreal in 1952. By an agreement dated September 11, 1952, (ex. 3) Dow transferred and assigned to the plaintiff exclusively, all its rights to televise over station CBFT or to distribute by wire service within the Province of Quebec, films or any part thereof of such games, such films, however, not to be televised by the plaintiff until the Friday following the dates when the games were played. The plaintiff was authorized to obtain from Dow's supplier one black-and-white copy of the film of each such game. By a supplementary agreement between the said parties dated October 17, 1952, (ex. 3) it was agreed that the rights granted to the plaintiff by the agreement of September 12 should include "the exclusive right to distribute and perform the television broadcasts of such films after receiving the same through the ether, by wire service or rediffusion."

7 The agreement between the plaintiff and the Broadcasting Corporation was duly carried out. The plaintiff sponsored the live telecast over station CBFT of the first four games played at Montreal. The plaintiff also obtained from Dow a cinematographic film of each of the first four games played by the Alouettes away from Montreal, furnished them to the Broadcasting Corporation, and telecasts thereof, without the assistance of a commentator, took place over station CBFT on the agreed dates. It is established that prior to the first of the four live telecasts and again prior to the first of the four film telecasts, the plaintiff, in writing, notified the defendant or its solicitors, of the rights which the plaintiff had acquired and forbade the defendant to rediffuse any of such telecasts. The defendant's solicitors, in each case, replied that their client could not agree that the relaying of the telecast programmes over their rediffusion circuits, in any way infringed the legal rights of the plaintiff.

8 By the agreement filed at the trial (ex. 5) it is admitted that the effect of the two agreements between the plaintiff and Dow Breweries was to vest in the plaintiff whatever copyright the latter had in the films of the games played by the Alouettes away from Montreal; that such cinematographic films were produced for valuable consideration by Briston Films Ltd. for Dow and were taken by employees of Briston Films Ltd.; and that the plaintiff by virtue of its agreement with Dow was entitled to and did obtain a black-and-white film of each of such games from Briston Films Ltd. to be used for telecast over station CBFT.

9 It is alleged that the defendant took each of the said telecasts off the ether and rediffused the same to its various subscribers and to its showroom and sales office at 1650 Berri Street, Montreal, and that thereby the defendant has infringed the copyright of the plaintiff in both the live and film telecasts. On October 24 these proceedings were commenced, the plaintiff claiming an injunction and damages, which by amendment at the trial, it fixed at $600.00.

10 On October 18, 1952, the plaintiff registered the telecast productions of the games played at Montreal and the cinematograph films reproducing the four games played out of Montreal in the Copyright office, all as unpublished artistic works; certified copies thereof are filed as ex. 4.

11 The defendant is a company incorporated under the Quebec Companies Act having its principal place of business at Montreal. It admits that its business consists in part in providing and maintaining equipment including an antenna in or near Montreal, which enables its subscribers to receive in private, by wire, in their homes and on their own and sole volition, and by wire only insofar as the defendant is concerned, telecast programmes emitted by the CBFT television transmitter. It alleges that its premises at 1650 Berri Street are used by it for private business purposes to demonstrate its services to potential subscribers, as is customary in all similar trades, and that for that purpose it there received the television programmes emitted by station CBFT. It denies that copyright subsists in any of the telecasts so sponsored by the plaintiff, and that if copyright did exist therein, no infringement resulted from the defendant's operations.

12 In the agreement filed (ex. 5) the defendant admitted that the four home games of the Alouettes were televised and that the films of the four out of town games were televised over station CBFT and that on each occasion the programmes were picked up from the ether by it and distributed by wire to its various subscribers and to its sales and showroom at Berri Street; that the said programmes were seen by members of the public on a terminal unit at the Berri Street room, except on four stated Sundays when the room was closed; and were also seen on terminal units in the homes of their subscribers, after having been picked up by the defendant's equipment and distributed by wire to such subscribers. It is also admitted that there were "over 100" such subscribers to the defendant's services.

. . .

55 As I have said, the plaintiff alleges that the defendant took its telecasts off the ether and "rediffused" the same to its subscribers and to its showrooms and sales office. It becomes necessary to describe in some detail just what the defendant does in this regard in order to understand what is meant by the process referred to as "rediffusion". I should note here that in addition to picking up the telecasts from Station CBFT, the defendant also initiates certain television programmes of its own, all of which are also transmitted through co-axial cables to the "terminal units" (that is the name given by the defendant to the receiving sets which are leased to its subscribers) in the homes of its subscribers.

56 Ex. 8 is a diagram of the defendant's studio setup. By means of an antenna which it provides and maintains, the defendant picks up from the ether the telecasts from Station CBFT which are then passed to a group of television receivers. These receivers are said to be a modification of the ordinary R.C.A. receivers, the modification enabling the video signal — which is the television picture information — to be transmitted through wires to the rest of the equipment. It then passes to a line clamp amplifier, the purpose of which is to clean up the signal within certain limits. The composite video signal is then passed to a selector switch bank and there it is possible to bring in other picture sources if desired. The output is then fed to a wired wireless transmitter which imposes the rediffusion signal on the outgoing co-axial cable, together with such other programmes as may have been added. The rediffusion signals are transmitted on a number of different frequencies (lower than those of the Station CBFT) so that they can be separated out again at the terminal unit. By means of the cable, the signals are conveyed to the subscribers' terminal units. These units include the same type of picture tube as is used in ordinary standard television receivers. There the process of amplification and detection, and the production of the image or picture are much the same as in the ordinary television receiver. The defendant supplies radio and television programmes to its subscribers by means of the equipment which I have described and leases to the subscribers a loudspeaker and a complete terminal unit "to give full Rediffusion service". Ex. 10 is a sample of the contract entered into with its subscribers.

57 The defendant says that in so rediffusing the telecasts of the plaintiff, there was no performance by them and that the only performance which took place

was the one by Station CBFT at the football stadium. They say that all that happened afterwards was merely an extension of the audience for that performance and a continuation of that performance. It follows, the defendants say, that the listeners saw the original performance put out by or on behalf of the plaintiff and that therefore nothing they did could constitute an infringement of the plaintiff's copyright.

58 Much the same submissions were advanced and rejected in the case of Performing Right Society, Ltd. v. Hammond's Bradford Brewery Co., [1934] 1 Ch. 121. That was a case under The Copyright Act, 1911 (England), involving a consideration of the terms of s. 35(1) defining "performance", which is identical to the definition of that word found in s. 2(q) of our Act, which is as follows:

> 2. In this Act, unless the context otherwise requires
>
> > (q) 'performance' means any acoustic representation of a work or any visual representation of any dramatic action in a work, including a representation made by means of any mechanical instrument or by radio communication;

59 The headnote in that case is as follows:

> On October 1, 1932, three songs of which the copyright was vested in the plaintiffs were performed with their consent at a cinema and the performance was broadcast by the British Broadcasting Corporation. By an agreement dated February 8, 1932, the plaintiffs had licensed the Corporation to broadcast songs from time to time in their repertoire, but the licence authorized and covered 'the audition or reception of copyright musical works by means of broadcasting for domestic and private use only'. By means of a receiving set and loud-speaker at a hotel belonging to the defendants the songs were made audible to visitors to the hotel. It was admitted that if what the defendants had done amounted to a performance, it was a performance to the public.
>
> Held, by the Court of Appeal (affirming the decision of Maugham J.), that by rendering the songs audible through their receiving set, the defendants had given or authorized a 'performance' within s. 35, subs. 1, of the Copyright Act, 1911; that, as the licence to the Corporation did not authorize the reception of the songs by means of broadcasting otherwise than for domestic and private use, the performance, being admittedly a performance to the public, was given without the plaintiffs' consent; and therefore that the performance constituted an infringement of the plaintiffs' copyright.

60 Lord Hanworth M.R., after referring to the applicable sections of the Act, said at p. 133:

> Bearing those sections in mind, what did the defendants do? By the use of what I have called an installation, they made this performance at Hammersmith audible to a larger number of persons than would otherwise have heard it and to persons outside the domestic circle of the George Hotel. It was at the instance of the management that steps were taken to provide this entertainment. It appears to me that that act on the part of the management constituted on their part either a performance or the authorization of a performance.

Maugham J. said in his judgment that the process employed was 'a reproduction and is not similar to the mere step of making distant sounds audible by some magnifying device. The sounds are produced by an instrument under the direct control of the hotel proprietor'; and it seems to me, as it did to Maugham J., that the act done at the volition of the hotel proprietor constituted an invasion of the rights of performance, or authorization of performance, which are granted to the owner of a copyright by s. 1, and is by virtue of s. 2 to be deemed to be an infringement unless consent can be proved. That it was a performance seems clear, because it was an acoustic representation of a work.

61 In the same case, Lawrence L.J. said at p. 137:

I find it impossible to escape from the conclusion that the owner of a receiving set who puts it into operation causes an acoustic representation of a musical work which is being broadcast to be given at the place where the receiving set is installed and is therefore himself performing or authorising the performance of the musical work within the meaning of the Copyright Act, 1911.

62 On the same page Romer L.J., as he then was, said:

In my opinion a man performs a musical composition when he causes it to be heard.

63 That decision was referred to and followed in Performing Right Society v. Gillette Industries Ltd., [1943] 1 A.E.R. 228 and 413; and in Canada in the case of Canadian Performing Right Society v. Ford Hotel, [1935] 2 D.L.R. 391.

64 The cases cited had to do with acoustic representations, but the principles there laid down on this point are in my opinion of equal application to a visual representation which is also included in the definition of "performance". I have no hesitation, therefore, in reaching the conclusion that the rediffusion of the film telecasts in question by the defendant in the manner which I have described constituted a "performance" of the plaintiff's work.

65 That, however, does not conclude the matter; mere performance is not enough; in order to find that the defendant infringed the plaintiff's right, I must find that the performance was "in public". The Act does not define "in public" and it would be undesirable for me to attempt to do so except to state that I regard it as the antithesis of "in private". Each case must depend on its own particular facts.

66 I have read the cases referred to by counsel and it seems to me that the test to be applied is, "What is the character of the audience?

67 In Duck v. Bates (1884), 13 Q.B.D. 843, a dramatic representation was given to the nurses and attendants of Guy's Hospital, together with the medical men and students and some of their families. Brett M.R. and Bowen L.J. held that the performance was a domestic or quasi-domestic and not a public performance, possibly because the audience was composed in the main of nurses who lived together at the hospital. Bowen, L.J. said in the course of his judgment:

Some domestic or quasi-domestic entertainments may not come within the Act. Suppose a club of persons united for the purposes of good fellowship gave a dramatic entertainment to its members; I do not say that the entertainment will necessarily fall within the prohibition of the statute.

68 In Harms Inc. and Chappel & Co. v. Martan's Club, [1927] 1 Ch. 526, there was a performance at the Embassy Club at which club members and some guests were present. It was held that the plaintiff's copyright was infringed. In that case Sargant L.J. said at p. 537:

> There has been an invitation to the members of the public capable of becoming members of the Club upon the terms of getting in return for their subscription the performance of music, so that you do really get an invitation to the public, and an invitation to the public to listen at a price or at a payment, though the payment is an annual one. Beyond that, there is, of course this, that the members of the public who have become members of the Club by passing through the not very severe test which is imposed, have also the privilege of bringing in other members of the public upon whom no test is imposed, who happen to be their friends and are invited on any particular evening.

69 In Performing Right Society Ltd. v. Hawthorn's Hotel (Bournemouth) Ltd., [1933] 1 Ch. 856, an orchestral trio played in the lounge of the defendant's hotel, there being present several guests of the hotel, among others. Bennett J. held that the performance by the hotel orchestra was a performance "in public" because it was open to any members of the public who cared to be guests of the hotel either by sleeping or dining there.

70 Again, the question was fully considered by the Court of Appeal in Jennings v. Stephens, [1936] 1 All E.R. 409, which reversed Crossman J., [1935] 1 Ch. 703. Romer L.J. in discussing the general question as to whether a performance was "in public", said at p. 416 ff.:

> No one, for instance, can doubt that the concerts given at the Albert Hall are, in general, performances 'in public,' or that music provided by a man for the entertainment of his guests after dinner or at a reception is performed 'in private'; and I think that the meaning of the two phrases can best be ascertained by considering what is the essential difference between the two performances. The difference in material for the present purpose lies, it seems to me, in this. In the latter case the entertainment forms part of the domestic or home life of the person who provides it, and none the less because of the presence of his guests. They are for the time being members of his home circle. In the former case, however, the entertainment is in no sense part of the domestic or home life of the members of the audience. It forms part of what may be called in contradistinction their non-domestic or outside life. In the one case the audience are present in their capacity as members of the particular home circle. In the other they are present in their capacity as members of the music-loving section of the public. The home circle may, of course, in some cases be a large one. The section of the public forming the audience may in some cases be a small one. But this can make no difference, though it may sometimes be difficult to decide whether a particular collection of persons can properly be regarded as constituting a domestic circle. In Duck v. Bates (1884), 13 Q.B.D. 843, the Court of Appeal seem to have regarded the nurses and medical staff of Guys' Hospital as forming a domestic circle, and a dramatic entertainment given before them and their guests as a private performance. Bennett J., on the other hand, in Performing Right Society v. Hawthorn's Hotel, [1933] 1 Ch. 855, treated,

and in my opinion rightly treated, a musical entertainment given to the residents in an hotel, to which any respectable member of the public could obtain admission merely by payment, as a performance in public. Nor, with all deference to those who think otherwise, can I agree that it makes any difference whether the actual performers are paid for their services or give them gratuitously, or whether the performers are strangers or members of the domestic circle. The performers at what is unquestionably a private performance are frequently paid. The performers at what is unquestionably a public performance frequently give their services for nothing. Nor can an entertainment that is private when given by the members of the home circle cease to be private when given by strangers.

I also find some difficulty in seeing why it is material to consider the nature of and the place where the entertainment is given. A private entertainment may be given in a public room. A public entertainment may be given in a private house. The question whether an entertainment is given in public or in private depends, in my opinion, solely upon the character of the audience. Suppose, for instance, that a number of people who are interested in the drama, band themselves together in a society or club for the purpose of providing by means of their subscriptions the performance before themselves from time to time of dramatic works. This would be something entirely outside their domestic lives, and they would, in my opinion, attend the performances merely as members of the public, and none the less because the section of the public which they represent may be limited by election, the social status of the members, or their capacity to pay a large subscription. I should regard any dramatic performance given before that society as a performance in public....

The teaching staff and pupils of a boarding school might, on the other hand, properly be regarded during the school term as forming a domestic circle, and a dramatic performance given before them might well be held to be a private performance, even though the parents or other relations of the pupils were present as guests. I cannot, indeed, think that a performance which would otherwise have been a performance in private could be turned into a performance in public by the mere presence of some guests. Guests were present at the entertainment that was the subject matter of the inquiry in Duck v. Bates (supra), to which I have already referred — a case which it must be confessed was somewhat near the line. It is easy to imagine other cases in which it is difficult to say whether they fall on the private or public side of the line. But the present case seems to me quite plainly to fall upon the public side.

71 The matter was again considered in Performing Right Society, Ltd. v. Gillette Industries, Ltd., [1943] 1 All E.R. 228 and 413. There the defendants installed in their factory a number of loudspeakers from which broadcast music was heard in various departments of the factory and about six hundred workers heard the broadcast, but all strangers were excluded from the factory. At the trial, Bennett J. pointed out the difficulty of obtaining from the authorities any real principle which could be said to govern every case and to lay down any general rule for defining what is meant by performance in public. He distinguished the case from Duck v. Bates (supra), holding that the performance of the music by the defendant could not be said to be for domestic purposes, and followed Jennings v. Stephens (supra). On appeal, Lord Greene M.R. affirmed the judgment of Bennett J., basing his judgment on the authority of the Court of

Appeal in Jennings v. Stephens, citing with approval the words of Lord Wright M.R. that, "The true criterion seems to be the character of the audience". In that case, the Master of the Rolls stated:

> The owner of the copyright is entitled to be paid for the use of his property unless and until the Legislature otherwise determines, and he is entitled to be paid for it even if the use that is made of it is a use which concerns the public welfare to a very considerable extent.... When the Legislature under The Copyright Act conferred upon the owner of copyright a monopoly, it no doubt intended that the monopoly should be a real and not an illusory right of property, and it is, therefore, in my opinion, important to consider whether a particular performance, the character of which is in question, is of a kind calculated to whittle down that monopoly to any substantial extent.

72 I think it may be said with some truth that the more recent cases have indicated a tendency to extend somewhat the protection afforded to the owners of copyright, since the case of Duck v. Bates. In none of these cases, however, can I find a suggestion that a performance in a private home where the performance is given, heard or seen by only members of the immediate household, could be considered as a performance in public.

73 As to the character of the audience in homes and apartments to which the telecasts of the live films were "rediffused" by the defendant, there is no evidence whatever except that they were seen by the defendant's subscribers, presumably only the householders. The character of the audience was therefore a purely domestic one and the performance in each case was not a performance in public. Counsel for the plaintiff, however, submits that even if one such "view" in the privacy of the owner's home does not constitute a performance in public, that in cases where a large number of people, each having a terminal unit in his home, performs the work by operating the terminal units, that such would constitute a performance in public. He says that from the point of view of the owner, a large number of such performances would constitute an interference with the owner's right of making copies of his work and might cause him to lose part of his potential market. I am unable to agree with that submission. I cannot see that even a large number of private performances, solely because of their numbers, can become public performances. The character of the individual audiences remains exactly the same; each is private and domestic, and therefore not "in public." Moreover, in telecasting the films, I think the plaintiff desired to have the telecasts seen by as many people as were within range and possessed the necessary receiving equipment in order that they might be informed of its product; so that I do not think that what was done by the defendant in so far as the private homes and apartments are concerned, interfered with his potential market in any way. It was stated and not denied that the films, including the commercial announcements of the plaintiff, were rediffused as a whole.

74 I find, therefore, that the performances in the homes and apartments of the subscribers of the defendant company were not performances "in public".

75 The situation, however, is quite different in regard to the defendant's Berri Street showroom. The evidence is that the showroom was operated by

the defendant for the purpose of demonstrating and selling its services which included the leasing of its terminal units. The showroom was open to the public, and members of the public there on various occasions saw the film telecasts of the plaintiff broadcast on Station CBFT. There was nothing there of a domestic or quasi-domestic nature and in my opinion it was a performance in public and an infringement of the copyright of the plaintiff in the cinematograph films. It was suggested by counsel for the defendant that a finding to that effect might seriously interfere with the operations of store salesmen of any type of television receiving sets, and that may be so. If, however, the plaintiff has established its right to copyright, it is entitled to the protection afforded by the Act for such right and to restrain the defendant from infringing that right no matter what the consequences to others might be.

76 My conclusion on this point, therefore, as regards the showing of the film telecasts by the defendant in its Berri Street showroom, is that there was an infringement by the defendant of the plaintiff's copyright in such cinematograph films.

Canadian Cable Television Assn. v. Canada (Copyright Board)

(1993), 46 C.P.R. (3d) 359 (Fed. C.A.)

Cameron J.:

1 This is an action for infringement of copyright, taken under the provisions of The Copyright Act, R.S.C. 1927, c. 32, as amended. In its Statement of Claim, the plaintiff also claimed an injunction and damages under the Unfair Competition Act, but at the opening of the trial these claims were dropped. By its Statement of Defence, the defendant in para. 22 alleged that for the reasons therein stated, the plaintiff had deprived itself of any right to relief in the action, but, at the trial, that paragraph, by consent, was struck out.

2 At the trial there was filed an agreement (ex. 5) in which, for the purposes of this action, the parties agreed on a substantial number of matters; there is little dispute as to the remaining facts.

3 The plaintiff is a company incorporated under the Dominion Companies Act, having its principal place of business at the Township of Toronto, in Ontario. It is engaged in the manufacture of television receiving sets, some of which are sold by dealers throughout the Province of Quebec. For the purpose of advertising its wares, the plaintiff decided to sponsor the telecast of the football games to be played in the Autumn of 1952 by the Montreal Football Club Inc., which operates a rugby football team called "The Alouettes" in the Inter-Provincial Football Union.

4 Accordingly, the plaintiff entered into an agreement with that football club (which I shall hereafter refer to as 'The Alouettes') on August 19, 1952, (ex. 1) and thereby, for the consideration mentioned, it was agreed that the plaintiff should have (a) the exclusive right to live telecasts of the six football games

to be played by the Alouettes in Montreal; and (b) an option to purchase the exclusive right to televise films in Montreal of the six games to be played by the Alouettes away from Montreal. The parties hereto have agreed that that agreement was duly executed and delivered by the parties thereto, that it was carried out according to its tenor, and that the option was taken up.

5 By an agreement dated August 27, 1952, between the Canadian Broadcasting Corporation and the plaintiff, the former for the consideration specified (a), agreed to furnish the personnel and all the facilities and equipment necessary to produce and telecast from Delorimier Stadium, Montreal over its television station CBFT Montreal the football games to be played by the Alouettes in Montreal during the 1952 season; (b) assigned and transferred to the plaintiff exclusively all of its right, title and interest in the copyright and any other property rights in the live telecast productions of the said games; and (c), agreed to supply the necessary facilities and the station time to telecast films provided by the plaintiff of the six games to be played by the Alouettes away from Montreal, such facilities to be available on the dates specified, namely, six days after the games were actually played. It was also agreed that the Broadcasting Corporation would not make available such telecast productions and film telecasts by direct wire to any other person, firm or corporation.

6 Dow Brewery Ltd. had acquired certain rights entitling it to make movie films of the league games to be played by the Alouettes away from Montreal in 1952. By an agreement dated September 11, 1952, (ex. 3) Dow transferred and assigned to the plaintiff exclusively, all its rights to televise over station CBFT or to distribute by wire service within the Province of Quebec, films or any part thereof of such games, such films, however, not to be televised by the plaintiff until the Friday following the dates when the games were played. The plaintiff was authorized to obtain from Dow's supplier one black-and-white copy of the film of each such game. By a supplementary agreement between the said parties dated October 17, 1952, (ex. 3) it was agreed that the rights granted to the plaintiff by the agreement of September 12 should include "the exclusive right to distribute and perform the television broadcasts of such films after receiving the same through the ether, by wire service or rediffusion."

7 The agreement between the plaintiff and the Broadcasting Corporation was duly carried out. The plaintiff sponsored the live telecast over station CBFT of the first four games played at Montreal. The plaintiff also obtained from Dow a cinematographic film of each of the first four games played by the Alouettes away from Montreal, furnished them to the Broadcasting Corporation, and telecasts thereof, without the assistance of a commentator, took place over station CBFT on the agreed dates. It is established that prior to the first of the four live telecasts and again prior to the first of the four film telecasts, the plaintiff, in writing, notified the defendant or its solicitors, of the rights which the plaintiff had acquired and forbade the defendant to rediffuse any of such telecasts. The defendant's solicitors, in each case, replied that their client could not agree that the relaying of the telecast programmes over their rediffusion circuits, in any way infringed the legal rights of the plaintiff.

8 By the agreement filed at the trial (ex. 5) it is admitted that the effect of the two agreements between the plaintiff and Dow Breweries was to vest in the plaintiff whatever copyright the latter had in the films of the games played by the Alouettes away from Montreal; that such cinematographic films were produced for valuable consideration by Briston Films Ltd. for Dow and were taken by employees of Briston Films Ltd.; and that the plaintiff by virtue of its agreement with Dow was entitled to and did obtain a black-and-white film of each of such games from Briston Films Ltd. to be used for telecast over station CBFT.

9 It is alleged that the defendant took each of the said telecasts off the ether and rediffused the same to its various subscribers and to its showroom and sales office at 1650 Berri Street, Montreal, and that thereby the defendant has infringed the copyright of the plaintiff in both the live and film telecasts. On October 24 these proceedings were commenced, the plaintiff claiming an injunction and damages, which by amendment at the trial, it fixed at $600.00.

10 On October 18, 1952, the plaintiff registered the telecast productions of the games played at Montreal and the cinematograph films reproducing the four games played out of Montreal in the Copyright office, all as unpublished artistic works; certified copies thereof are filed as ex. 4.

11 The defendant is a company incorporated under the Quebec Companies Act having its principal place of business at Montreal. It admits that its business consists in part in providing and maintaining equipment including an antenna in or near Montreal, which enables its subscribers to receive in private, by wire, in their homes and on their own and sole volition, and by wire only insofar as the defendant is concerned, telecast programmes emitted by the CBFT television transmitter. It alleges that its premises at 1650 Berri Street are used by it for private business purposes to demonstrate its services to potential subscribers, as is customary in all similar trades, and that for that purpose it there received the television programmes emitted by station CBFT. It denies that copyright subsists in any of the telecasts so sponsored by the plaintiff, and that if copyright did exist therein, no infringement resulted from the defendant's operations.

12 In the agreement filed (ex. 5) the defendant admitted that the four home games of the Alouettes were televised and that the films of the four out of town games were televised over station CBFT and that on each occasion the programmes were picked up from the ether by it and distributed by wire to its various subscribers and to its sales and showroom at Berri Street; that the said programmes were seen by members of the public on a terminal unit at the Berri Street room, except on four stated Sundays when the room was closed; and were also seen on terminal units in the homes of their subscribers, after having been picked up by the defendant's equipment and distributed by wire to such subscribers. It is also admitted that there were "over 100" such subscribers to the defendant's services.

. . .

55 As I have said, the plaintiff alleges that the defendant took its telecasts off the ether and "rediffused" the same to its subscribers and to its showrooms and

sales office. It becomes necessary to describe in some detail just what the defendant does in this regard in order to understand what is meant by the process referred to as "rediffusion". I should note here that in addition to picking up the telecasts from Station CBFT, the defendant also initiates certain television programmes of its own, all of which are also transmitted through co-axial cables to the "terminal units" (that is the name given by the defendant to the receiving sets which are leased to its subscribers) in the homes of its subscribers.

56 Ex. 8 is a diagram of the defendant's studio setup. By means of an antenna which it provides and maintains, the defendant picks up from the ether the telecasts from Station CBFT which are then passed to a group of television receivers. These receivers are said to be a modification of the ordinary R.C.A. receivers, the modification enabling the video signal — which is the television picture information — to be transmitted through wires to the rest of the equipment. It then passes to a line clamp amplifier, the purpose of which is to clean up the signal within certain limits. The composite video signal is then passed to a selector switch bank and there it is possible to bring in other picture sources if desired. The output is then fed to a wired wireless transmitter which imposes the rediffusion signal on the outgoing co-axial cable, together with such other programmes as may have been added. The rediffusion signals are transmitted on a number of different frequencies (lower than those of the Station CBFT) so that they can be separated out again at the terminal unit. By means of the cable, the signals are conveyed to the subscribers' terminal units. These units include the same type of picture tube as is used in ordinary standard television receivers. There the process of amplification and detection, and the production of the image or picture are much the same as in the ordinary television receiver. The defendant supplies radio and television programmes to its subscribers by means of the equipment which I have described and leases to the subscribers a loudspeaker and a complete terminal unit "to give full Rediffusion service". Ex. 10 is a sample of the contract entered into with its subscribers.

57 The defendant says that in so rediffusing the telecasts of the plaintiff, there was no performance by them and that the only performance which took place was the one by Station CBFT at the football stadium. They say that all that happened afterwards was merely an extension of the audience for that performance and a continuation of that performance. It follows, the defendants say, that the listeners saw the original performance put out by or on behalf of the plaintiff and that therefore nothing they did could constitute an infringement of the plaintiff's copyright.

58 Much the same submissions were advanced and rejected in the case of Performing Right Society, Ltd. v. Hammond's Bradford Brewery Co., [1934] 1 Ch. 121. That was a case under The Copyright Act, 1911 (England), involving a consideration of the terms of s. 35(1) defining "performance", which is identical to the definition of that word found in s. 2(q) of our Act, which is as follows:

   2. In this Act, unless the context otherwise requires

(q) 'performance' means any acoustic representation of a work or any visual representation of any dramatic action in a work, including a representation made by means of any mechanical instrument or by radio communication;

59 The headnote in that case is as follows:

On October 1, 1932, three songs of which the copyright was vested in the plaintiffs were performed with their consent at a cinema and the performance was broadcast by the British Broadcasting Corporation. By an agreement dated February 8, 1932, the plaintiffs had licensed the Corporation to broadcast songs from time to time in their repertoire, but the licence authorized and covered 'the audition or reception of copyright musical works by means of broadcasting for domestic and private use only'. By means of a receiving set and loud-speaker at a hotel belonging to the defendants the songs were made audible to visitors to the hotel. It was admitted that if what the defendants had done amounted to a performance, it was a performance to the public.

Held, by the Court of Appeal (affirming the decision of Maugham J.), that by rendering the songs audible through their receiving set, the defendants had given or authorized a 'performance' within s. 35, subs. 1, of the Copyright Act, 1911; that, as the licence to the Corporation did not authorize the reception of the songs by means of broadcasting otherwise than for domestic and private use, the performance, being admittedly a performance to the public, was given without the plaintiffs' consent; and therefore that the performance constituted an infringement of the plaintiffs' copyright.

60 Lord Hanworth M.R., after referring to the applicable sections of the Act, said at p. 133:

Bearing those sections in mind, what did the defendants do? By the use of what I have called an installation, they made this performance at Hammersmith audible to a larger number of persons than would otherwise have heard it and to persons outside the domestic circle of the George Hotel. It was at the instance of the management that steps were taken to provide this entertainment. It appears to me that that act on the part of the management constituted on their part either a performance or the authorization of a performance.

Maugham J. said in his judgment that the process employed was 'a reproduction and is not similar to the mere step of making distant sounds audible by some magnifying device. The sounds are produced by an instrument under the direct control of the hotel proprietor'; and it seems to me, as it did to Maugham J., that the act done at the volition of the hotel proprietor constituted an invasion of the rights of performance, or authorization of performance, which are granted to the owner of a copyright by s. 1, and is by virtue of s. 2 to be deemed to be an infringement unless consent can be proved. That it was a performance seems clear, because it was an acoustic representation of a work.

61 In the same case, Lawrence L.J. said at p. 137:

I find it impossible to escape from the conclusion that the owner of a receiving set who puts it into operation causes an acoustic representation of a musical work which is being broadcast to be given at the place where the receiving set is installed and is therefore himself performing or authorising the performance of the musical work within the meaning of the Copyright Act, 1911.

62 On the same page Romer L.J., as he then was, said:

> In my opinion a man performs a musical composition when he causes it to be heard.

63 That decision was referred to and followed in Performing Right Society v. Gillette Industries Ltd., [1943] 1 A.E.R. 228 and 413; and in Canada in the case of Canadian Performing Right Society v. Ford Hotel, [1935] 2 D.L.R. 391.

64 The cases cited had to do with acoustic representations, but the principles there laid down on this point are in my opinion of equal application to a visual representation which is also included in the definition of "performance". I have no hesitation, therefore, in reaching the conclusion that the rediffusion of the film telecasts in question by the defendant in the manner which I have described constituted a "performance" of the plaintiff's work.

65 That, however, does not conclude the matter; mere performance is not enough; in order to find that the defendant infringed the plaintiff's right, I must find that the performance was "in public". The Act does not define "in public" and it would be undesirable for me to attempt to do so except to state that I regard it as the antithesis of "in private". Each case must depend on its own particular facts.

66 I have read the cases referred to by counsel and it seems to me that the test to be applied is, "What is the character of the audience?

67 In Duck v. Bates (1884), 13 Q.B.D. 843, a dramatic representation was given to the nurses and attendants of Guy's Hospital, together with the medical men and students and some of their families. Brett M.R. and Bowen L.J. held that the performance was a domestic or quasi-domestic and not a public performance, possibly because the audience was composed in the main of nurses who lived together at the hospital. Bowen, L.J. said in the course of his judgment:

> Some domestic or quasi-domestic entertainments may not come within the Act. Suppose a club of persons united for the purposes of good fellowship gave a dramatic entertainment to its members; I do not say that the entertainment will necessarily fall within the prohibition of the statute.

68 In Harms Inc. and Chappel & Co. v. Martan's Club, [1927] 1 Ch. 526, there was a performance at the Embassy Club at which club members and some guests were present. It was held that the plaintiff's copyright was infringed. In that case Sargant L.J. said at p. 537:

> There has been an invitation to the members of the public capable of becoming members of the Club upon the terms of getting in return for their subscription the performance of music, so that you do really get an invitation to the public, and an invitation to the public to listen at a price or at a payment, though the payment is an annual one. Beyond that, there is, of course this, that the members of the public who have become members of the Club by passing through the not very severe test which is imposed, have also the privilege of bringing in other members of the public upon whom no test is imposed, who happen to be their friends and are invited on any particular evening.

69 In Performing Right Society Ltd. v. Hawthorn's Hotel (Bournemouth) Ltd., [1933] 1 Ch. 856, an orchestral trio played in the lounge of the defendant's hotel, there being present several guests of the hotel, among others. Bennett J. held that the performance by the hotel orchestra was a performance "in public" because it was open to any members of the public who cared to be guests of the hotel either by sleeping or dining there.

70 Again, the question was fully considered by the Court of Appeal in Jennings v. Stephens, [1936] 1 All E.R. 409, which reversed Crossman J., [1935] 1 Ch. 703. Romer L.J. in discussing the general question as to whether a performance was "in public", said at p. 416 ff.:

> No one, for instance, can doubt that the concerts given at the Albert Hall are, in general, performances 'in public,' or that music provided by a man for the entertainment of his guests after dinner or at a reception is performed 'in private'; and I think that the meaning of the two phrases can best be ascertained by considering what is the essential difference between the two performances. The difference in material for the present purpose lies, it seems to me, in this. In the latter case the entertainment forms part of the domestic or home life of the person who provides it, and none the less because of the presence of his guests. They are for the time being members of his home circle. In the former case, however, the entertainment is in no sense part of the domestic or home life of the members of the audience. It forms part of what may be called in contradistinction their non-domestic or outside life. In the one case the audience are present in their capacity as members of the particular home circle. In the other they are present in their capacity as members of the music-loving section of the public. The home circle may, of course, in some cases be a large one. The section of the public forming the audience may in some cases be a small one. But this can make no difference, though it may sometimes be difficult to decide whether a particular collection of persons can properly be regarded as constituting a domestic circle. In Duck v. Bates (1884), 13 Q.B.D. 843, the Court of Appeal seem to have regarded the nurses and medical staff of Guys' Hospital as forming a domestic circle, and a dramatic entertainment given before them and their guests as a private performance. Bennett J., on the other hand, in Performing Right Society v. Hawthorn's Hotel, [1933] 1 Ch. 855, treated, and in my opinion rightly treated, a musical entertainment given to the residents in an hotel, to which any respectable member of the public could obtain admission merely by payment, as a performance in public. Nor, with all deference to those who think otherwise, can I agree that it makes any difference whether the actual performers are paid for their services or give them gratuitously, or whether the performers are strangers or members of the domestic circle. The performers at what is unquestionably a private performance are frequently paid. The performers at what is unquestionably a public performance frequently give their services for nothing. Nor can an entertainment that is private when given by the members of the home circle cease to be private when given by strangers.
>
> I also find some difficulty in seeing why it is material to consider the nature of and the place where the entertainment is given. A private entertainment may be given in a public room. A public entertainment may be given in a private house. The question whether an entertainment is given in public or in private depends, in my opinion, solely upon the character of the audience. Suppose, for instance, that a number of people who are interested in the drama, band themselves together in

a society or club for the purpose of providing by means of their subscriptions the performance before themselves from time to time of dramatic works. This would be something entirely outside their domestic lives, and they would, in my opinion, attend the performances merely as members of the public, and none the less because the section of the public which they represent may be limited by election, the social status of the members, or their capacity to pay a large subscription. I should regard any dramatic performance given before that society as a performance in public....

The teaching staff and pupils of a boarding school might, on the other hand, properly be regarded during the school term as forming a domestic circle, and a dramatic performance given before them might well be held to be a private performance, even though the parents or other relations of the pupils were present as guests. I cannot, indeed, think that a performance which would otherwise have been a performance in private could be turned into a performance in public by the mere presence of some guests. Guests were present at the entertainment that was the subject matter of the inquiry in Duck v. Bates (supra), to which I have already referred — a case which it must be confessed was somewhat near the line. It is easy to imagine other cases in which it is difficult to say whether they fall on the private or public side of the line. But the present case seems to me quite plainly to fall upon the public side.

71 The matter was again considered in Performing Right Society, Ltd. v. Gillette Industries, Ltd., [1943] 1 All E.R. 228 and 413. There the defendants installed in their factory a number of loudspeakers from which broadcast music was heard in various departments of the factory and about six hundred workers heard the broadcast, but all strangers were excluded from the factory. At the trial, Bennett J. pointed out the difficulty of obtaining from the authorities any real principle which could be said to govern every case and to lay down any general rule for defining what is meant by performance in public. He distinguished the case from Duck v. Bates (supra), holding that the performance of the music by the defendant could not be said to be for domestic purposes, and followed Jennings v. Stephens (supra). On appeal, Lord Greene M.R. affirmed the judgment of Bennett J., basing his judgment on the authority of the Court of Appeal in Jennings v. Stephens, citing with approval the words of Lord Wright M.R. that, "The true criterion seems to be the character of the audience". In that case, the Master of the Rolls stated:

The owner of the copyright is entitled to be paid for the use of his property unless and until the Legislature otherwise determines, and he is entitled to be paid for it even if the use that is made of it is a use which concerns the public welfare to a very considerable extent... When the Legislature under The Copyright Act conferred upon the owner of copyright a monopoly, it no doubt intended that the monopoly should be a real and not an illusory right of property, and it is, therefore, in my opinion, important to consider whether a particular performance, the character of which is in question, is of a kind calculated to whittle down that monopoly to any substantial extent.

72 I think it may be said with some truth that the more recent cases have indicated a tendency to extend somewhat the protection afforded to the owners of

copyright, since the case of Duck v. Bates. In none of these cases, however, can I find a suggestion that a performance in a private home where the performance is given, heard or seen by only members of the immediate household, could be considered as a performance in public.

73 As to the character of the audience in homes and apartments to which the telecasts of the live films were "rediffused" by the defendant, there is no evidence whatever except that they were seen by the defendant's subscribers, presumably only the householders. The character of the audience was therefore a purely domestic one and the performance in each case was not a performance in public. Counsel for the plaintiff, however, submits that even if one such "view" in the privacy of the owner's home does not constitute a performance in public, that in cases where a large number of people, each having a terminal unit in his home, performs the work by operating the terminal units, that such would constitute a performance in public. He says that from the point of view of the owner, a large number of such performances would constitute an interference with the owner's right of making copies of his work and might cause him to lose part of his potential market. I am unable to agree with that submission. I cannot see that even a large number of private performances, solely because of their numbers, can become public performances. The character of the individual audiences remains exactly the same; each is private and domestic, and therefore not "in public." Moreover, in telecasting the films, I think the plaintiff desired to have the telecasts seen by as many people as were within range and possessed the necessary receiving equipment in order that they might be informed of its product; so that I do not think that what was done by the defendant in so far as the private homes and apartments are concerned, interfered with his potential market in any way. It was stated and not denied that the films, including the commercial announcements of the plaintiff, were rediffused as a whole.

74 I find, therefore, that the performances in the homes and apartments of the subscribers of the defendant company were not performances "in public".

75 The situation, however, is quite different in regard to the defendant's Berri Street showroom. The evidence is that the showroom was operated by the defendant for the purpose of demonstrating and selling its services which included the leasing of its terminal units. The showroom was open to the public, and members of the public there on various occasions saw the film telecasts of the plaintiff broadcast on Station CBFT. There was nothing there of a domestic or quasi-domestic nature and in my opinion it was a performance in public and an infringement of the copyright of the plaintiff in the cinematograph films. It was suggested by counsel for the defendant that a finding to that effect might seriously interfere with the operations of store salesmen of any type of television receiving sets, and that may be so. If, however, the plaintiff has established its right to copyright, it is entitled to the protection afforded by the Act for such right and to restrain the defendant from infringing that right no matter what the consequences to others might be.

76 My conclusion on this point, therefore, as regards the showing of the film tele-casts by the defendant in its Berri Street showroom, is that there was an infringe-ment by the defendant of the plaintiff's copyright in such cinematograph films.

---

4. Communicate Works to the Public by Telecommunication

(a) What is a "Communication"?

Section 3(1)(f) of the Act confers upon the copyright owner the sole right "in the case of any literary, dramatic, musical or artistic work, to commu-nicate the work to the public by telecommunication". This section together with Section 3(1) of the Act which gives the author the exclusive right to perform a work in public, implements Canada's obligations under Articles 11 and 11bis of the Berne Convention.[19] Section 3(1)(f) also implements Canada's obligations under the Free Trade Agreement with respect to the retransmission of local or distant signals that carry a literary, dramatic, musi-cal or artistic work.[20]

The term "telecommunication" is defined in the Act to mean "any trans-mission of signs, signals, writings, images or sounds or intelligence of any nature by wire, radio, visual, optical or other electromagnetic system." This definition is broad enough to include all conceivable forms and combinations of wired or wireless communications media, including transmission by hertz-ian waves (radio waves) satellite technology, wire and cable.

The word "communicate" has been defined to mean "to give to another as a partaker; to impart, confer, transmit, bestow." Each of these senses involves causing information or something comparable to reach or be imparted to another person.[21] The Supreme Court of Canada has also stated that a "communication" involves the passing of thoughts, ideas, words or information from one person to another."[22] However, most recently, the Court has ruled that downloading a digital copy of a work is not a "communication". In this context, the transmission is essentially a "delivery" of a copy made more efficient by technology, as opposed to a performance-based activity such as online streaming, which is a "communication" for the purposes of section 3(1)(f).

---

19   *Bishop v. Stevens*, [1990] 2 S.C.R. 467; *C.A.P.A.C. v. CTV Television Network Ltd.* (1968), 68 D.L.R. (2d) 98 (S.C.C.); *CTV Television Network Ltd. v. Canada (Copyright Board)* (1993), 46 C.P.R. (3d) 343 (Fed. C.A.); *Canadian Cable Television Association v. Copyright Board* (1993), 46 C.P.R. (3d) 359 (Fed. C.A.).

20   Canada — United States *Free Trade Agreement Implementation Act*, SS 61-65, CTV Television Network Ltd. v. Canada (Copyright Board), (1993), 46 C.P.R. (3d) 359 (Fed. C.A.).

21   *SOCAN v. Canadian Association of Internet Providers*, 2004 SCC 45.

22   *R. v. Goldman* (1979), 108 D.L.R. (3d) 17 (S.C.C.).

Composers, Authors & Publishers Assn. of Can. Ltd. v. CTV Television Network Ltd. (1966), 33 Fox Pat. C. 69 (Ex. Ct.), affirmed (1968), 68 D.L.R. (2d) 98 (S.C.C.)

Jackett P.

Judgment: March 25, 1966

The judgment of the court was delivered on April 1, 1968, by Pigeon J.:

1 The Plaintiff Appellant, Composers, Authors and Publishers Association of Canada Ltd. (hereinafter called "CAPAC") is a performing rights society contemplated in sections 48 to 51 of the Copyright Act (R.S.C. ch. 55) (hereinafter called the "Act"). In accordance with those provisions it has filed statements of fees which have been approved by the Copyright Appeal Board and published in the Canada Gazette. In those statements Tariff No. 3 entitled "Television Broadcasting" sets the fee payable for a general licence by an operator of television station other than the Canadian Broadcasting Corporation at 1 1/2% of the gross amount paid for the use of the operator's services or facilities.

2 Defendant CTV Television Network Ltd. (hereinafter called "CTV") has, since October 1, 1961, been operating a private television network in the following way. It acquires, or maybe produces, television programs recorded on videotape. It contracts with advertisers for payment in consideration of the addition of commercials. It also contracts with private affiliated television stations for having the programs broadcast at a proper time in consideration of stipulated payments. The programs are supplied to the affiliated stations in some cases by shipping a copy of the videotape but, in most cases, by using facilities provided by the Defendant The Bell Telephone Company of Canada (hereinafter called "Bell"). These facilities over short distances include cable only but, over long distances, the transmission is effected mostly by microwave.

3 It is obvious that CTV's gross revenue from the operations above described must be very substantially larger than the amount that it pays to the affiliated stations, seeing that this revenue has to cover the cost of the programs and the cost of transmission to the affiliated stations in addition to what is paid for broadcasting same and also provide for general expenses and profit. CAPAC has been trying to obtain a 1 1/2% fee on the larger amount. With that end in view, it has filed in November 1962 a tariff providing under the heading of "Television Broadcasting", in addition to the general licence above mentioned, for a general licence to CTV "for all network television broadcast". The fee for such licence is 1 1/2% of the gross amount paid to CTV for the use of the network less the amount in turn paid by CTV to its affiliated stations.

4 CTV objected to the tariff and, after it was approved, refused to take a licence. Thereupon CAPAC brought action in May 1963 alleging in substance the facts above recited and complaining of infringement of copyright in some seven named musical works by "communicating the same by radio communication throughout Canada, or by causing or authorizing the said musical works to be

communicated by radio communication throughout Canada without the licence or authority of the Plaintiff".

5 It is admitted that CAPAC is the owner of the copyright in the musical works in question. It is also admitted that these "musical numbers" as they are called in the admission were included in the programmes transmitted for broadcasting to the affiliated network stations and effectively broadcast by them. It is also admitted that the transmission in several cases was effected by means of cable and microwave facilities of Bell. The question is was this an infringement of CAPAC's copyright?

6 In the Exchequer Court it was held that there was no infringement for the reason that there was no transmission nor communication of the musical "works" from CTV to the affiliated stations and that the latter being authorized by licence from CAPAC to make use of the subject matter of the copyright, it could not be in infringement for CTV to authorize them to do it. As the learned President put it, "it cannot be a tort merely to authorize or cause a person to do something that that person has a right to do".

7 CAPAC's claim is based essentially on sub-paragraph (f) and the concluding words of sub-section (1) of section 3 of the Act, whereby it is enacted that "copyright" includes the sole right

> ...f) in case of any literary, dramatic, musical or artistic work, to communicate such work by radio communication; and to authorize any such acts as aforesaid.

In considering this provision, it is essential to note the following definitions in section 2 of the Act:

> (p) "musical work" means any combination of melody and harmony, or either of them, printed, reduced to writing, or otherwise graphically produced or reproduced;

> (q) "performance" means any acoustic representation of a work or any visual representation of any dramatic action in a work, including a representation made by means of any mechanical instrument or by radio communication.

. . .

It will be noted that where the Convention speaks of "radiodiffusion" i.e. radio broadcasting, the unfortunate translation reads "radiocommunication". The error in translation of the Convention was obviously carried into the statute intended to implement it, and, as happened in the case of the Hague Rules annexed to the Water Carriage of Goods Act, the English text was translated into French.

11 It is apparent that the above cited article of the Convention contemplates public performances by radio broadcasting. Such is the clear meaning of "la communication de leurs oeuvers au public par la radiodiffusion" (communication of their works to the public by radio broadcasting). In the Convention "oeuvres" (works) is not defined, therefore, as applied to musical works, it is properly taken in the primary sense of the composition itself, not its graphic representation as in the Act. Also, while "communication" does not usually mean "a performance" it is apt to include performances in its meaning along

with other modes of representation applicable to other kinds of artistic or literary works that are not "performed".

12 It must be noted that in the Convention it is doubly indicated by "au public" and by "radiodiffusion" that public performances or communications only are aimed at. This is consonant with the general definition of "copyright" which, as stated in sub-section 1 of section 3 of the Act, applies to any reproduction of the work but, as respect performances, applies only to those that are "in public". Is it to be inferred that Parliament intended to depart from this principle in enacting sub-section 2(f) (sic) simply because the words "to the public" are not found in it? Of course, if the provision was clear, if it could be applied literally to give this result, effect would have to be given to the intention. However, as previously noted, the material part of the provision does not read "to communicate a performance of such work by radio communication" but "to communicate such work by radio communication". In view of the statutory definitions of "musical work" and of "performance" the insertion of the word "performance" in the enactment is a very substantial departure from the text as written. Bearing in mind that the reproduction of a work as distinguished from a performance thereof is always within the definition of "copyright" while a performance is outside the scope of the definition if not in public, it is only through the insertion of the word "performance" without the words "in public" that a departure from principle would be effected.

13 On the assumption that the provision is not clear and that it must not be applied literally, it is not at all obvious that it must be read as suggested to give effect to CAPAC's contention. Once it is ascertained that interpretation has to be resorted to, the intention must be gathered from the statute as a whole and this certainly includes the Schedule that is referred to in the body of the Act and is printed with it. Upon such consideration it becomes apparent that sub-paragraph (f) is intended to achieve the result contemplated in paragraph 1 of article 11 bis. Bearing in mind that the Rome Convention is in French no other conclusion is possible but that the intent is to provide that copyright includes the exclusive right of public performance or representation by radio broadcasting ("communication au public par la radiodiffusion").

14 The contention advanced by CAPAC would have the anomalous result that the extent of the copyright with respect to the communication or transmission of performances of musical works, would depend on the means employed for such communication or transmission. If it was by physical delivery of magnetic tape or by transmission of an electrical signal by cable, there would be no monopoly in favour of the owner of copyright in the works performed. However, such monopoly would exist if the transmission was by microwave, although such transmission would be as private as the other cases.

15 I therefore come to the conclusion on the first point, that CAPAC's contention cannot be supported either on the literal meaning of the statute or on

construction in the light of the intention revealed by the whole Act, including the Schedule.

SOCAN v. Canadian Assn. of Internet Providers, 2004 SCC 45

Arbour J., Bastarache J., Binnie J., Deschamps J., Fish J., Iacobucci J., LeBel J., Major J., McLachlin C.J.C.

Heard: December 3, 2003
Judgment: June 30, 2004
Docket: 29286

Binnie J.:

1 This appeal raises the difficult issue of who should compensate musical composers and artists for their Canadian copyright in music downloaded in Canada from a foreign country via the Internet. In an era when it is as easy to access a website hosted by a server in Bangalore as it is to access a website with a server in Mississauga, where is the protection for the financial rights of the people who created the music in the first place? Who, if anyone, is to pay the piper?

. . .

II. Relevant Statutory Provisions

27 Copyright Act, R.S.C. 1985, c. C-42

2. ...

> "telecommunication" means any transmission of signs, signals, writing, images or sounds or intelligence of any nature by wire, radio, visual, optical or other electromagnetic system;
>
> 2.4 (1) For the purposes of communication to the public by telecommunication,
>
> . . .
>
> (b) a person whose only act in respect of the communication of a work or other subject-matter to the public consists of providing the means of telecommunication necessary for another person to so communicate the work or other subject-matter does not communicate that work or other subject-matter to the public; and
>
> . . .
>
> 3. (1) For the purposes of this Act, "copyright", in relation to a work, means the sole right to produce or reproduce the work or any substantial part thereof in any material form whatever, to perform the work or any substantial part thereof in public or, if the work is unpublished, to publish the work or any substantial part thereof, and includes the sole right
>
> . . .
>
> (f) in the case of any literary, dramatic, musical or artistic work, to communicate the work to the public by telecommunication,

and to authorize any such acts.

Loi sur le droit d'auteur, L.R.C. 1985, ch. C-42

2. [...]

télécommunication vise toute transmission de signes, signaux, écrits, images, sons ou renseignements de toute nature par fil, radio, procédé visuel ou optique, ou autre système électromagnétique.

[...]

2.4 (1) Les règles qui suivent s'appliquent dans les cas de communication au public par télécommunication:

[...]

b) n'effectue pas une communication au public la personne qui ne fait que fournir à un tiers les moyens de télécommunication nécessaires pour que celui-ci l'effectue;

. . .

3. (1) Le droit d'auteur sur l'uvre comporte le droit exclusif de produire ou reproduire la totalité ou une partie importante de l'uvre, sous une forme matérielle quelconque, d'en exécuter ou d'en représenter la totalité ou une partie importante en public et, si l'uvre n'est pas publiée, d'en publier la totalité ou une partie importante; ce droit comporte, en outre, le droit exclusif:

[...]

f) de communiquer au public, par télécommunication, une uvre littéraire, dramatique, musicale ou artistique;

Est inclus dans la présente définition le droit exclusif d'autoriser ces actes.

III. Judicial History

A. Decision of the Copyright Board

28 Tariff 22 proposed the amount and allocation of a royalty payable to copyright owners for the communication of music on the Internet. At the end of the first phase of its proceeding, geared to determining who might be liable to pay royalties, the Copyright Board held that a royalty can be imposed on content providers who post music on a server located in Canada that can be accessed by other Internet users. However, the Board also held that the normal activities of Internet intermediaries not acting as content providers do not constitute "a communication" for the purpose of the Copyright Act and thus do not infringe the exclusive communication rights of copyright owners. The parties did not frame an issue in relation to infringement of the right of reproduction, and its role, if any, did not play a significant part in the Board's decision.

29 In reaching its conclusions the Copyright Board considered a number of questions, including the following (p. 443):

1 When does a communication to the public occur on the Internet?

2 Who "communicates" (in the copyright sense) on the Internet? In particular, who can benefit from paragraph 2.4(1)(b) of the Act?

3 When does the act of "authorizing" a communication on the Internet occur?

4 When does a communication on the Internet occur in Canada?

30 After hearing 11 days of evidence and submissions and a subsequent period of reflection, the Board concluded that an Internet communication occurs at the time the work is transmitted from the host server to the computer of the end user, regardless of whether it is played or viewed at that time, or later, or never. It is made "to the public" because the music files are "made available on the Internet openly and without concealment, with the knowledge and intent that they be conveyed to all who might access the Internet" (at p. 445). Accordingly, "a communication may be to the public when it is made to individual members of the public at different times, whether chosen by them (as is the case on the Internet) or by the person responsible for sending the work (as is the case with facsimile transmissions)" (at p. 445). This is no longer contested.

31 In order to determine the level of intermediate participation in Internet transmission of musical works that could trigger liability for infringement under s. 3(1)(f) of the Copyright Act, the Board was required to interpret the scope of the limitation in s. 2.4(1)(b), which says that an Internet Service Provider does not "communicate" a copyrighted work if its "only act" is to provide "the means of telecommunication necessary for another person to so communicate the work" (emphasis added).

32 The Board rejected SOCAN's argument that s. 2.4(1)(b) should be narrowly construed as an exemption to copyright liability. The Board held that where an intermediary merely acts as a "conduit for communications by other persons" (at p. 453 (emphasis added)), it can claim the benefit of s. 2.4(1)(b). If an intermediary does more than merely act as a conduit, (for example if it creates a cache for reasons other than improving system performance or modifies the content of cached material), it may lose the protection. Insofar as the Internet Service Provider furnishes "ancillary" services to a content provider or end user, it could still rely on s. 2.4(1)(b) as a defence to copyright infringement, provided any such "ancillary services" do not amount in themselves to communication or authorization to communicate the work. Creation of an automatic "hyperlink" by a Canadian Internet Service Provider will also attract copyright liability.

33 As to "authorization", the Board found that knowledge by an Internet Service Provider that its facilities might be used for infringing purposes was not enough to incur liability. The Internet Service Provider needed to grant "the person committing the infringement a license or permission to infringe" (at p. 458).

34 In the result, the Board stated that an Internet communication occurs in Canada only if it originates from a server in Canada. Thus, a content provider is subject to a royalty approved by the Board if, but only if, the content is posted on a server located in Canada.

. . .

A. Communication Under the Copyright Act

42 It is an infringement for anyone to do, without the consent of the copyright owner, "anything that, by this Act, only the owner of the copyright has the right to do" (s. 27(1)), including, since the 1988 amendments, the right "to communicate the work to the public by telecommunication... and to authorize any such acts" (emphasis added) (s. 3(1)(f)). In the same series of amendments, "telecommunication" was defined as "any transmission of signs, signals, writings, images or sounds or intelligence of any nature by wire, radio, visual, optical or other electromagnetic system" (s. 2). The Board ruled that a telecommunication occurs when the music is transmitted from the host server to the end user. I agree with this. The respondent says that the appellants as intermediaries participate in any such transmission of their copyrighted works, and authorize others to do so, and should therefore be required to pay compensation fixed under Tariff 22.

43 In the United States, unlike Canada, detailed legislation has now been enacted to deal specifically with the liability of Internet intermediaries; see the Digital Millennium Copyright Act, 17 U.S.C. § 512 (1998). Australia has enacted its Copyright Amendment (Digital Agenda) Act 2000, No. 110 of 2000. The European Commission has issued a number of directives, as will be discussed. Parliament's response to the World Intellectual Property Organization's (WIPO) Copyright Treaty, 1996, ("WCT") and the Performances and Phonograms Treaty, 1996, remains to be seen. In the meantime, the courts must struggle to transpose a Copyright Act designed to implement the Berne Convention for the Protection of Literary and Artistic Works of 1886, as revised in Berlin in 1908, and subsequent piecemeal amendments, to the information age, and to technologies undreamt of by those early legislators.

44 The Board took the view that "[t]o occur in Canada, a communication must originate from a server located in Canada on which content has been posted" (at p. 459), except perhaps if the content provider has "the intention to communicate it specifically to recipients in Canada" (at p. 460). In my view, with respect, this is too rigid and mechanical a test. An Internet communication that crosses one or more national boundaries "occurs" in more than one country, at a minimum the country of transmission and the country of reception. In Dow Jones, supra, the defendant argued that the appropriate law should be that of the jurisdiction where the host server is located, but this was rejected in favour of the law of the State of reception by the High Court of Australia. To the extent the Board held that a communication that does not originate in Canada does not occur in Canada, I disagree with its decision.

45 At the end of the transmission, the end user has a musical work in his or her possession that was not there before. The work has, necessarily, been communicated, irrespective of its point of origin. If the communication is by virtue of the Internet, there has been a "telecommunication". To hold otherwise would not only fly in the face of the ordinary use of language but would have serious consequences in other areas of law relevant to the Internet, including Canada's

ability to deal with criminal and civil liability for objectionable communications entering the country from abroad.

46 The word "communicate" is an ordinary English word that means to "impart" or "transmit" (Shorter Oxford English Dictionary on Historical Principles (5th ed. 2002), vol. 1, at p. 463). Communication presupposes a sender and a receiver of what is transmitted; see R. v. Cremascoli (1979), [1980] 1 S.C.R. 976 (S.C.C.), at p. 995. The "communicator" is the sender, not the recipient. Thus, says SOCAN, all those entities located in Canada (other than Backbone Service Providers) who participate in the act of imparting or transmitting a copyrighted work across the Internet are guilty of infringement of the Canadian copyright. Any lesser protection, SOCAN says, would not strike an appropriate balance between the rights of copyright owners and the public interest in the encouragement and dissemination of their musical works (Théberge, at para. 30).

Entertainment Software Assn. v. SOCAN, 2012 SCC 34 (S.C.C.)

Present: McLachlin C.J. and LeBel, Deschamps, Fish, Abella, Rothstein, Cromwell, Moldaver and Karakatsanis JJ.

[1] Abella andMoldaver JJ. — In the video game publishing industry, the royalties for the reproduction of any musical works which are incorporated into the games are currently negotiated before the games are packaged for public sale. Once these rights have been negotiated, the owner of the copyright in the musical work has no further rights when the game is sold. The question in this appeal is whether the rights are nonetheless revived when the work is sold over the Internet instead of in a store. In our view, it makes little sense to distinguish between the two methods of selling the same work.

[2] The Copyright Board concluded that video games containing a musical work, the royalties to which have already been negotiated with the copyright owner, were nonetheless subject to a new fee when sold over the Internet ((2007), 61 C.P.R. (4th) 353). Its decision was upheld by the Federal Court of Appeal (2010 FCA 221, 406 N.R. 288). In our respectful view, the Board's decision misconstrues the provisions at issue in the Copyright Act, R.S.C. 1985, c. C-42, ignoring decades of legislative history, and violates the principle of technological neutrality, which requires that the Actapply equally notwithstanding the technological diversity of different forms of media.

Analysis

[3] The provision at issue in this appeal is s. 3(1)(f) of the Copyright Act, which states that copyright owners have the sole right

> in the case of any literary, dramatic, musical or artistic work, to communicatethe work to the public by telecommunication . . . .

[4] The focus of this appeal is on the meaning of the word "communicate" in s. 3(1)(*f*), a term which is not defined in the *Act*. The Society of Composers, Authors and Music Publishers of Canada (SOCAN), which administers the right to "communicate" musical works on behalf of copyright owners, applied to the Board for a tariff under this provision to cover downloads of musical works over the Internet. The Entertainment Software Association and the Entertainment Software Association of Canada (collectively, ESA), which represent a broad coalition of video game publishers and distributors, objected to the tariff, arguing that "downloading" a video game containing musical works did not amount to "communicating" that game to the public by telecommunication under s. 3(1)(*f*). Instead, a "download" is merely an additional, more efficient way to deliver copies of the games to customers. The downloaded copy is identical to copies purchased in stores or shipped to customers by mail, and the game publishers already pay copyright owners reproduction royalties for *all* of these copying activities.

[5] We agree with ESA. In our view, the Board's conclusion that a separate, "communication" tariff applied to downloads of musical works violates the principle of technological neutrality, which requires that the *Copyright Act* apply equally between traditional and more technologically advanced forms of the same media: *Robertson v. Thomson Corp.*, [2006] 2 S.C.R. 363, at para. 49. The principle of technological neutrality is reflected in s. 3(1) of the *Act*, which describes a right to produce or reproduce a work "in any material form whatever". In our view, there is no practical difference between buying a durable copy of the work in a store, receiving a copy in the mail, or downloading an identical copy using the Internet. The Internet is simply a technological taxi that delivers a durable copy of the same work to the end user.

[6] This argument is echoed by David Vaver in his book, *Intellectual Property Law: Copyright, Patents, Trade-marks* (2nd ed. 2011), where he appears to criticize the Board's decision in this particular case:

> In principle, *substitute delivery systems* should compete on their merits: either both or neither should pay. Copyright law should strive for technological neutrality.
>
>   . . .
>
> In the past, whether a customer bought a sound recording or video game physically at a store or ordered it by mail made no difference to the copyright holder: it got nothing extra for the clerk's or courier's handover of the record to the customer. Now, because of the telecommunication right, *copyright holders can and do charge extra for electronic delivery of identical content acquired off websites.* [Emphasis added; pp. 172-73.]

[7] ESA's argument is also consistent with this Court's caution in *Théberge v. Galerie d'Art du Petit Champlain inc.*, [2002] 2 S.C.R. 336, that the balance in copyright between promoting the public interest in the encouragement and dissemination of works and obtaining a just reward for the creator requires recognizing the "limited nature" of creators' rights:

> The proper balance among these and other public policy objectives lies not only in recognizing the creator's rights but in giving due weight to their limited nature. In crassly economic terms *it would be as inefficient to overcompensate artists and authors for the right of reproduction as it would be self-defeating to undercompensate them*. Once an authorized copy of a work is sold to a member of the public, it is generally for the purchaser, not the author, to determine what happens to it. [Emphasis added; para. 31.]

[8] The traditional balance between authors and users should be preserved in the digital environment: Carys Craig, "Locking Out Lawful Users: Fair Dealing and Anti-Circumvention in Bill C-32", in Michael Geist, ed., *From "Radical Extremism" to "Balanced Copyright": Canadian Copyright and the Digital Agenda* (2010), 177, at p. 192.

[9] SOCAN has never been able to charge royalties for copies of video games stored on cartridges or discs, and bought in a store or shipped by mail. Yet it argues that identical copies of the games sold and delivered over the Internet are subject to *both* a fee for reproducing the work *and* a fee for communicating the work. The principle of technological neutrality requires that, absent evidence of Parliamentary intent to the contrary, we interpret the *Copyright Act* in a way that avoids imposing an additional layer of protections and fees based solely on the *method of delivery* of the work to the end user. To do otherwise would effectively impose a gratuitous cost for the use of more efficient, Internet-based technologies.

[10] The Board's misstep is clear from its definition of "download" as "a file containing data . . . the user is meant to keep as his own" (para. 13). The Board recognized that downloading is a *copying* exercise that creates an exact, durable copy of the digital file on the user's computer, identical to copies purchased in stores or through the mail. Nevertheless, it concluded that delivering a copy through the Internet was subject to two fees — one for reproduction and one for communication — while delivering a copy through stores or mail was subject only to reproduction fees. In coming to this conclusion, the Board ignored the principle of technological neutrality.

[11] Justice Rothstein argues (at para. 126) that the Board can avoid such "double-dipping" by copyright owners by adjusting the two fees in a way that "divides the pie" between the collective societies administering reproduction rights, on the one hand, and communication rights, on the other. However, this seems to us to undermine Parliament's purpose in creating the collective societies in the first place, namely to efficiently manage and administer different copyrights under the *Act*. This inefficiency harms both end users and copyright owners:

> When a single economic activity implicates more than one type of right and each type is administered by a separate collective, the multiplicity of licences required can lead to inefficiency. . . . The result is that the total price the user has to pay for all complements is too high . . . .

. . .

. . . the fragmentation of licences required for single activities among several monopolist-collectives generates inefficiencies, from which copyright owners as a whole also suffer . . . .

(Ariel Katz, "Commentary: Is Collective Administration of Copyrights Justified by the Economic Literature?", in Marcel Boyer, Michael Trebilcock and David Vaver, eds., *Competition Policy and Intellectual Property* (2009), 449, at pp. 461-63)

[12] In our view, the Board improperly concluded that the Internet delivery of copies of video games containing musical works amounts to "communicating" the works to the public. This view is evidenced by the legislative history of the *Copyright Act*, which demonstrates that the right to "communicate" is histori- cally connected to the right to perform a work and not the right to reproduce permanent copies of the work.

[13] As this Court held in *Bishop v. Stevens*, [1990] 2 S.C.R. 467, at pp. 473-74, the 1921 Canadian *Copyright Act* was based on, and designed to implement, the following provisions of the 1886 *Berne Convention for the Protection of Liter- ary and Artistic Works*, as revised in the 1908 Berlin Revision:

Article 11

The stipulations of the present Convention shall apply to the *public representa- tion* of dramatic or dramatico-musical works and to the *public performance* of musical works, whether such works be published or not.

. . .

Article 13

The authors of musical works shall have the exclusive right of authorizing (1) the adaptation of those works to instruments which can *reproduce* them mechanically; (2) the *public performance* of the said works by means of these instruments.

. . .

Article 14

Authors of literary, scientific or artistic works shall have *the exclusive right of authorizing the reproduction* and public representation of their works by cinematography.

[14] These articles were reflected in the introductory paragraph to s. 3(1) of the *Copyright Act, 1921*, S.C. 1921, c. 24, which granted

the sole right to *produce or reproduce* the work or any substantial part thereof in any material form whatsoever, *to perform*, or in the case of a lecture to deliver, the work or any substantial part thereof in public; if the work is unpublished, to pub- lish the work or any substantial part thereof; . . .

[15] In the 1921 *Act*, "performance" was defined in s. 2(*q*) as

any acoustic representation of a work and any visual representation of any dramatic action in a work, including such a representation made by means of any mechanical instrument;

[16] The right to perform historically presupposed a live audience that would be present at the site where the performance took place. With the advent of radio broadcasting, however, a debate emerged about how this new technology should be treated under copyright law, reminiscent of the current debate over Internet technologies. The international consensus was that radio broadcasting should be treated as an extension of the existing performance right, in order to cover distant audiences: Paul Goldstein and P. Bernt Hugenholtz, *International Copyright: Principles, Law, and Practice*(2nd ed. 2010), at §9.1.4.3; Pierre-Emmanuel Moyse, *Le droit de distribution: analyse historique et comparative en droit d'auteur* (2007), at pp. 309-10. The Rome Revision (1928) of the *Berne Convention* therefore extended the Article 11 performance right. The new Article 11*bis*conferred on authors the "exclusive right of authorizing the *communication*of their works to the public *by radiocommunication*".

[17] Canada acceded to the amended *Berne Convention* in 1928, and enacted s. 3(1)(*f*) of the *Copyright Act*in 1931 to incorporate the new Article 11*bis*:

> (*f*) In case of any literary, dramatic, musical or artistic work, to *communicate* such work by *radio communication*.

(*Copyright Amendment Act, 1931*, S.C. 1931, c. 8, s. 3)

[18] At the same time, the 1931 *Copyright Amendment Act* amended the definition of "performance" to accommodate this new concept of performances at a distance:

> "performance" means any acoustic representation of a work . . . including a representation made by means of any mechanical instrument *or by radio communication*. [s. 2(3)]

[19] Like a performance, communicating a work by radio communication (i.e., a radio broadcast) under s. 3(1)(*f*) involved an "acoustic representation" of a work. Also like a performance, communication under s. 3(1)(*f*) did *not* contemplate the delivery of permanent copies of the work, since such a delivery was not possible through the means of Hertzian radio waves.

[20] This interpretation of the original s. 3(1)(*f*) is supported by the legislative debates. In explaining the purpose of this provision to Parliament, the Minister responsible for the amendments, C. H. Cahan, stated that s. 3(1)(*f*) was intended to bring the *Copyright Act*into conformity with the Rome Revision of the *Berne Convention* (*House of Commons Debates*, vol. 1, 2nd Sess., 17th Parl., April 23, 1931, at pp. 899-900), and that "radio communication" was a form of performance:

> In England, *the courts have decided that radio communication comes within the meaning of the word performance*; but in order to make it clear that the author's rights include not only the right of performance by acoustic representation and so forth, but also by radio communication, we have added those words "or by radio communication" to the present definition of performances as contained in the act. . .

.. I am simply adding the words "or by radio communication" to make it clear that *in respect of radio communication the author has exactly the same rights as he has in relation to other performances of his work.* [Emphasis added.]

(vol. 3, June 8, 1931, at p. 2399)

[21] This was also the interpretation of the original s. 3(1)(*f*) by this Court in *Composers, Authors and Publishers Assoc. of Canada Ltd. v. CTV Television Network Ltd.*, [1968] S.C.R. 676. The Court held that signals transmitted from CTV to its affiliates did not communicate "musical works" — at the time defined as "reduced to writing" — but instead communicated a "performance" of the works. In *obiter*, the Court went on to hold that Article 11*bis* of the *Rome Convention*, on which s. 3(1)(*f*) was based, was intended to cover public performances by radio broadcasting (pp. 680-82). Moreover, it held that "communication" is"apt to include performances in its meaning" (p. 681). As a result, the Court concluded that s. 3(1)(*f*) must include the exclusive right of public performance by radio broadcasting.

[22] After 1931, there were no changes to s. 3(1)(*f*) until 1988. In 1988, s. 3(1) (*f*) was amended to read as follows:

(*f*) in the case of any literary, dramatic, musical or artistic work, to communicate the work *to the public*by *telecommunication*. . . .

(*Canada-United States Free Trade Agreement Implementation Act*, S.C. 1988, c. 65, s. 62)

[23] SOCAN argues that the 1988 amendment from "radio communication" to "telecommunication" demonstrates Parliament's intent to remove *all* reference in s. 3(1)(*f*) to conventional performance or broadcasting activities, and to expand the communication right to technologies that involve transmitting data in a way that gives end users a permanent copy of the work.

[24] With respect, we disagree. The 1988 amendments to the *Copyright Act* found at ss. 61 to 65 of the *Canada-United States Free Trade Agreement Implementation Act*, were enacted in order to give effect to Articles 2005 and 2006 of the 1987 *Canada-U.S. Free Trade Agreement* (*CUFTA*): see *Canadian Wireless Telecommunications Assn. v. Society of Composers, Authors and Music Publishers of Canada*, 2008 FCA 6, [2008] 3 F.C.R. 539 (*CWTA v. SOCAN*), at para. 27. Before *CUFTA*, Canadian courts had held that "radio communication" under the former s. 3(1)(*f*) was limited to Hertzian radio waves and did *not* extend to communication by co-axial cables: *Canadian Admiral Corp. v. Rediffusion, Inc.*, [1954] Ex. C.R. 382, at p. 410. *CUFTA*, however, required Canada to compensate copyright owners for the retransmission of television signals that were sent over cable lines. The amendments were therefore designed to ensure that cable companies, and not just radio broadcasters, would also be captured under s. 3(1)(*f*): John S. McKeown, *Fox on Canadian Law of Copyright and Industrial Designs* (4th ed. (loose-leaf)), at pp. 21-86, 21-87 and 29-1.

[25] In this context, the replacement of the words"radio communication" with "telecommunication" should be understood as merely expanding the *means of*

communicating a work — that is, from radio waves ("by radio communication") to cable and other future technologies ("to the public by telecommunication"). In our view, by substituting the word "telecommunication" in 1988, Parliament did not intend to change the fundamental nature of the communication right, which had for over 50 years been concerned with performance-based activities. Instead, Parliament only changed the *means of transmitting* a communication. The word "communicate"itself was never altered.

[26] Parliament's addition of the phrase "to the public" to s. 3(1)(*f*) also supports this interpretation of the 1988 amendments. Before 1988, there was no doubt that all communications were "to the public", as the nature of a broadcast through radio waves was necessarily public. The term "telecommunication", however, risked introducing ambiguity into the *Act*, as telecommunication could also include private communications. By adding the phrase "to the public" with the term"telecommunication" in 1988, Parliament clarified its intent to maintain the communication right as a category of performance right.

[27] Therefore, we agree with Rothstein J. (at para. 98) that there is a "historic relationship" between the performance right and the communication right in the *Copyright Act*, but we disagree with his conclusion that Parliament intended to sever this relationship based on the 1988 amendments. In our view, this historical connection between communication and performance still exists today. With respect, the Board ignored this connection when it concluded that transmitting a download of a musical work over the Internet could amount to a"communication".

[28] The Board's conclusion was based in part on its erroneous view that a "download" is indistinguishable from a "stream". Although a download and a stream are both "transmissions" in technical terms (they both use "data packet technology"), they are not both "communications"for purposes of the *Copyright Act*. This is clear from the Board's definition of a stream as "a transmission of data that allows the user to listen or view the content at the time of transmission and that is not meant to be reproduced" (para. 15). Unlike a download, the experience of a stream is much more akin to a broadcast or performance.

[29] The Board also appears to have relied on Binnie J.'s observation in *Society of Composers, Authors and Music Publishers of Canada v. Canadian Assn. of Internet Providers*, [2004] 2 S.C.R. 427 (*SOCAN v. CAIP*), that a work has necessarily been "communicated" when, "[a]t the end of the transmission, the end user has a musical work in his or her possession that was not there before" (at para. 45), and on *CWTA v. SOCAN*, where Sharlow J.A. evoked *SOCAN v. CAIP* to hold that "[t]he word'communication' connotes the passing of information from one person to another"(paras. 19-20).

[30] As noted by Justice Rothstein, however, the comments in *SOCAN v. CAIP* were *obiter*, as the meaning of "communicate"in s. 3(1)(*f*) was not directly in issue in that case. Neither *SOCAN v. CAIP* nor *CWTA v. SOCAN* examined the legislative history behind the term "communicate" or the connection between communication and performance.

[31] For the same reason, we cannot agree with Justice Rothstein's dependence on the dictionary definition of the word"communicate" to mean *any* transmission of data, including a download which provides the user with a durable copy of the work. Dictionaries, while often offering a useful range of definitional options, are of little assistance in identifying what a word means when it is orphaned from its context: Ruth Sullivan, *Sullivan and Driedger on the Construction of Statutes* (4th ed. 2002), at p. 27; see also *Ontario v. Canadian Pacific Ltd.*, [1995] 2 S.C.R. 1031, at para. 67 (*per* Gonthier J.). In our view, using dictionary definitions in this case has the effect of ignoring a solid line of legislative history connecting the term "communicate" to performance-based activities.

[32] The Board's interpretation of s. 3(1)(*f*) also ignores the historic distinction between performance-based rights and reproduction-based rights, improperly extending the term "communicate" to capture the Internet delivery of permanent copies of a work. In our view, this interpretation goes far beyond what the term "communicate" was ever intended to capture.

[33] In enacting s. 3(1), Parliament distinguished between rights of reproduction and performance:

3.(1) For the purposes of this Act, "copyright" means the sole right to *produce or reproduce* the work or any substantial part thereof in any material form whatsoever, *to perform*, or in the case of a lecture to deliver, the work or any substantial part thereof *in public* . . . .

(*Copyright Act, 1921*)

[34] This distinction between reproduction and performance in s. 3(1) has been maintained all the way through to the current version of the *Act*.

[35] Performing a work is fundamentally different than reproducing it. As this Court concluded in *Bishop v. Stevens*, a performance is impermanent in nature, and does not leave the viewer or listener with a durable copy of the work:

> The right to perform (including radio broadcast), and the right to make a recording, are separately enumerated in s. 3(1). They are distinct rights in theory and in practice . . . . [T]he rights to perform and to record a work are considered sufficiently distinct that they are generally assigned separately, and administered by different entities.
>
> . . .
>
> . . . A *performance is by its very nature fleeting, transient, impermanent.* When it is over, only the memory remains. . . . Furthermore, *no imitation of a performance can be a precise copy. A recording, on the other hand, is permanent. It may be copied easily, privately, and precisely. Once a work has been recorded, the recording takes on a life of its own.* . . . Once the composer has made or authorized a recording of his work, he has irrevocably given up much of his control over its presentation to the public. *These are the reasons why the rights to perform and to record are recognized as distinct in the Act, and why in practice a composer may*

     wish to authorize performances but not recordings of his work. [Emphasis added; pp. 477-79.]

[36] In *Bishop*, the alleged infringer argued that the "right to broadcast" a musical work under s. 3(1)(*f*) included the incidental right to make an ephemeral copy for the sole purpose of facilitating the broadcast. This Court ultimately concluded that the right to perform — including the right to communicate — could not be understood to include the right to reproduce, since performing and communicating are different in nature from making a recording.

[37] Even though *Bishop* interpreted the pre-1988 version of the *Copyright Act* (before the "telecommunication"amendment), the distinction between performance-based and reproduction-based rights established in s. 3(1) is evidenced in the provisions of the current *Act*. For example, in s. 2.2(1), the term "publication" *includes* "making copies", but expressly *excludes* "the performance in public, or the communication to the public by telecommunication" of a work. Similarly, the educational institutions exception in s. 29.4(2) refers to the right to"reproduce" and the right to "communicate by telecommunication to the public"as distinct rights. The same is true of s. 15(1), which categorizes neighbouring rights under the *Act* into two categories: the right to"communicate" and "perform" a performance, and the right to "reproduce" a fixation of the performance.

[38] The distinction between performance and communication rights on the one hand and reproduction rights on the other is also evident in the collective administration of copyright tariffs under the *Copyright Act*. In 1993, SOCAN — a performing rights society — was put in charge of administering the communication right in s. 3(1)(*f*) in relation to musical works: S.C. 1993, c. 23, s. 3: see McKeown, at pp. 3-12, 27-2 and 27-3. These provisions are contained in a section of the *Act* entitled "Collective Administration of *Performing Rights and of Communication Rights*": ss. 67 to 68.2 (S.C. 1997, c. 24, s. 45): see McKeown, at p. 26-3. Even the Copyright Board itself categorizes its decisions relating to musical works into two categories: "Public Performance of Music" and "Reproduction of Musical Works":http://www.cb-cda.gc.ca/decisions/index-e.html.

[39] Therefore, the term "communicate" in s. 3(1)(*f*), which has historically been linked to the right to perform, should not be transformed by the use of the word "telecommunication" in a way that would capture activities akin to reproduction. Such transformation would result in abandoning the traditional distinction in the *Act* between performance-based rights and rights of reproduction. There is no evidence either in 1988 or in subsequent amendments to the *Act* that Parliament intended such abandonment.

[40] SOCAN submits that the distinction between reproduction and performance rights in *Bishop* actually supports its view that downloading a musical work over the Internet can attract two tariffs. Since reproduction and performance-based rights are two separate, independent rights, copyright owners should be entitled to a separate fee under each right. This is based on the Court's reliance in *Bishop*, at p. 477, on a quote from *Ash v. Hutchinson & Co. (Publishers), Ltd.*, [1936] 2 All E.R. 1496 (C.A.), at p. 1507, *per* Greene L.J.:

Under the Copyright Act, 1911 [on which the Canadian *Act* was based], . . . the rights of the owner of copyright are set out. A number of acts are specified, the sole right to do which is conferred on the owner of the copyright. The right to do each of these acts is, in my judgment, a separate statutory right, *and anyone who without the consent of the owner of the copyright does any of these acts commits a tort; if he does two of them, he commits two torts, and so on.* [Emphasis added.]

[41] In our view, the Court in *Bishop* merely used this quote to emphasize that the rights enumerated in s. 3(1) are distinct. *Bishop* does *not* stand for the proposition that a *single*activity (i.e., a download) can violate two separate rights at the same time. This is clear from the quote in *Ash v. Hutchinson*, which refers to "two acts". In *Bishop*, for example, there were two activities: 1) the making of an ephemeral copy of the musical work in order to effect a broadcast, and 2) the actual broadcast of the work itself. In this case, however, there is only one activity at issue: downloading a copy of a video game containing musical works.

[42] Nor is the communication right in s. 3(1)(*f*) a *sui generis* right in addition to the general rights described in s. 3(1). The introductory paragraph defines what constitutes "copyright". It states that copyright "means" the sole right to produce or reproduce a work in any material form, to perform a work in public, or to publish an unpublished work. This definition of "copyright" is exhaustive, as the term "means"confines its scope. The paragraph concludes by stating that copyright"includes" several other rights, set out in subsections (*a*) through (*i*). As a result, the rights in the introductory paragraph provide the basic structure of copyright. The enumerated rights listed in the subsequent subparagraphs are simply illustrative: Sunny Handa, *Copyright Law in Canada*(2002), at p. 195; see also *Apple Computer Inc. v. Mackintosh Computers Ltd.*, [1987] 1 F.C. 173 (T.D.), at p. 197. The rental rights in s. 3(1)(*i*) referred to by Justice Rothstein, for example, can fit comfortably into the general category of reproduction rights.

[43] In our view, therefore, the Board's conclusion that the Internet delivery of a permanent copy of a video game containing musical works amounted to a "communication" under s. 3(1)(*f*) should be set aside.

[44] We would therefore allow the appeal with costs.

THE REASONS OF LEBEL, FISH, ROTHSTEIN AND CROMWELL JJ. WERE DELIVERED BY

[45] Rothstein J. (dissenting) — Under the *Copyright Act*, R.S.C. 1985, c. C-42 (the "Act"), s. 3(1)(*f*), a copyright holder has the sole right to"communicate [his or her] work to the public by telecommunication" and to authorize any such communication. The question in this case is whether a musical work is "communicate[d] . . . by telecommunication" when a file containing the musical work is downloaded from the Internet.

[46] When files containing copyright protected works are downloaded, copyright holders are entitled to compensation for the reproduction of their works. This appeal concerns musical works contained in video games which may be downloaded from the Internet. The appellants, the Entertainment Software Association and the Entertainment Software Association of Canada (collectively, the

"ESA"), argue that works transmitted over the Internet by downloading should not give rise to further compensation under s. 3(1)(*f*). The respondent, Society of Composers, Authors and Music Publishers of Canada ("SOCAN"), says that reproduction and communication are different and independent rights under the Act and that copyright holders are entitled to remuneration for the communication of their works through Internet downloading.

[47] My colleagues Abella and Moldaver JJ. part company with me on some fundamental principles of copyright law. In my view, precedents of this Court have established the principles that must govern the analysis in this appeal. Copyright is a creature of statute (*Théberge v. Galerie d'Art du Petit Champlain inc.*, 2002 SCC 34, [2002] 2 S.C.R. 336, at para. 5; *Compo Co. v. Blue Crest Music Inc.*, [1980] 1 S.C.R. 357, at p. 373; *Bishop v. Stevens*, [1990] 2 S.C.R. 467, at p. 477). Copyright is comprised of a bundle of independent statutory rights (*Bishop v. Stevens*, at p. 477; *Compo Co. v. Blue Crest Music Inc.*, at p. 373). Courts must give effect to these independent rights as provided by Parliament. While courts must bear in mind that the *Copyright Act* "is . . . a balance between promoting the public interest in the encouragement and dissemination of works of the arts and intellect and obtaining a just reward for the creator",which balance requires "not only . . . recognizing the creator's rights but in giving due weight to their limited nature" (*Théberge*, at paras. 30-31), courts must still respect the language chosen by Parliament — not override it.

[48] In my respectful opinion, my colleagues'approach sweeps away these well-established principles. They start from the proposition that once the reproduction rights in the musical work contained in a video game are negotiated, "the owner of the copyright in the musical work has no further rights when the game is sold" (Abella and Moldaver JJ., at para. 1). They support their argument by reference to the principle of technological neutrality: because the production and sale of a *hard copy* of the video game would only engage the right to reproduce the musical works it contains, the sale of a *digital copy* of the game, by transmission over the Internet, must also not trigger protected rights other than the right to reproduce. For my colleagues, the "Internet is simply a technological taxi that delivers a durable copy of the same work to the end user" (para. 5). They say that the question in this appeal is "whether the rights are nonetheless revived when the work is sold over the Internet instead of in a store" (para. 1).

[49] Generally, a technologically neutral copyright law is desirable. However, technological neutrality is not a statutory requirement capable of overriding the language of the Act and barring the application of the different protected rights provided by Parliament. My colleagues' basic propositions pre-empt the application of other rights of the copyright holder to this set of facts and divest these rights of their independent content. There is no need to revive rights that have never been exhausted.

[50] In many respects, the Internet may well be described as a technological taxi; but taxis need not give free rides.

I. Facts and Procedural History

[51] On judicial review, the Federal Court of Appeal ("FCA") upheld the determination by the Copyright Board that the download of a file containing a musical work is a "communicat[ion] . . . to the public by telecommunication" within the meaning of s. 3(1)(*f*) of the Act, entitling SOCAN members to compensation in accordance with an approved tariff. The ESA appeals to this Court from the decision of the FCA.

[52] The ESA is a coalition of video game publishers and distributors. Video games are entertainment software consisting of millions of lines of software code. When installed and run on a computer, the software generates audiovisual effects in response to commands by the user. The audio component may include musical works as part of the game's soundtrack.

[53] Video games can be sold over the Internet. Customers navigate to the website of an online game provider where the video game program is offered for sale, pay the purchase price and download the program. The site transmits a permanent copy of the software to the customer's hard drive. This mode of delivery of the purchased program competes with the traditional model, where the video game is stored on a CD or in a cartridge, requiring the customer to buy it at a store.

[54] The customer must then install the program, either downloaded from the Internet or contained on the CD, on his or her computer. Only after the installation is complete may the customer run the game, at which point, the audio and the visual effects of the software become perceptible. The game and its audio and visual effects are not perceptible during the transmission of the file from the vendor to the video game user, a fact that is said to be of crucial significance in this case.

[55] It is standard practice within the video game publishing industry to negotiate clearance of copyright for the *reproduction* of the musical works incorporated in the games prior to their publication. There is no dispute that once reproduction rights are cleared, the owner of copyright in the musical work would have no further rights when the video game is sold to a customer at a bricks-and-mortar store or if a CD containing the game is shipped through regular mail.

[56] SOCAN is a collective society of composers, authors and publishers of music. It administers the right to perform in public and the right to communicate to the public by telecommunication the works covered by its members' copyrights. It files proposed tariffs with the Board and collects royalties, as set by the Board, on behalf of its members.

[57] These proceedings involve proposed tariffs first filed by SOCAN in 1995 for various uses of musical works constituting, in SOCAN's view, copyright protected communication of musical works to the public over the Internet. There were objections to the filed proposals. In 1996, the Board decided to deal with legal issues separately from the determination of the actual tariffs. The first step was to "determine which activities on the Internet, if any, constitute a protected use [of SOCAN's repertoire of music] targeted in the tariff" (*SOCAN Statement*

of Royalties, Public Performance of Musical Works 1996, 1997, 1998 (Tariff 22, Internet) (Re) (1999), 1 C.P.R. (4th) 417 ("Tariff 22 decision"), at p. 424).

[58] On October 27, 1999 (the Tariff 22 decision), the Board issued what it termed its Phase I decision, dealing with legal and jurisdictional issues. The Tariff 22 decision was ultimately appealed to this Court, but not on the issue of communication to the public by telecommunication now before this Court. However, in *Society of Composers, Authors and Music Publishers of Canada v. Canadian Assn. of Internet Providers*, 2004 SCC 45, [2004] 2 S.C.R. 427 ("*SOCAN v. CAIP*"), at para. 30, Binnie J. noted the Board's conclusion that "an Internet communication occurs at the time the work is transmitted from the host server to the computer of the end user, regardless of whether it is played or viewed at that time, or later, or never" (see Tariff 22 decision, at p. 450). He found that this particular issue was "no longer contested".

[59] In 2005, SOCAN modified its proposed Tariff to divide it into seven categories, each dealing with a different Internet-based activity. The sixth category applies to "Game Sites" and covers"communications of musical works as part of games, including gambling, from Sites or Services that consist predominantly of games . . ." (*Statement of Proposed Royalties to Be Collected by SOCAN for the Public Performance or the Communication to the Public by Telecommunication, in Canada, of Musical or Dramatico-Musical Works* (2005), 139 Can. Gaz. I (Supp.), at p. 18). When the Board proceeded to Phase II of the process to establish a tariff for the communication of musical works over the Internet for the years 1996 to 2006, the ESA argued that since the users can neither see, nor hear game software while it is being downloaded, "[t]he transmission solely involves a distribution of a <u>copy</u> of a work that is identical to copies available on discs in stores. The transmission [is] thus not a 'communication to the public'" (A.F., at para. 20 (emphasis in original)).

[60] The Board's Phase II determination was rendered in two decisions. In the first, issued on October 18, 2007 (61 C.P.R. (4th) 353) (the "Tariff 22.A decision"), the Board rejected the ESA's argument and confirmed its prior conclusion that a download is a "communication". While the Tariff 22.A decision dealt with the details of the tariffs applicable to uses of music by online music services that offer catalogues of songs for downloading upon payment of the purchase price, the Board held that the legal principles established in that decision would also apply to other uses of music on the Internet. The Board's second Phase II decision, issued on October 24, 2008, *SOCAN Statement of Royalties, Internet — Other Uses of Music, 1996-2006 (Tariffs 22.B-22.G)* (2008), 70 C.P.R. (4th) 81 (the "Tariff 22.B-G decision"),established the details of the tariffs applicable to other uses of music on the Internet, including use by game sites at issue in this appeal (Tariff 22.G).

[61] A number of objectors applied to the FCA for judicial review on different issues, which the FCA dealt with in separate decisions. *Bell Canada v. Society of Composers, Authors and Music Publishers of Canada*, 2010 FCA 220, 409 N.R. 102 ("*Bell Canada*"),was an appeal by online music services contesting the

Board's determination in the Tariff 22.A decision that a download of a music file from the online music service's website by the end consumer is a "communication to the public". The FCA held that the Board's determination was a reasonable interpretation of s. 3(1)(*f*) of the Act. The FCA considered that *SOCAN v. CAIP* had fully answered the question of what constitutes a "communication" and accordingly confirmed that a download is a communication (para. 5).

[62] As stated above, the ESA's application for judicial review of the Tariff 22.B-G decision was dismissed by the FCA. On the issue of whether downloads of video games are communications to the public of the musical works they contain, the FCA referred to its reasons in *Bell Canada*, that is, that a download of a file containing a musical work is a communication to the public by telecommunication (2010 FCA 221, 406 N.R. 288, at para. 13).

II. Issue

[63] The issue in this appeal is whether the transmission of a video game through an Internet download is a "communication" to the public within the meaning of s. 3(1)(*f*) of the Act. If it is, SOCAN is entitled to royalties for the communication of the included musical works.

III. Analysis

A. *Overview*

[64] The ESA submits that on reading s. 3(1)(*f*) in its entirety, considering it in the context of the entire Act and in light of its legislative history, the provision "creates an exclusive right of public performance (or representation for works that are not publicly performed) delivered by means of telecommunication". They say that to "communicate" must mean "to cause information in humanly perceivable form to be imparted to another person for <u>immediate</u> listening or viewing" (A.F., at para. 33 (emphasis added)). The communication right was never meant to cover situations where durable copies of the copyrighted works are made available, which are already covered by the *reproduction right* and for which copyright holders are already compensated. Since the users can *neither see nor hear* game software while it is being downloaded, the transmission from the online game provider to the user does not constitute a communication to the public. The ESA further argues that the Act uses both the terms "communicate" and "transmit" and that the two cannot have the same meaning. In their submission, the act of a game being downloaded by a user constitutes a transmission and not a communication. The ESA also relies on American jurisprudence and raises some "unintended consequences" of the decisions below.

[65] In this appeal, the ESA does not advance arguments on whether, should the transmissions be found to be "communications" within the meaning of s. 3(1)(*f*), such transmissions would be communications "*to the public*"; this issue is dealt with in the companion case *Rogers Communications Inc. v. Society of Composers, Authors and Music Publishers of Canada*, 2012 SCC 35, [2012] 2 S.C.R. 283.

[66] SOCAN says that the decisions of the Board and of the FCA were correctly decided. In SOCAN's view, to communicate means simply "to transmit, impart, make known or convey information" (R.F., at para. 32 (emphasis deleted)) and the ESA's submissions would artificially restrict the ordinary meaning of the word. Further, SOCAN says that the ESA's argument ignores the basic principle of copyright law that the copyrights granted in s. 3(1) for reproduction, performance and communication of a work are separate and distinct rights (R.F., at para. 9).

B. *Standard of Review*

[67] For the reasons explained in *Rogers*, at paras. 10-16, the applicable standard of review is correctness.

C. *Whether Transmitting Musical Works Through Downloads Over the Internet Is "Communicating"*

(1) Section 3(1)(f) and Section 2

[68] This appeal requires defining the right to"communicate . . . by telecommunication" in the *Copyright Act*. The ESA urges a definition of "communicate . . . by telecommunication" as "to cause information in humanly perceivable form to be imparted to another person for immediate listening or viewing" (A.F., at para. 33 (emphasis added)).

[69] The exclusive right of the copyright holder to"communicate . . . to the public by telecommunication" is provided in s. 3(1)(*f*) of the Act:

3. (1) For the purposes of this Act, "copyright", in relation to a work, means the sole right to produce or reproduce the work or any substantial part thereof in any material form whatever, to perform the work or any substantial part thereof in public or, if the work is unpublished, to publish the work or any substantial part thereof, and includes the sole right

. . .

(*f*) in the case of any literary, dramatic, musical or artistic work, to communicate the work to the public by telecommunication,

. . .

and to authorize any such acts.

[70] Section 2 of the Act defines "telecommunication":

"telecommunication" means any transmission of signs, signals, writing, images or sounds or intelligence of any nature by wire, radio, visual, optical or other electromagnetic system;

It is not disputed that transmissions in the digital environment are "telecommunications".

(2) The Approach to Statutory Interpretation

[71] The *Copyright Act* must be interpreted in accordance with the general rules of statutory interpretation: "the words of an Act are to be read in their entire context

and in their grammatical and ordinary sense harmoniously with the scheme of the Act, the object of the Act, and the intention of Parliament" (*CCH Canadian Ltd. v. Law Society of Upper Canada*, 2004 SCC 13, [2004] 1 S.C.R. 339, at para. 9, citing E. A. Driedger, *Construction of Statutes* (2nd ed. 1983), at p. 87).

(3) The Precedents

[72] The word"communicate" is not defined in the Act. I therefore start with the dictionary meaning of the word. The *Oxford English Dictionary* (online) defines the verb "communicate" as "[t]o impart (information, knowledge, or the like) . . .; to impart the knowledge or idea of (something), to inform a person of; to convey, express; to give an impression of, put across". The *Shorter Oxford English Dictionary on Historical Principles* (6th ed. 2007), vol. 1, at p. 466, includes the following definition: to "[i]mpart, transmit". The *Merriam-Webster's Collegiate Dictionary* entry is defined as "to convey knowledge of or information about: make known" ((11th ed. 2003), at p. 251). There is no suggestion in these definitions that "to communicate" cannot mean "to transmit", and indeed, the *Shorter Oxford English Dictionary* expressly includes in the definition of "communicate", "transmit".

[73] Although the question was not directly in issue in that case (see para. 30), Binnie J. in *SOCAN v. CAIP* endorsed the ordinary definition of"communicate" as the appropriate interpretation of the word in s. 3(1)(*f*) of the *Copyright Act*:

> The Board ruled that a telecommunication occurs when the music is transmitted from the host server to the end user. I agree with this.
>
> . . .
>
> The word "communicate"is an ordinary English word that means to "impart" or "transmit" (*Shorter Oxford English Dictionary on Historical Principles* (5th ed. 2002), vol. 1, at p. 463). [paras. 42 and 46]

[74] Since*SOCAN v. CAIP*, the FCA has had the occasion to deal directly with the meaning of the right to "communicate" under s. 3(1)(*f*) in *Canadian Wireless Telecommunications Assn. v. Society of Composers, Authors and Music Publishers of Canada*, 2008 FCA 6, [2008] 3 F.C.R. 539, leave to appeal refused, [2008] 2 S.C.R. vi ("*CWTA*"). The question in that case, answered in the affirmative, was whether a person communicates to the public the musical works contained in ringtones when members of the public download the ringtones for their mobile phones. Sharlow J.A. rejected the argument that a transmission is not the same thing as a communication because "'communication' must be understood to include only a transmission that is intended to be heard or perceived by the recipient simultaneously with or immediately upon the transmission" (para. 18). She wrote:

> In my view, the applicants are proposing a meaning of the word "communication"that is too narrow. The word "communication" connotes the passing of information from one person to another. A musical ringtone is information in the form of a digital audio file that is capable of being communicated. The normal mode of communicating a digital audio file is to transmit it. The wireless transmission of a musical

ringtone to a cellphone is a communication, <u>whether the owner of the cellphone accesses it immediately in order to hear the music, or at some later time</u>. The fact that the technology used for the transmission does not permit the cellphone owner to listen to the music during the transmission does not mean that there is no communication. In my view, in the context of a wireless transmission, it is the receipt of the transmission that completes the communication.

This conclusion accords with the [*SOCAN v. CAIP*] case (cited above). In that case Justice Binnie, writing for the majority, said that the transmission of information over the Internet is a communication once the information is received (see paragraph 45). . . . [I]t is undoubtedly a true statement. [Emphasis added; paras. 19-20.]

(4) The ESA's Arguments for Not Following SOCAN v. CAIP and CWTA

[75] The ESA argues that *SOCAN v. CAIP* (to the extent that it addressed the issue) and *CWTA* should not be followed.

(a) *"Communicate" and "Transmit"*

[76] The ESA first argues that there must be some difference between the words "communicate" and "transmit". The two words are not used interchangeably in the Act and if Parliament used both words, it intended them to have different meanings. On this basis, the ESA submits that to "communicate to the public" means "more than the [mere] transmission of a file from one point to another point without that file being seen or heard"(A.F., at para. 73). Therefore, a download is not a communication within the meaning of s. 3(1)(*f*), but a mere transmission.

[77] I do not find this argument compelling. Parliament is presumed to use words in their ordinary meaning: R. Sullivan, *Statutory Interpretation* (2nd ed. 2007), at p. 49. As noted above, to "communicate" means to "impart" or"transmit". The *Oxford English Dictionary* (online) defines "transmit"as: "[t]o cause (a thing) to pass, go, or be conveyed to another person, place, or thing; to send across an intervening space; to convey, transfer; . . . [t]o convey or <u>communicate</u> (usually something immaterial) *to* another or others" (emphasis added); and, in a more technical sense: "[t]o send out electric signals or electromagnetic waves corresponding to (an image, a programme, etc.)." The definitions of "transmit"in the *Merriam-Webster's Collegiate Dictionary* are:

to send or convey from one person or place to another . . .

to send out (a signal) either by radio waves or over a wire.

I see no reason why, having regard to context, the meaning of both words cannot overlap.

[78] As set out above, s. 2 of the Act defines "telecommunication" as "any transmission of signs, signals, writing, images or sounds or intelligence of any nature by wire, radio, visual, optical or other electromagnetic system". This definition equates the term "telecommunication"with the transmission of certain subject matter by electromagnetic system. The prefix "tele" simply means "to a distance". So, "telecommunication" means communicating to a distance by the means specified in the Act. It would seem odd that "telecommunication" and

transmission by electromagnetic system are interchangeable in the Act but that "to communicate" and "to transmit" would not be. The more obvious interpretation would be that for the purposes of s. 3(1)(f) of the Act, the exclusive right of the copyright holder to communicate works to the public by telecommunication is simply to transmit those works to the public by electromagnetic system, including the Internet.

[79] The above definitions of "communicate" and "transmit" and the context in which the words are used in the Act do not support the ESA's conclusion that to"communicate" in s. 3(1)(f) must necessarily mean to transmit information in a humanly perceptible form for *immediate* perceiving and listening. Even accepting that to communicate means to impart an idea, there is no requirement that the idea be perceived and heard *immediately*.

[80] The ESA supports its argument that the words "transmit" and "communicate"must have different meanings primarily by reference to s. 2.4(1) (c). Section 2.4(1)(c) provides:

2.4 (1) For the purposes of communication to the public by telecommunication,

. . .

(c) where a person, as part of

(i) a network, within the meaning of the *Broadcasting Act*, whose operations result in the communication of works or other subject-matter to the public, or

(ii) any programming undertaking whose operations result in the communication of works or other subject-matter to the public,

transmits by telecommunication a work or other subject-matter that is communicated to the public by another personwho is not a retransmitter of a signal within the meaning of subsection 31(1), the transmission and communication of that work or other subject-matter by those persons constitute a single communication to the public for which those persons are jointly and severally liable.

[81] The ESA argues that the words "transmit" and "transmission" appear twice and the word "communicate" five times, and that this means that they must have different meanings. It says that transmitting is merely delivery or receipt of information or data being conveyed; that the term "communicate" pertains to what happens after transmission; and that this implies that the difference is that a transmission is not the conveyance of information in a humanly perceivable form. As a result, a transmission does not implicate s. 3(1)(f), because s. 3(1)(f) uses the term communicate which, by contrast, does imply conveyance in humanly perceivable form. Therefore, since the communication only occurs after the transmission, a download does not give rise to any entitlement under s. 3(1)(f).

[82] This argument ignores the context and purpose of s. 2.4(1)(c). This section was introduced in 1988 in order to reverse the holding in *Composers, Authors and Publishers Assoc. of Canada Ltd. v. CTV Television Network Ltd.*, [1968] S.C.R. 676 ("*CAPAC*"), that CTV's transmissions of programs to its affiliated stations, for further broadcasting to the public by the affiliated stations, did not

engage the right to communicate to the public in s. 3(1)(*f*), because such transmissions remained within the private realm (see J. S. McKeown, *Fox on Canadian Law of Copyright and Industrial Designs* (4th ed. (loose-leaf)), at p. 21-90). In the context of s. 2.4(1)(*c*), a "transmission" describes conveying works within a network or programming undertaking before the work is conveyed to the public, while a "communication" is the conveyance of the work "to the public" by another actor within the network or programming undertaking. Without s. 2.4(1)(*c*), only the latter act — the communication to the public — would engage s. 3(1)(*f*); but a private transmission between affiliates would remain outside of copyright protection. The effect of s. 2.4(1)(*c*), where it applies, is to make the transmission and the communication a single act of communication to the public, so that both the person who transmits the work and the person who communicates the work to the public are jointly and severally liable for the act of communication to the public.

[83] All that can be teased out of s. 2.4(1)(*c*) is that "communication to the public" is the phrase used to designate instances where copyright protection is engaged, and not that "communication" means a conveyance of information in a humanly perceivable form. On the other hand, "transmit" or "transmission" are terms designating situations that do not engage copyright protection under s. 3(1)(*f*). I agree with the ESA that s. 2.4(1)(*c*) suggests that under the Act, the words "communicate" and "transmit" are not used interchangeably. But the provision does not suggest that the words refer to different types of conveyances. Rather, the distinction is that the words are used in conjunction with different types of recipient and different legal significance. Unless the transmission is combined with a communication to the public, s. 3(1)(*f*) would not attach to the transmission. When the transmission is ultimately a communication to the public, s. 2.4(1)(*c*) provides that the transmission and the communication to the public are a single communication to the public which does attract copyright under s. 3(1)(*f*). Indeed, the word "communicate" is consistently used in conjunction with the words "to the public" throughout the Act. The ESA's separating the word "communicate" from the words "to the public" to give it an independent meaning different from that of "transmit" is not supported by Parliament's intention in enacting s. 2.4(1)(*c*). The words of s. 2.4(1)(*c*), when read in context, do not support the distinction argued by the ESA.

(b) *The CAPAC Decision*

[84] The ESA relies on this Court's decision in *CAPAC* for the proposition that to communicate means disseminating performances to the public for immediate listening and not merely sending signals that may be perceived later. However, this jurisprudence is of little avail to the ESA.

[85] As noted above, in *CAPAC*, this Court was asked to determine whether the transmission of television programs containing musical works by CTV to its affiliated stations, for broadcasting to the public by the affiliates, constituted "communicating the same by radio communication" (at p. 679), an act protected under s. 3(1)(*f*) as it read at that time.

[86] It should first be noted that *CAPAC* interpreted provisions of the Act that have since been amended in a way relevant to the scope of s. 3(1)(*f*), as will be discussed later. In any event, in *CAPAC*, the *ratio* of the Court's decision was that CTV's transmissions of recorded TV programs containing music to its affiliates were not communications of musical *works* by radio-communication. Rather, as CTV was transmitting *performances* of musical works (e.g., in an ordinary TV program) and not the musical works themselves (e.g., the sheet of music), s. 3(1)(*f*), which did not apply to performances of musical works, was not engaged. It is important to note that this distinction arose from the definition of "musical work" in the Act as it read at the time and is no longer applicable.

[87] Nonetheless, the ESA relies on some comments of Pigeon J., at pp. 681-82 of *CAPAC*, involving an analysis of Article 11*bis* of the *Berne Convention for the Protection of Literacy and Artistic Works*, 828 U.N.T.S. 221, on which s. 3(1)(*f*) was based. The ESA says that this analysis demonstrates that a communication is more than sending signals, which is all that occurs when works are downloaded as in the case now before the Court. Rather, the ESA says that Article 11*bis* contemplates public performances by broadcasting, in other words, communications in humanly perceptible form. Therefore, a "communicat[ion]" within the meaning of s. 3(1)(*f*) must also be a conveyance of information in humanly perceptible form.

[88] However, the passages of Pigeon J.'s judgment note that "'communication' does not usually mean 'a performance' [but that] it is apt to include performances" (p. 681 (emphasis added)). The necessary implication of these words is that "communication" is a broader term than "performance". Therefore, Pigeon J.'s analysis does not support the ESA's contention that a communication is *necessarily* a performance or *necessarily* more than sending signals.

(5) Whether "Communicating" is "Performing" a Work at a Distance

[89] The ESA further argues, based on the legislative history of s. 3(1)(*f*), that the communication right is only a variation of the performance right, being the right to perform a work to a *distant* audience. Because a performance, in the ESA's submission, is, by nature, a transient event that cannot result in the transmission of a durable copy of the work to the audience, downloads cannot be performances and, therefore, cannot be communications.

[90] I digress briefly to point out that the structure of s. 3(1) implies that the communication right in paragraph (*f*) is a self-standing right independent of the performance right in the introduction of the section. The first lines of the English version of s. 3(1) provide that

> "copyright". . . means the sole right to produce or reproduce the work . . ., to perform the work . . . in public or . . . to publish the work . . . and includes the sole right . . .

There then follow specific rights listed as paragraphs (*a*) to (*i*). Paragraph (*f*) provides for the sole right to "communicate the work to the public by telecommunication".

[91] While the use of the word "includes" could indicate that the rights listed in paragraphs (*a*) to (*i*) are instances of one of the rights in the opening words of s. 3(1), the context indicates otherwise. Several of the listed rights are clearly outside of the right to produce or reproduce, perform or publish. For example, paragraph (*i*) provides for the right to rent out a sound recording embodying a musical work. It is difficult to see how this right fits within the right to produce or reproduce, perform or publish the work. Indeed, it would be contrary to *Théberge*, in particular at paras. 42 and 45, where the majority of this Court held that a "reproduction" within the meaning of the Act requires a *multiplication* of copies. All the prerogatives of the copyright holder in s. 3(1) are better considered as separate and distinct rights (*Bishop v. Stevens*, at p. 477, *per* McLachlin J.; *Compo Co. v. Blue Crest Music Inc.*, at p. 373, *per* Estey J.).

[92] This interpretation of the English version of s. 3(1) is consistent with the French version of the text, which states that "*[l]e droit d'auteur sur l'œuvre comporte le droit exclusif de produire ou reproduire . . . l'œuvre, [de la représenter ou de la publier]; ce droit comporte, en outre, [les droits énumérés aux al. a) à i)].*" The use of the phrase "*en outre*" — in addition — indicates paras. (*a*) to (*i*) are in addition to those in the opening words.

[93] Nonetheless, the ESA relies on legislative history in order to confine the scope of the right to communicate to the public to performing a work to a public in a distant place, in a humanly perceptible form, as distinct from a download.

[94] The Canadian Act was based on the *Berne Convention* of 1886, as revised in Berlin in 1908 (see *Bishop v. Stevens*, at p. 473). The revised *Berne Convention* comprised certain public performance rights in certain types of works. However, the advent of the radio warranted another revision of the Convention. In 1928, Article 11*bis* was added to the text, which guaranteed that:

Article 11*bis*

(1) Authors of literary and artistic works shall enjoy the exclusive right of authorizing the communication of their works to the public by radiocommunication.

[95] In 1931, Canada implemented the revision through the then s. 3(1)(*f*), which provided for a right, "[i]n case of any literary, dramatic, musical or artistic work, to communicate such work by radio communication" (*Copyright Amendment Act, 1931*, S.C. 1931, c. 8) (see *CAPAC*, at pp. 680-81).

[96] Section 3(1)(*f*) was again amended in 1988. According to *Canadian Admiral Corp. v. Rediffusion, Inc.*, [1954] Ex. C.R. 382, the radiocommunication right extended to radio and traditional over-the-air television broadcasting, leaving transmissions by *cable* outside of copyright protection. This technology-specific communication right was amended to the technologically *neutral* right to "communicate . . . to the public by telecommunication" to reflect the obligations entered into by Canada under the *North American Free Trade Agreement*, Can. T.S. 1994 No. 2 (*Canada-United States Free Trade Agreement Implementation Act*, S.C. 1988, c. 65, ss. 61 and 62). The change from radiocommunication to telecommunication and further amendments in 1993 meant that Canadian

cable companies which previously avoided any payment of royalties under the"radiocommunication" right, and other users, were now caught by the Act: S. Handa, *Copyright Law in Canada* (2002), at p. 320; D. Vaver, *Intellectual Property Law: Copyright, Patents, Trade-marks* (2nd ed. 2011), at p. 90.

[97] The ESA argues that from the outset, s. 3(1)(*f*), as well as its Berne progenitor Article 11*bis*, were meant to provide *broadcasting*rights the nature of which is "to deliver content [i.e. performances of works] to a public audience for immediate listening or viewing" (A.F., at para. 40). In the ESA's submission, the 1988 amendment from "radiocommunication" to "telecommunication"did not change the fundamental nature of the communication right, that is, that it was concerned with *broadcasting*. The word "communicate" in the English version was not amended, although the means by which the communication may be made were expanded (A.F., at para. 52). The verb "*transmettre*",used in the French version of s. 3(1)(*f*) prior to the 1988 amendments, was replaced by "*communiquer*".

[98] There is little doubt that a historic relationship between the right of public performance and the right to communicate to the public did exist:

> . . . as performance before a live audience was one of the first forms of exploitation to be covered by copyright, it made sense to create a right to provide protection when the performance took place at a distance through the use of Hertzian (radio) waves and the other types of communication technologies invented since then (television, cable, satellite and the internet).

(E. F. Judge and D. J. Gervais, *Intellectual Property: The Law in Canada* (2nd. ed. 2011), at pp. 166-67)

[99] The legislation has evolved to recognize the evolution of technologies. In 1988, the relevance of including transmissions by cable within the communication right had become obvious due to the prevalence of that mode of telecommunication.

[100] Even though the advent of cable may have been the catalyzing force for the 1988 amendment, the amendment did not only cover cable communications, in addition to radiocommunications, but adopted neutral language to encompass evolving but then unknown technological advances. In adopting the neutral language of "telecommunication", Parliament removed all reference to conventional broadcasting. The fact that in 1988 Parliament did not foresee, or could not have foreseen, the way in which modern technologies would evolve should not serve to limit the scope of the communication right when it is applied to one such new technology.

[101] On this basis, the historic relationship of s. 3(1)(*f*) with broadcasting-type industries does not support reading into the Act restrictions which are not apparent from and are even inconsistent with the current language of the Act. In particular, the historic relationship does not support adopting the ESA's proposition to read into the language of the Act the significant restriction that the transmission must be in a "humanly perceivable form for immediate viewing or listening" (A.F., at para. 74). While the rationale for the 1988 change from radio

to "telecommunication" was concerned with the technical *means* by which the communication to the public was made, nothing supports concluding that s. 3(1) (*f*) could not also apply to new technologies which operate in a manner different from traditional broadcasting. This includes a communication occurring in a manner which also provides durable copies of the works that the users may view at a later time. When transmitted over the Internet, whether works are perceptible immediately or at a later moment or whether or not the technology used involves producing temporary copies, as in the case of streams, or permanent copies of the work is irrelevant to whether a communication has occurred and the work will, or has the potential to be, viewed or listened to by the receiver. As stated at para. 45 of *SOCAN v. CAIP*:

> At the end of the transmission, the end user has a musical work in his or her possession that was not there before. The work has necessarily been communicated . .
> . . To hold otherwise would . . . fly in the face of the ordinary use of language . . . .

(6) American Jurisprudence

[102] The ESA relies on the decision of the United States Court of Appeals for the Second Circuit in *United States v. American Society of Composers, Authors and Publishers*, 627 F.3d 64 (2010) ("*U.S. v. ASCAP*"), *certiorari* denied (U.S.S.C., Octobre 3, 2011, No. 10-1337), where the Court of Appeals for the Second Circuit decided that the download of a copy of a work did not come within the scope of the right to perform in public, as defined in the U.S. *Copyright Act*, 17 U.S.C. §§ 101 and 106(4).

[103] This decision is of no avail to the ESA. The United States copyright law does not include an exclusive right in the copyright holder to communicate to the public. Rather, it recognizes a right of public performance (17 U.S.C. § 106(4)), which has been understood to include situations such as radio or television broadcasting where performances are made available to a distant public. This is a fundamental difference with the right to communicate a work by telecommunication in s. 3(1)(*f*) of the Canadian Act, as explained above. The two cannot be equated.

[104] This Court has recognized in the past important differences both in wording and in policy between Canadian and American copyright legislation. It has cautioned that "United States court decisions, even where the factual situations are similar, must be scrutinized very carefully"(see *Compo Co. v. Blue Crest Music Inc.*, at p. 367). The difference in statutory wording between the provisions of the American legislation and of the Canadian *Copyright Act* is sufficient to render the U.S. decisions of no assistance in the interpretive exercise engaged here. Indeed, following the American jurisprudence in interpreting Canada's copyright legislation would, in this case, amount to rewriting the Canadian Act.

(7) The Application of Section 3(1)(f) Does not Depend on the Purpose of the Communication

[105] The ESA's argument that the sole purpose of the transmissions in the case of downloads is just to *deliver copies*to the customers is not an answer to the

fact that a transmission by telecommunication to the public, and therefore, a communication within the meaning of s. 3(1)(*f*), effectively occurs.

[106] A similar argument was made in *Bishop v. Stevens*. That case dealt with whether a TV station that had paid the appropriate royalties for the right to broadcast a performance of a musical work had also acquired the right to make an "ephemeral" recording of the performance *for the sole purpose of facilitating the broadcast*. It was held that the right to perform did not include the right to make a recording, albeit an "ephemeral" one made only for technical reasons. McLachlin J. held that "s. 3(1)(*d*) contains no mention of purpose" (p. 479):

> Interpretation of a statute must always begin with the ordinary meaning of the words used, and nothing in this section restricts its application to recordings made for the purpose of reproduction and sale. A recording may be made for any purpose, even one not prejudicial to the copyright holder, but if it is not authorized by the copyright holder then it is an infringement of his rights. [p. 480]

[107] Similarly, the fact that the work is transmitted over the Internet, and therefore, "communicate[d] . . . by telecommunication"within the ordinary meaning of the words, for the purpose of delivering a copy of the video game containing the musical work to the user, does not change the fact that there *is* an Internet communication requiring authorization of the copyright holder.

(8) Unintended Consequences

[108] The ESA raises a number of "unintended consequences" that would flow from accepting that downloads are communications within s. 3(1)(*f*) of the Act.

[109] The ESA first refers to s. 2.2(1) of the Act, which defines the concept of "publication" for the purposes of the Act. Section 2.2(1) provides:

> **2.2** (1) For the purposes of this Act, "publication"means
>
> > (*a*) in relation to works,
> >
> > > (i) making copies of a work available to the public,
> >
> > . . .
>
> but does not include
>
> > (*c*) the performance in public, or the communication to the public by telecommunication, of a literary, dramatic, musical or artistic work or a sound recording, or . . .

[110] The ESA argues that adopting the "broad interpretation of 'communicate to the public' to include distribution of durable copies over networks" would mean that where copies of works are"distributed" over the Internet, these works would not be considered as"published", because publication, as defined by s. 2.2(1) of the Act, excludes works communicated to the public by telecommunication (A.F., at paras. 102-10).

[111] In my opinion, no conclusion concerning the scope of the right to communicate to the public by telecommunication in s. 3(1)(*f*) can be drawn on the basis of s. 2.2(1). Section 2.2(1) is only relevant in understanding the scope of

publication, in those sections where it appears in the Act. Where that word is used, the definition in s. 2.2(1) provides that it means "making copies of a work available to the public", but does not include the communication of a work to the public by telecommunication. On the other hand, s. 2.2(1) does *not* provide a comprehensive definition for all purposes of the Act whereby "making copies of a work available to the public" can never occur in connection with communication to the public by telecommunication. It cannot be inferred that the independent right of communication to the public by telecommunication in s. 3(1)(*f*) cannot be engaged where, at the same time, copies of a work are made available.

[112] As for the ESA's argument that this may render publication technologically non-neutral, as works distributed *only* by making them available for download on the Internet would not be considered as published, whether this is the inescapable conclusion about the meaning of s. 2.2(1) remains to be seen in a case where the issue arises. Indeed, there is some authority suggesting that "[w]ork available online or sitting in a public database may therefore be considered 'published'", and this notwithstanding the fact that a work conveyed over the Internet constitutes a communication to the public by telecommunication (Vaver, at pp. 157 and 172-73).

[113] ESA also argues that extending the s. 3(1)(*f*) right to include "digital delivery of copies of a work" would make the secondary infringement provisions in s. 27(2) "largely redundant" in the electronic environment (A.F., at para. 117). It says there would be little need for the secondary infringement provisions related to the electronic distribution of copies of works. I would note that this argument assumes that communication is equivalent to distribution under the Act without any supporting justification on the point. While it appears that such a redundancy point is a policy argument that should be addressed by Parliament if there is a view that any alleged overlap in the provisions is considered undesirable, I will deal with it briefly.

[114] The basic difference between primary and secondary infringement is that primary infringement under s. 3(1) may occur without the infringer knowing that infringement is occurring while secondary infringement only applies where the person has actual or constructive knowledge that what is being distributed constitutes an infringing copy of a work. Section 27(2) provides in relevant part for purposes of this case:

> It is an infringement of copyright for any person to
>
> . . .
>
> (*b*) distribute to such an extent as to affect prejudicially the owner of the copyright,
>
> . . .
>
> a copy of a work . . . that the person knows or should have known infringes copyright . . . .

[115] A secondary infringer may be the same person as the primary infringer, but need not be. The purpose of s. 27(2) is to widen the net for copyright infringement beyond those who engage in primary infringement to those who,

with knowledge or constructive knowledge, distribute to such an extent as to prejudicially affect the owner of the copyright, a copy of a work that already infringes copyright. A distributor who knows or should know that he is distributing an infringing copy of a work, for example because it was reproduced without authority of the copyright holder, may be liable for infringement even though he did not engage in the primary infringement. However, a distributor who distributes an authorized copy of the work will not be found liable under s. 27(2)(*b*).

[116] According to the evidence in this case, it is standard practice in the video game publishing industry to negotiate clearance of copyright for the reproduction of the musical works incorporated in the games prior to their publication. In the possession of the video game vendor and before the vendor takes any action with respect to communicating the game, there is no infringement of copyright because reproduction rights have been cleared. Unless authorized by the holder of the rights under s. 3(1)(*f*), however, the communication of the game will violate s. 3(1)(*f*) of the Act. But s. 27(2) will not be engaged.

[117] ESA has structured its examples in support of its redundancy argument carefully. However, they do not cover the facts of this case. Here the communication or distribution is of prior authorized copies, not infringing copies. Only s. 3(1)(*f*) is engaged, not s. 27(2).

(9) Policy Considerations

[118] The policy concern raised by the ESA is that a copyright holder should not be entitled to both a reproduction and a communication right in the context of Internet downloads.

[119] The answer to this concern is straightforward: the rights of copyright holders under s. 3(1) are distinct and separate rights. *Bishop v. Stevens* re-affirmed (at p. 477) the holding in *Compo Co. v. Blue Crest Music Inc.*, at p. 373, *per* Estey J., that the rights listed in s. 3(1) are distinct and separate rights:

> It is clear from an examination of s. 3(1) that it lists a number of distinct rights belonging to the copyright holder. As stated in *Ash v. Hutchinson & Co. (Publishers), Ltd.*, [1936] 2 All E.R. 1496 (C.A.), at p. 1507, *per* Greene L.J.:
>
> Under the Copyright Act, 1911 [on which the Canadian Act was based], s. 1(2), the rights of the owner of copyright are set out. A number of acts are specified, the sole right to do which is conferred on the owner of the copyright. The right to do each of these acts is, in my judgment, a separate statutory right, and anyone who without the consent of the owner of the copyright does any of these acts commits a tort; if he does two of them, he commits two torts, and so on. [Emphasis added.]

[120] The occurrence of one infringement therefore does not preclude the finding of another. As "[i]nfringement is the single act of doing something which 'only the owner of the copyright has the right to do'"(*Compo Co. v. Blue Crest Music Inc.*, at p. 375), if two protected acts occur without authorization of the copyright holder, there are two infringements. The fact that there are two protected rights does not restrict the protection afforded by each right.

[121] I cannot agree with my colleagues that the"principle of technological neutrality requires that ... we interpret the *Copyright Act* in a way that avoids imposing an additional layer of protections and fees based solely on the *method of delivery* of the work to the end user"(para. 9 (emphasis in original)). Characterizing the Internet transmission as a mere "method of delivery" of the work pre-empts the application of the right to communicate by telecommunication in s. 3(1)(*f*). Further, the proposition is inconsistent with the approach to media neutrality as described by the majority of this Court in *Robertson v. Thomson Corp.*, 2006 SCC 43, [2006] 2 S.C.R. 363, at para. 49, *per* LeBel and Fish JJ.:

> Media neutrality means that the *Copyright Act*should continue to apply in different media, including more technologically advanced ones. But it does not mean that once a work is converted into electronic data anything can then be done with it. . . . Media neutrality is not a licence to override the rights of authors — it exists to protect the rights of authors and others as technology evolves.

[122] A media neutral application of the Act to the facts of this case would mean that the right of reproduction continues to apply to copies made through downloads, notwithstanding the fact that they are *digital*copies. It would also support the proposition that the communication right must continue to apply to digital communications, notwithstanding that they may differ from traditional broadcasting technologies. A media neutral application of the Act, however, does *not* imply that a court can depart from the ordinary meaning of the words of the Act in order to achieve the level of protection for copyright holders that the court considers is adequate.

[123] Any concerns arising from the independent protected rights in the digital context are concerns of policy, which are properly within the domain of Parliament in defining the scope of copyright. "The *Copyright Act* is usually presented as a balance between promoting the public interest in the encouragement and dissemination of works of the arts and intellect and obtaining a just reward for the creator" (*Théberge*, at para. 30). While the "courts should strive to maintain an appropriate balance between these two goals" (*CCH Canadian Ltd.*, at para. 10), inferring limits into the communication right in the present case would be beyond the function of the courts. "In Canada, copyright [remains] a creature of statute . . ." (*SOCAN v. CAIP*, at para. 82). See also *CCH*, at para. 9; *Théberge*, at para. 5; *Bishop v. Stevens*, at p. 477; *Compo Co. v. Blue Crest Music Inc.*, at p. 373.

[124] Indeed, it would be hazardous for the courts to delimit the scope of broadly defined rights in the digital environment without the benefit of a global picture of the implications for all the parties involved. Binnie J. wrote in *SOCAN v. CAIP*, at para. 40:

> The capacity of the Internet to disseminate"works of the arts and intellect" is one of the great innovations of the information age. Its use should be facilitated rather than discouraged, but this should not be done unfairly at the expense of those who created the works of arts and intellect in the first place.

[125] In light of these considerations, providing exceptions to the right to communicate by telecommunication is properly left to Parliament. History has

shown that Parliament will indeed legislate when it considers copyright protection to be improperly balanced (for example, it introduced the ephemeral recordings exception in s. 30.8(1), following the ruling in *Bishop* (S.C. 1997, c. 24, s. 18); McKeown, at pp. 21-82 to 21-83).

[126] In addition, it should be borne in mind that SOCAN merely proposes tariffs, which must then be authorized by the Board. In doing so, it is within the power of the Board to adjust proposed royalty rates in a manner that it considers appropriate for a particular use. Specifically, when the same activity engages two protected rights, the Board is in a position to consider each of these rights in light of the type of use that causes users to engage in the activity. This is consistent with the core of the Board's mandate as an economic regulatory agency, which consists of "working out . . . the details of an appropriate royalty tariff" (*SOCAN v. CAIP*, at para. 49) based on the economic value of the different ways in which copyrighted works may be used. The Board's authority to determine royalty rates in factual circumstances addresses concerns about the relative value of services as between online game providers and bricks and mortar stores, and the overlapping of rights and alleged "double-dipping" by copyright holders.

IV. Conclusion — Meaning of "Communicate" in Section 3(1)(f)

[127] Communicating works to the public by telecommunication is an independent and distinct right from other rights in s. 3(1) that are included within copyright. It is complete when the communication is received, in this case, when the file is downloaded to the user's computer, even though it can be perceived only after the transmission, or whether or not it is ever perceived. As put by Professor Vaver, "[s]ending works by radio, television, cable, fax, modem, satellite, or microwave involves telecommunication"; if, in addition, the communication is "to the public", it will attract liability (p. 172).

[128] I would dismiss the appeal with costs.

(b) What is "To the Public"?

For the communication of a work to the public to be an infringing act, there must be a communication "to the public." The phrase "to the public" indicates that a communication must be aimed or targeted toward people in general or the community.[23]

In interpreting the meaning of the words "to the public", the courts in Canada, and in Commonwealth jurisdictions with similar legislation, have resorted to the authorities which have interpreted the word "public" in relation to the right to perform a work in public. The tests for determining what is the "public" — the character of the audience, the relation of the audience to the owner of the copyright, and whether permitting the performance would whittle down the value of the copyright to the owner — have been looked to.

---

23   *CCH Canadian Ltd. v. Law Society of Upper Canada* (2002), 18 C.P.R. (4th) 161 (Fed. C.A.).

Some authorities have suggested that the term "to the public" is broader than the term "in public" since it makes clear that the place where the relevant communication occurs is irrelevant. That is to say, there can be a communication to individual members of the public in a private or domestic setting which is nevertheless a communication to the public. A broadcast by a radio station is just such a communication.

CCH Canadian Ltd. v. Law Society of Upper Canada 2004 SCC 13

Arbour J., Bastarache J., Binnie J., Deschamps J., Iacobucci J., LeBel J., Major J., McLachlin C.J.C.

Heard: November 10, 2003
Judgment: March 4, 2004
Docket: 29320

The Chief Justice:

I. Introduction — The Issues To Be Determined

1 The appellant, the Law Society of Upper Canada, is a statutory non-profit corporation that has regulated the legal profession in Ontario since 1822. Since 1845, the Law Society has maintained and operated the Great Library at Osgoode Hall in Toronto, a reference and research library with one of the largest collections of legal materials in Canada. The Great Library provides a request-based photocopy service (the "custom photocopy service") for Law Society members, the judiciary and other authorized researchers. Under the custom photocopy service, legal materials are reproduced by Great Library staff and delivered in person, by mail or by facsimile transmission to requesters. The Law Society also maintains self-service photocopiers in the Great Library for use by its patrons.

2 The respondents, CCH Canadian Ltd., Thomson Canada Ltd. and Canada Law Book Inc., publish law reports and other legal materials. In 1993, the respondent publishers commenced copyright infringement actions against the Law Society, seeking a declaration of subsistence and ownership of copyright in eleven specific works and a declaration that the Law Society had infringed copyright when the Great Library reproduced a copy of each of the works. The publishers also sought a permanent injunction prohibiting the Law Society from reproducing these eleven works as well as any other works that they published.

. . .

5 The publishers have filed a cross-appeal in which they submit that, in addition to infringing copyright by reproducing copies of their works, the Law Society infringed copyright both by faxing and by selling copies of the publishers' copyrighted works through its custom photocopy service. The publishers also contend that the Great Library does not qualify for the library exemption under the Copyright Act and, finally, that they are entitled to an injunction to the extent that the Law Society has been found to infringe any one or more of

their copyrighted works. The four sub-issues that the Court must address on this cross-appeal are:

(1) Did the Law Society's fax transmissions of the publishers' works constitute communications "to the public" within s. 3(1)(f) of the Copyright Act so as to constitute copyright infringement?

(2) Did the Law Society infringe copyright by selling copies of the publishers' works contrary to s. 27(2) of the Copyright Act?

(3) Does the Law Society qualify for an exemption as a "library, archive or museum" under ss. 2 and 30.2(1) of the Copyright Act?

(4) To the extent that the Law Society has been found to infringe any one or more of the publishers' copyrighted works, are the publishers entitled to a permanent injunction under s. 34(1) of the Copyright Act?

6 With respect to the main appeal, I conclude that the Law Society did not infringe copyright by providing single copies of the respondent publishers' works to its members through the custom photocopy service. Although the works in question were "original" and thus covered by copyright, the Law Society's dealings with the works were for the purpose of research and were fair dealings within s. 29 of the Copyright Act. I also find that the Law Society did not authorize infringement by maintaining self-service photocopiers in the Great Library for use by its patrons. I would therefore allow the appeal.

7 On the cross-appeal, I conclude that there was no secondary infringement by the Law Society; the fax transmissions were not communications to the public and the Law Society did not sell copies of the publishers' works. In light of my finding on appeal that the Law Society's dealings with the publishers' works were fair, it is not necessary to decide whether the Great Library qualifies for the library exemption. This said, I would conclude that the Great Library does indeed qualify for this exemption. Finally, in light of my conclusion that there has been no copyright infringement, it is not necessary to issue an injunction in this case. I would dismiss the cross-appeal.

. . .

III. Analysis on Cross-Appeal

(1) Are the Law Society's fax transmissions communications to the public?

77 At trial, the publishers argued that the Law Society's fax transmissions of copies of their works to lawyers in Ontario were communications "to the public by telecommunication" and hence infringed s. 3(1)(f) of the Copyright Act. The trial judge found that the fax transmissions were not telecommunications to the public because they "emanated from a single point and were each intended to be received at a single point" (at para. 167). The Court of Appeal agreed, although it allowed that a series of sequential transmissions might constitute an infringement of an owner's right to communicate to the public.

78 I agree with these conclusions. The fax transmission of a single copy to a single individual is not a communication to the public. This said, a series of repeated fax transmissions of the same work to numerous different recipients might constitute communication to the public in infringement of copyright. However, there was no evidence of this type of transmission having occurred in this case.

79 On the evidence in this case, the fax transmissions were not communications to the public. I would dismiss this ground of cross-appeal.

Rogers Communications Inc. v. SOCAN, 2012 SCC 35 (S.C.C.)

The judgment of McLachlin C.J. and LeBel, Deschamps, Fish, Rothstein, Cromwell, Moldaver and Karakatsanis JJ. was delivered by

Rothstein J. —

I. Introduction

[1] Online music services offer permanent downloads, limited downloads and on-demand streams of files containing musical works. A download is the transmission over the Internet of a file containing data, such as a sound recording of a musical work, that gives the user a permanent copy of the file to keep as his or her own. A limited download allows the copy to be used as long as the user's subscription is paid up. A stream is a transmission of data that allows the user to listen to or view the content transmitted at the time of the transmission, resulting only in a temporary copy of the file on the user's hard drive. The Copyright Board was of the opinion that downloads and streams, among other uses of music that it examined as part of the certification process of a proposed tariff for the communication of musical works over the Internet, come within the scope of the exclusive right of copyright holders to communicate to the public by telecommunication provided by the Copyright Act, R.S.C. 1985, c. C-42 (the "Act"). Accordingly, it found that a claim for communication royalties by the holders of copyright in the communicated works was well founded, in addition to any reproduction royalties received when a work is copied through the Internet ((2007), 61 C.P.R. (4th) 353 ("Tariff 22.A decision")). On appeal, the Federal Court of Appeal agreed (2010 FCA 220, 409 N.R. 102).

[2] The sole issue in this appeal is the meaning of the phrase "to the public" in s. 3(1)(f) of the Act. The online music services brought this appeal on the basis that their uses of music do not engage the right to communicate to the public by telecommunication in s. 3(1)(f) because they do not come within the scope of the phrase "to the public". The issue of whether downloads can be "communication[s]" within the meaning of s. 3(1)(f) was left to be determined in the companion case Entertainment Software Association v. Society of Composers, Authors and Music Publishers of Canada, 2012 SCC 34, [2012] 2 S.C.R. 231 ("ESA"). In ESA, a majority of this Court determined that musical works

are not "communicated" by telecommunication when they are downloaded. This conclusion affects this appeal. The question of whether the online music services engage the exclusive right to "communicate . . . to the public by telecommunication" by offering downloads to members of the public has now become moot. However, the ESA did not contest the Board's conclusion that a stream constitutes a "communication" within the meaning of s. 3(1)(f) of the Act. As a result, the remaining issue here is whether, based on CCH Canadian Ltd. v. Law Society of Upper Canada, 2004 SCC 13, [2004] 1 S.C.R. 339 ("CCH"), such communication of protected works nevertheless does not engage the exclusive right to communicate to the public because a point-to-point transmission from the website of an online music service to any individual customer is a private communication.

II. Facts and Procedural History

[3] The appellants, Rogers Communications Inc., Rogers Wireless Partnership, Shaw Cablesystems G.P., Bell Canada and Telus Communications Company, offer online music services. Online music services provide catalogues of digital audio files that consumers can browse at their convenience. A consumer may select a song or an album and download or stream the digital audio file containing the musical work to his or her computer or mobile phone, or both.

[4] The respondent, Society of Composers, Authors, and Music Publishers of Canada ("SOCAN"), is a collective society of composers, authors and publishers of music. It administers the right to perform in public and the right to communicate to the public by telecommunication the works covered by its members' copyrights. It files proposed tariffs with the Board and collects licence royalties, as set in tariffs certified by the Board, on behalf of its members.

[5] The issue in the present appeal is now whether streaming of files from the Internet triggered by individual users constitutes communication "to the public" of the musical works contained therein by online music services who make the files available to the users for streaming.

[6] These proceedings involve proposed tariffs first filed by SOCAN in 1995 for various uses of musical works constituting, in SOCAN's view, communication of musical works to the public over the Internet. There were objections to the filed proposals. In 1996, the Board decided to deal with legal issues separately from the determination of the actual tariffs. The first step was to "determine which activities on the Internet, if any, constitute a protected use [of SOCAN's repertoire of music] targeted in the tariff" (SOCAN Statement of Royalties, Public Performance of Music Works 1996, 1997, 1998 (Tariff 22, Internet) (Re) (1999), 1 C.P.R. (4th) 417 ("Tariff 22 decision"), at p. 424). Issued on October 27, 1999, the Board termed this its Phase I decision, dealing with legal and jurisdictional issues. Some of its determinations are directly relevant to this appeal. The Tariff 22 decision was ultimately appealed to this Court, albeit on different issues. However, in Society of Composers, Authors and Music Publishers of Canada v. Canadian Assn. of Internet Providers, 2004 SCC 45, [2004] 2 S.C.R. 427 ("SOCAN v. CAIP"), at para. 30, Binnie J. noted the Board's interpretation

of the phrase "to the public", which was that a communication may be to the public when it is made to individual members of the public, regardless of whether they receive it at the same or at different times (Tariff 22 decision, at p. 435). He found that this particular issue was "no longer contested."

[7] After this Court's decision in SOCAN v. CAIP, the Board proceeded to Phase II of the process to establish a tariff for the communication of musical works over the Internet for the years 1996 to 2006. In these proceedings, the appellants argued both before the Board and subsequently on judicial review, that a point-to-point transmission of a musical work is not a communication "to the public". This argument is in large part based on CCH and on the finding in that case that fax transmissions of copyrighted works by the Great Library at Osgoode Hall to its patrons were private communications.

[8] The Board rejected this argument in its decision issued on October 18, 2007. The Tariff 22.A decision reiterates the Board's earlier-stated view that communications to individual members of the public through downloads or streams requested by them at different times are communications "to the public". Accordingly, finding SOCAN's claim to be valid in law, the Board proceeded to establish the tariffs it considered appropriate.

[9] The appellants' application for judicial review was unanimously dismissed by the Federal Court of Appeal. Pelletier J.A., writing for the court, considered that the application should be reviewed on the standard of reasonableness and found the Board's determination of what constitutes a "communication to the public" under the Act to be reasonable.

III. Analysis

A. Standard of Review

[10] The appropriate standard for reviewing the Board's determinations on points of law was considered by Binnie J. in SOCAN v. CAIP. In concluding that the correctness standard must apply, he wrote, at para. 49:

> There is neither a preclusive clause nor a statutory right of appeal from decisions of the Copyright Board. While the Chair of the Board must be a current or retired judge, the Board may hold a hearing without any legally trained member present. The Copyright Act is an act of general application which usually is dealt with before courts rather than tribunals. The questions at issue in this appeal are legal questions. [Emphasis added.]

[11] Since that decision, this Court has substantially revised the appropriate approach to judicial review. Dunsmuir v. New Brunswick, 2008 SCC 9, [2008] 1 S.C.R. 190, made clear that an administrative body interpreting and applying its home statute should normally be accorded deference on judicial review. See also Canada (Canadian Human Rights Commission) v. Canada (Attorney General), 2011 SCC 53, [2011] 3 S.C.R. 471 ("Canada (CHRC)"), at para. 16, and Smith v. Alliance Pipeline Ltd., 2011 SCC 7, [2011] 1 S.C.R. 160, at para. 26. In Alberta (Information and Privacy Commissioner) v. Alberta Teachers' Association, 2011 SCC 61, [2011] 3 S.C.R. 654 ("ATA"), at para. 39, the Court held

that "[w]hen considering a decision of an administrative tribunal interpreting or applying its home statute, it should be presumed that the appropriate standard of review is reasonableness." By setting up a specialized tribunal to determine certain issues the legislature is presumed to have recognized superior expertise in that body in respect of issues arising under its home statute or a closely related statute, warranting judicial review for reasonableness.

[12] As stated by Binnie J. in SOCAN v. CAIP, the core of the Board's mandate is "the working out of the details of an appropriate royalty tariff" (para. 49). Nevertheless, in order to carry out this mandate, the Board is routinely called upon to ascertain rights underlying any proposed tariff. In this, it is construing the Act, its home statute.

[13] However, as Binnie J. noted in SOCAN v. CAIP, the Act is a statute that will also be brought before the courts for interpretation at first instance in proceedings for copyright infringement. The court will examine the same legal issues the Board may be required to address in carrying out its mandate. On appeal, questions of law decided by the courts in these proceedings would be reviewed for correctness: Housen v. Nikolaisen, 2002 SCC 33, [2002] 2 S.C.R. 235, at para. 8.

[14] It would be inconsistent for the court to review a legal question on judicial review of a decision of the Board on a deferential standard and decide exactly the same legal question de novo if it arose in an infringement action in the court at first instance. It would be equally inconsistent if on appeal from a judicial review, the appeal court were to approach a legal question decided by the Board on a deferential standard, but adopt a correctness standard on an appeal from a decision of a court at first instance on the same legal question.

[15] Because of the unusual statutory scheme under which the Board and the court may each have to consider the same legal question at first instance, it must be inferred that the legislative intent was not to recognize superior expertise of the Board relative to the court with respect to such legal questions. This concurrent jurisdiction of the Board and the court at first instance in interpreting the Copyright Act rebuts the presumption of reasonableness review of the Board's decisions on questions of law under its home statute. This is consistent with Dunsmuir, which directed that "[a] discrete and special administrative regime in which the decision maker has special expertise" was a "facto[r that] will lead to the conclusion that the decision maker should be given deference and a reasonableness test applied" (para. 55 (emphasis added)). Because of the jurisdiction at first instance that it shares with the courts, the Board cannot be said to operate in such a "discrete . . . administrative regime". Therefore, I cannot agree with Abella J. that the fact that courts routinely carry out the same interpretive tasks as the board at first instance "does not detract from the Board's particular familiarity and expertise with the provisions of the Copyright Act" (para. 68). In these circumstances, courts must be assumed to have the same familiarity and expertise with the statute as the board. Accordingly, I am of the opinion that in SOCAN v. CAIP, Binnie J. determined in a satisfactory manner that the standard

of correctness should be the appropriate standard of review on questions of law arising on judicial review from the Copyright Board (Dunsmuir, at para. 62).

[16] I must also respectfully disagree with Abella J.'s characterization, at para. 62, of the holding in ATA as meaning that the "exceptions to the presumption of home statute deference are . . . constitutional questions and questions of law of central importance to the legal system and outside the adjudicator's specialized expertise". Dunsmuir had recognized that questions which fall within the categories of constitutional questions and questions of general law that are both of central importance to the legal system as a whole and outside the adjudicator's specialized area of expertise were to be reviewed on a correctness standard (paras. 58 and 60). ATA simply reinforced the direction in Dunsmuir that issues that fall under the category of interpretation of the home statute or closely related statutes normally attract a deferential standard of review (ATA, at para. 39; Dunsmuir, at para. 54). My colleague's approach would in effect mean that the reasonableness standard applies to all interpretations of home statutes. Yet, ATA and Dunsmuir allow for the exceptional other case to rebut the presumption of reasonableness review for questions involving the interpretation of the home statute.

[17] My colleague refers to pre-Dunsmuir decisions for the proposition that shared jurisdiction at first instance does not prevent reasonableness review of a tribunal's decision under its home statute. However, such precedents will only be helpful where they "determin[e] in a satisfactory manner the degree of deference to be accorded with regard to a particular category of question" (Dunsmuir, at para. 62).

[18] The recent examples raised by Justice Abella where reasonableness review was applied all involved bodies with exclusive primary jurisdiction under their home statute, constituting "discrete . . . administrative regime[s]". Canada (CHRC) concerned the Canadian Human Rights Act, R.S.C. 1985, c. H-6, which does not create shared primary jurisdiction between the administrative tribunal and the courts. In these circumstances, the Court simply found that the standard applicable on the facts of that case was the reasonableness standard and confirmed the presumptive rule that "if the issue relates to the interpretation and application of its own statute, . . . the standard of reasonableness will generally apply" (para. 24 (emphasis added)). Doré v. Barreau du Québec, 2012 SCC 12, [2012] 1 S.C.R. 395, involved the judicial review of a decision of a disciplinary body under a professional Code of ethics of advocates, R.R.Q. 1981, c. B-1, applicable to lawyers. There was no question of the constitutionality of the provision in the Code of ethics. The question, rather, was whether the adjudicator, making his fact-specific determination in the circumstances of that case, had "act[ed] consistently with the values underlying the grant of discretion, including Charter values" (Doré, at para. 24). In any case, the adjudicator was operating as part of a discrete administrative regime with exclusive jurisdiction over disciplinary matters under the Code of ethics.

[19] I wish to be clear that the statutory scheme under which both a tribunal and a court may decide the same legal question at first instance is quite unlike the scheme under which the vast majority of judicial reviews arises. Concurrent jurisdiction at first instance seems to appear only under intellectual property statutes where Parliament has preserved dual jurisdiction between the tribunals and the courts. However, I leave the determination of the appropriate standard of review of a tribunal decision under other intellectual property statutes for a case in which it arises. Nothing in these reasons should be taken as departing from Dunsmuir and its progeny as to the presumptively deferential approach to the review of questions of law decided by tribunals involving their home statute or statutes closely connected to their function.

[20] It should be equally clear that the Board's application of the correct legal principles to the facts of a particular matter should be treated with deference, as are the decisions of this nature by trial judges on appellate review. However, I cannot agree with Abella J. that the question arising in this appeal is a question of mixed fact and law (para. 74). The issue in this case has been argued by the parties as a pure question of law. The Court is asked to determine whether a point-to-point transmission can ever constitute a communication "to the public" within the meaning of s. 3(1)(f) of the Copyright Act (A.F., at para. 2). This is not a "questio[n] of mixed fact and law [that] involve[s] applying a legal standard to a set of facts" (Housen v. Nikolaisen, at para. 26); it is an extricable question of law.

B. Can a Point-to-Point Transmission Effected at the Request of the Recipient Be a Communication "to the Public"?

(1) Arguments of the Parties and Relevant Legislative Provisions

[21] Before this Court, the appellants maintain that a point-to-point communication by telecommunication of a discrete copy of a musical work is not a communication to the public, regardless of whether another copy of the same work is transmitted to a different customer at a different time. They argue that "the [Federal Court of Appeal's] decision is directly contrary to . . . CCH", where "all three Courts concluded that the Great Library's facsimile service did not infringe the right to communicate to the public by telecommunication — based on analyzing whether each transmission was a communication to the public" (A.F., at paras. 8 and 45 (emphasis in original)). The appellants further support their position by reference to the legislative history of s. 3(1)(f) of the Act and U.S. authorities. SOCAN views the decisions of the Board and of the F.C.A. as correct and consistent with relevant international copyright conventions.

[22] The legal question in this appeal involves the interpretation of s. 3 of the Act. The right to communicate to the public by telecommunication is set out in s. 3(1) (f) of the Act:

3. (1) For the purposes of this Act, "copyright", in relation to a work, means the sole right . . .

. . .

(f) in the case of any literary, dramatic, musical or artistic work, to communicate the work to the public by telecommunication,

. . .

and to authorize any such acts.

[23] Section 2 broadly defines "telecommunication" as "any transmission of signs, signals, writing, images or sounds or intelligence of any nature by wire, radio, visual, optical or other electromagnetic system". There is no dispute in this appeal that the communications in issue are "telecommunications" within the meaning of the Copyright Act.

(2) The Precedent in CCH: Interpreting "to the Public"

[24] The words "to the public" within the meaning of s. 3(1)(f) of the Act were considered in CCH. The Great Library offered the service of faxing reported judgments and excerpts of other legal materials to individual lawyers at the lawyer's request. The publishers holding copyrights in the transmitted works argued that the fax transmissions of copies of their works to individual lawyers were communications to the public by telecommunication by the Great Library. Contrasting this situation with telecommunications in the context of subscription or pay-per-view television, at trial, Gibson J. found no communication to the public since "the telecommunications, by facsimile, emanated from a single point and were each intended to be received at a single point" ([2000] 2 F.C. 451 (T.D.), at para. 167).

[25] The conclusion was affirmed on appeal by the Federal Court of Appeal (2002 FCA 187, [2002] 4 F.C. 213) and this Court. This Court, as did the F.C.A., held that "transmission of a single copy to a single individual is not a communication to the public": CCH (SCC), at para. 78; CCH (FCA), at paras. 101 and 253. Both sets of reasons in the Federal Court rely on the ordinary meaning of the phrase "to the public", as well as the definition of "public" in Art. 1721(2) of the North American Free Trade Agreement, Can. T.S. 1994 No. 2 ("NAFTA"), to conclude that "to be 'to the public' a communication must be targeted at an aggregation of individuals, which is more than a single person but not necessarily the whole public at large" (Linden J.A., at para. 100 (emphasis added)). This Court agreed with the F.C.A.'s conclusion (para. 78).

[26] However, this Court expressly limited its ruling to the facts in CCH. McLachlin C.J. wrote:

> The fax transmission of a single copy to a single individual is not a communication to the public. This said, a series of repeated fax transmissions of the same work to numerous different recipients might constitute communication to the public in infringement of copyright. However, there was no evidence of this type of transmission having occurred in this case.

On the evidence in this case, the fax transmissions were not communications to the public. [Emphasis added; paras. 78-79.]

(3) A Disagreement Based on Perspective

[27] Both parties in this appeal rely on CCH in support of their respective positions. They disagree, however, on the meaning of the caveat in CCH that "a series of repeated fax transmissions of the same work to numerous different recipients might constitute communication to the public in infringement of copyright". The appellants argue that all three courts in CCH ruled that each transmission must be analyzed on its own, as a separate transaction, regardless of whether another communication of the same work to a different customer may occur at a later point in time. They submit that a "series of repeated fax transmissions of the same work to numerous different recipients might constitute communication to the public in infringement of copyright" only where the series of transmissions to multiple users originate from a single act by the sender. They provide the example of multiple fax transmissions occurring successively as a result of a decision by the sender to fax to multiple recipients ("a broadcast fax" (A.F., at para. 70)). This is distinguishable in their view from discrete point-to-point transmissions which result from multiple unrelated acts by the sender. In SOCAN's view, there is no requirement in CCH that the series of transmissions originate from a single act of the sender.

[28] The disagreement is based on perspective. Where the appellants argue that we must consider the recipient of each transmission, SOCAN and the decisions below focused on the sender's activities in communicating a given work over time.

(4) Transmissions Must Be Looked at in Context

[29] In my respectful view, the appellants' proposition is untenable. Such a rule would produce arbitrary results. For example, where a copyright-protected work is sent to 100 randomly selected members of the general public by way of a single e-mail with multiple recipients, on the appellants' approach, this would constitute a communication "to the public". However, under the same approach, the sender could avoid infringing copyright simply by executing the same task through sending separate e-mails to each of the 100 recipients. If the nature of the activity in both cases is the same, albeit accomplished through different technical means, there is no justification for distinguishing between the two for copyright purposes.

[30] Focusing on each individual transmission loses sight of the true character of the communication activity in question and makes copyright protection dependant on technicalities of the alleged infringer's chosen method of operation. Such an approach does not allow for principled copyright protection. Instead, it is necessary to consider the broader context to determine whether a given point-to-point transmission engages the exclusive right to communicate to the public. This is the only way to ensure that form does not prevail over substance.

[31] Sharlow J.A. addressed this issue in Canadian Wireless Telecommunications Assn. v. Society of Composers, Authors and Music Publishers of Canada, 2008 FCA 6, [2008] 3 F.C.R. 539, leave to appeal refused, [2008] 2 S.C.R. vi ("CWTA"), holding that a person offering members of the public the opportunity to download ringtones for their mobile phones thereby communicates

the musical works contained in the ringtones to the public. She wrote that this approach is consistent with the language of [s. 3(1)(f) of the Act] and its context. It also accords with common sense. If a wireless carrier were to transmit a particular ringtone simultaneously to all customers who have requested it, that transmission would be a communication to the public. It would be illogical to reach a different result simply because the transmissions are done one by one, and thus at different times. [para. 43]

(5) The Appellants' Interpretation Would Exclude All On-Demand Transmissions

[32] In oral argument, counsel for the appellants seemed to go somewhat beyond the mere technicality of the transmissions by looking at the intention of the sender in accomplishing a given transmission. In the case of a "blas[t]" communication, he pointed out that the sender has "take[n] it upon [himself] to send [the work] out" (Transcript, at p. 24). By contrast, in the case of a one-to-one transmission, at least that from an online music service to a customer at the customer's request, or from the Great Library in CCH to a patron, he argued that there is no intention that the same work ever be transmitted again "because it is entirely at the request of the consuming public" (p. 26). In the appellants' view, this would justify differential treatment of the point-to-point transmission and the "blas[t]" communication.

[33] With respect, this proposition too must be rejected, for the same reason that focusing the analysis on the recipient of a transmission rather than on the overall context of the communication produces results inconsistent with the true character of the communication. The facts of this case underscore the point. The Board found that "[d]ownloads are 'targeted at an aggregation of individuals'" and are "offered to anyone with the appropriate device who is willing to comply with the terms" (para. 97). It is hardly possible to maintain that "there is no intention that the same work ever be transmitted again".

[34] In addition, the appellants' proposed rule that each transmission be analyzed in isolation because each is initiated at the request of individual members of the public would have the effect of excluding all interactive communications from the scope of the copyright holder's exclusive rights to communicate to the public and to authorize such communications. A stream is often effectuated at the request of the recipient. On-demand television allows viewers to request and view the desired program at the time of their choosing. By definition, on-demand communications — relating to the so-called "pull" technologies — are initiated at the request of the user, independently of any other user, and each individual transmission happens in a point-to-point manner. None of these telecommunications would be considered as being made "to the public" simply because the actual transmission occurs at the initiative and discretion of the consumer to accept the invitation to the public to access the content.

[35] Nothing in the wording of s. 3(1)(f) of the Act implies such a limitation. A communication is not restricted to a purely non-interactive context.

(6) Section 3(1)(f) Is Not Limited to Traditional "Push" Technologies; It Is Technology-Neutral

[36] The right to communicate to the public is historically linked to traditional media that operated on a broadcasting, or "push", model. As pointed out by the appellants, the predecessor to s. 3(1)(f) guaranteed copyright holders an exclusive right to communicate literary, dramatic, musical or artistic works by radio-communication. The predecessor section was introduced in 1931, implementing Article 11bis of the Berne Convention for the Protection of Literary and Artistic Works, 828 U.N.T.S. 221 (Rome Revision of 1928): J. S. McKeown, Fox on Canadian Law of Copyright and Industrial Designs, (4th ed. (loose-leaf), at p. 21-86); Composers, Authors and Publishers Assoc. of Canada Ltd. v. CTV Television Network Ltd., [1968] S.C.R. 676, at p. 681. Radio-communications were understood to include transmissions by microwave over the airwaves: Canadian Admiral Corp. v. Rediffusion, Inc., [1954] Ex. C.R. 382. As such, the radio-communication right extended to radio and traditional over-the-air television broadcasting, notably leaving transmissions by cable outside of copyright protection.

[37] This technology-specific communication right was amended to the technologically neutral right to "communicate . . . to the public by telecommunication" to reflect the obligations entered into by Canada under NAFTA (Canada-United States Free Trade Agreement Implementation Act, S.C. 1988, c. 65, ss. 61 and 62). The change from radio-communication to telecommunication meant that Canadian cable companies which previously escaped any payment of royalties under the "radio-communication" right, were now caught by the Act: S. Handa, Copyright Law in Canada (2002), at p. 320.

[38] The historic relationship between the right to communicate to the public and broadcasting-type, "push" technologies, and the 1988 amendment in particular, is evidence that the Act has evolved to ensure its continued relevance in an evolving technological environment. The historic relationship does not support reading into the Act restrictions which are not apparent from and are even inconsistent with the neutral language of the Act itself.

[39] In addition, this Court has long recognized in the context of the reproduction right that, where possible, the Act should be interpreted to extend to technologies that were not or could not have been contemplated at the time of its drafting: Apple Computer Inc. v. Mackintosh Computers Ltd., [1987] 1 F.C. 173 (T.D.), aff'd [1988] 1 F.C. 673 (C.A.), aff'd [1990] 2 S.C.R. 209. That the Act was to apply to new technologies was recently reaffirmed in Robertson v. Thomson Corp., 2006 SCC 43, [2006] 2 S.C.R. 363, at para. 49, per LeBel and Fish JJ.:

> Media neutrality is reflected in s. 3(1) of the Copyright Act which describes a right to produce or reproduce a work "in any material form whatever". Media neutrality means that the Copyright Act should continue to apply in different media, including more technologically advanced ones. . . . [I]t exists to protect the rights of authors and others as technology evolves.

Although the words "in any material form whatever" qualify the right to "produce or reproduce the work" in s. 3(1), the same principle should guide the application of the neutral wording of the right to "communicate . . . to the public by telecommunication". The broad definition of "telecommunication" was adopted precisely to provide for a communication right "not dependent on the form of technology" (SOCAN v. CAIP, at para. 90).

[40] Ultimately, in determining the extent of copyright, regard must be had for the fact that "[t]he Copyright Act is usually presented as a balance between promoting the public interest in the encouragement and dissemination of works of the arts and intellect and obtaining a just reward for the creator" (Théberge v. Galerie d'Art du Petit Champlain inc., 2002 SCC 34, [2002] 2 S.C.R. 336, at para. 30). This balance is not appropriately struck where the existence of copyright protection depends merely on the business model that the alleged infringer chooses to adopt rather than the underlying communication activity. Whether a business chooses to convey copyright protected content in a traditional, "broadcasting" type fashion, or opts for newer approaches based on consumer choice and convenience, the end result is the same. The copyrighted work has been made available to an aggregation of individuals of the general public.

(7) Developments at the International Level Are Consistent in Encompassing On-Demand Communications to the Public in Copyright Protection

[41] Developments at the international level are consistent with this conclusion. Article 11bis of the Berne Convention, of which Canada is a party, sets out certain communication rights in literary and artistic works:

> [Broadcasting and Related Rights]

(1) Authors of literary and artistic works shall enjoy the exclusive right of authorizing:

> (i) the broadcasting of their works or the communication thereof to the public by any other means of wireless diffusion of signs, sounds or images;
>
> (ii) any communication to the public by wire or by rebroadcasting of the broadcast of the work, when this communication is made by an organization other than the original one;
>
> (iii) the public communication by loudspeaker or any other analogous instrument transmitting, by signs, sounds or images, the broadcast of the work.

[42] As stated earlier, s. 3(1)(f) is based on Article 11bis of the Berne Convention.

[43] The advent of on-demand technologies, and the Internet in particular, led to questions as to whether such new telecommunication technologies were encompassed in the communication right existing under the Berne regime. While it was possible to interpret the relevant articles as extending to on-demand transmissions over the Internet, there was ambiguity: S. Ricketson and J. C. Ginsburg, International Copyright and Neighbouring Rights: The Berne Convention and Beyond (2nd ed. 2006), vol. I, at para. 12.48. For example, the word "broadcasting" used in Article 11bis(1) "may well imply widely sending a communication simultaneously to many recipients" (para. 12.49).

[44] In 1996, the WIPO Copyright Treaty, 2186 U.N.T.S. 121 ("WCT"), was entered into. The WCT is a special agreement within the meaning of Art. 20 of the Berne Convention, which stipulates that "[t]he Governments of the countries of the [Berne] Union reserve the right to enter into special agreements among themselves, in so far as such agreements grant to authors more extensive rights than those granted by the Convention, or contain other provisions not contrary to this Convention" (see Art. 1(1) of the WCT).

[45] Article 8 of the WCT reads:

> [Right of Communication to the Public] Without prejudice to the provisions of Articles 11(1)(ii), 11bis(1)(i) and (ii), 11ter(1)(ii), 14(1)(ii) and 14bis(1) of the Berne Convention, authors of literary and artistic works shall enjoy the exclusive right of authorizing any communication to the public of their works, by wire or wireless means, including the making available to the public of their works in such a way that members of the public may access these works from a place and at a time individually chosen by them.

[46] Ricketson and Ginsburg comment on the meaning and legislative history of Art. 8 in these terms:

> The WCT's principal innovation is its specification that the right of communication to the public includes a right of "making available to the public of [literary and artistic] works in such a way that members of the public may access those works from a place and at a time individually chosen by them". This right targets on-demand transmissions (whether by wire or wireless means), for it makes clear that the members of the public may be separated both in space and in time. [Emphasis added; para. 12.57.]

[47] The WIPO Intellectual Property Handbook: Policy, Law and Use, chapter 5, "International Treaties and Conventions on Intellectual Property", No. 489 (2nd ed. 2004), comments that the "WCT . . . clarifies that that right also covers transmissions in interactive systems" (para. 5.226 (emphasis added)).

[48] In the end, "[t]he core concept of 'making available' . . . can fairly be called neither a reaffirmation nor a novelty, for it resolves an ambiguity as to whether the old communication to the public rights accommodated or excluded 'pull technologies'" (J. C. Ginsburg, "The (new?) right of making available to the public", in D. Vaver and L. Bently, eds., Intellectual Property in the New Millennium: Essays in Honour of William R. Cornish (2004), 234, at p. 246).

[49] Canada has signed, but not yet ratified or legislatively adopted the WCT. Therefore, the WCT is not binding in this country. The WCT is only cited to demonstrate that the broad interpretation of s. 3(1)(f) of the Act, recognizing that a communication "to the public" subject to copyright protection may occur through point-to-point transmissions at the user's request, is not out of step with Art. 8 of the WCT and international thinking on the issue.

(8) American Jurisprudence

[50] The appellants' remaining argument is based on American jurisprudence. This argument must also be dismissed. They mainly rely on the decision of the

Court of Appeals for the Second Circuit in Cartoon Network v. CSC Holdings, Inc., 536 F.3d 121 (2008), in which it was held that the potential audience of each point-to-point transmission must be considered to determine whether a given transmission is "to the public". The Second Circuit Court of Appeals found in that case that the transmissions were not "to the public".

[51] This case is of no assistance to the appellants. The Court of Appeals for the Second Circuit relied on the specific language of the U.S. "transmit clause". It held that the language of the clause itself directs considering who is "capable of receiving" a particular "transmission" or "performance", and not of the potential audience of a particular "work" (p. 134). Quite to the contrary, our Copyright Act speaks more broadly of "communicat[ing a] work to the public". This Court has recognized in the past important differences both in wording and in policy between Canadian and American copyright legislation. It has warned that "United States court decisions, even where the factual situations are similar, must be scrutinized very carefully" (see Compo Co. v. Blue Crest Music Inc., [1980] 1 S.C.R. 357, at p. 367). The difference in statutory wording between the relevant provisions of the American legislation and of the Canadian Copyright Act is sufficient to render the U.S. decisions of no assistance in the interpretive exercise engaged here.

(9) Summary

[52] These considerations are sufficient to dispose of the appellants' argument that a point-to-point transmission is necessarily a private transaction outside of the scope of the exclusive right to communicate to the public. To quote Sharlow J.A., at para. 35 of CWTA,

> in determining whether paragraph 3(1)(f) applies to the transmission of a musical work in the form of a digital audio file, it is not enough to ask whether there is a one-to-one communication, or a one-to-one communication requested by the recipient. The answer to either of those questions would not necessarily be determinative because a series of transmissions of the same musical work to numerous different recipients may be a communication to the public if the recipients comprise the public, or a significant segment of the public.

CCH (SCC) determined that a "series of repeated . . . transmissions of the same work to numerous different recipients" may constitute a communication "to the public" within the meaning of s. 3(1)(f) of the Act (para. 78). Where such a series of point-to-point communications of the same work to an aggregation of individuals is found to exist, it matters little for the purposes of copyright protection whether the members of the public receive the communication in the same or in different places, at the same or at different times or at their own or the sender's initiative.

IV. Application to the Facts — Whether Online Music Services "Communicate to the Public"

[53] Although they occur between the online music provider and the individual consumer in a point-to-point fashion, the transmissions of musical works in this

case, where they constitute "communications", can be nothing other than communications "to the public".

[54] Online music services provide catalogues of musical works. It is open to any customer willing to pay the purchase price to download or stream the works on offer. The works in the catalogues could as a result be transmitted to large segments of the public — if not the public at large. Through the commercial activities of the online music services, the works in question have the potential of being put in the possession of an aggregation of customers. Indeed, the appellants' business model is premised on the expectation of multiple sales of any given musical work. Achieving the highest possible number of online sales is the very raison d'être of online music services. The number of actual transmissions depends only on the commercial success of a given work. The necessary implication of this business model is that there will be a "series of repeated . . . transmissions of the same work to numerous different recipients" (CCH (SCC), at para. 78). The conclusion that a communication "to the public" occurs is consistent with reality. As Professor Vaver explains,

> [i]f the content is intentionally made available to anyone who wants to access it, it is treated as communicated "to the public" even if users access the work at different times and places.

(D. Vaver, *Intellectual Property Law: Copyright, Patents, Trade-marks* (2nd ed. 2011), at p. 173)

[55] These facts are distinguishable from those in CCH and the holding in that case does not assist the appellants. The publishers alleging infringement in CCH had presented no evidence that the Great Library was communicating the same works in a serial fashion or that the Great Library had made the works generally available at any lawyer's request. The Great Library's employees examined and accordingly accepted or refused every request on its own merits, thus retaining control over access to the works.

[56] Following the online music services' business model, musical works are indiscriminately made available to anyone with Internet access to the online music service's website. This means that the customers requesting the streams are not members of a narrow group, such as a family or a circle of friends. Simply, they are "the public". In these circumstances, the transmission of any file containing a musical work, starting with the first, from the online service's website to the customer's computer, at the customer's request, constitutes "communicat[ing] the work to the public by telecommunication".

V. Conclusion

[57] The appeal is allowed in respect of downloads for the reasons set out by the majority in Entertainment Software Association v. Society of Composers, Authors and Music Publishers of Canada and dismissed in respect of music streamed from the Internet in accordance with these reasons. In view of the divided result, each party should bear its own costs.

The following are the reasons delivered by

[58] Abella J. — I agree with Justice Rothstein that in the case of streams only, not downloads, we ought not to disturb the Copyright Board's conclusion that a point-to-point communication from an online service provider, effected at the request of a customer, can be a communication "to the public". The focus of these concurring reasons, however, is on the standard of review.

[59] In my respectful view, the majority's conclusion about how to approach the standard of review overcomplicates what should be a straightforward application of the reasonableness standard. The Board, when interpreting its home statute in setting tariffs for the communication of new forms of digital media, should be accorded the same deference and be reviewed on the same standard as every other specialized tribunal in Canada.

[60] Since Dunsmuir v. New Brunswick, [2008] 1 S.C.R. 190, this Court has unwaveringly held that institutionally expert and specialized tribunals are entitled to a presumption of deference when interpreting their home statute. Applying a correctness standard of review on the sole basis that a court might interpret the same statute, in my view, takes us back to the pre-Dunsmuir focus on relative expertise between courts and tribunals and the view that courts prevail whenever it comes to questions of law. This effectively drains expert tribunals of the deference and respect they are owed, as is reflected in the language of Society of Composers, Authors and Music Publishers of Canada v. Canadian Assn. of Internet Providers, [2004] 2 S.C.R. 427 (SOCAN v. CAIP), which the majority's reasons rely on to conclude that the Board's legal determinations should be reviewed on a correctness standard:

> The Copyright Act is an act of general application which usually is dealt with before courts rather than tribunals. The questions at issue in this appeal are legal questions. . . . [T]he Board's ruling . . . addresses a point of general legal significance far beyond the working out of the details of an appropriate royalty tariff, which lies within the core of the Board's mandate. [Emphasis added; para. 49.]

[61] This Court recently held in Alberta (Information and Privacy Commissioner) v. Alberta Teachers' Association, [2011] 3 S.C.R. 654 (ATA), that deference on judicial review is presumed any time a tribunal interp rets its home statute:

> [U]nless the situation is exceptional, and we have not seen such a situation since Dunsmuir, the interpretation by the tribunal of "its own statute or statutes closely connected to its function, with which it will have particular familiarity" should be presumed to be a question of statutory interpretation subject to deference on judicial review. [Emphasis added; para. 34.]

[62] The existing exceptions to the presumption of home statute deference are, as noted in ATA, constitutional questions and questions of law of central importance to the legal system and outside the adjudicator's specialized expertise (ATA, at para. 30; Dunsmuir, at paras. 58 and 60). The Court in ATA also questioned the continued existence of another exception: the problematic category of true questions of jurisdiction or vires (paras. 33-34).

[63] In concluding that the Copyright Board's concurrent jurisdiction with all federal and provincial courts in Canada warrants a correctness standard of

review, the majority's reasons have added a new exception — shared jurisdiction with courts. This is not even hinted at in Dunsmuir. Nor is anything about this new category obviously analogous to the other exceptions to the presumption of home statute deference, which are essentially legal questions beyond the quotidian work of a tribunal. Nor is it obvious to me why shared jurisdiction should be seen to displace Parliament's attributed intention that a tribunal's specialized expertise entitles it to be reviewed with restraint. It appears to spring full panoplied from a different brow.

[64] We attribute expertise to a tribunal on the basis that Parliament has delegated decision making to it as an institutionally specialized body. Dunsmuir recognized the reality that "in many instances, those working day to day in the implementation of frequently complex administrative schemes have or will develop a considerable degree of expertise or field sensitivity to the imperatives and nuances of the legislative regime": at para. 49, citing David J. Mullan, "Establishing the Standard of Review: The Struggle for Complexity?" (2004), 17 C.J.A.L.P. 59, at p. 93. This idea was reinforced by this Court in Canada (Citizenship and Immigration) v. Khosa, [2009] 1 S.C.R. 339, where the majority held that express or implied statutory direction was not required before granting deference to a tribunal — deference flowed instead from the tribunal's "day to day" statutory familiarity (para. 25).

[65] The Board has specialized expertise in interpreting the provisions of the Copyright Act, R.S.C. 1985, c. C-42. The fact of shared jurisdiction does not undermine this expertise, the basis for institutional deference. The Board does not simply "wor[k] out . . . the details of an appropriate royalty tariff", despite what is suggested in SOCAN v. CAIP, at para. 49. It sets policies that collectively determine the rights of copyright owners and users, and plays an important role in achieving the proper balance between those actors: Margaret Ann Wilkinson, "Copyright, Collectives, and Contracts: New Math for Educational Institutions and Libraries", in Michael Geist, ed., From "Radical Extremism" to "Balanced Copyright" (2010), 503, at p. 514.

[66] The Board has highly specialized knowledge about the media technologies used to create and disseminate copyrighted works, such as the Internet, digital radio, satellite communications, as well as related economic issues: Copyright Board Canada, Performance Report for the period ending 31 March 2003 (online), at Section II: Departmental Context — Organization, Mandate and Strategic Outcomes. This specialized knowledge is precisely the kind of institutional expertise that Dunsmuir concluded was entitled to deference.

[67] In the case before us, the Board is tasked with determining whether downloading a musical work constitutes a "communicat[ion] . . . to the public" within s. 3(1)(f) of the Copyright Act. This question involves examining many facets, including how music is accessed (e.g., through a stream versus a download), recent changes and trends in the way that users and consumers access music, and how all of this impacts on the ability of copyright owners to obtain compensation for their work.

[68] In exercising its mandate, the Board must interpret the meaning of several provisions in the Copyright Act, including the exclusive rights of copyright owners listed in s. 3(1). The fact that a court might in another case be asked to interpret the same provisions of the Copyright Act does not detract from the Board's particular familiarity and expertise with the provisions of the Copyright Act. Nor does it make this legislation any less of a home statute to the Board. The Act may sometimes be home to other judicial actors as part of their varied adjudicative functions, but their occasional occupancy should not deprive the Board of the deference it is entitled to as the permanent resident whose only task is to interpret and apply the Act.

[69] The majority bases its conclusion that shared jurisdiction attracts a correctness standard on the possibility of inconsistent results stemming from a more deferential standard of review for the Board's interpretation of the Act. But this Court in Smith v. Alliance Pipeline Ltd., [2011] 1 S.C.R. 160, considered — and rejected — concerns over the possibility of multiple interpretations flowing from deference. Justice Fish noted that even prior to Dunsmuir, the standard of reasonableness was based on the idea that multiple valid interpretations of a statutory provision were inevitable, and ought not to be disturbed unless the tribunal's decision was not rationally supported (paras. 38-39).

[70] The majority's reasons also suggest that concurrent jurisdiction between tribunals and courts is rare, and therefore no threat to the integrity of the "home statute" presumption. Yet tribunals often share jurisdiction with courts in interpreting and applying the same statutory provisions. Both the Trade-marks Opposition Board and the Federal Court, for example, interpret and apply s. 6 of the Trade-marks Act, R.S.C. 1985, c. T-13, to determine whether a trade-mark is "confusing". The Board applies s. 6 in the context of opposition proceedings seeking to block registration of a trade-mark, while the Federal Court applies s. 6 in the context of actions for infringement or claims seeking the expungement of a registered trade-mark on the basis that it is invalid: see Chamberlain Group Inc. v. Lynx Industries Inc., 2010 FC 1287, 379 F.T.R. 270; Alticor Inc. v. Nutravite Pharmaceuticals Inc., 2005 FCA 269, 339 N.R. 56.

[71] Notwithstanding this shared jurisdiction, the Trade-marks Opposition Board's decisions are nevertheless reviewed on a reasonableness standard, as Rothstein J.A. concluded for the majority in Molson Breweries v. John Labatt Ltd., [2000] 3 F.C. 145 (C.A.):

> Having regard to the Registrar's expertise . . . I am of the opinion that decisions of the Registrar, whether of fact, law or discretion, within his area of expertise, are to be reviewed on a standard of reasonableness simpliciter . . . [unless] additional evidence is adduced in the Trial Division that would have materially affected the Registrar's findings of fact . . . . [Emphasis added; para. 51.]

[72] And in Canada (Canadian Human Rights Commission) v. Canada (Attorney General), [2011] 3 S.C.R. 471, this Court applied a reasonableness standard to the Canadian Human Rights Tribunal's conclusion that the terms "compensate . . . for any expenses incurred by the victim" in s. 53(2)(c) and (d) of the

Canadian Human Rights Act, R.S.C. 1985, c. H-6, gave it the authority to award costs. Justices LeBel and Cromwell, for the Court, noted that even though the issue of "costs" could arise before other adjudicative bodies, including the courts, this was not an automatic reason to apply a correctness standard. Instead, the Court found that the question was within the Tribunal's expertise, and therefore reviewable on a reasonableness standard of review:

There is no doubt that the human rights tribunals are often called upon to address issues of very broad import. But, the same questions may arise before other adjudicative bodies, particularly the courts. . . .

> . . . if the issue relates to the interpretation and application of its own statute, is within its expertise and does not raise issues of general legal importance, the standard of reasonableness will generally apply and the Tribunal will be entitled to deference. [Emphasis added; paras. 23-24.]

[73] There are other examples of the application of a reasonableness standard notwithstanding shared jurisdiction between tribunals and courts. Most recently, in Doré v. Barreau du Québec, [2012] 1 S.C.R. 395, this Court applied a reasonableness standard in determining whether a disciplinary board properly applied the Canadian Charter of Rights and Freedoms' guarantee of freedom of expression in disciplining a lawyer under Quebec's Code of ethics of advocates, R.R.Q. 1981, c. B-1. The fact that "freedom of expression" is concurrently interpreted by the courts did not in any way detract from the deference given to the discipline board in applying the Charter. If concurrent jurisdiction with the courts in interpreting and applying something as legally transcendent as the Charter does not affect the deference to which tribunals are entitled in interpreting their own mandate, surely it is hard to justify carving out copyright law for unique judicial "protection".

[74] Even if shared jurisdiction is accepted as a justification for reviewing the Board's legal determinations on a standard of correctness, the Board's mandate was to decide whether a particular activity — downloading a musical work — is the type of activity captured by the phrase "communicate . . . to the public" in s. 3(1)(f) of the Copyright Act, thereby triggering a tariff. This is a question of mixed fact and law which, according to Dunsmuir, attracts deference. The view that we can extricate a legal definition of "communicate . . . to the public" under s. 3(1)(f), from the context of the complex and interlocking facts and policies considered by the Board in setting a tariff, strikes me as unrealistic. The majority, however, sees two extricable legal questions: the definition of "communicate" and the definition of "to the public": see also the companion appeal, Entertainment Software Association v. Society of Composers, Authors and Music Publishers of Canada, [2012] 2 S.C.R. 231.

[75] "Extricating" legal issues from a question of mixed fact and law is an appellate review concept that was developed in Housen v. Nikolaisen, [2002] 2 S.C.R. 235. In the context of judicial review, however, extricating legal issues — sometimes referred to as "segmentation" — presents several problems. Unlike trial courts, which have no expertise relative to appellate courts when interpreting a statute, most tribunals are granted particular mandates, giving

them specialized expertise in interpreting and applying their home statute to a particular set of facts.

[76] In Dunsmuir, while Bastarache and LeBel JJ. for the majority did not define "mixed fact and law" questions, they did discuss the issue of "separat[ing]" legal and factual issues at paras. 51-53:

> Where the question is one of fact, discretion or policy, deference will usually apply automatically. We believe that the same standard must apply to the review of questions where the legal and factual issues are intertwined with and cannot be readily separated. [Emphasis added; citations omitted; para. 53.]

[77] This statement was recently affirmed by this Court in Rio Tinto Alcan Inc. v. Carrier Sekani Tribal Council, [2010] 2 S.C.R. 650, at para. 65. In that decision, the Chief Justice held that the B.C. Utilities Commission's conclusion that consultation with First Nations was not required for the approval of an Energy Purchase Agreement was a question of mixed fact and law (at para. 78). She declined to classify the Commission's decision within the scheme of the Administrative Tribunals Act, S.B.C. 2004, c. 45, as a "constitutional question" or question of law on the one hand, or a finding of fact on the other. Instead, citing Dunsmuir, she held that the mixed question "falls between the legislated standards and thus attracts the common law standard of 'reasonableness'" (para. 78).

[78] Moreover, this Court has repeatedly held that the application of multiple standards of review to different aspects of a tribunal's decision — one for questions of law and one for questions of fact — should be avoided, urging instead that the tribunal's decision be reviewed as a whole. As Iacobucci J. explained for the majority in Canadian Broadcasting Corp. v. Canada (Labour Relations Board), [1995] 1 S.C.R. 157 (CBC v. Canada):

> While the [Canada Labour Relations Board] may have to be correct in an isolated interpretation of external legislation, the standard of review of the decision as a whole, if that decision is otherwise within its jurisdiction, will be one of patent unreasonableness. Of course, the correctness of the interpretation of the external statute may affect the overall reasonableness of the decision. Whether this is the case will depend on the impact of the statutory provision on the outcome of the decision as a whole. [Emphasis added; para. 49.]

[79] And in Law Society of New Brunswick v. Ryan, [2003] 1 S.C.R. 247, at para. 56, Iacobucci J. confirmed that what should be reviewed are the "reasons, taken as a whole" (see also Newfoundland and Labrador Nurses' Union v. Newfoundland and Labrador (Treasury Board), [2011] 3 S.C.R. 708, at para. 14).

[80] In other words, even if an aspect of the tribunal's decision would otherwise attract a correctness standard, the decision "as a whole" should be reviewed on a deferential standard. As suggested by Iacobucci J. in CBC v. Canada (at para. 49 (emphasis added)), even when the tribunal incorrectly interprets an external statute, that would merely "affect the overall reasonableness of the decision", as opposed to being a completely extricable error of law.

[81] There are several other directives from this Court to the effect that the application of more than one standard of review to a tribunal's decision is an exceptional practice. In Toronto (City) v. C.U.P.E., Local 79, [2003] 3 S.C.R. 77, LeBel J. warned:

> This Court has recognized on a number of occasions that it may, in certain circumstances, be appropriate to apply different standards of deference to different decisions taken by an administrative adjudicator in a single case. This case provides an example of one type of situation where this may be the proper approach. It involves a fundamental legal question falling outside the arbitrator's area of expertise. This legal question, though foundational to the decision as a whole, is easily differentiated from a second question on which the arbitrator was entitled to deference: the determination of whether there was just cause . . . .

However, as I have noted above, the fact that the question adjudicated by the arbitrator in this case can be separated into two distinct issues, one of which is reviewable on a correctness standard, should not be taken to mean that this will often be the case. Such cases are rare; the various strands that go into a decision are more likely to be inextricably intertwined, particularly in a complex field such as labour relations, such that the reviewing court should view the adjudicator's decision as an integrated whole. [Emphasis added; citations omitted; paras. 75-76.]

[82] This view was endorsed in Council of Canadians with Disabilities v. VIA Rail Canada Inc., [2007] 1 S.C.R. 650, where the majority said:

> The Agency is responsible for interpreting its own legislation, including what that statutory responsibility includes. The Agency made a decision with many component parts, each of which fell squarely and inextricably within its expertise and mandate. It was therefore entitled to a single, deferential standard of review. [Emphasis added; para. 100.]

[83] And in Mattel, Inc. v. 3894207 Canada Inc., [2006] 1 S.C.R. 772, the Trade-marks Opposition Board concluded that use of the name "Barbie's" for a small Montreal restaurant chain would not create confusion in the marketplace with the Mattel doll of the same name. On judicial review and at this Court, Mattel argued that the Board wrongly interpreted a provision of the Trade-marks Act defining "confusion". Binnie J. for the majority refused to extricate a definitional legal question from the mixed question of whether the word "Barbie" created "confusion" in the marketplace. Concluding that the factual and legal issues were intertwined, he applied a deferential standard:

> The determination of the likelihood of confusion requires an expertise that is possessed by the Board (which performs such assessments day in and day out) in greater measure than is typical of judges. This calls for some judicial deference to the Board's determination . . . .

> . . .

> While the appellant frames its argument as a challenge to the correctness of the interpretation given to s. 6 . . . I think that in reality . . . its challenge is directed to the relative weight to be given to the s. 6(5) enumerated and unenumerated factors. The legal issue is not neatly extricable from its factual context, but calls

for an interpretation within the expertise of the Board. [Emphasis added; paras. 36 and 39.]

[84] Binnie J., rightly in my view, was reluctant to extricate a pure question of statutory interpretation from the Board's overall conclusion that the name "Barbie" did not create "confusion". The case before us raises the identical issue of reviewing statutory interpretation.

[85] Prof. David Mullan, persuasively in my view, has also warned against segmentation. In his view, "[o]ver-willingness" to see a question as a "court" question rather than a "tribunal" question (i.e., jurisdictional questions, questions of law or statutory interpretation), "can lead to excessive and wrong-headed intervention" (p. 74):

> In my view, it is quite inappropriate to place much, if any store in the context of a judicial review application on the fact that the tribunal might be resolving a "pure question of law" which will have "precedential value". To see that as an indicator of a need for correctness review would be to undercut seriously the philosophy of deference that prevails in judicial review . . . .
>
> . . .

To the extent that segmentation frequently involves the extraction of overarching legal principles, it will have a tendency to promote correctness review or greater intervention. [Emphasis added; pp. 77 and 79.]

[86] The Board was not tasked with definitively or even separately defining the terms "communicat[ion]" and "to the public" in its decision about whether s. 3(1)(f) applied to downloading music. It is not clear to me that Parliament intended this phrase to be defined categorically at all, as opposed to contextually depending on the facts of each case.

[87] Segmenting the definition of each word or phrase in a statutory provision into discrete questions of law is a re-introduction by another name — correctness — of the unduly interventionist approach championed by the jurisdictional and preliminary question jurisprudence, jurisprudence which this Court definitively banished in ATA. When that jurisprudence was in full flight, in Bell v. Ontario Human Rights Commission, [1971] S.C.R. 756 (Bell (1971)), this Court held that the Ontario Human Rights Commission exceeded its jurisdiction when it defined the term "self-contained dwelling unit" within the Ontario Human Rights Code, 1961-62, S.O. 1961-62, c. 93, to include a boarding house. In Halifax (Regional Municipality) v. Nova Scotia (Human Rights Commission), [2012] 1 S.C.R. 364, this Court overturned Bell (1971) on the basis that it represented an unduly interventionist approach on the part of the reviewing courts:

> Early judicial intervention . . . allows for judicial imposition of a "correctness" standard with respect to legal questions that, had they been decided by the tribunal, might be entitled to deference . . . . [para. 36]

[88] The Copyright Board's conclusion that a music download is a "communicat[ion] . . . to the public" was a decision entirely within its mandate and specialized expertise, involving a complex tapestry of technology, fact, and broadcast law and policy.

Pulling a single legal thread from this textured piece and declaring it to be the determinative strand for deciding how the whole piece is to be assessed strikes me, with great respect, as an anomalous jurisprudential relapse.

WNET, Thirteen v. Aereo, Inc., 2013 WL 1285591 (2d Cir., 2013)

CHIN and DRONEY, Circuit Judges, GLEESON, District Judge.*

DRONEY, Circuit Judge:

Aereo, Inc. ("Aereo") enables its subscribers to watch broadcast television programs over the internet for a monthly fee. Two groups of plaintiffs, holders of copyrights in programs broadcast on network television, filed copyright infringement actions against Aereo in the United States District Court for the Southern District of New York. They moved for a preliminary injunction barring Aereo from transmitting programs to its subscribers while the programs are still airing, claiming that those transmissions infringe their exclusive right to publicly perform their works. The district court (Nathan, J.) denied the motion, concluding that the plaintiffs were unlikely to prevail on the merits in light of our prior decision in Cartoon Network LP, LLLP v. CSC Holdings, Inc., 536 10 F.3d 121 (2d Cir. 2008) ("Cablevision"). We agree and affirm the order of the district court denying the motion for a preliminary injunction.[1]

BACKGROUND

The parties below agreed on all but one of the relevant facts of Aereo's system, namely whether Aereo's antennas operate independently or as a unit. The district court resolved that issue, finding that Aereo's antennas operate independently. The Plaintiffs do not appeal that factual finding. Thus the following facts are undisputed.

I. Aereo's System

Aereo transmits to its subscribers broadcast television programs over the internet for a monthly subscription fee. Aereo is currently limited to subscribers living in New York City and offers only New York area channels. It does not have any license from copyright holders to record or transmit their programs. The details of Aereo's system are best explained from two perspectives. From its subscribers' perspective, Aereo functions much like a television with a remote Digital Video Recorder ("DVR") and Slingbox.[2] Behind the scenes, Aereo's system uses antennas and a remote hard drive to create individual copies of the programs Aereo users wish to watch while they are being broadcast or at a later time. These copies are used to transmit the programs to the Aereo subscriber.

A. The Subscriber's Perspective

Aereo subscribers begin by logging on to their account on Aereo's website using a computer or other internet-connected device. They are then presented with a programming guide listing broadcast television programs now airing or that will air in the future. If a user selects a program that is currently airing, he is presented with two options: "Watch" and "Record." If the user selects "Watch," the program he selected begins playing, but the transmission is briefly delayed relative to the live television broadcast.[3] Thus the user can watch the program nearly live, that is, almost contemporaneously with the over-the-air broadcast. While the user is watching the program with the "Watch" function, he can pause or rewind it as far back as the point when the user first began watching the program.[4] This may result in the user watching the program with the "Watch" feature after the over-the-air broadcast has ended. At any point while watching the program with the "Watch" feature, the user can select the "Record" button, which will cause Aereo's system to save a copy of the program for later viewing. The recorded copy of the program will begin from the point when the user first began watching the program, not from the time when the user first pressed the "Record" button.[5] If a user in "Watch" mode does not press "Record" before the conclusion of the program, the user is not able to watch that program again later.

An Aereo user can also select a program that is currently airing and press the "Record" button. In that case, a copy of the program will be saved for later viewing. However, the "Record" function can also be used to watch a program nearly live, because the user can begin playback of the program being recorded while the recording is being made. Thus the difference between selecting the "Watch" and the "Record" features for a program currently airing is that the "Watch" feature begins playback and a copy of the program is not retained for later viewing, while the "Record" feature saves a copy for later viewing but does not begin playback without further action by the user. If an Aereo user selects a program that will air in the future, the user's only option is the "Record" function. When the user selects that function, Aereo's system will record the program when it airs, saving a copy for the user to watch later. An Aereo user cannot, however, choose either to "Record" or "Watch" a program that has already finished airing if he did not previously elect to record the program. The final notable feature of Aereo's system is that users can watch Aereo programing on a variety of devices. Aereo's primary means of transmitting a program to a user is via an internet browser, which users can access on their computers. Aereo users can also watch programs on mobile devices such as tablets or smart phones using mobile applications. Finally, Aereo subscribers can watch Aereo on an internet-connected TV or use a stand-alone device to connect their non-internet TVs to Aereo.

Aereo's system thus provides the functionality of three devices: a standard TV antenna, a DVR, and a Slingbox-like device. These devices allow one to watch live television with the antenna; pause and record live television and watch recorded programing using the DVR; and use the Slingbox to watch both live and recorded programs on internet-connected mobile devices.

B. The Technical Aspects of Aereo's System

Aereo has large antenna boards at its facility in Brooklyn, New York. Each of these boards contains approximately eighty antennas, which consist of two metal loops roughly the size of a dime. These boards are installed parallel to each other in a large metal housing such that the antennas extend out of the housing and can receive broadcast TV signals. Aereo's facility thus uses thousands of individual antennas to receive broadcast television channels.[6]

When an Aereo user selects a program to watch or record, a signal is sent to Aereo's antenna server. The antenna server assigns one of the individual antennas and a transcoder to the user. The antenna server tunes that antenna to the broadcast frequency of the channel showing the program the user wishes to watch or record. The server transcodes the data received by this antenna, buffers it, and sends it to another Aereo server, where a copy of the program is saved to a large hard drive in a directory reserved for that Aereo user. If the user has chosen to "Record" the program, the Aereo system will create a complete copy of the program for that user to watch later. When the user chooses to view that program, Aereo's servers will stream the program to the user from the copy of the program saved in the user's directory on the Aereo server. If the user instead has chosen to "Watch" the program, the same operations occur, except that once six or seven seconds of programming have been saved in the hard drive copy of the program in the user's directory on the Aereo server, the Aereo system begins streaming the program to the user from this copy. Thus even when an Aereo user is watching a program using the "Watch" feature, he is not watching the feed directly or immediately from the antenna assigned to him. Rather the feed from that antenna is used to create a copy of the program on the Aereo server, and that copy is then transmitted to the user. If at any point before the program ends, the user in "Watch" mode selects "Record," the copy of the program is retained for later viewing. If the user does not press "Record" before the program ends, the copy of the program created for and used to transmit the program to the user is automatically deleted when it has finished playing.

Three technical details of Aereo's system merit further elaboration. First, Aereo assigns an individual antenna to each user. No two users share the same antenna at the same time, even if they are watching or recording the same program.[7] Second, the signal received by each antenna is used to create an individual copy of the program in the user's personal directory. Even when two users are watching or recording the same program, a separate copy of the program is created for each. Finally, when a user watches a program, whether nearly live or previously recorded, he sees his individual copy on his TV, computer, or mobile-device screen. Each copy of a program is only accessible to the user who requested that the copy be made, whether that copy is used to watch the program nearly live or hours after it has finished airing; no other Aereo user can ever view that particular copy.

II. The Present Suits

Two groups of plaintiffs (the "Plaintiffs") filed separate copyright infringement actions against Aereo in the Southern District of New York. They asserted multiple theories, including infringement of the public performance right, infringement of the right of reproduction, and contributory infringement. ABC and its co-plaintiffs moved for a preliminary injunction barring Aereo from transmitting television programs to its subscribers while the programs were still being broadcast. The two sets of plaintiffs agreed to proceed before the district court in tandem, and the motion for preliminary injunction was pursued in both actions simultaneously.

Following expedited briefing and discovery and an evidentiary hearing, the district court denied the Plaintiffs' motion. Am. Broad. Cos., Inc. v. Aereo, 874 F. Supp. 2d 373, 405 (S.D.N.Y. 2012). The district court began its analysis with the first factor relevant to granting a preliminary injunction: whether the Plaintiffs have demonstrated a likelihood of success on the merits. Id. at 381 (citing Salinger v. Colting, 607 F.3d 68, 80 (2d Cir. 2010)). The district court found that this factor was determined by our prior decision in Cablevision, 536 F.3d 121. Aereo, 874 F. Supp. 2d at 381-82. After a lengthy discussion of the facts and analysis of that decision, the district court concluded that Aereo's system was not materially distinguishable from Cablevision's Remote Storage Digital Video Recorder system, which we held did not infringe copyright holders' public performance right. Id. at 385-86. The district court found unpersuasive each of the Plaintiffs' arguments attempting to distinguish Cablevision. See id. at 386-96. Thus the court concluded that the Plaintiffs were unlikely to prevail on the merits. Id. at 396.

The district court then considered the other three preliminary injunction factors. First, the court concluded that the Plaintiffs had demonstrated a likelihood that they would suffer irreparable harm in the absence of a preliminary injunction. Id. at 396-402. But second, the district court found that an injunction would severely harm Aereo, likely ending its business. Id. at 402-03. As such, the balance of hardships did not tip "decidedly" in favor of the Plaintiffs. Id. at 403. Finally, the district court concluded that an injunction "would not disserve the public interest." Id. at 403-04. Because the Plaintiffs had not demonstrated a likelihood of success on the merits or a balance of hardship tipping decidedly in their favor, the district court denied their motion for a preliminary injunction. Id. at 405. The Plaintiffs promptly filed an interlocutory appeal, and this case was briefed on an expedited schedule.

DISCUSSION

We review a district court's denial of a preliminary injunction for abuse of discretion. WPIX, Inc. v. ivi, Inc., 691 F.3d 275, 278 (2d Cir. 2012). A district court abuses its discretion when its decision rests on legal error or a clearly erroneous factual finding, or when its decision, though not the product of legal error or a clearly erroneous factual finding, cannot be located within the range of permissible decisions. Id. Our decisions identify four factors relevant to granting a preliminary injunction for copyright infringement. First, a district court may issue a preliminary injunction "only if the plaintiff has demonstrated either (a) a likelihood of success on the merits or (b) sufficiently serious questions going to the merits to make them a fair ground for litigation and a balance of hardships tipping decidedly in the plaintiff's favor." Salinger v. Colting, 607 F.3d 68, 79 (2d Cir. 2010) (internal citation and quotation marks omitted). Second, a plaintiff seeking a preliminary injunction must demonstrate "'that he is likely to suffer irreparable injury in the absence of'" an injunction. Id. at 79-80 (quoting Winter v. Natural Res. Def. Council, 555 U.S. 7, 20 (2008)). A court may not presume irreparable injury in the copyright context; rather the plaintiff must demonstrate actual harm that cannot be remedied later by damages should the plaintiff prevail on the merits. Id. at 80 (citing eBay Inc. v. MercExchange, L.L.C., 547 U.S. 388, 391 (2006)). Third, a district court "must consider the balance of hardships between the plaintiff and defendant andissue the injunction only if the balance of hardships tips in the plaintiff's favor." Id. Fourth and finally, "the court must ensure that 'the public interest would not be disserved' by the issuance of a preliminary injunction." Id. (quoting eBay, 547 U.S. at 391). The outcome of this appeal turns on whether Aereo's service infringes the Plaintiffs' public performance right under the Copyright Act. The district court denied the injunction, concluding, as mentioned above, that (1) Plaintiffs were not likely to prevail on the merits given our prior decision in Cablevision and (2) the balance of hardships did not tip "decidedly" in the Plaintiffs' favor. Aereo, 874 F. Supp. 2d at 405. Plaintiffs' likelihood of success on the merits depends on whether Aereo's service infringes Plaintiffs' copyrights. And, as we discuss further below, the balance of hardships is largely a function of whether the harm Aereo would suffer from the issuance of an injunction is legally cognizable, which in turn depends on whether Aereo is infringing the Plaintiffs' copyrights. See ivi, 691 F.3d at 287. As a result, a preliminary injunction can only be granted if Plaintiffs can show that Aereo infringes their public performance right. We now turn to that issue.

I. The Public Performance Right

The 1976 Copyright Act (the "Act") gives copyright owners several exclusive rights and then carves out a number of exceptions. The fourth of these rights, at issue in this appeal, is the copyright owner's exclusive right "in the case of literary, musical, dramatic, and choreographic works, pantomimes, and motion pictures and other audiovisual works, to perform the copyrighted work publicly." 17 U.S.C. § 106(4). The Act defines "perform" as "to recite, render, play, dance, or act [a work], either directly or by means of any device or process or, in the case of a motion picture or other audiovisual work, to show its images in any sequence or to make the sounds accompanying it audible." 17 U.S.C. § 101. The Act also states:

> To perform or display a work "publicly" means-
>
> 4 (1) to perform or display it at a place open to the public or at any place where a substantial number of persons outside of a normal circle of a family and its social acquaintances is gathered; or
>
> (2) to transmit or otherwise communicate a performance or display of the work to a place specified by clause (1) or to the public, by means of any device or process, whether the members of the public capable of receiving the performance or display receive it in the same place or in separate places and at the same time or at different times.

17 U.S.C. § 101. This appeal turns on the second clause of this definition (the "Transmit Clause" or "Clause").

The relevant history of the Transmit Clause begins with two decisions of the Supreme Court, Fortnightly Corp. v. United Artists Television, Inc., 392 U.S. 390 (1968), and Teleprompter Corp. v. Columbia Broadcasting System, Inc., 415 U.S. 394 (1974). These decisions held that under the then-current 1909 Copyright Act, which lacked any analog to the Transmit Clause, a cable television system that received broadcast television signals via antenna and retransmitted these signals to its subscribers via coaxial cable did not "perform" the copyrighted works and therefore did not infringe copyright holders' public performance right. Teleprompter, 415 U.S. at 408; Fortnightly, 392 U.S. at 399-401. Even before these cases were decided, Congress had begun drafting a new copyright act to respond to changes in technology, most notably, cable television.

These efforts resulted in the 1976 Copyright Act. The Act responded to the emergence of6 cable television systems in two ways. First, it added the Transmit Clause. The legislative history shows that the Transmit Clause was intended in part to abrogate Fortnightly and Teleprompter and bring a cable television system's retransmission of broadcast television programming within the scope of the public performance right. H.R. Rep. 94-1476, 1976 U.S.C.C.A.N. 5659, at 63 (1976) ("House Report") ("[A] sing[er] is performing when he or she sings a song; a broadcasting network is performing when it transmits his or her performance (whether simultaneously or from records); a local broadcaster is performing when it transmits the network broadcast; a cable television system is performing when it retransmits the broadcast to its subscribers; and any individual is performing when he or she plays a phonorecord embodying the performance or communicates it by turning on a receiving set."). Second, Congress recognized that requiring cable television systems to obtain a negotiated license from individual copyright holders may deter further investment in cable systems, so it created a compulsory license for retransmissions by cable systems.[8] See 17 U.S.C. § 111(d).

Plaintiffs claim that Aereo's transmissions of broadcast television programs while the programs are airing on broadcast television fall within the plain language of the Transmit Clause and are analogous to the retransmissions of network programing made by cable systems, which the drafters of the 1976 Copyright Act viewed as public performances. They therefore believe that Aereo is publicly performing their copyrighted works without a license.[9] In evaluating their claims, we do not work from a blank slate. Rather, this Court in Cablevision, 536 F.3d 121, closely analyzed and construed the Transmit Clause in a similar factual context. Thus the question of whether Aereo's transmissions are public performances under the Transmit Clause must begin with a discussion of Cablevision.

II. Cablevision's Interpretation of the Transmit Clause

In Cablevision, 536 F.3d 121, we considered whether Cablevision's Remote Storage Digital Video Recorder ("RS-DVR") infringed copyright holders' reproduction and public performance rights. Cablevision, a cable television system, wished to offer its customers its newly designed RS-DVR system, which would give them the functionality of a stand-alone DVR via their cable set-top box. 536 F.3d at 124-25. Before the development of the RS-DVR system, Cablevision would receive programming from various content providers, such as ESPN or a local affiliate of a national broadcast network, process it, and transmit it to its subscribers through coaxial cable in real time. Id. With the RS-DVR system, Cablevision split this stream into two. One stream went out to customers live as before. The second stream was routed to a server, which determined whether any Cablevision customers had requested to record a program in the live stream with their RS-DVR. If so, the data for that program was buffered, and a copy of that program was created for that Cablevision customer on a portion of a Cablevision remote hard drive assigned solely to that customer. Thus if 10,000 Cablevision customers wished to record the Super Bowl, Cablevision would create 10,000 copies of the broadcast, one for each customer. A customer who requested that the program be recorded could later play back the program using his cable remote, and Cablevision would transmit the customer's saved copy of that program to the customer. Only the customer who requested that the RS-DVR record the program could access the copy created for him; no other Cablevision customer could view this particular copy.[10] See 536 F.3d at 124-25.

Copyright holders in movies and television programs sued, arguing that Cablevision's RS-DVR system infringed their reproduction right by creating unauthorized copies of their programs and their public performance right by transmitting these copies to Cablevision customers who previously requested to record the programs using their RS-DVRs. The district court granted the plaintiffs' motion for summary judgment and issued an injunction against Cablevision. See Twentieth Century Fox Film Corp. v. Cablevision Sys. Corp., 478 F. Supp. 2d 607 (S.D.N.Y. 2007). The court found that the RS-DVR infringed the plaintiffs' reproduction right in two ways: (1) by creating temporary buffer copies of programs in order to create a permanent copy for each of its customers on its hard drives and (2) by creating a permanent copy of the program for each customer. Id. at 617-22. The court also found that Cablevision's transmission of a recorded program to the customer who had requested to record the program was a public performance under the Transmit Clause and therefore was infringing on that basis as well. Id. at 622-23.

This Court reversed on all three issues. Cablevision, 536 F.3d at 140. Because the Plaintiffs in the present cases did not pursue their claim that Aereo infringes their reproduction right in the injunction application before the district court, we need not discuss the two reproduction right holdings of Cablevision except where relevant to the public performance issue. Instead, we will focus on Cablevision's interpretation of the public performance right and the Transmit Clause, which the court below found determinative of the injunction application.

The Cablevision court began by discussing the language and legislative history of the Transmit Clause. 536 F.3d at 134-35. Based on language in the Clause specifying that a transmission may be "to the public . . . whether the members of the public capable of receiving the performance . . . receive it in the same place or in separate places and at the same time or at different times," 17 U.S.C. § 101, this Court concluded that "it is of no moment that the potential recipients of the transmission are in different places, or that they may receive the transmission at different times." 536 F.3d at 134. As the language makes plain, in determining whether a transmission is to the public it is important "to discern who is 'capable of receiving' the performance being transmitted." Id. (quoting 17 U.S.C. § 101). Cablevision then decided that "capable of receiving the performance" refers not to the performance of the underlying work being transmitted but rather to the transmission itself, since the "transmission of a performance is itself a performance." Id. The Court therefore concluded that "the transmit clause directs us to examine who precisely is 'capable of receiving' a particular transmission of a performance." 2 536 F.3d at 135 (emphasis added).

In adopting this interpretation of the Transmit Clause, Cablevision rejected two alternative readings. First, it considered the interpretation accepted by the district court in that case. According to that view, a transmission is "to the public," not based on the "potential audience of a particular transmission" but rather based on the "potential audience of the underlying work (i.e., 'the program') whose content is being transmitted." Id. at 135. The Cablevision court rejected this interpretation of the Transmit Clause. Given that "the potential audience for every copyrighted audiovisual work is the general public," this interpretation would render the "to the public" language of the Clause superfluous and contradict the Clause's obvious contemplation of non-public transmissions. Id. at 135-36.

Second, the Cablevision court considered "a slight variation of this interpretation" offered by the plaintiffs. Id. Plaintiffs argued that "both in its real-time cablecast and via the RS14 DVR playback, Cablevision is in fact transmitting the 'same performance' of a given work: the performance that occurs when the programming service supplying Cablevision's content transmits that content to Cablevision and the service's other licensees." Id. In this view, the Transmit Clause requires courts to consider "not only the potential audience [of a particular] transmission, but also the potential audience of any transmission of the same underlying 'original' performance." Id. This interpretation of the Transmit Clause would aggregate all transmissions of the same underlying performance, and if these transmissions enabled the performance to reach the public, each transmission, regardless of its potential audience, should be deemed a public performance. Cablevision rejected this view because it would make a seemingly private transmission public by virtue of actions taken by third parties. Id. For example, if a person records a program and then transmits that recording to a television in another room, he would be publicly performing the work because some other party, namely the original broadcaster, had once transmitted the same performance to the public. Id. The Cablevision court concluded that Congress could not have intended "such odd results"; instead, the Transmit Clause directed courts to consider only the potential audience of the "performance created by the act of transmission." Id. The Cablevision court found this interpretation consistent with prior opinions of this Court construing the Clause. Id.; see Nat'l Football League v. PrimeTime 24 Joint Venture, 211 F.3d 10 (2d Cir. 2000).

Finally, the Cablevision court considered Columbia Pictures Industries, Inc. v. Redd Horne, Inc., 749 F.2d 154 (3d Cir. 1984). In Redd Horne, the defendant operated a video rental store that utilized private booths containing individual televisions. Customers would select a movie from the store's catalog and enter a booth. A store employee would then load a copy of the movie into a VCR hard-wired to the TV in the customer's booth and transmit the content of the tape to the television in the booth. See 749 F.2d at 156-57. The Third Circuit, following an interpretation of the Transmit Clause first advanced by Professor Nimmer, held that this was a public performance because the same copy of the work, namely the individual video cassette, was repeatedly "performed" to different members of the public at different times. Id. at 159 (quoting 2 Melville B. Nimmer & David Nimmer, Nimmer on Copyright § 8.14[C][3], at 8.192.8(1) (Matthew Bender rev. ed.)). The Cablevision court endorsed this conclusion[11]; whether a transmission originates from a distinct or shared copy is relevant to the Transmit Clause analysis because "the use of a unique copy may limit the potential audience of a transmission and is therefore relevant to whether that transmission is made 'to the public.'" 536 5 F.3d at 138.

Applying this interpretation of the Transmit Clause to the facts of the RS-DVR, the Cablevision court concluded that Cablevision's transmission of a recorded program to an individual subscriber was not a public performance. Id. Each transmission of a program could be received by only one Cablevision customer, namely the customer who requested that the copy be created. No other Cablevision customer could receive a transmission generated from that particular copy. The "universe of people capable of receiving an RS-DVR transmission is the single subscriber whose self-made copy is used to create that transmission." Id. at 137. The transmission was therefore not made "to the public" within the meaning of the Transmit Clause and did not infringe the plaintiffs' public performance right. Id. at 138.

We discuss Cablevision's interpretation of the Transmit Clause in such detail because that decision establishes four guideposts that determine the outcome of this appeal. First and most important, the Transmit Clause directs courts to consider the potential audience of the individual transmission. See id. at 135. If that transmission is "capable of being received by the public" the transmission is a public performance; if the potential audience of the transmission is only one subscriber, the transmission is not a public performance, except as discussed below. Second and following from the first, private transmissions–that is those not capable of being received by the public–should not be aggregated. It is therefore irrelevant to the Transmit Clause analysis whether the public is capable of receiving the same underlying work or original performance of the work by means of many transmissions. See id. at 135-37. Third, there is an exception to this no-aggregation rule when private transmissions are generated from the same copy of the work. In such cases, these private transmissions should be aggregated, and if these aggregated transmissions from a single copy enable the public to view that copy, the transmissions are public performances. See id. at

137-38. Fourth and finally, "any factor that limits the potential audience of a transmission is relevant" to the Transmit Clause analysis. Id. at 137.

III. Cablevision's Application to Aereo's System

As discussed above, Cablevision's holding that Cablevision's transmissions of programs recorded with its RS-DVR system were not public performances rested on two essential facts. First, the RS-DVR system created unique copies of every program a Cablevision customer wished to record. 536 F.3d at 137. Second, the RS-DVR's transmission of the recorded program to a particular customer was generated from that unique copy; no other customer could view a transmission created by that copy. Id. Given these two features, the potential audience of every RS-DVR transmission was only a single Cablevision subscriber, namely the subscriber who created the copy.[12] And because the potential audience of the transmission was only one Cablevision subscriber, the transmission was not made "to the public."

The same two features are present in Aereo's system. When an Aereo customer elects to watch or record a program using either the "Watch" or "Record" features, Aereo's system creates a unique copy of that program on a portion of a hard drive assigned only to that Aereo user. And when an Aereo user chooses to watch the recorded program, whether (nearly) live or days after the program has aired, the transmission sent by Aereo and received by that user is generated from that unique copy. No other Aereo user can ever receive a transmission from that copy. Thus, just as in Cablevision, the potential audience of each Aereo transmission is the single user who requested that a program be recorded.

Plaintiffs offer various arguments attempting to distinguish Cablevision from the Aereo system. First, they argue that Cablevision is distinguishable because Cablevision had a license to transmit programming in the first instance, namely when it first aired the programs; thus the question was whether Cablevision needed an additional license to retransmit the programs recorded by its RS-DVR system. Aereo, by contrast, has no license. This argument fails, as the question is whether Aereo's transmissions are public performances of the Plaintiffs' copyrighted works. If so, Aereo needs a license to make such public performances; if they are not public performances, it needs no such license. Thus whether Aereo has a license is not relevant to whether its transmissions are public and therefore must be licensed. This argument by the Plaintiffs also finds no support in the Cablevision opinion. Cablevision did not hold that Cablevision's RS-DVR transmissions were licensed public performances; rather it held they were not public performances. It does not appear that the Cablevision court based its decision that Cablevision's RS-DVR transmissions were non-public transmissions on Cablevision's license to broadcast the programs live. Indeed, such a conclusion would have been erroneous, because having a license to publicly perform a work in a particular instance, such as to broadcast a television program live, does not give the licensee the right to perform the work again. That Cablevision had a license to transmit copyrighted works when they first aired thus should have no bearing on whether it needed a license to retransmit these programs as part of its RS-DVR system. Indeed, if this interpretation of Cablevision were correct, Cablevision would not need a license to retransmit programs using video-on-demand and there would have been no reason for Cablevision to construct an RS-DVR system employing individual copies.

Second, Plaintiffs argue that discrete transmissions should be aggregated to determine whether they are public performances. This argument has two aspects. Plaintiffs first argue that because Aereo's discrete transmissions enable members of the public to receive "the same performance (i.e., Aereo's retransmission of a program)" they are transmissions made "to the public." Br. of Pls.-Appellants Am. Broad. Cos., et al. at 19. But this is nothing more than the Cablevision plaintiffs' interpretation of the Transmit Clause, as it equates Aereo's transmissions with the original broadcast made by the over-the-air network rather than treating Aereo's transmissions as independent performances. See 536 F.3d at 136. This approach was explicitly rejected by the Cablevision court. See id.

Plaintiffs also argue that the Copyright Act requires that all of Aereo's discrete transmissions "be aggregated and viewed collectively as constituting a public performance." Br. of Pls.-Appellants WNET, Thirteen, et al. at 34. This is not contrary to Cablevision, they argue, because Cablevision only held that transmissions of the same performance or work made by different entities should not be aggregated. On their view, discrete transmissions of the same performance or work made by the same entity should be aggregated to determine whether a public performance has occurred. This argument is also foreclosed by Cablevision. First, Cablevision made clear that the relevant inquiry under the Transmit Clause is the potential audience of a particular transmission, not the potential audience for the underlying work or the particular performance of that work being transmitted. See 536 F.3d at 135. But the only reason to aggregate Aereo's discrete transmissions along the lines suggested by Plaintiffs is that they are discrete transmissions of the same performance or work. Thus Plaintiffs are asking us to adopt a reading of the Transmit Clause that is contrary to that adopted by Cablevision because it focuses on the potential audience of the performance or work being transmitted, not the potential audience of the particular transmission. Second, Plaintiffs provide no reason why Aereo's multiple, audience-of-one transmissions of unique copies of the same underlying program should be aggregated but not Cablevision's multiple, audience-of-one transmissions of unique copies of the same underlying program. Both Aereo and Cablevision are making multiple private transmissions of the same work, so adopting the Plaintiffs' approach and aggregating all transmissions made by the same entity would require us to find that both are public performances. While it does not appear that Cablevision explicitly rejected this view, interpreting the Transmit Clause as the Plaintiffs urge so as to aggregate Aereo's transmissions would, if fairly applied to the facts of Cablevision, require us to aggregate Cablevision's distinct RS-DVR transmissions. For these reasons, we cannot accept Plaintiffs' arguments that Aereo's transmissions to a single Aereo user, generated from a unique copy created at the user's request and only accessible to that user, should be aggregated for the purposes of determining whethe they are public performances.

Plaintiffs' third argument for distinguishing Cablevision is that Cablevision was decided based on an analogy to a typical VCR, with the RS-DVR simply an upstream version, but Aereo's system is more analogous to a cable television provider. While it is true that the Cablevision court did compare the RS-DVR system to the stand-alone VCR, these comparisons occur in the section of that opinion discussing Cablevision's potential liability for infringing the plaintiffs' reproduction right. See 536 F.3d at 131. No part of Cablevision's analysis of the public performance right appears to have been influenced by any analogy to the stand-alone VCR. Moreover, this Court has followed Cablevision's interpretation of the Transmit Clause in the context of internet music downloads. See United States v. Am. Soc'y of Composers, Authors & Publishers, 627 F.3d 64, 73-76 (2d Cir. 2010) ("ASCAP"); see also United States v. Am. Soc'y of Composers, Authors & Publishers (Application of Cellco P'Ship),2 663 F. Supp. 2d 363, 371-74 (S.D.N.Y. 2009) (following Cablevision's analysis of the Transmit Clause in the context of cellphone ringtones). Thus we see no support in Cablevision or in this Court's subsequent decisions for the Plaintiffs' argument that Cablevision's interpretation of the Transmit Clause is confined to technologies similar to the VCR.[13]

Plaintiffs' fourth argument for distinguishing Cablevision is that Cablevision's RS-DVR copies "broke the continuous chain of retransmission to the public" in a way that Aereo's copies do not. Br. of Pls.-Appellants Am. Broad. Cos., et al. at 39. Specifically, they argue that Aereo's copies are merely a device by which Aereo enables its users to watch nearly live TV, while Cablevision's copies, by contrast, could only serve as the source for a transmission of a program after the original transmission, that is the live broadcast of the program, had finished. As a result, Aereo's copies lack the legal significance of Cablevision's RS-DVR copies and are no different from the temporary buffer copies created by internet streaming, a process that this Court has assumed produces public performances. See, e.g., ivi, 691 F.3d at 278; ASCAP, 627 F.3d at 74.

This argument fails for two reasons. First, Aereo's copies do have the legal significance ascribed to the RS-DVR copies in Cablevision because the user exercises the same control over their playback. The Aereo user watching a copy of a recorded program that he requested be created, whether using the "Watch" feature or the "Record" feature, chooses when and how that copy will be played back. The user may begin watching it nearly live, but then pause or rewind it, resulting in playback that is no longer concurrent with the program's over-the-air broadcast.

Or the user may elect not to begin watching the program at all until long after it began airing. This volitional control over how the copy is played makes Aereo's copies unlike the temporary buffer copies generated incident to internet streaming. A person watching an internet stream chooses the program he wishes to watch and a temporary buffer copy of that program is then created, which serves as the basis of the images seen by the person watching the stream. But that person cannot exercise any control over the manner in which that copy is played–it cannot be paused, rewound, or rewatched later. As a result, the imposition of a temporary buffer copy between the outgoing stream and the image seen by the person watching it is of no significance, because the person only exercises control before the copy is created in choosing to watch the program in the first place. By contrast, the Aereo user selects what program he wishes a copy to be made of and then controls when and how that copy is played.[14] This second layer of control, exercised after the copy has been created, means that Aereo's transmissions from the recorded copies cannot be regarded as simply one link in a chain of transmission, giving Aereo's copies the same legal significance as the RS-DVR copies in Cablevision.[15]

Second, Plaintiffs' argument fails to account for Aereo's user-specific antennas. Each user-associated copy of a program created by Aereo's system is generated from a unique antenna assigned only to the user who requested that the copy be made. The feed from that antenna is not used to generate multiple copies of each program for different Aereo users but rather only one copy: the copy that can be watched by the user to whom that antenna is assigned. Thus even if we were to disregard Aereo's copies, it would still be true that the potential audience of each of Aereo's transmissions was the single user to whom each antenna was assigned. It is beyond dispute that the transmission of a broadcast TV program received by an individual's rooftop antenna to the TV in his living room is private, because only that individual can receive the transmission from that antenna, ensuring that the potential audience of that transmission is only one person. Plaintiffs have presented no reason why the result should be any different when that rooftop antenna is rented from Aereo and its signals transmitted over the internet: it remains the case that only one person can receive that antenna's transmissions.[16] Thus even without the creation of user-associated copies, which under Cablevision means that Aereo's transmissions are not public, there is significant reason to believe that Aereo's system would not be creating public performances, since the entire chain of transmission from the time a signal is first received by Aereo to the time it generates an image the Aereo user sees has a potential audience of only one Aereo customer.[17]

Finally, Plaintiffs argue that holding that Aereo's transmissions are not public performances exalts form over substance, because the Aereo system is functionally equivalent to a cable television provider. Plaintiffs also make much of the undisputed fact that Aereo's system was designed around the Cablevision holding, because it creates essentially identical copies of the same program for every user who wishes to watch it in order to avoid copyright liability, instead of using a perhaps more efficient design employing shared copies. However, that Aereo was able to design a system based on Cablevision's holding to provide its users with nearly live television over the internet is an argument that Cablevision was wrongly decided; it does not provide a basis for distinguishing Cablevision. Moreover, Aereo is not the first to design systems to avoid copyright liability. The same is likely true of Cablevision, which created separate user associated copies of each recorded program for its RS-DVR system instead of using more efficient shared copies because transmissions generated from the latter would likely be found to infringe copyright holders' public performance right under the rationale of Redd Horne, 749 F.2d 154. Nor is Aereo alone in designing its system around Cablevision, as many cloud computing services, such as internet music lockers, discussed further below, appear to have done the same. See Br. of the Computer & Commc'ns Indus. Ass'n & the Internet Ass'n as Amicus Curiae at 5-8. Perhaps the application of the Transmit Clause should focus less on the technical details of a particular system and more on its functionality, but this Court's decisions in Cablevision and NFL, 211 F.3d 10, held that technical architecture matters.

IV. The Legislative Intent Behind the 1976 Copyright Act

Plaintiffs also contend that the legislative history of the 1976 Copyright Act shows that Aereo's transmissions should be deemed public performances of the Plaintiffs' copyrighted works. They argue that cable retransmissions are public performances under the Transmit Clause and Aereo is functionally equivalent to a cable system. However, this reading of the legislative history is simply incompatible with the conclusions of the Cablevision court.

This view of the legislative history also ignores a contrary strand of the history behind the 1976 Copyright Act. Congress recognized when it drafted the 1976 Act that its broad definition of "performance" could create unintended results. The House Report states that under this definition, "any individual is performing whenever he or she plays a phonorecord embodying the performance or communicates the performance by turning on a receiving set."

House Report at 63. But because Congress did not wish to require everyone to obtain a license from copyright holders before they could "perform" the copyrighted works played by their television, Congress was careful to note that a performance "would not be actionable as an infringement unless it were done 'publicly,' as defined in section 101." id. "Private" performances are exempted from copyright liability. Id. This limitation also applies to performances created by a "transmission," since, as the Cablevision court noted, if Congress intended all transmissions to be public performances, the Transmit Clause would not have contained the phrase "to the public."[18] Cablevision, 536 F.3d at 135-36.

In the technological environment of 1976, distinguishing between public and private transmissions was simpler than today. New devices such as RS-DVRs and Slingboxes complicate our analysis, as the transmissions generated by these devices can be analogized to the paradigmatic example of a "private" transmission: that from a personal roof-top antenna to a television set in a living room. As much as Aereo's service may resemble a cable system, it also generates transmissions that closely resemble the private transmissions from these devices. Thus unanticipated technological developments have created tension between Congress's view that retransmissions of network programs by cable television systems should be deemed public performances and its intent that some transmissions be classified as private. Although Aereo may in some respects resemble a cable television system, we cannot disregard the contrary concerns expressed by Congress in drafting the 1976 Copyright Act. And we certainly cannot disregard the express language Congress selected in doing so. That language and its legislative history, as interpreted by this Court in Cablevision, compels the conclusion that Aereo's transmissions are not public performances.

V. Stare Decisis

Though presented as efforts to distinguish Cablevision, many of Plaintiffs' arguments really urge us to overrule Cablevision. One panel of this Court, however, "cannot overrule a prior decision of another panel." Union of Needletrades, Indus. & Textile Employees, AFL-CIO, CLC v. U.S. I.N.S., 336 F.3d 200, 210 (2d Cir. 2003). We are "bound by the decisions of prior panels until such time as they are overruled either by an en banc panel of our Court or by the Supreme Court." United States v. Wilkerson, 361 F.3d 717, 732 (2d Cir. 2004). There is an exception when an intervening Supreme Court decision "casts doubt on our controlling precedent," Union of Needletrades, 336 F.3d at 210, but we are unaware of any such decisions that implicate Cablevision. Plaintiffs have provided us with no adequate basis to distinguish Cablevision from the Aereo system.[19] We therefore see no error in the district court's conclusion that Plaintiffs are unlikely to prevail on the merits.

VI. The Other Preliminary Injunction Factors

We now turn to the remaining preliminary injunction factors. See Salinger, 607 F.3d at 79-80. Because the Plaintiffs are not likely to prevail on the merits, we consider whether the Plaintiffs have demonstrated "sufficiently serious questions going to the merits to make them a fair ground for litigation and a balance of hardships tipping decidedly in the plaintiff's favor." Id. at 79. Given our conclusion that Aereo's service does not infringe Plaintiffs' public performance right when it transmits a program still airing on broadcast television, we do not believe the Plaintiffs have demonstrated "sufficiently serious questions going to the merits to make them a fair ground for litigation." Id.

Moreover, we find no abuse of discretion in the district court's determination that the balance of hardships does not tip decidedly in the Plaintiffs' favor. The district court reached this decision based on its conclusions (1) that the Plaintiffs were likely to suffer irreparable harm in the absence of an injunction and (2) that Aereo would suffer significant hardship if an injunction should issue, since this would likely be the end of its business. See Am. Broad. Cos., Inc. v. Aereo, 874 F. Supp. 2d at 397-403. The parties do not appear to contest the district court's factual determinations supporting these conclusions and we see no clear error in them. Plaintiffs do argue that any harm suffered by Aereo should be disregarded in the balance of hardships analysis because Aereo's business is illegal and "[i]t is axiomatic that an infringer of copyright cannot complain about the loss of ability to offer its infringing product." ivi, 691 F.3d at 287. But this argument hinges on the conclusion that Aereo's business infringes the Plaintiffs' copyrights. Because we conclude that it does not—at least on the limited question before us of whether Aereo's transmissions of unique copies of recorded programs to the Aereo users who directed that they be created are public performances—the harms Aereo would suffer from an injunction are legally cognizable and significant. There is thus no reason to disturb the district court's conclusion that the balance of hardships does not tip "decidedly" in the Plaintiffs' favor.

CONCLUSION

We conclude that Aereo's transmissions of unique copies of broadcast television programs created at its users' requests and transmitted while the programs are still airing on broadcast television are not "public performances" of the Plaintiffs' copyrighted works under Cablevision. As such, Plaintiffs have not demonstrated that they are likely to prevail on the merits on this claim in their copyright infringement action. Nor have they demonstrated serious questions as to the merits and a balance of hardships that tips decidedly in their favor. We therefore affirm the order of the district court denying the Plaintiffs' motion.

CHIN, Circuit Judge:

I respectfully dissent.

Defendant-appellee Aereo, Inc. ("Aereo") captures over-the-air broadcasts of television programs and retransmits them to subscribers by streaming them over the Internet. For a monthly fee, Aereo's customers may "Watch" the programming "live" (that is, with a seven-second delay) on their computers and other electronic devices, or they may "Record" the programs for later viewing. Aereo retransmits the programming without the authorization of the copyright holders and without paying a fee.

The Copyright Act confers upon owners of copyrights in audiovisual works the exclusive right "to perform the copyrighted work publicly." 17 U.S.C. § 106(4). This exclusive right includes the right "to transmit or otherwise communicate a performance . . . to the public, by means of any device or process." Id. § 101. In my view, by transmitting (or retransmitting) copyrighted programming to the public without authorization, Aereo is engaging in copyright infringement in clear violation of the Copyright Act.

Aereo argues that it is not violating the law because its transmissions are not "public" performances; instead, the argument goes, its transmissions are "private" performances, and a "private performance is not copyright infringement." It contends that it is merely providing a "technology platform that enables consumers to use remotelylocated equipment . . . to create, access and view their own unique recorded copies of free over-the-air broadcast television programming."

Aereo's "technology platform" is, however, a sham. The system employs thousands of individual dime-sized antennas, but there is no technologically sound reason to use a multitude of tiny individual antennas rather than one central antenna; indeed, the system is a Rube Goldberg-like contrivance, over-engineered in an attempt to avoid the reach of the Copyright Act and to take advantage of a perceived loophole in the law. After capturing the broadcast signal, Aereo makes a copy of the selected program for each viewer, whether the user chooses to "Watch" now or "Record" for later. Under Aereo's theory, by using these individual antennas and copies, it may retransmit, for example, the Super Bowl "live" to 50,000 subscribers and yet, because each subscriber has an individual antenna and a "unique recorded cop[y]" of the broadcast, these are "private" performances. Of course, the argument makes no sense. These are very much public performances.

Aereo purports to draw its infringement-avoidance scheme from this Court's decision in Cartoon Network LP v. CSC Holdings, Inc., 536 F.3d 121 (2d Cir. 2008), cert. denied, 129 S. Ct. 2890 (2009) ("Cablevision"). But, as discussed below, there are critical differences between Cablevision and this case. Most significantly, Cablevision involved a cable company that paid statutory licensing and retransmission consent fees for the content it retransmitted, while Aereo pays no such fees. Moreover, the subscribers in Cablevision already had the ability to view television programs in real-time through their authorized cable subscriptions, and the remote digital video recording service at issue there was a supplemental service that allowed subscribers to store that authorized content for later viewing. In contrast, no part of Aereo's system is authorized. Instead, its storage and time-shifting functions are an integral part of an unlicensed retransmission service that captures broadcast television programs and streams them over the Internet.

Aereo is doing precisely what cable companies, satellite television companies, and authorized Internet streaming companies do — they capture over-the-air broadcasts and retransmit them to customers — except that those entities are doing it legally, pursuant to statutory or negotiated licenses, for a fee. By accepting Aereo's argument that it may do so without authorization and without paying a fee, the majority elevates form over substance. Its decision, in my view, conflicts with the text of the Copyright Act, its legislative history, and our case law.

For these and other reasons discussed more fully below, I would reverse the district court's order denying plaintiffs-appellants' motion for a preliminary injunction.

DISCUSSION

When interpreting a statute, we must begin with the plain language, giving any undefined terms their ordinary meaning. See Roberts v. Sea-Land Servs., Inc., 132 S. Ct. 1350, 1356 (2012); United States v. Desposito, 704 F.3d 221, 226 (2d Cir. 2013). We must "attempt to ascertain how a reasonable reader would understand the statutory text, considered as a whole." Pettus v. Morgenthau, 554 F.3d 293, 297 (2d Cir. 2009). Where Congress has expressed its intent in "reasonably plain terms, that language must ordinarily be regarded as conclusive." Negonsott v. Samuels, 507 U.S. 99, 104 (1993) (internal quotation marks and citation omitted); see Devine v. United States, 202 F.3d 547, 551 (2d Cir.2000). If we conclude that the text is ambiguous, however, we will look to legislative history and other tools of statutory interpretation to "dispel this ambiguity." In re Air Cargo Shipping Servs. Antitrust Litig., 697 F.3d 154, 159 (2d Cir. 2012).

I begin, then, by considering the text of the relevant sections of the Copyright Act. To the extent there is any arguable ambiguity in the statutory language, I next turn to its legislative history. Finally, I conclude with a discussion of Cablevision as well as other relevant precedents.

A. The Statutory Text

Section 106 of the Copyright Act sets out six exclusive rights held by a copyright owner; these include the right "to perform the copyrighted work publicly." 17 U.S.C. § 106(4).

As defined in section 101, "[t]o perform . . . a work 'publicly' means," among other things:

> to transmit or otherwise communicate a performance or display of the work . . . to the public, by means of any device or process, whether the members of the public capable of receiving the performance or display receive it in the same place or in separate places and at the same time or at different times.

Id. § 101. "To 'transmit' a performance" is "to communicate it by any device or process whereby images or sounds are received beyond the place from which they are sent." Id. Hence, the use of a device or process to transmit or communicate copyrighted images or sounds to the public constitutes a public performance, whether members of the public receive the performance in the same place or in different places, whether at the same time or at different times.

It is apparent that Aereo's system fits squarely within the plain meaning of the statute. See, e.g., Fox Television Stations, Inc. v. BarryDriller Content Sys., PLC, No. CV 12-6921, 2012 WL 6784498, at *1-6 (C.D. Cal. Dec. 27, 2012) (holding that a service "technologically analogous" to Aereo's was engaged in public performances). The statute is broadly worded, as it refers to "any device or process." 17 U.S.C. § 101 (emphasis added); see also id. (defining "device" and "process" as "one now known or later developed"). Aereo's system of thousands of antennas and other equipment clearly is a "device or process." Using that "device or process," Aereo receives copyrighted images and sounds and "transmit[s] or otherwise communicate[s]" them to its subscribers "beyond the place from which they are sent," id., that is, "'beyond the place' of origination," Columbia Pictures Indus., Inc. v. Prof'l Real Estate Investors, Inc., 866 F.2d 278, 282 (9th Cir. 1989). The "performance or display of the work" is then received by paying subscribers "in separate places" and "at different times." 17 U.S.C. § 101.

Even assuming Aereo's system limits the potential audience for each transmission, and even assuming each of its subscribers receives a unique recorded copy, Aereo still is transmitting the programming "to the public." Id. Giving the undefined term "the public" its ordinary meaning, see Kouichi Taniguchi v. Kan Pacific Saipan, Ltd., 132 S. Ct. 1997, 2002 (2012), a transmission to anyone other than oneself or an intimate relation is a communication to a "member[] of the public," because it is not in any sense "private." See Webster's II: New Riverside University Dictionary 951 (1994) (defining "public" as "[t]he community or the people as a group"); see also id. at 936 (defining "private" as, inter alia, "[n]ot public: intimate"). Cf. Cablevision, 536 F.3d at 138 ("[T]he identity of the transmitter . . . [is] germane in determining whether that transmission is made 'to the public.'"); Ford Motor Co. v. Summit Motor Prods., Inc., 930 F.2d 277, 299-300 (3d Cir. 1991) (construing "to the public" in section 106(3) and concluding that "even one person can be the public").

What Aereo is doing is not in any sense "private," as the Super Bowl example discussed above illustrates. This understanding accords with the statute's instruction that a transmission can be "to the public" even if the "members of the public capable of receiving the performance . . . receive it in the same place or in separate places and at the same time or at different times." 17 U.S.C. § 101. Because Aereo is transmitting television signals to paying strangers, all of its transmissions are "to the public," even if intervening "device[s] or process[es]" limit the potential audience of each separate transmission to a single "member[]" of the public." Id.

By any reasonable construction of the statute, Aereo is engaging in public performances and, therefore, it is engaging in copyright infringement. See id. §§ 106(4), 501(a).

B. The Legislative History

Even if the language of the transmit clause were ambiguous as applied to Aereo's system, see Cablevision, 536 F.3d at 136 ("[T]he transmit clause is not a model of clarity . . . ."), the legislative history reinforces the conclusion that Aereo is engaging in public performances. The legislative history makes clear that Congress intended to reach new technologies, like this one, that are designed solely to exploit someone else's copyrighted work. Just before the passage of the 1976 Copyright Act, the Supreme Court held in Fortnightly Corp. v. United Artists Television, Inc., 392 U.S. 390 (1968), and Teleprompter Corp. v. Columbia Broadcast Systems, Inc., 415 U.S. 394 (1974), that community antenna television ("CATV") systems — which captured live television broadcasts with antennas set on hills and retransmitted the signals to viewers unable to receive the original signals — did not infringe the public performance right because they were not "performing" the copyrighted work. See Teleprompter, 415 U.S. at 408-09; Fortnightly, 392 U.S. at 399-400. In reaching this conclusion, the Court reasoned that:

> If an individual erected an antenna on a hill, strung a cable to his house, and installed the necessary amplifying equipment, he would not be 'performing' the programs he received on his television set. . . . The only difference in the case of CATV is that the antenna system is erected and owned not by its users but by an entrepreneur.

Fortnightly, 392 U.S. at 400. This rationale is nearly identical to the justification advanced by Aereo: each subscriber could legally use his own antenna, digital video recorder ("DVR"), and Slingbox[20] to stream live television to his computer or other device, and so it makes no legal difference that the system is actually "erected and owned not by its users but by an entrepreneur." Id.[21]

But Congress expressly rejected the outcome reached by the Supreme Court in Fortnightly and Teleprompter. See Capital Cities Cable, Inc. v. Crisp, 467 U.S. 691, 709 (1984) ("Congress concluded that cable operators should be required to pay royalties to the owners of copyrighted programs retransmitted by their systems on pain of liability for copyright infringement."); see also WPIX, Inc. v. ivi, Inc., 691 F.3d 275, 281 (2d Cir. 2012); Fox Television Stations, 2012 WL 6784498, at *5. In the 1976 Copyright Act, Congress altered the definitions of "perform" and "publicly" specifically to render the CATV systems' unlicensed retransmissions illegal. See Sony Corp. of Am. v. Universal City Studios, Inc., 464 U.S. 417, 469 n.17 (1984); H.R. Rep. No. 94-1476, at 63, reprinted in 1976 U.S.C.C.A.N. 5659, 5676-77 ("[A] cable television system is performing when it retransmits the broadcast to its subscribers . . . ."); id. at 64, reprinted in 1976 U.S.C.C.A.N. at 5678 ("Clause (2) of the definition of 'publicly' in section 101 makes clear that the concept[] of public performance . . . include[s] . . . acts that transmit or otherwise communicate a performance or display of the work to the public . . . .").

Congress was not only concerned, however, with the then newly-emerging CATV systems. Recognizing that the Fortnightly and Teleprompter decisions arose in part because of the "drastic technological change" after the 1909 Act, Fortnightly, 392 U.S. at 396, Congress broadly defined the term "transmit" to ensure that the 1976 Act anticipated future technological developments:

> The definition of 'transmit' . . . is broad enough to include all conceivable forms and combinations of wires and wireless communications media, including but by no means limited to radio and television broadcasting as we know them. Each and every method by which the images or sounds comprising a performance or display are picked up and conveyed is a 'transmission,' and if the transmission reaches the public in [any] form, the case comes within the scope of clauses (4) or (5) of section 106.

H.R. Rep. No. 94-1476, at 64, reprinted in 1976 U.S.C.C.A.N. at 5678. Further anticipating that there would be changes in technology that it could not then foresee, Congress added that a public performance could be received in different places and at different times. This change was meant to clarify that:

> a performance made available by transmission to the public at large is 'public' even though the recipients are not gathered in a single place, and even if there is no proof that any of the potential recipients was operating his receiving apparatus at the time of the transmission. The same principles apply whenever the potential recipients of the transmission represent a limited segment of the public, such as the occupants of hotel rooms or the subscribers of a cable television service.

Id. at 64-65, reprinted at 1976 U.S.C.C.A.N. at 5678 (emphasis added).

While Congress in 1976 might not have envisioned the precise technological innovations employed by Aereo today, this legislative history surely suggests that Congress could not have intended for such a system to fall outside the definition of a public performance. To the contrary, Congress made clear its intent to include within the transmit clause "all conceivable forms and combinations of wires and wireless communications media," and if, as here, "the transmission reaches the public in [any] form, the case comes within the scope of clauses (4) or (5) of section 106." H.R. Rep. No. 94-1476, at 64, reprinted in 1976 U.S.C.C.A.N. at 5678. Aereo's streaming of television programming over the Internet is a public performance as Congress intended that concept to be defined.

C. Cablevision

Aereo seeks to avoid the plain language of the Copyright Act and the clear import of its legislative history by relying on this Court's decision in Cablevision. That reliance, in my view, is misplaced. Cablevision was a cable operator with a license to retransmit broadcast and cable programming to its paying subscribers. See Cablevision, 536 F.3d at 123-25; Twentieth Century Fox Film Corp. v. Cablevision Sys. Corp., 478 F. Supp. 2d 607, 610 (S.D.N.Y. 2007), rev'd sub nom., Cartoon Network LP v. CSC Holdings, Inc. (Cablevision), 536 F.3d 121 (2d Cir. 2008). The content providers sought to enjoin Cablevision from introducing a new Remote Storage DVR system (the "RS-DVR") that would "allow[] Cablevision customers who do not have a stand-alone DVR to record cable programming" and "then receive playback of those programs through their home television sets." Cablevision, 536 F.3d at 124. The lawsuit challenged only whether Cablevision needed additional licenses to allow its subscribers to record shows and play them back later through the RS-DVR system. See Twentieth Century Fox, 478 F. Supp. 2d at 609. If subscribers wanted to watch "live" television, they would watch it through Cablevision's licensed retransmission feed. See Cablevision, 536 F.3d at 124 (explaining that Cablevision split its programming data stream, sending one "immediately to customers as before"); Amicus Br. of Cablevision Sys. Corp. at 20.

The RS-DVR worked as follows. Cablevision split its licensed data stream, and sent a stream to a remote server, where the data went through two buffers. Cablevision, 536 F.3d at 124. At the first buffer, the system made a temporary copy of 0.1 seconds of programming while it inquired whether any subscribers wanted to copy that programming. Id. A customer could make such a request "by selecting a program in advance from an on-screen guide, or by pressing the record button while viewing a given program." Id. at 125. If a request had been made, the data moved to the second buffer and then was permanently saved onto a portion of a hard drive designated for that customer. Id. at 124. At the customer's request, the permanent copy was transmitted to the customer and played back to him. Id. at 125.

Cablevision held that the RS-DVR did not infringe either the reproduction or the public performance rights. Id. at 140. Unlike the majority here, I do not think we can view Cablevision's analyses of each right in isolation. See Majority Opin., supra, at 18. As Cablevision explained, "the right of reproduction can reinforce and protect the right of public performance." Cablevision, 536 F.3d at 138. "Given this interplay between the various rights in this context," id., Cablevision's holding that "copies produced by the RS-DVR system are 'made' by the RS-DVR customer," id. at 133, was critical to its holding that "each RS-DVR playback transmission . . . made to a single subscriber using a single unique copy produced by that subscriber . . . [is] not [a] performance[] "'to the public,'" id. at 139 (emphasis added); see also Amicus Br. of the United States at 17-19, Cable News Network, Inc. v. CSC Holdings, Inc., 129 S. Ct. 2890 (2009), denying cert., Cartoon Network LP v. CSC Holdings, Inc. (Cablevision), 536 F.3d 121 (2d Cir. 2008) [hereinafter "U.S. Cablevision Amicus Br."].

With this concept in mind, it is clear that Aereo's system is factually distinct from Cablevision's RSDVR system. First, Cablevision's RS-DVR system "exist[ed] only to produce a copy" of material that it already had a license to retransmit to its subscribers, Cablevision, 536 F.3d at 131, but the Aereo system produces copies to enable it to transmit material to its subscribers. Whereas Cablevision promoted its RS-DVR as a mechanism for recording and playing back programs, Aereo promotes its service as a means for watching "live" broadcast television on the Internet and through mobile devices. Unlike Cablevision, however, Aereo has no licenses to retransmit broadcast television. If a Cablevision subscriber wanted to use her own DVR to record programming provided by Cablevision, she could do so through Cablevision's licensed transmission. But an Aereo subscriber could not use her own DVR to lawfully record content received from Aereo because Aereo has no license to retransmit programming; at best, Aereo could only illegally retransmit public broadcasts from its remote antennas to the user. See, e.g., Fortnightly Corp., 392 U.S. at 400, overruled by statute as recognized in, Capital Cities Cable, 467 U.S. at 709; ivi, Inc., 691 F.3d at 278-79; see also U.S. Cablevision Amicus Br., supra, at 21 (arguing that the legality of a hypothetical unlicensed system that only allowed subscribers to copy and playback content "would be suspect at best, because [the subscriber] would be . . . copying programs that he was not otherwise entitled to view"). Aereo's use of copies is essential to its ability to retransmit broadcast television signals, while Cablevision's copies were merely an optional alternative to a set-top DVR. The core of Aereo's business is streaming broadcasts over the Internet in real-time; the addition of the record function, however, cannot legitimize the unauthorized retransmission of copyrighted content.

Second, subscribers interact with Aereo's system differently from the way Cablevision's subscribers interacted with the RS-DVR. Cablevision subscribers were already paying for the right to watch television programs, and the RS-DVR gave them the additional option to "record" the programs. Cablevision, 536 F.3d at 125. In contrast, Aereo subscribers can choose either "Watch" or "Record." Am. Broad. Cos. v. AEREO, Inc., 874 F. Supp. 2d 373, 377 (S.D.N.Y. 2012). Both options initiate the same process: a miniature antenna allocated to that user tunes to the channel; the television signal is transmitted to a hard drive; and a full-length, permanent copy is saved for that customer. Id. at 377-79. If the subscriber has opted to "Watch" the program live, the system immediately begins playing back the user's copy at the same time it is being recorded. Id. Aereo will then automatically delete the saved copy once the user is done watching the program, unless the subscriber chooses to save it. Id. at 379.

These differences undermine the applicability of Cablevision to Aereo's system. Cablevision found that the RS-DVR was indistinguishable from a VCR or set-top DVR because Cablevision's system "exist[ed] only to produce a copy" and its subscribers provided the "volitional conduct" necessary to make a copy by "ordering that system to produce a copy of a specific program." Cablevision, 536 F.3d at 131; see also U.S. Cablevision Amicus Br., supra, at 16 (noting that Cablevision turned on whether RS-DVR was more analogous to set-top DVR or video-on-demand service). The RS-DVR was not designed to be a substitute for viewing live television broadcasts. Aereo's system, however, was designed to be precisely that. It does not exist only, or even primarily, to make copies; it exists to stream live television through the Internet. Its users can choose to "Watch" live television instead of "Record" a program, but the system begins to produce a full-length copy anyway because, even under its own theory, Aereo cannot legally retransmit a television signal to them without such a copy.[22] Aereo's system is much different than a VCR or DVR — indeed, as Aereo explains, it is an antenna, a DVR, and a Slingbox rolled into one — and for that reason Cablevision does not control our decision here.

I note also that in Cablevision this Court "emphasize[d]" that its holding "does not generally permit content delivery networks to avoid all copyright liability by making copies of each item of content and associating one unique copy with each subscriber to the network, or by giving their subscribers the capacity to make their own individual copies." 536 F.3d at 139. Likewise, when the United States opposed the grant of certiorari in Cablevision, it argued that "the Second Circuit's analysis of the public-performance issue should not be understood to reach . . . other circumstances beyond those presented." U.S. Cablevision Amicus Br., supra, at 21.[23] Cablevision should not be extended to cover the circumstances presented in this case. Indeed, it is telling that Aereo declines to offer its subscribers channels broadcast from New Jersey, even though its antennas are capable of receiving those signals, for fear of being subject to suit outside the Second Circuit, i.e., outside the reach of Cablevision. Cf. Fox Television Stations, Inc. v. BarryDriller Content Sys., PLC, No. CV 12-6921, 2012 WL 6784498, at *3-4 (C.D. Cal. Dec. 27, 2012) (declining to follow Cablevision and enjoining an Aereo-like system based on plain meaning of § 101).

Finally, the majority's decision in my view runs afoul of other decisions of this Court. Although the issue was not even contested, in ivi we recognized that the retransmission of copyrighted television programming by streaming it live over the Internet constituted a "public performance" in violation of the Copyright Act. 691 F.3d at 278, 286, 287.[24] Similarly, in United States v. American Society of Composers, Authors, Publishers ("ASCAP"), where, again, the issue was not even contested, we observed that the streaming of a song, like the streaming of a "television or radio broadcast," is a public performance. 627 F.3d 64, 74 (2d Cir. 2010) (but holding in contrast that downloads of music do not constitute "public performances");[25] accord Infinity Broad. Corp. v. Kirkwood, 150 F.3d 104, 106-07, 111-12 (2d Cir. 1998) (holding that device allowing users to access private phone line to listen to public radio broadcasts infringed right of public performance, in the absence of a defense, and was not fair use).

In ivi, we addressed the need for a preliminary injunction to enjoin ivi from streaming copyrighted works over the Internet without permission:

> Indeed, ivi's actions — streaming copyrighted works without permission — would drastically change the industry, to plaintiffs' detriment. . . . The absence of a preliminary injunction would encourage current and prospective retransmission rights holders, as well as other Internet services, to follow ivi's lead in retransmitting plaintiffs' copyrighted programming without their consent. The strength of plaintiffs' negotiating platform and business model would decline. The quantity and quality of efforts put into creating television programming, retransmission and advertising revenues, distribution models and schedules — all would be adversely affected. These harms would extend to other copyright holders of television programming. Continued live retransmissions of copyrighted television programming over the Internet without consent would thus threaten to destabilize the entire industry.

691 F.3d at 286. These concerns apply with equal force here, where Aereo is doing precisely what ivi was enjoined from doing: streaming copyrighted works over the Internet without permission of the copyright holders. Today's decision does not merely deny the broadcasters a licensing fee for Aereo's activity; it provides a blueprint for others to avoid the Copyright Act's licensing regime altogether. See Appellant ABC, Inc. Br. at 10 (citing articles reporting on the rise of copycat services). Congress could not have intended such a result.

CONCLUSION

Based on the plain meaning of the statute, its legislative history, and our precedent, I conclude that Aereo's transmission of live public broadcasts over the Internet to paying subscribers are unlicensed transmissions "to the public." Hence, these unlicensed transmissions should be enjoined. Cablevision does not require a different result. Accordingly, I dissent.

Endnotes for WNET, Thirteen v. Aereo, Inc.

1   The two actions, although not consolidated in the district court, proceeded in tandem and the district court's order applied to both actions.

2   A Slingbox is a device that connects the user's cable or satellite set-top box or DVR to the internet, allowing the user to watch live or recorded programs on an internet-connectedmobile device, such as a laptop or tablet.

3   The technical operation of Aereo's system, discussed below, results in a slight delay in transmitting the program, which means that an Aereo subscriber using the "Watch" feature sees the program delayed by approximately ten seconds.

4   Thus if an Aereo user starts watching a program five minutes after it first began airing, he can rewind back to the five-minute mark, but not earlier.

5   Thus if an Aereo user starts watching a program five minutes after it first began airing and presses the "Record" button at the twenty-minute mark, the recorded copy will begin from the five-minute mark.

6   As mentioned in the text above, the lone factual dispute below was whether Aereo's antennas function independently or as one unit. The district court resolved this dispute in favor of Aereo, finding that its antennas operate independently. *American Broadcasting Companies, Inc. v. AEREO, Inc.*, 874. F. Supp. 2d 373 (S.D. N.Y., 2012) at p. 381. The Plaintiffs do not contest this finding on appeal.

7   Aereo's system usually assigns these antennas dynamically. Aereo users "share" antennas in the sense that one user is using a particular antenna now, and another may use the same antenna when the first is no longer using it. But at any given time, the feed from each antenna is used to create only one user's copy of the program being watched or recorded. Thus if 10,000 Aereo users are watching or recording the Super Bowl, Aereo has 10,000 antennas tuned to the channel broadcasting it.

8   Put briefly, the statute allows cable systems to retransmit copyrighted works from broadcast television stations in exchange for paying a compulsory license to the U.S. Copyright Office calculated according to a defined formula. The fees paid by cable systems are then distributed to copyright holders. See ivi, 691 F.3d at 281; *Eastern Microwave, Inc. v. Doubleday Sports, Inc.*, 691 F.2d 125 (2d Cir., 1982) at pp. 128-29.

9   Plaintiffs assert that Aereo's transmissions of recorded programs when the original program is no longer airing on broadcast television are also public performances and that Aereo's system infringes other exclusive rights granted by the Copyright Act, such as the reproduction right. Plaintiffs did not, however, present these claims as a basis for the preliminary injunction. They are therefore not before us and we will not consider them.

10   The RS-DVR was therefore unlike a video-on-demand service because it did not enable a customer to watch a program that had already been broadcast unless that customer had previously requested that the program be recorded and because it generated user-associated copies instead of using a shared copy or copies.

11   Aggregating private transmissions generated from the same copy is in some tension with the Cablevision court's first conclusion that the relevant inquiry under the Transmit Clause is the potential audience of the particular transmission. This interpretation of the Transmit Clause began with Professor Nimmer. He notes that it is difficult to understand precisely what Congress intended with the language in the Clause stating that a public performance can occur when the audience receives the work "at different times." See 2 Melville B. Nimmer & David Nimmer, Nimmer on Copyright § 8.14[C] [3], at 8.192.8 (Matthew Bender rev. ed.)). Arguing that this language on its face conflicted with other language in the statute and produced results Congress could not have intended, he proposed that by this language Congress wished to denote instances where the same copy of the work was repeatedly performed by different members of the public at different times.

See id. at 192.8(1)-192.8(6). The Cablevision court's focus on the potential audience of each particular transmission would essentially read out the "different times" language, since individuals will not typically receive the same transmission at different times. But Nimmer's solution–aggregating private transmissions when those transmissions are generated from the same copy– provides a way to reconcile the "different times" language of the Clause.

12 The Cablevision court concluded in its discussion of the reproduction right that Cablevision's customers, not Cablevision, "made" the RS-DVR copies. See 536 F.3d at 133.

13 And even if such analogies were probative, Aereo's system could accurately be analogized to an upstream combination of a standard TV antenna, a DVR, and a Slingbox.

14 It is true that an Aereo user in "Watch" mode will often not exercise volitional control over the playback of the program, because the program will automatically begin playing when selected and he will watch it through to the end. But that is not significant because the Aereo user can exercise such control if he wishes to, which means that the copy Aereo's system generates is not merely a technical link in a process of transmission that should be deemed a unity transmission. Moreover, the "Watch" feature's automatic playback is merely a default rule. The user can accomplish the same thing by using the "Record" feature, save that he must take the additional step of pressing "Play" once enough of the program has been recorded for playback. If this additional step were sufficient to break the chain of transmission, we see no reason why the "Watch" feature's default in favor of playback should change our analysis.

15 We also note that the Aereo system's use of copies gives it two features that would not be present were it simply to transmit the television programs its antennas receive directly to the user. First, it allows the Aereo user to pause and rewind seemingly live TV. This is because while the Aereo user has been watching the program "live," Aereo's system has in fact been creating a complete copy of the program. Thus if the user wishes to rewind thirty seconds or to the beginning of the program, he can easily do so. Second, if a user in "Watch" mode decides during a program he has been watching that he would like to save the program for later viewing, he can simply press the "Record" button. When the user does this, the entire program from the time he first began watching it is saved, not merely the portion beginning from the time when he pressed "Record." Were Aereo to transmit the signal from its antennas directly to each Aereo customers, neither of these features would be possible, because the image seen by the customer would be generated from a live feed, not a copy of the program. Aereo's users may well regard these two features as valuable and they provide an additional reason for regarding Aereo's copies as legally significant and not merely technical artifacts of a system to transmit live TV.

16   This makes Aereo's system unlike the early cable TV systems at issue in Fortnightly, 392 U.S. 390, and Teleprompter, 415 U.S. 394, because the signals from those community TV antennas were shared among many users. When Congress drafted the 1976 Copyright Act, it intended that such transmissions be deemed public performances. But, as discussed below, Congress clearly believed that, under the terms of the Act, some transmissions were private. The methodology Congress proscribed for distinguishing between public and private transmissions is the size of the potential audience, and by that methodology, the feed from Aereo's antennas is a private transmission because it results in a performance viewable by only one user. The 1976 Congress may not have anticipated that later technology would make it possible to mimic the functionality of early cable TV by means of private transmissions, but that unexpected result does not change the language of the statute.

17   Because Aereo's system uses both user-associated antennas and user-associated copies, we need not decide whether a system with only one of these attributes would be publicly performing copyrighted works.

18   This is particularly appropriate given that in 1976, when cable TV was still in its infancy, many Americans used rooftop antennas. Thus Congress would have certainly wished to avoid adopting language that would make millions of Americans copyright infringers because they transmitted broadcast television programs from their personal rooftop antennas to their own television sets.

19   Stare decisis is particularly warranted here in light of substantial reliance on Cablevision. As mentioned above, it appears that many media and technology companies have relied on Cablevision as an authoritative interpretation of the Transmit Clause. One example is cloud media services, which have proliferated in recent years. These services, which allow their users to store music on remote hard drives and stream it to internet-connected devices, have apparently been designed to comply with Cablevision. Just like Aereo's system and Cablevision's RS-DVR, they seek to avoid public performance liability by creating user associated copies of each song rather than sharing song files among multiple users. See Brandon J. Trout, Note, Infringers or Innovators? Examining Copyright Liability for Cloud-Based Music Locker Services, 14 Vand. J. Ent. & Tech. L. 729, 746-48 (2012).

20   A "Slingbox" is a set-top box that permits consumers to shift their television programming to their portable devices. Slingbox describes its service as "placeshifting": "Placeshifting is viewing and listening to live, recorded or stored media on a remote device over the Internet or a data network. Placeshifting allows consumers to watch their TV anywhere." See Placeshifting, Slingbox.com, http://www.slingbox.com/get/placeshifting (last visited March 5, 2013). The Slingbox thus enables a consumer to view on a remote device content that he is already entitled to receive from a licensed cable company or other authorized source to view on his television.

21   Aereo's contention that each subscriber has an individual antenna is a fiction because the vast majority of its subscribers are "dynamic users" who

are randomly assigned an antenna each time they use the system. Although each antenna is used only by one person at a time, it will be randomly assigned to another person for the next use. In other words, this is a shared pool of antennas, not individually-designated antennas.

22   Aereo's web page does contain a conspicuous notice under the "Watch" button that reads, "When you press 'Watch' you will start recording this show." Users thus have no choice but to record the show if they wish to watch it live, making it unlikely that the subscribers are voluntarily "ordering that system to produce a copy." Cablevision, 536 F.3d at 131.

23   By opposing the grant of certiorari, the government was not embracing Cablevision's construction of the transmit clause. To the contrary, the United States took the position that "scattered language in the Second Circuit's decision could be read to endorse overly broad, and incorrect, propositions about the Copyright Act." U.S. Cablevision Amicus Br., supra, at 6 (emphasis added). Specifically, the government was concerned with the suggestion "that a performance is not made available 'to the public' unless more than one person is capable of receiving a particular transmission" because it might "undermine copyright protection in circumstances far beyond those presented here, including with respect to . . . situations in which a party streams copyrighted material on an individualized basis over the Internet." Id. at 20-21. Despite these "problematic" aspects, id. at 22, the United States considered Cablevision an "unsuitable vehicle" for deciding these issues, due to the absence of any conflicting circuit court decisions at the time and the limitations imposed by the parties' stipulations, id. at 6.

24   There are companies in the market that stream television programming over the Internet pursuant to licenses, such as Hulu, Netflix, Amazon, and channel-specific websites like ComedyCentral.com. See Appellant WNET Br. at 12, 28, 43; Amicus Br. of Paramount Pictures Corp. et al. at 29. In general, however, these "negotiated Internet retransmissions . . . typically delay Internet broadcasts as not to disrupt plaintiffs' broadcast distribution models, reduce the live broadcast audience, or divert the live broadcast audience to the Internet." WPIX, Inc. v. ivi, Inc., 691 F.3d 275 (2d Cir., 2012) at p. 285.

25   In ASCAP, we left open "the possibility . . . that a transmission could constitute both a stream and a download." U.S. v. American Soc. of Composers, Authors, Publishers, 627 F.3d 64 (2d Cir., 2010) at p. 74 n.10. While streaming performances over the Internet constitutes a transmission "to the public," see ivi, Inc., 691 F.3d at 278-79; ASCAP, 627 F.3d at 74, allowing a consumer to download a copy so he can later play it back for himself does not, see ASCAP, 627 F.3d at 73, 75; Cablevision, 536 F.3d at 139. To the extent that Aereo's system immediately plays back from a copy that is still being recorded it is clearly "both a stream and a download," ASCAP, 627 F.3d at 74 n.10, and at a minimum the streaming portion constitutes an unlicensed public performance. If 50,000 Aereo subscribers choose to "Watch" the Super Bowl live, each subscriber receives a "performance or display" of the exact same broadcast on a seven second delay, even if Aereo is also simultaneously creating a unique copy for each subscriber so that each one has the option to pause,

rewind, or save the copy for later if they wish. Until the subscriber exercises that option, the existence of the copy is irrelevant; the broadcast is streaming "live" to each user at the same time just as it did in ivi.

(c) Making Available Right

Pursuant to the *Copyright Modernization Act*, Canada enacted making available rights for works, performers' performances and sound recordings. The rights were enacted to implement Article 8 of the WIPO Copyright Treaty (WCT) and Articles 10 and 14 of the WIPO Performances and Phonographs Treaty ("WPPT").

The WIPO Copyright Treaty requires contracting parties to enact a "making available" right. Article 8 of the treaty states the following:

> Without prejudice to the provisions of Articles 11(1)(ii), and 11bis (1)(i) and (ii), 11ter (1)(ii), 14(1)(ii) and 14bis (1) of the Berne Convention, authors of literary and artistic works shall enjoy the exclusive right of authorizing any communication to the public of their works, by wire or wireless means, including the making available to the public of their works in such a way that members of the public may access these works from a place and at a time individually chosen by them.

The WIPO Performances and Phonographs Treaty (WPPT) require members states to enact a Making Available Right for performers and phonograms. Articles 10 and 14 of the WPPT state the following:

Article 10

Right of Making Available of Fixed Performances

> Performers shall enjoy the exclusive right of authorizing the making available to the public of their performances fixed in phonograms, by wire or wireless means, in such a way that members of the public may access them from a place and at a time individually chosen by them.

Article 14

Right of Making Available of Phonograms

> Producers of phonograms shall enjoy the exclusive right of authorizing the making available to the public of their phonograms, by wire or wireless means, in such a way that members of the public may access them from a place and at a time individually chosen by them.

The rights of making available were introduced into the law of Canada pursuant to the *Copyright Modernization Act*.[24] In *Rogers Communications Inc. v. SOCAN*[25] the Supreme Court described attributes of the making available, emphasizing that its purpose is to confirm the applicability of communication rights to interactive, "pull" technologies. Notably, section 2.4(1.1)

---

[24] See Sections 2.4(1.1), 15(1.1), 18(1.1), and 19(1.1).
[25] *Rogers Communications Inc. v. SOCAN*, 2012 SCC 35 (S.C.C.) (decision reproduced at page 890 above).

includes the making available of work within the ambit of the right to communicate a work to the public by telecommunication. It will be interesting to see how Canadian courts interpret the making available right in light of the limits of the communication right as articulated by the Supreme Court in the *Entertainment Software Association* case. Would the making available right be infringed by a person who makes a work available to be downloaded over the Internet?[26]

Capitol Records Inc. v. Thomas (D Minn. Sept 24, 2008), 2008 WL 5423133 (D. Minn.)

. . .

II. BACKGROUND

Plaintiffs are recording companies that owned or controlled exclusive rights to copyrights in sound recordings, including 24 at issue in this lawsuit. On April 19, 2006, Plaintiffs filed a Complaint against Defendant Jammie Thomas alleging that she infringed Plaintiffs' copyrighted sound recordings pursuant to the Copyright Act, 17 U.S.C. §§ 101, 106, 501-505, by illegally downloading and distributing the recordings via the online peer-to-peer file sharing application known as Kazaa. Plaintiffs sought injunctive relief, statutory damages, costs, and attorney fees.

Trial on this matter began on October 2, 2007. The jury instruction regarding the definition of distribution under the Copyright Act was submitted as Plaintiffs' Proposed Jury Instruction No. 8. Thomas opposed inclusion of the instruction. After argument by the parties, the Court decided to give Plaintiffs' proposed jury instruction number 8, which became final Jury Instruction No. 15.

In Jury Instruction No. 15, the Court instructed: "The act of making copyrighted sound recordings available for electronic distribution on a peer-to-peer network, without license from the copyright owners, violates the copyright owners' exclusive right of distribution, regardless of whether actual distribution has been shown."

. . .

On May 15, 2008, the Court issued an Order stating that it was contemplating granting a new trial on the grounds that it had committed a manifest error of law in giving Jury Instruction No. 15. [Docket No. 139] The Court ordered the parties to brief the issue and also permitted the filing of amicus briefs. Five parties sought and gained permission to file amicus briefs: the Electronic Frontier Foundation, Public Knowledge, United States Internet Industry Association, and Computer & Communications Industry Association; the Copyright Law Professors; The Intellectual Property Institute at William Mitchell College of Law; the Motion Picture Association of America, Inc.; and The Progress & Freedom Foundation.

---

26 See paragraphs 44 to 49.

. . .

C. Statutory Framework

The Copyright Act provides that "the owner of copyright under this title has the exclusive rights to do and to authorize any of the following:... (3) to distribute copies or phonorecords of the copyrighted work to the public by sale or other transfer of ownership, or by rental, lease, or lending." 17 U.S.C. § 106(3). The Act does not define the term "distribute."

Courts have split regarding whether making copyrighted materials available for distribution constitutes distribution under § 106(3). The parties address four main arguments regarding the validity of the "making-available" interpretation: 1) whether the plain meaning of the term "distribution" requires actual dissemination of the copyrighted work; 2) whether the term "distribution" is synonymous with the term "publication," which, under the Copyright Act, does not require actual dissemination or transfer; 3) whether a defendant can be primarily liable for authorizing dissemination; and 4) whether U.S. treaty obligations and executive and legislative branch interpretations of the Copyright Act in relation to those obligations require a particular interpretation of the term "distribution."

D. Plain Meaning of the Term "Distribution"

There is a "strong presumption that the plain language of the statute expresses congressional intent [that] is rebutted only in rare and exceptional circumstances." United States v. Clintwood Elkhorn Mining Co., 128 S. Ct. 1511, 1518 (2008) (citations omitted). Each party asserts that the Court should adopt the plain meaning of the term "distribution;" however, they disagree on what that plain meaning is. Thomas and her supporters argue that the plain meaning of the statute compels the conclusion that merely making a work available to the public does not constitute a distribution. Instead, a distribution only occurs when a defendant actually transfers to the public the possession or ownership of copies or phonorecords of a work. Plaintiffs and their supporters assert that making a work available for distribution is sufficient.

1. Statutory Language

Starting with the language in § 106(3), the Court notes that Congress explains the manners in which distribution can be effected: sale, transfer of ownership, rental, lease, or lending. The provision does not state that an offer to do any of these acts constitutes distribution. Nor does § 106(3) provide that making a work available for any of these activities constitutes distribution. An initial reading of the provision at issue supports Thomas's interpretation.

2. Secondary Sources

The ordinary dictionary meaning of the word "distribute" necessarily entails a transfer of ownership or possession from one person to another. See, e.g., Merriam-Webster's Collegiate Dictionary (10th ed. 1999) (defining "distribute" as, among other things, "1: to divide among several or many: APPORTION... 2... b: to give out or deliver esp. to members of a group").

Additionally, the leading copyright treatises conclude that making a work available is insufficient to establish distribution. See, e.g., 2-8 Nimmer on Copyright, § 8.11[A] (2008); 4 William F. Patry, Patry on Copyright, § 13.11.50 (2008).

. . .

I. Implications of International Law

1. U.S. Treaty Obligations Regarding the Making-Available Right

The United States is party to the World Intellectual Property Organization ("WIPO") Copyright Treaty ("WCT") and the WIPO Performances and Phonograms Treaty ("WPPT"). S. Rep. No. 105-190, 5, 9 (1998). It is undisputed that the WCT and the WPPT recognize a making-available right that is not dependent on proof that copies were actually transferred to particular individuals. WCT art. 6(1), art. 8; WPPT art. 12(1), art. 14. Additionally, by ratifying and adopting the treaties, the legislative and executive branches indicated that U.S. law complied with the treaties by protecting that making available right.

Amici also note that the United States has entered various Free Trade Agreements ("FTA") that require the United States to provide a making-available right. See, e.g., U.S.-Australia Free Trade Agreement, art. 17.5, May 18, 2004.

. . .

b. Application of the Doctrine to Non-Self-Executing Treaties

The WIPO treaties are not self-executing and lack any binding legal authority separate from their implementation through the Copyright Act. 17 U.S.C. § 104(c), (d); Medellin v. Texas, 128 S Ct. 1346, 1365 (2008) (holding that non-self-executing treaties do not have binding domestic effect). Therefore, the fact that the WIPO treaties protect a making-available right does not create an enforceable making-available right for Plaintiffs in this Court. See, e.g., Guaylupo Moya v. Gonzales, 423 F.3d 121, 137 (2d Cir. 2005) ("This declaration [that the ICCPR is not self executing] means that the provisions of the ICCPR do not create a private right of action or separate form of relief enforceable in United States courts.") (citations omitted). Rather, the contents of the WIPO treaties are only relevant insofar as § 106(3) is ambiguous and there is a reasonable interpretation of § 106(3) that aligns with the United States' treaty obligations.

c. Application of the Doctrine in This Case

The Court acknowledges that past Presidents, Congresses, and the Register of Copyrights have indicated their belief that the Copyright Act implements WIPO's make-available right. The Court also acknowledges that, given multiple reasonable constructions of U.S. law, the Charming-Betsy doctrine directs the Court to adopt the reasonable construction that is consistent with the United States' international obligations. However, after reviewing the Copyright Act itself, legislative history, binding Supreme Court and Eighth Circuit precedent, and an extensive body of case law examining the Copyright Act, the Court concludes that Plaintiffs' interpretation of the distribution right is simply not reasonable. The Charming-Betsy doctrine is a helpful tool for statutory construction, but it is not a substantive law. It is always the case that "clear congressional action trumps customary international law and previously enacted treaties." Guaylupo-Moya, 423 F.3d at 136 (holding that it is improper to apply the Charming-Betsy canon when "the relevant provisions [of domestic law] are unambiguous"). Here, concern for U.S. compliance with the WIPO treaties and the FTAs cannot override the clear congressional intent in § 106(3).

(d) Who is Responsible for Acts of Infringement

The liability of Internet intermediaries such as internet service providers (ISPs) is complex. In determining their liability for any particular activities the function they play in relation to the internet must be considered. A key consideration is whether they can be characterised as the entity responsible for the communication of the content passing through their systems. Generally, a person who communicates material is the person who is responsible for sending it, not the person whose facilities are used to effect the transmission.[27] The relevant act is the initial act of making the work available, not the mere provision of server space, communication connections, or facilities for the carriage and routing of signals. To be liable for infringement there must also be an element of causation by the alleged infringer.[28] This element may be lacking where the basis of liability relates to an Internet intermediary's performance of a transport or access function or some other activities not related to procuring and propagating content to end users. Section 2.4(1)(b) reflects this principle.

SOCAN v. Canadian Association of Internet Providers, 2004 SCC 45

Arbour J., Bastarache J., Binnie J., Deschamps J., Fish J., Iacobucci J., LeBel J., Major J., McLachlin C.J.C.

Heard: December 3, 2003
Judgment: June 30, 2004
Docket: 29286

. . .

Binnie J.:

II. Relevant Statutory Provisions

27 Copyright Act, R.S.C. 1985, c. C-42

---

[27] *SOCAN v. Canadian Association of Internet Providers*, 2004 SCC 45.
[28] *Religious Technology Centre v. Netcom On-Line Communication*, 37 U.S.P.Q. (2d) 1545 (N.D. Cal., 1995).

2. ...

"telecommunication" means any transmission of signs, signals, writing, images or sounds or intelligence of any nature by wire, radio, visual, optical or other electromagnetic system;

> 2.4 (1) For the purposes of communication to the public by telecommunication,
>
> . . .
>
> (b) a person whose only act in respect of the communication of a work or other subject-matter to the public consists of providing the means of telecommunication necessary for another person to so communicate the work or other subject-matter does not communicate that work or other subject-matter to the public; and
>
> . . .
>
> 3. (1) For the purposes of this Act, "copyright", in relation to a work, means the sole right to produce or reproduce the work or any substantial part thereof in any material form whatever, to perform the work or any substantial part thereof in public or, if the work is unpublished, to publish the work or any substantial part thereof, and includes the sole right
>
> . . .
>
> (f) in the case of any literary, dramatic, musical or artistic work, to communicate the work to the public by telecommunication, and to authorize any such acts.

Loi sur le droit d'auteur, L.R.C. 1985, ch. C-42

. . .

III. Judicial History

A. Decision of the Copyright Board

. . .

32 The Board rejected SOCAN's argument that s. 2.4(1)(b) should be narrowly construed as an exemption to copyright liability. The Board held that where an intermediary merely acts as a "conduit for communications by other persons" (at p. 453 (emphasis added)), it can claim the benefit of s. 2.4(1)(b). If an intermediary does more than merely act as a conduit, (for example if it creates a cache for reasons other than improving system performance or modifies the content of cached material), it may lose the protection. Insofar as the Internet Service Provider furnishes "ancillary" services to a content provider or end user, it could still rely on s. 2.4(1)(b) as a defence to copyright infringement, provided any such "ancillary services" do not amount in themselves to communication or authorization to communicate the work. Creation of an automatic "hyperlink" by a Canadian Internet Service Provider will also attract copyright liability.

. . .

B. The Federal Court of Appeal

. . .

38 As to the limited protection of s. 2.4(1)(b), the majority opinion ruled that the Board erred in law when it held that an Internet Service Provider who caches material is thereby providing a means necessary for another to communicate it. The fact that the cache enhances the speed of transmission and reduces the cost to the Internet access provider does not render the cache a practical necessity for communication. To decide otherwise would further erode copyright holders' right to be compensated for the use of their works by others.

2 Sharlow J.A. (Dissenting in Part)

39 Sharlow J.A. disagreed with the majority on the interpretation of "necessary" in s. 2.4(1)(b), and found that in the context of that paragraph, something should be considered "necessary" for communication if it makes communication practicable or more practicable. Sharlow J.A. therefore agreed with the Board's conclusion that intermediaries who carry out caching activities are entitled to rely on s. 2.4(1)(b) of the Act.

. . .

a. The Section 2.4(1)(b) Protection

85 A telecommunication starts, as the Board found, at p. 450, with the content provider.

> The fact that [the communication] is achieved at the request of the recipient or through an agent neither adds to, nor detracts from the fact that the content provider effects the communication.

86 The 1988 amendments to the Copyright Act specify that participants in a telecommunication who only provide "the means of telecommunication necessary" are deemed not to be communicators. The section as presently worded provides as follows:

> 2.4 (1) For the purposes of communication to the public by telecommunication,

. . .

> (b) a person whose <u>only act</u> in respect of the communication of a work or other subject-matter to the public consists of <u>providing the means of telecommunication necessary</u> for another person to so communicate the work or other subject-matter <u>does not communicate</u> that work or other subject-matter to the public; and [Emphasis added.]

87 Parliament did not say that the intermediaries are engaged in communication of copyright content but enjoy an immunity. Instead, s. 2.4(1)(b) says that such intermediaries are deemed, for purposes of the Copyright Act, not to communicate the work to the public at all. Whether or not intermediaries are parties to the communication for legal purposes other than copyright is an issue that will have to be decided when it arises.

88 The respondent contends that s. 2.4(1)(b) is an exemption from liability and should be read narrowly; but this is incorrect. Under the Copyright Act, the

rights of the copyright owner and the limitations on those rights should be read together to give "the fair and balanced reading that befits remedial legislation" (CCH, supra, para. 48).

89 Section 2.4(1)(b) is not a loophole but an important element of the balance struck by the statutory copyright scheme. It finds its roots, perhaps, in the defence of innocent dissemination sometimes available to bookstores, libraries, news vendors, and the like who, generally speaking, have no actual knowledge of an alleged libel, are aware of no circumstances to put them on notice to suspect a libel, and committed no negligence in failing to find out about the libel; see Menear v. Miguna (1996), 30 O.R. (3d) 602 (Ont. Gen. Div.), rev'd on other grounds (1997), 33 O.R. (3d) 223 (Ont. C.A.); Newton v. Vancouver (City) (1932), 46 B.C.R. 67 (B.C. S.C.); Sun Life Assurance Co. of Canada v. W. H. Smith & Son, Ltd., [1933] All E.R. 432 (Eng. C.A.). See generally R. E. Brown, The Law of Defamation in Canada (2nd ed. (loose-leaf)), vol. 1, at §7.12(6).

90 The 1988 amendments, including the predecessor to s. 2.4(1)(b), followed on the recommendation of an all party Sub-Committee on the Revision of Copyright of the House of Commons Standing Committee on Communications and Culture. Its report, entitled A Charter of Rights for Creators (1985), identified the need for a broader definition of telecommunication, one that was not dependent on the form of technology, which would provide copyright protection for retransmissions. This led to the adoption of the broad definition of communication in s. 3(1)(f). In conjunction with this, the Committee recommended, at p. 80, that those who participate in the retransmission "solely to serve as an intermediary between the signal source and a retransmitter whose services are offered to the general public" should not be unfairly caught by the expanded definition. The ostensible objective, according to the Committee, was to avoid the unnecessary layering of copyright liability that would result from targeting the "wholesale" stage (p. 80).

91 The words of s. 2.4(1)(b) must be read in their ordinary and grammatical sense in the proper context. "Necessary" is a word whose meaning varies somewhat with the context. The word, according to Black's Law Dictionary,

> may mean something which in the accomplishment of a given object cannot be dispensed with, or it may mean something reasonably useful and proper, and of greater or lesser benefit or convenience, and its force and meaning must be determined with relation to the particular object sought. [Emphasis added.] (Black's Law Dictionary (6th ed. 1990), at p. 1029)

In context, the word "necessary" in s. 2.4(1)(b) is satisfied if the means are reasonably useful and proper to achieve the benefits of enhanced economy and efficiency.

92 Section 2.4(1)(b) shields from liability the activities associated with providing the means for another to communicate by telecommunication. "The means", as the Board found, "... are not limited to routers and other hardware. They include all software connection equipment, connectivity services, hosting and other facilities and services without which such communications would not occur" (at p. 452). I agree. So long as an Internet intermediary does not itself

engage in acts that relate to the content of the communication, i.e. whose participation is content neutral, but confines itself to providing "a conduit" for information communicated by others, then it will fall within s. 2.4(1)(b). The appellants support this result on a general theory of "Don't shoot the messenger!".

93 In rejecting SOCAN's argument on this point, the Board concluded (at p. 453):

> In the end, each transmission must be looked at individually to determine whether in that case, an intermediary merely acts as a conduit for communications by other persons, or whether it is acting as something more. Generally speaking, however, it is safe to conclude that with respect to most transmissions, only the person who posts a musical work communicates it. [Emphasis added.]

94 The Board also found, after its analysis of the activities of the various participants in an Internet transmission, that the person who "make[s] the work available for communication" is not the host server provider but the content provider (at p. 450):

> Any communication of a work occurs because a person has taken all the required steps to make the work available for communication. The fact that this is achieved at the request of the recipient or through an agent neither adds to, nor detracts from the fact that the content provider effects the communication. [Emphasis added.]

95 This conclusion, as I understand it, is based on the findings of fact by the Board of what an Internet intermediary, including a host server provider, actually does. To the extent they act as innocent disseminators, they are protected by s. 2.4(1)(b) of the Act. As the Board put it, at p. 452:

> As long as its role in respect of any given transmission is limited to providing the means necessary to allow data initiated by other persons to be transmitted over the Internet, and as long as the ancillary services it provides fall short of involving the act of communicating the work or authorizing its communication, it should be allowed to claim the exemption.

I agree with this approach. Having properly instructed itself on the law, the Board found as a fact that the "conduit" begins with the host server. No reason has been shown in this application for judicial review to set aside that conclusion.

96 A comparable approach to technology infrastructure was taken by this Court in a contract dispute involving telephone companies back in 1891:

> The owners of the telephone wires, who are utterly ignorant of the nature of the message intended to be sent, cannot be said within the meaning of the covenant to transmit a message of the purport of which they are ignorant. (Electric Despatch Co. v. Bell Telephone Co. (1891), 20 S.C.R. 83 (S.C.C.), at p. 91, per Gwynne J.)

97 Interpretation of s. 2.4(1)(b) in this way is consistent with art. 8 of the WIPO Copyright Treaty, 1996. In the accompanying Agreed Statements, the treaty authority states:

> It is understood that the mere provision of physical facilities for enabling or making a communication does not in itself amount to communication within the meaning of this Treaty or the Berne Convention.

98 Similarly, the European E-Commerce Directive provides, in clause 42 of its Preamble that Internet intermediaries are not liable where their actions are confined to

> the technical process of operating and giving access to a communication network over which information made available by third parties is transmitted or temporarily stored, for the sole purpose of making the transmission more efficient; this activity is of a mere technical, automatic and passive nature, which implies that the [Internet intermediary] has neither knowledge of nor control over the information which is transmitted or stored.

99 While lack of knowledge of the infringing nature of a work is not a defence to copyright actions generally (J. S. McKeown, Fox on Canadian Law of Copyright and Industrial Designs (4th ed. (loose-leaf)), pp. 21-4 and 21-5), nevertheless the presence of such knowledge would be a factor in the evaluation of the "conduit" status of an Internet Service Provider, as discussed below.

100 The Internet Service Provider, acting as an intermediary, does not charge a particular fee to its clients for music downloading (although clearly the availability of "free music" is a significant business incentive).

101 I conclude that the Copyright Act, as a matter of legislative policy established by Parliament, does not impose liability for infringement on intermediaries who supply software and hardware to facilitate use of the Internet. The attributes of such a "conduit", as found by the Board, include a lack of actual knowledge of the infringing contents, and the impracticality (both technical and economic) of monitoring the vast amount of material moving through the Internet, which is prodigious. We are told that a large on-line service provider like America Online delivers in the order of 11 million transmissions a day.

102 Of course an Internet Service Provider in Canada can play a number of roles. In addition to its function as an intermediary, it may as well act as a content provider, or create embedded links which automatically precipitate a telecommunication of copyrighted music from another source. In such cases, copyright liability may attach to the added functions. The protection provided by s. 2.4(1)(b) relates to a protected function, not to all of the activities of a particular Internet Service Provider.

103 On the other hand, as Evans J.A. pointed out, at para. 141, Internet Service Providers who operate a host server would not lose the protection of paragraph 2.4(1)(b) by providing their normal facilities and services, such as housing and maintaining the servers, and monitoring "hits" on particular Web pages, because these added services are merely ancillary to the provision of disk space and do not involve any act of communication.

b. The Liability of the Host Server

104 Having held quite specifically that "the content provider effects the communication" (at p. 450) and that "only the person who posts a musical work communicates it" (at p. 453 (emphasis added)), the Board added the further

limitation that to attract copyright liability "a communication must originate from a server located in Canada" (at p. 459).

105 This added limitation arose from a misreading by the Board of the earlier decision of the Federal Court of Appeal in Canadian Assn. of Broadcasters v. Society of Composers, Authors & Music Publishers of Canada (1994), 58 C.P.R. (3d) 190 (Fed. C.A.) ("CAB 1994"). The Board described what it conceived to be the effect of CAB 1994 as follows at p. 459:

> CAB 1994 makes it clear that communications occur where the transmission originates. The place of origin of the request, the location of the person posting the content and the location of the original Web site are irrelevant. As a result, the right to authorize must be obtained from the person administering the right in Canada only when the information is posted on a Canadian server, and the right to communicate must be obtained from that same person only when the transmission originates from a server located in Canada. [Emphasis added.]

I agree with Evans J.A. that CAB 1994 which dealt with the timing of a transmission, not its location, "does not support the Board's conclusion" (at para. 172). The correct view is that a content provider is not immunized from copyright liability by virtue only of the fact it employs a host server outside the country.

106 Conversely, a host server does not attract liability just because it is located in Canada. A simple "host server" test would catch communications that have no connection to Canada other than the location of a piece of physical equipment, serving a neutral role as a technological conduit. Indeed it may be "impossible for the user to predict the location of the [host] server"; see A. P. Reindl, "Choosing Law in Cyberspace: Copyright Conflicts on Global Networks" (1997-1998), 19 Mich. J. Int'l L. 799, at p. 820.

107 It is on this aspect of the test that I respectfully disagree with my colleague LeBel J., who accepts the Board's geographic limitation, i.e., that for copyright purposes there is no communication in Canada unless a communication "originates from a host server located in Canada.... [This] provides a straightforward and logical rule" (at para. 146). My colleague agrees that in the first instance the liability of a host server provider, as with any other Internet Service Provider, should be determined by whether or not the host server provider limits itself to "a conduit" function, as discussed above, and thereby qualifies for protection under s. 2.4(1)(b). However in my colleague's view even those participants in an Internet telecommunication who step outside the "conduit" role, and who would otherwise be liable for copyright infringement, will be exempt from liability for Canadian copyright unless the host server itself happens to be located here. In my view, with respect, such an added requirement would be unduly formalistic and would tilt the balance unfairly against the copyright owners. If there are to be formalistic rules they should be imposed by Parliament.

108 My colleague LeBel J., at para. 149, also relies on art. 8 of the WCT, which gives the copyright owner the exclusive right of "making available to the public... their works", but as previously noted, the Board found that in copyright terms it is the content provider, not the host server provider, that makes the work

available. Accordingly, as I see it, the issue of the relevance of art. 8 to the interpretation of the Copyright Act does not arise.

109   The Board found that a host server provider like AT&T Canada "merely gives the customer [i.e., the content provider] the right to place information on the servers" (at p. 441). Typically the host server provider will not monitor what is posted to determine if it complies with copyright laws and other legal restrictions. Given the vast amount of information posted, it is impractical in the present state of the technology to require the host server provider to do so. In any event, it is unrealistic to attribute to a provider an expertise in copyright law sufficient to "lawyer" all of the changing contents of its servers on an ongoing basis in the absence of alleged infringements being brought to their attention.

110   However, to the extent the host server provider has notice of copyrighted material posted on its server, it may, as the Board found, "respond to the complaint in accordance with the [Canadian Association of Internet Providers] Code of Conduct [which] may include requiring the customer to remove the offending material through a 'take down notice'" (at p. 441). If the host server provider does not comply with the notice, it may be held to have authorized communication of the copyright material, as hereinafter discussed.

111   Shorn of its misreading of the CAB 1994 case, the Board was correct in its general conclusion on this point, which for ease of reference I set out again (at p. 453):

> In the end, each transmission must be looked at individually to determine whether in that case, an intermediary merely acts as a conduit for communications by other persons, or whether it is acting as something more. Generally speaking, however, it is safe to conclude that with respect to most transmissions, <u>only the person who posts a musical work communicates it</u>. [Emphasis added.]

112   In my view, the Federal Court of Appeal was right to uphold this aspect of the Board's ruling.

c. The Use of Caches

113   The majority in the Federal Court of Appeal concluded that the use of caching amounts to a function falling outside s. 2.4(1)(b). Evans J.A. took the view, at para. 132, that protection is only available "when, without that person's activity, communication in that medium of telecommunication would not be practicable or, in all probability, would not have occurred". This is a high eligibility test which could inhibit development of more efficient means of telecommunication. SOCAN and others representing copyright owners would always be able to argue that whatever the advances in the future, a telecommunication could still have been practicable using the old technology, and that one way or the other the telecommunication would "in all probability" have occurred. In my view, with respect, Evans J.A. has placed the bar too high.

114   Parliament has decided that there is a public interest in encouraging intermediaries who make telecommunications possible to expand and improve their operations without the threat of copyright infringement. To impose copyright

liability on intermediaries would obviously chill that expansion and development, as the history of caching demonstrates. In the early years of the Internet, as the Board found, its usefulness for the transmission of musical works was limited by "the relatively high bandwidth required to transmit audio files" (at p. 426). This technical limitation was addressed in part by using "caches". As the Board noted, at p. 433: "Caching reduces the cost for the delivery of data by allowing the use of lower bandwidth than would otherwise be necessary." The velocity of new technical developments in the computer industry, and the rapidly declining cost to the consumer, is legendary. Professor Takach has unearthed the startling statistic that if the automobile industry was able to achieve the same performance-price improvements as has the computer chip industry, a car today would cost under five dollars and would get 250,000 miles to the gallon of gasoline: see Takach, supra, p. 21. Section 2.4(1)(b) reflects Parliament's priority that this entrepreneurial push is to continue despite any incidental effects on copyright owners.

115 In the Board's view, the means "necessary" under s. 2.4(1)(b) were means that were content neutral and were necessary to maximize the economy and cost-effectiveness of the Internet "conduit". That interpretation, it seems to me, best promotes "the public interest in the encouragement and dissemination of works of the arts and intellect" (Théberge, supra, at para. 30) without depriving copyright owners of their legitimate entitlement. The creation of a "cache" copy, after all, is a serendipitous consequence of improvements in Internet technology, is content neutral, and in light of s. 2.4(1)(b) of the Act ought not to have any legal bearing on the communication between the content provider and the end user.

116 As noted earlier, SOCAN successfully relied on the "exigencies of the Internet" to defeat the appellants' argument that they did not communicate a "musical work" but simply packets of data that may or may not arrive in the correct sequence. It is somewhat inconsistent, it seems to me, for SOCAN then to deny the appellants the benefit of a similar "exigencies" argument. "Caching" is dictated by the need to deliver faster and more economic service, and should not, when undertaken only for such technical reasons, attract copyright liability.

117 A comparable result has been reached under the U.S. Digital Millennium Copyright Act, which in part codified the result in Religious Technology Center v. Netcom On-Line Communication Services, 907 F. Supp. 1361 (U.S. N.D. Cal., 1995), where it was observed, at pp. 1369-70:

> These parties, who are liable under plaintiffs' theory, do no more than operate or implement a system that is essential if Usenet messages are to be widely distributed. There is no need to construe the Act to make all of these parties infringers. Although copyright is a strict liability statute, there should still be some element of volition or causation which is lacking where a defendant's system is merely used to create a copy by a third party.

> See also M. B. Nimmer, Nimmer on Copyright, (loose-leaf ed.), vol. 3, p. 12B-13.

118 The European E-Commerce Directive mandates member States to exempt Internet Service Providers from copyright liability for caching. (art. 13(1)).

119 In my opinion the Copyright Board's view that caching comes within the shelter of s. 2.4(1) is correct, and I would restore the Board's conclusion in that regard.

RecordTV Pte Ltd v. MediaCorp TV Singapore Pte Ltd., [2010] SGCA 43

Coram: Chan Sek Keong CJ, Andrew Phang Boon Leong JA and V K Rajah JA

Introduction

1 This is an appeal by the appellant, RecordTV Pte Ltd ("RecordTV"), against the decision of a High Court judge ("the Judge"), who dismissed its claim against the respondents, MediaCorp TV Singapore Pte Ltd, MediaCorp TV12 Singapore Pte Ltd, MediaCorp News Pte Ltd and MediaCorp Studios Pte Ltd (collectively referred to as "MediaCorp"), for making groundless threats to bring legal proceedings for copyright infringement. The Judge also held, *vis-à-vis*MediaCorp's counterclaim against RecordTV for copyright infringement, that RecordTV was liable in its use of an Internet-based digital video recorder ("iDVR") to record shows broadcast by MediaCorp.

2 This appeal raises an important policy issue as to how the courts should interpret copyright legislation in the light of technological advances which have clear legitimate and beneficial uses for the public, but which may be circumscribed or stymied by expansive claims of existing copyright owners. Bearing in mind that the law strives to encourage both creativity and innovation for the common good, in a case such as the present one, how should the courts strike a just and fair balance between the interests of all affected stakeholders, *viz*, consumers, content providers as well as technology and service vendors? If the law is not clear as to whether the use of improved technology which is beneficial to society constitutes a breach of copyright, should the courts interpret legislative provisions to favour the private rights of the copyright owner or the public's wider interests? This is the problem that we face and have to resolve in the present case. In the normal course of events, when enacting a statute, the Legislature balances the rights and interests of all affected stakeholders after considering the social costs and the economic implications. Where the statute is not clear, however, the courts have to perform this difficult task. In the present case, the Judge struck the balance in favour of MediaCorp, the copyright owner, by giving an expansive interpretation to the relevant provisions of the Copyright Act (Cap 63, 2006 Rev Ed). His detailed reasons can be found in *RecordTV Pte Ltd v Media-Corp TV Singapore Pte Ltd and others* [2010] 2 SLR 152 ("the Judgment").

The facts

Parties to the dispute

3 RecordTV was the owner of an Internet-based service that allowed its registered users (referred to hereafter as either "Registered Users" or a "Registered

User", as the context requires) to request the recording of MediaCorp's free-to-air broadcasts in Singapore. The broadcasts were recorded on RecordTV's iDVR, which functioned just like a traditional digital video recorder ("DVR"), *viz*, a Registered User could select a programme to record, play back and/or delete. The main difference between RecordTV's iDVR and a traditional DVR was that the former was a remote-storage DVR. This meant that the recording was made at RecordTV's premises, with the Registered Users operating the iDVR system remotely from home or elsewhere via a web browser.

4 MediaCorp is a state-owned group of commercial media companies in Singapore. It is the nation's largest media broadcaster and provider, and broadcasts a variety of free-to-air television programmes in Singapore. For present purposes, MediaCorp is also the copyright owner of the various free-to-air broadcasts and films particularised below (referred to hereafter as either the "MediaCorp shows" or a "MediaCorp show", as the context requires), whose copyright RecordTV is alleged to have infringed:

Broadcaster	Channel
First respondent	Channel 5, Channel 8 and Channel U
Second respondent	Central and Suria
Third respondent	Channel NewsAsia

Copyright owner(s) of film	Film
First and fourth respondents	My Sassy Neighbour III
	Live the Dream
	Dear, Dear Son-in-Law
	Say It If You Dare III
Third respondent	Amazing Asia
	Correspondent's Diary

RecordTV's iDVR service — a time-shifting service

5 RecordTV's iDVR service operated as follows. Members of the public had to first register with RecordTV (*ie*, they had to become Registered Users) before they could use its iDVR free-of-charge. Access to the iDVR was restricted to those Registered Users who were legally entitled to view and record the Media-Corp shows, all of which (as just mentioned) were broadcast on a free-to-air basis (see cl 3A of RecordTV's terms of use ("the Terms of Use"),[1] which is discussed in greater detail at [49] below). These Registered Users were, in the main, Registered Users based in Singapore who held valid television licences. In this regard, it should be noted that all members of the public in Singapore who hold valid television licences are in effect licensed by MediaCorp to view the MediaCorp shows as the Media Development Authority ("MDA") has granted a licence to MediaCorp to provide, *inter alia*, free-to-air broadcasts in Singapore, and this MDA-granted licence requires MediaCorp to provide shows to persons

in Singapore who hold valid television licences without requiring the payment of any subscription fees in return. By virtue of s 114 of the Copyright Act, persons in Singapore who hold valid television licences can also make copies of the MediaCorp shows for their own "private and domestic" use.

6 Reverting to RecordTV's iDVR service, upon a successful registration with RecordTV and a subsequent log-in using a unique username and password, a Registered User was able to access a database which listed the shows available for recording using RecordTV's iDVR, namely, the MediaCorp shows scheduled for broadcast over the coming week on Channel 5, Channel 8 or Channel News-Asia (this database was compiled by RecordTV using information from the public websites of the respective channels). The Registered User would select from this database the MediaCorp shows which he wanted to have recorded and enter the selected shows into a playlist. After making his selection, the Registered User would issue a request for RecordTV's iDVR to record the desired shows. This request would be updated in the iDVR's internal database. A control programme in RecordTV's recording computers, which were located away from the Registered User's computer, would continuously monitor the iDVR's internal database to check whether a request had been made. If the control programme detected that a Registered User had made a request for a particular MediaCorp show to be recorded, it would instruct the iDVR to record the said show.

7 RecordTV operated several television tuners (one per television channel) from which its iDVR captured and recorded those MediaCorp shows which Registered Users had requested to be recorded. Depending on the mode of storage in which the iDVR operated (which could be the "Single Instance Storage" ("SIS") mode, the "Mixed" mode or the "Multiple Copy" mode (see [9] below)), either one copy or multiple copies of the recording of a MediaCorp show would be stored in RecordTV's recording computers. After the recording had been made, the Registered User who had requested for the recording would be able to play it back on his computer.

8 It is important to note that each recording of a MediaCorp show could only be retrieved by the Registered User who had requested that that particular show be recorded. This recording would be "streamed" to the Registered User, rather than "downloaded" onto his computer (as to the difference between "streaming" and "downloading", see the Judgment at [97] — [98]; see also [62] below). The Registered User would then be able to view the recording until either RecordTV or the Registered User himself removed that recording from the latter's playlist. It was the practice of RecordTV to delete all recordings of the MediaCorp shows from its recording computers 15 days after the date of recording (which would also be the date of broadcast of the respective shows). In effect, RecordTV provided a time-shifting service to the Registered Users by means of its iDVR, such that a Registered User could view, for a period of up to 15 days after the date of broadcast, a MediaCorp show recorded at his request.

9 RecordTV's iDVR had three different phases of operation during its lifespan. When it was first launched in July 2007, it operated in the SIS mode. This

mode of file storage involved the storage in RecordTV's recording computers of one copy of the time-shifted recording of a MediaCorp show, regardless of the number of recording requests made for that show. By July 2008, RecordTV's iDVR was operating in the "Mixed" mode for Channels 5 and 8, and in the "Multiple Copy" mode for Channel NewsAsia. The "Mixed" mode was a hybrid mode of storage whereby multiple copies of the recording of a MediaCorp show were created based on the number of Registered Users who had requested the recording of that show. If, however, system resources were insufficient, then only one copy of the recording would be made. As for the "Multiple Copy" mode, it involved the making and storage of multiple copies of the recording of the same MediaCorp show, such that that show could be played back from different files. Finally, sometime around August to September 2008, RecordTV's iDVR was reconfigured to operate solely in the "Multiple Copy" mode for all channels. The one similarity among all three phases was that RecordTV would not make a recording of a MediaCorp show if it did not receive a recording request for that show. It should be noted that the third phase of operation of RecordTV's iDVR (*ie*, the phase during which only the "Multiple Copy" mode of storage was used) was implemented only after RecordTV had commenced its action against MediaCorp.

Litigation between the parties

10 The dispute between RecordTV and MediaCorp crystallised when the latter issued cease-and-desist letters to the former objecting to the former's introduction in July 2007 of its time-shifting service by means of its iDVR. MediaCorp alleged that the use of the iDVR infringed its copyright in the MediaCorp shows. In response, RecordTV commenced an action against MediaCorp for, *inter alia*, making groundless threats to bring legal proceedings for copyright infringement (see s 200(1) of the Copyright Act). MediaCorp in turn filed a counterclaim seeking, *inter alia*, injunctive relief for copyright infringement. At the conclusion of a long trial, the Judge reserved judgment. He eventually dismissed RecordTV's claim and allowed MediaCorp's counterclaim against RecordTV for copyright infringement. Dissatisfied with the Judge's decision, RecordTV appealed to this court.

Our approach in this appeal

11 In the present appeal, we are only concerned with MediaCorp's copyright in the MediaCorp shows in terms of the right to: (a) make copies of (*ie*, reproduce); (b) communicate to the public; and/or (c) authorise the copying and/or the communication to the public of those shows. The Judge found that RecordTV, in providing its iDVR service to Registered Users who held valid television licences such that they could access the MediaCorp shows on a time-shifted basis, had not infringed MediaCorp's right to reproduce those shows. However, he found that RecordTV had communicated the MediaCorp shows to the public and had also authorised them to copy the same, and was therefore liable for copyright infringement. He further held that RecordTV could not rely on any of the safe harbour or fair dealing provisions under, respectively, Pt IXA and s 109 of the

Copyright Act to escape liability for copyright infringement. In view of his ruling that MediaCorp's counterclaim against RecordTV for copyright infringement was made out, the Judge dismissed RecordTV's claim against MediaCorp for making groundless threats to bring infringement proceedings. In this appeal, we shall adopt the same approach as the Judge and likewise assess the merits of RecordTV's claim by reference to our ruling on MediaCorp's counterclaim.

MediaCorp's counterclaim against RecordTV for copyright infringement

The relevant provisions of the Copyright Act

12 For the purposes of MediaCorp's counterclaim, the relevant provisions in the Copyright Act which set out the nature of MediaCorp's copyright in the MediaCorp shows and the acts that infringe such copyright are ss 83, 84 and 103. These provisions read as follows:

Nature of copyright in cinematograph films

83. For the purposes of this Act, unless the contrary intention appears, copyright, in relation to a cinematograph film, is the exclusive right to do all or any of the following acts:

(*a*) to make a copy of the film;

. . .

(*c*) to communicate the film to the public.

Nature of copyright in television broadcasts and sound broadcasts

84. — (1) For the purposes of this Act, unless the contrary intention appears, copyright, in relation to a television broadcast or sound broadcast, is the exclusive right —

(*a*) in the case of a television broadcast insofar as it consists of visual images — to make a cinematograph film of the broadcast, or a copy of such a film;

. . .

(*d*) in the case of a television broadcast or a sound broadcast — to re-broadcast it or to otherwise communicate it to the public.

. . .

Infringement by doing acts comprised in copyright

103. — (1) Subject to the provisions of this Act, a copyright subsisting by virtue of this Part [ie, Pt IV of the Copyright Act] is infringed by a person who, not being the owner of the copyright, and without the licence of the owner of the copyright, does in Singapore, or authorises the doing in Singapore of, any act comprised in the copyright.

. . .

[emphasis added]

The issues to be decided in MediaCorp's counterclaim

13 In the light of the provisions of the Copyright Act reproduced above, three main issues arise for consideration before us *vis-à-vis* MediaCorp's counter-claim, namely:

(a) first, whether RecordTV copied the MediaCorp shows ("the First Issue");

(b) second, whether RecordTV communicated the MediaCorp shows to the public ("the Second Issue"); and

(c) third, whether RecordTV authorised the Registered Users to do in Singapore any act comprised in MediaCorp's copyright in the MediaCorp shows ("the Third Issue").

14 To summarise our rulings on the above issues in advance of our analysis, we find, *vis-à-vis* the First Issue, that RecordTV did not copy the MediaCorp shows; instead, it was the Registered Users requesting the recording of those shows using RecordTV's iDVR who did so. In respect of the Second Issue, we find that RecordTV did not communicate the MediaCorp shows to the public because the Registered Users who requested the recording of a particular MediaCorp show did not constitute "the public" for the purposes of ss 83 and 84 of the Copyright Act, and, in any event, the communication to them was not made by RecordTV. Finally, we find on the Third Issue that RecordTV did not authorise the Registered Users to do in Singapore any act comprised in MediaCorp's copyright in the MediaCorp shows. We shall elaborate on our reasons for making each of these findings after analysing the Judge's decision on the aforesaid issues.

The First Issue: Did RecordTV copy the MediaCorp shows?

15 In respect of the First Issue (*viz*, whether RecordTV copied the MediaCorp shows), the Judge found that RecordTV did not copy the MediaCorp shows within the meaning of the phrase "make a copy" in the Copyright Act, and that it was the Registered Users instead who copied the shows by their own actions in requesting the recording of those shows using RecordTV's iDVR. We agree with and affirm the Judge's finding that it was the Registered Users, and not RecordTV, who copied the MediaCorp shows.

16 In reaching the above-mentioned conclusion, the Judge relied on the inter-pretational (and policy) approach of the US Court of Appeals for the Second Circuit in *The Cartoon Network LP, LLLP v CSC Holdings, Inc* <u>536 F 3d 121</u> (2nd Cir, 2008) ("*Cartoon Network*"). At [22] of the Judgment, he said:

> In Cartoon Network, a three-judge panel of the US Court of Appeals for the Second Circuit held that [the defendant]'s proposed remote-storage digital video recording service ("RS-DVR"; this being the category under which [RecordTV]'s iDVR is classified, as opposed to set-top storage ("STS-DVR")) did not directly infringe the reproduction rights of those holding copyrights in the recorded materials. In overturning the decision of the district judge below, the [US] Court of Appeals for the Second Circuit held that (at 131 — 132):
>
>> ... There are only two instances of volitional conduct in this case: [the defendant]'s conduct in designing, housing, and maintaining a system that exists only to produce a copy, and a customer's conduct in ordering that system

to produce a copy of a specific program. In the case of a VCR [video cassette recorder], it seems clear — and we know of no case holding otherwise — that the operator of the VCR, the person who actually presses the button to make the recording, supplies the necessary element of volition, not the person who manufactures, maintains, or, if distinct from the operator, owns the machine. *We do not believe that an RS-DVR customer is sufficiently distinguishable from a VCR user to impose liability as a direct infringer on a different party for copies that are made automatically upon that customer's command.*

. . .

... In determining who actually 'makes' a copy, a significant difference exists between making a request to a human employee, who then volitionally operates the copying system to make the copy, and issuing a command directly to a system, which automatically obeys commands and engages in no volitional conduct. ... Here, by selling access to a system that automatically produces copies on command, [the defendant] more closely resembles a store proprietor who charges customers to use a photocopier on his premises, and it seems incorrect to say, without more, that such a proprietor 'makes' any copies when his machines are actually operated by his customers.

... we do not think it sufficiently proximate to the copying to displace the customer as the person who 'makes' the copies when determining liability under the Copyright Act [17 USC (US)]. [The defendant], we note, also has subscribers who use home VCRs or DVRs (like TiVo), and has significant control over the content recorded by these customers. But this control is limited to the channels of programming available to a customer and not to the programs themselves.*[The defendant] has no control over what programs are made available on individual channels or when those programs will air, if at all.* In this respect, [the defendant] possesses far less control over recordable content than it does in the VOD [video-on-demand] context, where it actively selects and makes available beforehand the individual programs available for viewing. For these reasons, we are not inclined to say that [the defendant], rather than the user, 'does' the copying produced by the RS-DVR system. As a result, *we find that the district court erred in concluding that [the defendant], rather than its RS-DVR customers, makes the copies carried out by the RS-DVR system.*

[emphasis in original]

17 In a nutshell, the court's finding in *Cartoon Network* that it was the customers of the defendant ("Cablevision"), and not Cablevision itself, who made the copies was premised on the concept of "volitional acts". There were two volitional acts in *Cartoon Network*. The first was that of Cablevision in designing, housing and maintaining a remote-storage digital video recorder ("RS-DVR") system that existed only to produce copies of specific programmes. The second volitional act was that of Cablevision's customers, who operated the RS-DVR system. The US Court of Appeals for the Second Circuit held that it was the customers who made the copies because the process in dispute was no different from that involved when a person used a video cassette recorder ("VCR") to copy a copyright-protected work.

18 At [23] of the Judgment, the Judge summarised the three factors considered by the court in *Cartoon Network* in concluding that the bulk of the relevant volitional conduct, "an important element of direct liability" (see *Cartoon Network* at 131), lay with the end-users (*ie*, Cablevision's customers) in that case:

(a) by analogy [with] the end-user of the ancient VCR, the end-user of an RS-DVR is the main volitional agent in requesting for certain programmes to be recorded;

(b) in relation to the end-user of an RS-DVR, who is able to choose specific programmes to record, Cablevision is only able to choose the channels of programming to be made available to a customer; and

(c) in determining who actually "makes" a copy, a significant difference exists between making a request to a human employee, who then volitionally operates the copying system to make the copy, and issuing a command directly to a system, which automatically obeys commands and engages in no volitional conduct.

[emphasis in original]

19 In relation to factor (c) of the above quotation, the Judge departed from the view adopted by the court in *Cartoon Network*. He held that *no* difference existed between "making a request to a human employee, who then volitionally operate[d] the copying system to make the copy, and issuing a command directly to a system, which automatically obey[ed] commands and engage[d] in no volitional conduct" (see sub-para (c) of [23] of the Judgment). He also ruled in RecordTV's favour on factor (b) of the above quotation, and, *vis-à-vis* factor (a) thereof, he was particularly persuaded by the analogy with "the end-user of the ancient VCR" (see sub-para (a) of [23] of the Judgment). At [33] of the Judgment, he said:

... [T]he end product we are concerned with here is a time-shifted recording. If the end-user is the maker of this time-shifted recording for the purposes of the VCR, it must remain that the end-user is the maker of the recording in the context of the DVR, remote or local. [emphasis in original]

20 Before this court, MediaCorp argued that the analogy which the Judge drew with "the ancient VCR" (see sub-para (a) of [23] of the Judgment) was flawed. We reject this argument and affirm, on two grounds, the Judge's conclusion that it was the Registered Users requesting the recording of a particular MediaCorp show who copied that MediaCorp show. First, we agree with the Judge that the iDVR is simply a digital version of the traditional DVR/VCR. Its functionality is essentially the same as that of the latter. Both are similar in the following ways:

(a) it is the user who chooses which show to record;

(b) the request to record a show is made to a recording device (the traditional DVR/VCR) or recording system (the iDVR); and

(c) it is the recording device/system which records the selected show.

21 No doubt, certain operational differences can be discerned between the iDVR and the traditional DVR/VCR, *eg*: (a) the traditional DVR/VCR is

located at the user's home, whereas the iDVR is located at the iDVR provider's premises; and (b) the vendor of the traditional DVR/VCR is unable to control the use of the DVR/VCR as a recording machine once it has been sold to the user, whereas the iDVR provider may stop the recording service as and when it wishes. However, in our view, these differences are immaterial as they are no more than variations of the same basic model of time-shifting. The fundamental objective of time-shifting is to allow a show to be recorded on a storage medium so that it may be viewed or listened to at the consumer's convenience after it is broadcast. This is a perfectly legitimate activity so long as it does not constitute copying copyright-protected material or communicating such material to the public contrary to copyright laws. We should add that in the present case, as mentioned at [5] above, the Registered Users had to be legally entitled to view and record the MediaCorp shows before they could avail themselves of RecordTV's iDVR service to record those shows; all that RecordTV did was merely to provide them with the advantages and convenience of a time-shifting service, which MediaCorp itself did not provide.

22 Our second reason for affirming the Judge's decision on the First Issue (namely, that RecordTV did not copy the MediaCorp shows) is that RecordTV's iDVR not only serves the same purpose as the traditional DVR/VCR (*viz*, to allow time-shifting), but is also a significant technological improvement over the latter with tangible benefits to users, in that RecordTV's iDVR is more convenient and user-friendly than the traditional DVR/VCR. Registered Users who may legitimately view and record the MediaCorp shows no longer need to know the start and end times of each MediaCorp show which they wish to record and the channel on which that show will be aired because RecordTV's iDVR has already been programmed with the relevant information. These Registered Users need only select from the iDVR's electronic programme guide the MediaCorp show which they wish to have recorded. Furthermore, they can even instruct RecordTV's iDVR to record all episodes of a particular MediaCorp show, regardless of when and/or on which channel the various episodes are to be broadcast.

The Second Issue: Did RecordTV communicate the MediaCorp shows to the public?

23 We turn now to the Second Issue, *viz*, whether RecordTV communicated the MediaCorp shows to the public. As mentioned at [11] above, the Judge ruled in MediaCorp's favour on this issue. With respect, we do not agree with his ruling. In our view, RecordTV did not communicate the MediaCorp shows to the public within the meaning of ss 83(*c*) and 84(1)(*d*) of the Copyright Act for two reasons: first, we are of the view that there have not been any communications to "the public"; and, second, we do not think that RecordTV was the party which made the communications in question in the present case.

Communications to "the public"

24 With regard to our first reason for departing from the Judge's decision on the Second Issue, the expression "the public" is not defined in the Copyright Act,

but, ordinarily, that word connotes all members of the community or a section of the public. A substantial number of persons can sometimes be "the public" in this sense. As the learned authors of Kevin Garnett, Gillian Davies & Gwilym Harbottle, *Copinger and Skone James on Copyright* (Sweet & Maxwell, 15th Ed, 2005) wrote at para 7-118:

> Although the Act [ie, the Copyright, Designs and Patents Act 1988 (c 48) (UK)] refers to the work being made available to "the public", in the usual way this does not mean that the restricted act is only committed when the public at large can obtain access to it. Where the work is only available to subscribers to an internet service, the subscribers will qualify as "the public" for this purpose. [emphasis added]

25   In the present case, the Registered Users who held valid television licences had an existing relationship with MediaCorp as they were licensed by the latter to watch the MediaCorp shows (see [5] above). To the extent that there was a contractual relationship between MediaCorp and those Registered Users arising from the former licensing the latter to view the MediaCorp shows, those Registered Users are arguably not members of "the public" for the purposes of ss 83(*c*) and 84(1)(*d*) of the Copyright Act.

26   In any case, in view of the *modus operandi* of RecordTV's iDVR service, we find that any communications made by RecordTV to Registered Users who had requested the recording of a particular MediaCorp show were made privately and individually. We see no reason why the aggregate of the private and individual communications made to each of the aforesaid Registered Users should transform the nature of such communications into "public" communications. Although any member of the public could register with RecordTV to become a Registered User, he had no immediate access to all (or any) of the MediaCorp shows already recorded by RecordTV. This was because RecordTV's iDVR service was not a video-on-demand service whereby RecordTV shared a library of recorded works with Registered Users. Rather, a Registered User was only allowed to access and view time-shifted recordings of the specific MediaCorp shows which he had requested to be recorded. Thus, each Registered User had to make a request for a particular MediaCorp show to be recorded for him, and only he could access the show recorded at his request. According to the court-appointed expert, Assoc Prof Roger Zimmermann:[2]

> Information about TV shows that are recorded on behalf of a [Registered] [U]ser's request is stored in [a] database table. Each record in the [database] table is associated with one [Registered] [U]ser. When a TV show is recorded into a file, the filename is also specific to the [Registered] [U]ser in that it includes the user identification in its name. When a [Registered] [U]ser logs into the RecordTV web site, the system will only present the recorded shows of this user under [his] ... [p]laylist and therefore access is implicitly [granted] only to those shows. [emphasis added]

27   Indeed, the Judge himself noted at [8] of the Judgment that a particular time-shifted recording of a MediaCorp show was made available for viewing to "the member of the public *who requested the recording* on the 'My Playlist' portion of [RecordTV's] [w]ebsite" [emphasis added]. Hence, the *only* recipient of that time-shifted recording would be the Registered User who had requested the making of

that recording and who later operated RecordTV's iDVR to play back that recording to himself, and no other Registered User. In other words, each transmission of a MediaCorp show recorded using RecordTV's iDVR was made to a single Registered User pursuant to his request. A Registered User did not have access to all (or any) of the MediaCorp shows which had already been recorded unless those shows were the subject of his prior *personal* recording requests.

28 Accordingly, the relevant question that ought to have been posed was not whether RecordTV's iDVR service was available to "the public" as comprising any group of Registered Users (even assuming (*cf* our view at [25] above) that Registered Users who are legally entitled to watch and record the MediaCorp shows can be regarded as "the public" for this purpose), which was the question that the Judge appeared to have asked himself when he said at [77] of the Judgment that "[i]t should not matter that [RecordTV's] service [was] available only to [R]egistered … [U]sers, when *any member of the public* with an Internet connection [could] register for free" [emphasis in original]. Rather, the question should have been whether a particular MediaCorp show had been transmitted to the public. Since Registered Users could only view those MediaCorp shows which they had requested to be recorded, those shows were communicated to the relevant Registered Users privately and individually. The aggregate of private communications to each Registered User is not, in this instance, a communication to the public.

29 MediaCorp argued that RecordTV's iDVR service allowed even a person who was not a Registered User (in essence, a hacker) to view recorded Media-Corp shows so long as he knew the URLs (universal resource locators) of the respective recorded shows. In this regard, MediaCorp's expert testified that no user names were appended to the filenames of the files containing recorded MediaCorp shows. Rather, those filenames were based on a numbering system which was not difficult to guess. A person who guessed the filenames correctly would be able to bypass the restrictions which RecordTV had put in place and thereby access recordings made for other Registered Users.

30 We cannot accept this argument. In our view, the average person would not, in all likelihood, know how RecordTV's naming convention for the files containing recorded MediaCorp shows worked. Such knowledge would be, to use the Judge's words at [98] of the Judgment, "beyond the ken of all but the most determined and technically gifted". The susceptibility of RecordTV's iDVR system to hackers would only mean that where a hacker managed to successfully guess or work out the filename of a file containing a recorded MediaCorp show, it would be the hacker himself who made the show accessible to himself, rather than RecordTV making the same accessible to him. We do not think RecordTV should be answerable for every abuse of its iDVR service as it has an essentially legitimate purpose. The nature of RecordTV's iDVR service is such that it can be, and is likely to have been, used significantly for legitimate, non-infringing purposes. This is plainly not a case where the technology employed by RecordTV is *bound to infringe* MediaCorp's copyright in the MediaCorp

shows. Hackers can hardly qualify as "the public" for the purposes of ss 83(*c*) and 84(1)(*d*) of the Copyright Act.

The communicator

31 We now turn to our second reason for disagreeing with the Judge's finding that RecordTV had communicated the MediaCorp shows to the public — namely, we do not think RecordTV was the communicator (*ie*, the party making the communications) in the present case. We are of the view that the Judge's finding was based on an overly technical reading of s 16(6) of the Copyright Act, which provides as follows:

> For the purposes of this Act, a communication other than a broadcast is taken to have been made by the person responsible for determining the content of the communication at the time the communication is made. [emphasis added]

32 In order to identify the communicator, s 16(6) of the Copyright Act requires a determination of: (a) the time of the communication ("limb (a) of s 16(6)"); (b) the content of the communication at the time of communication ("limb (b) of s 16(6)"); and (c) the identity of the person responsible for determining that content ("limb (c) of s 16(6)").

33 Considering limb (a) of s 16(6) (*viz*, the time of the communication) first, the earliest time at which the recorded MediaCorp shows could be regarded as being communicated would be the time when RecordTV's iDVR placed recordings of those shows on RecordTV's Internet server and made them accessible to those Registered Users who had requested the recording of those shows. This follows from the definition of "communicate" in s 7(1) of the Copyright Act, which includes the "making available of" a work:

> "communicate" means to transmit by electronic means ... a work or other subject-matter, ... and includes —
>
> . . .
>
> (c) the *making available* of a work or other subject-matter (on a network or otherwise) in such a way that the work or subject-matter *may be accessed* by any person from a place and at a time chosen by him ...
>
> [emphasis added]

The definition of "communicate" in s 7(1) of the Copyright Act is in substance the same as that in Art 8 of the World Intellectual Property Organization Copyright Treaty adopted in Geneva on 20 December 1996 ("the WIPO Copyright Treaty"). Indeed, the latter definition of "communicate" (*ie*, the definition in Art 8 of the WIPO Copyright Treaty) was implemented in our legislation via s 7(1) of the Copyright Act. Article 8 of the WIPO Copyright Treaty provides for a right of communication to the public which also includes, within that general right, the right of "making available" to the public copyright-protected works. That Article states, *inter alia*:

> ... [A]uthors of literary and artistic works shall enjoy the exclusive right of authorizing any communication to the public of their works, by wire or wireless means,

including the making available to the public of their works in such a way that members of the public may access these works from a place and at a time individually chosen by them. [emphasis added]

34 Ordinarily, the word "communicate" entails the communicator actively initiating an instance of communication. However, by designating, as a form of communication, the "making available" of a work in such a way that any person may access the work from a place and time so chosen by him, s 7(1) of the Copyright Act and Art 8 of the WIPO Copyright Treaty also regard transmissions initiated by recipients (as opposed to communicators) as a form of communication (see Susanna H S Leong & Yuanyuan Chen, "The Right of Communication in Singapore" (2010) 22 SAcLJ 602 at pp 606 — 607). Under this latter mode of communication, a work is said to be "made available" as soon as access to the work in question is provided. *Hence, on the basis of s 7(1) of the Copyright Act and Art 8 of the WIPO Copyright Treaty, it would seem that the recorded Media-Corp shows were communicated once they were made available for viewing by the Registered Users who had requested the recording of those shows.*

35 Turning next to limb (b) of s 16(6) (*viz*, "the content of the communication at the time the communication is made"), we find that the relevant content in the present case consisted of *specific MediaCorp shows* that had been recorded pursuant to the specific requests of a particular Registered User (these shows would subsequently be placed on RecordTV's Internet server and would appear on the playlist of that Registered User's account). The relevant "content of the communication" was not RecordTV's entire library or catalogue of recorded MediaCorp shows, as a Registered User was allowed to watch only those shows which he had requested to be recorded, and no other. If a Registered User had not requested that a particular MediaCorp show be recorded, that show would not be communicated to him. Indeed, if no request was made by any Registered User for a particular MediaCorp show to be recorded, no copy of that show would ever be made and, consequently, there would be no communication of that show to any Registered User.

36 In the light of our analysis as to how limb (a) of s 16(6) and limb (b) of s 16(6) apply in the present case, our ruling on how limb (c) of s 16(6) applies follows naturally, namely: since the only MediaCorp shows that were "communicated" were those shows that appeared on each Registered User's playlist, and since the exact make-up of each playlist depended on the specific shows which the Registered User in question had requested to be recorded, "the person responsible for determining the content of the communication at the time the communication [was] made" would be that Registered User himself. RecordTV would not have been the communicator of the MediaCorp shows for the purposes of s 16(6) of the Copyright Act. Accordingly, we do not accept Media-Corp's argument on this point and disagree with the Judge, who held that it was RecordTV which determined the content of the communication at the time of the communication because: (a) RecordTV pre-selected the channels whose programmes Registered Users could request to be recorded; and (b) RecordTV's iDVR system determined the start and stop times of each recording, such that

the Registered User did no more than merely put in a request for a particular MediaCorp show to be recorded.

37 In holding RecordTV to be the communicator of the MediaCorp shows for the purposes of s 16(6) of the Copyright Act, the Judge was influenced by the consideration that if he held that it was the Registered User who had control over the content of the communication because he had control over which MediaCorp shows to record, "the maker of unauthorised copies [would] *always* be the one to communicate the same to the public" [emphasis in original] (see the Judgment at [81]). The Judge's full analysis of this point is set out in the Judgment as follows:

> 80 Turning now to the issue of who made the communication to the public, ... [RecordTV] claims that it is not the party that "communicates" the work to the public within the meaning of s 16(6) of the Copyright Act. Section 16(6) states:
>
>> For the purposes of this Act, a communication other than a broadcast is taken to have been made by the person responsible for determining the content of the communication at the time the communication is made.
>
> Accordingly, since it is the end-user [ie, the Registered User who makes a recording request] who has control over what programmes to record, it is also the end-user who has control over the "content of the communication at the time the communication is made".
>
> 81 According to this line of reasoning, the maker of unauthorised copies will always be the one to communicate the same to the public (depending of course on permitting facts). I am not convinced by this argument. To my mind, there is an important distinction between the "making" and [the] "transmission" of copyrighted material. This distinction was noted by the US Solicitor General in her Amicus Curiae Brief for ... Cartoon Network ... at p 20:
>
>> c. The analogy between [Cablevision's] RS-DVR service and a set-top DVR is weakest with respect to the public-performance issue because the operation of the former, unlike the latter, would clearly involve a 'transmission.' ... (To 'transmit' a performance or display is to communicate it by any device or process whereby images or sounds are received beyond the place from which they are sent.) ... *Thus, even if the subscriber would 'make' the copies used in the RS-DVR system, [Cablevision] might still violate the Copyright Act [17 USC (US)] if [it] 'transmitted' those copies 'to the public'* ...
>
> 82 The key question is this: where exactly do the end-user's volition and control cease to operate? If we can say that the end-user has made the infringing copy and transmitted the infringing copy, there is little to prevent us from concluding that the end-user is, in fact, an RS-DVR in disguise. For where, in that analysis, would there be room for the implication of any properly culpable technology? If the RecordTV system neither copies nor transmits any material, how can it be said to have infringed any copyright?
>
> 83 The line, therefore, has to be drawn somewhere, and I think it sensible that it be drawn once the end-user has properly exercised his volition in making a choice. In other words, while I accept and have accepted that the end-user is the one who

has control over what programmes to record, the subsequent transmission of that content would be effected by a process governed entirely by [RecordTV].

84 Accordingly, I would read the words of s 16(6) technically. The section is concerned, after all, with a technical process. At the time the relevant communication is made, the end-user has already communicated [his] preference to [RecordTV] (this necessarily has to take place before any recording or transmission). [RecordTV] therefore is the one responsible for determining the content of the communication upon playback. One can easily envisage a situation whereby, after the end-user makes his selection, playback is somehow garbled due to a technical fault. It would be a stretch of the imagination to say that the end-user was the one who "determined" the content of the unintelligent static that was recorded.

85 In the light of the above, I find [RecordTV] liable for infringing [MediaCorp's] copyright in communicating the MediaCorp [shows] to the public.

[emphasis in original in italics; emphasis added in bold italics]

38 We disagree with the Judge's analysis (as reproduced above) for three reasons. First, we are not here dealing with the making of unauthorised copies of MediaCorp shows and the communication of the same to the public. In the present case, all the copies of recorded MediaCorp shows consisted of free-to-air broadcasts recorded for, transmitted to and viewed by Registered Users who represented that they had the legal right to view and record the MediaCorp shows (see [5] above). The only thing that RecordTV did was to provide those Registered Users with a facility to view the MediaCorp shows, which they were free to view at the original broadcast time, at a later time. In using RecordTV's iDVR to time-shift in this manner, the Registered Users were doing no more than what they could legally do when they used a traditional DVR/VCR to record the MediaCorp shows (which were free-to-air broadcasts received via television antennae) for their own subsequent viewing.

39 Second, the argument made by the US Solicitor-General in her *amicus curiae* brief for *Cartoon Network* (referred to by the Judge at [81] of the Judgment) is not relevant in the present context, not because there is no distinction between the "making" and the "transmitting" of a copyright-protected work (there is a distinction, of course), but because the issue here is whether RecordTV communicated the MediaCorp shows (by electronic means) *to the public* (see[24] — [30] above). The Judge was unnecessarily vexed by the consideration that if RecordTV's iDVR system was not somehow held culpable for communicating the MediaCorp shows, there would be "[no] room for the implication of any properly culpable technology [under the Copyright Act]" (see the Judgment at [82]). With respect, this consideration puts the cart before the horse as it assumes that RecordTV's iDVR system is illegal to begin with.

40 Third, it appears to us that the Judge's view that the volition of a Registered User ended once he made a request to RecordTV's iDVR system to make a recording (see the Judgment at [82] — [83]) was unjustifiably influenced by situations involving recording or transmission malfunctions. The Judge cited the example where a playback of a recording was garbled due to a technical fault to illustrate his point that the Registered User could not be said to have determined "the content of the unintelligent static that was recorded" (see the Judgment at

[84]). This appears to us to be an extreme analogy and is not particularly helpful in analysing the present issue.

41   In our view, where RecordTV's iDVR system operated normally as intended by RecordTV and the Registered Users, the Registered User's predetermined choices of the MediaCorp shows to be recorded governed the content of the communication from the time that content was made available all the way till the moment that content was received by that same Registered User during play-back. In situations involving recording or transmission malfunction, we are of the opinion that the Registered User did intend the same predetermined content to be communicated to him, but his intention was frustrated by the malfunction. In such situations, the Registered User could not be said to have "'determined' the content of the unintelligent static that was recorded" (see the Judgment at [84]) because he could not have intended such static to be recorded. However, it also cannot be said that RecordTV intended to transmit a garbled signal. After all, the aim of RecordTV's iDVR system was to allow the Registered Users to watch at their convenience those MediaCorp shows which they had requested to be recorded. Naturally, RecordTV's intention in the ordinary course of events would be to deliver to the Registered Users what they had requested for. The fact that RecordTV's iDVR system malfunctioned was not relevant to what a Registered User had determined to be the content of his request. The same rea-soning can be applied to MediaCorp's example of how a Registered User who wanted to watch "Amazing Asia" *only* might have to watch the end of the show preceding "Amazing Asia" if RecordTV's iDVR system did not behave as it was intended to — MediaCorp contended that in such a situation, the recording of the show preceding "Amazing Asia" would have been made by RecordTV's iDVR, and not by the Registered User.[3] In our view, the better analysis of this scenario is that it is a case of RecordTV's iDVR failing to deliver to the Regis-tered User what he had requested for. Accordingly, "the person responsible for determining the content of the communication at the time the communication [was] made" (*per s* 16(6) of the Copyright Act) in the present case was the Reg-istered User who requested that a particular MediaCorp show be recorded, and not RecordTV.

The Third Issue: Did RecordTV authorise the doing in Singapore of any act comprised in MediaCorp's copyright?

42   Thus far, we have ruled that:

(a) *vis-à-vis* the First Issue, RecordTV did not copy the MediaCorp shows; and

(b) *vis-à-vis* the Second Issue, RecordTV did not communicate the MediaCorp shows to the public as:

(i) the persons to whom the MediaCorp shows were communicated, being limited to those Registered Users who had requested the recording of the shows in question, did not constitute "the public"; and

(ii) RecordTV was not "the person responsible for determining the content of the communication at the time the communication [was] made" within the meaning of s 16(6) of the Copyright Act.

We now turn to the Third Issue, namely, whether RecordTV authorised "the doing in Singapore of ... any act comprised in the copyright [in the MediaCorp shows]" (see s 103(1) of the Copyright Act). In the present case, the relevant "act comprised in the copyright" would be the copying and/or the communication to the public of the MediaCorp shows.

The concept of authorisation liability

43 The concept of authorisation liability in s 103(1) extends the rights of copyright owners to cover acts of persons which are related, in some way, to an infringement of copyright. In *Ong Seow Pheng and others v Lotus Development Corp and another* [1997] 2 SLR(R) 113 ("*Ong Seow Pheng*"), this court held (at [27]) that the word "authorise" meant to grant or purport to grant, whether expressly or impliedly, to a third person the right to do the act complained of, regardless of whether the intention was that the grantee should do the act on his own account or only on account of the grantor. The court also said (which we reaffirm) that authorisation could only emanate from someone having or purporting to have authority to grant the right to do the act complained of; an act was not authorised by a person who merely enabled, possibly assisted or even encouraged another to do that act, but who did not actually have or who did not purport to have any authority which he could grant to justify the doing of that act (see *Ong Seow Pheng* at [28]).

44 Furthermore, in order for the authorisation of the doing of an act to be a tort, the act authorised must be an act restricted by the copyright. As Hoffmann LJ said at 660 of *ABKCO Music & Records Inc v Music Collection International Limited and Another* [1995] RPC 657 ("*ABKCO*"):

> It is true ... that the doing of an act restricted by the copyright and its authorisation are separate torts: see Ash v. Hutchinson and Co. (Publishers) Ltd. [1936] Ch. 489. But there is an overlap in the ingredients of the two torts in that "authorising" is a tort only if the act authorised is an act restricted by the copyright. [emphasis added]

In *ABKCO*, Hoffmann LJ was referring to s 16(2) of the Copyright, Designs and Patents Act 1988 (c 48) (UK) ("the CDPA"), which states that "[c]opyright in a work is infringed by a person who without the licence of the copyright owner does, or authorises another to do, *any of the acts restricted by the copyright*" [emphasis added]. Section 16(2) of the CDPA is *in pari materia* with s 103(1) of the Copyright Act, which likewise makes reference to the infringement of copyright via the doing in Singapore, or the authorisation of the doing in Singapore, of "*any act comprised in the copyright*" [emphasis added].

Our reasons for ruling in favour of RecordTV on the Third Issue

45 In the present case, as mentioned earlier (see, *inter alia*, [5] above), only those Registered Users who were authorised by MediaCorp to view the MediaCorp shows and record them for their own private viewing (*ie*, only those Registered Users based in Singapore who held valid television licences) were entitled

to use RecordTV's iDVR to record the MediaCorp shows. All that RecordTV did was to provide those Registered Users with a facility to time-shift their viewing of the MediaCorp shows. RecordTV could not have granted any right to the Registered Users to copy the MediaCorp shows and/or communicate them to the public as it did not itself have the right to copy and/or communicate to the public those shows.

46 In our view, the burden is on the copyright owner (*ie*, MediaCorp in the present instance) to prove that RecordTV had authorised the Registered Users to infringe MediaCorp's copyright in the MediaCorp shows. In this regard, the Judge was wrong in deciding that RecordTV had the burden of adducing evidence to show that "the [Registered] [U]sers, without exception, were all entitled to rely upon s 114 [*ie*, the defence of private and domestic use]" (see the Judgment at [45]).

47 The Judge also held that RecordTV had purported to authorise the copying of the MediaCorp shows because it had openly stated, via a statement in the "Frequently Asked Questions" section of its website, that it had "consulted with the Infocomm Development Authority (IDA) and [MDA] and [had] accordingly obtained all necessary licen[c]es from the Government of Singapore".[4] The Judge interpreted this statement as RecordTV representing that "it had the *actual* authority to provide its service to [the Registered] [U]sers" [emphasis in original] (see the Judgment at [42]), and held that "[t]o that end, [RecordTV] had purported to authorise the copies of the MediaCorp [shows] that were subsequently made at the behest of [the Registered Users]" (see likewise [42] of the Judgment). MediaCorp, unsurprisingly, supported the Judge's finding, and further contended that "the fact that the [aforesaid] authority appear[ed] to come from the Government and not [RecordTV] ma[de] [RecordTV's] position *worse*, not better"[5] [emphasis in original].

48 We find the Judge's and MediaCorp's position to be mistaken for two reasons. First, the reference to RecordTV having obtained all the necessary licences from the Infocomm Development Authority of Singapore ("IDA") and MDA did not and could not mean that RecordTV had obtained the requisite authority from MediaCorp to authorise the copying and/or the communication to the public of the MediaCorp shows. It was *MediaCorp's* approval, not IDA's and/or MDA's, which mattered, since copyright in the MediaCorp shows vested in MediaCorp, and not IDA and/or MDA.

49 Second, the statement by RecordTV that it had obtained "all necessary licen[c]es"[6] upon consultation with IDA and MDA could not possibly mean that it had obtained the requisite authority from MediaCorp to authorise the copying and/or the communication to the public of the MediaCorp shows. In fact, RecordTV had warned the Registered Users that the copying of certain shows might require permission and that it had no authority to grant the same. This was made clear in cl 3A of the Terms of Use, where RecordTV specifically stated that the Registered Users could use its iDVR service to record only those shows/programmes which they would otherwise be able to watch and record legally:[7]

> RecordTV hereby grants you permission to use the Website [ie, RecordTV's website] as set forth in [these] Terms of Service, provided that: ... (ii) you shall not record any shows/programs on the RecordTV.com website that you would otherwise not be able to legally see and record on ... another recording device, such as a personal video recorder, digital video recorder, video cassette recorder etc. ... [emphasis added]

Clause 3A of the Terms of Use shows that the right which RecordTV granted to the Registered Users was limited to the right to use the iDVR for non-infringing purposes. This clause would have come to the attention of all the Registered Users as they had to view and accept the Terms of Use before access to RecordTV's iDVR was granted. Accordingly, we conclude that no Registered User would reasonably deduce from the relevant portions of RecordTV's website, *viz*, the "Frequently Asked Questions" section and the Terms of Use, that RecordTV possessed or purported to possess authority to grant them the required permission to copy and/or communicate to the public the MediaCorp shows.

50 Further, we should add that there was also no evidence that RecordTV granted or purported to grant the Registered Users the right to copy and/or communicate to the public the MediaCorp shows. Upon considering the four factors listed below (collectively, "the authorisation liability factors"), which (in our view) the courts ought to take into account in determining whether authorisation to do an act comprised in the copyright has been granted illegitimately, we conclude that RecordTV did not authorise the Registered Users to do any act comprised in MediaCorp's copyright in the MediaCorp shows. The authorisation liability factors are as follows:

> (a) whether the alleged authoriser had control over the means by which copyright infringement was committed and, hence, a power to prevent such infringement ("the first authorisation liability factor");

> (b) the nature of the relationship (if any) between the alleged authoriser and the actual infringer ("the second authorisation liability factor");

> (c) whether the alleged authoriser took reasonable steps to prevent or avoid copyright infringement ("the third authorisation liability factor"); and

> (d) whether the alleged authoriser had actual or constructive knowledge of the occurrence of copyright infringement and/or the likelihood of such infringement occurring ("the fourth authorisation liability factor").

We should emphasise that the courts evaluate the authorisation liability factors in their totality in the context of the factual matrix of each case. Thus, proving one or even several of these factors in either the alleged authoriser's or the copyright owner's favour will not invariably be decisive on the question of authorisation liability.

51 *Vis-à-vis* the first authorisation liability factor (namely, whether the alleged authoriser had control over the means by which copyright infringement was committed and, hence, a power to prevent such infringement), in *Ong Seow Pheng*, the Court of Appeal found (at [33] — [35]) that even though the first

defendant might have facilitated or even incited the copying of the plaintiffs' computer manuals and programmes by (*inter alia*) a self-admitted dealer in pirated computer products, this did not amount to "authorisation" of such copying as once the defendants sold and delivered the infringing copies of the computer manuals and programmes to the dealer, they had no control over what the dealer would do with them.

52 The English and the Australian courts likewise take into account the first authorisation liability factor in determining whether the alleged authoriser ought to be held liable for illegitimately authorising others to do acts restricted by the copyright.

53 In the Australian High Court case of *The University of New South Wales v Moorhouse and another* [1975] HCA 26; (1975) 133 CLR 1 ("*Moorhouse*"), a graduate of the defendant university ("the University") used a photocopying machine in the University's library to make infringing copies of a book written by the first plaintiff and published by the second plaintiff (the latter had the exclusive right to print and sell that book in Australia). The plaintiffs sued the University for copyright infringement, alleging (*inter alia*) that it had authorised the copying of the aforesaid book without their permission. Gibbs J expressly stated (at 12) that "[a] person [could not] be said to authorize an infringement of copyright unless he ha[d] some power to prevent it". Following amendments to Australia's Copyright Act 1968 (Cth) in 2000, which amendments purportedly codified the principles of authorisation already developed under Australian common law, s 101(1A)(a) of the amended Act ("the Australian Copyright Act") now explicitly obliges the Australian courts to consider, in relation to authorisation liability, "the extent (if any) of the [alleged authoriser]'s power to prevent the doing of the act concerned". This obligation has been recognised more recently by Cowdroy J in *Roadshow Films Pty Ltd v iiNet Limited (No 3)* [2010] FCA 24 ("*iiNet*").

54 Turning to English law, the English cases of, *inter alia*, *CBS Inc and Another v Ames Records & Tapes Ltd* [1982] Ch 91, *CBS Songs Ltd and Others v Amstrad Consumer Electronics Plc and Another* [1988] UKHL 15; [1988] AC 1013 ("*Amstrad*") and, more recently, *Twentieth Century Fox Film Corporation and others v Newzbin Limited* [2010] EWHC 608 (Ch) ("*Newzbin*") indicate that the English courts similarly take into consideration the first authorisation liability factor when deliberating on authorisation liability. For instance, in *Amstrad*, which concerned the manufacture, advertisement and sale of twin-deck tape-recording machines that allowed users to copy the contents of one tape directly onto another, Lord Templeman held that the first defendant ("Amstrad") had not authorised breaches of copyright through its advertisement and sale of these tape-recording machines as, *inter alia*, it had "no control over the use of [its machines] once they [were] sold" (see *Amstrad* at 1054). The House of Lords held that without this power to control how its tape-recording machines were used after they were sold, Amstrad could not be held liable for authorising copyright infringement by purchasers of those machines.

55 Where the second authorisation liability factor (*ie*, the nature of the relationship, if any, between the alleged authoriser and the actual infringer) is concerned, the courts will consider in particular whether there was a direct and continuing relationship between the alleged authoriser and the actual infringer. The fact that there exists a commercial aspect to this relationship (for example, the alleged authoriser profits from the actual infringer's infringing activities) does not, however, have any definitive bearing on the issue of authorisation liability.

56 As for the third authorisation liability factor (*viz*, whether the alleged authoriser took reasonable steps to prevent or avoid copyright infringement), we find the Australian cases instructive in this regard. In *Moorhouse*, the High Court of Australia ruled that the steps taken by the University to prevent copyright infringement were not sufficient to amount to "reasonable or effective precautions against an infringement of copyright by the use of the [University's] photocopying machines" (at 17 *per* Gibbs J), and therefore held that the University had failed to adopt "measures reasonably sufficient for the purpose of preventing infringements taking place" (see *Moorhouse* at 17). In particular, Gibbs J considered the failure of the University to place "adequate notice ... on the [photocopying] machines for the purpose of informing users that the machines were not to be used in a manner that would constitute an infringement of copyright" (see *Moorhouse* at 17) to be "the fatal weakness in the case for the University" (see *Moorhouse* at 17).

57 More recently, in *Cooper v Universal Music Australia Pty Ltd* [2006] FCAFC 187; (2006) 237 ALR 714 ("*Cooper*"), an Australian case concerning a website owned and operated by one Stephen Cooper ("Cooper") which allowed users to download infringing music directly from other websites by clicking on hyperlinks provided on Cooper's website, Branson J considered s 101(1A)(c) of the Australian Copyright Act, which required the court to take into account "whether the [alleged authoriser] took any other reasonable steps to prevent or avoid the doing of the [infringing] act, including whether the [alleged authoriser] complied with any relevant industry codes of practice". Not only did Branson J find that Cooper had failed to take reasonable steps to prevent or avoid copyright infringement via the use of his website, he also found that Cooper had in fact deliberately designed his website to facilitate its use for copyright infringement, and that the latter's inclusion of various disclaimers was merely for cosmetic purposes.

58 Similarly, the English courts consider whether the alleged authoriser had taken reasonable steps to prevent or avoid copyright infringement, even though English copyright legislation does not mandate such a consideration. In *Newzbin*, Kitchin J said that even though he was not bound to consider this factor, he was of the view that *Cooper* and *iiNet* were consistent with the principles which he believed he had to apply (see *Newzbin* at [91] — [95]).

59 As for the fourth authorisation liability factor (*ie*, whether the alleged authoriser had knowledge, actual or constructive, of the occurrence of copyright infringement and/or the likelihood of such infringement occurring), we

should emphasise that the mere existence of such knowledge does not necessitate a finding that the alleged authoriser is therefore liable. In the Australian case of *Nationwide News Pty Ltd and Others v Copyright Agency Ltd* (1996) 136 ALR 273, for instance, Sackville J (with whom Jenkinson and Burchett JJ agreed) astutely observed (at 295) that:

> ... [A] person does not authorise an infringement merely because he or she knows that another person might infringe the copyright and takes no step to prevent the infringement.

60 We now apply each of the authorisation liability factors to the facts of this case. With regard to the first authorisation liability factor, it may be said that RecordTV did have the power to prevent potential infringement of MediaCorp's copyright in the MediaCorp shows by shutting down its iDVR service altogether. However, it was not necessary for RecordTV to take this drastic step as it had already expressly stated in cl 3A of the Terms of Use that the Registered Users could use its iDVR to record only those shows which they could otherwise legally view and record. In using RecordTV's iDVR to time-shift, the Registered Users were doing no more than what they, as holders of valid television licences, could do when they used a traditional DVR/VCR to record the MediaCorp shows (all of which were free-to-air broadcasts) for viewing at a more convenient time. Not unlike a VCR or a set-top DVR, RecordTV's iDVR responds directly and "automatically" to a Registered User's commands without any human intervention or decision-making by RecordTV's employees.

61 In respect of the second authorisation liability factor, RecordTV was at best a conduit enabling the Registered Users to time-shift their viewing of the MediaCorp shows. It could be said that there was a commercial relationship between RecordTV and the Registered Users, but, on the evidence, RecordTV did not profit commercially from that relationship, although the Registered Users did benefit socially. In any case, even if RecordTV profited from providing its iDVR service, that was not wrong. There was nothing to stop MediaCorp from providing an even better time-shifting service.

62 *Vis-à-vis* the third authorisation liability factor, we are of the view that RecordTV took adequate steps to prevent infringement of MediaCorp's copyright in the MediaCorp shows for three reasons. First, RecordTV restricted the use of its iDVR to personal, private and domestic use. This was made clear by cl 3A of the Terms of Use, which (apart from stipulating that RecordTV's iDVR could be used to record only those shows that the Registered Users could otherwise watch and record legally) stated that:[8]

> RecordTV hereby grants you permission to use the Website [ie, RecordTV's website] as set forth in [these] Terms of Service, provided that: (i) your use of the Website as permitted is solely for your personal, private and domestic use ...

Second, RecordTV designed its iDVR service such that the recorded MediaCorp shows were "streamed" to the Registered Users, rather than "downloaded" onto their computers (see [8] above). This went some way towards preventing illegal distribution of time-shifted recordings as the use of "streaming" ensured that a recording of a MediaCorp show was not saved in the Registered User's computer, thereby restricting the Registered User's ability to extract, modify and exploit the recording for further downstream transmission. As the Judge explained in the Judgment:

> 97 [RecordTV]'s system uses streaming as the technique to disseminate the television programme data from the server. With streaming, data is transferred from the server to the [Registered] [U]ser, but upon arrival the data is displayed as soon as possible. Once the data has been shown on the computer display, it is discarded. As a result of this, no local copy of the recorded programme is kept or created at the [Registered] [U]ser's computer and patrons of [RecordTV's] [w]ebsite therefore have little or no ability to store, edit or manipulate the recorded television programmes. …
>
> 98 The average lay person is, therefore, unable to extract recorded programmes … for further downstream transmission. …
>
> [emphasis in original]

Third, as we have already mentioned, RecordTV expressly stated in cl 3A of the Terms of Use that its iDVR service could be used to record only those shows which a Registered User could otherwise legally view and record. In effect, this meant that only those Registered Users living in Singapore who held valid television licences could use RecordTV's iDVR to record the MediaCorp shows (see [5] above). Registered Users who were located out of jurisdiction were not permitted to use RecordTV's iDVR to record the MediaCorp shows as they could not legally view and record those shows. Of course, Singapore-based Registered Users who did not hold valid television licences could in practice use RecordTV's iDVR to record the MediaCorp shows, but such activity would fall foul of cl 3A of the Terms of Use and thus would not be authorised by RecordTV where authorisation liability is concerned.

63 With regard to the fourth authorisation liability factor (*viz*, whether RecordTV had knowledge, actual or constructive, of the occurrence of copyright infringement and/or the likelihood of such infringement occurring), the answer is, in our view, clear. On this particular point, RecordTV had case law in its favour in the form of the decision in *Cartoon Network*. Given that RecordTV had expressly stated in cl 3A of the Terms of Use that the Registered Users could use its iDVR service to record only those MediaCorp shows which they could otherwise legally view and record, and given all the other precautions which RecordTV had taken to prevent copyright infringement, it would not be right to attribute knowledge of improper usage of the iDVR service to RecordTV in the absence of express proof of such knowledge.

64 Accordingly, for the reasons set out at [45] — [63] above, we find, *vis-à-vis* the Third Issue, that RecordTV is not liable under s 103(1) of the Copyright Act for authorising the doing in Singapore of any act comprised in MediaCorp's copyright in the MediaCorp shows. In our view, where the Copyright Act is unclear as to how much copyright protection ought to be granted to a copyright owner, the courts should not be quick to construe a statutory provision

so liberally as to deter or restrict technological innovations by preventing them from being applied in a manner which would benefit the public without harming the rights of the copyright owner. In the present case, one possible concern from MediaCorp's point of view could be that RecordTV's iDVR system might be hacked into by persons who do not hold valid television licences, thereby resulting in a loss of revenue for MediaCorp. Of course, the possibility of hacking exists, but no evidence of the likelihood of this possibility materialising was adduced before the court. In the circumstances, RecordTV cannot be held responsible for this possibility. In our view, the possibility of hacking is not a proper countervailing objection to the use of RecordTV's innovative recording system. After all, an ordinary DVR/VCR can be abused in a much more serious manner than RecordTV's iDVR (*eg*, the former can be used to make hundreds of pirated copies of a MediaCorp show for sale).

The provisions on safe harbour and fair dealing

65 As RecordTV is not liable to MediaCorp for infringing the latter's exclusive right to copy and/or communicate to the public the MediaCorp shows and is also not liable for authorising the Registered Users to do "any act comprised in [MediaCorp's] copyright" (see s 103(1) of the Copyright Act), it is not necessary for us to determine whether RecordTV can rely on any of the safe harbour or fair dealing provisions under Pt IXA and s 109 respectively of the Copyright Act. Accordingly, we now turn to RecordTV's claim against MediaCorp under s 200(1) for making groundless threats to bring legal proceedings for copyright infringement.

RecordTV's claim against MediaCorp under s 200(1) of the Copyright Act

66 Section 200(1) of the Copyright Act provides that where a person threatens another person with a copyright infringement action, the latter may bring an action against the former for (*inter alia*) a declaration that the threat is unjustifiable, unless the former satisfies the court that the alleged infringing acts "constituted, or, if done, would constitute, an infringement of copyright".

The full text of s 200(1) reads as follows:

Groundless threats of legal proceedings

200. — (1) Where a person, by means of circulars, advertisements or otherwise, threatens a person with an action or proceeding in respect of an infringement of copyright, then, whether the person making the threats is or is not the owner of the copyright or an exclusive licensee, a person aggrieved may bring an action against the first-mentioned person and may —

(*a*) obtain a declaration to the effect that the threats are unjustifiable;

(*b*) obtain an injunction against the continuance of the threats; and

(*c*) recover such damages, if any, as he has sustained,

unless the first-mentioned person satisfies the court that the acts in respect of which the action or proceeding was threatened constituted, or, if done, would constitute, an infringement of copyright.

Having regard to our findings that RecordTV has not infringed MediaCorp's exclusive right to copy and/or communicate to the public the MediaCorp shows and also has not authorised the Registered Users to do any of these acts (which are acts comprised in MediaCorp's copyright in the MediaCorp shows), it must follow that MediaCorp has made groundless threats against RecordTV for the purposes of s 200(1) of the Copyright Act.

Conclusion

67 In the result, we find that MediaCorp's threats to bring an action for copyright infringement against RecordTV are unjustifiable. Accordingly, the present appeal against the Judge's decision is allowed with costs here and below as well as the usual consequential orders. RecordTV is entitled to damages against MediaCorp (which shall be assessed by an assistant registrar), and an injunction restraining MediaCorp from making further threats against it.

Observations

68 As mentioned at [2] above, the present appeal requires us to balance the competing interests of several stakeholders (*viz*, consumers, content providers as well as technology and service vendors) in a manner which would result in the most benefits to and impose the least costs on society as a whole. It tests the boundaries of Singapore's copyright laws in protecting the exclusive rights of copyright owners to copy and/or communicate to the public, *inter alia*, cinematograph films, television broadcasts and sound broadcasts.

69 Although copyright law is intended to promote creativity and innovation by granting exclusive rights to copyright owners to exploit their rights for a specific period of time, there is also a public interest in not allowing copyright law to hinder creativity and innovation. Rights conferred on copyright owners are statutory rights. In our view, where the statute is not clear as to the ambit of an existing copyright owner's rights and the courts are asked to expand those rights so as to respond to novel technologies impinging on the copyright owner's interests, the courts must strive to strike the right balance between the copyright owner's private rights and the public interest in the use of new technology. Thus, unless the statutory words clearly reflect the legislative policy on the extent of the rights to be conferred on the copyright owner, the courts should not be quick to interpret the statutory words expansively if doing so may stifle technological advances which are in the public's interest.

70 In this connection, MediaCorp's counsel suggested that if RecordTV were not restrained from providing its iDVR service, it could one day monetise its service once it had acquired the requisite critical mass to sell advertisements. The suggestion is, therefore, that RecordTV would then be able to profit from its iDVR service at the expense of MediaCorp. This suggestion would be equally applicable to the use of traditional VCRs, DVRs and variations of those devices, such as Cablevision's RS-DVR in *Cartoon Network*. In *Cartoon Network*, the US Court of Appeals for the Second Circuit held that the public interest in Cablevision's innovative device prevailed over the private interests of the

copyright owners concerned. We are of the view that the same position should be adopted in the present case because, through its iDVR service, RecordTV provided a more convenient and/or more useful time-shifting facility than the time-shifting services that are currently available. The fact remains that so long as MediaCorp is prepared to broadcast the MediaCorp shows on a free-to-air basis to members of the public (including Registered Users) who hold valid television licences and who are thus legally entitled to view and record the same for their own private and domestic use, it has already factored in its alleged "loss" of revenue with respect to its copyright in those shows. That RecordTV, by virtue of its improved time-shifting facility, is able to exploit this relationship between MediaCorp and the aforesaid members of the public does not make RecordTV's actions unlawful or tortious under the Copyright Act.

71 To summarise our observations: in the present case, RecordTV's iDVR service represents a significant technological improvement over existing recording methods and facilitates the more convenient enjoyment of television viewing rights by those Registered Users living in Singapore who hold valid television licences. RecordTV's iDVR is simply a technological advance that is not addressed by the Copyright Act in the context of the copyright owner's exclusive right to copy (*ie*, reproduce), communicate to the public and authorise the copying and/or the communication to the public of copyright-protected material. Since RecordTV was doing no more than making it more convenient for the aforesaid Registered Users to enjoy the MediaCorp shows (which was something that these Registered Users were entitled to do as MediaCorp had licensed them to view those shows), we are of the view that the public interest is better served by encouraging rather than stifling the use of RecordTV's novel technology, especially given that MediaCorp has apparently not suffered any loss from RecordTV's provision of an additional and better time-shifting service to Registered Users who are licensed to view the MediaCorp shows.

Endotes to RecordTV Pte Ltd v. MediaCorp TV Singapore Pte Ltd.,

1   See the Appellant's Core Bundle of Documents dated 25 March 2010 ("ACB") at vol 2, tab 8.
2   See para 2.2.5 of the report by Assoc Prof Roger Zimmermann dated 20 March 2009 (at ACB vol 2, tab 7).
3   See the Respondents' Case dated 26 April 2010 ("the Respondents' Case") at paras 272 and 275.
4   See p 6 of MediaCorp's Supplemental Core Bundle dated 26 April 2010 ("SCB").
5   See the Respondents' Case at para 140.
6   See SCB at p 6.
7   See ACB at vol 2, tab 8.
8   See ACB at vol 2, tab 8.

National Rugby League Investments Pty Ltd v. Singtel Optus Pty Ltd., [2012] FCAFC 59 (F.C.A.)

FINN, EMMETT AND BENNETT JJ

INTRODUCTION

1 The Optus group of companies is a leading provider of communications services throughout Australia. Two of its members, Singtel Optus Pty Ltd and Optus Mobile Pty Ltd (referred to collectively here as "Optus"), devised a new subscription service — "TV Now" — which it offered, in the mainland State capitals, to private and to the employees (subject to conditions) of small to medium business customers from mid-2011. That service enabled a subscriber to have free to air television programmes recorded as and when broadcast and then played back at the time (or times) of the subscriber's choosing on the subscriber's compatible Optus mobile device or personal computer. The system which permits such "time-shifting" of programme viewing requires the copying and storing of each television broadcast recorded for a subscriber, hence the allegations of copyright infringement in this matter.

2 It has been agreed for the purposes of these proceedings that the Australian Football League, the National Rugby League partnership (which consists of the first and second appellants in NSD 201 of 2012) and Telstra have copyright interests in the free-to-air broadcasts of live and filmed AFL and NRL football games played on four specified days in September 2011 which were recorded for Optus subscribers using the TV Now system. The Australian Football League conducts a national Australian Rules competition. The National Rugby League partnership conducts a national Rugby League competition. Those entities have granted to Telstra an exclusive licence to communicate to the public, by means of the internet and mobile telephony enabled devices, free to air television broadcasts of football matches conducted by them.

3 The two primary issues raised in the appeals can be stated shortly. The first is: When a cinematograph film (or copy) and a sound recording (or copy) were made when a television broadcast of one of the AFL or NRL matches was recorded for a subscriber, who, for the purposes of the *Copyright Act 1968* (Cth) was the maker of that film, etc? Was it Optus or the subscriber (or both of them jointly)? The primary judge's answer to this was that the maker was the subscriber.

4 Ours is a different conclusion. The maker was Optus or, in the alternative, it was Optus and the subscriber. It is unnecessary for present purposes to express a definitive view as between the two. Optus could be said to be the maker in that the service it offered to, and did, supply a subscriber was to make and to make available to that person a recording of the football match he or she selected. Alternatively Optus and the subscriber could be said to be the maker for Copyright Act purposes as they acted in concert for the purpose of making a recording of the particular broadcast which the subscriber required to be made and of which he or she initiated the automated process by which copies were

produced. In other words, they were jointly and severally responsible for the act of copying.

5 The second question is: If Optus' act in making such a film would otherwise constitute an infringement of the copyright of AFL, NRL or Telstra, can Optus invoke what we would inaccurately, but conveniently, call the "private and domestic use" defence of s 111 of the Act? The primary judge did not have to consider this, given his answer to the first question.

6 Our answer is that Optus cannot in either of the above contingencies bring itself within the scope of the s 111 exception on its proper construction.

7 Our conclusions on these two matters are sufficient to resolve these appeals. They must be allowed. It is, in consequence, unnecessary to consider the various alternative grounds of appeal the appellants have raised.

8 We should also note at the outset that Audio-Visual Copyright Collecting Society Ltd — a declared collecting society for the purposes of Parts VA, VB and VC of the Copyright Act — sought leave pursuant to r 9.12 of the *Federal Court Rules 2011* to make short written and oral submissions on how s 111 should properly be interpreted having regard to the scheme of Part VC of the Act relating to the retransmission of free-to-air broadcasts. While this application was opposed by Optus (which nonetheless responded to the submissions made) it was an appropriate one in the circumstances and we have allowed the application on the limited basis sought. This said, we have in the event found it unnecessary to take account of those submissions.

9 Though our conclusions differ from those of the primary judge, we acknowledge the assistance we have derived from his reasons for decision. We have found the questions raised in the appeals to be of some difficulty and considerable uncertainty. His Honour conducted the proceeding at first instance in an expeditious manner, and reasoned cogently in his reasons for judgment. The primary judge has distilled very complicated technology and has crystallised complex issues in a way that has made the management of the appeal much easier than it might have been.

THE STATUTORY SETTING

10 The alleged copyright infringements relate primarily to the copying of television broadcasts but in the case of what has been called the "second AFL programme", the television broadcast in question was of a film of a match which had been pre-recorded on to film. Consequently it is necessary to refer to those provisions dealing with both the copyright in cinematograph films (s 86 of the Act) and copyright in television broadcasts and sound broadcasts (s 87).

11 There is a number of definitions in s 10 of the Act which require note at the outset. They are:

> **broadcast** means a communication to the public delivered by a broadcasting service within the meaning of the Broadcasting Services Act 1992 ...

> **cinematograph film** means the aggregate of the visual images embodied in an article or thing so as to be capable by the use of that article or thing:
>
> > (a) of being shown as a moving picture; or
> >
> > (b) of being embodied in another article or thing by the use of which it can be so shown;
>
> and includes the aggregate of the sounds embodied in a sound-track associated with such visual images.
>
> **copy**, in relation to a cinematograph film, means any article or thing in which the visual images or sounds comprising the film are embodied.
>
> **private and domestic use** means private and domestic use on or off domestic premises.
>
> **record** includes a disc, tape, paper, electronic file or other device in which sounds are embodied.
>
> **sound recording** means the aggregate of the sounds embodied in a record.
>
> **television broadcast** means visual images broadcast by way of television, together with any sounds broadcast for reception along with those images.

12 We would emphasise in passing the emphasis upon the requirement of physical embodiment in an article or thing in the definitions of "cinematograph", "copy", "record" and "sound recording".

13 Part IV Division 2 of the Act deals with the nature of copyright in (amongst other things) cinematograph films and television broadcasts, and sound broadcasts. Section 86 provides, insofar as presently relevant:

For the purposes of this Act, unless the contrary intention appears, copyright, in relation to a cinematograph film is the exclusive right to do all or any of the following acts:

> (a) to make a copy of the film;
>
> (b) to cause the film, in so far as it consists of visual images, to be seen in public, or, in so far as it consists of sounds, to be heard in public.

Section 87 provides for present purposes:

For the purposes of this Act, unless the contrary intention appears, copyright, in relation to a television broadcast or sound broadcast, is the exclusive right:

> (a) in the case of a television broadcast in so far as it consists of visual images — to make a cinematograph film of the broadcast, or a copy of such a film;
>
> (b) in the case of a sound broadcast, or of a television broadcast in so far as it consists of sounds — to make a sound recording of the broadcast, or a copy of such a sound recording.

14 Section 101(1) of the Act links infringement of copyright for present purposes to the doing of any of the "acts" specified in s 86(a) and s 87(a) and (b). It provides:

Subject to this Act, a copyright subsisting by virtue of this Part is infringed by a person who, not being the owner of the copyright, and without the licence of the owner of the copyright, does in Australia, or authorizes the doing in Australia of, any act comprised in the copyright.

15 Finally, s 111(1) and (2) provide:

(1) This section applies if a person makes a cinematograph film or sound recording of broadcast solely for private and domestic use by watching or listening to the material broadcast at a time more convenient than the time when the broadcast is made.

(2) The making of the film or recording does not infringe copyright in the broadcast or in any work or other subject-matter included in the broadcast.

16 There are two issues of construction which arise in relation to these various provisions. The first concerns the meaning of the words "to make" in s 86(a) and s 87(a) and (b). The second is whether the defence provided by s 111 applies only to the maker of the cinematograph film or sound recording or whether it can extend to a person who makes the copy not for his or her own "private and domestic use" etc, but the film etc is nonetheless made for such use by another.

17 To anticipate the second of these it is convenient to refer to the parliamentary evolution of the proposed s 111 in the *Copyright Amendment Bill 2006* (Cth) and the reasons for such changes as were made to the proposed section.

18 The Explanatory Memorandum to the 2006 Bill in its original form indicated that the major reforms it was making to the Copyright Act were guided by seven principles, the first four of which were:

- the need for copyright to keep pace with developments in technology and rapidly changing consumer behaviour

- recognising reasonable consumer use of technology to enjoy copyright material; Australian consumers should not be in a significantly worse position than consumers in similar countries

- reforms should not unreasonably harm or discourage the development of new digital markets by copyright owners

- Australia has a unique regime that should be maintained

19 One group of amendments was a response to the proposals made in the Government's "Fair Use and Other Copyright Exceptions" review. The EM (p 3) explained that the exceptions contained in the Bill would (inter alia) better recognise the rights of consumers to enjoy certain copyright material they have legitimately acquired where this does not significantly harm the interests of copyright owners.

20 The Regulation Impact Statement in the EM identified "time-shifting" and "format shifting" of copyright material as problems requiring address. Under the heading *"Private Copying"* it said in part (at pp 6-7):

One issue identified during the Fair Use review is the lack of provision in the Act of copying for private or personal use. This situation is increasingly out of step with consumer attitudes and behaviour. Technology is giving consumers new and more convenient ways to use copyright material, particularly for personal entertainment. Many consumer devices are designed so that users can easily copy and store copyright material.

. . .

A ... common example of private copying is recording a broadcast to watch or listen to at a later time. Video cassette recorders have been used to time-shift analogue television broadcasts in Australian homes since the 1970's. Today a range of new consumer devices (eg DVD recorders, Personal Video Recorders, and digital TV tuner cards for PCs) are being marketed to simplify and encourage the private copying of television broadcasts.

Legal action has not been taken by copyright owners in Australia to stop such private copying. Nevertheless, such acts usually infringe copyright. Many ordinary Australians do not believe that ... "time-shifting" a broadcast for personal use should be legally wrong with a risk of civil legal action, however unlikely. Failure to recognise such common practices diminishes respect for copyright and undermines the credibility of the Act.

The failure to recognise the reality of private copying is also unsatisfactory for industries investing in the delivery of digital devices and services. Eg, the supply of *personal recording devices* by broadcasters of subscription television services is proving to be important for the development of digital television. The availability of personal recording devices is also likely to be important for digital radio. (Emphasis added.)

21 What was proposed was a new specific exception which would legitimise this common form of private copying by (at p 8):

... allowing individuals *in their homes* to copy a broadcast for personal use to enable it to be viewed or listened to at a more convenient time. (Emphasis added.)

This exception, it said, would benefit domestic consumers who would be assured time-shifting did not infringe copyright. It would also provide legal certainty for industries that "provide products and services that assist consumers carry out these copying activities".

22 What requires emphasis is that this EM and its proposed s 111 had as their focus "private copying" by individuals in "domestic premises" using "private recording devices". So the proposed s 111(1) provided:

This section applies if a person makes a cinematograph film or sound recording of a broadcast:

(a) in domestic premises; and

(b) solely for private and domestic use by watching or listening to the material broadcast at a time more convenient than the time when the broadcast is made.

23 A subsequent amendment to the Bill resulted in a further amendment of relevance to s 111. The Supplementary Explanatory Memorandum indicated that the definition section (s 10) was now to include the definition of "private and domestic use" in the terms which are now in the Act. Such use could occur "on or off domestic premises".

24 A subsequent further amendment removed from s 111 the requirement that the *recording* of a broadcast for private and domestic use must be made "in domestic premises".

25 As the Further Explanatory Memorandum indicated (at [29]):

> This amendment provides greater flexibility in the conditions that apply to "timeshift" recording. The development of digital technologies is likely to result in increasing use of personal consumer devices and other means which enable individuals to record television and radio broadcasts on or off domestic premises. The revised wording of s 111 enables an individual to record broadcasts, as well as view and listen to the recording, outside their homes as well as inside for private and domestic use.

26 Section 111 had achieved the form in which it was enacted and now remains.

27 Because of its potential significance in this matter, reference needs to be made to an aspect of the law governing when two or more persons may be jointly and severally liable for a copyright infringement.

28 (i) Infringement of statutory copyright provisions has long been accepted as tortious. As such, infringement attracts the common law principles applied to joint tort feasors: see *WEA International Inc v Hanimex Ltd* (1987) 17 FCR 274 at 283; *Aristocrat Technologies Australia Pty Ltd v Global Gaming Supplies Pty Ltd* [2009] FCA 1495; (2009) 84 IPR 222 at [620]- [624].

29 (ii) Joint infringers are two or more persons who act in concert with one another in the infringement pursuant to a common design: *CBS Songs Ltd v Amstrad Consumer Electronics Plc* [1988] UKHL 15; [1988] 1 AC 1013 at 1057; *Universal Music Australia Pty Ltd v Cooper* [2005] FCA 972; (2005) 150 FCR 1 at [135].

30 (iii) That two or more persons assist or concur in, or contribute to, an act causing damage to another is not of itself sufficient to found joint liability. There must be some common design: *WEA International Inc* at 283; a "concurrence in the act or acts causing damage": *The "Koursk"* [1924] P 140 at 159-160; *Thompson v Australian Capital Television Pty Ltd* [1996] HCA 38; (1996) 186 CLR 574 at 580-581; something in the nature of "concerted action or agreed common action": *Universal Music Australia* at [135].

THE AGREED FACTS AND THE "TV NOW" SYSTEM

31 The parties have not disputed the accuracy of his Honour's narration of the primary facts and, in particular, of how the TV Now system ("the Service") is configured and works and of how it is activated by a subscriber to it. What

follows is drawn primarily from his Honour's reasons but in a much abbreviated form which suffices for present purposes.

32 (i) The decision to approve the capital expenditure to establish the infrastructure necessary for TV Now was taken at an Optus board meeting on 28 February 2011. The business case for the approval described this project as one enabling Optus "first to market with an innovative and *disruptive* TV & Video product to establish a leading position in the fast moving digital TV Industry": Emphasis added.

33 (ii) After its development the Service was made available to Optus 3G mobile prepaid and individual account customers and, subject to restrictions, to the employees of small and medium business customers who had mobile devices supported by the business' subscription. The Service is by a subscription and is available only in the five mainland State capital cities. Three plans are offered to a subscriber: a basic plan for 45 minutes free recording; a standard plan for about $7 a month for about 5 hours recording; and a premium plan for about $10 per month for 20 hours recording. Optus solicits eligible customers to subscribe to this Service through Optus' My Zoo homepage.

34 (iii) The process involved in subscribing is described in the trial judge's reasons in detail. It is done online, using a PC or compatible mobile device; there is a user ID requirement for use of the Service; and subscription requires intending subscribers to acknowledge they have read and agreed to the terms and conditions prescribed. Both the various descriptions of TV Now encountered as one navigates the TV Now website and the terms and conditions of subscription personalise what subscription provides as for example:

Optus TV Now allows you to record and store television shows.

The terms also address "special liability issues" the burden of which is to describe the limitations on the use which can be made of the recordings made. These crystallised in the concluding sentences:

> *You* are advised that it is a breach of copyright to make a copy of a broadcast other than to record it for your private and domestic use by watching the material broadcast at a more convenient time. You must not copy any information from Optus TV Now or from the Electronic Program Guide. Optus accepts no responsibility for copyright infringement. *You* indemnify Optus against claims for copyright infringement from copyright owners.

35 (iv) The recording and view service can be effected on any one *or more* of four Optus compatible types of device operated by the subscriber. They are (i) a personal computer; (ii) an iPhone or iPad; (iii) Android mobile devices; and (iv) most 3G mobile phones. In the process of recording a broadcast four copies are made. The reason for this is to allow the broadcast to be played back on any one of the above four types of device which the subscriber then happens to be using. There are examples in the evidence of a subscriber using one type of device when selecting the programme to be recorded and then using another, or several others, when viewing that programme. It is to be noted in passing that a

subscriber is not told that four copies are made and it is to be inferred that he or she would, as a rule, be unaware that such was the case.

36 (v) Once a subscriber has signed up for the Service, that person can log in and is then directed to an electronic programme guide which is used to look for and to select the programme to be recorded. As his Honour aptly put it (at [21]):

In essence, from the user's point of view, the TV Now system is simplicity itself. After logging in, he or she looks at the electronic program guide, decides what he or she wants to record and clicks the record button. Next, a pop up box appears on the screen displaying further information about the chosen program. This box invites the user to click on the "Record" button it displays to confirm that he or she wishes to record the program. That is the last the user does from then until he or she wants to play the recording. Users of the TV Now service can cancel a scheduled recording by clicking on an appropriate button.

When the subscriber later wants to view a recorded programme, he or she can do so on any of the four kinds of compatible device supported by the Service. Having logged in and selected the programme now to be watched, the TV Now system detects the particular kind of device the subscriber is then using and transmits a stream of data in the form suitable for that device from one of the four recordings of the programme held in Optus' data centre. If the subscriber later wishes to view some or all of the programme on another compatible device, the system will respond accordingly.

37 (vi) The essential features of TV Now's infrastructure system and of its components are described in eight paragraphs of the trial judge's reasons which, gratefully, can be reproduced here:

28. Australia uses a format known as DVB-T (digital video broadcasting — ter-restrial) for its digital free to air television broadcasts. These broadcasts are made using an audio visual compression computer format known as MPEG-2 (motion picture experts group). This format is used to send a stream of digitised data that reception equipment, such as television sets or set top boxes, can convert or pro-cess into what the viewer sees as a television program at, or nearly at, the same time as the data is received by the device. The data in a DVB-T signal are split into several streams using a number of frequencies in a particular range for that signal.

29. Optus has established TV antennae and three DVB-T receivers in each of the five capital cities in which it offers the TV Now service. The antennae receive the total of 15 digital signals broadcast in the MPEG-2 format by each free to air channel in each city. The antennae are connected by coaxial cable to the DVB-T receivers.

30. Each of the three DVB-T receivers is configured so that, between them, they will receive signals from the 15 free to air channels in each city. The receivers then convert the radio frequency DVB-T signal to a packet-based stream of data, also in MPEG-2 format, and transmit that stream of data to the transcode servers. Each of those transcode servers has significant RAM (random access memory) and hard drive memory capacity. Those servers run a program known as "transcod-ing". This digitally converts the MPEG-2 signal into four specifications that are

designed so that the program can be played back on the different types of users' devices that support the TV Now service. These data streams are called "**output profiles**". The transcoders convert the MPEG-2 signal into seven different data streams. One combined audio and video stream is for data in the QuickTime HTTP Live Streaming proprietary format used by Apple devices (**QuickTime Streaming**) ...The remaining six streams comprise three sets of an audio and a separate visual stream of data. Each set is in particular formats suitable for playback on one of the other three types of device capable of using the TV Now service.

31. Optus keeps a significant number of servers in its datacentre in Sydney. All the output profiles from Melbourne, Brisbane, Adelaide and Perth are sent as streams of data to the Sydney datacentre, as are the output profiles that are converted by the Sydney transcoders. The datacentre has the following equipment:

- two MACF [media application control framework] servers that control the TV Now service;

- routers that direct data from the network of computers in each of Brisbane, Melbourne, Perth and Adelaide (each known as a local area network (**LAN**)), to the LAN in Sydney, via a virtual private LAN;

- **recording controllers** or servers;

- a QuickTime Streaming server;

- a flash streaming server;

- a **network attached storage (NAS)** computer that is connected to and manages a large number of hard drives. The recording controllers and QuickTime Streaming server are connected and write data to the NAS;

- an electronic program guide engine;

- a user database.

32. The MACF servers display the electronic program guide for the TV Now service available in the five capital cities. When a user clicks on the "record" button for a program in the guide, that instruction is sent to the MACF servers which, in turn, enter this data in the user database. The MACF server enters or creates a schedule ID in respect of the program selected and the user's unique identifying number (**user ID**). Every time a user instructs the TV Now service to record a program the MACF server generates both a new schedule ID for that user's individual instruction and the user ID is entered against the schedule ID for each request.

33. The recording controllers ask or poll the user database once a minute enquiring whether any users have scheduled the recording of any programs due to be broadcast at the time of polling. If a user has instructed that a recording be made, the MACF server informs the recording controllers which then causes four recordings to be made on the NAS, one in each of the four output profiles for the user who gave that instruction. The recording controller notifies the MACF server, once a recording has begun, that the television program in relation to each particular schedule ID is being recorded. Thus, the user database contains the instructions of each user of the TV Now service to record a program for that user when it is later broadcast.

34. The MACF server then allocates an individual recording ID to each such recording and makes an entry in the user database linking the particular recording ID to the user ID associated with the instruction to make that recording. Thus, the MACF server is able to ascertain which particular recording was made for, and on the instruction of, which particular user. The MACF server will display information to the user about the recordings made for him or her or when the user next accesses the TV Now service. On the other hand, if no user has instructed that a program be recorded, no recording occurs (other than for no more than 60 seconds before deletion in the case of the Apple QuickTime Streaming server.

- The following occurs when a user decides to play a program he or she caused the TV Now service to record during the 30 day period before it is automatically deleted. The user clicks the "play" button for the desired program displayed in a list of recorded programs on the device he or she is using. This causes the MACF server to look up the recording ID associated with that user's ID in the user database. The equipment recognises the type of device that the user is then operating. It then causes the relevant streaming server to send to the device the compatible version of the output profile that is stored with the recording ID associated with the relevant user ID.

38 (vii) The parties have agreed certain facts for the purposes of the proceedings which are sufficient to found the controversy between them. These relate to the making of free-to-air broadcasts of AFL and NRL matches on specified days; the various copyright interests the appellants have in those broadcasts and films; the particular TV Now subscribers who selected and recorded football matches on those days and the time or times at which the respective subscribers viewed their recorded programme.

THE APPEAL ISSUES

1. Who "makes" the copy?

39 While s 86(a) and s 87(a) and (b) define the exclusive rights in relation to cinematograph films, television broadcasts and sound broadcasts respectively in understandably differing terms, for convenience in exposition those rights will be referred to in what follows as the right "to make a copy" of the film etc.

40 The present proceedings are yet another round in what has been described as the conflict between the electronic equipment industry and the entertainment industry: *CBS Songs Ltd v Amstrad Consumer Electronics PLC* at 1046; and see generally Ricketson, *The Law of Intellectual Property: Copyright, Designs & Confidential Information*, [9.600] ff. As is now characteristic in cases involving the allegedly infringing copying of films, television broadcasts and sound recordings, it is the entity which "facilitates" the copying — Optus — rather than the consumer who is the ben eficiary of it, whose acts have been called into question by the appellants.

41 The proper characterisation for copyright infringement purposes of what Optus — and, for that matter, a subscriber — does when a television broadcast is copied is made the less easy because the making of the copy utilises

very sophisticated technology, the process itself is highly automated and such communication as there is between a subscriber and Optus (and its technology), first, in subscribing and, then, in selecting what is to be recorded, is online.

(i) The trial judge's decision

42 The respective contentions of the parties at trial were, first (by AFL, NRL and Telstra) that Optus made the infringing copies of the broadcasts in issue and later communicated them to the subscribers who selected them; and, secondly (by Optus), that the respective subscribers made them and played them without any infringement of copyright because of the exception for private and domestic recording in s 111 of the Act. The trial judge accepted Optus' contention.

43 His Honour considered that the ordinary and natural meaning of "makes" and "making" as used in s 111(1) and (2) was "to create" by initiating a process utilising technology or equipment that recorded the broadcast. The subscriber made each of the copies in the four formats when he or she clicked on the "record" button on the electronic programme guide. The subscriber alone was responsible for the creation of the copies. No copies were made unless a subscriber required this to be done. The service that Optus offered was substantively no different from a VCR or DVR. This analogy, it should be noted, had been drawn in United States decisions and, notably for present purposes, *Cartoon Network LP, LLLP v CSC Holdings Inc* 536 F 3d 121 at 131-132 (2nd Cir 2008) which is considered later in these reasons. It was adopted as well by the Court of Appeal of Singapore in *Record TV Pte Ltd v MediaCorp TV Singapore Pte Ltd* [2011] 1 SLR 830 at [16] and [21]-[22]. His Honour referred approvingly to both decisions. We would note in passing that the appropriateness of the analogy itself as well as the broader reasoning in *Cartoon Network*, has been questioned in the US copyright scholarship: see Ginsburg, "Recent Developments in US Copyright Law — Part II, Caselaw: Exclusive Rights on the Ebb?" (2008) Columbia Public Law & Legal Theory Working Papers, Paper 08158.

44 His Honour further commented that the concept of "making a film or recording" in s 111 was not concerned with the technological or other means by which that result is created. Rather (at [64]) — It is unlikely that the Parliament intended to confine, in a presumptive way, the technology or other means available to be used by a person who wished to make a film solely for private or domestic use and subject to the other conditions in s 111.

45 To the extent that independent consideration was given to Optus' Service, it was said it provided a subscriber with the means to make a copy. Optus was in an analogous position to the University in *University of New South Wales v Moorhouse* [1975] HCA 26;(1975) 133 CLR 1 which supplied a photocopier for use by students in a library. As Gibbs J said in that case (at 11), it was "impossible to hold" that the University did the act of photocopying when the student copied part of a book in its library.

(ii) The parties' contentions

46 The issue of who made the copies is antecedent to the s 111 inquiries as to whether (a) the statutorily prescribed purpose informed their making and (b) the section could be invoked by the actual maker if it was not the user of the copies. The appellants in the two appeals now contend that the maker of a copy was Optus (or Optus and the subscriber jointly), the AFL going on to emphasise that the copies were made on, and stored in, the Service's NAS computer. They accept the term "make" can have nuanced differences in meaning depending on the context in which it is used: see the *Macquarie Dictionary*, "make". The proposed meanings they give it in the context of s 86(a), s 87(a) and (b), of s 101 (derivatively) and, for that matter, s 111 are (a) "To produce (a material thing) by giving a certain form to a portion of matter": AFL relying on *The Oxford English Dictionary's* primary usage of the senses in which the object of the verb "make" is a "product or thing": see OED Vol IX "make", 235 (2nd ed); and (b) variously, "to bring into existence by shaping material", or "to bring into a certain form", "to create": NRL and Telstra relying on the *Macquarie Dictionary*.

47 The appellants in substance contended that his Honour erred (i) in approaching the maker question through s 111; (ii) in finding that the subscriber alone did the acts involved in making a copy; (iii) in analogising the Service with a VCR, a DVR or a photocopier used by a third party; (iv) in disregarding Optus' heavy involvement in the creation of the copies, its responsibility for ensuring that a copy was made following a user's request and that Optus designed and maintained the system including its automation; (v) in relying upon US authority which, as will be seen, has a different jurisprudential context; (vi) in not concluding that Optus, rather than the subscriber, physically embodied the film etc copied (and hence "made" it) and, in any event, that Optus performed the last act necessary for the recording to be made (ie by its server informing its recording controller that the request to record had been made); (vii) in approaching the question as one of policy, as the overseas authorities relied upon appeared to, rather than as an orthodox question of statutory construction; and (viii) in not appreciating the significance of four copies, not one, being made.

48 Optus seeks to uphold the primary judge's findings. It emphasises that the person who made the copy was the person who did the act of making, eg by selecting the material to be copied and by initiating the other acts to create the copy. Optus merely provided the automated service by which the recording could be made. The dictionary definitions on which Optus relies in preference to the OED definition are drawn from the *Macquarie Dictionary*. They are "to produce by any action or causative agency", "to cause to be or become" and "to cause, induce or compel (to do something)". While Optus made four copies (none of which it used itself), this was to cover all of the contingencies of use of them the subscriber might make having regard to the compatible devices that, potentially, could be used to access the recordings. That Optus designed the Service and gave it its functionality, it is said, did not necessarily result in its being the maker of copies made using that functionality. Likewise the commercial nature of the Service provided is of no relevance to the identification of the maker of recordings using it.

(iii) Consideration

49 The question to be answered is easily stated: "Who 'does' the act of copying?": *Copinger and Skone James on Copyright*, 7-21 (16th ed, 2011). Its answering is the less easy because of the sophistication of the automated technologies used and the electronic communications made. Yet a legal person has to be identified who or which does that act. Considering the matter from the standpoint of s 101 of the Act, this identification requires an analysis both of who does what, when and where and of how the TV Now system itself functions. The rival contenders are Optus, the subscriber, or Optus and the subscriber jointly. Each can be advanced with varying plausibility in the circumstances as the person(s) who does the act of copying.

50 The first matter to be noted is Optus' TV Now Service itself. Optus designed it; gave it its functionality; owned the intellectual property in it (according to the board minutes of 28 February 2011); and marketed the service it provided to its customers. The system itself was configured so as to be able to receive, copy, store and permit the viewing of on compatible mobile and PC devices, the free-to-air broadcasts of the 15 TV channels in each of the five mainland State capitals. And it was fully automated. Its function in short was to receive, copy, store and stream to a subscriber's device, programmes required by a subscriber to the TV Now service.

51 It is unnecessary to describe again the process by which an individual Optus customer became a subscriber to this service and its three optional plans. What is clear is that the terms of the Optus-subscriber relationship were contractual in character. It again is unnecessary to consider here how these terms fitted into the larger contractual web between Optus and its customers. The terms and conditions to which the subscriber was required to agree personalised what the Service offers to a subscriber: it "allows you to record and store television shows. *You* can then access those recordings for a limited period"; it "is for *your* individual and personal use": italics in original. There is obvious licence and colloquialism in the language so used. The subscriber does not "store" television shows. Optus stores copies. To say that the subscriber "records" such shows and that Optus TV Now is for the subscriber's "use", are familiar and unexceptionable uses of language, but they by no means ordain the character of what a subscriber does (eg "records") and of the subscriber's relationship to the system itself (eg a "user" of it).

52 Before turning to how the act of copying fits within the Optus-subscriber relationship, one additional matter requires notice. Optus at all times retained possession, ownership and control of the physical copies made on the hard disc of its NAS computer until they were deleted by Optus after the expiry of 30 days from recording or by the subscriber before then. Viewing of the programmes copied was achieved by way of streaming the appropriate compatible version of playback data to the user's device. No data, no copies of the programme, were thereby stored in that device in any permanent form in that process.

53 There are four possible characterisations of the maker of the copies in this matter: (i) they were made by Optus but as agent for the subscriber; (ii) they were made by the subscriber as a principal using a facility made available by Optus pursuant to its contract with the subscriber; (iii) they were made by Optus as a principal using its own technology but subject to its contractual obligation to store and to allow subscriber viewing of the recordings so made at the time(s) of his or her choosing; or (iv) they were made jointly by Optus and the subscriber both of whom, consistent with their contract, acted in concert with one another pursuant to a common design to have a broadcast copied on Optus' technology and made available to be viewed by the subscriber.

(i) Agency

54 This possibility can be dismissed shortly. It seems only to have been raised by Optus in its appeal submissions and then only faintly. That the relationship of the subscriber and Optus in relation to the making of copies could be that of principal and agent, has no resonance at all either in the TV Now terms and conditions or, more generally, in the customer-service provider relationship of the parties. The invocation of agency here calls to mind Lord Herschell's comment in *Kennedy v De Trafford* [1897] AC 180 at 188 that "[n]o word is more commonly and constantly abused than the word 'agent'": see also *Scott v Davis* (2000) 204 CLR 333 at [227]. Even if Optus could properly be characterised as making the copy as agent, it would, nonetheless, "make the copy" and be jointly and severally liable with the subscriber for that making: see Dal Pont, *Law of Agency*, [24.8] (2nd ed, 2008).

(ii) The subscriber as principal

55 This is in essence what the primary judge has held and underpins Optus' submission. Put shortly, it is that Optus makes available to a subscriber a facility (a service) which enables the subscriber as and when he or she is so minded to use that facility to record broadcasts and later to view them. The copies that are made are the result of the subscriber's use of the facility though the actual making of them requires Optus' technology to function as it was designed to.

56 Underpinning this is a particular conception of what "make" means — a conception which robs the entirely automated copying process of any significance beyond that of being the vehicle which does the making of copies. As the primary judge put it, "make" means "to create" by selecting what is to be recorded and by initiating a process utilising technology or equipment that records the broadcast: Reasons [64]. Or, as Optus put it in submissions, it means "to cause, induce, or compel": the subscriber was the "causative agency" in the making of copies.

57 There are two additional matters relied upon in support of the contention that the subscriber is the maker. The *first* relates to the technology itself. It is that it is analogous, as his Honour suggested, to devices which can be used to make a copy of copyright material but which when so used by a third party do not result in the person who made, sold or hired out the device in question or in

whose possession or control the device remains, being held to be the "maker" of that copy. His Honour instanced the photocopier provided by the University to student copiers in *Moorhouse*, having earlier observed that the "service that TV Now offers the user is substantively no different from a VCR or DVR": Reasons [63]. The *second* matter, which flows from the facts that the subscriber both selects the programme to be copied and initiates the process of copying, is that the subscriber's is the last "volitional act" in the sequence of acts leading to a copy being made and, for that reason, is significant in determining the identity of the maker — the more so as a s 101 infringement requires a "person" to do or authorise the doing of, any "act" comprised in the copyright.

58 We consider that there are several reasons for rejecting the proposition that the subscriber was the maker for s 101, hence s 111, purposes. *First*, the meaning given "make" is, in our view, a contrived one. When s 86(a) refers to making a "copy" of a film, when s 87(a) refers to making a cinematograph film of a television broadcast or a copy of the film, when s 87(b) refers to making a sound recording or a copy of such, they each are referring to so acting as to embody images and sound in an "article or thing" (see the s 10 definitions of "cinematograph film" and "copy") or a "record". In our view "make", as it appears in s 86(a) and s 87(a) and (b), is a fundamental concept underpinning the Act and the essence of it is the idea of making (ie creating or producing) a physical thing (ie the embodiment of the copyright subject matter). We agree with the AFL's submission to this effect. The OED definition with its emphasis on producing a "material thing" is an apt one for the purposes of s 86(a) and s 87(a) and (b) — and hence for s 101(1) and s 111 of the Act. In saying this we do not discountenance the need for there to be a causative agency if a copy of a particular thing is to be made. The issue is not simply how something is made. It is by whom is it made. This, as will be seen, is of some importance when we come to consider whether copies were made by Optus and the subscriber jointly.

59 The *second* reason for rejecting the proposition that the subscriber alone is the maker relates to how the system itself works. This is better discussed when considering whether Optus itself is the maker. We merely note here that a subscriber's clicking on a button labelled "record" may trigger a sequence of actions which result in copies of a selected programme being made, but it does not necessarily follow that the subscriber alone makes that copy.

60 *Thirdly*, analogies are not necessarily helpful in this setting because they both divert attention from what the TV Now system has been designed to do and pre-suppose what is the function (albeit automated) it performs in the ongoing Optus-subscriber relationship. To anticipate matters, we consider that the system itself has been designed in a way that makes Optus the "main performer of the act of [copying]" (to adopt the language used in a recent Japanese decision involving a service relevantly similar to the present, which has been supplied to the Court in translation): see *Rokuraku II*, First Petty Bench of the Supreme Court, Japan, 20 January 2011.

61 *Fourthly,* there is some division between federal courts in the United States as how properly to differentiate between "direct" and "contributory" liability for copyright infringement where automated technologies are employed to make copies of copyright material: contrast eg *Cartoon Network LP, LLLP* and *Wolk v Kodak Imaging Network Inc* 2012 WL 11270 at 17-18 (SDNY) with *Arista Records LLC v Myxer Inc* 2011 US Dist Lexis 109668 at 12-13. In distinguishing the two forms of liability — a distinction which is of no concern to this Court in these appeals — the "volitional conduct" concept (and as well, the analogies with photocopier use by third parties and use of VCRs and DVRs) have been deployed.

62 So, in *Cartoon Network* (at 131-132) the United States Court of Appeals, Second Circuit, commented:

> [V]olitional conduct is an important element of direct liability ... In determining who actually "makes" a copy, a significant difference exists between making a request to a human employee, who then volitionally operates the copying system to make the copy, and issuing a command directly to a system, which automatically obeys commands and engages in no volitional conduct ... Here, by selling access to a system that automatically produces copies on command, Cablevision more closely resembles a store proprietor who charges customers to use a photocopier on his premises, and it seems incorrect to say, without more, that such a proprietor "makes" any copies when his machines are actually operated by his customers.

63 Whatever utility the volitional conduct concept has in distinguishing the two forms of infringement (given the need to do so in US jurisprudence), its adoption in this country would, in our view, require a gloss to be put on the word "make" in s 86(a) and s 87(a) and (b) of the Act. The need for so doing is not apparent to us, the more so because we have our own legislative and common law devices for imposing liability on third persons who are implicated or join in the infringing acts of another as, for example, by authorising the doing of such acts: see Copyright Act, s 101(1) and (1A) or by acting in concert with another to infringe copyright in pursuit of a common design: see eg *Aristocrat Technologies Australia Pty Ltd v Global Gaming Supplies Pty Ltd* at [620]-[624]; and see below *(iv) Optus and the subscriber jointly?*

64 It equally is not apparent to us why a person who designs and operates a wholly automated copying system ought as of course not be treated as a "maker" of an infringing copy where the system itself is configured designedly so as to respond to a third party command to make that copy: see generally the criticism of *Cartoon Network* in Ginsburg, at 15-18.

65 Although we have concluded that the subscriber cannot properly be said to be *the* maker of the copies in this matter, we return below to the question whether the subscriber can nonetheless be said to have acted jointly with Optus in making the copies.

(iii) Optus as the maker

66 It is the case that no copies will be made of a programme unless the subscriber selects that programme to be recorded and communicates his or her

confirmation of that selection to Optus, albeit by an electronic communication to its MACF servers. In at least this "but for" sense, the actions of the subscriber are causative of a recording later being made. Optus places emphasis on the necessity for that action of the subscriber, as well as the action of Optus, in setting up the system, in causing that recording to be made and, subsequently, causing the recording to be communicated to the subscriber. An Optus employee cannot press the record button. However, once that communication is made, the automated processes described by his Honour come into play — the server enters or creates a schedule ID in respect of the programme selected and the user's unique identifying number in the user database; the recording controllers poll that database once a minute enquiring whether any users have scheduled the recording of any programme due to be broadcast at the time of polling; when the poll so identifies that the user's selection is due to be broadcast, the MACF server informs the recording controllers which then cause four recordings to be made on the NAS hard disk — ie the timing of the recording coincides with Optus' recording controller causing the recording to be made, rather than when the subscriber communicates its selection to Optus.

67 Accepting as we do the appropriateness of the OED definition for the purposes of s 86, s 87 and s 101, we consider that Optus' role in the making of a copy — ie in capturing the broadcast and then in embodying its images and sounds in the hard disk — is so pervasive that, even though entirely automated, it cannot be disregarded when the "person" who does the act of copying is to be identified. The system performs the very functions for which it was created by Optus. Even if one were to require volitional conduct proximate to the copying, Optus' creating and keeping in constant readiness the TV Now system would satisfy that requirement. It should also be emphasised that the recording is made by reason of Optus' system remaining "up" and available to implement the subscriber's request at the time when its recording controllers poll the user database and receive a response indicating that a recording has been requested. What Optus actually does has — a nexus sufficiently close and causal to the illegal copying that one could conclude that the machine owner ... trespassed on the exclusive domain of the copyright owners: *CoStar Group Inc v LoopNet Inc* [2004] USCA4 133; 373 F3d 544 at 550 (4th Circ. 2004).

We would note this was quoted in *Cartoon Network* at 130.

68 Put shortly Optus is not merely making available its system to another who uses it to copy a broadcast: cf *CoStar Group Inc* at 550. Rather it captures, copies, stores and makes available for reward, a programme for later viewing by another: cf *New York Times Co Inc v Tasini* [2001] USSC 59; (2001) 533 US 483 at 504; and see Ginsburg at 15-16.

69 The real issue in consequence is whether Optus alone does the act of copying or whether Optus and the subscriber are jointly and severally responsible for that act.

(iv) Optus and the subscriber jointly?

70 The appellants' preferred characterisation of the Optus-subscriber relationship was that it was one in which Optus undertook to provide recordings of such free-to-air television programmes as the subscriber required to be recorded from time to time, the programmes after recording to be available to be viewed at the time or times of the subscriber's choosing on any one of four types of Optus compatible mobile phone or PC. It was, in short, a service for which Optus solicited subscribers and in which it was obliged to provide recordings for viewing of programmes the subscriber required to be recorded.

71 As the recording could only occur as and when the broadcast occurred of the programme sought but that programme itself had to be notified to Optus in advance, Optus established the wholly automated system, described above, which it so configured that the required recording did occur. If that part of the system embodied the steps taken by Optus to ensure that the required programme was recorded at the right time for the subscriber who required it, then the selection and notified confirmation by the subscriber of the programme required to be recorded could be said to be merely the necessary pre-condition to be satisfied to activate Optus' obligation to perform its service. If this be correct, then Optus can properly be identified as the maker of the copies of the recording. As the AFL has put it, Optus' data centre carries out the user's instruction to record a programme; it records that programme. In other words, if analogies are helpful in this particular setting (which we doubt), Optus is to be analogised with a commercial photocopier which copies copyright material provided to it for copying by it.

72 We would add that the circumstance of Optus making four copies to accommodate the four types of compatible playing devices on which a programme could be viewed lends support to this particular "service provision" conclusion. The parties ordinarily would not have agreed which device would be used to provide the viewing platform. Optus of necessity thus had to make four copies if it were to be able to discharge its obligation to provide the service required in all cases. It is difficult to characterise the subscriber, in using the service, as in all cases making four copies of the programme selected, some at least of which copies are likely to be of no use at all to him or her, in circumstances where the subscriber is probably unaware of the making of the four copies.

73 To view the matter in contractual terms, the terms and conditions of the Service are quite unyielding of any clear indication as to what actually is the true character of the parties relationship. Reference has already been made to the ambiguities, inaccuracies and colloquialism in formulae such as the system "allows you to record and store television shows". The system is "for your individual and personal use". Indeed the terms of the contract in this regard are in large measure unarticulated and must be inferred or implied if the agreement is to be given relevant content: cf *Hawkins v Clayton* (1988) 164 CLR 539 at 570-571. This said, it is more probable than not that a reasonable person, knowing the circumstances available to both parties, would characterise the relationship agreed between the parties (ie would infer or impute to them) that it was a contract by Optus to provide a service such as we have described above.

74 However, the contractual allocation of functions and responsibilities in making a copy of copyright material may, but does not necessarily, identify the person (or persons) who "make(s)" the copy for copyright infringement purposes. The making of the copy may be the product of the concerted action of both parties to the contract such that they together are the "makers" of the copy.

75 So one comes back to the question of construction raised by the word "make" and its application in the present setting. As we have indicated, Optus not only has solicited subscriber utilisation of its Service, it has also designed and maintained a sophisticated system which can effectuate the making of recordings wanted for viewing by subscribers. For s 101 purposes, it manifestly is involved directly in doing the act of copying. It counts as a maker of copies for the subscriber. Does the subscriber as well?

76 If one focussed not only upon the automated service which is held out as able to produce, and which actually produces, the copies but also on the causative agency that is responsible for the copies being made at all, the need for a more complex characterisation is suggested. The subscriber, by selecting the programme to be copied and by confirming that it is to be copied, can properly be said to be the person who instigates the copying. Yet it is Optus which effects it. Without the concerted actions of both there would be no copy made of a football match for the subscriber. Without the subscriber's involvement, nothing would be created; without Optus' involvement nothing would be copied. They have needed to act in concert to produce — they each have contributed to — a commonly desired outcome. The subscriber's contributing acts were envisaged by the contractual terms and conditions. How they were to be done were indicated by the prompts given on the Optus TV Now TV guide page. The common design — the production of the selected programme for transmission to the subscriber — informed the solicitation and the taking of a subscription by the subscriber; it was immanent in the service to be provided.

77 In consequence, they could both properly be said to be jointly and severally responsible for the act of making the copies.

78 While it is not strictly necessary for us to determine whether Optus alone is, or Optus and the subscriber are, the maker(s), our preferred view would be that both Optus and the subscriber, acting together, were the makers of the copies.

(iv) Conclusion

79 We have concluded that each cinematograph film and sound recording of the broadcasts and copies of the films in the Agreed Facts which was brought into existence after a subscriber had clicked the "record" button on that subscriber's Optus compatible device, was not made by the subscriber alone. It was made either by Optus alone or by Optus and the subscriber.

2. The s 111 exception

80 It is helpful at this point to reiterate the terms of s 111(1) and (2). They provide:

(1) This section applies if a person makes a cinematograph film or sound recording of broadcast solely for private and domestic use by watching or listening to the material broadcast at a time more convenient than the time when the broadcast is made.

(2) The making of the film or recording does not infringe copyright in the broadcast or in any work or other subject-matter included in the broadcast.

81 We have referred earlier both to various iterations of the s 111 exception in the sequence of drafts which culminated in the provisions enacted and to the various explanatory memoranda dealing with those iterations. We note this for this reason. If earlier draft provisions and explanatory memoranda are to be referred to (whether for the purposes of s 15AB of the Acts Interpretation Act 1901 (Cth) or as a matter of common law principle for the purposes of construction of the Act: see *CIC Insurance Ltd v Bankstown Football Club Ltd* (1997) 187 CLR 384 at 408) care must be taken to ensure that the observations in the explanatory memorandum being relied upon were not addressed to, and were to be understood by reference to, a version of the provision in question which was later amended in a relevantly operative way prior to its enactment: see Pearce and Geddes, *Statutory Interpretation in Australia*, [3.27] (7th ed, 2011) and see also *Avel Pty Ltd v Attorney-General for New South Wales* (1987) 11 NSWLR 126 at 128-129.

82 As we earlier observed, it was implicit in the terms of s 111 in its original draft form that, to attract the exception, the copy had to be made in domestic premises and the specified private and domestic purpose had to be that of the maker. As the matching explanatory memorandum made plain, the then provision would "allow individuals in their homes to copy a broadcast for personal use to enable it to be viewed or listened to at a more convenient time". The two subsequent amendments which directly affected s 111 and its interpretation were, first, the inclusion of a definition in s 10 of "private and domestic use" which allowed such use to be "on *or off* domestic premises" (emphasis added); and the requirement that copying itself be "in domestic premises" was removed.

83 There is one fundamental issue of construction which follows from the pre-enactment amendments made to s 111. The amendments ensured there was no prescribed *place of making or of viewing* a copy made solely for private and domestic etc purposes. But does the provision on its proper construction nonetheless prescribe a person (or class of persons) who can be the maker or viewer of the recording made?

84 One can put to one side any question relating to who are viewers whose watching is mandated by the section. That is not in issue here. We would note, though, that it seems to be accepted for present purposes that viewing by, say, close family members of the copy-maker could fall within the description "private and domestic".

85 In its original form the proposed s 111 addressed private copying by individuals in their own homes using personal recording devices. We emphasise that

for this reason. Optus has sought to draw comfort from an observation in the Explanatory Memorandum for the original form of s 111 which said:

> This [proposal] benefits domestic consumers who would be assured that time-shifting and format-shifting do not infringe copyright. *This option also provides legal certainty for industries that provide* products and *services that assist consumers carry out these copying activities.* It will also facilitate the growth of digital television and radio services. (Emphasis added.)

86 The emphasised passage, it is said, reveals that Parliament was alive to the possibility that these activities would be "outsourced" by consumers to business to conduct them, for them, without destroying the required purpose.

87 One need only repeat what we earlier said about the inappropriate use of an Explanatory Memorandum which relates to a version of a proposed section which materially differs from that enacted. Having regard to the terms of the original proposed s 111 and to its concern with private copying by individuals in their homes, the "certainty" being referred to in the above quoted passages was to industries that provided products and services to assist them so to carry out such copying. Further in the immediately following paragraph of that Explanatory Memorandum it was observed:

> This [proposal] impacts on the owners of the copyright in television program content. However, *in simply recognising present practices*, market impact is likely to be negligible. (Emphasis added.)

> This is hardly likely to have been said if outsourcing to commercial providers was in contemplation.

88 The changes made by the two pre-enactment amendments removed the requirements that the copies be made and watched in domestic premises. There is nothing to suggest that they in any way affected the clear premise of both the originally proposed s 111 and s 111 as enacted. They both were concerned with private copying done by individuals for the prescribed purpose. If the language of the section is said to raise any doubt about this, the explanation given in the Further Supplementary Explanatory Memorandum (dealing with the amendment eliminating the *place of making* requirement) dispels that doubt:

> 1. This amendment provides greater flexibility in the conditions that apply to "time-shift" recording. The development of digital technologies is likely to result in increasing use of personal consumer devices and other means which enable individuals to record television and radio broadcasts on or off domestic premises. *The revised wording of s 111 enables an individual to record broadcasts, as well as view and listen to the recording, outside their homes as well as inside for private and domestic use.*

(Emphasis added.)

89 There is nothing in the language, or the provenance, of s 111 to suggest that it was intended to cover commercial copying on behalf of individuals. Moreover, the natural meaning of the section is that the person who makes the copy is the person whose purpose is to use it as prescribed by s 111(1). Optus may well be

said to have copied programmes so that *others* can use the recorded programme for the purpose envisaged by s 111. Optus, though, makes no use itself of the copies as it frankly concedes. It merely stores them for 30 days. And its purpose in providing its service — and, hence in making copies of programmes for subscribers — is to derive such market advantage in the digital TV industry as its commercial exploitation can provide. Optus cannot invoke the s 111 exception.

90 This conclusion on the proper construction of s 111, when coupled with our conclusions on who is, or are, the maker(s) of the copies of a football match, is sufficient to dispose of this appeal.

91 If Optus alone was the maker, it has infringed the copyright interests of the AFL, the NRL partners and Telstra as claimed.

92 If both Optus and the subscriber were the makers of the copies made for that subscriber, a similar result ensues but for somewhat different reasons. But for the operation of s 111, they each would be jointly and *severally* liable for doing the acts comprised in the copyright of the respective owners. Each, we would emphasise, can be sued as *the* maker without joinder of the other. For present purposes we will assume that the subscriber in making his or her copies did so for the purposes prescribed by s 111 (there is an evidentiary dispute about this). If the subscriber was sued as a maker of the copies made to provide the programme he or she selected, that person could rely on s 111. No claim has been made against a subscriber, so there is no need to resolve whether any subscriber has been proved to have made a copy for the purpose prescribed in the section.

93 Section 111 offers no solace to Optus. It alone has been sued. It is severally liable as the person who did the acts of copying and that liability is not a secondary one dependent upon the primary liability of the subscriber: see Ginsburg, at 17 for the US position. It must bear the consequences of its actions.

Policy and a technologically neutral interpretation

94 Two matters bearing on interpretation have been themes in the case put by the respondent. They have some resonance both in the primary judge's reasons and in the United States and Singaporean case law on which he relied. The first is what has been described as "technologically neutral interpretation"; the second is what can be described as "interpretation informed by legislative policy".

95 The desirability of technological neutrality — of not limiting rights and defences to technologies known at the time when those rights and defences were enacted — has been acknowledged for some time. So it was, for example, that one declared objective stated in the Explanatory Memorandum to the *Copyright Amendment (Digital Agenda) Bill 1999* (Cth) was:

> To replace technology-specific rights with technology-neutral rights so that amendments to the Act are not needed each time there is a development in technology.

96 We are conscious that the construction which we are satisfied the language of s 111 requires is one that is capable of excluding, and does in fact in this instance exclude, a later technological development in copying. However, no

principle of technological neutrality can overcome what is the clear and limited legislative purpose of s 111. It is not for this Court to re-draft this provision to secure an assumed legislative desire for such neutrality: *R v L* (1994) 49 FCR 534 at 538.

97 This, in turn, brings into focus more generally what we have called interpretation informed by legislative policy. In varying guises and to differing extents, this has been a tool of statutory interpretation for many centuries. Its historical exemplar was the doctrine of the "equity of the statute": see *Nelson v Nelson* [1995] HCA 25; (1995) 184 CLR 538 at 552-554; *Comcare v Thompson* [2000] FCA 790; (2000) 100 FCR 375 at [40]- [43]. Its principal modern manifestation is in that form of purposive construction enjoined by s 15AA of the *Acts Interpretation Act 1901* (Cth). However, if the apparently confined words of a statute are to be given a more extended scope, not only must they be capable as a matter of language of sustaining such an extension, there must also be some indication in the legislation, its purpose and context of whether, and if so how, the legislature would wish to extend what, on its face, is the confined scope of the statute or of a section of it: see *Woodside Energy Ltd v Federal Commissioner of Taxation* [2009] FCAFC 12; (2009) 174 FCR 91 at [51].

98 What a court cannot do, as the plurality in the High Court recently emphasised in *Australian Education Union v Department of Education and Children's Services* [2012] HCA 3 at [28] is to adopt:

> ... a judicially constructed policy at the expense of the requisite consideration of the statutory text and its relatively clear purpose. In construing a statute it is not for a court to construct its own idea of a desirable policy, impute it to the legislature, and then characterise it as a statutory purpose.

And even if legislative purposes are discernible, it is salutary to remember, as was said in *Rodriguez v United States* [1987] USSC 36; 480 US 522 at 525-526 (1987):

> ... no legislation pursues its purposes at all costs. Deciding what competing values will or will not be sacrificed to the achievement of a particular objective is the very essence of legislative choice — and it frustrates rather than effectuates legislative intent simplistically to assume that *whatever* furthers the statute's primary object must be the law.

99 In the present matter such are the conflicting interests and values, such are the possible consequential considerations of which account might need to be taken that, if a choice is to be made to extend or otherwise modify an exception such as s 111, this requires a legislative choice to be made, not a judicial one.

CONCLUSION

100 We should emphasise that our concerns here have been limited to the particular service provider-subscriber relationship of Optus and its subscribers to the TV Now Service and to the nature and operation of the particular technology used to provide the service in question. We accept that different relationships

and differing technologies may well yield different conclusions to the "who makes the copy" question.

101 We will order that in both appeals:

(1) The appeal be allowed.

(2) The declarations and orders 1 to 5 made by the primary judge be set aside.

We will direct that, in each appeal, the respective appellants bring in draft minutes of consequential orders on or before 4 May 2012 to give effect to these reasons.

---

5. Authorizing Infringement

The *Copyright Act* grants the owner of a copyright the exclusive right to authorize the exercise of the copyright holder's exclusive rights.[29] It follows that anyone who authorizes the performance of an act that is the exclusive right of the owner of the copyright, absent a license to do so, infringes such right. As the right to authorize any of the exclusive rights provided by the Act constitutes a distinct right granted to the copyright owner, a person may be held liable for infringement of that right, regardless of whether or not the alleged infringer ultimately infringes the separate right.[30] Thus, for example, a person may be liable for authorizing the unlawful reproduction of a work, even if it is not established that the person given the authorization ultimately reproduced the work. However, the authorization of an ultimately non-infringing act will not give rise to liability; it is therefore not an infringement to authorize a person to perform an act that would constitute fair dealing, for example.

The term "authorize" has been judicially construed to include anyone who "sanctions, approves, or countenances" the infringing activity. It has been authoritatively settled in Canada, that the term "countenance" in the context of authorizing copyright infringement must be understood in its strongest dictionary meaning, namely, "give approval to, sanction, permit, favour or encourage".[31]

To authorize an act, the alleged infringer must grant or purport to grant, either expressly or by implication, the right to do the act complained of. Further, the grantor must have some degree of actual or apparent right to control the actions of the grantee before he will be taken to have authorized the act. An act is not authorized by somebody who merely enables or possibly assists or even encourages another to do that act, but who does not purport to have any authority which he can grant to justify the doing of the act. The

---

29 Section 3(1).

30 *CCH Canadian Ltd. v. Law Society of Upper Canada* (2002), 18 C.P.R. (Fed. C.A.), affirmed 2004 SCC 13.

31 *CCH Canadian Ltd. v. Law Society of Upper Canada*, 2004 SCC 13, at para. 38.

courts also presume that a person who authorizes an activity does so only so far as it is in accordance with law. This presumption may be rebutted if it shown that a certain relationship or degree of control existed between the alleged authorizer and the person who committed the copyright infringement.

It has consistently been held in Canada that it is not infringement to merely supply a person with equipment or other means of infringing a copyright even if the person supplying the equipment or other means of infringement knows that it will probably be used to infringe. This will be so particularly if the supplier has no control over how the means will be used. Where, however, a person retains control over the means in question, the facts may warrant a finding of implicit authorization. Similarly, infringement may occur where the means of infringement are supplied, and such supply is bound to lead to an infringement and was made specifically for that purpose.

CBS Songs Ltd. v. Amstrad Consumer Electronics TLC, [1988] A.C. 1013 (H.L.)

Lord Keith of Kinkel, Lord Templeman, Lord Griffiths, Lord Oliver of Aylmerton and Lord Jauncey of Tullichettle

1988 March 15, 16, 17, 21, 22, 23; May 12

. . .

LORD TEMPLEMAN.

My Lords, during the past half-century there have been continuous improvements in sciences and techniques concerned with the transmission, reception, recording and reproduction of sounds and signals. These developments were required for serious purposes such as war, espionage, safety and communications. The benefits of advances made for serious purposes have been employed for purposes of leisure and pleasure and have spawned two flourishing industries, the electronic equipment industry and the entertainment industry. The electronic equipment industry manufactures and sells sophisticated machines which enable individual members of the public to transmit, receive, record and reproduce sounds and signals in their own homes. The entertainment industry transmits and records entertainment on an enormous scale. Each industry is dependent on the other. Without the public demand for entertainment, the electronic equipment industry would not be able to sell its machines to the public. Without the facilities provided by the electronic equipment industry, the entertainment industry could not provide entertainment in the home and could not, for example, maintain orchestras which fill the air with 20th century cacophony or make gratifying profit from a recording of a group without a voice singing a song without a tune. Although the two industries are interdependent and flourish to their mutual satisfaction there is one area in which their interests conflict. It is in the interests of the electronic equipment industry to put on the market every facility which is likely to induce customers to purchase new machines made by the industry. It is in the interests of the entertainment industry to maintain a monopoly in the reproduction of entertainment. Facilities for recording and reproducing incorporated in machines sold to the public by the electronic equipment industry are capable of being utilised by members of the public to copy the published works of the entertainment industry, thus reducing the public demand for the original works and recordings of the entertainment industry itself. The electronic equipment industry invents and markets new and improved facilities which enable records to be made and copied. The public make use of those facilities to copy the recordings issued by recording companies and thus infringe the copyrights of the recording companies and of the composers, lyricists and others engaged in the entertainment industry. Hence arises the conflict between the electronic equipment industry and the entertainment industry which has resulted in these present proceedings.

This appeal is the climax of a conflict between the makers of records and the makers of recording equipment. The appellants, the British Phonographic Industry Ltd. ("B.P.I."), represent the makers of records while the respondents, Amstrad Consumer Electronics Plc. and Dixons Ltd., represent the makers and sellers respectively of recording equipment. B.P.I. argue that it is unlawful for Amstrad to make recording equipment which will be used by members of the public to copy records in which copyright subsists. In the alternative, B.P.I. argue that Amstrad must not advertise their equipment in such a way as to encourage copying. Amstrad and Dixons argue that they may lawfully make and sell to the public any recording equipment which ingenuity may devise and may lawfully advertise the advantages of such equipment.

. . .

Section 1(1) of the Act of 1956 confers on the copyright owners in a record the "exclusive right... to authorise other persons" to copy the record. B.P.I. submit that by selling a model which incorporates a double-speed twin-tape recorder Amstrad "authorise" the purchaser of the model to copy a record in which copyright subsists and therefore Amstrad infringe the exclusive right of the copyright owner. My Lords, twin-tape recorders, fast or slow, and single-tape recorders, in addition to their recording and playing functions, are capable of copying on to blank tape, directly or indirectly, records which are broadcast, records on discs and records on tape. Blank tapes are capable of being employed for recording or copying. Copying may be lawful or unlawful. Every tape recorder confers on the operator who acquires a blank tape the facility of copying; the double-speed twin-tape recorder provides a modern and efficient facility for continuous playing and continuous recording and for copying. No manufacturer and no machine confers on the purchaser authority to copy unlawfully. The purchaser or other operator of the recorder determines whether he shall copy and what he shall copy. By selling the recorder Amstrad may facilitate copying in breach of copyright but do not authorise it.

B.P.I.'s next submission is that Amstrad by their advertisement authorise the purchaser of an Amstrad model to copy records in which copyright subsists. Amstrad's advertisement drew attention to the advantages of their models and to the fact that the recorder incorporated in the model could be employed in the copying of modern records. But the advertisement did not authorise the unlawful copying of records; on the contrary, the footnote warned that some copying required permission and made it clear that Amstrad had no authority to grant that permission. If Amstrad had considered the interests of copyright owners, Amstrad could have declined to incorporate double-tape double-speed recorders in Amstrad's models or could have advertised the illegality of home copying. If Amstrad had deprived themselves of the advantages of offering improved recording facilities, other manufacturers would have reaped the benefit. The effect of double-tape double-speed recorders on the incidence of home copying is altogether speculative. If Amstrad had advertised the illegality of home copying the effect would have been minimal. Amstrad's advertisement was deplorable because Amstrad thereby flouted the rights of copyright owners. Amstrad's advertisement was cynical because Amstrad advertised the increased efficiency of a facility capable of being employed to break the law. But the operator of an Amstrad tape recording facility, like all other operators, can alone decide whether to record or play and what material is to be recorded. The Amstrad advertisement is open to severe criticism but no purchaser of an Amstrad model could reasonably deduce from the facilities incorporated in the model or from Amstrad's advertisement that Amstrad possessed or purported to possess the authority to grant any required permission for a record to be copied.

In Monckton v. Pathé Frères Pathephone Ltd. [1914] 1 K.B. 395 Buckley L.J. said, at p. 403: "The seller of a record authorises, I conceive, the use of the record, and such user will be a performance of the musical work." In that case a performance of the musical work by the use of the record was bound to be an infringing use and the record was sold for that purpose. In Evans v. E. Hulton and Co. Ltd. (1924) 131 L.T. 534, 535, Tomlin J. said that:

> "where a man sold the rights in relation to a manuscript to another with the view to its production, and it was in fact produced, both the English language and common sense required him to hold that this man had 'authorised' the printing and publication."

The object of the sale, namely publication, was bound to infringe. In Falcon v. Famous Players Film Co. [1926] 2 K.B. 474, the defendants hired to a cinema a film based on the plaintiff's play. It was held that the defendants infringed the plaintiff's exclusive right conferred by the Copyright Act 1911 to authorise a performance of the play. Here again, the hirer sold the use which was only capable of being an infringing use. Bankes L.J., at p. 491, following Monckton v. Pathé Frères Pathephone Ltd. and Evans v. Hulton, accepted that for the purpose of the Act of 1911 the expression "authorise " meant "sanction, approve, and countenance." Atkin L.J. said, at p. 499:

> "to 'authorise' means to grant or purport to grant to a third person the right to do the act complained of, whether the intention is that the grantee shall do the act on his own account, or only on account of the grantor;..."

In the present case, Amstrad did not sanction, approve or countenance an infringing use of their model and I respectfully agree with Atkin L.J. and with Lawton L.J. in the present case[FN3] [1986] F.S.R. 159, 207 that in the context of the Copyright Act 1956 an authorisation means a grant or purported grant, which may be express or implied, of the right to do the act complained of. Amstrad conferred on the purchaser the power to copy but did not grant or purport to grant the right to copy.

> FN3 Amstrad Consumer Electronics Plc. v. British Phonographic Industry Ltd. [1986] F.S.R. 159, 207.

In Moorhouse v. University of New South Wales [1976] R.P.C. 151 in the High Court of Australia where the facilities of a library included a photocopying machine, Gibbs J. said, at p. 159:

> "a person who has under his control the means by which an infringement of copyright may be committed — such as a photocopying machine — and who makes it available to other persons, knowing, or having reason to suspect, that it is likely to be used for the purpose of committing an infringement, and omitting to take reasonable steps to limit its use to legitimate purposes, would authorise any infringement that resulted from its use."

Whatever may be said about this proposition, Amstrad have no control over the use of their models once they are sold. In this country the duties of some libraries are defined by the Copyright (Libraries) Regulations 1957 (S.I. 1957 No. 868) made under section 15 of the Act of 1956.

In C.B.S. Inc. v. Ames Records & Tapes Ltd. [1982] Ch. 91, Whitford J. held that a record library which lent out records and simultaneously offered blank tapes for sale at a discount did not authorise the infringement of copyright in the records. He said, at p. 106:

> "Any ordinary person would, I think, assume that an authorisation can only come from somebody having or purporting to have authority and that an act is not authorised by somebody who merely enables or possibly assists or even encourages another to do that act, but does not purport to have any authority which he can grant to justify the doing of the act."

This precisely describes Amstrad.

In R.C.A. Corporation v. John Fairfax & Sons Ltd. [1982] R.P.C. 91 in the High Court of Australia, Kearney J., at p. 100, approved a passage in Laddie, Prescott & Vitoria, The Modern Law of Copyright (1980), para. 12.9, p. 403, in these terms:

> "a person may be said to authorise another to commit an infringement if the one has some form of control over the other at the time of infringement or, if he has no such control, is responsible for placing in the other's hands materials which by their nature are almost inevitably to be used for the purpose of infringement."

This proposition seems to me to be stated much too widely. As Whitford J. pointed out in the Ames case, at p. 107:

"you can home tape from bought records, borrowed records, borrowed from friends or public libraries, from the playing of records over the radio, and indeed, at no expense, from records which can be obtained for trial periods on introductory offers from many record clubs who advertise in the papers, who are prepared to let you have up to three or four records for a limited period of trial, free of any charge whatsoever."

These borrowed records together with all recording machines and blank tapes could be said to be "materials which by their nature are almost inevitably to be used for the purpose of an infringement." But lenders and sellers do not authorise infringing use.

For these reasons, which are to be found also in the judgments of the Court of Appeal, at pp. 207, 210 and 217, I am satisfied that Amstrad did not authorise infringement.

De Tervagne v. Beloeil (1993), 50 C.P.R. (3d) 419 (F.C.T.D.)

Joyal J.

Montréal: November 3, 1992
Montréal: November 24, 1992
Montréal: January 12, 1993
Ottawa: May 4, 1993
Docket: T-36-91

. . .

The following is the English version of the reasons for judgment rendered by Joyal J.:

1 This is an action for damages brought by the plaintiffs against the defendants for copyright infringement. The plaintiffs contend that the defendants authorized the public performance of the work Pique-Nique en Ville without their consent, which was presented at the Centre culturel de Beloeil from June 17 to August 25, 1990. Accordingly, the plaintiffs claim damages representing a lump sum for all of the performances or a sum representing all of the profits realized by the defendants.

. . .

(2) Review of the case law:

21 The fundamental doctrine in this area has been expressed as follows: "The legislator specifies that, besides the rights set out elsewhere in s. 3(1), the copyright owner holds the right to authorize any of these acts. Consequently, the authorization of any act reserved for the author without his consent constitutes infringement [at page 151]." "Thus, a person reproducing a work must first obtain the consent of the owner of the copyright or any other person authorized to consent [at page 240]." Otherwise, he or she commits an infringement. (See The Annotated Copyright Act 1991, Normand Tamaro, Carswell, 1991.)

22 The meaning which is to be given to the expression "authorize", as it is used by Parliament in subsection 3(1) of the Act, has been interpreted on a number of occasions in the case law.

23 First, in England, it was established in Falcon v. Famous Players Film Co., [1926] 2 K.B. 474 (C.A.), that the expression "authorize" must be interpreted in its ordinary sense as meaning "sanction, approve and countenance". In that decision, the author of a dramatic work had assigned the sole performing right in his work in the United Kingdom to the plaintiff. Subsequently, the author sold motion picture rights in his work throughout the world to the defendants. The defendants then produced a film based on the work in question and granted the owner of a theatre in the United Kingdom the right to exhibit the film. The Court of Appeal held that the defendants had authorized the owner of the theatre to exhibit the film, and were therefore liable for infringement of the plaintiff's performing right. Bankes L.J. stated, at page 491:

> In the present statute, that language has been deliberately dropped, and for the word "cause" has been substituted the word "authorise"; and the decision of Tomlin J. in Evans v. Hulton and the dictum of Buckley L.J. in Monckton v. Pathé Frères, both clearly indicate that in the opinion of these learned judges the present expression is to be understood in its ordinary dictionary sense of "sanction, approve, and countenance."

24 At page 499, Atkin L.J. restricted the definition of the expression "authorize" as follows:

> For the purposes of this case it appears to me that to "authorize" means to grant or purport to grant to a third person the right to do the act complained of, whether the intention is that the grantee shall do the act on his own account, or only on account of the grantor....

25 In Canada, three decisions in particular have interpreted the concept of authorization. In Underwriters' Survey Bureau Ltd. et al. v. Massie & Renwick Ltd., [1938] Ex.C.R. 103, affirmed [in this respect] by the Supreme Court of Canada at [1940] S.C.R. 218, Maclean J. confirmed, at page 122, that the definition of the expression "authorize" laid down in the English decision in Falcon's case, supra, applies in Canada:

> The word "authorize", in the last line of s. 3(1) of the Copyright Act has been judicially construed to include anyone who sanctions, approves, or countenances....

26 Another case, which is Canadian in origin although it was decided by the Privy Council, is Vigneux et al. v. Canadian Performing Right Society (1943), 4 Fox Pat. C. 183. In that decision the defendants Vigneux Brothers, had supplied a phono graph to the restaurant owned by the co-defendant Raes, for which they supplied records in return for a fixed monthly rental. The plaintiff C.P.R.S. asserted that the defendants had authorized the public performance of the musical piece Star Dust which had been played on the defendants' machine on one occasion. The Privy Council held that the defendants Vigneux Brothers could not be held liable for having authorized the public performance of the work in question, since they had no control over the use of the machine. At page 194 of

the decision, Lord Russell states that Vigneux Brothers did not give the alleged performance, nor did they authorize it:

> They had no control over the use of the machine; they had no voice as to whether at any particular time it was to be available to the restaurant customers or not. The only part which they played in the matter was, in the ordinary course of their business, to hire out to Raes one of their machines and supply it with records, at a weekly rental of ten dollars.

27 At page 152 of his work The Annotated Copyright Act 1991, the author Normand Tamaro, supra, interprets this passage from the reasons of Lord Russell as follows:

> The person authorizing the performance of a work by mechanical means, and not the one simply providing it, is the one who is in control of the instrument.
>
> . . .
>
> In other words, the person authorizing the performance is the person making it possible.
>
> . . .
>
> [TRANSLATION] It therefore cannot be argued that the person whose role is nothing more than to supply the means by which the public performance of the work is made possible authorizes a public performance.

28 In England, Whitford J. took the same position in CBS Inc v. Ames Records & Tapes Ltd, [1981] 2 All E.R. 812 (Ch. D.). In that case, Whitford J. decided that a record shop which rented out records and at the same time offered blank cassettes at discount prices was not authorizing copyright infringement. At page 821, he stated:

> Any ordinary person would, I think, assume that an authorisation can only come from somebody having or purporting to have authority and that an act is not authorised by somebody who merely enables or possibly assists or even encourages another to do an act, but does not purport to have any authority which he can grant to justify the doing of the act.

29 However, we should not forget two Australian decisions which adopted a somewhat different interpretation. First, in Moorhouse v. University of New South Wales, [1976] R.P.C. 151 (Aust. H.C.), a library had installed photocopying services in its premises. On that point, Gibbs J. held [at page 159]:

> ...a person who has under his control the means by which an infringement of copyright may be committed — such as a photocopying machine — and who makes it available to other persons, knowing, or having reason to suspect, that it is likely to be used for the purpose of committing an infringement, and omitting to take reasonable steps to limit its use to legitimate purposes, would authorise any infringement that resulted from its use. [Emphasis added.]

30 In another Australian case, RCA Corporation v. John Fairfax & Sons Ltd., [1982] R.P.C. 91 (N.S.W.S.C.), at page 100, Kearney J. approved the following passage taken from The Modern Law of Copyright (1980) by Laddie, Prescott and Victoria:

...a person may be said to authorize another to commit an infringement if the one has some form of control over the other at the time of infringement or, if he has no such control, is responsible for placing in the other's hands materials which by their nature are almost inevitably to be used for the purpose of an infringement.

31 This interpretation by the Australian courts must be rejected in Canada, in view of Vigneux, which clearly established that a defendant who simply supplies the means which make the infringement possible cannot be held liable for authorizing the infringement if he or she had no control over the means in question. However, we must note that the decision of the Privy Council in Vigneux has often been criticized since it is contrary to the English decisions which preceded it, such as Falcon's case. In his annotation preceding Vigneux at 4 Fox Pat. C. 183, Fox made the following comment [at page 184]:

> In the present case Vigneux supplied the gramophone and the record. It received payment for both services and gave into the hands of those who gave the performance the means of causing the copyrighted musical work to be performed. It is therefore difficult to ascertain the basis upon which the Board could hold that Vigneux did not authorise the performance. Authorisation does not need to be specific. Even an absence of effort to prevent infringement seems, on the cases, to be sufficient to bring a person within the meaning of the term "authorise". Of course, there must be some control by the person "authorising" over the person performing, but it cannot be said that Vigneux were strangers to the arrangement. It would seem, therefore, that this case may cast some doubt on the authority of such decisions as Performing Right Society v. Mitchell & Booker (Palais de Danse) Ltd., [1924] 1 K.B. 762; Canadian Performing Right Society Ltd. v. Canadian National Exhibition Association, [1934] O.R. 610; Canadian Performing Right Society Ltd. v. Canadian National Exhibition Association, [1938] O.R. 476.

32 Following the decision in Vigneux, the Supreme Court of Victoria decided to the contrary in Winstone v. Wurlitzer Automatic Phonograph Co. of Australia Pty. Ltd., [1946] V.L.R. 338 Vict. S.C. In that case, the defendant had installed a phonograph belonging to the defendant company in his restaurant. The plaintiff asserted that the musical work in which he owned the copyright had been played twice in the defendant's restaurant. The Court held that the owner of the restaurant and the defendant company had authorized the public performance of the work in question. The fact that the defendant company had supplied the records for the phonograph was sufficient to find that it had authorized the public performance of the work since, unlike the facts in Vigneux, the defendant company was to receive a share of the profits. This was therefore a joint venture by the defendants, while in Vigneux the relationship was simply in the normal course of the business of the defendants' rental firm.

33 The Supreme Court of Canada had occasion to comment on Vigneux in Muzak Corp. v. Composers, Authors, etc., [1953] 2 S.C.R. 182. In that case, the Supreme Court of Canada did not consider it appro priate to limit the scope of the decision in Vigneux or to criticize the decision rendered. Rather, Kellock J. clearly adopted the passage from the reasons of Lord Russell dealing with the element of control, thereby reaffirming the principle established by him. Accordingly, Vigneux applies in Canada.

34 Before moving on to an analysis of Muzak, supra, however, let us examine the decisions on which the plaintiffs rely in asserting that the defendants authorized the public performance of the play Pique-Nique en Ville.

35 First, in Canadian Performing Right Society Ltd. v. Canadian National Exhibition Association, [1934] O.R. 610 (H.C.), Rose C.J.H.C. held that the defendants had authorized the public performance of a substantial part of a musical work in which the plaintiffs owned the copyright, when the work in question was played during one of the performances organized by the defendants. Rose C.J.H.C. concluded that, despite the fact that the defendants had not specifically instructed the musicians to play the work in question, they had control over the band and were therefore liable for the negligence of their servants in the performance of their duty. At page 615, Rose C.J.H.C. added that the test for determining whether a person is a servant or an independent contractor was laid down in Performing Right Society v. Mitchell & Booker (Palais de Danse), Ld., [1924] 1 K.B. 762, by McCardie J., who stated at page 767: "the final test... and certainly the test to be generally applied, lies in the nature and degree of detailed control over the person alleged to be a servant." Also [at page 769]: "[b]y the employer is meant the person who has a right at the moment to control the doing of the act." In the case before him, Rose C.J.H.C. concluded that there was a master-servant relationship between the defendants and the bandmaster, given the degree of control exercised by the defendants over him. Despite the fact that there had been no agreement made between the parties as to the selection of musical works, it was clear that the defendants were able to dictate the conduct of the band.

36 In Canadian Performing Right Society Ltd. v. Canadian National Exhibition Association, [1938] O.R. 476 (H.C.), the defendant had hired Rudy Vallee and his orchestra to play at its dance hall. Greene J. found, at pages 483-484, that the contract between the parties did not give the defendants any control over the selection of musical works or the times when the orchestra was to play. Thus the defendants exercised no control over the orchestra, and under the test established by McCardie J. in Palais de Danse, supra, the orchestra was not a servant but an independent contractor. Greene J. held, however, that this was not sufficient to relieve the defendant of liability since the defendant had made no effort to ensure that the orchestra did not play works protected by copyright. Greene J. therefore held that the defendant had authorized the public performance, under subsection 3(1) of the Act, since the expression "authorize" had to be interpreted in its ordinary sense of "sanction, approve or countenance".

37 Finally, in Can. Performing Right Soc. v. Ming Yee, [1943] 4 D.L.R. 732 (Alta. Dist. Ct.), the defendant was the owner of a restaurant and had hired an orchestra to play dance music in his restaurant. No agreement had been made with the orchestra leader as to the selection of musical pieces, and the defendant was not aware in advance of what pieces would be played by the orchestra. The evidence revealed, however, that the orchestra leader played whatever piece the defendant called for, and on the other hand would not have played a piece forbidden by the defendant. Ford D.C.J., at pages 734-735, concluded that even

if the orchestra leader was not a servant in the strict sense of the word, under the test established by McCardie J. in Palais de Danse, supra, given the lack of practical control by the defendant over the orchestra, it was nonetheless clearly established that there was a principal-agent relationship. The orchestra leader had acted within the scope of his employment and for the benefit of the defendant. By giving total discretion to the orchestra leader, the defendant tacitly authorized the performance of the two pieces in question. Thus the defendant was liable for the infringement committed by his employee.

38 The final decision which we should examine is the decision of the Supreme Court of Canada in Muzak Corp. v. Composers, Authors, etc., supra. This is the leading decision in Canada interpreting the concept of authorization. Briefly, the facts are as follows. CAPAC was the owner of the sole right to perform certain musical works in public throughout Canada. CAPAC submitted that Muzak Corporation had authorized the performance of the works by leasing recordings containing the musical works in question to the Canadian ABC franchise (a broadcasting company); these recordings contained the musical pieces in question, which recordings were subsequently broadcast in public by ABC. In its decision, the Supreme Court rejected the authorization connection. First, Rand J. stated that the mere fact of supplying the means which permitted a person to commit an infringement did not amount to authorization. Kellock J. added that unless what was done by a defendant was to sanction, approve or countenance a performance, it cannot be established that such a defendant authorized a performance or representation.

39 In an article "Home Copying and Authorization" (1983), 67 C.P.R. (2d) 1983, pages 17-49, P.D. Hitchcock offers an excellent analysis of the decision in Muzak. At pages 29-33, the author sets out three principles which were applied and laid down by the Supreme Court of Canada in Muzak.

40 "The first principle that was applied in Muzak was that in order to 'authorize' within the meaning of the Copyright Act, a person must sanction, approve or countenance something more than the mere use of equipment that might possibly be used in an actual infringement of a copyright. Furthermore, the court makes the presumption that a person who authorized an activity authorized that activity only so far as the activity is in accordance with law." On this point, Rand J. stated, at page 189:

> Obviously, in one sense, Muzak authorizes Associated to make use of instruments which it owns but that use is to be in accordance with regulations dealing with it. There is not a syllable in the material to suggest that Muzak has made itself a party in interest to the performance either by warranting the right to perform without fee or by anything in the nature of a partnership or similar business relation. If by letting a device the owner is to be taken as engaging himself to its use in defiance of regulations, the very distinction between the right to make a record and the right to give a public performance by means of it which Mr. Manning made and the Act provides for, is wiped out. It would be as if a person who lets a gun to another is to be charged with "authorizing" hunting without a game license.

41 "The second principle establishes, as a matter of law, what constitutes the something more than mere use that must be sanctioned, approved or countenanced before a person has made an authorization within the meaning of the Act. [at page 30]" After a detailed examination of Falcon's case, supra, Kellock J. concluded that the principles laid down in that case could not apply in Muzak, given the distinction between the facts of the two cases. Rather, at page 193, Kellock J. relied on Vigneux to establish the following principle:

> In Falcon's case, Bankes, L.J., with whom Atkin L.J., agreed, approved of earlier expressions of opinion as to the meaning of "authorize", namely, that it is to be understood in its ordinary dictionary sense of "sanction, approve, and countenance". Unless what is done by a defendant is to sanction, approve or countenance actual performance, it cannot be said, in my opinion, that it has "authorized" performance. While it is true that to perform by means of such a mechanical contrivance as is here in question involves the use of recordings, and while the appellant, on the evidence, has authorized the use of the recordings in performing, it has not authorized the performance itself and has, therefore, not invaded any right of the respondent. Performance was clearly contemplated and authorized in Falcon's case, while in the case at bar the appellant is in the position of the appellant in Vigneux's case, as described by Lord Russell in the passage from the judgment above cited.

42 The position of Kellock J. may be summarized as follows: "[i]n order to 'authorize' a person must sanction, approve or countenance more than mere use of equipment that might possibly be used in an infringing performance but, on the other hand, a person need not go so far as to grant or purport to grant the right to perform" [at page 31].

> The third important principle to be found in the Muzak case is that it is possible to establish that a person has sanctioned, approved or countenanced an actual infringing activity (thereby rebutting the presumption that a person who authorizes an activity does so only so far as it is in accordance with the law), if it is shown that certain relationships existed between the alleged authorizer and the actual infringer, or that the alleged authorizer conducted himself in a certain manner [at page 32].

43 According to Hitchcock, at pages 32-33, this principle may be inferred from the decision in Muzak. First, Kellock J., at page 191 of his decision, adopts the passage from the reasons of Lord Russell from the Vigneux case, supra, in which Lord Russell states that the only part the defendants Vigneux Brothers played in the infringement may be summarized as, in the ordinary course of their business, to hire out one of their machines and supply it with records, at a weekly rental. "Similarly, Rand J. implies [at page 189, in the passage quoted supra] that certain conduct or relationships would have been sufficient to rebut the presumption that Muzak had authorized the use of the recordings only so far as that use was in accordance with regulations."

44 Hitchcock attempted, at pages 34-43, to define the type of conduct or relationship from which it can be concluded that a person in fact authorized the infringement, within the meaning of the Act, by his or her conduct or relationship with the person who infringed the copyright.

45 According to Hitchcock, this is primarily a question of fact which depends on the circumstances of each case. The first factor to be considered is the degree of control that the defendant exercised over the infringer. That control must be such that he or she could prevent the infringement from being committed. The second factor is that a reasonable person would be led to conclude that the defendant sanctions, approves or countenances the infringements, and that the defendant should have known that his or her words, actions or inaction would be seen as such by a reasonable person. It is Hitchcock's opinion that such authorization may be express or implied.

46 This concept of conduct was examined in the English decision Performing Right Society v. Ciryl Theatrical Syndicate, [1924] 1 K.B. 1 (C.A.). In that case, the managing director of a company which was the lessee of a theatre had, on behalf of the company, engaged a band to play music at performances of a play in the theatre leased by the company. In his absence and without his knowledge, the band performed certain musical works the copyright in which belonged to the plaintiffs. The plaintiffs then asserted that the defendant, which owned the theatre, had authorized the performance of the works or permitted the use of the theatre for that purpose. The Court of Appeal held that the defendant could not have authorized the performances since the band was the servant of the company and not of the defendant.

47 In his decision, at page 9, Bankes L.J. referred to the question of conduct as follows; this passage was also quoted by Whitford J. in CBS Inc. v. Ames Records & Tapes Ltd., [1981] 2 W.L.R. 973 (Ch. D.), at pages 987-988:

> I agree... that the court may infer an authorization or permission from acts which fall short of being direct and positive; I go as far as to say that indifference, exhibited by acts of commission or omission, may reach a degree from which authorisation or permission may be inferred. It is a question of fact in each case what is the true inference to be drawn from the conduct of the person who is said to have authorised the performance or permitted the use of a place of entertainment for the performance complained of.

48 Bankes L.J. concluded, at page 10, that the defendant had not exhibited indifference despite its refusal to take action against the orchestra after the plaintiffs had made it aware of the infringement. He held that since the musicians had been hired by the company and not by the defendant, and since the defendant was not present at the performances in question and was unaware of what pieces would be played by the orchestra, it could not be held liable for having authorized the performance, or for having permitted the use of the theatre for that purpose. At pages 12-13, Scrutton L.J. wrote:

> In my opinion, first, a man does not permit who cannot control, and secondly, a man does not permit the use of a place for the performance of a work if he does not know the work is being performed.

49 In Winstone v. Wurlitzer Automatic Phonograph Co. of Australia Pty. Ltd., supra, the Court held that it could be concluded that there was authorization

from the conduct of the defendants or the indifference they exhibited. At page 345, Herring C.J. stated:

> It is, of course, a question of fact in each case what is the true inference to be drawn from the conduct of the person said to have authorised the act complained of. And as the acts that may be complained of as infringements of copyright are multifarious, so, too, the conduct that may justify an inference of authorisation may take on an infinite variety of differing forms. In these circumstances any attempt to prescribe beforehand ready-made tests for determining on which side of the line a particular case will fall, would seem doomed to failure. So, too, will it be impossible to determine any particular case by reference merely to the relationship that may exist between the person said to have authorised the act complained of and the actual infringer, though, no doubt in the case of principal and agent an authorisation may be more readily inferred than in the case of vendor and purchaser. In the end the matter must in each case depend on a careful examination of all the relevant facts.

50   And, at page 347, the Chief Justice added:

> It would appear probable, however, that some measure of control of some sort by the person said to have authorised a public performance will usually be found in cases where the inference can properly be drawn that there has been an authorisation in fact. The type and measure of control, however, will vary from case to case according to the circumstances and particularly the nature of the act complained of, the relationship between the alleged "authoriser" and the actual infringer and the means by which the infringement is carried into effect.

ANALYSIS OF THE EVIDENCE

51   Having completed a survey of the case law relating specifically to the concept of "authorization" in respect of copyright, I find that each case essentially turns on its facts and that the Court must give judgment on those facts. This means that the case law is not always a faithful servant. We would note, for example, the decisions cited by the plaintiffs, in the two Canadian Performing Right Society Ltd. v. Canadian National Exhibition Association cases, and in Can. Performing Right Soc. v. Ming Yee.

52   In those three decisions, the degree of control exercised by the defendants over the people who committed the infringement was determined on the basis of the master-servant or employer-employee relationship that existed between the parties. In the case at bar, the town of Beloeil and Les Productions de la Coulisse Inc. exercised no control over the producer of the play, Mr. Bossac, or over his theatrical troupe. Moreover, there was no master-servant or employer-employee relationship. Rather, there was a strictly business relationship, which was limited, for Les Productions de la Coulisse Inc., to arrangements for renting the hall, and for the town of Beloeil to the fact that it is the owner of that Centre, the town of Beloeil having never had any transactions with Mr. Bossac. With respect to the other defendants, Mr. Ilial and Mr. Neveu, their relationship with Mr. Bossac was one of employer and employee, and therefore, following the reasoning in the three decisions referred to above, it was Mr. Bossac, in his capacity as employer, who was responsible for acts committed by these two

defendants in the course of their employment. I therefore cannot see how these three decisions assist the plaintiffs' case. In order for these decisions to apply in this case, the defendants would have had, for example, to have hired Mr. Bossac and the theatre troupe and/or exercised direct control over them or over the methods used in the infringement, which was not the case before me.

53 One final point which I would like to note relates to the issue of the joint liability of the defendants. In CBS Songs Ltd. v. Amstrad Consumer Electronics plc, [1988] 2 All E.R. 484 (H.L.), at page 495, Lord Templeman stated the following with respect to the defendants' joint liability in an action for copyright infringement:

> My Lords, joint infringers are two or more persons who act in concert with one another pursuant to a common design in the infringement.

54 In the case at bar, it cannot logically be said that the defendants acted in concert with Mr. Bossac to commit the infringement. It is therefore unnecessary to consider this question any further.

CONCLUSION

55 Based on the case law I have examined, I cannot find that the defendants have any liability for the copyright infringement committed. The defendants did not authorize the performances of the play Pique-Nique en Ville within the meaning of subsection 3(1) of the Act. The question of authorization is a question of fact in each case. In this case, the producer of the play, Mr. Bossac, alone had control over the play. The other defendants were not in such a position as would have enabled them to authorize the infringement. The mere fact that the town of Beloeil and Les Productions de la Coulisse Inc. rented the hall to Mr. Bossac, even though this in a way made possible or facilitated the infringement, does not support a finding that they authorized the performance of a play which infringed copyright. The defendants could reasonably have assumed that the purpose of renting the hall was to present a play in a lawful manner. Much more would be needed, according to the reasoning set out in Vigneux or in Muzak, for us to find the defendants liable. The participation of the defendants Ilial and Neveu was strictly in their relationship as employees of Mr. Bossac. They were at all times subject to his authority.

56 It was Scrutton L.J. in Ciryl (supra) who emphasized the absence of authority. Moreover, the evidence was that neither the town of Beloeil nor Les Productions de la Coulisse Inc. had any control whatsoever over the producer, Mr. Bossac, and over the play he staged. It would be difficult for me to find in the relationship between these parties any implied authority to present the play in such a way as would make them liable.

The potential significance of choosing between competing conceptions of authorization liability — and specifically in determining what kinds of acts *or omissions* amount to "sanctioning, approving or countenancing" infringement — can be seen in the *CCH Canadian Ltd.* case, below. It is interesting to note that, while having regard to the same jurisprudence, the Federal Court of Appeal arrived at a conclusion very different from that ultimately reached by the Supreme Court of Canada. Although the case dealt with the old technology of the photocopy machine, it seems fair to assume that the important implications for authorization liability in the Internet context were understood.

CCH Canadian Ltd. v. Law Society of Upper Canada
[2002] 4 F.C. 213, 18 C.P.R. (4th) 161 (Fed. C.A.),
reversed 2004 CarswellNat 446 (S.C.C.)
Federal Court of Appeal

Linden J.A.:

. . .

4 The Law Society [of Upper Canada] ... provides free-standing photocopiers in the Great Library, which are operated by patrons using coins or pre-paid cards. The Law Society does not monitor the use of these photocopiers, however, the following notice appears above each machine:

The copyright law of Canada governs the making of photocopies or other reproductions of copyright material. Certain copying may be an infringement of the copyright law. This library is not responsible for infringing copies made by users of these machines.

5 The Publishers [CCH Canadian Ltd., Thomson Canada Ltd. ... and Canada Law Book Inc. [who] produce legal materials] were aware of the Great Library's custom photocopying service but did not object to it until 1993 when, after delivering a cease and desist letter, they commenced this litigation. In essence, the Publishers assert that copyright subsists in their material, and that the Law Society infringes those copyrights through its custom photocopying service and by making free-standing copiers available in the Great Library.

. . .

c. Authorization

103 The Law Society maintains free-standing photocopiers in the Great Library, to which patrons have unrestricted access to make copies for a fee. In response to the Law Society's claim that making free-standing photocopiers available does not infringe any of the Publishers' copyrights, the Publishers argue, to the contrary, that the Law Society implicitly authorizes patrons to "produce or reproduce" their works. That is, the Publishers allege that the Law Society authorizes reproductions of their works, not through the custom photocopying service, but by maintaining free-standing photocopiers. Although there is no evidence of specific reproductions made using the self-service photocopiers, there is no

dispute the machines are used to reproduce works in the Great Library, including the Publishers' works.

104   Courts have consistently held that in order to authorize an act that only the copyright owner has the right to do, one must do more than merely provide the means with which to carry out the protected act. In *Vigneux v. Canadian Performing Right Society*, [1945] 2 D.L.R. 1 (Canada P.C.), rev'g [1943] 3 D.L.R. 369 (S.C.C.) ("*Vigneux* "), the Privy Council held that the supplier of a jukebox did not authorize public performances of musical works, since "they had no control over the use of the machine; they had no voice as to whether at any particular time it was to be available to the restaurant customers or not" (at 11).

105   The Supreme Court of Canada considered the right to authorize in *Muzak Corp. v. Composers, Authors & Publishers Assn. (Canada)*, [1953] 2 S.C.R. 182 (S.C.C.); ("*Muzak*"). The Court found that Muzak, an American company that merely leased a library of electrical transcriptions containing musical works to a Canadian franchise, did not authorize any public performance. According to Rand J., merely leasing a device that may be used to perform musical works did not constitute authorization, since there was nothing "to suggest that Muzak made itself a party in interest to the performance, either by warranting the right to perform without a fee or by anything in the nature of a partnership or similar agreement" (at 189). Rand J. remarked that one who merely lends a gun to another cannot be said to authorize that person to hunt without a license.

106   In *Muzak*, Kellock J. distinguished the British case of *Falcon v. Famous Players Film Co.*, [1926] 2 K.B. 474 (Eng. C.A.), on the grounds that, in *Falcon* , the defendant expressly purported to grant the right to exhibit a film, whereas in *Muzak*, there was insufficient evidence to suggest that Muzak gave such authorization. He then held (at 193) that "[u]nless what is done by a defendant is to sanction, approve or countenance actual performance, it cannot be said, in [his] opinion, that it has 'authorized' performance."

107   In *de Tervagne v. Beloeil (Town)* (1993), 50 C.P.R. (3d) 419 (Fed. T.D.), at 426-36 ("*de Tervagne* "), the Trial Division of this Court relied largely on *Muzak* to conclude (at 43) that merely owning or arranging for the rental of a hall in which a play was performed did not constitute authorization of that performance. Neither the owner of the hall in which a play was performed, nor the non-profit corporation that rented the hall authorized a performance of a certain play because they "exercised no control over the producer of the play" (at 436).

108   Similarly, the House of Lords refused to find a seller of dual cassette recorders liable for authorizing reproductions, since the seller had "no control over the use of their models once they are sold" (see *C.B.S. Songs Ltd. v. Amstrad Consumer Electronics PLC*, [1988] 2 All E.R. 484 (U.K. H.L.), at 492-4).

109   However, this case is distinguishable from those described above, since in those cases, the defendants merely supplied the means necessary to infringe copyright. The Law Society does much more than merely supply a device that may be used to "produce or reproduce" the Publishers' works, unlike for

example, manufacturers, distributors or retailers of photocopiers. Although the Law Society does not expressly purport to grant its patrons the right to make reproductions, no other inference can reasonably be drawn from the Law Society's provision of and control over its free-standing photocopiers, which are readily available to patrons of the Great Library, which is full of materials like the Publishers' works. It is clear, therefore, that the Law Society implicitly sanctions, approves or countenances its patrons to "produce or reproduce" the materials in the Great Library. To use a variation of the analogy of Rand. J. in *Muzak*, *supra*, it is as if the Law Society operates a game park, and provides each of its invited guests with a loaded gun. The Law Society is more akin to the restauranteur in *Vigneux* , on whose premises the juke-box was located, than to the distributor. In *de Tervagne* , one who not only arranged the performance of a play, but also provided the script, would almost surely have been be said to authorize its performance. Similarly, I doubt that the House of Lords would absolve the seller of dual cassette recorders of liability, had they facilitated copying of music provided by them on their premises.

110 The only effort by the Law Society to exercise its control or influence over the use of the photocopiers has been merely to post a notice that it "is not responsible for infringing copies made by the users of these machines." The Law Society has taken no additional steps to monitor, to police or to otherwise dissuade its patrons from infringing copyright or to ensure that its photocopiers are used legitimately. This stance, which might be described as, "see no evil, hear no evil", is insufficient to demonstrate that it does not authorize patrons to "produce or reproduce" the Publishers' works.

111 The Law Society argues that it is entitled to presume that the free-standing photocopiers will be used lawfully. Although it may be true that a person can initially presume that the protected act is carried out in accordance with the law, where the evidence suggests otherwise, such an assumption is unreasonable. In this case the evidence clearly shows that the Law Society has sufficient reason to suspect that not all patrons will use the free-standing photocopiers for legitimate purposes. Although the Publishers have not referred to specific occasions of illegitimate uses, the Law Society admittedly anticipates such activity. In fact, its notice expressly acknowledges that "certain copying may be an infringement of copyright law". This is distinct from the situation in *Muzak* where, since all other customers obtained their own licenses, it was reasonable to presume that the particular Canadian franchise would do the same. Similarly, in *de Tervagne* , there was no evidence whatsoever to suggest that the hall was to be used for an illegitimate purpose.

112 Patrons of the Great Library may indeed use the free-standing photocopiers for lawful purposes, for example to make copies of non-copyright material or to reproduce copyright material as permitted by the fair dealing exemptions of the *Act*. If copyright does not subsist in the reproduced material, then no exclusive authorization right exists and authorizing a reproduction of that material is, therefore, not an infringement of copyright. If, however, copyright does subsist in the copied work, then authorization constitutes a distinct right granted to the copyright owner and the Law Society may be held liable for infringement of that right, regardless of whether or not the patron ultimately infringes the separate right to reproduce the copied work. Importantly, section 30.3 of the *Act*, which will be discussed below, establishes a mechanism whereby the Law Society can avoid liability for offering free-standing photocopiers if it meets certain criteria.

113 In sum, it is clear that patrons of the Great Library will "produce or reproduce" the Publishers' works. The Law Society implicitly "authorize[s] any such acts" by providing both readily available photocopiers and a vast collection of the Publishers' works together in an environment that they control. Rather than attempting to exercise such control to prevent copyright infringement, the Law Society merely posted a notice indicating that it was not responsible, thereby implicitly sanctioning, approving and countenancing its patrons' reproductions. In this case, there is clearly sufficient evidence to alert the Law Society, and in fact, it acknowledges that the photocopiers may be used illegitimately. Therefore, the Law Society infringes the Publishers' right to authorize reproductions of their works.

114 I am comforted that the same result has been reached by the Australian High Court in *Moorehouse v. University of New South Wales*, [1976] R.P.C. 151 (Australia H.C.) where a university library made free-standing photocopiers available to its patrons. The Court noted that the university knew or had reason to suspect that the photocopiers were likely to be used for infringing purposes of committing an infringement. It is also expected that "UK courts would reach a similar conclusion" with respect to self-service photocopiers (see H. Laddie et al., *The Modern Law of Copyright and Designs*, 3rd ed. (London: Butterworths, 2000) at 1592).

. . .

CCH Canadian Ltd. v. Law Society of Upper Canada, 2004 SCC 13

Arbour J., Bastarache J., Binnie J., Deschamps J., Iacobucci J., LeBel J., Major J., McLachlin C.J.C.

Heard: November 10, 2003
Judgment: March 4, 2004
Docket: 29320

. . .

The Chief Justice:

I.   Introduction — The Issues To Be Determined

1 The appellant, the Law Society of Upper Canada, is a statutory non-profit corporation that has regulated the legal profession in Ontario since 1822. Since 1845, the Law Society has maintained and operated the Great Library at Osgoode Hall in Toronto, a reference and research library with one of the largest collections of legal materials in Canada. The Great Library provides a request-based photocopy service (the "custom photocopy service") for Law Society members, the judiciary and other authorized researchers. Under the custom photocopy service, legal materials are reproduced by Great Library staff and delivered in person, by mail or by facsimile transmission to requesters. The Law Society also maintains self-service photocopiers in the Great Library for use by its patrons.

2 The respondents, CCH Canadian Ltd., Thomson Canada Ltd. and Canada Law Book Inc., publish law reports and other legal materials. In 1993, the respondent publishers commenced copyright infringement actions against the Law Society, seeking a declaration of subsistence and ownership of copyright in eleven specific works and a declaration that the Law Society had infringed copyright when the Great Library reproduced a copy of each of the works. The publishers also sought a permanent injunction prohibiting the Law Society from reproducing these eleven works as well as any other works that they published.

3 The Law Society denied liability and counterclaimed for a declaration that copyright is not infringed when a single copy of a reported decision, case summary, statute, regulation or a limited selection of text from a treatise is made by the Great Library staff or one of its patrons on a self-service photocopier for the purpose of research.

4 The key question that must be answered in this appeal is whether the Law Society has breached copyright by either (1) providing the custom photocopy service in which single copies of the publishers' works are reproduced and sent to patrons upon their request or by (2) maintaining self-service photocopiers and copies of the publishers' works in the Great Library for use by its patrons. To answer this question, the Court must address the following sub-issues:

(1) Are the publishers' materials "original works" protected by copyright?

(2) Did the Great Library authorize copyright infringement by maintaining self-service photocopiers and copies of the publishers' works for its patrons' use?

(3) Were the Law Society's dealings with the publishers' works "fair dealing [s]" under s. 29 of the Copyright Act, R.S.C. 1985, c. C-42, as amended?

(4) Did Canada Law Book consent to have its works reproduced by the Great Library?

. . .

(2) Authorization: The Self-Service Photocopiers

(a) The Law

37 Under s. 27(1) of the Copyright Act, it is an infringement of copyright for anyone to do anything that the Act only allows owners to do, including authorizing the exercise of his or her own rights. It does not infringe copyright to authorize a person to do something that would not constitute copyright infringement. See C.A.P.A.C. v. CTV Television Network, [1968] S.C.R. 676 (S.C.C.), at p. 680. The publishers argue that the Law Society is liable for breach of copyright under this section because it implicitly authorized patrons of the Great Library to copy works in breach of the Copyright Act.

38 "Authorize" means to "sanction, approve and countenance": Muzak Corp. v. Composers, Authors & Publishers Assn. (Canada), [1953] 2 S.C.R. 182 (S.C.C.), at p. 193; de Tervagne v. Beloeil (Town), [1993] 3 F.C. 227 (Fed. T.D.). Countenance in the context of authorizing copyright infringement must be understood in its strongest dictionary meaning, namely, "give approval to, sanction, permit, favour, encourage": see The New Shorter Oxford English Dictionary (1993), vol. 1, at p. 526. Authorization is a question of fact that depends on the circumstances of each particular case and can be inferred from acts that are less than direct and positive, including a sufficient degree of indifference: C.B.S. Inc. v. Ames Records & Tapes, [1981] 2 All E.R. 812 (Eng. Ch. Div.), at pp. 823-24. However, a person does not authorize infringement by authorizing the mere use of equipment that could be used to infringe copyright. Courts should presume that a person who authorizes an activity does so only so far as it is in accordance with the law: Muzak Corp., supra. This presumption may be rebutted if it is shown that a certain relationship or degree of control existed between the alleged authorizer and the persons who committed the copyright infringement: Muzak Corp., supra; de Tervagne, supra: see also, J.S. McKeown, Fox Canadian Law of Copyright and Industrial Designs, 4th ed. (looseleaf), at p. 21-104 and P.D. Hitchcock, "Home Copying and Authorization" (1983), 67 C.P.R. (2d) 17, at pp. 29-33.

(b) Application of the Law to these Facts

39 For several decades, the Law Society has maintained self-service photocopiers for the use of its patrons in the Great Library. The patrons' use of the machines is not monitored directly. Since the mid-1980s, the Law Society has posted the following notice above each machine:

> The copyright law of Canada governs the making of photocopies or other reproductions of copyright material. Certain copying may be an infringement of the copyright law. This library is not responsible for infringing copies made by users of these machines.
>
> At trial, the Law Society applied for a declaration that it did not authorize copyright infringement by providing self-service photocopiers for patrons of the Great Library. No evidence was tendered that the photocopiers had been used in an infringing manner.

40 The trial judge declined to deal with this issue, in part because of the limited nature of the evidence on this question. The Federal Court of Appeal, relying in

part on the Australian High Court decision in Moorehouse v. University of New South Wales, [1976] R.P.C. 151 (Australia H.C.), concluded that the Law Society implicitly sanctioned, approved or countenanced copyright infringement of the publishers' works by failing to control copying and instead merely posting a notice indicating that the Law Society was not responsible for infringing copies made by the machine's users.

41 With respect, I do not agree that this amounted to authorizing breach of copyright. Moorhouse, supra, is inconsistent with previous Canadian and British approaches to this issue. See D. Vaver, Copyright Law (2000), at p. 27, and McKeown, supra, at p. 21-108. In my view, the Moorhouse approach to authorization shifts the balance in copyright too far in favour of the owner's rights and unnecessarily interferes with the proper use of copyrighted works for the good of society as a whole.

42 Applying the criteria from Muzak Corp., supra, and de Tervagne, supra, I conclude that the Law Society's mere provision of photocopiers for the use of its patrons did not constitute authorization to use the photocopiers to breach copyright law.

43 First, there was no evidence that the photocopiers had been used in a manner that was not consistent with copyright law. As noted, a person does not authorize copyright infringement by authorizing the mere use of equipment (such as photocopiers) that could be used to infringe copyright. In fact, courts should presume that a person who authorizes an activity does so only so far as it is in accordance with the law. Although the Court of Appeal assumed that the photocopiers were being used to infringe copyright, I think it is equally plausible that the patrons using the machines were doing so in a lawful manner.

44 Second, the Court of Appeal erred in finding that the Law Society's posting of the notice constitutes an express acknowledgement that the photocopiers will be used in an illegal manner. The Law Society's posting of the notice over the photocopiers does not rebut the presumption that a person authorizes an activity only so far as it is in accordance with the law. Given that the Law Society is responsible for regulating the legal profession in Ontario, it is more logical to conclude that the notice was posted for the purpose of reminding the Great Library's patrons that copyright law governs the making of photocopies in the library.

45 Finally, even if there were evidence of the photocopiers having been used to infringe copyright, the Law Society lacks sufficient control over the Great Library's patrons to permit the conclusion that it sanctioned, approved or countenanced the infringement. The Law Society and Great Library patrons are not in a master-servant or employer-employee relationship such that the Law Society can be said to exercise control over the patrons who might commit infringement: see, for example, De Tervagne, supra. Nor does the Law Society exercise control over which works the patrons choose to copy, the patron's purposes for copying or the photocopiers themselves.

46 In summary, I conclude that evidence does not establish that the Law Society authorized copyright infringement by providing self-service photocopiers and copies of the respondent publishers' works for use by its patrons in the Great Library. I would allow this ground of appeal.

---

6. Joint Liability for Copyright Infringement

In Canada, copyright law, like patent law, is neither tort law nor property law in classification, but is statutory law. Copyright legislation simply creates rights and obligations under the terms and in the circumstances set out in the statute. However, as in patent law, courts in Canada and elsewhere in the Commonwealth frequently resort to common law principles of tort law in determining who can be considered a party to infringement and thus subject to liability under the statute.[32] Thus, although Canada does not explicitly recognize a theory of "contributory infringement", as in the United States, courts have found liability on a joint tortfeasor basis.

CBS Songs Ltd v. Amstrad Plc, [1988] 2 All ER 484 at 495 (H.L.)

Lord Keith of Kinkel, Lord Templeman, Lord Griffiths, Lord Oliver of Aylmerton and Lord Jauncey of Tullichettle

1988 March 15, 16, 17, 21, 22, 23; May 12

. . .

Lord Templeman:

This appeal is the climax of a conflict between the makers of records and the makers of recording equipment. The appellants, the British Phonographic Industry Ltd. ("B.P.I."), represent the makers of records while the respondents, Amstrad Consumer Electronics Plc. and Dixons Ltd., represent the makers and sellers respectively of recording equipment. B.P.I. argue that it is unlawful for Amstrad to make recording equipment which will be used by members of the public to copy records in which copyright subsists. In the alternative, B.P.I. argue that Amstrad must not advertise their equipment in such a way as to encourage copying. Amstrad and Dixons argue that they may lawfully make and sell to the public any recording equipment which ingenuity may devise and may lawfully advertise the advantages of such equipment.

. . .

---

32   *CBS Songs Ltd v. Amstrad Plc,* [1988] 2 All ER 484 at 495 (H.L.); *Chappell & Co. Ltd. v. Associated Radio Co. of Australia Ltd* , [1925] V.L.R. 351 (Vict. S.C.). See, however, *Eros-Equipe de Recherche Opérationnelle en Santé Inc.* (2004), 35 C.P.R. (4th) 105 (F.C.).

B.P.I. next submitted that Amstrad were joint infringers; they became joint infringers if and as soon as a purchaser decided to copy a record in which copyright subsisted; Amstrad could become joint infringers not only with the immediate purchaser of an Amstrad model but also with anyone else who at any time in the future used the model to copy records. My Lords, Amstrad sell models which include facilities for receiving and recording broadcasts, disc records and taped records. All these facilities are lawful although the recording device is capable of being used for unlawful purposes. Once a model is sold Amstrad have no control over or interest in its use. In these circumstances the allegation that Amstrad is a joint infringer is untenable. In Townsend v. Haworth (1875) 48 L.J.Ch. 770n., decided in 1875 but reported in 1879 the defendant sold chemicals to be used by the purchaser in infringement of patent and agreed to indemnify the purchaser if the patent should prove to be valid. Mellish L.J. said, at p. 773:

> "Selling materials for the purpose of infringing a patent to the man who is going to infringe it, even although the party who sells it knows that he is going to infringe it and indemnifies him, does not by itself make the person who so sells an infringer. He must be a party with the man who so infringes, and actually infringe."

Mr. Kentridge on behalf of B.P.I. relied on the decision in Innes v. Short and Beal (1898) 15 R.P.C. 449. In that case the defendant Short sold powdered zinc and gave instructions to a purchaser to enable the purchaser to infringe a process patent. Bigham J. said, at p. 452:

> "There is no reason whatever why Mr. Short should not sell powdered zinc, and he will not be in the wrong, though he may know or expect the people who buy it from him are going to use it in such a way as will amount to an infringement of Mr. Innes' patent rights. But he must not ask the people to use it in that way, and he must not ask the people to use it in that way in order to induce them to buy his powdered zinc from him."

Assuming that decision to be correct, it does not assist B.P.I. because in the present case Amstrad did not ask anyone to use an Amstrad model in a way which would amount to an infringement.

In Dunlop Pneumatic Tyre Co. Ltd. v. David Moseley & Sons Ltd. [1904] 1 Ch. 164, 171; 21 R.P.C. 53; [1904] 1 Ch. 612; 21 R.P.C. 274, the defendant sold tyre covers which were an essential feature of a combination patent for tyres and rims. The tyre covers were adapted for use in the manner described in the patent, but not necessarily solely for use in that manner. Swinfen-Eady J. said, 21 R.P.C. 53, 60, that most of the "covers would probably ultimately be used in one or other of" the patented methods but that

> "those are not exhaustive of the purposes to which the covers may be put, and that they would be useful for other purposes in connection with other tyres... "

Swinfen-Eady J., upheld by the Court of Appeal, decided that the defendants did not infringe.

In The Koursk [1924] P. 140 where the question was whether the navigators of two ships had committed two separate torts or one tort in which they were both tortfeasors, Scrutton L.J., at p. 156, adopted the passage in Clerk & Lindsell on Torts, 7th ed. (1921), p. 59, to the effect that:

> "Persons are said to be joint tortfeasors when their respective shares in the commission of the tort are done in furtherance of a common design."

In the present case there is no common design between Amstrad and anybody else to infringe copyright.

In Rotocrop International Ltd. v. Genbourne Ltd. [1982] F.S.R. 241, Graham J. held, perhaps surprisingly, that there was novelty in a patent for a compost bin with removable panels and, less surprisingly, that a rival manufacturer who made and sold infringing bins in parts with assembly instructions was a joint tortfeasor with his customers. In that case, as in Innes v. Short and Beal, 15 R.P.C. 449, the vendor and the purchaser had a common design to carry out an infringing act.

In Belegging-en Exploitatiemaatschappij Lavender B.V. v. Witten Industrial Diamonds Ltd. [1979] F.S.R. 59, the defendants were alleged to have sold diamond grit for the sole purpose of making grinding tools in which it was to be embedded in a resin bond as part of a grinding material patented by the plaintiffs. Buckley L.J. held, at p. 66, that the defendants could not be infringers unless they

> "sold the grits in circumstances which in some way made them participants in their subsequent embodiment in resin bonded grinding wheels, or that they induced someone so to embody them..."

My Lords, joint infringers are two or more persons who act in concert with one another pursuant to a common design in the infringement. In the present case there was no common design. Amstrad sold a machine and the purchaser or the operator of the machine decided the purpose for which the machine should from time to time be used. The machine was capable of being used for lawful or unlawful purposes. All recording machines and many other machines are capable of being used for unlawful purposes but manufacturers and retailers are not joint infringers if purchasers choose to break the law. Since Amstrad did not make or authorise other persons to make a record embodying a recording in which copyright subsisted, Amstrad did not entrench upon the exclusive rights granted by the Act of 1956 to copyright owners and Amstrad were not in breach of the duties imposed by the Act.

B.P.I. submit, however, that if the Act of 1956 is defective to protect them, they are entitled to the protection of the common law. As a foundation for this submission B.P.I. seek to elevate the quality of the rights granted by the Act. They point out that in section 17(1) of the Act the owner of copyright in any action for infringement is entitled to all such relief as is available in any corresponding proceedings in respect of infringements of other proprietary rights; that copyright is an example of intellectual property; and that in Macmillan and Co. Ltd.

v. K. and J. Cooper (1923) L.R. 51 Ind.App. 109, 118, Lord Atkinson said that an infringer of copyright disobeyed the injunction "thou shalt not steal." My Lords, these considerations cannot enhance the rights of owners of copyright or extend the ambit of infringement. The rights of B.P.I. are derived from statute and not from the Ten Commandments. Those rights are defined by Parliament, not by the clergy or the judiciary. The rights of B.P.I. conferred by the Act of 1956 are in no way superior or inferior to any other legal rights; if B.P.I. prove that upon the true construction of the Act Amstrad and Dixons have infringed the rights conferred on B.P.I. by the Act, the court will grant appropriate and effective reliefs and remedies. But the court will not invent additional rights or impose fresh burdens.

MGM v. Grokster, Ltd., 125 U.S. S.Ct. 2764

Argued March 29, 2005.
Decided June 27, 2005.

Justice SOUTER delivered the opinion of the Court.

The question is under what circumstances the distributor of a product capable of both lawful and unlawful use is liable for acts of copyright infringement by third parties using the product. We hold that one who distributes a device with the object of promoting its use to infringe copyright, as shown by clear expression or other affirmative steps taken to foster infringement, is liable for the resulting acts of infringement by third parties.

I

A

Respondents, Grokster, Ltd., and StreamCast Networks, Inc., defendants in the trial court, distribute free software products that allow computer users to share electronic files through peer-to-peer networks, so called because users' computers communicate directly with each other, not through central servers. The advantage of peer-to-peer networks over information networks of other types shows up in their substantial and growing popularity. Because they need no central computer server to mediate the exchange of information or files among users, the high-bandwidth communications capacity for a server may be dispensed with, and the need for costly server storage space is eliminated. Since copies of a file (particularly a popular one) are available on many users' computers, file requests and retrievals may be faster than on other types of networks, and since file exchanges do not travel through a server, communications can take place between any computers that remain connected to the network without risk that a glitch in the server will disable the network in its entirety. Given these benefits in security, cost, and efficiency, peer-to-peer networks are employed to store and distribute electronic files by universities, government agencies, corporations, and libraries, among others.[FN1]

FN1. Peer-to-peer networks have disadvantages as well. Searches on peer-to-peer networks may not reach and uncover all available files because search requests may not be transmitted to every computer on the network. There may be redundant copies of popular files. The creator of the software has no incentive to minimize storage or bandwidth consumption, the costs of which are borne by every user of the network. Most relevant here, it is more difficult to control the content of files available for retrieval and the behavior of users.

Other users of peer-to-peer networks include individual recipients of Grokster's and StreamCast's software, and although the networks that they enjoy through using the software can be used to share any type of digital file, they have prominently employed those networks in sharing copyrighted music and video files without authorization. A group of copyright holders (MGM for short, but including motion picture studios, recording companies, songwriters, and music publishers) sued Grokster and StreamCast for their users' copyright infringements, alleging that they knowingly and intentionally distributed their software to enable users to reproduce and distribute the copyrighted works in violation of the Copyright Act, 17 U.S.C. § 101 et seq. (2000 ed. and Supp. II).[FN2] MGM sought damages and an injunction.

FN2. The studios and recording companies and the songwriters and music publishers filed separate suits against the defendants that were consolidated by the District Court.

Discovery during the litigation revealed the way the software worked, the business aims of each defendant company, and the predilections of the users. Grokster's eponymous software employs what is known as FastTrack technology, a protocol developed by others and licensed to Grokster. StreamCast distributes a very similar product except that its software, called Morpheus, relies on what is known as Gnutella technology.[FN3] A user who downloads and installs either software possesses the protocol to send requests for files directly to the computers of others using software compatible with FastTrack or Gnutella. On the FastTrack network opened by the Grokster software, the user's request goes to a computer given an indexing capacity by the software and designated a supernode, or to some other computer with comparable power and capacity to collect temporary indexes of the files available on the computers of users connected to it. The supernode (or indexing computer) searches its own index and may communicate the search request to other supernodes. If the file is found, the supernode discloses its location to the computer requesting it, and the requesting user can download the file directly from the computer located. The copied file is placed in a designated sharing folder on the requesting user's computer, where it is available for other users to download in turn, along with any other file in that folder.

FN3. Subsequent versions of Morpheus, released after the record was made in this case, apparently rely not on Gnutella but on a technology called Neonet. These developments are not before us.

In the Gnutella network made available by Morpheus, the process is mostly the same, except that in some versions of the Gnutella protocol there are no supernodes. In these versions, peer computers using the protocol communicate directly with each other. When a user enters a search request into the Morpheus software, it sends the request to computers connected with it, which in turn pass the request along to other connected peers. The search results are communicated to the requesting computer, and the user can download desired files directly from peers' computers. As this description indicates, Grokster and StreamCast use no servers to intercept the content of the search requests or to mediate the file transfers conducted by users of the software, there being no central point through which the substance of the communications passes in either direction.[FN4]

> FN4. There is some evidence that both Grokster and StreamCast previously operated supernodes, which compiled indexes of files available on all of the nodes connected to them. This evidence, pertaining to previous versions of the defendants' software, is not before us and would not affect our conclusions in any event.

Although Grokster and StreamCast do not therefore know when particular files are copied, a few searches using their software would show what is available on the networks the software reaches. MGM commissioned a statistician to conduct a systematic search, and his study showed that nearly 90% of the files available for download on the FastTrack system were copyrighted works.[FN5] Grokster and StreamCast dispute this figure, raising methodological problems and arguing that free copying even of copyrighted works may be authorized by the rightholders. They also argue that potential noninfringing uses of their software are significant in kind, even if infrequent in practice. Some musical performers, for example, have gained new audiences by distributing their copyrighted works for free across peer-to-peer networks, and some distributors of unprotected content have used peer-to-peer networks to disseminate files, Shakespeare being an example. Indeed, StreamCast has given Morpheus users the opportunity to download the briefs in this very case, though their popularity has not been quantified.

. . .

Grokster and StreamCast are not, however, merely passive recipients of information about infringing use. The record is replete with evidence that from the moment Grokster and StreamCast began to distribute their free software, each one clearly voiced the objective that recipients use it to download copyrighted works, and each took active steps to encourage infringement.

After the notorious file-sharing service, Napster, was sued by copyright holders for facilitation of copyright infringement, A&M Records, Inc. v. Napster, Inc., 114 F.Supp.2d 896 (N.D.Cal.2000), aff'd in part, rev'd in part, 239 F.3d 1004 (C.A.9 2001), StreamCast gave away a software program of a kind known as OpenNap, designed as compatible with the Napster program and open to Napster users for downloading files from other Napster and OpenNap users' computers. Evidence indicates that "[i]t was always [StreamCast's] intent to use [its OpenNap network] to be able to capture email addresses of [its] initial target market so that [it] could promote [its] StreamCast Morpheus interface to them," App. 861; indeed, the OpenNap program was engineered " 'to leverage Napster's 50 million user base,'" id., at 746.

StreamCast monitored both the number of users downloading its OpenNap program and the number of music files they downloaded. Id., at 859, 863, 866. It also used the resulting OpenNap network to distribute copies of the Morpheus software and to encourage users to adopt it. Id., at 861, 867, 1039. Internal company documents indicate that StreamCast hoped to attract large numbers of former Napster users if that company was shut down by court order or otherwise, and that StreamCast planned to be the next Napster. Id., at 861. A kit developed by StreamCast to be delivered to advertisers, for example, contained press articles about StreamCast's potential to capture former Napster users, id., at 568-572, and it introduced itself to some potential advertisers as a company "which is similar to what Napster was,"id., at 884. It broadcast banner advertisements to users of other Napster-compatible software, urging them to adopt its OpenNap. Id., at 586. An internal e-mail from a company executive stated: " 'We have put this network in place so that when Napster pulls the plug on their free service... or if the Court orders them shut down prior to that... we will be positioned to capture the flood of their 32 million users that will be actively looking for an alternative.' " Id., at 588-589, 861.

Thus, StreamCast developed promotional materials to market its service as the best Napster alternative. One proposed advertisement read: "Napster Inc. has announced that it will soon begin charging you a fee. That's if the courts don't order it shut down first. What will you do to get around it?" Id., at 897. Another proposed ad touted StreamCast's software as the "# 1 alternative to Napster" and asked "[w]hen the lights went off at Napster... where did the users go?" Id., at 836 (ellipsis in original).[FN7] StreamCast even planned to flaunt the illegal uses of its software; when it launched the OpenNap network, the chief technology officer of the company averred that "[t]he goal is to get in trouble with the law and get sued. It's the best way to get in the new[s]." Id., at 916.

> FN7. The record makes clear that StreamCast developed these promotional materials but not whether it released them to the public. Even if these advertisements were not released to the public and do not show encouragement to infringe, they illuminate StreamCast's purposes.

The evidence that Grokster sought to capture the market of former Napster users is sparser but revealing, for Grokster launched its own OpenNap system called Swaptor and inserted digital codes into its Web site so that computer users using Web search engines to look for "Napster" or "[f]ree file sharing" would be directed to the Grokster Web site, where they could download the Grokster software. Id., at 992-993. And Grokster's name is an apparent derivative of Napster.

StreamCast's executives monitored the number of songs by certain commercial artists available on their networks, and an internal communication indicates they aimed to have a larger number of copyrighted songs available on their networks than other file-sharing networks.Id., at 868. The point, of course, would be to attract users of a mind to infringe, just as it would be with their promotional materials developed showing copyrighted songs as examples of the kinds of files available through Morpheus. Id., at 848. Morpheus in fact allowed users to search specifically for "Top 40" songs, id., at 735, which were inevitably copyrighted. Similarly, Grokster sent users a newsletter promoting its ability to provide particular, popular copyrighted materials. Brief for Motion Picture Studio and Recording Company Petitioners 7-8.

In addition to this evidence of express promotion, marketing, and intent to promote further, the business models employed by Grokster and StreamCast confirm that their principal object was use of their software to download copyrighted works. Grokster and StreamCast receive no revenue from users, who obtain the software itself for nothing. Instead, both companies generate income by selling advertising space, and they stream the advertising to Grokster and Morpheus users while they are employing the programs. As the number of users of each program increases, advertising opportunities become worth more. Cf. App. 539, 804. While there is doubtless some demand for free Shakespeare, the evidence shows that substantive volume is a function of free access to copyrighted work. Users seeking Top 40 songs, for example, or the latest release by Modest Mouse, are certain to be far more numerous than those seeking a free Decameron, and Grokster and StreamCast translated that demand into dollars.

Finally, there is no evidence that either company made an effort to filter copyrighted material from users' downloads or otherwise impede the sharing of copyrighted files. Although Grokster appears to have sent e-mails warning users about infringing content when it received threatening notice from the copyright holders, it never blocked anyone from continuing to use its software to share copyrighted files. Id., at 75-76. StreamCast not only rejected another company's offer of help to monitor infringement, id., at 928-929, but blocked the Internet Protocol addresses of entities it believed were trying to engage in such monitoring on its networks, id., at 917-922.

. . .

MGM and many of the amici fault the Court of Appeals's holding for upsetting a sound balance between the respective values of supporting creative pursuits through copyright protection and promoting innovation in new communication technologies by limiting the incidence of liability for copyright infringement. The more artistic protection is favored, the more technological innovation may be discouraged; the administration of copyright law is an exercise in managing the tradeoff. See Sony Corp. v. Universal City Studios, supra, at 442, 104 S.Ct. 774; see generally Ginsburg, Copyright and Control Over New Technologies of Dissemination, 101 Colum. L.Rev. 1613 (2001); Lichtman & Landes, Indirect Liability for Copyright Infringement: An Economic Perspective, 16 Harv. J.L. & Tech. 395 (2003).

The tension between the two values is the subject of this case, with its claim that digital distribution of copyrighted material threatens copyright holders as never before, because every copy is identical to the original, copying is easy, and many people (especially the young) use file-sharing software to download copyrighted works. This very breadth of the software's use may well draw the public directly into the debate over copyright policy, Peters, Brace Memorial Lecture: Copyright Enters the Public Domain, 51 J. Copyright Soc. 701, 705-717

(2004) (address by Register of Copyrights), and the indications are that the ease of copying songs or movies using software like Grokster's and Napster's is fostering disdain for copyright protection, Wu, When Code Isn't Law, 89 Va. L.Rev. 679, 724-726 (2003). As the case has been presented to us, these fears are said to be offset by the different concern that imposing liability, not only on infringers but on distributors of software based on its potential for unlawful use, could limit further development of beneficial technologies. See, e.g., Lemley & Reese, Reducing Digital Copyright Infringement Without Restricting Innovation, 56 Stan. L.Rev. 1345, 1386-1390 (2004); Brief for Innovation Scholars and Economists as Amici Curiae 15-20; Brief for Emerging Technology Companies as Amici Curiae 19-25; Brief for Intel Corporation as Amicus Curiae 20-22.[FN8]

> FN8. The mutual exclusivity of these values should not be overstated, however. On the one hand technological innovators, including those writing file-sharing computer programs, may wish for effective copyright protections for their work. See, e.g., Wu, When Code Isn't Law, 89 Va. L.Rev. 679, 750 (2003). (Stream-Cast itself was urged by an associate to "get [its] technology written down and [its intellectual property] protected." App. 866.) On the other hand the widespread distribution of creative works through improved technologies may enable the synthesis of new works or generate audiences for emerging artists. See Eldred v. Ashcroft, 537 U.S. 186, 223-226, 123 S.Ct. 769, 154 L.Ed.2d 683 (2003) (STEVENS, J., dissenting); Van Houweling, Distributive Values in Copyright, 83 Texas L.Rev. 1535, 1539-1540, 1562-1564 (2005); Brief for Sovereign Artists et al. as Amici Curiae 11.

The argument for imposing indirect liability in this case is, however, a powerful one, given the number of infringing downloads that occur every day using StreamCast's and Grokster's software. When a widely shared service or product is used to commit infringement, it may be impossible to enforce rights in the protected work effectively against all direct infringers, the only practical alternative being to go against the distributor of the copying device for secondary liability on a theory of contributory or vicarious infringement. See In re Aimster Copyright Litigation, 334 F.3d 643, 645-646 (C.A.7 2003).

[1] One infringes contributorily by intentionally inducing or encouraging direct infringement, see Gershwin Pub. Corp. v. Columbia Artists Management, Inc., 443 F.2d 1159, 1162 (C.A.2 1971), and infringes vicariously by profiting from direct infringement while declining to exercise a right to stop or limit it, Shapiro, Bernstein & Co. v. H.L. Green Co., 316 F.2d 304, 307 (C.A.2 1963).[FN9] Although "[t]he Copyright Act does not expressly render anyone liable for infringement committed by another,"Sony Corp. v. Universal City Studios, 464 U.S., at 434, 104 S.Ct. 774, these doctrines of secondary liability emerged from common law principles and are well established in the law, id., at 486, 104 S.Ct. 774 (Blackmun, J., dissenting); Kalem Co. v. Harper Brothers, 222 U.S. 55, 62-63, 32 S.Ct. 20, 56 L.Ed. 92 (1911); Gershwin Pub. Corp. v. Columbia Artists Management, supra, at 1162; 3 M. Nimmer & D. Nimmer, Copyright § 12.04[A] (2005).

. . .

Despite the currency of these principles of secondary liability, this Court has dealt with secondary copyright infringement in only one recent case, and because MGM has tailored its principal claim to our opinion there, a look at our earlier holding is in order. In Sony Corp. v. Universal City Studios, supra, this Court addressed a claim that secondary liability for infringement can arise from the very distribution of a commercial product. There, the product, novel at the time, was what we know today as the videocassette recorder or VCR. Copyright holders sued Sony as the manufacturer, claiming it was contributorily liable for infringement that occurred when VCR owners taped copyrighted programs because it supplied the means used to infringe, and it had constructive knowledge that infringement would occur. At the trial on the merits, the evidence showed that the principal use of the VCR was for " 'time-shifting,' " or taping a program for later viewing at a more convenient time, which the Court found to be a fair, not an infringing, use. Id., at 423-424, 104 S.Ct. 774. There was no evidence that Sony had expressed an object of bringing about taping in violation of copyright or had taken active steps to increase its profits from unlawful taping. Id., at 438, 104 S.Ct. 774. Although Sony's advertisements urged consumers to buy the VCR to " 'record favorite shows' " or " 'build a library' " of recorded programs, id., at 459, 104 S.Ct. 774 (Blackmun, J., dissenting), neither of these uses was necessarily infringing, id., at 424, 454-455, 104 S.Ct. 774.

On those facts, with no evidence of stated or indicated intent to promote infringing uses, the only conceivable basis for imposing liability was on a theory of contributory infringement arising from its sale of VCRs to consumers with knowledge that some would use them to infringe. Id., at 439, 104 S.Ct. 774. But because the VCR was "capable of commercially significant noninfringing uses," we held the manufacturer could not be faulted solely on the basis of its distribution. Id., at 442, 104 S.Ct. 774.

[2][3] This analysis reflected patent law's traditional staple article of commerce doctrine, now codified, that distribution of a component of a patented device will not violate the patent if it is suitable for use in other ways. 35 U.S.C. § 271(c); Aro Mfg. Co. v. Convertible Top Replacement Co., 377 U.S. 476, 485, 84 S.Ct. 1526, 12 L.Ed.2d 457 (1964) (noting codification of cases); id., at 486, n. 6, 84 S.Ct. 1526 (same). The doctrine was devised to identify instances in which it may be presumed from distribution of an article in commerce that the distributor intended the article to be used to infringe another's patent, and so may justly be held liable for that infringement. "One who makes and sells articles which are only adapted to be used in a patented combination will be presumed to intend the natural consequences of his acts; he will be presumed to intend that they shall be used in the combination of the patent." New York Scaffolding Co. v. Whitney, 224 F. 452, 459 (C.A.8 1915); see also James Heekin Co. v. Baker, 138 F. 63, 66 (C.A.8 1905); Canda v. Michigan Malleable Iron Co., 124 F. 486, 489 (C.A.6 1903); Thomson-Houston Electric Co. v. Ohio Brass Co., 80 F. 712, 720-721 (C.A.6 1897); Red Jacket Mfg. Co. v. Davis, 82 F. 432, 439 (C.A.7 1897); Holly v. Vergennes Machine Co., 4 F. 74, 82 (C.C.D.Vt.1880); Renwick v. Pond, 20 F.Cas. 536, 541 (No. 11,702) (C.C.S.D.N.Y.1872).

[4][5] In sum, where an article is "good for nothing else" but infringement, Canda v. Michigan Malleable Iron Co., supra, at 489, there is no legitimate public interest in its unlicensed availability, and there is no injustice in presuming or imputing an intent to infringe, see Henry v. A.B. Dick Co., 224 U.S. 1, 48, 32 S.Ct. 364, 56 L.Ed. 645 (1912), overruled on other grounds, Motion Picture Patents Co. v. Universal Film Mfg. Co., 243 U.S. 502, 37 S.Ct. 416, 61 L.Ed. 871 (1917). Conversely, the doctrine absolves the equivocal conduct of selling an item with substantial lawful as well as unlawful uses, and limits liability to instances of more acute fault than the mere understanding that some of one's products will be misused. It leaves breathing room for innovation and a vigorous commerce. See Sony Corp. v. Universal City Studios, 464 U.S., at 442, 104 S.Ct. 774; Dawson Chemical Co. v. Rohm & Haas Co., 448 U.S. 176, 221, 100 S.Ct. 2601, 65 L.Ed.2d 696 (1980); Henry v. A.B. Dick Co., supra, at 48, 32 S.Ct. 364.

[6] The parties and many of the amici in this case think the key to resolving it is the Sony rule and, in particular, what it means for a product to be "capable of commercially significant noninfringing uses." Sony Corp. v. Universal City Studios, supra, at 442, 104 S.Ct. 774. MGM advances the argument that granting summary judgment to Grokster and StreamCast as to their current activities gave too much weight to the value of innovative technology, and too little to the copyrights infringed by users of their software, given that 90% of works available on one of the networks was shown to be copyrighted. Assuming the remaining 10% to be its noninfringing use, MGM says this should not qualify as "substantial," and the Court should quantify Sony to the extent of holding that a product used "principally" for infringement does not qualify. See Brief for Motion Picture Studio and Recording Company Petitioners 31. As mentioned before, Grokster and StreamCast reply by citing evidence that their software can be used to reproduce public domain works, and they point to copyright holders who actually encourage copying. Even if infringement is the principal practice with their software today, they argue, the noninfringing uses are significant and will grow.

We agree with MGM that the Court of Appeals misapplied Sony, which it read as limiting secondary liability quite beyond the circumstances to which the case applied. Sony barred secondary liability based on presuming or imputing intent to cause infringement solely from the design or distribution of a product capable of substantial lawful use, which the distributor knows is in fact used for infringement. The Ninth Circuit has read Sony's limitation to mean that whenever a product is capable of substantial lawful use, the producer can never be held contributorily liable for third parties' infringing use of it; it read the rule as being this broad, even when an actual purpose to cause infringing use is shown by evidence independent of design and distribution of the product, unless the distributors had "specific knowledge of infringement at a time at which they contributed to the infringement, and failed to act upon that information." 380 F.3d, at 1162 (internal quotation marks and brackets omitted). Because the Circuit found the StreamCast and Grokster software capable of substantial lawful use, it concluded on the basis of its reading of Sony that neither company could be held liable, since there was no showing that their software, being without any central server, afforded them knowledge of specific unlawful uses.

This view of Sony, however, was error, converting the case from one about liability resting on imputed intent to one about liability on any theory. Because Sony did not displace other theories of secondary liability, and because we find below that it was error to grant summary judgment to the companies on MGM's inducement claim, we do not revisit Sony further, as MGM requests, to add a more quantified description of the point of balance between protection and commerce when liability rests solely on distribution with knowledge that unlawful use will occur. It is enough to note that the Ninth Circuit's judgment rested on an erroneous understanding of Sony and to leave further consideration of the Sony rule for a day when that may be required.

C

[7][8] Sony's rule limits imputing culpable intent as a matter of law from the characteristics or uses of a distributed product. But nothing in Sony requires courts to ignore evidence of intent if there is such evidence, and the case was never meant to foreclose rules of fault-based liability derived from the common law.[FN10] Sony Corp. v. Universal City Studios, supra, at 439, 104 S.Ct. 774 ("If vicarious liability is to be imposed on Sony in this case, it must rest on the fact that it has sold equipment with constructive knowledge" of the potential for infringement). Thus, where evidence goes beyond a product's characteristics or the knowledge that it may be put to infringing uses, and shows statements or actions directed to promoting infringement, Sony's staple-article rule will not preclude liability.

> FN10. Nor does the Patent Act's exemption from liability for those who distribute a staple article of commerce, 35 U.S.C. § 271(c), extend to those who induce patent infringement, § 271(b).

The classic case of direct evidence of unlawful purpose occurs when one induces commission of infringement by another, or "entic[es] or persuad[es] another" to infringe, Black's Law Dictionary 790 (8th ed. 2004), as by advertising. Thus at common law a copyright or patent defendant who "not only expected but invoked [infringing use] by advertisement" was liable for infringement "on principles recognized in every part of the law." Kalem Co. v. Harper Brothers, 222 U.S., at 62-63, 32 S.Ct. 20 (copyright infringement). See also Henry v. A.B. Dick Co., 224 U.S., at 48-49, 32 S.Ct. 364 (contributory liability for patent infringement may be found where a good's "most conspicuous use is one which will co-operate in an infringement when sale to such user is invoked by advertisement" of the infringing use); Thomson-Houston Electric Co. v. Kelsey Electric R. Specialty Co., 75 F. 1005, 1007-1008 (C.A.2 1896) (relying on advertisements and displays to find defendant's "willingness... to aid other persons in any attempts which they may be disposed to make towards [patent] infringement"); Rumford Chemical Works v. Hecker, 20 F.Cas. 1342, 1346 (No. 12,133) (C.C.D.N.J.1876) (demonstrations of infringing activity along with "avowals of the [infringing] purpose and use for which it was made" supported liability for patent infringement).

[9] The rule on inducement of infringement as developed in the early cases is no different today.[FN11] Evidence of "active steps... taken to encourage direct infringement,"Oak Industries, Inc. v. Zenith Electronics Corp., 697 F.Supp. 988, 992 (N.D.Ill.1988), such as advertising an infringing use or instructing how to engage in an infringing use, show an affirmative intent that the product be used to infringe, and a showing that infringement was encouraged overcomes the law's reluctance to find liability when a defendant merely sells a commercial product suitable for some lawful use, see, e.g., Water Technologies Corp. v. Calco, Ltd., 850 F.2d 660, 668 (C.A.Fed.1988) (liability for inducement where one "actively and knowingly aid [s] and abet[s] another's direct infringement" (emphasis deleted)); Fromberg, Inc. v. Thornhill, 315 F.2d 407, 412-413 (C.A.5 1963) (demonstrations by sales staff of infringing uses supported liability for inducement); Haworth Inc. v. Herman Miller Inc., 37 U.S.P.Q.2d 1080, 1090, 1994 WL 875931 (W.D.Mich.1994) (evidence that defendant "demonstrate[d] and recommend[ed] infringing configurations" of its product could support inducement liability); Sims v. Mack Trucks, Inc., 459 F.Supp. 1198, 1215 (E.D.Pa.1978) (finding inducement where the use "depicted by the defendant in its promotional film and brochures infringes the... patent"), overruled on other grounds, 608 F.2d 87 (C.A.3 1979). Cf. W. Keeton, D. Dobbs, R. Keeton, & D. Owen, Prosser and Keeton on Law of Torts 37 (5th ed. 1984) ("There is a definite tendency to impose greater responsibility upon a defendant whose conduct was intended to do harm, or was morally wrong").

FN11. Inducement has been codified in patent law. Ibid.

[10][11] For the same reasons that Sony took the staple-article doctrine of patent law as a model for its copyright safe-harbor rule, the inducement rule, too, is a sensible one for copyright. We adopt it here, holding that one who distributes a device with the object of promoting its use to infringe copyright, as shown by clear expression or other affirmative steps taken to foster infringement, is liable for the resulting acts of infringement by third parties. We are, of course, mindful of the need to keep from trenching on regular commerce or discouraging the development of technologies with lawful and unlawful potential. Accordingly, just as Sony did not find intentional inducement despite the knowledge of the VCR manufacturer that its device could be used to infringe, 464 U.S., at 439, n. 19, 104 S.Ct. 774, mere knowledge of infringing potential or of actual infringing uses would not be enough here to subject a distributor to liability. Nor would ordinary acts incident to product distribution, such as offering customers technical support or product updates, support liability in themselves. The inducement rule, instead, premises liability on purposeful, culpable expression and conduct, and thus does nothing to compromise legitimate commerce or discourage innovation having a lawful promise.

III

A

The only apparent question about treating MGM's evidence as sufficient to withstand summary judgment under the theory of inducement goes to the need on MGM's part to adduce evidence that StreamCast and Grokster communicated an inducing message to their software users. The classic instance of inducement is by advertisement or solicitation that broadcasts a message designed to stimulate others to commit violations. MGM claims that such a message is shown here. It is undisputed that StreamCast beamed onto the computer screens of users of Napster-compatible programs ads urging the adoption of its OpenNap program, which was designed, as its name implied, to invite the custom of patrons of Napster, then under attack in the courts for facilitating massive infringement. Those who accepted StreamCast's OpenNap program were offered software to perform the same services, which a factfinder could conclude would readily have been understood in the Napster market as the ability to download copyrighted music files. Grokster distributed an electronic newsletter containing links to articles promoting its software's ability to access popular copyrighted music. And anyone whose Napster or free file-sharing searches turned up a link to Grokster would have understood Grokster to be offering the same file-sharing ability as Napster, and to the same people who probably used Napster for infringing downloads; that would also have been the understanding of anyone offered Grokster's suggestively named Swaptor software, its version of OpenNap. And both companies communicated a clear message by responding affirmatively to requests for help in locating and playing copyrighted materials.

[12] In StreamCast's case, of course, the evidence just described was supplemented by other unequivocal indications of unlawful purpose in the internal communications and advertising designs aimed at Napster users ("When the lights went off at Napster... where did the users go?" App. 836 (ellipsis in original)). Whether the messages were communicated is not to the point on this record. The function of the message in the theory of inducement is to prove by a defendant's own statements that his unlawful purpose disqualifies him from claiming protection (and incidentally to point to actual violators likely to be found among those who hear or read the message). See supra, at 2779-2780. Proving that a message was sent out, then, is the preeminent but not exclusive way of showing that active steps were taken with the purpose of bringing about infringing acts, and of showing that infringing acts took place by using the device distributed. Here, the summary judgment record is replete with other evidence that Grokster and StreamCast, unlike the manufacturer and distributor in Sony, acted with a purpose to cause copyright violations by use of software suitable for illegal use. See supra, at 2772-2774.

Three features of this evidence of intent are particularly notable. First, each company showed itself to be aiming to satisfy a known source of demand for copyright infringement, the market comprising former Napster users. StreamCast's internal documents made constant reference to Napster, it initially distributed its Morpheus software through an OpenNap program compatible with Napster, it advertised its OpenNap program to Napster users, and its Morpheus software functions as Napster did except that it could be used to distribute more kinds of files, including copyrighted movies and software programs. Grokster's name is apparently derived from Napster, it too initially offered an OpenNap program, its software's function is likewise comparable to Napster's, and it attempted to divert queries for Napster onto its own Web site. Grokster and StreamCast's efforts to supply services to former Napster users, deprived of a mechanism to copy and distribute what were overwhelmingly infringing files, indicate a principal, if not exclusive, intent on the part of each to bring about infringement.

[13] Second, this evidence of unlawful objective is given added significance by MGM's showing that neither company attempted to develop filtering tools or other mechanisms to diminish the infringing activity using their software. While the Ninth Circuit treated the defendants' failure to develop such tools as irrelevant because they lacked an independent duty to monitor their users' activity, we think this evidence underscores Grokster's and StreamCast's intentional facilitation of their users' infringement.[FN12]

> FN12. Of course, in the absence of other evidence of intent, a court would be unable to find contributory infringement liability merely based on a failure to take affirmative steps to prevent infringement, if the device otherwise was capable of substantial noninfringing uses. Such a holding would tread too close to the Sony safe harbor.

[14] Third, there is a further complement to the direct evidence of unlawful objective. It is useful to recall that StreamCast and Grokster make money by selling advertising space, by directing ads to the screens of computers employing their software. As the record shows, the more the software is used, the more ads are sent out and the greater the advertising revenue becomes. Since the extent of the software's use determines the gain to the distributors, the commercial sense of their enterprise turns on high-volume use, which the record shows is infringing.[FN13] This evidence alone would not justify an inference of unlawful intent, but viewed in the context of the entire record its import is clear.

> FN13. Grokster and StreamCast contend that any theory of liability based on their conduct is not properly before this Court because the rulings in the trial and appellate courts dealt only with the present versions of their software, not "past acts... that allegedly encouraged infringement or assisted... known acts of infringement." Brief for Respondents 14; see also id., at 34. This contention misapprehends the basis for their potential liability. It is not only that encouraging a particular consumer to infringe a copyright can give rise to secondary liability for the infringement that results. Inducement liability goes beyond that, and the distribution of a product can itself give rise to liability where evidence shows that the distributor intended and encouraged the product to be used to infringe. In such a case, the culpable act is not merely the encouragement of infringement but also the distribution of the tool intended for infringing use. See Kalem Co. v. Harper Brothers, 222 U.S. 55, 62-63, 32 S.Ct. 20, 56 L.Ed. 92 (1911); Cable/Home Communication Corp. v. Network Productions, Inc., 902 F.2d 829, 846 (C.A.11 1990); A&M Records, Inc. v. Abdallah, 948 F.Supp. 1449, 1456 (C.D.Cal.1996).

The unlawful objective is unmistakable.

B

In addition to intent to bring about infringement and distribution of a device suitable for infringing use, the inducement theory of course requires evidence of actual infringement by recipients of the device, the software in this case. As the account of the facts indicates, there is evidence of infringement on a gigantic scale, and there is no serious issue of the adequacy of MGM's showing on this point in order to survive the companies' summary judgment requests. Although an exact calculation of infringing use, as a basis for a claim of damages, is subject to dispute, there is no question that the summary judgment evidence is at least adequate to entitle MGM to go forward with claims for damages and equitable relief.

. . .

In sum, this case is significantly different from Sony and reliance on that case to rule in favor of StreamCast and Grokster was error. Sony dealt with a claim of liability based solely on distributing a product with alternative lawful and unlawful uses, with knowledge that some users would follow the unlawful course. The case struck a balance between the interests of protection and innovation by holding that the product's capability of substantial lawful employment should bar the imputation of fault and consequent secondary liability for the unlawful acts of others.

MGM's evidence in this case most obviously addresses a different basis of liability for distributing a product open to alternative uses. Here, evidence of the distributors' words and deeds going beyond distribution as such shows a purpose to cause and profit from third-party acts of copyright infringement. If liability for inducing infringement is ultimately found, it will not be on the basis of presuming or imputing fault, but from inferring a patently illegal objective from statements and actions showing what that objective was.

There is substantial evidence in MGM's favor on all elements of inducement, and summary judgment in favor of Grokster and StreamCast was error. On remand, reconsideration of MGM's motion for summary judgment will be in order.

The judgment of the Court of Appeals is vacated, and the case is remanded for further proceedings consistent with this opinion.

It is so ordered.

Justice GINSBURG, with whom THE CHIEF JUSTICE and Justice KENNEDY join, concurring

I concur in the Court's decision, which vacates in full the judgment of the Court of Appeals for the Ninth Circuit, ante, at 2782-2783, and write separately to clarify why I conclude that the Court of Appeals misperceived, and hence misapplied, our holding in Sony Corp. of America v. Universal City Studios, Inc., 464 U.S. 417, 104 S.Ct. 774, 78 L.Ed.2d 574 (1984). There is here at least a "genuine issue as to [a] material fact,"Fed. Rule Civ. Proc. 56(c), on the liability of Grokster or StreamCast, not only for actively inducing copyright infringe-ment, but also, or alternatively, based on the distribution of their software prod-ucts, for contributory copyright infringement. On neither score was summary judgment for Grokster and StreamCast warranted.

At bottom, however labeled, the question in this case is whether Grokster and StreamCast are liable for the direct infringing acts of others. Liability under our jurisprudence may be predicated on actively encouraging (or inducing) infringe-ment through specific acts (as the Court's opinion develops) or on distributing a product distributees use to infringe copyrights, if the product is not capable of "substantial" or "commercially significant" noninfringing uses. Sony, 464 U.S., at 442, 104 S.Ct. 774; see also 3 M. Nimmer & D. Nimmer, Nimmer on Copyright § 12.04[A][2] (2005). While the two categories overlap, they capture different culpable behavior. Long coexisting, both are now codified in patent law. Compare 35 U.S.C. § 271(b) (active inducement liability) with § 271(c) (contributory liability for distribution of a product not "suitable for substantial noninfringing use").

In Sony, 464 U.S. 417, 104 S.Ct. 774, the Court considered Sony's liability for selling the Betamax videocassette recorder. It did so enlightened by a full trial record. Drawing an analogy to the staple article of commerce doctrine from pat-ent law, the Sony Court observed that the "sale of an article... adapted to [a pat-ent] infringing use" does not suffice "to make the seller a contributory infringer" if the article "is also adapted to other and lawful uses." Id., at 441,104 S.Ct. 774 (quoting Henry v. A.B. Dick Co., 224 U.S. 1, 48, 32 S.Ct. 364, 56 L.Ed. 645 (1912), overruled on other grounds, Motion Picture Patents Co. v. Universal Film Mfg. Co., 243 U.S. 502, 517, 37 S.Ct. 416, 61 L.Ed. 871 (1917)).

"The staple article of commerce doctrine" applied to copyright, the Court stated, "must strike a balance between a copyright holder's legitimate demand for effective-not merely symbolic-protection of the statutory monopoly, and the rights of others freely to engage in substantially unrelated areas of commerce." Sony, 464 U.S., at 442, 104 S.Ct. 774. "Accordingly," the Court held, "the sale of copying equipment, like the sale of other articles of commerce, does not con-stitute contributory infringement if the product is widely used for legitimate, unobjectionable purposes. Indeed, it need merely be capable of substantial non-infringing uses." Ibid. Thus, to resolve the Sony case, the Court explained, it had to determine "whether the Betamax is capable of commercially significant noninfringing uses." Ibid.

To answer that question, the Court considered whether "a significant number of [potential uses of the Betamax were] noninfringing." Ibid. The Court homed in on one potential use-private, noncommercial time-shifting of television pro-grams in the home (i.e., recording a broadcast TV program for later personal viewing). Time-shifting was noninfringing, the Court concluded, because in some cases trial testimony showed it was authorized by the copyright holder, id., at 443-447,104 S.Ct. 774, and in others it qualified as legitimate fair use, id., at 447-455, 104 S.Ct. 774. Most purchasers used the Betamax principally to engage in time-shifting, id., at 421, 423, 104 S.Ct. 774, a use that "plainly satisfie[d]" the Court's standard, id., at 442, 104 S.Ct. 774. Thus, there was no need in Sony to "give precise content to the question of how much [actual or potential] use is commercially significant." Ibid.[FN1] Further development was left for later days and cases.

> FN1. Justice BREYER finds in Sony Corp. of America v. Universal City Studios, Inc., 464 U.S. 417, 104 S.Ct. 774, 78 L.Ed.2d 574 (1984), a "clear" rule permitting contributory liability for copyright infringement based on distribution of a product only when the product "will be used almost exclusively to infringe copyrights." Post, at 2791. But cf. Sony, 464 U.S., at 442, 104 S.Ct. 774 (recognizing "copyright holder's legitimate demand for effective-not merely symbolic-protection"). Sony, as I read it, contains no clear, near-exclusivity test. Nor have Courts of Appeals unanimously recognized Justice BREYER's clear rule. Compare A & M Records, Inc. v. Napster, Inc., 239 F.3d 1004, 1021 (C.A.9 2001) ("[E]vidence of actual knowledge of specific acts of infringement is required to hold a computer system operator liable for contributory copyright infringement."), with In re Aimster Copyright Litigation, 334 F.3d 643, 649-650 (C.A.7 2003) ("[W]hen a supplier is offering a product or service that has noninfringing as well as infringing uses, some estimate of the respective magnitudes of these uses is necessary for a finding of contributory infringement.... But the balancing of costs and benefits is necessary only in a case in which substantial noninfringing uses, present or prospective, are demonstrated."). See also Matthew Bender & Co. v. West Pub. Co., 158 F.3d 693, 707 (C.A.2 1998) ("The Supreme Court applied [the Sony] test to prevent copyright holders from leveraging the copyrights in their original work to control distribution of... products that might be used incidentally for infringement, but that had substantial noninfringing uses.... The same rationale applies here [to products] that have substantial, predominant and noninfringing uses as tools for research and citation."). All Members of the Court agree, moreover, that "the Court of Appeals misapplied Sony," at least to the extent it read that decision to limit "secondary liability" to a hardly ever category, "quite beyond the circumstances to which the case applied." Ante, at 2778.

The Ninth Circuit went astray, I will endeavor to explain, when that court granted summary judgment to Grokster and StreamCast on the charge of contributory liability based on distribution of their software products. Relying on its earlier opinion in A & M Records, Inc. v. Napster, Inc., 239 F.3d 1004 (C.A.9 2001), the Court of Appeals held that "if substantial noninfringing use was shown, the copyright owner would be required to show that the defendant had reasonable knowledge of specific infringing files." 380 F.3d 1154, 1161 (C.A.9 2004). "A careful examination of the record," the court concluded, "indicates that there is no genuine issue of material fact as to noninfringing use." Ibid. The appeals court pointed to the band Wilco, which made one of its albums available for free downloading, to other recording artists who may have authorized free distribution of their music through the Internet, and to public domain literary works and films available through Grokster's and StreamCast's software. Ibid. Although it acknowledged petitioners' (hereinafter MGM) assertion that "the vast majority of the software use is for copyright infringement," the court concluded that Grokster's and StreamCast's proffered evidence met Sony's requirement that "a product need only be capable of substantial noninfringing uses." 380 F.3d, at 1162.

. . .

This case differs markedly from Sony.Cf. Peters, Brace Memorial Lecture: Copyright Enters the Public Domain, 51 J. Copyright Soc. 701, 724 (2004) ("The Grokster panel's reading of Sony is the broadest that any court has given it...."). Here, there has been no finding of any fair use and little beyond anecdotal evidence of noninfringing uses. In finding the Grokster and StreamCast software products capable of substantial noninfringing uses, the District Court and the Court of Appeals appear to have relied largely on declarations submitted by the defendants. These declarations include assertions (some of them hearsay) that a number of copyright owners authorize distribution of their works on the Internet and that some public domain material is available through peer-to-peer networks including those accessed through Grokster's and StreamCast's software. 380 F.3d, at 1161, 259 F.Supp.2d 1029, 1035-1036 (C.D.Cal.2003); App. 125-171.

. . .

Even if the absolute number of noninfringing files copied using the Grokster and StreamCast software is large, it does not follow that the products are therefore put to substantial noninfringing uses and are thus immune from liability. The number of noninfringing copies may be reflective of, and dwarfed by, the huge total volume of files shared. Further, the District Court and the Court of Appeals did not sharply distinguish between uses of Grokster's and StreamCast's software products (which this case is about) and uses of peer-to-peer technology generally (which this case is not about).

In sum, when the record in this case was developed, there was evidence that Grokster's and StreamCast's products were, and had been for some time, overwhelmingly used to infringe, ante, at 2771-2773; App. 434-439, 476-481, and that this infringement was the overwhelming source of revenue from the products, ante, at 2773-2774; 259 F.Supp.2d, at 1043-1044. Fairly appraised, the evidence was insufficient to demonstrate, beyond genuine debate, a reasonable prospect that substantial or commercially significant noninfringing uses were likely to develop over time. On this record, the District Court should not have ruled dispositively on the contributory infringement charge by granting summary judgment to Grokster and StreamCast.[FN4]

> FN4. The District Court's conclusion that "[p]laintiffs do not dispute that [d] efendants' software is being used, and could be used, for substantial noninfringing purposes,"259 F.Supp.2d 1029, 1036 (C.D.Cal.2003); accord 380 F.3d, at 1161, is, to say the least, dubious. In the courts below and in this Court, MGM has continuously disputed any such conclusion. Brief for Motion Picture Studio and Recording Company Petitioners 30-38; Brief for MGM Plaintiffs-Appellants in No. 03-55894 etc. (CA9), p. 41; App. 356-357, 361-365.

If, on remand, the case is not resolved on summary judgment in favor of MGM based on Grokster and StreamCast actively inducing infringement, the Court of Appeals, I would emphasize, should reconsider, on a fuller record, its interpretation of Sony's product distribution holding.

Justice BREYER, with whom Justice STEVENS and Justice O'CONNOR join, concurring.

I agree with the Court that the distributor of a dual-use technology may be liable for the infringing activities of third parties where he or she actively seeks to advance the infringement. Ante, at 2770.I further agree that, in light of our holding today, we need not now "revisit" Sony Corp. of America v. Universal City Studios, Inc., 464 U.S. 417, 104 S.Ct. 774, 78 L.Ed.2d 574 (1984). Ante, at 2778-2779. Other Members of the Court, however, take up the Sony question: whether Grokster's product is "capable of 'substantial' or 'commercially significant' noninfringing uses." Ante, at 2783 (GINSBURG, J., concurring) (quoting Sony, supra, at 442, 104 S.Ct. 774). And they answer that question by stating that the Court of Appeals was wrong when it granted summary judgment on the issue in Grokster's favor. Ante, at 2784.I write to explain why I disagree with them on this matter.

I

The Court's opinion in Sony and the record evidence (as described and analyzed in the many briefs before us) together convince me that the Court of Appeals' conclusion has adequate legal support.

A

I begin with Sony's standard. In Sony, the Court considered the potential copyright liability of a company that did not itself illegally copy protected material, but rather sold a machine-a videocassette recorder (VCR)-that could be used to do so. A buyer could use that machine for non-infringing purposes, such as recording for later viewing (sometimes called " 'time-shifting,' " Sony, 464 U.S., at 421, 104 S.Ct. 774) uncopyrighted television programs or copyrighted programs with a copyright holder's permission. The buyer could use the machine for infringing purposes as well, such as building libraries of taped copyrighted programs. Or, the buyer might use the machine to record copyrighted programs under circumstances in which the legal status of the act of recording was uncertain (i.e., where the copying may, or may not, have constituted a "fair use," id., at 425-426, 104 S.Ct. 774). Sony knew many customers would use its VCRs to engage in unauthorized copying and " 'library-building.' " Id., at 458-459, 104 S.Ct. 774 (Blackmun, J., dissenting). But that fact, said the Court, was insufficient to make Sony itself an infringer. And the Court ultimately held that Sony was not liable for its customers' acts of infringement.

In reaching this conclusion, the Court recognized the need for the law, in fixing secondary copyright liability, to "strike a balance between a copyright holder's legitimate demand for effective-not merely symbolic-protection of the statutory monopoly, and the rights of others freely to engage in substantially unrelated areas of commerce." Id., at 442, 104 S.Ct. 774. It pointed to patent law's "staple article of commerce" doctrine, ibid., under which a distributor of a product is not liable for patent infringement by its customers unless that product is "unsuited for any commercial noninfringing use." Dawson Chemical Co. v. Rohm & Haas

Co., 448 U.S. 176, 198, 100 S.Ct. 2601, 65 L.Ed.2d 696 (1980). The Court wrote that the sale of copying equipment, "like the sale of other articles of commerce, does not constitute contributory infringement if the product is widely used for legitimate, unobjectionable purposes. Indeed, it need merely be capable of substantial noninfringing uses." Sony, 464 U.S., at 442, 104 S.Ct. 774 (emphasis added). The Court ultimately characterized the legal "question" in the particular case as "whether [Sony's VCR] is capable of commercially significant noninfringing uses " (while declining to give "precise content" to these terms). Ibid. (emphasis added).

It then applied this standard. The Court had before it a survey (commissioned by the District Court and then prepared by the respondents) showing that roughly 9% of all VCR recordings were of the type-namely, religious, educational, and sports programming-owned by producers and distributors testifying on Sony's behalf who did not object to time-shifting. See Brief for Respondents, O.T.1983, No. 81-1687, pp. 52-53; see also Sony, supra, at 424, 104 S.Ct. 774 (7.3% of all Sony VCR use is to record sports programs; representatives of the sports leagues do not object). A much higher percentage of VCR users had at one point taped an authorized program, in addition to taping unauthorized programs. And the plaintiffs-not a large class of content providers as in this case-owned only a small percentage of the total available un authorized programming. See ante, at 2786, n. 3 (GINSBURG, J., concurring). But of all the taping actually done by Sony's customers, only around 9% was of the sort the Court referred to as authorized.

The Court found that the magnitude of authorized programming was "significant," and it also noted the "significant potential for future authorized copying." 464 U.S., at 444, 104 S.Ct. 774. The Court supported this conclusion by referencing the trial testimony of professional sports league officials and a religious broadcasting representative. Id., at 444, and n. 24, 104 S.Ct. 774. It also discussed (1) a Los Angeles educational station affiliated with the Public Broadcasting Service that made many of its programs available for home taping, and (2) Mr. Rogers' Neighborhood, a widely watched children's program. Id., at 445, 104 S.Ct. 774. On the basis of this testimony and other similar evidence, the Court determined that producers of this kind had authorized duplication of their copyrighted programs "in significant enough numbers to create a substantial market for a noninfringing use of the" VCR. Id., at 447, n. 28, 104 S.Ct. 774 (emphasis added).

The Court, in using the key word "substantial," indicated that these circumstances alone constituted a sufficient basis for rejecting the imposition of secondary liability. See id., at 456, 104 S.Ct. 774 ("Sony demonstrated a significant likelihood that substantial numbers of copyright holders" would not object to time-shifting (emphasis added)). Nonetheless, the Court buttressed its conclusion by finding separately that, in any event, un authorized time-shifting often constituted not infringement, but "fair use." Id., at 447-456, 104 S.Ct. 774.

B

When measured against Sony's underlying evidence and analysis, the evidence now before us shows that Grokster passes Sony's test-that is, whether the company's product is capable of substantial or commercially significant non-infringing uses. Id., at 442,104 S.Ct. 774. For one thing, petitioners' (hereinafter MGM) own expert declared that 75% of current files available on Grokster are infringing and 15% are "likely infringing." See App. 436-439, ¶¶ 6-17 (Decl. of Dr. Ingram Olkin); cf. ante, at 2771-2772 (opinion of the Court). That leaves some number of files near 10% that apparently are noninfringing, a figure very similar to the 9% or so of authorized time-shifting uses of the VCR that the Court faced in Sony.

As in Sony, witnesses here explained the nature of the noninfringing files on Grokster's network without detailed quantification. Those files include:

- Authorized copies of music by artists such as Wilco, Janis Ian, Pearl Jam, Dave Matthews, John Mayer, and others. See App. 152-153, ¶¶ 9-13 (Decl. of Aram Sinnreich) (Wilco's "lesson has already been adopted by artists still signed to their major labels"); id., at 170, ¶¶ 5-7 (Decl. of Patricia D. Hoekman) (locating "numerous audio recordings" that were authorized for swapping); id., at 74, ¶ 10 (Decl. of Daniel B. Rung) (describing Grokster's partnership with a company that hosts music from thousands of independent artists)

- Free electronic books and other works from various online publishers, including Project Gutenberg. See id., at 136, ¶ 12 (Decl. of Gregory Newby) ("Numerous authorized and public domain Project Gutenberg eBooks are made available" on Grokster. Project Gutenberg "welcomes this widespread sharing... using these software products[,] since they assist us in meeting our objectives"); id., at 159-160, ¶ 32 (Decl. of Sinnreich)

- Public domain and authorized software, such as WinZip 8.1. Id., at 170, ¶ 8 (Decl. of Hoekman); id., at 165, ¶¶ 4-7 (Decl. of John Busher)

- Licensed music videos and television and movie segments distributed via digital video packaging with the permission of the copyright holder. Id., at 70, ¶ 24 (Decl. of Sean L. Mayers).

The nature of these and other lawfully swapped files is such that it is reasonable to infer quantities of current lawful use roughly approximate to those at issue in Sony. At least, MGM has offered no evidence sufficient to survive summary judgment that could plausibly demonstrate a significant quantitative difference. See ante, at 2771-2772 (opinion of the Court); see also Brief for Motion Picture Studio and Recording Company Petitioners i (referring to "at least 90% of the total use of the services"); but see ante, at 2786, n. 3 (GINSBURG, J., concurring). To be sure, in quantitative terms these uses account for only a small percentage of the total number of uses of Grokster's product. But the same was true in Sony, which characterized the relatively limited authorized copying market as "substantial." (The Court made clear as well in Sony that the amount of material then presently available for lawful copying-if not actually copied-was significant, see 464 U.S., at 444, 104 S.Ct. 774, and the same is certainly true in this case.)

Importantly, Sony also used the word "capable," asking whether the product is "capable of " substantial noninfringing uses. Its language and analysis suggest that a figure like 10%, if fixed for all time, might well prove insufficient, but that such a figure serves as an adequate foundation where there is a reasonable prospect of expanded legitimate uses over time. See ibid.(noting a "significant potential for future authorized copying"). And its language also indicates the appropriateness of looking to potential future uses of the product to determine its "capability."

Here the record reveals a significant future market for noninfringing uses of Grokster-type peer-to-peer software. Such software permits the exchange of any sort of digital file-whether that file does, or does not, contain copyrighted material. As more and more uncopyrighted information is stored in swappable form, it seems a likely inference that lawful peer-to-peer sharing will become increasingly prevalent. See, e.g., App. 142, ¶ 20 (Decl. of Brewster Kahle) ("[T]he [Internet Archive] welcomes [the] redistribution [of authorized films] by the Morpheus-Grokster-KaZaa community of users"); id., at 166, ¶ 8 (Decl. of Busher) (sales figures of $1,000 to $10,000 per month through peer-to-peer networks "will increase in the future as Acoustica's trialware is more widely distributed through these networks"); id., at 156-163, ¶¶ 21-40 (Decl. of Sinnreich).

And that is just what is happening. Such legitimate noninfringing uses are coming to include the swapping of: research information (the initial purpose of many peer-to-peer networks); public domain films (e.g., those owned by the Prelinger Archive); historical recordings and digital educational materials (e.g., those stored on the Internet Archive); digital photos (OurPictures, for example, is starting a P2P photo-swapping service); "shareware" and "freeware" (e.g., Linux and certain Windows software); secure licensed music and movie files (Intent MediaWorks, for example, protects licensed content sent across P2P networks); news broadcasts past and present (the BBC Creative Archive lets users "rip, mix and share the BBC"); user-created audio and video files (including "podcasts" that may be distributed through P2P software); and all manner of free "open content" works collected by Creative Commons (one can search for Creative Commons material on StreamCast). See Brief for Distributed Computing Industry Association as Amicus Curiae 15-26; Merges, A New Dynamism in the Public Domain, 71 U. Chi. L.Rev. 183 (2004). I can find nothing in the record that suggests that this course of events will not continue to flow naturally as a consequence of the character of the software taken together with the foreseeable development of the Internet and of information technology. Cf. ante, at 2770-2771 (opinion of the Court) (discussing the significant benefits of peer-to-peer technology).

There may be other now-unforeseen noninfringing uses that develop for peer-to-peer software, just as the home-video rental industry (unmentioned in Sony) developed for the VCR. But the foreseeable development of such uses, when taken together with an estimated 10% noninfringing material, is sufficient to meet Sony's standard. And while Sony considered the record following a trial, there are no facts asserted by MGM in its summary judgment filings that lead me to believe the outcome after a trial here could be any different. The lower courts reached the same conclusion.

Of course, Grokster itself may not want to develop these other noninfringing uses. But Sony's standard seeks to protect not the Groksters of this world (which in any event may well be liable under today's holding), but the development of technology more generally. And Grokster's desires in this respect are beside the point.

II

The real question here, I believe, is not whether the record evidence satisfies Sony.As I have interpreted the standard set forth in that case, it does. And of the Courts of Appeals that have considered the matter, only one has proposed interpreting Sony more strictly than I would do-in a case where the product might have failed under any standard. In re Aimster Copyright Litigation, 334 F.3d 643, 653 (C.A.7 2003) (defendant "failed to show that its service is ever used for any purpose other than to infringe" copyrights (emphasis added)); see Matthew Bender & Co. v. West Pub. Co., 158 F.3d 693, 706-707 (C.A.2 1998) (court did not require that noninfringing uses be "predominant," it merely found that they were predominant, and therefore provided no analysis of Sony's boundaries); but see ante, at 2784, n. 1 (GINSBURG, J., concurring); see also A&M Records, Inc. v. Napster, Inc., 239 F.3d 1004, 1020 (C.A.9 2001) (discussing Sony); Cable/Home Communication Corp. v. Network Productions, Inc., 902 F.2d 829, 842-847 (C.A.11 1990) (same); Vault Corp. v. Quaid Software, Ltd., 847 F.2d 255, 262 (C.A.5 1988) (same); cf. Dynacore Holdings Corp. v. U.S. Philips Corp., 363 F.3d 1263, 1275 (C.A.Fed.2004) (same); see also Doe v. GTE Corp., 347 F.3d 655, 661 (C.A.7 2003) ("A person may be liable as a contributory infringer if the product or service it sells has no (or only slight) legal use").

Instead, the real question is whether we should modify the Sony standard, as MGM requests, or interpret Sony more strictly, as I believe Justice GINSBURG's approach would do in practice. Compare ante, at 2784-2786 (concurring opinion) (insufficient evidence in this case of both present lawful uses and of a reasonable prospect that substantial noninfringing uses would develop over time), with Sony, 464 U.S., at 442-447, 104 S.Ct. 774 (basing conclusion as to the likely existence of a substantial market for authorized copying upon general declarations, some survey data, and common sense).

As I have said, Sony itself sought to "strike a balance between a copyright holder's legitimate demand for effective-not merely symbolic-protection of the statutory monopoly, and the rights of others freely to engage in substantially unrelated areas of commerce." Id., at 442,104 S.Ct. 774. Thus, to determine whether modification, or a strict interpretation, of Sony is needed, I would ask whether MGM has shown that Sony incorrectly balanced copyright and new-technology interests. In particular: (1) Has Sony (as I interpret it) worked to protect new technology? (2) If so, would modification or strict interpretation significantly weaken that protection? (3) If so, would new or necessary copyright-related benefits outweigh any such weakening?

A

The first question is the easiest to answer. Sony's rule, as I interpret it, has provided entrepreneurs with needed assurance that they will be shielded from copyright liability as they bring valuable new technologies to market.

Sony's rule is clear. That clarity allows those who develop new products that are capable of substantial noninfringing uses to know, ex ante, that distribution of their product will not yield massive monetary liability. At the same time, it helps deter them from distributing products that have no other real function than-or that are specifically intended for-copyright infringement, deterrence that the Court's holding today reinforces (by adding a weapon to the copyright holder's legal arsenal).

Sony's rule is strongly technology protecting. The rule deliberately makes it difficult for courts to find secondary liability where new technology is at issue. It establishes that the law will not impose copyright liability upon the distributors of dual-use technologies (who do not themselves engage in unauthorized copying) unless the product in question will be used almost exclusively to infringe copyrights (or unless they actively induce infringements as we today describe). Sony thereby recognizes that the copyright laws are not intended to discourage or to control the emergence of new technologies, including (perhaps especially) those that help disseminate information and ideas more broadly or more efficiently. Thus Sony's rule shelters VCRs, typewriters, tape recorders, photocopiers, computers, cassette players, compact disc burners, digital video recorders, MP3 players, Internet search engines, and peer-to-peer software. But Sony's rule does not shelter descramblers, even if one could theoretically use a descrambler in a noninfringing way. 464 U.S., at 441-442, 104 S.Ct. 774. Cable/Home Communication Corp., supra, at 837-850 (developer liable for advertising television signal descrambler), with Vault Corp., supra, at 262 (primary use infringing but a substantial noninfringing use).

Sony's rule is forward looking. It does not confine its scope to a static snapshot of a product's current uses (thereby threatening technologies that have undeveloped future markets). Rather, as the VCR example makes clear, a product's market can evolve dramatically over time. And Sony-by referring to a capacity for substantial noninfringing uses-recognizes that fact. Sony's word "capable" refers to a plausible, not simply a theoretical, likelihood that such uses will come to pass, and that fact anchors Sony in practical reality. Cf. Aimster, 334 F.3d, at 651.

Sony's rule is mindful of the limitations facing judges where matters of technology are concerned. Judges have no specialized technical ability to answer questions about present or future technological feasibility or commercial viability where technology professionals, engineers, and venture capitalists themselves may radically disagree and where answers may differ depending upon whether one focuses upon the time of product development or the time of distribution. Consider, for example, the question whether devices can be added to Grokster's software that will filter out infringing files. MGM tells us this is easy enough to do, as do several amici that produce and sell the filtering technology. See, e.g., Brief for Motion Picture Studio and Recording Company Petitioners 11; Brief for Audible Magic Corp. et al. as Amici Curiae 3-10. Grokster says it is not at all easy to do, and not an efficient solution in any event, and several apparently disinterested computer science professors agree. See Brief for Respondents 31; Brief for Computer Science Professor Harold Abelson et al. as Amici Curiae 6-10, 14-18. Which account should a judge credit? Sony says that the judge will not necessarily have to decide.

Given the nature of the Sony rule, it is not surprising that in the last 20 years, there have been relatively few contributory infringement suits-based on a product distribution theory-brought against technology providers (a small handful of federal appellate court cases and perhaps fewer than two dozen District Court cases in the last 20 years). I have found nothing in the briefs or the record that shows that Sony has failed to achieve its innovation-protecting objective.

B

The second, more difficult, question is whether a modified Sony rule (or a strict interpretation) would significantly weaken the law's ability to protect new technology. Justice GINSBURG's approach would require defendants to produce considerably more concrete evidence-more than was presented here-to earn Sony's shelter. That heavier evidentiary demand, and especially the more dramatic (case-by-case balancing) modifications that MGM and the Government seek, would, I believe, undercut the protection that Sony now offers.

To require defendants to provide, for example, detailed evidence-say, business plans, profitability estimates, projected technological modifications, and so forth-would doubtless make life easier for copyright holder plaintiffs. But it would simultaneously increase the legal uncertainty that surrounds the creation or development of a new technology capable of being put to infringing uses. Inventors and entrepreneurs (in the garage, the dorm room, the corporate lab, or the boardroom) would have to fear (and in many cases endure) costly and extensive trials when they create, produce, or distribute the sort of information technology that can be used for copyright infringement. They would often be left guessing as to how a court, upon later review of the product and its uses, would decide when necessarily rough estimates amounted to sufficient evidence. They would have no way to predict how courts would weigh the respective values of infringing and noninfringing uses; determine the efficiency and advisability of technological changes; or assess a product's potential future markets. The price of a wrong guess-even if it involves a good-faith effort to assess technical and commercial viability-could be large statutory damages (not less than $750 and up to $30,000 per infringed work). 17 U.S.C. § 504(c)(1). The additional risk and uncertainty would mean a consequent additional chill of technological development.

C

The third question-whether a positive copyright impact would outweigh any technology-related loss-I find the most difficult of the three. I do not doubt that a more intrusive Sony test would generally provide greater revenue security for copyright holders. But it is harder to conclude that the gains on the copyright swings would exceed the losses on the technology roundabouts.

For one thing, the law disfavors equating the two different kinds of gain and loss; rather, it leans in favor of protecting technology. As Sony itself makes clear, the producer of a technology which permits unlawful copying does not himself engage in unlawful copying-a fact that makes the attachment of copyright liability to the creation, production, or distribution of the technology an exceptional thing. See 464 U.S., at 431, 104 S.Ct. 774 (courts "must be circumspect" in construing the copyright laws to preclude distribution of new technologies). Moreover, Sony has been the law for some time. And that fact imposes a serious burden upon copyright holders like MGM to show a need for change in the current rules of the game, including a more strict interpretation of the test. See, e.g., Brief for Motion Picture Studio and Recording Company Petitioners 31 (Sony should not protect products when the "primary or principal" use is infringing).

In any event, the evidence now available does not, in my view, make out a sufficiently strong case for change. To say this is not to doubt the basic need to protect copyrighted material from infringement. The Constitution itself stresses the vital role that copyright plays in advancing the "useful Arts." Art. I, § 8, cl. 8. No one disputes that "reward to the author or artist serves to induce release to the public of the products of his creative genius." United States v. Paramount Pictures, Inc., 334 U.S. 131, 158, 68 S.Ct. 915, 92 L.Ed. 1260 (1948). And deliberate unlawful copying is no less an unlawful taking of property than garden-variety theft. See, e.g.,18 U.S.C. § 2319 (2000 ed. and Supp. II) (criminal copyright infringement); § 1961(1)(B) (2000 ed., Supp. II) (copyright infringement can be a predicate act under the Racketeer Influenced and Corrupt Organizations Act); § 1956(c)(7)(D) (2000 ed., Supp. II) (money laundering includes the receipt of proceeds from copyright infringement). But these highly general principles cannot by themselves tell us how to balance the interests at issue in Sony or whether Sony's standard needs modification. And at certain key points, information is lacking.

Will an unmodified Sony lead to a significant diminution in the amount or quality of creative work produced? Since copyright's basic objective is creation and its revenue objectives but a means to that end, this is the underlying copyright question. See Twentieth Century Music Corp. v. Aiken, 422 U.S. 151, 156, 95 S.Ct. 2040, 45 L.Ed.2d 84 (1975) ("Creative work is to be encouraged and rewarded, but private motivation must ultimately serve the cause of promoting broad public availability of literature, music, and the other arts"). And its answer is far from clear.

Unauthorized copying likely diminishes industry revenue, though it is not clear by how much. Compare S. Liebowitz, Will MP3 Downloads Annihilate the

Record Industry? The Evidence So Far 2 (June 2003), http://www.utdallas.edu/ liebowit/intprop/records.pdf (all Internet materials as visited June 24, 2005, and available in Clerk of Court's case file) file sharing has caused a decline in music sales), and Press Release, Informa Telecoms & Media, Steady Download Growth Defies P2P (Dec. 6, 2004), http://www. infor matm.com (citing Informa Media Group Reports, Music on the Internet (5th ed.2004)) (estimating total lost sales to the music industry in the range of $2 billion annually), with F. Oberholzer & K. Strumpf, The Effect of File Sharing on Record Sales: An Empirical Analysis 24 (Mar. 2004), www. unc. edu/ cigar/ papers/ File Sharing_ March 2004. pdf (academic study concluding that "file sharing has no statistically significant effect on purchases of the average album"), and McGuire, Study: File-Sharing No Threat to Music Sales (Mar. 29, 2004), http://www.washingtonpost.com/ac2/ wp-dyn/A34300-2004Mar29?language= printer (discussing mixed evidence).

The extent to which related production has actually and resultingly declined remains uncertain, though there is good reason to believe that the decline, if any, is not substantial. See, e.g., M. Madden, Pew Internet & American Life Project, Artists, Musicians, and the Internet 21 (Dec. 5, 2004), http://www.pewinternet. org/pdfs/PIP_Artists.Musicians_Report.pdf (nearly 70% of musicians believe that file sharing is a minor threat or no threat at all to creative industries); Benkler, Sharing Nicely: On Shareable Goods and the Emergence of Sharing as a Modality of Economic Production, 114 Yale L. J. 273, 351-352 (2004) ("Much of the actual flow of revenue to artists-from performances and other sources-is stable even assuming a complete displacement of the CD market by peer-to-peer distribution....[I]t would be silly to think that music, a cultural form without which no human society has existed, will cease to be in our world [because of illegal file swapping]").

More importantly, copyright holders at least potentially have other tools available to reduce piracy and to abate whatever threat it poses to creative production. As today's opinion makes clear, a copyright holder may proceed against a technology provider where a provable specific intent to infringe (of the kind the Court describes) is present. Ante, at 2782. Services like Grokster may well be liable under an inducement theory.

In addition, a copyright holder has always had the legal authority to bring a traditional infringement suit against one who wrongfully copies. Indeed, since September 2003, the Recording Industry Association of America (RIAA) has filed "thousands of suits against people for sharing copyrighted material." Walker, New Movement Hits Universities: Get Legal Music, Washington Post, Mar. 17, 2005, p. E1. These suits have provided copyright holders with damages; have served as a teaching tool, making clear that much file sharing, if done without permission, is unlawful; and apparently have had a real and significant deterrent effect. See, e.g., L. Rainie, M. Madden, D. Hess, & G. Mudd, Pew Internet Project and comScore Media Metrix Data Memo: The state of music downloading and file-sharing online 2, 4, 6, 10 (Apr. 2004), http://www.pewinternet.org/pdfs/ PIP_File sharing _April_04. pdf (number of people downloading files fell from a peak of roughly 35 million to roughly 23 million in the year following the first suits; 38% of current downloaders report downloading fewer files because of the suits); M. Madden & L. Rainie, Pew Internet Project Data Memo: Music and video downloading moves beyond P2P, p. 7 (Mar. 2005), http:// www.pewinternet.org/pdfs/PIP_Filesharing_March05.pdf (number of downloaders has "inched up" but "continues to rest well below the peak level"); Note, Costs and Benefits of the Recording Industry's Litigation Against Individuals, 20 Berkeley Tech. L. J. 571 (2005); but see Evangelista, File Sharing; Downloading Music and Movie Files is as Popular as Ever, San Francisco Chronicle, Mar. 28, 2005, p. E1 (referring to the continuing "tide of rampant copyright infringement," while noting that the RIAA says it believes the "campaign of lawsuits and public education has at least contained the problem").

Further, copyright holders may develop new technological devices that will help curb unlawful infringement. Some new technology, called "digital 'watermarking' " and "digital fingerprint[ing]," can encode within the file information about the author and the copyright scope and date, which "fingerprints" can help to expose infringers. RIAA Reveals Method to Madness, Wired News (Aug. 28, 2003), http://www.wired.com/news/digiwood/0,1412,60222,00.html; Besek, Anti-Circumvention Laws and Copyright: A Report from the Kernochan Center for Law, Media and the Arts, 27 Colum. J. L. & Arts 385, 391, 451 (2004). Other technology can, through encryption, potentially restrict users' ability to make a digital copy. See J. Borland, Tripping the Rippers, C/net News.com (Sept. 28, 2001), http://news.com./Tripping+the+rippers/2009-1023_3-273619.html; but see Brief for Bridgemar Services, Ltd. d/b/a iMesh.com as Amicus Curiae 5-8 (arguing that peer-to-peer service providers can more easily block unlawful swapping).

At the same time, advances in technology have discouraged unlawful copying by making lawful copying (e.g., downloading music with the copyright holder's permission) cheaper and easier to achieve. Several services now sell music for less than $1 per song. (Walmart.com, for example, charges $0.88 each.) Consequently, many consumers initially attracted to the convenience and flexibility of services like Grokster are now migrating to lawful paid services (services with copying permission) where they can enjoy at little cost even greater convenience and flexibility without engaging in unlawful swapping. See Wu, When Code Isn't Law, 89 Va. L.Rev. 679, 731-735 (2003) (noting the prevalence of technological problems on unpaid swapping sites); K. Dean, P2P Tilts Toward Legitimacy, Wired News (Nov. 24, 2004), http://www. wired. com/ news/ digiwood/0, 1412, 65836, 00.html; Madden & Rainie, March 2005 Data Memo, supra, at 6-8 (percentage of current downloaders who have used paid services rose from 24% to 43% in a year; number using free services fell from 58% to 41%).

Thus, lawful music downloading services-those that charge the customer for downloading music and pay royalties to the copyright holder-have continued to grow and to produce substantial revenue. See Brief for Internet Law Faculty as Amicus Curiae 5-20; Bruno, Digital Entertainment: Piracy Fight Shows Encouraging Signs (Mar. 5, 2005), available at LEXIS, News Library, Billboard File (in 2004, consumers worldwide purchased more than 10 times the number of digital tracks purchased in 2003; global digital music market of $330 million in 2004 expected to double in 2005); Press Release, Informa Telecoms & Media, Steady Download Growth Defies P2P (global digital revenues will likely exceed $3 billion in 2010); Ashton, [International Federation of the Phonographic Industry] Predicts Downloads Will Hit the Mainstream, Music Week, Jan. 29, 2005, p. 6 (legal music sites and portable MP3 players "are helping to transform the digital music market" into "an everyday consumer experience"). And more advanced types of non-music-oriented peer-to-peer networks have also started to develop, drawing in part on the lessons of Grokster.

Finally, as Sony recognized, the legislative option remains available. Courts are less well suited than Congress to the task of "accommodat[ing] fully the varied permutations of competing interests that are inevitably implicated by such new technology." Sony, 464 U.S., at 431, 104 S.Ct. 774; see, e.g., Audio Home Recording Act of 1992, 106 Stat. 4237 (adding 17 U.S.C., ch. 10); Protecting Innovation and Art While Preventing Piracy: Hearing before the Senate Committee on the Judiciary, 108th Cong., 2d Sess. (2004).

I do not know whether these developments and similar alternatives will prove sufficient, but I am reasonably certain that, given their existence, a strong demonstrated need for modifying Sony (or for interpreting Sony's standard more strictly) has not yet been shown. That fact, along with the added risks that modification (or strict interpretation) would impose upon technological innovation, leads me to the conclusion that we should maintain Sony, reading its standard as I have read it. As so read, it requires affirmance of the Ninth Circuit's determination of the relevant aspects of the Sony question.

. . .

For these reasons, I disagree with Justice GINSBURG, but I agree with the Court and join its opinion.

---

7. Enablement and Liability for Infringement in the Internet Context

SOCAN v. Canadian Association of Internet Providers, 2004 SCC 45

Arbour J., Bastarache J., Binnie J., Deschamps J., Fish J., Iacobucci J., LeBel J., Major J., McLachlin C.J.C.

Heard: December 3, 2003
Judgment: June 30, 2004
Docket: 29286

. . .

Binnie J.:

d. "Authorizing" Infringement

120 Authorizing a communication by telecommunication is a discrete infringement of s. 3(1); see Compo Co., supra, at pp. 373 and 376.

121 The respondent argues that even if the appellants did not themselves infringe the copyright, they were guilty of "authorizing" content providers to do so because Internet intermediaries know that material (including copyright material) placed on their facilities by content providers will be accessed by end users. Indeed as Evans J.A. pointed out, at para. 120: "Knowledge of the content available on the Internet, including "free" music, and of end users' interest in accessing it, are powerful inducements for end users to sign up with access providers, and content providers with operators of host servers."

122 Of course there is a good deal of material on the Internet that is not subject to copyright, just as there was a good deal of law-related material in the Great Library at Osgoode Hall that was not copyrighted in the recent CCH appeal. In that case, as here, the copyright owners asserted that making available a photocopier and photocopying service by the Law Society of Upper Canada implicitly "authorized" copyright infringement. This Court, however, held that authorizing infringement under the Copyright Act is not so easily demonstrated, at para. 38, per McLachlin C.J.:

> ...a person does not authorize infringement by authorizing the mere use of equipment that <u>could</u> be used to infringe copyright. Courts should presume that a person who authorizes an activity does so only so far as it is in accordance with the law. This presumption may be rebutted if it is shown that a certain <u>relationship or degree of control</u> existed between the alleged authorizer and the persons who committed the copyright infringement. [Emphasis added.]

See also Vigneux v. Canadian Performing Right Society, [1945] A.C. 108 (Canada P.C.); Muzak Corp. v. Composers, Authors & Publishers Assn. (Canada), [1953] 2 S.C.R. 182 (S.C.C.). SOCAN contends that the host server in essence acts as a commercial partner with the content provider when material is made available on the Internet, but there was no such finding of fact by the Board, and I do not think the rights and obligations of partnership can be so casually imposed.

123 The operation of the Internet is obviously a good deal more complicated than the operation of a photocopier, but it is true here, as it was in the CCH case, that when massive amounts of non-copyrighted material are accessible to the end user, it is not possible to impute to the Internet Service Provider, based solely on the provision of Internet facilities, an authority to download copyrighted material as opposed to non-copyrighted material.

124 On this point the Board concluded as follows (at p. 458):

> Even knowledge by an ISP that its facilities may be employed for infringing purposes does not make the ISP liable for authorizing the infringement if it does not purport to grant to the person committing the infringement a license or permission to infringe. An intermediary would have to sanction, approve or countenance more than the mere use of equipment that may be used for infringement. Moreover, an ISP is entitled to presume that its facilities will be used in accordance with law.

This conclusion is generally consistent with the decision of this Court in the CCH case, although I would point out that copyright liability may well attach if the activities of the Internet Service Provider cease to be content neutral, e.g. if it has notice that a content provider has posted infringing material on its system and fails to take remedial action.

125 Under the European E-Commerce Directive, access to cached information must be expeditiously curtailed when the Internet Service Provider becomes aware of infringing content. At that time, the information must be removed or access disabled at the original site (art. 13(1)(e)). Under the U.S. Digital Millennium Copyright Act, those who cache information are not liable where they act expeditiously to remove or disable access to material once notice is received that it infringes copyright (s. 512(b)(2)(E)). If the content provider disputes that the work is covered by copyright, the U.S. Act lays out a procedure for the resolution of that issue.

126 In the present appeal, the Federal Court of Appeal stated that, in the case of host servers, "an implicit authorization to communicate infringing material might be inferred from their failure to remove it after they have been advised of its presence on the server and had a reasonable opportunity to take it down" (at para. 160). Reference was made to Apple Computer Inc. v. Mackintosh Computers Ltd. (1986), [1987] 1 F.C. 173 (Fed. T.D.), aff'd [1990] 2 S.C.R. 209 (S.C.C.), at pp. 211 and 208, citing C.B.S. Inc. v. Ames Records & Tapes (1981), [1982] Ch. 91 (Eng. Ch. Div.), at p. 110, i.e., an Internet Service Provider may attract liability for authorization because "... indifference, exhibited by acts of commission or omission, may reach a degree from which authorisation or permission may be inferred. It is a question of fact in each case." See also Godfrey v. Demon Internet Ltd., [1999] 4 All E.R. 342 (Eng. Q.B.).

127 The knowledge that someone might be using neutral technology to violate copyright (as with the photocopier in the CCH case) is not necessarily sufficient to constitute authorization, which requires a demonstration that the defendant did "[g]ive approval to; sanction, permit; favour, encourage" (CCH, para. 38) the infringing conduct. I agree that notice of infringing content, and a failure to respond by "taking it down" may in some circumstances lead to a finding of "authorization". However, that is not the issue before us. Much would depend on the specific circumstances. An overly quick inference of "authorization" would put the Internet Service Provider in the difficult position of judging whether the copyright objection is well founded, and to choose between contesting a copyright action or potentially breaching its contract with the content provider. A more effective remedy to address this potential issue would be the enactment by Parliament of a statutory "notice and take down" procedure as has been done in the European Community and the United States.

128 In sum, I agree with the Court of Appeal that "authorization" could be inferred in a proper case but all would depend on the facts.

Cooper v. Universal Music Australia Pty Ltd., [2006] 156 FCR 380

Federal Court of Australia New South Wales District Registry French, Branson and Kenny JJ

7-9 August, 18 December 2006. Sydney

. . .

Branson J.

2 Stephen Cooper was the registered owner of the domain name "mp3s4free. net" and the originator, owner and operator of the now disabled "MP3s4FREE" website. Although that website did not contain any music files, it was structured to allow internet users ready access to music files of numerous popular sound recordings via hyperlinks. When an internet user clicked on a particular hyperlink, the music file in question was transmitted directly to his or her computer from a remote server. It is admitted that the overwhelming majority of the sound recordings the subject of the music files were the subject of copyright.

3 E-Talk Communications Pty Ltd ("E-Talk") and Com-Cen Pty Ltd ("Com-Cen") together conducted an internet service provider business under the name Comcen which hosted Mr Cooper's website. Liam Francis Bal is a director and, as the learned primary judge concluded, the controlling mind, of each of these companies. Chris Takoushis worked in the Comcen business. It seems that he is an employee of Com-Cen. Mr Takoushis was Mr Cooper's primary contact at Comcen and he provided assistance from time to time in relation to the establishment and operation of Mr Cooper's website.

4 A number of Australian record companies and other entities that own copyright in sound recordings, which I will together call the "Record Companies", instituted a proceeding in the Court in which they sought declaratory, injunctive and other relief against Mr Cooper, the two companies and Messrs Bal and Takoushis in respect of infringements of the Copyright Act 1968 (Cth) ("the Act"), the Trade Practices Act 1974 (Cth), the Fair Trading Act 1987 (NSW) and the Fair Trading Act 1989 (Qld).

5 On 22 December 2005 the primary judge granted declaratory and injunctive relief against each of Messrs Cooper, Bal and Takoushis, and against E-Talk and Com-Cen with damages to be later assessed.

6 These appeals challenge the orders made by his Honour on 22 December 2005 to the extent that the orders are founded on his Honour's conclusion that each of Messrs Cooper, Bal and Takoushis and E-Talk infringed the Record Companies' copyright in sound recordings by authorising the making of copies, and authorising the communication by operators of remote websites to the public, of those sound recordings. Com-Cen has not appealed from the orders made by the primary judge.

. . .

10 Section 101(1) which is in part IV, provides as follows:

"Subject to this Act, a copyright subsisting by virtue of this Part is infringed by a person who, not being the owner of the copyright, and without the licence of the owner of the copyright, does in Australia, or authorizes the doing in Australia of, any act comprised in the copyright. "

. . .

13 Section 101(1A) was inserted into the Act by the Copyright Amendment (Digital Agenda) Act 2000. It identifies certain matters that must be taken into account in determining, for the purposes of subsection (1), whether or not a person has authorized the doing in Australia of any act comprised in a copyright subsisting by virtue of Part IV. The matters so identified are not the only matters that may be taken into account.

14 Section 101(1A) may be assumed to have particular relevance in circumstances in which it is alleged that the act of infringement occurred in the online environment. This is because one of the objects of the Digital Agenda Act was to amend the Act so as to ensure the efficient operation of relevant industries in the online environment (s 3).

15 Section 101(1A) of the Act recognises that an element of judgment is involved in determining whether one person has, for the purposes of s 101(1), authorized another to do an act. It provides that:

"the matters that must be taken into account include the following:(a) the extent (if any) of the person's power to prevent the doing of the act concerned;(b) the nature of any relationship existing between the person and the person who did the act concerned;(c) whether the person took any other reasonable steps to prevent or avoid the doing of the act, including whether the person complied with any relevant industry codes of practice."

. . .

Orders Made by the Primary Judge

21 The primary judge made six declaratory orders and six restraining orders in similar terms against each of the appellants and Com-Cen. Each declaratory and restraining order relates to a particular schedule of sound recordings annexed to the orders.

22 A schedule of definitions, which forms part of the orders, provides the link between the terms of the orders and the schedules of sound recordings and additionally gives meaning to certain terms in the orders such as, for example, "Universal Catalogue" and "Universal Recordings".

23 The form of each of the six declaratory orders can be illustrated by setting out the terms of the first of them:

"1. The first, second, third, fourth and fifth respondents have infringed the copyright in sound recordings in the Universal Recordings, by:

(a) authorising the making of copies of; and

(b) authorising the communication to the public of,

the whole or a substantial part of those sound recordings without the licence of the first applicant or the owner of the copyright."

24 The form of each of the six restraining orders can also be illustrated by setting out the terms of the first of them:

"13. The first, second, third, fourth and fifth respondents, whether by themselves, their servants or agents or otherwise, be permanently restrained from:

(a) making a copy of;

(b) authorising the making of a copy of;

(c) communicating to the public; or

(d) authorising the communication to the public of,

the whole or a substantial part of any of the sound recordings in the Universal Catalogue including the Universal Recordings without the licence of the first applicant or the owner of the copyright."

25 Additionally the primary judge made orders permanently restraining the appellants and Com-Cen from operating or hosting the MP3s4FREE website and orders as to costs.

Mr Cooper's Notice of Appeal

. . .

27 As Mr Cooper's appeal was argued the sole issue for this Court's determination is the true meaning of the term "authorize" in s 13(2) of the Act and the related term "authorizes" in s 101(1) of the Act.

Did Mr Cooper Authorise?

28 The issue of whether Mr Cooper authorised internet users in Australia to copy, and operators of remote websites to communicate to the public, music files constituting sound recordings in which the Record Companies hold copyright must be determined primarily by reference to s 101(1A) of the Act (see [15] above). The appropriate starting point is to have regard to the matters identified in paras (a) to (c) of s 101(1A).

Power to Prevent (s 101(1A)(a))

29 Mr Cooper submitted that he did not have any power to prevent the doing of the acts comprised in the copyright of the sound recordings in issue because he did not have power to prevent:

(a) a person from making an MP3 file from a sound recording in another format (eg from a compact disc);

(b) a person from making an MP3 file generally accessible over the internet; and

(c) a person from accessing an MP3 file that another person had made generally accessible over the internet.

30 The above submission appears to overlook that the copyright in a sound recording is infringed each time that it is copied without proper authority. The making of a particular unauthorised copy is no less an infringement of the owner's copyright because other unauthorised copies are also made or are likely to be made.

31 Additionally, Mr Cooper submitted that to facilitate copying or communication is not to authorise it. He placed reliance on observations made by Lord Templeman in CBS Songs Ltd v Amstrad Consumer Electronics plc [1988] AC 1013 and by Sackville J, with whom Jenkinson and Burchett JJ agreed, in Nationwide News Pty Ltd v Copyright Agency Ltd (1996) 65 FCR 399 at 422. His Honour there observed that:

> "a person does not authorise an infringement merely because he or she knows that another person might infringe the copyright and takes no step to prevent the infringement."

> For the reasons given below (see in particular [37] and [43]) I conclude that Mr Cooper did not merely facilitate the infringements of copyright upon which the case of the Record Companies relied. He engaged in additional relevant conduct so as to take himself outside the purview of his Honour's observation.

32 Before considering the extent (if any) of Mr Cooper's power to prevent the copying or communication to the public of sound recordings in which the Record Companies hold copyright, it is necessary to determine what is meant by "power to prevent" in s 101(1A)(a). The appellants contended, in effect, that unless Mr Cooper had power, at the time of the making of an infringing copy of a sound recording, to prevent that copy being made, he had no power to prevent within the meaning of s 101(1A)(a). Unless s 112E of the Act, which is set out in [16] above, were enacted simply out of an abundance of caution, it presupposes that a person who merely provides facilities for making a communication might, absent the section, be taken to have authorised an infringement of copyright in an audio-visual item effected by use of the facility. This presupposition is inconsistent with the submission of the appellants. However, in my view, it is consistent with the ordinary understanding of authorisation. The following hypothetical situation may be considered. One person has a vial which contains active and highly infectious micro-organisms which are ordinarily passed from human to human by the coughing of an infected person. He or she authorises another person to break the vial in a crowded room knowing that this will result in some people in the room becoming infected with the micro-organisms. Most people would, I think, regard the first person as having authorised the infection not only of those in the room, but also the wider group thereafter directly infected by them, notwithstanding that he or she had no power to prevent those who were in the room from coughing.

33 In determining what is meant by "power to prevent" in s 101(1A)(a) it is appropriate then to turn to relevant authorities concerning authorisation in the context of copyright law, and in particular, to the Australian authorities as it is

these to which the legislature may be presumed to have given particular attention when enacting s 101(1A)(a).

34 In University of New South Wales v Moorhouse (1975) 133 CLR 1 the High Court unanimously held that the University had infringed Mr Moorhouse's copyright in a book of short stories by authorising the making of an infringing copy of one of the stories. The relevant circumstances were that a copy of Mr Moorhouse's book was held on open shelves in the University's library and the University placed a coin-operated photocopier in that library. Jacobs J, with whom McTiernan ACJ agreed, identified at 21 the real question to be determined as whether there was in the circumstances an invitation to be implied that the person who made the infringing copy might, in common with other users of the library, make such use of the photocopying facilities as he thought fit. His Honour found that such an invitation was to be implied. He concluded that it was immaterial that the library was not open to all comers, that use of the photocopier was not intended to generate a profit to the University and that the University did not know that users of the photocopier were doing acts comprised in authors' copyrights — and may even have been entitled to assume that users would obey the law of copyright.

35 In a separate judgment Gibbs J, after noting at 12 that a person cannot be said to authorise an infringement of copyright unless he or she has some power to prevent it, said at 13 that:

> "a person who has under his control the means by which an infringement of copyright may be committed — such as a photocopying machine — and who makes it available to other persons, knowing, or having reason to suspect, that it is likely to be used for the purpose of committing an infringement, and omitting to take reasonable steps to limit its use to legitimate purposes, would authorize any infringement that resulted from its use."

36 It seems to me that both Jacobs and Gibbs JJ concentrated on the behaviour of the University in making the photocopier available for use in the library rather than on the issue of the University's capacity to control the use of the photocopier once it had been made available to library users. The observation of Gibbs J that a person cannot be said to authorise an infringement unless he or she has some power to prevent it must be understood in this context. That is, the relevant power which the University had to prevent the copyright infringement must be understood to have been, or at least to have included, the power not to allow a coin-operated photocopier in the library.

37 Some support for this understanding of Moorhouse 133 CLR 1 can be found in Australian Tape Manufacturers Association Ltd v Commonwealth (1993) 176 CLR 480. In that case at 498 Mason CJ and Brennan, Deane and Gaudron JJ identified a distinction between the mere sale of an article, such as a blank tape or a video recorder, where there is a likelihood that the article will be used for an infringing purpose and the circumstances of Moorhouse 133 CLR 1. Their Honours noted that in Moorhouse 133 CLR 1 the University not only failed to

take steps to prevent infringement; it provided potential infringers with both the copyright material and the means by which it could be copied.

38 Some, albeit limited, support for understanding the reference in s 101(1A) (a) to "the person's power to prevent the doing of the act concerned" to include the person's power to avoid the means of infringement becoming available for use can, in my view, be found in Australasian Performing Right Association Ltd v Jain 26 FCR 53. In that case the Full Court, which concluded that Mr Jain had authorised the infringement of copyright in question, said at 61:

> "The judgment of the members of the High Court in the Moorhouse case establishes that one of the meanings of the word "authorize' in the context in which it is here used is "countenance'. It may be that not every act which amounts to the countenancing of something is an authorisation. Every case will depend upon its own facts. Matters of degree are involved. But the evidence in the present case reveals... a studied and deliberate course of action in which Mr Jain decided to ignore the appellant's rights and to allow a situation to develop and to continue in which he must have known that it was likely that the appellant's music would be played without any licence from it."

39 Additionally, as mentioned in [32] above, the introduction of s 112E into the Act suggests that, absent that section, a mere provider of facilities for making communications could have been held to have authorised copyright infringements effected by the use of those facilities. I do not accept, as Mr Cooper contended, that s 112E was introduced into the Act simply out of an abundance of caution. The supplementary explanatory memorandum for the Copyright Amendment (Digital Agenda) Bill 1999 (Cth) indicates otherwise by stating that the new s 112E:

> "has the effect of expressly limiting the authorisation liability of persons who provide facilities for the making of, or facilitating the making of, communications."

40 Mr Cooper placed considerable weight on a suggested analogy between his website and Google. Two things may be said in this regard. First, Mr Cooper's assumption that Google's activities in Australia do not result in infringements of the Act is untested. Perfect 10 v Google Inc 416 F Supp 2d 828 (2006) upon which Mr Cooper placed reliance is a decision under the law of the United States of America which includes the doctrine of "fair use". Secondly, Google is a general purpose search engine rather than a website designed to facilitate the downloading of music files. The suggested analogy is unhelpful in the context of Mr Cooper's appeal.

41 I therefore reject the contention that unless Mr Cooper had power, at the time of the doing of each relevant act comprised in a copyright subsisting by virtue of the Act, to prevent its being done, he had no relevant power within the meaning of s 101(1A)(a). I conclude that, within the meaning of the paragraph, a person's power to prevent the doing of an act comprised in a copyright includes the person's power not to facilitate the doing of that act by, for example, making available to the public a technical capacity calculated to lead to the doing of that act. The evidence leads to the inexorable inference that it was the deliberate

choice of Mr Cooper to establish and maintain his website in a form which did not give him the power immediately to prevent, or immediately to restrict, internet users from using links on his website to access remote websites for the purpose of copying sound recordings in which copyright subsisted.

42   I conclude that, within the meaning of s 101(1A)(a), Mr Cooper had power to prevent the copying in Australia of copyright sound recordings via his website. He had that power because he was responsible for creating and maintaining his MP3s4FREE website. As stated above, the principal content of the website comprised links to other websites and files contained on other servers. Senior counsel for Mr Cooper conceded that, in effect, the overwhelming majority of the files listed on the website were the subject of copyright. The website was structured so that when a user clicked on a link to a specific music file a copy of that file was transmitted directly to the user's computer.

43   It is immaterial, in my view, that Mr Cooper's website operated automatically in the sense that, although he could edit links on the site, he did not control the usual way in which links were added to the site. The evidence also leads to the inexorable inference that it was the deliberate choice of Mr Cooper to establish his website in a way which allowed the automatic addition of hyperlinks.

44   I also conclude that, within the meaning of s 101(1A)(a), Mr Cooper had power to prevent the communication of copyright sound recordings to the public in Australia via his website. Again he had that power because he was responsible for creating and maintaining his MP3s4FREE website with the characteristics referred to above.

45   For the above reasons, I find that, within the meaning of s 101(1A)(a), the extent of Mr Cooper's power to prevent copyright infringements via his website was considerable.

Nature of Relationship (s 101(1A)(b))

46   Mr Cooper submitted that he did not have any relationship with people who made MP3 files generally accessible over the internet or with people who downloaded such files from remote websites via hyperlinks on his website. The findings of the primary judge do not suggest any relationship between Mr Cooper and those who made MP3 files generally accessible over the internet. However, the same cannot be said of his Honour's findings concerning those who downloaded music files via Mr Cooper's website.

47   An aspect of the nature of the relationship existing between Mr Cooper and those users of the internet who obtained copyright sound recordings from the internet via his website is that the users were attracted to Mr Cooper's website and obtained the sound recordings by clicking on hyperlinks on that website. The primary judge found that Mr Cooper's website was user friendly and allowed internet users readily to select from a variety of catalogues of popular sound recordings.

48 His Honour also found that Mr Cooper benefited financially from sponsorship and advertisements on the website; that is, that the relationship between Mr Cooper and the users of his website had a commercial aspect. Mr Cooper's benefits from advertising and sponsorship may be assumed to have been related to the actual or expected exposure of the website to internet users. As a consequence Mr Cooper had a commercial interest in attracting users to his website for the purpose of copying digital music files.

Other Reasonable Steps Including Compliance With Industry Codes of Practice (s 101(1A)(c))

49 Mr Cooper did not suggest, other than by reference to disclaimers on his website, that he took any reasonable steps to avoid the infringements of copyright. As those disclaimers misstated Australian copyright law in a material way, the inclusion of them on the website did not constitute a reasonable step to prevent or avoid the infringement of copyright. In any event, I would have attributed little, if any, weight to them as, on his Honour's findings, their intended purpose was merely cosmetic.

50 The reasons for judgment of the primary judge make no reference to any relevant industry codes. It appears that the parties agreed at trial that there were no relevant industry codes to which his Honour could have regard.

51 I conclude that Mr Cooper did not establish that he took any reasonable steps to prevent or avoid the use of his website for copying copyright sound recordings or for communicating such recordings to the public.

Mr Cooper Authorised

52 Having taken into account the matters identified above, and the name of his website, I conclude that Mr Cooper infringed the Record Companies' respective copyrights in sound recordings by in Australia authorising internet users to do acts comprised in those copyrights, namely make copies of the sound recordings. I also conclude that Mr Cooper infringed the Record Companies' respective copyright in sound recordings by authorising operators of remote websites to communicate those sound recordings to the public in Australia.

. . .

Did E-Talk Authorise?

61 In determining whether E-Talk authorised the doing in Australia of any act comprised in the Record Companies' copyrights it is necessary to take into account, together with other relevant things, the matters identified in s 101(1A) of the Act (see [15] above).

62 As all of the relevant acts of copyright infringement took place via Mr Cooper's website, I conclude that E-Talk had power to prevent the doing of the acts concerned because, together with Com-Cen (of which Mr Bal was also the controlling mind), it had the power to withdraw the hosting of Mr Cooper's website (s 101(1A)(a)).

63 I would place no weight on the, at best, remote relationships between E-Talk, on the one hand, and the users of Mr Cooper's website and the remote providers of music files on the other hand (s 101(1A)(b)).

64 E-Talk could have, but did not, take reasonable steps to prevent or avoid the doing of the acts of infringement (s 101(1A)(c)). Rather than withdrawing hosting of Mr Cooper's website, or otherwise placing pressure on Mr Cooper to stop his website being used for the predominant purpose of copyright infringements, E-Talk sought to achieve a commercial advantage from advertising on Mr Cooper's website.

65 In the circumstances, in my view, no error has been shown to affect the conclusion of the primary judge that E-Talk and Mr Bal, its controlling mind, authorised the acts of copyright infringement which resulted from the use of Mr Cooper's website. At the least, E-Talk countenanced the acts of infringement (see Australasian Performing Rights Association Ltd v Jain 26 FCR 53 and [20] above).

Roadshow Films Pty Ltd v. iiNet Ltd., [2012] HCA 16 (H.C.A.)

1. FRENCH CJ, CRENNAN AND KIEFEL JJ. This appeal from the Full Court of the Federal Court of Australia (Emmett and Nicholas JJ; Jagot J dissenting) [1] concerns the authorisation of copyright infringement by a person who is neither the owner nor the licensee of a copyright under ss 101(1) and 101(1A) of the Copyright Act 1968 (Cth) ("the Copyright Act").

2. The 34 appellants are Australian and United States companies which either own or exclusively license the copyright in thousands of commercially released films and television programs, including a sample of 86 films in evidence before the courts below ("the appellants' films"). The respondent ("iiNet") is an Australian internet service provider ("ISP") which provides its customers with access to the internet in return for a monthly fee.

3. A number of parties sought leave to intervene or to appear as *amicus curiae*. Leave to appear as *amicus* was granted to the Australasian Performing Right Association Limited, which supported the appellants, and to the Communications Alliance Limited, which supported the respondent.

4. As will appear, some customers of iiNet have used the internet access provided by iiNet to infringe copyright in the appellants' films by making the films available online using the BitTorrent peer-to-peer file sharing system, explained below. The appellants claim that iiNet has infringed copyright in their films by authorising its customers' infringing acts.

5. The key question in the appeal, whether iiNet authorised its customers' infringing acts, "depends upon all the facts of the case"[2]. The facts and circumstances on which the appellants rely to support their contention that iiNet authorised its customers' infringing acts include the following:

- the provision by iiNet to its customers (and to other users of those customers' accounts) of access to the internet, which can be used generally and, in particular, to access the BitTorrent system;

- the infringement of the copyright in the appellants' films by customers of iiNet who have made the films available online in whole or in part using the BitTorrent system;

- the knowledge by iiNet of specific infringements, as drawn to its attention by notices from the Australian Federation Against Copyright Theft ("AFACT"), representing the appellants;

- the technical and contractual power of iiNet to terminate the provision of its services to customers infringing copyright; and

- the failure by iiNet to take reasonable steps to warn identified infringing customers to cease their infringements and, if appropriate, to terminate the provision of its services to them.

For the reasons that follow, in our opinion, the conduct of iiNet did not constitute authorisation of its customers' infringing acts.

Relevant statutory framework

6. Part IV of the Copyright Act (ss 84-113C), headed "Copyright in subject-matter other than works"[3], includes provisions in respect of "cinematograph films", which are defined in s 10(1)[4]. Section 86 provides that copyright in relation to a cinematograph film includes the exclusive right to make a copy of the film (s 86(a)), and to communicate the film to the public (s 86(c)). Under s 10(1), "communicate", in relation to a cinematograph film, means "make [the film] available online or electronically transmit [the film]".

7. By s 13(2), found in Pt II (headed "Interpretation"), an exclusive right of a copyright owner to do an act includes the exclusive right to authorise a person to do that act.

8. Section 101(1) provides that:

"Subject to this Act, a copyright subsisting by virtue of [Pt IV] is infringed by a person who, not being the owner of the copyright, and without the licence of the owner of the copyright, does in Australia, or authorizes the doing in Australia of, any act comprised in the copyright."

Accordingly, a primary infringement of a copyright in a cinematograph film occurs when a person, who is neither the owner nor the licensee, makes the film available online without the copyright owner's consent; a secondary infringement occurs when a person, who is neither the owner nor the licensee, authorises the making available online of the film without the copyright owner's consent.

9. Section 101(1A)[5] provides for three matters that must be taken into account when determining whether authorisation of infringing conduct has occurred:

"In determining, for the purposes of subsection (1), whether or not a person has authorised the doing in Australia of any act comprised in a copyright subsisting by virtue of this Part without the licence of the owner of the copyright, the matters that must be taken into account include the following:

(a) the extent (if any) of the person's power to prevent the doing of the act concerned;

(b) the nature of any relationship existing between the person and the person who did the act concerned;

(c) whether the person took any other reasonable steps to prevent or avoid the doing of the act, including whether the person complied with any relevant industry codes of practice."

Something more will be said later about the context in which s 101(1A) was introduced.

10. It is also necessary to note specific provisions relevant to the liability of an ISP in respect of a communication.

11. Section 22(6) provides:

"For the purposes of this Act, a communication other than a broadcast is taken to have been made by the person responsible for determining the content of the communication."

Accordingly, iiNet is not liable for any primary infringement in respect of the conduct of its customers[6].

12. Section 112E qualifies the operation of ss 101(1) and 101(1A) to the extent that they apply to a person (such as an ISP) who provides facilities for making communications. It provides:

"A person (including a carrier or carriage service provider) who provides facilities for making, or facilitating the making of, a communication is not taken to have authorised any infringement of copyright in an audio-visual item merely because another person uses the facilities so provided to do something the right to do which is included in the copyright."

As an ISP, iiNet is a "carriage service provider"[7]. A cinematograph film is an "audio-visual item" within the meaning of s 100A, and the meaning of the word "communication" in s 112E corresponds with the definition of "communicate" in s 10(1).

13. Sections 116AA to 116AJ limit the remedies available against carriage service providers for infringements of copyright which result from the carrying out of particular online activities by the carriage service provider, provided that the carriage service provider meets certain conditions. All of the members of the Full Court agreed that iiNet was not entitled to the benefit of these provisions in the circumstances of this case[8], and iiNet does not seek to rely on them in this appeal. What might be noted, however, is that s 116AG(3)(b), which limits

remedies against carriage service providers, empowers a court to make "an order requiring the carriage service provider to terminate a specified account".

Technical background

14. The technical background to the appeal has been explained in the courts below[9] and is not contested on the appeal. Nevertheless, it is convenient to summarise some aspects of the relevant technology before considering the submissions made on the appeal.

The Internet Protocol and IP addresses

15. Computers connected to the internet communicate with each other by means of a common language, or protocol, called the Internet Protocol ("IP"). Data sent by means of the IP is broken up into small "packets". Computers sending and receiving data are allocated IP addresses, which enable packets to be exchanged (in much the same way that postal addresses enable mail to be exchanged). Such IP addresses are sold in blocks to ISPs, and ISPs allocate IP addresses to their customers. The identity of the ISP to whom a particular block of IP addresses has been sold is publicly available information.

16. Where a customer's computer is directly connected to the internet (through a modem), the ISP will assign a public IP address to that computer. However, many computers are not directly connected to the internet, but are instead connected to a "router" — a device which can "route" data between a private network of computers. Where a customer's computer is connected to a router, the router will be directly connected to the internet (through a modem), and the ISP will assign a public IP address to the router. Where multiple computers are connected to a router, all of those computers will be able to access the internet — but only the public IP address assigned to the router will be visible to other computers on the internet. As such, a public IP address does not necessarily correspond to a specific person or computer.

17. iiNet allocates "dynamic" IP addresses to all of its non-business customers — this means that the IP address by which an iiNet customer's computer or router connects to the internet will change over time. Systems instituted by iiNet enable it to identify the customer account to which a particular IP address has been allocated at a particular time, but not necessarily the specific person or computer using that IP address (which may be several).

The BitTorrent system

18. The BitTorrent system[10] is designed to enable rapid and decentralised distribution of data across the internet, and operates differently from certain peer-to-peer file sharing systems which have been the subject of litigation in Australia[11] and the United States of America[12]. Types of data which might be distributed using the BitTorrent system include, for example, documents (usually .doc files), films and television programs (usually .avi files), and songs

(usually .mp3 files). Unlike traditional centralised methods of data distribution, the BitTorrent system operates on a peer-to-peer file sharing basis and all of the computers seeking the relevant data participate in its distribution.

19. The BitTorrent system has a number of parts, all of which must be employed before data can be distributed (that is, before a file can be downloaded). These parts are described below using the example of a person who wants to download a film (a .avi file):

> 1. BitTorrent client: A BitTorrent client is a computer program which allows a computer to access groups of computers sharing a particular .torrent file. These groups of computers are called "swarms", each computer in a swarm being a "peer". A person who wants to download a film using the BitTorrent system must first download and install a BitTorrent client.

>> 2. .torrent file: A .torrent file contains the information necessary for a Bit-Torrent client to contact and participate in a swarm — in this case, the swarm sharing the .torrent file associated with the relevant film. The .torrent file does not contain the underlying data associated with the film — that information is contained in the .avi file. Rather, the .torrent file contains the name of the .avi file sought, the size of the .avi file, the "hash value" of the .avi file, the "hash value" of the pieces of the .avi file, and the location of the "tracker". .torrent files are available from websites which allow users to search for the .torrent file associated with a particular underlying file (in this case, the film) which they wish to obtain.

>> 3. Hash value: Just as the IP breaks data into "packets", the BitTorrent system breaks data into "pieces". The hash value of a particular piece is unique, and identifies that piece. Hash values are important because the BitTorrent system distributes data (in this case, the film) in pieces. Pieces are downloaded out of sequence, rarest first, and must later be reassembled into a complete file.

>> 4. Tracker: A tracker is a computer program on a server which monitors the particular swarm with which it is associated. Instructions for locating the relevant tracker for a swarm are contained in the relevant .torrent file. Once located by the BitTorrent client, the tracker provides the BitTorrent client with the IP addresses of the peers in the swarm, enabling the BitTorrent client to participate in the swarm as a peer — that is, to send and receive pieces of the relevant file (in this case, the film).

20. In summary, a person who wants to download a film using the BitTorrent system must first download a BitTorrent client, and then locate and download a .torrent file associated with the relevant film. When the person opens the .torrent file, the BitTorrent client will use the instructions in the .torrent file to contact the tracker, and then start requesting and receiving pieces of the relevant .avi file — out of sequence — from peers in the relevant swarm. Once the BitTorrent client has received all of the pieces of the .avi file, it will use the instructions in the .torrent file to reassemble those pieces into the completed film and will save the file as instructed by the person who has downloaded the film.

21. As the BitTorrent client requests (and receives) pieces of the relevant .avi file that it has not yet obtained, it will receive requests from other peers in the

swarm for pieces of the relevant .avi file that they have not yet obtained. Generally, once it has received a piece of the .avi file, the BitTorrent client will share that piece with any peer from whom it receives a request. When the BitTorrent client has received all of the pieces of the .avi file, it will continue to share those pieces as long as the computer on which the .avi file has been downloaded is connected to the internet and the BitTorrent client is running. In most cases, this process of sharing will only end when the .torrent file is removed from the BitTorrent client by deliberate deletion by the person using the BitTorrent system. A user of the BitTorrent system who downloads a film, the subject of copyright, will infringe not only s 86(a) of the Copyright Act, but also s 86(c), because the BitTorrent system will automatically make that film available online on the user's computer until the .torrent file is removed from the BitTorrent client.

Legislative background

22. This Court has recognised on many occasions that ascertaining the meaning of the text of statutory provisions may require consideration of their context[13]. Section 101(1A) was part of a group of amendments to the Copyright Act made by the Copyright Amendment (Digital Agenda) Act 2000 (Cth) ("the 2000 amendments") described by the then Attorney-General, the Hon Daryl Williams, as the legislature's response to "rapid developments in communications technology, in particular the huge expansion of the Internet"[14]. The relevant Explanatory Memorandum contains echoes of those remarks[15] and, by reference to *Moorhouse*, explains that s 101(1A) partially codifies the principles in relation to authorisation which exist at common law[16].

23. The 2000 amendments followed the opening for signature by the World Intellectual Property Organisation ("WIPO") of the WIPO Copyright Treaty on 20 December 1996. Article 8 of the WIPO Copyright Treaty provides that "authors ... shall enjoy the exclusive right of authorizing any communication to the public of their works".

The agreed statement concerning Art 8 relevantly provides:

> "It is understood that the mere provision of physical facilities for enabling or making a communication does not in itself amount to communication within the meaning of this Treaty or the Berne Convention."

24. The 2000 amendments can usefully be summarised as follows:

- Sections 31, 85, 86 and 87 were all amended to add a new right, comprised in copyright in works and subject matter other than works, to communicate the work, sound recording, cinematograph film or television or sound broadcast to the public. The new right replaced the rights to broadcast and to transmit to subscribers to a diffusion service. Those rights had been overtaken by the availability of access to the internet. Section 10 was amended to include a definition of "communicate", as set out above.

- Section 101 was amended (as was s 36, in Pt III) to include a new sub-s (1A) to codify at least partially common law developments in relation to authorisation.

- Section 22(6) was inserted (as, later, was s 22(6A)[17]), effectively exempting ISPs from direct liability for communication of copyright material[18].

- Section 112E was inserted (as was s 39B, in Pt III), implementing the agreed statement in relation to Art 8 of the WIPO Copyright Treaty.

25. This statutory framework was subsequently added to:

- Sections 116AA to 116AJ, the "safe harbour" provisions, which correspond with cognate provisions in the United States[19], were introduced into Pt V (headed "Remedies and offences") by the US Free Trade Agreement Implementation Act 2004 (Cth) and the Copyright Legislation Amendment Act 2004 (Cth). Sections 116AB and 101(1A) (c) refer to industry codes. Regulation 20B of the Copyright Regulations 1969 (Cth) provides for the development of industry codes intended to represent a "consensus of copyright owners and carriage service providers".

- Sub-sections (5), (6), (7) and (8) of s 115, which were inserted into Pt V by Sched 4 to the Copyright Amendment Act 2006 (Cth), specify certain matters for courts to take into account when determining appropriate relief for electronic infringement on a commercial scale.

26. The 2000 amendments predated the release of the BitTorrent system. Their evident purpose was to respond to new communications technology by attempting to strike a balance between conflicting policy considerations. Access to internet technology is fostered by ss 22(6), 22(6A), 112E and 39B, and the "safe harbour" provisions, ss 116AA to 116AJ; the rights of copyright owners are enhanced by relevant amendments to ss 10, 31, 85, 86 and 87; the statutory clarification of the concept of authorisation in s 101(1A) is balanced against ss 22(6) and 112E. All three of those last-mentioned provisions can apply to a third party intermediary between copyright owners and copyright infringers (such as an ISP) although, as noted correctly by the primary judge (Cowdroy J), s 112E appears to provide protection where none is required[20].

Factual background

Contractual relationship with iiNet's customers

27. iiNet provides internet access to its customers under the terms of its Customer Relationship Agreement ("CRA"), which provides that an iiNet customer is responsible for the use of the customer's internet access by any other person. In October 2008, the CRA relevantly provided as follows[21]:

"Comply with all laws

4.1 In using the Service, you must comply with all laws and all directions by a Regulatory Authority and reasonable directions by us.

Prohibited Uses

4.2 You must not use, or attempt to use, the Service:

(a) to commit an offence or to infringe another person's rights;

. . .

(e) for illegal purpose or practices;

or allow anybody else to do so.

. . .

Cancellation or suspension by us

. . .

14.2 We may, without liability, immediately cancel, suspend or restrict the supply of the Service to you if:

. . .

(b) you breach a material term (other than a breach which separately gives rise to rights under this clause 14.2) and that breach is not capable of remedy;

(c) you breach a material term (other than a breach which separately gives rise to rights under this clause 14.2) and, where that breach is capable of remedy, you do not remedy that breach within 14 days after we give you notice requiring you to do so;

. . .

(i) you breach clause 4 ... or otherwise misuse the Service;

(j) we reasonably suspect fraud or other illegal conduct by you or any other person in connection with the Service;

. . .

14.3 If we suspend the Service under clause 14.2, then we may later cancel the Service for the same or a different reason."

Notices alleging infringement by iiNet customers

28. AFACT is an organisation which represents owners and exclusive licensees of copyright in films and television programs, including the appellants. From August 2007, AFACT employed a company called DtecNet Software APS ("DtecNet") to gather evidence of alleged copyright infringement by Australian internet users. From June 2008, DtecNet narrowed its investigations to target the use of the BitTorrent system by customers of four Australian ISPs, one of which was iiNet. DtecNet used a computer program ("the DtecNet Agent") to gather evidence that iiNet customers had used the BitTorrent system to download and share the appellants' films.

29. In essence, the DtecNet Agent is a BitTorrent client with an additional function — at the same time that it receives and shares pieces of a file, it gathers and records information about the peers in the swarm who are also receiving and sharing the pieces of that file. By using only .torrent files associated with the appellants' films (identified as such by hash values) and connecting only to peers with a public IP address that matched an IP address which had been sold to iiNet, DtecNet claimed that it was able to identify instances of copyright infringement by iiNet customers.

30. On 2 July 2008, the Executive Director of AFACT, Mr Neil Gane, sent iiNet the first of what would be many letters entitled "Notice of Infringement of Copyright" ("the AFACT notices"). The letter alleged infringement by customers of iiNet of the appellants' copyright in "movies and television shows" through the use of the BitTorrent system. The alleged infringements were said to involve "communication to the public of unauthorised copies of the motion pictures and television shows shared with other internet users via BitTorrent".

31. Attached to the letter was a spreadsheet said to contain the information relevant to infringing activities of iiNet customers occurring between 23 June 2008 and 29 June 2008.

32. The letter alleged that the attached spreadsheet showed that individual iiNet customers were involved in multiple infringements of copyright, and went on to state that iiNet's failure to prevent the alleged infringements from occurring "may constitute authorisation of copyright infringement by iiNet". iiNet was asked to "[p]revent the Identified iiNet Customers from continuing to infringe".

33. AFACT sent iiNet a second notice on 9 July 2008, including an almost identical letter relating to the period 30 June 2008 to 6 July 2008 and a corresponding spreadsheet. On 16 July 2008, AFACT sent iiNet a third notice, this time also enclosing three DVDs. These DVDs contained the spreadsheets attached to the earlier notices, as well as additional information said to be the underlying data gathered by DtecNet in its investigations.

34. AFACT sent iiNet a notice in similar terms (enclosing the same type of information) every week until August 2009. The AFACT notices did not contain information about how the data in the spreadsheets had been gathered, or how the DtecNet Agent operated. Responses by iiNet to the AFACT notices raised three issues: the desirability of AFACT referring its allegations to appropriate authorities; iiNet's inability to understand AFACT's data; and the insufficiency of an identification of an IP address to pinpoint a particular user of internet access provided by iiNet.

35. In the period 2008-2009, iiNet had approximately 490,000 customers, and was the third largest ISP in Australia. In the end, iiNet did not suspend or terminate any customer account in response to allegations of copyright infringement in the AFACT notices. It can be noted that, in responding to particular management or internet abuse issues (such as customers spamming or not paying bills), iiNet did,

in some cases, suspend or terminate customer accounts. However, the taking of those steps did not depend upon the accuracy of information provided by others.

36. When first sued, iiNet issued media releases on 20 November 2008 and 17 December 2008 asserting that it did not support or encourage any infringement of the appellants' copyright. iiNet also asserted in the media releases that it was for law enforcement agencies rather than iiNet to respond to the appellants' complaints about copyright infringement and that, in the absence of proof of the alleged infringements, iiNet was not prepared to disconnect any customer's internet service.

37. In addition to relevant clauses in the CRA, iiNet had other measures in place which it claims were designed to prevent or discourage copyright infringement by users of its internet services. These included a notice on iiNet's website which warned that the hosting or posting of illegal copyright material would constitute a breach of the CRA, and that such a breach may result in the suspension or termination of a customer's internet access. iiNet also provided and published an email address, facsimile number and postal address to which copyright owners could send copyright notices in accordance with the "safe harbour" provisions of the Copyright Act. Further, iiNet provided a service known as "Freezone", which allowed users of iiNet's internet services to download or stream a range of licensed, non-infringing material including films, sport, television programs, games, music and online radio stations.

38. By mid-2008, more than half the usage of iiNet's internet services by its customers (measured by volume) was represented by BitTorrent file sharing, and it was common knowledge that the BitTorrent system was used for infringing activities — although not solely for such.

Proceedings below

39. In the course of discovery in the proceedings before Cowdroy J, iiNet was provided with data from DtecNet which enabled iiNet to identify the accounts of 20 iiNet customers alleged in the AFACT notices to have repeatedly infringed the copyright in the appellants' films ("the R20 accounts"). Further, after the filing of expert reports which explained the DtecNet methodology, iiNet did not dispute the primary infringements by iiNet customers alleged in the spreadsheets attached to the AFACT notices between 23 June 2008 and 9 August 2009[22].

40. In concluding that iiNet did not authorise its customers' infringing acts, Cowdroy J did not have regard to the matters in s 101(1A). At the forefront of his Honour's reasoning was the fact that the BitTorrent system was the "means" of infringement, rather than iiNet's provision of access to the internet. His Honour observed that the evidence showed that iiNet had no connection with, or control over, the BitTorrent system[23]. Consequently, it could not be said to be incumbent upon iiNet to stop the infringements. The issue of a warning and the termination of customer accounts on the basis of the AFACT notices would not be a reasonable step to prevent or avoid infringements and would not constitute a relevant power to prevent infringements, his Honour held[24].

41. All members of the Full Court found that the statutory test for authorisation had not been applied correctly by his Honour. All agreed that a matter necessary to be taken into account in connection with s 101(1A) in this case was whether the exercise of any power on the part of iiNet to prevent acts of infringement was reasonable[25].

Authorisation

42. As explained in the reasons of Gummow and Hayne JJ[26], the concept of authorisation in copyright law has a long history in Australia and has existed since the *Copyright Act* 1905 (Cth)[27]. That Act was repealed by s 4 of the *Copyright Act* 1912 (Cth), which adopted the *Copyright Act* 1911 (UK) ("the Imperial Act")[28] as applying in Australia. Section 1(2) of the Imperial Act included in a copyright owner's statutory monopoly a right "to authorise" any of the sole rights constituting that monopoly, and it came to be recognised that authorisation of infringement was a separate statutory tort, distinct from primary infringement[29]. That amendment enlarged the copyright owner's protection in circumstances where the liability of a person for "causing" an infringement (a formulation found in prior legislation) had been construed as limited to situations involving employment and agency[30].

Relevant cases

43. In *Evans v E Hulton & Co Ltd*[31], Tomlin J relied on the Oxford English Dictionary's definition of "authorise" in connection with the authorisation of acts, "[t]o give formal approval to; to sanction; to approve; to countenance"[32]. His Honour did so in apparent rejection of counsel's contention that authorisation under the Imperial Act did not enlarge the copyright owner's protection in respect of infringement beyond employment and agency (as under the prior law). Tomlin J concluded that the scope of authorisation could not be so narrow[33]. That appears to be the first reference, in the context of authorisation of infringement, to synonyms to be found in the dictionary. The synonyms have been mentioned in numerous subsequent cases concerned with authorisation both in the United Kingdom and in Australia. However, in concluding that a defendant who sold a manuscript authorised its printing and publication, Tomlin J relied on an *obiter dictum* of Buckley LJ in *Monckton v Pathé Frères Pathephone Ltd*[34]:

> "The seller of a record authorizes ... the use of the record, and such user will be a performance of the musical work."

44. In *Falcon v Famous Players Film Co*[35], whilst the members of the Court of Appeal affirmed a judgment below that the defendants had infringed copyright in a play by authorising a theatre proprietor to perform the play, two differing approaches to the meaning of "authorise" emerged. Bankes LJ referred to *Evans v E Hulton & Co Ltd* and *Monckton v Pathé Frères Pathephone Ltd*, and then said[36]:

"in the opinion of those learned judges ['authorise'] is to be understood in its ordinary dictionary sense of 'sanction, approve, and countenance'."

That cumulative approach to the synonyms differed from the approach of Tomlin J.

45. Atkin LJ referred to the same cases after stating[37]:

"it appears to me that to 'authorize' means to grant or purport to grant to a third person the right to do the act complained of, whether the intention is that the grantee shall do the act on his own account, or only on account of the grantor".

46. The approach of Atkin LJ was applied by the House of Lords in *CBS Songs Ltd v Amstrad Consumer Electronics plc*[38]. Lord Templeman (with whom the other Law Lords agreed) found that the defendants (sellers of hi-fi systems which included facilities for tape recording) did not "sanction, approve or countenance" infringing use of these systems and went on to say that, by the sale of the products, the defendants "conferred on the purchaser the power to copy but did not grant or purport to grant the right to copy"[39].

47. Infringement under the Imperial Act included not only authorising the doing of an act within the copyright without the owner's consent (s 2(1)), but also permitting a theatre or place of entertainment to be used for the performance in public of a copyright work (s 2(3)). A managing director of a theatre company was sued in respect of both forms of infringement in *Performing Right Society Ltd v Ciryl Theatrical Syndicate Ltd*[40]. In that case, Bankes LJ stated that both forms of infringement might be inferred "from acts which fall short of being direct and positive", and went so far as to say that "indifference, exhibited by acts of commission or omission, may reach a degree from which authorization or permission may be inferred"[41].

48. By way of contrast, *Adelaide Corporation v Australasian Performing Right Association Ltd*[42] ("*Adelaide Corporation*") was concerned only with s 2(3) of the Imperial Act. Isaacs J (in the minority) saw s 2(3) as a "necessary complement" to s 2(1), and said that he understood the word "authorise" in the Imperial Act to import the sense of "sanction, approve and countenance"[43]. Higgins J (in the majority) appeared to agree, without expressly differentiating between the act of authorising and the act of permitting infringing conduct[44]. Higgins J went on to consider statements made by Atkin LJ in *Berton v Alliance Economic Investment Co Ltd*[45]. In that case, Atkin LJ said that "permit", in the context of a covenant in a lease, could mean "to abstain from taking reasonable steps to prevent the act where it is within a man's power to prevent it", although "sympathy" or even "assistance" with an act was not equivalent to permitting it to occur[46]. Higgins J considered that, for authorisation of infringement to be made out, there must be a direct power to prevent a specific act, such as a specific infringement of copyright, and not a power which would indirectly achieve that result only by putting an end to a relationship, such as that between lessor and lessee[47]. The other judges constituting the majority, Gavan Duffy and Starke JJ, said: "[p]ermission to do an act involves some power or authority

to control the act to be done"[48]; they also agreed that indifference does not necessarily establish permission to infringe[49].

49. In *Moorhouse*[50], a copyright owner of a literary work, a collection of short stories published under the title *The Americans, Baby*, alleged that a university was required to take positive steps to stop primary copyright infringement by library users photocopying library books on a photocopier located in the university library. It was contended that the university was indifferent to the occurrence of infringements through the use of the photocopier and had posted an inadequate notice concerning copyright infringement.

50. Jacobs J (with whom McTiernan ACJ agreed) spoke of the meaning of authorisation by reference to the dictionary sense of "sanction, approve, countenance"[51]. His Honour went on to find that an implied invitation to infringe could constitute authorisation despite the absence of knowledge of any actual act of infringement[52]. His Honour also found that providing a photocopier in a library was an unqualified invitation to users of the library which sufficiently caused the primary infringer to do the infringing acts comprised in the copyright[53].

51. Gibbs J likewise accepted as the meaning of authorise the dictionary sense, referred to in *Adelaide Corporation*, of "sanction, approve, countenance"[54]. His Honour then cited passages from that case to support the proposition that "[a] person cannot be said to authorize an infringement of copyright unless [the person] has some power to prevent it"[55]. His Honour went on to say[56]:

> "a person who has under his control the means by which an infringement of copyright may be committed — such as a photocopying machine — and who makes it available to other persons, knowing, or having reason to suspect, that it is likely to be used for the purpose of committing an infringement, and omitting to take reasonable steps to limit its use to legitimate purposes, would authorize any infringement that resulted from its use."

52. The derivation of the text of s 101(1A) — and in particular pars (a) and (c) — from these statements of Gibbs J is clear enough and, as already mentioned, this was acknowledged in relevant extrinsic material[57]. The effect of the *Moorhouse* decision on libraries was overcome by the introduction to the Copyright Act of s 39A[58]. Part VB of the Copyright Act (ss 135ZB-135ZZH) was subsequently introduced by the Copyright Amendment Act 1989 (Cth), instituting a system for the payment of equitable remuneration in respect of the copying of copyright works in educational and other institutions. Further, sub-ss (1A) and (1B) were added to s 40, exempting fair dealing for the purposes of research or study from copyright infringement.

53. *Australian Tape Manufacturers Association Ltd v The Commonwealth*[59] ("*Tape Manufacturers*") concerned the constitutional validity of a compulsory levy[60] imposed on vendors of blank cassette tapes. Citing Gibbs J in *Moorhouse*, among other cases, Mason CJ, Brennan, Deane and Gaudron JJ said[61]:

"The sale of a blank tape does not constitute an authorization by the vendor to infringe copyright. That is principally because the vendor has no control over the ultimate use of the blank tape".

Their Honours went on to say[62]:

"manufacture and sale of articles such as blank tapes or video recorders, which have lawful uses, do not constitute authorization of infringement of copyright, even if the manufacturer or vendor knows that there is a likelihood that the articles will be used for an infringing purpose such as home taping of sound recordings, so long as the manufacturer or vendor has no control over the purchaser's use of the article".

54. In 2000, a new Pt VC (ss 135ZZI-135ZZZE), headed "Retransmission of free-to-air broadcasts", was introduced by the Copyright Amendment (Digital Agenda) Act 2000 (Cth). The new Pt VC instituted a scheme for the payment of equitable remuneration in respect of retransmission of free-to-air broadcasts, including cinematograph films subject to copyright[63].

Submissions

Appellants

55. The appellants have brought no legal action against any individual user of the internet services provided by iiNet for any primary infringements of copyright under either s 86(a) or s 86(c), and it did not appear to be in contention that it would be somewhat impractical to do so[64]. The present proceedings do not cover those responsible for providing the BitTorrent system. No party doubted that the rationale for the separate tort of authorisation is economic — namely, cost-efficient enforcement of the rights of a copyright owner.

56. The appellants' complaint against iiNet is confined to alleging secondary infringement. The appellants contend that iiNet is liable for infringement of copyright in the appellants' films because it authorised users of its internet services to communicate those films to the public by making them available online to be downloaded by others through the use of the BitTorrent system, as prohibited by s 86(c).

57. In alleging the separate tort of authorisation, the appellants made it plain that their complaints were not complaints of contributory infringement; nor did they rely upon the principles applicable to joint tortfeasors. American authorities were referred to only as showing different approaches to dealing with the phenomenon of large-scale copyright infringements, occasioned by developments in communication technology including video recording[65] and peer-to-peer file sharing[66]. Accordingly, the appellants did not seek to show that iiNet had induced, incited or persuaded its customers to undertake acts of primary infringement.

58. The appellants relied on the second passage quoted above from the judgment of Gibbs J in *Moorhouse*[67]. The appellants equated the "control" referred to in that passage with the "power to prevent" referred to in s 101(1A)(a), and contended that iiNet's technical and contractual relationship with its customers

gave it the indirect power to control the use of its services — that is, to prevent continuing primary infringements (through warnings, suspension of services and termination of contractual relations). That led to the submission that, once iiNet had received credible information of past infringements sufficient to raise a reasonable suspicion that such acts of infringement were continuing, failure to enforce the terms of the CRA (through warnings, suspension and termination) amounted, at the very least, to "countenancing" the primary infringements. Further, applying the language used by Jagot J in the Full Court, it was contended that iiNet's media releases amounted to "tacit approval" of the primary infringements[68].

59. The appellants stated that, on any remitter to the Federal Court, they would seek injunctive relief to restrain iiNet from "continuing to provide internet services to each of [11 of the R20 accounts] without obtaining confirmation from the account holder ... that each of the cinematograph films identified ... in relation to that account has been removed from the BitTorrent system on that account". Accordingly (and consistently with the pleadings as amended from time to time), the appellants' case on authorisation ultimately was that iiNet could not avoid secondary infringement unless it implemented a system designed to achieve the removal of infringing material by iiNet customers from the BitTorrent clients on those customers' computers. The appellants did not identify any statutory warrant for the imposition of these obligations.

iiNet

60. iiNet's main contention was that the appellants' approach to s 101(1A) and the question of authorisation was inappropriately rigid. iiNet emphasised Jacobs J's statement in *Moorhouse* that "[i]t is a question of fact in each case what is the true inference to be drawn from the conduct of the person who is said to have authorized"[69], which was itself drawn from a passage in the judgment of Gavan Duffy and Starke JJ in *Adelaide Corporation*[70].

61. iiNet contended that authorisation cannot be determined on the basis that particular factors — such as knowledge or a power to prevent — are either present or absent. Rather, iiNet relied on the language of s 101(1A) and emphasised that each of those factors is a matter of degree, and that a court must consider the extent to which each factor exists before determining whether a person's "inactivity or 'indifference, exhibited by acts of commission or omission, [has reached] a degree from which authorization ... may be inferred'". iiNet also emphasised that questions of reasonableness ought to inform this process, and submitted that both *Moorhouse* and *Adelaide Corporation* leave room for legitimate inactivity or indifference. The facts in *Moorhouse* were said to be distinguishable because the university was responsible for the library, the books on its shelves and the photocopier, whereas iiNet is responsible for the provision of internet services but has no involvement in, or control over, the BitTorrent system.

62. iiNet further submitted that, when all of the relevant factors are considered, it cannot be inferred from iiNet's inactivity or indifference that it authorised

its customers' infringing acts. In particular, iiNet relied on the fact that it has no direct control over its customers' acts (only the ability to suspend or terminate their internet access completely). Further, iiNet argued that its ability to implement a system of warnings, suspension and termination depended on it first undertaking the complex and costly task of reviewing and analysing the allegations in the AFACT notices. That task raised questions — of expense and effort, and of the possible risks (as a proxy for copyright owners) of exposure to contractual liability to customers if the information in the AFACT notices turned out to be inaccurate. Such matters were said to bear on the reasonableness of taking no steps to warn its customers after receipt of the AFACT notices.

Questions

63. The appeal can be determined by asking interrelated questions informed by s 101(1A). Did iiNet have a power to prevent the primary infringements and, if so, what was the extent of that power (s 101(1A)(a))? Did reasonable steps to prevent those infringements (after receipt of the AFACT notices) include warnings and subsequent suspension or termination of the accounts of all customers identified as infringing the appellants' copyrights (s 101(1A)(c)), if such customers failed to cease communicating infringing material using the BitTorrent system? How does the relationship between iiNet and its customers (s 101(1A)(b)) bear on each of those questions? It will be observed that these are largely questions of fact and the ultimate question of whether iiNet authorised the infringements will be an inference to be drawn from those facts[71].

64. Before turning to those questions, some general observations as to matters of fact need to be reiterated. Access to the internet can be used for diverse purposes, including viewing websites, downloading or streaming non-infringing content, sending and receiving emails, social networking, accessing online media and games, and making voice over IP telephone calls. The BitTorrent system is also capable of being used for non-infringing purposes.

iiNet's power to prevent primary infringements

Technical power

65. It is important to note that iiNet has no involvement with any part of the BitTorrent system and therefore has no power to control or alter any aspect of the BitTorrent system, including the BitTorrent client. Further, iiNet is not a host of infringing material, or of websites which make available .torrent files relating to infringing material[72]. iiNet does not assist its customers to locate BitTorrent clients or .torrent files by any indexing service or database entries[73]. It cannot monitor the steps taken by users of its internet services under the BitTorrent system, it cannot directly prevent users of its internet services from downloading a BitTorrent client or .torrent files, and it cannot identify specific films to which users of its internet services seek access. Once infringing material is stored on a customer's computer iiNet cannot take down or remove that material, and cannot filter or block the communication of that material over its internet service.

Nor has iiNet any power to prevent its customers from using other internet services — and, as noted earlier, several users of an internet service may share an IP address. Whilst the relationship between iiNet and its customers involves the provision of technology, iiNet had no direct technical power at its disposal to prevent a customer from using the BitTorrent system to download the appellants' films on that customer's computer with the result that the appellants' films were made available online in breach of s 86(c).

Contractual power

66. Under the CRA, iiNet contracted to give its customers access to the internet (which carried with it power to use the internet for infringing or non-infringing purposes) on the basis (set out in cll 4.2(a) and (e) of the CRA) that iiNet was not thereby purporting to grant to the customer any right to use the internet to infringe another person's rights, or for illegal purposes.

67. Because the CRA, in its terms, indicated iiNet's express, formal and positive disapproval of using access to the internet for infringing or illegal purposes, the appellants were driven to rely on the notion that iiNet's inactivity (after receipt of the AFACT notices) amounted at least to "countenancing" acts of primary infringement.

68. "Countenance" is a long-established English word[74] which, unsurprisingly, has numerous forms and a number of meanings which encompass expressing support, including moral support or encouragement[75]. In both the United Kingdom and Canada, it has been observed that some of the meanings of "countenance" are not co-extensive with "authorise"[76]. Such meanings are remote from the reality of authorisation which the statute contemplates. The argument highlights the danger in placing reliance on one of the synonyms for "authorise" to be found in a dictionary. Whilst resort to such meanings may have been necessary in the past, attention is now directed in the first place to s 101(1A). That provision is intended to inform the drawing of an inference of authorisation by reference to the facts and circumstances there identified, and recourse must be had to it. That is an express requirement.

69. Even it if were possible to be satisfied that iiNet's inactivity after receipt of the AFACT notices, and its subsequent media releases, "supported" or "encouraged" its customers to continue to make certain films available online, s 101(1A) (construed with both s 22(6) and s 112E) makes it plain that that would not be enough to make iiNet a secondary infringer. An alleged authoriser must have a power to prevent the primary infringements[77]. *Australasian Performing Right Association Ltd v Jain*[78], *Tape Manufacturers*[79], *Kazaa*[80] and *Cooper*[81] all confirm that there must be such a power to prevent. So much had been recognised earlier, in any event, in *Adelaide Corporation*[82] and *Moorhouse*[83].

70. As explained, the extent of iiNet's power was limited. It had no direct power to prevent the primary infringements and could only ensure that result indirectly by terminating the contractual relationship it had with its customers.

Reasonable steps

71. The nature of the internet, the BitTorrent system, and the absence of any industry code of practice adhered to by all ISPs are all factors which are relevant to the statutory task of assessing whether iiNet took reasonable steps to prevent or avoid the primary infringements, given its indirect power to do so.

72. Conventionally, the efficacy of warnings to infringers from owners (or licensees) of copyright derives from, and is reinforced by, the potential for successful injunctive proceedings, including interim relief, coupled with an award of damages or an account of profits, and an order for costs against a proven infringer. Whether a non-responsive infringer is continuing to infringe after receipt of a warning notice from a copyright owner may often be checked with relative ease if infringing material is in the public market place.

73. Termination of an iiNet account with a customer who has infringed will assuredly prevent the continuation of a specific act of communicating a film online using a particular .torrent file on a particular computer. Regrettably, however, on receiving a threat of such termination, it is possible for a customer to engage another ISP for access to the internet on that computer or access the internet on another computer using a different ISP. Whilst any new infringement would be just as serious as the specific primary infringements about which the appellants complain, this circumstance shows the limitations on iiNet's power to command a response from its customers, or to prevent continuing infringements by them.

74. Whatever responses iiNet received to warnings, iiNet would be obliged to update the investigative exercise underlying the AFACT notices either itself or by reference to subsequent AFACT notices (allowing an appropriate interval for compliance with a request to cease infringement) before proceeding further.

75. Updating the investigative exercise in the AFACT notices would require iiNet to understand and apply DtecNet's methodology — which, among other things, involved a permission to DtecNet from AFACT to use the BitTorrent system to download the appellants' films. Before the filing of experts' reports in the proceedings, the information in the AFACT notices did not approximate the evidence which would be expected to be filed in civil proceedings in which interlocutory relief was sought by a copyright owner in respect of an allegation of copyright infringement. Also, any wrongful termination of a customer's account could expose iiNet to risk of liability. These considerations highlight the danger to an ISP, which is neither a copyright owner nor a licensee, which terminates (or threatens to terminate) a customer's internet service in the absence of any industry protocol binding on all ISPs, or any, even interim, curial assessment of relevant matters.

76. iiNet's inactivity after receipt of the AFACT notices was described by the appellants as demonstrating a sufficient degree of indifference to their rights to give rise to authorisation. However, the evidence showed that the inactivity was not the indifference of a company unconcerned with infringements of the appellants' rights. Rather, the true inference to be drawn is that iiNet was unwilling to

act because of its assessment of the risks of taking steps based only on the information in the AFACT notices. Moreover, iiNet's customers could not possibly infer from iiNet's inactivity (if they knew about it), and the subsequent media releases (if they saw them), that iiNet was in a position to grant those customers rights to make the appellants' films available online.

Conclusions

77. The appellants' submission, that iiNet should be taken to have authorised the infringements unless it took measures with respect to its customers, assumes obligations on the part of an ISP which the Copyright Act does not impose. A consideration of the factors listed in s 101(1A) does not permit a conclusion that iiNet is to be held liable as having authorised the infringements.

78. The extent of iiNet's power was limited to an indirect power to prevent a customer's primary infringement of the appellants' films by terminating the contractual relationship between them. The information contained in the AFACT notices, as and when they were served, did not provide iiNet with a reasonable basis for sending warning notices to individual customers containing threats to suspend or terminate those customers' accounts. For these reasons, iiNet's inactivity after receipt of the AFACT notices did not give rise to an inference of authorisation (by "countenancing" or otherwise) of any act of primary infringement by its customers.

79. This final conclusion shows that the concept and the principles of the statutory tort of authorisation of copyright infringement are not readily suited to enforcing the rights of copyright owners in respect of widespread infringements occasioned by peer-to-peer file sharing, as occurs with the BitTorrent system. The difficulties of enforcement which such infringements pose for copyright owners have been addressed elsewhere, in constitutional settings different from our own, by specially targeted legislative schemes, some of which incorporate co-operative industry protocols[84], some of which require judicial involvement in the termination of internet accounts, and some of which provide for the sharing of enforcement costs between ISPs and copyright owners.

80. The appeal should be dismissed with costs. This result renders it unnecessary to consider the issues raised in iiNet's notice of contention.

81. GUMMOW AND HAYNE JJ. This appeal from the Full Court of the Federal Court (Emmett and Nicholas JJ; Jagot J dissenting)[85] turns upon the question whether the respondent ("iiNet") has "authorised" the infringement of, and therefore itself infringed, certain film copyrights of the appellants. The Full Court dismissed an appeal from the decision of the primary judge (Cowdroy J) [86] in litigation which had been instituted on 20 November 2008.

82. In this Court, leave to be heard as amicus curiae was granted to Australasian Performing Right Association Limited ("APRA"), which supported the interests of the appellants, and to Communications Alliance Limited ("Alliance"), which supported the interests of the respondent[87].

83. For the reasons which follow the appeal should be dismissed.

84. It is convenient to begin with reference to some of the principal provisions of the legislation which bear upon the issues on the appeal.

Copyright in cinematograph films

85. Section 113 of the Copyright Act 1968 (Cth) ("the Act") distinguishes between, and treats as independent, copyright in literary, dramatic, musical and artistic works, for which provision is made in Pt III (ss 31-83), and copyright in other subject matter which subsists under Pt IV (ss 84-113C). The appellants are either the owners or exclusive licensees of "cinematograph films" ("films")[88] in which copyright subsists under Pt IV. Part V (ss 114-135AK) deals with remedies and offences. To an action for final relief for infringement under s 115 of the Act, an exclusive licensee would, in general, be a necessary party (ss 117-125).

86. The statutory monopoly conferred by the existence of copyright in relation to a cinematograph film includes the exclusive right "to communicate the film to the public" (s 86(c)). The term "communicate" means to "make available online or electronically transmit ... a work or other subject-matter" (s 10(1)). A communication other than a broadcast is taken to have been made by the person responsible for determining the content of the communication (s 22(6)). However, a person does not determine that content "merely because" that person takes one or more steps for the purpose of "gaining access to what is made available online by someone else in the communication", or of "receiving the electronic transmission of which the communication consists" (s 22(6A)).

The business of iiNet

87. These provisions in s 22 are important for an understanding of the business of iiNet and the complaint made against it by the appellants. The business was founded by Mr Michael Malone in 1993. It was incorporated in 1995 and in 1999 its shares were listed on the Australian Stock Exchange. iiNet is an internet service provider ("ISP"), which, for reward, contracts with its customers or "subscribers" to provide them with access to the internet. The Asia-Pacific Network Information Centre sells "IP addresses" in blocks to each Australian ISP to effect communication between computers. The ISP then allocates those IP addresses between subscribers to enable the subscribers to connect to the internet.

88. As an ISP, iiNet is a "carriage service provider" within the meaning of s 87 of the Telecommunications Act 1997 (Cth) ("the Telco Act") and that term has the same meaning in the Act (s 10(1)).

89. At the time of the trial before Cowdroy J in 2009, iiNet had 490,000 subscribers, making it the third largest ISP in Australia, after Telstra and Optus[89]. The agreements with iiNet subscribers prohibited the use of the iiNet service to infringe the rights of another and forbad the subscriber to "allow anybody else to do so". The agreements also empowered iiNet to cancel, suspend or restrict

the supply of the service if iiNet reasonably suspected illegal conduct by the subscriber, or any other person, in connection with the service[90].

The appellants' case

90. The appellants complain that computers in respect of the use of which iiNet provides its services are used (among other inoffensive activities) to make their films available online. The films have been assembled, or "downloaded", by the sharing of electronic files between users communicating directly ("peer-to-peer") and not by the mediation of an ISP such as iiNet. The appellants do not contend that iiNet is liable as having authorised the downloading by subscribers. Rather, they focus upon what was then made available online. The steps involved are fully explained in the reasons of Cowdroy J[91] and there is no dispute as to the treatment there of the relevant technology.

91. For many years iiNet has received by email from the United States "robot" notices alleging copyright infringement. Up to 350 have been received daily. Cowdroy J, however, did not regard these as reliable evidence of infringement[92].

92. The primary judge rejected what he described as a vigorous challenge to the credit of Mr Malone which had been made by the appellants[93]. In cross-examination Mr Malone did accept that it is "common knowledge" that peer-to-peer software (including that protocol which was created by Bram Cohen in 2001 and is identified as BitTorrent) is used for "infringing activities". He agreed that in the middle of 2008 more than half of the traffic over the internet and the iiNet service was represented by peer-to-peer downloads or uploads. It should be added that there is nothing unique about iiNet as an ISP that facilitates access to BitTorrent.

93. The effect of s 22 of the Act is that iiNet itself is not to be considered responsible for determining the availability online of the appellants' films. Accordingly, iiNet is not accountable as a "primary infringer" of the right conferred by s 86(c) of the Act. The "making available online" by the subscriber or other user of the computer is an act of primary infringement. But, rather than themselves pursue those multifarious wrongdoers for their primary infringements, the appellants seek to fix iiNet with the liability of a secondary infringer in relation to those primary infringements.

94. It is accepted that a secondary infringement is completed only when the primary infringement has taken place, but in the present case "making available online" involves a state of affairs the existence of which constitutes the primary infringement. Further, injunctive relief on a *quia timet* basis would be available in any event.

95. The Australian Federation Against Copyright Theft ("AFACT") is a body whose members include corporations engaged in the film production industry and it assisted the appellants in the provision of evidence of copyright infringement by iiNet subscribers. On 2 July 2008, some four months before the institution of proceedings by the appellants against iiNet, iiNet received the first of

what were to become weekly "AFACT Notices". The first AFACT Notice stated that it had investigated infringements of copyright by iiNet customers using the BitTorrent "peer-to-peer" protocol, and that the infringements "involve the communication to the public of unauthorised copies of the motion pictures and television shows shared with other internet users via BitTorrent". The attached spreadsheet related to activities between 23 June and 29 June 2008, and was said to include the time and date of infringements, the films in question, the names of the owners or exclusive licensees of the copyrights and the IP address used by customers of iiNet.

96. Cowdroy J noted that iiNet did not challenge that in the 59 weeks from 23 June 2008 to 9 August 2009, the spreadsheets attached to the weekly AFACT Notices recorded allegations of infringement by iiNet users[94]. The AFACT Notices "required" iiNet to prevent continuing infringement by iiNet customers of motion pictures and television shows controlled in Australia by the members of AFACT and to take "appropriate" action available under its agreements with its customers. However, in its first response on 25 July 2008, iiNet emphasised that the AFACT Notices did not identify any iiNet customers; IP addresses were supplied, but some of them iiNet did not recognise, and, in any event, IP addresses were not synonymous with persons or legal entities. Thereafter, on 12 August 2008, iiNet told AFACT that any service associated with an IP address might not be a computer in the sole use of an individual. Rather, the service could be a shared terminal at a school, library, internet café or "wi-fi hotspot". Whilst iiNet was ready to co-operate with law enforcement agencies in their prosecution of offenders, it had no obligation to employ staff in the pursuit of information for AFACT and would not take the responsibility of imposing penalties on its customers "purely on the allegations of AFACT"[95].

97. The appellants focus upon 20 particular (but not named) subscriber accounts ("the RC-20 Accounts") in respect of which during the process of discovery in the course of the litigation a list was compiled. This provided what Cowdroy J described as "the most specific evidence of copyright infringement by iiNet users in these proceedings"[96]. Forty-five IP addresses were utilised to derive the RC-20 Accounts, reflecting the circumstance that the one subscriber account may, over time, have multiple IP addresses.

98. If the appellants were to succeed in this Court, the declaratory and injunctive relief which they then would seek on remitter to the Federal Court would be limited to 11 of the RC-20 Accounts. The Schedule to the draft minute of that proposed order identifies 18 films in respect of which a declaration is sought that iiNet has infringed copyright from a specified date in the second half of 2008 by authorising communications to the public by making the films available online by users of the 11 specified accounts. These primary infringements are identified in these reasons as "the Scheduled Infringements". One film is said to have been so made available in respect of two accounts. Five of the specified accounts have more than one film listed against them. The appellants contend that the evidence shows that the films were made available online for at least seven days after receipt of a relevant AFACT Notice.

99. The appellants also would seek an injunction which from a specified date restrained iiNet from continuing to provide internet services to each of the 11 specified customer accounts without obtaining confirmation from each respective account holder that each of the relevant films has been removed from the BitTorrent system on that account.

The basis for the appellants' case

100. The appellants do not claim that iiNet has the liability of a joint tortfeasor with the relevant account holders in respect of the Scheduled Infringements. Such a joint liability for the one act of copyright infringement, treating this as a wrong which is tortious in nature, has been based upon agency[97], vicarious liability[98] and "common design"[99]. (With respect to vicarious liability, it should be noted that this Court has emphasised that from the case law there emerges no clear or stable principle which underpins this doctrine[100].)

101. Nor do the appellants rely upon United States authority, other than by way of comparison with the Australian law. In *Metro-Goldwyn-Mayer Studios Inc v Grokster Ltd*[101], decided in 2005, the United States Supreme Court treats as having "emerged from common law principles" an independent and distinct secondary liability for copyright infringement. This liability would appear to be part of "federal common law" or to arise as a matter of statutory implication[102]. Liability is founded upon "contributory infringement" constituted by "*intentionally inducing or encouraging* direct infringement" (emphasis added). Liability also is founded upon "vicarious infringement" constituted by "profiting from direct infringement while declining to exercise a right to stop or limit it"[103].

102. In *Sony Corporation of America v Universal City Studios Inc*[104], decided in 1984, it was said in the opinion of the Supreme Court that the Copyright Act of 1976 "does not expressly render anyone liable for [another's] infringement", but, as a leading treatise points out[105], such an express provision is made in the grant by §106 of the exclusive right "to authorize" any of the exclusive rights conferred upon copyright holders and §501(a) classifies as an infringer anyone who violates the exclusive rights of the copyright owner. In *Sony*, the Supreme Court did refer to these provisions[106], but went on to consider general law principles of vicarious liability and contributory infringement[107], and *Grokster* proceeds on the same basis.

103. In Australia, the effect of s 13(2) of the Act is that the exclusive right to communicate the appellants' films to the public, which is conferred by s 86(c), includes the exclusive right "to authorize" a person to do that act. Part IV Div 6 (ss 100A-112E) deals with infringement in copyrights such as those of the appellants, which subsist under Pt IV. Sub-section (1) of s 101 is the central provision[108]. It states:

> "Subject to this Act, a copyright subsisting by virtue of this Part is infringed by a person who, not being the owner of the copyright, and without the licence of the owner of the copyright, does in Australia, or *authorizes the doing in Australia* of, any act comprised in the copyright." (emphasis added)

It is upon the statutory criterion of authorisation that the appellants base their case.

Authorisation

104. The right of translation of the works of authors which appeared in Art V of the original Berne Convention of 1886 was identified as the "exclusive right of making or authorising"[109]. Professor Ricketson has shown that this was the most important right for an author seeking protection in jurisdictions where another language was in use and Art V responded to the long established practice of local publishers profiting from unauthorised translations of foreign works[110]. Thus, in its first appearance in modern copyright parlance, "authorisation" bore a fairly plain and simple meaning. This was not to remain the case.

105. In Australia, the reference to authorisation in s 13(2) of the Act may be traced to the provisions specifying the exclusive rights pertaining to books (including the right to translate), and pertaining to dramatic and musical works and artistic works, which were found respectively in s 13, s 14 and s 34 of the *Copyright Act* 1905 (Cth); these provisions included the term "authorize". That statute was repealed by s 4 of the *Copyright Act* 1912 (Cth), which saw the carriage into Australia of the *Copyright Act* 1911 (Imp) ("the Imperial Act"). Section 1(2) of the Imperial Act conferred the exclusive right "to authorise" the activities (including publication of a translation) which comprised the monopoly in respect of works. The corresponding provision with respect to works in the current Australian legislation, which is found in s 13(2), applies both to literary, dramatic, musical and artistic works subsisting under Pt III and to subject matter such as films protected under Pt IV.

106. The Imperial Act also introduced, by s 2(3), a species of infringement by "permitting" a public place of entertainment to be used for performance of a work. This provision now is represented by s 39 of the Act[111]. In *Performing Right Society v Ciryl Theatrical Syndicate*[112], Bankes LJ, in a passage cited in later cases[113], used "permission" and "authorization" as if they were synonymous[114]. The corporate defendant in that decision was the lessee of The Duke of York's Theatre in the West End of London and the second defendant was its managing director, who held the licence from the Lord Chamberlain to stage performances there. The orchestra engaged by the company performed two musical works without a licence from the copyright owners. Rowlatt J gave judgment against both defendants in an action based both upon authorisation within the meaning of s 1(2) of the Imperial Act and upon permission of performance at a public place of entertainment under s 2(3). Only the managing director appealed[115]. He did so on the basis that there was no evidence on either ground to support the decision against him, and his appeal succeeded. Today the primary significance of *Ciryl* in Australia rests in its treatment of the liability of a director for the torts of the company[116].

107. It often is said that infringement of copyright, including that constituted by "authorisation", may be seen as tortious[117]. That linkage between the statute

and the common law serves to highlight a basic issue for the present litigation. This concerns the scope of "authorisation".

108. Shortly after the enactment of the Imperial Act, Harrison Moore, in a passage referred to in *Brodie v Singleton Shire Council*[118] by Gaudron, McHugh and Gummow JJ, wrote[119]:

> "The cases in which men are liable in tort for pure omissions are in truth rare, as has been recently emphasized by Mr Jenks[120]. The common law of tort deals with causes which look backwards to some act of a defendant more or less proximate to the actual damage, and looks askance at the suggestion of a liability based not upon such a causing of injury but merely upon the omission to do something which would have prevented the mischief. Where tortious liability arises from some cause other than the commission of an unlawful act it is in general because the defendant has done something or *put himself in a position which though lawful in itself does expose the rights of others to risk and danger, unless he shows such care as the circumstances require*". (emphasis added)

109. Further, the several reasons of Gleeson CJ, Gaudron J, Hayne J and Callinan J in *Modbury Triangle Shopping Centre Pty Ltd v Anzil*[121] are recent reaffirmations of the general rule of the common law that in the absence of a special relationship one person has no duty to control another person to prevent the doing of damage to a third.

110. Liability as a secondary infringer of copyright has been said to have an economic rationale similar to that of the tort of inducing breach of contract, namely a lower cost of prevention of breach of the primary obligation[122]. But with respect to that tort, Jordan CJ emphasised in *Independent Oil Industries Ltd v Shell Co of Australia Ltd*[123]:

> "It is necessary to establish that the third party knew of the contract, knew that the doing of a particular act by one of the parties to it would be a breach of it, and with that knowledge procured the party to do the act. ... It may be that no tort is committed unless it is established that the doing of the act was procured either with intention to procure by its means the breach of the particular contract, or at least with knowledge that the doing of the act would necessarily and inevitably involve a breach of contract".

> Likewise, the equitable wrong of "knowing assistance" in a dishonest and fraudulent design for breach of fiduciary duty, a distinct species of liability[124], requires actual knowledge thereof, or wilful shutting of eyes, or wilful and reckless failure to make such inquiries as an honest and reasonable person would make, or, at least, knowledge of circumstances which would indicate the facts to such a person[125].

111. The appellants' case, in essence, is that iiNet "authorised" the Scheduled Infringements, and it did so by "standing by" and "allowing [this] to happen without doing anything about it". As noted above[126], these primary infringements are the making available online of the appellants' films. So long as the films are retained online they are "[made] available online" within the meaning of the definition of "communicate" in s 10(1) of the Act.

112. The appellants submit that these primary infringements are authorised by iiNet, notwithstanding that as the ISP: (i) iiNet had no power to modify the Bit-Torrent software; (ii) iiNet itself could not take down the infringing material because it was not acting as host[127]; and (iii) there was no "common design" as was found with respect to the Kazaa file sharing system[128], and it followed from the findings of Cowdroy J that iiNet had no intention or desire to see any primary infringement of the appellants' copyrights[129]. Further, s 112E of the Act[130] states:

> "A person (including a carrier or carriage service provider) who provides facilities for making, or facilitating the making of, a communication is not taken to have authorised any infringement of copyright in an audio-visual item *merely because* another person uses the facilities so provided to do something the right to do which is included in the copyright." (emphasis added)

> (The term "audio-visual item" is defined in s 100A in terms including a cinematograph film.)

113. The appellants submitted that while s 112E proceeds upon the assumption that the provision of facilities is relevant to the issue of authorisation, the result s 112E produces is that, without more, the provision of facilities by an ISP will not amount to authorisation merely because of the use to which another person puts the facilities. This may be accepted. The section seems to have been enacted from an abundance of caution. As Nicholas J observed, it is difficult to see how the activity it describes, without more, could amount to authorisation[131].

114. However, counsel for the appellants appeared to accept that their case posited a duty upon iiNet to take steps so as not to facilitate the primary infringements and that this duty was broken because, in particular, iiNet did nothing in that regard.

115. So expressed, the appellants' case resembles one cast as a duty of care owed to them by iiNet, which has been broken by inactivity, causing damage to the appellants. In *CBS Songs Ltd v Amstrad Consumer Electronics Plc*[132], the House of Lords rejected the proposition that the makers of recording equipment owed "to all owners of copyright a duty to take care not to cause or permit purchasers to infringe copyright" and held that the makers did not owe "a duty to prevent or discourage or warn against infringement". What, in the present case, the appellants in essence seek is so to interpret the "authorisation" species of infringement provided by the Act as to achieve the imposition of a duty of care upon iiNet which is owed to the appellants and would be discharged by the taking of steps in respect of its subscribers but is broken by the inactivity of iiNet.

116. It may be accepted that the application of the tort of negligence can render liable parties whose failure to take economically responsible precautions has resulted in harm to the plaintiff[133]. However, the width of the terms in which the proposed duty is cast would present iiNet and other ISPs with an uncertain legal standard for the conduct of their operations. Further, as counsel for Alliance submitted, this would achieve for copyright owners, but at the expense of the ISP, the suspension or disconnection by their ISP of subscribers from the

internet, a remedy which would not be available to the copyright owners were they themselves to sue the subscribers.

Technological change and copyright law

117. As was emphasised in *Stevens v Kabushiki Kaisha Sony Computer Entertainment*[134], given the complexity of the characteristics of modern copyright law it perhaps is inevitable that the legislation will give rise to difficult questions of construction. After a century, the selection of the term "authorise" to identify the activity constituting secondary infringement continues to give rise to difficulty. But the difficulties, which reflect both technological developments and changes in business methods, are unlikely to be resolved merely by recourse to a dictionary.

118. When enacted in 1968, the Act comprised about 100 pages. Reprint No 12, with amendments up to 2007, shows that the Act has grown to more than five times its original length. The Act has been amended and expanded on some fifty occasions, the most recent substantial changes being made by the US Free Trade Agreement Implementation Act 2004 (Cth), which introduced the "safe harbour" provisions to which further reference will be made later in these reasons[135].

119. An important feature of the introduction of Pt IV in the Act was the distinct treatment given copyright in some recordings, cinematograph films, and television and sound broadcasts. This responded to advances in technology since the framing of the Imperial Act. The terms of that statute had not been chosen so as to keep pace with those advances. Decisions such as *Gramophone Co Ltd v Stephen Cawardine & Co*[136] (concerning infringement of copyright in sound recordings by public performance) had given somewhat strained interpretations of the Imperial Act which attempted to meet a judicially perceived need to keep the statute law abreast of the times.

120. The history of the Act since 1968 shows that the Parliament is more responsive to pressures for change to accommodate new circumstances than in the past. Those pressures are best resolved by legislative processes rather than by any extreme exercise in statutory interpretation by judicial decisions.

The authorities dealing with "authorisation"

121. In 1924, in *Evans v E Hulton & Co Ltd*[137], Tomlin J held that "a man having a manuscript the copyright in which does not belong to him and in respect of which he has no authority to deal", but who "sells to another some right in relation to it with a view to that other producing it", has authorised the ensuing production. The object of such a sale, namely publication, was, as Lord Templeman later said in *Amstrad*[138], "bound to infringe". This would be so even though the seller did not "control" the steps in that ensuing production[139]. It was in this context that Tomlin J said he was content with the statement in the Oxford Dictionary that "to authorise a thing" is "To give formal approval to; to sanction; to approve; to countenance"[140].

122. Read without the subsequent accumulation of case law upon both the Imperial Act and the present Australian legislation, the term "to authorise" in a specification of copyright infringement would appear apt to apply to a person who, without authority from the copyright owner, purports to authorise the act constituting infringement. As a matter of ordinary usage "to authorise" is to clothe with authority, particularly legal authority, thereby giving a right to act; that act then may be said to have been authorised. This sense is conveyed by such expressions as "The Authorised Version" (the King James Bible), and the authorised capital of a corporation.

123. There would be some analogy here with the development of the action for breach of warranty of authority. This action involves: (a) representation by words or conduct that the defendant has the actual authority to act on behalf of another; and (b) the inducement of the plaintiff by such representation to act in a manner in which the plaintiff would not have acted (eg by infringing copyright) had the representation not been made[141]. The liability of the plaintiff to the copyright owner for that primary infringement would be the loss or damage then recoverable by the plaintiff from the defendant for the breach of warranty of authority.

124. However, in *University of New South Wales v Moorhouse*[142] Jacobs J (with whom McTiernan ACJ agreed) said of the case law which had its source in the construction of s 1(2) of the Imperial Act that:

> "It is established that the word is not limited to the authorizing of an agent by a principal. Where there is such an authority the act of the agent is the act of the principal and thus the principal himself may be said to do the act comprised in the copyright. But authorization is wider than authority."

125. Like Gibbs J[143], Jacobs J accepted as applicable to the current Australian legislation the meaning "sanction, approve, countenance" given to "authorise" as it appeared in s 1(2) of the Imperial Act in *Evans v E Hulton & Co Ltd* by Tomlin J and then in *Falcon v Famous Players Film Co* by Bankes LJ[144]. Two points should be made respecting that expression. The first is that it would be wrong to take from it one element, such as "countenance", and by fixing upon the broadest dictionary meaning of that word to seek to expand the core notion of "authorise". The second point is that, given the generality of that expression, there is force in the following statement by Herring CJ in *Winstone v Wurlitzer Automatic Phonograph Co of Australia Pty Ltd*[145]:

> "As the acts that may be complained of as infringements of copyright are multifarious, so, too, the conduct that may justify an inference of authorisation may take on an infinite variety of differing forms. In these circumstances any attempt to prescribe beforehand ready-made tests for determining on which side of the line a particular case will fall, would seem doomed to failure."

126. The first three defendants in *Falcon* had made a film of the plaintiff's play in the United States, then imported it into the United Kingdom and agreed with the fourth defendant, Mr Chetham, a cinema proprietor in Bedford, that he would show the film over three days, on terms that they would receive from him a share of the box-office receipts. The issue now relevant for the present appeal was whether the

first three defendants as well as Mr Chetham, the primary infringer, had infringed the plaintiff's sole right under s 1(2) of the Imperial Act to "authorise" the performance at the cinema. Bankes LJ held that evidence before McCardie J[146] had "amply justified" the finding that they had done so[147]. Scrutton LJ held that the first three defendants were liable as primary infringers although "[i]t may be" that they had authorised the performance by the fourth defendant[148]. Atkin LJ was the only member of the Court of Appeal fully to consider the issue of authorisation, and did so without joining Bankes LJ in the use of the expression "sanction, approve, countenance". Atkin LJ said[149]:

> "To my mind the hiring out of the film for three days on the terms of the contract of hiring, which is before us, amounts to an authorization by the defendants to Chetham to perform the play, and is an infringement of the right of the plaintiff, who alone has the right to give such an authorization. For the purposes of this case it appears to me that to 'authorize' means to grant *or purport to grant* to a third person the right to do the act complained of, whether the intention is that the grantee shall do the act on his own account, or only on account of the grantor". (emphasis added)

127. The phrase "or purport to grant" used by Atkin LJ has a significance not always appreciated in those later cases, including *Moorhouse*, which repeat the phrase "sanction, approve, countenance". What is important for the present case is the immediacy in *Falcon* of the relationship between the primary infringement and the secondary infringement.

128. In *Moorhouse*[150], Jacobs J adopted a passage in the judgment of Bankes LJ in *Ciryl*[151]. This was to the effect that indifference, exhibited by acts of commission or omission, "may reach a degree" from which there may be inferred authorisation. It is upon this notion of indifference to the requisite degree on the part of iiNet that the appellants rely for the proposition that iiNet sanctioned, in the sense of countenanced, the Scheduled Infringements. The contrast between the notion of indifference, and the requirement by the United States Supreme Court in *Grokster*[152] of intentional inducement or encouragement of "contributory infringement", will be apparent.

129. The appellants rely upon the notion of "countenancing" to encompass acts or omissions which are less precise or explicit than those involved in "sanctioning" or "approving". But in considering *Moorhouse*, and the adoption by Jacobs J of the statement by Bankes LJ in *Ciryl*, it should be emphasised that the University controlled access not only to the coin or token operated photocopying machines in a room close to the library but also to the book copied by Mr Paul Brennan and the premises containing the library and the machines.

130. The relief granted by this Court in *Moorhouse* was limited to a declaration that the University on a particular date had authorised the doing by Mr Brennan of the act of reproducing a particular literary work in a material form and thereby had infringed the copyright in that work of the respondents[153]. In *Australian Tape Manufacturers Association Ltd v The Commonwealth*[154], Mason CJ, Brennan, Deane and Gaudron JJ described as critical to the decision in *Moorhouse* the power of the University to control what was done by way of

copying; the University not only had failed to take steps to prevent infringement but had provided potential infringers with both copyright material and the use of its machines by which copies of the copyright material could be made. Their Honours referred in that regard to a passage in the reasons of Jacobs J, and distinguished the case before them as follows[155]:

> "manufacture and sale of articles such as blank tapes or video recorders, which have lawful uses, do not constitute authorization of infringement of copyright, even if the manufacturer or vendor knows that there is a likelihood that the articles will be used for an infringing purpose such as home taping of sound recordings, so long as the manufacturer or vendor has no control over the purchaser's use of the article".

The 2000 Act

131. An immediate response to *Moorhouse* and the use of copying machines installed in libraries and archives was the addition to the Act of s 39A. This was done by s 6 of the Copyright Amendment Act 1980 (Cth). The new s 39A provided that in certain circumstances neither the body administering the library or archives, nor the officer in charge, were to be taken to have authorised the making of an infringing copy "by reason only" that it was made on a machine installed there.

132. Thereafter, the Copyright Amendment Act 1989 (Cth) included Pt VB (ss 135ZB-135ZZH), headed "Copying of Works Etc by Educational and Other Institutions", added to the jurisdiction of the Copyright Tribunal to determine equitable remuneration (ss 153C, 153D), and amended the provision in s 40 respecting fair dealing for the purpose of research or study.

133. A further element of complexity for this appeal has been provided by an addition to s 101 of the Act apparently made as some further and general legislative response to *Moorhouse*. The introduction of the Copyright Amendment (Digital Agenda) Act 2000 (Cth) ("the 2000 Act") just preceded the advent of BitTorrent. The 2000 Act added sub-s (1A) both to s 36, dealing with infringement of copyright in works, and to s 101, dealing with infringement of copyright in other subject matter. The 2000 Act also added s 112E and s 86(c), with supporting definitions.

134. Section 101(1A) reads:

> "In determining, for the purposes of subsection (1), whether or not a person has authorised the doing in Australia of any act comprised in a copyright subsisting by virtue of this Part without the licence of the owner of the copyright, the matters that must be taken into account include the following:
>
> (a) the extent (if any) of the person's power to prevent the doing of the act concerned;
>
> (b) the nature of any relationship existing between the person and the person who did the act concerned;

(c) whether the person took any other reasonable steps to prevent or avoid the doing of the act, including whether the person complied with any relevant industry codes of practice."

Conclusions

135. Section 101(1A) is so drawn as to take an act of primary infringement and ask whether or not a person has authorised that act of primary infringement. In answering that question there will be "matters" that must be taken into account. These include, but are not confined to, the matters identified in pars (a), (b) and (c). Was there any relationship that existed between the primary infringer and the (alleged) secondary infringer? If so, what was its nature (par (b))? Did the secondary infringer have power to prevent the primary infringement; if so, what was the extent of that power (par (a))? Other than the exercise of that power, did the secondary infringer take any reasonable steps to prevent the primary infringement, or to avoid the commission of that infringement (par (c))?

136. In answering these questions an ISP is not to be taken to have authorised primary infringement of a cinematograph film "merely because" it has provided facilities for making it available online to a user who is the primary infringer (s 112E).

137. As indicated earlier in these reasons[156], the power of iiNet as an ISP with respect to the use of facilities provided to subscribers was limited by the nature of their commercial relationship; iiNet could not control the choice of its subscribers and other users to utilise the BitTorrent software, nor could iiNet modify the BitTorrent software or take down the appellants' films which were made available online.

138. At all material times iiNet had many thousands of account holders. Was it a reasonable step to require of iiNet that it monitor continually the activities of IP addresses to provide precise details of primary infringements that had been committed, and then take further steps to forestall further infringements? Warnings might or might not have that effect. Evidence was lacking of likely behaviour in that respect by users of ISP facilities. Further, with respect to the AFACT Notices, was it reasonable to expect iiNet to issue warnings or to suspend or terminate the contracts of customers when AFACT had not fully disclosed the methods used to obtain the information in the AFACT Notices? Those methods were disclosed only by the provision of expert evidence during the preparation of the case for trial[157].

139. In truth, the only indisputably practical course of action would be an exercise of contractual power to switch off and terminate further activity on suspect accounts. But this would not merely avoid further infringement; it would deny to the iiNet customers non-infringing uses of the iiNet facilities. And, in any event, in the absence of an effective protocol binding ISPs (and there is no such protocol) the iiNet subscribers whose agreements were cancelled by iiNet would be free to take their business to another ISP.

140. In her dissenting reasons Jagot J concluded that iiNet had "moved beyond mere indifference to at least tacit approval of [the] primary infringements"[158].

Her Honour relied particularly upon a press release by iiNet by which it "ensured [that] its customers knew that their accounts would not be terminated ... unless AFACT could prove in court the alleged copyright infringements"[159].

141. The press release was issued by iiNet on the day the litigation by the appellants was instituted, 20 November 2008. It was available for download from its website. The release referred to the intention of iiNet to defend the action and expressed the view that the AFACT Notices were not sufficient to require it to disconnect users of the iiNet service. The significance of the press release was overstated by her Honour.

142. The "key facts" as to the "indifference" of iiNet upon which the appellants relied in this Court were four in number. They were: (i) the provision by iiNet of the internet connections, a necessary but insufficient step for the acts of primary infringement; (ii) the technical ability of iiNet to control the use of its service and its contractual ability to issue warnings and suspend or terminate accounts; (iii) the evidence provided by the AFACT Notices given before and after suit; and (iv) the absence of action by iiNet in response to the AFACT Notices.

143. These matters, taken together, do not establish a case of authorisation of those primary infringements which are the Scheduled Infringements in respect of the authorisation of which the appellants seek relief in this Court. The progression urged by the appellants from the evidence, to "indifference", to "countenancing", and so to "authorisation", is too long a march.

144. The facts of this case are well removed from those which in *Moorhouse* led Jacobs J[160] to adopt what had been said on the subject of indifference by Bankes LJ in *Ciryl*[161]. The rhetorical question with reference to what had been said by Bankes LJ, which Whitford J posed in *CBS Inc v Ames Records & Tapes Ltd*[162], may be asked here:

> "Is this again a case of the indifference of somebody who did not consider it his business to interfere, who had no desire to see another person's copyright infringed, but whose view was that copyright and infringement were matters in this case not for him, but for the owners of the copyright? It must be recalled that the most important matter to bear in mind is the circumstances established in evidence in each case."

145. The position of iiNet also differs significantly from that of the respondent company director in *Australasian Performing Right Association Ltd v Jain*[163]. He was effectively the chief executive officer at the hotel owned by the company where there had been unlicensed performances of musical works. The Full Federal Court said of the respondent that it "was within his power to control what was occurring [but] he did nothing at all"; and that he had "countenanced" the infringements[164].

146. The present case is not one where the conduct of the respondent's business was such that the primary infringements utilising BitTorrent were "bound" to happen in the sense apparent in *Evans v E Hulton & Co Ltd*[165], and discussed earlier in these reasons[166]. Further, iiNet only in an attenuated sense

had power to "control" the primary infringements utilising BitTorrent. It was not unreasonable for iiNet to take the view that it need not act upon the incomplete allegations of primary infringements in the AFACT Notices without further investigation which it should not be required itself to undertake, at its peril of committing secondary infringement.

147. Accordingly, the appeal should be dismissed.

Further matters

148. This makes it unnecessary to enter upon two further matters. The first is the reliance by iiNet upon requirements of Pt 13 Div 2 (ss 276-278) of the Telco Act as an answer to the authorisation case presented against it. It was contended by iiNet that these provisions would have prohibited it from taking action in reliance on the AFACT Notices, for example, by warning, or by suspending or terminating the accounts of its subscribers. The second matter is the application in iiNet's favour of the "safe harbour" provisions in Pt V Div 2AA (ss 116AA-116AJ) of the Act. The term "safe harbour" was coined to describe the operation of the system established in 1998 by United States legislation**[167]**. Like the differently constructed Australian system, this does not determine issues of liability, but limits relief against "service providers" who fall within a "safe harbour" specified in the legislation.

149. The case presented by iiNet on these two grounds failed in the Full Court. In this Court iiNet did not rely on the "safe harbour" provisions, and did not press by oral argument its notice of contention respecting the Telco Act.

150. Nor is it appropriate to consider the schemes enacted in the United Kingdom by the *Digital Economy Act* 2010 (UK) and in New Zealand by the *Copyright (Infringing File Sharing) Amendment Act* 2011 (NZ), to the provisions in which for payments by copyright owners to ISPs reference was made by counsel for the appellants, iiNet, and Alliance.

Order

151. The appeal should be dismissed with costs.

The *Copyright Modernization Act* created a new action to address infringements in the internet context, called "Enablement". The new cause of action was enacted in the following terms:

> Infringement — provision of services
>
> 27. (2.3) It is an infringement of copyright for a person, by means of the Internet or another digital network, to provide a service primarily for the purpose of enabling acts of copyright infringement if an actual infringement of copyright occurs by means of the Internet or another digital network as a result of the use of that service.

Factors

(2.4) In determining whether a person has infringed copyright under subsection (2.3), the court may consider

> (a) whether the person expressly or implicitly marketed or promoted the service as one that could be used to enable acts of copyright infringement;

> (b) whether the person had knowledge that the service was used to enable a significant number of acts of copyright infringement;

> (c) whether the service has significant uses other than to enable acts of copyright infringement;

> (d) the person's ability, as part of providing the service, to limit acts of copyright infringement, and any action taken by the person to do so;

> (e) any benefits the person received as a result of enabling the acts of copyright infringement; and

> (f) the economic viability of the provision of the service if it were not used to enable acts of copyright infringement.

. . .

---

8. Secondary Infringement

(a) Selling or Distributing Copies

The owner of a copyright in the United States has the exclusive right to do and to authorize the distribution of copies of the copyrighted work to the public by sale or other transfer of ownership, or by rental, lease, or lending.[33] Until recently, the Canadian Copyright Act did not confer on the owner of the copyright an express right of distributing copies of works to the public.[34] The *Copyright Modernization Act* of 2012 has, however, enumerated a new exclusive right in section 3(1)(j): copyright includes the sole right "in the case of a work that is in the form of a tangible object, to sell or otherwise transfer ownership of the tangible object, as long as that ownership has never previously been transferred in or outside Canada with the authorization of the copyright owner."

After the first authorized sale or transfer of the tangible object, the section 3(1)(j) right is effectively "exhausted" and cannot then be exercised to

---

[33] 17 U.S.C., s. 106(3), subject to s. 109.

[34] Article 6 of the WIPO Copyright Treaty which Canada has signed contains certain requirements with respect to the right of distribution. In particular, it requires that "Authors of literary and artistic works shall enjoy the exclusive right of authorising the making available to the public of the original and copies of their works through sale or other transfer of ownership." It provides, however, that the Treaty shall not affect the freedom of Contracting Parties to determine the conditions, if any, under which the exhaustion of the distribution right applies after the first sale or other transfer of ownership of the original or a copy of the work with the authorization of the author.

restrict further sales or other transactions in respect of physical copy. The provision is thus consistent with what is known as the "first sale doctrine," according to which an intellectual property owner's rights to control use or sale of the physical article are exhausted with its first authorized transfer. Because the subject-matter of copyright is the intangible work as opposed to its physical embodiment, the policy of copyright law has been to enable members of the public to use and deal with works lawfully acquired by them free of restrictions imposed by copyright owners, as long as no exclusive copyright or other right is violated as a result.[35] The owner of a copy of a non-infringing work has been, and will continue to be, entitled to re-sell it, give it away, or destroy it without infringing the copyright of the owner.[36]

The Act does, however, address certain commercial acts knowingly done with *infringing* copies of a work. Specifically, it is an infringement of copyright for any person to (a) sell or rent out, (b) distribute to such an extent as to affect prejudicially the owner of the copyright, (c) by way of trade distribute, expose or offer for sale or rental, or exhibit in public, (d) possess for the purpose of doing anything referred to in paragraphs (a) to (c), or (e) import into Canada for the purpose of doing anything referred to in paragraphs (a) to (c), a copy of a work, sound recording or fixation of a performer's performance or of a communication signal that the person knows or should have known infringes copyright or would infringe copyright if it had been made in Canada by the person who made it.

The scope of this section was considered by the Supreme Court in the *CCH* case.

**CCH Canadian Ltd. v. Law Society of Upper Canada, 2004 SCC 13
(S.C.C.)**

**Arbour J., Bastarache J., Binnie J., Deschamps J., Iacobucci J., LeBel J.,
Major J., McLachlin C.J.C.**

**Heard: November 10, 2003
Judgment: March 4, 2004
Docket: 29320**

. . .

The Chief Justice:

5 The publishers have filed a cross-appeal in which they submit that, in addition to infringing copyright by reproducing copies of their works, the Law Society infringed copyright both by faxing and by selling copies of the publishers' copyrighted works through its custom photocopy service. The publishers also contend that the Great Library does not qualify for the library exemption

---

[35] See, *Galerie d'Art du Petit Champlain inc. c. Théberge*, 2002 SCC 34 (S.C.C.).
[36] *Galerie d'Art du Petit Champlain inc. c. Théberge* (2002), (*sub nom.* Théberge v. Galerie d'Art du Petit Champlain inc.) 17 C.P.R. (4th) 161 (S.C.C.).

under the Copyright Act and, finally, that they are entitled to an injunction to the extent that the Law Society has been found to infringe any one or more of their copyrighted works. The four sub-issues that the Court must address on this cross-appeal are:

(1) Did the Law Society's fax transmissions of the publishers' works constitute communications "to the public" within s. 3(1)(f) of the Copyright Act so as to constitute copyright infringement?

(2) Did the Law Society infringe copyright by selling copies of the publishers' works contrary to s. 27(2) of the Copyright Act?

(3) Does the Law Society qualify for an exemption as a "library, archive or museum" under ss. 2 and 30.2(1) of the Copyright Act?

(4) To the extent that the Law Society has been found to infringe any one or more of the publishers' copyrighted works, are the publishers entitled to a permanent injunction under s. 34(1) of the Copyright Act

. . .

(2) Did the Law Society infringe copyright in the publishers' works by selling copies contrary to s. 27(2) of the Copyright Act?

80 Under s. 27(2)(a) of the Copyright Act, it is an infringement of copyright to sell a copy of a work that the person knows or should have known infringes copyright, a practice known as secondary infringement. The majority at the Court of Appeal rejected the allegation of secondary infringement on the ground that it was not established that the Law Society knew or should have known it was dealing with infringing copies of the publishers' works. The publishers appeal this finding on cross-appeal.

81 At the Court of Appeal, Rothstein J.A., in his concurring judgment, properly outlined the three elements that must be proven to ground a claim for secondary infringement: (1) the copy must be the product of primary infringement; (2) the secondary infringer must have known or should have known that he or she is dealing with a product of infringement; and (3) the secondary dealing must be established; that is, there must have been a sale.

82 In the main appeal, I have concluded that the Law Society did not infringe copyright in reproducing the publishers' works in response to requests under its custom photocopy service. Absent primary infringement, there can be no secondary infringement. I would dismiss this ground of cross-appeal.

(b) Importing

Pursuant to section 27(2)(e) of the Act, it is secondary infringement of copyright for any person to import into Canada, for the purposes of sale or distribution (either for trade or to an extent prejudicial to the rightholder), any work that the person knows (or should have known) infringes copyright or would infringe copyright if it had been made in Canada by the person who made it. The effect of the section is to make it an infringement of copyright knowingly to import into Canada infringing copies of the work without the consent of the owner of the copyright in Canada, though they may have been made by or with the consent of the owner of the copyright in the place where there they were made. Potentially, this is an important limitation on the operation of the "exhaustion" principle at the international level.

In the following case, the Supreme Court grappled with the hypothetical inquiry necessitated by the phrase, "*if* it had been made in Canada by the person who made it." In light of the complicated split between members of the bench on the various issues at play, Kraft Canada was ultimately unsuccessful in this attempt to harness s. 27(2)(e) to prevent the parallel importation of lawfully acquired chocolate bars (the kind of "grey marketing" that trade-mark law does not restrict for good policy reasons). The ongoing effect of the Court's ruling on the secondary infringement issue, however, is to permit a Canadian owner or exclusive licensee of copyright in, e.g. a manufacturer's logo or a product instruction manual, to block the importation of otherwise lawful consumer goods by claiming secondary infringement of the accompanying and incidental copyright work.

Kraft Canada Inc. v. Euro Excellence Inc., 2007 SCC 37 (S.C.C.)

**Abella J., Bastarache J., Binnie J., Charron J., Deschamps J., Fish J.,
LeBel J., McLachlin C.J.C., Rothstein J.**

**Heard: January 16, 2007
Judgment: July 26, 2007
Docket: 31327**

. . .

Rothstein J.:

1 I have read the reasons of Bastarache J. While I agree with his conclusion, I am respectfully unable to agree with his analysis. I have three main concerns with his reasons.

. . .

(2) The Purposive Approach to the Copyright Act

Overview

14 In my view, this case turns on a straightforward application of s. 27(2)(e) of the Copyright Act. The Kraft companies allege that Euro-Excellence Inc. is liable for secondary infringement under s. 27(2)(e). However, Kraft Canada Inc. has failed to establish "hypothetical infringement", which is one of the three constitutive elements required to ground a claim under s. 27(2)(e). For Kraft Canada to succeed, it must show that Euro-Excellence imported works that

would have infringed copyright if they had been made in Canada by the persons who made them. It fails to do so.

15 Under the Kraft companies' argument, the putative "hypothetical infringers" (the persons who would have infringed copyrightif they made the impugned works in Canada) are the Kraft parent companies, Kraft Foods Belgium SA ("KFB") and Kraft Foods Schweiz AG ("KFS"). But KFB and KFS are also, respectively, the owners of the Côte d'Or and Toblerone copyrights at issue in this case. The copyright itself was not assigned to Kraft Canada. Therefore, to accept the Kraft companies'argument, this Court would have to find that copyright owners can infringe their own copyright if they have licensed copyright to an exclusive licensee despite their retention of the copyright. In my view, the Copyright Act does not permit exclusive licensees to sue the copyright owner-licensor for infringement of its own copyright. If KFS or KFB had reproduced Kraft labels in Canada in violation of its licensing agreement with Kraft Canada, Kraft Canada's only remedy would lie in breach of contract and not in copyright infringement. Because a copyright owner cannot be liable to its exclusive licensee for infringement, there is no hypothetical infringement and thus no violation of s. 27(2)(e) in this case by Euro-Excellence.

16 Bastarache J., at para. 75, suggests that on my reading of the Act, the Kraft companies could have circumvented the purposes of the Act by calling their agreements "assignments" rather than "exclusive licences". However, the distinction between assignments and exclusive licences is important and meaningful. By granting an assignment, the copyright owner intends to bestow upon the assignee the full panoply of rights and interests reserved for copyright owners. An exclusive licence, by contrast, permits owners to convey to licensees a more limited interest in the copyright. In my respectful view, an approach that conflates exclusive licences and assignments must be rejected. By enabling copyright owners to grant an interest in copyright either by assignment or exclusive licence, Parliament intended to provide copyright owners with two qualitatively different mechanisms by which to transfer their interests in whole or in part. Disregarding the distinctions between the two would lead to an unjustifiable narrowing of the owner's options in dealing with its interest.

Why there is no hypothetical infringement by KFS and KFB and therefore no secondary infringement by Euro-Excellence

17 Section 27 of the Copyright Act describes infringement under the Act. Section 27(1) describes what is known as "primary infringement". It provides that:

> It is an infringement of copyright for any person to do, without the consent of the owner of the copyright, anything that by this Act only the owner of the copyright has the right to do.

Section 3 sets out the catalogue of rights that the copyright owner possesses under the Act. These rights include the sole right to produce and reproduce copies of the copyrighted work. For the purposes of this case, primary infringement would have arisen if Euro-Excellence had produced copies of the Toblerone or Côte d'Or logos.

18 But Euro-Excellence does not want to produce labels with the Toblerone or Côte d'Or logos, and the Kraft companies have not alleged that it has done so. The Kraft companies seek to enjoin Euro-Excellence from importing into Canada works that have been produced lawfully in Europe by the Kraft parent companies, KFS and KFB.

19 The Kraft companies thus allege that Euro-Excellence has engaged in "secondary infringement" by importing for sale or distribution copies of KFS and KFB's copyrighted works into Canada. Secondary infringement is dealt with under s. 27(2) of the Act. In CCH, at para. 81, this Court held that three elements must be proven to establish secondary infringement: (1) a primary infringement; (2) the secondary infringer should have known that he or she was dealing with a product of infringement; and (3) the secondary infringer sold, distributed or exposed for sale the infringing goods. Perhaps the most straightforward form of secondary infringement arises when one sells a copy of an infringing work. Under s. 27(2)(a), "[i]t is an infringement of copyright for any person to... sell... a copy of a work... that the person knows or should have known infringes copyright".

20 Section 27(2)(e) stands out as an apparent exception to the rule in CCH that secondary infringement first requires primary infringement because, unlike s. 27(2)(a) to (d), it does not require actual primary infringement. Instead, it requires only hypothetical primary infringement. Under s. 27(2)(e),

> It is an infringement of copyright for any person to... import...a copy of a work... that the person knows...would infringe copyright if it had been made in Canada by the person who made it.

Section 27(2)(e) substitutes hypothetical primary infringement for actual primary infringement. It is possible that the infringing imports may have been lawfully made outside of Canada. Still, they are deemed to infringe copyright if the importer has imported into Canada works that would have infringed copyright if those works had been made in Canada by the persons who made the works abroad.

21 The apparent purpose of s. 27(2)(e) is to give Canadian copyright holders an added layer of protection where the Canadian copyright holder does not hold copyright in that work in foreign jurisdictions. Section 27(2)(e) protects Canadian copyright holders against "parallel importation" by deeming an infringement of copyright even where the imported works did not infringe copyright laws in the country in which they were made. Without s. 27(2)(e), the foreign copyright holder who could manufacture the work more cheaply abroad could flood the Canadian market with the work, thereby rendering the Canadian copyright worthless. Section 27(2)(e) thus represents Parliament's intention to ensure that Canadian copyright holders receive their just rewards even where they do not hold copyright abroad: see, e.g., Dictionnaires Robert Canada SCC v. Librairie du Nomade Inc. (1987), 11 F.T.R. 44 (Fed. T.D.); A & M Records of Canada Ltd. v. Millbank Music Corp. (1984), 1 C.P.R. (3d) 354 (Fed. T.D.); Fly by Nite Music Co. v. Record Wherehouse Ltd., [1975] F.C. 386 (Fed. T.D.); Clarke, Irwin & Co. v. C. Cole & Co. (1960), 33 C.P.R. 173 (Ont. H.C.).

22 On the facts of this case, the Kraft companies have not made out all of the constitutive elements of a claim under s. 27(2)(e). Hypothetical infringement has not been established. The Kraft companies cannot prove that the impugned works imported and distributed by Euro-Excellence would have infringed copyright if they had been made in Canada by the persons who made them in Europe.

23 The persons who made the impugned copies of the works in Europe were the Kraft parent companies, KFB and KFS. However, KFB and KFS would not have infringed copyright if they had produced the Côte d'Or and Toblerone logos in Canada.

24 This is because KFB and KFS are, respectively, the owners of the Canadian copyright in the Côte d'Or and Toblerone logos. On the Kraft companies'argument, KFB and KFS would be the hypothetical copyright infringers. The Kraft companies argue that KFB and KFS would have infringed copyright if they produced the copyrighted works in Canada because they had licensed the Toblerone and Côte d'Or copyrights to Kraft Canada. Accepting this argument would mean that KFB and KFS have infringed their own copyrights — a proposition that is inconsistent with copyright law and common sense. Under s. 27(1), infringement arises when a person, without the consent of the owner, does something that under the Act only the owner has the right to do. By definition, no person can simultaneously be owner and infringer of copyright: see also CCH, at para. 37.

25 The Kraft companies allege that KFB and KFS can, hypothetically, infringe copyright because they had licensed the exclusive rights to produce and reproduce the copyrighted works in Canada to Kraft Canada, their Canadian subsidiary. The Kraft companies thus assume that an exclusive licensee becomes the owner of the copyright and able to sue the licensor for infringement. This assumption is incorrect. Under the Copyright Act, exclusive licensees are not able to sue the owner-licensor for infringement. I arrive at this conclusion after considering the Copyright Act's provisions on copyright ownership and licensing.

. . .

FISH J. — I agree with the reasons of Justice Rothstein and would dispose of the appeal as he suggests.

53 Had it been necessary to do so, I would have been inclined to determine whether the appellant is in any event entitled to succeed on its alternative ground relating to the integrity of Canadian law regarding intellectual property rights.

54 Kraft Foods Belgium SA and Kraft Foods Schweiz AG manufacture and sell chocolate packaged in Europe. The issue in this case is whether the *Copyright Act*, R.S.C. 1985, c. C-42, entitles them to prevent the sale in Canada of that very same chocolate, packaged exactly as it was when they sold it. Their claim that it does is based on agreements between commonly owned corporations — agreements that have more to do with a monopoly on the sale in Canada of those chocolates than with copyright protection of the "works" that appear on the package. In virtue of identical and simultaneous agreements, and for a nominal

amount of $1,000 in each instance, Kraft Belgium and Kraft Schweiz granted Kraft Canada exclusive licences to use those "works".

55 I think it worth noting that the trial judge, in upholding Kraft's claim, proceeded on the assumption that "the sole purpose of [Kraft Belgium and Kraft Schweiz] registering copyright in Canada and then assigning rights to Kraft Canada Inc. was to mount the very attack upon [Euro-Excellence] which is currently before this Court" (*Kraft Canada Inc. c. Euro Excellence Inc.*, [2004] 4 F.C.R. 410, 2004 FC 652, at para. 44 (emphasis added)). For the true purpose of the *Copyright Act*, see *Robertson v. Thomson Corp.*, [2006] 2 S.C.R. 363, 2006 SCC 43, at para. 69.

56 Without so deciding, I express grave doubt whether the law governing the protection of intellectual property rights in Canada can be transformed in this way into an instrument of trade control not contemplated by the *Copyright Act.*

. . .

Bastarache J.:

. . .

C. The Purpose of Section 27(2)(e) of the Copyright Act

85 The Act protects only the legitimate economic interests of copyright holders. It protects the economic benefits of skill and judgment; it does not protect all economic benefits of all types of labour. Section 27(2) of the Act is meant to prohibit secondary infringement resulting from the wrongful appropriation of the gains of another's skill and judgment by way of the acts enumerated in paras. (a) to (c). Conversely, other economic interests — although they may seem to be closely associated with the interests legitimately protected as emanating from that skill and judgment — are not protected. In particular, if a work of skill and judgment (such as a logo) is attached to some other consumer good (such as a chocolate bar), the economic gains associated with the sale of the consumer good must not be mistakenly viewed as the legitimate economic interests of the copyright holder of the logo that are protected by the law of copyright.

86 Thus s. 27(2)(e) is meant to protect copyright holders from the unauthorized importation of works which are the result of their skill and judgment. It is not meant to protect manufacturers from the unauthorized importation of consumer goods on the basis of their having a copyrighted work affixed to their wrapper, this work being merely incidental to their value as consumer goods.

87 I should note here that, contrary to what was argued before this Court at the hearing, s. 27(2) is not meant to protect manufacturers from the importation of counterfeit versions of their consumer goods. The laws of trade-mark and passing off provide protection to manufacturers who fear the importation of cheap imitations of their products with a copy of the logo of the real product affixed to them. Indeed, this protection is central to the purpose of trade-mark law, as identified by LeBel J. in Kirkbi, at para. 39: "Trade-marks seek to indicate the source of a particular product, process or service in a distinctive manner, so that,

ideally, consumers know what they are buying and from whom." While it is certainly true that one work can be the subject of both copyright and trade-mark protection (see s. 64(3)(b) of the Act), it is equally certain that different forms of intellectual property protect different types of economic interests. To ignore this fact would be to ignore the "basic and necessary distinctions between different forms of intellectual property and their legal and economic functions", as noted by LeBel J. at para. 37 of Kirkbi.

88 This interpretation of s. 27(2) respects copyright's insistence that only legitimate economic interests receive copyright protection. To allow s. 27(2) to protect all interests of manufacturers and distributors of consumer goods would upset the copyright balance. Far from ensuring a "just reward" for creators of copyrighted works, it would allow a copyright to be leveraged far beyond the use intended by Parliament, allowing rights to be artificially enlarged into protection over consumer goods. This undue expansion of copyright would certainly be a failure to give heed to Binnie J.'s insistence, at para. 31 of Théberge, that the law give due weight to the limited nature of the rights of a copyright holder.

4. The Correct Interpretation of Paragraphs (a) to (c) of Section 27(2)

89 As mentioned above, para. (e) of s. 27(2) prohibits the importation into Canada of any copy of a work that would have infringed copyright had it been made in Canada by the person who made it, if that importation is for the purpose of doing anything referred to in paras. (a) to (c) of s. 27(2). Liability under para. (e) therefore relies on a finding that the defendant intended to commit on act enumerated in paras. (a) to (c), which prohibit the selling, renting out, distribution with a prejudicial effect, or dealing with by way of trade of copies of a work. How are we to interpret these prohibitions in light of the foregoing review of the purpose of s. 27(2)(e) and of the Copyright Act as a whole?

90 Paragraph (b) provides that "[i]t is an infringement of copyright for any person to distribute to such an extent as to affect prejudicially the owner of the copyright... a copy of a work". Parliament's inclusion of the word "prejudicially" here is another important key to the interpretation of s. 27(2) as a whole. One can imagine many ways that the distribution of a copyrighted work could prejudicially affect the copyright holder which surely would not be considered secondary infringement. As a somewhat trivial example, consider a book containing accurate and damning portrayals of the author's family, written under a pseudonym unbeknownst to the family of the author. Distribution of copies of this book — bought in full compliance with the Act — to the author's family would certainly tend to "affect prejudicially" the owner of the copyright; nevertheless, I am sure that this situation is not intended to fall within s. 27(2)(b). This hypothetical situation suggests that to "affect prejudicially" a copyright holder has a more limited meaning: this phrase limits protection to the interests of the copyright holder as author. That is, only those distributions which affect the legitimate economic interests protected by copyright will be held to affect prejudicially the owner of the copyright. Economic consequences of unauthorized importation of consumer goods are not, generally speaking, the types of

legitimate economic interests protected by the copyright in a work which is merely incidental to the sale or distribution of the consumer good to which it is attached. The effects of such importation do not meet the requirement of prejudice which is embedded in para. (b), which informs all of s. 27(2).

91 Paragraph (a) provides that "[i]t is an infringement of copyright for any person to sell or rent out" a copy of a work. Simply put, to sell a consumer good with a copyrighted work attached as a logo is not to sell that work. The work, qua work, is merely incidental to the consumer good, and thus a sale of the latter cannot be said in any real sense to be a sale of the former. While it is true that a logo affixed to a package can play an essential role in the sale of that package, that is the role of the logo as a trade-mark, not as a copyright. A finding that s. 27(2)(a) is violated requires that the work be sold as something more than a mere incident of the sale of some other item.

92 Similar logic applies to para. (c). It provides that it is an infringement to, "by way of trade distribute, expose or offer for sale or rental, or exhibit in public" a copy of a work. It must be noted that the modifier "by way of trade" clearly applies to all of the actions referred to in para. (c). This can be seen more clearly by referring to the French version of the provision which refers to "la mise en circulation, la mise ou l'offre en vente ou en location, ou l'exposition en public, dans un but commercial." When para. (c) is seen in this way, consistent with the purpose of the rest of s. 27(2) and the Act as a whole, it is clear that its protection is limited to those instances where the work itself is what is being distributed, exposed, offered for sale or exhibited in public. In other words, when the "trade" taking place, or the "but commercial" being sought, concerns the work itself; when the trade is a trade in some consumer good with which the work is only incidentally related, para. (c) is not triggered.

93 Each of paras. (a) to (c) must be interpreted in a manner consistent with the view that s. 27(2) is meant to protect authors from the unauthorized appropriation of the gains of their authorship; protection does not extend to include any and all economic gains claimed by an author or copyright owner. In each case, the wording of the provision, read in light of the purpose of s. 27(2) and the purpose of the Copyright Act as a whole, makes it clear that if the work in question is merely incidental to another consumer good, and it is that consumer good which is being sold or distributed, or dealt with by way of trade, s. 27(2) cannot be invoked. It is only when it is the work itself which is the subject of the sale or other commercial dealing that it can properly be said that the section applies and its protection becomes available.

94 The determination of when a work is merely incidental to a consumer good will not always be an easy one. Some factors which may be useful in making such a determination could include the nature of the product, the nature of the protected work and the relationship of the work to the product. If a reasonable consumer undertaking a commercial transaction does not think that the copyrighted work is what she is buying or dealing with, it is likely that the work is merely incidental to the consumer good.

95   Contrary to what Rothstein J. seems to argue at para. 4, the previous analysis does not suggest that the simple fact of a work being attached to a consumer good would preclude that work from copyright protection: the Act is clear that protection extends to, inter alia, works produced or reproduced "in any material form whatever" (s. 3(1)). The 'merely incidental' analysis goes to secondary liability under s. 27(2) only; rather than being about what is and is not copyrightable, its intention is to prevent that section from being improperly leveraged to use the Copyright Act as a protection of commercial interests completely unrelated to copyright's intended domain. Thus, the sale of a t-shirt with a reproduction of a painting on its front may constitute the sale of the work (the painting); on the other hand, the location of a small logo on the corner of a shirt pocket would not thereby transform an otherwise plain shirt into a copyrighted work, as the logo qua copyrighted work would be merely incidental to the shirt being sold (and, as noted above, any value the logo has as identifying a brand would be protected by trade-mark law, rather than by copyright). To take a slightly different example, a copyrighted instruction booklet included in the box of some consumer good would, as copyrighted work, be merely incidental to the good for the purposes of s. 27(2): see British Leyland Motor Corp. v. Armstrong Patents Co., [1986] 1 All E.R. 850 (U.K. H.L.).

5. Other Considerations

96   In my view, this purposive interpretation of s. 27(2), which views the provision in light of the purpose and scheme of the Copyright Act as a whole, is sufficient to deal with the problem of parallel importation. This interpretation means that two other arguments, raised before us by the appellant, become unnecessary. However, I think it would be useful to mention those arguments briefly.

97   The appellant argued that an attempt to extend copyright protection to prevent parallel importation of consumer goods could trigger the application of the civilian doctrine of abus de droit. This doctrine, which was recognized by this Court in Houle c. Banque Canadienne Nationale, [1990] 3 S.C.R. 122 (S.C.C.), provides that a party may not exercise a right in an unreasonable manner. (See also Wallace v. United Grain Growers Ltd., [1997] 3 S.C.R. 701 (S.C.C.), at para. 145, with respect to a similar concept in the common law.) Given the analysis above, I do not see an appeal to this doctrine as necessary to resolve this issue.

98   Similarly, the appellant argued that the newly developing American doctrine of "copyright misuse" applies to parallel importation of consumer goods. This doctrine is meant to act as a sort of equitable defence when "a copyright holder attempts to extend his copyright beyond the scope of the exclusive rights granted by Congress in a manner that violates federal antitrust law [or] the public policy embodied in copyright law": see K. Judge, "Rethinking Copyright Misuse" (2004), 57 Stan. L. Rev. 901, at pp. 903-4. The doctrine has been adopted by some Federal Circuit Courts of Appeal, but has not as of yet found favour at the United States Supreme Court (Judge, at pp. 902-3). As with the concept of abus de droit, my analysis renders an appeal to this developing doctrine unnecessary to deal with parallel importation of consumer goods. However, this is not to

comment on the possible application of this doctrine in Canada; a determination on that issue is best left for another day.

5. Application to the Facts

99 It is clear on the facts of the appeal before us that the protected works in question — the Côte d'Or and Toblerone logos, considered as copyrighted works — cannot be seen as anything other than merely incidental to the chocolate bars to which they are affixed. Therefore, Euro-Excellence's dealings with the chocolate bars are not caught within the language of s. 27(2) of the Act. I reach this conclusion on the basis of a consideration of the role of the logos as merely incidental to the sale of the chocolate bars in general.

100 As discussed above, to be brought within the protection of s. 27(2), a copyrighted work must be more than merely incidental to the consumer good to which it is affixed. Only when that condition is satisfied can it accurately be said that it is the copyrighted work itself which is the subject of one of the activities described in paras. (a) to (c) of s. 27(2).

101 In this appeal, the logos, considered as copyrighted works, are inarguably best described as merely incidental to the chocolate bars themselves. It cannot be reasonably maintained that in the course of a commercial transaction in which a customer buys a Côte d'Or or a Toblerone chocolate bar from a merchant, the customer is actually paying for a copyrighted work. This is not a situation in which the copyrighted work, as such, is an important aspect of the consumer transaction: it is a logo on a wrapper for a product which serves to identify the product's origins, nothing more.

102 Thus it cannot be said that Euro-Excellence is selling the copyrighted works themselves, as proscribed by para. (a); it cannot be said that Euro-Excellence is distributing those works to the extent of prejudicing KCI's interest as author or copyright holder, as prohibited by para. (b), when those interests are properly limited to the legitimate economic interests protected by the Act; and it cannot be reasonably maintained that Euro-Excellence is in contravention of para. (c) by dealing with those works "by way of trade" once it is understood that it is the works themselves which must be dealt with by way of trade rather than the chocolate bars to which they are attached. Thus, as Euro-Excellence's importation of the Côte d'Or and Toblerone bars was not done "for the purpose of doing anything referred to in paragraphs (a) to (c)" of s. 27(2), Euro-Excellence has not violated s. 27(2)(e).

103 The above does not imply that the Côte d'Or or Toblerone logos are not copyrightable works. Quite the opposite: the logos have been properly registered and there is no reason to dispute the trial judge's conclusions that the logos meet the Act's originality threshold and are therefore copyrightable works. KCI, as holder of those copyrights in Canada, would surely succeed in an action for copyright infringement against a defendant who produced and distributed posters of the logos, for example. However, it is necessary to ensure that this

legitimate copyright protection is not illegitimately leveraged into a protection for a market in consumer goods.

104 Similarly, I do not mean to suggest that logos play no role whatsoever in the sale of chocolate bars. So I think it is therefore useful to stress, once again, that in the s. 27(2) analysis the logos must be viewed strictly through the copyright lens as works. The analysis does not speak to the possibility — indeed, the certainty — that the logos, as trade-marks, can play a large role in the sale of the chocolate bars and are of great value to KCI. It is not disputed that part of the reason that a consumer buys a Côte d'Or bar or a Toblerone bar is because of the reputation and goodwill associated with each brand. But that is not a consideration which is relevant under the Copyright Act. It cannot be reasonably maintained that anyone buys a Côte d'Or or Toblerone because of the logos as works of art.

105 Côte d'Or and Toblerone are chocolate bars. When a consumer buys one of these bars, the bar is exactly what he or she is buying. The logo may play a role in that transaction qua trade-mark, but qua copyright it cannot be seen as anything other than a mere incident to the chocolate bars. Thus, Euro-Excellence did nothing for the purpose of selling the logos as copyrighted works, or dealing with those works by way of trade; nor did Euro-Excellence distribute the logos as works to the extent of prejudicially affecting the legitimate interests of KCI as copyright holder. In short, Euro-Excellence did not violate or intend to violate the terms of paras. (a) to (c) of s. 27(2), and therefore cannot be found liable under s. 27(2)(e).

. . .

Abella J.:

. . .

109 Resolving this appeal depends on the answers to two questions. First, is the copyrighted work being "sold" or "distributed" when it is printed on the wrapper of a consumer product? Second, can an exclusive licensee in Canada claim protection against secondary infringement when the copyrighted work was produced by the owner-licensor?

110 On the first issue, I agree with the conclusion reached by Rothstein J. There is nothing in the Act to endorse a restrictive definition of "sell". Section 64(3)(b) of the Act extends copyright protection to trademarks and labels. When a product is sold, title to its wrapper is also transferred to the purchaser. The Act is indifferent as to whether the sale of the wrapper is important to the consumer.

111 Like Bastarache J., I agree with the trial judge that the logos are copyrighted works. I respectfully disagree with his view, however, that no infringement is made out because the elephant and bear logos are incidental to the chocolate bars and are therefore not protected by s. 27(2). To inject an exception for logos on the basis that they are "incidental" would be to introduce unnecessary uncertainty, inviting case-by-case judicial explorations into the uncharted area of what is "merely" incidental, "somewhat" incidental, or not incidental at all. Such an

approach also takes insufficient account of the reality that many products are, to a significant extent, sold on the basis of their logo or packaging.

112 Nor do I share the view that s. 27(2)(e), which on its face appears to me to be applicable, "protects only the legitimate economic interests of copyright holders", that is, "the unauthorized importation of works which are the result of their skill and judgment" (paras. 85-86). It seems to me, with respect, that once a work falls within s. 27(2)(a) to (c) and otherwise meets the requirements established by the Act as prerequisites to copyright protection, there is no scope for a judicially created limit to that protection based on what might — or might not — be a "legitimate economic interest". I do not believe that Galerie d'art du Petit Champlain inc. c. Théberge, [2002] 2 S.C.R. 336, 2002 SCC 34 (S.C.C.), stands for such a proposition.

. . .

129 Copyright confers a limited monopoly to "produce or reproduce" the work in any material form whatever. In this case, KCI purchased the exclusive licence to the copyrighted work precisely because it wanted copyright on chocolate bar wrappers. Euro-Excellence purchased chocolate bars with labels displaying the copyrighted works; it imported those works into Canada after being notified of KCI's Canadian copyright interest; its purpose in importing the chocolate bars and the wrappers was to sell them or distribute them by way of trade. A s. 27(2) (e) infringement is therefore made out. KCI is entitled to the remedies provided by the Act.

Chapter 8

DEFENCES TO INFRINGEMENT

1. Fair Dealing and Public Interest

Pursuant to section 29, 29.1 and 29.2, it is not an infringement of copyright to deal fairly with a work for the purposes of research, private study, education, parody or satire, criticism, review or news reporting. Fair dealing for the purposes of criticism, review, or newspaper summary will not infringe copyright only if the source is mentioned, as well as the author's name if given in the source. In Canada, there are potentially three hurdles to be met by a defendant in order to make out a fair dealing defence: first, the use made of the work must be for an enumerated purpose; second, the use must be shown to be "fair" in the particular circumstances; and third, if applicable, sufficient acknowledgement of source and author must have been made. The scope of the "fair dealing" exception is impossible to define generally; it is a question of degree and depends on the facts of each case. A fair dealing is a reasonable use. What is reasonable must be judged by looking at the nature of the works themselves and the purpose for which the defendant dealt with them.

Canada's purpose-based approach to fair dealing is similar to that of the United Kingdom and much of the Commonwealth, but stands in contrast to the US doctrine of "fair use" (17 U.S.C. §107). Fair use is not limited to uses for specified purposes, but rather is available for uses "*such as* criticism, comment, news reporting, teaching (including multiple copies for classroom use), scholarship, or research", the fairness of which is determined in light of a non-exclusive list of statutorily enumerated factors for consideration. The significance of this difference between the Canadian and US approach arguably diminishes as Canada adds more fair dealing purposes to the Act ("parody", "satire" and "education" were all recent additions made by the *Copyright Modernization Act* 2012), and as Canadian courts interpret these purposes more liberally (following recent Supreme Court jurisprudence).

It is important to situate fair dealing in the context of the purposes of copyright law. While originally a judge-made and equitable doctrine, since its first legislative enactment in the United Kingdom in 1911, fair dealing has traditionally been narrowly interpreted by the Anglo-Canadian courts. This approach typically aligns with a view of copyright's primary purpose as being the protection of authors. However, the fair dealing exception, like other exemptions to infringement contained in the Act, reflects the mandate of copyright law to harmonize owners' rights with legitimate public interests.

Importantly, the Supreme Court of Canada has described fair dealing as a "user right" and one of the tools employed to achieve the proper balance between protection and access. Regarded in this way, it is an integral part of the copyright system that should not be interpreted restrictively.

Hubbard v. Vosper (1971), [1972] 1 All E.R. 1023, [1972] 2 Q.B. 84, [1972] 2 W.L.R. 389 (Eng. C.A.)

COURT OF APPEAL, CIVIL DIVISION

LORD DENNING MR. On 9th September a book was published called 'The Mind Benders'. It was written by Mr Cyril Vosper, the first defendant, and published by Neville Spearman Ltd, the second defendant. It was very critical of the cult of Scientology. On the same day the Church of Scientology of California issued a writ. They went to the judge and obtained ex parte an nterim injunction to restrain the publication of the book. Later on Mr Lafayette Ronald Hubbard was added as plaintiff. After hearing both sides, Kilner Brown J continued the injunction but, as the matter involved the public interest, he hoped it would be taken to appeal.

'Scientology' is a word invented by Mr Hubbard himself. He has invented a lot of other words too which he has set out in a Dictionary of Scientology. He defines it in this way:

> 'SCIENTOLOGY: An applied religious philosophy dealing with the study of knowledge, which, through the application of its technology can bring about desirable changes in the conditions of life.'

In addition to the dictionary, he has written many books about this philosophy or cult. They include 'Axioms and Logics', 'Introduction to Scientology Ethics', 'Scientology 8-80', 'Scientology 8-8008', and 'Scientology — A History of Man'. All of them contain a large number of his invented words. They cannot be understood by anyone who is not versed in the cult. In addition, Mr Hubbard has written numerous bulletins and letters which have been circulated to members of the cult. These give many descriptions of the workings of Scientology.

Mr Hubbard and his adherents occupy a big house near East Grinstead called Saint Hill Manor. They hold courses for those who wish to study Scientology and to acquire proficiency in it. Some of these courses, on their own admission, 'can be dangerous in untrained hands'.

Mr Vosper was a member of the Church of Scientology for 14 years. He worked at Saint Hill Manor as secretary, and such like. In 1967 he put his name down for a course which the authorities regarded as confidential. It was called the Saint Hill Special Briefing Course. He paid a fee of £ 150 and signed an undertaking 'relating to higher levels of knowledge'. He undertook (a) to use this knowledge for Scientology purposes only; (b) to refrain from divulging level VI materials to those not entitled to receive them or to discuss them within the hearing of such persons. Mr Vosper did not, however, complete the course. He became disillusioned with Scientology. Those in authority thought that he was actively seeking to suppress or damage Scientology. So in September 1968 they declared him to be a 'suppressive person', which meant that he was considered 'fair game', and they declared him to be in a condition of 'enemy'. In order to understand what that means, you have to look at the books. It means that in the eyes of Scientologists, Mr Vosper had no right 'to self, possessions or position', and that any Scientologist could take any action against him with impunity.

So Mr Vosper left Saint Hill Manor. He wrote 'The Mind Benders'. It said on the jacket that it was 'The first ever investigation into the cult of Scientology by an ex-Scientologist of 14 years' service'. It is this book of which the plaintiffs now seek to prevent publication. They do it on two grounds: first, infringement of copyright; secondly breach of confidence.

1 Infringement of copyright

Whatever one may think of Mr Hubbard's books, letters and bulletins, they are the subject of literary copyright. His name appears as author on every book, letter and bulletin. So he is presumed to be the owner of the copyright in them. In writing 'The Mind Benders' Mr Vosper has made free use of Mr Hubbard's books, letters and bulletins. He has taken very little from some, but from others he has taken very substantial parts. For instance, he has taken quite big extracts from the 'Introduction to Scientology Ethics', and put them into his book. He has also taken substantial parts of the letters and bulletins. The parts taken are so substantial that Mr Vosper will be guilty of infringement of copyright unless he can make good his defence. And his defence is that his use of them is fair dealing within s 6 (2) of the Copyright Act 1956. This provides:

> 'No fair dealing with literary, dramatic or musical work shall constitute an infringement of the copyright in the work if it is for purposes of criticism or review, whether of that work or of another work, and is accompanied by a sufficient acknowledgment.'

The last words of the section are satisfied. At the end of his book, Mr Vosper said: 'Criticisms are used from the following books by L Ron Hubbard' — setting them out.

The question is, therefore, whether Mr Vosper's treatment of Mr Hubbard's books was a 'fair dealing' with them 'for the purposes of criticism or review'. There is very little in our law books to help on this. Some cases can be used to illustrate what is not 'fair dealing'; It is not fair dealing for a rival in the trade to take copyright material and use it for his own benefit. Such as when the Times published a letter on America by Rudyard Kipling. The St James Gazette took out half-a-dozen passages and published them as extracts. This was held to be an infringement: see Walter v Steinropff. So also when the University of London published examination papers. The Tutorial Press took several of the papers and published them in their own publication for the use of students. It was held to be an infringement: see University of London Press Ltd v University Tutorial Press Ltd. Likewise when a band played 20 bars of 'Colonel Bogey' — to entertain hearers — it was not fair dealing: see Hawkes & Son (London) Ltd v Paramount Film Service Ltd n3.

In this case Mr Vosper has taken considerable extracts from Mr Hubbard's work and has commented freely on them. …Counsel for the plaintiffs says that what Mr Vosper has done is to take important parts of Mr Husbard's book and explain them and amplify them. That, he says, is not fair dealing. Counsel for the defendants says that Mr Vosper has, indeed, taken important parts of Mr Hubbard's book, but he has done it so so as to expose them to the public, and to criticise them and to condemn them. That, he says, is fair dealing.

It is impossible to define what is 'fair dealing'. It must be a question of degree. You must consider first the number and extent of the quotations and extracts. Are they altogether too many and too long to be fair? Then you must consider the use made of them. If they are used as a basis for comment, criticism or review, that may be a fair dealing. If they are used to convey the same information as the author, for a rival purpose, that may be unfair. Next, you must consider the proportions. To take long extracts and attach short comments may be unfair. But, short extracts and long comments may be fair. Other considerations may come to mind also. But, after all is said and done, it must be a matter of impression. As with fair comment in he law of libel, so with fair dealing in the law of copyright. The tribunal of fact must decide. In the present case, there is material on which the tribunal of fact could find this to be fair dealing.

Counsel for the plaintiffs took, however, another point. He said that the defence of 'fair dealing' only avails a defendant when he is criticising or reviewing the plaintiff's literary work. It does not avail a defendant, said counsel, when he is criticising or reviewing the doctrine or philosophy underlying the plaintiff's work. In support of this proposition, counsel for the plaintiffs relied on the words of Romer J in British Oxygen Co Ltd v Liquid Air Ltd [1925] Ch 383 at 393

> 'I am inclined to agree with [counsel for the plaintiffs] that, in this proviso [as to "fair dealing"] the word "criticism" means a criticism of a work as such.'

But, when you refer back to counsel for the plaintiffs' arguments, you will see that all he means is that the criticism must be a criticism of the plaintiff's work, and not of the plaintiff's conduct. I do not think that this proviso is confined as narrowly as counsel for the plaintiffs submits. A literary work consists not only of the literary style, but also of the thoughts underlying it, as expressed in the words. Under the defence of 'fair dealing' both can be criticised. Mr Vosper is entitled to criticise not only the literary style, but also the doctrine or philosophy of Mr Hubbard as expounded in the books.

Counsel for the plaintiffs took yet another point. This was on the bulletins and letters. These, he said, were not published to the world at large, but only to a limited number of people and, in particular, to those who took classes in Scientology. He said that, whilst it might be 'fair dealing' to criticise the books, it was not 'fair dealing' to take extracts from these bulletins and letters and criticise them. He quoted again the words of Romer J in the British Oxygen case [1925] Ch at 393

'... it would be manifestly unfair that an unpublished literary work should, without the consent of the author, be the subject of public criticism, review or newspaper summary. Any such dealing with an unpublished literary work would not, therefore, in my opinion, be a "fair dealing" with the work.'

I am afraid I cannot go all the way with those words of Romer J. Although a literary work may not be published to the world at large, it may, however, be circulated to such a wide circle that it is 'fair dealing' to criticise it publicly in a newspaper, or elsewhere. His happens sometimes when a company sends a circular to the whole body of shareholders. It may be of such general interest that it is quite legitimate for a newspaper to make quotations from it, and to criticise them — or review them — without thereby being guilty of infringing copyright. The newspaper must, of course, be careful not to fall foul of the law of libel. So also here these bulletins and letters may have been so widely circulated that it was perfectly 'fair dealing' for Mr Vosper to take extracts from them and criticise them in his book.

It seems to me, therefore, that Mr Vosper may have a good defence of 'fair dealing' to raise at the trial.

But here, although Mr Hubbard owns the copyright, nevertheless, Mr Vosper has a defence of fair dealing, and, although Mr Hubbard may possess confidential information, nevertheless, Mr Vosper has a defence of public interest. These defences are such that he should be permitted to go ahead with the publication. If what he says is true, it is only right that the dangers of this cult should be exposed. We never restrain a defendant in a libel action who says he is going to justify. So in a copyright action, we ought not to restrain a defendant who has a reasonable defence of fair dealing. Nor in an action for breach of confidence, if the defendant has a reasonable defence of public interest. The reason is because the defendant, if he is right, is entitled to publish it; and the law will not intervene to suppress freedom of speech except when it is abused.

I would, therefore, allow this appeal and remove the injunction.

. . .

MEGAW LJ. I agree. There are a few matters to which I wish to add some observations.

...The principal submission by counsel for the plaintiffs, related to the construction of s 6 (2) of the Copyright Act 1956. As I understand his argument, it was that criticism 'whether of that work of or another work' (words used in that subsection) cannot be taken to apply to criticism which is criticism of something other than the work itself. That may be an acceptable proposition, but it is only an acceptable proposition when one has defined with reasonable clarity what is meant by 'criticism of something other than the work itself'. Counsel for the plaintiffs did not suggest that 'criticism' in this subsection was confined to what I would call literary criticism; that is to say, criticism of the style — the literary style — of the work in question. But if it is not confined to that, it must surely then cover criticism of the ideas, the thoughts, expressed by the work in question — the subject-matter of the work. What is the subject-matter of the works which are relevant in this appeal? The subject-matter of each of them is some facet of the doctrine, the practice, the training, and the code of ethics or discipline of this organisation, the Church of Scientology of California. To my mind there can be no doubt that the criticism contained in the book, 'The Mind Benders', is, on a fair reading, a criticism of that subject-matter by reference, in part at least, to its exposition in those works. It is in that context that the quotations from those works are used.

It is then said that the passages which have been taken from these various works — in particular, from the one of them described as 'Introduction to Scientology Ethics' — are so substantial, quantitatively so great in relation to the respective works from which the citations are taken, that they fall outside the scope of 'fair dealing'. To my mind this question of substantiality is a question of degree. It may well be that it does not prevent the quotation of a work from being within the fair dealing subsection even though the quotation may be of every single word of the work. Let me give an example. Suppose that there is on a tombstone in a churchyard an epitaph consisting of a dozen or of 20 words. A parishioner of the church thinks that this sort of epitaph is out of place on a tombstone. He writes a letter to the parish magazine setting out the words of the epitaph. Could it be suggested that that citation is so substantial, consisting of 100 per cent of the 'work' in question, that it must necessarily be outside the scope of the fair dealing provision? To my mind it could not validly be so suggested. In this present case, having considered what we have been shown of the passages taken from the various works in relation (because I think this test must also be applied) to the nature and purpose of the individual quotations, I find myself unable to say that the plaintiffs have made out a case that the quotations are so substantial that this does not fall within the fair dealing provision. To my mind the plaintiffs have failed to establish to the required degree, in relation to an application of this sort and in relation to all the other factors that have to be taken into account, that they ought to be granted an interlocutory injunction in relation to the alleged breach of copyright.

. . .

DISPOSITION: Appeal allowed; injunction removed. Leave to appeal refused.

Beloff v. Pressdram Ltd., [1973] F.S.R. 33 (Ch. D.)

Before: Mr. Justice Ungoed-Thomas

6th, 7th, 11th to 14th, 17th, 18th July and 18th October, 1972.

. . .

UNGOED — THOMAS, J.

— This is an action for infringement of copyright. The plaintiff is Political and Lobby Correspondent of the Observer newspaper, which is owned by Observer

Ltd. The first defendant, Pressdram Ltd., is the publisher and the second defendant, Leo Thorpe Ltd., is the printer of Private Eye magazine. The infringement alleged is by the reproduction in an article in Private Eye of an internal Observer office memorandum written by the Plaintiff. The alleged infringement is in the case of Pressdram by publishing and in the case of Leo Thorpe by printing. ...

. . .

So in this case we have involved on the one side a long-established and highly reputable paper and on the other side a comparatively new magazine, apparently run largely by the comparatively young and doubtless largely for the comparatively young. They reflect different generations in their staff, their attitudes and their language. In such circumstances there is the danger of predilections. So I trust I will be forgiven for emphasising the obvious — that what we are concerned with here is the administration of the law and that that must be free of predilections; that this court is not concerned with taste, morals, or even public interest except as recognised by the law; that it is not a roving enquiry and cannot make its decisions on vague information. This court is concerned only with deciding specific issues according to the law on evidence that is admissible and advanced in this court. It is essential to bear constantly in mind that what we are concerned with in this case is not the conduct of Private Eye in general but only with the claims for breach of copyright by publishing the memorandum in an article by Mr. Foot, and to that this judgment is exclusively directed.

I come now to the events leading immediately to this action. Mr. Foot had for some time been concerned about Mr. Maudling's relations with Mr. Hoffman and his Real Estate Company of America, of which he was Chairman or President. Private Eye had published articles on this subject, and it appears that Mr. Foot was the person in Private Eye who dealt with the matter and that he wrote the "Footnotes" articles whose description indicated that they were by him. Mr. Hoffman, was I understand, sentenced this year to two years' imprisonment and fined £400 in the United States of America on fraud charges.

On 28th February 1971 the Observer published a very prominent article by the plaintiff making a slashing attack on Private Eye's attitude towards Mr. Maudling and accusing Private Eye in effect of smearing Mr. Maudling and amongst other things of "pure fabrication". On 12th March 1971 Mr. Foot replied by the Private Eye article in which the memorandum is incorporated. The memorandum and the article contain matters of whose publication the plaintiff complains, and I shall come to consider them later in some detail. The memorandum reads:

"From: Nora Beloff. 17th February, 1971. To: David Astor, Editor"

— and copies to Donald Trelford, Deputy Editor, John Silverlight, Assistant Editor, Laurence Marks, Chief Reporter, Tony Bambridge, Business Editor, Ivan Yates, Leader Writer, and John Lucas, News Editor. It is headed "Maudling", and the body of it reads:

"I had an interesting talk today with William Whitelaw, who drove me back from the Carlton Club to the House of Commons. I told him that the young Tory, that I had been lunching with, and I, had been speculating about who would take over if the P.M. ran under a bus. He said instantly there was no doubt at all it would be Reggie Maudling. He said this was not true when they were in opposition and when Reggie would hardly have been in the running, but it was overwhelmingly the fact that he had far more government experience and general confidence than anyone else in the Cabinet. He said that he talked the matter over recently with Robert Carr and they had agreed that neither of them would agree to support anyone else or would, themselves, stand against Maudling. He didn't know what other members of the Cabinet thought, but without boasting he felt that if he and Carr stood together that might have some weight.

I told him that the young Tory I had been speaking to thought Whitelaw himself would be a better choice and he said that in the present state he would never agree to oppose Maudling.

I asked him about the 'Private Eye' campaign and he conceded that in Maudling's place he probably already would have sued and he was sure that if it went on Maudling would have to. He did not, however, think the campaign had damaged Maudling as he thought 'Private Eye' had over-reached itself and lied on so many subjects about which everybody knew.

Whitelaw's remarks were, I thought, particularly interesting as a sidelight on just how little the Conservative Party leaders have really moved towards the Radical Right, and the move away from consensus politics, which is what Maudling really represents.

What I would like to suggest is that I do a study of Maudling instead of my usual political notebook, at some point soon when the Home Office is in the news, e.g. after the publication of the Immigration Bill, or some new development in Northern Ireland. If you will agree I will very carefully look at the evidence accumulated against Maudling by the 'Private Eye' people on the business side, and confront him frankly with the case to hear what he has to say. I still have to deal with it obviously within the restrictions imposed by the libel lawyer, but I will try also to put it into the wider context of his political personality and morality".

Information is not the subject of copyright, but only "the literary form in which the information is dressed". (Fraser v. Evans [1969] 1 Q.B. 349 at 362, *per* Lord Denning, M.R.). But the nub of this case is not the verbal quotation of the memorandum at all. As the plaintiff's counsel made quite clear in his reply, it is not even that the names of Mr. Whitelaw and Mr. Carr were revealed in the memorandum as the two Cabinet Ministers referred to in the plaintiff's article as supporting Mr. Maudling as the successor to Mr. Heath in the event of his ceasing to be Prime Minister; but the disclosure by the memorandum of Mr. Whitelaw as the source of the plaintiff's information. If it were not for that disclosure I am completely satisfied that this action would never have been brought. In that sense it is an action for breach of confidence under the guise of an action for infringement of copyright — an action springing from breach of confidence but framed in breach of copyright.

Public Interest and fair dealing.

In the course of this case, the defence of public interest has been interwoven with fair dealing. They are, however, separate defences and have rightly been separately pleaded. They are governed by separate considerations. Fair dealing is a statutory defence limited to infringement of copyright only. But public interest is a defence outside and independent of statutes, is not limited to copyright cases and is based upon a general principle of common law. I will deal first with public interest and then with fair dealing.

Public interest:

The most important recent cases referred to were the Court of Appeal cases of Initial Services Ltd. v. Putterill [1968] 1 Q.B. 396 and of Hubbard v. Vosper [1972] 2 W.L.R. 389 (where the claims were for infringement of copyright and also for breach of confidence).

The Initial Services case was on appeal to strike out certain provisions in the defence relying, in justification of disclosure of confidential information, on its exposure first of breach of statutory duty to register a restrictive trade agreement and secondly that a circular issued by the plaintiffs to their customers attributing increases in their charges to the Selective Employment Tax was misleading to the public.

Lord Denning said at page 405 that the exception to the obligation not to disclose confidential information

> "extends to any misconduct of such a nature that it ought in the public interest to be disclosed to others. Wood, V.-C. put it in a vivid phrase: 'There is no confidence as to the disclosure of iniquity.' In Weld-Blundell v. Stephens, Bankes, L.J. rather suggested that the exception is limited to the proposed or contemplated commission of a crime or a civil wrong. But I should have thought that was too limited. The exception should extend to crimes, frauds and misdeeds, both those actually committed as well as those in contemplation, provided always — and this is essential that the disclosure is justified in the public interest.*57 The reason is because 'no private obligations can dispense with that universal one which lies on every member of the society to discover every design which may be formed, contrary to the laws of the society, to destroy the public welfare': see Annesley v. Anglesea".

And Salmon, L.J. said at page 410:

> "I do not think that the law would lend assistance to anyone who is proposing to commit and to continue to commit a clear breach of a statutory duty imposed upon him in the public interest".

In that case publication, justifiable in the public interest, was considered to extend beyond exposure of what appears, at first blush, to have been meant by "contrary to the laws of the society" as stated in Annesley v. Anglesea, although not, as I see it, beyond "disclosure of iniquity" in Wood, V.-C.'s phrase.

In Hubbard v. Vosper, Lord Denning, M.R. treated material on scientology published in breach of confidence as susceptible to a defence of public interest on the ground that it was dangerous material, namely medical quackeries "dangerous in untrained hands".

The defence of public interest clearly covers and, in the authorities does not extend beyond, disclosure, which as Lord Denning emphasised must be disclosure justified in the public interest, of matters, carried out or contemplated, in breach of the country's security, or in breach of law, including statutory duty, fraud, or otherwise destructive of the country or its people, including matters medically dangerous to the public; and doubtless other misdeed of similar gravity. Public interest, as a defence in law, operates to override the rights of the individual, (including copyright), which would otherwise prevail and which the law is also concerned to protect. Such public interest, as now recognised by the law, does not extend beyond misdeeds of a serious nature and importance to the country and thus, in my view, clearly recognisable as such.

Witnesses for the plaintiff and for the defendants alike gave evidence of their own view of Press practice and conceptions of what justified publications not normally justifiable. They all involved "public interest" as the justification. This public interest was more permissive than is permissible as a defence in law. However, Mr. Astor and the plaintiff emphasised the seriousness of the national interest required. Nevertheless, the plaintiff's counsel in reply submitted that public interest as a defence in law should be given a wide meaning. Its meaning differed from witness to witness and, on occasion, even in different parts of the evidence of the same witness. All the witnesses considered that it was for the Editor to decide on balance whether publication was justifiable, although the plaintiff's counsel in reply recognised that the Press must, in this, be subject to the law.

The defendants submitted that the publication of the memorandum was in the public interest on such grounds as that the public should know what senior Minister had provided the plaintiff with the information appearing in the memorandum and in her article, what two key Ministers supported Mr. Maudling as Mr. Heath's successor, how the lobby correspondents obtained their information and how their system worked. On the other hand, the plaintiff maintained that, subject to narrow exceptions, it was not in the public interest in general, and indeed contrary to it, that Press sources of information should be disclosed, as otherwise the sources of information that should be available to the public would soon dry up. On the other hand, it might be thought that informants, particularly if public representatives or public officials speaking on public affairs, should not be concealed by anonymity. These considerations are, of course, all of public importance: but what has to be decided here is whether public interest, in the sense in which it is recognised as a defence in such a case as this, is established. The publication of the memorandum did not disclose any "iniquity" or "misdeed". It follows from the scope of public interest which I have ventured to indicate that the defence of public interest fails.

Fair dealing.

(1) The meaning of statutory "fair dealing".

The defence of fair dealing is governed by section 6 of the Copyright Act, 1956, and so far as is relevant to this case by subsections (2), (3) and (10). Subsection (2) reads:

> "No fair dealing with a literary . . . work shall constitute an infringement of the copyright in the work if it is for purposes of criticism or review, whether of that work or of another work, and is accompanied by a sufficient acknowledgment".

Subsection (3) reads:

> "No fair dealing with a literary . . . work shall constitute an infringement of the copyright in the work if it for the purpose of reporting current events — (a) in a newspaper, magazine or similar periodical, or (b). . ." (I need not read (b)) "and, in a case falling within paragraph (a) of this subsection, is accompanied by a sufficient acknowledgment".

"Sufficient acknowledgment" is defined by subsection (10), for present purposes, as

> "an acknowledgment identifying the work in question by its title or other description and . . . also identifying the author".

The defendants thus have to establish (1) fair dealing with the memorandum, (2) for purposes of criticism or review of the memorandum or of another work or for the purpose of reporting current events in a newspaper, magazine or similar periodical, and (3) sufficient identification of the work in question (i.e. the memorandum) by its title or other description and identifying the author. I will deal with these three matters in reverse order.

It seems to me that "the work" and the plaintiff as its author are so clearly identified that I will not pause to give reasons for this conclusion.

Defendants' counsel rightly submitted — and it was not disputed — that witnesses substantially agreed on what were the constituent elements of review and criticism of an article, namely, dealing with the article's literary merits, its truth, relevance, sources (including, as Mr. Foot expressed it, how the research has been done) and how it came to be written. Mr. Foot's evidence dealt with the question of whether his article was for such purposes. He said that the plaintiff's article was written four days after a Mr. Clarke had visited him on behalf of the Business Observer (not on behalf of the plaintiff as the plaintiff originally stated in her evidence which she returned to the box the next day to correct). This, he said, indicated that there had been no substantial enquiry into the matter. My notes of evidence (from which my quotations of evidence come throughout this judgment unless otherwise stated) are:

> "Plaintiff's article doesn't go into it in any depth — states nothing not available to anyone who looks into it for a moment — appeared just whitewash without dealing with revelations that had been made at all".

On the question whether Mr. Foot's article was for the purpose of reporting current events, the plaintiff was asked whether the fact that she had writtenher article in the Observer was news. She replied:

> "It is news in the sense that everything I write is news. The fact of my writing this article is news; and of my writing any other article in the Observer is news".

Mr. Foot said:

> "It was a very significant development that the political correspondent had written a large article on this. The Washington Post and the New York Times are constantly dealing with such matters. It was crucial that the Observer was doing so and in my view wrongly and shabbily, and had to be answered in sharp terms. Such an article is not far off editorial comment and is therefore very important".

And Mr. Howard likewise emphasised the importance of such a newspaper as the Observer "taking up the Maudling-Hoffman affair".

In his closing speech plaintiff's counsel, rightly in the light of the evidence, conceded that Mr. Foot's article was for the purposes of criticism and review and reporting current events within section 6.

I come now to the requirement, which I specified, of fair dealing with this memorandum. Fair dealing is not defined by the Act, although subject to the requirements which I have already stated including the purpose of criticism or review or reporting current events. The references to purposes, which I have just read, differ in their wording from the reference to purposes in subsection (1), which reads:

> "No fair dealing with a literary . . . work for purposes of research or private study shall constitute an infringement of the copyright in the work".

Thus "for the purpose" in subsection (1) and "if it is for the purpose" in the other subsections fundamentally have the same meaning and effect: and the difference in wording is explained by the inclusion in subsections (2) and (3) of additional provisions and requirements without parallel in subsection (1). It would, indeed, be whimsical if the relationship between fair dealing and the approved purposes were given a different significance in subsections (2) and (3) from subsection (1), in the absence of obvious reasons for making such a difference. The relevant fair dealing is thus fair dealing with the memorandum for the approved purposes. It is fair dealing directed to and consequently limited to and to be judged in relation to the approved purposes. It is dealing which is fair for the approved purposes and not dealing which might be fair for some other purpose or fair in general. Mere dealing with the work for that purpose is not enough; it must also be dealing which is fair for that purpose; whose fairness, as I have indicated, must be judged in relation to that purpose.

Thus public interest as such is outside the purpose of the section and of fair dealing. It is not of itself justification for infringement of copyright, except insofar as recognised by common law as a separate defence irrespective of the section, as already mentioned.

(2) Factors in the defence of fair dealing.

I come now to the relevant factors in determining fair dealing. A number of authorities were cited, but for present purposes, at any rate, the law is most conveniently stated in Hubbard v. Vosper [1972] 2 W.L.R. 389at 394D to 395D by Lord Denning, M.R. and at page 398F to H by Megaw, L.J. To summarise the statements:- Fair dealing is a question of fact and of impression, to which factors that are relevant include the extent of the quotation and its proportion to comment (which may be justifiable although the quotation is of the whole work); whether the work is unpublished: and the extent to which the work has been circularised, although not published to the public within the meaning of the Copyright Act.

In our case the memorandum was unpublished. Romer, J. in British Oxygen Co. v. Liquid Air Ltd.(1925) I Chancery 383 at 393, in dealing with a company's letter to a trade customer as a "literary work", said that publication without the author's consent would be "manifestly unfair" as it is not a "fair dealing" with the work. Romer, J.'s observations were made when the relevant statute was section 2 of the Copyright Act 1911, the percursor of section 6 of the 1956 Act. It was in wide terms into which limitations were introduced by section 6, but the differences are not material for present purposes. However, unpublished as well as published works are within the fair dealing provisions of both Acts: and what would otherwise be infringement cannot of itself, without regard to any other circumstances, be outside the exception to infringement made by those sections, as that would be to exclude from the sections what the sections in terms include. So I doubt if Romer, J. ever intended that his words should be read in the sense that an unpublished work should be automatically outside the provisions of the fair dealing defence rather than a factor, although doubtless an important factor, which with other factors have to be taken into consideration in considering fair dealing. And such a conclusion seems to me to be in accordance with the decision and observations of the Court of Appeal in Hubbard v. Vosper.

(3) Was the publication of the memorandum fair dealing within section 6?

The publication was of the whole memorandum. In extent it formed a quarter of the article which was published. But that article was throughout dealing with the relationship of Mr. Maudling and Mr. Hoffman and his companies; how the plaintiff's article came to be written replying to the plaintiff's criticisms of Private Eye's attitude towards Mr. Maudling: criticising the plaintiff's article on fact and on attitude; and in the course of doing so reflecting adversely on the plaintiff in the context of these matters.

The plaintiff submitted that Mr. Foot's article was not fair dealing, on the ground that it made a personal attack upon her and disclosed a competitor's confidential source of information. Whilst not lacking in respect for those submissions as for all the submissions made by the plaintiff's counsel, I will come immediately to what appears to me to be the greatest and simplest difficulty which the defendants have to face on fair dealing.

The memorandum was unpublished and indeed it was never intended to be published. This is therefore not just a case of quoting excessively from a work which had already been made available to the public generally. The law by bestowing a right of copyright on an unpublished work bestows a right to prevent its being published at all; and even though an unpublished work is not automatically excluded from the defence of fair dealing, it is yet a much more substantial breach of copyright than publication of a published work. And in our case all the contents of the memorandum were obtained and used without the author's consent in the correct conviction that, if consent had been sought, it would have been refused.

But receiving and using leaked information, in the sense of confidential information which someone who has it gives to someone not entitled to it appears to be common practice in the Press, and occurs in such a reputable paper as the Observer itself. An instance was even given in evidence of the publication by the plaintiff of such a leak. Distinctions were sought to be drawn by or on behalf of the plaintiff between different ways in which leaks occur. It was sought to distinguish between a leak by theft as contrasted with breach of confidence, and it was strongly maintained, particularly by the plaintiff in the early stages of the hearing, that the memorandum was stolen from the Observer's offices by someone from Private Eye; but Mr. Foot, who knew, said that the contents of the memorandum were disclosed by someone in the Observer who wanted the memorandum published; and I have no hesitation in accepting the evidence of Mr. Foot. A distinction was also sought to be drawn between, on the one hand, receiving and using a leak of a rival's confidential information (for example, by Private Eye of the confidential information of another newspaper) and, on the other hand, receiving and using confidential information of some other body not a rival (e.g. by Private Eye from a Government department, an industrial company or a private firm). Mr. Foot disagreed and so do I. A distinction was also suggested between a leak of information never intended by its owner to be published and a pre-empting leak in anticipation of authorised publication. The pre-empting leak might well be substantially prejudicial; and though the later such a leak takes place before authorised publication the less is apt to be the ill consequence, yet the less too is it apt to be in the public interest, which was mostly alone relied upon to justify the publication of leaked information. On all these distinctions there may well be differences of responsible views sincerely held: but for my part I am unable to make any decisive distinction between the unsought voluntary leak in this case by a person who wanted the leaked information published and other Press publications of leaks which were referred to in evidence.

Is then the publication of what was thus obtained by Private Eye by the leak to it fair dealing or compatible with fair dealing within section 6?

Defendants' counsel suggested that as the leak occurred before any infringement by publication it did not affect the fair dealing defence to such infringement and was outside the section. But the leak was clearly a dealing with the work in which copyright existed at the time of the leak, and the leak was given and accepted for the purpose of unauthorised publication. And, further, the publication itself was not just a publication in vacuo but a publication of information known to be leaked. which would not without the leak have been so published. The vice of the leak and publication in this case was, to my mind, clearly unjustifiable for the authorised purposes of criticism, review and news, and clearly in my view constituted dealing which was not fair within the statute. And this unfair dealing goes to the root of the publication — without it there would be no publication at all. This ground is ample to defeat the defence of fair dealing, and it is on this ground that I base my decision against the defendants on this issue.

R. v. James Lorimer & Co. Ltd., [1984] 1 F.C. 1065 (Fed. C.A.)

Heald, Mahoney and Ryan JJ.

Ottawa: November 29, 1983
Docket: A-831-82

. . .

2. The work subject of the Crown copyright here is a report entitled *The State of Competition in the Canadian Petroleum Industry*. The content of the work is the statement of evidence prepared by the Director of Investigation and Research under the *Combines Investigation Act*,[FN2] submitted to the Restrictive Trade Practices Commission pursuant to subsection 18(1) of that Act ensuing upon an inquiry instituted on application under subsection 7(1). The appellant caused the 1748-page work to be published in seven volumes and offered for public sale at $70 a set, $10 a volume. (Exhibit A-1.)

3 The respondent's infringing work is an abridgement of the Crown's work consisting, in the words of its publisher's introduction, of:

> ...the full text of Volume I — the findings and recommendations of the Director regarding the oil industry, together with much of the supporting discussion and information from Volumes II-VI. In the interests of keeping this volume to a reasonable length, some of the more technical sections have been omitted. But conclusions and summaries from all sections of the report have been reprinted....

> In this volume, the original volume, chapter and section heads from the full report have been retained, as have their letter and numerical designations.

> . . .

> Footnote numbers from the original report have been retained. Readers wishing to obtain footnote references can find them in Volume VII of the full report.

The infringing work, a single, 626-page volume, was retailed at $14.95. (Exhibits A-2 and A-3.)

. . .

22 The cross-appeal is concerned with defences raised by the respondent and rejected at trial and with the dismissal of the counterclaim. The first defence was that of fair dealing. The Act provides:

> 17. ...
>
> (2) The following acts do not constitute an infringement of copyright:
>
>> (a) any fair dealing with any work for the purposes of private study, research, criticism, review, or newspaper summary;

The respondent says its abridgement was a fair dealing for the purposes of review. After considering the authorities, the learned Trial Judge concluded [at page 11] that such fair dealing

> ...requires as a minimum some dealing with the work other than simply condensing it into an abridged version and reproducing it under the author's name.

23 (Appeal Book, page 150) The Trial Judge was right.

24 The second defence was that of public interest which is posed in the respondent's memorandum of fact and law in the following terms:

> Did the Respondent's publication further the disclosure to the public of facts and material relating to alleged misdeeds or other matters of a serious nature that are of importance to the country and to the public's welfare, such that the defence of public interest applies on the facts of this particular case?

Three copyright decisions were cited in support of the defence.

25 In *Hubbard et al. v. Vosper et al.* the alleged copyright infringement involved confidential documents of the Church of Scientology and, in *Beloff v. Pressdram Limited et al.*, the work subject of copyright was an unpublished document. Both deal with public interest in the context of information that ought to be public and is not, which is certainly not the situation here. The learned Trial Judge found [at page 19]:

> The extent of the disclosure in the report was very great. There was no suggestion that the public was suffering under any deprivation on the part of the authors of this report or those responsible for its distribution. Free copies were given out in very large numbers, put in libraries across the country and, therefore, there is not in the circumstances of this case any justification that relates to some concern that the public might not be fully informed of the subject-matter of this inquiry. Furthermore, it seems to me that Mr. Lorimer knew that.

26 (Appeal Book, page 158)

27 I have no doubt that a defence of public interest as enunciated in the English cases is available in proper circumstances against an assertion of Crown copyright. However, the facts here do not support its application and the learned Trial Judge was right to reject it.

28 In *Time Incorporated v. Bernard Geis Associates, et al.*, a United States District Court held that reproduction, in a book dealing with the assassination of President Kennedy, of individual frames of the plaintiff's copyrighted motion

picture film of the assassination constituted a "fair use" outside the limits of copyright protection. This is not a "public interest" case in the same sense as the English decisions nor, really, in the sense the defence was advanced here. Rather the U.S. Court applied an equitable doctrine similar in scope to the statutory defence of fair dealing already discussed. The judgment deals at some length with legislation then before Congress proposing to codify the doctrine.

Allen v. Toronto Star Newspapers Ltd. (1997), 36 O.R. 201

O'Driscoll, Flinn, Sedgwick JJ.

Heard: October 2, 1997
Judgment: November 3, 1997
Docket: Toronto 740/95

. . .

Sedgwick J.:

1 This is an appeal by the defendant (Toronto Star) from a judgment of the Ontario Court of Justice (General Division) released on October 13, 1995, [(1996), 26 O.R. (3d) 308 (Ont. Gen. Div.)], in favour of the plaintiff (Allen) for $900 general damages for infringement of copyright in a photograph. This appeal comes to the Divisional Court under ss. 19(1) (a) of the *Courts of Justice Act.*

2 Allen is a freelance photographer. His services were engaged by Saturday Night, a magazine with nation-wide circulation, to shoot a cover photo of a national political figure, Sheila Copps, M.P., then a member of an active group of opposition Members of Parliament known as the "Rat Pack".

3 The cover of the November 1985 issue of Saturday Night bore a photograph of Ms. Copps dressed in leathers astride a motorcycle, identified by counsel as a Harley-Davidson. The photo used on the cover was taken by Allen in the course of his engagement by Saturday Night.

4 On March 11, 1990, the Toronto Star, a daily newspaper, published a feature article about Ms. Copps, then a candidate for the national leadership of her party. The article was illustrated by two photographs. One of them was a photo of the cover of the November 1985 issue of Saturday Night. The other was a photo of Ms. Copps in 1990 in more conventional clothing speaking in Toronto to a group identified in the newspaper as Chinese Canadians.

5 The publication by the Toronto Star of that photograph resulted in this action being brought by Allen on October 16, 1991, for infringement of his copyright in the 1985 photo of Ms. Copps. Allen was successful at trial. The learned trial judge concluded:

> ...by reproducing the Saturday Night magazine cover of November 1985 the defendant infringed the copyright in the photograph owned by Allen and accordingly I will be awarding damages for such infringement. (*supra.* p.316).

6 Allen was awarded general damages in the amount of $900, calculated to be the amount of the fee to which he would have been entitled for the use of the photograph, according to the learned trial judge's view of the evidence as to the custom of the industry. Allen was awarded pre-judgment interest on that amount in accordance with section 128 of the *Courts of Justice Act*, from October 16, 1991 to October 26, 1995, together with his party/party costs fixed at $10,400 (plus GST). Allen's claim for aggravated or exemplary damages in the amount of $10,000 was dismissed.

7 Saturday Night has not objected to the reproduction of its November 1985 cover.

8 The Toronto Star appeals this judgment on three grounds:

(1) its reproduction of the 1985 magazine cover did not infringe the admitted copyright interest of Allen in the 1985 Copps photo itself, or any copyright interest in the magazine cover.

(2) its reproduction of the 1985 magazine cover does not infringe any copyright interest in the photo or the cover because the "fair dealing" defence set out in ss. 27(2)(a) of the *Copyright Act*, R.S.C. 1985, c. C-42, (then in force), applies.

(3) if the "fair dealing" defence does not apply, then ss. 27(2)(a) of the *Copyright Act* infringes s. 2(b) of the *Canadian Charter of Rights and Freedoms* and should be interpreted and applied in a manner consistent with s. 2(b) of the *Charter.*

. . .

(2) Fair Dealing

30 The second ground of this appeal is whether the defence of fair dealing protects the reproduction by the Toronto Star of the cover of the November 1985 issue of Saturday Night, regardless of the subsistence of copyright in the cover and its ownership.

31 On March 11, 1990, the "fair dealing" defence was set out in ss. 27(2) (a) of the *Copyright Act*, as follows:

(2) The following acts do not constitute an infringement of copyright:

(a) any fair dealing with any work for the purposes of private study, research, criticism, review or newspaper summary;

32 This provision has since been amended twice: by the *North American Free Trade Agreement Implementation Act*, S.C. 1993, c.44, s. 64(1), in force January 1, 1994, as ss. 27(2) (a.1); then by an Act to amend the *Copyright Act*, S.C. 1997, c.24, s. 18, in force September 1, 1997, as s. 29.2.

33 Submissions were addressed to us by both counsel on different points that were, to an extent, based on the amended provisions. In our view, the provisions

as amended are not germane to this appeal, either directly or indirectly as evidence of a previous legislative intent.

34 Section 29.2, which is the current provision of the *Copyright Act*, provides that fair dealing for the purpose of news reporting does not infringe copyright if the source and the author of the work reproduced are mentioned. At the time of the alleged infringement by the Toronto Star, however, there was no statutory or other legal requirement for crediting the author of a copyright or work (such as a photograph) in relation to the defence of fair dealing.

35 At trial, the Toronto Star contended that reproduction of the cover of Saturday Night constituted fair dealing as defined in s. 27(2) (a) of the *Copyright Act* as a "newspaper summary". According to the learned trial judge, Allen relied on the *ejusdem generis* rule of construction of s. 27(2) (a) and submitted that "publishing the whole photograph even in its Saturday Night magazine form does not fit the fair dealing defence" (*supra*, p. 315). The learned trial judge commented:

> The fair dealing defence raised by the defendant is an interesting issue which in my view has no application to the case at bar as I accept the plaintiff's submissions with respect to it. (*supra*, p. 316)

36 On a fair reading of the statute, we think that the fair dealing defence as expressed in s. 27(2) (a) of the *Copyright Act* in force on March 10, 1990, applies in this case.

37 The use by the Toronto Star on March 10, 1990 of a photographic reproduction of the November 1985 cover of Saturday Night was related to then current news, the leadership aspirations of Ms. Copps. The other photo used to illustrate the feature article on Ms. Copps portrayed her in a more traditional political appearance in 1990. It was apt for the newspaper to contrast the image she was willing to project in 1985. The change in her image was the thrust of the article.

38 The cover was not reproduced in colour as was the original. The cover was reproduced in reduced form. The news story and accompanying photos received no special prominence in the newspaper. They appeared on an inside page of an inside section. These factors are indications that the purpose of its reproduction of the cover was to aid in the presentation of a news story and not to gain an unfair commercial or competitive advantage over Allen or Saturday Night.

39 In our view, the test of fair dealing is essentially purposive. It is not simply a mechanical test of measurement of the extent of copying involved. We were referred to the case of *Zamacoïs v. Douville* (1943), 2 C.P.R. 270 (Can. Ex. Ct.), a decision of Angers J. in the Exchequer Court of Canada. To the extent that this decision is considered an authority for the proposition that reproduction of an entire newspaper article or, in this case, a photograph of a magazine cover can never be considered a fair dealing with the article (or magazine cover) for purposes of news summary or reporting, we respectfully disagree.

40 In *Hubbard v. Vosper*, [1972] 1 All E.R. 1023 (Eng. C.A.), the Court of Appeal of England considered the scope of the defence of fair dealing under s. 6(2) of the *(U.K.) Copyright Act* (1956), in relation to criticism or review of

literary works. The following passage from the judgment of Lord Denning M.R. has a broader application:

> It is impossible to define what is "fair dealing". It must be a question of degree. You must consider first the number and extent of the quotations and extracts. Are they altogether too many and too long to be fair? Then you must consider the use made of them. If they are used as a basis for comment, criticism or review, that may be a fair dealing. If they are used to convey the same information as the author, for a rival purpose, that may be unfair. Next, you must consider the proportions. To take long extracts and attach short comments may be unfair. But, short extracts and long comments may be fair. Other considerations may come to mind also. But, after all is said and done, it must be a matter of impression. (p. 1027)

Megaw L.J. considered the quantitative argument which appears to have been accepted by the learned trial judge in this case in determining the issue of fair dealing against the Toronto Star. Megaw L.J. said:

> It is then said that the passages which have been taken from these various works ... are so substantial, quantitatively so great in relation to the respective works from which the citations are taken, that they fall outside the scope of 'fair dealing'. To my mind this question of substantiality is a question of degree. It may well be that it does not prevent the quotation of a work from being within the fair dealing subsection even though the quotation may be of every single word of the work. Let me give an example. Suppose that there is on a tombstone in a churchyard an epitaph consisting of a dozen or of 20 words. A parishioner of the church thinks that this sort of epitaph is out of place on a tombstone. He writes a letter to the parish magazine setting out the words of the epitaph. Could it be suggested that that citation is so substantial, consisting of 100 per cent of the 'work' in question, that it must necessarily be outside the scope of the fair dealing provision? To my mind it could not validly be so suggested. In this present case, having considered what we have been shown of the passages taken from the various works in relation (because I think this test must also be applied) to the nature and purpose of the individual quotations, I find myself unable to say that the plaintiffs have made out a case that the quotations are so substantial that this does not fall within the fair dealing provision ... (p. 1031)

41 Similarly in *Williams & Wilkins Co. v. United States*, 417 U.S. 907 (U.S. Cl. Ct. 1974) in the U.S. Court of Claims, Judge Davis spoke to the quantitative point:

> It has sometimes been suggested that the copying of an entire copyrighted work, any such work, cannot ever be "fair use", but this is an overbroad generalization, unsupported by the decisions and rejected by years of accepted practice. There is, in short, no inflexible rule excluding an entire copyrighted work from the area of "fair use". Instead, the extent of the copying is one important factor, but only one to be taken into account, along with several others.

42 The decision of the Court of Claims was upheld on an equal division of the U.S. Supreme Court (Justice Blackmun taking no part in the decision), 420 U.S. 376 (U.S. Cl. Ct. 1975). At issue was the photocopying of journal articles for research workers by the National Library of Medicine and the National Institute of Health which was held not to infringe copyright in the photocopied articles.

(Referred to in B. Torno: *Fair Dealing: The Need for Conceptual Clarity on the Road to Copyright Revision*, Consumer & Corporate Affairs Canada, 1981.)

43 In our view, the learned trial judge erred in basing his decision that the defence of fair dealing did not apply solely on the factor that the Toronto Star used a photograph of the entire cover of the November 1985 issue of Saturday Night, without apparently considering other factors including the nature and purpose of the use.

44 Bearing in mind the nature and purpose of the use by the Toronto Star on March 10, 1990 of the photograph of the November 1985 cover of Saturday Night to illustrate a current news story, the defence of fair dealing applies in the circumstances of this case.

Extracts from the *CCH* case, from the trial division to the Supreme Court of Canada, reveal competing approaches to the interpretation and application of the fair dealing defence.

**CCH Canadian Ltd. v. Law Society of Upper Canada (1999),
2 C.P.R. (4th) 129 (Fed. T.D.), additional reasons 2000 CarswellNat 168
(Fed. T.D.), reversed 2002 CarswellNat 1000 (Fed. C.A.),
reversed 2004 CarswellNat 446 (S.C.C.)**

Federal Court, Trial Division

...ACTION for infringement of copyright by reason of the defendant making copies of reported judicial decisions, headnotes and other legal materials through the operation of its custom photocopy service; COUNTERCLAIM for a declaration that the operation of the defendant's custom photocopy services and the making available and use of the defendant's free-standing photocopy machines did not infringe any copyright of the plaintiffs.... ...

GIBSON J. :-

. . .

(iii) Fair Dealing

[174] The copying by the defendant in the course of its custom photocopy service was done in response to requests received, directly or indirectly, from members of the defendant; it was not done for the defendant's own use in research, private study, criticism or review. Prior to 1996, the defendant neither asked for, nor maintained a record of, the use to which the requesters proposed to put the copies. Commencing in 1996, requesters were required to identify the use to which they proposed to put the copies from among a list of possible uses, all of which were within the scope of "fair dealing". No alternative use, beyond the

scope of "fair dealing", was identified and a requester was provided no special opportunity to identify a use beyond the limits of "fair dealing".

[175] As noted earlier in these reasons, the Supreme Court of Canada has put beyond doubt the proposition that there is no requirement to show knowledge or mens rea to establish direct infringement of copyright; if the actions of the defendant are not themselves within the ambit of fair dealing, or if the actions of the requesters of copies from the custom photocopy service were not in fact within the ambit of fair dealing, then lack of knowledge on the part of the defendant of the ultimate use is not itself a defence. In Sillitoe v. McGraw-Hill Book Co. (U.K.) Ltd., [1983] F.S.R. 545 (Ch.) at 558., Justice Mervyn Davies wrote:

> The onus of showing that an exception applies is on the defendants. Mr. Jeffs contended that section 6(1) is widely drawn and not limited to the actual student, so that if a dealing is fair and for the purposes of private study the subsection applies whether the private study in mind is one's own or that of somebody else. Here, he said, the dealing was for the purpose of private study by the examinees who would acquire the notes. I do not accept that argument. To my mind section 6(1) authorises what would otherwise be an infringement if one is engaged in private study or research. The authors of the Notes, when writing the Notes and thus "dealing" with the original work, were not engaged in private study or research.

I am satisfied that the same might be said on the facts of this matter. The copying by the defendant in the course of its custom photocopy service was not for a purpose within the ambit of fair dealing notwithstanding that the ultimate use by the requester of the photocopying might itself be within the ambit of fair dealing. The conclusion in Sillitoe quoted above has been followed in both Australia and New Zealand. [FN103] I am satisfied that the fair dealing exception should be strictly construed.

[FN103] See De Garis v. Neville Jeffress Pidler Pty Ltd. (1990), 95 A.L.R. 625 (Aust. F.C.) at 629-30, and Longman Group Ltd. v. Carrington Technical Institute Board of Governors, [1991] 2 N.Z.L.R. 574 (N.Z.H.C.) at 584.

[176] While counsel for the defendant urged that the Sillitoe decision can be distinguished on its facts and that neither the Sillitoe decision itself nor the Australian and New Zealand decisions adopting its reasoning have been applied in Canada and should not be applied in Canada as they are contrary to the plain meaning of the fair dealing provisions of the Copyright Act, I am satisfied that those decisions are apt to the facts of this matter which, I acknowledge, are not identical to those of the cited decisions. I am satisfied that my conclusion in this regard is consistent with the "library exception" amendment to the fair dealing sections recently adopted by Parliament and now proclaimed in force.

. . .

CCH Canadian Ltd. v. Law Society of Upper Canada

(2002), 212 D.L.R. (4th) 385 (Fed. C.A.), reversed 2004 CarswellNat 446 (S.C.C.)

Federal Court of Apeal

Linden J.A.: ...

2 Upon request from lawyers, articling students, the judiciary or other authorized researchers the Law Society will photocopy legal materials from the Great Library's collection. Library users can pick up photocopies or have them forwarded by mail or facsimile. The photocopying service is intended to be carried out in accordance with the Law Society's "Access to the Law Policy", which states:

Access to the Law Policy

The Law Society of Upper Canada, with the assistance of the resources of the Great Library, supports the administration of justice and the rule of law in the Province of Ontario. The Great Library's comprehensive catalogue of primary and secondary legal sources, in print and electronic media, is open to lawyers, articling students, the judiciary and other authorized researchers. Single copies of library materials, required for the purposes of research, review, private study and criticism, as well as use in court, tribunal and government proceedings, may be provided to users of the Great Library.

This service supports users of the Great Library who require access to legal materials while respecting the copyright of the publishers of such materials, in keeping with the fair dealing provisions in Section 27 of the Canadian Copyright Act.

Guidelines to Access

1. The Access to the Law service provides single copies for specific purposes, identified in advance to library staff.

2. The specific purposes are research, review, private study and criticism, as well as use in court, tribunal and government proceedings. Any doubt concerning the legitimacy of the request for these purposes will be referred to the Reference Librarian.

3. The individual must identify him/herself and the purpose at the time of making the request. A request form will be completed by library staff, based on information provided by the requesting party.

4. As to the amount of copying, discretion must be used. No copies will be made for any purpose other than that specifically set out on the request form. Ordinarily, requests for a copy of one case, one article or one statutory reference will be satisfied as a matter of routine. Requests for substantial copying from secondary sources (e.g. in excess of 5% of the volume or more than two citations from one volume) will be referred to the Reference Librarian and may ultimately be refused.

5. This service is provided on a not for profit basis. The fee charged for this service is intended to cover the costs of the Law Society.

Jan. 28, 1996

> 3 When the Policy was put into writing in 1996 it was not intended to depart from the existing policy, although it did alter monitoring and compliance practices somewhat. The Law Society asserts that its guidelines are now strictly enforced.

. . .

C. Do Any Exemptions or Defences Apply to the Law Society?

122 Having established that the Law Society's custom photocopying service *prima facie* infringes the Publishers' exclusive right to reproduce their works, it is necessary for me to consider whether any exemptions or defences apply to the Law Society. The Law Society's primary argument is that it is not liable for copyright infringement by virtue of the fair dealing provisions in the *Act*....

1. Fair Dealing

123 The fair dealing analysis in this case is complicated by the fact that, unknown to it at the time, the Law Society dealt with the Publishers' works, on behalf of the Publishers' counsel, for the purpose of researching the Publishers' litigation against the Law Society. Thus, it is arguable that the reproductions by the Law Society of the Publishers' eleven specific works were implicitly authorized and, therefore, made fairly. However, little or no evidence or written or oral argument was directed at this problem or the fairness of any particular dealings. Rather, like the allegations of infringement, arguments were directed at the implications of the Law Society's activities under its Access to the Law Policy generally, not at specific actions or events. Because a full assessment of fair dealing can only be made in a fact-specific context, I cannot make any definitive pronouncement on the fairness in this case of the dealings by the Law Society with the Publishers' eleven specific works. However, since this is the central issue in the Law Society's cross-appeal and the Law Society relied so heavily on this defence and its Access to the Law Policy, this Court must consider the fair dealing exemption and the applicable principles in order to help resolve the dispute between these parties.

. . .

126 The Publishers first argument is that the *Act*'s exemptions, such as the fair dealing provisions, ought to be narrowly construed. It is true that the Supreme Court of Canada has indicated that courts ought not imply exceptions in addition to those expressly included in the *Act* by Parliament (see *Bishop v. Stevens*, *supra* at 480-1). However, this does not mean that we must narrowly interpret the exemptions that Parliament has established. The Trial Judge erred in law when he stated that exceptions to infringement must be "strictly construed" (at para 175). There is no basis in law or in policy for such an approach. An overly restrictive interpretation of the exemptions contained in the Act would be inconsistent with the mandate of copyright law to harmonize owners' rights with legitimate public interests (see Vaver, *Copyright Law*, *supra* at 170-1).

Instead, courts should employ the usual modern rules of purposive construction in the context (see R. Sullivan, *Driedger on the Construction of Statutes*, 3rd ed. (Toronto: Butterworths, 1994) at 131). As Professor Vaver has pointed out, "User rights are not just loopholes. Both owner rights and user rights should therefore be given [a] fair and balanced reading" (see *Copyright Law, supra* at 171). Simply put, any act falling within the fair dealing exemptions is not an infringement of copyright.

a. Allowable Purposes

127 The first task is to define the scope of each allowable purpose under section 29 in order to determine whether the Law Society's activities might fall within that scope. Importantly, the categories of allowable purposes under our *Act* are closed, unlike under the American doctrine of fair use (see 17 U.S.C. § 107). If the purpose of the dealing is not one that is expressly mentioned in the *Act*, this Court is powerless to apply the fair dealing exemptions. If the purpose of a dealing is an allowable purpose, this Court may then embark upon a separate, but related investigation as to the fairness of that dealing.

128 With respect to the purposes listed in section 29, "research" is not modified whereas "study" is required to be "private". Parliament's decision to expressly qualify "study" but not "research" indicates an intention to permit all fair research, whether in a private setting or not (see Vaver, *Copyright Law, supra* at 195-6; *Television New Zealand v. Newsmonitor Services Ltd.* (1993), 27 I.P.R. 441 (New Zealand H.C.)). Therefore, I do not agree with the Publishers' submission that research can never take place where a work is dealt with in a non-private context. Similarly, I do not agree with the Publishers that commercial research cannot be an allowable purpose. "Research" is not qualified in the *Act*, therefore, research for a commercial purpose, including legal research carried out for profit by entities such as law firms, is not automatically excluded from this exemption. Research for the purpose of advising clients, giving opinions, arguing cases, preparing briefs and factums is nonetheless research. Of course, if a copy is made for non-private or commercial research purposes, such a fact may affect the fairness of the dealing.

129 Section 29 qualifies "study", however, with the adjective "private". Therefore, non-private study is not an allowable purpose (see Vaver, *Copyright Law, supra* at 195-6). British courts have held that use in an educational institution was not for the purpose of private study (see *University of London Press, supra*). Thus, for example, if a law professor requests a copy of a work for the purpose of distributing it among his or her students, such a request would not be for the purpose of private study. If, on the other hand, an articling student requests a copy of a work for his or her own learning, that request could be for the purpose of private study.

130 The Publishers submit that one may deal fairly only for one's own purposes (see Vaver, *Copyright Law* at 193). The Law Society suggests that the statutory language speaks to the broader purpose of the dealing, and is not concerned

with who actually carries out the allowable purpose. The Trial Judge held that the Law Society's copying service was not for a purpose within the ambit of fair dealing, notwithstanding that the ultimate use of the works might have been (at para 175). He narrowly defined the Law Society's purpose as facilitating research, rather than research *per se*. Since there is little or no Canadian jurisprudence directly addressing this issue, I will examine the approach of foreign jurisdictions.

131   In the British case of *Sillitoe v. Mc-Graw Hill Book Co. (U.K.) Ltd.* , [1983] F.S.R. 545 (Eng. Ch.), the importer and distributor of study aids was not permitted to escape liability using the defence that the ultimate use of the infringing works was for students' private study or research. Similarly, the court in *University of London Press* , *supra* interpreted private study as not including educational purposes, and therefore did not allow professors to claim an exemption based upon their students' purposes. In *De Garis v. Neville Jeffress Pidler Pty. Ltd.* (1990), 95 A.L.R. 625 (Australia Fed. Ct.), the General Division of the Federal Court of Australia decided to extend the principle in *Sillitoe* to a situation where a commercial enterprise actively monitored certain subjects in the news and provided clients with photocopies of related media articles. Also, a New Zealand Court, in *Longman Group Ltd. v. Carrington Technical Institute Board of Governors*, [1991] 2 N.Z.L.R. 574 (New Zealand H.C.), stated in *obiter* that, if required to decide the issue, it would have relied upon earlier British decisions and agreed that the use for research or private study must be that of the compiler.

132   The Law Society is correct that these cases are all distinguishable on the facts. The Law Society has no purpose for copying the Publishers' works other than to fulfill the purpose of requesters. It does not perform this task for its own economic benefit, but as a service to researchers and studiers. Its only aim and design is to assist users of the Great Library in conducting research or private study, and it can, therefore, be said to have adopted that purpose as their own. The entities in the cases mentioned above had ulterior motives and simply tried to adopt customers' or students' purposes as their own in order to escape liability. Moreover, the otherwise infringing activity is carried out by the Law Society only in response to a patron's request. But for the end user's request, the Law Society would not carry out any of these allegedly infringing activities. In the foreign cases mentioned above, the otherwise infringing activity was initiated by the alleged infringer, rather than the end user.

133   Barry Torno, in *Fair Dealing: The Need for Conceptual Clarity on the Road to Copyright Revision*, Ottawa: C.C.A.C., 1981 at 45, has suggested that it is appropriate to consider:

> the party who initiates the duplication for the purpose of private study of research and not the agent who carries out the act of duplication ... If the use is "fair", it is not unreasonable to suppose that the means by which the single copy required is produced for the particular purpose and person concerned may be irrelevant.

134   Therefore, notwithstanding that the Law Society did not personally undertake research or private study, I am convinced that the Law Society shares the purposes

of individual patrons of the Great Library. However, this finding alone does not amount to an exemption from infringement, but merely crosses the threshold of fair dealing. This Court must still assess whether the dealings were fair.

. . .

c. Fairness

144 Necessarily, fairness depends upon the context and facts of each particular case, and for that reason, "fair" is not defined in the Act. In the case of *Hubbard v. Vosper* (1971), [1972] 2 Q.B. 84 (Eng. C.A.), at 94, Lord Denning recognized that "[i]t is impossible to define what is 'fair dealing.' It must be a question of degree. ... [I]t must be a matter of impression." In *Cie générale des établissements Michelin — Michelin & Cie v. CAW — Canada* (1996), 71 C.P.R. (3d) 348 (Fed. T.D.) ("*Michelin*") at 384, the Trial Division of this Court accepted that the overall use of the copyright must be fair and the copyright must be treated in a good faith manner. Like Lord Denning, the Court admitted that it was "a question of impression" (at 384). The Ontario Court (General Division) in *Allen v. Toronto Star Newspapers Ltd.* (1997), 78 C.P.R. (3d) 115 (Ont. Div. Ct.), at 123, viewed the test as "essentially purposive".

145 Despite these remarks, an assessment of fairness is not simply a subjective exercise, and there are a number of identifiable factors that might influence one's conclusion. A list of these factors has not been compiled by a Canadian court, nor is one contained in the *Act*. As our *Act* does not describe any specific factors to consider, it is incumbent upon this Court to do so as best it can.

146 In *Hubbard v. Vosper, surpa* Lord Denning described (at 94) some of the factors that may be relevant to a determination of the fairness of dealing for the purposes of criticism and review. He analysed the number and extent of quotations, the purpose of the dealing, whether the use was for a rival purpose, and the proportions of the extracts compared to independent comments. Some of these factors have been subsequently accepted and explained by the Court of Appeal in England in cases such as *Pro Sieben Media AG v. Carlton UK Television Ltd.*, [1999] F.S.R. 610 (Eng. C.A.) ("*Pro Sieben*"), and *Hyde Park Residence Ltd. v. Yelland*, [2000] E.W.J. No. 514 (Eng. C.A.). However, these considerations, which are related to fair dealing in the context of criticism or review or reporting current events, do not neatly apply in every situation. Nevertheless, they may provide guidance for this Court to explore the factors relevant to fair dealing under Canadian law.

147 17 U.S.C. § 107, which outlines the doctrine of fair use in the United States, directs American courts to consider a non-exhaustive list of factors, including the purpose and character of the use, the nature of the copyrighted work, the amount and substantiality of the portion used in relation to the copyrighted work as a whole and the effect of the use upon the potential market for or value of the copyrighted work.

148 I realize the differences in the American legislation as compared to our own *Act*. Generally, American law is more favourable to copyright users than is

Canadian law. In particular, 17 U.S.C. § 107 leaves open the types of purposes that may constitute fair use, unlike our *Act*, which specifies allowable purposes (see *Hager* , *supra* at 309; *Michelin*, *supra* at 379; and Vaver, *Copyright Law*, *supra* at 190). However, this fact alone does not mean that we cannot "find some assistance in examining the experience in the United States", as Estey J. suggested, and consider these factors in an analysis of fair dealing (see *Compo*, *supra* at 367). Importantly, the distinction between Canadian and American law regarding allowable purposes has limited bearing on a discussion of the factors that influence whether dealing is fair.

149 I am further comforted by the fact that Professor Vaver has described (in *Copyright Law*, *supra* at 191) many similar factors and implied that they may be applicable to Canadian law:

> Several factors have been used to determine whether a dealing is fair: the purpose and character of the dealing; the nature of the source work; what and how much has been dealt with; the effect of the dealing on the potential market for or value of the source work; whether the source work was available within a reasonable time at an ordinary commercial price; and any reasonable guidelines accepted by joint owner and user interests.

150 Assessing these observations in combination with the American and British factors, I have compiled a list of factors that should influence the fairness of the Law Society's dealings with the Publishers' works on behalf of patrons of the Great Library. Importantly, the elements of fairness are malleable and must be tailored to each unique circumstance. None of the factors are conclusive or binding, and additional considerations may well apply uniquely in the Canadian context. However, the following factors are usually among the non-exhaustive list of considerations: (1) the purpose of the dealing; (2) the nature of the dealing; (3) the amount of the dealing; (4) alternatives to the dealing; (5) the nature of the work in question; and (6) the effect of the dealing on that work.

i. The Purpose of the Dealing

151 The first factor to consider regarding fairness is the purpose of a dealing. This consideration may be less important in Canada than in the United States, since fair dealing, contrary to fair use, relates only to a closed set of purposes. Necessarily, under Canadian law, the purpose must be an allowable purpose, mentioned expressly in the *Act*. However, there may be varying degrees of fairness within allowable purposes. For example, philanthropic research is more likely to be fair than commercial research. Similarly, it might be unfair dealing to compile a library of copies of the Publishers' works regarding a general legal topic, although arguably such dealing is for the purpose of research. On the other hand, it might be fair dealing to make a copy of a work for the purpose of limited research regarding a specific legal topic.

ii. The Character of the Dealing

152 The character of the dealing, that is the way or ways in which the allegedly infringed work was dealt with, may also be relevant to the fair dealing

exemptions. The fact that reproduction of a single copy for a single requester, rather than general publication or widespread telecommunication for example, is the most significant activity typically carried out on behalf of patrons of the Great Library favours a finding of fairness. That is, it is more likely to be fair to deal with works privately than publicly.

iii. The Amount of the Dealing

153 The American reference to "the amount and substantiality of the portion used in relation to the copyrighted work as a whole", and Lord Denning's mention in *Hubbard v. Vosper* of "the number and extent of the quotations and extracts" may be more applicable to cases of criticism and review, since those purposes implicitly suggest that existing works will be somehow incorporated into new works. Yet this factor may also be applicable with respect to other allowable purposes.

154 Of course, one would not be required to analyse fair dealing if the portions taken from a work were not of sufficient quantity and quality to be considered substantial, for such dealing is not an infringement under Canadian law, regardless of section 29. For example, if a patron requested a part of a reported judicial decision that includes edited reasons for judgment, that may not constitute a substantial part of the work. If a patron requested only the headnote from a reported judicial decision, that would likely constitute a substantial part of the work. However, one may deal fairly with a substantial part of a work, or even with an entire work, without infringing copyright (see Vaver, *Copyright Law* at 191-2).

155 It is important to consider the number and types of requests made by a specific patron. It would be more unfair for one member of the Law Society or a single firm to frequently make requests for copies of a large number of works than to make only isolated requests for a copy of one work. To me, it would seem particularly unfair for one patron to request copies of multiple reported judicial decisions from the same series or volume over a short period of time; such a patron should be expected instead to purchase those works from the Publishers.

iv. Alternatives to the Dealing

156 Another important factor at this stage of our enquiry might be the availability of alternatives to the allegedly infringing dealing. The Publishers submit that it would be fair for patrons of the Great Library to achieve their purposes by buying the works they wish to copy. Alternatively, the Publishers argue that the Law Society should obtain a license to carry out the custom photocopying service. In response, the Law Society argues that the availability of a license should not be relevant to fair dealing, since activities that constitute fair dealing fall outside of the sphere of a copyright owner' rights. According to the Law Society, if fair dealing applies, then there is no infringement and no license is required. An offer of a license presupposes a copyright monopoly that can be licensed.

157 This may be true with respect to the Law Society's custom photocopying service in general, however, the purpose of this discussion is to enable an

analysis of the fairness of particular dealings by individual patrons of the Great Library. The fact that alternatives exist whereby patrons can otherwise obtain information contained in the Publishers' works cannot be ignored in an analysis of fairness. Broadly speaking, it is relevant to consider whether the material is reasonably available elsewhere, or whether the Publishers have an effective monopoly. The more alternative sources there are for material, the less fair it may be to reproduce copyright material. Thus, it might be more fair to reproduce an obscure foreign decision that cannot reasonably be obtained elsewhere than it would be to copy a domestic decision that is reported in several different publications or readily available from a court.

158 A related question is whether the dealing was reasonably necessary to achieve the ultimate purpose. For example, it would be unreasonable to expect all patrons to conduct their study or private research on the premises of the Great Library each time they wish to access the Publishers' works. This would be a heavy burden, especially for researchers outside of Toronto, who account for roughly 20% of the requests. Likewise, researchers are not permitted to remove materials contained in the Great Library's collection, due to the demand for works contained therein from other lawyers. Thus, the necessity of dealing with the Publishers' works by obtaining a copy thereof from the Great Library supports a finding of fairness, although such dealing may be less fair where it is reasonable for an individual to carry out his or her research without making a copy of the Publishers' work.

v. The Nature of the Work

159 It is generally in the public interest that access to judicial decisions and other legal resources not be unjustifiably restrained. The Law Society provides a valuable service in facilitating access to important legal publications. The justice system requires that lawyers, students, professors and judges can utilize these necessary research tools. However, the fact that access to legal publications is in the public interest does not imply that copying such publications is always fair dealing. On the contrary, these legal works must be protected to ensure that their authors are not deprived of financial incentives to continue producing original legal works. Of course, herein lies the challenge of interpreting the fair dealing exemption. However, whether easy public access outweighs the need for incentives to ensure that such works continue to be produced can only be assessed in the context of more specific facts.

vi. The Effect of the Dealing on the Work

160 The Publishers submit that the economic effect of the Law Society's dealing on the value of their works is a very important consideration. The United States Supreme Court has placed heavy emphasis on this factor (see *Campbell v. Acuff-Rose Music Ltd.*, 114 S. Ct. 1164 (U.S.S.C., 1994)). I also believe that this factor is significant, and am comforted that my British counterparts feel likewise. Lord Justice Robert Walker of the Court of Appeal stated, in *Pro Sieben, supra* at 619, that the "degree to which the challenged use competes with exploitation

of copyright by the copyright owner is a very important consideration, but not the only consideration." For example, it may be unfair for a patron to request a copy of the Publishers' works to incorporate into his or her own competing work. Thus, the fairness of particular dealing might be influenced by the degree to which the market for the reproduced work has been diminished. That determination, however, depends largely on a finding of fact that I am unable to make here.

d. The Access to the Law Policy

161 The Law Society seeks a ubiquitous declaration that fulfilling requests for single copies of reported judgments, statutes or regulations, or for limited selections of text from legal treatises, digests or other reviews of the law, for the purpose of research, in accordance with its Access to the Law Policy, constitutes fair dealing. This Court, however, cannot legitimize its entire photocopying operation with a blanket statement. Not only is it impossible to generalize with respect the Law Society's dealings because of the variability of the purposes the patrons of the Great Library, but likewise, one cannot categorically characterize all of the patrons' dealings as fair. Determining the fairness of a given dealing is enormously complex, and it must always be uniquely fact-specific. Just as the subsistence of copyright and allegations of infringement must be proven by copyright owners, the Law Society must establish, on a balance of probabilities, its vicarious reliance upon a patron's fair dealing exemption each time an infringement is alleged.
162 The Law Society attempts to fulfill an honourable mandate of providing the community with access to its extraordinary collection of legal resources. Indeed, the Great Library serves an important purpose in disseminating the knowledge and wisdom contained within its archives. Although it has not always done so since the inception of its photocopying service in 1954, the Law Society has made efforts since 1996, through its Access to the Law Policy, to ensure that its patrons' purposes were for research or private study, or other allowable purposes. There is no doubt that the Law Society generally acts in good faith and discourages abuses of its services.

163 However, even though the Law Society's purposes may be selfless, this does not mean that the same can always be said of all patrons of the photocopying service. Between 1988 and 1997, the number of requests per year ranged from 3,146 to 4,477, and in each year the Law Society copied an average of about 100,000 pages of material. Assuming that a not insignificant portion of the Law Society's copying might amount to *prima facie* infringement, the volume of such copying prevents me from making the declaration sought by the Law Society. Due to the potential breadth and scope of dealings of patrons of the Great Library, I cannot make a universal assessment of the Law Society's claims of fair dealing.

164 Although the Law Society may adopt the purposes of the Great Library's patrons as its own, those purposes might be different in each particular case. In a very large number of cases, a patron will request a work truly for research

or private study. Other times, however, a patron might misrepresent the purpose of the request and falsely indicate that it is for an allowable purpose. This unpredictability is compounded by the Law Society's inability to effectively ensure that requesters are honest or accurate. Notwithstanding its efforts to comply with copyright law through warnings and its adherence to its Access to the Law Policy, and that most requests will truly be for an allowable purpose, the Law Society cannot guarantee the legitimacy of the motives and dealings of its patrons in every case, nor can it ensure that its service will not be abused.

165 Furthermore, even if the Law Society could somehow ensure that persons who request materials are forthright in disclosing the true purpose of a request, the Law Society cannot verify the fairness of its patrons' dealing. A large proportion of requests may be from patrons whose dealings are nothing but fair, but there may be some that are not. It is impossible for me to conclude that each of the dealings by patrons of the Great Library is always fair, since undeniably, each otherwise infringing activity will have to be considered in light of its own particular circumstances.

166 Therefore, good faith reliance on its policy is insufficient to absolve the Law Society of all potential liability. The Publishers must recognize that if the Law Society strictly adheres to its policy and monitors requests, there will likely be only rare occasions where a request for an objectionable purpose would be filled. However, although the Policy is helpful to screen out potential requests that would not be for an allowable purpose or would not be fair, that only limits the Law Society's potential exposure to liability; it does not absolve it from all responsibility. The Policy is insufficient to categorically establish fair dealing with respect to every single request.

167 The Publishers seem to suggest that one of the factors that makes the Law Society's custom photocopying operation unfair is the volume of copying. However, in order to avoid liability, the Law Society does not rely upon its own fair dealing exemption, but upon the exemptions of its patrons. Notably, the Law Society can claim different patrons' fair dealing exemptions an infinite number of times, since it would be contrary to the purpose of the library exemptions to limit the number of times a library, archive or museum may copy a work on behalf of different persons. In fact, the library exemptions are intended to allow such institutions to disseminate works to a large number of different persons, on the condition that each dealing is fair....

179 The appeal, therefore, will be allowed in part and the cross-appeal dismissed. ...

Rothstein J.A. (Concurring):

. . .

Fair Dealing

292 I have read the analysis of Linden J.A. on fair dealing. I agree with him that there was no evidence or argument directed to the facts of any particular dealing.

293 The absence of a factual underpinning makes application of legal principles relating to fair dealing impossible. The traditional role of the Court is to resolve disputes based on the evidence provided. By failing to provide such evidence, the parties have precluded the Court from performing this role.

. . .

295 In view of the application of the library exemption to the Law Society and that there are no facts pertaining to the dealings that took place before enactment of the library exemption, I would prefer not to express an opinion on the general issue of intermediaries, other than libraries, adopting the end-user's purpose when considering the fair dealing exemption.

296 In all other respects, I am in agreement with the general approach to fair dealing set forth by Linden J.A. in his reasons.

CCH Canadian Ltd. v. Law Society of Upper Canada, 2004 SCC 13

Arbour J., Bastarache J., Binnie J., Deschamps J., Iacobucci J., LeBel J.,

Major J., McLachlin C.J.C.

Heard: November 10, 2003

Judgment: March 4, 2004

Docket: 29320

. . .

The Chief Justice:

I. Introduction — The Issues To Be Determined

1 The appellant, the Law Society of Upper Canada, is a statutory non-profit corporation that has regulated the legal profession in Ontario since 1822. Since 1845, the Law Society has maintained and operated the Great Library at Osgoode Hall in Toronto, a reference and research library with one of the largest collections of legal materials in Canada. The Great Library provides a request-based photocopy service (the "custom photocopy service") for Law Society members, the judiciary and other authorized researchers. Under the custom photocopy service, legal materials are reproduced by Great Library staff and delivered in person, by mail or by facsimile transmission to requesters. The Law Society also maintains self-service photocopiers in the Great Library for use by its patrons.

2 The respondents, CCH Canadian Ltd., Thomson Canada Ltd. and Canada Law Book Inc., publish law reports and other legal materials. In 1993, the respondent publishers commenced copyright infringement actions against the Law Society, seeking a declaration of subsistence and ownership of copyright in eleven specific works and a declaration that the Law Society had infringed copyright when the Great Library reproduced a copy of each of the works. The

publishers also sought a permanent injunction prohibiting the Law Society from reproducing these eleven works as well as any other works that they published.

3 The Law Society denied liability and counterclaimed for a declaration that copyright is not infringed when a single copy of a reported decision, case summary, statute, regulation or a limited selection of text from a treatise is made by the Great Library staff or one of its patrons on a self-service photocopier for the purpose of research.

4 The key question that must be answered in this appeal is whether the Law Society has breached copyright by either (1) providing the custom photocopy service in which single copies of the publishers' works are reproduced and sent to patrons upon their request or by (2) maintaining self-service photocopiers and copies of the publishers' works in the Great Library for use by its patrons. To answer this question, the Court must address the following sub-issues:

(1) Are the publishers' materials "original works" protected by copyright?

(2) Did the Great Library authorize copyright infringement by maintaining self-service photocopiers and copies of the publishers' works for its patrons' use?

(3) Were the Law Society's dealings with the publishers' works "fair dealing [s]" under s. 29 of the *Copyright Act*, R.S.C. 1985, c. C-42, as amended?

(4) Did Canada Law Book consent to have its works reproduced by the Great Library?

. . .

(3) The Law Society and Fair Dealing

47 The Great Library provides a custom photocopy service. Upon receiving a request from a lawyer, law student, member of the judiciary or authorized researcher, the Great Library staff photocopies extracts from legal material within its collection and sends it to the requester. The question is whether this service falls within the fair dealing defence under s. 29 of the *Copyright Act* which provides: "Fair dealing for the purpose of research or private study does not infringe copyright."

(a) The Law

48 Before reviewing the scope of the fair dealing exception under the *Copyright Act*, it is important to clarify some general considerations about exceptions to copyright infringement. Procedurally, a defendant is required to prove that his or her dealing with a work has been fair; however, the fair dealing exception is perhaps more properly understood as an integral part of the *Copyright Act* than simply a defence. Any act falling within the fair dealing exception will not be an infringement of copyright. The fair dealing exception, like other exceptions in the *Copyright Act*, is a user's right. In order to maintain the proper balance

between the rights of a copyright owner and users' interests, it must not be interpreted restrictively. As Professor Vaver, *supra*, has explained, at p. 171: "User rights are not just loopholes. Both owner rights and user rights should therefore be given the fair and balanced reading that befits remedial legislation."

49 As an integral part of the scheme of copyright law, the s. 29 fair dealing exception is always available. Simply put, a library can always attempt to prove that its dealings with a copyrighted work are fair under s. 29 of the *Copyright Act*. It is only if a library were unable to make out the fair dealing exception under s. 29 that it would need to turn to s. 30.2 of the *Copyright Act* to prove that it qualified for the library exemption.

50 In order to show that a dealing was fair under s. 29 of the *Copyright Act*, a defendant must prove: (1) that the dealing was for the purpose of either research or private study and (2) that it was fair.

51 The fair dealing exception under s. 29 is open to those who can show that their dealings with a copyrighted work were for the purpose of research or private study. "Research" must be given a large and liberal interpretation in order to ensure that users' rights are not unduly constrained. I agree with the Court of Appeal that research is not limited to non-commercial or private contexts. The Court of Appeal correctly noted, at para. 128, that "[r]esearch for the purpose of advising clients, giving opinions, arguing cases, preparing briefs and factums is nonetheless research". Lawyers carrying on the business of law for profit are conducting research within the meaning of s. 29 of the *Copyright Act*.

52 The *Copyright Act* does not define what will be "fair"; whether something is fair is a question of fact and depends on the facts of each case. See McKeown, *supra*, at p. 23-6. Lord Denning explained this eloquently in *Hubbard v. Vosper* (1971), [1972] 1 All E.R. 1023 (Eng. C.A.), at p. 1027:

> It is impossible to define what is 'fair dealing'. It must be a question of degree. You must consider first the number and extent of the quotations and extracts. Are they altogether too many and too long to be fair? Then you must consider the use made of them. If they are used as a basis for comment, criticism or review, that may be a fair dealing. If they are used to convey the same information as the author, for a rival purpose, that may be unfair. Next, you must consider the proportions. To take long extracts and attach short comments may be unfair. But, short extracts and long comments may be fair. Other considerations may come to mind also. But, after all is said and done, it must be a matter of impression. As with fair comment in the law of libel, so with fair dealing in the law of copyright. The tribunal of fact must decide.

53 At the Court of Appeal, Linden J.A. acknowledged that there was no set test for fairness, but outlined a series of factors that could be considered to help assess whether a dealing is fair. Drawing on the decision in *Hubbard*, *supra*, as well as the doctrine of fair use in the United States, he proposed that the following factors be considered in assessing whether a dealing was fair: (1) the purpose of the dealing; (2) the character of the dealing; (3) the amount of the dealing; (4) alternatives to the dealing; (5) the nature of the work; and (6) the effect of the

dealing on the work. Although these considerations will not all arise in every case of fair dealing, this list of factors provides a useful analytical framework to govern determinations of fairness in future cases.

(i)   The Purpose of the Dealing

54 In Canada, the purpose of the dealing will be fair if it is for one of the allowable purposes under the *Copyright Act*, namely research, private study, criticism, review or news reporting: see ss. 29, 29.1 and 29.2 of the *Copyright Act*. As discussed, these allowable purposes should not be given a restrictive interpretation or this could result in the undue restriction of users' rights. This said, courts should attempt to make an objective assessment of the user/defendant's real purpose or motive in using the copyrighted work. See McKeown, *supra*, at p. 23-6. See also *Associated Newspapers Group plc v. News Group Newspapers Ltd.*, [1986] R.P.C. 515 (Eng. Ch. Div.). Moreover, as the Court of Appeal explained, some dealings, even if for an allowable purpose, may be more or less fair than others; research done for commercial purposes may not be as fair as research done for charitable purposes.

(ii)   The Character of the Dealing

55 In assessing the character of a dealing, courts must examine how the works were dealt with. If multiple copies of works are being widely distributed, this will tend to be unfair. If, however, a single copy of a work is used for a specific legitimate purpose, then it may be easier to conclude that it was a fair dealing. If the copy of the work is destroyed after it is used for its specific intended purpose, this may also favour a finding of fairness. It may be relevant to consider the custom or practice in a particular trade or industry to determine whether or not the character of the dealing is fair. For example, in *Sillitoe v. Mc-Graw Hill Book Co. (U.K.) Ltd.*, [1983] F.S.R. 545 (Eng. Ch.), the importers and distributors of "study notes" that incorporated large passages from published works attempted to claim that the copies were fair dealings because they were for the purpose of criticism. The court reviewed the ways in which copied works were customarily dealt with in literary criticism textbooks to help it conclude that the study notes were not fair dealings for the purpose of criticism.

(iii) The Amount of the Dealing

56 Both the amount of the dealing and importance of the work allegedly infringed should be considered in assessing fairness. If the amount taken from a work is trivial, the fair dealing analysis need not be undertaken at all because the court will have concluded that there was no copyright infringement. As the passage from *Hubbard* indicates, the quantity of the work taken will not be determinative of fairness, but it can help in the determination. It may be possible to deal fairly with a whole work. As Vaver points out, there might be no other way to criticize or review certain types of works such as photographs: see Vaver, *supra*, at p. 191. The amount taken may also be more or less fair depending on the purpose. For example, for the purpose of research or private study, it may

be essential to copy an entire academic article or an entire judicial decision. However, if a work of literature is copied for the purpose of criticism, it will not likely be fair to include a full copy of the work in the critique.

(iv) Alternatives to the Dealing

57 Alternatives to dealing with the infringed work may affect the determination of fairness. If there is a non-copyrighted equivalent of the work that could have been used instead of the copyrighted work, this should be considered by the court. I agree with the Court of Appeal that it will also be useful for courts to attempt to determine whether the dealing was reasonably necessary to achieve the ultimate purpose. For example, if a criticism would be equally effective if it did not actually reproduce the copyrighted work it was criticizing, this may weigh against a finding of fairness.

(v) The Nature of the Work

58 The nature of the work in question should also be considered by courts assessing whether a dealing is fair. Although certainly not determinative, if a work has not been published, the dealing may be more fair in that its reproduction with acknowledgement could lead to a wider public dissemination of the work–one of the goals of copyright law. If, however, the work in question was confidential, this may tip the scales towards finding that the dealing was unfair. See *Beloff v. Pressdram Ltd.*, [1973] 1 All E.R. 241 at p. 264.

(vi) Effect of the Dealing on the Work

59 Finally, the effect of the dealing on the work is another factor warranting consideration when courts are determining whether a dealing is fair. If the reproduced work is likely to compete with the market of the original work, this may suggest that the dealing is not fair. Although the effect of the dealing on the market of the copyright owner is an important factor, it is neither the only factor nor the most important factor that a court must consider in deciding if the dealing is fair. See, for example, *Pro Sieben Media AG v. Carlton UK Television Ltd.*, [1999] F.S.R. 610 (Eng. C.A.), *per* Robert Walker L.J.

60 To conclude, the purpose of the dealing, the character of the dealing, the amount of the dealing, the nature of the work, available alternatives to the dealing and the effect of the dealing on the work are all factors that could help determine whether or not a dealing is fair. These factors may be more or less relevant to assessing the fairness of a dealing depending on the factual context of the allegedly infringing dealing. In some contexts, there may be factors other than those listed here that may help a court decide whether the dealing was fair.

(b) Application of the law to these facts

61 In 1996, the Law Society implemented an "Access to the Law Policy" ("Access Policy") which governs the Great Library's custom photocopy service and sets limits on the types of requests that will be honoured:

Access to the Law Policy

The Law Society of Upper Canada, with the assistance of the resources of the Great Library, supports the administration of justice and the rule of law in the Province of Ontario. The Great Library's comprehensive catalogue of primary and secondary legal sources, in print and electronic media, is open to lawyers, articling students, the judiciary and other authorized researchers. Single copies of library materials, required for the purposes of research, review, private study and criticism, as well as use in court, tribunal and government proceedings, may be provided to users of the Great Library.

This service supports users of the Great Library who require access to legal materials while respecting the copyright of the publishers of such materials, in keeping with the fair dealing provisions in Section 27 of the Canadian Copyright Act.

Guidelines to Access

1 The Access to the Law service provides single copies for specific purposes, identified in advance to library staff.

2 The specific purposes are research, review, private study and criticism, as well as use in court, tribunal, and government proceedings. Any doubt concerning the legitimacy of the request for these purposes will be referred to the Reference Librarian.

3 The individual must identify him/herself and the purpose at the time of making the request. A request form will be completed by library staff, based on information provided by the requesting party.

4 As to the amount of copying, discretion must be used. No copies will be made for any purpose other than that specifically set out on the request form. Ordinarily, requests for a copy of one case, one article or one statutory reference will be satisfied as a matter of routine. Requests for substantial copying from secondary sources (e.g. in excess of 5% of the volume or more than two citations from one volume) will be referred to the Reference Librarian and may ultimately be refused.

5 This service is provided on a not for profit basis. The fee charged for this service is intended to cover the costs of the Law Society.

When the Access Policy was introduced, the Law Society specified that it reflected the policy that the Great Library had been following in the past; it did not change the Law Society's approach to its custom photocopy service.

62 At trial, the Law Society claimed that its custom photocopy service does not infringe copyright because it is a fair dealing within the meaning of s. 29 of the *Copyright Act*. The trial judge held that the fair dealing exception should be strictly construed. He concluded that copying for the custom photocopy service was not for the purpose of either research or study and therefore was not within the ambit of fair dealing. The Court of Appeal rejected the argument that the fair dealing exception should be interpreted restrictively. The majority held that the Law Society could rely on the purposes of its patrons to prove that its dealings were fair. The Court of Appeal concluded, however, that there was not sufficient evidence to determine whether or not the dealings were fair and, consequently, that the fair dealing exception had not been proven.

63 This raises a preliminary question: is it incumbent on the Law Society to adduce evidence that every patron uses the material provided for in a fair dealing manner or can the Law Society rely on its general practice to establish fair dealing? I conclude that the latter suffices. Section 29 of the *Copyright Act* states that "[f]air dealing for the purpose of research or private study does not infringe copyright". The language is general. "Dealing" connotes not individual acts, but a practice or system. This comports with the purpose of the fair dealing exception, which is to ensure that users are not unduly restricted in their ability to use and disseminate copyrighted works. Persons or institutions relying on the s. 29 fair dealing exception need only prove that their own dealings with copyrighted works were for the purpose of research or private study and were fair. They may do this either by showing that their own practices and policies were research-based and fair, or by showing that all individual dealings with the materials were in fact research-based and fair.

64 The Law Society's custom photocopying service is provided for the purpose of research, review and private study. The Law Society's Access Policy states that "[s]ingle copies of library materials, required for the purposes of research, review, private study and criticism ... may be provided to users of the Great Library". When the Great Library staff make copies of the requested cases, statutes, excerpts from legal texts and legal commentary, they do so for the purpose of research. Although the retrieval and photocopying of legal works are not research in and of themselves, they are necessary conditions of research and thus part of the research process. The reproduction of legal works is for the purpose of research in that it is an essential element of the legal research process. There is no other purpose for the copying; the Law Society does not profit from this service. Put simply, its custom photocopy service helps to ensure that legal professionals in Ontario can access the materials necessary to conduct the research required to carry on the practice of law. In sum, the Law Society's custom photocopy service is an integral part of the legal research process, an allowable purpose under s. 29 of the *Copyright Act*.

65 The evidence also establishes that the dealings were fair, having regard to the factors discussed earlier.

(i) Purpose of the Dealing

66 The Access Policy and its safeguards weigh in favour of finding that the dealings were fair. It specifies that individuals requesting copies must identify the purpose of the request for these requests to be honoured, and provides that concerns that a request is not for one of the legitimate purposes under the fair dealing exceptions in the *Copyright Act* are referred to the Reference Librarian. This policy provides reasonable safeguards that the materials are being used for the purpose of research and private study.

(ii) Character of the Dealing

67 The character of the Law Society's dealings with the publishers' works also supports a finding of fairness. Under the Access Policy, the Law Society

provides single copies of works for the specific purposes allowed under the *Copyright Act*. There is no evidence that the Law Society was disseminating multiple copies of works to multiple members of the legal profession. Copying a work for the purpose of research on a specific legal topic is generally a fair dealing.

(iii) Amount of the Dealing

68 The Access Policy indicates that the Great Library will exercise its discretion to ensure that the amount of the dealing with copyrighted works will be reasonable. The Access Policy states that the Great Library will typically honour requests for a copy of one case, one article or one statutory reference. It further stipulates that the Reference Librarian will review requests for a copy of more than five percent of a secondary source and that, ultimately, such requests may be refused. This suggests that the Law Society's dealings with the publishers' works are fair. Although the dealings might not be fair if a specific patron of the Great Library submitted numerous requests for multiple reported judicial decisions from the same reported series over a short period of time, there is no evidence that this has occurred.

(iv) Alternatives to the Dealing

69 It is not apparent that there are alternatives to the custom photocopy service employed by the Great Library. As the Court of Appeal points out, the patrons of the custom photocopying service cannot reasonably be expected to always conduct their research on-site at the Great Library. Twenty per cent of the requesters live outside the Toronto area; it would be burdensome to expect them to travel to the city each time they wanted to track down a specific legal source. Moreover, because of the heavy demand for the legal collection at the Great Library, researchers are not allowed to borrow materials from the library. If researchers could not request copies of the work or make copies of the works themselves, they would be required to do all of their research and note-taking in the Great Library, something which does not seem reasonable given the volume of research that can often be required on complex legal matters.

70 The availability of a licence is not relevant to deciding whether a dealing has been fair. As discussed, fair dealing is an integral part of the scheme of copyright law in Canada. Any act falling within the fair dealing exception will not infringe copyright. If a copyright owner were allowed to license people to use its work and then point to a person's decision not to obtain a licence as proof that his or her dealings were not fair, this would extend the scope of the owner's monopoly over the use of his or her work in a manner that would not be consistent with the *Copyright Act*'s balance between owner's rights and user's interests.

(v) Nature of the Work

71 I agree with the Court of Appeal that the nature of the works in question—judicial decisions and other works essential to legal research — suggests that the

Law Society's dealings were fair. As Linden J.A. explained, at para. 159: "It is generally in the public interest that access to judicial decisions and other legal resources not be unjustifiably restrained." Moreover, the Access Policy puts reasonable limits on the Great Library's photocopy service. It does not allow all legal works to be copied regardless of the purpose to which they will be put. Requests for copies will be honoured only if the user intends to use the works for the purpose of research, private study, criticism, review or use in legal proceedings. This further supports a finding that the dealings were fair.

(vi) Effect of the Dealing on the Work

72 Another consideration is that no evidence was tendered to show that the market for the publishers' works had decreased as a result of these copies having been made. Although the burden of proving fair dealing lies with the Law Society, it lacked access to evidence about the effect of the dealing on the publishers' markets. If there had been evidence that the publishers' markets had been negatively affected by the Law Society's custom photocopying service, it would have been in the publishers' interest to tender it at trial. They did not do so. The only evidence of market impact is that the publishers have continued to produce new reporter series and legal publications during the period of the custom photocopy service's operation.

(vii) Conclusion

73 The factors discussed, considered together, suggest that the Law Society's dealings with the publishers' works through its custom photocopy service were research-based and fair. The Access Policy places appropriate limits on the type of copying that the Law Society will do. It states that not all requests will be honoured. If a request does not appear to be for the purpose of research, criticism, review or private study, the copy will not be made. If a question arises as to whether the stated purpose is legitimate, the Reference Librarian will review the matter. The Access Policy limits the amount of work that will be copied, and the Reference Librarian reviews requests that exceed what might typically be considered reasonable and has the right to refuse to fulfill a request. On these facts, I conclude that the Law Society's dealings with the publishers' works satisfy the fair dealing defence and that the Law Society does not infringe copyright.

(4) Canada Law Book's Consent

74 Under s. 27(1) of the Copyright Act, a person infringes copyright if he or she does something that only the owner of the copyright has the right to do without the owner's consent. On appeal to this Court, the Law Society submits that six of the items that the respondent publishers have claimed were copied in infringement of copyright were copied at the request of Jean Cummings, a lawyer who had been asked by Canada Law Book's Vice-President to obtain copies of these works from the Law Society. As such, the Law Society contends that the copies were made with the consent of Canada Law Book and therefore were not an infringement of copyright.

75 This issue was not really addressed in the courts below. In light of my findings on the issue of fair dealing, it is not necessary to answer this question to dispose of this appeal, and I decline to do so.

(5) Conclusion on Main Appeal

76 I would allow the appeal and issue a declaration that the Law Society does not infringe copyright when a single copy of a reported decision, case summary, statute, regulation or limited selection of text from a treatise is made by the Great Library in accordance with its Access Policy. I would also issue a declaration that the Law Society does not authorize copyright infringement by maintaining a photocopier in the Great Library and posting a notice warning that it will not be responsible for any copies made in infringement of copyright.

In the following cases, part of the so-called "copyright pentalogy", the Supreme Court reiterated, applied and expanded upon its earlier interpretation of fair dealing in the *CCH* case.

SOCAN v. Bell Canada, 2012 SCC 36 (S.C.C.)

[1] Abella J. — The purchase of musical works is increasingly carried out over the Internet. Some commercial Internet sites that sell music allow consumers to preview musical works before making a purchase. The issue in this case is whether those previews constitute "fair dealing" under s. 29 of the *Copyright Act*, R.S.C. 1985, c. C-42.

Background

[2] The Society of Composers, Authors and Music Publishers of Canada (SOCAN) represents composers, authors and music publishers and administers their performing and communication rights. Its arguments before this Court were supported by the Canadian Recording Industry Association and CMRRA-SODRAC Inc.

[3] Bell Canada, Apple Canada Inc., Rogers Communications Inc., Rogers Wireless Partnership, Shaw Cablesystems G.P. and TELUS Communications Inc. operate online music services that sell downloads of digital files of musical works. These services provide catalogues of digital audio files that allow users to identify musical works by title, album, genre and artist. The service providers also give consumers the ability to listen to free "previews" of those works before deciding which work to purchase. SOCAN seeks compensation for the provision of those previews over and beyond what would normally be paid for a music download or a CD.

[4] A preview consists of an extract taken from the work, usually 30 to 90 seconds of a musical track. Users are able to select and listen to the preview through an online "stream", meaning that a temporary copy of the excerpt is heard by the user in such a way that his or her computer does not store a permanent copy of the preview. The previews help users decide whether to purchase a permanent download of the work. Apple's iTunes service, for example, allows consumers to listen to previews as many times as they want, whether or not they make a purchase or have registered with the online service provider.

[5] As noted in the companion appeal (*Rogers Communications Inc. v. Society of Composers, Authors and Music Publishers of Canada*, [2012] 2 S.C.R. 283), SOCAN filed proposed tariffs targeting the years 1996 to 2006 with the Copyright Board of Canada in 1995 for the determination of royalties to be paid by users when musical works are communicated to the public over the Internet.

[6] In a decision released on October 18, 2007 (61 C.P.R. (4th) 353), the Board agreed that SOCAN was entitled to collect royalties for the downloading of musical works, but not for previews. In the Board's view, the use of previews was not an infringement of copyright since their use was "fair dealing" for the purpose of research under s. 29 of the *Copyright Act* based on the factors identified by McLachlin C.J. in *CCH Canadian Ltd. v. Law Society of Upper Canada*, [2004] 1 S.C.R. 339. Because the previews were not an infringement of copyright, no royalties were required to be paid to SOCAN for their use.

[7] The Federal Court of Appeal upheld the Board's decision (2010 FCA 123, 403 N.R. 57). As would I.

Analysis

[8] In *Théberge v. Galerie d'Art du Petit Champlain inc.*, [2002] 2 S.C.R. 336, this Court noted that copyright requires "a balance between promoting the public interest in the encouragement and dissemination of works of the arts and intellect and obtaining a just reward for the creator" (para. 30).

[9] *Théberge* reflected a move away from an earlier, author-centric view which focused on the exclusive right of authors and copyright owners to control how their works were used in the marketplace: see e.g. *Bishop v. Stevens*, [1990] 2 S.C.R. 467, at pp. 478-79. Under this former framework, any benefit the public might derive from the copyright system was only "a fortunate by-product of private entitlement":Carys J. Craig, "Locke, Labour and Limiting the Author's Right: A Warning against a Lockean Approach to Copyright Law" (2002), 28 *Queen's L.J.* 1, at pp. 14-15.

[10] *Théberge* focused attention instead on the importance copyright plays in promoting the public interest, and emphasized that the dissemination of artistic works is central to developing a robustly cultured and intellectual public domain. As noted by Professor David Vaver, both protection and access must be sensitively balanced in order to achieve this goal: *Intellectual Property Law: Copyright, Patents, Trade-marks* (2nd ed. 2011), at p. 60.

[11] *CCH* confirmed that users' rights are an essential part of furthering the public interest objectives of the *Copyright Act*. One of the tools employed to achieve the proper balance between protection and access in the *Act* is the concept of fair dealing, which allows users to engage in some activities that might otherwise amount to copyright infringement. In order to maintain the proper balance between these interests, the fair dealing provision "must not be interpreted restrictively": *CCH*, at para. 48.

[12] *CCH* sets out the test for fair dealing under s. 29 of the *Copyright Act*:

29. Fair dealing for the purpose of research or private study does not infringe copyright.

While not specifically in issue in the case before us, ss. 29.1 and 29.2 of the *Act* also permit"fair dealing" for the purposes of criticism, review or news reporting.

[13] The test for fair dealing articulated in *CCH*involves two steps. The first is to determine whether the dealing is for the purpose of either "research" or "private study", the two allowable purposes listed under s. 29. The second step assesses whether the dealing is "fair". The onus is on the person invoking "fair dealing" to satisfy both aspects of the test under *CCH*.

[14] To assist in determining whether the dealing is"fair", this Court set out the following six fairness factors for guidance: the purpose, character, and amount of the dealing; the existence of any alternatives to the dealing; the nature of the work; and the effect of the dealing on the work.

[15] The first inquiry in this case, therefore, is whether previews are provided for the allowable purpose of "research" under the first step of the *CCH* fair dealing test. While *CCH* did not define the word "research", it notably concluded that "'[r]esearch' must be given a large and liberal interpretation in order to ensure that users' rights are not unduly constrained" (para. 51).

[16] The Board defined "previews" as

> a marketing tool offered by online music services, among others. A preview is an excerpt (usually 30 seconds or less) of a sound recording that can be streamed so that consumers are allowed to "preview" the recording to help them decide whether to purchase a (usually permanent) download. [para. 18]

[17] Based on the evidence it heard about the purpose of previews and the way they were used by consumers, the Board concluded that previews were used "either to determine whether the track suits the user's tastes or to verify that the track is the one the user wants to buy" (para. 101). Listening to previews helped users identify what music to purchase. Since planning the purchase of a download involved "searching [and] investigation", the Board was of the view that previews amounted to "research"under s. 29 of the *Copyright Act* (para. 109).

[18] The Federal Court of Appeal endorsed the Board's view that listening to previews was part of planning the purchase of a download of a musical work and was therefore "for the purpose of research", concluding:

... it would not be unreasonable to give the word "research" its primary and ordinary meaning. The consumer is searching for an object of copyright that he or she desires and is attempting to locate and wishes to ensure its authenticity and quality before obtaining it. . . . "[L]istening to previews assists in this investigation". [para. 20]

[19] SOCAN argued that the Board and the Federal Court of Appeal misinterpreted the term "research" in two ways. It argued first that their interpretation of "research" was overly broad. Its second argument was that the purpose of "research" should have been analysed from the perspective of the online service provider and not the consumer. From this perspective, the purpose of the previews was not "research", but to sell permanent downloads of the musical works.

[20] SOCAN offers the definition of "research" as being "the systematic investigation into and study of materials and sources in order to establish facts and reach new conclusions" (A.F., at para. 96). Moreover, SOCAN argues, the goal of the "research" must be for the purpose of making creative works, since only uses that contribute to the creative process are in the public interest. As a result, previews do not amount to "research"since their primary purpose is not to foster creativity, but to enable users to purchase music online.

[21] It is true that an important goal of fair dealing is to allow users to employ copyrighted works in a way that helps them engage in their own acts of authorship and creativity: Abraham Drassinower,"Taking User Rights Seriously", in Michael Geist, ed., *In the Public Interest: The Future of Canadian Copyright Law* (2005), 462, at pp. 467-72. But that does not argue for permitting *only* creative purposes to qualify as "research" under s. 29 of the *Copyright Act*. To do so would ignore the fact that the dissemination of works is also one of the *Act*'s purposes, which means that dissemination too, with or without creativity, is in the public interest. It would also ignore that "private study", a concept that has no intrinsic relationship with creativity, was also expressly included as an allowable purpose in s. 29. Since "research" and "private study" both qualify as fair dealing purposes under s. 29, we should not interpret the term"research" more restrictively than "private study".

[22] Limiting research to creative purposes would also run counter to the ordinary meaning of "research", which can include many activities that do not demand the establishment of new facts or conclusions. It can be piecemeal, informal, exploratory, or confirmatory. It can in fact be undertaken for no purpose except personal interest. It is true that research can be for the purpose of reaching new conclusions, but this should be seen as only one, not the primary component of the definitional framework.

[23] In urging the Court to narrow the definition of"research" as requiring the creation of something new, SOCAN relied on American jurisprudence which looks to the requirement of a "transformative" purpose before the use is seen as fair. It cited as an example *United States v. American Society of Composers, Authors and Publishers*, 599 F.Supp.2d 415 (2009), where the New York District Court held that the use of music previews as a marketing tool to sell

musical ringtones was not "transformative" in nature and therefore could not be fairly described as "criticism, comment, news reporting . . . or research" under the fair use provisions in Title 17, § 107 of the U.S. Code, at pp. 424-25.

[24] The American approach is called "fair use". The U.S. Code provisions create an open set of purposes for fair use which include criticism, comment, news reporting, teaching, scholarship, or research: 17 U.S.C. § 107. The analysis proceeds straight to the assessment of fairness, an assessment based on factors enumerated in the Code or established by the case law. Although one of those fairness factors includes whether the use is transformative, it is not at all clear that a transformative use is "absolutely necessary" for a finding of fair use: *Campbell v. Acuff-Rose Music, Inc.*, 510 U.S. 569 (1994), at p. 579.

[25] But even if it were a requirement under American law, this Court has previously cautioned against the automatic portability of American copyright concepts into the Canadian arena, given the "fundamental differences" in the respective legislative schemes: *Compo Co. v. Blue Crest Music Inc.*, [1980] 1 S.C.R. 357, at p. 367. This caution has resonance in the fair dealing context.

[26] Unlike the American approach of proceeding straight to the fairness assessment, we do not engage in the fairness analysis in Canada until we are satisfied that the dealing is for one of the allowable purposes enumerated in the *Copyright Act*. Under the test set out in *CCH*,"fairness" is not considered until the second step of the test for fair dealing: see *CCH*, at para. 51; see also Giuseppina D'Agostino, "Healing Fair Dealing? A Comparative Copyright Analysis of Canada's Fair Dealing to U.K. Fair Dealing and U.S. Fair Use" (2008), 53 *McGill L.J.* 309, and *Century 21 Canada Limited Partnership v. Rogers Communications Inc.*, 2011 BCSC 1196, 338 D.L.R. (4th) 32, at para. 234.

[27] In mandating a generous interpretation of the fair dealing purposes, including "research", the Court in *CCH* created a relatively low threshold for the first step so that the analytical heavy-hitting is done in determining whether the dealing was fair. SOCAN's submission that "research" be restricted to the creation of new works would conflate the allowable purpose with the fairness analysis and unduly raise the bar for entering that analysis. Moreover, its restricted definitional scope of"research" contradicts not only the Court's admonition in *CCH* that "[i]n order to maintain the proper balance between the rights of a copyright owner and users' interests, [the fair dealing exception] must not be interpreted restrictively" (para. 48), but also its direction that the term "research" be given a "large and liberal interpretation" so that in maintaining that balance, users' rights are not unduly constrained (paras. 48 and 51).

[28] SOCAN's proposed definition of "research" as requiring "systematic investigation" and "new conclusions" is also at odds with its second submission about "research", namely, that "research" be analysed from the perspective of the purpose of the online service providers, and not that of the users. But its own proposed definition shows that it sees research as a user-focused undertaking, since the investigation and creation of new conclusions are clearly done *by* a user, not

a provider. The provider's purpose in making the works available is therefore not the relevant perspective at the first stage of the fair dealing analysis.

[29] This is consistent with the Court's approach in *CCH*, where it described fair dealing as a "user's right" (para. 48). In *CCH*, the Great Library was the provider, offering a photocopying service to lawyers requesting copies of legal materials. The Court did not focus its inquiry on the library's perspective, but on that of the ultimate user, the lawyers, whose purpose was legal research (para. 64).

[30] Similarly, in considering whether previews are for the purpose of "research" under the first step of *CCH*, the Board properly considered them from the perspective of the user or consumer's purpose. And from that perspective, consumers used the previews for the purpose of conducting research to identify which music to purchase, purchases which trigger dissemination of musical works and compensation for their creators, both of which are outcomes the *Act* seeks to encourage.

[31] The inquiry then moves to the second step, namely, determining whether the use of previews was "fair" in accordance with the *CCH* factors.

[32] Whether something is "fair" is a question of fact and depends on the facts of each case: *CCH*, at para. 52, citing *Hubbard v. Vosper*, [1972] 1 All E.R. 1023 (C.A.), at p. 1027. Based on all the factors, the Board concluded, properly in my view, that previews amounted to fair dealing.

[33] The first factor identified in *CCH* is the purpose of the dealing, where an objective assessment is made of the "real purpose or motive" behind using the copyrighted work (para. 54).

[34] SOCAN argued that the purpose of the previews in this case was purely commercial. This is an approach that looks at the purpose of the previews from the perspective not of the consumer, but of the service providers. I agree instead with the Board and the Federal Court of Appeal that the predominant perspective in this case is that of the ultimate users of the previews, and *their* purpose in using previews was to help them research and identify musical works for online purchase. While the service providers sell musical downloads, the purpose of providing *previews* is primarily to facilitate the research purposes of the consumers.

[35] The Board also noted that there were reasonable safeguards in place to ensure that the users' dealing in previews was in fact being used for this purpose: the previews were streamed, short, and often of lesser quality than the musical work itself. These safeguards prevented the previews from replacing the work while still fulfilling a research function.

[36] SOCAN also argued that even from the perspective of the consumers, the purpose of the previews was purely commercial, since their purpose was the potential purchase of musical works. Ultimately, however, the Board's approach is consistent with *CCH*'s observation that while research done for commercial reasons may be less fair than research done for non-commercial purposes (para. 54), the dealing may nonetheless be fair if there are "reasonable safeguards" in place to ensure that the works are actually being used for research (para. 66).

[37] The second factor discussed in *CCH* is the character of the dealing. The Court stated that a particular dealing might be unfair if multiple copies of works are being widely distributed (para. 55). But as the Court also pointed out, if a single copy of a work is used for a specific legitimate purpose, or if the copy no longer existed after it was used, this would favour a finding of fairness (para. 55).

[38] SOCAN's argument was based on the fact that consumers accessed, on average, 10 times the number of previews as full-length musical works. However, no copy existed after the preview was heard. The previews were streamed, not downloaded. Users did not get a permanent copy, and once the preview was heard, the file was automatically deleted from the user's computer. The fact that each file was automatically deleted meant that copies could not be duplicated or further disseminated by users.

[39] The third factor identified in *CCH* is the amount — or quantity — of the dealing. The Board characterized the "amount" of the dealing in terms of the length of each preview compared to the length of the work, concluding that streaming a preview of about 30 seconds was a modest dealing "when compared to purchasing the whole work [approximately four minutes] for repeated listening" (para. 113).

[40] SOCAN argued, however, that the proportion of the preview in relation to the length of the whole musical work was not the proper measure, and that the Board should have considered instead the *aggregate*number of previews that are streamed by consumers. Since the evidence showed that each user, on average, listened to 10 previews before purchasing a musical work for download, the overall amount of time spent listening to previews was so large that the dealing was unfair. SOCAN saw this factor as determinative in this case.

[41] There is no doubt that the aggregate quantity of music heard through previews is significant, but SOCAN's argument conflicts with the Court's statement in *CCH* that "amount" means the "quantity of the work taken" (para. 56). Since fair dealing is a "user's" right, the"amount of the dealing" factor should be assessed based on the individual use, not the amount of the dealing in the aggregate. The appropriate measure under this factor is therefore, as the Board noted, the proportion of the excerpt used in relation to the whole work. That, it seems to me, is consistent with the Court's approach in *CCH*, where it considered the Great Library's dealings by looking at its practices as they related to specific works requested by individual patrons, not at the total number of patrons or pages requested. The "amount of the dealing" factor should therefore be assessed by looking at how each dealing occurs on an individual level, not on the aggregate use.

[42] Moreover, the quantification of the aggregate dissemination is already considered under the "character of the dealing"factor, which examines whether multiple copies of works are being widely distributed. Reconsidering the same "aggregate" quantity under the "amount"factor would deprive that factor of any utility in the analysis, and would erase consideration of the proportion of the excerpt to the entire work.

[43] Further, given the ease and magnitude with which digital works are disseminated over the Internet, focusing on the "aggregate"amount of the dealing in cases involving digital works could well lead to disproportionate findings of unfairness when compared with non-digital works. If, as SOCAN urges, large-scale organized dealings are inherently unfair, most of what online service providers do with musical works would be treated as copyright infringement. This, it seems to me, potentially undermines the goal of technological neutrality, which seeks to have the *Copyright Act*applied in a way that operates consistently, regardless of the form of media involved, or its technological sophistication: *Robertson v. Thomson Corp.*, [2006] 2 S.C.R. 363, at para. 49.

[44] The fourth factor identified in *CCH* involves considering any alternatives to the dealing. A dealing may be less fair if there is a non-copyrighted equivalent of the work that could have been used, or if the dealing was not reasonably necessary to achieve the ultimate purpose (para. 57).

[45] SOCAN argued that there were other methods available, like advertising, to help users identify potential music for purchase. Many of the service providers, for example, offered album artwork, textual descriptions, and user-generated album reviews. In addition, some service providers offered return policies in the event that users accidentally downloaded the wrong musical work.

[46] But allowing returns is an expensive, technologically complicated, and market-inhibiting alternative for helping consumers identify the right music. And none of the other suggested alternatives can demonstrate to a consumer what previews can, namely, what a musical work *sounds* like. The Board found that "[l]istening to a preview probably is the most practical, most economical and safest way for users to ensure that they purchase what they wish" (para. 114). As a result, it concluded that short, low-quality streamed previews are reasonably necessary to help consumers research what to purchase. I agree.

[47] The fifth factor is the nature of the work, which examines whether the work is one which should be widely disseminated. SOCAN does not dispute the desirability of the sale and dissemination of musical works, but argues that since these works are easily purchased and disseminated without the use of previews, previews are of no additional benefit to promoting further dissemination. But the fact that a musical work is widely available does not necessarily correlate to whether it is widely disseminated. Unless a potential consumer can locate and identify a work he or she wants to buy, the work will not be disseminated.

[48] This observation is linked to the final factor: the effect of the dealing on the work and whether the dealing adversely affects or competes with the work. Because of their short duration and degraded quality, it can hardly be said that previews are in competition with downloads of the work itself. And since the effect of previews is to *increase* the sale and therefore the dissemination of copyrighted musical works thereby generating remuneration to their creators, it cannot be said that they have a negative impact on the work.

[49] All of this confirms the Board's conclusion that previews satisfy the requirements of fair dealing and that the online service providers do not infringe

copyright. In so concluding, the Board properly balanced the purposes of the *Act* by encouraging the creation and dissemination of works while at the same time ensuring that creators are fairly rewarded. Its approach was consistent with *CCH*, with the interpretative principles it set out, and with its test for fair dealing under s. 29 of the *Copyright Act*. The conclusion, as a result, should not be disturbed.

[50] I would dismiss the appeal with costs.

Alberta (Minister of Education) v. Canadian Copyright Licensing Agency, 2012 SCC 37 (S.C.C.)

[1] Abella J. — Many authors create textbooks and other literary works to sell to primary and secondary level educational institutions across Canada. Photocopying short excerpts of these works is a common practice in Canadian schools, and is often used as an important administrative and teaching tool by teachers. The issue in this appeal is whether photocopies made by teachers to distribute to students as part of class instruction can qualify as fair dealing under the *Copyright Act*, R.S.C. 1985, c. C-42.

Background

[2] Access Copyright represents authors and publishers of literary and artistic works in printed materials which are subject to copying. It administers the reproduction of published materials by issuing licences and collecting and distributing royalties to affiliated copyright owners. When Access Copyright does not reach a licensing or royalty agreement with users who photocopy published works in its repertoire, it can apply to the Copyright Board to certify a royalty in the form of a tariff.

[3] At elementary and secondary schools across Canada, teachers often make photocopies of portions of textbooks or other published works which are part of Access Copyright's repertoire. Between 1991 and 1997, Access Copyright reached royalty agreements with each of the provinces and territories (other than Quebec) with respect to the reproduction of its repertoire for use in these schools. In 1999, all the provincial parties and the Ontario School Boards (the "Coalition") signed a five-year agreement, providing for royalty increases based on a per student calculation, not on the number of pages copied.

[4] When the time came to renew the royalty agreement in 2004, Access Copyright wanted the royalties revised to reflect the volume and content of what was being copied. The parties were unable to reach an agreement, based largely on the fact that they could not agree on how a"volume study" was to be conducted. Access Copyright therefore filed a proposed tariff with the Copyright Board in accordance with s. 70.13(2) of the *Act*.

[5] During the course of the proceedings before the Board, the parties eventually agreed to the terms of a volume study. It was carried out between February

2005 and March 2006. In accordance with the agreed-upon terms, information was recorded by observers on stickers posted next to each photocopier, including who made the copy, who would be using the copy, and the purpose of the copy.

[6] Based on information collected from the stickers, each incident of photo-copying was divided into one of four categories. The first three dealt with copies made by teachers either for themselves or at the request of a student. All parties agreed that copies falling under these categories — about 1.7 million pages — constituted fair dealing.

[7] The fourth category (Category 4) dealt with copies of works made at the teachers' initiative with instructions to students that they read the material. Teachers would photocopy short excerpts from textbooks and distribute those copies to students as a complement to the main textbook the students used.

[8] At a hearing before the Board, Access Copyright argued that the Category 4 copies did not meet the test for fair dealing identified by McLachlin C.J. in *CCH Canadian Ltd. v. Law Society of Upper Canada*, [2004] 1 S.C.R. 339. The Coalition countered with the argument that the approximately 16.9 million pages in Category 4 should be excluded from any tariff because the copies constituted fair dealing under ss. 29 or 29.1 of the *Act*.

[9] Based on the evidence from the stickers used in the volume study, the Board concluded that the Category 4 copies were made for the allowable purpose of "research or private study" under s. 29 of the *Act*, but found, applying the *CCH* fairness factors, that the Category 4 copies did not constitute fair dealing and were therefore subject to a royalty. The Board also rejected the Coalition's argument that the Category 4 copies fell within the exception for educational institutions under s. 29.4 of the *Act*(online).

[10] On judicial review, the Federal Court of Appeal remitted the s. 29.4 issue back to the Board, stating that the Board failed to address an aspect of the "educational institutions" test. But the court found the Board's conclusion that the Category 4 copies were not fair dealing to be reasonable (2010 FCA 198, [2011] 3 F.C.R. 223).

[11] The Coalition appealed only the fair dealing issue to this Court, maintaining that the Board's conclusion was not in accordance with the *CCH* test and was therefore unreasonable. I agree and would therefore remit the matter to the Board for reconsideration in accordance with these reasons.

Analysis

[12] As discussed in the companion appeal *Society of Composers, Authors and Music Publishers of Canada v. Bell Canada*, [2012] 2 S.C.R. 326 (*SOCAN v. Bell*), the concept of fair dealing allows users to engage in some activities that might otherwise amount to copyright infringement. The test for fair dealing was articulated in *CCH* as involving two steps. The first is to determine whether the dealing is for the allowable purpose of "research or private study" under s. 29, "criticism or review" under s. 29.1, or "news reporting" under s. 29.2 of the *Act*.

The second step of *CCH* assesses whether the dealing is "fair". The onus is on the person invoking "fair dealing" to satisfy all aspects of the test. To assist in determining whether the dealing is "fair",this Court set out a number of fairness factors: the purpose, character, and amount of the dealing; the existence of any alternatives to the dealing; the nature of the work; and the effect of the dealing on the work.

[13] The Board accepted that where the photocopier stickers indicated that the copying was for an allowable purpose — "research" or "private study" — no further inquiry under the first step of the *CCH* test was required. The Board also found that where the sticker indicated that the purpose of the copy was "criticism or review", the purpose was also to be treated as "research or private study".

[14] Before this Court, there was generally no dispute that the first step in *CCH* was met and that the dealing — photocopying — was for the allowable purpose of research or private study. The dispute essentially centred on the second step of the test: whether the Category 4 copies were "fair" in accordance with the *CCH* factors. I have concerns over how the Board applied several of those factors.

[15] In my view, the key problem is in the way the Board approached the "purpose of the dealing" factor. The Board concluded that since the Category 4 copies were not made as a result of a student request, they were no longer for the purpose of research or private study at the second stage. This was based on its observation that in *CCH*, the Great Library was making copies at the request of lawyers. Because there was no such request for Category 4 copies, the Board concluded that the *predominant*purpose was that of the teacher, namely, "instruction" or "non-private study". The Board therefore found that this factor tended to make the Category 4 copies unfair. The Federal Court of Appeal, agreeing with the Board, stated that the real purpose or motive behind the copies was instruction, not private study.

[16] Access Copyright argued that the purpose of the dealing should be seen, as it was by the Board and the Federal Court of Appeal, from the copier's, or teacher's perspective. It relied particularly on three key Commonwealth cases which found the copier's purpose in reproducing the work to be determinative. In *Sillitoe v. McGraw-Hill Book Company (U.K.) Ltd.*, [1983] F.S.R. 545 (Ch. D.), an importer and seller of "study notes" which reproduced a substantial part of a literary work, argued that the notes were intended as a supplementary aid for students engaging in research and private study. The court held that the seller was unable to invoke the fair dealing exception since it was not *itself* engaged in private study or research, but was merely facilitating this activity for others (p. 558).

[17] The court in *Sillitoe* relied on *University of London Press, Ltd. v. University Tutorial Press, Ltd.*, [1916] 2 Ch. 601, where a publisher issued a publication reproducing old exams and sold it to students who were preparing for their own exams. The publisher argued that the publication amounted to fair dealing "for the purposes of private study" by university students preparing for exams. The court held that the company could not bring itself within the fair dealing

exception, rejecting the argument that the purpose of the publication was "private study":

> It could not be contended that the mere republication of a copyright work was a "fair dealing" because it was intended for purposes of private study; nor, if an author produced a book of questions for the use of students, could another person with impunity republish the book with the answers to the questions. Neither case would, in my judgment, come within the description of "fair dealing". [p. 613]

[18] In the New Zealand case *Copyright Licensing Ltd. v. University of Auckland*, [2002] 3 N.Z.L.R. 76 (H.C.), several universities provided copies of copyrighted works to students as part of course packs, and charged the students for these materials through various school fees. The universities argued that the copying constituted fair dealing for the purposes of research or private study. The court held that the "purpose"must be that of the person "doing the copying" (paras. 43 and 52). Since the copiers — the universities — were not themselves dealing with the work for the purposes of research or private study, the copying did not amount to fair dealing.

[19] With respect, I do not find these authorities particularly helpful. Firstly, courts in the U.K. have tended to take a more restrictive approach to determining the "purpose" of the dealing than does *CCH*. Based on s. 178 of the *Copyright, Designs and Patents Act 1988* (U.K.), 1988, c. 48, for example, which defines "private study" to exclude "a commercial purpose", courts in the U.K. have asserted that both research and private study must be for a non-commercial purpose: see G. D'Agostino, "Healing Fair Dealing? A Comparative Copyright Analysis of Canada's Fair Dealing to U.K. Fair Dealing and U.S. Fair Use" (2008), 53 *McGill L.J.* 309, at p. 339. This expressly contradicts the statement in *CCH* that the allowable purposes must be given a "large and liberal interpretation", and that"research" is not limited to non-commercial or private contexts (para. 51).

[20] More importantly, as noted by Linden J.A. of the Federal Court of Appeal in *CCH*, 2002 FCA 187, [2002] 4 F.C. 213, at para. 132 (reversed on other grounds), these "course pack" cases involved copiers with demonstrably ulterior — i.e. commercial — motives. They invoked the allowable purposes of "research" or "private study",in effect, in order to appropriate their customers' or students' purposes as their own and escape liability for copyright infringement.

[21] These cases, then, to the extent that they are germane, do not stand for the proposition that "research" and "private study"are inconsistent with instructional purposes, but for the principle that copiers cannot camouflage their own distinct purpose by purporting to conflate it with the research or study purposes of the ultimate user.

[22] As noted in the companion appeal *SOCAN v. Bell*, fair dealing is a "user's right", and the relevant perspective when considering whether the dealing is for an allowable purpose under the first stage of *CCH* is that of the user (*CCH*, at paras. 48 and 64). This does not mean, however, that the copier's purpose is irrelevant at the fairness stage. If, as in the "course pack" cases, the copier hides behind the shield of the user's allowable purpose in order to engage in a separate

purpose that tends to make the dealing unfair, that separate purpose will also be relevant to the fairness analysis.

[23] In the case before us, however, there is no such separate purpose on the part of the teacher. Teachers have no ulterior motive when providing copies to students. Nor can teachers be characterized as having the completely separate purpose of "instruction"; they are there to facilitate the students' research and private study. It seems to me to be axiomatic that most students lack the expertise to find or request the materials required for their own research and private study, and rely on the guidance of their teachers. They study what they are told to study, and the teacher's purpose in providing copies is to enable the students to have the material they need for the purpose of studying. The teacher/copier therefore shares a symbiotic purpose with the student/user who is engaging in research or private study. Instruction and research/private study are, in the school context, tautological.

[24] The Board's approach, on the other hand, drives an artificial wedge into these unified purposes by drawing a distinction between copies made by the teacher at the request of a student (Categories 1-3), and copies made by the teacher without a prior request from a student (Category 4). Nowhere in *CCH* did the Court suggest that the lawyer had to "request" the photocopies of legal works from the Great Library before those copies could be said to be for the purpose of "research". On the contrary, what the Court found was that the copies of legal works were "necessary conditions of research and thus part of the research process":

> The reproduction of legal works is for the purpose of research in that it is an *essential element of the legal research process*. . . . Put simply, [the Great Library's] custom photocopy service helps to ensure that legal professionals in Ontario can access the materials necessary to conduct the research required to carry on the practice of law. [Emphasis added; para. 64.]

[25] Similarly, photocopies made by a teacher and provided to primary and secondary school students are an essential element in the research and private study undertaken by those students. The fact that some copies were provided on request and others were not, did not change the significance of those copies for students engaged in research and private study.

[26] Nor, with respect, do I accept the statement made by the Board and endorsed by the Federal Court of Appeal, relying on *University of London Press*, that the photocopies made by teachers were made for an unfair purpose — "*non*-private study" — since they were used by students as a group in class, and not "privately". As discussed above, the holding was simply that the publisher could not hide behind the students' research or private study purposes to disguise a separate unfair purpose — in that case, a commercial one. The court did *not* hold that students in a classroom setting could never be said to be engaged in "*private* study".

[27] With respect, the word "private" in "private study" should not be understood as requiring users to view copyrighted works in splendid isolation. Studying and learning are essentially personal endeavours, whether they are engaged in with others or in solitude. By focusing on the geography of classroom

instruction rather than on the *concept* of studying, the Board again artificially separated the teachers' instruction from the students' studying.

[28] The Board's skewed characterization of the teachers' role as being independent and differently motivated from that of the student users, also led to a problematic approach to the "amount of the dealing" factor. In considering this factor, the Board accepted that teachers generally limit themselves to reproducing relatively short excerpts of each textbook. Having found that the teachers only copied"short excerpts", the Board was required to determine whether the proportion of each of the short excerpts in relation to the whole work was fair. Instead, it then cited a passage from *CCH*, at para. 68, that said "if a specific patron . . . submitted numerous requests for multiple reported judicial decisions from the same reported series over a short period of time",the dealing might not be fair. Relying on this quote, the Board concluded that a teacher was analogous to a specific patron, and that the repeated copying of the same "class set" of books — that is, a set shared by more than one class or by many students in the same class — tended to make the dealing unfair.

[29] This, with respect, was a flawed approach. First, unlike the single patron in *CCH*, teachers do not make multiple copies of the class set for their own use, they make them for the use of the*students*. Moreover, as discussed in the companion case *SOCAN v. Bell*, the "amount" factor is not a quantitative assessment based on aggregate use, it is an examination of the proportion between the excerpted copy and the entire work, not the overall quantity of what is disseminated. The quantification of the total number of pages copied, as the Court noted in *CCH*, is considered under a different factor: the"character of the dealing".

[30] The Board had, in fact, already considered the quantification of the dissemination when it assessed the character of the dealing, finding that multiple copies of the texts were distributed to entire classes. In reapplying this same quantitative concern when assessing the "amount of the dealing", it conflated the two factors, which had the effect of erasing proportionality from the fairness analysis.

[31] I also have difficulty with how the Board approached the "alternatives to the dealing" factor. A dealing may be found to be less fair if there is a non-copyrighted equivalent of the work that could have been used, or if the dealing was not reasonably necessary to achieve the ultimate purpose (*CCH*, at para. 57). The Board found that, while students were not expected to use only works in the public domain, the educational institutions had an alternative to photocopying textbooks: they could simply buy the original texts to distribute to each student or to place in the library for consultation.

[32] In my view, buying books for each student is not a realistic alternative to teachers copying short excerpts to supplement student textbooks. First, the schools have already purchased originals that are kept in the class or library, from which the teachers make copies. The teacher merely facilitates wider access to this limited number of texts by making copies available to all students who need them. In addition, purchasing a greater number of original textbooks to distribute to students is unreasonable in light of the Board's finding

that teachers only photocopy short excerpts to complement existing textbooks. Under the Board's approach, schools would be required to buy sufficient copies for every student of every text, magazine and newspaper in Access Copyright's repertoire that is relied on by a teacher. This is a demonstrably unrealistic outcome. Copying short excerpts, as a result, is reasonably necessary to achieve the ultimate purpose of the students' research and private study.

[33] The final problematic application of a fairness factor by the Board was its approach to the "effect of the dealing on the work", which assesses whether the dealing adversely affects or competes with the original work. Access Copyright pointed out that textbook sales had shrunk over 30 percent in 20 years. However, as noted by the Coalition, there was no evidence that this decline was linked to photocopying done by teachers. Moreover, it noted that there were several other factors that were likely to have contributed to the decline in sales, such as the adoption of semester teaching, a decrease in registrations, the longer lifespan of textbooks, increased use of the Internet and other electronic tools, and more resource-based learning.

[34] Despite this evidentiary vacuum, the Board nonetheless concluded that the impact of photocopies, though impossible to quantify, was "sufficiently important" to compete with the original texts to an extent that made the dealing unfair. The Board supported its conclusion with the finding that the schools copy "more than a quarter of a billion textbook pages each year", even though this total number included the pages for which the schools *already* pay a tariff. The Category 4 copies in dispute account for under 7% of those pages.

[35] In *CCH*, the Court concluded that since no evidence had been tendered by the publishers of legal works to show that the market for the works had decreased *as a result* of the copies made by the Great Library, the detrimental impact had not been demonstrated. Similarly, other than the bald fact of a decline in sales over 20 years, there is no evidence from Access Copyright demonstrating any link between photocopying short excerpts and the decline in textbook sales.

[36] In addition, it is difficult to see how the teachers' copying competes with the market for textbooks, given the Board's finding that the teachers' copying was limited to short excerpts of complementary texts. If such photocopying did not take place, it is more likely that students would simply go without the supplementary information, or be forced to consult the single copy already owned by the school.

[37] This Court in *CCH* stated that whether something is "fair" is a question of fact and "a matter of impression" (para. 52, citing *Hubbard v. Vosper*, [1972] 1 All E.R. 1023 (C.A.), at p. 1027). As a result, the Board's decision as to whether the photocopies amount to fair dealing is to be reviewed, as it was by the Federal Court of Appeal, on a reasonableness standard. Because the Board's finding of unfairness was based on what was, in my respectful view, a misapplication of the *CCH* factors, its outcome was rendered unreasonable.

[38] I would therefore allow the appeal with costs and remit the matter to the Board for reconsideration based on these reasons.

The reasons of Deschamps, Fish, Rothstein and Cromwell JJ. were delivered by

ROTHSTEIN J. (DISSENTING) —

I. Introduction

[39] This appeal is about fair dealing under s. 29 of the *Copyright Act*, R.S.C. 1985, c. C-42 ("Act"). Whether something is fair is a question of fact (*CCH Canadian Ltd. v. Law Society of Upper Canada*, 2004 SCC 13, [2004] 1 S.C.R. 339, at para. 52 ("*CCH*")). Fair dealing is"a matter of impression" (*CCH*, at para. 52, citing *Hubbard v. Vosper*, [1972] 1 All E.R. 1023 (C.A.), at p. 1027). In *CCH*, this Court found that the factors proposed by Linden J.A., at the Federal Court of Appeal (2002 FCA 187, [2002] 4 F.C. 213, at para. 150), to help assess whether a dealing is fair, provided a "useful analytical framework to govern determinations of fairness in future cases" (para. 53). While useful for purposes of the fair dealing analysis, the factors are not statutory requirements.

[40] The application of these factors to the facts of each case by the Copyright Board should be treated with deference on judicial review. A principled deferential review requires that courts be cautious not to inadvertently slip into a more intrusive, correctness review.

[41] Justice Abella finds that the Board misapplied several of the *CCH* factors and that its conclusion is, as a result, unreasonable. I respectfully disagree. In my view, the Board made no reviewable error in principle in construing the *CCH* factors and, with one relatively minor exception, its factual analysis, application of the *CCH* factors to the facts and its conclusions were not unreasonable. I would therefore dismiss the appeal.

II. Fair Dealing

A. *Purpose of the Dealing*

(1) Whose Purpose Is Relevant

[42] In my respectful opinion, it was not unreasonable for the Board to have considered that the teacher's purpose was relevant and *predominant on the facts in this case*. At para. 98 of its reasons (online), the Board stated:

> Conversely, with respect to copies of excerpts made on the teacher's initiative for his or her students or at the student's request with instructions to read them, we consider that the teacher's stated purpose must predominate. Most of the time, this real or predominant purpose is instruction or "non-private"study. We attribute a certain degree of importance to the fact that the teacher's role is scarcely comparable to that of staff at the Great Library, the subject of *CCH*. That staff makes copies at the clients' request. A teacher, in deciding what to copy and for whom, just as when directing students' conduct, is doing his or her job, which is to instruct students. According to this criterion, the dealing therefore tends to be unfair. [Emphasis added.]

[43] In my view, even if the selecting of passages and photocopying them carried out by teachers for their students were to be seen as an integral part of the students' private study, the teacher also has a purpose. It is to utilize the

photocopied excerpts in the process of instructing and educating the students, the essence of the job of teaching. This purpose cannot be ignored and was not by the Board. The teacher's role in selecting and photocopying excerpts of works is significantly different from the role of the Great Library staff in *CCH*, which was completely passive. The Board noted this difference at para. 98 and concluded that, *on the facts*, the teacher's purpose predominated in these circumstances. There is nothing unreasonable in this *factual* conclusion.

[44] Nor do I think that the Board's approach draws an artificial distinction between copies made by the teacher at the request of a student and those made at the teacher's own initiative. In my opinion, the distinction drawn by the Board remains consistent with and reasonable in light of *CCH*. It was quite clear in *CCH* that the photocopies made by the staff of the Great Library were made at the request of the lawyers. That is, without that request from the lawyers, there would have been no photocopies. Considering, as the Board did, that the fact that the initiative for a copy came from a teacher was an indicator that the photocopy would mainly serve the teacher's purpose of teaching is not artificial or unreasonable. This is a realistic assessment of the facts and circumstances of classroom teaching.

[45] At para. 88, the Board explained that since the dealing in issue was for more than one purpose, it would look, under the first step of *CCH*, at whether any one of the purposes was an allowable purpose for fair dealing under the Act; if so, it would proceed to assess the *predominant* purpose of the dealing in the analysis of whether the dealing is fair. The parties agreed that this appeal should be decided solely on the assessment of the Board's analysis of fairness under the second step of *CCH*. In these circumstances, there is no basis for the suggestion that the finding by the Board under the "purpose of the dealing" factor — that the copies were made predominantly for the teacher's purpose of instruction — contradicts its finding under the first step of the analysis — that Category 4 copies were made for an allowable purpose.

(2) The Meaning of "Private Study"

[46] I do not think that the Board and the Federal Court of Appeal erred in equating "instruction" with "*non*-private study", and that this tended to make the purpose of the dealing unfair (Board, at para. 98; 2010 FCA 198, [2011] 3 F.C.R. 223, at paras. 37-38).

[47] While I agree with Justice Abella that"[s]tudying and learning are essentially personal endeavours", in the sense that each individual applies his or her own mind to the acquisition of knowledge, studying may occur in different settings (para. 27). The *Copyright Act* itself requires that to be fair dealing, use of a copyrighted work must be for "private study", which indicates that the Act foresees private and non-private study (s. 29). This point was made in *CCH* by the majority of the Federal Court of Appeal at paras. 128-29. Parliament does not speak in vain (*Canada (Attorney General) v. JTI-Macdonald Corp.*, 2007 SCC 30, [2007] 2 S.C.R. 610, at para. 110). Words used by the legislator should

be construed to give them *some*meaning. The section cannot be interpreted to strip the word "private" in"private study" of *any* meaning.

[48] The Board relied on prior jurisprudence on this point (para. 90). The Federal Court of Appeal upheld the Board's conclusion as reasonable because

> "[p]rivate study" presumably means just that: study by oneself. . . . A large and liberal interpretation means that the provisions are given a generous scope. It does not mean that the text of a statute should be given a meaning it cannot ordinarily bear. When students study material with their class as a whole, they engage not in "private" study but perhaps just "study". [para. 38]

[49] I agree with the distinction made by the Federal Court of Appeal. When included in the Act, the expression "private study"arguably refers to the situation of a scholar or student dealing with a work for his individual study. This does not mean that the scholar or student may not collaborate with others. I would hesitate to endorse the Board's apparent view, at para. 90, that a copy made at the request of a teacher can *never*be for the purpose of private study. In my view, a copy made on a teacher's own initiative would indeed be for private study if, for example, the material is tailored to the particular learning needs or interests of a single or small number of students. However, "private study" cannot have been intended to cover situations where tens, hundreds or thousands of copies are made in a school, school district or across a province as part of an organized program of instruction. The Board's conclusion at para. 98 that, in the case of Category 4 copies, "[m]ost of the time, [the] real or predominant purpose is instruction or 'non-private' study" is reasonable on the facts of this case.

B. *Amount of the Dealing and Character of the Dealing*

[50] I agree with my colleague that as a matter of analytical coherence, the "amount of the dealing" factor is concerned with "the proportion between the excerpted copy and the entire work, not the overall quantity of what is disseminated" (para. 29). The number of copies and the extent of the dissemination are properly considered under the "character of a dealing" factor (*CCH*, at para. 55). I also agree that it is important to avoid double counting in assessing the fairness of a dealing by looking to the same aspect of the dealing under more than one factor.

[51] However, in my opinion, the Board's analysis under the "amount of the dealing" factor remained focused on the proportion of the photocopied excerpt to the entire work. In its factual assessment of the"amount of the dealing" factor, the Board found "that class sets will be subject to 'numerous requests for [. . .] the same [. . .] series'" (para. 104, citing *CCH*, at para. 68). I do not read the Board's reliance on this finding as indicating that it improperly considered the overall number of copies of the same excerpt distributed to a whole class.

[52] As I understand the Board's reasons, while teachers usually made short excerpts at any one time, this was offset by the fact that the teachers would return to copy other excerpts from the same books — the ones contained in class sets — thereby making the *overall proportion*of the copied pages unfair in relation to the entire work *over a period of time*. The Board found:

With respect to the copies made on the teacher's initiative for his or her students, there are factors weighing on each side. . . . [I]t seems that teachers generally limit themselves to reproducing relatively short excerpts from a work to complement the main textbook. On the other hand, in our view, it is more than likely that class sets will be subject to "numerous requests for [. . .] the same [. . .] series",which would tend to make the amount of the dealing unfair on the whole. [Emphasis added; para. 104.]

The Board's conclusion is consistent with the *CCH* direction that "the [amount of the] dealings might not be fair if a specific patron . . . submitted numerous requests for multiple reported judicial decisions from the same reported series over a short period of time" (para. 68). In this context, it was not unreasonable for the Board to compare a teacher with a specific patron of the Great Library, given its earlier conclusion that the teacher's purpose must predominate.

[53] Under the "character of the dealing" factor, the Board focused its analysis on the fact that multiple copies of the *same*excerpt are made, at any one time, to be *disseminated to the whole class*(Board, at para. 100). Accordingly, on my reading of the Board's reasons, there was no double counting; the Board's conclusions of unfairness under the"character of the dealing" and the "amount of the dealing" factors were arrived at independently, taking into consideration different aspects of the dealing.

[54] On the whole, unless it is shown that the Board's conclusion of fact that the books from the "class sets will be subject to 'numerous requests . . .'" was unreasonable — and I would observe that the appellants specifically state in their factum that "the Board's findings of fact are not in dispute" (para. 50) — I would not disturb the Board's assessment under the "amount of the dealing" and "character of the dealing"factors.

C. *Alternatives to the Dealing*

[55] According to my colleague's analysis, at para. 32, the Board also unreasonably assessed whether there were any alternatives to the dealing, because "buying books for each student is not a realistic alternative to teachers copying short excerpts to supplement student textbooks". I agree that buying books to distribute to all students does not seem like a realistic option if we are speaking of photocopies of short excerpts only, used to supplement the main textbooks already in possession of the students.

[56] However, on the premise that the same class sets of books will be subject to numerous requests for short excerpts, as found by the Board at para. 104, it was not unreasonable for the Board to consider, at para. 107, that from a practical standpoint, the schools had the option of buying more books to distribute to students or to place in the library or in class sets instead of photocopying the books. While buying books may not be a non-copyrighted alternative such as those envisaged in *CCH*, these were relevant facts for the Board to consider in a case where it found systematic copying from the same books. In addition, the Board considered the schools'resources and found that in this case, "[t]he fact

that the establishment has limited means does not seem to bar the recognition of this point" (para. 107). In a case where numerous short excerpts of the work are taken, the fact that there are no non-copyrighted alternatives to the dealing does not automatically render the dealing fair. Therefore, I am not persuaded that the Board's analysis under the "alternatives to the dealing" factor was unreasonable.

D.   *Effect of the Dealing on the Work*

[57] I agree with Justice Abella that the Board's conclusion that the photocopying of Category 4 copies "compete[s] with the original to an extent that makes the dealing unfair" seems unsupported by evidence (Board, at para. 111). Even accepting that it was reasonable for the Board to conclude, based on the evidence of declining book sales, that photocopying had a negative impact on the work, it appears from para. 111 that the Board came to this conclusion by referring to the *total* amount of photocopying across Canada — 250 million pages, the bulk of which is already paid for through the tariff — and not the 16.9 million Category 4 copies. Determining the effect of the Category 4 dealing on the work required relating *those*photocopies to the work and determining whether the effect of those copies was sufficiently important to "compete with the market of the original work" (*CCH*, at para. 59). I would be inclined to find this conclusion unreasonable.

[58] However, I do not think that an unreasonable observation under this one factor is sufficient to render the Board's overall assessment unreasonable. As noted in *CCH*, no one factor is determinative and the assessment of fairness remains fact specific (paras. 59-60). In the appellants' own submission, the Board in this case considered the "purpose of the dealing" and the "amount of the dealing" factors to be the most important (A.F., at para. 45). In light of my conclusion that the Board's assessment under those and other factors was reasonable, I would not find the entire decision unreasonable because of this one finding.

III. Conclusion

[59] Tribunal decisions can certainly be found to be unreasonable (see, e.g., *Canada (Canadian Human Rights Commission) v. Canada (Attorney General)*, 2011 SCC 53, [2011] 3 S.C.R. 471). However, I do not think it is open on a deferential review, where a tribunal's decision is multifactored and complex, to seize upon a few arguable statements or intermediate findings to conclude that the overall decision is unreasonable. This is especially the case where the issues are fact-based, as in the case of a fair dealing analysis.

[60] This Court has stated in *Dunsmuir v. New Brunswick*, 2008 SCC 9, [2008] 1 S.C.R. 190, that reviewing courts are to look for "justification, transparency and intelligibility within the decision-making process" of the tribunal and with"whether the decision falls within a range of possible, acceptable outcomes which are defensible in respect of the facts and law" (para. 47). In my respectful view, the Board's detailed and extensive analysis and decision in this case were intelligible, transparent and justifiable. Its conclusion cannot be said to fall

outside of a reasonable range of outcomes. For these reasons, I would dismiss the appeal with costs.

---

2. Fair Use

The doctrine of "fair use" in the United States is a broader one than the "fair dealing" exemption under the Canadian Act. Its scope is discussed below.

Campbell v. Acuff-Rose Music, Inc., 510 U.S. 569 (1994)

Argued Nov. 9, 1993.
Decided March 7, 1994.

. . .

SOUTER, J., delivered the opinion for a unanimous Court. KENNEDY, J., filed a concurring opinion, *post,* p. 1180.

. . .

In 1964, Roy Orbison and William Dees wrote a rock ballad called "Oh, Pretty Woman" and assigned their rights in it to respondent Acuff-Rose Music, Inc. See Appendix A, *infra,* at 1179. Acuff-Rose registered the song for copyright protection.

Petitioners Luther R. Campbell, Christopher Wongwon, Mark Ross, and David Hobbs are collectively known as 2 Live Crew, a popular rap music group. [FN1] In 1989, Campbell wrote a song entitled "Pretty Woman," which he later described in an affidavit as intended, "through comical lyrics, to satirize the original work...." App. to Pet. for Cert. 80a. On July 5, 1989, 2 Live Crew's manager informed Acuff-Rose that 2 Live Crew had written a parody of "Oh, Pretty Woman," that they would afford all credit for ownership and authorship of the original song to Acuff-Rose, Dees, and Orbison, and that they were willing to pay a fee for the use they wished to make of it. Enclosed with the letter were a copy of the lyrics and a recording of 2 Live Crew's song. See Appendix B, *infra,* at 1179-80. Acuff-Rose's agent refused permission, stating that "I am aware of the success enjoyed by 'The 2 Live Crews', but I must inform you that we cannot permit the use of a parody of 'Oh, Pretty Woman.' " App. to Pet. for Cert. 85a. Nonetheless, in June or July 1989,[FN2] 2 Live Crew released records, cassette tapes, and compact discs of "Pretty Woman" in a collection of songs entitled "As Clean As They Wanna Be." The albums and compact discs identify the authors of "Pretty Woman" as Orbison and Dees and its publisher as Acuff-Rose.

> FN1. Rap has been defined as a "style of black American popular music consisting of improvised rhymes performed to a rhythmic accompaniment." The Norton/

Grove Concise Encyclopedia of Music 613 (1988). 2 Live Crew plays "[b]ass music," a regional, hip-hop style of rap from the Liberty City area of Miami, Florida. Brief for Petitioners 34.

FN2. The parties argue about the timing. 2 Live Crew contends that the album was released on July 15, and the District Court so held. 754 F.Supp. 1150, 1152 (MD Tenn.1991). The Court of Appeals states that Campbell's affidavit puts the release date in June, and chooses that date. 972 F.2d 1429, 1432 (CA6 1992). We find the timing of the request irrelevant for purposes of this enquiry. See n. 18, *infra,* discussing good faith.

Almost a year later, after nearly a quarter of a million copies of the recording had been sold, Acuff-Rose sued 2 Live Crew and its record company, Luke Skyywalker Records, for copyright infringement. The District Court granted summary judgment for 2 Live Crew,[FN3] reasoning that the commercial purpose of 2 Live Crew's song was no bar to fair use; that 2 Live Crew's version was a parody, which "quickly degenerates into a play on words, substituting predictable lyrics with shocking ones" to show "how bland and banal the Orbison song" is; that 2 Live Crew had taken no more than was necessary to "conjure up" the original in order to parody it; and that it was "extremely unlikely that 2 Live Crew's song could adversely affect the market for the original." 754 F.Supp. 1150, 1154-1155, 1157-1158 (MD Tenn.1991). The District Court weighed these factors and held that 2 Live Crew's song made fair use of Orbison's original. *Id.,* at 1158-1159.

FN3. 2 Live Crew's motion to dismiss was converted to a motion for summary judgment. Acuff-Rose defended against the motion, but filed no cross-motion.

The Court of Appeals for the Sixth Circuit reversed and remanded. 972 F.2d 1429, 1439 (1992). Although it assumed for the purpose of its opinion that 2 Live Crew's song was a parody of the Orbison original, the Court of Appeals thought the District Court had put too little emphasis on the fact that "every commercial use ... is presumptively ... unfair,"*Sony Corp. of America v. Universal City Studios, Inc.,* 464 U.S. 417, 451, 104 S.Ct. 774, 792, 78 L.Ed.2d 574 (1984), and it held that "the admittedly commercial nature" of the parody "requires the conclusion" that the first of four factors relevant under the statute weighs against a finding of fair use. 972 F.2d, at 1435, 1437. Next, the Court of Appeals determined that, by "taking the heart of the original and making it the heart of a new work," 2 Live Crew had, qualitatively, taken too much. *Id.,* at 1438. Finally, after noting that the effect on the potential market for the original (and the market for derivative works) is "undoubtedly the single most important element of fair use,"*Harper & Row, Publishers, Inc. v. Nation Enterprises,* 471 U.S. 539, 566, 105 S.Ct. 2218, 2233, 85 L.Ed.2d 588 (1985), the Court of Appeals faulted the District Court for "refus[ing] to indulge the presumption" that "harm for purposes of the fair use analysis has been established by the presumption attaching to commercial uses." 972 F.2d, at 1438-1439. In sum, the court concluded that its "blatantly commercial purpose ... prevents this parody from being a fair use." *Id.,* at 1439.

We granted certiorari, 507 U.S. 1003, 113 S.Ct. 1642, 123 L.Ed.2d 264 (1993), to determine whether 2 Live Crew's commercial parody could be a fair use.

II

It is uncontested here that 2 Live Crew's song would be an infringement of Acuff-Rose's rights in "Oh, Pretty Woman," under the Copyright Act of 1976, 17 U.S.C. § 106 (1988 ed. and Supp. IV), but for a finding of fair use through parody.[FN4] From the infancy of copyright protection, some opportunity for fair use of copyrighted materials has been thought necessary to fulfill copyright's very purpose, "[t]o promote the Progress of Science and useful Arts...." U.S. Const., Art. I, § 8, cl. 8.[FN5] For as Justice Story explained, "[i]n truth, in literature, in science and in art, there are, and can be, few, if any, things, which in an abstract sense, are strictly new and original throughout. Every book in literature, science and art, borrows, and must necessarily borrow, and use much which was well known and used before." *Emerson v. Davies,* 8 F.Cas. 615, 619 (No. 4,436) (CCD Mass.1845). Similarly, Lord Ellenborough expressed the inherent tension in the need simultaneously to protect copyrighted material and to allow others to build upon it when he wrote, "while I shall think myself bound to secure every man in the enjoyment of his copy-right, one must not put manacles upon science." *Carey v. Kearsley,* 4 Esp. 168, 170, 170 Eng.Rep. 679, 681 (K.B.1803). In copyright cases brought under the Statute of Anne of 1710,[FN6] English courts held that in some instances "fair abridgements" would not infringe an author's rights, see W. Patry, The Fair Use Privilege in Copyright Law 6-17 (1985) (hereinafter Patry); Leval, Toward a Fair Use Standard, 103 Harv.L.Rev. 1105 (1990) (hereinafter Leval), and although the First Congress enacted our initial copyright statute, Act of May 31, 1790, 1 Stat. 124, without any explicit reference to "fair use," as it later came to be known,[FN7] the doctrine was recognized by the American courts nonetheless.

FN4. Section 106 provides in part:

"Subject to sections 107 through 120, the owner of copyright under this title has the exclusive rights to do and to authorize any of the following:

"(1) to reproduce the copyrighted work in copies or phonorecords;

"(2) to prepare derivative works based upon the copyrighted work;

"(3) to distribute copies or phonorecords of the copyrighted work to the public by sale or other transfer of ownership, or by rental, lease, or lending...."

A derivative work is defined as one "based upon one or more preexisting works, such as a translation, musical arrangement, dramatization, fictionalization, motion picture version, sound recording, art reproduction, abridgment, condensation, or any other form in which a work may be recast, transformed, or adapted. A work consisting of editorial revisions, annotations, elaborations, or other modifications which, as a whole, represent an original work of authorship, is a 'derivative work.' " 17 U.S.C. § 101.

2 Live Crew concedes that it is not entitled to a compulsory license under § 115 because its arrangement changes "the basic melody or fundamental character" of the original. § 115(a)(2).

FN5. The exclusion of facts and ideas from copyright protection serves that goal as well. See § 102(b) ("In no case does copyright protection for an original work of authorship extend to any idea, procedure, process, system, method of operation, concept, principle, or discovery ..."); *Feist Publications, Inc. v. Rural Telephone Service Co.,* 499 U.S. 340, 359, 111 S.Ct. 1282, 1294, 113 L.Ed.2d 358 (1991) ("[F]acts contained in existing works may be freely copied"); *Harper & Row, Publishers, Inc. v. Nation Enterprises,* 471 U.S. 539, 547, 105 S.Ct. 2218, 2223, 85 L.Ed.2d 588 (1985) (copyright owner's rights exclude facts and ideas, and fair use).

FN6. An Act for the Encouragement of Learning, 8 Anne, ch. 19.

FN7. Patry 27, citing *Lawrence v. Dana,* 15 F.Cas. 26, 60 (No. 8,136) (CCD Mass.1869).

[1] In *Folsom v. Marsh,* 9 F.Cas. 342 (No. 4,901) (CCD Mass. 1841), Justice Story distilled the essence of law and methodology from the earlier cases: "look to the nature and objects of the selections made, the quantity and value of the materials used, and the degree in which the use may prejudice the sale, or diminish the profits, or supersede the objects, of the original work." *Id.,* at 348. Thus expressed, fair use remained exclusively judge-made doctrine until the passage of the 1976 Copyright Act, in which Justice Story's summary is discernible:[FN8]

FN8. Leval 1105. For a historical account of the development of the fair use doctrine, see Patry 1-64.

"§107. Limitations on exclusive rights: Fair use

"Notwithstanding the provisions of sections 106 and 106A, the fair use of a copyrighted work, including such use by reproduction in copies or phonorecords or by any other means specified by that section, for purposes such as criticism, comment, news reporting, teaching (including multiple copies for classroom use), scholarship, or research, is not an infringement of copyright. In determining whether the use made of a work in any particular case is a fair use the factors to be considered shall include-

"(1) the purpose and character of the use, including whether such use is of a commercial nature or is for nonprofit educational purposes;

"(2) the nature of the copyrighted work;

"(3) the amount and substantiality of the portion used in relation to the copyrighted work as a whole; and

"(4) the effect of the use upon the potential market for or value of the copyrighted work.

"The fact that a work is unpublished shall not itself bar a finding of fair use if such finding is made upon consideration of all the above factors." 17 U.S.C. § 107 (1988 ed. and Supp. IV).

Congress meant § 107"to restate the present judicial doctrine of fair use, not to change, narrow, or enlarge it in any way" and intended that courts continue the common-law tradition of fair use adjudication. H.R.Rep. No. 94-1476, p. 66 (1976) (hereinafter House Report); S.Rep. No. 94-473, p. 62 (1975) U.S.Code Cong. & Admin.News 1976, pp. 5659, 5679 (hereinafter Senate Report). The fair use doctrine thus "permits [and requires] courts to avoid rigid application of the copyright statute when, on occasion, it would stifle the very creativity which that law is designed to foster." *Stewart v. Abend*, 495 U.S. 207, 236, 110 S.Ct. 1750, 1767, 109 L.Ed.2d 184 (1990) (internal quotation marks and citation omitted).

[2] The task is not to be simplified with bright-line rules, for the statute, like the doctrine it recognizes, calls for case-by-case analysis. *Harper & Row,* 471 U.S., at 560, 105 S.Ct., at 2230; *Sony,* 464 U.S., at 448, and n. 31, 104 S.Ct., at 792, & n. 31; House Report, pp. 65-66; Senate Report, p. 62. The text employs the terms "including" and "such as" in the preamble paragraph to indicate the "illustrative and not limitative" function of the examples given, § 101; see *Harper & Row, supra,* 471 U.S., at 561, 105 S.Ct., at 2230, which thus provide only general guidance about the sorts of copying that courts and Congress most commonly had found to be fair uses.[FN9] Nor may the four statutory factors be treated in isolation, one from another. All are to be explored, and the results weighed together, in light of the purposes of copyright. See Leval 1110-1111; Patry & Perlmutter, Fair Use Misconstrued: Profit, Presumptions, and Parody, 11 Cardozo Arts & Ent.L.J. 667, 685-687 (1993) (hereinafter Patry & Perlmutter).[FN10]

FN9. See Senate Report, p. 62 ("[W]hether a use referred to in the first sentence of section 107 is a fair use in a particular case will depend upon the application of the determinative factors").

FN10. Because the fair use enquiry often requires close questions of judgment as to the extent of permissible borrowing in cases involving parodies (or other critical works), courts may also wish to bear in mind that the goals of the copyright law, "to stimulate the creation and publication of edifying matter," Leval 1134, are not always best served by automatically granting injunctive relief when parodists are found to have gone beyond the bounds of fair use. See 17 U.S.C. § 502(a) (court "*may...* grant ... injunctions on such terms as it may deem reasonable to prevent or restrain infringement") (emphasis added); Leval 1132 (while in the "vast majority of cases, [an injunctive] remedy is justified because most infringements are simple piracy," such cases are "worlds apart from many of those raising reasonable contentions of fair use" where "there may be a strong public interest in the publication of the secondary work [and] the copyright owner's interest may be adequately protected by an award of damages for whatever infringement is found"); *Abend v. MCA, Inc.,* 863 F.2d 1465, 1479 (CA9 1988) (finding "special circumstances" that would cause "great injustice" to defendants and "public injury" were injunction to issue), aff'd *sub nom.Stewart v. Abend,* 495 U.S. 207, 110 S.Ct. 1750, 109 L.Ed.2d 184 (1990).

A

[3][4] The first factor in a fair use enquiry is "the purpose and character of the use, including whether such use is of a commercial nature or is for nonprofit

educational purposes." § 107(1). This factor draws on Justice Story's formulation, "the nature and objects of the selections made." *Folsom v. Marsh, supra,* at 348. The enquiry here may be guided by the examples given in the preamble to § 107, looking to whether the use is for criticism, or comment, or news reporting, and the like, see § 107. The central purpose of this investigation is to see, in Justice Story's words, whether the new work merely "supersede[s] the objects" of the original creation, *Folsom v. Marsh, supra,* at 348; accord, *Harper & Row, supra,* 471 U.S., at 562, 105 S.Ct., at 2231 ("supplanting" the original), or instead adds something new, with a further purpose or different character, altering the first with new expression, meaning, or message; it asks, in other words, whether and to what extent the new work is "transformative." Leval 1111. Although such transformative use is not absolutely necessary for a finding of fair use, *Sony, supra,* 464 U.S., at 455, n. 40, 104 S.Ct., at 795, n. 40,[FN11] the goal of copyright, to promote science and the arts, is generally furthered by the creation of transformative works. Such works thus lie at the heart of the fair use doctrine's guarantee of breathing space within the confines of copyright, see, *e.g., Sony, supra,* at 478-480, 104 S.Ct., at 807-808 (BLACKMUN, J., dissenting), and the more transformative the new work, the less will be the significance of other factors, like commercialism, that may weigh against a finding of fair use.

FN11. The obvious statutory exception to this focus on transformative uses is the straight reproduction of multiple copies for classroom distribution.

[5] This Court has only once before even considered whether parody may be fair use, and that time issued no opinion because of the Court's equal division. *Benny v. Loew's Inc.,* 239 F.2d 532 (CA9 1956), aff'd *sub nom.Columbia Broadcasting System, Inc. v. Loew's Inc.,* 356 U.S. 43, 78 S.Ct. 667, 2 L.Ed.2d 583 (1958). Suffice it to say now that parody has an obvious claim to transformative value, as Acuff-Rose itself does not deny. Like less ostensibly humorous forms of criticism, it can provide social benefit, by shedding light on an earlier work, and, in the process, creating a new one. We thus line up with the courts that have held that parody, like other comment or criticism, may claim fair use under § 107. See, *e.g., Fisher v. Dees,* 794 F.2d 432 (CA9 1986) ("When Sonny Sniffs Glue," a parody of "When Sunny Gets Blue," is fair use); *Elsmere Music, Inc. v. National Broadcasting Co.,* 482 F.Supp. 741 SDNY), aff'd, 623 F.2d 252 (CA2 1980) ("I Love Sodom," a "Saturday Night Live" television parody of "I Love New York," is fair use); see also House Report, p. 65; Senate Report, p. 61, U.S.Code Cong. & Admin.News 1976, pp. 5659, 5678 ("[U]se in a parody of some of the content of the work parodied" may be fair use).

[6] The germ of parody lies in the definition of the Greek *parodeia,* quoted in Judge Nelson's Court of Appeals dissent, as "a song sung alongside another." 972 F.2d, at 1440, quoting 7 Encyclopedia Britannica 768 (15th ed. 1975). Modern dictionaries accordingly describe a parody as a "literary or artistic work that imitates the characteristic style of an author or a work for comic effect or ridicule,"[FN12] or as a "composition in prose or verse in which the characteristic turns of thought and phrase in an author or class of authors are imitated in such a way as to make them appear ridiculous."[FN13] For the purposes of copyright law,

the nub of the definitions, and the heart of any parodist's claim to quote from existing material, is the use of some elements of a prior author's composition to create a new one that, at least in part, comments on that author's works. See, e.g., *Fisher v. Dees, supra,* at 437; *MCA, Inc. v. Wilson,* 677 F.2d 180, 185 (CA2 1981). If, on the contrary, the commentary has no critical bearing on the substance or style of the original composition, which the alleged infringer merely uses to get attention or to avoid the drudgery in working up something fresh, the claim to fairness in borrowing from another's work diminishes accordingly (if it does not vanish), and other factors, like the extent of its commerciality, loom larger.[FN14] Parody needs to mimic an original to make its point, and so has some claim to use the creation of its victim's (or collective victims') imagination, whereas satire can stand on its own two feet and so requires justification for the very act of borrowing.[FN15] See *ibid.;* Bisceglia, Parody and Copyright Protection: Turning the Balancing Act Into a Juggling Act, in ASCAP, Copyright Law Symposium, No. 34, p. 25 (1987).

> FN12. American Heritage Dictionary 1317 (3d ed. 1992).
>
> FN13. 11 Oxford English Dictionary 247 (2d ed. 1989).
>
> FN14. A parody that more loosely targets an original than the parody presented here may still be sufficiently aimed at an original work to come within our analysis of parody. If a parody whose wide dissemination in the market runs the risk of serving as a substitute for the original or licensed derivatives (see *infra* at 1177-1179, discussing factor four), it is more incumbent on one claiming fair use to establish the extent of transformation and the parody's critical relationship to the original. By contrast, when there is little or no risk of market substitution, whether because of the large extent of transformation of the earlier work, the new work's minimal distribution in the market, the small extent to which it borrows from an original, or other factors, taking parodic aim at an original is a less critical factor in the analysis, and looser forms of parody may be found to be fair use, as may satire with lesser justification for the borrowing than would otherwise be required.
>
> FN15. Satire has been defined as a work "in which prevalent follies or vices are assailed with ridicule," 14 Oxford English Dictionary, *supra,* at 500, or are "attacked through irony, derision, or wit," American Heritage Dictionary, *supra,* at 1604.

The fact that parody can claim legitimacy for some appropriation does not, of course, tell either parodist or judge much about where to draw the line. Like a book review quoting the copyrighted material criticized, parody may or may not be fair use, and petitioners' suggestion that any parodic use is presumptively fair has no more justification in law or fact than the equally hopeful claim that any use for news reporting should be presumed fair, see *Harper & Row,* 471 U.S., at 561, 105 S.Ct., at 2230. The Act has no hint of an evidentiary preference for parodists over their victims, and no workable presumption for parody could take account of the fact that parody often shades into satire when society is lampooned through its creative artifacts, or that a work may contain both parodic and nonparodic elements. Accordingly, parody, like any other use, has to work its way through the relevant factors, and be judged case by case, in light of the ends of the copyright law.

Here, the District Court held, and the Court of Appeals assumed, that 2 Live Crew's "Pretty Woman" contains parody, commenting on and criticizing the original work, whatever it may have to say about society at large. As the District Court remarked, the words of 2 Live Crew's song copy the original's first line, but then "quickly degenerat[e] into a play on words, substituting predictable lyrics with shocking ones ... [that] derisively demonstrat[e] how bland and banal the Orbison song seems to them." 754 F.Supp., at 1155 (footnote omitted). Judge Nelson, dissenting below, came to the same conclusion, that the 2 Live Crew song "was clearly intended to ridicule the white-bread original" and "reminds us that sexual congress with nameless streetwalkers is not necessarily the stuff of romance and is not necessarily without its consequences. The singers (there are several) have the same thing on their minds as did the lonely man with the nasal voice, but here there is no hint of wine and roses." 972 F.2d, at 1442. Although the majority below had difficulty discerning any criticism of the original in 2 Live Crew's song, it assumed for purposes of its opinion that there was some. *Id.*, at 1435-1436, and n. 8.

[7] We have less difficulty in finding that critical element in 2 Live Crew's song than the Court of Appeals did, although having found it we will not take the further step of evaluating its quality. The threshold question when fair use is raised in defense of parody is whether a parodic character may reasonably be perceived.[FN16] Whether, going beyond that, parody is in good taste or bad does not and should not matter to fair use. As Justice Holmes explained, "[i]t would be a dangerous undertaking for persons trained only to the law to constitute themselves final judges of the worth of [a work], outside of the narrowest and most obvious limits. At the one extreme some works of genius would be sure to miss appreciation. Their very novelty would make them repulsive until the public had learned the new language in which their author spoke." *Bleistein v. Donaldson Lithographing Co.,* 188 U.S. 239, 251, 23 S.Ct. 298, 300, 47 L.Ed. 460 (1903) (circus posters have copyright protection); cf. *Yankee Publishing Inc. v. News America Publishing, Inc.,* 809 F.Supp. 267, 280 (SDNY 1992) (Leval, J.) ("First Amendment protections do not apply only to those who speak clearly, whose jokes are funny, and whose parodies succeed") (trademark case).

> FN16. The only further judgment, indeed, that a court may pass on a work goes to an assessment of whether the parodic element is slight or great, and the copying small or extensive in relation to the parodic element, for a work with slight parodic element and extensive copying will be more likely to merely "supersede the objects" of the original. See *infra,* at 1175-79, discussing factors three and four.

While we might not assign a high rank to the parodic element here, we think it fair to say that 2 Live Crew's song reasonably could be perceived as commenting on the original or criticizing it, to some degree. 2 Live Crew juxtaposes the romantic musings of a man whose fantasy comes true, with degrading taunts, a bawdy demand for sex, and a sigh of relief from paternal responsibility. The later words can be taken as a comment on the naiveté of the original of an earlier day, as a rejection of its sentiment that ignores the ugliness of street life and the debasement that it signifies. It is this joinder of reference and ridicule that marks off the author's choice of parody from the other types of comment and criticism that traditionally have had a claim to fair use protection as transformative works. FN17

> FN17. We note in passing that 2 Live Crew need not label their whole album, or even this song, a parody in order to claim fair use protection, nor should 2 Live Crew be penalized for this being its first parodic essay. Parody serves its goals whether labeled or not, and there is no reason to require parody to state the obvious (or even the reasonably perceived). See Patry & Perlmutter 716-717.

[8][9] The Court of Appeals, however, immediately cut short the enquiry into 2 Live Crew's fair use claim by confining its treatment of the first factor essentially to one relevant fact, the commercial nature of the use. The court then inflated the significance of this fact by applying a presumption ostensibly culled from *Sony*, that "every commercial use of copyrighted material is presumptively ... unfair...." *Sony*, 464 U.S., at 451, 104 S.Ct., at 792. In giving virtually dispositive weight to the commercial nature of the parody, the Court of Appeals erred.

The language of the statute makes clear that the commercial or nonprofit educational purpose of a work is only one element of the first factor enquiry into its purpose and character. Section 107(1) uses the term "including" to begin the dependent clause referring to commercial use, and the main clause speaks of a broader investigation into "purpose and character." As we explained in *Harper & Row*, Congress resisted attempts to narrow the ambit of this traditional enquiry by adopting categories of presumptively fair use, and it urged courts to preserve the breadth of their traditionally ample view of the universe of relevant evidence. 471 U.S., at 561, 105 S.Ct. at 2230; House Report, p. 66, U.S.Code Cong. & Admin.News 1976, pp. 5659, 5679. Accordingly, the mere fact that a use is educational and not for profit does not insulate it from a finding of infringement, any more than the commercial character of a use bars a finding of fairness. If, indeed, commerciality carried presumptive force against a finding of fairness, the presumption would swallow nearly all of the illustrative uses listed in the preamble paragraph of § 107, including news reporting, comment, criticism, teaching, scholarship, and research, since these activities "are generally conducted for profit in this country." *Harper & Row, supra,* at 592, 105 S.Ct., at 2246 (Brennan, J., dissenting). Congress could not have intended such a rule, which certainly is not inferable from the common-law cases, arising as they did from the world of letters in which Samuel Johnson could pronounce that "[n]o man but a blockhead ever wrote, except for money." 3 Boswell's Life of Johnson 19 (G. Hill ed. 1934).

Sony itself called for no hard evidentiary presumption. There, we emphasized the need for a "sensitive balancing of interests," 464 U.S., at 455, n. 40, 104 S.Ct., at 795, n. 40, noted that Congress had "eschewed a rigid, bright-line approach to fair use,"*id.,* at 449, n. 31, 104 S.Ct., at 792, n. 31, and stated that the commercial or nonprofit educational character of a work is "not conclusive," *id.,* at 448-449, 104 S.Ct., at 792, but rather a fact to be "weighed along with other[s] in fair use decisions,"*id.,* at 449, n. 32, 104 S.Ct. at 792, n. 32, (quoting

House Report, p. 66) U.S.Code Cong. & Admin.News 1976, pp. 5659, 5679. The Court of Appeals's elevation of one sentence from *Sony* to a *per se* rule thus runs as much counter to *Sony* itself as to the long common-law tradition of fair use adjudication. Rather, as we explained in *Harper & Row, Sony* stands for the proposition that the "fact that a publication was commercial as opposed to nonprofit is a separate factor that tends to weigh against a finding of fair use." 471 U.S., at 562, 105 S.Ct., at 2231. But that is all, and the fact that even the force of that tendency will vary with the context is a further reason against elevating commerciality to hard presumptive significance. The use, for example, of a copyrighted work to advertise a product, even in a parody, will be entitled to less indulgence under the first factor of the fair use enquiry than the sale of a parody for its own sake, let alone one performed a single time by students in school. See generally Patry & Perlmutter 679-680; *Fisher v. Dees,* 794 F.2d, at 437; *Maxtone-Graham v. Burtchaell,* 803 F.2d 1253, 1262 (CA2 1986); *Sega Enterprises Ltd. v. Accolade, Inc.,* 977 F.2d 1510, 1522 (CA9 1992).[FN18]

> FN18. Finally, regardless of the weight one might place on the alleged infringer's state of mind, compare *Harper & Row,* 471 U.S., at 562, 105 S.Ct., at 2231 (fair use presupposes good faith and fair dealing) (quotation marks omitted), with *Folsom v. Marsh,* 9 F.Cas. 342, 349 (No. 4,901) (CCD Mass.1841) (good faith does not bar a finding of infringement); Leval 1126-1127 (good faith irrelevant to fair use analysis), we reject Acuff-Rose's argument that 2 Live Crew's request for permission to use the original should be weighed against a finding of fair use. Even if good faith were central to fair use, 2 Live Crew's actions do not necessarily suggest that they believed their version was not fair use; the offer may simply have been made in a good-faith effort to avoid this litigation. If the use is otherwise fair, then no permission need be sought or granted. Thus, being denied permission to use a work does not weigh against a finding of fair use. See *Fisher v. Dees,* 794 F.2d 432, 437 (CA9 1986).

B

[10] The second statutory factor, "the nature of the copyrighted work,"§ 107(2), draws on Justice Story's expression, the "value of the materials used." *Folsom v. Marsh,* 9 F.Cas., at 348. This factor calls for recognition that some works are closer to the core of intended copyright protection than others, with the consequence that fair use is more difficult to establish when the former works are copied. See, *e.g., Stewart v. Abend,* 495 U.S., at 237-238, 110 S.Ct., at 1768-1769 (contrasting fictional short story with factual works); *Harper & Row,* 471 U.S., at 563-564, 105 S.Ct., at 2231-2233 (contrasting soon-to-be-published memoir with published speech); *Sony,* 464 U.S., at 455, n. 40, 104 S.Ct., at 792, n. 40 (contrasting motion pictures with news broadcasts); *Feist,* 499 U.S., at 348-351, 111 S.Ct., at 1289-1291 (contrasting creative works with bare factual compilations); 3 M. Nimmer & D. Nimmer, Nimmer on Copyright § 13.05[A][2] (1993) (hereinafter Nimmer); Leval 1116. We agree with both the District Court and the Court of Appeals that the Orbison original's creative expression for public dissemination falls within the core of the copyright's protective purposes. 754 F.Supp., at 1155-1156; 972 F.2d, at 1437. This fact, however, is not much help in this case, or ever likely to help much in separating the fair use sheep from the

infringing goats in a parody case, since parodies almost invariably copy publicly known, expressive works.

C

[11] The third factor asks whether "the amount and substantiality of the portion used in relation to the copyrighted work as a whole,"§ 107(3) (or, in Justice Story's words, "the quantity and value of the materials used,"*Folsom v. Marsh, supra,* at 348) are reasonable in relation to the purpose of the copying. Here, attention turns to the persuasiveness of a parodist's justification for the particular copying done, and the enquiry will harken back to the first of the statutory factors, for, as in prior cases, we recognize that the extent of permissible copying varies with the purpose and character of the use. See *Sony, supra,* 464 U.S., at 449-450, 104 S.Ct., at 792-793 (reproduction of entire work "does not have its ordinary effect of militating against a finding of fair use" as to home videotaping of television programs); *Harper & Row, supra,* 471 U.S., at 564, 105 S.Ct., at 2232 ("[E]ven substantial quotations might qualify as fair use in a review of a published work or a news account of a speech" but not in a scoop of a soon-to-be-published memoir). The facts bearing on this factor will also tend to address the fourth, by revealing the degree to which the parody may serve as a market substitute for the original or potentially licensed derivatives. See Leval 1123.

The District Court considered the song's parodic purpose in finding that 2 Live Crew had not helped themselves overmuch. 754 F.Supp., at 1156-1157. The Court of Appeals disagreed, stating that "[w]hile it may not be inappropriate to find that no more was taken than necessary, the copying was qualitatively substantial.... We conclude that taking the heart of the original and making it the heart of a new work was to purloin a substantial portion of the essence of the original." 972 F.2d, at 1438.

The Court of Appeals is of course correct that this factor calls for thought not only about the quantity of the materials used, but about their quality and importance, too. In *Harper & Row,* for example, the Nation had taken only some 300 words out of President Ford's memoirs, but we signaled the significance of the quotations in finding them to amount to "the heart of the book," the part most likely to be newsworthy and important in licensing serialization. 471 U.S., at 564-566, 568, 105 S.Ct., at 2232-2234, 2234 (internal quotation marks omitted). We also agree with the Court of Appeals that whether "a substantial portion of the infringing work was copied verbatim" from the copyrighted work is a relevant question, see *id.,* at 565, 105 S.Ct., at 2232, for it may reveal a dearth of transformative character or purpose under the first factor, or a greater likelihood of market harm under the fourth; a work composed primarily of an original, particularly its heart, with little added or changed, is more likely to be a merely superseding use, fulfilling demand for the original.

Where we part company with the court below is in applying these guides to parody, and in particular to parody in the song before us. Parody presents a difficult case. Parody's humor, or in any event its comment, necessarily springs from recognizable allusion to its object through distorted imitation. Its art lies in the tension between a known original and its parodic twin. When parody takes aim at a particular original work, the parody must be able to "conjure up" at least enough of that original to make the object of its critical wit recognizable. See, e.g., Elsmere Music, 623 F.2d, at 253, n. 1; Fisher v. Dees, 794 F.2d, at 438-439. What makes for this recognition is quotation of the original's most distinctive or memorable features, which the parodist can be sure the audience will know. Once enough has been taken to assure identification, how much more is reasonable will depend, say, on the extent to which the song's overriding purpose and character is to parody the original or, in contrast, the likelihood that the parody may serve as a market substitute for the original. But using some characteristic features cannot be avoided.

[12] We think the Court of Appeals was insufficiently appreciative of parody's need for the recognizable sight or sound when it ruled 2 Live Crew's use unreasonable as a matter of law. It is true, of course, that 2 Live Crew copied the characteristic opening bass riff (or musical phrase) of the original, and true that the words of the first line copy the Orbison lyrics. But if quotation of the opening riff and the first line may be said to go to the "heart" of the original, the heart is also what most readily conjures up the song for parody, and it is the heart at which parody takes aim. Copying does not become excessive in relation to parodic purpose merely because the portion taken was the original's heart. If 2 Live Crew had copied a significantly less memorable part of the original, it is difficult to see how its parodic character would have come through. See Fisher v. Dees, supra, at 439.

[13] This is not, of course, to say that anyone who calls himself a parodist can skim the cream and get away scot free. In parody, as in news reporting, see Harper & Row, supra, context is everything, and the question of fairness asks what else the parodist did besides go to the heart of the original. It is significant that 2 Live Crew not only copied the first line of the original, but thereafter departed markedly from the Orbison lyrics for its own ends. 2 Live Crew not only copied the bass riff and repeated it,[FN19] but also produced otherwise distinctive sounds, interposing "scraper" noise, overlaying the music with solos in different keys, and altering the drum beat. See 754 F.Supp., at 1155. This is not a case, then, where "a substantial portion" of the parody itself is composed of a "verbatim" copying of the original. It is not, that is, a case where the parody is so insubstantial, as compared to the copying, that the third factor must be resolved as a matter of law against the parodists.

FN19. This may serve to heighten the comic effect of the parody, as one witness stated, App. 32a, Affidavit of Oscar Brand; see also Elsmere Music, Inc. v. National Broadcasting Co., 482 F.Supp. 741, 747 (SDNY 1980) (repetition of "I Love Sodom"), or serve to dazzle with the original's music, as Acuff-Rose now contends.

Suffice it to say here that, as to the lyrics, we think the Court of Appeals correctly suggested that "no more was taken than necessary,"972 F.2d, at 1438, but just for that reason, we fail to see how the copying can be excessive in relation to its parodic purpose, even if the portion taken is the original's "heart." As to the music, we express no opinion whether repetition of the bass riff is excessive copying, and we remand to permit evaluation of the amount taken, in light of the song's parodic purpose and character, its transformative elements, and considerations of the potential for market substitution sketched more fully below.

D

[14] The fourth fair use factor is "the effect of the use upon the potential market for or value of the copyrighted work." § 107(4). It requires courts to consider not only the extent of market harm caused by the particular actions of the alleged infringer, but also "whether unrestricted and widespread conduct of the sort engaged in by the defendant ... would result in a substantially adverse impact on the potential market" for the original. Nimmer § 13.05[A] [4], p. 13-102.61 (footnote omitted); accord, *Harper & Row,* 471 U.S., at 569, 105 S.Ct., at 2235; Senate Report, p. 65; *Folsom v. Marsh,* 9 F.Cas., at 349. The enquiry "must take account not only of harm to the original but also of harm to the market for derivative works." *Harper & Row, supra,* 471 U.S. at 568, 105 S.Ct., at 2234.

[15] Since fair use is an affirmative defense,[FN20] its proponent would have difficulty carrying the burden of demonstrating fair use without favorable evidence about relevant markets.[FN21] In moving for summary judgment, 2 Live Crew left themselves at just such a disadvantage when they failed to address the effect on the market for rap derivatives, and confined themselves to uncontroverted submissions that there was no likely effect on the market for the original. They did not, however, thereby subject themselves to the evidentiary presumption applied by the Court of Appeals. In assessing the likelihood of significant market harm, the Court of Appeals quoted from language in *Sony* that " '[i]f the intended use is for commercial gain, that likelihood may be presumed. But if it is for a noncommercial purpose, the likelihood must be demonstrated.'" 972 F.2d, at 1438, quoting *Sony,* 464 U.S., at 451, 104 S.Ct., at 104 S.Ct., at 793. The court reasoned that because "the use of the copyrighted work is wholly commercial, ... we presume that a likelihood of future harm to Acuff-Rose exists." 972 F.2d, at 1438. In so doing, the court resolved the fourth factor against 2 Live Crew, just as it had the first, by applying a presumption about the effect of commercial use, a presumption which as applied here we hold to be error.

FN20. *Harper & Row,* 471 U.S., at 561, 105 S.Ct., at 2230; H.R.Rep. No. 102-836, p. 3, n. 3 (1992).

FN21. Even favorable evidence, without more, is no guarantee of fairness. Judge Leval gives the example of the film producer's appropriation of a composer's previously unknown song that turns the song into a commercial success; the boon to the song does not make the film's simple copying fair. Leval 1124, n. 84. This factor, no less than the other three, may be addressed only through a "sensitive balancing of interests." *Sony Corp. of America v. Universal City Studios, Inc.,* 464 U.S. 417, 455, n. 40, 104 S.Ct. 774, 795, n. 40, 78 L.Ed.2d 574 (1984). Market harm is a matter of degree, and the importance of this factor will vary, not only with the amount of harm, but also with the relative strength of the showing on the other factors.

No "presumption" or inference of market harm that might find support in *Sony* is applicable to a case involving something beyond mere duplication for commercial purposes. *Sony*'s discussion of a presumption contrasts a context of verbatim copying of the original in its entirety for commercial purposes, with the noncommercial context of *Sony* itself (home copying of television programming). In the former circumstances, what *Sony* said simply makes common sense: when a commercial use amounts to mere duplication of the entirety of an original, it clearly "supersede[s] the objects," *Folsom v. Marsh, supra,* at 348, of the original and serves as a market replacement for it, making it likely that cognizable market harm to the original will occur. *Sony, supra,* 464 U.S., at 451, 104 S.Ct., at 793. But when, on the contrary, the second use is transformative, market substitution is at least less certain, and market harm may not be so readily inferred. Indeed, as to parody pure and simple, it is more likely that the new work will not affect the market for the original in a way cognizable under this factor, that is, by acting as a substitute for it ("supersed[ing] [its] objects"). See Leval 1125; Patry & Perlmutter 692, 697-698. This is so because the parody and the original usually serve different market functions. Bisceglia, ASCAP, Copyright Law Symposium, No. 34, at 23.

[16] We do not, of course, suggest that a parody may not harm the market at all, but when a lethal parody, like a scathing theater review, kills demand for the original, it does not produce a harm cognizable under the Copyright Act. Because "parody may quite legitimately aim at garroting the original, destroying it commercially as well as artistically," B. Kaplan, An Unhurried View of Copyright 69 (1967), the role of the courts is to distinguish between "[b]iting criticism [that merely] suppresses demand [and] copyright infringement[, which] usurps it." *Fisher v. Dees,* 794 F.2d, at 438.

This distinction between potentially remediable displacement and unremediable disparagement is reflected in the rule that there is no protectible derivative market for criticism. The market for potential derivative uses includes only those that creators of original works would in general develop or license others to develop. Yet the unlikelihood that creators of imaginative works will license critical reviews or lampoons of their own productions removes such uses from the very notion of a potential licensing market. "People ask ... for criticism, but they only want praise." S. Maugham, Of Human Bondage 241 (Penguin ed. 1992). Thus, to the extent that the opinion below may be read to have considered harm to the market for parodies of "Oh, Pretty Woman," see 972 F.2d, at 1439, the court erred. Accord, *Fisher v. Dees, supra,* at 437; Leval 1125; Patry & Perlmutter 688-691.[FN22]

> FN22. We express no opinion as to the derivative markets for works using elements of an original as vehicles for satire or amusement, making no comment on the original or criticism of it.

[17][18] In explaining why the law recognizes no derivative market for critical works, including parody, we have, of course, been speaking of the later work as if it had nothing but a critical aspect (*i.e.,* "parody pure and simple," *supra,* at 1177). But the later work may have a more complex character, with effects

not only in the arena of criticism but also in protectible markets for derivative works, too. In that sort of case, the law looks beyond the criticism to the other elements of the work, as it does here. 2 Live Crew's song comprises not only parody but also rap music, and the derivative market for rap music is a proper focus of enquiry, see *Harper & Row, supra,* 471 U.S., at 568, 105 S.Ct., at 2234; Nimmer § 13.05 [B]. Evidence of substantial harm to it would weigh against a finding of fair use,[FN23] because the licensing of derivatives is an important economic incentive to the creation of originals. See 17 U.S.C. § 106(2) (copyright owner has rights to derivative works). Of course, the only harm to derivatives that need concern us, as discussed above, is the harm of market substitution. The fact that a parody may impair the market for derivative uses by the very effectiveness of its critical commentary is no more relevant under copyright than the like threat to the original market.[FN24]

> FN23. See Nimmer § 13.05[A][4], p. 13-102.61 ("a substantially adverse impact on the potential market"); Leval 1125 ("reasonably substantial" harm); Patry & Perlmutter 697-698 (same).

> FN24. In some cases it may be difficult to determine whence the harm flows. In such cases, the other fair use factors may provide some indicia of the likely source of the harm. A work whose overriding purpose and character is parodic and whose borrowing is slight in relation to its parody will be far less likely to cause cognizable harm than a work with little parodic content and much copying.

[19] Although 2 Live Crew submitted uncontroverted affidavits on the question of market harm to the original, neither they, nor Acuff-Rose, introduced evidence or affidavits addressing the likely effect of 2 Live Crew's parodic rap song on the market for a nonparody, rap version of "Oh, Pretty Woman." And while Acuff-Rose would have us find evidence of a rap market in the very facts that 2 Live Crew recorded a rap parody of "Oh, Pretty Woman" and another rap group sought a license to record a rap derivative, there was no evidence that a potential rap market was harmed in any way by 2 Live Crew's parody, rap version. The fact that 2 Live Crew's parody sold as part of a collection of rap songs says very little about the parody's effect on a market for a rap version of the original, either of the music alone or of the music with its lyrics. The District Court essentially passed on this issue, observing that Acuff-Rose is free to record "whatever version of the original it desires,"754 F.Supp., at 1158; the Court of Appeals went the other way by erroneous presumption. Contrary to each treatment, it is impossible to deal with the fourth factor except by recognizing that a silent record on an important factor bearing on fair use disentitled the proponent of the defense, 2 Live Crew, to summary judgment. The evidentiary hole will doubtless be plugged on remand.

III

It was error for the Court of Appeals to conclude that the commercial nature of 2 Live Crew's parody of "Oh, Pretty Woman" rendered it presumptively unfair. No such evidentiary presumption is available to address either the first factor, the character and purpose of the use, or the fourth, market harm, in determining whether a transformative use, such as parody, is a fair one. The court also erred in holding that 2 Live Crew had necessarily copied excessively from the Orbison original, considering the parodic purpose of the use. We therefore reverse the judgment of the Court of Appeals and remand the case for further proceedings consistent with this opinion.

It is so ordered.

APPENDIX A TO OPINION OF THE COURT

"Oh, Pretty Woman" by Roy Orbison and William Dees

Pretty Woman, walking down the street,

Pretty Woman, the kind I like to meet,

Pretty Woman, I don't believe you, you're not the truth,

No one could look as good as you

Mercy

Pretty Woman, won't you pardon me,

Pretty Woman, I couldn't help but see,

Pretty Woman, that you look lovely as can be

Are you lonely just like me?

Pretty Woman, stop a while,

Pretty Woman, talk a while,

Pretty Woman give your smile to me

Pretty Woman, yeah, yeah, yeah

Pretty Woman, look my way,

Pretty Woman, say you'll stay with me

'Cause I need you, I'll treat you right

Come to me baby, Be mine tonight

Pretty Woman, don't walk on by,

Pretty Woman, don't make me cry,

Pretty Woman, don't walk away,

Hey, O.K.

If that's the way it must be, O.K.

I guess I'll go on home, it's late

There'll be tomorrow night, but wait!

What do I see

Is she walking back to me?

Yeah, she's walking back to me!

Oh, Pretty Woman.

APPENDIX B TO OPINION OF THE COURT

"Pretty Woman" as Recorded by 2 Live Crew

Pretty woman walkin' down the street

Pretty woman girl you look so sweet

Pretty woman you bring me down to that knee

Pretty woman you make me wanna beg please

Oh, pretty woman

Big hairy woman you need to shave that stuff

Big hairy woman you know I bet it's tough

Big hairy woman all that hair it ain't legit

'Cause you look like 'Cousin It'

Big hairy woman

Bald headed woman girl your hair won't grow

Bald headed woman you got a teeny weeny afro

Bald headed woman you know your hair could look nice

Bald headed woman first you got to roll it with rice

Bald headed woman here, let me get this hunk of biz for ya

Ya know what I'm saying you look better than rice a roni

Oh bald headed woman

Big hairy woman come on in

And don't forget your bald headed friend

Hey pretty woman let the boys

Jump in

Two timin' woman girl you know you ain't right

Two timin' woman you's out with my boy last night

Two timin' woman that takes a load off my mind

Two timin' woman now I know the baby ain't mine

Oh, two timin' woman

Oh pretty woman

Perfect 10 v. Google, Inc., 487 F.3d 701 (9th Cir. 2007)

Argued and Submitted Nov. 15, 2006.
Filed May 16, 2007.

. . .

IKUTA, Circuit Judge.

In this appeal, we consider a copyright owner's efforts to stop an Internet search engine from facilitating access to infringing images. Perfect 10, Inc. sued Google Inc., for infringing Perfect 10's copyrighted photographs of nude models, among other claims. Perfect 10 brought a similar action against Amazon.com and its subsidiary A9.com (collectively, "Amazon.com"). The district court preliminarily enjoined Google from creating and publicly displaying thumbnail versions of Perfect 10's images, *Perfect 10 v. Google, Inc.,* 416 F.Supp.2d 828 (C.D.Cal.2006), but did not enjoin Google from linking to third-party websites that display infringing full-size versions of Perfect 10's images. Nor did the district court preliminarily enjoin Amazon.com from giving users access to information provided by Google. Perfect 10 and Google both appeal the district court's order.

. . .

Background

Google's computers, along with millions of others, are connected to networks known collectively as the "Internet." "The Internet is a world-wide network of networks ... all sharing a common communications technology." *Religious Tech. Ctr. v. Netcom On-Line Commc'n Servs., Inc.,* 923 F.Supp. 1231, 1238 n. 1 (N.D.Cal.1995). Computer owners can provide information stored on their computers to other users connected to the Internet through a medium called a webpage. A webpage consists of text interspersed with instructions written in Hypertext Markup Language ("HTML") that is stored in a computer. No images are stored on a webpage; rather, the HTML instructions on the webpage provide an address for where the images are stored, whether in the webpage publisher's computer or some other computer. In general, webpages are publicly available and can be accessed by computers connected to the Internet through the use of a web browser.

Google operates a search engine, a software program that automatically accesses thousands of websites (collections of webpages) and indexes them within a database stored on Google's computers. When a Google user accesses the Google website and types in a search query, Google's software searches its database for websites responsive to that search query. Google then sends relevant information from its index of websites to the user's computer. Google's search engines can provide results in the form of text, images, or videos.

The Google search engine that provides responses in the form of images is called "Google Image Search." In response to a search query, Google Image Search identifies text in its database responsive to the query and then communicates to users the images associated with the relevant text. Google's software cannot recognize and index the images themselves. Google Image Search provides search results as a webpage of small images called "thumbnails," which are stored in Google's servers. The thumbnail images are reduced, lower-resolution versions of full-sized images stored on third-party computers.

When a user clicks on a thumbnail image, the user's browser program interprets HTML instructions on Google's webpage. These HTML instructions direct the user's browser to cause a rectangular area (a "window") to appear on the user's computer screen. The window has two separate areas of information. The browser fills the top section of the screen with information from the Google webpage, including the thumbnail image and text. The HTML instructions also give the user's browser the address of the website publisher's computer that stores the full-size version of the thumbnail.[FN2] By following the HTML instructions to access the third-party webpage, the user's browser connects to the website publisher's computer, downloads the full-size image, and makes the image appear at the bottom of the window on the user's screen. Google does not store the images that fill this lower part of the window and does not communicate the images to the user; Google simply provides HTML instructions directing a user's browser to access a third-party website. However, the top part of the window (containing the information from the Google webpage) appears to frame and comment on the bottom part of the window. Thus, the user's window appears to be filled with a single integrated presentation of the full-size image, but it is actually an image from a third-party website framed by information from Google's website. The process by which the webpage directs a user's browser to incorporate content from different computers into a single window is referred to as "in-line linking." *Kelly v. Arriba Soft Corp.*, 336 F.3d 811, 816 (9th Cir.2003). The term "framing" refers to the process by which information from one computer appears to frame and annotate the in-line linked content from another computer. *Perfect 10*, 416 F.Supp.2d at 833-34.

> FN2. The website publisher may not actually store the photographic images used on its webpages in its own computer, but may provide HTML instructions directing the user's browser to some further computer that stores the image. Because this distinction does not affect our analysis, for convenience, we will assume that the website publisher stores all images used on its webpages in the website publisher's own computer.

Google also stores webpage content in its cache.[FN3] For each cached webpage, Google's cache contains the text of the webpage as it appeared at the time Google indexed the page, but does not store images from the webpage. *Id.* at 833. Google may provide a link to a cached webpage in response to a user's search query. However, Google's cache version of the webpage is not automatically updated when the webpage is revised by its owner. So if the webpage owner updates its webpage to remove the HTML instructions for finding an infringing image, a browser communicating directly with the webpage would not be able to access that image. However, Google's cache copy of the webpage would still have the old HTML instructions for the infringing image. Unless the owner of the computer changed the HTML address of the infringing image, or otherwise rendered the image unavailable, a browser accessing Google's cache copy of the website could still access the image where it is stored on the website publisher's computer. In other words, Google's cache copy could provide a user's browser with valid directions to an infringing image even though the updated webpage no longer includes that infringing image.

> FN3. Generally, a "cache" is "a computer memory with very short access time used for storage of frequently or recently used instructions or data." *United States v. Ziegler,* 474 F.3d 1184, 1186 n. 3 (9th Cir.2007) (quoting MERRIAM-WEBSTER'S COLLEGIATE DICTIONARY 171 (11th ed.2003)). There are two types of caches at issue in this case. A user's personal computer has an internal cache that saves copies of webpages and images that the user has recently viewed so that the user can more rapidly revisit these webpages and images. Google's computers also have a cache which serves a variety of purposes. Among other things, Google's cache saves copies of a large number of webpages so that Google's search engine can efficiently organize and index these webpages.

In addition to its search engine operations, Google generates revenue through a business program called "AdSense." Under this program, the owner of a website can register with Google to become an AdSense "partner." The website owner then places HTML instructions on its webpages that signal Google's server to place advertising on the webpages that is relevant to the webpages' content. Google's computer program selects the advertising automatically by means of an algorithm. AdSense participants agree to share the revenues that flow from such advertising with Google.

Google also generated revenues through an agreement with Amazon.com that allowed Amazon.com to in-line link to Google's search results. Amazon.com gave its users the impression that Amazon.com was providing search results, but Google communicated the search results directly to Amazon.com's users. Amazon.com routed users' search queries to Google and automatically transmitted Google's responses (i.e., HTML instructions for linking to Google's search results) back to its users.

Perfect 10 markets and sells copyrighted images of nude models. Among other enterprises, it operates a subscription website on the Internet. Subscribers pay a monthly fee to view Perfect 10 images in a "members' area" of the site. Subscribers must use a password to log into the members' area. Google does not include these password-protected images from the members' area in Google's index or database. Perfect 10 has also licensed Fonestarz Media Limited to sell and distribute Perfect 10's reduced-size copyrighted images for download and use on cell phones.

Some website publishers republish Perfect 10's images on the Internet without authorization. Once this occurs, Google's search engine may automatically index the webpages containing these images and provide thumbnail versions of images in response to user inquiries. When a user clicks on the thumbnail image returned by Google's search engine, the user's browser accesses the third-party webpage and in-line links to the full-sized infringing image stored on the website publisher's computer. This image appears, in its original context, on the lower portion of the window on the user's computer screen framed by information from Google's webpage.

. . .

C. Fair Use Defense

Although Perfect 10 has succeeded in showing it would prevail in its prima facie case that Google's thumbnail images infringe Perfect 10's display rights, Perfect 10 must still show a likelihood that it will prevail against Google's affirmative defense. Google contends that its use of thumbnails is a fair use of the images and therefore does not constitute an infringement of Perfect 10's copyright. *See* 17 U.S.C. § 107.

The fair use defense permits the use of copyrighted works without the copyright owner's consent under certain situations. The defense encourages and allows the development of new ideas that build on earlier ones, thus providing a necessary counterbalance to the copyright law's goal of protecting creators' work product. "From the infancy of copyright protection, some opportunity for fair use of copyrighted materials has been thought necessary to fulfill copyright's very purpose ...." *Campbell,* 510 U.S. at 575, 114 S.Ct. 1164. "The fair use doctrine thus 'permits [and requires] courts to avoid rigid application of the copyright statute when, on occasion, it would stifle the very creativity which that law is designed to foster.' " *Id.* at 577, 114 S.Ct. 1164 (quoting *Stewart v. Abend,* 495 U.S. 207, 236, 110 S.Ct. 1750, 109 L.Ed.2d 184 (1990)) (alteration in original).

Congress codified the common law of fair use in 17 U.S.C. § 107, which provides:

Notwithstanding the provisions of sections 106 and 106A, the fair use of a copyrighted work, including such use by reproduction in copies or phonorecords or by any other means specified by that section, for purposes such as criticism, comment, news reporting, teaching (including multiple copies for classroom use), scholarship, or research, is not an infringement of copyright. In determining whether the use made of a work in any particular case is a fair use the factors to be considered shall include-

  (1) the purpose and character of the use, including whether such use is of a commercial nature or is for nonprofit educational purposes;

  (2) the nature of the copyrighted work;

  (3) the amount and substantiality of the portion used in relation to the copyrighted work as a whole; and

  (4) the effect of the use upon the potential market for or value of the copyrighted work.

The fact that a work is unpublished shall not itself bar a finding of fair use if such finding is made upon consideration of all the above factors.

17 U.S.C. § 107.

We must be flexible in applying a fair use analysis; it "is not to be simplified with bright-line rules, for the statute, like the doctrine it recognizes, calls for case-by-case analysis.... Nor may the four statutory factors be treated in isolation, one from another. All are to be explored, and the results weighed together, in light of the purposes of copyright." *Campbell,* 510 U.S. at 577-78, 114 S.Ct. 1164; *see also Kelly,* 336 F.3d at 817-18. The purpose of copyright law is "[t]o promote the Progress of Science and useful Arts,"U.S. CONST. art. I, § 8, cl. 8, and to serve "'the welfare of the public.'" Sony *Corp. of Am. v. Universal City Studios, Inc.,* 464 U.S. 417, 429 n. 10, 104 S.Ct. 774, 78 L.Ed.2d 574 (quoting H.R.Rep. No. 2222, 60th Cong., 2d Sess. 7 (1909)).

In applying the fair use analysis in this case, we are guided by *Kelly v. Arriba Soft Corp.,* which considered substantially the same use of copyrighted photographic images as is at issue here. *See*336 F.3d 811. In *Kelly,* a photographer brought a direct infringement claim against Arriba, the operator of an Internet search engine. The search engine provided thumbnail versions of the photographer's images in response to search queries. *Id.* at 815-16. We held that Arriba's use of thumbnail images was a fair use primarily based on the transformative nature of a search engine and its benefit to the public. *Id.* at 818-22. We also concluded that Arriba's use of the thumbnail images did not harm the photographer's market for his image. *Id.* at 821-22.

In this case, the district court determined that Google's use of thumbnails was not a fair use and distinguished *Kelly. Perfect 10,* 416 F.Supp.2d at 845-51. We consider these distinctions in the context of the four-factor fair use analysis, remaining mindful that Perfect 10 has the burden of proving that it will successfully challenge any evidence Google presents to support its affirmative defense.

Purpose and character of the use. The first factor, 17 U.S.C. § 107(1), requires a court to consider "the purpose and character of the use, including whether such use is of a commercial nature or is for nonprofit educational purposes." The central purpose of this inquiry is to determine whether and to what extent the new work is "transformative." *Campbell,* 510 U.S. at 579, 114 S.Ct. 1164. A work is "transformative" when the new work does not "merely supersede the objects of the original creation" but rather "adds something new, with a further purpose or different character, altering the first with new expression, meaning, or message." *Id.* (internal quotation and alteration omitted). Conversely, if the new work "supersede[s] the use of the original," the use is likely not a fair use. *Harper & Row Publishers, Inc. v. Nation Enters.,* 471 U.S. 539, 550-51, 105 S.Ct. 2218, 85 L.Ed.2d 588 (1985) (internal quotation omitted) (publishing the "heart" of an unpublished work and thus supplanting the copyright holder's first publication right was not a fair use); *see also Wall Data Inc. v. L.A. County Sheriff's Dep't,* 447 F.3d 769, 778-82 (9th Cir.2006) (using a copy to save the cost of buying additional copies of a computer program was not a fair use).[FN8]

FN8. We reject at the outset Perfect 10's argument that providing access to infringing websites cannot be deemed transformative and is inherently not fair use. Perfect 10 relies on *Video Pipeline, Inc. v. Buena Vista Home Entm't, Inc.,* 342 F.3d 191 (3d Cir.2003), and *Atari Games,* 975 F.2d at 843. But these cases, in essence, simply apply the general rule that a party claiming fair use must act in a manner generally compatible with principles of good faith and fair dealing. *See Harper & Row,* 471 U.S. at 562-63, 105 S.Ct. 2218. For this reason, a company whose business is based on providing scenes from copyrighted movies without authorization could not claim that it provided the same public benefit as the search engine in *Kelly. See Video Pipeline,* 342 F.3d at 198-200. Similarly, a company whose overriding desire to replicate a competitor's computer game led it to obtain a copy of the competitor's source code from the Copyright Office under false pretenses could not claim fair use with respect to its purloined copy. *Atari Games,* 975 F.2d at 843.

Unlike the alleged infringers in *Video Pipeline* and *Atari Games,* who intentionally misappropriated the copyright owners' works for the purpose of commercial exploitation, Google is operating a comprehensive search engine that only incidentally indexes infringing websites. This incidental impact does not amount to an abuse of the good faith and fair dealing underpinnings of the fair use doctrine. Accordingly, we conclude that Google's inclusion of thumbnail images derived from infringing websites in its Internet-wide search engine activities does not preclude Google from raising a fair use defense.

As noted in *Campbell,* a "transformative work" is one that alters the original work "with new expression, meaning, or message." *Campbell,* 510 U.S. at 579, 114 S.Ct. 1164. "A use is considered transformative only where a defendant changes a plaintiff's copyrighted work or uses the plaintiff's copyrighted work in a different context such that the plaintiff's work is transformed into a new creation." *Wall Data,* 447 F.3d at 778.

Google's use of thumbnails is highly transformative. In *Kelly,* we concluded that Arriba's use of thumbnails was transformative because "Arriba's use of the images serve[d] a different function than Kelly's use-improving access to information on the [I]nternet versus artistic expression." *Kelly,* 336 F.3d at 819. Although an image may have been created originally to serve an entertainment, aesthetic, or informative function, a search engine transforms the image into a pointer directing a user to a source of information. Just as a "parody has an obvious claim to transformative value" because "it can provide social benefit, by shedding light on an earlier work, and, in the process, creating a new one,"*Campbell,* 510 U.S. at 579, 114 S.Ct. 1164, a search engine provides social benefit by incorporating an original work into a new work, namely, an electronic reference tool. Indeed, a search engine may be more transformative than a parody because a search engine provides an entirely new use for the original work, while a parody typically has the same entertainment purpose as the original work. *See, e.g., id.* at 594-96, 114 S.Ct. 1164 (holding that 2 Live Crew's parody of "Oh, Pretty Woman" using the words "hairy woman" or "bald headed woman" was a transformative work, and thus constituted a fair use); *Mattel, Inc. v. Walking Mountain Prods.,* 353 F.3d 792, 796-98, 800-06(concluding that photos parodying Barbie by depicting "nude Barbie dolls juxtaposed with vintage kitchen appliances" was a fair use). In other words, a search engine puts images "in a different context" so that they are "transformed into a new creation." *Wall Data,* 447 F.3d at 778.

The fact that Google incorporates the entire Perfect 10 image into the search engine results does not diminish the transformative nature of Google's use. As the district court correctly noted, *Perfect 10,* 416 F.Supp.2d at 848-49, we determined in *Kelly* that even making an exact copy of a work may be transformative so long as the copy serves a different function than the original work, *Kelly,* 336 F.3d at 818-19. For example, the First Circuit has held that the republication of photos taken for a modeling portfolio in a newspaper was transformative because the photos served to inform, as well as entertain. *See Nunez v. Caribbean Int'l News Corp.,* 235 F.3d 18, 22-23 (1st Cir.2000). In contrast, duplicating a church's religious book for use by a different church was not transformative. *See Worldwide Church of God v. Phila. Church of God, Inc.,* 227 F.3d 1110, 1117 (9th Cir.2000). Nor was a broadcaster's simple retransmission of a radio broadcast over telephone lines transformative, where the original radio shows were given no "new expression, meaning, or message." *Infinity Broad. Corp. v. Kirkwood,* 150 F.3d 104, 108 (2d Cir.1998). Here, Google uses Perfect 10's images in a new context to serve a different purpose.

The district court nevertheless determined that Google's use of thumbnail images was less transformative than Arriba's use of thumbnails in *Kelly* because Google's use of thumbnails superseded Perfect 10's right to sell its reduced-size images for use on cell phones. *See Perfect 10,* 416 F.Supp.2d at 849. The district court stated that "mobile users can download and save the thumbnails displayed by Google Image Search onto their phones," and concluded "to the extent that users may choose to download free images to their phone rather than purchase [Perfect 10's] reduced-size images, Google's use supersedes [Perfect 10's]." *Id.*

Additionally, the district court determined that the commercial nature of Google's use weighed against its transformative nature. *Id.* Although *Kelly* held that the commercial use of the photographer's images by Arriba's search engine was less exploitative than typical commercial use, and thus weighed only slightly against a finding of fair use, *Kelly,* 336 F.3d at 818-20, the district court here distinguished *Kelly* on the ground that some website owners in the AdSense program had infringing Perfect 10 images on their websites, *Perfect 10,* 416 F.Supp.2d at 846-47. The district court held that because Google's thumbnails "lead users to sites that directly benefit Google's bottom line," the AdSense program increased the commercial nature of Google's use of Perfect 10's images. *Id.* at 847.

In conducting our case-specific analysis of fair use in light of the purposes of copyright, *Campbell,* 510 U.S. at 581, 114 S.Ct. 1164, we must weigh Google's superseding and commercial uses of thumbnail images against Google's significant transformative use, as well as the extent to which Google's search engine promotes the purposes of copyright and serves the interests of the public. Although the district court acknowledged the "truism that search engines such as Google Image Search provide great value to the public,"*Perfect 10,*

416 F.Supp.2d at 848-49, the district court did not expressly consider whether this value outweighed the significance of Google's superseding use or the commercial nature of Google's use. *Id.* at 849. The Supreme Court, however, has directed us to be mindful of the extent to which a use promotes the purposes of copyright and serves the interests of the public. *See Campbell,* 510 U.S. at 579, 114 S.Ct. 1164; *Harper & Row,* 471 U.S. at 556-57, 105 S.Ct. 2218; *Sony,* 464 U.S. at 431-32, 104 S.Ct. 774.

We note that the superseding use in this case is not significant at present: the district court did not find that any down loads for mobile phone use had taken place. *See Perfect 10,* 416 F.Supp.2d at 849. Moreover, while Google's use of thumbnails to direct users to AdSense partners containing infringing content adds a commercial dimension that did not exist in *Kelly,* the district court did not determine that this commercial element was significant. *See id.* at 848-49. The district court stated that Google's AdSense programs as a whole contributed "$630 million, or 46% of total revenues" to Google's bottom line, but noted that this figure did not "break down the much smaller amount attributable to websites that contain infringing content." *Id.* at 847 & n. 12 (internal quotation omitted).

We conclude that the significantly transformative nature of Google's search engine, particularly in light of its public benefit, outweighs Google's superseding and commercial uses of the thumbnails in this case. In reaching this conclusion, we note the importance of analyzing fair use flexibly in light of new circumstances. *Sony,* 464 U.S. at 431-32, 104 S.Ct. 774; *id.* at 448 n. 31, 104 S.Ct. 774 ("'[Section 107] endorses the purpose and general scope of the judicial doctrine of fair use, but there is no disposition to freeze the doctrine in the statute, especially during a period of rapid technological change.'") (quoting H.R.Rep. No. 94-1476, p. 65-66 (1976), U.S.Code Cong. & Admin. News 1976, p. 5659, at pp. 5678-80). We are also mindful of the Supreme Court's direction that "the more transformative the new work, the less will be the significance of other factors, like commercialism, that may weigh against a finding of fair use." *Campbell,* 510 U.S. at 579, 114 S.Ct. 1164.

Accordingly, we disagree with the district court's conclusion that because Google's use of the thumbnails could supersede Perfect 10's cell phone download use and because the use was more commercial than Arriba's, this fair use factor weighed "slightly" in favor of Perfect 10. *Perfect 10,* 416 F.Supp.2d at 849. Instead, we conclude that the transformative nature of Google's use is more significant than any incidental superseding use or the minor commercial aspects of Google's search engine and website. Therefore, the district court erred in determining this factor weighed in favor of Perfect 10.

The nature of the copyrighted work. With respect to the second factor, "the nature of the copyrighted work,"17 U.S.C. § 107(2), our decision in *Kelly* is directly on point. There we held that the photographer's images were "creative in nature" and thus "closer to the core of intended copyright protection than are more fact-based works." *Kelly,* 336 F.3d at 820 (internal quotation omitted). However, because the photos appeared on the Internet before Arriba used thumbnail versions in its search engine results, this factor weighed only slightly in favor of the photographer. *Id.*

Here, the district court found that Perfect 10's images were creative but also previously published. *Perfect 10,* 416 F.Supp.2d at 850. The right of first publication is "the author's right to control the first public appearance of his expression." *Harper & Row,* 471 U.S. at 564, 105 S.Ct. 2218. Because this right encompasses "the choices of when, where, and in what form first to publish a work,"*id.,* an author exercises and exhausts this one-time right by publishing the work in any medium. *See, e.g., Batjac Prods. Inc. v. GoodTimes Home Video Corp.,* 160 F.3d 1223, 1235 (9th Cir.1998) (noting, in the context of the common law right of first publication, that such a right "does not entail multiple first publication rights in every available medium"). Once Perfect 10 has exploited this commercially valuable right of first publication by putting its images on the Internet for paid subscribers, Perfect 10 is no longer entitled to the enhanced protection available for an unpublished work. Accordingly the district court did not err in holding that this factor weighed only slightly in favor of Perfect 10.[FN9] *See Perfect 10,* 416 F.Supp.2d at 849-50.

> FN9. Google contends that Perfect 10's photographic images are less creative and less deserving of protection than the images of the American West in *Kelly* because Perfect 10 boasts of its un-retouched photos showing the natural beauty of its models. Having reviewed the record, we conclude that the district court's finding that Perfect 10's photographs "consistently reflect professional, skillful, and sometimes tasteful artistry" is not clearly erroneous. *Perfect 10,* 416 F.Supp.2d at 849 n. 15. We agree with the district court that there is no basis for concluding that photos of the American West are more deserving of protection than photos of nude models. *See id.*

The amount and substantiality of the portion used. "The third factor asks whether the amount and substantiality of the portion used in relation to the copyrighted work as a whole ... are reasonable in relation to the purpose of the copying." *Campbell,* 510 U.S. at 586, 114 S.Ct. 1164(internal quotation omitted); *see also*17 U.S.C. § 107(3). In *Kelly,* we held Arriba's use of the entire photographic image was reasonable in light of the purpose of a search engine. *Kelly,* 336 F.3d at 821. Specifically, we noted, "[i]t was necessary for Arriba to copy the entire image to allow users to recognize the image and decide whether to pursue more information about the image or the originating [website]. If Arriba only copied part of the image, it would be more difficult to identify it, thereby reducing the usefulness of the visual search engine." *Id.* Accordingly, we concluded that this factor did not weigh in favor of either party. *Id.* Because the same analysis applies to Google's use of Perfect 10's image, the district court did not err in finding that this factor favored neither party.

Effect of use on the market. The fourth factor is "the effect of the use upon the potential market for or value of the copyrighted work." 17 U.S.C. § 107(4). In *Kelly,* we concluded that Arriba's use of the thumbnail images did not harm the market for the photographer's full-size images. *See Kelly,* 336 F.3d at 821-22. We reasoned that because thumbnails were not a substitute for the full-sized images, they did not harm the photographer's ability to sell or license his full-sized images. *Id.* The district court here followed *Kelly*'s reasoning, holding that Google's use of thumbnails did not hurt Perfect 10's market for full-size images. *See Perfect 10,* 416 F.Supp.2d at 850-51.

Perfect 10 argues that the district court erred because the likelihood of market harm may be presumed if the intended use of an image is for commercial gain. However, this presumption does not arise when a work is transformative because "market substitution is at least less certain, and market harm may not be so readily inferred." *Campbell,* 510 U.S. at 591, 114 S.Ct. 1164. As previously discussed, Google's use of thumbnails for search engine purposes is highly transformative. Because market harm cannot be presumed, and because Perfect 10 has not introduced evidence that Google's thumbnails would harm Perfect 10's existing or potential market for full-size images, we reject this argument.

Perfect 10 also has a market for reduced-size images, an issue not considered in *Kelly.* The district court held that "Google's use of thumbnails likely does harm the potential market for the downloading of [Perfect 10's] reduced-size images onto cell phones." *Perfect 10,* 416 F.Supp.2d at 851 (emphasis omitted). The district court reasoned that persons who can obtain Perfect 10 images free of charge from Google are less likely to pay for a download, and the availability of Google's thumbnail images would harm Perfect 10's market for cell phone downloads. *Id.* As we discussed above, the district court did not make a finding that Google users have downloaded thumbnail images for cell phone use. This potential harm to Perfect 10's market remains hypothetical. We conclude that this factor favors neither party.

Having undertaken a case-specific analysis of all four factors, we now weigh these factors together "in light of the purposes of copyright." *Campbell,* 510 U.S. at 578, 114 S.Ct. 1164; *see also Kelly,* 336 F.3d at 818("We must balance[the section 107] factors in light of the objectives of copyright law, rather than view them as definitive or determinative tests."). We note that Perfect 10 has the burden of proving that it would defeat Google's affirmative fair use defense, *see supra* Section II. In this case, Google has put Perfect 10's thumbnail images (along with millions of other thumbnail images) to a use fundamentally different than the use intended by Perfect 10. In doing so, Google has provided a significant benefit to the public. Weighing this significant transformative use against the unproven use of Google's thumbnails for cell phone downloads, and considering the other fair use factors, all in light of the purpose of copyright, we conclude that Google's use of Perfect 10's thumbnails is a fair use. Because the district court here "found facts sufficient to evaluate each of the statutory factors ... [we] need not remand for further fact-finding." *Harper & Row,* 471 U.S. at 560, 105 S.Ct. 2218(internal quotation omitted). We conclude that Perfect 10 is unlikely to be able to overcome Google's fair use defense and, accordingly, we vacate the preliminary injunction regarding Google's use of thumbnail images.

3. Private Copying

In 1997 the *Copyright Act* was amended to add a new part (Part VIII) dealing with private copying. Prior to the amendments, private copying of musical works for private enjoyment such as to listen to music in a car or while jogging was not fair dealing within the meaning of the Act. Unless copied for the purpose of research, private study, criticism, review or news reporting, copying of a musical work was not considered a fair dealing. The amendments to the Act were enacted to legalize private copying; to provide a system for the payment of royalties to those with copyrights to be imposed by way of levies on imports from manufacturers of blank tapes when sold by them; and to delegate to the Copyright Board the power to certify tariffs setting the levies on the sale of the blank tapes by importers and manufacturers. Its purpose is mainly an economic one – that is, to fairly compensate artists and the other creative people for their work by establishing fair and equitable levies.[1]

Section 80(1) of the Act exempts from infringement the copying of a musical work embodied in a sound recording or a sound recording of a musical work onto an "audio recording medium" such as audiocassettes or recordable CDs for the private use of the person that makes the copy. Section 80(2)(c) of the Act provides that the private copying defence does not apply if the act of copying is done for the purpose of communicating the work to the public by telecommunications or to distribute same (whether or not for purposes of trade).

The private copyright exemption in section 80 applies only when a copy is made for the private use for the person making it. This expressly excludes selling, renting out, exposing for trade or rental, distributing, communicating to public and telecommunication, or performing in public the copy made.

**Canadian Private Copying Collective v. Canadian Storage Media Alliance
(2004), 36 C.P.R. 289 (C.A.)**

Evans J.A., Linden J.A., Noël J.A.

**Heard: October 12-13, 2004
Judgment: December 14, 2004
Docket: A-9-04, A-10-04, A-11-04**

. . .

Noël J.A.:

1 These are three applications for judicial review of a decision of the Copyright Board of Canada (Board) which established the private copying levies to be

---

[1]   *AVS Technologies Inc. v. Canadian Mechanical Reproduction Rights Agency*, [2000] F.C.J. No. 960 (Fed. C.A.)

collected by the Canadian Private Copying Collective (CPCC) for the years 2003 and 2004. The applications were joined and heard together by order of the Court.

Background

2 The Board is an administrative tribunal created by the Copyright Act, R.S.C. 1985, c. C-42, (the Act). Among other things, the Board is responsible for the adoption of levies and their related terms and conditions in respect of the private copying of recorded musical works, performances and sound recordings (recorded music) on blank audio recording media (blank media or medium) that are sold or otherwise disposed of in Canada.

3 Part VIII of the Act legalizes copying recorded music for private use and thus provides a statutory exception to the exclusive reproduction rights of eligible authors, performers and makers of recorded music (rightsholders). At the same time, it entitles rightsholders to compensation for their loss of exclusivity by imposing a levy on media used to record music. For ease of reference, Part VIII is reproduced in full as Appendix 1 to these reasons.

4 Since the coming into force of Part VIII in March of 1998, the Board has certified three private copying tariffs, and one interim tariff. In 1999, the Board issued its first decision regarding the tariff for private copying levies (Private Copying I) and, in 2001, issued its second decision (Private Copying II). In 2002, the Board, on application, reconsidered its second decision on the ground that a material change had occurred in the rapidly evolving market for blank media, and amended the tariff accordingly. The present applications are directed against the latest decision dealing with private copying which was rendered on December 12, 2003 (Private Copying III).

5 CPCC is the "collecting body" designated by the Board under the Act to collect and distribute the levies to rightsholders. Manufacturers and importers of blank media sold in Canada must pay the levy to the CPCC. The collecting body must distribute the levy to the collective societies that represent the above-mentioned categories of rightsholders in the proportion determined by the Board.

6 Although manufacturers and importers are charged with the payment of the levy under the Act, they do not necessarily assume its cost. In the normal course, manufacturers and importers will include the amount of the levy in their sale price to purchasers, with the result that consumers usually bear the cost of the levy.

7 The Act authorizes the CPCC to file a proposed tariff with the Board for the benefit of rightsholders. After considering the proposed tariff and any objection to it, the Board must certify a tariff it determines to be fair and equitable.

8 In its proposed tariff for 2003-2004, the CPCC asked that levies be imposed for the first time on several new types of recording media used to copy music such as recordable or rewritable "digital versatile disks" (DVDs), removable electronic memory cards, and non-removable memory permanently embedded in "digital audio recorders", a term used by the Board to identify MP3 players and similar devices.

. . .

Application A-10-04–Digital Audio Recorder (MP3 Player) Levy and Rate Setting

133 The third judicial review application raises two issues. The first is whether a permanently embedded or non-removable memory, incorporated into a digital audio recorder (MP3 player), retains its identity as an "audio recording medium" and can be levied as such under Part VIII.

134 The second is whether the Board could set a levy on this embedded memory beyond that sought by the CPCC and, if so, whether the levy in question was set within the bounds of fairness. First Issue

135 The term "audio recording medium" (medium) is defined in section 79:

> "audio recording medium" means a recording medium, regardless of its material form, onto which a sound recording may be reproduced and that is of a kind ordinarily used by individual consumers for that purpose, excluding any prescribed kind of recording medium.« _support audio_ » Tout support audio habituellement utilisé par les consommateurs pour reproduire des enregistrements sonores, à l'exception toutefois de ceux exclus par règlement.

136 The levy is imposed on a "blank audio recording medium" (previously identified as "blank media" or "blank medium") which is defined, in its relevant part, as (section 79):

> (a) an audio recording medium onto which no sounds have ever been fixed, and
> (b) any other prescribed audio recording medium.

> Tout support audio sur lequel aucun son n'a encore été fixé et tout autre support audio précisé par règlement.

The Decision of the Board

137 The Board denied CPCC's request to establish a levy on recordable or rewritable DVDs, removable memory cards and removable micro hard drives. It found that these were not ordinarily used by individuals for the purpose of copying music (Private Copying III, pp. 42 and 43).

138 However, it held that digital audio recorders (MP3 players) were so used and that the memory embedded therein qualified as a medium within the meaning of the definition. The fact that this memory was incorporated into a device did not cause it to lose its identity so as to take it outside the statutory definition.

139 The Board's exact reasoning for holding that memory permanently embedded in a digital audio recorder was leviable rests on the above quoted definition of an "audio recording medium". The Board said (Private Copying III, p. 33):

> There are two aspects of [the definition] that are relevant to the Board in these proceedings. The first relates to the proper interpretation of the phrase "ordinarily used by individual consumers for that purpose". The second relates to the relevance of a medium's physical attributes ("a recording medium, regardless of its material form"), particularly the significance of its incorporation into a device.

140 Addressing the first aspect, the Board held that the intrinsic physical attributes of a digital audio recorder, including its size, convenience and compatibility, supported the conclusion that it was "ordinarily used by individual consumers" for copying music (Private Copying III, p. 45). It follows that the memory embedded therein was also so used. This conclusion so far as it goes is not contested.

141 The reasoning with respect to the second aspect of the definition is a function of substance over form (Private Copying III, pp. 36 and 38):

> A second aspect of the definition of an "audio recording medium" relates to the form of the medium. This issue is important because the Board was asked to establish a levy on memory in devices, although not on devices themselves. Hence, the question at this stage is whether or not the incorporation of a product into a device can affect its status as an audio recording medium.
>
> [...]
>
> As regards the physical characteristics of the product itself, the definition of an "audio recording medium" could hardly have been drafted more broadly. Specifically, the English version of the text contains the clause, "regardless of its material form". To the Board, the plain and ordinary meaning of this phrase rules out the possibility that the levy was intended to apply only to "removable" media, let alone only to audiocassettes.
>
> This language also demonstrates that it is not determinative whether the medium is affixed, incorporated or otherwise integrated in a device. Its breadth supports the conclusion that liability to pay a levy cannot be dependant [sic] upon physical characteristics alone. A medium that is incorporated into a device remains a medium.

Alleged Errors in Decision Under Review

142 The four members of the CSMA who appear as applicants in this judicial review application argue that the Board erred in law in holding that a permanently embedded memory in a digital audio recorder (MP3 player) is a medium and, as such, leviable under Part VIII.

143 The applicants argue that, when incorporated into a digital audio recorder, the embedded memory becomes integrated in, and inseparable from, this device, and thus loses its separate identity. Hence, it cannot be said that a manufacturer or importer who sells a digital audio recorder also sells the embedded memory.

144 In the alternative, the applicants submit that the Board has created an exemption from the scope of Part VIII of the Act, by only imposing a levy on memory when it is embedded in digital audio recorders, and not when the identical memory is embedded in other electronic devices (such as heart-rate monitors, digital cameras, personal digital assistants or telephones).

Analysis

145 It is not necessary to undertake a lengthy analysis to ascertain the applicable standard of review as it turns on the definitions set out in section 79 and

this Court has already held that the Board's interpretation of these definitions must be assessed against a standard of correctness.

146 In *Society of Composers, Authors & Music Publishers of Canada v. Canadian Assn. of Internet Providers* , supra, this Court said:

> [98] The heart of the Board's expertise is in the administration of those provisions of the Copyright Act pertaining to the setting and allocation of royalties. While necessary for enabling the Board to perform that function, its decisions defining Activities that infringe copyright have implications that "stray from the core expertise of the tribunal": Pushpanathan, supra, at paragraph 38.
>
> [...]
>
> [104] In my opinion, the scale is tipped decisively in favour of correctness review by the fact that the Copyright Board's interpretation of provisions of the Copyright Act in dispute here is not within its exclusive domain, but may arise in court proceedings other than judicial review applications. This is both because the Board's expertise on these issues cannot be said to be greater than the Court's and because, in the context of the administration of this statute, judicial deference is unlikely to serve the interests of consistency, adjudicative efficiency and economy.
>
> [105] Accordingly, in my respectful opinion, the Court was wrong in AVS, supra, to prescribe patent unreasonableness as the standard of review applicable to the Board's interpretation of those provisions [specifically, section 79] of the Copyright Act that are not within the Board's exclusive domain. Taken as a whole the scheme of the Copyright Act indicates that on an application for judicial review, the Court should apply a standard of correctness to the Board's interpretation of those provisions of the Copyright Act that could also be the subject of infringement proceedings in the courts.
>
> [emphasis added]

147 Although the CPCC maintains that the meaning of "audio recording medium" as defined in section 79 has no infringement implications, this is not so. If, indeed, digital audio recorders (or the memories embedded therein) fall outside the scope of the definition, copyright infringement could result from the use of such devices to private copy. Consistent with the proposition set forth in the above passage, the decision of the Board must be tested against the standard of correctness.

148 Applying this standard, I do not believe that it was open to the Board to establish a levy on memory embedded in digital audio recorders. In my respectful view, Part VIII of the Act and the definition of "audio recording medium" gave the Board no such authority.

149 The Board established the levy on the basis that it could, in effect, look through the device being sold and reach the permanently embedded memory found therein. The Board twice noted that the levy sought by the CPCC, and approved by it was on "memory in devices" but not on "devices" (Private Copying III, pp. 36 and 54).

150 The conceptual difficulty inherent in the exercise on which the Board embarked in certifying a levy on the memory embedded in a device, but not on the device itself, is illustrated by the tariff which it certified (Private Copying III, p. 63):

> For non-removable memory permanently embedded in a digital audio recorder, the Board adopts rates of $2 for each recorder that can record no more than 1 GB of data, 15$ for each recorder that can record more than 1 GB and no more than 10 GBs of data, and $25 for each recorder that can record more than 10 GBs of data.

[emphasis added]

151 Although the Board purported to establish a levy on the embedded memory, it acknowledged that this memory could not, looked at on its own, allow for the establishment of the levy; the device into which the memory was embedded had to be considered (Private Copying III, p. 44):

> Hard discs in personal computers are technically indistinguishable from those in some digital audio recorders. It appears therefore, inappropriate to generalize about the uses of all embedded memory. However, the distinction, in the Board's view, is that where a medium is permanently incorporated into a certain type of device, it becomes possible to categorize that medium and evaluate its use as a unique "kind" of "audio recording medium", based on the intrinsic characteristics of the device into which the medium has been incorporated.

[emphasis added]

Hence according to the Board, permanent memory embedded in an MP3 player comes within the definition, whereas the identical memory embedded into other devices does not (Private Copying III, p. 45).

152 It can be seen from the Board's own reasoning and from the tariff which it certified that it is the device that is the defining element of the levy and not the memory incorporated therein. The Board cannot establish a levy and determine the applicable rates by reference to the device and yet assert that the levy is being applied on something else.

153 One can readily understand why the Board wanted to go as far as it could to bring MP3 players within the ambit of Part VIII. The evidence establishes that these recorders allow for extensive private copying by individuals. Their use can potentially inflict on rightsholders harm beyond any "blank audio recording medium" as this phrase has been understood to date. However, as desirable as bringing such devices within the ambit of part VIII might seem, the authority for doing so still has to be found in the Act.

154 The Board found this authority in the definition of "audio recording medium". It focussed on the phrase "regardless of its material form" to hold that Parliament intended that a levy be established on a medium, regardless of its incorporation into a device. In the words of the Board, "A medium that is incorporated into a device remains a medium" (Private Copying III, p. 38).

155 There are a number of problems with the Board's analysis. First, according to the Board's own reasoning, a memory does not become an "audio recording

medium" unless and until it is incorporated into the appropriate device (Private Copying III, pp. 44 and 46). It is therefore difficult to see how such a memory can be said to remain a medium when embedded into a device.

156 Second, upon being incorporated into a device, a memory undergoes no change in form. It is therefore difficult to see how the Board can rely on the phrase "regardless of its material form" to justify its conclusion. Furthermore, to rely on this phrase, the Board first had to identify an "audio recording medium". According to its own reasons, a memory is not an "audio recording medium" unless and until embedded into a digital audio recorder.

157 It is apparent that the phrase on which the Board relied to "see through" a digital audio recorder and reach the memory embedded therein does not support its conclusion when regard is had to its own findings.

158 The Board acknowledges that, when it enacted Part VIII, Parliament could not have envisioned recent technological developments (Private Copying III, p. 38). Indeed, the legislative history of Bill C-32, which amended the Act to include Part VIII, shows that at the time, Parliament was looking at blank audio tapes as the cause of the harm to rightsholders and had been made aware of proposals in other countries (including the U.S.) to extend the levy to the hardware which recorded and played these blank audio tapes. Nevertheless, Parliament chose to limit the levy to blank medium (House of Commons, 35th Parl., 2nd Session, Standing Committee on Canadian Heritage, Meeting No. 24, October 9, 1996 at 2150, Application Record, Vol. III, Tab 5-B-13, pp. 651-662; House of Commons, 35th Parl., 2nd Session, Standing Committee on Canadian Heritage, see also Meeting No. 36, November 6, 1996 at 2035, where the Société Professionelle des Auteurs et des Compositeurs du Québec submitted as a flaw that "Bill C-32 makes no provision for the payment of levies by manufacturers of recorders," Application Record, Vol. III, Tab 5-B-15, p. 682; House of Commons, 35th Parl., 2nd Session, Standing Committee on Canadian Heritage, Meeting No. 27, October 22, 1996 at 1925 (B. Andriessen), Application Record, Vol. III, Tab 5-B-14, pp. 663-674; House of Commons, 35th Parl., 2nd Session, Second Report of the Standing Committee on Canadian Heritage, December 1996, Application Record, Vol. III, Tab 5-B-16, pp. 698- 717).

159 This shows that Parliament's definition of "audio recording medium" stands in contra-distinction with a recorder or similar devices as these were known to exist at the time and whose function it is to record and play blank audio tapes. No one has ever pretended that tape recorders came within the ambit of the definition.

160 A digital audio recorder is not a medium; the CPCC recognized so much when it asked that the levy be applied on the memory found therein but not on the recorder itself. The Board erred when it held that it could certify a levy on the memory integrated into a digital audio recorder.

161 Subsection 82(1) of the Act imposes a levy on manufacturers and importers of blank media. By the words of paragraph (a) thereof, the liability for the

payment of the levy can only arise "on selling or otherwise disposing of those blank audio recording media".

162 The Board therefore had to look at what was being sold or disposed of by the importers (it is common ground that there are no manufacturers of digital audio recorders in Canada), and determine whether the subject matter of the sale or disposition came within the ambit of the definition.

163 The Board did not ask itself that question. However, it seems clear that if it had, the subject matter of the sale or disposition was a digital audio recorder or a device as the Board called it, but not a medium as defined. In the absence of such a sale, no liability can arise for the levy.

164 In my respectful view, it is for Parliament to decide whether digital audio recorders such as MP3 players are to be brought within the class of items that can be levied under Part VIII. As Part VIII now reads, there is no authority for certifying a levy on such devices or the memory embedded therein.

165 I would therefore allow the judicial review application insofar as the first issue raised by the applicants is concerned. Second Issue

. . .

4. New Defences in Copyright Modernization Act

The *Copyright Modernization Act* added a series of new exceptions to the Act. These are described below:

(a) Exceptions for Network Service Providers and Search Engines

The *Copyright Modernization Act* added the following new sections to provide safe harbours to network service providers, hosting providers and providers of information location tools (search engines).

Network Services

31.1 (1) A person who, in providing services related to the operation of the Internet or another digital network, provides any means for the telecommunication or the reproduction of a work or other subject-matter through the Internet or that other network does not, solely by reason of providing those means, infringe copyright in that work or other subject-matter.

Incidental acts

(2) Subject to subsection (3), a person referred to in subsection (1) who caches the work or other subject-matter, or does any similar act in relation to it, to make the telecommunication more efficient does not, by virtue of that act alone, infringe copyright in the work or other subject-matter.

Conditions for application

(3) Subsection (2) does not apply unless the person, in respect of the work or other subject-matter,

(a) does not modify it, other than for technical reasons;

(b) ensures that any directions related to its caching or the doing of any similar act, as the case may be, that are specified in a manner consistent with industry practice by whoever made it available for telecommunication through the Internet or another digital network, and that lend themselves to automated reading and execution, are read and executed; and

(c) does not interfere with the use of technology that is lawful and consistent with industry practice in order to obtain data on the use of the work or other subject-matter.

Hosting

(4) Subject to subsection (5), a person who, for the purpose of allowing the telecommunication of a work or other subject-matter through the Internet or another digital network, provides digital memory in which another person stores the work or other subject-matter does not, by virtue of that act alone, infringe copyright in the work or other subject-matter.

. . .

Injunctive relief only — providers of information location tools

41.27 (1) In any proceedings for infringement of copyright, the owner of the copyright in a work or other subject-matter is not entitled to any remedy other than an injunction against a provider of an information location tool that is found to have infringed copyright by making a reproduction of the work or other subject-matter or by communicating that reproduction to the public by telecommunication.

Conditions for application

(2) Subsection (1) applies only if the provider, in respect of the work or other subject-matter,

(a) makes and caches, or does any act similar to caching, the reproduction in an automated manner for the purpose of providing the information location tool;

(b) communicates that reproduction to the public by telecommunication for the purpose of providing the information that has been located by the information location tool;

(c) does not modify the reproduction, other than for technical reasons;

(d) complies with any conditions relating to the making or caching, or doing of any act similar to caching, of reproductions of the work or other subject-matter, or to the communication of the reproductions to the public by telecommunication, that were specified in a manner consistent with industry practice by whoever made the work or other subject-matter available through the Internet or another digital network and that lend themselves to automated reading and execution; and

(e) does not interfere with the use of technology that is lawful and consistent with industry practice in order to obtain data on the use of the work or other subject-matter.

(3) [Not in force]

Exception

(4) Subsection (1) does not apply to the provision of the information location tool if the provision of that tool constitutes an infringement of copyright under subsection 27(2.3).

Factors — scope of injunction

(4.1) If it grants an injunction as set out in subsection (1), the court shall, among any other relevant factors, consider the following in establishing the terms of the injunction:

(a) the harm likely to be suffered by the copyright owner if steps are not taken to prevent or restrain the infringement; and

(b) the burden imposed on the provider and on the operation of the information location tool, including

(i) the aggregate effect of the injunction and any injunctions from other proceedings,

(ii) whether implementing the injunction would be technically feasible and effective in addressing the infringement,

(iii) whether implementing the injunction would interfere with the use of the information location tool for non-infringing acts, and

(iv) the availability of less burdensome and comparably effective means of preventing or restraining the infringement.

Limitation

(4.2) A court is not permitted to grant an injunction under section 39.1 against a provider who is the subject of an injunction set out in subsection (1).

Meaning of "information location tool"

(5) In this section, "information location tool" means any tool that makes it possible to locate information that is available through the Internet or another digital network.

(b) New Exceptions for End-Users

The *Copyright Modernization Act* also introduced new exceptions for individuals. Exceptions now provide a defense to enable individuals to engage in format shifting and time shifting, subject to the conditions in the Act. There is also a new exception to permit individuals to create and disseminate non-commercial user generated content.

i. Format Shift Exception

The *Copyright Modernization Act* introduced a new exception for reproduction for private purposes. The exception reads as follows:

Reproduction for private purposes

29.22 (1) It is not an infringement of copyright for an individual to reproduce
a work or other subject-matter or any substantial part of a work or other subject-
matter if

> (a) the copy of the work or other subject-matter from which the reproduction
> is made is not an infringing copy;

> (b) the individual legally obtained the copy of the work or other subject-
> matter from which the reproduction is made, other than by borrowing it or
> renting it, and owns or is authorized to use the medium or device on which it
> is reproduced;

> (c) the individual, in order to make the reproduction, did not circumvent, as
> defined in section 41, a technological protection measure, as defined in that
> section, or cause one to be circumvented;

> (d) the individual does not give the reproduction away; and

> (e) the reproduction is used only for the individual's private purposes.

Meaning of "medium or device"

(2) For the purposes of paragraph (1)(b), a "medium or device" includes digital
memory in which a work or subject-matter may be stored for the purpose of allowing the telecommunication of the work or other subject-matter through the Internet
or other digital network.

Marginal note: Limitation — audio recording medium

(3) In the case of a work or other subject-matter that is a musical work embodied
in a sound recording, a performer's performance of a musical work embodied in
a sound recording or a sound recording in which a musical work or a performer's
performance of a musical work is embodied, subsection (1) does not apply if the
reproduction is made onto an audio recording medium as defined in section 79.

Marginal note: Limitation — destruction of reproductions

(4) Subsection (1) does not apply if the individual gives away, rents or sells the
copy of the work or other subject-matter from which the reproduction is made
without first destroying all reproductions of that copy that the individual has made
under that subsection.

ii. Time Shifting Exception

The *Copyright Modernization Act* also introduced a new exception for
reproduction for later listening or viewing. This section reads as follows:

Reproduction for later listening or viewing

29.23 (1) It is not an infringement of copyright for an individual to fix a communication signal, to reproduce a work or sound recording that is being broadcast or to fix or reproduce a performer's performance that is being broadcast, in order to record a program for the purpose of listening to or viewing it later, if

(*a*) the individual receives the program legally;

(*b*) the individual, in order to record the program, did not circumvent, as defined in section 41, a technological protection measure, as defined in that section, or cause one to be circumvented;

(*c*) the individual makes no more than one recording of the program;

(*d*) the individual keeps the recording no longer than is reasonably necessary in order to listen to or view the program at a more convenient time;

(*e*) the individual does not give the recording away; and

(*f*) the recording is used only for the individual's private purposes.

Marginal note: Limitation

(2) Subsection (1) does not apply if the individual receives the work, performer's performance or sound recording under an on-demand service.

Marginal note: Definitions

(3) The following definitions apply in this section.

"broadcast"

« radiodiffusion »

"broadcast" means any transmission of a work or other subject-matter by telecommunication for reception by the public, but does not include a transmission that is made solely for performance in public.

"on-demand service"

« service sur demande »

"on-demand service" means a service that allows a person to receive works, performer's performances and sound recordings at times of their choosing.

In the United States, it has long been accepted that non-commerical time-shifting for later viewing qualifies as a "fair use" that generally does not infringe copyright in the recorded works. This was a central issue in the famous *Sony* case, below, in which the US Supreme Court refused to impose copyright liability on the distributors of the Betamax video-recorder. In Canada, uses for the purpose of time-shifting are highly unlikely to fall within the limited purposes for which a fair dealing defence in available; the new exception was therefore considered necessary to confirm the lawfulness of a common practice, made increasingly popular by new technologies, that does not harm the legitimate interests of the rightholders.

Sony Corp. of America v. Universal City Studios, Inc., 464 U.S. 417 (1984)

STEVENS, J., delivered the opinion of the Court in which BURGER, C. J., and BRENNAN, WHITE, and O'CONNOR, JJ., joined. BLACK-MUN, J., filed a dissenting opinion in which MARSHALL, POWELL, and REHNQUIST, JJ., joined, post, p. 457.

[1] Petitioners manufacture and sell home video tape recorders. Respondents own the copyrights on some of the television programs that are broadcast on the public airwaves. Some members of the general public use video tape recorders sold by petitioners to record some of these broadcasts, as well as a large number of other broadcasts. The question presented is whether the sale of petitioners copying equipment to the general public violates any of the rights conferred upon respondents by the Copyright Act.

[2] Respondents commenced this copyright infringement action against petitioners in the United States District Court for the Central District of California in 1976. Respondents alleged that some individuals had used Betamax video tape recorders (VTRs) to record some of respondents' copyrighted works which had been exhibited on commercially sponsored television and contended that these individuals had thereby infringed respondents' copyrights. Respondents further maintained that petitioners were liable for the copyright infringement allegedly committed by Betamax consumers because of petitioners' marketing of the Betamax VTR's. Respondents sought no relief against any Betamax consumer. Instead, they sought money damages and an equitable accounting of profits from petitioners, as well as an injunction against the manufacture and marketing of Betamax VTR's.

[3] After a lengthy trial, the District Court denied respondents all the relief they sought and entered judgment for petitioners. 480 F.Supp. 429 (1979). The United States Court of Appeals for the Ninth Circuit reversed the District Court's judgment on respondents' copyright claim, holding petitioners liable for contributory infringement and ordering the District Court to fashion appropriate relief. 659 F.2d 963 (1981). We granted certiorari, 457 U.S. 1116 (1982); since we had not completed our study of the case last Term, we ordered reargument, 463 U.S. 1226 (1983). We now reverse.

[4] An explanation of our rejection of respondents unprecedented attempt to impose copyright liability upon the distributors of copying equipment requires a quite detailed recitation of the findings of the District Court. In summary, those findings reveal that the average member of the public uses a VTR principally to record a program he cannot view as it is being televised and then to watch it once at a later time. This practice, known as "time-shifting," enlarges the television viewing audience. For that reason, a significant amount of television

programming may be used in this manner without objection from the owners of the copyrights on the programs. For the same reason, even the two respondents in this case, who do assert objections to time-shifting in this litigation, were unable to prove that the practice has impaired the commercial value of their copyrights or has created any likelihood of future harm. Given these findings, there is no basis in the Copyright Act upon which respondents can hold petitioners liable for distributing VTR's to the general public. The Court of Appeals' holding that respondents are entitled to enjoin the distribution of VTR's, to collect royalties on the sale of such equipment, or to obtain other relief, if affirmed, would enlarge the scope of respondents' statutory monopolies to encompass control over an article of commerce that is not the subject of copyright protection. Such an expansion of the copyright privilege is beyond the limits of the grants authorized by Congress.

. . .

IV

[40] The question is thus whether the Betamax is capable of commercially significant noninfringing uses. In order to resolve that question, we need not explore *all* the different potential uses of the machine and determine whether or not they would constitute infringement. Rather, we need only consider whether on the basis of the facts as found by the District Court a significant number of them would be noninfringing. Moreover, in order to resolve this case we need not give precise content to the question of how much use is commercially significant. For one potential use of the Betamax plainly satisfies this standard, however it is understood: private, noncommercial time-shifting in the home. It does so both (A) because respondents have no right to prevent other copyright holders from authorizing it for their programs, and (B) because the District Court's factual findings reveal that even the unauthorized home time-shifting of respondentss' programs is legitimate fair use.

. . .

B. Unauthorized Time-Shifting

[46] Even unauthorized uses of a copyrighted work are not necessarily infringing. An unlicensed use of the copyright is not an infringement unless it conflicts with one of the specific exclusive rights conferred by the copyright statute. *Twentieth Century Music Corp.* v. *Aiken*, 422 U.S., at 154-155. Moreover, the definition of exclusive rights in § 106 of the present Act is prefaced by the words "subject to sections 107 through 118." Those sections describe a variety of uses of copyrighted material that "are not infringements of copyright" "notwithstanding the provisions of section 106." The most pertinent in this case is § 107, the legislative endorsement of the doctrine of "fair use." That section identifies various factors that enable a court to apply an "equitable rule of reason" analysis to particular claims of infringement. Although not conclusive, the first factor requires that "the commercial or nonprofit character of an activity"

be weighed in any fair use decision. If the Betamax were used to make copies for a commercial or profit-making purpose, such use would presumptively be unfair. The contrary presumption is appropriate here, however, because the District Court's findings plainly establish that time-shifting for private home use must be characterized as a noncommercial, nonprofit activity. Moreover, when one considers the nature of a televised copyrighted audiovisual work, see 17 U. S. C. § 107(2) (1982 ed.), and that time-shifting merely enables a viewer to see such a work which he had been invited to witness in its entirety free of charge, the fact that the entire work is reproduced, see § 107(3), does not have its ordinary effect of militating against a finding of fair use. This is not, however, the end of the inquiry because Congress has also directed us to consider "the effect of the use upon the potential market for or value of the copyrighted work." § 107(4). The purpose of copyright is to create incentives for creative effort. Even copying for noncommercial purposes may impair the copyright holder's ability to obtain the rewards that Congress intended him to have. But a use that has no demonstrable effect upon the potential market for, or the value of, the copyrighted work need not be prohibited in order to protect the author's incentive to create. The prohibition of such noncommercial uses would merely inhibit access to ideas without any countervailing benefit. although every commercial use of copyrighted material is presumptively an unfair exploitation of the monopoly privilege that belongs to the owner of the copyright, noncommercial uses are a different matter. A challenge to a noncommercial use of a copyrighted work requires proof either that the particular use is harmful, or that if it should become widespread, it would adversely affect the potential market for the copyrighted work. Actual present harm need not be shown; such a requirement would leave the copyright holder with no defense against predictable damage. Nor is it necessary to show with certainty that future harm will result. What is necessary is a showing by a preponderance of the evidence that *some* meaningful likelihood of future harm exists. If the intended use is for commercial gain, that likelihood may be presumed. But if it is for a noncommercial purpose, the likelihood must be demonstrated.

[47] In this case, respondents failed to carry their burden with regard to home time-shifting. The District Court described respondents' evidence as follows:

"Plaintiffs' experts admitted at several points in the trial that the time-shifting without librarying would result in "not a great deal of harm." Plaintiffs' greatest concern about time-shifting is with "a point of important philosophy that transcends even commercial judgment." They fear that with any Betamax usage, invisible boundaries are passed: "the copyright owner has lost control over his program." 480 F.Supp., at 467.

[48] Later in its opinion, the District Court observed:

"Most of plaintiffs' predictions of harm hinge on speculation about audience viewing patterns and ratings, a measurement system which Sidney Sheinberg, MCA's president, calls a 'black art' because of the significant level of imprecision involved in the calculations." *Id.*, at 469.

[49] There was no need for the District Court to say much about past harm. "Plaintiffs have admitted that no actual harm to their copyrights has occurred to date." *Id.*, at 451.

[50] On the question of potential future harm from time-shifting, the District Court offered a more detailed analysis of the evidence. It rejected respondents' "fear that persons watching the original telecast of a program will not be measured in the live audience and the ratings and revenues will decrease," by observing that current measurement technology allows the Betamax audience to be reflected. *Id.*, at 466. It rejected respondents' prediction "that live television or movie audiences will decrease as more people watch Betamax tapes as an alternative," with the observation that "[there] is no factual basis for [the underlying] assumption." *Ibid.* It rejected respondents' "fear that time-shifting will reduce audiences for telecast reruns," and concluded instead that "given current market practices, this should aid plaintiffs rather than harm them." *Ibid.* And it declared that respondents' suggestion that "theater or film rental exhibition of a program will suffer because of time-shift recording of that program" "lacks merit." *Id.*, at 467. After completing that review, the District Court restated its overall conclusion several times, in several different ways. "Harm from time-shifting is speculative and, at best, minimal." *Ibid.* "The audience benefits from the time-shifting capability have already been discussed. It is not implausible that benefits could also accrue to plaintiffs, broadcasters, and advertisers, as the Betamax makes it possible for more persons to view their broadcasts." *Ibid.* "No likelihood of harm was shown at trial, and plaintiffs admitted that there had been no actual harm to date." *Id.*, at 468-469. "Testimony at trial suggested that Betamax may require adjustments in marketing strategy, but it did not establish even a likelihood of harm." *Id.*, at 469. "Television production by plaintiffs today is more profitable than it has ever been, and, in five weeks of trial, there was no concrete evidence to suggest that the Betamax will change the studios' financial picture." *Ibid.*

[51] The District Court's conclusions are buttressed by the fact that to the extent time-shifting expands public access to freely broadcast television programs, it yields societal benefits. In *Community Television of Southern California* v. *Gottfried*, 459 U.S. 498, 508, n. 12 (1983), we acknowledged the public interest in making television broadcasting more available. Concededly, that interest is not unlimited. But it supports an interpretation of the concept of "fair use" that requires the copyright holder to demonstrate some likelihood of harm before he may condemn a private act of time-shifting as a violation of federal law.

[52] When these factors are all weighed in the "equitable rule of reason" balance, we must conclude that this record amply supports the District Court's conclusion that home time-shifting is fair use. In light of the findings of the District Court regarding the state of the empirical data, it is clear that the Court of Appeals erred in holding that the statute as presently written bars such conduct. In summary, the record and findings of the District Court lead us to two conclusions. First, Sony demonstrated a significant likelihood that substantial numbers of copyright holders who license their works for broadcast on free television would not object to having their broadcasts time-shifted by private viewers.

And second, respondents failed to demonstrate that time-shifting would cause any likelihood of nonminimal harm to the potential market for, or the value of, their copyrighted works. The Betamax is, therefore, capable of substantial non-infringing uses. Sony's sale of such equipment to the general public does not constitute contributory infringement of respondents' copyrights.

V

[53] "The direction of Art. I is that *Congress* shall have the power to promote the progress of science and the useful arts. When, as here, the Constitution is permissive, the sign of how far Congress has chosen to go can come only from Congress." *Deepsouth Packing Co.* v. *Laitram Corp.*, 406 U.S. 518, 530 (1972).

[54] One may search the Copyright Act in vain for any sign that the elected representatives of the millions of people who watch television every day have made it unlawful to copy a program for later viewing at home, or have enacted a flat prohibition against the sale of machines that make such copying possible.

[55] It may well be that Congress will take a fresh look at this new technology, just as it so often has examined other innovations in the past. But it is not our job to apply laws that have not yet been written. Applying the copyright statute, as it now reads, to the facts as they have been developed in this case, the judgment of the Court of Appeals must be reversed.

---

iii. User Generated Content Exception

The *Copyright Modernization Act* introduced a new exception enabling individuals to create and disseminate user generated content (UGC). As with the previous end-user exceptions, this novel UGC exception is intended to ensure the lawfulness of everyday activities by end-users making use of new digital network technologies in personal and non-commercial ways. Sometimes referred to as "the Youtube exception," the government's fact sheet offers as examples "making a home video of a friend or family member dancing to a popular song and posting it online, or creating a 'mash-up' of video clips."[2] There are some important limitations on the UGC exception, however, that may give rise to some uncertainty. In light of the unpredictabity of the "viral-video effect," for example, it will be interesting to see how (and at what point in the process of making or disseminating UGN) the requirement of "solely non-commercial purposes" is assessed. It will also be interesting to see what kinds of adverse effects, other than financial ones, are considered sufficiently substantial to preclude the availability of the defence. The restriction to use of non-infringing works may also prove to be a significant one in light of the kinds or sources of content that the makers of UGC may use.

---

2   Balanced Copyright, *What the New* Copyright Modernization Act *Means for Consumers*, <http://www.ic.gc.ca/eic/site/crp-prda.nsf/eng/rp01186.html>.

This section reads as follows:

Non-commercial User-generated Content

29.21 (1) It is not an infringement of copyright for an individual to use an existing work or other subject-matter or copy of one, which has been published or otherwise made available to the public, in the creation of a new work or other subject-matter in which copyright subsists and for the individual — or, with the individual's authorization, a member of their household — to use the new work or other subject-matter or to authorize an intermediary to disseminate it, if

> (*a*) the use of, or the authorization to disseminate, the new work or other subject-matter is done solely for non-commercial purposes;

> (*b*) the source — and, if given in the source, the name of the author, performer, maker or broadcaster — of the existing work or other subject-matter or copy of it are mentioned, if it is reasonable in the circumstances to do so;

> (*c*) the individual had reasonable grounds to believe that the existing work or other subject-matter or copy of it, as the case may be, was not infringing copyright; and

> (*d*) the use of, or the authorization to disseminate, the new work or other subject-matter does not have a substantial adverse effect, financial or otherwise, on the exploitation or potential exploitation of the existing work or other subject-matter — or copy of it — or on an existing or potential market for it, including that the new work or other subject-matter is not a substitute for the existing one.

Definitions

(2) The following definitions apply in subsection (1).

"intermediary"

« intermédiaire »

"intermediary" means a person or entity who regularly provides space or means for works or other subject-matter to be enjoyed by the public.

"use"

« utiliser »

"use" means to do anything that by this Act the owner of the copyright has the sole right to do, other than the right to authorize anything.

It should be noted that many uses that could benefit from this defence may also constitute fair dealings for, e.g., criticism or parody purposes. In the United States, many such uses would be considered transformative fair use. Under fair dealing or fair use, there would be no absolute bar to the application of the defence in light of either a defendant's commercial purposes or any adverse consequences for the rightholder.

The following case considers the availability of fair use as a defence for UGC in the context of a notice-and-takedown order issued under the U.S. *Digital Millennium Copyright Act.* Notably, the Youtube post at issue would be unlikely to fit within Canada's fair dealing purposes — it might qualify, however, for the new UGC defence.

Stephanie LENZ, Plaintiff,

v.

UNIVERSAL MUSIC CORP., Universal Music Publishing, Inc., and Universal Music Publishing Group, Defendants.

United States District Court, N.D. California, San Jose Division. August 20, 2008.

JEREMY FOGEL, District Judge.

Defendants Universal Music Corp., Universal Music Publishing, Inc., and Universal Music Publishing Group (collectively, "Universal") move to dismiss the instant case for failure to state a claim upon which relief may be granted. *See* Fed.R.Civ.P. 12(b)(6). The Court has read the moving papers and has considered the oral arguments of counsel. For the reasons set forth below, the motion will be DENIED.

I. BACKGROUND

On February 7, 2007, Plaintiff Stephanie Lenz ("Lenz") videotaped her young children dancing in her family's kitchen. The song "Let's Go Crazy" by the artist professionally known as Prince ("Prince") played in the background. The video is twentynine seconds in length, and "Let's Go Crazy" can be heard for approximately twenty seconds, albeit with difficulty given the poor sound quality of the video. The audible portion of the song includes the lyrics, "C'mon baby let's get nuts" and the song's distinctive guitar solo. Lenz is heard asking her son, "what do you think of the music?" On February 8, 2007, Lenz titled the video "Let's Go Crazy # 1" and uploaded it to YouTube.com ("YouTube"), a popular Internet video hosting site, for the alleged purpose of sharing her son's dancing with friends and family. YouTube provides "video sharing" or "user generated content." The video was available to the public at http://www.youtube.com/watch?v=N1KfJHFW1hQ.

Universal owns the copyright to "Let's Go Crazy." On June 4, 2007, Universal sent YouTube a takedown notice pursuant to Title II of the Digital Millennium Copyright Act ("DMCA"), 17 U.S.C. § 512 (2000). The notice was sent to YouTube's designated address for receiving DMCA notices, "copyright@youtube.com," and demanded that YouTube remove Lenz's video from the site because of a copyright violation. YouTube removed the video the following day and sent Lenz an email notifying her that it had done so in response to Universal's accusation of copyright infringement. YouTube's email also advised Lenz of the DMCA's counter-notification procedures and warned her that any repeated incidents of copyright infringement could lead to the deletion of her account and all of her videos. After conducting research and consulting counsel, Lenz sent YouTube a DMCA counter-notification pursuant to 17 U.S.C. § 512(g) on June 27, 2007. Lenz asserted that her video constituted fair use of "Let's Go Crazy" and thus did not infringe Universal's copyrights. Lenz demanded that the video be re-posted. YouTube re-posted the video on its website about six weeks later. As of the date of this order, the "Let's Go Crazy # 1" video has been viewed on YouTube more than 593,000 times.

In September 2007, Prince spoke publicly about his efforts "to reclaim his art on the internet" and threatened to sue several internet service providers for alleged infringement of his music copyrights. Lenz alleges that Universal issued the removal notice only to appease Prince because Prince "is notorious for his efforts to control all uses of his material on and off the Internet." Lenz's Opposition Brief at 3. In an October 2007 statement to ABC News, Universal made the following comment:

> Prince believes it is wrong for YouTube, or any other user-generated site, to appropriate his music without his consent. That position has nothing to do with any particular video that uses his songs. It's simply a matter of principle. And legally, he has the right to have his music removed. We support him and this important principle. That's why, over the last few months, we have asked You-Tube to remove thousands of different videos that use Prince music without his permission. Second Amended Complaint ("SAC"), ¶ 30; *see also* J. Aliva et al., *The Home Video Prince Doesn't Want You to See,* ABC NEWS, Oct. 26, 2007, http://abcnews.go.com/ print?id + 3777651 (last viewed July 23, 2008). Lenz asserts in her complaint that "Prince himself demanded that Universal seek the removal of the ["Let's Go Crazy # 1"] video ... [and that] Universal sent the DMCA notice at Prince's behest, based not on the particular characteristics of [the video] or any good-faith belief that it actually infringed a copyright but on its belief that, as `a matter of principle' Prince `has the right to have his music removed.'" SAC ¶ 31.

On July 24, 2007, Lenz filed suit against Universal alleging misrepresentation pursuant to 17 U.S.C. § 512(f) and tortious interference with her contract with You-Tube. She also sought a declaratory judgment of non-infringement. Universal filed a motion to dismiss, which the Court granted on April 8, 2008, 2008 WL 962102. Lenz was given leave to amend her complaint to replead her first and second claims for relief. On April 18, 2008, Lenz filed the operative SAC, alleging only a claim for misrepresentation pursuant to 17 U.S.C. § 512(f). On May 23, 2008, Universal filed the instant motion.

III. DISCUSSION

The DMCA requires that copyright owners provide the following information in a takedown notice:

> ...(v) *A statement that the complaining party has a good faith belief that use of the material in the manner complained of is not authorized by the copyright owner, its agent, or the law....*

17 U.S.C. § 512(c)(3)(A) (emphasis added). Here, the parties do not dispute that Lenz used copyrighted material in her video or that Universal is the true owner of

Prince's copyrighted music. Thus the question in this case is whether 17 U.S.C. § 512(c)(3)(A)(v) requires a copyright owner to consider the fair use doctrine in formulating a good faith belief that "use of the material in the manner complained of is not authorized by the copyright owner, its agent, or the law."

Universal contends that copyright owners cannot be required to evaluate the question of fair use prior to sending a takedown notice because fair use is merely an *excused* infringement of a copyright rather than a use *authorized* by the copyright owner or by law. Universal emphasizes that Section 512(c)(3)(A) does not even mention fair use, let alone require a good faith belief that a given use of copyrighted material is not fair use. Universal also contends that even if a copyright owner were required by the DMCA to evaluate fair use with respect to allegedly infringing material, any such duty would arise only *after* a copyright owner receives a counternotice and considers filing suit. *See* 17 U.S.C. § 512(g)(2)(C).

Lenz argues that fair use *is* an authorized use of copyrighted material, noting that the fair use doctrine itself is an express component of copyright law. Indeed, Section 107 of the Copyright Act of 1976 provides that "[n]otwithstanding the provisions of sections 106 and 106A, the fair use of a copyrighted work ... is not an infringement of copyright." 17 U.S.C. § 107. Lenz asserts in essence that copyright owners cannot represent in good faith that material infringes a copyright without considering all authorized uses of the material, including fair use.

Whether fair use qualifies as a use "authorized by law" in connection with a takedown notice pursuant to the DMCA appears to be an issue of first impression. Though it has been discussed in several other actions, no published case actually has adjudicated the merits of the issue.

A. Fair Use and 17 U.S.C. § 512(c)(3)(A)(v).

...Even if Universal is correct that fair use only *excuses* infringement, the fact remains that fair use is a lawful use of a copyright. Accordingly, in order for a copyright owner to proceed under the DMCA with "a good faith belief that use of the material in the manner complained of is not authorized by the copyright owner, its agent, or the law," the owner must evaluate whether the material makes fair use of the copyright. 17 U.S.C. § 512(c)(3)(A)(v). An allegation that a copyright owner acted in bad faith by issuing a takedown notice without proper consideration of the fair use doctrine thus is sufficient to state a misrepresentation claim pursuant to Section 512(f) of the DMCA. Such an interpretation of the DMCA furthers both the purposes of the DMCA itself and copyright law in general. In enacting the DMCA, Congress noted that the "provisions in the bill balance the need for rapid response to potential infringement with the end-users [sic] legitimate interests in not having material removed without recourse." Sen. Rep. No. 105-190 at 21 (1998).

Universal suggests that copyright owners may lose the ability to respond rapidly to potential infringements if they are required to evaluate fair use prior to issuing takedown notices. Universal also points out that the question of whether a particular use of copyrighted material constitutes fair use is a fact-intensive inquiry, and that it is difficult for copyright owners to predict whether a court eventually may rule in their favor. However, while these concerns are understandable, their actual impact likely is overstated. Although there may be cases in which such considerations will arise, there are likely to be few in which a copyright owner's determination that a particular use is not fair use will meet the requisite standard of subjective bad faith required to prevail in an action for misrepresentation under 17 U.S.C. § 512(f)....

The Copyright Act unequivocally establishes the four factors used to determine fair use....17 U.S.C. § 107. Undoubtedly, some evaluations of fair use will be more complicated than others. But in the majority of cases, a consideration of fair use prior to issuing a takedown notice will not be so complicated as to jeopardize a copyright owner's ability to respond rapidly to potential infringements. The DMCA already requires copyright owners to make an initial review of the potentially infringing material prior to sending a takedown notice; indeed, it would be impossible to meet any of the requirements of Section 512(c) without doing so. A consideration of the applicability of the fair use doctrine simply is part of that initial review. As the Ninth Circuit observed in *Rossi,* a full *investigation* to verify the accuracy of a claim of infringement is not required....

The purpose of Section 512(f) is to prevent the abuse of takedown notices. If copyright owners are immune from liability by virtue of ownership alone, then to a large extent Section 512(f) is superfluous. As Lenz points out, the unnecessary removal of non-infringing material causes significant injury to the public where timesensitive or controversial subjects are involved and the counter-notification remedy does not sufficiently address these harms. A good faith consideration of whether a particular use is fair use is consistent with the purpose of the statute. Requiring owners to consider fair use will help "ensure[] that the efficiency of the Internet will continue to improve and that the variety and quality of services on the Internet will expand" without compromising "the movies, music, software and literary works that are the fruit of American creative genius." Sen. Rep. No. 105-190 at 2 (1998).

B.   The Sufficiency of Lenz's Second Amended Complaint

1.   The "Prince Policy"

The operative SAC contains sufficient allegations of bad faith and deliberate ignorance of fair use to survive the instant motion to dismiss. Lenz alleges that Universal is a sophisticated corporation familiar with copyright actions, and that rather than acting in good faith, Universal acted solely to satisfy Prince. SAC ¶ 31. Lenz alleges that Prince has been outspoken on matters of copyright infringement on the Internet and has threatened multiple suits against internet service providers to protect his music. *Id.* at ¶ 28. Lenz also alleges that Universal acted to promote Prince's personal agenda and that its actions "ha[ve] nothing to do with any particular [YouTube] video that uses his songs." *Id.* at ¶ 30. Although the Court has considerable doubt that Lenz will be able to prove that Universal acted with the subjective bad faith required by *Rossi,* and following discovery her claims well may be appropriate for summary judgment, Lenz's allegations are sufficient at the pleading stage.

2. Damages

Universal also contends that the SAC fails to allege a compensable loss under the DMCA. Universal Brief at 2. The SAC provides that:

> [Lenz's] injury includes, but is not limited to, the financial and personal expenses associated with responding to the claim of infringement and harm to her free speech rights under the First Amendment. Because Universal's notice was intimidating, Ms. Lenz is now fearful that someone might construe some portion of a new home video to infringe a copyright. As a result, she has not posted a single video on You-Tube since she received the takedown notice.

...Though damages may be nominal and their exact nature is yet to be determined, the Court concludes that Lenz adequately has alleged cognizable injury under the DMCA.

---

iv. New Fair Dealing Exceptions

As noted in Part 1 of this Chapter, the *Copyright Modernization Act* added newly enumerated purposes for which fair dealing is available. In addition to "private study and research," section 29 now includes "education, parody or satire." In one sense, these purposes are not exactly new. As the Supreme Court's ruling in the *Alberta v. Access Copyright* case (*supra.*) suggests, a large and liberal reading of "private study" could encompass many educational uses. Similarly, most parodies or satires would likely be considered "criticism or review" unless these categories are given an unduly restrictive interpretation. The following cases, however, underscore the narrow application of fair dealing in Canada that has previously excluded parodic uses from the scope of fair dealing, even following the *CCH* ruling. Such uses will now more readily meet the first fair dealing hurdle, and the defence will succeed or fail in light of the fairness of the use. This brings Canada's law significantly closer to the US position on parodies (see *Campbell v. Acuff-Rose Music*, *supra.*). Indeed, the inclusion of "satire" could potentially extend fair dealing beyond what would constitute fair use in the United States; in *Campbell*, Justice Souter drew a distinction between parodies that "target" the work *per se* and satires that that merely use the work as a "weapon" to criticize some other target or social issue.

Cie générale des établissements Michelin — Michelin & Cie v. CAW-Canada

(1996), 71 C.P.R. (3d) 348 (Fed. T.D.)
Federal Court, Trial Division
Teitelbaum J.
December 19, 1996

TEITELBAUM J.: —

FACTS:— This is an action for infringement of trademarks and copyrights with intriguing constitutional dimensions. The Plaintiff Compagnie Générale des Établissements Michelin-Michelin & Cie. (hereinafter "CGEM Michelin") is a French corporation with worldwide interests in the manufacture, distribution and sale of tires and automotive accessories. CGEM Michelin also provides tourism services, including the production of tourist guides and maps.

In February and March 1994, the Defendant, National Automobile, Aerospace, Transportation and General Workers Union of Canada (hereinafter "CAW") attempted to unionize the employees of Michelin North America (Canada) (hereinafter "Michelin Canada"), the wholly owned Canadian subsidiary of CGEM Michelin, at Michelin Canada's three tire plants in Granton, Waterville and Bridgewater, Nova Scotia. Defendant Larry Wark is the local CAW representative responsible for the Nova Scotia organizing campaign. Defendant Basil Hargrove is the National President of the CAW who approved the launching of the campaign. During the campaign, the CAW distributed leaflets, displayed posters and issued information sheets that reproduced the term "MICHELIN". The CAW also used in its campaign material CGEM Michelin's corporate logo, the Michelin Tire Man or "Bibendum" design, a drawing of a beaming marshmallow-like rotund figure composed of tires.

The Plaintiff CGEM Michelin holds trademarks and copyrights in the term "MICHELIN" and the "Bibendum" design. The Defendants did not obtain the permission of CGEM Michelin before they used the Plaintiff's intellectual property. The Plaintiff is now seeking damages on the grounds that its intellectual property rights were violated by the Defendants. The Plaintiff also wants a permanent injunction to restrain the Defendants from using its trademarks and copyrights in future organizing drives. The Defendants counter that they did not infringe the trademarks and copyrights of the Plaintiff....

The Leaflets and Poster

As I stated briefly above, the Defendant CAW conducted an organizing campaign at Michelin Canada's plants in Nova Scotia in February and March 1994. The Defendant CAW distributed 2500 leaflets to Michelin workers outside the factory gates at the three Nova Scotia Michelin Canada plants. The leaflet (Exhibit P-18) is included as Appendix II to this decision. The top right hand corner of the leaflet displays the CAW logo, a mark with the letters "CAW" and "TCA" separated by a stratified maple leaf and the word "CANADA" underneath a thinly drawn line. The contentious portion of the leaflet depicts a broadly smiling "Bibendum", arms crossed, with his foot raised, seemingly ready to crush underfoot an unsuspecting Michelin worker. In the same leaflet, another worker safely out of the reach of "Bibendum's" looming foot has raised a finger of warning and informs his blithe colleague, "Bob, you better move before he squashes you". Bob, the worker in imminent danger of "Bibendum's" boot has apparently resisted the blandishments of the union since a caption coming from his mouth reads, "Naw, I'm going to wait and see what happens". Below the roughly drawn figures of the workers is the following plea in bold letters, "Don't wait until it's too late! Because the job you save may be your own. Sign today for a better tomorrow." The leaflet also gives the phone number for the CAW office in Granton. Defendant Wark, the Defendant CAW's organizer for Nova Scotia, admitted that he had photocopied and prepared the leaflet with the offending "Bibendum" figure in the CAW office.

ISSUES The issues in this case force the Court to go beyond the straightforward question of whether the Defendants infringed the Plaintiff's trademarks and copyrights. Even the grounds of infringement under the Trade-marks Act and Copyright Act are not so clear cut in this instance. Both parties have urged the Court to consider novel interpretations of the law. ...On the copyright issue, the Defendant argued for an expanded and quite unprecedented notion of parody under Canadian copyright law....

. . .

II. Copyright Issues

The Defendants deny that there has been any infringement of copyright because the "Bibendum" on the leaflets and posters is an original work of the Defendants that does not substantially reproduce CGEM Michelin's copyright. The Defendants also argue that even if there has been reproduction of a substantial part, their "Bibendum" is a parody and therefore an exception to copyright infringement under Section 27(2)(a.1), fair dealing for the purpose of criticism.

(i) Substantial Part

I have no difficulty in finding that the Defendants have reproduced a substantial part of CGEM Michelin's "Bibendum" design on their union campaign posters and leaflets....

. . .

Counsel for the Defendants also argued that the "Bibendum" on the union leaflets and posters did not reproduce a substantial part of the original "Bibendum" because as a parody of the original, it constituted an entirely new work. Counsel cited Joy Music, Ltd. v. Sunday Pictorial Newspapers (1920), Ltd., [1960] 1 All E.R. 703, [1960] 2 Q.B. 60 (hereinafter "Joy Music" cited to All E.R.) in which Justice McNair at page 708 ruled that the test for infringement in regards to parody is whether the defendant "had bestowed such mental labour on what he has taken and subjected it to such revision and alteration as to produce an original work". The Defendants also cited Motel 6, Inc. v. No. 6 Motel Ltd. (1981), 127 D.L.R. (3d) 267, 56 C.P.R. (2d) 44 (F.C.T.D.) (hereinafter "Motel 6"), to argue that it is immaterial if there is evidence of reproduction of a substantial part as long as there is evidence of "independent creation".

I take issue with how the Defendants have framed the test for reproduction of a substantial part.

. . .

In short, the Defendant CAW has reproduced a substantial part of the "Bibendum" in the Plaintiff's registered copyrights and unregistered copyright. The addition of the roughly drawn workers and their cautionary dialogue on the union's leaflets and posters does not represent a significant difference in the use of the "Bibendum" copyright. ...The message purportedly behind the union's "Bibendum" cannot overcome the fact that a substantial part of the copyright original has been reproduced. The threshold for whether an act constitutes reproduction of a substantial part and thus infringement is not so low that an upraised boot is enough to constitute a new creation. It has been said that everyone is a critic, but I have no hesitation in dashing Counsel's arguments on the supposed creative spark found in the Defendant CAW's posters and leaflets.

(ii) Parody as an exception

As I have ruled that the Defendants have reproduced a substantial part of the Plaintiff's work and thus infringed the copyright, the burden now shifts to the Defendants to prove that they fall under an exception to copyright infringement. Like the Plaintiff in regards to the Trade-marks Act, the Defendants have offered a novel argument and radical interpretation of the law. In this case, the Defendants argue that parody is a form of "criticism" under Section 27(2)(a.1), the relevant exception to copyright infringement.

> 27(2) The following acts do not constitute an infringement of copyright:
>
> > ...(a.1) any fair dealing with any work for the purposes of criticism, review or newspaper summary, if
> >
> > > (i) the source, and
> > >
> > > (ii) the author's name, if given in the source are mentioned.

Parody is not explicitly discussed in the Copyright Act. The Defendants acknowledged that parody in previous cases had always been argued as an issue under Section 3(1) or that there had been no reproduction of a substantial part of the copyright because it constituted a new work (see Ludlow Music Inc. v. Canint Music Corp. (1967), 62 D.L.R (2d) 200 (Ex. Ct.) (hereinafter "Ludlow"), MCA Canada Ltd.-MCA Canada Ltée v. Gillberry & Hawke Advertising Agency Ltd. (1976), 28 C.P.R. (2d) 52 (F.C.T.D.) (hereinafter "MCA") and ATV Music Publishing of Canada Ltd. v. Rogers Radio Broadcasting Ltd. (1982), 65 C.P.R. (2d) 109 (Ont. H.C.J.) (hereinafter "ATV"). This long stream of Canadian cases held that parody is not an exception to acts of copyright infringement.

The Defendants attempted to distinguish the previous cases by arguing that they all discussed song parodies under Section 3(1) [FN9] or did not address the issue of whether the parody was a new work displaying original thought that did not infringe the copyright because they did not reproduce a substantial part of the work. Since words and music are so inextricably linked, the Court found in those cases that reproducing a substantial part of the music even with humorous parodic lyrics still constituted infringement of the copyright.

[FN9] In Ludlow, the song in question was "This Land is Your Land" by Woody Guthrie, in MCA the song was "Downtown", and in ATV the song was "Revolution" by the Beatles.

I am not satisfied that these cases are applicable to the current matter on the status of parody in Canadian law even if the fair dealing exception was not strictly pleaded. Under the Copyright Act, "criticism" is not synonymous with parody. Criticism requires analysis and judgment of a work that sheds light on the original. Parody is defined in the Collins dictionary (Second Edition) as "a musical, literary or other composition that mimics the style of another composer, author, etc. in a humorous or satirical way". In Zamacois v. Douville (1943), 3 Fox Pat. C. 44 (Ex. Ct.), Justice Angers at page 71 held that the Court will consider the wider context, both the quantity and quality of quotations from the original, in its evaluation of a work as "criticism": "The right of literary criticism includes the right of citation of passages from the work criticized and the number or the importance of the citations does not modify the character of the publication if they serve only to contribute to the demonstration of the criticism undertaken". In the Canadian and Commonwealth courts, parody has never been held to figure as criticism although the term criticism is not confined to "literary criticism".

The Defendants have added a twist to this usual reasoning by urging the Court to consider, in line with the recent decision of the American Supreme Court in Luther R. Campbell a.k.a. Luke Skywalker v. Acuff-Rose Music, Inc., 114 S. Ct. 1164 (1994) (hereinafter "Acuff-Rose"), that parody is a form of "criticism" under Section 27(2)(a.1). The Defendants submitted that even though their "Bibendum" constituted a reproduction of a substantial part of the Plaintiff's copyright, this was a type of parody that by the very definition of the term parody required substantial reproduction of the original to make its point. The addition of the men under "Bibendum's" upraised leg, the dialogue and the alteration in "Bibendum's" expression created a new, integrated "Bibendum" design that was meant to ridicule and mock "Bibendum's" usual corporate image as a benign, smiling and safe father figure. The Defendants further argued that they had no need to cite the source, a requirement under Section 27(2)(a.1) since in a parody, the source is implicitly known to the onlooker.

As with the Plaintiff's creative and novel interpretations of the Trade-marks Act, I have rejected the Defendants' submissions. The Defendants fall short because American case law permitting parody as criticism under the American doctrine of "fair use" is not applicable nor terribly persuasive in the Canadian context of a different legal regime and a longstanding trend to deny parody as an exception.

As well, exceptions to copyright infringement should be strictly interpreted. I am not prepared to read in parody as a form of criticism and thus create a new exception under Section 27(2)(a.1).

(iii) American case law and Strict Interpretation

The Defendants pointed to the recent unanimous decision of the American Supreme Court in Acuff-Rose (supra), as sole authority for reading in parody as a component of criticism or the exception to infringement. In effect, the Defendants are admitting, "Yes, we did infringe the Plaintiff's copyright by copying a substantial part of the original but as a defence, we can plead that we were parodying the original, a form of fair dealing for the purpose of criticism under Section 27(2)(a.1)". The Defendants admitted that they were urging the Court to accept a new interpretation of Section 27(2)(a.1) in the light of the American decision. In Acuff-Rose, the defendant had used the characteristic bass riff and opening line from Roy Orbison's classic rock song, "Pretty Woman" in its own rap song with new lewd and crude lyrics and distinctive rap background motifs. Justice Souter writing for the Court held at page 1173 that the Court of Appeal had erred in overstating the parodist's commercial motive to deny the fairness of the use: "In giving virtually dispositive weight to the commercial nature of the parody, the Court of Appeal erred." The rap version of "Pretty Woman" could still qualify as a parody or critique of the romantic fantasy embodied in the original song and could be considered an exception to copyright infringement as fair use for the purpose of criticism under Section 107 of the American Statute. The United States Supreme Court remanded the case to the trial level to reconsider the rap version of "Pretty Woman" against all of the factors for "fair use" in Section 107.

While the American case is most fascinating from both a cultural and legal perspective, I have not found it to be persuasive authority in the context of Canada's particular copyright regime. Chief Justice Laskin in Morgentaler v. The Queen, [1976] 1 S.C.R. 616, held at page 629 that a Court should be prudent in applying American precedents to the Canadian context and should take into consideration the particular rules of each system of law: "... they do not carry any authority beyond persuasiveness according to their relevance in the light of context, with due regard to the obvious differences that exist ...". American decisions are only persuasive to the extent that the laws in both jurisdictions are similar (see Compo Co. v. Blue Crest Music Inc., [1980] 1 S.C.R. 357 at page 367, 45 C.P.R. (2d) 1 (hereinafter "Compo")). The Plaintiff rightly pointed out many distinctions between Section 107 [FN11] of the American Copyright Act, 17 U.S.C., and our own system. Contrary to the opinion of James Zegers, author of an article entitled, "Parody and Fair Use in Canada after Campbell v. Acuff-Rose" in (1994) 11 C.I.P.R. 205, I hold that these distinctions are crucial. [FN12] First, the American system is open-ended when it comes to exceptions. In other words, the list of exceptions is not exhaustive but should be on a case-by-case basis since Section 107 reads, "for purposes such as criticism, comment ..." (emphasis added). As well, the four factors in Section 107 for determining whether use is fair are equally not exhaustive since they are prefaced by the phrase, "shall include". This is the not the case in Canada. The exceptions to acts of copyright infringement are exhaustively listed as a closed set in sub-sections 27(2) (a) to 27(2)(m) and 27(3) of the Copyright Act. They should be restrictively interpreted as exceptions. Justice McLachlin in Bishop v. Stevens, [1990] 2 S.C.R. 467 at pages 480-481, 31 C.P.R. (3d) 394 (hereinafter "Bishop"), cautioned the Court against reading in exceptions to copyright infringement given the detailed and explicit exemptions: "Furthermore, an implied exception to the literal meaning of s. 3(1)(d) is all the more unlikely, in my opinion, in light of the detailed and explicit exceptions in s. 17(2) (now s. 27(2)) of the Act, providing for matters as diverse as private study, research or critical review ...". I cannot accept that I should give the word "criticism" such a large meaning that it includes parody. In doing so, I would be creating a new exception to the copyright infringement, a step that only Parliament would have the jurisdiction to do.

Second, "fair use" in the American system is not equivalent to "fair dealing" in Canada. Unlike the explicit requirement in Section 27(2)(a.1), the American system does not require that the critic give the source and author of the copyright if this information is provided in the original. In sum, parody does not exist as a facet of "criticism", an exception to infringement in Canadian copyright law. I do accept that parody in a generic sense can be a form of criticism; however, it is not "criticism" for the purposes of the Copyright Act as an exception under the fair dealing heading.

In any event, the Plaintiff had argued that the "Bibendum" design on the leaflets and posters did not even qualify as a parody because the object of the parody or critical scorn has to be the original work, the original Michelin corporate "Bibendum" and not target CGEM Michelin's role as an employer. I do not intend to discuss at length this argument over what constitutes the proper object of parody. The American Supreme Court in Acuff-Rose (supra) held at page 1172 that to qualify as a parody, the commentary must have "critical bearing on the substance or style of the original composition". Since I have already ruled that parody does not exist as an exception to copyright infringement, it is immaterial to determine whether the proper target of the parody in this instance is the original work or the company represented by the original work. I will state, however, that I believe that the two are for all for intents and purposes equivalent in the public's perception. Michelin is the "Bibendum" and the "Bibendum" is Michelin, so any criticism of the "Bibendum" is criticism of Michelin and vice versa.

(iv) Mention Source and Fair Treatment

Thus, I hold, in line with the prevailing Canadian authorities, that parody does not exist as criticism, an exception to acts of copyright infringement. And even if I were to follow the American authority in Acuff-Rose and state that parody exists as a fair dealing exception to infringement, the Defendants would have failed under the two secondary elements of Section 27(2) (a.1). First, the Defendants did not mention the source and author's name of the original on their

"Bibendum" leaflets and poster. This is a condition of the fair dealing exception since Section 27(2)(a.1) states, "if (i) the source, and (ii) the author's name, if given in the source, are mentioned." The Defendants argued that by its very nature, every parody meets the criteria of mentioning the source and author since parody to succeed as parody must implicitly conjure up the heart of the original work. On the meaning of the term "mention", the Defendants were at pains to argue that mention is less stringent than another term like "cite" that Parliament could have used. The Defendants further submitted that "mention" means a casual allusion that is met by parody's implicit acknowledgement of the original by the mere fact of its necessary similarity to the original work.

With respect, I have difficulty accepting the Defendants' submissions on this issue. It is circular to argue that parody implicitly mentions the source and author because it is a parody. What if the source and author is not conjured up in the onlooker's mind because the parody is not very well executed, the parodist's target is particularly obscure or the recipient of the parody is dull-witted? Is it only "good" parodies that qualify under Section 27(2)(a.1)? The law cannot permit such distinctions. As well, the Defendants have to walk a very fine line in arguing that parody is a form of criticism that dispenses with the need to mention the source and author. Unfortunately for the Defendants, in walking this fine line, they have fallen into the abyss of logical inconsistency. According to the Defendants, the "Bibendum" depicted on the union leaflets and posters has to be similar enough to the Michelin original to implicitly "mention" the source but distinctive enough that it substantially reproduces the Michelin original but still constitutes a new work of criticism. The two facets of this argument are paradoxical and cannot be reconciled. The fact that the law requires mention of the source and author is yet another barrier to the Defendants' attempt to read in parody under the term "criticism". If parody does not require mention of the source because of its very nature as a parody, then parody cannot be included under the term "criticism" which so obviously requires mention of the source. The requirement to actively mention the source and author is there for a reason and not to be lightly skipped over. The need to require the source was added to amendments to the Copyright Act in An Act to Implement the North American Free Trade Agreement, S.C. 1993, c. 44, s. 64(1). There is no Canadian case law on what "mention" means but I am in agreement with the Plaintiff that it is more than a passive or implicit acknowledgement in parody. According to the Concise Oxford Dictionary (Eight Edition), mention means "to refer to briefly, to specify by name or to reveal or disclose ...". When the Plaintiff uses the "Bibendum", it gives Michelin as the source. The author or originator is not stated so at the very least the Defendants have to explicitly give the source and not the author if they hope to qualify under the fair dealing exception in Section 27(2)(a.1) when they use the "Bibendum" design. This they have not done.

In addition, the Defendants did not treat the original work in a fair manner, a further requirement of the "fair dealing" exception. The Defendants argued that as a parody, their work could not be held to treat the copyright in a kid glove fashion. Parody has to bite and in some way batter the reputation of the original.

However, once again, the Defendants have sought to dilute the usual rules of the fair dealing exception and defeat the wording of Section 27(2)(a.1) simply by labelling the "Bibendum" posters and leaflets a parody. It is not enough that because it is a parody, there is no need to mention the source. Now the Defendants would have the Court rule that by the mere fact of the parody label, the/ Defendants are permitted to forgo treating the Plaintiff's copyright in a fair manner, a requirement for all the existing exceptions like criticism, review and summary. To accept the Defendants' submissions on parody would be akin to making the parody label the last refuge of the scoundrel since the Court would have to do away with two of the usual strictures of Section 27(2)(a.1): mentioning the source and fair treatment. The term "fair dealing" is not defined in the Copyright Act but I accept the Plaintiff's submission that the overall use of the copyright must be "fair" or treat the copyright in a good faith manner. The Collins Dictionary defines "fair" as "free from discrimination, dishonesty, etc. just; impartial". The two secondary elements of mentioning the source and fair treatment are linked since the requirement that the critic mention the source and author's name is in some ways a testament to fair treatment. Whether the treatment of the original is in good faith is a question of degree and impression looking to the quality and quantity of the original work used (see Husband v. Vosper, [1972] 2 Q.B. 84 (C.A.)). Once again, as was the case in determining whether there has been reproduction of a substantial part, it is a question of impression. I have already ruled that the Defendants cannot avail themselves of the exception under Section 27(2)(a.1) but even if parody were to be read in as criticism, the Defendants would have to adhere to the bundle of limitations that go with criticism, including the need to treat the copyright in a fair manner. The Defendants held the "Bibendum" up to ridicule. Rather than the cuddly marshmallow creature of safety and responsibility, "Bibendum" became the boss's henchman about to stomp two workers into submission. The substantial quantity of the original work used in the leaflets and posters also casts doubt on the fairness of the Defendants' treatment.

(v) Conclusions on Copyright

I am not prepared to take the two leaps of faith urged by the Defendants. The first is that parody is synonymous with criticism. The second is that the Defendants can dispense with the need to mention the source and fair treatment because of the peculiar nature of parody with its implicit acknowledgement of the source. My role is not to create legislation but to apply the existing rules crafted by Parliament. If Parliament had wanted to exempt parody as a new exception under the fair dealing provision, it would have done so (see Bishop, supra, at pages 483-484). Since the Defendants have shown little creativity in depicting the "Bibendum", I do not accept the Defendants' contention that their creativity is being fatally stifled by a repressive copyright regime.

**Productions Avanti Ciné-Vidéo Inc. c. Favreau (1999), 1 C.P.R. (4th) 129
(Que. C.A.), reversing (1997), 79 C.P.R. (3d) 385 (Que. S.C.)**

Quebec Court of Appeal

Rothman and Gendreau JJ.A. and Biron J. (ad hoc)

August 4, 1999

The plaintiff produced a humorous, unique television program based upon a fictional couple: a mother, clearly played by a man, dressed in a flowered decorated robe and a father who sported a false long wide beard. The program was a caricature of a suburban Quebec family experiencing a variety of incidents. The program achieved unprecedented success on Quebec television.

The defendant used the characters from the plaintiff's program, recognisable in their costumes and mannerisms, in producing a pornographic film without appropriating any of the dialogue of the plaintiff's characters. The defendant claimed that the characters were not protected by copyright and that, if they were so protected, the defendant's use of the characters constituted a parody within the exception for fair dealing. The plaintiff secured an interlocutory injunction and applied to the court to uphold the interlocutory injunction in its favour. At trial the court concluded that the plaintiff's characters were not sufficiently original to be protected by copyright and, therefore, dismissed the action. The plaintiff appealed.

. . .

The defence of fair use

Notwithstanding my finding that Appellant's copyright has been infringed, the Respondent asks the Court to dismiss the appeal on the ground that the copied work is in fact a true parody, thus falling under the "fair use" exception contained in the Copyright Act.

The Respondent principally refers us to American law, which provides for a defence of "fair use" sufficiently large to include parody. The United States Supreme Court has acknowledged that parody is part of criticism and therefore may constitute a "fair use" defined by section 11 of the Copyright Act. That was decided in the Acuff-Rose affair.

In that case, the Court, during their review of the first component of section 107 of the American law concerning "the purpose and character of the use", expressed the opinion that the Court should examine "the nature and objects of the selections made" with a view to determining whether "the new work merely supersede(s) the objects of the original creation . . . or instead adds something new, with a further purpose or different character, altering the first with new expression, meaning, or message . . . in other words, whether and to what extent the new work is 'transformative'". The Court was of the view that parody clearly has a transformative value. That is why it added:

> For the purpose of copyright law, the nub of the definitions, and the heart of any parodist's claim to quote from existing material, is the use of some elements of a prior author's composition to create a new one that, at least in part, comments on that author's work.
>
> . . .
>
> If, on the contrary, the commentary has no critical bearing on the substance or style of the original composition, which the alleged infringer merely uses to get attention or to avoid the drudgery in working up something fresh, the claim to fairness in borrowing from another's work diminishes accordingly (if it does not vanish), and other factors, like the extent of its commerciality, loom larger.

In other countries, a separate exception has been created for parody. Thus, in France, article 122-5, paragraph 4 of the Code de la propriété intellectuelle [Intellectual Property Code] expressly provides for the exception of [translation] "parody, pastiche and caricature, based on the relevant laws". Frédéric Pollaud-Dulian writes that [translation] "the author cannot prevent parody or require remuneration for copies made of his work on such occasions, even if parody is in the nature of a derivative work". Nevertheless, not all copies are parody and the author specifies four conditions necessary so that parody be allowable [translation]:

[FN20] Juris-Classeur, Civil Annexes, Propriútú littúraire et artistique, Fasc. 1246 "Droits patrimoniaux, Droit de reproduction", by F. Pollaud-Dulian, 1995, no. 76, p. 19.

  a) parody must have a humoristic intention and effect, failing which there is infringement . . .

  b) parody may not create any risk of confusion with the works of the parodied author . . .

  c) parody generally has the purpose of amusing at the expense of the work or the parodied author. It is also possible that pastiche is used with a different intention, that of rendering homage to the work or the parodied author . . .

  d) parody may not intentionally aim to harm . . .

Since 1994, Belgium also has a similar provision in its laws. [FN22] This is also the case in Spain. [FN23]

[FN22] Loi du 30 juin 1994 relative au droit d'auteur et aux droits voisins, article 22 al. 6.

[FN23] Real decreto legislativo, 12 April 1996, Num. 1/1996, Propriedad intellectual, art. 39. The exception remains provided there is no risk of confusion or prejudice to the original work or its author.

Under Canadian law, the sole exception to these notions is contained within the notion of "fair use" provided for in the Copyright Act. Copyright is not infringed by unauthorized dealing or use of a work or substantial part of it for research or private study or for purposes of criticism, review or news reporting. Dealing for the purposes of criticism or reporting is possible for any type of work if the use is reasonable and complies with the purpose and if the source and name of the author are mentioned.

. . .

Several parallels may be drawn with the English Copyright, Designs and Patents Act 1988 (U.K.), c. 48, which allows a similar defence of fair dealing for the purposes of research, criticism, review and news reporting on current events and education, provided the work is accompanied by "sufficient acknowledgement" of the author of the original work. [FN24]

[FN24] Copyright Designs and Patents Act 1988, ss. 29 and 30.

The case law has not clearly determined the scope of the fair use exception up to now. However, it is possible to conclude that the purposes which are allowed as justifications for reproduction of an original work are restricted to those listed. The aim pursued by the person copying the work is at the heart of the analysis of fair use defined by sections 29 and 29.1 of Act and only certain well defined purposes are allowable purposes justifying fair use.

...[T]he purposes and motivation of a person who is reproducing the work are not relevant elements at the phase of determining of whether there is infringement of copyright. These elements, however, become very significant when reviewing the issue of fair use. ...

To what extent may parody constitute fair use of a work and also constitute an exception to protection of the original document? ...

It would seem that parody can be seen from two angles: an exception to copyright infringement under section 27(1) (now 29) of the Act, or an original work as such. In the first case, it is clear that the act is restrictive and that the exception will only be applied in the defined cases, particularly for purposes of criticism. Now, it is well known that criticism of an intellectual or artistic work is not necessarily serious or scholarly. It may also be humorous or comic due to amplification, deformation or exaggeration of the targeted work. In a word, it takes the avenues of caricature which allow it to be all the more scathing. In this sense, it may constitute an exception, provided that the requirements of the Act are satisfied. However, this is generally not the situation referred to, but rather the second, where parody is seen as a work in itself which is original, distinct and independent from the work being parodied, the creation of which requires labour, imagination and talent. This is what distinguishes it from colourable imitation. The authors, in particular Braithwaite, are inclined to acknowledge that this intellectual creation which constitutes true parody confers upon its author a true recognition, but are not ready to conclude that the rights of the parodied author have not been infringed, a step which was taken in England in the Joy Music, Ltd. case.

The absence of formal decision on this point in Canada, at least based on my research and that of the parties in the present matter, is perhaps due to the fact that in reality this vision of things is commonly accepted and that true parody is recognised. That means that if a creator produces authentic parody which creates a new work which pastiches or ridicules another work, or which relies upon another work to mock or criticise a social or political event — this is the situation in Joy Music, Ltd., where the song Rock-a-Billy was used to caricature Prince Philip — there is no copyright infringement. In my view, two criteria are met: the finality of borrowing from the other work and the originality of the new work. One can discuss the situation of "target parody" or that of "weapon parody", but the true question is, and remains, the following: what is the nature of the work produced? Parody and burlesque are literary and dramatic genres. Their purpose is to criticise by ridiculing a work, a situation or persons. As soon as a work is qualified as such, it takes on its own life. However, a parody must not be used as a shield to avoid intellectual work in order to benefit from the notoriety of the parodied work.

Nevertheless, in the present matter, whether the strict criterion of section 27 (now 29) of fair use for the purposes of criticism or a larger notion is relied upon, I am of the view that Favreau cannot succeed. As the Ontario Divisional Court underlined, the fair dealing rule refers to a purposive test. The Act furthermore requires that the object of appropriation must be criticism or reporting. On the basis of the evidence, La Petite Vite which Favreau estimates to produce 100,000 copies of (it would appear that this figure was determined based on the popular success of La Petite Vie) was not created, nor does it aim to be criticism or reporting of Meunier's work. The substantial borrowing from La Petite Vie, both in quantity and in substance, had the sole aim of providing maximum visibility to a video which would not have enjoyed such notoriety otherwise, while avoiding the inevitable labour of any literary or artistic creation. Nor is there any research or creation in fact. What constitutes the originality of La Petite Vite is its being a crass copy of substantial parts of Meunier's work.

Nor am I convinced that the purpose of Favreau was to ridicule the work of Avanti. In a word, Favreau borrowed everything he could possibly take from La Petite Vie (decor, characters, mannerisms, expressions, etc.) for the purpose of integrating it into his film. This is clearly neither parody nor criticism. The borrowings are neither subtle nor misleading, but are as accentuated as possible. Therefore in my view, the Respondent has infringed the rights of the Appellant.

For all the above grounds, I am of the view that the appeal should be allowed with costs...

Canwest v. Horizon

2008 BCSC 1609
[Aff'd 2009 BCSC 391]
October 28, 2008

Before: Master Donaldson

Reasons for Judgment

[1] This matter arises from the authoring, printing and distribution of "a fake edition of the *Vancouver Sun*" or a "parody" of the *Vancouver Sun* on the 7th of June, 2007. [The mock paper duplicated the masthead of the Vancouver Sun. It contained articles which, by their sarcasm, criticised, amongst other things, Israel's policy with respect to the Palestinians. The articles also criticised the plaintiff's reporting of Middle East issues. The mock papers were placed in Vancouver Sun vending machines.] The ...second motion in time is brought on behalf of the plaintiff seeking that certain paragraphs of Mr. Murray's statement of defence be struck, these being paragraphs 2, 3, 4 and 11. It is contended on the part of the plaintiff that those paragraphs disclose no reasonable defence and are unnecessary, scandalous, frivolous or vexatious or on the bases that they may prejudice or embarrass the proceeding....

[2] The defendant Mr. Murray characterizes the publication as being a parody and seeks extensive document production....

[4] Generally speaking the plaintiffs latest statement of claim makes four claims: 1. passing off; 2. injurious falsehood; 3. breach of copyright; and 4. breach of trademark.

[5] In his defence Mr. Murray claims that: 1. parody as a defence to the counter copyright claim, 2. freedom of expression as a defence to all claims....

[6] The defendant alleges media ownership in British Columbia is concentrated in the plaintiff; the plaintiff has a particular bias in relation to news matters that stem from the Middle East, that the plaintiff maintains a centralized editorial policy and that the action is motivated by an improper purpose.

Striking portions of the Statement of Defence

[7] I propose to deal firstly with the plaintiff's application to strike portions of the amended statement of defence of Gordon Murray. ...The paragraphs sought to be struck are:

> 2. Canwest is Canada's largest newspaper chain reaching 4.8 million readers on a weekly basis. It owns and operates the following newspapers, which together comprise approximately 84% of the daily paid newspaper circulation in British Columbia....Canwest describes itself as the dominant news organization in British Columbia.
>
> 3. Canwest newspapers and other Canwest media properties have a strong pro-Israel bias, particularly in their coverage of the Israeli occupation of the West Bank and the Gaza Strip. In Canwest publications, Israelis are usually portrayed

as innocent victims and Palestinians as inhuman terrorists. Israeli casualties and deaths are disproportionately reported and sympathetically described while Palestinian deaths are relatively underreported and unsympathetically described. Canwest takes the position that Israel is blameless and described the Palestinian people in one editorial as a single collective suicide bomber....

11. The defendant denies that Canwest suffered any loss of circulation or revenue as a result of the parody. The defendant says that this lawsuit is not intended to compensate Canwest for any losses. This lawsuit is intended to restrict publication and circulation of the Parody, to inflict economic and emotional harm on the defendants for the pro-Palestinian activities listed in paragraphs 10, 11 and 12 of the Statement of Claim, and to generally deter publication of the opinions expressed by the Parody. This purpose and effect of this lawsuit are inimical to the common law and to the Charter of Rights and Freedoms. This lawsuit represents a perversion of civil justice and an abuse of process and is contrary to Rule 19(24) of the Supreme Court Rules.

[8] *Rule 19(24)* of the *Rules of Court* is the applicable rule dealing with the striking of portions of a claim.

At any stage of a proceeding the court may order to be struck out or amended the whole or any part of an endorsement, pleading, petition or other document on the ground that

(a) it discloses no reasonable claim or defence as the case may be,

(b) It is unnecessary, scandalous, frivolous or vexatious,

(c) it may prejudice, embarrass or delay the fair trial or hearing or the proceeding, or

(d) it is otherwise an abuse of the process of the court,

and the court may grant judgment or order the proceeding to be stayed or dismissed and may order the costs of the application to be paid as special costs.

[9] The leading case on motions to strike pleadings is *Hunt v. Carey Canada Inc.,* [1990] 2 S.C.R. 959. In *Hunt* at page 980, Wilson, J. for the court set out the test:

...assuming that the facts as stated in the statement of claim can be proved, is it "plain and obvious" that the plaintiff's statement of claim discloses no reasonable cause of action?...

[10] Romilly, J. also discussed the "plain and obvious" rule in the context of subrules 19 (24) (c) and (d) in *Citizens for Foreign Aid Reform Inc. v. Canadian Jewish Congress* (1999), 36 C.P.C. (4th) 266 @ para 47. The theme throughout the definitions of scandalous, vexatious, unnecessary and frivolous allegations is relevance. That is, if the allegation is or may be relevant to a claim or defence, it must stay in; if not, it should be struck.

[11] The issue in this matter is whether the defendant's allegations are relevant to any of the defences. The media ownership, centralized editorial policy and

motivation allegations clearly do not go to any of the defences which the defendant has raised. Therefore, they should be struck.

[12] The defendant Mr. Murray contends that the defence of freedom of expression is appropriate and applicable to him in this matter. In *Compagnie Générale des Établissements Michelin — Michelin & Cie v. National Automobile, Aerospace, Transportation and Générale Workers Union of Canada (CAW — Canada)* (1996), 124 F.T.R. 192, (*sub nom. Cie Generale des Établissements Michelin-Michelin & Cie v. C.A.W.-Canada et al*) 71 C.P.R. (3d) 348 [*Michelin*], raised freedom of expression as a defence to both copyright and trade-mark infringement. Teitelbaum J. (as he then was) analyzed freedom of expression in relation to the *Copyright Act*, R.S. 1985, c. C-42, and held at Para. 76 that "the principles and outcome" also applied to the *Trade-marks Act*, R.S. 1985, c. T-13.

[13] Teitelbaum J. clearly found that freedom of expression is not a defence to copyright or trademark infringement. At Para. 79 he stated that:

> ... the defendants' right to freedom of expression was not restricted. The Charter does not confer the right to use private property — the plaintiff's copyright — in the service of freedom of expression...

He further held at Para. 109 that, if he had found an infringement, he would have held that the relevant provisions of the *Copyright Act* were justified under s. 1 of the *Charter.*

[14] In the statement of defence, the defendant seems to assert that the fake *Sun* is a parody, and therefore it does not infringe the *Copyright Act* due to the "fair use" exception for criticism in s. 29.1. However, Teitelbaum J held clearly in *Michelin* at Para. 63 that parody is not an exception to copyright infringement under the *Copyright Act*, and therefore does not constitute a defence.

[15] As parody is not a defence to a copyright claim, the defendant's allegations cannot be necessary to prove it....

[17] Thus I am satisfied that paragraphs 2 and 3 of the amended statement of defence filed the 21ˢᵗ of October 2008 should be struck....

[22] Paragraph 11 of the statement of defence should be struck....

---

v. Exceptions for Interoperability, Computer and Security Assessment, and Technological Processes

The Act contains several exceptions that permit copying of computer programs including for interoperability purposes, for the purposes of encryption research, computer and network security assessment and copying required as part of a technological process. The section reads as follows:

Permitted acts

30.6 It is not an infringement of copyright in a computer program for a person who owns a copy of the computer program that is authorized by the owner of the copyright, or has a licence to use a copy of the computer program, to

(a) reproduce the copy by adapting, modifying or converting it, or translating it into another computer language, if the person proves that the reproduced copy

(i) is essential for the compatibility of the computer program with a particular computer,

(ii) is solely for the person's own use, and

(iii) was destroyed immediately after the person ceased to be the owner of the copy of the computer program or to have a licence to use it; or

(b) reproduce for backup purposes the copy or a reproduced copy referred to in paragraph (a) if the person proves that the reproduction for backup purposes was destroyed immediately after the person ceased to be the owner of the copy of the computer program or to have a licence to use it.

Interoperability of computer programs

30.61 (1) It is not an infringement of copyright in a computer program for a person who owns a copy of the computer program that is authorized by the owner of the copyright, or has a licence to use a copy of the computer program, to reproduce the copy if

(a) they reproduce the copy for the sole purpose of obtaining information that would allow the person to make the program and another computer program interoperable; and

(b) they do not use or disclose that information, except as necessary to make the program and another computer program interoperable or to assess that interoperability.

No limitation

(2) In the case where that information is used or disclosed as necessary to make another computer program interoperable with the program, subsection (1) applies even if the other computer program incorporates the information and is then sold, rented or otherwise distributed.

Security

30.63 (1) Subject to subsections (2) and (3), it is not an infringement of copyright for a person to reproduce a work or other subject-matter for the sole purpose, with the consent of the owner or administrator of a computer, computer system or computer network, of assessing the vulnerability of the computer, system or network or of correcting any security flaws.

Limitation

(2) Subsection (1) does not apply if the person uses or discloses information obtained through the assessment or correction to commit an act that is an offence under the Criminal Code.

Limitation — computer program

(3) Subsection (1) applies with respect to a computer program only if, in the event that the assessment or correction reveals a vulnerability or a security flaw in the program and the person intends to make the vulnerability or security flaw public, the person gives adequate notice of the vulnerability or security flaw and of their intention to the owner of copyright in the program. However, the person need not give that adequate notice if, in the circumstances, the public interest in having the vulnerability or security flaw made public without adequate notice outweighs the owner's interest in receiving that notice.

32. The Act is amended by adding the following after section 30.7:

Temporary Reproductions for Technological Processes

Temporary reproductions

30.71 It is not an infringement of copyright to make a reproduction of a work or other subject-matter if

(a) the reproduction forms an essential part of a technological process;

(b) the reproduction's only purpose is to facilitate a use that is not an infringement of copyright; and

(c) the reproduction exists only for the duration of the technological process.

The UK Supreme Court recently considered the scope of a similar exception and its application to end-users viewing material online.

Public Relations Consultants Association Ltd. v. Newspaper

Licensing Agency Ltd.

[2013] UKSC 18 (U.K. S.C.)

17 April 2013

LORD SUMPTION (with whom Lord Neuberger, Lord Kerr, Lord Clarke and Lord Carnwath agree)

The issue

1. This appeal raises an important question about the application of copyright law to the technical processes involved in viewing copyright material on the internet. The owner of a copyright has the exclusive right to do or to authorise a number of acts defined in sections 16 to 26 of the Copyright, Designs and Patents Act 1988. Broadly speaking, it is an infringement to make or distribute copies or adaptations of a protected work. Merely viewing or reading it is not an infringement. A person who reads a pirated copy of a protected book or views

a forgery of a protected painting commits no infringement although the person who sold him the book or forged the painting may do.

2. The ordinary use of the internet will involve the creation of temporary copies at several stages. Copies will be created in the course of transmission in internet routers and proxy servers. Where a web-page is viewed by an end-user on his computer, without being downloaded, the technical processes involved will require temporary copies to be made on screen and also in the internet "cache" on the hard disk. The screen copy is self-evidently an essential part of the technology involved, without which the web-page cannot be viewed by the user. It will remain on screen until the user moves away from the relevant web-page. The function of the internet cache is somewhat more complex. It is a universal feature of current internet browsing technology. It would be possible to design browsing software without an internet cache, but in the present state of technology the result would be that the internet would be unable to cope with current volumes of traffic and would not function properly. The cache may be deliberately cleared by the end-user, but otherwise it will in the ordinary course be overwritten by other material after an interval which will depend on its capacity and on the volume and timing of the end-user's internet usage. The above is a crude, but for present purposes sufficient, description of the technical processes. Like most things in the digital world, their operation is capable of being modified. The capacity of the internet cache may within limits be modified by altering the browser settings on the user's computer. Deleted material can sometimes be retrieved by special software or highly proficient technicians. But this refinement is not characteristic of the ordinary use of the internet and can for present purposes be ignored. The important point is that in none of these cases does the end-user set out to make a copy of the web-page unless he chooses to download it or print it out. His object is to view the material. The copies temporarily retained on the screen or the internet cache are merely the incidental consequence of his use of a computer to do that. The question which arises on this appeal is whether they are nonetheless infringing copies unless licensed by the rights owner.

3. The appellant is a professional association of public relations professionals who, among other things, monitor news coverage on behalf of clients. One way of doing this is to use on-line monitoring or search services. This appeal is about the services provided to members of the association by the Meltwater group of companies. The Meltwater companies use automated software programmes to create anindex of words appearing on newspaper websites. Meltwater's customers provide them with search terms of interest to them, and Meltwater produces a monitoring report listing the results of a search of the index for those keywords. For each search hit, the monitoring report will present the opening words of the article, the keyword together with several words on either side of it, and a hyperlink (in the form of a reproduction of the headline) which enables the user to access the article on the relevant source website. It should, however, be noted that if that website has a paywall, the link will not enable the user to avoid it. He will have to pay for access to the material behind the paywall on the same terms

as anyone else. Meltwater sends the monitoring report to the customer by email or the customer accesses it on the Meltwater website.

4. A number of points are common ground. It is common ground that Meltwater agreed to take a licence from the publishers of the newspapers to provide their service on terms which have been settled by the Copyright Tribunal. It is also common ground, and has been from an early stage of these proceedings, that Meltwater's customers require a licence to receive the service in its present form. This is because in its present form the service automatically involves the transmission of the monitoring report by e-mail. The email copy is not temporary. It is stored on the recipient's hard drive until the end-user chooses to delete it. The real question on this appeal is whether Meltwater's customers would need a licence to receive its service if the monitoring report were made available only on Meltwater's website. Obviously, to the extent that the customer downloads the report from the website he is making a copy that will infringe the newspaper's copyright unless he is licensed. But what if he merely views the material on the website? Proudman J held that he also needed a licence for that, and the Court of Appeal agreed with her. The issue has reached this court because it affects the operation of a service which is being made available on a commercial basis. But the same question potentially affects millions of non-commercial users of the internet who may, no doubt unwittingly, be incurring civil liability by viewing copyright material on the internet without the authority of the rights owner, for example because it has been unlawfully uploaded by a third party. Similar issues arise when viewers watch a broadcast on a digital television or a subscription television programme via a set-top box.

Directive 2001/29/EC

5. Temporary copies created as part of the technical processes involved in viewing copyright material on a computer are dealt with by section 28A of the Copyright, Designs and Patents Act 1988. Section 28A was added to the Act by regulation in 2003 to give effect to Directive 2001/29/EC of 22 May 2001 on "the harmonisation of certain aspects of copyright and related rights in the information society." It is not disputed that the effect of the Directive and the English statutory provision is the same, and it is convenient to refer to the terms of the Directive.

. . .

9. Chapter II of the Directive deals with "Rights and Exceptions". The rights of the copyright owner are dealt with separately in articles 2, 3 and 4 under three heads: reproduction rights, communication rights and distribution rights respectively. Article 5 then qualifies these rights. Article 5.1 creates an exception for temporary copies which applies only to the reproduction right defined by article 2. It provides:

> "1. Temporary acts of reproduction referred to in Article 2, which are transient or incidental [and] an integral and essential part of a technological process and whose sole purpose is to enable:

(a) a transmission in a network between third parties by an intermediary, or

(b) a lawful use

of a work or other subject-matter to be made, and which have no independent economic significance, shall be exempted from the reproduction right provided for in Article 2.

. . .

5. The exceptions and limitations provided for in paragraphs 1, 2, 3 and 4 shall only be applied in certain special cases which do not conflict with a normal exploitation of the work or other subject-matter and do not unreasonably prejudice the legitimate interests of the rightholder."

Chapters III and IV then make extensive provision for the enforcement of copyright owners' rights in the digital world.

The effect of the CJEU decisions

26. The effect of this body of authority can be summarised as follows:

(1) Subject to the limitations which I shall summarise in the following subparagraphs, the exception in article 5.1 applies to copies made as an integral and necessary part of a "technological process", in particular the digital processing of data. For this purpose, the making of copies is a "necessary" part of the process if it enables it to function "correctly and efficiently": *Infopaq II*, at paras 30, 37.

(2) These copies must be temporary. This requirement is explained and defined by the words which follow, namely that the making of the copies must be "transient or incidental and an integral and essential part of a technological process". It means (i) that the storage and deletion of the copyright material must be the automatic consequence of the user's decision to initiate or terminate the relevant technological process, as opposed to being dependent on some further discretionary human intervention, and (ii) that the duration of the copy should be limited to what is necessary for the completion of the relevant technological process: see *Infopaq I*, at paras 62 and 64.

(3) The exception is not limited to copies made in order to enable the transmission of material through intermediaries in a network. It also applies to copies made for the sole purpose of enabling other uses, provided that these uses are lawful. These other uses include internet browsing: *Infopaq I*, at para 63 and *Infopaq II*, at para 49.

(4) For the purpose of article 5.1, a use of the material is lawful, whether or not the copyright owner has authorised it, if it is consistent with EU legislation governing the reproduction right, including article 5.1 itself: *Premier League*, at paras 168-173, *Infopaq II*, at para 42. The use of the material is not unlawful by reason only of the fact that it lacks the authorisation of the copyright owner.

(5) The making of the temporary copy must have no "independent economic significance". This does not mean that it must have no commercial value. It may well have. What it means is that it must have no *independent* commercial value, i.e. no value additional to that which is derived from the mere act of digitally transmitting or viewing the material: *Premier League*, at para 175, *Infopaq II*, at para 50.

(6) If these conditions are satisfied no additional restrictions can be derived from article 5.5.

Application to the present case

27. The first and fundamental question is whether article 5.1 applies at all to temporary copies generated by an end-user's use of the internet. Mr. Howe QC, who appeared for the Newspaper Licensing Agency, submitted that it did not. He argued that it applied only to copies made in the course of the transmission of the material within a network, for example in the caches of intermediate routers and proxy servers. In my opinion, this is an impossible contention. In the first place, it is clear from the Directive's recitals, and in particular from recital 33, that it was intended that the exception should "include acts which enable browsing as well as acts of caching to take place." Browsing is not part of the process of transmission. It is the use of an internet browser by an end-user to view web pages. It is by its very nature an end-user function. The "acts" referred to are the "acts of temporary reproduction" referred to at the outset of the recital, with which the whole recital is concerned. The acts of temporary reproduction which "enable" browsing to occur are accordingly the making of temporary copies in the internet cache of the end-user's hard drive and on his screen. It follows that the recital expressly envisages that the exception will apply to end-user viewing of web-pages. Secondly, if Mr Howe is right the scope of the exception corresponds only to that part of the process which is covered by article 5.1(a) ("transmission in a network between third parties by an intermediary"). In fact, caching is concerned with the transmission of material in a network, because its purpose is to make the operation of the internet more efficient by easing constraints on its capacity: see paragraph 2 above. But the exception in any event is wider than that, for it also extends to operations covered by article 5.1(b) ("lawful use"). Lawful "use" refers to the use of the work which is the subject of the copyright. It extends to use, as the Court of Justice made clear in the *Premier League* case and *Infopaq II*, whether or not authorised by the copyright owner, which is "not restricted by the applicable legislation". This necessarily includes the use of the work by an end-user browsing the internet. Third, Mr. Howe's submission is directly contradicted by the judgment in the *Premier League* case, where article 5 was applied to Mrs Murphy's use of the copyright material by displaying it on her television. She was the end-user. She and her customers were consuming the product. In the context of the fifth condition, that the copy should have no independent economic significance, the court considered at para 176 the status of the copy made on the television screen, because it had been suggested by the Advocate-General (at AG95) that the screen copy might have an independent economic significance that the cached copy lacked. At para 179, the court pointed out that if article 5.1 did not apply to the viewing of copyright material by a television end-user, such viewers "would be prevented from receiving broadcasts... in the absence of an authorisation from copyright holders", which would "impede and even paralyse the actual spread and contribution of new technologies in disregard of the will of the EU legislature as expressed in recital 31." For this purpose, there is no rational distinction to be made between

viewing copyright material on a television screen and viewing the same material on a computer.

28. Once it is accepted that part of the purpose of article 5.1 is to authorise the making of copies to enable the end-user to view copyright material on the internet, the various conditions laid down by that article must be construed so far as possible in a manner consistent with that purpose. It must, if the exception is to be coherent, apply to the ordinary technical processes associated with internet browsing.

29. There is, to my mind, no room for argument on the facts of this case about the third, fourth and fifth conditions in article 5.1. The third condition is that the making of copies in the internet cache and on screen should be an integral and essential part of a technological process. Manifestly it is. These were at the time of the Directive and remain today basic features of the design of modern computers. It would no doubt be possible to design computers that did not cache material in the course of internet browsing, but in the words of the judgment in *Infopaq II*, the technological processes required to browse the internet could not function "correctly and efficiently" without the acts of reproduction concerned: see paras 30 and 37. The fourth condition, as applied to end-users like Meltwater's customers, is that its use should be lawful. Once it is established, as it is by the decisions in the *Premier League* case and *Infopaq II*, that this means lawful apart from any lack of authorisation by the copyright owner, it is equally clear that this condition is satisfied. The fifth condition, that the copying should have no independent economic significance, is satisfied for the same reason as it was satisfied in the *Premier League* case, namely that it has no *independent* economic value to Meltwater's customers. This is because unless they download or print out the material (in which case it is not disputed that they require a licence), the sole economic value which they derive from accessing information on Meltwater's website is derived from the mere fact of reading it on screen.

30. These considerations no doubt explain why Mr. Howe's submissions were addressed mainly to the first two conditions, that the copies generated by the technical processes involved in browsing should be "temporary" and "transient or incidental". It is not suggested that "transient" means anything different from "temporary", and in my view they are the same. "Transience" is simply part of the elaborate explanation of "temporary" which follows that word.

31. If, as the Court of Justice has accepted, browsing copyright material on the internet is a method of using it which is within the scope of article 5.1, and if the making of copies in the internet cache or on screen is indispensable to the correct and efficient operation of the technical processes involved in browsing, it would be strange if the law said that the period of time for which these copies will exist in the ordinary course of that operation was insufficiently "temporary" or "transient" to qualify. As I have explained above by reference to the judgment in *Infopaq I*, the relevant requirements are (i) that the storage and deletion of the copyright material should be automatic, as opposed to being dependent on "discretionary human intervention", and (ii) that the duration of the copy

should be limited to what is "necessary for the completion of the technological processes in question": see paras 62 and 64. The "storage" of the material, i.e. the creation of copies in the cache or on screen, is the automatic result of browsing the internet. It requires no other human intervention than the decision to access the relevant web-page. Its deletion is the equally automatic result of the lapse of time coupled with the continuing use of the browser. The "technological processes in question" are those necessarily associated with web browsing, including the retention of material in the cache. It is retained there for no longer than the ordinary processes associated with internet use continue. Standing back for a moment from this fine verbal analysis of the language of the court, the purpose of these formulations is plain. It is to distinguish between the use of a computer or other equipment simply to view the relevant material, and its use to record it. The object of the restriction to "temporary" or "transient" copies is to ensure that the exception does not apply to protect downloading or other forms of digital or physical copying which will remain in existence until the user chooses to delete or destroy them and are therefore as permanent as he chooses to make them.

32. Mr Howe's argument was that cached material was not "temporary" or "transient" because the user could make a discretionary decision to close down the computer, thereby leaving the material in the cache indefinitely until the browser was used again. Or he could adjust the settings so as to enlarge the cache, thereby extending the period for which material might remain in it even while the browser was in use. He could also access a web page and leave his computer on with the web page on screen indefinitely. These are certainly examples of discretionary human intervention, but they are irrelevant because they do not involve a discretionary decision whether to retain the material in memory or not. They are merely rather artificial ways of extending the duration of the relevant "technological processes". They call for three comments in the present context. The first is that the effect of creating copies in the internet cache or on screen in the course of browsing, must be judged in the light of the normal operation of a computer or its browser. It is not enough that forensic ingenuity can devise a method of extending to some extent the life of copies which are by their nature temporary. Secondly, the question is whether human intervention is required to delete the material: see *Infopaq I* at para 66. There is a difference, which is fundamental to the object of article 5.1, between a discretionary decision to extend the duration of what remains an automatic process, and the storage of a copy of material in the course of the browsing in a manner which will ensure that it is permanent unless and until a discretionary decision is made to delete or destroy it. The decisions of the Court of Justice show that in principle the former satisfies the first two conditions in article 5.1 whereas the latter does not. Third, the Respondents' examples, as examples go, prove too much. If the mere fact that it is in principle possible to close down a computer, alter the browser settings to enlarge the internet cache or leave an image on screen indefinitely were enough to prevent article 5.1 from applying, then it would never apply to internet browsing. This would frustrate the purpose of the legislation.

33. If, as I consider, the copies made in the internet cache or on screen are "transient", it is strictly speaking unnecessary to consider whether they are also "incidental". But I think it clear that they are. The software puts a web-page on screen and into the cache for the purpose of enabling a lawful use of the copyright material, i.e. viewing it. The creation of the copies is wholly incidental to the technological process involved.

34. Once these matters are established, it follows that article 5.5 is also satisfied.

Consequences

35. It is the policy of the EU to maintain a "high level of protection of intellectual property". That policy is acknowledged both in the Directive itself (see recitals 4 and 9), and in the case law (for example, *Premier League* at para 186). We were pressed with the argument that if the viewing of copyright material on a web-page did not require a licence from the copyright owner, he would be exposed to large-scale piracy of a kind which would be difficult to detect or prevent.

36. I am not persuaded by this argument and nor, it is clear, was the Court of Justice on the successive occasions when it has dealt with this issue. Of course, any diminution in the rights of copyright owners necessarily narrows the scope of the protection which they enjoy for their works. But we need to keep this point in proportion. In the first place, article 5.1 is an exception to the copyright owner's right to control the reproduction of his work. It necessarily operates to authorise certain copying which would otherwise be an infringement of the copyright owner's rights. Secondly, it has never been an infringement, in either English or EU law, for a person merely to view or read an infringing article in physical form. This state of affairs, which is recognised in the enumeration of the copyright owner's rights in articles 2, 3 and 4 of the Directive, has never been thought inconsistent with a high level of protection for intellectual property. All that article 5.1 of the Directive achieves is to treat the viewing of copyright material on the internet in the same way as its viewing in physical form, notwithstanding that the technical processes involved incidentally include the making of temporary copies within the electronic equipment employed. Third, if it is an infringement merely to view copyright material, without downloading or printing out, then those who browse the internet are likely unintentionally to incur civil liability, at least in principle, by merely coming upon a web-page containing copyright material in the course of browsing. This seems an unacceptable result, which would make infringers of many millions of ordinary users of the internet across the EU who use browsers and search engines for private as well as commercial purposes. Fourth, nothing in article 5.1 affects the obligation of Meltwater to be licensed in order to upload copyright material onto their website or make non-temporary copies of it in some other way. At the moment, the licence fee payable by Meltwater is fixed on the basis that its customers need a licence of their own from the publishers and that the service will be supplied only to end-users who have one. It seems very likely (although I am not deciding the point) that the licence fee chargeable to Meltwater will be substantially higher if end-users do not need a licence because on that footing the

value of the rights for which Meltwater is licensed will be significantly higher. The respondents have lodged an alternative claim with the Copyright Tribunal on that basis. In my view it is altogether more satisfactory that a single large licence fee should be payable representing the value to the person who puts the material onto the internet, than that tiny sums should be separately collectable from hundreds (in other cases it may be millions) of internet viewers. Fifth, if merely viewing a web-page is not an infringement, that does not leave the copyright owner without effective remedies against pirates. It simply means that his remedy must be found against others who on the face of it are more obviously at fault. Nothing in article 5.1 impairs the copyright owner's right to proceed against those who unlawfully upload copyright material onto the internet, just as the copyright owner has always been entitled to proceed against those who make or distribute pirated copies of books, films, music or other protected works. The Directive itself contains in Chapters III and IV important provisions enlarging the range of procedures and sanctions available against piracy.

The decisions below

37. Proudman J decided that Meltwater's customers needed a licence both to receive the monitoring reports by email and to access them on Meltwater's website. Her reasons were (i) that the making of copies, however temporary, in the end-user's computer in the course of browsing was not part of the technological process because it was "generated by his own volition", i.e. by his voluntary decision to access the web-page; (ii) that it was outside the scope of the technological process for the additional reason that it was in reality the end result of that process since it was what the end-user viewed; and (iii) that the viewing of these copies did not constitute "lawful use" because they were not authorised by the copyright owner: see para 109. These reasons are of course related, and all three of them lead to the conclusion that, in the judge's words, the "kind of circumstance where the defence may be available is where the purpose of the copying is to enable efficient transmission in a network between third parties by an intermediary, typically an internet service provider" para 110. The Court of Appeal agreed with her, essentially on her ground (i). In their view the "acts of reproduction are those occasioned by the voluntary human process of accessing that web-page" para 35. For practical purposes, this amounted to an endorsement of Proudman J's view that unlicensed internet browsing could never satisfy the conditions in article 5.1. It will be apparent that Proudman J and the Court of Appeal could not have arrived at these conclusions if they had had the benefit of the judgments in *Premier League* and *Infopaq II*. In particular, the far broader meaning given by the Court of Justice in these cases to the concept of "lawful use" makes it impossible to confine the scope of the exception to the internal plumbing of the internet. Once it is accepted that article 5.1 extends in principle to temporary copies made for the purpose of browsing by an unlicensed end-user, much of the argument which the courts below accepted unravels.

Chapter 9

REMEDIES

Where a copyright is infringed, the owner of the copyright is entitled to various remedies including damages, and an accounting of profits, delivery of and injunctive relief. These remedies are discussed below.

1. Damages and Accounting of Profits

Pursuant to section 35 of the *Copyright Act*, where a person infringes copyright, the person is liable to pay such damages to the owner of the copyright as the owner has suffered due to the infringement, and in addition to those damages, such part of the profits that the infringer has made from such infringement and that were not taken into account in calculating the damages as the court considers just.

The amount of damages in cases of copyright infringement to which the plaintiff is entitled is an amount that will compensate the plaintiff for all foreseeable losses suffered by the plaintiff as a result of the infringing activities of the defendant.[1]

The right of an owner of a copyright to damages is not necessarily determined or measured by the amount of actual damage to him by reason of the infringement. Copyright is regarded as a right of property, and so the owner is entitled to come to court for the protection of that property even though he does not show or prove actual damage. If none can be established, the plaintiff is entitled to nominal damages. Damages for breach of copyright are at large, and may be dealt with broadly and as a matter of common sense without professing to be minutely accurate. Under section 38 of the Act a legal fiction is created and the plaintiff is considered to be the owner of the infringing copies of his work; the plaintiff may take proceedings for the recovery of the infringing copies or for damages for their conversion.[2] The amount of the conversion damages is not easy to determine when the infringing matter is inseparably mixed with non-infringing matter and in such cases the assessment of damage will depend upon the circumstances of each case and the requirements of just compensation. What has to be determined is the value of the part which has been converted at the time of the conversion.

While exemplary damages are not specifically mentioned as an available remedy in the *Copyright Act*, they are not excluded by subsection 34(1), and it is well established that they are, in appropriate circumstances, available, even in the absence of monetary loss, or of accountable profits. The

---

[1] *Prism Hospital Software Inc. v. Hospital Medical Records Institute* (1994), 57 C.P.R. (3d) 129 (B.C. S.C.).
[2] *Pro Arts Inc. v. Campus Crafts Holdings Ltd.* (1980), 28 O.R. (2d) 422 (Ont. H.C.).

amount of the exemplary damages should be commensurate with the gravity of the action committed and should reflect the indignation of the court at the conduct of the defendant.[3]

Mansell v. Star Printing & Publishing Co. of Toronto, [1937] A.C. 872 (P.C.)

Lord Atkin, Lord Macmillan, Lord Wright, Lord Alness, and Lord Maugham.

1937 July 28.

On Appeal from the Court of Appeal for Ontario.

. . .

July 28. The judgment of their Lordships was delivered by LORD MACMILLAN.

The plaintiff in these proceedings (now the appellant) is a publisher of fine art colour prints who resides in England and does business throughout the world. He complains that between the months of March and July, 1932, the respondents in infringement of his rights published in Toronto, in the illustrated section of a newspaper owned by them and known as the Star Weekly, a number of pictures of which he claims to be entitled to the copyright. The action related originally to thirty-eight pictures. In the course of the proceedings the appellant abandoned his claim to four of the pictures, and as regards three of them, which were painted after the Canadian Copyright Act, 1921, came into operation on January 1, 1924, the trial judge (Rose C.J.H.C.) held that the appellant was entitled to copyright, and awarded him $600 damages for infringement. As regards the remaining thirty-one pictures, all of which were painted before January 1, 1924, the trial judge held that the appellant had no copyright in them in Canada, and was consequently not entitled to any remedy against the respondents. This judgment was affirmed by the Court of Appeal for Ontario. The appellant says in his printed case that the appeal was dismissed "without reasons," and the respondents say that the Court of Appeal "gave no written reasons." It appears, however, from a newspaper report of the case which was supplied to their Lordships that the learned judges of the Court of Appeal in disposing of the case gave expression to their views on the questions raised, and their Lordships regret that no official record of these opinions has been made available to them, notwithstanding the requirement of r. 16 of the Judicial Committee Rules, 1925.

The only question between the parties at their Lordships' bar was whether the appellant was entitled to copyright in Canada in the thirty-one pictures painted or "made" before January 1, 1924. The appellant maintained that he was so entitled in virtue either of (1.) the Canadian Copyright Act, or (2.) the Imperial Copyright Act of 1911.

---

3   *Pro Arts Inc. v. Campus Crafts Holdings Ltd.* (1980), 28 O.R. (2d) 422 (Ont. H.C.).

. . .

Was the appellant immediately before January 1, 1924, entitled to copyright in Canada in the thirty-one pictures? If so, he must have acquired it under the previous Canadian Copyright Act of 1906. But the appellant never acquired copyright in Canada in the thirty-one pictures under the Act of 1906, for he never complied with the requirements of that Act. The condition for obtaining copyright in Canada under that Act in the case of works of art was prescribed by s. 6–namely, "that they shall be produced or reproduced in Canada," and the thirty-one pictures were never produced or reproduced there before January 1, 1924; nor did the appellant ever record the copyright thereof as required by the Act. As Lord Lindley said in giving the judgment of the Board in Graves & Co., Ld. v. Gorrie[FN9]: "Those who want copyright in Canada for paintings, drawings, and photographs must obtain such copyright by complying with the laws of that country." There was a substantial interval of time between the passing of the Canadian Copyright Act of 1921 and its coming into operation on January 1, 1924, during which the appellant, by compliance with Canadian law, could have protected himself, but he did not do so. The result is that the appellant's case so far as founded on the present Canadian Copyright Act therefore fails.

FN9 [1903] A. C. 496, 500.

2. Turning to the appellant's alternative submission under the Imperial Copyright Act of 1911, their Lordships are of opinion that the appellant can derive no aid from this quarter. The argument assumes that there can be simultaneously subsisting in Canada two independent copyrights–namely, copyright under the Canadian Act and copyright under the Imperial Act. Their Lordships would not readily reach so unlikely and so embarrassing a conclusion. Fortunately it is not necessary to do so. The Imperial Act, by s. 25, sub-s. 1, provides that it shall not extend to a self-governing Dominion unless declared by the Legislature of that Dominion to be in force therein. The Legislature of Canada has never declared that the Imperial Act of 1911 shall be in force therein. On the contrary, the Canadian Act of 1921 by s. 45 declared that no person should be entitled to copyright otherwise than under and in accordance with the provisions of that Act or of any other statutory enactment for the time being in force; and s. 47 enacted that "all the enactments relating to copyright passed by the Parliament of the United Kingdom are, so far as they are operative in Canada, hereby repealed."

The appellant, however, sought to rely on the second sub-section of s. 25 of the Imperial Act. Under that sub-section the Secretary of State may certify that "any self-governing Dominion has passed legislation under which works, the authors whereof were at the date of the making of the works British subjects resident elsewhere than in the Dominion or (not being British subjects) were resident in the parts of His Majesty's Dominions to which" the Imperial Act extended, "enjoy within the Dominion rights substantially identical with those conferred by" the Imperial Act. On the Secretary of State so certifying, as he did in the case of Canada on December 6, 1923, "then whilst such legislation continues in force the Dominion shall, for the purposes of the rights conferred by this Act, be treated as if it were a Dominion to which this Act extends." The certificate of the Secretary of State did not and could not extend the Imperial Act to Canada. His certificate had merely the effect of bringing into operation the provision that Canada should for the purposes of the rights conferred by the Imperial Act (but for those purposes only) be treated as if it were a Dominion to which the Act extended. The Imperial Act conferred no rights in Canada, and it was only for the purposes of the rights conferred by it that Canada was to be treated as if the Act extended to it. This can only mean that although under s. 1 a Canadian author writing in Canada would not, when the Imperial Act was passed, have any copyright under the Imperial Act, the effect of the certificate would be that such an author would become a person entitled to "the rights conferred" by the Imperial Act. That is to say, Canadian authors are to have the same rights under the Imperial Act, within the area to which that Act extends, as they would have if the Act extended to Canada, but they have no rights in Canada under the Imperial Act.

As the Imperial Act confers no rights in Canada on the appellant his second contention must share the fate of the first.

Their Lordships will accordingly humbly advise His Majesty that the appeal be dismissed, and the judgment of the Court of Appeal of Ontario of January 27, 1937, be affirmed. The appellant will pay the respondents' costs of the present appeal.

R. v. James Lorimer and Co. Ltd., [1984] 1 F.C. 1065 (Fed. C.A.)

Heald, Mahoney and Ryan JJ.

Ottawa: November 29, 1983

Docket: A-831-82

. . .

The following are the reasons for judgment rendered in English by Mahoney J.:

1 This is an appeal and cross-appeal from a judgment of the Trial Division [dated April 30, 1982, T-2216-81, not reported] which found the respondent had infringed the appellant's copyright in a certain work but denied the appellant costs as well as the injunctive relief and exemplary damages sought and dismissed the respondent's counterclaim without costs. The learned Trial Judge found that the Crown owned the copyright in its work (Appeal Book, page 142, lines 1 and 2). He rejected the defences of fair dealing, violation of Charter freedoms and public interest (page 159, line 24 to page 160, line 2). He characterized the infringing work as an abridgement (page 144, line 5) and the respondent's conduct as deliberate (page 159, lines 13 to 24) and a "blatant disregard" of the appellant's rights (page 164, lines 23 to 26). The infringement was done for a "primarily commercial" purpose (page 150, lines 28 and 29). It is agreed the appellant suffered no economic loss. The findings of fact by the learned Trial Judge are amply supported by the evidence and are not to be disturbed.

. . .

4 Dealing first with the appeal, the first point in issue is the refusal to grant the relief sought, which was:

(a) a permanent injunction enjoining and restraining the Defendant company, its officers, servants, agents and employees from producing or reproducing substantial portions of the Report of Robert J. Bertrand, Q.C., Director of Investigation and Research, Combines Investigation Act, entitled "The State of Competition in the Canadian Petroleum Industry" in a book entitled "Canada's Oil Monopoly" or in any other form whatsoever;

(b) a mandatory injunction requiring the Defendant company, its officers, servants, agents and employees to immediately deliver up to the Plaintiff all plates used or intended to be used for the production of the book entitled "Canada's Oil Monopoly";

(c) a mandatory injunction requiring the Defendant company, its officers, servants, agents and employees to immediately deliver up to the Plaintiff all copies of the book entitled "Canada's Oil Monopoly" which are presently in its possession or control;

(d) a mandatory injunction requiring the Defendant company, its officers, servants, agents and employees to reacquire all copies of the book entitled "Canada's Oil Monopoly" which have been distributed for retail or wholesale sale or distribution and to immediately deliver up said copies to the Plaintiff;

(e) an accounting of all monies received by the Defendant company from the publication and sale of the book entitled "Canada's Oil Monopoly" and payment over to the Plaintiff of the resulting profits from such publication and sale;

(f) exemplary damages;

As to (d), I know of no precedent for such an order. It was obviously intended to require recovery of copies no longer within the defendant's control as copies within its control were covered by (c). Compliance with such an order would not be entirely within the power of the person to whom it is directed. A prudent infringer might well attempt to do just that to reduce his exposure to damages but I do not think it a proper order by the Court and will not refer to it further. The claim for relief in paragraph (e) was withdrawn at trial. That claimed in paragraphs (a), (b), (c) and (f) was refused and, instead, a royalty of 8% of the retail selling price of the infringing work was awarded in respect of future sales and damages of $3,192.12, calculated on the basis of 8% of their retail selling price, awarded in respect of sales prior to judgment.

5 The learned Trial Judge, after reviewing the evidence, found [at page 20 of the reasons for judgment]:

All of that seems to confirm that Mr. Lorimer knew and acted at all times in a manner consistent with a person who knew that what he was doing was on the face of it an infringement of the plaintiff's copyright, and that he should either secure the consent or permission of someone to go ahead with it or expect to negotiate some kind of licence or royalty, and I therefore conclude that, if the copyright laws are to mean anything, then this defendant ought not to have done what it did in publishing this report in the form it did without the consent of the plaintiff.

6   (Appeal Book, page 159)

7 In denying exemplary damages and substituting what is, in effect, a compulsory licence for the injunctive relief, the learned Trial Judge said [at pages 21-23]:

Turning to remedies, I have found against the defendant on the basis that Mr. Lorimer, it seems to me, could have avoided the grief that visited him in this matter by the simple expedient of at least making some effort to secure permission before publication. He might be in a different position before this Court if he had demonstrated that he indeed did not assume that he would be tied in a bureaucratic tangle but rather at least offered to put his abridgement or proposed abridgement before someone who would have the opportunity to approve it, to authorize it, or license it or refuse it. But there was no evidence put forward of any effort in that regard on the part of Mr. Lorimer or any representative of his company. To that extent, therefore, he is the author of his own misfortune and that of his company in failing simply to take the expedient of attempting to secure authority which at least on the basis of Mr. Bertrand's evidence might very well have been forthcoming in some form or other. Furthermore, it might very well have been forthcoming in the form of what he described as a non-exclusive arrangement which might not have cost him anything.

On the other hand, I cannot overlook the fact that, by acting in the way that he did, he abrogated [*sic*] to himself what was in effect an exclusive right to publish an official abridgement of this report and, as such, was acting entirely in disregard of the copyright laws.

In terms of remedy, the plaintiff does not seek any accounting profits. I am relieved, therefore, of the burden of examining into the profit and loss information of the defendant company. I do not think that justice is served by having this Court attempt or either of the parties attempt at this time to withdraw from circulation or from publication a further distribution of copies of this work. It is not a situation, in other words, of the plaintiff's original work in its distribution or sale that the fact the plaintiff's economic position is adversely affected. Obviously, we have circumstances which mitigate the infringement of copyright to some extent. In the first place, the Crown is an unusual plaintiff and really is not greatly interested in income or revenue from this work. It could never approach the cost of the inquiry which ran for several years and undoubtedly cost many millions of dollars. The printing cost associated with the work was set upon the evidence by a very rough gauge to somehow cover printing costs which, I am sure, did not take place. So, the importance of the revenue or the significance of the revenue to this plaintiff is very minimal. Furthermore, I repeat that the defendant's publication did not then and certainly now is not having any adverse effect on further distribution or sales of the plaintiff's original work and, therefore, I see no purpose in ordering a recall or injunction by enjoining the defendant from further sales of this work at this time.

It not being, therefore, a situation in which the plaintiff should be compensated or even seeks compensation in the sense of loss of revenues from the sale of its own work, and not being one where I feel at this time the distribution of the plaintiff's work is adversely affected by the presence of the defendant's work in the marketplace, that injunction is not a proper remedy.

Again turning to the essential element of the defendant's transgression of the civil law, it is that it went ahead and did without seeking permission what it, in my opinion, either knew or should have known could not be done properly without permission or could not be done without some consequences without permission. It is, in my opinion, therefore, an appropriate case for compensation not by way of injunction or damages either exemplary or punitive, but rather by way of royalty.

8 (Appeal Book, pages 160 ff.) The pertinent provisions of the Act are:
17.(1) Copyright in a work shall be deemed to be infringed by any person who, without the consent of the owner of the copyright, does anything that, by this Act, only the owner of the copyright has the right to do.

. . .

20.(1) Where copyright in any work has been infringed, the owner of the copyright is, except as otherwise provided by this Act, entitled to all such remedies by way of injunction, damages, accounts, and otherwise, as are or may be conferred by law for the infringement of a right.

. . .

21. All infringing copies of any work in which copyright subsists, or of any substantial part thereof, and all plates used or intended to be used for the production of such infringing copies, shall be deemed to be the property of the owner of the copyright, who accordingly may take proceedings for the recovery of the possession thereof or in respect of the conversion thereof.

. . .

11 A computation of damages based on an appropriate royalty is acceptable where the copyright owner does not prove he would have made the sales the infringer did. However, I find no authority for requiring a copyright owner to acquiesce in a continuing infringement against payment of a royalty. That is tantamount to the imposition of a compulsory licence. In the absence of legislative authority, the Court has no power to do that.

12 I am of the opinion that the learned Trial Judge applied wrong principles and erred in law in denying the relief sought in paragraphs (a), (b) and (c) of the prayer for relief and substituting for that relief a royalty on the future sale of infringing copies.

13 The question of exemplary damages is more difficult. In addition to what has already been quoted, the learned Trial Judge [at page 25] characterized the respondent's conduct as a "blatant disregard of what was obviously the right of the plaintiff under our copyright laws ...". (Appeal Book, page 164.) He also found [at page 11] that "the defendant's purpose was primarily commercial" (page 150). Taken as a whole, the findings of fact are expressed in terminology that would lead one to think that an award of exemplary damages was in the offing.

14 While exemplary damages are not specifically mentioned as an available remedy in the *Copyright Act*, they are not excluded by subsection 20(1), and it is well established that they are, in appropriate circumstances, available. I see no reason why appropriate circumstances should be different in the case of copyright infringement than in the case of any other civil invasion of another's rights. I also see no reason in this case to express a settled view on whether the applicable principle in this Court is that enunciated by Lord Devlin in *Rookes v. Barnard et al.*, or that which appears to have been more generally accepted by provincial courts of appeal as enunciated, for example, by Clement J.A., in *Paragon Properties Ltd. v. Magna Investments Ltd.* In my opinion, the facts here do bring this matter within Lord Devlin's second category and, on application of either principle, exemplary damages could have been awarded.

15 In *Netupsky et al. v. Dominion Bridge Co. Ltd.*, Taggart J.A., for the Court, in sustaining a refusal of exemplary or punitive damages, held:

> ...I consider it sufficient to say that in this case I find absolutely no justification for such an award. I can find no fraud, malice, violence, cruelty, insolence or contemptuous disregard for the appellant's rights on the part of the respondent.

The grounds for refusing exemplary damages, unlike the grounds for refusing injunctive relief, are to be found in the conduct and motives of the infringer.

16 The absence of economic injury and the "unusual" nature of the Crown as a plaintiff are not good reasons to deny the Crown exemplary damages. The language of the reasons for judgment is difficult to reconcile with the conclusion that this is not an appropriate case for exemplary damages. It is manifest that the learned Trial Judge, notwithstanding his characterization of the unquestionably deliberate infringement, motivated by the respondent's marketing considerations, as "blatant", did not find it warranted punishment, nor did he see deterrence as a desirable object. It cannot be said that he clearly erred in so exercising his discretion and I do not feel it open to substitute my view of such an infringement for his.

Pro Arts Inc. v. Campus Crafts Holdings Ltd. (1980), 28 O.R. (2d) 422 (Ont. H.C.)

Labrosse J.

Heard: February 4, 5, 6, 7, 8, 11, 12, 13, 14, 15, 18 and 19, 1980

Judgment: March 27, 1980

Docket: 11045/77

. . .

Labrosse J.:

1 This is an action for infringement of copyright.

2 The plaintiff Pro Arts, Inc. is a corporation incorporated under the laws of the State of Ohio, having its head office in the city of Medina in the State of Ohio in the United States of America. The plaintiff manufactures and sells posters to distributors, retail stores and directly to customers through the mail.

3 The defendant Campus Crafts Holdings, Ltd. is a corporation incorporated under the laws of the province of Alberta having its head office in the city of Edmonton. Campus Crafts manufactures and sells posters to retail outlets in Canada.

4 The action has been settled or discontinued as against the remaining defendants named in the style of cause.

5 In June 1976, the plaintiff entered into an agreement with Farrah Fawcett-Majors (Farrah) who had appeared in numerous commercials and who was very well known by sight if not by name. The agreement granted the plaintiff the right, licence and privilege of utilizing her name and likeness in relation to the manufacture, sale and distribution of posters.

6 Farrah was photographed by a professional photographer hired by the plaintiff and Farrah and the plaintiff agreed on one photograph from which the plaintiff produced an off-set lithograph poster (hereinafter referred to as the poster). Production of the poster commenced in August 1976, and shortly thereafter, it was introduced on the market. Sales started off slowly but in the third week of September a television series titled "Charlie's Angels", in which Farrah was one of the stars, appeared on television. The program was soon rated as one of the top five in the United States and at times was number one. Its popularity had an effect on the poster which was now selling very well and by January 1977, the plaintiff believed that it had a "block-buster". The plaintiff registered the copyright to the poster in the United States on December 15, 1976, and in Canada on February 23, 1977. The poster turned out to be the best selling poster of all times. It sold over 4,000,000 copies.

7 In 1976 the defendant was the largest manufacturer and distributor of posters in Canada. It sold posters to numerous retail outlets including most of the chain stores. In January 1977, the defendant obtained the poster, had it photographed, and from the photograph it produced a copy of the poster deleting the plaintiff's copyright designatio7n. Such a copy is known in the trade as a counterfeit or bootleg poster (hereinafter referred to as the counterfeit). The counterfeit is of inferior quality. It has a washed out appearance, it is not as clear as the poster and when examined closely it has a checkerboard effect. The defendant produced 140,000 counterfeit copies and proceeded to sell them throughout Canada.

8 The defendant denies that the plaintiff is the owner of the copyright in the poster and states that if it did infringe any copyright owned by the plaintiff, the defendant was not aware and had no reasonable ground for suspecting the plaintiff's copyright in the poster. The defendant also denies that it has done acts or adopted business practices contrary to honest industrial or commercial usage in Canada.

. . .

Damages for Infringement

42 The evidence of Mr. Slawsky, president of the defendant company that the Farrah poster was only a mediocre seller and would have sold some 70,000 copies, cannot be accepted. It is against the evidence of all witnesses.

43 With respect to the Quebec market, I accept the evidence of Mr. Vanin who is the buyer for a department store which has 22 outlets in the province of Quebec. He stated that it was a good poster but that it was never given a chance to become a best-seller because it received no promotion. The television program "Charlie's Angels" was seen later in Quebec but it received a very high rating and the sales of the poster would probably have peaked later than in the rest of Canada. When Mr. Vanin said: "Give me a poster of Bo Derek and I will sell 1,000 during a weekend", the comparison was accurate. On the evidence, I am not satisfied that the Quebec market in this case should be treated any differently.

44 In my view, the plaintiff's estimate that the poster would have sold approximately 400,000 copies had there been no counterfeit, is much more reasonable than the estimate of the defendant. Mr. Slawsky stated that the best selling poster in Canada, a poster of Kiss, a rock group, sold 85,000 copies. However, he did not say how many had been printed or shipped out. The defendant had 140,000 copies of the counterfeit printed and before the granting of the injunction on March 4, 1977, sold 93,235 copies in a period of slightly more than one month. Invoices confirmed that some stores re-ordered three and four times during that short period of time. The defendant advertised the counterfeit as a "Hot Item" and "Best-Seller" and it sold more copies in one month that it did of its alleged best-seller, Kiss. All witnesses were in agreement that the life span of a celebrity poster is approximately six to nine months. The sales can be represented by a curve which rises quickly, reaches its peak and then comes down very quickly. As the defendant sold 93,235 in one month, which was the beginning of the life span of the counterfeit, and in view of the re-orders which had already started to come in, it would not have required many good months to sell 400,000 copies.

45 The grounds upon which the plaintiff bases its estimate were referred to earlier and in the circumstances, I consider the estimate of 400,000 copies to be reasonable and probable. The estimate is also reasonable in light of the fact that the plaintiff sold over 90,000 posters without the benefit of the chain stores which represent 70 per cent of the Canadian market.

46 Reference was made earlier to 2,330,500 posters which were printed by Western Publishing Company because the plaintiff required outside assistance in order to continue operating its normal business. It is reasonable to conclude that by the end of January 1977, the plaintiff's stock of posters had been exhausted. It is therefore probable that the Canadian market would have been supplied with the Western Publishing posters. The plaintiff is still left with a large stock of posters sufficient to have covered the Canadian market. The plaintiff's standard distributors' price was 40¢ U.S. per poster. Some were sold at a higher price and some at a lower price, but numerous posters were sold at a discount in an attempt to combat the counterfeit or break into the chain stores after the injunction. The

plaintiff should not suffer because of its attempt to mitigate its damages. In these circumstances, I accept the standard distributors' price of 40¢ U.S.

47 Four hundred thousand posters at 40¢ each represents $160,000. From that amount must be deducted the actual sales of the plaintiff of $25,462.60 and the royalty payable to Farrah representing 10 per cent or $16,000 leaving a balance of $118,527.40. Counsel for the plaintiff suggested that the amount be increased by 10 per cent or $11,852.70 which reasonably represents the difference in currency and which was not disputed. The total is $130,380.10. There should be no deduction for the costs of the posters which the plaintiff has already paid to Western Publishing Company. Any handling charges and overhead charges are counterbalanced by the storage costs of the excess posters.

48 Under this heading the plaintiff also claims damages for having been prevented from opening its subsidiary company, P.A. of Canada, and damages for loss of future sales from July 1977 to July 1979. I accept that the counterfeiting prevented the plaintiff from selling its poster to the Canadian market and that the position of the defendant with the chain stores made it very difficult for the plaintiff to break through. However, I cannot accept that the concept of the subsidiary company was abandoned as a result of the counterfeit. There is no proper basis for this part of the claim. It does not follow that because the plaintiff could not sell the poster to the chain stores it lost the opportunity to start a subsidiary company. There was no real attempt to form the subsidiary company and for reasons which I will refer to shortly, I doubt very much that the subsidiary company would have had the success that the plaintiff now says it should have had. In any event, I consider that part of the claim to be too remote.

49 After the injunction was granted, the plaintiff and its distributors had very little success in selling the poster. In my view, there were three reasons for this situation. Firstly, there was confusion amongst the chain stores as to who had the right to distribute the poster and who was distributing the counterfeit. The defendant had agreed to indemnify the other defendants and it clearly continued to represent that it had the right to distribute the counterfeit and other posters which were also counterfeits. Secondly, the chain stores were unhappy because they had been sued by the plaintiff. They were understandably reluctant to do business with the plaintiff. I recognize, however, that the necessity of this action was the direct result of the counterfeit. Thirdly, whatever may be said about the conduct of the defendant with respect to counterfeit posters, the defendant cannot be criticized for the manner in which it was handling the chain stores. It was providing them with excellent service which is what the stores really wanted. This was the defendant's strength across Canada. Retailers had been having unpleasant experiences with distributors who went out of business or failed to service the poster racks, until they dealt with the defendant.

50 As one witness suggested, there was no point in displaying a good selection of posters if the bins were empty and the stale posters were not replaced.

51 I have found that without the counterfeit, the Farrah poster would have been as successful in Canada as in the United States. I am prepared to accept that the

chain stores would have allowed the plaintiff to install other promotional displays when the plaintiff came out with a promising poster. But I am not prepared to find that it was probable that the plaintiff would break through with the chain stores and be permitted to install permanent displays. The defendant's reputation for providing excellent service would not be forgotten so easily. It should also be noted that very little is known of Greg Morry. He stayed in Canada for only a few months. It was indicated that he had financial problems and I am not aware of his background. The quality of the service provided by the defendant and the unknown quantity of Greg Morry were factors that I considered in arriving at my conclusion on the future of P.A. of Canada.

52 After Morry left Canada, Edward Mauro, under the firm name of Kedd Enterprises, became the exclusive distributor for the plaintiff. Kedd Enterprises has had limited success with the chain stores, but there was evidence that its service was not comparable to that provided by the defendant.

53 With repect to loss of future sales, I cannot accept the substantial estimates of the plaintiff for the period from July 1977 to July 1979. I accept that the plaintiff has suffered a loss which cannot be specifically ascertained. Unfortunately, the evidence did not reveal the actual sales of the plaintiff during this two-year period which may have been a helpful factor to consider. In 1977, the defendant sold 3,000,000 posters representing sales of $2,500,000. An officer of the plaintiff estimated the future sales from July 1977 to July 1979 at between 1,700,000 and 2,200,000 posters, provided that the plaintiff could get its posters into the chain stores. During argument, counsel for the plaintiff suggested that the loss of future sales be calculated at 1,100,000 representing 500,000 for the first year and 600,000 for the second year.

54 Having concluded from the evidence that the plaintiff would not have realized substantial sales in Canada during these two years as it would have had limited success with the chain stores, I consider that as a result of the counterfeit, the necessity of the injunction and the misrepresentations of the defendant to the chain stores, the plaintiff suffered a loss of sales of 200,000 posters, or approximately 10 per cent of the plaintiff's estimate. In my view, a 10 per cent breakthrough with the chain stores is, on the evidence, a realistic expectation. Calculated at the standard distributors' price of 40¢ U.S. per poster the plaintiff's profit, as supported by the evidence, would have been 20¢ per poster. I therefore assess the loss of sales from July 1977 to July 1979 at $40,000, to which I add 10 per cent for the difference in currency for a total of $44,000.

55 The total damages under the heading of infringement are therefore $174,380.10.

Profits of the Defendant

56 Pursuant to s. 20(4) of the Act, in addition to damages for infringement, the defendant is liable to pay such part of the profits that it has made from the infringement as the Court may decide to be just and proper.

57 The word "profit" is not defined in the Act and I propose to give it its ordinary meaning: the excess of the price received over the cost of purchasing and handling or producing and marketing foods. See Webster's Third New International Dictionary.

58 The plaintiff has proved that the defendant sold 93,255 counterfeits at prices of $1.55, $1.45 and $1. Most of the counterfeits were sold at $1.55 and I average the price at $1.45 for a total of $135,219.75.

. . .

69 In calculating the profit of the defendant, I take the total sales of counterfeits to be 93,255. From this figure I deduct 11,000 for posters removed and destroyed, leaving a balance of 82,255. At $1.45 per poster they represent an amount of $119,269.75 from which I deduct the elements of costs, proved at $33,251.33, and the overhead of $22,987.35, leaving a balance of $63,031.07 as the profit realized by the defendant. In the circumstances on this case, I consider that it is just and proper that the defendant pay back to the plaintiff all profits realized from the counterfeit.

Damages for Conversion

70 Under s. 21 of the Act a legal fiction is created and the plaintiff is deemed to be the owner of the counterfeits and the plaintiff may take proceedings for the recovery of the infringing copies or for damages for conversion. Based on the authority of *Sutherland Publishing Co. v. Caxton Publishing Co.*, [1936] Ch. 323, [1936] 1 All E.R. 177, affirmed [1939] A.C. 178, [1938] 4 All E.R. 389 (H.L.), the remedies available to the plaintiff are cumulative and not alternative and damages may be awarded for conversion as well as for infringement and for the profits realized by the infringer. Damages for conversion will usually be based on the value of the article converted at the time of its conversion. However, the Court must avoid any overlap or duplication: see also *Netupsky v. Dom. Bridge Co.* (1969), 70 W.W.R. 241, 43 Fox Pat. C. 14, 61 C.P.R. 150, 9 D.L.R. (3d) 182, a decision of the British Columbia Court of Appeal [reversed on other grounds [1972] S.C.R. 368, [1972] 1 W.W.R. 420, 3 C.P.R. (2d) 1, 24 D.L.R. (3d) 484].

71 There are two reasons why I cannot allow damages for conversion in the present case. Firstly, as I have allowed the plaintiff damages for infringement and the profits realized by the defendant from the counterfeit posters, the plaintiff has been adequately compensated. Secondly, in the circumstances of this case, an award of damages for conversion would be a complete duplication of damages already awarded to the plaintiff.

Punitive or Exemplary Damages

72 It was argued on behalf of the defendant that ss. 20 to 24 of the Act are a complete code of the remedies available in copyright actions and as there is no provision for exemplary damages, the Court has no authority to award any. It was pointed out that the English authorities on copyright cannot be of assistance because the English statute provides that the Court "shall have power to award

such additional damages by virtue of this subsection as the court may consider appropriate in the circumstances" which may include exemplary damages. The defendant relied on *Netupsky v. Dom. Bridge Co.* (1969), 68 W.W.R. 529, 41 Fox Pat. C. 154, 58 C.P.R. 7, 5 D.L.R. (3d) 195, varied, supra, where the British Columbia Court of Appeal stated at p. 186 [41 Fox Pat. C.]:

> Dealing with the latter, notwithstanding any doubt that may exist as to the propriety of awarding exemplary damages in infringement actions, I consider it sufficient to say that in this case I find absolutely no justification for such an award. I can find no fraud, malice, violence, cruelty, insolence or contemptuous disregard for the appellants' rights on the part of the respondent.

As can be seen from the above passage, the Court found that it was not a proper case for exemplary damages and I do not consider that case as an authority in support of the defendant's argument.

73 Section 20(1) of the Act was referred to earlier but for the sake of convenience, I wish to quote it again:

> 20.(1) Where copyright in any work has been infringed, the owner of the copyright is, except as otherwise provided by this Act, entitled to all such remedies by way of injunction, damages, accounts, and otherwise, as are or may be conferred by law for the infringement of a right.

There is certainly no prohibition in the Act to an award of exemplary damages and if the plaintiff is entitled to all such remedies by way of damages and otherwise as are or may be conferred by law for the infringement of a right, it is my view that it was not the intention to exclude exemplary damages. Exemplary damages are well recognized at common law. There have also been numerous Canadian decisions where exemplary damages have been awarded: see *Underwriters' Survey Bureau Ltd. v. Massie & Renwick Ltd.*, 2 Fox Pat. C. 39, [1942] Ex. C.R. 1, 8 I.L.R. 321, 1 C.P.R. 207 at 224, [1942] 1 D.L.R. 434; *Standard Indust. Ltd. v. Rosen*, [1955] O.W.N. 262, 14 Fox Pat. C. 173, 24 C.P.R. 41, [1955] 4 D.L.R. 363 (H.C.); *T.J. Moore Co. v. Accessoires de Bureau de Que. Inc.* (1973), 14 C.P.R. (2d) 113 (Fed. Ct.); and *MCA Can. Ltd. (Ltée) v. Gillberry & Hawke Advertising Agency Ltd.* (1976), 28 C.P.R. (2d) 52 (Fed. Ct.).

74 On February 4, 1977, when distribution of the counterfeit had barely commenced, the vice-president of the defendant emphatically denied that the defendant was involved with the counterfeit. Shortly thereafter, on February 17, 1977, the attorneys for the plaintiff wrote to the defendant a cease and desist letter. Not only did the letter not stop the defendant, it did not even slow it down.

75 After the injunction was granted on March 4, 1977, the defendant instructed its sales force as to what to do with the counterfeits. One memo directed the salesmen to remove the counterfeits from certain chain stores. With respect to other chains the salesmen were directed to leave it if it was still selling, and with respect to all other stores the salesmen were instructed to leave it. Another memo instructed the salesmen as to what to say when the counterfeit was removed and exchanged. It provided in part: "DO NOT get involved in legal discussions ... just say that there is lots of legal stuff going on in the United States because

Farrah is planning to leave the show ... and that we feel we should drop the 1 poster in question ..." The defendant thereby continued to represent that it had the right to distribute the counterfeit. The memo also provided with respect to one chain store: "... if they have 5 left in a rack leave it ... if they have a minipack or heavy stock TAKE IT OUT." The defendant clearly instructed its salesmen to ignore the terms of the injunction.

76 Numerous invoices confirm that the defendant sold the counterfeit after the date of the injunction. Having examined a box full of invoices, counsel for the plaintiff suggested to Mr. Slawsky that after March 4, 1977, there had been 69 sales of the counterfeit throughout Canada, including Ontario. Mr. Slawsky replied that it was possible. He had no explanation. Obviously, this was not an accident. Evidence which I accept, confirmed that in April 1978, the counterfeit was still being sold in the defendant's poster displays in Edmonton. It was still in the displays as late as January 1979 and by inference, it was still selling, otherwise it would have been removed.

77 One of the principles underlying the award of exemplary damages in cases such as this one, is that persons should be deterred from injuring the property of another in the belief that the material advantages to be gained by such injury will outweigh any compensatory damages which the wrongdoer might have to ultimately pay: see *Cassell & Co. v. Broome*, [1972] A.C. 1027, [1972] 1 All E.R. 801 (H.L.).

78 After the injunction, Mr. Slawsky ordered that the counterfeits which were removed be destroyed although the plaintiff, through its attorneys in their letter of February 17, 1977, demanded that the defendant account for all counterfeit copies and the statement of claim requested the delivery of all counterfeit posters.

79 When the counterfeit was removed from the stores, it was replaced by another counterfeit.

80 Considering the evidence in the most favourable light for the defendant, the inescapable conclusion is that the defendant demonstrated an exceptional degree of arrogance. Its actions constituted a callous disregard of the rights of the plaintiff and showed little more respect for the injunction granted by the Court.

81 In my opinion, this is a case which demands the granting of exemplary damages. The amount of exemplary damages should be commensurate with the gravity of the tort committed and should reflect the indignation of the Court. On the facts of this case, to assess exemplary damages at a nominal amount would be tantamount to a licence fee for having sold the counterfeits and for having ignored the terms of the injunction granted by the Court. I assess the exemplary damages at $35,000.

82 As a final word on the issue of damages, I recognize that the damages were difficult to ascertain and that under all heads of damages the assessments could have been calculated in different ways. I have attempted to calculate the damages in a manner which, in the circumstances of this case, is fair and just to both parties.

Prism Hospital Software Inc. v. Hospital Medical Records Institute, [1994]
10 W.W.R. 305 (B.C. S.C.)

Parrett J.

Heard: November 4-8, 14-15, 18-22, 25-27, December 2-4, 6, 9-13, 1991,
January

6-7, 9-10, 13-17, February 3-7, 10-14, 17-18 and July 9, 1992

Judgment: August 23, 1994

Docket: Doc. Vancouver C872267

. . .

The defendant was federally chartered non-profit company governed by a board of directors elected by its members, who were drawn from hospitals, provincial hospital associations, and provincial government health ministries. It funded itself mainly by charging fees to hospitals for its services. The defendant maintained a healthcare information database on a mainframe computer and member hospitals provided the defendant with details of patient visits on the death or discharge of the patient. The defendant stored the information "abstracts" so that they could be available for such purposes as analyzing resource use, management reviews, strategic planning, funding analyses and medical research. Collected data also provided a basis for comparing a particular hospital's data with national figures or with peer group hospitals. In addition to charging a per abstract collection fee, the defendant also charged for certain standard reports to all subscribing hospitals as well as other reports on request. The plaintiff started business in 1981 when its two principals began to create and market a computerized abstract collection and reporting system. Initially, the defendant received abstracts from hospitals on paper and it contracted with another company to have the information converted to electronic form for entry into its database. When that service ceased to be available, the defendant pushed member hospitals to submit abstracts electronically and it decided to contract for the preparation of a computer-based medical records abstracting system which it would distribute. In that regard, the defendant approached the plaintiff. The plaintiff offered to provide abstracting software to run on microcomputers and the parties agreed that the plaintiff would license the software to the defendant which the defendant would then sublicense to hospitals. The discussions culminated in 1985 in a contract reflected in the plaintiff's proposal and a licence agreement, which documents the parties referred to as "the contract documents." Under the contract, the plaintiff was to make its best efforts to provide a demonstration version of the software in 1985 for the defendant to show in December, and working versions incorporating edit requirements of different provinces were to be provided according to a schedule. The plaintiff provided a demonstration version in December 1985 and progressive working versions of the software from February 1986 to January 1987. At about that time, I., a programmer employed by the defendant, persuaded the defendant to authorize him to write a prototype replacement for the plaintiff's software on the basis that the software exhibited problems which the rewrite would not since it would be written in a more modern computer language. It was the "rewriting" of the plaintiff's software, without its knowledge or consent, that brought the parties' relationship to an end when discovered. While the defendant sought to justify its decision to pursue the rewrite of the plaintiff's software in a number of ways, central to its position was the thesis that as of October 1, 1986 the software was not a stable, maintainable product and that it was "deficient and inoperative" in many respects. The plaintiff sued the defendant and I. for damages for breach of contract and copyright infringement.

. . .

694....Damages for the infringement of copyright are generally determined as those which the owner of the copyright work may have suffered due to the infringement. Damages are specifically described in the Act and are to be found in s. 35(1) which provides:

> 35. (1) Where any person infringes the copyright in any work that is protected under this Act, the person is liable to pay such damages to the owner of the right infringed as he may have suffered due to the infringement, and in addition thereto such part of the profits that the infringer has made from the infringement as the court may decide to be just and proper.

695 The damages described are cumulative not alternative heads, but perhaps the most important feature underlying remedies available in copyright is that it is a right of property and the owner is, primarily, entitled to have his property rights protected. This is so even if the owner is unable to show actual damage at which point he may only be entitled, in addition to any protective orders, to an award of nominal damages.

696 The fact remains that the amount of damages in copyright infringement is not necessarily derived by the actual damage caused by the infringement. At pp. 3-314 and 3-315 Sookman puts it in these words:

> Damages for breach of copyright are at large, and may be dealt with broadly and as a matter of common sense without professing to be minutely accurate. Where the sum to be awarded is under consideration, the plaintiff, rather than the defendant, ought to have the benefit of any doubt there may be as to the amount of the award. [footnotes omitted]

697 The wording and concepts expressed by the author in this passage appear to originate in the language of Cozens-Hardy M.R. in *Meters Ltd. v. Metropolitan Gas Meters Ltd.* (1911), 28 R.P.C. 157 at 161-62:

> Therefore, in a case such as the present, where licences are not granted to anyone who asks for them for a fixed sum, it is a matter which is to be dealt with in the rough — doing the best one can, not attempting or professing to be minutely accurate — having regard to all the circumstances of the case, and saying what upon the whole is the fair thing to be done ... we must arrive at a conclusion as best we can, not tying ourselves down by any hard and fast rule, not requiring the Plaintiffs to establish before us that any definite number of retailers would have

come to the Plaintiffs if the Defendants had not supplied infringing instruments, but dealing with the matter broadly, and as best we can as men of common sense.

In addition it is clear and well established that exemplary damages are, in appropriate circumstances, available even in the absence of monetary loss or derived profits. Once again Sookman expresses the view, at p. 3-317, that "The amount of exemplary damages should be commensurate with the gravity of the action committed and should reflect the indignation of the court at the conduct of the plaintiff." At the risk of being overly technical I suggest the learned author meant "defendant" and suffered from a momentary programming error.

698   Returning for a moment to the underlying nature of copyright protection Robert Goff L.J. wrote in *Paterson Zochonis & Co. v. Merfarken Packaging Ltd.*, [1986] 3 All E.R. 522 at 538 (C.A.):

> The law of copyright is a self-contained branch of the law, concerned with the protection of a particular proprietary right. The provisions regulating the protection of that right, including, for example, those which provide for strict liability or liability based on fault, are framed with regard to a particular interest, viz the proprietary right in question. It would be undesirable as a matter of policy to extend the statutory remedies available for the protection of that interest to the recovery of damages in respect of the invasion of a different interest.

699   In their submissions on damages the defendants assert that "Profits which plaintiff's [sic] might have made had they obtained a contract which the infringer instead obtained are not recoverable." The defendants cite three authorities for this proposition: *British Insulated Wire Co. v. Dublin United Tramway Co.* (1899), 17 R.P.C. 14 at 21; *Meikle v. Maufe*, [1941] 3 All E.R. 144 at 154 (Ch. D.); and *Paterson Zochonis & Co. v. Merfarken Packaging Ltd.*, [1986] 3 All E.R. 522 at 538. With the greatest of respect, none of these decisions assert the general proposition which the defendants advance.

700   In the first of these decisions the court found on the facts that the plaintiff did not and may not have, in any event, obtained the contract in question. As a result they found that the profit margin the plaintiff may have made from a contract they neither entered nor performed was not the proper measure of damages. The heart of this decision is found in the passage immediately following that cited by the defendants where the court makes it clear that the defendant could have maintained its agreement with the American supplier and simply not brought the infringing cable into the country until after the date on which the plaintiff's patent expired.

701   In *Meikle* a similar situation existed; the plaintiff in that case argued that the measure of damages in a case where there was an infringement of copyright in the plans for a building was the fee he would have obtained if he had been hired as the architect. The court acknowledged that the fact the copyright was held by the architect was one of the factors to be considered but that the proper measure of damages was not the fee for performing a contract the architect never had nor performed.

702 The *Paterson* decision is even further removed. This decision, in my respectful view, stands for the narrow proposition that a person (in this case a printer) who infringes the plaintiff's copyright is not liable to him for the use made of the infringing material by a third party without his authority. These circumstances do not in my view support the general proposition advanced nor do they have application in the present case.

703 The critical difference in the present case is that the contract did exist and the infringing parties were one of the parties to the contract and an employee of that company. In addition the defendants in this case used their contractual relationship to enable them to both infringe the copyright and capture the potential market provided to Prism.

704 The general measure of damages to be awarded in cases of copyright infringement flow from the fact that it is a property right, the specific wording of s. 35 and the general principles that apply to the assessment of damages. What is recoverable by the copyright holder are damages to compensate him initially for all losses he suffered which flowed from the infringement. If the evidence establishes the necessary causal link to the infringement then a loss flows from it. If that loss is both foreseeable and not too remote it is recoverable.

705 On the second level contained within the wording of s. 35(1) an infringer may be, in appropriate circumstances, forced to surrender all or a portion of the profits which they have received from the infringing product.

706 What is different in the present case is that the infringement took place within a contractual setting and that the acts of infringement in this case also constituted breaches of the contract between the parties. Were it not for the difference between the liability of Imbert for copyright infringement and that of HMRI for both copyright infringement and breach of contract it would perhaps be possible to approach the damage issue on a more simplistic basis. It is important to recognize that in this case the infringing acts are not simply the individual sales of the infringing program itself but also the acts of Imbert in copying Prism's program itself.

707 A portion of the reasons for judgment of Fletcher Moulton L.J. in the *Meters Ltd. v. Metropolitan Gas Meters Ltd.* decision is both helpful and instructive in terms of the general principles to be followed in these cases and the dangers inherent in deviating from them. The passage beginning at p. 163 is lengthy but it is worthwhile to set it out fully:

> The Plaintiffs have, I think, done their duty to the Court in putting forward all the elements which enable the Court to judge of the magnitude and nature of the infringement. I take it that this is all they can be required to do. The Defendants seek to diminish the damages by a variety of affidavits intended to show that the particular purchasers for whom they manufactured these infringements were customers who would not have purchased from the Plaintiffs if they had not purchased from them. I am not for a moment going to say that evidence of that kind may not be relevant, but the argument based upon it was, that where a plaintiff proves the sale of infringing instruments by the defendants he does not establish any right to

damages unless he shows how many of those particular instruments would have been purchased from him if the defendant had not sold them; and the Counsel for the Defendants were bold enough to say that in this case of infringement on a large scale there ought to be only nominal damages. The estimation of damages in cases of breach of contract, or cases of tort, is often necessarily a most difficult matter. In some cases of contract, as is the case of the sale of articles capable of being purchased in the open market, there is, under ordinary circumstances, a method so obviously excellent of measuring the damages — measuring the injury done to the plaintiff by the breach of contract — that that method of estimating them has almost become a rule of the law. As soon as you leave that type of case the assessment of damages depends upon circumstances so various that in most instances there is no rule of law other than the very idea and principle of damages — that is an equivalent for the wrong done to the plaintiff. It is very dangerous to allow secondary rules to come in and be treated as rules of law unless you are certain that, whatever be the particular circumstances of the case, the nature of the breach, or the nature of the wrong is such that these secondary rules will always do justice between the parties. The Defendants have set up here — the burden of proof is on them — that there is this secondary rule of law, that where a defendant has sold infringing articles the plaintiff can only recover damages in respect of those which he can show would have been bought from him, if the defendant had not infringed. In my opinion there is no such secondary rule. I am quite aware that a good practical method of arriving at a fair estimate of the wrong done may, in some cases, be by forming a conception of how many sales of a particular article would have been made by the plaintiff, and then giving him the full manufacturing profit for that proportion, but there is no rule of law which requires the Court to do that in all circumstances, and there are innumerable cases in which such a rule of law would be quite inapplicable.

708 Once again returning to the general principle it is aptly summarized by Buckley L.J. in the same decision at p. 165:

> The matter to be ascertained is the pecuniary equivalent of the injury which the Plaintiffs have sustained by the wrongful acts done by the Defendants. In ascertaining that, we are not to include every injury, however remote; we have to find the pecuniary equivalent of the injury resulting as the natural consequence of the acts done by the Defendants. In order to answer that inquiry the proper mode is, I think, to ascertain, as far upon the evidence as it is possible to judge, the extent to which the trade of the Plaintiffs has been interfered with by the acts of the Defendants ...

709 The facts of this case involve the defendant HMRI placing the infringing work written by the defendant Imbert at 163 hospital sites in Canada, as at the date of trial. At approximately 80 of those sites they placed copies of a product called Q-Query which was a commercial report writer which served the same or similar purposes as the report writer developed by Prism and provided to HMRI for testing. There is no suggestion that Q-Query was an infringing work or that HMRI was restrained by a contractual term from offering to its hospital sites some other report writer.

710 It is not correct to say, however, that HMRI is not in the end responsible to account for profits earned through the supply of the Q-Query report writer. The Q-Query product was provided by HMRI to add functionality and features to the

infringing product and to manipulate the data collected by the infringing work. In this sense the product formed a part of HMRI's marketing strategy for the infringing product and represented both a profit they earned from the infringement and a portion of the appeal of the infringing work itself.

711 In addition, in so far as the actions of HMRI in marketing the infringing work forced Prism to reduce its price to compete that reduction is recoverable as flowing directly from the infringement. I can see no meaningful distinction between reducing the price of the copyright work and adding features which you would otherwise have charged separately for to achieve the same result. In this case the plaintiff bundled with its SuperMACS software both its Report Writer and a package of specialized reports. These two items are "extras" which are the equivalent of a price reduction forced on the plaintiff by HMRI's infringement. They are entitled to compensation for that "reduction".

712 I reject the defendant's submission that the plaintiff is restricted by any principle of the assessment of damages to the "paid up" lump sum licence fee and the per abstract royalties. Such an interpretation of copyright protection has the effect, in the present case, of limiting the damages recoverable for copyright infringement to the benefits directly receivable by the plaintiff under contract while permitting the defendant to breach the contract with impunity.

713 Those factors which forced the plaintiffs to effectively lower their price also restricted their market *for their add-on products*, and, in my view, are causally linked and flow directly from the infringing activity of the defendant HMRI and Imbert. These items, as such, are recoverable in copyright against both HMRI and Imbert. These categories are succinctly summarized by McLachlin J.A., then of our Court of Appeal, in *Houweling Nurseries Ltd. v. Fisons Western Corp.* (1988), 49 D.L.R. (4th) 205 at 210-11 [37 B.C.L.R. (2d) 2]:

> In my view, the law may be summarized as follows. The basic rule is that damages for lost profits, like all damages for breach of contract, must be proven on a balance of probabilities. Where it is shown with some degree of certainty that a specific contract was lost as a result of the breach, with a consequent loss of profit, that sum should be awarded. However, damages may also be awarded for loss of more conjectural profits, where the evidence demonstrates the possibility that contracts have been lost because of the breach, and also establishes that it is probable that some of these possible contracts would have materialized, had the breach not occurred. In such a case, the court should make a moderate award, recognizing that some of the contracts may not have materialized had there been no breach.

> The matter may be put another way. Even though the plaintiff may not be able to prove with certainty that it would have obtained specific contracts but for the breach, it may be able to establish that the defendant's breach of contract deprived it of the opportunity to obtain such business. The plaintiff is entitled to compensation for the loss of that opportunity. But it would be wrong to assess the damages for that lost opportunity as though it were a certainty.

714 The unique and distinguishing feature in the present action is that the acts of infringement and the licensing of the infringing work at 163 sites including those at which the plaintiff's work was already installed are inextricably and

inherently tied to the defendant HMRI's breach of its contractual obligation to market the plaintiff's software, in my view, with the exceptions I will set out; the damages flowing from the copyright breach, in this case, mirror those arising in contract.

---

2. Statutory Damages

Microsoft Corp. v. 9038-3746 Québec Inc. (2007), 57 C.P.R. (4th) 204 (F.C.T.D.)

S. Harrington J.

Heard: October 31–November 21, 2006
Judgment: January 17, 2007
Docket: T-1502-00

. . .

S. Harrington J.:

1 The first question in this copyright and trade-mark action is what the case is really about. The parties agree that it is about compact discs and related material which Microsoft alleges are counterfeit. The CDs contain copies of various Microsoft computer software programs. These programs are literary works, protected by copyright. The CDs and other material are also covered by such well-known trade-marks as "Microsoft", "Windows", "Office" and "Outlook". However Microsoft goes on to allege that even if the CDs and other material are genuine, the defendants' dealings in them were unlicensed and still constitute an infringement of its copyright and trade-marks. The defendants take the position that to the extent the items are genuine, even if unlicensed, they infringed nothing. They say they were dealing in the grey market which is perfectly legal.

2 I find that the CDs as well as the material related thereto, such as instruction manuals and certificates of authenticity, were counterfeit. By counterfeit I mean they were neither manufactured by Microsoft nor by any of its authorized replicators. It follows that the copies of the computer programs embodied in the CDs were unauthorized.

3 Consequently, Microsoft's position that dealing in genuine, but unlicensed, material infringes copyright and trade-mark is somewhat moot. Nevertheless, some consideration must be given thereto because of the wide-ranging scope of the permanent injunctive relief it seeks.

4 The evidence which leads me to the conclusion that the computer programs in question were not authorized by Microsoft to be copied, and that the CDs and related material are counterfeit, arises from a seizure by the Royal Canadian Mounted Police in November 1999, followed by another seizure by the Montreal Urban Community Police in March 2000. The items seized by the RCMP

were exhibited at trial and examined in extensive detail by a renowned expert retained by Microsoft. I accept his opinion that what he identified as counterfeit was counterfeit. The items seized by the Montreal police were returned to the defendants who then disposed of them under extremely suspicious circumstances. Fortunately, however, they had been examined by a Microsoft in-house expert while still in police custody. I accept her opinion that the items she identified as counterfeit were counterfeit. It follows that the copies of the computer programs embodied in the CDs were not authorized.

5 Although it is therefore a foregone conclusion that Microsoft is entitled to some judgmental relief, such as delivery up of the counterfeit material, the defendants say they did not know that the discs and related material were counterfeit and that the copies of the computer programs embodied therein were unauthorized. Indeed, by making Microsoft prove its case they made the point that it would be difficult, if not impossible, for someone to distinguish reality from illusion unless privy to Microsoft's closely-guarded confidential information. Knowledge, or lack thereof, has a considerable bearing on the personal liability of the two individual defendants who are, or were, directors of the corporate defendants and on the scope of the wide-ranging injunction, statutory damages, punitive damages and other remedies sought by Microsoft.

. . .

Damages

103 As a general rule, damages are awarded to put the plaintiff in the position it would have been in had it not been wronged by the defendants. The fact that damages may be difficult to calculate in a given case does not limit recovery to a nominal amount. This principle is not confined to infringement of intellectual property rights (*Penvidic Contracting Co. v. International Nickel Co.* (1975), [1976] 1 S.C.R. 267 (S.C.C.) and *Boutique Jacob Inc. v. Pantainer Ltd.*, 2006 FC 217 (F.C.)).

104 In addition, the Federal Court is a Court of Equity and, in cases such as this, may award a plaintiff the profit the defendant derived from its infringing activities. This remedy has been recognized in the field of trade-marks (*3925928 Manitoba Ltd. v. 101029530 Saskatchewan Ltd.*, 2005 FC 1465 (F.C.)), although not specifically mentioned in the *Trade-marks Act*.

Statutory Damages

105 However, the *Copyright Act* contains special statutory provisions which deal with profits and damages. Section 35 provides that in addition to the damages proved, a defendant is liable for "such part of the profits...made from the infringement...that were not taken into account in calculating the damages as the court considers just." A plaintiff may choose not to seek damages and an accounting. Section 38.1 allows him to elect instead to recover an award of statutory damages which normally ranges from $500 to no more than $20,000 with respect to each work which was infringed. That $500 minimum is subject to reduction to not less than $200 if the defendants were not aware and had

no reasonable grounds to believe they had infringed copyright. Furthermore, if more than one work has been infringed (25 were infringed in this case), the Court may reduce the award even more if it would otherwise be grossly out of proportion to the infringement.

106 In exercising its discretion, the Court is required to consider all relevant factors including:

    a.   Good or bad faith;

    b.   The conduct of the parties before and during the proceedings; and

    c.   The need to deter other infringements of the copyrights in question.

107 Finally, an election for statutory damages does not affect any right the copyright owner may have to exemplary or punitive damages.

108 Microsoft has not proved any special damages. In terms of copyright, it seeks the statutory maximum of $20,000 for each of the 25 copyrights which have been infringed. In addition, it seeks an accounting of profits under the *Trade-marks Act*, as well as punitive or exemplary damages.

109 The first factor I have taken into account in determining the amount of statutory damages is whether the defendants have satisfied the Court that they were not aware and had no reasonable grounds to believe that they had infringed copyright. If so, the Court may reduce the amount of the award to $200 per work. However, for the reasons previously given, the defendants have not satisfied me that they had reasonable grounds to believe they had not infringed copyright.

110 The next factor is whether the award of the minimum amount of $500 for each of the 25 works, or $12,500 all told, would be grossly out of proportion to the infringement. An award of $12,500 would be grossly out of proportion in the sense that it would be far too low. Had Microsoft not elected for statutory damages, the defendants would have, under section 35, been required to pay such part of their profits arising from the infringement. All the plaintiff had to prove were gross revenues, with the defendants then being required to prove every element of cost (*Kraft Canada Inc. v. Euro Excellence Inc.*, 2006 FC 453 (F.C.)).

111 Mr. Cerrelli's evidence is somewhat of a moving target. At the very least, according to his evidence at trial, Inter-Plus' annual gross was $3 million, 60 per cent of which was derived from the sale of Microsoft products. However, when it suited his purposes he swore that Inter-Plus' gross was in excess of $5 million, as he did in an affidavit filed in the Quebec Superior Court. I am not so naïve as to think that the only counterfeit items Inter-Plus ever had in its possession were those seized by the police. No evidence was led at trial as to Inter-Plus' expenses, but Microsoft had already elected for statutory damages. Nevertheless, a factor to be taken into account is that Inter-Plus had been under Court order to produce all its appropriate business records, receipts, purchase invoices, sales invoices and details of returned items through to 2005. Mr. Cerrelli said he was unable to do so because his records had been taken by a disloyal employee against whom he has taken action. However, when confronted with the fact that she had left

in mid-2003, and that he had been specifically ordered by the Court to provide documents through to 2005, he came up with the lame excuse that he must have misunderstood the question. Based on the facts proved and the conduct of the defendants, I infer that they continued to deal in counterfeit product. I say this mindful of the distinction to be drawn between inferences and conjecture. As Mr. Justice MacGuigan stated in *Satiacum v. Canada (Minister of Employment & Immigration)* (1989), 99 N.R. 171 (Fed. C.A.) at paragraphs 34 and 35:

> The common law has long recognized the difference between reasonable inference and pure conjecture. Lord Macmillan put the distinction this way in *Jones v. Great Western Railway Co.* (1930), 47 T.L.R. 39, at 45, 144 L.T. 194, at 202, (H.L.):
>
>> The dividing line between conjecture and inference is often a very difficult one to draw. A conjecture may be plausible but it is of no legal value, for its essence is that it is a mere guess. An inference in the legal sense, on the other hand, is a deduction from the evidence, and if it is a reasonable deduction it may have the validity of legal proof. The attribution of an occurrence to a cause is, I take it, always a matter of inference.

112 Twenty-five copyrights were infringed. At $20,000 per infringement, statutory damages work out to $500,000. I grant damages against the corporate defendants and Carmelo Cerrelli jointly and severally in that amount.

113 I have also taken into account the factors enumerated in section 38.1(5). The defendants have acted in bad faith. Their conduct both before and during these proceedings has been dismissive of law and order, and their failure to provide appropriate records, despite court order, demonstrates the necessity of deterring other infringements of the copyrights in question.

114 To give a further example of their behaviour, another company sharing office space with Inter-Plus was dealing in Microsoft product geared for the academic community. The contract permitted Microsoft to carry out audits. It gave notice that such an audit would be carried out. However, on arrival the accountant was met by someone calling himself Robert who refused him entry and threw him out. During discovery, and during his cross-examination at trial, Mr. Cerrelli claimed he had no knowledge of anyone by the name of Robert. When told that the accountant had been in the Court corridor, had seen him, and was going to testify that he was the Robert who threw him out, Mr. Cerrelli's memory improved. He had an overnight revelation and instructed his solicitors to stipulate that on reflection he recalled that he was the Robert who had shown the accountant the door.

115 Indeed, I very much doubt that $500,000 covers a full accounting of the profits the defendants have derived from infringing Microsoft's rights. However, Microsoft, which had also claimed an accounting of profits under the *Trade-marks Act*, said it was not seeking damages, apart from punitive or exemplary damages, however characterized, in excess of $500,000, and so I leave the matter there.

The *Copyright Modernization Act* amended section 38.1 of the *Copyright Act* with the effect that the statutory damages available to a copyright owner for infringing activities will depend on whether those activities were done for commercial or non-commercial purposes. Infringement for commercial purposes can result in an award of statutory damages "of not less than $500 and not more than $20,000" for each work infringed. However, the statutory damages available for non-commercial infringements are significantly reduced. Pursuant to s. 38.1(1)(b), where an infringement is carried out for non-commercial purposes (presumably meaning without motive of financial gain) an award of statutory damages can be "in a sum of not less than $100 and not more than $5,000 that the court considers just, with respect to all infringements involved in the proceedings for all works or other subject-matter...." No further statutory damages award may be sought against the defendant either by the plaintiff or any other copyright owner (see ss. 38(1.12), (1.2)) in respect of any other infringing activity for non-commercial purposes that occurred before the institution of the proceedings. The stated aim of this amendment was to prevent ordinary Canadians from facing "unreasonable penalties" for infringement, presumably along the lines of the controversial awards seen in US file-sharing cases. Defendants liable for enabling infringement under the new subsection 27(2.3), however, are deemed to have a commercial purpose and so cannot benefit from the s. 38.1(1)(b) cap (see s. 38(1.11), although they should be protected from a grossly disproportionate award under s. 38(3). In the case of infringements for non-commercial purposes, the court is to exercise its discretion with regard to "the need for an award to be proportionate to the infringements, in consideration of the hardship the award may cause to the defendant, whether the infringement was for private purposes or not, and the impact of the infringements on the plaintiff" (s. 38.1(5)).

3. Declaratory Relief

Research in Motion v. Atari (2007) 61 C.P.R. (4th) 193 (Ont. S.C.J.)

H. Spiegel J.

Heard: August 2, 2007
Judgment: August 16, 2007
Docket: C-1114-06

. . .

H. Spiegel J.:

Background

1 The plaintiff, Research in Motion Limited ("RIM") is an Ontario corporation with headquarters located in Waterloo. RIM is known around the world for its BlackBerry handheld wireless device. RIM claims it developed a video/computer game called BrickBreaker, which it includes on certain BlackBerry devices. RIM also claims it developed a video/computer game called Meteor Crusher

which is not included on BlackBerry devices but is available for download from its website.

2 The defendants (collectively referred to as "Atari") are affiliated corporations that develop, publish and licence video/computer games. They are headquartered in New York but carry on business in the U.S.A, Ontario and elsewhere. Atari has alleged that it owns copyrights around the world in two games, "Breakout" and "Asteroids".

3 RIM commenced this action against the defendants by way of statement of claim issued in the City of Kitchener on October 27, 2006. RIM claims a declaration that the copying, distribution, sales and communication to the public of RIM's BrickBreaker game do not infringe any copyright that the defendants Atari may have in the games Breakout and Super Breakout (hereinafter collectively referred to as "Breakout") under the laws of Canada or the United States. RIM also claims a declaration that the audio visual displays of Breakout do not constitute work protected by copyright under Canadian law and a declaration that Atari has no right to title or interest to Breakout under either the laws of Canada or the United States.

4 RIM's statement of claim alleges that in March 2006 Atari wrote to RIM claiming that RIM's BrickBreaker game infringes Atari's copyright in Breakout. RIM through its solicitors denied any infringement.

5 The statement of claim further alleges that in August 2006 Atari again wrote to RIM alleging that RIM infringed its copyright in Breakout. Atari enclosed a letter prepared by Atari's counsel which advised that it would be recommending that Atari initiate legal proceedings in the "relevant jurisdiction" if RIM did not accede to Atari's demands for production of all worldwide sales information of Blackberrys that feature BrickBreaker. RIM's counsel further stated, "due to worldwide distribution of Blackberry devices, our client is generally free to choose the forum in which it wishes to enforce its claims for copyright infringement". In September 2006 RIM's solicitor responded again denying any infringement.

6 RIM alleges that Atari has refused to retract its threats to sue RIM.

7 On December 6, 2006 Atari served this motion to strike, dismiss or stay the plaintiff's action.

. . .

Atari's Motion

13 Atari moves to strike the entire claim pursuant to Rule 21.01(1)(b) of the *Rules of Civil Procedure*[FN3] on the grounds that RIM's claim for a declaration of non-infringement discloses no reasonable cause of action, and/or under Rule 21.01(3)(b) on the basis that this Court has no jurisdiction to grant such a declaration. In the alternative, Atari seeks to stay the portion of RIM's claim related to United States copyright law on the basis that Ontario is *forum non conveniens*.

Does RIM's claim disclose no reasonable cause of action?

14 On a motion to strike a pleading under Rule 21.01(1)(b) the test is whether, accepting all of the allegations of fact in the statement of claim as true, it is plain and obvious that the action must fail[FN4]. Even if there is some chance that the plaintiff's case might succeed, the plaintiff must be permitted to pursue its claim. The novelty of the plaintiff's claim is not to militate against the plaintiff.[FN5]

15 Atari submits that RIM is seeking in essence a declaration of non-infringement and that no such remedy is found in the *Copyright Act*. The Supreme Court of Canada has recently affirmed the proposition that copyright is a creature of statute and the rights and remedies provided by the *Copyright Act* are exhaustive. Atari submits that therefore RIM's pleading discloses no reasonable cause of action.

16 In support of its submission Atari points to section 60(1) of the *Patent Act*, R.S.C. 1985, c. P-4 which does allow a party to commence an action in the Federal Court for a declaration of invalidity and section 60(2) which permits an action in the Federal Court for a declaration of non-infringement. Atari relies on the maxim *expressio unius est exclusio alterius* (to express one thing is to exclude others) as a rule of statutory interpretation that supports the conclusion that Parliament, by including the remedy of non-infringement in the *Patent Act*, must have intended to exclude it as a remedy under the *Copyright Act*. Atari submits that allowing the plaintiff's claim to proceed would "read into" the *Copyright Act* a cause of action Parliament expressly provided for with respect to patents but chose not to provide for with respect to copyrights.

17 RIM submits that the very relief that Atari says the court cannot grant because it is not found in the *Copyright Act* was granted by the Supreme Court of Canada in the *CCH Canadian Ltd.* case. CCH had claimed that the Law Society of Upper Canada (LSUC) was infringing on its copyright in law reports and other legal materials. LSUC counterclaimed for a declaration of non-infringement. The court found that there was no infringement and issued a declaration that LSUC does not infringe copyright when a single copy of a reported decision, case summary, statute regulation or limited selection of text from a treatise is made by the Great Library.

18 Counsel for Atari replies by pointing out that the reasons in the *CCH Canadian Ltd.* case indicate that there was no argument or discussion by the court addressed to the issue of whether a declaration of non-infringement is an available remedy under copyright law. Atari submits therefore that the *CCH Canadian Ltd.* case is not a binding authority for the proposition that such a remedy exists. I am inclined to agree with this submission, however it is not necessary for RIM to satisfy the court that the remedy exists but rather for Atari to demonstrate that it is plain and obvious that it does not exist. I think it can be fairly said that it was not plain and obvious to the Supreme Court in *CCH Canadian Ltd.* that a declaration for non-infringement is a remedy not known to the law. Otherwise it would not have granted the LSUC's counterclaim for a declaration of non-infringement.

19 RIM also submits that the courts in the United Kingdom, including the English Court of Appeal, have also endorsed the power to grant negative declarations in respect of copyright despite the absence of any explicit authority in the U.K. *Copyright Designs and Patents Act 1988* ("U.K. *Copyright Act*"). In *Point Solutions Ltd. v. Focus Business Solutions Ltd.* the plaintiff sought a declaration that it did not infringe the defendant's copyright in certain computer software. The trial judge, affirmed by the Court of Appeal, explicitly rejected the argument that the absence of a statutory right to make a negative declaration precluded the court from making such a declaration. Counsel for RIM advises me that the U.K. *Copyright Act* is virtually identical to the Canadian *Copyright Act*.

20 In response to Atari's statutory interpretation argument based on the maxim of *expressio unius est exclusio alterius* RIM submits that Atari has provided no authority for this proposition. RIM submits that such an argument cannot satisfy the burden on the moving party, who must show "that there is an existing bar in the form of a decided case directly on point from the same jurisdiction demonstrating that the very issue has been squarely dealt with and rejected by our courts." RIM submits moreover that the court's jurisdiction to issue declarations of non-infringement is found not in the *Copyright Act* but in this court's inherent jurisdiction, the *Courts of Justice Act* and the common law.

21 In my view there is much merit to this submission. The Superior Court is a court of general jurisdiction with all the powers that are necessary to do justice between the parties. This jurisdiction is unlimited and unrestricted in substantive law in civil matters except where specifically provided for to the contrary. In my view, there is nothing in the *Copyright Act* that specifically abrogates this court's general jurisdiction to grant such declarations.

22 Moreover this part of Atari's argument appears to have been dealt with in the English case of *Leco Instruments (U.K.) Ltd. v. Land Pyrometers Ltd.* In that case the court considered both the provision for a declaration of non-infringement in the U.K. *Patent Act* and the lack of a corresponding provision in the U.K. *Copyright Act*. The Court found that there was no reason in principle why, in the appropriate circumstances, the court should not provide an equally efficacious remedy by way of declaration in a copyright case.

23 Insofar as RIM's reliance on section 11 and section 97 of the *Courts of Justice Act*, Atari submits that section 97 does not create a right but simply provides a remedy with respect to a right where such a right arises under contract, agreement or statute. In the absence of such a right a declaration will be refused. Atari further submits that neither section 11 nor section 97 of the *Act* purports to confer a remedy with respect to copyright and if either of them did it would be *ultra vires* the Ontario Legislature, since under section 91(23) of the *Constitution Act* 1867 copyrights are solely within the jurisdiction of the Parliament of Canada.

24 I do not agree with this submission. Section 91(23) of the *Constitution Act* indeed provides Parliament with exclusive jurisdiction with copyright. However section 92(14) of the *Constitution Act* grants the provinces exclusive jurisdiction with the administration of justice. I am not persuaded that there is a conflict

between these two provisions. In my view this court is not prohibited from granting the relief sought on a constitutional basis.

---

4. Permanent Injunction

Since copyright is a species of property, the owner is entitled to protection of that property. Where infringement has been established, the owner of the copyright is *prima facie* entitled to an injunction restraining further infringement without proof of actual damages or prejudice. An injunction is, in principle, an equitable remedy and, thus, it is within the court's discretion to decide whether or not to grant an injunction.[4] An injunction need not be granted where the effect of the grant of the injunction would be oppressive.[5]

A permanent injunction will often be framed to require the defendant to deliver to the plaintiff infringing copies of the work in its possession or control. There is also authority that where the work has been widely distributed the injunction may be framed to compel third parties in possession of infringing copies to return such copies to the plaintiff. It has been held that such orders may provide for an orderly transition with a minimum of disruption to innocent third parties.[6]

R. v. James Lorimer and Co. Ltd., [1984] 1 F.C. 1065 (Fed. C.A.)

Heald, Mahoney and Ryan JJ.

Ottawa: November 29, 1983

Docket: A-831-82

. . .

Mahoney J.:

. . .

9 In exercising his discretion to refuse the injunctive relief, the learned Trial Judge found persuasive the facts that the infringement had not adversely affected distribution and sales of the appellant's infringed work nor adversely affected the revenue deriving from its sales as well as the unusual character of the appellant as a plaintiff. The characterization of the Crown as an "unusual plaintiff" lies, I take it, in his finding of fact that it was not much interested in income or revenue from its work and not, I trust, in a generalization that the Crown is to be treated differently than other litigants.

---

4   *CCH Canadian Ltd. v. Law Society of Upper Canada*, 2004 SCC 13, at para. 85.
5   *Navitaire Inc. v. Easy Jet Airline Co. Ltd.* (No. 2), [2005] E.W.H.C. 0282 (Ch.).
6   *Prism Hospital Software Inc. v. Hospital Medical Records Institute*, [1994] 10 W.W.R. 305 (B.C. S.C.).

10 The Act is clear. Infringement does not require that the infringing work compete in the marketplace with that infringed; it requires only that the infringer do something that the copyright owner alone has the right to do. It follows that, where infringement of copyright has been established, the owner of the copyright is *prima facie* entitled to an injunction restraining further infringement. It likewise follows that, where the infringing work is found to include any substantial part of a work in which copyright subsists, the copyright owner is to be deemed owner of all copies of the infringing work and all production plates and is *prima facie* entitled to the assistance of the Court in gaining possession of them. The onus is on the infringer to establish grounds upon which the Court may properly exercise its discretion against granting such relief. Those grounds must lie in the conduct of the copyright owner, not in the conduct or motives of the infringer. The fact that the copyright owner has suffered no damages as a result of the infringement is not a basis for refusing an injunction.

Navitaire Inc. v. Easy Jet Airline Co. Ltd. (No. 2), [2006] R.P.C. 4 (Ch. D)

Pumfrey J.

January 11-14 and March 11, 2005

. . .

Relief in respect of copyright infringement

101 The first question is that of injunctive relief. Generally, an injunction will be granted where the invasion of a property right is demonstrated, and where repetition is threatened. An injunction will not be granted where the effect of the grant of the injunction is oppressive: Jaggard v Sawyer [1995] 1 W.L.R. 269. I take the following statement of principle from the judgment of Millett L.J.:

> "When the plaintiff claims an injunction and the defendant asks the court to award damages instead, the proper approach for the court to adopt cannot be in doubt. Clearly the plaintiff must first establish a case for equitable relief, not only by proving his legal right and an actual or threatened infringement by the defendant, but also by overcoming all equitable defences such as laches, acquiescence or estoppel. If he succeeds in doing this, he is prima facie entitled to an injunction. The court may nevertheless in its discretion withhold injunctive relief and award damages instead. How is this discretion to be exercised? In a well known passage in Shelfer v. City of London Electric Lighting Co. [1895] 1 Ch. 287, 322-323, A. L. Smith L.J. set out what he described as 'a good working rule' that
>
> > '(1) If the injury to the plaintiff's legal right is small,
> >
> > (2) And is one which is capable of being estimated in money,
> >
> > (3) And is one which can be adequately compensated by a small money payment,

> (4) And the case is one in which it would be oppressive to the defendant to grant an injunction: — then damages in substitution for an injunction may be given.'

Laid down just 100 years ago, A. L. Smith L.J.'s check-list has stood the test of time; but it needs to be remembered that it is only a working rule and does not purport to be an exhaustive statement of the circumstances in which damages may be awarded instead of an injunction.

Reported cases are merely illustrations of circumstances in which particular judges have exercised their discretion, in some cases by granting an injunction, and in others by awarding damages instead. Since they are all cases on the exercise of a discretion, none of them is a binding authority on how the discretion should be exercised. The most that any of them can demonstrate is that in similar circumstances it would not be wrong to exercise the discretion in the same way. But it does not follow that it would be wrong to exercise it differently.

The outcome of any particular case usually turns on the question: would it in all the circumstances be oppressive to the defendant to grant the injunction to which the plaintiff is prima facie entitled? Most of the cases in which the injunction has been refused are cases where the plaintiff has sought a mandatory injunction to pull down a building which infringes his right to light or which has been built in breach of a restrictive covenant. In such cases the court is faced with a fait accompli. The jurisdiction to grant a mandatory injunction in those circumstances cannot be doubted, but to grant it would subject the defendant to a loss out of all proportion to that which would be suffered by the plaintiff if it were refused, and would indeed deliver him to the plaintiff bound hand and foot to be subjected to any extortionate demands the plaintiff might make. In the present case, as in the closely similar case of Bracewell v. Appleby [1975] Ch. 408, the plaintiff sought a prohibitory injunction to restrain the use of a road giving access to the defendants' house. The result of granting the injunction would be much the same; the house would not have to be pulled down, but it would be rendered landlocked and incapable of beneficial enjoyment."

102 At the same time, the jurisdiction to award damages in lieu of an injunction is not exercised merely because the defendant is willing to pay. In Shelfer's case, Lindley L.J. said:

> "But in exercising the jurisdiction thus given attention ought to be paid to well settled principles; and ever since Lord Cairns's Act was passed the Court of Chancery has repudiated the notion that the legislature intended to turn that court into a tribunal for legalizing wrongful acts; or in other words, the court has always protested against the notion that it ought to allow a wrong to continue simply because the wrongdoer is able and willing to pay for the injury he may inflict."

103 As Millett L.J. points out, the effect of refusing to grant an injunction in any given case is certainly to license the defendant, and provided the jurisdiction is exercised with caution, this is not of itself objectionable:

"References to the 'expropriation' of the plaintiff's property are somewhat over-done, not because that is not the practical effect of withholding an injunction, but because the grant of an injunction, like all equitable remedies, is discretionary. Many proprietary rights cannot be protected at all by the common law. The owner must submit to unlawful interference with his rights and be content with damages. If he wants to be protected he must seek equitable relief, and he has no absolute right to that. In many cases, it is true, an injunction will be granted almost as of course; but this is not always the case, and it will never be granted if this would cause injustice to the defendant. Citation of passages in the cases warning of the danger of 'expropriating' the plaintiff's property needs to be balanced by reference to statements like that of Lord Westbury L.C. in Isenberg v. East India House Estate Co. Ltd. (1863) 3 De G. J. & S. 263, 273 where he held that it was the duty of the court not

> 'by granting a mandatory injunction, to deliver over the defendants to the plaintiff bound hand and foot, in order to be made subject to any extortionate demand that he may by possibility make, but to substitute for such mandatory injunction an inquiry before itself, in order to ascertain the measure of damage that has been actually sustained.'"

104 Accordingly the grant or refusal of a final injunction is not merely a matter of the balance of convenience. Justice requires that the court observe the principles enunciated in Shelfer's case and remembers that if the effect of the grant of an injunction is not oppressive the defendant cannot buy his way out of it, even if the price, objectively ascertained, would be modest. My understanding of the word "oppressive" in this context is that the effect of the grant of the injunction would be grossly disproportionate to the right protected. The word "grossly" avoids any suggestion that all that has to be done is to strike a balance of convenience.

105 Recently in the copyright field, damages in lieu have been granted in a wholly exceptional case (Banks v CBS Songs [1996] E.M.L.R. 452, where the damage was not small) and refused where the grant of an injunction would not be oppressive: Ludlow Music v Williams [2002] F.S.R. 57 (p.868). These are cases on their own particular facts and provide no general guidance.

Icons and GUI screens

106 The works I have found to be infringed are (1) the icons and (2) the GUI screens. I see absolutely no reason why injunctive relief should not be granted in this case. There will be an enquiry as to damages in respect of the infringement.

Prism Hospital Software Inc. v. Hospital Medical Records Institute, [1994] 10 W.W.R. 305 (B.C. S.C.)

Parrett J.

Heard: November 4-8, 14-15, 18-22, 25-27, December 2-4, 6, 9-13, 1991, January 6-7, 9-10, 13-17, February 3-7, 10-14, 17-18 and July 9, 1992 Judgment: August 23, 1994 Docket: Doc. Vancouver C872267

. . .

The defendant was federally chartered non-profit company governed by a board of directors elected by its members, who were drawn from hospitals, provincial hospital associations, and provincial government health ministries. It funded itself mainly by charging fees to hospitals for its services. The defendant maintained a healthcare information database on a mainframe computer and member hospitals provided the defendant with details of patient visits on the death or discharge of the patient. The defendant stored the information "abstracts" so that they could be available for such purposes as analyzing resource use, management reviews, strategic planning, funding analyses and medical research. Collected data also provided a basis for comparing a particular hospital's data with national figures or with peer group hospitals. In addition to charging a per abstract collection fee, the defendant also charged for certain standard reports to all subscribing hospitals as well as other reports on request. The plaintiff started business in 1981 when its two principals began to create and market a computerized abstract collection and reporting system. Initially, the defendant received abstracts from hospitals on paper and it contracted with another company to have the information converted to electronic form for entry into its database. When that service ceased to be available, the defendant pushed member hospitals to submit abstracts electronically and it decided to contract for the preparation of a computer-based medical records abstracting system which it would distribute. In that regard, the defendant approached the plaintiff. The plaintiff offered to provide abstracting software to run on microcomputers and the parties agreed that the plaintiff would license the software to the defendant which the defendant would then sublicense to hospitals. The discussions culminated in 1985 in a contract reflected in the plaintiff's proposal and a licence agreement, which documents the parties referred to as "the contract documents." Under the contract, the plaintiff was to make its best efforts to provide a demonstration version of the software in 1985 for the defendant to show in December, and working versions incorporating edit requirements of different provinces were to be provided according to a schedule. The plaintiff provided a demonstration version in December 1985 and progressive working versions of the software from February 1986 to January 1987. At about that time, I., a programmer employed by the defendant, persuaded the defendant to authorize him to write a prototype replacement for the plaintiff's software on the basis that the software exhibited problems which the rewrite would not since it would be written in a more modern computer language. It was the "rewriting" of the plaintiff's software, without its knowledge or consent, that brought the parties' relationship to an end when discovered. While the defendant sought to justify its decision to pursue the rewrite of the plaintiff's software in a number of ways, central to its position was the thesis that as of October 1, 1986 the software was not a stable, maintainable product and that it was "deficient and inoperative" in many respects. The plaintiff sued the defendant and I. for damages for breach of contract and copyright infringement.

. . .

XVI. Relief

665 I have found the defendant HMRI in breach of the provisions of arts. 5, 6, 10 and 14 of the Licence Agreement. In addition I have found that both HMRI and the defendant Imbert by their actions have infringed Prism's copyright in Prism Savoir-Faire and as a consequence are jointly liable for damages flowing from that infringement. Mr. Imbert is not a party to the contract and cannot be liable as a result of the breaches I have found. The action as it proceeded before me did not proceed as against the defendants John Stenabaugh and Lynne Abbott.

666 There is no evidence or basis in law to justify an award to the remaining plaintiffs.

667 Prism seeks orders for prerogative relief, compensatory and punitive damages, interest, and costs on a special scale.

668 The thrust of the prerogative relief sought is to compel the removal of the infringing software from the market and to compel its return to the plaintiff. Prism is entitled to this relief but while some portions of this particular relief are easy to identify, others are more problematic. So far as possible the orders given should be tailored to attempt to place Prism back in the position they would have been in but for the breaches of contract and copyright. In achieving this it is necessary to recognize that the infringing software has been marketed widely by HMRI and has been installed in a large number of hospitals across Canada. Any orders made must provide for an orderly transition with a minimum of disruption to innocent third parties.

669 (1) There will be a declaration that Q-Pro-4 Savoir-Faire is an infringing work which violates Prism's copyright.

670 (2) There will be an injunction issued prohibiting HMRI and Imbert from further copying of either Prism's work or of the infringing software.

671 (3) The terms of the prohibition last described will permit, for a transitional period, HMRI to maintain the software at its existing sites. In the event the parties are unable to agree on the necessary transitional period either party may speak to the terms of such an exception.

672 (4) There will be an order directing HMRI to deliver up to Prism any and all infringing copies within their possession, save and except for materials reasonably necessary to enable them to maintain the existing software for

the transitional period. HMRI is to deliver up these materials forthwith and to provide Prism with a list of any materials they retain for the purpose mentioned together with a description sufficient to specifically identify all such material in their possession.

673 (5) There will be a further order directing the defendant Imbert to deliver up to Prism any and all infringing copies in his possession. This is to include any and all copies, paper or electronic, in his possession or control.

674 (6)   There will be an order directing that the infringing works in hospitals, under licence from HMRI, be withdrawn over a transitional period. Once again in the event counsel are unable to agree there is leave to speak to the details and time periods of the transition.

675 (7) HMRI will provide Prism forthwith with all necessary information, particulars, and data to enable Prism to convert Q-Pro-4 Savoir-Faire historical, current ancillary data files and any other necessary files to a compatible Super-MACS format and will pay all reasonable costs incurred by Prism to do so.

676 (8) HMRI will provide to Prism and/or a particular hospital, at no cost to them, historical data from their mainframe computer for that hospital if it elects to install the Prism software and wishes access to its historical data. The period provided will include that period for which data was submitted from that site by the Savoir-Faire program either Prism or Q-Pro-4.

677 (9) The defendant HMRI will pay all reasonable costs associated with the changing of any existing Savoir-Faire site to Prism SuperMACS. These costs will include the costs of conversion, installation and training. It may well be that these costs will as a result of SuperMACS' current incarnation include training in the use of a report writer. The bundling of the report writer with the software occurred as a result of Prism's attempt to survive in the market created by HMRI's wrongful acts and in no small measure by the fact that they were forced to compete in the market with a "version" of their own software. If that fact necessitates some modest cost for additional training it is one which flows from the defendants' wrongful acts.

678 (10) There will be an order that HMRI immediately cease marketing the infringing software.

679 (11) Upon the withdrawal of the infringing software from the market all remaining Savoir-Faire materials including user manuals, system diagrams, and source and object code whether in paper or electronic form within the control of HMRI is to be delivered to Prism forthwith.

680 (12) Where, to the knowledge of HMRI, copies, in paper or electronic form, of the infringing material have been delivered to individuals or organizations and are outside HMRI's direct control they will forthwith disclose to Prism the name, address and location of such individual or organization together with particulars of the materials in their possession.

681 In concluding this section of these reasons I wish to make clear that the "reasonable cost" of converting both data and sites will include compensation for the time of Prism's principals or employees to carry out these activities. The fixing of a specific fee for each site, as suggested by the plaintiff, does not in my view properly reflect the costs of the conversion process which may in fact be minimal in some cases and substantial in others.

682 Finally, I know of no principle which would permit me to or warrant the imposition, as the plaintiff suggests, of a form of licence fee based on existing sites electing to install a different system. Such an order would seek, in effect, to impose as a penalty what should properly be assessed as damages which flow from one or more of the defendants' breaches. It is proper, however, to recognize that during any transitional period, the continuing presence of an infringing work will be and remain a legitimate concern of Prism's; I will therefore impose an additional term during the transitional period.

. . .

5. Interlocutory Injunctive Relief

An interlocutory injunction is an extraordinary remedy designed to protect a very real threat to an enforceable right of the party and is a remedy that will not be granted lightly. It is a practical device or procedure by means of which a court may prevent what it perceives as a prima facie injustice causing continuing harm from being prolonged until the issue is finally determined.

Courts in Canada adopt a three-stage test when considering an application for an interlocutory injunction. First, a preliminary assessment must be made of the merits of the case to ensure that there is a serious question to be tried. Secondly, it must be determined whether the applicant would suffer irreparable harm if the application were refused. The cases establish that the possibility of collecting damages is not in all cases a sufficient answer to an action brought against an infringer when the plaintiff has shown a very strong prima facie case. Finally, an assessment must be made as to the balance of convenience between the parties.

Universal Studios Inc. v. Zellers Inc. (1983), 73 C.P.R. (2d) 1 (Fed. T.D.)

Walsh J.

Ottawa: June 15, 1983
Docket: T-617-83

. . .

The following are the reasons for order rendered in English by Walsh J.:

1 Plaintiffs move for an interlocutory injunction against defendant directing that all E.T. dolls and packaging therefor and advertising material relating thereto, in the care, custody or control of the defendant be delivered up into the interim

custody of plaintiffs' solicitors or of this Honourable Court until the final disposition of this action. These dolls and packaging are described in the motion. Plaintiffs also ask that all E.T. credit card keychains and packaging therefor and advertising material relating thereto similarly be delivered up, that defendant be restrained from manufacturing, importing, distributing, advertising, and offering for sale or selling any E.T. dolls and E.T. keychains which have not been authorized by plaintiffs and that defendant provide plaintiffs' solicitors with an accounting of the quantity of each unauthorized E.T. doll and E.T. keychain or any other unauthorized E.T. merchandise that is in the care, custody or control of the defendant. This motion was produced on March 4, 1983, and was adjourned until April 11, 1983, to allow for cross-examination. It was then again adjourned to April 18, simultaneous translation being requested by counsel for plaintiffs. It was finally heard on June 15 in Ottawa. The action arises out of the sale of allegedly counterfeit merchandise being sold by defendant in Canada in alleged infringement of plaintiffs' copyrights arising from the motion picture entitled "E.T. The Extra-Terrestrial". In March 1981 Universal retained Extra-Terrestrial Productions, Inc. to produce the motion picture. Universal was to own all rights in the motion picture and the mechanical creature known as "E.T." and the copyright in each. In the same month Extra-Terrestrial Productions, Inc. engaged Carlo Rambaldi Enterprises Inc. to design and create E.T. and it was understood that all copy right in E.T. was to belong to Extra-Terrestrial Productions, Inc. and hence to Universal. From March to August 1981 Carlo Rambaldi while in the employ of Carlo Rambaldi Enterprises Inc. as President created the original preliminary drawings of E.T. Copies of them were produced as well as photographs of the final E.T. The photography of the motion picture commenced in September 1981, the picture being produced by Steven Spielberg and Kathleen Kennedy, acting under contracts of service with them in the course of their employment by Extra-Terrestrial Productions, Inc. In November 1982 a set of confirmatory assignments was executed and confirmed the ownership by Universal of the copyright of E.T. and all photographs and drawings thereof, also of the motion picture. By virtue of these Carlo Rambaldi assigned his right as creator to Carlo Rambaldi Enterprises Inc. Carlo Rambaldi Enterprises Inc. assigned all their rights to Extra-Terrestrial Productions, Inc. Steven Spielberg and Kathleen Kennedy assigned their rights to Extra-Terrestrial Productions, Inc. and Extra-Terrestrial Productions, Inc. assigned their rights to Universal City Studios, Inc. the co-plaintiff. The copyrights in both the artistic work consisting of the sculpture E.T. and in the motion picture have been registered with the Canadian Copyright Office by Universal. Serial No. 318012 is the registration for the published dramatic work entitled "E.T. The Extra-Terrestrial" registered July 26, 1982, and No. 320738 is the registration of the published dramatic and artistic work entitled "E.T. The Extra-Terrestrial" registered December 3, 1982, and under No. 321014 is the registration for published artistic work entitled "E.T." (sculpture) registered December 17, 1982.

2 The motion picture was first exhibited to the public on or about June 11, 1982 and became an enormous box office success, becoming the most successful motion picture of all time as disclosed by its box office gross. As of February

17, 1983, the box office gross in the United States for the motion picture has been in excess of $293,241,000. It is estimated that there has been in excess of 104,365,000 admissions in the United States. As of the same date Universal had spent in excess of $6,300,000 U.S. in the United States advertising the motion picture, by media advertising, press kits and the like and some of such advertising has spilled over into Canada. The motion picture has also been extremely successful in Canada and has received substantial publicity in Canadian press and in U.S. newspapers and magazines which have substantial Canadian circulation. As a result of this the copyrights have become extremely valuable property. Plaintiff Universal has granted a number of licences authorizing manufacturers to manufacture and sell various goods representing or relating to E.T. The quality and design of each product produced under licence must first be approved by Universal through its licensing agent, Merchandising Corporation of America, Inc., the co-plaintiff.

3 The affidavit of John Nuanes on behalf of plaintiffs states that in October 1982 he became aware that the defendant Zellers Inc. was selling plastic E.T. dolls in plastic wrappers having a cardboard header on each side of which is a photograph of E.T. and Elliott. These were procured by Zellers through a company called International Games of Canada Ltd. and were made in Taiwan and are not authorized by Universal either itself or through its licensing agent Merchandising. On October 25, 1982 letters were written to both Zellers Inc. and International Games of Canada Ltd. advising of Universal's copyrights and requesting that they cease selling unauthorized E.T. merchandise. International Games of Canada Ltd. quickly undertook to cease all sales of unauthorized E.T. merchandise and supplied a written undertaking to such effect. Zellers however refused to stop selling the unauthorized E.T. dolls.

. . .

10 In the case of *Formules Municipales Ltee v. Pineault et al.* the Court refused to grant an interlocutory injunction on the grounds that there was no irreparable harm suffered by plaintiffs. Defendants operated a substantial and apparently prosperous business; any damages suffered by plaintiffs could be compensated by a monetary award. In making this finding however I concluded at page 146:

> It would appear, however, that plaintiff would not suffer any serious damage to its reputation by the alleged infringement of its copyright in the forms by defendants since it cannot be contended that defendants' forms are substantially different from or inferior to those of plaintiff so as to damage plaintiff's reputation should an unwary purchaser purchase them from defendants believing them to be plaintiff's forms.

In the case of *Fruit of the Loom, Inc. v. Chateau Lingerie Mfg. Co. Ltd.* Addy J. stated at page 54:

> As to the question of irreparable harm, the plaintiff has established that it would be most difficult to obtain a new licensee as long as the defendant is not enjoined from distributing the merchandise and the loss which might flow from that state of affairs would be very difficult to calculate; furthermore, the plaintiff would have

no control over quality and the possible loss of goodwill would again be very difficult to establish in damages.

This was a trade mark case however, in which loss of goodwill was an issue, and it has been held the mere difficulty in calculating damages does not make these damages irreparable. In the case of *Smith Kline & French Canada Ltd. v. Frank W. Horner, Inc.* I had occasion to state at page 53:

> I cannot accept plaintiff's argument that because it is impossible to segregate damages caused or profits resulting from the legally licensed sale of the drug Peptol from those resulting from the alleged infringement of plaintiff's copyright in the TAGAMET material prepared for use to enable these sales to be made, its damages are therefore irreparable. In other contexts it has frequently been held that the mere difficulty or even impossibility of calculating the quantum of damages by the use of any mathematical calculations does not justify a finding that no damages can be awarded when a finding of fault will result in entitlement to such damages, and the same would apply to an accounting of profits. The court must simply do the best it can under the circumstances and fix a global amount.

A similar finding was made in the Supreme Court case of *Webb & Knapp (Canada) Limited et al. v. The City of Edmonton* in which it was found that the assessment of damages for breach of appellant's copyright presented a question of difficulty, but the fact that the assessment was difficult was not a ground for awarding only nominal damages.

11 It is the question of irreparable harm which causes the most difficulty in the present proceedings. While it is somewhat difficult to conclude that sales of the dolls by the defendant and of the keychains if it should decide to put them on the market again would cause irreparable harm to plaintiffs which could not be compensated by damages, difficult as they would be to calculate since they would allegedly depend on loss of sales by licensees and possible loss of such licensees for want of adequate protection, and the amount of royalties or other payments which would flow through to plaintiffs as a result of these sales, there is no doubt that they would suffer serious harm. I do not believe that the possibility of collecting damages is in all cases a sufficient answer to an action brought against an infringer when the plaintiffs have a very strong *prima facie* case. The protection of industrial property rights from counterfeiting is an increasingly important question. In principle these rights should be protected whether or not breach of them causes serious damages. I therefore believe that the question of balance of convenience must be looked into. Plaintiffs have a very valuable property to protect both in their own interest and in that of their licensees, and their interest exceeds a mere monetary interest which can be compensated by payment of damages or an accounting of profits by Zellers on its sales of the offending merchandise. The general principle of protecting the extensive spin-offs of merchandise originating in a motion picture in which the creature E.T. has become an almost cult figure for contemporary youth is an important one, and the principle will also apply to merchandise derived from other motion pictures in future.

12 While defendant contends that plaintiffs waited nearly six months from October 1982 until March 1983 before bringing proceedings it was necessary for plaintiffs to fulfil certain legal requirements first by way of the formal assignments of the copyrights in November, and the registration of E.T. sculpture in December 1982. As soon as the alleged infringing sales were discovered letters to desist were written both to Defendant Zellers Inc. and to International Games of Canada Limited in October, and International Games responded positively, undertaking to withdraw any merchandising of the dolls. It was only in November that plaintiffs became aware of the sale by defendant of the keychains. I do not consider therefore that the delay in instituting proceedings constitutes acquiescence. Defendant also produced an affidavit of Marc André Filion which states that in April 1983, three keychains similar to those sold by Zellers were bought by him in various stores in the Montreal area, with plastic tabs depicting E.T. and other pictures purportedly taken from the motion picture E.T. The fact that other infringing sales are taking place is not a defence available to defendant nor is there any evidence before the Court in the present proceedings to indicate that steps have not also been taken by plaintiffs against the other vendors of such allegedly infringing merchandise as soon as these sales are ascertained. They may well be so common that it is difficult for plaintiffs to keep up with all such sales. In the case of small infringers it may well not be worth their while to institute proceedings against them. I do not believe however that on the evidence before me it can be said that plaintiffs have tolerated or condoned any such infringement.

13 Defendant contends that on balance of convenience it will suffer considerable loss if it is prevented from disposing of the remaining allegedly infringing merchandise in its hands, of which it has a considerable quantity, and it points out that there is a short life of sales of such products during the period while the motion picture and advertising emanating from it is in the forefront of the public's mind, after which the merchandise becomes difficult if not impossible to sell. This argument applies of course equally to plaintiffs' licensed vendors who also must realize their profits and pass on to plaintiffs their share of them as soon as possible, so any diminution of their sales resulting from counterfeit competing merchandise, sold most likely at a lower price, can also be damaging to them. Defendant argues that plaintiffs' witness even admits the possibility that the sale, even of infringing E.T. dolls and other products creates additional advertising and publicity for E.T. which might result in increased interest in purchasers in seeing the motion picture. Plaintiffs' witness points out, and I am inclined to agree, that it is more likely the other way around, and that it is people who have seen the motion picture who are interested in buying the spin-off products.

14 In any event it is not in my view acceptable for an alleged infringer (and there is a strong *prima facie* case of this in these proceedings) to contend that it should be allowed to continue to do so, as it will suffer financial loss if it is prevented from continuing allegedly infringing sales, or that it may be doing plaintiffs a favour by providing additional advertising for their product. While defendant is well able to pay damages which may be suffered by plaintiffs as the result of

continuing the sales if infringement is found, it is equally true that plaintiffs are well able to pay any damages the defendant may have suffered if it eventually succeeds on the merits but finds that it is unable to dispose of, or can only dispose of at a loss, merchandise remaining in its hands. Moreover plaintiffs are prepared to give an undertaking to this effect. It may be added that the sale of E.T. dolls and keychains represents a negligible part of defendant's business.

15 To summarize I therefore conclude as follows:

> 1. Plaintiffs have a strong *prima facie* case of infringement. While the affidavits identifying the infringing dolls and keychains with the E.T. character created for the motion picture and copyrighted in Canada are not as complete as they might be, there is a sufficient connection to satisfy me that an injunction application should not be refused at this stage of proceedings as a result of any minor defects in the proof. The overall evidence of infringement is fully adequate to make a *prima facie* case at this stage of the proceedings, although it will no doubt be elaborated and remedied by proof at trial on the merits. Defendant however has an arguable case as to whether the doll should have been registered under the *Industrial Design Act*, and on certain other issues.

> 2. On the question of irreparable harm, while the harm suffered by plaintiffs by allowing the sales to continue may not be irreparable in the strictest sense of the word, the consequences are so serious and the principle involved is so important, that, when it is apparent that continuing infringement, if in fact an infringement is taking place, will continue to cause serious damages, an interlocutory injunction should not be refused on this ground alone. As previously stated it is more important to plaintiffs to stop continuing infringement than to collect damages resulting from same.

> 3. The balance of convenience is strongly in favour of plaintiffs.

ORDER

16 An injunction is issued against defendant to remain in effect until final determination of the issue on the merits to restrain defendant from further purchases, other than from authorized licensees of plaintiffs, of E.T. dolls, keychains, or other merchandise related to E.T., and from any further sales of any such merchandise now in its possession and not acquired from said authorized licensees. Defendant shall provide plaintiffs' solicitors with an accounting of the quantity of such unauthorized items in its care, custody or control, but may remain in possession of them on undertaking not to advertise or dispose hereafter of any such items unless authorized to do so by plaintiffs or as a result of final judgment in its favour on the merits. This injunction is issued subject to plaintiffs undertaking to compensate defendant for any damages suffered as a result thereof, in the event of defendant succeeding on the merits.

17 Costs of this motion are in favour of plaintiffs.

6. Anton Pillar Orders

Anton Piller orders have now become established as part of the admin-istration of justice in civil cases. They play a part not unlike that played by search warrants in the area of crime and suspected crime. An Anton Piller order allows a request for entry and that request may be denied, but the denier faces contempt proceedings for failure to give permission that the court has ordered.[7]

In the *Celanese Canada* case,[8] the Supreme Court of Canada set out the following four essential conditions for the making of an *Anton Piller* order in Canada: First, the plaintiff must demonstrate a strong *prima facie* case. Second, the damage to the plaintiff of the defendant's alleged misconduct, potential or actual, must be very serious. Third, there must be convincing evidence that the defendant has in its possession incriminating documents or things; and fourthly, it must be shown that there is a real possibility that the defendant may destroy such material before the discovery process can do its work.

Celanese Canada Inc. v. Murray Demolition Corp., 2006 SCC 36

McLachlin C.J.C., Bastarache, Binnie, LeBel, Deschamps, Fish, Charron JJ.

Heard: December 12, 2005
Judgment: July 27, 2006
Docket: 30652

. . .

***Binnie J.*:**

1 An *Anton Piller* order bears an uncomfortable resemblance to a private search warrant. No notice is given to the party against whom it is issued. Indeed, defen-dants usually first learn of them when they are served and executed, without having had an opportunity to challenge them or the evidence on which they were granted. The defendant may have no idea a claim is even pending. The order is not placed in the hands of a public authority for execution, but authorizes a private party to insist on entrance to the premises of its opponent to conduct a surprise search, the purpose of which is to seize and preserve evidence to further its claim in a private dispute. The only justification for such an extraordinary remedy is that the plaintiff has a strong *prima facie* case and can demonstrate that on the facts, absent such an order, there is a real possibility relevant evi-dence will be destroyed or otherwise made to disappear. The protection of the party against whom an *Anton Piller* order is issued ought to be threefold: a

---

[7] *Celanese Canada Inc. v. Murray Demolition Corp.*, 2006 SCC 36; *Ontario Realty Cor-poration v. P. Gabriele & Sons Ltd.* (2000), 50 O.R. (3d) 539 (S.C.J. [Commercial List]).

[8] *Celanese Canada Inc. v. Murray Demolition Corp.*, 2006 SCC 36.

carefully drawn order which identifies the material to be seized and sets out safeguards to deal, amongst other things, with privileged documents; a vigilant court-appointed supervising solicitor who is independent of the parties; and a sense of responsible self-restraint on the part of those executing the order. In this case, unfortunately, none of these protections proved to be adequate to protect against the disclosure of relevant solicitor-client confidences. Inadequate protections had been written into the order. Those which had been provided were not properly respected. The vigilance of the supervising solicitor appears to have fallen short. Celanese's solicitors in the aftermath of the search seem to have lost sight of the fact that the limited purpose of the order was to *preserve* evidence not to rush to exploit it. In the result, the party searched (Canadian Bearings) now seeks the removal of Celanese's solicitors (Cassels Brock&Blackwell LLP ("Cassels Brock")) and to bar Celanese from making further use of their U.S. counsel (Kasowitz, Benson, Torres&Friedman LLP ("Kasowitz")).

. . .

I. Facts

5 The underlying litigation in this case, which does not directly affect the disposition of this appeal, involves alleged industrial espionage. Celanese operated a plant for the production of vinyl acetate in Edmonton. It decided for business reasons to demolish the facility rather than sell it. Celanese eventually retained the defendant, Murray Demolition, to undertake the demolition. Precautions were put in place to prevent the unauthorised disclosure during demolition of valuable proprietary information evident in the plant's design and processes. Celanese discovered in April 2003 that certain of the defendants, including Canadian Bearings, were engaged in what appeared to be an attempt, under the cover of the demolition, to copy in various ways proprietary processes and equipment. As a consequence, Canadian Bearings and others who had been given access to the site by Murray Demolition, were ordered off the property. Celanese is now suing Canadian Bearings, among others, for allegedly stealing technology discovered during the demolition and making unauthorized use of it in the construction of a vinyl acetate facility in Iran.

6 On June 19, 2003, the motions judge granted Celanese's *ex parte* application for an *Anton Piller* order against Canadian Bearings and others. The issue of how to deal with privileged documents was not considered in the draft order placed before the motions judge and his formal order did not contain such a provision. Nevertheless, all parties recognize that an *Anton Piller* order provides no authority whatsoever for access to a defendant's privileged documents.

7 The order was executed on June 20 and 21, 2003, in the presence of two police officers by an independent accounting firm, BDO Hayes Smith ("BDO") and was overseen by an independent supervising solicitor, Bernard Eastman, Q.C. At the outset, Mr. Eastman spoke at the search site with a senior executive of Canadian Bearings. He gave the executive a copy of the order and related documents, and explained its terms. Mr. Eastman advised the executive that, pursuant to the terms of the order, he would have one hour to seek legal advice.

Shortly thereafter, the solicitors for Canadian Bearings, Borden Ladner Gervais LLP ("BLG"), arrived at the scene. The search was conducted over a period of 18 hours in circumstances that could be described as mildly chaotic. Cassels Brock was not present at the search, but members of the firm were in frequent telephone communication with Mr. Eastman.

8 In the course of the search, privilege was claimed for certain paper documents which were then placed in a sealed folder in the custody of BDO until the merits of the claim could be resolved. The issue of privilege arises at this stage only in connection with the electronic documents seized.

9 When it became apparent that some of the electronic documents might be subject to solicitor-client privilege, the BDO representative enlisted the help of BLG lawyers to facilitate their identification. The process was rushed. Given the volume of electronic materials and the pace at which the search proceeded, BLG lawyers later complained that they were not given time to review the material adequately. Frequently, entire folders would be copied electronically without examination of individual documents. However, material that could be identified as potentially privileged was segregated into an electronic folder which was labelled "Borden Ladner Gervais".

10 In the course of the search, approximately 1,400 electronic documents thought to be relevant, but not as yet effectively screened for potential solicitor-client privilege claims, were downloaded by BDO onto a portable hard drive and "burned" onto CD-ROMs. These were placed in a plastic envelope and sealed. The seal was initialled by a BLG lawyer and by Mr. Eastman. The envelope was given to BDO. Contrary to the express provision in the *Anton Piller* order, no complete list of the seized records was made prior to their removal from the searched premises.

11 On June 23, 2003, lawyers from Cassels Brock and Kasowitz went to BDO to retrieve the seized documents. The Cassels Brock lawyer called the supervising solicitor, Mr. Eastman, to enquire about the sealed envelope containing the hard drive and CD-ROMs. Apparently satisfied there was no agreement that Cassels Brock would have to deal directly with BLG on the issue, he opened the envelope and directed BDO to copy the contents. After some delay, a CD containing copies of various e-mails was copied onto Cassels Brock's computer. A copy of the CD was not sent to BLG. Subsequently, a Cassels Brock lawyer e-mailed colleagues: "On June 24, 2003 representatives of Celanese, counsel from Kasowitz ... and I attended at the offices of BDO ... and reviewed all of the electronic documents seized from all of the defendants".

12 The CD turned out to contain privileged communications. The Cassels Brock lawyer admitted to having reviewed "a few dozen e-mail[s] in full", but said he did not recall reviewing "any e-mail that originated from or were sent to BLG".

13 A copy of the CD was also provided to Kasowitz and was reviewed by Todd Colvard, a Kasowitz lawyer based in Houston. He was directed to classify the electronic documents as "Relevant, Irrelevant, Proprietary, and Hot". Colvard

noticed that some of the e-mails were addressed to or from BLG, and so saved these in a separate fifth electronic folder which he marked "Privileged". He later found additional privileged documents in the folder marked "Relevant", thus evidencing a measure of misclassification. Other than for purposes of segregation, Colvard says he did not review "the substance of those messages".

14 When BLG discovered, on June 24, 2003, that the sealed envelope had been opened, some heated correspondence ensued. Cassels Brock declined to provide BLG with copies of the seized Canadian Bearings electronic documents until late Friday, June 27, 2003, after the motions judge so ordered.

15 On July 11 or 12, 2003, BLG became aware that privileged documents had been transferred to Cassels Brock and Kasowitz. BLG dispatched a letter dated July 14, 2003, enclosing a list of some 82 "privileged documents which were among those documents removed from my clients' computer system *and deleted from my clients' computer system* by those individuals executing the order of [Nordheimer J.] dated June 19, 2003" (emphasis added) and requesting the immediate return of the privileged documents "whether in print form or electronic" and identification of all individuals who may have reviewed them.

16 Eventually, Cassels Brock and Kasowitz, rather than returning the privileged electronic material as requested, advised BLG that the documents had been deleted from their respective systems. The Court of Appeal noted that "it is common ground that 13 lawyers, 3 clerks and 2 law students from Cassels [Brock] and 12 lawyers from Kasowitz would have been able to access the privileged electronic documents in the two to three week period that they remained in the possession of the law firms following the search".

17 Canadian Bearings brought a motion to disqualify Cassels Brock and Kasowitz from continuing to act for Celanese, which was dismissed by the motions judge. Canadian Bearings appealed to the Divisional Court, which allowed the appeal and ordered that Cassels Brock and Kasowitz be removed. Celanese, Cassels Brock and Kasowitz appealed to the Ontario Court of Appeal, which allowed the appeal, finding that neither of the courts below had applied the correct test for removal and remitted the matter back to the motions judge to be reconsidered on the basis of the appeal court's reasons. The appeal thus comes to this Court to determine the proper test and, in particular, which of the parties bears the onus to show (or rebut) the prejudice arising from disclosure of solicitor and client privileged documents.

. . .

III. Analysis

28 *Anton Piller* orders have been available in Canada for close to 30 years. Unlike a search warrant they do not authorize forcible entry, but expose the target to contempt proceedings unless permission to enter is given. To the ordinary citizen faced on his or her doorstep with an *Anton Piller* order this may be seen as a distinction without a meaningful difference.

29 Originally developed as an "exceptional remedy" in the context of trade secrets and intellectual property disputes, such orders are now fairly routinely issued in ordinary civil disputes, *Grenzservice Speditions GmbH v. Jans* (1995), 15 B.C.L.R. (3d) 370 (B.C. S.C.), in employment law, *Ridgewood Electric Ltd. (1990) v. Robbie* (2005), 74 O.R. (3d) 514 (Ont. S.C.J.), and *Netbored Inc. v. Avery Holdings Inc.*, [2005] F.C.J. No. 1723, 2005 FC 1405 (F.C.), and even in matrimonial litigation, *Neumeyer v. Neumeyer* (2005), 47 B.C.L.R. (4th) 162, 2005 BCSC 1259 (B.C. S.C. [In Chambers]). In one egregious case, a designated search team attempted to execute an *Anton Piller* order on the 10-year-old son of the defendant at a time when his parents were not at home: *Ridgewood Electric.*

30 With easier access to such orders, there has emerged a tendency on the part of some counsel to take too lightly the very serious responsibilities imposed by such a draconian order. It should truly be exceptional for a court to authorize the massive intrusion, without advance notice, of a privately orchestrated search on the privacy of a business competitor or other target party. As it was put by Lord Denning, M.R., in the original *Anton Piller* case:

> We are prepared, therefore, to sanction its continuance [i.e. of the order], but only in an extreme case where there is grave danger of property being smuggled away or of vital evidence being destroyed. [Emphasis added.]
>
> (*Anton Piller KG v. Manufacturing Process Ltd.* (1975), [1976] 1 Ch. 55 (Eng. C.A.), at p. 61)

Anton Piller orders, obtained *ex parte*, now regularly permit searches and seizures not only from places of business but from residential premises. While most *Anton Piller* orders are executed properly, they are capable of giving rise to serious abuse, as in *Ridgewood Electric*, mentioned earlier, where Corbett J. of the Ontario Superior Court of Justice protested the unacceptable conduct of those executing the order:

> Nigel Robbie arrived home on April 14, 2004, to find a neighbour barricading his front door. His ten-year-old son had been taken to another neighbour's house, distraught. The neighbourhood was in an uproar. A cadre in suits stood at the front of his house brandishing a thick wad of papers, demanding to be let in.
>
> . . .
>
> While everyone is taken to know the law, the Robbies and their neighbours might be excused for not knowing about *Anton Piller* orders. And so the Robbies and their neighbours were left to wonder what kind of country we live in, where one's former employer, acting secretly, may obtain a court order and then enter and search one's private residence. [paras. 1 and 4]

As Sharpe J.A., writing in a scholarly mode, has pointed out, "excessive zeal in this area is apt to attract criticism which will impair the ability of the courts to use injunctions in innovative ways in other areas" (R. J. Sharpe, *Injunctions and Specific Performance* (looseleaf ed.), at para. 2:1300).

31 The search in the present case was conducted by reputable and responsible people, under the supervision of a senior member of the Ontario bar. The

disclosure of solicitor-client confidences came about not by egregious mis-conduct, but through a combination of carelessness, overzealousness, a lack of appreciation of the potential dangers of an *Anton Piller* order and a failure to focus on its limited purpose, namely the *preservation* of relevant evidence.

32 Experience has shown that despite their draconian nature, there is a proper role for *Anton Piller* orders to ensure that unscrupulous defendants are not able to cir-cumvent the court's processes by, on being forewarned, making relevant evidence disappear. Their usefulness is especially important in the modern era of heavy dependence on computer technology, where documents are easily deleted, moved or destroyed. The utility of this equitable tool in the correct circumstances should not be diminished. However, such orders should only be granted in the clear rec-ognition of their exceptional and highly intrusive character and, where granted, the terms should be carefully spelled out and limited to what the circumstances show to be necessary. Those responsible for their implementation should conform to a very high standard of professional diligence. Otherwise, the moving party, not its target, may have to shoulder the consequences of a botched search.

33 Much of the argument before us about privileged documents turned on a supposed "spectrum" of situations. At one end of the spectrum, it was said, lie the "inadvertent disclosure" cases, where one party's counsel receives a privi-leged document due to an error of opposing counsel, for example a letter is faxed or e-mailed to the wrong party. In such cases, the remedy is often limited to an order requiring the document, which is clearly identified, to be deleted or returned and a direction that no use is to be made of it. At the other end of the spectrum is said to be the "moving solicitor" or "merging firm" cases, where counsel who has acted for a client ends up at a law firm that is acting for an opposing party — as in *MacDonald Estate* itself. In the latter cases, the precise confidences seen or heard by the moving solicitor may not be readily deter-mined. Unless adequate measures have been taken (usually in advance) to avoid "tainting" the new firm, the remedy is frequently disqualification. I agree with the intervener Advocates' Society that the emphasis on "inadvertence" is overly simplistic. As the Society submits:

> The notion of "inadvertence" is also analytically unhelpful because it conflates two questions that should be distinct: (a) how did the documents come into the possession of [Celanese] or its counsel; and (b) what did [Celanese] and its coun-sel do upon recognition that the documents were potentially subject to solicitor-client privilege?

34 Whether through advertence or inadvertence the problem is that solicitor-cli-ent information has wound up in the wrong hands. Even granting that solicitor-client privilege is an umbrella that covers confidences of differing centrality and importance, such possession by the opposing party affects the integrity of the administration of justice. Parties should be free to litigate their disputes without fear that their opponent has obtained an unfair insight into secrets disclosed in confidence to their legal advisors. The defendant's witnesses ought not to have to worry in the course of being cross-examined that the cross-examiner's ques-tions are prompted by information that had earlier been passed in confidence to

the defendant's solicitors. Such a possibility destroys the level playing field and creates a serious risk to the integrity of the administration of justice. To prevent such a danger from arising, the courts must act "swiftly and decisively" as the Divisional Court emphasized. Remedial action in cases such as this is intended to be curative not punitive.

A. Requirements for an Anton Piller Order

35 There are four essential conditions for the making of an *Anton Piller* order. First, the plaintiff must demonstrate a strong *prima facie* case. Second, the damage to the plaintiff of the defendant's alleged misconduct, potential or actual, must be very serious. Third, there must be convincing evidence that the defendant has in its possession incriminating documents or things, and fourthly it must be shown that there is a real possibility that the defendant may destroy such material before the discovery process can do its work: *Nintendo of America Inc. v. Coinex Video Games Inc.* (1982), [1983] 2 F.C. 189 (Fed. C.A.), at pp. 197-99; *Indian Manufacturing Ltd. v. Lo* (1997), 75 C.P.R. (3d) 338 (Fed. C.A.), at pp. 341-42; *Netsmart Inc. v. Poelzer* (2002), [2003] 1 W.W.R. 698, 2002 ABQB 800 (Alta. Q.B.), at para. 16; *Anton Piller KG*, at pp. 58-61; *Ridgewood Electric*, at para. 27; *Grenzservice*, at para. 39; *Pulse Microsystems Ltd. v. SafeSoft Systems Inc.* (1996), 67 C.P.R. (3d) 202 (Man. C.A.), at p. 208; *Ontario Realty Corp. v. P. Gabriele & Sons Ltd.* (2000), 50 O.R. (3d) 539 (Ont. S.C.J. [Commercial List]), at para. 9; *Proctor & Gamble Inc. v. John Doe*, [2000] F.C.J. No. 61 (Fed. T.D.), at para. 45; *Netbored Inc.*, at para. 39; *Adobe Systems Inc. v. KLJ Computer Solutions Inc.*, [1999] 3 F.C. 621 (Fed. T.D.), at para. 35.

36 Both the strength and the weakness of an *Anton Piller* order is that it is made *ex parte* and interlocutory: there is thus no cross-examination on the supporting affidavits. The motions judge necessarily reposes faith in the candour and complete disclosure of the affiants, and as much or more so on the professional responsibility of the lawyers participating in carrying out its terms. We are advised that such orders are not available in the United States (Transcript, at p. 70).

37 A troubling example in Canada is the *Adobe Systems* case, where a computer software company was tipped off that a small advertising firm in Halifax was using unlicensed versions of some of its software. The affiant swore that, in his opinion, the firm was likely to destroy its unlicensed copies of the software if it became aware of the pending litigation against it. The target firm was well established and its principals had an excellent reputation in the community. On subsequent cross-examination it was revealed that the source of the informant's opinion that the defendant was likely to destroy unlicensed copies was his "observation of human nature" and not any observation of that particular defendant. Upon a review of the order, Richard A.C.J. (now C.J. of the Federal Court of Appeal) found that the plaintiffs had not made sufficient inquiries of the facts before obtaining the order. Citing *Adobe Systems*, the Federal Court recently reiterated that "[i]n all proceedings taken *ex parte*, particularly in *Anton Piller* situations, there is a heavy obligation upon the moving party to make full and frank disclosure of all relevant facts to the Court" (*Netbored Inc.*, at para. 41).

38 At this stage, the challenge to the decision of Norheimer J. to grant the *Anton Piller* order is not before the Court.

B.   *Terms of the Anton Piller Order*

39 In *Grenzservice*, a case which dealt with an application to remove counsel who had seen privileged documents in the course of an *Anton Piller* execution, Huddart J. (later J.A.) observed: "This case suggests that safeguards cannot remain implicit in the supervision order. They must be specified" (para. 84). I agree. In *R. v. Lavallee, Rackel & Heintz*, [2002] 3 S.C.R. 209, 2002 SCC 61 (S.C.C.), Arbour J. for the majority set out at para. 49 a number of relevant concerns in the criminal law context, which may have some application by analogy. Notwithstanding the general recognition of the need for standard terms, many safeguards which one would expect to have become customary (such as a provision dealing with claims of privilege) are frequently omitted. Corbett J. commented in *Ridgewood Electric* that the *Anton Piller* order "has been with us for nearly 30 years, yet its 'standard terms' vary considerably across the province" (para. 3). In the United Kingdom, a set of standardized rules and a model order have been developed. In Australia, Order 25B of the *Federal Court Rules* and Practice Note No. 24 set out a number of standard safeguards for *Anton Piller* orders (5 May 2006). See also *Thermax v. Schott Industrial Glass*, [1981] F.S.R. 289 (Eng. Ch. Div.).

40 *Anton Piller* orders are often conceived of, obtained and implemented in circumstances of urgency. They are generally time-limited (e.g., 10 days in Ontario under Rule 40.02 (*Rules of Civil Procedure*, R.R.O. 1990, Reg. 194) and 14 days in the Federal Court, under Rule 374(1) (*Federal Court Rules, 1998*, SOR/98-106)). Despite the urgency, the more detailed and standardized the terms of the order the less opportunity there will be for misunderstandings or mischief. As noted by Lamer J. in *Descôteaux c. Mierzwinski*, [1982] 1 S.C.R. 860 (S.C.C.), at p. 889:

> Searches are an exception to the oldest and most fundamental principles of the common law, and as such the power to search should be strictly controlled.

Unless and until model orders are developed by legislation or recommended by law societies pursuant to their responsibility for professional conduct, the following guidelines for preparation and execution of an *Anton Piller* order may be helpful, depending on the circumstances:

(1)   Basic Protection for the Rights of the Parties

> (i) The order should appoint a supervising solicitor who is independent of the plaintiff or its solicitors and is to be present at the search to ensure its integrity. The key role of the independent supervising solicitor was noted by the motions judge in this case "to ensure that the execution of the Anton Piller order and everything that flowed from it, was undertaken as carefully as possible and with due consideration for the rights and interests of all involved". He or she is "an officer of the court charged with a very important responsibility regarding this extraordinary remedy". See also *Grenzservice*, at para. 85.

(ii) Absent unusual circumstances the plaintiff should be required to provide an undertaking and/or security to pay damages in the event that the order turns out to be unwarranted or wrongfully executed. See *Ontario Realty Corp.*, at para. 40; *Adobe Systems*, at para. 43; *Nintendo of America*, at pp. 201-02; *Grenzservice*, at para. 85; *Havana House Cigar & Tobacco Merchants Ltd. v. Jane Doe* (2000), 199 F.T.R. 12 (Fed. T.D.), aff'd (2002), 288 N.R. 198, 2002 FCA 75 (Fed. C.A.).

(iii) The scope of the order should be no wider than necessary and no material shall be removed from the site unless clearly covered by the terms of the order. See *Columbia Picture Industries Inc. v. Robinson* (1985), [1987] Ch. 38 (Eng. Ch. Div.).

(iv) A term setting out the procedure for dealing with solicitor-client privilege or other confidential material should be included with a view to enabling defendants to advance claims of confidentiality over documents before they come into the possession of the plaintiff or its counsel, or to deal with disputes that arise. See *Grenzservice*, at para. 85; *Ontario Realty Corp.*, at para. 40. Procedures developed for use in connection with search warrants under the *Criminal Code*, R.S.C. 1985, c. C-46, may provide helpful guidance. The UK practice direction on this point provides as follows:

> Before permitting entry to the premises by any person other than the Supervising Solicitor, the Respondent may, for a short time (not to exceed two hours, unless the Supervising Solicitor agrees to a longer period)–(a) gather together any documents he [or she] believes may be ... privileged; and (b) hand them to the Supervising Solicitor for [an assessment of] whether they are ... privileged as claimed.

> If the Supervising Solicitor decides that ... any of the documents [may be] privileged or [is in any doubt as to their status, he or she] will exclude them from the search ... and retain [them] pending further order of the court [(if in doubt as to whether they are privileged), or return them to the respondent and retain a list of the documents (if the documents are privileged)].

> [A] Respondent [wishing] to take legal advice and gather documents as permitted ... must first inform the Supervising Solicitor and keep him [or her] informed of the steps being taken.

> Experience has shown that in general this is a workable procedure. Counsel supporting the appellants suggested the basic "two-hour" collection period permitted in the U.K. is too short. This is a matter to be determined by the judge making the order, but it must be kept in mind that unnecessary delay may open the door to mischief. In general, the search should proceed as expeditiously as circumstances permit.

(v) The order should contain a limited use clause (i.e., items seized may only be used for the purposes of the pending litigation). See *Ontario Realty Corp.*, at para. 40; *Adobe Systems*, at para. 43; *Grenzservice*, at para. 85.

(vi) The order should state explicitly that the defendant is entitled to return to court on short notice to (a) discharge the order; or (b) vary the amount of security. See *Adobe Systems*, at para. 43; *Grenzservice*, at para. 85; *Nintendo of America*, at pp. 201-02.

(vii) The order should provide that the materials seized be returned to the defendants or their counsel as soon as practicable.

(2) The Conduct of the Search

(i) In general the order should provide that the search should be commenced during normal business hours when counsel for the party about to be searched is more likely to be available for consultation. See *Grenzservice*, at para. 85; *Universal Thermosensors Ltd. v. Hibben*, [1992] 1 W.L.R. 840 (Ch. D.).

(ii) The premises should not be searched or items removed except in the presence of the defendant or a person who appears to be a responsible employee of the defendant.

(iii) The persons who may conduct the search and seize evidence should be specified in the order or should specifically be limited in number. See *Adobe Systems*, at para. 43; *Grenzservice*, at para. 85; *Nintendo of America*, at pp. 201-02.

(iv) On attending at the site of the authorised search, plaintiff's counsel (or the supervising solicitor), acting as officers of the court should serve a copy of the statement of claim and the order and supporting affidavits and explain to the defendant or responsible corporate officer or employee in plain language the nature and effect of the order. See *Ontario Realty Corp.*, at para. 40.

(v) The defendant or its representatives should be given a reasonable time to consult with counsel prior to permitting entry to the premises. See *Ontario Realty Corp*, at para. 40; *Adobe Systems*, at para. 43; *Grenzservice*, at para. 85; *Sulphur Experts Inc. v. O'Connell* (2000), 279 A.R. 246, 2000 ABQB 875 (Alta. Q.B.).

(vi) A detailed list of all evidence seized should be made and the supervising solicitor should provide this list to the defendant for inspection and verification at the end of the search and before materials are removed from the site. See *Adobe Systems*, at para. 43; *Grenzservice*, at para. 85; *Ridgewood Electric*, at para. 25.

(vii) Where this is not practicable, documents seized should be placed in the custody of the independent supervising solicitor, and defendant's counsel should be given a reasonable opportunity to review them to advance solicitor-client privilege claims prior to release of the documents to the plaintiff.

(viii) Where ownership of material is disputed, it should be provided for safekeeping to the supervising solicitor or to the defendant's solicitors.

(3) Procedure Following the Search

(i) The order should make it clear that the responsibilities of the supervising solicitor continue beyond the search itself to deal with matters arising out of the search, subject of course to any party wishing to take a matter back to the court for resolution.

(ii) The supervising solicitor should be required to file a report with the court within a set time limit describing the execution, who was present and what was seized. See *Grenzservice*, at para. 85.

(iii) The court may wish to require the plaintiff to file and serve a motion for review of the execution of the search returnable within a set time limit such as 14 days to ensure that the court automatically reviews the supervising solicitor's report and the implementation of its order even if the defendant does not request such a review. See *Grenszervice*, at para. 85.

See also *Civil Procedure Act 1997* (U.K.), c. 12, s. 7; *Civil Procedure Rules 1998* (U.K.), SI 1998/3132 r. 25.1(1)(h); *CPR Part 25 — Practice Direction — Interim Injunctions* (U.K.); Sharpe, at para. 2:1100 and following.

41 It is evident that the draft order placed before the motions judge in this case was deficient in many respects. At issue here is the absence of any provision to deal with solicitor-client confidences. The absence of specific terms in the *Anton Piller* order does not relieve the searching solicitors from the consequences of gaining inappropriate access. Such consequences may include removal. A precisely drawn and clearly thought out order therefore will not only protect the defendant's right to solicitor-client privilege, but also protect the plaintiff's right to continue to be represented by counsel of choice by helping to ensure that such counsel do not stumble into possession of privileged information.

. . .

55 In summary, I agree with the Divisional Court that lawyers who undertake a search under the authority of an *Anton Piller* order and thereby take possession of relevant confidential information attributable to a solicitor-client relationship, bear the onus of showing there is no real risk such confidences will be used to the prejudice of the defendant. Difficulties of proof compounded by errors in the conduct of the search and its aftermath should fall on the heads of those responsible for the search, not of the party being searched. The onus was not met by the respondents in this case.

. . .

66 In view of all the circumstances, I agree with the Divisional Court that Cassels Brock and Kasowitz have not produced sufficient evidence to satisfy the *MacDonald Estate* test, namely "that the public represented by the reasonably informed person would be satisfied that no use of confidential information would occur" (p. 1260).

67 I also agree with the Divisional Court that the right of Celanese to choose counsel yields to what occurred in the execution of the *Anton Piller* order in this case and its aftermath, and that "[t]he reasonable perception of the integrity of the administration of justice would be adversely affected were Cassels Brock ... permitted to remain solicitors of record for [Celanese]". As to future role of Kasowitz however, I think the Divisional Court went too far in holding that "[Celanese] should be precluded in this litigation *or any related proceeding* from receiving advice or information directly and/or indirectly from the firm" (emphasis added). Celanese has worldwide interests and Kasowitz is its primary legal advisor. As the vinyl acetate plant is to be built in Iran, there may well be related litigation outside Canada. I think Canadian Bearings will be sufficiently protected if Celanese is ordered not to seek or receive advice or information directly or indirectly from Kasowitz in connection with any litigation *in Canada* arising out of the matters referred to in the amended statement of claim, or related thereto, provided Kasowitz files affidavit(s) satisfactory to the case management judge confirming that the firewalls it had undertaken to install were and are in place, and sworn confirmation that all of the material for which privilege

is claimed that came into Kasowitz's possession as a result of the *Anton Piller* order has been returned or destroyed.

Vinod Chopra Films Private Ltd. v. John Doe, 2010 FC 387 (F.C.)

[1] This is a review of a "rolling" type Anton Piller Order granted by the Court in these proceedings, *ex parte*, on January 26, 2010, which has been sought by several but not all of the parties that have been named as Defendants. This Order therefore will pertain only to those named Defendants who have sought this review, all others remain unaffected.

[2] For the reasons that follow I am setting aside the Anton Piller Order as it affects the Defendants who have sought this review, grant them their costs reasonably incurred on a full indemnity basis, and will Order that the action as against those Defendants be dismissed on terms.

THE DEFENDANTS WHO HAVE SOUGHT THIS REVIEW:

[3] Some, but not all of the persons and corporations that have so far been specifically identified as Defendants have sought this review. This Order shall only pertain to the Defendants seeking this review whom I will call Affected Defendants. They are:

- 1557768 Ontario Inc. o/a Golumbia Video
- Arangesan Paramsothy
- 1691731 Ontario Inc. o/a Bollywood 4 U
- Abulsama Jibhai
- 2148409 Ontario Inc. o/a Video Station
- Kulwant Kaur Singh
- 215151872 Ontario Inc. o/a Singh Video Station
- Mohan Singh
- 2031221 Ontario Inc. o/a Old Karachi Bazar
- Royal Paan Inc.
- Neerad Upadhyay
- Anmol Records Inc.
- Rajesh Syal
- 2122308 Ontario Inc. o/a Albion Audio & Video
- Kulbir Singh Mokha

[4] It must be noted that Tayyabi Huma appeared in person before me and filed an affidavit with this Court to the effect that she had nothing to do with Old Karachi Bazar and that her involvement was simply coincidental as she happened to be in the store when the Anton Piller enforcers arrived. She acted as an interpreter. After some discussion between Ms. Huma, the Court and counsel for the Plaintiffs it was agreed that Ms. Huma would no longer be troubled with anything to do with these proceedings. She has been inconvenienced by

the Plaintiffs who involved her in the proceedings and is entitled to reasonable out-of-pocket disbursements. I estimate they would be $250.00.

ANTON PILLER ORDERS

[5] An Anton Piller Order is a form of civil search warrant enabling representatives of a plaintiff to request entrance into premises occupied by persons named or to become named as defendants to search for and seize relevant documents and things pertinent to the proceedings subject to any further Order of the Court.

[6] The leading case is the recent decision of the Supreme Court of Canada in *Celanese Canada Inc. v. Murray Demolition Corp.*, 2006 SCC 36 (CanLII), 2006 SCC 36, [2006] 2 S.C.R. 189, in which Binnie J. delivered the unanimous decision for the Court. Binnie J. wrote at paragraphs 1, and 28 to 32:

> *1 BINNIE J.: — An Anton Piller order bears an uncomfortable resemblance to a private search warrant. No notice is given to the party against whom it is issued. Indeed, defendants usually first learn of them when they are served and executed, without having had an opportunity to challenge them or the evidence on which they were granted. The defendant may have no idea a claim is even pending. The order is not placed in the hands of a public authority for execution, but authorizes a private party to insist on entrance to the premises of its opponent to conduct a surprise search, the purpose of which is to seize and preserve evidence to further its claim in a private dispute. The only justification for such an extraordinary remedy is that the plaintiff has a strong prima facie case and can demonstrate that on the facts, absent such an order, there is a real possibility relevant evidence will be destroyed or otherwise made to disappear. The protection of the party against whom an Anton Piller order is issued ought to be threefold: a carefully drawn order which identifies the material to be seized and sets out safeguards to deal, amongst other things, with privileged documents; a vigilant court-appointed supervising solicitor who is independent of the parties; and a sense of responsible self-restraint on the part of those executing the order.*

> . . .

> *28 Anton Piller orders have been available in Canada for close to 30 years. Unlike a search warrant they do not authorize forcible entry, but expose the target to contempt proceedings unless permission to enter is given. To the ordinary citizen faced on his or her doorstep with an Anton Piller order this may be seen as a distinction without a meaningful difference.*

> *29 Originally developed as an "exceptional remedy" in the context of trade secrets and intellectual property disputes, such orders are now fairly routinely issued in ordinary civil disputes...*

[7] The Anton Piller Order originated from a decision of the English Court of Appeal in a case of that name *Anton Piller KG v. Manufacturing Process Ltd.*, [1976] Ch. 55, in which the Plaintiff, a manufacturer of sophisticated electric motors used in computers, had evidence from two former employees of the Defendant that the Defendant was stealing the Plaintiff's trade secrets and would be likely to destroy evidence to that effect if it had notice. The Court gave an Order permitting the Plaintiff to request that the Defendant allow an inspection

of its premises for the purpose of finding and securing such evidence. Refusal by the Defendant to allow such entry and inspection would be a contempt of court. The extraordinary nature of this Order was specifically addressed by Lord Denning M.R. at page 61 where he wrote:

> *This is not covered by the Rules of the Supreme Court and must be based on the inherent jurisdiction of the court. There are one or two old precedents which give some colour for it, Hennessy v. Rohmann, Osborne & Co. [1877] W.N. 14, and Morris v. Howell (1888) 22 L.R. Ir. 77, an Irish case. But they do not go very far. So it falls to us to consider it on principle. It seems to me that such an order can be made by a judge ex parte, but it should only be made where it is essential that the plaintiff should have inspection so that justice can be done between the parties: and when, if the defendant were forewarned, there is a grave danger that vital evidence will be destroyed, that papers will be burnt or lost or hidden, or taken beyond the jurisdiction, and so the ends of justice be defeated: and when the inspection would do no real harm to the defendant or his case.*
>
> *Nevertheless, in the enforcement of this order, the plaintiffs must act with due circumspection. On the service of it, the plaintiffs should be attended by their solicitor, who is an officer of the court. They should give the defendants an opportunity of considering it and of consulting with their own solicitor. If the defendants wish to apply to discharge the order as having been improperly obtained, they must be allowed to do so. If the defendants refuse permission to enter or to inspect, the plaintiffs must not force their way in. They must accept the refusal, and bring it to the notice of the court afterwards, if need be on an application to commit.*

[8] Thus an Anton Piller Order began as an extraordinary remedy, to be used only when it was *"essential"* and there was *"grave danger"* that the evidence might be destroyed such that the *"ends of justice be defeated"* and, from the defendant's point of view, no real harm would be done. The jurisprudence inCanada has culminated in the *Celanese*case, *supra*, where the Supreme Court of Canada has called the Order an *"extraordinary remedy"* to be used only when there is a *"real possibility that relevant evidence will be destroyed or otherwise made to disappear"*.

[9] There have been many cases in Canada dealing with Anton Piller Orders however it is appropriate to consider that the principal jurisprudence has now been established by the Supreme Court of Canada in *Celanese supra*. The requirements for obtaining such an Order were set out by Binnie J. at paragraph 35 of that decision:

> *35 There are four essential conditions for the making of an* Anton Piller*order. First, the plaintiff must demonstrate a strong* prima facie *case. Second, the damage to the plaintiff of the defendant's alleged misconduct, potential or actual, must be very serious. Third, there must be convincing evidence that the defendant has in its possession incriminating documents or things, and fourthly it must be shown that there is a real possibility that the defendant may destroy such material before the discovery process can do its work...*

I will return to these requirements later in these reasons.

WHAT IS A "ROLLING"ANTON PILLER ORDER?

[10] The Order under review here is what has become known as a "rolling" Anton Piller Order, Such an Order was discussed by Pelletier J. (as he then was) in *Club Monaco Inc. v. Woody World Discounts* (1994), 2 C.P.R. (4ᵗʰ) 4-36, [1999] F.C.J. No. 1645 at paragraph 6:

> 6 *The comments which follow are limited to the question of "rolling" Anton Piller orders in which the defendants are not known and which are issued against John Doe and Jane Doe. They are also limited to the case of itinerant sales or flea markets and do not deal with the particular problems which arise in the case of travelling celebrity attractions, to which other considerations may apply. These "rolling" orders are potentially binding upon all who carry on trade in certain types of consumer goods. It is therefore incumbent upon the Court to be satisfied that the potential interference with individual rights is justified by the evidence put before it as to the scope of the infringement of the plaintiff's rights.*

[11] There have been a few instances where such "rolling" Orders have also been directed toward permanent shops as well (e.g. *Viacom Ha! Holding Co. v. Doe* 2000 CanLII 15260 (FC), (2000), 6 C.P.R. (4ᵗʰ) 36 per Tremblay-Lamer J. at para 67).

[12] Professor Jeff Berryman of Windsor Law School (formerly the dean) has written extensively on the subject of Anton Piller Orders, particularly in the Canadian context. In his paper entitled *"Recent Developments in Anton Piller Orders"*appearing in the Oxford Intellectual Property Research Centre Working Paper series No. 4, Nov. 2001 he discussed the development of "rolling" Orders in Canada, particularly in the Federal Court (the "Oxford" paper). The following are excerpts from that paper. Prof. Berryman begins at page 2:

> *Rolling Anton Piller Orders*
>
> *It is difficult to discern a definite point in time when the rolling Anton Piller order was created in Canada although it is uniquely a creation of the Federal Court. Canada's Federal Court is a statutory court created pursuant to the constitutional powers accorded the Federal government to establish courts for the 'better administration of the laws of Canada'. Under the constitutional division of powers the Federal government has the exclusive responsibility to create and regulate copyright and patents, and pursuant to the trade and commerce power, to make provision for trademarks. While the jurisdiction of the Federal Court, and the reasons for maintaining it as a separate court, have often been challenged throughout its 126 year history, most critics have accepted the desire to have a specialist tribunal deal with, among other things, intellectual property as a valid reason for the court's continued existence. Pursuant to this specialized nature the Federal Court, during the eighties, built up a significant Anton Piller jurisdiction the majority of which involve breaches of copyright and trademark.*

[13] I move to the end of that paper where, at page 13 Prof. Berryman wrote:

> *Evaluation of the Federal Court's Position on Rolling Anton Piller Orders*
>
> *'New millennium', 'post-industrial', 'globalization', and the 'knowledge economy' are all terms often placed within close proximity to one another. Taken together*

they mark a paradigm shift in the underlying economic basis of western democracies. Information, knowledge, brand names and consumers associative memories that go with this material to generate goodwill, as well as the manipulation of the same, increasingly forms the main assets of modern enterprises. This new form of property is distinguished by one major characteristic, that it is capable of multiple use without a corresponding deprivation of use by the lawful owner. Thus, the primary wealth in the property is its 'use' value that can only be protected by remedies aimed at exclusion of others. The common law's presumptive remedy, damages, is substitutionary in effect, measuring and trading the plaintiff's loss for a damages equivalent. Equity's presumptive remedy, the injunction, is exclusionary in effect. Thus, as the knowledge economy takes hold, we can only expect an increasing reliance upon exclusionary remedies. The Federal Court's rolling order is a natural growth of this trend but it also portends other changes.

At page 14 he points out that the Federal Court is, in effect, filling in gaps in legislation:

By virtue of its statutory jurisdiction Canada's Federal Court has received the vast majority of Anton Piller suits. The court's cautious development has occurred at a time when the Federal government has spent considerable time in legislating changes to Canada's intellectual property statutes including the remedial provisions. Thus, the legislature has had the opportunity to address concerns with the direction that the court has been taking.

Certainly, one would expect and hope that government's legal advisors were aware of legislative initiatives in the United Kingdom during this period. On the other hand, the fact that the legislature did not make specific provision for a self-help right of seizure, as the United Kingdom had done with copyright in 1988, may cause pause for a court and whether it should 'gap fill' legislation. In this sense the Federal Court has been caught in a quandary over a lacuna in Canadian law.

The "Rolling Order" has never been fully litigated, a problem that concerned Professor Berryman as he wrote at page 15:

A common feature in most jurisdictions that have developed the Anton Piller order, but perhaps more so in Canada's Federal Court, have been the relative paucity of either 'strong' or willing defendants to mount concerted actions against the order. The conditions in which adjudication takes place are thus less than ideal. In Canada the number of plaintiffs, and their counsel engaged in arguing before the Federal Court, have been small in number. From a plaintiff's point of view, significant advances have been made, but have these been matched by sufficiently vigorous arguments for defendants?

. . .

Rolling Anton Piller orders and the exclusionary remedy they provide are both a work in progress and a principle derived from adjudication. The remedy is responsive to plaintiffs needs; it remains to be seen whether it proves to be an inconvenience along the way to a better developed set of coherent decision making principles. I do not believe the Federal Court should be faulted for trying. The conditions for adjudication are not ideal; nevertheless, the court does make participation in its processes by defendants and other voices representative of an extra-legal community an important focus.

[14] The situation remains today largely as expressed in 2001 by Prof. Berryman. There has not been a case, until the present, where sufficiently rigorous arguments have been raised by a defendant. The "rolling" Order as it has been developing is a remedy responsive to a plaintiff's needs but has a proper balance with respect to a defendant's concerns and the concerns of the public at large been considered? Has due regard been given to The Canadian Charter of Rights and Freedoms, section 8:

> 8. *Everyone has the right to be secure against unreasonable search or seizure.*

THE PLAINTIFFS AND RIGHTS ASSERTED

[15] It is not contested for the purposes of this review that the Plaintiff Vinod Chopra Films Private Limited is an Indian Company and owner of copyright in Canada in a motion picture film entitled "3 Idiots". A certificate of the registration of that copyright with the Canadian Copyright Office is in the record as registration number 1073886 registered January 13, 2010 which names Vinod Chopra Films Pvt. Limited as owner. (I do not consider that the abbreviation of Private to Pvt. is material at this stage). Under the provisions of the Copyright Act, R.S.C.1985, c. C-42, section 53(2) that certificate is evidence that copyright subsists in the work and that the person so registered is the owner. One of the Defendants'Counsel, Mr. Padda, raised an objection to the effect that the registration of copyright was secured after some of the allegedly infringing events occurred. It must be remembered that copyright subsists without registration, a registration is evidence as to the subsistence of copyright but is not necessary to create the right. Here we have that evidence by way of the registration. That evidence is not contested.

[16] The other Plaintiff, Reliance Mediaworks (USA) Inc. purports to be a licensee under that copyright with rights to exploit the work in Canada in motion picture theatres as well as by CD's, DVD's and the like. Counsel for some of the defendants, Mr. Schneiderman, invited me to find that this plaintiff had not sufficiently demonstrated his rights as licensee on the evidence provided to the Judge who granted the original *ex parte* Order, Justice Zinn. I have reviewed that evidence, which comprises the affidavit of Sumit Chadha sworn January 18, 2010 and in particular paragraphs 16 to 22. I am satisfied that this Plaintiff has sufficient status to claim as a licensee for the purpose of the Anton Piller Order. The full nature and extent of the license, if contested, may become more material as the action progresses into trial, if at all.

[17] For purposes of the Anton Piller Order I am satisfied that a strong *prima facie*case has been made and that copyright subsists in Canada in the motion picture filed entitled "3 Idiots", that the plaintiff Vinod Chopra Films Private Limited is the owner of that copyright and that the Plaintiff Reliance Mediaworks (USA) Inc. is a licensee in Canada in respect of that copyright. It has not been contested on the motion before me that such copies of "3 Idiots"has have been seized in execution of the Order are unauthorized copies.

REVIEW OF AN ANTON PILLER ORDER

[18] This is a review of an Anton Piller Order granted, *ex parte*, January 26, 2010. This is the first time that a defendant has an opportunity to challenge that Order. The law is clear that such a review is conducted *de novo* and that evidence in addition to that considered by the Judge granting the original Order may be taken into consideration. (*Adobe Systems Inc. v. KLJ Computer Solutions Inc.*, 1999 CanLII 7905 (FC), [1999] 3 F.C. 621 (T.D.); *Bell Express Vu v. Rodgers*(2007), 57 C.P.C. (6ᵗʰ) 312 (Ont. SC) at para 11).

[19] The original Order was granted *ex parte*. As Binnie J. wrote in *Celanese supra*at paragraph 36 there is a heavy onus on counsel and the parties seeking that Order to be candid and complete:

> 36. Both the strength and the weakness of an Anton Piller order is that it is made ex parte and interlocutory: there is thus no cross-examination on the supporting affidavits. The motions judge necessarily reposes faith in the candour and complete disclosure of the affiants, and as much or more so on the professional responsibility of the lawyers participating in carrying out its terms.

[20] There is a duty on a party, especially in *ex parte* proceedings, to make out its case. It should not take a position where it will put in enough evidence to persuade a Court to issue the Order, then "cooper up" any deficiencies later, if challenged. I am particularly concerned with two situations, one is directed to proof of a plaintiff's rights, something that is known to the plaintiff before the proceedings have been instituted and should be fully established in evidence before the Court in seeking the *ex parte* Order. The second is more insidious. An Anton Piller Order is to be granted only where there is grave danger that relevant material may be destroyed. For a plaintiff simply to allege that a defendant may destroy relevant material, obtain an Order, secure some material by a surprise search, then return to the Court with the material in hand should not mean that the fact that such material has been obtained can now be used as proof of the likelihood that it would have been destroyed. Such later acquired material may be evidence of the existence of such material, but not evidence that it would likely have been destroyed. Evidence as to the general conduct of a Defendant whose premises are being searched should be used with extreme caution when attempting to use such "post Order" evidence to support the "pre Order" assertion that the materials sought would likely be destroyed. There must be sufficient proof at the beginning of the process to support an allegation of likely destruction, not a simple allegation to be supported later by conduct of a party during execution of the Order or materials seized.

[21] Since an Anton Piller Order is an extraordinary remedy. I have no hesitation in drawing an analogy to a situation such as that considered in the context of criminal law. In Sopinka et al *"The Law of Evidence in Canada"*, 3ʳᵈ ed, Lexis Nexis, the authors wrote at paragraph 6.437:

> 6.347 It is therefore incumbent on the trial judge to carefully instruct the jury to ensure that such evidence is not misused. The jury should be told that after-the-fact conduct relied on by the Crown has only an indirect bearing upon the

issue of guilt and that the jury should exercise caution in inferring guilt because the conduct might be explained in an alternative manner. The jury should also be instructed that they must not use this conduct to support an inference of guilt unless they rejected any innocent explanation for the conduct.

[22] In short, post Order conduct of a defendant may be introduced but used with extreme caution if it is to be used in support of an allegation made at the *ex parte*hearing that the defendant would have been likely to destroy relevant material.

[23] A review of the *ex parte* Anton Piller Order is to be conducted so as to determine if the four criteria for obtaining such an Order as set out by the Supreme Court of Canada in *Celanese supra* at paragraph 35 have been met, to repeat:

- Has the plaintiff demonstrated a strong *prima facie* case
- Is the damage to the plaintiff potential or actual very serious
- Is there convincing evidence that the defendant has in its possessions incriminating documents or things
- Is there a real possibility that the defendant may destroy such material before the discovery process can do its work

[24] I add that there are further criteria discussed in *Anton Piller supra* and in cases such as *Netbored Inc. v. Avery Holdings Inc.*, 2005 FC 1405 (CanLII), 2005 FC 1405 at paragraphs 63 to 66, namely:

- Would the inspection do no harm to the defendant or its case
- Would the interests of justice be brought into disrepute

[25] As this case deals with a "rolling" Anton Piller Order the review must also consider criteria such as set out by Pelletier J. at paragraph 7 of *Club Monaco supra*:

As a result, it is my view that in future applications for a rolling Anton Piller order the evidence submitted in support of the application should reflect the following:

1) The affidavits should contain the personal knowledge of the affiant as to the nature and extent of the problem as it relates to the Plaintiff. It is, after all, the plaintiff's valuable property which it is sought to protect. If the officers of the plaintiff are not in a position to testify from their own personal knowledge as to the nature and extent of the problem, doubts are raised as to the need for the remedy. While counsel who habitually practice in this area no doubt acquire expertise and insight into the practices of counterfeiters, the unusually heavy reliance upon information provided by counsel which one often sees in these matters creates a risk of putting counsel's credibility in issue. This detracts from the independence which the Court is entitled to expect from counsel appearing before it.

2) Certain elements of the proof put before the Court are general in nature and cannot be easily be particularized, for example, the damage to the goodwill of the plaintiff from the existence of substandard counterfeit goods. This evidence can be given in the form of general statements of the plaintiff's understanding of the effect of counterfeiting upon the value of their intellectual properties.

3) Other elements of the proof can and should be particularized, specifically the instances of counterfeiting known to the plaintiff which would justify the granting of an order. In general it would not be sufficient to simply say that the plaintiff is aware of counterfeiting in a given city or region. Since these orders are applied for ex parte and often in camera, there is no obvious justification for not giving the Court particulars of known instances of counterfeiting which would justify the issuance of the order sought, especially when the counterfeiting activity is taking place at some distance from the centre where the order is sought.

4) In general, a number of instances of counterfeiting would be required to justify a "rolling" order for the simple reason that a specific instance would only justify a specific order. If the plaintiff wishes an order applicable to unlimited future instances, it is incumbent upon it to demonstrate that specific orders are not an appropriate remedy. The deponent's unsupported testimony as to his or her belief that such an order is required would not usually be sufficient.

5) In the same way, proof of a number of incidents of counterfeiting in Ontario would only justify an order which applied to Ontario. If a Canada wide order is sought, there should be some proof that the counterfeiting is not a local problem. This is not an insurmountable problem: an order tailored to the evidence submitted at the time of the hearing could be extended subsequently by amendment if further evidence of counterfeiting in other provinces or regions became available.

6) Since it is the allegation of counterfeiting which justifies the extraordinary interference with existing property rights, the grounds upon which it is believed that counterfeiting is occurring should be clearly stated. A simple assertion that the affiant believes the goods to be counterfeit is not sufficient. What observations or examinations support the affiant's belief? In general terms, evidence upon information and belief as to this issue would not be particularly persuasive. This evidence goes to the heart of the application and should receive critical attention.

7) In those cases where it is sought to renew an existing order, it is incumbent upon the plaintiff to demonstrate to the court the use which it has made of the order previously granted. An order which has not been enforced does not need to be renewed but the fact of enforcement does not, of itself, justify renewal of the order, though it may in some cases. As a courtesy to the Court, this information should be collated and summarized so as to enable the court to quickly review the plaintiff's past experience.

8) An assertion in an affidavit that the plaintiff agrees to be bound by an undertaking as to damages is not an undertaking as to damages just as a promise to agree is not an agreement. A separate undertaking as to damages, directed to the court, properly executed by corporate officers who have the authority to do so should accompany the application.

[26] A further point raised upon this review was the use of the "John Doe" designation of defendants in the "rolling" order. Was it a proper use of the "John Doe"procedure?

[27] Fortunately not all of these considerations need to be considered on this review. Counsel for all parties, Plaintiffs and Defendants, were extremely professional and helpful in reducing the number of issues and getting to the point particularly Ms. Danzig for the Plaintiffs and Mr. Toyne for some of the

Defendants. There is little real dispute, as to the rights asserted by the Plaintiffs, nor is there any real dispute that the copies of the "3 Idiots" motion picture embedded in the CD's and DVD's seized were unauthorized copies. The manner in which the execution of the Order, once granted, was carried out is not in dispute. The issues for consideration on this review are therefore those as set out in the following section.

ISSUES FOR REVIEW:

[28] The issues now before the Court, which will be considered in turn are:

1. Have the Plaintiffs established that the damage, potential or actual, is very serious?
2. Have the Plaintiffs provided convincing evidence that the defendants have in their possession incriminating documents or things?
3. Have the Plaintiffs established a real possibility that the Defendants may destroy such material before discovery?
4. Have the Plaintiffs provided a proper basis for a "John Doe" proceeding?
5. Have the interests of justice been brought into disrepute?

1. Have the Plaintiffs established that the damage, potential or actual, is very serious?

[29] It is to be noted at the outset that this requirement is not only that damage, potential or actual, exists or will exist, but that such damage is *very serious*.

[30] The evidence to that effect put before the Court on the *ex parte* application is found on the affidavit of Sumit Chadha sworn January 18, 2010. He is the US Operations Manager of the Plaintiff Reliance, a position that he has held for some three years. The issue of damage is discussed at paragraphs 32 to 44 of that affidavit. At paragraph 33 he states, with reference to a news report on the Al Jazeera Network (no copy provided) that the Indian pirated movie industry earns more than four times what the mainstream industry earns. At paragraph 34 he refers to a US India Business Counsel news release stating that the Indian economy has sustained huge job and revenue losses as result of piracy. A different report is also referred to in that paragraph. He purports to attach as Exhibit F a copy of the press release. In fact Exhibit F is another copyright registration certificate said to be erroneous (paragraphs 23 to 25). Nowhere is a copy of the news release or report provided. At paragraphs 35 to 38 he discusses how plans are made such that a motion picture is released in theatres with a planned later release of home video copies. At paragraph 38 he says that unauthorized copies "detrimentally impact" upon such plans. At paragraph 39 to 41 he discusses illegal sales of videos that "reduces attendance at theatres" referring to a 1999 report by an entity identified only as MPA respecting the movie "Star Wars". At paragraph 42 he says that his company's market for home video products will "diminish". At paragraph 44 he concludes that lost ticket sales and sales of video products will result.

[31] Nowhere does this evidence specifically direct itself to Canada, nor the motion picture "3 Idiots" nor to any particular potential defendant or group of defendants. Nowhere is the damage said to be "very serious".

[32] Even to look at the post-Order evidence, the results of the execution of the Order show that only a handful of unauthorized video copies of "3 Idiots" were seized. They are said to sell at between one and two dollars a copy. Even if statutory damages as permitted by the *Copyright Act*, *supra*, were assessed even at the high end, they would not amount to "very serious" damage.

[33] Plaintiffs'counsel submitted that the total quantity of unauthorized videos is still unknown and the market destruction is still unknown. That may be, but the onus was on the Plaintiffs to establish that the damage, actual or potential, was or would be "very serious". They have not done so.

2.   Have the Plaintiffs provided convincing evidence that the defendants have in their possession incriminating documents or things?

[34] I am satisfied that the Court had before it on the *ex parte* motion through the affidavits of Trehan, Parish and Archibald, sufficient evidence that a number of retail establishments, at the time identified only in a general way by city and unnumbered streets, were offering for sale unauthorized copies of"3 Idiots". The evidence later filed shows that, upon execution of the Order, some unauthorized copies were seized.

[35] There were no documents seized, other than a few business cards and cash register slips. No documents were recovered as to the source of such unauthorized copies. A later filed affidavit identifies a mysterious and untraceable Mansur Samji as the source of some of these copies. Inferences are raised that some shops may make copies on the premises using computers located there but no hard evidence to that effect was provided.

3.   Have the Plaintiffs established a real possibility that the Defendants may destroy such material before discovery?

[36] The evidence put before the Court on the *ex parte* application as to the likelihood of destruction is largely set out in the affidavit of Sumit Chadha referred to earlier (I will return to Trehan, Parish and Archibald later). The Chadha affidavit is peculiar in this regard. It begins at paragraph 46 by stating that, based on his experience at Reliance (some 3 years in the US) he has "come to learn" that certain persons may destroy or hide evidence. He says:

> *46. Based upon my experience at Reliance MediaWorks (USA) Inc. I have come to learn that persons engaged in the sale of Counterfeit Recordings, including street market vendors, flea market vendors and fixed location retail establishments, often move their operations on a moment's notice, and/or refuse to voluntarily identify themselves, and/or destroy or hide evidence of their wrongful conduct, and/or destroy or hide documents that might lead the Plaintiffs to the source of the Counterfeit Video Records or to their supplier, if given notice of the intended proceedings.*

[37] I give no weight to such a generalized statement. At paragraph 47 he gives hearsay evidence from Trehan. Trehan provided his own affidavit in these proceedings and could have said this himself. He did not.

> 47. I am advised by Tarun (Sunny) Trehan and believe that many fixed location retail establishments are engaged in the illicit sale of Counterfeit Recordings.

[38] I give no weight to this statement since Trehan gave evidence and did not say this anywhere.

[39] At paragraphs 48 and 49 Chadha gives hearsay evidence based on information received from Plaintiffs' counsel Mr. Lipkus:

> 48. I am advised by Mr. Lipkus and believe that the ever-changing and elusive practices engaged in by counterfeiters transcend the venue from which they carry on their trade. This position is sustainable when one considers the following examples of business practices, undertaken, from time to time, by persons carrying on business at fixed location retail establishments. I am advised by Lorne M. Lipkus and believe that all of these examples were extracted from Affidavits filed with this Honourable Court, and I believe each can be an indicator of impermanence and risk of loss of evidence of counterfeiting:
>
>> a) business permits not at business premises despite municipal by-laws mandating same;
>>
>> b) incorrect or expired or previous owners' business permit on premises;
>>
>> c) name on sign at the premises is different from the name appearing on receipts given to customers and/or from the name appearing on the business permit;
>>
>> d) generic cash register receipt with no reference to business name and/or no description of the item purchased;
>>
>> e) cash register receipt fails to contain GST number;
>>
>> etc. etc.
>
> 49. I am informed by Mr. Lipkus and believe that attempts are made from time to time to elicit the voluntary surrender of counterfeit merchandise, including, Counterfeit Video Recordings and the voluntary cessation of counterfeit activity. However, I am also informed by Mr. Lipkus, and believe that often the counterfeiters he encounters refuse to relinquish their rights to the counterfeit merchandise unless and until they are served with an Anton Piller Order. Even those served with Anton Piller Orders, from time to time, refuse to voluntarily surrender their counterfeit merchandise and refuse to voluntarily permit a search of their premises.

[40] It is highly improper for a Plaintiff's own lawyer, whether directly, or through information and belief adopted by another witness, to give evidence as to a contentious matter in a proceeding such as this. This is particularly so where the evidence is directed to an allegation that a person may hide or destroy evidence if notice were given. I contrast this situation with that considered by Justice Snider of this Court in *Chum Limited v. Stempowicz*, 2003 FCT 800 (CanLII), 2003 FCT 800 where Mr. Lipkus himself provided his affidavit

directed to similar points but a different law firm and different counsel appeared for the parties.

[41] As the Supreme Court of Canada said in *Celanese supra,* a plaintiff and counsel owe the highest degree of candour to the Court in matters of this kind in seeking an *ex parte* order. As stated by Pelletier J. in *Club Monaco supra* at paragraph 7, point 1:

> *The affidavits should contain the personal knowledge of the affiant as to the nature and extent of the problem as it relates to the Plaintiff. It is, after all, the plaintiff's valuable property which it is sought to protect. If the officers of the plaintiff are not in a position to testify from their own personal knowledge as to the nature and extent of the problem, doubts are raised as to the need for the remedy. While counsel who habitually practice in this area no doubt acquire expertise and insight into the practices of counterfeiters, the unusually heavy reliance upon information provided by counsel which one often sees in these matters creates a risk of putting counsel's credibility in issue. This detracts from the independence which the Court is entitled to expect from counsel appearing before it.*

[42] Counsel cannot avoid the issue by putting their opinions in the mouth of another witness speaking on information and belief (*Citifinancial Services of Canada v. 1472354 Ontario Inc.*, 2003 Carswell Ont. 507 at para 4).

[43] Rule 82 of this Court precludes Counsel from arguing a matter in which Counsel's own affidavit is in evidence. The Rule has been relaxed but only in respect of non-controversial matters. The Rule remains clear as stated by Pelletier J.A. in *Belmonte v. Syndicat des débardeurs,* 2004 FCA 141 (CanLII), 2004 FCA 141 at para 4:

> *4 The rule is clear and based on a consistent principle of professional ethics: counsel should not be the subject of the litigation himself. This rule is well known and must be observed for the protection of clients, if not of counsel himself. The Court finds that counsel's affidavit is inadmissible for purposes of the motion for an extension of time.*

[44] I rule that paragraphs 48 and 49 of the Chadha affidavit to be inadmissible. Even if admissible I would give it no weight as nowhere is it provided as to how Mr. Lipkus may have known about or gained expertise in such matters.

[45] The final paragraph of this Chadha affidavit, paragraph 50 is simply a conclusion based on the previous paragraphs. I give it no weight.

[46] Thus the Plaintiffs have led no probative evidence that the defendants would be likely to hide or destroy relevant documents or things.

[47] Turning to other evidence presented on the *ex parte* application, it consists of the affidavits of three private investigators, Trehan, Parish and Archibald, who visited several shops (only vaguely identified) and purchased unauthorized copies of "3 Idiots" recordings. Nowhere is it alleged that the shopkeepers were likely to hide or destroy such copies or other relevant materials.

[48] In fact the Plaintiffs' evidence is to the contrary. The affidavit of Parish states that he delivered a "cease and desist" letter (Exhibit A to his affidavit

sworn January 19, 2010) to a number of parties. His later affidavit identifies such parties so as to include many of the Affected Defendants. That letter, although not drafted with the skill of one practicing in the copyright area, requests that the recipient immediately cease selling "3 Idiots" unauthorized copies and preserve copies and relevant materials. In other words *notice had already been given* to many of the Affected Defendants as well as others.

[49] The evidence presented on the review indicates that after execution of the Order some of the Affected Defendants had unauthorized copies of "3 Idiots" for sale, others did not. There is *no evidence that after the notice*, any relevant copies of material had been hidden or destroyed.

[50] The Plaintiffs' evidence in this respect, particularly since it is directed to a state of mind or propensity to hide or destroy relevant documents and materials is woefully inadequate. At best it is careless, inadequate and a slipshod attempt to secure an Order whose real purpose is, and I am quoting a word used by the Plaintiffs' Counsel in argument before me, to "target" small shopkeepers. I view this as an abuse of the process of this Court. At worst it was an attempt to induce this Court to issue an Order for which there was no foundation.

4.   Have the Plaintiffs provided a proper basis for a "John Doe" proceeding?

[51] The"rolling" Anton Piller Order was granted in an action commenced by filing a Statement of Claim which does not name any particular defendant. They are identified in the style of cause as follows:

> JOHN DOE AND JANE DOE AND OTHER PERSONS, NAMES UNKNOWN,
>
> WHO DEAL IN COUNTERFEIT VIDEO RECORDINGS,
>
> AND OTHER PERSONS LISTED IN SCHEDULE "A" TO THE STATEMENT OF CLAIM

[52] Schedule"A" as it appears in the Statement of Claim as filed is simply a blank form, presumably to be filled in later with the names of persons identified and added pursuant to a subsequent Court Order. As such the Statement of Claim follows an established practice developed in this Court for actions of this kind.

[53] The Statement of Claim, as filed January 20, 2010, refers to the Defendants only in the following way:

5.   *The Defendants, John Doe and Jane Doe are persons whose names and identities are presently unknown to the Plaintiffs, who deal in Counterfeit Video Recordings.*

[54] This allegation, having regard to the evidence before the Court, is untrue. As of January 20, 2010 a number of persons and corporations said to deal in Counterfeit Videos were in fact known to the Plaintiffs. The affidavits of Trehan and Parish speak of a number of retailers whose identity they were"specifically not disclosing" at that time. Later affidavits of those persons disclose that visits were made to those premises late in December and very early in January. The

affidavit of Archibald discloses specific street addresses of premises he visited. The later of affidavits of these persons reveal that further information by way of corporate searches and the like, if required, was readily available.

[55] While the identity of all persons possibly dealing with Counterfeit Videos was not known, a great many persons were and could be identified. Mason J. of the Alberta Court of Queen's Bench addressed the "John Doe" situation in *Brochner v. MacDonald* 1987 CanLII 3231 (AB QB), (1987), 56 Alta. L.R. (2d) 72, 22 C.P.C. (2d) 4 and wrote:

> The replacement of John Doe as a Defendant by Dr. Anderson is permissible only in the case of misnomer as that principle has been defined at law. This is not a case of misnomer.
>
> The traditional procedure of suing John Doe as the unknown or unidentified person in a cause of action has long been accepted by the courts of this province as it has by the courts in other provinces of Canada where the person is real and is alleged to be part of the incident or transaction giving rise to the claim. A brief history of this traditional procedure is provided by Mr. Justice Bull of the British Columbia Court of Appeal in the case of Jackson v. Bubela 29 D.L.R. (3d) 500 at 502. See also Golden Eagle Liberia Limited and Westchester Marine Shipping Co. v. International Organization of Masters, Mates and Pilots, Marine Division, International Longshoremen's Association A.F.L.-C.I.O. et al (1974) 5 W.W.R. p. 49 and Dukoff et al v. Toronto General Hospital et al 54 O.R. (2d) p. 58 at 61 and following.
>
> An examination of the Statement of Claim reveals no action pleaded against a real person whose identity is or was for good reason unknown or unavailable to the Plaintiff. While the Statement of Claim names John Doe as a Defendant, he is not mentioned in any of the allegations set out in the Statement of Claim.
>
> At its best reading, the Statement of Claim refers only to the Defendant Dr. Malcolm MacDonald and the Defendant Hospital. Allegations of negligence and failure to use reasonable care are made only against those two named Defendants.
>
> The Plaintiff has, in paragraph 17 of the Statement of Claim, purported to reserve a right to add further particulars of negligence against "the said Defendants" in the following terms:
>
> > "17. The Plaintiff states that he is unable to give at this stage further particulars of negligence on the part of the Defendants, as the same are solely within the knowledge of the said Defendants and the Plaintiff reserves the right to add such further particulars of negligence as may be necessary."
>
> I am of the opinion that this reservation cannot possibly be used to bootstrap Dr. Anderson into the proceedings after the expiration of the limitation period as the real John Doe in these proceedings.
>
> The long established rule with respect to misnomer is stated in Davies v. Elsby Brothers Ltd. (1960) 3 All E.R. 672. That case states that the proper test to be applied in cases of determining whether or not there has been a misnomer is to ask the question — would a reasonable person reading the document understand that he is the person referred to therein but wrongly named or named under a psuedonym? If so, it is a matter of misnomer and the court will permit amendment of the

pleadings in order to properly identify the party. If such is not the case, the rule is that it is not a case of misnomer but simply an attempt to introduce a new party by way of addition or substitution.

[56] The fact that a number of defendants were known before the action was commenced and before the *ex parte* Order was sought, coupled with the fact that those persons had already been put on notice is yet another reason why this action and the resulting "rolling" Anton Piller Order is inappropriate.

5.   Have the interests of justice been brought into disrepute?

[57] From what has already been written it is clear that there was no proper foundation for the Anton Piller Order and that such an Order was inappropriate. The evidence was, in many respects, as discussed, careless, inadequate or misleading. The real purpose appears to have been to obtain an Order that would allow the Plaintiffs, through solicitors and other agents, to "target" certain persons selling what are described as "Counterfeit" Videos. In this case simply small shopkeepers.

SUMMARY AND REMEDIES

[58] In summary, having reviewed the *ex parte* Anton Piller Order, it cannot stand and must be set aside. There is insufficient evidence as to "serious damage" and no proper proof that the defendants would be likely to hide or destroy relevant documents or things. Further, since many potential defendants were known prior to the institution of the action, there was improper use of the "John Doe" process as well as a deliberate misleading statement made in paragraph 5 of the Statement of Claim.

[59] The Anton Piller Order in respect of the Affected Defendants must be set aside. Further, because of the misuse of the "John Doe" process the action against the Affected Defendants must be dismissed. This does not mean that a new action, specifically naming one or more of such Defendants could not be instituted, it can, however it would be improper to use the fruits of an improper Anton Piller Order to base such an action. Other evidence, if available, must be used.

[60] The *Copyright Act supra* is among the most generous of any intellectual property statute in Canada or elsewhere in providing for rights and remedies. Copyright subsists without the necessity for registration and is presumed in the absence of evidence to the contrary. Registration is cheap and easy and provides presumptive evidence as to copyright subsistence and ownership. Proceedings can be quickly brought as an application rather than an action. Damages can either be proved or an election to take statutory damages made. An injunction can extend to works not specifically put in issue. Allegedly infringing works can be taken into interim and final custody. An Anton Piller Order must be considered as an exceptional remedy to be used with caution and respect. It should not be considered as routine where so many other remedies and procedures are available.

[61] Given the manner in which the *ex parte* Order was obtained, including the insufficient, careless and misleading evidence as already discussed, it is

appropriate to award the Affected Defendants their reasonable costs on a full indemnity basis.

ORDER

FOR THE REASONS PROVIDED HEREIN:

THE COURT ORDERS THAT:

1. The Anton Piller Order granted January 26, 2010 herein is hereby set aside as against the following named Defendants, hereinafter the Affected Defendants:

- 1557768 Ontario Inc. o/a Golumbia Video
- Arangesan Paramsothy
- 1691731 Ontario Inc. o/a Bollywood 4 U
- Abulsama Jibhai
- 2148409 Ontario Inc. o/a Video Station
- Kulwant Kaur Singh
- 215151872 Ontario Inc. o/a Singh Video Station
- Mohan Singh
- 2031221 Ontario Inc. o/a Old Karachi Bazar
- Royal Paan Inc.
- Neerad Upadhyay
- Anmol Records Inc.
- Rajesh Syal
- 2122308 Ontario Inc. o/a Albion Audio & Video
- Kulbir Singh Mokha

2. This action as against the Affected Defendants is dismissed without prejudice to the right of the Plaintiffs to bring a further action based on evidence of alleged infringement other than the evidence of alleged infringement presented herein in respect of the original Anton Piller Order or the review thereof;

3. The Affected Defendants are entitled to their reasonable costs on a full indemnity basis;

4. Tayyabi Huma shall not be a named Defendant in this action and any proceedings as may involve her herein are dismissed. She represents herself and cannot recover a lawyer's costs but is entitled to recover her out-of-pocket disbursements. If she chooses not to tax such disbursements I award her the sum of $250.00.

Sharman License Holdings Pty. Ltd. v. Universal Music (Australia) Pty. Ltd., [2004] F.C.A. 183

20 February 2004, 4 March 2004. Sydney

Wilcox J.

1 Before the Court are two notices of motion seeking the discharge of Anton Piller type orders made by me on 5 February 2004. The orders were made in a proceeding intended to be instituted by six applicants, Universal Music Australia Pty Ltd, Festival Records Pty Ltd and Mushroom Records Pty Ltd trading as Festival Mushroom Records, EMI Music Australia Pty Limited, Sony Music Entertainment (Australia) Limited, Warner Music Australia Pty Limited and BMG Australia Limited. Although these six parties are respondents to the motions, it is convenient to refer to them in these reasons as "the applicants".

. . .

The Anton Piller orders

3 In accordance with usual practice, the Anton Piller orders were made on the ex parte application of counsel for the applicants. Counsel's application was supported by four volumes of material comprising the application proposed to be filed to commence the principal proceeding, two draft notices of motion (one of which was the motion seeking Anton Piller orders), a solicitor's undertaking, an outline of submissions, a draft order for ex parte relief and numerous affidavits.

4 The affidavit evidence indicated that all the applicants are Australian record companies with extensive catalogues of copyright sound recordings.

5 Paragraphs 3 to 6 of counsel's outline of submissions explained the background to the application:

> "These proceedings relate to large scale infringement of copyright in sound recordings by the operation of a so-called 'peer to peer' internet 'file sharing' system and associated computer software generally known as 'Kazaa'.

> Technological developments in recent years have greatly increased opportunities for, and the scale of, piracy of sound recordings. This has been particularly so with the availability of a range of technologies, including compact discs (CDs), personal computers and the internet, which have together enabled the copying and online transmission of digitally accessible versions of sound recordings.

> There is in Australia no right of private copying of copyright sound recordings. Accordingly, it is an infringement of copyright for an individual to 'rip' (copy) the content of a copyright commercial CD, or to download a digital music file that is a copyright sound recording, unless specifically authorised to do so.

> The developments described in paragraph 4 above have led to the promotion of various schemes designed to facilitate the exchange between computer users of copyright sound recordings, including the so-called 'peer to peer' technology."

6 Counsel went on to describe the "Kazaa" system. They described it as a scheme using software known as Kazaa Media Desktop (sometimes "KMD")

"that permitted users to distribute and receive digital music files to and from each other". They stated this software first appeared in the Netherlands. Legal proceedings were brought in the Netherlands, after which "there was a relocation of the entities apparently associated with supplying the software to countries outside the Netherlands".

7 In para 10 of their outline of submissions, counsel made a reference to legal proceedings in the United States. They said:

> "The second set of proceedings was commenced in the United States in relation to infringement of United States copyright. The applicants in those proceedings include but are not limited to five of the applicants in the present case. In October 2002, certain of the present respondents were joined to those proceedings. Those proceedings remain on foot. Ancillary proceedings (relating to a letter of request to obtain evidence and documents in Australia pursuant to the Hague Convention) are on foot in the Supreme Court of New South Wales. These are not substantive proceedings and they do not relate to Australian copyright."

. . .

11 It is not necessary for me to refer to all the material contained in the affidavits used to support the application for Anton Piller orders. None of that material is disputed, for present purposes. However, it is desirable to note the evidence put before me as to the nature of the risk of destruction of evidence, if Anton Piller type relief was not obtained.

12 Jorg Michael Speck is the Manager of Music Industry Piracy Investigations, an organisation apparently controlled by the applicants. Mr Speck has held that position for nine years. Prior to that time, he was a detective sergeant and senior investigator in the New South Wales Police Service. The material in his affidavit suggests he is well conversant with the problem of copyright piracy in the music industry. He has been deeply involved with investigations into the Kazaa system, the features of which he explained at length. He set out some information about each of the Kazaa Parties. At paras 185-187 of his affidavit, he said:

> "Information gained from files contained on the computers of the server or of the site operators is likely to reveal information about the structure, operation and monitoring of the Kazaa system and the infringement of copyright of the applicants occurring on that network or committed by Kazaa users.

> Based on my experience in the enforcement of copyright in cases of online copyright infringement, I believe that there is a very high risk of the destruction, dissipation or unavailability of documents and computer records in the event that notice is given to the respondents of the allegations of copyright infringement.

. . .

66 I am not in a position to form any view about the merits of the dispute between the parties as to the degree of co-operation shown by the respondents and the Brilliant Digital parties in disclosing material in the US proceedings. However, if it is correct to say this co-operation (whatever its degree) would have borne upon the desirability of making the Anton Piller orders, I accept the

co-operation ought to have been mentioned by counsel in seeking the Anton Piller orders. The question is whether it would have had such a bearing.

67 Counsel for both the respondents and the Brilliant Digital parties argue that, if there was material information known to the United States lawyers, non-disclosure of that information is not excused by the fact that Mr Williams was personally unaware of it. They point out that he was aware of the existence of the US proceedings and that Sharman Networks and LEF were parties to those proceedings. He was aware the US proceedings concerned allegations of infringement of copyright by those companies; in particular, through use of the Kazaa system. If Mr Williams did not have knowledge of any particular fact, they say, he needed only to ask. Counsel argue it is immaterial that the US proceedings concern infringement of United States copyright, whereas the present proceeding relates to Australian copyright. They say the significant point is that the behaviour of Sharman Networks, LEF and the Brilliant Digital parties, in relation to non-destruction of evidence, would have furnished guidance as to the likelihood that those companies would destroy evidence relevant to the present case.

68 I accept most of the submissions summarised in the last paragraph. I agree it would be no answer to an allegation of non-disclosure of a material fact for the applicants to say Mr Williams was personally unaware of that fact, if this was something about which he could have asked the United States lawyers.

69 However, the critical issue in the case is whether the conduct of Sharman Networks and LEF, in the US proceedings, was a fact material to the question whether or not it was appropriate for me to grant Anton Piller relief. This issue does not turn upon the circumstance that one proceeding is brought in the United States, under United States law, and the other in Australia, under Australian law; or upon any difference between the procedures, rights and remedies which those laws provide. The issue does not turn on differences between the identities of the moving parties in each proceeding, or the presence or otherwise of other responding parties. It is reasonable to work on the assumption that, if Sharman Networks and LEF conducted themselves in a particular way, in relation to non-destruction of evidentiary material in the US proceedings, they would be likely to conduct themselves in a similar way in respect of similar material relevant to the present proceeding. To put the matter at its lowest, if the purpose of the Anton Piller orders was to prevent the destruction of such material, information as to how they had conducted themselves in the US proceedings, in relation to similar material, ought to have been disclosed when the applicants applied for the Anton Piller orders.

70 Mr Lever put his finger on the critical issue when he invited a comparison between the material itemised in the United States subpoena addressed to his clients and the material authorised to be seized under the Anton Piller orders made by me on 5 February 2004. Although the subpoena is addressed to the Brilliant Digital parties, not the respondents, it seems the material sought of the respondents in the US proceedings was similar to that sought by the subpoena.

71 Mr Bermeister has asserted that he co-operated in providing the documents itemised in the United States subpoena. Whether or not that assertion is accepted, there is no suggestion that the Brilliant Digital parties, or anybody associated with them, has attempted to destroy any of the documents required by the subpoena. Consequently, I agree with Mr Lever that, if the material identified in Schedule 2 of the Anton Piller orders was similar in nature to the documents required by the United States subpoena, it would be reasonable to suppose that the Brilliant Digital parties would not attempt to destroy that material either. The same comment may be made in favour of the respondents. On the other hand, if the material sought to be preserved by the Anton Piller orders is of a different character to that required to be produced in the US proceedings, being material at risk of loss irrespective of the attitudes and intentions of the respondents and the Brilliant Digital parties, their conduct in relation to the US proceedings may fairly be regarded as irrelevant.

72 It will be recalled that counsel for the applicants argued the material sought to be preserved under the Anton Piller orders is different in kind to the documents required to be produced in the United States proceedings. This is not because the material covered by the Anton Piller orders comprises, or at least substantially includes, electronic information. The subpoena issued in the United States proceedings to the Brilliant Digital parties defines "documents" as including "writings in electronic form". The difference, according to counsel, is that the Schedule 2 material is "Perishable Material"; it is inherently transitory, rather than "Non-Perishable Material" that will continue to exist until it is deliberately destroyed.

73 With these thoughts in mind, I made the comparison urged upon me by Mr Lever. As I understand the list contained in the United States subpoena, the relevant "documents" are all documents relating to what Mr Bannon calls the "structure" of the Kazaa scheme. Item 1 refers to documents evidencing or referring to any version of the software, or the source or encryption code, that has a role in the functioning of KMD. Item 2 relates to documents evidencing or referring to the design, operation or capabilities of KMD. Item 3 is also concerned with documents relating to the design, operation or capabilities of software or code. Item 4 seeks documents relating to services or information proposed to be provided to Sharman Networks. Item 5 relates to documents that evidence or refer to the configuration of web servers, access log keepers and analysers. Item 6 requires documents relating to Sharman Network's policies and practices with regard to copyright infringement. Item 7 is concerned with Sharman Networks' "repeat infringer" policy. Item 8 relates to documents evidencing and referring to demographic information. Item 9 concerns financing information. Item 10 requires documents that evidence or refer to the content of available or downloaded files. Item 11 seeks documents relating to communications concerning KMD or alleged copyright infringements through KMD and item 12 requests documents that evidence or refer to communications between Sharman Networks and various other persons. Without going into further detail, the remaining items (13 to 23) all concern what might be called static business records.

74 The important point about this list is that none of the items includes material (even in electronic form) recording transitory information; that is, data concerning the moment to moment transactions undertaken by users of the Kazaa system.

75 On the other hand, Schedule 2 of the Anton Piller orders does just that. It authorises recovery of data that must be constantly changing: for example, the number and location of participants using the Kazaa system and the communications between them (items 1 and 2).

76 There may be elements of the information identified by the Schedule that are of a static nature. Perhaps the best example is item 4: information recording the administration, management or monitoring of the functions of participants in the Kazaa system. However, the possibility of picking up some static data was anticipated by order 13. Order 13(b) provides that order 8 extends to files that are in a static environment. In such a case, the files were to be extracted and copied and then held by a forensic expert, without further analysis, until further order of the Court. As I understand the position, the idea was that anything of a static nature would be treated like a discoverable document; it was not to be inspected until the appropriate time. However, to the extent that the seized material was of a dynamic nature, it could be copied and so preserved for future use as evidence.

77 In an ideal world, it would be preferable for parties not to need to resort to Anton Piller action. However, where the case sought to be made by a party depends upon demonstrating the operation of a dynamic scheme, it is difficult to see any alternative to the taking of "snapshots" of the scheme in operation, thereby preserving evidence of what the dynamic system was doing at the moment of inspection. This was the point made by Mr Speck when he said in his affidavit (see para 12 above) that he had previously found "that information [in a computer] is frequently overwritten or lost by the ordinary operation of computer systems". Although Mr Speck was also concerned with the possibility of deliberate destruction of electronic material, he was saying, as I understand him, that material may be lost without destructive intent. If that is so, it is not to the point that the respondents and the Brilliant Digital parties have not deliberately destroyed documents containing static data that are required for the US proceedings.

78 Because of the amount of material (evidence and submissions) that has been put before me in connection with these motions, I am now better informed of the problems and issues than I was on 5 February 2004. However, if I apply the test of asking myself whether I would today think it appropriate to make Anton Piller orders in similar terms to those of 5 February 2004, I find myself answering the question in the affirmative. I do so because it is obviously an essential part of the applicants' case to put evidence before the Court about the dynamic operation of the Kazaa system, as distinct from its structure. Evidence about dynamic operation is available on relevant computers, from moment to moment, as the transactions occur. If that evidence is to be available at the trial, there must be "snapshots", perhaps many snapshots, showing the changing data in the system from moment to moment. The scheme of the Anton Piller orders was to allow those snapshots to be taken, and thereby to preserve that changing data.

Analysis of the data will no doubt add to the experts' understanding of the operation of the Kazaa system, but that does not mean that the exercise permitted by the Anton Piller orders was an investigation. It was an exercise designed to preserve evidence. The situation seems unusual because it involves preserving data momentarily held in computer memory, rather than data recorded in a more permanent medium such as writing on paper. It is preservation nonetheless.

79 It might be argued that, if the respondents and the Brilliant Digital parties were willing not to destroy documents relevant to the United States proceedings, it should be assumed they would be willing to co-operate in an arranged demonstration of the Kazaa system in operation at a future date, so that evidence of its changing operational data could then be obtained without the necessity for any Anton Piller orders. However, it is one thing to expect parties to litigation not to destroy existing evidence; it is another thing to expect them conscientiously to co-operate in the creation and recording of evidence useful to their opponents. Moreover, as I understand the situation, the operation of the Kazaa system does not depend only (or even principally) upon action then being taken by the respondents or the Brilliant Digital parties, but upon the actions of countless other participants using the system the respondents have allegedly created. I do not understand how it could be ensured that these participants would act in a normal and natural way in an organised demonstration.

Disposition

80 Although the detail of the US proceedings was not disclosed to me on 5 February 2004, I have reached the conclusion that the non-disclosure was not material. The non-disclosed material would not have affected my decision to make the Anton Piller orders. Accordingly, there is no occasion for me to set aside those orders. Insofar as the notices of motion seek orders to that effect, they should both be dismissed. Insofar as the notices of motion seek other relief, they should be stood over to a later date.

. . .

---

7. Identifying Infringers

BMG Canada Inc. v. John Doe, 2005 FCA 193

Noël J.A., Richard C.J., Sexton J.A.

Heard: April 20-21, 2005

Judgment: May 19, 2005

Docket: A-203-04

. . .

Sexton J.A.:

Introduction

1 This case illustrates the tension existing between the privacy rights of those who use the Internet and those whose rights may be infringed or abused by anonymous Internet users.

2 Canada's music producers and recording industry are very concerned about infringement of copyright in their musical works through the use of Internet file sharing. They maintain that the industry, including the creators of the musical works, lose millions of dollars every year in sales due to the unauthorized downloading of files. They wish to bring action against the infringers but do not have their identity. They allege that the only means of ascertaining the identity is through the Internet Service Providers (ISPs), who provide the internet service to the infringers.

3 The ISPs, citing privacy concerns, have refused to provide the names of the Internet users, who are downloading files of the recording industry, without a court order.

4 Citizens legitimately worry about encroachment upon their privacy rights. The potential for unwarranted intrusion into individual personal lives is now unparalleled. In an era where people perform many tasks over the Internet, it is possible to learn where one works, resides or shops, his or her financial information, the publications one reads and subscribes to and even specific newspaper articles he or she has browsed. This intrusion not only puts individuals at great personal risk but also subjects their views and beliefs to untenable scrutiny. Privacy advocates maintain that if privacy is to be sacrificed, there must be a strong *prima facie* case against the individuals whose names are going to be released. Whether this is the correct test will be addressed in this decision.

5 Ultimately the issue is whether the identity of persons who are alleged to infringe musical copyright can be revealed despite the fact that their right to privacy may be violated. Each side presents compelling arguments and the difficulty lies in reaching a balance between the competing interests.

Facts

6 The plaintiffs consist of the largest musical providers in Canada and claim to collectively own the Canadian copyrights in more than 80% of the sound recordings sold to the public in Canada.

7 The plaintiffs claim that 29 internet users have each downloaded more than 1000 songs (the Songs) over which the plaintiffs have copyright onto their home computers and, by means of what is called a "peer-to-peer" (P2P) file sharing program, are infringing the plaintiffs' copyright by providing access to their files, thus reproducing or distributing the plaintiffs' Songs to countless other Internet users. The persons are alleged to be using 29 distinct Internet locations (IP addresses) to carry out their infringing activities.

8 The respondents are ISPs who administer the 29 IP addresses and are said to be the only entities who have information regarding the identity of the 29 persons.

9 The plaintiffs are unable to determine the name, address or telephone number of any of the 29 internet users in question as they operate under pseudonyms associated with software which they use; e.g., Geekboy@KaZaA. However, they have conducted an investigation, through which, they submit, it was discovered that these individuals used IP addresses registered with the ISPs. The plaintiffs sought an order, pursuant to Rules 233 and 238 of the *Federal Court Rules, 1998*, SOR/98-106 (Rules), to compel the ISPs to disclose the names of the customers who used the 29 IP addresses at times material to these proceedings. The respondents had previously refused to provide the information voluntarily.

10 The plaintiffs wish to pursue litigation against these 29 individuals but being unaware of their identities, they commenced this action against "John Doe, Jane Doe and all those persons who are infringing copyright in the plaintiffs' sound recordings" and then brought this motion before the Federal Court to identify these 29 individuals.

11 On the motion, the plaintiffs filed affidavits of Gary Millin, President of MediaSentry Inc. (MediaSentry), a company that provides online anti-piracy protection by specializing in automated detection of the unauthorized distribution of copyrighted materials on the Internet. The plaintiffs had retained Media-Sentry to investigate file-sharing of the Songs.

12 The affidavits explained that the plaintiffs provided a list of the Songs to MediaSentry. MediaSentry through its computer program then searched the Internet and identified 29 IP addresses as addresses from which large numbers of sound recordings, including the Songs, were being offered for copying. Screenshots were saved showing the numerous files being offered at these IP addresses. Copies of the files were then requested and received from these IP addresses. MediaSentry's program also matched each of the 29 IP addresses to the specific ISP who administered each IP address at the relevant time. Media-Sentry provided the files it received to a representative of the plaintiffs who confirmed that the contents of these files corresponded with the Songs.

13 The ISPs responded in different ways. Shaw, Bell and Telus argued that cross-examination showed that the affidavits were hearsay and not in compliance with Rule 81 of the Rules, maintaining *inter alia* that Mr. Millin had not done the investigation personally and had not revealed his sources of information and hence his evidence could not be accepted. Most importantly, they argued that because the evidence was hearsay, the plaintiffs had failed to establish any connection between the pseudonyms from which MediaSentry extracted the sound recordings on the Internet (i.e. Geekboy@KaZaA) and the IP addresses connected to the various respondent. Further, Shaw and Telus argued that under Rule 238 and the principles relating to equitable bills of discovery, that the plaintiffs had failed to establish a *prima facie* case of infringement and therefore no discovery could be ordered. They also argued that it would be burdensome and expensive to extract the information from their records. They along with the

respondent, Rogers, maintained that the information would be stale dated and hence unreliable due to the delay between the time they were being asked to provide the information and the time when MediaSentry did their investigation. This fed their concerns about protecting the privacy of their customers whom they were obliged to protect by virtue of the *Personal Information Protection and Electronic Documents Act*, 2000, c. 5 (PIPEDA). Videotron agreed with the plaintiffs' submissions on copyright infringement and adopted them as its own. Finally, while Bell and Videotron had privacy concerns, they indicated they were able to produce the information requested without difficulty but would not do so without a court order in view of PIPEDA.

14   The motion was dismissed by the Federal Court.

15   The Motions Judge held that:

   a)   Rule 233 was not applicable because it presupposes the existence of specified documents. Here, the documents that would reveal the identity of the 29 persons did not pre-exist. Rather, documents containing the information would have to be created by the respondents through the use of existing logs and tapes.

   b)   The affidavits filed in support of the motion were deficient in that the evidence failed to satisfy the requirements of Rule 81 because "major portions of these affidavits are based upon information which Mr. Millin gained from his employees. Accordingly they consist largely of hearsay.... Mr. Millin gives no reason for his beliefs."

   c)   Because of the conclusions in (a) and (b), there was no clear evidence that the requisite relationship between the IP addresses and the pseudonyms had been established.

   d)   Although the plaintiffs brought the motion pursuant to Rule 238, the legal principles applicable to equitable bills of discovery should apply to applications under Rule 238.

   e)   The test articulated by the Motions Judge for granting an equitable bill of discovery was as follows:

Equitable Bill of Discovery Requirements

   (a)   the applicant must establish a *prima facie* case against the unknown alleged wrongdoer;

   (b)   the person from whom discovery is sought must be in some way involved in the matter under dispute, he must be more than an innocent bystander;

   (c)   the person from whom discovery is sought must be the only practical source of information available to the applicants;

> (d) the person from whom discovery is sought must be reasonably compensated for his expenses arising out of compliance with the discovery order in addition to his legal costs;
>
> (e) the public interests in favour of disclosure must outweigh the legitimate privacy concerns.

. . .

Rule 233

17 I can find no palpable and overriding error in the conclusions of the Motions Judge with respect to Rule 233.

18 Rule 233(1) states,

233. (1) On motion, the Court may order the production of any document that is in the possession of a person who is not a party to the action, if the document is relevant and its production could be compelled at trial.

19 The information sought by the plaintiffs may be buried in logs and tapes but is not presently in a readable format. Since the documents in a readable format do not currently exist and would have to be created, Rule 233 has no application. The Rule contemplates the production of documents which are "in the possession of a person". It cannot be said that documents which do not exist are in the possession of a person.

Rule 81

20 I am of the view that the Motions Judge made no palpable and overriding error in concluding that the plaintiffs' material was deficient in that it failed to comply with Rule 81.

> 81. (1) Affidavits shall be confined to facts within the personal knowledge of the deponent, except on motions in which statements as to the deponent's belief, with the grounds therefor, may be included.
>
> (2) Where an affidavit is made on belief, an adverse inference may be drawn from the failure of a party to provide evidence of persons having personal knowledge of material facts.

21 Much of the crucial evidence submitted by the plaintiffs was hearsay and no grounds are provided for accepting that hearsay evidence. In particular, the evidence purporting to connect the pseudonyms with the IP addresses was hearsay thus creating the risk that innocent persons might have their privacy invaded and also be named as defendants where it is not warranted. Without this evidence there is no basis upon which the motion can be granted and for this reason alone the appeal should be dismissed.

22 However the reasons of the Motions Judge extend beyond merely dealing with the hearsay evidence issue. Rather the reasons address such matters as the appropriate procedure necessary to obtain the identities of the users, the proper test to be applied by the Court in granting orders compelling disclosure of the

identities, and vital copyright infringement issues. It is therefore necessary to address these issues.

Rule 238

23 In spite of the arguments of the respondents, I believe this proceeding could be brought pursuant to Rule 238 of the Rules.

> 238. (1) A party to an action may bring a motion for leave to examine for discovery any person not a party to the action, other than an expert witness for a party, who might have information on an issue in the action.
>
> (2) On a motion under subsection (1), the notice of motion shall be served on the other parties and personally served on the person to be examined.
>
> (3) The Court may, on a motion under subsection (1), grant leave to examine a person and determine the time and manner of conducting the examination, if it is satisfied that
>
> > (a) the person may have information on an issue in the action;
> >
> > (b) the party has been unable to obtain the information informally from the person or from another source by any other reasonable means;
> >
> > (c) it would be unfair not to allow the party an opportunity to question the person before trial; and
> >
> > (d) the questioning will not cause undue delay, inconvenience or expense to the person or to the other parties.

24 Rule 238(2) provides that notice of the motion must be served "on the other parties". Since the identities of the other parties are presently unknown to the plaintiffs, service is not possible and the respondents argued, therefore, that Rule 238 does not provide a procedure to discover the identities. Furthermore, they argued that Rule 238 is contained in a section under the general heading "Examination for Discovery" and that one would not normally expect the identity of each defendant to be revealed for the first time on an examination for discovery.

25 However, the plaintiffs argued that the main issue on the motion was the identity of each person who is committing infringement of the plaintiffs' copyrights. I agree and find that because this issue inevitably falls within the words in Rule 238(1) as being "an issue in the action", Rule 238 is broad enough to permit discovery in cases such as this.

26 As to the respondent's arguments, there is provision in the Rules to deal with the matter of service. Rule 136 allows the court to order substituted service or to dispense with service altogether. This Court has used the previously equivalent Rule to order substituted service where the persons whom the appellants sought to serve, had no address. The substituted service there consisted of providing notice of the appeal through newspaper publication (Indian Manufacturing Ltd. v. Lo (1996), 68 C.P.R. (3d) 174 (Fed. C.A.)). Also, although it is true that examinations for discovery of a third party are not routinely ordered, and should not become common place, they nevertheless are clearly applicable and

necessary in cases where the plaintiffs will be frustrated from pursuing their actions because they are unaware of the identity of the people they wish to sue. Furthermore, under Rule 238(3), the court may determine "the manner of conducting the examination". Thus a court could, in cases such as the present, limit the discovery to the submission of written questions which could be followed by written answers, limited to revealing only the identity of the users complained of, or such other limitations as the court might consider necessary.

27 It is worth noting that in Irwin Toy Ltd. v. Joe Doe, [2000] O.J. No. 3318 (Ont. S.C.J.), the Ontario Superior Court of Justice indicated that rules 30.10 and 31.10 of the Rules of Civil Procedure, R.R.O. 1990, Reg. 194, which are comparable to Rule 238, could be used to compel production of the identity of senders of e-mail from ISPs. There, the moving party successfully brought a motion to compel production of the identity of an individual who had sent an e-mail publication containing defamatory statements about the individual plaintiff. Similarly, in Loblaw Cos. v. Aliant Telecom Inc., [2003] N.B.J. No. 208 (N.B. Q.B.), the New Brunswick Court of Queen's Bench used Rule 32.12 of the New Brunswick Rules of Court, N.B. Reg. 82-73, also comparable to Rule 238, to compel production of the identity of an individual who had sent an e-mail containing confidential payroll information about a number of senior Loblaw employees to thirty-four other employees of Loblaw. Loblaw sought the identity of the person because spreading confidential information could have given rise to an action for damages or for an injunction against the individual who circulated the information.

Equitable Bills of Discovery

28 An equitable bill of discovery is an equitable remedy that is discretionary in nature. In Lord Denning's words in British Steel Corp. v. Granada Television Ltd., [1981] 1 All E.R. 417 (Eng. Ch. Div.) at p. 439, the bill of discovery "enables a person, who has been injured by wrongdoing, to bring an action to discover the name of the wrongdoer".

29 The concept has been accepted by this Court in Glaxo Wellcome plc v. Minister of National Revenue (1998), 81 C.P.R. (3d) 372 (Fed. C.A.) and was explained by Stone J.A. at paragraph 20:

> The equitable bill of discovery is in essence a form of pre-action discovery... It is of ancient origin. It developed alongside the procedures for discovery which are ordinarily available in the course of litigation and which, it is worth noting, also originated in the courts of equity.... This remedy permits a court, acting through its equitable jurisdiction, to order discovery of a person against whom the applicant for the bill of discovery has no cause of action and who is not a party to contemplated litigation. While it appears that an independent action for discovery cannot be brought against a person who is in the position of a "mere witness" or bystander to the cause of action, the case law suggests that a bill of discovery may be issued against an individual who is in some way connected to or involved in the misconduct.

30 The Motions Judge, while finding that the motion was brought pursuant to Rule 238, went on to hold that the criteria for determining whether an equitable bill of discovery should be issued, would be equally applicable to a proceeding brought under Rule 238. I agree. In my view, the plaintiffs could invoke either Rule 238 or equitable bills of discovery and in either case, the legal principles relating to equitable bills of discovery would be applicable. The same issues are at stake in both procedures and there would seem to be no reason for not applying the same legal principles.

31 While I agree that the criteria relating to granting an equitable bill of discovery can be applied to a Rule 238 motion in cases such as this, I disagree with the description of the first aspect of the test made by the Motions Judge. He said that the plaintiff has to provide evidence of a prima facie case. The plaintiffs argued that this was the wrong test and that the proper test should be whether the plaintiff has a bona fide claim against the proposed defendant. The respondents said that the plaintiffs had argued before the Motions Judge that the prima facie test was the correct one and that they should not be allowed to take a different position on appeal. If the respondents are correct as to what was argued before the Motions Judge, this might explain why he adopted the prima facie test. In any event, it is the duty of this Court to get the test right regardless of what was or is argued by counsel.

32 I am of the view that the proper test is whether the plaintiff has a bona fide claim against the proposed defendant. This is the test enunciated by this Court in Glaxo, supra, on very similar facts, after it considered Norwich Pharmacal Co. v. Customs & Excise Commissioners (1973), [1974] A.C. 133 (U.K. H.L.), where the test was reviewed by the House of Lords. In Glaxo, supra, the appellant sought disclosure of the names of individuals whose identity was unknown to Glaxo and who it was alleged had imported certain drugs into Canada, having the effect of infringing Glaxo's patent. Glaxo sought the names of the importers from Revenue Canada who were said to have the required information for the purposes of the Customs Act, R.S. 1985, c. 1 (2nd Supp.). An order was granted for disclosure. In his decision, Stone J.A. said at paragraphs 30 and 44:

It is of interest to note that several Canadian courts have adopted the Norwich Pharmacal approach to interpreting their own rules of civil procedure authorizing pre-action discovery.14 See for example Rule 18.02(c) of Nova Scotia's Civil Procedure Rules and Rule 18.02(1)(c) of Prince Edward Island's Rules of Civil Procedure.14 For instance, the Prince Edward Island Court of Appeal in Re Johnston and Frank Johnston's Restaurants Limited (1980), 33 Nfld. & P.E.I.R. 341 at pages 348, 351 and 353, specified three main criteria which an applicant must satisfy in order to be entitled to discover a third party before launching legal proceedings. The applicant must demonstrate that he or she has a bona fide claim. The Court added that the applicant's claim must be likely to succeed at trial, which according to my reading of the decision in Norwich Pharmacal was not an invariable requirement enunciated by the House of Lords. In an action for the infringement of patent rights, quite apart from a general denial, a defence of invalidity is often raised on the ground of lack of novelty, obviousness, insufficiency of specification or claims or some other recognized basis.15 See R.T. Hughes and J.H. Woodley, Hughes and Woodley on Patents (Toronto: Butterworths, 1984) at paragraph 36.15 It seems to me to go too far to insist that with respect to this kind of anticipated litigation, an applicant for a bill of discovery must show that he or she is likely to succeed at trial. As we have already seen, Lord Cross of Chelsea required that "the strength of the applicant's case" be considered as a factor, while Lord Kilbrandon spoke only of disclosing the names of persons "whom the appellants bona fide believe to be infringing" their patent rights. Finally, the applicant must also establish that he or she shares some sort of relationship with the third party against whom discovery is sought (i.e. that the person is in some way involved in the wrongdoing), and that the third party is the only practicable source of information available. These three requirements were likewise endorsed by the Nova Scotia Supreme Court in Comeau, Re (1986), 77 N.S.R. (2d) 57 at pages 59-60, and in Leahy v. Dr. A.B. (1992), 113 N.S.R. (2d) 417 at page 419. (emphasis added)

. . .

The next task is to determine whether the appellant has satisfied the criteria for issuing a bill of discovery. To my mind, the principles articulated in Norwich Pharmacal, supra, have direct application to the circumstances of the present case. Turning now to those principles, in my view the appellant has satisfied the threshold requirement for a bill of discovery in that it has a bona fide or legitimate claim against those who are importing RHCL into the country. (emphasis added).

33 The bona fide test was adopted by the Ontario Court of Appeal in Straka v. Humber River Regional Hospital (2000), 51 O.R. (3d) 1 (Ont. C.A.) where the respondent sought to compel production of confidential reference letters that had resulted in the respondent's failure to obtain an employment position. The Prince Edward Island Court of Appeal in Johnston v. Frank Johnston's Restaurants Ltd., [1980] P.E.I.J. No. 34 (P.E.I. C.A.) also adopted the bona fide test in a situation where the plaintiffs claimed they did not know the identity of persons they wished to sue.

34 In my view, it would make little sense to require proof of a prima facie case at the stage of the present proceeding. The plaintiffs do not know the identity of the persons they wish to sue, let alone the details of precisely what was done by each of them such as to actually prove infringement. Such facts would only be established after examination for discovery and trial. The plaintiffs would be effectively stripped of a remedy if the Courts were to impose upon them, at this stage, the burden of showing a prima facie case. It is sufficient if they show a bona fide claim, i.e. that they really do intend to bring an action for infringement of copyright based upon the information they obtain, and that there is no other improper purpose for seeking the identity of these persons.

Other Criteria relating to Equitable Bills of Discovery

35 As to the other criteria for granting an equitable bill of discovery, I agree with the conclusions of the Motions Judge. There should be clear evidence to

the effect that the information cannot be obtained from another source such as the operators of the named websites (KaZaA, et al). Also if an order for disclosure were granted, consideration would have to be given to the costs incurred by the respondents in assembling the information.

Privacy Issues

36 I agree with the Motions Judge's characterization of the 5th criteria–that is–the public interest in favour of disclosure must outweigh the legitimate privacy concerns of the person sought to be identified if a disclosure order is made.

37 All respondents raise the privacy issue. It is a an important consideration. Pursuant to PIPEDA, ISPs are not entitled to "voluntarily" disclose personal information such as the identities requested except with the customer's consent or pursuant to a court order. Indeed, pursuant to subsections 7(3)(c), 8(8) and 28 of PIPEDA, any organization that receives a request for the release of personal information must "retain the information for as long as is necessary to allow the individual to exhaust any recourse" under PIPEDA. Failure to comply could result in the organization being found guilty of an offence punishable on summary conviction or an indictable offence.

> 7. (3) For the purpose of clause 4.3 of Schedule 1, and despite the note that accompanies that clause, an organization may disclose personal information without the knowledge or consent of the individual only if the disclosure is
>
> . . .
>
> (c) required to comply with a subpoena or warrant issued or an order made by a court, person or body with jurisdiction to compel the production of information, or to comply with rules of court relating to the production of records;
>
> . . .
>
> 8. (8) Despite clause 4.5 of Schedule 1, an organization that has personal information that is the subject of a request shall retain the information for as long as is necessary to allow the individual to exhaust any recourse under this Part that they may have.
>
> . . .
>
> 28. Every person who knowingly contravenes subsection 8(8) or 27.1(1) or who obstructs the Commissioner or the Commissioner's delegate in the investigation of a complaint or in conducting an audit is guilty of
>
> (a) an offence punishable on summary conviction and liable to a fine not exceeding $10,000; or
>
> (b) an indictable offence and liable to a fine not exceeding $100,000.

38 Privacy rights are significant and they must be protected. In order to achieve the appropriate balance between privacy rights and the public interest in favour of disclosure, PIPEDA provides protection over personal information that is collected, held and used by organizations and allows disclosure of such information only in certain circumstances, enumerated in subsection 7(3). The purpose of

PIPEDA, which is the establishment of rules governing the "collection, use and disclosure of personal information", is articulated in section 3, which specifically states,

> 3. The purpose of this Part is to establish, in an era in which technology increasingly facilitates the circulation and exchange of information, rules to govern the collection, use and disclosure of personal information in a manner that recognizes the right of privacy of individuals with respect to their personal information and the need of organizations to collect, use or disclose personal information for purposes that a reasonable person would consider appropriate in the circumstances.

39 The delicate balance between privacy interests and public interest has always been a concern of the court where confidential information is sought to be revealed. Although PIPEDA had not been enacted at the time of the Glaxo decision, Stone J.A. nonetheless noted at paragraph 62:

> I am not persuaded that this is a sufficient justification for refusing to disclose the identity of the importers in the present case. While section 107 implies that information collected pursuant to the Act will be treated as confidential, section 108 indicates that it is susceptible to disclosure in certain situations. I am thus doubtful that importers have a high expectation of confidentiality regarding the information which they furnish to customs officials. More important, I am sceptical about the expectation and degree of confidentiality associated with the nature of the information which the appellant seeks. As the House of Lords observed in Norwich Pharmacal, supra, the names of the importers are likely to pass through many hands before reaching those of customs officials. It is therefore not reasonable to regard the identity of the importers as particularly sensitive information. In my opinion, in the circumstances of this case the public interest in ensuring that the appellant is able to pursue in the courts those who have allegedly violated its patent rights outweighs the public interest in maintaining the confidentiality of the importers' names.

He also approved, at paragraph 26, of the statement of Viscount Dilhorne in Norwich as follows:

> Subject to the public interest in protecting the confidentiality of information given to Customs, in my opinion it is clearly in the public interest and right for protection of patent holders, where the validity of the patent is accepted and the infringement of it not disputed, that they should be able to obtain by discovery the names and addresses of the wrongdoers from someone involved but not a party to the wrongdoing.

40 The reasoning in Glaxo and Norwich is compelling. Intellectual property laws originated in order to protect the promulgation of ideas. Copyright law provides incentives for innovators–artists, musicians, inventors, writers, performers and marketers–to create. It is designed to ensure that ideas are expressed and developed instead of remaining dormant. Individuals need to be encouraged to develop their own talents and personal expression of artistic ideas, including music. If they are robbed of the fruits of their efforts, their incentive to express their ideas in tangible form is diminished.

41 Modern technology such as the Internet has provided extraordinary benefits for society, which include faster and more efficient means of communication to wider audiences. This technology must not be allowed to obliterate those personal property rights which society has deemed important. Although privacy concerns must also be considered, it seems to me that they must yield to public concerns for the protection of intellectual property rights in situations where infringement threatens to erode those rights.

42 Thus, in my view, in cases where plaintiffs show that they have a bona fide claim that unknown persons are infringing their copyright, they have a right to have the identity revealed for the purpose of bringing action. However, caution must be exercised by the courts in ordering such disclosure, to make sure that privacy rights are invaded in the most minimal way.

43 If there is a lengthy delay between the time the request for the identities is made by the plaintiffs and the time the plaintiffs collect their information, there is a risk that the information as to identity may be inaccurate. Apparently this is because an IP address may not be associated with the same individual for long periods of time. Therefore it is possible that the privacy rights of innocent persons would be infringed and legal proceedings against such persons would be without justification. Thus the greatest care should be taken to avoid delay between the investigation and the request for information. Failure to take such care might well justify a court in refusing to make a disclosure order.

44 Also, as the intervener, Canadian Internet Policy and Public Interest Clinic, pointed out, plaintiffs should be careful not to extract private information unrelated to copyright infringement, in their investigation. If private information irrelevant to the copyright issues is extracted, and disclosure of the user's identity is made, the recipient of the information may then be in possession of highly confidential information about the user. If this information is unrelated to copyright infringement, this would be an unjustified intrusion into the rights of the user and might well amount to a breach of PIPEDA by the ISPs, leaving them open to prosecution. Thus in situations where the plaintiffs have failed in their investigation to limit the acquisition of information to the copyright infringement issues, a court might well be justified in declining to grant an order for disclosure of the user's identity.

45 In any event, if a disclosure order is granted, specific directions should be given as to the type of information disclosed and the manner in which it can be used. In addition, it must be said that where there exists evidence of copyright infringement, privacy concerns may be met if the court orders that the user only be identified by initials, or makes a confidentiality order.

. . .

Chapter 10

TECHNOLOGICAL PROTECTION MEASURES

1. Introduction and Background

A technological protection measure (TPM) or so-called "digital lock" is a technological means by which the access to or use of digital content is controlled. Common examples include password protections, pay walls and cryptography.

The concern with protecting TPMs as part of a digital copyright strategy traces back to a 1995 US government White Paper (Intellectual Property and the National Information Infrastructure, 1995), which recommended legislation to outlaw technologies having the primary purpose or effect of bypassing TPMs. The White Paper explained that, in the digital environment, copyright owners would increasingly turn to technology to protect their rights. The suggested prohibition on TPM-circumventing devices was thus "intended to assist copyright owners in the protection of their works" (White Paper, p. 231) and was proposed as an amendment to the U.S. Copyright Act. A draft treaty mirroring its proposals was distributed amongst members of the WIPO for consideration at the international diplomatic conference in Geneva in 1996. WIPO negotiations culminated in the WIPO Copyright Treaty (WCT) and the WIPO Performances and Phonograms Treaty (WPPT). Article 11 of the WCT, which is mirrored in article 18 of the WPPT states:

> Contracting Parties shall provide adequate legal protection and effective legal remedies against the circumvention of effective technological measures that are used by authors in connection with the exercise of their rights under this Treaty or the Berne Convention and that restrict acts, in respect of their works, which are not authorized by the authors concerned or permitted by law.

The United States enacted strong anti-circumvention laws (17 U.S.C. §1201) with the passage of the *Digital Millennium Copyright Act* in 1998. The European Union followed the United States' lead with *Directive 2001/29/EC on the Harmonisation of Certain Aspects of Copyright and Related Rights in the Information Society*).

Canada's first attempt to introduce anti-circumvention provisions was with Section 34.02(1) of Bill C-60:

> **34.02** (1) An owner of copyright in a work, a performer's performance fixed in a sound recording or a sound recording…are, subject to this Act, entitled to all remedies…that are or may be conferred by law for the infringement of a right against a person who, without the consent of the copyright owner…, circumvents, removes or in any way renders ineffective a technological measure

protecting any material form of the work, the performer's performance or the sound recording *for the purpose of an act that is an infringement* of the copyright in it or the moral rights in respect of it or for the purpose of making a copy referred to in subsection 80(1). [Emphasis added].

The effect of this provision would have been to make it an infringement to circumvent a TPM, but only if done for the purpose of an act constituting infringement of the copyright in the underlying work.

The new protections for TPMs enacted with the passage of the *Copyright Modernization Act* more closely resemble those found in the DMCA. Liability for circumvention is not tied to copyright infringing purposes in relation to the protected work; circumvention of an access-control is a separate and free-standing cause of action. The new Act prohibits, in addition to circumvention activities and services, devices or technologies that permit the circumvention of access- or use-control TPMs.

2.   New Protections for TPMs and RMI

The following is the Government Fact Sheet on the new digital lock provisions (http://balancedcopyright.gc.ca/eic/site/crp-prda.nsf/eng/rp01182.html)

What the *Copyright Modernization Act* Says About Digital Locks

The *Copyright Modernization Act* introduces legal protection for digital locks. These locks are sometimes used by copyright owners to prevent their works from being accessed or copied without permission. Examples include passwords, encryption software and access codes.

Key provisions include:

Prohibiting the hacking of digital locks: The Bill makes it illegal to circumvent or bypass technologies, such as password protection, used to prevent unauthorized access to copyrighted material. The manufacture, sale and distribution of devices that are primarily designed to hack digital locks, as well as the offering of services to do so, will also be prohibited and subject to civil remedies and criminal penalties.

Allowing specific exceptions in the public interest: The Bill includes a number of specific instances where hacking digital locks is permitted.

Digital locks can be hacked for the following purposes:

- law enforcement and national security activities;
- reverse engineering for software compatibility;
- security testing of systems;
- encryption research;
- personal information protection;
- temporary recordings made by broadcast undertakings;
- access for persons with perceptual disabilities; and
- unlocking a wireless device.

The Government will also retain the ability, through regulatory power, to provide new exceptions to the digital lock prohibition to ensure access where the public interest might be served or where anti-competitive behaviour arises.

Permitting unlocking of mobile devices: Consumers will be able to unlock their wireless devices, such as cell phones, in order to connect to another wireless network — to switch service providers, for example. However, this will not override any contractual or other agreement that may exist between consumers and their service providers.

Targeting those who promote and profit from infringement: The Bill prohibits the sale or import of tools and services that enable hacking. Civil and criminal penalties related to digital locks focus on those who profit from the manufacture and sale of hacking tools and services. However, the Bill exempts from statutory damages those who hack digital locks for non-commercial purposes. Statutory damages are pre-established damages used in civil litigation.

Prohibiting the removal of rights management information (RMI): RMI is the information often included in digital content that identifies the copyright owner and the terms and conditions of its use. The Bill prohibits its removal. RMI, such as digital watermarks, can help copyright owners track and prove illegal activity. It can also help consumers by giving them confidence in the authenticity of a work and certainty as to the conditions for its use.

The Bill recognizes that certain protections, such as restricted content on news websites or locked video games, are important tools for copyright owners to protect their digital works and are often an important part of online and digital business models.

Introducing legal protections for digital locks brings Canada in line with international partners, as it is one of the requirements of the World Intellectual Property Organization Internet treaties.

While the music industry has moved away from digital locks on CDs, they continue to be used in many online music services. Software producers, the video game industry and movie distributors also continue to use digital locks to protect their investments. Canadian jobs depend on their ability to make a return on their investment. Businesses that choose to use digital locks as part of their business models will have the protection of the law.

(Date modified: 2011-09-28)

The new protections for TPMs and RMI are enacted in the following provisions. Limited exceptions to specific circumvention prohibitions are found in ss. 41.11-41.18.

Technological Protection Measures and Rights Management Information

41. The following definitions apply in this section and in sections 41.1 to 41.21.

"circumvent"

« contourner »

　　"circumvent" means,

(*a*) in respect of a technological protection measure within the meaning of paragraph (*a*) of the definition *"technological protection measure"*, to descramble a scrambled work or decrypt an encrypted work or to otherwise avoid, bypass, remove, deactivate or impair the technological protection measure, unless it is done with the authority of the copyright owner; and

(*b*) in respect of a technological protection measure within the meaning of paragraph (*b*) of the definition *"technological protection measure"*, to avoid, bypass, remove, deactivate or impair the technological protection measure.

"technological protection measure"

« mesure technique de protection »

"technological protection measure" means any effective technology, device or component that, in the ordinary course of its operation,

(*a*) controls access to a work, to a performer's performance fixed in a sound recording or to a sound recording and whose use is authorized by the copyright owner; or

(*b*) restricts the doing — with respect to a work, to a performer's performance fixed in a sound recording or to a sound recording — of any act referred to in section 3, 15 or 18 and any act for which remuneration is payable under section 19.

41.1 (1) No person shall

(*a*) circumvent a technological protection measure within the meaning of paragraph (*a*) of the definition *"technological protection measure"* in section 41;

(*b*) offer services to the public or provide services if

(i) the services are offered or provided primarily for the purposes of circumventing a technological protection measure,

(ii) the uses or purposes of those services are not commercially significant other than when they are offered or provided for the purposes of circumventing a technological protection measure, or

(iii) the person markets those services as being for the purposes of circumventing a technological protection measure or acts in concert with another person in order to market those services as being for those purposes; or

(*c*) manufacture, import, distribute, offer for sale or rental or provide — including by selling or renting — any technology, device or component if

(i) the technology, device or component is designed or produced primarily for the purposes of circumventing a technological protection measure,

(ii) the uses or purposes of the technology, device or component are not commercially significant other than when it is used for the purposes of circumventing a technological protection measure, or

(iii) the person markets the technology, device or component as being for the purposes of circumventing a technological protection measure or acts in concert with another person in order to market the technology, device or component as being for those purposes.

(2) The owner of the copyright in a work, a performer's performance fixed in a sound recording or a sound recording in respect of which paragraph (1) (*a*) has been contravened is, subject to this Act and any regulations made under section 41.21, entitled to all remedies — by way of injunction, damages, accounts, delivery up and otherwise — that are or may be conferred by law for the infringement of copyright against the person who contravened that paragraph.

No statutory damages

(3) The owner of the copyright in a work, a performer's performance fixed in a sound recording or a sound recording in respect of which paragraph (1)(*a*) has been contravened may not elect under section 38.1 to recover statutory damages from an individual who contravened that paragraph only for his or her own private purposes.

Services, technology, device or component

(4) Every owner of the copyright in a work, a performer's performance fixed in a sound recording or a sound recording in respect of which a technological protection measure has been or could be circumvented as a result of the contravention of paragraph (1)(*b*) or (*c*) is, subject to this Act and any regulations made under section 41.21, entitled to all remedies — by way of injunction, damages, accounts, delivery up and otherwise — that are or may be conferred by law for the infringement of copyright against the person who contravened paragraph (1)(*b*) or (*c*).

. . .

Prohibition — rights management information

41.22 (1) No person shall knowingly remove or alter any rights management information in electronic form without the consent of the owner of the copyright in the work, the performer's performance or the sound recording, if the person knows or should have known that the removal or alteration will facilitate or conceal any infringement of the owner's copyright or adversely affect the owner's right to remuneration under section 19.

Removal or alteration of rights management information

(2) The owner of the copyright in a work, a performer's performance fixed in a sound recording or a sound recording is, subject to this Act, entitled to all remedies — by way of injunction, damages, accounts, delivery up and otherwise — that are or may be conferred by law for the infringement of copyright against a person who contravenes subsection (1).

Subsequent acts

(3) The copyright owner referred to in subsection (2) has the same remedies against a person who, without the owner's consent, knowingly does any of the following acts with respect to any material form of the work, the performer's performance fixed in a sound recording or the sound recording and knows or should have known that the rights management information has been removed or altered in a way that would give rise to a remedy under that subsection:

(*a*) sells it or rents it out;

(*b*) distributes it to an extent that the copyright owner is prejudicially affected;

(*c*) by way of trade, distributes it, exposes or offers it for sale or rental or exhibits it in public;

(*d*) imports it into Canada for the purpose of doing anything referred to in any of paragraphs (*a*) to (*c*); or

(*e*) communicates it to the public by telecommunication.

Definition of *"rights management information"*

(4) In this section, *"rights management information"* means information that

(*a*) is attached to or embodied in a copy of a work, a performer's performance fixed in a sound recording or a sound recording, or appears in connection with its communication to the public by telecommunication; and

(*b*) identifies or permits the identification of the work or its author, the performance or its performer, the sound recording or its maker or the holder of any rights in the work, the performance or the sound recording, or concerns the terms or conditions of the work's, performance's or sound recording's use.

---

3. TPMs and User Rights

Perhaps the greatest controversy around the introduction of the new protections for TPMs has been the interaction between the anti-circumvention provisions and the exemptions or defences available to users, which have been recognized as "user rights" that are integral to the *Copyright Act*. Because circumvention prohibitions are not tied to copyright infringement, it appears that fair dealing and other user exemptions offer no defence to circumvention liability. The use of TPMs can therefore render it unlawful to access the underlying protected work for fair dealing purposes, as well as to supply services or devices to facilitate fair dealing. Similarly, the user exceptions introduced by the *Copyright Modernization Act* are in most cases expressly subject to the condition that the user "did not circumvent, as defined in section 41, a technological protection measure, as defined in that section, or cause one to be circumvented" (see ss. 29.22(1)(c), 29.23(1)(b), 29.24(1)(c)).

The Act does contemplate, in s. 41.21(2)(a), the possibility of regulations by the Governor in Council prescribing circumstances in which the prohibition against circumvention will not apply, having regard to factors that include, most notably "(iii) "whether not being permitted to circumvent a technological protection measure that is subject to that paragraph could adversely affect criticism, review, news reporting, commentary, parody, satire, teaching, scholarship or research that could be made or done in respect of the work, the performer's performance fixed in a sound recording or the sound recording." It remains to be seen if or how this regulatory power will be exercised.

The need to safeguard permitted acts in the face of TPM protection has been a cause of concern internationally. Article 6(4) of the European *Information Society Directive* requires Member States "in the absence of voluntary measures taken by right holders" to "take appropriate measures to ensure that right holders make available to the beneficiary of an exception or limitation provided for in national law...the means of benefiting from that exception or limitation." This has produced various legislative and regulatory responses amongst Member States — ranging a right for mediation or arbitration to recourse to the courts or access to new administrative tribunals or complaints procedures — for would-be users unable to benefit from copyright exceptions.

The US DMCA authorizes the Librarian of Congress to assess the impact of the circumvention ban on traditional fair use practices and, if necessary, to issue rules exempting certain categories of works from the ban (§1201 (a)(1)(B)-(D)). The triennial rule-making proceeding yields temporary, narrowly crafted exemptions such as the following exempted class designated in 2012:

> "Motion pictures, as defined in 17 U.S.C. 101, on DVDs that are lawfully made and acquired and that are protected by the Content Scrambling System, where the person engaging in circumvention believes and has reasonable grounds for believing that circumvention is necessary because reasonably available alternatives, such as noncircumventing methods or using screen capture software as provided for in alternative exemptions, are not able to produce the level of high-quality content required to achieve the desired criticism or comment on such motion pictures, and where circumvention is undertaken solely in order to make use of short portions of the motion pictures for the purpose of criticism or comment in the following instances: (i) In noncommercial videos; (ii) in documentary films; (iii) in nonfiction multimedia ebooks offering film analysis; and (iv) for educational purposes in film studies or other courses requiring close analysis of film and media excerpts, by college and university faculty, college and university students, and kindergarten through twelfth grade educators. For purposes of this

exemption, "noncommercial videos" includes videos created pursuant to a paid commission, provided that the commissioning entity's use is noncommercial."

The US DMCA states in §1201(c)(1), "Nothing in this section shall affect rights, remedies, limitations, or defenses to copyright infringement, including fair use, in this title." However, as interpreted in the *Universal* case below, this is not a positive protection of fair use against restrictions imposed by TPMs; it simply clarifies that circumvention liability is not concerned with the use made of the work behind the "digital wall," whether fair or otherwise. The defendant challenged the constitutionality of the DMCA, arguing *inter alia* that it unduly obstructs the "fair use" of copyright materials. The US District Court held that fair use was not a defence to violations of the DMCA and issued injunctions. That ruling was upheld on appeal in the following judgment.

Universal City Studios, Inc. v. Corley, 273 F.3d 429 (2d Cir., 2001)

U.S. Court of Appeals Second Circuit
November 28, 2001

Newman, J.

When the Framers of the First Amendment prohibited Congress from making any law "abridging the freedom of speech," they were not thinking about computers, computer programs, or the Internet. But neither were they thinking about radio, television, or movies. Just as the inventions at the beginning and middle of the 20th century presented new First Amendment issues, so does the cyber revolution at the end of that century. This appeal raises significant First Amendment issues concerning one aspect of computer technology — encryption to protect materials in digital form from unauthorized access. The appeal challenges the constitutionality of the Digital Millennium Copyright Act ("DMCA"), 17 U.S.C. §1201 *et seq.* (Supp. V 1999) and the validity of an injunction entered to enforce the DMCA.

Defendant-Appellant Eric C. Corley and his company, 2600 Enterprises, Inc., (collectively "Corley," "the Defendants," or "the Appellants") appeal from the amended final judgment of the United States District Court for the Southern District of New York (Lewis A. Kaplan, District Judge), entered August 23, 2000, enjoining them from various actions concerning a decryption program known as "DeCSS." *Universal City Studios, Inc. v. Reimerdes*, 111 F. Supp. 2d 346 (S.D.N.Y. 2000) ("*Universal II*"). The injunction primarily bars the Appellants from posting DeCSS on their web site and from knowingly linking their web site to any other web site on which DeCSS is posted. *Id.* at 346-47. We affirm.

Introduction

Understanding the pending appeal and the issues it raises requires some familiarity with technical aspects of computers and computer software, especially software called "digital versatile disks" or "DVDs," which are optical media storage devices currently designed to contain movies. ...This appeal concerns the anti-trafficking provisions of the DMCA, which Congress enacted in 1998 to strengthen copyright protection in the digital age. Fearful that the ease with which pirates could copy and distribute a copyrightable work in digital form was overwhelming the capacity of conventional copyright enforcement to find and enjoin unlawfully copied material, Congress sought to combat copyright piracy in its earlier stages, before the work was even copied. The DMCA therefore backed with legal sanctions the efforts of copyright owners to protect their works from piracy behind digital walls such as encryption codes or password protections. In so doing, Congress targeted not only those pirates who would *circumvent* these digital walls (the "anti-circumvention provisions," contained in 17 U.S.C. §1201(a)(1)), but also anyone who would *traffic* in a technology primarily designed to circumvent a digital wall (the "anti-trafficking provisions," contained in 17 U.S.C. §1201(a)(2), (b)(1)).

Corley publishes a print magazine and maintains an affiliated web site geared towards "hackers," a digital-era term often applied to those interested in techniques for circumventing protections of computers and computer data from unauthorized access. The so-called hacker community includes serious computer-science scholars conducting research on protection techniques, computer buffs intrigued by the challenge of trying to circumvent access-limiting devices or perhaps hoping to promote security by exposing flaws in protection techniques, mischief-makers interested in disrupting computer operations, and thieves, including copyright infringers who want to acquire copyrighted material (for personal use or resale) without paying for it.

In November 1999, Corley posted a copy of the decryption computer program "DeCSS" on his web site, http://www.2600.com ("2600.com"). DeCSS is designed to circumvent "CSS," the encryption technology that motion picture studios place on DVDs to prevent the unauthorized viewing and copying of motion pictures. Corley also posted on his web site links to other web sites where DeCSS could be found.

Plaintiffs-Appellees are eight motion picture studios that brought an action in the Southern District of New York seeking injunctive relief against Corley under the DMCA. Following a full non-jury trial, the District Court entered a permanent injunction barring Corley from posting DeCSS on his web site or from knowingly linking via a hyperlink to any other web site containing DeCSS. *Universal II*, 111 F. Supp. 2d at 346-47. The District Court rejected Corley's constitutional attacks on the statute and the injunction. *Universal I*, 111 F. Supp. 2d at 325-45.

Corley renews his constitutional challenges on appeal. Specifically, he argues primarily that: (1) the DMCA oversteps limits in the Copyright Clause on the duration of copyright protection; (2) the DMCA as applied to his dissemination of DeCSS violates the First Amendment because computer code is "speech" entitled to full First Amendment protection and the DMCA fails to survive the exacting scrutiny accorded statutes that regulate "speech"; and (3) the DMCA violates the First Amendment and the Copyright Clause by unduly obstructing the "fair use" of copyrighted materials. Corley also argues that the statute is susceptible to, and should therefore be given, a narrow interpretation that avoids alleged constitutional objections.

Background

For decades, motion picture studios have made movies available for viewing at home in what is called "analog" format. Movies in this format are placed on videotapes, which can be played on a video cassette recorder ("VCR"). In the early 1990s, the studios began to consider the possibility of distributing movies in digital form as well. Movies in digital form are placed on disks, known as DVDs, which can be played on a DVD player (either a stand-alone device or a component of a computer). DVDs offer advantages over analog tapes, such as improved visual and audio quality, larger data capacity, and greater durability. However, the improved quality of a movie in a digital format brings with it the risk that a virtually perfect copy, *i.e.*, one that will not lose perceptible quality in the copying process, can be readily made at the click of a computer control and instantly distributed to countless recipients throughout the world over the Internet. This case arises out of the movie industry's efforts to respond to this risk by invoking the anti-trafficking provisions of the DMCA.

I.   CSS

The movie studios were reluctant to release movies in digital form until they were confident they had in place adequate safeguards against piracy of their copyrighted movies. The studios took several steps to minimize the piracy threat. First, they settled on the DVD as the standard digital medium for home distribution of movies. The studios then sought an encryption scheme to protect movies on DVDs. They enlisted the help of members of the consumer electronics and computer industries, who in mid-1996 developed the Content Scramble System ("CSS"). CSS is an encryption scheme that employs an algorithm configured by a set of "keys" to encrypt a DVD's contents. The algorithm is a type of mathematical formula for transforming the contents of the movie file into gibberish; the "keys" are in actuality strings of 0's and 1's that serve as values for the mathematical formula. Decryption in the case of CSS requires a set of "player keys" contained in compliant DVD players, as well as an understanding of the CSS encryption algorithm. Without the player keys and the algorithm, a DVD player cannot access the contents of a DVD. With the player keys and the algorithm, a DVD player can display the movie on a television or a computer screen, but does not give a viewer the ability to use the copy function of the computer to copy the movie or to manipulate the digital content of the DVD.

The studios developed a licensing scheme for distributing the technology to manufacturers of DVD players. Player keys and other information necessary to the CSS scheme were given to manufacturers of DVD players for an administrative fee. In exchange for the licenses, manufacturers were obliged to keep the player keys confidential. Manufacturers were also required in the licensing agreement to prevent the transmission of "CSS data" (a term undefined in the licensing agreement) from a DVD drive to any "internal recording device," including, presumably, a computer hard drive.

With encryption technology and licensing agreements in hand, the studios began releasing movies on DVDs in 1997, and DVDs quickly gained in popularity, becoming a significant source of studio revenue. In 1998, the studios secured added protection against DVD piracy when Congress passed the DMCA, which prohibits the development or use of technology designed to circumvent a technological protection measure, such as CSS. The pertinent provisions of the DMCA are examined in greater detail below.

II. DeCSS

In September 1999, Jon Johansen, a Norwegian teenager, collaborating with two unidentified individuals he met on the Internet, reverse — engineered a licensed DVD player designed to operate on the Microsoft operating system, and culled from it the player keys and other information necessary to decrypt CSS. The record suggests that Johansen was trying to develop a DVD player operable on Linux, an alternative operating system that did not support any licensed DVD players at that time. In order to accomplish this task, Johansen wrote a decryption program executable on Microsoft's operating system. That program was called, appropriately enough, "DeCSS."

If a user runs the DeCSS program (for example, by clicking on the DeCSS icon on a Microsoft operating system platform) with a DVD in the computer's disk drive, DeCSS will decrypt the DVD's CSS protection, allowing the user to copy the DVD's files and place the copy on the user's hard drive. The result is a very large computer file that can be played on a non — CSS — compliant player and copied, manipulated, and transferred just like any other computer file. DeCSS comes complete with a fairly user — friendly interface that helps the user select from among the DVD's files and assign the decrypted file a location on the user's hard drive. The quality of the resulting decrypted movie is "virtually identical" to that of the encrypted movie on the DVD. *Universal I*, 111 F. Supp. 2d at 308, 313. And the file produced by DeCSS, while large, can be compressed to a manageable size by a compression software called "DivX," available at no cost on the Internet. This compressed file can be copied onto a DVD, or transferred over the Internet (with some patience).

Johansen posted the executable object code, but not the source code, for DeCSS on his web site…. Within months of its appearance in executable form on Johansen's web site, DeCSS was widely available on the Internet, in both object code and various forms of source code.

In November 1999, Corley wrote and placed on his web site, 2600.com, an article about the DeCSS phenomenon. His web site is an auxiliary to the print magazine, *2600: The Hacker Quarterly*, which Corley has been publishing since 1984. As the name suggests, the magazine is designed for "hackers," as is the web site. While the magazine and the web site cover some issues of general interest to computer users — such as threats to online privacy — the focus of the publications is on the vulnerability of computer security systems, and more specifically, how to exploit that vulnerability in order to circumvent the security systems. Representative articles explain how to steal an Internet domain name and how to break into the computer systems at Federal Express. *Universal I*, 111 F. Supp. 2d at 308 — 09.

Corley's article about DeCSS detailed how CSS was cracked, and described the movie industry's efforts to shut down web sites posting DeCSS. It also explained that DeCSS could be used to copy DVDs. At the end of the article, the Defendants posted copies of the object and source code of DeCSS. In Corley's words, he added the code to the story because "in a journalistic world,...[y]ou have to show your evidence... and particularly in the magazine that I work for, people want to see specifically what it is that we are referring to," including "what evidence... we have" that there is in fact technology that circumvents CSS. Trial Tr. at 823. Writing about DeCSS without including the DeCSS code would have been, to Corley, "analogous to printing a story about a picture and not printing the picture." *Id.* at 825. Corley also added to the article links that he explained would take the reader to other web sites where DeCSS could be found. *Id.* at 791, 826, 827, 848.

2600.com was only one of hundreds of web sites that began posting DeCSS near the end of 1999. The movie industry tried to stem the tide by sending cease-and-desist letters to many of these sites. These efforts met with only partial success; a number of sites refused to remove DeCSS. In January 2000, the studios filed this lawsuit.

III. The DMCA

The DMCA was enacted in 1998 to implement the World Intellectual Property Organization Copyright Treaty ("WIPO Treaty"), which requires contracting parties to "provide adequate legal protection and effective legal remedies against the circumvention of effective technological measures that are used by authors in connection with the exercise of their rights under this Treaty or the Berne Convention and that restrict acts, in respect of their works, which are not authorized by the authors concerned or permitted by law." WIPO Treaty, Apr. 12, 1997, art. 11, S. Treaty Doc. No. 10517 (1997), available at 1997 WL 447232. Even before the treaty, Congress had been devoting attention to the problems faced by copyright enforcement in the digital age. Hearings on the topic have spanned several years. ...This legislative effort resulted in the DMCA.

The Act contains three provisions targeted at the circumvention of technological protections. The first is subsection 1201(a)(1)(A), the anti-circumvention provision. This provision prohibits a person from "circumvent[ing] a technological measure that effectively controls access to a work protected under [Title

17, governing copyright]." The Librarian of Congress is required to promulgate regulations every three years exempting from this subsection individuals who would otherwise be "adversely affected" in "their ability to make noninfringing uses." 17 U.S.C. §1201(a)(1)(B)-(E).

The second and third provisions are subsections 1201(a)(2) and 1201(b)(1), the "anti-trafficking provisions." Subsection 1201(a)(2), the provision at issue in this case, provides:

No person shall manufacture, import, offer to the public, provide, or otherwise traffic in any technology, product, service, device, component, or part thereof, that —

> (A) is primarily designed or produced for the purpose of circumventing a techno-logical measure that effectively controls access to a work protected under this title;
>
> (B) has only limited commercially significant purpose or use other than to circum-vent a technological measure that effectively controls access to a work protected under this title; or
>
> (C) is marketed by that person or another acting in concert with that person with that person's knowledge for use in circumventing a technological measure <273 F.3d 441> that effectively controls access to a work protected under this title. *Id.* §1201(a)(2). To "circumvent a technological measure" is defined, in pertinent part, as "to descramble a scrambled work... or otherwise to... bypass...a techno-logical measure, without the authority of the copyright owner."

Id. §1201(a)(3)(A).

Subsection 1201(b)(1) is similar to subsection 1201(a)(2), except that subsection 1201(a)(2) covers those who traffic in technology that can circumvent "a tech-nological measure *that effectively controls access* to a work protected under" Title 17, whereas subsection 1201(b)(1) covers those who traffic in technology that can circumvent "protection afforded by a technological measure *that effec-tively protects a right of a copyright owner* under" Title 17. *Id.* §1201(a)(2), (b) (1) (emphases added). In other words, although both subsections prohibit traf-ficking in a circumvention technology, the focus of subsection 1201(a)(2) is cir-cumvention of technologies designed to *prevent access* to a work, and the focus of subsection 1201(b)(1) is circumvention of technologies designed to *permit access* to a work but *prevent copying* of the work or some other act that infringes a copyright. *See* S. Rep. No. 105-190, at 11-12 (1998). Subsection 1201(a)(1) differs from both of these anti-trafficking subsections in that it targets the use of a circumvention technology, not the trafficking in such a technology.

The DMCA contains exceptions for schools and libraries that want to use circumvention technologies to determine whether to purchase a copyrighted product, 17 U.S.C. §1201(d); individuals using circumvention technology "for the sole purpose" of trying to achieve "interoperability" of computer programs through reverse-engineering, *id.* §1201(f); encryption research aimed at identi-fying flaws in encryption technology, if the research is conducted to advance the state of knowledge in the field, *id.* §1201(g); and several other exceptions not relevant here.

The DMCA creates civil remedies, *id.* §1203, and criminal sanctions, *id.* §1204. It specifically authorizes a court to "grant temporary and permanent injunctions on such terms as it deems reasonable to prevent or restrain a violation." *Id.* §1203(b)(1).

IV. Procedural History

Invoking subsection 1203(b)(1), the Plaintiffs sought an injunction against the Defendants, alleging that the Defendants violated the anti-trafficking provisions of the statute. On January 20, 2000, after a hearing, the District Court issued a preliminary injunction barring the Defendants from posting DeCSS. *Universal City Studios, Inc. v. Reimerdes*, 82 F. Supp. 2d 211 (S.D.N.Y. 2000).

The Defendants complied with the preliminary injunction, but continued to post links to other web sites carrying DeCSS, an action they termed "electronic civil disobedience." *Universal I*, 111 F. Supp. 2d at 303, 312. Under the heading "Stop the MPAA [(Motion Picture Association of America)]," Corley urged other web sites to post DeCSS lest "we . . . be forced into submission." *Id.* at 313.

The Plaintiffs then sought a permanent injunction barring the Defendants from both posting DeCSS and linking to sites containing DeCSS. After a trial on the merits, the Court issued a comprehensive opinion, *Universal I*, and granted a permanent injunction, *Universal II*.

The Court explained that the Defendants' posting of DeCSS on their web site clearly falls within section 1201(a)(2)(A) of the DMCA, rejecting as spurious their claim that CSS is not a technological measure that "effectively controls access to a work" because it was so easily penetrated by Johansen, *Universal I*, 111 F. Supp. 2d at 318, and as irrelevant their contention that DeCSS was designed to create a Linux — platform DVD player, *id.* at 319. The Court also held that the Defendants cannot avail themselves of any of the DMCA's exceptions, *id.* at 319 — 22, and that the alleged importance of DeCSS to certain fair uses of encrypted copyrighted material was immaterial to their statutory liability, *id.* at 322 — 24. The Court went on to hold that when the Defendants "proclaimed on their own site that DeCSS could be had by clicking on the hyperlinks" on their site, they were trafficking in DeCSS, and therefore liable for their linking as well as their posting. *Id.* at 325.

Turning to the Defendants' numerous constitutional arguments, the Court first held that computer code like DeCSS is "speech" that is "protected"(in the sense of "covered") by the First Amendment, *id.* at 327, but that because the DMCA is targeting the "functional" aspect of that speech, *id.* at 328-29, it is "content neutral," *id.* at 329, and the intermediate scrutiny of *United States v. O'Brien*, 391 U.S. 367, 377 (1968), applies, *Universal I*, 111 F. Supp. 2d at 329-30. The Court concluded that the DMCA survives this scrutiny, *id.* at 330-33, and also rejected prior restraint, overbreadth, and vagueness challenges, *id.* at 333-39.

The Court upheld the constitutionality of the DMCA's application to linking on similar grounds: linking, the Court concluded, is "speech," but the DMCA is content — neutral, targeting only the functional components of that speech. Therefore, its application to linking is also evaluated under *O'Brien*, and, thus evaluated, survives intermediate scrutiny. However, the Court concluded that a blanket proscription on linking would create a risk of chilling legitimate linking on the web. The Court therefore crafted a restrictive test for linking liability (discussed below) that it believed sufficiently mitigated that risk. The Court then found its test satisfied in this case. *Id.* at 339 — 41.

Finally, the Court concluded that an injunction was highly appropriate in this case. The Court observed that DeCSS was harming the Plaintiffs, not only because they were now exposed to the possibility of piracy and therefore were obliged to develop costly new safeguards for DVDs, but also because, even if there was only indirect evidence that DeCSS availability actually facilitated DVD piracy, the threat of piracy was very real, particularly as Internet trans-mission speeds continue to increase. *Id.* at 314 — 15, 342. Acknowledging that DeCSS was (and still is) widely available on the Internet, the Court expressed confidence in

the likelihood . . . that this decision will serve notice on others that "the strong right arm of equity" may be brought to bear against them absent a change in their conduct and thus contribute to a climate of appropriate respect for intellec-tual property rights in an age in which the excitement of ready access to untold quantities of information has blurred in some minds the fact that taking what is not yours and not freely offered to you is stealing.

The Court's injunction barred the Defendants from: "posting on any Internet web site" DeCSS; "in any other way... offering to the public, providing, or oth-erwise trafficking in DeCSS"; violating the anti — trafficking provisions of the DMCA in any other manner, and finally "knowingly linking any Internet web site operated by them to any other web site containing DeCSS, or knowingly maintaining any such link, for the purpose of disseminating DeCSS."

The Appellants have appealed from the permanent injunction. The United States has intervened in support of the constitutionality of the DMCA. We have also had the benefit of a number of *amicus curiae* briefs, supporting and opposing the District Court's judgment. After oral argument, we invited the parties to sub-mit responses to a series of specific questions, and we have received helpful responses.

Discussion

I. Narrow Construction to Avoid Constitutional Doubt

The Appellants first argue that, because their constitutional arguments are at least substantial, we should interpret the statute narrowly so as to avoid constitutional problems. They identify three different instances of alleged ambiguity in the statute that they claim provide an opportunity for such a narrow interpretation.

First, they contend that subsection 1201(c)(1), which provides that "[n]othing in this section shall affect rights, remedies, limitations or defenses to copyright infringement, including fair use, under this title," can be read to allow the circumvention of encryption technology protecting copyrighted material when the material will be put to "fair uses" exempt from copyright liability. We disagree that subsection 1201(c)(1) permits such a reading. Instead, it clearly and simply clarifies that the DMCA targets the *circumvention* of digital walls guarding copyrighted material (and trafficking in circumvention tools), but does not concern itself with the *use* of those materials after circumvention has occurred. Subsection 1201(c)(1) ensures that the DMCA is not read to prohibit the "fair use" of information just because that information was obtained in a manner made illegal by the DMCA. The Appellants' much more expansive interpretation of subsection 1201(c)(1) is not only outside the range of plausible readings of the provision, but is also clearly refuted by the statute's legislative history. *See Commodity Futures Trading Commission v. Schor*, 478 U.S. 833, 841 (1986) (constitutional doubt canon "does not give a court the prerogative to ignore the legislative will").

Second, the Appellants urge a narrow construction of the DMCA because of subsection 1201(c)(4), which provides that "[n]othing in this section shall enlarge or diminish any rights of free speech or the press for activities using consumer electronics, telecommunications, or computing products." This language is clearly precatory: Congress could not "diminish" constitutional rights of free speech even if it wished to, and the fact that Congress also expressed a reluctance to "enlarge" those rights cuts against the Appellants' effort to infer a narrowing construction of the Act from this provision.

Third, the Appellants argue that an individual who buys a DVD has the "authority of the copyright owner" to view the DVD, and therefore is exempted from the DMCA pursuant to subsection 1201(a)(3)(A) when the buyer circumvents an encryption technology in order to view the DVD on a competing platform (such as Linux). The basic flaw in this argument is that it misreads subsection 1201(a)(3)(A). That provision exempts from liability those who would "decrypt" an encrypted DVD with the authority of a copyright owner, not those who would "view" a DVD with the authority of a copyright owner. In any event, the Defendants offered no evidence that the Plaintiffs have either explicitly or implicitly authorized DVD buyers to circumvent encryption technology to support use on multiple platforms.

We conclude that the anti-trafficking and anti-circumvention provisions of the DMCA are not susceptible to the narrow interpretations urged by the Appellants. We therefore proceed to consider the Appellants' constitutional claims.

II. Constitutional Challenge Based on the Copyright Clause

In a footnote to their brief, the Appellants appear to contend that the DMCA, as construed by the District Court, exceeds the constitutional authority of Congress to grant authors copyrights for a "limited time," U.S. Const. art. I, §8, cl. 8, because it "empower[s] copyright owners to effectively secure perpetual protection by mixing public domain works with copyrighted materials, then locking both up with technological protection measures." Brief for Appellants at 42 n.30. This argument is elaborated in the *amici curiae* brief filed by Prof. Julie E. Cohen on behalf of herself and 45 other intellectual property law professors. *See also* David Nimmer, *A Riff on Fair Use in the Digital Millennium Copyright Act*, 148 U. Pa. L. Rev. 673, 712 (2000). For two reasons, the argument provides no basis for disturbing the judgment of the District Court.

First, we have repeatedly ruled that arguments presented to us only in a footnote are not entitled to appellate consideration. ...Although an *amicus* brief can be helpful in elaborating issues properly presented by the parties, it is normally not a method for injecting new issues into an appeal, at least in cases where the parties are competently represented by counsel.

Second, to whatever extent the argument might have merit at some future time in a case with a properly developed record, the argument is entirely premature and speculative at this time on this record. There is not even a claim, much less evidence, that any Plaintiff has sought to prevent copying of public domain works, or that the injunction prevents the Defendants from copying such works. As Judge Kaplan noted, the possibility that encryption would preclude access to public domain works "does not yet appear to be a problem, although it may emerge as one in the future." *Universal I*, 111 F. Supp. 2d at 338 n.245.

III. Constitutional Challenges Based on the First Amendment

A. Applicable Principles

. . .

1. *Code as Speech*

Communication does not lose constitutional protection as "speech" simply because it is expressed in the language of computer code. Mathematical formulae and musical scores are written in "code," *i.e.*, symbolic notations not comprehensible to the uninitiated, and yet both are covered by the First Amendment. ... If computer code is distinguishable from conventional speech for First Amendment purposes, it is not because it is written in an obscure language. *See Junger v. Daley*, 209 F.3d 481, 484 (6th Cir. 2000).

2. *Computer Programs as Speech*

Of course, computer code is not likely to be the language in which a work of literature is written. Instead, it is primarily the language for programs executable by a computer. These programs are essentially instructions to a computer. ... Whether computer code that gives a computer instructions is "speech" within the meaning of the First Amendment requires consideration of the scope of the Constitution's protection of speech....

. . .

Computer programs are not exempted from the category of First Amendment speech simply because their instructions require use of a computer. A recipe is no less "speech" because it calls for the use of an oven, and a musical score is no less "speech" because it specifies performance on an electric guitar. Arguably distinguishing computer programs from conventional language instructions is the fact that programs are executable on a computer. But the fact that a program has the capacity to direct the functioning of a computer does not mean that it lacks the additional capacity to convey information, and it is the conveying of information that renders instructions "speech" for purposes of the First Amendment....

3.   The Scope of First Amendment Protection for Computer Code

Having concluded that computer code conveying information is "speech" within the meaning of the First Amendment, we next consider, to a limited extent, the scope of the protection that code enjoys. As the District Court recognized, *Universal I*, 111 F. Supp. 2d at 327, the scope of protection for speech generally depends on whether the restriction is imposed because of the content of the speech. Content-based restrictions are permissible only if they serve compelling state interests and do so by the least restrictive means available.... A content-neutral restriction is permissible if it serves a substantial governmental interest, the interest is unrelated to the suppression of free expression, and the regulation is narrowly tailored, which "in this context requires... that the means chosen do not `burden substantially more speech than is necessary to further the government's legitimate interests.'" *Turner Broadcasting System, Inc. v. FCC*, 512 U.S. 622, 662 (1994)....

To determine whether regulation of computer code is content-neutral, the initial inquiry must be whether the regulated activity is "sufficiently imbued with elements of communication to fall within the scope of the First . . . Amendment[]." *Id.* at 409; *see also* *Name.Space*, 202 F.3d at 585. Computer code, as we have noted, often conveys information comprehensible to human beings, even as it also directs a computer to perform various functions. Once a speech component is identified, the inquiry then proceeds to whether the regulation is "justified without reference to the content of regulated speech." *Hill*, 530 U.S. at 720.

. . .

These realities of what code is and what its normal functions are require a First Amendment analysis that treats code as combining nonspeech and speech elements, *i.e.*, functional and expressive elements....

4.   The Scope of First Amendment Protection for Decryption Code

In considering the scope of First Amendment protection for a decryption program like DeCSS, we must recognize that the essential purpose of encryption code is to prevent unauthorized access. Owners of all property rights are entitled to prohibit access to their property by unauthorized persons. Homeowners can install locks on the doors of their houses. Custodians of valuables can place them in safes. Stores can attach to products security devices that will activate alarms if the products are taken away without purchase. These and similar security devices can be circumvented. Burglars can use skeleton keys to open door locks. Thieves can obtain the combinations to safes. Product security devices can be neutralized.

Our case concerns a security device, CSS computer code, that prevents access by unauthorized persons to DVD movies. The CSS code is embedded in the DVD movie. Access to the movie cannot be obtained unless a person has a device, a licensed DVD player, equipped with computer code capable of decrypting the CSS encryption code. In its basic function, CSS is like a lock on a homeowner's door, a combination of a safe, or a security device attached to a store's products.

DeCSS is computer code that can decrypt CSS. In its basic function, it is like a skeleton key that can open a locked door, a combination that can open a safe, or a device that can neutralize the security device attached to a store's products. DeCSS enables anyone to gain access to a DVD movie without using a DVD player.

The initial use of DeCSS to gain access to a DVD movie creates no loss to movie producers because the initial user must purchase the DVD. However, once the DVD is purchased, DeCSS enables the initial user to copy the movie in digital form and transmit it instantly in virtually limitless quantity, thereby depriving the movie producer of sales. The advent of the Internet creates the potential for instantaneous worldwide distribution of the copied material.

At first glance, one might think that Congress has as much authority to regulate the distribution of computer code to decrypt DVD movies as it has to regulate distribution of skeleton keys, combinations to safes, or devices to neutralize store product security devices. However, despite the evident legitimacy of protection against unauthorized access to DVD movies, just like any other property, regulation of decryption code like DeCSS is challenged in this case because DeCSS differs from a skeleton key in one important respect: it not only is capable of performing the function of unlocking the encrypted DVD movie, it also is a form of communication, albeit written in a language not understood by the general public. As a communication, the DeCSS code has a claim to being "speech," and as "speech," it has a claim to being protected by the First Amendment. But just as the realities of what any computer code can accomplish must inform the scope of its constitutional protection, so the capacity of a decryption program like DeCSS to accomplish unauthorized — indeed, unlawful — access to materials in which the Plaintiffs have intellectual property rights must inform and limit the scope of its First Amendment protection. *Cf. Red Lion*, 395 U.S. at 386 ("[D]ifferences in the characteristics of new media justify differences in the First Amendment standards applied to them.").

B.   First Amendment Challenge

...The validity of the posting and linking prohibitions must be considered separately.

1. *Posting*

. . .

Posting DeCSS on the Appellants' web site makes it instantly available at the click of a mouse to any person in the world with access to the Internet, and such person can then instantly transmit DeCSS to anyone else with Internet access. Although the prohibition on posting prevents the Appellants from conveying to others the speech component of DeCSS, the Appellants have not suggested, much less shown, any technique for barring them from making this instantaneous worldwide distribution of a decryption code that makes a lesser restriction on the code's speech component. It is true that the Government has alternative means of prohibiting unauthorized access to copyrighted materials. For example, it can create criminal and civil liability for those who gain unauthorized access, and thus it can be argued that the restriction on posting DeCSS is not absolutely necessary to preventing unauthorized access to copyrighted materials. But a content-neutral regulation need not employ the least restrictive means of accomplishing the governmental objective. *Id.* It need only avoid burdening "substantially more speech than is necessary to further the government's legitimate interests." *Id.* (internal quotation marks and citation omitted). The prohibition on the Defendants' posting of DeCSS satisfies that standard.

2. *Linking...*

...As they have throughout their arguments, the Appellants ignore the reality of the functional capacity of decryption computer code and hyperlinks to facilitate instantaneous unauthorized access to copyrighted materials by anyone anywhere in the world. Under the circumstances amply shown by the record, the injunction's linking prohibition validly regulates the Appellants' opportunity instantly to enable anyone anywhere to gain unauthorized access to copyrighted movies on DVDs.

IV. Constitutional Challenge Based on Claimed Restriction of Fair Use

Asserting that fair use "is rooted in and required by both the Copyright Clause and the First Amendment," Brief for Appellants at 42, the Appellants contend that the DMCA, as applied by the District Court, unconstitutionally "*eliminates* fair use" of copyrighted materials, *id.* at 41 (emphasis added). We reject this extravagant claim.

Preliminarily, we note that the Supreme Court has never held that fair use is constitutionally required, although some isolated statements in its opinions might arguably be enlisted for such a requirement. In *Stewart v. Abend*, 495 U.S. 207 (1990), cited by the Appellants, the Court merely noted that fair use "'permits courts to avoid rigid application of the copyright statute when, on occasion, it would stifle the very creativity which that law is designed to foster,'" *id.* (quoting *Iowa State University Research Foundation, Inc. v. American Broadcasting Cos.*, 621 F.2d 57, 60 (2d Cir. 1980)); see also *Harper & Row, Publishers, Inc. v. Nation Enterprises,* 471 U.S. 539, 560 (1985) (noting "the First Amendment protections already embodied in the Copyright Act's distinction between copy-rightable expression and uncopyrightable facts and ideas, and the latitude for scholarship and comment traditionally afforded by fair use"). In *Campbell v. Acuff-Rose Music, Inc.*, 510 U.S. (1994), the Court observed, "From the infancy of copyright protection, some opportunity for fair use of copyrighted materials has been thought necessary to fulfill copyright's very purpose, '[t]o promote the Progress of Science and useful Arts. . . .'" Id. at 575 (citation omitted); see generally William F. Patry, *The Fair Use Privilege in Copyright Law* 573-82 (2d ed. 1995) (questioning First Amendment protection for fair use).

We need not explore the extent to which fair use might have constitutional protection, grounded on either the First Amendment or the Copyright Clause, because whatever validity a constitutional claim might have as to an application of the DMCA that impairs fair use of copyrighted materials, such matters are far beyond the scope of this lawsuit for several reasons. In the first place, the Appellants do not claim to be making fair use of any copyrighted materials, and nothing in the injunction prohibits them from making such fair use. They are barred from trafficking in a decryption code that enables unauthorized access to copyrighted materials.

Second, as the District Court properly noted, to whatever extent the anti-trafficking provisions of the DMCA might prevent others from copying portions of DVD movies in order to make fair use of them, "the evidence as to the impact of the anti-trafficking provision[s] of the DMCA on prospective fair users is scanty and fails adequately to address the issues." *Universal I*, 111 F. Supp. 2d at 338 n.246.

Third, the Appellants have provided no support for their premise that fair use of DVD movies is constitutionally required to be made by copying the original work in its original format. Their examples of the fair uses that they believe others will be prevented from making all involve copying in a digital format those portions of a DVD movie amenable to fair use, a copying that would enable the fair user to manipulate the digitally copied portions. One example is that of a school child who wishes to copy images from a DVD movie to insert into the student's documentary film. We know of no authority for the proposition that fair use, as protected by the Copyright Act, much less the Constitution, guarantees copying by the optimum method or in the identical format of the original. Although the Appellants insisted at oral argument that they should not be relegated to a "horse and buggy" technique in making fair use of DVD movies, the DMCA does not impose even an arguable limitation on the opportunity to make a variety of traditional fair uses of DVD movies, such as commenting on their content, quoting excerpts from their screenplays, and even recording portions of the video images and sounds on film or tape by pointing a camera, a camcorder, or a microphone at a monitor as it displays the DVD movie. The fact that the resulting copy will not be as perfect or as manipulable as a digital copy obtained by having direct access to the DVD movie in its digital form, provides no basis for a claim of unconstitutional limitation of fair use. A film critic making fair use of a movie by quoting selected lines of dialogue has no constitutionally valid claim that the review (in print or on television) would be technologically superior if the reviewer had not been prevented from using a movie camera in the theater, nor has an art student a valid constitutional claim to fair use of a painting by photographing it in a museum. Fair use has never been held to be a guarantee of access to copyrighted material in order to copy it by the fair user's preferred technique or in the format of the original.

Conclusion

We have considered all the other arguments of the Appellants and conclude that they provide no basis for disturbing the District Court's judgment. Accordingly, the judgment is affirmed.

It will be interesting to see how the Canadian courts address the interaction of the new anti-circumvention provisions and copyright limits and exemptions in light of the principles of "balance" and "technological neutrality" articulated by the Supreme Court of Canada, and with respect to possible constitutional questions about federal jurisdiction and freedom of expression.

It will be interesting to see how the Canadian courts address the interaction of the new anti-circumvention provisions and copyright limits and exemptions in light of the principles of "balance" and "technological neutrality" articulated by the Supreme Court of Canada.

COPYRIGHT ACT

An Act respecting copyright

R.S.C. 1985, c. C-42 as am. R.S.C. 1985, c. 10 (1st Supp.), s. 1; R.S.C. 1985, c. 1 (3rd Supp.), s. 13; R.S.C. 1985, c. 41 (3rd Supp.), ss. 116, 117; R.S.C. 1985, c. 10 (4th Supp.), ss. 1–16, 17 (Fr.); S.C. 1988, c. 65, ss. 61–65, 149; 1990, c. 37, s. 33; 1992, c. 1, ss. 47–52; 1993, c. 15, ss. 2–11; 1993, c. 23, ss. 1–7; 1993, c. 44, ss. 52–80; 1994, c. 47, ss. 56–68; 1995, c. 1, s. 62; 1997, c. 24; 1997, c. 36, s. 205; 1999, c. 2, ss. 45, 46; 1999, c. 17, s. 119; 1999, c. 31, ss. 59–62; 2001, c. 27, ss. 235–241; 2001, c. 34, ss. 34, 35; 2002, c. 8, s. 131 (Fr.); 2002, c. 26; 2003, c. 22, ss. 154, 224(z.20), 225(s); 2004, c. 11, ss. 21, 25, 26; 2005, c. 38, ss. 139(b), 142(d), 145(2)(j); 2012, c. 20 [ss. 2(1), 5, 9(3), (4), 11(2), (4), (5), 12(2), 14, 15(2), (4), 16, 47 as it enacts 41.25, 41.26, 41.27(3), 50 not in force at date of publication.]

Short Title

1. Short title

This Act may be cited as the *Copyright Act*.

Interpretation

2. Definitions

In this Act,

"architectural work" means any building or structure or any model of a building or structure;

"architectural work of art" [Repealed 1993, c. 44, s. 53(1).]

"artistic work" includes paintings, drawings, maps, charts, plans, photographs, engravings, sculptures, works of artistic craftsmanship, architectural works, and compilations of artistic works;

"Berne Convention country" means a country that is a party to the Convention for the Protection of Literary and Artistic Works concluded at Berne on September 9, 1886, or any one of its revisions, including the *Paris Act* of 1971;

"Board" means the Copyright Board established by subsection 66(1);

"book" means a volume or a part or division of a volume, in printed form, but does not include

    (a)   a pamphlet,

    (b)   a newspaper, review, magazine or other periodical,

(c) a map, chart, plan or sheet music where the map, chart, plan or sheet music is separately published, and

(d) an instruction or repair manual that accompanies a product or that is supplied as an accessory to a service;

"broadcaster" means a body that, in the course of operating a broadcasting undertaking, broadcasts a communication signal in accordance with the law of the country in which the broadcasting undertaking is carried on, but excludes a body whose primary activity in relation to communication signals is their retransmission;

"choreographic work" includes any work of choreography, whether or not it has any story line;

"cinematograph" [Repealed 1997, c. 24, s. 1(2).]

"cinematographic work" includes any work expressed by any process analogous to cinematography, whether or not accompanied by a soundtrack;

"collective society" means a society, association or corporation that carries on the business of collective administration of copyright or of the remuneration right conferred by section 19 or 81 for the benefit of those who, by assignment, grant of licence, appointment of it as their agent or otherwise, authorize it to act on their behalf in relation to that collective administration, and

(a) operates a licensing scheme, applicable in relation to a repertoire of works, performer's performances, sound recordings or communication signals of more than one author, performer, sound recording maker or broadcaster, pursuant to which the society, association or corporation sets out classes of uses that it agrees to authorize under this Act, and the royalties and terms and conditions on which it agrees to authorize those classes of uses, or

(b) carries on the business of collecting and distributing royalties or levies payable pursuant to this Act;

"collective work" means

(a) an encyclopaedia, dictionary, year book or similar work,

(b) a newspaper, review, magazine or similar periodical, and

(c) any work written in distinct parts by different authors, or in which works or parts of works of different authors are incorporated;

"commercially available" means, in relation to a work or other subject-matter,

(a) available on the Canadian market within a reasonable time and for a reasonable price and may be located with reasonable effort, or

(b) for which a licence to reproduce, perform in public or communicate to the public by telecommunication is available from a collective society within a reasonable time and for a reasonable price and may be located with reasonable effort;

"communication signal" means radio waves transmitted through space without any artificial guide, for reception by the public;

"compilation" means

(a)   a work resulting from the selection or arrangement of literary, dramatic, musical or artistic works or of parts thereof, or

(b)   a work resulting from the selection or arrangement of data;

"computer program" means a set of instructions or statements, expressed, fixed, embodied or stored in any manner, that is to be used directly or indirectly in a computer in order to bring about a specific result;

"copyright" means the rights described in

(a)   section 3, in the case of work,

(b)   sections 15 and 26, in the case of a performer's performance,

(c)   section 18, in the case of a sound recording, or

(d)   section 21, in the case of a communication signal;

"country" includes any territory;

"defendant" includes a respondent to an application;

"delivery" [Repealed 1997, c. 24, s. 1(1).]

"dramatic work" includes

(a)   any piece for recitation, choreographic work or mime, the scenic arrangement or acting form of which is fixed in writing or otherwise,

(b)   any cinematographic work, and

(c)   any compilation of dramatic works;

"educational institution" means

(a)   a non-profit institution licensed or recognized by or under an Act of Parliament or the legislature of a province to provide pre-school, elementary, secondary or post-secondary education,

(b)   a non-profit institution that is directed or controlled by a board of education regulated by or under an Act of the legislature of a province and that provides continuing, professional or vocational education or training,

(c)   a department or agency of any order of government, or any non-profit body, that controls or supervises education or training referred to in paragraph (a) or (b), or

(d)   any other non-profit institution prescribed by regulation;

"engravings" includes etchings, lithographs, woodcuts, prints and other similar works, not being photographs;

"every original literary, dramatic, musical and artistic work" includes every original production in the literary, scientific or artistic domain, whatever may be the mode or form of its expression, such as compilations, books, pamphlets and other writings, lectures, dramatic or dramatico-musical works, musical works, translations, illustrations, sketches and plastic works relative to geography, topography, architecture or science;

"exclusive distributor" means, in relation to a book, a person who

(a) has, before or after the coming into force of this definition, been appointed in writing, by the owner or exclusive licensee of the copyright in the book in Canada, as

    (i) the only distributor of the book in Canada or any part of Canada, or

    (ii) the only distributor of the book in Canada or any part of Canada in respect of a particular sector of the market, and

(b) meets the criteria established by regulations made under section 2.6,

and, for greater certainty, if there are no regulations made under section 2.6, then no person qualifies under this definition as an **"exclusive distributor"**;

Editor's Note: S.C. 1997, c. 24, s. 62(1) replaced the definition of "exclusive distributor". S.C. 1997, c. 24, s. 62(2), however, provided as follows:

(2) The definition of "exclusive distributor" in section 2 of the Copyright Act, as enacted by subsection 1(5) of this Act [i.e. 1997, c. 24], did not apply from June 30, 1996 until the day that was sixty days after April 25, 1997, i.e., the day on which 1997, c. 24 received Royal Assent.

During the transition period, as noted above, the definition of "exclusive distributor" read as follows:

"exclusive distributor" means, in relation to a book, a person who has, before or after the coming into force of this definition, been appointed in writing, by the owner or exclusive licensee of the copyright in the book in Canada, as

    (a) the only distributor of the book in Canada or any part of Canada, or

    (b) the only distributor of the book in Canada or any part of Canada in respect of a particular sector of the market.

"Her Majesty's Realms and Territories" [Repealed 1997, c. 24, s. 1(1).]

"infringing" means

(a) in relation to a work in which copyright subsists, any copy, including any colourable imitation, made or dealt with in contravention of this Act,

(b) in relation to a performer's performance in respect of which copyright subsists, any fixation or copy of a fixation of it made or dealt with in contravention of this Act,

(c) in relation to a sound recording in respect of which copyright subsists, any copy of it made or dealt with in contravention of this Act, or

(d) in relation to a communication signal in respect of which copyright subsists, any fixation or copy of a fixation of it made or dealt with in contravention of this Act.

The definition includes a copy that is imported in the circumstances set out in paragraph 27(2)(e) and section 27.1 but does not otherwise include a copy made with the consent of the owner of the copyright in the country where the copy was made;

"lecture" includes address, speech and sermon;

"legal representatives" includes heirs, executors, administrators, successors and assigns, or agents or attorneys who are thereunto duly authorized in writing;

"library, archive or museum" means

 (a) an institution, whether or not incorporated, that is not established or conducted for profit or that does not form a part of, or is not administered or directly or indirectly controlled by, a body that is established or conducted for profit, in which is held and maintained a collection of documents and other materials that is open to the public or to researchers, or

 (b) any other non-profit institution prescribed by regulation;

"literary work" includes tables, computer programs, and compilations of literary works;

"maker" means

 (a) in relation to a cinematographic work, the person by whom the arrangements necessary for the making of the work are undertaken, or

 (b) in relation to a sound recording, the person by whom the arrangements necessary for the first fixation of the sounds are undertaken;

"Minister", except in section 44.1, means the Minister of Industry;

"moral rights" means the rights described in subsection 14.1(1);

> ### Proposed Amendment — 2 "moral rights"
>
> **"moral rights"** means the rights described in subsections 14.1(1) and 17.1(1);
> 2012, c. 20, s. 2(1) [Not in force at date of publication.]

"musical work" means any work of music or musical composition, with or without words, and includes any compilation thereof;

"perceptual disability" means a disability that prevents or inhibits a person from reading or hearing a literary, musical, dramatic or artistic work in its original format, and includes such a disability resulting from

 (a) severe or total impairment of sight or hearing or the inability to focus or move one's eyes,

 (b) the inability to hold or manipulate a book, or

 (c) an impairment relating to comprehension;

"performance" means any acoustic or visual representation of a work, performer's performance, sound recording or communication signal, including a representation made by means of any mechanical instrument, radio receiving set or television receiving set;

"performer's performance" means any of the following when done by a performer:

 (a) a performance of an artistic work, dramatic work or musical work, whether or not the work was previously fixed in any material form, and whether or not the work's term of copyright protection under this Act has expired,

 (b) a recitation or reading of a literary work, whether or not the work's term of copyright protection under this Act has expired, or

 (c) an improvisation of a dramatic work, musical work or literary work, whether or not the improvised work is based on a pre-existing work;

"photograph" includes photo-lithograph and any work expressed by any process analogous to photography;

"plaintiff" includes an applicant;

"plate" includes

(a) any stereotype or other plate, stone, block, mould, matrix, transfer or negative used or intended to be used for printing or reproducing copies of any work, and

(b) any matrix or other appliance used or intended to be used for making or reproducing sound recordings, performer's performances or communication signals;

"premises" means, in relation to an educational institution, a place where education or training referred to in the definition **"educational institution"** is provided, controlled or supervised by the educational institution;

"receiving device" [Repealed 1993, c. 44, s. 79(1).]

"Rome Convention country" means a country that is a party to the International Convention for the Protection of Performers, Producers of Phonograms and Broadcasting Organisations, done at Rome on October 26, 1961;

"sculpture" includes a cast or model;

"sound recording" means a recording, fixed in any material form, consisting of sounds, whether or not of a performance of a work, but excludes any soundtrack of a cinematographic work where it accompanies the cinematographic work;

"telecommunication" means any transmission of signs, signals, writing, images or sounds or intelligence of any nature by wire, radio, visual, optical or other electromagnetic system;

"treaty country" means a Berne Convention country, UCC country or WTO Member;

> **Proposed Amendment — 2 "treaty country"**
>
> **"treaty country"** means a Berne Convention country, UCC country, WCT country or WTO Member;
>
> 2012, c. 20, s. 2(1) [Not in force at date of publication.]

"UCC country" means a country that is a party to the Universal Copyright Convention, adopted on September 6, 1952 in Geneva, Switzerland, or to that Convention as revised in Paris, France on July 24, 1971;

"WCT country" means a country that is a party to the WIPO Copyright Treaty, adopted in Geneva on December 20, 1996;

"work" includes the title thereof when such title is original and distinctive;

"work of joint authorship" means a work produced by the collaboration of two or more authors in which the contribution of one author is not distinct from the contribution of the other author or authors;

"work of sculpture" [Repealed 1997, c. 24, s. 1(1).]

"WPPT country" means a country that is a party to the WIPO Performances and Phonograms Treaty, adopted in Geneva on December 20, 1996;

"WTO Member" means a Member of the World Trade Organization as defined in subsection 2(1) of the *World Trade Organization Agreement Implementation Act*.

R.S.C. 1985, c. 10 (4th Supp.), s. 1; 1988, c. 65, s. 61; 1993, c. 23, s. 1; 1993, c. 44, ss. 53, 79(1); 1994, c. 47, s. 56; 1995, c. 1, s. 62(1)(g); 1997, c. 24, s. 1; 2012, c. 20, s. 2(2)

Compilations

2.1 (1) A compilation containing two or more of the categories of literary, dramatic, musical or artistic works shall be deemed to be a compilation of the category making up the most substantial part of the compilation.

Idem

(2) The mere fact that a work is included in a compilation does not increase, decrease or otherwise affect the protection conferred by this Act in respect of the copyright in the work or the moral rights in respect of the work.

1993, c. 44, s. 54

Definition of "maker"

2.11 For greater certainty, the arrangements referred to in paragraph (b) of the definition **"maker"** in section 2, as that term is used in section 19 and in the definition **"eligible maker"** in section 79, include arrangements for entering into contracts with performers, financial arrangements and technical arrangements required for the first fixation of the sounds for a sound recording.

1997, c. 24, s. 2

Definition of "publication"

2.2 (1) For the purposes of this Act,

"publication" means

    (a) in relation to works,

        (i)   making copies of a work available to the public,

        (ii) the construction of an architectual work, and

        (iii) the incorporation of an artistic work into an architectual work, and

    (b) in relation to sound recordings, making copies of a sound recording available to the public,

but does not include

    (c) the performance in public, or the communication to the public by telecommunication, of a literary, dramatic, musical or artistic work or a sound recording, or

    (d) the exhibition in public of an artistic work.

Issue of photographs and engravings

(2) For the purpose of subsection (1), the issue of photographs and engravings of sculptures and architectual works is not deemed to be publication of those works.

Where no consent of copyright owner

(3) For the purposes of this Act, other than in respect of infringement of copyright, a work or other subject-matter is not deemed to be published or performed in public or communicated to the public by telecommunication if that act is done without the consent of the owner of the copyright.

Unpublished works

(4) Where, in the case of an unpublished work, the making of the work is extended over a considerable period, the conditions of this Act conferring copyright are deemed to have been complied with if the author was, during any substantial part of that period, a subject or citizen of, or a person ordinarily resident in, a country to which this Act extends.

1997, c. 24, s. 2

Telecommunication

2.3 A person who communicates a work or other subject-matter to the public by tele-communication does not by that act alone perform it in public, nor by that act alone is deemed to authorize its performance in public.

1997, c. 24, s. 2

Communication to the public by telecommunication

2.4 (1) For the purposes of communication to the public by telecommunication,

   (a) persons who occupy apartments, hotel rooms or dwelling units situated in the same building are part of the public, and a communication intended to be received exclusively by such persons is a communication to the public;

   (b) a person whose only act in respect of the communication of a work or other subject-matter to the public consists of providing the means of telecommunication necessary for another person to so communicate the work or other subject-matter does not communicate that work or other subject-matter to the public; and

   (c) where a person, as part of

   (i) a network, within the meaning of the *Broadcasting Act*, whose operations result in the communication of works or other subject-matter to the public, or

   (ii) any programming undertaking whose operations result in the communication of works or other subject-matter to the public,

transmits by telecommunication a work or other subject-matter that is communicated to the public by another person who is not a retransmitter of a signal within the meaning of subsection 31(1), the transmission and communication of that work or other subject-matter by those persons constitute a single communication to the public for which those persons are jointly and severally liable.

Communication to the public by telecommunication

(1.1) For the purposes of this Act, communication of a work or other subject-matter to the public by telecommunication includes making it available to the public by telecommunication in a way that allows a member of the public to have access to it from a place and at a time individually chosen by that member of the public.

Regulations

(2) The Governor in Council may make regulations defining **"programming undertaking"** for the purpose of paragraph (1)(c).

Exception

(3) A work is not communicated in the manner described in paragraph (1)(c) or 3(1) (f) where a signal carrying the work is retransmitted to a person who is a retransmitter within the meaning of subsection 31(1).

1997, c. 24, s. 2; 2002, c. 26, s. 1; 2012, c. 20, s. 3

What constitutes rental

2.5 (1) For the purposes of paragraphs 3(1)(h) and (i), 15(1)(c) and 18(1)(c), an arrangement, whatever its form, constitutes a rental of a computer program or sound recording if, and only if,

    (a)   it is in substance a rental, having regard to all the circumstances; and

    (b)   it is entered into with motive of gain in relation to the overall operations of the person who rents out the computer program or sound recording, as the case may be.

Motive of gain

(2) For the purpose of paragraph (1)(b), a person who rents out a computer program or sound recording with the intention of recovering no more than the costs, including overhead, associated with the rental operations does not by that act alone have a motive of gain in relation to the rental operations.

1997, c. 24, s. 2

Exclusive distributor

2.6 The Governor in Council may make regulations establishing distribution criteria for the purpose of paragraph (b) of the definition **"exclusive distributor"** in section 2.

1997, c. 24, s. 2

Exclusive licence

2.7 For the purposes of this Act, an exclusive licence is an authorization to do any act that is subject to copyright to the exclusion of all others including the copyright owner, whether the authorization is granted by the owner or an exclusive licensee claiming under the owner.

1997, c. 24, s. 2

Part I
Copyright and Moral Rights in Works (SS. 3–14.2)

Copyright

Copyright in works

3. (1) For the purposes of this Act, **"copyright"**, in relation to a work, means the sole right to produce or reproduce the work or any substantial part thereof in any material form whatever, to perform the work or any substantial part thereof in public or, if the

work is unpublished, to publish the work or any substantial part thereof, and includes the
sole right

    (a) to produce, reproduce, perform or publish any translation of the work,

    (b) in the case of a dramatic work, to convert it into a novel or other non-dramatic
work,

    (c) in the case of a novel or other non-dramatic work, or of an artistic work, to
convert it into a dramatic work, by way of performance in public or otherwise,

    (d) in the case of a literary, dramatic or musical work, to make any sound record-
ing, cinematograph film or other contrivance by means of which the work
may be mechanically reproduced or performed,

    (e) in the case of any literary, dramatic, musical or artistic work, to reproduce,
adapt and publicly present the work as a cinematographic work,

    (f) in the case of any literary, dramatic, musical or artistic work, to communicate
the work to the public by telecommunication,

    (g) to present at a public exhibition, for a purpose other than sale or hire, an artis-
tic work created after June 7, 1988, other than a map, chart or plan,

    (h) in the case of a computer program that can be reproduced in the ordinary
course of its use, other than by a reproduction during its execution in conjunction with a machine, device or computer, to rent out the computer program,

    (i) in the case of a musical work, to rent out a sound recording in which the work
is embodied, and

    (j) in the case of a work that is in the form of a tangible object, to sell or other-
wise transfer ownership of the tangible object, as long as that ownership has
never previously been transferred in or outside Canada with the authorization
of the copyright owner,

and to authorize any such acts.

Simultaneous fixing

(1.1) A work that is communicated in the manner described in paragraph (1)(f) is fixed
even if it is fixed simultaneously with its communication.

(1.2) [Repealed 1997, c. 24, s. 3(4).]

(1.3) [Repealed 1997, c. 24, s. 3(4).]

(1.4) [Repealed 1997, c. 24, s. 3(4).]

(1.5) [Repealed 1997, c. 24, s. 3(4).]

(2) [Repealed 1997, c. 24, s. 3(4).]

(3) [Repealed 1997, c. 24, s. 3(4).]

(4) [Repealed 1997, c. 24, s. 3(4).]
    R.S.C. 1985, c. 10 (4th Supp.), s. 2; 1988, c. 65, s. 62; 1993, c. 23, s. 2; 1993, c. 44,
s. 55; 1997, c. 24, s. 3; 2012, c. 20, s. 4

4. [Repealed 1997, c. 24, s. 4.]

Works in Which Copyright May Subsist

Conditions for subsistence of copyright

5. (1) Subject to this Act, copyright shall subsist in Canada, for the term hereinafter mentioned, in every original literary, dramatic, musical and artistic work if any one of the following conditions is met:

    (a) in the case of any work, whether published or unpublished, including a cinematographic work, the author was, at the date of the making of the work, a citizen or subject of, or a person ordinarily resident in, a treaty country;

    (b) in the case of a cinematographic work, whether published or unpublished, the maker, at the date of the making of the cinematographic work,

        (i) if a corporation, had its headquarters in a treaty country, or

        (ii) if a natural person, was a citizen or subject of, or a person ordinarily resident in, a treaty country; or

    (c) in the case of a published work, including a cinematographic work,

        (i) in relation to subparagraph 2.2(1)(a)(i), the first publication in such a quantity as to satisfy the reasonable demands of the public, having regard to the nature of the work, occurred in a treaty country, or

        (ii) in relation to subparagraph 2.2(1)(a)(ii) or (iii), the first publication occurred in a treaty country.

Protection for older works

(1.01) For the purposes of subsection (1), a country that becomes a Berne Convention country or a WTO Member after the date of the making or publication of a work shall, as of becoming a Berne Convention country or WTO Member, as the case may be, be deemed to have been a Berne Convention country or WTO Member at the date of the making or publication of the work, subject to subsection (1.02) and section 33.

Proposed Amendment — 5(1.01)

Protection for older works

(1.01) For the purposes of subsection (1), a country that becomes a Berne Convention country, a WCT country or a WTO Member after the date of the making or publication of a work is deemed to have been a Berne Convention country, a WCT country or a WTO Member, as the case may be, at that date, subject to subsection (1.02) and sections 33 to 33.2.

                     2012, c. 20, s. 5 [Not in force at date of publication.]

Limitation

(1.02) Subsection (1.01) does not confer copyright protection in Canada on a work whose term of copyright protection in the country referred to in that subsection had expired before that country became a Berne Convention country or WTO Member, as the case may be.

Proposed Amendment — 5(1.02)

Limitation

(1.02) Subsection (1.01) does not confer copyright protection in Canada on a work whose term of copyright protection in the country referred to in that subsection had expired before that country became a Berne Convention country, a WCT country or a WTO Member, as the case may be.

2012, c. 20, s. 5 [Not in force at date of publication.]

Application of subsections (1.01) and (1.02)

(1.03) Subsections (1.01) and (1.02) apply, and are deemed to have applied, regardless of whether the country in question became a Berne Convention country or a WTO Member before or after the coming into force of those subsections.

Proposed Amendment — 5(1.03)

Application of subsections (1.01) and (1.02)

(1.03) Subsections (1.01) and (1.02) apply, and are deemed to have applied, regardless of whether the country in question became a Berne Convention country, a WCT country or a WTO Member before or after the coming into force of those subsections.

2012, c. 20, s. 5 [Not in force at date of publication.]

First publication

(1.1) The first publication described in subparagraph (1)(c)(i) or (ii) is deemed to have occurred in a treaty country notwithstanding that it in fact occurred previously elsewhere, if the interval between these two publications did not exceed thirty days.

Idem

(1.2) Copyright shall not subsist in Canada otherwise than as provided by subsection (1), except in so far as the protection conferred by this Act is extended as hereinafter provided to foreign countries to which this Act does not extend.

Minister may extend copyright to other countries

(2) Where the Minister certifies by notice, published in the *Canada Gazette*, that any country that is not a treaty country grants or has undertaken to grant, either by treaty, convention, agreement or law, to citizens of Canada, the benefit of copyright on substantially the same basis as to its own citizens or copyright protection substantially equal to that conferred by this Act, the country shall, for the purpose of the rights conferred by this Act, be treated as if it were a country to which this Act extends, and the Minister may give a certificate, notwithstanding that the remedies for enforcing the rights, or the restrictions on the importation of copies of works, under the law of such country, differ from those in this Act.

(2.1) [Repealed 1994, c. 47, s. 57.]

(3) [Repealed 1997, c. 24, s. 5(3).]

(4) [Repealed 1997, c. 24, s. 5(3).]

(5) [Repealed 1997, c. 24, s. 5(3).]

(6) [Repealed 1997, c. 24, s. 5(3).]

Reciprocity protection preserved

(7) For greater certainty, the protection to which a work is entitled by virtue of a notice published under subsection (2), or under that subsection as it read at any time before the coming into force of this subsection, is not affected by reason only of the country in question becoming a treaty country.

1993, c. 15, s. 2; 1993, c. 44, s. 57; 1994, c. 47, s. 57; 1997, c. 24, s. 5; 2001, c. 34, s. 34

Term of copyright

6. The term for which copyright shall subsist shall, except as otherwise expressly provided by this Act, be the life of the author, the remainder of the calendar year in which the author dies, and a period of fifty years following the end of that calendar year.

1993, c. 44, s. 58

Anonymous and pseudonymous works

6.1 Except as provided in section 6.2, where the identity of the author of a work is unknown, copyright in the work shall subsist for whichever of the following terms ends earlier:

    (a)   a term consisting of the remainder of the calendar year of the first publication of the work and a period of `fifty years following the end of that calendar year, and

    (b)   a term consisting of the remainder of the calendar year of the making of the work and a period of seventy-five years following the end of that calendar year,

but where, during that term, the author's identity becomes commonly known, the term provided in section 6 applies.

1993, c. 44, s. 58

Anonymous and pseudonymous works of joint ownership

6.2 Where the identity of all the authors of a work of joint authorship is unknown, copyright in the work shall subsist for whichever of the following terms ends earlier:

    (a)   a term consisting of the remainder of the calendar year of the first publication of the work and a period of fifty years following the end of that calendar year, and

    (b)   a term consisting of the remainder of the calendar year of the making of the work and a period of seventy-five years following the end of that calendar year,

but where, during that term, the identity of one or more of the authors becomes commonly known, copyright shall subsist for the life of whichever of those authors dies last, the remainder of the calendar year in which that author dies, and a period of fifty years following the end of that calendar year.

1993, c. 44, s. 58

Term of copyright in posthumous works

7. (1) Subject to subsection (2), in the case of a literary, dramatic or musical work, or an engraving, in which copyright subsists at the date of the death of the author or, in the

case of a work of joint authorship, at or immediately before the date of the death of the author who dies last, but which has not been published or, in the case of a lecture or a dramatic or musical work, been performed in public or communicated to the public by telecommunication, before that date, copyright shall subsist until publication, or performance in public or communication to the public by telecommunication, whichever may first happen, for the remainder of the calendar year of the publication or of the performance in public or communication to the public by telecommunication, as the case may be, and for a period of fifty years following the end of that calendar year.

Application of subsection (1)

(2) Subsection (1) applies only where the work in question was published or performed in public or communicated to the public by telecommunication, as the case may be, before the coming into force of this section.

Transitional provision

(3) Where

> (a) a work has not, at the coming into force of this section, been published or performed in public or communicated to the public by telecommunication,
>
> (b) subsection (1) would apply to that work if it had been published or performed in public or communicated to the public by telecommunication before the coming into force of this section, and
>
> (c) the relevant death referred to in subsection (1) occurred during the period of fifty years immediately before the coming into force of this section,

copyright shall subsist in the work for the remainder of the calendar year in which this section comes into force and for a period of fifty years following the end of that calendar year, whether or not the work is published or performed in public or communicated to the public by telecommunication after the coming into force of this section.

Transitional provision

(4) Where

> (a) a work has not, at the coming into force of this section, been published or performed in public or communicated to the public by telecommunication,
>
> (b) subsection (1) would apply to that work if it had been published or performed in public or communicated to the public by telecommunication before the coming into force of this section, and
>
> (c) the relevant death referred to in subsection (1) occured more than fifty years before the coming into force of this section,

copyright shall subsist in the work for the remainder of the calendar year in which this section comes into force and for a period of five years following the end of the calendar year, whether or not the work is published or performed in public or communicated to the public by telecommunication after the coming into force of this section.

1993, c. 44, s. 58; 1997, c. 24, s. 6

8. [Repealed 1993, c. 44, s. 59.]

Cases of joint authorship

9. (1) In the case of a work of joint authorship, except as provided in section 6.2, copyright shall subsist during the life of the author who dies last, for the remainder of the calendar year of that author's death, and for a period of fifty years following the end of that calendar year, and references in this Act to the period after the expiration of any specified number of years from the end of the calendar year of the death of the author shall be construed as references to the period after the expiration of the like number of years from the end of the calendar year of the death of the author who dies last.

Nationals of other countries

(2) Authors who are nationals of any country, other than a country that is a party to the North American Free Trade Agreement, that grants a term of protection shorter than that mentioned in subsection (1) are not entitled to claim a longer term of protection in Canada.

1993, c. 44, s. 60(1)

10. [Repealed 2012, c. 20, s. 6.]

11. [Repealed 1997, c. 24, s. 8.]

Cinematographic works

11.1 Except for cinematographic works in which the arrangement or acting form or the combination of incidents represented give the work a dramatic character, copyright in a cinematographic work or a compilation of cinematographic works shall subsist

(a) for the remainder of the calendar year of the first publication of the cinematographic work or of the compilation, and for a period of fifty years following the end of that calendar year; or

(b) if the cinematographic work or compilation is not published before the expiration of fifty years following the end of the calendar year of its making, for the remainder of that calendar year and for a period of fifty years following the end of that calendar year.

1993, c. 44, s. 60(1); 1997, c. 24, s. 9

Where copyright belongs to Her Majesty

12. Without prejudice to any rights or privileges of the Crown, where any work is, or has been, prepared or published by or under the direction or control of Her Majesty or any government department, the copyright in the work shall, subject to any agreement with the author, belong to Her Majesty and in that case shall continue for the remainder of the calendar year of the first publication of the work and for a period of fifty years following the end of that calendar year.

1993, c. 44, s. 60(1)

Ownership of Copyright

Ownership of copyright

13. (1) Subject to this Act, the author of a work shall be the first owner of the copyright therein.

(2) [Repealed 2012, c. 20, s. 7.]

Work made in the course of employment

(3) Where the author of a work was in the employment of some other person under a contract of service or apprenticeship and the work was made in the course of his employment by that person, the person by whom the author was employed shall, in the absence of any agreement to the contrary, be the first owner of the copyright, but where the work is an article or other contribution to a newspaper, magazine or similar periodical, there shall, in the absence of any agreement to the contrary, be deemed to be reserved to the author a right to restrain the publication of the work, otherwise than as part of a newspaper, magazine or similar periodical.

Assignment and licences

(4) The owner of the copyright in any work may assign the right, either wholly or partially, and either generally or subject to limitations relating to territory, medium or sector of the market or other limitations relating to the scope of the assignment, and either for the whole term of the copyright or for any other part thereof, and may grant any interest in the right by licence, but no assignment or grant is valid unless it is in writing signed by the owner of the right in respect of which the assignment or grant is made, or by the owner's duly authorized agent.

Ownership in case of partial assignment

(5) Where, under any partial assignment of copyright, the assignee becomes entitled to any right comprised in copyright, the assignee, with respect to the rights so assigned, and the assignor, with respect to the rights not assigned, shall be treated for the purposes of this Act as the owner of the copyright, and this Act has effect accordingly.

Assignment of right of action

(6) For greater certainty, it is deemed always to have been the law that a right of action for infringement of copyright may be assigned in association with the assignment of the copyright or the grant of an interest in the copyright by licence.

Exclusive licence

(7) For greater certainty, it is deemed always to have been the law that a grant of an exclusive licence in a copyright constitutes the grant of an interest in the copyright by licence.

1997, c. 24, s. 10; 2012, c. 20, s. 7

Limitation where author is first owner of copyright

14. (1) Where the author of a work is the first owner of the copyright therein, no assignment of the copyright and no grant of any interest therein, made by him, otherwise than by will, after June 4, 1921, is operative to vest in the assignee or grantee any rights with respect to the copyright in the work beyond the expiration of twenty-five years from the death of the author, and the reversionary interest in the copyright expectant on the termination of that period shall, on the death of the author, notwithstanding any agreement to the contrary, devolve on his legal representatives as part of the estate of the author, and any agreement entered into by the author as to the disposition of such reversionary interest is void.

Restriction

(2) Nothing in subsection (1) shall be construed as applying to the assignment of the copyright in a collective work or a licence to publish a work or part of a work as part of a collective work.

(3) [Repealed 1997, c. 24, s. 11.]

(4) [Repealed R.S.C. 1985, c. 10 (4th Supp.), s. 3.]

R.S.C. 1985, c. 10 (4th Supp.), s. 3; 1997, c. 24, s. 11

Performers' Rights

14.01 [Repealed 1997, c. 24, s. 12.]

Moral Rights

Moral rights

14.1 (1) The author of a work has, subject to section 28.2, the right to the integrity of the work and, in connection with an act mentioned in section 3, the right, where reasonable in the circumstances, to be associated with the work as its author by name or under a pseudonym and the right to remain anonymous.

No assignment of moral rights

(2) Moral rights may not be assigned but may be waived in whole or in part.

No waiver by assignment

(3) An assignment of copyright in a work does not by that act alone constitute a waiver of any moral rights.

Effect of waiver

(4) Where a waiver of any moral right is made in favour of an owner or a licensee of copyright, it may be invoked by any person authorized by the owner or licensee to use the work, unless there is an indication to the contrary in the waiver.

R.S.C. 1985, c. 10 (4th Supp.), s. 4

Term

14.2 (1) Moral rights in respect of a work subsist for the same term as the copyright in the work.

Succession

(2) The moral rights in respect of a work pass, on the death of its author, to

(a)   the person to whom those rights are specifically bequeathed;

(b)   where there is no specific bequest of those moral rights and the author dies testate in respect of the copyright in the work, the person to whom that copyright is bequeathed; or

(c)   where there is no person described in paragraph (a) or (b), the person entitled to any other property in respect of which the author dies intestate.

Subsequent succession

(3) Subsection (2) applies, with such modifications as the circumstances require, on the death of any person who holds moral rights.

R.S.C. 1985, c. 10 (4th Supp.), s. 4; 1997, c. 24, s. 13

Part II
Copyright in Performers' Performances,
Sound Recordings and Communication Signals and
Moral Rights in Performers' Performances (ss. 15–26)

[Heading added 1997, c. 24, s. 14. Amended 2012, c. 20, s. 8.]

Performers' Rights

Copyright

[Heading added 2012, c. 20, s. 8.]

Copyright in performer's performance

15. (1) Subject to subsection (2), a performer has a copyright in the performer's performance, consisting of the sole right to do the following in relation to the performer's performance or any substantial part thereof:

(a) if it is not fixed,

    (i)   to communicate it to the public by telecommunication,

    (ii) to perform it in public, where it is communicated to the public by telecommunication otherwise than by communication signal, and

    (iii) to fix it in any material form,

(b) if it is fixed,

    (i)   to reproduce any fixation that was made without the performer's authorization,

    (ii) where the performer authorized a fixation, to reproduce any reproduction of that fixation, if the reproduction being reproduced was made for a purpose other than that for which the performer's authorization was given, and

    (iii) where a fixation was permitted under Part III or VIII, to reproduce any reproduction of that fixation, if the reproduction being reproduced was made for a purpose other than one permitted under Part III or VIII, and

(c) to rent out a sound recording of it,

and to authorize any such acts.

Copyright in performer's performance

(1.1) Subject to subsections (2.1) and (2.2), a performer's copyright in the performer's performance consists of the sole right to do the following acts in relation to the performer's performance or any substantial part of it and to authorize any of those acts:

(a) if it is not fixed,

    (i)   to communicate it to the public by telecommunication,

    (ii) to perform it in public, if it is communicated to the public by telecommunication otherwise than by communication signal, and

    (iii) to fix it in any material form;

(b) if it is fixed in a sound recording, to reproduce that fixation;

(c) to rent out a sound recording of it;

(d) to make a sound recording of it available to the public by telecommunication in a way that allows a member of the public to have access to the sound recording from a place and at a time individually chosen by that member of the public and to communicate the sound recording to the public by telecommunication in that way; and

(e) if it is fixed in a sound recording that is in the form of a tangible object, to sell or otherwise transfer ownership of the tangible object, as long as that ownership has never previously been transferred in or outside Canada with the authorization of the owner of the copyright in the performer's performance.

Conditions

(2) Subsection (1) applies only if the performer's performance

(a) takes place in Canada or in a Rome Convention country;

(b) is fixed in

    (i) a sound recording whose maker, at the time of the first fixation,

        (A) if a natural person, was a Canadian citizen or permanent resident within the meaning of subsection 2(1) of the *Immigration and Refugee Protection Act*, or a citizen or permanent resident of a Rome Convention country, or

        (B) if a corporation, had its headquarters in Canada or in a Rome Convention country, or

    (ii) a sound recording whose first publication in such a quantity as to satisfy the reasonable demands of the public occurred in Canada or in a Rome Convention country; or

(c) is transmitted at the time of the performer's performance by a communication signal broadcast from Canada or a Rome Convention country by a broadcaster that had its headquarters in the country of broadcast.

Conditions for copyright

(2.1) Subsection (1.1) applies if

(a) the performer's performance takes place in Canada;

(b) the performer's performance is fixed in

    (i) a sound recording whose maker, at the time of its first fixation,

        (A) was a Canadian citizen or permanent resident as defined in subsection 2(1) of the *Immigration and Refugee Protection Act*, in the case of a natural person, or

        (B) had its headquarters in Canada, in the case of a corporation, or

    (ii) a sound recording whose first publication in a quantity sufficient to satisfy the reasonable demands of the public occurred in Canada; or

(c) the performer's performance is transmitted at the time of its performance by a communication signal broadcast from Canada by a broadcaster that has its headquarters in Canada.

Proposed Addition — 15(2.2)

Conditions for copyright

(2.2) Subsection (1.1) also applies if

(a) the performer's performance takes place in a WPPT country;

(b) the performer's performance is fixed in

(i) a sound recording whose maker, at the time of its first fixation,

(A) was a citizen or permanent resident of a WPPT country, in the case of a natural person, or

(B) had its headquarters in a WPPT country, in the case of a corporation, or

(ii) a sound recording whose first publication in a quantity sufficient to satisfy the reasonable demands of the public occurred in a WPPT country; or

(c) the performer's performance is transmitted at the time of its performance by a communication signal broadcast from a WPPT country by a broadcaster that has its headquarters in that country.

2012, c. 20, s. 9(3) [Not in force at date of publication.]

Publication

(3) The first publication is deemed to have occurred in a country referred to in paragraph (2)(b) notwithstanding that it in fact occurred previously elsewhere, if the interval between those two publications does not exceed thirty days.

Proposed Addition — 15(4)

Publication

(4) The first publication of a sound recording is deemed to have occurred in a WPPT country, despite an earlier publication elsewhere, if the interval between the publication in that WPPT country and the earlier publication does not exceed 30 days.

2012, c. 20, s. 9(4) [Not in force at date of publication.]

1993, c. 44, s. 61; 1997, c. 24, s. 14; 2001, c. 27, s. 235; 2012, c. 20, s. 9(1), (2)

Contractual arrangements

16. Nothing in section 15 prevents the performer from entering into a contract governing the use of the performer's performance for the purpose of broadcasting, fixation or retransmission.

1994, c. 47, s. 59; 1997, c. 24, s. 14

Cinematographic works

17. (1) Where the performer authorizes the embodiment of the performer's performance in a cinematographic work, the performer may no longer exercise, in relation to the performance where embodied in that cinematographic work, the copyright referred to in subsection 15(1).

Right to remuneration

(2) Where there is an agreement governing the embodiment referred to in subsection (1) and that agreement provides for a right to remuneration for the reproduction, performance in public or communication to the public by telecommunication of the cinematographic work, the performer may enforce that right against

    (a) the other party to the agreement or, if that party assigns the agreement, the assignee, and

    (b) any other person who

        (i) owns the copyright in the cinematographic work governing the reproduction of the cinematographic work, its performance in public or its communication to the public by telecommunication, and

        (ii) reproduces the cinematographic work, performs it in public or communicates it to the public by telecommunication,

and persons referred to in paragraphs (a) and (b) are jointly and severally liable to the performer in respect of the remuneration relating to that copyright.

Application of subsection (2)

(3) Subsection (2) applies only if the performer's performance is embodied in a prescribed cinematographic work.

Exception

(4) If so requested by a country that is a party to the North American Free Trade Agreement, the Minister may, by a statement published in the *Canada Gazette*, grant the benefits conferred by this section, subject to any terms and conditions specified in the statement, to performers who are nationals of that country or another country that is a party to the Agreement or are Canadian citizens or permanent residents within the meaning of subsection 2(1) of the *Immigration and Refugee Protection Act* and whose performer's performances are embodied in works other than the prescribed cinematographic works referred to in subsection (3).

1994, c. 47, s. 59; 1997, c. 24, s. 14; 2001, c. 27, s. 236

Moral Rights

[Heading added 2012, c. 20, s. 10.]

Moral rights

17.1 (1) In the cases referred to in subsections 15(2.1) and (2.2), a performer of a live aural performance or a performance fixed in a sound recording has, subject to subsection 28.2(1), the right to the integrity of the performance, and — in connection with an act mentioned in subsection 15(1.1) or one for which the performer has a right to remuneration under section 19 — the right, if it is reasonable in the circumstances, to be associated with the performance as its performer by name or under a pseudonym and the right to remain anonymous.

No assignment of moral rights

(2) Moral rights may not be assigned but may be waived in whole or in part.

No waiver by assignment

(3) An assignment of copyright in a performer's performance does not by itself constitute a waiver of any moral rights.

Effect of waiver

(4) If a waiver of any moral right is made in favour of an owner or a licensee of a copyright, it may be invoked by any person authorized by the owner or licensee to use the performer's performance, unless there is an indication to the contrary in the waiver.

2012, c. 20, s. 10

Application and term

17.2 (1) Subsection 17.1(1) applies only in respect of a performer's performance that occurs after the coming into force of that subsection. The moral rights subsist for the same term as the copyright in that performer's performance.

Succession

(2) The moral rights in respect of a performer's performance pass, on the performer's death, to

    (a)   the person to whom those rights are specifically bequeathed;

    (b)   if there is not a specific bequest of those moral rights and the performer dies testate in respect of the copyright in the performer's performance, the person to whom that copyright is bequeathed; or

    (c)   if there is not a person as described in paragraph (a) or (b), the person entitled to any other property in respect of which the performer dies intestate.

Subsequent succession

(3) Subsection (2) applies, with any modifications that the circumstances require, on the death of any person who holds moral rights.

2012, c. 20, s. 10

Rights of Sound Recording Makers

Copyright in sound recordings

18. (1) Subject to subsection (2), the maker of a sound recording has a copyright in the sound recording, consisting of the sole right to do the following in relation to the sound recording or any substantial part thereof:

    (a)   to publish it for the first time,

    (b)   to reproduce it in any material form, and

    (c)   to rent it out,

and to authorize any such acts.

Copyright in sound recordings

(1.1) Subject to subsections (2.1) and (2.2), a sound recording maker's copyright in the sound recording also includes the sole right to do the following acts in relation to the sound recording or any substantial part of it and to authorize any of those acts:

  (a) to make it available to the public by telecommunication in a way that allows a member of the public to have access to it from a place and at a time individually chosen by that member of the public and to communicate it to the public by telecommunication in that way; and

  (b) if it is in the form of a tangible object, to sell or otherwise transfer ownership of the tangible object, as long as that ownership has never previously been transferred in or outside Canada with the authorization of the owner of the copyright in the sound recording.

Conditions for copyright

(2) Subsection (1) applies only if

  (a) the maker of the sound recording was a Canadian citizen or permanent resident within the meaning of subsection 2(1) of the *Immigration and Refugee Protection Act*, or a citizen or permanent resident of a Berne Convention country, a Rome Convention country or a country that is a WTO Member, or, if a corporation, had its headquarters in one of the foregoing countries,

   (i)   at the date of the first fixation, or

   (ii) if that first fixation was extended over a considerable period, during any substantial part of that period; or

  (b) the first publication of the sound recording in such a quantity as to satisfy the reasonable demands of the public occurred in any country referred to in paragraph (a).

Proposed Amendment — 18(2)

Conditions for copyright

(2) Subsection (1) applies only if

  (a) at the time of the first fixation or, if that first fixation was extended over a considerable period, during any substantial part of that period, the maker of the sound recording

   (i)   was a Canadian citizen or permanent resident as defined in subsection 2(1) of the *Immigration and Refugee Protection Act*,

   (ii) was a citizen or permanent resident of a Berne Convention country, a Rome Convention country, a WPPT country or a country that is a WTO Member, or

   (iii) had its headquarters in one of those countries, in the case of a corporation; or

> (b) the first publication of the sound recording in a quantity sufficient to satisfy the reasonable demands of the public occurred in any country referred to in paragraph (a).
>
> 2012, c. 20, s. 11(2) [Not in force at date of publication.]

Conditions for copyright

(2.1) Subsection (1.1) applies if

(a) at the time of the first fixation or, if that first fixation was extended over a considerable period, during any substantial part of that period, the maker of the sound recording

   (i) was a Canadian citizen or permanent resident as defined in subsection 2(1) of the *Immigration and Refugee Protection Act*, or

   (ii) had its headquarters in Canada, in the case of a corporation; or

(b) the first publication of the sound recording in a quantity sufficient to satisfy the reasonable demands of the public occurred in Canada.

Proposed Addition — 18(2.2)

Conditions for copyright

(2.2) Subsection (1.1) also applies if

(a) at the time of the first fixation or, if that first fixation was extended over a considerable period, during any substantial part of that period, the maker of the sound recording

   (i) was a citizen or permanent resident of a WPPT country, or

   (ii) had its headquarters in a WPPT country, in the case of a corporation; or

(b) the first publication of the sound recording in a quantity sufficient to satisfy the reasonable demands of the public occurred in a WPPT country.

2012, c. 20, s. 11(4) [Not in force at date of publication.]

Publication

(3) The first publication is deemed to have occurred in a country referred to in paragraph (2)(a) notwithstanding that it in fact occurred previously elsewhere, if the interval between those two publications does not exceed thirty days.

Proposed Addition — 18(4)

Publication

(4) The first publication of a sound recording is deemed to have occurred in a WPPT country, despite an earlier publication elsewhere, if the interval between the publication in that WPPT country and the earlier publication does not exceed 30 days.

2012, c. 20, s. 11(5) [Not in force at date of publication.]

1994, c. 47, s. 59; 1997, c. 24, s. 14; 2001, c. 27, s. 237; 2012, c. 20, s. 11(1), (3)

Provisions Applicable to Both Performers and Sound Recording Makers

Right to remuneration — Canada

19. (1) If a sound recording has been published, the performer and maker are entitled, subject to subsection 20(1), to be paid equitable remuneration for its performance in public or its communication to the public by telecommunication, except for a communication in the circumstances referred to in paragraph 15(1.1)(d) or 18(1.1)(a) and any retransmission.

Right to remuneration — Rome Convention country

(1.1) If a sound recording has been published, the performer and maker are entitled, subject to subsections 20(1.1) and (2), to be paid equitable remuneration for its performance in public or its communication to the public by telecommunication, except for

    (a) a communication in the circumstances referred to in paragraph 15(1.1)(d) or 18(1.1)(a), if the person entitled to the equitable remuneration is entitled to the right referred to in those paragraphs for that communication; and

    (b) any retransmission.

Proposed Addition — 19(1.2)

Right to remuneration — WPPT country

(1.2) If a sound recording has been published, the performer and maker are entitled, subject to subsections 20(1.2) and (2.1), to be paid equitable remuneration for its performance in public or its communication to the public by telecommunication, except for a communication in the circumstances referred to in paragraph 15(1.1)(d) or 18(1.1)(a) and any retransmission.

2012, c. 20, s. 12(2) [Not in force at date of publication.]

Royalties

(2) For the purpose of providing the remuneration mentioned in this section, a person who performs a published sound recording in public or communicates it to the public by telecommunication is liable to pay royalties

    (a) in the case of a sound recording of a musical work, to the collective society authorized under Part VII to collect them; or

    (b) in the case of a sound recording of a literary work or dramatic work, to either the maker of the sound recording or the performer.

Division of royalties

(3) The royalties, once paid pursuant to paragraph (2)(a) or (b), shall be divided so that

    (a) the performer or performers receive in aggregate fifty per cent; and

    (b) the maker or makers receive in aggregate fifty per cent.

1994, c. 47, s. 59; 1997, c. 24, s. 14; 2012, c. 20, s. 12(1), (3)

Deemed publication — Canada

19.1 Despite subsection 2.2(1), a sound recording that has been made available to the public by telecommunication in a way that allows a member of the public to access it from a place and at a time individually chosen by that member of the public, or that has been communicated to the public by telecommunication in that way, is deemed to have been published for the purposes of subsection 19(1).

2012, c. 20, s. 13

Proposed Addition — 19.2

Deemed publication — WPPT country

19.2 Despite subsection 2.2(1), a sound recording that has been made available to the public by telecommunication in a way that allows a member of the public to access it from a place and at a time individually chosen by that member of the public, or that has been communicated to the public by telecommunication in that way, is deemed to have been published for the purposes of subsection 19(1.2).

2012, c. 20, s. 14 [Not in force at date of publication.]

Conditions — Canada

20. (1) The right to remuneration conferred by subsection 19(1) applies only if

    (a) the maker was, at the date of the first fixation, a Canadian citizen or permanent resident within the meaning of subsection 2(1) of the *Immigration and Refugee Protection Act* or, if a corporation, had its headquarters in Canada; or

    (b) all the fixations done for the sound recording occurred in Canada.

Conditions — Rome Convention country

(1.1) The right to remuneration conferred by subsection 19(1.1) applies only if

    (a) the maker was, at the date of the first fixation, a citizen or permanent resident of a Rome Convention country or, if a corporation, had its headquarters in a Rome Convention country; or

    (b) all the fixations done for the sound recording occurred in a Rome Convention country.

Proposed Addition — 20(1.2)

Conditions — WPPT country

(1.2) The right to remuneration conferred by subsection 19(1.2) applies only if

    (a) the maker was, at the date of the first fixation, a citizen or permanent resident of a WPPT country or, if a corporation, had its headquarters in a WPPT country; or

    (b) all the fixations done for the sound recording occurred in a WPPT country.

2012, c. 20, s. 15(2) [Not in force at date of publication.]

Exception — Rome Convention country

(2) Despite subsection (1.1), if the Minister is of the opinion that a Rome Convention country does not grant a right to remuneration, similar in scope and duration to that provided by subsection 19(1.1), for the performance in public or the communication to the public of a sound recording whose maker, at the date of its first fixation, was a Canadian

citizen or permanent resident within the meaning of subsection 2(1) of the *Immigration and Refugee Protection Act* or, if a corporation, had its headquarters in Canada, the Minister may, by a statement published in the *Canada Gazette*, limit the scope and duration of the protection for sound recordings whose first fixation is done by a maker who is a citizen or permanent resident of that country or, if a corporation, has its headquarters in that country.

Proposed Addition — 20(2.1)

Exception — WPPT country

(2.1) Despite subsection (1.2), if the Minister is of the opinion that a WPPT country does not grant a right to remuneration, similar in scope and duration to that provided by subsection 19(1.2), for the performance in public or the communication to the public of a sound recording whose maker, at the date of its first fixation, was a Canadian citizen or permanent resident within the meaning of subsection 2(1) of the *Immigration and Refugee Protection Act* or, if a corporation, had its headquarters in Canada, the Minister may, by a statement published in the *Canada Gazette*, limit the scope and duration of the protection for sound recordings whose first fixation is done by a maker who is a citizen or permanent resident of that country or, if a corporation, has its headquarters in that country.

2012, c. 20, s. 15(4) [Not in force at date of publication.]

Exception

(3) If so requested by a country that is a party to the North American Free Trade Agreement, the Minister may, by a statement published in the *Canada Gazette*, grant the right to remuneration conferred by subsection 19(1.1) to performers or makers who are nationals of that country and whose sound recordings embody dramatic or literary works.

Application of section 19

(4) Where a statement is published under subsection (3), section 19 applies

    (a)   in respect of nationals of a country mentioned in that statement, as if they were citizens of Canada or, in the case of corporations, had their headquarters in Canada; and

    (b)   as if the fixations made for the purpose of their sound recordings had been made in Canada.

1994, c. 47, s. 59; 1997, c. 24, s. 14; 2001, c. 27, s. 238;
2012, c. 20, s. 15(1), (3), (5)

Rights of Broadcasters

Copyright in communication signals

21. (1) Subject to subsection (2), a broadcaster has a copyright in the communication signals that it broadcasts, consisting of the sole right to do the following in relation to the communication signal or any substantial part thereof:

    (a)   to fix it,

    (b)   to reproduce any fixation of it that was made without the broadcaster's consent,

    (c) to authorize another broadcaster to retransmit it to the public simultaneously with its broadcast, and

    (d) in the case of a television communication signal, to perform it in a place open to the public on payment of an entrance fee,

and to authorize any act described in paragraph (a), (b) or (d).

Conditions for copyright

(2) Subsection (1) applies only if the broadcaster

    (a) at the time of the broadcast, had its headquarters in Canada, in a country that is a WTO Member or in a Rome Convention country; and

    (b) broadcasts the communication signal from that country.

Exception

(3) Notwithstanding subsection (2), if the Minister is of the opinion that a Rome Convention country or a country that is a WTO Member does not grant the right mentioned in paragraph (1)(d), the Minister may, by a statement published in the *Canada Gazette*, declare that broadcasters that have their headquarters in that country are not entitled to that right.

1994, c. 47, s. 59; 1997, c. 24, s. 14

Reciprocity

Reciprocity

22. (1) Where the Minister is of the opinion that a country other than a Rome Convention country grants or has undertaken to grant

---

Proposed Amendment — 22(1) opening words

Reciprocity

(1) If the Minister is of the opinion that a country other than a Rome Convention country or a WPPT country grants or has undertaken to grant

2012, c. 20, s. 16(1) [Not in force at date of publication.]

    (a) to performers and to makers of sound recordings, or

    (b) to broadcasters

that are Canadian citizens or permanent residents within the meaning of subsection 2(1) of the *Immigration and Refugee Protection Act* or, if corporations, have their headquarters in Canada, as the case may be, whether by treaty, convention, agreement or law, benefits substantially equivalent to those conferred by this Part, the Minister may, by a statement published in the *Canada Gazette*,

    (c) grant the benefits conferred by this Part

        (i) to performers and to makers of sound recordings, or

        (ii) to broadcasters

as the case may be, that are citizens, subjects or permanent residents of or, if corporations, have their headquarters in that country, and

(d) declare that that country shall, as regards those benefits, be treated as if it were a country to which this Part extends.

Reciprocity

(2) Where the Minister is of the opinion that a country other than a Rome Convention country neither grants nor has undertaken to grant

> **Proposed Amendment — 22(2) opening words**
>
> **Reciprocity**
>
> (2) If the Minister is of the opinion that a country other than a Rome Convention country or a WPPT country neither grants nor has undertaken to grant
> > 2012, c. 20, s. 16(2) [Not in force at date of publication.]

(a) to performers, and to makers of sound records, or

(b) to broadcasters

that are Canadian citizens or permanent residents within the meaning of subsection 2(1) of the *Immigration and Refugee Protection Act* or, if corporations, have their headquarters in Canada, as the case may be, whether by treaty, convention, agreement or law, benefits substantially equivalent to those conferred by this Part, the Minister may, by a statement published in the *Canada Gazette,*

(c) grant the benefits conferred by this Part to performers, makers of sound recordings or broadcasters that are citizens, subjects or permanent residents of or, if corporations, have their headquarters in that country, as the case may be, to the extent that that country grants that those benefits to performers, makers of sound recordings or broadcasters that are Canadian citizens or permanent residents within the meaning of subsection 2(1) of the *Immigration and Refugee Protection Act* or, if corporations, have their headquarters in Canada, and

(d) declare that that country shall, as regards those benefits, be treated as if it were a country to which this Part extends.

Application of Act

(3) Any provision of this Act that the Minister specifies in a statement referred to in subsection (1) or (2)

(a) applies in respect of performers, makers of sound recordings or broadcasters covered by that statement, as if they were citizens of or, if corporations, had their headquarters in Canada; and

(b) applies in respect of a country covered by that statement, as if that country were Canada.

Application of Act

(4) Subject to any exceptions that the Minister may specify in a statement referred to in subsection (1) or (2), the other provisions of this Act also apply in the way described in subsection (3).

1994, c. 47, s. 59; 1997, c. 24, s. 14; 2001, c. 27, s. 239

Term of Rights

Term of copyright — performer's performance

23. (1) Subject to this Act, copyright in a performer's performance subsists until the end of 50 years after the end of the calendar year in which the performance occurs. However,

(a) if the performance is fixed in a sound recording before the copyright expires, the copyright continues until the end of 50 years after the end of the calendar year in which the first fixation of the performance in a sound recording occurs; and

(b) if a sound recording in which the performance is fixed is published before the copyright expires, the copyright continues until the earlier of the end of 50 years after the end of the calendar year in which the first publication of the sound recording occurs and the end of 99 years after the end of the calendar year in which the performance occurs.

Term of copyright — sound recording

(1.1) Subject to this Act, copyright in a sound recording subsists until the end of 50 years after the end of the calendar year in which the first fixation of the sound recording occurs. However, if the sound recording is published before the copyright expires, the copyright continues until the end of 50 years after the end of the calendar year in which the first publication of the sound recording occurs.

Term of copyright — communication signal

(1.2) Subject to this Act, copyright in a communication signal subsists until the end of 50 years after the end of the calendar year in which the communication signal is broadcast.

Term of right to remuneration

(2) The rights to remuneration conferred on performers and makers by section 19 have the same terms, respectively, as those provided by subsections (1) and (1.1).

Application of subsections (1) to (2)

(3) Subsections (1) to (2) apply whether the fixation, performance or broadcast occurred before or after the coming into force of this section.

Berne Convention countries, Rome Convention countries, WTO Members

(4) Where the performer's performance, sound recording or communication signal meets the requirements set out in section 15, 18 or 21, as the case may be, a country that becomes a Berne Convention country, a Rome Convention country or a WTO Member after the date of the fixation, performance or broadcast is, as of becoming a Berne Convention country, Rome Convention country or WTO Member, as the case may be, deemed to have been such at the date of the fixation, performance or broadcast.

Where term of protection expired

(5) Subsection (4) does not confer any protection in Canada where the term of protection in the country referred to in that subsection had expired before that country became a Berne Convention country, Rome Convention country or WTO Member, as the case may be.

1994, c. 47, s. 59; 1997, c. 24, s. 14; 2012, c. 20, s. 17

Ownership of Copyright

Ownership of copyright

24. The first owner of the copyright

    (a) in a performer's performance, is the performer;

    (b) in a sound recording, is the maker; or

    (c) in a communication signal, is the broadcaster that broadcasts it.

1994, c. 47, s. 59; 1997, c. 24, s. 14

Assignment of rights

25. Subsections 13(4) to (7) apply, with such modifications as the circumstances require, in respect of the rights conferred by this Part on performers, makers of sound recordings and broadcasters.

1993, c. 44, s. 62; 1994, c. 47, s. 59; 1997, c. 24, s. 14

Performers' Rights — WTO Countries

Performer's performance in WTO country

26. (1) Where a performer's performance takes place on or after January 1, 1996 in a country that is a WTO Member, the performer has, as of the date of the performer's performance, a copyright in the performer's performance, consisting of the sole right to do the following in relation to the performer's performance or any substantial part thereof:

    (a) if it is not fixed, to communicate it to the public by telecommunication and to fix it in a sound recording, and

    (b) if it has been fixed in a sound recording without the performer's authorization, to reproduce the fixation or any substantial part thereof,

and to authorize any such acts.

Where country joins WTO after Jan. 1, 1996

(2) Where a performer's performance takes place on or after January 1, 1996 in a country that becomes a WTO Member after the date of the performer's performance, the performer has the copyright described in subsection (1) as of the date the country becomes a WTO Member.

Performer's performances before Jan. 1, 1996

(3) Where a performer's performance takes place before January 1, 1996 in a country that is a WTO Member, the performer has, as of January 1, 1996, the sole right to do and to authorize the act described in paragraph (1)(b).

Where country joins WTO after Jan. 1, 1996

(4) Where a performer's performance takes place before January 1, 1996 in a country that becomes a WTO Member on or after January 1, 1996, the performer has the right described in subsection (3) as of the date the country becomes a WTO Member.

Term of performer's rights

(5) The rights conferred by this section subsist for the remainder of the calendar year in which the performer's performance takes place and a period of fifty years following the end of that calendar year.

Assignment of rights

(6) Subsections 13(4) to (7) apply, with such modifications as the circumstances require, in respect of a performer's rights conferred by this section.

Limitation

(7) Notwithstanding an assignment of a performer's right conferred by this section, the performer, as well as the assignee, may

    (a) prevent the reproduction of

        (i) any fixation of the performer's performance, or

        (ii) any substantial part of such a fixation,

where the fixation was made without the performer's consent or the assignee's consent; and

    (b) prevent the importation of any fixation of the performer's performance, or any reproduction of such a fixation, that the importer knows or ought to have known was made without the performer's consent or the assignee's consent.

1993, c. 44, s. 63; 1994, c. 47, s. 59; 1997, c. 24, s. 14

Part III
Infringement of Copyright and Moral Rights and Exceptions to Infringement (ss. 27–33)

[Heading added 1997, c. 24, s. 15.]

Infringement of Copyright

General

Infringement generally

27. (1) It is an infringement of copyright for any person to do, without the consent of the owner of the copyright, anything that by this Act only the owner of the copyright has the right to do.

Secondary infringement

(2) It is an infringement of copyright for any person to

    (a) sell or rent out,

    (b) distribute to such an extent as to affect prejudicially the owner of the copyright,

    (c) by way of trade distribute, expose or offer for sale or rental, or exhibit in public,

(d) possess for the purpose of doing anything referred to in paragraphs (a) to (c), or

(e) import into Canada for the purpose of doing anything referred to in paragraphs (a) to (c),

a copy of a work, sound recording or fixation of a performer's performance or of a communication signal that the person knows or should have known infringes copyright or would infringe copyright if it had been made in Canada by the person who made it.

Clarification

(2.1) For greater certainty, a copy made outside Canada does not infringe copyright under subsection (2) if, had it been made in Canada, it would have been made under a limitation or exception under this Act.

Secondary infringement related to lesson

(2.2) It is an infringement of copyright for any person to do any of the following acts with respect to anything that the person knows or should have known is a lesson, as defined in subsection 30.01(1), or a fixation of one:

(a) to sell it or to rent it out;

(b) to distribute it to an extent that the owner of the copyright in the work or other subject-matter that is included in the lesson is prejudicially affected;

(c) by way of trade, to distribute it, expose or offer it for sale or rental or exhibit it in public;

(d) to possess it for the purpose of doing anything referred to in any of paragraphs (a) to (c);

(e) to communicate it by telecommunication to any person other than a person referred to in paragraph 30.01(3)(a); or

(f) to circumvent or contravene any measure taken in conformity with paragraph 30.01(6)(b), (c) or (d).

Infringement — provision of services

(2.3) It is an infringement of copyright for a person, by means of the Internet or another digital network, to provide a service primarily for the purpose of enabling acts of copyright infringement if an actual infringement of copyright occurs by means of the Internet or another digital network as a result of the use of that service.

Factors

(2.4) In determining whether a person has infringed copyright under subsection (2.3), the court may consider

(a) whether the person expressly or implicitly marketed or promoted the service as one that could be used to enable acts of copyright infringement;

(b) whether the person had knowledge that the service was used to enable a significant number of acts of copyright infringement;

(c) whether the service has significant uses other than to enable acts of copyright infringement;

(d) the person's ability, as part of providing the service, to limit acts of copyright infringement, and any action taken by the person to do so;

(e) any benefits the person received as a result of enabling the acts of copyright infringement; and

(f) the economic viability of the provision of the service if it were not used to enable acts of copyright infringement.

Knowledge of importer

(3) In determining whether there is an infringement under subsection (2) in the case of an activity referred to in any of paragraphs (2)(a) to (d) in relation to a copy that was imported in the circumstances referred to in paragraph (2)(e), it is irrelevant whether the importer knew or should have known that the importation of the copy infringed copyright.

Plates

(4) It is an infringement of copyright for any person to make or possess a plate that has been specifically designed or adapted for the purpose of making infringing copies of a work or other subject-matter.

Public performance for profit

(5) It is an infringement of copyright for any person, for profit, to permit a theatre or other place of entertainment to be used for the performance in public of a work or other subject-matter without the consent of the owner of the copyright unless that person was not aware, and had no reasonable ground for suspecting, that the performance would be an infringement of copyright.

R.S.C. 1985, c. 1 (3rd Supp.), s. 13; 1985, c. 10 (4th Supp.), s. 5;
1993, c. 44, s. 64; 1997, c. 24, s. 15; 2012, c. 20, s. 18

Parallel Importation of Books

Importation of books

27.1 (1) Subject to any regulations made under subsection (6), it is an infringement of copyright in a book for any person to import the book where

(a) copies of the book were made with the consent of the owner of the copyright in the book in the country where the copies were made, but were imported without the consent of the owner of the copyright in the book in Canada; and

(b) the person knows or should have known that the book would infringe copyright if it was made in Canada by the importer.

Secondary infringement

(2) Subject to any regulations made under subsection (6), where the circumstances described in paragraph (1)(a) exist, it is an infringement of copyright in an imported book for any person who knew or should have known that the book would infringe copyright if it was made in Canada by the importer to

(a) sell or rent out the book;

(b) by way of trade, distribute, expose or offer for sale or rental, or exhibit in public, the book; or

(c) possess the book for the purpose of any of the activities referred to in paragraph (a) or (b).

Limitation

(3) Subsections (1) and (2) only apply where there is an exclusive distributor of the book and the acts described in those subsections take place in the part of Canada or in respect of the particular sector of the market for which the person is the exclusive distributor.

Exclusive distributor

(4) An exclusive distributor is deemed, for the purposes of entitlement to any of the remedies under Part IV in relation to an infringement under this section, to derive an interest in the copyright in question by licence.

Notice

(5) No exclusive distributor, copyright owner or exclusive licensee is entitled to a remedy under Part IV in relation to an infringement under this section unless, before the infringement occurred, notice has been given within the prescribed time and in the prescribed manner to the person referred to in subsection (1) or (2), as the case may be, that there is an exclusive distributor of the book.

Regulations

(6) The Governor in Council may, by regulation, establish terms and conditions for the importation of certain categories of books, including remaindered books, books intended solely for re-export and books imported by special order.

1997, c. 24, s. 15

28. [Repealed 1997, c. 24, s. 15.]

28.01 [Renumbered as s. 31: 1997, c. 24, s. 16.]

28.02 [Repealed 1997, c. 24, s. 17.]

28.03 [Repealed 1997, c. 24, s. 17.]

Moral Rights Infringement

Infringement generally

28.1 Any act or omission that is contrary to any of the moral rights of the author of a work or of the performer of a performer's performance is, in the absence of the author's or performer's consent, an infringement of those rights.

R.S.C. 1985, c. 10 (4th Supp.), s. 6; 2012, c. 20, s. 19

Nature of right of integrity

28.2 (1) The author's or performer's right to the integrity of a work or performer's performance is infringed only if the work or the performance is, to the prejudice of its author's or performer's honour or reputation,

(a) distorted, mutilated or otherwise modified; or

(b) used in association with a product, service, cause or institution.

Where prejudice deemed

(2) In the case of a painting, sculpture or engraving, the prejudice referred to in subsection (1) shall be deemed to have occurred as a result of any distortion, mutilation or other modification of the work.

When work not distorted, etc.

(3) For the purposes of this section,

(a) a change in the location of a work, the physical means by which a work is exposed or the physical structure containing a work, or

(b) steps taken in good faith to restore or preserve the work

shall not, by that act alone, constitute a distortion, mutilation or other modification of the work.

R.S.C. 1985, c. 10 (4th Supp.), s. 6; 2012, c. 20, s. 20

Exceptions
Fair Dealing

Research, private study, etc.

29. Fair dealing for the purpose of research, private study, education, parody or satire does not infringe copyright.

> R.S.C. 1985, c. 10 (4th Supp.), s. 7; 1994, c. 47, s. 61;
> 1997, c. 24, s. 18(1); 2012, c. 20, s. 21

Criticism or review

29.1 Fair dealing for the purpose of criticism or review does not infringe copyright if the following are mentioned:

  (a) the source; and

  (b) if given in the source, the name of the

   (i)   author, in the case of a work,

   (ii) performer, in the case of a performer's performance,

   (iii) maker, in the case of a sound recording, or

   (iv) broadcaster, in the case of a communication signal.

> 1997, c. 24, s. 18(1)

News reporting

29.2 Fair dealing for the purpose of news reporting does not infringe copyright if the following are mentioned:

  (a) the source; and

  (b) if given in the source, the name of the

   (i)   author, in the case of a work;

   (ii) performer, in the case of a performer's performance,

(iii) maker, in the case of a sound recording, or

(iv) broadcaster, in the case of a communication signal.

1997, c. 24, s. 18(1)

Non-commercial User-generated Content

[Heading added 2012, c. 20, s. 22.]

Non-commercial user-generated content

29.21 (1) It is not an infringement of copyright for an individual to use an existing work or other subject-matter or copy of one, which has been published or otherwise made available to the public, in the creation of a new work or other subject-matter in which copyright subsists and for the individual — or, with the individual's authorization, a member of their household — to use the new work or other subject-matter or to authorize an intermediary to disseminate it, if

(a) the use of, or the authorization to disseminate, the new work or other subject-matter is done solely for non-commercial purposes;

(b) the source — and, if given in the source, the name of the author, performer, maker or broadcaster — of the existing work or other subject-matter or copy of it are mentioned, if it is reasonable in the circumstances to do so;

(c) the individual had reasonable grounds to believe that the existing work or other subject-matter or copy of it, as the case may be, was not infringing copyright; and

(d) the use of, or the authorization to disseminate, the new work or other subject-matter does not have a substantial adverse effect, financial or otherwise, on the exploitation or potential exploitation of the existing work or other subject-matter — or copy of it — or on an existing or potential market for it, including that the new work or other subject-matter is not a substitute for the existing one.

Definitions

(2) The following definitions apply in subsection (1).

"intermediary" means a person or entity who regularly provides space or means for works or other subject-matter to be enjoyed by the public. (*"intermédiaire"*)

"use" means to do anything that by this Act the owner of the copyright has the sole right to do, other than the right to authorize anything. (*"utiliser"*)

2012, c. 20, s. 22

Reproduction for Private Purposes

[Heading added 2012, c. 20, s. 22.]

Reproduction for private purposes

29.22 (1) It is not an infringement of copyright for an individual to reproduce a work or other subject-matter or any substantial part of a work or other subject-matter if

(a) the copy of the work or other subject-matter from which the reproduction is made is not an infringing copy;

(b) the individual legally obtained the copy of the work or other subject-matter from which the reproduction is made, other than by borrowing it or renting it, and owns or is authorized to use the medium or device on which it is reproduced;

(c) the individual, in order to make the reproduction, did not circumvent, as defined in section 41, a technological protection measure, as defined in that section, or cause one to be circumvented;

(d) the individual does not give the reproduction away; and

(e) the reproduction is used only for the individual's private purposes.

Meaning of "medium or device"

(2) For the purposes of paragraph (1)(b), a **"medium or device"** includes digital memory in which a work or subject-matter may be stored for the purpose of allowing the telecommunication of the work or other subject-matter through the Internet or other digital network.

Limitation — audio recording medium

(3) In the case of a work or other subject-matter that is a musical work embodied in a sound recording, a performer's performance of a musical work embodied in a sound recording or a sound recording in which a musical work or a performer's performance of a musical work is embodied, subsection (1) does not apply if the reproduction is made onto an audio recording medium as defined in section 79.

Limitation — destruction of reproductions

(4) Subsection (1) does not apply if the individual gives away, rents or sells the copy of the work or other subject-matter from which the reproduction is made without first destroying all reproductions of that copy that the individual has made under that subsection.

2012, c. 20, s. 22

Fixing Signals and Recording Programs for
Later Listening or Viewing
[Heading added 2012, c. 20, s. 22.]

Reproduction for later listening or viewing

29.23 (1) It is not an infringement of copyright for an individual to fix a communication signal, to reproduce a work or sound recording that is being broadcast or to fix or reproduce a performer's performance that is being broadcast, in order to record a program for the purpose of listening to or viewing it later, if

(a) the individual receives the program legally;

(b) the individual, in order to record the program, did not circumvent, as defined in section 41, a technological protection measure, as defined in that section, or cause one to be circumvented;

(c) the individual makes no more than one recording of the program;

(d) the individual keeps the recording no longer than is reasonably necessary in order to listen to or view the program at a more convenient time;

(e) the individual does not give the recording away; and

(f) the recording is used only for the individual's private purposes.

Limitation

(2) Subsection (1) does not apply if the individual receives the work, performer's performance or sound recording under an on-demand service.

Definitions

(3) The following definitions apply in this section.

"broadcast" means any transmission of a work or other subject-matter by telecommunication for reception by the public, but does not include a transmission that is made solely for performance in public. (*"radiodiffusion"*)

"on-demand service" means a service that allows a person to receive works, performer's performances and sound recordings at times of their choosing. (*"service sur demande"*)

2012, c. 20, s. 22

Backup Copies

[Heading added 2012, c. 20, s. 22.]

Backup copies

29.24 (1) It is not an infringement of copyright in a work or other subject-matter for a person who owns — or has a licence to use — a copy of the work or subject-matter (in this section referred to as the "source copy") to reproduce the source copy if

(a) the person does so solely for backup purposes in case the source copy is lost, damaged or otherwise rendered unusable;

(b) the source copy is not an infringing copy;

(c) the person, in order to make the reproduction, did not circumvent, as defined in section 41, a technological protection measure, as defined in that section, or cause one to be circumvented; and

(d) the person does not give any of the reproductions away.

Backup copy becomes source copy

(2) If the source copy is lost, damaged or otherwise rendered unusable, one of the reproductions made under subsection (1) becomes the source copy.

Destruction

(3) The person shall immediately destroy all reproductions made under subsection (1) after the person ceases to own, or to have a licence to use, the source copy.

2012, c. 20, s. 22

Acts Undertaken without Motive of Gain

Motive of gain

29.3 (1) No action referred to in section 29.4, 29.5, 30.2 or 30.21 may be carried out with motive of gain.

Cost recovery

(2) An educational institution, library, archive or museum, or person acting under its authority does not have a motive of gain where it or the person acting under its authority, does anything referred to in section 29.4, 29.5, 30.2 or 30.21 and recovers no more than the costs, including overhead costs, associated with doing that act.

1997, c. 24, s. 18(1)

Educational Institutions

Reproduction for instruction

29.4 (1) It is not an infringement of copyright for an educational institution or a person acting under its authority for the purposes of education or training on its premises to reproduce a work, or do any other necessary act, in order to display it.

Reproduction for examinations, etc.

(2) It is not an infringement of copyright for an educational institution or a person acting under its authority to

(a) reproduce, translate or perform in public on the premises of the educational institution, or

(b) communicate by telecommunication to the public situated on the premises of the educational institution

a work or other subject-matter as required for a test or examination.

If work commercially available

(3) Except in the case of manual reproduction, the exemption from copyright infringement provided by subsections (1) and (2) does not apply if the work or other subject-matter is commercially available, within the meaning of paragraph (a) of the definition "commercially available" in section 2, in a medium that is appropriate for the purposes referred to in those subsections.

1997, c. 24, s. 18(1); 2012, c. 20, s. 23

Performances

29.5 It is not an infringement of copyright for an educational institution or a person acting under its authority to do the following acts if they are done on the premises of an educational institution for educational or training purposes and not for profit, before an audience consisting primarily of students of the educational institution, instructors acting under the authority of the educational institution or any person who is directly responsible for setting a curriculum for the educational institution:

(a) the live performance in public, primarily by students of the educational institution, of a work;

(b) the performance in public of a sound recording, or of a work or performer's performance that is embodied in a sound recording, as long as the sound recording is not an infringing copy or the person responsible for the performance has no reasonable grounds to believe that it is an infringing copy;

(c) the performance in public of a work or other subject-matter at the time of its communication to the public by telecommunication; and

(d) the performance in public of a cinematographic work, as long as the work is not an infringing copy or the person responsible for the performance has no reasonable grounds to believe that it is an infringing copy.

1997, c. 24, s. 18(1); 2012, c. 20, s. 24

News and commentary

29.6 (1) It is not an infringement of copyright for an educational institution or a person acting under its authority to

(a) make, at the time of its communication to the public by telecommunication, a single copy of a news program or a news commentary program, excluding documentaries, for the purposes of performing the copy for the students of the educational institution for educational or training purposes; and

(b) perform the copy in public before an audience consisting primarily of students of the educational institution on its premises for educational or training purposes.

(2) [Repealed 2012, c. 20, s. 25(3).]

1997, c. 24, s. 18(1); 2012, c. 20, s. 25

Reproduction of broadcast

29.7 (1) Subject to subsection (2) and section 29.9, it is not an infringement of copyright for an educational institution or a person acting under its authority to

(a) make a single copy of a work or other subject-matter at the time that it is communicated to the public by telecommunication; and

(b) keep the copy for up to thirty days to decide whether to perform the copy for educational or training purposes.

Royalties for reproduction

(2) An educational institution that has not destroyed the copy by the expiration of the thirty days infringes copyright in the work or other subject-matter unless it pays any royalties, and complies with any terms and conditions, fixed under this Act for the making of the copy.

Royalties for performance

(3) It is not an infringement of copyright for the educational institution or a person acting under its authority to perform the copy in public for educational or training purposes on the premises of the educational institution before an audience consisting primarily of students of the educational institution if the educational institution pays the royalties and complies with any terms and conditions fixed under this Act for the performance in public.

1997, c. 24, s. 18(1)

Unlawful reception

29.8 The exceptions to infringement of copyright provided for under sections 29.5 to 29.7 do not apply where the communication to the public by telecommunication was received by unlawful means.

1997, c. 24, s. 18(1)

Records and marking

29.9 (1) Where an educational institution or person acting under its authority

(a) [Repealed 2012, c. 20, s. 26.]

(b) makes a copy of a work or other subject-matter communicated to the public by telecommunication and performs it pursuant to section 29.7,

the educational institution shall keep a record of the information prescribed by regulation in relation to the making of the copy, the destruction of it or any performance in public of it for which royalties are payable under this Act and shall, in addition, mark the copy in the manner prescribed by regulation.

Regulations

(2) The Board may, with the approval of the Governor in Council, make regulations

(a) prescribing the information in relation to the making, destruction, performance and marking of copies that must be kept under subsection (1),

(b) prescribing the manner and form in which records referred to in that subsection must be kept and copies destroyed or marked, and

(c) respecting the sending of information to collective societies referred to in section 71.

1997, c. 24, s. 18(1); 2012, c. 20, s. 26

Literary collections

30. The publication in a collection, mainly composed of non-copyright matter, intended for the use of educational institutions, and so described in the title and in any advertisements issued by the publisher, of short passages from published literary works in which copyright subsists and not themselves published for the use of educational institutions, does not infringe copyright in those published literary works if

(a) not more than two passages from works by the same author are published by the same publisher within five years;

(b) the source from which the passages are taken is acknowledged; and

(c) the name of the author, if given in the source, is mentioned.

R.S.C. 1985, c. 10 (4th Supp.), s. 7; 1997, c. 24, s. 18(1)

Transitional Provision

1997, c. 24 provides:

18. (2) Section 30 of the Act, as enacted by subsection (1) of this section, does not apply in respect of collections referred to in section 30 that are published before the coming into force of section 30. Such collections continue to be governed by paragraph 27(2)(d) of the Act as it read before the coming into force of section 15 of this Act.

Meaning of "lesson"

30.01 (1) For the purposes of this section, **"lesson"** means a lesson, test or examination, or part of one, in which, or during the course of which, an act is done in respect of a work or other subject-matter by an educational institution or a person acting under its authority that would otherwise be an infringement of copyright but is permitted under a limitation or exception under this Act.

Application

(2) This section does not apply so as to permit any act referred to in paragraph (3)(a), (b) or (c) with respect to a work or other subject-matter whose use in the lesson constitutes an infringement of copyright or for whose use in the lesson the consent of the copyright owner is required.

Communication by telecommunication

(3) Subject to subsection (6), it is not an infringement of copyright for an educational institution or a person acting under its authority

(a) to communicate a lesson to the public by telecommunication for educational or training purposes, if that public consists only of students who are enrolled in a course of which the lesson forms a part or of other persons acting under the authority of the educational institution;

(b) to make a fixation of the lesson for the purpose of the act referred to in paragraph (a); or

(c) to do any other act that is necessary for the purpose of the acts referred to in paragraphs (a) and (b).

Participation by telecommunication

(4) A student who is enrolled in a course of which the lesson forms a part is deemed to be a person on the premises of the educational institution when the student participates in or receives the lesson by means of communication by telecommunication under paragraph (3)(a).

Reproducing lessons

(5) It is not an infringement of copyright for a student who has received a lesson by means of communication by telecommunication under paragraph (3)(a) to reproduce the lesson in order to be able to listen to or view it at a more convenient time. However, the student shall destroy the reproduction within 30 days after the day on which the students who are enrolled in the course to which the lesson relates have received their final course evaluations.

Conditions

(6) The educational institution and any person acting under its authority, except a student, shall

(a) destroy any fixation of the lesson within 30 days after the day on which the students who are enrolled in the course to which the lesson relates have received their final course evaluations;

(b) take measures that can reasonably be expected to limit the communication by telecommunication of the lesson to the persons referred to in paragraph (3) (a);

(c) take, in relation to the communication by telecommunication of the lesson in digital form, measures that can reasonably be expected to prevent the students from fixing, reproducing or communicating the lesson other than as they may do under this section; and

(d) take, in relation to a communication by telecommunication in digital form, any measure prescribed by regulation.

2012, c. 20, s. 27

Exception — digital reproduction of works

30.02 (1) Subject to subsections (3) to (5), it is not an infringement of copyright for an educational institution that has a reprographic reproduction licence under which the institution is authorized to make reprographic reproductions of works in a collective society's repertoire for an educational or training purpose

(a) to make a digital reproduction — of the same general nature and extent as the reprographic reproduction authorized under the licence — of a paper form of any of those works;

(b) to communicate the digital reproduction by telecommunication for an educational or training purpose to persons acting under the authority of the institution; or

(c) to do any other act that is necessary for the purpose of the acts referred to in paragraphs (a) and (b).

Exception

(2) Subject to subsections (3) to (5), it is not an infringement of copyright for a person acting under the authority of the educational institution to whom the work has been communicated under paragraph (1)(b) to print one copy of the work.

Conditions

(3) An educational institution that makes a digital reproduction of a work under paragraph (1)(a) shall

(a) pay to the collective society, with respect to all the persons to whom the digital reproduction is communicated by the institution under paragraph (1) (b), the royalties that would be payable if one reprographic reproduction were distributed by the institution to each of those persons, and comply with the licence terms and conditions applicable to a reprographic reproduction to the extent that they are reasonably applicable to a digital reproduction;

(b) take measures to prevent the digital reproduction from being communicated by telecommunication to any persons who are not acting under the authority of the institution;

(c) take measures to prevent a person to whom the work has been communicated under paragraph (1)(b) from printing more than one copy, and to prevent any other reproduction or communication of the digital reproduction; and

(d)   take any measure prescribed by regulation.

Restriction

(4) An educational institution may not make a digital reproduction of a work under paragraph (1)(a) if

(a)   the institution has entered into a digital reproduction agreement respecting the work with a collective society under which the institution may make a digital reproduction of the work, may communicate the digital reproduction by telecommunication to persons acting under the authority of the institution and may permit those persons to print at least one copy of the work;

(b)   there is a tariff certified under section 70.15 that is applicable to the digital reproduction of the work, to the communication of the digital reproduction by telecommunication to persons acting under the authority of the institution and to the printing by those persons of at least one copy of the work; or

(c)   the institution has been informed by the collective society that is authorized to enter into reprographic agreements with respect to the work that the owner of the copyright in the work has informed it, under subsection (5), that the owner refuses to authorize the collective society to enter into a digital reproduction agreement with respect to the work.

Restriction

(5) If the owner of the copyright in a work informs the collective society that is authorized to enter into reprographic agreements with respect to the work that the owner refuses to authorize it to enter into digital reproduction agreements with respect to the work, the collective society shall inform the educational institutions with which it has entered into reprographic reproduction agreements with respect to the work that they are not permitted to make digital reproductions under subsection (1).

Deeming provision

(6) The owner of the copyright in a work who, in respect of the work, has authorized a collective society to enter into a reprographic reproduction agreement with an educational institution is deemed to have authorized the society to enter into a digital reproduction agreement with the institution — subject to the same restrictions as a reprographic reproduction agreement — unless the owner has refused to give this authorization under subsection (5) or has authorized another collective society to enter into a digital reproduction agreement with respect to the work.

Maximum amount that may be recovered

(7) In proceedings against an educational institution for making a digital reproduction of a paper form of a work, or for communicating such a reproduction by telecommunication for an educational or training purpose to persons acting under the authority of the institution, the owner of the copyright in the work may not recover an amount more than

(a)   in the case where there is a digital reproduction licence that meets the conditions described in paragraph (4)(a) in respect of the work — or, if none exists in respect of the work, in respect of a work of the same category — the amount of royalties that would be payable under that licence in respect of those acts or, if there is more than one applicable licence, the greatest amount of royalties payable under any of those licences; and

(b) in the case where there is no licence described in paragraph (a) but there is a reprographic reproduction licence in respect of the work — or, if none exists in respect of the work, in respect of a work of the same category — the amount of royalties that would be payable under that licence in respect of those acts or, if there is more than one applicable licence, the greatest amount of royalties payable under any of those licences.

No damages

(8) The owner of the copyright in a work may not recover any damages against a person acting under the authority of the educational institution who, in respect of a digital reproduction of the work that is communicated to the person by telecommunication, prints one copy of the work if, at the time of the printing, it was reasonable for the person to believe that the communication was made in accordance with paragraph (1)(b).

2012, c. 20, s. 27

Royalties — digital reproduction agreement

30.03 (1) If an educational institution has paid royalties to a collective society for the digital reproduction of a work under paragraph 30.02(3)(a) and afterwards the institution enters into a digital reproduction agreement described in paragraph 30.02(4)(a) with any collective society,

(a) in the case where the institution would — under that digital reproduction agreement — pay a greater amount of royalties for the digital reproduction of that work than what was payable under paragraph 30.02(3)(a), the institution shall pay to the collective society to which it paid royalties under that paragraph the difference between

(i) the amount of royalties that the institution would have had to pay for the digital reproduction of that work if the agreement had been entered into on the day on which the institution first made a digital reproduction under paragraph 30.02(1)(a), and

(ii) the amount of royalties that the institution paid to the society under paragraph 30.02(3)(a) for the digital reproduction of that work from the day on which that paragraph comes into force until the day on which they enter into the digital reproduction agreement; and

(b) in the case where the institution would — under that digital reproduction agreement — pay a lesser amount of royalties for the digital reproduction of that work than what was payable under paragraph 30.02(3)(a), the collective society to which the institution paid royalties under that paragraph shall pay to the institution the difference between

(i) the amount of royalties that the institution paid to the society under paragraph 30.02(3)(a) for the digital reproduction of that work from the day on which that paragraph comes into force until the day on which they enter into the digital reproduction agreement, and

(ii) the amount of royalties that the institution would have had to pay for the digital reproduction of that work if the agreement had been entered into on the day on which the institution first made a digital reproduction under paragraph 30.02(1)(a).

Royalties — tariff

(2) If an educational institution has paid royalties to a collective society for the digital reproduction of a work under paragraph 30.02(3)(a) and afterwards a tariff applies to the digital reproduction of that work under paragraph 30.02(4)(b),

(a) in the case where the institution would — under the tariff — pay a greater amount of royalties for the digital reproduction of that work than what was payable under paragraph 30.02(3)(a), the institution shall pay to the collective society to which it paid royalties under that paragraph the difference between

    (i) the amount of royalties that the institution would have had to pay for the digital reproduction of that work if the tariff had been certified on the day on which the institution first made a digital reproduction under paragraph 30.02(1)(a), and

    (ii) the amount of royalties that the institution paid to the society under paragraph 30.02(3)(a) for the digital reproduction of that work from the day on which that paragraph comes into force until the day on which the tariff is certified; and

(b) in the case where the institution would — under the tariff — pay a lesser amount of royalties for the digital reproduction of that work than what was payable under paragraph 30.02(3)(a), the collective society to which the institution paid royalties under that paragraph shall pay to the institution the difference between

    (i) the amount of royalties that the institution paid to the society under paragraph 30.02(3)(a) for the digital reproduction of that work from the day on which that paragraph comes into force until the day on which the tariff is certified, and

    (ii) the amount of royalties that the institution would have had to pay for the digital reproduction of that work if the tariff had been certified on the day on which the institution first made a digital reproduction under paragraph 30.02(1)(a).

2012, c. 20, s. 27

Work available through Internet

30.04 (1) Subject to subsections (2) to (5), it is not an infringement of copyright for an educational institution, or a person acting under the authority of one, to do any of the following acts for educational or training purposes in respect of a work or other subject-matter that is available through the Internet:

(a) reproduce it;

(b) communicate it to the public by telecommunication, if that public primarily consists of students of the educational institution or other persons acting under its authority;

(c) perform it in public, if that public primarily consists of students of the educational institution or other persons acting under its authority; or

(d) do any other act that is necessary for the purpose of the acts referred to in paragraphs (a) to (c).

Conditions

(2) Subsection (1) does not apply unless the educational institution or person acting under its authority, in doing any of the acts described in that subsection in respect of the work or other subject-matter, mentions the following:

> (a)   the source; and
>
> (b)   if given in the source, the name of
>
> > (i)   the author, in the case of a work,
> >
> > (ii)   the performer, in the case of a performer's performance,
> >
> > (iii)   the maker, in the case of a sound recording, and
> >
> > (iv)   the broadcaster, in the case of a communication signal.

Non-application

(3) Subsection (1) does not apply if the work or other subject-matter — or the Internet site where it is posted — is protected by a technological protection measure that restricts access to the work or other subject-matter or to the Internet site.

Non-application

(4) Subsection (1) does not permit a person to do any act described in that subsection in respect of a work or other subject-matter if

> (a)   that work or other subject-matter — or the Internet site where it is posted — is protected by a technological protection measure that restricts the doing of that act; or
>
> (b)   a clearly visible notice — and not merely the copyright symbol — prohibiting that act is posted at the Internet site where the work or other subject-matter is posted or on the work or other subject-matter itself.

Non-application

(5) Subsection (1) does not apply if the educational institution or person acting under its authority knows or should have known that the work or other subject-matter was made available through the Internet without the consent of the copyright owner.

Regulations

(6) The Governor in Council may make regulations for the purposes of paragraph (4)(b) prescribing what constitutes a clearly visible notice.

2012, c. 20, s. 27

Libraries, Archives and Museums

Management and maintenance of collection

30.1 (1) It is not an infringement of copyright for a library, archive or museum or a person acting under the authority of a library, archive or museum to make, for the maintenance or management of its permanent collection or the permanent collection of another library, archive or museum, a copy of a work or other subject-matter, whether published or unpublished, in its permanent collection

    (a) if the original is rare or unpublished and is

        (i) deteriorating, damaged or lost, or

        (ii) at risk of deterioration or becoming damaged or lost;

    (b) for the purposes of on-site consultation if the original cannot be viewed, handled or listened to because of its condition or because of the atmospheric conditions in which it must be kept;

    (c) in an alternative format if the library, archive or museum or a person acting under the authority of the library, archive or museum considers that the original is currently in a format that is obsolete or is becoming obsolete, or that the technology required to use the original is unavailable or is becoming unavailable;

    (d) for the purposes of internal record-keeping and cataloguing;

    (e) for insurance purposes or police investigations; or

    (f) if necessary for restoration.

Limitation

(2) Paragraphs (1)(a) to (c) do not apply where an appropriate copy is commercially available in a medium and of a quality that is appropriate for the purposes of subsection (1).

Destruction of intermediate copies

(3) If a person must make an intermediate copy in order to make a copy under subsection (1), the person must destroy the intermediate copy as soon as it is no longer needed.

Regulations

(4) The Governor in Council may make regulations with respect to the procedure for making copies under subsection (1).

                    1997, c. 24, s. 18(1); 1999, c. 31, s. 59(E); 2012, c. 20, s. 28

Research or private study

30.2 (1) It is not an infringement of copyright for a library, archive or museum or a person acting under its authority to do anything on behalf of any person that the person may do personally under section 29 or 29.1.

Copies of articles for research, etc.

(2) It is not an infringement of copyright for a library, archive or museum or a person acting under the authority of a library, archive or museum to make, by reprographic reproduction, for any person requesting to use the copy for research or private study, a copy of a work that is, or that is contained in, an article published in

    (a) a scholarly, scientific or technical periodical; or

    (b) a newspaper or periodical, other than a scholarly, scientific or technical periodical, if the newspaper or periodical was published more than one year before the copy is made.

Restriction

(3) Paragraph (2)(b) does not apply in respect of a work of fiction or poetry or a dramatic or musical work.

Conditions

(4) A library, archive or museum may provide the person for whom the copy is made under subsection (2) with the copy only on the condition that

    (a)   the person is provided with a single copy of the work; and

    (b)   the library, archive or museum informs the person that the copy is to be used solely for research or private study and that any use of the copy for a purpose other than research or private study may require the authorization of the copyright owner of the work in question.

Patrons of other libraries, etc.

(5) Subject to subsection (5.02), a library, archive or museum, or a person acting under the authority of one, may do, on behalf of a patron of another library, archive or museum, anything under subsection (1) or (2) that it is authorized by this section to do on behalf of one of its own patrons.

Deeming

(5.01) For the purpose of subsection (5), the making of a copy of a work other than by reprographic reproduction is deemed to be a making of a copy of the work that may be done under subsection (2).

Limitation regarding copies in digital form

(5.02) A library, archive or museum, or a person acting under the authority of one, may, under subsection (5), provide a copy in digital form to a person who has requested it through another library, archive or museum if the providing library, archive or museum or person takes measures to prevent the person who has requested it from

    (a)   making any reproduction of the digital copy, including any paper copies, other than printing one copy of it;

    (b)   communicating the digital copy to any other person; and

    (c)   using the digital copy for more than five business days from the day on which the person first uses it.

Destruction of intermediate copies

(5.1) Where an intermediate copy is made in order to copy a work referred to in subsection (5), once the copy is given to the patron, the intermediate copy must be destroyed.

Regulations

(6) The Governor in Council may, for the purposes of this section, make regulations

    (a)   defining **"newspaper"** and **"periodical"**;

    (b)   defining scholarly, scientific and technical periodicals;

(c) prescribing the information to be recorded about any action taken under subsection (1) or (5) and the manner and form in which the information is to be kept; and

(d) prescribing the manner and form in which the conditions set out in subsection (4) are to be met.

1997, c. 24, s. 18(1); 2012, c. 20, s. 29

Copying works deposited in archive

30.21 (1) Subject to subsections (3) and (3.1), it is not an infringement of copyright for an archive to make, for any person requesting to use the copy for research or private study, a copy of an unpublished work that is deposited in the archive and provide the person with it.

[Editor's Note: According to s. 21(4) of the Library and Archives of Canada Act, *S.C. 2004, c. 11, this subsection applies in respect of unpublished works deposited in an archive on or before September 1, 1999, or at any time after that date.]*

Notice

(2) When a person deposits a work in an archive, the archive must give the person notice that it may copy the work in accordance with this section.

Conditions for copying of works

(3) The archive may copy the work only on the condition that

(a) the person who deposited the work, if a copyright owner, did not, at the time the work was deposited, prohibit its copying; and

(b) copying has not been prohibited by any other owner of copyright in the work.

Condition for providing copy

(3.1) The archive may provide the person for whom a copy is made under subsection (1) with the copy only on the condition that

(a) the person is provided with a single copy of the work; and

(b) the archive informs the person that the copy is to be used solely for research or private study and that any use of the copy for a purpose other than research or private study may require the authorization of the copyright owner of the work in question.

Regulations

(4) The Governor in Council may prescribe by regulation the manner and form in which the conditions set out in subsections (3) and (3.1) may be met.

(5) [Repealed 2004, c. 11, s. 21(3).]

(6) [Repealed 2004, c. 11, s. 21(3).]

(7) [Repealed 2004, c. 11, s. 21(3).]

1997, c. 24, s. 18(1); 1999, c. 31, s. 60(E); 2004, c. 11, s. 21; 2012, c. 20, s. 30

Machines Installed in Educational Institutions, Libraries, Archives and Museums

No infringement by educational institution, etc.

30.3 (1) An educational institution or a library, archive or museum does not infringe copyright where

    (a) a copy of a work is made using a machine for the making, by reprographic reproduction, of copies of works in printed form;

    (b) the machine is installed by or with the approval of the educational institution, library, archive or museum on its premises for use by students, instructors or staff at the educational institution or by persons using the library, archive or museum; and

    (c) there is affixed in the prescribed manner and location a notice warning of infringement of copyright.

Application

(2) Subsection (1) only applies if, in respect of a reprographic reproduction,

    (a) the educational institution, library, archive or museum has entered into an agreement with a collective society that is authorized by copyright owners to grant licences on their behalf;

    (b) the Board has, in accordance with section 70.2, fixed the royalties and related terms and conditions in respect of a licence;

    (c) a tariff has been approved in accordance with section 70.15; or

    (d) a collective society has filed a proposed tariff in accordance with section 70.13.

Order

(3) Where a collective society offers to negotiate or has begun to negotiate an agreement referred to in paragraph (2)(a), the Board may, at the request of either party, order that the educational institution, library, archive or museum be treated as an institution to which subsection (1) applies, during the period specified in the order.

Agreement with copyright owner

(4) Where an educational institution, library, archive or museum has entered into an agreement with a copyright owner other than a collective society respecting reprographic reproduction, subsection (1) applies only in respect of the works of the copyright owner that are covered by the agreement.

Regulations

(5) The Governor in Council may, for the purposes of paragraph 1(c), prescribe by regulation the manner of affixing and location of notices and the dimensions, form and contents of notices.

1997, c. 24, s. 18(1)

Libraries, Archives and Museums in Educational Institutions

Application to libraries, etc within educational institutions

30.4 For greater certainty, the exceptions to infringement of copyright provided for under sections 29.4 to 30.3 and 45 also apply in respect of a library, archive or museum that forms part of an educational institution.

1997, c. 24, s. 18(1)

Library and Archives of Canada

[Heading amended 2004, c. 11, s. 25.]

Permitted acts

30.5 It is not an infringement of copyright for the Librarian and Archivist of Canada under the *Library and Archives of Canada Act*, to

(a) make a copy of a work or other subject-matter in taking a representative sample for the purpose of preservation under subsection 8(2) of that Act;

(b) effect the fixation of a copy of a publication, as defined in section 2 of that Act, that is provided by telecommunication in accordance with subsection 10(1) of that Act;

(c) make a copy of a recording, as defined in subsection 11(2) of that Act, for the purposes of section 11 of that Act; or

(d) at the time that a broadcasting undertaking, as defined in subsection 2(1) of the *Broadcasting Act*, communicates a work or other subject-matter to the public by telecommunication, make a copy of the work ornother subject-matter that is included in that communication.

1997, c. 24, s. 18(1); 2004, c. 11, s. 25

Computer Programs

Permitted acts

30.6 It is not an infringement of copyright in a computer program for a person who owns a copy of the computer program that is authorized by the owner of the copyright, or has a licence to use a copy of the computer program, to

(a) reproduce the copy by adapting, modifying or converting it, or translating it into another computer language, if the person proves that the reproduced copy

(i) is essential for the compatibility of the computer program with a particular computer,

(ii) is solely for the person's own use, and

(iii) was destroyed immediately after the person ceased to be the owner of the copy of the computer program or to have a licence to use it; or

(b) reproduce for backup purposes the copy or a reproduced copy referred to in paragraph (a) if the person proves that the reproduction for backup purposes was destroyed immediately after the person ceased to be the owner of the copy of the computer program or to have a licence to use it.

1997, c. 24, s. 18(1); 2012, c. 20, s. 31

Interoperability of computer programs

30.61 (1) It is not an infringement of copyright in a computer program for a person who owns a copy of the computer program that is authorized by the owner of the copyright, or has a licence to use a copy of the computer program, to reproduce the copy if

(a) they reproduce the copy for the sole purpose of obtaining information that would allow the person to make the program and another computer program interoperable; and

(b) they do not use or disclose that information, except as necessary to make the program and another computer program interoperable or to assess that interoperability.

No limitation

(2) In the case where that information is used or disclosed as necessary to make another computer program interoperable with the program, subsection (1) applies even if the other computer program incorporates the information and is then sold, rented or otherwise distributed.

2012, c. 20, s. 31

Encryption Research

[Heading added 2012, c. 20, s. 31.]

Encryption research

30.62 (1) Subject to subsections (2) and (3), it is not an infringement of copyright for a person to reproduce a work or other subject-matter for the purposes of encryption research if

(a) it would not be practical to carry out the research without making the copy;

(b) the person has lawfully obtained the work or other subject-matter; and

(c) the person has informed the owner of the copyright in the work or other subject-matter.

Limitation

(2) Subsection (1) does not apply if the person uses or discloses information obtained through the research to commit an act that is an offence under the *Criminal Code*.

Limitation — computer program

(3) Subsection (1) applies with respect to a computer program only if, in the event that the research reveals a vulnerability or a security flaw in the program and the person intends to make the vulnerability or security flaw public, the person gives adequate notice of the vulnerability or security flaw and of their intention to the owner of copyright in the program. However, the person need not give that adequate notice if, in the circumstances, the public interest in having the vulnerability or security flaw made public without adequate notice outweighs the owner's interest in receiving that notice.

2012, c. 20, s. 31

Security

[Heading added 2012, c. 20, s. 31.]

Security

30.63 (1) Subject to subsections (2) and (3), it is not an infringement of copyright for a person to reproduce a work or other subject-matter for the sole purpose, with the consent of the owner or administrator of a computer, computer system or computer network, of assessing the vulnerability of the computer, system or network or of correcting any security flaws.

Limitation

(2) Subsection (1) does not apply if the person uses or discloses information obtained through the assessment or correction to commit an act that is an offence under the *Criminal Code*.

Limitation — computer program

(3) Subsection (1) applies with respect to a computer program only if, in the event that the assessment or correction reveals a vulnerability or a security flaw in the program and the person intends to make the vulnerability or security flaw public, the person gives adequate notice of the vulnerability or security flaw and of their intention to the owner of copyright in the program. However, the person need not give that adequate notice if, in the circumstances, the public interest in having the vulnerability or security flaw made public without adequate notice outweighs the owner's interest in receiving that notice.

2012, c. 20, s. 31

Incidental Inclusion

Incidental use

30.7 It is not an infringement of copyright to incidentally and not deliberately

   (a)   include a work or other subject-matter in another work or other subject-matter, or

   (b)   do any act in relation to a work or other subject-matter that is incidentally and not deliberately included in another work or other subject-matter.

1997, c. 24, s. 18(1)

Temporary Reproductions for Technological Processes

[Heading added 2012, c. 20, s. 32.]

Temporary reproductions

30.71 It is not an infringement of copyright to make a reproduction of a work or other subject-matter if

   (a)   the reproduction forms an essential part of a technological process;

   (b)   the reproduction's only purpose is to facilitate a use that is not an infringement of copyright; and

   (c)   the reproduction exists only for the duration of the technological process.

2012, c. 20, s. 32

Ephemeral Recordings

Ephemeral recordings

30.8 (1) It is not an infringement of copyright for a programming undertaking to fix or reproduce in accordance with this section a performer's performance or work, other than a cinematographic work, that is performed live or a sound recording that is performed at the same time as the performer's performance or work, if the undertaking

- (a) is authorized to communicate the performer's performance, work or sound recording to the public by telecommunication;

- (b) makes the fixation or the reproduction itself, for its own broadcasts;

- (c) does not synchronize the fixation or reproduction with all or part of another recording, performer's performance or work; and

- (d) does not cause the fixation or reproduction to be used in an advertisement intended to sell or promote, as the case may be, a product, service, cause or institution.

Record keeping

(2) The programming undertaking must record the dates of the making and destruction of all fixations and reproductions and any other prescribed information about the fixation or reproduction, and keep the record current.

Right of access by copyright owners

(3) The programming undertaking must make the record referred to in subsection (2) available to owners of copyright in the works, sound recordings or performer's performances, or their representatives, within twenty-four hours after receiving a request.

Destruction

(4) The programming undertaking must destroy the fixation or reproduction within thirty days after making it, unless

- (a) the copyright owner authorizes its retention; or

- (b) it is deposited in an archive, in accordance with subsection (6).

Royalties

(5) Where the copyright owner authorizes the fixation or reproduction to be retained after the thirty days, the programming undertaking must pay any applicable royalty.

Archive

(6) Where the programming undertaking considers a fixation or reproduction to be of an exceptional documentary character, the undertaking may, with the consent of an official archive, deposit it in the official archive and must notify the copyright owner, within thirty days, of the deposit of the fixation or reproduction.

Definition of "official archive"

(7) In subsection (6), **"official archive"** means the Library and Archives of Canada or any archive established under the law of a province for the preservation of the official archives of the province.

Application

(8) This section does not apply where a licence is available from a collective society to make the fixation or reproduction of the performer's performance, work or sound recording.

Telecommunications by networks

(9) A broadcast undertaking, as defined in the *Broadcasting Act*, may make a single reproduction of a fixation or reproduction made by a programming undertaking and communicate it to the public by telecommunication, within the period referred to in subsection (4), if the broadcasting undertaking meets the conditions set out in subsection (1) and is part of a prescribed network that includes the programming undertaking.

Limitations

(10) The reproduction and communication to the public by telecommunication must be made

(a) in accordance with subsections (2) to (6); and

(b) within thirty days after the day on which the programming undertaking made the fixation or reproduction.

Definition of "programming undertaking"

(11) In this section, **"programming undertaking"** means

(a) a programming undertaking as defined in subsection 2(1) of the *Broadcasting Act*;

(b) a programming undertaking described in paragraph (a) that originates programs within a network, as defined in subsection 2(1) of the *Broadcasting Act*; or

(c) a distribution undertaking as defined in subsection 2(1) of the *Broadcasting Act*, in respect of the programs that it originates.

The undertaking must hold a broadcasting licence issued by the Canadian Radio-television and Telecommunications Commission under the *Broadcasting Act*, or be exempted from this requirement by the Canadian Radio-television and Telecommunications Commission.

1997, c. 24, s. 18(1); 2004, c. 11, s. 26; 2012, c. 20, s. 33

Ephemeral recordings — broadcasting undertaking

30.9 (1) It is not an infringement of copyright for a broadcasting undertaking to reproduce in accordance with this section a sound recording, or a performer's performance or work that is embodied in a sound recording, solely for the purpose of their broadcasting, if the undertaking

(a) owns the copy of the sound recording, performer's performance or work and that copy is authorized by the owner of the copyright, or has a licence to use the copy;

(b) is authorized to communicate the sound recording, performer's performance or work to the public by telecommunication;

(c) makes the reproduction itself, for its own broadcasts;

    (d)   does not synchronize the reproduction with all or part of another recording, performer's performance or work; and

    (e)   does not cause the reproduction to be used in an advertisement intended to sell or promote, as the case may be, a product, service, cause or institution.

Record keeping

(2) The broadcasting undertaking must record the dates of the making and destruction of all reproductions and any other prescribed information about the reproduction, and keep the record current.

Right of access by copyright owners

(3) The broadcasting undertaking must make the record referred to in subsection (2) available to owners of copyright in the sound recordings, performer's performances or works, or their representatives, within twenty-four hours after receiving a request.

Destruction

(4) The broadcasting undertaking must destroy the reproduction when it no longer possesses the sound recording, or performer's performance or work embodied in the sound recording, or its licence to use the sound recording, performer's performance or work expires, or at the latest within 30 days after making the reproduction, unless the copyright owner authorizes the reproduction to be retained.

Royalty

(5) If the copyright owner authorizes the reproduction to be retained, the broadcasting undertaking must pay any applicable royalty.

(6) [Repealed 2012, c. 20, s. 34(3).]

Definition of "broadcasting undertaking"

(7) In this section, **"broadcasting undertaking"** means a broadcasting undertaking as defined in subsection 2(1) of the *Broadcasting Act* that holds a broadcasting licence issued by the Canadian Radio-television and Telecommunications Commission under that Act.

1997, c. 24, s. 18(1); 2012, c. 20, s. 34

Retransmission

Interpretation

31. (1) In this section,

"new media retransmitter" means a person whose retransmission is lawful under the *Broadcasting Act* only by reason of the *Exemption Order for New Media Broadcasting Undertakings* issued by the Canadian Radio-television and Telecommunications Commission as Appendix A to Public Notice CRTC 1999-197, as amended from time to time;

"retransmitter" means a person who performs a function comparable to that of a cable retransmission system, but does not include a new media retransmitter;

"signal" means a signal that carries a literary, dramatic, musical or artistic work and is transmitted for free reception by the public by a terrestrial radio or terrestrial television station.

Retransmission of local and distant signals

(2) It is not an infringement of copyright for a retransmitter to communicate to the public by telecommunication any literary, dramatic, musical or artistic work if

    (a) the communication is a retransmission of a local or distant signal;

    (b) the retransmission is lawful under the *Broadcasting Act*;

    (c) the signal is retransmitted simultaneously and without alteration, except as otherwise required or permitted by or under the laws of Canada;

    (d) in the case of the retransmission of a distant signal, the retransmitter has paid any royalties, and complied with any terms and conditions, fixed under this Act; and

    (e) the retransmitter complies with the applicable conditions, if any, referred to in paragraph (3)(b).

Regulations

(3) The Governor in Council may make regulations

    (a) defining "local signal" and "distant signal" for the purposes of subsection (2); and

    (b) prescribing conditions for the purposes of paragraph (2)(e), and specifying whether any such condition applies to all retransmitters or only to a class of retransmitter.

R.S.C. 1985, c. 10 (4th Supp.), s. 7; 1988, c. 65, s. 63;
1997, c. 24, s. 16; 2002, c. 26, s. 2

Network Services

[Heading added 2012, c. 20, s. 35.]

Network services

31.1 (1) A person who, in providing services related to the operation of the Internet or another digital network, provides any means for the telecommunication or the reproduction of a work or other subject-matter through the Internet or that other network does not, solely by reason of providing those means, infringe copyright in that work or other subject-matter.

Incidental acts

(2) Subject to subsection (3), a person referred to in subsection (1) who caches the work or other subject-matter, or does any similar act in relation to it, to make the telecommunication more efficient does not, by virtue of that act alone, infringe copyright in the work or other subject-matter.

Conditions for application

(3) Subsection (2) does not apply unless the person, in respect of the work or other subject-matter,

    (a) does not modify it, other than for technical reasons;

(b) ensures that any directions related to its caching or the doing of any similar act, as the case may be, that are specified in a manner consistent with industry practice by whoever made it available for telecommunication through the Internet or another digital network, and that lend themselves to automated reading and execution, are read and executed; and

(c) does not interfere with the use of technology that is lawful and consistent with industry practice in order to obtain data on the use of the work or other subject-matter.

Hosting

(4) Subject to subsection (5), a person who, for the purpose of allowing the telecommunication of a work or other subject-matter through the Internet or another digital network, provides digital memory in which another person stores the work or other subject-matter does not, by virtue of that act alone, infringe copyright in the work or other subject-matter.

Condition for application

(5) Subsection (4) does not apply in respect of a work or other subject-matter if the person providing the digital memory knows of a decision of a court of competent jurisdiction to the effect that the person who has stored the work or other subject-matter in the digital memory infringes copyright by making the copy of the work or other subject-matter that is stored or by the way in which he or she uses the work or other subject-matter.

Exception

(6) Subsections (1), (2) and (4) do not apply in relation to an act that constitutes an infringement of copyright under subsection 27(2.3).

2012, c. 20, s. 35

Persons with Perceptual Disabilities

Reproduction in alternate format

32. (1) It is not an infringement of copyright for a person with a perceptual disability, for a person acting at the request of such a person or for a non-profit organization acting for the benefit of such a person to

(a) make a copy or sound recording of a literary, musical, artistic or dramatic work, other than a cinematographic work, in a format specially designed for persons with a perceptual disability;

(b) translate, adapt or reproduce in sign language a literary or dramatic work, other than a cinematographic work, in a format specially designed for persons with a perceptual disability; or

(c) perform in public a literary or dramatic work, other than a cinematographic work, in sign language, either live or in a format specially designed for persons with a perceptual disability.

Limitation

(2) Subsection (1) does not authorize the making of a large print book.

Limitation

(3) Subsection (1) does not apply where the work or sound recording is commercially available in a format specially designed to meet the needs of any person referred to in that subsection, within the meaning of paragraph (a) of the definition **"commercially available"**.

R.S.C. 1985, c. 10 (4th Supp.), s. 7; 1997, c. 24, s. 19; 2012, c. 20, s. 36

Sending copies outside Canada

32.01 (1) Subject to this section, it is not an infringement of copyright for a non-profit organization acting for the benefit of persons with a print disability to make a copy, in a format specially designed for persons with a print disability, of a work and to send the copy to a non-profit organization in another country for use by persons with print disabilities in that country, if the author of the work that is reformatted is

(a) a Canadian citizen or permanent resident within the meaning of subsection 2(1) of the *Immigration and Refugee Protection Act*; or

(b) a citizen or permanent resident of the country to which the copy is sent.

Limitation

(2) Subsection (1) does not authorize a large print book or a cinematographic work to be sent outside Canada.

Work available in country

(3) Subsection (1) does not authorize a copy to be sent to a country if the organization knows or has reason to believe that the work, in the format specially designed for persons with a print disability, is available in that country within a reasonable time and for a reasonable price, and may be located in that country with reasonable effort.

Good faith mistake as to author's nationality

(3.1) If a non-profit organization that is relying on the exception set out in subsection (1) infringes copyright by reason only of making a mistake in good faith as to the citizenship or residency of the author of the work, an injunction is the only remedy that the owner of the copyright in the work has against the organization.

Royalty

(4) The organization making and sending the copy shall pay, in accordance with the regulations, any royalty established under the regulations to the copyright owner in the work.

If copyright owner cannot be located

(5) If the organization cannot locate the copyright owner, despite making reasonable efforts to do so, the organization shall pay, in accordance with the regulations, any royalty established under the regulations to a collective society.

Reports

(6) The organization making and sending the copy shall submit reports to an authority in accordance with the regulations on the organization's activities under this section.

Regulations

(7) The Governor in Council may make regulations

(a) requiring a non-profit organization that seeks to send a copy outside Canada to, before doing so, enter into a contract with the recipient non-profit organization with respect to the use of the copy;

(b) respecting the form and content of such contracts;

(c) respecting any royalties to be paid under subsections (4) and (5);

(d) respecting to which collective society a royalty is payable in relation to works or classes of works for the purposes of subsection (5);

(e) respecting what constitutes reasonable efforts for the purposes of subsection (5); and

(f) respecting the reports to be made, and the authorities to which the reports are to be submitted, under subsection (6).

Meaning of "print disability"

(8) In this section, **"print disability"** means a disability that prevents or inhibits a person from reading a literary, musical or dramatic work in its original format, and includes such a disability resulting from

(a) severe or total impairment of sight or the inability to focus or move one's eyes;

(b) the inability to hold or manipulate a book; or

(c) an impairment relating to comprehension.

2012, c. 20, s. 37

Statutory Obligations

No infringement

32.1 (1) It is not an infringement of copyright for any person

(a) to disclose, pursuant to the *Access to Information Act*, a record within the meaning of that Act, or to disclose, pursuant to any like Act of the legislature of a province, like material;

(b) to disclose, pursuant to the *Privacy Act*, personal information within the meaning of that Act, or to disclose, pursuant to any like Act of the legislature of a province, like information;

(c) to make a copy of an object referred to in section 14 of the *Cultural Property Export and Import Act*, for deposit in an institution pursuant to a direction under that section; and

(d) to make a fixation or copy of a work or other subject-matter in order to comply with the *Broadcasting Act* or any rule, regulation or other instrument made under it.

Limitation

(2) Nothing in paragraph (1)(a) or (b) authorizes a person to whom a record or information is disclosed to do anything that, by this Act, only the owner of the copyright in the record, personal information or like information, as the case may be, has a right to do.

Destruction of fixation or copy

(3) Unless the *Broadcasting Act* otherwise provides, a person who makes a fixation or copy under (1)(d) shall destroy it immediately on the expiration of the period for which it must be kept pursuant to that Act, rule, regulation or other instrument.

1997, c. 24, s. 19

Miscellaneous

Permitted acts

32.2 (1) It is not an infringement of copyright

    (a) for an author of an artistic work who is not the owner of the copyright in the work to use any mould, cast, sketch, plan, model or study made by the author for the purpose of the work, if the author does not thereby repeat or imitate the main design of the work;

    (b) for any person to reproduce, in a painting, drawing, engraving, photograph or cinematographic work

        (i) an architectural work, provided the copy is not in the nature of an architectural drawing or plan, or

        (ii) a sculpture or work of artistic craftsmanship or a cast or model of a sculpture or work of artistic craftsmanship, that is permanently situated in a public place or building;

    (c) for any person to make or publish, for the purposes of news reporting or news summary, a report of a lecture given in public, unless the report is prohibited by conspicuous written or printed notice affixed before and maintained during the lecture at or about the main entrance of the building in which the lecture is given, and, except while the building is being used for public worship, in a position near the lecturer;

    (d) for any person to read or recite in public a reasonable extract from a published work;

    (e) for any person to make or publish, for the purpose of news reporting or news summary, a report of an address of a political nature given at a public meeting; or

    (f) for an individual to use for private or non-commercial purposes, or permit the use of for those purposes, a photograph or portrait that was commissioned by the individual for personal purposes and made for valuable consideration, unless the individual and the owner of the copyright in the photograph or portrait have agreed otherwise.

Further permitted acts

(2) It is not an infringement of copyright for a person to do any of the following acts without motive of gain at any agricultural or agricultural-industrial exhibition or fair that receives a grant from or is held by its directors under federal, provincial or municipal authority:

(a) the live performance in public of a musical work;

(b) the performance in public of a sound recording embodying a musical work or a performer's performance of a musical work; or

(c) the performance in public of a communiation signal carrying

(i) the live performance in public of a musical work, or

(ii) a sound recording embodying a musical work or a performer's performance of a musical work.

Further permitted acts

(3) No religious organization or institution, educational institution and no charitable or fraternal organization shall be held liable to pay any compensation for doing any of the following acts in furtherance of a religious, educational or charitable object:

(a) the live performance in public of a musical work;

(b) the performance in public of a sound recording embodying a musical work or a performer's performance of a musical work; or

(c) the performance in public of a communication signal carrying

(i) the live performance in public of a musical work, or

(ii) a sound recording embodying a musical work or a performer's performance of a musical work.

1997, c. 24, s. 19; 2012, c. 20, s. 38

Interpretation

No right to equitable remuneration

32.3 For the purposes of sections 29 to 32.2, an act that does not infringe copyright does not give rise to a remuneration conferred by section 19.

1997, c. 24, s. 19

Compensation for Acts Done Before Recognition of Copyright of Performers and Broadcasters

Certain rights and interests protected

32.4 (1) Notwithstanding section 27, where a person has, before the later of January 1, 1996 and the day on which a country becomes a WTO member, incurred an expenditure or liability in connection with, or in preparation for, the doing of an act that would have infringed copyright under section 26 commencing on the later of those two days, had that country been a WTO member, any right or interest of that person that

(a) arises from or in connection with the doing of that act, and

(b)   is subsisting and valuable on the later of those days

is not prejudiced or diminished by reason only that that country has become a WTO member, except as provided by an order of the Board made under subsection 78(3).

Compensation

(2) Notwithstanding subsection (1), a person's right or interest that is protected by that subsection terminates if and when the owner of the copyright pays that person such compensation as is agreed to between the parties or, failing agreement, as is determined by the Board in accordance with section 78.

Limitation

(3) Nothing in subsections (1) and (2) affects any right of a performer available in law or equity.

1997, c. 24, s. 19

Certain rights and interests protected

32.5 (1) Notwithstanding section 27, where a person has, before the later of the coming into force of Part II and the day on which a country becomes a Rome Convention country, incurred an expenditure or liability in connection with, or in preparation for, the doing of an act that would have infringed copyright under section 15 or 21 commencing on the later of those days, had Part II been in force or had that country been a Rome Convention country, any right or interest or that person that

(a)   arises from or in connection with the doing of that act, and

(b)   is subsisting and valuable on the later of those days

is not prejudiced or diminished by reason only that Part II has come into force or that the country has become a Rome Convention country, except as provided by an order of the Board made under subsection 78(3).

Compensation

(2) Notwithstanding subsection (1), a person's right or interest that is protected by that subsection terminates if and when the owner of the copyright pays that person such compensation as is agreed to between the parties or, failing agreement, as is determined by the Board in accordance with section 78.

Limitation

(3) Nothing in subsections (1) and (2) affects any right of a performer available in law or equity.

1997, c. 24, s. 19

Certain rights and interests protected

32.6 Despite sections 27, 28.1 and 28.2, if a person has, before the day on which subsection 15(1.1), 17.1(1) or 18(1.1) applies in respect of a particular performers' performance or sound recording, incurred an expenditure or a liability in connection with, or in preparation for, the doing of an act that would, if done after that day, have infringed rights under that subsection, any right or interest of that person that arises from, or in connection with, the doing of that act and that is subsisting and valuable on that day is not, for two years after the day on which this section comes into force, prejudiced or diminished by reason only of the subsequent application of that subsection in respect of the performers' performance or sound recording.

2012, c. 20, s. 39

Compensation for Acts Done Before Recognition of Copyright or Moral Rights

Certain rights and interests protected

33. (1) Despite subsections 27(1), (2) and (4) and sections 27.1, 28.1 and 28.2, if a person has, before the later of January 1, 1996 and the day on which a country becomes a treaty country other than a WCT country, incurred an expenditure or liability in connection with, or in preparation for, the doing of an act that, if that country had been such a treaty country, would have infringed copyright in a work or moral rights in respect of a work, any right or interest of that person that arises from, or in connection with, the doing of that act and that is subsisting and valuable on the later of those days is not, except as provided by an order of the Board made under subsection 78(3), prejudiced or diminished by reason only of that country having become such a treaty country.

Compensation

(2) Notwithstanding subsection (1), a person's right or interest that is protected by that subsection terminates, as against the copyright owner or the author, if and when that copyright owner or the author, as the case may be, pays that person such compensation as is agreed to between the parties or, failing agreement, as is determined by the Board in accordance with section 78.

R.S.C. 1985, c. 10 (4th Supp.), s. 7; 1997, c. 24, s. 19; 2012, c. 20, s. 40

Certain rights and interests protected

33.1 (1) Despite subsections 27(1), (2) and (4) and sections 27.1, 28.1 and 28.2, if a person has, before the later of the day on which this section comes into force and the day on which a country that is a treaty country but not a WCT country becomes a WCT country, incurred an expenditure or liability in connection with, or in preparation for, the doing of an act that, if that country had been a WCT country, would have infringed a right under paragraph 3(1)(j), any right or interest of that person that arises from, or in connection with, the doing of that act and that is subsisting and valuable on the later of those days is not, except as provided by an order of the Board made under subsection 78(3), prejudiced or diminished by reason only of that country having become a WCT country.

Compensation

(2) Despite subsection (1), a person's right or interest that is protected by that subsection terminates as against the copyright owner if and when the owner pays the person any compensation that is agreed to between the parties or, failing agreement, that is determined by the Board in accordance with section 78.

2012, c. 20, s. 41

Certain rights and interests protected

33.2 (1) Despite subsections 27(1), (2) and (4) and sections 27.1, 28.1 and 28.2, if a person has, before the later of the day on which this section comes into force and the day on which a country that is not a treaty country becomes a WCT country, incurred an expenditure or a liability in connection with, or in preparation for, the doing of an act that, if that country had been a WCT country, would have infringed copyright in a work or moral rights in respect of a work, any right or interest of that person that arises from, or in connection with, the doing of that act and that is subsisting and valuable on the later of those days is not, except as provided by an order of the Board made under subsection 78(3), prejudiced or diminished by reason only of that country having become a WCT country.

Compensation

(2) Despite subsection (1), a person's right or interest that is protected by that subsection terminates as against the copyright owner if and when that owner pays the person any compensation that is agreed to between the parties or, failing agreement, that is determined by the Board in accordance with section 78.

2012, c. 20, s. 41

Part IV
Remedies (ss. 34–45)

[Heading added 1997, c. 24, s. 19.]

Civil Remedies

Infringement of Copyright and Moral Rights

[Heading added 2012, c. 20, s. 42.]

Copyright

34. (1) Where copyright has been infringed, the owner of the copyright is, subject to this Act, entitled to all remedies by way of injunction, damages, accounts, delivery up and otherwise that are or may be conferred by law for the infringement of a right.

Moral rights

(2) In any proceedings for an infringement of moral rights, the court may grant to the holder of those rights all remedies by way of injunction, damages, accounts, delivery up and otherwise that are or may be conferred by law for the infringement of a right.

Costs

(3) The costs of all parties in any proceedings in respect of the infringement of a right conferred by this Act shall be in the discretion of the court.

Summary proceedings

(4) The following proceedings may be commenced or proceeded with by way of application or action and shall, in the case of an application, be heard and determined without delay and in a summary way:

    (a) proceedings for infringement of copyright or moral rights;

    (b) proceedings taken under section 44.1, 44.2 or 44.4; and

    (c) proceedings taken in respect of

        (i) a tariff certified by the Board under Part VII or VIII, or

        (ii) agreements referred to in section 70.12.

Practice and procedure

(5) The rules of practice and procedure, in civil matters, of the court in which proceedings are commenced by way of application apply to those proceedings, but where those rules do not provide for the proceedings to be heard and determined without delay and in a summary way, the court may give such directions as it considers necessary in order to so provide.

Actions

(6) The court in which proceedings are instituted by way of application may, where it considers it appropriate, direct that the proceeding be proceeded with as an action.

Meaning of "application"

(7) In this section, **"application"** means a proceeding that is commenced other than by way of a writ or statement of claim.

R.S.C. 1985, c. 10 (4th Supp.), s. 8; 1993, c. 15, s. 3(E); 1993, c. 44, ss. 65(2), 78(b); 1994, c. 47, s. 62; 1997, c. 24, s. 20(1); 2012, c. 20, s. 43

Presumptions respecting copyright and ownership

34.1 (1) In any civil proceedings taken under this Act in which the defendant puts in issue either the existence of the copyright or the title of the plaintiff to it,

(a) copyright shall be presumed, unless the contrary is proved, to subsist in the work, performer's performance, sound recording or communication signal, as the case may be; and

(b) the author, performer, maker or broadcaster, as the case may be, shall, unless the contrary is proved, be presumed to be the owner of the copyright.

Where no grant registered

(2) Where any matter referred to in subsection (1) is at issue and no assignment of the copyright, or licence granting an interest in the copyright, has been registered under this Act,

(a) if a name purporting to be that of

(i)   the author of the work,

(ii) the performer of the performer's performance,

(iii) the maker of the sound recording, or

(iv) the broadcaster of the communication signal

is printed or otherwise indicated thereon in the usual manner, the person whose name is so printed or indicated shall, unless the contrary is proved, be presumed to be the author, performer, maker or broadcaster;

(b) if

(i)   no name is so printed or indicated, or if the name so printed or indicated is not the true name of the author, performer, maker or broadcaster or the name by which that person is commonly known, and

(ii) a name purporting to be that of the publisher or owner of the work, performer's performance, sound recording or communication signal is printed or otherwise indicated thereon in the usual manner,

the person whose name is printed or indicated as described in subparagraph (ii) shall, unless the contrary is proved, be presumed to be the owner of the copyright in question; and

(c) if, on a cinematographic work, a name purporting to be that of the maker of the cinematographic work appears in the usual manner, the person so named shall, unless the contrary is proved, be presumed to be the maker of the cinematographic work.

1997, c. 24, s. 20(1); 2012, c. 20, s. 44

Liability for infringement

35. (1) Where a person infringes copyright, the person is liable to pay such damages to the owner of the copyright as the owner has suffered due to the infringement and, in addition to those damages, such part of the profits that the infringer has made from the infringement and that were not taken into account in calculating the damages as the court considers just.

Proof of profits

(2) In proving profits,

(a) the plaintiff shall be required to prove only receipts or revenues derived from the infringement; and

(b) the defendant shall be required to prove every element of cost that the defendant claims.

1997, c. 24, s. 20(1)

36. [Repealed 2012, c. 20, s. 45.]

37. [Repealed 2012, c. 20, s. 45.]

Recovery of possession of copies, plates

38. (1) Subject to subsection (2), the owner of the copyright in a work or other subject-matter may

(a) recover possession of all infringing copies of that work or other subject-matter, and of all plates used or intended to be used for the production of infringing copies, and

(b) take proceedings for seizure of those copies or plates before judgment if, under the law of Canada or of the province in which those proceedings are taken, a person is entitled to take such proceedings,

as if those copies or plates were the property of the copyright owner.

Powers of court

(2) On application by

(a) a person from whom the copyright owner has recovered possession of copies or plates referred to in subsection (1),

(b)   a person against whom proceedings for seizure before judgment of copies or plates referred to in subsection (1) have been taken, or

(c)   any other person who has an interest in those copies or plates,

a court may order that those copies or plates be destroyed, or may make any other order that it considers appropriate in the circumstances.

Notice to interested persons

(3) Before making an order under subsection (2), the court shall direct that notice be given to any person who has an interest in the copies or plates in question, unless the court is of the opinion that the interests of justice do not require such notice to be given.

Circumstances court to consider

(4) In making an order under subsection (2), the court shall have regard to all the circumstances, including

(a)   the proportion, importance and value of the infringing copy or plate, as compared to the substrate or carrier embodying it; and

(b)   the extent to which the infringing copy or plate is severable from, or a distinct part of, the substrate or carrier embodying it.

Limitation

(5) Nothing in this Act entitles the copyright owner to damages in respect of the possession or conversion of the infringing copies or plates.

1997, c. 24, s. 20(1)

Statutory damages

38.1 (1) Subject to this section, a copyright owner may elect, at any time before final judgment is rendered, to recover, instead of damages and profits referred to in subsection 35(1), an award of statutory damages for which any one infringer is liable individually, or for which any two or more infringers are liable jointly and severally,

(a)   in a sum of not less than $500 and not more than $20,000 that the court considers just, with respect to all infringements involved in the proceedings for each work or other subject-matter, if the infringements are for commercial purposes; and

(b)   in a sum of not less than $100 and not more than $5,000 that the court considers just, with respect to all infringements involved in the proceedings for all works or other subject-matter, if the infringements are for non-commercial purposes.

Infringement of subsection 27(2.3)

(1.1) An infringement under subsection 27(2.3) may give rise to an award of statutory damages with respect to a work or other subject-matter only if the copyright in that work or other subject-matter was actually infringed as a result of the use of a service referred to in that subsection.

Deeming — infringement of subsection 27(2.3)

(1.11) For the purpose of subsection (1), an infringement under subsection 27(2.3) is deemed to be for a commercial purpose.

Infringements not involved in proceedings

(1.12) If the copyright owner has made an election under subsection (1) with respect to a defendant's infringements that are for non-commercial purposes, they are barred from recovering statutory damages under this section from that defendant with respect to any other of the defendant's infringements that were done for non-commercial purposes before the institution of the proceedings in which the election was made.

No other statutory damages

(1.2) If a copyright owner has made an election under subsection (1) with respect to a defendant's infringements that are for non-commercial purposes, every other copyright owner is barred from electing to recover statutory damages under this section in respect of that defendant for any of the defendant's infringements that were done for non-commercial purposes before the institution of the proceedings in which the election was made.

If defendant unaware of infringement

(2) If a copyright owner has made an election under subsection (1) and the defendant satisfies the court that the defendant was not aware and had no reasonable grounds to believe that the defendant had infringed copyright, the court may reduce the amount of the award under paragraph (1)(a) to less than $500, but not less than $200.

Special case

(3) In awarding statutory damages under paragraph (1)(a) or subsection (2), the court may award, with respect to each work or other subject-matter, a lower amount than $500 or $200, as the case may be, that the court considers just, if

    (a) either

        (i) there is more than one work or other subject-matter in a single medium, or

        (ii) the award relates only to one or more infringements under subsection 27(2.3); and

    (b) the awarding of even the minimum amount referred to in that paragraph or that subsection would result in a total award that, in the court's opinion, is grossly out of proportion to the infringement.

Collective societies

(4) Where the defendant has not paid applicable royalties, a collective society referred to in section 67 may only make an election under this section to recover, in lieu of any other remedy of a monetary nature provided by this Act, an award of statutory damages in a sum of not less than three and not more than ten times the amount of the applicable royalties, as the court considers just.

Factors to consider

(5) In exercising its discretion under subsections (1) to (4), the court shall consider all relevant factors, including

    (a) the good faith or bad faith of the defendant;

    (b) the conduct of the parties before and during the proceedings;

   (c)   the need to deter other infringements of the copyright in question; and

   (d)   in the case of infringements for non-commercial purposes, the need for an award to be proportionate to the infringements, in consideration of the hardship the award may cause to the defendant, whether the infringement was for private purposes or not, and the impact of the infringements on the plaintiff.

No award

(6) No statutory damages may be awarded against

   (a)   an educational institution or a person acting under its authority that has committed an act referred to in section 29.6 or 29.7 and has not paid any royalties or complied with any terms and conditions fixed under this Act in relation to the commission of the act;

   (b)   an educational institution, library, archive or museum that is sued in the circumstances referred to in section 38.2;

   (c)   a person who infringes copyright under paragraph 27(2)(e) or section 27.1, where the copy in question was made with the consent of the copyright owner in the country where the copy was made; or

   (d)   an educational institution that is sued in the circumstances referred to in subsection 30.02(7) or a person acting under its authority who is sued in the circumstances referred to in subsection 30.02(8).

Exemplary or punitive damages not affected

(7) An election under subsection (1) does not affect any right that the copyright owner may have to exemplary or punitive damages.

1997, c. 24, s. 20(1); 2012, c. 20, s. 46

Transitional Provision

1997, c. 24 provides:

> 20. (3) Section 38.1 of the *Copyright Act*, as enacted by subsection (1) of this section, only applies
>
>   (a)   to proceedings commenced after the date of the coming into force of that subsection; and
>
>   (b)   where the infringement to which those proceedings relate occurred after that date.

Maximum amount that may be recovered

38.2 (1) An owner of copyright in a work who has not authorized a collective society to authorize its reprographic reproduction may recover, in proceedings against an educational institution, library, archive or museum that has reproduced the work, a maximum amount equal to the amount of royalties that would have been payable to the society in respect of the reprographic reproduction, if it were authorized, either

   (a)   under any agreement entered into with the collective society; or

   (b)   under a tariff certified by the Board pursuant to section 70.15.

Agreements with more than one collective society

(2) Where agreements respecting reprographic reproduction have been signed with more than one collective society or where more than one tariff applies or where both

agreements and tariffs apply, the maximum amount that the copyright owner may recover is the largest amount of the royalties provided for in any of those agreements or tariffs.

Application

(3) Subsections (1) and (2) apply only where

    (a) the collective society is entitled to authorize, or the tariff provides for the payment of royalties in respect of, the reprographic reproduction of that category of work; and

    (b) copying of that general nature and extent is covered by the agreement or tariff.

1997, c. 24, s. 20(1)

Injunction only remedy when defendant not aware of copyright

39. (1) Subject to subsection (2), in any proceedings for infringement of copyright, the plaintiff is not entitled to any remedy other than an injunction in respect of the infringement if the defendant proves that, at the date of the infringement, the defendant was not aware and had no reasonable ground for suspecting that copyright subsisted in the work or other subject-matter in question.

Exception where copyright registered

(2) Subsection (1) does not apply if, at the date of the infringement, the copyright was duly registered under this Act.

1997, c. 24, s. 20(1)

Wide injunction

39.1 (1) When granting an injunction in respect of an infringement of copyright in a work or other subject-matter, the court may further enjoin the defendant from infringing the copyright in any other work or subject-matter if

    (a) the plaintiff is the owner of the copyright or the person to whom an interest in the copyright has been granted by licence; and

    (b) the plaintiff satisfies the court that the defendant will likely infringe the copyright in those other works or subject-matter unless enjoined by the court from doing so.

Application of injunction

(2) An injunction granted under subsection (1) may extend to works or other subject-matter

    (a) in respect of which the plaintiff was not, at the time the proceedings were commenced, the owner of the copyright or the person to whom an interest in the copyright has been granted by licence; or

    (b) that did not exist at the time the proceedings were commenced.

1997, c. 24, s. 20(1)

Transitional Provision

1997, c. 24 provides:

20. (4) Section 39.1 of the *Copyright Act*, as enacted by subsection (1) of this section, applies in respect of

(a) proceedings commenced but not concluded before the coming into force of subsection (1) of this section; and

(b) proceedings commenced after the coming into force of subsection (1) of this section.

No injunction in case of a building

40. (1) Where the construction of a building or other structure that infringes or that, if completed, would infringe the copyright in some other work has been commenced, the owner of the copyright is not entitled to obtain an injunction in respect of the construction of that building or structure or to order its demolition.

Certain remedies inapplicable

(2) Sections 38 and 42 do not apply in any case in respect of which subsection (1) applies.

1997, c. 24, s. 21

Technological Protection Measures and Rights Management Information

[Heading added 2012, c. 20, s. 47.]

Definitions

41. The following definitions apply in this section and in sections 41.1 to 41.21.

"circumvent" means,

(a) in respect of a technological protection measure within the meaning of paragraph (a) of the definition "technological protection measure", to descramble a scrambled work or decrypt an encrypted work or to otherwise avoid, bypass, remove, deactivate or impair the technological protection measure, unless it is done with the authority of the copyright owner; and

(b) in respect of a technological protection measure within the meaning of paragraph (b) of the definition "technological protection measure", to avoid, bypass, remove, deactivate or impair the technological protection measure.

(*"contourner"*)

"technological protection measure" means any effective technology, device or component that, in the ordinary course of its operation,

(a) controls access to a work, to a performer's performance fixed in a sound recording or to a sound recording and whose use is authorized by the copyright owner; or

(b) restricts the doing — with respect to a work, to a performer's performance fixed in a sound recording or to a sound recording — of any act referred to in section 3, 15 or 18 and any act for which remuneration is payable under section 19.

(*"mesure technique de protection"*)

R.S.C. 1985, c. 10 (4th Supp.), s. 9; 1997, c. 24, s. 22(1); 2012, c. 20, s. 47

Transitional Provision

1997, c. 24 provides:

22. (2) Subsection (1) applies in respect of

    (a) proceedings commenced but not concluded before this section comes into force; and

    (b) proceedings commenced after this section comes into force.

Prohibition

41.1 (1) No person shall

    (a) circumvent a technological protection measure within the meaning of paragraph (a) of the definition "technological protection measure" in section 41;

    (b) offer services to the public or provide services if

        (i) the services are offered or provided primarily for the purposes of circumventing a technological protection measure,

        (ii) the uses or purposes of those services are not commercially significant other than when they are offered or provided for the purposes of circumventing a technological protection measure, or

        (iii) the person markets those services as being for the purposes of circumventing a technological protection measure or acts in concert with another person in order to market those services as being for those purposes; or

    (c) manufacture, import, distribute, offer for sale or rental or provide — including by selling or renting — any technology, device or component if

        (i) the technology, device or component is designed or produced primarily for the purposes of circumventing a technological protection measure,

        (ii) the uses or purposes of the technology, device or component are not commercially significant other than when it is used for the purposes of circumventing a technological protection measure, or

        (iii) the person markets the technology, device or component as being for the purposes of circumventing a technological protection measure or acts in concert with another person in order to market the technology, device or component as being for those purposes.

Circumvention of technological protection measure

(2) The owner of the copyright in a work, a performer's performance fixed in a sound recording or a sound recording in respect of which paragraph (1)(a) has been contravened is, subject to this Act and any regulations made under section 41.21, entitled to all remedies — by way of injunction, damages, accounts, delivery up and otherwise — that are or may be conferred by law for the infringement of copyright against the person who contravened that paragraph.

No statutory damages

(3) The owner of the copyright in a work, a performer's performance fixed in a sound recording or a sound recording in respect of which paragraph (1)(a) has been contravened

may not elect under section 38.1 to recover statutory damages from an individual who contravened that paragraph only for his or her own private purposes.

Services, technology, device or component

(4) Every owner of the copyright in a work, a performer's performance fixed in a sound recording or a sound recording in respect of which a technological protection measure has been or could be circumvented as a result of the contravention of paragraph (1)(b) or (c) is, subject to this Act and any regulations made under section 41.21, entitled to all remedies — by way of injunction, damages, accounts, delivery up and otherwise — that are or may be conferred by law for the infringement of copyright against the person who contravened paragraph (1)(b) or (c).

2012, c. 20, s. 47

Law enforcement and national security

41.11 (1) Paragraph 41.1(1)(a) does not apply if a technological protection measure is circumvented for the purposes of an investigation related to the enforcement of any Act of Parliament or any Act of the legislature of a province, or for the purposes of activities related to the protection of national security.

Services

(2) Paragraph 41.1(1)(b) does not apply if the services are provided by or for the persons responsible for carrying out such an investigation or such activities.

Technology, device or component

(3) Paragraph 41.1(1)(c) does not apply if the technology, device or component is manufactured, imported or provided by the persons responsible for carrying out such an investigation or such activities, or is manufactured, imported, provided or offered for sale or rental as a service provided to those persons.

2012, c. 20, s. 47

Interoperability of computer programs

41.12 (1) Paragraph 41.1(1)(a) does not apply to a person who owns a computer program or a copy of one, or has a licence to use the program or copy, and who circumvents a technological protection measure that protects that program or copy for the sole purpose of obtaining information that would allow the person to make the program and any other computer program interoperable.

Services

(2) Paragraph 41.1(1)(b) does not apply to a person who offers services to the public or provides services for the purposes of circumventing a technological protection measure if the person does so for the purpose of making the computer program and any other computer program interoperable.

Technology, device or component

(3) Paragraph 41.1(1)(c) does not apply to a person who manufactures, imports or provides a technology, device or component for the purposes of circumventing a technological protection measure if the person does so for the purpose of making the computer program and any other computer program interoperable and

(a)   uses that technology, device or component only for that purpose; or

(b)   provides that technology, device or component to another person only for that purpose.

Sharing of information

(4) A person referred to in subsection (1) may communicate the information obtained under that subsection to another person for the purposes of allowing that person to make the computer program and any other computer program interoperable.

Limitation

(5) A person to whom the technology, device or component referred to in subsection (3) is provided or to whom the information referred to in subsection (4) is communicated may use it only for the purpose of making the computer program and any other computer program interoperable.

Non-application

(6) However, a person is not entitled to benefit from the exceptions under subsections (1) to (3) or (5) if, for the purposes of making the computer program and any other computer program interoperable, the person does an act that constitutes an infringement of copyright.

Non-application

(7) Furthermore, a person is not entitled to benefit from the exception under subsection (4) if, for the purposes of making the computer program and any other computer program interoperable, the person does an act that constitutes an infringement of copyright or an act that contravenes any Act of Parliament or any Act of the legislature of a province.

2012, c. 20, s. 47

Encryption research

41.13 (1) Paragraph 41.1(1)(a) does not apply to a person who, for the purposes of encryption research, circumvents a technological protection measure by means of decryption if

(a)   it would not be practical to carry out the research without circumventing the technological protection measure;

(b)   the person has lawfully obtained the work, the performer's performance fixed in a sound recording or the sound recording that is protected by the technological protection measure; and

(c)   the person has informed the owner of the copyright in the work, the performer's performance fixed in a sound recording or the sound recording who has applied the technological protection measure.

Non-application

(2) However, a person acting in the circumstances referred to in subsection (1) is not entitled to benefit from the exception under that subsection if the person does an act that constitutes an infringement of copyright or an act that contravenes any Act of Parliament or any Act of the legislature of a province.

Technology, device or component

(3) Paragraph 41.1(1)(c) does not apply to a person referred to in subsection (1) who manufactures a technology, device or component for the purposes of circumventing a

technological protection measure that is subject to paragraph 41.1(1)(a) if the person does so for the purpose of encryption research and

(a) uses that technology, device or component only for that purpose; or

(b) provides that technology, device or component only for that purpose to another person who is collaborating with the person.

2012, c. 20, s. 47

Personal information

41.14 (1) Paragraph 41.1(1)(a) does not apply to a person who circumvents a technological protection measure if

(a) the work, performer's performance fixed in a sound recording or sound recording that is protected by the technological protection measure is not accompanied by a notice indicating that its use will permit a third party to collect and communicate personal information relating to the user or, in the case where it is accompanied by such a notice, the user is not provided with the option to prevent the collection and communication of personal information without the user's use of it being restricted; and

(b) the only purpose of circumventing the technological protection measure is to verify whether it permits the collection or communication of personal information and, if it does, to prevent it.

Services, technology, device or component

(2) Paragraphs 41.1(1)(b) and (c) do not apply to a person who offers services to the public or provides services, or manufactures, imports or provides a technology, device or component, for the purposes of circumventing a technological protection measure in accordance with subsection (1), to the extent that the services, technology, device or component do not unduly impair the technological protection measure.

2012, c. 20, s. 47

Security

41.15 (1) Paragraph 41.1(1)(a) does not apply to a person who circumvents a technological protection measure that is subject to that paragraph for the sole purpose of, with the consent of the owner or administrator of a computer, computer system or computer network, assessing the vulnerability of the computer, system or network or correcting any security flaws.

Services

(2) Paragraph 41.1(1)(b) does not apply if the services are provided to a person described in subsection (1).

Technology, device or component

(3) Paragraph 41.1(1)(c) does not apply if the technology, device or component is manufactured or imported by a person described in subsection (1), or is manufactured, imported, provided — including by selling or renting — offered for sale or rental or distributed as a service provided to that person.

Non-application

(4) A person acting in the circumstances referred to in subsection (1) is not entitled to benefit from the exception under that subsection if the person does an act that constitutes an infringement of copyright or an act that contravenes any Act of Parliament or any Act of the legislature of a province.

2012, c. 20, s. 47

Persons with perceptual disabilities

41.16 (1) Paragraph 41.1(1)(a) does not apply to a person with a perceptual disability, another person acting at their request or a non-profit organization acting for their benefit if that person or organization circumvents a technological protection measure for the sole purpose of making a work, a performer's performance fixed in a sound recording or a sound recording perceptible to the person with a perceptual disability.

Services, technology, device or component

(2) Paragraphs 41.1(1)(b) and (c) do not apply to a person who offers or provides services to persons or organizations referred to in subsection (1), or manufactures, imports or provides a technology, device or component, for the purposes of enabling those persons or organizations to circumvent a technological protection measure in accordance with that subsection, to the extent that the services, technology, device or component do not unduly impair the technological protection measure.

2012, c. 20, s. 47

Broadcasting undertakings

41.17 Paragraph 41.1(1)(a) does not apply to a broadcasting undertaking that circumvents a technological protection measure for the sole purpose of making an ephemeral reproduction of a work, a performer's performance fixed in a sound recording or a sound recording in accordance with section 30.9, unless the owner of the copyright in the work, the performer's performance fixed in a sound recording or the sound recording that is protected by the technological protection measure makes available the necessary means to enable the making of such a reproduction in a timely manner in light of the broadcasting undertaking's business requirements.

2012, c. 20, s. 47

Radio apparatus

41.18 (1) Paragraph 41.1(1)(a) does not apply to a person who circumvents a technological protection measure on a radio apparatus for the sole purpose of gaining access to a telecommunications service by means of the radio apparatus.

Services or technology, device or component

(2) Paragraphs 41.1(1)(b) and (c) do not apply to a person who offers the services to the public or provides the services, or manufactures, imports or provides the technology, device or component, for the sole purpose of facilitating access to a telecommunications service by means of a radio apparatus.

Definitions

(3) The following definitions apply in this section.

"radio apparatus" has the same meaning as in section 2 of the *Radiocommunication Act.* (*"appareil radio"*)

"telecommunications service" has the same meaning as in subsection 2(1) of the *Tele-communications Act.* (*"service de télécommunication"*)

2012, c. 20, s. 47

Reduction of damages

41.19 A court may reduce or remit the amount of damages it awards in the circumstances described in subsection 41.1(1) if the defendant satisfies the court that the defendant was not aware, and had no reasonable grounds to believe, that the defendant's acts constituted a contravention of that subsection.

2012, c. 20, s. 47

Injunction only remedy

41.2 If a court finds that a defendant that is a library, archive or museum or an educational institution has contravened subsection 41.1(1) and the defendant satisfies the court that it was not aware, and had no reasonable grounds to believe, that its actions constituted a contravention of that subsection, the plaintiff is not entitled to any remedy other than an injunction.

2012, c. 20, s. 47

Regulations

41.21 (1) The Governor in Council may make regulations excluding from the application of section 41.1 any technological protection measure that protects a work, a performer's performance fixed in a sound recording or a sound recording, or classes of them, or any class of such technological protection measures, if the Governor in Council considers that the application of that section to the technological protection measure or class of technological protection measures would unduly restrict competition in the aftermarket sector in which the technological protection measure is used.

Regulations

(2) The Governor in Council may make regulations

(a) prescribing additional circumstances in which paragraph 41.1(1)(a) does not apply, having regard to the following factors:

(i) whether not being permitted to circumvent a technological protection measure that is subject to that paragraph could adversely affect the use a person may make of a work, a performer's performance fixed in a sound recording or a sound recording when that use is authorized,

(ii) whether the work, the performer's performance fixed in a sound recording or the sound recording is commercially available,

(iii) whether not being permitted to circumvent a technological protection measure that is subject to that paragraph could adversely affect criticism, review, news reporting, commentary, parody, satire, teaching, scholarship or research that could be made or done in respect of the work, the performer's performance fixed in a sound recording or the sound recording,

(iv) whether being permitted to circumvent a technological protection measure that is subject to that paragraph could adversely affect the market for the work, the performer's performance fixed in a sound recording or the sound recording or its market value,

(v)   whether the work, the performer's performance fixed in a sound recording or the sound recording is commercially available in a medium and in a quality that is appropriate for non-profit archival, preservation or educational uses, and

(vi)   any other relevant factor; and

(b)   requiring the owner of the copyright in a work, a performer's performance fixed in a sound recording or a sound recording that is protected by a technological protection measure to provide access to the work, performer's performance fixed in a sound recording or sound recording to persons who are entitled to the benefit of any of the limitations on the application of paragraph 41.1(1)(a) prescribed under paragraph (a). The regulations may prescribe the manner in which, and the time within which, access is to be provided, as well as any conditions that the owner of the copyright is to comply with.

2012, c. 20, s. 47

Prohibition — rights management information

41.22 (1) No person shall knowingly remove or alter any rights management information in electronic form without the consent of the owner of the copyright in the work, the performer's performance or the sound recording, if the person knows or should have known that the removal or alteration will facilitate or conceal any infringement of the owner's copyright or adversely affect the owner's right to remuneration under section 19.

Removal or alteration of rights management information

(2) The owner of the copyright in a work, a performer's performance fixed in a sound recording or a sound recording is, subject to this Act, entitled to all remedies — by way of injunction, damages, accounts, delivery up and otherwise — that are or may be conferred by law for the infringement of copyright against a person who contravenes subsection (1).

Subsequent acts

(3) The copyright owner referred to in subsection (2) has the same remedies against a person who, without the owner's consent, knowingly does any of the following acts with respect to any material form of the work, the performer's performance fixed in a sound recording or the sound recording and knows or should have known that the rights management information has been removed or altered in a way that would give rise to a remedy under that subsection:

(a)   sells it or rents it out;

(b)   distributes it to an extent that the copyright owner is prejudicially affected;

(c)   by way of trade, distributes it, exposes or offers it for sale or rental or exhibits it in public;

(d)   imports it into Canada for the purpose of doing anything referred to in any of paragraphs (a) to (c); or

(e)   communicates it to the public by telecommunication.

Definition of "rights management information"

(4) In this section, **"rights management information"** means information that

(a) is attached to or embodied in a copy of a work, a performer's performance fixed in a sound recording or a sound recording, or appears in connection with its communication to the public by telecommunication; and

(b) identifies or permits the identification of the work or its author, the performance or its performer, the sound recording or its maker or the holder of any rights in the work, the performance or the sound recording, or concerns the terms or conditions of the work's, performance's or sound recording's use.

2012, c. 20, s. 47

General Provisions

[Heading added 2012, c. 20, s. 47.]

Protection of separate rights

41.23 (1) Subject to this section, the owner of any copyright, or any person or persons deriving any right, title or interest by assignment or grant in writing from the owner, may individually for himself or herself, as a party to the proceedings in his or her own name, protect and enforce any right that he or she holds, and, to the extent of that right, title and interest, is entitled to the remedies provided by this Act.

Copyright owner to be made party

(2) If proceedings under subsection (1) are taken by a person other than the copyright owner, the copyright owner shall be made a party to those proceedings, except

(a) in the case of proceedings taken under section 44.1, 44.2 or 44.4;

(b) in the case of interlocutory proceedings, unless the court is of the opinion that the interests of justice require the copyright owner to be a party; and

(c) in any other case in which the court is of the opinion that the interests of justice do not require the copyright owner to be a party.

Owner's liability for costs

(3) A copyright owner who is made a party to proceedings under subsection (2) is not liable for any costs unless the copyright owner takes part in the proceedings.

Apportionment of damages, profits

(4) If a copyright owner is made a party to proceedings under subsection (2), the court, in awarding damages or profits, shall, subject to any agreement between the person who took the proceedings and the copyright owner, apportion the damages or profits referred to in subsection 35(1) between them as the court considers appropriate.

2012, c. 20, s. 47

Concurrent jurisdiction of Federal Court

41.24 The Federal Court has concurrent jurisdiction with provincial courts to hear and determine all proceedings, other than the prosecution of offences under sections 42 and 43, for the enforcement of a provision of this Act or of the civil remedies provided by this Act.

2012, c. 20, s. 47

Provisions Respecting Providers of
Network Services or Information Location Tools

[Heading added 2012, c. 20, s. 47.]

Proposed Addition — 41.25, 41.26

Notice of claimed infringement

41.25 (1) An owner of the copyright in a work or other subject-matter may send a notice of claimed infringement to a person who provides

(a) the means, in the course of providing services related to the operation of the Internet or another digital network, of telecommunication through which the electronic location that is the subject of the claim of infringement is connected to the Internet or another digital network;

(b) for the purpose set out in subsection 31.1(4), the digital memory that is used for the electronic location to which the claim of infringement relates; or

(c) an information location tool as defined in subsection 41.27(5).

Form and content of notice

(2) A notice of claimed infringement shall be in writing in the form, if any, prescribed by regulation and shall

(a) state the claimant's name and address and any other particulars prescribed by regulation that enable communication with the claimant;

(b) identify the work or other subject-matter to which the claimed infringement relates;

(c) state the claimant's interest or right with respect to the copyright in the work or other subject-matter;

(d) specify the location data for the electronic location to which the claimed infringement relates;

(e) specify the infringement that is claimed;

(f) specify the date and time of the commission of the claimed infringement; and

(g) contain any other information that may be prescribed by regulation.
2012, c. 20, s. 47 [Not in force at date of publication.]

Obligations related to notice

41.26 (1) A person described in paragraph 41.25(1)(a) or (b) who receives a notice of claimed infringement that complies with subsection 41.25(2) shall, on being paid any fee that the person has lawfully charged for doing so,

(a) as soon as feasible forward the notice electronically to the person to whom the electronic location identified by the location data specified in the notice belongs and inform the claimant of its forwarding or, if applicable, of the reason why it was not possible to forward it; and

(b) retain records that will allow the identity of the person to whom the electronic location belongs to be determined, and do so for six months beginning on the day on which the notice of claimed infringement is received or, if the claimant commences proceedings relating to the claimed infringement and so notifies the person before the end of those six months, for one year after the day on which the person receives the notice of claimed infringement.

Fees related to notices

(2) The Minister may, by regulation, fix the maximum fee that a person may charge for performing his or her obligations under subsection (1). If no maximum is fixed by regulation, the person may not charge any amount under that subsection.

Damages related to notices

(3) A claimant's only remedy against a person who fails to perform his or her obligations under subsection (1) is statutory damages in an amount that the court considers just, but not less than $5,000 and not more than $10,000.

Regulations — change of amounts

(4) The Governor in Council may, by regulation, increase or decrease the minimum or maximum amount of statutory damages set out in subsection (3).

2012, c. 20, s. 47 [Not in force at date of publication.]

Injunctive relief only — providers of information location tools

41.27 (1) In any proceedings for infringement of copyright, the owner of the copyright in a work or other subject-matter is not entitled to any remedy other than an injunction against a provider of an information location tool that is found to have infringed copyright by making a reproduction of the work or other subject-matter or by communicating that reproduction to the public by telecommunication.

Conditions for application

(2) Subsection (1) applies only if the provider, in respect of the work or other subject-matter,

(a) makes and caches, or does any act similar to caching, the reproduction in an automated manner for the purpose of providing the information location tool;

(b) communicates that reproduction to the public by telecommunication for the purpose of providing the information that has been located by the information location tool;

(c) does not modify the reproduction, other than for technical reasons;

(d) complies with any conditions relating to the making or caching, or doing of any act similar to caching, of reproductions of the work or other subject-matter, or to the communication of the reproductions to the public by telecommunication, that were specified in a manner consistent with industry practice by whoever made the work or other subject-matter available through the Internet or another digital network and that lend themselves to automated reading and execution; and

(e) does not interfere with the use of technology that is lawful and consistent with industry practice in order to obtain data on the use of the work or other subject-matter.

Proposed Addition — 41.27(3)

Limitation

(3) If the provider receives a notice of claimed infringement, relating to a work or other subject-matter, that complies with subsection 41.25(2) after the work or other subject-matter has been removed from the electronic location set out in the notice, then subsection (1) applies, with respect to reproductions made from that electronic location, only to infringements that occurred before the day that is 30 days — or the period that may be prescribed by regulation — after the day on which the provider receives the notice.

2012, c. 20, s. 47 [Not in force at date of publication.]

Exception

(4) Subsection (1) does not apply to the provision of the information location tool if the provision of that tool constitutes an infringement of copyright under subsection 27(2.3).

Factors — scope of injunction

(4.1) If it grants an injunction as set out in subsection (1), the court shall, among any other relevant factors, consider the following in establishing the terms of the injunction:

(a) the harm likely to be suffered by the copyright owner if steps are not taken to prevent or restrain the infringement; and

(b) the burden imposed on the provider and on the operation of the information location tool, including

   (i) the aggregate effect of the injunction and any injunctions from other proceedings,

   (ii) whether implementing the injunction would be technically feasible and effective in addressing the infringement,

   (iii) whether implementing the injunction would interfere with the use of the information location tool for non-infringing acts, and

   (iv) the availability of less burdensome and comparably effective means of preventing or restraining the infringement.

Limitation

(4.2) A court is not permitted to grant an injunction under section 39.1 against a provider who is the subject of an injunction set out in subsection (1).

Meaning of "information location tool"

(5) In this section, **"information location tool"** means any tool that makes it possible to locate information that is available through the Internet or another digital network.

2012, c. 20, s. 47 (part)

Criminal Remedies

Offences and punishment

42. (1) Every person who knowingly

(a) makes for sale or rental an infringing copy of a work or other subject-matter in which copyright subsists,

(b) sells or rents out, or by way of trade exposes or offers for sale or rental, an infringing copy of a work or other subject-matter in which copyright subsists,

(c) distributes infringing copies of a work or other subject-matter in which copyright subsists, either for the purpose of trade or to such an extent as to affect prejudicially the owner of the copyright,

(d) by way of trade exhibits in public an infringing copy of a work or other subject-matter in which copyright subsists, or

(e) imports for sale or rental into Canada an infringing copy of a work or other subject-matter in which copyright subsists

is guilty of an offence and liable

(f) on summary conviction, to a fine not exceeding twenty-five thousand dollars or to imprisonment for a term not exceeding six months or to both, or

(g) on conviction on indictment, to a fine not exceeding one million dollars or to imprisonment for a term not exceeding five years or to both.

Possession and performance offences and punishment

(2) Every person who knowingly

(a) makes or possesses any plate that is specifically designed or adapted for the purpose of making infringing copies of any work or other subject-matter in which copyright subsists, or

(b) for private profit causes to be performed in public, without the consent of the owner of the copyright, any work or other subject-matter in which copyright subsists

is guilty of an offence and liable

(c) on summary conviction, to a fine not exceeding twenty-five thousand dollars or to imprisonment for a term not exceeding six months or to both, or

(d) on conviction on indictment, to a fine not exceeding one million dollars or to imprisonment for a term not exceeding five years or to both.

Power of court to deal with copies or plates

(3) The court before which any proceedings under this section are taken may, on conviction, order that all copies of the work or other subject-matter that appear to it to be infringing copies, or all plates in the possession of the offender predominantly used for making infringing copies, be destroyed or delivered up to the owner of the copyright or otherwise dealt with as the court may think fit.

Circumvention of technological protection measure

(3.1) Every person, except a person who is acting on behalf of a library, archive or museum or an educational institution, is guilty of an offence who knowingly and for commercial purposes contravenes section 41.1 and is liable

    (a)   on conviction on indictment, to a fine not exceeding $1,000,000 or to imprisonment for a term not exceeding five years or to both; or

    (b)   on summary conviction, to a fine not exceeding $25,000 or to imprisonment for a term not exceeding six months or to both.

Limitation period

(4) Proceedings by summary conviction in respect of an offence under this section may be instituted at any time within, but not later than, two years after the time when the offence was committed.

Parallel importation of books

(5) No person may be prosecuted under this section for importing a book or dealing with an imported book in the manner described in section 27.1.

            R.S.C. 1985, c. 10 (4th Supp.), s. 10; 1997, c. 24, s. 24; 2012, c. 20, s. 48

Infringement in case of dramatic, operatic or musical work

43. (1) Any person who, without the written consent of the owner of the copyright or of the legal representative of the owner, knowingly performs or causes to be performed in public and for private profit the whole or any part, constituting an infringement, of any dramatic or operatic work or musical composition in which copyright subsists in Canada is guilty of an offence and liable on summary conviction to a fine not exceeding two hundred and fifty dollars and, in the case of a second or subsequent offence, either to that fine or to imprisonment for a term not exceeding two months or to both.

Change or suppression of title or author's name

(2) Any person who makes or causes to be made any change in or suppression of the title, or the name of the author, of any dramatic or operatic work or musical composition in which copyright subsists in Canada, or who makes or causes to be made any change in the work or composition itself without the written consent of the author or of his legal representative, in order that the work or composition may be performed in whole or in part in public for private profit, is guilty of an offence and liable on summary conviction to a fine not exceeding five hundred dollars and, in the case of a second or subsequent offence, either to that fine or to imprisonment for a term not exceeding four months or to both.

Limitation or Prescription Period

[Heading added 2012, c. 20, s. 49.]

Limitation or prescription period for civil remedies

43.1 (1) Subject to subsection (2), a court may award a remedy for any act or omission that has been done contrary to this Act only if

(a) the proceedings for the act or omission giving rise to a remedy are commenced within three years after it occurred, in the case where the plaintiff knew, or could reasonably have been expected to know, of the act or omission at the time it occurred; or

(b) the proceedings for the act or omission giving rise to a remedy are commenced within three years after the time when the plaintiff first knew of it, or could reasonably have been expected to know of it, in the case where the plaintiff did not know, and could not reasonably have been expected to know, of the act or omission at the time it occurred.

Restriction

(2) The court shall apply the limitation or prescription period set out in paragraph (1)(a) or (b) only in respect of a party who pleads a limitation period.

1997, c. 24, s. 25; 2012, c. 20, s. 49

Importation

[Heading amended 1997, c. 24, s. 26.]

Importation of certain copyright works prohibited

44. Copies made out of Canada of any work in which copyright subsists that if made in Canada would infringe copyright and as to which the owner of the copyright gives notice in writing to the Canada Border Services Agency that the owner desires that the copies not be so imported into Canada, shall not be so imported and are deemed to be included in tariff item No. 9897.00.00 in the List of Tariff Provisions set out in the schedule to the *Customs Tariff*, and section 136 of that Act applies accordingly.

R.S.C. 1985, c. 41 (3rd Supp.), s. 116; 1994, c. 47, s. 65; 1997, c. 36, s. 205; 1999, c. 17, s. 119; 2005, c. 38, s. 139(b)

Definitions

44.1 (1) In this section and sections 44.2 and 44.3,

"court" means the Federal Court or the superior court of a province;

"duties" has the same meaning as in the *Customs Act*;

"Minister" means the Minister of Public Safety and Emergency Preparedness;

"release" has the same meaning as in the *Customs Act*.

Power of court

(2) A court may make an order described in subsection (3) where the court is satisfied that

(a) copies of the work are about to be imported into Canada, or have been imported into Canada but have not yet been released;

(b) either

(i) copies of the work were made without the consent of the person who then owned the copyright in the country where the copies were made, or

(ii) the copies were made elsewhere than in a country to which this Act extends; and

(c) the copies would infringe copyright if they were made in Canada by the importer and the importer knows or should have known this.

Who may apply

(2.1) A court may make an order described in subsection (3) on application by the owner or exclusive licensee of copyright in a work in Canada.

Order of court

(3) The order referred to in subsection (2) is an order

(a) directing the Minister

(i) to take reasonable measures, on the basis of information reasonably required by the Minister and provided by the applicant, to detain the work, and

(ii) to notify the applicant and the importer, forthwith after detaining the work, of the detention and the reasons therefor; and

(b) providing for such other matters as the court considers appropriate.

How application made

(4) An application for an order made under subsection (2) may be made in an action or otherwise, and either on notice or *ex parte*, except that it must always be made on notice to the Minister.

Court may require security

(5) Before making an order under subsection (2), the court may require the applicant to furnish security, in an amount fixed by the court,

(a) to cover duties, storage and handling charges, and any other amount that may become chargeable against the work; and

(b) to answer any damages that may by reason of the order be incurred by the owner, importer or consignee of the work.

Application for directions

(6) The Minister may apply to the court for directions in implementing an order made under subsection (2).

Minister may allow inspection

(7) The Minister may give the applicant or the importer an opportunity to inspect the detained work for the purpose of substantiating or refuting, as the case may be, the applicant's claim.

Where applicant fails to commence an action

(8) Unless an order made under subsection (2) provides otherwise, the Minister shall, subject to the *Customs Act* and to any other Act of Parliament that prohibits, controls or regulates the importation or exportation of goods, release the copies of the work without further notice to the applicant if, two weeks after the applicant has been notified under subparagraph (3)(a)(ii), the applicant has not notified the Minister that the applicant has commenced a proceeding for a final determination by the court of the issues referred to in paragraphs (2)(b) and (c).

Where court finds in plaintiff's favour

(9) Where, in a proceeding commenced under this section, the court finds that the circumstances referred to in paragraphs (2)(b) and (c) existed, the court may make any order that it considers appropriate in the circumstances, including an order that the copies of the work be destroyed, or that they be delivered up to the plaintiff as the plaintiff's property absolutely.

Other remedies not affected

(10) For greater certainty, nothing in this section affects any remedy available under any other provision of this Act or any other Act of Parliament.

> 1993, c. 44, s. 66; 1997, c. 24, s. 27; 2005, c. 38, ss. 142(d), 145(2)(j)

Importation of books

44.2 (1) A court may, subject to this section, make an order described in subsection 44.1(3) in relation to a book where the court is satisfied that

    (a) copies of the book are about to be imported into Canada, or have been imported into Canada but have not yet been released;

    (b) copies of the book were made with the consent of the owner of the copyright in the book in the country where the copies were made, but were imported without the consent of the owner in Canada of the copyright in the book; and

    (c) the copies would infringe copyright if they were made in Canada by the importer and the importer knows or should have known this.

Who may apply

(2) A court may make an order described in subsection 44.1(3) in relation to a book on application by

    (a) the owner of the copyright in the book in Canada;

    (b) the exclusive licensee of the copyright in the book in Canada; or

    (c) the exclusive distributor of the book.

Limitation

(3) Subsections (1) and (2) only apply where there is an exclusive distributor of the book and the acts described in those subsections take place in the part of Canada or in respect of the particular sector of the market for which the person is the exclusive distributor.

Application of certain provisions

(4) Subsections 44.1(3) to (10) apply, with such modifications as the circumstances require, in respect of an order made under subsection (1).

1994, c. 47, s. 66; 1997, c. 24, s. 28

Limitation

44.3 No exclusive licensee of the copyright in a book in Canada, and no exclusive distributor of a book, may obtain an order under section 44.2 against another exclusive licensee of the copyright in that book in Canada or against another exclusive distributor of that book.

1997, c. 24, s. 28

Importation of other subject-matter

44.4 Section 44.1 applies, with such modfications as the circumstances require, in respect of a sound recording, performer's performance or communication signal, where a fixation or a reproduction of a fixation of it

   (a)   is about to be imported into Canada, or has been imported into Canada but has not yet been released;

   (b)   either

      (i)   was made without the consent of the person who then owned the copyright in the sound recording, performer's performance or communication signal, as the case may be, in the country where the fixation or reproduction was made, or

      (ii)   was made elsewhere than in a country to which Part II extends; and

   (c)   would infringe the right of the owner of copyright in the sound recording, performer's performance or communication signal if it was made in Canada by the importer and the importer knows or should have known this.

1997, c. 24, s. 328

Exceptions

45. (1) Notwithstanding anything in this Act, it is lawful for a person

   (a)   to import for their own use not more than two copies of a work or other subject-matter made with the consent of the owner of the copyright in the country where it was made;

   (b)   to import for use by a department of the Government of Canada or a province copies of a work or other subject-matter made with the consent of the owner of the copyright in the country where it was made;

   (c)   at any time before copies of a work or other subject-matter are made in Canada, to import any copies, except copies of a book, made with the consent of the owner of the copyright in the country where the copies were made, that are required for the use of a library, archive, museum or educational institution;

   (d)   to import, for the use of a library, archive, museum or educational institution, not more than one copy of a book that is made with the consent of the owner of the copyright in the country where the book was made; and

(e) to import copies, made with the consent of the owner of the copyright in the country where they were made, of any used books, except textbooks of a scientific, technical or scholarly nature for use within an educational institution in a course of instruction.

Satisfactory evidence

(2) An officer of customs may, in the officer's discretion, require a person seeking to import a copy of a work or other subject-matter under this section to produce satisfactory evidence of the facts necessary to establish the person's right to import the copy.

R.S.C. 1985, c. 41 (3rd Supp.), s. 117; 1993, c. 44, s. 67; 1994, c. 47, s. 67; 1997, c. 24, s. 28

Transitional Provision

1997, c. 24 provides:

62. (3) Notwithstanding paragraph (1)(d), paragraph 45(1)(e) of the *Copyright Act*, as enacted by section 28 of this Act, shall be read as follows for the period beginning on June 30, 1996 and ending on the day that is sixty days after the day on which this Act is assented to:

(e) to import copies, made with the consent of the owner of the copyright in the country where they were made, of any used books.

Part V
Administration (ss. 46–59)

Copyright Office

[Heading amended 1997, c. 24, s. 29.]

Copyright Office

46. The Copyright Office shall be attached to the Patent Office.

Powers of Commissioner and Registrar

47. The Commissioner of Patents shall exercise the powers conferred and perform the duties imposed on him by this Act under the direction of the Minister, and, in the absence of the Commissioner of Patents or if the Commissioner is unable to act, the Registrar of Copyrights or other officer temporarily appointed by the Minister may, as Acting Commissioner, exercise those powers and perform those duties under the direction of the Minister.

Registrar

48. There shall be a Registrar of Copyrights.

Registrar of Copyrights, certificates and certified copies

49. The Commissioner of Patents, the Registrar of Copyrights or an officer, clerk or employee of the Copyright Office may sign certificates and certified copies of the Register of Copyrights.

1992, c. 1, s. 47; 1993, c. 15, s. 4

Other duties of Registrar

50. The Registrar of Copyrights shall perform such other duties in connection with the administration of this Act as may be assigned to him by the Commissioner of Patents.

51. [Repealed 1992, c. 1, s. 48.]

Control of business and officials

52. The Commissioner of Patents shall, subject to the Minister, oversee and direct the officers, clerks and employees of the Copyright Office, have general control of the business thereof and perform such other duties as are assigned to him by the Governor in Council.

Register to be evidence

53. (1) The Register of Copyrights is evidence of the particulars entered in it, and a copy of an entry in the Register is evidence of the particulars of the entry if it is certified by the Commissioner of Patents, the Registrar of Copyrights or an officer, clerk or employee of the Copyright Office as a true copy.

Owner of copyright

(2) A certificate of registration of copyright is evidence that the copyright subsists and that the person registered is the owner of the copyright.

Assignee

(2.1) A certificate of registration of an assignment of copyright is evidence that the right recorded on the certificate has been assigned and that the assignee registered is the owner of that right.

Licensee

(2.2) A certificate of registration of a licence granting an interest in a copyright is evidence that the interest recorded on the certificate has been granted and that the licensee registered is the holder of that interest.

Admissibility

(3) A certified copy or certificate appearing to have been issued under this section is admissible in all courts without proof of the signature or official character of the person appearing to have signed it.

1992, c. 1, s. 49; 1993, c. 15, s. 5; 1997, c. 24, s. 30

Registration

Register of Copyrights

54. (1) The Minister shall cause to be kept at the Copyright Office a register to be called the Register of Copyrights in which may be entered

    (a) the names or titles of works and of other subject-matter in which copyright subsists;

    (b) the names and addresses of authors, performers, makers of sound recordings, broadcasters, owners of copyright, assignees of copyright, and persons to whom an interest in copyright has been granted by licence; and

    (c) such other particulars as may be prescribed by regulation.

(2) [Repealed 1997, c. 24, s. 31(1).]

Single entry sufficient

(3) In the case of an encyclopaedia, newspaper, review, magazine or other periodical work, or work published in a series of books or parts, it is not necessary to make a separate entry for each number or part, but a single entry for the whole work is sufficient.

Indices

(4) There shall also be kept at the Copyright Office such indices of the Register established under this section as may be prescribed by regulation.

Inspection and extracts

(5) The Register and indices established under this section shall at all reasonable times be open to inspection, and any person is entitled to make copies of or take extracts from the Register.

Former registration effective

(6) Any registration made under the *Copyright Act*, chapter 70 of the Revised Statutes of Canada, 1906, has the same force and effect as if made under this Act.

Subsisting copyright

(7) Any work in which copyright, operative in Canada, subsisted immediately before January 1, 1924 is registrable under this Act.

1992, c. 1, s. 50; 1997, c. 24, s. 31

Copyright in works

55. (1) Application for the registration of a copyright in a work may be made by or on behalf of the author of the work, the owner of the copyright in the work, an assignee of the copyright, or a person to whom an interest in the copyright has been granted by licence.

Application for registration

(2) An application under subsection (1) must be filed with the Copyright Office, be accompanied by the fee prescribed by or determined under the regulations, and contain the following information:

  (a) the name and address of the owner of the copyright in the work;

  (b) a declaration that the applicant is the author of the work, the owner of the copyright in the work, an assignee of the copyright, or a person to whom an interest in the copyright has been granted by licence;

  (c) the category of the work;

  (d) the title of the work;

  (e) the name of the author and, if the author is dead, the date of the author's death, if known;

  (f) in the case of a published work, the date and place of the first publication; and

  (g) any additional information prescribed by regulation.

1997, c. 24, s. 32

Copyright in subject-matter other than works

56. (1) Application for the registration of a copyright in subject-matter other than a work may be made by or on behalf of the owner of the copyright in the subject-matter, an assignee of the copyright, or a person to whom an interest in the copyright has been granted by licence.

Application for registration

(2) An application under subsection (1) must be filed with the Copyright Office, be accompanied by the fee prescribed by or determined under the regulations, and contain the following information:

    (a) the name and address of the owner of the copyright in the subject-matter;

    (b) a declaration that the applicant is the owner of the copyright in the subject-matter, an assignee of the copyright, or a person to whom an interest in the copyright has been granted by licence;

    (c) whether the subject-matter is a performer's performance, a sound recording or a communication signal;

    (d) the title, if any, of the subject-matter;

    (e) the date of

        (i) in the case of a performer's performance, its first fixation in a sound recording or, if it is not fixed in a sound recording, its first performance,

        (ii) in the case of a sound recording, the first fixation, or

        (iii) in the case of a communication signal, its broadcast; and

    (f) any additional information prescribed by regulation.

1993, c. 15, s. 6; 1997, c. 24, s. 32

Recovery of damages

56.1 Where a person purports to have the authority to apply for the registration of a copyright under section 55 or 56 on behalf of another person, any damage caused by a fraudulent or erroneous assumption of such authority is recoverable in any court of competent jurisdiction.

1997, c. 24, s. 32

Registration of assignment or licence

57. (1) The Registrar of Copyrights shall register an assignment of copyright, or a licence granting an interest in a copyright, on being furnished with

    (a) the original instrument or a certified copy of it, or other evidence satisfactory to the Registrar of the assignment or licence; and

    (b) the fee prescribed by or determined under the regulations.

(2) [Repealed 1992, c. 1, s. 5(1).]

When assignment or licence is void

(3) Any assignment of copyright, or any licence granting an interest in a copyright, shall be adjudged void against any subsequent assignee or licensee for valuable consideration

without actual notice, unless the prior assignment or licence is registered in the manner prescribed by this Act before the registering of the instrument under which the subsequent assignee or licensee claims.

Rectification of Register by the Court

(4) The Federal Court may, on application of the Registrar of Copyrights or of any interested person, order the rectification of the Register of Copyrights by

    (a)   the making of any entry wrongly omitted to be made in the Register,

    (b)   the expunging of any entry wrongly made in or remaining on the Register, or

    (c)   the correction of any error or defect in the Register,

and any rectification of the Register under this subsection shall be retroactive from such date as the Court may order.

1992, c. 1, s. 51; 1993, c. 15, s. 7; 1997, c. 24, s. 33

Execution of instruments

58. (1) Any assignment of copyright, or any licence granting an interest in a copyright, may be executed, subscribed or acknowledged at any place in a treaty country or a Rome Convention country by the assignor, licensor or mortgagor, before any notary public, commissioner or other official or the judge of any court, who is authorized by law to administer oaths or perform notarial acts in that place, and who also subscribes their signature and affixes thereto or impresses thereon their official seal or the seal of the court of which they are such judge.

Proposed Amendment — 58(1)

Execution of instruments

(1) Any assignment of a copyright, or any licence granting an interest in a copyright, may be executed, subscribed or acknowledged at any place in a treaty country, a Rome Convention country or a WPPT country by the assignor, licensor or secured or hypothecary debtor, before any notary public, commissioner or other official, or the judge of any court, who is authorized by law to administer oaths or certify documents in that place and who also subscribes their signature and affixes to, or impresses on, the assignment or licence their official seal or the seal of the court of which they are a judge.

2012, c. 20, s. 50 [Not in force at date of publication.]

Execution of instruments

(2) Any assignment of copyright, or any licence granting an interest in a copyright, may be executed, subscribed or acknowledged by the assignor, licensor or mortgagor, in any other foreign country before any notary public, commissioner or other official or the judge of any court of the foreign country, who is authorized to administer oaths or perform notarial acts in that foreign country and whose authority shall be proved by the certificate of a diplomatic or consular officer of Canada performing their functions in that foreign country.

Seals to be evidence

(3) The official seal or seal of the court or the certificate of a diplomatic or consular officer is evidence of the execution of the instrument, and the instrument with the seal or

certificate affixed or attached thereto is admissible as evidence in any action or proceeding brought under this Act without further proof.

Other testimony

(4) The provisions of subsections (1) and (2) shall be deemed to be permissive only, and the execution of any assignment of copyright, or any licence granting an interest in a copyright, may in any case be proved in accordance with the applicable rules of evidence.

1997, c. 24, s. 34

Fees

Fees regulations

59. The Governor in Council may make regulations

  (a) prescribing fees, or the manner of determining fees, to be paid for anything required or authorized to be done in the administration of this Act; and

  (b) prescribing the time and manner in which the fees must be paid.

1993, c. 15, s. 8

Part VI
Miscellaneous Provisions (ss. 60–65)
[Heading added 1997, c. 24, s. 35.]

Substituted Right
[Heading added 1993, c. 15, s. 9.]

Subsistence of substituted right

60. (1) Where any person is immediately before January 1, 1924 entitled to any right in any work that is set out in column I of Schedule I, or to any interest in such a right, he is, as from that date, entitled to the substituted right set out in column II of that Schedule, or to the same interest in the substituted right, and to no other right or interest, and the substituted right shall subsist for the term for which it would have subsisted if this Act had been in force at the date when the work was made, and the work had been one entitled to copyright thereunder.

Where author has assigned the right

(2) Where the author of any work in which any right that is set out in column I of Schedule I subsists on January 1, 1924 has, before that date, assigned the right or granted any interest therein for the whole term of the right, then at the date when, but for the passing of this Act, the right would have expired, the substituted right conferred by this section shall, in the absence of express agreement, pass to the author of the work, and any interest therein created before January 1, 1924 and then subsisting shall determine, but the person who immediately before the date at which the right would have expired was the owner of the right or interest is entitled at his option either

  (a) on giving such notice as is hereinafter mentioned, to an assignment of the right or the grant of a similar interest therein for the remainder of the term of the right for such consideration as, failing agreement, may be determined by arbitration, or

(b) without any assignment or grant, to continue to reproduce or perform the work in like manner as theretofore subject to the payment, if demanded by the author within three years after the date at which the right would have expired, of such royalties to the author as, failing agreement, may be determined by arbitration, or, where the work is incorporated in a collective work and the owner of the right or interest is the proprietor of that collective work, without any payment,

and the notice referred to in paragraph (a) must be given not more than one year or less than six months before the date at which the right would have expired, and must be sent by registered post to the author, or, if he cannot with reasonable diligence be found, advertised in the *Canada Gazette.*

Definition of "author"

(3) For the purposes of this section, **"author"** includes the legal representatives of a deceased author.

Works made before this Act in force

(4) Subject to this Act, copyright shall not subsist in any work made before January 1, 1924 otherwise than under and in accordance with the provisions of this section.

Clerical Errors

[Heading amended 1997, c. 24, s. 36.]

Clerical errors do not invalidate

61. Clerical errors in any instrument of record in the Copyright Office do not invalidate the instrument, but they may be corrected under the authority of the Registrar of Copyrights.

1992, c. 1, s. 52; 1993, c. 15, s. 10

Regulations

[Heading amended 1997, c. 24, s. 37(1).]

Regulations

62. (1) The Governor in Council may make regulations

(a) for the purposes of paragraph 30.01(6)(d), respecting measures, which may vary according to circumstances specified in the regulations;

(b) for the purposes of paragraph 30.02(3)(d), respecting measures, which may vary according to circumstances specified in the regulations;

(c) prescribing the form of a notice of claimed infringement referred to in subsection 41.25(2) and prescribing information to be contained in it;

(d) prescribing anything that by this Act is to be prescribed by regulation; and

(e) generally for carrying out the purposes and provisions of this Act.

Rights saved

(2) The Governor in Council may make orders for altering, revoking or varying any order in council made under this Act, but any order made under this section does not affect prejudicially any rights or interests acquired or accrued at the date when the order comes into operation, and shall provide for the protection of those rights and interests.

1997, c. 24, s. 37(2); 2012, c. 20, s. 51

Industrial Designs and Topographies

63. [Repealed 1997, c. 24, s. 38.]

Interpretation

64. (1) In this section and section 64.1,

"article" means any thing that is made by hand, tool or machine;

"design" means features of shape, configuration, pattern or ornament and any combination of those features that, in a finished article, appeal to and are judged solely by the eye;

"useful article" means an article that has a utilitarian function and includes a model of any such article;

"utilitarian function", in respect of an article, means a function other than merely serving as a substrate or carrier for artistic or literary matter.

Non-infringement re certain designs

(2) Where copyright subsists in a design applied to a useful article or in an artistic work from which the design is derived and, by or under the authority of any person who owns the copyright in Canada or who owns the copyright elsewhere,

    (a) the article is reproduced in a quantity of more than fifty, or

    (b) where the article is a plate, engraving or cast, the article is used for producing more than fifty useful articles,

it shall not thereafter be an infringement of the copyright or the moral rights for anyone

    (c) to reproduce the design of the article or a design not differing substantially from the design of the article by

        (i) making the article, or

        (ii) making a drawing or other reproduction in any material form of the article, or

    (d) to do with an article, drawing or reproduction that is made as described in paragraph (c) anything that the owner of the copyright has the sole right to do with the design or artistic work in which the copyright subsists.

Exception

(3) Subsection (2) does not apply in respect of the copyright or the moral rights in an artistic work in so far as the work is used as or for

    (a) a graphic or photographic representation that is applied to the face of an article;

(b)   a trade-mark or a representation thereof or a label;

(c)   material that has a woven or knitted pattern or that is suitable for piece goods or surface coverings or for making wearing apparel;

(d)   an architectural work that is a building or a model of a building;

(e)   a representation of a real or fictitious being, event or place that is applied to an article as a feature of shape, configuration, pattern or ornament;

(f)   articles that are sold as a set, unless more than fifty sets are made; or

(g)   such other work or article as may be prescribed by regulation.

Idem

(4) Subsections (2) and (3) apply only in respect of designs created after the coming into force of this subsection, and section 64 of this Act and the *Industrial Design Act*, as they read immediately before the coming into force of this subsection, as well as the rules made under them, continue to apply in respect of designs created before that coming into force.

R.S.C. 1985, c. 10 (4th Supp.), s. 11; 1993, c. 44, s. 68; 1997, c. 24, s. 39

Non-infringement re useful article features

64.1 (1) The following acts do not constitute an infringement of the copyright or moral rights in a work:

(a)   applying to a useful article features that are dictated solely by a utilitarian function of the article;

(b)   by reference solely to a useful article, making a drawing or other reproduction in any material form of any features of the article that are dictated solely by a utilitarian function of the article;

(c)   doing with a useful article having only features described in paragraph (a), or with a drawing or reproduction made as described in paragraph (b), anything that the owner of the copyright has the sole right to do with the work; and

(d)   using any method or principle of manufacture or construction.

Exception

(2) Nothing in subsection (1) affects

(a)   the copyright, or

(b)   the moral rights, if any,

in any sound recording, cinematograph film or other contrivance by means of which a work may be mechanically reproduced or performed.

R.S.C. 1985, c. 10 (4th Supp.), s. 11; 1997, c. 24, s. 40

Application of Act to topographies

64.2 (1) This Act does not apply, and shall be deemed never to have applied, to any topography or to any design, however expressed, that is intended to generate all or part of a topography.

Computer programs

(2) For greater certainty, the incorporation of a computer program into an integrated circuit product or the incorporation of a work into such a computer program may constitute an infringement of the copyright or moral rights in a work.

Definitions

(3) In this section, **"topography"** and **"integrated circuit product"** have the same meaning as in the *Integrated Circuit Topography Act*.

1990, c. 37, s. 33

65. [Repealed 1993, c. 44, s. 69.]

Part VII
Copyright Board and Collective Administration of Copyright (ss. 66–78)

[Heading added 1997, c. 24, s. 41.]

Copyright Board

Establishment

66. (1) There is hereby established a Board, to be known as the Copyright Board, consisting of not more than five members, including a chairman and a vice-chairman, to be appointed by the Governor in Council.

Service

(2) The members of the Board shall be appointed to serve either full-time or part-time.

Chairman

(3) The chairman must be a judge, either sitting or retired, of a superior, county or district court.

Tenure

(4) Each member of the Board shall hold office during good behaviour for a term not exceeding five years, but may be removed at any time by the Governor in Council for cause.

Re-appointment

(5) A member of the Board is eligible to be re-appointed once only.

Prohibition

(6) A member of the Board shall not be employed in the public service within the meaning of the *Public Service Labour Relations Act* during the member's term of office.

Members deemed public service employees

(7) A full-time member of the Board, other than the chairman, shall be deemed to be employed in

   (a)   the public service for the purposes of the *Public Service Superannuation Act*; and

(b) the federal public administration for the purposes of any regulations made pursuant to section 9 of the *Aeronautics Act*.

R.S.C. 1985, c. 10 (1st Supp.), s. 1(1); 1985, c. 10 (4th Supp.), s. 12; 2003, c. 22, ss. 154, 224(z.20), 225(s)

Duties of chairman

66.1 (1) The chairman shall direct the work of the Board and apportion its work among the members of the Board.

Absence or incapacity of chairman

(2) If the chairman is absent or incapacitated or if the office of chairman is vacant, the vice-chairman has all the powers and functions of the chairman during the absence, incapacity or vacancy.

Duties of vice-chairman

(3) The vice-chairman is the chief executive officer of the Board and has supervision over and direction of the Board and its staff.

R.S.C. 1985, c. 10 (4th Supp.), s. 12

Remuneration and expenses

66.2 The members of the Board shall be paid such remuneration as may be fixed by the Governor in Council and are entitled to be paid reasonable travel and living expenses incurred by them in the course of their duties under this Act while absent from their ordinary place of residence.

R.S.C. 1985, c. 10 (4th Supp.), s. 12

Conflict of interest prohibited

66.3 (1) A member of the Board shall not, directly or indirectly, engage in any activity, have any interest in a business or accept or engage in any office or employment that is inconsistent with the member's duties.

Termination of conflict of interest

(2) Where a member of the Board becomes aware that he is in a conflict of interest contrary to subsection (1), the member shall, within one hundred and twenty days, terminate the conflict or resign.

R.S.C. 1985, c. 10 (4th Supp.), s. 12

Staff

66.4 (1) Such officers and employees as are necessary for the proper conduct of the work of the Board shall be appointed in accordance with the *Public Service Employment Act*.

Idem

(2) The officers and employees referred to in subsection (1) shall be deemed to be employed in the public service for the purposes of the *Public Service Superannuation Act*.

Technical assistance

(3) The Board may engage on a temporary basis the services of persons having technical or specialized knowledge to advise and assist in the performance of its duties and the

Board may, in accordance with Treasury Board directives, fix and pay the remuneration and expenses of those persons.

R.S.C. 1985, c. 10 (4th Supp.), s. 12; 2003, c. 22, s. 225(s)

Concluding matters after membership expires

66.5 (1) A member of the Board whose term expires may conclude the matters that the member has begun to consider.

Decisions

(2) Matters before the Board shall be decided by a majority of the members of the Board and the presiding member shall have a second vote in the case of a tie.

R.S.C. 1985, c. 10 (4th Supp.), s. 12

Interim decisions

66.51 The Board may, on application, make an interim decision.

R.S.C. 1985, c. 10 (4th Supp.), s. 12

Variation of decisions

66.52 A decision of the Board respecting royalties or their related terms and conditions that is made under subsection 68(3), sections 68.1 or 70.15 or or [*sic*] subsections 70.2(2), 70.6(1), 73(1) or 83(8) may, on application, be varied by the Board if, in its opinion, there has been a material change in circumstances since the decision was made.

R.S.C. 1985, c. 10 (4th Supp.), s. 12; 1988, c. 65, s. 64; 1997, c. 24, s. 42

Regulations

66.6 (1) The Board may, with the approval of the Governor in Council, make regulations governing

(a) the practice and procedure in respect of the Board's hearings, including the number of members of the Board that constitutes a quorum;

(b) the time and manner in which applications and notices must be made or given;

(c) the establishment of forms for the making or giving of applications and notices; and

(d) the carrying out of the work of the Board, the management of its internal affairs and the duties of its officers and employees.

Publication of proposed regulations

(2) A copy of each regulation that the Board proposes to make under subsection (1) shall be published in the *Canada Gazette* at least sixty days before the proposed effective date thereof and a reasonable opportunity shall be given to interested persons to make representations with respect thereto.

Exception

(3) No proposed regulation that has been published pursuant to subsection (2) need again be published under that subsection, whether or not it has been altered as a result of representations made with respect thereto.

R.S.C. 1985, c. 10 (4th Supp.), s. 12

General powers, etc.

66.7 (1) The Board has, with respect to the attendance, swearing and examination of witnesses, the production and inspection of documents, the enforcement of its decisions and other matters necessary or proper for the due exercise of its jurisdiction, all such powers, rights and privileges as are vested in a superior court of record.

Enforcement of decisions

(2) Any decision of the Board may, for the purposes of its enforcement, be made an order of the Federal Court or of any superior court and is enforceable in the same manner as an order thereof.

Procedure

(3) To make a decision of the Board an order of a court, the usual practice and procedure of the court in such matters may be followed or a certified copy of the decision may be filed with the registrar of the court and thereupon the decision becomes an order of the court.

Effect of variation of decision

(4) Where a decision of the Board that has been made an order of a court is varied by a subsequent decision of the Board, the order of the court shall be deemed to have been varied accordingly and the subsequent decision may, in the same manner, be made an order of the court.

R.S.C. 1985, c. 10 (4th Supp.), s. 12

Distribution, publication of notices

66.71 Independently of any other provision of this Act relating to the distribution or publication of information or documents by the Board, the Board may at any time cause to be distributed or published, in any manner and on any terms and conditions that it sees fit, any notice that it sees fit to be distributed or published.

1997, c. 24, s. 43

Studies

66.8 The Board shall conduct such studies with respect to the exercise of its powers as are requested by the Minister.

R.S.C. 1985, c. 10 (4th Supp.), s. 12

Report

66.9 (1) The Board shall, not later than August 31 in each year, submit to the Governor in Council through the Minister an annual report on the Board's activities for the preceding year describing briefly the applications made to the Board, the Board's decisions and any other matter that the Board considers relevant.

Tabling

(2) The Minister shall cause a copy of each annual report to be laid before each House of Parliament on any of the first fifteen days on which that House is sitting after the Minister receives the report.

R.S.C. 1985, c. 10 (4th Supp.), s. 12

Regulations

66.91 The Governor in Council may make regulations issuing policy directions to the Board and establishing general criteria to be applied by the Board or to which the Board must have regard

    (a) in establishing fair and equitable royalties to be paid pursuant to this Act; and

    (b) in rendering its decisions in any matter within its jurisdiction.

1997, c. 24, s. 44

Collective Administration of Performing Rights and of Communication Rights

Public access to repertoires

67. Each collective society that carries on

    (a) the business of granting licences or collecting royalties for the performance in public of musical works, dramatico-musical works, performer's performances of such works, or sound recordings embodying such works, or

    (b) the business of granting licences or collecting royalties for the communication to the public by telecommunication of musical works, dramatico-musical works, performer's performances of such works, or sound recordings embodying such works, other than the communication of musical works or dramatico-musical works in a manner described in subsection 31(2),

must answer within a reasonable time all reasonable requests from the public for information about its repertoire of works, performer's performances or sound recordings, that are in current use.

R.S.C. 1985, c. 10 (1st Supp.), s. 1(2); 1985, c. 10 (4th Supp.), s. 12;
1993, c. 23, s. 3; 1993, c. 44, ss. 70, 79(3)(b); 1997, c. 24, s. 45

Filing of proposed tariffs

67.1 (1) Each collective society referred to in section 67 shall, on or before the March 31 immediately before the date when its last tariff approved pursuant to subsection 68(3) expires, file with the Board a proposed tariff, in both official languages, of all royalties to be collected by the collective society.

Where no previous tariff

(2) A collective society referred to in subsection (1) in respect of which no tariff has been approved pursuant to subsection 68(3) shall file with the Board its proposed tariff, in both official languages, of all royalties to be collected by it, on or before the March 31 immediately before its proposed effective date.

Effective period of tariffs

(3) A proposed tariff must provide that the royalties are to be effective for periods of one or more calendar years.

Prohibition of enforcement

(4) If a proposed tariff is not filed with respect to the work, performer's performance or sound recording in question, no action may be commenced, without the written consent of the Minister, for

    (a)   the infringement of the rights, referred to in section 3, to perform a work in public or to communicate it to the public by telecommunication;

    (b)   the infringement of the rights referred to in paragraph 15(1.1)(d) or 18(1.1)(a); or

    (c)   the recovery of royalties referred to in section 19.

Publication of proposed tariffs

(5) As soon as practicable after the receipt of a proposed tariff filed pursuant to subsection (1), the Board shall publish it in the *Canada Gazette* and shall give notice that, within sixty days after the publication of the tariff, prospective users or their representatives may file written objections to the tariff with the Board.

R.S.C. 1985, c. 10 (4th Supp.), s. 12; 1997, c. 24, s. 45; 2001, c. 34, s. 35; 2012, c. 20, s. 52

67.2 [Repealed 1997, c. 24, s. 45.]

67.3 [Repealed 1997, c. 24, s. 45.]

Board to consider proposed tariffs and objections

68. (1) The Board shall, as soon as practicable, consider a proposed tariff and any objections thereto referred to in subsection 67.1(5) or raised by the Board, and

    (a)   send to the collective society concerned a copy of the objections so as to permit it to reply; and

    (b)   send to the persons who filed the objections a copy of any reply thereto.

Criteria and factors

(2) In examining a proposed tariff for the performance in public or the communication to the public by telecommunication of performer's performances of musical works, or of sound recordings embodying such performer's performances, the Board

    (a)   shall ensure that

        (i)   the tariff applies in respect of performer's performances and sound recordings only in the situations referred to in the provisions of section 20 other than subsections 20(3) and (4),

        (ii)   the tariff does not, because of linguistic and content requirements of Canada's broadcasting policy set out in section 3 of the *Broadcasting Act*, place some users that are subject to that Act at a greater financial disadvantage than others, and

        (iii)   the payment of royalties by users pursuant to section 19 will be made in a single payment; and

    (b)   may take into account any factor that it considers appropriate.

Certification

(3) The Board shall certify the tariffs as approved, with such alterations to the royalties and to the terms and conditions related thereto as the Board considers necessary, having regard to

(a) any objections to the tariffs under subsection 67.1(5); and

(b) the matters referred to in subsection (2).

Publication of approved tariffs

(4) The Board shall

(a) publish the approved tariffs in the *Canada Gazette* as soon as practicable; and

(b) send a copy of each approved tariff, together with the reasons for the Board's decision, to each collective society that filed a proposed tariff and to any person who filed an objection.

R.S.C. 1985, c. 10 (4th Supp.), s. 13; 1993, c. 23, s. 5; 1993, c. 44, s. 72; 1997, c. 24, s. 45; 2012, c. 20, s. 53

Special and transitional royalty rates

68.1 (1) Notwithstanding the tariffs approved by the Board under subsection 68(3) for the performance in public or the communication to the public by telecommunication of performer's performances of musical works, or of sound recordings embodying such performer's performances,

(a) wireless transmission systems, except community systems and public transmission systems, shall pay royalties as follows:

(i) in respect of each year, $100 on the first 1.25 million dollars of annual advertising revenues, and

(ii) on any portion of annual advertising revenues exceeding 1.25 million dollars,

(A) for the first year following the coming into force of this section, thirty-three and one third per cent of the royalties set out in the approved tariff for that year,

(B) for the second year following the coming into force of this section, sixty-six and two thirds per cent of the royalties set out in the approved tariff for that year, and

(C) for the third year following the coming into force of this section, one hundred per cent of the royalties set out in the approved tariff for that year;

(b) community systems shall pay royalties of $100 in respect of each year; and

(c) public transmission systems shall pay royalties, in respect of each of the first three years following the coming into force of this section, as follows:

(i) for the first year following the coming into force of this section, thirty-three and one third per cent of the royalties set out in the approved tariff for that year,

(ii) for the second year following the coming into force of this section, sixty-six and two thirds per cent of the royalties set out in the approved tariff for that year, and

(iii) for the third year following the coming into force of this section, one hundred per cent of the royalties set out in the approved tariff for that year.

Effect of paying royalties

(2) The payment of the royalties set out in subsection (1) fully discharges all liabilities of the system in question in respect of the approved tariffs.

Definition of "advertising revenues"

(3) The Board may, by regulation, define **"advertising revenues"** for the purposes of subsection (1).

Preferential royalty rates

(4) The Board shall, in certifying a tariff as approved under subsection 68(3), ensure that there is a preferential royalty rate for small cable transmission systems.

Regulations

(5) The Governor in Council may make regulations defining **"small cable transmission system"**, **"community system"**, **"public transmission system"** and **"wireless transmission system"** for the purposes of this section.

1997, c. 24, s. 45

Effect of fixing royalties

68.2 (1) Without prejudice to any other remedies available to it, a collective society may, for the period specified in its approved tariff, collect the royalties specified in the tariff and, in default of their payment, recover them in a court of competent jurisdiction.

Proceedings barred if royalties tendered or paid

(2) No proceedings may be brought against a person who has paid or offered to pay the royalties specified in an approved tariff for

(a) the infringement of the right to perform in public or the right to communicate to the public by telecommunication, referred to in section 3;

(b) the infringement of the rights referred to in paragraph 15(1.1)(d) or 18(1.1)(a); or

(c) the recovery of royalties referred to in section 19.

Continuation of rights

(3) Where a collective society files a proposed tariff in accordance with subsection 67.1(1),

(a) any person entitled to perform in public or communicate to the public by telecommunication those works, performer's performances or sound recordings pursuant to the previous tariff may do so, even though the royalties set out therein have ceased to be in effect, and

(b) the collective society may collect the royalties in accordance with the previous tariff, until the proposed tariff is approved.

1997, c. 24, s. 45; 2012, c. 20, s. 54

Public Performances in Places Other than Theatres

69. (1) [Repealed R.S.C. 1985, c. 10 (4th Supp.), s. 14(1).]

Radio performances in places other than theatres

(2) In respect of public performances by means of any radio receiving set in any place other than a theatre that is ordinarily and regularly used for entertainments to which an admission charge is made, no royalties shall be collectable from the owner or user of the radio receiving set, but the Board shall, in so far as possible, provide for the collection in advance from radio broadcasting stations of royalties appropriate to the conditions produced by the provisions of this subsection and shall fix the amount of the same.

Expenses to be taken into account

(3) In fixing royalties pursuant to subsection (2), the Board shall take into account all expenses of collection and other outlays, if any, saved or savable by, for or on behalf of the owner of the copyright or performing right concerned or his agents, in consequence of subsection (2).

(4) [Repealed R.S.C. 1985, c. 10 (4th Supp.), s. 14(3).]

R.S.C. 1985, c. 10 (4th Supp.), s. 14; 1993, c. 44, s. 73

70. [Repealed R.S.C. 1985, c. 10 (4th Supp.), s. 15.]

Collective Administration in Relation to Rights under Sections 3, 15, 18, and 21

Collective Societies

Collective societies

70.1 Sections 70.11 to 70.6 apply in respect of a collective society that operates

(a) a licensing scheme, applicable in relation to a repertoire of works of more than one author, pursuant to which the society sets out the classes of uses for which and the royalties and terms and conditions on which it agrees to authorize the doing of an act mentioned in section 3 in respect of those works;

(a.1) a licensing scheme, applicable in relation to a repertoire of performer's performances of more than one performer, pursuant to which the society sets out the classes of uses for which and the royalties and terms and conditions on which it agrees to authorize the doing of an act mentioned in section 15 in respect of those performer's performances;

(b) a licensing scheme, applicable in relation to a repertoire of sound recordings of more than one maker, pursuant to which the society sets out the classes of uses for which and the royalties and terms and conditions on which it agrees to authorize the doing of an act mentioned in section 18 in respect of those sound recordings; or

(c)   a licensing scheme, applicable in relation to a repertoire of communication signals of more than one broadcaster, pursuant to which the society sets out the classes of uses for which and the royalties and terms and conditions on which it agrees to authorize the doing of an act mentioned in section 21 in respect of those communication signals.

R.S.C. 1985, c. 10 (4th Supp.), s. 16; 1997, c. 24, s. 46

Public information

70.11 A collective society referred to in section 70.1 must answer within a reasonable time all reasonable requests from the public for information abouts its repertoire of works, performer's performances, sound recordings or communication signals.

1997, c. 24, s. 46

Tariff or agreement

70.12 A collective society may, for the purpose of setting out by licence the royalties and terms and conditions relating to classes of uses,

(a)   file a proposed tariff with the Board; or

(b)   enter into agreements with users.

1997, c. 24, s. 46

Tariffs

Filing of proposed tariffs

70.13 (1) Each collective society referred to in section 70.1 may, on or before March 31 immediately before the date when its last tariff approved pursuant to subsection 70.15(1) expires, file with the Board a proposed tariff, in both official languages, of royalties to be collected by the collective society for issuing licences.

Where no previous tariff

(2) A collective society referred to in subsection (1) in respect of which no tariff has been approved pursuant to subsection 70.15(1) shall file with the Board its proposed tariff, in both official languages, of all royalties to be collected by it for issuing licences, on or before the March 31 immediately before its proposed effective date.

1997, c. 24, s. 46

Application of certain provisions

70.14 Where a proposed tariff is filed under section 70.13, subsections 67.1(3) and (5) and subsection 68(1) apply, with such modifications as the circumstances require.

1997, c. 24, s. 46

Certification

70.15 (1) The Board shall certify the tariffs as approved, with such alterations to the royalties and to the terms and conditions related thereto as the Board considers necessary, having regard to any objections to the tariffs.

Application of certain provisions

(2) Where a tariff is approved under subsection (1), subsections 68(4) and 68.2(1) apply, with such modifications as the circumstances require.

1997, c. 24, s. 46

Distribution, publication of notices

70.16 Independently of any other provision of this Act relating to the distribution or publication of information or documents by the Board, the Board shall notify persons affected by a proposed tariff, by

(a)   distributing or publishing a notice, or

(b)   directing another person or body to distribute or publish a notice,

in such manner and on such terms and conditions as the Board sees fit.

1997, c. 24, s. 46

Prohibition of enforcement

70.17 Subject to section 70.19, no proceedings may be brought for the infringement of a right referred to in section 3, 15, 18 or 21 against a person who has paid or offered to pay the royalties specified in an approved tariff.

1997, c. 24, s. 46

Continuation of rights

70.18 Subject to section 70.19, where a collective society files a proposed tariff in accordance with section 70.13,

(a)   any person authorized by the collective society to do an act referred to in section 3, 15, 18 or 21, as the case may be, pursuant to the previous tariff may do so, even though the royalties set out therein have ceased to be in effect, and

(b)   the collective society may collect the royalties in accordance with the previous tariff,

until the proposed tariff is approved.

1997, c. 24, s. 46

Where agreement exists

70.19 If there is an agreement mentioned in paragraph 70.12(b), sections 70.17 and 70.18 do not apply in respect of the matters covered by the agreement.

1997, c. 24, s. 46

Agreement

70.191 An approved tariff does not apply where there is an agreement between a collective society and a person authorized to do an act mentioned in section 3, 15, 18 or 21, as the case may be, if the agreement is in effect during the period covered by the approved tariff.

1997, c. 24, s. 46

Fixing of Royalties in Individual Cases

Application to fix amount of royalty, etc.

70.2 (1) Where a collective society and any person not otherwise authorized to do an act mentioned in section 3, 15, 18 or 21, as the case may be, in respect of the works, sound recordings or communication signals included in the collective society's repertoire are unable to agree on the royalties to be paid for the right to do the act or on their related terms and conditions, either of them or a representative of either may, after giving notice to the other, apply to the Board to fix the royalties and their related terms and conditions.

Fixing royalties, etc.

(2) The Board may fix the royalties and their related terms and conditions in respect of a licence during such period of not less than one year as the Board may specify and, as soon as practicable after rendering its decision, the Board shall send a copy thereof, together with the reasons therefor, to the collective society and the person concerned or that person's representative.

R.S.C. 1985, c. 10 (4th Supp.), s. 16; 1997, c. 24, s. 46

Agreement

70.3 (1) The Board shall not proceed with an application under section 70.2 where a notice is filed with the Board that an agreement touching the matters in issue has been reached.

Idem

(2) An agreement referred to in subsection (1) is effective during the year following the expiration of the previous agreement, if any, or of the last period specified under subsection 70.2(2).

R.S.C. 1985, c. 10 (4th Supp.), s. 16

Effect of Board decision

70.4 Where any royalties are fixed for a period pursuant to subsection 70.2(2), the person concerned may, during the period, subject to the related terms and conditions fixed by the Board and to the terms and conditions set out in the scheme and on paying or offering to pay the royalties, do the act with respect to which the royalties and their related terms and conditions are fixed and the collective society may, without prejudice to any other remedies available to it, collect the royalties or, in default of their payment, recover them in a court of competent jurisdiction.

R.S.C. 1985, c. 10 (4th Supp.), s. 16; 1997, c. 24, s. 47

Examination of Agreements

Definition of "Commissioner"

70.5 (1) For the purposes of this section and section 70.6, **"Commissioner"** means the Commissioner of Competition appointed under the *Competition Act*.

Filing agreement with the Board

(2) Where a collective society concludes an agreement to grant a licence authorizing a person to do an act mentioned in section 3, 15, 18 or 21, as the case may be, the collective society or the person may file a copy of the agreement with the Board within fifteen days after it is concluded.

Idem

(3) Section 45 of the *Competition Act* does not apply in respect of any royalties or related terms and conditions arising under an agreement filed in accordance with subsection (2).

Access by Commissioner

(4) The Commissioner may have access to the copy of an agreement filed in accordance with subsection (2).

Request for examination

(5) Where the Commissioner considers that an agreement filed in accordance with subsection (2) is contrary to the public interest, the Commissioner may, after advising the parties concerned, request the Board to examine the agreement.

R.S.C. 1985, c. 10 (4th Supp.), s. 16; 1997, c. 24, s. 48(1); 1999, c. 2, ss. 45, 46(a)

Examination and fixing of royalty

70.6 (1) The Board shall, as soon as practicable, consider a request by the Commissioner to examine an agreement and the Board may, after giving the Commissioner and the parties concerned an opportunity to present their arguments, alter the royalties and any related terms and conditions arising under the agreement, in which case section 70.4 applies with such modifications as the circumstances require.

Idem

(2) As soon as practicable after rendering its decision, the Board shall send a copy thereof, together with the reasons therefor, to the parties concerned and to the Commissioner.

R.S.C. 1985, c. 10 (4th Supp.), s. 16; 1999, c. 2, s. 46(6)

70.61 [Repealed 1997, c. 24, s. 50.]

70.62 [Repealed 1997, c. 24, s. 50.]

70.63 [Repealed 1997, c. 24, s. 50.]

70.64 [Repealed 1997, c. 24, s. 50.]

70.65 [Repealed 1997, c. 24, s. 50.]

70.66 [Repealed 1997, c. 24, s. 50.]

70.67 [Repealed 1997, c. 24, s. 50.]

70.7 [Repealed 1997, c. 24, s. 50.]

70.8 [Repealed 1997, c. 24, s. 50.]

Royalties in Particular Cases

Filing of proposed tariffs

71. (1) Each collective society that carries on the business of collecting royalties referred to in subsection 29.7(2) or (3) or paragraph 31(2)(d) shall file with the Board a proposed tariff, but no other person may file such a tariff.

Times for filing

(2) A proposed tariff must be

    (a)   in both official languages; and

(b) filed on or before the March 31 immediately before the date that the approved tariff ceases to be effective.

Where no previous tariff

(3) A collective society in respect of which no proposed tariff has been certified pursuant to paragraph 73(1)(d) shall file its proposed tariff on or before the March 31 immediately before its proposed effective date.

Effective period of tariffs

(4) A proposed tariff must provide that the royalties are to be effective for periods of one or more calendar years.

1997, c. 24, s. 50; 2012, c. 20, s. 55

Publication of proposed tariffs

72. (1) As soon as practicable after receipt of a proposed tariff filed pursuant to section 71, the Board shall publish it in the *Canada Gazette* and shall give notice that, within sixty days after the publication of the tariff, educational institutions or prospective retransmitters within the meaning of subsection 31(1), or their representatives, may file written objections to the tariff with the Board

Board to consider proposed tariffs and objections

(2) The Board shall, as soon as practicable, consider a proposed tariff and any objections thereto referred to in subsection (1) or raised by the Board, and

(a) send to the collective society concerned a copy of the objections so as to permit it to reply; and

(b) send to the persons who filed the objections a copy of any reply thereto.

1997, c. 24, s. 50; 1999, c. 31, s. 61; 2002, c. 26, s. 3

Certification

73. (1) On the conclusion of its consideration of proposed tariffs, the Board shall

(a) establish

(i)   a manner of determining the royalties to be paid by educational institutions and by retransmitters within the meaning of subsection 31(1), and

(ii) such terms and conditions related to those royalties as the Board considers appropriate;

(b) determine the portion of the royalties referred to in paragraph (a) that is to be paid to each collective society;

(c) vary the tariffs accordingly; and

(d) certify the tariffs as the approved tariffs, whereupon the tariffs become for the purposes of this Act the approved tariffs.

No discrimination

(2) For greater certainty, the Board, in establishing a manner of determining royalties under paragraph (1)(a) or in apportioning them under paragraph (1)(b), may not discriminate between owners of copyright on the ground of their nationality or residence.

Publication of approved tariffs

(3) The Board shall publish the approved tariffs in the *Canada Gazette* as soon as practicable and send a copy of each approved tariff, together with the reasons for the Board's decision, to each collecting society that filed a proposed tariff and to any person who filed an objection.

1997, c. 24, s. 50; 1999, c. 31, s. 62; 2002, c. 26, s. 4

Special case

74. (1) The Board shall, in establishing a manner of determining royalties under paragraph 73(1)(a), ensure that there is a preferential rate for small retransmission systems.

Regulations

(2) The Governor in Council may make regulations defining **"small retransmission systems"** for the purpose of subsection (1).

1997, c. 24, s. 50

Effect of fixing royalties

75. Without prejudice to any other remedies available to it, a collective society may, for the period specified in its approved tariff, collect the royalties specified in the tariff and, in default of their payment, recover them in a court of competent jurisdiction.

1997, c. 24, s. 50

Claims by non-members

76. (1) An owner of copyright who does not authorize a collective society to collect, for that person's benefit, royalties referred to in paragraph 31(2)(d) is, if the work is communicated to the public by telecommunication during a period when an approved tariff that is applicable to that kind of work is effective, entitled to be paid those royalties by the collective society that is designated by the Board, of its own motion or on application, subject to the same conditions as those to which a person who has so authorized that collective society is subject.

Royalties that may be recovered

(2) An owner of copyright who does not authorize a collective society to collect, for that person's benefit, royalties referred to in subsection 29.7(2) or (3) is, if such royalties are payable during a period when an approved tariff that is applicable to that kind of work or other subject-matter is effective, entitled to be paid those royalties by the collective society that is designated by the Board, of its own motion or on application, subject to the same conditions as those to which a person who has so authorized that collective society is subject.

Exclusion of remedies

(3) The entitlement referred to in subsections (1) and (2) is the only remedy of the owner of the copyright for the payment of royalties for the communication, making of copy or sound recording or performance in public, as the case may be.

Regulations

(4) The Board may, for the purposes of this section,

(a) require a collective society to file with the Board information relating to payments of royalties collected by it to the persons who have authorized it to collect those royalties; and

(b) by regulation, establish periods of not less than twelve months within which the entitlements referred to in subsections (1) and (2) must be exercised, in the case of royalties referred to in

(i) [Repealed 2012, c. 20, s. 56(2).]

(ii) [Repealed 2012, c. 20, s. 56(2).]

(iii) subsection 29.7(2), beginning on the making of the copy,

(iv) subsection 29.7(3), beginning on the performance in public, or

(v) paragraph 31(2)(d), beginning on the communication to the public by telecommunication.

1997, c. 24, s. 50; 2012, c. 20, s. 56

Owners Who Cannot be Located

Circumstances in which licence may be issued by Board

77. (1) Where, on application to the Board by a person who wishes to obtain a licence to use

(a) a published work,

(b) a fixation of a performer's performance,

(c) a published sound recording, or

(d) a fixation of a communication signal

in which copyright subsists, the Board is satisfied that the applicant has made reasonable efforts to locate the owner of the copyright and that the owner cannot be located, the Board may issue to the applicant a licence to do an act mentioned in section 3, 15, 18 or 21, as the case may be.

Conditions of licence

(2) A licence issued under subsection (1) is non-exclusive and is subject to such terms and conditions as the Board may establish.

Payment to owner

(3) The owner of a copyright may, not later than five years after the expiration of a licence issued pursuant to subsection (1) in respect of the copyright, collect the royalties fixed in the licence or, in default of their payment, commence an action to recover them in a court of competent jurisdiction.

Regulations

(4) The Copyright Board may make regulations governing the issuance of licences under subsection (1).

1997, c. 24, s. 50

Compensation for Acts Done Before Recognition of Copyright or Moral Rights

Board may determine compensation

78. (1) Subject to subsection (2), for the purposes of subsections 32.4(2), 32.5(2), 33(2), 33.1(2) and 33.2(2), the Board may, on application by any of the parties referred to in one of those provisions, determine the amount of the compensation referred to in that provision that the Board considers reasonable, having regard to all the circumstances, including any judgment of a court in an action between the parties for the enforcement of a right mentioned in subsection 32.4(3) or 32.5(3).

Limitation

(2) The Board shall not

    (a) proceed with an application under subsection (1) where a notice is filed with the Board that an agreement regarding the matters in issue has been reached; or

    (b) where a court action between the parties for enforcement of a right referred to in subsection 32.4(3) or 32.5(3), as the case may be, has been commenced, continue with an application under subsection (1) until the court action is finally concluded.

Interim orders

(3) Where the Board proceeds with an application under subsection (1), it may, for the purpose of avoiding serious prejudice to any party, make an interim order requiring a party to refrain from doing any act described in the order until the determination of compensation is made under subsection (1).

1997, c. 24, s. 50; 2012, c. 20, s. 57

Part VIII
Private Copying (ss. 79–88)

[Heading added 1997, c. 24, s. 50.]

Interpretation

Definitions

79. In this Part,

"audio recording medium" means a recording medium, regardless of its material form, onto which a sound recording may be reproduced and that is of a kind ordinarily used by individual consumers for that purpose, excluding any prescribed kind of recording medium;

"blank audio recording medium" means

    (a) an audio recording medium onto which no sounds have ever been fixed, and

    (b) any other prescribed audio recording medium;

"collecting body" means the collective society, or other society, association or corporation, that is designated as the collecting body under subsection 83(8);

"eligible author" means an author of a musical work, whether created before or after the coming into force of this Part, that is embodied in a sound recording, whether made before or after the coming into force of this Part, if copyright subsists in Canada in that musical work;

"eligible maker" means a maker of a sound recording that embodies a musical work, whether the first fixation of the sound recording occurred before or after the coming into force of this Part, if

(a) both the following two conditions are met:

   (i) the maker, at the date of that first fixation, if a corporation, had its headquarters in Canada or, if a natural person, was a Canadian citizen or permanent resident within the meaning of subsection 2(1) of the *Immigration and Refugee Protection Act*, and

   (ii) copyright subsists in Canada in the sound recording, or

(b) the maker, at the date of that first fixation, if a corporation, had its headquarters in a country referred to in a statement published under section 85 or, if a natural person, was a citizen, subject or permanent resident of such a country;

"eligible performer" means the performer of a performer's performance of a musical work, whether it took place before or after the coming into force of this Part, if the performer's performance is embodied in a sound recording and

(a) both the following two conditions are met:

   (i) the performer was, at the date of the first fixation of the sound recording, a Canadian citizen or permanent resident within the meaning of subsection 2(1) of the *Immigration and Refugee Protection Act*, and

   (ii) copyright subsists in Canada in the performer's performance, or

(b) the performer was, at the date of the first fixation of the sound recording, a citizen, subject or permanent resident of a country referred to in a statement published under section 85;

"prescribed" means prescribed by regulations made under this Part.

1997, c. 24, s. 50; 2001, c. 27, s. 240

Copying for Private Use

Where no infringement of copyright

80. (1) Subject to subsection (2), the act of reproducing all or part of any substantial part of

(a) a musical work embodied in a sound recording,

(b) a performer's performance of a musical work embodied in a sound recording, or

(c) a sound recording in which a musical work, or a performer's performance of a musical work, is embodied onto an audio recording medium for the private use of the person who makes the copy does not constitute an infringement of the copyright in the musical work, the performer's performance or the sound recording.

Limitation

(2) Subsection (1) does not apply if the act described in that subsection is done for the purpose of doing any of the following in relation to any of the things referred to in paragraphs (1)(a) to (c):

    (a) selling or renting out, or by way of trade exposing or offering for sale or rental;

    (b) distributing, whether or not for the purpose of trade;

    (c) communicating to the public by telecommunication; or

    (d) performing, or causing to be performed, in public.

1997, c. 24, s. 50

Right of Remuneration

Right of remuneration

81. (1) Subject to and in accordance with this Part, eligible authors, eligible performers and eligible makers have a right to receive remuneration from manufacturers and importers of blank audio recording media in respect of the reproduction for private use of

    (a) a musical work embodied in a sound recording;

    (b) a performer's performance of a musical work embodied in a sound recording; or

    (c) a sound recording in which a musical work, or a performer's performance of a musical work, is embodied.

Assignment of rights

(2) Subsections 13(4) to (7) apply, with such modifications as the circumstances require, in respect of the rights conferred by subsection (1) on eligible authors, performers and makers.

1997, c. 24, s. 50

Levy on Blank Audio Recording Media

Liability to pay levy

82. (1) Every person who, for the purpose of trade, manufactures a blank audio recording medium in Canada or imports a blank audio recording medium into Canada

    (a) is liable, subject to subsection (2) and section 86, to pay a levy to the collecting body on selling or otherwise disposing of those blank audio recording media in Canada; and

    (b) shall, in accordance with subsection 83(8), keep statements of account of the activities referred to in paragraph (a), as well as of exports of those blank audio recording media, and shall furnish those statements to the collecting body.

No levy for exports

(2) No levy is payable where it is a term of the sale or other disposition of the blank audio recording medium that the medium is to be exported from Canada, and it is exported from Canada.

1997, c. 24, s. 50

Filing of proposed tariffs

83. (1) Subject to subsection (14), each collective society may file with the Board a proposed tariff for the benefit of those eligible authors, eligible performers and eligible makers who, by assignment, grant of licence, appointment of the society as their agent or otherwise, authorize it to act on their behalf for that purpose, but no person other than a collective society may file any such tariff.

Collective body

(2) Without limiting the generality of what may be included in a proposed tariff, the tariff may include a suggestion as to whom the Board should designate under paragraph (8)(d) as the collecting body.

Times for filing

(3) Proposed tariffs must be in both official languages and must be filed on or before the March 31 immediately before the date when the approved tariffs cease to be effective.

Where no previous tariff

(4) A collective society in respect of which no proposed tariff has been certified pursuant to paragraph (8)(c) shall file its proposed tariff on or before the March 31 immediately before its proposed effective date.

Effective period of levies

(5) A proposed tariff must provide that the levies are to be effective for periods of one or more calendar years.

Publication of proposed tariff

(6) As soon as practicable after the receipt of a proposed tariff filed pursuant to subsection (1), the Board shall publish it in the *Canada Gazette* and shall give notice that, within sixty days after the publication of the tariff, any person may file written objections to the tariff with the Board.

Board to consider proposed tariffs and objections

(7) The Board shall, as soon as practicable, consider a proposed tariff and any objections thereto referred to in subsection (6) or raised by the Board, and

    (a) send to the collective society concerned a copy of the objections so as to permit it to reply; and

    (b) send to the persons who filed the objections a copy of any reply thereto.

Duties of Board

(8) On the conclusion of its consideration of the proposed tariff, the Board shall

    (a) establish, in accordance with subsection (9),

      (i)   the manner of determining the levies, and

      (ii) such terms and conditions related to those levies as the Board considers appropriate, including, without limiting the generality of the foregoing, the form, content and frequency of the statements of account mentioned in subsection 82(1), measures for the protection of confidential information contained in those statements, and the times at which the levies are payable,

  (b)   vary the tariff accordingly,

  (c)   certify the tariff as the approved tariff, whereupon that tariff becomes for the purposes of this Part the approved tariff, and

  (d)   designate as the collecting body the collective society or other society, association or corporation that, in the Board's opinion, will best fulfil the objects of sections 82, 84 and 86,

but the Board is not obligated to exercise its power under paragraph (d) if it has previously done so, and a designation under that paragraph remains in effect until the Board makes another designation, which it may do at any time whatsoever, on application.

Factors Board to consider

(9) In exercising its power under paragraph (8)(a), the Board shall satisfy itself that the levies are fair and equitable, having regard to any prescribed criteria.

Publication of approved tariffs

(10) The Board shall publish the approved tariffs in the *Canada Gazette* as soon as practicable and shall send a copy of each approved tariff, together with the reasons for the Board's decision, to the collecting body, to each collective society that filed a proposed tariff, and to any person who filed an objection.

Authors, etc., not represented by collective society

(11) An eligible author, eligible performer or eligible maker who does not authorize a collective society to file a proposed tariff under subsection (1) is entitled, in relation to

  (a)   a musical work,

  (b)   a performer's performance of a musical work, or

  (c)   a sound recording in which a musical work, or a performer's performance of a musical work, is embodied,

as the case may be, to be paid by the collective society that is designated by the Board, of the Board's own motion or on application, the remuneration referred to in section 81 if such remuneration is payable during a period when an approved tariff that is applicable to that kind of work, performer's performance or sound recording is effective, subject to the same conditions as those to which a person who has so authorized that collective society is subject.

Exclusion of other remedies

(12) The entitlement referred to in subsection (11) is the only remedy of the eligible author, eligible performer or eligible maker referred to in that subsection in respect of the reproducing of sound recordings for private use.

Powers of Board

(13) The Board may, for the purposes of subsections (11) and (12),

(a) require a collective society to file with the Board information relating to payments of moneys received by the society pursuant to section 84 to the persons who have authorized it to file a tariff under subsection (1); and

(b) by regulation, establish the periods, which shall not be less than twelve months, beginning when the applicable approved tariff ceases to be effective, within which the entitlement referred to in subsection (11) must be exercised.

Single proposed tariff

(14) Where all the collective societies that intend to file a proposed tariff authorize a particular person or body to file a single proposed tariff on their behalf, that person or body may do so, and in that case this section applies, with such modifications as the circumstances require, in respect of that proposed tariff.

1997, c. 24, s. 50

Distribution of Levies Paid

Distribution by collecting body

84. As soon as practicable after receiving the levies paid to it, the collecting body shall distribute the levies to the collective societies representing eligible authors, eligible performers and eligible makers, in the proportions fixed by the Board.

1997, c. 24, s. 50

Reciprocity

85. (1) Where the Minister is of the opinion that another country grants or has undertaken to grant to performers and makers of sound recordings that are Canadian citizens or permanent residents within the meaning of subsection 2(1) of the *Immigration and Refugee Protection Act* or, if corporations, have their headquarters in Canada, as the case may be, whether by treaty, convention, agreement or law, benefits substantially equivalent to those conferred by this Part, the Minister may, by a statement published in the *Canada Gazette*,

(a) grant the benefits conferred by this Part to performers or makers of sound recordings that are citizens, subjects or permanent residents of or, if corporations, have their headquarters in that country; and

(b) declare that that country shall, as regards those benefits, be treated as if it were a country to which this Part extends.

Reciprocity

(2) Where the Minister is of the opinion that another country neither grants nor has undertaken to grant to performers or makers of sound recordings that are Canadian citizens or permanent residents within the meaning of subsection 2(1) of the *Immigration and Refugee Protecton Act* or, if corporations, have their headquarters in Canada, as the case may be, whether by treaty, convention, agreement or law, benefits substantially equivalent to those conferred by this Part, the Minister may, by a statement published in the *Canada Gazette*,

(a) grant the benefits conferred by this Part to performers or makers of sound recordings that are citizens, subjects or permanent residents of or, if corporations, have their headquarters in that country, as the case may be, to the extent that that country grants those benefits to performers or makers of sound recordings that are Canadian citizens or permanent residents within the meaning of subsection 2(1) of the *Immigration and Refugee Protection Act* or, if corporations, have their headquarters in Canada; and

(b) declare that that country shall, as regards those benefits, be treated as if it were a country to which this Part extends.

Application of Act

(3) Any provision of this Act that the Minister specifies in a statement referred to in subsection (1) or (2)

(a) applies in respect of performers or makers of sound recordings covered by that statement, as if they were citizens of or, if corporations, had their headquarters in Canada; and

(b) applies in respect of a country covered by that statement, as if that country were Canada.

Application of Act

(4) Subject to any exceptions that the Minister may specify in a statement referred to in subsection (1) or (2), the other provisions of this Act also apply in the way described in subsection (3).

1997, c. 24, s. 50; 2001, c. 27, s. 241

Exemption from Levy

Where no levy payable

86. (1) No levy is payable under this Part where the manufacturer or importer of a blank audio recording medium sells or otherwise disposes of it to a society, association or corporation that represents persons with a perceptual disability.

Refunds

(2) Where a society, association or corporation referred to in subsection (1)

(a) purchases a blank audio recording medium in Canada from a person other than the manufacturer or importer, and

(b) provides the collecting body with proof of that purchase, on or before June 30 in the calendar year following the calendar year in which the purchase was made,

the collecting body is liable to pay forthwith to the society, association or corporation an amount equal to the amount of the levy paid in respect of the blank audio recording medium purchased.

If registration system exists

(3) If regulations made under paragraph 87(a) provide for the registration of societies, associations or corporations that represent persons with a perceptual disability,

subsections (1) and (2) shall be read as referring to societies, associations or corporations that are so registered.

1997, c. 24, s. 50

Regulations

Regulations

87. The Governor in Council may make regulations

    (a) respecting the exemptions and refunds provided for in section 86, including, without limiting the generality of the foregoing,

        (i) regulations respecting procedures governing those exemptions and refunds,

        (ii) regulations respecting applications for those exemptions and refunds, and

        (iii) regulations for the registration of societies, associations or corporations that represent persons with a perceptual disability;

    (b) prescribing anything that by this Part is to be prescribed; and

    (c) generally for carrying out the purposes and provisions of this Part.

1997, c. 24, s. 50

Civil Remedies

Right of recovery

88. (1) Without prejudice to any other remedies available to it, the collecting body may, for the period specified in an approved tariff, collect the levies due to it under the tariff and, in default of their payment, recover them in a court of competent jurisdiction.

Failure to pay royalties

(2) The court may order a person who fails to pay any levy due under this Part to pay an amount not exceeding five times the amount of the levy to the collecting body. The collecting body must distribute the payment in the manner set out in section 84.

Order directing compliance

(3) Where any obligation imposed by this Part is not complied with, the collecting body may, in addition to any other remedy available, apply to a court of competent jursdiction for an order directing compliance with that obligation.

Factors to consider

(4) Before making an order under subsection (2), the court must take into account

    (a) whether the person who failed to pay the levy acted in good faith or bad faith;

    (b) the conduct of the parties before and during the proceedings; and

    (c) the need to deter persons from failing to pay levies.

1997, c. 24, s. 50

Part IX
General Provisions (ss. 89–92)

[Heading added 1997, c. 24, s. 50.]

No copyright, etc., except by statute

89. No person is entitled to copyright otherwise than under and in accordance with this Act or any other Act of Parliament, but nothing in this section shall be construed as abrogating any right or jurisdiction in respect of a breach of trust or confidence.

1997, c. 24, s. 50

Interpretation

90. No provision of this Act relating to

(a) copyright in performer's performances, sound recordings or communication signals, or

(b) the right of performers or makers to remuneration

shall be construed as prejudicing any rights conferred by Part I or, in and of itself, as prejudicing the amount of royalties that the Board may fix in respect of those rights.

1997, c. 24, s. 50

Adherence to Berne and Rome Conventions

91. The Governor in Council shall take such measures as are necessary to secure the adherence of Canada to

(a) the Convention for the Protection of Literary and Artistic Works concluded at Berne on September 9, 1886, as revised by the *Paris Act* of 1971; and

(b) the International Convention for the Protection of Performers, Producers of Phonograms and Broadcasting Organisations, done at Rome on October 26, 1961.

1997, c. 24, s. 50

Review of Act

92. Five years after the day on which this section comes into force and at the end of each subsequent period of five years, a committee of the Senate, of the House of Commons or of both Houses of Parliament is to be designated or established for the purpose of reviewing this Act.

2012, c. 20, s. 58

Transitional Provision — General

1997, c. 24 provides:

> 53. The levies in the first tariffs certified under paragraph 83(8)(c) of the *Copyright Act*, as enacted by section 50 of this Act, become effective at the beginning of the first calendar year following the coming into force of that paragraph, regardless of when the tariffs are so certified, and are effective for a period of two calendar years.

> 53.1 Notwithstanding subsection 67.1(2) and section 70.13 of the *Copyright Act*, as enacted by sections 45 and 46 of this Act, the date for the filing of the first proposed tariffs under those sections shall be on or before September 1 of the year of the coming into force of this section.

54. For greater certainty, all notices published under subsection 5(2) of the *Copyright Act* before the coming into force of this section are deemed to have been validly made and to have had force and effect in accordance with their terms.

54.1 Section 6 of the *Copyright Act* applies to a photograph in which copyright subsists on the date of the coming into force of this section, if the author is

(a) a natural person who is the author of the photograph referred to in subsection 10(2) of the *Copyright Act*, as enacted by section 7 of this Act; or

(b) the natural person referred to in subsection 10(1.1) of the *Copyright Act*, as enacted by section 7 of this Act.

55. (1) Part II of the *Copyright Act*, as enacted by section 14 of this Act, shall be construed as a replacement for subsections 5(3) to (6) and section 11 of the *Copyright Act* as those provisions read immediately before the coming into force of subsection 5(3) and section 8, respectively, of this Act.

(2) The rights conferred by Part II of the *Copyright Act*, as enacted by section 14 of this Act, shall not be construed as diminishing the rights conferred by subsections 5(3) to (6) and section 11 of the *Copyright Act* as those provisions read immediately before the coming into force of subsection 5(3) and section 8, respectively, of this Act, in relation to records, perforated rolls and other contrivances by means of which sounds may be mechanically reproduced that were made before the coming into force of subsection 5(3) and section 8, respectively, of this Act.

(3) Where an assignment of copyright or a grant of any interest therein

(a) was made before the coming into force of Part II of the *Copyright Act*, as enacted by section 14 of this Act, and

(b) was made by the maker of a sound recording who was a natural person,

subsections 14(1) and (2) of the *Copyright Act* continue to apply in respect of that assignment or grant, with such modifications as the circumstances require, as if the sound recording was the work referred to in those subsections and the maker of the sound recording was its author.

56. Nothing in this Act shall be construed as diminishing the right conferred by section 14.01 of the *Copyright Act* as that section read immediately before the coming into force of section 12 of this Act.

57. For greater certainty, the amendments to the *Copyright Act* that eliminate references to **"British subject"** and **"Her Majesty's Realms and Territories"** do not affect any copyright or moral rights that subsisted in Canada immediately before the coming into force of those amendments.

58. Nothing in this Act shall be construed as reviving a copyright that expired before the coming into force of this section.

58.1 No agreement concluded before April 25, 1996 that assigns a right or grants an interest by licence in a right that would be a copyright or a right to remuneration under this Act shall be construed as assigning or granting any rights conferred for the first time by this Act, unless the agreement specifically provides for the assignment or grant.

Coming into Force

Coming into force

61. Except as provided by section 62, this Act or any provision of this Act, or any provision of the *Copyright Act* as enacted or amended by this Act, comes into force on a day or days to be fixed by order of the Governor in Council.

Coming into force

62. (1) The following provisions come into force or are deemed to have come into force on June 30, 1996:

  (a) the definitions **"exclusive distributor"**, **"educational institution"** and **"library, archive or museum"** in section 2 of the *Copyright Act*, as enacted by subsection 1(5) of this Act;

  (b) section 2.6 of the *Copyright Act*, as enacted by section 2 of this Act;

  (c) section 27.1 of the *Copyright Act*, as enacted by section 15 of this Act; and

  (d) section 45 of the *Copyright Act*, as enacted by section 28 of this Act.

(2) Notwithstanding subsection (1), the definition **"exclusive distributor"** referred to in paragraph (1)(a) shall be read as follows during the period beginning on June 30, 1996 and ending on the day that is sixty days after the day on which this Act is assented to:

"exclusive distributor" means, in relation to a book, a person who has, before or after the coming into force of this definition, been appointed in writing, by the owner or exclusive licensee of the copyright in the book in Canada, as

  (a) the only distributor of the book in Canada or any part of Canada, or

  (b) the only distributor of the book in Canada or any part of Canada in respect of a particular sector of the market.

(3) Notwithstanding paragraph (1)(d), paragraph 45(1)(e) of the *Copyright Act*, as enacted by section 28 of this Act, shall be read as follows for the period beginning on June 30, 1996 and ending on the day that is sixty days after the day on which this Act is assented to:

  (e) to import copies, made with the consent of the owner of the copyright in the country where they were made, of any used books.

63. (1) No exclusive distributor, within the meaning assigned to that expression by subsection 62(2) of this Act, copyright owner or exclusive licensee is entitled to a remedy referred to in the *Copyright Act* in relation to an infringement referred to in subsection 27.1(1) or (2) of that Act, as enacted by section 15 of this Act, during the period beginning on June 30, 1996 and ending on the day on which this Act is assented to, unless

  (a) before the infringement occurred, notice in writing has been given to the person referred to in subsection 27.1(1) or (2) of that Act, as enacted by section 15 of this Act, as the case may be, that

    (i) there is an exclusive distributor of the book in Canada, and

    (ii) section 27.1 of that Act came into force or was deemed to have come into force on June 30, 1996; and

  (b) in the case of an infringement referred to in section 27.1 of that Act, as enacted by section 15 of this Act, the remedy is only in relation to a book that was imported during that period and forms part of the inventory of the person referred to in section 27.1 of that Act on the day on which this Act is assented to.

(2) No exclusive distributor, copyright owner or exclusive licensee is entitled to a remedy referred to in subsection (1) against an educational institution, library, archive or museum.

(3) For greater certainty, the expiration of the period referred to in subsection 62(2) of this Act does not affect the right of an exclusive distributor to continue, after the expiration of that period, legal proceedings validly commenced during that period.

[Schedules]

The text in square brackets has been editorially added by Carswell and does not form part of the text of the legislation.

Schedule I
(Section 60)

Existing Rights

Column I	Column II
Existing Right	**Substituted Right**
Works other than Dramatic and Musical Works	
Copyright	Copyright as defined by this Act[1].
Musical and Dramatic Works	
Both copyright and performing right	Copyright as defined by this Act.
Copyright, but not performing right	Copyright as defined by this Act, except the sole right to perform the work or any substantial part thereof in public.
Performing right, but not copyright	The sole right to perform the work in public, but none of the other rights comprised in copyright as defined by this Act.

1   In the case of an essay, article or portion forming part of and first published in a review, magazine or other periodical or work of a like nature, the right shall be subject to any right of publishing the essay, article or portion in a separate form to which the author is entitled on January 1, 1924 or would if this Act had not been passed have become entitled under section 18 of *An Act to amend the Law of Copyright*, being chapter 45 of the Statutes of the United Kingdom, 1842.

For the purposes of this Schedule the following expressions, where used in column I thereof, have the following meanings:

"**Copyright**" in the case of a work that according to the law in force immediately before January 1, 1924 has not been published before that date and statutory copyright wherein depends on publication, includes the right at common law, if any, to restrain publication or other dealing with the work;

"**Performing right**", in the case of a work that has not been performed in public before January 1, 1924, includes the right at common law, if any, to restrain the performance thereof in public.

Schedule II

[Repealed 1993, c. 44, s. 74.]
[Repealed 1993, c. 44, s. 74.]

Schedule III

[Repealed 1997, c. 24, s. 51.]
[Repealed 1997, c. 24, s. 51.]

Transitional Provisions

— 2012, c. 20, ss. 59–62:

No revival of copyright in photograph

59. (1) The repeal of section 10 of the *Copyright Act* by section 6 does not have the effect of reviving copyright in any photograph in which, on the coming into force of that section 6, copyright had expired.

Cases where corporations were deemed to be authors

(2) In any case in which, immediately before the coming into force of section 6, a corporation is deemed, by virtue of subsection 10(2) of the *Copyright Act* as it read before the coming into force of that section 6, to be the author of a photograph in which copyright subsists at that time, the copyright in that photograph continues to subsist for the term determined in accordance with sections 6, 6.1, 6.2, 9, 11.1 or 12 of the *Copyright Act* as if its author were the individual who would have been considered the author of the photograph apart from that subsection 10(2).

Cases where individuals were deemed to be authors

(3) In any case in which an individual is deemed to be the author of a photograph, by virtue of subsection 10(2) of the *Copyright Act* as it read before the coming into force of section 6, the individual continues, after the coming into force of that section 6, to be the author of that photograph for the purposes of the *Copyright Act*.

Engraving, photograph or portrait

60. Subsection 13(2) of the *Copyright Act*, as it read immediately before the coming into force of section 7, continues to apply with respect to any engraving, photograph or portrait the plate or original of which was commissioned before the coming into force of that section 7.

No revival of copyright

61. Subsections 23(1) to (2) of the *Copyright Act*, as enacted by section 17, do not have the effect of reviving the copyright, or a right to remuneration, in any performer's performance

or sound recording in which the copyright or the right to remuneration had expired on the coming into force of those subsections.

Limitation or prescription period

62. (1) Subsection 43.1(1) of the *Copyright Act*, as enacted by section 49, applies only to proceedings with respect to an act or omission that occurred after the coming into force of that section.

Former limitation or prescription period continued

(2) Subsection 41(1) of the *Copyright Act*, as it read immediately before the coming into force of section 47, applies to proceedings with respect to an infringement that occurred before the coming into force of that section.

DATE DUE	RETURNED